FLEMISH PAINTERS
VOLUME ONE

FLEMISH
PAINTERS

1430-1830
by
R. H. WILENSKI

VOLUME ONE

A Reynal Book

THE VIKING PRESS

NEW YORK

To

RICHARD DE LA MARE

CONTENTS

CONTENTS

PART TWO: A DICTIONARY OF FLEMISH PAINTERS

NOTE TO THE GENERAL READER

In Part 1 of this book I am concerned with Flemish painters from the period of Philip the Good till 1830 when Belgium became an independent Kingdom; and painters born in Holland before the separation from the Southern Netherlands at the end of the sixteenth century are included.

My text is divided into chapters corresponding to the successive rulers of the country. Each chapter begins with historical notes designed to suggest the changing conditions, decade by decade, in the Netherlands and to recall the general 'feel' of each period by mention of some famous names and well-known happenings in other countries.

In each chapter I then try to answer the questions: What Flemish painters, old and young, were working in these years? How were they grouped in the various towns of the Netherlands? In what conditions did they work? To whom did they sell their pictures?

I have also tried to answer, where possible, the question: What Flemish painters were then working in France, England, Italy, Spain and Central Europe?

In other sections of each chapter I assemble the painters as producers of landscapes, townscapes, indoor and outdoor genre, still life, mythologies and allegories, topical comments, religious subjects and so forth.

The INDEX TO PART I, which is to be found at the end of VOLUME I, enables the reader to find the references to particular painters in the successive chapters.

The DICTIONARY OF FLEMISH PAINTERS which constitutes PART II of this volume records about 2500 Flemish painters from 1430 to 1900. Painters born in Holland before the separation from the Southern Netherlands are included as 'Flemish-Dutch'. Some living artists are included because it was against my conscience to work for a number of years on records of action by dead men without reference to the present continuance of that action.

Each entry records facts about the painter's life and groups of his signed, monogrammed or documented paintings in museums and other public places. By 'documented' I mean here paintings recorded by contemporary or near-contemporary writers or engravers as well as those recorded in archives, inventories and so forth. In recording pictures by nineteenth- and twentieth-century painters I have not divided them into 'signed', 'monogrammed' and 'documented' groups because questions of authorship very rarely arise in such cases.

The categories of pictures painted by each artist (e.g. landscapes, genre, religious subjects etc.) are indicated at the beginning of each entry.

Comments by contemporary or near-contemporary artists are occasionally quoted.

Many of the entries contain references to other entries when the painters are

ix

in one way or another connected. These cross-references which occurred to me when compiling or revising the entries are not systematic or in any degree complete. But as I found them useful when writing Part I of this book, I hope they may also be useful to others.

An asterisk * before a name in the DICTIONARY indicates that one or more of this artist's pictures can be found among the nine hundred and twelve reproductions in VOLUME II.

When a picture of unknown authorship is included in my reproductions in VOLUME II, I have invented a conventional reference name for the painter with a first word indicating the present location of the picture and the word 'Painter' at the end: e.g. **London Virgin with a Firescreen Painter** (Frontispiece). Some conventional reference names for pictures of unknown authorship are already current in art-historical writing; these always include the word 'Master'; in such cases I have used the current name when referring to the particular picture for which the name was invented: e.g. **Virgo inter Virgines Master** (Plate 128).

NOTE TO SPECIALIST STUDENTS

'Dat ik aan inlichtingen over de levens van de beroemde schilders minder
verkregen dan nagejaagd heb, zou men mij met een medelijdend hart gaarne
vergeven, als men maar merkte of wist, hoeveel ijver en moeite ik er naar mijn
vermogen of schier boven mijn vermogen aan besteed heb. Doch wie is er in
staat alles te volbrengen, wat hij zich met goeden wil ernstig voorneemt? Het
zijn er weinigen.'

KAREL VAN MANDER

This book only purports to take students of art history to the point where
work in a specialized art-historical library becomes unavoidable; and for those
entering on that study I have provided some NOTES ON THE LITERATURE on
pp. 725–759 of this first volume as preliminary guidance.

All the comments in the conspectus I have attempted in Part I are my own,
unless given as quotations.

Factual statements made there about particular painters can be checked by
consulting the books listed in the numbered BIBLIOGRAPHIC INDEX TO THE
DICTIONARY on pp. 695–724 (to which references are made by numbers at the
bottom of each entry in the DICTIONARY).

These references to books at the bottom of the entries are in chronological
order. The student who consults all those books, in that order, will thus be in a
position at the end to discover what additional factual information (as distinguished from conjecture and comment) is provided by books or other writings
later in date than the last I have recorded.

Except in the case of certain obituary notices I have excluded references to
specialist art-historical periodicals and art indices (some of which are listed in
my NOTES ON THE LITERATURE) because such references are inevitably out of date
by the time a book of this kind is printed, and the specialist student will have in
any event to consult the latest indices and also issues of periodicals later than
the latest indices.

When a conventional name of my invention (ending with the word 'Painter')
is used for the painter of a picture of unknown authorship, e.g. **London Virgin
with a Firescreen Painter** (Frontispiece), the authorship presumed by the compiler of the museum catalogue at the time of writing will be found in the
DICTIONARY entry for my invented name. When I use a conventional name
already in current use (**The So-and-So Master**) I restrict it to the picture for
which the name was originally invented; and I treat other pictures presumed by
some, on 'style' grounds, by that 'Master', as art-historically of unknown authorship.

xi

ACKNOWLEDGEMENTS

This is a personal book made possible by the generosity of my publishers who financed it and provided me with assistants over a period of years.

I am alone responsible for the text. My former secretary Miss Violet Glenn valiantly typed the whole of it (and most of it several times over in various drafts). My wife assisted me throughout in a number of ways.

I was much helped in the NOTES ON THE LITERATURE and the seventeenth-century entries in the DICTIONARY by Mr. Manfred Bräude.

The late Dr. Saxl, then Director of the Warburg Institute, was encouraging when I was planning the work.

My publishers have kindly provided the INDEX TO PART I.

PART ONE

FLEMISH PAINTERS

Notes on their Lives, Circumstances and Productions

CHAPTER I

Philip the Good

1419-1467

In 1419 Duke John the Fearless was murdered by the Dauphin's men at the bridge of Montereau, and his son Philip the Good became Duke of Burgundy and Count of Flanders. Duke Philip was then twenty-three and married to Michelle, daughter of Charles VI (Charles le Fou) of France. Henry V of England was then thirty-two and the English held all Normandy. John of Bavaria, de facto Count of Holland, was established at the Hague; Martin V was Pope; Tommaso Mocenigo was Doge in Venice and Giovanni dei Medici, founder of the family's wealth and influence, was a leading figure in Florence. John II was King of Castile, Alphonse V was King of Aragon, and John I, married to Philippa of Lancaster and allied to England by the Treaty of Windsor, was King of Portugal. Prince Henry the Navigator was twenty-five; René of Anjou was a child of ten; Sigismund, King of Hungary and titular King of Bohemia, was German King of the Romans and Holy Roman Emperor elect; Manuel II was Eastern Roman Emperor in Constantinople; and Mahommed I was Sultan in Adrianople.

In 1420 René of Anjou married Isabelle of Lorraine; Duke Philip, incensed against the Dauphin, was allied to England; Henry V married Catherine of Valois, daughter of Charles VI who disinherited the Dauphin by the Treaty of Troyes; and Duke Philip and Henry made a Pageant Entry into Paris. The Pope issued a Bull proclaiming a crusade for the destruction of the Wycliffites, Hussites and all heretics in Bohemia; King Sigismund besieged Prague; and the Hussite Jan Ziska defeated Sigismund at the battle of Penkrac. In 1421 Murad II became Sultan of Turkey; all Bohemia was in Hussite hands; and Duke Philip founded the University of Dôle. In 1422 Sigismund's army was again defeated by Jan Ziska at the battle of Nemecky; Henry V died and the infant Henry VI became King with Humphrey Duke of Gloucester as Regent in England and John Duke of Bedford as Regent in France; and the Duke of Gloucester married Jacqueline of Hainault, heiress of Holland and Zeeland who had left her husband the Duke of Brabant. Charles VI died; Henry VI was called King of France in the regions held by the English and Duke Philip; and the Dauphin, confined to the south of the Loire, claimed to be King of all France as Charles VII. Michelle of Valois died and Duke Philip married Bonne of Artois; **Jan van Eyck** was painter and 'valet de chambre' to John of Bavaria in the Hague; additions to the Doge's Palace were begun at the instance of Tommaso Mocenigo; and Sultan Murad laid siege unsuccessfully to Constantinople. In 1424 the Duke of Bedford, married to Duke Philip's sister Anne of Burgundy, defeated the French at Verneuil; and Gloucester invaded Hainault on behalf of Jacqueline. The Emperor Manuel II made peace with Sultan Murad and ceded to him a number of towns on the Black Sea; Jan Ziska died; and Prokop the Great became military leader of the Bohemian Taborite Hussites. In 1425 Constantine XI became Eastern Emperor on the death of Manuel; Duke Philip's second wife Bonne of Artois died; the Duke of Gloucester was driven from Hainault; and Jacqueline, abandoned by Gloucester, was captured by Duke Philip; John of Bavaria died; **Hubert van Eyck** (Meester Luberecht or Ubrechts) had an atelier with apprentices in Ghent; and **Jan van Eyck** became 'peintre et valet de chambre' to Duke Philip who installed him in Bruges and afterwards in Lille. In 1426 Duke Philip founded the University of Louvain where the faculty of Theology soon became supreme; **Hubert van Eyck** died; and Duke Philip sent **Jan van Eyck** on a pilgrimage and on journeys to 'certain places of which no mention must be made'. In 1427 the Duke bought the county of Namur and sent **Jan van Eyck** with Sir John de Lannoy, Sir Baldwin de Lannoy and other officials on a secret mission to Barcelona, perhaps in connection with a project of marriage with a Spanish princess. In 1428 the Duke of Bedford laid siege to Orléans; Jacqueline of Hainault's marriage with Gloucester was annulled and she was forced by Duke Philip to surrender her rights in Holland, Zeeland, Friesland and Hainault; **Jan van Eyck** visited Sandwich, Plymouth and Falmouth on a journey to Portugal as member of a diplomatic mission, led by Sir John de Lannoy, to arrange a marriage between John I's daughter Isabella and Duke Philip; Prince Henry the Navigator read 'The Book of Marco Polo' which his brother Peter had procured for him in Venice: and the Turks took Salonica from Venice, massacred the inhabitants, or sold them into slavery, and converted the churches into mosques. In 1429 Jeanne d'Arc relieved the siege of Orléans; Charles VII was crowned at Rheims, with René of Anjou among his military attendants; Giovanni dei Medici died; and Cosimo dei Medici, aged forty, inherited his wealth and power. A portrait of Isabella of Portugal by **Jan van Eyck** was sent from Lisbon to Duke Philip; the Duke's envoys (with **Jan van Eyck** presumably among them) made a pilgrimage to Santiago de Compostella and paid their respects to John II of Castile in Madrid and the Moorish King Mahommed in Granada; the marriage contract was signed in Lisbon; and the envoys returned, with Isabella and her suite, to Flanders.

In 1430 Duke Philip married Isabella and founded the Order of the Golden Fleece as climax of the celebrations; the Duke of Brabant died, and Philip took possession of Limburg, Brabant and Antwerp; a revolt in Liège was vigorously suppressed; and Jeanne d'Arc was captured at Compiègne by the Anglo-Burgundian army. In 1431 **Jan van Eyck** was at work on the *Altarpiece of the Mystic Lamb* (Pls. 9, 12); Jeanne d'Arc was burned at Rouen; Henry VI aged ten was crowned King of France in Paris; René of Anjou, now Count of Provence, tried to take possession of the Duchy of Lorraine and was captured and imprisoned by Duke Philip who supported the claim of the heir-male Antoine de Vaudemont. Pope Martin V died and Eugenius IV succeeded; the Council of Bâle began; and an army led by Frederick Margrave of Brandenburg, with Cardinal Cesarini as Papal Legate, invaded Bohemia and fled before the Hussites led by Prokop. In 1432 the Turks took Semendria in Serbia, invested Belgrade, and plundered Hungary as far as Hermannstadt; and **Jan van Eyck**, reestablished in Bruges, was visited by the Burgomaster and councillors, doubtless to inspect the *Altarpiece of the Mystic Lamb* which was finished in May and destined for the church of S. Bavon (then S. Jean) in Ghent. In 1433 there was a Hussite rising in Hungary; Cosimo dei Medici was exiled from Florence by political intrigues; and Portuguese mariners, encouraged by Prince Henry, sailed down the African coast to Cape Bogador in Rio de Oro. In 1434 Cosimo dei Medici went back to Florence; Eugenius IV, driven from Rome by political insurgents, took ship on the Tiber and was shot at and stoned as he sailed away; and the first consignment of negro slaves was brought to Lisbon.

2

In 1435 the Queen of Naples died and the title was disputed by René of Anjou and Alphonse of Aragon; Duke Philip suppressed a rising in Antwerp; **Rogier van der Weyden (Rogier de la Pasture)** was established in Brussels; and at a fruitless Peace Conference at S. Vaast d'Arras, attended by the Duke of Bedford, Duke Philip, Charles VII and representatives of the Pope and the Council of Bâle, the clerical delegates much admired four pictures painted by **Jacques Daret** for the church of S. Vaast. The Duke of Bedford died; Duke Philip, abandoning the English, joined Charles VII and, assisted by his chancellor, Nicolas Rolin, gained Auxerre, Mâcon, Bar-sur-Seine, Ponthieu and some towns on the Somme by the Treaty of Arras. In 1436 Charles VII entered Paris; the Bohemian Hussites secured the signing of tolerance 'compacts' from the Emperor Sigismund and the Roman church; and whole regions of Hungary were depopulated when Sigismund and the Inquisition destroyed the Hussite movement in that country. In 1437 the Emperor Sigismund died and the Hungarian general John Hunjadi expelled the Turks from Semendria. In 1438 Duke Philip and Duchess Isabella were driven out of Bruges by a popular rising and the Duke annulled a number of the city's privileges in reprisal. Pope Eugenius set up the Council of Ferrara and excommunicated the prelates assembled at the Council of Bâle; the Habsburg Albert of Austria became King of Hungary and Bohemia and German King of the Romans; and René of Anjou took possession of the Kingdom of Naples. In 1440 King Wladislas of Poland was elected King of Hungary; and the Habsburg Frederick of Styria, succeeding Albert of Austria, was elected German King at Frankfort.

In 1441 René of Anjou, driven from Naples by Alphonse of Aragon, went back to France and established his court at Aix-en-Provence; the new Duchess of Gloucester, Eleanor Cobham, was sentenced to public penance and life imprisonment for employing a witch to make and burn a waxen image of the King; and **Jan van Eyck** died and was buried in Bruges, S. Donatien. In 1442 John Hunjadi defeated a large Turkish army near Hermannstadt and won another victory at the Iron Gates. In 1443 Duke Philip bought Luxemburg; Alphonse 'the African' became King of Portugal; Pope Eugenius returned to Rome and launched a crusade against the Turks with John Hunjadi as military head of a confederacy representing Hungary, Poland, Serbia, Wallachia, the Duchy of Burgundy, Venice, Genoa, the Papacy and the Eastern Empire; and Hunjadi broke the Sultan's power in Bosnia, Herzegovina, Serbia, Bulgaria and Albania. In 1444 peace was made with the Sultan and violated by King Wladislas at the instigation of Cardinal Cesarini; and the Turks won the battle of Varna where Wladislas and Cesarini were both killed. In 1445 Portuguese mariners reached Cape Verde in Senegal; Henry VI married Margaret daughter of René of Anjou; Chancellor Rolin founded the Hospices de Beaune; and Frederick, the German king, made a secret treaty with the Pope whereby he pledged the obedience to Rome of the German church and people in return for money and the promise of the Imperial crown. In 1446 Edward Grymeston, Henry VI's ambassador to Duke Philip, had his portrait painted by **Petrus Christus**; and in 1447 **Dirk Bouts** from Haarlem was established in Louvain. In 1448 Duke Philip imposed a heavy salt tax and the city of Ghent declared war against him; the Concordat of Vienna, confirming the treaty between Frederick and Eugenius, was signed by Frederick as Emperor Elect and Pope Nicholas V, who had succeeded Eugenius; and John Hunjadi at the head of a large Hungarian army was heavily defeated by the Turks at Kossovo.

In 1450, the Jubilee year, **Rogerius Gallicus** and **Rogier of Bruges** were in Italy; many pilgrims made the journey to Rome from and through Duke Philip's territories; and Cardinal Torquemada (uncle of the Inquisitor) wrote his 'Summa Ecclesia' with section titles 'De universa Ecclesia', 'De Ecclesia Romana et pontificis primati', 'De universalibus conciliis' and 'De schismaticis et hereticis'. In 1451 Murad II died, and Mahommed II, the new Sultan in Adrianople, made preparations for a large-scale attack on Constantinople. In 1452 Frederick of Germany was crowned Emperor as Frederick III by Pope Nicholas. In 1453 the Turks captured Constantinople after a siege of fifty-three days in which Constantine XI, the last Eastern Emperor was killed; the Hundred Years' War ended with only Calais still in English hands; the Ghent rebels against Duke Philip were finally defeated at Gavre on the Scheldt; and Duke Philip annulled all the Gantois privileges, took a huge indemnity and made the leading citizens parade before him with halters round their necks and publicly beg for his pardon. In 1454 Henry IV became King of Castile; and Duke Philip invited European notables to a tremendous festival at Lille where he swore upon a pheasant to challenge the Sultan to single combat and lead a new crusade against the infidels—a vow which in fact was never fulfilled. In 1455 Calixtus III became Pope on the death of Nicholas V; the War of the Roses began with the battle of S. Albans; and Mahommed II prepared to retake Belgrade. In 1456 John Hunjadi destroyed a Turkish fleet, forced the Sultan to raise the siege of Belgrade, and died of the plague; and the Dauphin Louis, having quarrelled with his father, took refuge at the Court of Burgundy.

In 1458 Alphonse V died in Naples; John II became King of Aragon; Aeneas Silvius Piccolomini became Pope as Pius II; Prince Henry the Navigator sent a mission to convert the negroes of Gambia; and Duke Philip made a Pageant Entry into Ghent where the local Chamber of Rhetoric mounted a set piece titled *The Choir of the Blessed in the sacrifice of Paschal Lamb* which was based on the **van Eycks'** *Altarpiece of the Mystic Lamb* (Pls. 9, 12) and arranged on a three-tier stage some fifty feet high and twenty-eight feet wide.

In 1461 Edward IV became King of England; Louis XI became King of France; Duke Philip agreed to restore to France the towns on the Somme ceded by the Treaty of Arras in return for a payment envisaged in the treaty; and Duke Philip's son Charles, Count of Charolais, incensed at the concession, began to work for a new war with France. In 1462 Duke Philip being ill and ordered by his doctors to shave his head, five hundred of his nobles were commanded or requested by him to follow his example, and shaven heads were in fashion at his court till twelve months later when extra long hair was worn as a reaction. In 1464 Paul II became Pope; Cosimo dei Medici died and Piero dei Medici (Piero the Gouty) succeeded him in Florence; **Dirk Bouts** began his *Last Supper* (Pl. 58); and **Rogier van der Weyden** died. In 1465 **Hans Memlinc** was registered as a citizen in Bruges; Duke Philip, now sixty-nine, summoned deputies from all the Netherlands to a States General in Brussels and resigned the administration of all his domains to Charles, Count of Charolais; and Count Charles, who at once formed the League of the Public Weal (Ligue du bien public) against Louis XI, won the battle of Montlhéry and earned his sobriquet of Charles the Bold (Charles le téméraire) for his reckless military courage. In 1466 Louis XI restored the Somme towns by the Treaty of Conflans signed with Count Charles the Bold; Dinant and Liège revolted; and Count Charles made a truce with the Liégeois but drowned eight hundred of the Dinant rebels and savagely sacked the town. In 1467 Liège again revolted, Count Charles defeated the insurgents at S. Trond, entered the city and deprived it of many privileges as reprisal; Edward IV allied himself with Burgundy despite opposition from the Earl of Warwick; Duke Philip died; and Charles the Bold inherited his dominions.

As can be seen from the foregoing, Duke Philip had extended his domains till he ruled eventually over vast tracts of country from Holland to the Alps, interrupted only by Alsace and Lorraine. His territories included many prosperous manufacturing and trading centres and municipalities with long-established privileges and traditions of selfgovernment; and the revolts mentioned were protests against his fixed resolve to make all the towns obedient to his central government.

As a Valois, and greatgrandson of John the Good of France, the Duke spoke French as his native language; and the culture of his court was French. In the Walloon provinces, and Burgundy, French was exclusively spoken by all classes; but Dutch and Flemish were permitted in the provinces which normally spoke those languages and Flemish-Dutch was used there in the law courts, in official proclamations and so forth; and the country as a whole was thus bilingual.

The churchmen and the nobles had many privileges including exemptions from taxation. But the Duke took heavy taxes from the trading communities for his wars and pleasures and soon became notorious as one of the richest men in Europe. He loved pomp, parade and luxury; his apartments in Bruges, Lille and Brussels were hung with tapestries; his nobles were magnificently dressed; and at all his elaborate entertainments the most costly objects were lavishly displayed. He was also a genuine lover of the arts; he had his court musicians and court poets, he collected illuminated and other manuscripts, and he patronized both French and Flemish-speaking artists.

The organization of the painters followed the French pattern. There were firstly the painters attached, on salaries, as 'peintres et valets de chambre' to the households of rich nobles and prelates and of the Duke himself; these were expected to turn their hand on occasion to any kind of designing (documents show that they often painted banners and coloured statues by their sculptor confrères); and they were sometimes sent to foreign countries to draw portraits and also probably as secret agents to report on and make drawings of forts and waterways and so forth. Other painters were salaried by the municipalities as official painters to the several towns, and these and others were also employed by the local social and literary clubs, known as Chambers of Rhetoric, for the designing of civic ceremonies and on street decorations and the arrangement of tableaux vivants when the Duke or some foreign notable made a Pageant Entry.[1]

In ecclesiastical circles there were artist-monks and artist-nuns who illustrated manuscripts and painted devotional pictures for their monasteries and convents; and painters employed by the Cathedral Chapters or parish churches on decorative work. Altarpieces and religious paintings were usually commissioned by rich nobles or prelates or men of affairs who gave the pictures to the churches and were allowed by the theologians to have their own portraits as donors inserted in the pictures; but they were also sometimes commissioned by the occupational Guilds and the religious Fraternities who placed the pictures on their private altars in the churches.

The Court painters, the painters in the service of nobles and prelates, and the municipal painters, had recognized status as such. The rest had status as artist artisans within the appropriate craft Guilds established in the major towns at various dates in this period. Under the Guild régime the beginner was apprenticed to an experienced painter and worked under him till he qualified for the title of 'Master' in the Guild which gave him the right to

[1] New rulers in the Netherlands habitually made Pageant Entries into the most important towns and swore observance of the charter known as 'La Joyeuse Entrée' which had laid down the local privileges of Brabant in 1354 and given the municipalities the right to be consulted about wars and taxes (and was imitated by similar charters in other places). But the term 'Pageant Entry', as used throughout this book, is neither a translation of 'Joyeuse Entrée', nor restricted to this particular ceremony; it covers all the ceremonial entries with processions, pageants and so on, which were a feature of Flemish life at all periods.

practise and sell his work as an independent artist; and by the end of the period the majority of the painters, except the Duke's own painters, had status in that way. The licensed
'Master' could paint anything he liked and sell to anyone, and thus the moneyed classes—the
nobles and churchmen, the rich business men of Flanders and the representatives of the
many foreign firms (English, Italian, Portuguese, Spanish) established in Bruges and elsewhere, and the not-so-rich lawyers, doctors and civil servants, as well as the ladies of all
these classes, could take their choice of the works available from many artists or give commissions in their personal taste. The Guilds kept in touch with their 'Masters', elected them
'Dean' for a year when they wished to honour them, saw to it that painters from other regions did not impinge upon their territory, and arbitrated in disputes about delays or payments. They also saw to it that the materials used by the artists were good and permanent
—a necessary precaution as we know from a letter written by René of Anjou: 'A maître
Jeannot, le Flamand. Maître Jeannot, veuillez m'envoyer sans délai deux bons com-
pagnons peintres, au lieu des deux que vous m'avez envoyés, qui ne sont pas assez habiles
pour faire ce que je voulais et m'ont tout gâté. Sur le vieux tableau, ils n'ont pas bien gratté
l'ancienne peinture avant de repeindre, et pour le tableau de la Joute, ils n'ont pas choisi un
panneau bien sec, ou n'ont pas pris soin de le faire sécher, en sorte qu'il est déjà fendu. Et
pourtant le soleil ne manque pas dans ces contrées. Et on devra employer de meilleur bois.
C'est ce qui me détermine à les renvoyer, non pour les mettre dans une position fâcheuse
mais pour qu'ils apprennent mieux l'art de peindre. Et hâtez-vous de m'adresser deux
bons artistes, car j'en ai grand besoin, et ne mettez pas de négligence dans cette affaire.'

Duke Philip's Court painters ('peintres et valets de chambre') included **Hugues de
Boulogne, Jan van Eyck, Jehan de Boulogne, Pierre Coustain** and **Daniel Daret, Jehan
Dreux, Jehan Hennecart** and **Willem Vrelant.** Of these, **Hugues de Boulogne,** who died in
1449, had held the office under the Duke's father and grandfather; he was a pupil in his
youth of **Melchior Broederlam** of Ypres (designer of ceremonial costumes and ceramics and
painter of extant wings covering a sculptured altarpiece for Philip the Bold's Chartreuse de
Champmol at Dijon); since 1417 he had been Keeper of Château Hesdin where he is recorded as 'peintre et gouverneur de l'orloge, gayoles, verrières et engins d'esbatement'; in
1432 he painted arms for the Chapter of the Golden Fleece; and in 1437 he worked on the
decorations for one of Duke Philip's banquets to foreign potentates which contained as a
feature 'ung paon tout vif sur une trépasse et entouraoit dix lions dorez d'or qui tenoient
chascun une bannière armoyée des armes de tous les pais de mondit seigneur . . .'. **Jan van
Eyck** held the office from 1425 till 1441; the Duke treated him as a favourite and confidential
servant, sent him on the missions mentioned, stood godfather to one of his children, visited
his studio, and scolded the accountants when his salary was late. But oddly enough we
know next to nothing of the work done by **Jan van Eyck** on the Duke's instructions; he
doubtless painted one or more portraits of the Duke but none are known to survive or
seem to be mentioned in discovered records; and, indeed, in the sixteen years of this service
only one picture ordered from him by the Duke is named in such records—the portrait of
the Duke's third wife *Isabella of Portugal* painted in Portugal as noted in 1429. It is clear
that the Duke allowed him to paint for other employers; and most of the surviving pictures
known to be his work were outside commissions like the completion of the Ghent *Altarpiece
of the Mystic Lamb* (Pls. 9, 12) for Jodoc Vyt, a rich citizen and later Burgomaster of Ghent,
the *Van der Paele altarpiece* (Pl. 19) ordered by Georges van der Paele, canon of Bruges, S.
Donatien, and the portrait group *The marriage of Giovanni Arnolfini* (Pl. 18A) commissioned
by a silk merchant from Lucca established in Bruges; or else they were done for his own

pleasure like the *Margaret, wife of the painter* (Pl. 20) and the *Portrait of a young man* (*Timotheos*) (Pl. 10) which, the inscription suggests, was a present to a friend. **Jehan de Boulogne** became the Duke's painter on the death of his father **Hugues de Boulogne** in 1449 and he painted arms for the Chapter of the Golden Fleece in 1451. **Pierre Coustain** succeeded **Hugues de Boulogne** as 'peintre des princes' at Château Hesdin, continued the surveillance there of contraptions used in the Ducal entertainments, and painted a *Crucifixion* and a *Virgin and Child* placed in 1467 on the catafalque of the Duke in Brussels; **Daniel Daret,** who also became the Duke's painter in 1449, had been a pupil of his half-brother **Jacques Daret; Jehan Dreux** (or **de Rieue**) and **Jehan Hennecart** held the rank among the Duke's illuminators of fine books; and **Willem Vrelant** of Utrecht, a founder member of the Bruges Guild of S. John (Scribes, illuminators and booksellers) in 1454, provided sixty miniatures for a manuscript 'Chroniques de Hainault'.

Other artists patronized by the Duke, though not apparently Court painters, included **Ryck Broederlam,** who was charged by him with the direction of a ceramic factory, and **Jacques Daret** who painted the pictures for S. Vaast d'Arras already mentioned, made tapestry cartoons and book illustrations, and received exceptionally high wages when he was called to Lille, with numerous other artists, to contribute to the sumptuous Banquet of the Pheasant celebrations where tapestries depicting the 'Labours of Hercules' were hung round the walls, each course was ushered in by appropriate music, Olivier de la Marche recited his own verses, and *The Adventures of Jason* and *The Church assisted by Duke Philip in the fight against the Saracens* were among the themes of the richly costumed masques and interludes. **Rogier van der Weyden** though never, it seems, a Court painter, may nevertheless have worked for the Duke, and he is known to have directed the colouring of some sculpture which the Duke ordered in 1439 for a church in Brussels. **Hans Memlinc** is also not recorded as Court painter though a portrait *Isabella of Portugal* dated 1450 was listed as his work (possibly in error) in a Venetian catalogue before 1521.

The Duke's highest officers included several whose donations to churches are recorded. Thus his Chancellor Nicolas Rolin, whose son became Bishop of Autun, gave the Collegiate church there a famous picture, now in the Louvre, *The Virgin and Child with Chancellor Rolin as adorant donor* by an unrecorded artist (presumed by some to be **Jan van Eyck**); and as founder, with his second wife, of the Hospices de Beaune, he gave to the hospital chapel a polyptych *The Last Judgement with portraits of the donors on the wings* by an unrecorded artist here conventionally named the **Beaune Last Judgement Painter** (Pls. 34, 42, 136–139); and Peeter Bladelin, the Duke's Treasurer, gave the church in the village of Middelburg (near Bruges) a triptych with a central panel *The Nativity with portrait of the donor as adorant* (now in the Berlin Kaiser Friedrich Museum) by an unrecorded artist (presumed by some to be **Rogier van der Weyden**). Donations by rich prelates included the *Van der Paele altarpiece* (Pl. 19) by **Jan van Eyck** for Bruges, S. Donatien already referred to. The four pictures mentioned as painted by **Jacques Daret** for the church at S. Vaast d'Arras, were given to the church there by Jean du Clerq, Abbot of S. Vaast, in 1434. Henri de Werl, theologian and delegate at the Council of Bâle, who was in Tournai in 1435, ordered a triptych in 1438 from the unrecorded artist here conventionally named the **Madrid Werl Wings Painter** (Pls. 41, 44); and eleven pictures of unknown subjects were commissioned from **Rogier van der Weyden** by the Abbot of S. Aubert, Cambrai, in 1455.

Some of the municipal appointments and commissions are also known. **Rogier van der Weyden** was painter to the town of Brussels by 1436; and **Vrancke van der Stoct** succeeded him in 1464. **Hubert Stuerbout** was painter to the town of Louvain by 1454; **Ryck Broederlam** was town painter in Ypres; and **Simon Jansz** worked for the Town Hall in Leyden. **Hubert van Eyck** was employed by the magistrates of Ghent in 1425; **Jan Martins** and **Willem van Axpoele** worked there for the Scepenenhuus (Sheriff's Hall); and **Nabor Martins** and **Achille van den Bossche** also had municipal employment there.

We also have records of some of the commissions given by occupational Guilds and religious Fraternities. The Archers' Guild of Louvain ordered the *Descent from the Cross* (Pl. 46) from **Rogier van der Weyden** for their chapel in Notre Dame hors des Murs; the Louvain Confraternity of the Holy Sacrament commissioned the *Last Supper* polyptych (Pls. 59, 61) by **Dirk Bouts** for their chapel in S. Pierre; and the Antwerp Goldsmiths' Guild commissioned from **Petrus Christus** a S. *Eligius in his shop* in 1449.

Extant records and early chroniclers provide us with these names and also with the names of other painters active in Duke Philip's domains. Thus **M. van Ghestele** and **J. van Coudenberghe** worked together in Courtrai in 1430. In Antwerp, less important at this time than Bruges, Ghent and Ypres, **Jan Snellaert, Godefroid of Antwerp, Jean Thomas, Jacques Thonys, Henri Bastyn, Adrien Gerop, Lucas Adriaenssen, Jean Casyn Vinckaert** and **Guillaume Caddeman** were among the painters who founded the Guild of S. Luke there in 1453. The Bruges painters included **Jan van Eyck, Petrus Christus, Jehan Dreux, Rogier of Bruges** and **Hans Memlinc.** Of those in Tournai we have records of **Robert Campin, Rogelet van der Weyden, Jacques Daret** and **Daniel Daret.** In Brussels we know of **Rogier of Brussels, Rogier van der Weyden, Vrancke van der Stoct** and **Pierre Coustain**; in Malines of **Jean van Battel the elder, Gauthier van Battel** and **Baudoin van Battel**; in Ypres of **Ryck Broederlam** and **Pierquin Bernart**; and in Louvain of **Rogier of Louvain, Dirk Bouts** and **Hubert Stuerbout.** We also know of **Rogerius Gallicus** though no particular town in the Netherlands is mentioned in connection with his name. From records in Ghent where some of the archival entries are said (I think incredibly) to have suffered additions due to local patriotism, we know of **Hubert van Eyck, Margaret van Eyck, Jan Martins, Nabor Martins, Willem van Axpoele, Achille van den Bossche, Baldwin van Wytevelde, Daniel de Rycke, Gerard van der Meire, Joos van Wassenhove,** and **Hugo van der Goes.** In the northern provinces the painters included **Albert van Ouwater** and **Dirk Bouts** in Haarlem and **Symon Jansz** in Leyden.

What is known of these painters is, in most cases, no more than a few bald facts and even these are sometimes mutually conflicting. But occasionally enough has been discovered to suggest a human being or even a personality. The Antwerp painters are merely names to us, though one or two facts regarding **Jan Snellaert's** associations with the Guild survive and **Lucas Adriaenssen** is known to have been employed in the Cathedral in 1467. Of the Bruges men we know the facts already mentioned and some other details of **Jan van Eyck's** career but nothing shedding light upon him as a man. **Petrus Christus** was Master in the Guild in 1444 and a member from 1462 of the Fraternity of Our Lady of the Dry Tree (to which both Giovanni Arnolfini and his wife belonged); he was employed by the Comte d'Estampes and by religious Fraternities; and he was still alive in 1467. **Jehan Dreux** was also still living in Bruges at that date. **Rogier of Bruges**, a pupil of **Jan van Eyck**, painted an *Adam and Eve* and a *Lamentation* for Duke Leonello d'Este before 1449, was paid in Ferrara in 1450 for these (or other) pictures painted for the Duke and is said by Vasari (1550) to have had one 'Hausse' (presumed by some **Hans Memlinc**) as his pupil. **Hans Memlinc** described by Guicciardini (1567) and Vasari (1568) as a pupil of **Rogier van der Weyden,** was born at Seligenstadt (near Frankfort and not far from Mömling) at a date unknown and was a citizen of Bruges, as noted, by 1465.

Of the Tournai men **Robert Campin** comes to life more sharply as a personality than any other painter of the period; born at a place unknown he was an established artist in Tournai by 1410 when he received the freedom of the city, and he held offices in the Guild between 1423 and 1428; he had **Jacques Daret** as a member of his household from 1418, and between 1427 and 1432 both **Jacques Daret** and **Rogelet van der Weyden** were among his pupils or assistants; in 1429 he was fined for some unknown offence and sentenced to make a pilgrimage to S. Gilles-en-Provence and debarred from civic office; in 1432 he was banished for a year 'pour la vie ordurière et dissolue qu'il menait depuis longtemps, lui, homme marié, avec Laurence Polette' but the sentence was commuted to a fine at the instance of Jacqueline of Hainault (the ex-Duchess of Brabant and ex-Duchess of Gloucester); he was still at work in 1438; and he died in Tournai in 1444. **Jacques Daret** was Master in the Tournai Guild in 1432, worked in Arras from 1433 till 1435 and again in 1441 and 1452, was in Lille in 1454, and was still active in 1467 when he designed decorations for the Chapter of the Golden Fleece in Bruges; **Rogelet van der Weyden** was possibly identical with the **Rogier de la Pasture (Rogier van der Weyden)** who was Master in the Tournai Guild in 1432 and also with the **Rogier le Peintre** who received three commissions in Tournai in 1436 and 1437. **Daniel Daret,** already mentioned as pupil of his half-brother **Jacques Daret** and as among Duke Philip's Court painters from 1449, had acquired the rank of Master in the Tournai Guild in 1441 and he may have lived through the period, though the date of his death is not known. Of the Brussels painters **Rogier of Brussels** is recorded as painter of a *Self-portrait* (bust length) dated 1462, owned by a Venetian collector in 1531. **Rogier van der Weyden** (perhaps identical with **Rogier of Brussels** and **Rogier of Louvain**) was born at Tournai; by 1427 he was married to a Brussels girl and had a son; Brussels was his headquarters from 1435; he was official painter to the city, as noted, from 1436 and provided the 'Golden Chamber' of the Town Hall with four didactic 'Justice' subjects: *Trajan dispensing Justice to the widow, Pope Gregory obtaining the salvation of Trajan, Archamaud de Bourbon (Herkenbald) ill in bed and beheading his nephew for violating a girl,* and *The miracle of the Host that flew to the tongue of Archamaud from the hands of the Bishop who had refused him the Sacrament*—pictures which remained in position till destroyed by Marshal Villeroi's bombardment in 1695; in 1445 the Miraflores Charterhouse in Burgos received from King John of Castile a triptych, *Nativity, Descent from the Cross* and *Christ appearing to his Mother* described in their archives as by 'Master Roget, great and famous Flemish painter' which may refer to him; in 1450 he may have visited Italy (if the records of **Rogier of Bruges** and **Rogerius Gallicus,** as some suppose, refer to him); in 1459 his wife and workmen with cart and three horses delivered eleven pictures ordered by the Abbot of S. Aubert, Cambrai four years earlier; in 1460 at the request of Bianca Sforza, Duchess of Milan, he accepted an Italian, Zanetto Bugatti, as his pupil in Brussels and three years later he was thanked by the Duchess in a letter addressed to 'Maestro Rugerio de Tornay pictori in Burseles'; when he died in 1464 he was buried in Brussels, S. Gudule, and the Guild of S. Luke in Tournai placed candles on their altar in memory of 'Master Rogier de la Pasture born in Tournai but resident in Brussels'. **Vrancke van der Stoct,** already mentioned as his successor in the office of painter to the city of Brussels, was a Town Councillor in 1465 and lived beyond the end of the period; and **Pierre Coustain** was also active after 1467. **Rogier of Louvain** is referred to in the sixteenth century as 'Magister civis et pictor Lovaniensis' and as author of an altarpiece donated to S. Pierre in 1443 by W. Edelheer containing a version of *The Descent from the Cross* (Pl. 46) by **Rogier van der Weyden. Dirk Bouts** (Pls. 58, 61, 67, 69), born in Haarlem, was in Louvain and married to a rich woman (Catherina metten gelde) by 1447, and worked there through the period. **Hubert Stuerbout** was still town painter in

Louvain in 1467; in 1454 he designed two hundred and fifty bas-reliefs of religious subjects for the Town Hall and also decorations for various pageants including in 1463 an Omme-ganck procession where tableaux vivants on decorated cars toured the main streets and squares as in the Ommeganck (Pl. 513A) which toured the main streets of Brussels two centuries later. **Ryck Broederlam,** town painter in Ypres, provided decorative paintings for various public buildings and designed new clothes for the town officials, crossbowmen, archers and so forth in the month of July each year; in the fourteen-fifties he worked on windows for the Halles and in 1460 he restored a series of portraits of the Counts and Countesses of Flanders in the Cloth Hall and possibly added portraits of the reigning Duke and Duchess. Of the Malines painters **Jean van Battel the elder** seems to have been official painter to the city; in 1434 and 1437 he designed Ommeganck processions; in 1437 he painted a *S. Veronica with two angels* for the Malines Town Hall; and he probably died before 1467. His son **Gauthier (Wouter) van Battel** was also a designer of Ommeganck pro-cessions, worked for the Cathedral of S. Rombout and was active until after the period closed; **Baudoin van Battel,** a younger man, began his career as designer of an Ommeganck in 1465.

Of the Ghent men **Hubert van Eyck** remains a shadowy figure, despite most diligent searches; as 'Meester Luberecht' he was paid for two sketches by the Ghent magistrates in 1425; in the same year the apprentices of 'Ubrechts' were paid gratuities by the Council; in 1426 tax was paid in Ghent on his estate as 'Lubrecht van Heyke deceased'; and his tombstone bore the inscription:

> Hubrecht van Eyck was ick ghenant
> Nu spyse der wormen, voormals bekant
> In schilderye zeer hooge geeert.

For the rest we know that he began the *Altarpiece of the Mystic Lamb* (Pls. 9, 12) which was finished by his younger brother **Jan van Eyck** as an inscription on the picture records both facts. Sixteenth-century writers, who might easily have known the **van Eycks'** grand-children, inform us that **Margaret van Eyck** was a sister of **Hubert** and **Jan,** that she re-mained a spinster, devoted herself to painting, and lived with and was buried beside **Hubert.** **Jan Martins** was Master in the Ghent Guild in 1420 and Dean in 1449; with the help of **Willen van Axpoele** he painted about thirty life-size portraits of Counts and Countesses of Flanders to replace a faded series in the Scepenenhuus; he may be identical with the **Joao Martins** who worked for Lisbon Cathedral in 1441; and he probably died before 1467. We know that **Nabor Martins** and **Achille van den Bossche** also both received, as noted, muni-cipal commissions, that **Nabor Martins** was Master in the Guild in 1435, worked for churches in and near Ghent from 1443 to 1453, was fined for delay in completing pictures for Audenarde S. Walpurga in 1446, and died in Ghent in 1454. **Baldwin van Wytevelde** painted a *Temptation of S. Anthony* for Ghent S. Bavon in 1439, provided an altarpiece for Nieuwenbossche Abbey in Ghent at a date unrecorded and may have died before 1467. **Daniel de Rycke,** Ghent Master in 1440 and Dean in 1460, was still active in the following period; **Gerard van der Meire,** a younger man who was Ghent Master in 1452 and citizen of Brussels in 1467, is known to have painted a *Lucretia* at some stage in a long career that lasted beyond the end of the century. **Joos van Wassenhove,** Master in the Antwerp Guild in 1460, seems to have settled in Ghent where he was Master in 1464. **Hugo van der Goes,** we are told by Van Mander (1604), was a pupil of **Jan van Eyck** (i.e. before 1441); in 1467, sponsored by **Joos van Wassenhove,** he was Master in Ghent; in the same year with **Joos**

van Wassenhove, he worked on the decoration of S. Bavon (then S. Jean) for the reception of the Cardinal Legate of Pope Paul II, and he lived beyond the end of the period.

Of the painters in the Northern provinces **Albert van Ouwater** was a leading figure in Haarlem probably before 1440; in 1467 he buried there a daughter (age unspecified); he is known to have painted a picture for Haarlem Groote Kerk which was placed on the Roman altar (so-called because it was donated by pilgrims returned from Rome) and contained figures of S. Peter and S. Paul and a landscape with pilgrims walking, resting, eating and drinking; he also painted a *Resurrection of Lazarus* where (we are told by Van Mander (1604)) the miracle was depicted in a church with spectators looking through a choir screen (as in the picture reproduced here by the **Exhumation of S. Hubert Master** (Pl. 54)); and he seems to have still been active in the following decade. **Dirk Bouts** probably worked in his native Haarlem till he moved to Louvain in the middle forties. Of **Symon Jansz** we know only that he provided two portraits of *Duke Philip* and *Charles, Count of Charolais* for the Town Hall in Leyden in 1464.

These names represent, of course, but a fraction of the artists active in the seventeen provinces in these forty-eight years; and our knowledge of the commissions given them and the pictures they painted on their own initiative is also fragmentary. But together they form the basis for a concept of numerous painters at work on a varied production which was sold to various sections of the public. Some merchants, perhaps, bought genre subjects by men like **Petrus Christus** whose picture called *S. Eligius in his shop* (when completed with a halo for the Antwerp Goldsmiths' Guild), shows a goldsmith selling a ring to a young man and his betrothed; the intellectuals in the universities, the lawyers, writers, musicians, artists, architects, eccentric or reforming churchmen and so on, probably bought works of special sensibility or in new techniques or with new ideas by original, eccentric or satirical artists (the ancestors of **Hieronymus Bosch** and **Pieter Bruegel the elder**); there were ladies, I fancy, who bought landscapes and flowerpieces by assistants in the **van Eycks'** atelier where the flowered landscape in the *Altarpiece of the Mystic Lamb* (Pl. 23) was painted; and young Burgundian nobles may have bought pictures like *A woman sweating in a bath, spied on by two laughing youths, a dog beside the woman* by **Rogerius Gallicus**, *A woman bathing with attendant, a mirror on the wall* by **Jan van Eyck** (both owned by Italian nobles in the fifteenth century), and the *Lucretia* already mentioned by **Gerard van der Meire**.

But we know lamentably little, in fact, of the actual pictures painted by the artists whose names are recorded, as less than twenty-five pictures known to have been painted in Duke Philip's reign by particular artists are known to be extant. We have the *Altarpiece of the Mystic Lamb* (Pls. 9, 12) inscribed as the work of **Hubert van Eyck** and **Jan van Eyck** and nine pictures signed by **Jan van Eyck** who sometimes added to his signature a mock-humble motto 'Als ikh kan' (standing for a Flemish proverb 'As I can, not as I would'). We have six signed pictures by **Petrus Christus,** one more with what may be his signature incorporated in an inscription on the background, and one said to have had at one time 'Opus Petri Christophori' on the frame. There are no signed pictures by **Rogier van der Weyden,** but we have one documented work by him the *Descent from the Cross* (Pl. 46) sent to Spain from the Archers' Guild altar in Louvain, Notre Dame hor des Murs, recorded in the Escorial in 1574 and now in the Prado with the Archers' Guild stamp still on it, and one semi-documented pictures preserved in the Escorial since 1574. There are no extant pictures known to be by **Robert Campin.** There is one documented picture by **Jacques Daret,** his *Visitation with Abbot Jean du Clercq of S. Vaast as donor.* No pictures known to have been painted by **Hans Memlinc** or **Hugo van der Goes** before 1467 are known to be extant. Of the works

11

known to have been painted by **Dirk Bouts** in this period we have only *The Winding out of the entrails of S. Erasmus* inscribed 'Opus Theodorici Bouts Anno 1448' (which is too revolting to be reproduced here) and the *Last Supper* altarpiece (Pls. 58, 61) begun in 1464, finished by 1468 and still in Louvain, S. Pierre for which it was painted. There is one picture, a *Raising of Lazarus*, semi-documented to **Albert van Ouwater** in the sense that it corresponds closely to Van Mander's description mentioned above; but whether it was painted in this period or the next is not known.

All other extant pictures known or presumed to have been painted in this period are of unrecorded authorship; and when a name appears on the frame in a museum it is the result of a 'style-ascription', i.e. a guess. As such guesses are in their nature temporary, since each generation of style-ascribers rejects a large number of the preceding guesses, they bring much confusion to the study of the subject. In this inquiry I therefore leave all 'style ascriptions' on one side (without suggesting that they are wrong or right); and I treat all pictures of unrecorded authorship quite simply as pictures of which the authors are not known.[1]

As explained in the 'Note to the General Reader' at the beginning of this volume, when I reproduce a picture of unrecorded authorship I invent a conventional name for the unknown artist with 'Painter' as the last word and the place of the museum as the first. When a conventional name for an unrecorded artist is already in current use I use that name (the So-and-so Master) when referring to the particular picture for which the name was coined (while treating all pictures ascribed on style grounds to that 'Master' as works of unknown authorship).

My plates for the period include as pictures of known authorship the *Altarpiece of the Mystic Lamb*, with some details, by the **van Eyck** brothers (Pls. 9, 11, 12, 13, 14, 17, 23), seven works by **Jan van Eyck** (Pls. 10, 18, 18A, 19, 20, 21, 25), two by **Petrus Christus** (Pls. 27, 31), the *Descent from the Cross* by **Rogier van der Weyden** (Pl. 46) and two panels of the *Last Supper* altarpiece by **Dirk Bouts** (Pls. 58, 61). As pictures of unrecorded authorship I reproduce the works for which the conventional names **Flémalle Master** (Pls. 35, 36, 37), the **Redemption Master** (Pls. 51, 52, 53) and the **Exhumation of S. Hubert Master** (Pl. 54) were originally invented. Other pictures of unrecorded authorship reproduced here are referred to in my text as by the **London Virgin with a Firescreen Painter** (Frontispiece and Pl. 37), the **New York Crucifixion and Last Judgement Painter** (Pls. 1-8, 16, 96, 159, 160), the **Washington Annunciation in a Church Painter** (Pl. 15), the **Madrid Fountain of Grace Painter** (Pl. 22), the **New York Virgin in a Tabernacle Painter** (Pl. 24), the **New York Annunciation in a Porch Painter** (Pl. 26), the **Minneapolis Adoration Painter** (Pls. 28, 29, 75), the **Washington Nativity in a Sculptured Porch Painter** (Pl. 30), the **London Christ Appearing to His Mother Painter** (Pl. 32), the **New York Christ Appearing to His Mother Painter** (Pls. 33, 47),

---

[1] The temporary nature of 'style ascriptions' is shown by the history of style criticism in respect to **Gerard van der Meire** whose name appeared formerly in many museum catalogues; the pictures reproduced here by the **Exhumation of S. Hubert Master** (Pl. 54), the **Hoogstraeten Master** (Pls. 197, 198), the **The London Passion Scenes Painter** (Pl. 222) and **Aelbrecht Bouts** (Pls. 251, 252, 253) are among those formerly presumed by some his work; it is now, however, no longer the fashion to ascribe pictures to him and the Thieme-Becker Lexikon (1930) writes: 'Kein beglaubigtes Werk nachweisbar. Zuschreibungen unbegründet'. Other examples of such changes include **Margaret van Eyck** and **Robert Campin** to both of whom some pictures were formerly ascribed in museum catalogues; the **Danzig Last Judgement Master** who has been identified on style grounds as the **van Eycks**, **Jan van Eyck** alone, **Rogier van der Weyden**, **Albert van Ouwater** and **Hans Memlinc** by various ascribers; and the **Glasgow Saint and Donor Painter** (Pl. 154) similarly identified as **Memlinc**, **Hugo van der Goes**, **Jan Gossaert**, the French painter Jean Fouquet and the presumed French painter known as the Moulins Master.

the **London Woman in a Wimple Painter** (Pl. 40), the **London Magdalene Reading Painter** (Pl. 43), the **Madrid Werl Wings Painter** (Pls. 41, 44), the **Beaune Last Judgement Painter** (Pls. 34, 42, 136-9), the **Antwerp Philippe de Croy Painter** (Pl. 45), the **Boston S. Luke Painter** (Pls. 48, 49), the **New York d'Este Painter** (Pl. 50), the **Detroit S. Jerome Painter** (Pl. 55), the **London Young Woman in White Head Dress Painter** (Pl. 57), the **London Young Man in High Cap Painter** (Pl. 59) and the **New York Man in High Cap Painter** (Pl. 60).[1]

Despite five centuries of strife and destruction in the Netherlands we still have several hundred pictures known or presumed to have been painted in Duke Philip's time. But these extant works give a false idea of the character of the production as a whole because they consist, almost without exception, of portraits and religious subjects. These types of pictures have survived, while others have perished, because they belonged to individuals rich and powerful enough to transmit their property through several generations or because they were physically protected by public buildings like churches or reverently preserved in monasteries or convents. The pictures bought by the average business and professional men and their ladies and even by the minor nobles had no such protection from bricks and mortar; for the fortunes of these classes were unstable and their pictures, like their other property, were dispersed, neglected or destroyed if misfortune came through wars or bad trading or if the owners were 'liquidated' in some persecuting 'purge'. And these lost pictures, I feel certain, were as varied as the Flemish pictures of later ages, if not indeed as varied as the pictures of our day. For there have always been everywhere artists with all kinds of talent. Artists everywhere have always drawn and painted their wives and mistresses and children, they have always drawn and painted buildings, landscapes, animals and flowers, indoor and outdoor genre, erotic pieces, satires and caricatures (someone in Russia, as I write these words, is drawing a caricature of a Soviet leader and someone in Rome is drawing a cartoon on recent pronouncements by the Pope). Artists everywhere have always done much work on their own initiative as well as commissioned tasks; they have always set down their visual impressions and their imaginative ideas without waiting for commissions and sometimes they have used such drawings or paintings later when commissions came along. The social conditions of each time and place encourage some aspects of these independent creative activities and damp down or stamp out others; but *some* pictures of all these kinds have surely, everywhere, been always painted.

We have records of collaboration by some artists in this period; and we can, I think, be certain that collaboration took place between two or more artists in many of the more elaborate pictures. In the later periods such collaboration was notoriously frequent; surviving contracts show that some painters in the sixteenth century habitually deputed the execution of all but the heads and naked figures in their elaborate compositions and we know that **Frans Floris** in that century had a workshop with numerous assistants; we also know that in the seventeenth century **Rubens** and some of his followers and **Jan Brueghel the younger** had workshops where pupils and assistants were employed on special functions suited to their talents; and there was much collaboration also in the eighteenth century. In Duke Philip's time, when all established Masters had advanced pupils and assistants as well as apprentices in their workshops, it seems to me inevitable that they soon discovered the particular gifts and inclinations of their juniors and that, like the later artists, they left to them such parts of the picture as came within their specialist powers. In the later periods

[1] These conventional names are included in my Dictionary (pp. 481 to 694 in this Volume); and the authorship presumed for each picture in the museum catalogue at the time of writing is there indicated.

13

we know the names of such specialists in many fields of painting. But in Duke Philip's time (and throughout the fifteenth century) the specialists seem to have worked for the most part as anonymous auxiliary artists in the Master's studio where, for elaborate pictures, one was probably called on for the landscape or the architecture, another for the jewels and vestments, tiles and carpets, another for flowers and miscellaneous still-life and yet others for animals and for the minor figures including the genre episodes. The best of these auxiliary artists probably set up later on their own as independent specialists who were called in by various artists to fulfil their particular function or had the unfinished pictures sent to their own workshops for that purpose—just as in the eighteenth century clothes and backgrounds were added by London drapery experts to 'face paintings' sent them from all parts of the country; and thus perhaps it happened that the rug in the *Virgin and Child with SS. Jerome and Francis* (Pl. 27) by **Petrus Christus** appears to have been used again for another picture of the period known as the *Lucca altarpiece* by an unrecorded artist (presumed by some to be **Jan van Eyck**).

As so many works have perished, the characters of the production outside the fields of portraiture and religious subjects can only be deduced from the landscapes, architectural interiors and exteriors, genre scenes, animal, flower and still-life painting incorporated with other content in the surviving works; and this can be done, to some extent, by careful study of even the few pictures reproduced in my plates.

Landscapes, for example, appear as settings for the *Crucifixion* by the **New York Crucifixion and Last Judgement Painter,** for the adorational processions in the lower panels of the *Altarpiece of the Mystic Lamb* by **Hubert** and **Jan van Eyck,** for the *S. Barbara* by **Jan van Eyck,** the *Nativity* by the **Washington Nativity in a Sculptured Porch Painter,** the *Adoration of the Shepherds* by the **Minneapolis Adoration Painter** and the *Meeting of Abraham and Melchizedek* by **Dirk Bouts.** In the *Crucifixion* (Pl. 3), by the **New York Crucifixion and Last Judgement Painter,** a bare stony foreground goes back to a middle distance where the crosses have been set, beyond that, through a plain with trees, to a distant Jerusalem with imagined castellated buildings, and beyond that again to a river winding at the base of snow-capped mountains; the sky with tufted clouds curves down to the luminous horizon; and the definition, sharp throughout the foreground, becomes less and less sharp as we move to the horizon (Pls. 1, 2, 5, 6); the whole landscape is an integrated unit, complete in itself before the figures were put in; it is not in any degree a series of background fragments disposed around the figures to fill the panel, as in many Italian pictures of this period. We get the same thing in the lower panels of the **van Eycks'** *Altarpiece of the Mystic Lamb* (Pls. 9, 14, 23) where the artist who designed it, assisted perhaps by some landscape specialist, has imaged the whole space as a single landscape in depth with foreground of flowering meadow, a middle distance of flowering shrubs, a further distance with birds on the wing round trees in woods, and rocks and hillocks surrounding a city with towers and steeples, and ultimately snow-capped mountains on the horizon; the meadow is trampled by two hundred and nineteen figures but they have all come later to people this coherent integrated landscape which spreads outwards to right and left and recedes for miles into the distance; the definition, however, in this case is more uniform than in the picture by the **New York Crucifixion and Last Judgement Painter;** there is no suggestion here that less detail can be seen in the more distant parts, for in the distant woods the trees of all kinds, including cypress, palm and pine trees, are all sharply defined against the luminous sky, and the towers and temples in the distant city are architecturally constructed with precise details; and it is not till we reach the mountains that atmospheric perspective turns them into pale blue shapes. In the *S. Barbara* (Pl. 18), a tinted underpainting left unfinished and signed by **Jan van Eyck,** the huge upstanding tower and the plain with fields and border trees and hedges (anticipating **Pieter Bruegel's** *Tower of Babel* (Pls. 368, 371)) is so complete a unity without S. Barbara that this foreground figure, much too large in scale, seems thrust upon it by another hand. The **Washington Nativity in a Sculptured Porch Painter** (Pl. 30) takes us from a church interior, through the sculptured doorway and the stable, over a low wall, to a pleasant meadow, past a town with spires and castles, over a hill and away to the horizon and a clear bright sky. In the *Adoration of the Shepherds* (Pl. 75) by the **Minneapolis Adoration Painter** the stable, set diagonally, is a foreground structure (as in the altarpiece already referred to by the unrecorded painter employed by Peeter Bladelin to paint a *Nativity with portrait of the donor* for Middelburg church); and we pass behind it from the right into open country and a town with pointed steeples quite different from the more contiguous castellated town with central street by the other artist. Compared with these pictures the landscape setting in the *Meeting of Abraham and Melchizedek* (Pl. 61) by **Dirk Bouts** is much less integrated; indeed till we reach the distant city, it is quite perfunctory and seems the work, not of a landscape painter who sees a landscape as continuous space existing in its own right before the figures are inserted, but of a narrative figure painter content with a series of dull mounds and hillocks disposed around his figures; and the background town with its cathedral, the trees against the sky, and the smaller town on the horizon, is just an echo, without inspiration, of the distant townscape in the *Altarpiece of the Mystic Lamb.*

Views through windows or through doors or loggias occur in many Flemish pictures of this period. In some cases they probably show the actual streets and houses seen from the window of the room or studio where the artist worked; thus in the *Annunciation* on the exterior of the *Altarpiece of the Mystic Lamb* (Pl. 12) there are views through the window on to what may be the streets of Ghent where birds circle over houses and round a towered citadel or prison and a tall church spire. A fragment of a townscape, perhaps in Louvain, can be glimpsed through the window in the *Last Supper* (Pl. 58) by **Dirk Bouts;** and through the window in the peaceful interior by the **London Virgin with a Firescreen Painter** (Frontispiece and Pl. 39) we see a church behind a street of houses possibly on the outskirts of Brussels or Tournai, with a faithful rendering of the façades anticipating the *Street in Delft* which Vermeer painted about 1660. Through the columns of a loggia in the picture by the **Boston S. Luke Painter** (Pl. 48) we are shown a river with buildings on its banks (and a similar vista, with more wooded banks and a bridge across the river, is seen from a loggia in the picture, already mentioned, which Chancellor Rolin commissioned from an unrecorded artist for the church at Autun). Glimpses of the countryside are given through the window in the left-hand panel by the **Madrid Werl Wings Painter** (Pl. 41) and through the doorway in a picture by **Petrus Christus** (Pl. 27); and a winding stream with little figures on the bank is seen through the window in the picture by the **London Magdalene Reading Painter** (Pl. 43). Views through windows also occur, bringing light and air, in some of the portraits, as in the *Marriage of Giovanni Arnolfini and Giovanna Cenami* (Pl. 18A) where we see a cherry tree in fruit painted by **Jan van Eyck** in 1434, and in the *Portrait of a Young Man* (Pl. 59) painted by the **London Young Man in a High Cap Painter** in 1462. In some other works a window or doorway is inserted not only as architectural detail or to bring light and air to the apartment or to draw the eye to an infinity of space but also or mainly with illustrative intent. Thus in the picture reproduced by the **London Christ Appearing to His Mother Painter** (Pl. 32) the empty tomb with the angel and two sleeping soldiers can be seen through the window at the back, and the three Maries approach the sepulchre in the landscape through the window on the right; in the picture by the **New York Christ Appearing to His Mother Painter** (Pls. 33, 47) Christ rises from the tomb in the landscape seen through the central doors; in the *Expulsion from Eden* (Pl. 52) by the **Redemption Master** the Fall is represented in the Garden of Eden seen again through a central doorway; and in the *S. Barbara* panel (Pl. 44) by the **Madrid Werl Wings Painter** the landscape through the window is a setting for the building of the tower.

Some of the interiors which contain these windows show us living rooms in ordinary houses or apartments in religious institutions. Thus in the picture by the **London Virgin with a Firescreen Painter** (Frontispiece) the living room is simple—a tesselated floor, a large fireplace with metal grate and straw-plaited firescreen, shutters for the unglazed window, a three-legged stool, a wooden settle with dovetailed back-bar and small lions on the ends, and a carved chest (said to be a modern restoration); and in the *S. Barbara* by the **Madrid Werl Wings Painter** (Pl. 44) the room and its appointments are very much the same, though here there is leaded glass in the upper portion of the window, a metal vase with flowers is on the stool, the back-bar of the settle is not dovetailed to the end bar but fixed with a metal joint, and we suspect the presence of a bed against the unseen left-hand wall because a basin with metal ewer and a towel above it are on the right-hand wall. The dovetailed settle with the lions in the picture by the **London Virgin with a Firescreen Painter** is seen again in a similar apartment portrayed as setting for the *Annunciation* (not reproduced here) by an unrecorded painter known as the **Merode Master** (because the picture was for long owned by the Merode family); but there the furniture includes a faience jug with flowers on a circular table in the centre of the room. In the *S. Mary Magdalene* (Pl. 43)—a fragment of a picture—by the **London Magdalene Reading Painter** the reading lady is seated on a stool, and the artist (or his interior-and-furniture specialist assistant) has placed behind her the high chest on legs that also appears in the room with a lady reading by the **Madrid Werl Wings Painter** (Pl. 44). The curious interior shown in the left-hand panel (Pl. 41) by the **Madrid Werl Wings Painter,** appears to be a corner of the artist's studio with a door leading from another apartment on the right, and a wooden screen across the centre dividing the foreground from a smaller room behind; the unglazed lower panels of the windows have their shutters, the ground is covered with rectangular tiles, and on the screen there hangs a plain round convex mirror—mirrors being, it would seem, among the standard properties in the early painters' studios (and we shall see them again in pictures reproduced here from the first decades of the sixteenth century by the **London S. Luke Painter** (Pl. 186) and the **Fogg S. Luke Painter** (Pl. 260)). In **Jan van Eyck's** *Marriage of Giovanni Arnolfini* (Pl. 18A) we have a bedroom with plain wooden floor and one small Persian rug, a window with unglazed lower panels, a bed with canopy and curtains, a highbacked chair with S. Margaret and the dragon carved on the left-hand corner, a second chair or settle with lion ornament and cushion, and a side table with oranges upon it; from the ceiling hangs a brass chandelier with six branches and a lion's head with ring below; there is a convex mirror on the wall, and, left and right of it, suspended on nails, a string of amber beads and a little household dusting brush. The **London Young Man in High Cap Painter** (Pl. 59) shows only one corner of the room, and he has placed his model before a table by the window just as Vermeer was to place so many of his models two hundred years later. The shallow architecturally confused apartment in the *Annunciation* on the exterior of the **van Eycks'** *Altarpiece of the Mystic Lamb* (Pl. 12) suggests a first-floor corridor or lobby leading to some antechambers in a convent; the small rectangular floor panels seem to be of stone, a praying desk is on the right by a little window, two books, an unguent pot, a brass candlestick and a pewter ewer are in a niche behind, and an aquamanila with brass waterpot and basin and a towel hung on a bar, are further to the left. **The London Christ Appearing to His Mother Painter** (Pl. 32) shows an austere ground-floor bedroom in what may also have been a convent; the floor is tesselated and a small ambry with ewer and basin is in the foreground left; the Virgin is seated on an unseen stool or hassock; a bench and cushion are below the window which is again unglazed in the lower panels and protected by its folding shutters; and a settle bed without a canopy is by the wall behind. In the picture by **Petrus Christus** (Pl. 27) the Virgin and Child are enthroned in what seems to be a ground-floor hall or entrance chamber in a monastery, and here the protecting shutters are closed over all but one of the unglazed lower windows.

The *Last Supper* (Pl. 58) by **Dirk Bouts** probably depicts the refectory in the headquarters of the Louvain Confraternity of the Holy Sacrament by whom the picture was commissioned, as noted, in 1464; a serving hatch joins this dining chamber to the kitchen, an ambry (like the chest on legs in the picture by the **London Magdalene Reading Painter** (Pl. 43)), here used as a serving sideboard, is just within a passage on the right which leads into the garden, a square table in the centre is covered with a white cloth and surrounded by stools and benches, the floor is elaborately tesselated, and as in **Jan van Eyck's** *The Marriage of Arnolfini* a brass chandelier is suspended from the ceiling; there are windows on the left and cast shadows indicate more unseen windows nearer to us and also on the left. As interior painting this room, with its raftered ceiling by **Dirk Bouts** or some collaborating architectural specialist, is the climax of the series of pictures just referred to. As space delineation it gives us a whole cube (with only the front wall removed); it is complete in itself and was doubtless so painted before the figures were put in; and the figures as inserted are true in scale to the room thus prepared to receive them. These qualities can be appreciated if we look again at the other pictures mentioned. In the **van Eycks'** *Annunciation* on the exterior of the *Altarpiece of the Mystic Lamb* (Pl. 12) the raftered ceiling extending, not quite coherently, from left to right, makes the oblong corridor or lobby a token structure in the Gothic tradition, because this ceiling is so low that neither of the kneeling figures could possibly stand up. In the interior by the **London Virgin with a Firescreen Painter** (Frontispiece) the figure strikes us as true to the scale of the architectural setting, but that is because the artist has evaded definition of the height and area of the room, no side walls or ceilings being shown; and the same applies to the interior and its figures in the picture by **Petrus Christus** (Pl. 27). In **Jan van Eyck's** *Marriage of Arnolfini* (Pl. 18A) we have three sides of a room and a foot or so of the raftered ceiling where it joins the wall that faces us; the light coming sharply from the left upon the foreground figures suggests a second, nearer, unseen window on that side, but the effect none the less is of life-size figures in a room too small for them, as though the artist had begun in this case with the figures and added the details of the setting piecemeal as background without considering the scale of the apartment as a whole. In the picture by the **London Christ Appearing to His Mother Painter** (Pl. 32) we have three-quarters of a cube—two walls and a raftered ceiling—complete and coherent before the figures were put in; but the figures as we have them are still a shade too large for verisimilitude. In the panels by the **Madrid Werl Wings Painter** the height of the ceilings makes the figures appear life size; but as the rooms are only half cubes the problem of the whole-cube setting is to that extent evaded. This problem of interior space with related figures was variously handled by later Flemish painters including, as my plates will show, **Pieter Coecke van Aelst** (Pl. 307), **Hendrik van Steenwyck The Younger** (Pl. 537), **Henri Staben** (Pl. 518), **David Teniers** (Pls. 678, 679) and **Hieronymus Janssens** (Pl. 461); but, as my knowledge goes, Northern European painting had to wait for the seventeenth-century Dutchmen Pieter de Hooch and Jan Vermeer of Delft before this aspect of the *Last Supper* by **Dirk Bouts** was really surpassed or equalled.

Other interiors show actual or imagined loggias in palaces or mansions, church porticoes or cloisters; and yet others the interiors of churches. The palace loggia in the picture by the **Boston S. Luke Painter** (Pls. 48, 49) leads to an apartment on the right; the floor is tessel-ated, and thin Romanesque columns, with conventional capitals, support the structure without arches; and a more elaborate palace loggia, with Romanesque pillars, capitals carved into varied designs and figures, and round arches, is in the picture commissioned by Chancellor Rolin for Autun church. In the *Van der Paele altarpiece* (Pl. 19) by **Jan van Eyck,** the setting seems the apse of a Romanesque church choir, perhaps a part or adjunct of the Cathedral of S. Donatien for which the work was originally painted. In a small pic-ture (not reproduced here) in the Dresden Gallery, presumed by some by **Jan van Eyck,** the Virgin and Child are enthroned in the nave of a Romanesque church painted, I imagine, by some collaborating architectural specialist; and the same applies to the aisle or transept of the Romanesque church in the *Annunciation* (Pl. 15) by the **Washington Annunciation in a Church Painter** and to the lofty Gothic cathedral interior in the almost miniature *Virgin in a church* (not reproduced here) in the Berlin Gallery by an unrecorded artist presumed by some to be **Hubert** or **Jan van Eyck.** The **New York Christ Appearing to His Mother Painter** (Pl. 47) shows the round-arch doorway of a church with Gothic carvings and through it a tesselated portico or portion of a cloister. There is elaborate church architecture, again I imagine provided by a specialist, in the **Redemption Master's** central panel (Pl. 51) where the figures are in a shallow Gothic porch with tesselated floor, and behind, in the centre, there is a church interior—an arrangement which we also find in the fresco of *S. Laurence giving alms* painted by Fra Angelico in the Nicholas V chapel of the Vatican about 1450. The whole interior of a Gothic cathedral—perhaps S. Pierre in Louvain—is the setting for a *Seven Sacraments* (not reproduced here) in Antwerp Museum, by an unrecorded artist pre-sumed by some to be **Rogier van der Weyden.** In the picture by the **Exhumation of S. Hubert Master** (Pl. 54), probably commissioned for the chapel of S. Hubert consecrated in Brussels, S. Gudule, in 1440, the event takes place in the choir of a Gothic church, actual or imagined, and symbolizing S. Pierre in Liège where the remains of S. Hubert were exhumed in 852; and here again we may assume, I think, collaboration between the figure painter and the architectural draughtsman resulting, in this case, in logical scale relations between the figures and the building that contains them.

Very accomplished still-life painting, generally, I think, the work of specialists, occurs in these interiors and other Flemish pictures of this time. **Jan van Eyck,** the **Washington Annunciation in a Church Painter,** the **London Virgin with a Firescreen Painter,** the **Madrid Werl Wings Painter** and the **Redemption Master** were doubtless themselves efficient crafts-men in this field which, of course, is mainly a matter of infinitely patient handwork; but they probably trained their pupils and assistants to insert the glittering crowns and jewels, the brocaded vestments and cloths of honour, the pearl embroideries, the carved lecterns and illuminated books, the brazen chandeliers and ewers and basins, the mirrors with their reflections, the Gothic carvings, the nails in the shutters with rust marks beneath them, and the innumerable inscriptions which abound in these early pictures. Two standards in this field were set at the beginning by the painters of the still-life in the *Altarpiece of the Mystic Lamb* by **Hubert** and **Jan van Eyck.** In the first some humble objects are seen, at a distance, as shapes in a soft still even light and painted thus with quiet affection; in the second all kinds of objects and all the details of each object, with their surfaces and textures, are sub-jected to a lynx-eyed 'close-up' vision and vividly described in hard cold handling with the maximum of glittering highlights. The first standard is set by the aquamanila and the objects in the niche behind the Virgin in the *Annunciation* (Pl. 12) on the exterior panels; we find it in the still-life shown in the pictures by the **London Virgin with a Firescreen Painter** (Frontispiece), the **London Christ Appearing to His Mother Painter** (Pl. 32) and the **Madrid Werl Wings Painter** (Pl. 44); and it reappears in some pictures of the sixteenth cen-tury. The second standard is set by the upper panels of the interior of the **van Eycks'** altar-piece (Pls. 9, 13, 17) and by **Jan van Eyck's** *Van der Paele altarpiece* (Pl. 19); and this 'close-up' style in still-life with its inexorable concentration on illusionist completeness and varieties of surface texture was possibly launched by **Jan van Eyck** himself with assistants trained directly by him. Both the merit and the defect of the second style are indicated if we say that to describe these still-life passages we have to describe the actual objects painted. To describe, for example, the still-life in the *Singing Angels* (Pl. 17) of the *Altarpiece of the Mystic Lamb* we have to catalogue the vestments and church furniture depicted, to speak of 'a cope of crimson brocade, its orfreys embroidered with figures of saints in canopied com-partments, the closing morse quadriloped and set with jewels', and to speak of another cope with 'circular morse fastening showing a figure in high relief, another with orfreys orna-mented with repeating motifs of the Holy Face', and so on; and then we must speak of an oak lectern with a brass support, an open antiphoner upon the lectern, a book with clasps upon a stall surmounted by two carved seated figures, and so forth for each and every detail. In the same way in describing the still-life in the *Van der Paele altarpiece* (Pl. 19), we have to speak of S. Donatian's blue and gold brocaded cope with the apostles in the orfreys (which like Queen Elizabeth I's dresses could stand alone); of S. George's armour (that could be made from this picture) and of the rug (that could be woven), the capitals (that could be carved) and the Spanish tiles (that could be painted, glazed and fired from it); and when we get to the *Marriage of Arnolfini* (Pl. 18A) we have to describe each centimetre of the celebrated mirror in the background. Of 'close-up' illusionist technique in still-life painting Ruskin wrote: 'The most perfect ideas and pleasures of imitation are when one sense is contradicted by another . . . as when the eye says a thing is round and the finger says it is flat . . . these ideas and pleasures are the most contemptible that can be received from art.' But we must qualify this, I think, by observing that when this style is used the picture may acquire aesthetic and ethical values deriving from the aesthetic and ethical values of the objects shown. In illusionist still-life painting of this kind the aesthetic value is not derived from the aesthetic relations of the individual passages but from their sum when added together one by one, for the aesthetic value of the total depends on the aesthetic value of each brocade, each crown and carving and so on. We see this if we cover the head of *The Virgin* (Pl. 16) by the **New York Crucifixion and Last Judgement Painter** and then do the same to the heads of the *Singing Angels* (Pl. 17) in the upper panels of the *Altarpiece of the Mystic Lamb*; for in the first case there remains a portion of a picture with flowing lines and rhythms and relations of lights and darks and spaces with formal life apart from their representational content, and in the second we have only a series of objects with no aesthetic relations one to another in their shapes and volumes. In the same way the ethical values are affected by this intensely detailed illusionist technique because the ethical value of each object, when we are thus forced to apprehend it as an object, contributes to or detracts from the ethical value of the picture as a whole. In the crown worn by *The Virgin* (Pl. 13) in the upper panels of the *Altarpiece of the Mystic Lamb* for example, the snowdrops and lilies are factors in the picture's ethical value because they are objects that, whenever we meet them, we recognize as 'good' in terms of life; but the pearls and huge rubies and sapphires in the crown have no such ethical value in terms of life and they therefore bring nothing to the picture's ethical value unless the artist's view (or his compliance with a theologian's view) that the Virgin is appropriately arrayed in jewels of great earthly price be accepted as right, and the very different view of the **New York Crucifixion and Last Judgement Painter** (Pl. 16) be rejected as wrong. This 'close-up' illusionist still-life style, with its merits and defects, remained for long a feature of Flemish painting. In the sixteenth century we meet it in scores of details in the *Adoration of the Magi* by **Jan Gossaert** (Pl. 194), in the cold, hard accessories in pictures shown here by the **Princeton Christ Before Pilate Painter** (Pl. 174), **Marinus van Reymerswaele** (Pl. 237), and the **London Tax Collectors Painter** (Pl. 324) and in the vestments and crozier by **Jacobus de Punder** (Pl. 376); in the seventeenth century it persists in some aspects of the still-life painting—the drops of water on marble slabs round fish by **Alexander Adriaenssen** (Pl. 652), for example, and in works by **Jacob Foppens van Es** who painted the skins of grapes, his contemporaries tell us, with so skilful a transparency that it was possible to count the pips inside (Pl. 558); and it is still there at the end of the eighteenth century when **G. F. Ziesel** painted goldfish in a bowl reflecting the window of the room and the houses in the street outside.

Flower painting must always have been a special branch of study. It is recorded that **Gillis Congnet** in the later sixteenth century set a pupil to paint a flowerpiece; and many masters in the fifteenth century, selecting tasks for their apprentice pupils, must have anticipated the view expressed by Sir Joshua Reynolds that some time spent in painting flowers is 'no improper part of a painter's education'. The most successful of such student flower painters were doubtless soon established as local specialists; and there must always have been a market for flower paintings because people everywhere have always grown flowers in gardens, and everyone from childhood onwards has always reacted aesthetically to the shapes and colours of particular flowers (though it has probably been always the exclusive province of the painter to react aesthetically to the shapes of pots and pans and loaves of bread). In Duke Philip's day people walked in flowered gardens and the children of the Netherlands stretched out their hands in delight at posies of flowers, as the Christ-child does in **Jan van Eyck's** *Van der Paele altarpiece* (Pl. 19) and in the picture by **Petrus Christus** (Pl. 27) where a single rose is held towards him by the Virgin; bourgeois ladies at this time had flowers in vases in their living rooms, as we know from the **Madrid Werl Wings Painter** (Pl. 44) and the **Merode Master;** and in these conditions it is not surprising that flowers abound in the Flemish pictures. Thus in the great landscape of the **van Eycks'** *Altarpiece of the Mystic Lamb* (Pl. 9) the whole meadow is alive with various flowers most delicately observed and skilfully painted, and experts tell us that the flowers liking shade are set in shadowed corners while those needing sunlight are in the lightest parts; near the maiden saints, the lily-stems bear buds and flowers turned at their several angles; the iris, among their spear leaves, have flowers at the top and characteristic buds below; and behind them the peony roses are again all variously angled. Such flowers in verdure can be seen in other pictures of this period reproduced here; the **New York Annunciation in a Porch Painter** has filled a garden round a church with flowers and flowering shrubs, and flowers spring also from a chink in the Gothic buttress (Pl. 26); wild flowers are in the meadow shown by the **Washington Nativity in a Sculptured Porch Painter** (Pl. 30), flowers spring by the path leading from the tomb in the Resurrection shown through the window by the **New York Christ Appearing to His Mother Painter** (Pls. 33, 47), lilies of the valley, dandelions, forget-me-nots, violets and pinks grow round the feet of *S. Veronica* and daisies, anemones, violets and loosestrife round the feet of the *Virgin and Child* in the pictures by the **Flémalle Master** (Pls. 35, 36). We also get delicious glimpses of flowers in garden beds; in **Jan van Eyck's** small picture *The Virgin and Child by a fountain* (Pl. 25) there are flower-beds with roses and lilies, yellow iris, daisies, violets and lilies of the valley; the **Boston S. Luke Painter** puts flower-beds outside the loggia where the Virgin poses (Pls. 48, 49); and the **Washington Nativity in a Sculptured Porch Painter** shows a flower-bed in front of the low wall outside the stable (Pl. 30).

The animal painting of the period can also be, to some extent, examined in my plates. These show horses in the **van Eycks'** *Altarpiece of the Mystic Lamb*, in the *Crucifixion* by the **New York Crucifixion and Last Judgement Painter**, in **Jan van Eyck's** *S. Barbara*, and in the *Meeting of Abraham and Melchizedek* by **Dirk Bouts**; the ox and the ass in the pictures by the **Minneapolis Adoration Painter** and the **Washington Nativity in a Sculptured Porch Painter**; there is a famous little dog in the *Marriage of Arnolfini* by **Jan van Eyck**; and there are fantastic made-up beasts in the *Pit of Hell* by the **New York Crucifixion and Last Judgement Painter**. In the *Just Judges* and *Knights of Christ* panels of the *Altarpiece of the Mystic Lamb* (Pls. 9, 14) brown and black horses, of which little more than the heads are seen, are profiled behind white horses in conventional walking action also in profile; the bridles are jewelled, the horses' heads are pulled back hard with bearing reins and their mouths are worried by the bits; the gauntleted left hands of the Knights just touch the bearing reins, while the Judges use their bare right hands. The **New York Crucifixion and Last Judgement Painter** is more adventurous in his treatment of the eight horses ridden to the Crucifixion in his picture (Pls. 1, 3); of the two light horses in the foreground based, it would seem, on the horses in the *Altarpiece of the Mystic Lamb*, one, being guided upwards to the left, has his head and neck turned from us (Pl. 160); and of the others several are in back view with the inside of the raised hooves shown, while one, just behind the central cross, is foreshortened in a front view; and in the distant plain (Pl. 5) a galloping horse anticipates the horses in the background of the *Adoration of the Magi* (Pl. 157) by **Hieronymus Bosch**. In **Jan van Eyck's** *S. Barbara* (Pl. 18) four horsemen wheel towards us from the left and the foremost horse is shown foreshortened in a front view. In the *Meeting of Abraham and Melchizedek* (Pl. 61) by **Dirk Bouts** Melchizedek's light horse stands foreshortened in a front view and his retinue ride dark horses and a white one seen in profile as in the **van Eycks'** panels. The **Washington Nativity in a Sculptured Porch Painter** (Pl. 30) makes the ass reach upwards to nibble at his fodder; and, unusually for this period, the whole body of the ox is seen in the picture by the **Minneapolis Adoration Painter** (Pl. 75). The griffon terrier or Bolognese dog in **Jan van Eyck's** *Marriage of Arnolfini* (Pl. 18A) is a comic little statue in himself and he also completes the composition by repeating, below the figures, the juncture made above them by the chandelier—(cover him with your finger and the circular structure of the grouping goes). The fantastic beasts in the *Pit of Hell* by the **New York Crucifixion and Last Judgement Painter** are super-bears and pythons, bat-like monsters, whales and crocodiles, and seem to me the naïve inventions of a youthful mind (Pls. 4, 8).

In genre painting the Flemish artists showed intensive observation from the start. I have already referred to the studies of children reaching out to flowers in **Jan van Eyck's** *Van der Paele altarpiece* (Pl. 19) and the picture by **Petrus Christus** (Pl. 27); and we can add now the charming gestures in **Jan van Eyck's** *Virgin and Child by a fountain* (Pl. 25) where the Christ-child has one arm round his mother's neck and holds a rosary of corals in the other, and in the variant of the group by the **New York Virgin in a Tabernacle Painter** (Pl. 24) where the

21

child embraces his mother with both arms. We must note here also the gesture of the up-turned hands and feet of the child at his mother's breast in the picture by the **Boston S. Luke Painter** (Pl. 49)—a gesture found in works by many Flemish artists including the **London Virgin with Brocade Screen Painter** (Pl. 62); and the movement in the *Virgin and Child* (Pl. 36) by the **Flémalle Master** where the child, dressed in a blue fur-trimmed coat with a red girdle, is attracted by the gleam of the white pendant veil and turns from his mother's breast to grasp it. I have also referred, in speaking of the interior paintings, to the domestic scenes with ladies in their living-rooms by the **Madrid Werl Wings Painter** where the lady is reading on a settle with her back to a cheerful fire (Pl. 44) and by the **London Magdalene Reading Painter** (Pl. 43) where the lady sits upon a stool; and we must look again here at **Jan van Eyck's** genre portrait group now known as the *Marriage of Arnolfini* (Pl. 18A) where a betrothal or marriage seems to be taking place and other participants are reflected in the mirror, and the domestic atmosphere is increased by the dog, the bed, the oranges and the household dusting brush. We have also the tender domestic scene by the **London Virgin with a Firescreen Painter** (Frontispiece) which anticipates the nursery scene depicted for this devotional theme by the **Brussels Virgin with a Milk Bowl Painter** (Pl. 205) and shows what seems to be the noble model for the **Flémalle Master's** *Virgin and Child* (Pl. 36) in the same bluish-white mantle with grey fur cuffs—a studio property a little worn at the edges—at home in her apartment at the moment when, putting aside the book she has been reading, she offers the breast to her restless child. In the church interior by the **Exhumation of S. Hubert Master** (Pl. 54) a genre element is provided by the public peering through the screen and whispering humorous comments that have reached the sharp ears of the King of France's page. The picture by the **Boston S. Luke Painter** (Pl. 49), considered as a genre record, shows an artist in his patron's mansion at work on a portrait drawing to be copied in oil colours when he gets back later to his workshop; the **Detroit S. Jerome Painter** (Pl. 55) records the attitude of a scholar in his study, his head supported on his left hand while he turns with his right the pages of a book; the **Merode Master** shows S. Joseph as a carpenter making mouse-traps some of which he has set on a ledge outside the window giving on to the street; and I have already spoken of the goldsmith selling jewellery in his shop portrayed by **Petrus Christus.** In this series also I must mention again the *Woman sweating in a bath, spied on by two laughing youths, a dog beside the woman* recorded as the work of **Rogerius Gallicus** and the *Woman bathing with attendant, a mirror on the wall* known to have been painted by **Jan van Eyck.**

In outdoor genre painting we have chains of figures, knights and civic dignitaries, church-men, hermits, saints and martyrs inserted by the **van Eycks** in the flowered meadow of the *Altarpiece of the Mystic Lamb* (Pl. 9); inspired by church and civic ceremonies and plays, and by the Ducal pageants and processions, these figures wear contemporary clothes and vestments, and the maiden saints, with flowing hair, all stand in the fashionable posture of the period, with the back hollowed and the belly forward and the dress, if need be, padded on the belly to assist in the effect (Pl. 23); and some gather to their bellies the redundant yards of their Flemish mantles which trail on the ground around them as they trail round the ladies in **Jan van Eyck's** *S. Barbara* (Pl. 18) and the *Marriage of Arnolfini* (Pl. 18A). But though we find these records of contemporary pomp and fashion in the meadow scene of the *Altarpiece of the Mystic Lamb* there are here no genre touches, based on observation, of the men and girls as individual humans; in the *Crucifixion* of the **New York Crucifixion and Last Judgement Painter** on the other hand, there are scores of genre touches—a young man by the Cross cracks some joke to his friend beside him, a priest of the temple smiles into his

22

beard, a soldier chants a ditty while a bearded long-haired fellow turns round on his horse to laugh (Pls. 1, 2, 159); and even in the *Last Judgement* panel by this intriguing artist, the maiden saints who come towards us are a genre record of a girls' procession in a local church, and the smiling angel who receives the blessed kings and emperors and nobles is a friendly hostess of this earth (Pls. 4, 7). Other artists of the time—the **Washington Nativity in a Sculptured Porch Painter** (Pl. 30) and the **Minneapolis Adoration Painter** (Pls. 29, 75) for example—looked simply at the rural life around them when painting the shepherds approaching or adoring; and the second gives us a youthful shepherd in patched hose and damaged hood and an older peasant uncovering behind him. In **Jan van Eyck's** *S. Barbara* (Pl. 18) rustic artisans hew stones, trundle barrows and carry mortar for the building of the tower. **Petrus Christus** puts a man in a boat upon the river seen through the monastery doorway in the picture reproduced (Pl. 27); and **Dirk Bouts** puts a groom by the bridle of the riderless horse in the *Meeting of Abraham and Melchizedek* (Pl. 61).

Urban genre scenes are also present in some pictures. The townscape outside the window in the **van Eycks'** *Annunciation* (Pl. 12) in the *Altarpiece of the Mystic Lamb* is evidently seen by the artist standing close to a first-floor window and looking down upon the street where the townsfolk gossip in the doorways, take the air from their own windows or go about their business in the sunlight which casts their shadows on the cobblestones. Little figures promenade the quays seen through the loggia in the picture by the **Boston S. Luke Painter** (Pl. 48) and nearer, on the terrace of the palace, a man and woman with their backs to us, look down upon the river (as similar figures look down in the altarpiece donated to Autun church by Chancellor Rolin). In the townscape by the **London Virgin with a Firescreen Painter** (Pl. 39) horsemen and pedestrians move about the streets, two men with a ladder are replacing tiles in a leaking roof, and women in coifs and aprons of the period stand at their doorways and look on.

In figure painting, including figures in the nude, we have two style-standards from the outset—as in the still-life painting. In the first the figures are viewed from a certain distance and recorded with echoes of the two-dimensional aesthetic rhythm of the International Gothic manner which survived in Franco-Burgundian book illustrations and other works in the early years of the fifteenth century. These characters appear in the suave rhythm of the *Virgin* on the outside of the **van Eycks'** *Altarpiece of the Mystic Lamb* (Pl. 12), in the flowing lines of the *Virgin interceding* (Pls. 4, 7, 16) and *S. Michael* with his outstretched wings (Pls. 4, 96) in the *Last Judgement* by the **New York Crucifixion and Last Judgement Painter,** and in the swing of the *Impenitent Thief* (Pls. 1, 2, 6) in the same artist's *Crucifixion*. We meet these characters also in the simple silhouettes of the standing Virgin and the angel's wings in the picture by the **Washington Nativity in a Sculptured Porch Painter** (Pl. 30), in the stance and silhouette and down-flowing drapery of the *Virgin and Child* (Pl. 36) by the **Flémalle Master,** in the down-falling lines of the Christ in the same artist's *Holy Trinity* (Pl. 37), in Christ's flowing mantle in the polyptych by the **Beaune Last Judgement Painter** (Pl. 34), in the majestic two-dimensional pattern made by the figure and the fire-screen-halo in the picture by the **London Virgin with a Firescreen Painter** (Frontispiece); and this style arrives at an impressive climax in the two-dimensional rhythms of the *Descent from the Cross* by **Rogier van der Weyden** (Pl. 46), a composition in the nature of a coloured high-relief against a flat gold ground. In the International Gothic style the nude figures are sometimes lean with their limbs sharply angled in illustrative gestures; and this tradition is also continued in some pictures of our period; it appears for example in the nude child by the **London Virgin with a Firescreen Painter** (Frontispiece), in the nudes painted by the

23

Redemption Master in the *Expulsion from Eden* (Pl. 52) and the *Last Judgement* (Pl. 53), and also in the nudes by the **Beaune Last Judgement Painter** (Pls. 137, 138).

The second style-standard in the painting of figures, including nudes, is seen at its outset and its climax in the upper panels of the **van Eycks'** *Altarpiece of the Mystic Lamb* (Pl. 9). Here, as in the still-life portions, the artist paints with a close-up vision, his eye moving from point to point upon the surface of each small form, like a cinema camera moving across the surface of a high-relief; and his hand nevertheless miraculously achieves a three-dimensional record, life-like, complete and convincing. The face of the model for the Virgin (Pl. 13), for example, is constructed bit by bit in this close-up empirical fashion; the turn of each eyelid, and the upper lip of the half-open mouth projecting beyond the lower lip, are inexorably followed; and, between the lips, two teeth and the tip of the tongue are exactly reproduced in illusionist technique. The same close-up centimetre by centimetre vision and the same illusionist handling record for us the faces of the eight girls, surely sisters, in the *Singing Angels* panel (Pls. 9, 17), a record so intensively descriptive that the poet and painter **Lucas de Heere** (writing in the sixteenth century) declared himself able to detect the pitch of the different voices by the muscular movements of the mouths. In the *Adam* and *Eve* panels (Pl. 9) we see the method operating on two large full-length nudes; the lynx-eye moves across the surface of the component forms, one by one, with marvellous intensity; we are forced to follow as it records the veins on the male figure's hands, the hairs on legs and chest and round the nipples, and the toe-nails embedded in the fleshy toe-ends; and to follow also as it moves round the breasts of the female figure and dips into the navel and mounts the crown of the belly's form; and—as in the other figures in these panels—the result, unexpectedly, is coherent and majestically impressive, despite these wholly empirical procedures which amazed van Mander, a champion of Italian influence on Flemish painters, who wrote at the end of the sixteenth century: 'In early times painting as practised in the Netherlands can be described as an art without art (kunstig zonde kunst) in contrast with the later Italian painting based on study of the antique; but we must nevertheless marvel at the advanced skill in painting the human form which was shown by our early artists as though they had been taught by nature (als door de natuur geleerd).' But here we must observe, as we observed when considering the still-life painting in these panels and in the *Van der Paele altarpiece* (Pl. 19), that this technical procedure makes the ethical and aesthetic values of the picture to a large extent dependent on the values that we set upon each object shown. When we are forced to apprehend the painted noses and mouths, warts and wrinkles, limbs, breasts and bellies as actual parts of particular humans, the ethical value that we set upon the picture is influenced by our concepts of the ethical values of these human features; and thus it came that, rightly or wrongly, in 1781, the Emperor Joseph II, an admirer of Italian painting and an impetuous idealist, pronounced this *Adam* and *Eve* unsuited for a church interior and ordered their removal from S. Bavon. In the same way when each part of each figure is painted in this close-up illusionist technique the aesthetic impact of each figure is influenced by the aesthetic impact of each part; there is no denying, for example, that the physical beauty of the hands in the *Singing Angels* panel (Pl. 17)—and also in **Jan van Eyck's** *Marriage of Arnolfini* (Pl. 18A)—and the gouty swelling of the knuckles in the hands of *Jodoc Vyt* (Pl. 11) and the ugliness of the squat hands of *Canon van der Paele* (Pl. 19) affect us as physical parts of these particular people. No hands in other paintings surviving from this period thus physically impose themselves as portraits; in the *Annunciation* on the outside of the *Altarpiece of the Mystic Lamb* (Pl. 12), for instance, in **Rogier van der Weyden's** *Deposition* (Pl. 46), in the **Boston S. Luke**

Painter's picture (Pl. 49), in the **Redemption Master's** *Expulsion from Eden* (Pl. 52) and in the *Last Supper* by **Dirk Bouts** (Pl. 58) the hands are first and foremost instruments of gesture, integral factors in the illustrative meaning of the picture as a whole; in other pictures they speak mainly of the artist's formal prejudices—his personal pleasure in small tapering fingers, as in the works reproduced by the **Washington Nativity in a Sculptured Porch Painter** (Pl. 30) and the **Minneapolis Adoration Painter** (Pl. 75) or his pleasure in long-boned fingers as in the hands by the **London Virgin with a Firescreen Painter** (Frontispiece), the **Flémalle Master** (Pls. 35, 36) and the **Antwerp Philippe de Croy Painter** (Pl. 45); and in one case, the surely youthful **New York Crucifixion and Last Judgement Painter,** they speak mainly of the artist's inexperience (Pl. 16), though he can make them on occasion the vehicle of imaginative feeling to enhance the picture's illustrative content (Pls. 2, 160).

The portraits known or presumed to have been painted in this period include some studies of the artists' friends and members of their families as well as commissioned portraits. Examples of the first are **Jan van Eyck's** *Timotheos* and *Margaret, wife of the painter* and, probably, his *Man in a red turban*, the *Portrait of a Carthusian* by **Petrus Christus,** the portraits of women by the **London Woman in a Wimple Painter** and the **London Young Woman in White Headdress Painter** and a portrait of a man by the **London Young Man in a High Cap Painter.** The sitter for the *Timotheos* (Pl. 10) by **Jan van Eyck** may have been some other member of Philip the Good's establishment, perhaps his librarian, as we see him again, I think, standing behind a kneeling scribe in the frontispiece of a Burgundian manuscript, the 'Chroniques de Hainault', which depicts the Duke receiving a new book; the original of *Margaret van Eyck* (Pl. 20) with her long sharp nose and pointed chin, in a red gown with green girdle and a hideous horned headdress, was thirty-three when her husband painted her, though she looks some ten years older; and the original of the *Man in a red turban* (Pl. 21), a veritable hen's face with red comb, may have been, if we judge by the nose, her father. The *Portrait of a Carthusian* (Pl. 31) by **Petrus Christus,** to which the halo may have been added later, has the air of a self-portrait painted in a mirror, for the nose is a little more in profile than the eyes, as often happens in self-portraits when the artist's eyes 'pull the head round' and cause a change of pose as the work proceeds; the flat top to the head also argues for this theory because we find such flatness in the head of the Virgin in his Frankfort altarpiece (Pl. 27) and artists, as is well known, tend unconsciously to invest the figures in their pictures with characteristics of their own physique. The bourgeoise, in her heavy coif, painted by the **London Woman in a Wimple Painter** (Pl. 40) may have lived and kept the household linen carefully in carved chests in one of the houses shown in the plate printed opposite her portrait (Pl. 39); but the younger charmingly pretty lady painted in a cap covered with stiff transparent muslin by the **London Young Woman in White Headdress Painter** (Pl. 57) who might be her daughter, seems given to daydreaming and was probably forgetful of her household duties; and the young man, all brains and sensibility, painted beside the window by the **London Young Man in a High Cap Painter** (Pl. 59) has the look of a writer or an artist of some kind. To such uncommissioned portraits we must assimilate the studies of friends not infrequently inserted in figure compositions—some of the heads, I imagine, in the procession panels of the **van Eycks'** *Altarpiece of the Mystic Lamb* (Pls. 9, 14, 23) and all the faces in the upper panels of that picture (Pls. 9, 13, 17). Many of the faces in the *Crucifixion* (Pls. 1, 159) by the **New York Crucifixion and Last Judgement Painter** may likewise be based on drawings of the artist's friends; and the beautiful young woman who evidently posed for the Virgin in the pictures reproduced here by the **Flémalle Master** (Pl. 36) and the **London Virgin with a Firescreen Painter** (Frontispiece) can also be instanced in this category.

The commissioned portraits include full-length kneeling figures of donors inserted in altarpieces, small half-length portraits of the owners of portable diptychs, and portraits commissioned as independent objects, usually, it would seem, small head-and-hand pieces but occasionally also full-length figures. In the first category I have already mentioned the portraits of Jodoc Vyt and his wife in the **van Eycks'** *Altarpiece of the Mystic Lamb*, of Canon van der Paele in **Jan van Eyck's** *Van der Paele altarpiece*, of Chancellor Rolin and his wife in the *Last Judgement* polyptych at the Hospices de Beaune, of Chancellor Rolin in the *Autun Altarpiece*, of Peeter Bladelin in a triptych in Berlin, of Henri de Werl in a panel by the **Madrid Werl Wings Painter,** and of the Abbot of S. Vaast in a picture by **Jacques Daret.** In such pictures the figures are inserted in various places with varying degrees of prominence. In the *Altarpiece of the Mystic Lamb* (Pl. 11) the donors are on the outside of the wings and isolated, like the intervening statues, in carved niches; and they are also on the outside and isolated in the *Last Judgement* polyptych by the **Beaune Last Judgement Painter.** The **Madrid Werl Wings Painter** (Pl. 41) puts the donor on the left-hand inside panel with S. John the Baptist as presenting saint behind him, and both look towards the unknown action in the missing central panel. In the other pictures mentioned the donor appears as part of or in contact with the religious scene or devotional group which forms the subject of the altarpiece. Thus in the *Van der Paele altarpiece* (Pl. 19), which is otherwise a formal devotional image, the canon kneels between the Virgin's throne and S. George the presenting saint whose hand rests on his shoulder; in the *Autun altarpiece* the Chancellor kneeling at a prie-dieu on the left is actually larger and nearer than the Virgin and Child who face him on the right; in the *Nativity* commissioned by Peeter Bladelin, where the composition is like the delicate *Adoration of the Shepherds* (Pl. 75) by the **Minneapolis Adoration Painter,** S. Joseph and the donor kneel on the same plane left and right of the nativity group, while the apparition of the star to the Magi is relegated to the right-hand wing; and in the *Visitation,* ordered by the Abbot of S. Vaast, **Jacques Daret** makes the donor an incongruous intruder within hearing distance of the sacred confidences.

The portable diptychs of the period had habitually a devotional image on one panel and the portrait of the owner with hands folded as an adorant on the other; they were ordered for the altars of oratories in private houses and when closed with jewelled clasps they could accompany the owner on his travels and, eventually, be transmitted as mementoes to his heirs. The portraits reproduced here by the **Antwerp Philippe de Croy Painter** and the **New York Man in a High Cap Painter** are possibly from diptychs of this kind; the sitter for the first (Pl. 45) is a young noble with brown hair and green-blue eyes set rather close together, a sensitive mouth with full underlip, long nose and long narrow chin; put the characteristic headdress on him and he becomes a brother to Amenophis IV (Aknaton) the Egyptian reformer, whose portrait survives in Egyptian carvings; the reverse of the panel bears the name and arms of Philippe de Croy, Seigneur de Sempy who is thus identified as the sitter or the owner or as both. The name of the sitter painted by the **New York Man in a High Cap Painter** (Pl. 60) is not known.

Of the portraits commissioned as independent objects my plates show a head-and-hands piece by the **New York d'Este Painter** and the full-length *Marriage of Giovanni Arnolfini and Giovanna Cenami* by **Jan van Eyck**; and I have already mentioned the head of *Edward Grymeston* painted by **Petrus Christus** in 1446 when the sitter was Henry VI's ambassador to Duke Philip. Inscriptions and arms on the back of the picture by the **New York d'Este**

Painter (Pl. 50) indicate that it was owned at one time by a member of the d'Este family, and the sitter may be Leonello (whose portraits by Italian artists he resembles) or Francesco, or Meliadose who used a hammer at the opening ceremony of the 1450 Jubilee in Rome; since my plate was made the picture has been cleaned and the young man is now seen to hold a ring between his thumb and second finger which leads me to presume him some member of the family in the role of S. Eligius, the patron of goldsmiths and metal workers, whom he perhaps impersonated in some pageant. Giovanni Arnolfini, the man portrayed in **Jan van Eyck's** very celebrated picture (Pl. 18A) was a silk merchant from Lucca established in Bruges by 1421; by 1423 he was selling tapestries to Duke Philip, and in 1446 he lent him sums of money which, rather unusually in such transactions, were returned; ten years later he was the Duke's councillor, major-domo and chamberlain, and also Général de Finances en Normandie, and he died without issue in 1470 or 1472; Giovanna Cenami who is said to have had some royal French blood, was the daughter of a Lucchese merchant resident in Paris; the date of the marriage is unknown; she died in 1480 and was buried beside her husband in the church of the Rich Clares in Bruges.

Technically, the portraits in all these categories show again the two main style trends already noted in the still-life and figure paintings. In some the sitters are seen from a certain distance in a softening light and painted with echoes of the International Gothic two-dimensional aesthetic; in others we have a close-up vision and empirical illusionist technique. We have one aspect of the first manner in the beautiful oval of the sitter's face in the pictures by the **Virgin with a Firescreen Painter** (Frontispiece) and the **Flémalle Master** (Pl. 36) and in the *Annunciation* on the outside of the **van Eycks'** *Altarpiece of the Mystic Lamb* (Pl. 12); and we have other aspects of the Gothic tradition in some faces by the **New York Crucifixion and Last Judgement Painter** and in the portraits by **Petrus Christus**, the **Antwerp Philippe de Croy Painter**, the **New York d'Este Painter**, the **London Young Woman in White Headdress Painter** and the **London Young Man in a High Cap Painter**. The three faces reproduced here by the **New York Crucifixion and Last Judgement Painter** (Pl. 159) show a genius for shorthand portraiture in the Gothic miniature tradition—for the whole panel of the *Crucifixion* (Pl. 3) which contains these heads is less than two feet high. The head and shoulders in the little picture by **Petrus Christus** (Pl. 31) were evidently broadly drawn from a distance; but in the painting, where they are set in a softening light against a dark wall of varying tone, the mouth and beard are treated with delicate miniature technique, and the artist, to parade his skill in miniature handling, has perched a fly upon the bottom of the frame. The **Antwerp Philippe de Croy Painter** (Pl. 45) puts his sitter in purple doublet against a flat greenish textile divided into squares; and here the head is both broadly drawn and broadly painted in a softening light. The **New York d'Este Painter** (Pl. 50) conforms more closely to the two-dimensional tradition; for the sitter, in black doublet with brick-red collar and gold necklace, is seen in silhouette against a light cream ground and the features are recorded with a linear feeling. For the face and headdress in his little painting the **London Young Woman in White Headdress Painter** (Pl. 57) has evidently worked closely from a drawing made from life at a certain distance in a cool grey light; he has not forgotten the pin that holds the muslin headdress to the cap beneath or the pin that fastens the muslin at the breast; and these passages, most delicately coordinated in an even tone, are contrasted with the dark brown and green of the dress and the crimson stomacher. The still smaller portrait by the **London Young Man in High Cap Painter** (Pl. 59) is complex and fascinating from the technical standpoint; for if we cover the window and the shutters we have a high-relief silhouette against a flat light wall, a silhouette containing the half-length

27

figure in pinkish cap and doublet, the cap tight-fitting on the upper brow and falling back hollow above it, the tone of the face repeated in the hands, and the features most sensitively modelled (though the structure of the cheekbones has gone wrong); all this was doubtless based upon a drawing made from the sitter placed for the purpose by the window—though the window in the drawing was probably indicated by no more than a line or two; and the window, the landscape and the shutters with the rusting nails were probably added by the artist, or some assistant, in the painting stage; the result is thus a conflict between two different pictorial concepts—the initial concept of the two-dimensional high-relief against a plain flat ground (the concept seen in **Rogier van der Weyden's** *Descent from the Cross* (Pl. 46) and in the portrait by the **New York d'Este Painter** (Pl. 50)) and the concept of a figure seen in an interior, as in the various pictures in that category already discussed here.

Some portraits painted in the 'close-up' illusionist technique have just been mentioned in my comments on the figure painting of this time. On the outside of the **van Eycks'** *Altarpiece of the Mystic Lamb* we are forced to follow the lynx-eye of the artist in his voyage of discovery on the surface of the face of *Jodoc Vyt* (Pl. 11) from the indurated jaw gland, past the wart beneath the nose, to the pouches under the upturned eyes with the whites conspicuous against the sallow skin, and the lifted eyebrows and the wrinkles on the brow; we travel with **Jan van Eyck** from the drooping eyelids down the ugly snout of his *Arnolfini* (Pl. 18A), round the slightly twisting lips, across the tip of the squashed down nose, round the eye-case of each eye in his *Timotheos* (Pl. 10), and down the bald pate, over veins and in and out of wrinkles, past the swollen ear-lobe and the thin drawn mouth to the double chins of his *Canon van der Paele* (Pl. 19). As our knowledge goes this 'close-up' empirical vision, recorded with such patience in illusionist technique, was something new in European portraiture. No artist that we know of had done the thing before; and none that we know of has surpassed it since. For, as described already, the result, astonishingly, is not a series of disjointed bits and pieces—like the features in the portrait by the **London Woman in a Wimple Painter** (Pl. 40) who imitates the method—but a continuing coherent structure, an integral convincing mask; and even Sir Joshua Reynolds who disliked the 'hard manner' of **Jan van Eyck** allowed 'great character of nature' to the face of van der Paele.

The more elaborate religious pictures in this period were the joint products of the donors, the local theologians and the artists. I have referred already to the parts played by the magistratures, guilds and religious fraternities as initiators of such works, and by the rich individuals whose portraits were inserted in the paintings they had paid for. These services were simple and obvious. But the parts played by the theologians and the artists, and their mutual relations, were more various and complex.

From extant contracts for Flemish (as well as French and Spanish) religious pictures we know that local theologians gave detailed instructions to artists before the works were started. Thus **Hubert Stuerbout** when commissioned to make his two hundred and fifty bas-reliefs for Louvain Town Hall in 1449 was directed at the outset by Maître Jean de Phalizen, a priest of Louvain Cathedral and a Dominican named Jacques who chose the subjects to be treated; and the extant contract for the *Last Supper* (Pl. 58) by **Dirk Bouts** with its accompanying panels depicting episodes from the Old Testament related to the central subject—the *Meeting of Abraham and Melchizedek* (Pl. 61), the *Passover*, the *Gift of Manna* and *Elijah fed by the Angel*—enjoins upon the artist to depart in no particular from the instructions given to him by Jean Varenacker and Egidius de Bailleuil, both Professors of Theology in Louvain University. In the same way, to take a French example, the extant contract for a *Coronation of the Virgin* painted in 1453 for the Chartreuse of Avignon by

Enguerrand Charonton (reproduced in my 'French Painting' (Medici)) specifically directs the artist to clothe the Virgin in a robe of damask, and to paint the Father and the Son, who crown her, as identical figures; it also states that right and left in the heavenly zone there shall be assemblies of particular saints and churchmen, that on earth there shall be shown the cities of Rome and Jerusalem with particular happenings in each, and that below shall be shown the fate of the Blessed and the Damned on the Day of Judgement—the Blessed to be received by angels while the Damned remain among the tortures and fires of Hell. The three-tier arrangement prescribed for Charonton's picture is evidently related to the Mystery and Miracle plays habitually performed on three stages, the top stage for the figures in Heaven, the middle stage for a scene on earth, and the third, corresponding to the orchestra pit in a modern theatre, for the nether regions into which wrongdoers were sometimes ignominiously thrown down. This structure is followed in some early Flemish pictures; and it seems probable that the local theologians also ordered groupings of figures based on particular Mysteries, Miracles or tableaux vivants arranged on certain days in churches.

There is unfortunately no extant contract for the **van Eycks'** *Altarpiece of the Mystic Lamb* but the lower panels (Pls. 9, 14) are clearly an allegory on the theme of the Redemption of Mankind through the sacrifice of Christ. We know that originally there was also a predella (bottom panel), representing Hell or Purgatory, which was destroyed by an incompetent attempt to clean it in the middle of the sixteenth century; the whole altarpiece was thus designed as a three-stage composition, and it was so represented in the Pageant setpiece for Philip the Good in 1458, already mentioned; and the same structure is seen in the picture reproduced here by the **Madrid Fountain of Grace Painter** (Pl. 22). The scene on earth in the **van Eycks'** picture contains, in the foreground, two processions to the Fountain of Life; in the left-hand procession we have Just Judges, Knights of Christ, Gentile and Hebrew Prophets; in the other Pilgrims, Hermits, Saintly Churchmen, and Apostles. Behind the Fountain stands the rose-red altar with the Mystic Lamb upon it and a stream of blood from the Lamb's breast flows into a chalice; behind the altar are the cross and lance, the pillar and the reed with sponge; and angels with thuribles kneel round the altar to which rays descend from the Holy Ghost above. In the middle distance approaching from the left are male Saints and Martyrs, mostly churchmen, and approaching from the right there are female Saints and Martyrs, mostly maidens with some abbesses. The constitution of each group was doubtless within the theologians' province, and some figures can easily be recognized. Among the saintly Churchmen (Pl. 23) S. Stephen carries the stones that killed him, and S. Livin, Bishop and Patron of Ghent, who stands behind him, holds the pincers that tore out his tongue; the leaders of the Maiden Saints are S. Agnes with her lamb, S. Barbara with her tower and S. Dorothy with her basket of flowers; the two women hermits, behind the men, must be S. Mary Magdalene who holds her pot of unguent, and S. Mary of Egypt (though her loaves of bread, so clearly inserted in a later picture by the **Philadelphia Maria Egyptiaca Painter** (Pl. 131) cannot here be seen). The giant leading the pilgrims is obviously S. Christopher, and here, exceptionally, he really looks a giant, because he is contrasted with the men who follow him, and not with the little figure of the Christ-child (as in the pictures by the **Pearl of Brabant Master** (Pl. 92), the **Philadelphia S. Christopher Painter** (Pl. 132) and the **Lisbon Alexander VI Painter** (Pl. 202)). This processional adoration scene has Latin inscriptions at various points, selected, of course, by the theologians. The altar is inscribed: 'Ecce Agnus Dei, qui tollit peccata mundi'; the Fountain of Life bears the words 'Hic est fons aque vite procedens de sede dei et agni'; and the first Knight of Christ bears a shield inscribed 'Dominus fortis Adonai

Sabaot V. Emmanuel I.H.S. XRI. AGLA',—the four letters of the last word standing for Hebrew words with the meaning 'Thou art mighty for ever, O Lord'. In the zone of Heaven in this picture (Pl. 9) we have a theological concept *God the Father* or *God the Son* (or both in One) enthroned in a golden tabernacle; right and left in smaller golden tabernacles are the *Virgin* and *S. John the Baptist* flanked by groups of *Singing* and *Musician Angels*; *Adam* and *Eve*, whose Fall led to the Redemption, are in outer niches and above them grisailles, imitating carvings, show *The Sacrifice of Cain and Abel* and the *Murder of Abel*. The golden tabernacles are covered with inscriptions from the prophets, the psalms, the Apocrypha, the writings of S. Augustine and so forth; there are further inscriptions on the robe of the central figure; and the word 'Agla', already referred to, which is said to have been used as an exorcist symbol in the Middle Ages, is on some of the floor tiles in the tabernacles of the angels.

It is evident that the theologians wished the public to receive two dominant ideas from the **van Eycks'** polyptych when opened on the altar of the church in Ghent. They wished it to convey not only the idea of the Redemption of Mankind through the sacrifice of Christ, which is embodied in the scene on earth in the lower panels, but also the idea of the Church of Christ on earth as image of, and mystically united with, a Church of Christ in Heaven. This second idea is stressed in the structure and the details of the upper panels. For the figures in Heaven are not seated in the clouds but in man-constructed tabernacles, and the angels are placed in ecclesiastic chapels complete with lectern, organ and floor inlaid with decorated tiles; the central figure is crowned with the Pontifical tiara (as S. Peter is crowned in a picture painted later by Vasco Fernandez, the Portuguese painter, for Viseu Cathedral), he gives the Papal benediction, and the crown of earthly monarchs is placed below his feet; the Virgin and S. John the Baptist read the Church's sacred books; and the angels wear ecclesiastic vestments of sumptuous brocade with jewelled clasps and ornaments (Pl. 17).

The second of these theological concepts is the basis also of other pictures of this period. We find it in the *Seven Sacraments*, now in Antwerp Cathedral, by the unrecorded artist already mentioned; for there the Crucifixion is shown within an actual Cathedral (perhaps S. Pierre in Louvain) where Mass is being celebrated; and the sacraments are allegorized by contemporary genre scenes in side chapels. The church interior by the **Exhumation of S. Hubert Master** (Pl. 54) is, of course, in a different category because the happening there recorded did in fact take place within a church interior—S. Pierre in Liège. But the triptych by the **Redemption Master** is built on this theologic concept; for the central panel (Pl. 51) shows the *Crucifixion* in the porch of a Gothic cathedral, the Communion and the Elevation of the Host within the Cathedral, episodes from the Passion carved upon the soffits of the porch, and the sacraments carved in niches on the columns—the bottom figures of each column kneeling on the floor outside; on the wings, the *Expulsion from Eden* (Pl. 52) and the *Last Judgement* (Pl. 53) are also set in the carved porches of a Gothic church with the soffits of the first showing six scenes from *The Creation* and the seventh the *Creation of Eve*, for which there is no room, outside; and the soffits of the second showing six of the *Seven Works of Mercy* with the seventh, *Burying the Dead*, also placed outside to solve the same dilemma. The same idea directed some of the less elaborate pictures. The formal devotional image of the Virgin and Child with attendant saints by **Jan van Eyck** in the *Van der Paele altarpiece* (Pl. 19) is placed as noted in the apse of a Romanesque church choir; the **New York Virgin in a Tabernacle Painter** sets the Virgin and Child in a late Gothic shrine with a brocaded cloth of honour and canopy inscribed 'Domus Dei est et porta coeli' (Pl. 24); the **New York Annunciation in a Porch Painter** stands the Virgin Annunciate in a church porch inscribed 'Regina coeli letare' (Pl. 26); the **Washington Annunciation in a Church Painter** shows the Annunciation in a late Romanesque church with the signs of the zodiac and scenes from the Old Testament (*Samson and Delilah, David and Goliath* and *Saul in his tent*) on the tiles, and arrays the Archangel Gabriel in a gold and crimson cope, bordered with jewels, and crowns him with a coronet (Pl. 15). A church porch, with Old Testament subjects in the soffits, leads us to the stable in the *Nativity* by the **Washington Nativity in a Sculptured Porch Painter** (Pl. 30); and the **New York Christ Appearing to His Mother Painter** sets the scene in a church porch with episodes from the later life of the Virgin in the soffits (Pl. 47). We must note, too, that the **Beaune Last Judgement Painter** (Pls. 34, 42, 136-9)—in a panel not reproduced here—shows Heaven as a church where the Blessed are welcomed by an angel; and that S. Peter receives the Blessed on the steps of a cathedral in more than one *Last Judgement* of this period and also in a later picture by the **Antwerp Last Judgement Painter** (Pl. 135).

The artists' reactions to the theologians' requirements varied, of necessity, with each man. Some followed the instructions mechanically without individual thought or feeling, some were evidently fired by the mystic element in the theologians' ideas and some took the theology as starting points for excursions into visual experience of the life around them, for personal aesthetic experience, or for personal imaginative illustration of the Gospel themes.

We have, for example, nothing but the theologians' contribution and the artist's memory of a setpiece in a Mystery play in the picture by the **Madrid Fountain of Grace Painter** (Pl. 22) where the Princes of the Church and the Kings and other rulers form an ordered group on one side of the symbolic Fountain, and a blindfolded High Priest with attendant distraught Jews are shown in confusion on the other. **Dirk Bouts,** as I have suggested, seems to have begun his *Last Supper* (Pl. 58) as a complete and convincing study of a dining-chamber —or employed an architectural assistant to do this for him—and the theologians, rather strangely, have not insisted that the gathering should be shown in an 'upper' chamber (indeed this was not perhaps insisted on till the period of the Tridentine standards when we get the *Last Supper* (Pls. 423, 424) by **Adriaen Key**). In this picture by **Dirk Bouts** the figures round the table, posed and grouped perhaps on the model of a Mystery performance, are carefully painted without imaginative flights; the disciples sit quietly, and the central benediction is almost the only illustrative gesture; the four attendants are portraits, I imagine, of members of the Louvain Confraternity of the Holy Sacrament and thus come within the donors' part in the picture's form—for there is no evidence to support the notion that the man by the serving table is a portrait of the artist and that the youths in the serving hatch are portraits of his sons **Dirk Bouts the younger** and **Aelbrecht Bouts** who may have helped him with the picture, and it seems to me unlikely that the Flemish theologians of this period allowed the artists to put their own portraits in religious pictures (though **Lucas de Heere,** writing in 1559, refers to portraits of **Hubert van Eyck** and **Jan van Eyck** in the *Just Judges* panel (Pl. 14) of the *Altarpiece of the Mystic Lamb*).

In the lower panels of the **van Eycks'** *Altarpiece of the Mystic Lamb* (Pls. 9, 23) the theologians' orders seem to have moved the composing artist, at heart a landscape painter, to a grand imaginative vision of a radiant sky and a spreading and receding landscape as symbol of this earth with its flowers and trees and cities, a symbol consonant with the spirit of the allegory he was called on to give form to; and though the 'close-up' technique is used to describe the jewelled mitres and brocaded vestments on some churchmen shown as saints or martyrs, it does not clamour for attention—partly no doubt by reason of the smallness

31

of the scale in relation to such details on the panels above. We have also, I feel, the artist's own imaginative vision in the setting for the *Annunciation* on the outside of this altarpiece, in the lovely attitude of the Virgin and in the simplicity of the robes on both the figures (Pl. 12) contrasted, for example, with the setting and the attitudes of the figures and the sumptuous ornate vestments on the Archangel Gabriel in the picture by the **Washington Annunciation in a Church Painter** (Pl.15) which is all theology and manual skill. There is a similar contrast between the pictures by the **London Christ Appearing to His Mother Painter** (Pl. 32) and the **New York Christ Appearing to His Mother Painter** (Pl. 47), for in the first we have, I feel, the artist's own concept of a setting appropriate to the subject which contributes to the ethical content of the picture, while in the second, till we reach the subsidiary scene in the landscape (Pls. 47, 33), the artist seems bound by a theologian's script.

In the upper panels of the *Altarpiece of the Mystic Lamb* (Pl. 9) we find again an artist who seems to have accepted the script as handed to him and remained unmoved by it; he has not, I feel, been stirred till he began to paint the actual models in his studio with his 'close-up' vision and technique, and added, or trained his assistants to add for him, the brocaded robes and glittering crowns and other accessories demanded. In the event, accordingly, though the upper panels are in one sense all theology, we can only arrive at the theological content by coming to terms with the particular faces and bodies of the particular human beings who posed to the artist; we have to surmount the intrusion of the particular young woman who posed for the *Virgin* (Pl. 13) before we can think of her in the part she plays here; it is the same with the girls who posed for the *Singing Angels* (Pl. 17) and the *Musician Angels*, and with the men who posed for the central figure and S. John the Baptist; and, as already noted, there have been some, including the Emperor Joseph II, in whom the naked male and female figures quite failed to induce the theologic concept of *The Fall*. It is a case, to put it differently, of the actors 'stealing' our attention from the play. Something similar, but yet different, happens in the *Van der Paele altarpiece* (Pl. 19); for here **Jan van Eyck** has obeyed his script at every point, he has put Adam and Eve, the Death of Abel and Samson and the Lion, as instructed, on the Virgin's throne, he has inscribed 'Adonai' on S. George's gorget, and shown the seven candles on S. Donatian's wheel that miraculously marked the spot where the saint was drowned; but he was only stirred when he came to apply his 'close-up' method to the donor's face, which, for that reason, completely 'steals' the picture, as all visitors to Bruges have, for centuries, agreed. We must also observe at this point that even a minor degree of this 'close-up' vision and illusionist technique makes scenes of martyrdom and torture quite unbearable, even when the artist is wholly non-sadistic; I have already referred to *The Winding out of the entrails of S. Erasmus* by **Dirk Bouts** as too distressing to be reproduced here; the same can be said of some pictures of *Christ as the Man of Sorrows* where Christ's brow is bleeding from the crown of thorns; and it applies more especially to one example in the London National Gallery where a sadistic artist shows a large thorn driven like a nail through the eyebrow with the point directed to the eyelid.

In the great *Descent from the Cross* by **Rogier van der Weyden** (Pl. 46) we find, as dictated elements, the grouping, based probably on a Mystery tableau or a well-known work of sculpture, and the conventional gold background; and within these terms of reference the artist has created an imaginative illustration which is immensely moving, partly by reason of the aesthetic rhythms and partly by the artist's power to suggest the tragedy in terms of human grief. As van Mander, who knew the picture only from a copy, nevertheless quite accurately puts it: 'Hij legte een volmaakter kunstenaarschap aan den dag door de toepassing van zijn vindingen en behandeling, zoowel in houdingen als in compositie, door de uitbeelding van de menschelijke zieleroerselen, droefheid boosheid of vreugde, naar den eisch van het werk' (he displayed a perfect art in the correspondence of his design and treatment with his portrayal of the human emotions called for by his subject). The limp, dead Christ, the almost fainting Virgin, the lean, agonized contorted Magdalene are profoundly emotive figures; tears come from the Virgin's drooping eyelids and the wide open eyes of Joseph of Arimathea, and with touching realism they fall from the eyes in the down-bent face of the Magdalene not down the cheeks but across the nose; deep grief is here in abundance without rhetorical gestures to make it 'theatre'; no ill-considered lines or spaces destroy the aesthetic harmony; idea, pattern and feeling ring together in one chord.

Fusion of theologic idea with the artist's own imaginative concept appears again in the **Flémalle Master's** *Holy Trinity* (Pl. 37); the Christ here is dying but not dead—for the left leg still partly supports the body and the raised left arm with the sentient hand moves in a pathetic gesture to the side wound; there is tender sensibility in the invention of the turned long foot; and, as already noted, the long down-falling lines of the composition have the grand rhythm of Mediterranean aesthetic. This grisaille, where lateral cast shadows suggest the light effects of the modern photographer's arc lamp, was painted, I imagine, from a sculptured group where this fusion of theology and art was originally achieved and, as many early painters also worked as sculptors, the **Flémalle Master** may have carved the group himself; alternatively he may have used a well-known group in some cathedral of which small replicas were common—for a smaller version in fact appears on the wall above the fireplace of the living-room in the picture by the **Madrid Werl Wings Painter** (Pl. 44). Another beautiful fusion is attained in the *Virgin and Child by a Fountain* (Pl. 25) which **Jan van Eyck** signed in 1439, using, no doubt, a drawing made much earlier and perhaps by another hand; for here the youthful Virgin with her very human child, standing before, and upon, a cloth of honour upheld by angels, has floated down to an earthly garden where a fountain bird-bath is transmuted in concord to the Fountain of Life. The *Nativity* (Pl. 30) by the **Washington Nativity in a Sculptured Porch Painter** and the *Adoration of the Shepherds* (Pls. 28, 29, 75) by the **Minneapolis Adoration Painter** are both gentle, homely, imaginative illustrations, and both were probably based on the church tableaux vivants where the angels may well have been played by the local children; in both the Virgin looking down adores the tiny infant, protected by her mantle, on the ground; and in both we have aesthetic quality deriving from the artists' preferences for some delicate forms. But there are also elements that derive from theological instructions in both pictures—in the first the church porch carved with subjects already referred to, the ecclesiastic vestments on the angels and S. Joseph's pattens, and in the second, the lighted candle in S. Joseph's hand, the ruined pagan building transformed to the sacred stable, and the mysterious grating. As noted earlier at different points in my comments, theology and the artist's genre observation are equally evident in the formal devotional image by the **New York Virgin in a Tabernacle Painter** (Pl. 24); the *Virgin and Child* by the **Flémalle Master** (Pl. 36) is a perfect blend of aesthetic grandeur and genre tenderness, with the jewelled haloes and the gold and scarlet cloth of honour of theology completing the design; and no theology is apparent in the intimate and noble genre scene by the **London Virgin with a Firescreen Painter** if we regard the firescreen-halo quite simply as a firescreen (Frontispiece).

It remains to examine the fusion achieved by the **New York Crucifixion and Last Judgement Painter** who, as already indicated, I feel to be an adolescent artist. Theology has furnished inscriptions and the basic iconography of both his panels (Pls. 3, 4);

the frame of the first bears a Latin version of 'And the Lord hath laid on him the iniquity of us all...' from Isaiah; and the frame of the *Last Judgement* has inscriptions from Revelation: 'And Death and Hell delivered up the dead which were in them... and the sea gave up the dead which were in it...', and 'God shall wipe away all tears from their eyes...', and from Deuteronomy 'I will also send the teeth of beasts upon them, with the poison of serpents of the dust...'. Across the robe of Christ the Judge we read in Latin 'Come ye Blessed of my Father' and right and left of the Archangel Michael 'Depart from me ye cursed into everlasting fire'. Inscriptions in Greek lettering are on S. Michael's mail and the words 'Agla' and 'Adonai' are on his buckler (Pl. 96). The iconography of the *Last Judgement* has evident reference to the words of Christ as recorded by S. Matthew: 'And they shall see the Son of Man coming in the clouds of heaven with power and great glory; and he shall send his angels with a great sound of a trumpet and they shall gather together his elect from the four winds... and he shall separate them one from another.' The composition is an upright variant of the lateral polyptych by the **Beaune Last Judgement Painter** (Pls. 34, 42, 136-9) which was probably painted in the later fourteen-forties; and in certain aspects it seems to be based on a stark *Last Judgement*, an upright panel, dated 1452 and signed by **Petrus Christus.** As already mentioned, the landscape and townscape in the *Crucifixion* (Pls. 1, 3, 5, 6) recall the setting for the procession in the **van Eycks'** *Altarpiece of the Mystic Lamb*; the horses show acquaintance with the horses in the *Knights* and *Judges* panels and the artist seems resolved to 'go one better' by more varied movement in the animals just as **Hieronymus Bosch** was later to challenge **Jan van Eyck's** calligraphy on the wall of the *Marriage of Arnolfini* (Pl. 18A) by the Gothic flourishes round his *Operation for stone, or the cure of folly* (Pl. 161); and a memory of the Magdalene's agonized clasped hands in **Rogier van der Weyden's** picture (Pl. 46) may lie behind the Magdalene's gesture in the foreground (Pl. 160). But the essential quality of both panels, working through and permeating the theologic data, the standard iconographic features and the memories of other pictures, comes directly from the personal quality of the artist's mind and spirit. His genre observation (Pl. 1), his skill in shorthand portraiture (Pl. 159) and his delicate aesthetic (Pls. 5, 6, 16, 96) have already been the subjects of my comments; now we have to marvel at his feeling and his powers as imaginative illustrator of the sacred texts which fired him. With tremendous courage he has followed the Gospel account of the populace quite impervious to the tragedy at the Crucifixion; here the sponge is mounted and the spear is thrust from the midst of a crowd of passers-by, rulers and chief priests, who 'stand beholding' and make derisive comments 'wagging their heads' while only the centurion with back-flung head cries out his faith (Pls. 1, 59); right and left, the thieves, blindfolded and breeched (both unusual features) are tied not nailed to the crosses (Pls. 1, 5, 6) and 'afar off', in the foreground of the picture, we have the Virgin, her face almost hidden by her hood, collapsed in grief and supported by S. John, the other Maries behind her, while the Magdalene, the only gesture-making figure, looks up at the central torture with arms raised and hands clasped desperately together (Pls. 2, 3, 160). In the *Last Judgement* panel I have already referred to the charming group of the advancing maidens and to the smiling angel who welcomes the virtuous laymen (Pl. 7), and we must note now that the *Pit of Hell* (Pl. 8) is wholly innocent of sadism; there is no vicious delight here in cruel tortures wickedly devised by man; no clubs crash down on human faces (as in **Lucas van Leyden's** Hell scene (Pl. 292)), nor are there grim reminders of earthly judicial punishments, hangings and so forth (as in Giotto's *Last Judgement* in Padua); the artist tells us with simplicity that the wicked are being eaten because they have been wicked, and since he

34

had 'the teeth of beasts' in mind he has stressed especially, with naïve awe, the fangs and beaks and enormous teeth of his invented monsters.

Who was this astounding and enchanting artist? Were the panels painted, as I myself guess, about 1467 by a genius, about eighteen called **Hieronymus Bosch**? No one knows. For the pedigree of the panels begins in 1841 when they were owned by a Russian diplomat who had been in Spain where, he said, he had acquired them from a Spanish convent as the wings of a triptych, together with the central panel, an *Adoration of the Magi*, which was stolen from him.

CHAPTER II

Charles the Bold

1468-1477

DUKE CHARLES THE BOLD was a man of parts, speaking several languages, and fond of parade and pageantry. He was also an addict of music, having studied under an English musician, one Robert Morton. He composed some songs and motets and is said to have sung with a fine voice. On his accession he inherited a chapel of musicians, founded by his father, and much increased it; he had twenty-four singers including an Englishman John Stewart, with lutists and viola and oboe players; 'lorsqu'il avait mandé les expers musiciens de Rome' Jean Molinet, court chronicler informs us, '. . . le duc Charles recueilloit les plus fameux chantres du monde et entretenoit une chapelle estoffée de voix tant armonieuses et delectables que après la gloire céleste il n'estoit aultre liesse'; and these singers and musicians performed for him daily and he took them with him on some of his military campaigns. Though austere in his habits, he was obstinate, cruel, revengeful and subject to fits of violent fury at opposition or defiance. He was also superstitious, trusting to signs and omens, and believing that Tuesday was his lucky day. Convinced of his destiny to raise his inheritance to the status of a kingdom, he strengthened the centralized government established by Duke Philip, built up a mercenary army, the best trained and armed in Europe, and spent his fortune and the taxes of his subjects on futile warfare to add Alsace and Lorraine to his dominions and thus join the northern with the southern territories. But within ten years he was brought to defeat and ruin by the brains and perfidy of Louis XI and the unexpected valour of the Swiss Confederates.

In 1468 Duke Charles married Edward IV's sister Margaret of York as his third wife— (Isabella of Bourbon, his second wife and the mother of Maria of Burgundy, now a child of eleven, having died in 1465). The Duke at this date was thirty-five, Edward IV was twenty-six and Louis XI was forty-five; Frederick III was still Emperor and Paul II still Pope. The wedding took place with much pomp and pageantry in Bruges; Tommaso Portinari, Medici agent in Flanders, was among the countless foreigners attending, and Sir John Donne of Kidwell, Carmarthenshire, and his wife Elizabeth, also present for the occasion, commissioned an altarpiece from an unrecorded Flemish painter (presumed by some **Hans Memlinc**). Liège once more revolted in the autumn; and Charles, with Louis XI for the moment as his ally, led his storm troops to the city and sacked it in seven weeks of burning, pillaging and hideous slaughter. In 1469 Isabella of Castile, aged eighteen, married Ferdinand of Aragon, aged seventeen; Lorenzo dei Medici, aged twenty, conjointly with his brother Giuliano, aged sixteen, inherited the wealth and position of Piero dei Medici in Florence; the Earl of Warwick led rebellion against King Edward and defeated his forces at Edgecote where Sir John Donne was killed; the Archduke Sigismund of Austria pawned Alsace to

Duke Charles for 50,000 florins and a promise of aid against the disaffected Swiss Confederates; and Peter von Hagenbach sent by Charles as governor in Alsace, began there a régime of terror and rapacity. In 1470 Tommaso Portinari married Maria Baroncelli; Louis XI made a treaty with the Swiss; the Earl of Warwick was driven to France by Edward but returned with French aid to lead another revolt against him, and reached London; Edward fled to Holland and was welcomed by Duke Charles; and Henry VI, released from the Tower, was reinstalled as King with Warwick as de facto ruler. In 1471 Sixtus IV became Pope; the Portuguese captured Arzil and Tangiers from the Moors; Edward IV, back in England with troops provided by Duke Charles, won the Battle of Barnet where Warwick was killed; Henry VI died or was murdered in the Tower; Louis XI, again at war with Burgundy, seized a number of towns on the Somme; Duke Charles captured Nesle and butchered the inhabitants; and William Caxton translated the 'The Recuyelle of the Historyes of Troye' for the Duchess Margaret in Bruges. In 1472 Duke Charles failed to capture Beauvais in the war with France and made a truce with Louis. In 1473 Charles bought the duchy of Gelderland from the reigning duke and added 'Duke of Gelderland and Count of Zutphen' to his titles; at a meeting with the Emperor Frederick at Treves he offered Maria of Burgundy in marriage to the Emperor's son Maximilian, hoping to be nominated 'King of Belgian Gaul' or possibly King of the Romans; and the Emperor considered this, till, hearing that the Archduke Sigismund had allied himself with Louis, he stopped negotiations by leaving the town quite suddenly at night. In 1474 Isabella became titular Queen of Castile on the death of her brother Henry; William Caxton printed his first books in Bruges; Louis XI persuaded the Archduke Sigismund to sign the 'Everlasting Compact' renouncing all Austrian claims to the Swiss Confederates' lands; the towns of Alsace, oppressed by Hagenbach, produced the money to de-pawn the province but Charles refused to give it back to Sigismund; the Alsatians revolted and tried and executed Hagenbach; pretexting that some subjects of the Bishop of Cologne, his kinsman, had risen in rebellion, Charles launched war on Germany by besieging Neuss; and war was declared on him by the Swiss Confederates urged on by the Emperor and Sigismund. In 1475 René de Vaudemont, Duke of Lorraine, allied himself with Louis and declared war on Charles; the Swiss had numerous successes, capturing among other places Granson and Morat and also Estovayer where they massacred the garrison; Edward IV, allied to Charles, led an army into Picardy and was bought off by Louis with a large sum down and the promise of a pension (which was regularly paid thereafter); Charles, having failed to induce the famous condottiere Bartolomeo Colleone to send him troops and service, and faced with the approach of a large Imperial army, abandoned the siege of Neuss; the Emperor and Louis, alarmed at the Swiss successes, then made peace with him; and Charles' troops took Nancy. In 1476 'le bon roi' René of Anjou paid Nicolas Froment for an *Altarpiece of the Burning Bush*, with himself and his wife Jeanne de Laval as adorant donors, to be placed in the Eglise des Grands Carmes in Aix-en-Provence; the King of Portugal, Alfonso the African, was received in state by Louis XI in Tours on a dais designed by the French miniature painter Jean Fouquet; the burghers of the Netherlands, weary of Duke Charles' wars, began to withhold their subsidies; Charles, determined to subdue the Swiss, arrived at Granson which capitulated, and avenged Estovayer by hanging or drowning the whole garrison except two men compelled to act as executioners; the Swiss attacked him near Granson a few days later, destroyed his army and took enormous booty; Charles with a new army was defeated again at Morat where the Swiss had cavalry led by the Duke of Lorraine; Charles' troops evacuated Nancy and the Duke of Lorraine returned there; and

Charles with yet another army again laid siege to Nancy. In January 1477 Swiss and Lorraine troops came to the relief of Nancy, the Burgundians were defeated; and Charles himself was killed.

The painters in this period included **Petrus Christus** (Pls. 27, 31), **Jacques Daret, Hans Memlinc** (Pls. 85, 93, 111, 112), **Willem Vrelant** and **Jehan Dreux** in Bruges; **Jan Hennecart** and **Pierre Coustain** in Bruges and Brussels; **Vrancke van der Stoct** and **Pieter van der Weyden** in Brussels; and **Gerard van der Meire** in Brussels and possibly Ghent. In Ghent also there were **Clay Spierinc, Daniel de Rycke, Matthys van Roden, Hugo van der Goes, Joos van Wassenhove,** and, presumably, **Justus of Ghent. Jan Snellaert** and the other painter members of the Antwerp Guild mentioned in the last chapter, and presumably **Hugo of Antwerp** (Pls. 70, 76-8) were in Antwerp where **Lucas Adriaenssen** was Dean of the Guild in 1469; and another or the same **Jan Snellaert** was in Tournai. **Hubert Stuerbout** and **Dirk Bouts** (Pls. 67, 69) and his two sons **Dirk Bouts the younger** and **Aelbrecht Bouts** (Pls. 251, 252, 253) were in Louvain; **Arnould Raet** worked in Louvain and Léau; **Gauthier van Battel** and **Baudoin van Battel** in Malines; and **Albert van Ouwater** in Haarlem.

Of these **Jacques Daret** probably died in the seventies though the actual date is not known; **Jan Hennecart, Jehan Dreux, Willem Vrelant** and **Pierre Coustain** were confirmed by the Duke as Court painters for illuminations, decorative designing and other work; **Pierre Coustain** was prosecuted by the Bruges Guild for non-payment of dues in 1471 and successfully claimed immunity as a member of the Duke's establishment; **Petrus Christus,** who lived till 1472, was one of **Coustain's** prosecutors as Dean of the Guild at the time. There are no records that **Hans Memlinc** had Court employment; according to a seventeenth-century tradition (not confirmed so far by documents but probably true in outline though possibly erroneous in some details) he served as a soldier in one of Duke Charles' armies, was wounded, returned to Bruges and collapsed in the street near the Hôpital de S. Jean where he was nursed to health by the Hospitallers for whom he painted an altarpiece, refusing in gratitude to accept their payment; and this gift may have been the *S. John altarpiece* (Pl. 111) subscribed for by the men and women Hospitallers depicted as adorants (Pls. 114, 115) whose payment he may in fact have refused to accept. The *S. John altarpiece,* though painted in Mary of Burgundy's reign and not finished till 1479, was evidently commissioned by 1475 because one of the Hospitallers depicted as donor died that year; and **Memlinc** was doubtless employed on other pictures and some portraits in this period but none known to be his work are known to be extant. **Pieter van der Weyden (Rogier van der Weyden's** son) who was twenty-eight when his father died, is presumed to have continued his father's workshop in Brussels though no pictures by him are recorded; **Vrancke van der Stoct,** still official painter to the town of Brussels and a Town Councillor till 1475, visited Bruges in 1468 and was active through the period; and **Gerard van der Meire** was also still living in 1477. **Clay Spierinc,** illuminator and illustrator of books, was employed by the Duke as such; **Daniel de Rycke** visited Bruges in 1468 and decorated triumphal arches when the Duke made a Pageant Entry into Ghent. **Matthys van Roden** was Ghent Master in 1475. No pictures known to have been painted by **Hugo van der Goes** are known to be extant. But there are records of his status; he visited Bruges for the Duke's wedding in 1468, he did decorative work for the Duke's Pageant Entry into Ghent and other local ceremonies, and in 1474 and 1475 he was Dean of the Guild there; he then retired from public life and became a lay brother in the Rouge-Cloître (Roodendale) Augustinian Monastery in the Soignes Forest near Brussels where his brother was already an inmate. Of his pictures we know something from sixteenth-century chroniclers and also from van Mander and from later writers; van Mander speaks of a youthful work *The Legend of S. Catherine* painted for the Brothers of Our Lady in Ghent, of a small triptych with a *Virgin and Child* for the church of S. Jacques there, and of *Christ with the Thieves* (*Crucifixion* or *Deposition*) in Bruges, S. Jacques (and this was still in position when the art historian Descamps went there in 1769); **Lucas de Heere** wrote a poem on a *Meeting of David and Abigail* painted as an overmantel for a private house in Ghent, and van Mander also knew and praised this composition. There are no records of **Justus of Ghent's** career in his native town or elsewhere in Flanders; but by 1474 he is known to have been in Urbino where he painted for the Corpus Domini Fraternity an *Institution of the Eucharist* containing a portrait of the Fraternity's President Duke Federigo da Montefeltro; and the same Duke Federigo invited an unnamed Netherlander about this time to join Melozzo da Forli and Giovanni Santi (Raphael's father) then decorating his study with pictures of philosophers and poets and made payments later to 'Giusto da Guante' for his work there. **Joos van Wassenhove** seems to have been continuously in Ghent for the first six years of the period and we know from a document that he had left for Italy by 1475. **Jan Snellaert** visited Bruges with other Antwerp artists in 1468 but no details of his work in Antwerp or Tournai seem recorded. **Hugo of Antwerp** is known only as the painter of the large *Portinari altarpiece* (Pls. 76-8) commissioned by Tommaso Portinari for the church of the Hospital of Santa Maria Nuova in Florence with portraits of Portinari and his wife and their three eldest children as adorant donors on the wings; the clothes of the donor's wife (Pl. 70) suggest that the picture was in hand about 1475 but as the younger boy depicted (Pl. 79) was not born till 1474, it was probably not finished till 1477 or 1478; Vasari mentions this **Hugo of Antwerp**; and the altarpiece (which remained in Santa Maria Nuova till the Italian Government bought it for the Uffizi in 1897) was famous in the sixteenth century when Guicciardini described it as 'bellissima'; but strangely enough van Mander does not seem to have seen it or known of its existence when he visited Florence in 1573. **Dirk Bouts,** whose *Last Supper* altarpiece (Pls. 58, 61), completed in 1468, was discussed in the last chapter, became Town Painter in Louvain in that year; in 1472 he finished a *Last Judgement* triptych for the Town Hall; in 1473 he married as his second wife another rich woman, a burgomaster's widow; and in 1475 he had nearly finished the two 'Justice' pictures for the Town Hall—*The Unjust Judgement of Emperor Otho* (Pl. 67) and *The Ordeal by Fire* (Pl. 69)—when he died. His eldest son **Dirk Bouts the younger** was twenty-five in 1473 and **Aelbrecht Bouts** (Pls. 251, 252, 253), another son, was some years younger. **Hubert Stuerbout** was still at work in Louvain in 1477; and **Arnould Raet** painted for Léau church from 1460 to 1472 and died in Louvain after 1477. **Gauthier van Battel** and **Baudoin van Battel** continued their work as painters and designers for the Malines Ommeganck processions. **Albert van Ouwater** was continuously active as far as we know in Haarlem; and **Jansz Jacob** painted a *Crucifixion* for the Carriers Guild in Haarlem, S. Bavo in 1474.

As before, these names represent, of course, but a fraction of the painters active in the seventeen provinces in the period reviewed; and as before, though a number of pictures known or presumed to have been painted at this time are extant, we rarely know who painted them. Indeed I can think of but three pictures of known authorship surviving from this time—the two *Justice* panels by **Dirk Bouts** (Pls. 67, 69) and **Hugo of Antwerp's** *Portinari altarpiece* (Pls. 70, 76-81) and the last as noted was probably not finished till a year or so later. I reproduce all panels of these three works; and I also show pictures by unrecorded artists here referred to as by the **London Virgin with Brocade Screen Painter** (Pl. 62), the **Lille Path to Paradise Painter** (Pl. 63), the **Vienna Cruciform Lamentation Painter** (Pl. 64), the **London (Guicciardi) Entombment Painter** (Pl. 65), the **Vienna Adam and Eve Painter** (Pl. 66), the **Washington Man with an Arrow Painter** (Pl. 68), the **New York Lady with a Pink Painter** (Pl. 71), the **Ursula Legend Master** (Pls. 72-4, 97-101, 103, 120), the **Pearl of Brabant Master** (Pls. 86, 91, 92), the **Tiburtine Sibyl Master** (Pls. 87, 119), the **Dublin S. Augustine Painter** (Pl. 102), the **Philadelphia Adorant Painter** (Pl. 104), the **London (Layard) Virgin and Child Painter** (Pl. 105), the **Buckingham Palace Mystic Marriage Painter** (Pl. 106), the **Philadelphia S. Catherine Painter** (Pl. 108), the **New York S. Catherine Painter** (Pl. 109), the **Detroit Mystic Marriage Painter** (Pl. 110) and the **Minneapolis S. Catherine Painter** (Pl. 121) who may all have been active between 1467 and 1476.

All the works reproduced, except the didactic 'Justice' pictures by **Dirk Bouts,** are religious subjects, of various types, or portraits. But here, as before, we must assume an accompanying production of other kinds of painting which have disappeared for the reasons already suggested; and we must also remember that many artists were regularly employed on decorative work for the Ducal festivities and Pageants or other types of ceremonial designing.

Thus on Duke Philip's death artists were called on to design the memorial ceremonies all over his dominions; the catafalque in Brussels bore a *Crucifixion* and a *Virgin and Child* by **Pierre Coustain,** the catafalque in Ghent had armorial shields by **Hugo van der Goes,** and the final obsequies in Dijon gave work to other artists. Duke Charles' accession called for Pageant Entries to the major towns, with bas-reliefs and painted panels on the decorated arches. There were also elaborate pageants for the wedding celebrations, and others on gala occasions even in the midst of military campaigns—at the ten months' siege of Neuss, for example, the Duke had his singers, musicians, architects and painters with him in a grandiose encampment where ambassadors from a dozen states were entertained in elegant pavilions, with stained glass windows, specially erected to impress them. For the wedding celebrations scores of artists came to Bruges from other towns to reinforce the Brugeois artists; **Daniel de Ryck,** who received the highest payment of the whole team employed, and **Hugo van der Goes** were among the Gantois; **Vrancke van der Stoct, Pierre Coustain** and **Jan Hennecart** were there from Brussels; **Pierquin Bernart** came from Ypres; and **Jan Snellaert** came with his fellow painters of the Antwerp Guild **Godefroid of Antwerp, Jean Thomas, Henri Bastyn, Adrien Gérop, Lucas Adriaenssen, Jean Casyn Vinckaert** and **Guillaume Caddeman.** The veteran **Jacques Daret** (with the experience of the 'Oath of the Pheasant' ceremonies and work for the Chapter of the Golden Fleece behind him) led the Brugeois team; but **Hans Memlinc,** though as far as we know in Bruges at the time, does not seem to have been called on, nor apparently was **Petrus Christus.** There was plenty of work for all these artists, for these extravagant festivities included processions through streets hung with cloth of gold, tapestries and painted banners, and there were tableaux vivants on cars and on platforms at points of vantage. For the banquets there were specially constructed buildings (one was pre-fabricated in Brussels, sent by boat and then assembled); the fittings were directed by Jean Scalkin, an expert on light effects with mirrors and decorative fountains; plays, masques and episodes which drew upon mythology and the Old and New Testaments for their subjects, and topical allegories devised by Olivier de la Marche and the Chamber of Rhetoric, were performed in sumptuous costumes; and mechanical contrivances caused further entertainment—at one of the banquets the guests were confronted with 'une tour de quarente et un pieds de haut garnie de singes, de loups, de sangliers mécaniques dansant et chantant' while a huge whale crawled across the floor; and at another, a charade was performed showing monkeys stealing wares from a pedlar (a subject painted later by **Herri met de Bles**).

If my plates are carefully examined we find material for some concepts of this pageantry, and also, as before, for concepts of the landscapes, the town views, the interiors, genre, figure, animal, still-life and flower painting; and as before we must assume, I think, that specialists in these various studies were often called on as collaborators or as studio assistants.

Hints of contemporary pageants are in some of the pictures illustrated. Thus the **Ursula Legend Master** paints Charles the Bold and his Duchess as King and Queen of Holland receiving the Princess Ursula (Pl. 98) and there is another court scene in *King Agrippinus despatching the envoy* (Pl. 101); Court costume is also depicted by the **Tiburtine Sibyl Master** in a little procession from a palace (Pl. 87); and **Dirk Bouts** puts a huge winged headdress on the Empress in the *Unjust Judgement of the Emperor Otho* (Pl. 67) and a hennin on the kneeling lady, rich brocade upon the Emperor, and brocaded doublets and long pointed shoes upon his courtiers in the *Ordeal by Fire* (Pl. 69). The charming works by the **Buckingham Palace Mystic Marriage Painter** (Pl. 106) and the **Detroit Mystic Marriage Painter** (Pl. 110) were possibly related to tableaux vivants of S. Catherine receiving the ring from the Christ-child designed by artists for cars in the Ommeganck and other processions where all the parts were played by the local young ladies in 'fancy costume' closely influenced by prevailing fashions—as was still the case in the seventeenth century when **Denis van Alsloot** recorded an Ommeganck in detail (Pl. 513A).

The landscapes and townscapes follow the traditions of the earlier period; some, as before, are seen through loggias or windows; and some are used as settings for additional narrative details. We are in open country if we follow the horseman through the courtyard gate in the painting by the **Tiburtine Sibyl Master** (Pl. 119); a unified receding landscape with continuous space is the basic structure of the *Paradise* by the **Lille Path to Paradise Painter** (Pl. 63), and this landscape, from foreground meadow to horizon, with birds fluttering over rocks and trees, was complete in itself before the blessed, conducted by angels, began to arrive there; and in the same way the figures of S. John the Baptist and S. Christopher by the **Pearl of Brabant Master** seem almost intruders in the wonderful receding landscapes of meadows, rocks, trees and birds, distant town and estuary in the one case (Pl. 91) and wind-blown river bounded by bluffs with a setting sun or rising moon in the other (Pl. 92). Grey, muted blue and olive tones with delicate trees evoke a twilight atmosphere in the picture by the **London (Guicciardi) Entombment Painter** (Pl. 65) but, as in **Jan van Eyck's** *S. Barbara* (Pl. 18), the large figures, out of scale with the landscape setting, seem the work of a different artist; and this scale incongruity, suggesting collaboration, is found again in *The Fall* by the **Vienna Adam and Eve Painter,** for here the matter-of-fact garden with its tufted shrubs and foreground apple tree is a unit in itself and the figures, uncomfortably too large, seem thrust within it at a later stage (Pl. 66). In both these works the figures stand upon the foreground of the landscape; but in some other cases the landscape has the character of a painted backcloth hung behind them. We get this character in the wings of **Hugo of Antwerp's** *Portinari altarpiece* (Pls. 77, 78), in the compositions by the **Buckingham Palace Mystic Marriage Painter** (Pl. 106) and the **Detroit Mystic Marriage Painter** (Pl. 110), and also in the single-figure pieces by the **Minneapolis S. Catherine Painter** (Pl. 121), the **New York S. Catherine Painter** (Pl. 109) and the **Philadelphia S. Catherine Painter** (Pl. 108). In the right-hand wing of the *Portinari altarpiece* the backcloth landscape has mounds and hillocks as perfunctory as the similar forms in the *Meeting of Abraham and Melchizedek* by **Dirk Bouts** (Pl. 61), and one of the trees is awkwardly placed in relation to S. Margaret's shoulder (Pl. 78); but **Hugo of Antwerp** has redeemed this backcloth by the illustrative concept of the Magi's journey through a wintry landscape when the boughs are bare and few birds perch upon them (Pl. 81). In the left-hand wing of the *Portinari altarpiece* (Pl. 77) the backcloth shows a mountain pass with a scene subsidiary to the subject of the central panel, and the foreground has a wall which seems to be 'life size' because its top is not stated—a device already employed by Masaccio some fifty years earlier for *SS. Peter and John passing* in the Brancacci Chapel of the Carmine church in Florence which **Hugo of Antwerp** must, I think, have seen; and the **New York S. Catherine Painter** (Pl. 109) was another artist who probably went south as his landscape backcloth contains some cypress trees—though he may, of course, have taken them from the **van Eycks'** *Altarpiece of the Mystic Lamb* (Pl. 9). The backcloth by the **Minneapolis S. Catherine Painter** (Pl. 121) is a summary affair of tufted shrubs and fields with hedges; and the townscape by or provided for the **Philadelphia S. Catherine Painter** is curiously disturbing because the tower of one building seems to grow from the head of the pretty young lady who is posing for the saint (Pl. 108).

Some of the townscapes show particular places while others appear to be invented. The towers just mentioned in the picture by the **Philadelphia S. Catherine Painter** (Pl. 108) are the towers of Bruges, and they appear again in the backgrounds by or provided for the **Detroit Mystic Marriage Painter** (Pl. 110) and the **Philadelphia Adorant Painter** (Pl. 104). The monastery in the picture by the **Dublin S. Augustine Painter** (Pl. 102) can no longer be identified but it surely depicts some particular foundation; and the palace and courtyard, where the Emperor Augustus and the Sibyl had their vision of the Virgin, were probably painted from some local building and supplied by an architectural specialist to the **Tiburtine Sibyl Master** before the figures were put in (Pl. 87). Townscapes, apparently invented, are in the pictures by the **Ursula Legend Master** and the *Unjust Judgement of the Emperor Otho* by **Dirk Bouts.** Working in the manuscript tradition the **Ursula Legend Master** gives us charming little cities with pink and white walls and blue roofs and spires, to stand for Tiel, Cologne, Bâle and Rome and thus assist him in the telling of his story (Pls. 72, 73, 97-100, 101). The townscape in the *Unjust Judgement of the Emperor Otho* (Pl. 67) contains the Emperor's palace with its battlements and garden and one heavily barred window, perhaps the dungeon where the victim of the story was confined; further back there are other buildings with tall towers and spires; and all this, I fancy, was supplied complete by some architectural draughtsman to **Dirk Bouts** who made the figures near the buildings too large for the walls they stand by—a defect avoided, as noted, by **Hugo of Antwerp** in the left-hand panel of the *Portinari altarpiece* (Pl. 77) and also in the central panel where the top of the church depicted is again successfully 'life size' because there is no definition of its height (Pl. 76).

Landscapes and townscapes seen through doors and loggias are in several of my plates; and in others they are seen through windows. In the *Ordeal by Fire* by **Dirk Bouts** a hillside with church and town behind it are framed by the doorway of the Chamber of Justice (Pl. 69); a trim little garden with brick doorway is seen obliquely through a loggia in the *Envoy of King Agrippinus* by the **Ursula Legend Master** (Pls. 74, 101); a corner of another and more park-like garden with tufted and filigree trees is framed by a round arched loggia in the portrait by the **New York Lady with a Pink Painter** (Pl. 61); and a wall in the oddly constructed picture by the **Dublin S. Augustine Painter** suddenly becomes a parapet to reveal a monastery garden with open country and a cloud-swept sky (Pl. 102). The shutter of an unglazed window behind the figures by the **London Virgin with Brocade Screen Painter** opens on a wooded park or garden leading to a towered city (Pl. 62); a townscape and a stream winding between verdured bluffs appear through two unglazed windows, without shutters, in the portrait by the **Philadelphia Adorant Painter** (Pl. 104).

The interiors shown here are all unrealistic compared with those in earlier pictures; and none approach the three-dimensional completeness of the dining-chamber in the *Last Supper* by **Dirk Bouts** (Pl. 58) or the bedroom in **Jan van Eyck's** *Marriage of Arnolfini* (Pl. 18A) or the half-cube structures by the **London Christ Appearing to His Mother Painter** (Pl. 32) and the **Madrid Werl Wings Painter** (Pls. 41, 44). The interiors tend now to be token structures, suggesting rather than depicting a living-room in house or monastery, the hall or loggia of a palace, or a church interior. If we look back, for example, at the spacious room coming forward from window and fireplace in the devotional genre piece by the **London Virgin with a Firescreen Painter** (Frontispiece) and compare it with the setting for the same subject by the **London Virgin with Brocade Screen Painter** (Pl. 62) we find, in the second, a quite unaccountably small space between the foreground window frame and the back wall with the cloth of honour and the second window; and this has probably happened because the **London Virgin with Brocade Screen Painter** has added the back window, or caused it to be added, in the painting stage, though the picture—like the portrait by the **London Young Man in High Cap Painter** (Pl. 59)—had been conceived and drawn in the first place as a two-dimensional high-relief against a flat conventional background. A living-room is also no more than suggested in the portrait by the **Philadelphia Adorant Painter** which again recalls the portrait by the **London Young Man in High Cap Painter** though the sitter has now to suffer the draught from two unglazed windows instead of, as before, from one (Pl. 104). In the *Ordeal by Fire* (Pl. 69) by **Dirk Bouts** a canopied throne for the Emperor is at right angles to us on a tesselated floor; beyond, in the centre, we have a doorway with Gothic tracery, and beyond that what seems to be a terrace with stone wall and window; a few feet of wooden ceiling (partly obscured by the Gothic frame, a later addition) come forward from the top of the doorway well below the top of the window, thus suggesting an inner chamber, without walls, in a larger and loftier structure; but this token Chamber of Justice within a palace is far from coherent as we have it, perhaps because **Dirk Bouts** no longer had service from the architectural expert who constructed the dining-chamber for his *Last Supper* (Pl. 58) or because he was himself in process of altering the setting when he died, or by reason of later alterations or additions. In the *Envoy of King Agrippinus* (Pl. 101) by the **Ursula Legend Master** the palace loggia, whence the king despatches the envoy, is likewise a token structure, and the artist, to reveal the audience-chamber where the envoy delivers his message, has stripped the whole building of one wall. Two rooms in a monastery are indicated by the **Dublin S. Augustine Painter** (Pl. 102)—a bedchamber with only one wall which ends unaccountably, as noted, on the right-hand side, and a study with three walls, a ceiling and glazed window in the scene above; and the **Ursula Legend Master** suggests a church interior (Pl. 103) that is more convincing than his palace.

The still-life painting now tells us less than before of the furniture and equipment of the living-rooms. We have no more the large stone fireplaces, the studded shutters, the settles with cushions, the stools and curtained bedsteads, towels and washhand-basins, the chandeliers and mirrors and the statues of the *Holy Trinity* and the *Virgin and Child* so frequent in the earlier pictures (Frontispiece, Pls. 18A, 32, 41, 44, 58) though the tradition in respect of monastery equipment is continued by the **Dublin S. Augustine Painter** who puts a desk and cushioned settle in S. Augustine's study, and, in the chamber where the saint lies dying, a table with liturgic still-life, a metal ewer and basin and a lantern with other objects on the floor, and a painting of the *Holy Trinity* upon the wall behind him (Pl. 102); and the **Ursula Legend Master** shows some church equipment—an altar with a reliquary and little effigy, and votive offerings—in the *Veneration of the relics* (Pl. 103). But the artists, or their student-specialists, still give us rich brocades with elaborate patterns on cloths of honour, as in the picture by the **London Virgin with Brocade Screen Painter** (Pl. 62), on vestments worn by angels, as in the pictures by the **Lille Path to Paradise Painter** (Pl. 63) and **Hugo of Antwerp** (Pl. 76), and also, as already mentioned, on the robes of the Emperor Otho, his Empress and his courtiers as imaged by **Dirk Bouts** (Pls. 67, 69), on the robes of the Emperor Augustus in the picture by the **Tiburtine Sibyl Master** (Pl. 87), and on S. Catherine and her attendant saints by the **Buckingham Palace Mystic Marriage Painter** (Pl. 106), the **Philadelphia S. Catherine Painter** (Pl. 108), the **New York S. Catherine Painter** (Pl. 109), the **Detroit Mystic Marriage Painter** (Pl. 110) and the **Minneapolis S. Catherine Painter** (Pl. 121). In these S. Catherine pieces, the glittering crowns and jewelled headdresses recall the **van Eycks'** tradition in still-life painting; **Hugo of Antwerp** recalls it also in the necklaces worn by Madame Portinari (Pl. 70) and her daughter (Pl. 80) both so accurately painted that a jeweller could make them from the picture; and **Hugo of Antwerp's** S. Margaret holds a book with a triangle of legible text (Pl. 81) like the book held by the Virgin in the *Altarpiece of the Mystic Lamb* (Pl. 13).

Flowers abound in the pictures of these years; as before, they grow from verdure in the open and from bricked-round beds in gardens; they appear in vases as cut flowers; and single flowers are held by the sitters in some portraits. They spring from the meadow in the *Paradise* by the **Lille Path to Paradise Painter** (Pl. 63) and from the grass round S. Catherine's attendants in the picture by the **Buckingham Palace Mystic Marriage Painter** (Pl. 106); the **Detroit Mystic Marriage Painter** sets clusters of small flowers in the foreground grass, more flowers in beds on the walls round the figures, and roses in the hedge behind (Pl. 110); tall iris and aquilegias rise to hide the nakedness of Eve in the Garden of Eden by the **Vienna Adam and Eve Painter** (Pl. 66); and a lily grows from the foreground meadow in the wonderful landscape where the **Pearl of Brabant Master** has inserted his S. John the Baptist (Pl. 91). In the *Unjust Judgement of the Emperor Otho* by **Dirk Bouts** square beds of bush roses and other plants are behind the Emperor and Empress in their palace garden, and flowers rise in the foreground to conceal the victim's neck (Pl. 67); flowers with slim stems and delicate foliage are against the wall of the palace garden in the *Envoy of King Agrippinus* by the **Ursula Legend Master** (Pls. 74, 101); and flowers grow prettily up railings in the *Rest on the Flight* scene by the **Philadelphia Adorant Painter** (Pl. 104). Aquilegias in a glass and iris in a faience pot are in the foreground of **Hugo of Antwerp's** *Adoration of the Shepherds* (Pl. 76) just as cut flowers in vases were in the rooms shown by the **Madrid Werl Wings Painter** (Pl. 44) and the **Merode Master**; and the flowers held in the left hand of the Virgin in **Jan van Eyck's** *Van der Paele altarpiece* (Pl. 19) and the picture by **Petrus Christus** (Pl. 27) are recalled by the flower, perhaps a symbol of betrothal, in the right hand of the lady portrayed by the **New York Lady with a Pink Painter** (Pl. 71).[1]

The ox and the ass, horses and camels, a bear, monkeys, swans, peacocks, lizards, numerous dogs, a domestic cat and a dragon are among the animals depicted—in some cases perhaps by student specialists. In the central panel of **Hugo of Antwerp's** *Portinari altarpiece* (Pl. 76) the heads of the ox and the ass are above the manger, and the ass thinks only of his fodder, as in the earlier picture by the **Washington Nativity in a Sculptured Porch Painter** (Pl. 30); **Dirk Bouts** shows a dog asleep, impervious to the miracle, in the *Ordeal by Fire* (Pl. 69); and a cat sleeps in the foreground of the death-bed scene by the

---

[1] I am told that the flowers covering the neck in the picture by **Dirk Bouts** (Pl. 67) referred to in this paragraph have been removed, as a later addition, in a recent cleaning. [1958 note]

Dublin S. Augustine Painter (Pl. 102). In the right-hand wing of **Hugo of Antwerp's** altarpiece the Magi ride towards us on foreshortened horses while lively camels in profile form a silhouette behind (Pl. 81) and S. Margaret stands on the dragon that burst when he had swallowed her (Pls. 70, 78). In the panels by the **Ursula Legend Master** a knight rides a high-stepping destrier, while a greyhound trots beside him, in *S. Ursula leaving Rome* (Pl. 72), a greyhound plays with a monkey and another yaps at the arriving messenger in the *Envoy of King Agrippinus* (Pls. 74, 101), and swans, dear to all Brugeois artists, are in the Bâle scene (Pls. 73, 99). In the picture by the **Tiburtine Sibyl Master** (Pls. 87, 119) swans swim in the moat beside the entrance gate and lizards cross the distant roadway where a greyhound runs behind the horseman; the Emperor's own greyhound, with curling tail, is in the foreground, a peacock and a guinea fowl are further back, a monkey looks from a window in the palace, and a chained bear is sleeping at the foot of the steps that lead up to the palace door—(which reminds me that 'gardiens d'ours' were among the recipients of farewell 'tips' when Margaret of Austria left the Court of France some twenty years later).

In genre painting we have again some devotional genre pieces on the mother and child theme, some rural episodes and some town scenes. The **London Virgin with Brocade Screen Painter** (Pl. 62) shows the mother offering her breast to the child whose feet and hands are in eager action—a motif possibly invented by the **Boston S. Luke Painter** (Pl. 49). In the gentle picture by the **Buckingham Palace Mystic Marriage Painter** (Pl. 106) the prettily wriggling Christ-child, held firmly at his middle, puts the bridal ring on S. Catherine's finger while merrily cocking his head; and the youthful S. Barbara twinkles her delight with half-smiling eyes—just as, two hundred years later, an old woman will crow and smile at the new-born child in an *Adoration of the Shepherds* by **Jacob Jordaens** (Pl. 741); and in the devotional genre piece by the **London (Layard) Virgin and Child Painter** the same engaging Christ-child has both hands occupied with a rosary of coral (Pl. 105). Among the outdoor genre scenes the **Philadelphia Adorant Painter,** or a genre collaborator, presents us with a charming concept of the *Rest on the Flight*; for here the mother and child, guarded by musician angels, take their rest beneath the porch of a modest house beside a castle while S. Joseph draws water in a pitcher from a wayside pool (Pl. 104). The central panel of **Hugo of Antwerp's** *Portinari altarpiece* has a famous group of shepherds, acutely observed and characterized in genre terms, and here again the foremost figure smiles in delighted wonder at the child (Pl. 76); in the backcloth of the right-hand wing this artist has imaged the journey of the Magi as a genre episode, for a courier, sent ahead, inquires about the route from a group of peasants who are watching the strange procession from behind the trunks of the bare-boughed trees already referred to (Pls. 78, 81); and in the left-hand wing he shows a genre concept of the *Flight into Egypt*, for S. Joseph aids the Virgin down the steepness of a mountain path while the ass, with their mantles slung across the saddle, trots carefully behind them (Pl. 77). The **Ursula Legend Master** is a keen observer of the life around him; in his church interior a nun buys candles from a woman at the door (Pls. 103, 120); and in his outdoor genre scenes a beggar asks alms from a knight on horseback (Pl. 72), a procession of high churchmen comes forth from a cathedral (Pls. 73, 99) and, in one of the port scenes, a young woman with a travelling reticule is helped down the gangway by a port official while other officials, waiting to check their papers or to collect the port dues, peer out from 'guichets' at the entrance to the quay (Pl. 97). As an urban genre scene we have a conversation piece of Augustinian monks in the monastery garden by the **Dublin S. Augustine Painter** (Pl. 102); and we must also note that the picture by the **Tiburtine Sibyl**

Master and the 'Justice' pictures by **Dirk Bouts** are imaged as civic happenings in the artist's own environment, for **Dirk Bouts** is at pains to show the priest and civic dignitaries in the execution scene (Pl. 67), the Emperor's court attendants at the miracle, and the priest and other officials at the burning (Pl. 69), and the **Tiburtine Sibyl Master** surrounds the Emperor, the Sibyl and their suite by town and court officials, puts ladies watching from the palace windows, servants active at the palace door, and porters in the distance at the entrance to the courtyard (Pl. 87).

In figure painting the major works surviving are the 'Justice' pictures by **Dirk Bouts** where the figures are life size, and **Hugo of Antwerp's** *Portinari altarpiece* where many of the figures are also unusually large for Flemish painting of this time. In the 'Justice' pictures (Pls. 67, 69) **Dirk Bouts,** trusting to his eye and hand, paints figure by figure empirically, 'als door de natuur geleerd' in the **Jan van Eyck** tradition, but without excess of 'close-up' vision; the vertical rhythm of the figures which was marvellously in tune with the vertical lines of the containing chamber in the earlier *Last Supper* (Pl. 58) is now increased by a marked elongation of the figures, and there is less concordance now between them and the settings, as already noted. **Hugo of Antwerp,** on the other hand, has clearly tried with passionate valour to leave the Flemish empirical approach behind him and capture the secret of Italian Renaissance science; and at points in the *Portinari altarpiece* he succeeded —as would be very apparent if the altarpiece were housed in Bruges or Antwerp and surrounded with Flemish paintings of its date (though housed as it is in Florence and surrounded with Italian pictures its Flemish elements alone stand out). The heads and hands of the saints in both the wings (Pls. 77, 78, 81) and those of the Virgin and S. Joseph, and still more the heads and hands of the shepherds in the central scene (Pl. 76) are drawn in the spirit of Italian science—the science of Pollaiuolo, Verrocchio and others in Florence in his day; for **Hugo of Antwerp** was no lynx-eyed traveller on the surfaces of forms but an eager student of anatomy; and as a draughtsman he built his forms with linear construction and retained this feeling when he painted. Perhaps he was sent to Italy by Portinari to see what the Florentines were up to before he began this picture destined for a Florentine church; perhaps he saw Pollaiuolo at work on the *S. Sebastian* (now in the London National Gallery) and returned to Antwerp resolved to rival the open-mouthed archer by an open-mouthed peasant of his own; perhaps, as already suggested, he saw Masaccio's *S. Peter and S. John passing* in the Brancacci chapel of the Carmine church before he painted his S. Thomas and S. Anthony by the uprising 'life-size' wall; or perhaps he painted the whole or most of the altarpiece in Florence. Another contrast between the Flemish and a Flemish-Italian manner is seen, on a simpler plane, in the three single-figure pictures of S. Catherine reproduced here. For the **Philadelphia S. Catherine Painter** (Pl. 108) whose model was an elegant young lady of Bruges as she appeared in some church tableau, and the **Minneapolis S. Catherine Painter** (Pl. 121) who worked from a plump little bourgeoise, if not indeed a peasant, both followed the tradition of the maiden saints as painted in the meadow scene of the **van Eycks'** *Altarpiece of the Mystic Lamb* (Pl. 23) and both show the models in degrees of the old modish posture of the hollow back and protruding belly; but the **New York S. Catherine Painter** (Pl. 109), who had been, I suspect, to Italy or Avignon, had a less indigenous model or worked more probably without one; for the saint here, a two-dimensional concept in Mediterranean aesthetic, has no belly to thrust forward, she is non-corporeal and so much a ghost from the International Gothic that her face is an oval contrasted with the halo, and her hair a shape curving outwards to repeat the rhythm of her shoulders; or to make the point in a different way it is again the contrast between the **van Eycks'** *Singing*

Angels (Pl. 17) and the *Virgin interceding* by the **New York Crucifixion and Last Judgement Painter** (Pl. 16).

The most elaborate of the nude paintings of this time may well have been the *Last Judgement* commissioned from **Dirk Bouts** for Louvain Town Hall in 1468; but this triptych is unfortunately not known to be extant; and achievements in this field are suggested here by the nudes in pictures by the **Vienna Adam and Eve Painter,** the **Vienna Cruciform Lamentation Painter,** the **London (Guicciardi) Entombment Painter** and the **Lille Path to Paradise Painter.** Compared with the astonishing combination of inexorable surface naturalism and monumental grandeur of the *Adam* and *Eve* in the **van Eycks'** *Altarpiece of the Mystic Lamb* (Pl. 9) the figures by the **Vienna Adam and Eve Painter** (Pl. 66) seem the work of a beginner; but set beside the angular leanness and mincing movements of the *Adam* and *Eve* by the **Redemption Master** (Pl. 52) they are seen to have more dignity and substance, and appear the work of a gauche but earnest student of anatomy, who is worried by proportions and comes a cropper with the clumsy hands and enormous feet. No such gaucherie or trouble with proportions affects the **Vienna Cruciform Lamentation Painter** (Pl. 64) whose dead Christ, deeply emotive as a concept, is anatomically convincing in bone structure with normally proportioned feet and hands; and the same applies to the emotive nude, with the lengthened torso, slim hips and long lean thighs, by the **London (Guicciardi) Entombment Painter** (Pl. 65). In the attractive picture by the **Lille Path to Paradise Painter** (Pl. 63) the naked souls of the blessed form a vertical group in the right foreground (like the town officials, on the right, in the *Unjust Judgement of the Emperor Otho* by **Dirk Bouts** (Pl. 67)); modestly wrapped in their bath towels, they move inwards and upwards to the Fountain of Grace; and though all the figures are impeccably proportioned and indubitably walking, the artist, intent on the spirit of his subject, has not plagued himself, or us, with attempts to parade anatomical details.

In portraiture we can see the features, as before, of the artists' friends or members of their families, and portrait studies of other models in various compositions. We also have a number of small commissioned portraits and some portraits of adorant donors in altarpieces and portable diptychs; and what seem to be portrait groups of subscribers for certain pictures. In **Hugo of Antwerp's** *Portinari altarpiece* the faces of the Virgin and S. Joseph, and of SS. Thomas, Anthony Abbot, Margaret and Mary Magdalene are all evidently studies made from particular sitters, probably the artist's friends, and the faces of the shepherds are clearly adapted from portrait drawings of particular peasants brought into his studio and instructed to smile or keep quite still with their mouths half-open (Pls. 76, 77, 78, 81). As already remarked in my notes on the figure painting, the **Minneapolis S. Catherine Painter** (Pl. 121) provides a portrait of some young bourgeoise or peasant girl in his S. Catherine, and she may have been his daughter, wife or mistress, or the girl next door; while the picture by the **Philadelphia S. Catherine Painter** (Pl. 108) was probably a commission from the patrician Brugeois parents of the girl portrayed. SS. Barbara, Margaret and Agnes on the right of the tableau group by the **Buckingham Palace Mystic Marriage Painter** (Pl. 106) are evidently portrait studies of one and the same young girl, while another and slightly older and more delicately pretty girl has posed for the Virgin and for SS. Catherine and Ursula on the left of this picture—and also it would seem for the Virgin in the devotional genre piece by the **London (Layard) Virgin and Child Painter** (Pl. 105). The **Detroit Mystic Marriage Painter** (Pl. 110), on the other hand, gives the Virgin and the maiden saints conventional type faces, as was more usual in religious pictures. Type faces are also seen in the groups behind the dead Christ in the compositions by the **London (Guicciardi) Entomb-**

ment Painter (Pl. 65) and the **Vienna Cruciform Lamentation Painter** (Pl. 64); but in both these works the figures of Nicodemus and S. Mary Magdalene are evidently portraits, and they are also set a little apart from the other figures perhaps in echo of the Mystery plays and church tableaux vivants where these characters were possibly differentiated from the most sacred groups and placed on a lower level where they may have acted as narrators; the Nicodemus of the **London (Guicciardi) Entombment Painter** is a profile portrait of an ageing man, double-chinned and nearly bald, but still robust and vigorous, and the Magdalene is painted from the profile of a snub-nosed girl (like the girl in the portrait in the Milan Ambrosiana which used to be, and may still be, labelled '*Beatrice d'Este* by Ambrogio de Predis'); the Nicodemus by the **Vienna Cruciform Lamentation Painter** appears the portrait of some sturdy friend in the prime of life, and the Magdalene is a faithful study of a particular young woman as she sat on a studio stool in a simple frock revealing her small breasts —a daring stroke of anatomic realism at a time when no hint of the breasts was permitted in the clothes of fashionable ladies (as we know from the dresses worn by Madame Portinari (Pl. 70) and the sitter portrayed by the **New York Lady with a Pink Painter** (Pl. 71)). In the 'Justice' pictures by **Dirk Bouts** (Pls. 67, 69) the victim's wife in the fashionable gown and hennin was probably drawn from a Louvain lady in the artist's entourage for, as already mentioned, he had recently married a second rich wife (a burgomaster's widow) whose friends no doubt included such well-dressed bourgeois ladies. The male figures in these 'Justice' pictures are all broadly characterized as stiff upstanding individual portraits—(like the rows of portraits in the famous S. Vicente polyptych painted at just this time by the Portuguese Nuno Gonçalves); and here again the particular faces may well have been drawn from the artist's friends; but as these figures stand for civic and other dignitaries in the first scene and young nobles and court officials in the second, they may be portraits of Louvain notables who provided the Magistrates with money for these Town Hall pictures and wished to be seen in them, just as the donors of works to churches were seen there; and if this was so, they here anticipate the groups of subscribers that appear in many later paintings. The same applies to the portrait figures who play the parts of civic dignitaries and court officials in the picture by the **Tiburtine Sibyl Master** (Pl. 87); and also to the Augustinian monks in the scene by the **Dublin S. Augustine Painter** (Pl. 102), an artist with a very sharp eye for portraits, who may have been paid for his work by these particular inmates of the monastery, just as, a few years later, **Hans Memlinc** was paid or offered payment for the *S. John altarpiece* by four inmates of the Hospital depicted on the wings (Pls. 114, 115).

Of the portraits of the time showing adorant donors, I reproduce the *Portinari family* placed by **Hugo of Antwerp** on the wings of his altarpiece, and a *Young man in prayer* (probably the wing of a portable diptych with a *Virgin and Child* on the opposite panel) by the **Philadelphia Adorant Painter.** As already mentioned the *Portinari altarpiece* was commissioned for the church of the Hospital of Sta. Maria Nuova in Florence and the adorant donors (Pls. 77, 78) are Tommaso Portinari, Medici agent in Bruges, Maria Baroncelli whom he married in 1470, and their three eldest children, the younger boy born in 1474 being not less than three or four years old; and **Hugo of Antwerp** has used the earlier Mediterranean convention of small figures for the donors presented by much larger saints, perhaps because he was so instructed by his Italian patron who recalled the earlier Italian pictures or because he was himself recalling such pictures seen on a journey to Italy through France or in Italy itself. The Italianate and scientific elements in this artist's drawing give bite and interest to these portraits; Maria Portinari, tall and lean in her black gown trimmed with fur and her lofty hennin with muslin veil that falls behind her to the ground, has long and well-shaped fingers and a well-bred face with long blunt-ended nose and the skin drawn tightly round the jaw and cheekbones (Pl. 70); and Ghirlandaio and other contemporary Italian portraitists are recalled by the drawing of the children's faces (Pls. 79, 80). The **Philadelphia Adorant Painter** (perhaps a pupil of **Hugo of Antwerp**) has also drawn with science in the *Young man in prayer* (Pl. 104); the component factors in the head and hands show anatomic knowledge though the head as a whole is too large for the shoulders, and the artist, defeated by the problem of receding planes, has set the eyes and cheekbones too far apart and made the top of the head too low; the aureole was most probably added later by some dealer; but this passionate fanatical young man, with his spreading nostrils and far-gazing eyes, had perhaps within him the makings of a saint, for the aureole seems not incongruous. In contrast with these scientific portraits the **New York Lady with a Pink Painter** and the **Washington Man with an Arrow Painter** are purely empirical artists relying on their eye and hand to record their sensibility. Everything in the portrait by the **New York Lady with a Pink Painter** (Pl. 71) is exquisitely refined and delicate; the even tone of the face and breast is gently modulated to suggest the features, and the youth of the sitter is shown by her thin arms and tiny hands, themselves an emotive factor; the lady, perhaps the wife of a moderately well-off burgher, wears a quite small pendant on her necklace and an unpretentious ring on the middle joint of her second finger—and we may note in passing that rings in this century were often worn thus forward as well as sometimes at the base of the finger (Pls. 40, 45, 50, 57, 68, 70). We find great delicacy also in the portrait of what seems to be an aesthetic and musical young Jew by the **Washington Man with an Arrow Painter** (Pl. 68); there is no parade here of anatomic knowledge, no indication of bone structure beneath the outer forms; but the eyes, the corners of the mouth, and the dimple in the chin are all most sensitively seen and painted; and the artist, unless he flattered, has caught the sitter at his most attractive age before he coarsened and became too fat.

Considered as civic-didactic subjects the 'Justice' pictures by **Dirk Bouts** and *The Virgin appearing to the Tiburtine Sibyl and the Emperor Augustus* by the **Tiburtine Sibyl Master** had precedents in the 'Justice' pictures by **Rogier van der Weyden**, then still on the walls of the Brussels Town Hall—(and the tradition thus established was still alive in 1894 when the Brussels magistrates briefed **Xavier Mellery** to compose for the Town Hall an *Allegory of the virtues incumbent on a Burgomaster: Equity, Firmness and Kindness*). **Dirk Bouts,** as the official painter to the town of Louvain, was commissioned by the Magistrature to paint these pictures for the newly completed Town Hall; the Magistrates supplied him with the wooden panels (more than ten feet high) which they had bought in Antwerp, they chose the subjects, and they appointed Jan van Haecht, Professor of Theology in Louvain University as his theological adviser; as just suggested, some of their members and some other notables may have subscribed some money and thus acquired permission to have their portraits in the pictures. According to the legend chosen the Spanish wife of the Emperor Otho III, suffering unrequited love for a young married noble of the court, accused him to the Emperor of trying to seduce her; and the Emperor, without further inquiry, had him executed. But the victim's widow proved his innocence by holding a red-hot iron in her hand; the Emperor, convinced by the miracle, swore to atone in any way she dictated; and the lady declared that the perjured Empress must be burned alive. The theme is thus a sermon against the evil of false witness, and a warning to judges not to act on accusations whispered by their wives; and it was also possibly a crypto-protest against some gross miscarriage of justice by Charles the Bold inspired by Margaret of York who was rancorous and given to political intrigue. In the *Unjust Judgement of the Emperor Otho* (Pl. 67) **Dirk Bouts** shows three scenes of the drama; the Empress tells the Emperor her false story, her hand upon his shoulder; the innocent young noble, with bound wrists, comes forth in his shift for execution, his confessor before him, and his wife with officials behind; and, after the execution, the widow kneels with a napkin to receive the head from the executioner who holds it by the hair with his left hand while his right hand holds the sword; the last two scenes form a single diagonal in the picture's structure from the top of the left-hand corner to the bottom corner on the right, and this diagonal with a shorter one moving upwards to the right from the bottom left-hand corner makes a cruciform ground plan. There are no expressions of emotion in the figures; the noble and his wife make no gestures of fear or anguish; and the civic dignitaries, attending ex-officio, are impassive. In the *Ordeal by Fire* (Pl. 69) the widow, kneeling before the Emperor, holds the red-hot bar of iron in her left hand, and her husband's head, partly covered by the muslin of her hennin, in the right; the Emperor shrinks back in dismay at this proof of his wife's false witness; the courtiers are impassive or make minor gestures of surprise; and the lady with terrifying calm demands the frightful penalty. The last scene, the burning of the Empress on the hillside outside the town, is fortunately small and in the background; and here again the ex-officio spectators are apparently unmoved. It is not known who commissioned *The Virgin appearing to the Tiburtine Sibyl and the Emperor Augustus* (Pl. 87) from the **Tiburtine Sibyl Master** or where it was painted. The scene represents the moment when, the legend tells us, the Virgin and Child appeared to the Sibyl and Augustus and revealed to them the future site of the Sta. Maria d'Aracoeli Church in Rome; and the subject may be an allegoric reference to a local event in the town where the picture was commissioned, the choice of a site perhaps for some new church by Charles the Bold. As in the composition by **Dirk Bouts** the central figures form a diagonal procession to the foreground; the Sibyl points to the apparition, and the Emperor kneels; but the groups of civic and court officials, quietly engaged in discussion of their own affairs, seem unaffected by the vision, perhaps, as already suggested, because, as in **Dirk Bouts'** pictures, they are really portraits of subscribers to the picture.

Religious painting was still in part directed by local theologians, though their influence is no longer so widely evident. A theologian, for example, was certainly behind *The Fall* by the **Vienna Adam and Eve Painter** (Pl. 66) which considered as illustration presents unusual features; for Eve, it will be noted, holds two apples, one from which she has bitten and the other, destined for Adam, still attached to the tree; the serpent, woman-headed, as in the **Redemption Master's** picture (Pl. 52), is not yet a serpent crawling on its belly as a punishment, but a standing hybrid with frog's legs, the body of an otter, and a lizard's tail; and the second fruit tree behind Adam may be the Tree of Life which God feared that Adam now might eat of and thus 'live for ever'. A theologian was also, of course, responsible for the Fountain of Grace and the brocaded vestment on the angel in the picture by the **Lille Path to Paradise Painter** (Pl. 63); and another for the pillars of the pagan ruined temple, the church façade, the albs, dalmatics, copes and crowns upon the angels, and S. Joseph's patten in **Hugo of Antwerp's** *Portinari altarpiece* (Pl. 76). But all the artists whose works I reproduce here display their personal feeling in imaginative illustration of religious subjects, and also their personal observation and aesthetic. As already indicated the devotional image of the Virgin and Child was now habitually treated as a genre scene in the tradition launched by the **London Virgin with a Firescreen Painter** (Frontispiece) and others of that time; and the Mother and Child are sometimes presented, as by the **London Virgin with**

Brocade Screen Painter (Pl. 62) with intense vitality, and sometimes—as by the **London (Layard) Virgin and Child Painter** (Pl. 105) and the **Buckingham Palace Mystic Marriage Painter** (Pl. 106)—in terms of the gentlest domesticity. Among the more imaginative religious pictures the *Paradise* by the **Lille Path to Paradise Painter** (Pl. 63) is a poetic vision with the theologian's instructions merged within it. The twilight atmosphere in the *Entombment* by the **London (Guicciardi) Entombment Painter** (Pl. 65) may be due in part to a technical factor, as the picture is one of the few survivals of the very perishable paintings in tempera or distemper on linen which were common in this century and sometimes used as altar frontals or displayed in rooms like tapestries; but apart from this, the group of figures, as imaginative illustration of the subject, and also aesthetically, is extremely moving; the long straight torso is lowered slowly between the lateral straight lines of the tomb by Joseph of Arimathea in his brocaded coat, the Virgin's hands are clasped beneath the limp left wrist which the thumb of her left hand caresses, S. John supports the Virgin, the Maries weep behind, and in the foreground S. Mary Magdalene lifts the winding sheet to cover the left leg and Nicodemus gently lets down the feet; all the figures, except the weeping Maries, look towards the back-bent head from which the crown of thorns is not yet lifted; the bounding lines of the right-hand figures—curves flattened almost to straight lines—are slow and simple, and the rhythm quickens only with short sharp angles in the lower folds of the Magdalene's cloak. The *Lamentation* by the **Vienna Cruciform Lamentation Painter** (Pl. 64) is on panel and may have been originally half of a portable diptych. It measures only thirteen by nine inches, but within this space there is tremendous drama. The cruciform structure, with a double row of figures for the upright shaft and the three women at the cross shaft, makes it at once a Deposition and a Lamentation; for this Christ is deposed from a cross consisting of those most near to him. A structure so bold in mental and formal concept, with the figures so tightly packed in so steep a diagonal, might well have resulted in a disconcerting oddity; but though strange and physically impossible, this shaft of humans grips the spectator with a tragic tension that increases as the eye moves upward from the realistic portrait studies used for S. Mary Magdalene and Nicodemus in the foreground to the dead Christ and the Virgin, whose hands are folded below Christ's head, and thence to S. John supporting her and the Maries who kiss the nails passed back to them. In the central panel of the *Portinari altarpiece* (Pl. 76) **Hugo of Antwerp** began with the theologian's instructions, and he also remembered the church tableaux, with children, maybe, acting as the angels, just as the **Washington Nativity in a Sculptured Porch Painter** (Pl. 30) had doubtless remembered them earlier; and then with delightful lyric fancy he has filled the air with the rustle of more angels descending to adore the Christ-child. But the *Nativity* was not the subject given him; he had to go further and paint an *Adoration of the Shepherds*, and unlike the **Minneapolis Adoration Painter** (Pl. 75) he failed to do this and keep the lyric mood; his shepherds 'steal' the picture and destroy its ecstasy, not only because they are too large and placed too high for the balance of the design but also and still more because they are depicted with more insistent realism than the other figures. How did it happen that the artist spoilt his picture in this way? The answer, I feel sure, is, as already suggested, that **Hugo of Antwerp** embarked on this group and carried it through in passionate emulation of the scientific drawing of Florentine painters like Pollaiuolo whose works he must have seen and studied with excitement.

Subjects taken from the lives of the Saints became a feature in this period, partly, I suspect, because the theologians and the artists now had printed copies of the 'Legendae Sanctorum', better known as 'La Légende Dorée', or 'The Golden Legend' as a guide.

Written in Latin, about 1290 by the Genoese Dominican Jacques de Voragine, this book had been translated into French in the fourteenth century, and by about 1470 printed versions in Latin, French, Italian, English and other languages had become available and were widely read. In the Golden Legend there are countless stories of pious action with miracles and dramatic episodes; and as the sufferings and triumphs of the maiden saints appealed especially to pious women in hospitals and convents, the artists were often called on to paint them for the chapels in such places.

Thus the charming panels by the **Ursula Legend Master** were probably commissioned for the Couvent des Soeurs Noires in Bruges which still preserves them. According to the Golden Legend (and other sources) S. Ursula's story began when the heathen King of England wished to marry his son to the princess Ursula, daughter of the Christian King of Brittany—(but as Charles the Bold had just married an English princess, the artist, or his mentor, changed the King to Agrippinus, King of the Picts); and the first picture (Pl. 101) shows the handing of a written message to the envoy, then the envoy entering the palace of the King of Brittany from the garden (Pl. 74) and then the envoy delivering his message to the King. The princess Ursula made conditions for the marriage: the prince must be baptized and, before the ceremony, she herself, the prince's sister Florentina and nine other maidens each attended by a thousand others, must make a pilgrimage to Rome; and *The Departure of Florentina* is the subject of the second panel (not reproduced here). In the third, *The Arrival of S. Ursula at Tiel on the Vaal*, the princess is received by the rulers of Holland dressed as Charles the Bold and his English consort (Pl. 98). In the fourth, *The Arrival of S. Ursula at Cologne* (Pl. 97) the princess learns from an angel that she and her companions are destined to be martyrs. From Cologne the pilgrims sailed up the Rhine to Bâle whence they set out on foot for Rome; Pope Cyriacus had a vision that he was destined to be martyred with them; and in the fifth picture, *The Departure from Bâle* (Pl. 99), there is a subsidiary scene shown in my detail (Pl. 73) of the Pope in Rome. In the sixth picture, *The Departure from Rome*, the Pope, resolved to join their company and share their fate, is starting with them on the journey home. In the seventh, *The Martyrdom* (Pl. 100), the eleven thousand maidens are slaughtered by the Huns, an archer shoots his arrow at S. Ursula who has refused the advances of their King, and the Pope is killed by the sword in a boat by the quayside. In the last, the *Veneration of the relics of S. Ursula* (Pl. 100) we have the church interior with the candle-buying genre scene already referred to (Pl. 120). The whole story is imaged by the artist in terms of the life around him; and his engaging simplicity can be measured if we compare his panels with the series painted by Carpaccio for the Venetian orphanage the Scuola di devozione di Sta. Orsola; Carpaccio, for example, shows the angel who foretells her martyrdom appearing to S. Ursula asleep in bed; but to the **Ursula Legend Master** this was not a vision but an actual happening, and the angel just meets her on the quayside and gives her the tidings there (Pl. 97).

Paintings of S. Catherine of Alexandria, patron saint of schools and colleges, of ladies of noble birth and spinsters, were also in demand for women's religious houses; and S. Catherine appears in them sometimes as the Virgin Martyr and sometimes as the Bride of Christ. In the picture by the **New York S. Catherine Painter** (Pl. 109) she wears a turban surmounted by a crown as becomes a princess of the Orient; her right hand holds a sword as emblem of her martyrdom (depicted in the background) and her left hand holds a book as symbol of her holy learning which confounded and converted the pagan theologians summoned by the Emperor Maximin to instruct and refute her—(a scene painted by Pintoricchio in the Vatican for Alexander VI some twenty years later); beside her is the devilish machine with opposing sharp-spiked wheels invented for her torture which burst asunder when they tied her to it and killed scores of the assembled crowd; and the saint has one foot on the prostrate body of the Emperor, himself thrown down by the explosion. The **Philadelphia S. Catherine Painter** (Pl. 108) makes fewer references to the legend as he paints her crowned, but without the turban, and he leaves out the wheel; and the **Minneapolis S. Catherine Painter** (Pl. 121) shows her with only the crown, the sword and the book as attributes. The Golden Legend tells us that S. Catherine, at her martyrdom, heard a voice from Heaven crying 'Come my beloved Bride'; and, as already suggested, *S. Catherine receiving the ring from the Christ-child* was probably a frequent subject in church tableaux where other saints were added as S. Catherine's bridesmaids. In the delightful painting on this theme by the **Buckingham Palace Mystic Marriage Painter** (Pl. 106) the bridesmaids are SS. Barbara, Ursula, Margaret and Agnes; in the handsome group elaborately designed by the **Detroit Mystic Marriage Painter** (Pl. 110) they seem to be SS. Barbara, Ursula and Cecilia. Compositions of this type absorbed the earlier and beautiful *Hortus conclusus* concept of the Virgin and Child with saints or angels in a little garden enclosed by walls or hedges; and pictures with these two motifs which might have been titled *The Mystic Marriage of S. Catherine in a Hortus Conclusus* (and were indeed later titled *Virgo inter Virgines*) were perfectly in tune with the spirit of a convent; for they could easily be read as symbols of the shelter from mundane evils vouchsafed to chaste women with religious faith; and in the version by the **Detroit Mystic Marriage Painter** (Pl. 110) there seems also a reminder that all women in their homes are sheltered, for, beyond the rose-hedge, two horsemen canter forth from Bruges to work or fight in the world outside.

CHAPTER III

Maria of Burgundy 1477-1482: Regency of Maximilian 1482-1494

1477-1494

CHARLES THE BOLD's heir, Maria of Burgundy, daughter of his second wife Isabella of Bourbon, was a girl of eighteen. The States General and the trade corporations accordingly took charge and set out to break up the centralized government which Philip and Charles had constructed, to revive the local independencies, to make peace with Louis XI, and to marry Maria to the Dauphin Charles, then aged seven. But Maria, already betrothed by her father to the Archduke Maximilian, son of the Emperor Frederick III, now urged him to make good his claim; and Maximilian arrived to marry her. The sinister Habsburgs thus came into the history of the Netherlands; and the first result was renewal of the war with France which continued, with one or two truces, till Maria died.

When Charles the Bold was killed in January 1477, Louis XI was fifty-four, the Archduke Maximilian was eighteen, and Edward IV thirty-five; Sixtus IV was Pope; Alfonso the African was still King of Portugal; Isabella, Queen of Castile, was twenty-six and Ferdinand of Aragon was twenty-five. Early in the year Maria of Burgundy was in Ghent with her step-mother, the Dowager Duchess (Margaret of York); and, there, the States General representing Flanders, Brabant, Hainault, Namur, Artois, Holland and Zeeland obtained her signature to a democratic charter, known as the Great Privilege, whereby she undertook inter alia not to raise taxes or make war without consent of the States. The States General sent an embassy to Louis XI to arrange the marriage with the Dauphin; Maria also sent ambassadors to Louis, but these were arrested and beheaded on their return by order of the States though Maria personally pleaded for their lives (an episode made the subject of more than one 'costume-history' picture in the nineteenth century). Maria then summoned Maximilian in a secret letter; Maximilian came with a bodyguard of a thousand men; and the marriage took place in August. Louis XI sent troops to Burgundy which he claimed for France; Maximilian reorganized the remains of Charles the Bold's army for this new war; and Maria pawned jewels and plate from her father's treasure to equip the troops—Tommaso Portinari (the banker patron of **Hugo of Antwerp**) being among those who advanced the money. In 1478 Maria gave birth to Philip the Fair who later married Ferdinand and Isabella's daughter; Isabella asked the Pope for a Bull to introduce the Inquisition in Castile; and George Duke of Clarence, Edward IV's brother, imprisoned in the Tower, was drowned in a butt of malmsey. In 1479 Spain was united when Ferdinand became King of Aragon; Edward IV allied himself with Maximilian and betrothed his daughter Anne to the infant Philip the Fair; Maximilian defeated the French at Guinegatte; and

Hans Memlinc completed the *Floreins altar* (Pls. 82, 84, 85, 94, 95) and the *S. John altar* (Pls. 89, 90, 111, 114, 115). In 1480 Maria gave birth to Margaret of Austria, later Regent of the Netherlands; King René of Anjou died at seventy-one leaving Anjou, Maine, Provence and his titular kingdom of Naples to the Crown of France; and the **Lucy Legend Master** painted *Scenes from the Legend of S. Lucy* (Pls. 116, 117, 118). In 1481 six people were burned alive in the first auto-da-fé of the new Spanish Inquisition; Alfonso the African died, and John II became King of Portugal; Lodovico Sforza (Il Moro) became de facto ruler in Milan; Maximilian allied himself with Francis II, Duke of Brittany, against France; and **Hugo van der Goes** went mad. In March 1482 Maria fell from her horse and died; and her will appointed Maximilian Regent for and guardian of Philip the Fair.

The Archduke Maximilian was a man of parts; he kept on the chapel of musicians, inherited by Maria of Burgundy from Charles the Bold, though their wages were often left unpaid; he spoke several languages and in later life he wrote and inspired a series of books and was a patron of Albert Dürer. But his period in the Netherlands was continuously troubled, he was always pressed for money, and he held no settled court with attendant nobles as Philip the Good had done. Concerned with Habsburgian and Imperial affairs, he was out of the country for long periods, from the end of the eighties, fighting Hungarians and Turks; and he was glad to surrender the government of the Netherlands when Philip the Fair came of age in 1494.

By the terms of the Great Privilege the States General were not bound by Maria's will; but some accepted Maximilian as Regent—though Flanders (led by Ghent, Bruges and Ypres) and the chief nobles (the Princes du Sang) opposed it; and all pressed for peace with France. In these conditions Maximilian signed the Treaty of Arras with Louis XI in December 1482; by this instrument he surrendered Burgundy, sent his daughter Margaret of Austria, aged two, to France as fiancée of the Dauphin Charles, now aged twelve, and promised Artois and Franche-Comté as her dowry; at the same time he surrendered the guardianship of Philip the Fair to a Council of Nobles and agreed that Philip should live alternately in the major Flemish cities. In this year also **Hugo van der Goes** died; Leonardo da Vinci, aged thirty, went to Milan as protégé of Ludovico Sforza; and the Portuguese Diego Cam discovered the Congo. In 1483 Maximilian made himself Duke of Gelderland, though Charles of Egmont refused to surrender his claim; Louis XI died at sixty and Charles VIII aged thirteen succeeded with Anne de Beaujeu and her husband as the Regents; Cardinal Tomas de Torquemada became first Inquisitor-General in Spain; Edward IV died at forty-one; Richard III became King at thirty-one; and the Princes Edward and Richard were murdered in the Tower. In 1484 Maximilian defied the Council of Nobles, assumed the guardianship of Philip, and imported German landsknechten to fight the anti-Habsburg Flemings; Anne de Beaujeu, in Charles VIII's name, allied herself with Flanders against him; Pope Sixtus IV died; and Innocent VIII succeeded. In 1485 Maximilian captured Bruges and Ghent and was virtually master, for a moment, in the Netherlands; Mathias Corvinus King of Hungary drove the Emperor Frederick from Vienna; Maximilian went to Germany to be nominated King of the Romans, leaving Philippe de Cleves, chief of the Princes du Sang, Englebert of Nassau and Chancellor Carondelet as Governors in the Netherlands; Richard III was killed at Bosworth; and Henry VII, aged twenty-eight, succeeded. In 1486 Henry VII married Elizabeth of York and the red and white Tudor rose became the Tudor emblem; Lord Lovell, defeated in a revolt against Henry, fled to Flanders and was welcomed by Charles the Bold's widow, the Dowager Duchess Margaret a constant intriguer for all Yorkists; Maximilian came back from Germany, as King of the Romans elect, and made Pageant Entries into various towns; a visit from the Emperor followed; and Maximilian launched a new and unpopular offensive against France. In 1487 Maximilian was crowned King of the Romans at Aix-la-Chapelle and continued the war against France nominally in support of Francis II of Brittany; the Pretender Lambert Simnel, instigated by the Dowager Duchess Margaret, landed in Ireland with two thousand German mercenaries and Yorkist exiles, and was crowned King of England in Dublin by Lord Lovell and the Earl of Lincoln; and Henry VII defeated the rebels at Stoke near Nottingham, and pardoned Simnel who was employed thereafter as a turnspit in the royal kitchens. In February 1488 Maximilian, seeking money for the unpopular French war, summoned the States General to Bruges and went there with a token bodyguard of landsknechten; he found the guilds and trade corporations intensely hostile to himself and also despondent at the decline of Bruges prosperity—due partly to competition from Antwerp, now a rising and more modern city with capitalist ideas, and partly to the silting of the Zwyn which was already serious; fearing a popular rising Maximilian rode to the gates to summon more landsknechten whom he had left outside; but the gates were barred against him and he became a prisoner in a revolted town. Through the barred windows of the house where the Brugeois held him he saw the execution of magistrates who had favoured the Habsburg cause; and these bars and windows had been painted red by **Gerard David** (Pl. 195) while, round the corner, **Hans Memlinc** was at work on the *S. Ursula Shrine* (Pls. 93,112). While the Archduke was thus imprisoned, the Gantois formed a full alliance with the French against him; and the Princes du Sang were called on to form a government till Philip the Fair came of age. In May the Emperor led an army of twenty thousand to the Netherlands, and the Brugeois set Maximilian free on his oath to withdraw from the Netherlands forthwith. Once free, however, Maximilian joined the Emperor at Louvain and laid siege to Ghent; Brussels and other places joined the rebel patriots while Antwerp backed the Habsburgs; Henry VII and Ferdinand of Spain allied themselves with Maximilian against France; but the Habsburg forces failed to capture Ghent and, in October, the Emperor withdrew his troops. In 1489 there was a serious outbreak of the plague which claimed countless victims especially in Bruges and Brussels; Maximilian left for Germany and made Albert de Saxe general of the Habsburg forces in the Netherlands; Henry VII sent six thousand English troops to Brittany to fight for the Duchess Anne who, at the age of twelve, had succeeded her father Duke Francis; and Maximilian made peace with France from Frankfort. In 1490 Maximilian drove the Hungarians from Vienna and inherited Tyrol (where he was later financed by the wealthy Fuggers who had silver mines in the Tyrol and copper mines in Hungary); Albert de Saxe signed on his behalf the Treaty of Damme with the Brugeois; and Maximilian married the Duchess Anne of Brittany by proxy. In 1491 Maximilian signed the Treaty of Pressburg with Ladislaus King of Hungary, and Ladislaus agreed that the Habsburgs should inherit Hungary if he died without male issue; Anne of Brittany, under pressure from the French, broke her marriage with Maximilian and was married to Charles VIII; Margaret of Austria, betrothed to Charles from infancy, was sent back to the Netherlands; and Isabella d'Este the new Marchioness of Mantua, aged seventeen, began to plague Mantegna who was sixty. In 1492 Ferdinand and Isabella conquered Granada and expelled the Jews from Spain; Columbus discovered America; Pope Innocent VIII died and was succeeded by Rodrigo Borgia as Alexander VI; Henry VII landed at Calais but made peace with Anne of Beaujeu and Charles VIII in consideration of a money payment; the Flemish impostor Perkin Warbeck, claiming to be the younger of the Princes in the Tower, was received and acknowledged as her nephew by the

Dowager Duchess Margaret; Ghent made peace with Albert de Saxe and at last accepted Maximilian as Regent; Charles of Egmont, aided by the French, began to reconquer Gelderland; and Maximilian defeated the invading Turks at Villach. In 1493 Alexander VI made Cesare Borgia a Cardinal, and Lucrezia Borgia married Giovanni Sforza in a ceremony of great splendour; Maximilian agreed to the Peace of Senlis with Charles VIII who kept his hold on Burgundy but returned Artois and Franche-Comté to the Netherlands; the Emperor Frederick died; Maximilian, attending the funeral as Emperor Elect, was accompanied by Perkin Warbeck who was treated as King of England; and Henry VII broke off trade relations with the Netherlands. In 1494 Alexander VI gave Ferdinand and Isabella the title of the 'Catholic Monarchs'; the Treaty of Tordesillas confirmed the Pope's Bull dividing the New World between Portugal and Spain; and Savonarola drove Pietro dei Medici from power. Charles VIII led an army into Italy to enforce his inheritance of the Kingdom of Naples; the Emperor Maximilian married Bianca Sforza at Innsbrück, drove the Turks from Styria, returned to the Netherlands with Perkin Warbeck, and led an unsuccessful expedition against Charles of Egmont in Gelderland; and Philip the Fair, now of age at sixteen, became ruler of the Netherlands and began his Pageant Entries into various towns.

A regional conspectus of some of the painters known to have been working within these seventeen years shows **Pierre Coustain, Willem Vrelant, Hans Memlinc, Annekin Verhanneman, Paschier van der Mersch, Gerard David, Jan Provoost,** the **Lucy Legend Master,** the **Brussels Mystic Marriage Painter,** the **Bruges Virgin with the Apple Painter** and perhaps the **London S. Giles Mass Painter** in Bruges; **Pieter van der Weyden** and his son **Goswin van der Weyden, Vrancke van der Stoct** and his son **Bernaert van der Stoct, Colyn de Coter, Jan van Coninxloo the elder,** the **View of Sainte Gudule Master,** and perhaps the **Dublin S. Nicholas Painter** in Brussels; **Hugo van der Goes** in the Rouge-Cloître Monastery near Brussels; **Jan Snellaert,** some of the artists who had worked for Charles the Bold's wedding, **Quinten Massys, Jan Provoost, Colyn de Coter** and **Jacques van Lathem** in Antwerp; **Daniel de Ryke, Gerard van der Meire** and **Matthys van Roden** in Ghent; **Arnould Raet, Hubert Stuerbout,** his son **Gillis Stuerbout, Dirk Bouts the younger, Aelbrecht Bouts** and perhaps the **Philadelphia S. Christopher Painter** in Louvain; **Gauthier van Battel,** his son of the same name, and **Baudoin van Battel** in Malines; **Albert van Ouwater, Geertgen tot Sint Jans** and **Gerard David,** all probably in Haarlem; **Hieronymus Bosch** in Bois-le-duc (Hertogenbosch); **Cornelis Engelbrechtsz** in Leyden; **Jacob Cornelisz van Oostsanen** in Amsterdam; **Jan Joest** in Wesel and Calcar; and **Cornelis Buys the elder** probably in Alkmaar. Others probably working in the Northern provinces were the **London Nativity by Night Painter,** the **Virgo inter Virgines Master,** the **Liverpool Entombment Painter** and the **New York Lamentation Painter. Jean Hey** worked in a town unknown; and **Joos van Wassenhove** and **Justus of Ghent** may still have been active in Italy.

Among the Brugeois **Pierre Coustain** designed decorations for Maria of Burgundy's Pageant Entry into Bruges in 1477 and probably died in this period; the miniaturist **Willem Vrelant,** who lived till 1481 and was a friend and neighbour of **Hans Memlinc** in this period, gave the Guild of S. John (Scribes, illuminators and booksellers) a picture called *The Passion of Christ* by an unrecorded artist in 1478; and **Memlinc** who attended the presentation ceremony, was commissioned by the Guild to paint some unrecorded subjects on shutters to protect it. **Memlinc** himself married before 1480, had three sons before 1487 and died in 1494; in this period he completed the only extant works that are known to be by him—the *S. John altar* (Pls. 89, 90, 111, 114, 115) commissioned in the previous period, and the *Floreins alter* (Pls. 82, 84, 85, 94, 95) both installed in the Hôpital S. Jean in 1479, and the *S. Ursula shrine* (Pls. 93, 112) consecrated for the same institution in 1489 when Giles de Baerdemaker, Bishop of Sarepta and Suffragan of Tournai, placed within it some relics brought back from the Holy Land and given to the Hôpital by Anselme Adornes, councillor and ambassador of Charles the Bold. In 1480 **Memlinc** had a pupil called **Annekin Verhanneman** of whom nothing else is known; in the same year he bought himself a considerable house (domus magna lapidea); and in 1483 he had a pupil called **Passchier van der Mersch** of whom we know only that he lived beyond the end of this period. **Gerard David** (Pl. 195), born in Holland, was a newcomer in Bruges by 1484; as just mentioned, he was employed by the Bruges Town Council to decorate the window bars in the house where Maximilian was imprisoned in 1488; and he received a payment for a picture in the Town Hall in 1491; but no works known to have been painted by him in this period are known to be extant. **Jan Provoost,** also known as **Jean Prévost** (Pl. 283), who settled in Bruges at the end of the period in 1494, was born in Mons between 1462 and 1465; he had married in Valenciennes the widow of the French painter Simon Marmion, and had worked in Antwerp before coming to Bruges; no pictures known to have been painted by him in these years are known to be extant. The *Scenes from the Legend of S. Lucy* (Pls. 116-18) dated 1480 by an unrecorded artist known as the **Lucy Legend Master** were doubtless painted as a Bruges commission because the Belfry and S. Sauveur are seen in the background of the miracle picture. *The Virgin and Child* (Pl. 96A) by the unrecorded artist here referred to as the **Bruges Virgin with the Apple Painter** was painted in 1487; and the *Mystic marriage of S. Catherine* (Pl. 107) by an unrecorded artist here referred to as the **Brussels Mystic Marriage Painter** dates from 1489.

Of these Bruges commissions the three works by **Memlinc** were for a charitable foundation directed by the Church and both the altarpieces were commissioned by members of the Hôpital staff; the *S. Ursula shrine* was probably paid for by the two sisters of the Hôpital, Jossine van Dudzeele and Anna de Moortele portrayed upon it with the Virgin and Child as protectors. The altarpiece by the **Brussels Mystic Marriage Painter** was painted for the Confrérie des Trois Saintes (SS. Catherine, Barbara, and Mary Magdalene) and placed on their altar in Notre Dame; and the panels by the **Lucy Legend Master** were also doubtless originally ordered for some women's institution and paid for by the unidentified patrician whose arms appear in the window of the central panel. In the case of the picture by the **Bruges Virgin with an Apple Painter** (Pl. 96A) we know that this left-hand panel of a diptych was given to the Hospice de S. Julien by one of the guardians, the Bruges patrician Martin van Nieuwenhove, then twenty-three, and his portrait as an adorant forms the right-hand panel (not reproduced here). Rich Brugeois tradesmen are known to have paid for some other surviving works by unrecorded artists; and three such, Jean du Cellier, Jacques Floreins and Willem Moreel were all members of the Guild of Merchant Grocers. Of these Jacques Floreins (brother of Jean Floreins the donor of the Floreins altar) commissioned an altarpiece (now in the Louvre) in 1489 which shows himself, his Spanish wife and their eighteen children as adorants round the Virgin and Child with SS. James and Dominic. Willem Moreel, Burgomaster of Bruges in 1478 and 1483 and a sturdy opponent of Maximilian (who imprisoned him for five months in 1481) ordered a triptych for the funeral chapel of his family in S. Jacques in 1484; this altarpiece (now in the Bruges Museum) has *SS. Christopher, Giles and Maur* in the central panel, *Willem Moreel with five sons presented by S. William* on the left-hand wing and *Moreel's wife with eleven daughters presented by S. Barbara* on the right wing; and Descamps (artist and art historian) who saw the triptych in 1768, and records only two children, was shown it as a work then tradition-ally believed by 'Hemmelinck' (i.e. **Memlinc**).

In the Brussels group **Pieter van der Weyden** seems to have worked through these years, and his son **Goswin van der Weyden,** born in 1465, was probably active from the middle of the eighties though no records of pictures by either in this period have been found. We also know nothing of the pictures painted in these years by **Vrancke van der Stoct** who was probably still official painter to the city and was still alive in 1494, or those by his son **Bernaert van der Stoct** named as heir to some contents of his studio in a will made by his father in 1489. **Colyn de Coter** seems to have worked in Brussels where he owned a house which he mortgaged to the Confrérie de S. Eloi in 1479; he visited Antwerp in 1493; and he signed three extant pictures including *The Three Maries* (Pl. 280) painted in this period or later. **Jan van Coninxloo the elder,** recorded in Tournai as 'Jean de Royaulme, called Scernier, son of a Brussels painter' in 1483, was working in Brussels in 1491. The unidenti-fied painter known as the **View of S. Gudule Master** (Pl. 122) worked evidently in Brussels because his picture shows Sainte Gudule in the background, and the picture can be dated to Maximilian's period because one of the towers is unfinished; and the **Dublin S. Nicholas Painter,** unidentified author of *Two miracles of S. Nicholas of Bari* (Pl. 123), was clearly in some ways a similar artist.

As stated in my last chapter no pictures known to be by **Hugo van der Goes** are known to be extant. But we know that in 1478 he visited Louvain from the Rouge-Cloître Monastery near Brussels to value the *Justice* pictures (Pls. 67, 69) left unfinished by **Dirk Bouts;** he was then referred to as 'most famous' and 'a native of Ghent'; but he was not tempted to leave the monastery, and he seems to have returned to it at once. Of his life there we know some details because about 1872 the Belgian scholar Alphonse Wauters discovered and published a manuscript by Gaspard Ofhuys a fellow inmate of the monastery, who wrote as follows on the subject: 'The lay brother Hugo was so famous as a painter that no one "even" as they say "beyond the mountains" was his equal. Brother Hugo and I were fellow novices. When Hugo arrived, and while he was a novice, the Prior [Thomas de Vossem] allowed him sundry mundane privileges, whereby, in effect, he was more helped to contribute to the fame of the age than towards humility and repentance; and this greatly incensed some Brothers who maintained that novices should be humbled and not encouraged to be proud and arrogant. As Hugo was an excellent portrait painter many notable people, including the Archduke Maximilian came to visit him in order to see his pictures; and on such occasions Prior Thomas admitted him to the guest room and allowed him to dine with the visitors. About five or six years after his arrival [i.e. in 1480 or 1481] Hugo went with several Brothers to Cologne; and—as I learned from Brother Nicolas who went with him—he became mentally deranged on the journey back. He said incessantly that he was damned, and was only restrained by his companions from doing himself a horrible bodily injury. On reaching Brussels the Prior, who had been informed, came to meet them; he opined that Hugo was suffering from the malady of King Saul and that as King Saul had been calmed by David's harp, he gave permission for music to be played and other palliatives to be tried; but these measures were without avail; and when Hugo returned to the monastery he was still lamenting his inevitable damnation. The help and sympathy accorded to him by the Brothers, by day and night, are unforgettable. But, though unheeded by these Brothers, some other and much respected members expressed a different view of the matter; and there was no unity of opinion about the cause of the illness. Some held that he was suffering from a kind of madness; but according to others, he was possessed by a demon.

Symptoms supporting both opinions were discernible. But during the whole course of his illness he never attempted to injure anyone but himself—which is not usually the case either with the mad or the possessed. In my opinion only God knows the truth of the matter. If we assume a kind of natural madness then we must remember that there are various forms of this illness; some are brought on by certain diets conducing to melancholy, others by drinking strong wines which vitiate the humours, others by the pressure of the passions— such as worry, sorrow or too great addiction to work or to fear; sometimes also there is a predisposition to such illness which is increased by the affection of the humours. I know from sure sources that our Brother Hugo was much given to his passions; he was excessively worried about the execution of the pictures he had to paint, which, it was said, would take him nine years to finish; he read a lot in Flemish books; and as regards wine-drinking, the fact that he drank with his visitors, may have made his condition worse. All these circumstances may provide the causes which as time went on produced the major illness that befell him. From the other point of view it could be said that Hugo had a great reputation in our Order by reason of his talent and thus became much more famous that he would have been had he remained in the world outside, and being but a man like other men, he became overweening as result of his fame and of the homage paid to him and of the visits he received, and God to save him from complete destruction, laid this debasing illness on him and thereby humbled him; and Hugo himself seems to have thus understood it, for in lucid intervals, he behaved with great humility to everyone, voluntarily avoiding the Refectory and taking his meals most modestly with the other lay brothers. I give all these details because God, as I believe, permitted all this to happen not only as a punishment of sin for the betterment of the sinner but also for the edification of us all. Brother Hugo from inflaming of his imaginative powers was disposed to daydreaming fantasies and hallucinations and suffered in consequence an illness of the brain. For there is, I am told, a small delicate organ, near the brain, which is controlled by the creative and imaginative powers; if our imagination is too vivid or our fantasy too abundant, this little organ is affected, and if it is strained to breaking point madness or frenzy results. If we are to avoid falling into this irremediable danger, we must limit our fantasy, our imagination and our suspicions and exclude all other vain and useless thoughts which may excite our brains. We are but men; and the disaster that fell upon our Brother as result of his fantasies and hallucinations, could it not also fall on us? Hugo was buried in our monastery cemetery, in open ground, in 1482.'[1]

In the Antwerp group **Jan Snellaert** was Regent in the Guild in 1480 and may have died before 1494. **Quinten Massys** (Pls. 207, 235, 241), son of a Louvain smith, was himself a smith till he was just on twenty in 1485; from sixteenth-century chroniclers, writing in the lifetime of his son, we know that he began to paint while ill in bed when a friend brought him popular woodcuts to colour as distraction, and that he gave up his work as smith and became a professional painter in order to win a girl he was in love with who was about to yield to an artist suitor because she was reluctant to marry a humble smith; we also know that he married his first wife in Louvain in 1486 and that he moved to Antwerp where he

---

[1] The madness of **Hugo van der Goes** was unknown to **Lucas de Heere** who wrote a sonnet on his *David and Abigail* some eighty years later; it was also unknown to van Mander who collected the material for his 'Schilderboek' at the end of the sixteenth century; and it seems, with the visit to Cologne, to have been unknown to everyone till the publication of the account I have quoted. The interest aroused by the publication of this document was exploited by **Emile Wauters** in his costume-history picture *The Madness of Hugo van der Goes* (1872) now in the Brussels Museum.

became a Master at twenty-five in 1491; but we have no knowledge of pictures painted by him in Louvain or Antwerp in this period. **Jan Provoost** (Pl. 283) was Antwerp Master aged about twenty-eight in 1492 and moved to Bruges, as just noted, two years later. **Colyn de Coter** (Pl. 280), who visited Antwerp from Brussels in 1493 as also noted, became Master there, was employed by the Painters' Guild to paint angels on the ceiling of the Guild's chapel in Notre Dame, and may then have gone back to Brussels. **Jacques van Lathem,** later Court Painter to Philip the Fair, became Antwerp Master in 1493.

Of the painters active in Ghent, Louvain and Malines, **Matthys van Roden** contributed to the Pageant Entry into Ghent of Maria of Burgundy and the Archduke Maximilian on the occasion of their marriage in 1477; **Daniel de Rycke** was available there till sometime after 1482; and **Gerard van der Meire** worked there through the period. **Arnould Raet** died in Louvain in these years; **Hubert Stuerbout** carved a frame for a picture by **Dirk Bouts** in 1481 and died in Louvain in 1483; and his son **Gillis Stuerbout** was Town Painter there by 1482. **Dirk Bouts the younger** restored his father's *Last Supper* (Pl. 58) in Louvain S. Pierre in 1486 and died at fifty-two in 1490; his younger brother **Aelbrecht Bouts** (Pls. 251, 252, 253) an independent artist by 1479, collaborated with him in restoring the *Last Supper*; and the unidentified **Philadelphia S. Christopher Painter** (Pl. 132) was perhaps associated with the **Bouts** atelier at this time. **Gauthier van Battel** died in Malines about 1478; his son of the same name seems to have been at work there; and **Baudoin van Battel** who designed for Maria of Burgundy's Pageant Entry in Malines in 1477 and painted a *Last Judgement* for the Town Hall in 1481, was still alive in 1494. **Jean Hey,** whose habitat is not known, painted the *Christ crowned with thorns* (Pl. 134) in 1494 for Jean Cueillete, a secretary of Charles VIII; and an inscription on the picture describes him as 'Teutonicus', i.e. presumably, a Netherlandish artist.

In the Northern provinces **Albert van Ouwater** must have been still at work in Haarlem, though an old man, in the early eighties, for we know that **Geertgen tot Sint Jans** was his pupil there and **Geertgen** was probably about sixteen, the usual apprentice age, in 1483; and **Gerard David,** born at Oudewater, was possibly **van Ouwater's** pupil, as a boy, before he went to Bruges in 1484. Van Mander tells us that **Geertgen tot Sint Jans** died about the age of twenty-eight, that he had lived in Haarlem with the Brothers of S. John though he was not a member of the Order, and that he painted a large triptych for the Brothers with the *Crucifixion* as the central subject which was destroyed 'by the Iconoclasts or during the siege of Haarlem' except for one wing which had been sawn in two to show the inside and the outside pictures as two panels; and I reproduce these two panels which survive and correspond to van Mander's description of their subjects (Pls. 124, 127). **Hieronymus Bosch** (Pls. 156-8, 161, 163-71) is documented in Bois-le-duc (Hertogenbosch) by 1480 when the local Brotherhood of Our Lady (Lieve Vrouwe Broederschap) surrendered to him two panels left unpainted by his father—an artist of whom little else is known; **Bosch's** birthdate is unknown but he was probably over twenty by 1477 and old enough to have seen towns burned and sacked by Charles the Bold; in 1484 he inherited from his brother-in-law a small property near Oirschot, and by that time he had married a girl of a good Dutch family; in 1486 he himself became a member of the Brotherhood of Our Lady, and he was president at their banquet in 1488; in 1489 he painted the outside of the wings of an altarpiece in the Brotherhood's chapel then under construction in the church of S. John; in 1493, when he was perhaps about forty-four, he designed the windows for this chapel; and it is probable that some of his surviving pictures, which are all undated, were painted in this period. In Leyden **Cornelis Engelbrechtsz** (Pls. 210, 211, 213, 229, 230, 232, 233) had begun his career when the period closed as he was already twenty-six by then. **Cornelis Buys the elder** was probably at work in Alkmaar by the nineties; and his brother **Jacob Cornelisz van Oostsanen** (Pls. 265, 268, 302), about twenty-four in 1494, was probably by then an independent painter and established in Amsterdam. **Jan Joest** born probably at Wesel was at work there till 1480 when he seems to have moved to Calcar; and he returned to work in Wesel in 1490.

As can be seen from the foregoing, though we have the names of some of the artists active in these seventeen years and we know some facts about some of them, we have, again, few pictures extant which are known to be the work of particular recorded painters. Strictly speaking there seem, indeed, to be but four such extant works—the *Floreins altar* (Pls. 82, 84, 85, 94, 95), the *St. John altar* (Pls. 89, 90, 111, 114, 115) and the *S. Ursula shrine* (Pls. 93, 112) by **Memlinc**, and **Jean Hey's** *Christ crowned with thorns* (Pl. 134). The pictures reproduced by **Geertgen tot Sint Jans** (Pls. 124, 127) are known to have been painted by him, but as their date is not recorded it is not certain if they fall within this period or later; the same applies to the extant pieces by **Colyn de Coter** including the *Three Maries* (Pl. 280); and we have some dated pieces by unrecorded authors including the **Lucy Legend Master** (Pls. 116-18), the **Bruges Virgin with the Apple Painter** (Pl. 96A) and the **Brussels Mystic Marriage Painter** (Pl. 107). But, as before, we also have a number of works of quality or interest by unrecorded artists which can be presumed of this period by the style of the costumes or other factors. Of such works I have already mentioned the altarpieces ordered in Bruges by Jean du Cellier, Willem Moreel and Jacques Floreins and the pictures reproduced here by the **View of Sainte Gudule Master** (Pl. 122), the **Dublin S. Nicholas Painter** (Pl. 123) and the **Philadelphia S. Christopher Painter** (Pl. 132); and I also reproduce a *Mass of S. Giles* (Pls. 56, 83) by an unrecorded artist here referred to as the **London S. Giles Mass Painter** whom I take to be a Brugeois who visited Paris or employed a French assistant, and pictures probably painted in the Northern provinces by unrecorded artists here referred to as the **London Nativity by Night Painter** (Pl. 129), the **Virgo inter Virgines Master** (Pl. 128), the **Liverpool Entombment Painter** (Pl. 126) and the **New York Lamentation Painter** (Pl. 125).

As before, and for the reasons suggested, the pictures surviving from this period are mainly religious subjects and portraits. But again, if we examine the examples reproduced here, we can form some concept of the landscape and townscape painting, the interiors, the still-life and flowers, and animal painting, and the genre pieces; and those elements in the composition I assume to have been contributed in some cases by assistants or independent practitioners specializing in these fields.

Of the landscapes shown here the most elaborate are the settings for the figures in the *S. Christopher* by the **Philadelphia S. Christopher Painter** and in the two pictures by **Geertgen tot Sint Jans**. In this *S. Christopher* (Pl. 132)—as in the lovely picture of the subject by the **Pearl of Brabant Master** (Pl. 92) discussed in my last chapter—the whole landscape was complete in itself before the figures were inserted; as before, the sudden onset of the tempest is suggested by the agitated water in the foreground, contrasted with smooth expanse behind, and in this case, in the calmer portions swans swim peacefully and a man in a boat is fishing; moreover as the artist now has a broader panel there is more space between the river-banks and bluffs. This landscape, I fancy, was provided by a landscape specialist and one perhaps connected with the specialist landscape painter of the earlier picture. In the *Julian the Apostate burning the bones of S. John the Baptist* (Pl. 124) by **Geertgen** there is again an integrated landscape complete before the figures were inserted; but this was,

I think, designed by **Geertgen** himself because the sections are constructed to carry the four episodes that illustrate the story; the rocky plain has the monastery on the right and the tomb in the foreground and the burial scene behind; and trees and shrubs, very delicately observed and handled, are placed here and there to lead us to a mountain distance on the high horizon. In the *Lamentation* (Pl. 127) the landscape is also, I think, by **Geertgen,** and designed this time as setting for two scenes with a charming vista of wooded countryside between the rising mound that typifies Golgotha on the left side and the sepulchre on the right; the shrub behind the Holy Women ties the wooded landscape to the composition as a whole, but the foreground plain which includes the sepulchre, does not quite co-ordinate in the centre with the mound behind. In these three pictures the figures are veritably within the landscape and reasonably true to scale. This can also be said, to some extent, of *S. Lucy with her mother* (Pl. 117) by the **Lucy Legend Master** who shows the scene in the garden of a mansion with a wood beyond the castellated wall, and—since this artist was, I suspect, a Catalan visiting or domiciled in Bruges—there is a date-palm included in the wood; and this artist also sets his figures quite convincingly in a wooded park outside the town in his *Oxen failing to drag S. Lucy to a brothel* (Pl. 118). But in other pictures reproduced here known or presumed of this period, the landscape is no more than a painted backcloth hung behind the figures or inserted piecemeal to fill up spaces round the figures. Thus in **Memlinc's** *S. John altar* (Pl. 111) there is a landscape backcloth behind the colonnade; there are other such backcloths behind the arbour in the picture by the **Brussels Mystic Marriage Painter** (Pl. 107), behind the stable in **Memlinc's** *Adoration of the Magi* (Pl. 85) in the *Floreins altar*, and behind the convent cortile in the picture by the **Virgo inter Virgines Master** (Pl. 128). In **Memlinc's** *S. John the Baptist* and *S. Veronica* panels (Pls. 94, 95), on the outside wings of the *Floreins altar*, the saints sit on grassy mounds with perfunctory landscapes and awkwardly placed trees behind them to fill up the pictures; and there is also a perfunctory landscape seen through a window in the picture by the **Bruges Virgin with the Apple Painter** (Pl. 96A). As in the earlier pictures these landscape backcloths sometimes serve as setting for additional episodes connected with the central subject. Thus the landscape behind **Memlinc's** *Mystic Marriage of S. Catherine* (Pl. 111) has episodes from the lives of S. John the Baptist and S. John the Evangelist; among the first we see the preaching in the wilderness—a subject we shall meet again very variously treated in pictures by **Patinir** (Pl. 200), the **Bruges Baptism of Christ Painter** (Pl. 201) and crypto-Protestant painters; among the second we have the miracle of the cauldron of boiling oil, the transportation to Patmos and the baptism of the philosopher Crato. In the same way in his *Beheading of S. John the Baptist* (Pls. 89, 113) **Memlinc** adds in the background the baptism of Christ and the banquet of Herod. The landscapes in the pictures by the **Liverpool Entombment Painter** (Pl. 126), and the **New York Lamentation Painter** (Pl. 125) are basically backcloth 'fill-ups'; but both also contribute to the illustrative meaning of the pictures, since both show rising ground to typify Golgotha and both include the sepulchre.

Town views and streets, sometimes seen through doors or colonnades or windows, and sometimes identifiable, and the cloisters of monasteries, convents or hospitals still often appear. The austere cloisters of the convent or women's hostel in the picture by the **Virgo inter Virgines Master** (Pl. 128) cannot be identified though, as the artist was probably active in the Northern provinces, they may record a religious house in Haarlem, Delft, Amsterdam or Leyden. It is however clear that the **View of Sainte Gudule Master** (Pl. 122) has set his scene in a street running backwards to Sainte Gudule Cathedral in Brussels;

both the **Lucy Legend Master** (Pl. 118) and the **Brussels Mystic Marriage Painter** (Pl. 107) give us views of Bruges, like the earlier views by the **Philadelphia S. Catherine Painter** (Pl. 108), the **Detroit Mystic Marriage Painter** (Pl. 110) and the **Philadelphia Adorant Painter** (Pl. 104); and a part of Bruges with the Romanesque church of S. Jean is also seen in the landscape backcloth of **Memlinc's** *S. John altar* (Pl. 111). **Memlinc** who, we know from records, was a man of means from early in this period, seems to have had a specialist in townscapes among his studio assistants; and this specialist, using drawings or engravings, may well have provided the views of Cologne with the cathedral, the church of S. Martin the Great and the Bayenthurm, and also the imaginary buildings that help to illustrate the story told on the *S. Ursula shrine* (Pls. 93, 112); the same assistant may have painted the setting for the *Beheading of S. John the Baptist* where the execution takes place in a court-yard with adjacent buildings surrounding Herod's palace which has on the outside three nude sculptured figures set in niches (Pls. 89, 113); and we may also owe to him the inn, with symbolically closed door, glimpsed through the stable in the *Nativity* (Pl. 82) of the *Floreins altar*, the little street of pink and white houses seen through the door in the *Presentation in the Temple* (Pl. 84), the elaborate street scene with the gate of Bethlehem and the arrival of the Magi in the landscape backcloth of the central panel (Pl. 85), and the ecclesiastic doorway with sculptured figures of *Adam and Eve* and the *Expulsion from Eden* on the outside panels (Pls. 94, 95).

As interior painting we have again some living rooms in private houses, some palace chambers, church interiors, loggias, and symbolic structures for the *Nativity* stable. Among the living-rooms my plates again show nothing to rival the completeness of the dining-chamber in the *Last Supper* (Pl. 58) by **Dirk Bouts** or the bedroom by **Jan van Eyck** (Pl. 18A) or the half-cube interiors by the **London Christ Appearing to His Mother Painter** (Pl. 32) and the **Madrid Werl Wings Painter** (Pls. 41, 44). In the panel by the **Bruges Virgin with the Apple Painter** (Pl. 96A) the spatial concept is basically a two-dimensional high-relief of figures against a flat conventional background like the picture by the **London Virgin with Brocade Screen Painter** (Pl. 62) which I contrasted in my last chapter with the setting for this subject by the **London Virgin with a Firescreen Painter** (Frontispiece); like the **London Virgin with Brocade Screen Painter,** the **Bruges Virgin with the Apple Painter** gives variety to the flat conventional background by incidental factors—the view through the window on the right, the donor's arms in the left-hand window, the half-open shutters and the mirror (reflecting windows behind the spectator) oddly placed on another shutter; but these adventitious details seem illustrative additions in the painting stage, not essential parts of the picture's form as conceived in the initial plan. In *S. Lucy denounced as a Christian before the Consul* (Pl. 116) by the **Lucy Legend Master** the token chamber of Justice recalls the *Ordeal by Fire* (Pl. 69) by **Bouts** (and more closely, I think, a *SS. Cosmas and Damian before the Consul Lysias* painted about 1460 by a Catalan artist called Miguel Nadar). **Memlinc,** or his architectural assistant, has invented a Banqueting Hall of Herod, with a window, a vast cloth of honour behind the tetrarch, and a marble floor, and revealed it within the palace by removing a whole wall (Pl. 113)—a device already used by the **Ursula Legend Master** in the *Envoy of King Agrippinus* (Pl. 101) and by the **Dublin S. Augustine Painter** (Pl. 102); and the pillared loggia in **Memlinc's** *Mystic marriage of S. Catherine* (Pl. 111) is also quite traditional since it goes back, in fact, to the *Van der Paele altarpiece* (Pl. 19) by **Jan van Eyck.** Other loggias, too small for the figures placed within them, are used as token structures by the **View of Sainte Gudule Master** (Pl. 122) whose loggia seems a symbol for a cloister or religious meeting-house, and by the **Dublin S. Nicholas Painter** whose structure is a token baptistery with a Romanesque carved font (Pl. 123); and a token structure for S. Peter's Rome is in the third panel of **Memlinc's** *S. Ursula shrine* (Pl. 93). Realistically painted church interiors are in **Memlinc's** *Presentation in the Temple* (Pl. 84) and the *Mass of S. Giles* by the **London S. Giles Mass Painter** (Pl. 83); the corner of the lofty Romanesque church in **Memlinc's** picture may record a part of a church in Bruges or may be constructed from an architect's drawings; the Gothic interior by the **London S. Giles Mass Painter** shows the high altar of the ancient Abbey of S. Denis (north of Paris) and the south aisle of the choir behind it. In a *Holy Kinship* (not reproduced here) in the Amsterdam Museum an unrecorded artist, apparently of this period, and probably from the Northern provinces, has grouped the figures in a church with Gothic arches and a tessellated floor; and this may possibly record a church in Haarlem or the chapel of the Haarlem Brothers of S. John (the picture is catalogued as presumed by **Geertgen tot Sint Jans**). Examples of the Nativity stable appear in the *Nativity* by the **London Nativity by Night Painter** (Pl. 129) and in two panels of **Memlinc's** *Floreins altar* (Pls. 82, 85); and all continue the tradition of the thatched wooden structure imposed symbolically on portions of a ruined pagan temple already observed here in **Hugo of Antwerp's** *Portinari altarpiece* (Pl. 76) and in pictures like the *Adoration of the Shepherds* by the **Minneapolis Adoration Painter** (Pl. 75).

In still-life there is now again very little that records the equipment in bourgeois living-rooms; and of studio equipment my plates show nothing but the mirror, already mentioned, in the picture by the **Bruges Virgin with the Apple Painter** (Pl. 96A). But we still have church equipment, elaborate brocades, Near Eastern rugs, and contemporary clothes and jewellery to test the skill of the still-life painters. Church treasures in the Abbey of S. Denis are recorded with faithful patience in the picture by the **London S. Giles Mass Painter** (Pls. 56, 83); inserted perhaps by a Parisian still-life painter these treasures include a golden jewelled retable on the high altar and a large cross above it, a gothic structure supporting the coffin of S. Louis behind the altar, and on the right a tombal monument which still exists there; the King in this picture wears a jewelled crown presumed by some the Sainte Couronne which crowned the Kings of France till the end of the sixteenth century; the altar frontal is a rich brocade; and the Saint stands on a Near Eastern rug. In **Memlinc's** *Floreins altar* (Pl. 85) we have the golden gifts of the Magi, one of which, the chalice brought by the kneeling Magus, has been handed to S. Joseph—as also in the *Adoration of the Magi* by the **Pearl of Brabant Master** (Pl. 86). In **Memlinc's** *Mystic marriage of S. Catherine* in the *S. John altar* (Pl. 111), the monstrance and Host are contained in S. Barbara's Tower and S. John the Evangelist makes the sign of the cross above the chalice with the poisoned wine that proved fatal to the priest of Diana. Some specialist in textile painting may have collaborated with the **Lucy Legend Master** for the red and gold robe of the consul and the cloth of honour on his throne (Pl. 116), and **Memlinc's** chief drapery assistant was charged, I imagine, with the gold and green-blue brocaded tunic trimmed with ermine on the negro Magus in the *Floreins altar* and with the rug, the cloth of honour and S. Catherine's ermine corsage and black and gold brocaded gown in his *Mystic marriage of S. Catherine*. Contemporary clothes, like those worn by this S. Catherine, and armour and church vestments appear in other panels by **Memlinc** and also in the pictures by the **Lucy Legend Master** (Pls. 116-18) and the **London S. Giles Mass Painter** (Pl. 86). Knights in armour and a Pope in his vestments appear on **Memlinc's** *S. Ursula shrine* (Pls. 93, 112); S. Ursula herself wears her plaited hair coiled round her ears, a blue corsage with white surcoat and a violet skirt with ermine trimming; in his *Beheading of S. John the Baptist* a posturing courtier, with a small moustache, sports a red brocaded doublet with a handsome belt and Salome wears a gown of red and green and ermine and an elegant necklace (Pls. 89, 113); and the Brothers and Sisters of the Hôpital S. Jean, kneeling as donors on the outside of the wings of his *S. John altarpiece*, are shown in their professional habits (Pls. 114, 115). In the same way the **Lucy Legend Master** puts S. Lucy in a contemporary blue gown and mantle lined with ermine (Pls. 116-18). A curious mixture of contemporary clothes and of costumes fantasticated to suggest the pagan Orient is a feature of **Geertgen's** *Julian the Apostate burning the bones of S. John the Baptist* (Pl. 124); for the figures here wear the round-toed shoes that were just replacing the long pointed shoes seen in the earlier pictures while the rest of their clothes are invented and the Emperor himself is given an exotic hat, surmounted by his crown, and an ermine-hooded brocaded mantle with a train. This blend of actual and fantastic clothes, already encountered under Charles the Bold, is also seen to some extent in **Geertgen's** *Lamentation* (Pl. 121) and in other pictures reproduced here. Thus the **Virgo inter Virgines Master** (Pl. 128) arrays his saints and the Virgin herself in gowns of expensive fabrics with embroideries of gold thread and very large fur cuffs; the little of their hair that is seen is tightly plaited; and the foreground figures have jewelled turbans thrust far back to show the maximum of the ever-fashionable bald forehead (sometimes shaved, it would seem, to make it appear still balder and higher). Turbans and curious flat bonnets, similarly worn, and plaited hair are in the pictures by the **Liverpool Entombment Painter** (Pl. 126) and the **New York Lamentation Painter** (Pl. 125); and tall ornate headdresses of another kind are worn by the women in the picture by the **View of Sainte Gudule Master** (Pl. 122). We must note too that the attributes of the maiden saints are sometimes indicated by their clothes or jewels; thus in the picture by the **Virgo inter Virgines Master** the saints wear emblematic brooches—S. Catherine a little sword and wheel, S. Cecilia an organ, S. Barbara a tower and S. Ursula a heart pierced by the archer's arrow; and in the *Mystic marriage of S. Catherine* (Pl. 107) the **Brussels Mystic Marriage Painter** gives S. Catherine a gown embroidered all over with large wheels.

There are signs too of the flower painters in some of the pictures reproduced here; and **Memlinc** may have had such a specialist among his studio assistants, though flowers are not a feature in his authenticated works. The **Brussels Mystic Marriage Painter** (Pl. 107)—following the tradition of the **Detroit Mystic Marriage Painter** (Pl. 110)—sets the Virgo inter Virgines scene before an arbour of roses and vines in a flower-spangled meadow; the **Lucy Legend Master** puts lilies, narcissi and other flowers in the garden of S. Lucy's parents (Pl. 117); iris and other flowers grow round the loggia in the picture by the **View of Sainte Gudule Master** (Pl. 122) and tufts of iris and aquilegias are in the foreground of the *Miracles of S. Nicholas* by the **Dublin S. Nicholas Painter** (Pl. 123).

In the field of animal painting in addition to the ox and the ass in Nativity scenes and the lamb as emblem, we now have the Horses of the Apocalypse and a monster with gaping jaws in **Memlinc's** *S. John on Patmos* (Pls. 88, 90); and my plates show also terrestrial horses, other oxen, dogs, a camel, a pig, and swans upon a river. In the third panel by the **Lucy Legend Master** two oxen are in the foreground and three more are driven up the path behind them (Pl. 118). Large heads of the ox and ass form the centre of the lovely little picture by the **London Nativity by Night Painter** (Pl. 129); and the ass, with the ox behind him, bends down to the manger in the *Nativity* and in the *Adoration of the Magi* in **Memlinc's** *Floreins altar* (Pls. 82, 85). The Magi on horses and a camel are in the street behind the Virgin in the *Floreins altar*; and a boy rides a plump round-bellied horse in the courtyard of Herod's palace in **Memlinc's** *Beheading of S. John the Baptist* (Pls. 89, 113). S. John the Baptist's symbolic lamb is on the outside of a wing of the *Floreins altar* and in the central panel of the *S. John altar*, moving forward in the first case and static in the second; on the wings of the *S. John altar* (Pls. 114, 115) S. Anthony's pig and the lamb of S. Agnes are seen between the donors; and the **Brussels Mystic Marriage Painter** paints S. Agnes with her lamb upon her knee (Pl. 109). The **Philadelphia S. Christopher Painter** puts swans as noted in the placid distant reaches of the river (Pl. 132). The dogs are various and very oddly placed; **Geertgen tot Sint Jans** sets a greyhound and a funny little white-haired dog (more like a cat)—perhaps the pets of the Brothers of S. John—in the foreground of the *Julian the Apostate burning the bones of S. John the Baptist* (Pl. 124), and in his *Lamentation* a long-haired dog sits quietly on Golgotha's hilltop while the thieves are taken down (Pl. 127); a white greyhound is quite unperturbed by S. Ursula's martyrdom on **Memlinc's** *S. Ursula shrine* (Pl. 112); and a shaggy white puppy sniffs among the flowers and grass around the buildings suggested by the **View of Sainte Gudule Master** (Pl. 122).

In genre painting the mother and child theme is continued in gentle forms in devotional pictures; and there are genre touches in the narrative scenes by **Memlinc,** the **Lucy Legend Master** and **Geertgen tot Sint Jans.** In the treatment of the mother and child theme the most original concept is the eager movement of the child in the picture by the **Virgo inter Virgines Master** (Pl. 128); but there is nothing now to rival the enchantment of the central group by the **Buckingham Palace Mystic Marriage Painter** (Pl. 106). The **Bruges Virgin with the Apple Painter** (Pl. 96A) treats the theme in the tender spirit of the **London (Layard) Virgin and Child Painter** (Pl. 105). The **Brussels Mystic Marriage Painter** (Pl. 107) repeats the central group of the picture by the **Detroit Mystic Marriage Painter** (Pl. 110). **Memlinc** fails to suggest real intimacy in the central group of his *Mystic marriage of S. Catherine* (Pl. 111) because the mother's attention seems given to the book carried by an angel kneeling beside her like a page; but intimacy returns in his *Adoration of the Magi* (Pl. 85) in the *Floreins altar*, for there the Christ-child turns from the Magus at his feet to the glittering gift of the second Magus while the Virgin supports his left hand with a delicate movement; and **Memlinc** has also evolved a touching and most human gesture for the mother in the *Nativity* (Pl. 82) in that triptych. Among the other genre scenes **Memlinc's** *Presentation in the Temple* (Pl. 84) shows the mother fondly displaying her child to the strangers Simeon and the aged prophetess Anna, while S. Joseph takes the prescribed pair of turtle doves or pigeons from his basket. In the background of **Memlinc's** *Beheading of S. John the Baptist* (Pls. 89, 113) the baptism of Christ is depicted with the genre touch of an angel waiting with Christ's raiment, and musicians play reed instruments for Salome to dance to at the Banquet of Herod; and in the Bruges corner of the landscape backcloth in his *Mystic marriage of S. Catherine* there is a frankly contemporary genre scene with the town crane in operation and Jodoc Willems, Master of the Hôpital S. Jean, directing the gauging of the Hôpital's wine. **Memlinc's** *S. Ursula shrine* (Pls. 93, 112) is however far less interesting in genre details than the charming pictures by the **Ursula Legend Master** (Pls. 72-4, 97-101, 103, 120) discussed in my last chapter, though in the *Landing at Cologne* the princess's companions help her down the gangway, hold up her gown, and carry her reticule while porters follow with the heavy luggage, in the *Landing at Bâle* some sailors furl the sails, and, in the Rome scene, within the token structure for S. Peter's, a priest baptizes three adults in a font, another anoints two girls whose godmother stands beside them, and Ursula herself receives Communion. In **Geertgen's** *Lamentation* (Pl. 127) labourers with a ladder are about to take one thief down, while a soldier, with his pike, thrusts into a pit the corpse of the other already descended; the thieves are clothed not in loin cloths, as most commonly, or in drawers, as in the picture by the **New York Crucifixion and Last Judgement Painter** (Pls. 5, 6) but in shirts with belts; and beyond them on the hilltop, a soldier and two officials are set in silhouette against the sky line—just as later **Adriaen Brouwer** and **Joos van Craesbeeck** were to set their sentinels against the sky line on the ramparts of the Antwerp citadel (Pls. 623, 620). In **Geertgen's** *Julian the Apostate burning the bones of S. John the Baptist* (Pl. 124) a bearded labourer with apron and rolled-up shirt sleeves tends the log-fire while another throws the bones on from a long-handled spade. We can note too among these genre details that in *S. Lucy and her mother* (Pl. 117) by the **Lucy Legend Master** a group of beggars hold out their hands for gifts.

Of the portraits painted in these years my plates show the donor and others in **Memlinc's** *Floreins altar*, the donors of his *S. John altar*, and in **Geertgen's** *Julian the Apostate burning the bones of S. John the Baptist* a group of the Haarlem Brethren of S. John. In **Memlinc's** *Floreins altar* (Pl. 85) the donor, Jean Floreins, a Brother in the Hôpital since 1472, is not depicted on a wing but placed within the devotional scene in the tradition of **Jan van Eyck's** *Van der Paele altar* (Pl. 19); kneeling behind the second Magus he turns the pages of a missal and looks down towards it; he appears about forty or older but his actual age, thirty-six, is inscribed on the wall beside him. The identity of the young man behind the donor in this picture is not known; he may be an official of the hospital or the donor's brother Jacques Floreins; the bearded man who looks through the window on the right and the young man glimpsed behind the negro's upraised arm, may also be portraits perhaps of Hôpital officials, or they may indicate the shepherds who have remained or returned to watch the pageant arrival of the Magi—as we see the shepherds in pictures probably painted a few years later by the **New York Adoration in White Castle Painter** (Pl. 151) and the **Philadelphia Adoration of the Magi Painter** (Pl. 162). In the *S. John altar* the donors, i.e. the bursar and director of the Hôpital, the prioress and another nun—appear as adorants on the outside of the wings with their patron saints behind them; the figures in these panels *Brothers Anthony Seghers and Jacques de Kuenic with SS. Anthony and James the Great* (Pl. 114) and *Sisters Agnes Casembrood and Clare van Hulsen with SS. Agnes and Clare* (Pl. 115), are placed in token structures perhaps indicative of the Hôpital cloisters, and resemble sculptured groups in tabernacles; and their shadows cast on the walls behind them recall the outside panels of the **van Eycks'** *Altarpiece of the Mystic Lamb* (Pl. 12) and the *Holy Trinity* group by the **Flémalle Master** (Pl. 37). The donors, it will be observed, are here the same size as the saints behind them and not much smaller as in the donor panels of **Hugo of Antwerp's** *Portinari altar* (Pls. 77, 78); the heads and hands of **Memlinc's** donors are most delicately painted and must have pleased the sitters who, though not obviously flattered, are portrayed without any pejorative comment or romantic insistance on physical oddities or blemishes, and presented with an air of unpretentious piety; and **Memlinc** accordingly must have been, I think, much called on as a portrait painter in these years when many rich Brugeois merchants like Jean du Cellier, Jacques Floreins and Willem Moreel already mentioned, were ordering portraits of themselves with their wives and enormous families as adorant donors of pictures for churches and religious houses; such patrons were also ordering small head and shoulder or half-length portraits for portable diptychs and small independent portrait studies like the earlier examples reproduced here by the **London Woman in a Wimple Painter** (Pl. 40), the **Antwerp Philippe de Croy Painter** (Pl. 45), the **London Young Woman in White Headdress Painter** (Pl. 57), the **Washington Man with an Arrow Painter** (Pl. 68) and the **New York Lady with a Pink Painter** (Pl. 71); and surviving portraits in fact include a *Willem Moreel*, a *Barbara van Vlaendenbergh, wife of Willem Moreel*, and a *Mary, daughter of Willem Moreel* by unrecorded artists as well as the *Martin van Nieuwenhove* by the **Bruges Virgin with the Apple Painter** (Pl. 96A); there is no known record that **Memlinc** worked for any of these merchants but he may, of course, nevertheless have done so. **Geertgen tot Sint Jans** as a portrait painter is more inquisitive than **Memlinc**, and also sharper-eyed and more romantically moved by the oddities in particular faces. The twelve Brothers of S. John and some others in his *Julian the Apostate burning the bones of S. John the Baptist* (Pl. 124) can be presumed the subscription-donors of the triptych of which this panel was a wing, in the same way that the notables portrayed in the *Justice pictures* (Pls. 67, 69) by **Dirk Bouts** and in the picture by the **Tiburtine Sibyl Master** (Pl. 87), and the Augustinians portrayed by the **Dublin S. Augustine Painter** (Pl. 102) were probably subscribers to those works as I have already suggested in the previous chapter. In **Geertgen's** group the faces of the Brethren are sharply differentiated and indicative of particular characters; they are turned in different directions like a group of moderns posing to a battery of pressmen; the foremost Brother has a withered right arm or has lost his hand; the bearded Jewish-looking man behind him in a special cap may be a foreigner, perhaps the institution's doctor from Spain or Portugal.

In addition to these commissioned portraits we can discern, as before, some figures in the compositions which stand out as portraits from among the type or invented figures which surround them; thus the figure behind the mourners in **Geertgen's** *Lamentation* (Pl. 127), the man who holds a winding sheet, is quite evidently a portrait, and a portrait drawn with such quiet and sympathetic interest that if we look first at that point in the picture the mourners in the foreground seem all to be striking attitudes. As before, also, we can assume that some figures were drawn from the artist's friends or family or some neighbouring girls or rustics. The young man, for example, with the small moustache who posed for the second Magus in **Memlinc's** *Floreins altar* (Pl. 85) was probably a friend or neighbour, and another friend seems to have been used for the posturing courtier and the man with a turban in his *Beheading of S. John the Baptist* (Pl. 89) on the *S. John altar*, and for S. James the Great in the left-hand panel with the donors (Pl. 114); and **Geertgen's** bearded labourer in the foreground of *Julian the Apostate burning the bones of S. John the Baptist* (Pl. 124) may well have been drawn from a gardener employed by the Brethren. By this time, moreover, I suspect the use of professional models who worked for several artists as they do today; for S. Giles and the figure behind him in the picture by the **London S. Giles Mass Painter** (Pl. 83) and S. Joseph and Simeon in **Memlinc's** *Floreins altar* (Pls. 82, 84, 85) may all have been drawn from one model then available in Bruges; and the dark bearded figure who appears as the rich man of Arimathea in **Geertgen's** *Lamentation* (Pl. 127) and as S. Joseph in the picture by the **London Nativity by Night Painter** (Pl. 129) seems also to have worked for more than one artist—(unless, as some presume, the unrecorded author of the second picture was actually **Geertgen**).

In the pictures considered as religious subjects theological dictation is now hardly anywhere apparent; some artists had very personal concepts; and my plates show more incidents from the stories of the saints as recorded by the Golden Legend and other sources, some illustrations to the scriptures, some individual concepts of the *Nativity* and the *Lamentation*, and devotional images.

From the legends of the saints we have the burning of the bones of S. John the Baptist, scenes from the legends of S. Christopher, S. Giles and S. Nicholas, and, among the maiden saints, of S. Lucy, S. Ursula and S. Catherine. *Julian the Apostate burning the bones of S. John the Baptist* can be found, as an incident, in the background of **Memlinc's** *Mystic marriage of S. Catherine* (Pl. 111). But we see it more importantly as the central theme in

Geertgen's picture with that title (Pl. 124). The story, as related by **Geertgen,** begins high up in the centre where Herodias (with her back towards us) puts the Baptist's head in a hollow mound. On the left the headless body of the saint is lowered to the tomb with Christ himself beside it. The tomb reappears in the foreground and the bones are extracted from it by the Emperor's servants for the burning and by members of the Brotherhood of S. John as precious relics. Moving upwards to the right some of the Brothers of S. John take the relics to their monastery and others come forth processionally to receive them. In the foreground the Emperor, with his entourage of pagans, directs the exhumation and the burning; **Geertgen** gives all the pagan figures invented 'character' faces, some based perhaps on foreigners in Haarlem; he puts them in the fantasticated costumes already referred to and supplies the Emperor with two child-pages to hold up his train—just as other young pages were later to hold up the trains of the adorant Magi in pictures by **Pietro de Lignis** (Pl. 573) and **Cornelis de Baellieur** (Pl. 727). His picture thus has three characters in one; it is firstly a subscription portrait group of the Brothers of S. John at the moment, and secondly a story from the legend of the saint and, thirdly a costume-history picture purporting to record a past happening connected with the Brotherhood. As a subscription portrait group it had been heralded, as already suggested, by **Dirk Bouts** (Pls. 67, 69), the **Tiburtine Sibyl Master** (Pl. 87) and the **Dublin S. Augustine Painter** (Pl. 83); and as a costume-history picture, with local associations, it had precedent in the picture by the **Exhumation of S. Hubert Master** (Pl. 54). The **Philadelphia S. Christopher Painter** (Pl. 132) takes the usual moment in S. Christopher's story, when the giant, who transported passengers across the river, was beset one night by a sudden tempest and rising of the waters when he was carrying a child across; like the **Pearl of Brabant Master** (Pl. 92) the artist sets the saint amid-stream, staff in hand, and one end of his mantle trailing in the choppy waves; but, unlike the earlier painter, he shows the mantles of both saint and Christ-child lifted upwards by the sudden wind; night-time is suggested by the lighted lantern of the hermit on the bank. S. Christopher, as mentioned earlier, looks a veritable giant in the procession of hermits in the **van Eycks'** *Altarpiece of the Mystic Lamb* (Pl. 9), but here, though much larger than the hermit, he does not appear a giant because the smaller size of the hermit seems determined by the distance—(nor indeed does he look a giant in the later picture by the **Lisbon Alexander VI Painter** (Pl. 202)). The episode illustrated in the *Mass of S. Giles* by the **London S. Giles Mass Painter** (Pls. 83, 56) might also be titled *The Pardon of the King of France*; for the Golden Legend tells us that Charles Martel, King of France, having committed 'un vilain péché' which he was afraid to confess asked S. Giles to pray for him; the saint did so when celebrating Mass, and in response an angel brought down a written record of the royal sin and a promise of pardon if the King repented and confessed it. In character this church interior thus also continues the tradition of the picture by the **Exhumation of S. Hubert Master** (Pl. 54) since it illustrates an episode recorded as happening inside a church—as distinguished from pictures with symbolic ecclesiastic settings inspired by theologians like the **Redemption Master's** *Crucifixion in a church* (Pl. 51). Two stories from the legend of S. Nicholas are compressed within the token baptistery by the **Dublin S. Nicholas Painter** (Pl. 123). On the left S. Nicholas revives a dead man whom I take to be the rascal whose story is recorded as follows in the Golden Legend: A man borrowed money from a Jew and declared later falsely that he had returned it; summoned before the magistrate he put the money in a hollow cane which he handed to the Jew and then swore by S. Nicholas that the Jew had received the money; when judgement was given for him, he took back the cane from the unsuspecting Jew, but, on leaving the court, he was knocked down and killed by a passing chariot, the cane was broken and the coins all fell out; the Jew esteeming this a heaven-sent punishment for the perjury, declared that if S. Nicholas could bring back the sinner to life, he himself would become a Christian; S. Nicholas performed the miracle and the Jew (shown in the picture in a tall conical turban) was converted. The other scene depicts S. Nicholas, as Santa Claus, patron saint of children, reviving the three little scholars slaughtered by a wicked innkeeper who put them in a salt-tub intending to serve them to his customers as meat; the children are not shown in the tub (as is usual in illustrations of this story) but in the baptismal font which really illustrates the left-hand story.

The picture by the **View of Sainte Gudule Master** (Pl. 122) which I place beside the S. Nicholas scenes, may also tell some story connected with a saint; but it seems impossible to recognize the subject of the intriguing composition. Little figures, it will be observed, go up and down the steps of the entrance to the cathedral of Sainte Gudule whence a fat prelate comes towards us; in the foreground some fashionably dressed young men and others crowd into a porch where on the right a bearded man and a young woman kneel before a preacher; behind the kneeling figures a pretty and most elegantly dressed young lady appears to be seated on the knee of an old man in a 'Hamlet' chair; as already noted tall fantastic headdresses are worn by both the women; there is much play with gesticulating hands; and a bearded man and a laughing boy watch the scene from the church door, like the spectators in the picture by the **Exhumation of S. Hubert Master** (Pl. 54)—a motif that goes back to **Ouwater**. It is possible, I think, that this picture satirizes some heretical sect whose ministers were forbidden to preach in churches, just as later we see pictures of Lutherans and Calvinists preaching to their followers in token buildings adjacent to but outside churches (*The Sermon* (Pl. 187) by **Lucas van Leyden** for example). If this be so the building would be a token of their meeting-place—something equivalent to that 'certain tower of a magistrate of Brussels, outside the city walls', where the members of one such sect are known to have assembled 'for the celebration of their conventicle' much earlier in the century.

The three scenes from the story of S. Lucy by the **Lucy Legend Master** are fully explained by the Golden Legend. For S. Lucy, daughter of a noble Syracusan lady, was converted to Christianity and induced her mother to give the family's substance to the poor; and we see this happening in *S. Lucy and her mother* (Pl. 117) where swarthy beggars have arrived to receive the bounty. This dispersal of the family wealth drove Lucy's betrothed to denounce her as a Christian to the consul Paschasius; brought before Paschasius, as we see her in *S. Lucy before the Consul* (Pl. 116), she refused to sacrifice to idols and argued with the consul saying: 'I am the servant of God who has said "When you are before the Kings and princes, I will speak from within you" '; Paschasius, astounded at her confidence asked her: 'Have you then the Holy Ghost within you?' and Lucy said, 'Those who live chaste lives are filled with the Holy Ghost'. Then Paschasius said: 'I will have you taken to a brothel and you will be defiled and the Holy Ghost will leave you', and Lucy answered: 'The body cannot be defiled without the will's consent.' So Paschasius called his henchmen to take the saint to the house of prostitution; but the Holy Ghost made her stand so steadfast and so heavy that they could not drag nor carry her; and even when the consul had called for a thousand men and forty teams of oxen they all failed to move her. This miracle is depicted in *Oxen failing to drag S. Lucy to a brothel* (Pl. 118) where the unavailing oxen in the foreground are being reinforced by others; and the artist has placed the Holy Ghost within a nimbus on the young saint's head. There may have been three other panels in this

71

series, one showing the apparition of S. Agatha to Lucy which converted her, another S. Lucy's martyrdom (she was killed by a sword thrust through her throat), and a third of the deposition of Paschasius by the Emperor who had him executed for maladministration of his province.

S. Ursula's legend is told again in **Memlinc's** *S. Ursula shrine* and one aspect of S. Catherine's legend reappears in **Memlinc's** *Mystic Marriage of S. Catherine* and in the pictures of that subject by the **Brussels Mystic Marriage Painter** and the **Virgo inter Virgines Master. Memlinc's** version of the S. Ursula story is told in six panels in place of the eight used by the **Ursula Legend Master** (Pls. 72-4, 97-101, 103, 120). In the first three panels (Pl. 93), on one side of the carved oak casket, we have the *Arrival at Cologne*, the *Arrival at Bâle* and the *Arrival in Rome*. The Cologne scene incorporates a view into a bedroom of a house in the background where the angel foretelling her martyrdom appears to the princess in bed; **Memlinc,** like Carpaccio, thus treats this as a vision—a concept already contrasted with the simple and engaging conversation on the quayside imagined by the **Ursula Legend Master** (Pl. 97). The *Arrival at Bâle* contains two shiploads of the pilgrims and, in the background, some of Ursula's companions have begun to climb the mountains on their journey by land to Rome; and in the Roman scene the pilgrims enter the city gates from the distant landscape in the background, the foremost group headed by the princess have reached S. Peters where the Pope Cyriacus and cardinals receive them, while the genre episodes already referred to take place inside the token building for S. Peter's. On the opposite side of the casket we have three scenes on the journey back, the *Embarkation at Bâle*, the *Massacre of the Maidens* and the *Death of S. Ursula* (Pl. 112). Pope Cyriacus with cardinals and bishops join the pilgrims' vessel in the Bâle scene, and **Memlinc** shows this in two stages, the arrival on the ship and the departure of the ship with the Papal party in the bows and S. Ursula's party behind them. In the massacre scene, which takes place in Cologne, the two ships carrying the pilgrims and the Papal company fill the panel; two Hun archers on the quayside shoot at them, while another Hun with a sword kills one of the maidens who falls into S. Ursula's arms; and in the last scene, also, of course, in Cologne, we have the field headquarters of the King of the Huns where S. Ursula demurely rejects the King's advances and one of the King's knights kills her with bow and arrow. The subject known as the *Mystic marriage of S. Catherine*, discussed in my last chapter, is seen as part of a formal devotional image in **Memlinc's** *S. John altar* (Pl. 111), designed for the high altar of the Hôpital. This composition had also to include the institution's patron saints S. John the Baptist and S. John the Evangelist; and thus incorporated in a formal structure the charming Virgo inter Virgines theme is robbed of its particular flavour. Moreover in **Memlinc's** picture the mystic marriage itself is inadequately imagined; for the Virgin, as already mentioned, looks away from it to turn the pages of a book, and S. Catherine extending, most unusually, her left hand (not her right) pays no attention to the Christ-child and looks straight ahead of her with cold indifference. But the **Brussels Mystic Marriage Painter** (Pl. 107) continues the tradition of the delightful versions of this subject by the **Buckingham Palace Mystic Marriage Painter** (Pl. 106) and the **Detroit Mystic Marriage Painter** (Pl. 110); for here again we have the concept of the Hortus Conclusus, the garden where the Virgin among virgins is sheltered from the world, a concept appropriate for the Trois Saintes altar for which it was commissioned; and the artist has included SS. Catherine, Mary Magdalene, Ursula, Lucy, Apollonia, Cecilia, Margaret, Barbara, Agatha and Agnes, all with emblems of their martyrdoms or legends. The picture by the **Virgo inter Virgines Master** (Pl. 128) is again a Hortus Conclusus; but the garden has become an austere enclosure with the figures seated on low stools or benches, and this enclosure is set within the cortile of a convent, hospital or almshouse surrounded by its cloisters; the mystic marriage scene, though outdoor, is here in essence an interior; and in spirit, despite the oddness of the turbans worn by SS. Catherine and Ursula, it is fundamentally domestic; for these young ladies, plump beneath their fine apparel, and with large plump hands, might well be daughters of rich bourgeois families and patrons of the institution where the scene takes place; in temper the whole picture is very calm and static; and it is evident that the **Virgo inter Virgines Master** is not concerned with drama or emotion but delights in leisured quietude, bourgeois serenity and cloistered calm.

Among the illustrations of the scriptures we have **Memlinc's** *Beheading of S. John the Baptist*, *S. John the Evangelist on Patmos*, *S. John the Baptist in the Wilderness*, and *S. Veronica* as well as the little scenes from the lives of the two Saints John in the background of the *S. John altar* already referred to. In the *Beheading of S. John the Baptist* (Pl. 89) the drama is conveyed by the vigorous action of the executioner which makes the executioner's action in the *Unjust Judgement of the Emperor Otho* (Pl. 67) by **Dirk Bouts** seem relatively tame and static; and, surprisingly, for so discreet an artist, the bleeding neck of the victim's corpse is not concealed as in the earlier picture.[1] In *S. John the Evangelist on Patmos* (Pl. 90) the saint seated on the token island, looks up towards the vision described in Revelation, and the rest of the picture illustrates the details of that vision—the King of Kings enthroned and surrounded by the ancients, the mighty Angel that stood with rainbow on his head and his feet on land and sea, the Woman clothed with the sun and with the moon at her feet, the battle between the angels and devils, and, in the middle distance, reflected in the water, the Four Horsemen led by Death upon the pale horse and Hell with gaping jaws behind (Pl. 88). In the *S. John the Baptist in the Wilderness* (Pl. 94) and *S. Veronica* (Pl. 95) the church architecture which had theologic meaning in the pictures by the **New York Virgin in a Tabernacle Painter** (Pl. 24), the **Washington Nativity in a Sculptured Porch Painter** (Pl. 30), the **New York Christ Appearing to His Mother Painter** (Pl. 47) and the **Redemption Master** (Pls. 51-3), is here no more than a decorative frame with illusionist cast shadows; S. John, a sugared version of the standing figure by the **Pearl of Brabant Master** (Pl. 91) is not a prophet crying in the wilderness but a mild figure with cocked head, politely seated, and his flowing red mantle tied in a bow on his shoulder spreads right and left on the ground beside him. **Memlinc's** concept of *S. Veronica* daintily displaying the sudary is likewise essentially genteel—as we see if we compare it with the concepts of the compassionate woman by the **Cambridge Veronica Draughtsman** (Pl. 38) and the **Flémalle Master** (Pl. 35).

Among the pictures of the *Nativity*, I have already commented on the delicate gesture imagined by **Memlinc** for the Virgin in the *Floreins altar* (Pl. 82). Another concept, intensely original and moving, is provided by the **London Nativity by Night Painter** (Pl. 129) who follows S. Luke's words 'and laid him in a manger' for the first time in the pictures so far reproduced here—(for the **Washington Nativity in a Sculptured Porch Painter** (Pl. 30) has shown the child on a plaited mat or basket lid, the **Minneapolis Adoration Painter** (Pls. 28, 75) and **Memlinc** sheltered him from the ground by his mother's mantle, and **Hugo of Antwerp** has placed him on the ground (Pl. 76)). In this beautiful little picture, the Virgin in dark blue mantle bends down with hands in adoration; the child-angels opposite are in white robes shot with lilac-grey, S. Joseph in the half light has a dull red garment; a short-

---

[1] But *cf.* footnote on p. 44 above.

necked pot stands on a brick ledge in a corner of the stable and a basket, with white cloth protruding, hangs from a beam above it. The subject is treated as a night-piece which must have been done quite frequently by artists from early times after seeing taper-lit groups in church *tableaux vivants* or Nativity 'cribs' (though few such pictures have survived from the fifteenth century); but the **London Nativity by Night Painter** reveals a personal concept by illumining the scene with the radiance from the Christ-child, while outside on a distant hillside an angel appears as a flash of light to the shepherds who are illumined also by a fire of faggots.

Three pictures shown here in adjacent plates—the *Lamentation* by **Geertgen tot Sint Jans**, the *Entombment* by the **Liverpool Entombment Painter** and the *Lamentation* by the **New York Lamentation Painter** inevitably evoke our memories of **Rogier van der Weyden's** *Descent from the Cross* (Pl. 46), the *Lamentation* (Pl. 64) by the **Vienna Cruciform Lamentation Painter,** and the *Entombment* (Pl. 65) by the **London (Guicciardi) Entombment Painter.** In **Geertgen's** *Lamentation* (Pl. 127) a special atmosphere is created by the contrast between the serene and charming landscape in the upper right-hand corner and the agitation and emotions of the human and saintly figures; and within that there is a further contrast between the stillness of the sorrowful foreground group (where S. John's hand behind the Virgin is the one disturbing passage) and the brutal animation of the genre episodes behind—a contrast already observed in the *Crucifixion* by the **New York Crucifixion and Last Judgement Painter** (Pls. 1, 2, 3, 159, 160) and to be observed later in the *Road to Calvary* by **Pieter Bruegel** (Pls. 379, 381). The plan of **Geertgen's** picture is a symbolic cross with the line of figures as the shaft, and the body of Christ with the women right and left combining as the transept. This recalls the dramatic picture by the **Vienna Cruciform Lamentation Painter** (Pl. 64); but whereas the earlier picture, apart from the foreground figures, is a non-terrestrial vision, **Geertgen's** concept is a *tableau vivant* with all the figures firmly planted on this earth. The head of the dead Christ, with slightly open mouth, is supported on the Virgin's knee; Nicodemus has paused in his uncovering; the kneeling rich man of Arimathea has just completed the sign of the cross; one Holy Woman stands on the right of the picture; the Magdalene and another are kneeling on the left. Van Mander, speaking of this picture, praised **Geertgen**, as he had praised **Rogier van der Weyden,** for his power to portray the feelings (uitbeelding der affecten); 'the faces of the Holy Women' he writes 'show the deepest grief; and the Virgin, in mournful meditation is portrayed so full of sorrow that the picture astounds our present day artists and is highly prized by them.' But, as already suggested, if we come to the mourners from the portrait of the man behind them, they seem less mourners than actors posing in the attitudes of mourning; in the pictures by the **New York Crucifixion and Last Judgement Painter** (Pls. 3, 160) and **Rogier van der Weyden** (Pl. 46) the Magdalene wrings her hands from inner compulsion of despair; the gesture is the same in **Geertgen's** picture but it is now the gesture of a youthful actress obeying her producer's orders; and though the woman standing opposite makes the gesture of wiping tears away there are in fact no tears. It is true that if we look ahead to the flamboyant rhetoric in the treatment of this subject by **Van Dyck** (Pl. 608) and **Gaspar de Crayer** (Pl. 609), and then turn back to this *Lamentation* we find it a model of restraint and moderation and rejection of hyperbole; but there is none-the-less a coldness in **Geertgen's** imaginative concept, an absence of the warmth and passion that drove the **New York Crucifixion and Last Judgement Painter** to contort the brows of the veritably distressed S. John (Pl. 2) and drove **Rogier van der Weyden** to set tears down-streaming on the mourners' faces. The *Entombment* by the **Liverpool Entombment Painter** (Pl. 126) is really, I think, more deeply felt and more imaginative than **Geertgen's** *Lamentation.* For this artist shows a moment that is rare in pictures surviving from this time. The Virgin has not yet received the body; she has fallen to her knees, supported by S. John, while the dead Christ is brought towards her by Nicodemus, Joseph of Arimathea and the Magdalene. It is hard to follow the structure of the right-hand group; but this adds to rather than diminishes the drama since it helps us to focus on the central heads—the Christ, the Virgin and S. John—all most individual and appropriately expressive. Each figure indeed in this deeply moving picture seems affectionately drawn from a particular model; the body of Christ has substance and the finger touching it presses upon flesh. The **New York Lamentation Painter** (Pl. 125) is a very different artist—or rather, I fancy two different artists, the nondescript painter of the stock figures of the Virgin and S. John, and the curious and very personal painter, or rather, draughtsman of the rest. The artist who drew the standing Holy Women, the kneeling Magdalene and the dead Christ supported by the Virgin's knee has evidently worked entirely as the phrase goes 'from his head'. These figures are not drawn from nature but from memories and imagination coloured by a personal aesthetic reacting to lean lines and ornated elegance. The emaciated Christ, with upturned brows and down drawn mouth, may be a memory of some sculptured crucifix, some Gothic wood carving, seen perhaps in a wayside shrine; the Magdalene and the standing women are devoid of substance; they have long thin faces that haunt us because these features were a complex in the artist's sensibility; they wear their elaborate half-fashionable half-fantastic clothes on non-existent bodies; and the artist thus working solitary in his unreal world has immersed himself in surface decoration, in plaited hair, brocaded patterns, pearls and jewels and embroidery on caps and turbans; and I would give much to have seen this picture as a unity with the Virgin and S. John made equally expressive by this artist's most personal aesthetic.

Of the devotional images reproduced here by the **Bruges Virgin with the Apple Painter** (Pl. 96A) and **Jean Hey** I have already referred to the first in my comments on the genre and interior painting of this period. The *Christ crowned with thorns* (Pl. 134) painted by the 'Teutonicus' **Jean Hey** in 1494 is a variant of the *Christ as the Man of Sorrows* type of picture common in the Netherlands from the middle of the fifteenth century. Many of these pictures are too painful and near-sadistic for inclusion in my plates; and it was possibly such pictures that Michelangelo had in mind when he said in 1538 to the Portuguese painter Francisco da Hollanda 'Italian painting will never cause anyone to shed a tear, but Flemish painting will cause floods of tears'. But **Jean Hey's** picture is not of this type; it stands indeed less close to these Flemish treatments than to the tender version by a Portuguese painter of this time who covered the thorn-crown and also Christ's forehead with a cloth. In **Jean Hey's** most sensitively rendered head and torso and bound hands, our pity, it is true, is aroused by the blood that falls and trickles; but there is no insistence on the pain; the thorns are mingled with the aureole; and there are hints of it blossoming to flowers.

If all the extant Netherlandish pictures known or presumed to have been painted in these seventeen years were assembled in one row, it would be evident that no one style or aspect of aesthetic can properly be called the style or aesthetic of this period; and it would, of course, be still more impossible to do this if all the pictures painted had survived. The same applies to the pictures surviving from the periods discussed in my first two chapters; and it will be no less evident in the later periods from which many more pictures have come down to us.

There have always, for example, been some archaistic artists who, ill-at-ease with the originalities of their own day, hark back to earlier modes and idioms in a sentimental spirit of affection for Ye Olden Times. Thus in the period covered by this chapter both the **Dublin S. Nicholas Painter** (Pl. 123) and the **View of Sainte Gudule Master** (Pl. 122) are archaistic painters who cling to the Gothic habit of crowding figures into token buildings much too small to receive them; both, as noted, worked probably in Brussels; the Bruxellois **Colyn de Coter** was also archaistic, harking back in the *Three Maries* (Pl. 280) to **Rogier van der Weyden's** masterpiece (Pl. 46); and it may be that this reactionary feeling was encouraged by patrons in Brussels and that the unknown paintings by other Bruxellois of this time—**Pieter van der Weyden, Goswin van der Weyden, Vrancke van der Stoct** and **Bernaert van der Stoct**—were also archaistic. In Bruges **Memlinc** appears as an archaistic artist in the *S. Ursula shrine* where the crowded compositions recall some Gothic manuscripts (Pls. 93, 112); and the central panels of the *Floreins altar* (Pl. 85) and the *S. John altar* are both traditional in fundamental structure—as we see if we look back to **Jan van Eyck's** *Van der Paele altar* (Pl. 19) and the altarpiece by **Petrus Christus** (Pl. 27).

But **Memlinc** was not wholly a traditional artist; he was no mere academic stealing from others the products of their direct experience, passionate perception or imaginative adventure, and re-presenting them shrunk in the laundry of a cautious mind and ironed to a smooth urbane gentility. It is undeniable that his works seem unduly sweet and tame if we come to them from study of the **van Eycks'** *Altarpiece of the Mystic Lamb* (Pls. 9, 13), **Rogier van der Weyden's** *Descent from the Cross* (Pl. 46) and **Hugo of Antwerp's** *Portinari altarpiece* (Pls. 76-8); they evidently lack dramatic imagination if we set them beside the wholly personal concepts in the pictures by **Geertgen tot Sint Jans** (Pl. 127), the **London Nativity by Night Painter** (Pl. 129), the **Liverpool Entombment Painter** (Pl. 126) and the **New York Lamentation Painter** (Pl. 125); they seem unadventurous if compared with the **Lucy Legend Master's** *S. Lucy before the Consul* (Pl. 116) where the pale calm oval of the young saint's face is surrounded by the coarse and cunning faces of her enemies—as later Christ's face will be surrounded by cruel and evil faces in pictures by the **Princeton Christ before Pilate Painter** (Pl. 174) and the **London Christ Mocked Painter** (Pl. 175); and the scenes on the *S. Ursula shrine* lack undeniably the wit, the gaiety and the varied observation of the **Ursula Legend Master** (Pls. 72-4, 97-103, 120). But if we come to the *Floreins altar* and the *S. John altar* without any prejudice their superficial sweetness is seen to be the product of an unsentimental mind intent on capturing serenity; the beautifully even tone that unifies the flesh tints and the delicacy of some physical features—the hands of S. Agnes (Pl. 115) for example—reveal an artist of great refinement and keen aesthetic feeling; and when we study the compositions we find them imbued with geometric meaning. For the central panel of the *Floreins altar* is a semicircle of forms starting on the right with the small head thrust into the window and ending with the small head behind the donor on the left; the first part of the semicircle is doubled by the Negro and kneeling Magus, and the stable architecture running straight across and parallel with the picture plane is the semicircle's base. In the same way the central panel of the *S. John altar* is a semicircle in front of architecture parallel with the picture plane; but this time the semicircle is based on the front of the picture. Thus seen, these panels acquire the serene finality of geometric form; and **Memlinc** appears, like Fra Angelico, a link between the Gothic and the Renaissance epochs. For, somehow, perhaps from prints or drawings, he had captured the secret of the classic norm and Mediterranean measure and thus heralded the *Holy Kinship* (Pl. 207) by **Quinten Massys.**

Of the artists known or presumed to have been working in the Northern provinces, the

New York Lamentation Painter (Pl. 125) may have seen and been fired by prints from Botticelli's paintings or his drawings. But no hint of Mediterranean influence is discernible elsewhere. There is a Dutch rusticity in the curious small figures by the **Liverpool Entombment Painter** (Pl. 126); the bourgeois spirit already noted in the Hortus Conclusus picture by the **Virgo inter Virgines Master** (Pl. 128) is also eminently Dutch; and the **London Nativity by Night Painter** (Pl. 129) is so characteristically a Northern figure that he leads us to think of Rembrandt's passion for chiaroscuro and Vermeer's passion for forms rounded or flattened by effects of light. For **Geerten tot Sint Jans,** as a Haarlemer, the great names were his master **Albert van Ouwater** and **Dirk Bouts** who, we must remember, had been born in Haarlem and doubtless worked there before he settled in Louvain; and **Geertgen** may have made a pilgrimage to Louvain to see the *Justice* pictures—as the diagonal procession in the *Unjust judgement of the Emperor Otho* (Pl. 67) by **Dirk Bouts** occurs again in **Geertgen's** *Julian the Apostate burning the bones of S. John the Baptist* (Pl. 123) and also in his *Lamentation* where to carry the diagonal right back to the sepulchre he has added the portrait figure with the winding sheet and behind him the Magdalene's pot of unguent—which allowing for perspective must be more than three feet high (Pl. 127).

There are thus at any rate at least three or four styles obtaining in the Netherlands in these seventeen years; some are original and some are archaistic; the artists of the Northern provinces were different from those in Flanders and Brabant; there seems to have been a difference between the Brussels artists and the Brugeois; and the style of the Louvain production, centred probably in the atelier of **Dirk Bouts the younger,** and **Aelbrecht Bouts,** may also have been different.

CHAPTER IV

Philip the Fair and Joanna the Mad

1495-1506

THE ARCHDUKE PHILIP THE FAIR, handsome and pleasure-loving, was popular throughout the provinces and no one disputed his title. His advisers were chiefly the nobles who sought peace with France; and against this the Emperor Maximilian on the one hand, and Ferdinand and Isabella on the other, arranged two marriages—Philip to marry the Infanta Joanna, and his sister Margaret of Austria to marry the Infante John heir to the thrones of Castile and Aragon. But by 1500, as a result of the death of the Infante John and others, Joanna herself became heiress apparent to Castile and Aragon, with her son Charles, then five months old, as next in the succession. When Queen Isabella died the Archduke Philip and Joanna thus claimed the inheritance; this was opposed by King Ferdinand who wished to become Regent for his grandson Charles; and the matter was still unsettled when Philip died in Spain, at twenty-eight, in 1506.

In 1495 Philip, aged seventeen, made more Pageant Entries into towns in the various provinces; Maximilian called a Diet to Worms to raise money to fight the French in Italy; Charles VIII made a Pageant Entry into Naples but was driven out of Italy by the joint forces of the Emperor, Pope Alexander VI, King Ferdinand and others, and Mantegna painted the *Madonna della Vittoria* to celebrate the Marquis of Mantua's contribution to the fray. John the Perfect of Portugal died, and Emanuel I (Manoel the Fortunate) succeeded; and Perkin Warbeck, with two thousand Yorkists and German mercenaries tried to land at Deal and went thence to Ireland and Scotland where James IV acknowledged him. In 1496 Philip the Fair married the Infanta Joanna who was then seventeen; Henry VII licensed John and Sebastian Cabot to sail the Atlantic on a voyage of discovery, and signed a commercial treaty, the 'Magnus Intercursus', with the Netherlands which greatly benefited the herring fisheries of Holland and was recorded in a window with portraits of Henry and Elizabeth of York and Philip and Joanna in Antwerp Cathedral. In 1497 Vasco da Gama sailed from Lisbon for India; Margaret of Austria, aged seventeen, married the Infante John in April; and in October the Infante died. In 1498 Joanna gave birth to her daughter Eleanor; Charles VIII died, Louis XII succeeded, and Philip signed the Treaty of Paris with Louis which renewed the Treaty of Senlis. Erasmus went to England; and Savonarola was burned. In 1499 Joanna, who had taken kindly to the free and easy Court at Brussels, after the gloom of Torquemada's Spain, was sternly reproved by her mother for deviations from the Spanish standards of orthodoxy and decorum; and agents of Isabella were sent to spy and report on her conduct. Louis XII claimed the Duchy of Milan and successfully invaded it; Perkin Warbeck was executed; and the Emperor recognized the Independence of the Swiss. In 1500 Joanna gave birth in Ghent to her son Charles;

Miguel of Portugal, grandson of Ferdinand and Isabella, and heir apparent, died; and Joanna became heir apparent. Louis XII and King Ferdinand took joint possession of the Kingdom of Naples which they agreed to share; and the Portuguese Pedro Alvarez Cabral discovered Brazil. In 1501 Joanna gave birth to her daughter Isabella; France, Burgundy and Austria signed the Treaty of Lyons whereby Joanna's son Charles aged one and a half years and Louis XII's daughter Claude were betrothed and Claude was to bring Brittany, Milan and Naples in her dowry; Philip and Joanna left the Netherlands for Spain, travelling through France; and Margaret of Austria married Philibert II of Savoy. In 1502 the Cortes of Castile paid homage to Joanna as heiress to the throne and to Philip as her consort; and the Cortes of Aragon paid the same homage with proviso that if King Ferdinand remarried and had a son he might declare that son the King of Aragon. Isabella expelled from Castile all Moors who were not converted; and the Inquisition persecuted the converted Muslims (Moriscos) and sequestered their property if insincerity in conversion was alleged or suspected. Spain prepared for war on France to eject Louis XII from his share in the Kingdom of Naples; and Philip, who was a Francophil and detested the Inquisition, went to France on his way back to the Netherlands, leaving Joanna, again with child, in Spain. In 1503 the Borgia Pope died and was succeeded first by Francis Todeschini-Piccolomini as Pius III and before the year was out by Julian della Rovera as Julius II; James IV of Scotland married Margaret, daughter of Henry VII, and Joanna gave birth to her son Ferdinand. Isabella incessantly urged Joanna to remain in Spain and work for Spanish projects; but Joanna, moody and neurotic and passionately in love with Philip, wished only to return at once to Brussels, and Isabella, convinced that she was crazy, kept her in Spain, under constant supervision by her agents. In 1504 King Ferdinand drove Louis XII from Naples; and Philibert of Savoy, Margaret of Austria's husband, died. Joanna, now twenty-five, returned to Brussels to find that Philip had been unfaithful to her with a lady of the court; she assaulted the lady, made jealous scenes and went on hunger strike; and a treacherous courtier, agent of Isabella, kept a diary of her tantrums which Philip, to cover his misdemeanours, sent to Spain. The Emperor, Louis XII and Philip made a secret agreement that on Isabella's death Ferdinand should be regarded as King of Aragon only. Isabella died in November; and a codicil in her will appointed King Ferdinand Regent in Castile for her grandson Charles if Joanna 'should be absent, or lack desire or ability to rule'. In January 1505 Ferdinand called the Cortes of Castile and read them the diary to prove Joanna's 'inability' and procure his own appointment to the Regency; but the nobles hesitated; Philip put Joanna's and his own claims forward, styled himself King Philip I of Castile and announced his intention of coming with the Queen to Spain. Preparations for the journey lasted through the year; in May he wrote to the Archbishop of Seville, General of the Inquisition, to suspend all action by the Inquisition till he had arrived in Spain; and in September Joanna gave birth to her daughter Mary. In January 1506 Philip and Joanna sailed from Flushing; a storm dispersed their convoy, Philip had himself sewn in an inflated leather case with 'El Rey Don Felipe' painted in large lettering outside, while Joanna called calmly for her dinner 'diziendo que nunca Rey murió ahogado'; the storm drove them to Weymouth, whence Henry VII had them conducted with courtesy to Windsor and negotiations began for a marriage between Henry now a widower, with the widowed Margaret of Austria. In March King Ferdinand married Germaine de Foix; in April Philip and Joanna landed at Corunna; in the summer Philip marched with two thousand German mercenaries to meet Ferdinand; and the powerful Archbishop of Toledo and many Spanish nobles left Ferdinand and joined him. Joanna herself had no wish to surrender the throne of Castile to Philip; but both Philip and Ferdinand agreed on her inability to rule. Philip called the Cortes to ask them to pronounce the inability and acknowledge his own claim to be Philip I. Ferdinand on his part still claimed the Regency; and matters stood thus when Philip died in September of typhoid fever (or possibly of poison). Joanna, distracted by Philip's death and all the perfidies around her, became indubitably Juana la loca, Joanna the mad; and Ferdinand became Regent for the Infante Charles.[1]

The London National Gallery has a charming double portrait, *Philip the Fair and his sister Margaret of Austria* of unknown authorship, painted probably in 1495; and we see the young Archduke again in the left-hand wing of the triptych by the **Melbourne Miracles Painter** where the guests portrayed at the *Marriage Feast at Cana* (Pl. 149) are Philip the Good and his three wives, Charles the Bold with Isabella of Bourbon, Maximilian with Maria of Burgundy, and Philip himself still unmarried which dates the panel before 1496. Philip's court painters included **Pieter van Coninxloo (Pierre de Royaulme)** and also **Jacques van Lathem** who went with him to Spain in 1501 (and may have met there **Francis of Antwerp** known in Spain as **Francisco de Amberes** who was then at work in Toledo Cathedral). The **Brussels Zierickzee Master,** also possibly a court painter, put portraits of Philip and Joanna on the wings of a *Last Judgement* triptych, and their arms appear on the judge's throne in a *Judgement of Cambyses* by an unrecorded artist (presumed by some to be **Gerard David**). In 1504 the Archduke made a payment on account to **Hieronymus Bosch** for a large *Last Judgement* 'assavoir paradis et enfer' ordered by him 'pour son très noble plaisir', and it is possible, I think, that **Bosch** owed the commission to Erasmus who had spent two years in a school run by the Brothers of the Common Life in Bois-le-Duc and was in Louvain in 1504 when he was paid fifty livres by Philip for a panegyric on his Spanish visit. There was the usual work for the artists in the court ceremonies and pageants which had begun with Philip's Entry into Antwerp in 1494 when three almost naked girls posed as the goddesses in a *Judgement of Paris* tableau vivant; there were pageants for Philip's wedding and tremendous pageantry to celebrate the baptism of the infant Charles in Ghent. Such events were also doubtless chronicled in paintings and prints; and popular hand-coloured woodcuts of the sovereigns, the processions, the religious ceremonies and so forth were also doubtless abundant—like the hand-coloured woodcuts known to have been distributed in the Lazarite processions on Shrove Tuesday. Such popular productions, in perishable materials, and little regarded, do not normally survive; but we have perhaps an allusion to the Archduke's marriage in the picture by the **Toledo Marriage of Henry VI Painter** (Pl. 147) though this has been presumed to represent the marriage of Henry VI of England with Margaret of Anjou (daughter of King René), since Horace Walpole who owned it thus described it—adding that the queen is shown as pregnant, an error due to misunderstanding of the lady's stance which, as noted, had been considered elegant since the time of **Jan van Eyck** (Pl. 18A).

A regional conspectus includes some artists surviving from the last period and some new ones. In Bruges we have **Gerard David, Jan Provoost** and **Paschier van der Mersch.** In Antwerp **Goswin van der Weyden, Quinten Massys** and probably **Jan Gossaert** and **Joachim Patinir.** In Brussels **Pieter van der Weyden, Vrancke van der Stoct, Bernaert van der Stoct, Colyn de Coter, Jacques van Lathem, Jan van Coninxloo the elder, Pieter van Coninxloo**

---

[1] Joanna was interned thereafter for the rest of her life. But she remained the titular Queen and her name was used in official documents together with that of Charles as acting King of Spain till her death at seventy-six in 1555 (when Charles as Emperor was beginning his abdications).

and **Jean van Battel.** In Ghent, **Gerard van der Meire** and **Matthys van Roden.** In Louvain **Gillis Stuerbout** and **Aelbrecht Bouts,** and in Malines **Baudoin van Battel.** In the Northern provinces we have **Cornelis van Engelbrechtsz** in Leyden, and **Jacob Cornelis van Oostsanen** in Amsterdam; **Jan Joest** in Wesel and possibly Calcar, **Cornelis Buys the elder** in Alkmaar, and possibly **Albert van Ouwater** and **Geertgen tot Sint Jans** in Haarlem; and **Hieronymus Bosch** in Bois-le-Duc (Hertogenbosch).

Of these we know that **Gerard David** (Pl. 195) married a daughter of the Dean of the Bruges Goldsmiths' Guild when he was probably over thirty in 1496, that he received final payment for a picture in the Town Hall in 1499, and was himself Dean of the Painters' Guild in 1501. But no picture known to have been painted by **Gerard David** in this period is known to be extant; and the same applies to **Jan Provoost** (Pl. 283) who was assessor in the Bruges Guild in 1501 at about thirty-five, and carried out decorative work for the Knights of the Golden Fleece in S. Donatian in 1506; and to **Memlinc's** pupil **Paschier van der Mersch** who died in 1505. **Goswin van der Weyden** seems to have left Brussels at the beginning of the period; he worked in Lierre in 1497, and about 1498 he moved to Antwerp which was now attracting many artists; in Antwerp he was Master by 1504 and his pupils there included a Portuguese painter recorded as Simon Portugalois. His father **Pieter van der Weyden** may have stayed in Brussels or gone with him to Antwerp as no details of his later years are known. **Quinten Massys** (Pls. 207, 235, 241), aged about thirty in 1495, had an atelier in Antwerp where at this time or later a number of Portuguese painters including Eduardo o Portugues were among his pupils; but no pictures known to have been painted by **Massys** in these years are known to be extant. **Jan Gossaert** often referred to as **Mabuse** (Pls. 194, 238, 247, 255, 294, 297) was born near Utrecht or at Maubeuge in Hainault and is presumed the 'Jennyn van Hennegouwe' (Hainault) who was Master in Antwerp in 1503; but, again, no works known to have been painted by him in this period are known to be extant. **Joachim Patinir** (Pls. 216, 241, 244, 245) whose birthdate is unknown, was probably apprenticed to some master, possibly in Antwerp, before 1500. **Jacques van Lathem,** just mentioned as Court painter to Philip the Fair, seems to have moved from Antwerp to Brussels, the headquarters of the Court, by 1498 when he received his appointment as 'peintre et valet de chambre'; in 1500 he designed the ceremonies for a Chapter of the Knights of the Golden Fleece; and after his return from Spain (with the Archduke or with Joanna) he directed the designing of memorial ceremonies on the death of Queen Isabella. **Pieter van Coninxloo (Pierre de Royaulme),** also mentioned above as a Court painter, decorated the Archduke's coaches in 1499 and painted in 1505 a *Margaret of Austria* sent by Philip to Henry VII in connection with the marriage projected at that time. **Jan van Coninxloo the elder,** probably his father, may have died in Brussels before 1506. **Jean van Battel** (son of the Malines painter **Baudoin van Battel** who was still designing Ommeganck processions there in 1503) may have been established in Brussels by the end of 1504 when he took part in designing the memorial ceremonies on the death of Isabella; and thereafter he is known to have collaborated with **van Lathem. Colyn de Coter** (Pl. 280) who lived through the period was also perhaps continuously in Brussels. **Vrancke van der Stoct** died in 1495; and his son **Bernaert van der Stoct** left Brussels on a pilgrimage to Jerusalem in 1505. **Gerard van der Meire** was still working, as far as we know, in Ghent and was over seventy in 1506; and **Matthys Roden** also lived through the period and was thus presumably available as designer of the pageantry when the Infant Charles was baptized. **Gillis Stuerbout** may still have been town painter in Louvain in the nineties; and **Aelbrecht Bouts** (Pls. 251-3) who lived into the next period and beyond it, was probably the chief Louvain painter in this one, though no works known to have been painted by him in these years are known to be extant. Of the artists in the Northern provinces we know that **Cornelis Engelbrechtsz** (Pls. 210, 211, 213, 229, 230, 232, 233) was in the Leyden Civic Guard from 1499 for some twenty years and that he was thirty-eight in 1506; and that **Jacob Cornelisz van Oostsanen** (Pls. 265, 268, 302) was working in Amsterdam where he owned a house by 1500; but once again no pictures known to have been painted by either of these artists in this period are known to be extant. **Cornelis Buys the elder** (brother, as noted, of **Cornelisz van Oostsanen**) seems to have worked all the time in Alkmaar; and **Jan Joest** seems to have been in Wesel till 1505 when he received the commission for his only known extant work— twenty panels, *Scenes from the life of Christ* and two *Old Testament subjects* on wings to cover a carved wooden altarpiece in the Nicolai church in Calcar where he may have gone to execute them. In Haarlem **Albert van Ouwater** probably died over seventy before 1500 and **Geertgen tot Sint Jans** (Pls. 124, 127) died about twenty-eight also probably before 1500. **Hieronymus Bosch** (Pls. 156-8, 161, 163-73) is mentioned repeatedly in the records of the Bois-le-Duc Brotherhood of Our Lady between 1495 and 1502; and in 1504, Philip the Fair made him the payment on account for the *Last Judgement* with *Paradise* and *Hell* scenes already referred to. This *Last Judgement* is not known to be extant, and, as in the last period, we do not know what pictures **Bosch** painted in these years because his signed or documented works are all undated and no one therefore knows which are 'early' and which 'late'. I shall however discuss some products of his curious genius in this chapter as he was possibly between forty-five and fifty-five in this period and at something like the middle point of his activity.

There was certainly a large and varied production of pictures in Flanders, Brabant, Hainault and so on and also in the Northern provinces, for the country was at peace, commerce flourished and there was much free thinking, free admiration and free indignation—all incentives to creative action; and religious persecution had not yet set in. Many of the works were civic commissions or pictures for churches; many must have been commissioned or bought by rich private people and by intellectuals like the Humanists whose purchases were not recorded in the civic or ecclesiastic archives and failed to survive the troubled times which followed; and many, no doubt, were painted on the artists' own initiatives. But as can be seen from the foregoing there are hardly any extant pictures which are known to have been painted by any particular artist in this period; and my notes show only **Jan Joest's** *Scenes from the life of Christ* and these, though begun in 1505, were not finished till some years later.

On the other hand we have some dated or datable pictures of unidentified authorship. Thus the *Judgement of Cambyses* by an unrecorded artist, already referred to, with its companion piece the *Flaying of the unjust judge Sisamnes*, is dated 1498. The painter known as the **Bruges 1499 Master** is so-called because his picture is dated 1499. The *Last Judgement* triptych by the **Brussels Zierickzee Master** was commissioned in 1500 for the Zierickzee Town Hall though painted probably in Brussels. The **Lisbon Alexander VI Painter**, presumed a Fleming and possibly a Brugeois, must have produced his triptych, *The Virgin enthroned with saints and adorants* and the wings showing *S. Christopher* (Pl. 202) and *S. Sebastian* between 1500 and 1503 as the adorants include King Manoel the Fortunate of Portugal with his second wife Maria and Pope Alexander VI; and the **Alkmaar Master** inscribed 1504 on one panel of his *Seven Works of Mercy* (Pls. 182-5 and 188) probably painted for S. Laurentius in Alkmaar. The round shoes, small berets, full round capes and coats with deep lapels worn by figures in the **Alkmaar Master's** pictures were characteristic of the fashions which developed between the middle of the fourteen-nineties and the end of the first decade of the sixteenth century; and the presence of such fashions enables us to date to this period the pictures reproduced here by the **Brussels Man with a Rosary Painter** (Pl. 181), the **Oultremont Master** (Pl. 179), the **Giles Master** (Pl. 155), the **Worcester Saint and Donor Painter** (Pl. 153), the **Toledo Marriage of Henry VI Painter** (Pl. 147), and the **Philadelphia Marriage of the Virgin Painter** whose young dandy on the left wears all the latest fashions though the beard of the turbaned man behind him must surely be fantasticated to suggest an imposing Oriental magnate or rejected suitor (Pl. 152). Stripes on hose or jerkins appear in the pictures by the **Philadelphia Marriage of the Virgin Painter,** the **Giles Master** and the **Oultremont Master** and we find them also in works presumably of this period by the **Antwerp Last Judgement Painter** (Pl. 135), and the **New York Godelieve Legend Painter** (Pl. 144) and in the **Melbourne Miracles Painter's** *Raising of Lazarus* (Pl. 150) which may be a few years later than the *Wedding Feast at Cana* (Pl. 149) and perhaps by a different hand. Other pictures reproduced here, as probably of this period, are by unidentified artists here referred to as the **St. Louis Entombment Painter** (Pl. 130), the **Philadelphia Maria Egyptiaca Painter** (Pl. 131), the **Florence (Poggio Imperiale) Crucifixion Painter** (Pl. 133), the **New York Adoration in a White Castle Painter** (Pl. 151), the **Philadelphia Adoration of the Magi Painter** (Pl. 162), the **Princeton Christ before Pilate Painter** (Pl. 174) and the **London Christ Mocked Painter** (Pl. 175) who may all have worked in the Northern provinces, and by the **Malines Guild of S. George Master** (Pl. 146), the **Glasgow Saint and Donor Painter** (Pl. 154), the **London Wagner Ecce Homo Painter** (Pl. 177) and the **Hoogstraeten Master** (Pls. 197, 198) who probably painted in the Antwerp region or in Brabant or Flanders.

Some pictures of the period have didactic themes or make social protests or satiric comments; and some voice the stirrings of the Reformation and the growth of Humanism (Sebastian Brant had published his 'Ship of Fools' in 1494 and Josse Bade's 'Ship of Female Fools' dates from 1498). The *Judgement of Cambyses* with its companion piece the *Flaying of the unjust judge Sisamnes* (too sadistic to be reproduced here) are 'Justice' pictures in the tradition of commissions given by town authorities to **Rogier van der Weyden** and **Dirk Bouts** (Pls. 67, 69); the subject, taken from Herodotus and Valerius Maximus, is the story of the judge Sisamnes who was bribed to give an unjust verdict and was condemned by King Cambyses to be flayed alive; and the King further ordered that the judge's skin should be made into a covering for the chair of the Hall of Justice as a warning to succeeding occupants. The **Alkmaar Master** protests against the hideous tortures inflicted as punishments, or simply as 'questioning', by the Courts of Justice at this time; for in his *Releasing the prisoners* (Pl. 184) the reprieve brought by the foreground gentleman is too late to save the prisoner from the torture of the cord, where the victim, hands tied behind, was hoisted and questioned while his shoulders were dislocated and blows rained down upon him; in *Visiting the sick* (Pl. 185) a man sits by a patient's bedside and holds his hand while in the background a nurse and doctor put unguents on some poor miscreant who has doubtless just suffered some horrible maltreatment of this kind; and in the street scenes (Pls. 182, 183) crippled beggars are shown as victims of torture and of amputations of their hands or feet.

The **Alkmaar Master's** pictures can also be interpreted as propaganda, inspired by theologians, against the control of charity by the civil powers. For a bitter struggle between the Church and the civil authorities on this matter was launched at the turn of the century and continued through the next period and beyond; in the fifteenth century the care of the sick and destitute had been controlled by the Church which had collected large funds to build and run hospitals and charitable foundations; but these establishments were now for the most part badly managed and crowds of idle men and women, with their children, abused the charities so that the civil authorities wished to control the funds, reorganize their use and thus abate these evils. This movement was supported by the Humanists and also by the farmers and business men who wanted the children trained for landwork and for industry; but the Church opposed it as an infringement of its prerogatives and as born of reforming and anti-clerical ideas. The **Alkmaar Master's** *Seven Works of Mercy* and also the **Antwerp Last Judgement Painter's** version of the subject (Pl. 135), both destined for churches, may thus be part of the Church's protest in this field; for Christ appears in each scene of the *Works of Mercy* not only to illustrate the words 'In as much as ye have done it unto the least of these my brethren, ye have done it unto me', but also, perhaps, as a reminder that the organizing of these charities was the function not of laymen but the Church; and the **Antwerp Last Judgement Painter** further points the moral by attaching a saint or prophet to each category of good deed.

In pictures by **Hieronymus Bosch** we have abundance of satiric and social comment and also, quite evidently, some anti-clerical shafts and what I take to be protests against the Spanish Inquisition; for Torquemada's cruelties must then have been affecting all decent people in the Netherlands in much the same way that the Nazi cruelties in our own day affected such people in the neighbouring countries; and some Netherlanders must also have credited the dark rumours of Pope Alexander's vices (which probably led **Joachim Patinir** and others to paint *Lot and his daughters* as a gesture of crypto-protest). **Bosch** indicts all classes and conditions in the crowd that fights and scrambles in the *Haywain* (Pl. 165). We know the general meaning of this 'moralidad' from Father Sigüenza (late sixteenth-century historian of the Escorial and an earnest student of **Bosch's** works in the Spanish King's collection). It is based, he tells us, on Isaiah's 'All flesh is grass and all its glory like a flower of the field', and shows a laden hay cart, drawn by hybrid monsters, symbols of man's vices, and followed by Pope, Emperor and other powers that be; on the summit, lovers and musicians typify the pleasures of the senses; and Fame, a winged demon, trumpets forth 'grandeza y regalos'; round the cart all sorts and conditions struggle to grasp the transient glory, some using ladders and others grappling forks, some falling and others encumbering the wheels; and 'finally to show that nothing in this life is wholly removed from divine assistance, not even the greatest sinners in the midst of their sins, there is a guardian angel imploring God for them and the Lord Jesus Christ with arms extended and wounds manifest awaiting the converted'. But the picture may also illustrate the Flemish proverb 'De Werelt is een hooiberg; elk plukt ervan wat hij kan krijgen (the world is a haystack and each one plucks what he can from it); or it may symbolize the Seven Deadly Sins: Envy by the scrambling crowd, Gluttony by the fat abbot, Avarice by the quack doctor or dentist whose pocket bulges with his plunder and by the nuns who bring great sheaves to further fatten the fat abbot, Rage by the man committing murder, Sloth by the man sleeping at the feet of the nun with a baby, Lust by this nun, by the lovers on the summit of the haystack and by the well-dressed lady in the foreground who visits the gipsy womenfolk of the 'empiric' on some dark business (like Hogarth's *Visit to the Quack Doctor*), and Pride by the pope, the emperor and the kings—though as the pope shown is unmistakably the Borgia, he may typify some other vices also. The quack doctor with his table of instruments is also satirized in **Bosch's** *Christ driving the moneychangers from the Temple* (Pl. 164) and his wife again holds a child face downwards on her knee—(an attitude used later by

Jacob Jordaens in one of his riotous Twelfth Night parties, and by **Rubens** who makes it socially respectable and transforms the child into a Cupid (Pl. 662)); and **Bosch** shows a quack doctor yet again in the *Operation for Stone: or the Cure of Folly* (Pl. 161) where the funnel hat and the balanced book doubtless have relation to some local saws and fables. War, as practised in his day, and the Spanish Inquisition seem to me indicted in **Bosch's** *Hell* (Pls. 168, 173); for at the top armed horsemen, who have just sacked and burned some town or village, retire across a bridge above a blood and fire-stained river; and just below them naked figures are led to flaming stake and gallows by frantic gesticulating figures while more naked victims are driven towards them from the right by men in armour or in fantasticated monk-like habits. As anti-clerical shafts by **Bosch** we have the fat abbot and the lascivious nuns in the *Haywain* (Pl. 165), the monk and nun held up to ridicule in the *Operation for Stone: or the Cure of Folly* (Pl. 161) and, in the *Hell* (Pl. 168), monks with devil's horns and tails, and a sow accoutred as an abbess. Such anti-clerical gestures group him with satiric writers of the period and the Humanist precursors of the Reformation like Erasmus himself with whom, as mentioned, he may have been acquainted. A few years later, when the Inquisition reached the Netherlands, such comments would have been most dangerous; but in **Bosch's** lifetime the seats of power in the Netherlands were not yet committed to the repression of free thought, and the Church itself, not yet embarked on the Counter-Reformation in these regions, was still tolerant of comments on clerical abuses which it recognized and itself desired to rectify.

As our knowledge goes **Bosch** seems indeed the most original artist at work in this period. The **Princeton Christ before Pilate Painter** (Pl. 174) stands close to him in creative fire and spirit; and the **New York Adoration in a White Castle Painter** (Pl. 151) and the **St. Louis Entombment Painter** (Pl. 130) both have original concepts. On the other hand, **Colyn de Coter** (Pl. 280), the **Antwerp Last Judgement Painter** (Pl. 135), the **New York Godelieve Legend Painter** (Pls. 140-5), the **Malines Guild of S. George Master** (Pl. 146), the **Toledo Marriage of Henry VI Painter** (Pl. 147), the **Melbourne Miracles Painter** (Pls. 148-50), and the **Philadelphia Marriage of the Virgin Painter** (Pl. 152) are plainly archaistic; while the **Oultremont Master** (Pls. 176, 178-80), and the painter of the *Judgement of Cambyses* and the *Flaying of the unjust judge Sisamnes* were good traditional performers neither archaistic nor notably inventive.

If my plates for this period are examined we can again form some general impressions of the landscapes and townscapes, interiors and still-life, the genre and animal painting, the nudes and the portraits, in addition to the didactic and social comments already mentioned, the religious concepts in devotional pictures and the narrative treatments of scriptural subjects and the legends of the saints.

In landscape the **Malines Guild of S. George Master** (Pl. 146) may have called in a specialist for the background with its flat stretch of country and river on the outskirts of Malines; and the **Giles Master** (Pl. 155) probably employed another for the rocky Provençal countryside with the tree and thicket in the foreground. The **Melbourne Miracles Painter** sets his *Miracle of the loaves and fishes* in a desert place with rocks and trees receding to the seashore (Pl. 148); and the **Philadelphia Maria Egyptiaca Painter** (Pl. 131) puts a stream and shrubs to suggest a small oasis in a desert. A pastoral landscape sweeps behind the stable in the Adoration scene by the **Philadelphia Adoration of the Magi Painter** (Pl. 162); and a grey spreading plain against a delicate sunrise is background to the gentle composition, full of light and air, by the **New York Adoration in a White Castle Painter** (Pl. 151). There are woods right and left on Golgotha in the *Crucifixion* as imaged by the

Florence (Poggio Imperiale) Crucifixion Painter (Pl. 133); and in the St. Louis Entombment Painter's picture an emotive landscape recedes to the horizon between a bare bleak Golgotha on the left and, on the right, a wooded hill with the stone and sepulchre (Pl. 130). Naturalistic, semi-fantastic, and completely fantastic or symbolic details appear in various landscapes by Hieronymus Bosch; thus a flat stretch of countryside, with mill, church, gallows and torture wheel, is the setting for his *Operation for Stone: or the Cure of Folly* (Pl. 161); in his *Adoration of the Magi* (Pl. 157), when open as a triptych, all the foreground figures, including donors on the wings, are placed within a single vast receding grey-green and olive-silver landscape which occupies three-quarters of the picture; and behind the rural middle distance in the *Haywain* (Pl. 165) a blue estuary fades to the horizon. In the *Temptation of S. Anthony* (Pl. 163) the saint sits in the hollow of a large dead tree with an improvised thatch roof, and this shelter, on a small grass mound with a stream around it, is a little removed from a rural landscape with slim trees, woods, a monastery and a distant town with spires. In the *Creation of the World* (Pl. 172), on the outside of the wings of the *Garden of Delights*, rain descends on the rocks and verdure of the flat earth surface enclosed in a crystal sphere to symbolize the firmament; on the inside of one wing *The Creation of Eve* (Pl. 167) fantastic semi-phallic blue, salmon pink and golden cromlechs symbolize, I take it, mountains in Eden whence the river flowed to water the garden, and since Eden was 'eastward' there are two kinds of date-palm for the Tree of Knowledge and the Tree of Life. In the *Garden of Delights* itself (Pl. 166) the cromlechs are continued as semi-phallic structures of rock and crystal and stylized vegetable forms that resemble metal work and also suggest the armour and rigging of fantastic galleons; and the garden, geometrically constructed, has grey-green and olive sward, fruit-bearing shrubs and pools.

The townscapes in some cases follow the old tradition of topography and in others they are symbolic structures. Thus the Malines Guild of S. George Master shows four gates of Malines, the Blauwe Steen castle, and the tower of the Cathedral of S. Rombout in course of construction (Pl. 146); and the little town in the Giles Master's Provençal landscape (Pl. 155) may be Saint-Gilles-du-Gard. Walled towns on the horizon stand for Bethlehem in the pictures by the New York Adoration in a White Castle Painter (Pl. 151) and the Philadelphia Adoration of the Magi Painter (Pl. 162); and Bethlehem as tokened by Hieronymus Bosch (Pl. 157) is an exotic city with bottle-shaped towers and minarets and also a circular building which recalls the token Jerusalem by the New York Crucifixion and Last Judgement Painter (Pls. 1, 5, 6). Bosch's Jerusalem with the fantasticated temple in his *Christ driving the moneychangers from the Temple* (Pl. 164) is again a city with exotic bottle-shaped towers and minarets. But Jerusalem as depicted by the Florence (Poggio Imperiale) Crucifixion Painter (Pl. 133) is a Western town with a Netherlandish castle and smaller domestic buildings.

The tradition of street scenes and views through windows and into houses, is continued most notably by the archaistic painters, though we see it also in works by some with more contemporary taste. The Alkmaar Master gives us street scenes in *Feeding the Hungry* (Pl. 182), *Refreshing the Thirsty* (Pl. 183) and *Clothing the Naked* (Pl. 188); and we must note that all the windows in his street scenes have their shutters open but no curious inmates look out from them, though the London Virgin with a Firescreen Painter (Pl. 39) at the beginning of our story, Pieter Bruegel (Pls. 369, 370) and Denis van Alsloot (Pl. 513A) in the middle, and Jan Baptist de Jonghe (Pl. 892) at the end, all increased the actuality of their street scenes in that way. The New York Godelieve Legend Painter (Pls. 141-5) tells his elaborate tale of twenty episodes with the help of streets and peeps into rooms revealed by the old device of removing whole sections of the walls—a device already seen in pictures by the **Ursula Legend Master** (Pl. 101), the **Dublin S. Augustine Painter** (Pl. 102) and **Memlinc** (Pls. 93, 113). The same device is used here by the **Philadelphia Marriage of the Virgin Painter** who gives us a glimpse within the habitat of S. Anne, and the street outside the Temple with the Temple steps, all seen between the columns of the loggia where the marriage scene is set (Pl. 152); but the background of the marriage scene by the **Toledo Marriage of Henry VI Painter** is a cathedral front with a sculptured *Salvator Mundi* on the central pillar and *Moses, S. Peter, S. John the Evangelist* and other saints in niches (Pl. 147). **Hieronymus Bosch,** characteristically, uses townscape in a dramatic way; for he shows a town on fire (Pl. 168)—thus recording, I presume, his early memories of towns burned in savagery by Charles the Bold or in the civil wars of Maximilian. All these pictures—except perhaps the series by the **Alkmaar Master**—were done, I imagine, without help from architectural specialists. But some such specialist was probably called on for the architecture in the strange composition by the **Brussels Man with a Rosary Painter** (Pl. 181), for here the palace with its Italianate ornament and balcony and roof garden seems based on drawings made in Venice or elsewhere in Italy; and the painter of the *Judgement of Cambyses* (already several times referred to) must also I think, have been served by an architectural specialist acquainted with Mantegna's use of 'putti' holding swags of leaves and fruit and with the classical reliefs and cameos in Italian Renaissance art.

The interior painting seems for the most part unadventurous. Whoever painted the Hall of Justice in the *Judgement of Cambyses* remembered **Dirk Bouts'** *The Ordeal by Fire* (Pl. 69); but the standard of complete interior structure set by **Bouts,** or his architectural collaborator, in the *Last Supper* (Pl. 58) still seems generally ignored. The **Alkmaar Master** gives a coherent account of a hospital interior with a private cubicle and a general ward (Pl. 185); and the **Hoogstraeten Master** (Pls. 197, 198) may have had some help from an architectural draughtsman for his Temple scenes. But **Hieronymus Bosch** himself is content with an altar as token for a church interior in his *Mass of S. Gregory* (Pl. 156); and the archaistic painters provide no more than indications of interior settings. Thus the **New York Godelieve Legend Painter** provides an ingenious token church interior for his marriage ceremony (Pls. 140, 141) but his adjacent dinner party takes place in a chamber with no walls; the **Melbourne Miracles Painter** puts two pillars, a tessellated floor and a serving-hatch as setting for his *Marriage Feast at Cana* (Pl. 149) and leaves the rest of the room indeterminate; and the **Antwerp Last Judgement Painter** relies on a bed here and a window there to suggest the various apartments where certain of the sins or virtues are exhibited (Pl. 135).

The still-life painting—if **Bosch** be excepted—is mainly a matter of hack copying of textile patterns—as in the works reproduced by the **Antwerp Last Judgement Painter,** the **New York Godelieve Legend Painter,** the **Toledo Marriage of Henry VI Painter** (Pl. 147), the **Melbourne Miracles Painter,** the **Philadelphia Marriage of the Virgin Painter** (Pl. 152), the **Worcester Saint and Donor Painter** (Pl. 153), the **Glasgow Saint and Donor Painter** (Pl. 154), the **Giles Master** (Pl. 155) and **Colyn de Coter** (Pl. 282). But there is something more than hack work in the cruel glitter of the metals that is part and parcel of the spirit in the picture by the **Princeton Christ before Pilate Painter** (Pl. 174). **Bosch's** *Garden of Delights* is full of naturalistic, fantasticated or distorted still-life—for most beautifully painted giant lobster shells, enormous seed pods and glass cloches in addition to huge strawberries and other fruits abound in it (Pls. 18A, 170 and 171A); his ingeniously complex cromlechs are also in the nature of magnified still-life structures (Pls. 166, 167, 171); and astonishing objects are invented for his *Hell* (Pl. 168).

The flower painting in pictures surviving from these years seems unremarkable. But some flowers grow in a garden suggested by the **New York Godelieve Legend Painter** (Pl. 141) and in outdoor scenes by the **Melbourne Miracles Painter** (Pls. 148, 150); the **Giles Master** surrounds the hermit in his thicket with lilies, iris and a tangle of smaller plants (Pl. 155); and though flowers are rare in **Bosch's** compositions a few can be seen in the foreground meadow of S. Anthony's retreat (Pl. 163).

The genre painting provides some simple and pleasing records. In the **New York Godelieve Legend Painter's** panels a lady goes off to church accompanied by her little servant, and a page kneels to offer a fine dish to a distinguished guest at dinner (Pl. 141)—just as the angel kneels to offer the book to the Virgin in **Memlinc's** *Floreins altarpiece* (Pl. 85). In the *Miracle of the loaves and fishes* by the **Melbourne Miracles Painter** (Pl. 148) the loaves are distributed to men and women of all types and classes seated with their children in two rows—like the peasants at the picnic in the *Fête aux chaudrons* (Pl. 708) by **Teniers;** one child on the left holds up his arms in eager anticipation and another on the right looks up at his mother raising a glass or bottle to her mouth. In the *Seven Works of Mercy and the Seven Deadly Sins* (Pl. 135) by the **Antwerp Last Judgement Painter** children are provided with new shoes, tired travellers are having their feet washed, a vain lady, tempted by the Devil, spends the morning at her mirror while her lustful sister yields to amorous advances. In the **Alkmaar Master's** pictures (Pls. 182, 183) a shopkeeper and his wife give food to a strolling minstrel and, from another humble dwelling, drink is given to a blind man guided by his boy. From a window on the right in the background of the portrait by the **Brussels Man with a Rosary Painter** a man and woman lean forward and point excitedly to the vision of the Tiburtine Sibyl (Pl. 181). The **Philadelphia Marriage of the Virgin Painter** provides us with two charming genre scenes—the new-born child in its swaddling clothes held up by a ministering nun and an assistant while the mother lies in a bed behind, and the Virgin as a little girl welcomed to the Temple by the High Priest (Pl. 152). In the picture by the **New York Adoration in a White Castle Painter** (Pl. 151) the Christ-child is prettily attracted by the glitter of the Magi's gifts (again as in **Memlinc's** *Floreins altarpiece*) shepherds warm their hands by a small twig fire, and, outside in the country, peasants dance or stroll across the bridges and horsemen gallop. In the *Adoration of the Magi* (Pl. 157) by **Hieronymus Bosch** groups of horsemen scour the country, a man and woman, arm in arm, arrive at the Swan Inn, a peasant drives a donkey, and, in the foreground, peasants mount trees and peer through crannies of the stable while others clamber on the roof; and I have already drawn attention to the numerous genre episodes in **Bosch's** *Haywain* (Pl. 165).

The animal and bird painting covers an enormous range. There is a monkey in the foreground of the **Florence (Poggio Imperiale) Crucifixion Painter's** picture (Pl. 133); a family of rabbits and a shaggy dog are in the background behind the marriage scene by the **Philadelphia Marriage of the Virgin Painter** (Pl. 152) while in the foreground a greyhound looks across my pages to another greyhound, the ox, the hind quarters of the ass and the galloping horses by the **New York Adoration in a White Castle Painter** (Pl. 151); and the ox and the ass are delicately drawn by the **Philadelphia Adoration of the Magi Painter** (Pl. 162). A greyhound and a poodle are in the *Miracle of the loaves and fishes* (Pl. 148) by the **Melbourne Miracles Painter** who also shows an owl in a rocky mound; a hen picks up crumbs in *Feeding the Hungry* by the **Alkmaar Master** (Pl. 182); the **Brussels Man with a Rosary Painter** shows a dog, a chained-up monkey and a crane (Pl. 181), the **Giles Master** a charming hind (Pl. 155), and the **Malines Guild of S. George Master** (Pl. 146) an heraldic rocking-horse and a howling dragon which students of dragonology will compare with

Hugo of Antwerp's concept (Pl. 78) and with the beasts which the **New York Crucifixion and Last Judgement Painter** set upon the wicked in his Hell scene (Pl. 8). In **Bosch's** pictures there are all kinds of natural, mythical and invented animals, birds and fish; dogs run beside the galloping horses in his *Adoration of the Magi* (Pl. 157); in the *Temptation of S. Anthony* (Pl. 163) the saint has his routine pig beside him as in **Memlinc's** picture (Pl. 114), there is a pig beside the quack dentist's wife in the foreground of the *Haywain* (Pl. 165) and another in *Christ driving the moneychangers from the Temple* (Pl. 164) where farmer-traders leave the Temple with their livestock. In the *Creation of Eve* (Pl. 167) where we have 'every beast of the field and every fowl of the air and every thing that creepeth upon the earth' an elephant, a giraffe, a unicorn and a long-eared two-legged dog first attract attention; on the distant swards a sow with litter turns upon some prancing creature, a peacock croaks at the sow's young pigs and a lion devours a deer strayed from a neighbouring herd; ducks and swans swim in a pool round the elegant fountain and reptiles crawl from it; more reptiles and an otter crawl from the pool in the foreground where a duck-headed fish is reading a book; birds perch upon the fountain, cluster on the ground and swirl through and round the foremost cromlech; round the foreground pool we see birds pecking at the entrails of a frog, a three-headed bird, a frog-headed bird, and a cat passant, rat in mouth; behind Eve there is a solitary rabbit. The central panel of the *Garden of Delights* (Pls. 166, 169, 170, 171, 171A) has a procession of giant birds—wild duck, kingfisher, hoopoe, woodpecker and goldfinch—and left and right, huge owls seem sentinels; round an oval pool there is a cavalcade of horses, boars, oxen, deer, donkeys, goats, lions, panthers, bears, camels, unicorns and gryphons; some of the riders carry enormous fish, and another giant fish is in the foreground; apes crawl on all fours round one of the fantastic cromlechs and dolphin knights and mermaids are in water round the others; birds of normal size, including cranes, pelicans and flamingoes, perch on the riders and animals in the cavalcade and on the girls' heads in the central pool where one of the negresses is honoured by a peacock. In the *Hell* scene of this triptych (Pl. 168) hounds attack a prostrate knight in armour, a hybrid creature, half bird, half butterfly or moth intercepts a figure about to climb a ladder to the broken-egg-shell-rump of the central monster, lower down a giant hare accoutred as a sportsman carries a dead girl head downwards as a trophy of his hunting, and in the foreground, as already noted, a fat sow wears the headdress of an abbess.

In nude painting there is tender feeling in the limp dead Christ by the **St. Louis Entombment Painter** (Pl. 130). The figure of Christ by the **Florence (Poggio Imperiale) Crucifixion Painter** (Pl. 133) recalls the concept of the **New York Crucifixion and Last Judgement Painter** (Pl. 1), for the head is bent with down-hanging hair, and the legs are straight (not flexed at the knees as in the **Redemption Master's** concept (Pl. 51)); but the shoulders (as in the **Redemption Master's** picture) are lower in relation to the hands, and the body, which has swung a little, is made a unit by a flowing line from armpit to the feet. There is imagination in the taut gesture of the slight, but not emaciated, figure with thin arms and small clasped hands by the **Philadelphia Maria Egyptiaca Painter** (Pl. 131). This artist's aesthetic concept of the nude has points of contact with that of **Bosch** whose *Garden of Delights* reveals him as a delightful and most skilful painter in that field. If we look, for example, at the left-hand panel, the *Creation of Eve* (Pl. 167), **Bosch's** concept of Adam and Eve is seen to be quite different from such figures in earlier pictures reproduced in my plates; for in the **van Eycks'** *Altarpiece of the Mystic Lamb* Adam is mature and bearded, Eve is robust, and both are of the same height—perhaps for reasons of balance as they stand in two opposite niches (Pl. 9); in the **Redemption Master's** *Expulsion from Eden* both figures have lean limbs, and Adam, again mature and bearded, has much broader shoulders than Eve (Pl. 52); in *The Fall* by the **Vienna Adam and Eve Painter** Adam is much taller than Eve, has much broader shoulders, and is now a younger man with incipient beard; and both, as noted earlier, have clumsy hands and enormous feet (Pl. 66). In **Bosch's** concept, in this *Creation of Eve*, Adam is a slight and beardless adolescent; Eve is a delicately formed young girl with a broad domed head, high forehead and tiny chin—like the *Virgin* in the pictures by the **New York Crucifixion and Last Judgement Painter** (Pl. 16); her red-gold hair falls down to her thighs and creates a kind of cape behind her; and this hair is crimped into regular wavelets like the Virgin's hair in **Jan van Eyck's** *Van der Paele altarpiece* (Pl. 19), the hair of the Blessed in the vision by the **Lille Path to Paradise Painter** (Pl. 63), the saint's hair in the picture by the **Minneapolis S. Catherine Painter** (Pl. 121), the bride's hair in the picture by the **Philadelphia Marriage of the Virgin Painter** (Pl. 152), and the Virgin's hair in the Adoration scene by the **New York Adoration in a White Castle Painter** (Pl. 151). Adam and Eve occur again in the left-hand wing (See Pl. 164A) of **Bosch's** *Haywain* where a slim, beardless, adolescent Adam is about to take the apple from the woman-headed serpent, and Eve, who has already eaten, is slightly taller than he is, and much more resolute. The nudes in these two *Garden of Eden* panels correspond in character to the nudes in the *Garden of Delights* (Pls. 166, 169, 170, 171, 171A). Here countless naked figures are charmingly set down as formal units, uncomplicated by parade of anatomical details or effects of chiaroscuro; congruous, one with another, without disturbing particularizations, these little figures live and breathe without studio pose or affectation in all degrees of repose and movement and concerted acrobatics; their clear light forms sing out like daisies from a lawn or snowdrops from a garden bed; to these pale fair-haired figures, black girls, sometimes crowned with strawberries, make decorative contrasts; and there is something irresistibly engaging in these naked unembarrassed youths and girls who sit in fruit groves and eat oranges or apples while one brings to them a strawberry so large that he can hardly lift it, or who lie upon the grass like sunbathers by the Mediterranean, or climb in and out of oyster shells or talk together inside coral towers or crystal cloches while others, in the water, surround a giant blackberry or float inside fantastic seed pods whence, through crystal tubes, they gaze out at intruding mice. There are many nudes too in the *Hell* scene (Pl. 168); but they are less characteristic of **Bosch's** personal aesthetic; for here, the artist is creating a terrible nightmare where the charm of naked youths and maidens has no place.

In portraiture I have already referred to the youthful portraits of Philip the Fair and Margaret of Austria, and to portraits of the Archduke and Joanna in the picture by the **Brussels Ziericksee Master** in a window of Antwerp Cathedral; and one of the three standing figures in the foreground of the *Marriage Feast at Cana* by the **Melbourne Miracles Painter** (Pl. 149) is probably the donor of the triptych whose identity remains unknown. Other portraits shown in my plates for this chapter include a half-length by the **Brussels Man with a Rosary Painter,** a number of portraits of donors, and one subscription group. The identity of the mournful ascetic, with heavy eyelids and thin mouth, dressed in crimson velvet tunic with deep fur lapels, depicted by the **Brussels Man with a Rosary Painter** (Pl. 181) is not known, though some Dutch arms appear on the capital of the decorative pilaster; and the artist in providing—or calling on a specialist or assistant to provide—the outdoor scene in the background has followed a tradition already seen here in the portrait by the **Philadelphia Adorant Painter** (Pl. 104). The wonderfully sensitive picture by the **Worcester Saint and Donor Painter** (Pl. 153) was probably the wing of a diptych or triptych;

the donor's head was surely an admirable likeness, but his identity is not known—though some have suggested Claude de Toulongeon, Comte de la Baslie, a Franche Comté baron; the figure behind him in the character of the presenting saint is also, I presume, a portrait, and it has been suggested that the saint he impersonates is S. Claude, Bishop of Besançon who enforced the Benedictine rule in his abbey in the Jura. In this picture by the **Worcester Saint and Donor** the youthful donor is modestly attired while the bishop's official raiment is lavishly magnificent; on the other hand the donor portrayed by the **Glasgow Saint and Donor Painter** (Pl. 154) is more magnificent than the warrior saint—perhaps S. Victor or S. Maurice—who presents him; for this donor, who seems to be a prelate, wears costly rings on three fingers of his left hand, a jewelled brooch, and pearls, sapphires and rubies on the fillet round his head, while the saint behind has only one brooch which holds his laurel fillet; in general character this very competent but uninspired and derivative work is more evidently Flemish than the **Worcester Saint and Donor Painter's** picture which has a French or Spanish air; for this saint and donor are direct descendants of the S. George and Canon van der Paele by **Jan van Eyck** (Pl. 19); and laymen uncertain of what art critics mean when they call an artist 'academic' would find the answer if they could see the **Glasgow Saint and Donor's** picture hung beside **Jan van Eyck's.** Count Albert of Adrichem, donor of the triptych by the **Oultremont Master** (Pls. 176, 179-80, 231) appears as adorant in *The Road to Calvary* on the exterior wings (Pl. 179); he has uncovered, revealing his long fair hair, and has fallen to his knees as the procession passes; the falconer with the hawk and the jester in cap and bells behind him were, I take it, in his suite; and he is presented by S. Bavon, Patron of Haarlem, and S. Catherine perhaps in her quality of patroness of learning. The kneeling figures in *S. Giles and the hind* by the **Giles Master** (Pl. 155) have the character of portraits, and either the rich young man in his fashionable clothes or the cleric beside him, or both together, may therefore have donated an altarpiece of which this picture was perhaps a wing. The donors of **Bosch's** triptych *The Adoration of the Magi* (Pl. 157) are painted on the inside of the wings (not reproduced here); they seem simple bourgeois people, husband and wife, but their coats of arms which appear in the picture have not been positively identified; they kneel with clasped hands in the usual manner, and S. Peter and S. Agnes stand behind them; and on the outside of the wings, in the *Mass of S. Gregory* (Pl. 156), we have two more adorants, one of which, shown more clearly in my detail (Pl. 158) is a delicately touched-in impressionist portrait recalling some heads in the *Crucifixion* by the **New York Crucifixion and Last Judgement Painter** (Pl. 159). The subscription portrait group of thirty-two members of the Malines Crossbowmen's Guild by the **Malines Guild of S. George Master** (Pl. 146) is divided into two groups archaistically arranged in tight geometric formation; the artist has made the patron saints—an abbot and a bishop—much larger than the donors, a procedure already archaistic in **Hugo of Antwerp's** *Portinari altarpiece* (Pls. 77, 78); but as a portrait painter he was unquestionably brilliant; each face is an individual, unflattered likeness; and I know no picture where a physiognomist might have more fun. I have suggested earlier that the attendant officials in the 'Justice' pictures by **Dirk Bouts** (Pls. 67, 69) were portraits of magistrates and other notables who subscribed for the pictures; and this procedure may have been employed by the painter of the *Judgement of Cambyses* and the *Flaying of the Unjust judge Sisamnes* when depicting the officials round the King. As before we must assume, I think, that many painters put portraits of their family and friends in compositions with numerous figures. For though the highly characterized type faces round the head of Christ in the pictures by the **Princeton Christ before Pilate Painter** (Pl. 174) and the **London Christ Mocked Painter**

(Pl. 175) are obviously invented, the Nicodemus and other figures in the *Descent from the Cross* (Pl. 176) by the **Oultremont Master** would seem to be portraits, and most of the faces in the other panels (Pls. 178-80, 231) seem also drawn from particular people. There is also, I fancy, some further evidence of professional models working for several artists; for the turbaned Magus by the **New York Adoration in a White Castle Painter** (Pl. 151) seems drawn from the same man as the turbaned man with three-pronged beard in the picture by the **Philadelphia Marriage of the Virgin Painter** (Pl. 152). I must remark, too, that the nun in **Bosch's** *Operation for Stone: or the Cure for Folly* (Pl. 161) seems drawn from the same model as the turbaned woman in the *Crucifixion* by the **New York Crucifixion and Last Judgement Painter** (Pl. 160)—which would not be impossible if my guess that **Bosch** in his youth was the unrecorded painter of the earlier picture, should one day be discovered to be right.

As religious subjects my plates show episodes from the legends of S. Christopher, S. George, S. Anthony, S. Gregory, S. Giles, S. Godelieve and S. Mary of Egypt, and the *Vision of Augustus and the Tiburtine Sibyl*. We also have narrative paintings of the *Story of Joachim and Anne*, the *Childhood and marriage of the Virgin*, the *Presentation in the Temple*, *Christ among the Doctors*, *Christ driving the moneychangers from the Temple*, the *Raising of Lazarus*, and the *Miracle of the Loaves and Fishes*. The devotional pictures show the *Adoration of the Magi*, all the stages of the Passion from the *Agony in the Garden* to the *Crucifixion* and *Entombment*; and others symbolize the *Fall*, the *Seven Works of Mercy and the Seven Deadly Sins*, and the *Last Judgement* with *Resurrection* and *Hell* scenes.

In the *S. Christopher* (Pl. 202) by the **Lisbon Alexander VI Painter** the giant has come to the end of his stormy passage, the child is revealed as the Christ-child, and the saint's staff has begun to flower. The **Malines Guild of S. George Master** (Pl. 146) presents S. George as a skilful horseman with a long lance in his right hand and a buckler on his left arm while his left hand controls his charger; behind him is the Princess Cleodolinda of Silene who was next on the rota of human offerings to appease the dragon and had gone to the sacrifice in her most ceremonial clothes; and the Princess's parents, the King and Queen, watch the scotching of the dragon from a castle in the background. *S. Anthony assailed by the Devil to destroy his faith*, is seen here in the picture by **Hieronymus Bosch** (Pl. 163) who puts the saint in a peaceful retreat defiled by sinister spooks and little hybrid monsters and evil fascinations that rise up from the stream and creep about the meadows. A *Temptation of S. Anthony*, it will be remembered had been painted by **Baldwin van Wytevelde** for Ghent, S. Bavon, some sixty years earlier in 1439; and the subject seems to have become frequent from the end of the fifteenth century for some sixty or seventy years. **Bosch** himself who was famous in his lifetime, and all through the sixteenth century, for his strange disquieting inventions, produced a number of versions; and of these the most horrific, still extant, is a triptych now in the Lisbon Museum which belonged about 1530 to Damião de Goes, King Manoel the Fortunate's Ambassador in Flanders, and contains a Black Mass among the terrifying machinations of the Devil; and on one wing of this triptych the saint is seen exhausted by his struggle and carried away by the monastery brothers as described in the Golden Legend: 'Une fois qu'Antoine se réfugiait en un tombeau, une grande multitude de diables le tourmenta tant qu'un frère qui le servait fut obligé de l'emporter sur ses epaules'. We also know the subject illustrated by the **Giles Master** in *S. Giles and the hind* (Pl. 155); for S. Giles, the Golden Legend tells us, left Arles in Provence and became a hermit in the bare adjacent country where he found a thicket with a spring and where he had with him a pet hind which provided him with milk; caught wandering by the Royal Hunt of the King of France the hind fled back to the hermit's thicket and the hounds could not be driven to attack it—('aucun chien n'osa approcher de la distance d'un jet de pierre, mais ils aboyaient ensemble et retournaient vers les chasseurs'); but one huntsman shot at random into the thicket and the arrow struck the hand of the hermit who was caressing the trembling hind; and when the King heard of this he came with a bishop and begged pardon of the hermit and agreed as penance to found a monastery which S. Giles himself eventually directed.

The **New York Godelieve Legend Painter** tells the story of S. Godelieve in great detail (Pls. 140-5). This Flemish saint, martyred at Ghistelles near Bruges, was zealous in charitable actions; once, when guests were invited by her family, she had already given to the poor all the food prepared for the banquet, and angels miraculously appeared with substitute dishes (Pl. 141 left); later she married one Bertolf of Ghistelles (Pls. 140 and 141 centre), but she found herself hated and suspected of witchcraft by her husband and his mother to whom a little maidservant reported that her mistress had but to tell the crows to stay still while she went to Mass for the birds to obey her for an hour on end (Pl. 141 right); so the husband and the wicked mother-in-law hired two ruffians who dragged her from her bed and strangled her (Pl. 144 front and background); when she fell to the ground and her face became bloodstained the assassins thrust her head foremost in a well and then returned her to her bed (Pl. 145); and the water of the well thereafter had miraculous healing powers (Pl. 143).

The **Philadelphia Maria Egyptiaca Painter** (Pl. 131) shows S. Mary of Egypt, with her three loaves beside her, a small pathetic figure, clothed in long hair—not as a withered dark-skinned woman, approaching eighty, with short white hair, as her story demands. For the legend runs as follows: Zosimos, a Palestinian monk, going for a retreat into the desert beyond Jordan, came upon a naked figure burned dark brown, with short white hair, who called out to him: 'I am a woman, cast me your mantle that I may speak with you', and when covered with the mantle she told him of her life: 'I was born in Egypt and from the age of twelve I lived as a public harlot in Alexandria. In my twenty-ninth year I embarked on a ship with a company of pilgrims to Jerusalem, seeking only to continue my debauches and paying my passage in that way; in Jerusalem I accompanied the pilgrims to the door of the church where they went to venerate the True Cross; but I was held back by an invisible force though the others went within; I knew then that my evil life was the cause of this; and sitting in a corner of the cloister I wept and beat my breast till, perceiving an image of the Blessed Virgin in the porch, I prayed her humbly to forgive me, promising to live henceforth a life of chastity and penance. And thereafter I was able to pass into the church and there I heard a voice which said "If you go beyond the Jordan, you may find salvation." And I took three coins and bought three loaves and inquired of the baker which gate of the city led to Jordan; and I came here to this desert where I have lived for forty-seven years; my clothes have perished but by the Grace of God I have subdued the flesh'; Zosimos then blessed her and came next Lent and gave her the Holy Communion; he came also the year after, but he found her dead.

The *Vision seen by the Emperor Augustus and the Tiburtine Sibyl* which appears in the picture by the **Brussels Man with a Rosary Painter** (Pl. 181) corresponds to the treatment of the subject by the **Tiburtine Sibyl Master** (Pls. 87, 119) discussed in my second chapter; and its presence in the background of this portrait may mean that the panel was the right-hand wing of a triptych or diptych commissioned by the sitter. The *Story of Joachim and Anne* is related by the **Philadelphia Marriage of the Virgin Painter** (Pl. 152) in four scenes—

93

Joachim leaving the Temple when his sacrifice is refused, the *Meeting of Joachim and Anne at the Golden Gate*, the *Birth of the Virgin*, and *Joachim and Anne escorting the Virgin to the Temple*, and those who know the Arena Chapel in Padua will compare them with Giotto's concepts, and note that in the *Marriage of the Virgin* scene, this Northern artist makes no reference to the legend of S. Joseph's rod which flowered upon the altar when the other suitors' rods stayed bare, an episode indicated in Giotto's marriage scene and also in a picture of the subject by Niccolo di Buonaccorso in the London National Gallery and in Raphael's *Sposalizio* (painted in 1504 and now in the Brera Gallery, Milan). The **Hoogstraeten Master's** delightful *Presentation in the Temple* (Pl. 197) with the tiny Christ-child, and several figures unexplained by the scriptures, invites comparison with **Memlinc's** accurate illustration of S. Luke (Pl. 84); and his equally delightful *Jesus among the doctors* (Pl. 198) can be contrasted with the version of the subject painted a hundred years later by **Karel van Mander** (Pl. 472). The **Hoogstraeten Master** is so-called because these pictures were at one time in the Eglise S. Catherine at Hoogstraeten near Antwerp, but he was trained I imagine in the Northern provinces, as I feel an influence from **Geertgen** (Pl. 127). The *Christ driving the moneychangers from the Temple* (Pl. 164) signed **Hieronymus Bosch** has already been referred to in my comments on the didactic, architectural and animal painting of this time; the artist here has followed closely the several accounts in the Gospels —the kneeling figures in the centre, confronted with the surrounding rabble, proclaim that the house of prayer had become a den of thieves, the moneychangers' tables are overturned, and the traders with their sheep and oxen, all those that bought and sold, all quacks and scoundrels, are thrown out. We must however note that according to Don Felipe de Guevara (Spanish courtier and sixteenth century collector of **Bosch's** pictures) **Bosch** had a pupil who signed with his master's name, either from devotion to the master or to give credit to his own works; and this pupil may possibly be the author or copyist of this picture where characteristic pieces from other works by **Bosch** are assembled in the pastiche manner. The **Melbourne Miracles Painter** relates the *Raising of Lazarus* (Pl. 150) in two scenes and also follows closely the Gospel text: in the background Martha (or Mary) goes forth to meet Christ and the Disciples at Bethany and kneels to proclaim her faith; in the foreground Christ surrounded by the friends of Mary and Martha lifts up his eyes to give thanks to God, Lazarus rises, bound hand and foot by his grave clothes and with a napkin about his head, and Martha's words 'Lord, by this time he stinketh, for he has been dead four days' are also illustrated. In *The Miracle of the Loaves and Fishes* (Pl. 148)—strangely archaistic in its costumes and possibly by a different painter—the five thousand are set down in ranks by hundreds and by fifties, together with the children specifically mentioned by S. Matthew, and all twelve baskets are included.

The *Adoration of the Magi* by the **New York Adoration in a White Castle Painter** (Pl. 151) is most beautiful in colour and imbued with a poetic harmony born of the artist's feeling, his power to render light and air, and the perfect spacing of the design; there are traditional features in this charming picture—for the central landscape vista through the castle recalls the view through the porch and stable by the **Washington Nativity in a Sculptured Porch Painter** (Pl. 30), and the semicircle of figures sweeping forward from the shepherds' heads in the window on one side to the head in a window on the other is the semicircle in **Memlinc's** *Floreins altar* (Pl. 85) given greater elasticity and grandeur; but the whole work is none the less a most personal concept; birds nest in the crumbling windows of the ruined castle, symbol of a superseded era; the roof has perished but angels in rose and gold— repeating the rose and gold draperies of the foreground Magus—hold a grey-green cloth as canopy; a golden cloth is spread beneath the Virgin who sits sideways, the shepherds have remained or returned to watch the Magi's adoration, and S. Joseph has white hair and a small white beard. I have already mentioned the highly original genre details in this picture—the fire of faggots and the peasants in the distant country, symbols of the everyday world that surrounds the spiritual event; and I have also drawn attention to the little milk-white greyhound in the centre foreground—a brilliant link, aesthetically, in a circle of white spots, but unusual in early pictures of this subject. In the scene as painted by the **Philadelphia Adoration of the Magi Painter** (Pl. 162) the setting is a complete dilapidated stable—as in the picture by the **Minneapolis Adoration Painter** (Pl. 75)—not a token structure as in the pictures by **Hugo of Antwerp** (Pl. 76), the **Pearl of Brabant Master** (Pl. 86) and **Memlinc** (Pls. 82, 85); S. Joseph, here, has a full white beard, shepherds wait again in the background, the negro's white sleeve is embroidered with the *Gathering of the Manna* (not discernible in my plate) and, as another unusual feature, the Virgin's mantle, S. Joseph's drapery and the robe of the second Magus are all rose-red. The *Adoration of the Magi* by **Hieronymus Bosch** (Pl. 157) also has unusual features—fantastically accoutred figures from the Magi's retinue within the dilapidated stable and queer details in the Magi's gifts and in embroideries on the Magi's clothes; S. Joseph moreover is nowhere to be found unless he be a little figure on the left-hand wing (not reproduced here) who has his back towards us and dries some garment by a fire; and the companies of horsemen in the middle distance scouring the country for the Innocents, the unaffected peasants in the distant landscape and the inquisitive peasants round and on the stable roof are other exceptional concepts. We must observe, also, that the whole scene including the donors seems veritably set within the spreading landscape; and that standing before the actual triptych (which is some four and a half feet high), we seem to be looking down on all the foreground figures and the stable and directly beyond them to the landscape and the towers of Bethlehem. In the *Mass of S. Gregory* seen when the wings are closed (Pls. 156, 158) all is classical and calm; the design here has the grand simplicity and perfect spacing of Fra Angelico's frescoes in the S. Marco Monastery in Florence—though the central figure, very strangely, is divided in the middle when the wings are open; around the vision little grisaille paintings show *The Agony in the Garden, The Betrayal, Christ before Pilate, The Flagellation, The Crowning with thorns, The Road to Calvary* (with *S. Veronica*), *The Crucifixion, The Suicide of Judas* and *A devil departing with the soul of Judas*; and here and there some genre spectators are inserted to give more actuality of impact.

Father Sigüenza writing of a *Christ carrying the Cross* by **Bosch** speaks of 'Innocence which is Christ surrounded by furious, savage and scowling faces' (rostros furiosos, fieros, regañados). We see this contrast in the **Oultremont Master's** *Road to Calvary* (Pl. 178) where scowling soldiers shout insults at Christ and S. Veronica; we see it in the acid picture by the **Princeton Christ before Pilate Painter** (Pl. 174) where all, except the central figure, is bestial, cruel and cunning, the hands are thin and bony, and a brittle light plays on golden ewer and platter and the soldiers' mail; and the same contrast, much attenuated, marks the *Crowning with thorns* by the **London Christ Mocked Painter** (Pl. 175) a very different artist whose sense of form is uniformly softer and who gives his figures large fat hands. In **Bosch's** *Crowning with thorns* in the *Mass of S. Gregory* (Pl. 156) two jailors press the crown down with long rods and, to get more leverage, they straddle the bench Christ sits on—(a motif found much later in two well-known works by Titian). In the *Crowning with thorns* (Pl. 180) by the **Oultremont Master** the crown is pressed down by a ruffian with a battle axe; and the head of Christ from this picture, as repeated by the **London (Wagner) Ecce Homo**

95

Painter (Pl. 177), again recalls Michelangelo's dictum on the tear-provoking sentiment in some Netherlandish pictures which I have quoted in an earlier chapter.

The original imaginative concept in the *Crucifixion* by the **Florence (Poggio Imperiale) Crucifixion Painter** (Pl. 133) is gentle in feeling—though it is also dramatically arresting, especially when encountered in the Uffizi among the gracefully dancing angels and elegantly posturing gallants in Florentine Renaissance pictures; I have already remarked on the relation of the central figure to the Christ on the Cross by the **New York Crucifixion and Last Judgement Painter** (Pl. 1); in the foreground the swooning Virgin supported by S. John recalls the great picture by **Rogier van der Weyden** (Pl. 46) and forestalls this motif in groups by **Cornelis Engelbrechtsz** (Pls. 232, 233) and **Pieter Bruegel** (Pl. 379); and students of Italian painting will compare the anguished contorted Magdalene with the Magdalene at the foot of the Cross in a panel in Naples presumed to be part of Masaccio's *Crucifixion* altarpiece in Florence. The *Descent from the Cross* by the **Oultremont Master** (Pl. 176)—formerly owned by the Count Florent d'Oultremont—was probably a commission for Haarlem, S. Bavon where the Adrichem family had a chapel; but the artist was clearly acquainted with the composition of **Rogier van der Weyden's** great picture and he may therefore, I fancy, have been domiciled in Louvain; he was however no servile imitator, for his picture contains the original and impressive concept of the large white winding sheet that starts from the lap of the Virgin and spreads right across the foreground. The intense and wholly original *Entombment* by the **St. Louis Entombment Painter** (Pl. 130) is most tenderly imagined as a slow-moving circular procession that comes down from Golgotha and climbs towards the sepulchre; the short homely figures strike no dramatic attitudes and their small hands make simple gestures; in the head of the dead Christ the eyebrows are pulled up to the centre casting shadows on the hollows underneath, and this can be seen too, in the face of S. Mary by the **Philadelphia Maria Egyptiaca Painter** (Pl. 131) which may mean that both artists were acquainted with Masaccio's *Eve* in the Carmine church in Florence.

I have already spoken of the *Seven Works of Mercy* by the **Antwerp Last Judgement Painter** (Pl. 135) and the **Alkmaar Master** (Pls. 182-5, 188) in relation to the church and civic struggle for the control of charity. The **Antwerp Last Judgement Painter**, theologically directed and extremely archaistic, combines the theme with his *Last Judgement* and the *Seven Deadly Sins* to illustrate the whole context of Christ's dicta as recorded by S. Matthew; Satan appears as tempter in each of the Sin panels; and the saints and prophets with Christ in each of the others are Isaiah in *Feeding the hungry*, S. Willibrord in *Quenching the thirsty*, Abraham in *Succouring the poor*, S. Elizabeth of Hungary in *Clothing the naked*, S. Catherine of Siena in *Visiting the Sick*, S. Martin in *Comforting the prisoners* and S. Louis and Tobias in *Burying the dead*. His *Last Judgement* panel follows the tradition already seen here in pictures by the **New York Crucifixion and Last Judgement Painter** (Pls. 4, 7, 8), the **Beaune Last Judgement Painter** (Pls. 34, 42, 136-9) and the **Redemption Master** (Pl. 53); Heaven is theologically depicted as a church with S. Peter receiving the Blessed at the entrance; and the Hell scene follows Christ's words 'Depart from me, ye cursed, into ever-lasting fire, prepared for the devil and his angels'—as distinguished from the text in Deuteronomy 'I will also send the teeth of beasts upon them, with the poison of the serpents of the dust' which inspired the **New York Crucifixion and Last Judgement Painter** to invent his super-serpents and bears and monsters with huge teeth.

The conspicuous originality of **Hieronymus Bosch** as a religious painter has already been observed in his *Adoration of the Magi* (Pl. 157) and *Christ driving the moneychangers from* *the Temple* (Pl. 164); I have spoken of his fertility in inventing disquieting spooks and monsters as emissaries of the Devil to tempt S. Anthony as in the picture reproduced (Pl. 163) and the much more horrific *Temptation of S. Anthony* in Lisbon Museum; and I must now consider his two great didactic 'moralidades', the *Haywain* and the *Garden of Delights*, which are both in essence or to some extent religious pictures, as both have *Garden of Eden* and *Hell* scenes left and right of the central panels. The *Garden of Eden* (detail in Pl. 164A) on the left of the *Haywain* (Pl. 165) is constructed in four sections depicting the *Fall of the Rebel Angels* (imaged as a swarm of insect-devils), the *Creation of Eve* (where God the Father, white bearded, is crowned with a headdress resembling the Papal tiara worn by God the Father in the **van Eycks'** *Altarpiece of the Mystic Lamb* (Pl. 9)), the *Temptation and Fall* and the *Expulsion from Eden*; the *Hell* on the right of the *Haywain* picks up the theme of the Fallen Angels on the left-hand wing as the Devil and his angels, for whom the everlasting fire was originally prepared, now in their turn prepare this hell for the foolish sinners round the haywain, build a prison to receive them (Pl. 166A) and conduct them to it inflicting tortures on the way. In the *Garden of Delights* triptych the *Creation of the World* (Pl. 172) on the outside of the wings, should be, I take it, more properly titled *The Eighth Day: the Watering of the Ground* for it seems to illustrate the second chapter of Genesis. The *Creation of Eve* (Pl. 167) continues, I take it, the Eighth Day with the planting of the garden in Eden, the placing therein of Adam and all the animals which Adam named, and the giving of Eve to Adam as his wife; the Temptation and the Expulsion are not depicted here as the illustration stops at the last words of the chapter: 'They were both naked, the man and his wife, and were not ashamed'. The subject thus seems to me instinctive life before the Fall, and the abnormal animals may be there to symbolize abnormal instincts. The central panel, the *Garden of Delights* (Pls. 166, 169, 170, 171, 171A) is based, I think, on Chapters V and VI of Genesis, when man, after the Fall, still had his instincts but also knowledge of good and evil and 'every imagination of the thoughts of his heart was only evil continually'; and **Bosch's** elaborately sublimated Venusberg may thus be a symbolic presentation of the state of life, partly instinctive and partly imaginatively perverse, just before the Flood; the clothed man in the bottom right-hand corner may be Noah, and the instinctive animals and birds are perhaps there to illustrate the verse 'And the Lord said, "I will destroy man whom I have created from the face of the earth, both man and beast and the creeping thing and the fowls of the air; for it repenteth me that I have made them".' For the strawberries all over this picture we have Father Sigüenza's explanation that the picture is an allegory on the vanity of sensual delights of which the strawberry is a symbol because its taste and aroma are consumed at the instant of their savour (que apeñas se siente cuando ya es pasado). The *Hell* (Pl. 168), on the right-hand wing, contains, I think, a triple concept—(*a*) a Hell which illustrates the wickedness of **Bosch's** day (*b*) a Hell which punishes the same sins and follies as are satirized in the *Haywain* and (*c*) a Hell avenging the erotic sins and follies of the *Garden of Delights*. The burning town, the soldiers who fired it crossing the blood and fire stained river (Pl. 173), and the Spanish Inquisition scene, already referred to, form the first of these Hell concepts—the Hell on earth as **Bosch** himself had seen it. The sections repeating the motifs of the *Haywain* are explained by Father Sigüenza: 'Those', he says, 'who gave themselves to vanities like music and ribald singing, gambling, hunting, domination, revenge, hypocrisy and sham piety, find in this Hell their earthly satisfactions transformed, each in its own way, to everlasting torment'; and indeed we see wretches entangled in lutes and harps and other instruments, and gamblers raging amid cards and dice, and knights run through with swords and set on by their hounds; and we also see the anti-clerical passages—monks with devils' horns and tails (symbols of the hypocrites) and the sow with the headdress of the abbess already mentioned. **Bosch's** third concept seems to me the Hell of the pretty denizens of the Garden of Delights who find here the pleasures of the instincts and the imaginative perversities of that garden transformed to dreadful manias and sadistic vices which he has symbolized by obscene monsters and huge erotic emblems. For **Bosch** knew somehow all the secrets rediscovered by our psychologists; the emblems and monsters he invented correspond to obsessions now confessed by patients in the clinics of psycho-analysts (and perhaps in **Bosch's** day by penitents to their priests); and it is, of course, this aspect of this *Hell* that makes it so disquieting and horrific.[1]

The unusual features in the work of this obviously free-thinking artist made it inevitable that in the heretic-hunting sixteenth and seventeenth centuries there were those who looked upon him as tainted with heretical ideas. Though no charge of heresy was brought against him in his lifetime, the view had evidently been expressed by the end of the century because Father Sigüenza said quite plainly: 'I think those wrong who describe him as a heretic (pienso que sin razon le tienen infamado de herege) because if the Royal founder of the Escorial, so eminent in zealous piety, had known that to be so he would not have admitted his pictures to his private rooms, the chapter and the sacristy, which are all adorned with them'; and this defence seems to have left unconvinced Francisco Pacheco, master of Velazquez and Censor of Paintings to the Inquisition, who declared in 1649 that Father Sigüenza had done too much honour to **Bosch's** fantasies which were not recommendable to artists. The charge of heresy has recently been made again by a modern writer who presumes him a member of a secret Adamite sect which he presumes to have existed in Bois-le-Duc in **Bosch's** day, and which, he further presumes, cultivated nudism and sublimated sex and mixed up erotics, mysticism, ecstatic contemplation and various religious and philosophic notions; this writer further assumes that the *Garden of Delights* triptych was commissioned as an altarpiece for a secret meeting-place of these Adamites in Bois-le-Duc, that the central panel is a synthesis of their Millennium concepts, and that the whole design and all the details are cryptic references to their doctrines and to stages of initiation in their hocus pocus, all dictated to the artist by the Grand Master of these nudists whose portrait (fully clothed) is shown in the bottom right-hand corner of the central panel. But **Bosch's** continuous contacts with the orthodox Brotherhood of Our Lady in Bois-le-Duc and with the local Cathedral of S. John make it most improbable that he really belonged to an heretical sect; and it seems to me quite reasonable to abide by the statements of Father Sigüenza who described the *Haywain* and the *Garden of Delights* as painted satires on the sins and errors of mankind (satyras pintades de los pecados y desuarios de los hombres) and no less edifying than his nominally religious subjects though they seem more macaronic (no di menor prouecho, aunque parecen mas macarronicas). For Father Sigüenza, we must remember, was as close to **Bosch,** in time, as we are to Odilon Redon, and looked upon him simply as a highly original genius, and said of his *Seven Deadly Sins contrasted with the Sacraments* (now in the Prado) 'quien este pintava no sentia mal de nuestra fe'. We must also remember that **Bosch's** pictures were owned by distinguished and quite orthodox collectors in the sixteenth century; thus Margaret of Austria, as Regent of

[1] My suggestion that the *Garden of Delights* symbolizes the state of the world on the eve of the Flood, has some confirmation in the fact that the Archduke Ernest, at the end of the sixteenth century, owned a picture by **Bosch** which was then titled 'Sic erat in diebus Noë' (and was perhaps a version of this picture).

the Netherlands, owned in the painter's lifetime, a *Temptation of S. Anthony* and sent it to the chapel at Brou which contains her tomb; by 1521, five years after **Bosch's** death, Cardinal Grimani in Venice had a *Hell* 'con gran diversita de monstri' together with a *Dream* picture and a *Fortuna with Jonah and the Whale*; about 1530 Damião de Goes owned the *Temptation of S. Anthony* triptych, and Don Felipe de Guevara had the *Haywain*, a pictured called *The Witch* and the *Operation for Stone: or the Cure of Folly* before 1563; Philip II had the *Adoration of the Magi* and a *Christ carrying the Cross* in the Escorial by 1574 and about a dozen others when he died; and Philip III retained them in their places of honour. It is known moreover that Old and New Testament subjects by **Bosch** were still in the Cathedral of S. John in Bois-le-Duc at the beginning of the seventeenth century.

In any interpretation of **Bosch's** most curious pictures much must inevitably remain obscure to us. At four and a half centuries remove no one can understand the meanings of the countless strange conjunctions and 'disparates' as Sigüenza called them. Any detail may mean something precise or nothing—since the artist has evidently allowed the fullest licence to his fancy as he worked upon the panels inch by inch, and his appetite for invention clearly grew as he invented; he joins for example twenty youths in acrobatic postures, puts a seed pod above them, then a bird's head with a yard long beak, then a strawberry upon the bird's head, then a pair of human legs as a waving panache in the strawberry, and when all is done he sends a rabbit tight-rope walking down the beak (Pl. 166); or he makes youths the porters of a huge lobster claw, and puts more youths inside it and a bear cub, as a last idea, on top (Pl. 171A). We can but marvel at this incredibly fertile fancy—and suspect that in many details he just released his inhibitions and had fun. For though the *Adoration of the Magi* triptych was a commissioned picture destined perhaps for the private chapel of the donors painted on the wings, and though we know that he worked for churches in his native town, the two 'moralidades', the *Garden of Delights* and the *Haywain*, were doubtless painted on his own initiative as free expression of his personal aesthetic and of his witty and most brilliant intellect.

Bosch had many followers as will be seen in my later chapters. His 'spook' effects were imitated by **Jan Mandyn** (the master of **Gillis Mostaert**), **Frans Verbeeck, Pieter Huys** (Pls. 412, 413) and, in his early drawings by **Pieter Bruegel.** The burning buildings in his Hell scenes were imitated by **Joachim Patinir** whose *Lot and his daughters* was owned by Dürer, **Frans Mostaert, Gillis Mostaert,** the Calvinist **Lodewyck van den Bosch, Jan (Velvet) Brueghel** and **Pieter Brueghel the younger;** and also by **Pieter Schoubroeck** (Pl. 494), **Frederick** and **Gillis van Valkenborch** and **Louis de Caullery** (who all four painted *The Burning of Troy*), and by the **Brussels Sodom and Gomorrah Painter** (Pl. 495); and, in the seventeenth century, by **Daniel van Heil** (Pl. 713), **Theodore van Heil, Frans van Oosten** and others. These imitations began in fact in his lifetime; for Don Felipe de Guevara tells us that in addition to the pupil who signed his master's name there were forgers who painted monsters and grotesque fancies thinking that only this was needed to imitate his art, though **Bosch** himself never painted anything outside the bounds of nature (cosa fuera del natural) except in scenes of Purgatory or Hell or when showing demons sent from Hell (si no es que la pintura contenga en si purgatorio o infierno o materia de el); and Guevara adds that these forgeries were smoked by the fire to age them (ahuméndolas a las chimeneas para dalles autoridad y antiguedad).

CHAPTER V

Margaret of Austria

1507-1530

WHEN Philip the Fair died the States General appointed Maximilian Regent on behalf of his grandson Charles, and Maximilian deputed his daughter Margaret to act for him. The Duchess Margaret was a widow of twenty-seven; her second husband Philibert of Savoy having died, as noted, in 1504. She chose Malines as her headquarters, and lived there as guardian for Charles then seven and his sisters Eleanor, Isabella and Mary—the other sister Catherine being with her mother Joanna 'la Loca' now incarcerated at Tordesillas. Her Regency had a first period ending in 1515 when Charles came of age and a second ending politically with La Paix des Dames in 1529; the first was a time of prosperity for the Netherlands as their part in the international plots and counterplots and double-crossings was the making of money from several belligerents at once; in the second they were forced to disgorge large sums for Charles' warfares and they were disturbed by the rise of Lutherism and the launching of religious persecution to suppress it.

In 1507 the first year of the Regency, Holland and Brabant were invaded by Charles of Egmont, Duke of Gelderland. In 1508 Maximilian, Emperor in effect since 1493, was formally crowned; Pope Julius II, hoping to ruin Venice, formed the League of Cambrai with Maximilian, Louis XII and Ferdinand of Aragon; and Margaret was represented at the negotiations by Philippe Haneton, later donor to S. Gudule, Brussels, of the triptych by the **Brussels Haneton Lamentation Painter** (Pls. 239, 240, 279). In 1509 Henry VIII, aged eighteen, became King of England with Catherine of Aragon as Queen; and Erasmus aged forty-three was staying with Thomas More. In 1511 Raphael, aged twenty-eight, completed the *School of Athens*; Michelangelo, aged thirty-six, was still at work on the ceiling of the Sistine Chapel; and Henry VIII helped Margaret against Charles of Egmont and joined the Pope, Ferdinand of Aragon and the Swiss in converting the League of Cambrai into a 'Holy Alliance' against France. In 1513 Julius II died and Leo X (Giovanni dei Medici) became Pope; Henry VIII, in France with a considerable army, won the Battle of the Spurs against Louis XII and met Margaret of Austria with the Emperor and Charles aged thirteen at Lille; and Margaret made a four years truce with Gelderland. In 1514 Charles' sister Isabella aged thirteen was betrothed to Christian II of Denmark; Henry VIII made peace with France; and his sister Mary Tudor aged eighteen was married to Louis XII then fifty-two and decrepit. In 1515 Louis XII died and Francis I became King at twenty; Charles, now of age, was inaugurated as Count of Flanders, Duke of Brabant and so on in the various provinces; Francis I crossed the Alps and defeated the Swiss at Marignano; Wolsey was made Chancellor by Henry VIII and a Cardinal by Pope Leo; and Henry and the Cardinal intrigued with Maximilian and Ferdinand against Francis.

In 1516 Ferdinand of Aragon died; Charles was proclaimed King (on behalf of his mother) of Castile and Aragon and there was a solemn ceremony in Brussels, S. Gudule; Erasmus, appointed Councillor to Charles, took up residence in Brussels; Leonardo da Vinci took up residence in France; and Francis made peace with Pope Leo and the Swiss. In 1517 Martin Luther aged thirty-four nailed his ninety-five theses to the Wittenberg church door; Charles went to Spain taking **Jacques van Lathem** as Court Painter and a host of Flemish nobles and officials whose habits and rapacity were obnoxious to the Spaniards; and Selim I, Sultan of Turkey, became Caliph of Islam. In 1518 Lutherism was preached by Augustinians in the Northern provinces; Charles called on his mother in Tordesillas and removed his sister Catherine, till then her sole consolation in captivity; and his sister Eleanor married King Manoel the Fortunate of Portugal. In 1519 Erasmus settled in Louvain as director of the Collège des Trois Langues; Luther published his 'Address to the German Nobles'; Lutherism was preached by Augustinians in Antwerp; Charles made some Spanish grandees Knights of the Golden Fleece and thus procured their friendship; the Emperor Maximilian died; Charles, competing with Francis I and Henry VIII was elected Emperor as Charles V thanks largely to the banker Fugger's money; and Henry at the launching of the warship 'Princess Mary' played the part of pilot in 'a sailor's coat, and trousers of cloth of gold' and blew his whistle with much gusto. In 1520 Charles came to England to conclude a secret compact with Henry against Francis; Henry crossed to Calais for the Field of the Cloth of Gold; Luther was excommunicated and burned the Papal Bull; Charles made Pageant Entries as Emperor into the major cities of the Netherlands and issued his first 'placard' or Heresy Edict. In 1521 Charles was at war with France; Luther appeared before the Diet of Worms; and the Edict of Worms, which placed Luther under the ban of the Empire, was made applicable in the Netherlands. Charles issued a 'placard' ordering the burning of Luther's writings and the death penalty for printers who set up anything relating to the Faith without licence from a Faculty of Theology; Henry VIII wrote a treatise against Luther and was given the title of Fidei Defensor by the Pope; Erasmus was driven from Louvain to Bâle; Albrecht Dürer paid a visit to the Netherlands; Leo X died; and Sultan Suleiman the Magnificent declared war on the King of Hungary and captured Belgrade. In 1522 Adrian Dedel of Utrecht, tutor to Charles V, became Pope as Adrian VI; Charles introduced the Inquisition to the Netherlands, and then left for Spain; and King Manoel of Portugal died. In 1523 two Augustine Friars were burned alive for heresy in Brussels; Giuliano dei Medici became Pope as Clement VII; and Christian of Denmark, driven from his country, took refuge with his wife and family in the Netherlands. In 1525 Francis I was defeated by the Spaniards and taken prisoner at Pavia. In 1526 the Turks won the Battle of Mohacz and captured Budapest. In 1527 Pope Clement VII and Francis were allied against the Emperor; German troops of the Emperor sacked Rome; and Henry VIII began negotiations with the Pope for a divorce from Catherine of Aragon. In 1529 Charles made the Treaty of Barcelona with the Pope and the Treaty of Cambrai (La Paix des Dames) with Francis which surrendered Burgundy to France; and as Lutherism was widespread in the Netherlands and the Anabaptists were making converts among the poorer classes in the Northern provinces Charles issued a stronger Heresy Edict imposing the death penalty and confiscation of property on all who knew heretics and did not denounce them, for discussing religious questions, and for making or circulating 'images injurieuses pour Dieu, la Vierge et les Saints'; Cardinal Wolsey fell; and the Turks reached Vienna but failed to take it. In 1530 Francis married Charles' sister Eleanor widow of King Manoel of Portugal; and Margaret of Austria died.

Margaret, brought up at the French court and married in Savoy, had a French culture which increased her natural affection for the arts. She bewailed her misfortunes prettily in French verses, painted occasionally, using 'une petite boite d'argent et cinq pinceaux garnies d'argent', and all through her Regency she conferred with architects and artists on building and decorating the delicately flamboyant memorial church at Brou in Bresse which still has her tomb and Philibert's with cadavers beneath them and Italian putti on the top. Very rich (in possession of two dowries) she collected books, carvings, tapestries and paintings. An inventory of her collection, made about 1516, shows many family portraits, some by her court painters, others by unnamed artists; portraits of the male and female dwarfs of Christian II of Denmark are entered as the work of **Jan Gossaert;** a portrait of Charles is described as 'faicte par compas'; and two pictures portrayed young ladies with pet parrots (Margaret herself was much attached to a green parrot later celebrated in a poem by Jean Lemaire de Belges her court historian and author of 'La Couronne Margaritique'). There were pictures titled *Une belle fille esclave* and *David and Goliath*; one described as 'Ung homme et ung femme nuz, less pieds en l'eaue' was possibly by **Jan Gossaert** since it was given her by his patron, Philip, Bastard of Burgundy, Bishop of Utrecht; and a picture by **'Master Michiel'** is described as 'Une petite Notre Dame disant ses heures, que Madame appelle sa mignonne, et le petit dieu dort'. She also owned a *Temptation of S. Anthony* by **Hieronymus Bosch, Jan van Eyck's** *Marriage of Giovanni Arnolfini* (Pl. 18A) and *Virgin and Child by a fountain* (Pl. 25), and works by **Rogier van der Weyden, Memlinc, 'Dirick'** (possibly **Dirck Bouts**) and the French painter Jean Fouquet. Her library had manuscripts and printed books including *Aesop's Fables*, the *Golden Legend, Froissart's Chronicles, Ovid* and *Boccacio*.

Margaret's Court Painters at first included **Pieter van Coninxloo** of Brussels who had painted her portrait sent by Philip the Fair to Henry VII and who now painted Charles and his sisters; **Jean van Battel,** who worked for her palace in Malines and was also Court Painter to Charles himself by 1516; the Venetian Jacopo de' Barbari who painted a *Still-life with dead partridge, mail gauntlets and an arrow* in 1504 and was already an old man when he joined her service in 1510; **Jan Mostaert** appointed about 1512; **'Master Michiel'** formerly Court Painter to Isabella the Catholic (now presumed by some the Talinn—born Michel Zittow); the Malines painter **Paul Tubach** whom she made an Archer de Corps, **Frans Sanders** also of Malines, and **Jan van Roome (Jean de Bruxelles)** who worked for Brou. **Gerard Horenbout** of Ghent worked for her from 1516 to 1522. In 1516 she commissioned **Jan Gossaert,** then about thirty-six, to paint Charles' sister Eleanor; **Jean Schooff,** town painter to Malines since 1506, became her Court Painter in 1519; **Bernaert van Orley,** who became her Court Painter in 1518, was employed by her on 'certain agreeable services which she did not wish to be mentioned' and in 1521 she commissioned from him the *Job altarpiece* (Pls. 254, 256, 257-9) and gave it to her chevalier d'honneur Antoine de Lalaing, Count of Hoogstraeten, whom rumour spoke of, probably quite falsely, as her lover. In 1525 she made **Jan Cornelisz Vermeyen** (Pl. 323), then about twenty-five, a Court Painter and sent him later to paint Charles and his sister Mary of Hungary in Augsburg. In 1526 she had lodged in her palace the three children of the ex-King of Denmark, as their mother (her sister Isabella) had just died; their apartments were decorated by **Paul Tubach** and their portraits were painted in a group by **Jan Gossaert** showing Christina (later Holbein's *Duchess of Milan*) as the youngest of the three (Pl. 294). When Margaret died, **Paul Tubach** and **Jean van Battel** were among the artists who designed her catafalque.

Painters had their usual employment in connection with public ceremonies and pageants.

There were memorial ceremonies, for example, on the death of Philip the Fair; the memorial ceremony on the death of Henry VII included a catafalque in the Brussels Caudenberg church designed by **Jean van Battel,** and a memorial ceremony on the death of Manoel of Portugal was designed by **Jacques van Lathem.** There were street decorations and so forth for Margaret's Pageant Entries into various places and for Charles' inaugurations on his majority; and there were 'Ommeganck' processions in Malines and other towns. Above all there were the pageants connected with Charles V's Entries as Emperor into the major towns in 1520; in Antwerp on that occasion the arches and other decorations were designed by two hundred and fifty artists led by **Quinten Massys** (Pls. 207, 235, 241); in Bruges the team included **Jan Provoost** (Pl. 283), **Adriaen Ysenbrandt, Albert Cornelis** (Pl. 250) and **Lancelot Blondeel** (Pls. 270-2, 330); and **Jean Bellegambe** had a hand in the decorations at Douai.

A conspectus of some painters known, or presumed, to have worked in this period gives an idea of the activity in various regions.

In the Northern provinces **Hieronymus Bosch** (Pls. 156-8, 161, 163-71, 171A, 172, 173) was probably painting at Bois-le-Duc till he died in 1516, and some of his surviving pictures may therefore have been painted in these years; in Leyden **Cornelis Engelbrechtsz** (Pls. 213, 229, 232), thirty-nine when the period began, had **Lucas van Leyden** (Pls. 187, 189, 267, 277, 290-3) as his pupil about 1511 and **Aert Claesz** as his pupil about 1514; and his two sons **Cornelis Cornelisz** and **Lucas Cornelisz** also began their careers as his pupils. **Jacob Cornelisz van Oostsanen** (Pls. 265, 268, 302), about thirty-seven in 1507, was at work in Amsterdam, his son **Dirck Jacobsz** was active there after 1520, and **Cornelis Anthonisz** (Pl. 299) was another newcomer in the last decade. **Jacob Claessens (Trajectensis)** painted portraits in Utrecht and elsewhere; **Jan Gossaert** (Pls. 194, 238, 247, 294, 297), who was abroad from 1508 till 1510 and worked on his return in Middelburg and Utrecht with occasional visits to Brussels and Malines, seems to have had **Lambert Lombard** of Liège as his pupil in the middle twenties. **Marinus van Reymerswaele** (Pls. 237, 318), born probably in Zeeland and trained by a glass painter in Antwerp, was an established artist by 1521; **Jan van Scorel** (Pls. 284, 300, 301), pupil of **Jacob Cornelisz van Oostsanen** about 1515 and assistant to **Gossaert** in Utrecht in 1517, was abroad from 1518 till about 1523 and worked on his return in Utrecht and Haarlem; **Jan Joest** completed his *Scenes from the life of Christ* for the Nicolai Church in Calcar (mentioned in my last chapter) in 1508 and then settled in Haarlem where he died in 1519; **Ryckaert Aertsz,** known as **Ryck-met-de-Stelt** (Dick with the crutch) because one of his legs had been amputated, was a pupil of **Jan Mostaert** in Haarlem and painted *Scenes from the story of Joseph* on the wings of an altarpiece in S. Bavon before 1520 when he moved to Antwerp; and **Marten van Heemskerck** (Pls. 303, 304, 306, 354, 355, 365, 372) was **van Scorel's** assistant in Haarlem in 1527. **Jan Swart of Groningen,** who had already been abroad, was in Gouda about 1523; and others probably at work in the Northern provinces were the **Frankfort Master** (Pls. 209, 214, 215), the **London Delft Painter** (Pls. 221, 223-6, 234), the **Amsterdam Delft Painter** (Pls. 219, 220, 227, 228) the **Amsterdam Cadaver Painter** (Pl. 212) the **Hampton Court Cromatius Painter** (Pl. 266) and the **Detroit Crucifixion Painter** (Pl. 285).

In Bruges the senior artists included **Jan Provoost** (Pl. 283) who made topographic drawings for the magistrature in 1513, designed a domed ceiling for the choir of S. Jacques in 1516, painted pictures for the churches and died about sixty-five in 1529, and **Gerard David** who joined a patrician confraternity the Société de Notre Dame de l'Arbre Sec in 1508, painted the only authenticated example of his work known to be extant, the *Virgin and Child with SS. Catherine, Agnes and other saints* (Pl. 195), in 1509, and died about sixty in 1523. **Albert Cornelis**, who had his own stall in Bruges market-place for the sale of his pictures and prosecuted a man who had sold him bad colours in 1513, made good his own claim, in another action, to use assistants for all but the design and the faces in his six-foot composition *The Coronation of the Virgin* (Pl. 250) commissioned from him by the Fullers' Guild in 1517. **Adriaen Ysenbrandt**, perhaps a pupil of **Gerard David**, was Master in 1510 and held various offices in the Guild from 1516, but no pictures known to be by him are known to be extant; **Joannes Corvus (Jehan Raf)**, Master in 1512, was a portrait painter who went abroad before 1528; **Lancelot Blondeel**, painter, sculptor and architect and Master in 1519, painted a *Martyrdom of SS. Cosmas and Damian* triptych (Pls. 270-2) for the Barber-Surgeons Guild in 1523 and designed the fireplace of the Franc de Bruges, with statues of Maria and Maximilian, Ferdinand and Isabella, and Charles V, in 1529; **Ambrosius Benson** (Pl. 278), Master in 1519, and Guild Assessor in 1521, sold his works in the market from 1526 onwards; and others probably at work there included the **Bruges Death and the Miser Painter** (Pl. 236), the **Bruges Baptism of Christ Painter** (Pls. 196, 199, 201, 206, 218), the **New York Rest on the Flight Painter** (Pl. 201A), the **Brussels Virgin with a Milk Bowl Painter** (Pl. 205), the **Philadelphia Lamentation Painter** (Pl. 217), the **London Virgin with a Nun Painter** (Pl. 204), the **Seven Sorrows of the Virgin Master** (Pl. 281), the **Deipara Virgo Master** (Pl. 263), the **Saint Sang Master** (Pls. 262, 264), the **Fogg S. Luke Painter** (Pl. 260), the **Magdalene Legend Master** (Pl. 261), the **Bruges Birth of the Virgin Painter** (Pl. 269), and the **Brighton Assumption of the Virgin Painter** (Pl. 249).

All Margaret's Court Painters doubtless worked for long or short periods in Malines and Brussels. I have mentioned **Jean van Battel** and **Paul Tubach** in Malines, **Jacques van Lathem** who had headquarters in Brussels and **Jan van Roome** of Brussels who designed a tapestry *The Miraculous Communion of Herkenbald* for the Brotherhood of the Holy Sacrament in Louvain S. Pierre in 1513. **Jan Mostaert**, born in Haarlem, is known to have been in Margaret's continuous employment in Malines or Brussels for eighteen years and van Mander (1604) refers to pictures by him including a *Lineage of S. Anne*, an *Ecce Homo*, a *Banquet of the Gods*, a *Self-portrait with folded hands and a rosary before him in a naturalistic landscape with the Last Judgement in the sky*, a *West Indian landscape with many nude figures, rocks and strange huts*, and a *S. Hubert in a landscape*; but no work known to be by him is known to be extant. **Jean Schooff** painted a costume-history composition *The First Session of the Malines Parlement presided over by Charles the Bold 1473* with forty-six figures for the Malines Town Hall in 1516; **Frans Crabbe** painted religious subjects in Malines which, van Mander tells us, resembled works by **Lucas van Leyden** and **Quinten Massys; Frans Minnebroer**, who had **Frans Verbeeck** as his pupil at the end of the period, painted landscapes with religious subjects also in Malines; and the landscape painters **Hans Keynooghe** and **Claes Rogier** also worked there. In Brussels the landscape painter **Lucas Gassel** (Pls. 327, 328) was active from the early twenties; **Colyn de Coter** (Pl. 280) was employed by the Confrérie de S. Eloi in 1509 and seems to have worked through this period; and the **Brussels Haneton Lamentation Painter** (Pls. 239, 240, 279) produced his triptych for S. Gudule about 1520. **Bernaert van Orley** was commissioned to paint a *Last Judgement and Seven Works of Mercy* triptych (Pl. 282) by the Antwerp Almoners about 1518 and he sent it to them from Brussels about 1525; his *Job altarpiece* (Pls. 254, 256-9) dates from 1521 and his *Virgin and Child with S. Joseph and angels* (Pl. 248) from 1522. **Pieter Coecke van Aelst** (Pl. 307) was **Bernaert van Orley's** pupil for some years from probably about 1518. **Pieter van Coninxloo**, already mentioned as Court Painter, probably died in Brussels in the twenties; **Jan Cornelisz Vermeyen,** also mentioned above as Court

Painter from the middle twenties, was probably employed on portrait commissions both in Brussels and Malines; **Jan van Coninxloo** (Pl. 289) signed a *Nativity* probably in Brussels in 1530; **Cornelis van Coninxloo (Scernir)** signed the *Genealogy of the Virgin* (Pl. 276) in 1526; and **Pieter de Kempener** (Pl. 367)—later known as **Pedro de Campaña**—was active in Brussels by 1525 and went abroad soon after.

In Louvain **Aelbrecht Bouts** was at work on a picture for the chapel of the Brotherhood of the Holy Sacrament in S. Pierre in 1515; he restored a *Crucifixion* in the Town Hall in 1518; and he gave his *Assumption of the Virgin* triptych (Pls. 251-3), on which he had worked three years, to S. Pierre to join his father's pictures there probably about 1520. **Pieter van der Hofstadt** (Pl. 366) worked for S. Jacques in 1523; and **Jan van Rillaert** signed a grisaille *Judgement of Solomon* in 1528.

In Douai **Jean Bellegambe** painted a triptych donated to Anchin Monastery by Abbot Charles Coguin between 1511 and 1520, and made a map of the district between the Scarpe and the Somme presented by the town of Douai to Charles V in 1524.

Antwerp's growing affluence now attracted artists from all over the Netherlands since, as van Mander put it 'de Konst graag is waar rijkdom heerscht'; and there were also foreign artists at work there. The painters included a group of eclectic stylists known as the **Antwerp Mannerists** (Pls. 190-3) whose identities have not been discovered. Others there included **Adriaen van Overbeke** painter of religious subjects and Antwerp Master in 1508, and **Goswyn van der Weyden** who worked for Tongerloo Abbey from 1511 till 1515 perhaps assisted by his Portuguese pupils referred to in my last chapter, and was about sixty-five in 1530. **Joachim Patinir** (Pls. 200, 216, 241, 244-6), Antwerp Master in 1515, died apparently still young in 1524. **Quinten Massys** painted in Antwerp the *S. Anne altarpiece* (Pl. 207) for Louvain S. Pierre between 1507 and 1509 and another triptych the *Lamentation* with on one wing *Salome giving the head of S. John the Baptist to Herodias* and on the other the *Martyrdom of S. John the Evangelist* commissioned by the Cabinetmakers' Guild for Antwerp Cathedral in 1508; he was looked on as the leading Antwerp painter; and he continued his atelier with Portuguese and other students till he died in 1530. **Dirck Velaert,** chiefly active as glass painter, was Master as such in 1511, signed a glass panel *The Triumph of Time* in 1517 and may have been among Dürer's hosts in 1521. We know that **Jan de Beer,** Dean in 1515, signed an extant *Drawing of nine heads* in 1520, that **Jan de Cock** who had pupils in 1516 was Dean in 1520 and that **Joos van Cleve (Joos van der Beke),** Master in 1511 and Dean in 1519 and 1525, was a painter of religious subjects and of portraits; but no paintings known to be by any of these three artists are known to be extant. **Gerard Horenbout,** book illustrator from Ghent, was probably in Antwerp in 1521 when his daughter **Susanna Horenbout,** then about eighteen, sold Dürer a miniature *Salvator Mundi* for one florin and caused him to comment 'ist ein gross Wunder dass ein Weibsbild also viel machen soll'. **Jan Sanders van Hemessen** (Pls. 305, 317, 325), pupil of **Hendrik van Cleve the elder** in 1519, was Master in 1524; **Pieter Coecke van Aelst** (Pl. 307), pupil in Brussels of **Bernaert van Orley,** was Antwerp Master in 1527; **Jan van Amstel,** painter of religious subjects, was born in Amsterdam and became Antwerp Master by 1528; and **Lambert Lombard** of Liège, pupil of **Gossaert** in Middelburg about 1524, was in Antwerp aged about twenty-three and studying glass painting in 1529. Others possibly at work there included the **Chicago Man with a Pink Painter** (Pl. 208), the **London S. Luke Painter** (Pl. 186) and the **Dublin Flight Painter** (Pl. 203).

The period as a whole seems to have been propitious for the majority of artists, and the most successful figures became rich and lived in elegance. **Quinten Massys,** for example, had a fine house with outside frescoes which Dürer was taken to admire; **Bernaert van Orley** staged a banquet to welcome Dürer when he went to Brussels; **Jan Provoost** did the same for him in Bruges; and about 1527 **Jan Gossaert** and **Lucas van Leyden** went from Middelburg to Ghent, Malines and Antwerp and gave banquets to the local artists where **Gossaert** appeared in cloth of gold and **Lucas** in yellow silk.

There were, however, difficulties in some quarters. For though Charles V's Heresy Edicts were unpopular with the Netherlands' judiciary who were reluctant to inflict the major sentences, some artists were nevertheless affected in varying degrees by religious persecution after 1520. Thus **Adriaen van Overbeke** mentioned above as a painter of religious subjects was found guilty in 1521 of listening to Protestant sermons and of publicly reading and expounding the Bible and was sentenced to leave the town on a pilgrimage before nightfall on pain of having his right hand cut off. In 1527 **Bernaert van Orley** was arrested by the Inquisition in Brussels and charged with listening to Protestant sermons in the houses of two painters, members of his family; similar charges were made against the landscape painter and tapestry designer **Hans Tons** who collaborated with **van Orley** on tapestries known as '*Les Belles Chasses de Maximilian*' and against **Jan van Coninxloo**, painter of the *Marriage Feast at Cana* (Pl. 289), and some others; **van Orley**, possibly as Court Painter to the Regent, was acquitted, and the sentences in the other cases were light ones involving only attendance in S. Gudule at the same number of Catholic sermons.

Some Flemish artists including **Dirck Barendsz the elder** came to England about 1520 probably as a result of Protestant leanings. **Gerard Horenbout** came with his daughter **Susanna Horenbout** about 1522; his son or brother or cousin **Lucas Horenbout**, who instructed Holbein in the technique of miniature, followed soon after; and **Joannes Corvus (Jehan Raf)** of Bruges probably came about the same time and painted the blind *Richard Fox, Founder of Corpus Christi College Oxford* before 1528.

Visits to Italy, which were to become more and more *de rigueur* as the century advanced, were made in these years by a number of painters. **Jan Gossaert** accompanied his patron Philip, Bastard of Burgundy, to Rome in 1508; and **Bernaert van Orley** was probably there a few years later; **Pieter Coecke van Aelst** (Pl. 307) was in Rome probably before the end of the twenties; **Jan van Scorel**, who visited Venice on a pilgrimage to Jerusalem in 1520, was in Rome on his way back in 1522 when Adriaen VI made him keeper of the Belvedere gallery of antiquities and a Canon of Utrecht; **Jan Swart of Groningen** was in Venice in the early twenties; and **Pieter de Kempener** (Pl. 367) was in Bologna aged twenty-seven by 1530 when he worked on the arches for the Coronation Pageant of Charles V. There are no known records of Italian visits by **Quinten Massys** or **Lucas van Leyden;** but it is hard to believe that the serenity and measure and beautiful blond colours of the *Holy Kinship* (Pl. 207) by **Massys** were produced without personal experience of North Italian frescoes; though the Italianate qualities in **Lucas van Leyden's** *Last Judgement* (Pls. 290-3) may well have been absorbed at secondhand through prints.

As some Flemish and Flemish-Dutch artists had become acquainted with Graeco-Roman sculpture in Rome, mythologies and allegories and other themes with nude figures were now often chosen as subjects for easel pictures which were admired and bought by members of the upper classes who had visited Italy or were otherwise in touch with Renaissance culture. Thus **Jan Gossaert** painted a *Lucretia*, a *Danae* (Pl. 297), a *Mars and Venus*, a *Neptune and Amphitrite* (Pl. 247), a *Story of Hercules*, an *Adam and Eve* and probably a *Judith with the head of Holofernes* from which the pictures by the **Ottawa Judith Painter** (Pl. 295) and the **Grenoble Judith Painter** (Pl. 296) may have been derived.

In the *Neptune and Amphitrite* (Pl. 247) **Gossaert** evidently set out to keep the smooth charm and caressibility of Graeco-Roman statues and to give them more weight and majesty and the tang of Northern realism; and the hybrid result has bite and freshness and a bitter-sweet attraction revealing **Gossaert** in this picture as the only true precursor of **Rubens** (Pl. 601). Some German writers, moved no doubt by patriotism, have informed us that this *Neptune and Amphitrite* was inspired by Dürer's *Adam and Eve* engraving because the legs are in similar positions; but no artist, I imagine, would accept this supposition with the print before him or doubt that direct delight in Graeco-Roman statues was the artist's central inspiration for this work.

The religious pictures reproduced here include some theologically dictated compositions, and some personal interpretations and concepts.

In the Northern provinces **Jacob Cornelisz van Oostsanen** (Pls. 265, 268, 302) worked evidently to theological dictation in his *Worship of the Holy Trinity* of 1523 (not, I regret, reproduced here) where Adam and Eve, Moses, King David, the Evangelists, and scores of church dignitaries and male and female saints and martyrs are disposed on a central panel and two wings; there is theology also behind many details in **Jan Gossaert's** elaborate *Adoration of the Magi* (Pl. 194) begun, I imagine, before he went to Italy and finished after seeing **Hugo of Antwerp's** *Portinari altarpiece* (Pl. 76) in Florence; and theology dominates **Lucas van Leyden's** *Last Judgement* (Pls. 290-3) which is cold and academic in the central panel and crudely brutal in the *Hell* scene. But the Northern provinces, the centre of fermenting ideas and indignations, seem also to have produced the intensely personal religious pictures by the **London Delft Painter** and the **Amsterdam Delft Painter** who are both presumed to have lived at Delft, and by **Cornelis Engelbrechtsz** who is known to have lived in Leyden. There is throbbing vitality in the central *Crucifixion* of the **London Delft Painter's** triptych (Pl. 224); the mourners and the rulers and judges are in the foreground, the Magdalene with the centurion and a mocking soldier are round the foot of the central Cross, and the story of the Passion is in the background; behind the penitent thief, furtive men and officers with lanterns and weapons are led by Judas to the garden (Pl. 225); and behind the piteous plebeian impenitent thief, Christ is brutalized on the road to Calvary and Judas hangs himself (Pl. 226) as in the picture by **Hieronymus Bosch** (Pl. 156); all the figures are short, ungainly, ill-favoured and marvellously expressive; grief is suggested by pulled-up eyebrows as by the **St. Louis Entombment Painter** (Pl. 130) and the **Philadelphia Maria Egyptiaca Painter** (Pl. 131); and actuality is increased by the presence of genre spectators including a woman who leads a child to market near the Calvary procession (Pl. 226) and two boys whispering together in the foreground (as the young men joked together, wagging their heads, in the *Crucifixion* by the **New York Crucifixion and Last Judgement Painter** (Pl. 1)). The clothes are partly orientalized; but some are evidently local and of the moment, for the Holy Woman with raised hands behind the Virgin wears the same hat as the banker's wife by **Massys** (Pls. 234 and 235). The left-hand panel *Christ presented to the people* (Pl. 223) shows an unusual moment; the howling crowd has gone and the trumpet proclaims their victory over Pilate; only a woman and some children are there; Christ in his own clothes is led down roped to the waiting cross, a soldier shouts to him to hurry as the stripped thieves with their escort have already started. In the right-hand panel (Pl. 221) Christ with half-open mouth is descended from the Cross by a group recalling the picture by the **St. Louis Entombment Painter** (Pl. 130). Half-opened mouths are also seen on the fantastically accoutred saints in the Hortus Conclusus by the **Amsterdam Delft Painter** (Pl. 219); this includes a vision of one of the miracles when S. Gregory was celebrating Mass (as in **Bosch's** picture (Pl. 156)); the Christ-child here plays prettily with the Virgin's hair; and the outside wings have a beautifully designed *Annunciation* with a most engaging and unconventional Archangel (Pl. 220). In the Hortus Conclusus by the **Amsterdam Cadaver Painter** (Pl. 212) nothing but the setting of the theme remains as the foreground scene in this monastery garden is an *Allegory of the Vanity of Human Life*; but this picture also contains a curious and tender *Visitation* where S. Elizabeth affirms the Virgin's pregnancy by the pose of her right hand; and, in the cortile behind, the Virgin sits on the bricked-up base of a garden tree with musician angels in attendance. The **Amsterdam Cadaver Painter** was evidently employed by Augustinian prelates; and two elaborate and exciting altarpieces, with wings, by **Cornelis Engelbrechtsz** (Pls. 210, 211, 213, 229, 230, 232, 233) are known to have been painted for an Augustinian convent. Van Mander praised **Engelbrechtsz** (as he also praised **Rogier van der Weyden** and **Geertgen tot Sint Jans**) for portraying the emotions; and **Engelbrechtsz** is indeed a feeling and emotive painter; but he is also an eclectic mannerist, using, I imagine, Netherlandish, Italian and German prints and drawings; at times his figures droop in lovely rhythms that remind us of Botticelli; elsewhere the rhythms are angular and jagged, and there are long-drawn figures recalling the work of the German Matthias Grünewald—both in the striking and dramatic *Christ stripped* and *Christ mocked* on the outside of the *Crucifixion* triptych (Pl. 229) and in the *Crucifixion* itself (Pl. 232) where the figure of the older thief has a long nose and down-hanging hair. The clothes in these works by **Engelbrechtsz** are much fantasticated, but the Magdalene (Pl. 233) wears the small hat favoured by the current fashion as in the pictures by the **London Delft Painter** (Pl. 234) and **Quinten Massys** (Pl. 235) just mentioned. The **Detroit Crucifixion Painter** is a cruder and more rustic artist; but his *Crucifixion* (Pl. 285), where the sun is darkened and the Virgin swoons, shows personal imagination, deep feeling and dramatic power.

Some painters of religious subjects known or presumed to have been domiciled in Louvain, Brussels or Bruges, were less passionate and imaginative and more docile and derivative than these Northern artists. The *Assumption of the Virgin* triptych (Pls. 251, 253) by **Aelbrecht Bouts** is clearly the product of theological dictation, though the genre detail of the funeral procession in the background seems a personal feature. There are echoes of **Rogier van der Weyden's** *Descent from the Cross* (Pl. 46) in the picture by the **Brussels Haneton Lamentation Painter** (Pl. 279) and in **Colyn de Coter's** *The Three Maries* (Pl. 280); and the *Virgin and Child with S. Joseph and angels* (Pl. 248) by **Bernaert van Orley** is no more than a pastiche put together from Italian compositions. We find dignity and sentiment in the works reproduced by **Ambrosius Benson** (Pl. 278), the **New York Rest on the Flight Painter** (Pl. 201A), the **Seven Sorrows of the Virgin Master** (Pl. 281), and the **Saint Sang Master** (Pl. 262); but theology rules in **Jan Provoost's** academic *Last Judgement* (Pl. 283), in the *Virgin with Prophets and Sibyls* (Pl. 263) by the **Deipara Virgo Master** and in the archaistic *Coronation of the Virgin with choirs of angels* (Pl. 250) by **Albert Cornelis.** The **Brighton Assumption of the Virgin Painter** (Pl. 249) who seems inspired by the Maitre de Moulins (the unidentified presumably French painter of an altarpiece for the Cathedral at Moulins) has compromised successfully with theology in the charming group of the Virgin and Child with angels, and has used his eyes and sensibility in the landscape spread beneath (unless this was contributed by a landscape specialist). In **Gerard David's** *Virgin and Child with SS. Catherine, Agnes, Dorothy, Barbara, Godelieve and Lucy* (Pl. 195) the mother and child form a pretty group and the saints are nice young ladies posing with the serene gentility of **Memlinc's** figures; but **David's** concept lacks the simple poetry of the subject as imaged by the **Buckingham Palace Mystic Marriage Painter** (Pl. 106), the **Detroit Mystic Marriage Painter** (Pl. 110) and the **Brussels Mystic Marriage Painter** (Pl. 107). The **Bruges Baptism of Christ Painter** (Pl. 218), though technically most competent as a figure painter in the **Memlinc** tradition, seems also to lack fire and personal invention in his triptych which is chiefly remarkable for the wooded landscape probably provided by a landscape specialist, and for the episode of *S. John preaching in the Wilderness* in the background (Pl. 201). Bruges, declining into poverty as her port silted up and her commerce dwindled, seems, indeed, to have bred an especially unadventurous outlook to which the vivid actual Northern pictures must have seemed intolerably vulgar, and the cosmopolitan products of Antwerp disconcertingly newfangled. In Bruges we also find at this time an escapist impulse to defy the growing austerity of local conditions by precious unreality and ornamental art. Thus **Lancelot Blondeel** in his *Martyrdom of SS. Cosmas and Damian* (Pls. 272, 270, 271) diverts attention from the sufferings of the saints by the golden decoration that surrounds them; and the **Bruges Birth of the Virgin Painter** obscures the basically genre concept of his subject by elaborate costumes and the addition of canopies of delicate design (Pl. 269).

From the religious subjects painted in Antwerp my plates show the *Holy Kinship* from the *S. Anne altarpiece* by **Quinten Massys** and examples of Antwerp Mannerism by the **Munich S. Helena and Constantine Painter** and the **Antwerp Adoration Master.** The *Holy Kinship* (Pl. 207) by **Massys** is a noble composition with life-size figures; the design with the flattened semi-circle coming forward from the lateral loggia goes back to **Memlinc's** *S. John altarpiece* (Pl. 111); the medium is tempera and the colour is not the juxtaposition of rich jewelled notes characteristic of Flemish oil paintings but a blond harmony reminiscent of Italian frescoes; **Massys** indeed in this picture has captured Italian serenity and measure and combined them with Flemish tradition by his observation of genre details. Thus S. Anne in pink-red dress with black hood offers a grape with her right hand from a bunch held in her left; the Christ-child has a bird with a red string on his hand; a baby with a book is surrounded, on the ground, by coloured woodcuts; and tender feeling, serenity and personal imagination are also seen in the *Death of the Virgin* (not reproduced here) depicted on one of the wings of this altarpiece. The **Antwerp Mannerists** seem to have had a heyday from early in the century till the end of this period and longer. Some doubtless lived in cosmopolitan Antwerp; others may have worked in other cities (some being probably connected with glass designing and the tapestry factories in Brussels); some, I think, were Portuguese and others may also have been foreigners. All seem to have used prints and drawings from many quarters, and many were evidently inspired by **Cornelis Engelbrechtsz,** though unlike **Engelbrechtsz** they put style above ideas or feeling; they evolved an ornamental and aesthetic art that went beyond the Bruges and Brussel ornamentalists by distorting the actual figures into ingenious and lively rhythms and decorative conceits; and as they were aesthetically inventive their works have much vitality and attraction. These qualities, and fantasticated clothes and dancing rhythms are seen in the triptych reproduced by the **Antwerp Adoration Master** (Pls. 191-3); they also appear in the picture by the **Munich S. Helena and Constantine Painter** (Pl. 190) where the Empress Helena is formally charming in her strangely concocted garments though rather overburdened as a human with the True Cross, her sceptre, her draperies and the Imperial crown worn sideways on her bonnet (Pl. 190).

Some effects of the religious conflicts of the times can be seen, I fancy, in certain pictures. The struggle between the Church and the civil authorities for the control of charity, mentioned in my last chapter in connection with the **Antwerp Last Judgement Painter**

(Pl. 135) and the **Alkmaar Master** (Pls. 182-5, 188), may be referred to by **Lucas van Leyden** in his *Sermon* (Pl. 187), as a gentleman distributes bread there in the street scene; and by **Bernaert van Orley** in the *Last Judgement and Seven Works of Mercy* (Pl. 282) as lay almoners here replace the figure of Christ in the earlier pictures. The Protestant preachers in the woods and fields (preekers int groen) are probably referred to in the preaching scene by the **Magdalene Legend Master** (Pl. 261), in **Joachim Patinir's** *S. John preaching in the Wilderness* (Pl. 200)—a detail in the background of the *Baptism of Christ* (Pl. 216)—where S. John exhorts and prophesies the coming and Christ is seen approaching, and in the same subject by the **Bruges Baptism of Christ Painter** (Pl. 201) where the preacher argues and expounds. Protestant preachers in unconsecrated buildings may be referred to in the *Sermon* (Pl. 187) by **Lucas van Leyden** who, like the **View of S. Gudule Master** (Pl. 122), puts the congregation in a loggia. Conversion with mental reservations is doubtless the theme of the **Hampton Court Cromatius Painter's** picture (Pl. 266) where SS. Sebastian and Polycarp make the Prefect Cromatius confess the retention of a secret idol in his courtyard; and **Jacob Cornelisz van Oostsanen's** *Saul and the Witch of Endor* (Pl. 268), precisely dated November 29, 1526, may refer to some trial for witchcraft by Charles' new Inquisitors as it shows Saul at the witch's doorway, the Philistines' army that alarmed him on the hillside, and the witch with her familiars preparing brews and incantations as in the *Witches' Sabbath* (Pl. 496) by **Frans Francken,** painted eighty years later when witch-hunting was rampant.

The influence of Italian Renaissance pictures appears in some Flemish and Flemish-Dutch religious pictures at this time—we see it, as noted, in **Bernaert van Orley's** *Virgin and Child with S. Joseph and angels* (Pl. 248); we also see it in **Jan van Scorel's** *Baptism of Christ* (Pl. 284) where a man pulls off his shirt as in Piero della Francesca's *Baptism*, and in the drawing of the nudes in **Lucas van Leyden's** *Last Judgement* (Pl. 290-3). There are signs of the influence of Graeco-Roman sculpture on **Jan Gossaert** as also noted; and of Italian Renaissance architecture on **Gossaert** and **Bernaert van Orley.** But the main body of Flemish painting in the various provinces was scarcely affected by these modes; and native traditions continued in the great majority of paintings.

In portrait painting I have already referred to the Habsburg portraits by Margaret's Court painters **'Master Michiel', Jan Cornelisz Vermeyen, Jan Mostaert** and others, and to **Jan Gossaert's** arresting *Children of Christian II of Denmark* (Pl. 294) where the rhythm of the six small hands, arranged in groups of two and four, is in animated contrast with the static triangle of the three large heads. Replicas of these Habsburg portraits seem to have been made for various members of the family and for foreign princes whose friendship the Habsburgs were cultivating at the time; and some surviving portraits of *Margaret of Austria* and *Charles V* in his younger days may be replicas of this kind or productions by other Court painters. The Humanist world is evoked for us by extant portraits of *Erasmus* and *Aegidius* presumed the pictures known to have been painted by **Quinten Massys** in 1517, and by **Bernaert van Orley's** *Dr. George de Zelle* where the sitter, a physician, was a friend and neighbour of the artist. The tradition of the subscription portrait group continued; and my plates show *Twelve Jerusalem Pilgrims* (Pl. 300) painted in 1527 by **Jan van Scorel** for the Haarlem Brethren of S. John (descendants of **Geertgen tot Sint Jans'** patrons (Pl. 124)), and the **Amsterdam Cadaver Painter's** picture (Pl. 212) where the four Augustinians were doubtless the subscribers. In Amsterdam **Dirk Jacobsz** made his reputation in 1529 with a subscription group *Seventeen members of the Civic Guard* where the admirably painted hands, which attracted attention at the time, are factors in the formal structure (as in **Gossaert's** picture (Pl. 294)) though the figures are still placed unimaginatively in two

110

straight rows one above the other; and **Bernaert van Orley's** *Last Judgement and Seven Works of Mercy* (Pl. 282) contains portraits of some of the Antwerp Almoners who commissioned the picture. From the many portraits of adorant donors, sometimes with their families, I reproduce figures in works by **Cornelis Engelbrechtsz** (Pls. 210, 211) the **Frankfort Master** (Pls. 214, 215), the **Amsterdam Delft Painter** (Pls. 227, 228) and the **Brussels Haneton Lamentation Painter** (Pls. 239, 240). I also reproduce, as a detail, *The Four daughters of Elizabeth, first wife of Jean des Trompes, Burgomaster of Bruges* (Pl. 206) by the **Bruges Baptism of Christ Painter;** these little girls are shown with their mother and S. Elizabeth of Hungary as protecting saint on a wing of the triptych of which the *Baptism of Christ* (Pl. 218) is the central panel, and the artist was surely recalling the **van Eycks'** *Singing Angels* (Pl. 17) when he painted the sly child peeping behind the foreground figures from her corner on the right. **Gerard David's** *Virgin and Child with SS. Catherine, Agnes, Dorothy, Barbara, Godelieve and Lucy* (Pl. 195), given by the painter to the Bruges Sion Convent where his daughter was an inmate, has six portrait faces, right and left of the Virgin and the angels, which spoil the composition and were presumably inserted into an original design consisting of the central group and the six attendant saints. These portrait faces by **Gerard David** are affectionately characterized; and the same applies to the faintly smiling young women's faces by the **Vienna Catherine Painter** (Pl. 242) and **Jan van Scorel** (Pl. 301) and the men's heads by the **Brussels Young Knight Painter** (Pl. 243) and the **Chicago Man with a Pink Painter** (Pl. 208).

In genre painting we have congregations variously affected by sermons in pictures by **Lucas van Leyden** (Pl. 187), **Joachim Patinir** (Pl. 200) and the **Bruges Baptism of Christ Painter** (Pl. 201). The Magi's servants trundle their masters' luggage in the picture by the **Antwerp Adoration Master** (Pl. 193); a peasant waters his horse in a village stream in the picture by the **Brighton Assumption of the Virgin Painter** (Pl. 249); a young man with his arm round the pillar of a porch while he flirts with a young woman is wittily observed by the **Amsterdam Delft Painter** (Pl. 228), and, as noted, a woman takes her child to market in *The Crucifixion* by the **London Delft Painter** (Pl. 226). There are pleasing domestic scenes by the **Brussels Virgin with a Milk Bowl Painter** (Pl. 205), and by **Quinten Massys** whose children delighting in their picture books and coloured woodcuts (Pl. 207) remind us that, as mentioned in my last chapter, **Massys** began his career by colouring woodcuts distributed to children in the Lazarite processions on Shrove Tuesday. The **Amsterdam Cadaver Painter** portrays a child in a garden on a hobby horse (Pl. 212), and the **Bruges Birth of the Virgin Painter** shows the toilet of the new-born babe and visits to the mother by friends and relatives while her servant brings her a bowl of soup and her husband has his luncheon in the background (Pl. 269). **Bernaert van Orley** paints bourgeois interiors in *The rich man dining* (Pls. 254, 258) and *Death of the rich man* (Pls. 256, 259) and **Quinten Massys** in his *Salome giving the head of S. John the Baptist to Herodias* (not reproduced here) recalls and elaborates the Banquet hall of Herod provided by **Memlinc** (Pl. 113). Artists at work are depicted by **Jan Gossaert** (Pl. 238), the **London S. Luke Painter** (Pl. 186) and the **Fogg S. Luke Painter** (Pl. 260); a scholar's study is shown by **Marinus van Reymerswaele** (Pls. 237), **Quinten Massys** invents for us a banker's counting-house (Pl. 235), and the **Bruges Death and the Miser Painter** (Pl. 236) gives us a fat financier in his office. In **Jan Gossaert's** *S. Luke drawing the Virgin* (Pl. 238) the portrait painter, in his patron's mansion, is working on the drawing from which he will later make the painting in his studio; in an earlier picture of this subject by the **Boston S. Luke Painter** (Pl. 48) S. Luke, genuflecting, drew on a little board held uncomfortably in his left hand; and **Gossaert's** S. Luke though seated, still draws uncomfortably on unsupported paper on his knees. The painting stage, with the artist at work in his own studio, is depicted by the **London S. Luke Painter** (Pl. 186) and here the artist, warmly dressed, in a comfortable room with linen-fold panels as skirting, has a window and a mirror behind him and books and paint-pots on the shelves. The **Fogg S. Luke Painter** (Pl. 260) has fused the two stages; for the room is half a studio, with mirror and other tools of trade, and half a patron's palace adorned with Italian swags and putti; and though the artist has reached the painting stage the sitter is still posing. In the delicately painted *Banker and his wife* (Pl. 235) by **Quinten Massys** there is a nostalgic hark back to the past which seems to have prevailed in some quarters at this moment (**Jean Schooff**, it will be remembered, was commissioned in 1515 to produce a costume-history picture *The First Session of the Malines Parlement presided over by Charles the Bold 1473* for Malines Town Hall); for this scene by **Massys** (which recalls the *S. Eligius in his goldsmith's shop handing a ring to a young lady with her betrothed* painted by **Petrus Christus** for the Bruges Goldsmiths Guild in 1449) must surely depict not an actual Antwerp banker and his wife but two friends of the artist in fifteenth-century costumes posing for him as 'Ye Banker and his Wife in Olden Times'—though actuality has crept in at one point as the lady wears the fashionable bonnet already referred to.

In landscape painting the old traditions were continued and developed with occasional references to drawings made in Italy or the mountainous regions of France or on the Mediterranean coast as in the mountain landscape by **Quinten Massys** (Pl. 207), the vista by **Jan van Scorel** (Pl. 284) and the port scene by **Bernaert van Orley** (Pl. 248). The painters in this field included **Hieronymus Bosch** (Pls. 157, 161, 163) till 1516, **Joachim Patinir** (Pls. 200, 216, 241, 244-6) till 1524, **Patinir's** follower **Hans Keynooghe, Claes Rogier, Hans Tons** and **Lucas Gassel** (Pls. 327, 328); and landscape specialists probably provided the settings for the pictures by the **Bruges Baptism of Christ Painter** (Pl. 218), the **London Virgin with Nun Painter** (Pl. 205A), the **Philadelphia Lamentation Painter** (Pl. 217), the **New York Rest on the Flight Painter** (Pl. 201A), the **Brighton Assumption of the Virgin Painter** (Pl. 249), the **Magdalene Legend Master** (Pl. 261) and the **Antwerp Adoration Master** (Pls. 191, 192). The most celebrated of the landscape specialists was **Joachim Patinir**; Dürer praised him as such and (in **Pieter Bruegel's** lifetime) Don Felipe de Guevara named him and **Jan van Eyck** and **Rogier van der Weyden** as the three greatest painters which the Netherlands had produced. **Patinir** carried on the old Flemish concept of the deeply receding landscape and imbued it with personal affective qualities; he set craggy rock forms rising from smiling plains with trees and villages; and a smooth river generally winds to an estuary flanked with hills; his foreground is habitually warm grey, the middle distance green and the distances degrees of blue; and all combine in a single expansive panorama complete in itself before the figures were put in. The figures in **Patinir's** landscapes seem indeed to have been generally inserted by other artists; **Quinten Massys** is known to have painted the fashionably dressed girls in the *Temptation of S. Anthony* (Pl. 241); and some figure painter was doubtless responsible for the figures in the *Baptism of Christ* (Pl. 216). But **Patinir** himself may have inserted the quite small figures in the *Landscape with Flight into Egypt* (Pl. 244) where the Massacre of the Innocents takes place in a Flemish village in the background, and a heathen idol on a mountain pass collapses as the Holy Family approaches; and he may also have inserted the little figures and animals in the *Landscape with S. Jerome and the lion* (Pls. 245, 246) where the lion, who sits domestically with S. Jerome in the foreground, gallops off to meet the stolen donkey on the right and drives the caravan into the monastery on the hilltop in the centre. The rural aspects of **Patinir's** art appear in works by other painters in these years; and they are seen here in pictures by **Jacob Cornelisz van Oostsanen** (Pl. 265), the **London Virgin with Nun Painter** (Pl. 205A) and the **Brighton Assumption of the Virgin Painter** (Pl. 249); and the sharp upstanding rocks and the panoramic aspect of his art was much imitated by artists working in the following decades. The wooded landscape in the central panel by the **Bruges Baptism of Christ Painter** (Pl. 218) seems however quite uninfluenced by **Patinir**; for it follows the old tradition of the foreground meadow with wooded groves in the middle distance; the trees are of varied types, ivy grows up some of the trunks, and the tops of the trees are cut off by the frame— a device already seen here in works by the **Giles Master** (Pl. 155), **Hieronymus Bosch** (Pl. 163) and **Hugo of Antwerp** (Pl. 78), and also used by the **Magdalene Legend Master** (Pl. 261). A wood of this kind with tree-tops similarly cut off by the frame is in the charming picture by the **New York Rest on the Flight Painter** (Pl. 201A); and the bluffs crowned with verdure which form the foreground in that picture are a background motif in the *Lamentation* by the **Philadelphia Lamentation Painter** (Pl. 217).

In architectural painting we have a whole walled town on a distant hilltop and a castle with adjacent church and monastery in the background of the picture by the **Bruges Baptism of Christ Painter** (Pl. 218); and elsewhere we get street scenes and views through windows and loggias in the old traditions and also new elements that came from Southern travel or acquaintance with Southern prints or drawings. Street scenes are painted by, or supplied to, **Lucas van Leyden** (Pl. 187), the **Bruges Baptism of Christ Painter** (Pl. 199) and the **Amsterdam Delft Painter** (Pls. 227, 228); and the walled gardens of religious houses are in the pictures by the **Amsterdam Cadaver Painter** (Pl. 212) and the **Amsterdam Delft Painter** (Pl. 219). A window frames the Mediterranean port scene in the picture by **Bernaert van Orley** (Pl. 248); another in the picture by the **Brussels Virgin with a Milk Bowl Painter** (Pl. 205) frames a corner of old Bruges with the 'Lovers lake'; and **Quinten Massys** with the half-open door and glimpse of an inner room beyond in the *Banker and his wife* (Pl. 235) recalls the composition by the **New York Christ Appearing to His Mother Painter** (Pls. 33, 47) and anticipates some seventeenth-century Dutch painters. Loggias frame a Northern village and a Northern rocky landscape in pictures by **Jacob Cornelisz van Oostsanen** (Pl. 265) and **Lucas van Leyden** (Pl. 277) and another frames the mountain land-scape in the central panel by **Quinten Massys** (Pl. 207); **Lucas van Leyden** uses a round arch loggia for his *Sermon* (Pl. 187) and **Bernaert van Orley** a fantastic Italianate Renaissance structure for the banqueting hall in his *Job* composition (Pl. 257). **Gossaert** concocts an 'antique' architectural setting for his *Neptune and Amphitrite* (Pl. 247) and Italianate Renaissance structures for his *Virgin of Louvain* (Pl. 255) his *Danaë* (Pl. 297) and his *S. Luke drawing the Virgin* (Pl. 238)—using doubtless for these purposes some sketches made when wandering in delighted amazement about Rome. In this *S. Luke drawing the Virgin* by **Gossaert** the composition recalls the picture by the **Boston S. Luke Painter** (Pl. 48); but the token structure in the earlier picture has been transformed to a hall in an elaborate palace with vista on a courtyard, and though the architectural and sculptural motifs are flagrantly hybrid, the whole preposterous invention, as an exclamation of enthusiasm for Rome and the Italian Renaissance, is more arresting and intriguing than the buildings drawn with cold correctitude by later Romanists like **Michiel Coxie** (Pl. 308), **Lambert van Noort** (Pl. 402) and **Karel van Mander** (Pl. 472). Symbolic ruins replace the stable in the *Adoration of the Magi* by **Gossaert** (Pl. 194) and in the same subject by the **Antwerp Adoration Master** (Pl. 193); a flamboyant Gothic screen is background for **Cornelis van Coninxloo's** *Genealogy of the Virgin* (Pl. 276); and I have already referred to **Lancelot Blondeel's** inventive decorative fancy in the architectural ornaments that frame the figures in his *Cosmas and Damian* triptych (Pls. 270, 271, 272).

The continuance of animal painting can also be followed. Horses gallop and cavort across the plain in the **Detroit Crucifixion Painter's** concept of *Calvary* (Pl. 285) as, earlier, in the concepts by the **New York Crucifixion and Last Judgement Painter** (Pl. 4) and the *Adoration of the Magi* by **Hieronymus Bosch** (Pl. 157); a horse grazes and another champs on a tight rein and swishes his tail in the **London Delft Painter's** *Crucifixion* (Pls. 224, 226); and S. George rides a dancing horse as he slashes at the dragon in the picture by the **Antwerp Adoration Master** (Pl. 191). The ass in the *Flight into Egypt* is shown grazing by the **New York Rest on the Flight Painter** (Pl. 201A) and trotting, with the action well observed, by the **Dublin Flight Painter** (Pl. 203). The dog in the foreground of the *Adoration of the Magi* by the **New York Adoration in White Castle Painter** (Pl. 151) reappears in the foreground of the *Crucifixion* by **Cornelis Engelbrechtsz** (Pl. 232); dogs gnaw bones in the foreground of the *Adoration of the Magi* by **Jan Gossaert** (Pl. 194); the rich man's house-dogs snarl at the famished beggar in **Bernaert van Orley's** *Lazarus at the rich man's door* (Pl. 254); S. Jerome has his pet lion in the picture by **Joachim Patinir** (Pl. 245); and the ox, S. Luke's symbol, has also become a friendly pet in the studio interior by the **London S. Luke Painter** (Pl. 186). Peacocks and other birds are in the walled garden by the **Amsterdam Cadaver Painter** (Pl. 212); and swans are painted by the **Brussels Virgin with a Milk Bowl Painter** (Pl. 205) and the **Amsterdam Delft Painter** (Pl. 227).

The still-life which abounds and follows the main fifteenth-century traditions, was some-times, doubtless, the work of studio assistants or collaborating specialists. The Magi's gifts and the Negro's crown are painted in glittering detail by **Jan Gossaert** (Pl. 194); and in the *Banker and his wife* (Pl. 235) by **Quinten Massys** the book and mirror in the foreground recall the still-life by the **van Eycks** (Pls. 2, 18A) and the **Madrid Werl Wings Painter** (Pl. 41), and the brass-headed nails fixing the tablecloth recall the studs in the shutters by the **London Virgin with a Firescreen Painter** (Frontispiece) and at the same time herald the brass nails in chairs by Vermeer of Delft and in card tables by Chardin. The still-life in this *Banker and his wife* by **Massys** and in the studio and bourgeois interiors of this period (Pls. 186, 258, 259) is descriptive in character; but we get more formal meaning in the domestic still-life by the **Brussels Virgin with a Milk Bowl Painter** (Pl. 205), for here the gently painted bread, fruit, knife and milk bowl in the foreground, and the book, basket and cushion on the table in the background, are disposed in architectural relations forestalling the *Still-life with food and kitchen utensils* by **Hieronymus Francken** (Pl. 503); and, as earlier in the picture by the **Princeton Christ before Pilate Painter** (Pl. 174), we also get something more than illustration in the treatment of the still-life in **Marinus van Reymerswaele's** *S. Jerome in his study* (Pl. 237) because the sharp angles at which the objects are disposed and the hard light that shines upon them invest the scene with something cruel and sinister, an implication that this ecclesiast with his talons is a persecuting plotter—a suggestion in-creased by the relation of the skull-like head to the actual skull below.

The skull, signifying meditations upon death in this picture of S. Jerome, is related to the 'Vanitas' and 'Memento mori' motifs in many pictures of this time. The **Frankfort Master** puts a cadaver with 'Cogita Mori' on the outside of an altarpiece (Pl. 209) the **Amsterdam Cadaver Painter** shows a skeleton in an open grave with a Latin inscription 'Oh! passer-by, look round and weep. I am what you will be; I was what you now are; I beg you, pray for me' (Pl. 212); and **Cornelis Engelbrechtsz** in the predella to his *Crucifixion* altarpiece (Pls. 229, 232) shows the cadaver of Adam with the roots of the tree he planted in Eden whence—we read in S. Helena's legend—the True Cross was made. A cadaver as symbol for Death, is in the picture of the miser bribing Death for a new lease of life by the **Bruges Death and the Miser Painter** (Pls. 236). A skull signifying Golgotha, 'the place of the skull,' has already been seen here in the foreground of the *Crucifixion* by the **Florence (Poggio Imperiale) Crucifixion Painter** (Pl. 133), and skulls with that meaning are in pictures by the **Philadelphia Lamentation Painter** (Pl. 217) and **Cornelis Engelbrechtsz** (Pl. 232). Some works of this period show nothing but a skull as a symbolic still-life object; and in one, the back of a portrait by **Jan Gossaert,** the skull, with the jaw dissociated, is accompanied by the legend 'Facile contemnit omnia qui se semper cogitat moriturum Hieronymus, 1517'.

The flower painting of the time is seen here in several plates. Flowers in the old tradition grow from the meadows and an iris grows from the river bank in the landscape settings of the *Baptism* by the **Bruges Baptism of Christ Painter** (Pl. 218) and the triptych by **Aelbrecht Bouts** (Pls. 251-3); they grow round the feet of the mourners in the **London Delft Painter's** *Descent from the Cross* (Pl. 221) and in **Colyn de Coter's** *The Three Maries* (Pl. 280); and they grow as garden plants in the Hortus Conclusus pictures by the **Amsterdam Delft Painter** (Pl. 219) and the **Amsterdam Cadaver Painter** (Pl. 212). S. Dorothy hands a flower from her basket to the Virgin in the **Amsterdam Delft Painter's** picture and one of the angels scatters flowers from a basket in **Bernaert van Orley's** *Virgin and Child with S. Joseph and angels* (Pl. 248). Flowers in a vase appear at the foot of the throne in **Jan Gossaert's** *Virgin of Louvain* (Pl. 255) and in **Lucas van Leyden's** *Annunciation* (Pl. 267). There are no flowers on the rich man's dining-table by **Bernaert van Orley** (Pl. 258); but a vase of flowers is on the sideboard in the domestic interior by the **Brussels Virgin with a Milk Bowl Painter** (Pl. 205). Single flowers are held in the traditional manner by the sitter for the **Chicago Man with a Pink Painter** (Pl. 208), by several figures in the *Holy Kinship* (Pl. 207) by **Quinten Massys,** and by the Virgin posing to S. Luke in the picture by **Jan Gossaert** (Pl. 238).

CHAPTER VI

Mary of Hungary

1531-1555

IN 1531 Charles V appointed his sister, Mary of Hungary, as Regent of the Netherlands. Mary, the widow of Louis II of Hungary (who had been killed in 1526 at the Battle of Mohacz when the Turks conquered Hungary), was then twenty-five; Charles himself was thirty-one; Francis I was thirty-seven; and Henry VIII was forty. The period began by the re-enactment in the Netherlands of Charles' 1529 Edict against Lutherans, Anabaptists and other Protestants, and the acknowledgement by the English clergy of Henry VIII as Supreme Head of the Church in England; and in 1532 Charles left the Netherlands to drive the Turks back down the Danube. In 1533 Jan Matthijs of Haarlem launched the militant phase of Anabaptism; Rabelais published 'Pantagruel' in Lyons; Anne Boleyn was crowned Queen of England; Henry VIII was excommunicated; **Pieter Coecke van Aelst** went to Constantinople to offer Flemish tapestry designs to Suleiman the Magnificent and failed to sell them because they included human figures; and Atahualpa, ruler of Peru, was burned alive by Pizarro at Casamanca. In 1534 an order went out to expel all Anabaptists from Antwerp, men remaining after a given date to be burned alive and women to be drowned in the Scheldt; there were Anabaptist risings in Amsterdam and Münster; forty Protestants were burned alive in Paris; Calvin, aged twenty-five, fled from Paris to Bâle; Elizabeth Barton (the Nun of Kent) was beheaded at Tyburn; and Parliament confirmed King Henry as Supreme Head of the English Church. In 1535 militant Anabaptism collapsed with the fall of the Münster Anabaptists; there were wholesale executions of Anabaptists in Holland and Flanders; **Barent Dircksz** ('Doove Barent' father of **Dirck Barendsz**) painted pictures of this 'raving sect' (as van Mander describes them), and their appropriate punishments, in Amsterdam Town Hall; Henry VIII beheaded Sir Thomas More and Bishop Fisher and began to dissolve the monasteries; Khair-ad-Din, known as Barbarossa, was driven from Tunis by Charles V who had Andrea Doria as his admiral and **Jan Cornelisz Vermeyen** in attendance to make drawings for tapestries recording the occasion; and Francis I signed a treaty of commerce with Suleiman the Magnificent which gave French merchant ships monopoly of access to all Turkish ports. In 1536 Francis started a new war against the Emperor who led an army into Provence; Calvin published his 'Institution Chrétienne' in Latin; William Tyndale, translator of the Bible and chaplain to the British merchants in Antwerp, was strangled and burned as a heretic at Vilvorde by the Emperor's orders; Reginald Pole wrote 'Pro Ecclesiasticae Unitatis Defensione' in Italy and was made a Cardinal; Henry VIII was depicted holding a scroll inscribed 'Go ye into all the world and preach the gospel to all creatures' (referring perhaps to Miles Coverdale's translation of the Bible) in the

picture reproduced here by the **Hampton Court Henry VIII** (*c.* 1536) **Painter** (Pl. 312);
Holbein became Henry's Court Painter; and Anne Boleyn was beheaded. In 1538 the
French war ended with the Peace of Nice; and Henry who contemplated marriage with
Christina of Denmark sent Holbein to Brussels to make a drawing of her (which eventually
became the celebrated picture *The Duchess of Milan*). In 1539 the Ghent burghers refused
to subscribe to the Emperor's other wars and there was also a proletarian revolt there.
In 1540 Ignatius Loyola obtained a Bull from Pope Paul II approving a new order, the
Society of Jesus; and Charles went to Ghent, inflicted crushing punishment on the city and
staged a ceremony where the magistrates made public confession and pleaded for forgive-
ness—a scene depicted in a drawing reproduced here (Pl. 323) by **Jan Cornelisz Vermeyen.**
In 1541 Charles had **Cornelis Anthonisz** with him as official draughtsman when his fleet
was destroyed by a tempest off Algiers; John III of Portugal sent the Jesuit Francis Xavier
as a missionary to Goa; and Calvin, established in Geneva, published 'L'Institution
Chrétienne' in French. In 1542 Suleiman the Magnificent sent the Ottoman fleet to help
Francis who had again launched war against the Emperor; one van Rossem led Gelderland
troops in a fruitless attack on Antwerp—an episode painted about a hundred and fifty-five
years later by **Constantyn Francken;** and **Jan van Scorel** who had sold a picture to Gustavus I of Sweden received from him a signed letter announcing the dispatch as presents of
200 lbs. of cheese, an ice sledge, a case of furs and a ring, none of which in fact arrived. In
1543 Copernicus received the first printed copy of his 'De Revolutionibus Orbium
Coelestium'; Henry joined Charles in alliance against France; and Charles invaded Gelderland and annexed it to his Netherlands dominions. In 1544 Charles invaded Champagne
and made the Peace of Crépy when his troops were some thirty-five miles from Paris; and
Gerard Mercator, involved with forty others in a heresy trial in Antwerp, escaped with
minor consequences (thanks no doubt to his prestige as the Emperor's geographer)
though two of the others were burned, one was beheaded and two were buried alive. In
1545 three thousand Vaudois dissenters were massacred in the Vaucluse mountains and
their towns and villages burned; the Council of Trent began; and Boulogne was captured
for Henry VIII who was still at war with Francis. In 1546 Henry founded Trinity College
Cambridge and made peace with France. In 1547 Charles won the Battle of Mühlberg
against the German Protestants, and commissioned **Michiel Coxie** to design a tapestry to
record it; Francis I was succeeded by Henri II, Henry VIII was succeeded by Edward VI,
and Ivan the Terrible was crowned as the first Czar of Russia. In 1548 Archbishop Cranmer supervised the production of the first English prayer book; and Charles, who had
summoned Titian aged seventy from Venice to Augsburg to paint him in the armour that
he wore at Mühlberg, picked up the artist's brush which had fallen to the floor. In 1549
Charles toured the Netherlands with Prince Philip, then twenty-two, whom he introduced
to the provinces as his successor; and in England, Princess Mary, aged thirty-three, defied
the Act of Uniformity and refused to give up Mass. In 1550 **Jan van Scorel** went to Ghent
with **Lancelot Blondeel** to clean the **van Eycks'** *Altarpiece of the Mystic Lamb* (Pls. 9, 12),
and made plans with **Jan Cornelisz Vermeyen** for improving Harderwyk harbour and
damming the Zype (a project executed a hundred years later); Ronsard published his
'Odes' in Paris; and Charles issued the placard or Heresy Edict known as the Edict of
Blood which provided inter alia that any printer, seller, reader or owner of a work by
Luther, Zwingli or Calvin or 'other heretics reprobated by the Holy Church', and anyone
attending meetings of their followers or openly or secretly entertaining their opinions, was
to be burned or buried alive and that informers were to be rewarded by from ten to fifty

117

per cent of the property of the victim according to his means. In 1552 Henri II in alliance with the German Protestant princes, was at war against the Emperor who tried in vain with sixty thousand troops to capture Metz which the princes had recognized as French; and Anglican ritual was rigorously enforced in all English churches. In 1553 Queen Mary succeeded Edward VI; Charles, using his Secretary of State Bishop (later Cardinal) Granvella as intermediary, arranged her marriage with Prince Philip whose portrait by Titian he sent to recommend him; and **Cornelisz Anthonisz,** was present at the siege of Thérouanne and made woodcuts to commemorate it. In 1554 Queen Mary married Philip at Winchester; Cardinal Pole returned to England; and the realm was reconciled with Rome. In 1555 Bishops Ridley and Latimer were burned in Oxford; **Jan Cornelisz Vermeyen** engraved a *Portrait of Philip II* inscribed *Rex Anglorum*; the Plantin Press was founded in Antwerp; Charles V's mother Joanna 'la Loca' died; Charles abdicated in Brussels; and Philip came from London to attend the ceremonies.

Though personally disposed to religious toleration, Mary of Hungary was driven by Charles and his Inquisitors to increasing persecution as the years went on; and she needed no driving against the Anabaptists—for some of these were political communists and said to be polygamists as well as religious revivalists with everyone, including the Lutherans, against them, and the major cruelties went mainly in their direction. But the Lutherans and other Protestants had their share of martyrdoms and vexations; among the artists for example **Hans Tons** was again arrested for heresy in 1533, and **Jan Massys** (Pls. 315, 361-3), son of **Quinten Massys,** was banished as a suspected Protestant in 1544. Calvinism began to make progress in the forties; and, though the savage 1550 Placard was found impossible of full execution in Antwerp which relied on good relations with resident and visiting foreigners concerned with industry and commerce, many thousands of free thinkers of one kind or another were 'liquidated' in the seventeen provinces before the period closed. These conditions caused some emigrations among the artists and some local panics which affected them; and in 1550 the Bruges magistrates thought it prudent to order **Pieter Jansz Pourbus** (Pl. 334) to paint out a cartload of churchmen from the Hell scene in **Jan Provoost's** Town Hall *Last Judgement* (Pl. 283) which had been passed by the theologians in 1525.

In these circumstances there were inevitably some crypto-Protestant and crypto-political paintings and some so interpreted if not so intended. **Herri met de Bles** produced a landscape with a pedlar asleep while monkeys exposed his wares upon the trees which was interpreted, van Mander relates, as Lutherans exposing the Pope's claims 'which they call his wares' (though the subject was already in the repertoire of Flemish farce in the time of Charles the Bold, as noted); and there was doubtless crypto-Calvinist propaganda in the **Solomon Master's** choice of *The Idolatry of Solomon* as his subject (Pls. 286-8). As Holofernes was sent by Nebuchadnezzar to take vengeance on those who had refused assistance in his war against the Medes there may have been concealed applause of Ghent's defiance of the Emperor in *Judith with the head of Holofernes* as painted by the **Ottawa Judith Painter** (Pl. 295), the **Grenoble Judith Painter** (Pl. 296), **Jan Massys** (Pl. 315), **Cornelis Massys, Marcus Willems** and **Jan Sanders van Hemessen;** and as the struggle between the civil authorities and the church for the control of charity continued in these years, it was probably reflected in the *Feeding of the Poor* painted for Malines, S. Rombout by **Cornelis Enghelrams** (a protégé later of the Prince of Orange and already perhaps a crypto-Protestant) who, van Mander tells us, 'distinguished therein between the genuine poor and the professional fake beggars with their hurdy-gurdies and so forth'.

118

Mary of Hungary liked pomp and pageantry and built the Châteaux of Mariemont and Binche; she was also fond of music in which her subjects at this period excelled. Unlike Margaret of Austria she took relatively little interest in painting—possibly because she lacked Margaret's advantage of early contacts with French culture. But she bought from the executors the religious pictures left by Margaret to the memorial church at Brou; she owned **Jan van Eyck's** *Marriage of Giovanni Arnolfini* (Pl. 18A) which had belonged to Margaret, as noted, and had since then passed somehow to the possession of a barber (as we know from the contemporary historian van Vaernewyck); she acquired **Rogier van der Weyden's** *Descent from the Cross* (Pl. 46) from the Louvain Archers' Guild and sent it to Spain after **Michiel Coxie** had made a copy to replace it in Louvain, S. Pierre; and from her headquarters in Brussels she gave formal patronage to artists, choosing as her Court Painters **Bernaert van Orley** (Pls. 248, 254, 256-9, 282), **Jan Cornelisz Vermeyen** (Pl. 323), **Pieter Coecke van Aelst** (Pl. 307), **Guillaume Scrots, Catherina van Hemessen** (Pls. 340, 345, 346) and **Antonis Mor** (Pls. 332, 333, 341, 432, 350A, 408, 428). Charles himself was attracted by the arts and sciences; Gerard Mercator was his geographer, Vesalius was his anatomist and **Pieter Jansz Pourbus** (Pls. 331, 334, 336, 337) worked for him as cartographer; in the field of painting Titian was his favourite, but his Flemish Court Painters included **Jean van Battel, Philippe Vos, Cornelis Anthonisz** (Pl. 299), **Pieter Coecke van Aelst, Jan Vermeyen** and **Michiel Coxie** (Pls. 308, 310, 352). Of these artists thus personally patronized by Mary and/or the Emperor, **Bernaert van Orley** designed windows for Brussels S. Gudule in 1537 and died in 1541; and **Jan Vermeyen** (Barbalonga) a special protégé of the Emperor, was often seen at Court where his enormous beard which was said to have reached the ground made a great impression on the ladies. **Pieter Coecke van Aelst** who died in 1550 was very influential in this period as architect and designer for glass and tapestry in addition to his work as painter; back from Constantinople in 1534 he translated parts of Serlio's book on Vitruvius in 1539 and 1546, and he had **Pieter Bruegel The Elder, Nicolas van Neufchatel (Lucidel)** and probably **Willem Key** (Pl. 387) and **Jan Vredeman de Vries** (Pl. 462) among his pupils. The delightful talent of **Catherina van Hemessen** may have been brought to the Regent's notice when the artist married the musician Christian de Morien in 1554 at the age of twenty-six. **Antonis Mor**—Antwerp Master in 1547 after study in Utrecht under **Jan van Scorel** (Pls. 284, 300, 301)—was introduced to Court circles by Granvella for whom he was working by 1549; **Pieter Jansz Pourbus** was Bruges Master at twenty-three in 1543; and **Cornelis Anthonisz** whose home was Amsterdam, made a *View of Amsterdam* in twelve woodblocks for the Emperor in 1544. **Michiel Coxie,** after working in Rome, was Malines Master at the age of forty in 1539; he then moved to Brussels where he succeeded **Bernaert van Orley** as Director of the Tapestry Factory and painted four pictures *Christ bearing the Cross, The Virgin meeting Christ on the road to Calvary, The Crucifixion* and *The Virgin* which the Emperor acquired. **Jan Mostaert** living in retirement in Haarlem does not seem to have been re-appointed as Court Painter; but he was still in repute, van Mander tells us, and was visited by Knights of the Golden Fleece and other distinguished persons; he died about eighty at the end of the period.

The chief pageants were those designed for the tour made by Charles and Prince Philip in 1549 when Philip surrounded by Spanish grandees, including the Duke of Alva, may have appeared to his future subjects much as he was painted, probably soon after, by the **Madrid Philip II (Head) Painter** (Pl. 347). Decorations for his Pageant Entry into Amsterdam were designed by **Cornelis Anthonisz;** in Utrecht they were designed by **Jan van Scorel** (from whom Philip bought a *Sacrifice of Isaac* at this time); and in Louvain they were directed by **Jan van Rillaert** now Official Painter to the city; in Malines a triumphal arch with *Dido founding Carthage* was painted by **Marcus Willems** and other arches were designed by **Gerard Schoof the elder** and **Jan Vredeman de Vries** then beginning his career as painter of perspective vistas (Pl. 462); in Bruges **Lancelot Blondeel** (Pls. 270-2, 330) was consulted on the general design and his pupil and son-in-law **Pieter Jansz Pourbus** (Pls. 331, 334, 336, 337) devised a procession of the Rhetoricians; in Brussels **Michiel Coxie** was probably a chief designer and there, in one setpiece, a musician played upon an organ with the tails of live cats fastened to the keys so that the beasts howled and screeched as the chords were struck. In Antwerp **Pieter Coecke van Aelst** provided a polychrome figure of the giant Antigonus—mythical founder of the city who was reputed to have cut off the heads of all smuggling traders and thrown them into the Scheldt; and he led a team of more than two hundred artists including **Hieronymus Wellens de Cock,** just back from Rome, **Antonio van Palerme,** decorative painter, dealer and exploiter of young talents, **Frans Floris** (Pls. 335, 351, 353) Antwerp Master at about the age of thirty in 1547 who was co-director of the pageant and painted thirty-five figures in five weeks for this occasion, and probably the one-legged **Ryckaert Aertsz (Ryck-met-de-Stelt)** who was earning his living by painting nudes in allegories and mythologies for various artists and was a friend of **Floris.** In 1555 there was a Hanseatic Golden Fleece Pageant in Antwerp and designs were made for it by **Hubert Goltzius** who had been a pupil of **Lambert Lombard** and was thirty at that date.

As before, some painters were employed on civic commissions in the various towns; and the companies of civic guardsmen—archers, crossbowmen, fencers and so forth, more sporting clubs than para-military formations—and the trade guilds and corporations ordered portrait groups subscribed by the members. The business life of Bruges is evoked by **Pieter Jansz Pourbus** in his portraits of *Jan Fernaguut and his wife* (Pls. 336, 337) where the background shows shops in the Maison de la Coq and wine weighing on the Place de la Grue (an operation already seen in the background of **Memlinc's** *S. John altar* (Pl. 111)). But Bruges continued to decline while Antwerp became ever more the centre of shipping, commerce and banking and the point of attraction for artists; a whole new quarter was added to Antwerp in these years and speculators in real estate made fortunes—one such being a brewer named Gillis van Schoonbeke who employed the **Forties Master** to paint his portrait (Pl. 319); and another bourgeois patron in Antwerp at this time was one Jan van den Biest, a soapboiler and sheriff, who commissioned a triptych for an old women's almshouse from **Pieter Aertsen** in 1546. The trade in pictures offered publicly for sale was still controlled by the Painters Guilds in the various places and by dealers who operated under licence from the Guilds; and in Antwerp, as the old picture market, established in 1460 near the Cathedral, was now insufficient for requirements, a new market, the Schilders Pand, where pictures were all the time on sale, was installed on the upper floor of the Bourse in 1540.

Among the professional portraitists and other painters of portraits **Bernaert van Orley** was available in Brussels till 1541 and put figures of Charles V and his wife and Louis and Mary of Hungary in his S. Gudule windows and painted portraits of Charles, his brother the Archduke Ferdinand, Christina Duchess of Milan (also painted by **Gossaert** (Pl. 294) and by Holbein as noted), and several of the Regent. **Jan Vermeyen** was also available in Brussels in the intervals of his journeys abroad. **Jan van Scorel** (Pls. 300, 301) who declined an invitation from Francis I to become his Court Painter was available in Utrecht; his pupil or associate **Marten van Heemskerck**, a farmer's son, produced the vigorous uncompromising *Portrait of his father* (Pl. 306) in Haarlem in 1532 at the age of thirty-four; **Heemskerck's** pupil **Cornelis van Gouda** was taken up as a portraitist in Court circles, became a notorious drunkard and eventually, van Mander tells us, a dauber ('een knoeier'); **Cornelis Visscher** also of Gouda began his career there about 1540. In Amsterdam the **Amsterdam Armed Arquebusiers Painter** produced in 1531, the subscription group *Seventeen arquebusiers of the A company in armour* (Pl. 298) with a fantastic background of craggy rocks, viaducts and ruined buildings, and angels in the sky suggesting some connection with a pilgrimage; **Dirk Jacobsz** painted subscription groups of Civic guardsmen all through the period; **Jacob Cornelisz van Oostsanen** painted the taut *Portrait of a man* (Pl. 302), probably a self-portrait, a few months before he died at over sixty in 1533; in the same year **Cornelis Anthonisz**, just over thirty, painted a *Banquet of seventeen Civic Guardsmen* (Pl. 299) and infused variety and intimacy into the archaic formalism of the **Malines Guild of S. George Master** (Pl. 146) which was still adhered to by **Dirck Jacobsz;** and somewhere in Holland **Simon Jacobsz** was probably at work on portraits by 1545 when he was twenty-five. In Bruges **Pieter Jansz Pourbus** began his career about 1541; and in his fine portraits of *Jan Fernaguut and his wife* (Pls. 336, 337) painted some ten years later, when he was just over thirty, he achieved serenity by simple silhouetting of the figures. The Calvinist **Nicolas de Neufchatel (Lucidel)** seems to have been launched as a portrait painter in Mons from the middle of the forties. In Antwerp **Jan Gossaert** (Pl. 294) may have had some commissions in this period before he died about 1535; **Joos van Cleve (Joos van der Beke)** who died about 1540, was renowned as a portraitist (though no signed or documented examples are now known to be extant); **Sotte Cleve** (Crazy Cleve) seems also to have painted some portraits; **Willem Key** (Pl. 387) born at Breda, was available in Antwerp from 1542 when he became Antwerp Master; the **Forties Master** (Pl. 319) and the **Antwerp Forties Painter** (Pl. 320) seem also to have practised in Antwerp; and **Steven van der Meulen** started work there as a portraitist in 1552. **Antonis Mor** began his career in Antwerp at the end of the forties when he was just about thirty; he painted *Bishop (later Cardinal) Granvella* (Pl. 341) in 1549 when the Bishop, aged thirty-two, was already a trusted agent of the Emperor and already, as the portrait shows, a most formidable person; and perhaps about this time the **Paris Granvella's Dwarf Painter** portrayed Granvella's huge dog and his dwarf with the tormented soul (Pl. 339)—a composition known, I imagine, to Velazquez when he composed his famous *English dwarf with a dog* a hundred years later. **Mor's** *Archduke Maximilian* (later Emperor) (Pl. 332) and *Maria of Austria* (Pl. 333) were painted in Rome in 1550 and 1551; his *Catherine of Austria, Queen of Portugal* (Pl. 342) in Portugal the next year for Mary of Hungary, the Queen's sister; he was resident in Brussels in 1553 when he wrote a testimonial for **Conrad Schot** a former pupil and assistant probably employed on the clothes and jewels in his pictures; and his *Queen Mary of England* (Pl. 350A) was painted in London in 1554 for Prince Philip. All **Mor's** portraits exhibit grave immobility and horrifying pomp; there is grave pomp also in the portrait groups by the **Brussels Micault Triptych Painter** (Pls. 321, 322) which probably date from the early fifties; and it is pleasant to turn from these pomposities to the young bourgeoises so tenderly observed by **Catherina van Hemessen** who was only twenty-three when she produced the enchanting *Lady with a little dog* (Pl. 345) in 1551 and had already then been working for some years.

Landscapes by specialists, often with small religious and genre figures by other artists, were produced in numbers; but we know little about them as only a small proportion of this output has survived. In some of the extant pieces it is, however, possible to detect the influence of **Patinir** and the use of drawings made by the painters themselves or others in

Italy or the mountainous regions of France. Of the older landscape painters, **Claes Rogier,** died in Malines in 1534; **Hans Tons** also died early in the period; **Frans Crabbe,** whose landscapes and trees in his religious pieces were praised by van Mander, was at work in Malines till 1553; and his former pupil **Frans Verbeeck,** Malines Master in 1531, painted landscapes from that time onwards. **Anna de Smytere** of Ghent (mother of van Mander's master **Lucas de Heere**) painted miniature landscapes including one with a windmill, a miller, a horse and cart and people walking on the hillside 'so small that half an ear of wheat could cover it'. **Jan de Hollander,** whose birth and death dates are unknown, was praised by Lampsonius later in the century for having chosen to paint landscapes well rather than portraits, figure pieces and the Deity badly; he was followed, van Mander tells us, in some technical procedures by **Pieter Bruegel,** and he was often seen leaning from the window of his Antwerp studio examining the tones and colours of the sky; his wife, van Mander adds, travelled in Brabant and Flanders and sold his pictures in the markets there 'en verdiende daarmee veel geld'. **Hendrik (Herri) met de Bles** (Henry with the White Lock) of whom the records are confused, is described by van Mander as a follower of **Patinir;** he often inserted a little owl in his pictures; and he is perhaps identical with **Herri de Patinir** who was Antwerp Master in 1535. **Cornelis Massys,** son of **Quinten Massys** and Antwerp Master in 1531, painted rocks and plains in the *Return of the Prodigal* (Pl. 316) in 1538, the *Landscape with S. Jerome* (Pl. 329) in 1547 and died in the early fifties. **Lucas Gassel,** still active in Brussels, painted his *Mountainous landscape with mine workers* (Pl. 328) in 1544 and his panoramic *Landscape with Judith and Thamar* (Pl. 327) in 1548. **Patinir's** follower **Hans Keynooghe** moved from Malines to Antwerp in the thirties or forties. **Mathys Wellens de Cock,** who was Antwerp Master in 1540 and died young and in poverty in 1548, was regarded as an outstanding landscape specialist in his day; he was the first, van Mander tells us, to paint landscapes with more variety (met meer afwisseling) in the new Italian or 'antique' style and he was 'remarkably inventive in composition'; he had **Hans Keynooghe** as his associate for some time. **Christian van den Queborne,** active in Antwerp from 1545, had **Adriaen de Weerdt** among his pupils. The Brussels-born Calvinist **Joos van Liere** described by van Mander as an 'uitnemend meester' of landscape in oil and distemper and a tapestry designer, was established in Antwerp in the forties and Dean of the Guild there by 1546. **Jacob Grimmer** (Pls. 430, 444), pupil of **Mathys Wellens de Cock** and also of **Christian van den Queborne,** was Antwerp Master in 1547. **Hieronymus Wellens de Cock,** younger brother of **Mathys,** began as a landscape painter, was Antwerp Master, aged about thirty-five, in 1545 and then became a conspicuous engraver and publisher of prints. **Pieter Bom,** Antwerp painter of landscapes in distemper, was probably at work aged twenty by 1550 and **Hendrik van Cleve,** landscape painter and topographic draughtsman, from the early fifties. Some landscape specialist, whose identity is unknown, may have provided the landscape in a *Procession to Calvary* dated 1552 for **Pieter Aertsen** (Pls. 356, 357, 360) who painted the figures and signed it: **Frans Mostaert** (Pl. 371) a pupil of **Herri met de Bles,** and his twin brother **Gillis Mostaert** (Pl. 348) were both Antwerp Masters at twenty in 1554; and **Pieter Bruegel** (Pls. 381, 382, 390-3, 405, 407) who was Antwerp Master in 1551 and was abroad thereafter till the end of 1553 and became a staff draughtsman in the print-producing business of **Hieronymus Wellens de Cock** about 1554, made some landscape drawings in the last three years of this period.

In rural genre **Frans Verbeeck** is known to have painted a comic *Peasants' wedding* and similar subjects; and **Cornelis Massys** made drawings, for engravings, showing *Beggars and peasants eating, Peasant women fighting,* and '*The blind leading the blind*'. The peasants who

122

trundled barrows in the building scene by **Jan van Eyck** (Pl. 18) and gesticulated round **Bosch's** hay cart (Pl. 165) now work the mines and shear their sheep in pictures by **Lucas Gassel** (Pls. 327, 328); **Pieter Balten,** another painter of peasant scenes, was Antwerp Master by 1540; **Marten van Cleve** (Pls. 394, 396, 406) was active in Antwerp from 1551; and **Pieter Bruegel** (Pls. 381, 382, 390-3, 405, 407) may have made some peasant drawings in 1554 and 1555.

The genre painting also included high-life, bourgeois and professional scenes and low-life peasant interiors. The banqueting Burgundian princes and their wives in the picture by the **Melbourne Miracles Painter** (Pl. 149) are transformed in the *Allegorical love feast* (Pl. 331) by **Pieter Jansz Pourbus** to Flemish nobles with fashionable beards escaping from the Habsburg Court to a woodland picnic with light women. The devout young ladies reading missals by their firesides, recorded by fifteenth-century artists like the **Madrid Werl Wings Painter** (Pl. 44), and the **van Eycks'** church choir of singing and organ playing maidens (Pls. 9, 17) have become young bourgeoise ladies playing music of their choice; there is a young musician for example with large head and small chubby hands performing it would seem alone and listening intently to the chord she has struck in the picture reproduced here by the **Worcester Girl at Clavichord Painter** (Pl. 311). The **Female Half Lengths Master** (Pl. 314), an artist with a feeling for formal pattern, has grouped a trio of music loving ladies at a table in a panelled room and given all three, in the classical spirit, the same idealized type-face—(a type incidentally that seems related to the aesthetic favoured by some artists at the Court of Fontainebleau). In 1538 (with the *Miser in his Cabinet* (Pl. 236) by the **Bruges Death and the Miser Painter** and the *Banker and his wife in their counting house* (Pl. 235) by **Quinten Massys** as precedents) **Marinus van Reymerswaele** produced the *Moneychanger and his wife* (Pl. 318) where the banker's lady gently fingering her missal in the picture by **Quinten Massys** has become a usurer's wife turning the pages of a ledger with grasping, predatory hands; and the **London Tax Collectors Painter** gives us, possibly in this period, his *Two tax collectors* (Pl. 324) where the figures are again in archaistic clothes and the popular feeling against such people is relentlessly exploited in cold and glittering technique. The theme of the painter at work was continued in 1532 by **Marten van Heemskerck** who puts a bespectacled painter at his easel and the Virgin posing on the studio platform and imbues the scene with an imaginative quality by inserting a poet as inspirer of the painter and an angel with a flaming torch to illuminate the sacred figures (Pls. 303, 304); and **Lancelot Blondeel** in *S. Luke painting the Virgin* (Pl. 330) shows a painter at his easel and the Virgin before him, and a studio servant grinding colours in the background—a detail not included in the earlier works by the **London S. Luke Painter** (Pl. 186) and the **Fogg S. Luke Painter** (Pl. 260)—and invests this genre piece with a cere-monial and gracious air by surrounding the scene with decorative ornament in the precious taste of the Bruges intelligentsia already referred to in my last chapter. Kitchen scenes were painted by the **Brussels Kitchen Scene Painter** (Pl. 359) and by **Pieter Aertsen** (Pls. 356, 357, 360) who was Antwerp Master in 1535 and living with **Jan Mandyn** the 'spook' painter. Tavern and brothel scenes, discreetly labelled *The Prodigal Son*, and other pictures with low-life characters were produced by **Marten van Cleve,** by the **Brussels Piper Painter** (Pl. 326) and by **Jan Sanders van Hemessen** a most ingenious composer delighting in spon-taneous postures and intricate chains of arms, seen here in two tavern pieces *The Prodigal Son* dated 1536 (Pl. 305) and *The Prodigal Son* dated 1543 (Pl. 325). Similar scenes occur in the paintings reproduced by the **Prodigal Son Master** who tells the whole story of the prodigal's career in various corners of his picture and gives linear grace and elegance to all the figures including the strolling minstrels (Pl. 395), and by the **Brussels Prodigal Son Painter** (Pl. 358) who shows us a pretty prostitute wearing the same cape and headdress as the rich Bruges merchant's wife painted by **Pieter Jansz Pourbus** (Pl. 337).

Still-life continued to be a feature in many pictures and it was often produced by studio assistants or specialists called in from outside as we know from van Mander who describes the division of labour in Malines studios producing pictures on linen (imitating tapestries) where one painter was charged with the heads and hands, another with the clothes and accessories, another with the landscape and another with the lettering of inscriptions. Musical still-life, which goes back to the **van Eyck's** *Ghent Altarpiece* (Pls. 9, 17), is now seen in the picture by the **Female Half Lengths Master** (Pl. 314) where the ladies are provided with lute and flute and a legible score to perform from; in the picture by the **Brussels Prodigal Son Painter** (Pl. 358) where the prodigal, who has been singing to lute accompaniment, has the legible song book before him on the table while he fondles a girl, and a servant behind them puts clean linen on a bed; and in the *Allegorical love feast* (Pl. 331) by **Pieter Jansz Pourbus** where a sheet of music on the table has been identified as a song by Thomas Crecquillon. A clavichord of the time is shown in the room, with its curious bottles in the background, by the **Worcester Girl at Clavichord Painter** (Pl. 311); drum and fife appear in the tavern scene by the **Prodigal Son Master** (Pl. 395) and bagpipes in the low-life scenes by **Jan Sanders van Hemessen** (Pl. 305) and the **Brussels Piper Painter** (Pl. 325). Books, documents, half-burnt candles and piles of coins are painted in the sharpest imaginable detail in the pictures by **Marinus van Reymerswaele** (Pl. 318) and the **London Tax Collectors Painter** (Pl. 324). Bas-reliefs, the *Murder of Abel* and *David and Goliath*, are on the walls in **Pieter Coecke van Aelst's** *Last Supper* (Pl. 307); and **Marten van Heemskerck** sits his painter on a stool decorated with a bas-relief showing *Europa and the bull* and provides him with a fantastic term as central shaft for his easel (Pl. 304). The symbolic still-life on the square table in the *Last Supper* by **Dirk Bouts** (Pl. 58) has now been secularized in the *Banquet of Civic Guardsmen* (Pl. 299) by **Cornelis Anthonisz** and though the oblong table in *The Last Supper* (Pl. 307) by **Pieter Coecke van Aelst**—recalling the oblong table in Leonardo da Vinci's composition—bears the symbolic still-life, a basket with empty fish shells now appears as an addition on the floor. There are oblong tables also and appropriate still-life in *Christ in the House of Simon* (Pl. 274) by the **Abbey of Dilighem Master** and *The Marriage Feast at Cana* (Pl. 289) by **Jan van Coninxloo;** bowls of fruit and flagons of wine are disposed on round tables to refresh the Flemish nobles and the Prodigal Son in pictures shown here by **Pieter Jansz Pourbus** (Pl. 331) the **Brussels Prodigal Son Painter** (Pl. 358) and **Jan Sanders van Hemessen** (Pls. 305, 325); and **Pieter Aertsen** first won fame in the thirties by a *Butcher's Stall*, where a flayed ox, an ox's head, joints, sausages and other raw eatables were displayed. **Mathys Brill the elder** was active as a still-life and fruit painter by 1550.

Satirical and 'spook' pictures in the **Bosch** tradition were popular and the *Temptation of S. Anthony* was thus a subject in demand. **Jan Mandyn** of Haarlem who worked in **Bosch's** manner and painted a *Temptation of S. Anthony* was established in Antwerp from the early thirties. **Pieter Huys,** Antwerp Master in 1545, painted a *Temptation of S. Anthony* in 1547 and similar subjects in later years (Pls. 412, 413). **Frans Verbeeck** active in Malines, painted a *Temptation of S. Anthony* and a *S. Christopher* 'met veel gespook'. **Frans Mostaert,** who also painted such pictures may have produced some in 1554 and 1555; and **Pieter Bruegel** made 'spook' drawings in **Bosch's** manner for **Hieronymus Wellens de Cock** to publish as engravings.

Among the painters of religious subjects some were traditional or archaistic and others Romanist or mannerist. In Brussels **Cornelis van Coninxloo** (Pl. 276) was probably still active; the **Abbey of Dilighem Master** painted *Christ in the house of Simon* (Pls. 273-5) with its ornate setting about 1537; **Colyn de Coter** (Pl. 280) seems to have died about 1538; **Bernaert van Orley** (Pls. 248, 254, 256-9, 282) spent his last years on a triptych commissioned by Margaret of Austria's executors for the Church of Brou but never dispatched there because Charles V acquired it for himself and instructed Granvella to arrange for another to be painted to replace it; **Jan van Coninxloo,** who moved to Antwerp at sixty-three in 1552, continued the Romanist characters of his *Nativity* (Pl. 309) in an elaborate triptych *The Lineage of S. Anne* with wings showing *Joachim's sacrifice rejected* and *The Death of S. Anne* in 1546, and also in *The marriage feast at Cana* (Pl. 289) which was painted —the bride's clothes suggest—about 1550; **Michiel Coxie** (Pls. 308, 352) designed windows for S. Gudule, painted a *Christ crucified between the thieves* for Alsemberg and, probably in this period, a triptych showing *Scenes from the life of the Virgin* (Pl. 310) for S. Gudule as well as the religious subjects acquired by Charles V already recorded; and the **Brussels Micault Triptych Painter** produced an academic Romanist *Raising of Lazarus* for the Micault family altar in S. Gudule with the imposing portraits (Pls. 321, 322) already referred to, on the wings. In Bruges **Albert Cornelis** (Pl. 250) died in 1532; **Ambrosius Benson** (Pl. 278) was Dean of the Painters Guild in 1537 and died in 1550; **Adriaen Ysenbrandt** was active till 1551 (but as already mentioned, no pictures known to be by him are known to be extant); **Lancelot Blondeel** followed his *Martyrdom of SS. Cosmas and Damian* (Pls. 270, 271, 272) by a *Virgin and Child enthroned in an arch with SS. Luke and Eligius* painted for the Guild of S. Luke's chapel in S. Sauveur in 1545 and his *S. Luke painting the Virgin* (Pl. 330) already mentioned in its genre aspect, for the same Guild that year; and in 1551 **Pieter Jansz Pourbus** aged about thirty-two, was commissioned by the magistrates of the Franc to paint a *Last Judgement* (Pl. 334) where, doubtless directed by a theologian, he placed above Christ an angel with a lily on one side and an angel with a naked sword on the other, and, doubtless on his own initiative, gave the virtuous men rising from their graves the flowing beards in fashion at the moment. **Frans Minnebroer** was still working in Malines in 1540 and **Frans Crabbe** painted religious subjects for churches there and in the environs till 1553; **Vincent Sellaer** who painted a *Christ blessing children* in 1538 is recorded in Malines in 1544 and **Vincent Geldersman** painted a *Descent from the Cross* 'with the Magdalene washing the feet of Christ' for Malines, S. Rombout at this time or later. In Louvain both **Peter van der Hofstadt** (Pl. 366) and **Jan van Rillaert** were still working. In Ypres **Karel Foort (Karel van Yperen)** who had been to Italy and was painting religious subjects which made him famous by the end of the period, took **Simon Jacobsz** from Gouda as his pupil before 1540 and **Peter Vlerick** from Courtrai about 1554. In Liège **Lambert Lombard** who was in France and Germany in 1533 and 1534 and in Italy in 1537 and 1538, was influential as a Romanist teacher in the middle thirties, when **Lambert Suavius, Frans Floris** (Pls. 335, 351, 353) and **Willem Key** (Pl. 387) were his pupils, and again after his return from Rome with drawings of ancient monuments and sculpture, when **Hubert Goltzius, Jean Ramey** and **Domenicus Lampsonius** were among his later pupils; he was employed on frescoes and other paintings for churches in Liège, and his drawings or paintings recorded by engravings include a *Dead Christ on the knees of the Virgin* published in 1545, the *Last Supper* dedicated to Bishop Granvella and *S. Mary Magdalene anointing the feet of Christ* both engraved and published by **Hieronymus Wellens de Cock** in 1551, *Christ and the Adulteress* and *Esther and Ahasuerus* published in 1553, and *Moses striking water from the* *rock* published in 1555; but no paintings known to be by him are known to be extant.

In Antwerp religious subjects were still being painted by some mannerists including the **Solomon Master** whose animated triptych (Pls. 286-8) shows the Zidonian concubine posturing in a yellow gown of the 1550 fashion, King Solomon in a red mantle, the Queen of Sheba in gleaming gold, the King's dog asleep at his feet (like the dog at the feet of the Emperor Otho (Pl. 69)), and Solomon's attendant flamboyantly panached in the scene where God chides the King for his idolatry. **Pieter Coecke van Aelst** who painted *The Last Supper* (Pl. 307) before his visit to Turkey in 1533 and worked in Antwerp again from 1534, had **Pieter Bruegel** as a pupil living in his house in the later forties; and **Jan Mandyn** as noted was active through the period. **Jan van Amstel** who painted a *Crufixion* with more than two hundred figures seems to have died before 1544; **Joos van Cleve (Joos van der Beke)** continued to paint religious subjects till about 1540 and **Sotte Cleve** also painted some though no signed or documented religious pieces by either of these artists is known to be extant. **Jan van der Elburcht,** Master in 1535, produced a *Miraculous draught of fishes* for the Fishmongers Chapel in Antwerp Cathedral before 1553. **Jan Massys** (Pls. 315, 361-3) may have painted some religious subjects between 1531, when he became Antwerp Master, and his banishment in 1544. **Cornelis Massys** (or a figure painter working with him) gave touching illustration to the words 'But when he was yet a great way off his father saw him and had compassion and ran and fell on his neck and kissed him' in the *Return of the Prodigal* (Pl. 316) dated 1538. **Pieter Aertsen** (Pls. 356, 357) who painted his *Crucifixion* triptych for an Antwerp almshouse in 1546, had **Joachim Beuckelaer** (Pls. 398, 399, 400) his wife's nephew as a pupil about 1550; in 1552 he painted his *Road to Calvary* (where the procession is escorted by Spanish lancers, and genre episodes anticipate the later treatment of the subject by **Pieter Bruegel** (Pl. 379)); and, before 1555, he collaborated with **Jan Vredeman de Vries** (Pl. 462) in a *Calling of Matthew*. **Jan Sanders van Hemessen** worked in Antwerp till he moved to Haarlem about 1550, produced a *Christ driving the money-changers from the Temple* in 1536 and, in 1544, an *Ecce Homo* where Christ is surrounded by grimacing faces in the tradition of the **Princeton Christ before Pilate Painter** (Pl. 174) and where two children in the foreground caused Sir Joshua Reynolds to write 'This picture is not mentioned for its excellence but because we see many pictures of his and particularly his children which are attributed in every collection to Leonardo da Vinci'; and in the same year **Hemessen** painted the impressive *Virgin and Child* (Pl. 317) where the model for the foreground girl in his *Prodigal Son* of 1536 (Pl. 305) is transfigured to noble beauty for the Virgin in the vine-covered arbour (influenced perhaps by Albert Dürer) and the base of a majestic pyramid is constructed by the unusual placing of the legs. Newcomers painting religious subjects in Antwerp included **Willem Key, Jan van der Straet, Lambert van Noort, Marcellus Coffermans, Gillis Mostaert** and **Frans Floris.** Of these **Willem Key** (Pl. 387), was Antwerp Master in 1542 and signed a *Lamentation* in 1553; **Jan van der Straet** (known as **Stradanus**), a pupil of **Pieter Aertsen** was Antwerp Master in 1545 and went abroad in 1548; **Lambert van Noort** (Pl. 402), Master in 1549, painted a Romanist *Nativity with Adoration of the Shepherds* for the Painters' Guild in 1555; **Marcel Helmon** of whom nothing seems known except the *Adoration of the Shepherds* reproduced here (Pl. 401) may have painted it in Antwerp about 1550; **Marcellus Coffermans** (Pl. 403) was Master in 1549; and **Gillis Mostaert** (Pl. 348), a pupil of **Jan Mandyn,** was Master, as noted, in 1554. From 1547 onwards **Frans Floris** turned out Romanist compositions and designs for glass and tapestry from an atelier with numerous pupils and assistants who included **Hendrik van Cleve, Lucas de Heere, Marten van Cleve** (Pls. 394, 396, 406), **An-**

thonis Blocklandt (Pl. 420), **Marten de Vos** (Pls. 364, 397, 429), **Crispiaen van den Broeck** (Pl. 409), **Benjamin Sammeling** and **Hendrik van den Broeck**; in 1553 he visited Holland to instal an altarpiece commissioned by the Delft Confraternity of the Holy Cross, and he stopped for a time in Leyden; back in Antwerp in 1554 he was much applauded for the *Fall of the Rebel Angels* (Pl. 335) painted for the chapel of the Fencers in Antwerp Cathedral, with life-size muscular nude figures based on Michelangelo's *Last Judgement*; here, following some theologian's transcript of the passage in Revelation, he shows the Archangel Michael and his angels casting down Satan in the form of a seven-headed dragon, and Satan's legions in the form of humans with beasts' heads, while the Woman 'clothed with the sun and the moon under her feet' is in the firmament behind, and her Man-child is 'caught up unto God and to his throne'; and the student will find it intriguing to compare this picture with the *Hell* scene painted by the **New York Crucifixion and Last Judgement Painter** at the outset of our story (Pls. 4, 8).

In the Northern provinces **Lucas van Leyden** (Pls. 187, 189, 267, 277, 290-3) painted a *Healing of the blind man at Jericho* in 1531, was afflicted with persecution mania in his last years, and died in Leyden at thirty-nine in 1533; **Dammes Claes de Hoey** who married **Lucas van Leyden's** daughter in 1532 and inherited part of the contents of his studio, seems to have painted some religious subjects; **Cornelis Engelbrechtsz** (Pls. 210-13, 229, 230, 232, 233) died in Leyden aged sixty-five in 1533; **Cornelis van Oostsanen** (Pls. 265, 268, 302) died there the same year at about sixty-three; and **Cornelis Cornelisz** (son of **Engelbrechtsz**) died there at fifty-one in 1544. **Aert Claesz van Leyden,** active there through the period, painted a *Crucifixion*, a *Christ carrying the Cross*, a *Last Judgement* (with portraits of the Montvoort family on the wings), a *Crossing of the Red Sea* and a *Judgement of Solomon*; van Mander describes him as a bohemian of talent who spent his earnings on merry parties with his friends and played his German flute as he traversed the dark streets from one tavern to another; and at fifty-five in 1553 he declined an invitation from **Frans Floris** to join his circle in Antwerp preferring to continue his own mode of life. **Jan van Scorel** (Pls. 284, 300, 301) who worked in Breda Castle for the House of Nassau in 1541, still had his headquarters in Utrecht and may have painted some religious subjects recorded by van Mander in these years; and the intense and individual Haarlem painter **Marten van Heemskerck** who went abroad in 1532, after giving his *S. Luke painting the Virgin* (Pls. 303, 304) to the local guild, was back by 1537, produced a *Martyrdom of S. Lawrence* for the Alkmaar Church in 1540, a *Crucifixion* in 1543, wings for a sculptured altarpiece (later attached to the *Massacre of the Innocents* by Cornelis of Haarlem) for Haarlem, S. Bavon in 1546, a grisaille *Aaron and Moses with the brazen serpent* (Pl. 354) which shows him even more passionately impressed than **Gossaert** (Pl. 247) by antique sculpture, in 1551, and a *Last Judgement* in 1554.

Visits to Rome, Florence, Venice and other Italian cities were made by many of these painters of religious subjects as Italianate modes were favoured by the church; and these visits also helped the artists to give a Romanist air to mythologies with nudes which nobles and others bought for their collections. Some portrait, landscape and genre painters also went to Italy at this time. A stay of several years, with Rome as headquarters was now quite frequent; and in Antwerp there was a Romanist Fraternity of which only artists who had been to Italy could be members. **Pieter de Kempener** (Pl. 367), in Italy since 1530, was in Rome and Venice and patronized by Cardinal Grimani until 1536; **Michiel Coxie** arrived in Rome in 1531, met Vasari there in 1532, painted frescoes in Sta. Maria dell'Anima (the church of the Flemish Catholics) and returned to Flanders in 1539. **Marten van**

Heemskerck reached Rome at the end of 1532 and made many drawings of monuments and antique sculpture; in 1536 he joined a team of Flemish and German artists designing triumphal arches for Charles V's Pageant Entry into Rome when the Flemings, Vasari tells us, produced 'cose stupende' because they were 'riscaldoti dal furor del vino' when at work; and soon after that he returned to Haarlem—though he may have paid a second visit in the early fifties because his *Aaron and Moses with the brazen serpent* (Pl. 354) of 1551 shows an acquaintance, I think, with Michelangelo's *Last Judgement* (finished 1541) as well as an enthusiasm for antique sculpture like the 'Laocoon 'group, his picture titled *Bulls fighting in a Roman amphitheatre* is dated 1552 and his *Self-portrait with the Colosseum in the background* (Pl. 365) dates from 1553. **Karel Foort** came from Ypres probably in the early thirties, worked in Rome and probably in Venice (as a later picture is described by van Mander as 'een beetje Tintoretto-achtig') and seems to have returned before 1540. **Jan Stephen van Calcar** left the Netherlands about 1536 with a girl from Dordrecht whose parents kept an inn where travellers disappeared; he then went to Venice to study under Titian and subsequently to Naples where he met Vasari in 1545 and painted portraits in Titian's manner till he died about 1550. The eager archeologist, **Lambert Lombard,** who went to Rome with Cardinal Reginald Pole to collect antiques for the Prince Bishop of Liège in 1537, made drawings of Roman architecture and antique sculpture, and produced a painting for Pope Paul III before returning to Liège in 1539. **Frans Floris** arrived in Rome in 1541, made drawings of Michelangelo's *Last Judgement*, visited Venice, supplied a triptych for a church near Rapallo, returned to Antwerp in 1547 and painted in that year a *Mars and Venus in Vulcan's net* with gods and goddesses of Olympus as spectators. **Jan Massys** (Pls. 315, 361-3) may have visited Italy after his banishment in 1544. **Jan van der Straet** (Stradanus) was in Venice and Florence about 1550 and worked soon after with Vasari in Rome. **Antonis Mor** was in Rome in 1550-51 and painted there the *Maximilian II as Archduke* (Pl. 332) and *Maria of Austria* (Pl. 333) already referred to. **Hendrik van den Broeck** of Malines, already mentioned as a pupil of **Frans Floris,** went to Italy about 1551, worked first for the Medicis in Florence and then for churches in various places, and remained in Italy where he became known as **Arrigo Fiammingo,** or **Henricus Malinus** or **Henricus Paludanus.** His younger brother **Crispiaen van den Broeck** (Pl. 409) who also went to Italy, and probably at the same time, was back in Antwerp in 1555. **Marten de Vos** (Pls. 364, 397, 429) arrived in Italy, at about twenty, in 1552, visited Rome and Florence and then worked in Venice as assistant to Tintoretto. **Lambert van Noort** (Pl. 402) must have gone at some time to Italy unless his Romanism was entirely derived from Italian engravings and from paintings by other Romanists in Antwerp; the same applies to **Marcellus Coffermans** (Pl. 403); and it is possible to presume a visit also by **Vincent Geldersman** of Malines who painted, van Mander tells us, a half-length *Leda* with two eggs, a *Susanna* and a *Cleopatra with the asp* which became very popular and were frequently repeated.

The landscape painters and topographic draughtsmen visiting Italy in this period included **Herri met de Bles, Mathys Wellens de Cock, Hieronymus Wellens de Cock, Hendrik van Cleve, Michiel de Gast, Gregorius Beerings** and **Pieter Bruegel.** Of these **Herri met de Bles** was known as **Civetta** (Little Owl) and may have worked for the d'Este court at Ferrara. **Mathys Wellens de Cock** was in Italy just before or just after 1540. **Hieronymus Wellens de Cock** met Vasari in Rome in the early forties. **Hendrik van Cleve** made topographic drawings in Rome and other places in the fifties after becoming Antwerp Master in 1551. **Michiel de Gast** was drawing Roman landscapes with ruins from 1538 till the end of the period; and **Gregorius Beerings** arrived from Malines at the end of the forties, painted Roman ruins and a picture called *The Flood* 'showing only rain, the waters and the Ark', and returned to Malines about 1554. **Pieter Bruegel** went to Italy in 1552; he travelled there through France and I like to fancy that he talked with Rabelais and saw somehow Jean Fouquet's miniatures for the *Antiquités Judaïques* with their marvellous mountain landscapes; in Italy, and probably Savoy, he drew mountainous scenery and may have gone as far south as the Straits of Messina; he visited Rome where he met the miniaturist Giulio Clovio; he may also have gone to Venice, as he must have had, I think, some *Last Supper* or *Wedding Feast at Cana* by Tintoretto in his mind when he planned his *Peasant Wedding* (Pl. 405); and he was back in Antwerp, as mentioned, at the end of 1553. These landscape painters and draughtsmen were attracted to Italy because there was a vogue there for Flemish landscapes. In 1535, for example, more than three hundred Flemish landscapes were imported from the Netherlands by one dealer, and Duke Frederick II of Mantua had a number in his collection. This taste, understandably, was not shared by Michelangelo; and he protested against it in conversation with Vittoria Colonna and the Portuguese painter, Francisco de Hollanda, who tells us that he said: 'In Flanders they paint very green fields, shaded by trees, and rivers and bridges, which they call landscapes and in which they put many little figures here and there; such paintings may make a good effect on certain eyes but there is neither reason nor art in them; they lack symmetry and proportion, and no regard has been paid to selection and grandeur; there is no body in such painting and no strength . . . the artists try to depict perfectly so many things that they fail to succeed in perfecting any.' As this conversation took place in 1538 Michelangelo could only have been thinking of pictures imported before that date—works perhaps by **Joachim Patinir** (Pls. 200, 241, 244, 245, 246), **Claes Rogier, Hans Keynooghe** and **Jan de Hollander,** and the landscape adepts who provided the wooded scenes in pictures like those reproduced here by the **Florence (Poggio Imperiale) Crucifixion Painter** (Pl. 133) and the **Bruges Baptism of Christ Painter** (Pls. 201, 218); and he might possibly have seen some early works by **Lucas Gassel** (Pls. 327, 328) or **Herri met de Bles.** In any event his protest, which was private, was without effect on the contemporary market, for Flemish landscapes continued to be collected in Italy all through the period and they were widely admired, Vasari tells us, for their picturesque characters and their atmospheric perspective.

A number of Flemish painters also visited or settled in Portugal and Spain. One **Christoph of Utrecht** went to Portugal as a young man, worked with the Portuguese painter Figueiredo in Lamego in 1534 and settled soon after in Lisbon where his wife denounced to the Inquisition her coal merchant who had spoken disrespectfully of the King, the Pope and the Holy Office; and **Antonis Mor** went to Portugal, as noted, in 1552 to paint Queen Catherine (Pl. 342) Mary of Hungary's sister. **Pieter de Kempener (Pedro de Campaña)** (Pl. 367) who left Venice for Spain about 1536, was employed in Seville Cathedral when he was thirty-four in 1537 and remained in Seville for the rest of the period; in 1548 he painted for Santa Cruz chapel a *Descent from the Cross*, with life-size figures, which became very famous and is now in Seville Cathedral; and he had many commissions for the local churches. **Ferdinand Sturm** of Zierickzee was also in Spain (where he was known as **Esturme** or **Desturme**) by 1537 when he became a citizen of Seville, and he worked for churches there and in Cadiz and Arcos de la Frontera between 1539 and 1542; in 1547 he painted a polyptych commissioned by the Count of Oreña (later Duke of Osuna); and in 1555 an *Immaculate Conception* for the burial chapel of the Osuna family in Osuna, and a polyptych with the *Mass of S. Gregory*, the *Resurrection, The Four Evangelists* and *Saints* for the Capella de las Evangelistas in Seville Cathedral. **Francisco Frutet** is recorded as a Fleming working for religious houses in Seville in the middle forties and specifically as the painter of a triptych with the *Crucifixion* in the centre and *Christ bearing the Cross*, the *Virgin and Child*, the *Descent from the Cross* and *S. Bernard* on the wings, commissioned for the Hospital of SS. Cosmas and Damian (known as Las Bubas). **Jan Cornelisz Vermeyen** drew a *Tourney at Toledo* and signed it 'ut presens viderat Joannus Maius pictor' in 1539. The **Brussels Micault Triptych Painter** may have visited Spain as his picture (Pl. 322) is said to show the aqueduct at Segovia; and **Philippe Vos** seems to have gone to Spain at some time with the Emperor.

Of the painters who went to France **Joos van Cleve** was probably in Paris in the thirties as he is known to have been invited by Francis I to paint his portrait and that of Eleanor of Portugal his second Queen; and some Flemish painter probably painted the King's portrait reproduced here as by the **Philadelphia Francis I Painter** (Pl. 313). **Augustin Joris Verburcht** painter of religious subjects and allegories was five years in Paris in the later forties and was back in his native Delft by 1552 when he was drowned at twenty-seven in a well into which he had fallen in his cups. **Leonard Thiry** born at Deventer and trained in Malines worked at Fontainebleau under Rosso and Primaticcio between 1535 and 1550 and died in Antwerp. **Lucas de Heere** born at Ghent in 1534 and trained in Antwerp by **Frans Floris** (who employed him on cartoons for glass and tapestry) seems to have gone to Paris and Fontainebleau during Niccolo del Abbate's period probably in 1555; and **Jan Massys** (Pls. 315, 363) may well have been in Fontainebleau though no records of the visit have been found. **Jan van der Straet** (Stradanus) was in Lyons about 1548, worked with Cornelis de la Haye (Corneille de Lyon) before leaving for Italy; and various towns in France were also visited by other Flemings, including **Pieter Bruegel,** as they made their way to the South.

In England some Netherlanders already established continued their work. **Joannes Corvus (Jehan Raf)** was still active in the thirties and was naturalized in 1544; **Lucas Horenbout** was naturalized and became King's Painter in 1534 and died in London some ten years later; **Gerard Horenbout** left for Ghent sometime in the thirties and died there; and **Susanna Horenbout,** who remained in England, married a sculptor named Worsley, attached to the Royal Household, and died here in 1545. Of the newcomers the **Hampton Court Henry VIII** (*c.* 1536) **Painter** (Pl. 312) was probably here in the thirties and, like the **Philadelphia Francis I Painter** (Pl. 313) in France, may have drawn the sitter from life and employed some studio assistant or still-life specialist to paint the elaborate clothes; the miniaturist **Simon Bening** visited London from Bruges probably in the forties, and his daughter **Livina Teerlinck** came with her husband in 1545, held salaried Court posts as 'nurse' (presumably the equivalent of a French Court 'Gouvernante') and miniature painter under Henry VIII and Edward VI, was paid for a portrait *The Princess Elizabeth* in 1551, and remained a Court Painter to Queen Mary. **Lucas Cornelisz** (son of **Cornelis Engelbrechtsz**) came here from Leyden with his family in Henry VIII's reign before 1547 and died here or in Leyden in 1552; he painted religious compositions and portraits, signed his work 'Kunst', became famous here and may have painted a *Thomas Arundel, Archbishop of Canterbury* which Vertue saw at Penshurst in the eighteenth century. Guillim Stretes, King's Painter to Henry VIII in 1546, and to Edward VI, may also have been a Netherlander, and he is presumed by some identical with **Guillaume Scrots** already mentioned as one of Mary of Hungary's Court painters. **Hans Ewouts** (known here as **Eworth**), Antwerp Master in 1540, painter of portraits, allegories and allegorical portraits, arrived about 1545, and found employment in Edward VI's reign, and thereafter; in 1550 he portrayed *Captain Thomas*

Wyndham with his helmet and arms and some suggestion of a battle in the landscape background, and *Sir John Luttrell* in an allegoric piece where the knight wades naked through the sea with a shipwreck behind him and nude goddesses in the clouds above; he painted *Queen Mary* (Pl. 349) in 1554 and, also probably in this period, the formidable matriarch *Mary Nevill, Baroness Dacre* (Pl. 338). **Conrad Schot,** already mentioned as at some time a pupil of **Antonis Mor,** may have been here about 1550 as he painted a *Portrait of Edward VI* in collaboration with one **Jean Maes,** commissioned by the English Ambassador in Antwerp. **Antonis Mor** came, as noted, in 1554 and painted *Queen Mary* (Pl. 350A); **Jan Vermeyen** may also have been here at that time; and **Sotte Cleve** (Crazy Cleve) who came hoping to sell religious compositions and mythologies to King Philip and to obtain commissions for portraits, was quite unsuccessful, quarrelled violently with **Mor** (whom he advised to return to Utrecht to protect his wife from the Canons) and behaved in various eccentric ways till he eventually in fact went crazy.

CHAPTER VII

Philip II in the Netherlands 1556-1559;
Margaret of Parma 1559-1567

1556-1567

CHARLES V was fifty-five when he abdicated in Brussels on October 25, 1555, giving his Austrian possessions to his brother Ferdinand (who became Emperor as Ferdinand I) and his possessions in Spain, the Netherlands, Italy and the New World to Philip II. He went to Spain with Mary of Hungary in 1556; and when he retired to the monastery at Yuste the pictures in his apartments included some family portraits and religious subjects by Titian, **Mor's** *Queen Mary Tudor* (Pl. 350A) and the four religious subjects by **Michiel Coxie** acquired in Brussels. Mary of Hungary had **Catherina van Hemessen** (Pls. 340, 345, 346) and her musician husband in her suite and settled pensions on them; and she took with her **Jan van Eyck's** *The marriage of Arnolfini* (Pl. 18A) and gave instructions for its packing—('Cargasele mas una tabla grande con dos puertas, con que se cierra, y en ella un ombre e un mujer, que se tomaran las manas, con un espejo en que se muestran los dichos ombre e mujer . . . hecha por Juanes de Hec, anno 1434.')

Philip II was twenty-eight when he reached Brussels from England in September 1555. On his accession in 1556 he made the usual Pageant Entries in the various cities; his Entry into Brussels was recorded by **Jan Vermeyen;** and for his Entry into Antwerp a feature of the decorations was a *Victory trampling on fettered prisoners* painted by **Frans Floris** in one day. He was unpopular with the Netherlanders from the outset, as he could speak no Flemish and very little French; he made no efforts to make contacts with his new subjects and surrounded himself with Spanish courtiers, generals and officials. But he paid some attention to Flemish painting; he probably bought at this time one or more of the dozen pictures by **Hieronymus Bosch** which were later in the sacristy and his private rooms in the Escorial; and though, like his father, he thought Titian the greatest living artist, he named **Antonis Mor** and Charles's favourite **Michiel Coxie** his King's Painters, he ordered from **Coxie** a copy of the **van Eyck** *Altarpiece of the Mystic Lamb* (Pls. 9, 12), he took **Antoni Pupiler** of Antwerp into his service, and invited both **Mor** and **Pupiler** to follow him to Spain.

Philip began his reign in the Netherlands by introducing the Jesuits, by republishing his father's Heresy Edict of 1550 and urging the Courts and Inquisitors to apply it with more rigour; he also ordered a stricter censorship of books and of the Rhetoricians' plays and ballads. In this year 1556 there was a truce in the war between France and Spain; Pieter de Hondt (Peter Canisius) became first Provincial of the Jesuit Order in Germany; and Cranmer was burnt in London holding his right hand in the flames. In 1557 John III of

132

Portugal died and was succeeded by Sebastian, aged three, with his grandmother Queen Catherine (daughter of Isabella the Catholic) and his great uncle Cardinal Prince Henry, the Inquisitor General, as joint Regents; Henri II resumed the war against Spain; Philip's troops—led by his Lieutenant-General Emmanuel Philibert, Duke of Savoy, and by Dutch and Flemish nobles including Prince William of Orange and the young Count Egmont—won the Battle of S. Quentin; and Queen Mary sent English troops to help the Spaniards follow up their victory. In 1558 the Duc de Guise took Calais from the English; Charles V and Mary of Hungary died in Spain; the University of Louvain banned the writings of Erasmus; Queen Mary died; Elizabeth I, aged twenty-five, became Queen of England; and John Knox, in touch with Calvin in Geneva, published his 'Blast of the Trumpet against the Monstrous Regiment of Women'. In 1559 the war ended with the Peace of Câteau Cambresis, and *Apollo and the Muses* (Pl. 364) inscribed 'Musae loco Belli' by **Marten de Vos** may have been painted as an allegory of the event. Philip was betrothed to Isabel de Valois, Henri II was killed in the tournament celebrating the occasion, and Francis II, aged fifteen and married to Mary Queen of Scots, became King of France. The English Parliament passed the Acts of Uniformity and Supremacy; Calvin founded his Academy of Theology in Geneva; Emmanuel Philibert left the Netherlands for Savoy after sitting for his portrait to **Jacobus de Punder (Pindar)** (Pl. 376); the Chapter of the Golden Fleece held a festival in Ghent, S. Bavon for which **Lucas de Heere** painted an altarpiece and designed a roodscreen (painted by **Benjamin Sammeling**) and composed his 'Ode in honour of the Altarpiece of the Mystic Lamb'. Later in the year a Nationalist movement in the Netherlands led by the States General and Dutch and Flemish nobles demanded the withdrawal of all Spanish troops; Philip, much incensed, retired to Spain (in a fleet commanded by the young Flemish admiral Count Hoorn) and presided on arrival at an 'auto-da-fé' in Valladolid where he swore to uphold the Inquisition in all his dominions; and Margaret of Parma was appointed Regent of the Netherlands.

Margaret of Parma was Charles V's daughter by a Flemish mistress. Educated in Brussels she had married first a Medici (murdered in 1537) and then Ottavio Farnese Duke of Parma. She ruled in the Netherlands with a Council where Bishop Granvella and Viglius ab Aytta (who had drafted the 1550 Heresy Edict) represented Philip, and William of Orange and Count Egmont represented the local nobles. The *de facto* ruler was Granvella who became Archbishop of Malines and Primate of the Netherlands when Philip and Pope Paul IV created some fourteen new Bishoprics to tighten the machinery against Reformers and filled them in Bruges, Ypres, Bois-le-Duc, Ghent, Haarlem and Middelburg with men already notorious as officers of the Inquisition. The Lutherans in Margaret's reign were relatively unmolested by the Inquisition, as the Calvinists, the most conspicuous and aggressive among the Protestants, now attracted the major persecutions. But, despite the Inquisition, the Calvinists made progress especially in the Northern provinces; they established contacts with Huguenots in France and Protestants in England, they preached in fields against the 'idolatry' of Rome with the men of the congregation forming an armed guard in an outer circle and the women grouped round the preacher in the centre; and some nobles—Jean and Philip de Marnix, for example—went on visits to Calvin's Academy in Geneva and came back wholly or partly converted. In the Southern provinces the vast majority of the people were still Roman Catholics who had nothing to fear from the Inquisition if they kept away from Protestants; but all ranks detested its procedures; the educated who read Erasmus and Rabelais and Georges Cassander's pleas for the Union of the Churches (published in 1561) were opposed to its cruelty and intolerance; and the business worlds of Antwerp and Brabant disliked it as bad for international relations and as causing the emigration of textile and other workers to more tolerant places. As the country was not plagued by wars with its neighbours in this period there was still a large measure of prosperity; and Antwerp, with a population of a hundred and twenty-five thousand and hundreds of foreign firms established within it reached the height of its importance as a centre of industry and commerce.

In 1560 a French Huguenot plot to kidnap Francis II (the Conjuration d'Amboise) was discovered, and hideous executions were perpetrated in revenge; Francis II died in December; and Charles IX aged ten became King with Catherine de Médicis as Regent. In 1561 Granvella became a Cardinal; Titleman, the chief Inquisitor in the Netherlands, was howled at in the streets and refused asylum by innkeepers for fear of popular reprisals; the Flemish nobles made Philip withdraw all Spanish troops to Spain; and William of Orange, Stadholder of Holland and Zeeland, though still in name a Catholic, married Anna of Saxony, a Lutheran, and with Count Egmont and others formed a League of Nobles to rid the country of Granvella. In 1562 S. Theresa founded the first convent of Unshod Carmelites (Carmes Déchaussées) in Avila; some of Plantin's workmen in Antwerp printed an heretical pamphlet which caused a temporary closing of the Press; two Flemish Calvinists were rescued from the stake by the populace at Valenciennes; some of the rescuers were burnt in reprisals and died singing psalms which moved Philip to recommend the use of gags in burnings 'as formerly in England under Mary Tudor'; the Duc de Guise massacred French Huguenots at Vassy; and the French Wars of Religion started. In 1563 the Duc de Guise was murdered at Orléans; Catherine de Médicis issued the Edict of Amboise as a measure of toleration for the Huguenots; Queen Elizabeth promulgated the Thirty-nine Articles; the Council of Trent completed its work and published its Decrees; Philip II laid the first stone of the Escorial; and Count Hoorn, back from Spain, joined the Nationalist Flemish nobles. In 1564 Calvin died at fifty-five; Lorenzo da Villavicenzio railed at State and other lay organization of charity as 'a perfidious heresy' in his 'Oeconomica sacra circa pauperum curum'; the Emperor Ferdinand I died and was succeeded by Maximilian II (painted as Archduke (Pl. 332) by **Antonis Mor**); Granvella was made a scapegoat by Philip and withdrawn; and Philip demanded acceptance of the Tridentine Decrees throughout the Netherlands. In 1565 the Knights of S. John, assisted by a Spanish fleet, forced the Turks to abandon the siege of Malta; Mary Queen of Scots was married to Lord Darnley; **Lambert Lombard** wrote from Liège to Vasari asking for drawings or engravings after Margaritone, Gaddi and Giotto that he might compare them with glass paintings in Northern churches; Count Egmont went from Flanders to Spain to urge Philip not to press acceptance of the Tridentine Decrees; and Philip declared that he would rather sacrifice a hundred thousand lives than abate the Inquisition. In 1566 Suleiman the Magnificent died and was succeeded by Selim II (Selim the Drunkard); and the ex-Inquisitor Michele Ghislieri became Pope as Pius V. By the 'Compromise of the Nobles' the leading Dutch and Flemish nobles pledged themselves to fight for moderation of the Heresy Edicts and suppression of the Inquisition; referred to by their enemies contemptuously as The Beggars (Les Gueux) they adopted the title and took beggars' bowls and wallets as their emblems; Margaret of Parma promised to consult the King and to take steps to moderate the Edicts—which caused a false rumour that Protestant worship would be recognized and many crypto-Protestants, including some nobles, accordingly declared themselves; some political opportunists suggested that the **van Eycks'** *Altarpiece of the Mystic Lamb* (Pls. 9, 12) should be presented through the Prince of Orange to Queen

Elizabeth to encourage her assistance; Calvinist preachers petitioned the Regent for permission to preach in churches in the winter; and excited mobs of Calvinist Iconoclasts stormed churches all over the country, smashing sculpture and cutting and burning paintings as symbols of 'idolatry'. The nobles, in concert with the Regent, using Walloon troops (known as 'Habits Rouges'), put down the rioting; and Philip's agents drew up lists of Calvinists for future punishment—lists which included an Antwerp lawyer named Jan Rubens, later the father of **Peter Paul Rubens.** In 1567 the second French War of Religion started and Montmorency, leader of the Catholics, was killed in the Battle of S. Denis; Lord Darnley was murdered and Mary Queen of Scots married Bothwell; Justus Lipsius became Latin secretary to Cardinal Granvella, and went with him to Rome; Antonio Perez became a secretary to Philip II; the Infante Don Carlos accused of plotting against Philip was imprisoned; Philip ordered the Duke of Alva to march north from Italy with a large Spanish army to root out heresy and take vengeance on all Netherlandish rebels; William of Orange retired to Nassau to organize resistance and seek alliances; Alva reached Brussels, set up the 'Council of Troubles' (the Blood Council) with the help of Viglius ab Aytta, and arrested Counts Egmont and Hoorn; and Margaret of Parma asked and obtained the King's permission to resign.

The conflicts of these twelve years affected a number of artists, especially, of course, the Protestants; there were emigrations to England and Germany and, after the Edict of Amboise, to France; and **Karel Foort** who stabbed himself at a supper with artist friends in Courtrai in 1561 was doubtless not the only one who was driven melancholic. Some artists took part in the Iconoclast riots; the Calvinist flower painter **Lodewyck Jansz van den Bosch,** for example, was active in the Bois-le-Duc riot where pictures by **Hieronymus Bosch** may have been destroyed, and (unless there is some misreading of the records) the aged **Marinus van Reymerswaele** (Pls. 237, 318) was with the rioters in Middelburg and condemned to six years' banishment after public penance in his shirt. Others are recorded among the sufferers in the sense that their pictures were destroyed; a *Palm Sunday* by **Joachim Beuckelaer** (Pls. 398-400) and a *Come unto me* 'with portraits of many merchants' by **Willem Key** (Pl. 387) were destroyed in Antwerp Cathedral; an altarpiece by **Lucas de Heere** was destroyed in Ghent, S. Pierre; **Anthonis Blocklandt** (Pl. 420) had some paintings destroyed in Delft; a *Fall of Lucifer* by **Dirck Barendsz** (Pl. 389) was badly damaged in an Amsterdam church; and **Pieter Aertsen** (Pls. 356, 357, 360) lost a number of pictures in various Dutch churches, though a lady offered '100 pond' to the rioters to spare one, a gesture beside the point, as the Iconoclasts, bent only on smashing 'idols', were not out for money. There seems indeed to have been no looting of church treasure (ritual objects in gold and silver and so forth) and many pictures by living and dead artists were actually rescued. Thus the **van Eycks'** *Altarpiece of the Mystic Lamb* (Pls. 9, 12) in Ghent S. Bavon was hidden in the church tower two days before the Iconoclasts broke in; **Gossaert's** *Virgin and Child* (Pl. 255) was among the pictures saved at Louvain; the *Lamentation* triptych by **Quinten Massys** in Antwerp Cathedral was successfully hidden, and the *Fall of the Rebel Angels* (Pl. 335) by **Frans Floris** seems also to have been saved there; and a set of panels *Scenes from the life of S. Luke: with portrait of the donor Abbot Lucas and his dog* also by **Frans Floris** were rescued from Ghent S. Bavon and taken to the studio of **Lucas de Heere** for safe keeping.

Satiric comments, protests, open or concealed, against contemporary cruelties and vices, and Reformist propaganda were contained in many drawings for engravings as accompaniments of the verbal lampoons and pamphlets which abounded. **Hieronymus Wellens de**

Cock, whose publishing house 'Aux quatre vents' was very active, put out prints of all characters (since as he said himself 'a Cook must serve dishes to suit all tastes'). His prints included Romanist religious compositions after **Lambert Lombard** and Italian painters for the orthodox; landscapes by himself, his brother **Mathys Wellens de Cock** and **Pieter Bruegel;** perspectives of temples, palaces, gardens and interiors by **Jan Vredeman de Vries** (Pl. 462); Roman views by **Marten van Heemskerck** and others; peasant genre by various artists; and many social satires, moralities and 'spook' compositions and conflagrations after **Hieronymus Bosch** or by living artists in his manner. In 1556 **de Cock** published a set of *Triumphs of Charles V* after **Heemskerck** by the free-thinking religious philosopher and engraver Dirck Coornhert (closely associated later with the Prince of Orange); and in 1558 he published his own engraving of a *Battle between Carnival and Lent* drawn by the Protestant **Frans Hogenberg.** He had **Pieter Bruegel** working for him till 1563 when **Bruegel** moved to Brussels (on his mother-in-law's insistence that only thus would he get free from and forget a peasant girl who had been for some time his mistress); and **Bruegel** was certainly a free-thinker (if not indeed a crypto-Protestant) as he knew the free-thinking geographer Ortelius who wrote of him 'in omnibus eius operibus intelligitur plus semper quam pingitur' and he also knew the Protestant **Jan Vredeman de Vries** well enough to play a practical joke on him and he probably had contact with Dirck Coornhert and **Frans Hogenberg.** Social comments and protests are doubtless hidden in **Bruegel's** drawings (published by **de Cock**) *The Seven Deadly Sins* composed with multiple obscurities in the **Hieronymus Bosch** tradition, and also in another series called the *Virtues*; for the *Justice* in the second series shows an allegoric figure surrounded by wretches suffering death by burning, beheading and hanging, bodies broken on the wheel and victims of the cord and water tortures and other frightful cruelties inflicted by the courts and the Inquisition. Social protests may also have been concealed in the satiric and 'spook' pictures and *Temptations of S. Anthony* which were painted in this period by **Jan Mandyn,** by **Frans Verbeeck** and by **Pieter Huys** (Pls. 412, 413); and in the conflagrations by **Gillis Mostaert** (Pl. 348) and the Calvinist **Lodewyck van den Bosch** who occasionally painted conflagrations though he was mainly a flower painter.

We find such protests also, more or less concealed, in the satiric genre paintings by **Pieter Bruegel** including the *Battle between Carnival and Lent, Children's games* and the *Land of Cockayne*. In the *Battle between Carnival and Lent* (Pls. 368A, 370), a later composition than **Frans Hogenberg's,** there is reference, I think, to the still raging conflict between the Church and the civil authorities for the control of charity, as beggars confront the charitable before the church on the one side and before the inn on the other; like the **Alkmaar Master** (Pls. 182, 183) before him, **Bruegel** also protests in this picture against the horrible mutilations inflicted by the courts, for one beggar on the church side has had both feet and one arm cut off, and on the inn side the mutilated creatures move pitifully on crutches or drag themselves along on hand-blocks; there were also originally some protests on the church side which **Bruegel,** or some one later, thought it prudent to paint out, as we know from X-ray photographs that a half-nude corpse of a drowned man with swollen belly has been covered by the white sheet in the foreground on the right, that two sick people were formerly stretched out beneath the round table at the church door, and that towards the centre of the square there was formerly a skeleton figure in a barrow. *Children's Games* (Pl. 369) has been called Rabelaisian, and it does indeed remind me, in its cumulative method, of the two hundred and sixteen games listed as the child Gargantua's amusements; but **Bruegel** also had in mind, I think, the earlier chapter on Gargantua's childhood where achieving all counsels of imperfection, he sits between two stools, eats his cake and has it, leaps before he looks, thinks all gold that glitters, and beats the bushes while missing the birds; and the picture, thus interpreted, becomes a protest against the evils of the times, with each group an equivalent of some adult futility, cruelty or vice. In *The Land of Cockayne* (Pl. 414) we are shown a Fools' Paradise where a peasant, a soldier and a free-thinking young nobleman lie dreaming of a happier life in a country made of sausages, roast chicken and fruit tarts, with vista of a peaceful sea beyond; the peasant has his scythe as emblem, the soldier his lance and the young noble in a fur-lined mantle has a book beside him—perhaps by Calvin or Martin Luther; and **Bruegel** to point the harsh awakening ahead has disposed the three figures as spokes on the torture wheel where their limbs will eventually be broken. We find **Bruegel** protesting also in what purports to be a simple landscape with genre figures—the *Return of the Herd* (Pl. 393); for here the tranquillity of the scene is affronted by a gibbet and torture wheels on a hilltop opposite the village by the river.

Protests against conditions seem also to have been hidden in religious subjects. **Bruegel** in the *Road to Calvary* (Pl. 379) dated 1564, is evidently protesting against scenes he had witnessed when the Inquisition's victims were driven to the stake or gibbet under military escort and the Flemish peasants and townsfolk crowding round them were moved at times to attempt a rescue; for the hillside is dotted with torture wheels on poles and gibbets, Simon's wife tries to pull him from the soldiers (Pl. 381), and the procession is escorted not by Spanish troops in armour as in **Pieter Aertsen's** picture of 1552 (referred to in the previous chapter) but by the 'Habits Rouges' Walloons who had policed the country since Philip withdrew the Spaniards and were about to put down the Iconoclast riots. In his *Numbering at Bethlehem*, painted in 1566, **Bruegel** attacks the Spanish régime in its economic and police-state aspects; for here the peasants in a Flemish village are summoned to an inn where the representatives of Spain record their names and property and so on for taxation purposes and for use in lists of 'suspects'; **Bruegel's** *Conversion of S. Paul* (Pl. 378A), painted in 1567 when the Netherlands were awaiting Alva's troops from Italy, shows Saul, the persecutor, crossing the Alps with Alva's armoured lancers as his bodyguard; and his battle picture on the Old Testament subject *The Suicide of Saul* (Pl. 378) is crammed with Spanish lancers.

Much Protestant propaganda must also have been concealed in contemporary paintings, and some extant works may be possible examples. The crypto-Protestant subjects included, I think, *The Holy Family turned away from the Inn*, which could be interpreted as an allegory of Rome's refusal to admit the Protestants; *S. John preaching in the Wilderness* with its evocation of the open-air Protestant preachers (as already indicated in my references to versions of the subject in pictures by **Joachim Patinir** (Pl. 200) and the **Bruges Baptism of Christ Painter** (Pl. 201)); the *Healing of Tobit's blindness* probably an allegory of those whose eyes were opened by the Reformers; *Nebuchadnezzar worshipping idols* the equivalent, I take it, in this period of the **Solomon Master's** picture (Pl. 287); *The Queen of Sheba proving Solomon with hard questions* where Solomon, the rich and powerful idolator, may stand for Spain, the Roman Church and the Inquisition, and the Queen of Sheba for the Reformed Church fulfilling the words 'the queen of the south shall rise up in the judgement with this generation and shall condemn it: for she came from the uttermost parts of the earth to hear the wisdom of Solomon: and, behold, a greater than Solomon is here'; *The Conversion of S. Paul* which recalls the texts 'As for Saul, he made havock of the church, entering into every house and taking men and women committed them to prison' and 'Saul, yet breathing out threatenings and slaughter . . . came near Damascus: and suddenly there shined round about him a light from heaven; and he fell to the Earth and heard a voice saying unto him Saul, Saul, why persecutest thou me? And he said who art thou, Lord? And the Lord said I am Jesus whom thou persecutest; it is hard for thee to kick against the pricks'; and *The Tower of Babel*, Biblical equivalent of the Greek concept of the punishment of 'Hubris', perhaps interpreted by Protestants in this period as a prophecy of doom for Philip, or the Pope, who like Nimrod would have 'the whole earth of one language and one speech'. Among the pictures of these subjects **Jan Sanders van Hemessen,** working in Haarlem, produced a *Healing of Tobit's blindness* in 1555; **Jan Massys,** back from exile, but still apparently a crypto-Protestant, painted *The Holy Family turned away from the Inn* (Pl. 361) in 1558 and a *Healing of Tobit's blindness* (Pl. 362) in 1564; *S. John preaching in the Wilderness* was painted by **Henryck met de Bles,** by **Marten van Cleve,** by **Bruegel** (in 1566), by **Pieter Balten** in a picture where an elephant had been substituted for S. John when the Emperor Rudolf II owned it, and (later) by the Protestant **Karel van Mander. Pieter Aertsen** who moved from Antwerp to his native Amsterdam about 1556, probably for religious reasons, painted *Nebuchadnezzar worshipping idols* in 1560. **Lucas de Heere** later an avowed Protestant painted *The Queen of Sheba proving Solomon with hard questions* at twenty-five in 1559 for Ghent, S. Bavon and actually gave King Solomon a strong resemblance to King Philip. *The Conversion of S. Paul* was painted by **Karel Foort** in Ypres or Courtrai before 1562 and by **Bruegel** (Pl. 378A) as already mentioned in 1567. **Bruegel's** *Tower of Babel* (Pls. 368, 375) dated 1563, shows clouds breaking across the unfinished summit to illustrate the words 'Let us build us a city and a tower whose top may reach unto Heaven', and Nimrod, sceptre in hand, gives judgement on some presumably seditious or free-thinking workmen who kneel before him.[1]

Personal, as distinguished from ecclesiastic concepts of religious subjects, appear in this period as in the old days. Thus **Bruegel** in his *Adoration of the Magi* (Pl. 383), of 1564, surrounds the sacred happening with a semi-circle of everyday spectators—a Flemish magistrate and two officers, a notary or doctor in his spectacles, and an impervious young man whispering a comment in S. Joseph's ear (like the young men cracking jokes at the foot of the Cross in the **New York Crucifixion and Last Judgement Painter's** imaginative concept (Pl. 1) and the whispering boys in the **London Delft Painter's** picture (Pl. 224)); and beyond this semi-circle, peasant-soldiers from the Magi's retinue peer in with boorish amazement (like the peasants climbing on the thatch and peeping through the crannies in the *Adoration of the Magi* (Pl. 157) by **Hieronymus Bosch**). **Pieter Aertsen's** *Market scene with Christ and the adulteress* (Pl. 356), painted in 1559, is also a personal concept with the sacred episode placed in the midst of everyday Flemish life, as the scene is set before the steps of the Temple within the semi-circle of a fruit and vegetable market that fills the foreground. **Joachim Beuckelaer** (**Aertsen's** pupil and nephew) went further on these lines, for in several

---

[1] The Tower of Babel as a subject had appeared in fifteenth-century illustrated books, sometimes as a four-sided tower surrounded by spiral galleries; and it was painted before 1524 by **Joachim Patinir.** It seems to have become more frequent from the middle fifties to the end of the struggle against Spain. A version by the Protestant **Lucas van Valkenborch** shows the tower in a form suggesting the Papal tiara (Pl. 374); another version, with spiral galleries as in the early illustrations, appears on the wall of an interior by **Abel Grimmer** (Pl. 535); it was also painted by the Protestants **Martin van Valkenborch** and **Jan Vredeman de Vries,** by **Karel van Mander,** by **Rubens'** first master **Tobias van Haecht** in collaboration with **Jan (Velvet) Brueghel,** by **Nicolas van Cleve** in collaboration with **Josse de Momper** and **Juliaen Teniers the elder,** by **Roelandt Savery,** and by **Lodewyck Toeput.**

versions of *Christ in the house of Mary and Martha*, including one reproduced here (Pl. 399) of 1565, we are in the midst of the work in Martha's kitchen and see Christ with Mary and Martha as small figures in a vestibule beyond. Some artists were still more daringly free-thinking. **Gillis Mostaert,** who was active through the period and is represented here by an orthodox religious picture (Pl. 348), was, we know from van Mander 'niet zoo heel godsdienstig' and 'niet erg Spanisch gezind', and was given to scaring those whom the Inquisition haunted by adding scandalous details to religious subjects as when he painted himself and a friend playing backgammon in Hell in a *Last Judgement* and an unseemly brawl in a *Last Supper*; but he painted these details in a quickly removable medium over decorous passages beneath—a wise precaution in days when even the relatively mild Venetian Inquisition summoned Paolo Veronese before it for the animals and genre figures and German halberdiers in his *Supper in the house of Simon* and said firmly to him 'Are you not aware that in Germany, and in other places infected with heresy, they are in the habit of painting pictures full of scurrility for the purpose of ridiculing and degrading the Holy Church and teaching false doctrines to the ignorant and foolish?'

Orthodox religious pictures were painted, of course, by many artists including all or some of the free-thinkers and crypto-Protestants. In Antwerp **Frans Floris,** whose *Fall of the Rebel Angels* (Pl. 335) of 1554 was discussed in my last chapter, was forty in 1556 and now became extremely successful; he had Counts Egmont and Hoorn among his friends and patrons and lived in a handsome house adorned on the outside with figures of *The Liberal Arts* in golden grisaille imitating beaten brass (alsof het Koperfiguren waren); in the sixties he was known as Antwerp's stoutest drinker, and his later pupils, who had usually to see him to bed, included **Hieronymus Francken the elder** (Pl. 503), **Ambrosius Francken the elder, Frans Francken the elder** and **Frans Pourbus the elder** (Pl. 427); his output with the aid of his pupils and assistants was considerable, and his religious subjects included *Christ blessing little children*, *Adam and Eve driven from Paradise*, *Adam and Eve mourning Abel* and a *Last Judgement* for Notre Dame du Sablon in Brussels as well as the pictures for Antwerp Cathedral and Ghent S. Bavon mentioned above as saved from the Iconoclasts. **Jan Mandyn,** some fifteen years older than **Floris,** died in Antwerp about 1560; **Jan van Coninxloo** (Pls. 289, 309) seems to have died approaching seventy quite early in the period; and **Jan van den Elburcht** died in the sixties. The one-legged **Ryckaert Aertsz** who was painted at his easel, aged seventy-four, in 1556 (Pl. 351) was evidently still working at that time and was still alive in 1567. **Willem Key** (Pl. 387), who painted the *Come unto me* already mentioned for Antwerp Cathedral, produced a *Triumph of Christ* and *Lot and his daughters* before 1567. Others painting religious subjects in Antwerp included **Jan Massys** who was forty-seven when the period began, **Lambert van Noort** then thirty-six, **Marcellus Coffermans** and **Crispiaen van den Broeck** both twenty-seven, **Marten de Vos** twenty-five, **Joachim Beuckeleer** twenty-three, **Gillis Mostaert** twenty-two, and **Bernaert de Ryckere** twenty-one; and among the newcomers **Pieter Vlerick, Pauwels Frank** and **Jacques de Backer** all started in the sixties. **Jan Massys** seems to have painted three types of religious picture—orthodox subjects (a *S. Paul* and an *Elijah and the widow* for example) crypto-Protestant subjects like the *Holy Family turned away from the Inn* (Pl. 361) and *The healing of Tobit's blindness* (Pl. 362) already discussed, and pseudo-religious subjects like *Lot and his daughters* and *David and Bathsheba* which date from the early sixties. **Lambert van Noort** (Pl. 402), most frigid and orthodox of church painters in the 'Roman' style, produced a *Sibyl predicting the Church of Christ* and a series of *Scenes from the Passion* for the Chapel of the Guild of S. Luke between 1558 and 1565; **Marcellus Coffermans** (Pl. 403) also painted religious compositions in this orthodox manner; and **Bernaert de Ryckere** who settled in Antwerp in 1561, had already painted, in 1560, a *Christ falling beneath the Cross and succoured by S. Veronica* in the Romanist style with Roman soldiery in armour for S. Martin's church in his native Courtrai. **Crispiaen van den Broeck** (Pl. 409) a more spirited and adventurous artist who had been to Italy, as noted, and thus qualified for membership of the Antwerp Romanist Fraternity, was back before 1560 when he attracted attention with a *Last Judgement*, the first of several versions of this subject commissioned from him for various churches; and **Marten de Vos** (Pls. 364, 397, 429) back from Venice and Master in Antwerp Guild by 1558, painted a *Meeting of Isaac and Rebecca at the well* in 1562. **Joachim Beuckelaer** remained in Antwerp when his uncle returned to Amsterdam, became Master in 1560, painted many pieces in the manner of the *Kitchen scene with Christ in the house of Mary and Martha* (Pl. 399) mentioned above, and also some orthodox pictures—a *Four Evangelists*, for example, and *S. Anne and the Holy Kinship*; we know from van Mander that he was always, materially speaking, an unsuccessful artist, and it may be that the orthodox-minded suspected free-thinking even in his orthodox pieces and resented such personal touches as the puppy held up in the foreground of *S. Anne and the Holy Kinship* (Pl. 400). **Gillis Mostaert** drew or painted at various times a number of religious subjects recorded by engravers—*The Fall* among Old Testament themes and *The Adoration of the Shepherds, Christ mocked*, the *Deposition* and the *Entombment* from the New, as well as the *Last Supper* and the *Last Judgement* already mentioned; his *Christ on the Cross* (Pl. 348) made dramatic by the darkening of the sun (as in the picture by the **Detroit Crucifixion Painter** (Pl. 285)) is an impressive devotional picture where the figure of Christ appears to be based on an extant drawing ascribed by some to Michelangelo; but some especially sharp-eyed Inquisitor might have made complaint of the dog trotting past the Temple of Athene on the right. **Pieter Vlerick** who had moved from Malines to Antwerp was a pupil there of the glass-painter **Jacques Floris** (brother of **Frans Floris**) in the later fifties till he went abroad; **Pauwels Franck** was Antwerp Master in 1561 and went abroad soon after; and **Jacques de Backer** (Pl. 416) was pupil-apprentice in the house of the painter-dealer **Antonio van Palerme** who worked him, van Mander tells us, like a horse, and exported his paintings to France with much profit.

Among the painters of religious subjects in Brussels **Jan Vermeyen** (Barbalonga) (Pl. 323) died about sixty in 1559 after painting a *Resurrection* to be placed above his tomb. **Michiel Coxie** (Pls. 308, 310, 352) had headquarters there till the end of 1562 when he went back aged sixty-three to his native Malines; in high repute as King's Painter, he finished his cartoons for the windows of S. Gudule in 1556 and received commissions for Romanist triptychs to be placed there and in other churches. **Adriaen de Weerdt** back from Italy in the early sixties had developed by then from a landscape painter to a composer of pictures with religious themes in a landscape setting. **Aert Mytens** a talented and zealous young Bruxellois stole a corpse from the gallows to study its anatomy and went abroad in the early sixties; another young Bruxellois, **Joos van Winghe** (Pls. 457, 497), went abroad a year or so later; **Pieter de Kempener (Pedro de Campaña)** (Pl. 367) back from Spain at sixty in 1562 succeeded **Michiel Coxie** as Director of the Brussels tapestry factory in 1563; and **Pieter Bruegel** moved there, as noted, at about thirty-five in 1563. In **Bruegel's** *Road to Calvary* (Pl. 379), painted in Brussels in 1564, there is a striking contrast in style and spirit between the procession with the genre scenes descriptively handled and the treatment of the foreground group of sacred figures with the Virgin swooning and supported by S. John and the weeping Maries; and this group recalls the complex feeling in the mannerist groups of mourners by **Cornelis Engelbrechtsz** (Pls. 213, 232) and the simpler but equally emotive concept by the **New York Crucifixion and Last Judgement Painter** (Pl. 160). In the *Adoration of the Magi* (Pl. 383), also of 1564, **Bruegel** gives us the same contrast between the treatment of the genre figures and the foreground group; but here there is also a further contrast between the style of the Virgin and Child which seems inspired by memories of Italian High Renaissance pictures and the figures of the Magi which carry on the formal feeling of **Englebrechtsz** (Pl. 229) and the **Antwerp Mannerists** (Pl. 193). In **Bruegel's** *Numbering at Bethlehem* of 1566 there is however no style difference in the group of the Holy Family which is merged in the genre composition. There are no extant records that **Bruegel** received commissions for church paintings in this period (or earlier or later); and this is comprehensible in view of his highly personal approach to religious painting and his evident free-thinking; he probably sold his religious subjects, as he sold his other works, through dealers to private collections; and we know indeed from van Mander and other contemporary sources that a *Road to Calvary* was owned in 1565 by a rich collector, Nicolaes Jongelinck of Antwerp (brother of the sculptor Jacob Jongelinck), who also had other pictures by him.

Of the painters of religious subjects in other towns **Lancelot Blondeel** (Pls. 270, 271, 272, 330) was appointed Master of Works in the Bruges Convent of the Annunciation in 1557 and died about sixty-five in 1561; in Bruges also **Pieter Jansz Pourbus** (Pls. 331, 334, 336, 337) painted a series of religious subjects including *The Seven Sorrows of the Virgin*—a High Renaissance version of the picture by the **Seven Sorrows of the Virgin Master** (Pl. 281) —for S. Jacques in 1556, and a Romanist *Last Supper* for Notre Dame in 1562. **Jacques van den Coornhuuse** was Bruges Master in 1556; **Marcus Geeraerts the elder**, Master in 1558, worked for Bruges churches between 1561 and 1565; and **Gillis Claeissins**, son of a painter **Pieter Claeissins the elder**, was Master in 1566. In Malines **Gregorius Beerings**, Master at twenty-four in 1555 after his Italian visit, worked for local and other churches; **Cornelis Enghelrams** seems to have been there through the period; **Vincent Geldersman** and **Vincent Sellaer** were probably both still active; and **Pieter Stevens the elder** was Master in 1560 and had left for Rome by 1566. **Michiel Coxie**, re-established there by 1563, painted a *Last Supper* triptych with the *Footwashing* (Pl. 308) and an *Agony in the Garden* on the wings for Brussels S. Gudule in 1567; and his son and pupil **Raphael Coxie** was Master there in 1562. In Ghent **Lucas de Heere** painted *The Queen of Sheba proving Solomon with hard questions* for S. Bavon in 1559 and an altarpiece for S. Pierre (destroyed by the Iconoclasts as noted); in 1566 he took **Karel van Mander** (Pl. 472) aged sixteen as his pupil and was visited soon after by **Frans Pourbus the elder** (then nineteen and reluctant to go to Rome as he could not bear to part from Susanna, the niece of his master **Frans Floris).** **Michiel Coxie** seems to have been in Ghent for a year or more about 1557 to make his copy of the **van Eycks'** *Altarpiece of the Mystic Lamb* for King Philip. In Louvain **Jan van Rillaert,** who designed the memorial ceremonies on the death of Charles V, was still alive and approaching sixty in 1567, and **Pieter van der Hofstadt** (Pl. 366) then just over sixty was still producing some church pictures. **Karel Foort** painter of a *Conversion of S. Pau* and also of a *Resurrection* (on a chest or cupboard door) moved about 1560 from Ypres to Courtrai where (assisted by his pupil **Nicolas Snellaert**) he produced a *Last Judgement with Christ seated on the clouds, and, below, the symbols of the Evangelists* (described by van Mander as 'een beetje Tintoretto-achtig') for a church at Hooghlede near Roselaere; and he stabbed himself as related in 1562. **Karel Foort's** earlier pupil **Pieter Vlerick** returned from Venice to Courtrai aged twenty-eight in 1567. In Liège **Lambert Lombard** who drew or painted *The Miraculous draught of fishes* and *Christ rebuking Martha*, both engraved and published by **Hieronymus Wellens de Cock** in 1556, and *Christ crucified between the thieves* engraved and published in 1557, wrote the letter to Vasari already quoted in 1565, and died about sixty in 1566; his life was written in 1565 by his former pupil **Domenicus Lampsonius** who was chiefly active as an art historian and sent information to Vasari for his section on the Flemish painters.

Among the painters of religious subjects in the Northern provinces **Jan van Scorel** (Pls. 284, 300, 301) died in Utrecht at sixty-seven in 1562; **Dammes Claesz de Hoey** worked on the memorial ceremony for Charles V in Leyden, S. Peter, and seems to have died in 1560; and the genial bohemian **Aert Claesz van Leyden** fell into a Leyden canal one night and thus ended his career about 1566 when he was approaching seventy. In Delft **Anthonis Blocklandt van Montfoort** (Pl. 420), a young aristocrat who was followed by a footman when he walked the streets, painted large religious pictures including a *Beheading of S. James* for the church of S. John in Gouda, a *Last Supper* for Dordrecht, S. Nicolas and *Scenes from the Passion* for the chapel of the Dordrecht Civic Guards in these years or later; and in 1565 he had **Cornelis Ketel** (Pl. 451) aged eighteen as his pupil. In Amsterdam **Pieter Aertsen** painted the *Market scene with Christ and the adulteress* (Pl. 356) and *Christ in the house of Mary and Martha* (Pl. 357) when he was just over fifty in 1559; the Christ in the second picture recalls Titian's type, there are elements in both suggesting acquaintance with compositions by Bassano, and I suspect a visit to Venice a year or so before they were painted, though no such visit seems actually recorded. **Aertsen** also painted in these years the *Nebuchadnezzar worshipping idols* already mentioned and many pictures for churches including a large *Death of the Virgin* triptych with the *Adoration of the Magi* on the outside of the wings for the Amsterdam Oude Kerk, and a *Nativity* or *Adoration of the Shepherds* altarpiece with four wings and a *Beheading of S. Catherine* on the outside for the Nieuwe Kerk (both destroyed by the Iconoclasts); and probably in this period he also painted a series titled *Scenes from the life of Joseph*. **Dirck Barendsz,** seen here as a portraitist (Pl. 389), painted his *Fall of Lucifer* (damaged by the Iconoclasts in an Amsterdam church) in the early sixties. In Haarlem **Jan Sanders van Hemessen** (Pl. 317) was probably still at work in the sixties and died approaching seventy at the end of the period; and **Marten van Heemskerck,** fifty-eight in 1556 and immensely active, produced there among other things an *Ecce Homo* triptych in 1559 commissioned for a church in Delft, an *Entombment* triptych (Pl. 355) in 1559-60, a *S. Nicholas* for Amsterdam Oude Kerk and a *Jonah under the gourd* in 1561, a *Baptism of Christ* in 1563, *Death and Judgement* (known in his day as 'De Vier Uitersten' and bought by his ex-pupil the Amsterdam collector and amateur painter Jacob Rauwaert) in 1565, and *Christ on the sea of Tiberias* (Pl. 372) in 1567. I have suggested earlier that in his *Aaron and Moses with the brazen serpent* (Pl. 354) of 1551 **Heemskerck** had revealed a passion for antique sculpture and acquaintance with Michelangelo's *Last Judgement*; but the tense and noble *Entombment* (Pl. 355) seems to show an enthusiasm for the scientific drawing of the shepherds in **Hugo of Antwerp's** *Portinari altarpiece* (Pl. 76) and for pictures by Verrocchio and Luca Signorelli; and the student may find it salutary to recall this work when the field is held later by the soft sentiment and rhetoric of **Gaspar de Crayer** in his decadence (Pl. 609) and **Van Dyck** (Pl. 608). In *Christ on the Sea of Tiberias* (Pl. 372), painted at sixty-nine, **Heemskerck** is less passionate and tense, the figures are relatively small within the setting as a whole and the rhythm is almost suave; and these characters also appear in the *Death and Judgement*.

Mythologies and allegories, with nudes, were also produced by many of these painters, and others, sometimes as easel pictures or as drawings for engravers, sometimes as decorative panels for rich men's houses, sometimes on musical instruments or as cartoons for tapestries or as panels on arches and so forth in contemporary Pageants. Thus **Lambert Lombard** designed a series of allegoric figures *Spes*, *Fides* and *Caritas* which were engraved by 1558. **Marten de Vos** probably painted his *Apollo and the Muses* (Pl. 364)—which should be titled '*Triumph of Apollo*'—in 1559 when he was just under thirty and had memories of Venetian pictures still fresh in his mind; inscribed 'Musae loco Belli' the composition contrasts the group of instrumentalists and singers with the military conflict painted on the clavichord lid, and may have been connected with the celebration of the Peace of Câteau Cambresis as suggested above; alternately the picture itself may have decorated a panel on a clavichord lid, as **Marten de Vos**—like **Damiaen Oortelmans** (a specialist in this field)—is known to have painted a number of panels for such instruments. **Gillis Congnet** (Pl. 434) who had worked as a pupil in the house of the slave-driving dealer-painter **Antonio van Palerme** drew or painted, possibly in these years, a *Bacchus*, *Venus and Ceres*, a *Death of Cleopatra* and a *Phryne riding on the back of Aristotle* (a version presumably of the legend of Aristotle and the Indian girl) all recorded by engravings; the veteran **Ryckaert Aertsz** was still supplying nudes for allegories and mythologies by other painters; and **Vincent Geldersman** may have painted more pictures like the *Leda* and *Cleopatra* already referred to. **Jan Massys** painted his delicate *Flora* (Pl. 363) in 1561 and seems to have distilled there delighted memories of Fontainebleau and Venice and the Mediterranean seaboard. **Frans Floris,** after the sensational success of his *Victory trampling on fettered prisoners* in the Antwerp Pageant of 1556, painted the *Feast of the Sea Gods* (Pl. 353) in 1561 and thus used mythology to convert the social genre piece *An Allegoric Love Feast* (Pl. 331) by **Pieter Jansz Pourbus** to a similar genre scene with nude figures; and before 1565 he produced from his atelier seventeen pictures (ten titled *Scenes from the Story of Hercules* and seven titled *Allegories of the Liberal Arts*) which were hung in rooms known in their honour as 'The Chamber of Hercules' and 'The Chamber of the Arts' in the Antwerp house of the collector Jacob Jongelinck already mentioned as the owner of some paintings by **Bruegel.** In these years or later, **Marcus Geeraerts the elder** drew or painted *The Labours of Hercules*; **Crispiaen van den Broeck** (Pl. 409) drew or painted compositions titled *Venus and Adonis*, *The Judgement of Paris*, *Venus*, *Bacchus, Ceres and Amor*, *Pyramus and Thisbe* and *Allegories of the Virtues and Vices*, all recorded by engravings. **Abraham del Hele** painted a *Penelope and her maidens* in 1565. At this time also **Bernaert de Ryckere** may have produced some mythologies like his later *Diana and Actaeon*, **Dirck Barendsz** (Pl. 389) his *Venus* and *Perseus changing Polydectes and his guests to stone* and **Anthonis Blocklandt** (Pl. 420) his *Venus and Mars* and *Standing Venus*. **Dominicus Lampsonius** must also be included among the painters of nude figures because he wrote to Vasari in 1564: 'I draw and occasionally paint in oil the natural objects before me, more particularly figures nude or draped, but I have not courage to go further and attempt such things as require a firmer and more practised hand, landscapes, trees, water, clouds, conflagrations, etc. . . .'

Among the portrait painters **Antonis Mor** (Pls. 332, 333, 341, 342, 350A, 408) worked in Utrecht, Brussels and Antwerp both before and after 1559 when he passed some time, aged about forty, in Spain. **Willem Key** (Pl. 387), **Marten de Vos** (Pl. 429), **Steven van der Meulen, Cornelis de Zeeu** (Pls. 385, 386), **Ryckaert Aertsz** and **Frans Floris** (Pls. 335, 351, 353) were available in Antwerp all through or for part of the period; and both the **Chicago 1562 Painter** (Pl. 384) and the **Antwerp Jan van Wueluwe Painter** may also have worked there. **Jan Vermeyen** died, as noted, in Brussels in 1559. **Pieter Jansz Pourbus** (Pls. 331, 334, 336,

337) had portrait commissions in Bruges. **Pieter van der Hofstadt** (Pl. 366) worked in Louvain, **Jacques de Punder** (Pl. 376) probably in Malines, and **Nicolas de Neufchatel (Lucidel)** probably in Mons till he went abroad in 1560. In Ghent, from 1559, there was **Lucas de Heere** who painted many portraits from life and could draw recognizable portraits from memory; and **Domenicus Lampsonius** states in the letter to Vasari just mentioned that he had made some portraits in Liège. In the Northern provinces **Jan van Scorel** (Pls. 284, 300, 301) was available in Utrecht till 1562; **Marten van Heemskerck** (Pls. 303, 304, 306, 354, 365, 372) was the central portraitist in Haarlem where **Simon Jacobsz** of Gouda may also have been active. **Cornelis Visscher** of Gouda, described by van Mander as a good portraitist but sometimes out of his mind, was about thirty-five in 1556; the **Amsterdam Moucheron Family Painter** (Pl. 388) seems to have worked in Middelburg in 1563; **Adriaen van Cronenburch** (Pls. 343, 441, 443) began his career in Bergum near Leeuwarden in 1567; **Dirck Jacobsz** was still much employed in Amsterdam and **Dirck Barendsz** (Pl. 389) began to paint portraits there about 1561 after five years' training in Venice.

Of these portrait painters **Antonis Mor,** as King's Painter, had many commissions in Court circles and was ranked by his contemporaries as the leading artist in this field; in 1557 he painted *Alexander Farnese* the twelve-year-old son of Margaret of Parma; in 1559, in Utrecht or Madrid, he painted a *Self-portrait* for the Pitti Gallery in Florence; between 1560 and 1567 he seems to have had his headquarters in Utrecht; and in 1560 he made a portrait of *Jan van Scorel* placed, later, above Scorel's tomb. **Steven van der Meulen's** career in his own country was cut short in 1560 when he fled, as a Protestant, abroad; and **Cornelis de Zeeu** who was Antwerp Master in 1558 and produced the *Bearded man in a cap* (Pl. 386) in 1563 had also apparently emigrated before painting the *Man in a red chair* (Pl. 385) in 1565. **Frans Pourbus the elder** painted a remarkable head *Jan van Hembyze* when he was twenty-two in 1567; the sitter—whom I take to be the Gantois noble Hembyze (Imbizi) who was to lead anti-Catholic riots in Ghent some ten years later—is shown as a hook-nosed man with a high forehead, sparse light hair and beard, a thin mouth beneath a down-curling moustache and, though the inscription tells us, only thirty at the time, dissipation pouches round the eyes. Impressive portraits of donors in the old traditions survive on the wings of altarpieces painted by **Pieter Jansz Pourbus** and **Marten van Heemskerck** in the fifties and sixties. Van Mander praising the *Portrait of Abbot Lucas with his dog* on the wing of the *S. Luke* polyptych by **Frans Floris** said 'Het is een prachitg gelijkend portet, warmee Floris duidelijk heeft aangetoond dat hij, als hij maar wilde, de beste portretschilder kon zijn die er te vinden was'; and though **Floris** was never in regular practice as a portrait painter he produced some portraits of his friends which show this aspect of his talents — the *S. Luke painting* (Pl. 351) for example of 1556 contains a sympathetic portrait of the one-legged **Ryckaert Aertsz** at his easel with **Floris** himself behind him; and the sitters for *The Falconer* and *The Falconer's wife* (*Old lady with her dog*) painted with simple verity in 1558 were also probably his friends. **Willem Key,** ranked by his contemporaries as second only to **Mor,** painted, probably in these years his *Granvella in Cardinal's Robes* and the delicate *Portrait of an old woman* reproduced here (Pl. 387); his *Lazarus Spinola* painted in 1566 shows the uncle of the celebrated general portrayed later by **Rubens** and Velazquez; and he was also employed on subscription portrait groups including *Come unto me* (*with portraits of many merchants*) destroyed, as noted, by the Iconoclasts, and *The Antwerp Councillors* (*with Christ and Angels above*). Others who continued the tradition of the subscription portrait group were **Pieter Jansz Pourbus, Dirck Jacobsz, Dirck Barendsz,** and the **Amsterdam Moucheron Family Painter.** The sitters for the *Thirty-one members of* *the Bruges Confrérie du Saint Sang* painted in 1556 by **Pourbus** are shown in two serried groups like the members of the Crossbowmen's Guild in the earlier picture by the **Malines Guild of S. George Master** (Pl. 146). **Dirck Jacobsz** painted *Twelve members of the Amsterdam Civic Guard* when he was over sixty in 1563 four years before he died. **Dirck Barendsz** painted Jewish-looking sitters in *Fourteen members of the Amsterdam Civic Guard* (Pl. 389) for the Crossbowmen's Hall when he was twenty-eight in 1562 and *Eighteen members of the Amsterdam Civic Guard eating bullhead (perch)* for the Arquebusiers' Hall in 1566; he also painted other groups and many single portraits as he had made an advantageous marriage which brought him into contact with leading families in the town. In the charming conversation group of the Middelburg Moucheron family (Pl. 388) the **Amsterdam Moucheron Family Painter** shows Pierre de Moucheron aged fifty-five and his wife aged forty-five with their twenty children round the family dining-table, the sons in a descending semicircle on the one side and the daughters in similar arrangement on the other, and one of the daughters provides a little post-prandial music on the harpsichord. The curiously archaistic *Portrait of a Bishop (or Abbot)* (Pl. 376) was painted in the same year, 1563, by **Jacques de Punder (Pindar) (Poindre),** probably for a prelate with conservative taste who demanded a portrait in the style of the **Worcester Saint and Donor Painter** (Pl. 153); this artist, van Mander tells us, inserted many portraits in a *Crucifixion* and added prison bars to a *Portrait of an English captain* because the sitter had failed to pay him for his work; and, as already mentioned, he painted *Duke Emmanuel Philibert of Savoy* about 1559. I also reproduce **Pieter van der Hofstadt's** beautiful portrait *An old man in prayer* (Pl. 366) where the face and hands are most sensitively seen and modelled like the faces and hands in the portraits by **Catherina van Hemessen** (Pls. 345, 346).

Landscape painters were still employed on cartoons for the tapestry factories in Brussels, Tournai and elsewhere and for the Malines factories of painted linens. Other landscape specialists provided the figure painters with backgrounds and settings which often took the form of Mediterranean port scenes; and such specialists were possibly employed for the ivory-tinted city with towers and steeples round a little bay in *Christ on the Sea of Tiberias* (Pl. 372) signed by **Marten van Heemskerck;** for the town and bay in the picture by the **Brussels Icarus Painter** (Pl. 373); and for the elaborate landscape and coast scene—(recalling the earlier port scenes in pictures by **Pieter Jansz Pourbus** (Pl. 331) and **Bernaert van Orley** (Pl. 248)—in the *Flora* (Pl. 363) by **Jan Massys**. Of the landscape painters surviving from the last period **Henryck (Herri) met de Bles** was possibly still working in Belgium or abroad; **Frans Mostaert** (Pl. 371) died at twenty-six in 1560 and **Lucas Gassel** (Pls. 327, 328) over sixty soon after. **Christian van den Queborne,** who had **Denys Calvaert** aged about sixteen as a pupil from 1556, was official painter to Antwerp city at about forty-five in 1560; **Hans Keynooghe, Adriaen de Weerdt** and **Frans Verbeeck** were all approximately fifty in that year, **Hendrik van Cleve** was then about forty-five, **Michiel de Gast** about forty, and the Calvinist **Joos van Liere** also probably about forty; **Pieter Bom** was thirty, **Jacob Grimmer** (Pls. 430, 444) and **Gregorius Beerings** about thirty-four, **Pieter Bruegel** about thirty-one and **Gillis Mostaert** (Pl. 348) twenty-six. **Anna de Smytere** seems to have worked till after 1566; **Jan de Hollander** may also have still been painting; and **Leonard Kroes** whose birth and death dates are unknown was active in the sixties. The newcomers included the versatile **Marcus Geeraerts the elder** who was painting landscapes in Bruges from 1558 and **Cornelis van Dalem** Antwerp Master in 1556. **Martin van Valkenborch** (Pl. 439) was Malines Master in 1559, his elder brother **Lucas van Valkenborch** (Pls. 374, 432, 445, 446, 448-50) was Malines Master in 1560 and both were apparently in Antwerp by 1565. **Hans Bol** (Pl. 431) was Malines Master in 1560; **Pauwels Franck** and **Peter Goetkint** were both Antwerp Masters in 1561, **Gillis van Coninxloo** (Pls. 466, 476) was a pupil of **Leonard Kroes** (before 1562) and then of **Gillis Mostaert; Jan Sons** was another pupil of **Gillis Mostaert,** probably in the later sixties; **Frans Pourbus the elder** was established as an artist, after his time with **Floris,** by 1564; and **Cornelis Molenaer** known as Schele Neel (the Squinter) was also Antwerp Master in that year. Among these contemporaries of **Bruegel** it is clear from van Mander that **Frans Mostaert** (Pl. 371) had much influence, despite his early death, as his manner was followed for some time by **Jan Sons** and by **Adriaen de Weerdt. Gillis Mostaert** whose landscapes included moonlight effects, snow scenes, and compositions illustrating the *Months of the year* is represented in my plates by an imaginative reconstruction of Jerusalem seen from Golgotha (Pl. 348). **Frans Verbeeck's** landscapes included a *Winter scene* without snow or ice, with bare trees and fog-bound houses which made, van Mander tells us, 'een zeer natuurlijken indruk.' **Jacob Grimmer** (Pls. 430, 444) was described in 1567 by Guicciardini to Vasari as a painter of 'bellissimi paesi'; and van Mander wrote: 'he painted naturalistic views of the environs of Antwerp and was so excellent a landscape painter that in some aspects I know no better; for his skies, fine and full of light, were studied from nature, and the foregrounds, backgrounds and houses in his pictures were also faithfully observed and skilfully recorded'. **Gregorius Beerings,** in Malines through the period, was available for backgrounds with Italian ruins; **Michiel de Gast,** back from Rome with drawings and paintings of Italian ruins, was settled in Antwerp from 1558; and **Hendrik van Cleve** may have returned with topographic records of his Italian and other travels some time in the sixties or he may still have been working continuously abroad. **Cornelis van Dalem,** a rich amateur with an extensive library, was an occasional painter of rocky landscapes with figures inserted at various times by **Gillis Mostaert** and **Joachim Beuckelaer** and possibly also by **Bartholomaeus Spranger** (Pls. 458, 459) who became his studio-boy at fourteen in 1560 and remained for some years. **Pieter Bom,** painter of landscapes in distemper, was Antwerp Master at the unusually late age of thirty-four in 1564. **Peter Goetkint,** a pupil of the hard taskmaster **Antonio van Palerme,** survived the ordeal and married his master's daughter. In the sixties **Lucas van Valkenborch** (Pls. 432, 445, 446, 448-50), trained in the atmosphere of the Malines landscape painters on linen, was already an assured composer in the tradition of **Lucas Gassel** (Pl. 328) and perhaps a rival to **Jacob Grimmer. Hans Bol** (Pl. 431), who actually began as a painter on linen in the Malines workshops, produced a *Daedalus and Icarus* with sheep grazing in a wood and a distant harbour, perhaps before the period closed; and **Frans Pourbus the elder,** van Mander tells us, painted 'in his youth a *Paradise* (*Garden of Eden*) piece with many animals and trees from life where one could distinguish the pear, apple and nut trees' which suggests that he thus anticipated the *Earthly Paradise* pieces painted later by **Jan (Velvet) Brueghel** (Pl. 543), **Roelandt Savery** (Pl. 583), **Izaak van Oosten** (Pl. 584) and others.

Pieter Bruegel himself made landscape drawings for **de Cock** till he left Antwerp, and his achievements as a landscape painter in Brussels are seen here in the *Tower of Babel* (1563), the *Road to Calvary* (1564), *The Dark Day, The Harvesters, The Return of the Herd, Hunters in the Snow* (all 1565), the *Conversion of S. Paul* (1567) and the *Suicide of Saul* (indistinctly dated but painted, I presume, in 1567 or 1568). In the *Tower of Babel* (Pls. 368, 375) the tower rises by an estuary with a vast spreading plain behind; the sun catches the right-hand corner where the estuary joins the sea; a large town with houses, forts and other buildings and bridges over the river is in the middle distance; an aqueduct across the plain and the architecture of the tower show, I take it, that **Bruegel** travelled through Provence and made sketches of the amphitheatre and the Pont du Gard at Nimes. In the *Road to Calvary* (Pls. 379, 381) a plain intersected with a little stream is in the foreground sweeping up to the place of execution; a rock, in the **Patinir** tradition, crowned with a windmill, is in the middle distance; a walled town, with a domed temple to suggest Jerusalem, and rising country in a blue haze are behind it; storm-clouds cross the sky; and rooks fly and perch on the torture wheels and on the tree-tops as they perched in Mantegna's *Martyrdom of S. James* in Padua. *The Dark Day* (*March? or Spring?*) (Pl. 390), *The Harvesters* (*July? or Summer?*) (Pl. 392), *The Return of the Herd* (*November? or Autumn?*) (Pl. 393) and *Hunters in the Snow* (*February? or Winter?*) (Pl. 391), represent together a symbol of the seasons or are part of a series of twelve months like the calendars in the early manuscripts. In *The Dark Day* we look down from a height through tree trunks and bare boughs to a village by an estuary where shipping is tossed by the churned up waters; a tree blown down by the gale lies across the foreground on the right; it is not yet completely daylight; the sky is dark and there is light only on the line of the horizon and craggy snowtipped hills. In *The Harvesters* a half-reaped golden cornfield, with a leafy tree in the centre, occupies the foreground; a village with slate-roofed church is seen between trees behind it; pasture and more cornfields with farm dwellings form a vista on the left. In *The Return of the Herd* a river winds diagonally through a rocky bed; on the left bank there is a vineyard with ripe grapes; opposite, a small village lies round and within an upstanding bluff; in a central field a bird-net holds some captured birds; the foreground is an opening in a coppice with bare trees right and left and rooks upon the boughs; trees with copper leaves surround a farmhouse and other buildings near a ruined castle towards the distance on the left; clouds float across the sky and the air is sharp and still. *Hunters in the Snow* takes us to the depths of winter; the broad flat countryside and distant bluffs are snow and ice-bound; snow lies upon the roofs of a foreground village; and rooks perch on the bare boughs of the foreground trees. *The Conversion of S. Paul* (Pl. 378A) and *The suicide of Saul* (Pl. 378) with their pine-clad Alpine passes and vistas of plains and streams below, made a great impression on the artist's own contemporaries as we know from van Mander who records: 'It was said of him that while in the Alps he swallowed the mountains and rocks which he was thus able to spew forth (uit te spuwen) on his canvases and panels'; and it may be, as I have suggested earlier, that **Bruegel** not only studied nature on his travels but recalled some pages in Fouquet's 'Antiquités Judaiques' on journeys through Savoy and Italy. All these pictures are complete and integral as landscapes without the figures; they are in no sense figure compositions with landscape backgrounds to 'fill up'; and they thus continue the oldest traditions of Flemish painting shown here in the *Crucifixion* by the **New York Crucifixion and Last Judgement Painter** (Pls. 3, 5, 6) and the lower panels of the **van Eycks'** *Ghent altarpiece* (Pl. 9). But this old tradition is developed by **Bruegel's** subtle noting of seasonal sensations and of variations in the light and temperatures, and also by the placing of the figures within the formal pattern of the landscape which is actually enriched and stressed by their insertion.

Town views and street scenes were still being drawn and painted, and architectural perspectives of real and invented buildings, generally with small figures, were now in favour with collectors. **Hendrik van Cleve, Michiel de Gast** and **Gregorius Beerings** provided drawings and paintings of Italian towns and buildings as just noted; and **Antonio van Palerme** published a map of Antwerp in 1565. **Pieter Jansz Pourbus** (Pls. 331, 334, 336, 337), as town planner and cartographer to the city, painted a large bird's eye map of the Franc de Bruges from sketches made from the Belfry in 1562; and another detailed plan of Bruges was drawn and engraved the same year by **Marcus Geeraerts the elder. Pieter Bruegel** in the *Battle between Carnival and Lent* (Pl. 370) and *Children's games* (Pl. 369) continued the tradition of the **Tiburtine Sibyl Master** (Pl. 87) with records of local buildings round an open square complete before the figures were put in; but here, unlike his later landscapes just considered, the figures are not dovetailed into the formal pattern-structures of the pictures, but scattered pell-mell at all angles as though caught in action by a camera-obscura. Architectural perspectives were painted in Malines by **Cornelis van Vianen** who, van Mander tells us, was proficient in such pieces but 'too tight and laborious' (moeizaam) in his handling. After his death one of his pictures was finished in 1561 by **Jan Vredeman de Vries** (Pl. 462) then working in Malines. In 1563 **Jan Vredeman de Vries** himself was back, aged thirty-six in Antwerp; and there he provided architectural drawings for the print shop of **Hieronymus de Cock,** a trompe l'oeil perspective erected in the garden of the painter **Willem Key** (Pl. 387) and a trompe l'oeil garden vista in a room or passage for the shipowner Gilles Hoffman (Pl. 429) which deceived the Prince of Orange; in 1566 he painted a *Christ in the house of Mary and Martha* where the figures are traditionally recorded as by **Anthonis Blocklandt** (Pl. 420); and it must have been in these years also that he visited Brussels to paint there a trompe l'oeil summer house with an open door behind which, van Mander tells us, **Bruegel** inserted two love-making peasants in his absence. **Hendrik van Steenwyck the elder** (Pl. 488), who was later a pupil of **Jan Vredeman de Vries** and also painted architectural perspectives, was still under twenty in 1567.

In genre painting we get several types of picture by **Jan Massys;** his *Holy Family turned away from the Inn* (Pl. 361) of 1558 contains a glimpse of a farmyard with hens pecking grubs and crumbs as in the **Alkmaar Master's** *Feeding the hungry* (Pl. 182); in the sixties he painted variations on the Merry Company theme and a *Procuress* where the model for his *Flora* (Pl. 363) fondles a hideous old man while the procuress and another old woman leer behind them; and at the same time he was painting the pseudo-religious subjects *Lot and his daughters* and *David and Bathsheba* which are virtually genre pieces though embellished with decorative settings like the *Flora*. **Joachim Beuckelaer** (Pls. 398, 399, 400) signed a *Prodigal Son* in 1563 when he was approximately thirty; and **Jan Sanders van Hemessen** may have painted more *Prodigal Son* pictures (Pls. 305, 325) in his last ten years. In 1564 **Hieronymus Francken the elder,** then probably in Venice or Paris, signed a *Venetian Carnival* anticipating the social genre scenes by **Joos van Winghe** (Pl. 497) and **Frans Francken II** (Pl. 517); and in these years **Pieter Jansz Pourbus** may have painted more social genre pieces in the allegoric terms of his *Allegoric Love Feast* (Pl. 331), and **Marinus van Reymerswaele** may have made more social comments in the manner of his *Money-changer and his wife* (Pl. 318) till 1567 when he seems to have ceased work, or possibly died over seventy, after his possible connection with the Iconoclast raid on the Westminsterkerk in Middelburg referred to above. The old theme of the artist working at his easel with the studio assistant grinding colours in the background appears in the *S. Luke* (Pl. 351) by **Frans Floris;** and we have an outdoor genre scene in **Marten van Heemskerck's** *Christ on the Sea of Tiberias* (Pl. 372) where fishermen spread their nets on the beach and a two-horse cart or carriage is driven up the cliff to a house or inn with a soldier seated at the door.

Peasant genre was painted by **Pieter Aertsen, Joachim Beuchelaer, Frans Verbeeck, Pieter Huys, Pieter Balten, Marten van Cleve, Pieter Bruegel,** the **Detroit Wedding Dance Painter** and probably in his last years by **Lucas Gassel.** Of these **Pieter Aertsen** produced a *Peasants' wedding* in 1556, *The Cook* and *Market scene with Christ and the adulteress* (Pl.

356) in 1559, *The Cake Baker* in 1560, a *Kitchen piece with an ox's head on the table and his son Aert Pietersz as a boy in the foreground* also about 1560, *Peasants at market* in 1561, and the *Kitchen scene* (Pl. 360) in 1562. In these pictures **Aertsen** puts the peasants as large figures in the foreground; he treats them with respectful interest and invests them with human dignity; his peasants, grave, homely, resigned and static are more impressive than the inmates of **Hemessen's** taverns and anticipate the homely static peasants painted by the French realist Louis le Nain in the seventeenth century and by the Fleming **Pieter Snyers** in the eighteenth (Pl. 839); and his Martha shown as a genre figure just returned from market with her basket of provisions in *Christ in the house of Mary and Martha* (Pl. 357) is a large-boned, muscular, laborious ancestress of the dainty Parisian housewife in *La Pourvoyeuse* by Chardin. As already observed the Christ in **Aertsen's** *Christ in the house of Mary and Martha* seems reminiscent of Titian's type; and we can note here that the cook-maid in his *Kitchen scene* (Pl. 360) has the face of the model used by Titian in *La Bella* and the *Girl in a fur cape*. **Joachim Beuckelaer** painted several variants of a *Village Fair* (*Kermesse*) in 1563, a *Poultry market* in 1564, the *Kitchen scene with Christ in the House of Mary and Martha* (Pl. 399) in 1565, a *Market scene with Ecce Homo* in 1566 and a *Peasants with poultry, butter and eggs* in 1567. **Beuckelaer's** figures in these works have the quiet dignity of **Aertsen's** but the standing cook-maid on the right in his *Kitchen scene with Christ in the house of Mary and Martha* (Pl. 399), who might well be the daughter of **Aertsen's** Martha (Pl. 367), is less austere than **Aertsen's** figure, and the grave look which **Aertsen** gives his peasants is softened here to an incipient smile. **Frans Verbeeck,** already mentioned as a painter of a comic *Peasants' wedding* and similar themes, was a prolific worker and had a wide market, van Mander tells us, for his varied output. **Pieter Huys** (Pls. 412, 413) seems to have painted some genre pictures with half-length figures in addition to his satiric pieces. **Pieter Balten** among his 'boerenkermissen en dergelijke' made several versions of a *Feast of S. Martin* where peasants and beggars assail a huge barrel for free draughts of S. Martin's wine; and work in the fields is shown in **Hans Bol's** *Daedalus and Icarus* where a peasant drives a two-horse plough and in the *Landscape with fall of Icarus* (Pl. 373) by the **Brussels Icarus Painter** showing a peasant ploughing with one horse. **Marten van Cleve,** who added figures to some landscapes by **Jacob Grimmer** (Pl. 430, 444) and painted a brothel picture later owned by **Rubens,** is seen here in three plates. In the *Peasant household with cavalier* (Pl. 396) and *The Brawl* (Pl. 406) he anticipates some genre elements in works by **Adriaen Brouwer** (Pls. 617, 618), **Jordaens** (Pls. 658, 660) and **Teniers** (Pls. 678, 679, 680); the *Peasant household with Cavalier* takes us to crowded life in a farmhouse kitchen with women and children, cattle, pigs and hens, a flayed ox in the background, a dog begging for a bone, a cat asleep in the baby's cradle, while a youth fondles a young girl, a man puts a child to stool, and strolling minstrels play their fife and drum in the doorway to divert a gentleman who has stopped to call for a glass of wine and makes amorous advances to the girl who brings it; in *The Brawl* a similar farm kitchen is turned topsy turvy by a sudden quarrel ending in drawn knives and stabbing. In the third picture reproduced here, the *Flayed ox* (Pl. 394), a cook prepares some offal from the carcass, a cellar boy takes a long drink of beer and two children in the doorway have been given the bladder to play with. **Pieter Bruegel's** contributions to genre painting can be looked at in two groups—the pictures known or presumed to have been painted in Antwerp, and those painted later in Brussels. It was doubtless in the Antwerp period that he won his sobriquet of 'Peasant Bruegel'; for it is related by van Mander (who was already twenty-one when **Bruegel** died and has told us practically all we know about his life and habits) that, dressed as a peasant,

he frequented peasant fairs and weddings with an Antwerp friend; and his Antwerp peasant pictures include *The Battle between Carnival and Lent* (Pl. 370) dated 1559, *Children's games* (Pl. 369) dated 1560, and also probably the undated *Peasant wedding* (Pl. 405) and *Peasants' dance* (Pl. 407) painted, I imagine, in 1561 or 1562. Van Mander says that he reproduced the conduct of peasants eating, drinking, dancing, leaping, love-making or engaged in other jollities (hun manier van doen bij eten, drinken, dansen, springen, vrijen en ander grappig gedoe); and 'grappig gedoe' are indeed the appropriate words for these animated scenes. For here the peasants are not grave, silent, human beings as in **Aertsen's** pictures, or poverty-ridden underdogs as in **Marten van Cleve's** *Peasant household with cavalier* (Pl. 396); they are seen and presented as stage puppets, marionettes in clean brightly coloured clothes, capering, singing and grimacing to amuse their betters; they begin their antics as children in *The Battle between Carnival and Lent* and *Children's games* and continue them as adults in the *Peasants wedding* and the *Peasants dance*; and **Bruegel** thus launched or had a share in launching the 'Merry Peasant' myth. But in Brussels he becomes more credible because more simply descriptive as a genre painter. In *The Tower of Babel* (Pls. 368, 375) of 1563 we get men at work on building operations (inspired, I imagine, by Fouquet's *Building of the Temple* in the 'Antiquités Judaiques') who continue the tradition of the workmen in **Jan van Eyck's** *S. Barbara* (Pl. 18) and **Lucas Gassel's** *Mountainous landscape with mine workers* (Pl. 328); and in the landscapes of the *Seasons* (Pls. 390, 391, 392, 393) of 1565, the peasants pursue their rural occupations in the tradition of the calendars in Franco-Flemish manuscripts and go about their business quietly without grins or 'Merry Peasant' caperings.

In the painting of animals **Jan Massys** gives us a cock and hen and a rough-haired dog (Pls. 361, 362) and there are dogs and hens too in the pictures by **Marten van Cleve** (Pls. 394, 396); **Pieter Bruegel** painted *Two monkeys chained on a window sill with view of Antwerp and the Scheldt* presumed by some an illustration of the Flemish saw 'Wat vindt men ter wereld zeldzame kindern, zei de boer, en hij zag een aap in het vensten zitten', and we find horses, cattle, a mastiff and exhausted sporting dogs in his pictures reproduced here (Pls. 378A, 379, 381, 382, 391, 393). The **Brussels Icarus Painter** gives us sheep and a sheep dog and a ploughing horse (Pl. 373); and **Marcus Geeraerts the elder,** who had specialized skill in drawing animals and birds for engravings, produced a set of bear studies in 1559, and falling back on this aspect of his talents, he drew *Illustrations to Aesop's Fables* when he found himself without commissions after the disturbance caused by the Iconoclast riots in 1566.

Still-life of various kinds and flower painting appears in many pictures. Thus in the field of musical still-life the studies of the earlier periods are continued in *Apollo and the Muses* (Pl. 364) by **Marten de Vos** who shows us all the instruments current in concerted playing at this time. The antique relief on the sarcophagus, and the turban and crown of thorns before it, enhance the poetic quality in the drama of the *Entombment* (Pl. 355) by **Marten van Heemskerck** (just as the antique elements and the flaming torch contributed to the atmosphere of his *S. Luke painting the Virgin* (Pls. 303, 304)) and the semicircle of the winding sheet is no less emotive than the outspread sheet in the **Oultremont Master's** *Descent from the Cross* (Pl. 176). Some studio assistant or still-life specialist may have worked with **Jacques de Punder** on the vestments and accessories in his *Portrait of a Bishop (or Abbot)* (Pl. 376) where the meticulous rendering of these details continues the tradition of the **Worcester Saint and Donor Painter** (Pl. 153), the **Hampton Court Henry VIII (c. 1536) Painter** (Pl. 312) and the **Philadelphia Francis I Painter** (Pl. 313); and some student or specialist in flower painting may have been employed by **Jan Massys** for the charming flowerpiece in the foreground of his *Flora* (Pl. 363). Such flower specialists now included the draughtsman **Pieter van der Borcht** of Malines who made studies of flowers which were used for a *Florilegium* and *L'Herbier de Dodonoeus* published in Antwerp by the Plantin press; **Mathys Brill the elder** was probably still active as a painter of fruit and flowers; and thanks to van Mander we know the names also of the Calvinist **Lodewyck Jansz van den Bosch** and **Pauwels Coecke van Aelst** who both evidently continued the fifteenth-century painters and anticipated **Ambrosius Bosschaert** (Pls. 551, 552) and his contemporaries, as van Mander tells us that they painted flowers in glasses with great accuracy (groote nauwkeurigheid) and that **van den Bosch** put dewdrops, butterflies and insects on his flowers and foliage. Fruit also was painted by **van den Bosch;** small plates of fruit and cakes mark the end of the meal in the dining-room scene by the **Amsterdam Moucheron Family Painter** (Pl. 388) who follows the procedures of **Cornelis Anthonisz** (Pl. 299); fruit tarts and other pastries are in **Bruegel's** *Peasant wedding* (Pl. 405) and *The Land of Cockayne* (Pl. 414) and also in the *Battle between Carnival and Lent* (Pl. 370) where a fishwife in the centre slices salmon as Lenten fare. A giant lobster, eels and other sea fish refresh the revellers in the *Feast of the Sea Gods* (Pl. 353) by **Frans Floris;** baskets of fruit and vegetables in **Pieter Aertsen's** *Market scene with Christ and the Adulteress* (Pl. 356) prepare the way for the massed fruit and vegetables and so on in later decorative pieces by **Jacob Jordaens** (Pl. 545) and **Frans Snyders** (Pls. 655, 656, 657); the massed eatables in **Joachim Beuckelaer's** *Kitchen scene with Christ in the house of Mary and Martha* (Pl. 399), which takes us still further on this road, make credible van Mander's story that an Antwerp mint-master who had commissioned a *Kitchen scene* from **Beuckelaer** came each day with some further eatables to be included so that the fee agreed proved far too small for the time spent in painting this great variety of fruit, vegetables, game, fowls and joints of meat; and **Marten van Cleve's** study of a carcass in the *Flayed ox* (Pl. 394), though crudely descriptive and unpleasantly coloured, is of art-historical interest because **Abraham van den Hecken** made the subject dramatic by chiaroscuro about eighty years later (Pl. 684), **David Teniers** made it attractive by deft handling (Pl. 683) and Rembrandt raised it, with romantic vision, to a higher plane in the famous picture of 1655.

Artists abroad in this period included some painters who left the Low Countries to escape the religious persecutions and the political conflicts. Thus **Nicolas Neufchatel (Lucidel)** went to Nuremberg about 1561, painted there *The Nuremberg mathematician J. Neudorfer and his son* and portraits of the Emperor Maximilian II and his daughter Anne of Habsburg (later Queen of Spain), and was admonished by the Nuremberg Council for excessive Calvinist zeal in 1567; the Calvinist landscape painter **Joose van Liere** went to Germany in the sixties and settled in Frankenthal where the Elector Palatine Frederick III had established a colony for Protestant refugees; and the sitter for the picture shown (Pl. 344) by the **London Lady in a Flat Cap Painter** (probably a Flemish painter) would seem by her clothes to be German. **Lucas van Valkenborch** (Pls. 374, 432, 445, 446, 448-50) and his brother **Martin van Valkenborch** (Pl. 439), both Protestants, went via Liège to Aix-la-Chapelle in 1566 and **Lucas** may then have painted his *Landscape with ironworks* (Pl. 449) in the region of Liège; **Adriaen de Weerdt** left Brussels with his aged mother for Cologne in 1566; and the Calvinist **Lodewyck Jansz van den Bosch,** 'listed' for his part in the Iconoclast riots, fled to some town in Germany on Alva's approach in 1567.

Newcomers to England included the Liégeois **Cornelius de Vosse (Devosse),** his cousin **Arnold** (or **Arthur**) **van Brounckhurst,** the topographic draughtsman **Antonio van den**

Wyngaerde, the Protestant portrait painter **Steven van der Meulen** and probably **Cornelis de Zeeu** who may also have been a Protestant. Of these **Cornelius de Vosse,** described as a limner and a 'most cuninge pictur maker' was married here in 1558 and still here in the middle sixties; **Arnold van Brounckhurst** painted *Sir Henry Sidney* in 1565; **Antonio van den Wyngaerde** signed a drawing titled *Oatlands* in 1559 and another titled *Richmond* in 1562; **Steven van der Meulen** fled to London from the Inquisition in 1560, was naturalized in 1562 and may have been the 'Stevens' referred to by Vertue (before 1756) as the painter of portraits of the Lumley family with the 'pencil and manner' of Holbein but 'softer and tenderer'. **Cornelis de Zeeu** is presumed to have been here in 1565 as the sitter for the *Man in a red chair with a small black dog* (Pl. 385) was apparently English. Among the artists already established **Livina Teerlinck,** whose annuity from the Crown was continued through the period, gave Queen Mary a limning, *The Holy Trinity,* as a New Year's present in 1556 and Queen Elizabeth *The Queen's picture* 'painted finely on a card' as a New Year's present in 1558 and was rewarded for the second by a 'casting bottell guilt weighing two and three quarter ounces'. **Hans Ewouts (Eworth)** (Pls. 338, 349, 417) also worked here through the period; in 1559 he painted a double half-length portrait *Frances Brandon, Duchess of Suffolk and Adrian Stoke* where the mother of Lady Jane Grey, just remarried to her young and handsome master of horse, appears as formidable a matron as *Mary Nevill, Baroness Dacre* (Pl. 338); and his *Henry Stuart, Lord Darnley, aged eighteen with his brother Charles Stuart aged seven, later Earl of Lennox* (Pl. 350) painted in 1563 shows Lord Darnley two years before his marriage to Mary Queen of Scots and four years before he was murdered.

Some painters went to Paris and to Fontainebleau where there seem to have been special openings for pupils of **Frans Floris;** and after the Edict of Amboise many Protestants, and others, found conditions there more tolerant than in the Netherlands till about 1567 when Charles IX ordered the expulsion of such immigrants unless they could prove more than two years' residence in France. **Lucas de Heere,** in Paris and Fontainebleau in the later fifties, was employed on cartoons for tapestry for Catherine de Médicis and returned to his native Ghent aged twenty-five in 1559. One **Jacques de Backer the elder** (father of **Jacques de Backer)** is said to have gone to France from Antwerp in the later fifties to escape the results of an action for slander and to have remained and died there. **Hubert Goltzius,** who had just established his own printing press in Bruges, passed through France on the way to Italy to pursue his numismatic studies about 1558. **Joris Hoefnagel,** son of a rich Antwerp diamond merchant, began his career about 1561 when he travelled in France as agent for his father and made drawings of places visited and also, van Mander tells us, of 'agriculture, wine-making and waterworks', social and peasant festivities and national costumes. **Dirk Barendsz** (Pl. 389) passed through France on his way back from Italy about 1561. **Gillis van Coninxloo** (Pls. 466, 476) left the studio of **Gillis Mostaert** (Pl. 371) and visited Paris aged about twenty about 1563. **Bartholomaeus Spranger** (Pls. 458, 459) who had broken free from **van Dalem's** studio by 1565 spent some time in Paris and Lyons that year and then left for Italy. Three young men **Hieronymus Francken the elder, Hans de Maier** then about twenty-three, and **Aper Fransz van der Houve (Franssen)** of Delft, all formerly pupils of **Frans Floris,** were working in Fontainebleau with one **Denys van Utrecht** by 1566; and they all welcomed **Cornelis Ketel** (Pl. 451) who arrived at eighteen that year from the Delft studio of **Anthonis Blocklandt** (Pl. 420) and moved to Paris when the Court came to Fontainebleau in 1567. **Joos van Winghe** (Pls. 457, 497) who reached Paris from Rome towards the end of the period was about twenty-three in 1566, and he was possibly acquainted with the *Venetian Carnival* painted, as already mentioned, by **Hieronymus Francken** in 1564.

In Spain **Ferdinand Sturm** is recorded at work till 1557 and may have lived through the period though his death date is unknown; **Francisco Frutet** may also have still been working; and **Catherina van Hemessen** (Pls. 340, 345, 346) probably remained in Spain after Mary of Hungary's death. **Pieter de Kempener (Pedro de Campaña)** remained there till 1562; in 1556 he painted a polyptych (in conjunction with the Spanish painter Antonio de Alfian) for a Chapel in Seville Cathedral with striking portraits of the donor Mariscal Diego Caballero and his family; and in 1561 he was commissioned by Diego de Herrera to paint a new version of his earlier Santa Cruz *Descent from the Cross* for the Regina Angelorum convent in Seville. This second *Descent from the Cross* (Pl. 367) smaller than the earlier picture is also more dramatically emotive and more impressively composed and shows **Kempener** as the descendant of **Rogier van der Weyden** (Pl. 46), the **Flémalle Master** (Pl. 37), the **Oultremont Master** (Pl. 176) and the **Brussels Haneton Lamentation Master** (Pl. 279) with some elements contributed by Spain; the Christ is in the centre of a triangle, the left arm silhouetted against the light is down-hanging as in **Rogier van der Weyden's** picture, but the right arm makes a movement to display the wound within the hand and the fingers contracted round it, for (like the **Flémalle Master's** Christ whose left arm is lifted to his breast) this dead Christ still lives; below this triangle there is a wide semicircle of mourners culminating on the right in the figure of S. John who looks in anguish at the crown of thorns, an affective addition to the concept of the mourners in the earlier and more famous picture. As already mentioned **Antoni Pupiler** and **Antonis Mor** followed Philip II to Spain in 1559. **Pupiler** worked in the Pardo Palace and in 1567 the King sent him to Louvain for nine months to copy a celebrated altarpiece (perhaps *The Last Supper* (Pls. 58, 61) by **Dirk Bouts**). **Mor** (Pls. 332, 333, 341, 342, 350A, 408, 428) was much occupied with portrait painting at the Court and enjoyed high personal favour with the King who went often to his studio; but in 1560, van Mander relates, Philip, on such a visit, tapped him in a friendly way upon the shoulder, **Mor** riposted by touching the King with his maulstick, and being warned that the Inquisition (where he was suspect as coming from the heretical Netherlands) might use this offence as an opening against him, he left hurriedly for Utrecht and never ventured to return to Spain though Philip repeatedly invited him to do so. Of the newcomers to Spain in the sixties **Antonio van den Wyngaerde** obtained permission from Margaret of Parma to emigrate there in 1561, entered the King's service that year as topographic draughtsman, became known as **Antonio de las Viñas** and **Antonio de Bruselas,** and drew views of Spanish towns. **Izaak del Hele** came from Antwerp in 1562 and received commissions for frescoes in Toledo Cathedral; **Jan Floris** (brother of **Frans Floris**) painter, van Mander tells us, of 'allerlei sierlijke historietjes en figuurtjes' on faience, was invited to Spain by the King, employed in his various palaces, and made director of the Azulejos (painted tiles) factories in Madrid in 1563; **Joris Hoefnagel** came down from France still selling his father's jewels and making drawings; and **Simon Pereyns** painter of religious subjects came from Antwerp, worked in Toledo and left for Mexico in 1566. **Pereyns** also worked for a time in Lisbon, and may have met there **Christoph van Utrecht** who was made 'Examiner of Paintings' in 1556 and was still active and successful in 1565.

In Italy there were painters, established or on visits, in Venice, Florence, Rome, Parma, Naples and other cities and also in Sicily. **Marten de Vos** (Pls. 364, 396, 429) seems to have stayed in Venice as assistant to Tintoretto till 1558 when he was back again in Antwerp.

Dirck Barendsz (Pl. 389) aged twenty-two in 1556 was Titian's pupil and lived in his house from about that time till he went back to Amsterdam via France about 1561; and his *Fall of Lucifer*, slashed by the Iconoclasts, may have shown aspects of his training not seen in his portraits. As already suggested **Pieter Aertsen** (Pls. 356, 357, 360) may have gone from Amsterdam to Venice while **Barendsz** was at work there, though no such visit is recorded. **Pauwels Franck** known in Italy as **Paolo Fiammingo** reached Venice in the sixties and became a landscape assistant in Tintoretto's studio, after spending, it would seem, some time as a pupil in Titian's house. **Pieter Vlerick** went to Venice through France at the end of the fifties, was employed in Tintoretto's workshop, and was well thought of by Tintoretto whose daughter (van Mander who was later his pupil tells us) he might have married had he remained in Venice; in 1560 he left for Rome; there he made drawings from the antique and from Michelangelo's *Last Judgement*, collaborated with Girolamo Muziano on frescoes in Cardinal Ippolito d'Este's Villa d'Este in Tivoli, painted an *Adoration of the Magi* 'met mooie ruinen en veel beweging van kleine figuren', and drew panoramic vistas of Rome and the Tiber, the Castel S. Angelo and many ruins; about 1566 he visited Naples; and he went back via Germany to his native Courtrai in 1567. It is possible that **Hieronymus Francken the elder** was in Venice in 1564 when he painted his *Venetian Carnival* but it is also possible, of course, that the picture represents some carnival masquerade in Fontainebleau or Paris and was painted there. I have found no records of visits to Venice by **Ambrosius Francken the elder** or **Adriaen Thomas Key** (Pls. 423, 424, 425, 426, 437) presumed a nephew and pupil of **Willem Key** (Pl. 387) but both were possibly there in 1566 or 1567. **Michiel de Gast,** still making drawings of Roman landscapes with ruins in 1556, was back in Antwerp by 1558. **Hendrik van Cleve** seems also to have drawn and painted topographic works in Rome and elsewhere in this period. **Hubert Goltzius** arrived in Rome from France to continue his numismatic studies in 1559 and remained for some time before returning to his press in Bruges. **Adriaen de Weerdt** who arrived in Italy as a landscape follower of **Christian van den Queborne** and **Frans Mostaert,** probably in the later fifties, and became there, van Mander tells us, an enthusiast for the work of Parmigianino, was back in Brussels in the early sixties. **Hendrik van den Broeck (Arrigo Fiammingo, Henricus Malinus, Henricus Paludanus)** still established in Italy, worked in Orvieto in 1561, painted an *Adoration of the Magi* for the Montemelini Chapel in S. Francesco in Perugia between 1562 and 1564 and a *Descent from the Cross* for a church in Mongiovino in 1564, and visited Naples in 1567. **Jan van der Straet (Stradanus)** established in Florence, designed tapestry cartoons with religious, mythological and hunting subjects for Cosimo dei Medici in the later fifties, assisted Vasari on the decoration of Eleanor of Toledo's apartments in the Palazzo Vecchio in 1561, worked on Michelangelo's catafalque in 1564, and was among the numerous artists employed on the immensely elaborate pageantry and decorations for Francesco dei Medici's marriage with Joanna of Austria in 1565. **Federico di Lamberto Sustris** son of an Amsterdam artist and born in Italy or taken young there, was also associated with Vasari and employed on many of the same tasks as **Jan van der Straet;** in 1565 he designed some tapestries for Eleanor of Toledo's apartments; and in 1567 he was made a Councillor of the Accademia in Florence. **Gillis Congnet** (Pls. 434, 442) who came to Italy, possibly via Fontainebleau, either before or after 1561, went to Naples and Sicily, painted frescoes with 'grotesque' decoration in what van Mander calls the French manner (grotesken op de uitheemsch Fransche manier) in a villa at Terni, and also some religious subjects; and one 'Stello', possibly a Fleming, who worked with him at Terni was killed by a rocket when watching fireworks in Rome. **Anthoni Santvoort** from Malines, painter of religious subjects, seems to have been established in Rome by the middle sixties; **Aert Mytens** ('**Arnoldus**' or **Rinaldo Fiammingo**) who was his pupil and employed by him to make copies for the market of a favourite *Virgin and Child* in S. Maria Maggiore, came from Brussels in these years and left Rome about 1567 for Naples where he worked with a Fleming called **Cornelis Pyp** whose paintings are unknown. **Paul Schephen** who came from the Northern provinces worked in Naples from 1560 till 1567 when he painted frescoes in S. Severino. **Jan Speeckaert,** from Brussels, was a friend of **Aert Mytens** in this decade in Rome. **Pieter Stevens the elder,** from Malines, was in Rome by 1566 when he signed there an *Adoration of the Magi.* **Joos van Winghe** (Pls. 457, 497) spent four years in Rome before his visit to Paris at the end of the period. **Michel Joncquoy** from Tournai, was established in Rome by the middle sixties, painted many small crucifixions with black backgrounds repeated by means of stencils and sold mainly to devout Spaniards, and obtained some commissions for frescoes in churches. **Bartholomaeus Spranger** (Pls. 458, 459) went from France via Milan to Parma where at twenty in 1566 he was greatly impressed by Correggio's style; in Parma he assisted Bernardino Gatti (Il Sojaro) on frescoes in the cupola of S. Maria della Steccata, had a furious fight on the scaffolding with a rival assistant, and joined another master on decorations for the Pageant Entry of Margaret of Parma's son Alexander Farnese just married at twenty to Maria of Portugal; in 1567 he was working in Rome first as assistant to **Michel Joncquoy** and then independently; at this time he produced some landscapes and a 'spook' night piece 'with witches flying round a ruin like the Colosseum' which was bought by Giulio Clovio the miniaturist; and he was lodged before the year was out in the Cancelleria Palace of Cardinal Farnese to whom he had been introduced by Clovio. **Simon de Wobeck** reached Sicily from Haarlem before 1560 and seems to have remained there.

CHAPTER VIII

The Duke of Alva 1568-1573;
Don Luis de Requesens 1574-1575;
Don John of Austria 1576-1578

1568-1578

IN THE first months of 1568 ten thousand Spanish troops, with their auxiliaries and women, were quartered in various cities of the Netherlands; the building of the Spanish Citadel fortress in Antwerp (Pls. 433, 435) was begun; and the Duke of Alva's Terror was proceeding at full speed. Alva, assisted by Viglius ab Aytta and the Councillors Jacques del Rio and Juan de Vargas, worked seven hours a day examining and signing death warrants for his Council of Blood in Brussels; eighty-four patriots were executed on January 4, thirty-seven on February 21, fifty-five on March 20, and their confiscated property was applied to payment of the Spanish troops. There were also many victims of the Inquisition; and Alva wrote personally to the Rector of Louvain University for reports on the professors' religious and political trustworthiness. In April patriot forces under Louis of Nassau (Calvinist brother of William of Orange) launched unsuccessful military risings, and Alva replied by executing Counts Egmont and Hoorn on the Brussels market-place; in June and July Orange (now outlawed) led a military venture which also failed, and Alva ordered statues of himself as Victor over Heresy and Sedition to be made by the Flemish sculptor Jacob Jongelinck and erected in the Antwerp Citadel and in Brussels on the site of the Hôtel de Culembourg demolished by his troops because the Compromise of the Nobles had been signed there. In October Alva moved his headquarters to the Antwerp Citadel; and the lawyer Jan Rubens fled with his wife and first four children to Cologne where Anna of Saxony the drunken and unfaithful wife of William of Orange was established; and in December Alva defied Queen Elizabeth by arresting all English traders in the Netherlands. In this year also Mary Queen of Scots surrendered herself to Elizabeth; Philip II's son Don Carlos died or was murdered in prison; King Sebastian of Portugal, wholly guided by the Jesuits, came of age; the third French War of Religion started (after a short truce); Walter Raleigh served in the Huguenot armies defeated at Jarnac and Moncontour; and the Prince de Condé was assassinated. In 1569 the 'Northern Earls' were defeated in England and eight hundred of their followers were beheaded; Pius V expelled the Jews from the States of the Church; Philip II's bastard half-brother Don John of Austria aged twenty-four began the cruel suppression of a Morisco revolt in Granada; Alva demanded the imposition of new taxes in the Netherlands as the cash obtained from the Blood Council's victims was insufficient for his troops; and Orange issued letters-of-marque to the Beggars of the Sea (Gueux-de-Mer) whose vessels were to raid and plunder the Spaniards and their adherents on the coast. In 1570 Pope Pius V excommunicated Queen Elizabeth as a Calvinist and declared her a usurper; the third French War of Religion ended with the Peace of S. Germain, and Catherine de Médicis issued a new Edict of Pacification ceding four towns to the Huguenots as military centres; Justus Lipsius was Professor at the University of Jena where he passed as Lutheran; Turkish forces sent by Selim the Drunkard to capture Cyprus from the Republic of Venice took Nicosia and butchered the defenders; Cardinal Granvella was sent to Rome to work for an alliance between the Papacy, Venice and Spain against the Turks; Philip II married Anne of Austria (Pl. 408) and issued an Amnesty for offenders in the Netherlands with a list of exceptions that made it largely a façade; Alva, wearing a jewelled hat given him by the Pope as a 'Helmet of Righteousness', proclaimed this 'Amnesty' with elaborate pomp on the Town Hall Square in Antwerp; and many thousands of Dutch people lost their lives when the sea in tremendous gales broke the dykes and inundated large areas in Holland and Friesland. In 1571, while the Blood Council's persecutions continued, Alva imposed the Spanish 'Tenth Penny' (vendors') tax in the Netherlands which left the clergy and the nobles unaffected but caused widespread paralysis of commerce and misery among the workers whose salaries were reduced, and increased recruitments for the patriot Beggars of the Woods and Beggars of the Sea; Roberto Ridolfi (Florentine banker settled in England) visited Alva in Brussels and urged him to send troops to support a plot to marry Mary Queen of Scots to the Duke of Norfolk and to murder or dethrone Elizabeth; negotiations began for a marriage between Elizabeth, then thirty-eight, and François Duc d'Alençon (later Duke of Anjou), then seventeen; Jan Rubens was imprisoned in Dillenburg Castle by order of William of Orange and Count John of Nassau for adultery with Anna of Saxony; the Turks took Famagosta in Cyprus and mutilated and flayed alive Marc Antonio Bragadia who had led the defence for eleven months; Pius V and Philip II, now allied with Venice, sent Don John of Austria, aged twenty-six, to command a fleet which defeated the Turks at the Battle of Lepanto; and Miguel de Cervantes, aged twenty-four, had one hand permanently maimed in the course of the engagement. In 1572 Gregory XIII became Pope on the death of Pius V; and Francis Drake sailed to the Isthmus of Panama and cast eyes on the Pacific. In April the Beggars of the Sea captured Brill at the mouth of the Maas; in May and June, Flushing, Rotterdam and Gouda revolted, Luis of Nassau took Mons for the Calvinists, French Huguenots seized Valenciennes, there were risings in Dordrecht, Alkmaar, and Haarlem, and monks were cruelly ill-treated by the Beggars of the Sea at Gorcum. In the summer William of Orange became Stadholder of Holland and expecting Huguenot assistance marched on Mons where Alva's troops were besieging Louis; the Huguenot Henry of Navarre married Charles IX's sister Marguerite de Valois and abjured his religion; Catherine de Médicis and Charles IX launched the Massacre of S. Bartholomew; Coligny's head was sent to the Pope who ordered a commemorative medal; Philip II commanded a Te Deum; Charlotte of Bourbon, Abbess of Jouarre, fled to the court of the Elector Palatine and became a Protestant; and Orange retreated into Holland. In October Alva entered Malines (which had not revolted but given right of way to Orange) and set his troops to collect their pay in three days' unrestricted plunder; in November his bastard son Don Frederick of Toledo took Zutphen and Naarden and on Alva's orders killed all the male inhabitants and set the towns on fire; and in December Don Frederick laid siege to Haarlem. In 1573 Antonio Perez became chief secretary in Philip II's 'despacho universal'; Venice ceded Cyprus to the Turks; Don John captured Tunis; the Huguenots defended themselves in La Rochelle and Charles IX made concessions to them; Henri Duc d'Anjou, aged twenty-two, was elected King of Poland; William of Orange proclaimed himself a Calvinist; and a rich Spanish merchant endowed an Antwerp mansion as headquarters for the Jesuits who had acquired large funds and increased their influence in the later sixties though Alva himself disliked them. In July Haarlem, reduced to starvation, surrendered to the Spaniards after a resistance of six months with women fighting side by side with men, and the Spaniards executed two thousand of the inmates and publicly burned an effigy of Orange; Alkmaar successfully resisted a three-months' siege; Leyden was besieged from October onwards; the Beggars of the Sea captured Spanish treasure galleons and defeated Alva's fleet in the Zuyder Zee; and Alva left the Netherlands in December.

Don Luis de Requesens, Grand Commander of the Order of Santiago, who followed Alva as Governor General, had accompanied Don John of Austria at the Battle of Lepanto with instructions from King Philip to restrain the young commander's ardour and ambitions; and he came to the Netherlands as a keen supporter of the Jesuits. His first task there was to lead and control an army of some eight thousand Spaniards and some fifty thousand Walloons and German mercenaries which was difficult as their pay was in arrears and the Spaniards had evolved a technique of mutinous strikes; and his second task was to allay the passions and resentments caused by Alva's cruelties and blunders, which was still more difficult because Philip would not compromise on the religious question and Orange was demanding toleration and the removal of all foreign troops.

In 1574 Philip II ordered the remains of the Emperor Charles V to be transferred from Yuste to the Escorial which was now about half built; Henri Duc d'Anjou, who succeeded Charles IX as Henri III, came home from Poland via Venice where he passed under arches designed in his honour by Palladio and ornamented with panels by Tintoretto and Veronese, and was entertained at banquets decorated with statues made of sugar from designs by Sansovino; François Duc d'Alençon, the King's brother, became the Duke of Anjou and heir to the throne; and the fifth French War of Religion started with Anjou leading a party of Catholic nobles in political sympathy with Huguenot demands for more security and toleration. In the spring the Patriots in the Netherlands captured Middelburg and drove the Spaniards from Walcheren and Zeeland; Louis and Henry of Nassau were killed in the Battle of Mookerheide which the Spaniards won, and there was a large-scale mutiny among the Spanish troops. In May the siege of Leyden (abandoned since March) was resumed; the town held out despite appalling sufferings; Orange cut the dykes and opened the Rotterdam and Schiedam sluices, and in October Dutch ships sailed over the flooded fields and villages and reached the starving inmates. The University of Leyden was now founded to celebrate this triumph—(in 1615 **Pieter van Veen,** born in Leyden and eleven years old in 1574, painted *The Relief of Leyden by Admiral Boisot and the Beggars' Fleet* and gave it to the town). In 1575 the Archduke Albert, then eighteen (and later governor and sovereign of the Netherlands) was made a Cardinal; Anna of Saxony, divorced from William of Orange, was incarcerated as insane in a room with bricked-up windows; and Orange was married to Charlotte of Bourbon. The Spaniards who still held Amsterdam and Haarlem, captured Oudewater, burned most of the houses, massacred the garrison and sold the girls and women to the troops; Requesens personally planned the capture of the islands of Tholen and Duiveland and the siege of Ziericksee on Schouwen; Holland and Zeeland, now almost entirely Protestant, made plans for a political union under Orange and instructed Orange to seek foreign aid; and Orange sent envoys to Elizabeth inviting her to accept the protectorate of these provinces.

In 1576 Rudolf II became Emperor on the death of Maximilian II; the Huguenots, now led again by Henry of Navarre who had abjured his abjuration, together with appeasing Catholic nobles led by the Duke of Anjou, marched on Paris and forced Henri III to sign the Edict of Beaulieu which secured freedom of worship for the Huguenots everywhere in France except in Paris; the more ardent Catholics, led by the Duc de Guise, formed 'The League' in protest; and the sixth French War of Religion started. In March Requesens died; and the Council of State assumed the government of the Netherlands pending the arrival of a new Governor-General. In April Holland and Zeeland signed a formal Act of Federation; the envoys of Orange returned with vague promises from Elizabeth; and in May Orange opened negotiations with the Duke of Anjou. In June Ziericksee surrendered to the Spaniards and the Great Mutiny of the unpaid Spanish troops began; in July the mutineers were established in Alost; in September the Patriots instigated a coup d'état in Brussels which ejected the Council of State and proclaimed the Estates of Brabant and the Community of Brussels as a Provincial Government; and the Spanish mutineers were in touch with the garrisons in various citadel-fortresses. In October Maestricht revolted against the Spanish garrison, Don Frederick of Toledo sent troops who forced an entrance, with local women thrust before them, and butchered the insurgent burghers; attempts were made to dislodge the Spanish garrison from the Citadel in Ghent and Orange summoned a Congress there to devise a union of all the provinces; Don Sanchez d'Avila, Commander of the Antwerp Citadel, intimated that his garrison would help the Alost mutineers; and the Brussels Government sent five thousand Walloon militia to Antwerp to defend the citizens. On November 3 some three thousand Alost mutineers and others from other places marched into the Antwerp Citadel and with two thousand from the Citadel itself began the 'Spanish Fury' to collect their pay from the wealth and accumulated treasure of the city, which, despite the troubles, was still among the richest in the world; they easily routed the Walloon defenders and ran riot in five days of plunder, setting on fire a thousand buildings, including the Hotel de Ville and five hundred mansions, murdering eight thousand of the citizens and torturing others to extort their goods and money. On November 3 also Don John of Austria, the victor of Lepanto, sent from Naples by Philip to be Governor General, arrived in Luxemburg, disguised for safety as a Moorish slave; on November 8, the Spanish garrison was ejected from the Citadel of Ghent, and on that day also the Congress at Ghent was persuaded by Orange to sign the 'Pacification of Ghent'—an agreement between Holland and Zeeland and other provinces to unite for the expulsion of all Spanish troops, for the summoning of States-General, and for mutual tolerance between the Catholics and Protestants; and the Netherlands, thus temporarily united, made common cause in treating with Don John.

In 1577 Drake sailed for the Pacific; Danzig surrendered to Stephen Bathony, King of Poland and protector of the Jesuits; the sixth French War of Religion ended with the Peace of Bergerac after the Duke of Anjou, who had now abandoned the Huguenot side, had captured Issoire and butchered the inhabitants; and Henry of Navarre's wife, Marguerite de Valois, went to Spa nominally to take the waters but actually to further her brother Anjou's aspiration to become the Sovereign or Protector of the Netherlands. In January the Pacification of Ghent was confirmed by the Union of Brussels signed by thousands of leading men in all the provinces; Don John agreed to send away the Spanish troops but stipulated that they should leave by sea (as he intended to divert them for a raid on Britain where he hoped to marry Mary Queen of Scots and dethrone Elizabeth); and the States refused the stipulation. In February Don John signed the 'Perpetual Edict' whereby he undertook to send away the Spanish troops by land within forty days and to dismiss the German mercenaries when the States-General had paid their arrears of salary; the States agreed to uphold the Roman Catholic religion and to receive Don John as Governor General when the troops had actually left; and Orange led Holland and Zeeland to reject the Edict. In March Don John settled in Louvain where he shot down the popinjay in the annual festival of the Crossbowmen—as it was shot down later in Brussels by the Infanta Isabella, the Archduke Leopold Wilhelm and Prince Charles of Lorraine—and deployed his personal charm to attract the Flemish nobles whom he privately described as 'wine-skins' and detestable scoundrels. In April the Spanish troops left by land for Lombardy (though some twelve thousand German mercenaries remained in Antwerp and other places); and on May 1 Don John made a Pageant Entry as Governor-General in Brussels. In July Don John, fearing plots against his life, seized the Citadel of Namur with Walloon troops and German mercenaries and ordered other German mercenaries to eject the Flemish governor of the Antwerp Citadel; in August Patriot ships sailed up the Scheldt, the German mercenaries fled in panic, and the Patriots, now controlling the whole city, caused the demolition of the Citadel and the melting of Alva's statue into canon (Pls. 433, 435). In September Orange was acclaimed in Antwerp and went by canal to Brussels where half the population came to meet him; many crypto-Protestants now declared themselves, and emigrants began to return from various places; and some highly-placed Catholic nobles, in hostility to Orange, urged the Emperor's brother, the Archduke Mathias, then aged twenty, to come to the Netherlands to replace Don John as the Governor-General. In October Don John retired to Luxembourg whither Philip II sent troops collected secretly by Alexander Farnese (Margaret of Parma's son and, later, Duke of Parma); the Archduke Mathias arrived in Antwerp; Queen Elizabeth intimated her support of Orange; the States-General made Mathias Governor-General elect, and Orange, as Lieutenant-General and Ruuward of Brabant, the de facto ruler; and probably at this time **Marten de Vos** successfully protested to the Antwerp magistrates when the Cabinet Makers' Guild, owners of the *Lamentation* by **Quinten Massys,** proposed to offer it for sale to Queen Elizabeth. In November there was a Protestant rising in Ghent against the Catholic Governor the Duke of Aerschot and others alleged to be intriguing with Don John; the insurgents led by two young nobles Ryhove and Hembyze (Imbize) imprisoned the Bishops of Bruges and Ypres and many Catholic nobles, and Orange went in person to press for toleration—an episode recorded in 1818 in a costume-history picture by **Mattheus van Brée.** On December 7 the States General formally announced that Don John was no longer Governor-General and that all assisting him were rebels; on December 10 a new 'Act of Union' was signed in Brussels by which the Catholics and Protestants bound themselves to respect and protect each other with mutual guarantees against enemies of all kinds; and on December 18 Alexander Farnese reached Luxembourg to help Don John.

Early in 1578 Queen Elizabeth promised a subsidy and military assistance to the States; the Archduke Mathias made a Pageant Entry into Brussels as Governor-General and took a double oath of allegiance to King Philip and the States; the Patriots had an army of twenty thousand led by nobles (some of whom were disaffected); Don John also had some twenty thousand troops with Alexander Farnese and veteran Spanish generals on his staff; Gregory XIII issued a bull to bless the Spaniards in the terms used for crusades against the Turk; Don John went into battle beneath a banner with the Cross and 'In hoc signo vici Turcos in hoc Haereticos vincam' inscribed upon it; Alexander Farnese destroyed the Patriot army at Gemblours, near Namur, and Don John hanged the prisoners or drowned them in the Meuse. In March Juan de Escovedo was murdered in Madrid by agents of the King and Antonio Perez. In the early summer Don John captured some unimportant places; there were Protestant demonstrations in Amsterdam and Haarlem and also in Antwerp and Brussels; and Amsterdam, hitherto still Spanish, joined the State of Holland. The Calvinist John Casimir, brother of the Elector Palatine Louis VI, and a protégé of Queen Elizabeth, arrived at Zutphen with twelve thousand German mercenaries; and he also took command of a force of cavalry sent there from England. Later in the summer the Duke of Anjou, in league with Catholic nobles now known as the 'Walloon Malcontents', led an army into Mons; and Orange, who expected Anjou to marry Elizabeth, persuaded the States-General to give the Duke the title of 'Defender of the Liberty of the Netherlands against the Tyranny of the Spaniards and their adherents' and hinted at a later offer of the sovereignty of the Netherlands. In October Don John died; his corpse, divided into three parts and carried in bags by three troopers into Spain, was reassembled for interment in the Escorial; Philip appointed Alexander Farnese Governor of the Netherlands; and John Casimir in Ghent was hoping to be nominated Count of Flanders. In November the Walloon Malcontents intrigued with Farnese and Anjou and caused anti-Protestant risings; unpaid troops of all kinds—Spanish, Walloon, German, English and others—were living on the countryside and causing great distress; Ghent Calvinists rose in Iconoclast riots and drove Papists from the city till Orange went again himself to condemn and curb their excesses; and in December Duke Casimir returned to the Palatinate. In this year also King Sebastian of Portugal led an army to Morocco and was killed at the Battle of Al Kasr al Kebir; and his aged uncle Cardinal Prince Henry became king.

The effects on the artists of the happenings and conditions in the Netherlands were most various. I have found no records of painters executed among the eighteen thousand persons that Alva boasted he had 'liquidated' in his six years' rule—unless **Baptiste Floris** (a son of **Frans Floris**) murdered, van Mander tells us, by the Spaniards in Brussels, was one of the Blood Council's victims. But there are traces of sufferings. **Michiel Coxie** (Pls. 308, 310, 352) for example learned in 1574, when he was seventy-five, that his son, the painter **Guillaume Coxie,** accused of heresy by the Inquisition, had been condemned to ten years in the galleys, and saved him by direct appeal to King Philip who intervened on his behalf. Some artists perished in the various fightings; the portrait painter **Simon Jacobsz** was killed in the defence of Haarlem where **Pieter Pietersz** (Pl. 421), son of **Pieter Aertsen,** looked after the Dutch painter Cornelis of Haarlem whose parents had fled and left him as a boy of twelve in his care; others had their homes destroyed around them; **Marten van Heemskerck** (Pls. 303, 304, 306, 354, 355, 365, 372) aged seventy-four escaped from Haarlem to the house of his former pupil the collector Jacob Rauwaert in Amsterdam, and, driven paranoiac by the times, went about with a hoard of money sewn into his clothes; and the owner of **Albert van Ouwater's** *Raising of Lazarus* then in Haarlem was robbed of the picture which was sent by the Spaniards with other loot to Spain. When Malines was sacked, though **Michiel Coxie's** elegant house was specially exempt from billeting, the landscape painter **Hans Bol** (Pl. 431) and the draughtsman and engraver **Pieter van der Borcht** had to flee, quite destitute, to Antwerp; **Jan Snellinck** (Pl. 460) another Malinois who came to Antwerp soon after, was also, most probably, a refugee; and though **Pieter Bruegel,** commissioned by the Brussels Magistrature to paint pictures of the digging of the Antwerp-Brussels-Willebroeck Canal, secured exemption from billeting in 1568, he thought it wise to destroy a number of his 'al te bijtend of schimpend' compositions before he died in 1569 lest they should bring persecution on his wife. In the Spanish Fury in Antwerp the tapestry designer **Frans Spierinx** had his property severely damaged; the draughtsman and engraver **Joris Hoefnagel** saw his father's stock of diamonds, hidden in a well, betrayed to the marauders by a frightened servant girl; the printer Christopher Plantin had his press set on fire and was forced to pay an enormous ransom to procure his personal escape; and among those who left the city **Frans Badens,** aged five, was taken by his father into Holland. Some artists on the other hand weathered the storms by turning for a time to safer occupations; thus **Ambrosius Francken the elder** feathered his nest after the Spanish Fury by marrying a rich widow who owned a stone and chalk enterprise which he managed for some years; and **Pieter Jansz Pourbus** turned from painting for a time in 1578 to make plans for the defence of Bruges by flooding.

There were also, of course, more emigrations, mainly of Protestants, to Germany and England, as opportunities occurred, especially after the Amnesty of 1570 when some freedom of movement seems to have been allowed. Of the Protestants who remained, some are known to have exported their work to Germany, some sold to the steadily increasing numbers of rich Protestant burghers, and the more original were doubtless helped by Protestant professional men. After the Pacification of Ghent in 1576—when the Patriots were in power in Brussels, Antwerp and other places as well as in Holland and Zeeland— many of the émigrés returned; and one of them, the Protestant architectural draughtsman **Jan Vredeman de Vries** (Pl. 462) was made engineer in charge of the Antwerp fortifications.

Catholic painters, with nothing against them and willing to collaborate with the Spaniards, were normally immune from the Alva Terror and the Inquisition. But no one was safe from denunciations; and there is evidence that Catholics with pro-Spanish tendencies were cold-shouldered and sometimes molested or ill-treated by the Calvinists and Patriots, especially in the Northern provinces. In 1572, for example, when the Orange party ruled in Leyden, Cornelis van Veen, a former Burgomaster and still an official in 1571, was constrained to move to Antwerp taking with him his son **Otto van Veen** (Pls. 455, 510, 511, 570) who was then sixteen.

The Painters' and Craftsmen's Guilds and the Chambers of Rhetoric in the various places pursued their usual activities as far as circumstances allowed, and all the traditional modes of Flemish painting were continued. Thus in 1571 the officials of the Antwerp Guild included **Marten de Vos** as painter of religious pictures (Pl. 397), **Pieter Balten** as genre painter, and **Antonio van Palerme** as artist-dealer. There was even a certain amount of official patronage. Alva briefed **Antonis Mor** to paint his mistresses, made **Pieter de Kempener** (Pl. 367) his Master of Works, and sat for his portrait to **Willem Key** (Pl. 387) who overheard him order the execution of Counts Egmont and Hoorn and died himself, it is said from the shock, on the day that the sentence was fulfilled. Alva also gave work to the painters of allegories and mythologies when he staged his pompous ceremonials and pageants.

Records of and references to events, and, despite the danger, crypto-political allusions were made as always in popular prints and also in contemporary paintings. It was probably during Alva's Terror that **Frans Floris** (Pls. 335, 351, 353) painted *The Muses asleep in wartime* with half-nude figures recumbent in the foreground and a battle raging in the distant landscape; and that **Marten van Heemskerck** painted *The Flood*—with naked men and women and dead children still clasping their toys in the waters—as a gesture of despairing comment; and we know that **Karel van Mander** (Pl. 472), a Protestant and pupil of the Protestants **Lucas de Heere** and **Pieter Vlerick,** produced a play of his own composition called *Noah and the Flood*—with scenery painted by himself and water pumped in torrents round the ark—in Meulebeke at twenty-two in 1570. Some political prints may have been issued by **Hieronymus Wellens de Cock** before 1570 when he died—though he was mainly employed in his last years on a series of portraits of Flemish artists published in 1572 by his widow with verses by **Lampsonius.** Christopher Plantin seems to have run with the hare and hunted with the hounds, as he printed missals, breviaries and so forth and his 'Biblia polyglota' approved by the orthodox and also books illustrated by **Pieter Huys** (Pls. 412, 413) and **Lucas de Heere,** and, secretly, heretical tracts and, perhaps, political pamphlets. **Pieter Bruegel's** pictures painted in Brussels in his last two years are impregnated with the horrors around him; the *Misanthrope: or Perfidy of the World* of 1568 is inscribed 'Om dat de Werelt is soe ongetru/Daer om gha ic in den ru'; the *Five Crippled Beggars* of the same year shows pathetic wretches hideously maimed by tortures —(like the beggars in his *Battle between Carnival and Lent* (Pl. 370)); his *Blind leading the Blind* also of 1568 is another gesture of despair; and we know from van Mander that the *Magpie on the gallows with peasants dancing* was left to his wife as a warning that imprudent chatter might bring her to the gallows. The *Massacre of the Innocents* (Pl. 382), undated, was doubtless painted in these years to symbolize the Alva Terror—for Spanish lancers, with Alva himself at their head, are drawn up on a snow-covered village square, while soldiers batter down doors and the Netherlanders entreat in vain for mercy; and *Dulle Griet: (Mad Meg) calling up her legions* (with an undecipherable date) is surely a still more passionate protest against Alva—for here the central distracted creature, clad in the helmet and breast-plate of the Spaniards, is creating Hell on Earth in a landscape red from burning buildings and peopled with mad spooks and devils and Alva's lancers who come forth at her bidding from the Antwerp Citadel. There are obvious echoes of **Hieronymus Bosch's** concepts of Hell on Earth and Hell itself (Pls. 168, 173) in this *Dulle Griet* and we find both concepts also echoed in the *Battle between angels and demons, and torments in Hell* (Pl. 412) painted in 1570 by **Pieter Huys** with a flaming city in the distance and one of the Inquisition's victims lifted from the stake by angels while a savage lancer adds a final unnecessary blow. But the most terrible indictment of the whole Alva period is the picture reproduced here by the **Madrid Triumph of Death Painter** (Pls. 410, 415), for in this ghastly landscape where gibbets and torture wheels take the place of trees and a city burns once more on the horizon, Death collects his countless victims of all classes and transports them in cartloads while the bell of the Inquisition tolls. When Alva left, the tension to some extent abated—(though a city burns, a Spanish lancer's helmet is perched on a dead tree and a torture wheel still insults the sky in *The Temptation of S. Anthony* (Pl. 413) painted by Huys in 1577)—and direct recordings or pedantic symbolisms seem to have taken the place of these passionate protests and allusions. Thus in 1574 **Antoine Claeissins,** a pupil of **Pieter Jansz Pourbus** and official painter to the city of Bruges since 1570, produced an archaistic *Banquet of Ahasuerus* (Pl. 422) inscribed 'And the drinking was according to the law; none did compel'; but as Queen Vashti's feast to the women is inserted in the background, it is not clear whether the men's freedom to decline the wine or the punishment of Vashti for refusing to attend the major party, was the base of the topical meaning. The confused composition *Shadrach, Meshach and Abednego in the Fiery Furnace* (Pl. 421) painted in Haarlem in 1575 for the Bakers' Guild by the Protestant **Pieter Pietersz,** was perhaps deliberately confused to hide the meaning—for the Spaniards were then in Haarlem and the golden image that the young men refused to bow down to was surely taken by the Haarlemers to symbolize Alva's statue in the Antwerp citadel. A *Siege of Alkmaar*, to commemorate Alkmaar's successful resistance to Don Frederick, was commissioned some years later from **Pieter Adriaensz Cluyt** for the Alkmaar Civic Guardhouse. **Frans Pourbus the elder** made, I think, a crypto-anti-Spanish gesture in a triptych commissioned by Councillor del Rio in 1576; for here the central panel shows *Isaiah predicting the recovery of Hezekiah* which must have recalled to Patriot spectators 'Go and say thus saith the Lord: I will deliver thee and this city out of the hand of the King of Assyria'. **Crispiaen van den Broeck (Paludanus)** (Pl. 409) drew or painted *The Spanish Fury* for engravings, and the Antwerp Museum has an *Antwerp Town Hall in flames with fighting on the Place and Canal au Fromage in the Spanish Fury* by an unidentified artist. There were many records also of the *Demolition of the Antwerp Citadel* which was painted by **Marten van Cleve** and drawn or painted for engravings by **Jacob Jansz de Gheyn the elder** and other artists; the demolition was carried out by ten thousand Antwerp citizens including nobles, magistrates and burghers working side by side with the populace by day and night in improvised encampments, and this social aspect of the joyful task is stressed in the pictures reproduced here by the **Worcester Destruction of Citadel Painter** (Pl. 435) and the **Antwerp Destruction of Citadel Painter** (Pl. 433). At the end of the period the Prince of Orange briefed **Cornelis Enghelrams** of Malines to paint a series of panels *The Story of David* from designs by **Lucas de Heere** with architectural motifs by **Jan Vredeman de Vries** (Pl. 462) for an apartment reserved for him in Antwerp, and this probably included a *David and Goliath* panel where David symbolized the Patriots and Goliath the Might of Spain; and **Pieter Vlerick** (back from Italy and working in Tournai) made propaganda gestures with a *Massacre of the Innocents* and a *Martyrdom of the Maccabees*—Judas Maccabaeus being at this time a recognized symbol for Orange in the Rhetoricians' repertories.

Pictures with what seems to have been open or crypto-Protestant propaganda and some personal unorthodox pieces were still being painted; and in this connection we may note that other plays by **Karel van Mander** produced between 1570 and 1573 were a *Nebuchadnezzar* and a *Story of Solomon* with the Queen of Sheba's visit and the King's idolatry as episodes. In 1570 **Joachim Beuckelaer** painted in Antwerp the *Fishmarket with Ecce Homo and the Crucifixion in the background* (Pl. 398) with his old unorthodox placing of the sacred figures and must have sold it, I imagine, into Holland where his work was collected by, among others, Jacob Rauwaert (owner also of pictures by **Gerard van der Meire, Pieter Aertsen, Dirck Barendsz** and **Marten van Heemskerck**). More Protestant subjects like those reproduced here (Pls. 361, 362) may have been painted by **Jan Massys** who lived till 1575; and **Gillis Mostaert** (Pl. 348) who lived through the period, still 'niet zoo heel godsdienstig' and 'niet erg Spaansch gezind' may have painted his *Christ mocked* and the *Massacre of the Innocents* at this time and may have risked more of his jocular affronts to orthodoxy—to be washed off at the approach of danger. In 1571 **Frans Pourbus the elder** painted a triptych for Ghent S. Bavon commissioned by Viglius ab Aytta; in the main panel *Jesus among the doctors* we have the Child Jesus in the centre with the doctors, the High Priest behind, and in the left foreground Charles V, Philip II and Alva; *Jesus among the Doctors* can easily, of course, be read as a crypto-Protestant subject with the Child Jesus symbolizing the initial purity of Christian doctrine; **Frans Pourbus the elder,** who later avowed himself a Protestant, may have been a crypto-Protestant at this date; and the picture may thus have been a crypto-Protestant gesture with Charles V, Philip and Alva and the doctors symbolizing corrupted doctrines in state and church, produced as it were beneath the very nose of Viglius, Alva's collaborator and abettor.

The orthodox religious painters were guided by Tridentine theologians who favoured the Romanist manner and frowned on the old traditions of the Netherlands where the door had been open to personal imaginative concepts and simple delight in the stories of the Golden Legend; the nude was discouraged in religious pictures except in the *Last Judgement* where, as the Venetian Inquisitors had pointed out to Veronese, the figures being 'disembodied spirits' could be properly shown without clothes or draperies; and in 'De picturis et imaginibus' published in 1570 by Jean Molanus, Professor in Louvain University, the painters were given rules to work by and forbidden, inter alia, to show S. Joseph as an old man—as we have seen him in the lovely picture by the **New York Adoration in a White Castle Painter** (Pl. 151), or to paint the Virgin swooning at the Crucifixion—as she appears in the moving works by the **New York Crucifixion and Last Judgement Painter** (Pl. 160), **Rogier van der Weyden** (Pl. 46), the **Florence (Poggio Imperiale) Crucifixion Painter** (Pl. 133), **Cornelis Engelbrechtsz** (Pls. 232, 233), the **Detroit Crucifixion Painter** (Pl. 285), and also **Bruegel's** *Road to Calvary* (Pls. 379, 381).

Of the Antwerp painters of religious subjects **Bernaert de Ryckere** seems to have worked through the period painting Romanist pictures; and **Izaak del Hele** back from Spain was in Antwerp from 1571. **Lambert van Noort,** who died under fifty in 1571, must have pleased the Tridentine theologians with the orthodox Romanism of his *Adoration of the Shepherds* (Pl. 402) painted in the first year of the Alva Terror; and the defects of this guidance are embodied in the *Penitent Magdalene* (Pl. 403) painted the same year by **Marcellus Coffermans**—as we can see if we contrast the marble complacency of this long-limbed figure with the pathetic penitent by the **Philadelphia Maria Egyptiaca Painter** (Pl. 131). **Marten de Vos,** who was much employed to replace altarpieces destroyed by the Iconoclasts and took **Wenzelas Coebergher** (Pl. 493) as a pupil in 1573, painted as eminently orthodox propaganda subjects *S. Paul at Ephesus: the burning of the books* (Pl. 397) at about thirty-seven in 1568 and *The Incredulity of S. Thomas* for the Furriers' Altar in the Cathedral in 1574. **Frans Floris** (Pls. 335, 351, 353), who died under sixty in 1570, was engaged in his last years on an *Adoration of the Magi* triptych and on two panels twenty-seven feet high—a *Crucifixion* and an *Ascension* commissioned by the Grand Prior of Spain: like **Rubens** later, it was his custom to make drawings of his compositions and hand them to his pupils and assistants who enlarged and painted them with the aid of studio studies of heads and so forth, and thereafter, presumably, he did some final retouching; his last undertakings had apparently reached the second of these stages when he died, and it is known that his former pupil **Hieronymus Francken the elder** came to Antwerp from Paris to finish the triptych and that other former pupils, including **Frans Pourbus the elder** and **Crispiaen van den Broeck,** completed the Grand Prior's panels and also the wings for them which, at that time, were scarcely begun and still in monochrome 'lay in' ('nauwelijks begonnen en gedoodverfd'); **Hieronymus Francken the elder** then thirty-one may have then stayed in Antwerp for some years or gone back immediately to Paris. **Frans Pourbus the elder,** citizen and Master in both Bruges and Antwerp at twenty-four in 1569 when he married his mistress Susanna Floris, had a number of commissions for religious pictures in addition to the *Jesus among the Doctors* of 1571 and *Isaiah predicting the recovery of Hezekiah* of 1576 already referred to; these included a *Raising of Lazarus* for Tournai Cathedral, a *S. Matthew inspired by an angel* in 1573, and a *S. George* triptych (which may have topical allusions) for the Abbaye des Dunes in 1577. **Crispiaen van den Broeck** painted the *Last Judgement* reproduced here (Pl. 409) at forty-seven in 1571, and may have been, I think, the author later of the *Last Judgement* owned by Vermeer of Delft and inserted as background to his *Woman weighing Gold* (or *Pearls*). Of other **Floris** pupils **Frans Francken the elder,** much employed for churches, took **Gortzius Geldorp** (Pls. 454, 486) and

165

Herman van der Mast (Pl. 453) as pupils about 1570; and **Ambrosius Francken the elder** worked for the Bishop of Tournai in 1569, went abroad in 1570, settled in Antwerp in 1573, and directed a stone and chalk enterprise, as mentioned, from 1577. **Joachim Beuckelaer** whose admirable *Fishmarket with Ecce Homo and the Crucifixion in the background* (Pl. 398) of 1570 has already been referred to, and who may have painted a *Raising of Lazarus* in these years, was now more than ever unsuccessful in his native Antwerp and was reduced on occasion to hack painting as assistant to other artists before his death, in poverty, in 1574; and both **Gillis Mostaert** (Pl. 348) and **Jan Massys** (Pls. 361, 362) may have painted some orthodox pictures. Among the newcomers **Jacques de Backer,** released from his bondage to **Antonio van Palerme,** painted the imposing *Last Judgement* (Pl. 416) in the manner of **Crispiaen van den Broeck** (Pl. 409) when he was round about twenty in 1571. **Adriaen Thomas Key,** Antwerp Master in 1568, after the visit to Venice presumed in my last chapter, painted *The Last Supper* (Pls. 425, 426) on the exterior wings of an altarpiece for the Recollets church in 1575 when he was just over thirty; some theologian probably instructed him to indicate the 'upper chamber' by the servant in the foreground climbing up the stairs; but otherwise the composition seems to me quite evidently based on two versions of the subject by Titian (the picture now in the Ducal Palace at Urbino and the picture painted in 1564 for the Escorial). **Jan Snellinck** (Pl. 460), in Antwerp at about twenty-six by 1574, had a number of pupils by 1577; **Cornelis Floris,** son of the sculptor of that name and nephew of **Frans Floris,** began his career as Antwerp Master at the same age in 1577 after training in Paris; and **Gerard Schoof** who had come from Malines was Antwerp Master in 1575.

Among the painters of religious subjects in the other towns **Pieter Jansz Pourbus** (Pls. 331, 334, 336, 337), Dean of the Bruges Guild at about fifty in 1569, signed a grisaille triptych with a *Deposition* (*and Entombment in the background*) as the centre panel for the Hospice de Damme in 1570, an *Adoration of the Shepherds* for Notre Dame in 1574 and a *Resurrection* for S. Jacques in 1578; **Marcus Geeraerts the elder,** probably a Protestant, went abroad from Bruges in 1568; **Antoine Claeissins** (Pls. 422, 492) worked for various churches in the archaistic spirit favoured by the Brugeois; his brother **Pieter Claeissins the younger,** Master in 1571, collaborated with his father **Pieter Claeissins the elder** on a *Resurrection* for S. Sauveur in 1572; **Gillis Claeissins** was also still working in Bruges; and **Jacques van den Coornhuuse** made a free copy of **Jan Provoost's** *Last Judgement* (Pl. 283) for the Prévôté of S. Donatien in 1578. In Brussels production appears to have diminished; **Joos van Winghe** (Pls. 457, 497) may have painted some religious subjects as he returned there from Paris in these years; and the same applies to **Aert Mytens** who seems to have visited his native Brussels from Naples at this time. But **Adriaen de Weerdt** was abroad all through the period and **Pieter Bruegel** is not known to have painted such subjects in his last two years. **Pieter de Kempener** (Pl. 367) was still alive in 1578 but as he was already sixty-five in 1568 and occupied thereafter with his posts as Master of Works to Alva and Director of the Tapestry Factory he may have painted little and declined commissions. In Malines **Cornelis Enghelrams,** protégé as noted of the Prince of Orange and evidently a Protestant, was just over forty in 1568; **Gregorius Beerings** died about 1570, and both **Vincent Geldersman** and **Vincent Sellaer** may also have died before 1578. **Raphael Coxie,** about twenty-eight in 1568, was now receiving some commissions and had **Chrétien de Bruyne** as his assistant for decorative adjuncts in 1571; and **Michiel Coxie,** still King's Painter and persona gratissima with the Spaniards, painted *S. Cecilia* (Pl. 352) in or before 1569 and dated a *Martyrdom of S. Sebastian* painted for the Vieux Serment altar in

Antwerp Cathedral '1575 aetatis suae 76'. **Pieter Vlerick** moved from Courtrai to Tournai in 1568, had **Karel van Mander** (Pl. 472) as his pupil till 1569, became a member of the Guild there despite the restrictive measures against non-local artists and painted, van Mander tells us, for a nunnery a *Crucifixion* triptych with a *Road to Calvary* with light and shade effects in the manner of his master Tintoretto which displeased the nuns, another *Crucifixion* where the body of Christ was veritably collapsed like a corpse, a *Resurrection* as a memorial panel on a tomb, and other religious subjects in addition to the *Massacre of the Innocents* and the *Martyrdom of the Maccabees* already referred to as propaganda pieces; and **Michel Joncquoy** back in Tournai from Rome about 1575 made **Vlerick** furious by disparaging an arm in his *Resurrection* and actually altering it with paint. **Jan van Rillaert** died in Louvain in 1568; and **Pieter van der Hofstadt** (Pl. 366) who painted, presumably there, his triptych *Christ as the Man of Sorrows* with *The Agony in the garden* and *Christ carrying the Cross* at about sixty-five in 1569, may have lived there (or abroad) till 1578 as the date and place of his death are unknown. **Jean Baptiste Saive,** twenty-eight in 1568, was painting religious subjects in Namur. In Ghent, where conditions were constantly in ferment and the vast majority of the burghers were ardent Calvinists by 1578, I find no records of religious paintings though some were, no doubt, produced. In Liège **Otto van Veen** (Pls. 455, 510, 511, 570), aged seventeen in 1573, was being trained first by **Domenicus Lampsonius** and then by **Jean Ramey** who painted a *Last Supper* for a funeral monument in S. Pierre in 1576. In the Northern provinces **Marten van Heemskerck** (Pls. 303, 304, 306, 354, 355, 365, 372) died in Haarlem at seventy-six in 1574, and **Pieter Aertsen** (Pls. 356, 357, 360) in Amsterdam at about sixty-seven in 1575. **Pieter Pietersz** working in Haarlem painted a *Martyrdom of SS. Peter and Paul* for a Gouda church before 1569 and the *Shadrach, Meshach and Abednego in the Fiery Furnace* (Pl. 421) mentioned above at thirty-three in 1575. **Aert Pietersz** (Pl. 485) a younger son of **Pieter Aertsen** was an independent artist in Amsterdam by 1570 and painted some religious subjects; and **Dirck Barendsz** (Pl. 389) also established in Amsterdam, and thirty-four in 1568, may have painted in these years his *Nativity* triptych for the Fratershuis in Gouda described by van Mander as 'zeer goed op de Italiaansche wijze', and drawn his *Story of Jonah* and other religious subjects for engravers. **Anthonis Blocklandt** (Pl. 420), thirty-six in 1568, worked in Delft till he went to Italy in 1572, returned the same year and then settled in Utrecht where he was Master in 1577; in Utrecht he painted *The Legend of S. Catherine* for Hertogenbosch, a *Pentecost* and an *Ascension*; and he had there **Adriaen Cluyt** (son of **Pieter Adriensz Cluyt**), later a portrait painter, as his pupil and assistant.

Alva as mentioned gave work to the designers of allegories, mythologies and Olympian groups for his various pageants. Girls in classical draperies symbolizing Righteousness and Peace stood right and left of the throne in his 'Amnesty' performance on the Town Hall Square in Antwerp; and there was work the same year for artists in these categories when Anne of Austria (Pl. 408) daughter of the Emperor Maximilian II (Pl. 332), passing through Antwerp on her way to Spain, was given a Pageant Entry where one of the arches was provided by the largely Protestant German colony who employed **Jan Vredeman de Vries** (Pl. 462) to design it. When Don John made his Pageant Entry into Brussels rows of arches decorated with figures and painted panels were set up, and the Rhetoricians concocted ingenious allegories translated by the artists into tableaux vivants on numerous cars and stages. When Orange went from Antwerp by canal to Brussels three barges were filled with allegoric tableaux in his honour. On his visit to Ghent to curb the Hembyze anti-Catholic riots he was given a Pageant Entry for which **Lucas de Heere,** member as artist-poet of the local Chamber of Rhetoric known as 'Jesus met de balsembloeme', designed cars and tableaux where Orange was symbolized by Judas Maccabaeus, and a group called *The Pacification of Ghent* showed the Catholic and Protestant religions as maidens bound together by chains of amity while Discord in a corner devoured his own evil heart. When the Archduke Mathias was given his Pageant Entry into Brussels there were twenty-four stages on the Town Hall Square; and Juno, Cybele and Hebe, Wisdom, Constancy and Prudence, Fame and Glory, Quintus Curtius and Scipio Africanus were shown in various conjunctions to symbolize his powers and virtues. All the painters of allegories and mythologies with nude and draped figures were of course available for such tasks. In Antwerp they included **Frans Floris** (Pls. 335, 353) till 1570, **Abraham del Hele** probably till some time in the early seventies, **Jan Massys** (Pl. 363) till 1574, **Marten de Vos** (Pl. 364), **Gillis Congnet** (Pl. 434), **Crispiaen van den Broeck** (Pl. 409), **Jacques de Backer** (Pl. 416), **Bernaert de Ryckere, Gortzius Geldorp** (Pls. 454, 486) in the later seventies, and **Cornelis Floris** from 1577. **Joos van Winghe** (Pl. 457, 497) was available in Brussels; and it was probably there that **Antonis Mor** painted nudes titled *Venus* and *Mars*, possibly for Alva, before 1574. **Jan van der Straet (Stradanus)** is said to have come to Flanders from Italy in the service of Don John and to have stayed till 1578; and both the **Vienna Feast of the Gods Painter** (Pl. 419) and the **Dublin Rebecca Painter** (Pl. 418) were probably active in these years. The Bruges men included **Pieter Jansz Pourbus** (Pls. 331, 334) and **Gerard Pietersz** and **Antoine Claeissins** (Pls. 422, 492) official painter to the city from 1570. **Pieter Vlerick** joins this category in Tournai with a *Susanna and the Elders*. **Lucas de Heere** was available in Ghent from 1577. **Domenicus Lampsonius** may have painted some nude figures in Liège and **Otto van Veen** (Pls. 455, 510, 511, 570) was working there, as noted, from 1573 till he went abroad at twenty in 1576. **Anthonis Blocklandt's** *Diana and Actaeon* (Pl. 420) with its Titian and Bronzino echoes, and the punishment of Actaeon mercifully tiny on the distant hills, was painted in 1573 immediately after his Italian visit. **Dirck Barendsz** (Pl. 389) was available in Amsterdam; and **Cornelis Ketel** (Pl. 451) who had a passion for allegoric subjects was back from Fontainebleau and in Gouda from 1568 when he was twenty till 1573.

Among the portrait painters **Willem Key** (Pl. 387) died in Antwerp in 1568 and **Antonis Mor** died there in 1576. Others available in Antwerp included **Marten de Vos, Frans Pourbus the elder, Adriaen Thomas Key, Benjamin Sammeling, Gillis Congnet** (Pl. 442) and from the middle seventies two newcomers **Gortzius Geldorp** (Pls. 454, 486) and **Daniel van den Queborne.** Of these **Antonis Mor,** working in Utrecht and Brussels as well as in Antwerp, painted Alva's mistresses, as noted, and was still King's Painter; his impressive *Gentleman with a dog* (Pl. 428) dates from 1569 when he was approximately fifty; in 1570 he painted the fair-haired *Anne of Austria* (Pl. 408) in a black dress with yellow sleeves, when she passed through Antwerp, as mentioned, aged twenty-one to become the fourth wife of Philip II then forty-three; in 1576, some months before he died, he painted in one hour—van Mander tells us—his *Hubert Goltzius* and gave it to the sitter, an old friend, in exchange for one of his books on medals; and up to 1573 he seems to have given the indigent **Joachim Beuckelaer** employment as assistant on the clothes and accessories in some portraits. Despite the troubles of the time rich burghers still commissioned family groups— sometimes as conversation pieces with indications of their wealth and social status, and sometimes in the old way as adorants on the wings of altarpieces donated to some church Thus in 1570 **Marten de Vos** painted *The Antwerp shipowner Gilles Hoffman and his wife* (Pl. 429) where Hoffman, who had establishments in Antwerp and Middelburg and whose ships went as far afield as Russia, and his wife, Margaretha van Nispen, holding her pomander chain, stand in front of a table with a lantern clock, a rare possession at that date; and in 1577 he painted *The family of Antoine Anselmo* where the sitter, a brother-in-law of Hoffman and later a sheriff of Antwerp, is seated with his wife and two children before a table with a pot of flowers including a tulip, then a novelty as tulip growing began in Holland about 1560. **Frans Pourbus the elder** painted *An old lady in an armchair with a pet dog in her arm* in 1568, and, in 1571, when he was twenty-six, *The Family of Joris Hoefnagel*, an elaborate conversation piece with twenty portraits where **Hoefnagel**, who had returned from abroad to get married, is shown at his wedding party, with some members of the family round a buffet and others playing lutes and virginals, and a small child enchanted with the colours of a parakeet; in these years also he portrayed *Councillor del Rio* and *Councillor Viglius ab Aytta* as adorant donors in the altarpieces of 1571 and 1576 already referred to, and he also painted a portrait inscribed *The Duc d'Alençon (Duc d'Anjou)*? (Pl. 427) in 1574. In 1575 the widow of Gillis de Smidt, syndic of the Antwerp Recollets, who died in 1574, gave an altarpiece to the Recollets which contained **Adriaen Thomas Key's** *Last Supper* (Pls. 423, 424), and on one wing *Gillis de Schmidt with a daughter and six sons as adorants* (Pl. 425) and on the other *Maria de Deckere his second wife with her daughter as adorants* (Pl. 426) with the arms of both families conspicuously displayed on the prie-dieu covers. The same spirit is observable in Bruges where **Pieter Jansz Pourbus** (Pls. 336, 337) painted three groups of rich burghers with their large families as adorant donors—*Anselmo Boetius and his wife with their ten children, Josse de Damhoudere with his wife and nine children* on the wings of pictures for Notre Dame in 1573 and 1574 and *Soyer van Male with his two wives and sixteen children* on the wings of a picture for S. Jacques in 1578. Of the portrait painters in the other towns **Nicolas Snellaert** was available in Courtrai, **Pieter van der Hofstadt** may have painted more sensitive studies like the one reproduced here (Pl. 366) in Louvain or elsewhere, and **Lucas de Heere** may have produced some in Ghent in 1578. **Cornelis Visscher** painted *William of Orange* somewhere in Holland at this time and, in 1574, *An elderly man*, inscribed 'Ars probat virum', which probably shows us a musician. The portrait painter **Simon Jacobsz** was killed at fifty-three in the siege of Haarlem, as mentioned, in 1573; and **Pieter Pietersz**, in Haarlem from 1572, was mainly occupied with portraits because, van Mander tells us, commissions for compositions like his *Shadrach, Meshach and Abednego in the Fiery Furnace* (Pl. 421) were rare there in these years. In 1575 **Aert Pietersz** (Pl. 485) was beginning to paint portraits at twenty-five in Amsterdam where **Dirck Barendsz** (Pl. 389) the most conspicuous portrait painter may have painted more Civic Guard groups though I have found no records of particular commissions; **Cornelis Ketel** (Pl. 451) probably produced some portraits in Gouda between 1568 and 1573; **Jacob Willemsz Delff** (Pl. 440) was a newcomer in Gouda from soon after 1570; and the admirable portraitist **Adriaen van Cronenburch** (Pls. 343, 441, 443) was probably active in Bergum near Leeuwarden all through the period.

The landscape painters who could leave the urban centres and draw or paint in the wooded suburbs or open country were, no doubt, relatively unaffected by many of the distresses and obstructions of the period. In Antwerp the new men included the brilliant **Gillis van Coninxloo** (Pls. 466, 476), back from Paris and Antwerp Master at twenty-six in 1570, who remained in the city through the troubles ('maakte alle beroerten mee'), sold many of his works to dealers who found buyers in various places, and made in these years some joint compositions with **Marten van Cleve** (Pls. 394, 396, 406), seventeen years his senior, who painted the figures. **Pieter Goetkint**, about twenty-eight in 1568, seems to have combined landscape and genre painting with picture-dealing, probably in connection with his father-in-law **Antonio van Palerme. Jan Sons,** twenty in 1568, painted a picture with 'a foreground road and a hedge of fine trees' and other landscapes in the style of **Frans Mostaert** improved, van Mander tells us, 'by his own industry and observation of nature', and went abroad in 1573. **Mathys Brill,** also about twenty in 1568, seems to have worked in Antwerp till 1572 or 1573 when he too went abroad. **Paul Brill** (Pls. 473, 474), some five years younger than his brother, was a pupil of **Damiaen Oortelmans,** the specialist painter on musical instruments, and went abroad in 1574; and beginners at the end of the period included two pupils of **Hans Bol,** his stepson **Frans Boels** and **Jacques Savery the elder** (Pl. 438). **Cornelis Molenaer (Schele Neel),** who worked in Antwerp through the period, was about twenty-eight in 1568 and an able but feckless fellow as we know from van Mander who writes: 'Although there have been many gifted landscape painters who excelled in painting trees and other landscape features, no one painted foliage with so painterly (schilderachtig) a touch—that I believe to be the truth and I hope that this judgement will not be taken amiss. As regards the composition of his landscapes and the backgrounds I can only say that painters admire everything they see of his. He had however no disposition to paint figures. He worked in the manner of the distemper painters without a maulstick and his style was free. He hired himself out to various people on a daily wage and could paint a large fine landscape in a day; he would receive a "daalder" for a whole day's work and seven "stuivers" for a landscape background. He was a very good-natured fellow and many painters exploited him to their own profit while he himself lived in great poverty in a wretched home. He had in fact no self-control and was very fond of the bottle. As often happens the blame for this was laid on his wife, who used to take any money that was paid him in advance and often the picture remained unfinished in his studio'; and elsewhere van Mander tells us that **Gillis Congnet** (Pls. 434, 442) was among the artists who employed him to add landscape backgrounds to their pictures. Of the older men **Hans Bol,** in Antwerp from Malines at thirty-eight in 1572, gave up his Malines manner of painting in distemper on linen and canvas because he said his pictures were bought and copied and the copies then sold as originals, and developed a personal manner in small landscapes with miniature figures, generally on paper or parchment mounted on wood, which he was confident that nobody could copy; and I reproduce one delicately detailed painting of this kind, his *Panorama of Antwerp from a suburb* (Pl. 431) with villages and woods, a bridge across the river, and a castellated mansion on the right. **Jacob Grimmer,** about forty-two in 1568, was looked on as the leading landscape painter of the time and his quality appears in the intriguing picture of 1578 *The Outskirts of Antwerp (Kiel)* (Pl. 430), showing a country house surrounded by its orchards, gardens and home farm, roads bordered with trees and hedges leading to the town, the Scheldt beyond, and the towers of Antwerp silhouetted against a cloud-swept sky. **Hans Keynooghe,** whose death date is unknown, was still alive and probably painting, though over sixty, in 1570; the rich amateur **Cornelis van Dalem,** whose death date is also unknown, may still have occasionally painted a rocky landscape and sent it round to **Joachim Beuckelaer** or **Gillis Mostaert** for the insertion of small figures; and **Gillis Mostaert** (Pl. 348) himself probably painted more snow scenes, moonlight pieces and conflagrations. **Christian van den Queborne,** who died over sixty in 1578, and **Pieter Bom** seem also to have worked through the period; and some landscapes may have been painted in the Antwerp region in 1578 by **Lucas van Valkenborch** (Pls. 374, 432, 445, 446, 448, 449, 450) back from Germany and a protégé of the Archduke Mathias in that year. There seem only fragmentary records of the landscape painters outside Antwerp at this time. But we know that **Frans Verbeeck** died in Malines over sixty-five in

1570, and that **Pieter Bruegel** painted three landscapes in his last two years in Brussels—a meadow with large foreground trees and a thatched farmhouse in the distance in a 'proverb' picture, *The Birds' Nest* of 1568, a meadow with stream and barn and large church in the distance in *The Blind leading the Blind*, and a panoramic landscape with foreground woods and watermill in his *Magpie on the Gallows*.

Among the painters of town views, architectural interiors and trompe l'oeil perspectives, **Jan Vredeman de Vries** (Pl. 462) was abroad from the end of 1570, in Liège in 1574, and back in Antwerp by 1575; and in 1577, as noted, when he was fifty, he was made engineer in charge of the Antwerp fortifications, doubtless by reason of his architectural equipment. His pupil **Hendrik van Steenwyck the elder** (Pl. 488) went abroad about twenty-one in 1571 and was back in Antwerp by 1577 as a specialist in church interiors. Roman views and ruins and Italianate architectural features could still be supplied by **Hendrik van Cleve;** and also by **Michel de Gast** who may have died in the later seventies. Architectural specialists may have helped with the town view in the background of **Joachim Beuckelaer's** *Fishmarket with Ecce Homo* (Pl. 398), with the Renaissance palace in the *Banquet of Ahasuhuerus* (Pl. 422) by **Antoine Claeissins,** with the fantastically hybrid palaces and temples and carved obelisks suggesting Ephesus in the *Burning of the books* (Pl. 397) by **Marten de Vos,** and with the ruined temple and town view in the *Adoration of the Shepherds* (Pl. 402) by **Lambert van Noort.** It is possible that **Pieter Vlerick,** using his Roman sketch books, may have worked on occasion for other artists in this way, for van Mander describes him as an expert in architecture, perspective, and the painting of temples with columns and marbles, carved flutes and fillets and so forth; and **Nicolas Snellaert** may have been available in Courtrai as we know from van Mander that he had begun his career by assisting his master **Karel Foort** with architectural backgrounds.

In genre painting social, musical, market, kitchen, peasant and low-life pieces seem to have been continued though I have found few specifically named and dated. **Michiel Coxie's** *S. Cecilia* (Pl. 352) is virtually a musical genre piece in the tradition launched by the *Musician Angels* and *Singing Angels* (Pl. 17) in the **van Eycks'** *Ghent altarpiece*; **Joos van Winghe** (Pl. 457) probably produced some social scenes like his *Night banquet and masquerade* (Pl. 497) before or after he left Paris for Brussels; and it was possibly at this time that **Dirck Barendsz** painted the social genre piece described by van Mander as a 'modern festmahl' with a harp-player in the foreground and a woman singing, inspired perhaps by visits to Fontainebleau and Paris when he passed through France in 1561. **Pieter Aertsen** (Pls. 356, 357, 360) may have painted more large grave serious figures in market and kitchen pieces in his last years at Amsterdam. **Joachim Beuckelaer's** *Fishmarket with Ecco Homo* (Pl. 398) of 1570, considered as a genre piece, shows a fine compact group of large foreground figures more rhythmic in design than the figures in his earlier *Kitchen scene with Christ in the house of Mary and Martha* (Pl. 399); and there is evidently intentional contrast between the gentle composure of the passing ladies and the passionate though restrained disquiet of the bearded man who conveys his desire to the girl in the foreground, while the fishmonger, distressed and hesitant, husband perhaps, or lover of the girl, looks on. In 1571 **Pieter Huys** (Pls. 412, 413) signed a *Bagpiper and old woman* closely recalling the picture reproduced here by the **Brussels Piper Painter** (Pl. 326); **Jan Massys** (Pls. 315, 361, 362, 363) may have painted more subjects like his *Procuress* and 'Merry Company' pieces in *The Prodigal Son* tradition between 1568 and 1575; and in Malines more genre subjects like his *Comic Peasants' Wedding* were possibly produced in his last two years by the veteran **Frans Verbeeck.** In **Hans Bol's** *Panorama of Antwerp from a suburb*

(Pl. 431) of 1575 there are scores of tiny genre figures—an elegant lady is being helped into the foreground boat by an old boatman nude to the waist while a young man strumming on his lute awaits her in the bows; an elegant gentleman comes from the castle door while a boy relieves himself against the castle wall; other boys skylarking on the path recall the archers by a castle in the **Ursula Legend Master's** picture (Pl. 100); horses, one mounted by a boy clinging round his neck, swim across the river; in the wooded country on the left, peasants and their womenfolk walk arm in arm as in the background landscape of **Hieronymus Bosch's** *Adoration of the Magi* (Pl. 157), and some angry boors wave sticks at one another in a brawl. A great variety of genre is also seen in pictures of the encampments improvised for the demolition of the Antwerp Citadel; thus the **Worcester Destruction of Citadel Painter** (Pl. 435) shows in the foreground a rich burgher in a decorated tent, a cavalier saluting an elegant lady and gentleman in a carriage and, in the background, working parties round the citadel itself; while the **Antwerp Destruction of Citadel Painter** (Pl. 433) takes us to a more rustic encampment with a quack doctor's booth and a peasant woman combing her son's hair for lice—a genre detail repeated a hundred years later by **Jan Siberechts** (Pl. 788). **Marten van Cleve** who also painted *The Demolition of the Antwerp Citadel* and whose *Flayed ox* (Pl. 394), *Peasant household with cavalier* (Pl. 396) and *The Brawl* (Pl. 406) have been discussed in my last chapter, seems to have worked all through in Antwerp and may have painted there his *Twelfth Night* (*Le roi boit*) before 1578. **Pieter Balten,** mentioned in my last chapter as the painter of several variants on the *Feast of S. Martin* theme with wine-drinking peasants, was still in Antwerp in 1571; but he may have gone abroad thereafter, for van Mander tells us that he visited 'verschillende landen' as distinguished from **Marten van Cleve** who never left his own. **Jacob Grimmer,** with perhaps a collaborating figure painter, put intriguing genre scenes in his *Outskirts of Antwerp* (*Kiel*) *with peasants and covered waggons* (Pl. 430) where some burghers with a lolling lute-strumming young spark ride in the foremost waggon on their way home from a village kermesse; peasants accompany them on foot and follow in a second waggon and other peasants seated by the roadside watch the procession pass; at the head of the procession a mounted town-official waves his baton at two gentry quarrelling with drawn swords (one mounted and one on foot) and women restrain a furious fellow from joining in the fracas; two inmates of the mansion in the centre look out above the high walls and hedges, the owner gives instructions to a gardener in the orchard, a woman feeds the chickens in the distant farmyard, and on the side roads market carts with produce calmly trundle into town. There are no Merry Peasants 'putting on an act', as we now say, to amuse their betters in the surviving pictures dated by **Pieter Bruegel** in his last two years; his *Bird's Nest* dated 1568 shows indeed a fat and flaccid peasant in the foreground and a boy in the tree behind, but the picture clearly illustrates some proverb like 'A bird in the hand is worth two in the bush' and is not a soi-disant record of contemporary genre life; the *Blind leading the Blind* and *Five Crippled Beggars* are essentially deeply-felt political protests, as already indicated; and though peasants caper in the *Magpie on the Gallows* the sinister conjunction of the cross and gallows that dominates the picture gives tragic irony to their mindless antics and insouciance.

In the field of still-life and flower painting I have already drawn attention to the lantern clock (Pl. 429) and the flower piece with tulip in portraits by **Marten de Vos,** and to the embroidered prie-dieu covers inserted by **Adriaen Thomas Key** into portrait groups (Pls. 425, 426) to suggest the patrons' wealth and status; and students of music will compare the instrument in **Michiel Coxie's** *S. Cecilia* (Pl. 352) with the instruments in the pictures reproduced by the **Worcester Girl at Clavichord Painter** (Pl. 311) and **Marten de Vos** (Pl. 364), and the legible scores and words in the song books with the scores in the pictures by the **Female Half Lengths Master** (Pl. 314), **Pieter Jansz Pourbus** (Pl. 331) and the **Brussels Prodigal Son Painter** (Pl. 358). **Joachim Beuckelaer** shows his skill again with fish, whole and sliced, disposed across the foreground of the *Fishmarket with Ecce Homo* (Pl. 398); and he may have painted the clothes and jewels in **Antonis Mor's** *Anne of Austria* (Pl. 408). **Pieter Aertsen** probably included still-life in his final pictures. The **Vienna Feast of the Gods Painter** (Pl. 419) provides his gods with sea-fish fare of the kind already seen in the *Feast of the Sea-Gods* by **Frans Floris** (Pl. 353), and elaborate ewers of types to be frequent in later Flemish paintings and a table covered with a lace-trimmed cloth are other still-life features in this al fresco banquet—(where we may note in passing the huge dog couchant and partly covered by the cloth). In the opposite spirit **Frans Pourbus the elder** drew or painted a *Vanitas: Memento Mori* picture with death's head, flowers and hour-glass in the tradition which is seen here in works by the **Amsterdam Cadaver Painter** (Pl. 212) and the **Frankfort Master** (Pl. 209) and goes back to **Jan Gossaert;** and students of the difference between trite descriptive painting and passionate subjective realism can compare the book, crucifix and pot of unguent in the *Penitent Magdalene* (Pl. 403) by **Marcellus Coffermans** with the book, guttering candle, skull, crucifix and other still-life in **Marinus van Reymerswaele's** *S. Jerome in his study* (Pl. 237), discussed in an earlier chapter. Of the specialist flower painters **Lodewyck Jansz van den Bosch** was abroad through the period; but **Pauwels Coecke van Aelst** seems to have been throughout in Antwerp and presumably still painting his flowers in glasses; and the draughtsman and engraver **Pieter van der Borcht the elder,** mentioned in my last chapter as author of studies used in the *Florilegium* and *L'Herbier de Dodonoeus* published by Plantin in Antwerp, was there from 1572 and working again for the Plantin Press.

The painters working abroad included the Protestants and others who had left the Netherlands on Alva's approach or earlier to escape the Inquisition; these were now joined by other refugees; many of both groups went back, as noted, about 1577, when the Orange party were dominant in Brussels and Antwerp; and about that time also Vienna and Prague became points of attraction for some artists on their travels.

Of the painters in Central Europe we have thus first the earlier emigrés to Germany including the portrait painter **Nicolas Neufchatel (Lucidel)** who seems to have remained all through in Nuremberg; and the Calvinist flower painter **Lodewyck van den Bosch** who was also in some German town where he may now have painted the *Conflagrations*, recorded by van Mander, as symbols of the Alva Terror. The Calvinist landscape painter **Joos van Liere** established in the Calvinist colony at Frankenthal, was citizen there in 1574, town councillor in 1576 and still there in 1578; he ceased to paint, van Mander tells us, when he left the Netherlands so that his pictures were later sold as rarities for high prices. **Martin van Valkenborch,** established in Aix-la-Chapelle and citizen there by 1573, painted, probably in Alva's day, a series *The Twelve Months* with scenes from the life of Christ and illustrations of the Parables in the foregrounds and subsidiary episodes in the landscape settings; and he alludes unequivocally to the Alva Terror in the *February: Flight into Egypt* (Pl. 439) where in the middle distance Spanish soldiery in armour raid a village to massacre the innocents, and one company (immediately behind S. Joseph), led by Alva himself with his long white beard, is defied by peasants armed only with their pitchforks in the doorway of their cottage. **Lucas van Valkenborch,** also established in Aix-la-Chapelle, painted in 1568 the old propaganda subject *The Tower of Babel* (a later version is reproduced here (Pl. 374), in 1570 the *Landscape with village and peasants* (Pl. 432) a remarkably modern composition where from a wooded hillside we look down upon a village street running diagonally across the picture and above that to the opposite hillside crowned with adjacent churches, in 1574 some *Landscapes with peasant scenes* and in 1577 a gouache *Landscape with inn and peasants*. **Adriaen de Weerdt** who had begun as a landscape follower of **Frans Mostaert** and then gone to Italy where he was much attracted by Parmigianino, was now established in Cologne, and there, van Mander tells us, 'he published a number of prints including a *Raising of Lazarus*, the *Story of Ruth* with some pleasing landscape settings, the *Life of the Virgin*, *The Nativity*, and so forth; and also composed some allegories for Coornhert—[Dirck Volckertsz Coornhert, Dutch humanist, free-thinker and engraver then resident in Cleve and Xanten]—*The Four Pursuits of the Spirit* where one pursues property, another shameless pleasure and so on, while the last one gives himself to the pursuit of God'.

New arrivals in Germany included **Jan Vredeman de Vries, Hendrik van Steenwyck the elder** (Pl. 488), **Nicolas van der Perre, Hans van Coninxloo the elder, Federico di Lamberto Sustris, Engelhart van Pee, Joris Hoefnagel, Abraham del Hele, Frans Hogenberg.** Of these **Jan Vredeman de Vries** (Pl. 462) went from Antwerp to Aix-la-Chapelle, with his sons Salomon and Paul, in 1570 when it became clear that the exceptions to the Amnesty made his life as a Protestant unsafe; and van Mander tells us that he stayed over two years in Aix-la-Chapelle and went thence for a year and a half to Liège. **Hendrik van Steenwyck the elder** (Pl. 488) followed him to Aix-la-Chapelle, became his pupil there in 1571, married there a daughter of **Martin van Valkenborch** in 1573, and signed in that year an *Interior of Aix-la-Chapelle Cathedral*. The portrait painter **Nicolas van der Perre** escaped from Antwerp in 1569, reached Leipzig with his wife and infant son **Jan van der Perre** in 1570 and remained there. **Hans van Coninxloo the elder** (a painter of mythologies and son of the **Jan van Coninxloo** who had been fined for listening to Protestant sermons under Margaret of Austria) left Antwerp in 1571, went to Emden and remained there. **Federico di Lamberto Sustris** left Florence for Augsburg at Hans Fugger's invitation in 1569, painted allegoric decorations in the Fugger mansions and castles till 1573 and then worked at Landshut for Duke Albert of Bavaria's son (later Duke William V). **Engelhart van Pee** from Brussels worked at Landshut from 1570 till 1577. **Joris Hoefnagel** left Antwerp after the Spanish Fury with the geographer Ortelius, went to Augsburg (where Hans Fugger introduced him to Duke Albert who made him a Court artist) and thence to Venice in 1577; **Abraham del Hele** was also in Augsburg, probably as a refugee, in these years, and was painting portraits and perhaps mythologies in Regensburg in 1576. **Frans Hogenberg** reached Cologne, after two years in England, in 1570, contributed to Braun's 'Civitates Orbis Terrarum' published there in 1572, and was still at work there in 1578. One **Jerrigh** of whom little is known, was in Cologne in 1568 when the Cologne-born Hans van Achen, then sixteen, was his pupil.

Jan Rubens, who had been listed as a Calvinist before Alva's arrival, arrived in Cologne with his wife in 1568 and was imprisoned in Dillenburg Castle for adultery with Anna of Saxony (Orange's first wife) in 1571 as already related; in 1573 he was released from prison but confined to the town of Siegen where he and his wife renounced their Calvinism for Lutheran doctrine; in 1577 **Peter Paul Rubens** was born at Siegen; and in 1578 the family was allowed to leave there and settle in Cologne where Jan Rubens now declared himself a Catholic.

The attraction to Vienna seems to have begun in 1575 when **Bartholomaeus Spranger**

(Pls. 458, 459), recommended by the sculptor Giovanni da Bologna, went there from Rome to work for the Emperor Maximilian II on a monthly wage; in 1576 he painted there a *Mercury bringing Psyche to the Council of the Gods* 'uitstekend gecomponeerd en uitgevoerd' with 'een mooi doorkijkje door de wolken' and an *Allegory of Rome with the Tiber and the Wolf*; and in 1577 he painted large allegoric figures of *The Virtues*, in grisaille imitating bronze, on the triumphal arch erected for the new Emperor Rudolf II's Pageant Entry— work completed in twenty-eight days despite continuous rain. **Karel van Mander** (Pl. 472) left Rome in 1577 for Krems where he painted frescoes in the Cemetery Chapel and then went to Vienna to help **Spranger** with his figures for the arch.

The homeward movement of many of these refugees and travellers began soon after the death of Requesens and increased in the next three years. Thus **Jan Vredeman de Vries** returned to Antwerp aged forty-eight in 1575; **Hendrik van Steenwyck the elder** was back, about twenty-seven, with his wife, by 1577; **Lucas van Valkenborch** was back about forty-five by 1578; **Martin van Valkenborch** seems to have returned either then or very soon after; and **Karel van Mander** returned to Meulebeke from Vienna via Nuremberg in 1578.

Of the artists already in England **Arnold** (or **Arthur**) **van Brounckhurst** who painted an *Andromeda* about 1572 was granted a licence in that year—together with his cousin **Cornelius de Vosse (Devosse)** and the English miniaturist Nicholas Hilliard—to prospect for gold in Scotland; the licencees 'searched sundry moors' and claimed to have found gold in various places; but nothing more seems to have come of it and **van Brounckhorst** stayed in Scotland where he painted portraits and, later, had contact with Court circles. **Hans Ewouts (Eworth),** settled in London and still engaged on portraits (Pls. 338, 349, 350), was also occupied as designer of Court masques and so on for Queen Elizabeth's Office of Revels between 1572 and 1574 and he was probably still active in 1578, though his death date is unknown. Two intriguing extant pictures show his decorative manner at this time. In the first, *Queen Elizabeth eclipsing Juno, Minerva and Venus* dated 1569, the goddesses are routed by the wisdom, power and beauty of Elizabeth in a landscape with Windsor Castle in the background, and an inscription on the picture reads:

> Juno potens sceptris et mentis acumine Pallas
> Et roseo Veneris fulget in ore decus;
> Adfuit Elizabeth: Juno perculsa refugit;
> Obstupuit Pallas erubuitque Venus.

The second, *The Wise and Foolish Virgins* (Pl. 417) painted in 1570, is really an illustration to the whole twenty-fifth chapter of S. Matthew, as a prone figure in the background would seem to be the owner of the single talent, the separation of the sheep and goats is in the middle distance, and the wise and foolish virgins form groups in the foreground; a feature of this composition is a landscape on the right with a bridge across a river and some large buildings among the trees which may have been contributed by a topographic landscape painter also perhaps responsible for the Windsor landscape in *Queen Elizabeth eclipsing Juno, Minerva and Venus*. **Livina Teerlinck,** who lived till 1576, painted, possibly in 1570, two charming miniatures *Little girl with an apple* and *Little girl with a red carnation* as we know from inscriptions formerly upon them which gave Greenwich as the place of their production and 1590—an evident error—as their date. **Steven van der Meulen** may still have been at work here; and **Cornelis de Zeeu** (Pls. 385, 386) who signed portraits painted here or elsewhere in 1569 and 1570 may have stayed on in this period or gone back to the Northern provinces. The new arrivals included **Lucas de Heere, Marcus Geeraerts** the elder, **Marcus Geeraerts the younger, Frans Hogenberg, Joris Hoefnagel,** and **Cornelis Ketel.** Of these **Lucas de Heere,** reported on to Alva as a Protestant but described at the same time as 'een constich schilder ende zeer verstendich en studiues', was banished from Ghent in 1568 and came, aged thirty-four, to London; in 1570 he was commissioned by the Lord High Admiral Edward Lord Clinton, Earl of Lincoln, to make a series of watercolours titled 'Théâtre de tous les peuples et nations de la terre avec leurs habits et ornements divers tant anciens que modernes' and for this he drew an Englishman wearing nothing but a loin cloth, with large scissors in his right hand and uncut cloth in the other because, he explained to the High Admiral, the tools of tailoring were essential in England where the fashions of one day were out of date the next—an explanation which, van Mander tells us, was reported to the Queen who said: 'We are indeed in a foolish pass, when our nation is so feather-brained (wispelturig) that foreigners can justly hold us up to ridicule' (though the same satiric comment had in fact been made by Andrew Boorde, an Englishman, in his 'Fyrst Boke of the Introduction to Knowledge', 1542, where a drawing of a naked Englishman is captioned:

'I am an Englishman and naked I stand here,
Musing in my mind what raiment I shall wear.
For now I will wear this and now I will wear that,
And now I will wear—I cannot tell what'.)

Of **Lucas de Heere's** other work in England there seem to be no records, though he may also have been occupied as poet, translator, portrait and 'history' painter, or tapestry designer; persona grata with the Prince of Orange and his entourage (and later, if not already, on the Prince's pay list) he may have acted here as secret agent; he went back to Ghent in 1577 and designed the Prince's Pageant as related, and it is perhaps significant that he was also denizened that year in Middelburg where the Prince had his headquarters. **Marcus Geeraerts the elder** came as a refugee from Bruges in 1568 and three years later he married as his second wife Susanna de Critz (daughter of an Antwerp jeweller Troilus de Critz established here and naturalized by 1552 and founder of a family of painters who rank among the English School); with his varied experience in religious and allegoric-mythological subjects, landscapes, topographic and animal painting and drawing, and his experience also as engraver and designer of glass windows and decorative objects, he doubtless found some kind of employment (it is tempting, for example, to guess him the author of the landscapes in the *Queen Elizabeth eclipsing Juno, Minerva and Venus* and *The Wise and Foolish Virgins* by **Hans Ewouts**); but apart from a *Procession of the Sovereign and Knights of the Garter* (engraved in 1576) there seem no records of his productions here; and he went back to Belgium, where he settled in Antwerp, in 1577. **Marcus Geeraerts the younger** was brought here by his father, at the age of seven; at fifteen in 1576 he was an apprentice-pupil of **Lucas de Heere:** and when both his father and his master had gone back to Belgium he probably worked under Jan de Critz his stepmother's brother. **Frans Hogenberg,** Protestant painter and engraver, was driven by Alva from Malines or Antwerp and came to England with his brother, the engraver Remigius Hogenberg, in 1568; he engraved here some portraits including *Sir William Cecil (Burleigh)*, *The Earl of Leicester* and *Queen Elizabeth*, contributed to the 'Bishops' Bible', and left for Cologne, as mentioned, in 1570. **Joris Hoefnagel,** here by 1569, painted a *Wedding at Horsleydown in Bermondsey*, made twenty-five drawings for a 'Traité de la patience par les emblemes' (dated London 1569) and also made drawings of some English towns engraved in Braun's 'Civitates Orbis

176

Terrarum' published three years later; and he returned after the 'Amnesty' of 1570 to Antwerp where his wedding party in 1571 was painted by **Frans Pourbus the elder** in the picture already referred to. **Cornelis Ketel** (Pl. 451) came from Gouda where 'door den oorlog niet veel te schilderen viel' in 1573 at twenty-five; in London he was welcomed by a Dutch or Flemish sculptor-architect who knew his family; he soon sent for a girl from Holland whom he married; and he was still here at the end of the period. Van Mander, who had the details from him personally, informs us that **Ketel** painted portraits here of the German merchants in the Hansa Steelyard soon after his arrival and sold some pictures brought with him from Holland; that he painted portraits of the *Earl of Oxford* and of many nobles with their wives and children, some being full-length life-size figures; and that in 1578 he painted *Queen Elizabeth* from life for the Earl of Hertford to celebrate the Queen's visit to Hanworth—(just as Sir Henry Lee employed an artist later to celebrate the Queen's visit to Ditchley in 1592 (Pl. 462A)); he also tells us that he received no commissions in England for 'history' pieces (i.e. mythologies and allegories), which were his natural bent (and for which his stay in Fontainebleau had, of course, equipped him), though to show his skill in this department he painted here a *Victory of Wisdom and Foresight over Force* with over life-size figures which was bought by a young English merchant 'Mr. Pieter Hachten' who gave it to Sir Christopher Hatton. **Ketel** also painted here *Sir Robert Tyrwhit and his wife Elizabeth Oxenham* in 1573 and a full-length *Martin Frobisher* in 1577; Horace Walpole (1762) refers to portraits of *Sir Christopher Hatton*, *The Earl of Arundel*, the *Earl of Pembroke* and *Lord Admiral Lincoln* as his work.

In France the Wars of Religion and the Massacre of S. Bartholomew caused some interruptions in the work at Fontainebleau. We know that **Cornelis Ketel** (Pl. 451) went back to Gouda in 1568, and that **Aper Fransz van der Houve (Franssen)** went back to Delft, gave up painting and became a brewer and collector; but it is not known whether **Hans de Maier** and **Denys van Utrecht** stayed on in France or returned to the Netherlands in these years. **Gillis van Coninxloo** (Pls. 466, 476) was back in Antwerp from Paris by 1570; **Joos van Winghe** (Pls. 457, 497) returned to Brussels at some time in the period; and **Hieronymus Francken the elder** was in Paris till 1571 when he visited Antwerp to finish the altarpiece by Frans Floris, already referred to, and he was probably back in Paris before 1578. Of the new arrivals **Cornelis Floris** was a pupil in Paris of **Hieronymus Francken the elder** at seventeen in 1568; **Ambroise Dubois** (Pl. 491), later much employed at Fontainebleau, went from Antwerp to Paris aged twenty-five in that year or soon after, though nothing is known of his work there in this period; **Ambrosius Francken the elder** was in Fontainebleau for a while in 1570. **Jan de Hoey**, grandson of **Lucas van Leyden** and later a painter of religious subjects, reached France from Leyden at twenty-six in 1571 and settled in Troyes. **Paul Brill** (Pls. 473, 474) stayed for some time in Lyons, and possibly in Paris, on his way to Italy, in 1574. **Wenzelas Coebergher** (Pl. 493) who arrived in Paris at the end of the period, had left Antwerp, about twenty, hoping by foreign travel to cure an unrequited passion for **Marten de Vos's** daughter. **Herman van der Mast** (Pl. 453) trained first by **Frans Floris** and then a fellow-pupil with **Gortzius Geldorp** (Pls. 454, 486) of **Frans Francken the elder**, reached Paris at about twenty-two in the early seventies, joined the establishment of the Archbishop of Bourges and painted a *S. Sebastian* which included, van Mander tells us, the Archbishop's mule and trodden-down grass so faithfully rendered that the King's doctor could differentiate the herbs and grasses; he then joined the establishment of the Attorney-General De La Queste and occupied the post of shield-bearer (schild-knaap) to De La Queste's wife, a lady-in-waiting to the Queen. **Jan de Wael**, another pupil of **Frans**

Francken the elder, and later a painter of religious pictures, was in Paris, aged about twenty, probably in the later seventies, and seems to have stayed there for some time.

In Spain **Izaak del Hele,** still in Toledo, painted for the Cathedral in 1568 his *Scenes from the life of Bishop Micasius of Reims*—(an orthodox propaganda subject as the Bishop was killed by an invading horde of infidels from Germany)—and went back to Antwerp in 1571; **Rodrigo Diriksen,** a newcomer, was at work on religious and decorative paintings for King Philip in the Escorial by 1572; **Antonio van den Wyngaerde** had evidently ceased making drawings of Spanish towns by 1572 when he was over seventy and the King gave him a disability pension as both his hands were crippled; and he probably died before the end of this period or soon after. **Jan Floris** continued his work as a genre and decorative painter on faience and as Director of the Azulejos factories in Madrid; and **Antoni Pupiler** may have returned to Spain after copying the Louvain altarpiece for Philip though there seem to be no records of him in this period. The King also continued to make some show of patronage of the painters resident in Belgium; **Michiel Coxie** and **Antonis Mor** were still King's Painters, as noted, and he gave **Raphael Coxie** the same rank in 1570. He bought **Michiel Coxie's** *S. Cecilia* (Pl. 352) in 1569 and hung it in the Escorial church; and attracted doubtless by its affinities with pictures by **Hieronymus Bosch** he also bought and hung in the Escorial *The Battle of angels and demons and the torments of Hell* (Pl. 412) by **Pieter Huys** though the **Huys** composition was probably a crypto-protest against conditions as already suggested.

In Italy a number of new men came to join the established painters. **Jan Kraeck (Caracca)** of Haarlem, Court Painter in Turin to Duke Emmanuel Philibert by 1568, painted there the *Duchess Margaret of Valois* in 1577 and a *Holy Family* for Annecy, S. Maurice, in 1578. In Rome **Pieter de Witte (Candido), Denys Calvaert** and **Hendrik van den Broeck** assisted Vasari on the *Battle of Lepanto* and other frescoes in the Sala Regia of the Vatican from 1572; **Pieter de Witte** had just come from Florence where he had gone about twenty-two in 1570 with his father, a bronze caster from Bruges; he went back to Florence in 1573, worked there with Vasari on the cupola of the Duomo, and designed tapestries for Duke Francesco dei Medici, and was appointed Court Painter by Duke Albert of Bavaria in 1578. **Denys Calvaert** had reached Rome about thirty by 1570 after working under Prospero Fontana and Lorenzo Sabbatini in Bologna; back in Bologna about 1574 he painted a *Flagellation* for S. Leonardo, founded an art school (some eight years before the Carracci's institution) and soon had a number of pupils whom he is said to have bullied and cuffed with some vigour. **Hendrik van den Broeck (Arrigo Fiammingo, Henricus Paludanus)** had arrived in Rome from Naples just over fifty at the end of the sixties; in Rome he painted a *Resurrection* over a damaged fresco of the subject by Ghirlandaio in the Sistine Chapel; and he seems to have become a member of the Rome Accademia di S. Luca in 1577, the year of its foundation. **Jan Sons** and **Mathys Brill** worked on frescoes in the Sala Ducale of the Vatican from 1573 both being then about twenty-five; **Jan Sons** stayed in Rome till about 1575 when he left for Parma to become Court Painter to Ottavio Farnese; in Rome he painted small landscapes with figures as easel pictures in his earlier Antwerp manner, and his Vatican frescoes included a *Landscape wth a cock in the foreground* in an oval panel (surrounded by large decorative ornaments and figures probably by an Italian artist) and a *S. Augustine and the child by the seashore* where, van Mander tells us, the sea was 'wonderfully well painted in natural perspective, light and shade and flatness'; the Italians complained that his touch was rough and muddy (ruw en niet zuiver genoeg) though the effect from a distance was admitted to be good. From 1575 **Mathys Brill** painted landscape frescoes in other apartments in the Vatican where Lorenzo Sabbatini was in charge of the decorative scheme. **Paul Brill** (Pls. 473, 474) reached Rome about twenty in 1576 and was working soon after as assistant to his brother. **Bartholomaeus Spranger** (Pls. 458, 459), twenty-two in 1568, painted frescoes *The Last Supper* and the *Four Evangelists* in a church at S. Oreste (in collaboration with **Michel Joncquoy** who went back to Tournai in 1575); in 1570 as a protégé of Cardinal Farnese he joined Federico Zuccaro on landscape frescoes with figures in the Villa Farnese at Caprarola, and was introduced by the Cardinal to Pius V who lodged him in the Belvedere and made him a Painter to the Papal Court despite attempts by Vasari to discredit him; in 1572, when the Pope was ill, he took to his bedside a small *Agony in the Garden* on copper and the Pope commissioned a whole series of *The Passion*—(pen sketches of the compositions to be first approved by him); in Rome also he painted a *Last Judgement* on copper with five hundred faces later placed on a memorial monument to the Pope, a *Martyrdom of S. John the Evangelist in boiling oil* for the high altar of S. Giovanni alla Porta Latina, and a *Portrait of a Lady* done from memory for her lover; and in 1575 he left for Vienna as related. **Gaspar Heuvick** from Audenarde reached Rome about twenty-five in 1575 after working in Mantua under Lorenzo Costa the younger who was then providing large pictures for the churches there. One **Herder** from Groningen, painter of 'history' and allegories, arrived in Rome at the same age at that time. In 1575 also **Anthoni Santvoort** and **Jan Speeckaert** were prosecuted in Rome for painting in a church there without being members of the local guild; in 1577 **Santvoort** became a member of the guild (or of the new Accademia di S. Luca) and had the German painter Hans van Achen as a pupil in his house; and **Speeckaert** who painted a *Joseph and Potiphar's wife* and a *Portrait of the engraver Cornelis Cort* died young in that year or soon after. **François Stellaert** of Malines, painter, later, of landscapes and religious subjects, reached Rome as a quite young man about 1576. **Karel van Mander** (Pl. 472) went from Meulebeke to Italy aged twenty-one in 1573 and his first biographer reminds us that the long slow journey south was in itself an education, for he tells us that Karel's parents gave him clothes and money and sent him first to an uncle in Ghent who had already made the journey; Karel then started with a group of young gentlemen who soon became impatient because he stopped to look at works of art in various places and to call on artists and eventually left him to find his way without them; in Florence before the end of the year he met **Pieter de Witte** and saw the sights with him ('ging daar met hem om'); in Terni he was commissioned by a nobleman, perhaps a Flemish crypto-Protestant, to paint *The Massacre of S. Bartholomew with Admiral Coligny thrown from the window* in fresco for his villa, and he became associated with an Italian artist skilled in decorative painting in the 'grotesque' style; he reached Rome in 1574, and there he painted landscapes in fresco in the Flemish manner, studied Roman ruins and antiques and drew in the newly discovered catacombs; and he met **Santvoort, Speeckaert, Heuvick, Herder,** and **Jan Sons** who took him up the scaffolding to see his *Landscape with a cock*, and also **Bartholomaeus Spranger** who became his intimate and whom he followed as related in 1577 to Vienna. **Frans van den Kasteele (Francesco da Castello)** painter of religious subjects and miniatures, provided altarpieces for churches in Pisa and Orte either now or later, and settled in Rome where he was elected a member of the Accademia di S. Luca at thirty-seven in 1577. **Otto van Veen** (Pls. 455, 510, 511, 570) in Italy from Liège at twenty in 1576, was a pupil in Rome of Federico Zuccaro (who had recently returned from a visit to England in 1574-75). **Anthonis Blocklandt** (Pl. 420) who toured Italy in 1572 and was more impressed, van Mander tells us, by Parmigianino than by Michelangelo, went probably to Venice as well as Florence, Parma and Rome. In Venice **Gaspar Rem** from Antwerp was established as a painter of portraits and religious subjects by 1572 when he was just about thirty; in 1574 he refused to take Hans van Achen (then twenty-two) as his pupil on the ground that the 'Moffen' (Germans) had no capacity for art, but he relented when van Achen painted a *Laughing Self-portrait* which impressed him. **Pauwels Franck (Paolo Fiammingo),** twenty-eight at the outset of the decade, was still landscape assistant to Tintoretto when work began on new pictures for the Large Council Chamber in the Doges' Palace after the fire there in 1577; and in these years or later he also painted some religious subjects. **Joris Hoefnagel,** in Venice from Augsburg in 1577, saw the fire in the Doges' Palace and left the next year for Naples after passing through Rome where, on account of his post as Court painter to Duke Albert of Bavaria, he had to decline an offer from Cardinal Farnese to take the place of the miniaturist Giorgio Clovio who had recently died. **Lodewyck Toeput** of Malines (known in Italy as **Pozzoserrato**) was in Venice, just over twenty-five, by 1577 when he too saw the fire and made a drawing or painting recording the event. **Pietro Mera** presumed from Brussels who signed a *Nativity* in Florence in 1570 may have moved to Venice by 1578 as he is known to have lived there later. The **Vienna Feast of the Gods Painter** (Pl. 419), presumed as noted a Fleming, may have painted the picture reproduced here when living in or after touring Italy. In Florence **Jan van der Straet (Stradanus)** was the most conspicuous Flemish painter in this decade after **Federico di Lamberto Sustris** had left for Augsburg in 1569; in that year **van der Straet** provided a *Crucifixion* for S. Annunziata and an *Ascension* for S. Croce, and in 1570 when he was forty-seven he painted, among other panels of occupational subjects, a *Chemists at work* commissioned for his 'studiolo' in the Palazzo Vecchio by Francesco dei Medici who was deeply interested in chemistry; in 1576 he was invited to Naples by Don John of Austria 'per dipingere i suoi fatti militari'; he is said to have followed him to the Netherlands, as noted, and to have gone back to Naples after Don John's death. **Paul Schephen** was probably active in Naples at this time and **Cornelis Pyp** may have died there before 1578; **Aert Mytens,** now established in Naples, and known as **Rinaldo,** visited Bruges and The Hague possibly in these years and then returned there. **Dirck Hendricksz** from Amsterdam was in Naples by 1574; he became known there as **Errico Fiammingo** and painted for the local churches; his friend **Cornelis Smet,** who married there in 1574, was working for S. Eligio by 1578; and the topographic draughtsman **Jan van Stinemolen** documented there a few years later may already have arrived in this period. **Simon de Wobeck,** established in Sicily, was engaged on devotional pictures for religious houses; and he may have started before 1578 his *Assumption of the Virgin with the Trinity, Apostles, and S. Nicholas* (completed by 1581) for the Palermo Oratory of S. Nicholas del Borgo.

CHAPTER IX

The Patriot Régime; The Union of Utrecht;
The Duke of Anjou; The Act of Abjuration;
and Alexander Farnese, Duke of Parma

1579-1592

ALEXANDER FARNESE, usually known as the Duke of Parma (which he became in 1586), was nominally Governor General in all the provinces for Philip II from 1579 till 1592. But, as related in the last chapter, confused conditions had prevailed in the Netherlands since 1577 when he had arrived to help Don John. In 1579 the Patriots held most of the Northern provinces, now predominantly Protestant, and also the chief cities in Flanders and Brabant, including Bruges, Ghent, Brussels and Antwerp where the Protestants were minorities. In all these regions there was toleration at this time for the Catholics thanks to the Prince of Orange who stood for freedom of worship and continuously urged both sides to avoid provocative gestures and to abstain from 'mutual jeerings' by 'pictures, ballads, books or otherwise'—though paintings and satiric drawings and engravings with open or crypto-propaganda were nevertheless produced. The confusion increased in the first few years of Parma's governorship when the Northern provinces achieved their independence under Orange, the Walloon malcontent provinces were reconciled to Spain, and the rest were under the nominal sovereignty of the Duke of Anjou; and it was probably at this time that an unrecorded artist painted *The Milch Cow* (preserved in the Amsterdam Museum) where the Netherlands are represented by a cow ridden by Philip of Spain, milked by the Prince of Orange, fed by Queen Elizabeth and having its tail pulled by the Duke of Anjou, as we know from English quatrains inscribed upon it:

> Not long time since I sawe a cow
> Did Flaunders represente
> Upon whose back Kinge Philippe rode
> As being Malcontent.

> The Queene of England giving hay
> Wheareon the cow did feede
> As one that was her greatest helpe
> In her distress and neede.

> The Prince of Orange milked the cow
> And made his purse the payle
> The cow did . . . in Monsieur's hand
> While he did hold her tayle.

These confused conditions, the military operations, and the revival of religious feuds caused immense displacement of persons. Thus, under the Protestant régime, some two thousand Catholics moved from Brussels to the Walloon provinces; later, when Parma was in control of all but the Northern provinces, there were large scale movements of Protestants to Germany and Holland; eleven hundred Calvinists went to Middelburg alone in 1585; and nine thousand persons left Ghent, when Parma conquered it. Antwerp, which had numbered a hundred and twenty-five thousand inhabitants when Alva arrived, was reduced to eighty-five thousand when Parma conquered it in 1585, and four years later, the exodus of traders, caused by the Dutch closing of the Scheldt and by Parma's expulsion of Protestants, had further reduced it to fifty-five thousand. For Parma expelled all Protestants, unless they recanted, from the towns he conquered; to encourage recantations he organized a conference of Jesuits at Louvain to discuss ways and means of conversion; he allowed a time limit of a year or two in most cases; and in Antwerp, where many Protestants were commercially important, he extended the period to four years. Some opportunists inevitably recanted; but hosts of Calvinists, including many artists, emigrated. For all these reasons most of the towns in the Spanish Netherlands now suffered from commercial difficulties; and in the countryside there was much disorder and highway brigandage. In the Northern provinces, on the other hand, there was increasing organization and prosperity. By the middle of this period the fortunes of the Northern and Southern provinces had become in fact distinct; and the Dutch Republic was virtually in being. From that time the story of the Spanish Netherlands is the separate story of what we now call Belgium; and for that reason I have not included in this survey any artists born in Holland after 1581.

In 1579 Parma was thirty-four, the Prince of Orange and Queen Elizabeth were both forty-six, the Duke of Anjou was twenty-five, Henri III was twenty-eight, Henry of Navarre was twenty-six, Philip II was fifty-two, the Emperor Rudolf II was twenty-seven, and the Archduke Mathias was twenty-two. The aged Cardinal Prince Henry was King of Portugal, Ivan the Terrible was Czar, Louis VI, a Lutheran, was Elector Palatine, Gregory XIII was Pope and Murad III was Sultan. In this year Hainault and Artois, the Walloon provinces of Flanders, formed the 'League of Arras' to defend the Roman Catholic faith and maintain allegiance to King Philip; and Holland, Zeeland, Utrecht, Gelderland and Zutphen signed the 'Union of Utrecht' to uphold their rights and liberties and freedom in religion. Maestricht was besieged and captured by Parma and thousands of the inhabitants, men, women and children were hideously slaughtered; a Peace Conference in Cologne between the Walloon provinces and the Spaniards was attended by Philip's Ambassador Charles of Aragon, Duke of Terranova, who had the young Louvain painter **Gortzius Geldorp** (Pls. 454, 486) in his suite; the Seventh French War of Religion started; and Justus Lipsius began a ten years stay in the University of Leyden where he now conformed to Calvinist doctrines. In 1580 the Jesuits Campion and Parsons landed in England; Drake returned from his voyage round the world; Queen Elizabeth went down to Deptford to knight him; and capitulations were signed between England and Sultan Murad. The Seventh French War of Religion ended; King Henry of Portugal died and Philip II claimed the Portuguese crown; King Philip issued his ban on the Prince of Orange, expelling him from his dominions, forbidding his subjects to give him food, drink or fuel, and promising twenty-five thousand crowns of gold and a title of nobility for his capture or assassination—a document composed by Cardinal Granvella and published in the Netherlands by Parma; the Catholics of Gronigen and Overijssel announced their defection from the Union of Utrecht; and, prompted by Orange, the States-General—with Holland and Zeeland abstaining—made the Treaty of Plessis-les-Tours with the Duke of Anjou (heir to the French throne) inviting him to become sovereign of the United Provinces with limited powers. In 1581 King Stephen of Poland was invading Russia; the Jesuit Campion was tortured and executed in England and Parsons escaped to make new plots against Elizabeth inspired by King Philip and the Duc de Guise; the Archduke Matthias resigned his post as nominal Governor General for the United Provinces and retired to Linz taking with him **Lucas van Valkenborch** (Pls. 374, 432, 445, 446, 448-50) as his Court painter; the representatives of Brabant, Flanders, Utrecht, Gelderland, Holland and Zeeland signed the 'Act of Abjuration' formally renouncing their allegiance to King Philip; Orange agreed to act as sovereign of Holland and Zeeland 'till the end of the war'; and the Antwerp New Crossbowmen's Guild commissioned the Protestant **Gillis Congnet** to paint a *S. George and the Dragon* (Pl. 434) where, I take it, the nude maiden rescued is not Cleodolinda but Belgica, the dragon stands for Spain, and S. George in golden armour with a silver shield is a symbol for the Prince of Orange. Anjou appeared with French troops at Cambrai which Parma was besieging, relieved it and then went to England to court Elizabeth who showed signs of yielding; Philip II became King of Portugal (after Alva had defeated opposition at the Battle of Alcantara) and made Cardinal the Archduke Albert aged twenty-four his viceroy; and Parma captured Tournai. In 1582 Ivan the Terrible had to cede large territories to Poland; Anjou left England and landed at Flushing escorted by Robert Dudley Earl of Leicester, Sir Philip Sidney and other English gentleman; in Antwerp Anjou was inaugurated as Duke of Brabant with elaborate pageantry of which **Crispiaen van den Broeck** (Pl. 409) was one of the designers; the Prince of Orange was shot in the head by the servant of a Spanish merchant, but his life was saved by the devotion of relays of attendants who staunched a haemorrhage with thumb-pressure day and night till the wound was healed; Parma captured Audenarde and other places, and procured some sixty thousand troops from Spain as reinforcements; two assassins, hired by Parma, tried unsuccessfully to poison Orange and Anjou when both were in Bruges for Anjou's inauguration as Count of Flanders; and when Anjou entered Ghent **Lucas de Heere** designed the decorations in his honour. In 1583 Anjou, resenting limitations placed on his power and jealous of the Prince of Orange, planned military coups d'état in a number of towns; his troops assaulted Antwerp in the 'French Fury' and most of them were killed by the citizens who resisted in street fighting; pressed by Catherine de Médicis and Elizabeth to condone Anjou's bad faith, the States-General made only verbal protests; Anjou intrigued with Parma and left for France; Orange married Louise de Coligny; the States-General moved the government of the United Provinces from Antwerp to Holland and offered the sovereignty to Orange who refused it; Parma captured a number of places some by arms and some through the treachery of the men in charge; and the Calvinist John Casimir became de facto Elector Palatine on behalf of his nephew Frederick IV. In 1584 Elizabeth sent the Spanish Ambassador out of England, and granted Sir Walter Raleigh a patent to take unknown lands in America in the Queen's name; Jan Huyghen van Linschoten of Haarlem who had sailed to Goa with the Portuguese East India fleet began his notes and charts and maps; and Ivan the Terrible died. Ypres surrendered to Parma in April; Bruges surrendered in May and **Pieter Claeissins the younger** designed the decorations for Parma's Pageant Entry and painted the *Convention of Tournai* (Pl. 436) which celebrates his treaty with Bruges and shows Hispanophil Belgian nobles escorting a chariot where Peace, Charity and Justice are surmounted by the Holy Ghost and the arms of Philip II, while Violence, Jealousy and

Discord are driven from the country or trampled underfoot; and Parma began the siege of Antwerp in the summer. The Duke of Anjou died in June leaving Henry of Navarre the heir to the throne of France; and The League, headed by the Duc de Guise and assisted by the clergy, fomented opposition to this Huguenot succession and put up Cardinal de Bourbon as a Catholic candidate. In July the Prince of Orange was assassinated at Delft by Balthasar Gerard, a Catholic fanatic who had been in touch with some Jesuits and Parma; in September Ghent surrendered to Parma; and in December Philip II signed the Treaty of Joinville with the Duc de Guise and the French Catholics against the Huguenots and Henry of Navarre's succession. In 1585 Pope Gregory XIII died and was succeeded by Sixtus V; the Eighth French War of Religion started; Henri III declined an offer of the Sovereignty of the United Provinces; Prince Maurice of Nassau succeeded his father as Stadholder of Holland; Brussels surrendered to Parma and **Joos van Winghe** (Pls. 457, 497) was among the burghers sent to negotiate the terms; Malines surrendered soon after; Antwerp fell in August after Parma had constructed a bridge across the Scheldt and held it against Gianibelli's fireships, and Philip II, who received the news in the middle of the night, leaped at once from his bed to inform his daughter Isabella (then nineteen and later sovereign of the Spanish Netherlands). Parma made a Pageant Entry into Antwerp surrounded by partisan Belgian nobles; the United Provinces cut Antwerp from the sea by closing the Scheldt against her; Elizabeth made a formal alliance with the United Provinces and sent the Earl of Leicester with fifty ships and an English force to Flushing; and Raleigh sent out colonists to Virginia. In 1586 Jan van Olden Barneveldt became Land's Advocate of Holland; Leicester made a Pageant Entry in The Hague and was invested Governor of the United Provinces in a ceremony drawn by **Jacques Savery the elder** (Pl. 438); Prince Maurice of Nassau and Sir Philip Sidney distinguished themselves in raids on Axel (across the Honte from Flushing); Sidney was killed near Zutphen in fighting where the Earl of Essex showed great courage; Spenser wrote 'Astrophel'; and Zutphen and Deventer were betrayed by their English governors to Parma who now became master of all the Netherlands except Holland, Zeeland, Friesland, Utrecht and part of Gelderland. The Babington plot to murder Queen Elizabeth was discovered; Mary Queen of Scots was brought to trial; Drake returned from Virginia; and tobacco and potatoes were introduced into England. In 1587 Henry of Navarre won the Battle of Coutras against the forces of The League; and The League planned to depose Henri III in favour of the Duc de Guise. Leicester made a Pageant Entry into Amsterdam through arches decorated by **Dirck Barendsz** (Pl. 389) and **Cornelis Ketel** (Pl. 451); and the Dutch picture dealers were intrigued when Englishmen in Leicester's suite asked for works by **Lucas Cornelisz** who had been in England in Henry VIII's reign, as related, and had now become, it would seem, an artist in demand among English collectors. Philip II instructed Parma to build landing barges for the invasion of England; Drake 'singed the King of Spain's beard'; Mary Queen of Scots was beheaded and her Protestant son James became heir to the throne of England; and Leicester was recalled from the Netherlands. In 1588 the Spanish Armada was destroyed; Maria Rubens arrived in Antwerp with her children from Cologne (bringing with her a false certificate that she and her late husband had lived there continuously from 1569 to 1587); Parma was repulsed from Bergen-op-Zoom by Prince Maurice of Nassau; a new persecution of Anabaptists was started in Flanders; and the Duc de Guise was murdered by the order of Henri III. In 1589 the people of Paris, instigated by The League, revolted against Henri III and a rebel Government arraigned him as 'assassin' and 'ennemi de la patrie'; Henri III and Henry of Navarre joined forces and tried to capture the capital by arms; Henri III was assassinated; Henry of Navarre, now legally Henri IV, won the Battle of Arques against the forces of The League; Philip II ordered Parma to send troops to France to fight against him; Elizabeth sent men and money to support him; Drake sacked Corunna and set fire to Vigo in support of a claimant against Philip to the Portuguese crown; Antonio Perez, convicted of the murder of Escovedo, escaped from prison and took refuge in Aragon; and Lipsius scandalized Leyden by his 'Politicorum Libri Sex' which declared that a government must recognize but one religion and extirpate dissent by fire and sword. In 1590 **Peter Paul Rubens,** aged thirteen, became page to the Countess Marguerite de Ligne-Arenberg; Spenser published three books of his 'Faerie Queen'; Lipsius left Leyden and was publicly reconciled with the Roman church; Gregory XIV became Pope; Prince Maurice captured Breda; Henri IV won the Battle of Ivry; and Parma, in France with an army of sixteen thousand, forced Henri to retire from Paris which he was then blockading. In 1591 **Peter Paul Rubens** became a pupil of **Tobias van Haecht** (Pl. 377), and Shakespeare, aged twenty-seven, wrote 'Romeo and Juliet'. Innocent IX became Pope; Antonio Perez was declared a heretic by the Inquisition and escaped from Aragon to France; Prince Maurice captured Zutphen, Deventer, Hulst (near Antwerp) and Nijmwegen; Elizabeth sent more money and a force led by Essex to help Henri IV and the Huguenot cause; and Parma again led an army into France. In 1592 Sir Walter Raleigh was committed to the Tower in the affair of Elizabeth Throgmorton; Clement VIII became Pope and issued the Clementine Vulgate; the United Provinces sent three thousand men to help Henri IV who was besieging Rouen; and Parma, who forced Henri to raise the siege, was mortally wounded at Caudebec and died in Arras, at forty-seven, in December.

The thousands of persons displaced by the conditions in the Netherlands included many artists who have already appeared in our story and a number of new ones. There was first a movement inwards of Protestants returning during the Patriot régime in the major towns; then came local displacements due to the fighting; and then a large-scale exodus abroad. As related in my last chapter, of the Protestants and others who had gone abroad in Alva's time **Jan Vredeman de Vries** (Pl. 462), **Hendrik van Steenwyck the elder** (Pl. 488), **Lucas van Valkenborch** (Pls. 374, 432, 445, 446, 448-50) and probably **Martin van Valkenborch** (Pl. 439) had all come back from Germany to Antwerp by 1579; **Marcus Geeraerts the elder** had returned there from England and **Gillis van Coninxloo** (Pls. 466, 476) from Paris; **Joos van Winghe** (Pls. 457, 497) had come back from Paris to Brussels, and **Karel van Mander** (Pl. 472) from Vienna via Nuremberg to Meulebeke. Such returns continued in the early eighties both to Flanders and Brabant and to the Northern provinces. Thus the landscape painter **Joos van Liere** came back from Frankenthal in 1580 or 1581 to his birthplace Swyndrecht (near Antwerp) where he was chiefly active as a Calvinist preacher till he died there in 1583; **Herman van der Mast** (Pl. 453) left Paris about 1580 and settled in Delft; and **Cornelis Ketel** (Pl. 451) left London for Amsterdam in 1581. Between 1581 and 1583 the rural populations of the Walloon provinces were 'zwaar belast en overbelast' by the military operations of both sides; they were plundered by marauding soldiery including Walloon Malcontents and German mercenaries; and many were driven from their homes. **Karel van Mander,** now just over thirty, newly married with an infant son, was stripped of his possessions and had to leave Meulebeke for Courtrai and then to take refuge in Bruges. In Ghent **Lucas de Heere** was among the sufferers as he seems to have disappeared on Parma's approach and to have died at a place unknown in 1584; and **Godefroid van Steynemolen,** Dean of the Malines Guild in 1581, had to flee the town for opposition to the Spaniards in 1586. Others were called on for military or para-military service; in 1584 during the siege of Antwerp **Frans Pourbus the elder** (Pl. 427), now avowedly a Protestant, served as ensign in the Civic Guard and died at thirty-six of typhoid fever contracted through resting by an open drain after a military exercise; and **Jan Vredeman de Vries** worked through the siege as an engineer on the fortifications.

After Parma's conquests of Bruges, Brussels and Antwerp, many Protestant artists emigrated to Holland (which must now be regarded as a foreign country); others went to Germany, and some came probably to England; and much Flemish painting of this period was thus produced abroad.

In Holland the artists established from the last period included **Dirck Barendsz** (Pl. 389), **Pieter Pietersz** (Pl. 421), **Aert Pietersz** (Pl. 485) and **Frans Badens** in Amsterdam; **Jacob Willemsz Delff** (Pl. 440) and possibly the **Amsterdam Little Girl with Dog Painter** (Pl. 452) in Delft; **Pieter Adriaensz Cluyt** in Alkmaar; his son **Adriaen Cluyt** as assistant to **Anthonis Blocklandt** (Pl. 420) in Utrecht; and **Adriaen van Cronenburch** (Pls. 343, 441, 443) in Bergum. The newcomers in Amsterdam included **Cornelis Ketel** (Pl. 451) from 1581, and **Gillis Congnet** (Pls. 434, 442) who came from Antwerp in 1586. **Hans Bol** (Pl. 431) left Antwerp in 1584 and settled in Amsterdam at the end of the period after working in Bergen-op-Zoom and Dordrecht (where his son **Jacques Bol the younger** was already established and **Nicolas Snellaert** had arrived from Courtrai by 1586); **Hans Bol** also worked in Delft and The Hague, and his stepson **Frans Boels** who had left Antwerp with him was probably also with him in some of or all these places. **Herman van der Mast** (Pl. 453) arrived in Delft as just mentioned in 1580; **Hans Jordaens the elder** escaped from Antwerp and seems to have reached Delft about 1587; and **Frans Spierinx,** also from Antwerp, arrived in Delft about 1590. **Karel van Mander** (Pl. 472) escaped from Bruges to Haarlem in 1583; **Jacques de Gheyn the younger** (Pl. 484) came to Haarlem from Antwerp in 1585 and had moved on to Amsterdam by 1591. **Daniel van den Queborne** reached Middelburg, from Antwerp, with his wife (the engraver Barbara van den Broeck) and **Crispiaen van den Broeck** (Pl. 409) in 1585; at the same time **Gillis van Coninxloo** (Pls. 466, 476) left Antwerp for Zeeland (doubtless Middelburg); and **Jacques Savery the elder** (Pl. 438) left Antwerp for The Hague. **Otto van Veen** (Pls. 455, 510, 511, 570) went from Liège to Leyden for some months in 1584.

To these adult arrivals we must add a number of painters of the next generation who were taken to Holland as children by their refugee Protestant parents. These included **Roelandt Savery** (Pls. 525, 564, 583, 585, 586) of Courtrai, younger brother of **Jacques Savery the elder; Joos Goeimare** also of Courtrai and also a painter later of landscapes with figures and animals; **Ambrosius Bosschaert** (Pls. 550, 551, 552) of Antwerp, **Cornelis van der Voort** of Antwerp later a portrait painter; and **Gillis de Hondecoeter,** of Malines or Antwerp, founder of a dynasty of Dutch bird painters. Others taken as children from Antwerp were **Adriaen van Stalbemt** (Pls. 479, 562), **Willem van Nieulandt** (Pl. 475), **Adriaen van Nieulandt** (Pls. 515, 647) and **David Vinckeboons** (Pl. 533). **Adam Willaerts** (Pl. 688) born in Antwerp in 1577 was also probably taken to Holland at this time as he is first recorded as an artist in Utrecht where **Joachim Uytewael** (Pls. 490, 498, 524) who was born there began his activities in the early eighties.

In the Amsterdam group **Dirck Barendsz** (Pl. 389), who became so corpulent in these years that no carriage could be found to drive him about, was doubtless still painting portraits and possibly groups and he sat to **Cornelis Ketel** for his own portrait in 1590; he may also have painted more mythologies with nude figures and he took part, as noted, in designing the decorations for Leicester's Pageant Entry into Amsterdam in 1587; he was working on a *Last Judgement with the Seven Works of Mercy* for the Amsterdam Hospital when he died at fifty-eight in 1592. **Pieter Pietersz** moved from Haarlem to Amsterdam when he was something over forty in 1585; he was mainly employed on portraits, probably, in both places, though he may also have produced more religious subjects like his *Shadrach, Meshach and Abednego* (Pl. 421) discussed in my last chapter; and **Aert Pietersz**, thirty-five when his brother joined him, may have obtained some commissions in these years for group portraits like the later example reproduced here (Pl. 485). **Frans Badens,** who later painted mythologies with nudes and social scenes including masquerades, began his career at the end of the period as he was twenty-one in 1592. **Cornelis Ketel,** thirty-three in 1581, and enjoying the prestige of his success in England, was immediately employed on portraits of Amsterdam notables and on groups of Civic Guardsmen; an early commission was *The Company of Captain Herman Rodenbergh Beths in a gallery with allegoric figures*; in 1588 he printed his *Company of Captain Rosencranz and Lieutenant Pauw* (Pl. 451) where the officers swagger in elegant postures (just as others swaggered some fifty years later in Frans Hals' *Company of Captain Reael and Lieutenant Blaeuw*) and a little dog catches the light in a framework of the guardsman's legs (just as the little girl catches the light among the legs of the guardsmen in Rembrandt's *Night Watch* of 1642). In 1587 **Ketel** had a hand, as mentioned, in the decorations for Leicester's Entry into Amsterdam; and these years he also produced a number of allegoric pieces with nudes in the Fontainebleau style, described by van Mander as '*Naked Truth guarded by Virtue against Deceit*', '*Intelligence disarmed by Wine, Venus and Avarice*', '*Love as the Fountain of the Arts*' and so on—compositions crowded with ingenious conceits which the artist explained in accompanying poems. After moving to Amsterdam when he was approximately fifty **Gillis Congnet** (Pls. 434, 442) doubtless continued to paint portraits, mythologies with nudes, and pictures with landscape settings; but he seems above all to have specialized there in genre pieces with night effects like his *Drawing of the Lottery for the Benefit of the Amsterdam Lunatic Asylum in an Amsterdam street in August 1592* where the scene is lit by torches; van Mander tells us that in certain of these pictures he used gold to suggest the light of lamps and torches, a trick which some people looked on as a violation of oil painting; and van Mander also tells us that others complained because he sold copies of his pictures, almost wholly by his pupils, as though they were originals by his hand. **Hans Bol,** fifty when he escaped into Holland, was still producing his delicate and elaborate miniature landscapes, with small figures, on parchment like the Antwerp example (Pl. 431) discussed in my last chapter; these now included two versions of *Fish spearing at The Hague* in 1585 and 1586, a *David and Abigail* in 1587 and a *Park landscape with buildings and figures* in 1589. **Frans Boels,** working in his stepfather's manner, signed several pieces titled *Mountainous landscape with mythological figures* in 1588. In the Delft group—where **Frans Boels** was de passage— **Jacob Willemsz Delff,** who had moved there from **Gouda** aged about thirty-two in 1582, was mainly employed on portraits, though his curious composition *The Reconciliation of Jacob and Esau* (Pl. 440) dates from 1584; he had **Pieter Cornelisz van Ryck,** painter of kitchen interiors, as his pupil in the middle eighties; and in 1592 he painted *Paulus Cornelisz van Beresteyn, Burgomaster of Delft* and a *Group of Thirty-one Civic Guardsmen* for the Delft Town Hall; there may have been some political allegory in his *Reconciliation of Jacob and Esau* (Pl. 440) which follows the Genesis story in every detail, or it may refer to some reconciliation within the family of the ugly old lady in the corner who commissioned it; and considered in relation to the style-developments in Flemish-Dutch painting it intrigues by the juncture of realism inherited from the **London Delft Painter** (Pls. 224, 226, 234) and **Pieter Aertsen** (Pls. 356, 357) with the mannerist elements which have appeared here in *S. Paul at Ephesus* (Pl. 397) by **Marten de Vos** and were destined to persist in works by **Joachim Uytewael** (Pls. 490, 498, 524) and also by **Ambroise Dubois** (Pl. 491). The bourgeois quietude of Delft, where the Prince of Orange had a mansion, seems to lie behind **Herman van der Mast's** sober *Portrait of a Lady* (Pl. 453) which anticipates the categoric portraits by the later Dutch painters; and the delightful picture by the **Amsterdam Little Girl with Dog Painter** (Pl. 452) is at once a genre piece and that rare phenomenon a formal but vital portrait of a very young child which students may find it instructive to compare with **Peter van Lint's** *Portrait of a baby with a rattle and a dog* (Pl. 697) painted some sixty years later in Antwerp. **Hans Jordaens the elder,** painter of miscellaneous genre scenes, came to Delft with his wife (the widow of **Frans Pourbus the elder**); and **Frans Spierinx** founded there a tapestry factory about 1591. In Haarlem **Karel van Mander** was a respected figure for twenty years from 1583; he produced there grisaille compositions, including a *Deluge*, drawings for engravers, paintings of religious subjects (Pl. 472), 'history', allegories and mythologies, and also portraits and genre; he sold pictures including a *Kermesse* to the Dutch collector Jacob Rauwaert (already referred to as owner of works by **Gerard van der Meire, Pieter Aertsen, Joachim Beuckelaer, Dirck Barendsz** and **Marten van Heemskerck**). With the Dutch painter Cornelis of Haarlem (who had returned there aged twenty-two in 1583 after working in Antwerp under **Gillis Congnet**) and the Dutch engraver Hendrick Goltzius, **van Mander** now founded an 'Academy' i.e. art school; and in 1592 he signed a *Portrait of a gentleman* showing a blond full-bearded man, in black robe and white ruffle, standing by a table with a green cover. **Jacques de Gheyn the younger** (Pl. 484) was twenty when he left Antwerp as a Protestant and arrived in Haarlem in 1585; in Antwerp he had practised as engraver and glasspainter and he had finished some windows begun by his father (**Jacques Gheyn the elder** who died in 1582); in Haarlem he joined the new 'Academy' and worked under Goltzius for engraving from 1585 till 1587; in 1591 his repute as an engraver was so high that the Jesuits in Antwerp invited him to return there and engrave the plates for an important book—hoping, it has been suggested, to convert him in the process; but he seems to have declined the offer and to have gone to Amsterdam instead; his first pictures were flower studies and it is possible that he began to paint in this period, but no dated examples are recorded. In the Utrecht group **Anthonis Blocklandt** (Pl. 420) painted an *Assumption of the Virgin* in 1579, had the Dutch portrait painter Michiel Miereveld as his pupil in 1581, and died, about fifty, in 1583 leaving unfinished a set of *Scenes from the story of Joseph* and a monochrome underpainting of *Bathsheba at the bath*; and the newcomer **Joachim Uytewael** (Pls. 490, 498, 524), son of a Utrecht glasspainter, and pupil about 1582 of **Joos de Beer** (painter, ex-pupil of **Frans Floris** and collector of pictures by **D. Barendsz** and **Anthonis Blocklandt**) went abroad at twenty in 1586 and was back by 1592. In Alkmaar **Pieter Adriaensz Cluyt** painted a *Siege of Alkmaar 1573* for the Civic Guard House in 1580. We know hardly anything of **Adriaen van Cronenburch** who was born before 1540, made a joint will with his wife in 1590 and seems to have worked as an isolated provincial figure in Bergum near Leeuwarden where he was still alive when the period closed; his beautifully designed and most tenderly experienced double portrait *Young lady with girl holding carnations* (Pl. 443), surely an arresting work in any collection of sixteenth-century pictures, bears an almost illegible date which the Prado catalogue transcribes as 1587 (though the clothes suggest an earlier decade and some read the date as 1567); the two other portraits by this artist reproduced here, the *Lady in*

Dutch dress (Pl. 343) and the *Lady holding a yellow flower* (Pl. 441) are also of outstanding quality, and both may also have been painted in the previous period or early in this one. In The Hague—where **Hans Bol** (probably accompanied by **Frans Boels**) was de passage in 1585 and 1586—his pupil **Jacques Savery the elder** drew in 1586 the *Pageant Entry of the Earl of Leicester* as already mentioned; sometime in the eighties **Savery** produced the miniature *Landscape with Jephthah's daughter* and in 1591 a *Landscape with Tobias and the angel*; his *Landscape with Jephthah's daughter* (Pl. 438), about seven by twelve inches, is a delicate panorama where Mizpeh is shown as a wooded town with partly invented and partly actual buildings and outlying farmlands; on the left Jephthah's unsuspecting daughter, with two companions, is the first to come from the main gate to welcome her father just arrived with his victorious army; in the centre there is boating on a stream and a crane is perched upon a rock; on the right, beyond an inn with a thatched porch and hanging sign, a covered waggon proceeds along a country road; and in the distance there is shipping on an estuary with mountains on each side. Many of the artists who went to Middelburg moved later to other towns because Middelburg was established by Leicester as a place of reception for the Calvinist refugees; thus the portrait painter **Daniel van den Queborne** went on, perhaps in this period, to The Hague where he became court painter to Prince Maurice; **Crispiaen van den Broeck** (Pl. 409) who was threatened by the Antwerp Magistrature with confiscation of his property as an émigré, returned to Antwerp for a time in 1588, and died either there or more probably back in Holland at sixty-seven before the beginning of 1591; and **Gillis van Coninxloo** (Pls. 466, 476), just over forty when he crossed the frontier, had moved from Zeeland into Germany by 1587. **Otto van Veen** was twenty-eight when he visited his native Leyden in 1584; he had been back in Liège from Italy for a year or more and become page to the Prince Bishop, Ernest of Bavaria; he went to Leyden to see his family who had returned there from Liège, and he recorded the visit in a *Self-portrait with members of his family* showing himself at his easel with his mother, father and sixteen other figures including five children one of whom strokes a recalcitrant cat in the foreground; this conversation piece, where no Italian influence is discernible, is a crowded composition like the *Family of Joris Hoefnagel* painted in 1571 by **Frans Pourbus the elder** described in my last chapter; an inscription upon it states that it was dedicated to the holy memory of God and was to remain in the family as long as there were any male descendants.

In Germany there were Flemish artists already established and many newcomers including refugees. Of the artists already there **Frans Hogenberg** remained in Cologne till he died at something over fifty in 1590; and **Adriaen de Weerdt**, nearly seventy when the period began, seems also to have died in Cologne about 1590. **Gortzius Geldorp** reached Cologne in 1579 not as refugee but as protégé of the Spanish Ambassador, the Duke of Terranova, as already related, and he stayed there painting biblical subjects (*Esther and Ahasuerus*), nudes (*Venus, Lucretia, Diana, Susanna*) and engaging portraits (Pls. 454, 486). **Jan (Velvet) Brueghel** (Pls. 464, 465, 467, 470, 480-3, 521) passed through Cologne on his way to Italy either in 1588, when he was twenty, or a year or so earlier. **Hans van Coninxloo the elder** was still in Emden in 1592 when he painted mythologies called *The Gods on Olympus* and *Hercules on Olympus*; **Nicolas de Perre** continued as a portraitist in Leipzig where he became a citizen in 1582; **Abraham del Hele** seems to have been still in Augsburg; **Nicolas Neufchatel** probably died in Nuremberg in 1590; and the Calvinist flower painter **Lodewyck Jansz van den Bosch** may also have died in Germany before the end of this period. **Cornelis Visscher** who, it will be recalled, had painted *William of Orange* and is described by van Mander as a good portraitist but sometimes mentally deranged, seems to have been in

Hamburg in the eighties and is known to have been drowned when returning thence over sixty in 1586. In Munich Duke William V's Court painters now included **Federico de Lamberto Sustris** as architect and painter of religious subjects and mythologies, **Pieter de Witte (Candido)** who had arrived from Italy by 1586 or earlier and also painted religious subjects and mythologies, **Engelhart van Pee** as portrait painter and **Joris Hoefnagel** who left for Vienna in 1590 after producing a missal with five hundred miniatures and a hundred decorated borders for the Archduke Ferdinand of Tyrol. Protestants expelled by Parma were not attracted to Munich because the Jesuits were in power there; they went especially to Frankfort or to Frankenthal where John Casimir welcomed Calvinists, and they included many of the painters who had gone home from Germany at the end of the last period or early in this one and become refugees again during Parma's campaigns or after his captures of Antwerp and Brussels. Thus **Jan Vredeman de Vries** (Pl. 462), **Hendrik van Steenwyck the elder** (Pl. 488), **Martin van Valkenborch** (Pl. 439), and his sons **Frederick van Valkenborch** (Pl. 502) and **Gillis van Valkenborch** had all gone from Antwerp to Frankfort by 1586; **Joos van Winghe** (Pls. 457, 497), arrived there from Brussels the same year; and to Frankfort, also from Brussels, **Hendrik van der Borcht the elder** was now taken as a child by his Protestant parents. **Gillis van Coninxloo** (Pls. 466, 476) arrived in Frankenthal from Zeeland in 1587; **Pieter Schoubroeck** (Pl. 494), son of a Protestant minister who had fled from Alva's persecutions, was then already in Frankenthal; and there too was **Antonie Mirou** (Pl. 469) as a child recently born of Flemish parents who had gone as emigrants in the earlier period. Of the new refugees to Frankfort **Jan Vredeman de Vries,** fifty-nine in 1586, was probably accompanied by his son **Paul Vredeman de Vries** as van Mander tells us that he went from Antwerp 'met zijn gezin'; **Paul Vredeman de Vries** then twenty-one, was like his father, a specialist in architectural perspectives and so forth, and he had already collaborated with **Joos van Winghe.** Armed with an introduction to the Duke of Brunswick **Jan Vredeman de Vries** moved on to Wolfenbüttel where he worked, probably with his son, for some years; in 1591 he went to Hamburg where, doubtless aided by a figure specialist, he painted a large perspective piece *Christ trampling on the Devil, Death and Hell* for the tomb of a jeweller in the Church of S. Peter; a staircase seen through two half open doors was in the lower half of this picture and a lighted lamp was painted above the figures, and visitors made heavy bets, van Mander tells us, that the doors, stairs and the lamp were real; in 1592 he moved on to Danzig, and there both he and his son were employed by the town authorities. His former pupil **Hendrik van Steenwyck the elder**—whose son **Hendrik van Steenwyck the younger** (Pls. 487, 489, 536, 537) was born about 1580—became a citizen of Frankfort aged about thirty-six in 1586; in 1588 he painted there a *Palace room with musicians*; in 1591 he is said to have worked in Carlsruhe; his *Night scene in a crypt* reproduced here (Pl. 488), which became a model for Flemish pictures of *The Liberation of S. Peter* (Pl. 489), may represent Protestants hiding in a crypt, and as its date is not known it may have been painted earlier in Antwerp, or at this period, or later, in Frankfort. **Martin van Valkenborch** whose *February: Flight into Egypt* (Pl. 439) was discussed in my last chapter, was fifty-one when he became an émigré again and arrived in Frankfort, and he was still there in 1592; **Frederick van Valkenborch** (Pl. 502) was about sixteen in 1586 and left Frankfort about 1591 on a study visit to Rome; and his brother **Gillis van Valkenborch** also, later, a landscape painter, was about the same age and went with him to Rome. **Joos van Winghe** (Pls. 457, 497) remained in Frankfort from 1586 and painted there, probably soon after his arrival, a large allegory *Justice protecting Innocence against Tyranny* and a *Belgium's Ordeal* where, van Mander tells us, 'Belgica, a nude figure, is chained to a

190

rock, Time flies down to break the fetters, while Religion with the Bible is trampled underfoot by Tyranny in armour with sword in hand'. In the Frankenthal colony **Gillis van Coninxloo,** forty-three when he arrived, was at once influential as a landscape painter; in 1588 he signed a *Landscape with King Midas judging between Apollo and Marsyas* where the figures, probably by a collaborator (possibly **Pieter Schoubroeck** (Pl. 494), then about nineteen), are set in a panorama with rising hills and estuary framed by a wooded foreground; and this foreground anticipates the landscapes with magnificent trees which **van Coninxloo** painted in his later years (Pls. 466, 476).

In Austria we have **Bartholomaeus Spranger** (Pls. 458, 459) already established, **Otto van Veen** (Pls. 455, 510, 511, 570) on a brief visit, and as newcomers **Joris van Hoefnagel, Pieter Stevens the younger** (Pl. 468) and **Lucas van Valkenborch** (Pls. 374, 432, 445, 446, 448-50). The Emperor Rudolf II was a neurotic intellectual who surrounded himself with astronomers, scientists and artists; like other Habsburgs he had a menagerie and aviaries and he collected miscellaneous rarities and ingenious machines in a 'Wunderkammer'. His picture gallery already included a number of works by **Pieter Bruegel the elder;** and in contemporary painting he especially favoured the Italianate art of **Bartholomaeus Spranger** whom he made a Court painter in 1584. **Spranger** at that date was thirty-eight and living in Prague where he had frescoed the outside of his house with figures imitating copper or brass reliefs; he had accompanied the Emperor to the Diet of Augsburg in 1582 and worked in his Vienna palace in 1583; after 1584 he was employed exclusively for the palaces in Prague and Vienna where the Emperor had studios fitted up for him and came repeatedly to watch him at work; in 1588 he was publicly honoured by the gift of a gold chain which the Emperor placed upon him at a banquet; and in 1592 he painted the *Allegory of the Virtues of Rudolf II* (Pl. 459) where, with Correggio in his mind, he surrounded the Emperor with Olympian deities while Fame blasts abroad his glory with two trumpets—a conceit which recalls to us the winged demon trumpeting 'grandeza y regalos' in **Bosch's** *Haywain* (Pl. 165). **Otto van Veen** visited Prague in an embassy from the Prince Bishop of Liège to Rudolf II in 1584 (either before or after his visit to Leyden). **Joris Hoefnagel** reached Prague from Munich aged forty-eight in 1590 and then settled in Vienna; and van Mander records a series of *Natural History* drawings in four books—quadrupeds, reptiles, birds and fishes—which the Emperor acquired and doubtless placed in his Wunderkammer. **Pieter Stevens the younger,** painter of landscapes with figures (Pl. 468), reached Prague from Antwerp in 1590 at about twenty-three and also settled down there. **Lucas van Valkenborch** whose remarkable *Landscape with village* (Pl. 432) was discussed in my last chapter, went to Linz in 1581 with the Archduke Mathias as mentioned above. In 1582, at about forty-eight, he painted the imposing *Mountain landscape* (Pl. 450) developing more naturalistically a tradition launched by **Patinir** (Pl. 244) and followed by **Lucas Gassel** (Pl. 328). In 1585 he produced a *Summer landscape: Harvesters* and also his *Autumn landscape: Fruit gathering* (Pl. 445) where the fruit gathering occupies the foreground, a team of farm horses draws a waggon from wooded country to a village and rustics perform aquatic sports on a castle moat or disport themselves with round dancing and bowls benevolently watched by the lord of the manor and his lady. The figures in these outdoor genre pieces by **Lucas van Valkenborch** may be the work of a collaborator and they recall the outdoor genre scenes by **Jacob Grimmer** (Pl. 430) and anticipate the *Village Fair* by **Jan (Velvet) Brueghel** (Pl. 467) and village scenes by **Pieter Stevens the younger** (Pl. 468), **David Vinckeboons** (Pl. 533) and **David Teniers** (Pl. 708). In 1586 he produced a *Winter landscape: Village in a snowstorm* where the whole air is full of snowflakes falling on the peasants, the village church and other buildings and the leafless trees. In 1587 he painted the charming *Spring landscape: Picnic with elegant company* (Pl. 446) where the picnickers, in a wood with castle and gardens and winding stream in the distance, recall the picnickers by **Pieter Jansz Pourbus** (Pl. 331) and anticipate the picnickers by Watteau; and the humour of the seventeenth-century genre painters is forestalled here by the cavalier just descended from his horse who respectfully kisses the hand of his hostess while his servant relieves himself against the castle wall. In 1590 he painted a *Wooded landscape with the Archduke Mathias fishing*; and he was still in Linz in 1592.

Of the Flemish and Flemish-Dutch artists established in England **Hans Ewouts (Eworth)** (Pls. 338, 349, 350, 417) probably died about sixty quite early in this period; and **Cornelis Ketel** (Pl. 451) left for Amsterdam in 1581 as already related. There are no records of paintings by **Marcus Geeraerts the younger** at this time; but he was probably launched as a portrait painter in the early eighties and he may have painted the Queen before 1592; it is known that in 1590 he married Magdalena de Critz, whose elder sister Susanna was the second wife of his father **Marcus Geeraerts the elder** who may have re-emigrated to England from Antwerp after 1587 as van Mander tells us that he died here at a date which his son, on enquiry, declined to disclose 'meenende dat het hem niet paste mij iets loffelijks over zijn vader te schrijven'. Rather strangely there seem indeed to be no records of Flemish or Flemish-Dutch painters among the refugees to England when Parma expelled the Pro-testants; but **Hieronymus Custodis** who came from Antwerp and worked in London in the later eighties may have been among them. This **Hieronymus Custodis** practised here as a portrait painter till about 1592 (as his wife is described as a widow in 1593); his sitters in 1589 included *Sir John Parker* and *Giles Bruges (Brydges) 3rd Lord Chandos*. In the same year **Custodis** painted the daughter of Giles Brydges *Elizabeth Bruges (Brydges)* who a little later was Maid of Honour to Queen Elizabeth and incurred her displeasure by attracting the attention of Essex; the picture shows her aged fourteen in an embroidered gown with embroidered cuffs and upstanding embroidered collar, a white Maltese dog is beside her and a white finch with a briar rose is above her in the background; the face is delicately drawn but Walpole described the colouring as 'flat and chalky' a description still accurate today; it is however possible that some carmine glazes had already faded from the cheeks and lips when Walpole saw the picture, and it is more than likely that they will reappear there some day replaced by a restorer. In Scotland **Arnold** (or **Arthur**) **van Brounkhurst,** after the failure of his search for gold recorded in my last chapter, became Court Painter to James VI in 1580 'to draw all the small and great pictures for his majesty'; and a precept signed by the King referring to him as 'our lovit servitour Arnold Bronckhorst our painter' contains commissions for portraits including several of himself and one of George Buchanan who was then seventy-four and had published 'De Jure Regni apud Scotos' in 1579.

Of the painters in France **Wenzelas Coebergher** (Pl. 493) left Paris for Italy about 1579; **Herman van der Mast** (Pl. 453), who was knighted by Catherine de Médicis at a Carnival ball, went to Delft, as mentioned, about 1580; and **Jan de Wael** was back in Antwerp from Paris at twenty-five by 1583. **Jan de Hoey,** still in Troyes, at forty, in 1585, was appointed painter to Henry of Navarre before the end of the period. **Hieronymus Francken the elder** had the young Dutchman Abraham Bloemaert as his pupil in Paris in 1582, painted there an *Adoration of the Shepherds* for the Église des Cordeliers in 1585, and married a French girl soon after. It was probably at this time also that he produced his *Evening Party with a lady at the harpsichord* which shows figures of Henri III's period and continues his work in

192

the social genre field begun with his *Venetian Carnival* of 1564 discussed in my last chapter; for social pieces, depicting Court and other festivities, were now much in vogue in Paris and van Mander speaks of one 'Bolerij' (doubtless Hieronymus Bollery or his son Nicolas Bollery) who excelled in 'nachttafereelen, maskeraden, vasten avonden en zulke feesten' with echoes of Bassano—(a tradition continued in the *Night banquet and masquerade* (Pl. 497) by **Joos van Winghe**). Owing to the Wars of Religion and the political conflicts there was still a lull in decorative work at Fontainebleau; but **Ambroise Dubois** (Pl. 491) seems to have been employed there probably on the staff of the directing artist Toussaint Dubreuil who, van Mander tells us, had Flemish painters as assistants. From about 1589 the brilliant **Joachim Uytewael** (Pls. 490, 498, 524), then twenty-three, spent two years in France with the Bishop of S. Malo on his way back from Italy; and he may have met **Ambroise Dubois** and French followers of Primaticcio and Niccolo del Abbate in the ateliers at Fontainebleau, and the French mannerist Jacques Bellange then a youth, in Nancy, and Antoine Caron painter of allegoric fêtes and ballets, in Paris.

In Spain there seem to have been but few Flemish artists at this time. But **Rodrigo Diriksen** married to a daughter of **Antonio van den Wyngaerde** was still in the King's service and still at work in the Escorial; in 1581 he finished an *Ecce Homo* left unfinished at his death by the Spanish painter J. F. Navarete (El Mudo); he is known to have painted a *S. Mary Magdalene* for the tomb of the King's fool Miguel de Antona; and in 1589 a team of Spanish artists produced a fresco in the Sala de Batallas *The Battle of Higueruela* based on his cartoons. **Jan Floris**, probably still director of the Faience Factory in Madrid, became Superintendent of the Pardo Palace in 1581 and may have died before 1592. **Jan Kraeck (Caracca)** in Spain from Turin on affairs of his patron Duke Charles Emmanuel of Savoy in 1585 and 1591, became known there as **Juan Carraza**; and he probably took with him on his second visit his *Portrait of Philip of Savoy aged five* which was painted in that year.

The newcomers in Italy included the two first teachers of **Rubens**—**Tobias van Haecht** (Pl. 377) and **Adam van Noort; Joachim Uytewael** (Pls. 490, 498, 524); and **Jan (Velvet) Brueghel** (Pls. 464, 465, 467, 470, 480-3, 521). Of these **Tobias van Haecht** arrived from Antwerp at eighteen in 1579 and was back in Antwerp by 1590; an inscription on the engraving of his portrait in De Bie's 'Gulden Cabinet' (1661) tells us that he worked in Florence for the Duke of Tuscany and that in Rome he painted some frescoes showing *Landscapes with ruins* and also a *Tower of Babel* which was particularly admired; he was quite unaffected by Italian painting and his later picture reproduced here (Pl. 377) shows him an imitator of **Pieter Bruegel's** Alpine landscapes (Pls. 378, 378A). **Adam van Noort** on the other hand, as a painter of religious subjects, was more concerned with Italian painting; he reached Italy from Antwerp about 1582, when he was twenty, and was back in Antwerp by 1587. **Joachim Uytewael** arrived from Utrecht, at twenty, in 1586; in Padua, van Mander says, he met and was taken up by the Bishop of S. Malo with whom he travelled about Italy from 1587-89; he thus laid the foundation for his life's work by study of the local mannerist concepts and also, evidently, of Graeco-Roman statues; and thereafter as just mentioned he enlarged his experience by two years travel through France. **Wenzelas Coebergher** went to Italy, from France, probably in 1579 when he was approaching twenty, and he worked in Naples, painting pictures for churches, from 1580 till the end of the period. **Jan (Velvet) Brueghel** who arrived in Italy from Cologne about 1589, reached Naples in 1590 and he is known to have been painting rural landscapes by 1591. In Naples the newcomers found **Jan van Stinemolen, Dirck Hendricksz, Cornelis Smet, Aert Mytens** and **Jan van der Straet (Stradanus).** Of these **Jan van Stinemolen** signed a *Panorama of Naples* in 1582; **Dirck Hendricksz (Errico Fiammingo)** active there through the period, painted then or later an *Execution of S. John the Baptist* and other works for S. Gregorio, a *Flagellation*, a *Virgin in Glory* and a *King Totilla and S. Benedict* for S. Maria Donnaromita and a *Virgin of Purity* for S. Paolo Maggiore; his friend **Cornelis Smet** (who became a friend also of **Wenzelas Coebergher**) contracted to produce a *Virgin of the Rosary* for S. Giovanni in Mercato Sanseverino in 1579, a *Circumcision* for S. Domenico Maggiore in Naples in 1580 and a *Virgin of the Rosary* for a church in Muro Lucano in 1590; and he seems to have died in Naples about 1592. **Aert Mytens (Rinaldo Fiammingo),** about thirty-eight in 1579, worked in Naples with a number of pupils through the period, and married there, as his second wife, the widow of his former master **Cornelis Pyp;** in 1584 he painted a *Virgin of the Rosary with the Fifteen Mysteries* for S. Severino in Naples, in 1586 he repeated the *Virgin of the Rosary* theme for S. Giovanni in Mercogliano, and perhaps at this time also he painted three pictures for Naples churches recorded by van Mander—an *Assumption of the Virgin* with over life-size figures, a *Torture of S. Catherine* showing the wheel bursting asunder and a torturer struck by a splinter and screaming with mouth wide open 'zeer natuurgetrouw afgebeeld', and a *S. Maria del Soccorso striking a prostrate devil with a club.* **Jan van der Straet (Stradanus)** was in Naples in 1579; he drew there a *Battle of Saul and the Philistines* that year and painted there some pictures for churches; in the middle eighties he was back in Florence where he painted an *Adoration of the Shepherds* in 1586 and an *Adoration of the Magi* in 1587; he designed some of the pageantry occasioned by the marriage of the Grand Duke Ferdinand dei Medici with Christina of Lorraine in 1589, and was still active there at sixty-nine in 1592. In Rome **Hendrik van den Broeck (Arrigo Fiammingo, Henricus Paludanus)** was elected Councillor of the Accademia di S. Luca in 1580 when he was just over sixty; in 1581 or 1585 he provided pictures for churches in Perugia with **Johannes Wraghe** as his assistant; in 1585 he also supplied a *Holy Family* for the church at Mongiovino for which **Wraghe** supplied a *Visitation* at this time or later; in 1588 he painted the *Second Lateran Council* for the Sala Sistina in the Vatican Library; and in 1590 he painted panels in S. Maria Maggiore. **Mathys Brill** painted *Views of Rome behind processions bringing the relics of S. Gregory of Nyssa to S. Peter's* on the walls of Loggias in the Vatican in 1580 (with figures by the Italian Antonio Tempesta); in 1581 he became a member of the Accademia di S. Luca; a year or so later, assisted by **Paul Brill,** he painted landscape frescoes in the Torre dei Venti; and he died under forty in 1583 or 1584. **Paul Brill** (Pls. 473, 474) became a member of the Accademia di S. Luca at about twenty-seven in 1582; he probably finished his brother's frescoes in 1583 or 1584; between 1585 and 1590 he painted landscapes and seascapes for the Scala Santa of the Vatican (*Jonah thrown into the sea* and *Jonah cast up by the whale*) and *Landscape with hermits* for the Lateran, all commissioned by Sixtus V; and he also painted some easel pictures. In Rome also **François Stellaert (Stella)** who signed a *Cascade in Tivoli* in 1587 was perhaps the author of an *Entombment* in S. Pietro in Montorio—as an eighteenth-century engraving of this picture is inscribed 'd'après le tableau de F. Stellaert'. **Frans van den Kasteele (Francesco da Castella),** about thirty-nine in 1579, held offices in the Accademia di S. Luca in 1588 and 1591; he continued to paint miniature compositions of religious subjects and pictures for churches; and he may also have produced some decorative panels with mythologies at this time. **Anthonie Santvoort** still a member of the Academy seems to have been in Rome through the period; **Otto van Veen** (Pls. 455, 510, 511, 570) left Zuccaro's atelier in the early eighties and was back in Liège aged twenty-seven by 1583. **Frederick** van Valkenborch (Pl. 502) and his brother **Gillis van Valkenborch** both visited Rome when they were just over twenty about 1591; and **Gaspar Heuvick** may have left to paint for churches in Bari by 1592 or soon after. In Parma **Jan Sons** remained Court Painter to Duke Ottavio Farnese till 1586 and was confirmed in the office by Alexander Farnese on his accession; he probably continued his easel pictures with landscapes and small figures, and in 1590 he signed a *Resurrection* for S. Francesco del Prato. In Bologna **Denys Calvaert's** art school was now flourishing and his pupils included Guido Reni who came aged nine in 1584 and was still there in 1592. **Calvaert** was also occupied with many commissions for churches; thus in 1582 he painted an *Annunciation* for S. Maria dei Bulgari in Bologna, in 1583 a *Martyrdom of S. Lawrence* for S. Lorenzo church in San Lorenzo, and in 1590 a *Mystic Marriage of S. Catherine*. In Turin Duke Charles Emmanuel I continued **Jan Kraeck (Caracca)** in his post as Court Painter when he succeeded Duke Emmanuel Philibert in 1580; **Kraeck** painted the new Duke's portrait in that year; in the early eighties he had the Dutch marine painter Hendrik Cornelisz Vroom as a pupil for some time; in 1586 he was paid for pictures titled *The Prodigal Son, Fruit piece, Landscape* and *S. Mary of Egypt*; and in 1585 and 1591 he visited Spain as related above. In Venice **Pauwels Franck (Paolo Fiammingo)** continued for some years as associate of Tintoretto in the Doges' Palace where *Pope Alexander III blessing the Fleet 1176* is traditionally recorded as his work; he also painted religious pictures, including a *Pietà with S. John and Joseph of Arimathea*, numerous decorative pieces for Pietro Gradenigo's Venetian palace and for the banker Hans Fugger's Schloss Kirchheim in Swabia, and two compositions for or acquired by Rudolf II; the pictures for the Emperor were *Landscapes with allegories of Fortune and the Virtues*; those for Gradenigo and Fugger were *Landscapes with allegories of the Seasons, the Elements, the Senses, the Four Quarters of the World, the Planets and so forth*, titles which reveal him as an early exponent of a type of subject soon to be frequently painted by **Jan (Velvet) Brueghel** (Pl. 542) and **Jan Brueghel the younger** (Pl. 605) and by many others. **Lodewyck Toeput (Pozzoserrato)** continued in Venice for some years; he paid visits to Rome and Florence and moved, perhaps before 1592, to Treviso; like **Pauwels Franck** he painted some pictures for churches; but he seems to have specialized in landscapes with gardens, Venetian villas and small figures; in 1584 or 1587 he painted a *Tower of Babel* for Hans Fugger's Kirchheim castle; he drew or painted a *Portrait of Tintoretto* (engraved in 1588); and a *Masked ball on a terrace* and a *View of S. Mark's Venice* are recorded by engravings. Others in Venice in these years were **Pietro Mera, Gaspar Rem** and **P. C. van Ryck** painter of genre and portraits.

At home in Belgium Parma was too occupied with his military commitments to concern himself much with art; but he was called on to show respect to **Michiel Coxie** (Pls. 308, 310, 352), **Raphael Coxie** and **Marten de Vos** (Pls. 364, 397, 429) who all remained King's Painters; and he extended his patronage to some other artists. Thus he made **Jean Baptiste Saive** of Namur a Court painter, transferred him to Brussels, made him 'Concierge des vignobles' and sat to him for his portrait; and in Bruges he favoured **Gillis Claeissins, Antoine Claeissins** (Pl. 422) and **Pieter Claeissins the younger** (Pl. 436). He made **Joos van Winghe** (Pls. 457, 497) a Court painter either before 1585 or on entering Brussels, and when **van Winghe,** as van Mander puts it, had been 'driven by his conscience' to emigrate to Frankfort, he appointed **Otto van Veen** (Pls. 455, 510, 511, 570) to replace him.

Commissions for religious pictures seem to have been relatively rare during the Patriot and Anjou occupations of the major towns. But they were numerous under Parma when a religious revival called for altarpieces directed by Tridentine rules and executed in the

Romanist manner. Parma, in conjunction with the Jesuits and the Catholic hierarchy, launched a campaign to revive enthusiasm for all orthodox doctrines; and, as special efforts were made to indoctrinate the children, *The Lineage of S. Anne* and *Suffer little children . . .* increased in favour as subjects for commissioned pictures.

The painters available for religious subjects when Parma entered Antwerp in 1585 included **Michiel Coxie** (Pls. 308, 310, 352) who had a studio there as well as in Malines and was then eighty-six and still active, **Crispiaen van den Broeck** (Pl. 409) then aged sixty-one, **Marten de Vos** (Pls. 364, 397, 429) then about fifty-four, **Michel Joncquoy** about fifty-three, **Gillis Mostaert** (Pl. 348) then fifty-one, **Bernaert de Ryckere** about fifty, **Raphael Coxie** about forty-five, **Frans Francken the elder** forty-three, **Ambrosius Francken the elder** forty-one, **Adriaen Thomas Key** (Pls. 423, 424) about forty-one, **Jan Snellinck** (Pl. 460) about forty, **Cornelis Floris** thirty-four, **Gerard Schoof** about thirty and **Jan de Wael** twenty-seven. **Marcellus Coffermans** (Pl. 403) and **Jacques de Backer** (Pl. 416) whose death dates are uncertain may still have been living in 1585, the first about fifty-five and the second under thirty; **Frans Pourbus the elder** (Pl. 427) had died at thirty-six in 1581; **Adam van Noort** was probably still in Italy in 1585 though he was back aged twenty-five by 1587; **Abraham de Ryckere** (son and pupil of **Bernaert de Ryckere**) was nineteen; **Pieter Brueghel the younger** (Pls. 380, 411) was twenty-one and **Jan (Velvet) Brueghel** (Pl. 470) was seventeen; **Marten Pepyn** (Pls. 569, 571, 572), **Abraham Janssens** (Pl. 509) and **Hendrik van Balen** (Pls. 507, 508) were boys of ten; and **Peter Paul Rubens** (still with his mother in Germany) was eight. Of the established artists **Michiel Coxie** and **Crispiaen van den Broeck** had received, in 1582, a joint commission from the Antwerp Magistrature to paint two pictures for the Town Hall; but it is not known whether this called for religious subjects like **Crispiaen van den Broeck's** *Last Judgement* (Pl. 409) or for secular themes, and it is also not known whether the pictures were completed or not when **van den Broeck** left Antwerp for Middelburg after Parma's conquest. **Michiel Coxie** probably came to Antwerp from Malines to work on them; he was back to Malines in the later eighties; and he died in Antwerp at ninety-two in 1592 as a result of falling from a scaffold in the Town Hall when restoring a *Judgement of Solomon*. Contemporary references to religious pictures by **Jacques de Backer** tell us that a *Last Judgement* by him was placed in the church of the Carmes Chaussés on the funeral monument of **Pieter Goetkint** who died in 1583, and that another picture of the same subject, also by him, was placed in Antwerp Cathedral on the funeral monument of Christopher Plantin who died in 1589; but the dates when he painted the pictures are not known. Van Mander, who was **Jacques de Backer's** contemporary wrote of Him: 'Hij ist weel een van de beste coloristen die Antwerp heeft gehad; hij schilderde de naakten geheel in vleeschkleur, zonder zich bij het aanbrengen van de licht partijen van wit te bedienen'; of the Carmes Chaussés picture Descamps wrote in 1769: 'Le dessein en est correct, mais la composition en est confuse et les figures sur le second plan sont plus grandes que celles du premier, il est d'une bonne couleur et touché avec esprit, c'est un joli tableau'; of the other picture (which is still in Antwerp Cathedral and can be compared with **de Backer's** 1571 *Last Judgement* reproduced here (Pl. 416)) Descamps wrote: 'Le tableau est d'un dessein fin et correct, d'une très bonne couleur, mais un peu sec' and Sir Joshua Reynolds who saw it in 1781 wrote 'correctly drawn but without any skill in disposition of light and shadow'. **Marten de Vos** (who took the talented young Bruxellois **Hendrik de Clerck** as his pupil about 1586) had many commissions for church pictures in these years, his atelier was staffed with assistants, and many of his pictures were disseminated in engravings; in 1585 he painted a *Lineage of S. Anne*, before 1588 a

196

'*Suffer little children . . .*' and in 1589 *Christ on the sea of Tiberias* and *Jonah swallowed by the whale*. In 1590 **de Vos** produced a triptych *The Triumph of Christ, The Baptism of Constantine* and *Constantine building a church in Constantinople dedicated to S. George* for the altar of the Old Crossbowmen's Guild in Antwerp Cathedral; Descamps commenting on this wrote 'La correction du dessein et des têtes belles et bien peintes y font un grand plaisir, mais il n'y a point d'effet', but Reynolds dismissed it as 'not worth attention'. **Michel Joncquoy** came from Tournai to Antwerp in the early eighties and was citizen there by 1584. **Gillis Mostaert** as our knowledge goes, was in Antwerp through the period: he was still 'niet zoo heel godsdienstig' and 'niet erg Spaansch gezind', but after Parma's arrival he may have concentrated for a time on orthodox pieces like his *Christ on the Cross* (Pl. 348) discussed in an earlier chapter; among the artists, at any rate, he now held considerable status, for in 1589 he acted as assessor (with **Marten de Vos** and **Bernaert de Ryckere**) in a dispute about the price of a *Last Judgement* by **Raphael Coxie**. **Bernaert de Ryckere** painted a triptych *Pentecost, The Baptism of Christ, The Creation of Adam* and sent it in 1587 from Antwerp to the church of S. Martin in his native Courtrai; this was evidently produced without the aid of studio assistants as he signed it 'Bernardus de Ryckere pinxit et solus fecit', and it is still in the church at Courtrai where it can be compared with his Romanist *Christ falling beneath the Cross and succoured by S. Veronica* painted in 1560; his picture titled *The Finding of Moses* may also have been painted in these later years when, van Mander tells us, 'he changed his style and thought he had improved it;' **Bernaert de Ryckere** also acted as copyist and probably as dealer; and when he died in 1590 among some five hundred and twenty pictures in his studio there were originals by **Quinten Massys, Marinus van Reymerswaele** and **Gillis van Coninxloo** and copies from them, and also copies of works by **Frans Floris, Marten de Vos, 'Sotte' Cleve, Willem Key** and others. **Raphael Coxie** moved from Malines and was Antwerp Master by 1585; his *Last Judgement*, mentioned above, was commissioned by the Ghent City Council for the Sheriffs Hall in 1588; when the price dispute arose the assessors secured for him an additional thousand florins which were welcome as he was in debt at this time as result of gambling and disordered habits; these financial difficulties were revealed in the course of the dispute and to counteract the bad impression he presented a *Resurrection* to a Ghent religious house next year. **Frans Francken the elder,** who held high rank in the Guild in 1585, was another artist who collected (and possibly dealt in) pictures; in 1586 he began a triptych *Jesus among the Doctors* (set within a Romanist temple), *S. Ambrose baptizing S. Augustine* and *Elijah reviving the widow's son at Sarepta* commissioned by Archdeacon Reynier Bervoets de Brakel for the altar of the Schoolmasters Guild in Antwerp Cathedral; Reynolds wrote of the central panel: 'There are some fine heads in this picture; particularly the three men that are looking on one book are admirable characters; the figures are well drawn and well grouped: the Christ is but a poor figure'—and he might have added that **Jordaens** repeated this motif of grouped doctors 'looking on one book' in a *Jesus among the Doctors* painted some seventy-six years later. **Ambrosius Francken the elder** made money from his wife's stone and chalk business between 1579 and 1581 when he supplied materials for public buildings; his wife died in 1582; he married in 1583 another rich widow and made over the stone and chalk business to his first wife's children; in 1585 he became an alderman; and it was not till after Parma's conquest that he resumed, or continued more vigorously, his practice as a painter of church pictures; no surviving works known to be by him are actually dated in this period, but his triptych *The Last Supper, The Disciples at Emmaus* and *SS. Paul and Barnabas called to the Apostolate by the Holy Spirit* commissioned for the altar of the Holy Sacrament in Antwerp S. George, may well have been painted to theological dictation under Parma. **Adriaen Thomas Key** was available for religious subjects like his *Last supper* (Pls. 423, 424) till 1589 and possibly later as his death date is unknown; but he seems as before to have chiefly worked as portraitist. **Jan Snellinck** (Pl. 460) whose *Suffer little children . . .* was probably painted in these years, registered **Abraham Janssens** (Pl. 509) as his pupil in 1585 and was probably training him by 1590. **Cornelis Floris,** active as sculptor as well as painter, left Antwerp for an unrecorded reason in 1586 but was back and working for the Cathedral by 1589; **Gerard Schooff** who had **Jacob de Hase** among his numerous pupils in 1588 was Treasurer of the Guild in 1589. Among the younger men **Jan de Wael,** back from Paris and Antwerp Master by 1584, became brother-in-law to **Jan Snellinck** in 1588 when he married Gertrude de Jode, a lady known to us in the picture *Jan de Wael and his wife* painted later by **Van Dyck. Adam van Noort,** Master by 1587, painted a '*Suffer little children . . .*' probably at this time; he had an atelier with many pupils including **Hendrik van Balen** (Pls. 507, 508), **Sebastiaan Vrancx** (Pls. 531, 532, 534) and **Ferdinand van Apshoven the elder** by 1592. **Abraham de Ryckere** painted a *Christ crucified between the thieves* donated to Antwerp, S. Jacques by one Jan Doncker in 1591. **Pieter Bruegel's** sons **Pieter Brueghel the younger** and **Jan (Velvet) Brueghel** were in Antwerp from Brussels by the early eighties; the first became Antwerp Master at twenty-one in 1585 and remained there for the rest of the period, and the second left for Italy, as related, about 1589.

Among the Brussels painters of religious subjects **Pieter de Kempener** (Pl. 367) was seventy-six in 1579 and probably died soon after. **Jean Baptiste Saive** had moved from Namur to Brussels at Parma's invitation by the end of the eighties and he may have painted there his *Crucifixion* placed in Brussels, S. Catherine. **Joos van Winghe** (Pls. 457, 497) painted a *Last Supper* (with **Paul Vredeman de Vries** as collaborator) for Brussels, S. Géry before he emigrated; van Mander describes this as his best work in Belgium and also records a *Delila cutting Samson's hair* and a *Conversion of S. Paul.* **Otto van Veen** (Pls. 455, 510, 511, 570) had left Liège and established himself in Brussels when he became Court Painter to Parma at the age of thirty in 1586, and in 1589 he painted the *Mystic Marriage of S. Catherine* reproduced here (Pl. 455) as a commission from a member of the d'Arenberg family for the Capucins church; Descamps who saw this picture in the sacristy dismissed it as 'un assez beau tableau', but another French painter Eugène Fromentin who saw it about a hundred years later (in 1875) was more appreciative as he wrote in his 'Maîtres d'autrefois': 'Ce tableau m'a beaucoup frappé . . . il est tout imbibé de le suc italien dont le peintre s'était profondément nourri. . . . A voir une certaine tendresse dans les types, un chiffonage arbitraire dans les etoffes, un peu de manière dans les mains, on sent Corrège introduit dans du Raphael. Des anges sont dans le ciel et y forment une jolie tache; une draperie jaune sombre en demi-teinte est jetée comme une tente à plis relevés a travers les rameaux des arbres . . . les cheveux blonds qui se noient dans les chairs blondes, les linges blanc-gris qui passent l'un dans l'autre, des couleurs qui se nuancent ou s'affirment, se fondent ou se distinguent très capricieusement d'après des lois nouvelles et suivant des fantaisies propres a l'auteur, tout cela c'est le pur sang italien transfusé dans une veine capable d'en faire un sang neuf. Tout cela prépare Rubens, l'annonce, y conduit'. Fromentin might have added that this picture is also an ancestor of the rhetoric and religiosity of **Van Dyck's** religious pieces at their worst—(the *Blessed Herman Joseph before the Virgin* for example)—and we must observe here also that iconographically it breaks entirely with the Pre-Tridentine Hortus Conclusus concept of this subject which had produced the charming works by the **Buckingham Palace Mystic Marriage Painter** (Pl. 106), the **Detroit Mystic Marriage Painter** (Pl. 110), the **Brussels Mystic Marriage Painter** (Pl. 107), the **Amsterdam Delft Painter** (Pl. 219) and the less personal but still attractive picture by **Memlinc** (Pl. 111); for the Mystic Marriage which formerly showed us the Virgin Mother among the maiden saints in a secluded garden or flowered arbour or convent cortile is now set in a handsome landscape with verdure in the Titian-Tintoretto-Veronese style, and SS. Joseph and Francis now replace the maiden saints as attendant figures. There is a charm in the rhythm of the carefully composed and executed triptych which **Hendrik de Clerck** painted at twenty for Brussels, Église de la Chapelle, in 1590; this has *The Lineage of S. Anne* (Pl. 456) in the centre and on the inside and outside of the wings *S. Yves Patron of Lawyers*, *Joachim's sacrifice rejected*, *The Judgement of Solomon* and *Joachim and Anna at the Golden Gate*; in the *Lineage of S. Anne* **de Clerck** has enriched the blond serenity and classical measure of *The Holy Kinship* (Pl. 207) by **Quinten Massys** with complexities provided by Tridentine theology and Romanist rules of balance and design; and it may, I think, have been recalled by **Jacob Jordaens** when he planned the design of his *Jesus among the Doctors* for Furnes, S. Walpurga at the age of seventy in 1663. I reproduce also a detail from the *Suffer little children* . . . (Pl. 471) painted by **de Clerck** some two years later for Brussels, S. Gudule; this contains, as a personal concept, a woman in striped mantle with a sun hat that suggests a halo and thus converts the group she stands in to a Virgin and Child with S. Anne.

Among the painters of religious subjects in other places **Josse van der Baren** was now beginning his career in Louvain with pictures for the local churches. In Malines **Cornelis Enghelrams** died in 1580 or 1583; and a newcomer **Rombout van Avont** became Master in 1581. **Michiel Coxie** (Pls. 308, 310, 352) who was mainly resident in Malines and was paid compensation by Parma for war damage to his handsome house, signed a *Martyrdom of S. George* for S. Rombout 'aetatis suae 89' in 1588; and four years later he signed his last picture *Scenes from the life of S. Gudule* for Brussels, S. Gudule 'pictor regius fecit anno salutis 1592 vero aetatis suae 92'. Among the Bruges painters of religious subjects **Pieter Jansz Pourbus** (Pls. 331, 334, 336, 337) who visited Antwerp from Bruges in 1581 and 1582, outlived his son **Frans Pourbus the elder** by three years and died in Bruges at sixty-four in 1584. **Jacques van den Coornhuuse** seems to have died in Bruges at some date after 1584. **Antoine Claeissins** (Pls. 422, 492) who remained official painter to the city till 1581 signed a *Virgin and Child with donors* for Notre Dame in 1584 and restored the *Last Judgement* (Pl. 334) of his former master **Pieter Jansz Pourbus** when he was something over fifty in 1589. **Pieter Claeissins the younger** succeeded his brother as city painter in 1581, worked for various churches in the archaistic manner of his allegoric *Convention of Tournai* reproduced here (Pl. 436) and restored in 1586 the *Resurrection* which his father **Pieter Claeissins the elder** had painted with his aid for S. Sauveur in 1572; and **Gillis Claeissins**, author of an undated *Holy Trinity*, was Court Painter to Parma after 1584. **Lucas de Heere** disappeared from Ghent, as noted, and died, aged fifty, at a place unknown in 1584. **Pieter Vlerick** died in Tournai of the plague, aged forty-two, in 1581; **Michel Joncquoy** was in Tournai when the period began and had moved to Antwerp by 1584; and **Karel van Mander** signed a *Martyrdom of S. Catherine* in Courtrai for S. Martin's church when he was thirty-four in 1582 before moving to Bruges and thence to Holland.

Allegories and mythologies with nudes were painted for Pageant ceremonies and as easel pictures and decorations. I have referred above to the Pageant contributions by **Crispiaen van den Broeck, Lucas de Heere, Pieter Claeissins the younger, Dirck Barendsz, Cornelis**

Ketel, Jacques Savery the elder and **Jan van der Straet (Stradanus)**. I have spoken also of the pro-Spanish allegory the *Convention of Tournai* (Pl. 436) by **Pieter Claeissins the younger,** the anti-Spanish allegories by **Gillis Congnet** (Pl. 434) and **Joos van Winghe,** the elaborate didactic allegories by **Cornelis Ketel,** the Olympian scenes by **Hans van Coninxloo the elder,** the emblematic figures of the Seasons, the Planets and so forth in landscapes by **Pauwels Franck (Paolo Fiammingo),** the *Judgement of Midas* in a landscape by **Gillis van Coninxloo,** the nudes by **Gortzius Geldorp,** the *Bathsheba at the bath* by **Anthonis Blocklandt** and the *Allegory of the Virtues of Rudolf II* (Pl. 459) by **Bartholomaeus Spranger.** Some other works in these fields must now be added. **Jacques de Backer** (Pl. 416) painted a composition (or three pictures) titled *Venus, Juno* and *Minerva* with half-life-size standing figures and, van Mander tells us, the attributes of each goddess; he also painted a *Danae* and an *Adam and Eve*; and Descamps saw a *Justice and Peace* by him in the Antwerp Academy's apartments. **Bernaert de Ryckere** painted a *Diana and Actaeon* in 1582 and, before 1590, a *Feast of the Gods* which was later owned by **Rubens;** and **Cornelis Floris** painted a *Feast of Bacchus* at a date unrecorded but possibly in this period. **Otto van Veen** (Pls. 455, 510, 511, 570) made an allegoric portrait of Parma in full armour with Jupiter's thunderbolt in his hand which his brother **Gijsbert van Veen** engraved and surrounded with a frame of allegoric figures. **Pieter Jansz Pourbus** was available for more pseudo-allegoric pieces like his earlier *Allegoric Love Feast* (Pl. 331) till 1584; and **Marten de Vos** was available for more decorative compositions like *Apollo and the Muses* (Pl. 364). **Joachim Uytewael** (Pls. 490, 498, 524) and **Adam van Noort** may have produced mythologies with nudes on their travels or after they returned; and **Karel van Mander** who made allegoric drawings for engravers including an *Allegory of a Wise King*, an *Allegory of a Foolish King* and *The Four Times of the Day typified by Aurora, Phoebus, Venus and Morpheus* may well have begun the series soon after his arrival in Holland.

In portraiture the specialists and others had a good many commissions in the relative quiet of Holland in these years; I have already mentioned the portrait activity in the Dutch towns of **Dirck Barendsz** (Pl. 389), **Pieter Pietersz** (Pl. 421), **Aert Pietersz** (Pl. 485), **Cornelis Ketel** (Pl. 451), **Herman van der Mast** (Pl. 453), **Jacob Willemsz Delff** (Pl. 440), the **Amsterdam Little Girl with Dog Painter** (Pl. 452), **Adriaen van Cronenburch** (Pls. 343, 441, 443), **Karel van Mander** and **Daniel van den Queborne;** and I have also mentioned the *Self-portrait with members of his family* which **Otto van Veen** painted on his visit to Leyden. In the harassed conditions of the Belgian provinces portrait commissions seem to have been less frequent. But during the Patriot and Anjou régimes **Frans Pourbus the elder,** who may have portrayed Anjou when Duke of Alençon in 1574 (Pl. 427), was available in Antwerp till 1581; **Pieter Jansz Pourbus** (Pls. 331, 334, 336, 337) produced there a *Portrait of the Duc d'Anjou* in 1582 which van Mander tells us was 'naar het leven geschilderd'; and, in Bruges, the year before he died, he painted his *Portrait of J. van der Gheenste, Sheriff of Bruges, aged seventy* a striking head-study of a long-nosed man, with sunken eyes and skin drawn tight over brow and cheekbones, wearing a small-skull-cap and full ruffle. **Benjamin Sammeling** seems to have worked in Antwerp in these years, and in 1580 **Adriaen Thomas Key** produced the *Portrait of a man with a pointed beard* (Pl. 437) which recalls his striking earlier portrait groups (Pls. 425, 426). In 1581 the Antwerp Old Crossbowmen's Guild commissioned from **Gillis Congnet** the souvenir portrait *Pierson la Hues, drummer of the Crossbowmen for thirty-one years*—a full length figure with an enormous drum (Pl. 442); and **Congnet** was available in the next four years for other portraits till he emigrated. **Daniel van den Queborne** was also available till he emigrated; and **Marten de Vos** was there to paint more portraits like his admirable *Gilles Hoffman and his wife* (Pl. 429) discussed in my last chapter. In Antwerp under Parma **Marten de Vos** was still available, and **Adriaen Thomas Key** is recorded till 1589 when he may have moved from Antwerp or emigrated or died under fifty. In 1591 **Benjamin Sammeling**, aged seventy-one, provided a portrait group *Members of the Plantin family with SS. John and Roch* for the funeral monument of Christopher Plantin in Antwerp Cathedral—(a monument also furnished, as noted, with a *Last Judgement* by **Jacques de Backer**). Newcomers in Antwerp now included **Abraham de Ryckere, Frans Pourbus the younger** (Pls. 539, 540) and **Bernaert van Somer.** Of these **Abraham de Ryckere** portrayed as donors *Jan Doncker and his wife* on the wings of his triptych for S. Jacques when he was twenty-five in 1591. **Frans Pourbus the younger** who inherited money from his grandmother (wife of **Pieter Jansz Pourbus**) when he was nineteen in 1588, moved soon after from Bruges to Antwerp where he was Master in 1591; and a portrait by him dated in that year is signed 'Francisco Pourbus' an indication, it has been suggested, that he was already in contact with Spanish Court circles. **Bernaert van Somer,** who was later to paint some portraits, was a pupil in Antwerp of one **Philip Lisaert** in 1588. Under Parma in Brussels **Jean Baptiste Saive** painted an official portrait *Alexander Farnese, Duke of Parma, with the Scheldt in the background* after 1586; and I have mentioned above the allegoric *Portrait of the Duke of Parma* produced there by **Otto van Veen** as Court Painter. In the *Convention of Tournai* (Pl. 436) by the Brugeois **Pieter Claeissins the younger** the portraiture is more archaic than in portraits of this period in Antwerp or Brussels, the heads of the Hispanophil nobles being massed like the heads more acutely characterized by the **Malines Guild of S. George Master** a hundred years earlier (Pl. 146).

The landscape painters who worked at home under the Patriot régime and then went abroad included **Hans Bol** (Pl. 431), **Frans Boels, Jacques Savery the elder** (Pl. 438), **Hans Jordaens the elder, Lucas van Valkenborch** (Pls. 374, 432, 445, 446, 448-50), **Martin van Valkenborch** (Pl. 439) and **Gillis van Coninxloo** (Pls. 466, 476). All these had left the country by 1587 and I have already mentioned paintings done by some of them in Germany, Austria or Holland. Among the works produced by them at home between 1579 and 1585 **Hans Bol** signed a *Landscape with Meleager and Atalanta* in 1580 and a *Landscape with Hagar and Ishmael* in 1583. **Lucas van Valkenborch** painted a *Mountain landscape with mine workers* in 1580 and probably then or in 1581 his *Landscape with iron works* (Pl. 449); these pictures seem to indicate a visit to the region of Liège just before or after his departure with the Archduke Mathias, and both, like the *Mountain landscape* (Pl. 450) of 1582, show this interesting artist continuing and developing the art of **Lucas Gassel** (Pl. 328). No pictures dated in these years by **Martin van Valkenborch** or **Gillis van Coninxloo** appear to be recorded though both were active in Antwerp till they emigrated. The landscape painters who worked at home during the Patriot régime and continued under Parma included **Cornelis Molenaer, Pieter Goetkint, Jacob Grimmer** (Pls. 430, 444), **Gillis Mostaert** (Pl. 348), **Pieter Bom, Artus van Uden, Kerstiaen de Keuninck** (Pl. 501), **Josse de Momper** (Pl. 500) and also **Cornelis van Dalem** if he survived into this period. Of these **Pieter Goetkint** died in Antwerp in 1583. **Cornelis Molenaer (Schele Neel)** was available there till 1589 or later as a specialist in landscape backgrounds for figure painters; and some such specialist was probably employed in Brussels in 1590 by **Hendrik de Clerck** for the landscape vista in his *Lineage of S. Anne* (Pl. 456). **Jacob Grimmer,** who died in Antwerp over sixty in 1590, painted *Landscape with festival* and a *Landscape with castle* (Pl. 444) in 1583, a *Landscape with village* in 1586, a *View on the Scheldt* in 1587 and was still at work in 1588; his *Landscape with castle* (Pl. 444) shows a castle approached by a double bridge with lodge in the middle distance, a surrounding countryside with trees and windmill, and genre episodes across the foreground; and his *View on the Scheldt*—less panoramic than his *Outskirts of Antwerp (Kiel)* (Pl. 430) discussed in my last chapter—shows the river and a windmill in the distance, a castle and other buildings in surrounding country in the middle plane, and, again, genre incidents across the foreground. **Gillis Mostaert,** forty-five when the period began and still working at the close, probably painted landscapes with snow scenes and conflagrations as before; and **Pieter Bom,** who was four years older was also still living in 1592. **Artus van Uden** Antwerp Master in 1587 was the father of **Lucas van Uden** (Pls. 561, 566, 567, 602) who was not yet born. **Kerstiaen de Keuninck** who was about to develop a characteristic style of wooded and mountain landscapes with metallic colour and dramatic light effects (Pl. 501) came from his native Courtrai to Antwerp at the end of the seventies and was Master there aged about twenty in 1580; and **Josse de Momper** (Pl. 500) was Antwerp Master at seventeen in 1581. Landscape painters who began their careers in Parma's period included **Pieter Brueghel the younger** (Pls. 380, 411) and **Jan (Velvet) Brueghel** (Pls. 464, 465, 467), **François Borsse, Pieter Stevens the younger** (Pl. 468), **Pieter van der Hulst, Abel Grimmer** (Pls. 447, 535) and **Tobias van Haecht** (Pl. 377). Of these **Pieter Brueghel the younger** was active in Antwerp from 1585 and **Jan (Velvet) Brueghel** went to Italy about 1589 as related; both had received instruction in drawing and watercolour painting from their grandmother **Marie Bessemers** in Brussels; thereafter, van Mander tells us, **Pieter Brueghel the younger** was a pupil of **Gillis van Coninxloo** (Pls. 466, 476), and **Jan (Velvet) Brueghel** of **Pieter Goetkint;** but it seems to me probable that both were pupils of **Goetkint** till he died in 1583 and then of **van Coninxloo** till he emigrated. **François Borsse,** who painted landscapes with mythologic figures sometimes as decorations for musical instruments, was Antwerp Master in 1587. **Pieter Stevens the younger,** born probably at Malines about 1567, was Antwerp Master in 1589 and left for Prague soon after; and **Pieter van der Hulst** also, probably, a Malinois was Antwerp Master the same year. **Abel Grimmer,** Antwerp Master at approximately twenty in 1592, probably completed some pictures planned or left unfinished by his father, and the *Landscape with castle (The Fortune teller)* (Pl. 447), dated 1592, may have been a joint production of this kind; this attractive composition shows a castle reflected in a moat or river and farm buildings right and left in the middle plane, a wood with genre figures is in the foreground, and a panoramic landscape—with a city and cathedral on rising ground, and shipping on a river—recedes to the horizon against a handsome cloud-swept sky. **Tobias van Haecht** (Pl. 377) was back from Italy at twenty-nine by 1590 when he became Antwerp Master; and in 1591, as noted, he took **Rubens** aged fourteen as his pupil.

Among the painters of town views, architecture and trompe l'oeil perspectives **Jan Vredeman de Vries** (Pl. 462) may have found time to compose some architectural perspectives in the intervals of his engineering duties before he left Antwerp in 1586; and his son **Paul Vredeman de Vries** had by that time begun his career by providing such features for a picture by **Joos van Winghe.** **Hendrik van Steenwyck the elder** whose *Night scene in a crypt* (Pl. 488) has already been referred to, produced an *Interior of Antwerp Cathedral* in 1585 before he emigrated; his son **Hendrik van Steenwyck the younger** (Pls. 487, 489, 536, 537) with him in Frankfort was still a child at the end of the period. **Pieter Neeffs the elder** (Pls. 649, 650), born in Antwerp about 1578, was also still a child in 1592. **Hendrik van Cleve,** who died at sixty-four in 1589, either at home or abroad, signed that year a *Landscape view of Rome* which was probably painted from an earlier drawing as it shows an incomplete S. Peters. **Pieter Vlerick** may have supplied some architectural features for pictures by contemporaries in his last two years in Tournai before 1581; and in 1590 some architectural specialist in Antwerp was possibly responsible for the elaborate church in course of construction in the *Constantine building a church dedicated to S. George* by **Marten de Vos.**

Among the genre paintings we have high-life and low-life genre scenes and rural pieces with peasants and artisans. **Joos van Winghe** (Pls. 457, 497) may have painted his *Night banquet and masquerade* (Pl. 497) before he left Brussels in 1586; in this picture—which it is intriguing to compare on the one hand with the Allegoric *Love Feast* (Pl. 331) by **Pieter Jansz Pourbus** and, on the other, with **Joachim Uytewael's** *Diana and Actaeon* (Pl. 498) and also, of course, with Hogarth's *Orgy* in the 'Rake's Progress'—**Joos van Winghe** has evidently called up his memories of high-life genre pieces seen in Paris and his memories of mannerist attitudes and devices seen on his Italian tour; the company is depicted in three groups—in the background young gentlemen and forthcoming ladies play at backgammon, drink wine and have supper while one reluctant young lady is urged by an older woman to join them; in the centre a lady and gentleman dance with affected elegance to an improvised din made with bellows and tongs and other household utensils; on the right a gentleman reclining on his lady's knee sings her a ditty and twangs a guitar; and in the foreground, by the wine-jug in its inevitable cooler, a boy points inwards at the dancers with a Tintoretto gesture; as the scene is lit by candlelight it can be grouped with a *Night masquerade* painted, probably at this time, by **Jooris van Cleve** (who, van Mander tells us, died young from loose living and whose pictures were later admired by **Adriaen Brouwer**) and with the outdoor night scene lit by torches the *Drawing of a Lottery in an Amsterdam Street* by **Gillis Congnet** already mentioned. The figures in the *Landscape with castle* (Pl. 444) by **Jacob Grimmer** seem to illustrate a village custom; at the entrance to the bridge across the stream some gentry stand to receive a procession headed by a drummer and a crowned woman with two children; on the left we have peasants dancing, drinking, and so on, outside an inn; on the right we have a family group with a woman in a sun hat—(as in pictures reproduced here by **Hendrik de Clerck** (Pl. 471) and **Karel van Mander** (Pl. 472))—and a peasant prone upon the ground with a jug of wine beside him; a woman with guitar or lute is in a boat on the stream, and peasants in pastoral occupations are in the background. The genre episodes in **Jacob Grimmer's** *View on the Scheldt* of 1587 (not reproduced here) include on one side covered waggons with rich farmers and their wives driving to or from a fair or market while boys tumble and stand on their heads for coins as they pass, and peasants dance in a circle outside the village inn; and on the other side in a wooded meadow elegant ladies and gentlemen are in amorous dalliance round a picnic luncheon spread upon the ground. In the *Landscape with castle: (The Fortune teller)* (Pl. 447)— probably, as suggested, a joint composition by **Jacob** and **Abel Grimmer**—a group of gentry dressed in the latest fashions submit their palms to a wandering gipsy and, partly concealed by a mound of grass (a device used later by Watteau) we see the backs of a gentleman and lady wearing upstanding ruffs, the man with his arm round the lady's waist; by the stream a peasant youth is fishing and a peasant woman is seated with a child in her lap; and in the distance there are beggars and farmyard scenes. As already mentioned there are high-life genre figures in the *Spring landscape: Picnic with elegant company* (Pl. 446) which **Lucas van Valkenborch** painted in Linz and peasant genre scenes in his *Autumn landscape: Fruit gathering* (Pl. 445) which belongs to the same series. In the *Musical company in a loggia* (Pl. 462) painted in the next period by **Jan Vredeman de Vries** we have high-life figures doubtless inserted by a collaborator, and it is probable that such figures were also in architectural compositions produced by this artist both in Antwerp and Germany in this period. There were also little genre figures in the miniature compositions by **Hans Bol** (Pl. 431) and **Frans Boels** and perhaps also by **Jacques Savery the elder** (Pl. 438) before they emigrated. **Marten van Cleve** (Pls. 394, 396, 406) signed a *Peasant girl led to her bridal bed* in 1580 the year before he died at fifty-four; and his pupil **Hans Jordaens the elder** may have painted some genre pieces in the early eighties before he left for Holland. **Gillis Mostaert** (Pl. 348) signed a *Peasant fair* in 1579. **Pieter Huys** (Pls. 412, 413) may have produced more pictures with peasants like his *Bagpiper and old woman* before he died about 1581. **Pieter Balten** who was still alive and approaching seventy in 1592 may have painted more genre pieces like his *Feast of S. Martin*—though it is not known whether he worked in Antwerp or abroad in this period. **Peter Goetkint** may have painted genre pieces when **Jan (Velvet) Brueghel** and probably **Pieter Brueghel the younger** were his pupils before 1583. **Sebastiaan Vrancx** (Pls. 531, 532, 534), painter later of outdoor genre scenes, was **Adam van Noort's** pupil probably at about seventeen in 1590; and **Pieter Stevens the younger,** launched on his career in 1589, probably began with peasant jollities in landscape like the later picture reproduced here (Pl. 468). Occupational scenes with artisans at work, touches of domestic genre and occasional echoes of contemporary fashions can be found in some paintings of religious subjects at this time as in the earlier periods. **Marten de Vos** gives us sculptors and labourers in his *Constantine building a church* where a mason, his head covered with cloth against the stone-dust, works with mallet and chisel on a block of stone or marble in the foreground, and, round the rising church, sculptors carve statues for the pediment and niches, and labourers swarm up ladders, operate the cranes, and so forth as in earlier pictures shown here by **Pieter Bruegel** (Pl. 368) and **Jan van Eyck** (Pl. 18). Domestic genre is found in **Hendrik de Clerck's** *Lineage of S. Anne* (Pl. 456) where two boys play with a dog in the foreground and remind us of the boy and puppy in the foreground of **Joachim Beuckelaer's** picture of this subject (Pl. 400); and I have drawn attention to the sun hat of the moment which appears in **Hendrik de Clerck's** *Suffer little children . . .* (Pl. 471) and reminds us of the smaller hat in an earlier fashion used by **Cornelis Engelbrechtsz** (Pl. 233), the **London Delft Painter** (Pl. 234), and **Quinten Massys** (Pl. 235).

In the field of animal and bird painting I have alluded to the dogs in pictures painted in Holland by the **Amsterdam Little Girl with Dog Painter** (Pl. 452) and **Cornelis Ketel** (Pl. 451) and to the farm horses drawing a waggon in *Autumn: Fruit gathering* (Pl. 445) painted by **Lucas van Valkenborch** in Linz. I must add here the horses, camels and sheep in the *Reconciliation of Jacob and Esau* (Pl. 440) by **Jacob Willemsz Delff** and the warriors' horses on the left of **Jacques Savery the elder's** *Landscape with Jephthah's daughter* contrasted with the peasants' horses and farm animals on the right-hand side of that picture (Pl. 438). In Antwerp, before he emigrated **Gillis Congnet** set his S. George on a plumed and prancing rocking-horse above a snake-tailed dragon already wounded by a lance-thrust (Pl. 434); and **Hans Bol** (Pl. 431) produced a book of natural history drawings with all kinds of animals, birds and fishes 'naar het leven'. **Marcus Geeraerts the elder** who had, it will be remembered, special skill in the drawing of animals and birds, may have worked in this field in Antwerp between 1579 and 1586 when, at approximately sixty-five, he seems to have gone for a second time to England as related. In the pictures by artists who worked throughout these years in Antwerp I have just referred to the dog in the *Lineage of S. Anne* (Pl. 456) by **Hendrik de Clerck;** and many animals occur in the genre scenes which the landscape painters inserted or caused to be inserted by collaborators. Thus we have cattle, sheep, dogs, swans, other waterfowl and pigeons in **Jacob Grimmer's** *Landscape with a*

ou vrages datés et signés, ont amené les historiens d'art, depuis Waagen, à attribuer à un seul artiste, appelé par eux « Le Protée de la peinture », une vingtaine d'ouvrages

✠ PETRVS·XPĪ · ME· FECIT · I͡X̄i7·

dont ceux même qui portent des dates très voisines sont très divers de facture. Mais ces ouvrages peuvent être facilement divisés en deux groupes très homogènes ; c'est pourquoi nous avons cru devoir les attribuer à deux peintres différents, de même nom et de même prénom, très probablement le père et le fils. Voici tous les faits et les dates que l'on a pu réunir jusqu'ici sur « Petrus Christus » : 1443 : Petrus Christus achète une maison à Bruges — 1444 : « Pieter Christus, fils de Pieter, né à Baerle, a acheté son droit de bourgeoisie (à Bruges) le 6 juillet 1444 ; (présenté) par Joos van der Donc pour être peintre ». — 1446 : Le portrait d'*Edward Grimeston* (collect. de lord Verulam) porte, au revers du panneau, la signature :
PETRVS. XPI. ME. FECIT. A° 1446.
— 1449 : *Le Saint Eloi* de la collection Oppenheim, exposé à Bruges en 1902, porte l'inscription en gothique cursive :
petr. xpi me fecit a° 1449.
— 1450 : Petrus Christus est mentionné comme membre de la gilde de Saint-Luc de Bruges. — 1452 : Le diptyque du Musée de Berlin représentant l'*Annonciation*, la *Nativité* et le *Jugement dernier* porte l'inscription en lettres gothiques :
petrus xpi. me. fecit. anno. domini. m. cccc. lij.
— 1453 ou 1454 : Petrus Christus fait, à Cambrai, pour le duc d'Etampes, trois copies d'une *Vierge* miraculeuse que la cathédrale avait reçue de Rome. — 1457 : *La Vierge entre deux saints* du Musée Staedel de Francfort-sur-le-Mein est signée : ✠ PETRVS. XPI. Me. FECIT. 1457. On avait lu cette date, par erreur, 1417 et 1447. — 1462 : Petrus Christus et sa femme sont inscrits comme membres de la Confrérie de N.-D. de l'Arbre Sec, à Bruges. — 1463 : La ville de Bruges charge « Pieter Christus et Maître Pieter Nachtegale » de faire un grand arbre de Jessé avec le petit Jésus pour la procession annuelle. — 1467 : Petrus Christus est chargé de repeindre l'arbre de Jessé. — 1471 : Il est notable de la gilde de Saint-Luc à Bruges. — 1472 : Il est juré du métier de peintre à Bruges. — Novembre 1473 : Il est inscrit comme défunt dans l'obituaire de la gilde. Voici maintenant la liste complète des ouvrages attribués à un seul Petrus Christus, mais que nous avons divisés entre le vieux et le jeune, en ajoutant à l'œuvre de chacun d'eux, mais surtout de ce dernier, plusieurs chefs-d'œuvre méconnus, attribués par l'opinion à d'autres grands artistes :

Christus (Petrus) le vieux. — 1416-1417 : *La Vierge entre les saintes*. Miniature des *Heures* de Turin. Très probablement (selon nous) par P. C. le vieux d'après un patron et sous la surveillance d'Hubert van Eyck. — 1416-141? : *Pieta*. Miniature des *Heures*. Idem. — En ou après 1426 : *Donateur avec saint Antoine*. Copie d'après Hubert van Eyck. Musée de Copenhague. — Peu avant 1428 : *La Vierge aux Chartreux*. Imitation de celle de la collection du baron G. de Rothschild par Hubert van Eyck. — 1449 : *La Vierge allaitant l'Enfant*. Collection du comte Matuschka-Greiffenklau, Allemagne. Signé et daté sur le cadre. Découvert tout récemment. — 1452 : *Annonciation, Nativité, Jugement dernier*. Diptyque du Musée de Berlin, signé et daté. — 1457 : *La Vierge et l'Enfant entre deux saints*. Musée de Francfort. Signé et daté. — Date inconnue (peu postérieure à 1440 ?) : *Portrait d'un jeune homme*, légué par M. Salting à la National Gallery de Londres. Date inconnue, plus probablement du temps d'Hubert van Eyck : *La Fontaine de vie*, copie d'un tableau perdu d'Hubert, probablement par P. C. le vieux. Musée du Prado. — Date inconnue, plus probablement de la première période : *La Vierge avec l'Enfant devant un tabernacle*. Copie avec variantes d'une *Vierge à la Fontaine*, tableau perdu d'Hubert van Eyck. Musée métropolitain de New-York. — Date inconnue, plutôt de la première période : *Pieta* de la collection de M. Schloss, Paris. — Date inconnue, plutôt du milieu du siècle : *Saint Jean-Baptiste et Sainte Catherine*. Volets, Musée de Berlin. — Date inconnue, postérieure à 1454 : *Calvaire* de la collection du duc d'Anhalt, à Woerlitz. — Date inconnue, probablement vers 1460 : *La Vierge avec l'Enfant sous un portique*, avec fond de paysage. Exécuté peut-être avec la collaboration d'un très bon élève. Collection de M. J. Dollfus, Paris. — Date inconnue, probablement vers 1460 : Répétition ou copie du précédent. Collection du comte Strogonof,

Saint-Pétersbourg. — Date inconnue, vers 1460 ? : *La Vierge et l'Enfant sur un trône*, avec fond de paysage. Prado.

Christus (Petrus) le jeune. — Vers 1440-1445 : *Portrait de Philippe le Bon*. Musée de Lille. Vers 1440-1445 ? : *La Vierge et l'Enfant dans un intérieur*. Musée de Turin. — Date inconnue, vers 1440-1445 ? : L'original perdu, d'une miniature d'un *Livre d'heures* latin de la collection du prince d'Arenberg : *La Vierge cousant avec l'Enfant en robe assis à sa droite*. — 1446 : Portrait d'*Edward Grimston*. Collection de lord Verulam. Signé et daté au dos. — 1446 : Portrait de lady Grimston (autrefois censé représenter lady Talbot). Pendant du précédent. Musée de Berlin. — 1449 : *Saint Eloi*. Collection du baron Oppenheim. Cologne. — 1460 ou très peu après : *Le Christ pleuré*, Musée de Bruxelles. Vers 1464 : *Scènes de la vie de Marie*. Prado. — Vers 1467 : *Mise au tombeau*. National Gallery. — 1472 et avant novembre 1473 : Grand triptyque de la Chapelle royale de Grenade, *Crucifixion, Descente de croix, Résurrection.* — Avant novembre 1473 : Petit triptyque du Collège du Patriarche, à Valence. Répétition du précédent. — Vers 1473 ? : *Portraits de deux époux*. Diptyque. Offices. — La *Mise au tombeau* de Londres et les triptyques de Grenade et de Valence, que nous avons rendus à Petrus Christus et qui étaient attribués à Thierry Bouts par de bons critiques, sont datés par la présence et l'âge d'un modèle qui avait déjà posé en 1449 pour le *Saint Eloi* et vers 1460 pour une des figures de la *Mise au tombeau* de Bruxelles. D'après toutes les vraisemblances, Petrus le vieux est le père de Petrus le jeune. Collaborateur, très probablement, d'Hubert van Eyck vers 1416-1417, il a dû naître vers 1390 ; il vivait encore en 1457, date du diptyque de Berlin. Les documents d'archives paraissent tous se rapporter à Petrus le jeune, né à Baerle, où son père est sans doute établi. Ayant acheté le droit de bourgeoisie à Bruges en 1444, il avait donc au moins trente ans en ce moment-là, ce qui le fait naître en ou avant 1414, date bien concordante avec notre hypothèse sur celle de la naissance de Petrus Christus le vieux. Les caractères des ouvrages de celui-ci sont : une composition assez habile, quoique un peu éparpillée, avec des attitudes parfois gauches dans les figures ; une exécution assez simple et solide, mais plus sommaire et moins souple que chez le fils ; les ombres des chairs un peu lourdes et brunes ; l'ovale des visages large aux pommettes, avec menton souvent pointu ; le nez droit, parfois proéminent, toujours un peu relevé ; le front haut et carré, à deux pointes le plus souvent ; les chevelures à petites ondes très brillantes, un peu trop régulières ; le paysage avec arbres lointains en pain de sucre, les plus proches déchiquetés sur le ciel, avec feuillé en touches un peu lourdes. Le fils compose mieux, il est beaucoup plus élégant dans les attitudes ; plus noble dans les types et dans les draperies ; plus expressif, non sans un léger maniérisme chez les femmes ; excellent dessinateur et modeleur, avec une exécution légère et des ombres délicates ; et, tandis que son père garde le syle eyckian, le fils se laisse influencer par Rogier de la Pasture et surtout par Thierry Bouts, à qui l'on a attribué ses meilleurs ouvrages. L'œuvre de Petrus le jeune, tel que nous l'avons reconstitué, rivalise donc dans une assez large mesure avec celui de plusieurs Flamands de premier ordre.   E. DURAND-GRÉVILLE.

PRIX. — PARIS. Vte duc de Tallard, 1756 : *Deux allégories* (esquisses) : 10 fr. — COLOGNE. Vte Weyer, 1862 : *La Naissance du Sauveur* : 450 fr. — PARIS. Vte Paul Demidoff, 1869 : *Sainte Famille* : 580 fr.

CHRISTUS ou Cristus III (Petrus).
Ce peintre est appelé Petrus II par J. Weale, qui n'admet qu'un Petrus Christus peintre au xve siècle. C'est sans doute un des trois fils de Sébastien Christus. C'est vraisemblablement cet artiste qui travailloit en 1507, 1516, 1528 et 1530 à Grenade sous le nom de Pedro de Christo.

CHRISTUS ou Cristus (Sebastian), *peintre et miniaturiste à Bruges, mort entre 1495 et 1499* (Ec. Flam.).
Les archives de Bruges mentionnent ce peintre comme un fils naturel de « Petrus Christus » — évidemment de Petrus Christus le jeune — qui fut admis à la franchise du métier de peintre le 8 mars 1475. Il avait pour élève, en 1483, un certain Thomas de Clerc. Dans l'inventaire des objets d'art ayant appartenu à la duchesse Anne de Bretagne figure : *Une Vierge tenant son Enfant ; et le fist ung nommé Sebastianus, quondam filius Petri Christi.*

castle (Pl. 444) of 1583; his *View on the Scheldt* of 1587 shows a cow being milked, teams of farm horses drawing waggons, and cavaliers' horses; and the *Landscape with castle:* (*The Fortune Teller*) (Pl. 447) painted, or completed, by **Abel Grimmer,** contains a cavorting horse ridden by a gentleman among the trees on the left and farmyard animals across the river on the right.

Some idea of the still-life, fruit and flower painting can also be gathered from my plates. We can note in the supper party by **Joos van Winghe** (Pl. 497) the pictures on the wall and also the elaborate ewers already seen in the allegoric banquet by the **Vienna Feast of the Gods Painter** (Pl. 419); the basket of fruit held by the child in the portrait by the **Amsterdam Little Girl with Dog Painter** (Pl. 452); the eatables spread out and the fashionable clothes in **Lucas van Valkenborch's** *Spring landscape: Picnic with elegant company* (Pl. 446); the still more elegant clothes in the **Grimmer** *Landscape with castle* (*The Fortune teller*) (Pl. 447); and in **Adriaen van Cronenburch's** double portrait (Pl. 443) the flowers held by the younger lady and the 'Memento mori' motif of the skull that can be traced back through **Marinus van Reymerswaele** (Pl. 237), the **Amsterdam Cadaver Painter** (Pl. 212), and the **Frankfort Master** (Pl. 209) to **Jan Gossaert.** Of the flower specialists named in my last chapter the Calvinist **Lodewyck Jansz van den Bosch** may have died in these years in Germany as noted; **Pauwels Coecke van Aelst,** who died in Antwerp at a date unknown, may still have been working in 1592 when he was something over sixty; and **Pieter van der Borcht the elder** though chiefly occupied at this time with miscellaneous engraving, may have nevertheless continued his studies of flowers like the early pieces he had produced for Plantin. **Jan (Velvet) Brueghel** (Pls. 521, 541) probably made flower studies as part of his training in Brussels and Antwerp; for this was customary as we know from van Mander who tells us that when the Dutch painter Cornelis of Haarlem was a pupil of **Gillis Congnet** in Antwerp, about 1580, he was set to paint a vase of flowers without verdure (bijna zonder groen) as a studio exercise; and we know that when **Jacques de Gheyn the younger** turned later from engraving to painting he began with studies of flowers. The next generation of still-life, fruit and flower painters was still in embryo—for **Ambrosius Bosschaert** (Pls. 550, 551, 552) born in 1573 was still a boy when his parents took him from Antwerp to Middelburg; **Osias Beet the elder** (Pl. 506) was still adolescent in 1592, **Frans Snyders** (Pls. 554, 555) was thirteen in that year, and **Jacob van Hulsdonck** (Pl. 556) was ten.

A sidelight on bourgeois patronage at this time is furnished by an inventory of 1588 which details some paintings owned by an Antwerp merchant—one Peter du Moulin; for we find there a *Suffer little children . . .* by **Marten de Vos** and pictures by **Adriaen Thomas Key** and **Jacob Grimmer.**

CHAPTER X

Archduke Ernest 1593-1595;
Archduke Albert 1596-1598;
Archduke Albert and Infanta Isabella to the
Twelve Years Truce 1599-1609

1593-1609

THE ARCHDUKE ERNEST, brother of the Emperor and nephew of Philip II, was appointed Governor of the Netherlands in 1593. He had been educated by the Jesuits in Spain and when he reached Brussels in 1594, middle-aged and plagued by gout and other maladies, his chief concern was to strengthen the Jesuits' position and further their aims in his territories. But he exercised his office for no more than a year before succumbing to his ailments. His brother the Cardinal-Archbishop Archduke Albert, who followed him, arrived in Belgium in February 1596. He too had been educated by the Jesuits in Spain; he had been made a Cardinal at eighteen; he had been Viceroy of Portugal and he had recently been appointed Archbishop of Toledo. He was very devout and his first act on arrival was to visit the shrine of Notre Dame de Hal. He brought troops and credits with him for the prosecution of the War; and he took the field in person with a measure of success. He remained sole Governor for about two years; he then left to make arrangements for his wedding; and when he returned as the husband of the Infanta Isabella he had royal status because Philip II had appointed Isabella and her husband joint Sovereigns of the Netherlands, and this of course included the nominal sovereignty of the Northern provinces as well as of Belgium till the Truce of 1609.

When they began their joint rule the Archduke was forty and the Infanta was thirty-three. The Infanta, daughter of Isabelle de Valois, was much respected by her father and the creation of this sovereignty in the Netherlands was mainly a gesture in her honour. We know her appearance from childhood in various portraits; for we can see her in the Prado in Sanchez Coello's portrait painted in her thirteenth year; in the Prado also we can see her about eighteen in an unforgettable picture by an unknown artist, with her pet monkeys and a Court fool Magdalena Ruiz (who had accompanied Philip II to Spain in 1582 and was often referred to in his letters). We can see her soon after her marriage in a portrait, with her dwarf, at Hampton Court. Like the Archduke she was very devout and much influenced by the Jesuits from the outset.

Thus favoured by the sovereigns the Jesuits much increased their power in Belgium in this period. But there was no active persecution of Protestants, the sadism of the time being chiefly directed to witch-hunting and the occasional torture of an Anabaptist. The Protestants in fact had now been almost 'liquidated' in the Southern Netherlands, the few rich Calvinists and Lutherans established there were treated as tolerable eccentrics, and Protestantism was virtually impossible for the needy because only the orthodox had any claim on Church or other charities. There was however a strict censorship of plays and books and pamphlets; and a watch was kept against the importation of unorthodox literature from England, France or Holland.

In 1593 Belgium was administered, pending the Archduke Ernest's arrival, by the Comte de Fuentes (a brother-in-law of Alva) who believed in ferocity and ordered that all prisoners captured in the war against Holland should be forthwith hanged; Prince Maurice of Nassau captured Geertuidenberg and laid siege to Groningen; Philip II sent troops to Paris and claimed the throne of France for the Infanta Isabella who was then twenty-seven; Henri IV abjured the Huguenot faith and publicly became a Catholic; three Brownist Separatists were hanged in England; and the Long War began in Hungary. At this time Philip II was sixty-six, Queen Elizabeth was sixty, Henri IV was forty, Olden Barneveldt was forty-six and Prince Maurice was twenty-six. Rudolf II was still Emperor, Clement VIII was Pope, and Murad III was still Sultan. In 1594 Barents and Linschoten sailed from Holland to explore the Arctic, reached Nova Zembla, and returned with tales of bears and seals and walruses. Prince Maurice captured Groningen; the Archduke Ernest made Pageant Entries into Antwerp and other places, the Antwerp Pageant being seen by **Peter Paul Rubens** aged seventeen and a pupil of **Adam van Noort.** Henri IV was acclaimed in Paris; and Antoine Arnauld published an attack upon the Jesuits. Antonio Perez, established in England, wrote 'Pedazos de Historia' dedicated to the Earl of Essex; Richard Hooker published the first four volumes of his 'Laws of Ecclesiasticall Politie'; and Hugh O'Neill, Earl of Tyrone, led the Irish in rebellion. In 1595 the Archduke Ernest died in February; and soon after Philip II chose the Archduke Albert to succeed him. Henri IV declared war on Spain and won the battle of Fontaine-Française. Sultan Murad III died and Mahommed III succeeded; Sigismund Bathory, persecutor of the Transylvanian Sabbatarians, defeated the Turks in Walachia; Cornelius Houtman sailed from Holland round the Cape of Good Hope to the East Indies using maps and charts provided by Linschoten; Drake and Hawkins went on their fatal expedition to the West; and Raleigh failed to find Manoa.

In 1596 the Turks, led by Mahommed III in person, captured Erlau and won a three days' battle on the plain of Keresztes; the Archduke Ferdinand of Styria aged eighteen began a violent persecution of his Lutheran subjects; England and Holland were allied with Henri IV; the Archduke Albert captured Calais; Philip II sent a second Armada against England which a gale destroyed; Anglo-Dutch naval forces under Raleigh, Lord Howard of Effingham and the Earl of Essex took Cadiz and sacked it; Philip II repudiated his debts and claimed back lands, revenue and taxes pledged for the payment of their interest; Barents and Jacob van Heemskerck found and named Spitzbergen in another attempt to reach China by the North East passage and Barents died after wintering in Ice Haven; Linschoten published his 'Itinerario. Voyage ofte Schipvaert naar Oost ofte Portuguels Indien'; and **Rubens** was a pupil of **Otto van Veen** (Pls. 455, 510, 511, 570). In 1597 Duke William V of Bavaria abdicated and his son Maximilian I succeeded. Prince Maurice won the battle of Turnhout and captured various places; the Spaniards took Amiens and lost it; Anna Hove, an Anabaptist, was buried alive in Brussels; Houtman returned to Holland after making a treaty with the Sultan of Bantam in Java; and Raleigh and Essex attacked the Azores. In 1598 **Rubens** became Antwerp Master; Boris Godunov became

Czar of Russia; and Henri IV issued the Edict of Nantes granting religious and political toleration to the Huguenots. Philip II made peace with France in the Treaty of Vervins which surrendered Calais; he announced the forthcoming marriage between the Infanta Isabella and the Archduke Albert and their sovereign status—with the proviso that if there were no children of the marriage the Netherlands should revert to the crown of Spain on the death of either Sovereign; and he died in the Escorial at seventy-one after enjoining Isabella on his death-bed to propagate the Catholic faith in her dominions. Philip III son of Anne of Austria became King of Spain at the age of twenty; the Archduke Albert left Belgium to obtain the Pope's dispensation for his marriage; and the marriage took place by procuration at Ferrara.

In 1599 Essex was Governor-General of Ireland; the Archduke and the Infanta made a Pageant Entry in August into Brussels when the Infanta's jewels and her horse's accoutrements incrusted with pearls made a great impression on the populace; and Vincenzo Gonzaga, Duke of Mantua, present at these festivities invited **Frans Pourbus the younger** (Pls. 539, 540) then thirty to become his Court Painter. In the autumn the Archduke and the Infanta made Pageant Entries into Antwerp, Ghent, Louvain, Malines and other places; and in Louvain they called at the University to bestow their approval on Justus Lipsius in his final most orthodox phase. In 1600 **Rubens,** aged twenty-two, left Antwerp for Venice and was invited by Duke Vincenzo Gonzaga to become his Court Painter. The Turks took Kamizsa; Queen Elizabeth gave a charter to the East India Company which began with a capital of £72,000; Henri IV, aged forty-seven, married Marie de Médicis, aged twenty-seven, by proxy in Florence and sent her a set of dolls dressed in the latest French fashions that she might know what gowns to bring with her to Paris; Prince Maurice invaded the Belgian coast to occupy the ports; the Archduke took the field against him; Isabella exhorted the Spanish troops and promised to sell jewels to guarantee their pay; and Prince Maurice won the battle of Nieuport where the Archduke's white Spanish war horse was captured and given to the victor, as we know from the inscription on **Jacques de Gheyn's** picture reproduced here (Pl. 484). In 1601 a Spanish expedition to help the rebel Irish was defeated by Lord Mountjoy; Essex was executed as a traitor; the Archduke Albert began the Siege of Ostend which was garrisoned by Dutch and English troops commanded by Sir Frances Vere; and the Infanta vowed not to change her linen till the place was captured. The Belgian Chambers of Rhetoric were required to submit all their productions to censorship to ensure strict orthodoxy in all matters of religion; and the Malines painter **Jan Ghuens the younger** gave evidence against Anna Deckers who was being tried for witchcraft. In 1602 the Sultan Mahommed's Grand Vizier forced the Archduke Mathias, who had taken Pest, to raise the siege of Buda. Lord Mountjoy used starvation to subdue the Irish; and Shakespeare's 'Hamlet' was performed. There was an outbreak of the plague in Amsterdam which killed **Jacques Savery the elder** (Pl. 438) and was recorded in an allegoric painting by **Cornelis Ketel** (Pl. 451); the Dutch East India Company was started with a capital of £550,000; and the Dutch founded the town of Batavia in Java. The siege of Ostend continued; and the Genoese Ambrosius Spinola, aged thirty-three, took service under Philip III with nine thousand men and was sent to Flanders where Philip's Minister, the Duke of Lerma, hoped to employ him in new plans for the invasion of England. In 1603 Queen Elizabeth died at sixty-nine; James I succeeded at thirty-seven; Sir Walter Raleigh, accused of treason, was condemned to preventive detention in the Tower; and Tyrone surrendered to Mountjoy. The Archduke Albert put Spinola in charge of the siege of Ostend; and **Rubens** spent eight months in Spain. In 1604

Henri IV renewed the capitulations of François I with the Sultan; the Emperor's General George Basta subdued Transylvania and launched a terror there; James I made peace with Spain; and Arabella Stuart (Pl. 463?) wrote in a letter 'Count Arenberg was here within these few days and presented to the Queene the Archduke and the Infanta's pictures most excellently drawn' (i.e. presumably the portraits by **Otto van Veen** recorded by van Mander as so presented, or originals—or copies of originals—by **Frans Pourbus the younger**). **Karel van Mander** designed a title page with allegoric figures of Fame, History, Painting and so on for the first edition of his 'Schilderboek' which was published in Haarlem and contained no reference to **Rubens.** Prince Maurice captured the port of Sluys; Spinola captured Ostend; and Isabella changed her linen. In 1605 the Gunpowder Plot was discovered; Sir Francis Bacon published 'The Advancement of Learning'; Spinola led his troops into Overijsseel; Stephen Bocskay was elected Prince of Transylvania; and Pope Clement VIII died. In 1606 Sir Edward Michelbourne returned to Portsmouth from the East Indies where he had gone under the King's licence 'to discover the countries of Cathay, China, Japan, Corea and Cambay and the islands and countries thereto adjoining and to trade with the people there'—an event recorded later by the marine painter **Adam Willaerts;** the Long War in Hungary ended when Stephen Bocskay secured religious liberty for Transylvania by the Treaty of Vienna; and the Truce of Sitvatorok was made between the Emperor and the Turks; Spinola and Prince Maurice continued their war with indecisive fighting; Albert and Isabella issued an edict against witches and sorcerers; and Shakespeare finished 'Macbeth'. In 1607 **Frans Francken the younger** painted *The Witches' Sabbath* (Pl. 496); Jacob van Heemskerck now an Admiral was killed in action after destroying the Spanish fleet off Gibraltar—a victory later recorded in several pictures by **Adam Willaerts** (Pl. 688); an eight months' armistice to discuss a truce was arranged between the Spaniards and the Dutch; the Earl of Tyrone in flight from Ireland, took refuge in the Netherlands and was welcomed by the Archduke and the Infanta; and English colonists established plantations on the James river in Virginia. In 1608 Samuel Champlain established a 'habitation' in Quebec; and a group of English Separatists, later to be known as the Pilgrim Fathers, left England for Holland. The Archduke Mathias was elected King of Hungary, and the Emperor also ceded Austria and Moravia to him; Spinola went in pomp to The Hague to meet the Ambassadors of England, France and other countries for discussions about truce terms with the Dutch; Jan Lippershey invented the telescope in Middelburg; **Frans Snyders,** aged twenty-nine, nursed **Jan (Velvet) Brueghel,** aged forty, through an illness; and **Rubens** aged thirty-one returned to Antwerp from Italy in December. In 1609 the Emperor issued a Majestätsbrief granting religious freedom in Bohemia; the Archduke Mathias was forced to grant some measure of religious freedom in Austria; and Maximilian of Bavaria formed the German Catholic League. Philip III decreed the expulsion of the Moors from Spain; and the Twelve Years Truce was signed between Spain and the Northern provinces 'in the quality of free States over whom the Archdukes made no pretensions'—no mention being made of freedom of worship for Roman Catholics in Holland or of freedom of trade for the Dutch in the Indies (though Philip agreed in a secret treaty to place no hindrance on Dutch trade in any quarter).

Court patronage under the successive rulers was given to established painters and some new ones. Of the surviving King's Painters **Marten de Vos** (Pls. 364, 397, 429) was widely reputed till he died over seventy in 1603, and **Raphael Coxie** was still painting in 1609. The newcomer **Frans Pourbus the younger** (Pls. 539, 540), twenty-four in 1593, seems to have worked for Court circles till he went to Italy in 1600. The Archduke Ernest authorized the drawing and painting of his portrait by **Otto van Veen** (Pls. 455, 510, 511, 570) and engravings from these works by **Gysbert van Veen;** he made **Jan Snellinck** (Pl. 460) a Court painter and confirmed the Brugeois **Gillis Claeissins** in that rank. In 1595 he bought a *Moonlight landscape* and a *Conflagration* by **Gillis Mostaert** (Pl. 348) who was then sixty-one, and pictures titled *The Four Seasons* and *Market scene* by Parma's protégé the Namurois **Jean Baptiste Saive;** he owned another set of pictures titled *The Seasons*, including the *Spring: Picnic with elegant company* (Pl. 446), by **Lucas van Valkenborch** which he had probably acquired in Austria; and he also owned three paintings by **Hieronymus Bosch** which were titled *The Cure of Folly* (perhaps a version of Pl. 161), *'Sic erat in diebus Noë'* (perhaps a version of the central panel of *The Garden of Delights* (Pl. 166)), and a *Crucifixion* with *Christ in the Underworld* on the predella. There are few records of the Archduke Albert's action as art patron in the two years of his sole Governorship before he left to make arrangements for his marriage. But it is known that he sat to **Otto van Veen** for his portrait in 1596, that he continued **Jan Snellinck** as Court Painter and employed both **van Veen** and **Snellinck** as designers of Audenarde tapestries depicting his military achievements; and he also gave tapestry commissions to **Josse de Momper** (Pl. 500) who was thirty-two in 1596.

After their marriage the Archduke and the Infanta began a conspicuous patronage of artists. The Infanta's taste at this time must have been influenced by her memories of Spanish painters and especially of the Court painter Pantoja de la Cruz who had just painted a most delicate full length portrait of Philip III as Infante. She made however no attempt to surround herself with Spanish painters, but joined the Archduke in honouring the status of **Marten de Vos** and **Raphael Coxie** and in allotting favours to other Belgians. The new sovereigns thus authorized official portraits of themselves by **Otto van Veen** and **Frans Pourbus;** they made **van Veen** a Court painter before the end of 1599, they confirmed **Jan Snellinck** (Pl. 460) in that rank and they probably confirmed **Gillis Claeissins** as he made a miniature portrait of the Infanta before he died in 1607. Other Court painters were **Jan (Velvet) Brueghel** (Pls. 464-7, 470, 480-3, 521), **Denis van Alsloot** (Pls. 477, 513, 513A) and **Antonio de Succa** who all seem to have been appointed about 1600; **Wenzelas Coebergher** (Pl. 493) and **Pierre Noveliers** were appointed in 1605; **Hendrik de Clerck** (Pls. 456, 471, 477, 587) was appointed in 1606; and **Rubens** was appointed at the end of the period.

Of these Court Painters **Jan Snellinck,** now about fifty, was clearly influential as painter of religious subjects (Pl. 460) and battle pieces and as designer of tapestries with military subjects; and he was also director of an art school where **Abraham Janssens** (Pl. 509) was his pupil for some years. **Otto van Veen** (some eight years younger than **Snellinck**) was also influential as director of an art school where **Rubens** was his pupil from 1596 till 1598. **Jan (Velvet) Brueghel** back from Rome aged twenty-eight in 1596 had a letter of recommendation from Cardinal Borromeo to Laevinus Torrentius, Bishop of Antwerp; he was Antwerp Master in 1597 and soon became a Member of the Antwerp Society of Romanists and of the Violiere Chamber of Rhetoric; in 1599 he married Elizabeth, daughter of the successful engraver Gerard de Jode and thus became related to **Jan de Wael** (married to Gertrude de Jode) and to **Jan Snellinck** (whose first wife had been Helena de Jode and who was principal witness at the wedding); by 1601 he was Dean of the Antwerp Guild, and as Court Painter he travelled repeatedly from Antwerp to Brussels where he was given access to the palace aviaries, menageries and gardens to study birds and animals and rare flowers; in 1603 his first wife died and by 1604 he was so successful as an artist that he built himself the large house in Antwerp known as De Meerminne (The Siren) 'met poorte, plaetse, sale, coeckere, neercamere, hove, diversche appercameren, keldere, pompe, regenbaeke, gronde' and so forth; in 1605 he married as second wife Catherina van Marienberghe; and in 1606 the Archduke and the Infanta specially exempted him from various taxes. **Denis van Alsloot** (Pls. 477, 513, 513A), probably a Bruxellois, was Brussels Master aged about twenty-nine in 1599. **Antonio de Succa** born in Antwerp of a noble Italian family, and Master in 1598, was 'genealogical Court painter' and as such was charged with the copying of royal and other portraits in the palaces. **Wenzelas Coebergher** (Pl. 493) was back in Antwerp from Italy in 1604 (after a possible visit in 1601); in his official capacity he was employed as architect and engineer to the Archduke whom he instructed in mathematics and for whom he constructed fountains in the gardens of the palace at Tervueren; he was also an antiquary and numismatist and advised the sovereigns as collectors in those fields. **Pierre Noveliers** held the office of Keeper of the pictures in the Archducal palaces in Brussels and Tervueren—pictures which then included **Jan Gossaert's** *Adoration of the Magi* (Pl. 194) bought for their collection in 1601 from the Abbot of S. Adrian's, Grammont, and installed in the Chapel of the Brussels Palace in 1603. **Hendrik de Clerck** whose early talent evidenced in his *Lineage of S. Anne* (Pl. 456) and *Suffer little Children . . .* (Pl. 471) was referred to in my last chapter, was an outstanding artist in Brussels when he received his appointment at thirty-six. **Rubens** was thirty-two when he received his Court appointment in September 1609; in June he had been officially received into the Antwerp Society of Romanists by **Jan (Velvet) Brueghel** then Dean of the Society, and he found there as fellow members, **Abraham Janssens** then aged thirty-four and **Hendrik van Balen** (Pls. 507, 508) both back from Italy by that time, and his former master **Otto van Veen.** Shortly before this, the Antwerp Magistrates had commissioned pictures for the Town Hall from **Abraham Janssens** (Pl. 509) and from **Rubens;** and a month later **Rubens** married Isabella Brant then just under eighteen and the daughter of a lawyer who held the office of First Secretary of Antwerp.

The Pageant Entries of the period (paid for as always by the magistratures and arranged by the local Guilds and Chambers of Rhetoric who chose the artists, actors, orators and poets) began with the Archduke Ernest's Pageant Entry into Antwerp. In this elaborate affair, largely devised by the poet and rhetorician Jean Baptist Houwaerts, half-naked girls in classical draperies were posed to typify the Archduke's virtues—Piety, Audacity, Virility, Equity, Alacrity and so on, and other tableaux showed the Archduke as Apollo destroying the Python and as Perseus rescuing Andromeda; the artists who designed this pageant and painted decorations for it were led by **Marten de Vos** and **Ambrosius Francken the elder** assisted by **Cornelis Floris, Artus van Uden** now official painter to the city, **Otto van Veen, Josse de Momper, Tobias van Haecht** now Dean of the Guild, and **Gerard Schoof** who had come from Malines. The Antwerp Pageant Entry of the Archduke Albert and the Infanta seems to have been chiefly designed by **Otto van Veen** who had **Rubens** among his assistants. For their Ghent Entry the designers included **Jacques de Liemakere** (Master there by 1597), **Pierre van der Meulen the elder** and the Bruges painter **Gerard Pietersz.** In Tournai the aged **Michel Joncquoy** made decorations for the arches including portraits of the Archduke and the Infanta; and in Malines the panels of the arch were painted by **Jacob Stevens.**

There were, as usual, some pictures with topical comment and I reproduce, as examples, *Mars with the Arts and Sciences overcoming Ignorance* (Pl. 492) by **Antoine Claeissins** and the *Witches' Sabbath* (Pl. 496) by **Frans Francken the younger** which were both of a nature to be officially approved; and I also show two pictures by **Pieter Brueghel the younger,** the *Triumph of Death* (Pl. 411) and *The Road to Calvary* (Pl. 380) which seem to be crypto-anti-Spanish protests. The Brugeois **Antoine Claeissins** was just on seventy in 1605 when he painted this *Mars and the Fine Arts overcoming Ignorance* (Pl. 492) as an allegory on the benefits of the Archducal régime with special reference to Bruges whose Minnewater and towers appear in the background. **Frans Francken II** was twenty-six when he painted the *Witches' Sabbath* (Pl. 496)—a print of which must have been known, I fancy, to Hogarth; this propaganda illustration of the new Archducal Edict against witches and sorcerers is much richer in episode than the *Saul and the witch of Endor* (Pl. 268) of 1526 by **Jacob Cornelisz van Oostsanen,** and only an expert in the literature of witchcraft could explain the multiple hocus-pocus and give the meanings of all the cabalistic names and signs inscribed upon it. **Pieter Brueghel the younger** seems to have been mainly occupied in this period with variants of his father's genre pictures; and he also produced some variants of the protests against tyranny made by his father and others in the days of Granvella and Alva; thus his *Triumph of Death* (Pl. 411) signed 'Bruegel' and painted in 1597 when he was thirty-three, is a free copy of the horrific indictment of the Alva period by the **Madrid Triumph of Death Painter** (Pl. 410)—(and the Forchoudt firm of Antwerp dealers were surely wrong when they described it in 1672 as the work of his brother **Jan (Velvet) Brueghel** who was too eminently 'bien pensant' to have risked incurring official displeasure in that way); his *Road to Calvary* (Pl. 380) is based on his father's picture of this subject (Pls. 379, 381) but is nevertheless in no sense just a copy; and we must note here that the procession is escorted not by the Walloon 'Redcoats' seen in his father's picture but by Alva's lancers who had not arrived in the Netherlands when the earlier picture was painted. These pictures by **Pieter Brueghel the younger** could not have been openly sold, I imagine, in Belgium at this time; they could only have been sold clandestinely to free-thinking or anti-Spanish collectors, or exported by dealers to Holland.

Owing to the displacements under Parma, recorded in my last chapter, many Flemish-born artists were working in Holland, Germany and elsewhere abroad at the outset of this period; most of them, being Protestants, remained there; and in Holland there were also of course the Dutch-born artists who rank as Flemish-Dutch in this record as they started their careers before 1581.

Of the Flemish-Dutch painters in Holland **Adriaen van Cronenburch** (Pls. 343, 441, 443) was still in Bergum, over sixty, in 1604 and probably died soon after; **Jacob Willemsz Delff** (Pl. 440) continued to paint portraits in the nineties and died in Delft in 1601; **Herman van der Mast** (Pl. 453) painted portraits in Delft through the period; and **Pieter Cornelisz van Ryck** (son of a Delft brewer and pupil of **Jacob Willemsz Delff**) signed in Haarlem in 1604 a *Kitchen piece* with figures and dogs, masses of meat, game and shellfish and a biblical subject in the background in the **Aertsen-Beuckelaer** manner. In Amsterdam **Cornelis Ketel** (Pl. 451), forty-five in 1593, was still painting portraits, allegories and occasional religious subjects and writing poems; in 1595 he began to model in clay; and from 1599 he experimented in painting without brushes, using only his hand or his foot to spread the colours on the canvas, though he also painted some portraits—including *Admiral Jacobus van Neck* and his wife *Griete van Neck* (dated 1605)—in the normal way. Pictures painted by his hand and fingers included a *Self-portrait*, and *Democritus and Heraclitus* and heads of *Mary, S. John and Christ as the Man of Sorrows*; a picture titled *Hippocrates* was painted with his foot; *Self-portrait*, and an *Allegory of Painting without tools* were done partly with his hand and partly with his foot; and he also used these methods for large panels with allegoric subjects disposed as decorations in his house; van

Mander, who knew him intimately, tells us that he sold such pictures as curiosities to Dutch collectors and visiting foreign notables including the Duke of Nemours and a Polish Count of the Leczinski family, and he comments: 'Most people looked on these procedures as the products of ridiculous unnatural impulses like a pregnant woman's cravings for strange or uncooked food . . . but we have no right to condemn those who prove that what seems impossible is possible . . . there are people who walk on tight-ropes though it is far more natural to walk upon the ground'; and I may add here the comment that Ketel's experiments were doubtless an inspiration to the nineteenth-century armless Belgian **Charles François Felu** who held his brush with one foot and his palette with the other. **Ketel's** style in his allegoric subjects shows his memories of Fontainebleau mannerism; and **Joachim Uytewael** (Pls. 490, 498, 524), back from his travels now evolved his personal combination of Italian and French mannerism in his native Utrecht. Thus by 1597, when he was thirty-one **Uytewael** had already produced a brilliantly accomplished *David and Abigail*; about 1598 he painted an *Apollo and the Muses on Parnassus*; before 1604 (when van Mander described him as worthy to be named 'onder onze beste Nederlandsche schilders') he produced the brilliant *Annunciation to the Shepherds* (Pl. 490) where the shepherds sleeping in a farmyard are awakened by a radiant flight of angels—(a composition with which Samuel Palmer was perhaps, I think, in some way acquainted by 1833); before 1604 he also painted some portraits, a *Lot and his daughters*, a *Feast of the Gods* and a *Mars and Venus surprised by Vulcan*; in 1605 he painted a *Kitchen piece with parable of the great supper* in the **Aertsen-Beuckelaer** tradition; and in 1607 the delightful *Diana and Actaeon* (Pl. 498) where Actaeon is half changed to a stag in the centre distance and the foreground nudes are in prettily contorted attitudes and one points into the picture with a Tintoretto gesture like the boy with the wine-cooler in the *Night Banquet and masquerade* by **Joos van Winghe** (Pl. 497). **Uytewael** in these years was a successful artist, but he found time to devote himself also to a flourishing flax business which led van Mander to express amazement that 'Pictura' in the circumstances should extend such favours to him.

Of the Flemish-born painters active in Amsterdam **Hans Bol** (Pl. 431) died there at fifty-nine in 1593 and **Frans Boels** who painted a *Four Seasons* in 1594 seems to have died somewhere in Holland soon after; **Jacques Savery the elder** (Pl. 438) was thirty-two when he died of the Amsterdam plague in 1602; **Gillis Congnet** (Pls. 434, 442) died in 1599 in Hamburg having gone there on a visit from Amsterdam; and **Pieter Pietersz** (Pl. 421) worked in Amsterdam till he died there in 1603. **Aert Pietersz** active through the period was mainly occupied with subscription portrait groups in the old tradition; thus in 1599 he painted *The Company of Captain Jan Philipsz de Bischop and Lieutenant Egbertsz Vinck* nineteen half-length figures in two formal rows, and in 1603, when he was fifty-three, he painted his *Anatomy lesson of Dr. Sebastiaan Egbertsz* (Pl. 485) which anticipates Rembrandt's first picture of this subject by twenty-nine years and shows twenty-eight Master Surgeons assembled to hear Dr. Egbertsz lecture on a corpse. **Frans Badens,** who had been taken to Holland as a child by his parents after the Spanish Fury in Antwerp in 1576, went from Amsterdam to Italy aged twenty-two in 1593 and returned in 1597 when he called himself Francesco and painted social scenes, masquerades, mythologies and portraits; van Mander (in Amsterdam from 1604 till 1606) went to his studio and saw a *Bathsheba at the bath* with a procuress handing Bathsheba a letter from the King and whispering in her ear; he also saw in Amsterdam a genre piece *Lovers in Italian clothes, the man playing on a flute,* and his comments on this artist are revealing for he says: 'Painting in Holland has recently changed and developed to its advantage particularly in respect of colouring and flesh tints and shadows as the artists have more and more abandoned the former stone-grey or cold fishlike colouring and now generally render the warmth and glow of flesh. Francesco Badens has played a large part in this and he is known as "The Italian" among the younger artists because he was the first to use this splendid manner in Amsterdam; and he has indeed an engaging and glowing style and is an excellent artist.' **Jacques de Gheyn the younger** (Pl. 484) was in Amsterdam in the first years of the period and acted in a Rhetoricians' play there in honour of Prince Maurice in 1594; in 1595 he married into the Hague aristocracy; he worked in Leyden for a year or two from 1596, and in 1598 he settled in The Hague where he designed gardens for the Stadholder's palace. Up to 1603 when he was thirty-eight **de Gheyn** was still chiefly active as an engraver of portraits and compositions drawn by himself and of drawings and paintings by other artists including **Crispiaen van den Broeck, Dirck Barendsz** and **van Mander**; but thereafter he more or less abandoned this for painting, and van Mander describes the steps he took to train himself as a painter: 'As he had at first some difficulty in distinguishing the exact characters of the various colours, he covered a board with a hundred squares of different colours adding the appropriate shadow tint for each colour; and he numbered the squares in a note book for reference.' His first pictures van Mander tells us were flowerpieces, one of which was bought by Rudolf II; at the same time he produced a book with miniature paintings of flowers and insects also bought by the Emperor; and he then embarked on the life-size painting *A groom leading the white Spanish war horse captured from the Archduke Albert at the battle of Nieuport and presented to Prince Maurice* (Pl. 484); this picture pleased Prince Maurice but **de Gheyn,** van Mander tells us, was dissatisfied and went forward with his studies by producing a *Still life with a skull* and a life-size *Sleeping Venus with satyrs.* By 1606 **de Gheyn** was so successful as a flower painter that the States-General of Holland commissioned him to paint a flowerpiece for official presentation to Marie de Médicis; and it was also perhaps before 1609 that his undated *Venus and Cupid* was painted.

New arrivals of Flemings in Amsterdam included **Gillis van Coninxloo** and **Jan Vredeman de Vries** who both ended their careers in Holland, **Paul Vredeman de Vries, Pieter Stalpaert, Bernaert van Somer, Paul van Somer, Hans van Coninxloo the younger** and **Jeremias van Winghe.** Of these **Gillis van Coninxloo** left Frankenthal in 1596 and was settled in Amsterdam by 1597 when he was fifty-three, and he died there in 1607; at the height of his powers in these last ten years he painted the splendid *Wooded landscape with huntsman crossing bridge* (Pl. 466) in 1598, a *Wooded landscape with staghunt* in 1600 and the *Wooded landscape with duckshooters* (Pl. 476) in 1604; and van Mander writes of him 'I know no better landscape painter of the present time; he has many followers in Holland, so that trees that used to be bare now tend to be verdured in his manner—though some painters are loath to admit this.' **Jan Vredeman de Vries** left Prague after painting his *Musical party in a loggia* reproduced here (Pl. 462) and went in 1598 to Hamburg where **Gillis Congnet** advised him to settle in Holland; he arrived accordingly in Amsterdam in 1601 when he was seventy-four and van Mander tells us that he brought with him a *Tower of Babel* 'so rich in detail that he had damaged his eyesight in producing it'; he then went for a time to The Hague with his son **Paul Vredeman de Vries** and revisited Hamburg; back in Holland in 1604 he was recommended by Prince Maurice for the post of Professor of Architecture in the University of Leyden but he was not elected and he seems to have died soon after. **Paul Vredeman de Vries,** who worked independently as well as in collaboration with his father, remained in Holland for the rest of the period. **Pieter Stalpaert** was a young Bruxellois painter of landscapes and marines who had settled in Amsterdam by 1599.

214

Bernaert van Somer painter of portraits, religious subjects, and mythologies with nudes was later an innkeeper and art dealer; he arrived from Rome, about thirty, in 1604 bringing with him a large *Christ crowned with thorns* by his father-in-law **Aert Mytens;** his brother **Paul van Somer** (Pl. 538) was also in Amsterdam, aged about twenty-eight, by 1604 and van Mander describes him as good at portraits and 'alle ondedeelen der kunst' including works 'van eigen vinding'. **Hans van Coninxloo the younger,** who had been taken to Emden by his parents in flight from Alva, was in Amsterdam for some years from 1603 and active chiefly as art dealer. **Jeremias van Winghe,** a son of **Joos van Winghe** (Pls. 457, 497), was born in Brussels and had gone with his father to Frankfort; he arrived in Amsterdam after his father's death in 1603, or perhaps in 1598 when he was twenty; he worked for a time as a pupil of **Frans Badens** and later specialized in portraits.

In Amsterdam also many of the Flemings who had been taken to Holland as children by their parents in flight from or expelled by Parma were now working as art-students or beginning their careers. Thus by 1599 **Roelandt Savery, Joos Goeimare, David Vinckeboons** and **Cornelis van der Voort** were all about twenty-three, **Willem van Nieulandt** was fifteen and **Adriaen van Nieulandt** was twelve. Of these **Roelandt Savery** (Pls. 525, 564, 583, 585, 586), pupil probably of **Hans Bol** in 1592 and 1593 and then of **Jacques Savery the elder,** was a talented and precocious artist who is said to have gone to France and worked for Henri IV (possibly soon after 1600); and by 1604 he is known to have entered the service of Rudolf II in Prague; he began as a painter of landscapes with animals and of flower-pieces, and works painted before he left Holland for Prague include a *Tower of Babel* dated 1602, a *Wooded landscape* dated 1603 and a *Vase of flowers in a niche with lizards, snails and insects* also dated 1603; an *Orpheus charming the animals* dated 1604, perhaps the first version of a subject that he painted often in later years, may also have been painted in Amsterdam before his departure that year. **Joos Goeimare** was in the Savery circle as he married a member of the family in 1600; this connection appears in his choice of subject in a picture titled *Orpheus charming the animals* possibly painted in this period; but he seems to have been also influenced by the **Aertsen-Beuckelaer** tradition as he is known to have painted a *Christ in the house of Mary and Martha* with a mass of provisions. **David Vinckeboons** (Pl. 533) began as a watercolour painter instructed by his father who worked in this medium; he had, van Mander tells us, another master for oil painting and this was probably **Gillis van Coninxloo** as a picture by **van Coninxloo** with figures by him is recorded; he was painting in oils by 1602 when he signed a *Wooded landscape with staghunt;* in 1603 he signed a *Wooded landscape with robbers* and in that year also (inspired perhaps by **Gillis Congnet's** picture of 1592) he produced a large composition eight feet by fourteen, *The drawing of a lottery for the benefit of the Amsterdam Old Men's Hostel* commissioned by or given to that Hospital, and van Mander describes it as a night scene on a square in the city with a varied crowd carrying lanterns and torches; in 1604 he painted a *Landscape with Christ bearing the Cross,* described by van Mander as containing a great concourse of figures, a *Christ healing the blind man,* exported, van Mander tells us, to Frankfort, and a *Christ preaching by the Lake of Gennesaret;* we know too that he was also painting outdoor scenes with peasant genre by 1604 as van Mander speaks of two pictures titled *Peasant wedding;* he was thirty-three at the end of the period and already established as a versatile painter of several kinds of outdoor picture. **Cornelis van der Voort** had a practice as a portrait painter, with pupils, by 1604; he was also already active as collector (or dealer) and owned at that time **Joos van Winghe's** *Justice protecting Innocence against Tyranny,* the *Lovers in Italian clothes* by **Frans Badens** and a sketch by the Dutch painter Abraham

Bloemaert. **Willem van Nieulandt** (Pl. 475) a pupil of **Jacques Savery the elder** left Amsterdam for Italy in 1602. **Adriaen van Nieulandt** (Pls. 515, 647) who remained in Amsterdam worked first under the Dutch painter Pieter Isaaksz and then before 1607, when he was twenty, with **Frans Badens**.

Of the Flemings in the other Dutch towns **Daniel van den Queborne** the portrait painter, about fifty-five in 1600, was conspicuous in The Hague as Court Painter to Prince Maurice; the architectural and perspective painter **Salomon Vredeman de Vries** died there in 1604; and I have already mentioned **Jacques de Gheyn** as active there from 1598. In Middelburg the Flemings included **Adriaen van Stalbemt** (Pls. 479, 562) and the flower painter **Ambrosius Bosschaert** who had both been brought there by their Protestant parents after Parma's conquest of Antwerp. **Adriaen van Stalbemt,** probably acquainted with **Gillis van Coninxloo's** Amsterdam landscapes (Pls. 466, 476), may have painted his undated *Wooded landscape with hunters and dogs* (Pl. 479) by 1609 when he was just under thirty. **Ambrosius Bosschaert** (Pls. 550, 551, 552) was a member of the Middelburg Guild of S. Luke by 1593 when he was twenty; and he was well established as a flower (and occasionally fruit) painter by 1609 when he painted a *Flowers in a porcelain vase on a silver-gilt stand*; in this picture (not reproduced here) there are insects and a butterfly on the slab or table where the vase is placed, the background is a plain dark wall, and the flowers include tulips, roses, narcissi, daffodils, iris, lilies of the valley, and a light red carnation in the centre. The same juxtaposition of flowers of different seasons can also be seen in **Bosschaert's** later pictures reproduced here (Pls. 551, 552); and it is thus evident that he constructed his flowerpieces from individual flowers separately painted and not from a bouquet actually before him at the time; in some cases indeed he may have worked from watercolour studies or from prints of exemplary blossoms by botanical experts like those in the books produced by Plantin with plates by **Pieter van der Borcht the elder** referred to in previous chapters. **Jacques de Gheyn** and **Roelandt Savery** also quite evidently worked in the same way; and it was probably thus also that the earlier flower specialists including **Pauwels Coecke van Aelst** and **Lodewyck Jansz van der Bosch** had proceeded. Flowerpieces by these earlier painters may indeed have been known to this new generation; and **Ambrosius Bosschaert** was perhaps acquainted with examples by **Lodewyck van den Bosch** then owned by a Middelburg Mintmaster named Melchior Wijntgens whose collection I shall chronicle below. In Utrecht the Flemings included **Adam Willaerts** (Pl. 688), marine painter, who was twenty-three in 1600, and **Gillis de Hondecoeter,** painter of landscapes with animals, who was a little younger (and the father by 1604 of Gysbert de Hondecoeter Dutch landscape and bird painter, father in his turn of the more famous bird painter Melchior de Hondecoeter). In Delft **Hans Jordaens the elder** painted a *Beach scene with whale and many figures* in 1598 at approximately forty; before 1604 he had produced a number of works which led van Mander to describe him as a clever and inventive painter of 'boeren, soldaten, schippers, visschers, nachttafereelen, branden, rotsen en dergelijk mooi werk'; and before 1604 also he was employed by Prince Maurice to copy **Bernaert van Orley's** cartoons for tapestries *Equestrian portraits of the House of Orange*. In Delft too **Frans Spierinx** was having success with his tapestry factory which received a commission from the Earl of Nottingham (Lord High Admiral Lord Howard of Effingham) for tapestries depicting *The Defeat of the Spanish Armada in 1588*; **Spierinx** invited **Karel van Mander** to make the cartoons but **van Mander** not feeling competent transferred the commission to the Dutch marine painter Hendrik Cornelisz Vroom (who went to England to gather material, was given £100 by the Admiral, and sat to Isaac Oliver for a miniature portrait);

and in 1604 **van Mander's** son **Karel van Mander the younger** joined **Spierinx** as assistant. In Dordrecht **Nicolas Snellaert** painted a subscription portrait group *The Regents of the Dordrecht mint* and died over sixty in 1602; and in Rotterdam **Jan Porcellis** (born in Ghent before Parma's conquest) was painting marines by 1605.

In Haarlem (where **Porcellis** had been trained by Hendrick Cornelisz Vroom) **Karel van Mander** was continuously patronized by a number of Dutch collectors; he painted an *Annunciation* in 1593, a *S. John preaching in the wilderness* in 1597, his *Jesus leaving the Temple with his parents* (Pl. 472) in 1598, a *Village Fair* in 1600, a *Battle between Hannibal and Scipio* with a number of elephants in 1602 and about the same time a *Bathing house* with nudes and a picture called *Amor omnibus idem*. His *Jesus leaving the Temple with his parents* (Pl. 472) gives imaginative illustration to two subjects—first *Jesus among the Doctors* where the little figure in the grand pulpit facing the adults appeals by its smallness as in the picture of the subject by the **Hoogstraeten Master** (Pl. 198), and then *Jesus leaving the Temple with his parents* where the smallness of the central figure is unhappily not maintained; the Temple, evidently based on **van Mander's** memories of the vast interior of St. Peter's Rome has a certain spacious grandeur but its cold correctitude is much less exciting than the architecturally preposterous interior invented by **Jan Gossaert** from his Roman memories for *S. Luke drawing the Virgin* (Pl. 238)—a picture, incidentally, which **van Mander** himself had seen in Prague; and we may also note in passing that a figure on the right of this picture wears the large sun hat of the eighties and nineties which I referred to in my last chapter when discussing **Jacob Grimmer's** *Landscape with castle* (Pl. 444) of 1583 and **Hendrik de Clerck's** *Suffer little children . . .* (Pl. 471) of 1592. In these years **van Mander** continued the direction of his Academy (founded as noted, with Hendrik Goltzius and Cornelis van Haarlem) and Frans Hals was his pupil there in the later nineties. In 1602 he entertained his old friend **Bartholomaeus Spranger** (Pls. 458, 459) who was visiting the Netherlands after an absence of thirty-seven years and was fêted by the artists with a banquet and a Rhetoricians' play called 'Homage to Painting' when he stayed in Haarlem. From about 1600 **van Mander** had been collecting material for his 'Schilderboek' and in 1603 he moved to Zevenbergen (between Haarlem and Alkmaar) where he wrote the greater part of it. In 1604 he moved to Amsterdam; but before leaving Zevenbergen he produced a comedy of his own in honour of his artist friends; this was acted by his pupils and staged within a proscenium adorned by Italian decorative motifs, 'trophies' contrived with painters' tools, and other conceits new and strange 'voor hen die nooit buitenslands geweest waren'. He finished the 'Schilderboek' in 1604 in Amsterdam after calling on collectors and visiting studios to gather information for the section on contemporary painters; but though he found out much, to our very great advantage, some artists were uncooperative, protesting that they were not good enough to be recorded in a book with important masters—'so that' he laments 'between the deceased artists who cannot talk and the living ones who don't want to, I have not had an easy passage'. When his book had gone to Haarlem to be published he resumed his painting; and he had produced a large picture *The Israelites committing whoredom with the Moabite women* before he died at fifty-eight in 1606. *A Vase of wildflowers* was among the unfinished pictures in his studio.

Sidelights on the taste of Dutch collectors in this period can be extracted from the 'Schilderboek' as van Mander names the owners of many of the pictures he had personally seen. I have already referred in earlier chapters to the collection of the amateur artist Jacob Rauwaert of Amsterdam who died in 1597 and had pictures by **Gerard van der Meire, Pieter Aertsen, Joachim Beuckelaer, Marten van Heemskerck, Dirck Barendsz** and

Karel van Mander himself; and I have mentioned above the collection of the young portrait painter **Cornelis van der Voort.** I must now add some details of the collections of Bartholomaeus Ferreris a painter in Leyden, of Jan Gerritsz Buytewegh who also lived in Leyden, of Herman Pilgrim and Jacques Razet and Hendrik van Os in Amsterdam and of Melchior Wijntgens, Mintmaster, in Middelburg. Ferreris had works by **Lucas van Leyden, Quinten Massys,** Holbein, the Dutch portraitist Michiel Miereveld, who was much in favour with the House of Orange and the Dutch aristocracy from the turn of the century onwards, and the Dutch Romanist Cornelis of Haarlem. Jan Gerritsz Buytewegh had pictures by **Dirk Bouts** and **Aert Claesz van Leyden.** Herman Pilgrim had a *Peasant's wedding* by **Pieter Bruegel,** landscapes by **Gillis van Coninxloo** and a *Venus and Mercury teaching Cupid to read* by **Bartholomaeus Spranger.** Jacques Razet, a close friend of van Mander's and with him on his death-bed, owned works by **Van Mander, Miereveld, Cornelis Ketel, Dirck Barendsz, Hans Bol, Joris Hoefnagel,** the flower painter **Lodewyck van den Bosch** and Holbein. Hendrik van Os had *Democritus and Heraclitus* painted by **Cornelis Ketel** with his fingers without brushes, a *Peace triumphing over War* by Rudolf II's German painter Hans van Achen, a *Flowers in a vase* by **Jacques de Gheyn** and landscapes by **Gillis van Coninxloo** and **Paul Brill.** The very large collection of the Mintmaster Melchior Wijntgens included a *Lucretia* by Dürer and the same subject by **Jan Gossaert,** and pictures by **Patinir, Hendrik met de Bles, Joos van Cleve, Jacques de Backer, Frans Floris, Joachim Beuckelaer, Marten van Heemskerck, Marinus van Reymerswaele, Lodewyck van den Bosch, Joos van Winghe, Gillis van Coninxloo, Joachim Uytewael, Otto van Veen, van Mander** and Cornelis of Haarlem.

In Germany there were Flemish painters in Frankfort, Nuremberg, Frankenthal, Cologne and Munich and several paid short visits to Hamburg. **Joos van Winghe** (Pls. 457, 497) seems to have worked throughout in Frankfort till he died there about sixty in 1603; but it is possible, I think, that he visited Prague, was commissioned there to paint one of the Emperor's mistresses and did so in his *Apelles painting Campaspe* (Pl. 457) which is known to have been in Rudolf's collection and which may thus be an allegoric genre piece with himself as Apelles painting Alexander's favourite as Venus rising from the sea and Alexander as symbol of the Emperor Rudolf. Considered as a 'Painter in his studio' genre piece this *Apelles painting Campaspe* inevitably recalls the series which began with the **Boston S. Luke Painter** (Pl. 48) and continues through works by the **London S. Luke Painter** (Pl. 186), **Jan Gossaert** (Pl. 238) and the **Fogg S. Luke Painter** (Pl. 260) to **Marten van Heemskerck** (Pls. 303, 304), **Lancelot Blondeel** (Pl. 330) and **Frans Floris** (Pl. 351); the painter's tools of trade reappear here but the studio mirror is now held by a studio servant; the artist himself has now become the hero of the picture, for the angel casting light upon the sacred sitter and the poet inspiring the painter in **van Heemskerck's** picture have become a muse inspiring the painter who is no longer a humble bespectacled student but a confident master in bravura attitude; the Cupid now directs his arrow at the artist's breast; and Alexander has come to the studio to watch the magic growth of the picture, as Rudolf II went frequently to watch his painters at work—which reminds us that fifty years had passed since the Emperor Charles V gained kudos by bending down to pick up a brush for Titian, and that forty had passed since Philip II had frequented the studio of **Antonis Mor.** Others in Frankfort were **Martin van Valkenborch,** his sons **Frederick van Valkenborch** and **Gillis van Valkenborch, Lucas van Valkenborch, Hendrik van der Borcht the elder, Hendrik van Steenwyck the elder** (Pl. 488) and probably **Hendrik van Steenwyck the younger.** Of these **Martin van Valkenborch** (Pl. 439) painted a *Tower of Babel* at sixty in 1595, visited Italy between 1602 and 1604 and then returned to Frankfort. **Frederick van Valkenborch** was back in Frankfort from Italy by 1595 when he painted a *Village Feast*; in 1597 when he was approximately twenty-seven he was accepted as a citizen of Frankfort after an examination in Lutheran doctrine; in 1602 he moved to Nuremberg where he became a citizen after giving up his Frankfort rights in 1605; in his *Mountain landscape with robbers attacking peasants* (Pl. 502) painted in Nuremberg in 1605 a corpse hangs from a gallows and another is on a wheel recalling similar details in quite different landscapes by **Pieter Bruegel the elder** (Pls. 379, 393); and there is also comment on the horrors of the times in his *Burning city* of 1607. **Gillis van Valkenborch,** also back from Italy, became a citizen of Frankfort after the same examination in Lutheran doctrine in 1597 and remained in Frankfort; he seems to have concentrated on pictures symbolic of contemporary conflicts as a *Burning of Troy* is recorded and he signed a *Defeat of King Sennacherib* in 1597. **Lucas van Valkenborch** (Pls. 374, 432, 445, 446, 448, 449, 450) moved from Linz to Frankfort where he settled at the end of 1593 when he was approximately sixty; he became a Frankfort citizen in 1594 and died there in 1597; he painted a *View of Linz with man painting* in 1593 and a *Tower of Babel* (Pl. 374), where the tower has the form of the Papal tiara, in 1594; he finished his career with the rocky coast piece *The Gergesene Demoniacs* (Pl. 448)—a highly remarkable picture where the landscape is complete in itself before the figures were put in, and the figures though small, with Christ and the demoniacs the smallest of all, are a faithful illustration of all the details in S. Matthew's text from the landing in the centre to the departure of the ship in the distance on the right. **Hendrik van der Borcht the elder,** taken to Frankfort as a child by his Protestant parents as related in my last chapter, was a pupil of **Gillis van Valkenborch** probably when he was sixteen in 1599; and he left there for Italy, possibly with **Martin van Valkenborch,** in 1602 and was later a portrait painter and antiquarian. The architectural painter **Hendrik van Steenwyck the elder** (Pl. 488) was in Frankfort from the outset of the period; and in 1598 he signed a *Market-place* where the scene is crowded with genre figures in various occupations; these figures were doubtless contributed by an unrecorded collaborator who thus links **Pieter Bruegel** (Pl. 370) with the genre painters **David Vinckeboons** (Pl. 533) and **Sebastiaan Vrancx** (Pl. 534), **Adriaen van Nieulandt** (Pl. 515), **Pieter Bout** (Pl. 796), **Pieter Gysels** (Pl. 799) and **Jan Anton Garemyn** (Pl. 860). Nothing seems known of the movements in these years of **Hendrik van Steenwyck the younger,** but he may have gone from Frankfort to Holland before 1609; he was signing church interiors with figures by collaborators by 1603; and his skill as an architectural draughtsman is well seen in the *Interior of a Gothic church* (Pl. 487) painted in 1605 at about twenty-five. The Frankenthal colony was weakened when **Gillis van Coninxloo** went to Amsterdam in 1595; but the younger Flemings **Pieter Schoubroeck** and **Antonie Mirou** show some influence from him in the treatment of trees and verdure. **Pieter Schoubroeck** visited Nuremberg in 1597 and painted there a *Village landscape with peasants, farm animals, and a beggar asking alms at a farmhouse* but was back in Frankenthal soon after; in 1603 he signed a *Battle of the Amazons*; like the other Protestants **Frederick van Valkenborch** and **Gillis van Valkenborch** he also painted burning cities symbolic of contemporary conflicts and his style in such work is shown here in *Troy burning and Aeneas carrying his father* (Pl. 494) where the destroying army crossing the bridge can be compared with the destroying army near a burning city by **Hieronymus Bosch** (Pls. 173); he died under forty in 1607. **Antonie Mirou** (possibly a pupil of **Schoubroeck**) was married in Frankenthal perhaps under twenty in 1602; and in 1608 he signed a *Village and foreground wood with sportsmen shooting game and a beggar asking alms of* *cavaliers,* a tight rather tentative work much less accomplished than his *Landscape with Abraham and Hagar* (Pl. 469) which was probably painted some ten or more years later.

In the Catholic German centres **Goltzius Geldorp** lived through the period in Cologne; he was forty-three when he painted *Hortensia del Pardo* (Pl. 454) in 1596; his *Catherine Fourmenois as a child* (Pl. 486) dates from 1604; and both pictures appeal by a combination of grand simplicity in design with a gentle intimate study of the faces recalling the gentle intimate face-studies by **Catherine van Hemessen** (Pls. 345, 346), **Pieter van der Hofstadt** (Pl. 366) and **Adriaen van Cronenburch** (Pls. 343, 441). In Munich there was still the Court architect and painter **Federico di Lamberto Sustris** till he died about sixty in 1599. **Pieter de Witte (Candido)** continued as Court Painter to Duke William V and thereafter to Duke Maximilian by whom he was appointed superintendent of all artists working in the palaces; he also painted many religious subjects for the Munich and other churches, and in 1595 an *Annunciation* for the Carmelite Church in Brescia; at the same time he painted decorative mythologies for the Ducal palaces and from 1604 he designed tapestries with historical and allegoric subjects for a tapestry factory then newly founded in Munich. **Engelhart van Pee,** still a leading portraitist in Court circles, painted *Duke Maximilian aged twenty-seven* in 1600 and his sister *Duchess Magdalena aged fourteen* in 1601; in that year after long disputes with the Painters Guild he became a Munich Master; and he died in Munich in 1605.

In Austria there were also Flemish painters as before. In Prague the Emperor Rudolf continued to shower honours on **Bartholomaeus Spranger** (Pls. 458, 459); he ennobled him as 'van den Schilde' in 1595 and gave him a thousand guilders in 1602 for the journey to the Netherlands which was nominally a private visit but may have included some secret political tasks in Antwerp, Holland or Cologne; **Spranger** signed a *Venus and Mercury teaching Cupid to read* in 1595 and he told van Mander in 1602 that he had much improved his colouring in recent years after seeing some pictures by the Emperor's German Court Painters Joseph Heinz and Hans van Achen. **Joris Hoefnagel** also retained the Emperor's favour till he died at fifty-eight in 1600 after producing an elaborate set of miniatures (town views, portraits, animals, plants, etc.) in G. Bocskay's 'Examples of Calligraphy (Schriftmonsterboek)'. **Pieter Stevens,** in Prague since 1590, became a Court painter in 1594; like the Emperor he was evidently an admirer of **Pieter Bruegel the elder** and the delicate tree painting in his *Village fair* (Pl. 468) of 1596 suggests direct influence from **Pieter Bruegel's** *Harvesters* (Pl. 392) and *Peasants' dance* (Pl. 407)—though the peasants are cruder in their amorous amusements than in extant works by **Bruegel.** Of the newcomers to Prague **Paul Vredeman de Vries** arrived from Danzig at twenty-seven in 1594 and painted several ceilings with trompe l'oeil architecture and figures in perspective, and also a trompe l'oeil courtyard and fountain on the wall of a small room which delighted the Emperor who declared himself deceived by it. **Jan Vredeman de Vries** followed his son to Prague when he was sixty-nine in 1596 and left, with him, as already related in 1598; he signed, with his son, a *Marble pillared hall with cavaliers and ladies* and he produced with his own signature a *Palace courtyard with fountain, dwarf and goose and elegant company and a table set for a banquet* in 1596. In another picture of this type the *Musical party in a loggia* (Pl. 462) also painted by **Jan Vredeman de Vries** in 1596, the fantastic invented architecture would make an admirable setting for Shakespeare's 'Twelfth Night' and the elegant music-making ladies and gentlemen (perhaps inserted by a collaborator) are not only descendants of the elegant folk in pictures by **Abel Grimmer** (Pl. 447) and **Lucas van Valkenborch** (Pl. 446) but also ancestors of the elegant companies in similar groups by Watteau; and students of music can compare the instruments they play on with the instruments in pictures shown here by **Marten de Vos** (Pl. 364), **Frans Floris** (Pl. 352), the **Female Half Lengths Master** (Pl. 314) and the **Worcester Girl at Clavichord Painter** (Pl. 311). **Jan Vredeman de Vries** also worked as an architect in Prague designing cabinets to display the Emperor's curiosities and pictures and van Mander tells us that he devised an arrangement whereby the Emperor could move secretly all over his palace 'zonder dat hij gezien werd'. **Jacob Hoefnagel,** a miniature draughtsman like his father, and a skilful engraver, was in Prague from Antwerp by 1602 at twenty-seven; and the Emperor set him to draw this, that and the other in his gardens, aviaries and Wunderkammer. Another young man **Philip van den Bossche,** a topographic draughtsman, joined Rudolf's artists in 1604 and drew a *View of Prague* for him soon after. **Roelandt Savery** arrived in Prague in 1604 at about twenty-seven; within the next year or so he may have painted the undated *Birds in a forest* (Pl. 583) from specimens in Rudolf's aviaries, and the little company of nude girls bathing in the background of this picture may record his memories of the Fontainebleau School; in 1606 he was sent by his patron to the Tyrol where he painted pine woods and mountain landscapes and made drawings eventually used in some later pictures like the *Stag and boar hunt in a rocky landscape* reproduced here (Pl. 564); the exact date of his return to Prague does not seem to be recorded but he was probably back by 1609. In the Tyrol we also find **Frans Pourbus the younger** (Pls. 539, 540) on visits to Innsbruck to paint portraits in 1603 and 1608. In Styria a Fleming whose earlier history is almost unknown, **Aegidius de Rye,** is recorded in Graz in 1596 as Court Painter to the Archduke Ferdinand by whom he was commissioned to paint frescoes in the castle; he had worked as topographic draughtsman and contributed drawings of Cracow, Klausenburg and Kaschau to Braun's *Civitates Orbis Terrarum*; in 1597 he signed a miniature painting on copper *S. Catherine buried by angels*; in 1602 he was granted an annual pension by the Archduke; and he died in Graz in 1605.

In England **Marcus Geeraerts the younger (Marcus Gerard)**—was thirty-two in 1593; after 1596 he was employed by the Royal Wardrobe on various decorative work for coaches and so on which he doubtless had executed by his studio assistants; in 1598 he was named among the notable painters in the 'Wit's Commonwealth' by Francis Meres; in 1607 he monogrammed a *Head and shoulders of a dead man*; and in 1609 he was paid by James I 'for makeinge the picture of Phillipp late Kinge of Spaine'. He seems to have had a considerable practice as a painter of the full length portraits with elaborate clothes (probably painted by specialist assistants) which became increasingly fashionable as decorations for the long galleries of Elizabethan houses at the turn of the century; and some English private houses still own collections of such portraits traditionally ascribed to him—(I saw a number at Charlton some thirty years ago). I reproduce two full length portraits of this time both probably painted by Flemings at work here; the first is the superbly monumental *Portrait of Queen Elizabeth* (Pl. 462A) by an unrecorded artist here called the **London Queen Elizabeth at Ditchley Painter;** this was probably painted in 1593 as it commemorates the Queen's visit in 1592 to the Oxfordshire house of Sir Henry Lee (her Master of the Armoury and some time Personal Champion in many tilts)—an occasion on which her host staged many ingenious diversions including one where a choir of maidens sang:

'Happie houre, happie daie
That Eliza came this waie'.

The picture shows the Queen, aged about sixty, standing on a Sheldon tapestry map of

Oxfordshire with her feet on Ditchley; and the first four lines of the poem in the panel on the right are:

> 'The Prince of Light, the Sun by whom things live
> Of heaven the glorye and of earth the grace
> Hath no such glorye as your grace to give
> Where correspondencie may have no place'.

The archaistic character of the painting—which may remind some readers of certain portraits by the Douanier Rousseau—was due to the Queen's well-known dislike of chiaroscuro which she pronounced unsuitable for portraits unless the sitter had some blemish to be concealed by shadows. The painting also irresistibly recalls the comments on the Queen's portraits made by Horace Walpole: 'The profusion of ornaments with which they are loaded are marks of her continual fondness for dress, while they entirely exclude all grace and leave no more room for a painter's genius than if he had been employed to copy an Indian idol totally composed of hands and necklaces; a pale Roman nose, a head of hair loaded with crowns and powdered with diamonds, a vast ruff, a vaster fardingale, and a bushel of pearls, are the features by which everybody knows at once the pictures of Elizabeth'. In the second picture reproduced here, a charming work by an unrecorded painter here called the **Hampton Court Lady in a Persian Dress Painter** (Pl. 463), the lady is depicted in a white 'exotic' gown embroidered with birds and flowers; standing in a conventionally treated wooded landscape she places a garland of flowers on the stag beside her; and the various inscriptions include the lines:

> With pensive thoughtes my weepinge stagg I crowne,
> Whose melancholy tears my cares expresse;
> Her teares in sylence, and my sighes unknowne
> Are all the physicke that my harmes redresse'.

The sitter is presumed by some to be Arabella Stuart, who, as by pedigree next in succession to the throne after James I, was always the centre of Catholic intrigue and was confined at Hardwick by the Queen's orders in 1602.

In France **Hieronymus Francken the elder** held the rank of Peintre du Roy in this period; in 1600 he produced a *Beheading of S. John the Baptist* which shows the event just after the execution when attendants pass the head to Salome; and in 1604 he painted a subscription portrait group *The Sheriffs of Paris* for the Hotel de Ville. In 1607 when he was sixty-seven he may have painted the *Still-life with food and kitchen utensils* (Pl. 503) signed 'Jeronimus Francken'; in this most interesting picture there is a print on the wall showing an owl, a pair of spectacles and a candle in a candlestick inscribed 'Al heeft hij kaers en bril . . . uyl niet zien will'; and the objects on the table are disposed in formal relationships that anticipate much later concepts of still-life painting. **Jan de Hoey,** already Peintre du Roy as noted in my last chapter, produced a *Last Judgement* for Notre Dame in this period; in 1603 the eventual reversion of his post was granted to his son Claude; in 1608 when he was sixty-three he held the post of Keeper of the King's Pictures in Fontainebleau; and it was probably at this time that he painted an *Assumption of the Virgin* and a *Church militant* for Fontainebleau chapel. **Ambroise Dubois** obtained the rank of Peintre du Roy about 1594 when he was just over fifty, and before 1599 he painted *Gabrielle d'Estrées as Diana*; in 1601 he married **Jan de Hoey's** sister (as his second wife) and became a naturalized Frenchman; on the death of the French painter Toussaint Dubreuil in 1602 he was put in charge of all the decorative painting in Fontainebleau palace; in 1606 he was appointed

Court Painter to Marie de Médicis and he then painted a series of panels including the *Baptism of Clorinda* (Pl. 491) in the mannerist style for the Queen's Fontainebleau apartments. Among the newcomers **Roelandt Savery** (Pls. 525, 564, 583, 586) was possibly in Paris and Fontainebleau about 1600 as already mentioned. The Malineois **Lucas Franchoys the elder,** painter of portraits and religious subjects, was in France for some time from 1600 when he was twenty-six and he then went on to Spain. Another Malineois **Ferdinand Elle** reached Paris about 1607 at a little over twenty and was at work by 1609 on a subscription portrait group *Provosts, Sheriffs and other Municipal notables* for the Hotel de Ville. **Frans Pourbus the younger** (Pls. 539, 540) visited Paris in 1606 and again in 1609 when he definitely settled there; on the first visit when he was thirty-seven he was sent by the Duke of Mantua to join the suite of his wife Duchess Eleonora Gonzaga (sister of Marie de Médicis) then in Paris for the baptism of her godson the Dauphin, and he was instructed to make portraits of the King and Queen and the Dauphin (who was already six years old); and on the second occasion his services were particularly asked for by Marie de Médicis. In the provinces **François Stellaert** who had been in Italy was established in Lyons by 1596 (when his son François Stella was born there); he worked for churches in Lyons and may also have painted more landscapes like the *Cascade in Tivoli* of 1587, already referred to, as van Mander calls him an 'uitneemend meester in landschappen, figuren, compositie, portretschilderen naar het leven en teekenen'; he died in Lyons at forty-two in 1605.

In Italy there were Flemish painters established from the last period and many new ones including **Frans Pourbus the younger** (Pls. 539, 540) and **Rubens.** All of course visited a number of towns on the routes to and from their central habitat which was frequently Rome, and we have the itineraries, or some details from them, in some cases. In other cases we know only that the artist visited Italy without more precise location; but we can, I think, assume that all painters contrived if possible to visit Venice then at the height of her beauty and offering tourists the spectacle of pictures by Titian, Veronese and Tintoretto as well as a variety of gay-life entertainments.

Milan was visited by **Jan (Velvet) Brueghel** in the suite of Cardinal Borromeo in 1595 and **Brueghel** painted there a *Christ on the Lake of Gennesaret* and a *Landscape with hermits*; **Frans Snyders** arrived there with an introduction from **Brueghel** to the Cardinal in 1608 and returned to Antwerp in 1609. Genoa was visited by **Rubens** in 1606 or 1607 when he collected material for a book (published later) on the Genoese palaces and painted an altarpiece for S. Ambrogio commissioned by the Marquis Niccolo Pallavicini (the Duke of Mantua's banker), and also possibly some portraits; and **Abraham Matthys,** a pupil of **Tobias van Haecht** (Pl. 377) and son of a fishdealer (with interests in whale fisheries) may have called at Genoa when travelling in Italy from 1603. In Turin we find **Frans Pourbus the younger** (Pls. 539, 540) on a visit from Mantua in 1605 and also **Jan Kraeck (Caracca)** who remained the Duke of Savoy's Court Painter till he died there approaching seventy and was buried in the Cathedral in 1607. **Lodewyck Toeput (Pozzoserrato),** now established in Treviso, painted a *Mountain landscape with the fall of Phaeton* at approximately fifty in 1599 and died in Treviso before 1609. In Bologna **Denys Calvaert** painted an *Entombment* in 1595, a *Paradise* in 1602 and a *Descent from the Cross* in 1609 when he was nearly seventy; Guido Reni was still his pupil at the beginning of the period, Francesco Albani came soon after and both left for the Carracci Academy about 1595; Domenichino came as a pupil about 1596 and left for the Carracci Academy probably before 1600. In Parma **Jan Sons** was confirmed in his post of Court Painter by the new Duke Ranuccio I whose portrait he painted in 1600; with the experience of his landscape frescoes in the Vatican behind him, he worked with Italian artists on paintings for the palace; he also continued to work for local churches including S. Maria Bianca where his pictures were much admired by Annibale Carracci; and in 1607 he signed a *Holy Family* for S. Maria della Steccata at approximately sixty. **Ernest Schayck the younger** was in Italy, from Utrecht, by 1600 when he signed a *Virgin in glory with saints and donors* for Lugo, S. Rocco, and in 1609 he was working for S. Maria Assunta at Filottrano (Ancona). **Theodore van Loon** from Brussels, who was certainly in Italy later, was probably there on a first visit about nineteen about 1604. In Florence **Jan van der Straet (Stradanus)** may still have been active in the later nineties and he died there at eighty-two in 1605. The Naples Flemish colony lost both **Aert Mytens (Rinaldo Fiammingo)** and **Wenzelas Coebergher** in this period. For **Aert Mytens,** who had now lived there for some twenty-five years, was driven away, van Mander tells us, by his second wife's 'onbeschaamdheid' and left with his children and assistants at the end of the nineties; he went to Abruzzo and Aquila and was in Rome by 1600 when he was just on sixty; in Naples he painted in this period a *Four Evangelists* for S. Annunziata; and in Aquila he painted a *Crucifixion* and began a *Christ crowned with thorns* which he took with him to Rome. **Wenzelas Coebergher** (Pl. 493) painted a *Resurrection* for S. Domenico Maggiore in 1594; he had then been in Naples for fourteen years and he moved to Rome in 1597 or 1598 at approximately forty. **Dirck Hendricksz (Errico Fiammingo)** remained in Naples still occupied with pictures for local and other churches till 1604; and he too seems to have left before 1609 when he was approaching sixty and had been in Naples for nearly thirty years. **Frans Pourbus the younger** (Pls. 539, 540) visited Naples from Mantua for some months in the autumn of 1607; and he tried, unsuccessfully, to persuade Duke Vincenzo Gonzaga to acquire the *Virgin of the Rosaries* by Caravaggio (who had just left for Malta) as the picture was then for sale there.

In the Venetian colony **Pauwels Franck (Paolo Fiammingo)** died at fifty-six in 1596. This may have left **Gaspar Rem** the doyen of the colony as he was fifty-eight in 1600 and painted soon after a *S. Jerome in the desert striking his breast with a stone* engraved by 1603 with a dedication to his friend **Frans van den Kasteele** then living in Rome. **Pietro Mera,** about fifty in 1600, seems to have worked in these years for Venetian churches including S. Maria dell'Orto, SS. Giovanni e Paolo and S. Nicolo di Lido. **Martin van Valkenborch** (Pl. 439) visited Venice from Frankfort at sixty-seven in 1602; and he may have been accompanied, as suggested above, by **Hendrik van der Borcht the elder** who was then nineteen and remained in Italy for some years working mainly as an antiquary and collector of antiques. **Henri Staben,** painter later of *A visit to the studio of Rubens* (Pl. 518), reached Venice from Antwerp in the middle nineties and worked as a youth in Tintoretto's atelier then directed by his son Domenico; and he was probably still there aged twenty-two when **Rubens** arrived in July 1600. **Rubens** at this time was just twenty-three (he had celebrated his birthday in the middle of the two months journey from Antwerp) and he was accompanied by **Deodatus Delmont** then eighteen as pupil and assistant; he must have been thunderstruck with the colour in Venetian painting, and he probably met most of the Flemish painters named above including **Gaspar Rem** by whom he may have been furnished with a letter to the influential **Frans van den Kasteele.** He had with him some examples of his painting which were shown to Duke Vincenzo Gonzaga then in Venice; and he accepted an offer from the Duke to go to Mantua and join his Court Painters.

In Mantua **Rubens** had at first two Flemish colleagues as Court Painters **Frans Pourbus the younger** (Pls. 539, 540) who was then thirty-one, and a painter recorded simply as

'Jan'; and **Deodatus Delmont** worked under him there and remained his assistant for the next eight years in Italy. Duke Vincenzo, now thirty-eight, had been Duke since he was twenty-five; he had two palaces with frescoes by Mantegna, Giulio Romano, Primaticcio, Niccolo dell'Abbate and so on, collections of antique sculpture and of pictures, and a special gallery of portraits of pretty women to which he was continually adding; he had the usual accumulation of miscellaneous objets d'art including Flemish tapestries and Chinoiseries; his gardens contained Dutch tulips and his menagerie lions, tigers and a crocodile. In the autumn of 1600 he took **Rubens** in his suite to Florence to be present at the marriage by proxy of Henri IV to Marie de Médicis and **Rubens** noted the details of the ceremony where the Grand Duke Ferdinand dei Medici was the 'stand in' for King Henri and Cardinal Aldobrandini gave the nuptial blessing. In 1601 the Duke sent **Rubens** to Rome with a letter of introduction to Cardinal Montalto and instructions to copy some pictures; and he set **Frans Pourbus** to work on portraits of himself and his family. In 1603 he allowed **Frans Pourbus** to go to Innsbruck to paint Anna of Tyrol and he sent **Rubens** to Spain with a shipload of presents to Philip III and the Duke of Lerma because he had hopes at the moment of obtaining the post of Admiral in the Spanish service. In 1604 both **Pourbus** and **Rubens** were in Mantua, and **Rubens** began *The Gonzaga Family adoring the Trinity* for the Mantuan Jesuit church. In 1605 **Pourbus** painted the Duke's daughter Margherita Gonzaga for Rudolf II who had thoughts of marrying her; he was then sent by the Duke to Turin to paint portraits of Charles Emmanuel's two daughters in order that the Duke's son Francesco Gonzaga might choose one of them as his bride; and while in Turin he also painted some portraits commissioned by Charles Emmanuel. In 1606 the Duke instructed **Pourbus** to join the suite of the Duchess Eleanora in Nancy (where Margherita Gonzaga was being married to Henri, Duc de Bar) and thence to accompany her to Paris and paint portraits of Henri IV, the Queen and the Dauphin on the occasion of the Dauphin's baptism as related above. At the same time, or a few months earlier, he gave **Rubens** permission to return to Rome to continue his studies and execute some work there, and he thereby lost him as Court Painter—for **Rubens** never came back to Mantua though he was nominally the Duke's servant for two years more. In 1607 the Duke sent **Pourbus** to Naples to paint Neapolitan beauties 'of any rank' for his gallery of pictures of pretty women, and **Pourbus** painted two such pictures on this visit. In 1608 the Duke took **Pourbus** to Turin for the marriage of Francesco Gonzaga with Margaret of Savoy; and later in the year he allowed him to revisit Innsbruck. In 1609 he yielded to the request of Marie de Médicis for his services and thus lost him also as Court Painter—for **Pourbus** transferred his allegiance to the Queen soon after his arrival in Paris.

In Rome the Flemish artists already established included **Hendrik van den Broeck (Arrigo Fiammingo, Henricus Paludanus)** who was still on the Council of the Accademia till he died at seventy-eight in 1597; **Anthoni Santvoort** who died in 1600; and **Frans van den Kasteele** and **Paul Brill** both active through the period. **Frans van den Kasteele** continued to paint religious pictures for various churches including a *Christ and the Virgin receiving souls from Purgatory* signed in 1599 for a church in Spello; and he must have been officially the central figure of the Flemish colony from 1600 when he was elected Principe of the Accademia at the age of sixty. **Paul Brill** continued to paint large frescoes with landscapes and marine subjects and small landscapes as easel pictures; about 1600 when he was forty-five he produced a series of frescoes *Saints and hermits in rugged landscapes* in S. Cecilia and collaborated with the Italian Baglione in S. Giovanni in Lateran; in 1602 he covered a whole wall in the Sala Clementina of the Vatican with his *S. Clement* *cast into the sea*; and thereafter he provided landscapes for frescoes by various Italians. **Brill's** easel pictures of these years included a *Waterfall in Tivoli* of 1595 and two pictures reproduced here—the *Rocky landscape* (Pl. 473) of 1602 which shows a decorative alternation of dark and light areas in a panoramic landscape and the *Italian landscape with ruins* (Pl. 474) which may be the picture owned in 1604 by Hendrik van Os in Amsterdam and described by van Mander as 'een mooi stukje op koper met practige ruinen en figuurtjes dat overeenkomst vertoont met de Campo Vaccino, de oude markt van Rome'; and such works reveal him as an early exponent of the picturesque-classical landscape with Roman ruins and campagna vistas—a tradition which passed through Claude le Lorrain to **Adriaen Baudewyns** (Pl. 815) and **Jan Frans van Bloemen** (Pls. 818, 819) and to Richard Wilson in England.

New arrivals in Rome included **Jan (Velvet) Brueghel, Sebastiaan Vrancx, Wenzelas Coebergher, Abraham Janssens, Pietro de Lignis, Louis Finson (Finsonius), Aert Mytens, Bernaert van Somer, Hendrik van Balen, Jacob de Hase, David Teniers the elder, Jan Snellinck the younger, Willem van Nieulandt, Balthasar Lauwers, Marten Pepyn, Willem Backereel, Jacques Francart** and **Rubens.** Of these **Jan (Velvet) Brueghel** (Pls. 464, 465, 467, 470, 480-3, 521) was in Rome from Naples by 1593 when he was twenty-five and he stayed through 1594; he inscribed his name in the Adam and Eve chamber of the catacombs of S. Domitilla and became a protégé of Cardinal Federigo Borromeo for whom he painted a number of pictures; when the Cardinal became Archbishop of Milan he went with him to Milan as mentioned above; and he was back in Antwerp in 1596. **Sebastiaan Vrancx** (Pls. 531, 532, 534) reached Italy from Antwerp aged twenty-four in 1597; he seems to have worked some time in Rome and possibly in Parma where he may have met **Jan Sons** before returning to Antwerp at the end of 1600; and while in Italy he painted a *S. John preaching in the wilderness* and a *Battle of Centaurs and Lapiths.* **Wenzelas Coebergher** (Pl. 493) had reached Rome from Naples, as noted, by 1598; before 1600 he painted a *Martyrdom of S. Sebastian* commissioned by the Antwerp Crossbowmen for their altar in the Cathedral and sent it to Antwerp where it was damaged by a rival or a lunatic who cut out the heads of two women and he had to repair this passage (probably on a visit to Antwerp for the purpose) in 1601; in 1603 he completed a *Pentecost* for S. Maria in Vallicella (Chiesa Nuova) in Rome; and he was back in Antwerp in 1604. **Abraham Janssens** (Pl. 509) arrived in Rome at the age of twenty-three in 1598 and was back in Antwerp by 1601. **Pietro de Lignis** (Pl. 573) was in Rome by 1599; he decided to stay there; and he was made a member of the Accademia by 1607. The Brugeois **Louis Finson (Finsonius)** was a pupil of Caravaggio in Rome at the age of twenty in 1600; he seems to have been still in Rome in 1609; and at this time or later he became the owner of Caravaggio's *Virgin of the Rosaries* (which was for sale in Naples in 1607 as mentioned above). **Aert Mytens** when he returned to Rome from Naples viâ Aquila in 1600, brought with him his large night piece *Christ crowned with thorns* and finished it; and he died in 1602 at approximately sixty. **Bernaert van Somer** was in Rome from Antwerp by 1600 or earlier; in 1602 he married there the eldest daughter of **Aert Mytens;** and he had left for Amsterdam, taking with him his father-in-law's *Christ crowned with thorns*, by 1604. **Hendrik van Balen** (Pls. 507, 508) reached Rome probably in the later nineties before he was twenty-five and he was back in Antwerp (after, I suspect, a visit to Venice) by 1604 or earlier. **Jacob de Hase** (known in Italy as **Giacomo Fiammingo** and **di Assa**) was established in Rome by 1601 when he was twenty-six or younger; he was married to an Italian girl with **Paul Brill** as a witness in 1602; he painted religious pictures for churches and also battle pieces and he was made a member of the Accademia in 1604. **David Teniers the elder,** who may have been a pupil of **Rubens** in Antwerp in 1599, went to Rome about 1602 when he was twenty and worked there under the young German painter Adam Elsheimer (and perhaps again under **Rubens**) till he returned to Antwerp about 1605. **Jan Snellinck the younger** was a pupil of **Jacob de Hase** in 1603 when he was twenty-three, and was back in Antwerp by 1606. **Willem van Nieulandt** (Pl. 475) known in Italy as **Guglielmo Terranova,** reached Rome from Amsterdam at eighteen in 1602 and lodged with his uncle a painter of the same name; he worked for a year or more as a pupil of **Paul Brill** and went back not to Amsterdam but to Antwerp in 1604. **Balthasar Lauwers,** known in Italy as **Baldassare Lauri,** came from Antwerp about 1600 in his early twenties and worked first as pupil and then as assistant to **Paul Brill;** he married a French girl before 1603; and by 1604 he was commissioned by Don Francisco Pacheco to paint twelve pictures—*Hunting pieces* and *Landscapes with hermits* 'in the style of Tempesta'. **Marten Pepyn** (Pls. 569, 571, 572) is known to have been in Rome at the same time as **Rubens** and he was probably there between 1603 when he was twenty-eight and 1612 as he seems to have been absent from Antwerp in these years; his *Entombment* dated 1603 was therefore probably painted in Rome; and he must also, I think, have visited both Florence and Venice. The landscape painter **Willem Backereel** reached Rome after 1605 and remained there. **Jacques Francart** (whose sister was married to **Wenzelas Coebergher**) was both painter and architect; he is known to have been in Rome in 1607 and 1608 when he was about twenty-five and he was probably still there in 1609.

Rubens, as noted, had two periods in Rome—the first from the middle of 1601 till the middle of 1602 and the second from the beginning of 1606 till the end of 1608 (with one or more absences in Genoa). He is known to have frequented **Frans van den Kasteele** and to have been much impressed by the work of **Marten Pepyn;** he probably met all the established Flemish painters and those elected to the Accademia at this time; and his letters show him a friend and admirer of Adam Elsheimer. When he reached Rome in 1601 he was doubtless still under the spell of the great colouring in Venetian pictures—an enthusiasm which never left him; but he now joined this to an enthusiasm for the naturalism of Caravaggio and in 1607 he encouraged Duke Vincenzo to buy Caravaggio's intensely original picture *The Death of the Virgin* which had been painted for S. Maria della Scala in Trastavere and rejected by the church authorities as unseemly. On his first visit to Rome he copied pictures for the Duke and received permission from him to paint an altarpiece for the church of S. Croce in Gerusalemme (a commission sent him from Brussels by the Archduke Albert who had been connected as Cardinal with that church). On the second visit he painted a *Saints adoring a picture of the Virgin and Child* for S. Maria in Vallicella (Chiesa nuova) where **Wenzelas Coebergher's** *Pentecost* was already installed as noted; the subject of the composition was selected by the church authorities who instructed him to make a much-revered picture of the *Virgin and Child* already in the church the central feature of his work. In the event this altarpiece by **Rubens** was not installed there; **Rubens** stated in a letter to the Duke that he had withdrawn it after placing it in position because light-reflections made it virtually invisible; but it seems more probable that the church authorities were displeased with it possibly, I think, because he had inserted a half-length nude of himself as one of the saints; and **Rubens** in fact replaced the picture by a triptych on the same theme. In October 1608 learning that his mother was in extremis he left Rome hurriedly for Antwerp which he reached in December as related; his faithful assistant **Deodatus Delmont** went with him and the first version of the *Saints adoring a picture of the Virgin and Child* was sent after them to Antwerp.

Of the Flemish painters in Spain **Rodrigo Diriksen** was granted a retirement pension by Philip III in 1599, and he was probably still living in the Escorial (where his son **Felipe Diriksen** was born in 1594) when **Rubens** went there in 1603. **Lucas Franchoys the elder** is said to have worked for the Spanish Court when he went there from France about 1603; and he was back in Malines at thirty-one by 1605. **Justus Tiel,** of whom little is known, was a Court painter to Philip II and probably to Philip III; he provided a *Portrait of Pope Urban VII* and a *Portrait of Pope Clement VIII* for the Escorial in 1593; he also painted a *Panoramic landscape with hawks on trees* which was in Philip II's collection; and about 1594 he signed the picture reproduced here *Allegory of the Education of Philip III* (Pl. 461) where Time drives Cupid from the young Prince in armour and advances Justice who provides him with a sword. **Jan van der Hamen** from Brussels was settled in Madrid by 1596 (when his son, the Spanish still-life painter, Juan van der Hamen y Léon was born there); and he appears to have practised as an amateur flower painter in the later years of the period.

Rubens was just under twenty-six when he arrived at Alicante in April 1603. The gifts which he brought from the Duke for the King included a coach and seven horses, a number of special firearms, and a rock-crystal vase filled with perfume; for the Duke of Lerma he brought two gold vases and a silver vase filled with perfume and many paintings including sixteen copies of pictures by Raphael made by an Italian Pietro Facchetti; and he also brought various gifts for other persons. From Alicante he went to Valladolid and delivered the presents to Annibal Iberti the Duke's official representative in Spain. The journey, with the coach and horses and the numerous crates and cases, had been much more difficult and expensive than had been foreseen and **Rubens** had to restore a number of the pictures which had been damaged in transit by rain. After various delays the gifts were handed over to the King by Iberti in July; **Rubens** who was not presented, watched the ceremony from a nearby garden; but he was presented to the Duke of Lerma when the pictures and vases brought for him were delivered a few days later. He remained in Spain till the end of the autumn as Duke Vincenzo had instructed him to paint some portraits of Spanish Court ladies for his gallery of pretty women; he painted an *Equestrian portrait of the Duke of Lerma* in October in the sitter's country mansion at Ventosilla where the King was then staying; and he also painted a series of pictures *The Saviour and the Twelve Apostles* and two panels *Heraclitus weeping* and *Democritus laughing*. In these months he was able to study the splendid pictures in the Royal Palaces and the Escorial; he must also, I think, have visited Toledo; and he wrote in a letter 'The grand works by Titian, Raphael and others in the Royal Palace and the Escorial have astounded me as much by their number as their perfection whereas by modern painters there is nothing here of worth'—and this though Pantoja de la Cruz was still painting his delicate portraits and El Greco, who was now sixty-two, had produced *The Burial of the Conde Orgaz* in 1586 and more recently the *S. Martin sharing his cloak with the beggar* for Toledo S. José, and though **Rubens** himself was evidently influenced by El Greco as can be seen in the second version of the S. Maria in Vallicella picture and also in the *Equestrian portrait of the Duke of Lerma* (if the picture now presumed by some the original of this portrait is in fact that work). Duke Vincenzo desired him to proceed to Paris to paint there more pretty Court ladies for his gallery; but **Rubens** protested in a letter to his employer's secretary: 'Why should I waste time, journeys, expenses and salaries (which I should do in spite of His Highness's generosity) on works which I think ignoble and which any painter can execute to His Highness's satisfaction? . . . I implore him to make use of my services,

228

whether at home or abroad, on work more in keeping with my gifts', and as a result the project was abandoned and **Rubens** was allowed to return to Mantua without the Parisian détour.

At home in Belgium the artists continued to paint religious subjects, mythologies, portraits, landscapes, genre pieces, animals, still-life and flower pieces, though the teams in several categories were much weakened by the absence abroad of so many talents.

Paintings of religious subjects were ordered for churches all over the country; some commissions went to local artists; but the majority were executed by painters established in Brussels or Antwerp. **Raphael Coxie** moved from Antwerp to Brussels in 1594; he painted there the wings for an altarpiece in Antwerp Cathedral in 1601 when he was just over sixty and the contract specified a money payment and a handkerchief (presumably of lace) for his wife. **Jean Baptiste Saive** worked in Brussels in the nineties, painted there a *Crucifixion* for the Town Hall of his native Namur in 1597 and settled in Malines at sixty-three in 1603. **Wenzelas Coebergher** was back in Antwerp from Italy in 1604 and soon moved to Brussels to be near his Archducal patrons. In his imposing *Entombment* (Pl. 493) painted in 1605 for the altar of Our Lady of Sorrows in Brussels, S. Géry, the figure on the right adoring the crown of thorns continues a motif already seen here in **Pieter de Kempener's** *Descent from the Cross* (Pl. 367), the light falls downwards from a studio roof-window recalling Caravaggio's *Death of the Virgin* which **Coebergher** may have seen in Rome, and the setting anticipates some concepts of Rembrandt's teacher the Dutchman Jan Pynas and of Rembrandt himself. Descamps wrote of this work (in 1769): 'Le fond de cette composition est beau, les têtes n'en sont pas belles; une figure vêtue d'une draperie bleue à la gauche du tableau ressemble à un porte-manteau sans aucune forme distinguée'; but Sir Joshua Reynolds described it as 'equal to the best of Domenichino' and followed this judgement with: 'the fascinating power of **Rubens'** pencil has prevented this picture from possessing such reputation as it undoubtedly deserves: simplicity is no match against the splendour of **Rubens**, at least at first sight and few stay to consider longer. The best pictures of the Italian school, if they ornamented the churches of Antwerp would be overpowered by the splendour of **Rubens**; they certainly ought not to be overpowered by it; but it resembles eloquence which bears down everything before it and often triumphs over superior wisdom and learning'. In Brussels, also, **Hendrik de Clerck** was much employed for churches through this period when the careful balance of his Tridentine-Romanist style, seen here in his *Lineage of S. Anne* (Pl. 456) discussed in my last chapter, had not yet suffered the disturbing influence of **Rubens** (Pl. 587). **Gaspar de Crayer** (Pls. 598, 607, 609, 642) was **Raphael Coxie's** pupil at the turn of the century and became Brussels Master at twenty-five in 1607; **Geeraert Snellinck** (son of **Jan Snellinck**) was Brussels Master in 1603 and moved to Antwerp by 1608; and **Theodore van Loon** began his career in Brussels (after his probable first visit to Italy) at about twenty-four in 1609. In Bruges **Gillis Claeissins** died in 1607 at approximately sixty-two. **Antoine Claeissins** (Pls. 422, 492) painted a *Last Supper* for S. Gilles in 1593 and a triptych with a delicately mannerist *Descent from the Cross* for S. Sauveur at seventy-three in 1609. **Pieter Claeissins the younger** (Pl. 436) still official painter in the city and much employed by public bodies, made a contract in 1606 with the Notre Dame de l'arbre sec Fraternity to provide a triptych for S. Walpurge and received three canettes of French wine and a capon for his wife to seal the bargain; in 1608 he finished a *SS. Crispin and Crispinian* for the Shoemakers' altar in S. Sauveur, and for the Hospice de la Poterie an archaistic *Notre Dame de l'arbre sec* with God the Father and the Holy Ghost; and in 1609 he painted an *Ecce Homo* in a triptych for S. Sauveur. In Louvain

Josse van der Baren painted a triptych with *The Beheading of S. Dorothy* for S. Pierre in 1594 and a *Martyrdom of S. Sebastian* for the Louvain Archers Guild in 1597; he became a friend of Justus Lipsius in his last years and drew plates for his 'Lovanium' in 1604. In Malines **Michiel Coxie the younger,** Master in 1598, produced a triptych *The Temptation of S. Anthony* for Notre Dame in 1607; **Rombout van Avont** was also available; and **Lucas Franchoys the elder,** Master in 1599 was back from his travels in France and Spain by 1605. **Michel Joncquoy** back in his native Tournai from Antwerp by 1594 was given free lodging by the Tournai Magistrature in order to retain him there; and he remained a local figure till he died there over seventy-five in 1606. The Liégeois **Denis Pesser** painted a fresco *The Resurrection* in Liége S. Jacques in 1598. An example of sadism by **Antoine Ferrer,** a painter otherwise unknown and presumed a Fleming who worked at this period, is a triptych seen by Descamps in the Nieuport Parish church and described by him as showing in the centre *Hérodiade qui perce la langue de Saint Jean dont elle porte la tête* on one wing *S. Sebastien dont l'on perce le corps avec des flèches* and on the other wing *S. Sebastian mourant.*

In Antwerp the older painters of religious subjects included **Marten de Vos** (Pls. 364, 397, 429) who directed his atelier till he died at seventy-two in 1603; in 1593 he sent out a *Presentation in the Temple* and a *Raising of Lazarus*; in 1594 he provided S. Anthony's altar in Antwerp Cathedral with a *Temptation of S. Anthony* where the saint's faith is assaulted by Woman, Wealth, Music and Dancing and also by a monk with a pig's head and riders on giraffes and elephants that recall the inventions of **Hieronymus Bosch** (Pls. 163, 168, 171); in 1601 he provided S. André with a triptych *Render unto Caesar, S. Peter finding the tribute money* and *The widow's mite*; and in 1602 he painted a *S. Luke painting the Virgin* (later furnished with wings by **Marten Pepyn** and **Otto van Veen**) for the chapel of S. Luke's Guild in Antwerp Cathedral. **Gillis Mostaert** (Pl. 348) was evidently still practical joking at the expense of the Spaniards till he died at sixty-four in 1598; for in 1594, van Mander tells us, having painted a *Virgin and Child* for a Spanish patron who declined to pay him the full sum agreed, he decorated the Virgin with a frivolous headdress and gave the face a lewd expression (using some temporary medium); the Spaniard rushed off to denounce him as a blasphemer; **Mostaert** then removed the alterations and when the authorities arrived he obtained from them enforcement of the Spaniard's bargain. In 1597 at fifty-five **Frans Francken the elder** painted a *Road to Calvary* (*with S. Veronica*) and had perhaps the aid of a landscape specialist for the spreading landscape and the stormy sky; and in 1603 he provided a *Crucifixion* for S. André. In 1598 at fifty-four **Ambrosius Francken the elder** may have painted the *Miracle of the loaves and fishes* installed that year on the Millers' and Bakers' altar in Antwerp Cathedral. **Jan Snellinck** painted his *Crucifixion* (Pl. 460) in 1597. In this large picture, commissioned by one Octavian Michaelis for an unrecorded church, the figure of the Magdalene suggests acquaintance with works by Palma Vecchio and Titian, though I can find no record that he visited Venice; there is much parade of anatomy in the nudes, and the mourners are disposed in conventional Tridentine postures; the whole concept seems indeed to be theologically dictated; there is no personal imagination of the tragedy as human drama—as we see if we compare it with the concepts of earlier artists like the **New York Crucifixion and Last Judgement Painter** (Pls. 1-3, 160), the **Florence (Poggio) Imperiale Crucifixion Painter** (Pl. 133) or the **London Delft Painter** (Pls. 224, 226) and **Cornelis Engelbrechtsz** (Pl. 232). **Jan Snellinck** was also called on for other church commissions—a triptych with *The Resurrection* for Malines S. Rombout for example in 1601, a *Pentecost* for Malines S. Catherine in 1606 and, in 1608 when he was approximately sixty, an *Allegory of the Franciscan Order* for the Maestricht Franciscan Monastery and a triptych with the *Creation and Fall of Man* for a church in Audenarde. The next generation included **Cornelis Floris, Jan de Wael, Adam van Noort, Gerard Schoof** and **Otto van Veen.** Of these **Adam van Noort** was much in demand as a teacher; he had **Rubens** as a pupil as noted about 1594, he registered five new pupils in 1595, three more in 1598, eight more between 1602 and 1605; he had **Jacob Jordaens** (Pls. 545, 546, 588, 658, 660, 741, 774) aged fourteen as his pupil in 1607; and his pictures included a *S. John the Baptist preaching* in 1601. **Gerard Schoof** also continued his art school in these years. **Otto van Veen** (Pls. 455, 510, 511, 570)—some six years older than **Adam van Noort**—had **Rubens** as pupil and assistant in the later nineties as also noted; he worked in Antwerp through the period with occasional visits to Brussels in connection with his Court appointment; among other pictures for churches he produced a *Martyrdom of S. Andrew* for Antwerp S. André (described by Descamps as 'beau et bien coloré') before 1599 and an *Assumption of the Virgin* paid for by the Magistrates in 1602; in Antwerp he frequented Latinists and divines and served **Rubens** as example of the urbane gentleman-and-scholar type of artist as distinguished from **van Noort** who is said to have been ill-tempered and uncouth. In the next age-group **Abraham de Ryckere** died at thirty-three in 1599. **Pieter Brueghel the younger** painted his *Road to Calvary* (Pl. 380) already discussed as a crypto-anti-Spanish protest, when he was twenty-nine in 1603. **Jan (Velvet) Brueghel** painted *Christ delivering souls from Purgatory* in 1597; *The Adoration of the Magi* (Pl. 470) in 1598, *The Temptation of S. Anthony*, a night piece with spooks on the ground and flying in the air, in 1604, *Christ preaching in the ship* in 1606, and *The calling of Peter and Andrew* in a landscape with numerous figures and animals in 1608. His *Adoration of the Magi* reproduced here (Pl. 470) shows groups based on versions of the subject by **Hieronymus Bosch** (Pl. 157) and **Pieter Bruegel the elder** (Pl. 383); the shepherds have remained as in the pictures by the **New York Adoration in a White Castle Painter** (Pl. 151) and the **Philadelphia Adoration of the Magi Painter** (Pl. 162); in the distance on the left the Magi's couriers ask the way of peasants as in **Hugo of Antwerp's** picture (Pl. 81); and the middle distance on the right is filled with a crowd of orientals in turbans and exotic garments. Among the younger men **Juliaen Teniers the elder,** the eldest of the family, was Antwerp Master at twenty-two in 1594. **Abraham Janssens,** formerly **Jan Snellinck's** pupil, was back from Rome, Antwerp Master, a member of the Violiere Chamber of Rhetoric and of the Antwerp Romanists at twenty-six by 1601; by 1606 he was Dean of the Guild with an atelier and pupils; and by 1609 he received the commission for the Town Hall (Pl. 509) already referred to. **Hendrik van Balen** (Pls. 507, 508), the same age and a former pupil of **Adam van Noort,** was back from Rome by 1604 and also a member of the Antwerp Romanists; and **Marten Pepyn** (Pls. 569, 571, 572) also the same age was Antwerp Master at twenty-five in 1600, active there in 1601 and 1602 and probably in Rome, as suggested above, for the rest of the period. **Ferdinand van Apshoven** a former **van Noort** pupil, was Master at twenty in 1596 and began to take pupils soon after. **Frans Francken II** whose *Witches' Sabbath* (Pl. 496) of 1609 has been mentioned as a political picture, was Antwerp Master at twenty-four in 1605; in the following year he painted a *Crucifixion* and in 1608 a *Seven works of Mercy* with the *Feeding the Hungry* in the foreground and the other subjects behind. **David Teniers the elder** was back from Italy and working for Antwerp churches from 1606 when he was twenty-four and about to marry a rich wife; and a Malineois **Adam de Coster** was Antwerp Master at twenty-two in 1608. The adolescents included **Gerard Seghers** (Pl. 527) who was Antwerp Master at eighteen in 1609 after working with **Hendrik van Balen** and **Janssens;** and **Jacob Jordaens** who was sixteen that year and still a pupil of **Adam van Noort.**

Allegories, mythologies and 'history' pieces were painted by many of these artists; and I have already recorded the painters employed on the Pageant Entries of the Archduke Ernest and of the Archduke Albert and the Infanta. The *Mars and the Fine Arts overcoming ignorance* (Pl. 492) by **Antoine Claeissins**—mentioned above as a propaganda picture—is typical of the archaistic standards of impoverished Bruges; the hollow stomach and swelling thorax of the Mars continues the style of the male figures in the *Banquet of Ahasuerus* (Pl. 422) of 1574, and the lean elegance of the faded Fontainebleau beauties who symbolize the Arts and Sciences was doubtless admired by Brugeois dilettanti still hostile to the Romanist and Baroque standards of Antwerp and Brussels. My plates in this category show also a *Wooded landscape with Cephalus and Procris* painted in Brussels in 1608 by **Hendrik de Clerck** and **Denis van Alsloot,** and **Jan (Velvet) Brueghel's** *Latona mocked by the Lycian peasants* painted in Antwerp in 1601. In the *Wooded landscape with Cephalus and Procris* (Pl. 477) the landscape was painted by **Denis van Alsloot** (Pls. 513, 513A) and the charming foreground group a little too large in scale, was inserted, evidently later, by **Hendrik de Clerck** (Pls. 456, 471, 587) perhaps to please a dealer or customer with a taste for the fable which tells us that Procris unjustly jealous of her husband Cephalus spied upon him when he rested after hunting in a wood and Cephalus, who heard the rustle of her footsteps and suspected wild beasts, cast his javelin or shot an arrow at the bushes and thus killed her; and in this picture we see him vainly extracting the arrow from her breast. Two stages of Latona's story are illustrated in **Jan (Velvet) Brueghel's** *Latona mocked by the Lycian peasants* (Pl. 465); for Latona, with her children Apollo and Diana, seeking refuge in Lycia from Juno's anger, was insulted by the local peasants who stirred up the mud in a pool from which she was hoping to drink; and Jupiter then changed the peasants into frogs (one is shown thus changed behind the mud-stirring peasant in the centre of this picture). Others working in this field were **Otto van Veen** (Pls. 455, 510, 511, 570), **Hendrik van Balen** (Pls. 507, 508) and **Abraham Janssens** (Pl. 509). Of these **Otto van Veen** painted a *Triumph of Bacchus* in 1604 and perhaps at this time a picture acquired by the Emperor Rudolf—an *Allegory of the Temptations of Youth* where a semi-nude youth stretched upon the ground is protected by Minerva from Venus, Bacchus, a Faun and others attempting to lead him to excesses; **Hendrik van Balen** signed a *Judgement of Paris* in 1608; and **Abraham Janssens** began his *Allegory of Antwerp and the Scheldt* (Pl. 509) for Antwerp Town Hall in 1609. We must also recall here the allegoric paintings of the *Tower of Babel* and the conflagration allegories on contemporary conditions produced abroad by the Protestant Painters **Jan Vredeman de Vries, Frederick van Valkenborch, Pieter Schoubroeck** (Pl. 494) and probably the **Brussels Sodom and Gomorrah Painter** (Pl. 495); the *Diana and Actaeon* (Pl. 498) by **Joachim Uytewael** and the allegoric works by **Cornelis Ketel, Frans Badens, Karel van Mander** and **Jacques de Gheyn** all painted in Holland; **Roelandt Savery's** *Orpheus charming the animals* painted in Holland or Prague; and the works in these categories by **Bartholomaeus Spranger** (Pl. 458) in Prague, **Joos van Winghe** (Pl. 457) in Frankfort, **Pieter de Witte (Candido)** in Munich, **Ambroise Dubois** (Pl. 491) in Fontainebleau and **Justus Tiel** (Pl. 461) in Spain.

In portraiture the Archduke Ernest was painted, as mentioned, by **Otto van Veen;** and the Archduke Albert and Infanta Isabella were painted by **van Veen** and **Frans Pourbus the younger.** In Antwerp **van Veen** was available for other portraits through the period; **Abraham de Ryckere** was available till 1599 and **Marten de Vos** (Pl. 429) till 1603. **Paul van**

Somer (Pl. 538) may have had some commissions between 1596 and 1604 when he had already moved to Holland. **Abraham Janssens** drew or painted *Justus Lipsius* in Antwerp or Louvain between 1601 and 1606; and **Cornelis de Vos** (Pls. 599, 600) arrived on the scene in 1608. In Brussels commissions went to **Raphael Coxie** who produced a series of portraits —*Philip II, Anne of Austria, Isabelle de Valois* and the *Infanta Isabella* for the Elector Frederick William of Saxony in 1596; **Frans Pourbus the younger** (Pls. 539, 540) was there at the end of the nineties till he left for Mantua; and **Gaspar de Crayer**, later an admirable portrait painter (Pls. 598, 607, 642) may have had some commissions by 1607. **Jean Baptiste Saive** was available in Brussels and Malines, and **Lucas Franchoys the elder** in Malines by 1605. The veteran **Benjamin Sammeling**, seventy-three in 1593, was still living in Ghent in 1604; and **Antonio de Succa**, whose work as 'Genealogical Painter' to the Sovereigns took him to a number of places as copyist of old pictures, may also have painted some portraits from life. Among the Brugeois the aged **Antoine Claeissins** (Pls. 422, 492) painted *Bishop Charles-Philippe de Rodoan* as adorant donor kneeling before a prieu-dieu on the right-hand wing of his *Descent from the Cross* for S. Sauveur in 1609; **Gillis Claeissins** made a miniature portrait of the Infanta Isabella in 1607 the year of his death; and **Pieter Claeissins The Younger** (Pl. 436) painted *Twenty-two members of the Shoemakers Guild* as subscribing donors of an altarpiece in S. Sauveur in 1608 and *Jean van den Berghe (Montanus) Abbot of L'Eekhout* as donor of an *Ecce Homo* for S. Sauveur in 1609. The old custom of inserting portraits of relatives and friends in religious compositions was continued in some cases; there are evident portraits for example among the spectators on the left in **Jan (Velvet) Brueghel's** *Adoration of the Magi* (Pl. 470); but such particularization was doubtless not encouraged by Tridentine-Romanist standards and there are thus no heads which are evidently portraits in **Jan Snellinck's** *Crucifixion* (Pl. 460) or **Coebergher's** *Entombment* (Pl. 493).

In landscape the team at home was weakened by the absence of **Gillis van Coninxloo, Lucas van Valkenborch, Paul Brill** and others abroad. But it included for some of or all the period **Pieter Bom, Gillis Mostaert** and **Artus van Uden** in the older generation; **Kerstiaen de Keuninck, Tobias van Haecht, Josse de Momper, Pieter Brueghel the younger, Jan (Velvet) Brueghel, Abel Grimmer, François Borsse, Pieter van der Hulst, Denis van Alsloot, Pieter Stalpaert** and **Sebastiaan Vrancx** among the younger men; and as newcomers in the later years **Balthasar Lauwers, Willem van Nieulandt, Jan Snellinck the younger, Jacques Fouquier, Jan Wildens, Pieter de Witte the younger, Charles de Cauwer, Abraham Govaerts, Andreas Snellinck, Marten Ryckaert** and **Jan Tilens.** Of the older men **Pieter Bom** lived till 1607 when he died at seventy-seven; and **Gillis Mostaert** (Pl. 348), who may have painted in 1593 the *Moonlight landscape* and *Conflagration* acquired by Archduke Ernest, died, as noted, in 1598. **Artus van Uden**, forty-nine in 1593, was active through the period and probably still official painter to the city of Antwerp at the end. **Kerstiaen de Keuninck**, about the same age, may have painted his dramatic *Landscape with a shipwreck and saint* (Pl. 501), which is undated, before 1609. **Tobias van Haecht** (Pl. 377) thirty-two in 1593 and **Josse de Momper** (Pl. 500), twenty-nine that year, were both active as painters of mountainous landscapes who collaborated with a number of figure painters. **Pieter Brueghel the younger** is seen here in his *Road to Calvary* (Pl. 380) as a painter of trees recalling his master **Gillis van Coninxloo** (Pl. 466) and of plains studded with towns and villages recalling some works by his father (Pl. 368). **Jan (Velvet) Brueghel's** small delicately drawn and brightly coloured landscapes with unaffected genre figures were bought for high prices by dealers and collectors as well as by his official patrons the Archduke and the Infanta (and the taste for them persisted, with some fluctuations, till well into the eighteenth century when they were still being imitated by **Joseph van Bredael** (Pl. 840), **Theobald Michau** (Pl. 841) and others). Some aspects of his landscape talent can be seen in the pictures reproduced here. In the *Landscape with Tobias and hunting party* (Pl. 464) of 1598, the *Village Fair* (Pl. 467) of 1600 and the *Wooded landscape with Latona persecuted by the Lycian peasants* (Pl. 465) of 1601 the handsome decorative tree painting follows **Gillis van Coninxloo** under whom, as already suggested, he had probably worked in his youth; but in the *River landscape* (*The Ferry*) (Pl. 481) of 1603 and the *Village on river bank* (Pl. 480) of 1604 the landscape observation is quite personal; and the same applies to the rural vistas in *The road to the market* (Pl. 482) and the *Landscape with a covered waggon* (Pl. 483) both painted in 1603. **Abel Grimmer,** who was about twenty-three in 1593 and whose part in the charming *Landscape with cattle* (*The Fortune Teller*) (Pl. 447) was discussed in my last chapter, painted a *View of the country round Antwerp* about 1600 with country roads and trees and genre figures in the foreground and shipping on the river which recalls his father's *Outskirts of Antwerp* (Pl. 430) of 1598; and he also painted winter pieces including *The moat of the ramparts round the Porte S. Georges with people skating* dated 1602. **François Borsse,** about twenty-six in 1593, had **Balthasar Lauwers** as his pupil in Antwerp in the middle nineties; and **Pieter van der Hulst** had **Jan Wildens** (Pls. 628, 629) inscribed as his pupil in 1596 and **Pieter de Witte the younger** as pupil from round about 1602. **Denis van Alsloot** (Pls. 477, 513, 513A) a year or two younger than **Jan (Velvet) Brueghel,** must have met him about 1600 in Brussels when they were both Court Painters; and the evident influence of **Gillis van Coninxloo** in the splendid tree painting of his *Wooded landscape with Cephalus and Procris* (Pl. 477) was possibly due to that contact. **Pieter Stalpaert,** twenty-one in 1593, was at work in Brussels in the middle nineties till he left for Amsterdam; and **Sebastiaan Vrancx,** a year younger and later an attractive painter of trees and open spaces (Pls. 531, 532), was in Antwerp till he left for Italy about 1596 and again on his return in 1600 or 1601. Of the newcomers in the later years **Balthasar Lauwers,** pupil of **François Borsse,** as just mentioned, left for Rome about 1600; **Willem van Nieulandt** (Pl. 475) arrived in Antwerp from Italy at twenty in 1604; and **Jan Snellinck the younger** was back there from Rome at twenty-six in 1606. **Jacques Fouquier** (Pl. 563) still a child in 1593 was a pupil of some Antwerp landscape painter between 1600 and 1609; **Jan Wildens** (Pls. 628, 629) was Antwerp Master at eighteen or twenty in 1604; **Willem Backereel** was Antwerp Master at thirty-five in 1605 before his migration to Italy; and **Pieter de Witte the younger** was twenty-three and about to become Master in 1609. **Charles de Cauwer** was a pupil of **Juliaen Teniers The Elder** in 1601 and Antwerp Master in 1609. **Abraham Govaerts** (Pl. 478), possibly a pupil of **Jan (Velvet) Brueghel,** was Antwerp Master at eighteen in 1607. **Andreas Snellinck** was Antwerp Master at twenty-one in 1608. **Marten Ryckaert,** who seems to have been a pupil of **Tobias van Haecht,** probably about 1605, was twenty-two in 1609 but not yet Antwerp Master; and **Jan Tilens** (Pl. 499) was twenty in 1609 and also not yet Master.

The team of specialists in architectural interiors, town views, and trompe l'oeil perspectives was weakened by the absence abroad of **Jan Vredeman de Vries** (Pl. 462), **Paul Vredeman de Vries, Hendrik van Steenwyck the elder** (Pl. 488), **Hendrik van Steenwyck the younger** (Pl. 487) and **Karel van Mander** (Pl. 472). But a new generation was led in Antwerp by **Pieter Neeffs the elder** (Pls. 649, 650) who signed an *Interior of a Gothic church* in 1605 at approximately twenty-seven and became Master in 1609; it is sometimes assumed that this artist visited Frankfort at the end of the nineties to work under **Hendrik** van Steenwyck the elder, but this seems to me unlikely as he was evidently a Catholic and devoutly impressed by the Catholic ritual. For secular interiors Frans Francken II (Pl. 517) was available from 1605 when he became Antwerp Master at twenty-four; Henri Staben (Pl. 518) was perhaps back from Italy by 1609; and Abel Grimmer or an architectural collaborator may have painted some interiors like the one shown here in his *Christ in the house of Mary and Martha* (Pl. 535) which dates from the next period. Among the town views we have a Flemish city with two large churches and a castle on two sides of a river as a symbol for Bethlehem in Jan (Velvet) Brueghel's *Adoration of the Magi* (Pl. 470) of 1598; Abel Grimmer portrayed the Porte S. Georges in the Antwerp ramparts in 1602 and probably more buildings like the castle reflected in the water in the *Landscape with castle* (*The Fortune teller*) (Pl. 447); and I have already referred to the view of Bruges which Antoine Claeissins included in his *Mars with the Arts and Sciences overcoming Ignorance* (Pl. 492) thus continuing a tradition that goes back to the Philadelphia Adorant Painter (Pl. 104), the Detroit Mystic Marriage Painter (Pl. 110) and the Lucy Legend Master (Pl. 116).

The genre scenes included, as before, peasant and urban figures and groups of gentry in elegant clothes; and the old subject of the artist at work is also continued. Among the painters of peasant genre Pieter Balten died about seventy-three in 1598—the same year as Gillis Mostaert. Abel Grimmer symbolized the *Four Seasons* by peasant occupations, in the old Calendar tradition, using prints after drawings by Pieter Bruegel the elder and Hans Bol; Jean Baptiste Saive was the author of a *Four Seasons* and a *Market scene;* and the originality of Pieter Brueghel the younger in his variants of his father's pictures can be seen if the genre figures in his *Road to Calvary* (Pl. 380) be compared in detail with his father's concept of the subject (Pl. 379). Sebastiaan Vrancx on his return from Italy began to watch the frequenters of markets and horse fairs whom he painted later with much skill (Pls. 532, 534) and in these years he may have inserted figures in some landscapes by Tobias van Haecht (Pl. 377) and also perhaps in some by Jan (Velvet) Brueghel; and Denis van Alsloot must have been already a student of the crowds attending contemporary pageants and processions (Pls. 513, 513A). Social conversation pieces were painted by Jacob van der Lamen, Antwerp Master in 1605; and Frans Francken II, who will be seen in the next chapter as painter of a high-life social scene (Pl. 517), appears as a student of mixed genre in his *Seven Works of Mercy* of 1608. Mixed genre is also seen in the work of Jan (Velvet) Brueghel who was looked on as the outstanding composer of outdoor scenes then active in Flanders. In the *Landscape with Tobias and hunting party* (Pl. 464), painted when Brueghel was thirty, Tobias with the angel beside him draws the fish from the river in the foreground on the right, and the rest of the picture is peopled with gentry and peasants more or less connected with a stag hunt in the middle distance on the left; on the river bank behind Tobias a peasant casts his line for fish while others clean fish in a large round tub; further back three youths haul a rope to help the landing of a ferry boat; and across the river there are little figures in a wood which remind us that Jan (Velvet) Brueghel was among the ancestors of Watteau. No figures in this picture show the influence of Pieter Bruegel the elder; but in the *Village Fair* (Pl. 467) Jan (Velvet) Brueghel recalls his father's 'Merry Peasant' formula in the backviews of some dancing figures and there are groups of children which recall the *Children's games* (Pl. 369); in the middle distance of this *Village Fair* there is a group of elegant gentry and behind them a procession moves towards a church. Both the *Landscape with Tobias and hunting party* and the *Village Fair* were probably painted for the Archduke and the Infanta; and the same is doubtless true of a *Peasant dance before the Archduke and the Infanta* (not reproduced here) where the

Sovereigns watch village girls performing a serpentine dance in a meadow. In all these pieces and in the simpler rural scenes—the *River landscape* (*The Ferry*) (Pl. 481), the *Road to the market* (Pl. 482) and the *Landscape with covered waggon* (Pl. 483)—the figures are perfectly in scale within the charming landscapes; and in the rural scenes the peasants go about their business quite quietly without affected gestures—they cross the river to a village or take their produce to the town, and a farmer and his family driving across open country give their names and addresses without protest when stopped and interrogated by excise officials. There are genre features also in **Jan (Velvet) Brueghel's** *Adoration of the Magi* (Pl. 470) where one of the shepherds holds a bagpipe and peasants and burghers dispute and ask questions round the mounted soldiers in the middle distance. It is known that **Brueghel** employed collaborators for some figures in his genre pictures; and as some of the gentry in the *Landscape with Tobias and hunting party* are very like the figures in **Grimmer's** *Landscape with castle* (*The fortune teller*) (Pl. 447) it seems to me possible that **Abel Grimmer** had a hand in them; and **Denis van Alsloot** (Pls. 513, 513A) was perhaps responsible for the little girls in ruffles in the *Village Fair* and for the figures in the *Landscape with covered waggon* (Pl. 483). The theme of the artist at work, brought up to date in Frankfort (or Prague) by **Joos van Winghe** in his *Apelles painting Campaspe* (Pl. 457) already discussed, is also found in the *S. Luke painting the Virgin* (not reproduced here) which **Marten de Vos** painted in 1602; the artist here is seated in an armchair before his easel, his left hand holds a stock of brushes and his maulstick, and his right the brush in service; like Apelles in **Joos van Winghe's** picture, he is painting from life; the sitter's palace invented by earlier painters like the **Boston S. Luke Painter** (Pl. 48), **Jan Gossaert** (Pl. 238) and the **Fogg S. Luke Painter** (Pl. 260) has become his own palatial studio with stairs and doorways to further chambers and marble pillars and niches prepared for statues; a globe and an open book upon a table covered with a near-Eastern rug show the scholarly nature of his mind; his studio assistant grinds colours behind him in the old tradition, and, as a modern development, a maidservant awaits his summons from a first floor landing at the top of the stairs.

Military genre pieces, including battle pictures, which were to be much in demand in the seventeenth and eighteenth centuries, were now produced both as easel pictures and as designs for tapestry. This type of genre, like the others, can be traced from the outset of our story. For mounted warriors ride in procession in the **van Eycks'** *Altarpiece of the Mystic Lamb* (Pl. 9), they gallop on their chargers in the picture by the **New York Crucifixion and Last Judgement Painter** (Pls. 1, 5), they face one another in opposing groups in **Hieronymus Bosch's** *Adoration of the Magi* (Pl. 157), they gallop again across country in the picture by the **Detroit Crucifixion Painter** (Pl. 285), and later they assault a fortress in the background of a portrait group by the **Brussels Micault Triptych Painter** (Pl. 321). **Jan Cornelisz Vermeyen** who accompanied Charles V on his expedition to Tunis made tapestry designs of the sieges and battles, and **Pieter Bruegel the elder** portrayed the Walloon 'Redcoats' in his *Road to Calvary* (Pls. 379, 381) and Alva's lancers in his battle piece *The Suicide of Saul* (Pl. 378) and in his picture showing Alva's army climbing the mountains on the way from Italy to Flanders (Pl. 378A). In this period the Malineois **Jan Ghuens** painted as a bird's eye panorama *The relief of Lierre by Malines troops in 1595*; **Sebastiaan Vrancx** —seen here in a later military piece (Pl. 531)—painted *Leckerbetken's fight with Breauté at Bois-le-Duc on Jan. 5 1600* in 1601; and I suspect him as collaborator in the battle piece with countless figures called *Alexander the Great's victory at Arbela* monogrammed by **Jan (Velvet) Brueghel** probably about 1602; and **Pieter Brueghel the younger** put Alva's lancers in his *Road to Calvary* (Pl. 380) in 1603. We must recall too in this connection the Archduke Albert's commissions to **Otto van Veen** and **Jan Snellinck** to depict his battles as designs for tapestry in 1596, the *Defeat of King Sennacherib* painted by **Gillis van Valkenborch** in Frankfort in 1597, the picture called the *Battle between Hannibal and Scipio* (with a number of elephants) which **Karel van Mander** produced in Haarlem in 1602 and a *Battle of the Amazons* painted by **Pieter Schoubroeck** in Frankenthal in 1603.

In animal painting we have horses in the military pieces, the Crucifixions and Adorations; and the ox and the ass are of course in the Nativities. There are numerous animals and birds in many pictures of this period by **Jan (Velvet) Brueghel;** thus in his *Adoration of the Magi* (Pl. 470) a large mastiff-type dog stands in the foreground on the left and a piebald greyhound in the foreground on the right, a cat looks out from the stable window and farmyard fowl peck at the thatch on the dilapidated roof; in his *Landscape with Tobias and hunting party* (Pl. 464) we have a herd of swine and a donkey in the left foreground, horses and hounds among the hunting party, the same large mastiff and piebald greyhound, a half a dozen more miscellaneous dogs, and birds in the air and on the verdure; several of the same dogs and a number of pigs appear in the foreground of his *Village Fair* (Pl. 467); a rough-haired terrier leaps barking behind the rustics in his *Latona mocked by the Lycian peasants* (Pl. 466); and we have draught horses in his *Road to the market* (Pl. 482) and *Landscape with a covered waggon* (Pl. 483). An owl is perched above the foreground group in the *Cephalus and Procris* (Pl. 477) by **Denis van Alsloot** and **Hendrik de Clerck,** and other birds and waterfowl inhabit the trees and pools. **Frans Snyders** later a specialist in this field (Pls. 630, 632, 634, 635) was established as Antwerp Master at twenty-three in 1602; before that he had worked first as a pupil of **Pieter Brueghel the younger** and then as pupil or assistant of **Hendrik van Balen. Snyders** himself, before 1609, had a pupil called **Jan Roos** who later painted animals and was associated with **Van Dyck;** and **Sebastiaan Vrancx** probably painted animals in some works of this period as in his later pictures (Pls. 531, 532). The production in this category, as in others, was nevertheless weakened by the absence of some able practitioners abroad—as can be seen if we look at the animals and birds in pictures reproduced here by **Joachim Uytewael** (Pls. 490, 498), **Jacques de Gheyn** (Pl. 484), **Karel van Mander** (Pl. 472), **Jan Vredeman de Vries** (Pl. 462), **Paul Brill** (Pls. 473, 474) and **Roelandt Savery** (Pl. 583).

In still-life, fruit and flower painting I have drawn attention to the intriguing *Still-life with food and kitchen utensils* (Pl. 503) apparently painted by **Hieronymus Francken the elder** in Paris, and also to the flowerpieces produced in Holland by **Ambrosius Bosschaert, Jacques de Gheyn** and **Roelandt Savery.** In Antwerp **Jan (Velvet) Brueghel** was painting flowerpieces probably in the later nineties and certainly by 1606 when he was making studies in the Archducal gardens and wrote from Antwerp to his patron Cardinal Federigo Borromeo in Milan: 'I have commenced a bouquet of flowers for your eminence. It should be beautiful for its truth to nature and on account of the unusual beauty of the flowers, many of which are unknown or seldom seen here; I have indeed been to Brussels to copy some blooms which are not to be found in Antwerp. . . . There will be more than a hundred life-size flowers in the picture including ordinary ones like lilies, roses, violets and carnations and others quite rare or never seen before in this country.' I reproduce his astonishing *Bouquet of flowers* (Pl. 521) possibly the picture referred to in this letter; here a multitude of blooms, each separately and exquisitely portrayed, is combined to a decorative whole impossibly lofty for the tub which contains it; and **Brueghel** like the Flemish painters of the time in Holland—and **Petrus Christus** at the outset of our story (Pl. 31)—has perched a dragonfly on the side of the tub as a final touch in virtuosity. Among others working in this field in Antwerp **Pieter van der Borcht the elder** died at sixty-three in 1607, **Jacob Hoefnagel** may have made some drawings of plants and so forth before leaving for Prague in 1602 and **Juliaen Teniers the elder** may have painted flowerpieces from 1594. **Osias Beet (or Beert) the elder** (Pl. 506) began his career as a still-life painter when he became Antwerp Master in 1602; **Jacob van Hulsdonck**, who painted mainly fruit in baskets (Pl. 556), was Antwerp Master at twenty-seven in 1609; **Frans Snyders** who was later to paint swags of fruit and flowers (Pl. 554) and miscellaneous still-life (Pls. 555, 655-7) may have painted flowers and fruit while a pupil of **Hendrik van Balen** (Pls. 507, 508), and he was certainly in touch with **Jan (Velvet) Brueghel** by 1608. **Clara Peeters** (Pls. 504, 522, 523), domiciled in Holland in the next period, was born in Antwerp about 1589; she was signing still-life pieces by 1608, but whether she was then in Antwerp or had already migrated is not known.

It was into this mass of varied, interesting and in many ways able production that **Rubens** irrupted in 1609. Visitors to his studio saw his *Saints adoring a picture of the Virgin and Child* (with the half-length nude of himself) withdrawn from S. Maria in Vallicella, and the beginning of a large composition the *Adoration of the Magi* for the Antwerp Town Hall. By the end of the year they probably saw there the completed *Peter Paul Rubens and Isabella Brant, his wife* (Pls. 512, 516); this life-size, arresting, immensely competent and intolerably smug and flattering double portrait was infallibly a 'winner'; but the special verve and rhythm that **Rubens** was to bring to painting is not to be found in it, as Sir Joshua Reynolds observed when he saw it in Düsseldorf in 1781 and noted in his diary: 'Rubens and his wife, when he was a young man, for his portrait here appears not above two or three and twenty: his wife is very handsome and has an agreeable countenance: she is much the best part of the picture which is rather in a hard manner. The linen is grey: he was at this period afraid of white.' Reynolds shows here his habitual care and justice when assessing works by **Rubens;** but he did not know, or had forgotten, that grey linen had been made fashionable as the 'couleur Isabelle' at the time of the Ostend siege; and it was typical of **Rubens** on arrival at the Infanta's court to do everything possible to please her.

CHAPTER XI

Archduke Albert and Infanta Isabella to the death of the Archduke and the end of the Twelve Years Truce

1610-1621

THE ARCHDUKE ALBERT and the Infanta Isabella continued the pattern of their joint régime in the period of the Twelve Years Truce. As became sovereign rulers they maintained a sumptuous, dignified court in Brussels where the Spanish language and Spanish modes in dress for men and women were de rigueur. They had several palaces with parks and gardens and the aviaries and menagerie referred to in my last chapter; they organized Court masques and balls recorded by **Frans Francken** (Pl. 517) and other painters; and they took part in outdoor fêtes and processions painted by **Denis van Alsloot** (Pls. 513, 513A) and **Antoine Sallaert** (Pl. 514). As there was no drain for war expenditure the trade of the country to some extent recovered. The Archduke and the Infanta favoured the luxury industries such as silk spinning and tapestry, and they also favoured some new crafts—gold leather on the Cordovan model (later in the century **Erasmus Quellinus** (Pls. 639, 671) and **Jan Baptist Borkens** had apartments hung with such leather) and glass in the Venetian style (early pieces, perhaps, are shown in the *Still-life with oysters* by **Osias Beet the elder** (Pl. 506)). To combat usury they encouraged the foundation of State Pawn Shops, with money provided by religious bodies, and they made **Wenzelas Coebergher** (Pl. 493) the first Director General of these establishments. But, as before, their chief and most passionate concern was the furtherance of the religious revival. Guided by the Jesuits they encouraged the creation of new Jesuit colleges whence educational writings of all kinds were disseminated; they also encouraged other religious orders and the founding of new monasteries and convents and the building of many new churches in the so-called 'Jesuit' style. A sharp watch was kept on all expressions of free thought; new statutes were established for the University of Louvain to ensure strict orthodoxy in the curriculum; and Jean Baptiste van Helmont, denounced as a heretic for his 'De magnetica vulnerum curatione' (observations on animal magnetism held by the Jesuits to derogate from certain miracles) found it wise to retract before the Episcopal court in Malines. But in 1616 Cornelius Jansen (Jansenius), aged thirty-one, became director of the Theological college of S. Pulcheria in Louvain and began his struggle against the Jesuits which created Jansenism; and Antoine Arnauld the elder died in Paris in 1619 when his son Antoine Arnauld, later a leading Jansenist, was seven years old. Witch-hunting continued; and a new edict against witches and sorcerers

239

issued in 1612, exempted only girls and boys below the age of puberty from the death penalty for such connivance with the Devil.

In 1610 the Archduke Albert was fifty-one and the Infanta was forty-four; Philip III was thirty-two and the Duke of Lerma fifty-eight; Henri IV was fifty-seven and Marie de Médicis thirty-seven; James I was forty-three and Prince Charles ten; Prince Maurice of Nassau was forty-three, Prince Frederick Henry twenty-six and Olden Barneveldt sixty-three; the Emperor Rudolf was fifty-eight, the Archduke Mathias fifty-three and Ferdinand of Styria thirty-two; Paul V was Pope and Ahmed I was Sultan. In this year Henri IV made preparations for a war against the Emperor and Spain and was murdered by a Catholic fanatic; Louis XIII, aged nine, succeeded with Marie de Médicis as Regent; and Philip III's Edict expelling the Moors from Spain was put into effect. In 1611 the Archduke Mathias became King of Bohemia; and Papal officials in the gardens of the Quirinal examined the stars through Galileo's telescope. In 1612 the Emperor Rudolf died; the Archduke Mathias succeeded; and the city of Antwerp gave the *Adoration of the Magi* by **Rubens** from the Antwerp Town Hall to the King of Spain's envoy Roderigo Calderon, Count of Oliva, who was high in the favour of Lerma. In 1613 James I's daughter Elizabeth married Frederick V, Elector Palatine, leader of the German Calvinists; Concino Concini, Marquis d'Ancre, became Marshal of France and Premier Ministre; and the Romanov dynasty began in Russia with Michael Romanov. In 1616 Sir Walter Raleigh, released from his detention in the Tower, was sent by James I to find gold in Orinoco and given strict instructions to make no attacks on Spaniards; Concini made Richelieu Secretary of State for War; and Galileo, admonished by the Pope after the Inquisition had condemned his theories, undertook to refrain from publicly repeating them. In 1617 George Villiers aged twenty-five became Duke of Buckingham; Louis XIII came of age; Concini was murdered, his wife Leonora Galigai was burnt as a sorceress, the Duc de Luynes, Dresseur d'oiseaux de chasse to the King became Premier Ministre, Marie de Médicis retired to Blois, and Richelieu went with her. In 1618 Sir Francis Bacon became Lord Chancellor; Sir Walter Raleigh was executed for permitting the destruction of a Spanish settlement at San Tomas; Prince Maurice and the Calvinists procured the arrest of Olden Barneveldt; the Duke of Lerma was driven from power and became a Cardinal; and the Thirty Years War began when Bohemian Protestants, revolting against oppressive measures by King Mathias, threw two of his ministers from a window of the Hzadshin fortress-palace. In 1619 the Manneken-Pis statue was made by the sculptor Jerome Duquesnoy the elder for the city of Brussels. Marie de Médicis was reconciled with Louis XIII; the Duke of Buckingham became Lord High Admiral; Olden Barneveldt at seventy-two was beheaded in The Hague; the Emperor Mathias died; Ferdinand of Styria, persecutor of Protestants, became Emperor as Ferdinand II; and the Bohemian Protestants, rejecting him as King, chose James I's son-in-law Frederick Elector Palatine to replace him. In 1620 the Pilgrim Fathers sailed from Delftshaven to England and from Plymouth in the *Mayflower* to Plymouth, Massachusetts; a Spanish army under Spinola invaded the Palatinate where English volunteers were established in some fortresses; and the Elector Frederick (known in England as the Palsgrave) fled from Bohemia after his defeat on the White Hill by Maximilian of Bavaria and Count Tilly. In 1621 Lord Chancellor Bacon was tried and condemned for corruption; the Duc de Luynes died after failing to suppress a Huguenot revolt; Lerma's former protégé the Count of Oliva was beheaded; Philip III died and Philip IV succeeded at sixteen; Pope Paul V died; the Twelve Years Truce ended; and the Archduke Albert died.

As before there were Flemish-born artists at work in France, England, Holland, Central Europe and Italy.

In France **Ambroise Dubois** (Pl. 491) was still probably Director of Painting in Fontaine-bleau Château when he died there at about seventy in 1614; and **Jan de Hoey** still Keeper of the King's pictures died there also aged seventy in 1615. In Paris **Hieronymus Francken the elder** (Pl. 503), still Court Painter, died at seventy in 1610. **Frans Pourbus**, established as Court Painter to Henri IV and Marie de Médicis and, after 1610, to Louis XIII, was now a naturalized Frenchman and occupied one of the studios in the Louvre which Henri IV had installed for the Court Painters; he produced ceremonial state portraits *Marie de Médicis* and *Henri IV* in 1610 and took **Justus Sutterman**, aged twenty, as his pupil in 1617. In a less ceremonial portrait, the *Marie de Médicis* reproduced here (Pl. 539), **Frans Pourbus** shows the Queen Mother at forty-four holding a lace kerchief in her left hand as had now become the fashion, and the fat lady looks fat in spite of the raised little finger of her right hand—though the gesture seems graceful and delicate in the same artist's *Isabella of Bourbon, Queen of Philip IV* (Pl. 540) where the daughter of Marie de Médicis is exquisitely portrayed about eighteen or younger with a favourite lap dog. Familiar with Italian High Renaissance portraiture, **Pourbus** placed Marie de Médicis on a palace terrace, and Isabella of Bourbon stands in a small room with outlook onto open country through the window; and students of the development of style in portraiture will compare this beautifully patterned portrait of Isabella of Bourbon with the picture of her riding one of her favourite white horses which Velazquez began about ten years later. The portraitist **Ferdinand Elle** now became Court Painter to Louis XIII and had Nicolas Poussin aged about nineteen as his pupil about 1612. **Rudolf Schoof** (son of **Gerard Schoof**) was Court Painter to Louis XIII about 1612 and had **Adriaen de Bie** from Lierre as his pupil from 1612 till 1614. **Willem van Haecht**, known later as a painter of interiors with collections of pictures, was in Paris at twenty-two in 1615. **Jacques Fouquier** (Pl. 563) arrived in Paris at about thirty-six in 1621 and his pupil **Philippe de Champaigne** (Pls. 742, 750) came in the same year aged nineteen. The Bruges-born **Louis Finson (Finsonius)** was in Aix-en-Provence from Rome at about thirty in 1610 and painted a *Resurrection* for S. Jean; he was there again in 1613 when he painted an *Incredulity of S. Thomas* for the Cathedral and a *Self-portrait with bare chest and feathered cap*; in 1614 he produced an *Adoration of the Magi* for Arles, S. Tro-phine; in the following years he made portraits of Aix magistrates and was friendly with the antiquarian Claude Fabri de Peiresc (who lived there and was also a friend and correspondent of **Rubens**); and after 1616 he left for Amsterdam.

In England **Marcus Geeraerts the younger** was continuously Court Painter and prob-ably much employed on the full length portraits with elaborate clothes (doubtless painted by assistants) which were still in demand here; he is known to have painted as full length portraits *James I*, *Anne of Denmark*, the *Duke of York* and *Princess Elizabeth* at this time; in 1619 he was mentioned in a list of tradesmen and artificers present at the Queen's funeral; and at sixty in 1621 he painted *Sir Henry Savile*. **Paul van Somer** came to England at the end of 1616 and died here at forty-five in 1621; he became Court Painter soon after his arrival and painted *James I*, *Anne of Denmark*, *Prince Charles*, *The Earl of Pembroke* and *Lord Windsor* and worked for the Earls of Dorset and Rutland; and in 1619 he is named as a 'picture maker' who received black material for the Queen's funeral which suggests that he had a hand in constructing a catafalque. I reproduce **van Somer's** *Queen Anne of Denmark, with horse, negro groom, and dogs* (Pl. 538), a handsome composition (possibly in **Van Dyck's** mind when he painted the famous *Charles I with horse, equerry and groom* (Pl.

644)); the palace in the distance is believed to be Oatlands; the dogs are Italian greyhounds and the Queen's initials are on their collars; a ribbon floating in the sky is inscribed 'La mia grandezza dal eccelso'. One **Abraham van Blyenbergh** seems to have come from Antwerp to England for a short time about 1618; he painted *James I* and *Prince Charles* and was back in Antwerp in 1622. The Antwerp born marine painter **Adam Willaerts** (Pl. 688) was probably here on a visit from Holland at thirty-six in 1613 when he painted *The Elector Palatine leaving England with his bride the Princess Elizabeth of England on the 'Prince Royal', the largest ship of her time, with the 'Disdain', a miniature ship built for Prince Henry, in attendance.* **Hendrick van Steenwyck the younger** (Pls. 487, 489, 536, 537) reached London, where he settled, in 1617; and my plates show two pictures he produced here in these years. His night piece *The liberation of S. Peter* (Pl. 489) recalls his father's *Night scene in a crypt* (Pl. 488) referred to in an earlier chapter as a Protestant propaganda picture. In his *Christ in the house of Mary and Martha* (Pl. 537), where the figures are probably by a collaborator, the kitchen scene is not the subject of the foreground—as in the picture of 1565 by **Joachim Beuckelaer** (Pl. 399)—but is glimpsed through the central doorway of a foreground chamber where Christ is shown with the contrasted sisters; and this foreground chamber is a whole-cube complete interior of a type not seen in my plates since **Dirk Bouts** (or his architectural assistant) constructed the dining-chamber for his *Last Supper* (Pl. 58) between 1464 and 1467. **Van Dyck** came here from Antwerp at the invitation of the Earl of Arundel at twenty-one in the autumn of 1620; he became a Court Painter and was granted a yearly salary in November; and he probably painted some portraits before February 1621 when he was paid £100 by the King for an unknown 'special service' and given eight months' leave of absence which he used, in the first place, to return to Antwerp.

In Holland there were still some Dutch-born painters who have figured in my story and also the emigrants or sons of emigrants from Belgium. Of the Flemish-Dutch painters **Herman van der Mast** (Pl. 453) died in Delft about sixty in 1610 and **Cornelis Ketel** (Pl. 451) died in Amsterdam at sixty-eight in 1616 leaving by will a *Self-portrait* painted 'by fingers, thumb and foot' to his wife. **Joachim Uytewael** was in Utrecht as painter (and possibly still as flax merchant); in 1611 he became a member of the newly founded Painters and Sculptors Guild distinct from the Saddlers Guild to which Utrecht artists had formerly belonged; in 1614 his name appears as 'inventor' on an *Adam and Eve* (Pl. 524) where the large figures, rhythmically joined by a chain of arms and set in an Eden verdured in the **Gillis van Coninxloo** tradition (Pls. 466, 476), are surrounded by cattle, rams, goats, stags and dogs more static in treatment than the animals in his earlier pictures (Pls. 490, 498); in 1618 he signed a *S. John preaching in the wilderness* where the congregation includes some horsemen in plumed hats and there are mannerist backviews of figures in the foreground; and he signed a *Suffer little children . . .* at fifty-five in 1621. **Pieter Cornelisz van Ryck,** probably in Haarlem through the period, signed a *Kitchen piece with venison, poultry, fish, vegetables and a man jesting with a woman in the background* in 1621. The marine painter **Jan Porcellis** may have been in Rotterdam till about 1615 when he was working in Antwerp.

Among the Flemish painters in Amsterdam **Joos Goeimare** died at thirty-five in 1610, **Frans (Francesco) Badens** died there in high repute at forty-seven in 1618, and **Dirck Hendricksz (Errico Fiammingo)** was in Amsterdam (from Naples) in these years and died there, approaching seventy, in 1618. **Louis Finson (Finsonius)** who had come from Provence by 1617 made his will in Amsterdam that year leaving his part ownership of Caravaggio's *Virgin of the Rosaries* to a German-Dutch painter A. Vinck; and he probably died there, still under forty, soon after. **Bernaert van Somer,** who owned the night piece *Christ crowned with thorns* by **Aert Mytens,** as related, was there as painter and dealer; and his brother **Paul van Somer** (Pl. 538) was there till 1612. **Aert Pietersz,** whose *Anatomy lesson of Dr. Egbertsz* (Pl. 485) was discussed in my last chapter died there at sixty-two in 1612. **Cornelis van der Voort,** continuing the old Flemish-Dutch tradition of the subscription portrait group, was employed by the Arquebusiers to paint *Fifteen members of Captain Witsen's Company* with their standards and so on, a year or two before Frans Hals began to receive such commissions in 1616; and in 1618, when he was forty-two, he followed this with *The Guardians of the Old Men's and Women's Almshouse*—five bearded and hatted burghers round a table with the hatless secretary behind them (a direct antecedent of Rembrandt's *Syndics of the Cloth Hall* of 1662). The architectural and perspective painter **Paul Vredeman de Vries** and the landscape painter **Pieter Stalpaert** seem both to have worked there through the period. The gifted still-life painter **Clara Peeters** was established in Amsterdam by 1611 and in that year, when she was little over twenty, she signed the *Still-life with fish and artichokes* (Pl. 504), the *Still-life with flowers, dried fruits and cakes* (Pl. 522) and a *Still-life with dead birds and a pyramid of dishes on a larder table*. Her *Still-life with fish and shells* (Pl. 523) and some other extant undated pieces may have been painted about the same time or later; she is documented in The Hague in 1617; and as nothing seems known of her thereafter, she may have married and given up painting before 1621. Her jug with flowers in the *Still-life with flowers, dried fruits and cakes* (Pl. 522) is a graceful arrangement of individual blossoms more opulently decorative than the vase with flowers which an earlier specialist probably contributed to the *Flora* (Pl. 363) by **Jan Massys** in 1561; a long thin leaf curving outwards from the iris in this picture makes an arch with the ewer on the right; and in the same way the eels enlarge and add rhythm to the form of the perch in the *Still-life with fish and shells* (Pl. 523); but in general the remarkably varied objects depicted by **Clara Peeters**—the glasses and vessels of metal and faience, the candlesticks and baskets, the fruit and cakes, the table birds, the soft and crustacean fishes and the East Indian seashells—are painted individually with little or no interest in their formal relations one to another, and the artist is content to display her skill in illusionist imitation of the shape, tints and texture of each object in the oldest of Flemish traditions. In Amsterdam also the versatile **Adriaen van Nieulandt** (Pls. 515, 647) signed in 1616 at twenty-nine a *Kitchen piece with swan, venison, lobster and figures* which continues the tradition of **Pieter Aertsen** (Pl. 356) and **Joachim Beuckelaer** (Pls. 398, 399) as there are serving women in the foreground among the still-life and a little scene with Dives and Lazarus behind. **David Vinckeboons,** another versatile artist, continued the Flemish 'Merry Peasant' tradition of **Pieter Bruegel the elder** (Pl. 407), **Jacob Grimmer** (Pl. 430) and emigrants like **Lucas van Valkenborch** (Pl. 445). In the *Village Fair* (Pl. 533), which **Vinckeboons** painted at thirty-four in 1610, some gentry look on while peasants and children dance and frolic and a family sits round a table at a meal between two taverns in the foreground; further back there are actors skylarking before their booth to attract attention (the 'Parade' motif common in later fair scenes); pictures and musical instruments are displayed for sale in one of the booths; in the left-hand distance there is boating on the river; and a large building, probably a town hall, dominates the landscape setting where the trees are verdured in formulae taken from **Gillis van Coninxloo** (Pl. 466). Other works signed by **Vinckeboons** in this period include *Christ carrying the Cross* where the procession with numerous small figures moves from right to left across the landscape (instead of the usual movement to the right) and a *S. John* *preaching in the wilderness,* dated 1621, which invites comparison with **Uytewael's** 1618 version of the subject; he also signed or monogrammed at this time some rustic pieces with a few large genre figures in the foreground, and in 1612 he monogrammed a composition with large foreground figures *The wife of Herakles abducted by the centaur Nessos.* **Vinckeboons** would seem to have had collaborators as the figures in his pictures exhibit varieties in style; and some collaborator may also have supplied the architecture in his *Village Fair* (Pl. 533) as the towers of Antwerp appear there in the background—though **Vinckeboons** may, of course, have visited Antwerp (the frontiers being open) in the year that it was painted. **Roelandt Savery** (Pls. 525, 564, 583, 585, 586) was in Amsterdam, after nine years absence in Austria, at about thirty-seven in 1613; he went back to Vienna in 1614 and left again for Amsterdam in 1616; in Amsterdam he painted some flowerpieces, an *Orpheus charming the animals* in 1617, and a *Round tower in a wood with pool and birds* in 1618; he then moved to Utrecht where he settled; in Utrecht he painted a *Birds in a forest* in 1619, *Noah and the animals round the Ark, Stag and boar hunt in a rocky landscape* and *Vase of flowers in a niche with grasshopper and lizard* in 1620, and another *Landscape with staghunt* in 1621; in the *Noah and the animals round the ark* there is a marked use of light and dark contrast in the composition as the main mass of animals is in a darkened foreground and Noah praying on his knees by the Ark is in full light in the middle distance; the same contrast of dark and light occurs in his *Stag and boar hunt in a rocky landscape* (Pl. 564) where the light is concentrated on a castle in the rocky background; and in *Flowers in a niche with grasshopper and lizard* the light is focussed on two large flowers at the base of the bouquet and the whole interior of the niche is dark. In Utrecht **Savery** found **Joachim Uytewael** (Pls. 490, 498, 524) as mentioned, the marine painter **Adam Willaerts** then forty-two and the flower painter and dealer **Ambrosius Bosschaert** then forty-six. **Adam Willaerts** (Pl. 688) had taken part, with **Uytewael,** in the foundation of the new Painters and Sculptors Guild in 1611; he was probably in England as noted above in 1613; he painted a dramatic *Ships in a storm with a whale* in 1614, *The Dutch under Heemskerck defeating the Spaniards off Gibraltar 1607* with a foreground of land troops in 1617, *Dutch ships in a rocky bay* in 1620 and *English warships in harbour off a rocky coast with castle and fishmarket on the shore* in 1621. **Ambrosius Bosschaert** (Pls. 550, 551, 552) was in Middelburg till 1614 and his two sons were born there—**Ambrosius Bosschaert the younger** in 1609 and **Abraham Bosschaert** in 1613; he was in Bergen-op-Zoom in 1615, in Utrecht where he joined the new Painters Guild from 1616 till 1619, and thereafter in Breda; in 1621 having painted a flowerpiece for the Cupbearer of the Prince of Orange, he delivered it himself in The Hague and he was taken ill and died there. In my last chapter I described a flowerpiece produced by **Bosschaert** in Middelburg in 1609; and my plates for this period show three eminently skilful examples all probably painted in Utrecht—a *Glass of flowers in a niche* (Pl. 551) of 1618, a *Flowers on a window sill* (Pl. 552) and a *Flowers in a faience vase* (Pl. 550); round the base of the glass pot in the first there are shells from the Indies which were now much collected, a fly, a butterfly and a fallen rose; on the window sill in the second there are other shells from the Indies, a bumble bee and a carnation, and the flowers here are against a landscape background as in some modern flowerpieces by Henri Matisse, André Derain, Marc Chagall and Paul Nash; in the third picture a butterfly approaches a rose on the left and there are dewdrops on a leaf by the metal mount round the neck of the vase; in all three, as in **Bosschaert's** earlier picture, the bouquets are obviously put together from individual specimens, not painted from an actual arrangement before him, as the flowers are again of different seasons and some are repeated or almost repeated in all three pictures; in the first two the mass of flowers seems tall for the container (as in **Jan (Velvet) Brueghel's** flowerpiece (Pl. 521) discussed in my last chapter) but in the third the relation between flowers and container seems more reasonable and the bold pattern on the faience pot appears to have led the artist to a less intricate and elaborate but more imposing composition with fewer flowers and more space between them. In The Hague some flowerpieces were still being painted with success by **Jacques de Gheyn** (Pl. 484) who signed a *Glass vase in a niche with tulips, roses, lilies of the valley and other flowers* in 1612; but flower painting was only one aspect of **Jacques de Gheyn's** activities; and in 1611 he signed a *Christ revealing the True Cross to the Empress Helena* which moved Descamps (who saw it in 1769 in the Dominican church in Bruges) to write 'Il y a du mérite, même de la finesse dans la couleur, mais tout y est dur, sec et tranchant sur les bords'. In The Hague also **Clara Peeters** was established or on visit in 1617 as mentioned above; and the portrait painter **Daniel van den Queborne** died there under sixty before 1618. **Paul van Somer** (Pl. 538) was in Leyden from Amsterdam from 1612 till 1614. The landscape painter **Jan Snellinck the younger** was in Rotterdam from Antwerp by 1614 and seems to have remained in Holland. **Frans Spierinx** was still running his tapestry factory in Delft; and in 1615 his chief designer **Karel van Mander the younger** founded a rival factory where twenty-two tapestries were made from his designs for Christian IV of Denmark.

Of the Flemings in Central Europe **Gortzius Geldorp** (Pls. 454, 486) died in Cologne at sixty-three in 1616. **Jacques Fouquier** (Pl. 563) was in Heidelberg about 1617. **Deodatus Delmont** worked as painter and architect for, and was ennobled by, the Duke of Pfalz-Neuburg between 1612 and 1620. **Martin van Valkenborch** (Pl. 439) died in Frankfort at seventy-seven in 1612. **Gillis van Valkenborch** worked there through the period and **Frederick van Valkenborch** (Pl. 502), who was all the time in Nuremberg, designed the triumphal arch for the Pageant Entry of the Emperor Mathias in 1612. In Frankenthal **Hendrik van der Borcht the elder** made drawings for engravers of *The Entry into Frankenthal of the Elector Palatine Frederick V with Princess Elizabeth of England in 1613*. **Antonie Mirou** signed there a *Wooded landscape with huntsmen* in 1611 and a *Wooded landscape with beggars* in 1612; and he also painted a series of landscapes in the region of Bad Schwalbach before 1620. His curious undated *Landscape with Abraham and Hagar* (Pl. 469) probably painted in this period shows towering trees in the foreground, Abraham's house perched on a rock in the centre and a city with bridges and castle receding in the distance; the landscape here was evidently completed before the figures were inserted and these figures, perhaps the work of a collaborator, show Abraham in the centre surrounded with farmyard animals—cattle, swine, hens, ducks and a shepherd with his dog—while Sarah and Isaac watch the dismissal of Hagar and Ishmael; in the left foreground Hagar in the wilderness is comforted by the angel; and (inexplicably to me) a coach escorted by pack mules is driven to a bridge in the distance. In Munich **Pieter de Witte (Candido)** was still Court Painter, and painted an *Assumption of the Virgin* for the Frauenkirche in 1620. It was also probably in Munich that the **Munich Duchess Magdalena Painter** produced the enthralling picture believed to be a portrait of the Duchess Magdalena, daughter of William V of Bavaria (Pl. 520); the face here is studied and set down with the sensitive intimacy of **Catherine van Hemessen** (Pls. 345, 346) and **Pieter van der Hofstadt** (Pl. 366), and the elaborate pink and silver gown, the jewels and the up-tilted ruff edged with pink ribbon, all in the Spanish mode, are exquisitely painted as symbols of royal status by this delicate portraitist or his still-life-and-drapery assistant. In Austria **Bartholomaeus Spranger** (Pls. 458, 459) died in Prague at sixty-five in 1611; **Pieter Stevens the younger** (Pl. 468) seems to have worked there all through; and the topographic draughtsman **Philip van den Bossche** signed a *Mountain landscape with towns and villages* in 1615. **Jacob Hoefnagel** as Court Painter to the Emperor Rudolf was paid for pictures of his rare birds in 1610 and became a citizen of Prague in 1614; some years later he was accused of financial irregularities and/or seditious political action and he fled, probably to Holland, before 1621. **Roelandt Savery** (Pls. 525, 564, 583, 585, 586) was confirmed as Court Painter by the Emperor Mathias in 1612; he visited Amsterdam, as noted, in 1613, and worked in Vienna from 1614 till 1616 when he went back to Holland; in his circular *Cowshed* (Pl. 525) dated 1615, painted in Vienna, the semi-darkness of the interior is contrasted with the bright light on the farmhouse outside, a woman milks a cow in the foreground, a boy plays a flute in the doorway and witches on broomsticks are painted on the frame—an allusion perhaps to the renewed Archducal campaign in Belgium against sorcerers and witches (like **Frans Francken's** picture (Pl. 496) of 1607 discussed in my last chapter).

In Italy there was now the beginning of a Flemish colony in Genoa; the central figure was **Cornelis de Wael,** a versatile painter of picturesque military scenes, marines, genre and religious subjects, who arrived from Antwerp at twenty-one in 1613 and remained there. His associates at this time included his brother **Lucas de Wael**, painter of landscapes with mountains and waterfalls, and **Jan Roos (Giovanni Rosa)**, painter of animals, still-life with flowers and fruit, and religious subjects who was settled there by 1616 at twenty-five after working in Antwerp under **Snyders;** and when **Van Dyck** reached Genoa from Antwerp or Saventhem in November 1621 he lodged with **Cornelis de Wael** and painted, then or later, the double portrait *Cornelis de Wael with his brother Lucas de Wael behind him.* **Jan Sons** died over sixty in Parma or Cremona between 1611 and 1614; and **Denys Calvaert** died in Bologna approaching eighty in 1619. **Ernest Schayck the younger** signed a *Virgin in glory with saints* for Lugo, S. Maria, in 1615. **Theodoor Rombouts** (Pls. 581, 596, 597) went to Italy from Antwerp at nineteen in 1616 visiting Pisa, Florence and Rome; his chief success there would seem to have been in Florence where he worked for Duke Cosimo II and for Duke Ferdinand II. **Justus Sutterman** left his master **Frans Pourbus** in Paris at twenty-two in 1619 and joined a company of tapestry workers who were travelling to Florence to work for Duke Cosimo; in Florence he painted a portrait of the Doyen of this company which impressed the Duke who made him a Court Painter in 1620; in the following year he painted *Homage of the Florentine Senate to Duke Ferdinand II aged eleven* commissioned by Duke Cosimo's widow Maria Magdalena of Austria (sister of the Emperor Ferdinand II); and Duke Ferdinand confirmed him in his Court appointment. In Venice **Pietro Mera** painted a *S. James the Less, S. Lawrence and S. Stephen* for Cividale Cathedral at something over sixty in 1611 and probably died before 1621; and **Gaspar Rem** signed a *Self-portrait at seventy-two* in 1614 and seems to have died soon after. **Louis Finson (Finsonius)** was in Naples in 1612 and painted there an *Annunciation* before moving to Provence. In Rome, where the Principe of the Accademia **Frans van den Kasteele** died over eighty in 1621, **Paul Brill** (Pls. 473, 474) continued to produce landscape and marine frescoes, in collaboration with other painters, for Roman churches and private villas, and also easel pictures; in 1610 he painted a seapiece for Cardinal Borromeo; and in 1617 a *Landscape with the Emmaus pilgrims* which appears in the gallery interior painted some ten years later by the **Hague Studio of Appelles Painter** (Pl. 580); in 1621, when he was sixty-six, his reputation in Antwerp was so high that one of his landscapes was assessed in a collection at the price then current for **Jan (Velvet) Brueghel**—(the assessors being **Pieter Goetkint, Adriaen van Stalbemt** and **Hendrik van Balen**). **Pietro de Lignis** worked in Rome through the period and I reproduce his *Adoration of the Magi* (Pl. 573) which he painted at approximately forty in 1616; in this very interesting composition the star casts rays down to the Virgin and Child, the Virgin and S. Joseph are both haloed, and pages hold up the train of the kneeling Magus—as they held the train of Julian the Apostate in **Geertgen tot Sint Jans's** picture (Pl. 124); the Magi's camels (that thrust their heads right into the stable in the *Adoration of the Magi* which **Rubens** painted eight years later (Pl. 574)), are here discreetly silhouetted in the background, and though **Rubens** would doubtless have thought the composition of no interest, Rembrandt with a pot of umber and some ochre, could have turned it into mystic drama. **Jacob de Hase (di Assa)** in Rome through the period, had Flemish and also Italian pupils. A newcomer **Nicholas Regnier,** pupil of **Abraham Janssens** in Antwerp, became a pupil of Bartholomeo Manfredi in Rome about 1610 when he was approximately twenty and stayed on in Rome. **Marten Pepyn** (Pls. 569, 571, 572) and **Jacques Francart** were probably in Italy till 1613 when both were back in Antwerp. **Adam de Coster,** painter of religious subjects, 'history' and genre pieces with torch and candlelight effects, may have visited Rome and Naples in these years; and the same applies to the **Madrid Judith Painter** (Pl. 582). **Adriaen de Bie** painter of religious subjects, portraits and pictures on jasper, agate and porphyry, reached Rome from Paris in 1615 and stayed for eight years; and **Willem van Haecht** seems to have come to Italy from Paris in 1619. **Gerard Seghers** (Pl. 527) arrived in Rome from Antwerp in his early twenties probably before 1615; he was patronized there by the Spanish ambassador Cardinal Zapata y Mendoza by whom he was sent to Spain with an introduction to the King; and he returned to Antwerp in 1620. **Justus van Egmont** (Pl. 722) left Antwerp for Italy at seventeen in 1618 and was also back about 1620. **Anton van den Heuvel,** painter of religious subjects, reached Rome from Ghent after 1618 and seems to have stayed for nine years. Of the Flemish landscape painters **Willem Backereel** died in Rome at forty-five in 1615, **Paul Brill's** former assistant **Balthasar Lauwers** was still much employed there, **Marten Ryckaert,** in Italy from Antwerp, signed a *Waterfall at Tivoli* in 1616, **Jan Wildens** (Pls. 628, 629) in Italy from 1613 till 1618 was back in Antwerp by 1619, and **Jacques Fouquier** (Pl. 563) was in Rome and Venice before or after his Heidelberg visit of 1617 and was probably in Brussels in 1620 before his migration to Paris. The Liégeois painter **Simon Damery** was active as dealer in Rome in 1616; and **Adriaen van Utrecht** (Pls. 693, 694) seems to have reached Italy from France and Germany about 1619 when he was just about twenty.

At home in Belgium the period as a whole was propitious to artists and a bird's eye conspectus would show an animated scene. In 1610 for example **Van Dyck** (Pls. 579, 604, 608, 612, 644, 663) aged eleven was a pupil of **Hendrik van Balen** (Pls. 507, 508) who was then thirty-five and collaborating with **Jan (Velvet) Brueghel;** the still-life painter **Alexander Adriaenssen** (Pls. 559, 652, 653) became Antwerp Master at twenty-three; **Adriaen van Stalbemt** (Pls. 479, 562) returned aged thirty from Middelburg to Antwerp where he became a Catholic and joined the Guild; and **Wenzelas Coebergher** (Pl. 493) began the building of Notre Dame de Montaigu in the Jesuit style. In 1611 the flower painter **Daniel Seghers** (Pls. 692, 757) became Antwerp Master and **Frans Snyders** (Pl. 555) aged thirty-two married a sister of **Cornelis de Vos** (Pls. 590, 599, 600, 641) then twenty-six. In 1612 **Gerard Schoof** presented a *Descent from the Cross* to Hoboken Church on condition that he and his wife were taken every year by carriage to the kermesse and given a good dinner; and **Pieter Brueghel the younger** (Pls. 380, 411), in money difficulties, sold his share in his grandmother's property to **Jan (Velvet) Brueghel.** In 1613 **Sebastiaan Vrancx** (Pls. 531, 532, 534) married a sister of the second wife of **Tobias van Haecht** (Pl. 377); and his pupil

Peeter Snayers (Pls. 627, 700, 701) became Antwerp Master. In 1614 **Daniel Seghers** joined the Jesuit Order and the architect Pieter Huyssens began the Antwerp Jesuit church (Pls. 782, 783). In 1615 **Jacques Fouquier** (Pl. 563), **Jasper van der Lanen** (also a landscape painter) and **Jacob Jordaens** (Pls. 545, 546, 588, 658, 660, 741, 774), aged twenty-two, became Antwerp Masters; Isabella Brant, wife of **Rubens**, stood godmother to daughters of **Marten Pepyn** (Pls. 569, 571, 572) and **Jan (Velvet) Brueghel**; and **David Teniers the elder** bought three houses in Antwerp with borrowed money—a transaction which caused his ruin. In 1616 **Cornelis de Vos** (Pls. 590, 599, 600, 641) acquired the right to trade as an art dealer in Antwerp; and **Jordaens** married a daughter of his former master **Adam van Noort.** In 1617 **Jacques Francart** (inventor of an alarum clock that also struck a light) published a part of a 'Livre d'architecture' (designs for doorways, etc.); the marine painter **Jan Porcellis** became Antwerp Master; **Jan (Velvet) Brueghel,** in some degree of financial difficulty, moved to a smaller house in Antwerp and **Rubens** painted figures in several of his pictures possibly to help him. In 1618 **Van Dyck** aged nineteen and **Cornelis Schut** (Pl. 669) aged twenty-one became Antwerp Masters. In 1619 **Rubens** was a witness at the marriage of **Jan Wildens** (Pls. 628, 629) who had just come back from Italy; the landscape painter **Alexander Keirincx** (Pls. 610, 611, 613) became Antwerp Master, and the portrait painter **Pieter van der Plas** (Pl. 676) became Master in Brussels; **Cornelis de Vos** sold pictures in the foreign artists section of the Paris S. Germain fair; and, probably in that year, **Philippe de Champaigne** (Pls. 742, 750) aged seventeen refused his father's offer to buy him apprenticeship with **Rubens** and became a pupil in Brussels of **Michel de Bordeau.** In 1620 **Van Dyck** was assistant to **Rubens** and living in his house; **Philippe de Champaigne** was probably a pupil of **Jacques Fouquier** (Pl. 563) in Brussels; **Simon de Vos** (Pls. 673, 674, 687) aged seventeen and **Paul de Vos** (Pls. 633, 636) aged twenty-four became Antwerp Masters; **Peeter van Avont** (Pl. 605) became Master in Malines; **Justus van Egmont** (Pl. 722) aged nineteen was back in Antwerp from Italy; and **Gerard Seghers** (Pl. 527) aged twenty-nine was back from Spain. In 1621 **Jacob van Oost the elder** (Pls. 715, 729, 740) was Master in Bruges; and **Van Dyck** back in Antwerp from England began his career as successful independent artist.

Among the Court Painters of the Archduke and the Infanta **Jan (Velvet) Brueghel** (Pls. 464, 465, 467, 470, 480-3, 521) remained a first favourite; he was promoted to Painter of the Household in 1610 and delivered sixteen pictures to the Sovereigns in 1616. Others continued from the last period were **Jan Snellinck** (Pl. 460), **Otto van Veen** (Pls. 455, 510, 570), **Hendrik de Clerck** (Pls. 456, 471, 477, 587) **Wenzelas Coebergher** (Pl. 493), **Denis van Alsloot** (Pls. 477, 513, 513A) and **Rubens;** and these were now joined by **Antoine Sallaert** (Pl. 514), **Gaspar de Crayer** (Pls. 598, 607, 609, 642) who bought works of art for the Archducal collection, **Peeter Snayers** (Pls. 627, 700, 701) who began as a painter of processions, **Nicolaus van der Horst** painter and draughtsman of portraits, processions and town views who was made an Archer de la Garde, **Jacques Francart** also active as an architect, **Willem van Deynum** a miniature painter and **Salomon Noveliers** who succeeded his father **Pierre Noveliers** as keeper of pictures in the palaces and received some revenues from wine and beer duties and exemption from certain taxes as his salary. Albert and Isabella seem to have been gracious and friendly with their artists. **Jan (Velvet) Brueghel** had the entrée to their aviaries, gardens and menageries to make drawings and **Henri Staben** has left us a record of a visit they paid to the studio of **Rubens** (Pl. 518).

Rubens, thirty-three in 1610, had no special privileges in these years and no more favours than other Court Painters; he made portrait sketches of the Archduke and the Infanta in

1616 but he seems to have been less employed by them than **Jan (Velvet) Brueghel, Wenzelas Coebergher** and **Jacques Francart,** and indeed some of his pictures with life-size nude figures may well have shocked these pious and austere Sovereigns; he supplied the Archduke with a painting for his private oratory but the Infanta's oratory had a series of pictures by **Jacques Francart** from whom she also commissioned a *Mysteries of the Rosary* series to be presented to Pope Paul V; and **Rubens** was not in the Infanta's personal confidence till the next period, i.e. till after the Archduke's death. His aim was to capture the commissions for the new churches in the Jesuit style where large altarpieces with life-size figures were required as points of focus above the high altar; and after the success of his first church pictures the Jesuits decided that he was, in all respects, their man. He also aimed at supplying the richest collectors in Europe with paintings of secular subjects for their palaces and mansions, and here too he captured his market in these years when his magnificent house, with a number of studios and with galleries for his collections of pictures and antique sculpture, was built and organized as a mass production factory. He had numerous premium pupils and also specialist assistants for landscape, still-life, animals and so forth. These assistants, who worked, it would seem, on salaries for a period or were called in on special contracts for particular assignments, included, probably in these years, **Frans Snyders** (Pls. 554, 555, 655-7) for still-life and dead animals; **Daniel Seghers** (Pls. 692, 757) for flower painting; **Jacques Fouquier** (Pl. 563), **Lucas van Uden** (Pls. 561, 566, 567, 602), **Jan Wildens** (Pls. 628, 629) and **Alexander Keirinx** (Pls. 610, 611, 613) for landscape; and **Jacob Jordaens** (Pls. 545, 546), **Van Dyck** (Pls. 579, 604, 608, 612), **Gerard Seghers** (Pl. 527) and **Cornelis Schut** (Pl. 669) for figures. In some cases **Rubens** painted the whole picture himself and charged accordingly; but as a rule he drew the composition and made some small colour sketches which he handed to his factory to be enlarged and executed; after this he sometimes 'retouched' the enlarged versions which no doubt meant some unifying work all over the picture and the repainting of certain dominant passages or areas; sometimes, already in this period and still more later, there was no 'retouching' and the whole work was executed in the factory from designs by him or by his chief assistants under his direction. **Rubens** was a man of parts, speaking several languages, and he was urbane with other artists; **Jan (Velvet) Brueghel, Hendrik van Balen, Marten Pepyn** and **David Teniers the elder** were among his friends and with the first two he formed a syndicate (about 1618) to buy Caravaggio's *Virgin of the Rosary* from the heirs of **Louis Finson** and presented it to the Antwerp Dominican church. He also knew how to impress his customers and visitors to his house and studios. At the end of this period, for example, his factory was described by a Danish doctor who went there and was also admitted to the private studio: 'We found him at work', the doctor wrote later, 'Tacitus was being read aloud to him and he was also dictating a letter; we hesitated to interrupt him but he himself addressed us and then answered our questions while continuing his work and the dictation and without stopping the Tacitus reader.' By these procedures **Rubens** and his atelier had turned out by 1621 a series of huge pictures with life-size figures as altarpieces and ceiling panels for churches in addition to cartoons for tapestry, hunting pieces with horses and wild animals, and mythologies and allegories with nude figures. One setback only is recorded—the return to him by Prince Charles of England of a picture on the ground that the Prince judged it a studio production scarcely touched by the master's hand, a judgement which **Rubens** admitted, in a letter, to be right.[1]

[1] Unless some document defining it survives, it is impossible now to disentangle with certainty the work done by **Rubens** himself on any particular picture because all 'style' judgements in such

As indicated by my plates and the brief conspectus above, the output of the **Rubens** atelier were only one factor in a copious production in Belgium at this time; and, despite the absence of the many talents abroad, scores of artists continued all the main aspects of Flemish painting—topical and other genre scenes with figures and animals, portraits, landscapes, town views, interiors and still-life pieces, as well as religious subjects, allegories and mythologies; and it is noteworthy that in this period most of the painters were quite unaffected by the rhythmic flamboyance and bravura of the **Rubens** style.

Among the topical paintings some events of 1615 and 1616 were recorded in a number of works. This happened because in 1615 the Infanta shot down the popinjay from the steeple of Notre Dame du Sablon in the annual festival in Brussels and the magistrature voted her some twenty-five thousand florins as a gift; with this money she made a fund to dower each year six well-conducted girls of indigent parents; **Antoine Sallaert** was commissioned to record the shooting episode and also to paint *The 1616 procession of the dowered maidens* (Pl. 514) where the six girls then chosen were accompanied by the six who had received the bounty the first year—(and this dowering by Isabella may also be referred to in **Otto van Veen's** picture *The charity of S. Nicholas to the daughters of the poor gentleman* (Pl. 570)). The shooting at the popinjay was followed each year by an Ommeganck procession to Notre Dame du Sablon; this procession included decorated cars with tableaux vivants of religious subjects and mythologies; in 1615 the Ommeganck was especially elaborate and contained a car representing *Diana and archers* to celebrate the Infanta's skill, and I reproduce this car (Pl. 513A) as painted by **Denis van Alsloot** who recorded the whole procession in a series of intriguing pictures. Another topical pageant was also recorded by **Denis van Alsloot**—*The Feast of Our Lady in the Wood* (*Vivier d'Oye Fête in Tervueren Forest*) (Pl. 513) which shows the state barge of the Archduke and the Infanta on Tervueren lake and in the centre of the lake the small figure of Vivier d'Oye, who, according to a popular tale, had announced his intention of walking on the water.

In portraiture the Archduke and the Infanta were painted for the Brabant chambre des Comptes by **Paul van Somer** (Pl. 538) who was in Brussels for some months in 1616 and had **Everard van Remonde** as collaborator; and as just mentioned they were also painted in this year by **Rubens.** In 1621 they were painted for the Chartreuse de Marlagne by **Otto van Veen** who was then sixty-five; they appear in the *Visit of the Archduke and the Infanta to Rubens' studio* (Pl. 518) by **Henri Staben** and in the *Ball at the Court of Albert and Isabella* (Pl. 517) by **Frans Francken II,** and also of course in the procession and festival pictures just mentioned by **Antoine Sallaert** (Pl. 514) and **Denis van Alsloot** (Pls. 513, 513A). Outside Court circles the tradition of the subscription group was continued in Brussels by **Gaspar de Crayer** a most able and gifted portraitist as can be seen in his undated *The Virgin protecting the Crossbowmen's Guild* (Pl. 598) possibly painted before 1621 when he was just under forty; **Pieter van der Plas** who was later to paint such groups (Pl. 676) was a newcomer in 1619; and in Bruges the veteran **Pieter Claeissins the younger** (Pl. 436) portrayed *Sixteen nobles of the Confrérie de Notre Dame de l'Arbre sec* as donors on the wings of an altarpiece in 1620. In Malines **Lucas Franchoys the elder** painted *Burgomaster Philip Snoy*

cases are just guesses. For the same reason sketches should not be catalogued as 'by **Rubens**' unless there is factual support for the statement—as there often is. Some small paintings catalogued as sketches by **Rubens** are not sketches properly so-called by **Rubens** or anyone else but either (*a*) working models ('modellos') based on a **Rubens** sketch and made in his workshop probably by the chief executant as a stage in construction of the final picture or (*b*) small copies of the final picture made in the shop as record, or (*c*) small copies made at the time or later by some student for himself or (*d*) by some copyist for the international art trade.

in 1619. In Antwerp **Cornelis de Vos** (Pls. 599, 600), now rising as a portrait painter, was commissioned by the Guild of S. Luke to paint *Abraham Grapheus, Messenger of the Guild, with silver and other trophies of the Guild* in 1620; and in 1621 he painted his *Portrait of the artist aged thirty-six with his wife and two children* an agreeable and 'lifelike' domestic group which must have brought him many orders from rich burghers to paint family groups and portraits of children. **Rubens** seems to have found time to carry out some portrait commissions and to paint some portraits of his friends including perhaps the famous *Susanna Fourment: (Le Chapeau de Paille)*; after 1618 **Van Dyck** may also have had some commissions or painted some portraits of his friends; and the superlatively 'life-like' head by an unrecorded artist here referred to as the **London van der Geest Painter** (Pl. 560) was possibly painted about 1620.

Among the landscape painters **Abel Grimmer** (Pl. 447) died under fifty before 1619; but many of the specialists recorded in the previous period were still at work at the end of this one. Thus in 1621 **Kerstiaen de Keuninck** (Pl. 501) was about sixty-one and **Tobias van Haecht** (Pl. 377) was sixty; **Josse de Momper** (Pl. 500) and **Pieter Brueghel the younger** (Pls. 380, 411) were fifty-seven; **Jan (Velvet) Brueghel** (Pls. 464, 465, 467, 480-3) was fifty-three; **Denis van Alsloot** (Pls. 477, 513) was about fifty-one and **Sebastiaan Vrancx** (Pls. 531, 532, 534) and **Pieter van der Hulst** were a few years younger. **Adriaen van Stalbemt** (Pls. 479, 562) was forty-one, **Willem van Nieulandt** (Pl. 475) thirty-seven, **Jan Wildens** (Pls. 628, 629), **Jacques Fouquier** (Pl. 563) and **Charles de Cauwer** all about thirty-six, and **Pieter de Witte the younger** thirty-five. **Marten Ryckaert** and **Andreas Snellinck** were thirty-four; **Abraham Govaerts** (Pl. 478) and **Jan Tilens** (Pl. 499) were thirty-two; and among the newcomers **Peeter Snayers** (Pls. 627, 700, 701) was twenty-nine, **Lucas van Uden** (Pls. 561, 566, 567, 602) twenty-six, **Jasper van der Lanen** about the same age, **Alexander Keirincx** (Pls. 610, 611, 613) twenty-one and **Jan Brueghel the younger** (Pl. 605) twenty. Of these **Kerstiaen de Keuninck** may have painted in these years his curious undated *Landscape with Diana and Actaeon* where half the picture is a landscape with craggy mountains (like his *Landscape with a shipwreck and saint* (Pl. 501)) while in the right-hand foreground Actaeon surprises Diana and her nymphs protected by a tasselled curtain hung from tree stumps as they bathe in water from an ornate marble fountain at the base of a dilapidated palace. **Tobias van Haecht** recalls two pictures by **Pieter Bruegel the elder** (Pls. 378, 378A) in his *Mountain landscape with hunting adventure of the Archduke Maximilian* (Pl. 377) where the figures may have been inserted by his brother-in-law **Sebastiaan Vrancx**; and though it is hard to discover the story from the painting it in fact relates an episode when Maximilian I (as Archduke or Emperor) became isolated on a rocky peak when hunting in the Tyrol and was rescued by the prayers of a priest, surrounded by the courtiers and attendants, in the valley below. **Josse de Momper** whose *Mountain landscape* reproduced here (Pl. 500) was possibly painted before 1621, continued to collaborate with figure painters, and his landscapes were popular with contemporary collectors; but as he rarely signed or dated he is not really known to be the author of many of the pictures that are catalogued as his work today. **Pieter Brueghel the younger** continued to paint landscape settings of his own in his variants of his father's pictures; **Jan (Velvet) Brueghel** painted more rural pieces like those discussed in my last chapter (he signed among others a *Plain with two windmills* in 1611, a *Landscape with wood, animals and gipsies* in 1614, and a *Country road with figures* in 1619); and about 1617 he painted a charmingly wooded Garden of Eden in his *Adam and Eve in Paradise* (Pl. 543) where the figures were inserted by **Rubens.** His son **Jan Brueghel the younger** was at first his pupil and then worked for some time under **Abraham Janssens** (Pl. 509). **Denis van Alsloot** had thrown off the influence of **Gillis van Coninxloo**—(that had characterized his *Wooded landscape with Cephalus and Procris* (Pl. 477))—by 1616 when he signed his *Feast of Our Lady of the Wood* (*Vivier d'Oye Fête in Tervueren Forest*) (Pl. 513) where the landscape has naturalistic woods and shrubs on rising banks round Tervueren lake. In the same year **Sebastiaan Vrancx** set an *Attack on a convoy* (Pl. 531) in a deep receding plain (as **Jan (Velvet) Brueghel** had set his *Landscape with covered waggon* (Pl. 483)); and his undated *Horsemarket* (Pl. 532), also perhaps of this period, is set in a village market-place with delicately painted trees. **Adriaen van Stalbemt** was still true to the **Gillis van Coninxloo** tradition (Pls. 466, 476) already observed in his *Wooded landscape with hunters and dogs* (Pl. 479); for we see it also in the noble trees round a silent pool in his *Wooded landscape with the fables of the fox and the eagle, the rabbits and the frogs, the stork and the frogs, and the two men with a bear* (Pl. 562) painted in Antwerp in 1620. This tradition also persists in the *Oakwood with gipsies* (Pl. 478) signed in 1612 at twenty-three by **Abraham Govaerts** who painted a *Wooded landscape with Abraham and Isaac* in 1615 and a *Wooded landscape with rape of Europa* in 1621. **Willem van Nieulandt's** *View of Rome* (Pl. 475) dated 1611 was doubtless composed from drawings made in the suburbs of Rome when a pupil of **Paul Brill** (Pl. 474) some nine years earlier; **Jan Tilens,** as noted, must have visited Italy for his *Landscape near Tivoli* (Pl. 499); and **Marten Ryckaert** whose *Waterfall at Tivoli* of 1616 has also been referred to was working in Antwerp from 1620. **Rubens** is not known to have concerned himself with landscape at this time; and the landscape backgrounds in his pictures known to be or presumed of this period—the large *Cimon finding the sleeping Iphigenia* (Pl. 548) for example—can therefore be presumed by his assistants. There are however no precise records of the dates when his several landscape assistants began to work with him. **Jacques Fouquier** may have been in his atelier before he left for Germany and Italy in 1616; and he was probably in Brussels in 1620 when he painted the *River landscape with bluffs* (Pl. 563) evidently constructed from sketches made on his travels. **Lucas van Uden** may have been in the **Rubens** atelier from about 1615 onwards; and his undated *River landscape with sunset* (Pl. 561) was possibly painted about 1620 and influenced by **Jacques Fouquier. Jan Wildens** was probably in the **Rubens** atelier before he went to Italy in 1613 and after his return in 1619; and he signed a *Landscape with rainbow* in 1621; and **Alexander Keirincx** (Pls. 610, 611, 613) who signed a *Wooded landscape with fishpond* in 1620 may have joined the atelier soon after.

Among the marine painters **Andries van Ertvelt** (Pl. 704) had begun his career as Antwerp Master at nineteen in 1609 and seems still to have been there in 1621. **Adam Willaerts** (Pl. 688) was domiciled in Utrecht as mentioned. **Jan Porcellis** a gifted and original painter was in Antwerp from Holland by 1615; in that year when already thirty, he was still compelled to do hack work and agreed with an Antwerp dealer to supply forty seapieces with shipping within twenty weeks, two to be delivered weekly and the proceeds shared; in 1617 he achieved independence as an Antwerp Master; he was declared a bankrupt the following year; but he managed to survive and both **Rubens** and Rembrandt were eventually owners of his work. **Abraham Matthys,** already mentioned as son of a fishdealer with interests in whale fishing, was back from Italy by 1619 when he became an Antwerp Master and he went off on a voyage with the whaling fleet that year.

In genre painting we again see several types of figures in rural and urban settings. **Jan (Velvet) Brueghel** (Pls. 467, 481-3) was still a leader in this category; there are Flemish peasants in **Lucas van Uden's** *River landscape with sunset* (Pl. 561) possibly painted, as suggested above, about 1620; and Italian peasants in **Jacques Fouquier's** *River landscape*

(Pl. 563) and in **Willem van Nieulandt's** Roman scene (Pl. 475). Farmers and gentry appraise the horses offered them by dealers in the spirited *Horse market* (Pl. 532) by **Sebastiaan Vrancx;** and in the *Oakwood with gipsies* (Pl. 478) by **Abraham Govaerts** a gipsy in a large sunbonnet tells the fortunes of some sportsmen (as a gipsy told the fortunes of some gentry in **Abel Grimmer's** picture (Pl. 447)) and a naked corpse hangs from a tree in the forest (perhaps an allusion to the witch-hunting edicts of this time). In his *Feast of Our Lady of the Wood* (Pl. 513) **Denis van Alsloot** shows a huge gathering of many kinds of people (as **Jan (Velvet) Brueghel** had done in his *Landscape with Tobias and the angel* (Pl. 464)); here the banks and woods are crowded with spectators; two elegant ladies seated sideways in their coach look out at the proceedings; civic guardsmen come down in procession from the hill, and mounted militia are present to keep order while peasants wheel their barrows and, in the foreground on the right, a family of peasants eat their luncheon in their own back garden ignoring the official happening—(just as, much later, other peasants gossip from a punt with a servant girl and ignore the procession of the Tailors' Guild in **Jean Beerblock's** picture of 1788 (Pl. 859). In 1613 **Otto van Veen** (Pls. 455, 510, 511, 570) included a genre scene *The Supper in the wood* (Pl. 511) in a series of 'history' subjects for the Assembly Chamber of the Dutch States-General; but no genre observation appears in this picture because **van Veen,** pretentious and literary, was immersed in 'costume-history' ideas; there are echoes here of the *Allegorical Love Feast* (Pl. 331) by **Pieter Jansz Pourbus** which **van Veen** no doubt despised as 'Gothic', but we miss the contemporary costumes that gave actuality to the earlier picture, and **van Veen's** flabby figures anticipate the Royal Academic nineteenth-century 'costume-history' manner against which the Pre-Raphaelites, who liked early Flemish pictures, so vigorously rebelled. Among the outdoor urban scenes **Sebastiaan Vrancx** shows a dozen episodes in his *Market-place with flogging and a funeral* (Pl. 534); here the flogging takes place before a Town Hall in the centre and the funeral procession advances up a side street; in the foreground housewives buy eggs, vegetables, fruit, fish and grain from the peasants, oysters are opened and eaten, a peasant woman is infuriated by a pony cart that has driven over her crockery spread out on the ground, and a woman smacks the bottom of an offending child. In **Antoine Sallaert's** *The 1616 procession with the maidens dowered by the Infanta Isabella* (Pl. 514) musicians lead churchmen surrounding the image of the Virgin, the Brussels townsfolk watch the procession from their windows, boys take up positions on the wall of the Sablon church, and the coach of the Archduke and the Infanta awaits their return in a space protected by a temporary screen. In **Denis van Alsloot's** *Ommeganck procession 1615* of which my colour plate (Pl. 513A) shows only a detail, the Brussels townsfolk line the streets and look out from the windows at the parade of churchmen, magistrates, the five military and the forty-nine crafts guilds and the cars with religious and allegoric tableaux vivants; while marshals on horseback attempt in vain to prevent small boys from running on the square. Among the indoor genre painters **Jacob van der Lamen** seems to have worked in Antwerp till 1616 when he settled in Brussels. In the *Ball at the Court of Albert and Isabella* (Pl. 517), painted by **Frans Francken II** in 1611, a minuet is danced by a lady and gentleman in the centre and musicians play for them in a gallery on the right. As a contrast we have a *Peasant wedding* painted in 1620 by **Pieter Brueghel the younger** which takes place in an inn or peasants' living-room and seems to be based on a lost watercolour drawing by **Pieter Bruegel the elder** referred to by van Mander as depicting the peasant custom of bringing gifts of money to the bride.

The popularity of the military genre piece continued to increase; and in this field **Jan**

Snellinck (seen here only as a religious painter (Pl. 460)) was available through the period and **Jan Ghuens** was still living in 1618. **Sebastiaan Vrancx**—whose *Leckerbetkens fight with Breauté* of 1601 was mentioned in my last chapter—painted his *Attack on a convoy* (Pl. 531) in 1616 and this shows his manner in these subjects which influenced his pupil **Peeter Snayers** (Pl. 701) and others as the century advanced.

In animal painting I have already referred to the animals and birds in works produced abroad by **Joachim Uytewael** (Pl. 524), **Roelandt Savery** (Pl. 525), **Paul van Somer** (Pl. 538), **Frans Pourbus** (Pl. 540), **Jan Roos** and others; and I have also mentioned the animals from Aesop's fables in **Adriaen van Stalbemt's** *Wood* (Pl. 562). In **Hendrik van Balen's** undated *Rape of Europa* (Pl. 507) the bull-Jupiter is perhaps the work of his former pupil **Jan Snyders.** Birds and beasts of all kinds (some in pairs) are in **Jan (Velvet) Brueghel's** *Garden of Eden* (Pl. 543) and the little long-haired dog at the feet of Eve must not be missed there. We see dogs in the military and genre pieces by **Sebastiaan Vrancx** (Pls. 531, 532, 534), in the pageant scenes by **Denis van Alsloot** (Pl. 513A) and **Antoine Sallaert** (Pl. 514) and in the landscapes by **Jacques Fouquier** (Pl. 563) and **Lucas van Uden** (Pl. 561). A greyhound leaps up to be fondled by a youth in **Henri Staben's** studio interior (Pl. 518) and a dog sleeps through the dialogue with Mary and Martha as shown by **Abel Grimmer** (Pl. 535)—just as dogs slept through the *Ordeal by Fire* as shown by **Dirk Bouts** (Pl. 69) and through the *Queen of Sheba's visit to Solomon* as shown by the **Solomon Master** (Pl. 286). A large shaggy dog pants with open mouth in the foreground of the *Raising of the Cross* by **Rubens** (Pl. 528), a small dog yaps in the *Flagellation* by **Frans Francken** (Pl. 519), a puppy yaps at Cimon intruding upon Iphigenia in the composition by **Rubens** (Pl. 548) and a dog takes refuge from a turkey while a parrot squawks above them in *The daughters of Cecrops finding Erichthonius* by **Jordaens** (Pl. 546). **Jan (Velvet) Brueghel** puts a monkey in his *Allegory of Sight* (Pl. 542), **Frans Snyders** puts one in his *Terms: and a garland round a bust of Ceres* (Pl. 554) and **Rubens** or an assistant (perhaps **Frans Snyders**) puts one in the foreground of *Cimon finding the sleeping Iphigenia* (Pl. 548). There are horses, static and in action, in the pictures reproduced by **Jan (Velvet) Brueghel, Sebastiaan Vrancx, Sallaert** and **Denis van Alsloot;** and **Rubens** brought a new standard of muscular spring and snorting animation in the horses that rear and tumble in the *Battle of the Amazons* (Pl. 576). Letters written by **Rubens** at this time refer to hunting pieces painted without his collaborators, to a picture with 'leopards, taken from the life, with satyrs and Nymphs, original by my hand except a most beautiful landscape done by the hand of a master skilful in that genre' and to a 'Daniel amidst many lions, which are taken from life, original the whole by my hand'. This may mean that like **Jan (Velvet) Brueghel** he had access to the Archducal menagerie of wild animals, unless the pictures were painted from studies made earlier from lions and leopards belonging to the Duke of Mantua; and these studies may also have been used by the **Vienna Daniel Painter** (Pl. 526) who was possibly **Frans Snyders.** A newcomer who later excelled in animal painting was **Paul de Vos** (Pls. 633, 636) who was launched as an independent artist at about twenty-four in 1620.

In architectural and interior painting we have urban buildings (possibly by specialist collaborators) and church and domestic interiors and collectors' galleries. Notre Dame du Sablon and adjacent buildings are in **Antoine Sallaert's** *Procession of the dowered maidens* (Pl. 514); the streets of Brussels are also in **Denis van Alsloot's** *Ommeganck* (Pl. 513A); and **Sebastiaan Vrancx** (or an architectural collaborator) is clearly topographic in *Market place with flogging* (Pl. 534). The invented loggia and buildings in **Hendrik van Steenwyck's** *Open square with figures* (Pl. 536) were painted in 1614 either in Germany or Holland or else in Belgium before he went to England; and I have already referred to his *Christ in the house of Mary and Martha* (Pl. 537) and *Liberation of S. Peter* (Pl. 489) both painted in England. In Antwerp the devout **Pieter Neeffs the elder** (Pls. 649, 650) was now conspicuous as a painter of church interiors; and in 1618, at approximately forty, he signed a *Mass in a Flemish church* where the figures by some collaborator move about in a vast interior with rows of altars and altarpieces right and left all down the nave as in Antwerp Cathedral. In 1614, a few years before his death, **Abel Grimmer** signed his *Christ in the house of Mary and Martha* (Pl. 535) where the handsome foreground chamber is a strangely all-purposes affair as it contains an altar, a bed, a dining-table and a doorway without, it would seem, a door, giving on to a courtyard; the room has also something of the air of a collector's gallery (as the paintings on the walls include a *Rest on the Flight* an *Adam and Eve* and a *Tower of Babel* with spiral galleries that seem to be collapsing and is thus a variant of the concepts by **Pieter Bruegel the elder** and **Lucas van Valkenborch** (Pls. 374, 375)); as in **Hendrik van Steenwyck's** picture of the subject (Pl. 537), the architectural structure—a whole cube with side walls and raftered ceiling—goes right back to the whole-cube interior in the *Last Supper* (Pl. 58) by **Dirk Bouts** (which had evolved from the half-cube concepts of the earlier fifteenth-century painters); but **Abel Grimmer** is not only concerned here to invent an appropriate setting for the subject, he is also concerned with the exact placing of the dog and the pitcher as signposts in recession and thus forestalls procedures used later by the Dutch interior painters Pieter Janssens and Vermeer of Delft.

There was now a growing vogue for pictures with interiors of collectors' galleries; and early examples were produced by the versatile **Frans Francken** (who signed an interior of this kind with a book of drawings, coins and so forth on a table and pictures round the walls, at thirty-eight in 1619), by **Hans Jordaens III**, Antwerp Master at about twenty-five in 1620, and by **Henri Staben**, then just over forty. **Staben's** *Visit of the Archduke Albert and the Infanta Isabella to Rubens' studio* (Pl. 518) must be ranked as a scene in a collector's gallery because it depicts or purports to depict a room full of pictures in **Rubens'** mansion, with a doorway to his gallery of antique statues; as none of the paintings visible (landscapes, seascapes, still-life pieces, religious subjects, a composition with nude figures, and a portrait) appear to be by **Rubens,** they must be taken to represent a part of his collection, and the large work inspected by the Sovereigns, to whom he bows his reverence, was presumably one of his more valuable possessions. A collector's gallery is also suggested by the astonishing conglomeration of bric-à-brac brought together by **Jan (Velvet) Brueghel** in his *Allegory of Sight* (Pl. 542) where the point is driven home by optical instruments, various globes and by works of art of all kinds—a large cabinet with painted panels, tapestries, goldsmiths' work, busts, statues, and prints and paintings which include a double portrait *The Archduke Albert and the Infanta Isabella*, an allegory in the style of Titian, a seapiece with shipping (perhaps by **Andries van Ertvelt** (Pl. 704) or **Jan Porcellis**), a still-life in the style of **Jacob van Hulsdonck** (Pl. 556) a hunting or battle piece and a bacchanal in the style of **Rubens,** and the *Virgnd and Child in a garland of flowers* by **Jan (Velvet) Brueghel** and **Rubens** (Pl. 541).

In the field of flower painting and other types of still-life I have already mentioned the Flemings active in Holland—**Ambrosius Bosschaert** (Pls. 550, 551, 552), **Jacques de Gheyn, Roelandt Savery** and **Clara Peeters** (Pls. 504, 522, 523). In Belgium the flower painters were still led by **Jan (Velvet) Brueghel** whose *Bouquet of flowers* (Pl. 521) was discussed in my last chapter; in 1617 he inserted a large pot of flowers in his *Allegory of Sight* (Pl. 542); in his *Allegory of Smell* in that series he painted a garden packed with roses, lilies, tulips, carnations, iris, narcissi, hollyhocks and other flowers growing from beds and pots or disposed in baskets and vases; he scattered flowers in his Garden of Eden (Pl. 543); he possibly provided the chain of flowers which decorates the bull in the *Rape of Europa* (Pl. 507) by **Hendrik van Balen** with whom he is known to have collaborated; and in 1618 he hung a flower garland round a metal fruit stand in a still-life. In this period also **Jan (Velvet) Brueghel** launched a fashion for compositions with a flower garland surrounding a circular or oval panel like the *Virgin and Child in a garland of flowers* (Pl. 541) where the figures are by **Rubens;** and of this he wrote to the purchaser Cardinal Borromeo: 'This is the most beautiful and choice work I have ever done in my life; and Sieur **Rubens** has also done his best to show his skill with a lovely Madonna in the central panel.' The garland in this picture is indeed a triumph of most delicate and fanciful workmanship and the flowers are interspersed with birds, lizards, a monkey and insects painted he told the Cardinal 'd'après ceux qui sont en la possession de la Clarissime Infante'. This vogue for flower garlands round a central panel continued through the century and the young Jesuit **Daniel Seghers** who had been trained by **Jan (Velvet) Brueghel** and was later to excel in such pictures (Pls. 692, 757) was in the **Rubens** atelier as assistant about 1620. The motif was converted to a fruit garland or a fruit and flower garland by **Frans Snyders** who had been in touch with **Jan (Velvet) Brueghel** since 1608; but whereas the older artist aimed at delicacy in the delineation of each flower, **Snyders,** through the new influence of **Rubens,** aimed at and achieved an effect of massed richness in his *Terms: and a garland round a bust of Ceres* (Pl. 554) and also perhaps in the *Nature adorned by the Graces* (Pl. 544) as the garland there is possibly his work. In the miscellaneous still-life painting of these years I have just referred to the immense array of symbolic illustrative objects in **Jan (Velvet) Brueghel's** interior the *Allegory of Sight* (Pl. 542), and there are other conglomerations to symbolize the Senses in that series—musical instruments and clocks in *Hearing*, piles of armour and military weapons in *Touch* and all kinds of eatables in *Taste*. On occasion **Jan (Velvet) Brueghel** also painted 'straight' still-life pieces with objects disposed on a table for the pleasure of imitating their shapes, tints and textures; and in his *Still-life* of 1618 with the flower garland on a metal fruit stand just mentioned, there are coins, rings, pearls and other jewels like the objects on the table in *The banker and his wife* (Pl. 235) by **Quinten Massys** and *The moneychanger and his wife* (Pl. 318) by **Marinus van Reymerswaele.** Other still-life painters of this time painted tables with food and vessels like those produced by **Clara Peeters** (Pls. 504, 522, 523) in Holland; and sometimes an attempt is made to give formal meaning to the picture by throwing strong light on the nearer objects and gradually reducing it to darkness in the background as can be seen in two unsigned attractive pieces probably of this time by painters here referred to as the **Grenoble Artichoke Painter** (Pl. 505), and the **Grenoble Strawberry Painter** (Pl. 553). The hard brittle glittering 'close-up' technique that goes back to the still-life painting in the upper panels of the **van Eycks'** *Ghent altarpiece* (Pls. 9, 13, 17) is seen in the *Still-life with oysters* (Pl. 506) by **Osias Beet** (or **Beert**) **the elder** who had his nephew **Frans Ijkens** (Pl. 695) as pupil in 1614 and was still at work in 1621. The *Basket of fruit* (Pl. 556) by **Jacob van Hulsdonck,** also active through this period, is closely related to a basket of flowers in the centre foreground of **Jan (Velvet) Brueghel's** *Allegory of Smell* which indicates, I assume, some contact between these artists. **Alexander Adriaenssen** who later specialized in arrangements of fish (Pls. 652, 653) was launched as a still-life painter by 1610 and his *Still-life with cheese, bread and fish* (Pl. 559) may well have been painted by 1621. Another newcomer **Jacob Foppens van Es** (Pls. 557, 558), later to be praised for rendering the skin of grapes with such delicacy that the pips could be discerned within them, was Antwerp Master at just over twenty in 1617. The **Rubens** influence on the table-of-food type of still-life ('bancketgen' as they were called) is discernible in the undated *Still-life with fruit and game* (Pl. 555) painted by **Frans Snyders** probably in these years; for here the objects are not set out as single independent entities but massed together and superimposed; we find this also in the still-life of fruit in the foreground of the *Cimon finding the sleeping Iphigenia* (Pl. 548) produced by **Rubens** and his atelier; and we have it with still more richness and exuberance in the massed fruit and vegetables in the *Allegory of Abundance* (Pl. 545) by **Jordaens**.

The difference between the aesthetic of **Rubens** and that of **Jan (Velvet) Brueghel** is evident in the paintings on which they worked together. In the *Virgin and Child in a garland of flowers* (Pl. 541) the clash between the flowing unified rhythm of the figures and the static separated forms in the garland does little harm to the picture because the garland is frankly a decorative frame distinct from the central panel; but in *Adam and Eve in Paradise* (Pl. 543) where an over-large sculptural group of two figures by **Rubens** is thrust upon a setting conceived as a series of small units, the conflict in aesthetic destroys the picture's unity; and this is made more manifest when we compare this hybrid picture with the same subject painted some twenty-five years later by **Izaak van Oosten** (Pl. 584) one of **Jan (Velvet) Brueghel's** imitators, for here the little figures of Adam and Eve are veritably within the Paradise; and there is also more formal relation between the figures, the animals and the landscape in the composition (Pl. 524) by **Joachim Uytewael**.

Religious subjects were commissioned as usual for churches all over the country. In Malines **Lucas Franchoys the elder** painted a *Pietà* for Ghent, S. Bavon in 1610; **Michiel Coxie the younger** was available till 1616 and **Rombout van Avont** till 1619; **Jean Baptiste Saive** was still alive, over eighty, in 1621; and **Peeter van Avont** (Pl. 605) was a newcomer in 1620. In Brussels **Wenzelas Coebergher** was much occupied as architect and engineer-consultant to the Archduke and as Director General of the new Belgian pawnshops, but he probably produced more religious paintings in the manner of the fine *Entombment* (Pl. 493) discussed in my last chapter. **Hendrik de Clerck** (Pls. 456, 471, 477, 587) collaborated with **Denis van Alsloot** in a *Christ tempted in the desert* for Louvain Jesuit College in 1611. **Gaspar de Crayer** (Pls. 598, 607, 609, 642) whose splendid portraits in the *Virgin protecting the Crossbowmen's Guild* (Pl. 598) have been mentioned above, was some twenty-five years younger than **Coebergher** and twelve years younger than **de Clerck**; at thirty-seven in 1619 he received a commission for a *Virgin with Saints* for the tomb of Sheriff Jan van der Meersche in Alost, S. Martin, and about 1620 he painted his *Judgement of Solomon*, a measured concept that can be profitably compared with a brutal illustration of the subject produced about this time in the atelier of **Rubens**. **Jacques Francart,** the same age as **de Crayer** and established in Brussels or Antwerp, painted pictures for the Infanta's private oratory between 1614 and 1618 and a *Mysteries of the Rosary* series commissioned by her as a present to Pope Paul V already chronicled. **Theodore van Loon** some three years younger and thus twenty-five in 1610 was also established in Brussels and working for churches there and elsewhere. In Bruges **Antoine Claeissins** (Pls. 422, 492) died about seventy-seven in 1613; **Pieter Claeissins the younger** (Pl. 436) painted a *Christ bearing the Cross* in 1616, and in 1620 at approximately seventy he finished his triptych for S. Walpurge *Notre Dame de l'arbre sec* (commissioned in 1606) which shows the Virgin on the bare tree flanked by Moses and Gideon. **Ghislain Vroilynck** painted pictures for Notre Dame and S. Sauveur between 1613 and 1621; and a talented new man **Jacob van Oost the elder** (Pls. 715, 729, 740) began his career at twenty in 1621.

In Antwerp **Cornelis Floris** and **Juliaen Teniers the elder** died in 1615, and **Frans Francken the elder** and **Raphael Coxie** in 1616; **Ambrosius Francken the elder** painted pictures for Ghent Recollets and Antwerp, S. Jacques in 1610 and 1611 and died in 1618; and **Abel Grimmer** (Pl. 535) died before 1619. Among the older men who worked all through, **Jan Snellinck** (Pl. 460), **Jan de Wael, Otto van Veen** (Pls. 455, 570), **Gerard Schoof, Adam van Noort** and **Pieter Brueghel the younger** (Pls. 380, 411) were all born before 1570; **Abraham Janssens, Marten Pepyn** (Pls. 569, 571, 572), **Hendrik van Balen, Geeraert Snellinck** and **Rubens** were born in the seventies; **Deodatus Delmont, Frans Francken the younger, David Teniers the elder, Adam de Coster** and **Artus Wolfordt** (Pl. 606) who began late at thirty-five in 1616, were born in the eighties; **Gerard Seghers** (Pl. 527), **Jordaens** (Pl. 588), **Cornelis Schut** and **Van Dyck** were born in the nineties; **Simon de Vos** (Pl. 673), a precocious artist born in 1603, was on the scene at seventeen as Antwerp Master in 1620; and two painters (not otherwise known) **Arnold Vinckenborch** and **Mathieu Voet** were among those who contributed to a *Mysteries of the Rosary* series for Antwerp S. Jacques. As a religious painting **Abel Grimmer's** *Christ in the house of Mary and Martha* (Pl. 535) shows the same concept as **Hendrik van Steenwyck's** picture (Pl. 537) painted in England and already considered in relation to **Joachim Beuckelaer's** concept (Pl. 399). The small *Flagellation* (Pl. 519) some fourteen inches high by **Frans Francken the elder** or **Frans Francken II** is vividly imagined as a night piece without sadism or rhetoric, and the contrast between the tenderly drawn expressive central figure and the loutish surrounding types recalls the more biting contrast by the **Princeton Christ before Pilate Painter** (Pl. 174). **Jan Snellinck** whose *Crucifixion* (Pl. 460) was discussed in my last chapter, painted frescoes, in three days, for the Fraternity of Married Men in 1610 and *Scenes from the Passion* in 1611 and 1612. **Otto van Veen's** *Charity of S. Nicholas* (Pl. 570) probably painted about 1620 when he had moved back from Antwerp to Brussels, is a steep descent from his *Mystic marriage of S. Catherine* (Pl. 455) of 1589; it illustrates the Golden Legend which tells us that S. Nicholas began the distribution of his inherited riches by thrusting three bags of gold (now the pawnbroker's symbol) into the window of a house where the three daughters of an impoverished nobleman were being tempted into prostitution as their father was unable to dower them; the plight of the girls is explicitly described in **van Veen's** picture, for the first has taken to spinning, the second to sewing and the third who holds gold in her hand is evidently tempting her sisters; in a small most engaging fifteenth-century Flemish picture of this subject (presumed by some by **Gerard David**) the three girls are prettily tucked up in bed; but there is nothing engaging in **van Veen's** large concoction where the flaccid life-size figures in their 'timeless' clothes have the curious nineteenth-century English air already remarked in his genre picture *The Supper in the Wood* (Pl. 511); and I feel that these ladies might well have visited Lord Leighton's soirées and sat for their portraits to George Frederick Watts. Among the younger men the outstanding newcomer was **Jacob Jordaens** who produced at twenty-five in 1618 a monumental *Adoration of the Magi* with half-length figures massed together in one group. In that year **Rubens,** struck doubtless by the prodigious talent of this young man sixteen years his junior, procured him for his atelier and perhaps put him in charge of it soon after. **Van Dyck,** six years younger than **Jordaens,** was acquired by **Rubens** as assistant by 1619 or earlier; in 1620 before leaving for England he painted *Christ carrying the Cross* as a commission of his own for the Dominican church (S. Paul); and in 1621 on his return to Antwerp he painted *S. Martin dividing his cloak* for the church at Saventhem before he left for Genoa. **Cornelis Schut** (Pl. 669) and **Gerard Seghers** (Pl. 527) were both working for **Rubens** by 1620.

258

The **Rubens** commissions in this period included a large *Adoration of the Magi* completed in 1610 for Antwerp Town Hall (and given two years later, as related above, to the Count of Oliva), the *Raising of the Cross* (Pl. 528) for Antwerp, S. Walpurgis completed in 1611, the *Descent from the Cross* (Pl. 529) for the Crossbowmen's altar in Antwerp Cathedral completed in 1614 and the *Miraculous Draught of Fishes* ordered by the Fishermen's Guild for Malines Cathedral, on which **Jordaens** collaborated about 1618. In 1619 came commissions for the new Jesuit church in Antwerp—*S. Ignatius Loyola healing the possessed* and *Miracles of S. Francis Xavier* which alternated on the high altar, and also the commission for the *Last communion of S. Francis* for the Recollets church. In March 1620 **Rubens** contracted to deliver, within nine months, thirty-nine ceiling panels for the Jesuit church to be executed from his sketches by **Van Dyck** (named in the contract) and his other assistants; and in that year also he was commissioned by Burgomaster Nicholas Rockox to paint for the Recollets the *Crucifixion*, generally referred to as *Le coup de lance*, and the Prince of Arenberg ordered a *Dead Christ on the knees of the Virgin with S. Francis and other saints* for Brussels Capucins church. A *Last Judgement* and a *Fall of the Rebel Angels* also issued from his studio in these years; and he signed a *Lamentation* (Pl. 530) apparently painted on his own initiative. Both the *Raising of the Cross* and the *Descent from the Cross* were painted before his mass production factory was really in full swing and both for that reason may be largely his own work. In the *Raising of the Cross* (Pl. 528) he parades his ability to draw muscular nudes in violent action; the diagonal composition, as Sir Joshua Reynolds observed, may have been inspired by Tintoretto, though diagonal compositions had been long ago produced by the **Vienna Cruciform Lamentation Painter** (Pl. 64), **Geertgen tot Sint Jans** (Pl. 127) and others; the upturned eyes are religiosity; and the blood streaming from the tortured hands continues the aspect of the Flemish tradition that had led Michelangelo to speak of the 'floods of tears' caused by some Flemish paintings. The *Descent from the Cross* (Pl. 529) is more restrained in action; the central figure is admirably pathetic; and the concentration of light on this figure and the drapery almost unifies the design, though the waving hands of the Virgin and the arms of the half-nude man with carefully trimmed beard and silken hair bending down from above the Cross are disconcerting details; as imaginative illustration the picture as a whole rings false largely, I think, because the figures grouped round the central passage are too evidently painted from models dramatically posed in the studio; for just as the **van Eycks'** *Virgin* in the upper panels of the *Ghent altarpiece* (Pls. 9, 13) can only be apprehended as the Virgin after we have come to terms with the model as such, so the Magdalene in this picture is first seen as a particular pretty and plump girl in a silk dress and can only thereafter be transformed by the spectator to the part she plays. As imaginative illustration the small *Lamentation* (Pl. 530), inspired I imagine by Mantegna's famous foreshortened *Dead Christ*, is surely on a higher plane; the figures here, unconscious of the spectator, are within the drama, and the gesture of the Virgin, who is not closing the eyelids but lifting them to look again upon the eyes, is a memorable invention; the upturned head on the right is a disturbing note of religiosity and this head is also redundant in the linear design and destroys its balance and serenity; but we get a measure for the concept as a whole if we look at the subject as painted later by **Van Dyck** (Pl. 608) and **Gaspar de Crayer** (Pl. 609) largely as result of later works from the **Rubens** workshop. This small signed *Lamentation* of 1614, which I take to be wholly his own work, was perhaps in fact, his greatest religious painting; for the commissions which poured in on him after his first successes encouraged the rhetorical aspects of his talents; the Jesuits, who knew their business, set him to paint propaganda pictures of miracles performed by the recent saints, and he was thus decoyed to design huge theatrical scenes in architectural decors which were to hold their own in the gold and marble settings of the palatial new churches in the Jesuit style; and in such contributions, though he could and did display enormous technical talent, immense fertility of invention and exciting bravura in design, neither simplicity nor deep feeling were called for or forthcoming.

Among the 'history' paintings, mythologies and allegories I have mentioned the compositions provided for the Assembly Chamber of the Dutch States-General by **Otto van Veen** in 1613, the allegoric tableaux vivants in the Ommeganck procession of 1615 recorded by **Denis van Alsloot,** and the *Allegories of the Senses* painted by **Jan (Velvet) Brueghel** in 1617. **Otto van Veen's** uninspired compositions were twelve scenes titled *The Insurrection of the Batavians against the Romans* of which I show *Brinio acclaimed chief of the Canini-fates* (Pl. 510) and the *Supper in the Wood* (Pl. 511) where Brinio seems one of the participants. From **Denis van Alsloot's** pictures of the 1615 Ommeganck we know that one car had an allegoric tableau of *King Psapho of Libya with the birds trained to speak his name and thus spread his fame* and that another symbolized *The Virtues of Isabella*; the three cars shown in my colour reproduction (Pl. 513A) are *Diana and the archers* (symbolic of the Infanta's skill as already explained) *Apollo and the Muses* (the Muses here being all musicians) and the *Ship of Charles V* with sea-horses, sea-elephants and rigging (a traditional feature in these processions since its construction for the Brussels Pompe Funèbre of Charles V in 1558); and other features in the procession were Amazons on chargers and children mounted on decorated camels. The allegoric figures in the five *Allegories of the Senses* by **Jan (Velvet) Brueghel** were inserted by **Rubens** (a fact recorded in a document of 1636) and as can be seen from the *Allegory of Sight* reproduced (Pl. 542) they again point the contrast between the aesthetic of these two artists already remarked in the *Adam and Eve in Paradise* (Pl. 543); the allegoric meaning of these pictures is conveyed not only by the figures and the still-life but also in some cases by paintings on the walls; thus *The Marriage Feast at Cana* and a *Peasants feast* appear in *Taste, The Flagellation* appears in *Feeling,* and *Orpheus charming the animals* in *Hearing.* Other painters of allegories and mythologies at this time were **Hendrik van Balen, Abraham Janssens** and **Jordaens.** Of these **Hendrik van Balen,** a friend of **Jan (Velvet) Brueghel** and **Frans Snyders,** may have had their aid, as suggested above, in his charming, small undated *Rape of Europa* (Pl. 507) where he seems to have remembered Paolo Veronese's picture in the Doges' Palace. **Abraham Janssens** delivered his *Allegory of Antwerp and the Scheldt* (Pl. 509) to the Antwerp Town Hall in 1610 and we see there traces of anatomical instruction from **Jan Snellinck** (Pl. 460) reinforced by memories of his stay in Rome and of Michelangelo's Medici tomb in Florence. **Jordaens** painted his superb composition *The Daughters of Cecrops finding Erichthonius* (Pl. 546) at twenty-four in 1617, and the picture renders credible the statement made by the German art historian Sandrart in his lifetime that **Rubens** was jealous of **Jordaens.** The picture shows the moment when the daughters of Cecrops, having disobeyed Athene's orders by opening the chest where the child Erichthonius was hidden, find him surrounded by a serpent (or afflicted with a serpent's tail in lieu of legs), and **Jordaens** has imaged it by three nude figures and an old peasant attendant, a veritable Juliet's nurse, who looks at the baby with smiling affection; the noble design, with figures grouped on a shallow stage, goes back to the high-relief picture-concept of **Rogier van der Weyden's** *Descent from the Cross* (Pl. 46); and the massive nudes are deployed across the foreground where we can stretch out our hand and touch them like the figures in the foregrounds of pictures by **Pieter Aertsen** (Pls. 356, 357) and **Joachim Beuckelaer** (Pls. 399, 400). **Jordaens** here reveals himself equipped to paint large figures in light and shade, foreshortening and so on, and also as a classical artist impelled to transform rich sensual experience to ordered architectural form; the faces and bodies of the models are indeed, by classical standards, too much particularized, but even so the picture is a prodigious classical achievement. His undated *Allegory of Abundance* (Pl. 545), again a rich high-relief composition with figures massed in the foreground and particularized models, is less classical in impulse, less nobly simple in its rhythm, and more popular in appeal as the uninhibited sensual experience is less transmuted to linear design and related volumes; I presume it painted between 1618 and 1620 when he was associated with the **Rubens** factory, for in the *Daughters of Cecrops* of 1617 the models used have no connection with those then serving that establishment, but in the *Allegory of Abundance* the smiling negro in the background on the right appears twice in *Nature adorned by the Graces* (Pl. 544) by **Rubens** and assistants, and the plump short-necked fair-haired woman in the centre (evidently the Magdalene in **Rubens'** *Descent from the Cross* some five or six years older) is on the left there; the man crouching beneath the splendid still-life of vegetables and fruit is the model for Cimon in *Cimon finding the sleeping Iphigenia* (Pl. 548) by **Rubens** and assistants, and the brown-haired woman crouching in the foreground is similarly posed in the *Cimon*.

Of the 'history' paintings, mythologies and allegories by **Rubens** and his assistants a number are known or presumed to have been painted in this period. The allegories include *Nature adorned by the Graces*, the mythologies *Cimon finding the sleeping Iphigenia* and the *Rape of the daughters of Leucippus by Castor and Pollux*, and the 'histories' a series of designs for tapestries *The History of Decimus Mus* and paintings titled *Queen Tomyris receiving the head of Cyrus* and the *Battle of the Amazons*. The composition of *Nature adorned by the Graces* (Pl. 544) is related to the *Virgin and Child in a garland of flowers* (Pl. 541) by **Rubens** and **Jan (Velvet) Brueghel** and to *Terms; and a garland round a bust of Ceres* (Pl. 554) by **Snyders** and the theme is the same as the *Allegory of Abundance* (Pl. 545) by **Jordaens**; but the picture as a whole is a decorative concept and may be a design for tapestry. The *Cimon finding the sleeping Iphigenia* (Pl. 548) was also possibly a design for tapestry; here **Rubens** set out to rival the Venetians and Correggio as a painter of female beauty—as **Jan Massys** had set out to rival the nude painting of the Fontainebleau School in his *Flora* (Pl. 363) and **Joachim Uytewael** had challenged the Fontainebleau artists and the Italian mannerists with the charmingly posturing figures in his *Diana and Actaeon* (Pl. 498). We have seen, much earlier in our story, that **Jan Gossaert** added weight and a tang of Northern realism to the caressibility of Graeco-Roman sculpture in his *Neptune and Amphitrite* (Pl. 247); and now **Rubens** adds an over-life-size quality, a muscular structure and a nervous tension to the ripe pearl-decked loveliness of Veronese's female types, and to the soft hedonism of Correggio's sleeping Antiope (well known to him no doubt in Gonzaga's Mantua collection) and of Titian's sleeping Antiope (which he had seen, I presume, in the Pardo palace on his Spanish visit). In this picture **Rubens,** I fancy, must himself have painted or extensively 'retouched' the two recumbent figures which are pearly in the flesh tints and elegantly seductive in pose; and I assume that he also painted the central head (Pl. 549) where we learn as much about the mouth of his favourite blonde model who had posed for the Magdalene in the *Descent from the Cross* (Pl. 529) as we learned in the **van Eycks'** *Ghent altarpiece* about the mouth of the model who posed there for the Virgin (Pl. 13); and though undeniably erotic, this head is sublimated to great art—as we should see if it were set beside the *Ariadne in Naxos* by Jean-Baptiste Greuze. But this huge *Cimon finding the sleeping Iphigenia* as a whole is less majestically designed than the *Daughters of Cecrops* (Pl. 546) by **Jordaens** and it is built with parts that do not coalesce; it is all too evidently a factory product with the empty spaces round the figures filled in by the studio specialists for landscape, still-life and so on, and the group of nudes, compared with the group in the *Daughters of Cecrops* or even with the group of nudes by **Anthonis Blocklandt** in *Diana and Actaeon* (Pl. 420), is ill-composed as a formal unit—for a thin poor space divides the two front figures and the projecting sequence of leg-arm-leg makes a weak and spiky base. In the *Rape of the daughters of Leucippus* (Pl. 547A) four figures, two horses, and a cupid are confined within a diamond quadrilateral poised on one foot of the foreground nude (which is perhaps why Sir Joshua Reynolds described the composition as 'too artful'); here again **Rubens,** I imagine, must himself have painted the nudes of Hilaeira raised aloft by Castor, and Phoebe seized by Pollux; and the foreshortened head of Hilaeira (Pl. 547) is again a study from the girl who posed for the Magdalene in the *Descent from the Cross* but treated this time with a rhetorical expressiveness equivalent to the religiosity of upturned eyes in the religious subjects. The *Battle of the Amazons* (Pl. 576) represents the battle on the bridge of Thermodon between Theseus King of Athens and Hippolyta Queen of the Amazons whom Theseus took prisoner (and then married as we know from Shakespeare's 'Midsummer Night's Dream'). This is wholly I presume by **Rubens** and must surely be ranked among his finest works; the composition is a perfect unity, with the semi-circle of nude figures at the base completing the circle with the figures on the bridge; there is no question here of models posing in a studio, all is seen in the mind's eye and set down swiftly and with genius; some drawings of rearing horses by Leonardo da Vinci for his famous battle piece may have been, I think, a starting point (as Titian's *Bacchus and Ariadne* may have been the starting point for many of his *Bacchanals*, and Michelangelo's *Last Judgement* the spur for his own *Last Judgement* and *Fall of the Rebel angels*); but Leonardo's science was soon felt too restricting as the scene took rhythmic form and the grouping became more intricate and the action wilder and wilder till **Rubens** had given us in painting what Wagner was to give us later in the Ride of the Valkyries. There is erotic savagery in this scene of armed men slashing at women with bare breasts (as there is savagery in the hunting pieces by **Rubens** of this period); but all is absorbed here in the driving rhythm; and Reynolds must have had this picture in his memory when he wrote: 'The productions of Rubens seem to flow with a freedom and prodigality as if they cost him nothing; and to the general animation of the composition there is always a correspondent spirit in the execution of the work; the striking brilliancy of his colours, and their lively opposition to each other, the flowing liberty and freedom of his outline, the animated pencil with which every object is touched, all contribute to awaken and keep alive the attention of the spectator, to awaken in him, in some measure, correspondent sensations and make him feel a degree of that enthusiasm with which the painter was carried away.'

Only princes and nobles and exceptionally rich bourgeois could afford the 'histories', mythologies, allegories and hunting pieces produced by **Rubens** and his atelier in this period; only such collectors had palaces and mansions with space to display them; and only such, it may be, had the sumptuous taste which admired them. The *Cimon finding the sleeping Iphigenia* was bought by the Duke of Buckingham, the *Battle of the Amazons* was sold or given to the millionaire Cornelius van der Geest (Pl. 560) whose immense collection was visited by the Archduke and the Infanta in 1615, and the tapestry designs for the *History of Decimus Mus* were commissioned by the Pallavicini or some other noble family to decorate their Genoese palace. But there were many art lovers in Belgium with smaller purses and quite different tastes; and sidelights on the preferences of some are revealed in extant inventories of Antwerp collectors. We have for example an assessment by **Hendrik van Balen, Adriaen van Stalbemt** and a dealer son of **Pieter Goetkint** of the collection of one Nicolaes Cornelis Cheeus of Antwerp who died in 1621 owning a number of landscapes by **Jan (Velvet) Brueghel, Jacob Grimmer, Jacques Savery, Cornelis van Coninxloo, Lucas van Valkenborch, Josse de Momper, Paul Brill** and **Hendrik van Cleve,** flower pieces by **Jan (Velvet) Brueghel** and **Jacques de Gheyn,** a conflagration piece by **Mostaert (Gillis or Frans),** a winter scene by **Pieter Brueghel the younger,** battle pieces by **Sebastiaan Vrancx,** a *Flora* by **Jan Massys** (perhaps the charming picture reproduced here (Pl. 363)), Old Testament subjects and a *Last Judgement* by **Crispiaen van den Broeck** and, as 'Old Masters', a *S. Mary Magdalene* by **Quinten Massys** and a *Virgin and Child* which the assessors recorded as 'na der estimeerders ordeel' by 'Meester Ghear van Brugge' which may mean that they 'ascribed' it to **Gerard David** (Pl. 195). Another extant inventory shows that Jacques Snel, an Antwerp taverner who died in 1623, left a number of musical instruments decorated by **François Borsse, Otto van Veen, Jan Snellinck, Marten de Vos,** his son **Daniel de Vos** and 'Ruckaert' (perhaps the one-armed landscape painter **Marten Ryckaert)** and more than fifty paintings, many of large size, distributed in seven rooms; the paintings included a *Landscape with Daedulus and Icarus* by **Josse de Momper** (the figures by another hand), a landscape, a *Baptism of S. John* and an *Emmaus* by **Charles de Cauwer,** a *S. John preaching* by **Pieter Balten,** a *Tower of Babel* in which **Josse de Momper, Juliaen Teniers** and **Nicolas van Cleve** were collaborators and a *Preaching on the sea* the combined work of **Josse de Momper, Tobias van Haecht** and **Ambrosius Francken;** there were still-life and flower pieces by **Juliaen Teniers** and a *Larder scene ('banket') with a pickled herring* by an unnamed painter; the genre pictures included a *Kermesse,* a *Bride* and a *Blind man* by 'Pieter Brugel' and an *Attack on a baggage waggon* by **Josse de Momper** and **Sebastiaan Vrancx** which may have resembled the picture reproduced here (Pl. 531); and there were also *Scipio and Hannibal,* a *Crucifixion* and an *Orpheus* by **Lazarus van der Borcht,** a *Venus and Cupid* and a *Judgement of Paris* by unnamed painters, religious subjects by **Marten de Vos** and **Jan Snellinck** and portraits of the wine taverner and his wife by **Frans Francken.**

CHAPTER XII

Infanta Isabella, Governor-General

1622-1633

AFTER the Archduke Albert's death, the Infanta Isabella cut her hair, donned the Clarissan habit which she wore for the rest of her life, and entered the Tertiary Order of S. Francis; as there were no children of the marriage, the sovereignty of the Netherlands reverted, under the terms of its creation, to the crown of Spain; and she therefore ruled as Governor-General for her nephew Philip IV who was inaugurated by proxy as King of the Netherlands in the Belgian provinces in 1622. More devout than ever, the Infanta took part in many pilgrimages and religious processions and encouraged the establishment of more and more convents. Orthodoxy was complacently triumphant; but Jansen, who continued his fight against the Jesuits, became regius professor of scriptural interpretation in Louvain university and began his book 'Augustinus' in 1630, and Angélique Arnauld, Abbess of the Port Royal Convent, which moved to Paris from the country in 1626, was converted to Jansenism by Jansen's friend Duvergier de Hauranne, Abbot of S. Cyran, in this period. In state affairs the Infanta was officially guided by the Bishop of Segovia formerly confessor to the Archduke Albert, by Cardinal de la Cueva sent from Spain to fill the part formerly played by Granvella with Margaret of Parma, and, in the last years, by the Marquis d'Aytona sent to replace de la Cueva; but privately she now discussed her state affairs with **Rubens** who won her confidence perhaps in the ways that Disraeli won Queen Victoria's. The Thirty Years War continued through the period; and the Spanish war against Holland was resumed at the end of the Twelve Years Truce.

In 1622 the German Protestant adventurer Count Mansfeld defeated Count Tilly at Wiesbach and was himself defeated at Höchst; the Spaniards defeated Mansfeld at Fleurus (an event recorded later by **Pieter Meulener**), and Marquis Spinola leading Spanish-Belgian forces was driven from the siege of Bergen-op-Zoom by Mansfeld. In 1623 Urban VIII succeeded Gregory XV as Pope; the Infanta Isabella sent her own carriages to instal Annunciad nuns in a new establishment at Ghent and welcomed to Belgium Anna of S. Bartholomew sometime secretary and infirmarian and last companion of S. Theresa. Prince Charles aged twenty-three and George Villiers now Duke of Buckingham aged thirty-one arrived in Madrid as 'Mr. Smith' and 'Mr. Brown' to court Philip IV's sister the Infanta Maria; the project failed; Charles went back to England with the promise of some pictures by Titian as a consolation; and **Jan Porcellis** recorded his departure in his *Prince Charles leaving Santander*. In 1624 James I promised the Dutch assistance; Richelieu (restored to power by Louis XIII) sent them money; and Isabella reviewed the Spanish troops before Breda which Spinola was besieging. In 1625 James I died; Charles I was married by proxy in Paris to Henrietta Maria (sister of Louis XIII) and formed alliances with France and Denmark against Spain; English troops were sent to serve under Mansfeld; and Sir Edward Cecil failed to take Cadiz and intercept the Spanish treasure ships. Richelieu waging war against the Huguenots began the siege of La Rochelle; Prince Maurice of Nassau died and Frederick Henry succeeded as Stadholder; and Isabella triumphantly entered Breda which Spinola had captured. In 1626 Mansfeld was defeated by Wallenstein at the Bridge of Dessau; Charles IV of Denmark was defeated by Tilly at Lutter; and Buckingham sent an emissary to the Netherlands to broach secret negotiations for a peace with Spain. In 1627 there was war between England and France; and Buckingham leading an expedition to relieve La Rochelle was defeated on the Isle de Ré. In 1628 Charles I agreed to the Petition of Right; Buckingham was murdered; La Rochelle was taken by Richelieu; Wallenstein failed in the siege of Stralsund; a Spanish silver fleet was captured by the Dutch; Spinola was recalled to Spain; and Henri de Bergh became generalissimo of the Spanish-Belgian forces in the Netherlands. In 1629 Richelieu signed La Grace d'Alais with the Huguenots; Charles I made peace with France; Christian of Denmark signed the Peace of Lübeck; and Gustavus Adolphus of Sweden joined the German Protestants. Spanish forces had brief successes in Gelderland and the province of Utrecht, the Dutch West Indian Company financed the national resistance, Frederick Henry captured Bois-le-Duc, Isabella pawned her jewels for 566,000 florins which helped the Treasury to pay some troops but drained the resources of the Flemish State Pawnshops (of which **Wenzelas Coebergher** was still, it would seem, director), and Philip IV and the Count Duke Olivarez took steps about a peace with England. In 1630 Spinola died; England made peace with Spain; and Marie de Médicis tried vainly to persuade Louis XIII to thrust Richelieu from power. In 1631 Gustavus Adolphus, financed by Richelieu, took Frankfort-on-Oder; Tilly sacked Magdeburg; and Gustavus defeated Tilly at the first Battle of Breitenfeld. Henri de Bergh was replaced to his great indignation by the Marquis de Santa Cruz as generalissimo of the Spanish-Belgian forces; a Spanish fleet left Antwerp with an army for an attack on Zeeland and was destroyed by the Dutch; Prince Frederick Henry invaded Flanders; and Marie de Médicis, exiled by Richelieu and Louis XIII, took refuge in the Infanta's territories. In 1632 Galileo published his 'Dialogo dei due massimi sistemi del mondo' at sixty-eight in Florence and was cited to Rome by the Inquisition. Gustavus Adolphus won the battle of Lech (where Tilly was mortally wounded) and occupied Augsburg and Munich; Wallenstein defeated Gustavus at Alte Veste; Gustavus was killed at the battle of Lützen; and his daughter Christina aged six became Queen of Sweden. Prince Frederick Henry captured Maestricht; some Flemish nobles, long dissatisfied through their exclusion from influence by the Spanish caucus, formed a nationalist plot known as the Conspiration des Nobles; Henri de Bergh went over to the Dutch; Isabella summoned the Belgian States-General, appealed to the country, and was supported; and the Belgian States-General sent envoys to Holland in the hope of negotiating peace. In 1633 Wallenstein won the battle of Steinau; Bishop Laud became Archbishop of Canterbury; the Earl of Newcastle spent £20,000 in entertaining Charles I at Welbeck; Philip IV took possession of the Casa del Buen Retiro (presented to him by Olivarez) and wore for the festivities a suit of brown velvet embroidered in silver in which Velazquez painted him; Galileo recanted (with the verbal or mental reservation 'eppur si muove'); and the Infanta Isabella died at sixty-seven with Marie de Médicis aged sixty by her bedside.

Thanks to his personal friendship with the widowed Infanta, **Rubens** now reached the apex of his social progress and became involved in politics. In 1622 he went to Paris to arrange about pictures for the Luxembourg Palace and took a little dog and a necklace with twenty-four enamelled plaques as presents from the Infanta to Marie de Médicis. In 1624 the Infanta made him a Gentleman of the Household; the Bishop of Segovia, President of the Netherlands Council, inspired no doubt by the Infanta, obtained for him a title of nobility from Philip IV (urging among other things in his favour that he 'lived splendidly' and had the means to maintain that state); and the Infanta began to employ him in secret negotiations for a new truce with Holland. In 1625 he met Buckingham in Paris at the wedding by proxy of King Charles and Henrietta Maria, and Buckingham went to his studio in Antwerp. In 1626 when Buckingham wished to negotiate peace between England and Spain he chose as emissary the painter-dealer Balthasar Gerbier and ordered him to address himself to **Rubens** as a fellow painter and a man in the Infanta's confidence. In 1627 **Rubens** was empowered by the Infanta to discuss these secret peace proposals under cover of the sale to Buckingham of paintings and other works of art, and for these purposes he met Gerbier in Holland, a proceeding which angered Philip IV who wrote to the Infanta: 'I much regret that you have recourse to a painter to treat of such important affairs. It is the cause of great discredit, as may be imagined, for this monarchy, since there necessarily follows a loss of prestige when a man of such little importance is the minister whom ambassadors must seek out in such weighty matters. Though we cannot actually refuse to allow the proposer his choice of intermediary, since we are engaged to it from the beginning, and since England does not consider it harmful that that intermediary should be **Rubens,** none the less it is very harmful to our country.' In 1628 the King followed this by summoning **Rubens** to Spain to report in detail on his political actions to himself and to the Count Duke Olivarez; **Rubens** went, placated them both, was made Secretary of the Netherlands Privy Council, and was sent in 1629 to England to propose an exchange of ambassadors for peace talks (he went as the Infanta's envoy but had orders to report in detail to Olivarez). On the way he passed through Brussels where he paid his respects to the Infanta. He reached England on June 5 accompanied by his brother-in-law Hendrik Brant and attendants, and was given an interview by Charles I at Greenwich the next day; the exchange of ambassadors was arranged after many long delays; and before he left in March 1630 he was knighted by the King and given a diamond hatband (bought from Gerbier for £500) and Gerbier was given a hundred and twenty-eight pounds two shillings and elevenpence as refund for expenses incurred in procuring his comforts. In 1631 he was one of the Infanta's representatives to welcome Marie de Médicis in the Netherlands and when she was installed there he helped her to pawn her jewels; and in the same year, as secret personal envoy of the Infanta, he had an interview with Prince Frederick Henry at The Hague. He went again to Holland in 1632 and took to the Stadholder's camp near Maestricht the Infanta's own proposals for peace or truce terms with Holland—a proceeding which this time caused much anger among the official Belgian State envoys (led by the Primate Archbishop of Malines, the Prince of Arenberg and the Duke of Aerschot). But **Rubens** kept his head despite the success of his social climbing. He knew that kings, courtiers and ministers looked upon him as a parvenu; and when he married his second wife at fifty-three in 1630 he chose a girl of sixteen, daughter of an Antwerp silk merchant and wrote of the event; 'I have married a young woman of honourable though humble birth, though everyone advised me to choose a lady about the Court. I feared "commune illud nobilitatis malum superbiam praesertim in illo sexu" and for that reason I chose one who would not blush to see me take up my brushes. Also I loved my liberty too much to give it up for the embraces of any old woman.' From soon after 1630 he seems indeed to have drawn back to some extent from the world of kings and princes; and he now painted for his personal pleasure his *Helena Fourment nude with a fur coat* (Pl. 601) which he gave to his young wife and possibly the *Peasants' dance* (Pl. 666) which was also never put upon the market.

Van Dyck was also now progressively successful as a social figure. In a six years stay in Italy he was a favoured guest in the palaces of Italian nobles and much admired by the Italian ladies for his handsome appearance, elegant clothes and engaging manners; back in Antwerp he became Court Painter to the Infanta in 1630; he was visited in his studio by Marie de Médicis in 1631; and he was launched as Charles I's Court Painter and knighted by 1633.

The reputation of Flemish painting was now very high in various countries, thanks to the foreign travels of **Rubens** and **Van Dyck** and to the work of many other painters resident or visitors in France, Italy, Holland, England and elsewhere.

In Paris the Court Painters of Louis XIII included **Frans Pourbus** (Pls. 539, 540), **Rudolf Schoof, Ferdinand Elle** and **Jacques Fouquier** (Pl. 563). Of these **Frans Pourbus** died at fifty-three in 1622; **Ferdinand Elle** continued to paint portraits; and **Jacques Fouquier**, commissioned to fill the spaces between the windows of the Grande Galerie du Louvre with paintings of the principal French cities, set off on travels through the country to make sketches for this purpose. In 1622 Marie de Médicis began the adornment of the Luxembourg Palace just built for her by Salomon de Brosse; she put one Nicolas Duchesne in charge of the decorations and both **Philippe de Champaigne** (Pls. 742, 750), then just over twenty, and Nicolas Poussin, just under thirty, were employed there on panels before 1624. At the same time—having heard perhaps that Louis XIII had commissioned a set of tapestries depicting the *History of Constantine* from **Rubens** and wishing to outdo him as a patron—she herself ordered from **Rubens** a series of huge historico-allegoric pictures recording and celebrating her own life up to date; and she summoned him to Paris to decide upon the subjects. **Rubens** arrived in January and before he left, six weeks later, twenty-one subjects were agreed upon; these included: *The Birth and Education of Marie de Médicis; Henri IV ravished by her portrait; The Marriage by proxy in Florence; The Landing at Marseilles; The second Marriage in Lyons; The Birth of Louis XIII; Henri IV entrusting the Queen with the government of France before departing for the war with Germany; The Queen's Coronation in S. Denis; The Apotheosis of Henri IV; The Good government of the Queen; The Journey to Ponts de Cé; France receiving Anne of Austria betrothed to Louis XIII and Spain receiving Isabella of Bourbon betrothed to Prince Philip; The Queen leaving Paris after the murder of Concini* (later changed to *Prosperity under the Queen's rule); The Majority of Louis XIII; The escape of the Queen from the Château de Blois; The Queen deciding on reconciliation with Louis XIII; The Queen celebrating the 1619 Peace; The meeting between the Queen and Louis XIII in 1619;* and *The Queen and Louis XIII united by the publication of the Truth.* By May 1623 **Rubens** was back in Paris bringing nine finished pictures, all about thirteen feet high; Marie de Médicis was delighted; Richelieu commissioned a painting for himself; and it was perhaps at this time that **Rubens** painted his *Portrait of Marie de Médicis* (Pl. 575) a smug, superficial, flattering concoction —(compare it with the searching and sensitive portrait by the **Munich Duchess Magdalena Painter** (Pl. 520))—which became an archetype for countless flattering portraits of fat ladies. By February 1625 the remaining twelve pictures of the Marie de Médicis series were finished in Antwerp and transported to Paris; **Rubens,** with **Justus van Egmont** (Pl. 722) then twenty-four among his assistants, supervised the erection of the whole series in the Luxembourg gallery; he had finally retouched them in situ by May when the King and his

Court, and Buckingham (in Paris for Charles I's wedding) were invited to see them; and he returned to Antwerp with **Justus van Egmont** in June. In 1625, also, **Jan Brueghel the younger** (Pl. 605) was in Paris on his way home from Italy. In the following years Nicolas Duchesne and **Philippe de Champaigne** continued the decoration of other parts of the Luxembourg Palace; and in 1628, when Duchesne died, Marie de Médicis made **Philippe de Champaigne** her Premier Peintre, installed him in a studio in the palace, and commissioned from him some religious subjects for the Carmelite convent; Louis XIII not to be outdone then ordered **Philippe de Champaigne** to paint *Louis XIII crowned by Victory* (*with La Rochelle in the background*) and in 1633 he commissioned from him *Louis XIII conferring the Order of the Saint Esprit on the Duc de Longueville in 1633* a composition like a later picture reproduced here (Pl. 750). **Justus van Egmont** (Pl. 722) returned to Paris as an independent artist in 1628 and painted portraits after collaborating for a time with the French painter Simon Vouet. **Henri Staben** (Pl. 518) also moved from Antwerp to Paris probably in the later twenties; and three newcomers in 1631 were **Pieter van Mol** then thirty-two who was at work soon after on mural paintings for the Carmelite church, **Peeter Franchoys** (Pl. 654) then twenty-five, and **Theodor van Thulden** (Pls. 589, 753) who was also twenty-five and worked first for the Trinitarians and then went to Fontainebleau to make etchings of Niccolo del Abbate's frescoes in the Ulysses Gallery. The marine painter **Mathieu van Plattenberg** (known in France as **Platte-Montagne**) was in Paris before 1633; he studied there under **Jacques Fouquier** (Pl. 563) after earlier instruction in Antwerp or Genoa from the marine painter **Andries van Ertvelt** (Pl. 704); and the still-life painter **Frans Ijkens** (Pl. 695) nephew and former pupil of **Osias Beet** (Pl. 506) was in Aix-en-Provence and Marseilles in 1629.

In Italy there were resident Flemings in Genoa, Florence, Rome and elsewhere and the usual visitors. **Jan Brueghel the younger** (Pl. 605) arrived in Milan aged twenty-one in 1622 with a letter from his father **Jan (Velvet) Brueghel** to Cardinal Borromeo. In Genoa the Flemings round **Cornelis de Wael** included **Van Dyck** in the spring of 1622 and at various times later, **Lucas de Wael** who went back to Antwerp in 1628, and the animal painter **Jan Roos.** The newcomers there included **Jan Brueghel the younger, Vincent Malo, and Andries van Ertvelt;** of these **Jan Brueghel the younger** came from Milan and went on to Rome; **Vincent Malo,** painter of genre pictures (Pl. 615) and of religious subjects for Genoese churches, came from Antwerp, where he had worked under **Rubens,** and lodged with **Cornelis de Wael; Andries van Ertvelt** (Pl. 704) reached Genoa from Antwerp about 1628 and went home about 1630. In 1625 **Ernest Schayck the younger** painted a *Virgin of the Rosary* and in 1631 a *Virgin in Glory with Saints* for churches in San Severino and seems then to have died there. In Florence **Justus Sutterman** was still Court portrait painter to Duke Ferdinand dei Medici and **Theodoor Rombouts** (Pls. 581, 596, 597) was probably there till he went back to Antwerp in 1625. In Rome (where Poussin was settled by 1624 and Claude le Lorrain by 1627) the Flemish painters founded a Schildersbent (Artists club) in 1623 and this, known later as the 'Bent', became the recognized centre for the welcoming of newcomers. Among the older artists already established there **Paul Brill** (Pls. 473, 474) lived till 1626 and is said by his contemporary Baglione to have worked with undiminished skill in his last years and to have sold his easel pictures to Flemish dealers for high prices. **Pietro de Lignis** (Pl. 573) lived till 1627, **Anton van den Heuvel** went back to Ghent in 1628, **Jacob de Hase** and **Balthasar Lauwers** remained through the period, and **Nicolas Regnier** now painting religious pictures was a member of the Congregazione dei Virtuosi in 1623 and left for Venice in 1626. Of the new arrivals in Rome **Jan Brueghel the**

younger came down from Genoa in 1623 and went thence to Malta, Palermo and Milan before going back to Antwerp in 1625; **Cornelis Schut the younger** arrived in Rome in 1624, was nicknamed 'Brotsack' in the Bent and seems to have gone back to Antwerp in 1628. **Louis Cousin (Luigi Primo)** painter of portraits and religious subjects came from Brussels via Paris at about twenty about 1626 and stayed on; **Karel Spieringh** who also came from Brussels was in Rome at twenty-two in 1631. **Jacob van Oost the elder** (Pls. 715, 729, 740) came from Bruges some time in the early twenties and was home again by 1629. **Gillis Backereel** (Pl. 594) was in Rome for some time in the middle twenties. **François Walschartz** from Liège seems to have come soon after. **Theodore van Loon,** who had already worked for Brussels and Louvain churches, came at a few years over forty in 1628 and stayed till 1632; **Matthias Stom (Stomer)** came from Utrecht where he had worked under the Dutchman Gerard Honthorst (Gerardo della Notte) at approximately thirty in 1630 and moved on to Naples in 1632; and **Peter van Lint** (Pls. 677, 697) reached Rome at twenty-four in 1633 and was helped by Cardinal Ginnasio.

Van Dyck was in Genoa, Florence, Rome, Venice (where he studied portraits by Titian and Tintoretto and Veronese's pictures in the Doges' Palace) Mantua, Parma, Naples and Palermo at various times between 1622 and 1627. He was in Rome in the summer of 1622; he then returned to Antwerp on family affairs; and he was back in Rome in the summer of 1623 when he stayed in the palace of the historian Cardinal Guido Bentivoglio and painted his portrait. In Rome, though on terms of friendship with **Jan Brueghel the younger** (two years his junior) and with the Belgian sculptor François Duquesnoy, he seems to have been unpopular with his countrymen in the Schildersbent who resented his fine clothes, his cavalier manners and the servants who walked behind him in the street. In Palermo he drew the Italian woman painter Sofonisba Anguissola then ninety-six years old; and wherever he went he made drawings of pictures by Venetian and other High Renaissance artists. After 1623 he was mainly in Genoa at work on portraits for the Balbi, Pallavicini, Grimaldi, Adorno, Spinola, Brignole-Sale, Lomellini, Durazzo and other families; and I reproduce his *Elena Grimaldi, Marchesa Cattaneo* (Pl. 579) where a negro page in 'Titian' pink holds a red parasol above the black-gowned lady who strolls majestically, flower in hand, to the terraced gardens of the Cattaneo palace.

In Holland (where Frans Hals was forty in 1621 and Rembrandt was fifteen) **Cornelis van der Voort** continued to paint groups of civic guardsmen and other portraits in Amsterdam till he died, under fifty, in 1625. **Adriaen van Nieulandt** (Pls. 515, 647) painted his *Prince Maurice with Prince Frederick Henry and his suite by the seashore* before 1625; and I reproduce his *Procession of the lepers in Amsterdam on 'Kopper Maandag'* (Pl. 515) where the annual procession on the second Monday after New Year's day comes towards us in a townscape showing the Waag, the Nieuwe Kerk, the old Raadhuis and the Damrak, while two drummers warn a crowd of genre figures disposed haphazard on the Dam in the Flemish tradition of the crowd caught, as it were, by a camera-obscura—a tradition going back to **Pieter Bruegel the elder's** *Children's games* (Pl. 369) and *Battle between Carnival and Lent* (Pl. 370). **David Vinckeboons,** who had followed this tradition in his *Village Fair* (Pl. 533) of 1610, discussed in my last chapter, was at work in Amsterdam till he died there in 1629; his *Christ preaching at Gennesaret* of 1623 has young children and a dog at play in the foreground; and his *Village Fair* of 1629 has large figures of feasting and romping peasants combined across the foreground in a single chain of animated movement. **Willem van Nieulandt** (Pl. 475) moved from Antwerp to Amsterdam about 1629. **Adriaen Brouwer** (Pls. 617, 618) who had been a pupil of Frans Hals in Haarlem (at the same time as the Dutch painter Adriaen van Ostade) was in Amsterdam in 1626 and lodging with the painter-dealer-innkeeper **Bernaert van Somer;** he seems to have been back in Haarlem in 1627; his *Peasants and soldiers brawl by wayside inn* (Pl. 617) and *Boors' carouse* (Pl. 618) were possibly painted in Holland before he settled in Antwerp at about twenty-five in 1631. **Bernaert van Somer** himself stood godparent, with the Dutch woman painter Judith Leyster, to a daughter of Frans Hals in 1631, and died in Amsterdam in 1632. The marine painter **Jan Porcellis** moved from Antwerp to Haarlem in 1622; he was mainly at sea in 1624 perhaps gathering material for his *Prince Charles leaving Santander in 1623* already referred to; he settled in Amsterdam in 1625, and died in Leyden at forty-seven in 1632. **Jan Coelenbier** painter of landscapes and river scenes reached Haarlem from Courtrai at something over thirty in 1632; and the painter of kitchen pieces, **Pieter Cornelisz Ryck,** probably died in Haarlem before 1633. **Jacques de Gheyn** (Pl. 484) died in The Hague at sixty-four in 1629. **Adriaen Lucasz Fonteyn** painter of peasant and social genre scenes reached Rotterdam probably from his native Ypres in 1626 and remained there. In Utrecht **Joachim Uytewael** (Pls. 490, 498, 524), **Adam Willaerts** (Pl. 688) and **Roelandt Savery** (Pls. 525, 564, 583, 585) were all still working in 1633 when the first was sixty-seven, the second fifty-six and the third fifty-seven; **Savery** was chosen by the city to present personally on their behalf a number of his pictures as a gift to Amalia van Solms on her marriage with Prince Frederick Henry in 1626; and in 1628 he painted the *Orpheus charming the animals* reproduced here (Pl. 586). Other Flemings working in Holland through the period were the flower painters **Abraham Bosschaert** and **Ambrosius Bosschaert the younger,** the landscape painters **Pieter Stalpaert** and **Willem van Bundel** and the architectural painter **Paul Vredeman de Vries** who probably died about 1633.

Van Dyck went to The Hague about 1628 on the invitation of Prince Frederick Henry to make portraits of the Prince and Amalia van Solms; he also painted the poet Constantyn Huygens then private secretary to the Stadholder; and on this visit (or on his way to England in 1632) he called on Frans Hals, drew or painted his portrait, and received his own portrait by Hals in exchange.

Rubens is not known to have painted any pictures on his month's visit to Holland in 1627 or his nine- and eight-day visits in 1631 and 1632. But it is known that on the 1627 visit he met Gerbier in Delft, went from town to town upon what the British ambassador called 'the pretence of pictures' to be acquired for Buckingham, and further masked his political action by calling on the Dutch painters Gerard Honthorst, Abraham Bloemaert and Cornelis van Poelenburgh in Utrecht and by confiding to his escort, the young German painter and art historian Joachim van Sandrart, that he had come to Holland to forget his sorrow at the death of his much loved wife.

Jordaens made a journey in Holland with his father-in-law **Adam van Noort** in 1632, and may then have become a crypto-Calvinist; no pictures painted by him on this journey seem to be recorded.

In Spain there was much demand now for pictures by Flemish painters, and dealers imported landscapes, marines, genre and allegoric pieces and religious subjects. In Court circles **Jan (Velvet) Brueghel** was in high repute as the Infanta Isabella had sent a number of his pictures to both Philip III and Philip IV and the royal palaces had others acquired by Philip IV's Queen, Isabella of Bourbon. **Rubens** was also now very famous in Court circles; and the King owned his huge picture the *Adoration of the Magi* (painted as related in 1609 for the Antwerp Town Hall, given in 1612 by the city of Antwerp to the Spanish envoy Roderigo Calderon, Count of Oliva, and acquired by Philip after Oliva's execution in 1621). In 1603 **Rubens** had not been presented to Philip III when he came in charge of the Duke of Mantua's presents; but in 1628 he was treated as a second Titian by Philip IV who ordered from him an equestrian picture *Philip II crowned by Victory* and also an equestrian portrait of himself. **Rubens** on his side wrote about the King: 'This Prince is evidently very fond of painting and in my opinion has excellent qualities. I know him personally as my rooms are in the palace and he comes to see me nearly every day'; and in another letter 'I have nothing but pity for the King. He is gifted by nature with all qualities of mind and body . . . he could certainly be capable of governing under any difficulties if he did not distrust himself and put too much trust in his ministers'. It took Philip and Olivarez eight months to decide to send **Rubens** to England; he thus had time to enlarge and extensively repaint his early *Adoration of the Magi*, to paint portrait heads of all the Royal Family (a commission from the Infanta Isabella), and to make a free copy in his own manner of Titian's *Adam and Eve*. He also had time to go to the Escorial with Velazquez (then thirty and thus twenty-two years his junior) and to make a drawing *View of the Escorial with deer in the foreground* which was painted by one 'Verhulst' (**Pieter van der Hulst?**) either later in Antwerp or at the time in Spain if he was there as an assistant.

In England the established Flemings included **Marcus Geeraerts the younger** and **Hendrik van Steenwyck the younger** (Pls. 487, 489, 536, 537) both active through the period; and the newcomers included **Jacques de Gheyn** (Pl. 484), **Jorge Geldorp, Alexander Keirincx** (Pls. 610, 611, 613), **Abraham van Diepenbeeck, Rubens, Van Dyck, Remigius van Leemput, Jan van Reyn** (Pls. 592, 651), **Adriaen van Stalbemt** (Pls. 479, 562) and **Jan van Belcamp.** Of these **Marcus Geeraerts** signed his *Elizabeth, Lady Russell* when he was sixty-four in 1633. **Hendrik van Steenwyck** signed a *Court of a Renaissance Palace* like the earlier outdoor perspective reproduced here (Pl. 536) in 1623, and a *Liberation of S. Peter* in the style of the night piece (Pl. 489) in 1626. **Jacques de Gheyn** paid a visit with his son, an engraver of the same name, in 1622 and then went back to Holland. **Jorge Geldorp,** portrait painter and possibly a son of **Gortzius Geldorp** (Pls. 454, 486), arrived from Antwerp after 1623, became curator of Charles I's collections and had a house in Drury Lane where he 'entertained Ladies and Gentlemen with wine and hams and other curious eatables and carried on intreagues between them'. **Alexander Keirincx** came to London from Antwerp (probably from the **Rubens** atelier) in 1625; he was known in England as **Carings**; and his *Oakwood with staghunt* (Pl. 611)—a personal enrichment of the **Coninxloo-Govaerts** tradition (Pls. 466, 478)—was painted here in 1630. **Abraham van Diepenbeeck** seems to have been here (also from the **Rubens** atelier) in 1629 and may then have painted a series of life-size portraits of the Earl of Newcastle's Barbary horses with the Earl's several mansions in the backgrounds.

Rubens had time to paint some pictures here and make plans and sketches for decorative projects as it took Charles and Philip ten months to agree arrangements for the exchange of ambassadors. The chief pictures were *Peace and War* (Pl. 591A)—originally titled *Peace and Plenty*—a sumptuous composition with life-size figures, including a group of children apparently painted from Gerbier's family, which **Rubens** presented to the King as an allegory of their peacemaking efforts; and a *S. George and the Dragon* set in a Thames-side valley with small figures including the King as S. George and Henrietta Maria as Cleodolinda, which Charles acquired through Endymion Porter. The chief decorative enterprise undertaken here was a commission from the King for ceiling paintings in the Banqueting House of Whitehall palace, the subject being in general terms *The Apotheosis of King James I* with a series of allegories in separate panels; and **Rubens** made sketches for some of these panels and showed them to the King. He also possibly made sketches here for a set of tapestries *The History of Ulysses* commissioned by an unrecorded patron. It is not known what assistants worked with him on this English visit; he may have called on **Abraham van Diepenbeeck** and **Alexander Keirincx** or summoned others from his Antwerp atelier when he saw that his stay was likely to be long; but a contemporary letter says: 'MONS. **Rubens** in honour of our nation hath drawn with his pencil the history of S. George wherein (if it be possible) he hath exceeded himself; but the picture he hath sent home into Flanders to remain as a monument of his abode and employment here'—which suggests that, in fact, he made a sketch-painting for *S. George and the Dragon* and sent it to Antwerp to be enlarged and executed in the usual way.

Van Dyck arrived here from Antwerp aged thirty-three in the spring of 1632; he lodged with **Jorge Geldorp** till the King gave him a house in Blackfriars and made him 'Principal Painter to their Majesties' in July; and before the end of 1633 he had painted several portraits of the King and Queen and among some portraits of nobility his *Venetia, Lady Digby as Prudence* and the *Philip Lord Wharton* reproduced here (Pl. 612). **Van Dyck** was soon joined by one of his pupils from Antwerp the able **Jan van Reyn** (Pls. 592, 651) who worked here as his assistant, and by another young Anversois **Remigius van Leemput** who lived here in his house and copied his pictures. **Jan van Belcamp** a pupil of **Hendrik van Balen** (Pls. 507, 508) seems also to have come about 1632 and worked in **Van Dyck's** studio; and **Adriaen van Stalbemt** (Pls. 479, 562), here for ten months in 1633, signed a *View of Greenwich Park* with figures of the King and Queen and courtiers inserted by **van Belcamp.**

In Central Europe the Flemish portrait painter **Anton van Opstal** was working for the Archduke Charles in Silesia from 1622 till 1624. **Pieter Stevens the younger** (Pl. 468) died probably in Prague after 1624. **Gillis van Valkenborch** died in Frankfort in 1622 and **Frederick van Valkenborch** (Pl. 502) in Nuremberg in 1623. **Hendrick van der Borcht the elder** moved from Frankenthal to Frankfort in 1627; **Pieter de Witte (Candido)** died in Munich in 1628; and **Willem Panneels** (Pl. 668) toured Germany in 1630–32.

At home in the Belgian art world there were unions by marriage, and arrangements with dealers, and collaborations as in the previous period; and though we read of financial and other distresses in some cases, the majority of painters appear to have prospered. Thus by 1623 the marine painter **Abraham Matthys** was back in Antwerp from his expeditions with the whaling fleet and soon after he became a brother of the Tertiary Order of S. Francis and turned to religious subjects. In 1625 **Cornelis Schut** (Pl. 669), **Hendrik van Balen** (Pls. 507, 508) and **Rubens** became executors of **Jan (Velvet) Brueghel's** will and guardians of his younger children; and **Jan Brueghel the younger** (Pl. 605) aged twenty-four took over his father's studio and made plans to run it as a mass production factory with collaborators and assistants. In 1626 Isabella Brant, the first wife of **Rubens,** died; **Jan Brueghel the younger** married Sara Janssens daughter of **Abraham Janssens** (Pl. 509) and niece of Antoon Goetkint a painter-dealer active in Antwerp and later in Paris where he was known as Bonenfant; **Abraham Janssens,** now over fifty, is said to have worked little in later life and to have spent his time in taverns, but his paintings were still in demand and a *Crucifixion* by him was sold this year for the high price of 1000 guilders. In 1627 **Rubens** bought the Château d'Ursele at Eeckeren, north of Antwerp, as a country house; **Theodoor Rombouts** (Pls. 581, 596, 597) married a sister of **Jan Philip van Thielen** (Pl. 754) later a successful painter of flowers; and **Cornelis de Vos** (Pls. 590, 599, 600, 641) was Antwerp representative of a Seville dealer Chrysostom van Immerseel (a cousin of **Jan Brueghel the younger**) who was now buying shiploads of Flemish pictures for customers in Spain, Portugal and the New World. In 1628 Cornelius van der Geest made **Willem van Haecht** the keeper of his picture gallery; **Jan Brueghel the younger** became Antwerp agent for Van Immerseel; **Rubens** in an affidavit praised his former assistant **Deodatus Delmont** as painter, architect, engineer and 'zealot of the true Catholic religion'. **Willem Panneels** (Pl. 668) was in charge of **Rubens'** house in Antwerp when **Rubens** went to Spain; the still-life painter **Adriaen van Utrecht** (Pls. 693, 694) aged twenty-nine married the poetess Constantia van Nieulandt daughter of **Willem van Nieulandt** (Pl. 475) himself the author of a number of plays including an 'Anthony and Cleopatra' and a 'Solomon' for the 'Olyfetak' drama Society; and **Simon de Vos** (Pls. 673, 674, 687) aged twenty-five married **Adriaen van Utrecht's** sister. In 1629 **David Teniers the elder** was in prison for the fraudulent raising of a second mortgage on his house property and was rescued by sales of pictures by himself and his son **David Teniers** (Pls. 567, 678-80, 682, 683) who was then nineteen and had organized the sales. In 1630 Helena Fourment a niece of the wife of **Jan Wildens** (Pls. 628, 629) was married to **Rubens**. In 1631 **Adriaen Brouwer** (Pls. 595, 617, 618, 623, 625) became Antwerp Master at about twenty-five having somehow crossed the Dutch frontier without the necessary passport; **Jacques Moermans** began to sell engravings and prints by various artists to Antoon Goetkint (Bonenfant) in Paris; and **Jan Brueghel the younger,** who had just inherited his stepmother's collection of pictures containing works wholly by his father and some partly by his father and partly by himself, sent those wholly by his father to Paris to be sold there after copies had been made of them. In 1632 when pictures in the estate of **Abraham Janssens** were put up to auction the bidding was interrupted by the noise of gunfire from a naval battle on the Scheldt; **Jan Brueghel the younger** exhibited in his studio a set of *The Five Senses* which were inspected and admired, he tells us, by countless visitors (duysent menschen); **Rubens,** called as witness in a lawsuit, expressed a respect for **Brouwer's** pictures which were already then being copied and forged; and Jan van der Bosch a silk merchant paid **Brouwer's** debts in exchange for the contents of his studio which included eleven sketches by **Brouwer** himself, two landscapes by **Josse de Momper** (Pl. 500), two grisailles by **Jooris van Cleve,** a landscape on marble by **Jacques Fouquier** (Pl. 563), a map of the Siege of Breda, a lay figure and some books. In 1633 **Brouwer** was imprisoned, probably as a suspected spy, in the Antwerp Citadel where the prison baker **Joos van Craesbeeck** (Pls. 616, 619, 620, 626) became his friend; and his release was procured by **Rubens** who introduced him in his mansion to good company which he found more constraining than the Citadel; and by this time Albert the eldest son of **Rubens** had been married to a daughter of **Deodatus Delmont.**

Speaking generally we find, as before, a group of Court painters, a much larger group associated with the Guilds and the Chambers of Rhetoric, and a third group associated with the **Rubens** factory; and the subjects of the pictures, as before, include topical pieces, portraits and portrait groups, and social, domestic and gay-life genre, landscapes and marines, rural and military outdoor scenes, interiors of churches and collectors' galleries, still-life and flowerpieces as well as allegories, mythologies, 'history', and religious subjects mainly commissioned for churches.

The Infanta's Court Painters for the whole or part of the period included **Jan (Velvet) Brueghel** (Pls. 464, 465, 467, 470, 480, 481-3, 521), **Denis van Alsloot** (Pls. 477, 513, 513A), **Otto van Veen** (Pls. 455, 510, 511, 570), **Wenzelas Coebergher** (Pl. 493), **Jan Snellinck** (Pl. 460), **Hendrik de Clerck** (Pls. 456, 471, 477, 587), **Rubens, Jacques Francart, Gaspar de Crayer** (Pls. 598, 607, 609, 642), **Peeter Snayers** (Pls. 627, 700, 701), **Antoine Sallaert** (Pl. 514), **Nicolaus van der Horst, Salomon Noveliers, Anton van Opstal** and **Van Dyck.** Of these

Jan (Velvet) Brueghel died in 1625, Denis van Alsloot in 1627 and Otto van Veen in 1629. Jan Snellinck already over seventy in 1622 was still alive in 1633. Jacques Francart was high in the Infanta's favour; she chose him, and not Rubens, to design the Archduke's cata- falque; when she felt herself dying she sent for him to discuss the details of her tomb; and she allowed him to introduce to her his niece the painter Anna de Bruyns and commissioned from her a *Mysteries of the Rosary* series to be presented to Pope Gregory XV or Urban VIII. She made Gaspar de Crayer an Archer de la Garde, a rank already held by Nicolaus van der Horst; and she commissioned Hendrik de Clerck to copy a picture by Michiel Coxie (Pls. 308, 310, 352) which she gave to the church of S. Josse-ten-Noode. The portrait painter Anton van Opstal came back from Silesia to Brussels about 1625 and obtained her patronage soon after. She sat to Rubens in his studio for her portrait in Clarissan habit in 1625; and in 1629 when Rubens called on her on his way to England she seems to have commissioned him to paint *S. Ildephonse receiving a chasuble from the Virgin with portraits of the Archduke and the Infanta as adorants* as a gift for the Brussels branch of the Fraternity of S. Ildephonse (founded in Lisbon by the Archduke in 1588). Van Dyck, as noted, became her Court Painter in 1630.

Topical events were painted (or drawn for engravers) by several of these Court artists. Thus Nicolaus van der Horst recorded *The Procession of the Infanta Isabella with four hundred nuns, her court and Archers de la Garde to Notre Dame de Laeken to ask blessing on the Spanish army in 1623* and *The Ceremonial entry into Antwerp of Marie de Médicis in 1631. The Arrival of Marie de Médicis with the Infanta Isabella at the port of Antwerp* was painted in a panorama picture possibly by Jan Wildens. Peeter Snayers painted *The Infanta Isabella's Procession to Laeken* and *The Infanta Isabella and Marquis Spinola at the Siege of Breda.* Antoine Sallaert recorded *The Funeral Procession of the Infanta Isabella*; and Denis van Alsloot may have painted some topical happenings between 1621 and 1627. We can also note here that records of the siege of Breda were made by the French engraver Jacques Callot who went to Brussels from Nancy for the purpose, that Philip IV com- missioned Velazquez some years later to paint his *Surrender of Breda* ('*Las Lanzas*') for the Buen Retiro palace, that Marten Pepyn's *S. Elizabeth giving her jewels to the poor* (Pl. 572) painted in 1629 was perhaps an allegoric reference to the Infanta's sacrifice in pawning her jewels, and that the *Judith with the head of Holofernes* (Pl. 582) by the Madrid Judith Painter and other pictures of the subject probably painted at this time may also be allegoric tributes to the Infanta.

Among the portrait painters Jacob van Oost the elder (Pl. 715) was back in Bruges from Italy in 1629; Lucas Franchoys the elder was available in Malines; and Anton van Opstal, Pieter van den Plas (Pl. 676) and Gaspar de Crayer (Pls. 598, 607, 642) were available in Brussels. Cornelis de Vos (Pls. 599, 600) continued his practice among the Antwerp bour- geoisie. A *Family group* now in the Prado and recorded in the eighteenth century as by Jordaens, may date from early in this period and show the painter himself aged about thirty with his wife and child and servant. Van Dyck, whose portraits painted at this time in Italy (Pl. 579), in Holland and in England (Pl. 612), have already been referred to, seems to have painted some others on his Antwerp visit in 1621; between 1627 and 1632 his com- missions there included *Jean Malderus Bishop of Antwerp, Adriaen Stevens Treasurer of Antwerp* and *The Infanta in Clarissan habit*; at the same time he made drawings and grisaille sketches of Antwerp artists to be engraved as an 'Iconography'; he also made half and three-quarter length paintings of some artists including *Marten Pepyn, Petrus Stevens* a collector and amateur landscape painter, and *Quinten Simon* an obscure 'history' painter whose portrait was later described by Sir Joshua Reynolds as 'a perfect pattern of portrait painting'. **Rubens,** as mentioned, painted *Marie de Médicis* (Pl. 575) probably in Paris in 1623, *The Infanta Isabella in Clarissan habit* in 1625, and the *Archduke Albert and the Infanta Isabella in ceremonial costume as adorant sovereigns* (on the wings of the *S. Ildephonse* altarpiece) in 1630; and soon after his second marriage he painted *Helena Fourment in her wedding dress* (Pl. 591) and *Helena Fourment nude in a fur coat* (Pl. 601). Among the portraits reproduced here **Gaspar de Crayer's** *Burgomaster H. de Dongelberghe* in the *Pietà* (Pl. 607) probably painted in this period is surely a masterpiece in feeling and unaffected record; for the sitter does not seem to be posing for his portrait but veritably observed unawares at his devotions. **Cornelis de Vos** appears as an affectionate observer of children's gestures in the tilt of the boy's head among the family of donors in *S. Norbert recovering the Sacred Vessels* (Pl. 599); and his *Family group* (Pl. 600)—a conversation piece in the tradition going back through **Adriaen Key** (Pls. 425, 426), the **Amsterdam Moucheron Family Painter** (Pl. 388) and the **Brussels Micault Triptych Painter** (Pls. 321, 322) to **Hugo of Antwerp** (Pls. 77, 78)—shows the father and sons on one side and the mother with the girls on the other while the baby half smiles at fruit and shells held up to her as the Christ-child smiled at S. Catherine in the charming picture by the **Buckingham Palace Mystic Marriage Painter** (Pl. 106). **Rubens** was undoubtedly at his best in portraiture in *Helena Fourment in her wedding dress* (Pl. 591) for it pleased him to pile jewels and finery on his young wife 'of honourable though humble birth' and to record her soft rotundities; it pleased him also to paint her moving forward with the spring of youth in *Helena Fourment nude in a fur coat* (Pl. 601) and as she had knobby knees and ugly feet he truthfully set down the blemishes.

The old subject of the artist at work, which can be followed in my plates from the **Boston S. Luke Painter** (Pl. 48) to **Joos van Winghe** (Pl. 457) is now seen in the foreground of a picture by an unrecorded artist here called the **Hague Studio of Apelles Painter** (Pl, 580) which may have been painted between 1628 and 1633; as in **Joos van Winghe's** *Apelles painting Campaspe* Alexander himself is witness of the artist's labours and in this case he is clearly giving him instructions; the sitter now is not Campaspe nude but Campaspe clothed as a fashionable lady, and the sitting takes place in the main gallery of the patron's immense collection of paintings and sculpture.

In the field of social, domestic and gay-life genre **Rubens** may have painted *Young people disporting in a castle park* (Pl. 661) on his own estate the Château d'Ursele soon after his return from England. It is probable—though not certain—that **Jordaens** now painted some domestic conversation pieces like his later *The old sing and the young pipe* (Pl. 660) and some animated feasts like his later *Twelfth Night* (*Le roi boit*) (Pl. 658); **Theodoor Rombouts** (Pls. 581, 596, 597) became conspicuous and successful as a gay-life painter on his return from Italy at twenty-eight in 1625; **Adam de Coster's** *Men and women playing backgammon by candlelight* may date from this period; and, at fifty-two in 1633, **Frans Francken** (Pls. 496, 517, 519) signed a *Prodigal Son* where the whole story is told as a series of social genre scenes (as earlier by the **Prodigal Son Master** (Pl. 395)). The 'Bad company' motif in the Prodigal Son tradition, as we had it in pictures by **Jan van Hemessen** (Pls. 305, 325) and the **Brussels Prodigal Son Painter** (Pl. 358), is continued by **Theodoor Rombouts** in his *Card players* (Pl. 581); but the style of the picture is now Italianate, as **Rombouts** was recalling genre pictures by Caravaggio and the 'Tenebrosi' seen on his Italian visit; and these Italian memories are still more evident in his *Quack Dentist* (Pl. 596) with its vivid contrasts of light and shadow.

Of the landscape painters **Jan (Velvet) Brueghel** worked till 1625 and **Denis van Alsloot** till 1627; the gifted **Abraham Govaerts** (Pl. 478) died at thirty-seven in 1626 (many pictures left in his studio being finished by **Frans Francken, Gaspar van der Lanen, Hans Jordaens III,** and **Jasper Adriaenssen**); **Jan Tilens** (Pl. 499) died at forty-one in 1630, **Marten Ryckaert** at forty-four in 1631 and **Tobias van Haecht** (Pl. 377) at seventy also in 1631. But **Kerstiaen de Keuninck** (Pl. 501) over seventy in 1633, **Sebastiaan Vrancx** (Pls. 531, 532), **Pieter Brueghel the younger** (Pls. 380, 411), **Josse de Momper** (Pl. 500), **Marten Ryckaert, Willem van Nieulandt** (Pl. 475), **Adriaen van Stalbemt** (Pls. 479, 562), **Peeter Snayers** (Pls. 627, 700, 701), **Pieter de Witte the younger, Charles de Cauwer** and **Andreas Snellinck** were active through the period. **Antonie Mirou** whose *Landscape with Abraham and Hagar* (Pl. 469) was discussed in my last chapter, seems to have come back to Antwerp from Frankenthal or Bad Swalbach in the twenties or thirties; **Lucas de Wael** came back from Genoa in 1628; and newcomers included **Peeter van Avont** (Pl. 605), **Jan Brueghel the younger** (Pl. 605), **Jacob van Uden, Frans Lucas Peters, Artus Wolfordt** (Pl. 606), **Lodewyck de Vadder** (Pl. 685), **Daniel van Heil** (Pls. 709, 713, 714), **Frans de Momper, Teniers** and **Brouwer.** Of the younger men the Bruxellois **Lodewyck de Vadder** (Pl. 685) trained, I imagine, in the first place by **Denis van Alsloot** (Pl. 513), was Brussels Master at twenty-three in 1628, and **Daniel van Heil** (Pls. 709, 713, 714) also a Bruxellois was twenty-four that year. In Antwerp **Frans de Momper** was Master at twenty-six in 1629. **Jacob van Uden** (perhaps a brother of **Lucas van Uden**) was associated with **Jan Brueghel the younger** by 1627. **Frans Lucas Peters** was twenty-five by 1631. **Peeter van Avont** collaborated with **Jan Brueghel the younger,** and their joint picture *Flora in a garden* (Pl. 605) may have been painted before 1633 when **van Avont** was thirty-four and **Brueghel** thirty-two; in this picture the charming garden of a mansion in the Antwerp suburbs—recalling the mansion and orchard painted more than fifty years earlier by **Jacob Grimmer** (Pl. 430)—was doubtless provided by **Brueghel** as his extant Daybook has many records of landscapes painted into pictures with figures by other artists—('Gemaakt eenen gront achter een . . . van . . .'); and the garden in the *Rest on the Flight* (Pl. 606) by **Artus Wolfordt** who was over fifty in 1633 may also be **Brueghel's** work though there seems no record of collaborations in this case and **Wolfordt** himself may have painted the whole picture. **Gillis Peeters** signed a *Rocky landscape with waterfall* at twenty-one in 1633. **Teniers** known to have been painting by 1629, was Antwerp Master at twenty-three in 1633 and it was perhaps in that year that he painted the figures and animals in **Lucas van Uden's** *Wooded landscape with peasants dancing* (Pl. 567) which is signed by both artists. The landscape in **Brouwer's** *Peasants and soldiers brawl by wayside inn* (Pl. 617) has the air of a Dutch village which may mean, as suggested above, that he painted this picture in Holland; but his *Peasants and Spanish soldiers at a table* (Pl. 623) was painted in the grounds of the Antwerp citadel during his stay there in 1633.

In the **Rubens** entourage **Alexander Keirincx** may have been in the factory till he left for England about 1625, as the composition and some details of his *Landscape with shepherds* (Pl. 613) have evident relation to a *Landscape with shepherd* by **Rubens** (or **Rubens** and assistants) in the National Gallery in London. **Vincent Malo,** whose inn-porch with feathered trees beyond it in his *Peasants before an inn* (Pl. 615) seems to have relation to the landscapes in **Rubens'** *Kermesse* (Pl. 665) and *Peasant Dance* (Pl. 666), was Antwerp Master at about twenty-three in 1623 and probably in the **Rubens** atelier till he went to Italy. **Jan Wildens,** who worked for **Rubens** through the period, also painted landscapes of his own including a winter scene with bare tree stumps *Landscape with a sportsman and dogs* signed by him at forty in 1624 and acquired by the collector Cornelius van der Geest, and a pair of coppices with tall upstanding verdured trees in a *Landscape with dancing peasants* (Pl. 629) in 1631. **Lucas van Uden** whose *River landscape with sunset* (Pl. 561) was discussed in my last chapter, seems also to have worked with **Rubens** in these years; and his own undated *Flat landscape with peasants and horses* (Pl. 602) and *Wooded landscape with peasants dancing* (Pl. 567) just mentioned may all have been painted at this time. **Rubens** is not known to have concerned himself with landscape in these years and the landscape backgrounds in some rural subjects known or presumed to have been painted before the end of 1633 can again be presumed to be partly or wholly the work of his landscape assistants; these pictures include the Thames valley landscape in his *S. George and the Dragon* partly painted in England and discussed in my notes on his English visit, the *Landscape with cattle* (Pl. 603), the *Farm at Laeken*, the *Summer* (Pl. 568) sold to the Duke of Buckingham before 1628 (and described by **Rubens** as his own work 'un poco ajutato', i.e. carried out by assistants in some parts), and, I imagine, the *Rainbow landscape* sold to the Balbi Palace in Genoa. The *Young people disporting in a castle park* (Pl. 661) as suggested above, the *Kermesse* (Pl. 665) and *Peasant dance* (Pls. 666, 668A) may also date from the end of this period.

Rural figures appear in most of the landscapes at this time and collaboration was so much the rule that in 1624 the dealer Goetkint wrote in astonishment of **Sebastiaan Vrancx** (Pls. 531, 532, 534) then engaged on six paintings: 'He refuses all help and will not have his pictures copied.' The capering figures in **Jan Wildens'** *Landscape with dancing peasants* (Pl. 629) and in the *Wooded landscape with peasants dancing* (Pl. 567) by **van Uden** and **Teniers,** are in **Pieter Bruegel the elder's** 'Merry Peasant' formula; but in other pictures reproduced here—**van Uden's** *Flat landscape with peasants* (Pl. 566) and his *Flat landscape with peasants and horses* (Pl. 602), for example—the peasants go about their country business without play-acting or self consciousness: they carry turnips in their baskets and wash their linen in the stream as simply as **Jan van Eyck's** peasants wheeled barrows to S. Barbara's tower (Pl. 18), as shepherds drove their flocks in the picture by the **Washington Nativity in a Sculptured Porch Painter** (Pl. 30) and sheared their sheep while Judah tempted Tamar in the picture by **Lucas Gassel** (Pl. 327), and drove their produce in covered carts to market or ferried it across the river in pictures by **Jan (Velvet) Brueghel** (Pls. 482, 483). In these two pictures by **van Uden** the little figures were clearly inserted after the landscape was complete and they are perfectly in scale within it; but **Vincent Malo** evidently began his *Peasants before an inn* (Pl. 615) with the three large figures in the foreground anecdotically engaged in a game of cards, the other figures and the landscape being built around them; and he painted them from models serving in the **Rubens** workshop—as can be seen if the youth on the left be compared with the youth in *A young lord renouncing the world* (Pl. 589) by **Theodor van Thulden.** In **Brouwer's** *Peasants and soldiers brawl by wayside inn* (Pl. 617) and *Boors' carouse* (Pl. 618) the peasants seem more Dutch than Flemish and of the race and type portrayed by the Dutchman Adriaen van Ostade (sometime fellow pupil with **Brouwer** of Frans Hals); and these stunted quarrelsome besotted figures, recalling the realism and pathetic actuality of the *Penitent thief* by the **London Delft Painter** (Pl. 226), are grouped in pyramids like the figures in many of Van Ostade's works. In contrast the figures in **Brouwer's** *Peasants and Spanish soldiers at a table in the grounds of the Antwerp Citadel* (Pl. 623) are calmly seated in a quiet corner of the prison grounds; and the picture is not only a genre record but also and still more a plein-air study; the genre observation of the smiling man's face, the man passing water and the man in the privy, is excellently veracious, but the picture as a whole—including the main group with a man's back in the foreground and the guards on the mound seen against the sky (like the soldiers on the hilltop in **Geertgen's** *Lamentation* (Pl. 127))—is formally perceived in terms of light diffusion and thus forestalls the silvery plein-air naturalism in some later paintings by **Teniers** (Pls. 707, 708).

The exact date when **Rubens** began to concern himself with genre subjects is not known; and we are not helped by an early biographer who tells us the unlikely story that he began to paint scenes with rural genre and animals after hearing **van Uden** and **Snyders** boasting that he could not do without them for such work. He may, I think, have produced some rural subjects in the lifetime of **Jan (Velvet) Brueghel** and withheld them from the market from motives of generosity till his old friend was dead; and examples wholly or partly by him, dating from this period may include the *Landscape with cattle* (Pl. 603), the *Farm at Laeken*, the *Summer* (Pl. 568), the *Rainbow landscape* and a farmyard scene called the *Return of the Prodigal* (suggested perhaps by his call in Utrecht on Abraham Bloemaert who painted the subject in similar terms). As remarked above, the *Kermesse* (Pl. 665) and the *Peasant dance* (Pl. 666) were painted, I imagine, soon after his marriage with Helena Fourment and both perhaps about 1633. The figures and animals in these rural pieces by **Rubens** (or **Rubens** and assistants) are larger in relation to the landscape than in the pictures shown here by **Jan Wildens** (Pl. 629), **Lucas van Uden** (Pls. 566, 602) and in the joint picture by **van Uden** and **Teniers** (Pl. 567); but the peasants are not set in the absolute foreground and inspected as grave and static human entities as they were set and inspected by **Pieter Aertsen** (Pls. 356, 360) and **Joachim Beuckelaer** (Pl. 399); still less are they thrust to the foreground as grotesque beings in the manner of **Jan van Hemessen** (Pl. 325) and the **Brussels Piper Painter** (Pl. 326); they are seen as it were from a middle distance and descriptively reported as typical incidents in rural prospects. I say 'incidents' and 'prospects' because these pictures are all at bottom in some degree theatrical or aesthetic concepts and, as such, stand nearer the pastoral fantasies by Boucher than to the matter of fact records by **Pieter Bruegel the elder** at his highest level in the *Landscapes of the Seasons* (Pls. 390-3), or to the rural pieces by **Jan (Velvet) Brueghel** (Pls. 481-3); for these peasants by **Rubens** (or **Rubens** and assistants), even in the simpler pictures, attitudinize a little as they milk the cows which in their turn 'play up' to them (Pl. 603); they urge on their horses at the turn of the road with exaggerated shouts and gestures (Pl. 568); and when we reach the *Kermesse* (Pl. 665) and *Peasant dance* (Pl. 668A) we are not at village feasts in Flanders but back on the Bridge of Thermodon in the *Battle of the Amazons* (Pl. 576); for in the *Kermesse* the rough-and-tumble dancing, drinking and love-making peasants are mere excuses for renewal of the swift torrential rhythm in the earlier picture, a rhythm now controlled by chains of intertwined curves that bind the leaping and the reeling forms; and in the *Peasant dance* the figures are frankly 'dressed up' as Italian peasants and the round dance is wholly an abstract fantasia of concerted movement, continuous rhythm and gay colour.

Among the marine painters **Adam Willaerts** (Pl. 688) and **Jan Porcellis** were in Holland and **Mathias de Plattenberg (Platte-Montagne)** was in Paris as noted above. In Antwerp in 1623 before turning to religious subjects **Abraham Matthys** signed a *Whale fishing* with a fleet of ships and several huge whales being hauled to the shore. **Andries van Ertvelt** (Pl. 704) was in Antwerp till he left for Genoa about 1628 and after his return in 1630; and **Gaspar van Eyck** (Pl. 703) worked there as his pupil till 1632 when he became a Master at nineteen.

The painters of military genre included **Sebastiaan Vrancx** (Pls. 531, 532), **Peeter**

Snayers (Pls. 627, 700, 701) who was twenty-four in 1622, and a newcomer **Pieter Meulener** (Pl. 698) then twenty.

Animals were painted in Antwerp by **Sebastiaan Vrancx** and the other military painters; a newcomer **Jan Fyt** (Pls. 719, 733), a pupil of **Snyders,** was Antwerp Master at nineteen in 1630; and I have already chronicled the *Orpheus charming the animals* (Pl. 586) painted by **Roelandt Savery** in Holland, the Barbary horses in pictures painted in England possibly at this time by **Abraham van Diepenbeeck** and the *Oakwood with staghunt* (Pl. 611) painted in England by **Alexander Keirincx.** In the **Rubens** atelier **Frans Snyders** (Pls. 630, 632, 634, 635) forty-three in 1622 and **Paul de Vos** (Pls. 633, 636) about twenty-six, were leading specialists in the animal department; **Abraham van Diepenbeeck,** also twenty-six that year, may have worked there till he left for England about 1629; and all three may have had a hand in the *Marie de Médicis* series where the Queen rides an arab horse (taken from El Greco's *S. Martin*) in the *Journey to Ponts-de-Cé*, lions draw the chariot emblematic of the town of Lyons in the *Marriage* allegory, a fantastic many-headed Monster of Discord is overcome in the *Reconciliation*, the Queen's pet spaniels and other dogs appear in several pieces, and peacocks preen themselves as emblems of Juno and the Queen. **Rubens** himself, I fancy, must have been responsible for the fluently drawn cows in the *Landscape with cattle* (Pl. 603); there are horses and dogs in the *Summer* (Pl. 568), a donkey and a trotting lapdog in his *Flight of Lot* (Pl. 577), an ox in the foreground and camels at the rear in the *Adoration of the Magi* (Pl. 574), a handsome leopard in the *Peace and War* (Pl. 591A) and careering dogs that extend the circle in the *Peasant Dance* (Pl. 666). A farmer's horses graze in a meadow in **Lucas van Uden's** landscape (Pl. 602)—as a Prince's horses graze in the plain depicted a hundred years later by **John George Hamilton** (Pl. 850); there are sheep and dogs in the *Wooded landscape with Peasants dancing* (Pl. 567) by **van Uden** and **Teniers** and sheep and goats in the *Landscape with dancing peasants* (Pl. 629) by **Wildens; Brouwer** puts a sow in the grounds of the Antwerp Citadel (Pl. 623), and a sow and her litter in his *Peasants' and soldiers' brawl* (Pl. 617). The sitter's pet spaniel yaps at Apelles in the studio scene by the **Hague Studio of Apelles Painter** (Pl. 580), a dog gnaws a bone in the foreground of **Vincent Malo's** *Peasants playing cards* (Pl. 615) as his ancestor gnawed one in the foreground of **Gossaert's** *Adoration of the Magi* (Pl. 194); a sporting dog tempts Adonis from his lady in the *Venus and Adonis* (Pl. 593) by **Josse de Paepe;** and a child holds a rough-haired dog in *S. Martin curing a demoniac* (Pl. 588) by **Jordaens.**

Among the flower painters **Jacques de Gheyn** died in 1629 in Holland where **Roelandt Savery, Abraham Bosschaert** and **Ambrosius Bosschaert the younger** were still at work in 1633 as noted above. In Antwerp **Jan (Velvet) Brueghel** (Pls. 521, 541, 543) himself was still available till 1625, and his manner was continued by **Jan Brueghel the younger** author, doubtless, of the foreground flowers in the *Flora in a garden* (Pl. 605) painted with **Peeter van Avont.** Flower and fruit pieces were painted by **Jacob van Uden** after 1627; and by **Frans Lucas Peters** from about the same time. Flower garlands round grisaille or coloured centres (usually by other artists) in the tradition probably launched by **Jan (Velvet) Brueghel** (Pl. 541) were painted by **Jan Brueghel the younger** and by the Jesuit **Daniel Seghers** (Pls. 692, 757) who was forty-three in 1633. In Brussels a newcomer **Leo van Heil** who was trained as an architect and painted flowerpieces with small insects was twenty-eight in 1633. There was little or no call for flower painting in the **Rubens** factory as swags or piles of fruit—probably by **Frans Snyders** (Pls. 544, 548, 554) and sometimes possibly by **Jordaens** (Pl. 545)—were always preferred there as decorative features; but occasional flowers—inserted perhaps by **Daniel Seghers**—can be found here and there in the *Marie de Médicis* series.

Of the painters of general still-life, of tables with food and utensils and of kitchen and larder pieces **Osias Beet the elder** (Pl. 506) died in Antwerp at thirty-nine in 1624; **Jacob van Hulsdonck** (Pl. 556) forty in 1622, **Alexander Adriaenssens** (Pls. 559, 652, 653) thirty-five and **Jacob Foppens van Es** (Pls. 557, 558) about twenty-six, all worked there through the period; and it was perhaps at this time that **Rubens** acquired the '*Petite pièce avec un verre et quelques tranches de jambon* and '*Un banquet sur fond de bois*' by **van Es** which were still in his collection when he died. Among the new men **Martin Verhoeven,** a fruit painter, appeared in Malines in 1623; **Adriaen van Utrecht** (Pls. 693, 694) back from Italy was Antwerp Master at twenty-five in 1624; **Mathieu Matheussens** painter of kitchen pieces (after working as a pupil of **Marten Pepyn**) was Master there in 1629; **Frans Ijkens** (Pl. 695) was back from Provence and Antwerp Master at twenty-nine in 1603; and **Jan Fyt** began his career as a still-life as well as an animal painter in 1630. In the **Rubens** entourage the kitchen and larder pieces were soon to become conglomerations of piled up meat, vegetables, dead game, swans, and so on, painted by **Frans Snyders** (Pls. 655, 656) and possibly by **Jordaens** (Pl. 658) and others; and it would seem that compositions of this kind were already on the market in this period as one with dead swan, peacock, venison, etc., is seen among the pictures in the gallery interior by the **Hague Studio of Apelles Painter** (Pl. 580).

The vogue for gallery interiors was now steadily increasing. The pictures, statues, shells and so on shown in them were sometimes an actual collection, sometimes an ideal collection, and sometimes a dealer's stock; and when figures depicting the owners and some visitors are included, these gallery interiors are also an aspect of the social conversation piece. **Henri Staben,** whose *Visit of the Archduke Albert and the Infanta Isabella to Rubens' studio* (Pl. 518) was discussed in my last chapter, was no longer at hand in Antwerp for such pictures having moved to Paris; but **Willem van Haecht** back from Italy by 1628, the **Hague Studio of Apelles Painter, Frans Francken, Hans Jordaens III, Cornelis de Baellieur** (Pls. 645, 727) son of an art dealer and Master in 1627, and **Frans Francken III** (Pl. 728), twenty-six in 1633, were all available. When the millionaire collector Cornelius van der Geest (seen here in the portrait by the **London van der Geest Painter** (Pl. 560)) made **Willem van Haecht** the keeper of his gallery in 1628 he commissioned him to paint *The visit of the Archduke Albert and the Infanta Isabella to the Van der Geest collection in 1615*; the picture, which is extant, shows the collection as it was in 1615 with some recent acquisitions; and we are thus informed that by 1628 Van der Geest's sculpture included life-size copies of the Apollo Belvedere, the Farnese Hercules and many Graeco-Roman statues, and among the countless paintings the *Battle of the Amazons* (Pl. 576) by **Rubens**, the *Winter landscape with huntsman* by **Jan Wildens**, a kitchen scene in the style of **Joachim Beuckelaer**, a *Judith killing Holofernes* in the light-and-shade 'Caravaggio' manner of the **Madrid Judith Painter** (Pl. 582), and a *Woman bathing with attendant and a mirror on the wall* (presumed by some a now lost work by **Jan van Eyck**). The ideal collection of Alexander the Great as depicted by the **Hague Studio of Apelles Painter** (Pl. 580) forestalls the eclectic taste of the Archduke Leopold Wilhelm recorded later in pictures by **Teniers** (Pls. 724, 725, 726); for Alexander is here allegorically presented as owner of a version of the Apollo Belvedere and many Graeco-Roman statues, of Italian High-Renaissance paintings including Titian's *Venus binding Cupid's eyes* (*The Education of Cupid*), Correggio's *Jupiter and Antiope*, Albani's *Apollo and Daphne* and Domenichino's *Diana hunting*, and among Flemish pictures of the *Banker and his wife* (Pl. 235) by **Quinten Massys**, a *Rape of Europa* in the manner of **Hendrik van Balen** (Pls. 507, 508), a *Judith killing Holofernes* in the manner of the **Madrid Judith Painter** (Pl. 582), a gay-life genre piece by candlelight (*The Prodigal Son* or *S. Peter's denial*) in the manner of **Theodoor Rombouts** (Pls. 581, 596) or **Adam de Coster,** a large still-life with dead swan, venison and so forth in the manner of **Frans Snyders** (Pls. 655, 656, 657), a *Samson and Delilah* in the manner of **Van Dyck** and the *Battle of the Amazons* (Pl. 576) by **Rubens.**

There was still a vogue for church interiors and 'perspectives'. **Hendrik van Steenwyck the younger** (Pls. 487, 489, 536, 537) was absent in England and **Paul Vredeman de Vries** in Holland. But **Peeter Neeffs the elder** (Pls. 649, 650) was painting his church interiors, with services in progress, through the period; and it was perhaps at this time that **Sebastiaan Vrancx** signed an *Interior of the Jesuit church in Antwerp* where **Rubens'** *S. Ignatius Loyola healing the possessed* is shown on the high altar.

For altarpieces in churches the Jesuits and others now encouraged subjects extolling the piety and miracles of recent or recently canonized saints—S. Francis Xavier (canonized 1622), S. Ignatius Loyola (canonized 1622), S. Theresa (canonized 1622), and S. Carlo Borromeo (canonized 1610); S. Felix of Cantalicio (beatified 1625) and Aloysius Gonzaga (beatified 1605). S. Rosalia appears because, I imagine, her relics were found in 1624, the Blessed Herman Joseph because the Emperor Ferdinand II was applying for his canonization as a German saint, and S. Norbert because, though he had been canonized by 1582, his bones were moved from Magdeburg to Prague in 1627. **Rubens** it will be recalled had orders for altarpieces with S. Ignatius Loyola and S. Francis Xavier for Antwerp Cathedral in 1619 (three years before their canonizations). **Gerard Seghers** painted *S. Theresa's vision* (Pl. 527), *The Blessed Aloysius de Gonzaga renouncing his rank to become a Jesuit* and *S. Norbert receiving the habit from the Virgin*; and the Blessed Aloysius is probably represented in the *Young lord renouncing the world* (Pl. 589) by **Theodor van Thulden.** S. Norbert appears in pictures by **Abraham van Diepenbeeck** and **Cornelis de Vos** (Pl. 599). **Van Dyck** painted S. Rosalia and the Blessed Herman Joseph. **Gaspar de Crayer** was commissioned in 1633 to paint *S. Carlo Borromeo invoked against the plague-stricken* for Anderlecht, S. Guidon; and some years later **Gillis Backereel** painted scenes from the lives of S. Felix and S. Carlo Borromeo. We must note too that the *Israelites crossing the Red Sea* was also now favoured as a subject for some reason; for it was painted by **Frans Francken, Marten Pepyn, Hendrik van Balen** and **Hans Jordaens III.**

A regional conspectus of the painters of religious subjects shows in Louvain **Theodore van Loon** who moved there from Brussels in 1623 and worked there till he left for Rome in 1628. In Malines **Jean Baptiste Saive** till he died in 1624, **Lucas Franchoys the elder,** and **David Herregouts** Malines Master in 1624. In Bruges **Pieter Claeissins the younger** (Pl, 436) who died over seventy in 1623, **Jacob van Oost the elder** (Pls. 715, 729, 740) on his return from Italy in 1629, and probably **Ghislain Vroilynck.** In Ghent **Jan Janssens, Anselmus van Hulle,** and **Anton van den Heuvel** on his return from Rome in 1628. In Tournai **Mathieu van Negre** who painted an altarpiece for Notre Dame in 1623 and worked with **Ambrosius Francken the younger** on pictures for Louvain, S. Pierre. In Namur **Frans Saive** recorded there in 1627. In Liège **François Walschartz** till he went to Italy, **Jean Taulier** (said to have been a crypto-Protestant) and his pupils **Renier Lairesse** and **Gerard Douffet** painter of *Pope Nicholas V opening the tomb of S. Francis to verify the stigmata in 1449* in 1627 and **Alexander de Horion.** The Brussels group included **Hendrik de Clerck** (Pls. 456, 471, 477, 587), **Otto van Veen** (Pls. 455, 510, 511, 570) till 1629, the veteran **Wenzelas Coebergher, Gaspar de Crayer** (Pls. 598, 607, 609) fifty-one in 1633, and **Jacques Francart** who had moved there at some time from Antwerp. Of these **Hendrik de**

Clerck painted a *Descent from the Cross* (Pl. 587) for Anderlecht church in 1628; here the prancing horses in the background and the over-large central figure show the fatal influence of **Rubens** on an artist whose lyrical *Lineage of S. Anne* (Pl. 456) painted in his youth in 1590 had been congruous throughout and scrupulously controlled by classical measure. **Gaspar de Crayer's** *Pietà with Burgomaster H. de Dongelberghe and his wife as adorants* (Pl. 607) with the wonderful portrait of the donor already referred to, is likewise destroyed by the **Rubens** influence in the Pietà group, as will be evident if this overweighted group be compared with the vision of the Virgin in **de Crayer's** *The Virgin protecting the Crossbowmen's Guild* (Pl. 598) discussed in my last chapter; and we know in fact that **de Crayer** was soon to establish a mass-production factory for church pictures on the **Rubens** model with numerous pupils and assistants.

In Antwerp the painters of religious subjects who died in this period included **Gerard Schoof** till 1624, **Abraham Janssens** (Pl. 509) whose *Crucifixion* sold in 1626 has been mentioned above, **Hendrik van Balen** (Pls. 507, 508) till 1632, and **Jan de Wael** till 1633. Of the older men who survived into the next period **Jan Snellinck** (Pl. 460) was over eighty in 1633, **Adam van Noort** was seventy-one and **Pieter Brueghel the younger** (Pls. 380, 411) was sixty-nine. In the next age group we have **Marten Pepyn** (Pls. 569, 571, 572), **Rubens, Frans Francken** (Pls. 496, 517, 519, 648), **Artus Wolfordt** (Pl. 606), **Abraham Matthys** and **Deodatus Delmont**. Then come **Cornelis de Vos** (Pls. 590, 599, 600, 641), **Gaspar van den Hoecke, Adam de Coster, Gerard Seghers** (Pl. 527), **Gillis Backereel** (Pl. 594) and **Jordaens**. The young men included **Hans Jordaens III, Abraham van Diepenbeeck, Cornelis Schut** (Pl. 669), **Theodoor Rombouts** (Pls. 581, 596, 597), **Van Dyck, Pieter van Mol, Pieter de Witte the younger, Eduaert Snayers, Jan Brueghel the younger** (Pl. 605), **Jan Cossiers** (Pl. 640), **Peeter van Avont** (Pl. 605), and **Simon de Vos** (Pls. 673, 674, 687). And in a still younger group we have **Theodor van Thulden** (Pls. 589, 753), **Erasmus Quellinus** (Pls. 639, 671), **Peter van Lint** (Pls. 677, 697), **Jan van den Hoecke** (Pls. 716, 721) and **Balthasar van Cortbemde**. Of these **Marten Pepyn** painted *The Passage of the Red Sea* mentioned above in 1626; he also completed in that year two altarpieces with wings for the Antwerp Hospital of S. Elizabeth—the first showing *Scenes from the life of S. Augustine* with *Sick people going to hospital* on one wing and the second having *S. Elizabeth giving her jewels to the poor* (Pl. 572) in the centre, the *Death of S. Elizabeth* and *S. Elizabeth received in Heaven* on the wings and on the outside in grisaille *S. Elizabeth tending the sick* (Pl. 569) and *A poor family going to hospital* (Pl. 571); and before 1632 he had painted pictures titled *Adam and Eve*, *Joseph and Potiphar's wife, Sarah and Hagar, Esther and Ahasuerus, The Triumph of David*, *Bathsheba* and *The Judgement of Solomon*. In his *S. Elizabeth giving her jewels to the poor* (Pl. 572) **Marten Pepyn's** concept of the saint is very different from that of the **Antwerp Last Judgement Painter** who followed the Golden Legend and showed her in Franciscan habit giving shoes to poor children (Pl. 135); for S. Elizabeth, who affected the simplest of garments, now wears an elegant robe and a coronet indicating her father's status when she hands out jewels to be scrambled for by naked beggars and cripples; and she still wears her coronet when she tends the sick in the hospital she founded (Pl. 569); there is evidence in this triptych of **Pepyn's** study of Italian paintings in Rome—and also, I fancy, in Venice and Florence—for the central panel has a markedly Venetian air and the *Poor family going to hospital* (Pl. 571) seems inspired by Masaccio's *S. Peter and S. John passing* in the Carmine Church in Florence (a composition which may also have influenced **Hugo of Antwerp** (Pl. 77) as suggested earlier). We may note too in passing that the patients in **Pepyn's** hospital scene are in curtained cubicles as we saw them earlier in the hospital scene by the

Alkmaar Master (Pl. 185). **Abraham Matthys** in his new role of religious painter produced a large *Death of the Virgin* in 1632 for Antwerp Cathedral where it was hung behind the high altar immediately at the back of the *Assumption of the Virgin* by **Rubens. Deodatus Delmont** painted, probably in these years, a *Transfiguration* placed near the Baptismal Font in Antwerp Cathedral, a *Christ carrying the Cross* for the Jesuit College, and for the church of the 'Facon' nuns an *Adoration of the Magi* where the attendants in the foreground held bales of merchandise as gifts—on which Descamps commented 'Cette idée très ridicule n'empêche pas que le tableau ne soit avec du merite et d'une grande manière'. **Frans Francken** painted *The Four crowned Martyrs* for the altar of the Serment des Maçons in Antwerp Cathedral in 1624. His pupil **Artus Wolfordt** painted religious subjects like *The Rest on the flight* (Pl. 606). **Cornelis de Vos** had now established a considerable workshop and he certified in 1627 that six pictures exported by him to Spain were by himself and assistants; his *S. Norbert recovering the sacred vessels* (Pl. 599) was painted in 1630 for the memorial chapel of the Snoeck family in the Abbaye de S. Michel, where one of the family was a monk; the picture represents an episode in the history of this Premonstratensian Abbey of S. Michel founded by S. Norbert, for it is related that in the year 1115 one Tankelin (or Thankhelm) 'a bold and eloquent heretic openly asserted that the institution of the priesthood is a fiction and that the eucharist and other sacraments are of no service in salvation . . . he practised the most filthy abominations of the Gnostics and lured the people with magnificent banquets', but S. Norbert was appealed to, the heretic was killed in a riot, and S. Norbert recovered for the Abbey the sacred vessels which the faithful had hidden while the heresy held sway. **Gaspar van den Hoecke** painted a *Mystic Marriage of S. Catherine* in 1624 and possibly worked for the **Rubens** atelier before the end of the period. **Adam de Coster** declared in January 1627 that he had painted pictures titled *Christ on the Cross*, the *Liberation of S. Peter, S. Peter's denial, S. Francis at a table with books* and a *S. Francis with an angel* all within three months; he was known as 'pictor noctium' and among these pictures the *Liberation of S. Peter* was probably a night effect with torches. **Gillis Backereel** was back from Rome at about thirty-seven by 1629. **Gerard Seghers** who had visited Spain after Italy and worked under **Rubens** on the ceiling panels for the Antwerp Jesuit Church in 1621, was thirty-one in 1622; he painted in 1630 an *Adoration of the Magi* for Bruges, Notre Dame, of which Descamps wrote 'la figure on roi placée sur le devant est de la plus grande beauté', and also perhaps in this period his *S. Norbert receiving the habit from the Virgin* for the Abbaye de S. Michel, *The Blessed Aloysius de Gonzaga renouncing his rank to become a Jesuit* for the Jesuit Collegiate Church and *S. Theresa's vision* for the Carmes Déchaussées. The impressive picture of S. Theresa (Pl. 527) which can be more fully titled *S. Theresa's vision of the angel with the flame-tipped spear that pierced her heart* may well have been commissioned soon after the canonization and some twenty years before Bernini's sculptured group in S. Maria della Vittoria in Rome; in my monochrome plate a fold in the drapery suggests an alternative and better position for the saint's left hand, but even with the hand raised the concept is emotionally restrained and quite free from the equivocal eroticism that disfigures Bernini's famous rendering of the subject. **Jordaens** is known to have painted his *Four Evangelists* before 1632 and may have painted it in the early or middle twenties; his *S. Martin curing a demoniac* (Pl. 588), dated 1630, was painted for the church of S. Martin's monastery in Tournai; here the naked possessed man is held by three men and a young woman in the foreground, the Saint in mitre and golden dalmatic performs the exorcising, and the Roman proconsul (in a black and red Flemise costume) attended by a negro slave with parrot, surveys the scene from the raised balustrade of a palatial building; **Jordaens** thirty-seven when he painted this picture was already concerned here with problems of formal massing in recession which from this time onward were to occupy him incessantly both in religious paintings and in genre subjects (Pl. 658); and the use of the negro model from the **Rubens** atelier—already seen in his *Allegory of Abundance* (Pl. 545) and in the *Nature adorned by the Graces* (Pl. 544) by **Rubens** and assistants discussed in my last chapter—suggests that he still had connections with that workshop and was possibly still in general charge of it. **Hans Jordaens III** signed an *Israelites crossing the Red Sea* in 1624 and made other versions of the subject with hundreds of genre figures. **Abraham van Diepenbeeck,** as stated above, was probably associated with the **Rubens** atelier before his visit to England about 1629 and also after his return in 1631; and his *S. Norbert consecrating the first Abbot of S. Michel* commissioned for the Abbaye de S. Michel may date from the early thirties. **Cornelis Schut** (Pl. 669) seems also to have worked in the **Rubens** atelier in these years. But **Theodoor Rombouts** remained an independent artist outside the **Rubens** circle as can be seen in his *Christ driving the money-changers from the Temple* (Pl. 597) where he has used the same young man as model for a foreground figure that he used for a figure in his genre piece (Pl. 596); and the curious can compare the backward-falling figure in this picture with the centurion in the *Crucifixion* by the **New York Crucifixion and Last Judgement Painter** (Pl. 159) and the whole composition with the fantastic concept by **Hieronymus Bosch** (Pl. 164) and the later most elaborate and complex structure by the **Paris Expulsion of Traders Painter** (Pl. 659). **Van Dyck** painted some intolerably rhetorical pictures for churches between 1628 and 1630; these included *Christ crucified: with S. Dominic and S. Catherine of Siena in adoration* (given to the Antwerp Dominicans who had nursed his father in his last illness) where S. Catherine swoons at the foot of the cross and a cherub is seated in the foreground, *S. Rosalia receiving a chaplet from the Infant Christ* (commissioned by the Jesuit Fraternity of Unmarried Men of which he was himself a member) and *The Blessed Herman Joseph presented to the Virgin by an angel* (commissioned by the same Fraternity). **Pieter van Mol,** Antwerp Master at twenty-four in 1623 and then probably for some time in the **Rubens** atelier, seems to have had commissions for churches in Antwerp and elsewhere before his departure for Paris in 1631; Descamps saw an *Epiphany* by him ('assez dans la manière de son maître **Rubens**') in the Groenendael Priory Church, an *Adoration of the Magi* on the Tailors' altar in Antwerp Cathedral ('ce peintre a pillé la composition d'après les ouvrages de son maître, tout y est assez bien coloré, mais les ombres sont poussées au noir'), and in Ghent, S. Jacques a *Descent of the Holy Spirit on the Apostles* ('la couleur est fausse et les ombres trop noires)— which may all have been painted in these years. **Jan Cossiers** a pupil of **Cornelis de Vos** was Antwerp Master in 1629. **Pieter de Witte the younger** painted an *Agony in the Garden* for Antwerp Town Hall at forty-six in 1632. **Peeter van Avont,** Antwerp Master at twenty-two in 1622, signed undated pictures titled *Wooded landscape with Holy Family and angels* and *Wooded landscape with Virgin and Child, S. John and angels* possibly in this period when he worked in conjunction with **Jan Brueghel the younger** (Pl. 605) as related in my comments on the landscape painters. **Eduaert Snayers,** also probably associated with **Jan Brueghel the younger,** painted a *Dying Magdalene* before 1627 and *Four scenes from the life of Adam* before 1633. **Simon de Vos** (Pls. 673, 674, 687) joined the **Rubens** factory at nineteen in 1622 and may have had assignments there in the later twenties and early thirties. Of the quite young men **Theodor van Thulden** (Pl. 589) was a pupil of **Abraham van Blyenberch** (who was back from England by 1622); he was Master at twenty in 1626 and then probably worked in the **Rubens** atelier till he went to Paris in 1631. **Erasmus Quellinus** (Pls. 639, 671) was Master at twenty-six in 1633 possibly after training in the **Rubens** atelier. **Peter van Lint** (Pls. 677, 697) pupil at fifteen of **Artus Wolfordt** in 1624 was Antwerp Master in 1632. **Jan van den Hoecke** (son of **Gaspar van den Hoecke**) was twenty-two in 1633 and probably attached to the **Rubens** atelier; and the gifted **Balthasar van Cortbemde** whose early training is unknown was Antwerp Master at twenty in 1632.

Rubens painted and signed his *Flight of Lot from Sodom* (Pl. 577) in 1625 possibly in Paris; and though preposterous as illustration of the subject the picture charms aesthetically by its pretty blond colouring and the rhythmic movement in the chain of figures. His deliveries for churches included the *Adoration of the Magi* (Pl. 574) commissioned by Abbot Yrsselius for the Abbaye de S. Michel in 1624, the *Assumption of the Virgin* commissioned for Antwerp Cathedral by Jan Delrio (then Dean of the Cathedral) about 1625 and placed in position in 1626, *The Mystic Marriage of S. Catherine* (sometimes called the *Virgin and Child adored by Saints*) commissioned for Antwerp Augustins about 1627 and finished in 1628 possibly before **Rubens** left for Spain; *S. Ildephonse receiving a chasuble from the Virgin* commissioned by the Infanta Isabella, as mentioned above, for the altar of the Fraternity of S. Ildephonse in Brussels S. Jacques-sur-Coudenberg in 1629 and delivered in 1632; and, possibly by 1633, *S. Theresa interceding for the deliverance of Bernardin de Mendoza* (*patron of the Theresian convent in Valladolid*) *and other souls from Purgatory* for the Antwerp Carmes Déchaussées. Of these the *Adoration of the Magi* (Pl. 574) is a huge picture with over life-size figures and life-size camels; there is an old tradition that it was painted in sixteen days, but that was surely impossible even if all hands in the factory were called on for the effort. In the sketch for this picture, doubtless made by **Rubens** himself, the kneeling Magus, baldheaded and grey-bearded, is in the foreground and pages behind hold up his train as in the picture by **Petro de Lignis** (Pl. 573); in the final picture the kneeling Magus is brown bearded and is placed further back and the pages are replaced by the standing grey bearded Magus of whom Sir Joshua Reynolds wrote: 'One of the Kings, who holds a cup in his hand, is loaded with drapery, his head appears too large, and upon the whole he makes but an ungraceful figure'; and indeed this change (with most of the others, for there are many) gives us cause to wish that **Rubens** had stuck to his first design; for the small sketch was a flash of flamboyant imaginative vision while the final picture, altered as result of indecisions and executed in the atelier, shows the disadvantage of a method that allowed so many loopholes where the first inspiration could escape. *The Mystic Marriage of S. Catherine* (or *The Virgin and Child adored by saints*), not reproduced here, is vastly different from the early 'Hortus Conclusus' concepts of the subject as seen in the picture by the **Buckingham Palace Mystic Marriage Painter** (Pl. 106) and other fifteenth-century artists, and even from the concept painted by his former master **Otto van Veen** (Pl. 455) in 1589; for the Virgin and Child and S. Catherine are now perched aloft on a marble throne, and from the ground upwards a dozen male and female saints from S. John the Baptist to S. George and S. Sebastian and from S. Mary Magdalene to S. Claire and S. Apollonia gesticulate and posture in a circle so that Reynolds could write of it with accuracy: 'The whole appears as much animated and in motion as it is possible for a picture to be where nothing is doing. . . . Rubens' manner is often too artificial and picturesque for the Grand Style: Titian knew that so much formality and regularity as to give the appearance of being above all the tricks of art, which we call picturesque, is of itself grandeur.' Of the *S. Theresa interceding* Reynolds wrote: 'The whole has great harmony of colouring and freedom of pencil: it is in his best manner', and Descamps wrote of it 'C'est un tableau d'un dessein coulant, partout clair et argentin, du plus bel effet, les têtes sont de la plus grande beauté', but in the nineteenth century Lafenestre had a different reaction: 'Ce tableau n'est pas entièrement de la main de Rubens; c'est l'oeuvre d'un élève, Van Thulden peut-être, que le maître a retouchée dans les deux figures principales.'

Among the 'history' subjects, allegories and mythologies **Jan (Velvet) Brueghel** may have painted some allegories in his last three years before 1625; and after his death sets of pictures titled *The Seasons* and *The Senses* and landscapes with allegoric figures were staple products in the atelier of **Jan Brueghel the younger** whose *Flora in a garden* (Pl. 605) painted with **Peeter van Avont** has been mentioned above in its landscape and floral aspects and can now be compared as an allegoric concept with the *Flora* (Pl. 363) by **Jan Massys**. Between 1625 and 1632 both **Abraham Janssens** (Pl. 509) and **Hendrik van Balen** (Pls. 507, 508) provided figures for small pictures which **Jan Brueghel the younger** completed with landscape and accessories; and a newcomer in this milieu was **Frans Wouters** (Pl. 667) pupil at seventeen of **Peeter van Avont** in 1629. **Frans Francken** (Pls. 496, 517, 519) signed a *Croesus showing his treasures to Solon* in 1633 and may have painted by then his *Neptune and Amphitrite* (Pl. 648). Pictures of *Judith and Holofernes* (probably allegoric of the Infanta's services as suggested above) were painted by **Jean Baptiste Saive** for Malines, S. Rombout, by 1624, by **Pieter van Mol**, by **Jan Cossiers**, possibly by **Adam de Coster**, and also by the unrecorded artist here referred to as the **Madrid Judith Painter** whose *Judith and servant with the head of Holofernes* (Pl. 582) can be compared with earlier hedonist concepts of the subject by the **Ottawa Judith Painter** (Pl. 295), the **Grenoble Judith Painter** (Pl. 296) and **Jan Massys** (Pl. 315). In 1629 **Van Dyck** painted, in Antwerp, a *Rinaldo and Armida* commissioned by Endymion Porter for Charles I's collection; and about the same time he must also have painted, with Titian in his memory, his *Venus at the forge of Vulcan demanding arms for Achilles* (Pl. 604) where the model for the Virgin in his religious pieces for the Jesuit Fraternity of Unmarried Men is depicted as Venus and the foreground cherub in his *Christ crucified: with S. Dominic and S. Catherine of Siena in adoration* has become a foreground Cupid. There are very few records of **Van Dyck's** pupils, assistants and collaborators in this Antwerp period; but **Jan van Reyn** (Pls. 592, 651) is known as a pupil aged about twenty about 1630; **Remigius van Leemput** some three years older was probably an assistant between 1628 and 1630; and other assistants or collaborators may have included **Gillis Backereel** who was back from Italy in 1629 and whose *Hero and Leander* (Pl. 594) has a **Van Dyck** air, and also **Josse de Paepe** who had not yet gone to Italy and whose *Venus and Adonis* (Pl. 593) is described as follows in the 1927 Amsterdam catalogue 'Venus draped in a light red robe is seated before a highly coloured landscape against a brown rock; Adonis, holding his arms round her waist, is filled with secret longing to go hunting with his dogs'. **Jordaens** author of the noble *Daughters of Cecrops* (Pl. 546) in 1617 does not seem to have dated his mythologies and allegories between 1622 and 1633; but his *Allegory of Abundance* (Pl. 545), discussed with the *Daughters of Cecrops* in my last chapter, and other undated pictures in this category may have been painted in this period when I assume him largely occupied as de facto director of the **Rubens** atelier; and though no painters are entered as his pupils in these years **Jan Boeckhorst** (Pl. 720) known as **Lange Jan** is said to have worked under him before becoming Antwerp Master at twenty-eight in 1633.

The output of allegories, mythology and 'history' from the **Rubens** atelier was staggering in quantity—especially when we recall the collateral production for churches and the fact that **Rubens** himself was away from Antwerp for nearly two years (if we add up his visits to Paris and Holland and his absence in Spain and England from August 1628 till

March 1630). For it included the twenty-one huge pictures in the *Marie de Médicis* series where all the gods of Olympus and countless allegorical conceits were combined to flatter the patron; the cartoons for three sets of tapestries—the *History of Constantine* for Louis XIII, the *Triumph of the Eucharist* (treated as allegory) commissioned by the Infanta Isabella for the Descalzas Reales in Madrid, and a *History of Achilles* for an unrecorded purchaser; most of the panels for the Whitehall ceiling *The Apotheosis of James I*; and the two pictures acquired by Charles I in 1630, the *Peace and War* (Pl. 591A) and the *Allegory of Peace: S. George and the Dragon* which may also have passed through the Antwerp workshop as already suggested. It is clear that **Rubens** himself made rapid preliminary sketches for everything—and I reproduce his sketch *The arrival at Marseilles* (Pl. 578) from the *Marie de Médicis* series; but once such sketches had passed into the atelier the procedure was still what it had been when he first organized his mass factory as described in my last chapter. The identity of the chief executants who made the first more detailed 'modellos' from his sketches in these years is not known; **Van Dyck** had left before the period began; but it seems to me likely, as suggested above, that **Jordaens** was director of all the executive departments and responsible for the some of the 'modellos' and in general charge of the enlargements to the scale required. For the rest we know, as mentioned earlier, that **Jan Wildens** (Pls. 628, 629) and **Lucas van Uden** (Pls. 561, 566, 567, 602) were there as landscape specialists and it is possible that **Alexander Keirincx** (Pls. 610, 611, 613) and **Vincent Malo** (Pl. 615) may have worked in that department for some time; **Frans Snyders** (Pls. 630, 632, 634, 635), **Paul de Vos** (Pls. 633, 636), and probably for some time **Abraham van Diepenbeeck,** were there for animals; **Frans Snyders** was still the atelier specialist for decorative swags and garlands of fruit and piled up fruits as still-life additions (Pls. 554, 555, 655, 656, 657); **Adriaen van Utrecht** (Pls. 693, 694)—through his connection with **Simon de Vos**—may also have worked in that section; and **Daniel Seghers** (Pls. 692, 757), as already suggested, may have been called on for the very occasional flowers. In figure painting the more important work may well have been done by **Jordaens** (Pls. 545, 546, 588) directing at various times **Deodatus Delmont, Gerard Seghers** (Pl. 527), **Gaspar van den Hoecke, Cornelis de Vos** (Pls. 590, 641), **Cornelis Schut** (Pl. 669), **Abraham van Diepenbeeck, Justus van Egmont** (Pl. 722), **Willem Panneels** (Pl. 668), **Jan Boeckhorst** (Pl. 720), **Simon de Vos** (Pls. 673, 674, 687), **Jacques Moermans** registered as a **Rubens** pupil at twenty in 1622 and as Master in 1630, and **Theodor van Thulden** (Pls. 589, 753) before his departure for Paris; and towards the end **Erasmus Quellinus** (Pls. 639, 671), **Jan van den Hoecke** (Pls. 716, 721), **Jan Cossiers** (Pl. 640), **Jan de Ceustere, Gerard Weri, Peeter Symons** (Pl. 638), **Jacob Peter Gowi** (Pl. 637) and possibly **Jan Thomas (van Ypern). Rubens** himself, when in Antwerp, presumably looked in at various stages to give advice and order alterations; and when the chief executants had completed their work, he may often still have 'retouched' the whole picture or some details.

These products of the **Rubens** atelier were admired and acquired exclusively, as before, by Princes and nobles; and the taste of other rich collectors has been indicated in my accounts of the pictures in the van der Geest gallery and in the ideal gallery portrayed by the **Hague Studio of Apelles Painter** (Pl. 580). Side-lights on the choices made by average collectors with less sumptuous tastes are again provided by Antwerp inventories of this period and by records of pictures exported. Thus an inventory of 1627 details the collection of Antoinette Wiael, widow of one Jans van Haecht (who seems to have been a relation of **Tobias van Haecht** (Pl. 377) and perhaps a dealer, as many of the widow's pictures were in the hands of dealers in Paris); this collection contained a flowerpiece by **Osias Beet** and several fruit pieces by **Adriaen van Utrecht** (who was under thirty at that date); landscapes, including a hunting piece by **Tobias van Haecht** and two works a *Conversion of S. Paul* and *Diana hunting* by **Tobias van Haecht** in collaboration with **Sebastiaan Vrancx**; a *Judgement of Paris* and a *Nausicaa* by **Hendrik van Balen**, a *Venus and Adonis* by **Frans Francken** in a landscape by **Abraham Govaerts**, also religious pictures by **Lucas van Leyden, Wenzelas Coebergher, Marten Pepyn, Lazarus van der Borcht, Hendrik de Clerck** and **Adriaen van Nieulandt.** The painter **Steven Wils** (a pupil of **Abraham Janssens**), who was Dean in the Guild in 1625 and died in 1628, left hundreds of prints and drawings, including some by Dürer and Aldegrever, about a hundred models of classical sculpture, and among the paintings some copies of works by Caravaggio, a *Pan and Syrinx* by **Paul van Somer**, a *Seapiece with shipping* by **Jan Porcellis**, a *Judith* by **Jan van Hemessen**, an *Adam and Eve* by **Frans Floris**, a *Taking chestnuts from the fire* by **Marten van Cleve**, a *Portrait of Michiel Coxie with a death's head in his hand*, a *Temptation of S. Anthony* by **Frans Verbeeck**, a *Portrait of a man* by **Willem Key** and among earlier pieces 'A young man taking an old man's purse' by '**Master Quinten**' (perhaps **Quinten Massys**); his own works left in the studio included a *Justice asleep*, and *Justice triumphant*, a *Pan and Apollo*, a *Satyr admiring the beauty of Diana*, a *David offering the head of Goliath to Saul* and a *S. John in the wilderness*. Details of exports are contained in the records of dealing by **Cornelis de Vos** and **Jan Brueghel the younger** who sent pictures to Chrysostom van Immerseel in Seville for sale in Spain, Portugal and the New World as related above: **Cornelis de Vos** sent him pictures by himself and by **Sebastiaan Vrancx, Abraham Janssens** and others; **Jan Brueghel the younger** sent pictures by himself and his collaborators including sets of *The Seasons, The Months* and *The Senses*, a *History of Adam*, several pictures called *Flora*, fruit pieces and tables with food and vessels by one of his assistants ('knechten'), seapieces by **Andries van Ertvelt** (thirty-six in one consignment), landscapes and fruit pieces by **Jacob van Uden**, religious pictures and mythologies by **Marten Pepyn, Hendrik van Balen, Frans Francken** and **Abraham Janssens,** and many works by artists unknown today. In 1632 he offered a copy of a *Fruit garland with figures* 'the finest work my father ever painted with figures by **Rubens** which was sold to the Prince of Poland for 1600 gulden', and a *Noli me tangere in a landscape with fruit and flowers and in the background the Maries going to the sepulchre* from the **Rubens** atelier retouched ('overdaen') by the master 'for some prince or crowned head'; but his correspondence shows that he hardly expected van Immerseel to buy these particular pictures as he recognized that pictures by **Jan (Velvet) Brueghel** and **Rubens** were too expensive for his market.

CHAPTER XIII

Cardinal Infante Ferdinand

1634-1641

THE Cardinal Infante Ferdinand, Isabella's successor as Governor of the Spanish Nether-lands, was Philip IV's brother. He had been a cardinal from the age of ten, he was twenty-five in 1634, and thirty-two when he died of smallpox. During his Governorship the Thirty Years War was continued; the Dutch gained France as an ally in their war against Spain; the Jesuits maintained their power in Belgium; and the Jansenist movement grew.

In 1634 Charles I was thirty-four, Louis XIII was thirty-three, Philip IV twenty-nine and the Stadholder Prince Frederick Henry fifty. Ferdinand II was still Emperor and Urban VIII still Pope. Wallenstein was murdered at Eger; the Cardinal Infante Ferdinand, before taking up his post in Belgium, served the Emperor handsomely by defeating the Protestant leader Bernard of SaxeWeimar at the Battle of Nordlingen when Octavio Piccolomini was one of his commanders; and, pending the Cardinal Infante's arrival, Prince Thomas Francis of Savoy was acting Governor in Belgium. In 1635 the Cardinal Infante made his Pageant Entry into Antwerp; Octavio Piccolomini became one of his commanders in Belgium; Richelieu formed an alliance with the Dutch, declared war on Spain and made the Treaty of Rueil with the Alsatians; Jansen published 'Mars Gallicus'; and the Académie Francaise was founded. In 1636 Jansen became Bishop of Ypres; the Cardinal Infante's armies invaded France and reached Compiègne; and Charles I sent the Protestant Thomas Howard, Earl of Arundel to Vienna to urge the restoration of the Palatinate to his nephew Charles Louis. In 1637 the Emperor Ferdinand II died and Ferdinand III succeeded; Prince Frederick Henry recaptured Breda; Piccolomini led Imperial troops in Alsace; Descartes, aged forty-one and living in Holland, published his 'Discours de la méthode'; the Dutch went crazy about tulip bulbs; and Philip IV made Calderón de la Barca, aged thirty-seven, a Knight of the Order of Santiago. In 1638 John Hampden refused to pay shipmoney to Charles I; Milton aged twenty-nine wrote 'Lycidas' and published 'Comus'; Jansen died; his follower Duvergier de Hauranne, Abbot of S. Cyran and author of 'Petrus Aurelius', was im-prisoned by Richelieu; and Antoine Lemaître, grandson of Antoine Arnauld the elder, became the first Port Royal 'solitaire' or hermit. Prince Frederick Henry marched on Antwerp in spite of protests from the Amsterdam merchants who secretly supplied the enemy with food and munitions as they preferred an Antwerp blockaded at the mouth of the Scheldt to an Antwerp incorporated in the Dutch Republic as a rival; the Cardinal Infante organized resistance; and the Dutch were defeated at the Battle of Calloo. In 1639 Piccolomini defeated the French at Thionville and was recalled by the Emperor to act as 'ad latus' to the Archduke Leopold Wilhelm; Hesdin surrendered to the French; and van Tromp destroyed a Spanish fleet off the English coast. In 1640 Jansen's 'Augustinus' was posthumously published; and the Belgian Jesuits published 'Imago primi saeculi' to celebrate the Jesuit centenary. The Long Parliament assembled in London; the Dutch destroyed a Spanish fleet off the coast of Pernambuco; the French captured Arras; the Catalans in revolt against Philip IV invited Louis XIII to become their King; and Portugal, revolting more permanently against Spain, acclaimed the Duke of Braganza as King John IV. In 1641 Strafford was beheaded; William of Orange married Charles I's daughter Mary; the Cardinal Infante lost La Bassée, Lens and Bapaume but resisted the French elsewhere; the French entered Barcelona but were defeated at Tarragona; and the Cardinal Infante died.

Some of these events gave rise to topical paintings. Thus **Rubens** painted *The Cardinal Infante Ferdinand at the Battle of Nordlingen* (Pl. 643) and the victory was referred to in the decorations for the Cardinal Infante's Pageant Entry into Antwerp. The Battle of Calloo was painted for the Antwerp Town Hall in a joint composition by **Gillis Peeters** and his brother **Bonaventura Peeters**; the subject was also painted by **Jan Brueghel the younger** and probably by **Peeter Snayers** (Pls. 627, 700, 701); **Rubens** as official painter to the city of Antwerp was commissioned to design a *Victory of Calloo triumphal car* to be used in processions and received as part payment a cask of French wine; and **Gerard Weri** painted *The Virgin handing a sword to the Cardinal Infante Ferdinand* for Calloo church. **Peeter Snayers** was chosen by Piccolomini as official recorder of his military campaigns and began a series of military pieces amounting in the end to some twenty pictures.

As always there were Flemings at work abroad. In Paris **Philippe de Champaigne** (Pls. 742, 750) was now Court Painter to Louis XIII and high in Richelieu's favour; in 1634 he finished the *Louis XIII conferring the Order of the Saint Esprit on the Duc de Longueville, 1633* and painted *Louis XIII in adoration* (*Le voeu de Louis XIII*) as an ex-voto commissioned by the King for Notre Dame; he then painted a full-length *Portrait of Richelieu* and began works for the Palais Royal and the Sorbonne on the Cardinal's orders; he also designed some tapestries *The Life of the Virgin* for Notre Dame and painted altarpieces for various churches. The portraitist **Justus van Egmont** (Pl. 722) remained among the King's Court Painters, but **Ferdinand Elle** died about 1638 and **Gerard Schoof** may have died before 1641. **Pieter van Mol,** who finished his murals for the Carmelite church about 1635, was Court Painter to Queen Anne of Austria at forty-one in 1640 and may have painted at this time his signed *Entombment* for the Augustins Déchaussés (Petits Pères). **Theodor van Thulden** (Pls. 589, 753) was back in Antwerp from Paris and Fontainebleau by 1635, and by then **Peeter Franchoys** (Pl. 654) had also left for his native Malines. **Henri Staben** (Pl. 518) was still painting interiors and **Mathieu van Plattenberg** marines. The animal and still-life painter **Jan Fyt** (Pls. 719, 733) was in Paris at twenty-two in 1633 and left for Italy some two years later. **David Teniers the elder** was in Paris in 1635 selling pictures by himself and his sons **David Teniers** and **Juliaen Teniers the younger** (Pl. 681) at the S. Germain Fair. **Jan van Reyn** (Pls. 592, 651) went from Antwerp to Paris at twenty-seven on the invitation of the Comte de Gramont about 1637 but soon left in dudgeon for his native Dunkirk because a lacquey had stolen a shirt from him; and his sensitively observed and beautifully designed *Lady in black dress with red ribbons* (Pl. 651) of that year was possibly painted in Paris. **Jacques Fouquier** (Pl. 563) was still concerned with his landscape panels for the Grande Galerie of the Louvre till 1641 when he quarrelled with Nicolas Poussin who had returned from Rome and been put in charge of all the Louvre decorations. A landscape and fruit-and-flower painter **Jean Michel Picart,** in Paris from Brabant by 1640, was chiefly active as dealer; and in the South **Jean Daret** of Brussels settled at Aix-en-Provence in 1637 and painted for the Cathedral a *Salvator de Horta healing the sick* in 1637, a *Crucifixion: with the Virgin of the Seven Sorrows* in 1640 and a *S. Theresa* in 1641.

In Holland **Joachim Uytewael** (Pls. 490, 498, 524) died in Utrecht at seventy-two in 1638. **Roelandt Savery** (Pls. 525, 564, 583, 585) painted an *Elijah fed by ravens* and yet another *Orpheus charming the animals* in 1634 and died insane in Utrecht at about sixty-three in 1639. **Adam Willaerts,** whose headquarters was Utrecht, painted his *Coast scene with stormy sea and ships* (Pl. 688) at sixty-one in 1638 and may have visited England to paint his *Return of Sir Edward Michelbourne from the East Indies to Portsmouth 1606* dated 1640. **Abraham Bosschaert** was painting flowerpieces first in Amsterdam and, after 1637, in Utrecht; and **Ambrosius Bosschaert the younger** was also in Utrecht. The landscape painter **Jan Coelenbier** was active, chiefly as dealer, in Haarlem; **Adriaen Lucasz Fonteyn** was painting his peasant and social genre scenes in Rotterdam; and **Frans de Momper** seems to have moved from Antwerp to the Hague before 1641. **Pieter Stalpaert** painted a *Rural landscape with farmhouses and horseman* in Amsterdam at sixty-three in 1635 and probably died there about 1637. **Willem van Nieulandt** (Pl. 475) died in Amsterdam just over fifty about 1635; **Adriaen van Nieulandt** (Pls. 515, 647), there through the period, signed a *Landscape with huntsmen* at fifty-three in 1640 and a *Landscape with Diana and Nymphs* in 1641; **Samuel van den Hecken** was in Amsterdam in 1635 and **Alexander Keirincx** (Pls. 610, 611, 613) was there from England in 1636.

In England **Marcus Geeraerts the younger** painted *Mrs Anne Hoskins* in 1629 and died at seventy-four in 1635. **Hendrik van Steenwyck the younger** (Pls. 487, 489, 536, 537), fifty-three in 1633 and still active in 1641, signed a *Sacristy interior* in 1634, a *Charles I beneath a triumphal arch in a garden* with figures by an unrecorded artist in 1637, and another *Liberation of S. Peter* in 1638. **Walther (Gauthier) Damery** of Liège, painter of religious subjects, visited England about 1635 aged about twenty-five. **Teniers** (Pls. 682, 708) came to Dover aged twenty-six in 1636 to meet the Seville dealer van Immerseel who ordered some pictures. **Frans Wouters** (Pl. 667), who had visited the Court of Ferdinand II in Vienna, came at twenty-four in 1636 in the suite of the Emperor's ambassador to London whence he wrote to the Antwerp dealer William Forchoudt: 'I cannot complain as I ride here daily in a carriage with six horses and dine at the ambassador's table with twenty-one footmen behind'; he became painter to Charles, Prince of Wales, soon after; and he may have painted here his *Landscape with Diana resting* signed in 1636 and his *Landscape with rainbow and man at plough* before returning to Antwerp in 1641. **Cornelis de Neve** was here from Antwerp under thirty by 1637 when he painted a double full-length portrait of the Earl of Dorset's sons *Richard Sackville (Lord Buckhurst) and the Hon. Edward Sackville.* The Dutchman Cornelis van Poelenburgh came about 1637 and put figures in some architectural pieces by **van Steenwyck.** Alexander Keirincx (known in England as **Carings**) was back here from Holland perhaps about 1637 and certainly by 1640 when he painted prospects and castles in Scotland for the King; he collaborated with van Poelenburgh in some pictures they both signed, and his *Landscape with bathing women* (Pl. 610) may have been painted here, with van Poelenburgh, at this time. One **Cornelis Bol,** from Antwerp, a friend of **Keirincx** in 1640, was possibly the author of some extant Thames views with London buildings. **Gonzales Coques** (Pls. 764, 773) may have come on a visit before 1641 when he was twenty-seven. **Hendrik van der Borcht the younger** arrived from Italy aged twenty-six about 1640 and may have painted some portraits here; one **Weesop** presumed a Fleming came in 1640 or 1641; **Philippe Vleughels,** pupil of **Cornelis Schut** (Pl. 669)—and father of Watteau's friend Nicolas Vleughels—came for a time in 1641; **Jorge Geldorp,** who still had his London house, was the banker Jabach's agent in the matter of a *Crucifixion of S. Peter* commissioned from **Rubens** in 1638, and was host to the young Dutchman Peter Lely when he arrived here shortly after **Van Dyck's** death.

Van Dyck reached the height of his success here in this period. He was away from England, in Antwerp and Brussels, in the autumn and winter of 1634; he went again to Antwerp in the later part of 1640 and visited Paris in 1641 before his death here at forty-two in December of that year; but except for these absences he was continuously at work here and painting more portraits of the King and Queen and the Royal Family, elegant full length and half-length likenesses of nobles and rich gentry and their ladies, and a number of mythologies or allegoric pieces. He also reached the height of his extravagance in these years and, hoping to balance his expenditure, he established a laboratory for an alchemist who claimed to be able to make gold. He married the Queen's lady, Mary Ruthven, in 1639; and the King recoiled from the price he asked for a *History of the Order of the Garter* to be painted as murals in the Whitehall Banqueting Hall beneath the ceiling provided by **Rubens.** To represent **Van Dyck's** portraits of this time I reproduce his celebrated *Charles I with horse, equerry and groom* (Pl. 644), and also the *Diana Cecil, Countess of Oxford* (Pl. 663) which reminds me that Walpole said: 'his ladies are so little flattered that one is surprised he had so much custom' for the lady in this picture seems as formidable a matron as the sitter for the *Mary Nevill, Baroness Dacre* by **Hans Ewouts** (Pl. 338). His studio assistants here are known to have included two Dutchmen David Beck and A. Hanneman, a Spaniard named P. Moya and possibly the Englishman William Dobson; **Jan van Reyn** (Pls. 592, 651) probably went back with him to Antwerp in 1634 and remained there till he left again for Paris; but between 1635 and 1641 **Remigius van Leemput** was again his assistant and copyist; and another assistant was probably **Jan van Belcamp** who had now become copyist of family and other portraits in the Royal Collections and inserted figures of the King and Henrietta Maria in a perspective scene by **van Steenwyck. Frans Wouters** (Pl. 667), I suspect, assisted **Van Dyck** with some landscape backgrounds and with his mythologies including a *Cupid and Psyche*; **Alexander Keirincx** may also have collaborated; and **Theodor Boeyermans** had probably come from Antwerp as pupil-assistant aged nineteen by 1639.

In Italy the Flemish colony in Genoa lost **Jan Roos** who died in 1638; but **Cornelis de Wael** was still there in 1641 and the young marine painter **Gaspar van Eyck** (Pl. 703) was there for some time probably in the early thirties. In Florence **Justus Sutterman** painted his *Portrait of Galileo* in 1636; and a Liégeois **Bertholet Flémalle** (pupil of **Gerard Douffet**) arrived about twenty-six, after visiting Rome, in about 1640. **Vincent Malo** (Pl. 615) seems to have gone down from Genoa to Florence and Rome. **Jan Boeckhorst (Lange Jan)** (Pl. 720) went to Italy from Antwerp at thirty-one in 1636 but did not reach Rome and was back in Antwerp before 1639. **Jan Claret** painter of religious subjects was working for churches in Turin and Savigliano. **Hendrik van der Borcht the younger** arrived in Italy about 1637 to buy antiques for Thomas Howard Earl of Arundel whom he had met in Frankfort; and **Jan van den Hoecke** (Pls. 716, 721) arrived at twenty-six at about the same time. **Pieter de Coster** was a new arrival in Venice; **Nicolas Regnier** was still there and now had four daughters who were to be famed for their beauty ; **Michele Desubleo** his halfbrother was in Bologna; and **Matthias Stom (Stomer)** was in Naples and then in Sicily where he signed a *Miracle of S. Isidore* for the Augustine church in Caccamo (Palermo) in 1641. **Abraham van Diepenbeeck** seems to have made an Italian journey, probably to Rome, about 1636 accompanied by **Jan Thomas (van Ypern)** then nineteen, and to have gone back to Antwerp by 1638. In Rome **Jacob de Hase** died just under sixty in 1634, **Cornelis Schut the younger** died there under thirty in 1636, and **Karel Spieringh** died at thirty in 1639 when he was painting frescoes in the Flemish church S. Maria dell' Anima. **Balthasar Lauwers** visited Milan about 1634 but was soon back in Rome and still painting landscapes at the end of the period; and **Louis Cousin (Luigi Primo)**, still painting religious subjects and portraits, supplied a fresco *S. Dominic ordering the burning of the books* for SS. Domenico e Sisto and was elected member of the Accademia di S. Luca in 1638. The Liégeois **François Walschartz** seems to have left for Rome about 1634. **Peter van Lint** (Pls. 677, 697) who painted frescoes *The Finding of the True Cross by S. Helena* and *Heraclius carrying the Cross* for S. Maria del Popolo, and a portrait of his patron *Cardinal Ginnasio* in 1639, returned to Antwerp at thirty-one in 1640. Among the newcomers, doubtless welcomed in the 'Bent', **Jan Fyt** (Pls. 719, 733) arrived in Rome from Paris at twenty-four in 1635 and visited Venice before returning to Antwerp in 1641 or earlier. **Frans Luyckx** painter of portraits and occasional religious subjects was also in Rome, just over thirty in 1635. **Jan Miel** (Pl. 772) arrived in Rome from Antwerp at thirty-seven in 1636, painted figures in some landscapes by Claude le Lorrain, joined the Italian Andrea Sacchi as an assistant in the Barberini Palace in 1641 and became a member of the Congregazione dei Virtuosi the same year; **Josse de Paepe** (Pl. 593) reached Rome from Antwerp in 1634 and became a member of the Guild of S. Luke in 1641; and **Vincent Leckerbetien** painter of landscapes and battle pieces, who was known as **Manciolla** (because he had lost his right hand and painted with his left), appears to have been acquainted with Poussin before 1640.

Visits to Spain seem to have been made in this period by **Gaspar de Crayer** (Pls. 598, 607, 609, 642), **Cornelis Schut** (Pl. 669), who painted there a *S. Francis Xavier baptising Indians*, and the marine painter **Gaspar van Eyck** (Pl. 703).

In Central Europe **Hendrik van der Borcht the elder** was in Frankfort where he signed an allegorical piece *Germany entreating the Emperor Ferdinand III to make peace* at fifty-six in 1639. **Frans Wouters** (Pl. 667) visited Vienna at twenty-three in 1635 and became Court Painter to Ferdinand II but left soon after for England as related. **Frans Luyckx** who went to Vienna from Rome about 1637, became Court Painter to Ferdinand III in 1638. **Jan Hulsman** was working for Cologne Cathedral in 1639.

At home in Belgium the artists were loosely grouped, as before, into Court Painters, the general community of painters connected with the Guilds, and painters regularly or occasionally employed by the **Rubens** atelier.

The Cardinal Infante's Court Painters included **Gaspar de Crayer** (Pls. 598, 607, 609, 642), **Gerard Seghers, Peeter Snayers** (Pls. 627, 700, 701) **Rubens** and probably **Antoine Sallaert**; and **Jacques Francart** was confirmed in the post of Court architect. From **Peeter Snayers** the Cardinal Infante commissioned a series of hunting pieces for Philip IV's hunting lodge the Torre de la Parada which included a *Hunting party of Cardinal Infante Ferdinand* and the *Philip IV killing a wild boar* reproduced here (Pl. 627); and he commissioned his portrait in Cardinal's robes (Pl. 642) from **Gaspar de Crayer**. With **Rubens** his relations were close and cordial from the start; learning that, prostrate with gout, he had not been present at the Antwerp Pageant Entry, he called upon him at his house to congratulate him on the decorations; he commissioned him, as noted, to paint his portrait as victor at the Battle of Nordlingen (Pl. 643); he kept in touch with him in connection with a series of mythologies commissioned by Philip IV to go with the hunting pieces in the Torre de la Parada; and at the end of the period he sent to Philip IV the *Judgement of Paris* (Pl. 670) with a letter saying 'All the painters here consider this his best work. It has however one fault—the excessive nudity of the figures. But I have not been able to get him to make any concession as he said this was the essence of the picture's excellence. The Venus in the centre is a good likeness of his wife, the prettiest woman here.' **Van Dyck** was never Court Painter to the Cardinal Infante; there seems no evidence that he painted his portrait on his Belgian visit at the end of 1634; and when he revisited Antwerp, after the death of **Rubens** in 1640, his price and conditions for a proposed continuation of the **Rubens** commissions for the Torre de la Parada were rejected by the Cardinal Infante as too pretentious to be seriously considered.

In the general community of artists **Adriaen Brouwer** (Pl. 595, 617, 618, 623, 625) lived first with the baker **Joos van Craesbeeck** (Pls. 616, 619, 620, 626) and gave him painting lessons, and then for a time with the engraver Paul Pontius; and **Jan Brueghel the younger** (Pl. 605) continued his factory of small pictures in several categories. In 1635 **Theodor van Thulden** (Pls. 589, 753) aged twenty-nine married **Hendrik van Balen's** daughter Maria, a godchild of **Rubens**. In 1636 **Jan Baptist Borkens (Borrekens)** aged twenty-five married **Jan (Velvet) Brueghel's** daughter Catherine, a ward of **Rubens** who was witness at the wedding; **Brouwer** became friendly with the still-life painter **Jan Davidsz de Heem** who had recently arrived from Holland; **Jan Brueghel the younger** quarrelled with the Seville dealer van Inmerseel and one Antoon Cossiers replaced him as Antwerp agent; **Teniers** who met van Immerseel in Dover, as mentioned, agreed to paint some pictures for him and deliver them to Cossiers; and the Vienna branch of the Forchoudt firm of Antwerp dealers asked for pictures by **Brouwer** to be sent to them. In 1637 **Teniers** aged twenty-seven married **Jan (Velvet) Brueghel's** daughter Anna, the contract being witnessed by **Rubens, Jan Brueghel the younger** and **Jan Baptist Borkens (Borrekens)** and signed in the house of **Hendrik van Balen's** widow; **Gerard Weri** married the widow of **Theodor Rombouts**; **Balthasar van Cortbemde** married a sister of **Jan van den Hoecke**; and **Jacques Moermans** testified that since 1631 he had made 1200 guldens a year out of pictures and engravings by various artists exported to Antoon Goetkint now trading as 'Bonenfant' in Paris. In 1638 **David Teniers the elder** and Helena Fourment stood godparents at the baptism of **Teniers'** first son; **Abraham van Diepenbeeck** hitherto affiliated with the Glassmakers' Guild became a member of the Painters' Guild and began long quarrels with that body; **Pieter Brueghel the younger** (Pls. 380, 411) died at seventy-four; and **Brouwer** died at thirty-five or younger. In 1639 **Jordaens**, through Balthasar Gerbier, was commissioned by Charles I to paint the *Story of Cupid and Psyche* in a series of wall and ceiling pictures for the Queen's villa at Greenwich; **Ambrosius Brueghel** (younger brother of **Jan Brueghel the younger**) testified himself the owner of a *Christ on the Cross* by **Jan (Velvet) Brueghel** and of a *Portrait of Jan (Velvet) Brueghel and his wife* by **Rubens**: and Antoon Goetkint (Bonenfant) made payments from Paris to numerous Antwerp engravers and painters including **Adriaen van Stalbemt** (Pls. 479, 562). In 1640 Edward Norgate on a visit to **Rubens** chose the *View of the Escorial with deer in the foreground* (painted by 'Verhulst' (**Pieter van der Hulst?**) from a **Rubens** drawing) for Charles I's collection, and **Rubens**, after supervising some retouching, sent the picture to Gerbier with explanation of its genesis and the comment 'Plaise à Dieu que l'extravagance du sujet puisse donner quelque récréation à sa Majesté'; and on May 30 of that year **Rubens** died, paralysed in both hands, at sixty-three. In 1641 **Frans Snyders, Jan Wildens** and **Jacques Moermans** were executors of **Rubens'** estate; **Frans Wouters** back from England for the purpose was valuing pictures at the Château de Steen; **Gaspar de Crayer** (Pls. 598, 607, 609, 642) was made Philip IV's Court Painter and received a *S. Benedict* from the **Rubens** estate; and **Erasmus Quellinus** (Pls. 639, 671) aged thirty-four succeeded **Rubens** as official painter to the city of Antwerp.

In his last seven years **Rubens** suffered intermittently with gout. He took no more part in politics and now concerned himself with his household and friends and his enormous art collections. He continued to organize commissions carried out in his atelier, to paint on some compositions and to make occasional portraits of his wife and children. But his chief delight now was landscape painting as we know from Norgate who wrote in his 'Miniatura' in 1648: 'Landscape is an art . . . wherewithal Sir P. P. Rubens was soe delighted in his latter time as he quitted all his other practices in picture and story, whereby he got a vast estate (150,000 crowns), to study this, wherof he hath left the worlde the best that are to be seene.' Thus in 1635 he did not go to London to install the completed Whitehall pictures explaining to a friend that he now abhorred court life; and in that year he bought a new country home, the Château de Steen, a castellated mansion with ten acres of woodland and farm land. He spent much of his time at Steen but died in his house in Antwerp.

A conspectus of the allegories, mythologies, religious subjects, portraits, landscapes, genre pieces and so on, shows the continued diversity of Flemish production in these years.

In the field of 'history', allegory and mythology, for example, the period began with the decorations for the Cardinal Infante's Pageant Entry into Antwerp which had been fixed for January 1635 but was postponed till April as the winter was abnormally cold. These decorations cost the city some seventy-eight thousand gulden; **Rubens** was put in charge of them and designed a *Stage of Welcome* and a series of *Triumphal Arches* with allegoric statues and decorative paintings which were executed from his sketches by his workshop staff and by collaborators called in for the occasion. The team for this work included **Jordaens** (Pls. 545, 546, 588, 658, 660, 741, 774) who may have been in charge of the executants, **Cornelis de Vos** (Pls. 590, 599, 600, 641), **Jan Wildens** (Pls. 628, 629), **Cornelis Schut** (Pl. 669), **Gerard Seghers** (Pl. 527) who worked on an *Arch of Philip IV* and contributed a panel titled '*The Infanta Isabella descending from Heaven to advise Philip IV to appoint the Cardinal Infante Ferdinand Governor*', **Gaspar van den Hoecke** and **Jan van den Hoecke** (Pls. 716, 721) who enlarged sketches for an 'Arch of Ferdinand', **Jan Boeckhorst (Lange Jan)** (Pl. 720), **Jan de Ceustere** who collaborated with **Jordaens**, the still-life painter **Alexander Adriaenssen** (Pls. 559, 652, 653), **Jan Cossiers** (Pl. 640), **Jan Eyck, Gerard Weri, Artus Wolfordt** (Pl. 606), **Frans Wouters** (Pl. 667) who was then twenty-three and had not yet gone abroad, and **Gaspard van Balen** (son of **Hendrik van Balen**) who was twenty. A good deal of the work was also done by **Erasmus Quellinus** (Pls. 639, 671) aged twenty-eight and **Theodor van Thulden** (Pls. 589, 753) aged twenty-nine who were both active as executants in the **Rubens** workshop from this date. The whole Pageant Entry was recorded in etchings titled 'Pompa Introitus Ferdinandi' by **Theodor van Thulden** (published in 1641); and my plates show a detail of *Sea-horses* (Pl. 631) from **Rubens'** sketch for a painting titled *Wrath of Neptune (Quos Ego)* (Virgil, *Aeneid*, I, 136) which represented *Neptune calming the waves for the Cardinal Infante* and was enlarged for a side panel on the *Stage of Welcome* and balanced by a *Meeting of Cardinal Infante Ferdinand with Ferdinand of Hungary before the Battle of Nordlingen* (with Danubius and various allegoric females in the foreground). The allegoric panels for the Whitehall ceiling begun in the early thirties from sketches by **Rubens** were finished in the workshop by 1634 and dispatched, as just noted, in 1635. The mythologies for the Torre de la Parada, produced in the workshop from 1636 onwards, were also all based on sketches by **Rubens** but in most cases they were signed by the executants—perhaps because the collaborators had struck against the system of anonymity or because **Rubens** thought the signatures would help them or because he thought some of their works so feeble that he wanted to disown them. My plates show in this Torre de la

Parada series *Bacchus and Ariadne* (Pl. 639) by **Erasmus Quellinus**, the *Marriage of Peleus and Thetis* (Pl. 592) by **Jan van Reyn** (in Antwerp between his visits to England and France), *Narcissus* (Pl. 640) by **Jan Cossiers**, *Hippomene and Atalanta* (Pl. 637) by **Jacob Gowi,** *Cephalus spied upon by Procris* (Pl. 638) by **Peter Symons**, and two paintings by **Cornelis de Vos**—the *Triumph of Bacchus* (Pl. 641) a sad decline from Titian's radiant vision and *Apollo and the python* (Pl. 590) where the Apollo, based on the Apollo Belvedere, was evidently painted from the young model in the **Rubens** workshop also seen in the *Young lord renouncing the world* (Pl. 589) by **Theodor van Thulden** and *Peasants before an inn* (Pl. 615) by **Vincent Malo** as pointed out in my last chapter. Other mythologies contributed to this series included *Apollo and Marsyas* by **Jordaens**, *Hercules discovering the purple dye* by **Theodor van Thulden**, the *Fall of Phaeton* by **Jan Eyck**, the *Apotheosis of Hercules* by **Jan Baptist Borkens** and one or more pictures by **Thomas Willeboirts** (known as **Bosschaert**) who is represented here by a later work (Pl. 672). In addition to the sketches for the Antwerp Pageant Entry and the Torre de la Parada scenes **Rubens** painted the *Judgement of Paris* (Pl. 670) mentioned above for Philip IV and probably at this time *The Three Graces* which the King acquired from his estate; and he designed and 'retouched' a tumultuous *Allegory of the outbreak of war* sent in 1638 to **Justus Sutterman** in Florence for the collection of Duke Ferdinand II. The influence of the **Rubens** style in this field was very considerable at this moment but by no means universal; some painters, even among those closely associated with his atelier, were able to escape from it; and elsewhere in Antwerp allegories and mythologies with nude figures were produced in quite different styles. This can be seen, for example, in the quietly imagined, gentle, static composition *Diana and her nymphs* (Pl. 668) painted in 1640 by **Willem Panneels** who had long been attached to the **Rubens** workshop and had looked after the Antwerp mansion when **Rubens** was abroad in 1628 and 1629; **Simon de Vos** (Pls. 673, 674, 687), who signed a *Sine Baccho et Cerere friget Venus* at thirty-two in 1635, had worked under **Rubens** on the *Marie de Médicis* series but shows little of his influence in this period; pleasant unpretentious small allegories of *The Seasons*, *The Senses* and so on were still being sold from the workshop of **Jan Brueghel the younger** in the style of his *Flora in a garden* (Pl. 605) painted in conjunction with **Peeter van Avont**, and such pictures were also being painted by **Jan Boots**. **Frans Francken** was still painting mythologies with small nudes like his *Neptune and Amphitrite* (Pl. 648); and a similar mythology with small nudes is a feature in *The Visit to an art gallery* (Pl. 645) painted in 1637 by **Cornelis de Baellieur**. Outside Antwerp the **Rubens** influence though considerable was again not universal. Thus in Ghent, when the Cardinal Infante made his Pageant Entry, the decorations were produced not only by **Gaspar de Crayer** (Pls. 598, 607, 609, 642) who had gone there from Brussels probably for the purpose and by **Cornelis Schut** (Pl. 669) who came from the **Rubens** circle, but also by **Nicolas de Liemaker** a Gantois and by **Theodoor Rombouts** (Pls. 581, 596, 597) who had gone there from Antwerp but was quite unaffected by the **Rubens** manner and received a commission for an *Allegory of Justice* for the Ghent Town Hall.

Among the portrait painters **Jacob van Oost the elder**, thirty-two in 1633, was available in Bruges for quiet, serious and sympathetic records (Pl. 715). In Malines **Peeter Franchoys**, back from Paris and Fontainebleau, signed at thirty-three in 1639, his able and arresting *Young man with wine glass* (Pl. 654) sometimes referred to as *Le rubis sur l'ongle* because the sitter in his yellow jerkin and black sleeves is tilting the last drop of wine from a goblet to his thumbnail. **Jan van Reyn**, whose charming *Lady in black dress with red ribbons* (Pl. 651) of 1637 has already been referred to, was available in Dunkirk from about 1638. In Brussels

Antoine Sallaert (Pl. 514) continued the old tradition of the subscription group in his *Brussels magistrates presented to the Virgin by S. Michael* painted at about forty-four for the Brussels Town Hall in 1634; **Pieter van der Plas** (Pl. 676) about thirty in 1634 also painted civic groups as well as single portraits; **Anton van Opstal**, 'pictor Bruxellensis iconum' already recorded as among the Infanta Isabella's Court Painters, was possibly but not certainly still working in 1641. **Gaspar de Crayer** whose skill in portraiture has been seen in his earlier pieces (Pls. 598, 607, 609) was back in Brussels from Ghent by 1636 and signed at fifty-seven in 1639 his simple and imposing *Cardinal Infante Ferdinand in cardinal's robes* (Pl. 642) which continues the tradition of **Frans Pourbus** (Pl. 540) and lends interest to a statement that he visited Spain in the 1630's before Philip IV appointed him Court Painter in 1641. A newcomer in Brussels **Jan Baptist van Heil** was twenty-five in 1634, and **Peter Meert** painter of single portraits and subscription groups was Brussels Master at about twenty-one in 1640.

In Antwerp portraits were painted by, among others, **Cornelis de Vos, Simon de Vos, Frans Denys, Gysbrecht Thys, Philip Fruytiers, Gonzales Coques, Van Dyck** (in the winter of 1634-35) and **Rubens**. Of these **Cornelis de Vos**, whose skill in bourgeois portraiture (Pls. 599, 600) was discussed in my last chapter, was still much employed in this category; he is said to have had many portrait commissions passed on to him by **Rubens** and to have made a fortune by his portrait practice. **Simon de Vos** was evidently an admirable portraitist when the sitter's personality appealed to him, as we see in his *Lady with a dish of fruit* (Pl. 687) which was probably painted after 1641. **Frans Denys** who worked through the period signed a *Portrait of a cleric* (with arms and the device 'Non in solo pane') at about thirty in 1640. **Gysbrecht Thys**, whose portraits the seventeenth-century art historian Arnold Houbraken informs us were often taken for **Van Dyck**'s, arrived on the scene as Antwerp Master in 1637. **Philip Fruytiers**, a pupil of **Rubens,** and twenty-three in 1633 signed a miniature group *Rubens and his family* before the middle of 1640. **Gonzales Coques** (Pls. 764, 773) who began a brilliant career at about twenty-five was Antwerp Master in 1641. **Van Dyck** painted several portraits on his 1634 visit to Belgium; these included a formal equestrian *Prince Thomas Francis of Savoy* and a half length of the same sitter then Deputy Governor of Belgium as noted above, and a full length of the wife of Gaston, Duke of Orléans, *Marguerite de Lorraine.* **Rubens** in his private capacity painted *Jan Brant* showing the father of his first wife at seventy-five in 1635, *Helena Fourment and her eldest child* about the same time, and a few years later *Helena Fourment and two children*—a sketch portrait that Fragonard must surely have known and admired. As Court Painter **Rubens** produced the *Cardinal Infante Ferdinand at the Battle of Nordlingen* (Pl. 643) which he embellished with an Austrian eagle and an allegoric female as Victory in the spirit of the *Marie de Médicis* series (Pl. 578); seen in the Prado the composition of this picture is inevitably compared with the formal equestrian portraits *Philip IV* and *Count Duke Olivarez* by Velazquez; the face of Cardinal Infante Ferdinand is also inevitably compared there with the *Cardinal Infante Ferdinand with sporting gun and dogs* painted by Velazquez (from an earlier study when the Infante was clean shaven) for the Torre de la Parada at about the same time; and the second comparison tells us that the Cardinal Infante was really a thick-nosed ugly fellow much flattered by the courtier **Rubens**.

In genre painting we have the artist at work in his studio, interiors with bourgeois, domestic, peasant, low-life and gay-life scenes, high-life genre gatherings and studies of peasants in rural settings.

The artist at work is seen in *A painter in his studio* (Pl. 646) signed by **David Ryckaert III** at twenty-six in 1638; here the artist is not camouflaged as S. Luke or Apelles and there is also nothing to remind us that **Rubens** worked in a palatial mansion and that **Van Dyck** entertained his English sitters with musical performances and luxurious luncheons; for the picture quite frankly records the humble studio where an unimaginative genre painter has his model before him in the pose seen in the canvas on the easel, while a pupil copies a drawing pinned up on a screen and a studio assistant grinds colours in exactly the attitude portrayed by **Frans Floris** in *S. Luke painting* (Pl. 351) and before that by **Lancelot Blondeel** (Pl. 330).

In domestic genre **Jordaens** painted his monumental composition *The old sing and the young pipe* (Pl. 660) at forty-five in 1638— the title being the Flemish saw 'Soo de ouden songen, soo peepen de jongen'; the figures here are almost in the foreground and removed from us only by the still-life, as in the earlier pictures by **Pieter Aertsen** (Pls. 356, 357, 360) and **Joachim Beuckelaer** (Pls. 398, 399); the pyramid-group on the left is grandly balanced by the old lady in her high basket chair on the right; and the gesture of the old lady peering through her spectacles can be compared with the old gambler peering at his cards in the tavern piece by **Rombouts** (Pl. 581). It was also probably in these years that **Jordaens** painted the stupendous scene of bourgeois feasting *Twelfth Night: Le roi boit* (Pl. 658) where a cylinder of laughing, shouting, drinking figures shows a side of Flemish life that moved the Cardinal Infante to write to Philip IV 'the people in this country really live like beasts'— though the origin of the picture, I imagine, was just an urge to go one better than Frans Hals in his groups of feasting archers (seen on his trip to Holland in 1632). **Theodoor Rombouts** (Pls. 581, 596, 597), who died in Antwerp at forty in 1637, has left us a *Five Senses* that is virtually a genre piece in this category as a youth in contemporary clothes smokes and holds onions to signify 'Smell', another plays a lute for 'Sound' and a blind man caresses a sculptured head for 'Touch'. **Joos van Craesbeeck's** *Homecoming by night* (Pl. 620) records, I take it, a domestic episode—his own homecoming with his wife to the Antwerp citadel; and we can note here the sentry pacing on the rampart as in **Brouwer**'s *Peasants and Spanish soldiers in the grounds of Antwerp citadel* (Pl. 623) compared in my last chapter with the figures silhouetted on the skyline in the *Lamentation* (Pl. 127) by **Geertgen tot Sint Jans**. **David Ryckaert III** (Pls. 646, 705) signed in 1639 *The old sing and the young pipe* with six old people on one side and six young ones on the other; in that year he also signed a *Butcher's shop with man offering beer to a woman* and in 1640 a subject which was now to be popular *The chemist (or alchemist) engaged on his researches*. Someone—(**Simon de Vos** (Pls. 673, 674), I imagine)—inserted the spirited anecdotic figures in the larder scene by **Snyders** now known as *The market stall* (Pl. 655); and some genre pieces in this domestic category may have been painted before 1641 by **Teniers** (Pls. 678, 682, 683) who was two years older than **David Ryckaert III**, and by **Juliaen Teniers the younger** (Pl. 681) Antwerp Master at twenty in 1636.

The painters of rural and urban peasants in indoor and outdoor settings and of low-life genre subjects included **Sebastiaan Vrancx** (Pls. 532, 534) just over sixty in 1634 and still alive in 1641, **Adriaen Brouwer** till 1638, **van Craesbeeck**, the **Munich Tobacco Den Painter**, the **London (Wallace) Sleeping Boor Painter, David Ryckaert III, Teniers, Anthoni Victoryns** and **Antoon Goubau**. The simple, veracious *Outdoor Dentistry* (Pl. 625) by **Brouwer** invites comparison with the fantasticated but nevertheless veracious scene of the quack dentist in **Bosch**'s *Haywain* (Pl. 165) and makes the performance in the *Quack Dentist* (Pl. 596) by **Rombouts**—discussed in my last chapter as a gay-life picture—seem theatrical and concocted. **Van Craesbeeck**, who outlived **Brouwer** by some twenty years, eventually developed as an independent artist with ideas and vision of his own; but his early training under **Brouwer** is apparent when his *Landscape with soldiers and women* (Pl. 616) is considered in relation to **Brouwer**'s Citadel picture (Pl. 623); and in his *Boors' Concert* (Pl. 626), which in some ways anticipates both Hogarth and Chardin, he has caricatured the models drawn (or the types remembered) by **Brouwer** in his *Outdoor Dentistry*. **David Ryckaert III** painted an *Interior with peasants by a fire* in 1638; **Teniers** signed a *Peasants in a barn* in 1634 and versions of the old theme *Peasants dancing before an inn* in 1640 and 1641. **Anthoni Victoryns**, a follower of **Brouwer**, signed an *Interior of an inn* in 1637 and may have painted the boors in his *Peasant interior* (Pl. 624) before or after 1640 when he was Antwerp Master. **Antoon Goubau** who went later to Rome (Pls. 775, 776) began as a genre painter in Antwerp where he was Master at twenty in 1636, and his undated rural picture *Farmyard with figures* (Pl. 614) may indicate his manner in this period. In this category also we have some unknown collaborator with **Jan Wildens** who added to his *View of Antwerp from the countryside* (Pl. 628) the peasants and farmers working on their land and contrasted urban and rural traffic on the country roads in the tradition of **Jacob Grimmer** (Pl. 430) and **Hans Bol** (Pl. 431). A new theme in peasant genre is the subject of **Brouwer**'s *Smoker* (Pl. 595) and of the works reproduced by the **Munich Tobacco Den Painter** (Pl. 621) and **London (Wallace) Sleeping Boor Painter** (Pl. 622); for these pictures represent what were then called 'pipe drunkards' i.e. smokers who stupefied themselves with the strong doped tobacco provided in the newly established tobacco dens; and both **Brouwer** and **van Craesbeeck** probably had occasion to make first-hand studies of the process as both are said to have been addicts of this new vice.

In gay-life painting **Theodoor Rombouts** may have produced more tavern pieces like his *Card players* (Pl. 581) and *Quack Dentist* (Pl. 596) in his last three years before 1637, **Adam de Coster** some pieces like his *Man and woman playing backgammon by candlelight* and **Frans Francken** more pieces on the *Prodigal Son* theme. **Teniers** signed an *Officers and women at a supper* (*The dinner party*) as a gay-life scene in 1634 and, probably soon after, a *Five Senses* where the theme is treated as a supper party in a tavern with officers and women eating, drinking, singing, lute playing, smelling lemons and discreetly adventuring on amorous advances. The *Lute player* (Pl. 619) painted, possibly about 1640, by **van Craesbeeck** is a highly interesting design with compositional devices used later by Vermeer (born 1632); and it shows us the Prodigal Son (in a large hat) collapsed, it may be from doped drink, while an old villain whispers to the lute player that the time has come to go through his pockets. In his *Gipsy woman telling a young man's fortune* (Pl. 674) **Simon de Vos** reminds us of the figures in **Jan van Hemessen**'s *Prodigal Son* (Pl. 325) and of the setting in the *Peasant household and cavalier* (Pl. 396) by **Marten van Cleve**; and though little influenced by **Rubens** he must still have had contacts with the atelier where the dark young man with curly hair on the left of this picture was evidently a model in the thirties as we see him making love to a blonde young woman in the *Market stall* (Pl. 655) by **Snyders** already referred to and again with the same young woman in the left foreground of **Rubens**' *Kermesse* (Pl. 665) discussed in my last chapter.

In high-life genre the newcomers included **Christoffel van der Lamen** Antwerp Master in 1637 who painted conversation pieces with elegant gentry in indoor and outdoor settings and **Gonzales Coques** (Pls. 764, 773) who signed a conversation piece *A young man with a book and a young woman playing a painted harpsichord* at twenty-six in 1640. **Frans Francken** (Pl. 517) was still available for social scenes; **Cornelis de Baellieur** puts the fashionable clothes of the moment on a lady and gentleman inspecting pictures in 1637 (Pl. 645).

Rubens appears in this category with the famous decorative conversation piece the *Garden of Love* (Pl. 662) which allegorizes his happiness with Helena Fourment and was probably painted at the outset of this period; here a flight of Cupids bearing the doves of Venus, torches, and chaplets of roses, drive strapping gentry in expensive clothes to amorous diversions; and this social concept with its rich and glamorous colour and palatial setting can be art-historically placed as the middle link in a chain leading back through **Abel Grimmer** (Pl. 447) and **Lucas van Valkenborch** (Pl. 446) to **Pieter Jansz Pourbus** (Pl. 331) and leading forward through **Hieronymus Janssens** (Pl. 730, 731) to the exquisite delicacy of Watteau.

The painters of military genre pieces included **Sebastiaan Vrancx** (Pl. 531) sixty-one in 1634, **Peeter Snayers** (Pls. 700, 701) then forty-two and **Pieter Meulener** (Pl. 698) then thirty-two. A newcomer **Lambert de Hondt** (Pl. 699) was signing pictures by 1636; another newcomer **Nicolaas van Eyck** (Pl. 785) was Antwerp Master at twenty-four in 1641; and some assistant in the **Rubens** atelier put a cavalry charge in the background of *The Cardinal Infante Ferdinand at the Battle of Nordlingen* (Pl. 643). In this category we now get guard-room scenes with officers or soldiers playing cards or tric-trac; and **Teniers** signed some pictures of this kind in the later years of the period.

Among the painters of marines and naval combats **Andries van Ertvelt** (Pl. 704) was fifty-one in 1641; his former pupil **Gaspar van Eyck** (Pl. 703) twenty-eight in 1641 was probably back by then from Genoa after a visit to Spain; and the newcomers included **Gillis Peeters** Antwerp Master at twenty-two in 1634 and **Bonaventura Peeters** (Pls. 689, 690, 702) Master at twenty the same year.

In animal painting, in addition to the horses in the military pieces there are horses, dogs and cattle in the rural scenes and a flock of sheep in *The View of Antwerp from the country-side* (Pl. 628) by **Wildens**. Dogs appear in the riotous *Twelfth Night* (Pl. 658) by **Jordaens**, in the *Gipsy woman telling a young man's future* (Pl. 674) by **Simon de Vos** and in **Cornelis de Baellieur**'s *Visit to an art gallery* (Pl. 645). **David Ryckaert III** puts a curled-up cat in the *Painter in his studio* (Pl. 646) and in other pictures of this period; and **Teniers** shows a monkey on the floor in his gay-life supper scenes and cocks and hens in his *Old woman peeling potatoes* (Pl. 682). **Rubens** himself seems to have painted the sea-horses in the sketch called *Wrath of Neptune* (Pl. 631) already referred to; but **Frans Snyders** may have supplied the dogs and sheep for *The Judgement of Paris* (Pl. 670) as he was still associated with the **Rubens** atelier. In the mythologies sent to the Torre de la Parada **Cornelis de Vos** painted the prescribed team of leopards for the chariot of Bacchus (Pl. 641). In the hunting pieces for the Torre de la Parada horses, dogs and boar are in *Philip IV killing a wild boar* (Pl. 627) by **Peeter Snayers**. The revolting *Staghunts* reproduced here by **Snyders** (Pl. 635) and **Paul de Vos** (Pl. 636) were also painted for this series; and **Snyders** supplied a *Boar Hunt* which is still more revolting. Both **Snyders** and **Paul de Vos** are seen, however, more agreeably in other pieces from the series—**Snyders** in *Waterbirds and ermines* (Pl. 632), *Wildcat, monkey, fox and ermine* (Pl. 634) and the *Fable of the hare and tortoise* (Pl. 630) and **de Vos** in his *Greyhound in flat landscape* (Pl. 633). **Jan Fyt** (Pls. 719, 733) in Paris, Rome and Venice for most of the period, as mentioned above, was back in Antwerp at thirty in 1641 and may then have resumed his contacts with **Snyders** his sometime teacher.

Of the painters of general still-life, of fruit pieces, tables with food and vessels (banketjen) and of kitchen and larder pieces **Snyders**, fifty-five in 1634, was now the senior exponent; **Jacob van Hulsdonck** (Pl. 556) was three years younger, **Alexander Adriaenssen** (Pls. 559, 652, 653) was forty-seven, **Jacob Foppens van Es** (Pls. 557, 558) about thirty-eight, **Adriaen** van Utrecht (Pls. 693, 694) thirty-five, **Mathieu Matheussens** about thirty-four and **Frans Ijkens** (Pl. 695) thirty-three. **Snyders** himself seems now to have painted a series of larder compositions with figures inserted by painters in or on the fringe of the **Rubens** atelier circle; and these monstrous accumulations of meat, venison, dead game, swans, fish, piled-up vegetables, baskets of fruit and so on (Pls. 655, 656, 657) carry the still-life arrangements by **Aertsen** (Pls. 356, 360) and **Beuckelaer** (Pls. 398, 399) to a vulgar and otiose climax. **Alexander Adriaenssen**'s fish piece (Pl. 652) reminds us that Chardin's *La raie* was to be mistaken in his day for a Flemish painting of the seventeenth century; and **Adriaen van Utrecht** reveals his personal aesthetic in 1640 in the fine tonality of his *Garland of fruits suspended from a wall* (Pl. 694). Among the newcomers in these categories **Hendrik Andriessen** known as 'Mancken Heyn' (Limping Henry) was probably active in Antwerp by 1634; **Jan Davidsz de Heem** thirty in 1636 when he settled in Antwerp from Holland, painted tables with shell fish, vessels and fruit in this period; **Cornelis Mahu** Antwerp Master at about twenty-five in 1638 and **Andries van Benedetti** Master there in 1640 both painted tables with food and vessels; **Jan Fyt** (Pls. 719, 733) was back in Antwerp as just noted, in 1641; **Jan Boots** who had **Pieter Gysels** (Pl. 806) as his pupil in 1641 is known to have painted a *Still-life with dead birds* before 1642; and **Martin de Paepe** worked in Malines as a specialist in still-life arrangements with fruit. Piles of armour, gauntlets and other military equipment—already encountered in **Jan (Velvet) Brueghel**'s *Allegory of Touch of* 1617—are disposed in the foreground of the guard-room scenes by **Teniers** in this period; but whether he painted these still-life additions or trained a pupil to provide them is not known.

Among the flower painters **Daniel Seghers** (Pls. 692, 757) forty-four in 1634, and **Jan Brueghel the younger** (Pl. 605) thirty-three that year, were established specialists; **Charles de Cauwer** collaborated with **Jan Brueghel the younger** and **Adriaen van Stalbemt** in a large flowerpiece for the Spanish market at about fifty in 1635; **Jacob van Uden** was about thirty-four in 1634; **Frans Lucas Peters** was twenty-eight that year, and the newcomers included **Jan Philip van Thielen** (Pl. 754)—a pupil of **Daniel Seghers**—who was twenty in 1638; Canon **Jean Antoine van der Baren** of Brussels who seems to have painted the charming garlands and vases in the *Flowers round a mystic marriage of S. Catherine* reproduced here (Pl. 675) at twenty-six in 1641; and the Liégeois **Gerard Goswin** a pupil of **Gerard Douffet**. The **Rubens** atelier does not seem to have needed a flower specialist in these years, though a clumsy swag of roses appears in *The Three Graces* and Cupids bear roses in *The Garden of Love* (Pl. 662).

Among the landscape painters there were three rising men in Brussels **Daniel van Heil** (Pls. 709, 713, 714) thirty in 1634, who painted some winter scenes and also urban conflagrations, **Lodewyck de Vadder** (Pl. 685) twenty-nine in 1634 and making a reputation with wooded landscapes of the Soignes forest, and his follower **Jacques D'Arthois** (Pls. 686, 710, 736) Antwerp Master at twenty-one in 1634 and soon to be famous for similar subjects. In Antwerp **Josse de Momper** (Pl. 500) died at seventy-one in 1635; **Kerstiaen de Keuninck** (Pl. 501) died also over seventy at about the same time; and **Artus Wolfordt** (Pl. 606) died at sixty in 1641. **Frans de Momper** seems to have gone to The Hague as noted before 1641; but **Sebastiaan Vrancx** (Pls. 531, 532, 534) was still active in 1641; and others who worked through the period were **Antonie Mirou** (Pl. 469) about fifty in 1634, **Andreas Snellinck** who was then forty-seven and provided at some time a landscape setting for a *Virgin and Child* by **Cornelis de Vos**, **Lucas de Wael** then forty-three and **Gillis Peeters** Master that year at twenty-two and already referred to as painter of marines. Landscapes with a variety of small figures were still produced in the atelier of **Jan Brueghel the younger** (Pl. 605) and by artists associated with him including **Adriaen van Stalbemt** (Pls. 479, 562) fifty-four in 1634 and much in demand among the dealers, **Charles de Cauwer, Jacob van Uden, Jan Boots, Ambrosius Brueghel** twenty-four in 1641 and **Pieter Gysels** (Pl. 799) then twenty. **Brouwer** painted a number of landscapes with genre figures probably in his last four years; these include *Peasants in a moonlight landscape with cottage and trees in foreground and a distant sea, Landscape with peasants playing bowls* and *Landscape with seated peasant playing a shawn* which reveal him as descendant of the **Pearl of Brabant Master** (or whoever painted the romantic landscapes in his admirable pictures (Pls. 91, 92)) and as ancestor of the nineteenth-century romantic landscapists as in these works the peasants are no longer the centre of attention brawling, gesticulating or besotted with drink or tobacco as in many of his genre pictures (Pls. 617, 618) but are now disposed quite quietly within the landscape (as in his *Peasants and Spanish soldiers at a table in the grounds of the Antwerp citadel* (Pl. 623)) and subordinated to a lyric mood that permeates the scene. In the **Rubens** entourage **Lucas van Uden** (Pls. 561, 566, 567, 602) was thirty-nine in 1634 and **Jan Wildens** (Pls. 628, 629) was forty-eight. **Van Uden** whose *River landscape with sunset* (Pl. 561), *Flat landscape with peasants and horses* (Pl. 602) and *Wooded landscape with peasants dancing* with figures by **Teniers** (Pl. 567) were discussed in earlier chapters, may now have painted his *Flat landscape with peasants* (Pl. 566) in the neighbourhood of Steen, and may also have collaborated with **Rubens** in his *Autumn: Château de Steen. The View of Antwerp from the countryside* (Pl. 628) was commissioned from **Wildens** by the Antwerp magistrates; and **Wildens** may have supplied the landscapes in *The Judgement of Paris* (Pl. 670) by **Rubens** as suggested above and also in *Philip IV killing a wild boar* (Pl. 627) by **Peeter Snayers**, the *Fable of the hare and the tortoise* (Pl. 630) by **Snyders** and the horrible *Staghunts* (Pl.s 635, 636) by **Snyders** and **Paul de Vos**.

Rubens himself, as already stated, is known to have produced a number of landscapes in this period. Examples were in his studio when he died; and these included a *Flooded landscape with Philemon and Baucis* (Een groote Diluvie of zondvloed met de Historie van Philemon en Baucis) later in the Archduke Leopold Wilhelm's collection, a *Landscape with Atalanta hunting* on panel (Een groot stuk nae't leven of ter plaetze geteekend, met de Jagd van Athalanta, in beldekens op doek), and also a *Hunting piece with Atalanta and Meleager* (De Jagt van Athalanta en Meleager) which I take to be the picture (on canvas) reproduced here as *Landscape with Atalanta hunting* (Pl. 664). This exciting *Landscape with Atalanta hunting* was perhaps his first inspiration for an equally exciting larger version (also on canvas) owned by Philip IV by 1636 and now in the Prado; in rhythmic movement it recalls the *Battle of the Amazons* (Pl. 576) the *Kermesse* (Pl. 665) and the *Peasants' dance* (Pl. 666); but here the actual landscape is caught up in the rhythm and its richness and beauty remind me that Walpole wrote: '**Rubens** was never greater than in landscape: the tumble of his rocks and trees, the deep shadows in his glades and glooms, the watery sunshine, and dewy verdure, show a variety of genius which are not to be found in the inimitable but uniform glow of Claude Lorrain' and that Constable said 'In no other branch of the art is **Rubens** greater than in landscape . . . dewy light and freshness, the departing shower, with the exhilaration of the returning sun, are effects which he, more than any other painter, has perfected on canvas.'

Altarpieces were ordered in these years for churches and religious houses all over the country. In Brussels where **Frans Francart** designed the catafalque for the Infanta Isabella and the veteran **Wenzelas Coebergher** (Pl. 493) died in 1634, **Antoine Sallaert** (Pl. 514) painted

The Brussels magistrates presented by S. Michael to the Virgin—already referred to as a portrait group—for the Brussels Town Hall in 1634, and (perhaps with assistance from his son **Jan Baptist Sallaert**) a *Beheading of S. John the Baptist* for Releghem church; and **Theodore van Loon** back from his second visit to Italy was also probably working for Brussels churches in this period. **Gaspar de Crayer** (Pls. 598, 607) now directing a mass production factory on the **Rubens** model, may have painted in these years his *Lamentation* (Pl. 609) where a further stage in the destruction of his talents by the **Rubens** influence can be seen. In Ghent the church painters included **Jan Janssens, Nicolas de Liemaker, Anselmus van Hulle, Anton van den Heuvel** and for a time in 1635 **Theodoor Rombouts** (Pl. 597); in Bruges **Paul Ryckx**, Master there in 1635 and **Jacob van Oost the elder** whose *S. Martin dividing his cloak* (Pl. 729) recalling the famous picture by **Van Dyck** was probably painted at this time; in Malines **Lucas Franchoys the elder** sixty-seven in 1641, **Lucas Franchoys the younger** till he went to Antwerp to join the **Rubens** atelier, **Peeter Franchoys** (Pl. 654) after 1635, **David Herregouts,** and **Nicolas Smeyers** pupil of **Lucas Franchoys the elder** and Master there in 1632; in Tournai **Mathieu van Negre**; in Namur **Frater Jacques Nicolai** and possibly still **Frans Saive**; in Liège **Jean Taulier** who died about 1640, **François Walschartz** back from Italy by 1635, **Renier Lairesse, Gerard Douffet** who painted a *Martyrdom of S. Catherine* in 1640 commissioned by Walthère de Liverloo for Liège, S. Catherine, and **Douffet's** pupil **Bertholet Flémalle** who left Italy at twenty-four in 1638. In Dunkirk the gifted **Jan van Reyn** (Pls. 592, 651) was available from approximately 1638. Many of these artists provided religious pictures also for other places; thus **Gaspar de Crayer** finished his *S. Carlo Borromeo invoked against the plague-stricken* and other works for Anderlicht in 1634; **Jan Janssens** painted a *Resurrection* which Descamps described as 'comme de **Van Dyck**' for Bruges, S. Sauveur in 1640; **Nicolas de Liemaker** also worked for Bruges; and altarpieces were sent in all directions by the painters of Antwerp.

Among the Antwerp painters of religious subjects a number died before 1641. Thus **Theodoor Rombouts** (Pls. 581, 596, 597) was forty when he died in 1637; **Pieter Brueghel the younger** (Pls. 380, 411) died at seventy-four in 1638 and **Jan Snellinck** (Pl. 460) at about ninety the same year; **Rubens** died at sixty-three in 1640; **Adam van Noort** died at seventy-nine in 1641 and **Artus Wolfordt** (Pl. 606) at sixty the same year. **Van Dyck** who died in England as noted at forty-two in 1641 painted some religious subjects in Antwerp in 1634. Among the older men who worked through the period and into the next, we have **Marten Pepyn** (Pls. 569, 571, 572), **Frans Francken** (Pls. 496, 517, 519, 648), **Abraham Matthys, Deodatus Delmont, Cornelis de Vos** (Pls. 590, 599, 600, 641) **Gaspar van den Hoecke, Pieter de Witte the younger,** and **Adam de Coster**; in the next age group there were **Gerard Seghers** (Pl. 527), **Jordaens** (Pls. 588, 660, 741), **Gillis Backereel** (Pl. 594), **Hans Jordaens III, Abraham van Diepenbeeck, Cornelis Schut** (Pl. 669), **Eduaert Snayers, Peeter van Avont** (Pl. 605) **Jan Brueghel the younger** (Pl. 605) **Jan Cossiers** (Pl. 640) and **Simon de Vos** (Pls. 673, 674, 687); and the men under thirty in 1634 included **Theodor van Thulden** (Pls. 589, 753) **Erasmus Quellinus** (Pls. 639, 671), **Gerard Weri, Jan Boeckhorst (Lange Jan)** (Pl. 720), **Cornelis de Baellieur** (Pls. 645, 727), **Peter van Lint** (Pls. 677, 697), **Jan van den Hoecke** (Pls. 716, 721), **Balthasar van Cortbemde, Thomas Willeboirts (Bosschaert)** (Pl. 672) and **Victor Wolfvoet**.

Theodoor Rombouts painted a *Mystic marriage of S. Catherine* for Antwerp S. Jacques in 1634 before he went to Ghent and a *S. Augustine washing the feet of Christ as pilgrim* for Malines Augustine church in 1636. **Van Dyck's** rhetorical *Lamentation* (Pl. 608)—reproduced here above **Gaspar de Crayer's** picture of this subject (Pl. 609)—was commissioned by the Abbé Scaglia for Recollets church in 1634 and painted in Antwerp that year; Descamps wrote of this; 'Les têtes sont belles et la douleur y est exprimée avec sentiment'; Reynolds wrote of it; 'This has been one of his most chaste pictures but the colouring has gone. The expression of the Virgin is admirable, at least equal to that of Annibale Carracci in the Duke of Orléans' collection, it conveys an idea that she is petitioning with an earnest agony of grief. S. John is showing or directing the attention of an angel to Christ, the other angel is hiding his face'; and modern students of the Baroque style and the Jesuit influence on painting may find it profitable to compare these pictures by **Van Dyck** and **de Crayer** with the deeply felt *Lamentation* (Pl. 530) painted twenty years earlier by **Rubens** and then to turn back to pictures shown here by **Pieter de Kempener** (Pl. 367), **Martin van Heemskerck** (Pl. 355), the **Brussels Haneton Lamentation Painter** (Pl. 279), **Cornelis Engelbrechtsz** (Pl. 213), the **Oultremont Master** (Pl. 176), the **Liverpool Entombment Painter** (Pl. 126), **Geertgen tot Sint Jans** (Pl. 127), the **Vienna Cruciform Lamentation Painter** (Pl. 64), and **Rogier van der Weyden** (Pl. 46). **Marten Pepyn** painted a *S. Norbert kneeling before the Ostensorium* for Antwerp Cathedral in 1634 before he went to Ghent, and an *Adoration of the Magi* in 1641. **Jordaens** painted his *Martyrdom of S. Apollonia* for the Antwerp Augustine church before 1639. Of **Gerard Seghers** his contemporary Sandrart tells us that he changed his early style (shown here in *S. Theresa's vision* (Pl. 527) discussed in my last chapter) and used lighter colours in imitation of **Rubens** in order to make money. **Gerard Weri,** whose topical picture *The Virgin handing a sword to the Cardinal Infante Ferdinand* has been mentioned above, painted an *Adoration of the Magi* for Verrebroek church in 1639; and **Victor Wolfvoet** painted a *Visitation* for Antwerp S. Jacques of which Descamps wrote: 'C'est un élève de Rubens; on reconnoit la manière de l'école mais la couleur en est froide et noire dans les ombres.' **Simon de Vos** signed a *Queen of Sheba before Solomon* in 1641. **Gillis Backereel** may have painted in these years *The Virgin appearing to S. Felix* for the Brussels Capucins, and his *S. Carlo Borromeo administering the Viaticum to victims of the plague* of which Descamps wrote: 'il est composé avec sentiment et noblesse, de la plus belle couleur et argentine, du plus beau pinceau; je l'ai cru de **Rubens,** mais il est bien plus fin de dessein et mieux drapé.' **Cornelis de Baellieur** may have painted some religious subjects like his undated *Adoration of the Magi* (Pl. 727) before 1641; **Peeter van Avont** and **Eduaert Snayers** seem to have still worked in the circle of **Jan Brueghel the younger**; and **Peter van Lint** was back from Italy in 1640.

Rubens himself may have done all or most of the work on the *Virgin and Child with S. George, S. Jerome and other Saints* designated by him for his tomb in Antwerp, S. Jacques. His atelier probably finished in 1634 the *S. Theresa interceding for souls in Purgatory* for the Carmes Déchaussés discussed in my last chapter; and other works delivered from the atelier in this period included a *Christ falling beneath the Cross, with S. Veronica* for Afflighem Abbey, a *Martyrdom of S. Livin* for Ghent Jesuit church, a *Crucifixion of S. Peter* commissioned by the banker Jabach for S. Peter's church in Cologne, and two Augustinian subjects commissioned by the Countess Helena Martinitz for a church in Prague. It is not known whether **Jordaens** had a hand in any of these later pictures; but **Theodor van Thulden** (Pl. 589) and **Erasmus Quellinus** (Pl. 671), who signed a *Holy Family* at thirty-two in 1639, were both certainly employed in the factory at this time; and others who may have worked there on the religious subjects were **Deodatus Delmont, Gerard Seghers, Cornelis de Vos, Abraham van Diepenbeeck, Gaspar van den Hoecke, Cornelis Schut** before and after his visit to Spain, **Jan Boeckhorst** before and after his visit to Italy, **Jan van der Hoecke** till he went to Italy, **Simon de Vos, Thomas Willeboirts, Gerard Weri, Jan Cossiers** and **Victor Wolfvoet.**

Church interiors were still being painted in Antwerp by **Peeter Neeffs the elder** who was about fifty-six in 1634; and I reproduce his *Church interior with candlelight effect* (Pl. 649) of 1636 and *Interior of Antwerp Cathedral* (Pl. 650) of 1638 which show him still concerned not only with the architecture but also with organizing dramatic effects of light and shade and mysterious recessions to capture the atmosphere pervading the churches when the tapers burn and service is in progress at the high altar or in one of the side chapels. The figures in his church interiors were always it would seem inserted by collaborators; **Adriaen van Stalbemt** and **Frans Francken** are known to have provided some in 1635 and **Teniers** was possibly called upon for others. **Lodewyck Neeffs** and **Peeter Neeffs the younger** may have worked with their father on the architecture from about 1640 as the first was twenty-three that year and the second twenty.

The painters of collectors' galleries still included **Frans Francken, Willem van Haecht** till he died in 1637, **Hans Jordaens III, Cornelis de Baellieur** (Pls. 645, 727) and **Frans Francken III** (Pl. 728) who was Antwerp Master at thirty-two in 1639. Of these **Hans Jordaens III** painted the *Interior of an art dealer's gallery* about 1637 when he was something over forty, and shows us there an old dealer displaying to four elegant young customers his varied stock of sculpture, books of drawings, shells, a globe atlas and so forth and many pictures including a *Raising of Lazarus*, a *Joseph and Potiphar's wife*, a *Roman charity*, a *Salome receiving the head of S. John the Baptist* and several mythologies with nudes, landscapes, and still-life pieces with tables of food or dishes of vegetables and fruit or pots of flowers. In the *Visit to an art gallery* (Pl. 645) painted by **Cornelis de Baellieur** at thirty in 1637 we see the stock of another dealer, probably the painter's father; here again we have a table laden with shells, a globe and miscellaneous objets d'art; and the pictures shown include a *Neptune and Amphitrite*—to be compared with versions of the subject reproduced here by **Frans Francken** (Pl. 648) and **Adriaen van Nieulandt** (Pl. 647)—a bird piece with parrots in the style of the decorative panels supplied for the Torre de la Parada by **Frans Snyders** (Pls. 632, 634), a landscape in the style of **Jan Wildens** (Pl. 629), two large still-life compositions and two heads in circular frames that appear to be Dutch (and might be by the Dutchman Jan Lievens who was in Antwerp and a friend of **Brouwer** in 1636).

Other sidelights on collectors' taste are again provided by dealers' records and by inventories of estates. Thus in 1635 the Seville dealer van Immerseel bought works by **Frans Wouters** and **Andries van Ertvelt**; a *Virgin and S. Catherine* by **Cornelis de Vos**; an *Interior of Antwerp Jesuit church* by **Peeter Neeffs** and **Frans Francken** and another *Church interior* by **Peeter Neeffs** and **Adriaen van Stalbemt**; he paid **Adriaen van Stalbemt** for thirteen landscapes, a series of thirty-two pictures titled *Morael ofte die Histori van den Geltduvel* and for another series of twenty-one pieces titled *Histori van Pallas oft de Wysheyt*; in 1636 he ordered twelve religious subjects and a **Brouwer** pastiche from **Teniers** at the meeting in Dover already chronicled, and his new Antwerp agent Antoon Cossiers made payments to **Jan Boots, Bonaventura Peeters, Andries van Ertvelt, Adriaen van Stalbemt, Simon de Vos** and **Teniers**. The Antwerp dealer William Forchoudt received orders in 1636 from his partner in Vienna for pictures by **Brouwer** as mentioned above and also for copies after **Rubens**, for landscapes and for two thousand small pictures of unnamed subjects on parchment; in 1638 he paid an artist in cash, beer and cheese for a group of paintings including two versions of a *Battle of Nordlingen*, a *Twelve Months* series, and paintings on a cabinet; and in 1639 he bought large numbers of battle pieces, sieges and hunting pieces from another dealer. When **Jan Snellinck** died in 1638 pictures by **Sebastiaan Vrancx** and **Paul de Vos** were sold with his effects; and the inventory of pictures owned in 1640 by Nicolas Rockox, sometime Burgomaster of Antwerp and friend of **Rubens**, lists family portraits, landscapes, religious pictures, a military piece by **Sebastiaan Vrancx**, a *Peasant wedding* and other pictures by **'Breugel'** and two works by **Rubens**—*Three lions* on panel and a *Samson and Delilah*.

After the death of **Rubens** his Antwerp house and studio and the Château de Steen contained about eighty of his own paintings (ten of which were bought by Philip IV) and copies by him of works by Titian and others. His immense collection included pictures by Italian 'Old Masters' and among the Flemish 'Old Masters' he had pictures by **Marten van Cleve, Jan van Hemessen** and **Pieter Bruegel**; there were also works by Dürer, Holbein and Adam Elsheimer. The Flemish contemporaries represented were **Alexander Adriaenssen, Paul Brill, Jan (Velvet) Brueghel, Van Dyck, Jacob Foppens van Es, Frans Ijkens, Jordaens, Jan Porcellis, Daniel Seghers, Peeter Snayers, Frans Snyders, Paul de Vos, Simon de Vos, Sebastiaan Vrancx, Jan Wildens** and **Adriaen Brouwer** by whom he had sixteen pictures including landscapes titled *Landscape in moonlight, Landscape with a flash of lightning* and *Landscape with villagers dancing*.

CHAPTER XIV

Don Francisco de Melo 1642-1644;
Don Manuel de Moura (Marquis of Castel Rodrigo)
1644-1646;
Archduke Leopold Wilhelm 1647-1655

1642-1655

IN 1642 Don Francisco de Melo, a protégé of the Count-Duke Olivarez, succeeded the Cardinal Infante as Governor-General and had some military success against the French and Dutch; Richelieu died, Cardinal Mazarin became Premier Ministre, Chancellor Séguier succeeded Richelieu as active protector of the Académie Francaise, and Jansen's 'Augustinus' was condemned by Pope Urban VIII. The Civil War began in England and the greater part of the second Duke of Buckingham's collection was sent across to Antwerp where **Frans Wouters** (Pl. 667) eventually assisted in its sale. In 1643 Louis XIV aged seven became King of France with Anne of Austria as Regent and Mazarin as her Chef du Conseil; Condé (then Duc d'Enghien and aged twenty-two) defeated de Melo's troops at the battle of Rocroi; the Count-Duke Olivarez was disgraced and banished; John Milton aged thirty-five wrote 'The Doctrine and Discipline of Divorce' when his wife had left him after a month of marriage; Antoine Arnauld published his Jansenist 'De la Fréquente Communion'; de Melo incurred the enmity of the Jesuits by supporting the Archbishops of Malines and Ghent and the University of Louvain in resistance to the Bull against Jansen's 'Augustinus'; and the Flemish State Pawnshops, short of funds, tried to recoup by selling the Infanta Isabella's jewels (on which, as noted, they had advanced 566,000 florins in 1629) and were ruined by the small sum they recovered.

In 1644 the French and Dutch gained further victories; risings instigated by the Jesuits took place in Ghent, Bruges and Brussels against de Melo who was superseded as civil governor by Don Manuel de Moura, Marquis of Castel Rodrigo, a friend of the Jesuits, and as military commander by Ottavio Piccolomini who had returned to Belgium; Christina of Sweden (nominally Queen since 1632) became active ruler at the age of eighteen; Urban VIII died and Innocent X became Pope; and Descartes published his 'Principia Philosophiae' in Amsterdam. In 1645 Piccolomini's Spanish-Belgian troops were unable to prevent more French and Dutch successes; Cromwell's Ironsides won the battle of Naseby; and negotiations for the end of the Thirty Years War were begun at Münster and Osnabrück in Westphalia. In 1646 the French captured Courtrai and Dunkirk; a proposal by Mazarin that Prince Frederick Henry should blockade Brabant and Flanders by occupation of the canal from Ghent to Bruges was vetoed by the Dutch merchants as interference with their grain trade; and Dutch envoys at Münster were instructed to negotiate a separate peace with Spain.

In 1647 the Amalfi fisherman Masaniello led a sensational revolt in Naples; William II of Orange, married to Charles I's daughter Mary, succeeded Prince Frederick Henry as Stadholder of Holland; and the Archduke Leopold Wilhelm arrived in Brussels as Governor-General of the Spanish Netherlands with full civil and military powers. The new Governor, brother of the Emperor Ferdinand III and cousin of Philip IV, was now thirty-three; educated by the Jesuits he was a keen opponent of the Jansenists; he was also a soldier who had led troops in the Thirty Years War; and he now brought reinforcements with him and recaptured some places from the French before the year was out. In January 1648 Holland and Spain signed a separate peace at Münster which permanently closed the Scheldt against Antwerp and gave the Dutch all they had fought for since the days of Titelman and Alva. Thanks partly to Queen Christina of Sweden, the Treaty of West-phalia which ended the Thirty Years War was concluded in October; and in November the Queen received five shiploads of pictures from the collection made by Rudolf II and others in Prague which the Swedish General Count Königsmark had captured shortly before the peace was signed. France and Spain remained none-the-less at war; the Spaniards laid siege to Courtrai—an episode recorded by **Peeter Snayers** (Pl. 700)—and, in August, they were defeated by Condé at Lens. In this year also Don John of Austria, natural son of Philip IV from an actress, and now nineteen, suppressed a second rising in Naples instigated by the French and led by the Duc de Guise. In 1649 Condé captured Paris for the Royalists in the Fronde Parlementaire; the Archduke Leopold Wilhelm led an army into France to support the Frondeurs; the University of Paris condemned five propositions in Jansen's 'Augustinus' which it sent to Rome, backed by eighty-five bishops, for endorsement by Innocent X; Queen Christina sent a naval vessel to Holland to fetch Descartes to Stockholm where he gave her lessons in philosophy at five in the morning; Charles I cast perhaps a last look at the **Rubens** Ceiling as he stepped out to the scaffold from a window in the Whitehall Banqueting House; **Jan van Belcamp** was appointed a Trustee for the sale of the King's effects; and Parliament sequestered what remained of the second Duke of Buckingham's collection and ordered the sale of all his pictures except those 'with representations of the Second Person of the Trinity or the Virgin Mary' which were to be 'forthwith burnt'. In 1650 the Commonwealth began the sale of Charles I's pictures; Descartes died in Stockholm; the Fronde des Princes began after Mazarin and Anne of Austria had arrested Condé; the Archduke after indecisive fighting withdrew his troops for the winter; and John De Witt aged twenty-five was imprisoned as an active opponent of the House of Orange by the Stadholder William II who died that year. In 1651 Condé, released from prison, went over to the Spaniards; Prince Charles was defeated at Worcester and hid in the celebrated oak; and Cromwell made his triumphal entry into London. In 1652 Condé occupied Paris till the Fronde des Princes collapsed; Prince Charles, at S. Germain, was given an allowance by Louis XIV; naval war began between the Commonwealth and Holland; Don John of Austria suppressed a rising in Barcelona instigated by the French; and two Jesuits went secretly to Stockholm to instruct Queen Christina in the Roman Catholic faith. In 1653 Condé and the Spaniards attacking Arras were repulsed by the Vicomte de Turenne who commanded the Royal forces; Louis XIV, the Regent and Mazarin were all now firmly in the saddle; the Commonwealth completed the sale of Charles I's pictures; Samuel Pepys, aged twenty, undergraduate in Magdalene College

Cambridge, was publicly admonished for being 'scandalously overserved with drink'; John De Witt aged twenty-eight became Grand Pensionary of Holland; Pope Innocent X declared the five propositions in Jansen's 'Augustinus' heretical, and the Archduke ordered the Bull ('Cum occasione') to be published in Belgium. In 1654 Cromwell obtained the use of Lisbon harbour for the British navy by an Anglo-Portuguese alliance and made a peace with De Witt which excluded William III the young half-Stuart Prince of Orange from the office of Stadholder. Christina of Sweden after abdicating at Upsala, was received in Brussels by the Archduke; and while there she presented a gold chain and a medal with her portrait to **Teniers** and sat to **Justus van Egmont** for her portrait in armour. In 1655 Cromwell made a Treaty with France against Spain; Christina went to Innsbruck to be publicly converted to Catholicism and thence to Rome to which many of her tapestries and her pictures by Titian, Veronese and other Italians, and a flowerpiece by **Daniel Seghers**, were dispatched on her instructions; **Teniers** applied to Philip IV for title of nobility and was told that any selling of pictures—his own or other people's—must be renounced as a condition; and the Archduke, after ordering the removal of Jansen's tombal stone from Ypres Cathedral, asked and obtained the King's permission to retire next year to Vienna on the ground of failing health.

In the five years under Francisco de Melo and Castel Rodrigo the Court patronage of painting seems to have been only formal and routine. But, despite the war, some artists were favoured by the House of Orange; the young **Gonzales Coques** (Pls. 764, 773) for example painted some portraits for them, **Thomas Willeboirts** provided Prince Frederick Henry with *Venus arming Mars* (Pl. 672) an allegory on his military prowess, and the Jesuit **Daniel Seghers** (Pl. 692) painted a flowerpiece for the same Prince and refused money payment for it, demanding and receiving instead official permits for a group of Jesuits to travel in Holland. In the field of civic and guild patronage **Erasmus Quellinus** (Pls. 639, 671) was now official painter to the city of Antwerp; and **Teniers** painted a *Fête of the Cross-bowmen of S. Sebastian on Antwerp Grande Place* with two hundred and sixty figures for the Crossbowmen's Guild. There were, as usual, commissions for church paintings; thus **Cornelis Schut** (Pl. 669) painted *S. George refusing to sacrifice to Apollo* in successful competition against **Thomas Willeboirts** for the Junior Crossbowmen's altar in Antwerp Cathedral, **Gaspar de Crayer** (Pls. 598, 607, 609, 642) supplied the Brussels Augustines Church with a *Virgin and child enthroned with saints, and the artist and members of his family as adorants* based, as Sir Joshua Reynolds observed, on the *Mystic marriage of S. Catherine* which **Rubens** had provided for the Antwerp Augustines; and **Paul Ryckx** painted a *S. Jerome and the trumpets of the Last Judgement* for Bruges, S. Sauveur in 1644. Many artists also worked for or sold pictures to dealers in these five years; **Gerard Seghers** (Pl. 527) sent fourteen pictures by himself and/or others to the Seville dealer van Immerseel in 1642, and the Antwerp dealer Forchoudt who was now exporting to Portugal and Spain as well as to Vienna received orders for dozens of landscapes, battle pieces and seapieces from a Lisbon dealer who especially approved of **Pieter Meulener** (Pl. 698) and upbraided Forchoudt for sending him bad examples of seapieces by **Andries van Ertveldt** (Pl. 704) in 1643.

Under the Archduke Leopold Wilhelm Court patronage was conspicuously increased. For the Archduke, though voracious as a collector of old masters and of antiquities—(he had the English or Scottish-born portrait painter and numismatist Michael Wright as his antiquary for some time)—was also a collector of contemporary work and bought or commissioned pictures from some sixty-five artists active in Belgium in his day. When he arrived in 1647 he had with him as Court Painter in Ordinary **Jan van den Hoecke** (Pls. 716, 721) who was then thirty-six and had gone to Vienna from Italy; and he found among the painters surviving from the **Rubens** period **Frans Snyders** then sixty-eight, **Gaspar de Crayer** sixty-five, **Jan Wildens** about sixty-three, **Cornelis de Vos** sixty-two, **Gillis Backereel** probably about sixty, **Daniel Seghers** and **Andries van Ertvelt** fifty-seven, **Gerard Seghers** fifty-six, **Peeter Snayers** fifty-five, **Jordaens** fifty-four, **Lucas van Uden** fifty-two, **Paul de Vos** and **Abraham van Diepenbeeck** fifty-one, **Cornelis Schut** fifty, **Jan Cossiers** and **Peeter van Avont** forty-seven, **Jan Breughel the younger** forty-six, **Daniel van Heil** forty-three, **Leo van Heil** forty-two, **Theodor van Thulden, Joos van Craesbeeck, Jan Davidsz de Heem** and **Frans Lucas Peters** all forty-one, **Erasmus Quellinus** forty, **Peeter van Lint, Jan Boeckhorst** and **Jan Baptist van Heil** thirty-eight, **Teniers** thirty-seven, **Jan Fyt** thirty-six, **David Ryckaert III** and **Frans Wouters** thirty-five and **Thomas Willeboirts** thirty-four. All these and others were patronized by the Archduke in one way or another, and many of the pictures he acquired from them are now in the Vienna Kunsthistorisches Museum. His Pageant Entry into Antwerp was directed by **Erasmus Quellinus** with **Leo van Heil** as architectural assistant. He was painted in representations of the *Shooting at the Popinjay at Brussels* by **Peeter Snayers** and by **Teniers** (Pl. 712)—as the Infanta Isabella had been painted by **Antoine Sallaert**—and **Teniers** also painted him in his gallery of Italian pictures (Pls. 724, 725, 726). From **Justus van Egmont** (who came to Brussels from Paris in 1649 and settled in Antwerp in 1653) he ordered his portrait in golden armour with his hand upon a lion and a laurel-bearing eagle in the background (Pl. 722); from **Jan van den Hoecke** he ordered his portrait at prayer with the Virgin and Child appearing to him, and an equestrian portrait with allegoric figures (Pl. 721); and he also commissioned his portrait from **Abraham van Diepenbeeck** and **Jan Baptist van Heil**. His mythologies and allegories included the *Hero and Leander* (Pl. 594) by **Gillis Backereel**, *Diana returning from the chase* (Pl. 719) by **Thomas Willeboirts** with animals by **Jan Fyt**, the pretty composition *Mercury enamoured of Herse on her way to the Temple of Minerva with her sisters* (Pl. 720) by **Jan Boeckhorst (Lange Jan)**, an *Allegory of the return of Peace* by **Theodor van Thulden**, a *Triumph of Time* and *Bacchus and his train* (Pl. 669) by **Cornelis Schut**, a *Triumph of Silenus* by **Frans Wouters**, an *Amor vincit omnia* by **Jan van den Hoecke** (with dogs and still-life by **Paul de Vos**), and designs for tapestry by **Jan van den Hoecke** including the *May and June* reproduced here (Pl. 716). His religious pictures included the *Lamentation* (Pl. 609) by **Gaspar de Crayer**, an *Anointing of Solomon* by **Cornelis de Vos**, a *Virgin and Child with S. John* by **Gerard Seghers**, a version (without the donors) of **Peter van Lint's** *The Pool of Bethesda* (Pl. 677), a *Crossing of the Red Sea* by **Cornelis de Wael** who was fifty in 1647 and still living in Italy, and an *Adam and Eve with the murdered Abel* by **Philippe de Champaigne** who visited Brussels from Paris aged fifty-four in 1656 just before the Archduke left the city. His genre purchases included the splendid *Twelfth Night* (Pl. 658) by **Jordaens**, a *Fishmarket* by **Snyders**, the *Landscape with soldiers and women* (Pl. 616) by **Joos van Craesbeeck**, *The goatherd* (Pl. 679), a *Peasants' dance, Soldiers plundering a village* (Pl. 706) and other pieces by **Teniers**, and the two genre scenes in which **David Ryckaert** typified peace by a *Village Kermesse* and war by *Soldiers plundering a village* (Pl. 705). He acquired military pieces by **Peeter Snayers** and the *Harbour with Spanish warships* (Pl. 704) by **Andries van Ertvelt**. His landscapes included a *Wooded landscape with hunstmen* painted by **Jan Wildens** in 1649, a *Wooded landscape with Holy Family and angels* by **Peeter van Avont**, wooded landscapes with biblical figures by **Frans Wouters,** and a *Winter landscape* (like the picture reproduced here (Pl. 709)) by **Daniel van Heil**. He bought a *Flower garland round a mons-*

trance by **Daniel Seghers**, a similar piece by **Jan Davidsz de Heem**, flowerpieces by **Frans Lucas Peters** and a miniature showing a *Stagbeetle with unequal horns* by **Leo van Heil**. He appointed, among others, **Gerard Seghers, Peeter Snayers, Jan van den Hoecke** and **Teniers** his Court Painters and he made **Teniers** curator of his gallery and ordered from him small copies of many of the pictures for the use of engravers who were to record the collection.

The Archduke also patronized the younger generation which included **Gonzales Coques** (Pls. 764, 773) who was thirty-three in 1647, Canon **Jean Antoine van der Baren** (Pl. 675) who was about thirty-two and became his chaplain and Court Painter, **Jan Thomas van Ypern** who was thirty, **Michaelina Wautier** about thirty, **Peeter Neeffs the younger** twenty-seven, **Robert van den Hoecke** twenty-five, **Peeter Thys** and **Jan Peeters** twenty-three, and **Alexander Coosemans** (Pls. 744, 800) twenty. He bought two half lengths *S. Joachim reading* and *S. Joseph with a lily* from **Michaelina Wautier**; he had his portrait painted by **Gonzales Coques**, by **Jan Thomas (van Ypern)** and by **Peter Thys** (Pl. 723); he is seen with his suite in an *Interior of Notre Dame in Antwerp* by **Pieter Neeffs the younger** where the figures are by **Bonaventura Peeters**, and in a *Camp scene* and a *Conflagration* piece and *Watching skaters on the Brussels moat* (Pl. 711) by **Robert van den Hoecke**. He commissioned **Peter Thys** to make the tapestry cartoons *Night* (Pl. 717) and *Day* (Pl. 718) based on designs by **Jan van den Hoecke**, and he bought a *Bacchanal* from **Jan Thomas (van Ypern)**. His landscapes by the younger men included a *View of Ostend from the countryside* by **Robert van den Hoecke**, and his marines included two pieces by **Jan Peeters**. He owned a *Still-life* by **Andries van Benedetti** and a *Fruitpiece* by **Alexander Coosemans**.

Concurrently with this patronage of living Flemish painters the Archduke bought pictures by recently deceased Flemish artists and the Flemish Old Masters, and when he left the Netherlands he had not only five hundred and seventeen Italian pictures but also nearly nine hundred Flemish pictures many of which **Teniers** would have copied for engravers if the Archduke had not taken them with the others to Vienna. The Archduke's pictures by recently deceased Flemish artists included the beautiful *Lamentation* (Pl. 530), three landscapes, and one or two other works by **Rubens**, a *Venus and Vulcan* and a *Samson and Delilah* by **Van Dyck** and the *Infanta Isabella in Clarissan habit* (shown in Pl. 725) by or after **Rubens** or **Van Dyck**, the *Rape of Europa* (Pl. 507) by **Hendrik van Balen**, the *Bouquet of Flowers* (Pl. 521) by **Jan (Velvet) Brueghel**, the *Diana and Actaeon* (Pl. 498) by **Joachim Uytewael**, the *Troy burning and Aeneas carrying his father* (Pl. 494) by **Pieter Schoubroeck**, the *Landscape near Tivoli* (Pl. 499) by **Jan Tilens**, the *Mountain landscape* (Pl. 500) by **Josse de Momper**, a *Croesus showing his treasures to Solon* by **Frans Francken II**, a *Church interior with the liberation of S. Peter* by **Hendrik van Steenwyck the younger** (in the style of his picture reproduced here (Pl. 489)), an *Interior of Antwerp Jesuit church with Rubens' S. Ignatius Loyola healing the possessed on the high altar* by **Sebastiaan Vrancx** (like the pictures reproduced here by **Anton Gheringh** (Pl. 782) and **Wilhelm van Ehrenberg** (Pl. 783)) and the *Interior of a picture gallery with a dealer displaying his wares to customers* by **Hans Jordaens III** described in my last chapter. Of the sixteenth-century painters he had a *Last Judgement* by **Frans Floris**, a *Lot and his daughters* by **Jan Massys**, the same subject with a background conflagration of Sodom and Gomorrah by **Gillis Mostaert**, the *Peasant household and cavalier* (Pl. 396) by **Marten van Cleve**, the picture reproduced here by the **Prodigal Son Master** (Pl. 395), and seven pictures by **Pieter Bruegel the elder** including the *Seasons or Months* (Pls. 390-3), the *Tower of Babel* (Pls. 368, 375) and *Peasant wedding* (Pl. 405). Of the earlier painters he had the *Lamentation* (Pl. 127) and *Julian the Apostate burning* *the bones of S. John the Baptist* (Pl. 124) by **Geertgen tot Sint Jans**, the *Lamentation* (Pl. 64) by the **Vienna Cruciform Lamentation Painter** and *The Fall* (Pl. 66) by the **Vienna Adam and Eve Painter**, a *S. Luke drawing the Virgin* by an unrecorded artist (seen in the foreground of the **Teniers** interior Pl. 725) and pictures now catalogued in the Vienna museum as by **Memlinc, Gerard David, Rogier van der Weyden** and **Jan van Eyck**.

In the Archduke's time, as under Melo and Castel Rodrigo, there was patronage for some artists by the House of Orange. The Stadholder William II summoned **Peter Thys** to paint his portrait; and when Amalia van Solms widow of Prince Frederick Henry, employed, a troup of Dutch painters to decorate an octagonal hall in her newly built Huis ten Bosch (House in the Wood) near The Hague, she ordered panels from **Gonzales Coques**—who seems to have passed on the commission to **Theodor van Thulden**—and she reserved the two main panels for **Jordaens** who provided a *Triumph of Time* and a *Triumph of Prince Frederick Henry*. All the paintings in the Huis ten Bosch (still extant and in situ) glorify the House of Orange in the exuberant **Rubens** style, and the effect was thus described in 1781 by Sir Joshua Reynolds: 'The Hall is painted on every side, and every recess has some allegorical story. . . . The different hands that have been here employed make variety, it is true; but it is variety of wretchedness. A *Triumphal Entry* by **Jordaens** is the best, and this is but a confused business; the only part which deserves any commendation is the four horses of the chariot which are well painted: it is remarkable that the foreleg of each of the horses is raised, which gives them the formality of trained soldiers.'

Many painters in the Archduke's time sold their pictures to bourgeois collectors and to the richer artists—sometimes directly and sometimes through dealers. Among the artists who bought pictures, **Erasmus Quellinus, Gerard Seghers, Jan Boeckhorst,** and **Justus van Egmont** had large collections; **Jan Wildens** left seven hundred paintings when he died in 1653 and **Victor Wolfvoet**, painter of religious subjects and 'history', owned in 1652 some five hundred pictures including works by his contemporaries **Frans Wouters, Peter van Avont, Gerard Seghers, Pieter Meulener, Lucas van Uden, Jacques d'Arthois, Andries van Ertvelt, Alexander Adriaenssen, Jacob Foppens van Es, Ambrosius Bosschaert** and **Adriaen van Utrecht** and by men as young as **Christiaan Luyckx** (Pl. 696) and **Joris van Son** (Pls. 743, 745) both then under thirty and **Jan Philip van Thielen** (Pl. 754) who was then thirty-four. The dealer Forchoudt employed **Pieter de Witte III**, brother of **Gaspar de Witte** (Pl. 781), as a painter of landscape and hunting pieces and as restorer and 'toucher up', and bought battle scenes and sieges from **Jan** and **Geeraert Verschueren** of Malines and did business with 'à la mode' pictures by **Christoffel van der Lamen**; in 1652 he received an order from one Ralph Harrison ('in Blackfriars at the 3 Fishes on the backside of Ludgate') for three cabinets with pictures and 'a perspective' on them; in the same year he sent ten dozen watercolours to a dealer in Amsterdam and sold in Antwerp to an Englishman a *Battle piece* by **Pieter Meulener** (Pl. 698) and a picture by **Jan Fyt** (Pl. 719, 733); in 1653 he sold a *Large painting with flowers* by **Frans Ijkens** (Pl. 695) to the Duchess of Lorraine and received orders from a Seville dealer for as many landscapes as possible, for military and seapieces representing Don John's recent success at Barcelona and fighting round Dunkirk, and for four pictures 'with little figures of people dancing, shepherds and satyrs' by **Adriaen van Stalbemt** (Pls. 479, 562) who was seventy-three that year.

The foregoing notes on patronage and commerce show the continued variety of Flemish painting in this period 1642–1655; and my plates give some indications of styles employed in religious subjects, mythologies, portraits, landscapes and marines, military pieces and other types of outdoor genre, interiors with peasants, church and gallery interiors, and still-life and flowerpieces. The influence of **Rubens**, it must be noted, was confined to some of the older painters of religious subjects and mythologies and to men who had actually worked with him, and even there, it soon evaporated; and the main production in most fields continued the traditions of the periods before his arrival.

From the religious subjects my plates include the *Queen of Sheba before Solomon* by **Erasmus Quellinus** probably painted at this time, an *Adoration of the Shepherds* by **Jordaens** and the *Beheading of S. Paul* by **Simon de Vos**. Of these the *Queen of Sheba before Solomon* (Pl. 671) by **Erasmus Quellinus** is clearly influenced by the **Rubens** atelier. The engaging *Adoration of the Shepherds* (Pl. 741) by **Jordaens** is perhaps a sketch for his picture of the subject seen by Descamps in 1768 in the church of the Chanoinesses de Sion in Courtrai and thus described by him 'L'Enfant endormi est soulevé par sa Mère pour le faire voir à ceux qui venaient pour l'adorer; les figures très jolies, sont bien variées et intéressent par les expressions naives et simples; le boeuf broute à côté de la crèche'; and, if so, the eighteenth-century critic has seized upon the point of it; for though the design and the pictorial idiom remind us that **Jordaens** played a part in some church commissions executed in the **Rubens** atelier, the spirit of the concept, with the old woman crooning repturously at the new-born baby, is not ecclesiastic but personally imaginative and basically genre—as appears if we compare it with the orthodox Romanist concepts by **Marcel Helmon** (Pl. 401) and **Lambert van Noort** (Pl. 402); **Jordaens** at this time had abandoned more or less openly the official faith and become a Calvinist which may explain why to find a comparable concept of the subject in my plates we must go back behind the Jesuit and Tridentine periods to the years when **Hugo of Antwerp** gave us the genre shepherds in the *Portinari altarpiece* (Pl. 76). **Simon de Vos** had quite shaken off the **Rubens** influence by 1648 when he was forty-five and painted *The Beheading of S. Paul* (Pl. 673) which contains some traditional genre features, for the Emperor surveys the execution from a throne (as the Roman Proconsul watched S. Martin curing a demoniac in the picture by **Jordaens** (Pl. 588) and the Emperor Otho and his wife had surveyed an execution from their palace garden in the picture by **Dirk Bouts** (Pl. 67)), and an urchin has climbed upon the pedestal of a nearby pillar to watch the happening (as urchins climb trees in the *Archduke Leopold Wilhelm shooting at the popinjay* (Pl. 712) by **Teniers** and children were among the spectators in the **London Delft Painter's** *Crucifixion* (Pl. 224) and *Christ presented to the people* (Pl. 223)). I have already mentioned pictures painted for Antwerp Cathedral by **Cornelis Schut**; and others now painting religious subjects in Antwerp more or less in the **Rubens** manner were **Deodatus Delmont** and **Gerard Weri** who both died in 1644, **Gerard Seghers** (Pl. 527) who died in 1651, **Victor Wolfvoet** who died in 1652, **Gaspar van der Hoecke** who probably died in this period, **Cornelis de Vos** (Pl. 599), **Abraham van Diepenbeeck**, **Jan van der Hoecke** (Pls. 716, 721) from 1647 till his death at forty in 1651, **Jan Boeckhorst (Lange Jan)** (Pl. 720), **Theodor van Thulden** who signed *The Netherland provinces worshipping the Virgin* in 1654 and sent pictures from Antwerp to Malines and Bruges churches and the Trinitarian church in Paris, **Gillis Backereel** who sent them to Bruges and Lierre and **Jan Cossiers** who sent an *Adoration of the Shepherds* to Louvain. Of the completely non-Rubensian painters of religious subjects in Antwerp **Frans Francken** (Pls. 496, 517, 519, 648) died at sixty-one in 1642, **Marten Pepyn** (Pls. 569, 571, 572) died at sixty-eight in 1643 and **Adam de Coster** at fifty-seven the same year. **Jan Brueghel the younger** continued his workshop with various associates including **Peeter van Avont** (Pl. 605) who died in 1652 and **Eduaert Snayers**. In 1642 **Peter van Lint**, quite uninfluenced by **Rubens**, built his *Pool of Bethesda* (Pl. 677) at thirty-three with his own Roman memories (as **Karel van Mander** had built his *Jesus leaving* *the Temple* (Pl. 472) and **Gossaert** his *S. Luke drawing the Virgin* (Pl. 238)). In 1647 at thirty-five **Balthasar van Cortbemde** provided the Antwerp Guild of Surgeons with his *Good Samaritan* a remarkable and highly individual picture where the naked victim of the robbers is tended by the Samaritan in a handsome decorative landscape; **Cornelis de Baellieur** probably painted in these years his *Adoration of the Magi* (Pl. 727) which recalls the version of the subject reproduced here by **Pietro de Lignis** (Pl. 573) and contains a curious genre detail of two peasants seated at a table commenting on the happening (in the spirit of the whispering youth in **Bruegel's** *Adoration of the Magi* (Pl. 383) and the jesting onlookers at the *Crucifixion* as imagined by the **New York Crucifixion and Last Judgment Painter** (Pl. 1)). A newcomer **Frans Goubau** Antwerp Master at twenty-seven in 1649 painted a *S. Norbert adoring the Sacrament* for the Abbaye de S. Michel in 1650 and an *Entombment* for S. Jacques in 1655. Some pictures for Antwerp churches may also have been painted between 1650 and 1655 by **Antoon Goubau** (Pls. 614, 775, 776) President of the Fraternity of Unmarried Man in 1653 and President of the Fraternity of the Holy Name of Jesus in 1655 who became a Jesuit for a few weeks in that year and then retracted.

Of the painters working for churches in the other towns **Gaspar de Crayer** (Pls. 598, 607, 609) continued his factory in Brussels, and I have already referred to his large composition for the Augustines' church in 1646; **Antoine Sallaert** (Pl. 514) drew or painted there his *Innocent X extending his hand to weeping Religion* between 1644 and 1655; and **Theodore van Loon** provided pictures there for local and other churches. In Ghent, where **Nicolas de Liemaker** died in 1646, **Anton van den Heuvel** was working for churches through the period and **Jan Janssens** till he died about 1650. In Bruges the chief church painters were **Paul Ryckx** whose *S. Jerome and the trumpets of the Last Judgement* painted for S. Sauveur in 1644 has been mentioned above and **Jacob van Oost the elder** (Pls. 729, 740) who signed a *David victorious over Goliath* in 1645 and had many commissions. In Malines **Lucas Franchoys the elder** died in 1643, **Nicolas Smeyers** in 1645 and **Peeter Franchoys** (Pl. 654) in 1654; **Lucas Franchoys the younger** worked for local churches and sent a *Beheading of S. John* to Tournai, S. Quentin in 1650: and others available were **David Herregouts** and two newcomers **Jan Verhoeven,** Master in 1642 and **Jacques de Hornes** Master in 1648. **Mathieu van Negre** died in Tournai about 1644. In Ypres (or Antwerp) **Jan Thomas (van Ypern)** back from Italy signed a *Francisco de Mannez before the Virgin* for S. Martin at thirty-two in 1645. The Jesuit **Frater Jacques Nicolai** was painting through the period in Namur. The Liège group of church painters included **Gerard Douffet, François Walschartz, Renier Lairesse, Walther (Gauthier) Damery, Alexander de Horion** and also **Bertholet Flémalle** back from Italy in 1647. In Dunkirk **Jan van Reyn** (Pls. 592, 651) thirty-two in 1642 may have painted for S. Eloi in these years his *Four crowned martyrs* and *S. Alexander freed from prison by an angel* which Descamps ranked with 'les plus beaux ouvrages de **Van Dyck**'; and in Furnes near Dunkirk **Victor Boucquet** (Pl. 767) was probably active by 1650.

Mythologies and allegories were produced by **Gysbrecht Thys**, by a newcomer **Jan de Duyts**, Antwerp Master in 1648, and by **Charles Wautier** who painted a *Bacchus crowned with vine leaves* in 1652. There is some influence from **Rubens** in the surviving works by **Duyts**, but my plates show the absence or disappearance of this influence on most of the painters at this time. It is evident that **Jan Boeckhorst** still owes much to **Rubens** in *Mercury enamoured of Herse on the way to the Temple of Minerva* (Pl. 720) and that **Thomas Willeboirts (Bosschaert)** owes him a little in *Diana returning from the chase* (Pl. 719) with animals by **Jan Fyt** (though the composition here goes back to **Hendrik van Balen** (Pls. 507, 508)) and he also owes him something in *Venus arming Mars* (Pl. 672) where the Venus has ankles as elegant as Juno's in Tintoretto's *Origin of the Milky Way*. But there is more of Titian than of **Rubens** in the *Bacchus and his train* (Pl. 669) where **Cornelis Schut** combines some elements from the *Triumph of Bacchus* (Pl. 641) by **Cornelis de Vos** (from a **Rubens** sketch or drawing) with Titian's *Bacchus and Ariadne* which inspired it. The **Rubens** three-dimensional rhythm, parched and patchy in **Theodor van Thulden's** *Love and Music* (Pl. 753), has almost vanished from the two-dimensional cartoons for tapestry *Night* (Pl. 717) and *Day* (Pl. 718), executed by **Peter Thys** from drawings by **Jan van den Hoecke** who made them after seven years in Italy and tied his cupids into garlands round a central figure (in the tradition of the fruit garlands by **Frans Snyders** and others in the **Rubens** atelier (Pls. 544, 554) and the flower garlands by **Daniel Seghers** (Pl. 692) and **Jan (Velvet) Brueghel** (Pl. 541)). **Van Dyck** more than **Rubens** is behind the *Hero and Leander* (Pl. 594) which **Gillis Backereel** painted in this period or earlier; and **Frans Wouters**—like **Willem Panneels** (Pl. 668)—is wholly free from the **Rubens** influence in his charming *Landscape with Venus and Adonis* (Pl. 667).

In portraiture my plates reproduce a *Baby with dog and rattle* by **Peter van Lint**, a *Boy with a muff* by **Jacob van Oost the elder**, a *Lady with a dish of fruit* by **Simon de Vos**, a subscription group by **Pieter van der Plas** and seven portraits of *The Archduke Leopold Wilhelm*. Sir Joshua Reynolds, more than a century later, tried his hand at the rough and tumble of the **Rubens** rhythm in his *Princess Sophia Matilda of Gloucester as a baby with a dog* (reproduced in my 'English Painting'), but five years after the death of **Rubens** there is nothing of this rhythm in **Peter van Lint's** picture where the baby, poised on a red cushion, is a static monumental form (Pl. 697), or in the *Boy with a muff* (Pl. 715) by **Jacob van Oost the elder** who portrayed the boy in 1650 as quietly and gravely as **Hugo of Antwerp** had portrayed the Portinari children (Pls. 79, 80) and the **Bruges Baptism of Christ Painter** the four little daughters of Jean des Trompes (Pl. 206); and though **Simon de Vos** had worked as noted under **Rubens**, he is brother to the Dutchman Metsu and ancestor of Jean Baptiste Chardin in his quiet and sensitive *Lady with a dish of fruit* (Pl. 687) which is undated and may have been painted either earlier or in this period or later. The *Virgin and Child with syndics of a Brussels Guild* (Pl. 676) by **Pieter van der Plas** goes back through **Gaspar de Crayer** (Pl. 598) and the Flemish-Dutch civic groups to the **Malines Guild of S. George Master** (Pl. 146); for the old tradition of the subscription group was still obtaining; and **Peter Meert**, who also worked in Brussels, was among the painters employed on such pictures by the guilds and corporations. The tradition of the conversation portrait group was also much alive and such pieces were painted at this time by **Peter Meert**, by the very successful **Gonzales Coques** (Pls. 764, 773) forty-one in 1655, and by **Leandre van Dalen** follower of **Van Dyck**; and two artists who were soon to paint such conversation pictures, **Gillis van Tilborgh** (Pls. 762, 763) and **Theodor Boeyermans** became Antwerp Masters in 1654. Of the portraits of the *Archduke Leopold Wilhelm* reproduced here, **Teniers** portrays him as he appeared at the *Shooting of the Popinjay* (Pl. 712) in large hat and cape, and, wearing the same clothes, in the Italian section of his gallery in Brussels (Pls. 724, 725, 726). The other portraits of the Archduke show him accoutred as a warrior; the timid, silly, full-length on horseback by **Jan van den Hoecke** (Pl. 721) designed perhaps to evoke the *Cardinal Infante Ferdinand at the Battle of Nordlingen* (Pl. 643) by **Rubens**, evokes in fact the *Allegory of the Virtues of Rudolf II* (Pl. 459) by **Bartholomaeus Spranger**; and the half-length in golden armour with an eagle and a lion (Pl. 722) by **Justus van Egmont** is no more impressive—though it doubtless caught the fancy of Christina of Sweden (who sat to **van**

Egmont for her portrait in armour as mentioned above) for she later ordered another painter to portray her with a lion when he had proposed a fan. Neither **Jan van den Hoecke** nor **Justus van Egmont** convince me that their warrior is a faithful portrait of the Archduke; but the face in the half-length in armour (Pl. 723) by **Peter Thys** with its typically Habsburg structure was, I imagine, a good likeness. Others painting portraits at this time were **Cornelis de Vos** (Pl. 600), **Peeter Franchoys** (Pl. 654), **Jan van Reyn** (Pl. 651), **Gysbrecht Thys, Jacob van Reesbroeck, Frans Denys, Michaelina Wautier** and **Philip Fruytiers** who made a water-colour *The family of the Earl of Arundel* in 1643 in Antwerp from a drawing by **Van Dyck**.

Of the painters of marines and naval warfare **Andries van Ertvelt**, active in Antwerp till his death over sixty in 1652, is represented here by his *Harbour with Spanish warships being loaded with munitions* (Pl. 704) painted at this time or earlier. **Gaspar van Eyck** painted the *Naval battle between Turks and Maltese* (Pl. 703) at thirty-six in 1649 and lived beyond the end of the period. **Bonaventura Peeters** is represented here by *The Scheldt with shipping round a pier* (Pl. 689) and *Stormy sea and shipwreck* (Pl. 690) both of which anticipate Turner, and by the *Dutch men-of-war off an East Indian coast with natives on the foreshore* (Pl. 702) which may be the picture exported to Vienna fifty years later by the dealer Forchoudt and described as 'De Hollanders de eerste reys in Oost Indien comen en van de Indiaenen wel onthaelt worden'. **Bonaventura Peeters** left Antwerp about 1648, when this East Indian picture was painted, to escape the enmity of the Jesuits whom he had satirized, and settled at Hoboken where he died at thirty-eight in 1652; his brother **Jan Peeters**, Antwerp Master at twenty-one in 1645, who is seen here in *Stormy sea and shipwreck* (Pl. 691), and his sister **Catherina Peeters**, also a sea painter, both went with him to Hoboken and both returned to Antwerp in 1654. **Jan Peeters** seems to have visited the Mediterranean and drawn various Near Eastern ports, and **Gaspar van Eyck** visited Spain as well as Genoa as already related, but it is not known whether **Bonaventura Peeters** visited all or any of the foreign ports he depicted or whether he relied on drawings or prints by others for the local features.

Of the painters of battle pieces, sieges and other military genre **Sebastiaan Vrancx** (Pl. 531) died at seventy-four in 1647. I reproduce two works by **Peeter Snayers** who worked through the period *The Spaniards besieging Courtrai in 1648* (Pl. 700) where the disposition of the Spanish forces is set out and *Cavalry skirmish between Spanish and Dutch troops* (Pl. 701) showing terrified horses and thrown riders. **Pieter Meulener**, whose *Cavalry Skirmish* (Pl. 698) of 1644 is less sensitively imaged, signed a *Battle of Fleurus 1612* in 1646, an *Occupation of Magdeburg by Tilley's troops 1631* in 1650 and died at fifty-two in 1654. **Nicolaas van Eyck** (Pl. 785) and a newcomer **Simon van Douw** Antwerp Master in 1654 were also available in this field. **Adam van der Meulen**, pupil of **Peeter Snayers**, began his career in Brussels about 1652 with pictures of skirmishes and other military pieces like the *Halt of horsemen* (Pl. 737) perhaps painted in the sixteen-fifties. **Lambert de Hondt**, who worked in Malines, may have painted in these years his spirited *Horsemen in pursuit of baggage waggons* (Pl. 699) which is more a scene of brigandage in a rural setting than a military genre piece properly so-called; and **Anton Crussens** of Brussels, of whom hardly anything is known, signed a drawing *Mountain landscape with soldiers and officers on horseback* in 1655. War as it affects the peasants was painted by **Teniers** in *Soldiers plundering a village* (Pl. 706), and, more elaborately, by **David Ryckaert III** in *Peasants' distress* (*Soldiers plundering a village*) (Pl. 705) where the troops burn and pillage in the countryside and tie an old man to a horse's tail while the bad girl of the village is perched on the officer's knee; and more guard-room pieces were painted by **Teniers**.

Outdoor genre scenes with peasants and village festivals, sometimes attended by gentry, and indoor scenes with peasants at work and boors or housewives in a kitchen, were painted in this period by **Teniers** and, in his manner, by his brothers **Juliaen Teniers** (Pl. 681) six years his junior and **Abraham Teniers** Antwerp Master in 1646, by **Matthys van Helmont** and **Thomas van Apshoven** both Antwerp Masters the same year, and by **David Ryckaert III** who was two years his junior. **Teniers** himself was thirty-four in 1643 when he painted the *Village fête with cauldrons (Fête aux chaudrons)* (Pl. 708) where the peasants are seated on the ground in rows like the figures in the *Miracle of the loaves and fishes* by the **Melbourne Miracles Painter** (Pl. 148). In his outdoor genre pieces **Teniers** had learned something from **Sebastiaan Vrancx** (Pl. 532, 534), **David Vinckeboons** (Pl. 533), **Jan (Velvet) Brueghel** (Pl. 467, 482, 483) and their antecedents; but he was personal in his delicate cool colour which anticipates the silvery tones of Corot; and though, in his youth, he had been personally intimate with **Rubens** and his family, he was quite unaffected by the *Kermesse* (Pl. 665) and *Peasant dance* (Pl. 666) compared with which his village festivals have been described by Élie Faure as 'des danses immobiles, des orgies silencieuses et des kermesses mortes dans des paysages gris et doux'; his *Village fête with cauldrons* (Pl. 708) shows indeed the accuracy of the modern French critic's comments but it also reminds us that Sir Joshua Reynolds wrote with equal accuracy; 'The works of **Teniers** are worthy the closest attention of a painter who desires to excel in the mechanical knowledge of his art; his manner of touching, or what we call handling, has perhaps never been equalled; there is in his pictures that exact mixture of softness and sharpness which is difficult to execute.' In his indoor genre paintings **Teniers** owes something to the **Munich Tobacco Den Painter** (Pl. 621) to **Brouwer** (Pls. 595, 618) and to **Brouwer's** associates the Dutchman Adriaen van Ostade and **Joos van Craesbeeck** (Pls. 619, 626), but the lusty animation of **Jordaens** in his *Twelfth Night* manner (Pl. 658) was foreign to his nature and the peasants in such pictures as *The Goatherd* (Pl. 679) and the *Flayed ox* (Pl. 683) are as dutiful and sober as the bourgeoise housewife preparing a huge dinner in the *Kitchen scene with swan* (Pl. 678); some genre features in these pictures were already in the *Peasant household with cavalier* (Pl. 396) and the *Flayed ox* (Pl. 394) which **Marten van Cleve** produced in 1566, but the inmates of the **Teniers** interiors no longer throw up their sweaty night caps and clap their chapped hands, they are less rank scented and more domesticated, and they are unified in the pictures with all around them by the skilful dispositions of the light. The veritable antecedents of these interiors by **Teniers** are the domestic scenes of the fifteenth century—the room with the artist's wife or mistress and her baby by the **Virgin with a Firescreen Painter** (Frontispiece) and the room with the bourgeoise reading by the fireside by the **Madrid Werl Wings Painter** (Pl. 44).

High-life genre pieces were painted by **Christoffel van der Lamen** till he died under forty about 1652; by his pupil **Hieronymus Janssens** (Pls. 730, 731, 761) who was later to excel in them and began his career as Antwerp Master at twenty in 1644; and throughout the period by **Gonzales Coques** (Pls. 764, 773).

Among the landscape painters **Jan Wildens** (Pls. 628, 629) was about sixty-eight when he died in Antwerp in 1653; **Andreas Snellinck** died the same year at sixty-six and **Gillis Peeters** at forty-two. **Antonie Mirou** (Pl. 469) signed a *Forest scene with duckhunter* in 1653 and probably died soon after. **Lucas van Uden** (Pls. 561, 566, 567, 602), **Lucas de Wael** and **Jan Brueghel the younger** with his associates were all still working in 1655, and I must refer again here to the admirable landscape in the *Good Samaritan* by **Balthasar van Cortbemde** perhaps by that artist who signed it or by some landscape specialist collaborating with him.

Winter landscapes were painted by the versatile **Robert van den Hoecke** who produced the *Skating on Brussels moat* (Pl. 711) in 1649, and by **Daniel van Heil** (Pl. 709) who also painted *Conflagrations* (Pls. 713, 714) recalling the burning towns in **Bosch's** *Hell* scenes (Pls. 168, 173). Newcomers in Antwerp included **Gillis Neyts** Master there at twenty-five in 1647, **Jan Siberechts** (Pls. 787-92) later a most personal artist who was Master there at twenty-one in 1648, **Pieter Gysels** (Pl. 799) Master at twenty-nine in 1650 and **Isaak van Oosten** (Pl. 584)—probably an associate of **Jan Brueghel the younger**—who signed a *Wooded landscape* in 1650. Some picturesque Italianate landscapes in a tradition going back to **Paul Brill** (Pls. 473, 474), through Claude, were also painted; and three artists later successful with such pictures **Pieter van Bredael** (Pl. 778), **Gaspar de Witte** (Pl. 781) and **Jan Frans Soolmaker** (Pl. 780) were beginning their careers as Antwerp Masters respectively in 1650, 1651, and 1654. In the Brussels group of landscape painters **Lodewyck van Vadder** (Pl. 685) died at fifty in 1655 when one of his pupils **Lucas Achtschellinck** was twenty-nine and another **Ignatius van der Stock** (Pls. 738) was twenty; **Jacques d'Arthois** who painted winter landscapes (Pl. 710) as well as forest pieces (Pls. 686, 736) and was forty-two at the end of the period was now selling many pictures to dealers and collectors; he was nevertheless fast approaching bankruptcy through improvidence, and he was probably much helped in his work at this time by his brother **Nicolas d'Arthois**, Antwerp Master at twenty-three in 1640, who is known to have collaborated with him.

Of the animal and bird painters **Frans Snyders** (Pls. 630, 632, 634, 635) and **Paul de Vos** (Pls. 633, 636) were both still working in 1655. **Jan Fyt** (Pls. 719, 733) collaborated with **Thomas Willeboirts**; **Jan van Kessel the elder**, Antwerp Master in 1645, was making compositions like the one reproduced here (Pl. 732) in the middle fifties; and **Peeter Boel**, pupil of **Snyders** and of **Fyt**, was Master at twenty-eight in 1650. All kinds of animals in pairs are in **Izaak van Oosten's** *Garden of Eden* (Pl. 584) painted possibly by 1655. Horses appear in many of the outdoor pictures including, of course, the military pieces where they are often drawn in formulae used by **Sebastiaan Vrancx** (Pls. 531, 532)—though **Peeter Snayers** (Pl. 701) developed these formulae and broke through them. Absurdly shorn dogs are in **Peter van Lint's** portrait of 1645 (Pl. 697) and in a large composition by **Adriaen van Utrecht** (Pl. 693) who also shows a monkey and a parrot. **Cornelis de Baellieur** puts a strange mongrel dog in his *Adoration of the Magi* (Pl. 727) and **Christiaan Luyckx**, Master in 1645, shows a cat marauding in a larder (Pl. 696). **Frans Francken III** paints two parrots, a monkey and a dog as pets in the picture gallery of some Antwerp gentry (Pl. 728); and **Teniers** with the manual dexterity described by Reynolds paints his own pet dog (Pls. 678, 683), the pets of the Archduke Leopold Wilhelm (Pls. 724-6), and goats and hens in the light and shade of a farmyard outhouse (Pl. 679).

In still-life painting piles of military equipment, armour and so on continued as incidents in guard-room military pieces by **Teniers** and others. **Snyders** was probably still painting compositions with massed food (Pls. 655, 657); the commonplace and heavy handed **Jan Fyt**, much influenced by **Snyders**, was concocting larder pieces with dead birds and other food and miscellaneous objects; and dead birds were also features in still-life pieces by **Jan Boots** and by **Peeter Boels** after 1650. **Alexander Adriaenssen**, sixty-nine when the period closed, was still at work on his handsome arrangements of wet fish like those reproduced here (Pls. 652, 653); **Teniers** proved himself a skilful naturalistic still-life painter in his *Kitchen scene with swan* (Pl. 678) and many later pictures (though he probably used some assistants). **Adriaen van Utrecht**, who died just over fifty about 1652, applied his personal feeling for design in chiaroscuro to his large composition with fruit, ham, lobster, pie, vessels and musical instruments (Pl. 693). **Hendrik Andriessen (Mancken Heyn)** who died under fifty in 1655 was painting 'Vanitas' pictures with skull, hour-glass and so forth in these years; **Jan Davidsz de Heem** signed elaborate compositions with miscellaneous still-life; and **Andries van Benedetti** painted a *Still-life with lobster, lemons, vessels and lute* probably in the early sixteen-fifties. **Frans Ijkens** followed the early sober works by **Snyders**—like the *Still-life with fruit and game* (Pl. 555)—in his *Still-life with hare, asparagus and dead birds* (Pl. 695) painted at forty-five in 1646, and the same spirit seems to pervade the *Cat and dead birds* (Pl. 696) by **Christiaan Luyckx** a pupil of **Frans Francken III** and Antwerp Master at twenty-one in 1645. Others at work were **Jacob Foppens van Es** (Pl. 557, 558) who was still alive in 1655, **Matthew Matheussens, Cornelis Mahu** and **Pieter Gysels** (Pl. 806). Among the painters of fruit, **Jacob van Hulsdonck** (Pl. 556) died at sixty-five in 1647. **Jan Davidsz de Heem** signed a fruit and vegetable piece in 1653, and his pupil **Alexander Coosemans** (Pls. 744, 800) was Antwerp Master in 1645. Fruit pieces often with flowers, were painted most delicately by **Joris van Son** (Pls. 743, 745) Antwerp Master at twenty-one in 1644; **Christiaan Luyckx** paid a doctor with a *Still-life with fruit* in 1648; and **Theodor Aenvanck**, possibly the author of many unsigned pictures 'ascribed' to more famous names, signed the beautifully balanced *Still-life with grapes and other fruit* (Pl. 747) at the age of twenty in 1653.

Among the flower painters there was **Jan Brueghel the younger** (Pl. 650) as before. But the leading specialist was still the Jesuit **Daniel Seghers** who signed the enchanting *Garland of Flowers round a statue of the Virgin* (Pl. 692) at fifty-five and lived beyond the end of the period. Garlands round grisaille and other centres were now being painted by his pupils **Frans Lucas Peters** and **Jan Philip van Thielen** (Pl. 754) Antwerp Master in 1642 and also by **Canon van der Baren** (Pl. 675), **Andries Bosman** (Pl. 756), **Jan Davidsz de Heem, Alexander Coosemans** and **Peter Willebeeck** Antwerp Master in 1646. **Gaspar Pieter Verbruggen the elder**, later a flower painter (Pl. 810), was Antwerp Master at twenty-five in 1650 after working with **Cornelis Mahu.**

Among the painters of collectors' galleries and interiors with art dealers' wares, **Frans Francken** died in 1642 and **Hans Jordaens III** in 1643. But **Teniers, Cornelis de Baellieur** (Pl. 645) and **Frans Francken III** were all available in these years; and I reproduce three glimpses of the Archduke Leopold Wilhelm's gallery (Pls. 724, 725, 726) by **Teniers** and a view of a bourgeois collection (Pl. 728) by **Frans Francken III.** As the Archduke left Belgium with his huge collection before **Teniers** had copied his Flemish pictures the works shown in these interiors are all Italian with the exception (for some unknown reason) of a sixteenth-century *S. Luke drawing the Virgin* and a *Portrait of the Infanta Isabella in Clarissan habit* by or after **Rubens** or **Van Dyck** which occur on the ground in *The Archduke Leopold Wilhelm in his picture gallery at Brussels with Conde Fuensaldaña and others* (Pl. 725); the Italian pictures there include Titian's *Diana and Callisto, Nymph and Shepherd* and *Danae* and works by or ascribed to Giorgione, Raphael, Palma Vecchio, Veronese and so on. The picture placed above it in my plates (Pl. 724) purports to show another chamber in the gallery; here the walls are hung with Titian's *Danae* and *Diana and the death of Actaeon* and other identifiable High Renaissance works; and in *The Archduke Leopold Wilhelm in his picture gallery at Brussels with the dwarfish flower painter Canon van der Baren and others* we have Titian's *Jacopo de Strada*, some of the same pictures as before, and a number of new ones. In the *Family group in a picture gallery* (Pl. 728) by **Frans Francken III** the living room adjoins a bedroom on the right with a dog curled up on the floor; the figures in clothes of an earlier date may be posthumous portraits of the owner's parents and inserted by a portrait painter as collaborator; and the pot of flowers on the table, perhaps inserted by **Jan Brueghel the younger** or some other flower specialist, reminds us that the Flemish bourgeoisie had always had pots of flowers on their tables as we know from fifteenth-century Annunciation scenes with such interiors; the modest collection shown in this picture contains one piece of sculpture on the table and the walls are hung with an *Adoration of the Magi* in the style of **Cornelis de Baellieur** (Pl. 727), a *Neptune and Amphitrite* recalling the versions of the subject by **Frans Francken II** (Pl. 648) and **Adriaen van Nieulandt** (Pl. 647), mountainous and wooded landscapes, a winter landscape, a conflagration and a seapiece; and there are two unframed pictures—a church interior and an *Apelles painting Campaspe for Alexander* much less dashing than the concepts of **Joos van Winghe** (Pl. 457) and the **Hague Studio of Apelles Painter** (Pl. 580).

Church interiors were still being painted by **Peter Neeffs the elder** (Pls. 649, 650) who signed a *Liberation of S. Peter* at about seventy-three in 1651 and was still alive in 1655; they were also painted by his sons **Lodewyck Neeffs** who became a monk and signed in 1648 an *Interior of Antwerp Cathedral* (which is also signed by **Frans Francken III** as painter of the figures) and **Peeter Neeffs the younger**; and by **Jacob Lidts.**

As usual there were Flemish painters in England, Holland, France, Italy, Spain and Central Europe.

In England **Hendrik van Steenwyck the younger** (Pls. 487, 489, 536, 537) died about seventy about 1649. **Alexander Keirincx (Carings)** (Pls. 610, 611, 613) left for Holland in 1643 and **Cornelis Bol** may well have gone with him. **Hendrik van der Borcht the younger** who worked for the Earl of Arundel till the Earl died in 1646, was patronized thereafter by the Prince of Wales and left for Holland in 1652. **Jorge Geldorp** stored some of the King's pictures in his house when the Civil War began and was still in London in 1655. **Cornelis de Neve** was here and painting portraits through the period; **Weesop** who painted some portraits here (which Vertue tells us were 'passing for **Van Dyck**' at the beginning of the eighteenth century) left in protest at the King's execution and painted a picture of the happening. **Van Dyck's** former assistant and copyist **Remigius van Leemput** was now working for Lely whose Flemish assistants also included **Prosper Henricus Lankrink** provider of landscape backgrounds and decorative accessories and, after 1649, **Jan Baptiste Gaspers** (a pupil of **Thomas Willeboirts** (Pls. 672, 719)). When Charles I left Whitehall he gave instructions about the disposal of a *Princess Mary of Orange* by **Jan van Belcamp** and when Parliament ordered the sale of the King's pictures **van Belcamp**, as noted, was partly in charge of the arrangements. Buyers at the sale included **Remigius van Leemput** who bought **Van Dyck's** *Charles I on horseback*, **Jan Baptiste Gaspers** who bought as an agent for an unrecorded principal, and the Archduke Leopold Wilhelm (represented by agents). **Teniers** who visited England about this time to buy Italian pictures for Count Fuensaldaña (seen with him in the Archduke's gallery (Pl. 725)) may also have been present at this sale.

In Holland **Ambrosius Bosschaert the younger** died in Utrecht at thirty-six in 1645; **Abraham Bosschaert** continued to paint flowers in Amsterdam or Utrecht; and **Adam Willaerts** (Pl. 688) still domiciled at Utrecht signed a *Harbour with fishmarket* at seventy-four in 1651. **Alexander Keirincx** (Pls. 610, 611, 613) was back in Holland from England as just mentioned by 1643 and died in Amsterdam at fifty-two in 1652; and **Hendrik van der Borcht the younger** was in Amsterdam from England from 1652 till 1654 when he left for Antwerp. **Wallerant Vaillant** (a pupil of **Erasmus Quellinus** and later a painter of trompe l'oeil still-life, portraits and genre) was in Middelburg aged twenty-four in 1647 and in Amsterdam a few years later. In Amsterdam also **Adriaen van Nieulandt** (Pls. 515, 647) signed his *Neptune and Amphitrite* (Pl. 647) at sixty-four in 1651. **Adriaen Lucasz Fonteyn** was still painting peasant and social genre scenes in Rotterdam. **Frans van Momper** moved from The Hague to Haarlem in 1647 and thence to Amsterdam in 1638. **Jan Coelenbier** was still active as a dealer in Haarlem and **Jan Baptist Wolfordt** (son of **Artus Wolfordt**) was there from Italy in 1647. **Eduard Dubois**, portrait, landscape and 'history' painter from Antwerp, was in the Haarlem Guild at twenty-nine in 1648, his brother **Simon Dubois** aged sixteen was a pupil there of C. P. Berchem (father of the famous Nicolas) and both left for Italy about 1653. **Peter Thys** (Pls. 717, 718, 723) visited The Hague about 1649, as mentioned, to paint the Stadholder and other members of the House of Orange; both **Jordaens** and **Theodor van Thulden** must have paid visits there in connection with their work for the Huis ten Bosch; and **Willem van den Bundel** was there in 1642.

In Paris **Pieter van Mol** signed an *Adoration of the Shepherds* in 1642 or 1643 and died at fifty-one in 1650. **Philippe Vleughels** arrived from London (where he had gone as noted at the end of the last period), was introduced by **van Mol** to the Flemish colony's club 'La Chasse' and met there **Jacques Fouquier** (Pl. 563) now over sixty and the marine painter **Mathieu van Plattenberg** whose daughter he married. **Nicasius Bernaerts** (a pupil of **Snyders**) was painting animals and still-life with dead game by 1643; **Walther (Gauthier) Damery** who had been kidnapped by Algerian pirates on his way back from Italy and rescued by the Recollets, arrived in Paris about 1644. **Bertholet Flémalle**, who came from Italy about the same time, was patronized by Chancellor Séguier and painted for Paris churches before returning to Liège in 1647. **Vincent Leckerbetien** invited, perhaps on Poussin's recommendation, to contribute to the decoration of the Louvre, came from Italy to Paris in 1642 and produced a series of pictures titled *The Battles of Alexander* for the Château de Vincennes in the following years. **Philippe de Champaigne** (Pls. 742, 750), now in touch with the Port Royal 'Solitaires' and himself an open or crypto-Jansenist, retained none the less the favour of Court circles and was much employed on religious subjects and on portraits; by 1644 he had provided a *Nativity* for Rouen Cathedral, in 1648 he completed a *Last Supper* for the Port Royal convent, and later in the period he produced a series of pictures *The Lives and martyrdoms of SS. Gervasius and Protasius* which were translated into tapestries; his portraits of this time include the Jansenists *Robert Arnauld d'Andilly* and *Duvergier de Hauranne, Abbot of S. Cyran*, an official group *The Provost and sheriffs of Paris* painted in 1648 and *Jean Antoine de Mesme, President of the Parlement de Paris* painted in 1653; and in 1648 he became a Foundation Member of the Académie Royale des Beaux Arts and gave the institution a *S. Philip* painted the next year. Other Flemish artists elected to the new Académie Royale at this time were **Justus van Egmont** (Pl. 722) who left for Brussels, as related, in 1649, **Mathieu van Plattenberg, Pieter van Mol** and the flower painter and tapestry designer **Gerard Goswin** from Liège. **Jean Baptiste de Champaigne** (**Philippe de Champaigne**'s nephew) joined his uncle as a boy of twelve from Brussels in 1643 and was naturalized French in 1655; **Gaspar de Witte** (Pl. 781) travelled through France on his way back from Italy to Antwerp in 1651 or earlier; **Eduard** and **Simon Dubois** passed through Paris on their way to Italy from Holland about 1653; **Henri Staben** (Pl. 518) was still in Paris aged seventy-seven in 1655; and **Jean Daret** was still painting pictures for churches in Provence.

In Italy **Cornelis de Wael** was sixty-three when the period closed and still in Genoa; he was joined there for a time by his nephew **Peeter Boel** from Antwerp; and another pupil was **Jan Lambertsz Houwaert** also from Antwerp who may have painted in these years his *Saint with three nuns* for Genoa, S. Maria Maddalena. **Justus Sutterman** fifty-eight in 1655 was still portraying the nobility and notables in various places from his headquarters in Florence. **Matthias Stom (Stomer)** was still in Sicily working for churches till 1651 and seems to have died soon after. **Pieter van Bredael** (Pl. 778) may have visited Italy at this time; **Vincent Malo** (Pl. 615) may have gone back to Antwerp; and **Jan Claret** may have died in Savigliano or Turin. **Eduard Dubois** reached Turin from Paris about 1653 and remained there to work for Duke Charles Emmanuel II of Savoy; **Simon Dubois** came with him but left soon after for Rome. In Venice **Enrico Falange** was working for churches by 1650; **Nicolas Regnier** was still painting religious subjects and using his pretty daughters as models, and his half brother **Michele Desubleo** joined him from Bologna about 1655. In Rome **Balthasar Lauwers** died at sixty-seven in 1645 and **Josse de Paepe** (Pl. 593), probably under forty, in 1646; **Vincent Leckerbetien (Manciolla)** died there (or in France) about fifty in about 1650. **Louis Cousin (Luigo Primo),** now a figure in the Flemish colony, became Princeps of the Accademia in 1651 and a member of the Roman Confrérie de Saint-Julien l'Hospitalier in 1653. **Jan Miel** continued to work with Andrea Sacchi in the Barberini Palace till 1643 when he left because Sacchi disapproved of his genre tendencies; he then had success as a painter of Italian scenes with genre figures like his *Roman Carnival* (Pl. 772) of 1653 (which shows the influence of the Dutchman Pieter van Laer, known as Bamboccio or Bamboche who had worked in Rome in the sixteen-thirties): and he became a member of the Accademia in 1648. Among the newcomers **Michael Sweerts** came to Rome from Brussels in about 1644 and was elected a member of the Accademia at twenty-two in 1646; in 1652 he signed a *Young man playing draughts* and I reproduce his *In the studio, young artists with plaster casts* (Pl. 768) which was painted the same year. **Antoon Goubau** (Pls. 614, 775, 776) was probably in Rome between 1642 and 1650 when he seems to have gone back for a time to Antwerp. **Gaspar de Witte** (Pl. 781) was probably there from about 1645 when he was twenty-one and was back in Antwerp by 1651. **Jan Baptist Wolfordt** was there aged twenty-one in 1646 when he signed an *Italianate landscape with shawmplayer;* he then visited Haarlem, as just mentioned, and returned to Italy perhaps by 1650 when he signed a *Mountainous landscape with figures.* **Andries Smit,** landscape painter, was in Rome in 1650 and acquainted with Velazquez; and **Simon Dubois** came down from Turin at the end of the period.

In Spain **Adriano Rodriguez (Adriaen Dierickx)** of Antwerp entered the Jesuit order in Madrid in 1648 and painted for the refectory of the Jesuit College there; another Jesuit from Antwerp, **Ignacio Raeth,** pupil of **Daniel Seghers,** was also attached to the Madrid Jesuit College and began there a series of thirty-six scenes from the life of S. Ignatius Loyola in 1655. **Christiaan Luyckx** (Pl. 696) was in Spain for some time in 1646, became a Court Painter to Philip IV, and was back in Antwerp by 1648. **Pieter van Bredael** (Pl. 778) seems to have visited Spain as well as Italy in this period. **Anton van de Pere** arrived in Madrid about 1650 and worked for various churches and religious houses. **Andries Smit** who reached Madrid from Rome after 1650 had success with his landscapes and may have renewed his acquaintance with Velazquez; **Cornelis Schut III,** nephew of **Cornelis Schut** (Pl. 669), was established in Seville as a painter of religious pictures in the early sixteen-fifties; and **Miguel Manrique** was in Malaga.

In Central Europe **Hendrik van der Borcht the elder** was still in Frankfort at seventy-two in 1655. **Jan Thomas (van Ypern)** went from Antwerp to Mainz and became Court Painter to the Prince Bishop at about thirty-seven about 1654; and there soon after he took as pupil **Jan Baptiste de Ruel** who had come from Antwerp as a youth and began his career (as a singer) in the Prince Bishop's service. The Liégeois **François Walschartz** seems to have visited Westphalia in 1655 and painted decorative pictures for Raesfeld Castle. **Jan van den Hoecke** (Pls. 716, 721) went to Vienna from Rome at thirty-four in 1645, became Court Painter in Ordinary to the Archduke Leopold Wilhelm and accompanied him to Belgium in 1647 as related above. **Frans Luyckx,** Court Painter to Ferdinand III, was ennobled by the Emperor in Prague or Vienna in 1645, travelled in Germany painting portraits of Electors between 1648 and 1650, visited his native Antwerp in 1652 and returned to Vienna after working for Regensburg Cathedral in 1653 and 1654. The Gantois **Anselmus van Hulle,** who had entered the service of the Stadholder of Holland in 1642, was sent to Münster to make portraits of the delegates at the peace conference in 1648; he then worked at various German courts; and he too was ennobled by the Emperor.

CHAPTER XV

Don John of Austria 1656-1658;
Marquis of Caraçena 1659-1664;
Marquis of Castel Rodrigo 1664-1668;
Don Inigo de Velasco 1669;
Count de Monterey 1670-1674;
Duke of Villa Hermosa 1674-1680

1656-1680

IN 1656 the Archduke Leopold Wilhelm retired to Vienna taking with him his pictures and his other collections; **Canon van der Baren** (Pl. 675) who went with him was appointed curator and ordered to compile, with others, an inventory of the pictures; and Don John of Austria (the younger) became Governor-General and Commander-in-Chief in the Netherlands.

Don John had served the King from the age of eighteen by suppressing risings in Naples and Barcelona as related, and also by showing skill in pacification. Now, at twenty-seven, gay, self-confident and handsome he soon made himself popular and roused the jealousy of Condé who had to fight under him in the war against the French and English. Their first joint military exploit, which drove Turenne from Valenciennes, was none the less successful and this was recorded in a surviving picture, possibly by **Teniers**, where the disposition of the troops is shown and portraits of Philip IV, Don John and Condé are inserted. Condé in this year was thirty-five and Philip IV was fifty-one; Velazquez, fifty-seven, was painting *Las Meninas*; Prince Charles of England, twenty-six, was in Bruges where he was elected King of the Crossbowmen (Roi des Arbalétriers) a ceremony recorded by the Bruges painter **Jean Baptiste van Meunincxhove**; Alexander VII confirmed Innocent X's anathema (Cum occasione) on the five propositions in Jansen's 'Augustinus', the Jansenist Antoine Arnauld was deprived of his degree in the University of Paris, and Blaise Pascal published the first of his 'Petites lettres à un Provincial' in defence of Arnauld and against the Jesuits. In 1657 Leopold I succeeded Ferdinand III as Emperor; Blake destroyed sixteen Spanish ships in the harbour of Santa Cruz (Teneriffe); Cromwell, standing beneath the ceiling painted by **Rubens** in the Whitehall Banqueting House, refused the crown of England, and later sent six thousand Ironsides and a fleet to France in fulfilment of his pact with Mazarin; Don John called upon the Belgian Estates to furnish special funds to resist this French alliance with 'heretics' out to destroy 'la seule et vraye religion'; Pascal continued his 'Provincial letters'; and Christopher Wren, aged twenty-five, became professor of astronomy at Gresham College. In 1658 Don John, at instance of the Jesuits, urged the Brabant Council to act against the Belgian Jansenists who were much encouraged by the 'Provincial Letters'; John De Witt was re-elected Grand Pensionary of Holland; Prince Charles went from Bruges to Brussels where he called upon **Teniers** and made a treaty with Don John promising to mobilize his Royalist supporters in return for an allowance; Dunkirk, promised by Mazarin to Cromwell as a permanent possession, was handed to the English in July after Turenne (with the Ironsides in his army and the English vessels co-operating from the harbour) had defeated Don John and Condé (with English Royalists in their forces) at the Battle of the Dunes; Cromwell died in September; and Philip IV recalled Don John for his failure at Dunkirk.

In 1659 the Marquis of Caraçena who had accompanied Don John to the Netherlands became Governor-General in his stead; Philip IV ordered republication of Innocent X's anathema on Jansen's five propositions; Louis XIV by the Peace of the Pyrenees became betrothed to the Infanta Maria Theresa, Philip IV's daughter from his first wife Isabella of France; and Molière scored his first success with 'Les Précieuses Ridicules'. In 1660 Condé left the Spaniards and was pardoned by Louis XIV; the King married the Infanta, both he and his bride being then twenty-two; Charles II became King of England; and England made peace with Spain. In 1661 Cromwell's body was hanged at Tyburn and the head set up upon Westminster Hall (where it remained till 1684); Mazarin died; Louis XIV personally assumed the government and, influenced by the Jesuits, began to persecute the Jansenists; Pascal's 'Provincial Letters' were publicly burnt in Paris, and leading Jansenists were soon forced into hiding or imprisoned. In 1662 there was an alliance between France and Holland; Colbert reorganized the Gobelins factory and Charles Le Brun was chosen as Director; Charles II sold Dunkirk to the French and married Catherine of Braganza, daughter of John IV of Portugal, who brought Tangier and Bombay in her dowry; Samuel Pepys was clerk to the Navy Board; Milton was finishing 'Paradise Lost'; John Locke was lecturing in Christ Church, Oxford; a Corpus Christi play by Calderón de la Barca was censured by the Spanish Inquisition; Cartesian philosophy was condemned by the Faculty of Theology in Louvain University at the instance of the Papal Internuncio; the Archduke Leopold Wilhelm died in Strasbourg; and envoys sent by the Marquis of Caraçena to Ratisbon failed to get help for isolated Belgium from the Emperor who countered with a request for money against aggression by the Turks. In 1663 Louis XIV made a Pageant Entry in Dunkirk and **Jan van Reyn** (Pls. 592, 651) designed the decorations. In 1664 the Imperial general Count Raimond Montecucculi defeated the Turks at St. Gotthard on the Raab; New Amsterdam on Manhattan Island, raided by an English fleet, was rechristened New York in honour of James, Duke of York, who had sent out the expedition; and Philip IV recalled the Marquis of Caraçena.

In 1665 the Marquis of Castel Rodrigo succeeded Caraçena as Governor of the Netherlands; Philip IV died and was succeeded by Charles II aged four, with his mother Mariana of Austria as Regent; and war was declared between England and Holland. In 1666 the Marquis de Louvois, apostle of Frightfulness, became secretary of war to Louis XIV, and the French gave some naval assistance to the Dutch; the English lost a four days' fight against Admiral de Ruyter; London suffered the Plague and the Great Fire; Isaac Newton aged twenty-four watched apples falling in his garden; Antoine Arnauld's nephew the Jansenist Isaac Le Maistre de Saci, translator of the New Testament, was imprisoned in the

325

Bastille; and Castel Rodrigo received the allegiance of the Estates of Flanders to the new Spanish King in ceremonies recorded by **François Duchatel** (Pl. 777) and other artists. In 1667 Louis XIV claimed the Spanish Netherlands as his Queen's inheritance by the Law of Devolution; French armies marched into Flanders; and the King, with the Queen and her ladies in their coaches, entered town after town in triumph while **Adam van der Meulen** (Pls. 737, 759, 766), in attendance for the purpose, made sketches for eventual pictures; Racine wrote his 'Andromaque' at the age of twenty-eight; the English and Dutch signed the Peace of Breda after De Ruyter had burnt the docks at Chatham; Wren was appointed Surveyor-General and Principal Architect for rebuilding the city of London; John Locke published 'An Essay on Toleration'; Clement IX succeeded Alexander VII as Pope; and Le Maistre de Saci's translation of the New Testament, which the Jansenists at Port Royal were afraid to publish, was printed nominally at Mons but actually by the Elzeviers in Holland. In 1668 John De Witt was again elected Grand Pensionary of Holland; England, Holland and Sweden formed a Triple Alliance against Louis XIV; Le Vau designed the façade of the new vast extension of Versailles palace; French armies led by Condé and the King overran the Franche Comté in a fortnight; the Treaty of Aix-la-Chapelle between France and Spain gave Lille, Douai, Tournai, Audenarde and other towns to France and returned the Franche Comté to Spain: and Madrid recalled the Marquis of Castel Rodrigo.

In 1669 Don Inigo Fernandez de Velasco y Tovar, an old, effete and frivolous person, arrived as Governor-General in the Netherlands where the War of Devolution had caused widespread wretchedness and poverty; Clement IX achieved a temporary placation of the Jansenist disputes; the Turks entered Candia (besieged since 1648) and thus mastered Crete; and John Sobieski, Commander-in-Chief of the Polish army, began to conspire against Michael Wisniowiecki, the new king.

In 1670 the Count de Monterey succeeded Don Inigo de Velasco as Governor of the Netherlands and made great efforts to organize the national defences: Louis XIV destroyed the Triple Alliance by diplomatic actions which included secret treaties with Charles II of England; and de Monterey and John De Witt drafted terms for an alliance between Spain and Holland which the Queen Mother Mariana, as Regent, signed for Spain next year. In 1672 Louis XIV crossed the Rhine with **Adam van der Meulen** present to record the operation; French armies overran Holland; Dutch concessions were rejected; John De Witt was lynched by a Dutch mob; William III of Orange was appointed Stadholder at twenty-two; de Monterey sent troops to help him; and the Turks stormed Kamienic and gained the whole of the Ukraine by the Peace of Buczacz. In 1673 French troops marched, pillaging, through Belgium to the siege of Maestricht; the Emperor Leopold I and the Hohenzollern Frederick William of Brandenburg, the 'Great Elector', joined the Stadholder; De Ruyter defeated an Anglo-French fleet; John Sobieski defeated the Turks at Khoczim; and Charles II knighted Christopher Wren and commissioned him to submit a model for the new St. Paul's.

In 1674 de Monterey was recalled and the Duke of Villa Hermosa, a cavalry officer, became the Governor. England made peace with Holland; Condé checked the Stadholder, advancing towards Paris, at the Battle of Seneffe; Turenne drove the Germans from Alsace; and John Sobieski became King of Poland. In 1675 the French, led again by Louis XIV in person, captured many towns in Belgium and inflicted great hardship in some regions; Villa Hermosa appealing desperately to Madrid for troops and money was ordered to send some singing birds desired by the Queen Mother; Pierre Bayle, aged twenty-eight, was Professor of Philosophy in the Protestant University of Sedan; Sir Christopher Wren began

Greenwich Observatory; and Sarah Jennings became Maid of Honour to Princess Anne. In 1676 Sobieski recovered two-thirds of the Ukraine from the Turks in the Treaty of Zaravno. In 1677 the Stadholder married Mary, daughter of James, Duke of York; the French had more successes in the war; Racine produced his 'Phèdre'; and Don John of Austria, bitter enemy of the Queen Mother since his return from the Netherlands, forced her to retirement at Toledo and became Prime Minister to Charles II now sixteen and thus by Spanish law of age. In 1678 the Treaty of Nymwegen gave to France the Franche Comté and, on her north-eastern frontier, a chain of towns including Valenciennes where Antoine Watteau's father was working as a tiler; Charles II of Spain announced that he had placed the Netherlands under the protection of S. Joseph; Titus Oates, expelled from the Jesuit College at Valladolid, concocted the Popish plot; Dryden produced his 'All for Love'; Colonel Churchill married Sarah Jennings; and **Erasmus Quellinus** (Pls. 639, 671) died in Antwerp leaving rooms hung with gold leather, a large collection of pictures, and a library including Descartes' 'Principia Philosophiae', van Mander's 'Schilderboek', Ovid's 'Metamorphoses' in French, and books on music, coins, pharmacy and optics. In 1679 Charles II of Spain married Marie Louise de Bourbon daughter of Philippe d'Orléans, and Calderón aged eighty wrote his last play in honour of the occasion; Don John of Austria died; the Quaker William Penn wrote 'An Address to Protestants of all Persuasions'; persecution of the Jansenists was resumed in France; and Antoine Arnauld, forced to leave Paris at sixty-seven, took refuge first at Mons and afterwards in Brussels. In 1680 a woman named Voisin was burned alive in France for poisoning by witchcraft; Louis XIV began annexing towns and regions as 'dependencies' of places ceded by the Peace of Nymwegen; Villa Hermosa was recalled; and Alexander Farnese II, second son of the Duke of Parma, was sent as his successor.

In these twenty-five years 1656-80 there was a measure of Court and civic patronage of painters despite the wars and the invasions. Don John's Court Painters included **Peeter Snayers** (Pls. 627, 700, 701) now sixty-four who designed and portrayed his Pageant Entry into Brussels, **Erasmus Quellinus** (Pls. 639, 671) forty-nine, designer of his Entry into Antwerp, **David Teniers** aged forty-six, and **Gonzales Coques** (Pls. 764, 773) aged forty-two. Though France was politically the Public Enemy there was a cultural influence from Paris; and Don John tried to emulate the modes and gaiety of the French Court—as we see in *A Ball at the Court of Don John of Austria* (Pl. 730) and *La main chaude* (Pl. 731) by **Hieronymus Janssens** who was thirty-two in 1656 and had some favour from Don John and was known as 'Le Danseur et Peintre à la Mode' which suggests that he was or had been a professional dancer or teacher of dancing. Under the Marquis of Caraçena **Teniers** was continued as Court Painter; his 'Theatrum Pictorium'—engravings of two hundred and forty-four Italian pictures in the Archduke Leopold Wilhelm's collection—was published in 1660; and the Marquis stood godfather to a child of his second wife, the richly dowered daughter of the Secretary to the Brabant Council. Caraçena also doubtless confirmed the position of **Erasmus Quellinus** who drew at this time *The marriage of Louis XIV and the Infanta Maria Theresa* for an engraving and was most highly thought of, as we know from the 'Gulden Cabinet' published in 1661 by Cornelis de Bie: 'Zou dunkt my dat de geest van Zeuxis of Urbin, gemengt is met de ziel in't lichaam van Quellin.' The *Allegory in honour of the birth of a prince* (Pl. 751), with Spain and her colonies shown upon the globe, painted by **Jan Ijkens** in 1659 records the birth in 1657 of the short-lived Prince Philip Prosper; and Caraçena's appeals to Leopold I may be recorded in *Antwerp begging the Emperor to reopen the Scheldt* (Pl. 786) by **Huybrecht Sporckmans**. The Marquis of Castel Rodrigo was portrayed by **François Duchatel**, a pupil of **Teniers**, and by **Erasmus Quellinus** who added Mercury and Athene as attendants; **Quellinus** designed his Pageant Entry into Antwerp and recorded the Turks' renewed attack on Crete in a drawing called *Peace driving Mars and Bellona to the defence of Candia*. In Malines **Jacques de Hornes** designed the local ceremonies for the Pageant of Allegiance to Charles II. In Ghent an *Allegory of Charles II receiving the homage of Flanders* was painted by **Jan van Cleef** and the actual Ghent Pageant of Allegiance was drawn by **Jacques van Werden** and painted in detail by **François Duchatel** whose picture reproduced here (Pl. 777) shows the Marché de Vendredi with its statue of the Emperor Charles V on a pillar in the centre and is accurately described by Descamps :— 'Le fond représente une des principales places de la Ville, où sont les arcs de Triomphe, des amphithéatres ; la noblesse et la bourgeoisie sous les armes sont en parade ; on y compte plus de mille figures, toutes bien variées, bien dessinées, bien peintes et touchées avec esprit, aussi beau à bien des égards que de **Teniers**.' In the Count de Monterey's time the Antwerp authorities ordered a *Portrait of Charles II of Spain* from **Peter Thys** (Pls. 717, 718, 723) for the Town Hall; and de Monterey's attempts to stiffen the national resistance may have called forth the '*William Tell performed before the S. Sebastian's Guild in Antwerp* (Pl. 784) ordered by the Guild in 1672 from **Charles Emmanuel Biset** and *The 1673 Review of the Antwerp Civic Guard on the Place de Meir* (Pl. 785) by **Nicholaas van Eyck**. De Monterey himself continued **Gonzales Coques** and also doubtless **Erasmus Quellinus** as Court Painters and he patronized **Biset** and **Abraham Genoels** (Pls. 817, 826) from whom he commissioned tapestry cartoons. **Genoels**, thirty-two at this moment, had worked for the Gobelins in Paris, and he called in **Nicasius Bernaerts** and **Peeter Boel** whom he had known in Paris to assist him respectively with the animals and birds in this commission. Collaborations of this kind, common, I have suggested, from the outset of our story, and documented more and more frequently from the middle of the sixteenth century onwards, were still common at this time; and in the *William Tell* (Pl. 784) by **Biset**, just referred to, **Wilhelm Schubert van Ehrenberg** (Pl. 783) is known to have painted the architecture and **Philips Augustyn Immenraet** the trees and sky. While the Duke of Villa Hermosa was Governor the Brabant authorities ordered a *Charles II of Spain* from **François Duchatel** (Pl. 777) and the King was also painted by **Willem de Ryck** and by **Louis van Schoor** in a design for tapestry; **Duchatel** painted a portrait of the Duke; and **Lucas Achtschellinck** was granted exemption from beer tax for designing landscape tapestries for the Brussels Magistrature.

Conditions for artists were changed to some extent in Castel Rodrigo's period by the foundation of the Antwerp Academy in imitation of the Académie Royale in Paris. The Guild régime had hitherto controlled the education of the members and their procedures in selling their own and other artists' pictures (as many artists also acted as dealers), and was on occasion undoubtedly vexatious. Many artists had long resented this. **Abraham van Diepenbeeck** for example had a standing feud with the Antwerp Painters' Guild. When **Jan Cossiers** (Pl. 640) was engaged in Don John's time on a large *Golgotha* triptych, twenty-nine feet high, for the Malines Béguinage, he painted it in his Antwerp studio but wished to finish it in the final position in Malines; this the Malines Guild would not permit on the ground that non-residents were not allowed to paint in the town, and they maintained this refusal though a group of Antwerp artists including **Frans Francken III** (Pl. 728), **Jan Brueghel the younger, Ambrosius Brueghel** and **Cornelis de Baellieur** (Pls. 645, 727) all ex-deans of the Antwerp Guild, declared on his behalf that it was customary in Antwerp and also in Brussels, Louvain, Ghent and Bruges for non-resident artists to adjust or finish such commissioned pictures in situ. The Guild régime was also out of favour with some artists who thought its educational principles restrictive and old fashioned; and for this too there seems to have been some reason, for when **Michael Sweerts** (Pl. 768) returned to Brussels from Italy and tried in 1656 to launch an art school for drawing from the nude, he had soon to abandon the endeavour probably from opposition instigated by the Guild. In Antwerp the project for the Academy was set on foot in Caraçena's period by **Teniers** who had been proceeded against by the Brussels Guild for selling his own and other artists' pictures by auction in conditions against the rules; money for eight professorships was later raised by an auction where the eight highest bidders secured exemption from taxes; Philip IV became the official founder and patron; and rooms were provided by the city on the first floor of the Bourse where the inauguration took place in 1664. Classes for students—in which drawing from the nude was still forbidden—began in 1665. The Academy thus founded had considerable trouble with the Guilds and there were various legal actions; but it survived the storms and eventually became a recognized factor in the Antwerp art world. Pictures were given to the headquarters at the outset by **Jordaens** (Pl. 774), by the marine painter **Hendrik van Minderhout** (Pls. 793, 794) and by **Theodor Boeyermans**; **N. M. Fierlants** gave an allegoric work in 1670; and in 1674 **Abraham Genoels** gave his *Landscape with Minerva and the Muses* (Pl. 826).

All the traditional aspects of Flemish painting were continued in these decades when scores of artists sold their pictures to dealers and private persons and received commissions for churches in addition to the patronage from the Court, the civic bodies, guilds and so on.

Among the painters of religious subjects the stupendous **Jordaens** was still painting for Catholic churches in the sixties, though his Calvinism was known; in 1663 he provided S. Walpurga in Furnes with a *Christ among the doctors*—constructed on classical geometric principles like the *Lineage of S. Anne* (Pl. 456) by **Hendrik de Clerck**—which Descamps in 1769 assessed among the finest of his pictures; in 1665 he painted *S. Carlo Borromeo interceding for the plague-stricken* for Antwerp S. Jacques; and when he died at eighty-one in 1678 he bequeathed a *Descent from the Cross* to the Antwerp Hospice Civil. **Jan Boeckhorst (Lange Jan)** (Pl. 720) died in 1668, **Abraham van Diepenbeeck** in 1675 and **Simon de Vos** (Pls. 673, 674, 687) in 1676. **Theodor Boeyermans**, who died in 1678, painted a *Martyrdom of S. Rombout* for the Malines Béguinage in 1660, a *Vow of S. Aloysius Gonzaga* in 1671 and a *Pool of Bethesda* for the Antwerp Soeurs Noires in 1675. **Jan Cossiers** (Pl. 640) painted his large *Golgotha*, just referred to, for the Malines Béguinage between 1655 and 1662, an *Adoration of the Magi* for the Antwerp Soeurs Noires in 1666 and other religious subjects before he died in 1671. **Antoon Goubau** (Pls. 614, 775, 776) who seems to have been in Antwerp from Rome about 1670 signed an *Adoration of the Magi* in that year. **Peter Thys** (Pls. 717, 718, 723) painted *The Virgin, SS. Roch and Anne with the plague-stricken* for Termonde church in 1661 and a *Martyrdom of S. Catherine* for the same church in 1665 and died in 1677. **Huybrecht Sporckmans** (Pl. 786) painted *S. Carlo Borromeo interceding for the plague-stricken* and *The Order of the Carmelites confirmed by the Pope* for the Antwerp Carmelites. **Erasmus Quellinus** (Pls. 639, 671) painted an *Adoration of the Shepherds* for Malines Cathedral in 1669 and died in 1678; his son **Jan Erasmus Quellinus** (Pl. 821), back from Rome in 1661, produced an enormous *Pool of Bethesda* for the Antwerp Abbey of S. Michel in 1672, and either he or his father, invited by the dealer Forchoudt to paint a *S. Sebastian* for a Viennese customer, agreed to do so on condition that the time to be taken would be dependent on the price—'want men moet meer winnen op twee maanden dan op eene'. **Peter van Lint** (Pls. 677, 697), **Cornelis de Baellieur** (Pls. 645, 727), who died in 1671 and **Lucas Smout the elder** who died in 1674, also sold religious subjects in this period to

Forchoudt. Among the newcomers **Godfried Maes**, pupil of **Peter van Lint**, became Antwerp Master in 1672; **Willem de Ryck** pupil of **Erasmus Quellinus** (or of **Jan Erasmus**) was Antwerp Master in 1673 and painted a *S. Matthew* for Antwerp Cathedral soon after; and **Peter Ijkens**, also Antwerp Master in 1673, painted an *Elisha carried up to heaven* in a landscape by **Jan Baptist Wans** for the Carmes Dechaussés. **Jan Baptist Herregouts** came back from Italy in 1673 and began to be employed for churches. A *Visitation* by **Charles Wautier** seen by Descamps in Antwerp Augustines and described by him as 'composé avec feu et génie' may have been painted in these years; and it was perhaps at this time also that **Teniers** painted a *Temptation of S. Anthony* which recalls the *Temptation of S. Anthony* (Pl. 241) by **Joachim Patinir** and **Quinten Massys** as the hermit is distracted by spooks and a young lady in contemporary dress. In Bruges, where **Paul Ryckx** died in 1668, **Pierre Bernaerdt** painted a *Trinity* for Notre Dame in 1660 and a *Virgin interceding for souls in Purgatory* for S. Jacques in 1674. **Jacob van Oost the elder** continued to be employed for Bruges churches till he died in 1671; and his deeply felt *Christ crowned with thorns* (Pl. 740) painted in 1661 (and evidently influenced, I should say, by **Van Dyck's** version of the subject then in the Abbaye des Dunes near Bruges) might advantageously be studied between the picture shown here by the **London Christ Mocked Painter** (Pl. 175) and Manet's version of the subject (reproduced in my 'French Painting' (Medici)). **Jacob van Oost the younger** (Pls. 769, 771) who went abroad at twenty in 1659 was back in Bruges before 1668 when he painted *The Virgin giving a stole to S. Hubert* for S. Sauveur. In Ghent, religious pictures for churches were painted by **Pieter Le Plat** who worked through the period; by **Anton van den Heuvel** who restored the **van Eycks'** *Altarpiece of the Mystic Lamb* in 1663 and died in 1677; by **Gaspar de Crayer** (Pls. 598, 607, 609) who moved there from Brussels in 1664, signed a *Martyrdom of S. Blaise* at eighty-six in 1668 and died there aged eighty-seven in 1669; and by **Jan van Cleef** who came aged eighteen as **de Crayer's** assistant and was much employed on altarpieces from 1670 onwards. In Brussels an *Entombment* was painted for the Riches Claires convent by **Lancelot Volders** who was Brussels Master in 1657 and had **Victor Honoré Janssens** (Pls. 812, 827) as his pupil in 1675; and **David Teniers III**, produced a *S. Dominic adoring the Virgin* for the Church at Perck where his father owned the Dry Toren Château (Pl. 707). **Antoine Sallaert** (Pl. 514) died in Brussels approaching seventy in about 1658, and **Theodore van Loon** died probably in Brussels or Louvain at about seventy-five about 1660. From Bois-le-Duc, where he died in 1669, **Theodor van Thulden** (Pls. 598, 753) sent an altarpiece in 1660 to the Jesuit Church in Bruges. **Jan van Reyn** (Pls. 592, 651) died in Dunkirk at sixty-eight in 1678. From Furnes, near Dunkirk, **Victor Boucquet** (Pl. 767) sent altarpieces to Loo parish church between 1658 and 1660, a *Christian slaves freed by Trinitarians* to the church at Nieuport and a *Descent from the Cross* to the Ostend Capucins before he died in 1677. In Malines the church painters included **David Herregouts** who died in 1662, his son-in-law **Gilles Smeyers**, **Henri Herregouts** who painted for churches in Malines and Antwerp in the sixties and seventies, **Jan Verhoeven**, **Jacques Le Pla** and **Lucas Franchoys the younger** who sent a *Resurrection of Christ* to Tournai Cathedral in 1657 and had an influential studio with **Sebastiaen van Aken** among his pupils in the sixties. In Audenarde **Simon de Pape** painted a *Ransoming of Christian slaves* and a *S. Helena finding the True Cross*. **Nicolas Stramot** painted a *Samson killing the lion* for the monastery of the Cross Bearers in his native Diest in 1677. The Jesuit **Frater Jacques Nicolai** died in Namur at seventy-three in 1678. In Liège **Gerard Douffet** died in 1660, **Walther Damery** in 1672 and **Bertholet Flémalle**—poisoned it was said by the Marquise de Brinvilliers then in the city—in 1675. **Flémalle's** pupil **Gerard de Lairesse**

(Pls. 813, 814) painted a *Martyrdom of S. Ursula* for Aix-la-Chapelle Cathedral at the age of nineteen in 1660; **Lambert Blendeff**, another pupil of **Flémalle**, left the city in 1677, settled in Louvain and worked there for the churches; **Jean Gilles Delcour** came back from Rome some time after 1660 and **Englebert Fisen** was back by 1679.

Among the 'history' pieces, mythologies and allegories, **Victor Boucquet** (Pl. 767) painted a *Judgement of Cambyses* for Nieuport Town Hall in 1671; **Erasmus Quellinus** (Pls. 639, 671) and **Jan Erasmus Quellinus** (Pl. 821) both painted *Achilles discovered among the daughters of Lycomedes*—a subject shown here in a picture by **Gérard de Lairesse** (Pl. 814); **Jan Erasmus Quellinus** painted an *Anthony and Cleopatra* before 1670 and either he or his father an *Artemisia drinking the ashes of Mausolus* owned in the seventies by Forchoudt. Mythologies were painted by **Frans Wouters** (Pl. 667) who died at forty-seven in 1659, by **Jan de Duyts** who died in 1676, and also by **Jan Brueghel the younger** (Pl. 605) till he died at seventy-seven in 1678, by **Jan Boeckhorst** (Pl. 720) till 1668, by **Peter Thys** (Pls. 717, 718) till 1677, and by **Gysbrecht Thys** till the end of the period. **Abraham Genoels** was clearly influenced by his contacts with the Gobelins in the pretty *Landscape with Minerva and the Muses* (Pl. 826); a *Landscape with Diana sleeping* by **Peter van Halen** was sold about 1674 to Count Carl von Liechtenstein, and a series called *The Twelve Months* by **Gaspar de Witte** (Pl. 781) was also exported to Vienna. **Daniel Janssens** Malines Master in 1660 and Antwerp Master in 1667 designed arches for the S. Rombout Jubilee that year; and **David Teniers III** was designing tapestries with mythologies by 1680. In the *Allegory in honour of the birth of a Prince* (Pl. 751) by **Jan Ijkens** an elegant gentleman—in the posture of figures by **Cornelis Engelbrechtsz** (Pl. 230) and the **Oultremont Master** (Pl. 231)—hands a golden bit with red leather bridle to a page, and War, Fame, Time, Abundance, Art and Power are in attendance. In his *Allegory of Commerce and Industry* (Pl. 774), presented, as noted, to the Antwerp Academy, **Jordaens** shows the Fine Arts protected and nourished by Industry and Commerce—a concept which sociologists will contrast with *Mars and the Fine Arts overcoming Ignorance* (Pl. 492) by **Antoine Claeissins** and the Parnassian Utopia by **Marten de Vos** (Pl. 364). In *Antwerp as Foster-Mother of the Painters*, which **Theodor Boeyermans** presented to the Academy, there are portraits of **Rubens** and **van Dyck** with Envy in the background, and the city of Antwerp is symbolized by a figure traditionally described as a portrait of **Van Dyck's** wife, Mary Ruthven, whom **Boeyermans** may have known in England in his youth.

Among the Antwerp portrait painters **Cornelis de Vos** (Pls. 599, 600) died at seventy-two in 1657. The water-colourist **Philip Fruytiers** was active till 1666, the prosperous **Justus van Egmont** (Pl. 722) till 1674, **Simon de Vos** (Pl. 687) till 1676, **Peter Thys** (Pl. 723) till 1677 and **Theodor Boeyermans** till 1678. **Peter van Lint** (Pl. 697), **Gonzales Coques** (Pl. 764) now at the height of his reputation as 'The little van Dyck', and **Hieronymus Janssens** (Pl. 761) were all available through the period; and others active in Antwerp were **Gysbrecht Thys** whose portraits as already mentioned were often ascribed to **Van Dyck** in the early eighteenth century, **Michiel Engel Immenraet** who portrayed two young ladies as shepherdesses in 1661 and went abroad in the early seventies, **Jacob van Reesbroeck, Charles Wautier** and a newcomer **Jan van Helmont**, Master in 1676. In Brussels **Peter Meert** was available for portraits, conversation pieces and subscription groups till he died in 1669; **Gillis van Tilborgh** (Pls. 762, 763) returned there from Antwerp and worked there till approximately 1678, and **François Duchatel** (Pl. 777) who portrayed both Castel Rodrigo and Villa Hermosa, was still at work in 1680. In Bruges, **Jacob van Oost the elder** (Pl. 715) was available till 1671 and **Jacob van Oost the younger** echoed **Van Dyck's** urbane depicting of urbane clerics in his *Jacques Matyn, Canon of Bruges, S. Donatien* (Pl. 769). In Ghent, Jonkheer **Frans van Cuyck de Mierhop**, a Bruges aristocrat who had settled there, made a portrait group *The Members of the Butchers' Guild, with the vision of S. Hubert* in 1678 and had **Robert van Audenaerd** (Pl. 823) as his pupil by 1680. In Namur **Pierre de Bourguignon**, twenty-six in 1656, probably painted some portraits till he left for Paris before 1671. In Dunkirk **Jan van Reyn** doubtless painted more portraits like the sensitive *Lady in black dress with red ribbons* (Pl. 651) before the end of his career; and in Furnes **Victor Boucquet** painted the vigorous and impressive *Standard Bearer* (Pl. 767) which was doubtless the portrait of a young volunteer in the Civic Guard.

Subscription portrait groups in the tradition going back to the fifteenth century were still as frequent as ever. Thus Civic Guardsmen in festive finery appear in *The 1673 review of the Antwerp Guard* (Pl. 785) by **Nicolaas van Eyck**. **Charles Emmanuel Biset** painted twenty-four members of the Antwerp S. Sebastian's Guild and the Guild's standard bearer, halberdiers and messengers as the audience in his *Performance of William Tell* (Pl. 784); and **Huybrecht Sporckmans** shows members of the Fishermen's and Fishmongers' Guilds in his *Antwerp begging the Emperor to re-open the Scheldt* (Pl. 786) but may have called in some hack archaistic portraitist for the purpose as the burghers, set in serried formation, are stylistically different from the allegoric figures.

Conversation pieces and portrait groups in domestic settings illustrated in my plates include *The Cradle* (Pl. 787) by **Jan Siberechts** which gives us a pretty bourgeois interior with the artist's wife and baby, a servant sweeping, and several of the artist's pictures on the walls; the charming *Family group (The Betrothal)* (Pl. 761) by **Hieronymus Janssens** where a little boy brings a rose with cavalier grace to his child fiancée who awaits him fan in hand; the *Family group with a young lady at a harpsichord* (Pl. 762) by **Gillis van Tilborgh** where the young lady strikes the tinkling chords, her beau leans upon her chair behind her, the mother and a younger sister make lace on cushions, and the father weighs gold coins while his secretary takes down the figures and his son is thus instructed in a proper reverence for money; and **van Tilborgh's** *Family group round a dining table* (Pl. 763) where the little girl in the foreground has just put flowers from her bouquet in her grandmother's lap and the young man on the left is about to take snuff from a snuff box. The three last named interiors are all spatially constructed on principles that go back through **Cornelis de Baellieur** (Pl. 645), **Hendrik van Steenwyck** (Pl. 537) and **Abel Grimmer** (Pl. 535) to **Dirk Bouts** (Pl. 58); and the domestic settings are rooted in the tradition launched at the outset of our story by **Jan van Eyck** (Pl. 18A) and the **London Virgin with a Firescreen Painter** (Frontispiece); for these seventeenth-century artists describe the furnishings of their day, the gold leather on the walls, the painted cabinets, the pictures and the harpsichords as faithfully as the fifteenth-century artists described the studded shutters, the candelabra, the ewers, towels, rugs and cushions and the flowers in vases on tables by ladies seated on carved benches and turning the pages of their books.

Among the high-life genre records the *Ball at the Court of Don John of Austria* (Pl. 730) and *La main chaude* (Pl. 731) by **Hieronymus Janssens** lead on to the fêtes galantes by Watteau; and some aspects of Watteau's art are also foreshadowed in the charming conversation piece *The Verbiest family on a terrace* (Pl. 764) painted by **Gonzales Coques** in 1664. In the *Château with figures and a greyhound* (Pl. 707) **Teniers** puts a lady and gentleman, perhaps himself and his daughter, with their gardener in the foreground; some gentry of the time are seen in **Guillaume van Schoor's** *L'Hôtel de Nassau at Brussels* (Pl. 760) where the young lady with the cavalier plays a guitar initialled 'T. B.' which may mean that the figures were inserted by **Theodor Boeyermans** whose occasional social pieces include one with a Jesuit dignitary calling upon a patrician family seated on a terrace—a record of the Jesuit influence in the Belgian upper classes; and gentry in decorous deportment are inserted by some high-life genre painter in the *Interior of Antwerp Jesuit Church* (Pl. 782) by **Anton Gheringh**. Ladies greeting one another from their coaches and a horseman riding through the gateway to his house are seen in *Antwerp: Place de Meir* (Pl. 765) by **Erasmus de Bie**. The elaborate *Open air performance in the Place du Grand Sablon, Brussels* (Pl. 759), painted by **Adam van der Meulen** before he left for Paris, records a whole range of fashions about 1660; and we note here that the ladies sit facing outwards in their coaches as earlier in **Denis van Alsloot's** *Feast of Our Lady of the Wood* (Pl. 513). The brilliant *Village fair with actors on a stage* (Pl. 796) painted by **Pieter Bout** at eighteen is in the genre tradition of **Sebastiaan Vrancx** (Pls. 532, 534) and **David Vinckeboons** (Pl. 533) and shows all sorts and conditions of people—gentry, soldiers, farmers, stall keepers, pedlars, beggars and a turbaned Jew who seems to have strayed from Rembrandt's Amsterdam.

The landscapes of this time included winter scenes, often with skaters, Italianate and wooded compositions, flat river pieces, and rural backgrounds to genre scenes. Winter landscapes were painted by, among others, **Erasmus de Bie, Daniel van Heil** (Pl. 709), **Jacques d'Arthois** (Pl. 710), **Robert van den Hoecke** (Pl. 711) and **Pieter Bout** (Pl. 797). Italianate compositions were painted by **Adriaen Frans Baudewyns** (Pl. 815) pupil of **Ignatius van der Stock** (Pl. 738) and Brussels Master in 1665 who then went to Paris till 1674, by **Jan van den Hecke, Philips Augustyn Immenraet**, his pupil **Peter Rysbraeck** who left for England aged about twenty in 1674, by **Pieter Spierinckx, Jan van Buken** (Pl. 779), **Abraham Genoels** (Pls. 817, 826) who was in Antwerp from 1672 to 1674, **Antoon Goubau** (Pls. 614, 775, 776), **Pieter van Bredael** (Pl. 778), **Gaspar de Witte** whose *Landscape with fortune teller in the Roman Campagna* (Pl. 781) was painted in Antwerp in 1667 from drawings made twenty years earlier in Rome, by **de Witte's** pupil **Cornelis Huysmans** (who worked with **Jacques d'Arthois**) and by **Jan Baptist Huysmans** (Pl. 825) Antwerp Master in 1677. Wooded landscapes were painted by **Jacques d'Arthois** (Pls. 686, 710, 736) who was imprisoned for debt at forty-five in 1658, provided Brussels, S. Gudule, with a *Landscape with Holy Family in Flight* in 1664 and was still working in Soignes forest at the end of the period; by **Lucas Achtschellinck, Daniel van Heil** (Pls. 709, 713, 714) and **Ignatius van der Stock** (Pl. 738) who all painted such landscapes with small religious figures for Brussels S. Gudule; by **François Coppens** who worked for Brussels Notre Dame de la Chapelle; by **Renier Megan** of Brussels (a pupil of **Leo van Heil**) till he left for Vienna in 1670; and by **Jan Baptiste van Meunincxhove** who worked with two monks **Donatien van den Bogaerde** and **Balthasar d'Hooghe** for the Abbaye des Dunes. **Gillis Neyts** painted landscapes with towns and both flat and mountainous landscapes with trees and river valleys. **Lucas van Uden** (Pls. 561, 566, 567, 602) was probably active till he died over seventy about 1672. Wooded landscapes with fords and streams as rural setting for large genre figures were painted by **Jan Siberechts** in Antwerp till he left for England in 1672; **Siberechts** owes something to **Jacques d'Arthois** (Pl. 736) and **Jan (Velvet) Brueghel** (Pl. 482) in his *Market cart with animal at a ford* (Pl. 790) but the landscape here with its effects of light anticipates the naturalism of early nineteenth-century rural pieces such as those reproduced by **Eugène Joseph Verboeckhoven** (Pl. 895) and **Adolphe Engel** (Pl. 896). Village landscapes with small figures recalling **Jan (Velvet) Brueghel** (Pls. 467, 481-3) were painted by the able and versatile **Pieter Gysels** (Pl. 799).

The genre figures in the various types of landscape were often inserted by some figure painter; and in many cases the figures are the conventional merrymakers shown here in the *Market outside an Italian town* by **Pieter van Bredael** (Pl. 778). But sometimes the figure painter was a personal artist. **Pieter Bout** (Pls. 796), for example, who is known to have collaborated with **Adriaen van Baudewyns** (Pl. 815), gives us merrymakers in his *Skating scene* (Pl. 797) as vividly observed as the merrymakers in **Jacob Grimmer's** *Outskirts of Antwerp* (Pl. 430) painted a century before. **Jan Siberechts** seems to have painted both the landscape and figures in his pictures and was very distinctive in his treatment of the figures; thus in *Peasant girls at a ford* (Pl. 791) and *Peasant girls with cart and cattle at a ford* (Pl. 792) he invites us to inspect his peasant girls at close quarters and to take them seriously as individual humans, thus proclaiming his descent from **Pieter Aertsen** (Pls. 356, 360) and **Joachim Beuckelaer** (Pl. 399); in one of his realistic farm scenes he portrays a woman examining her child's hair (Pl. 788) and elsewhere in the picture he sets lambs trotting behind a juvenile farm hand (Pl. 789) as prettily as the **Ursula Legend Master** set a barking dog behind the messenger (Pl. 74). Others painting peasant genre in this period were **David Ryckaert III** (Pls. 646, 705) who died under fifty in 1661, **Simon van Douw** who painted in that year (perhaps in Holland) a *Horseman and peasant girl with cattle at a ford*, **Teniers** who was seventy when the period ended, **Juliaen Teniers the younger** (Pl. 681), **Thomas van Apshoven** who died about 1665, **Abraham Teniers** who died in 1670, **Matthys van Helmont, Gillis van Tilborgh, Vincent Malo** (Pl. 615) who died of apoplectic rage at an insult in 1668 and **Guilliam van Herp** who took bits and pieces from both **Jordaens** and **Teniers** and worked till 1677. Curiosities of the time are oriental landscapes with camel caravans by **Nicolas Ryckx** of Bruges who went (like **Michael Sweerts** (Pl. 768)) to Palestine and was back by 1667.

Some artists revealed the old affections for panoramas, town views and other topographic pieces. **Jan Baptist Bonnecroy** painted a *Panorama of Antwerp and the Scheldt* with varied activities in the foreground in the tradition of **Jacob Grimmer** (Pl. 430), **Hans Bol** (Pl. 431) and **Jan Wildens** (Pl. 629); **Gillis Neyts** made a water-colour *Panorama of Brussels*; **Guillaume van Schoor** portrayed the Hôtel de Nassau in Brussels with its formal gardens and adjacent street (Pl. 760); **Teniers** portrayed his own 'Dry Toren' château (Pl. 707); and **Theodore van Heil** son of **Daniel van Heil** (Pls. 713, 714) recalled his father's conflagrations in a *Fire in the Brussels Palace 1674* where peasants in the foreground rush desperately to a fountain with their buckets. Among the town views **Jan Baptist van Meunincxhove** painted picturesque views in Bruges; **Adam van der Meulen** the Place du Grand Sablon in Brussels (Pl. 759)—already seen here in *The 1615 Procession of the maidens dowered by the Infanta Isabella* (Pl. 514) by **Antoine Sallaert**; **Erasmus de Bie** records the Calvary in the Antwerp Place de Meir (Pl. 765) which is seen from another angle in the picture reproduced (Pl. 785) by **Nicolaas van Eyck**; and all these pictures continue the tradition of the street scenes seen through windows in the works shown by the **London Virgin with a Firescreen Painter** (Pl. 39) and other fifteenth-century artists and of the town views by the **Alkmaar Master** (Pls. 182, 183), **Pieter Jansz Pourbus** (Pls. 336, 337), **Pieter Bruegel** (Pls. 369, 370, 382) and **Denis van Alsloot** (Pl. 513A).

Of the painters of church interiors **Peeter Neeffs the elder** (Pls. 649, 650) died about 1660, **Frans Francken III** in 1667 and **Peeter Neeffs the younger** about 1657. **Anton Gheringh**, Antwerp Master in 1662, seems to have specialized in pictures of the Antwerp Jesuit church and to have died in great poverty in 1668 after painting the fine example here reproduced (Pl. 782) where **Rubens'** *S. Ignatius Loyola healing the possessed* is seen on the high altar and some of the ceiling panels produced by the **Rubens** atelier are discernible through the upper arches on the right. **Wilhelm Schubert van Ehrenberg**, who painted the same church from the same angle (Pl. 783) in 1667 and an *Interior of Malines S. Rombout* in 1673, died about 1676; and **W. de Smet** painted *The Interior of Louvain S. Pierre* in 1667.

There was still a demand for naval and military pieces which were produced in considerable numbers. Among the marine painters **Jan Verhuyck** of Malines painted a series of works called *Naval combat*; **Gaspar van Eyck** (Pl. 703) lived till 1673; **Jan Peeters** (Pl. 691) lived till approximately 1677; **Catherina Peeters** who signed a *Naval combat* in 1657 was still living in the middle seventies; **Hendrik van Minderhout,** painter of the *Port of Bruges* with sailors perched perilously in the rigging of the ships and an elegant company arriving by coach in the foreground (Pl. 793), was Bruges Master at thirty in 1662, moved to Antwerp in 1672 and gave a *Levantine port* to Antwerp Academy in 1675; and **Peter van der Velde** who painted *The burning of the English fleet off Chatham,* and sold many marines to the dealer Forchoudt for export to Vienna, also worked in Antwerp through the period. Military scenes, including sieges, were drawn by **Anton Crussens** who produced an *Attack on Valenciennes* in 1656 and by **Jacques van Werden** active from early in the period onwards. Military pieces were also painted by **Adam van der Meulen** (Pl. 737) in Brussels before he left for Paris about 1661, by **Jan Verhuyck, Alexander Casteels, Pauwels Casteels, Peeter Snayers** (Pls. 627, 700, 701) who lived till the middle sixties and **Lambert de Hondt** (Pl. 699) who also lived till approximately 1665. **Robert van den Hoecke,** represented here in another aspect (Pl. 711), painted *Bivouacs* with numerous figures in the sixties and died in 1668; and **Simon van Douw** painted *Cavalry skirmishes* and *Combats with Turks* till approximately 1677. Many pictures of this kind were sold to dealers for export; the dealer Forchoudt for example bought two dozen *Military combats* and as many *Naval combats* from **Jan Verhuyck** in the middle sixties and he exported scores of battle pieces by **Alexander Casteels** and **Pauwels Casteels** to his Vienna branch which also received from him seventy-seven battle pieces and thirty-three sieges (in watercolour) by various artists in one consignment in 1667. Guard room pieces were also still painted; and **Gillis van Tilborgh** signed an example in 1669.

The animal painting of the time appears in the military pieces, in hunting and sporting pictures and in other works. Horsemarkets in the tradition of **Sebastiaan Vrancx** (Pl. 532) were painted by **Simon van Douw** (mostly in Holland); **Izaak van Oosten** may have painted more *Garden of Eden* scenes like the one reproduced here (Pl. 584) between 1656 and his death at forty-eight in 1661; animals and birds were painted by **Jan Sloots** of Malines till he left for Italy sometime in the period; and sporting dogs and birds by **Jan van den Hecke** back from Italy by 1659, by **Jan Fyt** (Pls. 719, 733) till he died at fifty in 1661, by **Nicasius Bernaerts** till he returned to Paris in the early sixties, by **Peeter Boel** till he went to Paris in 1668, by **David de Coninck**—whose *Hawk and dogs attacking water fowl* (Pl. 734) is clearly influenced by **Fyt**—till he left for Italy in 1670, by **Ferdinand van Kessel** and by **Jan van Kessel the elder** (Pl. 732) who died in 1679. Mock genre pieces with monkeys instead of humans were painted by **Teniers, Jan van Kessel the elder** and **Abraham Teniers.** Hunting pieces, exported in numbers to Vienna, seem to have followed the tradition of **Frans Snyders** (Pl. 635) who died at seventy-eight in 1657 and **Paul de Vos** (Pl. 636) who died at eighty-two in 1678. Conventional cattle, sheep and goats appear in the Italianate landscapes by **Pieter van Bredael** (Pl. 778) and others. **Hieronymus Janssens** shows a formula for greyhounds in his high-life genre scenes (Pls. 730, 731), **Adam van der Meulen** gives us various lap dogs of the gentry and a large dog dragging three women in a cart (Pl. 759); **Erasmus de Bie,** who painted many market scenes with animals, gives us dogs and horses in his *Antwerp: Place de Meir* (Pl. 765); and **Jan Siberechts** shows his almost nineteenth-century naturalism in horses, dogs and cattle (Pls. 787–92).

Of the still-life pictures, much collected and exported, compositions with dead game and trophies of the chase were painted by **Guilliam Gabron, Jacobus Biltius** and **Pieter Gysels**; and they were also produced by the painters of sporting subjects including **Jan Fyt, Peeter Boel, David de Coninck** and **Nicasius Bernaerts**. The veteran **Alexander Adriaenssen** signed a fish piece reproduced here (Pl. 653) at seventy-three in 1660; and fish pieces were also painted by **Frans van Cuyck de Mierhop**. Tables bearing fruit, vegetables and other food and vessels were painted by **Jacob Foppens van Es** (Pls. 557, 558) who lived till 1666, by **Joris van Son** (Pls. 743, 745) an artist of delicate talent who delighted in the tints of oysters and peeled lemons and died at forty-four in 1667, by **Alexander Coosemans** (Pl. 744) and **Cornelis de Heem** (Pl. 748) who were both fond of introducing watches, by **Jan Davidsz de Heem** who was over seventy in 1680, **Cornelis Mahu, Jan Pauwel Gillemans** (one of many who inserted lobsters), by **Frans Ijkens** (Pl. 695), **Theodor Aenvanck** (Pl. 747) and **J. D. Coosemas** (Pl. 749) of whom hardly anything is known but who seems to have imitated **Joris van Son**.

In flower painting the charming style of **Daniel Seghers** (Pls. 692, 757), who died at seventy-one in 1661, was continued by **Andries Bosman** (Pl. 756) canon of Antwerp S. Jacques from 1657 till 1664 when he went to Rome, by **Gaulterus Gysaerts** (Pl. 755) who entered a Franciscan friary in 1674, by **Hieronymus Galle,** by **Jan Philip van Thielen** (Pl. 754) who died in 1667 and by his daughters **Maria Theresa** and **Anna Maria**. A newcomer **Nicolas van Verendael** who lived in poverty 'renfermé vis-à-vis des fleurs qu'il copiait' may have painted before 1680 the exquisite *Flowers round an antique bust* (Pl. 758) which achieves a Surrealist poetry; and he seems to have begun in the sixties by painting flowers into compositions by other artists as we know of one picture where the kitchen still-life was painted by **Christiaan Luyckx** (Pl. 696) and the figures by **Teniers,** and another with figures by **Jan Boeckhorst**. Flowerpieces and garlands were also painted by **Gerard Goswin** (in Liège from 1660), by **Jan van den Hecke,** by **Joris van Son,** by his pupil **Frans van Everbroeck** and by **Gaspar Pieter Verbruggen the elder** whose *Vase of flowers with allegoric figures* (Pl. 810) may have been known to Sir Joshua Reynolds when he designed *The Graces decorating Hymen*. Garlands of fruit in the tradition of **Frans Snyders** (Pl. 554) and **Adriaen van Utrecht** (Pl. 694) were painted by **Jan Davidsz de Heem**, and fruit and flowerpieces, sometimes with butterflies and insects by **Joris van Son,** by **Abraham Brueghel** (Pls. 746, 807) till he left for Rome in 1670, by **Jan van Kessel the elder** (Pl. 732), **Ferdinand van Kessel, François van Aken, Leo van Heil** and **Elias van den Broeck** Antwerp Master in 1673 who worked for some years on a salary for the painter-dealer **Bartholomeus Floquet**.

The 'Vanitas' motif, which goes back to the fifteenth century and can be traced in my plates from the **Frankfort Master** (Pl. 209) and the **Amsterdam Cadaver Painter** (Pl. 212) to the **Bruges Death and the Miser Painter** (Pl. 236) and **Marinus van Reymerswael,** (Pl. 237) was common in this period in a form described by Houbraken at the end of the century as a conglomeration of books, letters, hour-glasses, death's heads and other objects which might strike terror by flickering lamplight into 'een vreesagtig of bygeloovig mensch'; such pieces were painted by **Pieter van der Willigen,** by **Cornelis Norbertus Gysbrechts** (Pl. 802) who was Antwerp Master in 1659 and later went to Denmark, by **Jan Davidsz de Heem,** and by **de Heem's** pupil **Alexander Coosemans** whose *Vanitas* (Pl. 800) inscribed '... nihil mortem vincit ...' contains a crown and rich vessels as well as an hour-glass, a dying candle, a crucifix and a death's head; the same moral, without the death's head, was suggested by **Peeter Boel** and **Guilliam Gabron** in compositions with heaped-up globes, mitres, turbans, gold and silver statues and so on in a palace loggia or hall; and we get the 'Vanitas' motif in its simplest form in the picture reproduced here by the **Hague Vanitas Painter** (Pl. 801).

Among the painters of gallery interiors **Frans Francken III** (Pl. 728) was available till 1667, **Cornelis de Baellieur** (Pls. 645, 727) till 1671, and those available through the period included **Teniers** (Pls. 724, 725, 726), **Gillis van Tilborgh** and **Gonzales Coques**. The example reproduced (Pl. 773) by **Gonzales Coques** is a document of major interest because the pictures shown are all by painters working about 1670-71 when the interior was composed as a gift to a lawyer who had rendered some service to the Painters' Guild or the new Academy; what we see is thus an invented collection like the one put together by the **Hague Studio of Apelles Painter** (Pl. 580); but in this case most of the pieces are signed or monogrammed by the individual artist who either painted them into the picture or certified them in that way as reputable copies; there are two religious subjects—a small *Lamentation* monogrammed by **Jan van den Hecke** and a large unsigned *Christ and the Centurion* in a style recalling *The Pool of Bethesda* (Pl. 677) by **Peter van Lint,** with foreground figures silhouetted in the manner of the *Allegory in honour of the birth of a prince* (Pl. 751) by **Jan Ijkens**; the mythologies include *Sleeping nymphs* by **Jan de Duyts**, a *Triumph of Bacchus* by **Jan Cossiers** (Pl. 640), *The Four Seasons* by **Theodor Boeyermans**, a *Persephone and Aesculapius*(?) with an almost illegible signature, possibly that of **Charles Emmanuel Biset,** allegorical figures of *Earth*, monogrammed E.Q. (**Erasmus** or **Jan Erasmus Quellinus**(?)) and *Water* monogrammed T.B. (**Theodor Boeyermans** (?)), a large unsigned *Judgement of Paris*, a *Hero and the Naiads* also unsigned, and a *Venus and Adonis* added in 1706 by **Gaspar Jacob van Opstal** who was about sixteen in 1670; the Italianate landscapes, with shepherds, shepherdesses, cattle, sheep, goats and so on are by **Pieter van Bredael** (Pl. 778), **Antoon Goubau** (Pls. 775, 776) home apparently on a visit from Rome, and the versatile **Jan van den Hecke** who is seen in several such pieces, including one with men and horses bathing, and may also have contributed the floral swags and ornaments; **Pieter Spierinckx** is represented by a village fair with actors on a stage, and the marine painter **Jan Peeters** (Pl. 691) by a ship entering rocky narrows in a storm; the still-life pieces include a study of butterflies and insects in the style of **Jan van Kessel the elder** (Pl. 732), a composition with dead game on a block of stone with a sporting gun and game bag by **Pieter Gysels** and a large unsigned arrangement of fruit and flowers disposed round a fountain in the manner of **Gysels**' picture reproduced here (Pl. 806); there is a large unsigned boar hunt in the tradition of **Frans Snyders** (Pl. 635) and **Paul de Vos**; and the architecture may be the work of **Wilhelm Schubert van Ehrenberg** (Pl. 783).

Despite the wars the glamour of French culture led some Belgian artists to collaborate with the invaders and a number were residents or visitors in Paris as before. **Charles de Somme** of Brussels, fruit and flower painter, was 'peintre de la reine' from about 1657 till he died aged thirty-six in 1673; **Jacques Fouquier** (Pl. 563) died in poverty at seventy-nine in 1659 and his funeral was paid for by his former pupil the marine painter **Mathieu van Plattenberg** (Platte-Montagne); **Wallerant Vaillant** (Pl. 770) was brought to Paris from Frankfort by the Comte de Gramont in 1659 and had favour in Court circles for the next four years as painter of portraits, genre and trompe l'oeil still-life and also as pastellist and mezzotinter. His half brother **Bernard Vaillant** was there at the same time. **Charles Emmanuel Biset** (Pl. 784) came from Malines to Paris at the end of the sixteen-fifties and was employed by Court circles till he left for Antwerp in 1661; **Jacob van Oost the younger** (Pls. 769, 771) came at the same time from Bruges, aged about twenty, and stayed for two years. **Adam van der Meulen** who seems to have arrived about 1661 was soon employed by

Charles Le Brun at the Gobelins and made a Court Painter with a stipend and lodgings in the factory; his *Hunting party with coach* (Pl. 766) may represent Louis XIV and be one of his earliest French pictures; as mentioned earlier he accompanied the King on the Flemish and Dutch invasions as official painter of the campaigns and the Louvre has pictures titled *The King's army before Tournai, Entry of Louis XIV and the Queen into Douai, The march to Courtrai, Entry of Louis XIV and the Queen into Arras, Battle near Bruges Canal* and others from the 1667 campaign, *The Surrender of Dôle* from the Franche Comté invasion, the *Passage of the Rhine* and *Arrival of the King at the siege of Maestricht* and others from the war with Holland, and also the *Capture of Valenciennes in 1677.* **Adam van der Meulen** was joined soon after 1665 by **Adriaen Baudewyns** (Pl. 815) who was then about twenty-two and provided landscape backgrounds for the Gobelins and married **Adam van der Meulen's** sister; and **François Duchatel** after finishing his record of the *Ghent Pageant of Allegiance* (Pl. 777) also came for a time to work with him. **Van der Meulen** was elected a member of the French Académie des Beaux Arts in 1673. Other Belgians who were members in this period included **Mathieu van Plattenberg, Gerard Goswin, Abraham Genoels, Jean François (Francisque) Millet, Ferdinand Voet, Philippe Vleughels, Philippe de Champaigne, Nicasius Bernaerts, Bertholet Flémalle** and **Pierre de Bourguignon.** Of these **Mathieu van Plattenberg** died in 1660; **Gerard Goswin** was Professor in the Academy in 1659 and returned to his native Liège in 1660; **Abraham Genoels** (Pls. 817, 826) arrived aged nineteen in 1659, painted landscape backgrounds for Le Brun's 'Alexander' tapestries, was sent by Louis XIV with **Adriaen Baudewyns** (Pl. 815) to draw Mariemont Castle in 1669 and returned to Antwerp in 1672. **Jean François (Francisque) Millet,** born in Antwerp, went to Paris, aged seventeen, in 1659, worked there with **Genoels** (who extolled his exceptional visual memory) copied pictures by Poussin (then owned by the banker Jabach) and made so great a reputation as a painter of picturesque landscapes with figures that his madness and death in 1679 were said to be due to poison administered by a rival. **Ferdinand Voet,** portrait painter, was elected to the Academy when he was twenty-five in 1664 but was soon after expelled for some technical breach of the rules. **Philippe Vleughels,** launched earlier in the Flemish club 'La Chasse', as related in my last chapter, became a naturalized Frenchman in this period and painted pictures for the Carmelites of S. Denis and for Parisian churches. **Philippe de Champaigne** continued in Court favour despite his contacts with the Jansenists from the outset of the period till his death at seventy-two in 1674; his portrait of the Jansenist *Isaac Le Maistre de Saci* is dated 1658; his best known and most impressive picture the *Mother Catherine Agnes Arnauld of Port Royal and the artist's daughter Sister Catherine de Suzanne* (Pl. 742) bears an inscription stating that this daughter was cured of paralysis by the prayers of the Port Royal nuns in 1662; his *Louis XIV conferring the Order of the Saint Esprit on the Duc d'Anjou* (Pl. 750) was commissioned by the King in 1665. **Nicasius Bernaerts** was a member of the Academy in 1663, provided Le Brun with cartoons of animals for the Gobelins from 1667, had the French animal painter François Desportes as his pupil about 1673 and died in poverty in 1678. **Bertholet Flémalle,** who paid a second visit to Paris from Liège in 1670, produced there an *Allegory of Religion protecting France* for the Tuileries and then went back to Liège where his pupil **Jean Guillaume Carlier** who painted religious pictures and had been with him in Paris is said to have died of distress on learning that Liège had been surrendered to the French in 1675; and **Pierre de Bourguignon** who came from Namur was a member as a portraitist by 1671 when he painted *Mlle. de Montpensier as Minerva* as his reception piece. Others who went to Paris were **Pieter Spierinckx** whose Italianate landscapes with genre figures and designs for tapestry found favour with the King in the early sixties; **Peeter Boel** who arrived about 1668, worked with Le Brun at the Gobelins, became a Court Painter and continued his animals pieces and 'Vanitas' and other still-life compositions till he died in 1674; **Jan van Cleef** who completed some tapestry cartoons ordered by the King from **Gaspar de Crayer**, brought them from Ghent to Paris in the seventies and was fêted by French painters and the Court; and **Peter Rysbraeck** painter of Italianate landscapes who arrived from London about 1679. In 1670 **Jacob van Oost the younger** (Pls. 769, 771) paid a second visit to France and married in Lille where he provided S. Étienne with an *Infant Jesus on the knees of the Virgin showing angels the instruments of the passion* in 1680.

There were also Belgian painters at work in England, Holland, Denmark, Central Europe, Spain and Italy.

In England **Jeremias van der Eyden** became drapery assistant to Lely after 1658 and then settled in Northamptonshire where he painted portraits for the Earls of Rutland and Gainsborough and others. **Jan Baptist Gaspers** known in this period as 'Lely's Baptist' painted draperies and furnished 'postures' for Lely's Restoration portraits and painted *Charles II* and *Catherine of Braganza*. **Prosper Henricus Lankrink** continued as Lely's assistant for landscape backgrounds, flowers and other accessories and also painted portraits and pictures titled *Nymph bathing her feet* and *Narcissus*; and Vertue records him as 'not only a good bottle companion and excellent company but also a great favourite with the ladies through his exceeding complaisance and comely appearance'. **Remigius van Leemput** copied the figures of *Henry VIII, Jane Seymour, Henry VII* and *Elizabeth of York* from Holbein's Whitehall fresco in 1668, was ordered by the courts to surrender to the Crown the *Charles I on horseback* by **Van Dyck**—which he had bought at the Commonwealth sales as related—and died here in 1675. **Cornelis de Neve** painted *Elias Ashmole* (whose name lives in the Oxford Ashmolean Museum) in 1664 before returning to Antwerp where he died in 1678. The newcomers included **Jacob Huysmans, Peter Rysbraeck, Pierre van der Meulen, Jean Baptiste van den Lantscroon, Balthasar van Lemens, Daniel Boone, Jan Siberechts, Edouard Dubois** and **Simon Dubois**. Of these **Jacob Huysmans**, pupil in Antwerp of **Frans Wouters** (Pl. 667), came soon after the Restoration, became the Queen's favourite portraitist and painted an altarpiece in her chapel in S. James's; Pepys wrote in his diary in 1664: 'To see some pictures by one Huysmans . . . which is said to exceed Lely; and indeed there is both of the Queen's and Maids of Honour, particularly Mrs. Stuart's [Frances Stuart, Duchess of Richmond] in a buff doublet like a soldier, as good pictures I think as ever I saw. The Queen is drawn in one like a shepherdess, in the other like S. Catherine, most like and most admirably'—and I reproduce the delightful *Queen Catherine of Braganza as a shepherdess with cupids* (Pl. 752) referred to in this passage. This **Jacob Huysmans** was a witness at the trial of the presumed Catholic murderers of Sir Edmund Berry Godfrey, the Magistrate who had received depositions from Titus Oates; and the Titus Oates affair affected **Peter Rysbraeck** who came to London about 1674 with the French painter Nicolas de Largillière and returned to Paris with Largillière as a result of the anti-Catholic disturbances about 1679. **Pierre van der Meulen** painter of military pieces (and brother of **Adam van der Meulen**) came here from Brussels, where he had worked as a sculptor, in 1670 and remained till the end of the period. **Jean Baptiste van den Lantscroon** came from Malines in 1677 and worked from 1678 at Windsor under the Italian Antonio Verrio who was painting large decorations there with mythologies and allegories in the baroque style. **Balthasar van Lemens,** painter of mythologies, came from Antwerp soon after 1660 and worked chiefly as assistant to other painters and as designer for engravers;

Daniel Boone, an Antwerp pasticheur of **Brouwer's** type of peasant genre, arrived in 1666 from Amsterdam, where he had been working for ten years, and remained here. **Jan Siberechts** (Pls. 787-92) was brought to London by the Duke of Buckingham in 1672 and continued here his rural landscapes with peasant figures; he also painted river views and prospects of noblemen's estates and mansions including a *View of Longleat* painted in 1675; and he was still at work here in 1680. **Wallerant Vaillant** (Pl. 770) may have come for a year about 1664; **Francisque Millet** came for a while at a date unknown; **Eduard Dubois** came on from Holland at the end of the period; and his brother **Simon Dubois** came at the same time probably from Rome.

In Holland the Antwerp-born **Jan Frans Soolmaker** (Pl. 780) was a pupil at twenty of Nicolas Berchem (the famous Dutch painter of Italianate landscapes with cattle, goats and so on) by 1658 and seems to have stayed there till he left for Italy about 1655. The genre painter **Jan van Pee** worked as pasticheur for dealers in Amsterdam and Leyden till he escaped to Antwerp where he kept himself on a visit by making copies of pictures by **Rubens** and **Van Dyck** which deceived the experts. **Adriaen van Nieulandt** (Pls. 515, 647) died in Amsterdam aged seventy-one in 1658; **Adam Willaerts** (Pl. 688) died in Utrecht at eighty-seven in 1664; **Wallerant Vaillant** (Pl. 770) settled in Amsterdam in 1665 and died there in 1677; **Jacques Vaillant** visited Holland after 1666 on his way to Berlin; **Bernard Vaillant** worked there from 1664 and drew delegates to the Peace Conference at Nymwegen in 1678. **Michael Sweerts** (Pl. 768) went in 1661 from Brussels to Amsterdam where he had success as a portrait painter till he joined a French missionary society and followed the Bishop of Heliopolis to Palestine in 1662; **Simon Dubois** was in Haarlem in 1661 and then seems to have gone to Italy; his brother **Eduard Dubois** was in Holland from 1662 till the end of the period when he came to England as related. **Simon van Douw,** already recorded as a painter of military pieces, horse markets and other outdoor genre scenes, worked at Middelburg and other places in the middle fifties and sixties; and **Gerard de Lairesse** (Pls. 813, 814) after stabbing a girl in Liège fled to Bois-le-Duc at twenty-three in 1664 and then settled in Amsterdam where he painted an *Allegory of Virtue* in 1670 and other allegories, mythologies and 'history' pieces.

In Denmark **Cornelis Norbertus Gysbrechts** was Court Painter to the King from about 1670; he specialized, as noted, in *Vanitas* still-life pieces with a death's head, and also in trompe l'oeil arrangements of objects disposed on a flat board; and the aesthetic of the examples reproduced here (Pls. 802-5) anticipates the flat-pattern Cubist compositions of the early twentieth century where the board or canvas worked on was frankly taken as the most distant plane and forms in low relief were disposed on the surface. **Gysbrechts** seems to have remained in Denmark and he probably died there after 1675.

In Central Europe **Hendrik van der Borcht the elder** died in Frankfort at seventy-seven in 1660; **Wallerant Vaillant** (Pl. 770), who went from Holland to Heidelberg and Frankfort before his Parisian visit, painted in Frankfort a trompe l'oeil still-life of letters disposed in a letter rack (in the manner of the pictures reproduced here by **Gysbrechts** (Pls. 803-805)) and portraits of the Emperor Leopold I and notables at the Emperor's coronation ceremonies in 1658; and he met there Prince Rupert who collaborated with him in the new technique of mezzotint. **Jan Thomas (van Ypern)** moved from Mainz to Vienna at the outset of the period, painted there the *Archduke Leopold Wilhelm with a red sash,* became Court Painter to the Emperor whom he accompanied to Frankfort for the coronation, painted an allegoric *Leopold I receiving the homage of his provinces* in 1663 and died in Vienna in 1678. **Jan Baptist van Ruel,** pupil of **Jan Thomas** in Mainz, painted a *S. Elizabeth* for Würzburg Cathedral in 1659 and a *Legend of S. Cunegund* for the Prince Bishop of Bamberg in 1667. **Frans de Hamilton**, painter of animals, still-life with game, and compositions with flora, reptiles and insects (like **Leo van Heil** and **Jan van Kessel the elder**) was in Cleve, Potsdam and Hanover in the sixties and seventies. **Frans de Neve the elder** Antwerp painter of religious subjects, mythologies, landscapes with pastoral figures and portraits, was in Salzburg, after Italy, by 1672. **Michiel Engel Immenraet** of Antwerp was in Idstein (Hesse-Nassau) working for Count John of Idstein from 1673 till 1675 and seems then to have gone to Holland. **Victor Honoré Janssens** (Pls. 812, 827) went from Brussels to Flensburg at the end of the period and became Court Painter of the Duke of Holstein. **Jacques Vaillant** was Court Painter to Frederick William, the 'Great Elector', in Berlin in 1672 and visited Vienna to paint the Emperor's portrait. **Frans Luyckx,** who was confirmed as Court Painter by Leopold I, made a portrait of the Archduke Leopold Wilhelm, accompanied him to Strasbourg, drew him on his death-bed in 1662 and died himself in Vienna in 1668; and **Canon van der Baren** (Pl. 675) became Court Painter to the Emperor after the Archduke's death. Others in Vienna in these years were **Nicolas van Hoy** who painted pictures for churches and was patronized by the Emperor and died in 1679, **Jan de Herdt** painter of 'history', genre and religious subjects, **Renier Megan** landscape painter from Brussels, who was Court Painter by 1670 and **Jan Erasmus Quellinus** (Pl. 821) who visited Vienna about 1680 and became a Court Painter.

In Spain **Ignacio Raeth** completed his paintings in the Madrid Jesuit College about 1658 and left soon after for Germany or Flanders. **Cornelis Schut III**, with Murillo, Francisco de Herrera, J. Valdés Leal and other Spanish painters, was a founder member in 1660 of the Seville Academy where the students were fined for swearing or talking of anything not pertaining to their studies; as demonstrating professor in this academy **Schut** used nude models though these, as noted, were not then permitted in the Antwerp art schools; and he painted some pictures for churches including a *S. Theresa* for the Cathedral in Cadiz. **David Teniers III** was in Spain for some five years from 1661 and probably worked for churches and made tapestry designs; **Adriano Rodriguez** died in the Madrid Jesuit College in 1669; and **Anton van de Pere** worked for the Madrid Church of S. Martin and painted a *S. Theresa* in 1676. **Jan van Kessel the younger** was in Madrid by 1677 at the age of twenty and in that year he is said to have accompanied the Queen Mother Mariana in her exile at Toledo; his brilliant *Family in a garden with portrait of the artist at a window* (Pl. 808) with its fearless portraiture, its elegance and decorative conceits, was painted three years later, and the figure of the servant at the fountain is said to be a caricature of Charles II—though this seems unlikely as he became, soon after, a Court Painter to the king.

As always there were Flemish painters who visited Italy and some who remained there; and the old lure of Rome still competed successfully with the new lure of Paris. The Flemish colony's club the 'Bent' was now very much frequented; and in describing an initiation feast when newcomers were given their 'Bentnamen', i.e. nicknames, Houbraken commented, 'Ik geef den Lezer te denken, hoe veel Wyn er op dit Bentfeest wel over de lippen gestort is, en hoe veel spys door de tanden vermaalt eer de kakebeenen vermoeit waren.' The painters were of many categories and came from all parts of Belgium. **Henri Herregouts** of Malines was there in the fifties till 1661; the Liégeois **Jean Gilles Delcour** arrived at twenty-five in 1657 to work with Andrea Sacchi and stayed for some years; **Gilles Hallet** another Liégeois came early in the period, remained there, and provided pictures for various Roman churches; **Jan Erasmus Quellinus** (Pl. 821) arrived aged twenty-six in 1660, after visiting Venice, Florence and Naples, was nicknamed **'Sederboom'** at the 'Bent' festivity and returned to Antwerp the next year; **Frans de Neve the elder** joined the 'Bent' in 1660, remained till 1666 and went thereafter, as noted, to Salzburg; **Andries Bosman** (Pl. 756) arrived from Antwerp in 1664 and remained; **Jan van Buken** (Pl. 779) came in the early sixties and probably remained some years; **Lievin Cruyl**, architectural draughtsman from Ghent, drew the Forum and other buildings about 1666; and **Jacob van Oost the younger** who arrived from Paris about 1662 went back to his native Bruges either before or after painting his *Children drawing from a cast* (Pl. 771) in 1666. **Jan Baptist Herregouts** from Termonde who arrived in the sixties was back in Antwerp by 1673. **Jan Frans Soolmaker** came from Holland perhaps via Portugal about 1665 and settled in Rome painting Italianate landscapes with shepherds, cattle and so forth like the *Meeting with Jacob and Esau* (Pl. 780); the animals and figures in some of his pictures are conventional but sometimes he shows a keener interest and painted cattle in the spirit of **Jan Siberechts** (Pl. 790) and in a technique anticipating the Englishman James Ward. **Nicolas la Fabrique** of Namur seems to have arrived by 1670 and to have stayed some years. **Antoon Goubau** painted *Artists drawing antiques in the Roman Campagna* (Pl. 775) in 1662 and the *Piazza Navona, Rome* (Pl. 776) in 1680. **Ferdinand Voet**, who frescoed the 'Bent's' headquarters with portraits of the members, had come on from Paris, painted Clement IX and Cardinal Azzolini and became Court Painter to Christina of Sweden before being expelled from Rome for an unknown reason in 1678 and taking refuge in Turin. **David de Coninck** (Pl. 734) came in 1670 received his 'Bent' name of **Ramelaer** (Buck-rabbit) and was later arrested and interrogated by the Inquisition as the presumed ringleader of alleged heretical practices in the colony. **Abraham Brueghel**, initiated in the 'Bent' in 1670, became a member of the Accademia di San Luca the same year and painted, before leaving for Naples, the *Still-life with pomegranates and white grapes* (Pl. 746), a *Flower garland round a picture by Carlo Maratta* and the *Young lady picking grapes* (Pl. 807) which anticipates a picture called *Young lady with flowers by a trellis* painted two centuries later by Gustave Courbet. His brother **Jan Baptist Brueghel** was also in Rome in the seventies and went with him to Naples about 1680. **David de Coninck, Abraham Brueghel** and one **Gillis du Mont** nicknamed 'Brybergh' were 'Bent' sponsors for **Abraham Genoels** (Pls. 817, 826) who came via Venice and Bologna aged thirty-four in 1674, was nicknamed **'Archimedes'** and stayed for the rest of the period making drawings of ruins, painting Campagna landscapes and working for Cardinal Rospigliosi. Other newcomers in 1674 were **Anthoni Schoonjans** painter of religious subjects, history and portraits, then about twenty and nicknamed **'Parrhasius'**, who also stayed for the rest of the period, and **Robertus de Mol** (son of **Pieter van Mol**) who became a member of the Accademia and painted a *Charles II of Spain* for its headquarters. Two painters of religious subjects **Englebert Fisen** and **Sebastiaen van Aken** came respectively from Liège and Malines to work in the studio of Carlo Maratta in the early seventies; and **Simon Dubois**, apart from his visit to Haarlem, seems to have been in Rome till he came to England at the end of the period. Elsewhere in Italy **Jan Miel** (Pl. 772) worked for Duke Charles Emmanuel II of Savoy in Turin from 1658 till he died at sixty-four in 1663; and **Eduard Dubois** worked for the same Duke till about 1661 when he left Italy for Holland. **Robert la Longe** of Brussels worked for churches in Cremona in the seventies; and **Jan Sloots** of Malines was in various parts of Italy and the Tyrol. **Frans Denys** (or **de Nys**) painter of portraits and allegoric pieces who left Antwerp, over forty, in 1656, was Court Painter in Parma to Ranuccio Farnese II and then worked in Mantua for Isabella Clara of Austria till he died in 1670; his son **Jacob Denys** (Pl. 811) who arrived in Italy about 1666 painted religious subjects in Mantua for Isabella Clara and portraits in Florence for Duke

Cosimo III, went to Venice in 1674 and was back in Antwerp about 1679. **Lieven Mehus** of Audenarde, who had been taken young to Italy by his parents and worked in Florence with Pietro da Cortona, was in Florence in these years, painting cabinet pictures and making drawings of outdoor scenes with small figures for the Medici Court and religious subjects for churches in Florence and Prato which were greatly admired by eighteenth-century critics; and **Justus Sutterman,** still in Florence and still painting the Medici family in 1678 when he was eighty-one, was still alive when the period closed. **Pieter de Coster** was still in Venice and may have painted in these years a *Religion presenting the Venetian Republic to the Virgin* traditionally recorded as his work. **Daniel van den Dyck** who had married one of **Nicolas Regnier's** daughters in Venice became Curator of the Duke of Mantua's Gallery in 1658; **Regnier** himself died in Venice approaching eighty in 1667 and **Valentin Le Febre** made a copy of Veronese's *Feast in the house of Simon* presented to Louis XIV by the Signoria in 1665. **Jan de Herdt** was in Brescia from about 1660 till he left for Vienna before 1670. **Cornelis de Wael** moved from Genoa to Rome after 1656 and died there in 1667; his pupil **Jan Lambertsz Houwaert** remained in Genoa and died there in 1668.

CHAPTER XVI

Alexander Farnese (II) 1681-1682;
Marquis de Grana 1682-1685;
Don Francisco Antonio de Agurto
(Marquis de Gastañaga) 1685-1691;
Maximilian Emmanuel, Elector of Bavaria
1692-1700

1681-1700

THE NEW Governor Alexander Farnese II, a vast fat man, portrayed by **Charles Emmanuel Biset,** was unpopular with the Belgians because he paraded a Spanish luxury at a time of national distress when unpaid soldiers were robbing travellers on the highways and many were deserting to the French; and he held office only through 1681 and the first three months of 1682. During his Governorship new combines were begun against Louis XIV who had occupied Strasbourg; the Jansenist Pasquier Quesnel was banished from Paris; the Protestant University of Sedan was suppressed and Pierre Bayle moved to Rotterdam; Dryden published his 'Absalom and Achitophel'; Wren designed Tom Tower for Christ Church, Oxford; Purcell composed his 'Dido and Aeneas' for a girls' school in Chelsea; and the Turks advanced towards Vienna.

In 1682 the Marquis de Grana, a professional diplomat, was sent to replace Farnese with some military reinforcements. He made a stand against indiscipline and tried to relieve the prevalent distresses. Louis XIV moved his court to Versailles and, faced with a coalition of Spain, the Empire, Holland and Sweden against him, made conciliating gestures; Pierre Bayle published his 'Pensées diverses sur la Comète de 1680'; the inhabitants of Vienna were ordered to lay in a year's provisions and pay a one per cent tax on their property against the threat of a Turkish siege; William Penn sailed from Deal in the 'Welcome' with a hundred Quakers to organize his settlement in Pennsylvania; and Colonel Churchill became Baron Churchill of Aymouth. In 1683 Louis XIV married Madame de Maintenon; his troops suddenly invaded Belgium ravaging North Flanders and Brabant; and the Turks who had besieged Vienna for two months were driven off and defeated by Duke Charles V of Lorraine and John III of Poland (Sobieski). In 1684 John Locke, expelled from England for alleged complicity in Shaftesbury's plots, took refuge in Holland; Lord St. Albans commissioned Wren to build St. James' church in Piccadilly; Louis XIV made

344

his enemies agree to the Truce of Ratisbon (Regensburg) which confirmed the occupation of Strasbourg and gave France a chain of Flanders forts, Luxembourg and the Franche Comté; and a member of the Forchoudt firm of art dealers in Antwerp wrote in a letter: 'Times are so bad here that it is impossible to make a penny. Antwerp is like a village; there is hardly anyone to be seen on the Place de Meir' (Pls. 765, 785). In 1685 an altar erected on the Place de Meir and elaborate ceremonies marked the centenary of Parma's capture of Antwerp from the Protestants; Louis XIV revoked the Edict of Nantes; Huguenot refugees began to flock to Holland and England; the Jansenist Pasquier Quesnel joined Antoine Arnauld in Brussels; Charles II of England died confessing himself a Roman Catholic on his death-bed; the Monmouth Rebellion against James II was destroyed by Lord Churchill at Sedgemoor; Judge Jeffreys conducted the Bloody Assize; Anne, now Princess of Denmark, and Lady Churchill her Lady of the Bedchamber began corresponding as 'Mrs. Morley' and 'Mrs. Freeman'; and Don Francisco Antonio de Agurto, better known by his later rank of Marquis de Gastañaga, arrived as Governor of the Netherlands to replace the Marquis de Grana who died at Mariemont in June.

In 1686 Gastañaga made a good impression in his provinces by leaving the Belgians to manage their own affairs; the Kings of Spain and Sweden, the Emperor, William III of Orange, the Electors of Bavaria and Saxony and some other princes formed the League of Augsburg against Louis XIV; and Budapest was taken from the Turks by Charles of Lorraine and Maximilian Emmanuel, Elector of Bavaria. In 1687 at the Diet of Pressburg, the crown of Hungary was made hereditary in the House of Habsburg and formally bestowed on the Emperor's son Prince Joseph then aged nine; Charles of Lorraine and Maximilian Emmanuel defeated the Turks at Mohacz; a Venetian army under Morosini bombarded the Parthenon (then a Turkish powder magazine) and partially destroyed it; Turkish privateers captured eight Dutch and one English ship (with eighty passengers) off the coast of Holland; James II issued the Declaration of Indulgence and turned Magdalen College Oxford into a Roman Catholic seminary; Dryden, converted to Catholicism, published 'The Hind and the Panther' as an apologia; and Lord Churchill began negotiations with the Prince of Orange. In 1688 Maximilian Emmanuel captured Belgrade from the Turks; William of Orange landed with an army near Tor Bay and was joined by the Prince of Denmark and Lord Churchill; Lady Churchill and the Bishop of London smuggled the Princess Anne to Nottingham; James II escaped to France; and Louis XIV went to war with Germany and Holland and built the Grand Trianon for Madame de Maintenon. In 1689 Charles II of Spain married Mariana of Neuburg; Guillaume de Precipiano, a violent anti-Jansenist, became Archbishop of Malines; William and Mary became joint sovereigns of England and Purcell played the organ at the Coronation; James landed with French troops in Ireland where the King's cause was upheld in Londonderry and Enniskillen; William declared war on France and sent Churchill, now Lord Marlborough, with an army into Flanders; and Spanish-Belgian forces defeated a French army at Walcourt (South of Charleroi). In 1690 John Locke, back from Holland, published 'An Essay concerning Human Understanding'; an Anglo-Dutch fleet was defeated by a French fleet off Beachy Head; King William at the head of allied forces won the Battle of the Boyne; Marlborough captured Cork; Patrick Sarsfield held out for James in Limerick; and French troops making mass levies of food and fodder drove back Spanish-Belgian forces between Ghent and Audenarde and marched across country to defeat an allied army at Fleurus (near Namur). In 1691 Louis XIV conducted the siege of Mons in person and entered the town in April; French forces bombarded Liège and Hal, and Marshal Villars defeated the allies near

Leuze (a battle recorded by **Jan Pieter** or **Joris van Bredael**); Lord Marlborough intrigued with James at S. Germain; the Jacobites in Ireland lost the Battle of Aughrim; and the Margrave Louis of Baden defeated the Turks at Slankamen.

In 1692 Maximilian Emmanuel, aged thirty and married to the Emperor's daughter Maria Antonia, arrived in Brussels to replace Gastañaga as Governor; he was greeted with triumphal arches and illuminations as a military hero (as the two Don Johns and the Infante Ferdinand had been greeted) and he brought with him German troops to help the allies and two million florins provided by his Bavarian subjects. Pasquier Quesnel published the first complete edition of his 'Réflexions morales sur le Nouveau Testament', and Maximilian Emmanuel made the Jansensist Ruth d'Ans an almoner to the Electress which much enraged the Jesuits and Archbishop Precipiano. Louis XIV captured Namur and entered there in triumph; King William at the head of an allied army was defeated at Steenkirk; the British navy won the Battle of La Hogue which put an end to French plans for invading England; and Marlborough was dismissed his offices and imprisoned for two months in the Tower. In 1693 the French took Furnes and Dixmude, William was defeated in the Battle of Neerwinden (Landen) where twelve thousand allied troops and eight thousand French were killed; and Maximilian Emmanuel visited the Antwerp Academy, then in financial straits, and granted it new Letters Patent as a gesture of assistance. In 1694 there was indecisive fighting in Belgium; Maximilian Emmanuel married as second wife Thérèse Cunégonde daughter of the King of Poland (Sobieski); Antoine Arnauld died in Brussels leaving Pasquier Quesnel as leader of the Jansenists; Queen Mary died of smallpox and Congreve wrote a memorial ode; and Sir John Houblon, a descendant of a Flemish refugee from Alva, was appointed the first Governor of the Bank of England, founded this year to provide the Government with a loan of £1,200,000 which the public subscribed in the first ten days. In 1695 Archbishop Precipiano declared that more than half the secular clergy in Belgium were infected with Jansenist notions; William with an allied army laid siege to Namur and took it in a final assault by the 'British grenadiers'; and Maximilian Emmanuel showed high spirit in Brussels when the French Marshal Villeroi bombarded the city with red-hot shot which damaged the Town Hall and other historic buildings on the Grand Place and burnt down sixteen churches and three thousand eight hundred houses without military result. In 1696 there was only desultory fighting in Belgium as both sides were weary of the war; John Sobieski died; Frederick Augustus, Elector of Saxony, became King of Poland as Augustus III after defeating seventeen competitors and renouncing Lutheranism for Roman Catholicism for the purpose; and Czar Peter the Great, aged twenty-four, ordered day and night building of a Russian fleet to fight the Turks in the Sea of Azov and personally laboured in the shipyards. In 1697 Louis XIV agreed by the Treaty of Ryswick to restore to Spain the duchy of Luxembourg, Charleroi, Mons, Courtrai and all the places taken since the Treaty of Nymwegen; Spain allowed the Dutch to put garrisons in Courtrai, Nieuport, Audenarde, Mons, Charleroi, Namur and Luxembourg as barrier fortresses; Pierre Bayle completed his 'Dictionnaire historique et critique'; the choir of St. Paul's Cathedral was opened with a Thanksgiving Service for the Peace of Ryswick; and Prince Eugene of Savoy, aged thirty-four and in the service of the Emperor, defeated the Turks at Zenta on the Theiss. In 1698 the Count de Bergeyck, Treasurer General for Maximilian Emmanuel, set up trading restrictions and protective tariffs for the benefit of Belgian industry and commerce—which roused local opposition and also incensed the English and the Dutch; Maximilian Emmanuel patronized the opera in Brussels, held a gay court in Caudenberg Palace with **Dominique Nollet** as his chief

Court Painter, provided three million florins from his private fortune towards the reparation of war damage, and, advised by **Nollet,** bought from one Gisbert van Ceulen for his Schleissheim gallery one hundred and five pictures including twelve by **Rubens,** fifteen by **Van Dyck** and eleven by **Brouwer.** Peter the Great spent three months at Sayes Court, rented from the diarist Evelyn, to study English shipbuilding at Deptford and left the house and garden a considerable wreck before going back to Moscow to take savage vengeance for the revolt of the Stryeltsy; Charles II made a will leaving all his domains to Ferdinand Joseph the six year old son of Maximilian Emmanuel by the Emperor's daughter—to the dismay of England, France and Holland who wished to divide the territories among Ferdinand-Joseph, the Dauphin and the Archduke Charles the Emperor's second son. In 1699 Maximilian Emmanuel's son, the boy Ferdinand-Joseph, died; the Turks signed the Peace of Karlowitz which gave all Hungary and Transylvania to Austria, and all Podolia, the Ukraine and the fortress of Kamenets Podolski to Poland; Maximilian Emmanuel persuaded the Emperor to make Belgium a party to the Treaty that the country might profit by clauses governing trade with the Levant; and local opposition to the new protective tariffs caused demonstrations outside Bergeyck's house in Brussels. In 1700 Maximilian Emmanuel caused Bergeyck to withdraw the tariffs—mainly to placate the Dutch; England, France and Holland agreed to divide the Spanish succession between the Archduke Charles (to whom Belgium was allotted) and the Dauphin; Charles II died and left the whole inheritance to the Dauphin's son Philip of Anjou (the Papal candidate); Louis XIV accepted the inheritance; there were fireworks and fountains playing wine outside the Jesuit college in Brussels; Philip instructed the Belgian Privy Council to obey all orders coming to them from the King of France; and Maximilian Emmanuel asked Versailles to appoint him Perpetual Governor in the Bourbon Netherlands.

In these years many pictures were commissioned for churches all over the country. In Antwerp where **Peter van Lint** (Pls. 677, 697) and **Huybrecht Sporckmans** (Pl. 786) died in 1690, **Peter Ijkens** painted *S. Catherine disputing with the heathen scholars* for the cathedral in 1684, gave an *Abraham and Hagar* to the Guild in 1689 and died in 1695; **Willem Borremans,** a van Lint pupil, was active in the early nineties till he went to Italy; and **Godfried Maes,** another **van Lint** pupil, provided the church of S. George with a *Martyrdom of S. George* in 1684. **Gaspar Jacob van Opstal** worked for various churches and organized an atelier with pupils and assistants where copies and pastiches of compositions by **Rubens** and **Van Dyck** were turned out. **Willem de Ryck** was available through the eighties till he left for England. **Jacob van Hal,** a **van Opstal** pupil, started work independently in 1692; and **Jean Pierre Tassaert** Master at thirty-nine in 1690, painted eight large panels *Scenes from the lives of SS. Peter and Paul* for the Diamond Polishers' Guild probably before 1700. **Jan Erasmus Quellinus,** back in Antwerp from Vienna by 1685, painted pictures commissioned for the Carthusian monastery at Lierre and others for S. Rombout and the Béguinage in Malines; in his *Miracle of S. Hugh, Bishop of Lincoln* (Pl. 821) the saint, accompanied by a swan as his emblem, resuscitates a child while the Christ-child appears in the chalice, and the scene is set in a garden loggia with term and fountain such as **Van Dyck** (Pl. 579) and **Gonzales Coques** (Pl. 764) had used in backgrounds for their high-life portraits and as Watteau, born in 1684, was to use in *Gilles and his family* about 1716. In Brussels many artists were employed at the end of the period on altarpieces for churches being reconstructed after Marshal Villeroi's 1695 bombardment; and these included **Jean van Orley** who was thirty in that year and **Victor Honoré Janssens** who had come back from Rome at thirty-one in 1689 and may have painted his *S. Carlo Borromeo interceding for the plague-*

stricken (Pl. 812) for the Carmes Déchaussés before 1700. In Ghent some commissions went to **Jan Serin** who also worked for Tournai churches till he left for Holland towards the end of the period; other commissions went to **Pieter Le Plat** who painted a *Marc d'Aviano preaching in Ghent during the plague epidemic of 1681, with members of the Heynderickx family as donors* and to his son **Gilles Le Plat** who provided S. Jacques with a *S. Nicholas baptising an old woman* in 1684 and the Town Hall with a *Seven Works of Mercy* in 1691; but the favourite for church paintings in Ghent was still **Jan van Cleef** who had **Robert van Audenaerd** (Pl. 823) as his pupil about 1683 and **Victor Verspilt** as a landscape assistant and painted many large altarpieces, including *A Soeur Noire succouring victims of the plague* for the Soeurs Noires convent which was much admired by eighteenth-century critics and which he himself considered his outstanding picture. In Bruges many churches received new altarpieces; S. Anne for example received a *Christ before Caiaphas* by **Jean Baptiste van Meunincxhove**, a *Last Judgement* by **Henri Herregouts** with over-life-size nudes which Descamps observed 'might with advantage have been draped', a *Landscape with the Visitation* by **Dominique Nollet**, *Scenes from the life of Christ* and a *Flight into Egypt* by **Jan Anthonie van der Leepe** (with figures by other Brugeois) and a *S. Sebastian* by **Lodewyck de Deyster** who painted altarpieces with dramatic chiaroscuro after 1688 when he came back from Rome and Venice; S. Jacques received thirteen *Landscapes with the life of S. James* by **Dominique Nollet**, three pictures by **Lodewyck de Deyster** and, in 1700, a *Nativity of the Virgin* by **Nicolas Vleys** (Master in 1694 after working in Rome) and an *Assumption of the Virgin* by **Marcus van Duvenede** a pupil of **Jan Baptist Herregouts** and Antwerp Master at twenty-six that year. In Bruges also the Carmelite received a *S. Louis embarking for the Holy Land* by **Dominique Nollet** and Notre Dame an *Esther before Ahasuerus* by **Lodewyck de Deyster** and an *Elijah on the mountain* by **Dominique Nollet**. Yet other commissions went in Bruges to **Jan Baptist Herregouts** who had moved there from Antwerp by 1684 and, after 1695, to **Joseph van den Kerckhove** who had worked in France after early study with **van Meunincxhove** and **Jan Erasmus Quellinus**. In Malines **Gilles Smeyers** and his son **Jacques Smeyers** (Master in 1688) both painted for the churches and **Jacques Le Pla** died at a date unknown; **Lucas Franchoys the younger** died in 1681; and his pupil **Pierre Simon Verlinden** was active from 1690. In Louvain **Charles Wautier** painted a *Christ handing the Keys to Peter* for S. Pierre in 1685, and **Lambert Blendeff,** who became iconographer to the University in 1684, may also have continued to paint religious pictures. In Liège **Englebert Fisen** was much employed and kept a record of his prolific output; the Namurois **Nicolas la Fabrique** who was back from Rome via Paris and seems to have settled in Liège about 1690 signed a *Raising of the Cross* for one of the Namur churches; **Jean Gilles Delcour** was active in Liège till he died in 1695; and others working for the Liège churches included **Philippe Coclers, A. Dumoulin** (after 1695) and **N. J. Riga** who produced inter alia a *S. Anthony of Padua kneeling before Christ with the Virgin and Trinity above and an old man as donor*. **G. F. Ladam** worked for churches in Tournai.

Allegories and mythologies were produced as easel pictures, decorative panels and designs for tapestry. In Antwerp **Abraham Genoels**, back from Rome by 1682, may have painted at this time the *Landscape with Diana hunting* (Pl. 817) inspired, it would seem, by Poussin's later pictures; **Jan Claudius de Cock** made drawings of classical subjects for engravers; **Gaspar Jacob van Opstal, Jacques Leyssens** and **Jacob van Hal** provided classical figures for decorative still-life arrangements like the *Still-life with peacock, parrot and cupids in a loggia* (Pl. 806) painted by **Pieter Gysels** shortly before his death in 1690, for flowerpieces by **Jan Baptist Bosschaert** and **Simon Hardimé** and for compositions like the

Vase of flowers with allegoric figures (Pl. 809) by **Gaspar Pieter Verbruggen the younger** who was much employed to decorate ceilings and overdoors in Maximilian Emmanuel's period. Cartoons for tapestry were made by **Abraham Genoels, Adriaen Frans Baudewyns** (Pl. 815), **Pieter Spierinckx** and **Louis van Schoor**, and many tapestries were exported to Vienna by the Forchoudts who offered some to Prince Montecuccoli in 1688. **Pieter Spierinckx** painted a ceiling panel for the Academy which also received an *Allegory of Painting, Sculpture and Poetry* by **Godfried Maes** who died about 1700 and an *Allegory of the study of the nude* by **Jacob Denys** who was back from Italy by 1681, worked probably as portraitist for Alexander Farnese II, married a widow with a number of children and then fled from her to a destination never discovered in 1695. This *Allegory of the study of the nude* (Pl. 811) by **Denys** was presumably painted to celebrate the introduction of 'life' study in the Academy's schools as we see there students working from a nude man and professors instructing them, while 'Sculpture' holds up a modelled figure, 'Poetry' provides inspiring titles, 'Painting' copies the posing model (with much less gusto than the artist displayed in **Joos van Winghe's** *Apelles painting Campaspe* (Pl. 457)) and 'Abundance' showers medals and money on the students' heads; and the picture may also celebrate Maximilian Emmanuel's visit to the Academy, already referred to, in the year that it was painted. In Brussels **Richard van Orley** drew a gouache miniature *Pandora opening the box* in 1692; cartoons for tapestry were made by **David Teniers III** who died in 1685, by **Jean van Orley**, **Richard van Orley** and **Victor Honoré Janssens** whose *Dido building Carthage* (Pl. 827), probably designed for tapestry, shows the Queen and her attendants and her pet dog round the skull of the bull whose hide was the measure of the first foundation, Juno with her peacock on a cloud, and, in the background, a building scene with masons climbing ladders in the genre tradition that goes back through **Pieter Bruegel** (Pl. 375) to **Jan van Eyck** (Pl. 18) and the **London Virgin with a Firescreen Painter** (Pl. 39). Commissions were also allotted to most of these artists for decorative paintings in the Brussels Town Hall and in rich men's houses reconstructed after the 1695 bombardment. In Malines **Daniel Janssens** painted a ceiling for the Town Hall in 1681 and died the next year; and both **Jacques Smeyers** and **Pierre Simon Verlinden** provided allegoric decorations for various public buildings in the second decade of the period.

There were the usual records of contemporary ceremonies and official portraits of the sovereign; and there were also some costume-history pieces extolling the national heroes of the past. **Nicolas Stramot** painted *The members of the Louvain All Souls Brotherhood of S. Gertrude at the Mass in celebration of their 50th anniversary* for Louvain University in 1682; and **Alexander van Bredael**, Antwerp Master in 1685, painted in that year *The Place de Meir Centenary Celebration of Parma's capture of Antwerp* (*1585*) already mentioned and an *Ommeganck*—such as **Denis van Alsloot** had painted (Pl. 513A)in 1696. The Antwerp magistrates ordered a *Charles II* from **Peter Ijkens** in 1686, the Malines magistrates ordered one from **Antoine Coxie** in 1691, **Jean van Orley** painted a *Charles II on horseback* for the Brussels Town Hall in 1698 and **Willem de Ryck** painted *Charles II on horseback* for Courtrai Cathedral. Among the costume history pieces **Jan Erasmus Quellinus** (Pl. 821) produced in 1687 a *Coronation of Charles V as Roman Emperor in Bologna 1530* in a series of fifteen panels commissioned by the Emperor for the Hofburg.

The tradition of the subscription portrait group continued; and conversation pieces were also in demand. **Jan van Helmont** painted groups for the Antwerp Magistrates and provided the Soeurs Noires convent with a life-size *Twelve nuns adoring the Cross*; **Jean van Orley** painted *Members of the Brussels Clothmakers' Guild*; and **Gilles Smeyers** is traditionally recorded author of a group showing *The Directors of the Malines Tailors' Guild*. Of the painters of conversation pieces **Gonzales Coques** (Pls. 764, 773) died at seventy in 1684 and **Hieronymus Janssens** (Pls. 730, 731, 761) at sixty-nine in 1693. Among the other portrait painters **Gysbrecht Thys** died in poverty at seventy-two in Antwerp in 1684. **Charles Emmanuel Biset** (Pl. 784) painted *Alexander Farnese II* in 1682, married his servant soon after, became idle, degenerate and destitute and left Antwerp for Holland about 1686. **Peter Ijkens** painted *J. B. Greyns, President of the Antwerp Guild of S. Luke* in 1690 and died in 1695. **Franciscus de Cock**, canon and cantor of Antwerp Cathedral, painted portraits of bishops and *Count Kaunitz, Imperial Ambassador at the Peace of Ryswick* in 1697. **Gaspar Jacob van Opstal** painted *J. K. N. Hove, President of the Guild of S. Luke and of the Olyftak Chamber of Rhetoric* and *Andries-Eugeen van Valckenisse, Secretary of the City of Antwerp* in 1699. Portraits were also painted in Antwerp by **Ferdinand Voet** who returned from Turin in 1684 and died about 1700, by **Jacob van Reesbroeck** who moved to Hoog-straeten, and by newcomers including **Frans van Stampert**, Master at seventeen in 1692, and the brilliant **Balthazar van den Bossche** (Pl. 832) who was Master at sixteen in 1697 after working under **Gerard Thomas** (Pl. 833). In Brussels **Jean van Orley** received some commissions, **Louis Volders** painted *Hendrik Casimir II*, and **Augustin Coppens** anticipated some aspects of English eighteenth-century portraiture in his *Self-portrait with buildings damaged by the 1695 bombardment and the steeple of the Hôtel de Ville* (Pl. 822). Local notables were painted by **Antoine Coxie** and **Gilles Smeyers** in Malines and by **Nicolas Stramot** in Louvain. **Jean Gilles Delcour** and **Englebert Fisen** were available in Liège where **Nicolas la Fabrique** signed a *Self-portrait in a feathered hat* in 1685; and the Liégeois **Philippe Coclers** back from Italy in the nineties, worked for some years in Maestricht as Court Painter to Joseph Clement of Bavaria the Prince Bishop.

Among indoor genre scenes there seems to have been a fashion for interiors with alchemists in the manner of **Teniers** who died at eighty in 1690 after suffering embarrassments from legal actions set on foot by the children of his first wife, one of whom was married to **Jan Erasmus Quellinus**. There were the usual interiors with peasants also in his manner, and **Jan van Pee** who had moved permanently to Antwerp from Holland painted an *Old woman baking cakes with her family round her* in 1682 and had **Jan Joseph Horemans** (Pls. 836-8) among his many pupils at the end of the period. Satiric genre scenes with monkeys replacing humans were painted in the eighties, probably as potboilers, by the flower painter **Nicolas van Verendael** (Pl. 758) who died in poverty in 1691; and there was a growing vogue in the nineties for studio interiors which were painted by among others **Gerard Thomas** (Pl. 833) Antwerp Master in 1688, and **Jan Thielens**.

Among the painters of outdoor genre pieces, **Peter Bout**, working all through the period, produced some coast scenes with fishmarkets and more village scenes like the examples shown here (Pls. 796, 797) and continued on occasion to paint the figures in landscapes by **Adriaen Frans Baudewyns** (Pl. 815). **Teniers** may have painted some outdoor genre scenes in his last years; and many were painted by others in his style. There was also a vogue for Flemish fairs and markets following more closely the tradition that went back through **David Vinckeboons** (Pl. 533) and **Sebastiaan Vrancx** (Pls. 532, 534) to **Jan (Velvet) Brueghel** (Pl. 467). Thus **Mathieu Schoevaerdts** a pupil of **Baudewyns** in 1682 and Brussels Master in 1690, painted the *Procession of the fat ox in front of the Swan Inn* (Pl. 798); **Theobald Michau** (Pl. 841) who worked in this way, was a pupil of **Lucas Achtschellinck** in the early nineties and Brussels Master in 1698; **Jan van Buken** (Pl. 779) was available till 1694; **Peter Gysels** who died in 1690 produced, at sixty-six, the brilliant *Village Fair* (Pl. 799) with peasants selling river fish to pompous gentry in the foreground and booths behind on the village square. In 1700 the Vienna branch of the Forchoudt firm in Antwerp asked especially for such pictures with peasants clothed in the Brueghel style saying that collectors there would not buy some genre pictures by **Jan Baptist van der Meiren** (who was Antwerp Master at twenty in 1685 and signed an *Oriental market* in 1698) because the figures had feathered headdresses and fantastic clothes; and we may add here that the Oriental note complained of may also have been seen in these years in more Palestinian landscapes with caravans, camels and so forth by the Brugeois **Nicolas Ryckx** who lived till 1695.

Wooded landscapes as settings for such genre scenes, or for hunting meets or episodes, or for religious subjects with small figures, were produced in Brussels, Bruges and Antwerp. In Bruges some churches received landscapes with religious subjects by **Dominique Nollet** as noted; **Balthasar d'Hooghe** painted a *Landscape with Flight into Egypt* for Bruges, S. Anne in 1691 and died in the Abbaye des Dunes in 1697; **Donatien van den Bogaerde** died in the Abbey in 1695; and **Antoine Coxie** signed a large wooded landscape for Bruges S. Jacques in 1698. **Jacques d'Arthois** (Pls. 686, 710, 736) died indigent in Brussels at seventy-three in 1686; and **Lucas Achtschellinck**, for whom **Lodewyck de Deyster** now sometimes provided figures, was active there till 1699. In Antwerp **Gillis Neyts** signed a *Wooded landscape with cavaliers and ladies* in 1681 and died in 1687; and **Peter Verdussen** was among the newcomers by 1697.

Among the painters of Italianate landscapes and Roman ruins with genre figures **Antoon Goubau** (Pls. 775, 776) who seems to have finally returned from Rome to Antwerp in 1681, had **Jan Frans van Bloemen** (Pls. 818, 819, 820) as his pupil in that year and died at eighty-two in 1698; **Gaspar de Witte** (Pl. 781) died in 1681; **Abraham Genoels** (Pls. 817, 826) returned from Italy via Paris in 1682; **Pieter van Bredael** (Pl. 778) was Director of the Academy at sixty in 1689 with **Hendrik Frans van Lint** (Pls. 864, 865) as his pupil about 1700; **Pieter van Bloemen** returned from Italy in 1694; and both **Pieter Spierinckx** and **Peter Rysbraeck**, who had **Joseph Vervoort** as a pupil in the middle nineties, were active all through the period. In Bruges in the later eighties **Jan Anthonie van der Leepe** painted Italianate landscapes into which, after 1695, **Joseph van den Kerckhove** sometimes inserted figures of religious or other subjects. In Brussels **Peter van Orley** was Dean of the Guild in 1688 and **Adriaen Frans Baudewyns** (Pl. 815) had a nephew of the same name as his pupil in the nineties. **Mathieu Schoevaerdts** painted Italianate port scenes with round towers and fishmarkets, the *Italianate landscape with mounted figures and peasants* reproduced here (Pl. 816) as well as the Flemish village scenes (Pl. 798) already referred to; and like **Peter Bout** he sometimes inserted figures in landscapes by **Adriaen Baudewyns**. Newcomers included **Lambert Dumoulin** after 1685 in Liège, **Jean Baptiste Juppin** after 1695 in Namur and **Jacques de Rooster**, who may have visited Italy, in Malines.

Some eclectic landscapes with wooded and Italianate characters were produced in Antwerp by **Jan Baptist Huysmans** and **Cornelis Huysmans** and in Brussels by **Adriaen Baudewyns**. **Jan Baptist Huysmans** was forty-three when he painted the *Landscape with cattle and two herdsmen* (Pl. 825); **Cornelis Huysmans**, who was six years older, worked in Malines as well as Antwerp, and Descamps (who saw many of his pictures in his daughter's house) informs us that he retouched many landscapes by **Jacques d'Arthois**, **Achtschellinck** and others.

Panoramas, views and street scenes were still being painted. **Jan Baptist van Meuninxhove** signed a *Place du Bourg, Bruges* in 1682 and another in 1696; **Gillis Neyts** was working in Brussels in 1687; and in 1692 **Theodore van Heil** signed a *Panorama of Brussels* seen from

S. Gilles with the Nid-du-Chien lake in the foreground and the city shown surrounded by its walls.

Military scenes (warfare and picturesque genre) and marines (port scenes and naval combats) were also painted as before. **Joris van Bredael**, Antwerp Master at twenty-three in 1684, sold a *Relief of Vienna*, a *Capture of Buda*, a *Capture of Belgrade* and other battle pieces to the dealer Forchoudt in 1690; **Dominique Nollet** painted some military subjects, probably for Maximilian Emmanuel, in the nineties; **Pieter van Bloemen,** back from Rome aged thirty-seven in 1694, painted officers on prancing horses with Roman ruins in the background. **Jacques van Werden** continued to draw sieges and so forth till 1696. **Constantyn Francken** (Pl. 828), back from Paris in 1695, painted that year a *Siege of Namur with William III and his generals* and took **Carel van Falens** (Pl. 846) aged fourteen as his pupil in 1697. **Jan Baptist van der Meiren** had **Jasper Broers** as his pupil in 1695 and painted *Coblenz besieged by Turenne* and a *Military camp in a mountain landscape* in 1698; **Peter Verdussen** became an independent artist in 1697; and **Carel Breydel** (Pls. 831, 842) was a pupil in the nineties first of **Peter Ijkens** and then of **Peter Rysbraeck.**

Of the marine painters **Jan Anthonie van der Leepe,** already mentioned in other aspects, worked in Bruges from the later eighties. In Antwerp **Hendrick van Minderhout** was active till 1696; at sixty-three in 1695 he painted an *Antwerp fishmarket* where canons from the Abbaye S. Michel are shown among the buyers; seven years earlier he had painted the *Disembarkation* (Pl. 794) where an elegant lady landing from a barge is received by a bowing young man while porters carry her trunk, ladies give alms to a beggar, a lady and gentleman drive off in a cabriolet, and a peasant girl, pitcher on head, crosses a footbridge to the quay with its obelisk-fountain in the centre; and the student may find it intriguing to contrast this composition with *S. Ursula landing at Cologne* as imaged by the **Ursula Legend Master** (Pl. 97) and **Hans Memlinc** (Pl. 93). In Antwerp also **Lucas Smout the younger** was **Minderhout's** pupil at fifteen in 1686; **Peter van der Velde** continued to paint naval combats and other seapieces till the end of the eighties; **Minderhout's** son **Antoon van Minderhout,** painter of sea ports, was active from the middle nineties; and **Jan Baptist van der Meiren** signed an *Oriental seaport* in 1700.

There were the usual painters of animals and birds who often painted still-life arrangements with trophies of the chase set sometimes in landscape or surrounded by plant forms with reptiles and insects. Of these **Jan Sloots** of Malines, back from Italy and the Tyrol in 1684, painted animals and birds till he died in 1690. **Elias van den Broeck** left Antwerp for Amsterdam in the early eighties when rivals had accused him of sticking live butterflies in his plant and insect compositions. **Bernaert de Bridt,** painter of dead birds and swans and live animals, was Antwerp Master in 1688. **Pieter Gysels** produced the large decorative *Dead swan, fruit, vegetables and live parrot and peacock in a loggia setting* (Pl. 806) in 1690 just before he died at seventy. **Frans Ijkens** (Pl. 695) died, over ninety, about 1693; and **Jan Pieter van Bredael the elder,** active as dealer and painter, produced dead game studies and fruit and flower pieces in the nineties. **Adriaen de Gryef** (Pls. 735, 847) appeared as Ghent Master in 1687 and then worked in Brussels—possibly with **David de Coninck** (Pl. 734) who died there in 1699; and **Andries Verhoeven,** another painter of trophies of the chase in landscape, began in Antwerp in 1687. **Philip Ferdinand de Hamilton** (son of a Scottish still-life painter and born in Brussels about 1664) began as fruit and insect painter, signed a *Hound and dead hare* in 1698, and then specialized in animal painting (Pls. 849, 851); his brother **Charles William de Hamilton** born in Brussels a few years later was painting horses and other animals and also compositions with lizards, insects and so forth among plants and thistles by the middle nineties; and a yet younger brother **John George de Hamilton** born in Brussels in 1672, painter of birds and animals including horses (Pl. 850), was also active in the early nineties till he went to Vienna in 1698.

Flower pieces and garlands, tables with fruit, food and vessels, fish pieces and 'Vanitas' pictures were still produced in numbers and, as inventories show, collected. Of the older painters of flowers and fruit **François van Aken** worked in Antwerp through the period; **Nicolas van Verendael** (Pl. 758) died in poverty in Antwerp in 1691; **Gerard Goswin** died in Liège in 1691; and **Jan Christoph Lotyn** returned from England to Brussels after 1695. Newcomers painting flowers and fruit garlands included **Jacob Seldenslach** who had been a pupil of **Gaspar Pieter Verbruggen the elder** (Pl. 810); **Christiaen de Knodder** Antwerp Master in 1685; **Anthonie van Eeckhout** active in Bruges from 1688 till 1691 when he went abroad; **Gaspar Pieter Verbruggen the younger** (Pl. 809) and **Jean Baptiste Morel** (pupil of Verendael) both much employed under Maximilian Emmanuel; and **David Cornelisz de Heem** and **Pieter Hardimé** who both left Antwerp for Holland in 1697. The flower painter **Jan Baptist van Crépu** was an officer in the Spanish service who retired about the age of forty, was Antwerp Master in 1685, and moved before 1689 to Brussels, where going home one night in his cups he killed the governor's pet hind mistaking it for a footpad; **Jan Baptist Bosschaert** and **Simon Hardimé** were his pupils for flower painting in the Antwerp period. Of the painters of tables with fruit, food and vessels **Jan Davidsz de Heem** died in 1683, **Alexander Coosemans** (Pls. 744, 800) and **Cornelis Mahu** were active till 1689, **Theodor Aenvanck** (Pl. 747) till approximately 1690 and **Cornelis de Heem** (Pl. 748) till 1695. The fish painter **Frans van Cuyck de Mierop** lived till 1689; and the 'Vanitas' painter **Pieter van der Willigen** till 1694.

In France (where **Adam van der Meulen** lived till 1690) there were other Belgian painters established or on visits. The Italianate landscape painter **Peter Rysbraeck** who had come back with Largillière from England to escape the Titus Oates anti-Catholic disturbances, was in Paris for some time in the early eighties. **Pierre de Bourguignon**, portraitist and Academician, was in Paris till he left for Holland soon after the Revocation of the Edict of Nantes. **Peter Sperwer**, portraitist, worked in Paris for some years at the beginning of the eighties. **Philippe Vleughels**, Academician and naturalized Frenchman, painted pictures for Parisian churches till 1694; and **Matthieu Elias**, painter of portraits and religious subjects, who had arrived at about twenty by 1681, became a Member of the old Academy of S. Luke in this period and was still in Paris in 1700. **Pierre van der Meulen**, painter of contemporary warfare, seems to have come from England about 1689 and may have died in Paris in the nineties; **Constantyn Francken** (Pl. 828) painter, as noted, of contemporary warfare, arrived aged twenty at the outset of the period and worked in Paris and at Versailles till he returned to Antwerp in 1694. **Joseph van den Kerckhove** worked in Paris, Angers and Nantes in the early nineties and returned to Bruges in 1695. **Perpète Delcloche** had probably arrived in Paris from Dinant by 1700 when nearly thirty. **Jacob van Oost the younger** (Pls. 769, 771) was all the time in Lille and worked for churches there and at Tournai; and **Balthazar van den Bossche** (Pl. 832) arrived under twenty before 1700 and worked for some time in Paris, Douai and Nantes.

In Holland there were Flemish painters at work in a number of places. In Amsterdam **Gérard de Lairesse** (Pls. 813, 814) was at the height of his reputation in the eighties when his studio was full of pupils, his house was a rendezvous for men of parts, and he was much employed on allegories and mythologies commissioned by patricians for their mansions; in 1684 he visited the Hague to paint a series of panels for the Council Chamber of the

Courts of Justice; at the end of the eighties he designed, in pastel, an *Apotheosis of William III, King of England* and at forty-nine in 1690 he went blind; thereafter he dictated 'Het Groot Schilderboek' where he attacked the naturalists and Rembrandt whom he had described elsewhere as 'a master capable of nothing but vulgar and prosaic subjects . . . who merely achieved an effect of rottenness'—a dictum to be contrasted with that of Sir Joshua Reynolds on **Lairesse's** own *Death of Cleopatra*—'The figure of Cleopatra is well drawn and in an attitude of great grace, but the style is degraded by the naturalness of the white satin which is thrown over her.' **Gérard de Lairesse** was assisted by two sons; and **Jacques Lairesse**, his brother, supplied flowers and other motifs for some of his pictures. Others in Amsterdam were **Elias van den Broeck** who arrived in 1685 and cultivated a garden with plants, flowers, insects and reptiles for use in his still-life pieces; and **Antoine Coxie** who came from Malines at the end of the period. **Charles Emmanuel Biset** (Pl. 784) arrived in poverty at Breda about 1686 and died there in 1691. His son **Jean Andreas Biset** who had come with him from Antwerp and was approximately twenty in 1691, painted portraits and mythologies in Breda and worked in Middelburg about 1698. King William employed two Belgian painters in his Breda palace—**Jan Claudius de Cock** who had begun as a sculptor in Antwerp about 1688 and worked in the palace in 1696, and **Ferdinand van Kessel**, painter of animals, birds and flowerpieces who had the Dutch flower painter and art historian Jacob Campo (Campovivo) Weyerman as his pupil; **Ferdinand van Kessel** was also Court Painter to John III (Sobieski) of Poland and painted for him *The Four Elements* and *The Four Quarters of the Globe*; and he died in Breda in 1696. **Pierre de Bourguignon** reached The Hague from Paris about 1687 and left for London two or three years later: **Jan Serin** arrived at a date unknown and may have died there before 1700; and the flower painters **Pieter Hardimé** and **Simon Hardimé** were both active there at the end of the nineties. **Michiel Engel Immenraet** died in Utrecht in 1683; and **Bernard Vaillant** made portraits in oil and pastel in various places till he died in Leyden at sixty-six in 1698.

In England **Jacob Huysmans** (Pl. 752), Queen Catherine's favourite, continued as a portrait painter in his Jermyn Street studio; in 1685 he painted *Father John Hudleston aged 78* (showing the Queen's chaplain who received the dying Charles II into the Roman Church that year); and he died in London in 1696. **Willem de Keyser**, Antwerp painter of portraits and religious subjects (in oil, watercolour and enamel), arrived about 1685, worked for James II's Court, painted a *S. Catherine* for the Queen Dowager's Somerset House chapel, and died, ruined by the revolution, in 1692. **Jan Siberechts** (Pls. 787-92), who was still living aged seventy in 1700, produced in 1684 his splendid *Huntsmen setting out* with a huge spreading oak tree and a distant prospect seen beneath it; he made drawings of Chatsworth in 1686 and worked for Lord Middleton in the nineties; in 1695 he painted *Wollaton House* with the mansion in the distance and in the foreground a carriage crossing a country stream near a cottage with laundry spread out on the hedge to dry; and some Belgian critics have suggested, perhaps correctly, that his pictures had influence on Gainsborough and also on Constable who is said to have owned one. **John Baptist Medina** (son of a Spanish officer serving in the Netherlands and pupil of **François Duchatel** (Pl. 777)) arrived in 1686, went to Edinburgh about 1689 where he executed £500 worth of portrait commissions in one year having equipped himself beforehand with 'postures' for heads and half lengths, and remained there producing a family of twenty children 'which prevented his growing rich'. **Jan Peeters the younger** came to London from Antwerp about 1685, became drapery assistant to Godfrey Kneller, and was also active as dealer and 'restorer' especially of old drawings 'giving them the masterly stroak and Air of genuine drawings so that many of the Prime Connoisseurs or Vertuose purchased at great prices'—an accomplishment which earned him the sobriquet of 'Doctor Peeters'. **Jan Baptist Gaspers** ('Lely's Baptist') assisted John Riley after Lely's death and then became assistant to Kneller; he was also active as designer of tapestries; and he died here in 1691. **Simon Dubois**, now launched in portrait practice, painted *Sir William Jones, Solicitor General* and *Lady Jones* in 1682, the daughters of the Dutch Ambassador in 1693, collaborated in some way with the Dutch marine painter Willem van der Velde at the end of the period and concocted 'bambochades' in the Italian manner which he sold as by Italian artists. **Jeremias van der Eyden** continued to paint portraits in the provinces till 1695 when he died at Staplefort in Leicestershire where he had been working for Lord Sherard. **Prosper Henricus Lankrink** bought pictures with borrowed money at the sale of Lely's collection and seems to have fallen on bad days under William and Mary and to have died in poverty in 1692. The landscape painter **Cornelis Huysmans** came to London, probably at this time, had frames made by Grinling Gibbons and gave him pictures in payment. **Daniel Boone**, who lived till the end of the period, produced a *Beggars carousing* as a wall decoration for a London tavern called 'The Beggars' Cellar'. **Balthasar van Lemens** seems to have continued to make drawings of mythologies for London engravers; and **Jan Baptist van den Lantscroon** probably worked through the period as assistant to Verrio, first at Windsor, then at Whitehall, then at Chatsworth (where Verrio went when he refused to serve King William) and finally on the Great Staircase at Hampton Court (which Verrio began, when he relented, about 1699). **Jan Frans van Son** (son of **Joris van Son** (Pls. 743, 745)) arrived in the early eighties, married a niece of Charles II's Sergeant Painter Robert Streater and remained here painting large decorative still-life pieces with fruit, flowers, vessels, carpets and gold-fringed curtains described by Walpole (following Descamps) as 'medleys of familiar objects that strike the ignorant vulgar' though they were much admired in his period by Lords Radnor, Ranelagh and Dover who bought them in numbers for their mansions. **Jan Pieter van Bredael the elder** was in London for a while as painter and dealer in 1685. **Jan Christoph Lotyn** arrived as flower painter and tapestry designer under William and Mary, was patronized by the Queen and returned, as noted, to Brussels about 1695; and **Simon Hardimé** came as flower painter from The Hague and established himself here about 1700. **Willem de Ryck** arrived from Antwerp about 1689, painted a conversation piece *Alexander Pittfield and all his family* and other portraits, and died here about 1700. **Nicolas Stramot** came from Louvain about 1695 and may have remained some years painting portraits and conversation pieces or making architectural drawings; and the battle painter **Pierre van der Meulen**, who had arrived as noted in the previous period, was employed by King William in 1689 but seems thereafter to have gone away to Paris.

In Spain **Cornelis Schut III** continued a figure in the Seville Academy till he died in or soon after 1685. In Madrid **Perpète Évrard** from Dinant, painter of portraits and miniatures, had Court employment as a young man some time in the eighties; and **Jan van Kessel the younger**—whose intriguing *Family in a garden* (Pl. 808) was discussed in my last chapter—became a Court Painter without salary to Charles II in 1683, applied successfully two years later for the salaried post left vacant by Don Juan Carreño de Miranda (who had painted most admirable portraits of the King and the Queen Mother), decorated the northern gallery of the Alcazar with *Scenes from the story of Cupid and Psyche* at the instance of Queen Maria Louisa, and held the favour of Mariana of Neuburg, Charles' second Queen, after 1690.

In Central Europe **Victor Honoré Janssens** (Pls. 812, 827) left the Duke of Holstein's court in Flensburg before 1684 for Rome; **Jan Baptist van Ruel** provided an *Assumption of the Virgin* for Mainz Cathedral in 1684 and died in Würzburg in 1685; and **Jacques Vaillant** continued to paint Court portraits in Berlin till he died there in 1691. **Frans de Hamilton** was working for the Court in Munich in the eighties and may have died there or in Augsburg. **Hendrik Goovaerts** painter of single and group portraits, social genre (Pl. 845) and 'history', left Malines about twenty at the outset of the nineties and worked in Frankfort, Prague, Vienna and Hungary before 1700 when he returned to Antwerp; **Abraham Godyn**, painter of 'history' and decorative compositions, went to Prague from Italy about 1687 and decorated Troja Castle there between that date and 1694, and **Izaack Godyn**, presumed his brother, also worked at Troja. **Frans de Neve the elder** worked in this period in Vienna and in Salzburg where he probably died. **Perpète Évrard** seems to have gone to Vienna after his Spanish visit and to have stayed there till the end of the period; **Canon van der Baren** (Pl. 675) died as Court Painter in Vienna at seventy-one in 1686; and the landscape painter **Renier Megan** died there also as Court Painter in 1690. **Jan Erasmus Quellinus** (Pl. 821) Court Painter from the early eighties remained in Vienna for some time and was commissioned by the Emperor to paint ceiling panels, as noted, for the Hofburg. **Anthoni Schoonjans** went to Vienna from Italy in the early nineties, had social success there (assisted by his wife who was a singer), became a Court Painter in 1695 and left suddenly for Copenhagen in 1696. **Jacques Ferdinand Saey**, painter of architectural pieces and pupil of his uncle **Wilhelm Schubert van Ehrenberg** (Pl. 783), arrived in Vienna aged thirty-six in 1694 and remained there. **John George de Hamilton** (Pl. 850) went there from Brussels aged twenty-six in 1698 and painted an *Equestrian portrait of King Joseph of Hungary* that year. **Frans van Stampart**, portrait painter, arrived from Antwerp, under twenty-five about 1698 and soon became Court Painter; the battle painter **Joris van Bredael** was there on a visit in 1699 and may have remained there; and both **Joannes de Cordua** painter of genre and still-life (including 'Vanitas' pieces) and his brother **Johan Baptist de Cordua** were active in Vienna from early in the period till the end.

Of the Flemish artists in Rome, **Andries Bosman** (Pl. 756) died in 1681, **Gilles Hallet** in 1694, and **Gillis du Mont** in 1697. **Jan Frans Soolmaker** (Pl. 780) whose death date is unknown may also have died in Rome in this period. **Antoon Goubau** (Pls. 614, 775, 776) seems to have left for Antwerp in 1681, and **Abraham Genoels** (Pls. 817, 826) returned there in 1682. **David de Coninck** (Pl. 734) became a member of the Accademia in 1686 and left for Antwerp aged fifty-one in 1687. **Anthoni Schoonjans** may have been continuously in Rome till he left for Vienna. **Sebastiaen van Aken** was still in Italy, and still perhaps connected with Maratta's atelier, in 1697; and newcomers in Maratta's atelier included **Robert van Audenaerd** (Pl. 823) who arrived from Ghent aged twenty-two in 1685, started work as an engraver and remained for the rest of the period, and **Nicolas Vleys**, Bruges Master in 1694, who was in Rome before or after that year and back in Bruges painting for the churches by 1700. **Jan Frans van Bloemen**, his elder brother **Pieter van Bloemen**, and his younger brother **Norbert van Bloemen** were all in Rome at this time. Of these **Jan Frans van Bloemen** (Pls. 818, 819, 820), pupil at nineteen of **Antoon Goubau**, arrived in the early eighties and declared that when he visited the Campagna it all looked like familiar pictures; he was nicknamed **Orizonte** (Horizon) at the 'Bent' initiation, and remained painting Italianate landscapes with figures and cattle much influenced by Claude (who died in 1682) and Poussin (who had died in 1665). **Pieter van Bloemen** arrived in 1681, was nicknamed **'Standaart',** painted battle pieces showing combats with the Turks (sometimes in collaboration with a German named Reder) and returned in 1694 to Antwerp where he specialized, as noted, in military pieces with Roman ruins in the background. **Norbert van Bloemen**, painter of genre and portraits, arrived in the nineties, was nicknamed **'Cephalus'**, and returned to Antwerp on foot, sleeping in monasteries and begging his way (as was not, it would seem, uncommon since Houbraken records one **Spalthof**, a painter of market scenes and Roman landscapes, who made the journey to Rome three times on foot). Others there for a time included **Lodewyck de Deyster** who came from Bruges in the eighties and was back by 1688; his brother-in-law the flower painter **Anthonie van den Eeckhout** who left for Lisbon about 1692 and was shot dead there in his coach by a rival; **Philippe Coclers** who came in the eighties from Malines; **Victor Honoré Janssens** (Pls. 812, 827) who came from Brussels in the eighties and returned in 1689; **Jacques Leyssens** nicknamed **Nootenkraaker** (Nut cracker) there probably in the early nineties; **Anthony Barbiers** who came about 1693 aged about seventeen and began as a pupil of **Pieter van Bloemen**; and **Gomar Wouters**, 'history' painter and **Jan Carel van Eyck**, painter of landscapes with genre figures, both from Antwerp. Elsewhere in Italy **Justus Sutterman** died in Florence aged eighty-four in 1681 and **Lieven Mehus** seems to have continued his pictures for churches in Florence and Prato till he died in Florence in 1691. **Ferdinand Voet** was in Turin till 1864 when he left for Antwerp; and **Robert la Longe** moved from Cremona to Piacenza and worked there for many of the churches. **Abraham Brueghel** (Pls. 746, 807) was still in Naples till he died there about 1690; and either he or his brother **Jan Baptist Brueghel,** nicknamed **'Meleager'** in Rome, painted flowers in Naples in some pictures by Luca Giordano. **Willem Borremans** came to Italy in the nineties and worked for Neapolitan churches; **Pieter de Coster** was still in Venice; and **Andries Immenraet** travelling in Italy in the middle eighties with the amateur A. de Leyen (to whom De Bie's 'Gulden Cabinet' had been dedicated) was required to draw anything his patron selected.

CHAPTER XVII

Maximilian Emmanuel 1701-1706;
Régime of the Maritime Powers pending
installation of the Archduke Charles 1706-1715;
Count von Königsegg 1715-1716;
Marquis de Prié (for Prince Eugene) 1716-1725

1701-1725

PHILIP V was not acknowledged by the Emperor Leopold who claimed the crown of Spain and all Spanish dominions for the House of Habsburg and put forward the Archduke Charles as the Habsburg heir. But in Belgium Philip was welcomed by the Jesuits and other churchmen because he had been the Papal candidate and because Louis XIV was an active enemy of the Jansenists. The Belgian people as a whole accepted Charles II's testament; and Maximilian Emmanuel, after bargaining with both sides, threw in his lot with Louis and continued as Governor-General for Philip.

In 1701 Louis XIV announced that Philip V would not tolerate the Dutch garrisons which had occupied the Barrier towns since the Treaty of Ryswick, and sent Marshal Boufflers to replace the garrisons with French troops—an operation completed in four days. Philip V married Marie Louise of Savoy. Maximilian Emmanuel went to Bavaria to prepare against military action by the Emperor and took with him **Dominique Nollet** as Court Painter and curator of his collection; the Marquis de Bedmar became Military Governor of Belgium in his absence; and the Count de Bergeyck, collaborating with French envoys, began to reorganize the administration on the French authoritarian pattern. The English Parliament passed the Act of Settlement vesting the succession after William and Anne in the Protestant house of Hanover; Ex-King James II died at S. Germain and Louis XIV proclaimed James's son, the Old Pretender, King James III; England and Holland joined the Emperor in a Grand Alliance against France; and Frederick, Elector of Brandenburg, became King of Prussia. In 1702 Bergeyck went forward with a new constitution for Belgium which abolished many local privileges and included the French systems of farming out taxes and recruiting for the army by lot. William III died; and Queen Anne gave high appointments to the Duchess of Marlborough. The Emperor, England and Holland officially began the War of the Spanish Succession against France and Spain; Marlborough forced some French armies back from the Dutch border and captured Liège; Maximilian Emmanuel led an army to the Black Forest; the French General

Villars crossed the Rhine and won the battle of Friedlingen; Admiral Sir George Rooke carried 5000 troops in an Anglo-Dutch fleet to Cadiz in a fruitless attempt to start an Andalusian revolt against Philip; and Jean Cavalier, a baker's assistant, aged twenty-one began to lead the Protestant peasants of the Cevennes (Gard) in the Camisard insurrection against dragonnades and conversions by torture. In 1703 Bergeyck reorganized the Belgian cloth trade on Colbertian lines and revised the customs system for the benefit of Franco-Belgian commerce; Louis XIV wrote to Pope Clement XI proposing a joint offensive to put an absolute end to Jansenism; Philip V urged Precipiano, still Archbishop of Malines, to ensure that no Jansenist adherent held any post in the University of Louvain; Precipiano had Pasquier Quesnel and other Jansenists illegally imprisoned in Malines (whence Quesnel escaped to Amsterdam some three months later) and the Jansenist Ruth d'Ans was expelled from the country on personal orders from Philip. Bedmar and the French general Boufflers defeated a Dutch army advancing against Antwerp at the Battle of Eeckeren; Maximilian Emmanuel and Marshal Villars won the Battle of Hochstett against the Austrians; the Archduke Charles was formally proclaimed King Charles III of Spain by the Emperor and given a seat of civil government in Limbourg just won for the Allies; Portugal joined the Alliance against France and Spain; French troops burned four hundred and sixty-six villages in the Cevennes where Cavalier and his Camisards received some supplies from an English fleet; Antoine Watteau aged nineteen, and recently arrived in Paris, was given assistance by the Flemish painter **Jan Jacques Spoede** and others in the Flemish colony; and Peter the Great founded S. Petersburg as the new capital of Russia. In 1704 Bergeyck ordered the construction of new roads joining Brussels to Mons and Ghent; a Dutch army bombarded Bruges; the Archduke Charles, hoping to invade Spain, went across Belgium to England and thence in an Anglo-Dutch fleet under Rooke and Sir Clowdesley Shovell to join Anglo-Dutch and Portuguese troops in Lisbon; Rooke and Shovell took Gibraltar; Marlborough laid waste parts of Maximilian Emmanuel's Bavaria and with Prince Eugene won the Battle of Blenheim; Maximilian Emmanuel returned with the remnants of his army to Brussels where he planned to resume his easy-going Court; and Vanbrugh was ordered to build Blenheim Palace as a present from Queen Anne and Parliament to Marlborough. In 1705 Maximilian Emmanuel and Marshal Villeroi led the French King's forces in minor combats against Marlborough in Belgium; Catalonia and Aragon declared for the Archduke Charles who made a formal entry as Charles III into Barcelona which Lord Peterborough and Sir Clowdesley Shovell had captured for him; the Emperor Leopold died; and the new Emperor Joseph I was harassed in Hungary by Rakoczy's revolt. In 1706 Philip V marched through Aragon to Catalonia, brutally ill-treated the Carlist partisans, failed to recapture Barcelona, and retired to Perpignan; the Allies occupied Madrid; the Castilians, hostile to Charles with his Portuguese and 'heretic' supporters, embarked on guerrilla warfare; Marlborough defeated Villeroi at Ramillies and entered Brussels, Antwerp, Ostend, and other places till the French held only Hainault, Namur and Luxembourg; Maximilian-Emmanuel retired to Mons; the Estates of Brabant and Flanders acknowledged Charles in place of Philip; Marlborough refused the Regency of the Netherlands to placate the Dutch; and England and Holland set up a Régime of the Maritime Powers to administer the country till Charles could effectively govern.

In 1707 **Rubens'** palatial house in Antwerp was rented by the dealer Forchoudt whose Vienna branch was selling Flemish pictures and 'Teniers' tapestries to Prince Adam von Liechtenstein and complaining that he bargained about prices; the Duc de Vendôme replaced Marshal Villeroi as head of the French armies in Belgium; Maximilian Emmanuel held Mons, Namur and Luxembourg; the Maritime Powers set up a Conference of Allied Representatives as an executive body, abolished most of the French reforms, and announced that the religion of the country would be respected and local autonomies restored. Allied troops in Spain under the Huguenot Earl of Galway were defeated at Almanza by Franco-Spanish forces under the Duke of Berwick; Philip V became master of all Spain except Catalonia where Charles was still established; a French fleet was destroyed at Toulon; and England signed the Act of Union with Scotland. In 1708 Maximilian Emmanuel made a futile attempt to capture Brussels; and Marlborough and Prince Eugene defeated Vendôme at Audenarde. In 1709 Marlborough and Eugene won the Battle of Malplaquet and entered Mons; Maximilian Emmanuel retired to Compiègne where he amused himself, as usual, with the ladies; Louis XIV closed the Port Royal convent and ejected the Jansenist nuns; the Emperor's envoy, the Marquis de Prié, persuaded Clement XI to recognize Charles as King of Spain; and Peter the Great won the Battle of Poltava against Charles XII of Sweden. In 1710 it was estimated that one tenth of the French population was indigent; the art dealer Sirois drew the attention of the millionaire Pierre Crozat to Watteau's talents; Louis XIV had the Port Royal convent razed completely to the ground; Marlborough's armies captured Douai, Béthune and other towns in France; Allied troops in Spain won the battles of Alménara and Saragossa; Charles was reinstated in Madrid; the Bourbon supporters resumed guerrilla warfare; Vendôme, sent to Spain by Louis XIV, won the battles of Brihuega and Villa Viciosa; and Charles went back to Barcelona. In 1711 Joseph I died and Charles became Emperor as Charles VI; Louis XIV (in the name of Philip V) proclaimed Maximilian Emmanuel Sovereign of the Catholic Netherlands; Marlborough captured Bouchaca in a campaign against Marshal Villars, and was dismissed the service when his party fell from power in England; the Duchess of Marlborough, supplanted by Lady Masham, was ejected from her appointments by Queen Anne; the South Sea company was granted a monopoly of the British trade with South America and the Pacific Islands; and at the Queen's Theatre, Haymarket, Handel aged twenty-six heard his opera Rinaldo much applauded. In 1712 the Belgian population was in great distress; Guillaume van Espen, Jansenist jurist in the University of Louvain, published his 'Tractatus de promulgatione legum ecclesiasticarum'; Ruth d'Ans, recalled from exile, became Dean of Tournai Cathedral; England officially withdrew her troops from Belgium and thousands mutinied at the decision and enlisted under Prince Eugene; Villars defeated Eugene and the Allied armies at Denain; and Maximilian Emmanuel made triumphal entries as sovereign in Namur and Luxembourg, had money struck with his effigy and began to organize a new gay court with theatres, ladies and so forth.

In 1713 Belgium ceased to be the Spanish Netherlands and became the Austrian Netherlands by the Treaty of Utrecht which ended the war leaving Philip V King of Spain and ceding Belgium to the Emperor Charles VI subject to his agreement to Dutch garrisons in the Barrier towns; Frederick I of Prussia was succeeded by Frederick William; Pope Clement XI published the Bull 'Unigenitus' which condemned Quesnel's 'Réflexions morales . . .' as heretical; and Jansenist and nationalist opposition prevented official publication of the Bull in Belgium. In 1714 Queen Anne died and George I succeeded; Philip V married Elizabeth Farnese of Parma and entered Barcelona captured for him by the Duke of Berwick; the Emperor Charles VI signed the Treaty of Rostadt with Louis XIV; Bavaria was restored to Maximilian Emmanuel who retired there; the Emperor's plenipotentiary the Count van Königsegg negotiated with the Dutch on the Barrier towns and their demand for religious toleration in Belgium; and Belgian private enterprise equipped some ships for trade with the New World. In 1715 Louis XIV died and Louis XV succeeded at the age of five with Philip Duke of Orleans as Regent; James Edward the Old Pretender was defeated at Preston; and von Königsegg, acting for the Emperor, agreed to Dutch garrisons in Namur, Tournai, Menin, Furnes, Warneton, Ypres and other places and the continued closing of the Scheldt against Antwerp, but refused toleration of the Protestant religion except for the garrisons of these towns. In 1716 a deputation of the Estates of Brabant and Flanders protested to the Emperor in Vienna against the Barrier garrisons and attempts by von Königsegg to re-establish a centralized régime; the Emperor appointed Prince Eugene nominal Governor of Belgium and, allied to Venice, started war against the Turks. Prince Eugene defeated the Turks at the Battle of Peterwardein; England joined France in an alliance to watch Elizabeth Farnese's plans for the aggrandisement of Spain; John Law founded the Banque Générale in Paris; and Belgian ships trading with the Indies were looked on with disfavour by the English and Dutch.

In 1717 the Marquis de Prié became acting Governor of Belgium as Minister Plenipotentiary for Prince Eugene; and Belgrade was captured by Eugene from the Turks. In Brussels trade associations claiming ancient privileges made demonstrations under François Anneessens, Dean of the Cabinetmakers' Guild; and in Bruges **Jan Baptist Herregouts, Joseph van den Kerckhove** and **Marcus van Duvenede** founded an Academy whose members were released from the restrictions imposed for centuries on artists by the various trade guilds (as had been done in Antwerp by **Teniers** and others in 1664). In Paris John Law floated the Compagnie d'Occident (the Mississippi Scheme); Voltaire aged twenty-three was imprisoned in the Bastille for eleven months for a lampoon on the Regent (which he did not write); and Watteau completed *L' Embarquement pour Cythère*. In 1718 Thomas Philippe d'Alsace, a new Archbishop of Malines, declared acceptance of the Bull 'Unigenitus' an article of faith; the jurists led by van Espen declared this illegal; and thirteen professors of the Arts Faculty in Louvain University protested to Prince Eugene and the Emperor, though the Faculty of Theology supported the Archbishop. The Emperor made the Treaty of Passarowitz with the Turks and joined France and Holland in alliance against Spain; Admiral Sir George Byng destroyed the Spanish navy off Cape Pissaro; and George I became Governor of the South Sea company. In 1719 François Anneessens was executed in Brussels for sedition; Pasquier Quesnel died in Amsterdam; all Paris was wildly speculating in Law's Mississippi and other schemes; and the South Sea company arranged to take over the National Debt. In 1720 the Mississippi Bubble burst in Paris; and in London the South Sea shares, after months of fantastic booming, also suddenly collapsed. In 1721 de Montesquieu published his 'Lettres Persanes'. In 1722 the Emperor gave a thirty years' monopoly of trade with the West and East Indies and Africa to a new corporation called the Compagnie d'Ostende to operate with his Imperial protection from Ostend. In 1723 the Regent, Philip of Orleans, died and the Duc de Bourbon became nominal ruler for Louis XV with Fleury, Bishop of Fréjus, as the power behind the throne; and the Emperor declared his support for the Archbishop of Malines in the 'Unigenitus' dispute but counselled appeasing tactics. In 1724 the first three ships of the Compagnie d'Ostende left Ostend flying the Imperial colours. In 1725 Czar Peter the Great died; Louis XV aged fifteen married Marie Leczinska of Poland; the Emperor in a ceremony in Brussels proclaimed the Pragmatic Sanction appointing his daughter Maria Theresa, then aged eight, the heir to all the Habsburg territories, and named his sister Maria Elisabeth as new Governor of the Austrian Netherlands to replace Prince Eugene who had resigned; the Marquis de Prié, guilty of financial irregularities, was disgraced; and Philip V in a Treaty with the Emperor gave the Compagnie d'Ostende the same trading rights in the Spanish overseas possessions as those enjoyed by the English and Dutch while the Emperor for his part renounced at last all claim to the throne of Spain.

Many of these events occasioned contemporary paintings and some commissions given show how the winds were blowing. Thus in 1703 the Belgians still thought that the Franco-Spaniards would remain in power and the Battle of Eeckeren, won by that side, was painted by **Constantyn Francken** in the picture reproduced here (Pl. 828) and also by **Peter Verdussen** and **Jasper Broers**; and in that year the Antwerp magistrates ordered a *Portrait of Philip V* for the Town Hall from **Peter Sperwer** a French-trained artist with a Parisian wife. Between Blenheim and Ramillies Marshal Villeroi ordered a copy of **Rubens'** *Descent from the Cross* from the all-purposes atelier run by **Gaspar Jacob van Opstal** and sent it to Versailles. In 1706, after Ramillies, Marlborough became a patron of the gifted **Balthazar van den Bossche** (Pl. 832) then twenty-five, and sat to him for an equestrian portrait to which **Pieter van Bloemen** contributed the horse. In 1707, when the Estates of Brabant and Flanders had accepted Charles as King of Spain, the Antwerp authorities ordered **Gaspar Jacob van Opstal** to provide his portrait as *Charles III* for the Town Hall (presumably in place of **Sperwer's** *Philip V*); and in the year of Audenarde **Victor Honoré Janssens** (Pls. 812, 827) painted an *Allegory of the year 1708* for the Brussels Town Hall. A picture called an *Allegory of the Peace of Utrecht* by **Hendrik Goovaerts** (Pl. 845) was seen by Descamps in 1768 in the Crossbowmen's Chamber of the Antwerp Town Hall and described by him as follows: 'Le Temps en l'air fait voir le portrait de l'Empereur Charles VI, soutenu par l'Amour, l'Union et la Force; une belle femme y personnifie la Ville d'Anvers, et S. Georges, Protecteur de la maison d'Autriche, y est environné d'Anges; les Vices sont terrassés; a côté sont les portraits des Chefs de cette compagnie pour lors vivans.' Prince Eugene's defeat of the Turks at Peterwardein was recorded by **Jan Pieter van Bredael** in the picture reproduced here (Pl. 830); the same artist painted his capture of Belgrade; and combats with the Turks were also painted by **Carel Breydel** (Pl. 831). In 1718 a *Charles VI proclaimed Count of Flanders in 1717* was ordered from **Jan Baptist van Volsum** in Ghent; in that year also **Victor Honoré Janssens** designed a tapestry titled *The Inauguration of Charles VI as Duke of Brabant 1718* for the Brussels Town Hall; and in 1720 the Tournai Council ordered portraits of the *Emperor Charles VI* and *Prince Eugene* from **Dominique Joseph van Oost** who was domiciled at Lille.

In addition to the topical allegories, there was continued production of allegories and mythologies, mostly in the French taste, for decorative panels, ceilings and so forth in public buildings and private mansions and also as easel pictures. In Antwerp **Gaspar Jacob van Opstal** added a *Venus and Adonis* dated 1706 to the *Gallery Interior* (Pl. 773) by **Gonzales Coques**; a newcomer **Balthazar Barbiers** was much employed on decorations for public buildings after 1708; **Jan Claudius de Cock** drew a *Boreas and Oreithyia* in 1709; **Abraham Godyn**, back from Prague, was employed on decorative commissions from about 1710 and had **Marten Joseph Geeraerts** (Pl. 855) as his pupil in 1723; **Jacques Ignatius de Roore**, who began as an assistant to **Gaspar Jacob van Opstal**, painted allegories on the ceilings of the Council and Treasury Chambers of the Town Hall in 1715 and also worked for private mansions; **Louis Rysbraeck**, presumed a son of **Peter Rysbraeck**, and perhaps a pupil of **Abraham Genoels** (Pls. 817, 826), signed a *Diana and her nymphs in a wooded landscape with a temple* in 1716; and figures of *Flora* or *Pomona* and so forth were inserted in compositions by flower painters like **Jan Baptist Bosschaert, Gaspar Pieter Verbruggen the younger** (Pl. 809), **Jacques Leyssens, Jacob van Hal** and **Gaspar Jacob van Opstal**. In Brussels the Town Hall received a ceiling-painting titled *Meeting of the Gods on Olympus* by **Victor Honoré Janssens** (Pls. 812, 827) who went abroad again in 1718; another ceiling was painted with allegoric subjects by **Jean van Orley**; and **Richard van Orley** continued to draw miniatures with classical subjects. Malines Town Hall received ceiling-paintings with allegories by **Pierre Simon Verlinden**; and in the Town Hall of Liège **Jean Riga** painted a *Justice, Prudence and Strength* for the Chamber of Marriages and a *Faith, Hope and Charity* for the Council Chamber.

As the demand for tapestries continued a number of painters were still employed on cartoons. In Antwerp, where the veteran **Abraham Genoels** (Pls. 817, 826) died at eighty-three in 1723, **Louis van Schoor** was available all through the period; and the Forchoudts sent to Vienna an *Orpheus* tapestry designed by **Pieter Spierinckx** who died in 1711. In Brussels, cartoons were made by **Jean van Orley**, by **Victor Honoré Janssens**, by a newcomer **Zeger Jacob van Helmont** and perhaps still by **Adriaen Frans Baudewyns** (Pl. 815) who died in poverty at sixty-seven in 1711; and **Arnold Smitsens**, a newcomer, was available in Liège in the second decade.

Costume-history compositions recalling past events in Belgian history or in the history of the religious orders or of particular churches were also produced. **Richard van Orley** for example was commissioned to paint a *Return to Rome of Pope Innocent II, 1133* for the Benedictine Tongerloo Abbey (as Innocent II had been a Benedictine Abbot); **Constantyn Francken** painted a *Martin van Rossem after his attempts on Antwerp in 1542*; **Victor Honoré Janssens** designed tapestries showing *The inauguration of Philip of Burgundy as Duke of Brabant* and the *Abdication of Charles V* for the Brussels Town Hall; and in 1720 **Willem Ignatius Kerricx** contributed two pictures to a series commissioned for display in the Brussels celebration of the fifth centenary of the founding of S. Gudule Cathedral.

Among the painters of religious pictures the newcomers **Willem Ignatius Kerricx** and **Jacques Ignatius de Roore** were both highly successful in Antwerp. **Kerricx** was Master there in 1704, gave the Guild of S. Luke a *S. Luke painting the Virgin* in 1718 and was commissioned by Tongerloo Abbey to paint two enormous compositions *Passover in Egypt* and *The Adoration of the Lamb* in 1725. **Jacques Ignatius de Roore** painted a large *Liberation of Christian slaves by Trinitarian monks* with many half-nudes and some figures in Oriental costumes, for Antwerp, S. Jacques, in 1709 and was much employed till he went abroad about 1720. Of the older church painters in Antwerp **Henri Herregouts** died in 1704 and **Gaspar Jacob van Opstal** in 1717; **Jean Pierre Tassaert**, abroad in 1717, was otherwise available for church paintings till he died at sixty-four in 1725; and **Jacob van Hal** and **Jan Claudius de Cock** were also both available all through the period. In Brussels many artists were still employed on pictures for churches and other buildings reconstructed after Marshal Villeroi's bombardment; **Victor Honoré Janssens** provided S. Nicolas with *S. Roch healing the plague-stricken* and S. Madeleine with *The anointing of Christ's feet;* **Jean van Orley** painted a *Christ on the Cross* for the Alderman's Chamber in the Town Hall in 1712; **Zeger Jacob van Helmont**, Master in 1711 at twenty-eight, painted a *Christ and the woman of Canaan* for S. Nicolas, *The Martyrdom of S. Catherine* (described by Descamps as 'bien dans la manière de Guide') for S. Madeleine; also *Christ on the Cross*, very famous in its day, for the Carmelite church in Ghent. **François Eisen** began to paint pictures destined for Valenciennes churches when he was twenty-one in 1716; **Philips Karel Marissal** of Ghent who had studied in Paris joined **van Helmont** in Brussels as assistant about 1723 when he was about twenty-five; and **Jean Baptist Millé** was **van Helmont's** pupil from about 1724. In Ghent itself **Robert van Audenaerd,** back from Italy aged forty in 1703 was author of the impressive *Assembly of Bernardine monks in Baudeloo Abbey before a fresco of the Virgin presenting the habit of the Order* (Pl. 823) and also painted *S. Peter enjoining a group of Carthusian monks to stay in their monastery* for the local Chartreux, a *Martyrdom of S. Catherine* for S. Jacques and a *Christ among the Doctors* for the Petit Béguinage all probably commissioned at this time; his pupil **Jan Baptist van Volsum,** Master at twenty-seven in 1706, painted a *S. Nicholas overthrowing the idols* for Alost, S. Martin, probably before 1725; and of the older generation of Gantois **Jan van Cleef** died at seventy in 1716 and **Gilles Le Plat** at about the same age in 1724. In Bruges **Nicolas Vleys** died under forty in 1703 and **Jan Baptiste van Meunincxhove** about eighty in 1704; and **Lodewyck de Deyster** who painted a *Road to Calvary* and a *Descent from the Cross* as a night effect, perhaps with the aid of his daughter **Anna de Deyster,** in 1704, was mainly occupied thereafter with the making of musical instruments till he died, it seems in poverty, in 1711. Of the other Bruges painters of religious subjects surviving from the last period **Jan Baptist Herregouts** worked till 1721 after founding the Bruges Academy, as noted, with **Joseph van den Kerckhove** who worked till 1724 and **Marcus van Duvenede** who was abroad for the first few years and painted little if at all after 1718 when he married a wealthy lady in the lace trade. A newcomer, later influential, **Mathias de Visch** was a pupil of **van den Kerckhove** in the Academy and left for Paris aged twenty-one in 1723; **Dominique Nollet** was not in Bruges in this period as he followed the fortunes and peregrinations of his patron Maximilian Emmanuel. In Malines **Jan Erasmus Quellinus** (Pl. 821) spent his last years in poverty living with a daughter; **Sebastiaen van Aken,** back from his travels soon after 1701, painted again some pictures for the churches till he died at seventy-four in 1722; **Pierre Simon Verlinden** worked for the Jesuit Church and the Soeurs Noires convent and died in 1725. A newcomer **Gilles Joseph Smeyers** went abroad at twenty-one in 1715; his grandfather **Gilles Smeyers** died in 1710; and his father **Jacques Smeyers** became blind at the end of the period. In Louvain there was **Lambert Blendeff** till 1721; and in Namur there was **Pierre Delcloche** from Dinant. In Liège **Englebert Fisen** continued his copious output; **Nicolas la Fabrique,** already fifty-two when the period started, **A. Dumoulin** and **Philippe Coclers** were all still available; and **N. J. Riga** was presumably working till he died at sixty-four in 1717. Among the newcomers in Liège, **Renier Panhay de Rendeux** went abroad at eighteen in 1702 and returned in 1712; **Olivier Pirotte,** his pupil at seventeen in 1716, went abroad in 1721; **Edmond Plumier** pupil of **Englebert Fisen** went abroad about twenty-one about 1715 and was back by 1719; **Jean Baptiste Coclers** son and pupil of **Philippe Coclers** also went abroad as a young man probably before 1720; and **Jean Riga** who painted a *Marriage Feast at Cana* for S. Nicolas, died at forty-five in 1725.

Among the portrait painters a new generation appeared in Antwerp painting conversation pieces, subscription groups and single portraits. These newcomers included **Balthazar van den Bossche** (Pl. 832) who returned to Antwerp from France about 1701, painted Marlborough, as noted, in 1706, and died at thirty-four in 1715 from striking his head on a window frame while lecturing to his students; **Jan Baptist Nollekens,** who painted conversation pieces, went abroad in 1716 or earlier; **Pieter van Angellis** who came from his native Dunkirk just under twenty about 1704, went abroad about 1711, was back in Antwerp in 1715 and then went abroad again; **Jan Joseph Horemans the elder** (Pls. 836-8) was Master at twenty-four in 1706; **Pieter Snyers** (Pls. 839, 856), Master at twenty-six in 1707, went abroad about 1720 or earlier; **Francois Xavier Verbeeck** was Master at twenty-four in 1710; **Ignace van der Beken** (Pl. 834) went abroad at twenty-three in 1712 and came back about ten years later; and **Pieter Jacob Horemans** and **Joseph Francis Nollekens** (son of **Jan Baptist Nollekens**) both began about 1720. Of the older portrait painters **Franciscus de Cock** died in Antwerp in 1709 and the Cathedral chaplains, alluding to his varied activities, wrote the following epitaph in their register:

> Si Cocum cognovisses,
> Non vere ut cocum, sed ut pictorem amasses:
> Si Cocum mecum audisses,
> Non cocum, sed cantorem dilexisses:
> Nunc pictor, cantor, Cocus
> Coxit sibi cibos in oevum. Echo: verum!

Jan van Helmont died about 1714, **Gaspar Jacob van Opstal** in 1717, and **Hendrik Goovaerts** (Pl. 845) in 1720; both **Jean Pierre Tassaert** and **Jan Baptist Nollekens** were available till 1717 when both went abroad, and **Tassaert**, as noted, was there again about 1718. The conversation pieces of this time continued the tradition of **Gonzales Coques** (Pl. 764) and **Jan van Kessel the younger** (Pl. 808) as can be seen in **Jan van der Beken's** *Portrait group on the terrace of a park* (Pl. 834) where the setting is perhaps the work of **Jan van der Straeten**; and students of English portrait painting may find it fruitful to compare this picture painted in 1722 with conversation groups in gardens by Dandridge, Devis, Hogarth, Mercier and so forth. The subscription groups ordered by the guilds and corporations now had a character of their own; my plates have shown groups of various members of fraternities and public bodies incorporated in religious scenes by **Geertgen** (Pl. 124) the **Malines Guild of S. George Master** (Pl. 146) and others in the fifteenth century, and placed under the protection of the Virgin by **Gaspar de Crayer** (Pl. 598) and **Pieter van der Plas** (Pl. 676) in the seventeenth: they also show such subscribers arranged in rows by **Jan van Scorel** (Pl. 300) or grouped round a dining-table by **Cornelis Anthonisz** (Pl. 299) and **Dirck Barendsz** (Pl. 389); but now some contemporary episode in the corporation's history is made the nominal occasion for these groups which thus continue the *Performance of William Tell before the S. Sebastian Guild* (Pl. 784) commissioned from **Charles Emmanuel Biset** in 1672. **Balthazar van den Bossche** for example painted *The Reception of J. B. del Campo Burgomaster of Antwerp by the Junior Crossbowmen's Guild* (Pl. 832), **Hendrik Goovaerts** *The Junior Crossbowmen's Guild inaugurating the portrait of their Captain Jan Carel de Corde* and **Francois Xavier Verbeeck** *The Reception of J. B. Vermoelen Abbot of S. Michel by the Corporation of Fencers*. In **Balthazar van den Bossche's** picture (Pl. 832) the elaborate architectural setting is known to be the work of **Jan van der Straeten,** and the park beyond of **Cornelis Huysmans,** and the fat Burgomaster appears with his thumb inside his hand because he had been backward in producing his share of the picture's price. In **Verbeeck's** picture painted in 1713 the numerous portraits are displayed with grandiose architecture in the background and a garden vista, a parrot is perched on a stay rod, and a huge curtain is looped across the top of the picture as in Rigaud's *Louis XIV* of 1700 and Hogarth's *Beggar's Opera* of 1728. In Brussels portraits were now being painted by **Louis Volders** and **Jean van Orley**; in Bruges by **Jan Baptist Herregouts** and **Joseph van den Kerckhove** and perhaps in his last years by **Jacob van Oost the younger** (Pls. 769, 771) who came back from Lille in 1710 and died at seventy-four in 1713. In Ghent there was the able **Robert van Audenaerd** whose thirty-five life-size portraits in his *Assembly of the Bernardine monks in Baudeloo Abbey* (Pl. 823) have just been referred to, and **Gilles Le Plat** who also painted an *Assembly of Bernardine monks* for Baudeloo Abbey. **Jacques Beernaert** painted corporation groups in Ypres. **Nicolas Stramot** back from England early in the period may have painted some portraits in Montaigu before he died there at seventy-two in 1709; **Gilles Smeyers** probably painted some in his last ten years in Malines; and in Liège where **Englebert Fisen** was most in demand, **Nicolas la Fabrique** and **Philippe Coclers** were available all through the period and **Edmond Plumier** from 1720.

In social genre painting there was now a vogue for carnival and party scenes. One **C. J. de Crec**, pupil of **Gaspar Jacob van Opstal** in 1707, signed, for example, a *Carnival scene* in 1717; and I reproduce a picture titled *Carnival in a Palace* (Pl. 845) painted by **Hendrik Goovaerts** in 1714. In **Goovaerts'** picture the setting—a terrace with statues, urns and so forth and a large looped curtain at the top—is in much the same style as the settings for the portrait groups by **Balthazar van den Bossche** (Pl. 832) and **Ignace van der Beken** (Pl. 834) and it was possibly provided by **van der Straeten** or some other specialist; the figures suggest not an elegant high-life fête but a rather drunken art students' fancy-dress party; for a young woman in the large hat of a shepherdess pours wine from an Italian *fiasco* into the glass of a young man lying at her feet (who recalls the young man at the feet of the nun in **Bosch's** *Haywain* (Pl. 165)) and in the foreground another young man, overcome with drinking, clasps a wine-jug in his arms; some of the company play fiddles as they move about the room and on the right a young man and a girl face one another in a dance (as in the very different pictures in Edinburgh and Dulwich which Watteau painted perhaps in this same year.)

The vogue for studio interiors continued; and the painters included **Gerard Thomas** who lived till 1720, **Balthazar van den Bossche**, **François Xavier Verbeeck**, **Pieter van Angellis** till he went abroad, and probably **Jan Thielens**. In *The Painter's studio* (Pl. 833) by **Gerard Thomas** there is nostalgic hark back to 'ye olde times' (as in the *Moneychanger and his wife* (Pl. 318) by **Marinus van Reymerswaele**); for the lady whose portrait is being painted wears clothes of the time of Albert and Isabella, and the artist himself is provided with a ruff; the studio is the usual architectural structure of this period with columns, urns and looped up curtain; and the student at this point may find it instructive to trace this theme of the artist at his work as shown in pictures reproduced here by the **Boston S. Luke Painter** (Pl. 48), the **London S. Luke Painter** (Pl. 186), **Jan Gossaert** (Pl. 238), the **Fogg S. Luke Painter** (Pl. 260), **Marten van Heemskerck** (Pl. 304), **Lancelot Blondeel** (Pl. 330), **Frans Floris** (Pl. 351), **Joos van Winghe** (Pl. 457), **Henri Staben** (Pl. 518) and **David Ryckaert III** (Pl. 646). This tradition was often combined at this time with the theme of the collector's gallery or an interior containing an invented collection of miscellaneous objets d'art; and it was then usually titled *Allegory of Painting and Sculpture* or *Allegory of the Fine Arts* thus recalling the pictures reproduced here by **Jan (Velvet) Brueghel** (Pl. 542) and the **Hague Studio of Apelles Painter** (Pl. 580). There are elements of this in the *Painter's studio* by **Gerard Thomas** as 'Painting' in the foreground holds a circular framed picture and 'Sculpture' is symbolized by the *Farnese Hercules* (which, it will be recalled, was one of the antique statues drawn by the students in **Antoon Goubau's** picture (Pl. 775)); and in an *Allegory of the Fine Arts* of this kind by **Balthazar van den Bossche** the Muse of Painting is at work on a canvas (as in the *Allegory of the study of the nude* (Pl. 811) by **Jacob Denys**)—and 'Sculpture' is symbolized by Giovanni Bologna's *Rape of a Sabine woman*.

Interiors with peasant and bourgeois genre were painted by **Jan van Pee** who died in 1710, and by his pupil **Jan Joseph Horemans the elder** (Pls. 836-8) who was Antwerp Master in 1706 and inherited **van Pee's** drawings and sketchbooks. In *The Shoemaker's* *shop* (Pl. 836) by **Horemans** the central group of a standing woman with a child looking over its shoulder anticipates the gentle observation of Chardin (who was thirteen when this picture was painted in 1712) and the group of the cobbler's wife and her family on the right is also agreeably seen and composed; the *Poacher denounced* (Pl. 837) reminds us that Hogarth, born two years before Chardin, was fifteen years younger than **Horemans** and may have been acquainted with his work; and we find something like Hogarth's protests against cruelty in a *Village School* painted by **Horemans** in 1712, for there a child about to be chastised by the clerical schoolmaster shrinks and writhes in screaming terror on the floor. Other interior genre pictures painted at this time were in the tradition of **Teniers** whose subjects were still repeated; and **Jacques Smeyers** of Malines signed an *Old woman with an old man counting money* in 1710.

The taste for outdoor genre scenes in the style of **Jan (Velvet) Brueghel** (Pls. 480-3) already noted in the previous period, was now at its height; there was also a vogue for pastiches in the manner of the Dutch painter Philips Wouverman; and an Antwerp dealer named De Witte especially catered for these tastes. **Joseph van Bredael** who painted *Riverside village with gentry and cattle* (Pl. 840) at twenty-five in 1723 was employed for nine years by this dealer; **Jan Frans van Bredael**, probably his cousin, was employed in the same way till he went abroad in 1715 and Descamps wrote of him (in 1763): 'S'il etait presque impossible de distinguer ses copies, bientôt on eut la même peine à distinguer ses imitations'. **Theobald Michau**, who moved from Brussels to Antwerp at thirty-five in 1711, also served the **Jan (Velvet) Brueghel** fashion as can be seen in his *Riverside village with peasants and cattle* (Pl. 841); and the Wouverman influence is apparent in the work of **Carel van Falens** (Pl. 846) who went abroad at twenty in 1703. Other young men painting outdoor genre scenes continously or on occasion included **Jan Joseph Horemans the elder** just referred to as a painter of genre interiors (Pls. 836-8), **Pieter Snyers** Antwerp Master at twenty-six in 1707 whose serious and imposing *Market vendors with fruit, fish and ram* (Pl. 839) may have been painted before he went abroad a few years later, **Jan Baptist Lambrechts** active in Antwerp from 1709 when he was twenty-nine, **Pieter van Angellis** for part of the period, **Frans Breydel** Antwerp Master in 1712 who painted a *Carnival dance amid Roman ruins* and went abroad about forty about 1720, and the brilliant **Arnold Frans Rubens** who was Antwerp Master at twenty-two in 1709, died ten years later, and is re-presented here by *Merrymaking outside a tavern* (Pl. 843) and the *Carnival in an Italian landscape* (Pl. 844) where what seems to be the Campo Vaccino in Rome is enlivened by dancers, quacks and actors and a dog barking at a boy astride a hobby-horse. Of the older outdoor genre painters **Jan Baptist van der Meiren** died about 1708; **Pieter van Bredael** (Pl. 778) signed a *Landscape with kermesse* (probably assisted by his son **Jan Pieter van Bredael**) in 1715 and died at ninety in 1719; **Pieter Bout** (Pls. 796, 797) died at sixty-one the same year; and **Mathieu Schoevaerdts** (Pls. 798, 816), whose death-date is unknown, may still have been living in 1725.

Among the specialists in landscapes, sometimes with small figures and cattle by others, **Cornelis Huysmans** produced wooded and eclectic compositions till the end of the period and **Jan Baptist Huysmans** (Pl. 825) died at sixty-two in 1716. Italianate landscapes were painted by **Peter Rysbraeck** who became Director of Antwerp Academy in 1713 and moved to Brussels at sixty-five in 1720, by **Jan Anthonie van der Leepe** who had **Joseph van den Kerckhove** and **Marcus van Duvenede** to help him with the figures and held civic offices in Bruges till he died in 1718; by **Joseph Vervoort**; by **Hendrik van Lint** (Pls. 864, 865) who was a pupil in Antwerp of **Pieter van Bredael** (Pl. 778) and went abroad quite early in the period and never came back; by **Jean Baptiste Juppin**, born in Namur, who went abroad aged thirty-seven in 1712 and came back in 1717 to work in Liège and Namur; and by **Lambert Dumoulin** who seems to have worked continuously in Liège. Of the older painters of Italianate landscape **Peter van Orley** who signed two *Arcadian landscapes* (miniatures on parchment) at sixty-four in 1702, and **Jacques de Rooster** both probably died before 1725; and, as already mentioned, **Adriaen Frans Baudewyns** (Pl. 815) died at sixty-seven in 1711, **Pieter van Bredael** (Pl. 778) at ninety in 1719, **Pieter van Bloemen** at sixty-three in 1720 and **Abraham Genoels** (Pls. 817, 826) at eighty-three in 1723.

Marines, coast scenes and naval combats were painted by **Jan Baptist van der Meiren** who signed a *Sea battle with Barbary pirates* in 1701; by **Jan Anthonie van der Leepe**; by **Antoon van Minderhout** who died at thirty in 1705; and by **Lucas Smout the younger** who died at forty-three in 1713 after producing a *Sea battle at Kjogebucht* in 1710 and the *Beach scene at Scheveningen* (Pl. 795) where static uprights of masts and buildings are contrasted with bustling groups of figures and animals in the foreground and with rolling clouds above.

Of the pictures of military combats I have already mentioned the contemporary battles painted by **Constantyn Francken** who died at sixty-three in 1720, by **Peter Verdussen** who died about fifty after 1710, by **Jasper Broers** who died at thirty-four in 1716, and by **Jan Pieter van Bredael** and **Carel Breydel** who both lived through the period. In the *Battle of Eeckeren* (Pl. 828) by **Constantyn Francken** the Marquis de Bedmar and the French Marshal Boufflers direct operations in the foreground and, beyond, we have a plan-of-battle composition like the *Siege of Courtrai* (Pl. 700) by **Pieter Snayers** and similar pieces by **Adam van der Meulen**. In **Jan Pieter van Bredael's** *Prince Eugene's victory over the Turks at Peterwardein* (Pl. 830) the Prince followed by his trumpeter directs fresh Austrian reinforcements to the central battle; and the complex composition shows how military painting had developed from the earlier examples reproduced here by **Sebastiaan Vrancx** (Pl. 531), **Pieter Meulener** (Pl. 698) and **Pieter Snayers** (Pl. 701). **Carel Breydel's** pictures of the Turkish war in the style of his *Cavalry attack* (Pl. 831) represent more generalized military combats in landscape settings probably provided by some landscape specialist; and indeed the extensive landscape in his *Military movements by a river* (Pl. 842) is monogrammed by the Dutch painter Jan Robert Griffier. Others painting military pieces in these years were **Peter Tillemans** (Pl. 829) who went abroad in 1708, **Joris van Bredael** till about 1706, **Jan Baptist van der Meiren** till 1708, **Arnold Frans Rubens** (Pls. 843, 844) till 1719, **Pieter van Bloemen** till 1720, and **Dominique Nollet** of whose work in this category (for Maximilian Emmanuel) Descamps wrote in 1763: 'Ses batailles, ses campements, ses sièges de villes, ses marches d'armées sont traités avec feu et avec une grande vérité; on ne peut avoir plus de facilité; il semble de près que quelques-uns de ses tableaux ne soient qu'à moitié faits, à peine la toile ou le panneau sont-ils couverts de couleur, mais à une certaine distance on est frappé de l'harmonie et de la chaleur qui règnent partout; son dessein est correct et spirituel; sa manière approche de celle de **van der Meulen**; quant au mérite de l'idée et de l'exécution, il y a peu de différence entre **van der Meulen** et **Nollet**: je donnerai cependant la palme au premier.'

Compositions with animals and birds or trophies of the chase with dead game were still much painted. **Adriaen de Gryef** who died in 1715 shows French influence in his *Huntsman and trophies in a landscape* (Pl. 847) though in his *Eagle attacking poultry* (Pl. 735) he followed the tradition seen here in pictures by **Jan van Kessel the elder** (Pl. 732), **Jan Fyt** (Pl. 733) and **David de Coninck** (Pl. 734). **Bernaert de Bridt** who probably died before 1725 signed a *Still-life with dead swan, hare, monkey and dog* in 1712. **Philip Ferdinand van Hamilton** (Pls. 849, 851) and his brothers **Charles William de Hamilton** and **John George de Hamilton** (Pl. 850) all left for Central Europe quite early in the period; and **Andries Verhoeven** left, probably in the first decade, for Rome. Among the newcomers **Jan Baptist Bouttats**, who had **Pieter van Angellis** as his pupil before 1705, signed a *Cocks fighting* and a *Cock attacked by a vulture* in the manner of **Jan Fyt**. **Peter Andreas Rysbraeck**, Antwerp Master in 1709, painted dead game in landscape and other still-life till he went abroad in 1720. **Jan Baptist Govaerts** represented here by *Game piece with dead boar in a landscape* (Pl. 848) was a pupil of **Alexander van Bredael** in 1713; **Pieter Jan Snyers** was a pupil of his uncle **Pieter Snyers** in 1713; and **Arnold Smitsens** painted *Trophies of the chase* as a set of overdoors in Liège Town Hall in 1721.

There were also still painters of tables with food, vessels, fruit and flowers; and painters of garlands round grisaille panels or in compositions with allegoric figures supplied by others. A whole generation in the first category had died at the end of the century, but the new men included the admirable **Pieter Snyers**, already referred to as portraitist and genre painter, whose feeling for still-life, much developed later, can be seen in his *Market vendors with fruit, fish and ram* (Pl. 839) where the crocus-pot and the leafless trees proclaim the season of the year. Flowers and fruit and garlands were now painted in Antwerp by **Jan van der Borght**, by **François van Aken**, by **Gaspar Pieter Verbruggen the younger** (Pl. 809) till he went to Holland in 1706 and after his return in poverty in 1723, by **Jacob Seldenslach**, by **Jan Baptist Bosschaert** who lived in indigence, exploited by dealers, till 1710, and possibly by **Christiaen de Knodder** who may have lived into this period. In Brussels **Jean Baptiste Morel** was much employed by the rich families on decorative flowerpieces for houses reconstructed in the first decade after Marshal Villeroi's bombardment, and he was still at work there in 1725. **Jan Christoph Lotyn**, whose death date is unknown, may also have still been at work there.

In France there were Belgian painters active in the last years of Louis XIV's reign, and through the Regency and after. **Matthieu Elias** painted *The sons of Sceva tormented by demons* for Paris, Notre Dame, in 1702, drew a *Cistercian monks before the Pope* in 1707, was Rector of the old Academy of S. Luke in 1709, and then settled at Dunkirk where he worked for the local churches. **Jean Jacques Spoede**, painter of animals, still-life with game and also of allegories and mythologies, arrived in Paris aged about twenty-three about 1703, met Watteau soon after at the Confrérie Flamande de S. Germain des Prés and introduced him to the dealer Sirois. **Perpète Delcloche** from Dinant, probably there by 1700, was Laureate of the Academy of S. Luke in 1723 and is said to have worked at some time with Nicolas Lancret (who was twenty years his junior). **Carel van Falens** arrived aged twenty in 1703, stayed on and became Court Painter to Louis XV in 1724 and was successful with picturesque genre pieces like the *Hunters assembling* (Pl. 846) painted a few years later. **Joseph van Bredael** whose *Riverside village with gentry and cattle* is reproduced here (Pl. 840) was in Paris, probably in this period, and became a member of the Academy. **Jan Frans van Bredael** came from London as pasticheur and dealer for a short while in 1719 when **Jan Pieter van Bredael** was also there as dealer. **Joseph Francis Nollekens**, Antwerp painter of conversation pieces, genre and decorations, seems to have arrived under twenty about 1720 and is said to have worked under Watteau (who died in the summer of 1721). The Brugeois **Mathias de Visch** came aged twenty-one in 1723 and left soon after for Rome, the Liégeois **Edmond Plumier** worked for some time about 1715 under Largillière and then went to Rome. **Jacques François Delien** of Ghent, another pupil of Largillière, painted portraits and occasional genre and remained to become a member of the Academy and Court Painter to Louis XV in 1725; and the Liégeois **Olivier Pirotte** reached Paris aged twenty-six in 1725, after study in Rome, and worked with Noël-Nicolas Coypel who was then much employed as a painter of religious subjects and mythologies. Elsewhere in France **Dominique Joseph van Oost** (son of **Jacob van Oost the younger** (Pls. 769, 771)) was established in Lille and painted religious subjects for the churches there; and **Jacques Smets** of Malines was established in Auch and painting for the town authorities and churches in the twenties.

In England the newcomers in Queen Anne's reign included **Anthoni Schoonjans, Peter Tillemans, Peter Casteels III** and **Pieter van Angellis**. Of these **Schoonjans** came here from Holland, aged about fifty-two about 1707 and painted a staircase in Little Montague House and a portrait of **Jan Peeters** ('Doctor' Peeters) before leaving for Düsseldorf a year or two later. **Peter Tillemans**, already referred to as a painter of military pieces, came on a dealer's invitation when he was about twenty-four in 1708 and was at first employed as a copyist or pasticheur of pictures by **Teniers** and similar painters and of battle pieces by the Frenchman Jacques Courtois; but he soon developed as a military painter in pictures like the *Attack on a Convoy* (Pl. 829) which recalls the same subject by **Lambert de Hondt** (Pl. 699), and also as a painter of landscapes and topographic views with mansions, of race horses and other animals and of equestrian portraits; in 1711 he was a foundation member of Kneller's Academy and later he was Steward of the Virtuosi of S. Luke (known as Van Dyck's club) and was patronized by the Duke of Devonshire, Lord Derby, Lord Byron and others; in 1719 he drew views for Bridges' 'History of Northamptonshire', in 1725 he painted *Thoresby Hall with the Duke of Kingston and a shooting party* and he painted scenery at various times for the Haymarket Opera House. His brother-in-law **Peter Casteels III** who came to London at the same time and was also a member of Kneller's Academy and also remained here, painted decorative flowerpieces with birds and so forth in the tradition of **Pieter Gysels** (Pl. 806) as can be seen in the example reproduced *Flowerpiece on a terrace with parrot and monkey* (Pl. 857). **Pieter van Angellis**, here from Antwerp by 1712, and described by Vertue as 'a man of affable temper and genteel manners' painted an *Installation of the Knights of the Garter in Kensington Palace on August 4th 1713*, conversation pieces and social genre scenes anticipating Hogarth, studio interiors with the customary collector's bric-a-brac, and market scenes with piles of vegetables, fish and fruit; he had considerable success and was established by 1725 in the fashionable artists' quarter, the Covent Garden Piazza. Of the older Flemish painters already here in Queen Anne's reign **Jan Siberechts** (Pls. 787-92) died in 1703 and **Balthasar van Lemens** in 1704. **Simon Dubois** married Willem van der Velde's daughter at seventy-five in 1707 and died the next year leaving battle pictures to his wife and portraits of his parents by **Van Dyck** to his patron the Lord Chancellor Lord Somers. **Jan Peeters** ('Doctor' Peeters) continued as Kneller's drapery assistant till 1712; thereafter he was in diminished circumstances as gout interfered with his 'doctoring' of old drawings; but, Vertue tells us, having been before 'a proper lusty man of a free open temper, a lover of good company and his bottle' and being still 'of a high spirit with a little of the Spanish blood in him' he 'rather bore his misfortunes to himself than acquaint his friends to the last'. **Jean Baptiste van Lantscroon**, here throughout the period, signed some decorations in Arno's Grove, Southgate in 1723; **Simon Hardimé**, also here throughout the period, had Lord Scarborough among other patrons for his flowerpieces; **Jan Frans van Son** continued his decorative flowerpieces till he died here about 1718. In Edinburgh **John Baptist Medina**, knighted by the Lord High

Commissioner of Scotland just before the Union, continued to paint portraits and 'history' till he died in 1710.

Newcomers in the first ten years of George I's reign included **David Cornelisz de Heem** and **Pieter Snyers** (who may both have arrived before Queen Anne died), **Jan Frans van Bredael, Giuseppe Grisoni, Joseph van Aken, Peter Andreas Rysbraeck, Victor Honoré Janssens,** and **Frans Breydel**. Of these **David Cornelisz de Heem** painted fruit and flowerpieces in the family tradition and died here soon after 1718. **Pieter Snyers** seems to have been mainly employed here as a portraitist, though he may also have painted still-life pieces and genre subjects like his *Market vendors with fruit, fish and ram* (Pl. 839). **Jan Frans van Bredael** already mentioned as copyist, pasticheur and painter of landscapes with genre figures, came at the beginning of the reign, was patronized by James Radcliffe, Earl of Derwentwater whom he visited in prison before his execution for his part in the Jacobite rising; and he is said to have worked for the King before returning to Antwerp in 1725. **Giuseppe Grisoni** (or **Grison**), born probably at Mons, had some training in Italy at an early age, was brought here about 1715 by John Talman (son of the architect of Chatsworth and himself first Director of the Society of Antiquaries) became a member of John Vanderbank's Academy in St. Martin's Lane, painted *Colley Cibber* in one of his star parts, and other portraits, and was still here in 1725. **Joseph van Aken (van Haecken)** described by Vertue as 'a man of good complexion, a good round fat face and a small cast with one eye' came from Antwerp about twenty about 1719 and remained here painting 'history' and genre pieces for some years and then began specializing in posture-designing and drapery painting for the portraitists. **Peter Andreas Rysbraeck** came with his brother the sculptor John Michael Rysbraeck in 1720 and remained as a successful painter of still-life with game, fruit and fish sometimes with a landscape background. **Victor Honoré Janssens** (Pls. 812, 827) was here for a time about 1722. **Frans Breydel** painter of portraits, conversation pieces and carnival scenes, arrived before 1724 after working in Germany and remained for some years; and **Jan Baptist Nollekens** was here and painting conversation and genre pieces from about 1719 till the end of the period.

Among the Flemish painters in Holland, **Jean Andreas Biset** a friend of Campo Weyerman, worked in Delft in 1703 and thereafter for some years in Breda where he painted portraits of English officers and their wives then quartered there and produced a picture in 1709 called *Anna Maria de Salis on her death bed*; and **Jan Claudius de Cock** was in Breda till he left for Antwerp at a date unknown. **Anthoni Schoonjans** was in The Hague about 1704; **Gaspar Pieter Verbruggen the younger** (Pl. 809) came to The Hague in 1706 and painted flower garlands and other motifs in compositions by the Dutch decorator Matthaus Terwesten till he lost this employment through irresponsibility and idleness in 1722; **Pieter Hardimé**, who then obtained the post with Terwesten, had been in The Hague from the outset of the period with perhaps a visit to Antwerp in 1718 when he painted fruit and flower pieces symbolizing *The Seasons* for the Abbey of S. Bernard; **Perpète Evrard** reached The Hague about 1707 and remained painting portraits and miniatures; **Harmen Serin**, portrait painter from Ghent, was Master in The Hague in 1718; and **Jan Baptist Nollekens** was in Middelburg that year. In Amsterdam **Antoine Coxie** was active till he left for Berlin in 1705; **Anthoni Schoonjans** arrived from The Hague in 1706; **Elias van den Broeck** died in 1708; **Anthony Barbiers** painter of 'history' arrived from Rome about 1711; **Gerard de Lairesse** (Pls. 813, 814) died in 1711; **Carel Breydel** (Pls. 831, 842) arrived from Germany, worked for a dealer for some years, and left for Brussels about 1723; and **Jacques Ignatius de Roore** who arrived about 1720, and also worked at Rotterdam and

The Hague, was much employed on ceilings and decorative panels for the houses of the rich.

In Spain the gifted **Jan van Kessel the younger** (Pl. 808) painted a portrait of Philip V, which the King disliked, and died at fifty-four in 1708; and **Sebastiaen van Aken** arrived from Italy about 1700 and went on to Portugal before returning to Malines.

In Central Europe there were Flemish painters in Berlin, Munich, Düsseldorf and other German cities and, as always, in Vienna; and **J. Philipp van Santvoort** painter of social scenes, was probably in Poland as he signed a *Polish manners in the time of Augustus the Strong* in 1718.

Anthoni Schoonjans was in Berlin in 1702 and painted for Frederick I a *David and Goliath* showing the Crown Prince Frederick Wilhelm, then aged fourteen, as David. **John George de Hamilton** the horse painter (Pl. 850) also worked about this time for Frederick I; **Antoine Coxie**, who came from Amsterdam was Frederick's Court Painter from 1705 till 1713; and **Charles Sylva Dubois**, a native of Brussels, became his Court dancing master in 1707 and began to paint landscapes, with figures by the Frenchman Antoine Pesne, under Frederick William. **Dominique Nollet** went with Maximilian Emmanuel to Munich, as already mentioned, at the outset of the war; and **Jean Pierre Tassaert** visited Munich and painted some portraits there in 1717. **Charles William de Hamilton** seems to have been in Baden-Baden early in the period painting lizards and so forth among plants and thistles and also birds and animals; and thereafter he settled in Augsburg where he became Court Painter to Bishop Alexander Sigismund and painted his horses. **Frans de Backer** painter of religious subjects and portraits, **Ignace van der Beken** (Pl. 834) and **Anthoni Schoonjans** all spent some time in Düsseldorf at the Court of the Elector Palatine Johann Wilhelm (who also patronized the Dutch painters Jan Frans van Douven, Adriaen van der Werff, Godfried Schalcken, Jan Weenix and Rachel Ruysch); **Schoonjans** painted a portrait of the Electress and may also have painted there his *Job tormented by his wife* which is dated 1710. **Gilles Joseph Smeyers** went from Malines to Düsseldorf at twenty-one in 1715, worked there for three years under Jan Frans van Douven and then went to Rome. **Carel Breydel** (Pls. 831, 842) and his brother **Frans Breydel**, who painted portraits and conversation pieces, worked for some time at the Court of Hesse-Cassel. In Vienna **Joris van Bredael, Perpète Evrard, Victor Honoré Janssens, Frans van Stampart, Philip Ferdinand de Hamilton, John George de Hamilton, Jan Pieter van Bredael, Anthoni Schoonjans** and **Jacques Ferdinand Saey** were all active on long or short visits or all through the period. Of these **Joris van Bredael** probably died about 1706, **Perpète Evrard** left for Holland about 1707, **Victor Honoré Janssens** (Pls. 812, 827) paid a visit about 1718. **Frans van Stampart** continuously Court Painter under Leopold I, Joseph I and Charles VI painted portraits of all three Emperors and many of Austrian and German nobles, and Descamps wrote of him: 'Lorsqu'il peignoit des personnes de considération, qui n'avoient ni le temps, ni la patience d'attendre, il dessinoit leur tête aux crayons noir, blanc et rouge: d'après ce dessein il peignoit et il ne se servoit plus de la nature que pour finir. . . . Un auteur respectable assure qu'avant d'ébaucher une tête, il donnoit une couche de couleur de chair à la place même ou il la posoit.' **Philip Ferdinand de Hamilton** Court Painter to Joseph I and Charles VI signed his *Wolves and dead hind* (Pl. 849), in the savage tradition of **Frans Snyders** (Pls. 634, 635), in 1720 and his gentle *Deer and porcupine* (Pl. 851), which recalls the *Greyhound in flat landscape* (Pl. 633) by **Paul de Vos**, in 1724. **John George de Hamilton** arrived from Berlin before 1711, painted *The Imperial riding school with Charles VI on a white horse* and groups of horses in the style of the picture reproduced here (Pl. 850) for Prince von Liechtenstein, Prince von Schwarzenberg and other owners whose estates he visited for the purpose. **Jan Pieter van Bredael** whose battle pieces for Prince Eugene,

372

including the *Battle of Peterwardein* (Pl. 830) and the *Capture of Belgrade*, have already been mentioned, worked in Prague and Vienna and painted his *Ladies watching an elegant sportsman killing wild boars in an enclosure* at thirty-four in 1717. **Anthoni Schoonjans** returned, over sixty, to Vienna from Düsseldorf about 1716; he was much employed there and also at Brünn on church paintings and portraits, and he drew or painted at some time a *Joseph I on horseback with Fortuna and Justice in the clouds*. **Jacques Ferdinand Saey** had headquarters in Vienna all through the period and signed a *Hall with columns and figures* at sixty-seven in 1725.

In Rome whence Maratta's pupil **Robert van Audenaerd** (Pl. 823) returned to Ghent about 1703, the newcomers in Maratta's atelier included **Marcus van Duvenede** who came about twenty-seven soon after 1700 and visited Naples before returning to Bruges, and **Renier Panhay de Rendeux** who came at eighteen in 1702, remained in Italy till 1712 and then returned to Liège. Among the painters of the Italianate landscapes in the Poussin-Claude tradition **Jan Frans van Bloemen (Orizonte)**, praised by Descamps for his mists and rainbows, signed his *Campo Vaccino* (Pl. 820) with its admirable cattle (perhaps inserted by a specialist) in 1704 when he was forty-two and provided Prince Camillo Pamphili with a series of pictures in the style of the other examples reproduced here (Pls. 818, 819) in 1711. A newcomer **Hendrik van Lint** (Pls. 864, 865), already mentioned as a pupil of **Pieter van Bredael** (Pl. 778), arrived in Rome aged about twenty about 1704, was nicknamed 'Studio' at the 'Bent' initiation feast, remained throughout the period and was nearly lynched as a sorcerer in 1711 when a house which he was drawing in the Campagna mysteriously collapsed for no apparent reason. Others in Rome included the fruit and flower painter **Jan Baptist Brueghel** who was back there from Naples in 1700 and died there in 1719; **Anthony Barbiers** who had studied under **Pieter van Bloemen** and seems to have stayed till he went to Amsterdam about 1711; **Andries Verhoeven** nicknamed **Distelbloem** (Thistle) who signed there a *Hunting trophies in a landscape* in 1716; **Gilles Joseph Smeyers** who came on from Düsseldorf about 1719; and **Frans de Backer** who accompanied the Electress Anna-Louise de Médicis on a visit to her father Duke Cosimo III in Florence after the Elector Palatine's death in 1716, and painted his own portrait for the Uffizi when he reached Rome in 1721. The 'Bent' (the Schildersbent) which had existed since 1623, was dissolved by Pope Clement XI in 1720. But there was now a recognized concentration of Liégeois artists in Rome as a philanthropist has just founded a hostel for them and all new arrivals from Liège went to live there; these included **Edmond Plumier** who came from Paris about 1717 and stayed for two years, **Olivier Pirotte**, one of **Renier Panhay de Rendeux's** pupils, who arrived at twenty-two in 1721 and worked under Benedetto Luti and Pietro Bianchi till 1725; and **Jean Baptiste Coclers** who probably arrived before 1720 and worked for Sebastiano Conca and Marco Benefial. Elsewhere in Italy **Dominique Nollet** accompanied the Electress of Bavaria on a visit to Venice in 1706; **Robert la Longe** died in Piacenza in 1709; **Willem Borremans** (Guglielmo il Fiammingo) worked for churches in Cosenza from 1703 till 1705 and for churches in Palermo from 1715 onwards; and the Italianate landscape painter **Jean Baptiste Juppin** saw and drew an eruption of Vesuvius when visiting Naples between 1712 and 1717.

The Roman ruins in pictures of this period by **Frans Breydel** and in the *Carnival in an Italian landscape* (Pl. 844) by **Arnold Frans Rubens** may be evidence of Italian visits by both artists; but no such visits seem to be recorded; and these settings may have been painted from other pictures or from prints, or by landscape specialists who had been to Italy and were therefore called on to provide them.

CHAPTER XVIII

The Archduchess Maria Elizabeth 1726-1741;
Counts Harrach and von Königsegg 1741-1743;
Prince Charles of Lorraine 1744-1746;
Marshal de Saxe 1747-1748

1726-1748

THE NEW Governor-General, the Archduchess Maria Elizabeth, was a spinster of forty-five when she arrived in Brussels; and, as sister of the Emperor Charles VI, she maintained a formal quasi-regal court surrounded by officials from Vienna. Militantly pious, and driven by the Jesuits, she encouraged a new campaign against the Jansenists; and before she died she boasted with some reason that Jansenism had at last been 'liquidated' in her provinces.

As there was no war on Belgian territory during the sixteen years of Maria Elizabeth's rule, agriculture to some extent recovered; but Belgium was still economically exhausted by the War of the Spanish Succession and hampered by Dutch restrictions on her commerce. When the War of the Austrian Succession began the people were again required to contribute to war expenditure; and in the last years of the period the whole country was once more overrun by fighting and marauding troops.

In 1726 Maximilian Emmanuel died and his son Charles Albert became Elector of Bavaria; Cardinal Fleury became Premier Ministre for Louis XV; Voltaire was again imprisoned in the Bastille and then came aged thirty-two to England; and Swift published 'Gulliver's Travels' which **Giuseppe Grisoni (Pierre Joseph Grison)** began to illustrate soon after. In 1727 George II became King of England; and the Emperor Charles VI, yielding to Dutch, English and French protests against the Compagnie d'Ostende, caused financial panic in Belgium by suspending the company for the next seven years. In 1729 de Montesquieu came to England with Lord Chesterfield then British Ambassador at The Hague. In 1730 Charles Emmanuel III became Duke of Savoy and King of Sardinia on the abdication of his father; the University of Louvain ruled that all candidates for any academic grade must adhere to the Bull 'Unigenitus' (against Quesnel's 'Réflexions morales'); the Parlement de Paris united to oppose compulsory acceptance of the Bull; and Jansenist convulsionists caused excited scenes at the tomb of the French Jansenist Pâris in the churchyard of S. Médard. In 1732 the Compagnie d'Ostende was finally wound up. In 1733 the War of the Polish Succession began, and France, Spain and Charles Emmanuel of Sardinia were allied against the Austrians after Austro-Russian armies had installed Frederick Augustus II, Elector of Saxony (nephew of the Emperor) as Augustus III in Poland where Stanislas

Leczinski (father-in-law of Louis XV) had just been legally elected King. In 1734 Voltaire's 'Lettres anglaises' were burned by the Public Executioner in Paris; Hogarth was painting the *Rake's Progress* series in Leicester Fields; Charles Emmanuel defeated the Austrians at the battle of Guastalla, an event painted later by **Jan Peter Verdussen**; and Charles Emmanuel had other successes eventually painted by **Hyacinth de La Pegnia**. In 1735, the Polish war ended; Prince Francis, Duke of Lorraine, affianced to Maria Theresa the Emperor's daughter, renounced Lorraine for the Grand Duchy of Tuscany and the prospect of the Imperial crown; and Lorraine was ceded to Ex-King Stanislas Leczinski for his lifetime with reversion to the Crown of France. In 1736 David Hume, aged twenty-five, was writing his 'Treatise of Human Nature' at La Flèche; De Montesquieu's 'Lettres Persanes' were banned by the Sheriffs of Mons as 'un ouvrage impie et blasphématoire'; Johann Sebastian Bach, aged fifty-one and completing his B minor Mass in Leipzig, was appointed Court Composer by Frederick Augustus; and Samuel Johnson aged twenty-seven had David Garrick aged nineteen as his pupil at Edial. In 1739 Voltaire, visiting Brussels, described it as 'le séjour de l'ignorance' and 'l'éteignoir de l'imagination'; John Wesley, aged thirty-six, turned a disused gun-factory in London into a Methodist chapel; and England declared war on Spain about Captain Jenkins' ear. The Turks were rapidly successful in a new war waged against them by the Emperor some of whose troops were led by Prince Francis and his younger brother Prince Charles of Lorraine; and large areas were ceded to the Turks by the Treaty of Belgrade. In 1740 Frederick II, aged twenty-eight became King of Prussia; the Emperor Charles VI died; and the War of the Austrian Succession began when Charles Albert, Elector of Bavaria, challenged Maria Theresa's claim to the hereditary Habsburg dominions. In 1741 Frederick of Prussia attacked Maria Theresa and overran Silesia; France, Saxony and others also attacked her in support of Charles Albert; England voted her a subsidy of £300,000; the Hungarians provided her with 100,000 men; Prince Charles of Lorraine became a Field Marshal in the Austrian army; Prague fell to Franco-Bavarian forces; Elizabeth Petrovna became Empress of Russia; and the Archduchess Maria Elizabeth died in the Mariemont palace.

In 1742 Belgium was administered provisionally first by Count Harrach and later by the Count von Königsegg; the Duc d'Arenberg raised an army there for Maria Theresa; and fortifications were built round Brussels. Charles Albert of Bavaria was crowned Emperor as Charles VII in Frankfort; Munich was captured by the Austrians; and the French were besieged in Prague. In 1743 England, Holland and Sardinia were Maria Theresa's allies; Charles Emmanuel of Sardinia won the Battle of Casteldelfino; Anglo-Belgian troops with George II in command won the Battle of Dettingen, and Prince Charles of Lorraine was successful as a military leader and became affianced to Maria Theresa's sister the Archduchess Maria-Anna.

In 1744 Prince Charles and the Archduchess Maria-Anna arrived in Belgium as Joint Governors-General; in Brussels the Archduchess charmed the crowd by publicly wearing the costume of Brabant; and in Antwerp they were welcomed under arches designed by **Willem Ignatius Kerricx**. French troops assembled at Dunkirk to support the claim of Charles Edward the Young Pretender; Louis XV led troops into Belgium and captured Menin and Ypres; Prince Charles crossed the Rhine at Philipsbourg and entered Alsace; Frederick of Prussia overran Bohemia; Prince Charles arrived from Alsace and ejected Frederick from Prague; and the Archduchess Maria-Anna died in Brussels. In 1745 Belgium was administered by the Count von Kaunitz in the absence of Prince Charles who was twice defeated by the Prussians; Prince Francis, Maria Theresa's husband, was elected

Emperor as Francis I on the death of Charles VII (Charles Albert); Catherine of Anhalt-Zerbst aged sixteen was married to the Grand Duke Peter of Holstein-Gottorp, aged sixteen, grandson of Peter the Great and nephew of the Empress Elizabeth; and Frederick of Prussia finally secured Silesia. The Young Pretender landed in Scotland and marched south; Charles Emmanuel of Sardinia was defeated at Bassignano; French troops led by Marshal de Saxe, with Louis XV in the field, won the Battle of Fontenoy against George II's son the Duke of Cumberland; Marshal de Saxe captured Tournai, Ghent, Bruges, Audenarde, Termonde, Ostend and Nieuport; Louis XV made a Pageant Entry into Bruges through arches designed by **Jan Anton Garemyn** (Pls. 858, 860); and Madame de Pompadour was established at Versailles. In 1746 the Duke of Cumberland, with troops withdrawn from Belgium, defeated the Young Pretender at Culloden; and William Pitt aged thirty-eight refused all perquisites as Governor-General of the Forces. Charles Emmanuel of Sardinia won the Battle of Piacenza recorded in a drawing by **Jan Peter Verdussen** who was present as field artist; Marshal de Saxe captured Brussels without bombardment after courteously imploring von Kaunitz not to defend the suburbs; von Kaunitz and the Government retired to Antwerp; Louis XV slept in Brussels in a room adorned for the occasion with 'Don Quixote' Gobelins tapestries, and the Mannekin-Pis statue arrayed, in his honour, in a French suit and white cockade, was invested by the King with the Order of S. Louis. The actor Favart and his company were brought from Paris to entertain de Saxe's officers at their field headquarters and de Saxe lent them for some days to entertain Prince Charles who now opposed him with Austro-Belgian forces; Antwerp surrendered; von Kaunitz retired to Aix-la-Chapelle; and Prince Charles was defeated at Raūcourt (Roucoux) by de Saxe who commissioned the Liégeois **Paul Delcloche** to record his triumph.

In 1747 Marshal de Saxe was de facto Governor-General of Belgium for the King of France; French troops invaded Holland; de Saxe defeated an Anglo-Dutch army at the Battle of Laufeld (Laeffelt), a victory also recorded by **Delcloche**; and Bergen-op-Zoom was captured. Between the victories de Saxe paid court to the actress Madame Favart, French singers from the Paris opera performed for his officers in Brussels, and **Jan Frans van Bredael**, back from England by 1726, was patronized by the Prince de Clermont (French Governor in Antwerp) and sold to Louis XV a *Landscape with Christ preaching on the seashore* and a *Christ performing miracles*. In 1748 Ensign Clive fought gallantly against the French at the siege of Pondicherry; Hume published his 'Inquiry concerning Human Understanding' and went, as secretary to General St. Clair, in an embassy to Vienna and Turin; and de Montesquieu published his 'L'Esprit des Lois'. The War of the Austrian Succession ended; and Belgium was restored to Maria Theresa by the Treaty of Aix-la-Chapelle.

A feature of the period was the number of Belgian painters who were residents or visitors abroad.

Thus in England **Pieter van Angellis** painted more conversation groups in the manner of **Balthazar van den Bossche** (Pl. 832) and **Ignace van der Beken** (Pl. 834), and a *Covent Garden market with figures in contemporary clothes* as observed from his studio in the Piazza; and he left for Rome in 1728 (the year in which Hogarth began his conversation pieces). Before leaving England **Angellis** copied two *Market scenes* by **Snyders** in the Walpole Gallery at Houghton and Walpole wrote of him: 'His manner was a mixture of Teniers and Watteau with more grace than the former and more nature than the latter; his pencil was easy, light and flowing but his colouring too faint and nerveless; he afterwards adopted the habits of **Rubens** and **Van Dyck**, more picturesque indeed but not so proper to improve his productions in what their chief beauty consisted, familiar life';

and we may note in passing that such Rubens-Van Dyck costumes have already been seen here in the *Painter's studio* (Pl. 833) by **Gerard Thomas**, and that the fashion, spreading to English portraiture in the seventeen-thirties, when John Vanderbank painted his wife in what Vertue calls 'a habit somewhat like a picture of Rubens' wife', reached an aesthetic climax in the blue Van Dyck suit of Gainsborough's *Edward Bouverie* which, I imagine, was left in the studio by the sitter and used again later for the celebrated *Blue Boy*. **Peter Tillemans** (Pl. 829), who had Arthur Devis the English painter of small portraits and conversation pieces as his pupil, was living at Richmond in the first years of the period and probably painted his *View of Chelsea Hospital with Walpole House from across the river* and a charming small equestrian portrait *John 2nd Earl of Ashburnham* at this time; he was a frequent visitor in Lord Radnor's house at Twickenham where Alexander Pope, in his absence, made some alterations 'with glee' to one of his pictures then in progress there; about 1730 he was commissioned by the wealthy Dr. Cox Macro (chaplain to George III) to draw a handless and footless German dwarf called Buchinger who despite his infirmities could dance a hornpipe, play the hautboy and make drawings in one of which, a composition with a self-portrait, quotations from the psalms were ingeniously entwined within the curls of the peruke. **Tillemans** was also commissioned by Dr. Macro to decorate a staircase and paint some pictures at Little Haugh, Norton near Bury-St-Edmunds; and he died at Norton aged about fifty in 1734. **Joseph Francis Nollekens** (son of **Jan Baptist Nollekens** who left for France at a date unknown) arrived here from France in 1733 and was welcomed and helped at first by **Tillemans**; he painted conversation and genre pieces with small figures, groups of children, decorative pieces and pastiches after Panini and Watteau (from whom as noted in my last chapter he is said to have had some training); he worked for Lord Cobham at Stowe and Lord Castlemain (Lord Tilney) at Wanstead; he died at forty-six in 1748; and Vertue describes him as 'a little sprightly man' but another contemporary, the sculptor Banks, records him as a miser (like his son the sculptor Joseph Nollekens) and prostrated by fear lest his house should be looted in the anti-Catholic demonstrations after the Young Pretender's venture in 1745. **Peter Casteels III** (Pl. 857) brother-in-law of **Peter Tillemans**, published a set of bird prints in 1726, painted a series of *Twelve flowerpieces in vases representing the months* engravings of which were published by Robert Furber, a Kensington seedsman, in 1730; from 1735 onwards he made flower designs for a firm of Tooting calico printers and he moved with this firm to Richmond in the forties. **Peter Andreas Rysbraeck** who lived till 1748 continued to paint his still-life arrangements with game and so forth which Vertue tells us were 'paid for by Noblemen and Gentlemen at as high a rate as any contemporary painter in that kind'. **Joseph van Aken** (Van Haecken), here since 1719, was busily employed as posture-designer and drapery painter for the portraitists in the thirties and forties when he became known as 'Tailor Vanaken'; he worked thus for Highmore, Hudson, Ramsay, Dandridge and others including the Lancashire portraitist Hamlet Winstanley from whom he received heads which he returned completed as half-length or whole-length portraits; he was assisted in this work by his brother **Alexander van Haecken** and both were friends of Hogarth who declared that any 'phiz-monger' without a ray of genius could make more money in a week from the work of his drapery painter than 'a man of first professional talents' could make in three months, and who went with the brothers—and Hayman and Hudson—on the famous expedition of 1748 to Calais where Hogarth was arrested for sketching Calais Gate. Of the other Flemings already here in the previous period **Pieter Snyers** (Pls. 839, 856) and **Jan Frans van Bredael** returned to Antwerp in 1726 and **Frans Breydel** in 1727. **Jan**

Peeters ('Doctor' Peeters) died about sixty in 1727. **Giuseppe Grisoni** left for Italy in 1728. **Simon Hardimé** died about seventy in 1737; and **Jan Baptist van Lantscroon** died the same year at eighty-four. Among the newcomers, the Liégeois **Jean Latour**, painter of religious and 'history' subjects, was probably here in the later forties on his way back from Rome; and the Gantois **Petrus Johannes Reysschoot**, who seems to have arrived from Paris in the thirties or early forties, produced a genre piece titled *The Happy man* and a portrait *The Duchess of Norfolk* already engraved by 1746.

In Paris the established artists continued their careers and there were new arrivals in both decades. In the circle of the Académie Royale, **Jacques François Delien** worked throughout the period, **Carel van Falens** till he died at fifty in 1733, and **Joseph van Bredael** till he died at forty-one in 1739. Of these, **Delien**, a regular contributor to the Salons, sent a genre piece titled *La lanterne magique* in 1740 and *Un buveur sous une treille* in 1745. **Carel van Falens**, elected to the Académie Royale in 1726, deposited as reception-piece a cold, eclectic but ingeniously concocted *Hunters assembling* (Pl. 846) clearly influenced by the Dutch painter Philips Wouverman still much in favour in the international art trade at that time; and the student will find it instructive to compare this picture with Watteau's *Rendez-vous de Chasse* (London, Wallace Collection) painted in 1720. **Joseph van Bredael**, Court Painter to the Duke of Orleans in 1736, was still painting outdoor genre scenes in the **Jan (Velvet) Brueghel** tradition like the *Riverside village with gentry and cattle* (Pl. 840) referred to in my last chapter; and he was probably the artist 'Van Breda' employed as restorer of some passages in **Rubens'** *Marie de Médicis* series in 1730—a task for which his early experience as a dealer's pasticheur had to some extent equipped him. A newcomer **Gerard Rysbraeck**, from Antwerp, was selling hunting scenes, and still-life with fish and game, in Court circles by 1747. In the studios of the French artists of the Académie Royale the Liégeois **Olivier Pirotte** was still a pupil of Noël-Nicolas Coypel in 1726; he then joined the studio of François Lemoine; and he left for Liège about 1728 to try his fortune as painter of 'history' and religious subjects. The Gantois **Petrus Johannes van Reysschoot** was probably the 'Reyschoot' inscribed as a pupil in the Académie Royale in 1730 and he may have worked there for some years before leaving for England. The versatile **Hyacinth de La Pegnia** painter of contemporary warfare, designer of military tapestries, and occasional painter of topographic views, came from Brussels to Paris as 'ingénieur-dessinateur' about 1740, and I reproduce his attractive and interesting *Pont Neuf from the Quai de la Mégisserie* (Pl. 854) and *Pont Neuf from the Quai de l'Horloge* (Pl. 853) of 1743 both painted, I presume, with the aid of a camera obscura in the mode launched before 1730 by Luca Carlevaris in Venice. The well-born Liégeois **Nicolas de Fassin**, painter, later, of picturesque landscapes and social genre scenes, arrived aged twenty in 1748 and became an officer in the 'mousquetaires gris'. In the circle of the old Academy of S. Luc, Watteau's friend the animal and game-piece painter **Jean Jacques Spoede** was a figure all through the period and **Perpète Delcloche** was a teacher till he died at a date unknown. Newcomers in that circle included **Paul Joseph Delcloche** who worked under **Perpète Delcloche** and Lancret in the thirties, returned to his native Liège in 1740 and painted the battle pieces already mentioned for Marshal de Saxe in 1747. **Charles Joseph Redouté** (father of three celebrated flower painters) came from Dinant aged twenty-two in 1737, worked in the S. Luc Academy till 1743 and then settled at S. Hubert in Luxembourg where he painted religious subjects. **Jan Nollekens** painter of religious subjects, allegories and genre (and uncle of the sculptor Joseph Nollekens) reached Paris from Antwerp at the end of the twenties, sent his work to the S. Luc Academy's exhibitions and remained beyond the end of the period. Others in Paris in these

378

years were the veteran **Dominique Nollet** who came after his patron Maximilian Emmanuel's death and died over ninety in 1736; the portrait painter **Guillaume de Spinny** (Pl. 862) who arrived from Brussels in 1740; **François Eisen** who had worked for Valenciennes churches, and came via Brussels in 1745; and **Jacques de Soignie** of Mons, painter of religious subjects and portraits, who also came in the forties after study in Antwerp and Brussels. Elsewhere in France **Jan Peter Verdussen** of Antwerp, painter of military pieces and also of horse and cattle markets in the **Sebastiaan Vrancx** tradition (Pls. 532, 534), was domiciled in Marseilles till Charles Emmanuel of Sardinia called him to Turin in 1744; the Liégeois **Jean Baptiste Coclers** was in Marseilles, aged about thirty-five, on his way home from Rome about 1731. **Jacques Smets** continued his work for churches in Auch and the environs. **Pieter van Angellis** went from Rome to Rennes about 1731 and died there in 1734; **Dominique Joseph van Oost** died in Lille in 1738, **Matthieu Elias** in Dunkirk in 1741, and **Jan Baptist Nollekens** at Roanne about 1748.

In The Hague, where **Perpète Evrard** died in 1727, **Harmen Serin** continued his portrait practice all through the period; and **Pieter Hardimé** is said to have become melancholic in the later years as the demand for his fruit and flowerpieces and decorative paintings had declined. **Jacques Ignatius de Roore** left The Hague for Antwerp in 1728 but returned a year or two later and painted four large panels *The History of Pandora* for an Amsterdam sheriff, and other mythologies and 'histories' for rich patrons in The Hague; he was also active in art dealing, and in 1739, in association with another dealer, he bought **Van Dyck's** *S. Martin and the Beggar* from Saventhem church but was forced by a local riot in protest to return it; he died at sixty-one in 1747 when the sale of his remaining pictures and his acquisitions brought considerable money to his heirs. In Middelburg **Jan Andreas Biset** was still painting mythologies and portraits in the later twenties and died there, or elsewhere, about 1730. In Amsterdam the 'history' painter **Anthony Barbiers** died at fifty in 1726; and **Norbert van Bloemen**, still an unsuccessful artist, arrived from Antwerp, painted a portrait of the art dealer Jan Pietersz Somer for whom he probably produced some genre pieces at low prices, and died, at seventy, in 1746.

In Central Europe **Ignace van der Beken** (Pl. 834) visited Mainz to paint the Kurfürst, the Archbishop and other local notables in 1733; and **Jan Baptist Govaerts** who probably died there in 1746 was Court Painter from 1740 to 1745 when he produced some kitchen interiors as well as trophies-of-the-chase compositions like the picture reproduced here (Pl. 848). **Frans de Backer,** arriving from Italy, was Court Painter to the Prince Bishop in Breslau from 1726 and painted there an *Immaculate Conception* for S. Maurice and other religious pieces for S. Adalbert and the Cathedral. In Munich **Pieter Jacob Horemans** (younger brother and pupil of **Jan Joseph Horemans the elder**) became Court Painter at twenty-seven to Charles Albert Elector of Bavaria (later the Emperor Charles VII) in 1727—and worked there for the rest of the period painting fruit and flower pieces, numerous portraits of court ladies and elaborate records of court festivities beginning with the *Carrousel celebrating the birth of Kurfürst Max-Joseph 1727*. **Charles William de Hamilton**, still established in Augsburg, continued his animal and plant pieces with lizards and so forth and signed a *Dead fox* at seventy in 1739; and **Jan Baptist Lambrechts** may have died there before 1748. **Charles Sylva Dubois** approaching sixty in 1726 remained in Berlin under Frederick William and Frederick II and had figures painted in his landscapes not only by the Frenchman Antoine Pesne but also in the later years by the German George Wenceslaus Knobelsdorff who worked as a painter in the intervals of designing palaces and theatres for the King and laying out gardens in the forties. In Vienna **Anthoni Schoonjans** and **Jacques**

Ferdinand Saey both died, about seventy, in the first years of the period. **Jan Pieter van Bredael**, the recorder of Prince Eugene's victories (Pl. 830) and painter also of hunting pieces, signed a *Boarhunt* in 1727 and died in 1735 a year before the Prince. **John George de Hamilton** (Pl. 850) painted the *Imperial stables at Lipizza* in 1727 and a *Riding school* in 1735 and died at sixty-five in 1737. **Philip Ferdinand de Hamilton** (Pls. 849, 851) who continued to paint animals and birds and still-life with game, fruit and insects, was Court Painter to Maria Theresa in the forties; and the successful portraitist **Frans van Stampart** painted *Prince Charles of Lorraine*, contributed to an engraved repertoire of works of art in the Imperial collections, and was Court Painter to Maria Theresa at seventy-three when the period closed.

Of the artists established in Rome the veteran **Jan Frans van Bloemen** (Pls. 818, 819, 820) was made a member of the Accademia di S. Luca to celebrate his eightieth birthday in 1742 and lived for another six years; and **Hendrik van Lint** (Pls. 864, 865) signed a *Landscape with procession crossing a bridge* in 1726, became a member of the Congregazione dei Virtuosi in 1744, and signed an *Italian house seen from the garden with hounds being fed, while a beggar asks for food in vain* when he was sixty-four in 1748. Among the newcomers in Italy **Pieter van Angellis** arrived in Rome from England in 1728 in the company of two Belgian sculptors Laurent Delvaux and Pieter Schaemaeckers the younger; he was there till approximately 1731 when he left to return to England but stopped at Rennes and died there as related; in Rome, Vertue tells us, **Angellis** used a peasant youth as model for both male and female figures in his genre pictures and 'caused much sport and laughter' among the local artists by the sight of this 'rustic ill-shaped mortal' dressed in women's habits for the purpose; he also astonished the Italian painters by his transparent colouring in the Flemish tradition which led them to assume, quite wrongly, that he was using some special Flemish and not ordinary Italian pigments; but he was shy of exhibiting his pictures and the Pope's Antiquary remarked of him 'this man is surely touched to leave Rome and not let his works be seen when he could achieve such success here'. The Brugeois **Mathias de Visch,** in Rome at the beginning of the period, went to Venice for some years and studied with Piazzetta before returning in 1732 to paint religious pictures for Bruges churches. **Maximilian de Haese** who also painted religious pictures came from Brussels, about thirty, about 1739 and was made a Member of the Accademia di S. Luca in 1746. **Giuseppe Grisoni** (Grison) went in 1728 from London to Florence; he worked there for various churches and painted there a *Self portrait in a landscape*; in 1740 he was commissioned by the Compagnía dei Tedeschi e Fiamminghi to paint a *S. Barbara in a landscape* in competition with Vincenzo Meucci; and soon after he went to Rome and stayed there. **Jean Baptiste Coclers** finished his studies with Sebastiano Conca and Marco Benefial and left Rome about 1730 to paint religious pictures and 'history' in Maestricht and his native Liège; and **Jean Latour** (who had been **Coclers'** pupil in Liège) reached Rome at twenty-one in 1740 and worked there under Corrado Giaquinto till 1745. Other newcomers from Liège were **Henri Deprez** who became Giaquinto's pupil at nineteen in 1746, and **Engelbert Panhay de Rendeux** who came with **Deprez**, became a pupil of the French landscape and marine painter Joseph Vernet and developed as a painter of marines. **Willem Borremans** was still established in Palermo and working for churches there and for Catania Cathedral till he died in 1744. **Jan Peter Verdussen** and **Hyacinth de La Pegnia** (Pls. 853, 854) were both employed as military painters by Charles Emmanuel in Turin; **Verdussen** accompanied him for the purpose on his 1745 and 1746 campaigns (as **Adam van der Meulen** had accompanied Louis XIV and **Jan Cornelisz Vermeyen** had accompanied the Emperor Charles V) and **La Pegnia** who arrived from Paris about 1744 seems to have stayed for three years and then gone to Rome where the Accademia di S. Luca elected him a member in 1748.

At home in Belgium the main production seems to have been for the churches and religious houses. In Antwerp **Willem Ignatius Kerricx** completed his huge *Passover in Egypt* and *Adoration of the Lamb* for Tongerloo Abbey in 1731; he then supplied a composition for the Antwerp Jesuit church and a *S. Augustine inspired by the Holy Spirit* and an *Angel attacking Heresy* (described by Descamps, 1768, as 'dans la manière de **Gaspar de Crayer**') for a convent in Lierre; and he died at sixty-three in 1745. **Jacques Ignatius de Roore** may have had some commissions for religious subjects on his visit from Holland about 1728. **Jacob van Hal** worked all through the period and supplied Antwerp, S. Jacques, with a *Collecting of the Manna* in 1742 and *The Holy Sacrament adored by the Four Quarters of the World* in 1743. **Jan Claudius de Cock**, who died approaching seventy in 1736, signed drawings of Biblical subjects in 1728; and **Marten Joseph Geeraerts** (Pl. 855), Antwerp Master in 1731, and teacher without fee in the Antwerp Academy to help that institution in a financial crisis in 1741, may also have painted some religious subjects at this time. **Balthasar Beschey** who began (under the name of 'Boscaye') as a dealer and pasticheur of works by **Teniers** and **Rubens**, painted a *Landscape with the Holy Family* in 1734 at twenty-six, *The Flood* in 1737, and *Joseph sold to his brethren* (with camels taken from **Rubens'** *Adoration of the Magi* (Pl. 574)) and *Joseph Viceroy of Egypt* for the Soeurs Noires convent in 1744. His brothers **Jacques Andries Beschey** and **Jean François Beschey** collaborated with him. **Pierre Joseph Verhaghen** (Pls. 872, 873) pupil in Antwerp Academy aged thirteen in 1741, became **Balthasar Beschey's** pupil in 1744 and kept himself by designing lace; his younger brother **Jean Joseph Verhaghen** was also a pupil in Antwerp Academy in the forties; and **Karel Ijkens the younger**, who also painted some religious subjects, was a pupil of **Pieter Snyers** (Pls. 839, 856) and Antwerp Master in 1746. In Brussels the new men included **Maximilien de Haese**, pupil of his uncle **Jean van Orley** and Master in 1726, **Jean Baptiste Millé** Master in 1729 and **Nicolas Emmanuel Pery** Master in 1736. **Millé's** teacher **Zeger Jacob van Helmont** died at forty-three in 1726. **François Eisen** was back from Valenciennes by 1745 but soon left again, as result of the war, for Paris; and of the older men **Jean van Orley** died at seventy in 1735 and **Victor Honoré Janssens** (Pls. 812, 827) died about 1736 when he was nearly eighty. In Bruges **Mathias de Visch** was back from Italy in 1732; he provided S. Jacques with an *Adoration of the Shepherds* soon after, was much employed on altarpieces for various churches and very influential as a teacher at first in his own art school and from 1739 as Director of the Bruges Academy to which he presented many drawings and pictures collected in Rome and Venice. **Jan Anton Garemyn** (Pls. 858, 860) his pupil at twenty in 1732 and later himself a Director of the Academy, and **Paul Joseph de Cock** his pupil about 1742 and also later a Director, may both have painted some religious pictures before 1748. In Ghent to which **Philips Karel Marissal** returned from Brussels in 1726, **Jan Baptist van Volsum** lived till 1735 or later and **Robert van Audenaerd** (Pl. 823) till 1743. Newcomers in Ghent included **Emanuel Petrus van Reysschoot** who was twenty in 1733 and **Jean Baptiste Simons** who painted a *Christ and the Woman of Samaria* and a *Disciples at Emmaus* for S. Étienne in 1743. Malines churches received pictures from **Gilles Joseph Smeyers** back from Rome about 1726 to support the family after the blindness of his father **Jacques Smeyers** (who lived till 1732); and also probably from **Pierre Simon Verlinden** who was just over sixty in 1726 and died at a date not recorded. In Mons there was a newcomer **Jacques Joachim de Soignie** who studied in Brussels, Antwerp and, as noted, in Paris in the early forties, and then returned to work for the churches and religious houses. In S. Hubert (Luxembourg) **Charles Joseph Redouté** was working for the Abbey soon after 1743. In Namur **Pierre Delcloche** was probably still active till he died in 1729. In Liège his son **Paul Joseph Delcloche**, already mentioned as battle painter for Marshal de Saxe, was also a painter of religious pictures for the churches when he returned there from Paris aged thirty-nine in 1740. **Jean Baptiste Coclers**, back from Rome via Marseilles about 1731, worked at Maestricht till 1737, became Court Painter to the Prince Bishop, contributed religious subjects to the churches and was very influential as a teacher, (**Jean Latour** war his pupil about 1738 and **Nicolas de Fassin** about 1745.) **Olivier Pirotte**, back from Paris aged twenty-nine in 1728, had commissions for churches in Liège, Wandre and Flores (near Namur). **Henri Deprez** pupil of **Renier Panhay de Rendeux** at sixteen in 1743 left for Rome in 1746; and **Edmond Plumier** died at thirty-nine in 1733. Among the older men **Nicolas la Fabrique** died at eighty-four in 1733. **Englebert Fisen** died at seventy-eight in 1733 leaving a diary which recorded six hundred and fifty-two pictures painted by him between 1679 and 1729 when he probably ceased work. **Philippe Coclers** died over seventy in 1736, **A. Dumoulin** at sixty-five in 1740 and **Renier Panhay de Rendeux** at sixty in 1744.

A relatively small number of 'history' paintings, allegories, mythologies and decorative compositions were painted by some of these church painters and also by some specialists. In Antwerp **Willem Ignatius Kerricx, Jacob van Hal** and **Jan Claudius de Cock** were available in these fields for the whole or part of the period; and **Marten Joseph Geeraerts** (Pl. 855) began to specialize in the thirties in decorative allegoric compositions with nudes and cupids in grisaille imitating wood or stone reliefs. Similar grisaille compositions were painted by an Antwerp newcomer **Michiel Frans van der Voort** who was twenty in 1734 and by **François Eisen** in Valenciennes and Brussels. In Bruges **Mathias de Visch** was available for 'history' subjects from 1732; **Jan Anton Garemyn** (Pls. 858, 860) was employed on decorative pieces for private mansions in the forties; and **Garemyn's** pupil **Bernard Verschoot** later active as a decorative painter, was twenty by 1748. In Ghent **Philips Karel Marissal** painted decorative pieces for private mansions. In Liège the versatile **Paul Joseph Delcloche** supplied decorative paintings for the Château Colonster and for the Prince Bishop's Palace; and **Jean Baptiste Coclers** was also employed on decorative work for the Palace.

Portrait groups and conversation pieces were still being painted in Antwerp by **Ignace van der Beken** (Pl. 834) and **François Xavier Verbeeck; Jan Joseph Horemans the elder** (Pls. 836-8) was commissioned to paint *The Reception of the Abbot of S. Michel by the Confraternity of Fencers at the entrance to their Headquarters* in 1746 and was assisted in the work by **Jan Joseph Horemans the younger** (Pls. 824, 835, 861) then thirty-two. Some portraits were probably painted by **Pieter Snyers** (Pls. 839, 856) back from England in 1726 and professor without fee in the Antwerp Academy from 1741; and others were produced by many of the church and 'history' painters. In Brussels two new men were available **Jean Baptiste Millé** from 1729 and **Jean Pierre Sauvage** from 1736. In Bruges some portraits were probably painted by **Mathias de Visch** and **Jan Anton Garemyn** (Pls. 858, 860) who is said to have been influenced by **Jacques Beernaert** painter of subscription groups in Ypres who was living in Bruges about 1730. In Ghent there was still the admirable **Robert van Audenaerd** (Pl. 823) who was sixty-three in 1726 and lived as noted till 1743. **Jan Baptist van Volsum** completed his *Charles VI proclaimed Count of Flanders in 1717* in 1728. **Philips Karel Marissal** was available through the period and the newcomer **Emanuel Petrus van Reysschoot** from the middle of the thirties. In Malines **Gilles Joseph Smeyers** is traditionally recorded author of a subscription group *The Directors of the Malines Tailors'*

Guild dated 1735. In Liège **Edmond Plumier** portrayed *Prince Bishop Lewis de Berg* in 1728, and portraits were also produced there by the church and 'history' painters.

Among the painters of indoor genre **Jan Joseph Horemans the elder** (Pls. 836, 837) still successful and popular may have painted his *Kitchen interior* (Pl. 838) before 1748; and **Jan Joseph Horemans the younger**, who signed with an identical signature, may have painted all or part of the *Interior with figures* (Pl. 835) which so closely resembles the *Kitchen interior*. **François Xavier Verbeeck** continued his studio interiors; and his pupil **Melchior Brassauw**, Antwerp Master in 1737, a copyist of **Teniers** and an imitator of the seventeenth-century Dutchmen, painted genre subjects including a *Man caressing a woman* and a *Prodigal son* where the 'merry company' is dressed for the occasion in a mixture of 'olde' styles.

In the field of outdoor genre, riverside landscapes with figures in the tradition of **Jan (Velvet) Brueghel** were still being painted by **Theobald Michau** (Pl. 841) who was fifty in 1748, and by **Jan Frans van Bredael** who also painted assemblies of huntsmen. The engaging *Landscape with duckpond and children pointing to a bird's nest* (Pl. 856) by **Pieter Snyers**, more freely handled and less monumental than his *Market vendors with fruit, fish and ram* (Pl. 839), was probably produced about 1748 when he was sixty-seven. **Jan Baptist Lambrechts** painted more outdoor genre scenes including markets with piles of vegetables, between 1726 and 1731 when he went abroad. **Gerard Rysbraeck** (son of **Peter Rysbraeck**) Antwerp Master in 1726, painted hunting scenes till he went to Paris.

Wooded and Italianate landscapes seem to have been out of fashion. Many of the leading practitioners had died in the previous period and of the survivors **Cornelis Huysmans** died in 1727, and **Peter Rysbraeck** and **Jean Baptiste Juppin** in 1729. **Lambert Dumoulin** though living in Liège till 1743 probably ceased work some years earlier as he was nearly eighty when he died; and **Hendrik van Lint** (Pls. 864, 865) who painted Italianate landscapes all through the period was away, as noted, in Rome. But the tradition of the country house picture with gentry strolling in the formal gardens and cornfields and meadows with cattle in the country right and left (seen here in paintings by **Jacob Grimmer** (Pl. 430) and **G. van Schoor** (Pl. 760)) seems to have been continued; and **Jan Baptist Bouttats** signed a picture of this kind called *Mansion seen from the garden* in 1730.

Among the painters of contemporary battles and other military pieces **Hyacinth de La Pegnia**, **Jan Peter Verdussen** and **Paul Joseph Delcloche** have already been referred to. **Jan Pieter van Bredael** (Pl. 830) and **Dominique Nollet** both finished their careers, as noted, the first in Vienna in 1735 and the second in Paris in 1736; and **Carel Breydel** (Pls. 831, 842) who moved from Brussels to Ghent at just under fifty in 1726 became crippled with gout and probably gave up painting some years before his death in Antwerp in 1733 (or in Ghent in 1744).

Animals and birds, trophies of the chase and still life with dead game, were still being painted by specialists and by some of the outdoor genre painters, including as usual, the painters of hunting and military pieces. Thus game pieces were produced by **Gerard Rysbraeck** and by **Pieter Jan Snyers**, painter of a picture called *Swan and cygnets with dead game* and a prominent member of the Antwerp Guild at this time. **Jan Baptist Govaerts** painter of *Gamepiece with dead boar* (Pl. 848) was active in Antwerp till he went to Mainz in 1740. **Jan Baptist Bouttats** who seems to have lived beyond 1738 (and may or may not be identical with the painter of the *Mansion seen from the garden* just mentioned) probably painted more bird pieces like his *Cocks fighting* and *Cock attacked by vulture* in the manner of **Jan Fyt** (Pl. 733) and **Adriaen de Gryef** (Pl. 735). But **Jan Pieter van**

Bredael the elder, who lived till 1745 and had painted some game pieces earlier, is not likely to have added to them in this period as he was seventy-two in 1726 and over ninety when he died.

Other traditions in still-life were also continued and tables with fruit, flowers, vessels and so forth were still painted. **Pieter Snyers** (Pls. 839, 856) signed a composition with fruit, pheasant, partridge, and francolin against a landscape with mountains and castle at sixty-three in 1743. **Jean Joseph Verhaghen** began to paint the still-life pieces with kitchen utensils, which earned him his nickname 'Pottekens', about 1746. **Jacobus Plasschaert,** Bruges Master in 1739, painted a *Still-life with skull and engravings* (Pl. 852) going back in its 'close-up' vision of surfaces, through **Cornelis Norbertus Gysbrechts** (Pls. 802-5) and **Wallerant Vaillant** to the studded shutters by the **London Virgin with a Firescreen Painter** (Frontispiece) and also to the 'Vanitas' and 'Memento Mori' motifs in sixteenth-century pictures by the **Frankfort Master** (Pl. 209) and **Jan Gossaert.**

Fruit and flower pieces, sometimes with birds and insects, and flower garlands, were also continued. In Antwerp **Cornelis Lens** worked in this field from 1738 and also decorated coaches; and of the older men **Gaspar Pieter Verbruggen the younger** (Pl. 809), employed as a servant of the Guild in his indigent last years, died at sixty-six in 1730, **Jacob Seldenslach** died at eighty-three in 1735 and **Jan Baptist Bosschaert** at seventy-nine in 1746. In Brussels **Jean Baptiste Morel** lived till 1732. In Tournai there was a new flower painter **Regnier Joseph Malaine** who was twenty in 1731. **Charles Bigée,** who also decorated musical instruments, was a new flower painter in Malines; and in Liège **Jean Georges Coclers** painted flowers, fruit, birds and insects from the age of twenty in 1735 and became official painter to the City in 1743.

CHAPTER XIX

Charles of Lorraine

1749-1780

PRINCE CHARLES OF LORRAINE was thirty-seven when he returned to Brussels in April 1749; and he soon became the best liked and the most successful of the foreign governors. He was amiable and easy-going and devoted to the slaughter called hunting in his day; he never remarried and he conducted amorous intrigues in a merry Court where his close friend the young Prince de Ligne led the social gaieties in the second half of the period. As the first French-speaking Governor since Margaret of Parma, he encouraged the French language at his Court, and French in these years was generally spoken by the upper and upper middle classes—Flemish being used only by the peasants and the petite bourgeoisie and for judicial and other procedures in Flanders. The influence of the French philosophers and encyclopaedists thus penetrated into Belgium, for though the censors seized some works by Jean Jacques Rousseau as subversive they seem to have admitted Voltaire's writings and de Montesquieu's and the Encyclopaedia itself. French culture was also a directive for the decorative arts and for the theatre and opera in Brussels where Prince Charles was a regular attendant; and though his interest in the theatre was partly an interest in the actresses (including the wife and daughters of the actor J. N. Servandoni d'Hannetaire whose company became his Comédiens Ordinaires in 1767) he insisted on high standards of performance and sometimes paid the players' fares to Paris to see the French productions. Policy, in major affairs, was controlled throughout the period by the Empress Maria Theresa and executed by Ministers Plenipotentiary acting in the Governor's name. But Charles himself was much more than a figure-head and often used his influence with the Empress to modify the form if not the fundament of the authoritarian system which the Plenipotentiaries were instructed to build up—'Ces pays-ci' he wrote her on one occasion 'sont très attachés à leurs privilèges, et même j'ose dire qu'ils poussent cela jusqu'à la folie: mais ils sont tous élevés dans ce préjugé et il serait fort dangereux de toucher cette corde.' As the country was at peace (except during the Seven Years War) there was a gradual recovery from the economic prostration prevailing at the outset, and prosperity returned in the later years though business was hampered throughout by lack of capital—as all the big fortunes were in the hands of the Church, the religious houses, individual prelates and nobles. The Church as an ultramontane power reached the apogee of its influence in the early years but suffered onslaughts from Febronian ideas and the expulsion of the Jesuits in the later decades. There were countless ecclesiastical processions and jubilees and so forth; some new churches were built and many old ones were enlarged and adorned with expensive altars, screens and pulpits. There was also much civic building especially in Brussels where the Prince had the Hôtel de Nassau reconstructed as his central residence.

2 B   385   W.F.P. I

In the country official help was forthcoming for the making of new roads and waterways including the Bruges-Ghent canal, an event depicted by **Jan Anton Garemyn** in a picture reproduced here (Pl. 858) which the Count de Cobenzl commissioned in 1753.

In 1749 Prince Charles made Pageant Entries into Brussels, Antwerp, Malines, Namur and other cities. In Brussels he entered in a triumphal car surrounded by allegoric figures of the Elbe and Danube, Olympian deities, fauns and dryads, and regiments of hussars, and when he arrived at the gates of Antwerp a young woman symbolic of the city knelt before him with the magistrates assembled behind her, as recorded in a picture reproduced (Pl. 824) by **Jan Joseph Horemans the younger**. Other processions and ceremonies took place in Bruges, with **Jan Anton Garemyn** (Pls. 858, 860) as designer, to celebrate the Sixth Centenary of the Saint Sang Chapel (founded in 1149 to enshrine drops of the Holy Blood brought from Jerusalem by Theodoric of Alsace, Count of Flanders). The first Minister Plenipotentiary was the Marquis de Botta-Adorno; and the first act of policy was a message to the Dutch that the Belgian territories of the Empress would no longer pay subsidies for the upkeep of garrisons in the Barrier towns. In this year also Madame de Pompadour sent her brother (later Marquis de Marigny) to Italy to study classical architecture; and Buffon began publication of his 'Histoire naturelle'. Diderot, in prison for his 'Lettre sur les Aveugles', was visited there by Jean Jacques Rousseau and Voltaire; Dr. Johnson's 'Irene' was produced at Drury Lane; and Joshua Reynolds aged twenty-six was taken to the Mediterranean by Commodore Keppel. In 1750 Jean Jacques Rousseau published 'Discours sur les Sciences et les Arts'; and Voltaire went to the Court of Frederick of Prussia. In 1751 Captain Clive aged twenty-six captured Arcot, capital of the Carnatic, and held it against large numbers of Indian and French troops. Maria Theresa, courting a French alliance, wrote to Madame de Pompadour as 'Madame ma très chère soeur'; and Diderot and d'Alembert published the first volume of the Encyclopaedia. In 1752 Botta-Adorno worked out a scheme to make Belgium a transit country for Western European commerce; Prince Charles shot down the popinjay from the spire of Notre Dame du Sablon in Brussels, an event recorded at the time by the Gantois **Emanuel Petrus van Reysschoot** (or later by his son **Petrus Norbertus**)—as **Teniers** (Pl. 712) had recorded the same feat by the Archduke Leopold Wilhelm a hundred years earlier and **Antoine Sallaert** (Pl. 514) and **Denis van Alsloot** (Pl. 513A) had celebrated its performance by the Infanta Isabella in 1615. Voltaire published 'Le Siècle de Louis XIV'; and the Venetian adventurer Jacopo Casanova, aged twenty-eight and visiting Vienna, was indignant at maltreatment there of plebeian prostitutes by Maria Theresa's Chastity Police. In 1753 the French drove English traders from the Ohio Valley and erected Fort Duquesne (later Pittsburg) to prevent their return; the Empress Elizabeth of Russia lost four thousand dresses in a palace fire and the Grand Duchess Catherine, enceinte with the future Paul I, was reading the fourth volume of Bayle's 'Dictionnaire'; Voltaire left the King of Prussia's Court; the Count de Cobenzl succeeded Botta-Adorno as Minister Plenipotentiary in Brussels; and **Emmanuel Petrus van Reysschoot** was employed to paint commemorative pictures when ceremonies and processions for the sixth jubilee of S. Bernard were organized by Baudeloo Abbey (where **Jan van Cleef** and **Robert van Audenaerd** (Pl. 823) had worked). In 1754 George Washington aged twenty-two was sent against the French in Fort Duquesne; Hume published his 'History of England during the reign of James I and Charles I'; and Rousseau published 'Discours sur l'origine et les fondements de l'inégalité'. In 1755 Lisbon was almost destroyed by an earthquake; Admiral Boscawen attacked a French fleet bound for Canada; General Braddock was ambushed by the French and Red Indians at Monangahela; George Washington was commissioned Colonel and charged with the defence of the frontier against French and Indian attacks; Dr. Johnson's 'Dictionary' was published; and the French painter Jean-Baptiste Greuze aged thirty became famous with '*Un père de famille qui lit la Bible à ses enfants*' exhibited in the Paris Salon.

In 1756 Frederick of Prussia launched the Seven Years War by invading Saxony; and Maria Theresa instructed Prince Charles of Lorraine to defend Bohemia against him. Suraj-ud-Dowlah, Nawab of Bengal, took Calcutta from the English and threw his prisoners into the Fort William jail (the 'Black Hole' of Calcutta); Burke published 'On the Sublime and Beautiful'; Voltaire published 'Essai sur les moeurs'; and Casanova escaped from the 'Piombi' prison in Venice. In 1757 Frederick had England as ally, and Austria was supported by Sweden, Russia and France; Prince Charles, in Prague and Breslau for a spell, lost both after Frederick's victories at Rossbach and Leuthen, and found time to send some bottles of Tokay to the Duchesse de Mirepoix as a present to Louis XV; Pitt aged forty-nine was director of British policy, and Clive defeated Suraj-ud-Dowlah at Plassey. In 1758 Charles of Lorraine went back to Brussels; the British captured Fort Duquesne and Louisbourg; the Empress Elizabeth founded the Russian Academy of Arts in S. Petersburg and sat to the French painter Louis Tocqué for her portrait; Madame de Pompadour read the manuscript of Casanova's account of his escape from the 'Piombi'; and Casanova became Director of the French State Lotteries. In 1759 Frederick won the Battle of Minden with the help of British contingents; French fleets were destroyed by the British off Lagos and Quiberon; the British captured Quebec; the Jesuits were expelled from Portugal; Voltaire published 'Candide'; Johnson wrote 'Rasselas'; and Diderot launched journalistic art criticism with his article on the Paris Salon. In 1760 George III became King of England; the French surrendered Montreal; Coote won the Battle of Wandiwash; and Frederick won the battles of Leignitz and Torgau. In 1761, Charles of Lorraine visited Vienna to become Grand Master of the Teutonic Order; Coote captured Pondicherry; and 'l'affaire Lavalette' caused a public agitation against the Jesuits in Paris. In 1762 the Empress Elizabeth was succeeded by Peter III and then by Catherine II; Frederick won the Battle of Schweidnitz; and Jean-Jacques Rousseau published 'Le Contrat Social' and 'Émile' and fled to Switzerland when 'Émile' was condemned to be burned by the Parlement de Paris. In 1763 when the Seven Years War ended Louis XV signed the Treaty of Paris ceding Canada and all territories on the left bank of the Mississippi to England and renounced political pretensions in India; and Maria Theresa signed the Treaty of Hubertsburg ceding Silesia to Frederick. Febronius published 'De Statu Ecclesiae'; Descamps published his 'Vie des peintres flamands, allemands et hollandais'; Sterne and Garrick went to Paris; and Hume taken to Paris by the Ambassador Lord Hertford was fêted by the Encyclopaedists and in the salons of the Comtesse de Boufflers and Madame Geoffrin.

In 1764 the Archduke Joseph became King of the Romans; and Stanislas Poniatowski became King of Poland. Pope Clement XIII condemned the doctrine of Febronius; and Maria Theresa forbade publication of the Pope's ban in Austria and Belgium. Louis XV issued an Edict against the Jesuits; Madame de Pompadour died at forty-three; Hogarth died at sixty-seven; and Reynolds founded the Literary Club. In 1765 Francis I died and Joseph II became Emperor with Maria Theresa retaining the active power; Grenville imposed the Stamp Tax in the American colonies; and Boswell on his travels called on Voltaire and Jean-Jacques Rousseau and was foully cruel to his dog Jachone. In 1766 ex-King Stanislas (Leczinski) died and Lorraine reverted to the French Crown; Diderot's

Encyclopaedia was completed; Mozart aged ten improvised on the clavichord at a 'thé à l'anglaise' in the mansion of the Prince de Conti; Goldsmith published 'The Vicar of Wakefield' and Jean Jacques Rousseau went to England. In 1767 **Petrus Norbertus van Reysschoot** was employed as designer when the seventh centenary of S. Macarius, protector of Ghent against the plague, was celebrated in that city; the publication in Belgium of a Jansenist 'Life of Espen' was authorized by Count Cobenzl; and the Jesuits were expelled from France and Spain. In 1768 Madame du Barry became the mistress of Louis XV; France bought the Island of Corsica from Genoa; Descamps toured Belgium to record the pictures there in the churches and religious houses and the rooms of the Antwerp Academy; **Jan Anton Garemyn**, Director of the Bruges Academy, obtained permission from the Chapter of S. Donatien to inscribe an epitaph in memory of **Jan van Eyck**; and the Royal Academy was founded in England. In 1769 Napoleon Bonaparte was born in Corsica; Burke published his 'Observations on the Present State of the Nation'; Descamps published his 'Voyage' with tributes to Prince Charles of Lorraine and Cobenzl as art patrons and a dedication to the Marquis de Marigny; there were Jubilee celebrations throughout Belgium to mark the twenty-fifth year of Prince Charles' Governorship; and the Estates of Brabant commissioned the Ghent sculptor Pierre Verschaffelt to make an eleven-foot bronze statue of the Prince on a pedestal of Italian marble. In 1770 Cobenzl died; the Prince de Stahremberg, who succeeded him, escorted to Paris the Archduchess Marie Antoinette aged fifteen to marry the Dauphin aged sixteen, and Maria Theresa wrote to the Dauphin: 'Votre épouse vient de se séparer de moi, comme elle faisait mes délices, j'espère qu'elle fera votre bonheur. Je l'ai élevée en conséquence, parce que dès longtemps je prévoyais qu'elle devait partager votre destinée.' In 1771 news reached Bruges that the Brugeois **Joseph Benoit Suvée** (Pl. 883) aged twenty-eight had won the Prix de Rome in Paris, and the Municipality invited him to attend a fête to celebrate his triumph; when he reached Bruges he was driven in a coach and six in a procession of twenty-seven coaches, with Fame blowing a trumpet at their head, to the Academy's headquarters, and at a luncheon in the Town Hall a hundred guests assembled in his honour. In 1772 Frederick of Prussia and Catherine of Russia signed the First Partition of Poland. In 1773 Pope Clement XIV suppressed the Jesuits ('Dominus ac Redemptor'), Maria Theresa ordered obedience to the breve in her dominions, and all Jesuit establishments and colleges in Belgium were closed. The inhabitants of Boston threw shiploads of tea into the harbour in protest against taxation; Warren Hastings aged forty-one became the first Governor-General of India; Johnson and Boswell went to Scotland; Goldsmith's 'She Stoops to Conquer' was produced at Covent Garden; and Diderot went to S. Petersburg and sold his library to Catherine II.

In 1774 Louis XVI became King of France; Maria Theresa issued an edict in Belgium forbidding the publication of any religious book without a Government licence; and Catherine II signed a treaty with Turkey. In 1775 the American War of Independence began with the fighting at Lexington; Verschaffelt's statue of Prince Charles was erected on the Brussels Place de Lorraine (Place Royale) with fêtes and ceremonies; and the millennary of S. Rombout, celebrated in Malines, occasioned pictures by **Willem Jacob Herreyns** (Pl. 867) in that city, **Maximilien de Haese** and **Nicolas Emmanuel Pery** in Brussels, **Jan Anton Garemyn** in Bruges, **Andreas Cornelis Lens** in Antwerp and **Pierre Joseph Verhaghen** in Louvain. In 1776 the American colonies issued their Declaration of Independence; Gibbon published the first volume of his 'Decline and Fall of the Roman Empire'; Maria Theresa bought *S. Ignatius Loyola healing the possessed* and *Miracles of*

S. Francis Xavier by **Rubens**, together with the original sketches, from the Antwerp Jesuit church, and, incensed at the continuance of Belgian local privileges, wrote to Prince Charles 'Je dois protection et justice à mes sujets; ils me doivent obéissance et contributions. . . . La faculté de consentir ne donne pas le droit de refus, inséparable de la monstrueuse idée d'une obéissance précaire.' In 1777 General Burgoyne surrendered at Saratoga; the Emperor Joseph II sent by his mother to Paris as 'Count von Falkenstein' to urge Marie Antoinette to give up her gambling habits, found time to call at the studio of Greuze who had just completed *La cruche cassée* and was painting his portrait of Benjamin Franklin; and Maria Theresa founded new secular schools in Belgium (Collèges Thérésiens) where history, geography and mathematics were stressed in the curriculum, Latin was relegated to a minor place and corporal punishment was forbidden. In 1778 France joined the American colonists against Britain; William Blake aged twenty-one was a student in the Royal Academy schools; Voltaire died; and the Belgian Conseil Privé praised the 'De Statu Ecclesiae' of Febronius as refuting 'le système absurde de la domination de la cour de Rome, incompatible avec les lumières du siècle.' In 1779 Spain joined France against Britain and a Franco-Spanish fleet sailed up the Channel. In 1780 Gibraltar was besieged by a Franco-Spanish fleet; London suffered the Gordon Riots; England declared war on Holland; Jacques Necker the French Controller General of Finance published his Compte-Rendu exposing Court expenditures and inequalities of taxation; Prince Charles of Lorraine died; and Maria Theresa died after appointing Duke Albert of Saxe-Teschen and the Archduchess Maria Christina Joint Governors of Belgium.

Charles of Lorraine liked sumptuous textiles and tapestries, mechanical curiosities and decorative bibelots; he collected miniatures and landscapes by some earlier Flemish artists and he also took an interest in contemporary painting in Belgium. He owned a gold fountain pen and thirty-five French and English clocks, by famous makers, with temperature indicators, calendars and other special features; he had a hundred and fifty jewelled snuff boxes, fifty gold and enamel flacons and innumerable rings and ornamental canes; his miniatures included works by **Perpète Evrard**, his landscapes about twenty by **Jacques d'Arthois** (Pls. 686, 710, 736) and a joint work by **Adrian Frans Baudewyns** (Pl. 815) and **Pieter Bout** (Pls. 796, 797); he also owned **Jan Gossaert's** *Adoration of the Magi* (Pl. 194) which seems to have remained in Brussels since Albert and Isabella acquired it in 1601 (and was sold on Prince Charles' death as a work by Dürer). As a patron of contemporary Belgian painting he gave decorative commissions for his palaces, he concerned himself with the affairs of the Antwerp Academy, he founded or gave titles of royal patronage to academies in Brussels, Ghent, Bruges, Courtrai, Audenarde, Ypres, Malines and Mons, and he caused the Empress to issue an edict to enhance the status of artists in the body politic. After 1753 he was encouraged in this by Cobenzl, himself a patron of living artists (and also a voracious collector of pictures by **Rubens** and **Van Dyck** some of which he acquired by very doubtful means as when on appointing a 'Monsieur V . . .' Superintendent of the Bollandist Library he 'reserved' for himself 'le beau tableau de **Van Dyck** qui est dans la salle de la sodalité').

The Court Painters, appointed at various times in this long reign, included **Philip Joseph Tassaert, Louis Legendre, Jean Pierre Sauvage, Joseph Gregoire Sauvage, Bernard Verschoot, Andreas Cornelis Lens** (Pl. 871), **Johannes Jacobus Lens** (Pl. 867), and **Pierre Joseph Verhaghen** (Pls. 872, 873). Of these **Philip Joseph Tassaert** was a painter of landscapes with animals, and of religious and allegoric pieces (and later a pasticheur, restorer and dealer). **Louis Legendre** painted the Prince's official portrait for engravings. **Jean Pierre Sauvage** painted him as Grand Master of the Teutonic Order. **Joseph Gregoire Sauvage** made miniature portraits of his favourite ladies including Madame d'Ursel, the Marquise de Deyns (wife of the Capitaine des Archers de la Garde Noble) and one of the Hannetaire sisters. **Bernard Verschoot** painted a ceiling on the grand staircase of the Château Mariemont, designed decorations for stage performances and fêtes and was Director of the Brussels Academy (which received its deed of Royal patronage in 1767). **Andreas Cornelis Lens** (Pl. 871), trained in the Antwerp Academy by **Balthasar Beschey** and professor himself in the Academy at twenty-four in 1763, was sent by the Prince with a scholarship to Italy in 1764 and became his mentor in the politics of the art world; and **Johannes Jacobus Lens** (Pl. 869) his younger brother was also sent to Italy. **Pierre Joseph Verhaghen**, another pupil of **Balthasar Beschey**, settled in Louvain in 1749 and painted religious subjects for local churches till he was discovered at forty-one by Cobenzl in 1769; Cobenzl commissioned from him *S. Stephen King of Hungary receiving the Pope's Ambassadors* (Pl. 872) and died before the picture was delivered; Prince Charles sent it to Maria Theresa who bought it partly, no doubt, on its merits and partly by reason of her interest, as Queen of Hungary, in the subject—since the picture shows Duke Stephen of Hungary receiving confirmation of his pious foundations and the crown of Hungary from Pope Silvester II in 1003; and thereafter **Verhaghen** became a protégé of the Empress and was sent to Italy at her charge.

The Prince also patronized or helped a number of artists in addition to these Court Painters. In 1759 when he came back from fighting in the Seven Years War he visited the Antwerp studio of **Marten Joseph Geeraerts** (Pl. 855) and on **Geeraerts'** recommendation he sent his pupil **François Joseph Lonsing** then aged twenty, and later a portrait painter, with a scholarship to Rome; and later he employed **Jean Baptiste Simons**, then twenty-seven, to paint overmantels for Château Mariemont. He was also, I suspect, responsible for introducing to the Empress a number of painters, draughtsmen and designers; in the fifties he probably introduced **Hyacinth de La Pegnia** (Pls. 853, 854) who was then designing camp scenes and other military subjects as a cartoonist in the Brussels tapestry factory with the rank of 'peintre extraordinaire de l'Impératrice', and the young painters **Herman Gillis** and **Pierre Joseph Lion** and the draughtsman-engraver **Antoine Alexandre Cardon** who all visited Vienna; in the sixties he was doubtless behind a commission given by Maria Theresa to **Philippe Lambert Spruyt** to make engravings of works of art in Belgian churches and religious houses, and also behind an Imperial command that a set of drawings recording notable events in the history of the Netherlands made in 1767 by **Willem Jacob Herreyns** (Pl. 867), aged twenty-four, for the magistrates of Malines should be sent to Vienna for exhibition in the Academy there; in 1774, when the Archduke Maximilian visited Antwerp, the Academy staged an exhibition in his honour with many pictures by **Lens** and **Geeraerts** and the landscape and topographic painter **Hendrik de Cort**, and the Archduke, probably prompted by Prince Charles, made **Hendrik de Cort** his personal painter; and in the later seventies it was perhaps the Prince's doing that **Gertrude de Pélichy** (Pl. 868) was brought to the notice of the Empress.

In his dealings with the Antwerp Academy Prince Charles was caught up in the politics of the local art-world. He went there first in 1750, inspected a working séance where two models were posing for the students, established some annual prizes, and found the professors in a state of feud with the old Guild of S. Luke which, nominally amalgamated with the Academy at its foundation by **Teniers**, had never been absorbed or liquidated and still stood for various vexatious controls on artists by the trade and craft corporations—**Cornelis Lens** for example, flower painter and coach decorator (and father of **Andreas Cornelis**

Lens) was prosecuted in this period for doing his own gilding without a licence from the appropriate trade body. Some of the Academicians asked the Prince's help against these restrictions, pointing out, doubtless, that the Bruges Academicians had become more free than the Antwerp Academicians since they founded their own Academy led by **Jan Baptist Herregouts** and **Joseph van den Kerckhove** in 1717. As the policy of the Austrian Government was to curb the Belgian passion for long established local privileges the Prince supported the Academy against the Guild and corporations; but the Guild successfully opposed him for some twenty years. The point was raised again by **Andreas Cornelis Lens** back from Italy in 1768 and incensed at the prosecution of his father; and this time it was coupled by a demand to reorganize the teaching system in the Academy by greatly increasing the time spent on drawing from the antique, as **Lens** was a champion of the Neo-Classic movement. **Lens** wrote memoranda to the Prince and offered his resignation from the Academy to force the issue to a point; the Prince replied 'Nous observerons qu'il ne saurait desconvenir qu'il y ait de l'indécence à confondre les arts liberaux avec les arts mécaniques . . . . C'est avilir les peintres . . . que de les obliger à se faire inscrire dans un corps de métier quelconque'; and by 1773 he had procured from the Empress an 'Ordonnance pour affranchir les Arts', which stressed the dignity of the liberal arts and stated inter alia: 'La peinture, la sculpture, la gravure et l'architecture ne dérogent point à la noblesse; tout le monde peut exercer librement ces arts et vendre ses ouvrages sans être sujet à se faire inscrire dans les métiers, corps ni compagnies quelconques, pourvu que l'artiste se borne à l'exercice de son art sans se mêler d'ouvrages mécaniques ou de débits réservés aux métiers.'

In official portraiture in addition to the portraits of the Prince by **Louis Legendre** and **Jean Pierre Sauvage** already referred to, there were pictures of the Empress and the successive Emperors commissioned by the court or by public bodies in various places; thus **Jean Baptiste Millé** painted *The Empress Maria Theresa on horseback* for Brussels Town Hall before 1768; **Jean Pierre Sauvage** painted the *Empress Maria Theresa* and the *Emperor Francis I* in 1765; **Balthasar Beschey** provided Louvain Town Hall with *The Empress Maria Theresa* before 1768; **Herman Gillis** painted *The Emperor Joseph II* for the same Hall in 1777; and **Gertrude de Pélichy** painted the *Empress Maria Theresa wearing a gown covered with Brussels lace* (Pl. 868) for Bruges Town Hall which procured her honorary membership of the Vienna Academy probably at the end of the seventies. It is doubtful if any of these portraits were based on drawings made actually from the sitters, except perhaps the *Joseph II* by **Herman Gillis** who may have drawn the Emperor in Vienna or on his way to or from Paris. The others were presumably based on engravings from official prototypes supplied from Vienna; and the elegant picture of Marie Theresa by **Gertrude de Pélichy** would appear to be based on a standard composition by the Swede Martin van Mytens, a favourite Court Painter of the Empress.

Other portraits were painted, of course, by these and other artists; and group portraiture in the old tradition was continued. In Antwerp—where **Pieter Snyers** (Pls. 839, 856) died in 1752, **François Xavier Verbeeck** in 1755 and **Jan Joseph Horemans the elder** (Pls. 836-8) in 1759—**Ignace van der Beken** (Pl. 834) probably painted some portraits between the beginning of the period when he was sixty and 1774 when he died at eighty-five, **Philip Joseph Tassaert** was available between 1756 and 1769 when he went abroad, and **Jan Joseph Horemans the younger** (Pls. 824, 835, 861) painted conversation groups all through the period. **Balthasar Beschey** who lived till 1776, painted a *Reception of the Rector of the Guild of S. Luke* in 1756, a *Self-portrait in powdered wig, yellow silk suit and red mantle*, *working at his easel* presented to the Academy in 1763 and a pastel *Portrait of the artist Martin Joseph Geeraerts*. In 1762, at twenty-three, **Andreas Cornelis Lens** (Pl. 871) painted *The engraver Peter Frans Martenasie, Director of the Academy 1762, engaged on an engraving of Rubens' Rape of the Sabines* presented to the Academy by the sitter who was one of his earliest admirers, and two years later **Lens** painted *Marie Catherine de Villegas de Borsbeke*. **Andreas Bernardus de Quertenmont** drew and painted portraits in Antwerp from soon after 1770; and **Willem Jacob Herreyns** (Pl. 867) from 1766 till he left for Malines in 1771. **Herman Gillis** was available in Antwerp and Malines as well as in Louvain from the end of the sixties; and **Gilles Joseph Smeyers** probably painted some groups in Malines in this period though he passed his last years in an almshouse where he died about eighty about 1774. In Brussels **Jean Pierre Sauvage** painted *Count F. de Coswarem, Chamberlain to the Empress in the service of Prince Charles of Lorraine* in 1761 and died at eighty-one in 1780. **Jean Baptiste Millé**, teacher in the Brussels Art School (later the Academy) in the fifties, was probably available till 1768 when **Bernard Verschoot** (born and trained in Bruges) replaced him as Director of the school. **Louis Legendre** active from early in the sixties painted the *Count de Cobenzl*, his mistress *Mlle. Murray* and made pastel portraits for Cobenzl of his two sons, the actress *Angelica d'Hannetaire* (mistress of the Prince de Ligne) and her sister *Eugénie d'Hannetaire*. **Joseph Gregoire Sauvage** was available from the middle sixties for miniature, pastel and enamelled portraits; **François Joseph Lonsing** (born in Brussels but trained by **Marten Joseph Geeraerts** in Antwerp) went abroad with his scholarship at twenty in 1759; and **Guillaume de Spinny** (Pl. 862) also born in Brussels was abroad all through the period. In Bruges **Jacques Beernaert** painted some subscription groups and died at a date unknown; **Joseph Benoit Suvée** (Pl. 883) gave a *Self-portrait* to the Academy in 1772 in return for the festivities in 1771 and also painted a *Portrait of the painter Paul Joseph de Cock*. **Jan Anton Garemyn** (Pls. 858, 860), Director of the Bruges Academy from 1765-75, was available for portraits all through the period; his pupil **C. Noel** who painted his portrait in 1777 was a member of the Lille Academy and seems to have settled there; and another pupil who later became a portraitist **Joseph Angelus van der Donckt** (Pl. 889) went abroad at twenty-three in 1780. In Ghent **Philips Karel Marissal** founded and directed the Art School (later the Academy) and died at seventy-two in 1770; **Petrus Johannes van Reysschoot** died at fifty-nine in 1772; and **Bernard Paul** painted some portraits and conversation pieces before 1763 when he went abroad and after 1771 when he was again in Ghent. In Liège **Jean Latour** was back from Italy at the outset of the period; **Pierre Joseph Lion**, born in Dinant in 1729, was trained in Liège before leaving for Paris in 1754; **Leonard Defrance**, abroad until the middle sixties and organizer of the Academy in 1773 and Director in 1778, made the intimate study of a geometer known as *Portrait of a member of the Jalheau family* (Pl. 874) in 1768 when he was thirty-three. **Louis Bernard Coclers** (Pl. 866) may also have worked in his native Liège in the middle sixties though he lived abroad till 1763 and again from early in the seventies.

The painters of religious subjects had continuous employment as the wealth and power of the clergy caused many commissions to be given. In Antwerp where **Jacob van Hal** died at seventy-eight in 1750 and **Karel Ijkens the younger** at thirty-four in 1753, some commissions went to **Balthasar Beschey** professor in the Academy from 1755 till 1776, and others to **Jacques Andries Beschey** who painted a *Holy Family* in 1751 and a *Raising of the Cross* based on the **Rubens** composition (Pl. 528). **Marten Joseph Geeraerts** (Pl. 855), now a senior professor in the Academy, painted *Seven scenes from the Old and New Testament* in grisaille imitating sculptured bas-reliefs for Afflighem Abbey and an *Assump-*

tion of the Virgin in colour for the church of the English Benedictines in Brussels before 1768; his pupil **Herman Gillis** painted *Scenes from the Legend of the Holy Blood* for Hoogstraeten Church about 1770; and another pupil **Piat Joseph Sauvage**, from Tournai, painted *S. Carlo Borromeo and the plague stricken* for Brussels S. Gilles at twenty-one in 1765. **Andreas Cornelis Lens** (Pl. 871), at work again in Antwerp aged thirty in 1769 after his Italian studies, produced a *Presentation in the Temple* for Antwerp, Augustines, *Scenes from the life of S. Romualdus* for Malines, S. Rombout in 1775, and *Scenes from the life of S. Mary Magdalene* in 1777. His stay in Rome had made **Lens** an enthusiast for Neo-Classic doctrines; on the way back in Paris he had doubtless seen pictures by Nicolas Poussin; and in 1776 he published his treatise 'Le Costume, ou Essai sur les Habillements et les Usages de plusieurs Peuples de l'Antiquité prouvé par les monuments' with drawings made from antique statues; this laid down archaeological exactness as a first principle in Neo-Classic painting—('Les connoisseurs verront toujours avec regrets les disciples de Jésus-Christ représentés avec des mitres comme nos evêques, Tarquin vêtu d'un pourpoint espagnol, les femmes grecques et romaines avec les robes de nos aieules, les Patriarches avec un turban, les Mages enveloppés dans un manteau de brocard, et la reine de Carthage expirante sur un bûcher au milieu d'une garde suisse')—and described the principal object of Painting as the representation of 'Les faits mémorables de l'antiquité, les personnages illustres et les exemples de la Sublime Vertu'; it also contained the maxim 'Suivre les anciens c'est suivre la nature'—the author's translation of Pope's 'Learn hence for ancient rules a just esteem. To copy nature is to follow them.' **Jean Baptiste Pauwels**, a follower of **Lens**, was a pupil in the Academy at nineteen in 1773; **Joseph François**, another follower, was a pupil there in 1777; and **Willem Jacob Herreyns** (Pl. 867), who refused to subscribe to Neo-Classic doctrines, was professor in the Academy from 1766 till 1771 when he moved to Malines as related. In Brussels **Jean Baptiste Sévin** painted a ceiling for the sacristy of Notre Dame de la Chapelle in 1753; **Jean Baptiste Millé** provided the Jacobin church with a *Flight into Egypt* and a *Holy Family*, S. Gudule with a *Resurrection* and the Abbaye de Ninove with *Scenes from the life of S. Cyprian* all before 1768 when Descamps saw them in position; and **Nicolas Emmanuel Pery** painted a *Birth of the Virgin* and an *Assumption of the Virgin* for the Église des Cordeliers and pictures for the Jacobins before 1768, an *Apotheosis of S. Romualdus* for Malines S. Rombout in 1775, and probably died before 1780. **Maximilien de Haese**, back in Brussels from Italy and very successful throughout the period, signed a *Supper at Emmaus* (as 'DHase') in 1754, painted a *Martyrdom of S. Barbara* for Alost, S. Martin, a *Christ carrying the Cross* for Dilighem Abbey, the *Wedding Feast at Cana* for Brussels, Jacobins, *The Purification* for Brussels, S. Gudule, *The Adoration of the Shepherds* and *The Adoration of the Magi* for the Madeleine, *The Resurrection* for the Grand Béguinage and the *Marriage of the Virgin* for the Carmes Déchaussés all before 1768; he also painted *Scenes from the life of S. Romualdus* for Malines S. Rombout in 1775 and made cartoons for tapestries, *The Miracles of the Host*, executed for Brussels, S. Gudule.

Among the painters in other towns, religious subjects were painted in Ghent by **Frans de Lange**, by **Philips Karel Marissal** and by **Philippe Lambert Spruyt** who followed him in 1770 as Director of the Ghent Art School which was given Academic status by Charles of Lorraine soon after; and others were probably painted there by **Jean Baptiste Simons** who died after 1777. **Emanuel Petrus van Reysschoot**, who lived till 1772, painted fourteen panels *The Saviour*, *The Virgin* and *The Twelve Apostles*, with over-life-size figures for the Bernardine Jubilee in Baudeloo Abbey in 1753. His Brother **Petrus Johannes van Reysschoot** back from a long stay in England and known accordingly as 'The Englishman', painted

The Twelve Apostles with over life-size figures for the Ghent Augustines after 1768 and also died in 1772; and his son **Petrus Norbertus van Reysschoot,** back from Italy and professor of architecture in the Academy after 1770, painted *The Annunciation, S. Bernard at the feet of Christ* and *S. Theresa in ecstasy* for the Carmelite church and began a series of grisaille pictures *Old and New Testament subjects related to the Eucharist* for S. Bavon in 1774. In Bruges **Jacques de Smidt,** master in 1754, began an altarpiece for the chapel of Notre Dame des Sept Douleurs in S. Sauveur in 1756 and worked through the period. **Mathias de Visch,** who died at sixty-three in 1765, painted an *Elijah's offering* and *S. Joseph supporting the Christ-child on a globe* for the Bruges Carmes Déchaussés and *Christ washing the disciples' feet* for S. Jacques; as professor and director of the Academy he was still an influential teacher and his later pupils included **Joseph Benoit Suvée** (Pl. 883). His earlier pupil the versatile **Jan Anton Garemyn** (Pls. 858, 860) painted a *Christ on the Cross* for S. Sauveur and *Six Old Testament subjects* for S. Anne in 1760, *S. Anne teaching the Virgin to read* for S. Anne in 1768, and *Ten scenes from the Passion* for Notre Dame; he also painted *The calling of S. Romualdus* for Malines S. Rombout in 1775 and began a series of *Scenes from the History of the Order of the Trinitarians* for Bruges, S. Gilles in 1778; and his pupils included **Antoine Ignace Steyaert** and **Augustin van den Berghe** in the later years. In Malines **Gilles Joseph Smeyers** died nearly eighty in an almshouse about 1772 after supplying information for the 'Vie des peintres...' to Descamps who saw works by him in S. Rombout, the Recollets, in Asch Paris church and in the Abbaye de Ninove in 1768. **Willem Jacob Herreyns** (Pl. 867) who became the first director of the Malines Academy when he arrived there aged twenty-eight in 1771, painted *Scenes from the life of S. Romualdus* for S. Rombout in 1775, became Court Painter to Gustavus III of Sweden at the end of the period and signed as such a *Christ on the Cross*, commissioned for the Abbaye de S. Bernard, which goes back to the tradition of **Jan Snellinck** (Pl. 460) via the *Coup de lance* of **Rubens.** In Louvain religious subjects were painted by **Pierre Joseph Verhaghen** (Pls. 872, 873) who moved there from Antwerp aged twenty-one in 1749 and copied pictures by **Gaspar de Crayer** (Pls. 598, 607, 609, 642), **Rubens** and **Van Dyck** and obtained some decorative employment while his wife helped to keep things going by a draper's shop; in 1753 he painted a *Purgatory* for Louvain, S. Quentin, in 1765 an *Abraham and Melchisedek*, in 1766 a *Last Supper*, and in 1767 a *Presentation in the Temple* which led some to acclaim him the successor of **Rubens** and **Jordaens**; in 1770 he finished *S. Stephen King of Hungary receiving the Pope's Ambassadors* (Pl. 872) which was bought, as noted, by the Empress; returning from Italy as 'First Painter to the Empress' in 1773 he was given an official reception by the city and a number of commissions for local churches; in 1775 he painted *Scenes from the life of S. Romualdus* for Malines, S. Rombout, and in the later seventies a *Supper at Emmaus* for Hasselt Béguinage and a *Wedding Feast at Cana* and *Christ in the House of Simon* with nine other compositions for Tongerloo Abbey; and in 1780 he began an *Adoration of the Magi* commissioned by the Empress. His brother **Jean Joseph Verhaghen,** also settled in Louvain, collaborated with him on occasion and himself received some commissions for churches; and **Antoine Clevenbergh** born there in 1755 seems to have copied a number of **Verhaghen's** pictures from soon after 1775. In Mons **Jacques Joachim de Soignie** painted *Scenes from the life of S. Jeanne Françoise de Chantal, foundress of the Order of Visitants* and *Scenes from the life of S. Angela, foundress of the Institute of S. Ursula* for local convents and applied in 1780 for the post of Director in the newly founded Academy. **Charles Joseph Redouté** worked for the Benedictine Abbey at S. Hubert in Luxembourg and died there in 1776. In Liège the painters available for religious subjects included **Jean Latour** and **Henri Deprez, Paul Joseph Delcloche** who died at thirty-nine in 1755, **Olivier Pirotte** who died in 1764, and **Jean Baptiste Coclers** who employed **Henri Deprez** as a collaborator, took **Leonard Defrance** (Pls. 874, 879, 880) as a pupil in 1752, and died at seventy-six in 1772 leaving some sixteen children including the painters **Philippe Henri Coclers** and **Louis Bernard Coclers** (Pl. 866).

Allegories and mythologies and 'history' pieces, were produced by many of the painters of religious subjects and also by some others. Thus **Marten Joseph Geeraerts** painted grisaille compositions with cupids and so on symbolizing this and that, a grisaille *Allegory of the Fine Arts* presented to the Academy in 1760 and the *Allegory of Peace* (Pl. 855) one of his rare pictures in colour where the student can find a 'Mercury' based on Giambologna's statue, an 'Abundance' copied from a figure in *Hercules and Omphale* by the French painter François Lemoine, and a rhythm in the twining arms anticipating Etty and Renoir. A ceiling and panels on the theme of *Apollo and the Muses* were painted for the Antwerp Salle de Concert by **Michiel Frans van der Voort (Vervoort)** who was Director of the Academy from 1752 till 1762 and died insane at sixty-three in 1777. **Theodor de Bruyn**, Antwerp Master in 1758, painted some allegories and decorative pieces in grisaille imitating sculptured bas-reliefs and went abroad about 1767. **Andreas Cornelis Lens** (Pl. 871) chose *Hercules protecting the Muse of Fine Art against Jealousy and Ignorance* as the subject for the picture he gave to the Academy in 1763, an allusion doubtless to the Academy's battle against the Guild's restrictive claims; and students of sociology will compare this theme with the themes of some earlier allegoric pieces—*Mars and the Fine Arts overcoming Ignorance* (Pl. 492) by **Antoine Claeissins**, *Commerce and Industry protecting the Fine Arts* (Pl. 774) by **Jordaens** and the *Allegory of the Study of the Nude* (Pl. 811) presented by **Jacob Denys** in 1694. **Johannes Jacobus Lens** (Pl. 869) who came back with his brother from Rome in 1768 is said to have painted pictures with such subjects in his brother's style. **Jean Pierre Borrekens**, a pupil of **Lens** whose sister he married, began work in these categories after winning the Academy's prize for nude painting at twenty-five in 1772; **Jean Baptiste Sévin** painted a ceiling of the Salle d'Assemblée in the Antwerp Maison des Bouchers before 1768; **Piat Joseph Sauvage**, who seems to have abandoned religious subjects after 1765, specialized in grisaille decorations imitating bas-reliefs in the manner of his master **Geeraerts** till he left for Paris in 1774; and **Pieter Jan Balthasar de Grée**, pupil of **Geeraerts** in 1773, also specialized in such grisaille decorations. In Bruges **Andreas Peter de Muynck**, later a 'history' painter, was a pupil of **Mathias de Visch** in the later fifties and went to Paris with his fellow student **Joseph Benoit Suvée** (Pl. 883) in the early sixties; **Pieter Mathias Goddyn**, who also worked later in this field, was a pupil of **Garemyn** at the end of the sixties till he too left for Paris; **Augustin van den Berghe**, already mentioned as **Garemyn's** pupil, left Bruges for Paris aged twenty-four in 1780; and I have already referred to the work of the Brugeois **Bernard Verschoot** (a former pupil of **Garemyn**) who went to Paris in 1754 and to Italy at the end of the fifties and was summoned to Brussels by Charles of Lorraine in 1765 to paint ceilings and so forth for Château Mariemont and make designs for the theatre and for the Prince's fêtes. In Malines the decorations for the S. Rombout millenary in 1775 were directed by **Willem Jacob Herreyns** and the emblematic cars designed by him were distinguished, a contemporary tells us, by 'stoutheid van behandeling en rijkdom van verbeelding.' Decorative works with gatherings of Olympian gods and goddesses were painted for Ghent mansions by **Petrus Norbertus van Reysschoot** from the early sixties; and **Emanuel Petrus van Reysschoot** designed a *Chariot of the Unicorn* in a procession organized by the Ghent Guild of S. Luke in 1766. The Liégeois painters of decorative works in private houses and the Bishop's Palace included **Paul Joseph Delcloche** till 1755, **Jean Baptiste Coclers, Henri Deprez, Jean Latour**, and **Joseph Dreppe** who was a pupil of **Latour** in the fifties, went abroad in 1758 and was back by 1761. In the field of costume-history I have already mentioned the drawings of notable events in Netherlands history made in 1767 by **Willem Jacob Herreyns** for the magistrates of Malines; and, about 1780, **Herreyns** began a series of pictures *Scenes from the life of Gustavus Vasa* for the King of Sweden after he had become his Court Painter.

Among the painters of landscape and outdoor genre scenes, there were survivors from the last period and a new generation beginning their careers. In Antwerp **Pieter Snyers** died over seventy in 1752, and his *Landscape with duckpond and children pointing to a bird's nest* (Pl. 856) was bought from his widow by the Antwerp Academy for the Directors' Chamber in 1763; **Jan Frans van Bredael** died at sixty-seven in 1750; **Theobald Michau** (Pl. 841) died at eighty-nine in 1765; and **Gerard Rysbraeck** returned there from Paris about 1754 and died blind and in poverty at seventy-seven in 1773. A newcomer **Hendrik Joseph Antonissen**, Antwerp Master at eighteen in 1755, painted picturesque landscapes with figures and animals in the style of the picture reproduced here (Pl. 863) and was very influential as a teacher; thus **Jacques André Trachez**, his pupil in the sixties, became Antwerp Master in 1771, worked for some years in Ghent, and signed a *Winter landscape in Holland* in 1780; **W. J. L. Spoor**, painter later of landscapes with animals, was another pupil; **Hendrik de Cort** already mentioned as Antwerp Master in 1770 and protégé of the Archduke Maximilian, was also his pupil in the sixties, and **Balthasar Paul Ommeganck** (Pl. 876) later himself influential, became a pupil, at fourteen, in 1769; **Hendrik Blomaerts** and **Simon Joseph Denis** were fellow pupils with **Ommeganck** about 1772; and **Petrus Johannes van Regemorter**, pupil in the Academy (also probably of **Antonissen**) before 1775, collaborated in some early pictures with **Hendrik de Cort**. Other newcomers who painted landscapes were **Theodor de Bruyn** active in Antwerp from 1758 till 1767, **Philip Joseph Tassaert** in Antwerp from England by 1756, **Nicolas de Fassin** who became a student in the Academy at the late age of thirty-four in 1762 and stayed till 1769, and **Simon d'Argonne (Dargonne)** who came to Antwerp from Dieppe about 1772, assumed the name of Pierre Simon Gautier, gave music and dancing lessons (like **Hieronymus Janssens** (Pls. 730, 731) and **Charles Sylva Dubois**) and took up landscape painting, in which he later specialized, perhaps before the end of the period. In Bruges **Jan Anton Garemyn** produced his remarkable *Building the Ghent Canal* in 1753 and *The vegetable market* in 1778; the *Building the Ghent Canal* (Pl. 858) commissioned, as noted, by Cobenzl, has hundreds of figures and scores of genre episodes in the tradition going back through **Sebastiaan Vrancx** (Pls. 531, 534) and **Jan (Velvet) Brueghel** (Pls. 467, 483) to the **Antwerp Destruction of the Citadel Painter** (Pl. 433) and **Jacob Grimmer** (Pl. 430) and beyond that to the building operations in the *S. Barbara* (Pl. 18) by **Jan van Eyck**; *The vegetable market* (Pl. 860), with the inevitable street charlatan on a platform in the background, follows the same tradition and also shows the old affection of all Brugeois for their city and its daily life, already seen in the backgrounds of pictures by the **Detroit Mystic Marriage Painter** (Pl. 110), **Hans Memlinc** (Pls. 111, 113), the **Lucy Legend Master** (Pl. 118), the **Brussels Virgin with a Milk Bowl Painter** (Pl. 205) and **Pieter Jansz Pourbus** (Pls. 336, 337); and this affection appears again in views of Bruges painted at this time by **Jean Beerblock** (Pl. 859) who began as a house-painter and went to the Academy with funds provided by a gentleman who discovered him in the early sixties, by **Pierre François Ledoulx** (a pupil of **Mathias de Visch** and **Garemyn**), by **Jean Charles Verbrugge** (also a pupil of **Garemyn**) who signed a *Porte d'Ostende*, a

Porte Sainte-Croix and a *Porte Saint-Leonard* in 1780, and by others who specialized in views of the Lac d'Amour and the Ghent canal with the famous 'barge' which all travellers admired. **Paul Joseph de Cock**, painter of picturesque landscapes and port scenes, professor in Bruges Academy by 1766 and Director on **Garemyn's** retirement in 1775, was influential as a teacher; and his many pupils included **Joseph François Ducq** who was eighteen in 1780. **Jean François Legillon,** pupil in the Academy about 1755, was almost continuously abroad from 1759 to the end of the period when he produced the *Stable in Switzerland* (Pl. 877) which anticipates some paintings of the nineteenth century; and **Jacques Albert Sénave**, born in 1758, and painter later of rural genre, was a student in the Ypres and Bruges academies at the end of the seventies. In Ghent **Jan Lodewyck de Wouters** painted landscapes with moonlight effects and **Petrus Norbertus van Reysschoot** landscapes with genre figures. **Hyacinth de La Pegnia**, shown here as a topographic painter (Pls. 853, 854), was in Brussels from 1755 till 1759. **Antoine Clevenbergh** painted landscapes in Louvain. **Joseph Dreppe** produced some in Liège after 1761; and **Nicolas de Fassin** was back from travel and at work there in 1773 when he organized the new Academy with **Leonard Defrance**.

Of the painters of military pieces **Hyacinth de La Pegnia** designed military tapestries in Brussels between 1755 and 1757 for Maria Theresa as already mentioned; **Paul Joseph Delcloche** was active till 1755 when he died in Liège; and **Jan Peter Verdussen** was abroad till he died in 1763.

Among the painters of marine and port scenes **Englebert Panhay de Rendeux** was abroad till he died in 1777; and the newcomers **Charles Greuzen** from 1750 and **Frans Balthasar Solvyns** a pupil of **Quertenmont** in Antwerp Academy at the end of the seventies.

Genre pictures, including interior subjects, were produced by **Jan Joseph Horemans the younger** who dressed his models in clothes recalling seventeenth-century works in his *Music Party* (*The New Song*) where a woman singing at the virginals regales a 'merry company' in the tradition of tavern subjects by Jan Steen—(a hark back to 'ye olde' costumes already affected by **Gerard Thomas** (Pl. 833), **Pieter van Angellis** and **Melchior Brassauw** as related in my last chapter). In his *Landlord and tenant* (Pl. 861) on the other hand, **Horemans the younger** shows the costumes, furniture and interior decoration of soon after 1760 when he painted the picture for the Antwerp mansion of Count de Hamale in a series of contemporary genre subjects which incorporated portraits of the Hamale family and included a *Fish market*, a *Horse pond*, *Spring*, *Summer*, *Autumn* and *Winter* (all contemporary genre scenes) and some hunting pieces. Costume genre pieces in the Dutch tradition were painted in the sixties by **Jacob Andries Brassauw** author of a *Card Players* and a *Girl with a copper pail* described as pastiches of Gerard Dou; and genre subjects were still probably produced by **François Xavier Verbeeck** who died at sixty-nine in 1755, **Melchior Brassauw** who died about fifty before 1760 and **Jan Joseph Horemans the elder** (Pls. 836-8) who died at seventy-seven in 1759. In Louvain kitchen interiors were painted by **Jean Joseph Verhaghen (Pottekens)**. In Liège **Leonard Defrance** (Pls. 874, 879) developed as a genre painter in the sixties and **Nicolas de Fassin** painted *The Four Times of the Day* and *A lady drinking tea* among similar pieces in the early seventies. In Bruges **Jacobus Johannes Lauwers**, later a genre painter, was pupil in the Academy about 1770 till he left for Rome after 1772; and **Jean Beerblock** (Pl. 859) produced *The Interior of the Hôpital S. Jean* with many small figures commissioned for the hospital in 1778.

Some fruit and flower pieces were painted in Antwerp by the landscape painter **Hendrik Joseph Antonissen** (Pl. 863); and newcomers there who specialized in flower studies and fruit and flower pieces with insects and so forth included **Pierre Joseph Thys** pupil in the

Academy about 1765 till he left for Paris (with the Dutch painter Gerard van Spaendonck) in 1770, **Pieter Faes** (Pl. 887) pupil in the Academy in the later sixties, **George Frederick Ziesel** in Antwerp from Hoogstraeten at the age of twenty in 1776, **Jan Frans Eliaerts** (Pl. 888) pupil in the Academy about 1777 and **Jan Frans van Dael** (Pl. 886) apprenticed to a coach painter in the later seventies and a pupil in the Academy by 1780. In Bruges **Pierre François Ledoulx** made hundreds of flower studies, many in watercolour, and also miniatures of all kinds of insects from the middle fifties onwards. **Martin van Dorne** appeared in Louvain about 1760 and **Michel Joseph Speeckaert** some years later. In Tournai **Joseph Laurent Malaine** was active from approximately 1765 and **Antoine Plateau** from the later seventies. In S. Hubert in Luxembourg **Antoine Ferdinand Redouté** was a pupil of his father **Charles Redouté** till he left for Paris just over twenty in 1776; and his younger brother **Pierre Joseph Redouté** had the same training till he followed his brother a year or two later. Of the painters established from the previous period **Cornelis Lens** painted flowers in the portrait of *Marie Catherine de Villegas de Borsbeke* by his son **Andreas Cornelis Lens** in 1764 and worked till the later sixties. **Jean Georges Coclers** died in 1751, **Charles Bigée** after 1759 and **Regnier Joseph Malaine** in 1762.

Among the painters of miscellaneous still-life **Jean Joseph Verhaghen (Pottekens)** produced many of the arrangements of pots and pans that earned him his nickname. **Antoine Clevenbergh** painted some still-life including game pieces after 1775. **Gerard Rysbraeck** may have painted some still-life with fish and game pieces in Antwerp in the later fifties and early sixties. **Pieter Snyers** (Pls. 839, 856) died in Antwerp at seventy-one, as noted, in 1752. His nephew **Pieter Jan Snyers** died there at sixty-one in 1757; and the trompe l'oeil painter of 'Vanitas' still-life **Jacobus Plasschaert** (Pl. 852) died in Bruges in 1765.

The immense repute of French art all over Europe in this period drew artists from many countries to Paris. The schools of the Académie Royale received two hundred and seventy-five foreign students, of whom sixty-two came from Belgium, between 1758 and 1787; and there were other students who worked in the old Academy of S. Luc or as private pupils of French painters. Belgian newcomers in the fifties included **Philippe Lambert Spruyt, Pierre Joseph Lion, Bernard Verschoot, Jean Baptiste Simons, Jean François Legillon,** and **Paul Joseph de Cock**. In the sixties they included **François Luc Peters, Leonard Defrance, Philippe Henri Coclers, Andreas Peter de Muynck, Joseph Benoit Suvée, Gertrude de Pélichy, Theodor de Bruyn, Andreas Cornelis Lens** and **Johannes Jacobus Lens**; and in the seventies **Pierre Joseph Thys, Jean Louis Demarne, Pieter Matthys Goddyn, Piat Joseph Sauvage, Hendrik de Cort, Antoine Ferdinand Redouté, Pierre Joseph Redouté, François Joseph Lonsing** and **Joseph Angelus van der Donckt**. Of these **Philippe Lambert Spruyt** came from Ghent about 1750 and worked under Charles van Loo till 1757 when he went aged thirty to Rome. The portrait painter **Pierre Joseph Lion** was a pupil of Joseph Vien from about 1754 and left for Vienna at thirty in 1759. The decorative painter **Bernard Verschoot** came from Bruges at twenty-six in 1754 and remained till 1757 when he left for Rome. The landscape painter **Jean François Legillon** (Pl. 877), who seems to have made the acquaintance of the French painter-historian Jean Baptiste Descamps in Bruges, worked under him in Rouen from 1759 for some years, moved for a time to Marseilles where he became a member of the Academy in 1769, and left for Italy at thirty-one in 1770. **Paul Joseph de Cock** came from Bruges probably in the early fifties, worked in Paris and Valenciennes and was back by the middle sixties to teach in the Bruges Academy. **François Luc Peters** was in Paris from Brussels about 1760 making genre compositions for engravers titled *L'amour materneal, La jeune dévideuse, La petite marchande de carpes, La jardinière en* *repos, Le vigneron galant* and so forth. **Leonard Defrance** (Pls. 874, 879) reached the south of France from Italy aged twenty-six in 1761 and worked at Montpellier, Castres, Toulouse and Bordeaux before returning to Liège, a keen Francophil, in 1764. **Philippe Henri Coclers** painter of portraits, miniatures and still-life arrived in Marseilles from Italy aged about twenty-two about 1760 and seems to have remained there. **Andreas Peter de Muynck** who came at twenty-six in 1763 from Bruges to Paris with **Joseph Benoit Suvée**, spent some years in the study of 'history' painting and then left for Rome. **Joseph Benoit Suvée** (Pl. 883), twenty in the year of his arrival, worked first under Jean-Jacques Bachelier (painter of a famous *Cimon in prison* and associated with the Sèvres china factory) and later in the Académie Royale under Joseph Vien; in 1764 he attracted attention with his *Raising of the young man at Nain*; in 1767 he became an instructor in the newly founded École gratuite de dessin; in 1771 he won the first Prix de Rome against Louis David with a composition titled *The Conflict of Mars and Minerva before Troy* and visited Bruges in triumph as related; back from Italy in 1778, he exhibited *The Birth of the Virgin, S. Sebastian. The Death of Cleopatra* and *Erminia and Clorinda* in the Salon of 1779 and became an Associate of the Académie Royale; and in 1780, at thirty-seven, he became a full member and Peintre du roi and deposited as his reception piece *Freedom restored to the Fine Arts by Louis XVI through the good offices of M. d'Angiviller*—a subject celebrating the annihilation of the Guild of S. Luc (the old Maîtrise) as a teaching institution competing with the Academy. **Gertrude de Pélichy** (Pls. 868, 870) came aged twenty-four in 1767, lodged in the Pensionnat des Dames de l'Instruction Chrétienne, attended **Suvée's** classes in the École gratuite and returned to Bruges in the middle seventies. **Theodor de Bruyn**, already referred to as a painter of landscapes and decorative grisailles, came from Antwerp about 1767 and left for England about 1769. **Andreas Cornelis Lens** (Pl. 871) and his brother **Johannes Jacobus Lens** (Pl. 869) travelled through France on their way home from Italy in 1768. The flower painter **Pierre Joseph Thys** reached Paris at twenty-one in 1770 and remained for ten years. **Jean Louis Demarne** (Pls. 875, 894) of Brussels, a pupil at eighteen of Gabriel Briard in the Académie Royale in 1772, shared defeat with Louis David in the Prix de Rome competition (won by Pierre-Charles Jombert) that year; and he remained in Paris through the period attempting unsuccessfully to attract attention as a painter of costume-history. **Pieter Mathias Goddyn** came from Bruges at twenty in 1772 and left for Rome about 1780. **Piat Joseph Sauvage** arrived aged thirty in 1774, became a member of the old Académie de S. Luc where he deposited a grisaille *Death of Germanicus* as his reception piece, had similar successes in the academies of Toulouse and Lille in 1776 and remained in France with headquarters in Paris. **Hendrik de Cort** reached Paris at thirty-four in 1776, became painter to the Prince de Condé (who commissioned topographic pictures of Chantilly) and was elected an Associate of the Académie Royale in 1779; and the flower-painters **Antoine Ferdinand Redouté** and **Pierre Joseph Redouté** came respectively in 1776 and 1779 as already recorded. **François Joseph Lonsing** went to Lyons in 1778, when he was just under forty, after nineteen years in Italy, and remained painting portraits for some years; and **Joseph Angelus van der Donckt** (Pl. 889) was in a business house in Marseilles aged twenty-three in 1780.

Of the older men still in France from the last period **Gerard Rysbraeck** seems to have held Court favour with his hunting scenes and still-life with fish and game till he went back to Antwerp at fifty-eight in 1754. **Jean Jacques Spoede**, the former friend of Watteau, sent game pieces, mythologies and allegories to the Academy of S. Luc's exhibitions in the early fifties and died approaching eighty in 1758. **Guillaume de Spinny** (Pl. 862) seems to have left Paris for Holland aged thirty-five in 1756. **Nicolas de Fassin**, 'mousquetaire du roi' till he went back to Belgium in 1754, passed through France on his travels in 1769 when he called on Voltaire at Ferney and drew his portrait in his robe de chambre. **Jacques François Delien**, who painted *M. Berryer, Lieutenant general of Police* (a protégé of Madame de Pompadour) soon after 1750 and died at seventy-seven in 1761, sent no genre pictures to the Salons in this period, and seems to have found the market for his work diminished as he engraved a plate where the art-inspecting public is depicted as a donkey. **Jan Peter Verdussen** was back in Marseilles from Turin by 1758, deposited a *Cavalry battle* as his reception piece when the Academy elected him a member in 1759, and died over sixty at Avignon in 1763; **Jacques Smets** died in Auch at eighty-four in 1764; and **Jacques Rysbraeck** died in Paris at eighty in 1765. **François Eisen** employed in the fifties and sixties on hack production of genre subjects and grisaille panels with cupids and flowers for the dealers, sent a *Corps de garde* to the Academy of S. Luc's exhibition in 1762 and died in an alms-house over eighty at the end of the period; and **Jan Nollekens** sent works titled *A drawing academy*, *The Woman taken in adultery*, *Samson and Delilah* and *The Four Seasons* to the same exhibitions between 1752 and 1774, received in 1760 an unwelcome visit from his nephew Joseph Nollekens the sculptor (then twenty-three and on his way to Rome) and was still alive at eighty-five in 1780.

Of the Belgians in England surviving from the last period **Peter Casteels III** (Pl. 857) died aged sixty-five at Richmond in 1749; **Joseph van Aken (Tailor Vanaken)** died at fifty the same year and Hogarth caricatured the despair of the portrait painters at losing his assistance; **Alexander van Haecken (Aken)**, his successor as drapery painter to Thomas Hudson, died about fifty-seven about 1758; and **Petrus Johannes van Reysschoot (The Englishman)** seems to have remained till 1768 and to have returned then at sixty-six to Ghent. Newcomers in the period included **Philip Joseph Tassaert, Bernard Paul, Louis Paul, Jean Latour, Pierre Joseph Lion** and **Theodor de Bruyn.** Of these the eclectic **Philip Joseph Tassaert** worked here with **Alexander van Haecken** in the early fifties, went to Antwerp in 1756 where he became a Court Painter to Charles of Lorraine as related, and came back in 1769; as a Member of the Society of Artists where he exhibited landscapes, genre pictures and 'history' pieces from 1769 onwards, and as its President in 1775, he played a part in the English art-world, and he much incensed the Society in 1777 by arranging what he called The Grand Museum where he exhibited, probably for sale, both contemporary paintings and Old Masters and also curiosities of various kinds. **Bernard Paul** and his brother **Louis Paul** were in London from Ghent making portrait drawings for a year or two round 1766. **Jean Latour** seems to have visited London from Liège in 1767 when three figure pieces and a portrait by 'Latour' were exhibited in the Free Society of Artists. **Pierre Joseph Lion** seems to have come here from Vienna in 1772 when he sent a portrait drawing to the Academy and drew or painted *The daughters of General Carpenter* which was subsequently engraved in mezzotint. **Theodor de Bruyn** arrived from Paris in 1769, took a studio in Castle Street, Cavendish Square and remained here; he exhibited grisaille compositions *Allegory of Painting* and *Allegory of Sculpture* (painted for the Duke of Norfolk at Worksop Manor) and *Bacchanalian groups* in the Free Society in 1769, 1770 and 1771; and he also sent landscapes to the Free Society, the Society of Artists and the Royal Academy in the seventies.

In Holland the flower painter **Pieter Hardimé** died at eighty-one in 1758; and **Harmen Serin** who signed a portrait 'aetatis 77' in 1754 probably died soon after. **Guillaume de Spinny**, who arrived from Paris and settled in The Hague about 1765, painted *Members of the Hague Town Council* in 1759 and was much employed as a portraitist by the upper bourgeoisie; his carefully designed and cautiously executed *Lady with a rose* (Pl. 862) of 1762 shows the influence of French fashions in Holland as well as the influence of Parisian painting; at the end of the sixties he was patronized by the House of Orange and his *Fredericka Sophia Wilhelmina of Prussia, wife of the Stadholder William V* dates from 1769. **Bernard Paul** of Ghent arrived in The Hague aged twenty-six in 1763 and seems to have worked there as portraitist till he left for London some three years later. **Leonard Defrance** (Pls. 874, 879, 880) was in Holland with **Nicolas de Fassin** in 1773. **Louis Bernard Coclers** who worked in various Dutch towns in the seventies produced the engagingly simple *Catherine Six, wife of Jan Bicker seated by a table with a trinket box and flowers* (Pl. 866), probably in Amsterdam, in 1776. The landscape and animal painter **Jean Baptiste de Roy** of Brussels was in Holland as a youth at the end of the period; and the landscape painter **Jacques Trachez** was there on a visit in 1780.

In Central Europe **Charles Sylva Dubois** died at eighty-five in Berlin in 1753, **Charles William Hamilton** at about the same age in Augsburg in 1754, and **Frans de Backer**, over seventy, soon after 1750, probably in Breslau. **Pieter Jacob Horemans**, who continued in favour at the Bavarian Court, painted *The Concert, Quadrille and Coffee Party celebrating the Visit to Munich of Augustus III of Poland*, which included thirty-two portraits, in 1761; in the following years he was much employed on portraits of Court ladies for the Amalienburg and also signed some fruit pieces, a *Self portrait* and a *Portrait of a Sculptor*; his *Portrait of a Court musician* dated 1774 was probably his last picture as he died almost blind at seventy-six soon after. In Vienna **Philip Ferdinand de Hamilton** (Pls. 849, 851) died about eighty-six in 1750 and the portraitist **Frans van Stampart** at seventy-five the same year. **Hyacinth de La Pegnia** (Pls. 853, 854) 'peintre extraordinaire' of the Empress reached Vienna in 1759, stayed till 1762, and then left for Rome. **Antoine Alexandre Cardon** went from Brussels to Vienna aged about twenty in 1759, became a pupil of **La Pegnia** and was sent to Rome with a stipend from the Empress in 1762. **Pierre Joseph Lion** who arrived from Paris, probably via Brussels, was Court Painter to the Empress at thirty-one in 1760 and painted a full length portrait of her and a set of pastel landscapes for her private apartments; he was also employed on portraits of the Esterhazy, Poniatowski and other families and seems to have worked continuously in Vienna and the region (except in 1772 when he made his visit to London). **Herman Gillis** reached Vienna from Antwerp just under thirty in 1762, painted *Field Marshal Loudon* there soon after, and went back to Antwerp about 1768. **Pierre Joseph Verhaghen** (Pls. 872, 873) visited Vienna on his way home from Italy in 1773 and presented a *S. Theresa* to the Empress who hung it in her bedroom. **Gertrude de Pélichy** (Pls. 868, 870) though an Honorary Member of the Imperial Academy in Vienna at the end of the seventies, does not seem to have actually gone there.

In Rome **Hendrik van Lint** became Regent of the Congregazione dei Virtuosi in 1752, signed the picturesque landscapes *Italian lake with boats and fishermen* (Pl. 864) and *Italian landscape with figures and cattle* (Pl. 865) in 1756 and died at seventy-nine in 1763. **Giuseppe Grisoni** was presumably active till he died over seventy in 1769. **Henri Deprez** remained with Corrado Giaquinto till 1751 and then returned to Liège. **Maximilien de Haese** seems to have returned to Brussels soon after 1750. **Englebert Panhay de Rendeux** continued his marine compositions till he died in 1777; and **Jacob Vermoelen** was still painting his game pieces when the period closed. **Hyacinth de La Pegnia** (Pls. 853, 854) back in Turin from Rome in 1749 painted *The handing over of Milan to Charles Emmanuel III King of Sardinia 1734* and *The Siege of Tortona 1734* for Charles Emmanuel in 1752, and went to Rome again, after the Brussels and Vienna periods, in 1762; in Rome he became a protégé of Cardinal Albani and held the office of Provisor of the Flemish Foundation of S. Julien (established in Rome for the benefit of Brugeois artists) from 1768 till his death at sixty-six in 1772. **Jan Pieter Verdussen**, also in Turin in the early fifties, was still painting battle pieces for Charles Emmanuel till he left for Provence and died there in 1763. Of the newcomers in the fifties **Leonard Defrance** (Pls. 874, 879, 880) came on foot from Liège aged eighteen in 1753 and visited Milan, Padua, Florence, Naples, Bologna and Venice before leaving for France about 1760; in Rome he kept himself by hack devotional pictures and portraits of Popes and Cardinals painted for dealers, and worked for a time under the French 'history' and portrait painter Laurent Pécheux (who had studied under the German Raphael Mengs, the leader, with Madame de Pompadour's brother, the Marquis de Marigny, and the German writer Johann Winckelmann, of the Neo-Classic movement). Two other Liégeois **Philippe Henri Coclers** who arrived in Rome aged twenty in 1758 and **Joseph Dreppe** who arrived the same year aged twenty-one were also pupils of Laurent Pécheux; and **Louis Bernard Coclers** (Pl. 866) who arrived aged eighteen in 1759 may also have worked with him before leaving for Holland in 1762. **Philippe Lambert Spruyt** arrived from Paris aged thirty in 1757, was a pupil of Mengs till 1760 and then worked in Naples before returning to Ghent in 1761. **François Joseph Lonsing** came from Antwerp aged twenty with his scholarship from Prince Charles in 1759, worked there under Mengs till 1761, made drawings and engravings for Sir William Hamilton's 'Etruscan, Greek and Roman Antiquities' (published in Naples in 1767) and for Gavin Hamilton's 'Schola Italica Picturae' (published in Rome in 1773) and had left for France by 1778. **Bernard Verschoot** who came from Paris at the end of the fifties, worked in Rome and Naples before returning to Brussels to work for Prince Charles in 1765. Of the newcomers in the sixties **Antoine Alexandre Cardon** reached Rome from Vienna, with his stipend from Maria Theresa, in 1762, went thence to Naples where, abandoning painting, he engraved some *Views of Naples* in 1764 and also contributed to Sir William Hamilton's 'Etruscan, Greek and Roman Antiquities' before returning to Brussels in 1769. **Andreas Cornelis Lens** (Pl. 871) arrived at twenty-five, with his stipend from the Prince, in 1764, made drawings of antique sculpture, ruins and so forth in Rome, Naples and Florence and went back to Antwerp via France in 1768; his brother **Johannes Jacobus Lens** (Pl. 869) was with him in Rome and went back with him. **Petrus Norbertus van Reysschoot** came from Ghent in the early sixties, collected drawings and art historical books and was back as a lecturer on architecture in Ghent Academy by 1770. The Brugeois **Andreas Peter de Muynck** came from Paris, probably in the later sixties, copied Italian pictures which he sold to English visitors and became Provisor of the S. Julien Foundation after the death of **Hyacinth de La Pegnia** in 1772. **Nicolas de Fassin** was in Rome and Naples in 1768 or 1769 either before or after his visit to Voltaire at Ferney. In the seventies **Pierre Joseph Verhaghen** (Pl. 872, 873) was in Italy with the funds provided by Maria Theresa from 1771 to 1773; he reached Rome via Paris, Versailles, Turin and Milan and later visited Florence, Parma, Bologna, Venice, Naples and Sicily; in Rome he painted a *S. Peter* for the Belgian Franciscans and, for the Empress, an *Ecce Homo* and a *Disciples at Emmaus* as well as the *S. Theresa* already referred to; and he won the favour of Pope Clement XIV who accorded him a plenary indulgence, at the hour of death, for himself, his relations and connections to the third degree, and for thirty persons of his nomination. **Jean François Legillon** (Pl. 877) arrived from Marseilles in 1770, produced a *Self-portrait in Rome* in 1772 and was back in Bruges by 1774. **Joseph Benoit Suvée** (Pl. 883) came from Paris as Prix de Rome winner in 1772, worked in the French Academy in Rome under Charles Joseph Natoire till 1775 and under

Joseph Vien (with Louis David as fellow student and personal enemy) till 1777; and he visited Naples, Sicily and Malta on his way back to Paris in 1778. Another Brugeois the genre painter **Jacobus Johannes Lauwers** came on foot (like **Leonard Defrance**) as a pilgrim in the middle seventies, arrived destitute, was befriended by **Suvée** and, at the S. Julien Foundation, by **Andreas de Muynck** and then kept himself for some time by producing cheap portraits of the Pope and Cardinals in a workshop which catered for the peasants. Yet another Brugeois **Pieter Matthias Goddyn** came from Paris in the middle seventies. **Michel d'Argent** arrived from Liège aged twenty-four in 1775; and **Joseph François** came from Antwerp aged nineteen in 1778.

CHAPTER XX

Duke Albert of Saxe-Teschen and The Archduchess Maria Christina (Joseph II) 1781-1789; Brabant Revolution 1789-1790; Restoration 1791-1792; General Dumouriez 1792; French Commissaries 1793; Archduke Charles 1793-1794; French Representatives en Mission 1794-1795; Union with France 1795

1781-1795

IN THE first nine years of this period Belgium was ruled by the Emperor Joseph II who made the Minister Plenipotentiary and the military commander directly responsible for execution of his edicts and left the Governors, Duke Albert of Saxe-Teschen and the Archduchess Maria-Christina, as purely decorative figures. The Emperor set out to transform the traditional civil institutions, with their complicated local privileges, to a single authoritarian structure conforming to 'les lumières du siècle'; and, on Febronian principles, to integrate the Church within this structure, thus reducing the powers of the clergy and the Pope. His reforms pleased the Belgian business and professional men and also intellectuals and free-thinkers influenced by English and French ideas; but they incensed the old privileged classes—the Church, the nobles, the Estates and also the trade and artisan corporations; and when he died, at the beginning of 1790, they had been swept away by the Brabant Revolution which expelled the Habsburgs and made Belgium a Federal Republic.

This new Republic, reactionary and incompetent, collapsed before an Austrian army which restored the Habsburgs some twelve months later. But the Restoration also was shortlived, and from 1792, with one brief interval, the country was overrun and dominated by the troops and emissaries of the French Republic which officially absorbed it in 1795.

In 1781 the Emperor Joseph II came to Belgium travelling incognito as 'Count von Falkenstein'; he arrived in May refusing all pageantry of welcome, and left on July 6 convinced that the Belgian people were 'arriéré', their traditional institutions and governing procedures absurd, and the influence of French culture upon them no more than a veneer.

The new Governors Duke Albert and the Archduchess Christina arrived on July 10 and carried out the usual inauguration pageants on the Emperor's behalf. In October Joseph published an Edict of Toleration for all religions in all his territories; and in November he ordered the Dutch to remove their garrisons from the Belgian Barrier towns. In this year also a woman condemned for witchcraft by the Inquisition was burned alive in Seville; Sir Joshua Reynolds toured the Netherlands and wrote his brilliant 'Character of Rubens' in a subsequent account of his impressions; William Blake and the painter Stothard were arrested as French spies for sketching on the Medway; Gibraltar was still besieged by the French and Spanish; and Lord Cornwallis surrendered Yorktown. In 1782 the Dutch removed their garrisons from the Barrier towns; an Imperial decree forbade mention of the old 'Unigenitus' Bull (against Quesnel's 'Réflexions morales') in Belgian educational establishments; and the defenders of Gibraltar drove off the besiegers by burning their floating batteries. In 1783 England recognized the independence of the United States of America and made peace with France, Spain and Holland; Joseph issued a decree dissolving a hundred and sixty-three Belgian monasteries and convents 'où l'on ne mène qu' une vie purement contemplative et parfaitement inutile à la religion, à l'État et au prochain' —an event recorded in a panegyric painting by the francophil and anti-clerical Liégeois **Leonard Defrance** (represented here as portrait and genre painter (Pls. 874, 879)); and another Imperial edict abolished hermits 'des bois et de la campagne' which affected **Jean Henri Gilson**, a painter of religious subjects, then living as a hermit in the Ardennes. In 1784 the younger Pitt was Prime Minister of England at the age of twenty-five; Joseph told the Dutch that the Scheldt must be considered open; and Imperial edicts made marriage a civil contract, forbade the use of torture by the Belgian courts without permission from the Privy Council, and authorized employers to engage their workmen without reference to the rules of the guilds or corporations. In 1785 Joseph ordered Belgian priests to read his edicts from the pulpit, and signed reluctantly the Treaty of Fontainebleau which confirmed the clôture of the Scheldt as Louis XVI had intimated that he would not tolerate its opening. Cardinal de Rohan was sent to the Bastille in the Affair of the Diamond Necklace; Mrs. Siddons played Lady Macbeth and was painted by Gainsborough in a 'picture' hat; and Sir Joshua Reynolds in Brussels and Antwerp to buy pictures on sale from the monasteries and convents had the Antwerp painter **Pieter Jan Balthasar de Grée** as his agent and assistant and wrote to the Duke of Rutland: 'The pictures of the suppressed religious houses are the saddest trash that ever were collected together; the *Adoration of the Magi* and *S. Justus* by **Rubens** and a *Crucifixion* by **Van Dyck** were the only tolerable pictures but these are not the best of those masters; I was shown some reserved for the Emperor which were not an iota better than the common run of the rest of the collection.' In 1786 Mozart composed the 'Marriage of Figaro' in Vienna; Frederick II died and Frederick William II became King of Prussia; and Imperial edicts curtailed the traditional Belgian religious processions with the carrying of statues and so forth, made sermons subject to the ordinary rules of censorship, and founded a State-controlled Central Seminary at Louvain to replace the existing Episcopal Seminaries for the training of theological students. In 1787 the Turks declared war on Russia; the French notables met at Versailles; Louis XVI said in the Parlement de Paris 'C'est légal parce que je le veux'; a 'Patriot' party in Holland deposed the Stadholder William V who was reinstated by his brother-in-law the King of Prussia; Joseph dissolved the Belgian administrative and judicial systems, replaced them by new structures, and sent General d'Alton and Count von Trauttmansdorff to deal firmly with the opposition which was now fomented by the clergy among the peasants and by the lawyer Henri van der Noot as mouthpiece of the corporations among the urban artisans. Mozart had Beethoven aged seventeen as his pupil in Vienna and became Court Composer to Joseph; and Sheridan spoke for six hours in the House of Commons against Warren Hastings. In 1788 the spirit of the old Belgian corporations was expressed in the picture *'The 1788 Procession of the Bruges Tailors' Guild, with the thirteen poor people traditionally clothed by them, to the annual service in the church of Notre Dame* (Pl. 859) commissioned from **Jean Beerblock** for the Bruges Tailors' Hall; the new Louvain Seminary was an obvious failure with only eighteen students; the Estates of Hainault and Brabant refused to vote the taxes; there were riots suppressed by d'Alton's troops; hundreds of people were arrested; Henri van der Noot fled to Breda; and von Trauttmansdorff wrote to the Emperor: 'Je ne saurais dissimuler à Votre Majesté que les coeurs ne sont pas ramenés encore comme je le désirerais pour n'avoir plus à s'attendre à l'égarement des faibles esprits de ces pays-ci où on attache plus de valeur à une procession, à une bannière ou à un petit habit de gala dont on décorait un saint destiné à etre exposé à la vénération du public dans de certains jours qu'aux affaires les plus conséquentes pour le bien total du pays. ...' In 1789 the French States-General assembled at Versailles; a Brussels lawyer Jean-François Vonck, in correspondence with Mirabeau, formed a Belgian Patriots Party with a progressive liberal-democratic programme supported by the business and professional classes and a few of the nobles; Cardinal de Franckenberg, Archbishop of Malines, condemned the teaching in the new Louvain Seminary as unorthodox; and van der Noot at Breda attracted those who wished to put the clock back to the old régime of local privileges. In June the French States-General became the National Assembly. In July the National Assembly became the Constituent Assembly and the Bastille was stormed. In August the Constituent Assembly published the Déclaration des Droits de l'Homme; insurgents in Liège forced the Prince Bishop to abscond; high ranking Belgian clergy, hostile to the Vonckist Patriots, joined van der Noot in Breda; and General van der Mersch, an old professional soldier, became the leader of armed Vonckist volunteers. In October the women of Paris marched to Versailles and Louis XVI was brought to Paris; Vonck went to Breda to make common cause with van der Noot, and Belgian Patriot forces under General van der Mersch took possession of Turnhout and drove off d'Alton's troops. In November the Constituent Assembly decreed the sale of Church property and the issue of 'assignats' in payments; Belgian Patriot forces under the Prince de Ligne captured and held Ghent; and Duke Albert and the Archduchess Maria Christina left Brussels and retired to Bonn. In December there was fighting in the streets of Brussels, d'Alton withdrew his troops to Luxembourg, von Trauttmansdorff and the Austrian officials fled and van der Noot returned to Brussels as the hero of the hour. The Estates of Brabant, supported by the clergy, the corporations and most of the nobles, declared themselves the Government of Belgium, thrusting on one side the Vonckist Patriot Party who desired a National Assembly to decide the form the Government should take; and the Manneken-Pis in Brussels was dressed in the colours of Brabant. In this year also Jeremy Bentham published his 'Principles of Morals and Legislation' at forty-one, and Robert Burns wrote 'Tam O'Shanter' and 'Auld Lang Syne' at thirty.

In 1790 Joseph II died and his brother Leopold II succeeded; the French celebrated the Fête de la Fédération (Quatorze Juillet) and established the civil constitution of the clergy which took the appointment of French bishops from the Pope and drastically reduced their numbers; and Belgium became a Federal Republic led by van der Noot and Pierre van Eupen, Penitentiary of Antwerp, both pledged to restore old privileges in all fields. In the spring the Vonckists made demonstrations against the 'reactionary' Belgian Government, the clergy organized processions against the Vonckist 'enemies of religion', a Government army marched against General van der Mersch still at the head of Vonck's Patriot Volunteers, and the General made a personal surrender to avoid a civil war. In the summer the King of Prussia made a Treaty of Alliance with the Emperor, an Austro-Prussian army under General Bender was built up in Luxembourg, and the Belgian Government called for a forced loan and a mass levy of volunteers against an Austrian invasion. In the autumn General Bender entered Namur and Mons, the Belgian army melted in desertions, van Eupen and van der Noot fled to Holland, and the Belgian Republic disappeared in chaos. In December the country was once more Austrian, the Emperor proclaimed a general amnesty, and there were in fact no acts of revenge or punishment.

In 1791 Duke Albert and the Archduchess Maria Christina returned to Brussels; **Johannes Jacobus Lens** painted, doubtless for the Antwerp inauguration ceremonies, *The Emperor Leopold II as Peacemaker and apostle of Justice* (Pl. 869) with a lion couchant at his feet and Justitia holding scales behind him; **Willem Jacob Herreyns** (Pl. 867) designed inauguration ceremonies in Malines; and **Antoine Brice** of Brussels drew a *Glorification of Leopold II* engraved the next year by **Antoine Alexandre Cardon**. The French Constituent Assembly became the Legislative Assembly; Belgian Vonckists assembled at Lille and founded clubs on the French Revolutionary model; French Royalist emigrés swarmed into Belgium, joined the King's brothers in Coblenz and sought military aid from the Austrians and Prussians; and Louis XVI and Marie Antoinette were in secret communication with the Austrians. In 1792 Catherine of Russia signed the Treaty of Jassy with the Turks; Leopold II died and was succeeded by Francis II who was eager to fight for the French émigrés' cause; France declared war on Austria; Prussia declared war on France; and Louis XVI betrayed to the Austrians the military dispositions of the French. A Parisian mob stormed the Tuileries; Louis XVI and his family were imprisoned in the Temple; Duke Albert laid siege to Lille; and Austro-Prussians besieged Verdun. A Parisian mob incited by Marat's 'L'Ami du Peuple' broke into prisons and massacred royalists and suspects; the Legislative Assembly became the National Convention; and the First French Republic was established. A French army under General Kellerman and General Dumouriez defeated the Prussians at Valmy; General Dumouriez entered Belgium from Valenciennes with a regiment of Belgians (Vonckists and others) in his army, and decisively defeated the Austrians at Jemappes; the French émigrés disappeared into Germany and Holland; the Austrians abandoned Brussels; Duke Albert and the Archduchess fled; and Dumouriez entering Mons, Brussels, Antwerp, and Liège was acclaimed as 'Saviour of the Belgians'. The Convention declared the Scheldt an open waterway; the trial of Louis XVI began; and General Dumouriez, a moderate Revolutionary in sympathy with the Vonckists, advised the Belgians to elect a National Assembly as a middle course between the church-and-privilege party and the Belgian Jacobins who now set up 'Sociétés des Amis de la Liberté et Egalité' in all towns and who in Liège, urged on by **Leonard Defrance** (Pls. 874, 879), were calling for the destruction of the Cathedral of S. Lambert as an anti-clerical gesture.

In 1793 the fate of Belgium depended on the ebb and flow of the French Republic's progress. In January Louis XVI was guillotined; the French envoy was expelled from England; and General Dumouriez was replaced in Belgium by Commissaries of the Convention instructed to support the Belgian Jacobins, to liquidate the property of the privileged classes and to circulate French assignats at par. In February France declared war on England and Holland; General Dumouriez captured Breda; the French Commissaries robbed Belgian churches of their argenterie; and Belgian Jacobins destroyed the statue of Charles of Lorraine 'ci-devant tyran' in Brussels. In the spring Pitt began to organize a Coalition against France; French priests incited a Royalist rising in the Vendée; Belgian Jacobins and French troops made sacrilegious gestures in the Brussels Cathedral of S. Gudule; General Dumouriez was driven from Holland by the Austrians and was also defeated at Neerwinden and Louvain; Austrian armies entered the principal Belgian cities; the Archduke Charles arrived in Brussels as the new Governor of Belgium; Dumouriez disgusted by the 'impious brigandage' of the Convention's Commissaries, deserted to the Austrians; and the Convention set up in Paris the Revolutionary Tribunal for Summary Judgement and the Committee of Public Safety (with nine members including Danton). In the summer the French Jacobin Montagnards seized power from the moderate Girondins in Paris; there were Girondin risings in Lyons, Bordeaux, Marseilles and other places; the Royalists were still in revolt in the Vendée; Marat was assassinated by Charlotte Corday; Prince Josias of Saxe-Coburg leading Austrian, English, Hanoverian, Hessian, Dutch and Prussian troops took Condé and Valenciennes; the Duke of York besieged Dunkirk; Saxe-Coburg besieged Maubeuge; Spanish troops took Bayonne and Perpignan; and French Royalists surrendered Toulon to the English. In the autumn Robespierre took the place of Danton in the Committee of Public Safety and organized the Terror; and Carnot in charge of military problems declared the whole French nation requisitioned for the war; Marie-Antoinette was guillotined, and Philippe Egalité, Duke of Orléans, with scores of others followed to the scaffold; new French armies defeated Anglo-Hano-verians at Hondschoote, relieved Dunkirk from the English, routed the Dutch at Menin, and drove Saxe-Coburg from Maubeuge; Jean-Baptiste Carrier, who had been a Com-missary in Belgium, suppressed a revolt in Nantes and drowned his prisoners by hundreds in the river; the Royalists in La Vendée were defeated at Le Mans and Savenay; General Hoche drove invaders out of Alsace; and Toulon was recaptured from the English by General Napoleon Bonaparte.

In this year also the painter Louis David, Jacobin member of the Convention and leading member of its Comité d'Instruction and Commission des Arts, abolished the Académie Royale, the provincial academies and the French Academy in Rome; Fragonard, aged sixty, who had done David a kindness many years before, was put in charge of the Musée National des Arts established in the Louvre to safeguard paintings sequestered from royal palaces, the churches and the houses of the émigrés; Alexandre Lenoir, employed by the Convention to assemble sculpture and applied art from nationalized French buildings, held an exhibition of the works collected (which included Goujon's *Diane Chasseresse*) in a former convent in the rue des Petits Augustins; and the dealer-painter Jean-Baptiste Le Brun (husband of the painter Madame Vigée le Brun), authorized by the Convention to buy works of art at private sales for the Musée National, acquired a portrait by **Rubens** and Rembrandt's *Ménage du Menuisier* (for 7,750 and 17,120 livres) at the sale of pictures formerly owned by the Duc de Choiseul-Praslin recorded as 'deceased'.

In 1794 Tadeusz Kosciuszko leading a Polish revolt was defeated by Marshal Suvorov; and Goya depicted contemporary victims of the Inquisition in Madrid. The Emperor Francis II came to Brussels to be inaugurated and found the majority of Belgians hostile or apathetic to the Austrian régime; Robespierre's Terror reached its climax; and Robes-pierre in a Deist ceremony burned a statue of Atheism on the Champs de Mars. In the summer the Terror ceased; Robespierre was guillotined and Louis David was imprisoned; French armies swept into Belgium taking Ypres and Charleroi; General Jourdan won the decisive Battle of Fleurus against Saxe-Coburg; and the Habsburg rule in Belgium ended when the French occupied Antwerp and Brussels after capturing Tournai, Bruges, Ostend, Audenarde and Ghent. From August to November Belgium was administered by Representatives on Mission from the Committee of Public Safety; Committees of Surveillance and Summary Tribunals were set up; hostages were taken; there were wholesale requisitions for the French army's needs and rapacious levies on the clergy and nobles; assignats were tendered to civic bodies when their funds and properties were impounded; a church in each town was converted into a 'Temple of Reason'; and gestures of tolerance were restricted to collaborators and the Belgian Jacobins who outdid the French in Revolutionary ardour—in Ghent for example the carillon of the Beffroi played the 'Marseillaise', the 'Carmagnole', the 'Danse Républicaine' and 'Ça ira', and in Liège **Leonard Defrance's** plan to pull down the Cathedral was put into effect. In the autumn the Representatives were instructed to pursue a policy of cajolement and appeasement; hostages were released, the Committees of Surveillance were abolished, civil marriage was introduced for all who might desire it, judicial torture was forbidden, and efforts were made to induce the country to seek Union with France.

When the Representatives on Mission first arrived in Belgium they had orders to send home sculptures and argenterie to Lenoir's Museum in the rue des Petits Augustins and to send paintings to the Louvre for the Musée National—as such objects in 'pays conquis', in the Convention's ruling, should be impounded 'pour embellir Paris'. Most of the pictures, sculptures and so on in the Governors' palaces had been taken to Vienna by Duke Albert and the Archduchess; but there were still immense numbers owned by churches and civic bodies all over the country, and before this year 1794 was out some two thousand works of art had been brought to a central Bureau established in Brussels to receive them. From this agglomeration the selections were made for Paris. The argenterie from the Antwerp Painters' Guild preserved in the Academy's headquarters (and depicted in the *Portrait of the Guild's messenger Abraham Grapheus* by **Cornelis de Vos**) was sent in an early consignment; and some two hundred and seventy paintings went in the next few months. The Representatives' advisers in the choice of paintings included **Leonard Defrance** (Pls. 874, 879), another Liégeois artist **Joseph Dreppe** and, in Antwerp, **Simon Pierre d'Argonne** who was now given the rank of 'officier municipal' as reward for his collaboration. The central panels of the **van Eycks'** *Altarpiece of the Mystic Lamb* went from Ghent, S. Bavon, and **Jean van Eyck's** *Van der Paele Altarpiece* (Pl. 19) from Bruges, S. Donatien; the *Moreel altarpiece* (*with SS. Christopher, Maur and Giles*) then described as by 'Hemmelinck' (Memlinc) went from the Bruges Hôpital de Saint Julien, and the *S. Anne altarpice* (*The Holy Kinship*) (Pl. 207) by **Quinten Massys** from Louvain S. Pierre. Some other early pictures were also selected; but the taste of the time was for seventeenth-century art and the main consignments included sixty-two pictures by **Rubens** (and the **Rubens** atelier), twenty-five by **Van Dyck**, fifteen by **Jordaens**, twenty-six by **Gaspar de Crayer** as well as the *Portrait of Abraham Grapheus* by **Cornelis de Vos** from the Antwerp Academy's headquarters and the same artist's *S. Norbert recovering the Sacred Vessels* (Pl. 599) from the Antwerp Abbaye de S. Michel, and **Antoine Sallaert's** *The 1616 procession with the maidens dowered by the Infanta Isabella* (Pl. 514), from Brussels, Notre Dame du Sablon. *S. Martin curing a demoniac* (Pl. 588) by **Jordaens** went from the church of the monastery of S. Martin in Tournai. The **Gasper de Crayer** series included *The Virgin protecting the Brussels Crossbowmen's Guild* (Pl. 598) from Brussels, Notre Dame du Sablon, *SS. Paul and Anthony* *hermits* from the Brussels Alexian monastery and *The Virgin and Child with S. Dominic receiving the Rosary* from Anderlecht church. **Van Dyck's** *S. Martin and the beggar* went from Saventhem church, his *Crucifixion with SS. Catherine and Dominic* from the sacristy of the Dominican church in Antwerp, and his *Lamentation* (Pl. 608) from the chapel of Notre Dame des Sept Douleurs in Antwerp, Recollets. The **Rubens** series included the *Virgin with the Parrot* from the Antwerp Academy's headquarters, the *Adoration of the Magi* (Pl. 574) and *Saints adoring a picture of the Virgin and Child* from the Antwerp Abbaye de S. Michel, *S. Theresa delivering Bernardin de Mendoza from Purgatory* from the Antwerp Carmes Déchaussés, *Christ crucified between the thieves* (*Le coup de lance*) from the Antwerp Recollets, the *Virgin and Saints interceding for sinners* from the Antwerp Jacobins, the *Raising of the Cross* (Pl. 528) from Antwerp, S. Walpurgis, the *Descent from the Cross* (Pl. 529) and the *Assumption of the Virgin* from Antwerp Cathedral, the *Road to Calvary* from the Abbey of Afflighem, the *Entry of Christ into Jerusalem* and *Christ washing the feet of the Apostles* from Malines S. Rombout, the *Dead Christ on the knees of the Virgin* from the Brussels Capucins and others from Ghent, Tournai and elsewhere.

In 1795 the Third Partition of Poland took place. The French Republic was successful in all fields; and there was widespread lethargy, distress and indigence in Belgium, though some nests were feathered by collaborators, blackmarket dealers and other profiteers. Amsterdam was entered by General Pichegru who had led his troops over snow and ice; the Stadholder William V fled with his son Prince William Frederick to England and was lodged at Hampton Court; the Stadholder's collection of pictures was sent to join the works of art in Paris; and the Dutch signed the Treaty of The Hague which confirmed the opening of the Scheldt and made Holland as the 'Batavian Republic' an ally of France. Prussia and Spain made peace with France; a landing of Royalist emigrés from England at Quiberon Bay was a total fiasco; and a Royalist rising in Paris was dispersed by General Bonaparte with a 'whiff of grapeshot'. The Convention, declaring its work completed, proclaimed the Constitution of Year III (with two legislative bodies and an executive Directorate); and before dispersing in October it decreed the absorption of Belgium in the French Republic, the right of the inhabitants to all the privileges of 'citoyens français', and the abolition of all customs barriers.

Both before the French Revolution and after 1789 there were Belgian painters as usual in Paris, some already established there and others who arrived in this period. Under the old régime only members and agréés of the Académie Royale could exhibit in the biennial Salons; but in 1791 the Assembly decreed that the Salons should be open to all artists, and the number of pictures shown in that year increased as a result from three hundred and fifty to seven hundred and ninety-four; in 1793, when the Terror began, the Salon was exhibiting a thousand pictures; the 1795 Salon had just above three thousand; and thus Belgian members of the Academy exhibited in the eighties and many others in the 'open' Salons of the later years.

Of the Belgians remaining from the last period **Jan Nollekens** died at eighty-three in 1783; and **Hendrick de Cort** painted *Chantilly seen from La Pelouse* and *Chantilly seen from La Vertugadin* in 1781 and returned to Antwerp the year after. **Piat Joseph Sauvage,** who followed **Hendrick de Cort** as painter to the Prince de Condé, became Associate of the Académie Royale in 1781, Member in 1783 (when he deposited a *Still-life* as his reception piece) and Court Painter to Louis XVI soon after; in the later eighties he provided grisaille panels imitating sculptured bas-reliefs (in the tradition of his former master **Marten Joseph Geeraerts** (Pl. 855)) for Compiègne Palace—*Justice* and *Prudence* for the King's

Private Cabinet, *Anacreon and Lycoris* and *Bacchus and Ariadne* for the Salle du Grand Couvert; he did similar work for the Salon des jeux de la Reine at Fontainebleau; in 1791 he made a grisaille profile portrait, like an antique cameo, of William Beckford who was then in Paris; later he destroyed his diplomas as Court Painter and Academician, proclaimed Republican sentiments and served in the National Guard where he commanded a battalion in 1795. **Jean Louis Demarne** (Pls. 875, 894), still seeking fame as a costume-history painter, produced a *Louis XV after the Battle of Fontenoy* and *Bravery rewarded* (*Scene from the American War of Independence*) at twenty-seven in 1781; he was elected an Associate of the Académie Royale in 1783, began to show picturesque outdoor genre scenes in the Salons, and weathered the Revolution by becoming a member of an approved artists' group known as the Société Populaire et Républicaine des Arts. The Brugeois **Jean François Legillon** (Pl. 877) who returned to France in 1783 and established himself in Paris and Fontainebleau forest became an Associate of the French Académie Royale in 1788, a Member the year after, exhibited *A derelict barn in sunlight with women and animals* as his reception piece in 1789, a *View of Fontainebleau forest with figures and animals by a fountain* in 1791, and was either at Fontainebleau or in Bruges during the last three years of the period. **Antoine Ferdinand Redouté** supplied flowerpieces and decorative panels for private mansions in the eighties, continued as a flower and fruit painter under the Assembly and the Convention, sent *Une corbeille remplie de fleurs*, *Deux plantes étrangères*, and *Un cadre renfermant des fruits et champignons* to the Salon of 1793 and *Branche de rose*, *Branche de jacinthe* and *Fruits sur une table de marbre* to the Salon of 1795. **Pierre Joseph Redouté** who worked at first as assistant to his brother, and then made stage designs for the Italian Comedians, became a specialist plant draughtsman early in the eighties after meeting the botanist C. L. Lhéritier de Brutelle for whose 'Stirpes novae ...' (published in 1784) he drew some plates; by 1787 he was working for the Dutch flower painter G. van Spaendonck at the Jardin du Roi (which became the Musée National d'Histoire Naturelle in 1794 and more generally known as the Jardin des Plantes); and in 1788 he was appointed 'dessinateur du cabinet de la reine'; he too continued his work under the successive governments of the Revolution and was given the title of 'Flower painter to the Nation' when he was thirty-four in 1793. **Joseph Benoit Suvée** (Pl. 883), thirty-eight in 1781 and Assistant Professor in the Académie Royale with a studio in the Louvre and many pupils, was a regular exhibitor in the Salons where he sent *The Visitation* and the *Vestal Emilia maintaining her innocence* in 1781, a *Fête at Palès* in 1783, *The Resurrection* and *Aeneas amid the ruins of Troy* in 1785 and *The Death of Coligny* (a design for tapestry) in 1787; in the last months of the Académie Royale in 1792 he was elected Director of the French Academy in Rome (in succession to the French painter François-Guillaume Menageot) and he was about to go there when Louis David closed that institution with the others; in 1794, he was denounced as a suspect on the instigation of David, a rancorous personal enemy since his defeat in the 1771 Prix de Rome competition; and he was then imprisoned in S. Lazare where he remained till the end of the Terror; in S. Lazare he drew portraits of fellow prisoners including the poet André Chénier, author of 'Le Jeu de Paume à David Peintre' who was among those taken to the guillotine; and by 1795 he was back in his own studio where he painted *Cornelia, mother of the Gracchi* for the Salon of that year.

New arrivals in Paris included three Brugeois **Augustin van den Berghe, François Jacques Wynckelman** and **Joseph François Ducq** who all became pupils of **Suvée**. Of these **Augustin van den Berghe** came at twenty-five in 1781, made copies during the eighties of Old Masters in the Orléans gallery, competed unsuccessfully for the Prix de Rome with a *Corialanus* *and his family* in 1786 and returned to Bruges in 1791; **Wynckelman** who was to become a landscape painter and is portrayed in a picture shown here by **Joseph Dionysius Odevaere** (Pl. 882), was **Suvée's** pupil at nineteen in 1781 and left for Rome in 1784; **Joseph François Ducq** painter, later, of 'history' and allegories and portraits, came at twenty-four in 1786, left for Bruges in 1792 and returned to Paris in 1795. Another **Suvée** pupil **Jacques Albert Senave**, born at Loo but trained in Bruges, arrived aged twenty-three in 1781, began as a painter of outdoor genre, market scenes and landscapes, exhibited a *View of Paris from the Jardin de l'Arsenal* in the Salon of 1791 and remained all through the Revolution. A number of Belgians including **Frans Balthasar Solvyns** and **Antoine Ansiaux** were attracted to the studio of the French Neo-Classic 'history' painter and portraitist François-André Vincent who had portrayed Fragonard's patron the financier Bergeret de Grancourt in Rome and was a favourite teacher in the Académie Royale from the end of the seventies; **Solvyns** came to him from Antwerp early in the eighties, served at the same time or later in the corps du génie, painted some marines and harbour pieces and returned to work for the Archduchess Maria Christina at Château Laeken; **Antoine Ansiaux**, a Liégeois who had worked in the Antwerp Academy, arrived at nineteen in 1783, chose 'history' and portraiture as his fields of study, exhibited in the Salon of 1793, became a member of the Société Populaire et Républicaine des Arts (where he probably met **Jean Louis Demarne)** and stayed on in Paris. The new arrivals also included some flower painters. **Henri Joseph Redouté** joined **Pierre Joseph Redouté** at nineteen in 1785, drew flower studies for a print publisher in 1786, assisted his brother in his work for Lhéritier de Brutelle, specialized as a draughtsman of birds, fish, and other natural history subjects at the Jardin du Roi, and was still thus employed in 1795 when he exhibited fish studies in watercolour at the Salon. **Jan Frans van Dael** (Pl. 886) came from Antwerp at twenty-two in 1786, was successful both before and during the Revolution, exhibited in the Salon from 1793 and, doubtless on Louis David's orders, was given a studio in the Louvre by the Convention in that year. **Joseph Laurent Malaine** of Tournai was employed as designer at the Gobelins in the eighties, became flower painter to the King in 1787 when he was forty-two, exhibited in the Salon in 1791, received his last commission from the Gobelins in April 1792 and left in 1793 for Alsace where he made his living for a time as designer of wallpapers and textiles. **Jan Frans Eliaerts** (Pl. 888), twenty in 1781, arrived from Antwerp in this period and painted flowerpieces reproduced by the Gobelins; and **George Frederick Ziesel**, painter of flowers and fruit and other still-life, who was five years older then **Eliaerts**, is also known to have worked in Paris for some time. Other newcomers included **Simon Joseph Denis** (already mentioned as a pupil of **Hendrik Joseph Antonissen** (Pl. 863) in Antwerp) who arrived as a painter of picturesque landscapes with figures and animals about twenty-six in 1781, worked for a time with the painter-dealer Jean-Baptiste Le Brun and left for Italy in 1786. The portrait painter, pastellist, and miniaturist **Joseph Angelus van der Donckt** (Pl. 889) came from Bruges about twenty-five about 1782, copied old masters in the Orléans Gallery (where he may have met **Augustin van den Berghe**) remained till 1785 when he went back to Bruges, returned to Paris in 1789 to escape the Brabant Revolution, and left again for Italy soon after to escape the conditions in Paris. The Liégeois genre and portrait painter **Louis Bernard Coclers** (Pl. 866), now also active as dealer and restorer, arrived in Paris from London about 1786, became a friend of Greuze (then sixty) and left again for Holland, after a sale of the contents of his studio and his stock as dealer, in 1789. **Germain Joseph Hallez** arrived from Mons aged eighteen in 1787, travelled through France as assistant to a dealer, and returned to Belgium in 1789. **Pierre**

Joseph Lafontaine, painter of church interiors, came from Courtrai in the eighties, became a member of the Académie Royale at thirty in 1789, and stayed on apparently in contact with **Jean Louis Demarne** who sometimes inserted figures in his pictures. **J. F. Depelchin,** painter of architectural views, church interiors, landscapes and genre, who seems to have come from Courtrai aged about twenty about 1790, sent a *View of the Église des Bernardins* to the Salon of 1791, painted an *Interior of Notre Dame* in 1792 and a *View of the Tuileries and the Port Royal* and then seems to have gone to Italy whence he sent Italian landscapes to the Salons of 1793 and 1795.

In the French provinces **Philippe Henri Coclers,** established in Marseilles, signed a picture called *The Stall* in 1784, was Director there of the Académie Royale and seems to have remained there unmolested when the Academy was suppressed; and **François Joseph Lonsing,** after leaving Lyons, settled in Bordeaux in 1783, painted portraits of the local notables in a style influenced by his former master Raphael Mengs, produced a *Mirabeau on the rostrum* in 1790 or 1791, and was still there in 1795.

Of the Belgians established in London **Theodor de Bruyn** supplied grisaille panels imitating sculptured bas-reliefs for the new Greenwich College Chapel opened in 1789 and exhibited *Views of the Mansion of Paris Hill, seat of B. Bond Hopkins Esq.* in the Royal Academy Exhibitions of 1790 and 1791. **Philip Joseph Tassaert** sent two small full length portraits to the Academy in 1785, went to Rome for some years, was back in London by 1791 when Christie's sent him to Paris to report on the Orléans collection which Philippe Egalité was offering for sale, and seems to have been mainly occupied for the rest of the period in dealing and restoring—(a contemporary, the English painter and art historian Edward Edwards wrote of him 'as an artist this gentleman cannot be ranked as an original, his works being mostly pasticios, frequently copies; he was also a picture-dealer and cleaner which last profession if not an art is at least an artifice by which more money is frequently obtained for scowering a picture than the original master was able to obtain as the first price for its design'). A newcomer **Pieter Jan Balthasar de Grée,** already referred to as Antwerp agent for Sir Joshua Reynolds, was here at the end of 1785 and introduced by Reynolds to the Duke of Rutland as 'a very excellent painter in chiaro oscuro in imitation of bas relievos', and also as a painter of portraits in oil and crayons, and a connoisseur; in 1787 he was employed in Dublin by the Lord Lieutenant, the first Marquis of Buckingham, and by the Dublin Society which rewarded him with a silver palette for a grisaille *Ceres and Triptolemus* painted for their headquarters; and when he died at thirty-eight in 1789 he was buried with imposing ceremony by the Roman Catholic authorities. Among other newcomers **Louis Bernard Coclers** (Pl. 866) seems to have arrived from Holland in 1784 and to have stayed, probably engaged in dealing, till he left for Paris in 1787. **Hendrik de Cort** settled here after the Brabant Revolution, exhibited *The Maritime Cornmarket of Antwerp, The Brussels Canal near Vilvorde* and *View from Highgate Hill* in 1790, *Windsor Castle from Eton* and *Lord Cremorn's seat at Chelsea* in 1791, *Knoll Castle, Glamorganshire* in 1792, and views of parks and buildings in various English counties in 1794 and 1795. **Pierre Joseph Redouté** came for some months from Paris with Lhéritier de Brutelle in 1787, made drawings for Lhéritier's 'Sertum Anglicum' and experimented in colour printing. **P. de Glimes** of Brussels, painter of *A young man in a hat* (Pl. 878), was apparently in England about 1786 as a portrait by him *General Eliott (Lord Heathfield of Gibraltar)* was engraved in 1787; and **Joseph François** who sent a *Judgement of Paris* to the Academy in 1788 may have been here in that year.

In Holland the portrait painter **Guillaume de Spinny** (Pl. 862) died in The Hague at sixty-four in 1785. **W. J. L. Spoor,** landscape painter and former pupil of **Hendrik Joseph Antonissen** (Pl. 863), was now employed at Eindhoven as steward to the Stadholder William V and made copies of animal pieces by Paul Potter and other pictures in the Stadholder's collection before it was sent to Paris from The Hague. **Jean Baptiste de Roy** landscape and animal painter, was probably still in Holland in the eighties and back in his native Brussels soon after 1790. The Brugeois **Jacobus Johannes Lauwers** came to Amsterdam from Rome via Paris some time in the eighties, married and settled there, worked as copyist and pasticheur of Gerard Dou and other Dutchmen, collaborated with the Dutch painter of landscapes and designer of painted wall-hangings Pietersz Barbiers, and also painted indoor and outdoor genre compositions of his own; and **Louis Bernard Coclers** (Pl. 866) reached Amsterdam from Paris in 1789 and stayed for the rest of the period.

In Vienna **Joseph François** painted a *Bacchus and Ariadne* during a six months' visit on the way home from Italy about 1782; and **Pierre Joseph Lion,** who remained as Court Painter to Joseph II after Maria Theresa's death, signed portraits of both in 1784 and left about 1786 to return to Belgium.

Of the artists in Italy from the last period the game and still-life painter **Jacob Vermoelen** died in Rome about seventy in 1784. **Michel d'Argent** left Rome at thirty in 1781 and went back to his native Liège. **Pieter Matthias Goddyn,** working in Rome, won a prize offered by the Parma Academy for a picture of *Sinon counselling Priam and the Trojans to admit the wooden horse* in 1782 and went back to Bruges aged thirty-two in 1784. **Joseph François** left Rome for Antwerp in 1781 and came back at forty in 1789; in Rome he painted a *Virgin of the Rosaries* and a *Purgatory* for Prince Lambertini; and he left Italy again for Belgium in 1792. **Andreas de Muynck** was in Rome throughout the period and still Provisor of the S. Julien Foundation and still selling his copies of Italian pictures to English visitors—a profitable profession since, Gibbon tells us, there were forty thousand English gentry travelling in Italy in 1785. Among the new arrivals in Italy the landscape painter **François Jacques Wynckelman** came to Rome from **Suvée's** atelier in Paris in 1784; he evidently visited Naples as a *Neapolitan landscape* is recorded and he returned to Bruges in 1789. **Philip Joseph Tassaert** came from London about 1785 and was probably engaged in dealing till he went back to London in 1790. **Simon Joseph Denis** came from Paris, with help from the painter-dealer Jean Baptiste Le Brun, at thirty-one in 1786, established himself in Rome as a painter of picturesque landscapes, signed a *Cascade* in 1793, and was still there in 1795. **Jean Baptiste Pauwels** arrived in Rome from the Brussels atelier of **Andreas Cornelis Lens** in the middle eighties, painted religious subjects—including a *Christ* for Pope Pius VI—and was probably still there in 1795. The portrait painter **Joseph Angelus van der Donckt** (Pl. 889) came from Paris aged thirty-two in 1789, toured the principal cities and went back to Bruges in 1791. **J. F. Depelchin** seems to have been in Italy in the early nineties and painting landscapes which he sent, as mentioned, to the Paris Salons.

At home in Belgium the Emperor Joseph II, the Governors Duke Albert and the Archduchess Maria Christina and the Emperor Leopold II all gave patronage to painters. When Joseph II toured the country in 1781 he was conducted round the artistic sights of Antwerp by **Andreas Cornelis Lens** (Pl. 871) whom he treated with marked courtesy, giving him a seat in his own coach and inviting him, without success, to go to Vienna as Court Painter; in Antwerp also he sat to **Andreas Bernardus de Quertenmont** for a portrait (placed in the Town Hall in 1784 and publicly burned as an effigy of a 'ci-devant tyran' in 1794) and he agreed that **Quertenmont** should copy Caravaggio's *Virgin of the Rosaries* for the Antwerp Dominicans from whom he bought the original for his own collection in

Vienna. In Malines Joseph visited the studio of **Willem Jacob Herreyns** (Pl. 867) who painted his portrait (engraved by **Antoine Alexandre Cardon**); another portrait was painted by **Jacques Joachim de Soignie** in Mons; and the elegant full length with sportive cupids and a cornucopia reproduced here (Pl. 870) was painted in Bruges by **Gertrude de Pélichy** probably in this year. In Ghent the Emperor visited the cathedral of S. Bavon to see the **van Eycks'** *Altarpiece of the mystic Lamb* (Pl. 9) and, as mentioned earlier, he ordered the removal of the *Adam and Eve* panels as unsuitable for exhibition in a church—(a removal which saved them later from transportation to the Louvre). Back in Vienna he was painted, as just noted, by **Pierre Joseph Lion** in 1784 and the picture went eventually, with the posthumous portrait of Maria Theresa, to the Town Hall in Ypres. His suppression of the Belgian religious houses was celebrated, as also noted, in an allegoric picture by **Leonard Defrance** (Pls. 874, 879) always eager to applaud an anti-clerical gesture. Duke Albert of Saxe-Teschen was an enthusiast for drawings and prints; his collection, which amounted to twelve thousand examples, became the nucleus of the Albertina Gallery in Vienna which commemorates his name; and he is said to have himself designed the Château Laeken near Brussels built for him and the Archduchess between 1782 and 1784. The Governors' Pageant Entry into Brussels in 1781 was recorded by **Piat Joseph Sauvage** who may have come from Paris for the purpose; and **Antoine Alexandre Cardon** drew and engraved a *Fête given by the Governors at Château Laeken to the Brussels Guilds in 1785*. The Archduchess visited the Louvain studio of **Jean Joseph Verhaghen** (Pls. 872, 873) in 1784 and she inspected the pictures painted by the ex-hermit **Jean Henri Gilson** in Orval Abbey in 1787. The marine painter **Frans Balthasar Solvyns**, back from Paris, was appointed Captain of Château Laeken, painted a *View of Ostend Harbour* for the Archduchess, and went abroad about 1790; **Andreas Cornelis Lens** (Pl. 871) provided Château Laeken with a *Jupiter on Mount Ida put to sleep by Juno* and a *Minerva in discord with Mars and Venus* which the Governors took with them to Vienna; **Joseph François** was also represented in the Château probably by mythologies; and flowerpieces were supplied by **Pieter Faes** (Pl. 887), **Antoine Plateau**, and **Pierre Joseph Thys** who had returned from Paris by 1781. There was not much time for Belgian artists to record the reign of Leopold II; but his portrait was painted by **Germain Joseph Hallez** and by **Johannes Jacobus Lens** in the picture already referred to (Pl. 869); and **Antoine Brice**, as also noted, drew a *Glorification of Leopold II* in 1791.

There were, of course, commissions for portraits outside the Habsburg circles. The heroes of the Brabant Revolution—Henri van der Noot, the Penitentiary Pierre van Eupen, General van der Mersch, Cardinal de Franckenberg, many members of the Estates of Brabant and many ex-heads of the suppressed religious houses were drawn by **Andreas Bernardus de Quertenmont** in 1790 for a collection of engravings partially completed in the next few years; active on the staff of the Antwerp Academy from the middle seventies **de Quertenmont** was Director there from 1791 but lost the post in 1794 when **Simon Pierre d'Argonne** enjoyed the favours of the French Representatives. **Frans Marcus Smits**, a pupil of **de Quertenmont**, began to practise as a young man about 1781 and painted a portrait of his friend the still-life painter **George Frederick Ziesel**; and **Jan Joseph Horemans the younger** still living in Antwerp at seventy-six in 1790 may have painted more conversation portraits like *The Landlord and his Tenant* (Pl. 861) in the eighties. In Brussels **Bernard Verschoot** died in 1783; **Louis Legendre** was available till he died (probably before 1790); **Joseph Grégoire Sauvage** collapsed with a 'maladie nerveuse' in 1787 and his mother petitioned the Governors to grant him refuge, as former Court Portraitist to Charles of Lorraine, in the newly founded Hôpital de S. Pierre 'afin de terminer sa déplorable carrière aux frais de la caisse de religion'. **Germain Joseph Hallez,** back from France, began a career as portrait painter in Brussels in 1790 but left for his native Mons when the French regained Brussels in 1792. **Andreas Cornelis Lens** (Pl. 871) who moved to Brussels from Antwerp in 1781 and **Johannes Jacobus Lens** (Pl. 869) were both available for portraits in Brussels; and though **Andreas Cornelis Lens** refused to co-operate with the French Representatives on Mission he was not molested by them because his 'Costumes of Antiquity' was famous in the studios of Paris and Louis David knew him as a champion of the Neo-Classic theories. **P. de Glimes** who drew or painted *Henri van der Noot* in Brussels probably in 1789 or 1790, and may have seen pictures by George Morland on his visit to England, signed the freely painted *Young man in a hat* (Pl. 878) in 1793. In Bruges **Jan Anton Garemyn** (Pls. 858, 860) who continued painting in the eighties, married a girl of twenty-four at seventy-nine in 1791 and was still living in 1795. **Gertrude de Pélichy** seems also to have worked through the period. **Joseph Angelus van der Donckt** (Pl. 889) returned from Paris aged twenty-eight in 1785, drew portraits in pastel, painted miniatures including a *Paul Joseph de Cock* which he gave to the Academy in 1789, left again for Paris, as related, when the Brabant revolution started and succeeded **Paul Joseph de Cock** as Director of the Academy when he came back to Bruges in 1791. **De Cock's** pupil **Joseph François Ducq** came from **Suvée's** atelier aged thirty in 1792 and probably painted some portraits in Bruges before returning to Paris in 1795. **Louis Gerbo,** painter of portraits and religious subjects, was thirty-four in 1795 and by that time or soon after a Professor in the Academy's drawing school; and both **van der Donckt's** pupil **Joseph Dionysius Odevaere** (Pl. 882) about twenty in 1795 and **François Joséphe Kinson** (Pls. 881, 884, 885) then twenty-four were then beginning their careers. In Malines **Willem Jacob Herreyns** (Pl. 867) painted *The priest Jan Jacob de Brandt* in 1790, *Jos. Ghesquière ex-Jesuit and Bollandist in Tongerloo Abbey* in 1793, and *Godfried Hermans, forty-fourth and last Abbot of Tongerloo* among other portraits; and **Peter van Huffel** was at work there before 1790. **Louis Paul** and **Bernard Paul** were available through the period in Ghent. **Leonard Defrance** doubtless painted more portraits of the calibre of *A member of the Jalheau family* (Pl. 874) in Liège. **Pierre Joseph Lion,** back in his native Dinant from Vienna, painted portraits at Château Sorinne hard by in 1787 but went down with paralysis about 1790 and was ruined financially by the French régime.

Many established painters of religious subjects died in this period; and conditions also limited production. Joseph II's suppression of the monasteries and convents was a severe setback; there was little demand for such pictures in the first and second periods of French rule; and the Restoration periods were too shortlived and troubled for any considerable revival of commissions. In Antwerp **Jacques Andreas Beschey** died at seventy-six in 1786 and **Marten Joseph Geeraerts** (Pl. 855) at eighty-three in 1791; but some religious subjects were probably painted there by **Andreas de Quertenmont** and **Joseph François** before 1789. **Jacques Joachim de Soignie** died in Mons at sixty-three in 1783. In Bruges, where **Jacques de Smidt** died in 1787, **Jan Anton Garemyn** (Pls. 858, 860) completed his *Scenes from the History of the Trinitarians* for Bruges, S. Gilles in 1782 and a picture for Bruges, S. Walpurgis in 1783; **Antoine Ignace Steyaert** was a prize-winning student of **Paul Joseph de Cock** in the Academy in 1784; and **Garemyn's** former pupil **Augustin van den Berghe** back from Paris in 1791 produced a *Vision of S. Anthony of Padua* for Zweveghem church at about thirty-six that year. In Louvain **Pierre Joseph Verhaghen** finished the *Adoration of the Magi* commissioned, as noted, by Maria Theresa before she died; in 1781 he provided Tongerloo Abbey with a *Dismissal of Hagar* (Pl. 873) which students may find intriguing to compare with versions of the subject by Rembrandt, Jan Steen and Adriaen van der Werff (all reproduced in my 'Dutch Painting'); in 1784, when he was fifty-six, he finished a *Belshazzar and Daniel* which had been commissioned for the refectory of Bornhem Abbey and shows the Writing on the Wall behind the King—probably a crypto-comment on the conflict between Joseph II and the Church; for the rest of the period he painted religious subjects for private patrons; and when the Convention's Representatives arrived in Louvain he was not, apparently, molested by them. In Louvain also **Antoine Clevenbergh** probably copied more of **Verhaghen's** pictures and is said to have painted a *Christ at Gethsemane* at thirty-eight in 1793; and **François van Dorne** became **Verhaghen's** pupil about that time. In Brussels **Maximilien de Haese** died at eighty in 1787; **Johannes Jacobus Lens** (Pl. 869) signed a *Virgin and Child* in 1793; **Andreas Cornelis Lens** (Pl. 871), who doubtless painted some religious subjects in this period, had **Jean Baptiste Pauwels** as his pupil in the early years and **Cornelis Cels** as a pupil in 1794; and his former pupil and associate **Joseph François** was available for such subjects when he settled in Brussels on his second return from Italy in 1792. In Malines **Willem Jacob Herreyns** was still the leading figure (with **Henri Bernaerts** and **Peter van Huffel** as new pupils); his *Adoration of the Magi* (Pl. 867) painted probably in the eighties has an ox's head in the foreground recalling the *Adoration of the Magi* (Pl. 574) by **Rubens** and a procession group recalling the composition reproduced here (Pl. 573) by **Pietro de Lignis**; and his other pictures of this time include a *Disciples at Emmaus* painted for Malines, S. Jean, in 1793. In Ghent **Petrus Norbertus van Reysschoot** completed his series of seventeen *Old and New Testament subjects* in grisaille for S. Bavon in 1791 and died at fifty-nine in 1795. Religious subjects may also have been painted in Ghent by **Philippe Lambert Spruyt**, who remained Director of the Academy and published a book on drawing 'Beginselen der Teekenkunst' in 1792 and an art critical book 'Konstlievende Mengelingen' in 1794; and others who may have had commissions there were **Charles Spruyt** who began his career about 1789 and **Bernard Paul** who was approaching sixty in 1795. The ex-hermit **Jean Henri Gilson** (also known as **Brother Abraham d'Orval**) painted a series of religious pictures for Orval Abbey (near Florenville in the Ardennes) which were destroyed by fire in 1793. In Liège, where the anti-clerical movement was active from the middle eighties, **Henri Deprez**, fifty-four when the period began, seems to have been almost alone as occasional painter of religious works.

A number of allegories and mythologies were commissioned as decorations in the eighties and Neo-Classic compositions seem to have increased in the nineties. Thus **Andreas Cornelis Lens** (Pl. 871) whose work for Château Laeken has already been referred to, produced a series of panels on the *Bacchus* legend for a private house in Brussels; **Johannes Jacobus Lens** (Pl. 869) also continued to paint such subjects; and **Joseph François** was available after 1792. In Antwerp **Joseph François** had painted a gallery of pictures on the *Venus* theme for the mansion of a man named Vinck and also a *Diana and Callisto* before he went to Italy in 1789. **Jean Pierre Borrekens**, another **Lens** pupil, also painted mythologies and 'history' in these years. **Pieter de Grée** produced grisaille compositions in the tradition of his master **Marten Joseph Geeraerts** (Pl. 855). A new man who later painted 'history' **Louis Adrien Moons**, a pupil of **Quertenmont**, was a first-prize winner for nude painting in Antwerp Academy by 1792. In Bruges there were festivities in 1784 when **Pieter Mathias Goddyn** came back at thirty-two after winning the Parma competition referred to above— the church bells were rung, there was a cavalcade to a Town Hall banquet, and the artist presented the Academy with his *Allegories of Geometry amd Mathematics*; **Augustin van den Berghe** painted a *Venus mourning the death of Adonis* and an *Oedipus at Colonus* soon after 1791; and **Joseph François Ducq,** in Bruges from Paris between 1792 and 1795, painted *Oedipus at Colonus* in 1794. **Antoine Plateau** provided decorative pieces for houses in Tournai and Brussels. In Ghent **Petrus Norbertus van Reysschoot** and his sister **Anna Maria van Reysschoot** were available for grisaille compositions imitating bas-reliefs. **Michel d'Argent** back from Rome in 1781 painted 'history' pieces in Liège; and decorative works for the Bishop's Palace and for mansions there were produced by **Henri Deprez** and by **Joseph Dreppe** Director of the Academy from 1784.

The landscape and outdoor genre painters, accustomed to work on their own volition without waiting for commissions, were evidently less affected by the disturbed conditions than the painters of religious subjects, decorative mythologies and portraits—as had also been the case in the troubled times two hundred years earlier. In Antwerp **Hendrick Joseph Antonissen** signed the pleasant *Wooded landscape with figures and cattle* (Pl. 863) in 1787 and died at fifty-seven in 1794. His pupil **Balthasar Paul Ommeganck** painted the *Landscape with cattle, goats and sheep* reproduced here (Pl. 876) at twenty-six in 1781; when the French were fighting in Belgium he was arrested as a suspect for sketching in the region of Dinant and he was not released till his sketchbooks, sent to Paris, had been examined by the censor there; in 1788 he had founded an Antwerp Society for the Encouragement of Art (Genootschap ter aenmoediging der Schoone Kunsten generally known as the Kunstmaatschappij) with **Antonissen's** other pupils the landscape painters **Hendrik de Cort** who came back from Paris aged forty in 1782 and left for England after the Brabant Revolution as related, and **Hendrik Blomaerts** who moved to Brussels at thirty-five in 1790; another Foundation Member of the Society was **Ommeganck's** pupil **Hendrik Aarnut Myin** who had married **Ommeganck's** sister **Maria Jacoba** (herself a landscape painter and imitator of her brother) when he was twenty-six in 1786. The Society held annual exhibitions to which the members sent their works; **Simon Pierre d'Argonne** and **Pieter Faes** (Pl. 887) became members in 1789; **Jean Pierre Borrekens** who, in addition to his mythologies, had begun to paint landscapes with animals inserted by **Ommeganck** and others, was elected in 1791. **Jacques André Trachez,** who is said to have worked sixteen hours a day in the summer months, collapsed with eye trouble and abandoned painting probably in this period. **Petrus Johannes van Regemorter** who held offices in the Antwerp Guild in the later eighties and was forty by 1795, produced some moonlight landscapes and outdoor genre scenes and also worked as restorer and pasticheur. **Martin Verstappen** was **van Regemorter's** pupil about 1790 and then worked under **Hendrik Myin. Frans Balthasar Solvyns** the marine painter, whose appointment as Captain of Château Laeken has been mentioned above, left Belgium after the Brabant Revolution and sailed with Sir Horne Riggs Popham (probably from Ostend in 1790) to India where he met the English artist Thomas Daniell about 1792, drew some views for Daniell's 'Antiquities of India' and later made drawings for a book of his own called 'Manners, Customs and Dresses of the Hindoos'. In Brussels **Jean Baptiste de Roy** was making a reputation from about 1790 as a painter of landscapes with cattle much influenced by Paul Potter whose works he had seen in Holland; and **Henri van Assche,** twenty in 1794, was one of the earliest of his many pupils. In Bruges **Paul Joseph de Cock** fifty-seven in 1781 may have painted more italianate landscapes; **Jean François Legillon** (Pl. 877) was abroad, as noted, from 1783; and **François Jacques Wynckelman** abroad from early in the eighties was back aged twenty-eight and painting landscapes by 1790. In Ghent **Jan Lodewick Wouters,** whose death date is unknown, may have painted more moonlight landscapes and **Petrus Norbertus Reysschoot** probably painted more landscapes with genre figures. **Antoine Clevenbergh** is said to have imitated **Ommeganck** in landscapes with cattle painted in the nineties in Louvain. In Liège **Joseph Dreppe** exhibited landscapes and marines at the local Société d'Émulation in the eighties. **Nicolas de Fassin** was away from Liège for some time in Spa—(very fashionable then with its 'Waux-Hall' and gaming tables)—and sold there his picturesque landscapes to the English visitors.

There was continued production also of town views and street scenes with genre figures in the tradition that can be followed in my plates from the pictures by the **London Virgin with a Firescreen Painter** (Pl. 39). Topographic pieces were painted in Antwerp by **Hendrik de Cort** till he went abroad. **Nicolas de Fassin** painted some views of Liège. In Bruges **Jean Charles Verbrugge** and **Pierre François Ledoulx** were still active in this field though the latter spent much time on the compilation of a history of Brugeois painters (left in manuscript and used by Immerzeel in his 'Levens en Werken der Hollandsche en Vlaamsche Kunstschilders . . .). **Jan Anton Garemyn** probably painted more genre scenes with topographic setting like the *Bruges vegetable market* reproduced here (Pl. 860); and I have already mentioned **Jean Beerblock's** *The 1788 Procession of the Bruges Tailors' Guild* (Pl. 859) which shows the Place du Braamberg (Marché aux Poissons), the Tailors' Hall, the church of the Frères Mineurs, the tower of Notre Dame and in the right-hand lower corner a subsidiary genre scene where a young woman in a doorway chaffs two fellows in a boat—(like the subsidiary genre scene in the right-hand lower corner of the *Feast of Our Lady of the Wood* (Pl. 513) painted in 1616 by **Denis van Alsloot**, and the little scene in the background of the **Amsterdam Delft Painter's** picture (Pl. 228) where a young man twines his arm round a pillar while chatting with a girl.)

Among the painters of indoor genre pieces **Jean Joseph Horemans the younger** (Pls. 824, 835, 861) was still exhibiting at seventy-six in 1790; **Anna Maria Reysschoot**, who painted genre as well as her grisaille decorative pieces, exhibited *A young mother by the cradle of her child* in the Ghent exhibition of 1792; and **Jean Joseph Verhaghen (Pottekens)** died at sixty-nine in 1795. **Petrus Johannes van Regemorter** may have painted some indoor genre pieces with candle-light effects and others in the Dutch tradition, and **Nicolas de Fassin** some indoor social scenes in addition to his outdoor pieces. **Leonard Defrance** produced, probably in these years, *The Interior of a prison during the Revolution*, *The Prisoners in the Temple*, *The Rope Dancer* and *The Forge*; of these *The Rope Dancer* (Pls. 879, 880) painted—the costumes suggest—about 1792 or a few years earlier, continues the seventeenth-century tradition of the village fair with 'saltimbanques' performing —(as in the pictures by **David Vinckeboons** (Pl. 533), **Adam van der Meulen** (Pl. 759) and **Pieter Bout** (Pl. 796))—and anticipates the circus, 'parade' and saltimbanque pieces by nineteenth-century and later painters—(Degas, Seurat, Toulouse-Lautrec, Picasso); the performers' tent seems to have been rigged up at the entrance to some farm building and children peep in from outside, like the crowd behind the screen in the picture by the **Exhumation of S. Hubert Master** (Pl. 54) and the shepherds in the *Adoration of the Magi* by **Hieronymus Bosch** (Pl. 157); an abbé (evidence of the painter's anti-clerical obsession) puts a spy glass to his eye to see as much as may be of the girl performers, while a small boy in the background is more intrigued by the trio of musicians playing flute, violin and viol da gamba; most of the audience, small bourgeoisie and artisans, wear clothes in the fashion of the eighties, but some figures in the foreground are dressed in the latest English or Parisian style.

In the field of miscellaneous still-life **Jean Joseph Verhaghen** worked till the end of the period as just mentioned; and the versatile **Antoine Clevenbergh** is said to have painted a number of game pieces including a *Fox and poultry*. Among the flower painters a number of young men including **Jan Frans Dael** (Pl. 886), **Jan Frans Eliaerts** (Pl. 888) and **Henri Joseph Redouté** left for Paris in the eighties as mentioned above. But **Antoine Plateau** was working in Tournai, **Pierre Joseph Thys** in Brussels, **Martin van Dorne** in Louvain, **Michel Joseph Speeckaert** probably in Malines, **Pierre François Ledoulx** in Bruges, and **Pieter Faes** and **George Frederick Ziesel** in Antwerp. The *Flowers and Fruit* (Pl. 887) painted by **Pieter Faes** in 1794 when he was forty-four is evidently inspired by the light and shade artifices and favourite arrangements of the Dutch seventeenth-century painters from Jacob van Walscapelle to Jan van Huysum and thus departs not only from the Flemish tradition of descriptive recording of exemplary flowers (shown here in works by **Jan (Velvet) Brueghel** (Pl. 521) and **Ambrosius Bosschaert** (Pl. 550)) but also from the decorative manners of **Daniel Seghers** (Pl. 692), **Nicolas van Verendael** (Pl. 758) **Gaspar Verbruggen** (Pl. 809) and **Pieter Casteels III** (Pl. 857). **Georges Frédéric Ziesel** a friend of **Pieter Faes** and **Balthasar Paul Ommeganck** was twenty-five in 1781 and sometimes worked on glass and in miniature; in his *Flowers and fruit with insects and a bowl of fish on a marble table*, probably painted in these years, windows of the houses opposite the studio window are reflected on the curved surface of the glass bowl and we are thus reminded of the mirrors in the *Banker and his wife* (Pl. 235) by **Quinten Massys** and in the *The Marriage of Arnolfini* (Pl. 18A) by **Jan van Eyck**.

CHAPTER XXI

The Directorate 1796-1799;
The Consulate 1800-1804;
The Empire 1804-1814

1796-1814

BELGIUM throughout this period was a part of France and benefited from free access to French markets and from many administrative, social and educational reforms imposed by the French. In the Flemish regions the peasants and urban workers still habitually spoke Flemish, and a few Flemish newspapers were published; but French, the official language, was spoken everywhere by upper and middle class people who absorbed French ideas from French books and newspapers and from French theatrical performances in Antwerp and Brussels and other towns. There was much encouragement of artists; commissions were given, new Art Societies in a number of places began to hold annual Salons and give prizes and travelling scholarships; and museums were founded with pictures sent from Paris and by drawing on the stores of works sequestered from churches and religious houses. The Church lost money and influence in the first years, recovered some power beneath the Consulate and Empire, applauded Napoleon when he seemed a Church supporter and turned against him when he tried to force the Church to act as agent for his policies and when he bullied and defied the Pope. There were no military operations on Belgian soil till the very last year of the period; but when the Imperial régime began to crumble, Belgium inevitably shared the sufferings of France—the incessant and ever-increasing demands for man-power for the army, the economic losses resulting from the 'Continental System', and, towards the climax, intolerable censorship and persecution from the secret police.

In 1796 France was ruled by the Directorate. George III was fifty-eight, Pitt thirty-seven and General Bonaparte twenty-seven. Holland (as the Batavian Republic) was a satellite of France. Charles IV of Spain was forty-eight, Queen Maria Luisa forty-five, her favourite Godoy (the 'Prince of the Peace') thirty-one and the Infante Ferdinand a boy of twelve. Queen Maria of Portugal was insane and Don John was acting Regent. Ferdinand IV (married to Maria Carolina, sister of Marie Antoinette) was King of Naples; Frances II was Holy Roman Emperor; Pius VI was Pope; Selim III was Sultan; Catherine of Russia died and Paul I succeeded; Frederick William II was King of Prussia; Victor Amadeus III was succeeded by Charles Emmanuel IV as King of Sardinia; and Lodovico Manin was Doge of Venice. France was at war with England, Austria, Sardinia and the Pope. General Bonaparte married Josephine de Beauharnais and began his campaign in Italy where he defeated the Papal troops and behaved with heroism at the Bridge of Arcola. Madame de Stael aged thirty wrote 'De l'influence des passions sur le bonheur des individus et des nations' and became the mistress of Benjamin Constant aged twenty-nine and author this year of 'De la force du gouvernement actuel et de la nécessité de se rallier'. Commissaries sent by the Directorate to organize Belgium divided the country into nine administrative Departments which included the Deux-Néthes with Antwerp as centre, Dyle round Brussels, La Lys round Bruges, L'Escaut round Ghent, Jemappes round Mons, L'Ourthes round Liège and Sambre-et-Meuse round Namur. New taxes, graduated on income, made no exemption for the nobility or clergy; civil marriages and divorce by mutual consent were recognized; believers, dissenters and atheists were given equal status; and civil hospitals were established. Much church property was sequestered or ear-marked for public sale; most of the surviving religious houses, Baudeloo Abbey and Tongerloo Abbey for example, were closed and their buildings relegated to some civil purpose (Baudeloo Abbey for which **Robert van Audenaerd** (Pl. 823), **Jan van Cleef, Gilles le Plat** and **Emanuel van Reysschoot** had provided pictures, was made a central library for all books and manuscripts from monasteries and convents and its grounds were allocated for a Jardin des Plantes); expelled monks and nuns were compensated by vouchers expendable in 'biens nationaux'; and as an anti-monarchical and anti-Austrian gesture the statue of the Emperor Charles V was removed from the Marché du Vendredi in Ghent. In 1797 Écoles Centrales (incorporating the local academies and art schools) were established in the nine Departments, and the University of Louvain was abolished. All literate Belgians, who were above twenty-one and direct tax-payers, were given the right to vote for the Belgian representatives in the French Assemblies; voters in all elections were required to take an oath of 'Haine à la royauté', and Cardinal de Franckenberg still Primate as Archbishop of Malines, refused the oath and retired to Emmerich to join some Dutch and Belgian émigrés. Frederick William II of Prussia was succeeded by Frederick William III. Admiral Jervis and Commodore Nelson won the Battle of S. Vincent against the Spaniards; and Admiral Duncan beat the Dutch at Camperdown. General Bonaparte made Pope Pius VI sign the Treaty of Tolentino which ceded a hundred works of art to the French Republic for transport to the Louvre Museum; and the French painter Antoine Gros was made head of a Commission to choose works from the Vatican and others from other places. Doge Lodovico Manin abdicated on the approach of Bonaparte; and the Republic of Venice ended when the Peace of Campo Formio gave Venice and most of her dependencies to Austria who renounced, in return, her hereditary claims on Belgium. In 1798 the French military conscription law (claiming all single men between twenty and twenty-five) was applied to Belgium; and peasants in various parts of Flanders, incited by the clergy, rose in the revolt of the 'Roomsch Katholijke Jonkheid' which was drastically put down. **Willem Jacob Herreyns** (Pl. 867) was now Director of the Art School in the École Centrale of the Deux-Néthes Department; the school was located in the secularized convent of the Carmes Déchaussés and with the help of **Simon d'Argonne,** still in high favour with the French, **Herreyns** contrived to procure some three hundred pictures from churches—including the *Entombment* by **Quinten Massys**—as material of service to the students and as the nucleus of a possible museum. At the same time the Batavian Republic began to assemble pictures abandoned in their castles by the Orange émigrés for the nucleus of a national collection in the Huis ten Bosch (decorated, as related earlier, by **Jordaens** and others for Amalie van Solms). The French general Berthier, pretexting revenge for a French diplomat's murder, led his troops into Rome, proclaimed the Papal territories a Republic and took the Pope prisoner. General Bonaparte, planning to strike England by invading India and helping Tippoo Sahib, Sultan of Mysore, to revolt, set sail from Toulon, took Malta from the Knights of S. John, landed at Aboukir, captured Alexandria, won the Battle of the Pyramids against the Mamelukes (recorded by **Pierre Jean Baptiste Leroy** in 1805) and entered Cairo; Admiral Nelson destroyed the French fleet at the Battle of the Nile; Ferdinand of Naples, urged on by Queen Maria Carolina, declared war on France; and the Sultan Selim signed a treaty against France with Paul of Russia. In 1799 Wordsworth aged twenty-nine settled at Grasmere with his sister Dorothy; and William Cockerill constructed wool-carding and wool-spinning machines at Verviers. The French Commissaries in Belgium took vengeance on the peasants and clergy for the late revolt; hundreds of peasants were executed and seven thousand four hundred clergy were listed for deportation—(but the clergy were hidden by their followers in the countryside and less than five hundred were eventually found.) A new Coalition of England, Austria, Russia, Turkey and Naples was formed againt France. Marshal Suvorov drove the French from Italy, the Austrians won a battle on the Rhine and Anglo-Russian forces entered Holland. The French took Naples and proclaimed the Parthenopaean Republic; Cardinal Ruffo organized a counter-revolution of the populace as an 'Esercito Cristiano della Santa Fede'; Nelson (accompanied by Sir William and Lady Hamilton) went to Naples; Francesco Garaciolo was hanged; and Ferdinand was reinstated. General Masséna defeated Suvorov's armies near Zurich; Bonaparte fought the Turks in Syria and returning to Egypt won the Battle of Aboukir; Russia left the alliance and the English retired from Holland; Tippoo Sahib was killed when the English stormed Seringapatam; and Bonaparte became First Consul.

In 1800 Pius VI died and Pius VII succeeded. Goya aged fifty-four painted *Charles IV, Queen Maria Luisa and their family*; Louis David aged fifty-two painted *Madame Récamier*; Joseph Mallord William Turner aged twenty-five drew Fonthill Abbey, then in course of construction, and Nelson (with the Hamiltons) was entertained there with fantastic pageantry by Beckford; and William Blake aged forty-three met Hayley and went to Felpham. The French 'Constitution de l'An VIII' was applied to Belgium; Prefects, sub-prefects, mayors and so on took charge of the Departments; and the metric system was introduced for weights and money. A Museum of Fine Arts was founded in Brussels as one of fifteen in the provincial cities of the French Republic destined to receive the overflow of pictures from the Louvre, and Guillaume Bosschaert (an amateur painter and sometime pupil of **Andreas Cornelis Lens** (Pl. 871)) was appointed head of a Commission to apply for pictures to be sent there. Bonaparte, now called Napoleon, crossed the Alps and beat the Austrians at Marengo, General Moreau won the Battle of Hohenlinden, and the English drove the French from Malta. In 1801 Chateaubriand published 'Atala' at thirty-three. **Herreyns** supported by d'Herbouville, the Prefect of the Deux-Néthes, procured the return from France to Antwerp of two pictures by **Rubens** (or **Rubens** and assistants)—*The Virgin and Child with Saints* (taken from S. Jacques) and *The Virgin with the Parrot* (taken from the Antwerp Academy) as objects for special study in his art school. Napoleon made peace with Austria and with Ferdinand of Naples and drafted a Concordat with the Pope; England and Ireland were united; British troops drove the French from Egypt; Russia, Sweden and Denmark formed the Northern Confederacy against the English Right of Search; Nelson won the Battle of Copenhagen; Paul I was murdered and the new Czar Alexander I gave way on the Right of Search. In 1802 Napoleon founded the Legion of Honour and signed the Peace of Amiens with England. Chateaubriand published 'Le génie du Christianisme'; and Benjamin Constant was removed by Napoleon from the

Tribunate. The Concordat was applied to Belgium and **Joseph François** drew or painted an *Allegory of the Concordat* which was popularized in an engraving. Many churches were now reopened; and French bishops for four new Bishoprics established to cover the nine Belgian Departments were nominated by Napoleon and appointed by the Pope. Education in Belgium was concurrently reorganized and Lycées were established in Brussels, Ghent, Bruges and Liège. In 1803 France and England were again at war; the French took Hanover and sold Louisiana to the United States; and Napoleon went to Belgium to advance preparations for the invasion of England. On this Belgian visit Napoleon accompanied by Josephine made an excellent impression; all ceremonies were conducted with the pomp and pageantry that had always appealed to the Belgians; business men were confident that the new conditions would bring them extended markets; and pious Catholics were won over when the First Consul went publicly to Mass in Ghent. In Brussels Napoleon held military reviews, attended fêtes, ordered new fortifications and adornments for the city, and acquired Château Laeken as a personal palace. In Antwerp he mainly concentrated on enormous extensions of the port. Both Napoleon and Josephine made a point of patronizing Belgian artists; thus Napoleon commissioned a huge picture *The Entry of Napoleon, First Consul, into Antwerp in 1803* from **Mattheus Ignatius van Brée** and also ordered from him two ancient history compositions for the Antwerp palace; and Josephine expressed delight in the landscapes with cattle by **Balthasar Paul Ommeganck** (Pl. 876) and began a habit of buying one or more of them each year. At the same time the new Museum of Art in Brussels was formally opened to the public; this now had a subsidy from the Conseil Municipal for maintenance and purchases and owned officially about two hundred and fifty pictures. The star places in the Museum's exhibition went to a group of works acquired the year before by Bosschaert from the authorities in Paris; these included *The calling of SS. Peter and Andrew* by Baroccio, some pictures then ascribed to Raphael, Leonardo, Andrea del Sarto, Veronese and Velazquez, some pictures by the French artists Jouvenet, van Loo and Vouet (represented by *S. Carlo Borromeo interceding for the plague-stricken in Milan*), a *Presentation in the Temple* painted by **Philippe de Champaigne** (Pls. 742, 750) for the Carmelites in Paris, and three pictures by **Rubens** (or **Rubens** and assistants) which had been taken from Belgium and were now returned—*The Virgin and S. Francis interceding to avert the Divine Thunderbolts* from the Recollets in Ghent where Reynolds had written of it 'The Christ which is ill-drawn, in an attitude affectedly contrasted, is the most ungracious figure that can be imagined', *The Adoration of the Magi* (taken from Tournai, Capucins) and *The Coronation of the Virgin* (taken from Antwerp, Recollets); to these was added *The Martyrdom of S. Liven* which had been painted by **Rubens** (or **Rubens** and assistants) for the Jesuit church in Ghent and had been bought from there by Louis XVI in 1777. The remaining works, the bulk of the exhibition, had come to the Museum from the store of pictures assembled in Brussels by **Leonard Defrance** (Pls. 874, 879), **Joseph Dreppe** and **Simon d'Argonne** from churches and private ownership in 1749 (as related in my last chapter) and judged at that time as unworthy of transference to Paris; the Museum's holdings from this source included some pictures by fifteenth- and sixteenth-century painters but, as the taste of the time disliked them, they were shown with apologies and described as examples of 'the first stages of the slow and difficult progress of art'. In 1804 the swineherd Kara George led a Serbian revolt against the Turks; Mehemet Ali began his rise to power in Egypt; the Jesuits reappeared in Naples at Ferdinand's request and with permission from the Pope; the French Code Civil was applied to Belgium; the Duc d'Enghien was shot as a scapegoat when a plot against Napoleon was discovered; Napoleon, aged thirty-five, crowned himself Emperor in Notre Dame with Pius VII in attendance; Louis David was commissioned to record him crowning Josephine; and one aspect of Belgian opinion was expressed by the head of the Seminary of Malines who wrote to the Ministry of the Interior that 'Le grand Bonaparte' had been 'envoyé de Dieu comme un autre Cyrus pour rétablir la religion et la paix tant dans l'ancienne France que dans les départements réunis'—an enthusiasm perhaps not unconnected with a recent order exempting the Belgian seminarists from military conscription. In this year also Beethoven wrote the 'Eroica Symphony' at thirty-four and Schiller wrote 'William Tell' at forty-five. **Herreyns,** supported by the Mayor of Antwerp and again by the Prefect d'Herbouville, obtained the use of the Recollets church (which had not been reopened) as headquarters for a provisional Antwerp Museum and also for his art school (now known again as the Antwerp Academy); and the Prefect took steps to procure some seventeen pictures from Tongeloo Abbey including *The Dismissal of Hagar* (Pl. 873) by **Pierre Joseph Verhaghen,** the large *Passover in Egypt* and *Adoration of the Lamb* by **Willem Ignatius Kerricx,** two portraits of Tongerloo Abbots by **Herreyns,** and a *Miraculous deliverance of the Emperor Maximilian from his hunting mishap* (a subject painted also by **Tobias van Haecht** (Pl. 377)) of unrecorded authorship.

In 1805 the Prefect d'Herbouville authorized and patronized an Antwerp Exhibition of contemporary Belgian art; Napoleon crowned himself King of Italy in Milan; French troops were massed at Boulogne for the invasion of England; Pitt completed the Third Coalition of England, Austria and Russia which Ferdinand of Naples soon joined; Nelson won the Battle of Trafalgar; Napoleon won the Battles of Ulm and Austerlitz; and Austria lost Venetia to the new Kingdom of Italy by the Treaty of Pressburg. In 1806 a new Université Impériale, charged with the unification of education, became the titular head of all teaching establishments in Belgium; and pressure was put upon the clergy to conform to the central policies of Paris. A French force drove Ferdinand of Naples to Palermo, and Joseph Bonaparte became King of Naples. Pitt died. William V Ex-Stadholder of Holland died and William Frederick became Prince of Orange. Napoleon put an end to the Batavian Republic and made Louis Bonaparte King of Holland; he also put an end to the Holy Roman Empire and let Francis II continue as Frances I Emperor of Austria. Frederick William III of Prussia allied himself with Russia and England; Napoleon destroyed two Prussian armies at Jena and Auerstadt; and the Berlin Decree set on foot the Continental System as a blockade of all ports against England. In 1807 Napoleon fought the Russians at Eylau and Friedland; Czar Alexander signed the Peace of Tilsit; the Grand Duchy of Warsaw was established; Jérôme Bonaparte became King of Westphalia; the Peninsular War started when Napoleon sent an army to Portugal under Junot; and Great Britain replied to Napoleon's Continental System by Orders in Council declaring a blockade against France and her allies. Two classes of conscripts (1807 and 1808) were called up in Belgium —a measure that fell hardest on the poorer classes as the rich could now buy exemptions; Fouché, Napoleon's Chief of Police, tightened the press censorship and all articles in Belgian newspapers were henceforth submitted to the local Prefects before printing. In 1808 Louis Bonaparte, who was popular in Holland, moved the Royal residence from Utrecht to Amsterdam and founded the Rijksmuseum first known as the 'Grand Musée Royal'; and in Belgium a new Société pour l'Encouragement des Arts was established in Ghent and began to hold annual Salons and give prizes and travelling scholarships in the manner of the Antwerp Art Society (founded in 1788 as related in my last chapter). Napoleon, incensed against the Vatican for non-cooperation in his policies, sent General

Mothis to occupy Rome and join Ancona and other places to his Kingdom of Italy. Murat, married to Caroline Bonaparte, went to Spain with an army of eighty thousand; Charles IV and the Infante Ferdinand surrendered the throne to Napoleon at Bayonne; Murat suppressed the Madrid Revolt of the Dos de Mayo; Joseph Bonaparte became King of Spain and Murat King of Naples; a Central Junta (Council) of patriotic Spaniards was established at Aranjuez; General Dupont was defeated by the Spaniards at Baylen and Junot by Wellesley at Vimeiro; the French actor Talma, whose famous antique costumes were based on drawings by **Andreas Cornelis Lens** (Pl. 871), was taken by Napoleon to Erfurt and played 'La Mort de César' to an audience of crowned heads; Napoleon joined his army in Madrid in December and suppressed the Inquisition; and the Spanish Central Junta retired to Seville. In 1809 Napoleon was faced by the Fifth Coalition of England, Austria, Spain and Portugal. In January Sir John Moore was killed at Corunna; in February the French took Saragossa; in May Napoleon annexed the Papal States to France; in June he was excommunicated; on July 5 General Radet broke into the Quirinal and made the Pope a prisoner; on July 6 Napoleon fought the Battle of Wagram (where William Frederick, Prince of Orange, was wounded fighting for the Austrians); on July 29 Wellesley won the Battle of Talavera; in August the English took Flushing but could do no more and went back next month; in October the Treaty of Vienna made Austria cede large territories to the Duchy of Warsaw; and, at the end of the year, the Empress Josephine was divorced and retired to her Château at Malmaison. The French Code de Commerce was applied this year to Belgium; the Belgian textile trade was hit by the Continental System and the loss of the Spanish market; a hundred and ten thousand Belgians were conscripted while press gangs seized and imprisoned the parents or 'petites amies' of evaders or deserters; and Napoleon was now looked on as a sacrilegious monster by the Belgian clergy and their followers. In 1810 Napoleon aged forty-one married Marie Louise of Austria who was then eighteen; and an allegoric picture of the marriage was painted in Mons by **Germain Joseph Hallez**. Pius VII was held a prisoner at Savona; Napoleon commissioned a series of decorations for the Quirinal Palace; and S. Mark's Square in Venice was completed, on his orders, by the Nuova Fabbrica forming the west side. Holland became a part of France after Louis Napoleon had been deposed for his opposition to the Continental System; and France was further extended along the coast of Germany as far as Hamburg. In the Peninsular War Marshal Soult was reinforced in Spain where the Central Junta was now established at Cadiz; and Marshal Masséna was sent to Portugal where Wellesley, now Lord Wellington, built the Lines of Torres Vedras to resist him. In June, before annexing Holland, Napoleon and the Empress went to Belgium with the usual pageantry; but there was no enthusiasm in the public welcome and the clergy with their followers made open parade of their hostility. Though mainly occupied on this visit with military matters—the fortifications of Antwerp and the building of warships—the Emperor found time to confirm the use of the Recollets church and monastery as a provisional Antwerp Museum with **Herreyns** as Director; and some commissions as before were given to Belgian artists. The ceremonies connected with this Imperial visit were recorded in some propaganda pictures; thus *The Entry of the Emperor Napoleon into Brussels 1810*, *The Triumphal Arch at the Porte de Laeken with a numerous company* and *The Place Royale Brussels with the Promenade of Giants* were painted by **Pierre Jean Baptiste Leroy**, and **Mattheus van Brée** produced *Napoleon and Marie Louise visiting a naval squadron anchored in the Scheldt* and *The 'Friedland' piloted into Antwerp Harbour*. In this year also Sir Francis Burdett, imprisoned for the Jones affair, became a London hero and 'Burdett for

426

ever' appeared upon the beer jugs; Lord Byron swam the Hellespont at twenty-two; Scott published 'The Lady of the Lake' at thirty-nine; Benjamin Haydon aged twenty-four drew the Elgin marbles illumined by a candle-lantern at Burlington House; Goethe aged sixty-one published his 'Pandora' and the treatise 'Farbenlehre' and was at work on 'Aus meinem Leben!...'; and Canova (who had already made a bust of Napoleon as First Consul, a full-length classical nude of him as Emperor and a portrait of Pauline Borghese as *Venus victrix*) was summoned aged fifty-three from Rome to Fontainebleau where he modelled a portrait of Marie Louise while Napoleon lectured him on the proper limits of Papal jurisdiction and stressed his determination to make Paris the world's art centre by still further gathering of all major works of art there. In 1811 the Peninsular War continued; George III went mad; the Prince of Wales became Regent; and Shelley aged nineteen was sent down from University College Oxford for circulating 'The Necessity of Atheism'. Russia retired from the Continental System; the Empress Marie Louise gave birth to the Roi de Rome; Napoleon visited Holland; **Mattheus van Brée** was commissioned to paint a huge picture *The Emperor Napoleon entering Amsterdam on October 5, 1811*; the Bishops of Ghent and Tournai were imprisoned at Vincennes for protesting at the Concile National de Paris against the Emperor's church policy; clergy in the Belgian rural districts inflamed the peasants against the modern 'Anti-Christ' by tales of miraculous signs and portents; and Savary, Napoleon's new Chief of Police, sent a host of secret police to spy and report on everyone in Belgium. A new Société des Beaux Arts—on the model of the Antwerp and Ghent societies—held its first salon in Brussels this year; and Bosschaert, supported by the Mayor of Brussels, secured a windfall for the Brussels Museum, as Denon, Director of the Musée Napoléon, now sent him thirty-one pictures from Paris, including among other national works **Antoine Sallaert's** *The 1616 Procession with the maidens dowered by the Infanta Isabella* (Pl. 514) originally in Notre Dame du Sablon, and **Jordaens's** *S. Martin curing a demoniac* (Pl. 588) originally in S. Martin's monastery at Tournai and also a number of Italian pictures of which the most important were Tintoretto's sketch for the *Martyrdom of S. Mark* (sent from the former collection of Louis XVI), Veronese's *Juno showering gifts on Venice* (taken from a ceiling in the Doge's Palace) and Albani's *Adam and Eve (The Fall)* (taken from the collection of Eugene of Savoy in Turin). In 1812 the number of Belgian conscripts was a hundred and twenty thousand; and as disaffection among the Flemish-speaking populace was reported widespread, a campaign that had been brewing for some years was brought to a head with the prohibition of all Flemish printed matter, the removal of Flemish street names and so forth. In Spain the Central Junta proclaimed a Liberal Constitution of three hundred and eighty articles which abolished the Inquisition, established a parliamentary system with freedom of the press and personal security for all classes but confined the suffrage to Roman Catholics. In the Peninsular War Wellington took Ciudad Rodrigo and Badajoz and won the Battle of Salamanca. The United States of America declared war on England about the Right of Search; Detroit surrendered to English forces based on Canada; and American ships had a series of successes. Napoleon allied with Austria and Prussia declared war on Russia from Château Laeken; the crossing of the Niemen with an army of three hundred and sixty thousand (of whom two-thirds were allies and satellites) took place in June; Moscow was reached in September; the Retreat from Moscow began in October, the Beresina was crossed in November, and the remnants of the army were back in France at the end of the year. In 1813 fighting continued on the Canadian frontier in the American war; and Captain Philip Bowes Broke in the 'Shannon' took the American frigate 'Chesapeake'. The results of the Continental System were evidenced in Belgium by unemployment and many bankruptcies. The Belgian conscription figure rose to a hundred and sixty thousand, another hundred thousand were pressed into the National Guard, and a new category, the Garde d'Honneur, claimed the sons of the richest citizens in all the nine Departments—though even now it was possible to buy exemptions, the Seminarists seem to have been still exempted, and we find exemption granted to **Joseph Chrétien Nicolié** a student of twenty-two in the Antwerp Art School for a set of architectural drawings. In January Pius VII, now seventy, was transported from Savona and sumptuously lodged, though still a prisoner, at Fontainebleau where Napoleon extracted from him a new Concordat with large concessions. In March the Pope retracted his concessions, Prussia and Sweden joined Russia against France, and Austria was non-committal. In April the Bruges conscripts mutinied, killed the Chef du Bureau Militaire and tore up the recruiting register; and 'A bas le tyran' was scrawled on the walls in Brussels. In May Napoleon defeated Russian-Prussian armies at Lützen and Bautzen. In June Wellington won the Battle of Vittoria against Joseph Bonaparte. In August Wellington took S. Sebastian, Austria joined the final Coalition against France, and Napoleon won the battle of Dresden. In the autumn Napoleon lost the battle of Leipzig; the French armies were driven from Spain; there was insurrection in Holland where Prince William Frederick (supported by England and the Allied Powers) was acclaimed as Sovereign Prince; and by the end of December Uhlans and Cossacks were in Belgium. At the beginning of 1814 there were clashes in Belgium between French troops and the invading Allied forces and the Belgian populace was brutalized by Russian and Prussian troops and officials; Napoleon fought desperately in France till the Allies entered Paris; Chateaubriand published his pamphlet 'De Bonaparte, des Bourbons, et de la necessité de se rallier à nos princes légitimes'; Napoleon abdicated and retired to Elba; and Louis XVIII, acclaimed King of France by Talleyrand and the Senate, promulgated a Constitutional Charter as a grant from himself and had it dated 'la dix-neuvième année du règne' to mark the continuity of the ancien régime. Provisional peace was made by the Powers; the Congress of Vienna was set up by the Treaty of Paris; the Ex-Empress Josephine died; and the Ex-Empress Marie Louise took her son to Vienna. Pius VII went back to Rome and reconstituted the Jesuit order (disbanded by Clement XIV in 1773) with his 'Sollicitudo omnium Ecclesiarum'. The Infante Ferdinand went back to Spain as Ferdinand VII, rejected the 1812 Constitution, restored the Inquisition and launched savage persecution of the Liberals. The American war ended in December with the English holding Canada after Sir Alexander Cochrane had raided Washington and burned the Capitol; the Powers by the Treaty of Paris joined Belgium to Holland; and Prince William Frederick became King William I of the United Netherlands.

Many Belgian painters worked in this period in France where they now had the rights and duties of citoyens français. The majority were regular contributors to the Salons; and a number were patronized by Napoleon and Josephine who bought their pictures or gave them commissions for portraits or propaganda pieces. Josephine probably sat for her portrait to several of these Belgian painters; Napoleon habitually refused to do this because he wished all artists to represent him in general terms as an Augustine type—(he sat to Louis David for three hours on the eve of his departure for Egypt in 1798 and he gave Canova five sittings for a bust in 1802, but he would not sit to Ingres or Greuze who both had commissions from provincial municipalities for portraits of him as First Consul, and when he became Emperor the most an artist could hope for was permission to come to one of his palaces and see him at close quarters for a very short time.)

Of the painters already established in France **Joseph Benoit Suvée** continued his Neo-Classic compositions like *The daughter of Butades drawing the shadow of her lover* (or *The Origin of drawing*) (Pl. 883) which he took from Paris to Bruges in 1799 and presented to the Academy; about the same time he painted a portrait of his father-in-law *Louis Rameau formerly Court jeweller to Louis XVI*; in 1800 or 1801 he painted *Napoleon as First Consul* and *Josephine Bonaparte* and in 1801 at fifty-eight he left Paris for Rome to take up the post of Director of the École Française recently reopened by Napoleon. **Suvée's** friend the landscape painter **Jean François Legillon** (Pl. 877) died at fifty-eight in 1797 leaving some thirty-five pictures and a thousand drawings in his studio. **Suvée's** former pupil **Joseph François Ducq** thirty-four in 1796 sent unsuccessfully an *Oedipus cursing his son Polynices* from Paris to Ghent for a competition organized by the Ghent Society of Artists; in 1800 he won a prize given by the French Académie des Beaux Arts (reorganized as the Institute) and was given lodgings in the Louvre as part of the prize conditions; at the same time he was commissioned to paint allegories of *Nightfall* and *Daybreak* as ceilings in the Palace of S. Cloud; his prize-winning picture *Scipio receiving the ambassadors of Antiochus* and a *Meleager taking arms to free Calydon from the boar* shown in the Salon of 1804 were bought by Fouché, the Chief of Police; in 1807 he went to Rome; and he was back in Paris in 1813. **Jacques Albert Senave**, also a former **Suvée** pupil, was thirty-eight in 1796 and seems to have continued his genre pictures and panoramic landscapes through the Consulate and Empire. **Piat Joseph Sauvage** fifty-two in 1796 resumed his career after his service in the National Guard recorded in my last chapter; he made some grisaille medallions of *Napoleon as First Consul*, continued his allegories and mythologies, generally in grisaille imitating marble or bronze reliefs, exhibited in most of the Salons till 1804, and returned to his native Tournai in 1808. **Antoine Ansiaux** thirty-two in 1796 sent a *Citizen B . . . architect teaching his brother to draw* to the Salon of that year; in 1799 he exhibited *General Kléber*, in 1800 *General Kellerman*, in 1801 *Sappho and Leda*, in 1810 *Le Comte de Champmol, Minister of the Interior* and a much admired *Angelica and Medor*; in 1812 he exhibited *The Assumption of the Virgin* and in 1814 *The Conversion of S. Paul* commissioned for the church of S. Paul which had been the cathedral of his native Liège since 1802. **Jean Louis Demarne**, forty-two in 1796, became highly successful from about 1800 onwards when he owned a country house at S. Denis in addition to his Paris studio and specialized in pictures of genre scenes on the 'grandes routes' in the environs of Paris; a topical piece, painted about 1806, is described as *A farm interior with a soldier returned from Austerlitz*; in 1808 (or possibly in 1813) he exhibited an official propaganda picture *Napoleon and Pius VII in Fontainebleau Forest*; in 1814 his Salon exhibits included *Townsmen visiting a farm* and two typical 'grandes routes' subjects—*A country road* (P. 875) and a *Fair in front of an inn* (Pl. 894) which reveal him a descendant of **Sebastian Vrancx** (Pls. 531, 532, 534); the trees in his *Napoleon and Pius VII in Fontainebleau Forest* were the work of the French landscape painter Alexandre Hyacinthe Dunouy who had been his fellow student some twenty years earlier in the atelier of Gabriel Briard, and it is possible that the landscapes in the pictures reproduced here were also by Dunouy while **Demarne** himself was responsible for the cattle, dogs and the genre and anecdotic aspects of the pictures. **Pierre Joseph Lafontaine** thirty-eight in 1796 continued his church interiors with figures by **Demarne** and various French artists; he was also active as a dealer and probably frequented the Café Caveau in the Palais Royal where the dealers assembled to make arrangements for handling the copious production of **Demarne**. Among the established painters of flowers and decorative still-life **Joseph Laurent Malaine** came back to Paris from Alsace in 1798, had success with

429

still-life pieces of flowers in vases with butterflies and insects, exhibited at the Salon in 1808, and died at sixty-four in 1809 (or a few years later). **Jan Frans van Dael** in high repute during the Consulate and Empire painted three pictures for the Empress Josephine —*Tombeau d'une jeune fille décoré par ses amies* (exhibited in the Salon in 1804), *Offrande à Flore*, and a large composition called *La Croisée* on which he worked for three years and bought back from Malmaison after Josephine's death; in 1806 he signed a *Fleurs dans une corbeille d'osier* and in 1807 *La tubéreuse cassée* (both acquired by the Musée de Lyons founded by the Consulate in 1800); and in 1810 when he was forty-six he signed the picture reproduced here *Flowers in a vase, with grapes and peaches on a marble slab* (Pl. 886) which gives the measure of his skill and industry. **Jan Frans Eliaerts,** whose *Flowers in a vase with bas-relief figures, bird's nest and bullfinch on a marble slab, and insects on the flowers* is also reproduced here (Pl. 888), was thirty-five in 1796, exhibited in the Salon in 1800 and was still in Paris when the Empire fell. **Antoine Ferdinand Redouté** was officially employed as flower painter and decorator in the Salle du Tribunal of the Palais-Royal (where Napoleon was declared Emperor) and in the Palais de l'Élysée (reconstructed for Caroline Murat in 1805); he also worked at Compiègne and for Josephine's Château de Malmaison (remodelled by the architects Percier and Fontaine in 1799) and he died in Paris at fifty-three in 1809. **Pierre Joseph Redouté** exhibited drawings of plants and flowers in the Salon of 1796 and frequently thereafter; in 1799 he was appointed official draughtsman in the natural science section of the Institute and in 1800 he became an official painter in the Jardin des Plantes; in 1802 he published the first volume of 'La famille des Liliacées', depicting rare flowers in Josephine's garden at Malmaison, which was given by the Emperor to European sovereigns and leading scholars and artists to celebrate his coronation; and he followed this with 'Les plantes du jardin de la Malmaison' in 1803; he lived in affluence during the Empire with a studio in the rue de Seine and a villa at Fleury; and after 1810 he gave lessons in flower drawing to the Empress Marie Louise. **Henri Joseph Redouté** continued his practice as a natural history draughtsman with special interest in fish; he accompanied Napoleon on the Egyptian campaign as member of an official Arts and Sciences Commission (which became the Institut d'Egypte) and he seems to have stayed in Egypt till 1802 when he returned to Paris with numerous drawings which he later used as book illustrations. The marine landscape and ethnographic draughtsman **Frans Balthasar Solvyns** who had been to Paris in his youth and had gone since then to India, as related in my last chapter, returned to Paris in 1806 and prepared French and English editions of his book 'Two hundred and fifty etchings descriptive of the Manners, Customs and Dresses of the Hindoos' which General Wellesley (Governor of Seringapatam from 1799 till 1802) had helped him to publish in Calcutta; and he was still in Paris in 1814.

Among the newcomers in Paris a number of young men were pupils of Louis David in these years. Of these the Brugeois **Joseph Dionysius Odevaere** (Pl. 882), who sent an *Ajax* and a *Young man with a horse* to the Salon in 1799, was helped at first by **Suvée** and then became David's pupil; in 1802 when the subject was *Sabinus and Eponina* he competed unsuccessfully for the Prix de Rome; in 1804 he won the prize with a *Phocion, condemned to death with four companions, drinking from the poisoned cup*, was congratulated by Napoleon and left for Bruges where he stayed some months on his way to Rome; in 1812 he came back from Rome to Paris with a group of pictures *Pietà* (*Christ on the knees of the Virgin with S. John and Mary Magdalene*), *The arrival of Iphigenia in Aulis* which was eight by fourteen feet, and *The King of Rome at the Capitol* which won him a medal in the Salon; he then painted *The Reception of Napoleon by Baron Croeser, Burgomaster of Bruges* recording an episode in the 1803 or 1810 visit, and he left France for Belgium when the Empire fell. **Albert Jacob Gregorius**, another Brugeois, was David's pupil at twenty-eight in 1802; he competed unsuccessfully for the Rome prize with a *Prodigal Son* in 1805, drew in the Musée Napoléon for engravers, and made a copy of Holbein's *Portrait of Erasmus* which he sent to the Ghent Exhibition in 1808; he also painted portraits including *The Emperor Napoleon;* and he received a medal in the Salon of 1814. The Gantois **Joseph Paelinck,** some seven years younger, was David's pupil about the same time; in 1804, without David's knowledge, he sent a *Judgement of Paris* to an exhibition in Ghent and won a prize with it; in 1807 (the year of the canonization of S. Colette) he was still in Paris where he painted *S. Colette obtaining permission to found a convent in Ghent* for Ghent, S. Bavon; he also painted *The Empress Josephine*; and he left for Ghent about 1808. **Pieter van Hanselaere** (Pl. 891) came from Ghent to work under David at twenty-three in 1809; and he went back to Ghent in 1814. **Jean Baptiste Bastiné**, painter later of religious and history subjects, arrived from Louvain to work in David's atelier at twenty-one in 1804; he stayed in Paris till 1811 and then went to Aix-la-Chapelle where he founded an art school. Another Louvainais **Henri van der Haert** who was twenty in 1810 and began as a portrait painter, was in Paris in the later years of the Empire and probably worked under David with whom he was certainly associated later. A third Louvainais **François van Dorne,** son of the fruit and flower painter **Martin van Dorne** and pupil of **Pierre Joseph Verhaghen** (Pls. 872, 873) as noted in my last chapter, came to David's atelier at thirty in 1806 and he seems to have stayed for some years before returning to Louvain. **Melchior Gommar Tieleman** born in Lierre came to Paris under twenty, worked in David's atelier and painted *Napoleon as First Consul* presumably before 1805. **Cornelis Groenendael,** also of Lierre, is said to have been David's pupil some years later; in Paris he painted *Le Comte de Fresnell* and *La Comtesse Thalouet* and portraits of some Belgian compatriots and he was working on a portrait *Le Roi de Rome* (then aged three) when the Empire fell and he returned to Antwerp. The gifted **François-Joseph Navez** (Pl. 890) reached David's atelier with a scholarship from the Brussels Société des Beaux Arts at twenty-six in 1813; he copied pictures by **Rubens** in the Louvre, was still in Paris in 1815, and became eventually the most famous of David's Belgian followers.

Other newcomers in Paris were **Mattheus Ignatius van Brée, Philip Jacob van Brée, Louis Ricquier, Louis Adrien Moons, Jean Baptiste Berré, Ignatius Josephus van Regemorter** and **Martinus Spey** from Antwerp; **François Josèphe Kinson** (Pls. 881, 884, 885), **Louis Gerbo** and **François Simonau** from Bruges; **Cornelis Cels** and **Alexandre de La Tour** (or **Delatour**) from Brussels; and **Peter van Huffel** from Malines. Of these **Mattheus Ignatius van Brée** came at about twenty-three at the outset of the period and worked with the French painter François André Vincent (with whom **Frans Balthasar Solvyns** and **Antoine Ansiaux** had worked in the previous period); in 1797 he was second in the competition for the Prix de Rome with a *Death of Cato*; he stayed till 1803 when he returned to Antwerp and witnessed the visit of the First Consul and Josephine; and later he again came several times to Paris to make portrait studies for his official picture of Napoleon's entry. His brother **Philip Jacob van Brée** came at twenty-five in 1811, worked with the French painter A. L. Girodet-Trioson, painted perhaps at this time *The atelier of the flower painter Jan Frans van Dael* and was still in Paris in 1814. **Louis Ricquier** came to Paris in 1811 and worked with **Philip Jacob van Brée**; in 1812 when he was twenty he painted there an *Androcles and the Lion* and in 1813 he sent his *Virgil reciting the Aeneid to Augustus and Octavia* together with a *S. Joseph and the Infant Jesus* to the Antwerp Salon. **Louis Adrien Moons** painter of religious and 'history' subjects was in Paris at thirty-two in 1801 on a visit from Dresden; and he went back to Dresden soon after. **Jean Baptiste Berré** came to Paris at thirty-one in 1808 and specialized in the painting (and occasional modelling) of animals; he drew in the menagerie of the Jardin des Plantes and seems to have been soon presented to the Empress Josephine who commissioned from him a *Lioness with her cubs* which was finished in 1810 and shown in the Salon of that year; he remained in Paris and exhibited there *An eagle about to lift a lamb* and *An antelope in the clutches of a lion* in 1812, and *Romulus and Remus suckled by the wolf* (with figures by **Philip Jacob van Brée**) in 1814. **Ignatius Josephus van Regemorter,** painter of landscape, genre and costume history, visited Paris aged twenty-four in 1809 to see the Musée Napoléon. **Paul Joseph Noël** came to Paris probably at twenty in 1809 with **Regemorter** from whom he is said to have received some instruction; he kept himself in Paris by copying pictures in the Musée Napoléon, went back to Belgium before 1812 and returned to Paris in 1814 to work with the French landscape, military genre and contemporary history painter Jacques Swebach. **Martinus Spey,** painter of portraits and still-life, reached Paris at about thirty-five in 1809 and was still there in 1812. The Brugeois **François Josèphe Kinson,** painter of portraits (Pls. 884, 885) and occasional 'history' (Pl. 841) came at twenty-seven in 1798 with an introduction to **Suvée** who helped him to exhibit his portraits; in 1799 he won a prize for the best portrait in the Salon; in 1801 he married the daughter of an architect who possessed a considerable income and also drew portraits as an amateur; in 1804 he exhibited *General Leclerc*, and in 1806 *Senator de Viry Prefect of the Department of La Lys* painted for the Bruges Academy; by 1808 he had become a favourite portraitist of the Imperial family and he exhibited *Laetitia Bonaparte* (*Madame Mère*), *Joseph Bonaparte* and *Pauline Borghese* in the Salon of that year; he was then appointed Court Painter to Jérôme Bonaparte, King of Westphalia and he left Paris for Cassel in 1810. **Louis Gerbo** did decorative work in Paris probably in this period and drew *The Empress Josephine* and *The Empress Marie Louise* for engravers. **François Simonau,** who studied under the French painter Baron Gros and became a painter of portraits and genre figures, probably arrived at twenty-five in 1808 after Gros had achieved his cardinal success with the propaganda picture *The Emperor at the Battle of Eylau*—(though he may have come some years earlier); and he was back in Belgium by 1812. **Cornelis Cels** came at twenty-two in 1800 to work under **Suvée**; he prepared a composition for the Prix de Rome but generously withdrew it after seeing the picture submitted by Ingres who was then twenty and stood in more need of the stipend; and in 1801 he left for Rome with **Suvée**. **Pieter van Huffel,** painter of religious subjects and portraits, came at just over thirty about 1800, painted a *Napoleon as First Consul* and seems to have left for Ghent about 1803. **Alexandre de La Tour** painter of portrait miniatures came probably about 1805 when he was twenty-five and worked under Jean Baptiste Augustin, a favourite miniaturist in Imperial circles.

In the French provinces **François Joseph Lonsing** died at sixty in 1799 at Léognan near Bordeaux; and **Philip Henri Coclers** died in Marseilles at sixty-five in 1803. **Augustin van den Berghe,** a former pupil of **Suvée,** as related in my last chapter, went from Bruges to Beauvais at just over forty about 1797 to take up a French government appointment as professor in the Beauvais art school (then a branch of the École Centrale du Département de l'Oise); in 1802 he designed an *Allegory of the Peace of Amiens* commissioned by the Consulate for a tapestry to be made in the Beauvais factory; he also painted landscapes and exhibited some portraits in the Salons from 1806; and he was still in Beauvais in 1814.

In England the established Belgians included **Théodor de Bruyn, Hendrik de Cort** and

Philip Joseph Tassaert; and newcomers were **Jean Pierre Borrekens** and **Melchior Gommar Tieleman**. Of these **Théodor de Bruyn,** thirty years in London by 1796, sent a *Landscape with figures* and a *Winter scene* to the Academy in 1797, a *View from Donnington Park, Leicestershire* in 1799, a *View near Rochford, Essex* in 1800, and landscapes with cattle and figures between 1801 and 1803; and he died here probably over seventy in 1804. **Hendrik de Cort,** here since 1790, continued to send pictures to the Academy till 1803 and died in London at sixty-eight in 1810; his Academy exhibits in 1796 included pieces titled *Corfe Castle, East view of Wells Cathedral, Lulworth Castle, Dorset,* and *The effects of the storm, the 14th October last at Giltsham, Devon;* in 1797 he sent *Winchester College* and *Salisbury Cathedral,* in 1798 *Clieveden ruins near Taplow Court and Maidenhead Bridge,* in 1800 *Castle Howard, Yorkshire* and views in Wales, in 1801 *A remarkable old oak in Burton Park, Sussex,* and *Farnham Castle in Surrey,* and in 1803 *Crocomb Vale near the river Tyngh with an additional Gothic bridge.* **Philip Joseph Tassaert** whose varied activities in the London art world have been described in my last two chapters, was probably still dealing and possibly still restoring when he died here at seventy-one in 1803. **Jean Pierre Borrekens** appears to have been here on a visit, despite the war, in 1797 at the age of fifty, as two pictures by him— a *Rape of Proserpina* and a *Rape of Europa*—in the Royal Academy that year were sent from an address in Marylebone. **Melchior Gommar Tieleman** may have come from Paris in 1814 after the fall of the Empire and was certainly here the year after.

Of the Belgians in Holland **Louis Bernard Coclers** whose engaging *Catherine Six, wife of Jan Bicker, seated by a table with a trinket box and flowers* (Pl. 866) was discussed in an earlier chapter, was still in Amsterdam where he exhibited in the newly established Salon at seventy-two in 1813 and again in the following year. **Jacobus Johannes Lauwers** was also still in Amsterdam where he signed in 1799 a *Flemish farmyard with peasant girl drawing water from a well near a cottage door with a boy and dog in foreground,* a curious blend of elements from de Hooch, Fragonard and Chardin; and he died there at forty-seven in 1800. Of **W. J. L. Spoor** in this period we know only that he was still alive in 1810; he may still have been painting in Holland; but as a former protégé of Prince William he was possibly elsewhere with the Orange émigrés. Newcomers to Holland who came on visits included **Constantin Fidèle Coene, Pierre Joseph Thys** and **Petrus Johannes van Regemorter.** Of these **Constantin Coene** was born at Vilvorde and came from Brussels at twenty in 1800 to work in Amsterdam under Pietersz Barbiers (with whom **Jacobus Lauwers** had collaborated as noted in my last chapter); he stayed in Amsterdam till 1802 and then went back to paint genre and costume-history in Brussels. The flower painter **Pierre Joseph Thys,** who had been in Paris and worked for Château Laeken as related, was in Rotterdam for some time at fifty-eight in 1797; he restored 'Old Masters' there for a collector named van der Pot and then went back to Brussels. **Petrus Johannes van Regemorter,** some six years younger, was in Rotterdam from Antwerp the same year. Rotterdam at the moment was clearly a centre for the restoring and faking of seventeenth-century Dutch pictures, and **Regemorter,** an expert restorer and pasticheur, was employed there by a dealer, one Marneffe, for whom he made pastiches in the manner of the Dutch painters Ruisdael, Both and Pynacker which (**Pierre Thys** alleged) were destined to be later marketed as originals; he seems however to have stayed but a short time in Rotterdam, and was back in Belgium by 1800.

In Central Europe we find Belgian painters in Dresden and Cassel. **Louis Adrien François Moons** left Antwerp for Dresden in 1798 and was there (except for the 1801 visit to Paris recorded above) till about 1805; he then went to S. Petersburg where he was working in 1807 and may have remained for the rest of the period. **Martin Verstappen** went from Antwerp to Dresden at the turn of the century and worked under the German painter of landscapes with figures and animals Johann Christian Klengel (then Professor of landscape in the Dresden Academy) who set him to copy pictures by Claude le Lorrain and the Dutchman Wouverman; by 1802 he was himself painting picturesque landscapes with figures and animals; in 1803 he travelled the Rhine and he then went via Switzerland to Rome. **François Josèphe Kinson** (Pls. 881, 884, 885) arrived in Cassel from Paris as Court Painter to Jérôme Bonaparte at thirty-nine in 1810; and his wife, already mentioned as an amateur painter, was appointed portrait-draughtsman to the Queen; in Cassel he embarked on two large ceremonial portraits: *King Jérôme of Westphalia* showing the King seated in a park with the Castle of Wilhelmshöhe in the background and *Queen Catherine of Westphalia and her son* also in a landscape setting; but both pictures were still unfinished in 1813 when the French were driven from Westphalia and he himself left hurriedly for Paris.

Of the Belgians established in Italy **Andreas de Muynck** was still Provisor of the S. Julien Foundation in Rome; he continued his help to young compatriots arriving in the city; and died at seventy-six in 1813. **Simon Joseph Denis** continued to paint picturesque landscapes and was resident in Rome till 1801; he then moved to Naples (where Ferdinand IV had just made peace with Napoleon as noted) and stayed there till 1805 when he went for some time to Rome; in 1806 he was back in Naples as Court Painter to Joseph Bonaparte and he stayed there under Murat; he sent pictures to the Paris Salons in 1802, 1804 and 1806 and died at fifty-eight in Naples in 1813. **Jean Baptiste Pauwels** left Rome for his native Brussels at a date not known. **J. F. Depelchin** who was still painting townscapes and church interiors in Italy in the early years is said to have worked for a tapestry factory and to have visited Switzerland at the end of the nineties and then returned to Belgium. Among the new arrivals in Rome **Joseph Suvée** took up his post as Director of the École Française in 1801; in 1803 he became a member of the Accademia di S. Luca; in 1804 he superintended the transfer of the École Française from the Palazzo Mancini to the Villa Medici and spent large sums from his own purse for the benefit of the students; he died at sixty-four in 1807 and his friends and pupils subscribed for a bust to be placed in the Pantheon. His protégé **Cornelis Cels,** who came with him from Paris as related above, had headquarters in Rome for the next six years and received help and advice from Canova and **Andreas de Muynck** as well as from **Suvée** himself; in 1803 he visited Florence; back in Rome he painted a *Cincinnatus taking leave of his wife and children to assume the Dictatorship* which was sent to Ghent and won a gold medal; he then produced a *Visitation* with over life-size figures for the Antwerp Augustines; in 1805 he received encouragement from **Simon Denis** and he visited Naples probably in 1806; in 1807 he painted *The Descent from the Cross* for Antwerp, S. Paul, which was exhibited in the Pantheon and procured him the rank of Professor in the Accademia di S. Luca; and shortly afterwards he went back to Belgium and settled in Antwerp. **Martin Verstappen** reached Rome at a little over thirty about 1805 and settled down there painting landscapes (including some with sunset or moonlight effects), views of the environs of Rome with monuments, and also architectural pieces; like **Cels** he received encouragement at first from **Simon Denis**; in 1810 he had success with a picture sent to the Paris Salon; and he became a member of the Accademia di S. Luca before 1814. **Joseph François Ducq,** forty-five when he reached Rome from Paris in 1807, was given a studio in the Villa Medici by **Suvée** (or his successor Guillaume Guillon Lethière) at the instance of Napoleon's Viceroy Eugène de Beauharnais who was now his especial patron and paid him an annual stipend; for the Viceroy he painted a *Cyparissus with his stag, Psyche, Toxaris* (*The Devo-*

tion of a Scythian), *Lot and his daughters* and *David and Abishag*; he also produced small idylls and mythologies for other patrons before his return to France in 1813. Napoleon's plans for the adornment of the Quirinal Palace, which included commissions for a sculptured frieze *The entrance of Alexander the Great into Babylon* by the Danish sculptor Thorwaldsen and frescoes titled *Ossian's dream* and the *Temple of Romulus* by Ingres, were also of benefit to two Belgians: **Joseph Dionysius Odevaere** and **Joseph Paelinck** who were both in Rome at the time. **Joseph Odevaere** (Pl. 882) was a few years under thirty when he arrived at the Villa Medici as Prix de Rome winner in 1805; in the following years he painted *A Roman Girl in her bath* and *The Fountain of the Villa Borghese*; his *Coronation of Charlemagne* sent from Rome to the Paris Salon in 1810 was much approved of by Napoleon as it showed the Pope genuflecting to the Emperor; in 1811 he completed two frescoes *Romulus receiving the spoils of war* and *Greeks and Trojans fighting over the corpse of Patroclus* as his share in the Quirinal commission; and he left Rome for Paris in 1812. **Joseph Paelinck** was in Rome aged twenty-nine by 1810 with a travelling scholarship from the Ghent authorities; in 1811 he was commissioned to paint *Augustus adorning Rome* as a fresco in the Quirinal series and he began this but did not complete it; in Rome he also painted *The Finding of the True Cross by the Empress Helena*, *Christ on the Cross*, a *Holy Family* and a genre study *An old man of the Roman Campagna* which were all exhibited in Ghent; and he was back in Ghent at the end of the period.

At home in Belgium the conditions for artists were at first disturbed, but they steadily improved during the Consulate and Empire until 1814 when the country had become impoverished, things generally were again unsettled, and most people were in one way or another discontented. The art schools functioned as heretofore; and the curriculum seems to have remained for the most part what it had been since **Andreas Cornelis Lens** reorganized the Antwerp Academy under Charles of Lorraine—though **Herreyns** probably reduced the time spent on drawing from the antique. The official titles of the schools were several times altered and the term 'Academy' was not officially restored till the later years of the Empire though it was always in colloquial use among the artists and students. Young painters found it easier than before to attract attention as they could now exhibit in new or reorganized Salons in Ghent, Brussels, Antwerp and elsewhere; after a few successes in these Salons many painters were given teaching posts in the art schools which provided a basic income; and the new Societies for the Encouragement of Art, which gave prizes and travelling scholarships, replaced to some degree the diminished patronage by rich nobles and clerics. The churches by the end of the Directorate were almost denuded of paintings, and all through the Consulate and Empire the national heritage of pictures could only be studied in the Louvre; but after the Concordat a number of painters received commissions for reopened churches; and the official founding of the Brussels Museum and the unofficial founding of the Antwerp Museum were encouraging events for the type of artist who draws sustenance or inspiration from the paintings of earlier ages.

In the field of religious painting **Andreas Cornelis Lens** (Pl. 871) was still a respected figure in Brussels with a number of pupils; in 1809 when he was seventy he was commissioned to paint an *Annunciation* for S. Michel in Ghent; but his picture displeased the church authorities because the Angel was depicted as a youth without wings and the Virgin was given a classical garment that to some extent revealed the figure; the church wardens accordingly demanded the addition of wings to the Angel and adjustments in the Virgin's drapery; **Lens** added the wings but refused to touch the Virgin's drapery: 'Je ne puis' he wrote 'que louer le zèle des ecclésiastiques qui font leur devoir pour arrêter la corruption de nos moeurs. La beauté est un don de Dieu; la Sainte Écriture l'attribue aux personnes les plus saintes; devrions nous la cacher? Alors les arts d'imitation doivent être condamnés et défendus. Alors les belles personnes devraient se défigurer'; and referring doubtless to Joseph II's visit to Ghent, S. Bavon, he went on: 'Je ne dis pas qu'il faut copier Adam et Ève dans les églises, mais leur représentation n'est pas défendue: Honi soit qui mal y pense'. His former pupil **Joseph François,** Professor in the Brussels Art School from the time of the Consulate, produced an *Assumption of the Virgin* for Ghent, S. Michel (probably at the same time as the *Annunciation* commissioned from **Lens**) and a *S. Germain blessing S. Geneviève* (probably a commission from a Paris-born cleric) for Notre Dame du Sablon in Brussels; he was now much regarded as a teacher, and his pupils included **François-Joseph Navez** (Pl. 890) from about 1804 to 1808 and **Jean Baptiste Madou** from about 1811. Another former pupil of **Lens, Jean Baptiste Pauwels,** back in Brussels from Rome, painted pictures for churches in S. Josse-ten-Noode and Everberg (near Louvain); later he ceased painting and entered the business world. **Johannes Jacobus Lens** (Pl. 869), who may have painted more religious subjects in this period, was still exhibiting in the Brussels Salon in 1813 and he died in Brussels at sixty-eight next year. In Louvain **Josse Pierre Geedts** became a professor at thirty in the new École de Dessin in 1800 and worked later for the Louvain churches; **Pierre Joseph Verhaghen** (Pls. 872, 873) accepted the Honorary Presidency of the new Louvain school and died at eighty-three in 1811; **Antoine Clevenbergh,** associated with **Verhaghen** and copyist of his religious subjects as related earlier, died in Louvain at fifty-five in 1810; **Verhaghen's** former pupil **François van Dorne** returned from David's atelier in Paris to paint pictures for Louvain churches possibly by 1808 but probably some years later; **Jan Baptist van der Hulst,** who painted later for Louvain churches, was a pupil of **Josse Pierre Geedts** in the Louvain school about 1808 and was beginning his career at twenty-four by 1814; and **Pierre Paul Geedts** (son and pupil of **Josse Pierre**) was another beginner at about the same time. In Malines **Herreyns** (Pl. 867) was the leading figure till 1798 when he moved at fifty-five to Antwerp. His former pupil **Henri Bernaerts** painted in the following years *S. Martin dividing his cloak, The Disciples at Emmaus, The Temptation of S. Anthony* and *The Arrogance of Haman* (perhaps a crypto-comment on some local Prefect) and also *The Woman taken in adultery* dated 1813 when he was forty-five. A new man **Jean Joseph Vervloet** a native of Malines and painter later of religious subjects was twenty-four in 1814. In Bruges **Jan Anton Garemyn** (Pls. 858, 860) died at eighty-seven in 1799; and **Paul Joseph de Cock** died at seventy-seven in 1801. The Brugeois **Augustin van den Berghe** won a prize in Ghent in 1796 and then left for Beauvais as related above. **Joseph Odevaere** (Pl. 882) visited his native Bruges on his way from Paris to Italy as Prix de Rome winner in October 1804 and stayed till September 1805. **Louis Gerbo** in Bruges, except for his Parisian visit, was still a Professor in the École de Dessin and produced a *Holy Family* for Ghent, S. Jacques, at forty-nine in 1810. **Antoine Ignace Steyaert** was in Bruges till 1802 and then moved at forty-one to Ghent. In Mons **Germain Joseph Hallez** who became Professor in the Art School of the École Centrale of the Jemappes Department at twenty-seven in 1796, was Director of the establishment by 1802, and painted perhaps in this period, a *S. Barbara* for the church of his native Frameries. In Tournai **Piat Joseph Sauvage,** back from France at sixty-four in 1808, became Professor in the Art School in 1810, painted an *Annunciation* for Baugnies church in 1811 and was still at work in 1814. In Ghent **Philip Lambert Spruyt** died at seventy-four in 1801; **Charles Spruyt,** twenty-seven in 1796, painted *A dying man receiving the consolations of the Church* for Ghent, S. Nicolas, and *S. Theresa interceding for some souls in Purgatory* for the Ghent church of the Carmes Déchaussés between 1802 and 1815; **Bernard Paul** sent a *Judith and Holofernes* to the Ghent Exhibition in 1796 when he was fifty-seven and painted a *Nativity* in 1806 or later. **Antoine Ignace Steyaert** became Professor in the Art School on his arrival in Ghent in 1802; by 1809 he was made Director and in that year he painted *S. Anthony preaching at Limoges* for Ghent, S. Nicolas, commissioned by the Ghent Society for the Encouragement of Art. **Peter van Huffel,** who settled in Ghent from Paris about 1803, painted the *Miracle of S. Landoald* (the saint who evangelized Belgium and North Eastern France) for Ghent, S. Bavon, and other religious subjects placed in churches probably in this period; he became a Professor in the Art School soon after his arrival and seems to have succeeded **Steyaert** as Director in 1814. **Pieter van Hanselaere** (Pl. 891) was **van Huffel's** pupil about 1804 when he went to work with David in Paris; back in Ghent at twenty-eight in 1814 he exhibited an *Abel's offering* and this won him a scholarship for Rome presented by the Ghent Society. **Charles Remes,** painter later of pictures for Ghent churches, was **van Huffel's** pupil about 1812. **Joseph de Cauwer** painter of a *Baptism of Christ* for Ghent, S. Bavon, and a *S. Elizabeth giving alms*, was attracting attention in the Ghent exhibitions from 1802 when he was twenty-three; in 1807 he became a Professor in the Ghent Art School; and in 1812 the Ghent Society awarded him a medal for his exhibited pictures. **Joseph Paelinck** whose *S. Colette obtaining permission to found a convent in Ghent* sent from Paris for Ghent, S. Bavon, in 1807 and *The Finding of the True Cross by the Empress Helena* for Ghent, S. Michel, sent with other religious subjects from Rome have already been referred to, had been a pupil in the Ghent Art School before he went to David; between his return from Paris and his departure for Rome he held a teaching post in the Ghent Academy for a short time about 1809 when **Joseph Geirnaert** was his pupil; and he was much acclaimed when he came back from Rome at thirty-three in 1814. In Antwerp **Louis Adrien Moons** was a teacher in the Art School at twenty-eight in 1797 till he went abroad. From 1798 the establishment was taken over by **Herreyns** (Pl. 867) whose activities in its service and in assembling pictures as basis for a Museum have been chronicled above; as teacher **Herreyns** stood for the **Rubens** tradition against the Neo-Classic doctrines of **Lens** in Brussels and of David in Paris (though his pupils showed a tendency to desert to the enemy's camp); as artist he continued to paint religious subjects when commissions were forthcoming after 1802; his *Disciples at Emmaus* for Antwerp Cathedral was painted in 1808 and a *S. John the Baptist in the Wilderness* for Malines, S. Jean, is said to have been painted in 1813 (after he was seventy). **Josse Pierre Geedts** was a pupil of **Herreyns** till he left Antwerp for Louvain in 1800. **Jean Baptiste Berré,** also a pupil in the Antwerp Art School under **Herreyns,** began his career at twenty-five with a *Mater Dolorosa* exhibited in Antwerp in 1802; he followed this with other such pieces in 1802 and 1807, and then left for Paris where he specialized in animal painting with much success as noted. **Melchior Gommar Tieleman** and **Cornelis Groenendael** were other pupils of **Herreyns** till they left for Paris to work under David. **Mattheus van Brée** back in Antwerp from Paris by 1803 was Professor in the Art School at thirty-one in 1804, and he may have painted some of his religious subjects, including his *Baptism of S. Augustine* for Antwerp, Augustins, concurrently with his Napoleonic propaganda pictures; he is described as an inspiring teacher and his pupils at this time included his brother **Philip Jacob van Brée** and **Louis Ricquier** till they went to Paris, and **Ferdinand de Braekeleer** (Pl. 893) from about 1809. **Cornelis Cels** who had worked under **Lens** in Brussels till 1800 when he went to Paris and whose pictures sent from Rome to Antwerp, Augustins, and Antwerp, S. Paul, have already been mentioned, had headquarters in Antwerp from 1808, when he was thirty; in

1809 he painted a *Beheading of S. John the Baptist* for Lierre, S. Gommaire, and in 1811 a *Martyrdom of S. Barbara* for the Cathedral in Bruges.

Mythologies and classical 'history' compositions were produced in numbers by artists of all ages because such pictures were still much reputed and because the prizes and scholarships offered by the art schools and the various Art Societies were generally for classical 'history' subjects. Thus in 1796 the open competition organized by the Ghent Art Society prescribed as subject *Oedipus cursing his son Polynices while his daughter Antigone vainly attempts to assuage his wrath*; this was won at forty by the Brugeois **Augustin van der Berghe** who was acclaimed with a public procession and a banquet organized by the Bruges authorities and given a pair of candlesticks by the Bruges Academy to celebrate the event. **François Josèphe Navez** (Pl. 890) had success at twenty-four in the first Salon of the Brussels Société des Beaux Arts in 1811 with a *Vow of Brutus* and he won a medal in the Ghent Exhibition with his *Virgil reading the Aeneid to Augustus* in 1812 before leaving Brussels to work under David in Paris. **Ferdinand de Braekeleer** (Pl. 893) won a prize offered by the Antwerp Society for the Encouragement of Art when he sent at twenty-one to the 1813 Antwerp Salon his *Aeneas rescuing his father Anchises from burning Troy*—a subject that goes back in our story to the conflagration pieces painted by **Pieter Schoubroeck** (Pl. 494) and others at the turn of the sixteenth to the seventeenth century; in the Ghent *Oedipus* competition of 1796 the runner-up against **van der Berghe** was **Joseph François Ducq** then thirty-four who submitted his work from Paris; and I have already chronicled *The daughter of Butades drawing the shadow of her lover* (or *The Origin of Drawing*) (Pl. 883) given by **Joseph Suvée** to Bruges Academy on a visit from Paris at fifty-six in 1799, the *Cincinnatus taking leave of his children to assume the Dictatorship* sent from Rome to the Ghent exhibition in 1803 by **Cornelis Cels** at twenty-five, the *Judgement of Paris* which was sent from Paris and won the Ghent prize for **Joseph Paelinck** at twenty-three in 1804 and the *Androcles and the Lion* and *Virgil reading the Aeneid to Augustus and Octavia* sent from Paris to the Antwerp Salon by **Louis Ricquier** at twenty-one in 1813. **Mattheus van Brée**, whose *Death of Cato* was painted in Paris at twenty-five in 1796, resumed work in this field concurrently with his religious subjects and Napoleonic propaganda pieces after his return to Antwerp in 1803, and when Napoleon commissioned him to paint two large pictures for the Antwerp Palace the subjects selected were *Regulus returning from Carthage* and *Theseus coming to the rescue of Athenian youths and maidens about to be sacrificed to the Minotaur*. **Bernard Paul** sent a *Venus and Adonis* to the Ghent Exhibition at fifty-nine in 1796 and **Louis Paul** sent *Oedipus at Colonus* and *Venus crowned with flowers* to the Exhibition there in 1810 when he was seventy-seven. **Germain Joseph Hallez** had a *Waking of Jupiter* in the Brussels Exhibition of 1811 and **Josse Pierre Geedts** sent there that year a Homeric subject presumably misrecorded as *Telemachus on the island of Calypso*. **Johannes Jacobus Lens** (Pl. 869) painted pictures titled *The Birth of Venus*, *The Death of Cleopatra* and *Marchande d'amours* which seem to have been exhibited in this period; and **Andreas Cornelis Lens** (Pl. 871) himself may have produced some final mythologies between 1796 and 1810 when he ceased to paint and gave his time to the preparation of his second book on the theory of aesthetic—'Traité du bon goût ou la Beauté de la peinture considérée dans toutes ses parties'—which was published in Brussels in 1811 when he was seventy-two. Some pictures in these categories were also painted by **Jean Pierre Borrekens** whose mythologies exhibited in London in 1797 have been mentioned, by **Joseph de Cauwer** who painted an *Antigone: or sisterly devotion* and *Anacreon with Polycrates* at dates unrecorded, by **Pieter Goddyn** between 1796 and his death in 1811, by **François Kinson** who may have painted a few such pictures (heralding his later *Belisarius* (Pl. 881)) before he went to Paris in 1798, by **Jean François Thys** (son and pupil of the flower painter **Pierre Joseph Thys** and also pupil of **Antoine Cardon**) and author of an *Aeneas fighting Diomedes* at about twenty-two in 1804, by **Henri Bernaerts** who painted a *Cimon and Pero* (*Roman Charity*) before 1813, and by **Paelinck's** pupil **Joseph Geirnaert** who was twenty-three in 1814. There were also compositions with cupids and draped or nude allegoric figures used as decorations for mansions or public buildings. Thus **Joseph François,** though resident in Brussels, painted *The Story of Psyche* as a frieze in a house designed by the successful architect Jean Baptiste Pisson who worked mainly in Ghent; **Anna-Maria van Reysschoot** was probably still painting grisailles imitating bas-reliefs in Ghent and **Piat Joseph Sauvage** was again available for this type of decoration in Tournai after 1808. **Antoine Plateau,** known to have done some decorative work in Brussels, may also have done some in Tournai, **Michel d'Argent** may have done some in Brussels and Liège and **Joseph Dreppe** was available in Liège till he died there at seventy-three in 1810.

Costume-history pictures showing events in the past history of Belgium and other countries seem to have been little painted in these years. But **Paul Godefroid Joseph Noël,** later successful with landscapes and anecdotic genre, received an Honourable Mention at twenty-three in 1812 for a *Rudolf of Habsburg giving his horse to a priest carrying the viaticum* exhibited in a competition organized by the Ghent Society of Artists; **Constantin Fidèle Coene** back in Brussels from Holland at twenty-two in 1802 won a prize in the Ghent Exhibition of 1808 with his *Rubens receiving from Charles I the sword with which the King had knighted him,* an early example of the anecdotic costume history pieces showing episodes in the lives of artists which were to become a vogue—an epidemic even—in the following decades; and of the later producers of costume history **Ignatius Josephus Regemorter** and **Willem Hendrik Franquinet** were twenty in 1805, **Jean François Thys** was two or three years older and **Antonis van Bedaff,** trained in the Antwerp École Centrale, was twenty in 1807.

In portraiture I have already referred to the success of **François Kinson** in Paris and Cassel and to portraits painted in Paris by **Antoine Ansiaux, Cornelis Groenendael** and others. Of the production in Belgium I reproduce two characteristic pieces by **Joseph van der Donckt** and **Joseph Odevaere** both painted in Bruges. **Joseph van der Donckt** thirty-nine in 1796 was Director of the Bruges Art School through the period; his *Silvie de la Rue and her dog* (Pl. 889) painted about 1810 shows the sitter at about fourteen and heralds the feeling of nineteenth-century domestic portraiture as can be seen if we compare it with the *Isabella of Bourbon* (Pl. 540) by the Brugeois **Frans Pourbus the younger** and the *Wife of Jan Fernaguut* (Pl. 337) by the still earlier Brugeois **Pieter Jansz Pourbus.** The *Self portrait with F. J. Wynckelman President of the Council of Administration of the Bruges Academy and the Director J. van der Donckt* (Pl. 882) painted by **Odevaere** at about thirty in the spring of 1805, was given by him to the Academy when he visited Bruges on his way to Rome; in this scrupulously drawn and carefully balanced composition, revealing his training under **Suvée** and Louis David, we see the artist's portrait on the wall, the landscape painter **François Jacques Wynckelman** seated in an empire chair and **van der Donckt** standing by the table with his hand on a document inscribed 'Programme de la fête de M. Odevaere le 7 Brum an 13 . . . par l'Académie de Bruges', an allusion to the entertainment offered to **Odevaere** as Prix de Rome winner when the usual procession through the streets was provided by the Municipality and the Academy gave him a banquet and a gold medal. Before leaving for Rome **Odevaere** also painted in the same style a full-length portrait *The Marquis de Chauvelin, Prefect of La Lys Department* where the Prefect in his official uniform stands on a jetty with a view of Ostend harbour and its lighthouse in the background; and this picture was presented by the sitter to Bruges Academy. **François Kinson** (Pls. 881, 884, 885) doubtless painted some portraits in Bruges as a young man before 1798 and he may have visited Bruges from Paris to paint his *Senator de Viry, Prefect of La Lys Department* exhibited in Paris in 1806, as the Senator succeeded the Marquis de Chauvelin in that year and the picture was either commissioned by the Bruges Academy or given to it by the Prefect. Some portraits may also have been painted in Bruges by **P. J. Remaut**, by **Albert Jacob Gregorius** before he left in 1802 to work under David in Paris and again in 1807 when he is said to have been back on a visit, and by **François Simonau** before his period in Paris and after his return in 1812, by **Louis Gerbo** also before or after his Parisian visit and by **Gertrude de Pelichy** (Pls. 868, 870) who was fifty-three in 1796 and still alive in 1814. In Antwerp **Andreas van Quertenmont** fifty-six in 1796 had a much frequented art school in his own house after **Simon d'Argonne** had taken charge of the Academy in 1794; and he doubtless continued to draw and paint portraits of Belgian notables. His pupil **Frans Marcus Smits**, thirty-six in 1796, exhibited *The landscape painter B. P. Ommeganck* in 1805 and painted, probably at this time, his *Willem Jacob Herreyns*, a half-length study showing the sitter over sixty with a palette in his hand. **Herreyns** himself, **Balthasar Paul Ommeganck** (Pl. 876) and **Cornelis Cels,** after his return from Rome in 1808, all produced occasional portraits. **Martinus Spey** painted some in Antwerp between 1796 and his departure for Paris in 1809 and he sent one to the Ghent Exhibition in 1812. **Mattheus van Brée** had portrait commissions in addition to his other activities in Antwerp after 1803 and went back several times to Paris to make portrait studies for his Napoleonic propaganda pictures as noted above. In Brussels **Johannes Jacobus Lens** (Pl. 869) sent portraits as well as his religious and 'history' subjects to the Belgian exhibitions; **P. de Glimes** probably painted more portraits like the one recorded in my last chapter (Pl. 878). **François-Joseph Navez** (Pl. 890) made some portrait studies in the years when he exhibited his first classical 'history' pieces before leaving for Paris in 1813. **Charles Pierre Verhulst,** twenty-one in 1796, became some years later a Professor in the Brussels École de Dessin; in 1805 he painted *Gilles Lambert Godecharle* (showing the successful sculptor who had made allegoric groups for the façade of Château Laeken in 1783 and a bust of *Napoleon as First Consul* and was then fifty-five); and his portrait *The musician Tuerlinckx* was probably produced in this period. Occasional portraits seem also to have been painted in Brussels by **Joseph François, Alexandre Boens, Hendrik Blomaerts** and a newcomer **Ignace Brice** nineteen in 1814. In Ghent **Bernard Paul** exhibited about 1806 an *Interior with an English family* perhaps connected with his visit to London recorded in an earlier chapter; **Louis Paul,** eighty-one in 1814, may have painted some portraits in the earlier years; **Joseph de Cauwer** and **Antoine Ignace Steyaert** were available from 1802; **Joseph Paelinck** painted *The Prefect Faipoult* between his return from Paris and his departure for Italy in 1810; and **Peter van Huffel,** who received commissions for portraits as well as for religious subjects on his return from Paris about 1803, painted *Cardinal de Franckenberg, Archbishop of Malines* and *Mgr. Fallot de Beaumont, Bishop of Ghent* probably before 1807 and *John Quincy Adams, American Ambassador at the Congress of Ghent* in the later part of 1814. The Malineois **Henri Bernaerts** also painted *Cardinal de Franckenberg*; and the precocious **Charles Brias** was showing portraits in the Malines exhibitions from 1812 when he was only fourteen. **Germain Joseph Hallez** was building up a portrait practice in Mons in the second half of the period; **François van Dorne** did the same in Louvain in the later years; and **Leonard Defrance,** who died in Liège at seventy in 1805, may have painted some final portraits on the level of his earlier *Member of the Jalheau family* (Pl. 874).

Indoor genre subjects, out of favour since the eighties, were again more frequent towards the end of this period. **Petrus Johannes van Regemorter** was available for pastiches in the manner of earlier Flemish and Dutch painters both before and after his Rotterdam visit; and his son **Ignatius van Regemorter** also produced some indoor genre scenes. **P. de Glimes** (Pl. 878) painted *A young girl with a bird on her hand* before 1810. **Germain Joseph Hallez** sent *The devoted young mother,* where a young woman bathes a child in a spring within a grotto, to the Brussels Exhibition in 1813. **Jean François Thys** exhibited *The Card players* in 1814; and in 1814 also **Antoine Ignace Steyaert** painted *A young girl by a window with candle-light effect.* **François Simonau** doubtless made genre studies before his visit to Paris and after his return in 1812. **Leonard Defrance** (Pls. 879, 880) and **Nicolas de Fassin** (who died at eighty-three in 1811) probably continued in their last years to paint such subjects as they had done before. **Joseph Geirnaert, Leopold Boens** and **Ignace Brice** were young men who painted them later.

Among the painters of still-life and flowers I have already recorded the strong team absent from Belgium in Paris—**Joseph Laurent Malaine, Jan Frans van Dael** (Pl. 886), **Jan Frans Eliaerts** (Pl. 888), **Antoine Ferdinand Redouté** and **Pierre Joseph Redouté.** Others were working at home. Thus in Antwerp **Pieter Faes** (Pl. 887) was a figure in the circle of **Ommeganck** in the Antwerp Art Society of which he had been a member since 1789; he sent his flowerpieces to the Society's exhibitions up to 1813 and died at sixty-four in 1814. **Georges Frédéric Ziesel,** who belonged to the same circle, was presumably still painting his elaborate arrangements of flowers, fruit and accessories till he died at fifty-three in 1809; and **Martinus Spey** painted flowers and game pieces in Antwerp as well as portraits before 1809. **Pierre François Ledoulx** died in Bruges at seventy-seven in 1807. **Pierre Joseph Thys,** whose visit to Rotterdam in 1797 has been mentioned above, was back in Brussels during the Consulate and Empire and working again as flower painter and restorer. **Antoine Plateau** was still painting flowerpieces in Tournai with perhaps some visits to Brussels for his decorative work there. **Michel Joseph Speeckaert** seems to have worked through the period in Brussels or Malines. The flower painter **Martin van Dorne** was in Louvain till he died there at seventy-two in 1808. **Antoine Clevenbergh** may have painted more game pieces in Louvain between 1796 and 1810. By 1814 **Charles Antoine Clevenbergh (Antoine Clevenbergh's** son) was painting still-life in Louvain at twenty-three when his brother **Joseph Clevenbergh,** also later a still-life painter, was eighteen. **Adèle Evrard,** later successful as a painter of flowers and fruit and game pieces, was twenty-two in 1814 and living in Ath where her father was a merchant and landowner.

Among the painters of topographic pieces (sometimes with ceremonial happenings) and architectural views (including church interiors) **Pierre Jean Baptiste Leroy** produced an *Interior of the 1812 Ghent Exhibition* which can also be regarded as an interior genre piece; and his large watercolours *Porte de Laeken* and *Place Royale in Brussels* showing them in festive garb for Napoleon's visit in 1810 (already referred to) continued the tradition of pictures reproduced here by **Antoine Sallaert** (Pl. 514), **Denis van Alsloot** (Pl. 513A) and **Adam van der Meulen** (Pl. 759). Of the painters of town views named in my last chapter **Jean Beerblock** (Pl. 859) died in Bruges at sixty-seven in 1806 and **Pierre François Ledoulx** died there at seventy-seven in 1807. **Jean Charles Verbrugge,** forty in 1796, continued his drawings of buildings in Bruges which included *The Recollets Church* in 1809 and the *Porte d'Ostende* about 1814. A newcomer **Seraphin Vermote,** who began as a topographic draughtsman in Bruges, was commissioned by the Brugeois Baron de Huerne to make drawings of buildings, monuments and ruins in many Flemish towns and villages when he was twenty-four in 1812; and this series included the *Abbaye des Dunes* showing the 1813 appearance of this Abbey (now the Episcopal Seminary) which had pictures in the seventeenth century by **Lucas Achtschellinck, Donatien van den Bogaerde, Balthasar d'Hooghe, Jan Baptist van Meunincxhove** and **Pieter van Bredael** as noted in earlier chapters. **J. F. Delpelchin** back from his travels in France, Italy and Switzerland about 1800, when he was round about thirty, became a Professor in the Courtrai Art School and continued to paint church interiors and other architectural pieces. **Jan Baptist de Jonghe** (Pl. 892), born at Courtrai and said to have been influenced by **Delpelchin,** was probably painting town views as well as landscapes before 1814. **Joseph Chrétien Nicolié,** who later specialized in church interiors, studied architecture and drawing in the Antwerp Art School where his work done between 1811 when he was twenty and 1813 procured his exemption from military service at the height of Napoleon's demands for conscripts as already recorded. **Pierre François de Noter** trained as a sculptor in Malines was a late starter as a painter at twenty-eight in 1807 when he began to paint views of churches and church interiors. **François Vervloet** nineteen in 1814 and trained in the Art Schools of Malines and Antwerp was also later a specialist in church interiors; and **Ange de Baets** trained as architect and painter in the Ghent Art School began to specialize in architectural painting from about the end of the period when he was just over twenty.

Among the painters of landscapes, or landscapes with cattle, and outdoor genre scenes, we find a number who have already appeared and a number of new ones. Among the older men I have already chronicled the deaths of **Jan Anton Garemyn** (Pls. 858, 860) in 1799, **Joseph Dreppe** in 1810 and **Nicolas de Fassin** in 1811. **Balthasar Paul Ommeganck,** whose *Landscape with cattle, goats and sheep* (Pl. 876) of 1781 was referred to in my last chapter, became Professor in the Antwerp École Spéciale at forty-one in 1796; in 1797 he was awarded the landscape prize in the first Paris Decennial Competition for a picture submitted without his knowledge by a friend; this was followed by a vogue for his work among French collectors (led by Josephine Bonaparte as noted) and under the Consulate and Empire the French called him 'Le Racine des moutons' (as a pendant to their designation of **Pierre Joseph Redouté** as 'Le Raphael des fleurs'); in 1808 he received a Medal of Honour from Napoleon, and in 1809 he was appointed Corresponding Member of the Institut de France; but he was not tempted to go and live in Paris, preferring to remain in Antwerp where he was still a leading member of the Art Society and, from 1804, a member with **Herreyns** of the Council of Administration in the Antwerp School; the sheep and cattle in his pictures were as much admired in Belgium as in France, and he often painted animals in landscapes by other artists thus continuing the old Flemish tradition of collaboration by specialists. His brother-in-law and former pupil **Hendrik Aarnut Myin,** thirty-six in 1796 and also a teacher in the Antwerp École Spéciale from that date, had considerable success with pictures in the **Ommeganck** style; and as **Maria Jacoba Myin** also continued to paint in this manner, the family constituted a small factory for such landscapes with animals. **Jean Pierre Borrekens** already nearly fifty in 1796 was also associated with this group, being one of the artists into whose landscapes **Ommeganck** occasionally inserted the cattle; but as a man of means with amateur rather than professional status he played no part in the main production or commercial marketing of such pictures. **Petrus Johannes van Regemorter,** the same age as **Ommeganck,** probably painted more moonlight landscapes and outdoor scenes with peasants after 1800. **Martin Verstappen** (pupil of **van Regemorter** and of **Hendrik Myin**) went abroad, as noted, at about twenty-seven about 1800. **Simon Pierre d'Argonne,** whose aid to **Herreyns** in procuring pictures from churches in 1798 has also been noted, seems to have retired from administrative cooperation with the French authorities in the second half of this period; and in 1811 he settled at Vilvorde near Brussels to devote himself to landscape painting. Among the newcomers in Antwerp **Johannes Carolus Carpentero** began to show pictures in the style of **Ommeganck** from about 1802; **Frédéric Théodore Faber** came from Brussels at seventeen in 1799 to work under **Ommeganck** and was launched as a painter of landscapes and genre before 1814; **Julien Ducorron** born at Ath and twelve years older than **Faber,** was a moneyed amateur till the end of the nineties when he too went to **Ommeganck** in Antwerp; in 1802 at thirty-two he became a professional, lived for a time at Lens near Mons, and began to paint landscapes with pastoral figures; by 1812 he had won a prize with a landscape in the Ghent Exhibition and become a member of the Ghent Society of Artists; in 1813 he received a medal for a picture exhibited in Brussels; and he may have been back in Ath by 1814. **Ignatius Josephus van Regemorter** pupil of his father and of **Ommeganck** was twenty in 1805 and began as a landscape painter before turning to the various types of genre already mentioned. **Jan Baptist de Jonghe** (Pl. 892) also twenty in 1805 had come a few years earlier from Courtrai to work under **Ommeganck**; and in 1812 he won the first prize in the Ghent Exhibition with a landscape titled *The Approach of the Storm.* **Henri Joseph van der Poorten,** pupil of **Herreyns** and then, for landscape, of **Hendrik Aarnut Myin,** had a first success at twenty-five in the Salon organized in 1813 by the Antwerp Society, and his *Country road with figures* was in the Ghent Exhibition of 1814. **Jan Frans Lentzen (Lenzen)** another pupil of **Myin** attracted attention at about twenty-three in the 1813 Antwerp Exhibition with a picture called *The Comet seen at 7 p.m. on October 7, 1811*; and **Paul Godefroid Joseph Noël** sent a *View on the Meuse* to the Brussels Salon at twenty-four in 1813. In Brussels **Jean Baptiste de Roy** had many pupils in these years and was now the most successful painter there of landscapes with animals; in 1803 when he was forty-four he exhibited a *Bull standing in a meadow with Château Laeken in the background* where the bull was life-size as a challenge to the famous picture by Paul Potter; and a picture described as *Four cows and a bull with herdsman coming from a wood to a meadow with a pool* acquired by the Ghent Academy is also recorded. **Simon Pierre d'Argonne** who was just over sixty when he settled at Vilvorde in 1811, became **de Roy's** pupil, painted wooded landscapes and river scenes and exhibited in Brussels from 1813. **P. de Glimes** (Pl. 878) painted a *Landscape with four bathing shepherdesses* and similar subjects probably in Brussels before 1814. **Hendrik Bloemaerts,** also established in Brussels and now more occupied with landscape than mythology, was the author of a *Hilly and wooded landscape with animals and figures* at forty-seven in 1802. Most of the young newcomers in Brussels were pupils of **de Roy.** Of these **Henri van Assche** twenty-four in 1796 signed a *Storm scene with terrified animals* in 1805; in 1808 he painted a *View of the Château at Montaigle* and began to send pictures to the Ghent Exhibitions, and in 1813 he became a member of the Ghent Society of Artists; he worked in the environs of Brussels and also round Dinant and Namur making studies of wind and water mills which were used in his *Mill at Éprave* in 1810, *Watermill near Brussels* in 1812, and *Mill at Salzinnes* in 1814; he also painted forges including a *Forge at Fumay* in 1814. **Henri Voordecker,** twenty-four in 1803, began as a painter of landscapes with animals and received a medal from the Brussels Society in 1813. **Pierre Jean Baptiste Leroy** began as a painter of open-air scenes with horses, and appeared at twenty-one in the Antwerp Salon of 1805 with the *Cavalry combat between the French and Mamelukes* celebrating the Battle of the Pyramids already referred to; in the Brussels Salon of 1811 he received a medal from the Brussels Society for his records of Brussels en fête for Napoleon's entry; and in 1812 he sent to the Ghent Exhibition a *Horse-race scene* and was made a member of the Ghent Society of Artists. **Pierre Jean Hellemans,** who became a painter of wooded landscapes at the end of the period, had probably finished his training with **de Roy** by 1810 when he was twenty-three. Other newcomers in Brussels were **François de Marneffe** twenty-one in 1814 who began as a landscape painter, **Maximilian Lambert Gelissen** (a pupil of **Henri van Assche** about 1806) who was twenty-eight in 1814, **Isabella Kindt** (niece and pupil of **Henri van Assche**) who had exhibited watercolour landscapes in Ghent and Bruges before she was twenty in 1814, and **Antoine Payen** of Tournai who went to Brussels to work with **van Assche** about 1805 and exhibited a *Petite chaumière* in Ghent at twenty-nine in 1814. In Bruges **François Jacques Wynckelman** was still active. **Antoine Ignace Steyaert** began to paint landscapes, including some by moonlight (in addition to his religious and genre subjects) from his Ghent headquarters after 1802. **Antoine Pierre Steyaert,** eighteen in 1796, taught drawing in the Ghent School doubtless through his father's influence after 1802, and had a *Landscape with cottages* in the Ghent Exhibition of 1810. **Pierre François de Noter,** mentioned above as a painter of churches and church interiors from 1807, began to paint landscapes (including winter scenes) and also some marines at about the same time; he seems to have settled in Ghent towards the end of the period; and in 1813 he won a medal in the Ghent Exhibition.

CHAPTER XXII

William I. King of the United Netherlands

1815-1830

WILLIAM I was forty-three when he began his reign in the dual Kingdom arranged by the Powers. A portrait of him painted at the end of the reign by the Dutchman Jan Adam Krusemann is inscribed 'Hersteller van den Koophandel, Zeevaart, Scheepsbouw en Nijverheid' a merited tribute which might have added a reference to his work as patron of learning and the arts. He worked, in fact, hard and ceaselessly, especially in Belgium, to advance the material welfare of his subjects; he founded banks and factories, encouraged industry and commerce, started important new canals, founded schools and universities and employed a number of artists. But behind a constitutional façade he ruled as a bene-volent despot, and being half Dutch and half German (his mother was a Prussian) he never understood the Belgians. Moreover as a Calvinist and a Febronian he was always persona ingratissima with the Catholic Church which worked against him, openly or secretly, throughout his reign, and he was finally defeated when influences from Left and Right in France led young Liberals and young Catholics in Belgium to combine in the nationalist revolt which ended the dual Kingdom.

At the beginning of 1815 the Congress of Vienna was in session with Metternich, Castlereagh and Talleyrand as the leading figures. On March 1 Napoleon landed at Golfe Juan from Elba; on March 13 the Congress of Vienna declared him 'hors la loi' and the Powers agreed to raise armies of 600,000 men against him; on March 19 Louis XVIII took refuge in Ghent (King William affecting ignorance of his presence), and on March 20 Napoleon reached the Tuileries. In May Napoleon promulgated the new Constitution for France known as 'Acte Additionnel aux Constitutions de l'Empire' drafted by Benjamin Constant and supported by Lafayette. In June he marched into Belgium and was defeated at Waterloo where sixty thousand men were killed and King William's son the Prince of Orange aged twenty-three was among the wounded. In July Anglo-Prussian troops re-occupied Paris, Louis XVIII resumed the throne and Napoleon surrendered to Captain Maitland on the Bellerophon. In August the 'Chambre introuvable' was returned in France and a White Terror led by the King's brother the Comte d'Arthois began the persecution of Liberals and of many signatories of Napoleon's Acte Additionel; King William sent **Joseph Odevaere** (Pl. 882) to Paris to redeem the pictures from his family collection which the French had taken from The Hague in 1795; the Municipality of Antwerp, incited by **Jacob Herreyns** (Pl. 867) and the Antwerp Society for the Encouragement of Art, sent **Balthasar Paul Ommeganck** (Pl. 876) and **Petrus Johannes van Regemorter** to reclaim the pictures taken from Belgium; and a British officer, one Colonel Hay, convalescing from a Waterloo wound, saw **Jan van Eyck's** *The Marriage of Giovanni Arnolfini* (Pl. 18A) in a

445

Brussels house and bought it. In October Napoleon reached S. Helena; and ex-King Joachim Murat went to Pizzo in Calabria and was at once arrested and shot. In November, by the Second Treaty of Paris, France surrendered Savoy and Nice and the Saar Valley and had to finance the installation of fortresses against her on the coast at Ostend and Nieuport, on the Scheldt at Antwerp, Termonde, Ghent, Audenarde and Tournai, on the Meuse at Liège, Namur and Dinant and also in Ypres, Menin and Ath, Mons, Charleroi, Philippeville and Marienbourg. In December Marshal Ney was shot; and before the end of the year Louis David was banished as a regicide and signatory of the Acte Additionnel despite the personal support of Louis XVIII who had bought his *Leonidas* and *Rape of the Sabines*.

In this year also King William proclaimed the Fundamental Law as the Constitution of the United Netherlands. This established two Chambers, one appointed by the King and the other elected by the propertied classes, half the deputies in the Second Chamber being Dutch and half Belgian—though Belgium had a population of some three and a half million and Holland had only two. All religious creeds were given equal rights, the control of education was vested in the King, and the ministers were responsible to the King alone. The press was nominally free though a special court had already been set up to deal with misdemeanours from that quarter. The King, on his part, undertook to live alternate years with his Government and Court in The Hague and Brussels. For the rest the Departmental system surviving from the French Directorate was maintained in Belgium (though the Departments were rechristened Provinces and the Prefects were now called Governors). The Roman Catholics were fiercely opposed to this Fundamental Law because it gave equal rights to 'Truth' and 'Error' and placed education in the hands of a Calvinist; and Mgr de Broglie, Bishop of Ghent and leader of the Catholics (as the See of Malines was vacant) at once put out a 'Pastoral Instruction' forbidding his followers to approve it.

In 1816 Byron aged twenty-eight went through Belgium and the Rhine country to Geneva and travelled in Switzerland with Shelley aged twenty-four; and Keats aged twenty-one was a dresser in Guy's Hospital. Louis David took up residence in Brussels; Louis de Potter, a young Belgian Radical, attacked the Roman Church in 'Considérations sur l'histoire des principaux conciles'; Mgr de Broglie forbade the clergy to take the Oath of Fidelity required by the Fundamental Law; King William reopened the Brussels Académie de Sciences et Belles Lettres (founded in 1772 and disbanded by the first French Commissaries) and the Prince of Orange married the Grand Duchess Anna Paulowna (sister of the Czar Alexander). Louis XVIII dissolved the 'Chambre introuvable'; and Ferdinand IV of Naples proclaimed himself Ferdinand I, King of the Two Sicilies. In 1817 the French electors gave a majority in the Chamber to the Constitutional Royalists; and F. R. de Lamennais published the first volume of his 'Essai sur l'indifférence en matière de religion'. The English Government suspended the Habeas Corpus Act after riots caused by distress among industrial workers; Jeremy Bentham aged sixty-nine published his 'Catechism of Parliamentary Reform'; Walter Scott wrote 'Rob Roy' at forty-six; and Waterloo Bridge was opened with a military pageant sketched in oils by John Constable aged forty-one. In Belgium a trade depression caused great distress among industrial workers (the unemployed in Ghent alone numbered fifteen thousand); and King William installed the Château de Seraing (former pleasure palace of the Prince Bishops of Liège) as a new centre for the construction of industrial machines with John Cockerill (William Cockerill's son) as the director. The Princess of Orange gave birth to a son, and Mgr de Broglie forbade thanksgiving in Catholic churches because the Grand Duchess was schismatic. King William established a series of model schools (Écoles royales) and founded new State Universities in Ghent, Louvain and Liège (to replace the old Louvain University suppressed in 1797); the Professors in these Universities were nominated by the Government after consultation with the University Trustees; there were Faculties of Philosophy, Letters, Law, the Sciences and Medicine but no Faculty of Theology. The Church campaigned against the new foundations; and the Abbé de Foere who attacked 'les absurdes prétentions anti-religieuses du Gouvernement' in the 'Spectateur Belge' was condemned to two years' imprisonment. Mgr de Broglie was cited before the Cour d'Assises by van Maanen, the King's Minister of Justice, for 'manoeuvres against the State'; the Bishop denied the Court's competence, took refuge in France and was condemned to exile in his absence. The Government suspended clergy nominated by Mgr de Broglie and withdrew the exemption from military service hitherto granted to Belgian seminarists; and the vacant Primacy of Malines was filled by Mgr de Méan, Prince Bishop of Liège, who expressed himself willing to take the Oath of Fidelity 'in a civic sense'—a compromise which secured the Pope's approval. In 1818 Shelley, living at Marlow, met Keats and published political pamphlets; Keats recited part of 'Endymion' to Wordsworth; Byron began 'Don Juan' in Venice; and King William commissioned **Mattheus van Brée** to paint the costume-history picture *William of Orange urging the release of the Bishops of Bruges and Ypres and the Catholic nobles imprisoned in Ghent by Hembijzi and the anti-Catholic faction in 1577* as a propaganda gesture symbolizing his own stand for tolerance in the religious field. In 1819 King William decreed that Dutch would be the official language in the Flemish regions of Belgium from 1823 onwards when it would become compulsory in the law courts and all administrative offices. This blunder was widely resented because French which had long been the language of the upper classes was now in general use among all classes—except the peasants who spoke a Flemish-Dutch patois—as a legacy of the French occupation; and there was a natural suspicion that the rule would later be applied to the Walloon provinces as well. In 1820 Lamartine published his 'Méditations'; the Duc de Berri (second son of the Comte d'Arthois) was murdered on the steps of the Opera by a fanatic enemy of the Bourbons; and the French moderates were driven from power. George III died; the Regent became George IV; the leaders of the Cato Street conspiracy were executed; and Sir Francis Burdett was imprisoned for public censure of the Government. In Spain the capriciously cruel and reactionary government of Ferdinand VII caused a revolution led by Colonel Riego (who had learned liberal doctrines when a prisoner in France); the 1812 Constitution was partially revived, the Inquisition was once more abolished and Ferdinand was virtually a prisoner. In Naples the parallel misrule of Ferdinand I of the Sicilies caused a Liberal rising fomented by the Carbonari; the Spanish Constitution of 1812 was adopted there; and Austria, Prussia and Russia signed the Troppau Protocol affirming the right of 'collective Europe' to crush dangerous internal revolutions. In Belgium the new fortresses against France prescribed in the Second Treaty of Paris were completed; trade revived; six hundred manufacturers took part in a highly successful Industrial Exhibition in Ghent and many Catholic business men became supporters of the Government. In 1821 the Neapolitan Liberals were defeated by an Austrian army sent to restore the autocracy of King Ferdinand; and Ferdinand launched a persecution of Carbonari and all Liberal adherents. The Greeks rose against the Turks, won victories in the Peloponnesus (Morea), captured Athens and blockaded the Turks in the Acropolis; the Turks executed the Patriarch Gregorius; and there were hideous atrocities on both sides. Napoleon died of cancer at fifty-two on S. Helena; Keats died at twenty-six in Rome; Shelley wrote 'Adonais' in Pisa; and Heinrich Heine attended

Hegel's lectures in Berlin. In 1822 the Comte de Villèle was Premier Ministre in France, the press censorship was made more vigorous, the Liberals were hunted down, the Church and the Jesuits (who had returned in 1814) considerably increased their power, and Alfred de Vigny published his 'Poèmes antiques et modernes' at twenty-five. A Turkish army was driven back by the Greek defenders of Missolonghi in Aetolia, another was starved out in the mountains of Argolis, and the Turks massacred the Greeks in Chios (which led Eugène Delacroix then twenty-five to begin 'Le Massacre de Scio' in the following year). Lord Castlereagh committed suicide; Canning became Foreign Minister; and the Duke of Wellington, at the Congress of Verona, refused English aid to restore the autocracy of Ferdinand VII. In Belgium, where business prosperity continued, there was heavy taxation including milling and slaughtering taxes which increased food prices and thus pressed most heavily on the poorest classes; there was much agitation among the lawyers and civil servants against the language Law due to take effect next year; and the Church was incensed by a decree forbidding primary school teachers to practise till they had obtained a State licence to do so. But industry and commerce were much helped and encouraged by the King's foundation in Brussels of credit institutions, the Syndicat d'Amortissement and the central bank called the Société Générale des Pays Bas pour favoriser l'industrie nationale (Algemeene Nederlandsche Maatschappij ter begunstiging der volksvlijt). In 1823 Leo XII succeeded Pius VII; and General Dumouriez died at Turville Park near Henley. A French fleet and army known as 'The Sons of S. Louis' and led by the Duc d'Angoulême (eldest son of the Comte d'Arthois) restored the autocracy of Ferdinand VII in Spain; Ferdinand had Colonel Riego hanged, revived the Inquisition, and took such savage vengeance on the Liberals that the Duc d'Angoulême refused in disgust the Spanish decorations offered him. In Belgium the Church, working underground, was now persuading Belgian youths of good family to study in the Jesuit establishments in Paris and in the Jesuit College at Saint-Acheul near Amiens; and King William's Government dissolved the Catholic Society for the Propagation of Religious Literature as a dangerous and seditious body. The English Parliament passed Peel's law reducing the number of crimes punishable by death from two hundred to about a hundred; Daniel O'Connell and the Irish Catholic priests formed the Catholic Association to organize agitation for the admission of Roman Catholics to Parliament; Canning recognized the South American Republics; and President Monroe announced the 'Monroe Doctrine'. Byron sailed from Genoa to help the Greek insurgents; and Mehemet Ali, Pasha of Egypt, sent his son-in-law Hussein Bey to help the Turks in Crete. In 1824 King William founded the Nederlandsche Handelsmaatschappij, with headquarters in The Hague, as a bank to finance the Dutch and Belgian exports to the Indies and elsewhere. In England the Radical tailor Francis Place (through Joseph Hume in Parliament) achieved the repeal of the laws against workmen's combinations, and Trade Union action became legal in wage disputes. In France Louis XVIII died at sixty-nine, the Comte d'Arthois succeeded as Charles X at sixty-seven, and the reactionary Ultras triumphed. In the Greek War Byron landed at Missolonghi and died of fever, Hussein Bey took Crete, and Ibrahim Pasha adopted son of Mehemet Ali sailed with an army from Alexandria for Morea. In 1825 Ibrahim Pasha landed at Modon and began to devastate Morea, slaughtering the men and selling the women into slavery; Missolonghi was invested; Czar Alexander in command of an army formed to fight against the Turks died suddenly in December and Nicholas I succeeded. Ferdinand of Naples died and Francis I, who succeeded, continued repression of Liberal ideas. Charles X made the French Chambers vote huge indemnities to landowners whose properties had been confiscated in the revolutionary period and pass a sacrilege law prescribing penal servitude for life for the theft of ritual vessels and death for public profanation of a consecrated host; and de Lamennais published the first volume of 'De la religion considérée dans ses rapports avec l'ordre civil et politique'. In Belgium King William founded a School of Mines in Liège and a Collège Philosophique in Louvain; he also issued a decree refusing entry into the State University of students trained abroad (which meant in this connection France); and other decrees prescribed State registration and inspection of secondary educational bodies, civil and religious, and made a University degree a condition for the teachers. In the new Collège Philosophique the teachers were to be nominated by the Ministry of the Interior (after consultation with the Archbishop of Malines who was offered the office of Curator); and all candidates for seminaries were required to take a preliminary course there. Mgr de Méan who had hitherto compromised with the King's Febronian principles declared himself unable to approve the College and refused the office of Curator; the King opened it, nevertheless, in October, and a hundred and sixty-seven students were forthcoming—to use accommodation planned to receive twelve hundred. In 1826 Missolonghi and the town of Athens were occupied by the Turks; and Canning sent the Duke of Wellington to S. Petersburg where Czar Nicholas agreed that the Turks should be urged to recognize Greece as a vassal and tributary state. In France there was popular resentment at new reactionary proposals by Villèle. In Belgium King William opened the new building of the Ghent University; prosperity continued with a balanced budget; Antwerp was recognized by the Dutch as in fact the leading port of the dual Kingdom, and more and more Amsterdam firms of standing set up branches there. Transport was improved by work on the Terneuzen Canal, by the completion of the Pommeroeul-Antoing canal, and by the inception of the Charleroi canal (planned but not begun by Napoleon). But the King's benevolent despotism was challenged from a new direction when a group of young Liberals launched the paper 'Le Belge' in Brussels. In 1827 the Turks took the Acropolis after a bombardment that badly damaged the Erectheum; England, France and Russia formed a Triple Alliance (Treaty of London) to impose the 'Vassal State' solution of the Greco-Turkish problem by mediation if possible and if not by force; and the Turko-Egyptian fleet was destroyed in Navarino Bay by a fleet of the Triple Alliance. King William signed a Concordat with Pope Leo which neither side in Belgium made serious efforts to put into effect. Heinrich Heine published his 'Buch der Lieder' at thirty and spent some months in England; and Victor Hugo wrote the 'Preface' to his 'Cromwell' at twenty-five. In 1828 a revolt against the misrule of Francis I in the Two Sicilies was savagely suppressed. Wellington was Prime Minister in England with Peel as Home Secretary. The relatively moderate Martignac was Prime Minister in France; French troops occupied Morea; and de Lamennais published 'Le progrès de la révolution et de la guerre contre l'église'. In Belgium young Liberals influenced by Benjamin Constant's ideas of constitutional and parliamentary government, and young ultramontane Catholics influenced by de Lamennais, made a marriage of convenience against King William's Government; and Louis de Potter was sent to prison for a seditious article in the 'Courier des Pays Bas'. In 1829 Leo XII died and Pius VIII succeeded. The Catholic Emancipation Act admitted Irish and other Roman Catholics to the English Parliament and most public offices. A London protocol established Greece as an autonomous tributary state to be governed by an hereditary prince to be chosen by the Powers; and Russia made Turkey endorse this in the Adrianople Treaty. The Prince de Polignac, a fanatical reactionary, became Prime Minister of France; Talleyrand aged seventy-five and Thiers aged thirty-two began propaganda for a new régime under Louis Philippe, Duke of Orléans; Balzac published 'Le dernier Chouan' at thirty, and Alfred de Musset published his 'Contes d'Espagne et d'Italie' at nineteen. In Belgium the young Liberals gave Louis de Potter the status of a martyr; the clergy collected three hundred and sixty thousand signatories for a Petition to the King against his Government; and the King gave seminarists the option of declining the course at the Collège Philosophique, and promised abolition of the slaughter tax—but spoilt the effect of these concessions by public reference to the opposition's conduct as 'infâme'.

In 1830 the young French Romantics yelled their applause at Hugo's 'Hernani' performed for three months from February at the Théâtre Français; and Théophile Gautier published his poem 'Albertus' at nineteen. In January six Belgian functionaries were dismissed from their offices for voting against the Budget in the Second Chamber; a public subscription was organized in their favour and de Potter, in the 'Courier des Pays Bas', called for a confederation to support resistance to the Government. In March over two hundred and twenty-one members of the French Chambers sent an Address to Charles X protesting against the government of de Polignac, and Charles X dissolved the Chamber. In April de Potter with the Liberal Tielemans and two Catholics were exiled from Belgium. In June King William repealed the Language Law of 1819; George IV died and William IV succeeded; and a French army sent to deal with piracy attacked and took Algiers. In July elections for a new French Chamber showed a large increase in the opposition; Charles dissolved the Chamber and issued ordinances imposing fresh restrictions on the press and curtailing the electorate in defiance of the Louis XVIII Charter; there was fighting in the streets of Paris, and Louis Philippe, Duke of Orléans was proclaimed Lieutenant-General of the Kingdom by Deputies meeting in the Palais Bourbon. In the first ten days of August Charles X fled to England and Louis Philippe became King of the French; and King William opened an Industrial Exhibition in Brussels without any hostile incidents. But on August 25, the anniversary of King William's accession, the Belgian Revolution started at a performance of Auber's opera 'La Muette de Portici' (dealing with Masaniello's 1647 revolt in Naples) in the Théâtre de la Monnaie when young people in the audience excited by the duet 'L'amour sacré de la patrie' emerged into the streets, joined other demonstrators, invaded the office of the Chief of Police, and set fire to the house of van Maanen the unpopular Minister of Justice. On the following days the revolt spread to other places and hastily improvised Burgher Guards took charge of local affairs. On August 31 the King sent the Prince of Orange from The Hague to attempt conciliation and on September 3 van Maanen was dismissed and the Prince of Orange, back in The Hague, reported to the King that nothing but separation from Holland would satisfy the Belgians. On September 12 'La Brabançonne' (the 'Marseillaise' of this uprising) was sung at the Théâtre de la Monnaie; on September 20 the Brussels rioters got out of hand and on September 23 Prince Frederick, the King's second son, invited by bourgeois elements, came to restore order with Dutch troops. On September 27 Prince Frederick's troops were driven away after six hundred Belgian volunteers had lost their lives in fighting in the streets of Brussels; on September 28 de Potter returned from exile and a Provisional Government was set up with de Potter and the Catholic noble Count Felix de Mérode on the Executive Committee. On October 5 the Prince of Orange came again to Brussels hoping to be elected King of Belgium (a solution favoured by King Louis Philippe). On October 10 the Provisional Government appointed a Commission to draw up a Constitution and resolved on elections for a National Congress; and on October 26 the Prince of Orange finally left Brussels. On October 27 troops of the Provisional Government advanced on Antwerp where King William's troops were now commanded by Duke Bernard of Saxe-Weimar; the Belgians fired on the Royalist troops who retired to the citadel; and on October 28 Saxe-Weimar ordered a futile bombardment of the town from the citadel and from ships of war on the Scheldt causing widespread fires and the destruction of many buildings. In November a Conference of the Powers in London decided on non-intervention in Belgium and arranged a truce between the Provisional Government and King William; and the new Belgian National Congress proclaimed the Independence of the Belgian people, the institution of an hereditary monarchy and the exclusion of the House of Orange. In February 1831 the Belgian Congress adopted a constitution described by the historian Pirenne as 'le type le plus complet et le plus pur que l'on puisse imaginer d'une constitution parlementaire et libérale ... un chef d'oeuvre de sagesse politique'; and in June Leopold of Saxe-Coburg, recommended by the Powers, was accepted by the Belgians as the first King of independent Belgium.[1]

When **Joseph Odevaere** (Pl. 882), **Balthasar Paul Ommeganck** (Pl. 876) and **Petrus Johannes Regemorter** reached Paris in August 1815 to reclaim the pictures from the Musée Napoléon, they found passions running high in the Louvre. For the French most violently resented the dispersal of this huge collection which they considered French property legitimately acquired as spoils of war or by agreements like the Treaty of Tolentino which had ceded the Vatican marbles; and they were not in fact then bound by any Treaty obligations to return these works (as this was not imposed on them till November in the Second Treaty of Paris when the emissaries of the various nations had made it a fait accompli). But Wellington had insisted on the restorations in a personal interview with Talleyrand; and when the Belgian emissaries arrived angry groups muttering against the Allies were gathered round the Louvre each day, English, Prussian and Russian troops were required to guard the entrances and more Allied troops were inside the galleries to keep order while the various claimants eventually removed between them some two thousand pictures and statues. The French painters were naturally among those who most bitterly regretted these departures and their feelings were shared by many foreign artists who had come to see the collection while it was still accessible in Paris. Thus the Aberdeen-born miniature painter Andrew Robertson met there Baron Gros, Sir Thomas Lawrence and the sculptor Chantrey, and also Canova sent from Rome to recover the Vatican marbles (including the *Laocoon* and the *Apollo Belvedere*) and other objects from the Papal States; and when the *Medici Venus* was carried away, the artists, he tells us, were moved to tears while a German officer just laughed at them and kissed her. Of the two hundred and seventy pictures taken from Belgium and The Hague in 1794 and 1795 about two hundred were now identified and removed; a few distributed in the new Provincial Museums founded by Napoleon were not recovered; and a few, as noted, had already been returned to Brussels. The emissaries stood by while porters, assisted by British troops, took down the reclaimed paintings; they had them packed for the journey and themselves escorted them to Belgium.

There seems to have been no feeling in France against the Belgians as such and the Belgian artists already established there; even those who had worked for Napoleon and the Imperial court were all able to continue their careers as none of them had concerned themselves with politics. There was however resentment at the choice of **Ommeganck** as emissary to

[1] King William who refused to accept the fait accompli sent military forces into Belgium in August 1831 and his troops were not finally ejected from Antwerp citadel till France and England took action for the purpose in the autumn of 1832 when the French bombarded the citadel with results portrayed by **Ferdinand de Braekeleer** in the picture reproduced here (Pl. 893).

collect the pictures from the Louvre because this artist, the French said truly enough, had especially profited from French Court patronage; and one of his landscapes then on view in a Paris gallery was slashed with a knife by an indignant visitor.

Among the established painters **Jean Louis Demarne** (Pls. 875, 894) sixty-one in 1815, continued his successes at the Salons till he died in 1829; his pictures reproduced here were bought by Louis XVIII, his *Seashore with fishermen* was a Salon exhibit in 1817 and his *Landscape with man and dancing dog* in 1824; and in 1828 Charles X gave him the Legion of Honour. **Pierre Joseph Lafontaine**, fifty-seven in 1815 and associated with **Demarne,** was still painting church and other interiors and also still active in profitable dealing; and he was presumably the 'Lafontaine' (no initial) who exhibited a *S. Pierre de Beauvais* and *Fire in a village near Beauvais* in the Salon of 1817 and an *Interior of Gothic church* (*with candle-light effects*) in 1827. Josephine's former protégé the animal painter **Jean Baptiste Berré** received a medal at the 1817 Salon for an officially commissioned picture *The Duc and Duchesse de Berri, accompanied by ladies in waiting and the professors of the establishment visiting the elephant in the Jardin des Plantes*; in 1821 he sent *A Herd of deer and hinds in a wood* to the Brussels Exhibition, and in 1822 he sent to the Amsterdam Exhibition a *Lioness and serpent*; he had official lodgings in the Jardin des Plantes from 1822 onwards and his works were sought after by leading collectors in Restoration society. **François Kinson** despite his former close association with the Bonapartes (Pls. 884, 885) became Court Painter to the Duc d'Angoulême in 1817; in that year, at forty-six, he exhibited in the Salon his *Belisarius, General of the Emperor Justinian, released from prison where his eyes had been put out, returning home at the moment when his wife Antonina died* (Pl. 881)—a subject taken from Marmontel's 'Bélisaire' and painted in the Neo-Classic manner of **Joseph Suvée** (Pl. 883); in 1819 he sent to the Salon *The Duc d'Angoulême as Grand Admiral* (*with the port of Bordeaux in the background*); in 1820 he sent seven works to the Ghent Exhibition and his Salon exhibits included *The Duchesse de Berri and her infant daughter before a bust of her murdered husband* which so moved Louis XVIII that he appointed him Court Painter and gave him the Legion of Honour; in 1821 he visited Brussels to paint *The Prince of Orange* and the *Princess of Orange*; in 1822 he sent a full-length *Lady Montgomerie* to the London Royal Academy; in 1824 he was appointed Court Painter to Charles X; and he went back to his native Bruges after the July Revolution in 1830. **Antoine Ansiaux,** fifty-one in 1815, again adjusted his production to the climate of patronage around him; he continued to paint portraits and as there was now a vogue for costume-history pictures with subjects taken from the earlier history of France (because Louis XVIII encouraged the idea that France had resumed her normal Bourbon course after the interruption of the Revolution and the Empire) he responded with *Richelieu presenting Poussin to Louis XIII* exhibited in the 1817 Salon; at the same time he appealed to a different taste with a *Renaldo and Armida* followed by a *Sleeping nymph* in 1819; and as the Church and the Jesuits resumed power and incited commissions for the existing Paris churches and some new ones (such as La Madeleine begun in 1804 but not yet completed, Notre Dame de Lorette begun in 1823 and S. Vincent de Paul begun in 1824) **Ansiaux** responded with a series of religious subjects including *The Return of the Prodigal* in 1819, *S. John rebuking Herod* in 1822 and *S. John preaching* in 1824. **Jacques Albert Senave** painted more genre pieces and gave a *Seven Works of Mercy* to the church of his native Loo in 1820; in 1821 he was made Honorary Director of the Ypres Academy, where he had studied; and he gave the Academy on this occasion a costume-history composition *Rembrandt* (*and other artists*) *in his atelier* but he did not return to Ypres and he died in Paris at seventy-one in

1829. **Philip Jacob van Brée** who painted, probably in 1815, his *Atala found by Père Aubry* and exhibited a *Portrait of Louis Ricquier* in the 1816 Salon, took his friend **Louis Ricquier** to Italy that year; he was back in Paris in the twenties and probably painted then his *Queen Blanche with her children*; and he seems to have been in Brussels by 1830 when he painted *The Great fire in the Entrepôt* (*formerly Abbaye de S. Michel*). **Louis Ricquier,** twenty-three in 1815 (and six years younger than **Philip van Brée**) sent his *Fernando Cortez triumphing over Montezuma* to the Salon in 1816; he too came back from Italy in the twenties (after working some time in Antwerp) and he exhibited *Columbus discovering the New World* in 1830. Among the established painters of flowers and fruit and natural history **Henri Joseph Redouté** made drawings for illustrated books through the period. **Pierre Joseph Redouté** published the last volume of *La Famille des Liliacées* in 1816, the first volume of *Les Roses* in 1817, the last volume of *Les Roses* in 1824 and the first volume of the *Choix des Plus Belles Fleurs et des Plus Beaux Fruits*—a selection from what he considered his best drawings—in 1827; he was now patronized by the Duchesse de Berri, he received the Legion of Honour from Charles X in 1825, and he was still working at seventy-one in 1830. **Jan Frans van Dael** (Pl. 886) fifty-one in 1815 was also patronized by the Duchesse de Berri; he spent the summers at his country house where he grew flowers for his pictures; he won a gold medal with a flowerpiece in the Salon of 1819; and he too received the Legion of Honour from Charles X in 1825. **Jan Frans van Eliaerts** (Pl. 888) continued to exhibit in the Salons; he was still working and exhibiting at sixty-nine in 1830 and probably still resident in Paris; and **Martinus Spey** of whom nothing seems known after 1818, when he was still under fifty, may have continued to paint his flowerpieces and still-life with game.

Of Louis David's pupils still in Paris **Albert Jacob Gregorius,** forty-one in 1815, was commissioned to paint *Louis XVIII* and *Charles X* as full-length portraits and he sent them with many other portraits to the Salons in these years; and **François-Joseph Navez** (Pl. 890) twenty-eight in 1815 followed David to Brussels in 1816. David's art school was taken over by Baron Gros who was forty-five in 1816 and had more than three hundred pupils, including a number of Belgians, in this period. Thus **Jodocus Sebastiaen van den Abeele** came to Gros from Ghent at twenty-two in 1819 and painted in Paris *Homer abandoned*, *The Oracle declaring Socrates the wisest of men* (sent from Paris to the Ghent Exhibition in 1820) and *Portrait of the painter Gros* before he left for Rome in 1824. **Henri de Caisne** (or **Decaisne**) of Brussels who had worked under Girodet-Trioson in 1819 and then revisited Brussels, came back to Paris to work under Gros at twenty-one in 1820; he then settled in Paris and exhibited costume-history pictures at the Salons from 1824; he had for some reason a preference for English subjects such as *Murder of the Princes in the Tower* (1824), *Milton dictating 'Paradise Lost' to his daughter* (1828), *Charles I taking leave of his children* (1829) and *Cromwell and his daughter* (1830); he also painted portraits including *Madame Malibran Garcia as Desdemona* sent from Paris to the London Royal Academy in 1830. The Brugeois **Dominique François du Bois (Dubois)** came from Antwerp to work under Gros probably in 1820 at the age of twenty and stayed for some time before returning to Belgium to paint contemporary and costume history. **Charles Louis Saligo** came to Gros from Ghent about 1823 and then settled in Paris where he painted portraits and 'classical' history subjects; he won a prize at twenty-three with his *Briseis taken from the tent of Achilles by Agamemnon's envoys* sent from Paris to the Brussels Exhibition of 1827; and his *Mgr Fallot de Beaumont* probably painted in this period shows the Bishop of Ghent whom Mgr de Broglie superseded in 1807.

Among other newcomers to Paris the topographic draughtsman **Seraphin Vermote,** financed by one of his patrons the Vicomte de Winnzeele, was there for some time to study figure painting at twenty-seven in 1815. **Willem Hendrik Franquinet** came to Paris at thirty-two in 1817 and remained through the period; in 1821 he sent a *Bacchanal* with nine figures to the Brussels Exhibition; his *Henri IV visiting Sully wounded at Ivry*, conforming to the Bourbon costume-history vogue, was also painted before 1830, and for ten years from 1823 he was engaged on a publication called 'La Galerie des Peintres' which appeared in portfolios with lithographed reproductions of pictures by French seventeenth-century painters and other 'Old Masters' and text by the critic V. Chabert. **Jan Baptist van der Hulst,** successful painter of portraits and religious subjects, came from Louvain at twenty-nine in 1819, remained some years, and then left for Rome. The architectural painter **François Vervloet,** who is known to have studied in Paris, was probably there at twenty in 1815; and he was back in his native Malines by 1817. **Charles Brias,** painter later of contemporary history, anecdotic genre and portraits, reached Paris from Malines at twenty-one in 1819 and stayed till 1822 when he left for Brussels taking with him an *Entrée d'une maison à Paris* exhibited in Ghent in 1823. **Pierre Antoine Verlinde** came from Antwerp, perhaps about 1823 when he was twenty-two, and worked for some time with Paulin-Guérin then much in favour as a teacher; he painted portraits for a branch of the Montmorency family, and his *Death of S. Louis* exhibited in Brussels in 1827 was possibly sent there from Paris. The landscape and horse painter **Joseph Jodocus Moerenhout** worked for a year at twenty-four with Horace Vernet in 1825. The Louvainais **François Verheyden** painter later of anecdotic genre pieces came to work under Jérôme Martin Langlois at about twenty about 1826. **Guillaume van Bomberghen** came from Antwerp under twenty about 1826, sent portrait miniatures to the Belgian exhibitions and was still in Paris in 1830. **Gustave Wappers,** soon to be famous as a leader of the Belgian Romantics, visited Paris at twenty-three in 1826; and he was there again in 1829 in the midst of the controversy aroused by Delacroix's *Mort de Sardanapole* (which had been inspired by Byron and exhibited in 1827 and 1828). **Theodor Schaepkens** another Romantic was in Paris at nineteen in 1829 as a pupil of Louis Hersent and stayed till after the July Revolution of 1830; and the remarkable **Antoine Wiertz,** son of a Dinant gendarme, came from Antwerp at twenty-three in 1829, lived there in poverty for three years and was greatly excited by Géricault's *Radeau de la Méduse* which the Louvre had acquired in 1824.

In the French provinces **Augustin van den Berghe** lost his post as professor in the Beauvais art school when the École Centrale was closed at the Restoration, and he then opened a private art school which was much frequented; after about 1825 he signed his pictures 'Van den Berghe père' to avoid confusions with the work of his son Charles Auguste van den Berghe (who was born in Beauvais in 1798 and trained by Girodet-Trioson and Gros); and he was still active at seventy-four in 1830. **Jan Baptist de Jonghe** (Pl. 892) who began as a landscape painter and topographic draughtsman visited France between 1815 and 1820; **Henri van Assche,** landscape painter, visited the Vosges from Brussels in 1818; **Eugène Verboeckhoven** (Pl. 895) travelled in France as a young man before 1824; **Jules Victor Génisson** painter of church and other interiors began a tour in France at twenty-four in 1829; and **Edouard Delvaux,** landscape painter, made a tour the same year. **Michel Ghislain Stapleaux** painter of portraits and costume-history is also known to have travelled in France; and his *S. Vincent de Paul removing a galley slave's chains to his own wrists* was probably painted in Paris before 1830 when he was thirty-one.

In England we find in the first years **Melchior Gommar Tieleman** who soon left for Hanover, **Jan Baptist de Jonghe** (Pl. 892) who was here between 1815 and 1820, and the genre painter **Paul Godefroid Joseph Noël** here for some months in the summer of 1820. **Eugène Verboeckhoven** (Pl. 895), who visited London at twenty-seven in 1826, drew animals in the Royal Menagerie in the Tower and may have had access also to George IV's menagerie at Sandpit-Gate, Windsor and to the newly founded Zoological Gardens in the Regent's Park (though these were not open to the public until 1828). **François Simonau**, who had worked under Gros in Paris as related in my last chapter, reached London from Belgium at thirty-two in 1815 and stayed on, living first in the East End and later in Greek Street, Soho; taken up by Sir Thomas Lawrence and introduced by him to London society he acquired a considerable practice as a portrait painter and became known as 'The Flemish Murillo'; he exhibited portraits at the Royal Academy from 1818 onwards and he also exhibited at the British Institution; his *Jewish Rabbi* was in the Academy in 1822, his *Polish Jew* in 1823, his *Monsieur J. Ancot, Composer and Professor of the Pianoforte* in 1824; and his *Young Italian, in tall hat, playing a hand-organ* shown in the British Institution in 1829 explains the Murillo sobriquet. **Jules Victor Génisson** (who exhibited in the British Institution in 1851) is said to have been here between 1829 and 1834. **Louis Haghe** son of a Tournai architect was in London at about twenty by about 1826; he was soon launched as a watercolour draughtsman of architectural and genre subjects and as lithographer and publisher of lithographs; he continually travelled but made London his headquarters and he was later the President of the New Water Colour Society (where he began to exhibit in 1835).

In Central Europe **Willem Hendrik Franquinet** went to Frankfort from Maestricht in 1816 and painted there a *S. John in the Wilderness* commissioned by Baron von Aretin (then Bavarian representative in Frankfort); in 1817 he was expelled for some reason by the Frankfort Guild and he then established himself successfully in Paris. **Melchior Gommar Tieleman** was in Hanover from some time after 1816 as Court Painter to the Governor Adolphus Frederick, Duke of Cambridge, and he seems to have stayed till 1829 when he went back to his native Lierre. **François Vervloet** painted interiors and other views of churches on the Rhine between 1819 and 1822; **Louis Adrien Moons** was in Munich and Stuttgart on his way back from Italy in 1823; **Philip Jacob van Brée** made a tour in Germany in 1827; and **Eugène Verboeckhoven** (Pl. 895) was there in 1828.

In Italy **Martin Verstappen** forty-two in 1815 was very successful in this period as Professor in the Accademia di San Luca in Rome and a prominent figure in the Flemish colony; he now sent his views of the environs of Rome and picturesque paintings of Roman churches and monuments to exhibitions in Belgium and Holland, and his local patrons included Ferdinand I of the Two Sicilies and many foreign notables visiting Rome. **Charles Spruyt** came to Rome from Ghent at forty-six in 1815 and may have painted there his *Disciples at Emmaus*; but he was chiefly occupied with picturesque architectural pieces, mostly interiors, including *The interior of S. Silvestro-in-capite* and an *Interior of a grotto in a Franciscan monastery*; he returned to Belgium and settled in Brussels in 1821. **Henri van Assche** visited Italy from Brussels at the end of 1815 and painted a *View of Perugia and Lake Trasimene* in 1816. **Pieter van Hanselaere** arrived at thirty in 1816 with his scholarship from the Ghent Society for the Encouragement of Art, and was soon elected member of the Accademia on Canova's recommendation; he had commissions for portraits including *Baron Steengracht* and *M. Reinholds, Netherlands Ambassador to the Holy See*, he made genre studies including a *Roman beggar* exhibited in the Palazzo Caffarelli in 1819 and a *Roman woman in prayer*, and in 1820 he painted his *Susanna and the elders* reproduced here (Pl. 891); in Rome he seems also to have painted a *S. Sebastian* before moving to Naples probably in 1823 after the Austrian intervention; he became a member of the Naples Academy and Court Painter to Ferdinand I; he provided altarpieces for new churches then being built in Naples and painted many portraits there including *Princess Scylla* and *Count Ascoli*; after 1825 he painted *King Francis I* and *Queen Isabella* and he returned to Ghent in 1829. Other new arrivals were **Philip van Brée** and **Louis Ricquier** who came together from Paris aged thirty and twenty-four in 1816 and left together in 1819; **Philip van Brée** painted his *Procession in S. Peter's* and *A Cardinal in his villa* on this Roman visit (and he seems to have been back in Rome in 1832 when he painted *The youth of Sixtus V* much admired by some present day critics); **Louis Ricquier** painted a *View of Naples* on this visit (and he too seems to have gone back to Rome about 1832 and painted there *A family of brigands* in 1833). **François-Joseph Navez** (Pl. 890) reached Rome at thirty in 1817 with a scholarship from the Brussels Society for the Encouragement of Art and he stayed in Italy till 1821; he impressed many artists in Rome and his friends there included Ingres (who was thirty-seven in 1817 with *La grande odalisque* commissioned by Caroline Murat in 1814 still in his studio and about to paint *Christ giving the keys to S. Peter* for S. Trinita dei Monti, *Pius VII in the Sistine Chapel* and *Roger delivering Angelica*). **Navez** was also friendly with the French painter Léopold Robert who arrived at twenty-four in 1818 (trained like Ingres and **Navez** himself by Louis David) and started a vogue for genre pictures featuring Italian banditti and their families studied from life in a concentration camp near the Thermae of Diocletian. In Rome **Navez** painted *Hagar and Ishmael in the Desert* in 1820 and sent it to the Brussels Society in return for his scholarship, and in 1821 he sent to the Brussels Exhibition his *Elisha raising the Shunammite woman's son*, a composition with ten life-size figures which was bought by the Government; at the same time, influenced by Léopold Robert, he painted some genre studies of Italian types and a *Fortune teller with a family of Italian brigands*, a composition with four life-size half-length figures. **Ferdinand de Braekeleer** (Pl. 893) was in Rome with his scholarship from the Antwerp Academy by 1819 when he was twenty-seven; he painted there *Faustulus showing Romulus and Remus to his wife* which he sent to the Antwerp Exhibition in 1819 and *Esau seeking his father's blessing* sent to the Amsterdam Exhibition in 1822, he also painted a *Murder of Abel*, a *Magdalene*, a *Holy Family* and probably some genre subjects and landscapes; and he went back to Antwerp in 1823. **Louis Adriaen Moons** came from Antwerp as a widely travelled and experienced artist at fifty-one in 1820 and stayed till 1823; he painted in Rome *The Disciples at Emmaus* for Antwerp, S. Jacques and sent it to the Antwerp Exhibition in 1822; he also painted there *Aeschylus writing* sent to the Malines Exhibition the same year and *Isaac blessing Jacob* sent to the Ghent Exhibition in 1823. **Mattheus van Brée** was also in Rome exceptionally late as he came on a visit in 1821 at forty-eight and then only stayed some months; he was entertained there by his former pupil **Ferdinand de Braekeleer** (as **Philip van Brée** had already left); he was fêted everywhere as a celebrated artist, received the Cross of the Golden Spur from Pius VII (who sat to him for his portrait at seventy-nine) and before leaving he painted or made studies for his small picture *The Tomb of Nero with lazzaroni and musicians* exhibited in Antwerp in 1830. **François Vervloet** reached Rome after his tour on the Rhine in 1822; he was then twenty-seven and had a scholarship (probably from the Society for the Encouragement of Art in his native Malines); in 1823 he visited Subiaco, Naples and Trani making studies of churches; in 1824 he painted his *Interior of S. Peter's, Rome, looking towards the High Altar* which was sent to the Hague Exhibition and bought by the Government; after 1825, with Naples as headquarters, he made expeditions to Apulia and Calabria; and in 1826 he painted his *Naples, Sta. Maria la Nuova*. **Jan Baptist Lodewyck Maes (Maes-Canini)** came to Rome with a scholarship at twenty-eight in 1822; he sent a *S. Sebastian* and a *Roman woman in prayer* to the Antwerp Exhibition in 1823; his *Good Samaritan* sent to the Amsterdam Exhibition in 1825 was bought by the Government; he visited Ghent in he painted a *Holy Family* for Ghent, S. Michel, in 1827 and other pictures for Ghent churches 1826; in 1827 after marrying a daughter of the engraver Canini he settled in Rome where in the following years; (and after 1830 he had success with his *Roman woman with her child in a church* and similar genre pieces). **Pierre François Charles Leroy** (known as **Leroy Fils**) seems to have been in Rome at over twenty about 1825 and to have followed Léopold Robert in painting banditti; an *Italian shepherd caressing a lamb* by him is also recorded. **Jodocus Sebastiaen van den Abeele** reached Rome from Paris at twenty-seven in 1824; his *Orpheus after the death of Eurydice*, *A young Greek artist in his studio*, and *Anthea with her maidens* were probably painted there, and he is said to have painted for the Ara-coeli monastery; he gave drawing lessons in Rome to Prince Louis Napoleon (later Napoleon III) and he was still there in 1830. **Jan Baptist van der Hulst** was in Rome at thirty-six by 1826 having come directly from Paris or after a period in Belgium; he probably painted both portraits and religious subjects in Rome and returned to his native Louvain after visiting Naples, Florence, Bologna and Venice in 1827. The Malineois **Charles van Beveren** was in Rome at twenty-one in 1830 and he painted there *The Malineois sculptor Louis Royer seated in his studio* and *Carolina Kerst, wife of Louis Royer seated by a table, wearing a straw hat*.

At home in Belgium the return of the national pictures from the Musée Napoléon in 1815 was a stimulus to the public and also, of course, to certain artists. The pictures reached Brussels in ten large waggons with military escort at the end of November and were ceremoniously received by the Mayor who set aside a group belonging to the King and another group belonging to the churches and claimed the rest, including all taken from the suppressed religious houses, as national property for the national Brussels museum. But the King, apprised by the Antwerp Society for the Encouragement of Art, gave formal orders that such pictures must be sent to the central town of the region from which they had been taken. Thus in the event the **van Eycks'** *Altarpiece of the Mystic Lamb* (Pls. 9, 12) went back to Ghent, **Jan van Eyck's** *Van der Paele altarpiece* (Pl. 19) to Bruges and the *S. Anne altarpiece* (Pl. 207) by **Quinten Massys** to Louvain. Some forty paintings went to Antwerp where they were welcomed at the Porte S. Georges by **Herreyns** as Director of the Academy and by a long procession of civic dignitaries; the waggons were dragged by students through cheering crowds to the Town Hall; there were fireworks in the evening; **Petrus Johannes van Regemorter** and his son **Ignatius van Regemorter** were charged with the restoration and conditioning of some damaged works; and the whole series was shown to the public in Antwerp Museum in 1816.

The presence of Louis David in Brussels was another stimulus from his arrival in January 1816 (bringing with him his *Death of Marat*) till his death at seventy-seven in December 1825. There was the influence, too, of David's former pupil the Lyonnais Philippe Hennequin, painter of a celebrated *Orestes pursued by the Furies* and an avowed anti-Bourbon who thought it prudent to work from 1815 in Belgium where he succeeded **Cornelis Cels** as Director of the Tournai Academy in 1827 and had **Louis Gallait** as his pupil. Some artists also benefited from the presence of François Rude, a favourite sculptor of Napoleon and his marshals, who took refuge in Brussels in 1815, made a portrait bust of King William and a series of reliefs (*Meleager hunting* and *Scenes from the life of Achilles*) for Tervueren castle and returned in 1827 to Paris (where he made *Le Départ* for the Arc de Triomphe between 1833 and 1836). David was soon surrounded by his former pupils led by **Joseph Odevaere** (Pl. 882) and **Joseph Paelinck,** both now established in Brussels, and many young men came as new pupils or seeking his advice or assistance. **Odevaere** painted a full-length portrait of him standing in his studio, and also a picture titled *Louis David refusing to paint the Duke of Wellington* and wrote of his visits to the studio; 'Je voyais David le plus souvent que je pouvais et quand j'avais passé quelques heures avec lui, je rapportais chaque fois de ces entretiens de nouvelles lumières. . . .' **François-Joseph Navez** (Pl. 890), back from Paris, also painted David and signed the portrait 'Navez discipulus faciebat' at thirty in 1817 before leaving for Rome; and when a banquet was given in his honour on his return from Rome in 1822 he took from his head the crown of laurels given him by his admirers and placed it on the head of his former master who was present. The Louvainais **Henri van der Haert**, who had probably already worked with him in Paris, was David's pupil in Brussels from 1817 when he was twenty-seven (and also working, for sculpture, under Rude). The Gantois **Jodocus Sebastiaen van den Abeele** was David's pupil at twenty-one in 1818 before going to Paris with an introduction from him to Gros; **Michel Ghislain Stapleaux** was in his atelier probably from 1817 at eighteen and also stayed till he went to France; **Henri de Coene,** painter later of indoor and outdoor genre, was there at about the same age at about the same time; **Henri de Caisne** though not it would seem his pupil had an introduction from him to Gros in 1820; **Marie Adelaide Kindt,** later successful with costume-history pictures, was his pupil at nineteen from 1823; **Henri Voordecker** was encouraged by him to turn from landscape to outdoor genre and portrait painting; and the Louvainais **François Verheyden** was his pupil at about eighteen probably by 1824 and may have met in his studio the French painter Jérôme Martin Langlois who came that year from Paris to paint David's portrait and had **Verheyden** later as his pupil. David wished to be buried in France but Charles X's Government refused permission and **Odevaere** replied by opening a subscription for a monument to be placed on his tomb in Brussels and by proclaiming in a manifesto: 'David est mort au milieu de nous. . . . Que le ministère de France lui accorde ou non un peu de terre, refusée à Molière, à Voltaire, à tant d'autres grands hommes, c'est parmi nous que ces cendres précieuses doivent être honorées, doivent rester à jamais. C'est nous qui lui devons, après de nobles funérailles, un mausolée.dépositaire de nos regrets et de notre reconnaissance.'

The Belgian artists were also encouraged by King William's zeal as collector of Old Masters and as patron of contemporary painters. The King's family pictures recovered from Paris were sent to The Hague and arranged in the Mauritshuis; and when his Government opened this mansion as a museum in 1821 the public saw there the *Salome with the head of John the Baptist* (Pl. 265) by **Jacob Cornelisz van Oostsanen,** the *Interior of a collector's gallery* (Pl. 773) by **Gonzales Coques,** the *Kitchen Scene with swan* (Pl. 678) by **David Teniers** and a great many excellent Dutch pictures including Paul Potter's *The young bull* and Terborch's *The message.* The King moreover bought in this period and added to the Mauritshuis collection a fifteenth-century *Lamentation* (presumed the work of **Rogier van der Weyden** by some modern students), **Gillis van Tilborgh's** *Family group round a dining table* (Pl. 763), Vermeer's *View of Delft* (acquired at auction for three thousand seven hundred florins), Rembrandt's *The Anatomy lesson of Professor Tulp* (which cost him thirty-two thousand florins), a signed *Magdalene repentant* by the seventeenth-century Spaniard Mateo Cereso and some Italian pictures; and he also bought for the gallery, or caused his Government to buy, a hundred and forty-three works by living Dutch and Belgian painters. In Amsterdam he reorganized Louis Napoleon's Musée Royal, renamed it the Rijksmuseum and bought for it, or caused his Government to buy, some sixty pictures by living painters who again included a number of Belgians. In 1828 he ordered the installation of the Welgelegen Pavilion in Haarlem as a Museum of Contemporary Painting; and all the acquisitions of pictures by living Belgians made in his reign were eventually transferred to it. He bought and gave to Antwerp Museum Titian's *Jacopo Pesaro, Bishop of Paphos presented to S. Peter by Pope Alexander VI* which had once belonged to Charles I of England. He was also an active patron of the Brussels Museum (which procured the *Allegory of Abundance* (Pl. 545) by **Jordaens** from a private collection in 1827); he acquired *The Unjust Judgement of the Emperor Otho* (Pl. 67) and the *Ordeal by Fire* (Pl. 69) by **Dirk Bouts,** and **Bernaert van Orley's** *Job Triptych* (Pl. 257) and had them placed in the Brussels residence of the Prince of Orange. He encouraged and sometimes cooperated with the Societies for the Encouragement of Art which now existed in Amsterdam, Ghent, Brussels, Antwerp, Malines and other places. In 1818 he established the Order of the Netherlands Lion for civil merit and bestowed it in the following years on **Andreas Cornelis Lens** (Pl. 871), **Joseph François Ducq, Joseph Odevaere** (Pl. 882), **Balthasar Paul Ommeganck** (Pl. 876), **Mattheus van Brée, François Kinson** (Pls. 881, 884, 885) and **Joseph Paelinck.** In 1820 he provided an extra stipend for **François-Joseph Navez** (Pl. 890) to prolong his stay in Rome; in 1821 he gave a small scholarship to **Antoine Wiertz** who was brought to his notice as a talented beginner then fifteen; and in 1822 he provided the Rome scholarship for **Jan Baptist Lodewyck Maes (Maes-Canini)** referred to above. He employed **Henri van der Haert** to paint grisaille decorations imitating bas-reliefs in the eighteenth-century Flemish tradition at Tervueren and in his Brussels Palace; and he is said to have employed **Gustave Adolph Diez** (a pupil of **Odevaere**) at Tervueren. He ordered portraits of himself and Queen Wilhelmina from **Joseph Paelinck** in 1815 and sent versions to The Hague, Berlin and London; he also commissioned or authorized portraits of himself by **Mattheus van Brée, Joseph François Ducq, Odevaere, Navez, Désiré Donny, Charles Pierre Verhulst, Jan Baptist van der Hulst** and **Cornelis Cels;** and we can note here that **Eugène Verboeckhoven** (Pl. 895) began his career in 1820 with a small picture titled *King William I on horseback returning from a military review near a wood on the outskirts of Ghent.*

Like Louis XVIII King William cherished the idea of linking his reign to the period before the Revolution and the Empire, which in his case meant linking it to the earlier history of the House of Orange; and propaganda subjects embodying this idea were painted by some of his Court Painters who thus launched a vogue for costume-history pictures like the similar vogue in France. His chief Court Painters were **Joseph François Ducq, Odevaere, Mattheus van Brée,** and **Jan Baptist van der Hulst.** Of these **Joseph François Ducq,** back from Paris and Director of the Academy in his native Bruges, was given the appointment in 1815; he restored **Memlinc's** *S. John Altar* (Pl. 111) in the Hôpital S. Jean, probably at the King's instigation, in 1817; he was working in 1820 and died at sixty-seven in 1829 after suffering a stroke a year or two before. **Odevaere** (Pl. 882), appointed at about forty in 1815, had been introduced to the King in 1814 when he submitted a drawing for a symbolic propaganda subject *The Union of Utrecht 1579*; after his return from the Louvre with the King's collection he settled in Brussels and painted for the King *The Prince of Orange wounded at the Battle of Waterloo* and this was followed by *Prince Maurice at the Battle of Nieuport 1600* as a companion composition; in 1823-24 he converted his earlier drawing *The Union of Utrecht* to a painting called *The Foundation of the Principality of Orange 1579* which was twenty-four feet by sixteen and was hung by the King in his Brussels Palace. In 1826 **Odevaere** painted *The Last Defenders of Missolonghi April 22, 1826* which was exhibited in Ghent and bought by the State; in 1829 he defied the prevailing political climate by producing a huge panorama *The Inauguration of William I as King of the United Netherlands in Brussels in 1815* which he exhibited to the public in a hall rented from the Messageries, defending this popularizing gesture by the precedent of David who had shown his *Sabines* on the Paris Boulevards; and he was still loyal to his patron when he died in 1830. **Mattheus van Brée** was appointed Court Painter at forty-four in 1817 and painted that year *The patriotism of P. A. van der Werff, Burgomaster of Leyden 1576* commissioned by the King and given by him to the Town Hall in Leyden; this was followed in 1818 by *William of Orange urging the release of the Bishops of Bruges and Ypres and of the Catholic nobles imprisoned in Ghent by Hembijzi and the anti-Catholic faction in 1577*— the propaganda picture already mentioned which the King commissioned and gave to the city of Ghent; and in or after 1826 he too painted *The Last Day of the Missolonghi siege*. **Jan Baptist van der Hulst** became Court Painter about 1828; like **Odevaere** he remained faithful to his patron; and in 1830 he settled at The Hague where he was eventually confirmed in his post by William II. Some of these painters and others were patronized by members of the Royal Family. Thus pictures by **Joseph François Ducq** and others were bought by the Prince of Orange. **Joseph Paelinck** was Court Painter to Queen Wilhelmina from 1815, and the Queen had a painting by **François-Joseph Navez** in her oratory. **Charles Pierre Verhulst** who died at forty-five in 1820 had then been Court Painter for some years to the Prince of Orange and had painted his portrait and that of his brother Prince Frederick. **Peter van Huffel** was Court Painter to the Princess of Orange from 1819 and supplied her with devotional pictures eventually placed in her oratory in The Hague. **Cornelis Cels** painted *The Dowager Princess of Orange* (the King's mother). **Odevaere** painted *The Prince of Orange in Hussar's uniform* in 1817; **François Kinson** (Pls. 881, 884, 885) visited Brussels from Paris to paint *The Prince of Orange* in 1821; and a picture titled *William II as Prince of Orange giving a standard to the Garde Nationale of Bois-le-Duc* was painted either before or after 1830 for Bois-le-Duc Town Hall by **Dominique François du Bois** Director of the Bois-le-Duc Academy from 1828.

Current political and military events were recorded by a number of artists. **Jean Joseph Vervloet** Professor in Malines Academy at twenty-eight in 1818 composed *The Prince of Schwartzenberg bringing the news of the Battle of Leipzig to the Allied Princes*. **Joseph Odevaere's** panorama *The Inauguration of King William* (in which he was possibly assisted by his pupil **Gustave Diez**) has already been referred to; and **Pierre Jean Baptiste Leroy,** who had made a watercolour of Napoleon's entry into Brussels in 1810, made a series of drawings *Fêtes in Brussels for the Entry and Inauguration of King William I in 1815* which were engraved and much collected. Engravings of **Odevaere's** composition *The Prince of Orange wounded at the Battle of Waterloo* were also widely distributed and the picture itself was shown at special exhibitions in Ghent, Brussels and other places, the 'gate money' being given to charitable causes. A large watercolour *The Battle of Waterloo at seven in the evening* by **Leroy** won a medal in the 1816 Ghent Exhibition and was later exhibited in Brussels and London; **Constantin Coene's** *The Battle of Waterloo* was exhibited in London and bought by the Prince Regent; **Joseph de Cauwer** painted *Belgian humanity; an episode of the Battle of Waterloo* at thirty-eight in 1817. In the same year **Charles Brias** aged nineteen sent *General Chassé driving back Napoleon's Old Guard at*

Waterloo to the Ghent Exhibition; and pictures titled *The Battle of Waterloo* were also painted by **Joseph Paelinck** and **Jean François Thys**. The Prince of Orange was much liked in Belgium from Waterloo onwards and his popularity was increased or exploited by the painters. Thus **Jan Baptist Maes (Maes-Canini)** won a prize offered by the Malines Society for the Encouragement of Art at twenty-two in 1816 with an *Allegory on the marriage of the Prince of Orange with Grand Duchess Anna Paulowna*; **Joseph François** composed an *Allegory on the Birth of the Crown Prince of Orange* in 1817; **Peter van Huffel** exhibited in Ghent *The Prince of Orange inspecting the Ghent manufactures*; and **Mattheus van Brée** painted *The Prince of Orange visiting victims of the flood in the Amsterdam orphanage* (*Aalmoezeniers Weeshuis*) *in 1825*. **Maes-Canini,** who was evidently out to earn favours by propaganda service, won a prize offered by the Netherlands Institute with his *Allegory on the Union of the Dutch and Belgian Schools of Painting* exhibited in Ghent in 1818, and in 1819 he won a prize, given by the Antwerp Society for the Encouragement of Art, with his *Vaccination Station* presumably a propaganda piece related to a new Belgian law about vaccination (which had just been made compulsory in several German States). In 1817 **François Vervloet** made his reputation at twenty-two when he exhibited *The interior of Malines Cathedral with the installation of the Prince-Bishop Mgr de Méan as Archbishop.* The Greek Revolution inspired pictures by **Odevaere** and **Mattheus van Brée** as mentioned above. The street fighting in Brussels and other events in the September Revolution of 1830 were recorded in a number of pictures—mostly painted a few years later and so strictly speaking outside the limits of my story. **Joseph Paelinck's** pupil **Charles Picqué** began in 1830 his *Meeting of the Provisional Government on Sept 24, 1830* (exhibited in Ghent in 1832). **Joseph Lodewyck Geirnaert,** teacher in Ghent Academy by the end of the period, painted *Belgium before the 1830 rising* and *Belgium after the 1830 rising* and a *Signing the petition* which was lithographed and widely distributed. **Edouard de Biefve,** pupil in Brussels of **Joseph Paelinck** from 1828 when he was twenty, exhibited in 1830 a *Masaniello 1647* inspired by the historic performance of Auber's opera which launched the Revolution as noted. Certain painters, **Charles Brias** and **Eugène Verboeckhoven** (Pl. 895) for example, are known to have been involved in the actual fighting; and there are portraits of **Verboeckhoven**, of **François Bossuet** (painter of architectural pieces who was thirty-two in 1830), **Alexandre Joseph Thomas** (twenty in 1830 and later a painter of dramatic religious pictures) and **Henri Leys** (then fifteen) in the famous *Episode of the September Days in 1830* which was exhibited by **Gustave Wappers** in 1835 and purported to depict a group of insurgents receiving the Proclamation of the Provisional Government on the Grand' Place near the Brussels Town Hall after a day of fighting. *The death of Count Frédéric de Mérode 1830* was painted by **Théodor Schaepkens** who was twenty in 1830 and back from Paris in time to witness and perhaps take part in the Revolution. The same subject was painted by **Ferdinand de Braekeleer** who also painted *Fire in Antwerp 1830* and *Antwerp citadel after the bombardment of 1832* (Pl. 893).

The popularity of the Orangist costume-history pictures led the Court Painters to seek further subjects from the earlier periods and, as other painters followed their example, there was a big increase in costume-history painting all through the period and also during the first decades after 1830. I have already referred to works in this category produced in Paris by **Antoine Ansiaux, Philip van Brée, Louis Ricquier, Henri de Caisne** and **Willem Franquinet** and I must add here some examples painted in Belgium. Thus **Charles Spruyt,** in Brussels from 1821, exhibited *John Duke of Brabant proclaiming the innocence of his imprisoned sister* and sold it to the Government in 1826. **Louis Ricquier,** in Antwerp for some years between his return from Rome in 1819 and his second departure for Paris, painted, probably at that time, *Francis of Borselen taking leave of Jacqueline of Bavaria before starting out to hunt in 1432* and *Jacqueline of Bavaria surrendering her domains*; and 'mediaeval' subjects were painted later by **Theodor Schaepkens**, the Gantois **Félix de Vigne** (pupil of **Joseph Paelinck** in Brussels in this period) and **François de Marneffe**. Among subjects connected with the struggle against Spain **Louis Ricquier** painted *The surrender of Brill to the Beggars of the Sea*; **Mattheus van Brée's** *The patriotism of Burgomaster van der Werff at the Siege of Leyden in 1575* already mentioned was painted in 1816; and another composition on this subject with fifty life-size figures launched a wide reputation for **Gustave Wappers** at twenty-seven in 1830. **Ferdinand de Braekeleer** painted *The Patriotism of the Antwerp Magistrates in 1576* soon after his return from Italy (and later a huge composition *The Spanish Fury in Antwerp* which was bought by the city of Antwerp). **Antonis van Bedaff**, who was Director of the Art School in Bois-le-Duc in the twenties and died there at forty-two in 1829, produced *The Meeting of the States General at Dordrecht in 1572* and *The Compromise of the Nobles in 1566* both bought by the Government; and *The Compromise of the Nobles* was painted later by **Edouard de Biefve**. **Mattheus van Brée** painted *Count Egmont comforted by Bishop Trost*; **Antonis van Bedaff** a *Last Meeting of William of Orange and Count Egmont*, acquired by the Government; **Edouard de Biefve** *The Countess of Egmont begging for the release of her husband* and *Alva at the execution of Counts Egmont and Hoorn*. **Constantin Fidèle Coene**, Professor in the Brussels Academy at forty in 1820, composed and lithographed *Prince William of Orange swearing vengeance for the death of Count Hoorn*; **Joseph Geirnaert** contributed *The arrest of Count Egmont*; **Marie Adelaide Kindt** won a prize at the Ghent Academy at twenty-two in 1826 with *Count Egmont taking a last farewell from his wife*; **Petrus Kremer,** twenty-nine in 1830, painted *The Duke of Alva handing to the Bishop of Ypres the death sentence on Counts Egmont and Hoorn* and *Count van der Marck swearing vengeance for the deaths of Egmont and Hoorn* which was bought by the Government; (and **Louis Gallait**, twenty in 1830, painted his celebrated *Last honours to the decapitated Egmont and Hoorn* some twenty years later). **Marie Adelaide Kindt** followed her early success on the 'Egmont and Hoorn' theme with other costume-history pieces including *Queen Elizabeth deciding on the death of Mary Stuart* exhibited in Brussels in 1827 and bought by the Government, *Melancthon foretelling the future of Prince William of Orange* exhibited in Ghent in 1828 and also bought by the Government, *Mary Stuart at Loch Leven* (a moonlight scene) exhibited in Ghent in 1829 and *Francis I and Eleanor of Austria* exhibited in 1830. Among 'New World' costume-history subjects **Louis Ricquier** painted *Christopher Columbus at the Court of Ferdinand and Isabella* in 1822, **Philip van Brée** exhibited a *Captain Barents with his companions at sunrise in Nova Zembla 1594* in 1828, and **Petrus Kremer** painted *Captain Heemskerck meditating on his plan for the Nova Zembla venture*.

Large numbers of pictures illustrating episodes in the lives of the painters of the past—a sub-division of the costume-history category—were produced in this period and the following decades. Early examples suggest that the mode began as an aspect of the link-up with Pre-Revolution-and-Empire history encouraged by the Bourbons in France and by King William in the Netherlands; for in Paris, as noted, **Antoine Ansiaux** painted his *Richelieu presenting Poussin to Louis XIII* in 1817, and in Belgium in 1821 **Jean François Thys** provided a political link up with Orangist history in his *Daniel Seghers while painting a garland round a picture of the Virgin is presented with a golden palette brought him by Thomas Willeboirts as a gift from Prince Frederick Henry of Orange*. The painters generally chose anecdotes related by the early biographers but they sometimes invented scenes and brought together people in non-historical conjunctions; the *Rembrandt and other artists in his studio*, for example, sent from Paris to Ypres by **Jacques Albert Senave** in 1821, depicted an imaginary birthday luncheon in Rembrandt's studio with **David Teniers**, Jan Steen, **Brouwer** and **Craesbeeck** as the most conspicuous guests, and models dressed as Anthony and Cleopatra for a picture then in hand. **Rubens** and **Van Dyck** were, of course, obvious choices for such pictures. Thus **Louis Ricquier** painted *Rubens presenting Adriaen Brouwer to his wife* exhibited in Amsterdam in 1824 and bought by the Government, **Ferdinand de Braekeleer** contributed *Rubens painting Le Chapeau de Paille*; and **Mattheus van Brée** *Rubens painting Marie de Médicis, Rubens introduced to Justus Lipsius by Madame Moretus* and, in 1827, the ten-foot high *Death of Rubens* bought by King William and given by him to the Antwerp Museum. After 1830 *Rubens painting in his garden surrounded by his family* and *Van Dyck taking leave of Rubens* were contributed by **Philip van Brée**, and **Petrus Kremer** painted *Rubens and his wife calling on Daniel Seghers*, **Jean François Thys** *Rubens visiting Van Dyck at Saventhem while Van Dyck was painting Anna van Ophem* and **Edouard Biefve** *Rubens in London*. In 1827 **Gustave Wappers** then twenty-four exhibited in The Hague his *Van Dyck making love to the peasant girl who was acting as his model in Saventhem* which was bought by the Government (and would rank high today in any list of ludicrous pictures in public museums); later **Marie Adelaide Kindt** painted *Van Dyck showing his picture of S. Martin dividing his cloak to the peasant girl at Saventhem*; and before or after 1830 **Petrus Kremer** painted *The peasant girl of Saventhem weeping for the departure of Van Dyck* and *Van Dyck on his deathbed*. Other Flemish painters recalled in such pictures either before 1830 or in the following decades were **Teniers, Jan (Velvet) Brueghel, Craesbeeck, Memlinc** and **Hubert van Eyck**; but rather strangely despite the material provided by van Mander I have found no **Pieter Bruegel** episodes. Among the Dutchmen I have found Jan Steen, Paul Potter, Jan van Huysum and Rembrandt as noted; and among the Italians Antonello da Messina, Leonardo da Vinci, Raphael and Francesco Francia. Thus **Ignatius van Regemorter** exhibited *Jan Steen sending out his son to sell his pictures* in Amsterdam in 1828 and sold it to the Government and in the same year he exhibited in the London Royal Academy a picture titled *Jan Steen having exhausted his finances and the contents of his cellar by his generosity to his fellow artists, takes down his sign, ceases to sell beer and wine, and resumes his profession of painter while Frans van Mieris offers his disconsolate wife a portion of the last bottle*; he also painted *Jan Steen's marriage, Jan Steen painting the sign for his tavern and showing it to his wife for her approval, The baker and painter Joos van Craesbeeck putting the love and fidelity of his wife to the test;* and in 1832 he exhibited in Ghent his *Rembrandt painting his monkey in a family portrait group* which illustrates the following passage in Houbraken's chapter on Rembrandt: 'At one time Rembrandt had a commission for a large portrait group of a man and his wife and children. When the picture was half-finished his pet monkey died, and as there was no other canvas at hand he painted the corpse of the monkey on the canvas containing the group. His patrons quite naturally refused to have a disgusting dead monkey in their family picture. But Rembrandt was so passionately attached to the creature that he refused to remove its portrait and kept the canvas which subsequently served for a long time as a partition in the studio where his pupils worked.' **Petrus Kremer** painted *Jan Brueghel in his studio, Paul Potter painting from nature, Jan van Huysum in his studio* and *David Teniers drawing a village fair from life*; and **Louis Ricquier** *Queen Christina of Sweden visiting the studio of David Teniers*. **Joseph François Ducq** exhibited in 1820

Antonello da Messina in Jan van Eyck's studio (an episode recorded by Vasari but considered unlikely by most present-day historians). **Joseph Geirnaert's** pupil, the Brugeois **Edouard Wallays,** seventeen in 1830, painted in one of the following decades *Memlinc at work on the S. Ursula shrine as a gift of gratitude to the Hôpital S. Jean.* **Geirnaert** himself produced *Albert Dürer accompanied by his wife and maidservant visiting the tomb of Hubert van Eyck in Ghent, S. Jean*; and he also painted *Leonardo da Vinci completing his portrait of La Gioconda* which was bought by the Government. **Joseph Odevaere** painted a *Triumph of Cimabue* in 1821 and exhibited in Brussels before 1830 his *Raphael introduced by Bramante to Pope Julius II*; and **Charles Spruyt** painted in 1829 *Francesco Francia painter of Bologna dying at the sight of a picture by his friend Raphael* illustrating Vasari's story that Francia saw Raphael's *S. Cecilia* sent from Rome to a church in Bologna and died of chagrin at recognizing his own inferiority as an artist. Episodes in the lives of Netherlandish poets of the past formed another sub-division in the costume-history category. Thus **Mattheus van Brée** painted *Johannes Secundus presented to Charles V* and **Geirnaert** *Johannes Secundus reading his poems to his mistress* which was bought by the Government.

Mythologies and other classical subjects were called forth as before by the Academies which still habitually chose them for scholarship competitions, and by the new Societies for the Encouragement of Art which gave prizes for them in the exhibitions. In Antwerp the Academy's subject for the Rome scholarship in 1821 was *Alexander and Diogenes*; in 1823, when **Gustave Wappers** aged twenty unsuccessfully competed, the subject was *The Departure of Coriolanus*; in 1832, when **Anton Wiertz** won the scholarship at twenty-six, the subject was *Scipio Africanus receiving back his son from the hands of the ambassadors of King Antiochus*; (and **Wiertz** himself, strangely enough, was to choose *Greeks and Trojans fighting for the body of Patroclus* as his theme when he set out to rival Géricault's *Radeau de la Méduse* in 1835). In Antwerp **Mattheus van Brée** as leading Professor in the Academy and a Director from 1827 (after the death at eighty-four of **Herreyns** (Pl. 867)) was an influential mentor for such pictures; **Ferdinand de Braekeleer** was available there for more pieces like his *Faustulus showing Romulus and Remus to his wife* after his return from Rome in 1823; some were probably painted by **Germain Joseph Hallez** Director of the Mons Academy who was made a member of the Antwerp Academy in 1817, and by **Louis Ricquier** whose *Androcles and the Lion* and *Virgil reading the Aeneid to Augustus and Octavia* were recorded in my last chapter; and it was probably in Antwerp before his Italian visit that **Louis Adrien Moons** (whose *Aeschylus writing* has been mentioned) produced his *Alexander and his physician Philippus*. In Brussels the Neo-Classic doctrine lost a life-long champion by the death of **Andreas Cornelis Lens** (Pl. 871) at eighty-three in 1822 (when a body of admirers inscribed on his tombal monument: 'Régénérateur de la Peinture de Belgique et parfait chrétien, il réunit la pratique de toutes les vertus à un talent enchanteur'). His former pupil **Joseph François** fifty-six in 1815 was senior Professor in the Brussels Academy through this period. Louis David's pupil **Joseph Paelinck** Professor in Brussels from 1817 won the Ghent Academy's prize with his *Anthea on the way to Ephesus* which he sold to the Government at thirty-nine in 1820; and he was much acclaimed for his *Psyche in Amor's palace attended by slaves* in 1823. Other Davidian influences in Brussels came from **Odevaere** (Pl. 882) who exhibited in 1820 a *Narcissus*, a *Phaedra confessing her sin to Theseus*, in 1826 a *Devotion of Themistocles and the Athenians to the Freedom of Greece* (bought by the Government at the same time as his *Last Defenders of Missolonghi*) and a *Galatea* in 1827. **François-Joseph Navez** (Pl. 890) built himself a handsome house in the rue Royale where he had many private pupils after his return from Rome in 1822; and he painted there about 1830 a *Hope and Faith* and *The Fountain nymph of Salmacis joined in embrace with Hermaphroditus* both with life-size figures. **Odevaere's** pupil **Gustave Adolph Diez** painted a *Rosecrowned Hebe in the clouds holding a beaker for Jupiter in the guise of an eagle* which was bought by the Government. A *Hebe* was also painted by **Paelinck's** pupil **Charles Picqué** who was thirty-one in 1830; and **Paelinck's** pupil **Edouard de Biefve** began his career in 1828 with a *Telemachus and Eucharis hunting* before turning to costume-history. In Brussels also some classical subjects were possibly painted by **Jean François Thys** whose *Fight between Aeneas and Diomedes* was mentioned in my last chapter; and I must recall here the grisaille decorations painted for Terveuren and the Brussels Palace by David's pupil **Henri van der Haert.** In Bruges **Joseph François Ducq** passed on the tradition of **Joseph Suvée** (Pl. 883) to his pupils in the Bruges Academy and himself painted *The Marriage of Angelica and Medor* in 1820; and the tradition was reinforced there by **François Kinson** (Pl. 881), also it will be remembered a **Suvée** pupil, who returned to his native Bruges from Paris at sixty-nine in 1830. In Louvain **Josse Pierre Geedts** painter of a Homeric subject recorded in my last chapter was Professor in the Academy through this period. In Tournai **Piat Joseph Sauvage** was Director of the Academy till he died at seventy-four in 1818; **Cornelis Cels** (trained it will be remembered by **Lens** and **Suvée** and encouraged by Canova in Rome) became Director at forty-two in 1820 after five years in The Hague where he had painted a *Venus* and a *Sapho* in 1816; and the French exile Philippe Hennequin, successor to **Cels** as Director in 1827, was author of the *Orestes pursued by the Furies* already referred to. In Liège **Joseph Barthélemy Vieillevoye** (who also painted costume-history, genre and religious subjects) produced a *Nymph of Salmacis and Hermaphroditus* at thirty-two in 1830. In Ghent, where **Louis Paul** died at eighty-four in 1817 and **Bernard Paul** at eighty-three in 1820, **Peter van Huffel** was Director of the Academy from 1815. **Joseph de Cauwer,** Professor in the Ghent Academy and also director of a private art school, presumably produced some classical subjects in these years between his earlier *Antigone: or sisterly devotion* and *Anacreon with Polycrates* and 1832 when he exhibited a *Liberation of Prometheus.* Among the younger Gantois **Joseph Geirnaert** signed a *Phaedra and Hippolytus* at twenty-eight in 1819; **Jan Baptist Maes (Maes-Canini),** whose political allegories have been mentioned, won a prize at twenty-four in 1818 with *Alexander and his physician Philippus* and secured his Rome scholarship with *Alexander and Diogenes* in 1821; and I must recall here that **Jodocus Sebastiaen van den Abeele** trained by **van Huffel** and David, sent classical subjects from Paris and Rome to the Ghent and other exhibitions, that **Charles Louis Saligo,** another pupil of **van Huffel,** sent a Homeric subject from Paris to Brussels in 1827, and that classical subjects were painted in Paris by **Antoine Ansiaux** and **Willem Franquinet.**

Religious subjects were now painted as demonstration pieces for the exhibitions and also, as before, as commissions for churches. In Antwerp **Herreyns** (Pl. 867) may have painted some more religious pictures in his last years before 1827; and two by **Mattheus van Brée** a *Christ healing the sick* and a *Suffer little children* may date from this period. **Louis Adrien Moons,** whose religious subjects sent from Rome between 1820 and 1823 have been mentioned, was back in Antwerp by 1823 where he painted *Job and his three friends* and *Hagar and Ishmael in the wilderness* exhibited in Brussels in 1824, *The Annunciation to the Shepherds* and *The Incredulity of S. Thomas* exhibited in Antwerp in 1825, *Jacob with Joseph's blood-stained raiment* exhibited in Amsterdam in 1826, *The Rest on the Flight* exhibited in Antwerp in 1828 and *The Conversion of S. Paul* exhibited in Ghent in

1829; by 1830 when he was sixty-one he was a member of the Antwerp and Amsterdam Academies and of the Antwerp Society for the Encouragement of Art and he thus rivalled **Mattheus van Brée** (who was four years younger) as an official leader of the Antwerp art world. Louis David's former pupil **Cornelis Groenendael,** established in Antwerp at thirty by 1815 on his return from Paris, produced an *Education of the Virgin* some three or four years later for a church in his native Lierre and the picture was mutilated by a religious fanatic who judged the clothes or draperies indecorous (as other zealots had judged the draperies in the 1809 *Annunciation* by **Lens**); but **Groenendael** was supported by the Archbishop of Malines (Mgr de Méan) who pronounced the spirit of the picture full of piety and the design quite decorous. **Ferdinand de Braekeleer,** who won his Rome prize with his *Healing of Tobit* and sent *Esau seeking his father's blessing* and other religious subjects from Rome between 1819 and 1823, may have painted more such subjects on his return to Antwerp though he was mainly occupied with the contemporary and costume-history pieces recorded above. **Gustave Wappers,** who was to exhibit an *Entombment* in 1833, may have painted some religious subjects between 1823, the end of his studentship, and 1830; and **Pierre Anton Verlinde** (two years older than **Wappers** and a pupil first of **Joseph François Ducq** in Bruges and then of **Mattheus van Brée** in Antwerp before his Paris visit) produced a *Rest on the Flight* and *Christ and the woman of Samaria* probably before 1829 when he was back in Antwerp at twenty-eight and teacher there in the Academy. In Brussels **Joseph Odevaere** exhibited a *Martyrdom of S. Laurence* and worked for various churches in these years; **Joseph François,** whose *Assumption of the Virgin* and *S. Germain blessing S. Geneviève* for Brussels churches were mentioned in my last chapter, produced a *Four Evangelists* for the Minimes probably before 1830 when he was seventy-one; and **Charles Spruyt** was available for such subjects on his return from Rome at fifty-two in 1821. **Joseph Paelinck** in his Brussels headquarters was much employed on commissions for churches and religious houses all over the country; in 1817 he gave a *Christ on the Cross* to the city of Ghent and received in exchange a gold medal of honour from the Ghent Society for the Encouragement of Art; his sixteen-feet high *The Disciples on the Way to Emmaus* was painted for a church at Everghem and his *Flight into Egypt* for a church in Malines. **François-Joseph Navez** (Pl. 890) was chiefly employed on religious subjects after his return from Rome; by the end of 1823 he had completed three pictures *The Incredulity of Thomas, The Marriage of the Virgin* and a *Holy Family* for the Jesuit church of S. Francis Xavier in Amsterdam, in 1824 he painted a *Massacre of the Innocents*, in 1825 a *S. Cecilia* (much admired by Louis David), and in 1826 *The Meeting of Isaac and Rebecca* exhibited in Brussels and bought by the Government; by 1830 his status in the art world had begun to diminish as a result of the Romantic movement, and his *Athaliah and Joash* with over-life-size figures shown that year in the Brussels Salon was eclipsed in public favour by *The Patriotism of the Burgomaster of Leyden* by **Gustave Wappers. Charles Picqué** painted a *Tobit blessing Tobias* at twenty-four in 1823; **Michel Stapleaux's** *S. Vincent de Paul removing a galley slave's chains to his own wrists* has already been referred to as painted probably in Paris before 1830; **Jean Baptiste van Eycken,** later much employed for churches, was a pupil of **Navez** and twenty-one by 1830; and **Henri van der Haert** painted a *Dismissal of Hagar* either before 1830 in Brussels or later in Ghent. **Antoine Ignace Steyaert** now settled in Ghent painted *The Disciples at Emmaus* and *The Last Supper* for S. Michel there in 1824 and a *Rest on the Flight* in 1830. **Peter van Huffel** painted for Doorseele Abbey a *Presentation of the Virgin* much admired in the Ghent Exhibition of 1817, the eight pictures for the Oratory of the Princess of Orange already mentioned, and other commissions for various churches. **Joseph de Cauwer** whose *Baptism of Christ* and *S. Elizabeth giving alms* were recorded in my last chapter, produced a *Christ healing the blind* for Ghent S. Michel before 1823, a *Descent from the Cross* for S. Nicholas and other works for churches before 1830. **Pieter van Hanselaere** (Pl. 891), back from Rome and Professor in the Ghent Academy at forty-three in 1829, exhibited a *Lamentation* in 1830 and may have begun that year his *Jesus among the Doctors* completed in 1831. **Charles Remes** (a pupil of **van Huffel**) painted a *Christ on the Cross* at twenty-two in 1817, a *S. Dominic receiving a rosary from the Virgin* for the Ghent Grand Béguinage in 1820, became a teacher in the art school of his native Wetteren in 1823 and later provided many village churches with versions of *The Road to Calvary*. **Jan Baptist Maes (Maes-Canini)** painted a *Hagar and Ishmael in the desert* at twenty-seven in 1821 before leaving Ghent for Rome; and on his visit to Ghent from Rome in 1826 he had much success with *The Virgin presenting the Infant Jesus to S. Anne*. **Joseph Geirnaert** though chiefly occupied with genre and occasional classical subjects may have painted his *Finding of Moses* and *Chastity of Joseph* before 1830 when he moved from Ghent to The Hague. In Malines **Henri Bernaerts** painted *Christ on the Cross* in 1818, *The Last Supper* and *S. Francis* in 1825 when he became Professor in the Academy at fifty-seven, and an *Abraham's offering* and *David's last charge to Solomon* before 1830. **Jean Joseph Vervloet,** Professor in the same Academy at twenty-eight in 1818, painted a *Repentant Magdalene* for the village church at Reeth, an *Assumption* for the chapel of a country house, *Abraham dismissing Hagar, S. George and the Dragon* and *S. Vincent de Paul rescuing a child abandoned in the snow* either in this period or later. In Louvain **Josse Pierre Geedts** sent a *Christ crucified between the thieves* to the Malines Exhibition at fifty-two in 1822 and painted *The Archbishop of Cologne handing over a miraculous host to the Prior of an Augustine monastery* for a series of Sacrament pictures in Louvain S. Jacques in 1824; his pupil **Jan Baptist van der Hulst** painted a *Miracle of the Holy Sacrament* for the same Sacrament series on his return from Italy in 1827; and his son, pupil and assistant **Pierre Paul Geedts** also contributed to this series. **François van Dorne** (who wrote a life of his former master **Pierre Joseph Verhaghen**) was in Louvain through the period and painted three pictures *The Crowning with thorns, The Flagellation* and *Christ carrying the Cross* for the Dominican church there at fifty in 1826. **Melchior Gommar Tieleman,** back from Hanover and Director of the Academy in his native Lierre by 1829, painted *The Pilgrims to Emmaus* for Lierre Cathedral in this period or later. In Tournai **Cornelis Cels** painted an *Incredulity of S. Thomas* (commissioned for a church in The Hague) at forty-four in 1822; and **Louis Gallait** who worked under him in the Tournai Academy as a youth (and was later trained there by Philippe Hennequin) had his first success with *The Tribute money* completed at twenty-one in 1831. In Liège **Joseph Barthélémy Vieillevoye** painted *The repentant Magdalene* and *The Flood* in 1830 at the same time as his *Nymph of Salmacis and Hermaphroditus*.

In portraiture I have mentioned some works painted by **François Josèphe Kinson, Antoine Ansiaux, Henri de Caisne, Charles Louis Saligo** and **Pierre Antoine Verlinde** in Paris, by **François Simonau** in London, by **Pieter van Hanselaere** (Pl. 891) in Rome and Naples and **Mattheus van Brée** on his visit to Rome; and of the production in Belgium I have referred to portraits of King William and other Orange Royalties and portraits of Louis David by **Odevaere** and **Navez**. In Brussels **Navez** was faithful to the Davidian style in *The Hemptinne Family* (Pl. 890) painted at twenty-nine in 1816 before his Roman visit; he was living then in the house of August Donat de Hemptinne (later Director of the École de Pharmacie in Brussels University and shown here with his wife and child); and after his return to Brussels he painted a *Self-portrait* against a light background and a number of commissioned portraits including *Prince Charles Rasso de Gavre, Grand Marshal at the Court of William I* and *The geologist Engelspach-Larivière.* In 1830 **Odevaere** painted a full-length *Portrait of the artist's wife* showing Sylvie de la Rue (sitter some twenty years earlier for the picture reproduced (Pl. 889) by **Joseph van der Donckt**) who had been married to him since 1818 when she was twenty-two and he was over fifty; looser in handling and much less carefully composed as a linear design than his portrait group of 1805 (Pl. 882) this picture illustrates his retreat from the David-Suvée manner, a retreat recorded in his dictum of this time: 'Il faut le dire, les systèmes académiques ont ruiné les arts et il a fallu de grands efforts pour les affranchir, même à ceux qui en ont subi l'absurdité, tant l'habitude a de pouvoir sur les hommes. . . . J'ai gardé des compositions pour faire voir à mes élèves à quelle raideur mène la mauvaise habitude de faire des *traits* . . . de mauvais conseils enseignent cette méthode vicieuse qui ne peut qu'engendrer un dessin raide, sans vie et sans souplesse.' Others painting portraits in Brussels (a good centre as a seat of the Court) included **Hendrik Blomaerts, Joseph François, Alexandre Boens, Jean François Thys, Charles Pierre Verhulst, Henri Voordecker, Joseph Paelinck, Henri van der Haert, Cornelis Cels, Jan Baptist van der Hulst, Ignace Brice, Charles Brias, Charles Picqué, Marie Adelaide Kindt** and possibly **P. de Glimes.** Of these **Hendrik Blomaerts,** though chiefly occupied with landscapes, was still exhibiting portraits in 1830 when he was seventy-five; **Charles Pierre Verhulst,** whose portraits *The sculptor Godecharle* and *The musician Tuerlinckx* were mentioned in my last chapter, died at forty-five in 1820 after painting the *Prince of Orange* and *Prince Frederick.* **Joseph Paelinck** in addition to his Royal commissions painted *Lord Clancarty, British Ambassador to the Kingdom of the Netherlands* and may or may not have known that Clancarty described the Belgians as 'vain, futile and never satisfied'. **P. de Glimes** whose death-date is unknown may still have been painting portraits like the *Young man in a hat* reproduced here (Pl. 878). **Cornelis Cels** was available for portraits when he moved in 1828 to Brussels from Tournai. In 1828 also **Jan Baptist van der Hulst** seems to have moved from Louvain to Brussels and painted there a series of portraits for the Duc d'Arenberg as well as his Royal commissions before settling in The Hague in 1830. **Ignace Brice** exhibited portraits in Brussels, Antwerp, Ghent and Amsterdam between 1821 and 1828 and lithographed his *Thérèse Langhendries, Mother Superior of the Brussels Hôpital* at twenty-eight in 1823. **Charles Brias** back from Paris at twenty-four in 1822 and available thereafter in Brussels, had exhibited portraits in Malines in 1816, and his *General Chassé at Waterloo* in Ghent, before his Parisian visit. **Charles Picqué,** a year younger, painted *Joseph Paelinck* probably in the twenties and in 1830 made the portrait studies for his *Meeting of the Provisional Government on Sept. 24, 1830.* **Marie Adelaide Kindt** painted portraits concurrently with her costume-history pictures and produced her *Portrait of Professor Baron* at twenty-two in 1826. **Henri van der Haert** was mainly occupied with portrait-lithographs but he also painted some portraits including *The Terwagne Family* either before or after 1830 when he was forty. In 1826 soon after Louis David's death **Jean Baptist Madou** lithographed a *Full-length portrait of David in an overcoat* from a drawing made in a café, and in the same year he lithographed *A Portrait of the actor Talma* also based on a drawing made in a café or restaurant in Brussels where Talma in his last years was a frequent visitor; **Madou,** who was later most successful with genre subjects, was already thirty at this time but not yet a painter; held back by poverty he had worked as a clerk in his youth and he seems then to have had some instruction from **Joseph François** in Brussels; in 1817 he had been employed as Government cartographer in Courtrai and Mons, and he had been working as a draughtsman and lithographer in Brussels since 1820.

In Antwerp, in 1815, **Mattheus van Brée** painted *The art patron Johannes Hermanus Molkenboer* (showing the collector seated on an Empire chair with a drawing in his right hand and a smirking self-satisfied air); and his *Jean-Mathieu de Moor formerly Curé of Antwerp, S. Jacques* may have been painted before or after his visit to Rome. **Cornelis Groenendael** was available in Antwerp through the period; and **Pierre Antoine Verlinde** on his return from Paris about 1827. **Frans Marcus Smits** whose *G. F. Ziesel, B. P. Ommeganck* and *W. J. Herreyns* have been mentioned in earlier chapters, seems to have sunk into poverty at the end of the twenties and, probably by 1830 when he was seventy, he was installed by his friends in the S. Elizabeth Almshouse (where he died in 1833). Occasional portraits were produced by the landscape painter **Balthasar Paul Ommeganck** (Pl. 876) before 1826; and **Andreas van Quertenmont,** eighty in 1830, may have still had some sitters for portrait drawings in the early years of the period. In Ghent **Peter van Huffel** painted a full-length *Mgr de Broglie Bishop of Ghent* before 1818 and other portraits of prelates; **Joseph de Cauwer** painted *Count Delafaille President of the Ghent Academy, The composer Verheyen* and many commissioned portraits; and **Pieter van Hanselaere** (Pl. 891) was highly regarded as a portrait painter when he came back from the Court of Naples in 1829. In Bruges **Louis Gerbo** died in 1818, **Joseph van der Donckt** (Pl. 889) in 1821, and **P. J. Remaut** in 1826. **Joseph François Ducq** painted some portraits in addition to the Royal commissions before suffering the stroke which crippled him, as noted, in the later twenties. **Jean Baptiste van Acker,** who had worked under **Ducq,** was twenty-one in 1815 when he began to specialize in miniature portraits with which he had great success; he worked in Bruges in this period and went later to Paris (where he contributed to Gavarni's 'Journal des Gens du Monde'). **Désiré Donny** painted *Dr Crommelinck* in Bruges at twenty-eight in 1826; and **François Josèphe Kinson** (Pls. 884, 885) began a new phase in his career as portraitist after his return there in 1830. In Malines **Henri Bernaerts** was available for portraits through the period; **Gustave Adolph Diez** probably returned there before 1830 when he was twenty-nine after working under **Odevaere** in Brussels and painting there his master's portrait; and **Michel Joseph Speeckaert,** sixty-seven in 1815, was still living in Malines (or Brussels) in 1830. In Louvain **François van Dorne** had a number of commissions and his *Burgomaster Plasschaert* and *Van Laere, Secretary of the Academy* may both have been painted before 1830. In Tournai **Cornelis Cels** painted some portraits between 1820 and 1828; and before 1830 **Louis Gallait** produced his *Portrait de Lepez* as a juvenile work. **Germain Joseph Hallez** was still an active portraitist in Mons. **Joseph Barthélemy Vieillevoye** had many commissions in Liège and signed in 1820 his *Jan Lodewyck Bourcenet, State Secretary of Antwerp* (possibly painted on a visit or a stay in Antwerp). In The Hague, alternative with Brussels as seat of the Government, the portrait painters were mostly Dutchmen. But **Cornelis Cels,** there, as noted, from 1815 to 1820, had a number of commissions in official circles including *J. C. van den Hoop Minister of Marine, C. F. van Maanen Minister of Justice, M. Ferrier British Consul in Rotterdam* and *Count G. K. van Hogendorp.* **Petrus van Schendel,** who worked later in The Hague, went from Antwerp to Amsterdam at twenty-three in 1829 and painted there that year his *Adriana Johanna van Wijck, wife of J. Ploos van Amstel* and other portraits.

Among the younger painters of still life and flowers **Joseph Clevenbergh** was in Louvain where his eldest brother **Charles Antoine Clevenbergh** was also active, and **Henri Robbe** of Courtrai may have begun his practice as a painter of fruit and flowers by 1830 when he was twenty-three. The woman painter **Adèle Evrard** was very successful in these years; after working under the landscape painter **Julien Ducorron** in her native Ath she won a medal or honourable mention at an exhibition in Douai at twenty-nine in 1821; she was made a member of the Brussels Academy in 1825, and the Government bought her *Fruit and flower piece* sent to the Ghent Exhibition in 1827. In Ghent **Annette de Noter** and **Josephine de Noter** were both launched as painters of fruit and flowers before 1830 when the first was twenty-seven and the second twenty-five. **Augustina Vervloet**, another woman painter of fruit and flowers and sometimes of game pieces, exhibited pictures in Brussels and Malines from soon after 1830; she is said to have been the wife of **François Vervloet** and her pictures would therefore have been sent from Italy; but she may have been the wife of **Jean Joseph Vervloet** who was active as noted in Malines.

Indoor genre subjects, often with an anecdotic basis, were now as numerous as in the days of **Jan Joseph Horemans the elder** (Pls. 836, 837, 838) and **Jan Joseph Horemans the younger** (Pls. 835, 861); and some practitioners, **Ferdinand van Braekeleer** (Pl. 893) for example, dressed their models in seventeenth-century clothes as had been done on occasion by **Horemans the younger, Jacob Andries Brassauw, Melchior Brassauw** and more recently by **Petrus Johannes van Regemorter** (who seems to have been wholly occupied by restoring in these years). In 1816 **Jean François Thys** painted *The interior of a cabinet maker's workshop* and followed this with other interior genre subjects. **Paul Godefroid Joseph Noël** scored a popular success at twenty-seven with his *Soldiers painting a moustache on a sleeping girl* exhibited in the Brussels Salon of 1816; his *Merry company in a Flemish smokers' tavern* was exhibited in 1819; and he continued such pictures when he moved next year to Holland. In 1818 when he was twenty-seven **Joseph Geirnaert** won a prize in the Brussels Exhibition with his *Belgian officer introducing to his family a comrade in arms who had saved his life*; in 1820 he won the Ghent Academy's prize with *A young girl taking a lesson on the harp in the presence of her mother*; in 1821 he was given a medal of honour by the Douai Society for the Encouragement of Art; in 1827 his *Visit of the doctor* was exhibited and much admired in Ghent; and he also painted pictures called *The card players* and *Children blowing soap bubbles.* **Charles Spruyt,** though mainly occupied with religious subjects and costume-history pieces after his return from Rome, exhibited a picture called *The anger of a paintbrush vendor* at fifty-five in 1824 and other genre subjects later. **Cornelis Cels,** who rarely painted genre subjects, produced his *Swiss peasant girl with a partridge, an Alpine stick and her left hand outstretched towards a dog* which was bought by the Government from an exhibition in The Hague in 1821. **Pierre François Charles Leroy** began his career at twenty with *A young man preparing breakfast* exhibited in Ghent in 1823. **Marie Adelaide Kindt** painted *A young girl visiting a hermit* at eighteen in 1822, *The music lesson* in 1826 and *Waiting for the fisherman's return* in 1828. **Jean Baptiste van Eycken** (later a painter of religious subjects for Brussels churches as mentioned above) began as an anecdotic genre painter at eighteen in 1827 with *A boy who wants to be a painter taken by his mother to an artist's studio* exhibited in The Hague and bought by the Government. In 1827 also **Pierre Antoine Verlinde** painted at twenty-six (in Paris or Antwerp) his *Interior of the artist's studio* which was also bought by the Government. **Ignatius van Regemorter** painted pictures titled *Cardplayers quarrelling* and *Interior with a pair of lovers* and sent *The Old Gallant* from Antwerp to the London Royal Academy in 1828. In that year **Seraphin Vermote** who had taken to occasional figure painting produced a picture on a theme immortalized by **Jordaens** (Pl. 658) *Twelfth Night (Le roi boit)*; **Charles van Beveren** began his career at nineteen with *The soldier's farewell to his parents*; **Gustave Wappers** painted *A fallen girl by the side of her child's cradle* about the same time; and **Charles Brias** sent *The interior of a French Cabaret* to the London Royal Academy in 1830.

Occasional works in this category were still being painted by established artists like **Antoine Ignace Steyaert** who often added interest by candlelight effects, by **Germain Hallez** whose *Devoted young mother* was mentioned in my last chapter and, possibly, by **P. de Glimes** (Pl. 878) whose *Girl with a bird in her hand* was also mentioned there. Newcomers not named above included **Leopold Boens** and **Charles Remes** both twenty in 1815; **Henri de Coene** who was seventeen in 1815 and later successful with humorous anecdotic pieces such as *Friday* (peasants eating meat on Friday surprised by the curé); **Petrus van Schendel** who painted genre interiors by candlelight and was twenty-four in 1830; **François Verheyden** also twenty-four in 1830, **Julie Anne Marie Noël** (later the wife of **Jean Baptiste van Eycken**) who was eighteen in 1830 and was exhibiting pictures called *Young mother by a cradle* and *Girl asleep by a spinning wheel* by 1833; and **Emmanuel Noterman,** twenty-two in 1830 but not launched till some years later when in addition to bourgeois and village genre he painted *A monkey as dentist* and *A monkey as painter* in the tradition of **David Teniers** and **Verendael.** **Jean Baptiste Madou** whose interior genre scenes were often treated with a touch of humour, was still a lithographer as mentioned above; and he contributed to a publication called 'Costumes du peuple de toutes les provinces du royaume des Pays Bas' before the end of the period.

Topographic drawings and watercolours of picturesque buildings and church interiors were now produced in numbers for lithographed publications and **Madou** contributed to a 'Voyage Pittoresque dans le Pays Bas'. There were also oil painters who specialized in this field as at all periods in our story. Thus in the Ghent group **Pierre François de Noter** who seems to have moved from Malines to Ghent by 1820 exhibited *The Ghent Sassentor with skaters* at forty-seven in 1826 and sold it to the Government; and in 1829 he painted *The interior of Ghent S. Bavon with the altarpiece of the Mystic Lamb*; he was very successful in the later years of the period when he taught in the Ghent Academy, exhibited in Brussels, Tournai, Cambrai and elsewhere and was made a member of the Academy in Antwerp. His brother **Jean Baptiste de Noter** who painted a *View of the underground passage in the Old Castle in Ghent with the tomb of S. Macarius* in 1822 seems also to have divided his time between Ghent and Malines. **Ange de Baets,** thirty-three in 1826, sent *The Vestibule of the new Ghent University* to the Ghent Exhibition of that year and sold it to the King who gave it to the town; and in 1830 he sent his *Staircase of the Ghent University* to the Brussels Exhibition and sold it to the Brussels Society for the Encouragement of Art. A newcomer **Pierre Poelman** who died at twenty-five in 1826 went from his Ghent headquarters to make topographic pictures in various places; in 1820 he painted a *View of Ghent, S. Michel*, in 1822 a *View of Mons taken from the Groote Markt*, in 1824 *Audenarde Town Hall with Cossacks by the fountain in the Square* (perhaps a childhood memory) which was exhibited in Brussels and bought by the Government, and in 1826 *The Saint Sang chapel in Bruges* and *The Place S. Pharäilde in Ghent with the entrance of the Old Castle of the Counts of Holland.* **Ivo Ambros Vermeersch** (a pupil of **Pierre François de Noter** in Ghent Academy) painted *The Fishmarket in Ghent* at sixteen in 1810, *The church and cloister of the Dominicans in Ghent* in 1829, *The ruins of the church of S. Macarius and the Old Citadel of Ghent* and *The ruins of the Abbey of S. Bavon* in 1830; and the last named motif was also used by the Brussels landscape painter **Henri van Assche** who seems to have visited Ghent for the purpose in 1828. In Brussels (where the tradition of topographic painting goes back through **Denis van Alsloot** (Pl. 513A) and **Antoine Sallaert** (Pl. 514) to **The View of Sainte Gudule Master** (Pl. 122)) **Constantin Fidèle Coene** now painted or caused an architectural collaborator to paint the streets there for his outdoor genre scenes; **Pierre Jean Baptiste**

Leroy's *Fête in Brussels for the Entry and Inauguration of King William I* had a topographic setting; and **Charles Spruyt** (whose architectural interiors painted in Rome have been mentioned) may have painted such works in Brussels concurrently with his religious and costume-history subjects after 1821; **Alexandre Boens** made paintings and lithographs of old monuments and picturesque corners in Brussels after a period as lithographer with **Leopold Boens** and **Madou** in Courtrai; **François Antoine Bossuet,** who had been a naval cadet and an Admiralty official, began a career as topographic painter with his *View of Brussels S. Gudule* exhibited in Brussels when he was thirty-two in 1830; and in that year **François Stroobant** and **Jean Baptiste van Moer,** both painters later of old Brussels buildings, were boys of eleven. In Courtrai **J. F. Delpelchin** was still painting architectural pieces at about sixty in 1830. **Jan Baptist de Jonghe** was back there from his foreign travels by about 1820 and then toured Belgium making topographic drawings for lithographed collections of picturesque views; in 1826 at forty-one he became Professor in the Courtrai Academy; and his skill as an architectural painter is well seen in his *Market day at Courtrai* (Pl. 892) exhibited in Amsterdam in 1828 and bought by the Government. **Louis Haghe** began his career with *Interior of S. Quentin in Tournai* and other drawings contributed to a lithographed publication 'Vues pittoresques de Tournai . . .' before leaving for England about 1826. In Malines **François Vervloet,** whose first success *Interior of Malines Cathedral with the installation of the Prince-Bishop Mgr de Méan as Archbishop* painted in 1817 has been mentioned above, was painting interiors of churches and other architectural pieces till he left for Italy at twenty-seven in 1822; **Charles van Beveren** painted a *View of the Porte de Louvain in Malines* and *View of the Town gate at Aerschot* before leaving for Italy at twenty-seven in 1830; and **Jean Baptiste de Noter** whose work in Ghent has just been mentioned produced a *View of the Towers of Malines, S. Rombout* in 1823 and other Malines views before 1830. In Antwerp **Joseph Chrétien Nicolié** was now conspicuous in this category and sold many of his works to English visitors with the help of his father an art dealer; and his *Interior of Antwerp, S. Jacques with the tomb of Rubens* showing mass being celebrated at a side altar in the tradition of **Peter Neefs the elder** (Pls. 649, 650), was bought by the Government from the Ghent Exhibition when he was thirty-four in 1825. **Jules Victor Génisson** painted his first church interiors in Antwerp before starting his foreign tour at twenty-four in 1829. **Jan Michiel Ruyten** who painted such pictures later was a pupil of **Ignatius van Regemorter** at seventeen in 1830; and **A. Blom** of whom little seems known painted an *Interior of Antwerp S. Georges* with figures by **Petrus van Regemorter** before the end of the period. In Bruges—(where devoted painters of the monuments have appeared in our story from the days of the **Philadelphia S. Catherine Painter** (Pl. 108), the **Detroit Mystic Marriage Painter** (Pl. 110) and **Memlinc** (Pl. 111))—**Jean Charles Verbrugge** was probably active till he died at seventy-four in 1831; and **Seraphin Vermote** who worked in Bruges and Ypres among other places between 1816 and 1830 painted *Bruges, Notre Dame* in grisaille at twenty-eight in 1816 and *Bruges, Place Van Eyck* before 1820.

Among painters of landscapes, and landscapes with animals, there were groups, as always, in Antwerp, Brussels, Ghent and elsewhere; and all now sent their work to exhibitions in various places. In Antwerp **Balthasar Ommeganck** (Pl. 876) was active till his death at seventy-one in 1826; and in 1824 his *Landscape with farm carts, animals and figures* exhibited in Brussels was bought by the Government. **Hendrik Aarnut Myin** died at sixty-six in 1826, **Jean Pierre Borrekens** died at eighty in 1827, and **Petrus Johannes van Regemorter** died at seventy-five in 1830. **Maria Jacoba Myin** worked through the period in the **Ommeganck** manner, **Jan Frans Lentzen (Lenzen)** made many copies of **Ommeganck's** pictures, and **Jean Charles Carpentero** who exhibited a *Mountainous and wooded landscape with sheep and cattle* at thirty-five in 1819 was now imitating **Ommeganck** so closely that some of his pictures were sold under **Ommeganck's** name. **Ommeganck's** former pupil **Ignatius van Regemorter** was still painting landscapes as well as outdoor genre scenes. **Hendrik Myin's** former pupil **Henri Joseph van der Poorten** painted landscapes with moonlight effects which he sent to the Antwerp and Brussels exhibitions; and, he sold a *Landscape with Animals* to the Government before 1830. Among the newcomers in Antwerp **Josephus Jodocus Moerenhout**, a pupil of **van der Poorten** from 1817 till 1820, had two landscapes in the Antwerp Salon at twenty-one in 1822; he visited The Hague in 1824, and worked for a time with Horace Vernet in Paris as related; he then specialized in outdoor scenes with horses and sold a *Racecourse scene* to the Government at twenty-eight in 1829. **Guillaume van Bomberghen** trained in the Antwerp Academy and, successful later with moonlight landscapes, was still painting portrait miniatures in Paris at twenty-three in 1830. **Petrus van Schendel**, another painter, later, of moonlight landscapes, was a pupil of **Mattheus van Brée** in Antwerp Academy from 1822 till 1828 when he left for Holland (and began his career there by painting some portraits as noted above). **Jan Michiel Ruyten,** seventeen in 1830 as just mentioned, painted snow scenes and other landscapes later in addition to his topographic pieces.

Among the landscape painters in Brussels **Jean Baptiste de Roy** was still a central figure; in 1815 the Brussels Society for the Encouragement of Art chose him with **André Cornelis Lens** (Pl. 871) and the sculptor Gilles Lambart Godecharle for special medals of honour; in 1827 a contemporary wrote of him; '**De Roy** nous a donné des foires de bestiaux, parcs de boeufs, des combats de taureaux, des hardes dans des gras pâturages, des incendies, des coups de vents, des brouillards, là tout un troupeau qui quitte la ferme vers la prairie ou qui regagne l'étable, et toujours des sites spacieux et romantiques'; and he was still exhibiting at seventy-one in 1830. Among his former pupils **Henri van Assche,** who followed his Italian visit of 1815 by tours at various times in the Vosges, Switzerland and Germany, was a member of the Brussels Society of Artists by 1818, of the Amsterdam Society in 1822 and of the Antwerp Academy by 1823; his *Forge near Stavelot* was painted in 1820; his *Mountain stream in the Ardennes at sunset* dated 1821 was shown in the Amsterdam Exhibition in 1828 and bought by the Government; and he painted *The Reichenbach Falls* at fifty-six in 1836. **Henri Voordecker** won a medal from the Brussels Society at thirty-six in 1815 and then turned to outdoor genre and portraits. **Pierre Jean Hellemans** thirty-six in 1823 and well known by then as a painter of wooded landscapes and sunrise effects in misty valleys was a member of the Brussels Society by 1825, collaborated with **Eugène Verboeckhoven** for animals and **Charles Brias** for figures, and exhibited an *Outskirts of the forest of Soignes* in 1830. **Pierre Jean Baptiste Leroy** worked in Brussels till 1830 when he went abroad at forty-six and visited Paris, London and Vienna. **Simon d'Argonne** was still signing himself 'Pupil of J. B. de Roy' when he exhibited wooded and river landscapes at seventy-two in 1821. **Hendrik Blomaerts** was still exhibiting landscapes painted in the environs of Brussels at seventy-two in 1827. **Paul Godefroid Joseph Noël** painted a *View of the Château de Rey on the Meuse at Dinant* in 1816 and died at thirty-three in 1822. **Frédéric Théodore Faber** opened a porcelain factory at thirty-seven in 1819 but continued his landscape and genre painting; and in 1820 he sent to the Ghent Industrial Exhibition a dinner service with views of beauty spots in the United Netherlands which the Queen had commissioned. **François de Marneffe** painted wooded landscapes, hunting pieces, waterfalls and sunsets at various times, exhibited in Brussels, Ghent and Antwerp, and was thirty-seven by 1830. When the Ghent Society organized a competition for a landscape titled *Sunset behind a watermill in September* in 1820 one of the prizes went to **van Assche's** former pupil **Maximilian Lambert Gelissen** then thirty-four and working in Brussels. **Edouard Delvaux (van Assche's** pupil from 1824 to 1827) was probably back from his foreign tour at twenty-four by 1830 when he sent wooded landscapes to the exhibitions in Brussels and Liège and sold to the Government his *Banks of the Sambre with ruins in the distance* exhibited in Amsterdam. **Laurence Petronilla Kindt** (who was to marry **Edouard Delvaux** in 1838) was a sister of **Marie Adelaide Kindt** and a pupil of **van Assche** from about 1828 when she began to exhibit at twenty-three; **Claire Kindt** (another sister of **Marie Adelaide Kindt**) was also a **van Assche** pupil; and **Isabella Kindt** (née **van Assche**) mentioned in my last chapter, exhibited in Ghent in 1826 and 1829, married C. L. Kindt at thirty-four in 1828 and painted a *Farm near Watermael* with figures by **Leroy** in 1830. In Ghent **Antoine Ignace Steyaert** gave much of his time to moonlight and other landscapes in this period. **Antoine Pierre Steyaert** sold to the Government his *Ruins of a Gothic castle in a mountainous landscape* at thirty-five in 1823. **Pierre François de Noter,** whose topographic pieces have just been mentioned, won a prize in 1820 with his *Sunset behind a watermill in September* (in the same competition as **Maximilian Lambert Gelissen**) and also painted winter landscapes. **Herman August de Noter** began painting landscapes at twenty in 1826. **Eugène Joseph Verboeckhoven,** son of a sculptor of Warneton in West Flanders, was at first the pupil of his father and of the Ghent sculptor A. J. Voituron and began by modelling animals; from about 1818 he worked for a time in Antwerp under **Ommeganck**; by 1820 he was living in Ghent and he exhibited there *King William I on horseback returning from a military review* already referred to; in 1821 he collaborated with **Pierre François de Noter** in a *Cattle market in Ghent*; his *Boy and cattle in a field* (Pl. 895) was painted in Ghent at twenty-five between his French and English visits; and by 1827 he seems to have moved to Brussels where he painted animals in landscapes by various artists including **Pierre Jean Hellemans, Louis Pierre Verwée** (who moved to Brussels from Courtrai to become his pupil) and **Henri de Coene** who supplied the figures in a picture called *The Veterinary Surgeon* in 1834. **Adolphe Charles Maximilian Engel** was a pupil of **Jean Baptiste de Noter** in Ghent Academy and a graduate of Ghent University; he began to exhibit in 1820, worked in the regions of Dinant, Liège, Namur and the Ardennes, and painted his *Wooded landscape with cattle* (Pl. 896) at twenty-six in 1827; he had considerable success at the end of the period and committed suicide at thirty-two in 1833. His pupil **Jan Bernard de Vriendt** (or **Devriendt**) was hampered by poverty in his early years but began work at twenty-nine in 1830; and **Edouard de Vigne** pupil in Ghent Academy about 1826 was another beginner in this field by 1830 when he was twenty-two. In Bruges **François Jacques Wynckelman** was sixty-eight by 1830; and **Désiré Donny** thirty-two that year had begun to paint rivers in moonlight. **Jan Baptist de Jonghe** (Pl. 892) of Courtrai, whose topographic skill has just been mentioned, painted wooded landscapes and made forty drawings for a Brussels publication 'Principes de Paysage' in 1826; and in this period or later **Verboeckhoven** provided animals for some of his pictures. **Louis Pierre Verwée** was de Jonghe's pupil in Courtrai before he went to Brussels; and **Louis Robbe** another pupil obtained a doctorate in Ghent University with a Latin thesis on divorce at twenty-four in 1830 and practised as a lawyer in addition to his work as a painter of animals in landscape. **Julien Ducorron** now founded the Ath Academy, became its Director at forty-nine in 1819, exhibited much admired landscapes with animals and figures in Brussels, Douai, Cambrai, Arras and Holland, and became a member of several Academies in Belgium and Holland before 1830. The Tournaisian **Antoine Payen** won a prize at thirty in the Brussels exhibition of 1815 with *The Château de Marche-les-Dames* (*between Namur and Huy*) *by moonlight* and was then sent by the Government to record the flora and landscape of Java; in 1818 he painted there his *Residence at Buitenzorg with a range of mountains in the background* exhibited in Ghent in 1820; he returned from Java to Brussels in 1827 and exhibited *The volcano Gounong-Gountow with coconut palms, 'Kamiri' and other Javanese growths* which the Government acquired. **Pierre Louis Kuhnen** painter later of landscapes with sunsets and twilight effects was born at Aix-la-Chapelle, worked there under Louis David's former pupil **Jean Baptiste Bastiné** (now Director of the Aix-la-Chapelle Art School) and went later to Brussels where **Verboeckhoven** painted animals in some of his landscapes.

Some of these landscape painters also produced marines and coast scenes in the tradition going back through **Lucas Smout the younger** (Pl. 795), **Hendrik van Minderhout** (Pl. 793), **Bonaventura Peeters** (Pl. 690), **Adam Willaerts** (Pl. 688), and so on to the fifteenth and sixteenth centuries painters of estuaries and harbours. Such pieces were occasionally painted by **Pierre François de Noter** and **Désiré Donny**. Specialists in the field included **Dominique de Bast** a merchant who studied the sea and ships in the course of his business travels, contributed to the Ghent exhibitions from 1817, and sold a *Coast scene with shipping* to the Government before 1830; **Louis Verboeckhoven** (brother and pupil of **Eugène Verboeckhoven**) who began to paint at eighteen in 1820 and worked on the coasts of Holland, France and England; and **Joseph Maes** who exhibited a *Coast scene with stormy sea* in Antwerp in 1828 and other seascapes later.

We may note too that the landscape painters were still more numerous in the decades which followed despite the continued popularity of costume-history; and of these **Théodore Fourmois** was sixteen in 1830, **Alfred de Knyff** was eleven, **François Roffiaen** ten, **Joseph Quinaux** and **Jean Baptiste Kindermans** eight, **Edmond de Schampeleer** six and **François de Lamorinière** two. The animal painters **Charles Tschaggeny** and **Edmond Tschaggeny** were then fifteen and twelve; and the marine painter **Paul Jean Clays** was seventeen.

There were also painters of military pieces continuing the tradition that can be traced back in my plates through the skirmishes and battle scenes by **Carel Breydel** (Pls. 842, 831), **Jan Pieter van Bredael** (Pl. 830), **Constantyn Francken** (Pl. 828), **Adam van der Meulen** (Pl. 737), **Pieter Meulener** (Pl. 698), **Peeter Snayers** (Pls. 700, 701) and **Sebastiaan Vrancx** (Pl. 531) to the charging horsemen by the **Brussels Micault Triptych Painter** (Pl. 321) and **Hieronymus Bosch** (Pl. 157). Among the pictures in this category I have referred above to the Waterloo and Missolonghi pieces and to the scenes from the September fighting in Brussels in 1830. I must add here that **Pierre Jean Baptiste Leroy** was among the painters of cavalry skirmishes; and that **Paul Godefroid Joseph Noël** painted *Bavarian cavalry halting at a farm* in 1817. Cossacks are shown, as mentioned, on the Square near Audenarde Town Hall in a picture by **Pierre Poelman**; and Horace Vernet's pupil **Josephus Jodocus Moerenhout** sent *Cossack advance guards* (one mounted and one on foot by his horse) from Antwerp to the Amsterdam Exhibition in 1828 and sold it to the Government. **Pierre François Charles Leroy** (son of **Pierre Jean Baptiste Leroy**) visited Spain and painted costume-history reconstructions of guerrilla fighting in the Peninsular War; and in 1827 when he was twenty-four he exhibited *French soldiers firing on two Spanish guerrillas in a bare landscape* in the Brussels Salon. His son **Joseph Anne Jules Leroy** (a pupil of **Verboeckhoven**) was eighteen in 1830; he had success in the following decades with small military pieces generally in watercolour; and he became eventually Professor of Drawing in the École Militaire.

Outdoor genre painting (as distinguished from landscapes with cattle and peasants and from the military pieces) included some dramatic snow scenes, village and country scenes with peasants, beggars and children, humorous anecdotic episodes, village fairs and market pieces. Thus **Paul Godefroid Joseph Noël** painted *A traveller attacked by wolves* before 1822, **Verboeckhoven** (Pl. 895) a *Group of riders attacked by wolves in a Polish wood* in 1836, and **Charles Picqué** *A woman with her unconscious child rescued from the snow by a S. Bernard dog* which the Government acquired in 1827. **Henri de Coene,** perhaps influenced by **Demarne,** painted *News from the Market: Peasants meeting on a country road* in 1827 and sold it to the Government in 1829. **Henri Bernaerts** painted a *Kermesse* in 1827. **Pierre Antoine Verlinde** painted a *Blind man led by his daughter along Antwerp harbour,* and **Charles Remes** a *Blind man led by a beggar* (a theme going back in our story to the **Alkmaar Master** (Pl. 183)). **Charles van Beveren** painted *A tramp with his children,* and **Antoine Ignace Steyaert** *Children coming from school.* **Constantin Coene** sold his *Peasant family seated before their cottage* to the Government; and a similar subject was painted in 1826 by **Henri Voordecker** in *Hunter and his family with fowls and pigeons by the vineclad doorway of his cottage* which was also bought by the Government and continues on the one hand the peasant and farmyard studies by **Jan Siberechts** (Pls. 787–92) and anticipates on the other the English Pre-Raphaelites by its brilliant hard sunlight and cast shadows. **Seraphin Vermote** produced a *Poachers' encampment;* and the humorous note with which **Jean Baptiste Madou** was later to win much applause, was also struck by **Joseph Barthélemy Vieillevoye** whose *Teasing the poacher* is admired by some present-day critics, and by **Charles Brias** whose *Boys stealing a chicken from a sleeping vendor and substituting a cat* gained the genre prize at the Brussels exhibition in 1824. **Ignace Brice,** successful in this period with genre figures of market types, sold his *Poultry seller offering a partridge to a servant girl and squeezing her arm* to the Government in 1827; and this picture where the figures are thrust to the front of the canvas goes back in one aspect to the grave market scene by **Pieter Snyers** (Pl. 839) and the market peasants by **Pieter Aertsen** (Pl. 356) and **Joachim Beuckelaer** (Pl. 398) though in spirit it stands closer to the figures in the *Market stall* (Pl. 655) by a collaborator with **Frans Snyders.** In the same way *The fishmarket in Antwerp* which **Ignatius van Regemorter** sold to the Government about 1830 can be compared and contrasted with *The Fishmarket* (Pl. 398) by **Beuckelaer.** Combined effects of candlelight inside market stalls and moonlight above were a feature of market pictures painted by **Petrus van Schendel** from soon after 1830. **Julien Ducorron** painted *A man with a handcart in conversation with a youth by the side of a canal with cottages*; and **Seraphin Vermote** an *Arrival of the diligence on the Grand' Place at Ypres,* a subject probably suggested by Léopold Boilly's *L'arrivée de la diligence* which he may have seen in the painter's studio in Paris. Some of these, and other, artists also painted general impressions of market day life more or less in the tradition which my plates carry back through **Jan Garemyn's** *Vegetable market in Bruges* (Pl. 860) to market scenes by **David Vinckeboons** (Pl. 533) and **Sebastiaan Vrancx** (Pls. 532, 534). Among such pictures **Paul Godefroy Noël's** *Vegetable market in Amsterdam with a drunkard falling on a stall* painted in 1821 was lithographed by **Madou** and later bought by the Government from an exhibition in The Hague; and **Constantin Coene's** *The Porte de Hal, Brussels, with market carts, many figures, two men fighting, and a runaway horse* painted in 1823 was sold to the Government in 1824. **Jan Baptist de Jonghe's** *Market day in Courtrai* (Pl. 892) referred to above in its topographic aspect is also in this category, and most admirably sets down a unified visual impression with many wittily observed subordinate details; readers of my story will see many traditional features in this market piece and compare the lady and gentleman buying flowers at the foot of the Town Hall steps with the woman buying candles by the **Ursula Legend Master** (Pl. 120), the janitor on guard at the top of the steps with the servants on the steps of the palace by the **Tiburtine Sibyl Master** (Pl. 87) and the loungers on the café terrace and woman at the window with the women lounging at the doorways and looking out from windows by the **London Virgin with a Firescreen Painter** (Pl. 39, Frontispiece). But this *Market day at Courtrai* is also essentially a nineteenth-century picture; painted in 1828, some ten years before the camera was invented, it already speaks the camera's language; and **de Jonghe** by making the aesthetic subject of his picture the sunlight streaming from the left, was an unpretentious herald of the French Impressionist painters and their followers.

A word in conclusion on collectors' taste in Belgium in this period. I have spoken above of King William's installation of the Mauritshuis in The Hague for his family pictures, of his gifts to the Antwerp Museum and Amsterdam Museum and his purchases for the Brussels Palace; and I must add here that the Chevalier Florent van Ertborn, at one time Burgomaster of Antwerp, was collecting Flemish pictures of the fifteenth and sixteenth centuries in the eighteen-twenties with the help of the topographic painter **Joseph Chrétien Nicolié.** Van Ertborn's collection which he bequeathed to the Antwerp Museum included **Jan van Eyck's** *S. Barbara* (Pl. 18) and *Virgin and Child by a fountain* (Pl. 25), *Philippe de Croy, Seigneur de Sempy as an adorant* (Pl. 45) by the **Antwerp Philippe de Croy Painter,** **Patinir's** *Landscape with the Flight into Egypt* (Pl. 244), *The Temptation of S. Anthony* (Pl. 163) by **Hieronymus Bosch,** *The Presentation in the Temple* (Pl. 197) and *Jesus among the Doctors* (Pl. 198) by the **Hoogstraeten Master,** *The Virgin with Prophets and Sibyls* (Pl. 263) by the **Deipara Virgo Master,** and *The Holy Family turned away from the Inn* (Pl. 361) and *The healing of Tobit* (Pl. 362) by **Jan Massys.** It also included the *Triptych with the Seven Sacraments* now presumed by some by **Rogier van der Weyden** and pictures now presumed by some the work of **Dirk Bouts, Albrecht Bouts, Hans Memlinc, Gerard David, Justus of Ghent, Quinten Massys, Cornelis Engelbrechtsz, Lambert Lombard** and **Marinus van Reymerswaele.**

PART TWO

A DICTIONARY
OF FLEMISH PAINTERS

A

Abbey of Afflighem Master. Presumed Flemish Sch. 15th/16th cent. Name for painter of BRUSSELS Mus. (552) *Scenes from the life of Christ and the Virgin,* ten pictures, on eight panels, from the Abbey of Afflighem, one inscribed 'Te Bruesele'. Presumed by some identical with the Joseph Master *q.v.,* and by some with the Brussels Zierickzee Master *q.v.* [Fl. 892, Fl. 316, Fl. 124, Fl. 798.]

*Abbey of Dilighem Master. Presumed Flemish Sch. 16th cent. Name for painter of BRUSSELS Mus. (560) Triptych: centre: *Christ in the house of Simon,* wings: *Raising of Lazarus, Assumption of the Magdalene (with donor Canon Jean Teugele),* exterior wings: *Christ appearing to the Magdalene* (grisaille) from the Abbey of Dilighem (destroyed 1794) to which it was donated by the abbot *c.* 1537. Presumed by some identical with Cornelis van Coninxloo *q.v.* and by some with Fifteen-Eighteen Master *q.v.* [Fl. 120, Fl. 316, Fl. 124, Fl. 798.]

Abeele, Albyn (Binus) van den. Flemish Sch. *b* 1835 *d* 1918. *Landscapes.* Civil servant in the village of Laethem-Saint-Martin and amateur painter associated with artists who worked there (*cf.* V. de Saedeleer, A. Servaes, G. v. d. Woestyne also F. v. d. Berghe, C. Permeke). [Fl. 388, Fl. 296, Fl. Bib. 19th cent.]

Abeele, Jodocus Sebastiaen van den. Flemish Sch. *b* Ghent 1797 *d* Ghent 1855. '*History*' (*classical and mythological subjects*), *landscapes, genre, portraits.* Pupil in Ghent of P. v. Huffel, in Brussels of L. David, and in Paris of Baron Gros (*cf.* H. de Caisne, C. L. Saligo, F. Simonau) 1819; went to Italy 1824; was for some years in Rome where Prince Louis Napoleon (later Napoleon III) was his pupil; Professor in Ghent Acad. 1836. Represented in BELGIAN Royal Coll. *Family at evening prayers.* A *Homer,* an *Answer of the Delphic Oracle* (in Ghent Salon 1820), an *Orpheus after the death of Eurydice* and paintings in the Ara Coeli monastery in Rome are recorded. [Fl. 451, Fl. 612, Fl. 481, Fl. 892, Fl. 798.]

Abeloos, Sonia. Flemish Sch. *b* Brussels 1876. *Ports, beach scenes, genre.* Exhibited Paris Salons; also London exhibitions (1909-18). [Fl. 465.]

Abeloos, Victor. Flemish Sch. *b* Brussels 1881. *Landscapes, animals, figure pieces, portraits.* Pupil of A. Cluysenaar (*cf.* J. de Lalaing); exhibited Glasgow Royal Institute 1901, Paris Salon and Artistes Français. Titles recorded include *The king of the Flemish prairie (a stallion)* 1901, *Tiger destroying a serpent* 1904, *Circe* 1931, *The man with the heron* 1932. [Fl. 440, Fl. 73.]

Abry, Léon (Léon Eugène Auguste). Flemish Sch. *b* son of a general, Antwerp 1857 *d* Antwerp 1905. '*History*', *military genre, animals, landscapes, portraits; also posters and engravings.* Pupil in Antwerp Acad. of N. de Keyser. Member of the Dertien (XIII) group (*cf.* E. Farasyn) 1891; Knight of the Order of Leopold. Represented in ANTWERP *Grooming horses in a barracks* 1887, *Rocks at Laroche* 1891 and others. BRUSSELS *Infantry rally after battle.* A *Leopold II on horseback at manoeuvres* was exhibited 1903. [Fl. 440, Fl. 17.]

Abshoven, see **Apshoven.**

Acar, Charles Louis. Flemish Sch. *b* Audenarde 1804. *Religious subjects for churches, portraits, landscapes and genre.* Pupil in Brussels Acad. of J. D. Odevaere. Visited Holland. [Fl. 892.]

Achtschellinck, Lucas. Flemish Sch. *b* Brussels 1626 *d* Brussels 1699. *Wooded landscapes (with figures, religious and genre, sometimes by other artists); also designs for tapestry (cf.* A. F. Baudewyns and A. Genoels). Pupil of P. van der Borcht the younger and L. de Vadder *q.v.*; Master Brussels Guild 1657; was paid for pictures in Brussels S. Gudule (*cf.* J. d'Arthois) D. v. Heil, I. v. d. Stock) 1659 and 1666; was granted exemption from beer tax for designing tapestries for Brussels Magistrature 1680; cartoons for landscape tapestries 'van goeden meester van Achtschellinck' were exported to Vienna by the Forchoudt firm (*cf.* A. Casteels and A. Coppens) *c.* 1702; T. Michau was his pupil. **Documented Example:** BRUGES Mus. *Landscape with S. Dominic and angels* (formerly Dominican Church where seen 1768 by Descamps who records W. (Guillaume) van Oost as painter of the figures); Descamps also records in Bruges S. Anne *Flight into Egypt,* with figures by L. de Deyster, and other examples in churches and religious houses in Brussels and Malines. A *Clearing in a forest* (now in Bruges Mus.) comes from the Abbaye des Dunes (*cf.* D. v. d. Bogaerde). Dresden has *Road through a wood with figures and animals* and *House in a wood with canal and figures* recorded his work by 1742; the figures and animals in both pictures are presumed by some the work of P. Bout *q.v.* [Fl. 86, Fl. 425, Fl. 215, Fl. 216, Fl. 576, Fl. 440, Fl. 301, Fl. 212.]

Acker, Florimond van. Flemish Sch. *b* Bruges 1858 *d* after 1935. *Landscapes, picturesque corners of old Bruges, genre, portraits, religious subjects (including murals for churches cf.* J. Swerts); *also posters.* Pupil in Bruges Acad.; then in Antwerp of C. Verlat and in Brussels of J. Portaels; travelled widely; visited England; Director Bruges Acad. 1910-26. Represented in BRUGES *Bruges from the ramparts* 1903 and two *Portraits.* Murals in OSTEND, BRUGES, BASSEVELDE, HARLEBEKE, HOLLEBEKE and other churches. [Fl. 440, Fl. 114.]

Acker, Jean Baptiste van (or Vanacker). Flemish Sch. *b* Bruges 1794 *d* Bruges 1863. *Miniatures.* Pupil in Bruges Acad. of J. F. Ducq *q.v.*; went Paris, 1834; painted many miniatures there and contributed to Gavarni's *Journal des Gens du Monde.* Later patronised by Leopold I in Brussels (*cf.* A. v. Assche); visited England. Represented in BRUGES Mus. [Fl. 892, Fl. 114, Fl. 73.]

*Adriaenssen, Alexander. Flemish Sch. *b* son of a musician Emanuel A., Antwerp 1587 *d* Antwerp 1661. *Still life with birds, fruit, cheese, flowers, but mainly fish and sometimes with a cat (cf.* C. Peeters, J. F. van Es, T. van Apshoven, F. Cuyck de Mierhop, C. Luyckx, F. Snyders, A. van Utrecht, H. Andriessen). Master (as water colour painter *cf.* J. Jordaens) in Antwerp Guild 1610; worked under Rubens on Pageant Entry into Antwerp of Cardinal Infante Ferdinand (*cf.* G. Weri) 1635; friend of P. Snayers and of Rubens who owned a *Bird piece* and a *Basket of fruit* and whose first wife Isabella Brant stood godmother to one of his children (*cf.* M. Pepyn and Jan (Velvet) Brueghel). His works in contemporary Antwerp collections (*cf.* V. Wolfvoet) included a *Fish market,* a *Bird's nest with birds* (*cf.* P. Snyers) and a *Hambone;* some were exported by the Forchoudt firm of dealers (*cf.* A. Casteels) to

Vienna. F. Denys painted his portrait which was engraved. **Signed Examples:** AMSTERDAM Rijks. *Still life with lobster, haddock and other fish* 1660. BUDAPEST *Fish* 1640. MADRID Prado *Still life with cheese, bread and fish, Still life with cod, salmon, other fish and a cat,* and two others. VIENNA K. *Dead game and cat.*
[Fl. 86, Fl. 425, Fl. 215, Fl. 107, Fl. 892, Fl. 440, Fl. 212, Fl. 213.]

Adriaenssen, Antoon. Flemish Sch. *b* Antwerp (?) before 1595 *d* Rome (?) 1649 (?). Pupil in Antwerp of H. v. Balen (*cf.* J. v. Belcamp and A. van Dyck) 1605; Master Antwerp Guild 1614; went Rome (?) and remained there (?) (*cf.* W. Backereel.)
[Fl. 617, Fl. 892.]

Adriaenssen, Jasper (Gaspar). Flemish Sch. *b* Antwerp (?) before 1605 *d* Antwerp (?) 1632. *Landscapes.* Master Antwerp Guild 1620; completed a number of pictures left unfinished by A. Govaerts *q.v.* at his death (*cf.* J. v. d. Lanen, F. Francken II, H. Jordaens III) 1626. [Fl. 107.]

Adriaenssen (or **Adriaens**), **Lucas.** Flemish Sch. *b* Antwerp before 1450 *d* before 1493. *Decorative paintings; religious subjects* (?). Employed in Antwerp Cathedral 1467; worked in Bruges on decorations for marriage ceremonies of Duke Charles the Bold with Margaret of York (*cf.* P. Bernart, P. Coustain, J. Daret, H. v. d. Goes, D. de Rycke, V. v. d. Stoct also H. met de Bles) 1468; Dean in Antwerp Guild 1469, 1475, 1480, 1483. [Fl. 892, Fl. 440, Fl. 150.]

Adriaensz, Anthonis. Flemish (Dutch) Sch. *b* son of burgomaster, Alkmaar before 1590 *d* 1642. Van Mander (1604) records him as a 'goed schilder' living in Alkmaar. [Fl. 559.]

Adriano, see **Rodriguez.**

Aeken, Hieronymus van, see **Bosch.**

Aelst, P. C. van, see **Coecke.**

*Aenvanck, Theodor. Flemish Sch. *b* Antwerp 1633 *d* place unknown *c.* 1690. *Still life with fruit and vessels* (*cf.* A. Benedetti, A. Brueghel, J. v. Buken, A. Coosemans, J. D. Coosemas, G. Gabron, J. P. Gillemans, P. Gysels, C. de Heem, J. D. de Heem, C. Luyckx, C. Mahu, M. de Paepe, J. M. Picart, C. de Somme, J. v. Son, J. F. v. Son, A. v. Utrecht, also J. v. Hulsdonck). Master Antwerp Guild 1670; presumed to have worked most of his life abroad. **Signed Example:** ANTWERP *Still life with grapes and other fruit* 1653.
[Fl. 107, Fl. 892, Fl. 16.]

Aerdenberg, W. S., see **Ehrenberg.**

Aertsen, A. and D., see **Pietersz.**

*Aertsen (or **Aartsen**). **Pieter,** called 'Lange Peer' or 'Pier' (Pietro Lungo) on account of his height. Flemish (Dutch) Sch. *b* son of a weaver specializing in stockings, Amsterdam *c.* 1508 *d* Amsterdam 1575. *Religious subjects, some combined with genre scenes* (*cf.* J. Beuckelaer), *kitchen scenes* (*cf.* P. C. v. Ryck), *market pieces, peasant genre* (*cf.* P. Bruegel the elder, M. v. Cleve, P. Balten, J. (Velvet) Brueghel, F. Verbeeck); *also designs for glass windows* (*cf.* J. de Gheyn and P. A. Cluyt). Pupil in Amsterdam of Allaert Claesz; went Antwerp where lived with J. Mandyn; Master Antwerp Guild 1535; citizen Antwerp 1542; returned Amsterdam *c.* 1556; his pictures painted for churches in Amsterdam, Delft, Louvain, Diest and Warmenhuyzen, described by van Mander (1604), were destroyed by the Iconoclasts (*cf.* A. Blocklandt and J. Cornelisz v. Oostsanen) 1566 although in one case a lady offered the rioters '100 pond' to spare it (*cf.* J. Gossaert); his religious paintings were admired by M. Coxie; his genre pictures were collected by J. Rauwaert in Amsterdam (*cf.* M. v.

Heemskerck); his pupils included his sons A., D., and P. Pietersz *q.v.*, his wife's nephew J. Beuckelaer and J. v. d. Straet (Stradanus). **Monogrammed Examples:** (Initials and/or a woolcomb to indicate his family's trade *cf.* A. and P. Pietersz and L. Blondeel): ANTWERP Mayer v. d. Bergh *Peasant wedding* (*cf.* P. Bruegel the elder) (*m.*) 1556. BERLIN K.F. *Landscape with the road to Calvary* (*cf.* P. Bruegel the elder) (*m.* and comb) 1552. BRUSSELS *Christ in the house of Mary and Martha* (*cf.* J. Beuckelaer and J. Goeimare) (*m.* and comb) 1559, *The cook* (*m.* and comb) 1559. BUDAPEST *Peasants at market* (comb) 1561. FRANKFORT Städel. *Market scene with Christ and the Adulteress* (*m.*) 1559. GENOA Pal. Bianco *Cook* (*m.*) 1559. LILLE *Peasant woman* (comb). ROTTERDAM Boymans *The cake baker* (comb) 1560, *Nebuchadnezzar worshipping idols* (comb). STOCKHOLM *Kitchen scene* (comb) 1562. **Documented Example:** ANTWERP (851-853) Triptych: centre: *Crucifixion,* wings: *Donor Jan v. d. Biest (soapboiler and sheriff) with S. John the Baptist, S. John the Evangelist with the Virgin destroying a seven headed dragon in the clouds,* exterior wings: grisaille *Twelve kneeling old women with SS. Francis of Assisi and William of Mateval* (commissioned for an Antwerp Almshouse 1546 and initialled 'A' on a soldier's shield in the centre panel. Van Mander records a *Kitchen piece with a head of an ox* (later copied by the Dutch painter A. Bloemaert), a *Joseph,* an *Emmaus* and among subjects painted for Amsterdam Nieuwe Kerk a *Beheading of S. Catherine.* Antwerp 17th cent. collectors' inventories and invoices of the Forchoudt firm of Antwerp exporting dealers record a *Brothel scene,* a *King with a man, The Calling of Matthew* (with J. V. de Vries), *Rebecca, S. Mary Magdalene, The Story of Joseph* (*cf.* R. Aertsz, A. Blocklandt, Joseph Master, A. Claesz van Leyden, M. Pepyn), kitchen and market pieces. ROTTERDAM (Boymans) has a *Christ in the house of Mary and Martha* dated 1553. Amsterdam Rijks. has *Ox's head with shepherd* (fragment) presumed by some part of a *Nativity* recorded by van Mander painted for Amsterdam Nieuwe Kerk and destroyed by the Iconoclasts. Other pictures presumed by some his work are in various museums (*cf.* Brussels Kitchen scene Painter).
[Fl. 371, Fl. 818, Fl. 559, Fl. 107, Fl. 892, Fl. 765, Fl. 445, Fl. 885, Fl. 212, Fl. 213, Fl. 316, Fl. 631 (1936), Fl. 421.]

Aertsen, P. the younger, see **Pietersz, P.**

Aertsz (Aartsz), Ryckaert. Flemish (Dutch) Sch. *b* son of a fisherman, Wyck-aan-Zee 1482 *d* aged ninety-five and nearly blind, Antwerp 1577. Known as Ryck-met-de-Stelt (Dick-with-the-crutch) because he had lost a leg. *Religious subjects; also nudes, some in works by other painters.* Pupil in Haarlem of J. Mostaert *q.v.*; went Antwerp where member of artists' Chamber of Rhetoric 'Violiere' 1520. Van Mander (1604) describes him as an amiable, peaceful and pious man with a paintable (schilderachtig) head, content in later life to do nothing but paint the nudes in pictures by other artists for a small wage; he also records that F. Floris *q.v.* painted his portrait as *S. Luke painting* and gave it to the Guild in 1556. His son Lambert A. was Master in Antwerp Guild 1555. **Signed Examples:** None. **Documented Examples:** None. His *Joseph's brothers appealing for corn* and *Joseph as governor* (wings recorded by van Mander as added to a *Crucifixion* by Jansz Jacob *q.v.* in Haarlem S. Bavo) were extant till 1784 (*cf.* P. Aertsen). [Fl. 559, Fl. 892.]

Agneesens, Édouard. Flemish Sch. *b* son of a proof reader, Brussels 1842 *d* (insane) Uccle 1885. *Portraits, genre, and cartoons for compositions.* Pupil in Brussels Acad. and of J. Portaels *q.v.* Visited Russia 1869; J. de Lalaing was his pupil. Represented in ANTWERP *Juliette Quénel.* BRUSSELS *The painter I. Verheyden, The sculptor G. Marchant, The woman with the glove* 1874, *The children of M. Colard* 1874, *Maternity* 1875, *The botanist Prof. Bommer* 1875, *Sleeping boy* (painted at the age of seventeen); GHENT, TOURNAI

Woman knitting 1882. A full length portrait *The tragedian Samoiloff* and a group *The children of M. Samoiloff* painted in S. Petersbourg are recorded.

[Fl. 160 (1885), Fl. 440, Fl. 296, Fl. Bib. 19th cent.]

Aken, Alexander van, see **Haecken.**

Aken, Anthonis van. Flemish (Dutch) Sch. *b* 's Hertogenbosch before 1430 *d* 's Hertogenbosch 1478. Father of Hieronymus Bosch *q.v. Religious subjects.* Worked for Brotherhood of Our Lady (Lieve Vrouwe Broederschap) 's Hertogenbosch. Two panels of an altarpiece for the Brotherhood left unfinished at his death, were handed over to Hieronymus Bosch 1480.

[Fl. 595, Fl. 60, Fl. 133 (1950).]

Aken, Arnold (Arnout) van. Flemish Sch. *b* Antwerp (?) date unknown *d* London 1736. Brother of J. van Aken (?). *Small figures, landscapes and conversations; also active as engraver.* Vertue (1736) records a set of prints of fish 'or wonders of the deep' (*cf.* H. J. Redouté). Strutt (1785) records 'frontispieces to plays and to other small works for booksellers'.

[Fl. 826, Fl. 782, Fl. 856.]

Aken, François van. Flemish Sch. *b* Antwerp (?) before 1652 *d* after 1714. *Fruit and flowers* (*cf.* J. B. de Crépu, A. Brueghel, J. v. d. Hecke, N. Verendael). Master Antwerp Guild 1667. M. Blommaerdt was his pupil 1697. [Fl. 892.]

Aken, Hieronymus van, see **Bosch.**

Aken (or Vanaecken or Van Haecken), Joseph van, known as 'Tailor Vanaken'. Flemish Sch. *b* Antwerp 1699 *d* London 1749. *'History' genre and portraits, but mainly drapery and compositions for other portrait painters* (*cf.* J. B. Gaspers). Came London (*cf.* P. v. Angellis and P. Tillemans) *c.* 1719; employed as drapery painter by the English portrait painter T. Hudson, the Scottish painter A. Ramsay and many others, and added figures to heads sent him from all over the country; made much money and formed a collection of objets d'art; with the English painters W. Hogarth, F. Hayman and Hudson and his brother (*cf.* A. v. Haecken) visited France (where Hogarth was arrested for sketching Calais Gate) 1748; Hogarth caricatured the despair of the portrait painters at 'the Tailor's death'; Vertue who describes him as 'a man of good complexion, a good round fat face and a small cast with one eye' saw (1749) his portrait in Ramsay's studio 'mighty well and very like him'.

[Fl. 826, Fl. 729, Fl. 856, Fl. 223, Fl. 880, Fl. 18 (1936).]

Aken, Léon van. Flemish Sch. *b* Antwerp 1857 *d* Antwerp 1904. *Peasant genre and interiors.* Pupil of P. Beaufaux in Antwerp Acad. Member Antwerp group De Dertien (XIII) (*cf.* E. Farasyn) 1891. Represented in ANTWERP *The Archers* 1901, *The Invalid.* [Fl. 440.]

Aken, Sebastiaen van. Flemish Sch. *b* Malines 1648 *d* Malines 1722. *Religious subjects for Malines churches and religious houses* (*cf.* D. and H. Herregouts, G. Smeyers and G. J. Smeyers, J. Verhoeven). Pupil in Malines of L. Franchoys the younger (*cf.* P. S. Verlinden); Master 1666; went Italy where pupil of Carlo Maratta (*cf.* R. v. Audenaerd, E. Fisen and R. P. de Rendeux); went Spain (*cf.* J. v. Kessel the younger and A. Smit) *c.* 1700; also visited Portugal; Descamps (1769) records an *Assumption of the Virgin* (by 'v. Aeken') in Malines Hanswyck Church; a *S. Norbert receiving the Habit of his Order from the Virgin* in Duffel (near Malines) is also recorded. [Fl. 216, Fl. 613, Fl. 892.]

Albert, Ernest. Flemish Sch. *b* Berchem (Antwerp) 1900. *Landscapes, town pieces, marines, portraits, still life, nudes.* Pupil in Antwerp Higher Institute of F. Courtens. Represented in ANTWERP *Evening on the Scheldt, The lighthouse.*

[Fl. 17.]

Albert, Joseph. Flemish Sch. *b* Brussels 1886. *Landscapes, figure pieces, still life, portraits.* Pupil S. Josse-ten-Noode

(Brussels) Acad. Represented in ANTWERP *Still life* 1923. BRUSSELS *Kitchen garden* 1927. GHENT *Landscape.*

[Fl. 388, Fl. 296, Fl. 17.]

Alé, see **Hallet.**

★Alkmaar Master (or Seven Works of Mercy Master). Presumed Flemish (Dutch) Sch. 16th cent. Name for painter of AMSTERDAM Rijks. *The Seven Works of Mercy* (seven panels, in one frame, dated 1504, from Alkmaar, S. Laurentius (*cf.* Cornelis Buys the elder). Pictures presumed by some his work are in various museums. [Fl. 316, Fl. 798.]

★Alsloot, Denis van. Flemish Sch. *b c.* 1570 *d c.* 1627. *Landscapes with religious and mythological subjects (figures sometimes by others including H. de Clerck q.v.), winter scenes (cf. P. Bruegel the elder, L. van Valkenborch and J. d'Arthois), processions and other contemporary fêtes (cf. A. Sallaert also F. Duchatel).* Master Brussels Guild 1599; Court Painter to Archduke Albert and Infanta Isabella (*cf.* J. (Velvet) Brueghel, G. Claeissens, H. de Clerck, G. v. Deynum, A. v. Dyck, J. Francart, N. v. d. Horst, M. Joncquoy, J. de Liemakere, P. v. d. Meulen, P. and S. Noveliers, A. v. Opstal, G. Pietersz, F. Pourbus the younger, P. P. Rubens, A. Sallaert, P. Snayers, J. Snellinck, P. v. Somer, Jacob Stevens, O. v. Veen also G. de Crayer) from *c.* 1599; commissioned by Archduchess to paint a series of pictures recording Ommeganck procession in 1615 when the Archduchess shot down the popinjay (*cf.* P. N. v. Reysschoot and D. Teniers the younger). **Signed Examples:** ANTWERP *Landscape with Tobias and the Angel* 1610. BRUSSELS *Bird's eye view of the Castle and Park at Mariemont* 1620, *Cambre Abbey* (*winter scene*) 1616, *Groenendael Abbey in Soignes Forest* 1612. LONDON Vic. and Alb. *Two scenes from the 1615 Ommeganck procession series* 1616. LOUVAIN Jesuit College *Jesus tempted in the Desert* 1611 (also signed by H. de Clerck). MADRID Prado *Two scenes from 1615 Ommeganck procession series* 1616, *Feast of Our Lady of the Wood* (*Vivier d'Oye Fête in Tervueren Forest*) 1616. MOSIGKAU (nr. Dessau) *Winter landscape* 1614. NANTES *Cambre Abbey* 1609. SCHLEISSHEIM *Earthly Paradise* (also signed by H. de Clerck; *cf.* R. Savery). VIENNA K. *Landscape with Cephalus and Procris* (A's signature recorded but no longer legible; also signed by H. de Clerck; *cf.* P. Symons) 1608; Harrach *Marshy landscape.* **Documented Example:** BRUSSELS Mus. *Vivier d'Oye Fête in presence of Archduke Albert and Archduchess Isabella* (same subject as Madrid: *Feast of Our Lady of the Wood;* Tervueren Inventory 1677).

[Fl. 86, Fl. 866, Fl. 892, Fl. 440, Fl. 25 (1922), Fl. 508.]

Amberes, Francisco de, see **Antwerp, F. of.**

Amberes, Miguel de, see **Manrique.**

Amstel (Aertssone), Jan van. Flemish (Dutch) Sch. *b* Amsterdam before 1507 *d* Antwerp before 1544. Brother of P. Aertsen (?). *Religious subjects.* Master Antwerp Guild 1522 or 1528; citizen of Antwerp 1536; Guarienti in his edition of Orlandi's Abecedario (1753) records a *Crucifixion* with more than two hundred figures. Presumed by some identical with J. de Hollander *q.v.* [Fl. 628, Fl. 107, Fl. 892, Fl. 421.]

★Amsterdam Armed Arquebusiers Painter. Presumed Flemish (Dutch) Sch. 16th cent. Name for painter of AMSTERDAM Rijks. (366) *Seventeen Arquebusiers of the 'A' company in armour* (an A and T incorporated are on a shield) 1531. Presumed by some identical with C. Anthonisz (Teunissen) *q.v.* and by others with J. v. Scorel *q.v.* [Fl. 7, Fl. 8, Fl. 316.]

★Amsterdam Cadaver Painter. Presumed Flemish (Dutch) Sch. 15th/16th cent. Name for painter of AMSTERDAM Rijks. (43a) *Allegory: Vanity of Human Life* (*cf.* C. Engelbrechtsz, E. Schayck the elder, Frankfort Master, F. Pourbus the elder, A. J. Verburcht also C. N. Gysbrechts). Presumed by some identical with Delft Master *q.v.*

Amsterdam Death of the Virgin Master. Presumed Flemish (Dutch) Sch. 15th/16th cent. (Not to be confused with the Death of the Virgin Master *q.v.*). Name for painter of AMSTERDAM Hofje der Zeven Keurvorsten *Death of the Virgin*. Pictures presumed by some his work are in various museums. [Fl. 421, Fl. 316.]

*****Amsterdam Delft Painter.** Presumed Flemish (Dutch) Sch. early 16th cent. Name for painter of AMSTERDAM Rijks. (774a) Triptych: *Holy Family with SS. Dorothy and Catherine and angels in a walled garden, Donor with Bishop as patron saint, Donor's wife with S. Barbara*, and (on exterior) *Annunciation*. Presumed by some identical with Delft Master *q.v.*

*****Amsterdam Little Girl with Dog Painter.** Presumed Flemish (Dutch) Sch. 16th cent. Name for painter of AMSTERDAM Rijks. (773) *Little girl with dog* (*cf.* C. v. Hemessen, F. Pourbus the elder, F. Pourbus the younger) inscribed 1581. Presumed by some identical with J. W. Delff *q.v.*

*****Amsterdam Moucheron Family Painter.** Presumed Flemish (Dutch) Sch. 16th cent. Name for painter of AMSTERDAM Rijks. (152) *Pierre de Moucheron, his wife Isabeau and their twenty children* dated 1563. Presumed by some identical with Cornelis de Zeeu *q.v.*

André Virgin Master. Presumed Flemish Sch. 15th/16th cent. Name for painter of PARIS Jacquemart-André Mus. *Virgin and Child*. [Fl. 316.]

Andriessen (Andriesz), Hendrik called 'Mancken Heyn' (Limping Henry). Flemish Sch. *b* Antwerp 1607 *d* Zeeland 1655. *Still life (including 'Vanitas' compositions)* (*cf.* A. Adriaenssen, C. Peeters, P. Boel and C. N. Gysbrechts). Paintings presumed by some his work are in various museums. [Fl. 86, Fl. 892, Fl. 632.]

Anethan, Alix (Alice). Flemish Sch. *b* Brussels 1848 *d* Paris 1921. *Allegories, religious subjects, genre*. Pupil of E. Wauters and in Paris of A. Stevens and the French painter Puvis de Chavannes. Represented in BRUSSELS *Holy Women at the Tomb* and drawings. GHENT *Woman's head*. An allegory titled *The Garden* was exhibited in the Paris Salon 1894. [Fl. 123, Fl. Bib. 19th cent.]

Angellis (or Angillis or Anchilus), Pieter van. Flemish Sch. *b* Dunkirk 1685 *d* Rennes 1734. *Outdoor genre, market scenes, landscapes with small figures, conversation pieces* (*cf.* I. v. d. Beke), *interiors*. Went Antwerp and worked with J. B. Bouttats; visited Düsseldorf; came England (*cf.* F. Breydel, J. van Aken, P. Tillemans, A. Schoonjans, S. Dubois, P. Snyers, and Jan Peeters the younger). *c* 1712; may have revisited Antwerp where Master in Guild 1715; Vertue (before 1754) describes him as 'a man of affable temper and genteel manners' who had a studio in Covent Garden Piazza the fashionable artists' quarter 1726; made small copies of *Market scenes* by F. Snyders *q.v.* (then at Houghton now Leningrad Hermitage); went Rome with the sculptors Scheemakers and Delvaux 1728; in Rome used male model for both male and female figures in his genre pictures; settled Rennes *c.* 1731. **Signed Examples:** BERLIN K.F. *The Approach (young man and peasant girl before a cottage)* 1725. LONDON Nat. Portrait Gallery *Installation of the Knights of the Garter in Kensington Palace August 4th 1713.* STOCKHOLM *Interior of a sculptor's studio* 1716 (*cf.* B. van den Bossche and G. Thomas). Vertue records a *Covent Garden Market with figures in contemporary clothes* 1726. [Fl. 353, Fl. 826, Fl. 856, Fl. 612, Fl. 223, Fl. 892, Fl. 92.]

Ansiaux, Antoine (Jean Joseph Eléonore Antoine). Flemish Sch. *b* Liège 1764 *d* Paris 1840. *Portraits (some in miniature) religious subjects, 'history', costume history; also contemporary history* (*cf.* M. I. v. Brée). Studied Liège and Antwerp; went Paris where pupil in Académie Royale (*cf.* P. Lafontaine and P. Sauvage, also P. van Mol) 1783; worked also under the French painter F. A. Vincent; remained Paris and became member during Revolution of Société Populaire et Républicaine des Arts (*cf.* J. L. Demarne); popular Salon exhibitor under Directorate, Consulate and Empire (*cf.* L. Gerbo, P. J. Redouté and J. B. Suvée); officially patronized during Restoration when many of his works were acquired by the French State. **Documented Examples:** BORDEAUX *Richelieu presenting Poussin to Louis XIII* 1817. CASTRES *Mme Bonet*. LIÈGE Cathedral *Conversion of S. Paul* 1814; Town Hall *Return of the Prodigal Son* 1819. LILLE *S. John rebuking Herod* 1822. PARIS S. Étienne du Mont *S. Paul preaching* 1824. VERSAILLES *General Kléber* 1799, *General Kellerman* 1800, *Comte de Champmol* 1810. Others in cathedrals of Angers, Arras, Le Mans, and Metz. Recorded works include *Citizen B... architect teaching his brother to draw* (Salon 1796); *Renaldo and Armida* (Salon 1817), *The clemency of Napoleon to the Princess de Hatzfeld* (Salon 1833), *Christ dying on the Cross* (Salon 1835). [Fl. 66, Fl. 612, Fl. 197.]

*****Anthonisz (or Teunissen), Cornelis.** Flemish (Dutch) Sch. *b* Amsterdam *c.* 1500 *d* after 1554. *Group portraits* (*cf.* D. Jacobsz, D. Barendsz, J. W. Delff); *town views; contemporary warfare* (*cf.* P. Bruegel the elder, Antwerp Destruction of Citadel Painter also J. de Gheyn and P. Snayers); *also active as engraver (copper and wood) and cartographer*. Member of Amsterdam Archers Guard 1536; served as official draughtsman in Emperor Charles V's fleet during Algerian campaign (*cf.* J. van Battel and J. C. Vermeyen) 1539-41; worked on Pageant Entry into Amsterdam of Charles V and Philip (*cf.* L. Blondeel, F. Floris, P. J. Pourbus, J. v. Rillaert, J. Scorel and J. Vredeman de Vries) 1549; city councillor 1547; was present at siege of Terwaenen (Thérouanne) and made woodcuts 1553. **Monogrammed Examples:** AMSTERDAM Rijks. *Banquet of Civic Guardsmen* (initials C. and T. on either side of S. Anthony's bell and 1533; from Amsterdam Lodge of the Crossbowmen of S. George); Town Hall *View of Amsterdam* (initials C. and T. with bell and 1536; his woodcuts of this subject (on 12 blocks) were presented to Charles V 1544). His engravings and woodcuts include many allegorical subjects (*cf.* J. de Backer and C. Ketel) and a *Destruction of the Tower of Babel* (*cf.* M. v. Valkenborch). *Cf.* also Amsterdam Armed Arquebusiers Painter. [Fl. 425, Fl. 53, Fl. 892, Fl. 421.]

*****Antonissen, Henricus Josephus.** Flemish Sch. *b* Antwerp 1737 *d* Antwerp 1794. '*History at first, then picturesque landscapes with figures and animals* (*cf.* J. F. Legillon); *occasional still life with fruit and flowers*. Pupil of B. Beschey (*cf.* A. C. Lens) 1753; Master in Antwerp Guild 1755; member of Jesuit Brotherhood of Married Men. His pupils included S. Denis *q.v.*, H. Blomaerts, H. J. F. de Cort, B. P. Ommeganck, W. J. L. Spoor and J. A. Trachez. **Signed Examples:** ANTWERP *Landscape* 1776. CAMBRIDGE Fitz. *Wooded landscape with figures and cattle* 1787. FRANKFORT Staedel: *Landscape with cattle* 1792. VIENNA Harrach *Landscape with ruins and figures* 1780. [Fl. 451, Fl. 107, Fl. 892, Fl. 440.]

Antwerp, Francis of (known in Spain as Francisco de Amberes). Flemish Sch. *b* Antwerp (?) before 1475 *d* Toledo 1512. *Religious subjects* (?); *worked as polychromer and decorator*. Went Spain (*cf.* J. v. Lathem); worked with Spanish artists Juan de Borgoña and others in Toledo Cathedral 1493-1512. [Fl. 153, Fl. 668.]

*****Antwerp Adoration Master.** Presumed Flemish Sch. early 16th cent. Name for painter of ANTWERP Mus. (208-210) Triptych: *Adoration of the Magi, S. George, S. Margaret and donor;* exterior wings: *Archangel Gabriel* and *Virgin Annunciate*. Pictures presumed by some his work are in various museums. [Fl. 13, Fl. 316, Fl. 16.]

Antwerp Crucifixion Master. Presumed Flemish Sch. early 16th cent. Name for painter of ANTWERP Mus. (649-651) Triptych: *Crucifixion, Carrying of the Cross, Resurrection.* [Fl. 13, Fl. 740 (1934), Fl. 316.]

*Antwerp Destruction of Citadel Painter. Presumed Flemish Sch. 16th cent. Name for painter of ANTWERP Mus. (670) *Demolition of the Spanish Citadel in Antwerp 1577.* Presumed by some identical with P. Goetkint *q.v.* (*Cf.* Worcester Destruction of Citadel Painter, F. Pourbus the elder, J. V. de Vries, P. A. Cluyt and C. Verlat).

*Antwerp Forties Painter. Presumed Flemish Sch. 16th cent. Name for painter of ANTWERP (697) *Elizabeth, wife of G. van Schoonbeke* dated 1544. Presumed by some identical with Forties Master *q.v.*

*Antwerp Last Judgement Painter. Presumed Flemish Sch. 15th/16th cent. Name for painter of ANTWERP Mus. (680) *Last Judgement with Seven Works of Mercy* and *Seven Deadly Sins.* [Fl. 13, Fl. 16.]

'Antwerp Mannerists'. Generic name for Antwerp painters active *c.* 1500-*c.* 1530 whose identities are not known. [Fl. 316.]

*Antwerp Philippe de Croy Painter. Presumed Flemish Sch. *c.* 1459. Name for painter of ANTWERP Mus. (254) *Philippe de Croy, Seigneur de Sempy, as an adorant.* (Philippe de Croy bore the title of Seigneur de Sempy 1459-1460). Presumed by some identical with R. v. d. Weyden *q.v.*

Antwerp Triptych of the Virgin Master. Presumed Flemish (Dutch) Sch. 15/16th cent. Name for painter of ANTWERP Mus. (561-563) Triptych: *Virgin and Child enthroned with musician angels, S. George, S. Christopher.* [Fl. 316.]

Apshoven, Ferdinand van the elder. Flemish Sch. *b* Antwerp 1576 *d c.* 1653. *'History' and portraits.* Pupil of A. van Noort *q.v.* at the same time as Rubens (*cf.* H. v. Balen); Master Antwerp Guild 1596. (*Cf.* J. van Kessel the elder). [Fl. 107, Fl. 892, Fl. 440.]

Apshoven, Ferdinand van the younger. Flemish Sch. *b* son of Ferdinand van A. the elder, Antwerp 1630 *d* Antwerp 1694. *Peasant genre and interiors* (*cf.* D. Ryckaert III); *also active as dealer* (*cf.* P. v. Avont). Presumed by some pupil of D. Teniers the younger. In Antwerp Guild as dealer 1657. A *Genre scene with soldiers* (*cortegaarde*) by 'van Ophoven' was exported to Vienna by the Forchoudt firm of Antwerp dealers 1690 (*cf.* T. van A.) [Fl. 107, Fl. 892, Fl. 440, Fl. 212.]

Apshoven, Thomas van. Flemish Sch. *b* son of Ferdinand van A. the elder, Antwerp 1622 *d* Antwerp *c.* 1665. *Indoor and outdoor genre* (*cf.* D. Ryckaert III), *still life* (*cf.* A. Adriaenssen). Presumed by some pupil of D. Teniers the younger; Master in Antwerp Guild 1646; standard bearer Antwerp Civic Guard 1652; his sister married J. van Kessel the elder *q.v.* His son Willem van A. (1664-94) was also a painter. **Signed Examples:** DARMSTADT *Cottage with peasants and girl drawing water from a well* 1656. DRESDEN *Oysters, fruit and vessels.* Landscapes and copies of pictures by Teniers are recorded in Antwerp 17th cent. inventories (*cf.* F. van A. the younger). [Fl. 107, Fl. 892, Fl. 440, Fl. 213.]

Archimedes, see Genoels, A.

Arden, Charlotte Léonie. Flemish Sch. *b* Antwerp 1860 *d* Uccle (near Brussels) 1904. *Genre.* Pupil of Alfred Stevens; exhibitor Paris Salon. Represented BRUSSELS *Et je suis resté seul.* [Fl. 160 (1904), Fl. 123.]

Argent, Marie Josèphe d' (**Mme Hebbelinck**). Flemish Sch. *b* daugher of Michel A., Liège 1789 *d* Uccle (nr. Brussels) 1863. *Miniatures* (signed Joséphine). [Fl. 892.]

Argent (Dargent), Michel d'. Flemish Sch. *b* Liège 1751 *d* Liège 1824. *'History' and miniatures.* In Rome 1775-81 (*cf.* H. Deprez and J. Dreppe); then Liège and Brussels. He signed 'Dargent'. [Fl. 892.]

Argonne (Dargonne), Simon Pierre d'. Flemish Sch. *b* Dieppe 1749 *d* Brussels 1839. *Landscapes round Vilvorde (near Brussels)* (*cf.* H. Bloemaerts). Went Antwerp where recorded as Pierre Simon Gautier and as a dancing and music master (*cf.* C. S. Dubois) 1772; member of Antwerp Soc. of Artists (*cf.* B. P. Ommeganck) 1789; after French occupation of Antwerp (1794) collaborated with French and became Commissaire du Directoire exécutif with authority over the Academy (*cf.* L. Defrance, W. J. Herreyns, L. Moons and P. J. Regemorter; but also A. B. de Quertenmont); as painter chiefly active after 1811 when settled at Vilvorde; signed himself (1821) pupil of J. B. de Roy *q.v.* [Fl. 104, Fl. 107, Fl. 892, Fl. 440.]

Armanno, Vincenzo, called Monsù Armanno. Flemish Sch. *b* Flanders *c.* 1599 *d* aged 50, Venice 1649. *Landscapes and frescoes.* Went Italy and remained there (*cf.* W. Backereel and J. Sutterman); worked Rome in palaces of the nobility; Passeri (1772) records him denounced to the Inquisition for eating meat on Fast days and imprisoned in a Dominican monastery (*cf.* D. de Coninck); after his release he set out for home but succumbed to a fever in Venice. **Documented Example:** ROME Sta. Maria sopra Minerva (Fresco) *Landscape with hermits* (recorded by Passeri). Presumed by some identical with V. Malo *q.v.* [Fl. 642, Fl. 505, Fl. 892, Fl. 798, Fl. 678.]

Arrigo Fiammingo, see Broeck, H. v. d.

Art, Berthe. Flemish Sch. *b* Brussels 1857. *Portraits, flowers, birds, landscapes (some of the French Riviera); sometimes used pastel.* Pupil in Paris of A. Stevens. Exhibited London R.A. 1896-8 and Paris Salon. Represented in ANTWERP *Blue macaws.* BRUSSELS *Poppies* (pastel). TOURNAI *Chrysanthemums.* [Fl. 440.]

Artan de Saint-Martin, Louis. Flemish Sch. *b* son of a Belgian diplomat, The Hague 1837 *d* Nieuport 1890. *Marines* (*cf.* P. J. Clays) *and landscapes.* Brought Brussels by his father 1842; pupil there of E. Delvaux; later worked with A. Marcette; and in Paris; contributed to 'Uylenspiegel' edited by F. Rops *q.v.*; member of Société Libre des Beaux Arts (*cf.* E. Lambrichs and L. Dubois) 1868; Chevalier of the Order of Leopold. A monument to him by the sculptor Van der Stappen was erected at Oost-Duinkerke near Furnes in 1895. Represented in ANTWERP *Climbing the mast, After fishing, Snow, Stormy sea* and two other seapieces. BRUSSELS *The North Sea, The wrecked boat, Day, Night* and others. [Fl. 440, Fl. 388, Fl. 296, Fl. Bib. 19th cent.]

*Arthois (or Artois), Jacques d'. Flemish Sch. *b* Brussels 1613 *d* in poverty, Brussels 1686. *Wooded landscapes* (*cf.* A. Keirincx, L. de Vadder, B. Peeters the younger, J. Siberechts) *many of Soignes forest* (*cf.* F. Coppens, I. v. d. Stock, also H. Boulenger and J. de Greef); *some with religious and genre figures, including horsemen* (*cf.* S. J. v. Douw) *painted by others; some in winter* (*cf.* E. de Bie and D. v. Alsloot). Master Brussels Guild 1634; successful but improvident and imprisoned for debt (though he had refused an offer of a fixed stipend to work regularly for a patron (*cf.* J. Porcellis)) 1658; his assistants included his brother Nicolas d'A. and his son Jean Baptiste. C. Huysmans *q.v.* was his pupil. **Signed Examples:** ANTWERP *Wooded landscape with figures and cattle.* BOSTON *The road through the woods.* BRUSSELS Mus. *Winter landscape, The return from the fair, The outskirts of the forest,*

Landscape; S. Gudule *Landscape with Holy Family on the Flight* 1664 (*cf.* L. Achtschellinck); DRESDEN, LILLE, MADRID Prado, MONTPELLIER (with figures by Teniers, monogram D. T.), STOCKHOLM and VIENNA K. **Monogrammed Examples:** FRANKFORT Staedel. *Lake with trees and horsemen.* V. Wolfvoet *q.v.* and other contemporary Antwerp collectors owned examples; Prince Charles of Lorraine owned nineteen in 1753. Descamps (1769) records landscapes with religious subjects in churches in Brussels, Ghent and Malines. Pictures presumed by some his work are in many museums.
[Fl. 86, Fl. 425, Fl. 878, Fl. 215, Fl. 216, Fl. 892, Fl. 440, Fl. 301, Fl. 213.]

Arthois, Jean Baptiste d'. Flemish Sch. *b* son of Jacques d'A. Brussels 1638 *d* place and date unknown. *Landscapes.* Master in Brussels Guild 1657; assisted his father *q.v.*
[Fl. 892, Fl. 440.]

Arthois, Nicolas d'. Flemish Sch. *b* Brussels 1617 *d* place and date unknown. *Landscapes.* Master in Brussels Guild 1640; assisted his brother Jacques d'A. *q.v.* [Fl. 892, Fl. 440.]

Artvelt see Ertvelt.

Assche, Amélie van. Flemish Sch. *b* daughter of H. van A., Brussels 1804 *d* after 1848. *Portraits in miniature and pastel.* Court painter to Queen Marie Louise of Belgium 1839. A portrait *King Leopold I* is recorded. (*cf.* J. B. van Acker)
[Fl. 451, Fl. 440.]

Assche, Henri van. Flemish Sch. *b* son of an amateur painter, Brussels 1774 *d* Brussels 1841. *Landscapes, often with waterfalls, mills or castles (animals sometimes by B. P. Ommeganck q.v. cf.* J. P. Borrekens); *also worked as lithographer.* Pupil of J. B. de Roy (*cf.* S. P. d'Argonne); Italy 1815-16, then the Vosges, Switzerland, Germany and Holland; member of Ghent and Brussels Soc. of Artists, and of Amsterdam and Antwerp Academies; his funeral was conducted with much pomp by his brother artists. E. Delvaux and A. Payen were his pupils. **Signed Examples:** AMSTERDAM Rijks. *Mountain stream in the Ardennes at sunset* 1821. ANTWERP *Storm scene with lightning and terrified animals* 1805. BRUGES *Brabant landscape in a thunderstorm* 1837. [Fl. 451, Fl. 440.]

Asselbergs, Alphonse. Flemish Sch. *b* Brussels 1839 *d* Uccle 1916. *Landscapes.* Pupil of E. Huberti; member of Tervueren School (*cf.* H. Boulenger); worked at one time at Barbizon; visited Algiers 1873. Represented in AMSTERDAM *Sunset in the Campine.* ANTWERP *Dawn, Marsh in the Campine.* BRUGES *The 'Mare aux Fées' at Fontainebleau.* BRUSSELS, LIÈGE, MONS, NAMUR.
[Fl. 114, Fl. 296, Fl. Bib. 19th cent.]

Aubée, Martin. Flemish Sch. *b* Liège 1729 *d* Paris 1805. Pupil of J. B. P. Coclers *q.v.*; Professor and later Director of Liège Academy. His son Jean Martin A. painted portraits, 'history' and genre. [Fl. 409.]

*****Audenaerd (or Oudenaerd), Robert van.** Flemish Sch. *b* Ghent 1663 *d* Ghent 1743. *Group portraits (cf.* M. Elias, I. v. d. Beke, and F. Verbeeck) *and religious subjects; but chiefly active as engraver.* Pupil of F. van Cuyck de Mierhop and J. van Cleef *q.v.*; went Italy 1685; in Rome joined the Italian painter Carlo Maratta's workshop (*cf.* S. v. Aken, M. v. Duvenede, E. Fisen, R. P. de Rendeux, N. Vleys) as engraver; remained Italy till *c.* 1703 (*cf.* G. J. Smeyers); then returned Ghent. J. F. Delien *q.v.* was his pupil *c.* 1702. **Documented Examples:** GHENT Mus. *Assembly of monks in Baudeloo Abbey, Ghent, before a fresco of the Virgin presenting the Habit of the Order* (*cf.* E. P. v. Reysschoot); S. Jacques *Martyrdom of S. Catherine;* Petit Béguinage *Christ among the Doctors* (all recorded by

Descamps 1763). Descamps also saw (1768) a *S. Peter prevailing upon a group of Carthusian monks to stay in the monastery* (Ghent Église des Chartreux) and a *Resurrection* (Lille Hôpital de la Conception). The *Group portrait of the Corporation of butchers* (now Ghent Mus.) recorded his work by Descamps is signed by F. v. Cuyck de Mierhop *q.v.*
[Fl. 215, Fl. 216, Fl. 892, Fl. 440.]

Augustine Master. Presumed Flemish Sch. 15th cent. Name for painter of BRUGES Mus. *Bishop enthroned with a city* (Bruges?) *in background.* Pictures presumed by some his work are in Dublin (*cf.* Dublin S. Augustine Painter) and other collections. [Fl. 316, Fl. 143.]

Averecht (Aurecht), Jacob. Flemish Sch. 15th cent. *Decorative paintings and sculpture.* Recorded Bruges 1382-1416. *Cf.* 'Awerchs'. [Fl. 892.]

Averecht, Jan. Flemish Sch. 15th cent. Recorded Bruges 1405-17. *Cf.* 'Awerchs'. [Fl. 892.]

Averecht, Willem. Flemish Sch. 15th cent. Recorded Bruges 1420-40. *Cf.* 'Awerchs'. [Fl. 892.]

Avondt, van den. Presumed Flemish Sch. 17th cent. Painter of ANTWERP Mus. (792) *Daniel and the Priests of Baal s* Van Den Avondt F. 1677. Presumed by some identical with T. van Loon *q.v.* [Fl. 13, Fl. 16.]

Avont, Augustin van. Flemish Sch. *b* Malines *c.* 1602 *d* Brussels (?) after 1624. *Paintings and book illustrations.* Brother of Peter van A. Went Germany 1622, robbed of all his possessions by highwaymen near Cologne 1624; later recorded in Brussels. [Fl. 613, Fl. 892.]

*****Avont, Peeter van.** Flemish Sch. *b* son of sculptor Hans van A. or of Rombout A., Malines 1599 or 1600 *d* in poverty, Deurne (Antwerp) 1652. *Religious subjects and 'history' in landscape and garden settings (cf.* A. Wolfordt); *also worked as engraver and dealer (cf.* F. v. Apshoven the younger) *and print publisher.* In Malines Guild 1620; settled Antwerp and member of Guild 1622; member of Antwerp Chamber of Rhetoric (Violiere) 1632; resigned from Violiere 1634; collaborated with Jan Brueghel the younger, L. v. Uden, F. Wouters (his pupil) and others; was friend of the Bohemian engraver W. Hollar. **Signed Examples:** VIENNA K. *Flora in a garden* (landscape and flowers by J. Brueghel the younger whose signature was also recorded on it 1796), *Wooded landscape with Holy Family and angels, Wooded landscape with Virgin and Child, S. John and angels;* Liechtenstein *Wooded landscape with Virgin and Child, S. John and angels* (landscape by F.Wouters; bought 1671 by Prince Karl von Liechtenstein from the Forchoudt firm of Antwerp art exporters (*cf.* A. Casteels)). A *Landscape with sleeping Venus (cf.* F. Wouters) was sold 1678 by Forchoudt to 'Fransoys Michiel Chevalier' at Venice (former Venetian ambassador at Vienna). V. Wolfvoet *q.v.* owned a small *S. Mary Magdalene.* Drawings for a 'Livre de satyres et grotesques' are recorded by engravings.
[Fl. 86, Fl. 613, Fl. 892, Fl. 440, Fl. 212, Fl. 213.]

Avont, Rombout van. Flemish Sch. *b* Malines before 1570 *d* Malines 1619. *Religious subjects; and MS. illustrations; also worked as sculptor.* Master in Malines Guild 1581; worked for a time in Brussels. [Fl. 613, Fl. 892.]

'Awerchs'. Presumed Flemish (or French) Sch. 15th cent. Painter of MOULINS Mus. *Scenes from the lives of SS. Stephen and Laurence* inscribed 'Awerchs'. Presumed by some identical with Jacob, Jan or W. Averecht *q.v.* [Fl. 778.]

Axpoele, Willem (Guillaume) van. Flemish Sch. Recorded Ghent 1402-36 (*cf.* Hubert van Eyck); with J. Martins *q.v.* painted *Counts and Countesses of Flanders* 1419-20.
[Fl. 385, Fl. 892.]

B

Backer, François Joseph Thomas de. Flemish Sch. *b* Gheel (Antwerp) 1812 *d* Antwerp 1872. *Religious subjects for churches in Antwerp region; genre.* A painting titled *The unhappy family* 1843 is recorded. [Fl. 892.]

Backer, Frans (Jan Frans) de. Flemish Sch. *b* Antwerp (?) before 1680 *d* after 1749. *Religious subjects, portraits; also active as engraver.* Went Düsseldorf where court painter to Elector Palatine Johann Wilhelm (*cf.* I. v. d. Beken and A. Schoonjans) *c.* 1704; in Rome 1721; recorded Breslau 1725, 1727 and 1733. **Signed Examples:** BRESLAU S. Maurice *Immaculate Conception.* FLORENCE Uffizi *Self portrait.* His engravings include *Cain killing Abel, The corpse of Abel* and *Cimon and Pera* all from paintings or drawings by A. Schoonjans. [Fl. 481, Fl. 612, Fl. 440, Fl. 892.]

Backer, J. de the elder. Flemish Sch. *b* Antwerp (?) before 1550 (?) *d* France after 1571 (?). Presumed by some the unnamed artist recorded by van Mander (1604) as the father of Jacques de Backer *q.v.* and as 'a good painter who, because of an action for slander (om het een of andere beleedigingsproces) went to live in France and died there' (*cf.* H. Francken the elder and L. Thiry). ANTWERP Mus. *Last Judgement* signed D. O. M. J. de Backer 1571 is presumed by some his work and by others the work of his son. [Fl. 559.]

*Backer, Jacques de (known as van Palermo). Flemish Sch. *b* son of a painter (who fled to France following an action for slander) Antwerp before 1555 (?) *d* of consumption or cancer, Antwerp before 1585 (?). *Religious subjects including several versions of 'The Last Judgement'* (*cf.* B. v. Orley, L. v. Leyden, J. Provoost, J. v. d. Coornhuuse, F. Floris, J. v. Hemessen, P. J. Pourbus, H. v. Balen, C. v. d. Broeck), *mythologies and allegories with nudes.* Pupil of artist-dealer A. van Palerme *q.v.* (*cf.* G. Congnet and P. Goetkint); Van Mander (1604) records that he was made to work there 'like a horse' while Van P sold his paintings for much profit in France; went to live later with H. v. Steenwyck the elder *q.v.*; died, Van Mander (1604) records, in the arms of van Palerme's daughter (i.e. Catherine then wife or widow of P. Goetkint or Lucretia wife of V. Wolfvoet's father) before the age of thirty. Houbraken (1718), acquainted only with a *Last Judgement*, describes him as 'een groot meester'. Van Mander records that he painted his nudes entirely 'in flesh colour without white in the light parts'. **Signed Example:** ANTWERP Mus. *Last Judgement* (*s* D. O. M. J. de Backer 1571; *cf.* J. de Backer the elder). **Documented Examples:** ANTWERP Notre Dame *Last Judgement* placed on funeral monument of Christopher Plantin (*d* 1589) (*cf.* B. Sammeling); recorded there by Descamps (1769), seen there (1781) by Sir Joshua Reynolds who wrote 'correctly drawn but without any skill in disposition of light and shadow', taken Paris for Musée Napoléon and recovered 1815 (*cf.* J. D. Odevaere). Another *Last Judgement* placed on the funeral monument of P. Goetkint (*d* 1583) in the church of the Carmes Chaussés was also taken to Paris but disappeared on the way back; Descamps also records a *Justice and Peace* in the Antwerp Academy's apartments in the Bourse; Van Mander records standing figures of *Venus, Juno* and *Pallas* 'in charming poses, with their attributes, clothing and animals . . .'; also an *Adam and Eve* and a *Caritas;* allegories with nudes are recorded by engravings (*cf.* C. Anthonisz); a 1614 Antwerp inventory records an *Adam and Eve* 'after Jacques de Backer'; V. Wolfvoet *q.v.* owned (1652) a grisaille *Golden rain,* a *S. John baptising* and a *Caritas;* 17th

cent. invoices of the Forchoudt firm of Antwerp dealers record an *Andromeda,* a *Devil sowing while the peasants sleep,* a *Vanitas with nude* and a *Judgement of Midas* (landscape by J. (Velvet) Brueghel) which may have been his work. [Fl. 559, Fl. 425, Fl. 216, Fl. 702, Fl. 107, Fl. 892, Fl. 212, Fl. 213.]

Backer, John James, see Baker.

*Backereel, Gillis. Flemish Sch. *b* Antwerp *c* 1592 (?) *d* Antwerp before 1662. *Religious subjects and 'history'.* Studied Rome (*cf.* J. and W. B.); returned Antwerp where Master in Guild 1629. **Documented Examples:** BRUGES S. Sauveur *S. Carlo Borromeo administering the Viaticum to victims of the plague* (painted after the saint's canonisation in 1616 (*cf.* V. H. Janssens); Descamps (1769) says: 'il est composé avec sentiment et noblesse, de la plus belle couleur et argentine, du plus beau pinceau; je l'ai cru de Rubens, mais il est bien plus fin de dessein et mieux drapé'. BRUSSELS *The Virgin appearing to S. Felix* (from Brussels Égl. des Capucins; taken to Paris Louvre 1794 and returned 1815). VIENNA K. *Hero and Leander* (Leopold Wilhelm inventory 1659). Descamps saw religious subjects in Antwerp: S. Jacques and Église des Augustins, Bruges: Église des Carmes Chaussés and Lierre: Église des Chartreux. A *Four Evangelists* was sent to Vienna by the Forchoudt firm of Antwerp dealers in 1668. [Fl. 425, Fl. 216, Fl. 892, Fl. 212.]

Backereel, Jacques. Flemish Sch. *b* Antwerp (?) before 1600 *d* Antwerp after 1658. *'History'* (?), *landscape* (?). Pupil of T. v. Haecht (Rubens' first master (*cf.* C. Bol)) 1612; Master in Antwerp Guild 1618; A. Genoels *q.v.* was his pupil. May have visited Rome as Houbraken writes (1718) 'There have always been artists of this name living in Rome and no sooner has one died than one or two more have come from Antwerp to take his place; Sandrart relates that he has known seven or eight during his lifetime who all made money and spent it merrily'. *Cf.* G. and W. B. [Fl. 425, Fl. 215.]

Backereel, Willem (or Guiliam). Flemish Sch. *b* Antwerp 1570 *d* Rome 1615. Brother of Gillis B. *q.v. Landscapes.* Master in Antwerp Guild 1605; went Italy and remained there (*cf.* V. Armanno, Jacques B., F. v. d. Kasteele, P. de Lignis, J. de Paepe, N. Regnier, and J. Sutterman). Landscapes by 'Backereel' one 'with birds' are recorded in 17th cent. inventories of the Forchoudt firm of Antwerp dealers. [Fl. 425, Fl. 212, Fl. 213.]

Badens, Frans (Francesco). Flemish Sch. *b* son of an artist, Antwerp 1571 *d* Amsterdam (?) 1618. *Social scenes, including masquerades* (*cf.* J. v. Winghe), *mythologies, portraits, religious subjects.* Taken by his father from Antwerp to Holland soon after the Spanish Fury 1576 (*cf.* J. Badens also J. Hoefnagel, F. Spierinx); in Italy with the engraver J. Matham 1593-7; then settled Amsterdam (*cf.* P. Stalpaert). Van Mander (1604) records him as called 'the Italian' by the younger Dutch painters because he introduced the Italian warm flesh tones. A. v. Nieulandt and Jeremias v. Winghe were his pupils. C. v. d. Voort *q.v.* owned one of his pictures. Van Mander records a *Bathsheba* (*cf.* A. Blocklandt) and a *Loving couple with a flute player* in Italian costume; a *S. Jerome in adoration* and a *Bacchus, Venus and Ceres* are recorded by engravings; an Antwerp inventory (1642) records a *Judith* (*cf.* M. Willems). [Fl. 559, Fl. 892, Fl. 213.]

BADENS—BALEN

Badens, Jan. Flemish Sch. *b* son of an artist two weeks after the Spanish Fury, Antwerp 1576 *d* 'of languor', Netherlands 1603. Brother of Frans B. Travelled Italy and Germany and met with success; but (Van Mander (1604) records) returning to Netherlands 'well dressed, riding his own horse and with much money' he was robbed of everything and imprisoned by 'ruwe soldaten'. [Fl. 559.]

*Baellieur, Cornelis de. Flemish Sch. *b* son of an art dealer, Antwerp 1607 *d* Antwerp 1671. *Religious subjects, interiors of picture galleries* (*cf.* W. v. Haecht). Master Antwerp Guild 1625; as an ex-dean testified with E. Snayers *q.v.* and others in favour of J. Cossiers *q.v.* in connection with difficulties about his large pictures for Malines Béguinage 1656. Had a son of the same name. **Signed Examples:** BRUNSWICK *The woman taken in adultery.* BRUSSELS *Adoration of the Magi.* PARIS Louvre *Visit to an art gallery* 1637 (*cf.* P. v. Boons and A. de Baets). [Fl. 520, Fl. 107, Fl. 214.]

Baerdemaeker, Félix de. Flemish Sch. *b* Louvain 1836 *d* Ghent 1878. *Landscapes.* A professional soldier who painted as an amateur. Represented in GHENT. [Fl. 466 (1878), Fl. 892, Fl. 440.]

Baertsoen, Albert. Flemish Sch. *b* Ghent 1866 *d* Ghent 1922. *Landscapes, coast pieces, canals, picturesque corners of old Ghent and other towns* (*many in snow*). Pupil of J. Delvin and G. den Duyts and in Paris of the French painter A. Roll; member of the 'Essor' group (*cf.* A. Hamesse), and of the 'Libre Esthétique' (*cf.* G. Buysse); in England during German invasion 1914-18 (*cf.* L. de Smet, C. Permeke, E. Tytgat). Represented in ANTWERP *Village square* 1897. BRUGES *Canal quay* 1895. BRUSSELS *Barges in the snow.* GHENT *Snowy morning in Flemish town* 1895 and sixteen others. PARIS State Collection *The thaw.* [Fl. 299, Fl. 388, Fl. 114, Fl. 296, Fl. Bib. 19th cent.]

Baes, Edgar A. Flemish Sch. *b* Ostend 1837. *Marines, landscapes, costume history, genre.* Also active as engraver and art historian. [Fl. 892, Fl. 798.]

Baes, Émile. Flemish Sch. *b* Brussels 1879. *Costume history, nudes, figure pieces;* also active as writer on art. Pupil in Brussels Acad.; then in Paris of J. Stallaert; regular exhibitor in Paris Salons; Chevalier of the Order of Leopold; Chevalier of the Légion d'honneur. Represented in French State Collection. [Fl. 892, Fl. 465.]

Baes, Firmin. Flemish Sch. *b* son of decorative painter H. B., St.-Josse-ten-Noode (Brussels) 1874. *Genre, landscapes, nudes, still life, portraits* (*many in pastel*). Pupil of Léon Frédéric in Brussels Acad.; worked in the region of Condroz. Represented in ANTWERP *Unrest.* BRUGES *The cleaner* (*l'écureuse*) 1910. BRUSSELS *Maternity;* LOUVAIN, OSTEND. [Fl. Bib. 19th cent., Fl. 114, Fl. 296.]

Baes, Rachel. Flemish Sch. *b* Brussels 1912. *Landscapes, still life, flowers, interiors with figures* (*many painted in Paris*). Her work has been praised by the French Surrealist poet Paul Eluard. Represented in ANTWERP *Garden with flowers.* [Fl. 17, Fl. 73.]

Baesten, Maria, née **Ommeganck.** Flemish Sch. 18/19th cent. Daughter, pupil and imitator of B. P. Ommeganck *q.v.* Not to be confused wtih Maria Jacoba Myin *q.v.* [Fl. 481.]

Baets, Ange de. Flemish Sch. *b* Everghem 1793, *d* Ghent 1855. *Interiors, architectural views, portraits.* Pupil and later teacher in Ghent Acad. Represented in LYONS *Picture exhibition in Ghent 1839* (*cf.* P. J. B. Leroy). [Fl. 451, Fl. 481, Fl. 88, Fl. 798.]

Baker (Bakker or **Backer), John James** (or **Nicholas?**). Flemish Sch. *b* Antwerp (?) 1648 *d* London after 1697. *Portraits and draperies.* Came London where worked as assistant to the Anglo-German painter G. Kneller (*cf.* Jan Peeters the younger). Vertue, who acknowledges kindness and help from him in his student days, records (before 1737) that he copied Kneller's *Self portrait* sent to the Duke of Florence and accompanied Kneller to Brussels when he painted the Elector of Bavaria on a white horse *c.* 1697. Walpole (1771) records him as a brother of the Dutch painter Adriaen Backer. A *Portrait of Sir Stephen Fox* engraved 'after J. Baker' is presumed by some to record his work. [Fl. 826, Fl. 878, Fl. 215, Fl. 856, Fl. 892.]

Baldissera (Balthazar) De Ana (called il Fiammingo). Flemish Sch. *b* after 1560 *d* after 1639. *Religious subjects.* Went Venice (*cf.* L. Toeput, H. Staben; also H. Francken the elder) and worked for Treviso and Venetian churches. **Signed Example:** VENICE S. Maria Formosa *The Pope approving liberation of slaves* (dated 1619). [Fl. 305.]

Balen, Gaspard van. Flemish Sch. *b* son of Hendrik van B. the elder, Antwerp 1615 *d* Rome 1641. Pupil of his brother Jan van B.; Master Antwerp Guild 1632; worked under Rubens on Pageant Entry into Antwerp of Governor General Cardinal Infante Ferdinand (*cf.* G. Weri) 1635; went Italy with Jan van B. 1639. [Fl. 107, Fl. 440, Fl. 892.]

*Balen, Hendrik van. Flemish Sch. *b* Antwerp 1575 *d* Antwerp 1632. *Religious and mythological subjects* (*some with landscapes and accessories by others*); *also designs for tapestry and glass.* Pupil of Rubens' master A. van Noort *q.v.*; Master Antwerp Guild when 18 years old 1593; travelled Italy and visited Rome; back in Antwerp by 1604; was friend of Jan (Velvet) Brueghel and Jan Brueghel the younger; with P. Goetkint *q.v.* and A. v. Stalbemt *q.v.* assessed an Antwerp collection 1622; executor with Rubens, C. Schut and others of Jan (Velvet) Brueghel's will 1625; member of Antwerp Chamber of Rhetoricians 'De Violiere' and of the Society of 'Romanists'; A. van Dyck (1610), G. Seghers (?) and F. Snyders were among his many pupils. T. v. Thulden *q.v.* married his daughter; Van Dyck drew his portrait for the 'Iconography'. **Signed Examples:** BRIGHTON Art Gall. *Pluto and Persephone.* CAMBRIDGE Fitz. *The Adoration of the Shepherds.* CASSEL *Diana and Actaeon.* DRESDEN *Marriage of Peleus and Thetis* 1608, *Marriage of Bacchus and Ariadne.* HERMANNSTADT Gymnasium *Judgement of Paris* 1608. VIENNA Liecht. *Rape of Europa* (*cf.* A. v. Nieulandt and A. Snellinck). **Documented Examples:** ANTWERP Mus. *Blazon of Antwerp Chamber of Rhetoricians 'De Violiere' Antwerp 1618* (figures by H. v. B. and F. Francken II, flowers and decorations by J. (Velvet) Brueghel, animals by S. Vrancx). CAMBRIDGE Fitz. *The Judgement of Paris* (landscape by J. (Velvet) Brueghel) corresponding to a description by Houbraken (1718). VIENNA K. *Rape of Europa* (with landscape by Jan (Velvet) Brueghel, in Archduke Leopold Wilhelm inventory 1659). ANTWERP Cathedral *Virgin and Child with SS. Joseph and John the Baptist,* (and wings *Concert of Angels* and *SS. Philip and Anne* now in Antwerp Mus.) recorded by Descamps 1769; S. Jacques *Resurrection* and *Portraits of himself and his wife* (recorded by Descamps who suspected van Dyck author of the portraits); *Adoration of the Magi, Annunciation, Visitation;* Mus. S. *John preaching in the wilderness* (formerly in the Cathedral). Descamps also saw pictures in S. Quentin, Malines, Bruges and Antwerp: Carmes Chaussés and Jacobins. Jan Brueghel the younger's day book records the sale (1628) of a large *Summer* with figures by H. v. B. to the Prince of Orange; Antwerp 17th cent. collections included pictures with landscape by J. de Momper, a *Virgin and Child* (with flower garland and insects by Jan (Velvet) Brueghel) a *Rape of the Sabines* and a *Nausicaa;* also a *Last Judgement* (*cf.* J. de Backer). V. Wolfvoet *q.v.* owned 'a

small picture by Van Balen and Coninxloo'; the Forchoudt firm of Antwerp dealers owned a *Feast of the Gods* (*cf.* F. Floris and P. Boel) with accessories by J. (Velvet) Brueghel; Houbraken (1718) records *The Deluge* (*cf.* G. Beerings), *Moses striking the rock* and *The Passage of the Red Sea* 'the Israelites in full light with shadowed figures in the foreground' (*cf.* M. Pepyn). Pictures presumed by some his work are in various museums. (*cf.* H. v. B. the younger).
[Fl. 559, Fl. 452, Fl. 215, Fl. 216, Fl. 892, Fl. 440, Fl. 212, Fl. 213, Fl. 214.]

Balen, Hendrik van the younger. Flemish Sch. *b* son of Hendrik van B. the elder, Antwerp 1623 *d* Antwerp 1661. *Religious subjects, some in landscapes by others.* Pupil of his brother Jan; then of Jan Wildens 1638; Master Antwerp Guild 1640; lived with T. van Thulden who was married to his sister; went France (*cf.* C. E. Biset) 1645; in Tours 1648; in Rome 1653; then returned Antwerp. A *Holy Family in a landscape* and a *Crucifixion* are recorded in Antwerp inventories 1689 and 1691; the Forchoudt firm of Antwerp dealers owned four pictures with landscapes by G. de Witte *q.v.*
[Fl. 892, Fl. 440, Fl. 212, Fl. 213.]

Balen, Jan van. Flemish Sch. *b* son of Hendrik van B. the elder, Antwerp 1611 *d* Antwerp 1654. *'History' compositions with children and angels, and copies after Rubens.* Pupil of his father; worked under Rubens on Pageant Entry into Antwerp of Governor-General Cardinal Infante Ferdinand (*cf.* G. Weri) 1635; with his brother Gaspard van B. went Italy 1639; back Antwerp 1642.
[Fl. 86, Fl. 425, Fl. 215, Fl. 107, Fl. 892, Fl. 440, Fl. 83.]

Balen (or **Balem**), **Pieter.** Flemish Sch. *b* Liège 1580 *d* Liège after 1656. *Religious subjects (mainly in small format).* Pupil of J. Ramey (*cf.* O. v. Veen); visited Italy; then returned Liège; married daughter of L. Lombard *q.v.* A *Holy Trinity* painted for Liège S. Christophe is recorded.
[Fl. 451, Fl. 892, Fl. 88, Fl. 440.]

Balten (Balthazar) de Costere or **Custodis, Pieter.** Flemish Sch. *b* son of sculptor B. Janszone Costere (Custodis), Antwerp *c.* 1525 *d* Antwerp (?) *c.* 1598. *Landscapes* (*cf.* F. Mostaert and L. Toeput, A. Mirou) *some with religious and mythological subjects; peasant genre* (*cf.* F. Verbeeck, P. Bruegel the elder, M. v. Cleve); *portraits; also worked as engraver.* Master Antwerp Guild 1540; Dean 1569; senior member of Guild with A. v. Palerme *q.v.* and M. de Vos 1571. Van Mander (1604) records that he visited many countries, followed the style of Pieter Bruegel and was friend of C. Ketel. The engraver D. Custos was his son. **Signed Examples:** ANTWERP *The Feast of S. Martin* (a different version also signed in AMSTERDAM). **Monogrammed Examples:** ANTWERP *Ecce Homo.* DARMSTADT *Landscape.* A *Landscape with Juno discovering Jupiter and Io* and *portraits of notables* are among his engravings. Van Mander says: 'The Emperor (Rudolf II) has a painting by him *S. John preaching in the Wilderness* (*cf.* M. v. Cleve and K. v. Mander), but he had somebody paint an elephant instead of S. John and now it looks as if all the people came to see the elephant'. The same subject is recorded in a 1623 Antwerp inventory.
[Fl. 559, Fl. 892, Fl. 213.]

Bamesbier, Hans. Flemish (Dutch) Sch. *b c.* 1500 (?) *d* Amsterdam *c.* 1598. *Portraits.* Van Mander (1604) records him as 'a High German'. Pupil of L. Lombard *q.v.* (*cf.* L. Suavius, J. Ramey, P. Balen, F. Floris); he adds that though a heavy drinker he lived to be nearly a hundred. [Fl. 559.]

Baptist, see **Gaspers.**

Barbara Legend Master. Presumed Flemish Sch. 15th cent. Name for painter of BRUSSELS (1037) *Scenes from the life*

of S. Barbara. Pictures presumed by some his work are in various museums (*cf.* Dublin S. Nicholas Painter).
[Fl. 316, Fl. 798.]

Barbiers, Anthony. Flemish Sch. *b* Rousselaere 1676 *d* Amsterdam 1726. *'History'.* Visited Rome where was pupil of P. v. Bloemen before 1694; in A'dam by 1711. [Fl. 892.]

Barbiers, Balthazar. Flemish Sch. *b* Antwerp 1685 *d* Antwerp (?) after 1728. *Decorative paintings for Antwerp public buildings.* Brother of Anthony B.; Master Antwerp Guild 1708. [Fl. 107.]

Bard (or **Bart**), **Oliver.** Flemish Sch. *b* Bruges before 1545. Was friend of K. Foort (Karel van Ypern) *q.v.* whom he nursed in Courtrai after he had stabbed himself at a banquet 1562. [Fl. 559.]

*__Baren Jean Antoine (Johannes Antonius) van der.__ Flemish Sch. *b* Brussels (?) 1615 *d* Vienna 1686. *Flowers and garlands round pictures by other artists* (*Cf.* D. Seghers). Canon (*cf.* F. de Cock) and chaplain to Archduke Leopold Wilhelm when Governor of the Netherlands (1647-56); Court painter to the Archduke (*cf.* J. B. v. Heil, F. L. Peeters, F. Snyders); went with Archduke to Vienna 1656; curator in Vienna of the Archduke's collection (as D. Teniers the younger *q.v.* had remained in Brussels); collaborated on inventory of the collection 1659; after Archduke's death entered service of the Emperor Leopold I (*cf.* E. de Bie, J. de Cordua, P. Evrard, F. Luyckx, R. Megan, J. Schoonjans, F. Stampart, J. Thomas 'van Ypern') 1662; made his will (extant) 1679. Teniers painted him as a very short man, almost a dwarf, in the *Archduke Leopold Wilhelm in his gallery at Brussels* (Vienna version). **Signed Example:** VIENNA K. *Flower garland round a Virgin and Child.* Documented Examples: VIENNA K. Twelve *Flower pieces.* **Inscribed Example:** BRUSSELS *Flowers round a mystic marriage of S. Catherine* 1641. [Fl. 631 (1907), Fl. 892, Fl. 124.]

Baren, Josse van der. Flemish Sch. *b* Louvain (?) before 1560 *d* Louvain (?) after 1604. *Religious subjects; also drawings of Louvain.* Friend of Justus Lipsius in his last years and illustrated his 'Lovanium' 1604. A *Beheading of S. Dorothy* painted for Louvain S. Pierre 1594, and a *Martyrdom of S. Sebastian* (*s* and dated 1597) painted for the Louvain Archers' Guild are recorded. [Fl. 269, Fl. 88, Fl. 892.]

*__Barendsz, Dirck.__ Flemish (Dutch) Sch. *b* son of the deaf painter Barent Dircksz *q.v.*, Amsterdam 1534 *d* Amsterdam 1592. *Portraits, including groups* (*cf.* C. Anthonisz, Allaert Claesz, J. W. v. Delff, C. Ketel, D. Jacobsz, A. Pietersz, C. v. d. Voort), *religious subjects, mythologies.* Pupil of his father; went Italy (*cf.* J. v. d. Straet) *c.* 1555; worked Venice (*cf.* Baldissera de Ana, J. S. v. Calcar, P. Franck, G. Rem, P. C. de Rycke, J. v. Scorel, J. Swart van Groningen, H. Staben, L. Toeput) where pupil of Titian and lived in his house; returned Amsterdam by way of France (*cf.* H. Francken the elder and L. Thiry) *c.* 1561; with C. Ketel worked on Pageant Entry of Earl of Leicester into Amsterdam (*cf.* L. Cornelisz and J. Savery the elder) 1587; sat to Ketel for his portrait 1590. Van Mander (1604) describes him as a man of parts, a musician, a good Latinist, a friend of Lampsonius *q.v.* and of Philips Marnix (Lord of Aldegonde, Burgomaster and defender of Antwerp against Parma 1584); he also describes him as too heavy to be able to travel in a carriage. **Documented Examples:** AMSTERDAM *Fourteen Civic Guardsmen* 1562 (one man holding paper inscribed 'in vino veritas'; from the Hall of the Crossbowmen whose cipher G appears in the corner); *Banquet of eighteen Civic guardsmen eating bullhead* (*perch*) 1566 (known as 'the Pos (or Pors) Eaters' and so described by Van Mander; from the Hall of the Arquebusiers whose cipher 'L' is incorporated in the date). GOUDA Mus. Triptych: *Nativity* (recorded by Van

Mander in Gouda). Van Mander also records a *Judith* (*cf.* M. Willems), a *Venus*, a *Fall of Lucifer* (almost entirely destroyed by the Iconoclasts) a *Self portrait*, a *Portrait of his wife*, a *Portrait of Titian*, a *Crucifixion*, a *Perseus changing Polydectes and his guests to stone* and a *Bathsheba* and a *Last Judgement with seven works of mercy* (both unfinished at his death); he further records a *Portrait Group of Archers with a drummer*. [Fl. 127, Fl. 559, Fl. 48, Fl. 892.]

Barendsz, Dirck (Theodoricus Bernardi) the elder. Flemish (Dutch) Sch. *b* Amsterdam (?) *c.* 1500 (?) *d* England (?) after 1519. '*History*'. Worked for Robert Sherborne Bishop of Chichester. Some paintings in Chichester Cathedral and the neighbourhood have been presumed by some his work. His son Anthony died in Chichester at the reputed age of 105 in 1619. [Fl. 451, Fl. 892, Fl. 798.]

Barent, Doove, see **Dircksz.**

Baron, Théodore. Flemish Sch. *b* Brussels 1840 *d* St.-Servan, nr. Namur 1899. *Landscapes* (*many of the Meuse banks*). Pupil of L. Dubois *q.v.* and member of Société Libre des B. A. 1868; influential in the Tervueren group (*cf.* H. Boulenger); worked at Calmpthout; Director Namur Acad. Represented in ANTWERP *The Meuse at Profondeville* 1872, *In the Dunes*, *Rocks* (*evening*), *Fontainebleau Forest* (*Autumn evening*). BRUSSELS *Rouat valley in winter*, *Arm of the Scheldt*, *Rainy weather*. GRONINGEN, LIÈGE, MONS, NAMUR, TOURNAI *The Dunes*.
[Fl. 160 (1899), Fl. Bib. 19th cent., Fl. 388, Fl. 296.]

Baroncelli Master. Presumed Flemish Sch. 15th cent. Name for painter of FLORENCE Uffizi *Pierantonio Baroncelli*, *Medici agent in Bruges, and his wife*, diptych with *Annunciation* on reverse. [Fl. 316.]

Baseleer, Richard. Flemish Sch, *b* Antwerp 1867. *Marines, port and coast scenes, landscapes, portraits*. Pupil in Antwerp Acad. of A. Verlat; worked mainly on Lower Scheldt; visited Holland and Venice; member of L'Art Contemporain (Kunst van Heden) (*cf.* R. Strebelle); teacher in Antwerp Higher Institute. Represented in ANTWERP *The cemetery, Shrimpers on the Lower Scheldt, Coast scene, Evening*. BRUSSELS *Morning* (*w*). [Fl. Bib. 19th cent., Fl. 17.]

Bast, Dominique de. Flemish Sch. *b* Ghent 1781 *d* Ghent 1842. *Marines, landscapes, portraits*. Was a travelled merchant and painted as an amateur; contributed to Ghent exhibitions 1817-35. [Fl. 451, Fl. 612, Fl. 126, Fl. 892, Fl. 88.]

Bastien, Alfred T. J. Flemish Sch. *b* Brussels 1873 or 1875. *Portraits, figure pieces, landscapes, costume history*. Pupil in Brussels Acad. of J. Portaels; then in Ghent; member of Sillon group (*cf.* A. Pinot); won Charleroi prize 1897; travelled in North Africa and the East 1905-8; with P. Mathieu *q.v.* painted *Panorama of the Congo* for Ghent International Exhibition 1912; Director of Brussels Academy; wrote a book on J. de Greef *q.v.* 1932. Represented in GHENT *Portrait of the artist's mother*. PHILADELPHIA *The sculptor Kerfyzer*. SAN FRANCISCO *Portraits*. A *Symbol of Christian humility* (for Charleroi prize) 1897 is recorded. [Fl. Bib. 19th cent. Fl. 798, Fl. 296, Fl. 17.]

Bastiné, Jean Baptiste Joseph. Flemish Sch. *b* Louvain 1783 or 1785 *d* Aix-la-Chapelle 1844. *Religious subjects, 'history'*. Went Paris where pupil of L. David (*cf.* J. Paelinck, M. G. Stapleaux and F. J. Navez) 1804. Went Aix-la-Chapelle where founded an art school 1811. Represented in AIX-LA-CHAPELLE *Return of Tobias*. [Fl. 892, Fl. 798.]

Battel, Baudoin van (real name B. van der Wyct). Flemish Sch. *b* Malines (?) before 1450 *d* Malines (?) after 1508. *Religious*

subjects; decorative painting. Designed for Ommeganck processions in Malines (*cf.* G. van B., J. v. B. the elder and H. Stuerbout) 1465-1503; worked on Pageant Entry into Malines of Maria of Burgundy 1477 (*cf.* P. Coustain, M. v. Roden and J. Snellaert). A *Last Judgement* painted for Malines Town Hall 1481 is recorded. [Fl. 613.]

Battel, Gauthier (Wouter) van. Flemish Sch. *b* son of J. van B. the elder, Malines (?) before 1420 *d* Malines (?) *c.* 1478, *Decorative paintings and designs for glass*. Worked on Malines Ommeganck processions (*cf.* B. van B.) and for Malines S. Rombaut. His son of the same name collaborated with him and *d* Malines 1506. [Fl. 613, Fl. 892.]

Battel, Jacques van (real name J. van der Wyct). Flemish Sch. *b* son of Jean van B. (van der Wyct), Malines before 1510 *d* Malines (?) before 1557. *Religious subjects, decorative painting, heraldic designs, MS. illustrations, portraits*. Worked in Malines for Emperor Charles V (*cf.* C. Anthonisz, P. Coninxloo, J. v. Lathem, J. C. Vermeyen); employed by City of Malines to paint a portrait of Charles V (*cf.* B. v. Orley); painted decorations for Golden Fleece Chapters at Tournai 1531 and Utrecht 1546 (*cf.* Jean van B. also Jacques Daret). A *S. Anthony* and a *Crucifixion* are recorded.
[Fl. 88, Fl. 892, Fl. 798.]

Battel, Jean van the elder. Flemish Sch. *b* Malines (?) before 1400 *d* Malines (?) after 1443. *Religious subjects and decorative painting*. Designed for Malines Ommeganck processions 1434-7 (*cf.* B. van B.). A *S. Veronica with two angels* (*cf.* Flémalle Master) for Malines Town Hall 1437 is recorded.
[Fl. 613.]

Battel, Jean van (real name J. van der Wyct). Flemish Sch. *b* son of Baudoin van B., Malines 1477 *d* Malines 1557. *Decorative painting, designs for ceremonies, MS. illustrations. portraits*. Designed memorial ceremonies for Isabella of Castile in Brussels S. Gudule 1504; collaborated with J. van Lathem *q.v.* 1505; designed memorial ceremonies for King Henry VII in Brussels Église de Caudenberg 1509; worked for Emperor Charles V 1516; worked in Malines palace for Margaret of Austria Regent of the Netherlands (*cf.* G. Schooff); Court painter to Charles V (*cf.* C. Anthonisz and J. C. Vermeyen) 1520; with P. Tubach *q.v.* designed catafalque of Margaret of Austria in Malines 1530; decorated official registers of the Order of the Golden Fleece for which he received high payment 1525-52; visited Utrecht and The Hague on affairs of the Golden Fleece (*cf.* Jacques van B.).
[Fl. 613, Fl. 88, Fl. 892, Fl. 798.]

*Baudewyns (or Bauduin or Boudewyns), Adriaen Frans. Flemish Sch. *b* Brussels 1644 *d* Brussels 1711. *Italianate and wooded landscapes, some with figures and animals by others* (*cf.* P. v. Bredael, J. F. v. Bloemen, A. Crussens, J. P. Spalthof and J. B. Juppin); *also worked as engraver* (*mainly of works by A. F. v. d. Meulen) and as tapestry designer* (*cf.* L. Achtschellinck, F. Baudewyns, A. Coppens, V. H. Janssens, A. Smitsens, L. van Schoor, D. Teniers III, G. de Witte, P. de Witte III). Pupil of I. v. d. Stock *q.v.*; Master Brussels Guild 1665; went Paris (*cf.* C. E. Biset and M. Elias); designed tapestry cartoons for Louis XIV (*cf.* N. Bernaerts, P. Boel, A. Flamen, A. Genoels, A. F. v. d. Meulen) and went with Genoels to draw the Château Mariemont (Hainault) on the King's order 1669; married A. F. v. d. Meulen's sister 1670; returned Brussels after 1674. His nephew Adriaen Baudewyns and M. Schoevaerdts *q.v.* were his pupils. Pictures by him with figures by P. Bout, J. B. v. d. Meiren and C. E. Biset were recorded in his lifetime by invoices of the Forchoudt firm of Antwerp dealers (*cf.* A. Casteels) which exported to Vienna and Spain. The art historian Campo Weyerman (1729), who knew him in Brussels, records him as an eccentric then living in poverty, **Signed Example:** AMSTERDAM *Italianate*

landscape with foreground figures. **Monogrammed Example:** BRUNSWICK *Mediterranean port.* **Documented Examples:** DRESDEN and MADRID Prado (works recorded before 1750). For VIENNA example *cf.* P. Bout.
[Fl. 425, Fl. 878, Fl. 215, Fl. 892, Fl. 212.]

Baudewyns (or **Boudewyns**), **Frans.** Flemish Sch. *b* Brussels (?) *c.* 1700 *d* 1766. *Designs for Brussels tapestry works.* Recorded in Brussels Guild 1720. **Signed Examples** (drawings): HAMBURG *Italianate landscape* 1740. VIENNA Albertina 1725.
[Fl. 892, Fl. 798.]

Baugniet, Charles. Flemish Sch. *b* Brussels 1814 *d* Sèvres 1886. *Portraits, genre; also many portrait drawings and lithographs of contemporary artists, musicians and other notabilities.* Pupil in Brussels Acad. and of J. Paelinck. Court portrait draughtsman to the King of the Belgians 1835; visited London where drew the Prince Consort, Charles Dickens and many others; devoted himself mainly to painting after 1860. Represented in BRUSSELS *Visiting the widow;* Bibliothèque royale *Portrait drawings and Lithographs.* LONDON British Museum *Portrait drawings* and *Lithographs.* Pictures titled *Madame Céleste as Cynthia in the 'Flowers of the Forest'* 1847, *Herr Pishek as Don Juan* 1847, *Which shall I choose?* 1862, *The embarrassing reply* 1870 and others were exhibited in the London R.A.
[Fl. 466 (1886), Fl. 361, Fl. 440.]

Beaufaux, Polydore. Flemish Sch. *b* Court-St.-Étienne 1829 *d* Waver 1904. *Religious subjects, costume history.* Pupil in Antwerp Acad.; later teacher in the Acad., L. van Aken was his pupil. Represented in ANTWERP *Salome watching the beheading of S. John the Baptist* 1873. A *Finding of the corpse of S. Stephen* is recorded. [Fl. 892, Fl. 17.]

*Beaune Last Judgement Painter. Presumed Flemish Sch. 15th cent. Name for painter of BEAUNE Hospices: Polyptych: *The Last Judgement.* on exterior wings: *Annunciation, SS. Sebastian and Anthony* (grisaille): *Chancellor Nicolas Rolin* and *Guigone de Salins* founders of the hospital (1443) who donated the picture. Presumed by some identical with R. v. d. Weyden *q.v.* All the nudes were draped or covered with flames by a restorer at the end of the eighteenth century; these additions were removed by a restorer in 1876; the present condition is due to recent restoration.

Bedaff, Antonis A. E. van. Flemish Sch. *b* Antwerp (?) 1787 *d* Brussels 1829. *Costume history, portraits.* Professor and Director Bois-le-Duc School of Art. Recorded works include *Meeting of the States General in Dordrecht 1572*, and *The last meeting of William of Orange and Count Egmont.* (*Cf.* D. F. du Bois). [Fl. 451, Fl. 88.]

Beeck (**Peecks**), **Jan.** Flemish Sch. *b* Looz 1457 *d* Liège (?) 1516. *Religious subjects.* Monk and later Abbot of S. Laurentius monastery nr. Liège. Pictures and MS. illustrations for the monastery are recorded.
[Fl. 451, Fl. 409, Fl. 410, Fl. 88.]

Beeckman, Baron Fernand de. Flemish Sch. *b* Brussels 1845 *d* Brussels 1918. *Landscapes and city views.* Represented in BRUSSELS *Venice scenes* 3 w. [Fl. 123.]

Beer, Arnould (**Aert**) **de.** Flemish Sch. *b* son of Jan de B., Antwerp before 1514 *d* Antwerp 1542. *Designs for glass paintings* (*cf.* P. Cornelisz, P. Cluyt, A. P. Crabeth, D. J. Velaert). Master Antwerp Guild 1529; Lambert Lombard *q.v.* was his pupil *c.* 1529. [Fl. 559, Fl. 892, Fl. 316.]

Beer, Jan de. Flemish Sch. *b* Antwerp (?) before 1480 *d* Antwerp (?) after 1520. Apprenticed in Antwerp as 'Henneken de B.' to G. van Everen 1490; Master Antwerp Guild 1504; Dean 1515. **Signed Example:** LONDON B. M. (drawing)

Nine heads dated (indistinctly) 1520. Paintings presumed by some his work are in various museums. [Fl. 316.]

Beer, Joos de. Flemish (Dutch) Sch. *b* Utrecht before 1535 *d* Utrecht *c.* 1593. Van Mander (1604) records him as pupil in Antwerp of F. Floris and later in service of the Bishop of Tournai; in Utrecht and Master in Guild 1550; J. Uytewael *q.v.* and the Dutch painter A. Bloemaert were his pupils. Van Mander records pictures by D. Barendsz *q.v.* and A. Blocklandt *q.v.* in his possession *c.* 1567. His wife was referred to as his widow in 1593. [Fl. 559, Fl. 892.]

*Beerblock Jean (**Johannes**). Flemish Sch. *b* son of a butcher, Bruges 1739 *d* Bruges 1806. *Interiors, town views and decorative panels.* Worked first as house painter; 'discovered' by a Bruges gentleman and sent to Bruges Acad. where pupil of M. de Visch; continued as house painter for some years painting pictures in spare time. **Signed Example:** BRUGES Mus. *Procession of the Tailors' Guild on Bruges, Place du Braamberg, with the thirteen poor people clothed by the Guild each year* 1788 (painted for the Tailors' Guild). An *Interior of the hospital* painted (1778) for Bruges Hôpital S. Jean is recorded.
[Fl. 451, Fl. 207, Fl. 88, Fl. 892, Fl. 114.]

Beerings (or **Beerincx**), **Grégoire** (**Gregorius**) known as 'B. in de Schaer' ('Scissors' presumed name of house where he was born). Flemish Sch. *b* Malines 1526 *d* Malines 1570 or 1573. *Religious subjects and landscapes* (*cf.* F. Mostaert). Went Rome where known as Gregorio nelli Forbici and where, Van Mander (1604) records, he painted ruins (in distemper) and *The Flood* (*cf.* H. v. Balen) showing rain, the waters and the Ark, and when asked why no figures were included answered 'they are all drowned except those in the Ark'; made many replicas of this picture which was popular; back in Malines where Master in Guild by 1555; worked for Louvain and Malines churches. [Fl. 559, Fl. 48, Fl. 613, Fl. 892.]

Beerings (or **Beerincx**), **Gregorius the younger.** Flemish Sch. *b* son of painter Paul B. (and grandson of G. B.), Malines before 1585 *d* Malines 1669. In Malines Guild 1604; Dean 1629; was visited in his atelier by Van Dyck. His son Cornelis B. (*b* 1605) was the master of T. Egret. Other painters named Gregorius B. (*b* 1619, 1649, 1653) are recorded. Jan Baptist B., son of Cornelis (*b* 1634) was Dean of Malines Guild 1702.
[Fl. 613, Fl. 892.]

Beernaert, Euphrosina. Flemish Sch. *b* Ostend 1831 *d* Ixelles (Brussels) 1901. *Landscapes.* Pupil of L. Robbe. Worked in Belgian Campine and travelled Holland and Norway. Represented in ANTWERP, BRUGES, BRUSSELS, COURTRAI, GHENT, LOUVAIN, NAMUR, OSTEND. (*cf.* G. Guffens). [Fl. 160, (1901) Fl. 892, Fl. 114, Fl. 17.]

Beernaert, Jacques. Flemish Sch. 18th cent. *b* Ypres *d* Bruges. *Group portraits and interiors.* Worked Ypres till 1730; thereafter Bruges. J. A. Garemyn *q.v.* is recorded influenced by his colouring. [Fl. 451, Fl. 892, Fl. 296.]

Beernaert, P. see **Bernaerdt.**

Beers, Jan van. Flemish Sch. *b* son of poet Jan v. B., Lierre 1852 *d* Fay-aux-Loges (Loiret) 1927. *Costume history, genre portraits, landscapes.* Pupil Antwerp Acad.; worked mainly in Paris after 1880. Represented in AMSTERDAM *Funeral of Count Charles the Good.* ANTWERP *Maerlant on his death bed* triptych 1879, *Henri Rochefort* (in London R. A. 1890), *Lady in white, Peter Benoit, The poet J. van B. and his wife, The youth of Emperor Charles, The fallen star.* BRUSSELS *Sarah Bernhardt.* ROUEN *Parisienne.* Pictures titled *A smile* and *Come back* were in the London R. A. 1890 and 1891. *cf.* G. Vanaise. [Fl. Bib. 19th cent., Fl. 388.]

Beert, O., see **Beet.**

*Beet (or Beert), Osias the elder. Flemish Sch, *b* Antwerp before 1585 *d* Antwerp 1624. *Still life with food and sometimes flowers* (*cf.* L. J. v. d. Bosch, A. Bosschaert, Pauwel Coecke van Aelst, G. Congnet, J. F. v. Es, J. v. Hulsdonck, Clara Peeters, Grenoble Strawberry Painter); *also active as cork merchant.* In Antwerp Guild 1596; Master 1602; F. Ijkens *q.v.* was his nephew and pupil. **Signed Example:** MADRID *Still life with oysters.* Brussels Mus. has *Still life with oysters and plates of fruits and cakes* monogrammed DB (or OB?) presumed by some his work. A *Flowerpiece* is recorded in an Antwerp collection 1627. (*cf.* O. B. the younger).

[Fl. 107, Fl. 892, Fl. 213, Fl. 1 (1938).]

Beet (or Beert), Osias the younger. Flemish Sch. *b* son of painter and cork merchant Osias B. the elder *q.v.*, Antwerp 1622 *d* Antwerp (?) *c.* 1678. *Still life.* Master Antwerp Guild 1645; recorded in Antwerp 1657 when a *Kiss of Judas* by V. Malo *q.v.* after van Dyck belonging to an Antwerp collector was in his house (for repair?). May have painted some of the pictures listed under his father's name.

[Fl. 107, Fl. 231, Fl. 1 (1938).]

Behaeghel, Théophile. Flemish Sch. *b* Ypres 1795 *d* France (?) date unknown. *Interiors, portraits.* Went Paris where pupil of L. David (*cf.* F. J. Navez) and also worked under other French painters. Remained in France. [Fl. 892.]

Beke, Joos van der, see **Cleve, J. van.**

*Beken, Ignace van der. Flemish Sch. *b* Antwerp 1689 *d* Antwerp 1774. *Portrait groups and conversation pieces* (*cf.* P. v. Angellis, R. v. Audenaerd, B. v. d. Bossche, H. Goovaerts, P. J. Horemans, J. F. Nollekens, G. and G. J. Smeyers, F. X. H. Verbeeck). Pupil of G. v. Herp the younger; went Düsseldorf to work for the Elector Palatine Johann Wilhelm (who also employed F. de Backer *q.v.*, A. Schoonjans *q.v.* and the Dutch painters A. v. d. Werff, G. Schalcken, J. Weenix and Rachel Ruysch) 1712; returned Antwerp where Dean in Guild 1722; visited Mainz 1733; again Dean in Antwerp Guild 1738 and 1749. **Signed Examples:** COPENHAGEN *A gentleman returning from hunting* 1722, *Portrait group on the terrace of a park* 1722. [Fl. 768, Fl. 481, Fl. 892, Fl. 170.]

Belcamp (Belkamp, Belchamp, Belcom), Jan van. Flemish Sch. *b* Antwerp (?) 1610 *d* London 1653. *Copyist of old pictures to King Charles I.* Pupil in Antwerp of H. v. Balen before 1631; came England (*cf.* R. v. Leemput) and worked under the Anglo-Dutch painter C. Janssens van Ceulen (Cornelius Johnson) and A. van Dyck (*cf.* T. Boeyermans); as copyist was directed till 1640 by Abraham van der Dort, keeper and cataloguer of the Royal Cabinet; appointed by vote of the House of Commons a Trustee for the sale of the King's effects 1649; witnessed directions for the sale 1650; made purchases on his own account (*cf.* J. B. Gaspers). **Monogrammed Example:** WINDSOR Royal Coll.: *Charles I and Queen Henrietta-Maria with members of the court in Greenwich Park* (landscape signed by A. van Stalbemt *q.v.*). **Documented Examples:** HAMPTON COURT Royal Coll. *Louis XIII of France* (in James II's inventory), *Edward IV* (in Commonwealth's and James II's inventories; both copies of earlier originals; the latter described by Walpole (1771) as 'whole length in his night gown and slippers ... the face, profile, probably taken from the ancient original' and as then over the chimney in the antechamber in St. James's). Recorded works include a copy of a portrait of *Princess Mary of Orange* which Charles I before he escaped from Whitehall directed should be restored to the owner the Countess of Anglesey; *The King and Queen in little in a perspective by H. van Steenwyck the younger, with figures by Belcamp* (in Charles I's collection); a *Stag*, a *Last Supper*, *Queen Anne of Denmark in a white hat with a red feather* (*cf.* P. v. Somer), *Edward III in armour*, *The Black Prince* (all in James II's inventory, the last two seen in

S. James's Palace by Walpole). Vertue (before 1756) records a series of portrait heads at Whaddon (near Wimpole) presumed his work; and Walpole records at Drayton *Henry VI* and *Henry VIII* copied by Belcamp from Holbein's large Whitehall picture (burned 1698).

[Fl. 826, Fl. 856, Fl. 451, Fl. 730, Fl. 892.]

Bellegambe, Jean. Flemish Sch. *b* son of wood worker, Douai before 1490 *d* Douai before 1540. *Religious subjects; designs for church ornaments, vestments and glass* (*cf.* P. Cornelisz and D. J. Velaert); *also worked for civil authorities.* Master in Douai Guild by 1504; married daughter of a grocer, Douai 1504; employed by churches and religious establishments in Douai and Cambrai and the Flines convent near S. Omer; designed a crown in Douai celebrations for Charles V's accession as emperor 1519; made plan of district between the Scarpe and the Somme presented by Douai City to Charles V (*cf.* P. J. Pourbus) 1524; his son Martin B. was also a painter. **Signed Examples:** None. **Monogrammed Example:** NEW YORK Met. Triptych *Virgin and Child enthroned with musician angels, donors, saints and adorants;* exterior *Virgin and Child* and *S. Bernard.* **Semi-Documented Example** (recorded 1600): DOUAI Mus. polyptych: *Adoration of the Holy Trinity,* exterior: *Adoration of the Holy Cross* with *Charlemagne* and *Portrait of the donor Abbot Charles Coguin* painted for Anchin Monastery (between 1511 and 1520) where it was dismantled in the Revolution; reassembled in Douai Cathedral 1857. Paintings presumed by some his work are in various museums.

[Fl. 895, Fl. 88, Fl. 200, Fl. 892, Fl. 316, Fl. 778.]

Bellis, Hubert. Flemish Sch. *b* Brussels 1831 *d* Brussels 1902. *Still life (flowers and fruit), portraits, decorative compositions.* Pupil of F. Navez and H. de Coene. Chevalier of the Order of Leopold 1894. Represented in AMIENS, AMSTERDAM, BRUSSELS *Chrysanthemums.* LIÈGE *Strawberries.*

[Fl. 160 (1902), Fl. 440.]

Benedetti, Andries. Flemish Sch. *b* Antwerp (?) before 1620 *d* Antwerp (?) after 1649. *Still life with food, vessels, musical instruments* (*cf.* C. Mahu and T. Aenvanck), *'vanitas' subjects some with skull and hourglass* (*cf.* C. N. Gysbrechts). Master in Antwerp Guild 1640; recorded there 1649. **Documented Example:** VIENNA K. *Still life with lobster, lemons, vessels and lute* (in Archduke Leopold Wilhelm inventory 1659 as 'Original von Benedetti van Antorff'). A signed *Still life with chest of drawers, clay pipes, death's head, hourglass, pack of cards, grapes and half filled wine glass* is recorded in an English private collection. A *Still life* in Budapest monogrammed A. B. is presumed by some his work. V. Wolfvoet *q.v.* owned 1652 a *Still life with food* (banketken).

[Fl. 892, Fl. 213.]

Bening, Alexander (Sanders). Flemish Sch. *b* Ghent (?) before 1455 *d* after 1518. *MS. painter.* In Ghent Guild 1469; in Bruges Guild 1486; married Catharina v. d. Goes (sister? of Hugo v. d. Goes). MS. illustrations presumed by some his work are in various museums. [Fl. 247, Fl. 892, Fl. 798.]

Bening (Benninck), Livina, see **Teerlinck.**

Bening, Paul. Flemish Sch. 15th/16th cent. *d* after 1519. Son of Alexander B. MS. painter (?). [Fl. 892, Fl. 798.]

Bening (or Benninck), Simon. Flemish Sch. *b* son of Alexander B., Ghent (?) 1483 *d* Bruges 1561. *MS. paintings and portrait miniatures* (*cf.* A. de Smytere and M. Bessemers). In Bruges Guild of S. Luke 1508; citizen of Bruges 1519; Dean of Bruges Guild 1524; executed a *Mount Calvary* for Dixmude town council 1530; commissioned by the Infante Don Fernando of Portugal to paint genealogical tree of the House of Portugal and received for the purpose a series of drawings by the Por-

tuguese miniaturist Antonio de Hollanda 1530; Damião de Goes, King Manoel the Fortunate's ambassador to Flanders, informed Don Fernando that 'Maître Simon' had given up all other work for the Infante's commission 1530; Dean in Bruges Guild 1536; visited London (?) (cf. L. Teerlinck, L. and S. Horenbout, L. Cornelisz); Dean in Bruges Guild 1546; Francisco de Hollanda (son of Antonio) records (1548) in his list of outstanding MS. painters (following his list of 'Eagles') 'Master Simon the most agreeable colourist among the Flemings and the best for trees and distances'. Vasari (1568) and Guicciardini (1582) also praise him. **Signed Example:** LONDON V. & A. *Self portrait, holding spectacles, before a miniature painting on an easel* ('Seipsū pīgebat ano aetatis 75, 1558'). **Semi-Documented Example:** LONDON B. M. *Genealogical Tree of the House of Portugal* (presumed the work referred to by D. de Goes left unfinished on death of D. Fernando 1534). Miniatures presumed by some his work are in various museums.
[Fl. 414, Fl. 818, Fl. 371, Fl. 692, Fl. 892, Fl. 798, Fl. 887, Fl. 28.]

***Benson, Ambrosius.** Flemish Sch. *b* place unknown, of Lombard origin, before 1505 *d* Bruges 1550. *Religious subjects.* Master Bruges Guild 1519; assessor (vinder) in Guild 1521, 1539 and 1545; Dean 1537; president (gouverneur) 1540; exhibited and sold works in Bruges market 1526-30. His son Guillaume, Master in Bruges Guild 1551, died 1585; his son Jean was Master in Antwerp Guild 1550 and in Bruges Guild 1551. **Signed Examples:** None. **Documented Examples:** None. **Monogrammed Examples** ('AB' presumed his monogram): BRUSSELS Triptych centre: *S. Anthony of Padua*, wings: *Rest on the Flight* and S. *Secundus Bishop of Avila*, exterior wings: *Annunciation* (formerly Madrid Count of Valencia collection). MUNICH A. P. *Holy Family* (formerly Nuremberg Germ. Mus.). Pictures presumed by some his work are in various museums (*cf.* Deipara Virgo Master and Ottawa Judith Painter).   [Fl. 892, Fl. 316, Fl. 530, Fl. 668, Fl. 575.]

Berchmans, Émile. Flemish Sch. *b* son of a decorative painter, Liège 1867. *Decorative paintings (murals and ceilings for theatres in Liège and Verviers), posters, lithographs and illustrations.* Contributed to 'La Plume'; founder of 'Revue Caprice'. Represented in AIX-LA-CHAPELLE S. Michel (ceiling). BRUSSELS *Twilight* (*w.*). LIÈGE *Youth.*
[Fl. 440, Fl. 296.]

Bergh (or Berg), Matthys van den. Flemish Sch. *b* son of J. v. d. B. (*b* Alkmaar 1588 employed as bailiff by Rubens), Ypres 1615 *d* Alkmaar 1687. *Portraits and copies (paintings and drawings) after Rubens, Van Dyck and others.* Pupil of Rubens. Houbraken (1718) records that he went Alkmaar and was Master in Guild there 1646. **Signed Example:** HAARLEM Bisschoppelijk Mus. *The priest Jod. Verkampen.*
[Fl. 425, Fl. 892.]

Bergh, Nicolas van der. Flemish Sch. *b* Antwerp (?) 1725 *d* Antwerp 1774. *Copies; also active as engraver after Rubens.* Pupil of B. Beschey *q.v.*; exempted from military training and from obligations to Antwerp Guild for a copy of the *Fête of the Crossbowmen of S. Sebastian* by D. Teniers the younger (now Leningrad Hermitage) 1750; Master in Antwerp Guild by 1752; Dean 1760. Had many pupils. Descamps saw a copy by him of a picture by Teniers in Antwerp Town Hall 1768.
[Fl. 216, Fl. 481, Fl. 892.]

Berghe, Augustin van den. Flemish Sch. *b* Bruges 1756 or 1757 *d* Beauvais 1836. *'History', religious subjects, landscapes, portraits.* Pupil of J. A. Garemyn in Bruges Acad. before 1776; went Paris 1780; pupil there of J. B. Suvée in Paris Acad. from 1781; returned Bruges 1791; won prize in Ghent Acad. competition and was given festive reception by Bruges authorities to celebrate success (*cf.* J. B. Suvée, P. M.

Goddyn, J. D. Odevaere, P. J. Verhaghen) 1796; settled Beauvais to take up French government appointment as professor in Beauvais art school *c.* 1797; commissioned by French Government to design *An Allegory of the Peace of Amiens* (executed as tapestry at Beauvais) 1802; exhibited Paris Salon 1806-35 (*cf.* L. Gerbo); in later years signed 'Van den Berghe père' to avoid confusion with his son the French painter Charles Auguste v. d. B. (*b* Beauvais 1798). **Documented Examples:** BRUGES Notre Dame *The Vision of S. Anthony of Padua* (painted for Zweveghem Church 1791). GHENT Mus. *Oedipus cursing Polynices* (Ghent prize picture). Pictures titled *Oedipus at Colonus* and *The Death of Adonis* are recorded.   [Fl. 451, Fl. 440.]

Berghe, Frits van den. Flemish Sch. *b* son of a librarian, Ghent 1883 *d* Ghent 1939. *Landscape and figure compositions in Post Impressionist, Expressionist and Surrealist conventions; still life, illustrations.* Pupil Ghent Acad. of J. Delvin (*cf.* L. de Smet); associated with second generation of Laethem-St. Martin (*cf.* C. Permeke and A. Servaes, also A. v. d. Abeele and G. v. d. Woestyne); visited United States 1907; in Holland during 1914-18 German invasion (*cf.* G. de Smet, J. Smits and R. Wouters) contributed drawings to Ghent 'Vooruit' 1929-39; illustrated F. Villon: 'Le petit et le grand Testament' and E. Langui: 'Un fils de Dieu'. Represented in ANTWERP *The tree, Life.* BRUSSELS *Sunday.* GHENT *Fall of the Saints.* GRENOBLE *Man in the Clouds.*
[Fl. 388, Fl. 708, Fl. 399, Fl. 448, Fl. 296, Fl. 449, Fl. Bib. 20th cent.]

Bernaerdt, Pierre. Flemish Sch. 17th cent. *Religious subjects.* **Signed Examples:** BRUGES Notre Dame *The Trinity* 1660 (seen by Descamps 1769); S. Jacques *The Virgin interceding for souls in Purgatory* 1674.   [Fl. 216, Fl. 892.]

Bernaerts, Henri. Flemish Sch. *b* Malines 1768 *d* Malines 1849. *Religious subjects, 'history', portraits.* Pupil in Malines Academy; visited Italy (?); professor Malines Academy 1825. His son Joseph Hubert B. was chiefly active as a restorer of 17th cent. pictures in Malines churches
[Fl. 451, Fl. 892, Fl. 440.]

Bernaerts (Beernaerts), Nicasius (known in France as Nicaise and Nicasius). Flemish Sch. *b* Antwerp 1620 *d* in indigence, Paris 1678. *Animals, and still life (some with dead game)* (*cf.* P. Boel, D. de Coninck, J. Fyt). Apprenticed pupil to F. Snyders at age of fourteen 1634; travelled Italy; in Paris (*cf.* P. Vleughels, J. Fouquier and C. Biset) 1643; in Antwerp where Master in Guild 1654; in Paris and member of French Acad. roy. (*cf.* P. v. Mol) 1663; worked as animal painter under the French painter C. Le Brun in the Gobelins tapestry factory (*cf.* A. Baudewyns and A. Genoels) from 1667; the French animal painter F. Desportes was his pupil *c.* 1673. A *Fruit and flower piece* is recorded as his Academy reception work. A *Dog and cat fighting* and a *Ferret* are recorded by engravings.
[Fl. 287, Fl. 142, Fl. 440.]

Bernard, Adolph. Flemish Sch. *b* Ghent 1812 *d* after 1844. *Genre, portraits.* Pupil in Ghent Acad. of P. van Hanselaere *q.v.*; in Rome (where won prize in Accad. di San Luca 1835) 1833-8. Pictures titled *The artist in Italy* and *Banditti* are recorded.   [Fl. 451, Fl. 440, Fl. 798.]

Bernart, Pierquin. Flemish Sch. *b* Ypres before 1454. Recorded in Bruges among the painters who worked on decorations for the marriage of Duke Charles the Bold with Margaret of York (*cf.* L. Adriaenssen, J. Daret, P. Coustain, H. v. d. Goes, D. de Rycke, V. v. c. Stoct) 1468.   [Fl. 440.]

Bernier, George. Flemish Sch. *b* Namur 1862 *d* Brussels 1918. *Animals (race horses and cattle), landscapes.* Pupil Brussels Acad. Represented in BRUGES and BRUSSELS.
[Fl. 123, Fl. 114.]

Berré, Florent. Flemish Sch. *b* Antwerp 1821 *d* Antwerp (?) after 1854. *Marines.* Pupil in Antwerp Acad. of J. Jacobs; travelled in the East and later entered the shipping trade.
[Fl. 892.]

Berré, Jean Baptiste. Flemish Sch. *b* Antwerp 1777 *d* Paris 1838. *First some religious subjects; then animals* (*cf.* J. B. de Roy); *occasional still life with game* (*cf.* M. Spey also B. de Bridt); *also worked as sculptor of animals.* Pupil in Antwerp Acad.; went Paris 1808 where was patronized by Empress Josephine (*cf.* J. F. v. Dael, B. P. Ommeganck and L. Gerbo) and by Restoration collectors; regular exhibitor in Paris Salons; had lodgings in Jardin des Plantes from 1822 (*cf.* P. J. Redouté); J. J. Eeckhout *q.v.* lithographed his portrait. **Signed Example:** MONTPELLIER *Landscape with animals* 1821. **Documented Example:** PARIS State collection *Animals at rest* (Paris Salon 1834). Recorded works include *A lioness with cubs* commissioned by Empress Josephine (Salon 1810); *An eagle about to lift a lamb* (Salon 1812); *An antelope in the clutches of a lion* (Salon 1812); *Romulus and Remus suckled by the wolf* (Salon 1814); *The Duke and Duchess of Berry accompanied by ladies in waiting and professors of the establishment visiting the elephant in the Jardin des Plantes* (State commission, Salon 1817).
[Fl. 451, Fl. 107, Fl. 66, Fl. 88, Fl. 440.]

Bervoets, Leo. Flemish Sch. *b* Antwerp 1892. *Landscapes, port scenes, genre.* Pupil in Antwerp Acad. of I. Opsomer. Represented in ANTWERP *The inn.* [Fl. 17.]

Beschey, Balthasar. Flemish Sch. *b* son of a tailor, Antwerp 1708 *d* Antwerp 1776. *Landscapes with genre figures; religious subjects, 'history', portraits.* Under the name of 'Biscaye' produced and dealt in pastiches and copies of earlier Flemish and Dutch pictures including works by D. Teniers the younger and small versions of pictures by Rubens (*cf.* his brothers J. A. and J. F. Beschey, N. v. d. Bergh, J. F. v. Bredael the elder, J. P. v. Bredael the elder, Joseph van Bredael, G. v. Opstal); painted religious subjects for Antwerp churches and religious houses from *c.* 1744; Master in Antwerp Guild 1753; professor-director Antwerp Academy 1755; Dean Antwerp Guild 1756. P. J. Verhaghen, then working as lace designer, was his pupil 1744; A. C. Lens and H. J. Antonissen were also his pupils. **Signed Examples:** ANTWERP *Joseph sold by his brothers* 1744, *Joseph Viceroy of Egypt* 1744, both from Église des Sœurs Noires; *Self portrait* (*painting*) (presented to Antwerp Acad. 1763). BUDAPEST *Portrait of a woman.* DESSAU Amalienstift *Landscape with Holy Family* 1734. LENINGRAD *Three senses: Hearing, Smell and Taste* 1733, *Two senses: Sight and Touch.* MANNHEIM *The Flood* 1737. PARIS Louvre *Family group* 1751, **Documented Example:** ANTWERP *Portrait of the painter M. J. Geeraerts* (pastel). Recorded works include *Reception of the Rector of S. Luke's Guild* 1756, *Moses and the burning bush, The crossing of the Red Sea,* (both for Louvain Town Hall) and *Portrait of the Empress Maria Theresa* (*cf.* G. de Pélichy) seen by Descamps (1768) in Louvain Town Hall.
[Fl. 481, Fl. 107, Fl. 717, Fl. 88, Fl. 892, Fl. 440.]

Beschey, Charles. Flemish Sch. *b* Antwerp (?) 1706 *d* Antwerp (?) date unknown. Brother of Balthasar B. *Landscapes with figures.* Pupil of H. Goovaerts. **Signed Examples:** STOCKHOLM University Gall. *Landscapes with figures* (two). [Fl. 107, Fl. 892.]

Beschey, Jacques Andries (Jacob Andreas). Flemish Sch. *b* Antwerp 1710 *d* Antwerp 1786. Brother of Balthasar B. *Religious subjects, landscapes* (?), *still life* (?). Pupil of and associated in pastiche making and dealing with Balthasar B.; Master in Antwerp Guild 1727 (?); Dean 1766. **Signed Examples:** MADRID Prado *Elevation of the Cross* (based on Rubens' picture in Antwerp Cathedral). SCHWERIN Gall. *Holy Family* 1751. [Fl. 107, Fl. 892, Fl. 440, Fl. 555.]

Beschey, Jean François (Jan Frans). Flemish Sch. *b* Antwerp 1717 *d* Antwerp 1799. Brother of Balthasar B. *Landscapes, genre, interiors, religious subjects* (?). Pupil of and associated in pastiche making and dealing with Balthasar B.; Dean in Antwerp Guild 1767. [Fl. 451, Fl. 481, Fl. 107.]

Beschey, Joseph Hendrik. Flemish Sch. *b* Antwerp 1714 *d* Antwerp (?) date unknown. Brother of Balthasar B. [Fl. 481, Fl. 107.]

Bessemers, Marie (also known as Mayken Verhulst). Flemish Sch. *b* Malines *c.* 1520 *d c.* 1600. *Miniatures.* Second wife of Pieter Coecke van Aelst 1537; mother-in-law of Pieter Bruegel the elder; first teacher of Jan (Velvet) Brueghel. Guicciardini (1581) records her as one of the most famous women painters of her time (*cf.* L. Teerlinck, S. Horenbout, A. de Smytere and C. David).
[Fl. 371, Fl. 559, Fl. 613, Fl. 892.]

*Beuckelaer (Bueckelaer, Buekelaar), Joachim. Flemish Sch. *b* Antwerp *c.* 1533 *d* in poverty, Antwerp 1573 or 1574. *Religious subjects; market and kitchen scenes some with religious subjects in background* (*cf.* P. Aertsen and P. C. van Ryck); *peasant genre* (*cf.* F. Verbeeck, M. v. Cleve, P. Bruegel the elder); *portraits.* Pupil in Antwerp of P. Aertsen whose wife was his aunt; Master Antwerp Guild 1560; Van Mander (1604) records that he painted figures in landscapes by C. van Dalem *q.v.* (*cf.* G. Mostaert and B. Spranger), received a daily wage as clothes-painter for A. Mor (*cf.* C. Schut) and died aged forty while working for a general on the staff of the Duke of Alva (*cf.* A. Mor, M. Coxie, P. de Kempener, C. v. d. Perre also W. Key); he adds that he sold his pictures for very small sums, that a mintmaster of Antwerp and the collector J. Rauwaert of Amsterdam (*cf.* M. v. Heemskerck) bought some and that the prices rose tenfold after his death. **Signed Examples:** ANTWERP *Fishmarket with man and women in foreground* 1574 or 1571. STOCKHOLM *Fishmarket with Ecce Homo in background* 1570 (from the collection of the Emperor Rudolf II (*cf.* P. Stevens the younger) in which van Mander records a picture of this subject). **Monogrammed Examples:** AMSTERDAM *Kitchen scene; with Christ in the house of Mary and Martha in the background* (*cf.* P. Aertsen) 1566. ANTWERP *The Prodigal Son* (*cf.* J. S. v. Hemessen, C. Massys, P. C. v. Ryck and Prodigal Son Master) 1563, *Still life* 1564. BRUSSELS *Fair scene* 1563, *Poultry market* 1564, *Christ in the house of Mary and Martha* 1565. COPENHAGEN *S. Anne and the Holy Kinship* (Van Mander records a 'Sint Anna te Drieën') 1567. DRESDEN *The Four Evangelists* (Van Mander records a picture of this subject) 1567. FLORENCE Uffizi *Ecce Homo* 1566. LENINGRAD *Village feast* (a 'Kermesse' is recorded in an Antwerp collection 1614) 1563. NUREMBERG *Market scene with Ecce Homo* 1566. STOCKHOLM *Kitchen scene: Christ with Mary and Martha* 1565, *Vegetable market with Ecce Homo* (from collection of Rudolf II; recorded by Van Mander) 1565. VIENNA Kunsthist. *Peasants with poultry, butter and eggs* 1567. Pictures of all these types are recorded in 17th cent. Antwerp inventories and a *Butcher's shop* is among pictures exported 1690 to Vienna by the Forchoudt firm of Antwerp dealers. The dealer H. de Neyt whose large collection included many 16th cent. pictures owned at his death (1642) a *Man's portrait* and a *Woman's portrait.* Jan van Moers, Sheriff of Antwerp owned a *Fruitmarket* 1652 and Jeremias Wildens *q.v.* owned 1653 a *Raising of Lazarus.* A *Palm Sunday* recorded by Van Mander in Antwerp Notre Dame was destroyed by the Iconoclasts (*cf.* A. Blocklandt).
[Fl. 559, Fl. 892, Fl. 780, Fl. 212, Fl. 213.]

Beucken, J. van, see **Buken.**

Beughem, Charles Ferdinand, Vicomte de. Flemish Sch. *b*

Brussels 1828 *d* Château Steenhault 1882. *Landscapes and marines.* Worked in the Alps, the Ardennes and the Pyrenees.
[Fl. 440.]

Beurden, Alfons van. Flemish Sch. *b* Antwerp 1878. (Not to be confused with sculptor of same name *b* 1854). *Landscapes, figures, decorative panels, still life.* Pupil in Antwerp Acad.; and later teacher there. Represented in ANTWERP *Gladioli and dahlias.*
[Fl. 17.]

Beveren, Charles van. Flemish Sch. *b* Malines 1809 *d* Amsterdam 1850. *Portraits, genre, religious subjects, city views.* Pupil Malines and Antwerp Academies; im Italy 1830; settled Amsterdam. Represented in AMSTERDAM Mus. *The soldier's farewell* 1828, *The sculptor L. Royer in his studio* Rome 1830, *The wife of Louis Royer in a straw hat;* Church of Moses and Aaron *Death of S. Anthony Hermit.* MALINES *View of Aerschot* 1828. MUNICH *The invalid* 1844. STUTTGART.
[Fl. 451, Fl. 88, Fl. 440.]

Bicke, Jan, see Miel.

Bie, Adriaen de. Flemish Sch. *b* Lierre 1593 *d* Lierre 1668. Houbraken (1718) records that his father was born by a Caesarian operation ('en mirakeleus by't leven behouden'). *Religious subjects, portraits and paintings on precious metals, jasper, agate and porphyry.* Houbraken records that he went Paris and worked there under R. Schoof *q.v.* 1612-14; then Rome for eight years; returned Lierre 1623; buried in Lierre S. Gomaire. Father of the poet biographer of artists, Cornelis de B., whose 'Gulden Cabinet' contains an engraving of his portrait by P. Meert *q.v.* **Signed Example:** DARMSTADT *Old lady in a black dress* 1652. A *S. Eligius* (triptych) painted 1626 for Lierre S. Gomaire is recorded.
[Fl. 86, Fl. 425, Fl. 215, Fl. 440, Fl. 892.]

*Bie, Erasmus de. Flemish Sch. *b* son of painter Frans de B., Antwerp 1629 *d* Antwerp 1675. *Genre, market scenes (cf.* D. Vinckeboons, S. Vrancx, S. J. v. Douw, D. Teniers the younger, G. v. Tilborgh, J. Siberechts, J. v. Buken, M. Schoevaerdts, P. Bout, A. F. v. d. Meulen), *street views, winter landscapes with skating scenes (cf.* D. v. Alsloot, J. d'Arthois, D. v. Heil, R. v. d. Hoecke), *marines, occasional religious subjects.* Pupil of D. Ryckaert III *q.v.;* Master Antwerp Guild 1654. (His sons Frans and Jan Baptist were also painters; the latter was recorded in Vienna (*cf.* J. A. v. d. Baren and P. Evrard) 1691.) **Signed Example:** ANTWERP *Place de Meir at Antwerp with coaches and promenaders.* **Monogrammed Examples:** IXELLES *Antwerp fair,* YPRES *Winter landscape.* A *Place de Meir in winter* and a *Skating on the Scheldt* 1670 are recorded. His father's collection (1671) contained a *Temptation of S. Anthony* and two *Pictures with animals* ('met beestkens') by E. de Bie and works by D. Ryckaert, Jan Fyt and Sebastian Vrancx. Other 17th cent. Antwerp collections (1657, 1679 and 1688) contained *Market scenes* and *Marines* by 'de Bie'.
[Fl. 481, Fl. 107, Fl. 892, Fl. 440, Fl. 213.]

Biefve, Édouard (Edmond Jean François) de. Flemish Sch. *b* Brussels 1808 *d* Brussels 1882. *Costume history, religious subjects, genre, portraits.* Pupil of J. Paelinck 1828-30; in Paris where influenced by P. Delaroche 1831-41; on return received official presentations from Brabant Council and Brussels Council for his *Compromise of the Nobles* 1841; member of L'Essor group (*cf.* A. Hamesse) *c.* 1875; left his fortune to Brussels Hospices. Represented in ANTWERP, BERLIN, BRUSSELS *Compromise of the Nobles 1566* 1841 commissioned by Belgian government, and sent (with *Abdication of Charles V* by L. Gallait *q.v.*) on tour of German towns. Senate: *Allegory of the Belgian Provinces.* Other titles recorded include *The Flagellation* 1834, *Ugolino and his sons* 1836, *Raphael composing the Transfiguration* 1845, *Rubens in London (cf.* P. Kremer)

1848, *Alva at the execution of Counts Egmont and Hoorn (cf.* L. Gallait also W. Key) 1850, *Alexander Farnese and his council of war at the siege of Antwerp* and *The Countess of Egmont begging for the liberation of her husband.*
[Fl. 451, Fl. 440, Fl. Bib. 19th cent., Fl. 296.]

Bigée, Charles. Flemish Sch. *b* Malines before 1733 *d* Malines (?) after 1759. *Flowers and decorative paintings (cf.* G. P. Verbruggen the younger, C. W. de Hamilton, R. J. Malaine, P. and S. Hardimé; also J. v. d. Borght and P. Faes), *genre.* **Signed Example:** BRUSSELS Mus. Instrumental on Conservatoire *Sportsmen and anglers* (painting on clavichord *cf.* F. Borsse).
[Fl. 613, Fl. 440.]

Billoin, Charles. Flemish Sch. *b* Brussels 1813 *d* Ixelles (Brussels) 1869. *Costume history, genre, portraits; also active as lithographer and engraver.* Pupil in Brussels of J. Paelinck and H. v. d. Haert. A painting titled *Charles V visiting Joanna the Mad (cf.* W. Geets) 1860 and a *Portrait of M. Fischer Chef d'orchestre of the Brussels Société royale de la Grande Harmonie* are recorded.
[Fl. 451, Fl. 892, Fl. 440.]

Biltius (van der Bilt), Jacobus. Flemish Sch. (?) *b* before 1640 *d* Antwerp (?) after 1679. *Still life with game (cf.* F. Snyders, F. Ijkens, C. Luyckx, and B. de Bridt), *also trompe-l'œil arrangements of game and trophies of the chase hanging against the wall (cf.* C. N. Gysbrechts). Pupil in The Hague of Valenciennes born C. Hardy 1651; member of Hague Guild 1660; in Antwerp where member of a Calvinist society (*cf.* J. Jordaens also B. v. Orley) 1671; Master Antwerp Guild 1672. **Signed Examples:** COLOGNE *Dead game and hunting equipment* 1673. COPENHAGEN *Dead hare* 1670, *Dead game and trophies of the chase* 1674, *Dead game and hunting equipment* 1679. THE HAGUE Gem. Mus. *Dead game* 1673 and 1676. A signed example dated 1655 is recorded in a private collection.
[Fl. 481, Fl. 892, Fl. 798, Fl. 170.]

Binje, Frans. Flemish Sch. *b* Liège 1835 *d* Brussels 1900. *Landscapes (o. and w.).* Began as civil servant in railway or telegraph service. Then pupil of H. v. d. Hecht *q.v.;* associated with Tervueren School (*cf.* H. Boulenger); worked in Brabant, the Ardennes and on the coast. Represented in ANTWERP *At Dunkirk, Evening,* BRUSSELS *Ardennes, Autumn morning,* COURTRAI, GHENT, LIÈGE *Rainy evening.*
[Fl. 892, Fl. 798, Fl. 296, Fl. 17, Fl. Bib. 19th cent.]

Biscaye, see Beschey.

*Biset, Charles (Karel) Emmanuel. Flemish Sch. *b* son of decorative painter Georges B., Malines 1633 *d* Breda 1691 or later. *Social genre, conversation pieces (cf.* G. Coques), *portraits.* Pupil of his father (?). Went Paris (*cf.* A. F. Baudewyns, A. de Bie, N. Bernaerts, J. B. de Champaigne, P. de Champaigne, Jan v. Cleef, L. Cousin, F. Duchatel, J. v Egmont, A. Flamen, B. Flemalle, J. Fouquier, P. Franchoys, L. Franck, C. Francken, A. Genoels, G. Goswin, V. Leckerbetien, A. F. v. d. Meulen, J. F. Millet, P. v. Mol, M. v. Plattenberg, J. v. Reyn, P. Rysbraeck, R. Schoof, H. Staben, P. Sperwer, P. Spierincx, B. and W. Vaillant, P. Vleughels, F. Voet, J. v. Werden); Houbraken (1718) records that he worked there for court circles till *c.* 1661; back in Antwerp where friend of P. Spierincx and Master in Guild 1661; married Maria daughter of L. v. Uden *q.v.* 1662; citizen of Antwerp 1663; after death of his wife had illegitimate daughter by her sister Anna 1666; in Malines where re-married 1670; patronized by Comte de Monterey, Governor of the Netherlands (*cf.* A. Genoels and G. Coques) 1670-74; sold four pictures to the Duc d'Orléans 1671; Dean in Antwerp Guild 1674; married his servant 1682; Weyerman, who knew him, records (1729) that he lived an irregular life, was dirty and lazy, and quite indigent in his last years; his house was sold for his mortgages 1686; thereafter he went to Breda. His sons

Jean Charles (in Antwerp Guild 1732) and Jean Andreas *q.v.* were painters. **Signed Example**: THE HAGUE Mauritshuis *Aesculapius transformed to an owl* (in *Interior of a picture gallery* by G. Coques). **Documented Example**: BRUSSELS *'William Tell' performed before the S. Sebastian's Guild at Antwerp* (commissioned by the Guild 1672; completed *c.* 1674; the architecture recorded as by W. S. v. Ehrenberg *q.v.*; the landscape as by P. A. Immenraet *q.v.*; originally in the Guild headquarters in the Antwerp Hôtel de Ville where seen by Descamps 1768). A *Portrait of Alexander Farnese Prince of Parma* (Governor of the Netherlands 1680-82) and a *Portrait of the Prince's son* are recorded painted in 1682. The figures in architectural pieces by W. S. v. Ehrenberg and versions of *The Five Senses* (*cf.* G. Coques and D. Teniers the younger) are recorded in contemporary Antwerp collections. *Landscapes with figures* by A. F. Baudewyns and B. were owned by the Vienna branch of the Forchoudt firm of Antwerp dealers 1707.
[Fl. 425, Fl. 878, Fl. 215, Fl. 216, Fl. 88, Fl. 107, Fl. 892, Fl. 212, Fl. 213.]

Biset, Jean Andreas (not Jean Baptist). Flemish Sch. *b* son of C. E. B., Antwerp 1672 *d* place unknown after 1729. *Mythologies and portraits.* Worked Breda, Hertogenbosch, Middelburg and Delft. Friend of the Dutch flower painter and art historian J. Campo Weyerman who records him of irregular habits like his father *q.v.* **Signed Example**: BRUNSWICK *Venus weeping.* Recorded works include a *Jupiter and Danaë,* a *Judgement of Paris, Anna Maria de Salis, wife of Count K. W. von Erbach, on her death bed 1709,* and portraits of many English officers and their wives painted in Breda during the war of the Spanish succession. Lyons Mus. has *Portrait of a man in black* catalogued as his work.
[Fl. 878, Fl. 481, Fl. 892, Fl. 798, Fl. 547.]

Bisson, Willem de. Flemish Sch. 16th cent. **Documented Example**: LANCUSI (prov. Salerno) S. Martino *Immaculate Conception with Saints* painted for this church 1572. [Fl. 305.]

Blendeff, Lambert (or **Martin**). Flemish Sch. *b* Liège *c.* 1650 *d* Louvain 1721. *Religious subjects, portraits.* Pupil in Liège of B. Flemalle; went Louvain and became painter to the city by 1677; iconographer to Louvain University 1684. Descamps (1769) records *S. Margaret and the dragon with the Trinity in the sky* ('la couleur m'a paru lourde et peu vraie') in Louvain S. Quentin and others in Louvain Jesuit church.
[Fl. 216, Fl. 267, Fl. 613, Fl. 88, Fl. 798.]

Bles, Henryck, Henry or Herri, met de, (also referred to as Civetta, (Little Owl), Maître Chouette, Henri à la Houppe). Flemish Sch. *b* Bouvines (nr. Dinant) *c.* 1500 (?) *d* Flanders (?) *c.* 1550 (?) or Ferrara (?) 1584 or later. *Landscapes with small figures* (*cf.* F. Boels, H. Bol and F. Mostaert), *religious subjects.* Lampsonius under his portrait with an owl in background engraved 1572 writes:

Henrico Blesio, Bovinati, Pictori,
Pictorem urbs dederat Dionatum Eburonia, pictor
Quem proximis dixit poeta versibus.
Illum adeo artificem patriae situs ipse, magistro,
Aptissimus, vix edocente fecerat.
Hanc laudem invidit vicinae exile Bovinum
Et rura doctum pingere Henricum dedit
Sed quantum cedit Dionato exile Bovinum,
Joachime, tantum cedit Henricus tibi.

(The Joachim here referred to is Joachim Patinir *q.v.*; the third edition of Lampsonius (1600) adds after the name: 'Bubonem pro nota tabulis suis appinxit, vixitque, circa an. 1550); Lanzi (1816) based on Lomazzo (1584) records him as 'Civetta or perhaps Enrico de Bles a Bohemian ('boemo' mistranslation of Bovinas?) living about 1590; died at Ferrara' and adds: 'known under the name of Civetta, from the frequent introduction of an owl in his landscapes; he lived for a long

time in the Venetian state'. Van Mander (1604) records him as a follower of J. Patinir and the master of F. Mostaert, and adds 'He was called Henryck met de Bles ('with the forelock') because he had a patch of white hair on the front of his head; he was a painstaking artist and painted landscapes with little trees, rocks, little cities and many small figures; he was the 'Master with the owl', as he painted a little owl in all his pictures, though it is sometimes so well hidden that people bet one another that they cannot find it ... The Emperor owns a number of his pictures and his works are much sought after in Italy where the Owl Master is famous'. Presumed by some identical with Herri de Patenir *q.v.* **Signed Examples**: None (a signature 'Henricus Blesius F' on a picture in Munich A. P. was found to be a forgery during cleaning operations in 1911 *cf.* Pseudo-Blesius and Munich Adoration Master). **Documented Example**: BÂLE *Mountain landscape with castle and river and Holy Family with S. John in the foreground* (recorded 1568 as the work of 'Heinrich Blesii Bovinatis'; figures presumed by some by another hand); **Semi-Documented Example**: DRESDEN *Mountain landscape with sleeping pedlar and monkeys stealing his wares* (owl in tree; corresponds to the picture described by Van Mander: 'A large fine and choice landscape with a pedlar sleeping under a tree while a lot of monkeys steal his wares and hang them about on the trees; some interpret the subject as a satire on the Pope, the monkeys being 'Martinists' i.e. Lutherans, who expose the papal doctrines which they describe as his wares; but they may be wrong and Henryck had no such intention, because art has no business to be mocking'; the subject was performed in the marriage festivities of Charles the Bold 1468; the picture was engraved by H. Cock 1562 as by P. Bruegel the elder). Van Mander records a *Road to Emmaus* (with the *Supper at Emmaus* and *Scenes from the Passion* in other parts of the picture) and *The story of Lot.* Lanzi records 'Landscapes to be met with in Venice which all present traces of old fashioned crudeness', 'a *Nativity* for Brescia San Nazaro recalling Bassano's composition, with a bluish tone all over, and a foreign look in the faces' and small cabinet pictures with a multitude of small figures known as fantastic witch pictures ('chimere e stregozzi') *cf.* H. Bosch, J. Mandyn, Cornelisz van Oostsanen and P. Huys. Rubens owned 1640 a *Virgin in a landscape;* other 17th cent. Antwerp collectors owned a *S. Christopher,* a *Hell piece* and a *S. John.* The Forchoudt firm of Antwerp exporting dealers owned pictures titled *S. John preaching, Orpheus* (*cf.* L. v. d. Borcht), *S. Jerome, Temptation of Christ* (tondo), *Descent from the Cross,* also a *Temptation of S. Anthony* 'na Bles' and landscapes. His portrait 'van Moor' (A. Mor?) was owned 1642 by the Antwerp dealer H. de Neyt. The following pictures with an owl are presumed by some his work: Berlin K. F. *Mountain landscape with river;* Copenhagen *Landscape with the Flight into Egypt;* Dresden *Landscape with S. John the Baptist preaching;* Namur *The good Samaritan;* Prague *Landscape with ironworks* (*cf.* L. v. Valkenborch and L. Gassel); Strasbourg *Landscape with Diana;* Vienna Kunsthist. *Landscape with S. John preaching;* Vienna Academy *The road to Calvary.* Pictures without an owl presumed by some his work are in various museums.
[Fl. 503, Fl. 371, Fl. 818, Fl. 526, Fl. 559, Fl. 892, Fl. 798, Fl. 440, Fl. 150, Fl. 212, Fl. 213, Fl. 316.]

Blieck, Maurice. Flemish Sch. *b* Laeken 1876 *d* Brussels 1922. *Marines, port scenes, landscapes, portraits, genre.* Pupil in Brussels Acad.; in Paris 1896. Visited London. Represented in ANTWERP *Antwerp Port* (winter), *Marine.* BRUGES *Sailing ship in port.* IXELLES *The Tide.*
[Fl. 2 (1909), Fl. 440.]

Block, Eugène F. de. Flemish Sch. *b* Grammont 1812 *d* Antwerp 1893. *Genre, religious subjects, portraits.* Pupil of P. van Huffel in Ghent and of F. de Braekeleer in Antwerp; lived Brussels and later Antwerp where curator of Museum. Represented in ANTWERP *Returning from school.* AMSTER-

DAM Rijks. *Sunny room with figures.* BRUSSELS *The Bible lesson, Consolation.* GHENT *The quarrel.* A picture titled *Sportsman starting out* was in the London R. A. 1845.
[Fl. 451, Fl. 361, Fl. 892, Fl. 440, Fl. Bib. 19th cent.]

*Blocklandt van Montfoort, Anthonis.** Flemish (Dutch) Sch. *b* of noble family, Montfoort *c.* 1533 *d* Utrecht 1583. *Religious subjects; mythologies with nudes; occasional portraits.* Pupil in Antwerp of F. Floris before 1552; then worked Delft where C. Ketel was his pupil 1565; went Italy, where Van Mander (1604) records him more impressed by Parmigiano then by Michelangelo, 1572; returned Holland before end of year; Master in Utrecht Guild 1577; Van Mander writes: 'when he walked the streets he was always followed by a footman as his noble descent required'; he records that a number of his pictures were seen by the Dutch painter A. Bloemart in the house of his master Joos de Beer *q.v.* in Utrecht *c.* 1577 and that many painted for churches were destroyed by the Iconoclasts (*cf.* P. Aertsen, J. Beuckelaer also M. de Vos). A. P. Cluyt was his pupil and assistant; the Dutch painter M. J. Miereveldt was his pupil. **Signed Examples:** None. **Monogrammed Example** ('B' presumed his monogram): VIENNA Kunsthist. *Diana and Actaeon* (*cf.* J. Uytewael and B. de Ryckere) 1573. **Documented Examples:** GOUDA *Martyrdom of S. James* (from S. John's church). HAARLEM Bisschoppelijk Mus. *Entombment* (both described by Van Mander). DORDRECHT Town Hall (from S. Nicholas church) *Last Supper* (engraved). A *Crucifixion* in Dordrecht Civic Guards' House, an *Assumption of the Virgin, Pentecost* and *Ascension* in Utrecht, *Scenes from the life of Joseph* (*cf.* P. Aertsen and Joseph Master) in Amsterdam and *Scenes from the legend of S. Catherine* painted for Hertogenbosch are among religious subjects recorded by Van Mander; an *Assumption of the Virgin* 1579 is recorded by an eighteenth century engraving; a *Bathsheba at the bath* (*cf.* F. Badens) and a *Venus* are among pictures with nudes recorded by Van Mander; a *Standing Venus*, a *Mars and Venus* and a *Lot with his daughters* are recorded in 17th cent. inventories; other *Scenes from the life of Lot* are recorded by engravings (*cf.* J. V. de Vries).
[Fl. 559, Fl. 481, Fl. 892, Fl. 631 (1931), Fl. 212, Fl. 213, Fl. 421.]

Blocq (Block), Pierre Balthasar de. Flemish Sch. *b* son of a painter M. J. de B., Antwerp 1729 *d* Charleroi 1795. *Religious subjects for Charleroi churches, portraits, decorative paintings.* In Antwerp till 1762; then travelled abroad; settled Charleroi 1766. His son Jean Joseph and his grandson Louis were also painters. **Signed Example:** CHARLEROI S. Fiacre *Scene from the life of S. Fiacre.* A *Portrait of Joseph II* (*cf.* G. de Pélichy) is recorded. [Fl. 440.]

*Bloemen (Blommen), Jan Frans van,** called Orizonte or Horizonte. Flemish Sch. *b* Antwerp 1662 *d* Rome 1748 or 1749. *Italianate landscapes* (*cf.* J. B. Juppin and J. P. Spalthof) *some with figures by others; also worked as engraver.* Brother of N. and P. van B. *q.v.* Pupil of A. Goubau 1681; went Italy and remained there (*cf.* R. la Longe, J. X. Vermoelen, H. v. Lint); given his nickname in Flemish colony in Rome; commissioned by Prince Camillo Pamphili to paint a series of pictures 1711; member Accad. de S. Luca 1742. Descamps (1763) records that on reaching Rome he declared that he could only see the environs in terms of pictures already painted; Descamps describes his work as 'des vues de Tivoli et des environs; des chutes d'eau; une vapeur d'eau bien représentée; un arc-en-ciel qui s'entrevoyait au travers des brouillards ou d'une pluie fine; ces temps sont représentés à tromper'. Lanzi (1792) writes: 'the palaces of the Pope and nobility in Rome abound with his landscapes in fresco and oil ... he commonly imitated Poussin'. **Signed Examples:** COPENHAGEN *Arcadian landscape with sculpture* (F. v. Blommen-Orizonte). GLASGOW *Italian landscape with pastoral figures* (Blommen

Roma). MADRID Prado *Campo Vaccino Rome* H. v. . . . 1704 (in Philip V's collection before 1746). **Documented Example:** MADRID Prado *Italian landscape with foreground figures* (*in* Philip V's collection before 1746). Rome Doria-Pamphili Gallery has a number of pictures traditionally presumed the pictures commissioned 1711. London British Museum has *Drawings of buildings in Rome and environs.* Pictures presumed by some his work are in many museums.
[Fl. 353, Fl. 215, Fl. 505, Fl. 451, Fl. 612, Fl. 107, Fl. 892, Fl. 678.]

Bloemen (Blommen), Norbert van, called Cephalus. Flemish Sch. *b* Antwerp 1670 *d* Amsterdam 1746. *Peasant and social genre, portraits, religious subjects* (?). Brother of P. and J. F. van B. Went Rome where given his nickname in Flemish colony; returned Antwerp on foot, begging his way and sleeping in monasteries (*cf.* J. P. Spalthof); later settled Amsterdam. **Signed Example:** AMSTERDAM Rijks. *J. P. Somer, art dealer of Amsterdam.* **Monogrammed Example:** LENINGRAD *Peasants playing cards in the open air* (NO. V. B.). [Fl. 425, Fl. 353, Fl. 215, Fl. 892.]

Bloemen (Blommen), Pieter van, called Standaart. Flemish Sch. *b* Antwerp 1657 *d* Antwerp 1720. *Military pieces* (*cf.* J. Broers and J. B. van der Meiren) and *Italianate landscapes with genre figures and animals* (*cf.* J. B. Juppin). Brother of Norbert and J. F. van B. *q.v.* Pupil of S. J. van Douw *q.v.* when ten years old 1667; Master Antwerp Guild by 1673; went Rome (*cf.* A. Barbiers) where was given his nickname in Flemish colony; Lanzi (1789) records that the German painter C. Reder collaborated with him in scenes of battles between Christians and Turks, in fashion after taking of Buda 1686 (*cf.* J. P. v. Bredael also A. and P. Casteels); returned Antwerp 1694; Dean in Antwerp Guild 1699. Descamps (1763) records that many of his pictures show horse markets, 'caravannes' and oriental figures with 'débris d'architecture' in the landscape. **Monogrammed Examples:** COPENHAGEN *Horsemen at a smithy* 1705. DRESDEN *Market amid Roman ruins* 1710, *Riding school amid Roman ruins.* LENINGRAD *Riding school* 1712. NANTES *Horsemen at a smithy* 1711. ROME Corsini *Halt of horsemen* 1708. STOCKHOLM *Cavalry camp, Bivouac.* TROYES *Landscape with woman on a white horse, cowherd, cattle and goats.* VIENNA Liecht. *Italian peasants playing cards.* Vienna Albertina and Haarlem Teyler have monogrammed drawings. *cf.* A. F. Rubens.
[Fl. 425, Fl. 353, Fl. 215, Fl. 505, Fl. 84, Fl. 107, Fl. 892, Fl. 678.]

Blom, A. Flemish Sch. 18th/19th cents. *Architectural interiors.* **Signed Example:** ANTWERP *Interior of Old S. George's church, Antwerp* (with figures by P. J. van Regemorter *q.v.*).
[Fl. 17.]

Blomaerts (or Blommaerts), Hendrik. Flemish Sch. *b* Antwerp 1755 *d* Brussels 1837. *Landscapes with animals and figures, views of country round Brussels,* (*cf.* S. P. Argonne), *portraits.* Pupil of H. J. Antonissen *q.v.*; founder-member of Antwerp Soc. des Beaux-Arts (*cf.* B. P. Ommeganck) 1788; exhibited there regularly from 1789; settled Brussels 1790.
[Fl. 451, Fl. 107, Fl. 440.]

Blommaerdt, Maximilian. Flemish Sch. 17th/18th cent. *Genre.* Pupil in Antwerp of flower painter F. van Aken 1697. **Signed Example:** BRUNSWICK *Music making company.* [Fl. 892.]

*Blondeel, Lancelot.** Flemish Sch. *b* Poperinghe *c.* 1496 *d* Bruges 1561. *Religious subjects in floriated architectural settings; also active as architect* (*cf.* P. Coecke van Aelst), *designer for sculpture, pageantry and tapestry* (*cf.* B. v. Orley), *decorative painter; also engineer* (*cf.* J. v. Scorel and J. C. Vermeyen). Presumed by some the 'Lancilotto' referred to by Vasari (1568) as 'eccellente in far fuochi, notti, splendori,

diavoli e cose somiglianti'. Van Mander (1604), following an inscription on his tomb, records him as in youth a mason, who signed his pictures accordingly with a trowel (*cf*. P. Aertsen, A. and P. Pietersz) and excelled in depicting 'bouwkundige ornamenten' and 'antieke ruinen', Master, as painter, in Bruges Guild 1519; commissioned to paint an altarpiece by the Guild of Barber-Surgeons 1523; commissioned by the city of Bruges to design the fireplace in the Council Room of the Franc de Bruges (executed with renaissance ornaments, 'putti' and life-size statues of Maximilian of Austria and Maria of Burgundy, Ferdinand and Isabella of Spain and the emperor Charles V by several sculptors, and now in Bruges Palais de Justice), 1528-31; took P. J. Pourbus as a pupil before 1540; submitted scheme (not executed) for construction of a new port and canals against the silting up of the Zwyn (*cf*. P. J. Pourbus) 1546; consulted by the city authorities about designs for a triumphal arch for the Pageant Entry into Bruges of Charles V and Philip II (*cf*. P. J. Pourbus also C. Anthonisz) 1549; went Ghent with J. v. Scorel to clean and restore the *Adoration of the Mystic Lamb* by Hubert van Eyck *q.v.* and Jan van Eyck *q.v.* (*cf*. A. v. d. Heuvel and J. v. d. Veken); they left certain parts 'which had merely become pale' untouched and on concluding their work kissed the picture reverently 1550; appointed Master of Works to Convent of the Annunciation (built by Margaret of Austria) 1557. His daughter married P. J. Pourbus. **Signed Examples** (LAB and trowel): BRUGES Mus. S. *Luke painting the Virgin* 1545 (painted for the Guild of S. Luke); S. Jacques Triptych: centre: *Martyrdom of SS. Cosmas and Damian*, wings: *S. Cosmas, S. Damian* 1523 (painted for the Barber-Surgeons' Guild); S. Sauveur *Virgin and Child enthroned on an arch with SS. Luke and Eligius* 1545 (painted for the Guild of S. Luke). A *Last Judgement* commissioned by the Blankenberghe Magistrature 1540 is recorded.
[Fl. 818, Fl. 371, Fl. 752, Fl. 559, Fl. 896, Fl. 58, Fl. 892, Fl. 113, Fl. 161, Fl. 316, Fl. 296, Fl. 174.]

Blyenberch (or **Blyenburch**), **Abraham** (van). Flemish Sch. *b* Antwerp before 1605 *d* after 1623. *Portraits*. Came England and painted *James I* and *Charles Prince of Wales* (*cf*. P. v. Somer, J. de Gheyn the younger and C. de Neve) *c*. 1618. T. van Thulden was his pupil in Antwerp 1622.
[Fl. 748, Fl. 107, Fl. 892, Fl. 899.]

Boch, Anna. Flemish Sch. *b* La Louvière 1848 *d* after 1914. *Landscapes, coast scenes, flower pieces in Impressionist conventions*. Pupil in Brussels of I. Verheyden. Member of Brussels group 'Les Vingt' (*cf*. J. Ensor) 1884; and of 'Vie et Lumière' (*cf*. G. Morren) 1914; travelled widely; worked in France and Holland. Represented in BRUSSELS *Brittany coast*.
[Fl. 123, Fl. 388, Fl. 296.]

Bocquet, V., see **Boucquet.**

*****Boeckhorst** (**Bockhorst**), **Jan,** known as Lange Jan (Langhenjan). Flemish Sch. *b* Münster 1605 *d* Antwerp 1668. *Religious subjects, mythologies, portraits; also designs for tapestry*. Went young to Antwerp where pupil of J. Jordaens; Master Antwerp Guild 1633; employed under Rubens on decorations for Pageant Entry into Antwerp of Cardinal Infante Ferdinand (*cf*. G. Weri) 1635; went Italy 1636; made a will in Antwerp recording himself about to return to Italy because he had not seen Rome (*cf*. T. Boeyermans) 1639; made later wills in Antwerp 1654 and 1668 disposing of his considerable collection of pictures, engravings, drawings and books (*cf*. E. Quellinus); referred to by some as painter of figures in pictures by F. Snyders *q.v.*; collaborated with Jan Wildens. **Documented Example:** VIENNA K. *Mercury enamoured of Herse on her way to the Temple of Minerva with her sisters Agraulos and Pandrosos* (Archduke Leopold

Wilhelm's inventory 1659). Descamps saw (1768), by 'Langhenjan', Antwerp: Annonciades *Angels holding the sudary of S. Veronica* ('aussi beau que van Dyck'); Carmes Déchaussés *Flight into Egypt* (landscape by P. de Witte the younger); Religieuses Façons *Flight into Egypt* (landscape by J. Wildens) and others; Béguinage: Triptych *Resurrection of Christ, Annunciation, Ascension* (Funeral monument of the Béguine Maria Snyders; 'il y a une finesse de couleur aimable et la touche la plus facile'); Church of the Cordeliers *Finding of the True Cross*. Bruges: Jacobins *Adoration of the Magi* ('je ne sais pourquoi un chien occupe le coin du tableau sans aucun rapport avec le reste; c'est une cheville'); Ghent: S. Jacques *Martyrdom of S. James* ('les figures sur le premier plan sont trop grandes pour le Saint et pour les bourreaux'); S. Michel *S. Hubert adoring the stag with the mystic Cross* ('un très beau tableau qui a, je crois, un peu noirçi' *cf*. P. Boel), *Allegory of the Old and New Testaments* ('la couleur y est argentine'), *The Virgin and the Holy Trinity with Zacharias and S. Elizabeth, Adam and Eve*, Lille: S. Maurice *Martyrdom of S. Maurice and the Theban Legion* ('nettoyé depuis peu et repeint assez mal'); and others elsewhere. Jeremias Wildens *q.v.* owned (1653) a *Herse, Four Quarters of the World, Twelve Sibyls* and copies of pictures by Rubens and Van Dyck (all as by 'Brouckhorst'); J. B. Borkens *q.v.* owned (1668) a *Landscape by J. Wildens with figures by Langen Jan after Rubens*; the inventory (1678) of the collection of E. Quellinus *q.v.* records a *Caritas* and a copy by Quellinus of a *Diana hunting*; and other 17th cent. inventories record portraits, *Samson and Delila, Courtship of Neptune, Adam and Eve driven from Paradise*, and (1655) a *Silenus* 'by myn Heer Rubens geretocceert'. The Forchoudt firm of Antwerp dealers refer in a letter (1658) to a picture by Van Dyck and 'Jannis Bincoerst genaent Langhe Jan' and in another (1668) to the death of 'Joannes Bockhoerst die men noemden Langhen Jan'. An inventory (1691) records collaboration with N. v. Verendael *q.v.*
[Fl. 86, Fl. 215, Fl. 216, Fl. 892, Fl. 113, Fl. 212, Fl. 213.]

Boel, Jan Baptist. Flemish Sch. *b* son of Peeter B. *q.v.* Antwerp 1650 *d* Antwerp 1689. *Still life with 'Vanitas,' emblems* (*cf*. B. de Bridt, N. v. Steenwyck, C. N. Gysbrechts). Master Antwerp Guild 1675. **Documented Example:** ANTWERP *'Vanitas' still life with dead swan, peacock, globe, violoncello, carpet, bronzes and sunflowers* painted for the Olyftak Chamber of Rhetoric 1679 and hung in the Chamber of the Guild of S. Luke. [Fl. 107, Fl. 440, Fl. 13.]

Boel (Boels), Louis (Lodewyk). Flemish Sch. *b* Bruges (?) before 1465 *d* Bruges 1522. Pupil in Bruges Guild 1477; Master 1485; held other offices 1513-18; acquired H. Memlinc's house 1509. **Signed Examples:** None. **Documented Examples:** None. [Fl. 870, Fl. 892.]

Boel, Peeter. Flemish Sch. *b* son of engraver Jan B., Antwerp 1622 *d* Paris 1674. *Large decorative still life compositions some with 'Vanitas' emblems* (*cf*. J. B. Boel, P. Gysels, J. F. v. Son, A. v. Utrecht), *still life with dead birds and game, trophies of the chase and animals* (*cf*. N. Bernaerts, D. de Coninck, J. B. Govaerts, J. Fyt, P. A. Rysbraeck, F. v. Schney, F. Snyders, J. J. Spoede); *also designs for tapestry and some engravings*. Recorded by his contemporary E. Quellinus *q.v.* as pupil of J. Fyt and by his contemporary Félibien as pupil of F. Snyders (whose widow, Félibien states, he married); went Italy where worked in Genoa with his uncle C. de Wael *q.v.* and in Rome; in Antwerp where Master in Guild 1650; went Paris and worked there with the French painter C. Le Brun for the Gobelins factory (*cf*. A. F. Baudewyns) *c*. 1668; Court painter to Louis XIV (*cf*. A. F. v.d. Meulen). D. de Coninck was his pupil in Antwerp; E. Quellinus painted his portrait with a dog. **Signed Examples:** LILLE *Still life with 'Vanitas' emblems* (globe, mitre, crown, armour and metal vessels) *in a palace setting*. MADRID

Prado *Game, fish and dog on a seashore.* MUNICH A. P. *Dead boar, hind and swan with greyhounds in a landscape.* ROTTERDAM *Trophies of the chase.* **Monogrammed Examples:** BERLIN K.F. *Dead birds and hare with cat* (*cf.* C. Luyckx). BRUSSELS *Game piece.* CASSEL *Donkey laden with kitchen utensils, and two dogs.* MADRID Prado *Armour, vessels and a sporting dog, Dead birds, swan and rabbit in a landscape with greyhound and two other dogs.* VIENNA Acad. *Globe, vessels, carpet, musical instruments and small dog in a terrace setting.* The Forchoudt firm of Antwerp dealers sent (1670) to their Vienna branch a series of hunting pieces in which A. J. v. Diepenbeeck *q.v.* collaborated with the horses and the landscapes, and (1671) a *Feast of the sea gods* (*cf.* F. Floris and H. v. Balen) with figures by E. Quellinus, and other examples of this collaboration; E. Quellinus had in his own collection a *Noah's ark* (*cf.* C. de Wael) painted by himself with 'de beesten van Boel'; Anna Colyns, widow of a Treasurer General of Antwerp owned 1667 a *Bird piece.* Descamps (1769) records hounds and stag painted by him in a *S. Hubert adoring the stag with the mystic Cross* (*cf.* J. Boeckhorst) by G. de Crayer with landscape by L. de Vadder *q.v.* in Louvain S. Jacques. Pictures presumed by some his work are in various museums.
[Fl. 86, Fl. 287, Fl. 773, Fl. 878, Fl. 215, Fl. 216, Fl. 107, Fl. 892, Fl. 440, Fl. 212, Fl. 213.]

Boels (or **Bols**), **Frans** (**François**). Flemish Sch. *b* Malines (?) *d* Holland *c* 1594. *Miniature landscapes, some with figures.* Van Mander (1604) records him as stepson and pupil of Hans Bol *q.v.*; fled with him as Protestant to Holland after Parma's capture of Antwerp (*cf.* D. v. d. Queborne) 1584. **Signed Examples:** HERMANNSTADT *Mountainous landscapes with mythological figures* three examples on parchment 1588. STOCKHOLM *The Four Seasons* 1594 gouache on paper (*cf.* L. v. Valkenborch). An example was recorded in the Archduke Leopold Wilhelm's inventory 1659.
[Fl. 559, Fl. 892.]

Boens, Alexandre. Flemish Sch. *b* Charleroi 1760 *d* Charleroi 1835. '*History, landscapes, portraits; also lithographs for books.* Pupil of P. B. Blocq and A. Lens in Antwerp Academy; worked mainly in Brussels. [Fl. 440.]

Boens, Alexandre the younger. Flemish Sch. *b* son of Alexandre B., Tournai 1793 *d* after 1837. *Landscapes and town views* (*many as lithographs*). Pupil of J. François (*cf.* F. J. Navez and J. B. Madou) in Brussels; in Courtrai as cartographer 1819; thereafter mainly Brussels. [Fl. 440.]

Boens, Léopold. Flemish Sch. *b* son of Alexandre B., Tournai 1795 *d* Brussels 1837. *Interiors and genre, also lithographs.* Pupil in Brussels of J. François (*cf.* A.B. the younger).
[Fl. 440.]

Boeyermans, Theodor. Flemish Sch. *b* Antwerp 1620 *d* Antwerp 1678. *Religious subjects, 'history', allegories, portraits and conversation groups* (*cf.* G. Coques, P. Fruytiers, H. Janssens, P. Meert). Made a will at the age of fourteen (usual when leaving for abroad (*cf.* J. Boeckhorst and Ambrosius Brueghel) and presumed by some to have gone London (taken by Van Dyck (?)) 1634; presumed pupil and assistant of Van Dyck (*cf.* J. v. Belcamp, R. v. Leemput, J. v. Reyn) and acquainted thus with his wife Mary Ruthven 1639; in Antwerp (having returned with van Dyck and his family (?)) 1640; visited Italy (?); Master Antwerp Guild 1654; associated with the opening of the Antwerp Academy founded by Philip IV (*cf.* J. Jordaens and D. Teniers the younger) 1665; took Marcus Forchoudt of the Forchoudt family of dealers (*cf.* A. Casteels) as his pupil 1670; commented in a letter to Marcus Forchoudt (then in the Vienna branch) on the international situation and recorded the results of disputes between the Academy, the Guild of S. Luke and

the painters: 'Het process dat tussen de schilders ende de gilden gehangen heeft soo langen tijt, is ten lesten geweszn, in faveur van de schilders die het met costen ende al hebben gewonnen, soo dat de camer meer als ooyt te voren floreren sal . . .' 1677. **Signed Examples:** ANTWERP *The pool of Bethesda* (*cf.* P. v. Lint) 1675 (from Antwerp Sœurs Noires convent), *Patrician family receiving a church dignitary and a Jesuit father on a terrace.* THE HAGUE Mauritshuis (in *Interior of a picture gallery* by G. Coques) *The Four Seasons.* MALINES Béguinage *Martyrdom of S. Rombout* 1660. NANTES *The vow of S. Aloysius Gonzaga* 1671 (taken to France in 1794 and not returned (*cf.* G. de Crayer and J. D. Odevaere)). **Documented Example:** ANTWERP *Antwerp as Foster-mother of the Painters* 1665 (showing Rubens and van Dyck behind a table with a bust of Homer and the City of Antwerp symbolised by a figure traditionally recorded as representing Mary Ruthven; painted for the ceiling of the new Antwerp Academy headquarters in Antwerp Bourse where seen by Descamps (1768); *cf.* A. Genoels, H. v. Minderhout also P. Spierincx, M. Sweerts and J. Denys; rewarded by a silver-gilt cup and a panegyric poem). Descamps (1768) saw *The Virgin interceding for the plague stricken* ('bien composé, d'une grande finesse de couleur') in Malines S. Pierre, and *Scenes from the life of the Virgin* and other pictures in Malines Béguinage; in Antwerp S. Jacques an *Assumption* ('du plus beau pinceau à égaler aux ouvrages de van Dyck.' (*cf.* J. v. Reyn), in Antwerp Augustins *Flagellation* ('d'une mauvaise couleur, crue et lourde'), in Antwerp Jacobins *Martyrdom of S. Paul* (*the Virgin binding his eyes*) and *The history of the Rosary* (six pictures); in Ypres Jesuits *S. Francis Xavier converting an Indian prince* ('ce tableau, argentin . . . est, je crois, le chef d'œuvre de ce maître trop peu connu') and *Apparition of the Virgin to S. Ignatius Loyola;* and in Ypres Religieuses du Bois *Assumption.* The Antwerp collector J. van Weerden owned (1686) an *Apollo* and '*Zeetriumphe*' (*Neptune and Amphitrite* (?) or *Quos ego* (?)); and a Forchoudt invoice (1670) records a *Belshazzar's Feast.*
[Fl. 216, Fl. 613, Fl. 614, Fl. 88, Fl. 107, Fl. 892, Fl. 646, Fl. 440, Fl. 212, Fl. 213, Fl. 679.]

Bogaerde, Donatien van den. Flemish Sch. *b* Bruges 1644 *d* Bruges 1695. *Wooded landscapes* (*cf.* J. d'Arthois). A monk and lived in the Abbaye des Dunes from 1664. **Documented Examples:** BRUGES Séminaire Épiscopal (formerly Abbaye des Dunes), *Landscapes* (in collaboration with B. R. d'Hooghe *q.v.*). (*Cf.* also L. Achtschellinck, J. B. van Meunincxhove and P. v. Bredael.)
[Fl. 892, Fl. 113, Fl. 114.]

Bois (**Dubois**), **Dominique François du.** Flemish Sch. *b* Bruges 1800 *d* Bois-le-Duc 1840. *History and decorative compositions.* Pupil in Bruges of J. F. Ducq *q.v.* and in Antwerp of M. I. v. Brée *q.v.*; then studied Paris (*cf.* J. S. v. d. Abeele, H. de Caisne, C. L. Saligo, F. Simonau); director Bois-le-Duc Academy 1828. A *William II as Prince of Orange giving a standard to the Garde-Nationale of Bois-le-Duc* painted for the Town Hall and compositions in the King's Palace in The Hague are recorded. (*Cf.* A. v. Bedaff.)
[Fl. 451, Fl. 892, Fl. 440.]

Boks, Evert Jan. Flemish Sch. *b* Beekbergen (Holland) 1838 *d* Antwerp 1914. '*History', and portraits; but chiefly anecdotic genre.* Pupil in Antwerp of N. de Keyser; settled Antwerp; exhibited Antwerp, Paris Salons and London. Represented in ANTWERP *Self portrait* 1898. A picture titled *The sleep of the just* was in the London Royal Academy 1879. Other titles recorded are '*When the cats are away . . .*' and *Servants frolicking surprised by their masters.*
[Fl. 892, Fl. 361, Fl. 440.]

Bol, Cornelis. Flemish Sch. *b* Malines after 1534 *d* Antwerp (?) after 1577. Brother of Hans Bol *q.v.* He had a son of the same name. [Fl. 440.]

Bol, Cornelis. Flemish Sch. *b* Antwerp before 1595 *d* Haarlem (?) after 1649 (?). Pupil in Antwerp of T. v. Haecht (Rubens' first master; *cf.* J. Backereel) 1607; Master Antwerp Guild 1615; recorded in Antwerp 1623; presumed by some identical with a marine painter of this name who settled Haarlem after visiting England (where was friend of A. Keirincx *q.v.* 1640). Not to be confused with an engraver of this name who worked in Richmond in 1611.

[Fl. 892, Fl. 440, Fl. 798.]

Bol, Cornelis. Flemish (?) or Dutch (?) Sch. Vertue (before 1741) records him as painter of Thames scenes showing Arundel House, Somerset House and the Tower 'before the Great Fire' (i.e. before 1666). Dulwich has a *View on the Thames with Somerset House and the Savoy and distant views of Whitehall and Westminster Abbey* monogrammed 'C.B.' presumed by some his work.

[Fl. 826, Fl. 856, Fl. 892, Fl. 440.]

*Bol, Hans (Jan). Flemish Sch. *b* Malines 1534 *d* Amsterdam 1593. *Landscapes with small figures* (*cf.* H. met de Bles, P. Bom, P. Bruegel the elder, L. Gassel, J. Grimmer, F. Mostaert); *miniature compositions* (*cf.* A. de Smytere); *also active as draughtsman and engraver.* Van Mander (1604) records him as beginning among the numerous Malines painters of linen wall hangings (*cf.* J. Jordaens); presumed by some pupil of his uncles Jacques and Jan B. *q.v.*; Van Mander records that he went Germany and worked two years in Heidelberg; visited Italy (?); in Malines Guild 1560; Van Mander records that he 'invented' there many landscapes and other compositions in watercolour till he had to flee destitute from the Spanish sack of Malines (*cf.* P. v. d. Borcht the elder, also M. Coxie) 1572; went Antwerp where Master in Guild 1574; van Mander records that in Antwerp he illustrated a book with all kinds of animals, birds and fish 'naar het leven' and evolved a personal style in miniature painting on parchment because his watercolours on linen were extensively copied and then sold as his work; fled from Antwerp as Protestant after Parma's conquest (*cf.* D. v. d. Queborne) 1584; went Bergen-op-Zoom, then Dordrecht (*cf.* Jacques Bol the younger), then Delft and Amsterdam. His pupils included his stepson Frans Boels *q.v.*, Jacques Savery the elder and J. Hoefnagel. The Dutch engraver H. Goltzus engraved his portrait. **Signed Examples:** BERLIN K.F. (miniatures) *Landscape with Hagar and Ishmael* 1583 gouache on parchment, *Park landscape with buildings and figures* 1589 gouache on parchment, *Fish spearing at The Hague* 1585 watercolour on parchment, *Landscape with gallows and the Good Samaritan* gouache on parchment. BRUSSELS *Panorama of Antwerp* (*cf.* J. B. Bonnecroy and A. Grimmer) 1575. DRESDEN *Fish spearing at The Hague* 1586, *Village Kermesse* 1580, *David and Abigail* 1587, *Meleager and Atalanta* 1580; all in tempera on parchment mounted on wood. **Monogrammed Example:** VIENNA Kunsthist. *Flemish village scene.* **Documented Examples:** DRESDEN *Jacob's dream, Moses and the daughters of Jethro* (both in 1587 inventory). STOCKHOLM *Daedalus and Icarus* (*cf.* Brussels Icarus Painter; formerly in Prague; composition corresponding to Van Mander's description of a water colour picture of this subject belonging to his nephew). Brussels has signed drawings. Van Mander records a *Crucifixion*; the Antwerp collector Alexander Voet owned (1689) a *Peasant kermesse* in watercolour. Many compositions are recorded by engravings.

[Fl. 371, Fl. 818, Fl. 559, Fl. 613, Fl. 892, Fl. 440, Fl. 301, Fl. 213.]

Bol, Jacques. Flemish Sch. *b* Malines before 1525 *d* Malines (?) date unknown. Master Malines Guild 1540. [Fl. 613.]

Bol, Jacques the younger. Flemish Sch. *b* Malines after 1534 *d* Holland after 1581. Brother of Hans B. *q.v.*; Master Malines Guild 1558; left Malines 1572 (?); Master Antwerp Guild 1574; left Antwerp for religious reasons and went Dordrecht where recorded 1578; in Dordrecht Guild 1581.

[Fl. 613, Fl. 892, Fl. 440.]

Bol, Jan. Flemish Sch. *b* Malines (?) before 1500 *d* Malines (?) date unknown. Recorded Malines 1507. [Fl. 613.]

Bols, see **Boels.**

Bom, Pieter. Flemish Sch. *b* Antwerp 1530 *d* Antwerp 1607. *Landscapes* (*cf.* H. Bol). In Antwerp Guild 1560; Master 1564. Van Mander (1604) records him as a good painter in watercolour. [Fl. 559, Fl. 892.]

Bomberghen, Daniel van. Flemish Sch. *b* Antwerp (?) before 1500 *d* Venice 1549. *Painter and printer of Hebrew books in Antwerp.* Van Mander (1604) records him as 'schilder' and 'schilderkunst liefhebber' who befriended J. v. Scorel in Venice 1520. [Fl. 559, Fl. 892.]

Bomberghen, Guillaume van. Flemish Sch. *b* Antwerp 1807 *d* Brussels 1882. *Landscapes including moonlight effects* (*cf.* P. v. Schendel and J. L. de Wouters), *portraits, miniatures.* Pupil in Antwerp Acad.; then in Paris; returned Belgium 1834. Represented in LEIPZIG *Moonlight landscape* 1850.

[Fl. 440.]

Bonet, Jacques Louis. Flemish Sch. *b* Grand Ménil (Namur) 1822 *d* Belgrade (Namur) 1894. *Religious subjects for Namur churches, 'history', portraits.* Pupil in Brussels Acad. of F. J. Navez; professor and later director of Namur Academy. Represented in NAMUR Hôtel de Ville *The Judgement of Solomon.* An *Allegory of painting* designed as a ceiling decoration is recorded. [Fl. 440.]

Bonnecroy, Jan Baptist. Flemish Sch. *b* son of Willem (Guillaume) B., Antwerp 1618 *d* Brussels 1676. *Panoramic town and river views* (*cf.* H. Bol, A. Grimmer and J. Wildens); *also worked as engraver.* A frère mineur in Order of S. Francis 1638 but gave up orders and married the next year; pupil in Antwerp of L. v. Uden; sent landscapes to his great-uncle the Seville dealer C. v. Immerseel (*cf.* J. Boots) 1642; Master in Antwerp Guild 1645; in Brussels Guild 1665. **Signed Examples:** ANTWERP Mus. *Large panorama of Antwerp and the Scheldt with part of the Tête de Flandre* 1658 (shows shipping and a foreground with cattle in the fields, peasants and gentry; bought from the artist by the Antwerp Magistrature and formerly in Hôtel de Ville). BRUGES Séminaire *Same subject* dated 1656. [Fl. 107, Fl. 892, Fl. 440, Fl. 214.]

Bonnecroy, Philippe. Flemish Sch. *b* Antwerp 1720 *d* Antwerp (?) after 1771. Pupil of J. A. Beschey; Dean in Antwerp Guild in 1762 and 1771. [Fl. 440.]

Boogh, Hans in den. Flemish Sch. *b* Antwerp (?) before 1545 *d* 1586. Van Mander (1604) records that he left Antwerp with P. Vlerick *q.v.* [Fl. 559.]

Boom, Charles. Flemish Sch. *b* Hoogstraten 1858 *d* Antwerp 1939. *Costume history, genre, portraits, decorative murals* (*cf.* L. Delbeke, J. Swerts, N. de Keyser, C. Ooms, P. v. d. Ouderaa, F. Pauwels, A. and J. de Vriendt). Pupil in Antwerp Acad. of C. Verlat; later teacher in the Academy. Represented in ANTWERP Mus. *Within the walls of Antwerp 1550* 1901, *Self portrait* (pastel); Town Hall; *murals* (*cf.* E. Farasyn, H. Houben, E. de Jans, V. Lagye and P. Verhaert).

[Fl. 440, Fl. 741, Fl. 16.]

Boone (or Boon), Daniel. Flemish Sch. *b* Burgerhout nr. Antwerp *c.* 1632 *d* London (?) 1698 or 1700. *Peasant genre* (*cf.* A. Brouwer, J. v. Craesbeeck, M. v. Helmont, D. Teniers the younger, A. Victorijns, A. Wouwer). Worked Amsterdam

1654-65; then in London (*cf.* J. Siberechts). **Signed Examples:** AMSTERDAM Rijks. *Peasants playing cards, Peasant laughing and eating from a bowl.* J. C. Weyerman saw, when in London, *c.* 1718, a comic *Judgement of Paris* and, in a tavern called 'The Beggars' Cellar' a *Beggars carousing* on the wall; Vertue records (1743) *A man with a candle, laughing, squeezing a lemon, Diogenes and his lantern* and a mezzotint representing a *Man playing the fiddle.*
[Fl. 878, Fl. 826, Fl. 856, Fl. 451, Fl. 892.]

Boons, P. van. Presumed Flemish Sch. 17th cent. Signature on VIENNA Harrach *Interior of a gallery with cavalier examining a picture of the Virgin* dated 1627 (*cf.* C. de Baellieur, B. v. d. Bossche and W. v. Haecht). [Fl. 892.]

Boots (Boets, Boits), Jan. Flemish Sch. *b* Antwerp before 1620 *d* date and place unknown. *Landscapes with allegorical figures (four seasons, elements, etc. cf.* J. (Velvet) Brueghel, R. Savery, S. de Vos), *outdoor genre markets* (*cf.* S. Vrancx), *still life with dead birds* (*cf.* F. Snyders). Worked for Seville dealer C. van Immerseel who also imported pictures by J. B. Bonnecroy, A. v. Ertvelt, Jacques van Eyck, G. Franck, G. Seghers, A. v. Stalbemt, D. Teniers the younger, J. v. Uden, S. de Vos, S. Vrancx, F. Wouters and others (*cf.* also J. Brueghel the younger) 1636-41; P. Gysels *q.v.* was his pupil 1641; A. de Wael *q.v.* was his pupil in 1642. Pictures of the types listed above are recorded in Antwerp invoices of the Forchoudt firm of dealers (*cf.* A. Casteels) 1653-71; the very large collection of the Antwerp dealer H. de Neyt included 1642 a *Still life with dead birds* by 'Boot'.
[Fl. 717, Fl. 212, Fl. 213, Fl. 214.]

Borcht, Hendrik van der, the elder. Flemish Sch. *b* Brussels 1583 *d* Frankfort 1660. '*History*', *still life* (*antiques and curios cf.* F. Francken II and III, also P. Boel); *also active as engraver, antiquary, collector and dealer.* Taken to Germany by his parents after the Parma conquests (*cf.* D. v. d. Queborne) 1586; pupil of G. v. Valkenborch *q.v.* (and of Martin van V.?) in Frankfort; went Italy where worked as antiquary; went Frankenthal (*cf.* A. Mirou and J. v. Liere); published there engravings of official entry into Frankenthal of the Elector Palatine Frederick V and Princess Elizabeth of England 1613; went Frankfort 1627; sold collection of gems and other antiques to Thomas Howard, Earl of Arundel; visited England (?). **Monogrammed Example:** LENINGRAD *Antique statues, bronze vases, cameos, medals and other collectors' objects.* A signed allegorical composition *Germany beseeching the Emperor Ferdinand III to make peace* 1639 (*cf.* H. Sporckmans) is recorded in a private collection. Both pictures are possibly the work of his son H. v. d. B *q.v.*
[Fl. 86, Fl. 425, Fl. 878, Fl. 215, Fl. 892, Fl. 659, Fl. 440.]

Borcht, Hendrik van der the younger. Flemish Sch. *b* son of Hendrik van der B. the elder, Frankenthal 1614 *d* Antwerp 1665 (?). *Portraits; but mainly active as engraver.* Pupil of his father; in Frankfort with his father and made there the acquaintance of the Protestant Thomas Howard, Earl of Arundel (then on the way to Vienna to urge restitution of the Palatinate to Charles I's nephew) 1636; sent by the Earl to Italy to join his agent then buying antiques for him; came England (*cf.* A. van Dyck, J. v. Belcamp, H. v. Steenwyck the younger and C. de Neve); engraved works of art in Arundel collections; after the Earl's death (1646) entered service of the Prince of Wales; in Amsterdam 1652-4; then Antwerp. His *Portrait of H. v. d. Borcht the elder* is recorded by an engraving. The pictures listed as by H. v. d. B. the elder *q.v.* are possibly his work.
[Fl. 86, Fl. 826, Fl. 856, Fl. 892, Fl. 659, Fl. 440.]

Borcht, Lazarus van der. Flemish Sch. *b* Antwerp (?) before 1585 *d* Antwerp (?) after 1611. *Religious subjects and 'history', some in landscape.* Master Antwerp Guild 1601.

Signed Example: BRUNSWICK *Orpheus charming the animals* 1604 (*cf.* H. met de Bles, F. Borsse, P. Coecke van Aelst, J. Goeimare, A. de Gryef, Jacob Hoefnagel, G. C. de Hondecoeter, H. Jordaens III, F. Pourbus the elder, R. Savery, J. V. de Vries). An Antwerp collector owned (1614) a *Battlepiece* (batalje), an *Adam and Eve* and a '*hermitagie*' (*S. Jerome*?); the Antwerp wine taverner Jacques Snel (*cf.* F. Snyders and G. Seghers also C. de Cauwer) owned (1623) a large *Scipio and Hannibal.* A *Crucifixion* and an *Orpheus* were in other 17th cent. Antwerp collections. A series *The Twelve Months* (*cf.* P. Bruegel the elder and M. van Valkenborch) copied by S. Vrancx *q.v.* is also recorded. [Fl. 714, Fl. 213.]

Borcht, Pierre (Pieter) van der the elder. Flemish Sch. *b* Malines 1545 *d* Antwerp 1608. *Figures, landscapes; but chiefly active as draughtsman and engraver of landscape, genre and flowers.* Fled destitute from Spanish pillage of Malines (*cf.* H. Bol, also M. Coxie) 1572; went Antwerp where employed by Plantin Press (for which he had already worked 1565 and 1567) (*cf.* C. v. d. Broeck); Master in Antwerp Guild 1580; Dean 1589 to 1592. Flower studies by him were used in publications by Plantin. His brother Paul, and his sons Pierre and Frans were painters. [Fl. 440, Fl. 632.]

Borcht, Pierre (Pieter) van der. Flemish Sch. 17th cent. *Landscapes with figures.* In Brussels Guild as pupil of D. v. Alsloot 1604. A Pierre van der B. the younger (his son?) was Master in Brussels Guild 1625 and L. Achtschellinck *q.v.* was his pupil. Landscapes with figures by an artist of this name were recorded in the Archduke Leopold Wilhelm's inventory 1659. [Fl. 86, Fl. 892.]

Bordeau, Michel de. Flemish Sch. 16th–17th cent. *Religious subjects.* Worked Brussels where P. de Champaigne and A. Sallaert were his pupils. [Fl. 287.]

Borght (Burgt), J. van der. Flemish Sch. late 17th or 18th cent. *Flowers and fruit* (*cf.* C. Bigée, E. v. d. Broeck, P. Casteels III, J. B. de Crépu, A. v. d. Eeckhout, J. P. Gillemans the younger, P. and S. Hardimé, J. C. Lotyn, J. Seldenslach, G. P. Verbruggen the younger). Presumed distinct from the tapestry designer Jacques van der Borght (*d* 1794) and identical with the painter described as equal to the Italian flower painter Michelangelo di Campidoglio by J. Campo Weyerman (1729) who saw a number of his flower pieces in Dilighem Abbey and also copies of works by Luca Giordano. **Signed Example:** UTRECHT *Flower piece.*
[Fl. 878, Fl. 768, Fl. 892, Fl. 798, Fl. 296.]

Borkens (Borrekens), Jan Baptist. Flemish Sch. *b* Antwerp 1611 *d* Antwerp 1675. '*History*'. Master in Antwerp Guild 1630; married Catherine, daughter of Jan (Velvet) Brueghel (Rubens being witness at the wedding) 1636; worked on pictures from Rubens' sketches for Philip IV's hunting lodge La Torre de la Parada (*cf.* J. P. Gowi) *c.* 1636; Rubens was godfather to his son 1637; witness, with Rubens, Jan Brueghel the younger and others to contract at the marriage of D. Teniers the younger with another daughter of Jan (Velvet) Brueghel 1637; quarrelled with Teniers and expressly excluded him from guardianship of his children in will dated 1644; gave up painting, made a fortune in commerce, and had handsome house and large collection of pictures by Rubens, van Dyck, Brueghel, Teniers and other contemporaries (including a *Mater Dolorosa* by J. B. Gaspers *q.v.*); an inventory of the contents of his house (1688) shows that several rooms were hung with gold leather (*cf.* E. Quellinus). The engraver Mattheus B. was his brother. **Signed Example:** MADRID Prado *Apotheosis of Hercules* (*Hercules in a chariot drawn by four horses*) from a sketch by Rubens now in Brussels Mus.
[Fl. 107, Fl. 892, Fl. 440, Fl. 213, Fl. 214, Fl. 555.]

Borrekens, Jean Pierre. Flemish Sch. *b* Antwerp 1747 *d* Antwerp 1827 '*History*', and, later, landscapes (*some with figures and animals by B. P. Ommeganck* (*cf.* H. v. Assche) *and others*). Pupil of A. C. Lens *q.v.*; with B. P. Ommeganck *q.v.* a member of Antwerp Society of Artists; married sister of A. C. Lens; visited London. Pictures titled *Rape of Proserpina* and *Rape of Europa* were in the London Royal Academy 1797.

[Fl. 451, Fl. 107, Fl. 88, Fl. 361, Fl. 440.]

Borremans, Willem (Guglielmo il Fiamingo). Flemish Sch. *b* Antwerp (?) 1670 *d* Sicily (?) 1744. *Religious subjects, landscapes*. Pupil in Antwerp of P. v. Lint 1688–9; went Italy, worked in Naples and Cosenza; then settled Sicily (Palermo) where much employed as church painter. His son Luigi and his nephew Guglielmo were also painters and worked in Sicily. **Signed Examples:** CACCAMO S. Annunziata 1725. CALTANISETTA Cathedral 1720. COSENZA S. Catarina 1705; Cathedral 1703; S. Maria di Costantinopli 1704. DIANO (prov. Cosenza) Assunta 1706. NICOSIA S. Vincenzo Ferreri 1717. PALERMO S. Maria del Cancelliere 1717; S. Maria della Volta 1715; Oratorio della Carita 1728. S. MARTINO DELLA SCALE (prov. Palermo) 1727. **Monogrammed Example:** CATANIA Cathedral 1730. Other works are recorded by 18th century writers.

[Fl. 571, Fl. 305.]

Borsse (Borse, Borst, Bors), François. Flemish Sch. *b* Antwerp before 1570 *d* Antwerp (?) after 1595. *Landscapes, religious subjects, mythologies and decorations on musical instruments* (*cf.* C. Bigée, P. Brill, P. Meulener, D. Oortelmans, P. Schey, J. Snellinck, A. v. Stalbemt, D. de Vos, M. de Vos). Master Antwerp Guild 1587; B. Lauwers was his pupil. Jacques Snel, Antwerp wine taverner (*cf.* F. Snyders and G. Seghers)—who had a number of musical instruments and paintings by J. Snellinck, J. Teniers the elder, C. de Cauwer *q.v.* and other contemporaries—owned (1623) an organ painted by him, with figures by O. v. Veen and the 'foot by Snellincx'; also an *Orpheus* (*cf.* L. v. d. Borcht) with figures by 'Roelken' (R. Savery?) painted on a clavichord, and a *Christ healing the blind*. [Fl. 107, Fl. 213.]

Bosch, Édouard Corneille van den. Flemish Sch. *b* Antwerp 1828 *d* Brussels 1878. *Animals, still life, flowers and fruit*. Represented in BRUSSELS *Le chat s'amuse* (a cat spilling ink on a manuscript). [Fl. 440.]

*__Bosch Van Aken (Aeken), Hieronymus (Jeronimus) Anthonissen.__ Flemish (Dutch) Sch. *b* son of Anthonis van Aken *q.v.*, 's Hertogenbosch (Bois-le-Duc) before 1460 *d* 's Hertogenbosch 1516. *Religious subjects, symbolic compositions with fantastic inventions* (*cf.* J. Mandyn, F. Verbeeck, P. Bruegel the elder, and P. Huys). No known records of his apprenticeship or Guild degrees; acquired from the 's Hertogenbosch Brotherhood of Our Lady (Lieve Vrouwe Broederschap) two altar panels which his father had left unpainted 1480–81; inherited from his brother-in-law a small property near Oirschot 1484; married a girl of good family between 1475–84; became member of the Brotherhood of Our Lady (as Jheronimus Anthonissen van Aken) 1486; presided over the Brotherhood's banquet 1488; painted outside wings for altarpiece in their chapel then being built in S. John's church 's Hertogenbosch 1489; designed windows for the Brotherhood's chapel (*cf.* P. Cornelisz, J. Bellegambe, D. J. Velaert and P. A. Cluyt) 1493; mentioned repeatedly in the Brotherhood's records 1491–99 and 1501–02; received a payment on account from Duke Philip the Fair for a *Last Judgement* ('un grant tableau ... de IX pieds de hault un XI pieds de long, où doit estre le Jugement de Dieu, assavoir paradis et enfer, que Monseigneur lui avait ordonné faire pour son très noble plaisir') 1504; designed for the Brotherhood a copper chandelier 1511; and a cross 1512; memorial services were held in the Brotherhood's chapel on

his death; an entry in their records reads: 'Obitus fratrum; Ao. 1516: Hieronymus Aquen alias Bosch, insignis pictor.' Margaret of Austria, Regent of the Netherlands, owned (before 1516) 'ung moien tableau de Sainct Anthoine qui n'a couverture ne feullet qui est fait de Jheronimus Bosch' also recorded as 'Sainct Anthoine tenant ung livre et un bericle en sa main et ung baston soubz son bras, le fond de bocaige et estranges figures de personnages' given to her by 'Jhoane femme de chambre de Madame Lyonor' and sent by her to the 'prieurs et religieux' of Brou for her memorial chapel (*cf.* J. v. Eyck, R. v. d. Weyden, D. Bouts, Michiel (Master Michel), also J. Schooff). Philip II who had a passion for his works, placed a number in the Escorial and his private apartments, and wrote (1581) from Lisbon to his daughters (including the Infanta Isabella later Governor of the Netherlands) 'I am sorry that you and your brother (later Philip III) could not see the procession (Corpus Christi) here, although there were some devils resembling those in the pictures by Hieronymus Bosch which I think would have frightened him'. Don Felipe de Guevara, courtier and collector, owned (before 1563) a number of his pictures (later acquired by Philip II) and informed the King: (1) that pictures showing any monstrosity or anything exceeding the bounds of nature, except in hell or purgatory scenes, are not by Bosch himself even though signed, but by one of his many imitators (Bosco nunca pintó cosa fuera del natural en su vida, sino fuese en materia de infierno o purgatorio; sus invenciones estribaron en buscar cosas rarísimas pero naturales: de manera que puede ser regla universal, que qualquiera pintura, aunque firmada de Bosco, en que hubiera monstruosidad alguna, o cosa que pase los limites de la naturaleza, que es adulterada y fingida, si no es, como digo, que la pintura contenga en si infierno o materia de él); (2) that among the imitators of Bosch there was one who was his pupil and, either from devotion to his master or in order to give credit to his own works, signed his pictures with Bosch's name and not his own. Guicciardini (1567) records him as 'Girolamo Bosco di Bolduc, inventore nobilissimo et maraviglioso di cose fantastiche et bizarre'. D. Lampsonius *q.v.*, describes him (beneath an engraving of his portrait published 1572 by the widow of H. Cock *q.v.*) as haunted by the spirits of hell:

> Hieronymo Boschio. Pictori.
>
> Quid sibi vult, Hieronyme Boschi
> Ille oculus tuus attonitus? quid
> Pallor in ore? velut lemures si,
> Spectra Erebi volitantia coram
> Aspiceres? Tibi Ditis avari
> Crediderim patuisse recessus,
> Tartareasque domos: tua quando
> Quicquid habet sinus imus Averni
> Tam potuit bene pingere dextra.

Van Mander, acquainted with a number of his pictures, writes (1604): 'Who can chronicle all the strange fantasies of spirits from hell (wondelijke fantasiën van spooksels en hellegedrochten) that he had in his head and set down with his brush, fantasies more gruesome than pleasant to behold?' and adds 'his treatment of drapery was different from the prevailing way of painting it with many wrinkles and folds; his handling was broad, free and skilful; he usually worked alla prima (er zette dikwijls zyn tafereelen en eens op) but his pictures have lasted well; he drew on a white ground and glazed on his colours and let the white ground contribute in places to the effect.' Fr. José de Sigüenza, historian of the Escorial (1600–05), defends him against imputations of heresy, stressing his evident respect for all Catholic dogma and hierarchies and adding 'the Royal founder of the Escorial, so eminent in zealous piety, would not have admitted his pictures to his private rooms, the chapter and the sacristy which are all adorned with them, if he had known him to be a heretic'; he distinguishes three aspects of his work in the Escorial: (1) religious subjects from the Life of Christ where there is nothing monstrous or extravagant (donde no se vee ninguna monstruosidad ni disparate) though the forces of false wisdom 'that would kill innocence, which is Christ', are shown with furious, savage and scowling faces (con rostros furiosos, fieros, regañados); (2) pictures such as the *Temptation of S. Anthony* (of which he records versions in the Chapter, in the Prior's cell, in the Infanta's gallery (two), in his own cell and elsewhere) where the serene confidence of the hermit is contrasted with the countless fantasies and monsters conjured up by the enemy, and pictures like that in the King's closet with his books, showing the *Seven Deadly Sins* contrasted with the *Seven Sacraments* the Church's remedies against them; (3) the two symbolic compositions: the triptych based on Isaiah 41 'All flesh is grass and all its glory like a flower of the field' (*The Haywain*) and the triptych (*The Garden of Delights*) based 'on the words of David: El hombre es como heno y sus glorias como la flor del campo' (Psalm 102? My days are consumed like smoke . . . I am like a pelican of the wilderness: I am like an owl of the desert . . . My days are like a shadow that declineth; and I am withered like grass') which symbolises the vanity of earthly pleasures by the brief delights brought to the senses by the strawberry 'que apenas se siente cuando ya es pasado'. F. Pacheco, Spanish painter, master of Velàzquez, and Censor of Paintings to the Inquisition, writes (1649): 'In my opinion he has been too much honoured by Father Sigüenza, who has made mysteries out of those licentious fantasies which are unsuitable for painters.' **Signed Examples:** ANTWERP *Temptation of S. Anthony* (version of centre of Lisbon triptych). BERLIN *S. John on Patmos* (on reverse circular composition in grisaille: *Scenes from the Passion round a central circle with a pelican on a rock* (signature partly obliterated). BONN *Temptation of S. Anthony* (version of Lisbon Triptych). BRUGES Triptych: centre: *Last Judgement (or Purgatory)*, left wing: *Rise of the Blessed from a garden with the Fountain of Life*, right wing: *Fall of the damned into Hell.* BRUSSELS *Temptation of S. Anthony* (version of Lisbon triptych). GLASGOW *Christ driving the moneychangers from the Temple.* LISBON Triptych *Temptation of S. Anthony*, exterior of wings: grisaille *The Betrayal (with S. Peter and Malchus in the foreground)* and *Christ carrying the Cross (with the thieves and priests in the foreground)* from Lisbon Palacio das Necessidades; originally owned by Damião de Goes, King Manoel the Fortunate's ambassador in Flanders (*cf.* S. Bening) 1530. MADRID Prado Triptych: centre: *Adoration of the Magi*, left wing: *Landscape with donor and S. Peter*, right wing: *Landscape with donor's wife and S. Agnes*, exterior: mainly grisaille *The Mass of S. Gregory with donors and scenes from the Passion* (from the Escorial; acquired by Philip II 1568, sent to Escorial 1574); Triptych: centre *The Haywain*, left wing: *Creation of Eve, The Fall, Expulsion from Paradise*, right wing: *Hell*, exterior *Life's pilgrimage (a vagrant and the perils of the road)* (an unsigned version is in the Escorial). *Table with the Seven Deadly Sins grouped in circle round a Christ in the tomb and the words 'Cave, cave, Dominus videt'* in the corners: *The Last Sacrament, The Last Judgement, Heaven and Hell* (from the Escorial; recorded (1563) in Philip II's possession by Guevara who means it is an example of work by a pupil who signed with Bosch's name; described not quite accurately signed with Bosch's name; described not quite accurately (1600–05) by Sigüenza). *Temptation of S. Anthony* (from the Escorial; version of wing of Lisbon triptych). VENICE Doges' Palace Triptych: centre : *S. Jerome in the desert*, left wing: *Temptation of S. Anthony*, right wing: *S. Aegidius wounded by the arrow with the hind* (*cf.* Giles Master) (from Vienna where taken from Venice during Austrian domination). Triptych: centre: *Crucifixion of S. Julia*, left wing: *Temptation of S. Anthony*, right wing: *Landscape with ship in harbour of Capo Corso and a knight led by a monk in foreground* (also from Vienna). **Documented Examples:** MADRID Prado *The Operation for stone or The Cure of folly* inscribed 'Meester suijt (or mijt) die Reye (or Keye) ras, Myne name

is bibbert das' (acquired by Philip II from the widow and son of Felipe Guevara); Triptych: centre: *The Garden of Delights (The Millennium?)* left wing: *The creation of Eve*, right wing: *Hell*, exterior: *Creation of the World* (sometimes referred to as La Lujuria or La pintura del Madroño (the strawberry picture); from the Escorial where recorded as 'Una pintura de la variedad del Mundo cifrada con diversos disparates de Hierónimo Bosco que llaman del Madroño' 1593; described and interpreted by Sigüenza (1600–05); presumed by some to have been painted for a heretical Adamite sect and to represent cryptically their millennium concepts; *Temptation of S. Anthony* (from the Escorial where sent by Philip II 1574). ESCORIAL *Christ carrying the Cross*; *The Arrest* (both sent by Philip II to the Escorial 1574).

Morelli's Anonimo records (1521) a *Hell*, a *Dream picture* and a *Fortuna with Jonah and the whale* in the collection of Cardinal Grimani in Venice. An Antwerp collection inventoried 1552 records 'Een personnagie van een groot hoot met andere phisolonnyen'; pictures titled *The leader of the blind, Flemish dance, Blind men on a wild boar hunt* and *The witch* (*cf.* J. Cornelis van Oostsanen and F. Francken the younger), *The Haywain* and the *Cure of Folly* were recorded (1570) as acquired by Philip II from Guevara's heirs; the widow of an Antwerp mintmaster owned 1574 a *Seven Deadly Sins*; Gerard von Haen, Canon of Bonn bought (1584) from a Flemish refugee a triptych with centre: *Christ's entry into Jerusalem* and wings: *Nativity* and *Resurrection* (destroyed by fire 1590); a Spaniard Sr. Marco Nunez Perez owned (before 1603) in Antwerp a picture 'en que ay un hombre que con cierta folles y lanternas'; Van Mander (1604) records having seen a *S. Dominic testing the heretical books*, a *Christ carrying the Cross*, a *Flight into Egypt* (with *S. Joseph in the foreground questioning a peasant about the way and in the background figures with a dancing bear and a strange rock in some way resembling an inn*), a *Hell (Purgatory?)* (*with the freeing of the patriarchs while Judas is hanged*), and a *Miracle* (*with a king and various figures falling down in consternation (een koning en anderen die ter aarde gevallen zijn zeer verschrikt kijken*). Van Mander also records (without titles) a number of pictures in 's Hertogenbosch church. Pictures titled *The creation of the world, Abigail before David and Solomon honouring his mother, Adoration of the Magi, The murder of Holofernes and the rout of the Assyrians, Mordecai and Esther and the Triumph of the liberated Jews* seen in S. John's church 's Hertogenbosch 1610 by J. B. Gramaye were removed from the church by permission of Prince Frederick Henry in 1629. A number of compositions are recorded by engravings. Pictures presumed by some his work are in various museums (*cf.* London Christ mocked Painter, New York Adoration in a white castle Painter, Philadelphia Adoration of Magi Painter, Princeton Christ before Pilate Painter).

[Fl. 370, Fl. 371, Fl. 767, Fl. 559, Fl. 636, Fl. 612, Fl. 355, Fl. 892, Fl. 319, Fl. 493, Fl. 604, Fl. 212, Fl. 213, Fl. 316, Fl. 805, Fl. 450, Fl. 167, Fl. 144, Fl. 194, Fl. 314, Fl. 595, Fl. 60, Fl. 143, Fl. 900.]

Bosch (or **Bos**), **Lodewyck Jansz van den** (real name **Valkenborch**). Flemish (Dutch) Sch. *b* 's Hertogenbosch (Bois-le-Duc) before 1530 *d* after 1568. *Religious subjects, conflagrations* (*cf.* H. Bosch, Brussels Sodom and Gomorrah Painter, P. Huys, J. Mandyn, P. Schoubroeck), *but mainly fruit and flowers* (*cf.* Mathys Brill, Pauwels Coecke van Aelst, G. Congnet, also Ambrosius Bosschaert). Active as Calvinist (*cf.* J. v. Liere) and a leading agitator in the Iconoclast riots in Bois-le-Duc (*cf.* Marinus van Reymerswaele also P. Aertsen) 1566; fled to Germany (?) on approach of Alva (*cf.* C. Ketel, N. Neufchatel; also M. v. Valkenborch) 1567. Van Mander (1604) records him 'good at painting lifelike fruit, and flowers in glasses, with insects and dew drops on the flowers'; he also records examples in Dutch collections, and a *S. Jerome* and four *Conflagrations* in tondos.

[Fl. 559, Fl. 892, Fl. 631 (viii), Fl. 798.]

Bosman (or **Bosmans**), **Andries.** Flemish Sch. *b* Antwerp 1621 *d* Rome *c.* 1681. *Flowers* (*cf.* J. B. de Crépu) *and garlands* (*cf.* D. Seghers). Pupil in Antwerp Guild 1636; recorded (as Antoine) in Rome 1649; Chaplain to Bishop Antonin Triest; canon of Antwerp S. Jacques (*cf.* F. de Cock) 1657; resigned position and went Rome 1664. **Signed Examples:** COPEN-HAGEN *Flower garland round a sculptured high relief* ('A Bosman Canon S. Jacobi' 1659). MADRID Prado *Flower garland round a Virgin and Child with S. Anne.*

[Fl. 107, Fl. 892, Fl. 440.]

Bosschaert, Abraham. Flemish (or Dutch) Sch. *b* Middelborg 1613 *d* after 1643. *Flowers* (*cf.* Ambrosius B.) *and 'Vanitas' still life* (*cf.* H. Andriessen). Recorded in Amsterdam as having come from Utrecht 1637. Brother of Ambrosius B. the younger. **Signed Example:** UTRECHT *Flowers in a glass; with fly on table* 1635. A '*Vanitas*' signed and dated 1643 is recorded. Some pictures monogrammed AB listed as by Ambrosius B. are presumed by some his work.

[Fl. 481, Fl. 892, Fl. 798, Fl. 83, Fl. 146.]

*Bosschaert, Ambrosius. Flemish Sch. *b* Antwerp 1573 *d* The Hague 1621. *Flowers* (*cf.* Abraham B., L. J. v. d. Bosch, O. Beet, J. (Velvet) Brueghel, Pauwels Coecke van Aelst, G. Congnet, J. de Gheyn the younger, Grenoble Strawberry Painter, C. Peeters, F. L. Peters, R. Savery, also J. B. Bosschaert and J. v. d. Hecke). In Antwerp Guild 1588?; in Middelburg 1593-1613; Bergen-op-Zoom 1615; Utrecht Guild 1616. His three sons Ambrosius, Abraham and Jan were also flower painters. **Monogrammed Examples:** AMSTERDAM Rijks. *Flowers in a faience vase* 1619. COPENHAGEN *Glass of flowers in a niche* 1618. DETROIT *Flowers in a glass with frog upon the table* 1627. THE HAGUE *Flowers on a window sill with view on distant landscape.* LENINGRAD *Flowers.* OXFORD Ashmolean *Flowers in a silver gilt mounted faience vase, with butterflies and insects and a shell upon the table.* STOCKHOLM *Flowers in a vase with insects and drops of water; other flowers on the table.* VIENNA Kunsthist. *Flowers in a silver gilt mounted faience vase* 1609. The painter V. Wolfvoet *q.v.* was among 17th cent. Antwerp collectors who owned his work. The Antwerp Councillor de Rop owned 1690 'A fruit piece with five apples in a porcelain dish and flowers, shells, etc.; an excellent original by Ambrosius Boschaert bought at the sale of Bishop van den Bosch and before that in the sale of the old Duke of Aerschot'.

[Fl. 892, Fl. 401, Fl. 780, Fl. 170, Fl. 632, Fl. 146.]

Bosschaert, Ambrosius the younger. Flemish (Dutch) Sch. *b* Arnemusden (nr Middelburg) 1609 *d* Utrecht 1645. *Flowers.* In Utrecht by 1634. **Signed Example:** UTRECHT *Flowers in a vase with fly on the table* 1635 (presumed by some by Abraham B. *q.v.*)

[Fl. 146.]

Bosschaert, Jan Baptist. Flemish Sch. *b* Antwerp 1667 *d* 1746. *Flowers* (*cf.* G. P. Verbruggen the younger). Fellow pupil with S. Hardimé *q.v.* of J. B. de Crépu *q.v.* 1685; Master Antwerp Guild 1693 (or 1703); collaborated with J. Leyssens *q.v.* J. Campo Weyerman who knew him, records (1729) that dealers exploited him (*cf.* B. v. d. Bossche, E. v. d. Broeck and J. Porcellis) and that he lived in indigence.

[Fl. 878, Fl. 107, Fl. 892, Fl. 440.]

Bosschaert, T., see **Willeboirts.**

Bossche, Achille van den. Flemish Sch. *b* Ghent (?) before 1414 *d* Ghent (?) 1452. *Decorative paintings* (*banners, etc.*). Master in Ghent Guild 1428; collaborated with N. Martins *q.v.* (*cf.* also W. v. Axpoele, H. v. Eyck and S. v. d. Bossche, J. Martins). His daughter Agnes and his son Livinus were also painters.

[Fl. 135, Fl. 385, Fl. 440.]

*Bossche (or **Bosch**), **Balthazar van den.** Flemish Sch. *b* son of a cooper, Antwerp 1681 *d* Antwerp (from striking his head

on a window frame while instructing his pupils) 1715. *Portrait groups, conversation pieces, interiors of studios and collectors' galleries* (*cf.* P. v. Angellis, I. v. d. Beken, H. Goovaerts, P. J. Horemans, J. F. Nollekens, G. and G. J. Smeyers, G. Thomas, F. X. H. Verbeeck), *some with figures emblematic of the arts* (*cf.* J. Denys). Pupil in Antwerp of G. Thomas; Master (?) in Antwerp Guild 1697; went France (*cf.* C. v. Falens and J. J. Spoede) and worked Paris, Nantes and Douai; back in Antwerp after 1700; worked some time for a dealer (*cf.* J. P. Bosschaert); patronised by Duke of Marlborough in Antwerp after Battle of Ramillies 1706; successful thereafter till his death. Descamps (1763) records that the figures in his luxurious interiors were more elegant than those of G. Thomas; Sir Joshua Reynolds referring (1774) to the French painter Antoine Coypel (1661-1722) wrote: 'The modern affectation of grace in his works, as well as in those of Bosch and Watteau, may be said to be separated by a very thin partition from the more simple and pure grace of Correggio and Parmegiano.' One Vierpyl *q.v.* was his pupil. **Signed Examples:** ANTWERP *Reception of J. B. del Campo, Burgomaster of Antwerp at the headquarters of the Junior Guild of Crossbowmen* 1711 (painted for the Guild to secure exemption from civic guard duties; Descamps records the architecture by J. v. d. Straeten *q.v.* and the landscape by C. Huysmans *q.v.*; he adds that the painter has shown the Burgomaster with his thumb inside his hand because he had not paid his appropriate share for the picture). GOTHA *Studio of an artist.* POMMERSFELDEN *Entertainment with dancing in an elegant mansion* 1709. SCHWERIN *Company at luncheon on the terrace of a mansion, Soldiers in a palace quarrelling over cards.* Descamps records: *Interior of a sculptor's studio with pupils* and *Interior of a painter's studio* ('le peintre, assis devant son chevalet, travaille, un élève montre un tableau de fleurs à un jeune seigneur qui accompagne une jolie personne, un petit domestique nègre lui porte la queue') (*cf.* C. de Baellieur) and *Equestrian portrait of the Duke of Marlborough* (the horse by P. v. Bloemen *q.v.*). Pictures titled *Terrace of a mansion with figures emblematic of Astronomy and Architecture* and *Terrace of a mansion with figures emblematic of the Fine Arts* are also recorded.

[Fl. 878, Fl. 215, Fl. 703, Fl. 612, Fl. 481, Fl. 107, Fl. 892, Fl. 440, Fl. 341, Fl. 296.]

Bossche (**Bosch**), **Philip van den.** Flemish (or Dutch) Sch. *b* before 1590 *d* after 1615. *Topographic drawings* (*also embroideries and engravings*). Worked Prague for Emperor Rudolf II (*cf.* J. V. de Vries and P. Stevens the younger) 1604. A signed drawing *Mountain landscape with towns and villages* 1615 and a *View of Prague* (engraved 1606) are recorded.

[Fl. 892, Fl. 798.]

Bossche, Simon van den. Flemish Sch. **b** Ghent (?) before 1410 *d* Ghent (?) after 1444. Master in Ghent Guild 1422; Dean 1428 and 1444. His son, of the same name, born Ghent 1425, painted portraits. (*Cf.* H. v. Eyck and A. v. d. Bossche.)

[Fl. 440.]

Bossuet, François Antoine. Flemish Sch. *b* Ypres 1798 or 1800 *d* Brussels 1889. *Town and architectural views and genre.* Began as a naval cadet and admiralty official; pupil of W. Herreyns in Antwerp Acad.; travelled in Europe and Morocco; professor of perspective at Brussels Acad. 1832-74; Commander of the Order of Leopold; J. B. v. Moer was among his pupils. G. Wappers *q.v.* included his portrait in '*September* 1830'. Represented in ANTWERP *The Old Fishmarket in Antwerp* 1833, *Seville Cathedral* 1843. BRUGES *Spanish town* 1875. BRUSSELS *Tour de Saint-Amand at Rouen, Seville procession* 1843. LIÈGE *Granada.* MONTPELLIER, YPRES. A *Granada: Entrance Gate* was bought by Queen Victoria (*cf.* G. Wappers and C. Baugniet); Napoleon III bought a *Granada: Roman Towers* and the Lord Mayor of London a *Seville Cathedral* from the Paris International Exhibition 1855. A *View of Brussels: S. Gudule* 1830 is recorded. [Fl. 451, Fl. 440.]

*Boston S. Luke Painter. Presumed Flemish Sch. Name for painter of BOSTON Mus. (93. 153) *S. Luke drawing the Virgin.* Presumed by some identical with R. v. d. Weyden *q.v.* (*cf.* also Fogg S. Luke Painter, J. Gossaert, M. v. Heemskerck, F. Floris and L. Blondeel).

*Boucquet (Bocquet), Victor. Flemish Sch. *b* son of a painter Marcus B., Furnes 1619 or 1629 *d* Furnes 1677. *Religious subjects, military portraits* (*cf.* F. Duchatel and J. A. Bisett) **Signed Example:** PARIS Louvre *The standard bearer* dated Furnes 1664. Descamps saw (1768) in Loo Parish Church *S. Roch interceding for the plague stricken* ('tableau composé avec génie, d'un dessein un peu lourd') and *Seven scenes from the life of the Virgin* painted 1658, 1659 and 1660 ('plusieurs têtes ont le mérite de l'expression mais le dessein est sans finesse et d'une nature courte'); in Nieuport Parish Church *The freeing of Christian slaves by Trinitarians* and Town Hall *The Judgement of Cambyses* painted 1671 ('le meilleur tableau peint par V.B.; mais les figures sont courtes et la couleur en est crue'); in Ostend Capucins *Descent from the Cross* ('le dessein est court, les têtes peu belles et il y a de la crudité dans la couleur'). Brussels Mus. has *Portrait of an officer* presumed by some his work. *cf.* V. van Heede. [Fl. 215, Fl. 216, Fl. 892, Fl. 440, Fl. 640, Fl. 787, Fl. 124.]

Boudewyns, A. F., see **Baudewyns.**

Boulenger, Hippolyte. Flemish Sch. *b* son of an officer and a French mother, Tournai 1837 *d* of spinal affection, Brussels 1874. *Landscapes.* Educated in Paris; then Brussels Acad. under F. J. Navez and J. Quinaux; helped financially by C. v. Camp *q.v.*; settled Tervueren 1863; visited Paris 1867; a leading member of the Tervueren school (*cf.* A. Asselbergs, T. Baron, F. Binje, A. Bouvier, J. Coosemans, L. Crépin, H. v. d. Hecht, E. Huberti, J. Montigny, J. Raeymackers). Represented in ANTWERP *Cow by a ditch* 1864, *Sheep by a wood* 1864, *La Vallée de Josaphat* 1868. BRUSSELS *Edge of the wood* 1865, *Dinant* 1870, *Autumn morning* 1873, *Allée des vieux charmes* 1871, *Mare au cochon, Messe de S. Hubert, The Flood* 1871. GHENT, TOURNAI *Spring at Boitsfort* and others. [Fl. Bib. 19th cent., Fl. 440, Fl. 165, Fl. 296.]

Boulogne (Boulongne), Hugues (Hue) de. Flemish Sch. *b* son of Laurent B. keeper of Hesdin Castle, Hesdin (?) before 1390 *d* 1449. *Decorative paintings and pageant designs.* Pupil of M. Broederlam *q.v.* in Ypres; Court painter to Duke Philip the Bold of Burgundy 1398; recorded as painter and keeper of Hesdin Castle in charge of clocks, bird cages and machinery for practical jokes (?) ('peintre et gouverneur de l'orloge, gayoles, verrières et engins d'esbatement') for Duke John the Fearless 1417; painted arms for Chapter of Golden Fleece (founded by Duke Philip the Good 1430) 1432; worked on decorations for a banquet given by Philip the Good to the King of Sicily where one of the 'entremets' was 'ung paon tout vif sur une trespasse et entour avoit X lions dorez d'or qui tenoient chascun une bannière armoyée...' 1437 (*cf.* J. Daret); held rank of 'peintre et varlet de chambre' to Philip the Good (*cf.* Jan van Eyck, P. Coustain, D. Daret, Jehan de Boulogne; also J. Dreux, J. Hennecart, S. Jansz, J. Martins, W. Vrelant and Rogier v. d. Weyden). [Fl. 490, Fl. 199, Fl. 179, Fl. 150.]

Boulogne, Jehan de. Flemish Sch. *b* son of Hugues de B. *q.v.* before 1415 *d* after 1451. *Decorative paintings.* Succeeded his father as 'peintre et varlet de chambre' to Duke Philip the Good 1449; painted arms for Chapter of Golden Fleece, Mons 1451 (*cf.* J. Daret and J. v. Battel). [Fl. 490, Fl. 179.]

Bource, Henri Jacques. Flemish Sch. *b* Antwerp 1826 *d* Antwerp 1899. *Costume history, genre, landscapes, coast scenes with fisher folk, portraits.* Pupil of G. Wappers, J. Dyckmans and in Paris of the Franco-Dutch painter Ary Scheffer. Received many Academic medals and honours; was in London 1876 and 1877; Officer of the Order of Leopold. Represented in ANTWERP *The Return* 1878. BRUSSELS *Fatal tidings* 1868. GHENT *The fisherman's widow* 1865. THE HAGUE *Summer evening on the coast* 1862. LIÈGE *The empty cradle* 1867. MONS, SHEFFIELD *On Scheveningen beach.* A picture titled 'So like his Daddy' 1871 was among those exhibited at the London Royal Academy 1870–77. Pictures titled *Jeptha's daughter* and *Marie-Antoinette taking leave of her family* 1857 (bought by the Grand Duchess Marie of Russia) are also recorded. [Fl. 440, Fl. 361.]

Bourguignon (or Bourgonjon), Pierre de. Flemish Sch. *b* Namur 1630 *d* London 1698. *Portraits.* Went Paris (*cf.* P. Vleughels and C. E. Biset); admitted to Paris Acad. Roy. (*cf.* B. Flemalle and P. v. Mol) 1671; went Holland (after Revocation of the Edict of Nantes); in The Hague Guild as 'foreigner' 1687; then London (*cf.* J. C. Lotyn and J. B. Medina). **Documented Example:** VERSAILLES *Mlle. de Montpensier as Minerva* (Acad. reception piece 1671). [Fl. 878, Fl. 892.]

Bourlard, Antoine Joseph. Flemish Sch. *b* Mons 1826 *d* Mons 1899. *Costume history, religious subjects, portraits.* Pupil of A. v. Ysendyck; then studied Paris. Lived 18 years in Italy; professor Mons Acad. 1871–99. Represented in BRUSSELS, LIÈGE, MONS *The Fallen Angels ...* 1852; Town Hall *Leopold I.* Pictures titled *Perugino in Florence* (*cf.* P. Kremer), *Diana huntress* and *The death of Cleopatra* are recorded. [Fl. 440.]

Bourson, Amadée (Georges Paul Amadée). Flemish Sch. *b* son of director of 'Moniteur belge', Brussels 1833 *d* Etterbeek (Brussels) 1905. *Portraits.* Pupil of F. J. Navez and E. Slingeneyer; director of Art School in S. Josse ten Noode. A *Portrait of P. J. Proudhon* is recorded. [Fl. 440.]

*Bout, Pieter. Flemish Sch. *b* Brussels 1658 *d* Brussels 1719. *Landscapes and coast scenes with genre figures, fair and market pieces and skating scenes* (*cf.* E. de Bie, L. Smout the younger, T. Michau, M. Schoevaerdts, J. B. v. d. Meiren, D. v. Heil, R. v. d. Hoecke); *some landscapes with religious subjects; also some engravings.* Apprentice in Brussels Guild 1671; worked for some years in Paris (?) (*cf.* P. de Bourguignon); presumed by some to have visited Italy; recorded in Brussels 1677, 1695, and 1702; painted figures in some pictures by A. F. Baudewyns *q.v.*, J. d'Arthois (?) and L. Achtschellinck (?). **Signed Examples:** AMSTERDAM Rijks. *Halt of horsemen with dogs before a grotto.* ANTWERP *Village fair* 1686. AUGSBURG *Village market.* BRUNSWICK *Annunciation to the Shepherds.* BRUSSELS *Village fair with actors on a stage* (*cf.* J. v. Buken, A. v. d. Meulen, P. Spierinckx also L. Defrance) 1676. CARLSRUHE *Fishmarket on the coast* 1683. FRANKFORT Staedel. *Return from fishing* 1677. MADRID Prado *Skating scene* 1678. *Village square* 1678. Dresden has examples recorded 1722 and 1742 as joint work with A. F. Baudewyns. Vienna K. has a landscape by Baudewyns with figures by Bout from the estate of Prince Charles of Lorraine (1780). [Fl. 878, Fl. 612, Fl. 892, Fl. 440.]

*Bouts, Aelbrecht. Flemish Sch. *b* son of Dirk B. *q.v.*, Louvain (?) after 1451 *d* Louvain 1549. *Religious subjects.* Recorded 1473 and referred to as under 25 in 1476; referred to as painter 1479; married 1481; with D. Bouts the younger restored his father's Louvain S. Pierre altarpiece 1486; married a second wife 1490; worked for Louvain S. Pierre

1515. Signed Example (An 'A' with crossbow bolts (i.e. 'bouts') on arms of Louvain Guild of Painters): BRUSSELS Triptych: centre: *Assumption of the Virgin,* wings: *Donor, angels and saints, Donor (portrait of the artist?) with kneeling woman (his wife? or mother?) angel and saints* (Molanus (*c.* 1575) records that he worked for three years on an *Assumption of the Virgin* which he gave to Louvain S. Pierre). Pictures presumed by some his work are in various museums. [Fl. 589, Fl. 269, Fl. 120, Fl. 316, Fl. 757, Fl. 530, Fl. 124.]

*Bouts, Dirk, (Dierick, Thierry). Flemish (Dutch) Sch. *b* Haarlem before 1432 *d* Louvain 1475. Father of Dirk B. the younger and Aelbrecht B. *Religious subjects, portraits.* Vasari (1568) knew of 'Dirick d'Harlem'; also of 'Divik da Lovanio' (*cf.* D. Bouts the younger); Van Mander (1604) records a Dirck van Haarlem whose little house there with a decorated façade—'kleine woning met een ouderwetsch geveltje, versierd met eenige gebeeldhouwde koppen' (*cf.* Q. Massys, K. Foort, F. Floris, M. Ponteau, B. Spranger)—was known to him and who later lived in Louvain. Married a rich woman (known as Catherina metten gelde) Louvain 1447; town painter to Louvain (*cf.* Jan Spaden, A. Raet and H. Stuerbout) 1468; married as second wife a rich burgomaster's widow 1473; made his will 1475. **Signed Examples:** None. **Documented Examples:** LOUVAIN S. Pierre: Triptych: centre: *The Last Supper,* wings: *The Four Mystic Meals: Passover; Elijah in the Desert; The meeting of Abraham and Melchizedek; The gathering of the Manna* (commissioned for Louvain S. Pierre 1464 with detailed programme supplied by the theologians Jean Varenacker and Egidius de Bailleuil; finished 1468; the wings formerly in Berlin and Munich were returned Louvain under the Treaty of Versailles 1920; *cf.* A. Bouts and A. Pupiler). BRUSSELS *The unjust judgement of Emperor Otho, The Ordeal by Fire* (the victim's widow passes the ordeal; the perjurer is burned) two of four panels commissioned for Louvain Town Hall 1468; the painter died before executing the other two; extant receipts refer to a Dierick Stuerbout). **Inscribed Example:** LOUVAIN S. Pierre: Triptych: centre: *The winding out of the entrails of S. Erasmus;* wings: *S. Jerome, S. Bernard* (inscribed 'Opus Theodorici Bouts. Anno 1448' and recorded by Molanus (*c.* 1575)). Van Mander records a triptych seen by him in Leyden (*The Saviour* in the centre and *S. Paul* and *S. Peter* on the wings) inscribed in Latin in 'letters of gold' 'In 1462 Dirck, born in Haarlem, made me in Louvain'; he adds 'the heads about life size were remarkably skilful for the time they were painted, the hair and beards being beautiful.' A *Last Judgement* commissioned for Louvain Town Hall 1468 (*cf.* B. v. Battel), finished 1472 and restored by one Jean Willems 1543 is recorded. Margaret of Austria, Regent of the Netherlands (1507–30) owned 'une petite Nostre Dame fait de la main de Dierick' (*cf.* Jan van Eyck and Rogier v. d. Weyden). Pictures presumed by some his work are in various European and American museums (*cf.* Lille Path to Paradise Painter, London (Guicciardi) Entombment Painter, London Young Man in High Cap Painter, London Virgin with a brocade screen Painter, New York Man in High Cap Painter, Pearl of Brabant Master and Philadelphia S. Christopher Painter). [Fl. 371, Fl. 818, Fl. 589, Fl. 559, Fl. 861, Fl. 863, Fl. 349, Fl. 120, Fl. 892, Fl. 316, Fl. 757, Fl. 530, Fl. 615.]

Bouts, Dirk the younger. Flemish Sch. *b* son of D. Bouts *q.v.* Louvain *c.* 1448 *d* Louvain 1490. *Religious subjects.* Vasari (1568) and Guicciardini (1581) knew of 'Dirik da Lovanio' as well as 'Dirick d'Harlem'. Recorded as twenty five years old in 1473; married in Louvain 1476; with his younger brother Aelbrecht B. *q.v.* restored his father's *Last Supper* in Louvain S. Pierre 1486. **Signed Examples:** None. **Documented Examples:** None. (*cf.* Pearl of Brabant Master). [Fl. 818, Fl. 371, Fl. 269, Fl. 88, Fl. 892, Fl. 757, Fl. 530.]

Bouts, Jan. Flemish Sch. *b* son of Dirk B. the younger, Louvain before 1490 *d* 1531. Recorded in Louvain 1501 and 1505; and in Malines 1516 and 1518 (*cf.* Jean van Battel and J. Schooff). [Fl. 88.]

Bouts, Thierry, see **Bouts, D.**

Bouttats (or Boutats), Jacob. Flemish Sch. 17th–18th cent. BAMBERG Gall. has *Paradise (Garden of Eden) s* 1700. [Fl. 798.]

Bouttats, Jan Baptist. Flemish Sch. *b* Antwerp (?) before 1700 *d* after 1738. Presumed member of Antwerp artist family of this name which included several engravers. *Landscapes with views of houses, game and bird pieces, copies of earlier pictures and engravings (?);* with the engraver Filibert B. painted coats of arms commissioned by the Forchoudt firm of Antwerp dealers for a customer 1701. Master in Antwerp Guild 1706; P. v. Angellis *q.v.* worked with him in Antwerp before 1710. **Signed Examples:** GATESHEAD Shipley Art Gall. *Dutch or Flemish mansion seen from the gardens* 1730 (*cf.* G. v. Schoor). GREENWICH Maritime Mus. *The arrival of Charles II at The Hague, May 15, 1660, on his way to Scheveningen to embark for England* 1738 (copy of an earlier picture or engraving?). LEIPZIG *Cocks fighting, Cock attacked by a vulture* (*cf.* J. Fyt, D. de Coninck, A. de Gryef). **Documented Example:** DRESDEN *Bird piece* (Inventory 1754). The signatures and records may refer to more than one artist. [Fl. 826, Fl. 612, Fl. 481, Fl. 892, Fl. 212, Fl. 364.]

Bouvier, Arthur. Flemish Sch. *b* of rich family, Brussels 1837 *d* S. Gilles (Brussels) 1921. *Landscapes and marines.* Associated with Tervueren School (*cf.* H. Boulenger); Chevalier of the Order of Leopold; exhibited Paris and Chicago. Represented in BRUSSELS *Marine, Break in the clouds* 1880. LIÈGE *Approaching storm.* NAMUR *The hurricane.* [Fl. 440, Fl. 123.]

Bouvignes, Henri de, see **Bles.**

Bouvy, Firmin. Flemish Sch. *b* Deynze 1822 *d* San Francisco 1881. *Costume genre.* Pupil of H. Dillens; gave up painting and devoted himself to colouring photographs after *c.* 1855; visited Paris, Spain, Australia, South America; then settled San Francisco 'dans l'aisance mais oublié'. Represented in LEIPZIG *Episode from Gil Blas.* Pictures titled *Flemish kermesse in the 15th cent.* 1843 and *Don Quixote disputing with the curé and the barber* 1846 are recorded. [Fl. 440.]

Bouwens, Gabriel. Flemish Sch. *b* before 1520. Master Antwerp Guild 1536. J. Grimmer *q.v.* was his pupil in 1539. [Fl. 892.]

Bovie, Jean Félix Lambert. Flemish Sch. *b* Brussels 1812 *d* Brussels 1880. *Landscapes (mainly in the Ardennes);* also active as poet. Pupil of E. Verboeckhoven. [Fl. 451, Fl. 440.]

Boyermans, T., see **Boeyermans.**

Braekeleer, Adrien de. Flemish Sch. *b* Antwerp 1818 *d* Antwerp 1904. *Costume history, genre with horses and dogs; also active as sculptor.* Nephew and pupil of F. de B.; received state award for shooting a tiger escaped from the Zoo in the streets of Antwerp 1868. Represented in ANTWERP *The blacksmith* 1878. HAMBURG, MONTREAL, RENNES, STUTTGART. [Fl. 440.]

*Braekeleer, Ferdinand de. Flemish Sch. *b* Antwerp 1792 *d* Antwerp 1883. *Religious and classical subjects, contemporary and costume history, anecdotic genre, town views, portraits.* Pupil of M. van Brée *q.v.*; won prize for 'history' composition in Antwerp Salon 1813; Rome prize 1817; in Rome 1819; entertained there van Brée 1821; returned Belgium 1823; was successful with genre pictures; president of commission for restoring Rubens' pictures in Antwerp Cathedral 1836; Chevalier of Order of Leopold 1839; his many pupils included E. de Block and H. Leys whose sister he married; in last years lost his fortune through bad speculation by one of his sons; was still painting in his ninety-first year. Represented in AMSTERDAM *Antwerp citadel after the bombardment* 1832. *Courtship in the 17th century* 1848. ANTWERP *Antwerp citadel after the bombardment* 1832. *The Spanish Fury 1576* 1837, *Death of Count Frédéric de Mérode 1830* (*cf.* T. Schaepkens), *Fire in Antwerp 1830, Arc de Triomphe erected in Antwerp for the second centenary of the death of Rubens 1840, The school master* 1854; Academy *The healing of Tobit* (*cf.* J. Massys. Rome prize picture 1817). BERLIN *The quarrel*. BRUSSELS *The golden wedding* 1839, *Mi-Carême in the school* 1839. *A Patriotism of the Antwerp Magistrates 1576* painted *c.* 1824 is also recorded.

[Fl. 451, Fl. 481, Fl. 107, Fl. 440, Fl. Bib. 19th cent.]

Braekeleer, Ferdinand de, the younger. Flemish Sch. *b* son of F. de B., Antwerp 1828 *d* Antwerp 1857. *Interiors and 17th cent. genre; also some religious subjects.* Pupil of his father. Painted few pictures and went New York where acted unsuccessfully as dealer in contemporary Belgian pictures 1852–55. Represented in ANTWERP *Young artist in his studio*, 1851.

[Fl. 440.]

Braekeleer, Henri de. Flemish Sch. *b* son of Ferdinand de B. the elder, Antwerp 1840 *d* paralysed, Antwerp 1888. *Interiors, genre, landscapes, still life (at first in traditional and later more Impressionist technique); also etchings and lithographs.* Pupil of his father and of his uncle H. Leys; lived and worked to some extent as a recluse; Chevalier of the Order of Leopold and given medal of honour by the City of Antwerp (*cf.* E. de Biefve) 1883; retrospective exhibition (fifty pictures) Brussels 1892. Paul Fierens writes (1947): 'aujourd'hui tenu pour un maître de premier ordre'. Represented in ANTWERP *The man in a chair* 1875 *The printer of engravings* 1875, *The wine shop, Dining room in Leys' house* 1869, *Kitchen garden, Strawberries and champagne* 1883, *Still life with jug* 1884, *Woman reading* 1886 and others. BRUSSELS *The geographer* 1872, *The man at the window* 1876, *Interior of Hydraulic House, Woman spinning, A woman of the people, Flowers, Medlars, Scheldt village, View of Antwerp* and others. BELGIAN Royal Coll. *Antwerp Cathedral*. PARIS State Coll., TOURNAI *The laundry* 1861, *Studio interior*.

[Fl. Bib. 19th cent., Fl. 160 (1888), Fl. 514, Fl. 440, Fl. 911, Fl. 706, Fl. 388, Fl. 96, Fl. 398, Fl. 296.]

Brassauw (Brisschau or Brisjouw), Jacob Andries Melchior. Flemish Sch. *b* son of Melchior B., Antwerp 1739 *d* Antwerp (?) after 1763. *Genre, portraits and copies of pictures by Teniers and others.* In Antwerp Guild 1763. A portrait group *Mieris and his wife* (the Dutch painter F. v. Mieris the younger (?)) and pictures titled *Card players* and *Girl with a copper pail* ('in the manner of the Dutch painter G. Dou') are recorded.

[Fl. 481, Fl. 107.]

Brassauw (Brisschau or Brisjouw), Melchior. Flemish Sch. *b* Malines 1709 *d* Antwerp (?) after 1757. *Genre, and copies of pictures by Teniers and others.* Pupil in Antwerp of F. X. H. Verbeeck; Master in Antwerp Guild 1737. **Signed Example:** AMSTERDAM Rijks. *The prodigal son (musical company on a terrace)*. Recorded pictures include *A man caressing a woman* and *Baker blowing a horn* (a picture of this subject by A. v. Ostade is in the Amsterdam Museum).

[Fl. 481, Fl. 613, Fl. 107, Fl. 892, Fl. 7.]

Brauwer, A., see Brouwer.

Bredael (or Breda), Alexander van. Flemish Sch. *b* son of Pieter van B. *q.v.,* Antwerp 1663 *d* Antwerp 1720. *Official*

celebrations and processions (*cf.* A. Sallaert, D. v. Alsloot, F. Duchatel, N. v. Eyck) *and outdoor genre scenes.* Master Antwerp Guild 1685; married daughter of H. Sporckmans *q.v.;* P. Snyers, J. B. Govaerts and his son Jan Frans van B. the elder were his pupils. **Signed Examples:** ANTWERP Town Hall *'Ommeganck' procession in Antwerp Grande Place* 1696. LILLE *A fête in Antwerp.* NANCY *Farm scene.* A *View of the altar in the Place de Meir, Antwerp* with many figures, painted 1685 for the centenary celebrations of the capture of Antwerp by Alexander Farnese Duke of Parma (*cf.* D. v. d. Queborne and E. de Bie), is recorded.

[Fl. 215, Fl. 481, Fl. 107, Fl. 892.]

Bredael (or Breda), Guillaume van. Flemish Sch. *b* Antwerp (?) before 1630 *d* date and place unknown. *Italianate landscapes with markets* (*cf.* P. v. B.). Hermannstadt has *Roman market* signed G. van Breda. [Fl. 440.]

Bredael (or Breda), Jan Frans (Jean François) van. Flemish Sch. *b* son of Alexander van B. *q.v.,* Antwerp 1686 (or 1683) *d* Antwerp 1750. *River landscapes with genre figures* (*cf.* T. Michau and C. Breydel); *some with religious subjects; picturesque military and hunting pieces* (*cf.* C. v. Falens). Pupil of his father; then worked nine years for art dealer J. de Witte as copyist and pasticheur of works by J. (Velvet) Brueghel, P. Wouwerman and others (*cf.* Joseph van B.), and Descamps (1763) records: 'S'il étoit presque impossible de distinguer ses copies, bientôt on eut la meme peine à distinguer ses imitations'; went England (*cf.* Jan Peeters the younger) where patronized by James Radcliffe, Earl of Derwentwater, whom he visited in prison before his execution 1716; worked for George I; visited Paris (*cf.* J. J. Spoede and Joseph v. B. and J. P. v. B. the elder) 1719; in England again where friend of the sculptor J. M. Rysbrack (who came 1720); married in England 1723; returned Antwerp 1725; Dean in Antwerp Guild from 1726; patronized by Louis XV and his entourage in Antwerp (*cf.* J. A. Garemyn and G. de Spinny also J. J. Horemans the younger, and W. I. Kerricx) 1746; also patronized by Prince de Clermont (governor of Antwerp during French occupation until 1748). **Documented Examples:** DRESDEN *Horsemen in front of a forge* and *Start of the hunt* (companion pieces, recorded by 1765). Descamps records landscapes with *Christ preaching on the seashore* and *Christ performing miracles* sold to Louis XV, pictures titled *Winter* and *Summer* and others.

[Fl. 215, Fl. 481, Fl. 107, Fl. 440.]

Bredael (or Breda), Jan Frans (François) van, the younger. Flemish Sch. *b* son of J. F. v. Bredael *q.v.,* Antwerp 1729 *d* after 1763. Descamps (1763) records him as pupil and follower of his father. [Fl. 215, Fl 107.]

Bredael (or Breda), Jan Pieter van the elder. Flemish Sch. *b* son of Pieter van B. *q.v.,* Antwerp 1654 *d* Antwerp 1745. *Still life; with fruit and flowers* (*cf.* Abraham Brueghel and P. Casteels III) *and game pieces* (*cf.* J. B. Govaerts, A. de Gryef and B. de Bridt); *but chiefly active as dealer and restorer* (*cf.* Joseph van B.). Visited Italy; Master Antwerp Guild 1680; visited London (*cf.* W. de Keyser and J. B. Medina) 1685; Dean in Antwerp Guild 1689; sold three pictures by Rubens and Snyders to Forchoudt firm of Antwerp dealers (*cf.* Joris van B.) 1699; in Paris as dealer (*cf.* J. F. v. Bredael and J. J. Spoede) 1719. **Signed Example:** LYONS *Still life with dead game*. The Antwerp collector Guillaume Potteau 'Commissaris ordinaris van de monsteringhe van den volcke van orloghe ten dienste van syne Catholycke Majesteyt' owned 1692 a *Fruit and flower piece* by 'Joan Peeter van Bredael'.

[Fl. 107, Fl. 440, Fl. 212, Fl. 213.]

*Bredael (or Breda), Jan Pieter van. Flemish Sch. *b* son of Joris van B., Antwerp 1683 *d* Vienna 1735. *Contemporary warfare* (*cf.* Joris van B., P. v. Bloemen, C. Breydel, J. Broers, P. J. Delcloche, C. Francken, J. v. d. Meiren, H. de La Pegnia, P.

Tillemans, J. P. and P. Verdussen) *also hawking and hunting pieces* (*cf.* C. v. Falens). Pupil of his father; went Prague *c.* 1706; painted war records there for Prince Eugene; in Antwerp and member of Guild 1720; returned Vienna at invitation of Prince Eugene and remained there (*cf.* J. G. and P. F. de Hamilton); left his estate to his brother Joseph van B. *q.v.* who gave possession of his house to F. v. Stampart *q.v.* 1736. **Signed Examples:** BRESLAU *Boar hunt* 1727. VIENNA K. *Prince Eugene's victory over the Turks at Peterwardein 1716, Prince Eugene's capture of Belgrade from the Turks 1717. Ladies watching an elegant sportsman killing wild boars in an enclosure 1717* (*cf.* P. Snayers), *The hawking party.* **Documented Example:** AIX-EN-PROVENCE *The Marquis de Villars at the Battle of Leuze 1691* (painted for the Duc de Villars. Probably by Joris v. B.).
[Fl. 107, Fl 828, Fl. 440.]

Bredael, Joris (Georges) van. Flemish Sch. *b* son of Pieter v. B. *q.v.*, Antwerp 1661 *d* Vienna (?) *c.* 1706. *Contemporary warfare* (*cf.* P. v. Bloemen, A. and P. Casteels). Pupil of his father; married daughter of A. J. v. Diepenbeeck *q.v.* 1681; Master Antwerp Guild 1684; in Vienna (*cf.* A. Schoonjans) where called upon the dealer Marcus Forchoudt (who was then selling pictures to Prince von Liechtenstein) and showed him sketches of three paintings by Rubens and Snyders owned 'by his brother the captain' (J. P. v. Bredael the elder) 1699. Jan Pieter van B. the younger *q.v.* and Joseph van B. were his sons. Guillaume Forchoudt in Antwerp sent (1690) to his brothers in Vienna six battlepieces by Joris van Bredael including a *Relief of Vienna*, a *Capture of Buda*, a *Capture of Belgrade* and a *Capture of Gran*. [Fl. 107, Fl. 892, Fl. 212.]

*Bredael (or Breda), Joseph van. Flemish Sch. *b* son of Joris van B. *q.v.*, Antwerp 1688 *d* Paris 1739. *Landscapes with genre figures* (*cf.* T. Michau). Employed for some years by dealer J. de Witte to make pastiches of works by J. (Velvet) Brueghel, P. Wouwerman and others (*cf.* J. F. v. Bredael, B. v. d. Bossche, J. P. Bosschaert, B. Beschey, G. v. Opstal, P. J. v. Regemorter, J. I. de Roore); went Paris (*cf.* J. F. v. Bredael, J. Delien, C. J. Redouté, also P. J. Sauvage); became member of Acad. Royale; inherited from his brother J. P. v. B. 1735; Court painter to the Duc d'Orléans 1736. **Signed Example:** AMSTERDAM Rijks. *Riverside village with gentry and peasants* 1723. A painter 'van Breda' restored Rubens' pictures in the Luxembourg *c.* 1730. [Fl. 612, Fl. 107, Fl. 892.]

*Bredael (or Breda), Pieter van. Flemish Sch. *b* Antwerp 1629 *d* Antwerp 1719. *Italianate landscapes with genre figures* (*cf.* G. v. Bredael, A. F. Baudewyns, P. v. Bloemen, J. v. Buken, J. de Rooster, A. F. Rubens, M. Schoevaerdts, P. Spierinckx, G. de Witte). Pupil of D. Ryckaert III 1640; visited Spain (*cf.* C. Luyckx and A. Smit); also Italy (?); in Antwerp 1648; Master Antwerp Guild 1650; Director Antwerp Academy 1689; H. v. Lint *q.v.* was his pupil. Jan Pieter, Joris and Alexander B. were his sons. **Signed Examples:** BARNARD Castle *Italian market.* BRUGES *Landscape with figures, Italian market* (both from Abbaye des Dunes *cf.* D. Bogaerde and B. R. de Hooghe). STOCKHOLM *Market outside an Italian town.* VIENNA Liecht. *Landscape with kermesse* 1715 (perhaps completed by Jan Pieter van B.). Gonzales Coques' *Interior of a gallery* in The Hague (Mauritshuis) contains a *Landscape with shepherds and dog* monogrammed P. V. B. F.
[Fl. 86, Fl. 215, Fl. 612, Fl. 107, Fl. 892.]

Brée, Mattheus Ignatius van. Flemish Sch. *b* son of a painter, Antwerp 1773 *d* Antwerp 1839. *Contemporary history* (*cf.* A. Ansiaux, J. L. Demarne, I. J. v. Regemorter also C. Picqué), *costume history, religious subjects, mythologies, portraits.* Pupil in Antwerp Acad. till 1794 then of P. J. van Regemorter; in Paris of French painter F. A. Vincent; painted Greek and Roman 'history' subjects Paris 1798; Court painter to the Empress Josephine (*cf.* J. F. v. Dael, B. P. Ommeganck and

L. Gerbo); commissioned by Napoleon to paint pictures for Antwerp palace; professor in Antwerp Acad. from 1804; Court painter to William First King of United Netherlands (*cf.* J. D. Odevaere) 1817; joined his pupil F. de Braekeleer *q.v.* in Rome where given the Cross of the Golden Spur by Pope Pius VII 1821; succeeded W. J. Herreyns *q.v.* as Director Antwerp Acad. 1827; pallbearers at his ceremonial funeral (when six orations were pronounced) included his pupils G. Wappers, F. de Braekeleer and N. de Keyser; other pupils were D. F. du Bois, P. J. v. Brée, L. Ricquier *q.v.*, J. C. Carpentero, P. v. Schendel, A. v. Ysendyck and A. J. Wiertz. Represented in AMSTERDAM Rijks. *Self portrait, The art patron J. H. Molkenboer 1815, The Prince of Orange visiting victims of the 1825 flood* (sketch). ANTWERP Mus. *The death of Rubens* (*cf.* P. Kremer) 1827; Augustins *Baptism of S. Augustine.* BRUSSELS *Regulus returning from Carthage* (commissioned by Napoleon). CAMBRAI *Rubens painting Marie de Médicis.* LEYDEN Town Hall *The patriotism of Burgomaster P. A. van der Werff 1576* (exhibited Ghent 1817). ROME Vatican *Pius VII.* VERSAILLES *Entry of Napoleon Bonaparte as first consul into Antwerp; Napoleon and Marie Louise visiting a naval squadron anchored in the Scheldt; The 'Friedland' piloted into Antwerp harbour.* Recorded pictures include *The death of Cato* 1797, *Young Athenians to be sacrificed to the Minotaur* (commissioned by Napoleon and exhibited Amsterdam 1812), *William of Orange interceding for the Bishops of Bruges and Ypres* 1818, *Count Egmont comforted by Bishop Trost, The tomb of Nero in Rome with lazzaroni and musicians*, and a portrait *William I of the United Netherlands.* [Fl. 451, Fl. 612, Fl. 336, Fl. 481, Fl. 440.]

Brée, Philip Jacob van. Flemish Sch. *b* son of a painter, Antwerp 1786 *d* Brussels 1871. *Costume and contemporary 'history', genre, town views.* Pupil in Antwerp of his brother M. I. v. B. *q.v.* from *c.* 1804, and in Paris of the French painter A. L. Girodet-Trioson 1811; in Italy with L. Ricquier *q.v.* 1816; in Antwerp after 1819; patronised by William I of United Netherlands; again in Paris then Brussels; visited Germany 1827; in Italy 1832 and England 1839; Keeper of Brussels Museum. V. J. Génisson was among his pupils. Represented in ANTWERP *Abdication of Charles V, The great fire in the Entrepôt (formerly Abbaye S. Michel) 1830, The ruins of the Entrepôt after the great fire.* BRUSSELS *The youth of Sixtus V 1832, Procession in S. Peter's Rome, Rubens surrounded by his family, painting in his garden* (*cf.* P. Kremer) 1833. Recorded works include *Portrait of L. Ricquier* 1816, *Petrarch and Laura, Van Dyck taking leave of Rubens, The rescue of Marie Leczinska, The Spanish nun* and *Captain Barends with his companions in Novazembla at sunrise* 1828.
[Fl. 451, Fl. 612, Fl. 440, Fl. 296.]

Breughel see **Bruegel** and **Brueghel.**

*Breydel, Carel (known as Le Chevalier). Flemish Sch. *b* Antwerp 1677 or 1678 *d* after long suffering with gout, Antwerp 1733 (or Ghent 1744). *Landscapes with genre figures* (*cf.* Joseph van Bredael and T. Michau); *contemporary warfare and other military pieces* (*cf.* J. P. v. Bredael the younger, J. Broers, J. B. v. d. Meiren also A. v. d. Meulen). Pupil of Peter Ijkens (before 1695) then of P. Rysbraeck; in Antwerp where married 1703; Master Antwerp Guild 1704; Descamps (1763) records that he went Frankfort and Nuremberg and then to the court of Hesse-Cassel where his brother Frans B. *q.v.* was working; then to Amsterdam where copied Rhine landscapes by the Dutch pasticheur Jan Robert Griffier (son of the Dutch river painter and pasticheur Jan Griffier who lived for some time on a yacht on the Thames) for a dealer named J. de Vos (*cf.* J. F. v. Bredael the elder); left wife and family and went Brussels where lived with Z. J. v. Helmont *q.v.* and made friends with P. K. Marissal *q.v. c.* 1723; followed P. K. Marissal to Ghent where set up house with a 'gouvernante' 1726. **Signed Examples:** ANTWERP *River landscapes* *with peasants and market carts* (two). BRUSSELS *Cavalry attack, Cavalry battle against the Turks, Cavalry skirmish.* CAMBRIDGE Fitz. *Cavalry skirmish,* GOTHA *Cavalry combat* 1722. HERMANNSTADT *Cavalry combat.* STOCKHOLM *Cavalry attack.* VIENNA Liecht. *Mountain landscape with military movements by a river* (also monogrammed J. R. G. (Griffier)), *River landscape with cavalry battle* (also signed J. R. Griffier), *Cavalry battle against the Turks.*

[Fl. 215, Fl. 612, Fl. 107, Fl. 892, Fl.440.]

Breydel, Frans. Flemish Sch. *b* Antwerp 1679 *d* Antwerp 1750. *Portraits, conversation pieces* (*cf.* B. v. d. Bossche) *and masquerades* (*cf.* H. Goovaerts). Master Antwerp Guild 1712; Descamps (1763) records that he went to Hesse-Cassel and was made Court painter (*cf.* C. Breydel); in London (*cf.* P. v. Angellis, J. F. v. Bredael, P. Casteels III, G. Grisoni, V. H. Janssens, P. Tillemans) before 1724; friend there of the Dutch painter Herman van der Myn (in London 1727); later returned Antwerp. **Signed Examples:** DRESDEN *Carnival amid Roman ruins, Carnival dance amid Roman ruins* (*cf.* A. F. Rubens). Descamps saw (1768) a group portrait *Officials of the S. Sebastian Archers* in Antwerp Town Hall; he also records two *Masquerades* owned by an Antwerp Burgomaster and a *Conversation piece on the terrace of a mansion, with much game, and sportsmen seen through an alley of trees* (*cf.* I. v. d. Beken) owned by the Dordrecht collector J. van der Linden van Slingeland (collection dispersed 1785).

[Fl. 215, Fl. 216, Fl. 107, Fl. 892.]

Brias, Charles. Flemish Sch. *b* Malines 1798 *d* Brussels 1850 or 1884. *Contemporary history, anecdotic and petit-bourgeois genre, portraits.* Studied Paris 1819, back Brussels 1822; fought in Belgian War of Independence 1830; Croix de Fer 1833; Cross of the Order of Leopold 1840. A *Robbing the poultry vendor* (boys stealing a chicken from a sleeping vendor and substituting a cat (*cf.* H. met de Bles)) won a Brussels prize 1824; an *Interior of a French cabaret* by 'Brias' (surname only) was in London R.A. 1830. A *General Chassé driving back the French Guard at Waterloo* 1817 is also recorded.

[Fl. 451, Fl. 612, Fl. 892, Fl. 361, Fl. 440.]

Brice, Ignace. Flemish Sch. *b* son of an artist Antoine B., Brussels 1795 *d* St. Josse-ten-Noode (Brussels) 1866. *Genre, portraits and portrait lithographs.* Founder member Brussels Soc. des Beaux Arts. Represented in AMSTERDAM *The poultry seller* 1827 (half length figures: recorded by Nagler (before 1850): 'Ein Bauer in natürlicher Grösse gemalt, der einer Köchin eine Taube zum verkaufe anbietet und sie lüstern im Arm kneipt; es herrscht darin die grösste Wahrheit.' A drawing by his father *The glorification of the Emperor Leopold II* was engraved by A. Cardon *q.v.*

[Fl. 612, Fl. 440.]

Bridt, Bernaerdt de. Flemish Sch. *b* Antwerp (?) before 1674 *d* Antwerp (?) after 1722. *Still life with animals and birds* (*cf.* J. Biltius, J. P. v. Bredal, A. Clevenbergh, D. de Coninck, J. B. Govaerts, A. de Gryef, P. A. Rysbraeck, J. F. v. Son, J. J. Spoede, A. Smitsens, A. Verhoeven, J. X. Vermoelen also M. Spey). Master in Antwerp Guild 1688. **Signed Example:** DESSAU Amalienstift *Still life with dead bird.* A signed *Still life with dead swan, hare, monkey and dog* (*cf.* P. Gysels, J. B. Boel and P. J. Snyers) 1712 is recorded.

[Fl. 612, Fl. 892, Fl. 798.]

*Brighton Assumption of the Virgin Painter. Presumed Flemish Sch. 16th cent. Name for painter of BRIGHTON Mus. *Assumption of the Virgin.* Presumed by some identical with A. Cornelis *q.v.*

Brill (or Bril), Mathys. Flemish Sch. *b* son of a still life and fruit painter Mathys B. the elder (*cf.* L. J. v. d. Bosch), Antwerp or Breda 1548 or 1550 *d* Rome 1583 or 1584. *Landscapes and town views in fresco.* Went Italy and remained there (*cf.* J. v. d. Straet); in Rome during Pontificate of Gregory XIII from 1573; worked in the Vatican with Jan Sons *q.v.* 1573-5; painted landscapes under the Italian Lorenzo Sabbatini in the apartments looking on the Loggia della Conserva in the Vatican 1575-7; in Accad. di San Luca (*cf.* F. v. d. Kasteele) 1581; van Mander, his contemporary in Rome, records: 'he worked in the rooms and loggias of the Vatican; in one of the upper loggias he painted in fresco some fine landscapes and views (vergezichten) with processions such as habitually take place in Rome'. His brother Paul B. *q.v.* worked with him in the last years. **Documented Examples:** ROME Vatican (Frescoes) *Views of Rome behind processions bringing the relics of S. Gregory of Nyssa to S. Peter's* 1580 (figures documented as by the Italian Antonio Tempesta). Landscapes in fresco in the loggia of the Torre dei Venti are recorded. Vienna Albertina has a drawing *Buildings in Rome* monogrammed with an 'M' and spectacles (bril). Landscapes and town views are recorded by engravings 1614.

[Fl. 559, Fl. 36, Fl. 800, Fl. 84, Fl. 892, Fl. 574, Fl. 440, Fl. 715 (1928 and 1934), Fl. 678.]

*Brill (or Bril), Paul. Flemish Sch. *b* son of still life and fruit painter Mathys B. the elder, Antwerp or Breda 1554 or 1556 *d* Rome 1626. Brother of Mathys B. *q.v. Landscapes and port-scenes with small figures* (*cf.* M. Ryckaert, L. and M. v. Valkenborch, L. Toeput, J. (Velvet) Brueghel, A. Govaerts, A. v. Stalbemt, K. de Keuninck, and A. Mirou); *some in fresco with figures by Italian painters* (*cf.* Lamberto (Tedesco) and P. Franck); *also worked as engraver.* His contemporary van Mander records (1604) that he began as pupil in Antwerp of D. Oortelmans *q.v.* and painted on musical instruments (*cf.* F. Borsse); that he went Lyons (*cf.* F. Stella) at the age of twenty and later joined Mathys B. in Rome; remained Italy (*cf.* J. v. d. Straet); in Rome Accademia di San Luca (*cf.* F. v. d. Kasteele and P. de Lignis) 1582; his contemporary Baglione records (1642) that he collaborated with Mathys B. in his last works in the Vatican and completed his commissions; worked in the Vatican and the Lateran for Sixtus V 1585-90; married 1592; worked in S. Cecilia in Trastevere, S. Giovanni in Lateran and Palazzo Rospigliosi *c.* 1600; in Sala Clementina in the Vatican for Clement VIII 1602; collaborated with Baglione and other Italian painters. His pupils and assistants included the Italian A. Buonamici (i.e. 'Tassi', the master of Claude le Lorrain), B. Lauwers *q.v.*, W. v. Nieulandt *q.v.*, K. Spieringh *q.v.* and J. Sons *q.v.* Van Mander records landscapes on canvas and copper; Baglione referring to the work of his last years writes: 'Continuamente lavorava per mercatanti Fiamminghi che gli davano ciò ch'egli chieder sapeva; è contutto chè fosse molto vecchio, non dimeno lavorava paesi picciole in rame, con tal diligenza fatti che un giovane formar più non avrai potuto'; E. Norgate the English scribe and illuminator writes (*c.* 1648) of 'his old friend Paulo Brill' as excelling in landscape 'an Art soe new in England as all the Language within our fower Seas cannot find it a name but a borrowed one', and mentions the German Adam Elsheimer, J. de Momper *q.v.*, G. v. Coninxloo *q.v.*, Brueghel and Rubens as other exponents. **Signed Examples:** AMSTERDAM Rijks. *Italian landscape with ruins and figures.* ANTWERP *Rocky landscape with trees, lake, castle and figures.* AUGSBURG *Landscape with S. Peter* 1600. BERLIN *Landscape with Latona and the peasants* (*cf.* J. (Velvet) Brueghel). BRUSSELS *Mediterranean port scene.* DRESDEN *Landscape with Roman ruins and an inn, figures and castle* 1600 (signature and spectacles ('bril') on inn sign), *Mountain landscape with waterfall, village and figures* 1608 (signature, and spectacles on inn sign), *Wooded landscape with Tobias and the Angel* 1624 (*cf.* D. v. Alsloot, J. (Velvet) Brueghel). FLORENCE Uffizi. GLASGOW *Rocky landscape* 1602. LENINGRAD. PARIS Louvre *Landscape with fishermen* 1624. ROME Borghese *Waterfall at Tivoli* 1595. ROTTERDAM

Landscape with S. Jerome. TURIN, VIENNA Kunsthist. *River landscape with ruined tower on rock* 1600. DETROIT has a *Harbour scene* (with spectacles rebus). **Documented Examples:** ROME (frescoes) Vatican, Sala Clementina S. *Clement cast into the sea* 1602 (recorded by van Mander; Sala del Consistorio *Landscapes with abbeys under Papal direction* (recorded by van Mander); Scala Santa *Jonah thrown into the sea, Jonah cast up by the whale* (recorded by Baglione); Lateran *Landscapes with hermits* (payments made 1589 and 1590); Santa Maria Maggiore *Landscapes* (recorded by Baglione); S. Cecilia *Landscapes with saints and hermits* (recorded by Baglione); S. Giovanni in Lateran *Landscapes in Scenes from the Life of Constantine* (in collaboration with Baglione and other Italian painters; recorded by Baglione). Van Mander records 'a small picture on copper with figures and ruins recalling the Campo Vaccino in Rome'; also six large landscapes with distant castles painted for Hasdrubal Mattei brother of Cardinal Mattei for whom he decorated a whole room with landscapes and grotesques. Rubens owned a *Landscape with the Story of Psyche;* a landscape in an Antwerp collection 1621 was assessed by P. Goetkint *q.v.,* H. v. Balen *q.v.* and A. v. Stalbemt *q.v.* at 120 gulden (about the same as landscapes in the same collection by J. (Velvet) Brueghel); Erasmus Quellinus *q.v.* owned (1678) 'een curieuse lantschapken van Pauwels Bril', Jeremias Wildens *q.v.* owned (1653) an original and a number of copies. A *Landscape with the Prodigal son among the swine* (*cf.* C. Massys and Prodigal Son Master) is among subjects recorded by engravings. The Forchoudt firm of Antwerp dealers sold (1671) a *Landscape* to Prince Liechtenstein for 80 Ryxd (as compared with 90 Ryxd for a *Landscape with dancing peasants* by Jan Brueghel). Pictures in many museums are presumed by some his work.
[Fl. 559, Fl. 36, Fl. 618, Fl. 800, Fl. 22, Fl. 215, Fl. 84, Fl. 289, Fl. 892, Fl. 574, Fl. 440, Fl. 305, Fl. 212, Fl. 213, Fl. 678.]

Brisschau see **Brassauw.**

*Broeck, Crispiaen (Crispin) van den** (known as Paludanus). Flemish Sch. *b* Malines 1524 *d* Holland or Antwerp (?) *c.* 1591. *Religious subjects, mythologies, nudes; also active as engraver and draughtsman for engravers and as architect.* Guicciardini (1581) records that he visited Rome (*cf.* his brother H. v. d. Broeck); van Mander (1604) records him as pupil of F. Floris and a good composer, painter of large nudes and architect, who died in Holland; Master Antwerp Guild 1555; married daughter of the engraver A. de Bruyn; citizen Antwerp 1559; member of Antwerp Romanist Fraternity; worked for Plantin press (*cf.* P. v. d. Borcht) from 1566; finished a work by F. Floris after his death, 1570 (*cf.* H. Francken the elder and F. Pourbus the elder); worked on decorations for the Duke of Anjou's entry into Antwerp 1582; commissioned with M. Coxie *q.v.,* then eighty-three, to paint a picture for Antwerp Town Hall 1582; in Antwerp during French Fury 1583; went Middelburg after Parma's capture of Antwerp (*cf.* D. v. d. Queborne) 1585; his daughters Barbara, an engraver, married to D. v. d. Queborne, and Isabella, mother of C. and P. de Vos, also went Middelburg; threatened by Antwerp Magistrature with confiscation of his property as an emigré; promised to return when he had completed work contracted for in Holland; recorded in Antwerp 1588; his wife recorded as his widow 1591. **Signed Examples** (Crispian or Crispiaen): ANTWERP *Last Judgement* 1571 (*cf.* J. de Backer). BRUSSELS *Last Judgement* 1560 (another version in Arras). MADRID Prado *Holy Family* (signature recorded but now illegible). He drew the frontispiece to Guicciardini's 'Descrizione' 1581. Works recorded by engravings include *The Spanish Fury in Antwerp* (*cf.* F. Badens and Worcester Destruction of Citadel Painter), *The Judgement of Paris, Venus and Adonis, Venus, Bacchus and Ceres* and religious subjects. Antwerp inventories (1614, 1621 and 1642) record analogous subjects, also a *Tobias* (*cf.* J. v. Scorel, J. Massys, J. Savery the elder and J. (Velvet) Brueghel), and

(1663) a *Rebecca* (*cf.* Dublin Rebecca Painter and C. Buys the younger); the Forchoudt firm of Antwerp exporting dealers sent (1690) to their Vienna branch a *Wise and Foolish Virgins* (*cf.* H. Ewouts) and (1700) a *Seetriomf* (Neptune and Amphitrite?) *cf.* F. Francken the younger and A. v. Nieulandt.
[Fl. 371, Fl. 559, Fl. 613, Fl. 612, Fl. 107, Fl. 892, Fl. 440, Fl. 212, Fl. 213.]

Broeck, Elias van den. Flemish Sch. *b* Antwerp *c.* 1653 (or Amsterdam (?) 1650) *d* Amsterdam 1708. *Flowers with butterflies, insects, lizards and snakes* (*cf.* J. v. Kessel the elder, L. v. Heil, N. Schneider, J. Sloots, J. v. d. Borght, F. and C. W. de Hamilton and J. B. Crépu) *and other still life.* Pupil in Amsterdam of Dutch flower painter C. Kick 1665-9, then in Antwerp of J. D. de Heem; Antwerp Master 1673; delivered paintings to B. Floquet *q.v.* at an annual salary (*cf.* J. B. Bosschaert) 1674; suffered from a legend that he stuck living butterflies to his pictures, went Amsterdam 1685, where Houbraken (1718) records he cultivated flowers, insects, etc. in a private garden (like the Dutch painter O. Marseus van Schrieck *cf.* also J. Francart). **Signed Examples:** AMSTERDAM, COPENHAGEN, OXFORD Ashmolean, ROTTERDAM, SCHWERIN, STOCKHOLM, VIENNA K. and Liecht.
[Fl. 425, Fl. 878, Fl. 215, Fl. 107, Fl. 892, Fl. 440, Fl. 213.]

Broeck, Hendrik van den (known as Paludanus). Flemish Sch. *b* Malines *c.* 1519 *d* in poverty, Italy 1597. Presumed identical with the artist known in Italy as Arrigo Fiammingo, Henricus Malinis and Henricus Paludanus. *Religious subjects; also worked as designer of windows.* Pupil of Frans Floris; went Italy and remained there (*cf.* J. v. d. Straet); worked for the Medicis in Florence *c.* 1551; in Orvieto 1561 and Perugia 1564 and later; in Naples (*cf.* C. Pyp) 1567; also worked in Rome and (as Arrigo Fiammingo) assisted Vasari on frescoes in the Sala Regia of the Vatican (*cf.* P. de Witte (Candido)) before 1573; on the council of Rome Accad. di S. Luca (*cf.* F. v. d. Kasteele) from 1580. J. Wraghe *q.v.* was his assistant in Perugia. *Cf.* also C. v. d. Broeck. **Signed Examples:** PERUGIA Pinacoteca *Adoration of the Magi* ('Henricus Malinis' 1564) commissioned for the Montemelini chapel in S. Francesco 1562; S. Agostino *Christ and S. Andrew* ('Henricus Paludanus' 1581). MONGIOVINO (nr. Perugia) Church *Descent from the Cross* ('Henricus Malinis' 1564). **Monogrammed and Documented Example:** ROME Vatican Sistine Chapel *Resurrection* (Baglione (1642) records this commissioned in the Pontificate of Gregory XIII 1572-85 (*cf.* M. Brill and J. Sons) and as replacing a fresco by Dom. Ghirlandajo). **Documented Examples:** MONGIOVINO *Holy Family* 1585, *Assumption of the Virgin.* ROME Vatican Library: Sala Sistina *The second Lateran Council* (painted under the direction of the Italian D. Fontana 1588; described by Baglione as 'historia grande che occupa una facciata, un concilio con quantità di vescovi, di prelati et di gran personaggi'); S. Maria Maggiore *Hesron and Aram* and *Aminadab and Naasa* 1590 (recorded by Baglione); S. Maria degli Angeli *S. Michael driving the rebel angels from Paradise* (*cf.* F. Floris; recorded by Baglione).
[Fl. 818, Fl. 371, Fl. 36, Fl. 800, Fl. 440, Fl. 305, Fl. 878.]

Broederlam, Melchior. Flemish Sch. *b* Ypres before 1365 *d* Ypres (?) *c.* 1410. *Religious subjects, portraits, paintings on banners; also designs for ceremonial costumes, jewels and ceramics.* Had atelier in Ypres *c.* 1381-1409; in service of Louis de Mâle Count of Flanders 1381; 'peintre et valet de chambre' of Philip the Bold, Duke of Burgundy 1385; designed ceramics for Château de Hesdin 1387; visited Paris 1390, Ghent 1395 and Dijon 1399. H. de Boulogne *q.v.* was his pupil. **Documented Examples:** DIJON Mus. wings covering a reredos carved by J. de Baerse of Termonde for the Dijon Charteuse de Champmol *Annunciation and Visitaion, Presentation and Flight into Egypt* (commissioned by Philip the Bold

1392; painted Ypres; installed by the artist in Dijon and paid for 1399).

[Fl. 199, Fl. 490, Fl. 892, Fl. 440, Fl. 244, Fl. 334, Fl. 150, Fl. 548, Fl. 256, Fl. 778, Fl. 710.]

Broederlam, Ryck (Richard). Flemish Sch. *b* son of Melchior B. (?) Ypres (?) before 1410 *d* Ypres (?) after 1460. *Portraits, decorative paintings; designs for glass and ceremonial costumes.* Recorded as painter in Ypres 1436, 1450 and 1460; charged by Duke Philip the Good of Burgundy with the superintendence of a ceramic factory (*cf.* Melchior B. and H. de Boulogne). [Fl. 892, Fl. 440.]

Broerman, Eugéne. Flemish Sch. *b* Brussels 1860 or 1861. '*History*', *portraits, genre, landscapes, murals, posters.* Pupil in Brussels Acad. under J. Portaels; visited Italy and Provence. Represented in BRUSSELS Mus. *Oliva* 1887; S. GILLES (nr. Brussels), Town Hall *Allegorical murals with figures in modern dress.* A book *Célébrités nationales* reproducing a series of his portraits was published in Antwerp 1893. Pictures titled *Filial devotion (Cleobis and Biton)* 1883, *Dante* 1888, *Allegorical portrait of Baron Lambermont* 1903 and *Ave Maria of the Fishermen* 1910 are recorded. [Fl. 440.]

Broers, Jasper (or Gaspar). Flemish Sch. *b* Antwerp 1682 *d* Antwerp 1716. *Contemporary warfare and picturesque military pieces* (*cf.* P. v. Bloemen, Joris v. Bredael, J. F. v. Bredael, J. P. v. Bredael, C. Breydel and J. B. v. d. Meiren). Houbraken (1718) records him as painter of *peasant genre and market scenes* (*cf.* J. B. Spalthof and J. v. Buken). Pupil in Antwerp of J. B. v. d. Meiren 1695; Master Antwerp Guild 1703. **Signed Examples:** ANTWERP Plantin *The battle of Eeckeren* 1703 (*cf.* C. Francken and P. Verdussen). CAMBRIDGE Fitz. *Cavalry skirmish by a river* 1715. DRESDEN *Skirmish in the mountains, Skirmish in a valley.* VIENNA Liechtenstein *Military pieces* (two).

[Fl. 425, Fl. 481, Fl. 107, Fl. 892, Fl. 440.]

Brounckhurst (or Bronckhorst), Arnold or **Arthur van.** Flemish Sch. *b* before 1550 *d* Scotland (?) after 1580. *Portraits and miniatures.* Came England by 1565 (*cf.* C. Ketel, S. v. d. Meulen); with the English miniaturist N. Hilliard and one Cornelius de Vosse 'a most cuninge pictur maker' obtained licence to prospect for gold in Scotland 1572; he 'searched sundry moors and found gold in sundry places' but was refused permission by the Regent acting for James VI of Scotland (then 6 years old) to export the gold to England; remained Scotland and entered the King's service 'to draw all the small and great pictures for his Majesty'; a precept signed by the King referring to him as 'our lovit servitour Arnold Bronckhorst our painter' contains commissions for portraits including one of George Buchanan 1580; a portrait *Sir Henry Sidney* 1565 and an *Andromeda* 1572 are recorded.

[Fl. 882, Fl. 535, Fl. 887, Fl. 28.]

*****Brouwer (or Brauwer), Adriaen.** Flemish Sch. *b* son of a tapestry draughtsman and his wife who sold linen drapery, Audenarde (or Haarlem?) 1605, 1606 or 1608 *d* of the plague, Antwerp 1638. *Peasant genre* (*cf.* D. Boone), *landscapes with small figures* (*cf.* L. de Vadder) *some with moonlight, occasional religious subjects; also some engravings.* In early youth drew foliage and birds on linen for embroidered caps and stomachers sold by his mother to the peasants; presumed by some to have gone Antwerp and learned painting there from *c.* 1622; Houbraken (1718), informed about him from a document owned by the Dutch painter Karel de Moor (*b.* 1656) records him in Haarlem from his youth as pupil of Frans Hals and exploited by him, till, encouraged by the Dutch painter A. van Ostade, a fellow pupil, he left for Amsterdam and worked there for the painter, innkeeper and dealer B. van Somer *q.v.* with whom he lodged; documented in Van Somer's inn Het Schild van Frankryck (named by Houbraken) 1626;

in Haarlem Chamber of Rhetoric 'In Liefd Boven Al' 1626; referred to as living Haarlem 1627; in Antwerp where Master in Guild 1631; took one Jan Dandoy as his pupil 1631; records of an Antwerp lawsuit in which he and Rubens appeared as witnesses (1632) show that his work was already being forged and copied and that Rubens admired it; deeply in debt, made over his whole property (including his painting materials, clothes, a map of the siege of Breda, a lay figure, two landscapes by Josse de Momper *q.v.*, two grisailles by Jooris van Cleve, a landscape on marble by J. Fouquier *q.v.*, a painting of the Emperor Theodosius and a few books and prints) together with 11 sketches of his own to a patron Jan van der Bosch, silk merchant, who paid his debts (*cf.* J. d'Arthois) 1632; imprisoned in Antwerp Citadel (reason unknown; Houbraken states that he had come from the United Provinces to Antwerp without procuring necessary papers and was arrested as a spy) 1633; was lent money by van der Bosch on two more occasions 1633; made friends with the prison baker J. van Craesbeeck *q.v.*; Houbraken records that Rubens, (informed of his detention by the Duc d'Arenberg, then a privileged prisoner in the citadel (?)), procured his release, took him to his house and introduced him to good company 'which he found more constraining than the prison he had left' (*cf.* L. Ricquier); lived for a time with Craesbeeck, taught him painting and became the lover of his wife; member of the Antwerp Chamber of Rhetoric, (Violiere), and acted as shipwrecked sailor in one of their plays 1634; had further trouble with creditors and was helped by the engraver P. Pontius with whom he was then living 1635; recorded friend of J. D. de Heem *q.v.* and of the Dutch painter Jan Lievens (in Antwerp since 1634 and friend of P. Pontius) 1636; Houbraken, who describes him as all his life a dissolute frequenter of the disreputable company that he painted, records a visit to Paris and his death as follows 'Na dat hy eenigen tyd te Parys en elders om gezworven had, en Venus en Bacchus teffens te yverig gedient had, kwam hy ziek zynde te rug tot Antwerpen, en arm zynde tot het Gasthuis, daar hy na verloop van twee dagen kwam te sterven, en voorts by de dooden in den pestput geworpen met stroo en kalk gedekt werd.' De Bie (1661) records that his body was later exhumed and buried within the Carmelite church. Houbraken relates that Rubens began a model for a monument to be placed above the tomb but died before it was completed. Van Dyck drew his portrait for his iconography. **Signed Examples:** BRUSSELS *Peasants and Spanish soldiers at a table in the grounds of Antwerp citadel* (corresponds to a picture recorded by Houbraken as painted in Antwerp citadel for the Duc d'Arenberg (?) and described by him as 'Sommige Spanjaarden die zig om een hoek neerzetten om een kaartje te spelen', which much pleased 'om den ernst dien zy in't speelen betoonden, en de natuurlyke verbeelde magere getaande Spaansche troonien. En inzonderheid om een die in't verschiet zat te kakken, waar in het drukken, als wilde het zig niet gemakkelyk ontlasten, zoo natuurlyk en potsig vertoont was, dat men't zelve zonder te lachen niet konde aanzien'.) DESSAU Amalienstift *Peasents singing.* THE HAGUE (Steengracht) *Four smokers* 1630. **Monogrammed Examples (AB):** AMSTERDAM Rijks. *Boors' carouse, Peasants' and soldiers' brawl by wayside inn.* BERLIN *Woman before a mirror* (as 'Superbia' in series of *Seven Deadly Sins* in a 17th century engraving), *Landscape with peasants playing bowls, Landscape with seated shepherd playing a shawm. Peasants in a moonlight landscape with cottage and trees in foreground and distant sea.* CARLSRUHE *Boor asleep (Pipe drunkard).* FRANKFORT *Taste (the bitter drink)* (Houbraken records a series *The Five Senses, The Twelve Months* and 'similar subjects' (*cf.* J. (Velvet) Brueghel and D. Teniers the younger and Berlin and Munich examples) painted in the early days in Hals's atelier), *Village doctor operating on a peasant's back.* LENINGRAD *The drinker.* MUNICH *Taste (three smokers)* (initial B. only; *cf.* Frankfort and Vienna Czernin examples). PARIS Louvre *The smoker,.* PHILADELPHIA Johnson

The smoker; Tavern scene, Peasant's cottage, Road near a house. VIENNA Czernin *Village doctor operating on a peasant's arm (Feeling) (cf.* Frankfort and Munich examples), *The Miser with a sack of gold* (as 'Avarice' in a 17th century engraving). Kunsthist *Old peasant singing, and holding pipe and pot, seated on a cask.* Liechtenstein *Old man with pipe in his hat and jug in his hands, Old man at table with bread and sausage, Village dentistry.* **Documented Examples:** AIX-LA-CHAPELLE *Village doctor plastering an old man's foot* (recorded by 17th century engraving). MUNICH *Soldiers quarrelling over cards one striking another with a pot, one drawing a short sword* (corresponds to a picture recorded by Houbraken as painted in Amsterdam). Pictures title*d S. Francis reading* and other pictures of the saint are recorded by 17th century engravings. The Vienna branch of the Forchoudt firm of Antwerp dealers was asking for his pictures by 1636 and received the next year from Antwerp a *Self portrait with a pipe and a beerglass in his hand,* a *Man cutting a pen* and others (of which some were sold later to Prince Carl von Liechtenstein); the Seville dealer Immerseel ordered (1636) copies of his works to be made by D. Teniers the younger *q.v.*; Rubens (before 1640) owned a *Temptation of S. Anthony* and pictures with the following titles: *Drunkards fighting, one dragging another by the hair; Tavern with company round a fire; Peasants making music; The jealous peasant; A fight where one man is held by the throat; Three men fighting, one striking with a pot (cf.* Munich documented example); *Peasant concert round a fire; Lute player; Peasant with a glass of wine and pot; Tobacco smokers; Landscape with a peasant fastening his shoe; Two peasants looking out of a window; Landscape in moonlight; Landscape with a flash of lightning; Landscape with villagers dancing* and another *landscape.* Rembrandt owned six of his pictures; copies of his pictures are recorded in Antwerp collectors' inventories by 1642; *Moonlight landscapes* were owned (1659) by Susanna Willemsen widow of an Antwerp cloth merchant and (1652) by the Antwerp Sheriff J. van Meurs who also owned a *Temptation of S. Anthony* (and the same subject by H. Bosch *q.v.*); the widow of an Antwerp 'Commis Postmeester' owned (1663) 'Seven small pictures of the *Seven Deadly Sins*' and copies of the same; the large collection of J. B. Anthoine, Antwerp Postmaster assessed (1691) by J. E. Quellinus *q.v.* and P. v. d. Willigen *q.v.* contained a *Twelfth Night (Le roi boit)* and a number of others. Paintings presumed by some his work are in various museums *(cf.* London (Wallace) Sleeping Boor Painter and Munich Tobacco Den Painter).
[Fl. 86, Fl. 753, Fl. 652, Fl. 141, Fl. 425, Fl. 353, Fl. 22, Fl. 215, Fl. 19, Fl. 788, Fl. 108, Fl. 631 (1884), Fl. 605, Fl. 756, Fl. 413 (1910), Fl. 91, Fl. 879, Fl. 212, Fl. 213, Fl. 214.]

*Bruegel, Pieter the elder (known as Peasant Bruegel and Droll Bruegel). Flemish Sch. *b* Brueghel (near Eindhoven twenty miles from 's Hertogenbosch) (?) or Breda (?) before 1535 *d* Brussels 1569. *Symbolic and satirical compositions (cf.* H. Bosch, H. met de Bles, J. Mandyn, P. Huys and P. Brueghel the younger); *landscapes (cf.* J. Patinir, C. Massys, M. W. de Cock, H. Bol, J. de Hollander, G. Mostaert and F. Mostaert), *some with religious and military subjects, and some with genre figures (cf.* P. Aertsen, M. v. Cleve, F. Verbeeck, P. Balten and J. (Velvet) Brueghel), *some with crypto-protests against the Spanish persecutions in the Netherlands (cf.* F. Hogenberg and A. de Weerdt); *some representing months or seasons (cf.* F. Boels, P. Stevens the younger, L. and M. v. Valkenborch, J. Grimmer and L. v. d. Borcht); *also drawings and compositions for engravers and occasional engravings.* Van Mander (1604) records him pupil of P. Coecke van Aelst *q.v.* and living in his house; and as working thereafter with the Antwerp engraver and publisher H. W. de Cock *q.v.*; Master in Antwerp Guild 1551; went Italy, Van Mander records, through France *(cf.* L. Thiry and A. Dubois); in Rome *(cf.* G. Beerings, M. de Gast, M. v. Heemskerck) 1553; met there and collaborated with the miniaturist Giulio Clovio *(cf.* B. Spranger and J.

Hoefnagel); went down to Straits of Messina (?); Van Mander writes: 'On his travels he painted many pictures from nature so that it was said of him that while in the Alps he had swallowed the mountains and rocks which he was able on his return to bring out (uit te spuwen) on his canvas and panels, so faithfully did he follow nature in this and other aspects'; back in Antwerp by 1554; made many drawings engraved and published by H. W. de Cock; friend of J. V. de Vries *q.v.*; Van Mander records him as working much for a Nuremberg merchant Hans Franckert (in Antwerp Guild 1546) and adds that, disguised as peasants, they attended peasant fairs and weddings together; lived with a girl who was so inveterate a liar that he would not marry her; married Maria daughter of of P. Coecke van Aelst whom he had known as a child; moved to Brussels at the instance of his mother-in-law *(cf.* M. Bessemers) who made this a condition 'opdat hij het vorige meisje zou verlaten en vergeten' 1563; his house was exempted from billeting of troops *(cf.* M. Coxie) 1568; died, Van Mander records, before executing a commission from the Brussels Magistrature to paint pictures of the digging of the Antwerp-Brussels Willebroeck canal *(cf.* J. Garemyn); destroyed on his deathbed, Van Mander records, a number of his drawings inscribed with biting comments which might have brought persecution on his wife to whom he left his *Magpie on a gallows* (as a warning against imprudent chatter). At the instance of J. (Velvet) Brueghel, Rubens painted a *Christ giving the Keys to S. Peter* for his tomb in Brussels N. D. de la Chapelle (sold 1765 and replaced by a copy). 'He was', Van Mander writes, 'a quiet pleasant man, who spoke little, but liked to make jokes in company and frighten his friends and pupils with ghost nonsense . . . and strange noises (spokerij en lawaai) . . . nature chose him among peasants to be the painter of peasants . . . , he had made a good study of the manner of Hieronymus Bosch and himself made many similar 'spook' designs (spookachtige tafereelen) and drolleries many of which are reproduced in prints'; he also records that he made many pen drawings from nature, that he followed J. de Hollander *q.v.* in his technique of painting thinly and allowing the ground to show through and be part of the pictures (doorschijnen en medewerken) *(cf.* H. Bosch), and he names P. Balten as a follower. B. Spranger drew his portrait (engraved 1606); Lampsonius beneath a profile portrait (published by H. W. de Cock's widow 1572) describes him as a second and more amusing Hieronymus Bosch; Guicciardini (1581) writes: 'Pietro Bruegel de Breda, grande imitatore della scienza et fantasie di Girolamo Bosco'. The geographer Ortelius *(cf.* Joris Hoefnagel and F. Hogenberg) wrote (before 1598): 'Multa pinxit, hic Brugelius, quae pingi non possunt, quod Plinius de Apelle. In omnibus eius operibus intelligitur plus semper quam pingitur'; Sir Joshua Reynolds (1781) wrote: 'Old Bruegel was totally ignorant of all the mechanical art of making a picture but in the *Massacre of the Innocents* there is a great quantity of thinking, a representation of variety of distress, enough for twenty modern pictures. In this respect he is like Donne as distinguished from the modern versifiers, who carrying no weight of thought, easily fall into that false gallop of verses which Shakespeare ridicules in 'As You like it'. There is the same difference between the old portraits of Albert Dürer or Holbein and those of the modern painters: the moderns have certainly the advantage in facility, but there is a truth in the old painters, though expressed in a hard manner, that gives them a superiority'. **Signed Examples** (Bruegel): BERLIN *The Blue Cape (the Cuckold) and other Flemish Proverbs* 1559, *Two monkeys chained on a window-sill with view of Antwerp and the Scheldt* 1562 (presumed by some an illustration of the Flemish proverb 'Wat vindt men ter wereld zeldzame kinderen, zei de boer, en hij zag een aap in het venster zitten'). BRUSSELS *S. Michael and the Rebel Angels* 1562 *(cf.* F. Floris and New York Crucifixion and Last Judgement Painter), *The numbering at Bethlehem* 1566. BUDAPEST *S. John preaching in the Wilderness (with gipsies in foreground* 1566 *(cf.* Bruges Baptism of Christ Painter, J.

Patinir, H. met de Bles, M. van Cleve, P. Balten and K. v. Mander; for gipsies *cf.* J. (Velvet) Brueghel). DARMSTADT *Magpie on a gallows with peasants dancing* 1568 (recorded and explained by Van Mander; presumed by some to illustrate a proverb). LONDON N.G. *Adoration of the Magi* 1564. MUNICH *The Land of Cockayne* 1567. NAPLES *The blind leading the blind* 1568 (*cf.* Cornelis Massys), *The Misanthrope (or Perfidy of the World)* 1568 (tondo; inscribed 'Om dat de Werelt is soe ongetru/ Daer om gha ic in den ru,' date indistinct). NEW YORK Met. *The harvesters (July? or August? or Summer?)* '65 (presumed from a series of months or seasons; *cf.* Vienna examples). PARIS Louvre *Five crippled beggars in capes with fox-tails (Les Gueux?)* 1568. VIENNA Kunsthist. *Battle between Carnival and Lent* 1559 (recorded by Van Mander; *cf.* F. Hogenberg); *Children's games* 1560 (recorded by Van Mander); *Suicide of Saul (Battle of the Israelites and Philistines)* 1562 (last figure of date indistinct; inscribed 'Saul XXXI capit' (*cf.* L. v. d. Borcht and J. (Velvet) Brueghel)); *The Tower of Babel* 1563 (Van Mander records in the collection of the Emperor Rudolf II (*cf.* P. Stevens the younger) 'a large picture of the Tower of Babel with many well painted details, shown so that one can look down into it from above; and a small version of the same subject' (*cf.* J. Patinir, C. Anthonisz, M. v. Valkenborch, L. v. Valkenborch, R. Savery, N. v. Cleve, T. v. Haecht, A. Grimmer, L. Toeput, J. V. de Vries, J. de Momper, S. Dubois and K. v. Mander); *The road to Calvary* 1564 (Van Mander records two versions in the collection of Rudolf II 'which make a very natural effect and have some droll episodes' (*cf.* P. Aertsen, H. met de Bles, London Delft Painter); *Massacre of the Innocents* ('Brueg . . .'; recorded by Van Mander as in the collection of Rudolf II 'with much action in it; a whole family entreating for the life of a peasant child which the murderous soldiers have seized to kill, the grief and swooning of the mothers and other arresting scenes (pakkende voorstellingen) are well shown'); *Conversion of S. Paul (the road to Damascus)* 1567 (recorded by Van Mander as 'with a fine mountain landscape' in Rudolf II's collection (*cf.* K. Foort, M. v. Cleve, J. de Momper, A. Snellinck, G. Snellinck, P. Snayers); *Hunters in the snow (February? or Winter?)* 1565 (with the two following presumed from a series of Months or Seasons, *cf.* New York example), *The dark day (March? or Spring?)* 1565, *Return of the Herd (November? or Autumn?)* 1565; *The bird's nest* 1568 (presumed illustration of proverb 'He who knows where the nest is, has the knowledge, he who steals it, has the nest'; *cf.* P. Snyers); *Peasant dance* (*cf.* J. (Velvet) Brueghel, P. Stevens the younger, P. P. Rubens, D. Teniers the younger). **Documented Examples:** ANTWERP Mayer van den Bergh Mus. *Dulle Griet (Mad Meg storming Hell)* 156 . (the date, indistinct, is presumed by some false; recorded by Van Mander: 'There is also by him a Mad Meg who is calling up her legions to storm hell, (die een roof voor de hel doet) she has a wild staring look and is strangely accoutred; I think it is among the Emperor's pictures'). VIENNA Kunsthist. *Peasant wedding* (Archduke Leopold Wilhelm's inventory 1659; *cf.* Detroit Wedding Dance Painter, F. Verbeeck and J. (Velvet) Brueghel).

Van Mander records a *Temptation of Christ* 'in which, as though standing in the Alps, one looks down on a landscape with cities through rents in the clouds'; a *Triumph of Truth* 'which he himself spoke of as his best work'; a *Peasant wedding* 'showing among those bringing presents an old peasant who counts out his money, from a purse hanging from his neck' (*cf.* P. Brueghel the younger), and a *Remedies against Death*. Compositions with social protest recorded by engravings (published by H. W. de Cock) include a series *The Vices* and plates titled *Hope, Faith, Charity, Temperance, Justice, Prudence* and *Strength*. A *Peasants quarrelling over cards* is recorded by an engraving (*cf.* P. Brueghel the younger and J. (Velvet) Brueghel). Nicolaas Jongelinck, brother of the sculptor Jacob Jongelinck, owned (1565) in Antwerp (together with ten pictures by F. Floris *q.v.* and one by Albert Dürer) sixteen pictures by Bruegel 'onder de welke is den Thoren van

Babilonyen, eenen Cruysdrager, de Tweelf maenden'. The miniaturist G. Clovio owned (1577) a *Tower of Babel*, two other pictures by Bruegel and 'un quadretto di miniatura' partly by B. and partly by himself. Rubens owned (1640) pictures titled *The Flight into Egypt, Mount S. Gothard, The Death of the Virgin* (grisaille), *Two small heads* (in tondos), *A man yawning, A beggar's head* (tondo), *A ship piece* (tempera), *Landscape with conflagration* (tempera), *Battle between Turks and Christians* (*cf.* the *Suicide of Saul* above), all by 'Oude Bruegel'. The Antwerp collector P. van Valckenisse owned (1614) a *Triumph of Death* 'van Bruegel'. Jeremias Wildens *q.v.* owned (1653) a *Triumph of Death* by J. (Velvet) Brueghel 'after Oude Bruegel'. The head of the Forchoudt firm of Antwerp dealers wrote (October 1672) to his sons in the Vienna branch 'I have here a *Triumph of Death* by Velvet Brueghel 'is meer als dobbel doek groet, men seyt van den ouden Brueghel het eerste te sijn by oft int Cabinet van den Keyser, twelck Ul eens wilt adviseren, anders sout Ul toesenden, het cost ons 350 gulden' and two months later 'I am glad to hear you have sold one of the two works by van Heemskerck, God grant other good opportunities . . . I am sending you the important work by the Old Brueghel the *Triumph of Death*' (*cf.* Madrid Triumph of Death Painter and P. Brueghel the younger). The banker Jabach owned (1695) an *Adoration of the Magi* (*with snow falling and a child on a little sledge on the ice*) by 'vieil Brugel' (*cf.* P. Brueghel the younger and L. van Valkenborch). Many of the other references to pictures by 'Oude Bruegel', 'Peter Bruegel' and 'Bruegel' (with various spellings) in 17th century Antwerp inventories and records may refer either to him or to one of his sons or grandsons. A *Christ and the adulteress* is recorded by an engraving; a grisaille painting of the subject, signed and dated 1565 was recorded in commerce 1952. Drawings (some signed) and paintings presumed by some his work are in various museums (*cf.* Brussels Icarus Painter, Detroit Wedding Dance Painter and Madrid Triumph of Death Painter).

[Fl. 503, Fl. 371, Fl. 559, Fl. 753, Fl. 702, Fl. 331 (1890), Fl. 602, Fl. 456 (1905), Fl. 55, Fl. 56, Fl. 892, Fl. 78, Fl. 440, Fl. 383, Fl. 257, Fl. 313, Fl. 596, Fl. 803, Fl. 251, Fl. 180, Fl. 899, Fl. 345, Fl. 212, Fl. 213, Fl. 214, Fl. 582, Fl. 804, Fl. 166, Fl. 110, Fl. 316, Fl. 460, Fl. 797 (1942), Fl. 615, Fl. 378.]

Brueghel (Breugel), Abraham (called Rhyngraef and Il Napolitano). Flemish Sch. *b* son of Jan B. the younger, and grandson of A. Janssens, Antwerp 1631 *d* Naples *c.* 1690. *Still life with fruit and flowers* (*cf.* T. Aenvanck, F. v. Aken, J. P. Bredael the elder, J. B. Brueghel, J. P. Brueghel, P. Casteels III, P. Gysels) *some with figures.* Pupil of his father; went Rome where Houbraken (1719) records he received his nickname in Flemish artists' colony 1670; member of Accad. di S. Luca 1670; present, Houbraken records, at the inauguration of A. Genoels *q.v.* as 'Archimedes' in the Flemish colony 1674; went Naples (*cf.* J. B. Brueghel) where, Dominici (1742) records, he painted still life in pictures by the Neapolitan Luca Giordano; made much money but lost it through speculation and the dishonesty of his business adviser. **Signed Examples:** AMSTERDAM *Still life with pomegranates and white grapes* (Rome) 1670. ROTTERDAM Boymans *Fruit and flowers.* STOCKHOLM *Young lady picking grapes with fruit and flowers on a table* (Rome). TURIN Pinac. *Fruit and flowers* 1671. An inventory of theo collection of the Antwerp postmaster J. B. Anthoine compiled 1691 by J. E. Quellinus *q.v.* records '*A woman and child in a garland of flowers, the woman by Carlo Maratti* (*cf.* R. v. Audenaerd) *and the flowers by Abraham Brueghel*' (*cf.* D. Seghers).

[Fl. 425, Fl. 353, Fl. 564, Fl. 232, Fl. 215, Fl. 107, Fl. 892, Fl. 213, Fl. 678.]

Brueghel, Ambrosius. Flemish Sch. *b* son of Jan (Velvet) B., *q.v.* Antwerp 1617 *d* Antwerp 1675. *Landscapes with figures;*

flowers. Pupil of his brother J. B. the younger and of H. v. Balen. Inherited a share of his father's property under his will (of which Rubens, H. v. Balen and C. Schut were among the executors) distributed 1627; made his own will (presumed to indicate that he was going abroad *cf.* T. Boeyermans and J. Boeckhorst) witnessed by J. v. Hulsdonck *q.v.* and bequeathing to his brother-in-law D. Teniers the younger a *Christ on the Cross* by Jan (Velvet) B., to his other brother-in-law J. B. Borkens (Borrekens) *Portrait of his father and mother* by Rubens, and to Jan Wildens *q.v.* the repayment of a debt of 300 gulden 1639; in Antwerp where settled accounts with his former guardians, his brother Jan Brueghel the younger and D. Teniers 1641; Master in Antwerp Guild 1645; married in Antwerp 1649; member of Violiere Chamber of Rhetoric; Dean in Guild 1654; as ex-Dean testified with his brother Jan Brueghel, C. de Baellieur, E. Snayers, F. Francken III and others that the request of Jan Cossiers *q.v.* to be allowed to finish his picture for the Malines Béguinage *in situ* was in accordance with common usage 1656. J. B. Borkens *q.v.* owned (1668) a *Landscape with figures.* A *Mountain landscape* signed and dated 1653 was recorded (1876) in a private collection. [Fl. 602, Fl. 892, Fl. 213, Fl. 214.]

Brueghel, Ferdinand. Flemish Sch. *b* son of Jan B. the younger, Antwerp 1637. Recorded as 'painter' in Antwerp 1662.

[Fl. 107.]

***Brueghel, Jan** (known as **'Velvet'**). Flemish Sch. *b* son of P. Bruegel the elder *q.v.*, Brussels 1568 *d* of cholera, Antwerp 1625. *Landscapes with genre figures and animals (cf.* F. and G. Mostaert, H. Bol, W. v. d. Bundel, G. v. Coninxloo, A. Govaerts, J. Grimmer, A. Grimmer, D. v. Alsloot, A. v. Stalbemt, J. Stevens, P. Stalpaert, D. Vinckeboons, S. Vrancx, A. Mirou; also J. Brueghel the younger, Ambrosius Brueghel, J. Hulmans, P. Gysels, C. Greuzen, T. Michau and J. F. v. Bredael); *flower pieces (cf.* Ambrosius B., J. B. the younger, L. J. van den Bosch, M. Brill, P. Coecke van Aelst, G. Congnet, J. de Gheyn the younger, R. Savery and Ambrosius Bosschaert); *flower garlands round pictures by other artists (cf.* D. Seghers); *flowered gardens (cf.* J. Brueghel the younger, P. v. Avont, A. Wolfordt); *decorative compositions symbolising the* '*Five Senses*' (*cf.* J. Brueghel the younger, A. Govaerts, A. Brouwer, J. Teniers the younger), '*The Elements*' (*cf.* J. Boots, J. Breughel the younger, R. Savery, S. de Vos, F. v. Kessel), '*Earthly Paradise*' (*cf.* J. Bouttats, H. de Clerck, I. van Oosten, R. Savery, A. Snellinck, J. Uytewael); *also in earlier years occasional religious subjects, battle pieces (cf.* P. Bruegel the elder, S. Vrancx) *and hell scenes and conflagrations (cf.* H. Bosch, P. Brueghel the younger, Madrid Triumph of Death Painter, J. Sons, F. v. Oosten, P. Schoubroeck, Brussels Sodom and Gemorrah Painter, P. Huys). On his father's death taken to live with his grandmother Marie Bessemers *q.v.*. Van Mander (1604) records him pupil for watercolour of Marie Bessemers; and for oil of P. Goetkint *q.v.* (in Antwerp); presumed by some pupil of G. van Coninxloo *q.v.* in Antwerp or Frankenthal; Van Mander records that he went Cologne (*cf.* F. Hogenberg and A. de Weerdt); in Italy from *c.* 1589; recorded in Naples (*cf.* A. Mytens, D. Hendrickx, W. Coebergher, C. Pyp, C. Smet) 1590; in Rome (*cf.* P. Brill, H. v. d. Broeck, F. v. d. Kasteele) 1593; in Rome visited the catacomb of S. Domitilla where his name survives among the graffiti; and worked for Cardinal Federigo Borromeo (nephew of S. Carlo Borromeo and founder of Ambrosiana Library); went Milan when the Cardinal was appointed Archbishop of Milan 1595; returned Antwerp with letter of recommendation from the Cardinal to L. Torrentius, Bishop of Antwerp 1596; Master Antwerp Guild 1597; married daughter of engraver Gérard de Jode (Jan Snellinck *q.v.* being a winess) 1599; became successful and honoured and maintained a correspondence with Cardinal Borromeo for whom he continued to paint pictures; Dean of Antwerp Guild 1601; Member of Antwerp Society

of Romanists and Catholic Chamber of Rhetoricians the Violiere; worked continuously for Archduke Albert (*cf.* G. de Crayer) and the Infanta Isabella (*cf.* D. v. Alsloot); went repeatedly from Antwerp to Brussels to draw flowers, birds and animals in the court gardens, aviaries and menagerie, and objets de luxe in their collections; bought large house in Antwerp 1604; married a second wife 1605; exempted from some taxes at instance of the Archduke and the Infanta 1606; nursed in illness by F. Snyders *q.v.* and gave him an introduction to Cardinal Borromeo when he went Italy 1608; Dean of the Antwerp Society of Romanists, and as such received Rubens into the Society on his return from Italy 1609; became close friend of Rubens who took part in his correspondence with the Cardinal; officially appointed 'peintre et domestique' of the Archduke and the Infanta 1610; further tax exemption granted him 1613; Rubens' first wife Isabella Brant stood godmother to his daughter 1615; painted sixteen small pictures for the Archduke and the Infanta 1616; became involved in financial difficulties and moved to smaller house; Rubens painted figures in some of his pictures (*cf.* Hague and Paris examples); the Infanta Isabella and Cardinal Borromeo godparents to one of his children 1623. Rubens with C. Schut *q.v.* and H. v. Balen *q.v.* were among the executors of his will and guardians of his children; Rubens painted his portrait for his tomb and composed the inscription. Rubens also painted him with his wife (*cf.* Ambrosius Brueghel). Van Dyck drew his portrait engraved as 'pictor florum et ruralium prospectum'. Of his nine children J. Brueghel the younger and Ambrosius Brueghel were painters; one of his daughters married H. van Kessel *q.v.*; another J. B. Borkens (Borrekens) *q.v.*; and a third D. Teniers the younger. J. de Backer *q.v.* collaborated with him in his youth; the German painter H. Rottenhammer collaborated in some works in Rome; H. v. Steenwyck the younger (1609), H. v. Balen, F. Francken II and J. de Momper were among those who collaborated with him after his return to Antwerp. His pupils included J. Brueghel the younger, D. Seghers and L. de Wael. Many of his pictures were copied and imitated by J. Brueghel the younger and by many others in the 17th and 18th centuries (*cf.* J. F. v. Bredael). D'Argenville (1745) writes: 'Ce maître étoit extrêmement laborieux à en juger par le grand nombre de tableaux qui sont sortis de sa main . . . sa touche légère et spirituelle, la correction de ses figures, les animaux et les voitures dont il ornait ses paisages, sont des choses qu'on ne scauroit trop admirer . . . il seroit seulement à souhaiter qu'il eût moins mis de bleu dans ses lointains.' **Signed Examples** (Brueghel or J. Brueghel): AMSTERDAM *Riverside village* 1604. ANTWERP *Adoration of the Magi* 1600, *River landscape* (*The Ferry*) 1603 (*cf.* Hartford example). AUGSBURG *Landscapes* dated 1597, 1615, 1622. BRUSSELS *Still life* (*vessel with flower garland and box of jewels*) 1618. BUDAPEST *Aeneas in the underworld* 1600 (*cf.* P. B. the younger and P. Schoubroeck). CASSEL *Landscape with village* 1597, *River landscape* 1598, *Winter landscape* 1599 (*cf.* P. B. the elder, L. van Valkenborch, D. v. Alsloot, J. d'Arthois, E. de Bie). DRESDEN *Juno in the underworld* 1592 or 1598, *Temptation of S. Anthony* 1604, *River scene in mountain landscape* 1604, *Port scene with round tower* 1605, *Landscape with sportsmen shooting waterfowl* 1605, *Country road through tall trees with river landscape and many figures* 1605, *Landscape with the calling of SS. Peter and Andrew* 1608, *River landscape with woodcutter* 1608, *Country road with market cart and horse's skeleton and river landscape* 1608, *Plain with two windmills* 1611, *Road through a village* 1611. FRANKFORT *Latona and the peasants* 1601. FLORENCE Uffizi *River landscape* 1607, *Calvary* 1604 (based on a composition by A. Dürer). THE HAGUE *Christ delivering souls from purgatory* 1597; *Adam and Eve in Garden of Eden* (also signed by Rubens 'Petri Pauli Rubens Figr' and recorded by Houbraken 1718). HARTFORD (U.S.A.) Wadsworth Ath. *River landscape* (*The Ferry*) variant of Antwerp example. LENINGRAD *Wooded landscape* 1607. LONDON N.G. *Adoration of the Magi* 1598 ('Brueghel in';

version of Vienna Kunsthist. example). Royal Collection (Windsor) *Village Fair* 1600. MADRID Prado *Landscape with a covered waggon* 1603 (*cf.* J. Grimmer); *The Five Senses: (Sight)* 1617 (Gallery interior (*cf.* Hague Studio of Apelles Painter, W. v. Haecht and H. Staben) with nude allegorical figure recorded as by Rubens), *The Five Senses: (Smell)* (garden scene in mansionpark with flowers growing and in pots, nude allegorical figure recorded as by Rubens; *cf.* Documented examples), *Landscape with wood, animals and gipsies* 1614 (for gipsies *cf.* P. Bruegel the elder, A. Govaerts, A. Grimmer, S. de Vos, G. de Witte), *Wooded landscape outside a village with peasants dancing at a wedding* 1623 (*cf.* P. Bruegel the elder; brought to Spain from Flanders by Isabella of Bourbon, first Queen of Philip IV (*cf.* F. Pourbus the younger); recorded in the King's summer bedroom 1636); MUNICH *Wooded landscape with S. Jerome* 1597, *River scene* 1602, *Landscape with windmills* 1608, *View of a port with Scipio and Allucius* 1609, *Landing place* 1615, *Country road with figures* 1619 and others. PARIS Louvre *Landscape with a windmill* 1600, *The Bridge of Talavera* 1610, *The Air* 1621 (decorative composition with many birds on the ground and on trees; nude allegorical figure presumed by some by H. v. Balen; from series *The Elements* painted for Cardinal Borromeo; taken from Milan Ambrosiana by Napoleon 1796 and not returned; *cf.* Documented examples). STOCKHOLM *Christ preaching in the ship* 1606, *Rural landscape with figures and white horse, distant mountains and port* 1609 (signature indistinct). VIENNA Kunsthist. *The Adoration of the Magi* 1598, *The road to market* 1603, *Landscape with figures symbolising Earth, Air and Water* 1604; Liechtenstein *Landscape with windmill, country road with figures and covered waggons* 1597, *Landscape with Tobias and a hunting party* (*cf.* C. v. d. Broeck, J. v. Scorel, Jacques Savery, J. Massys), 1598, *River landscape with high trees and distant castle* 1604. **Monogrammed Example:** PARIS Louvre *Alexander the Great's victory at the battle of Arbela* (bequeathed to Louis XIV 1693). **Documented Examples:** ANTWERP *Blazon of the Violiere Chamber of Rhetoricians* (in collaboration with H. van Balen, F. Francken II and Sebastian Vrancx; presented by the artists to the Chamber 1618). MILAN Ambrosiana *Water, Fire* (from series *The Elements* painted for Cardinal Borromeo and documented by correspondence; taken Paris by Napoleon and returned 1815; *cf.* Paris examples), *Christ on the Lake of Genesareth* 1595, *Landscape with hermits* 1595 (both painted, with other pictures for Cardinal Borromeo). MADRID Prado *The Five Senses: (Touch, Taste and Hearing)* (from series with allegorical figures recorded as by Rubens; *cf.* Madrid signed examples), *Landscape with serpentine dance of peasant girls before the Archduke Albert and the Infanta Isabella* (*cf.* D. v. Alsloot, A. Sallaert, F. Francken II, and H. Staben); perhaps companion to *Landscape with peasants dancing at a wedding* (*cf.* Madrid signed examples), *Country life* (*Flat landscape with figures and cattle*) several groups of figures and cattle based on Rubens' *Landscape with cattle* in Munich; taken from Flanders to Spain by Isabella of Bourbon; in Madrid Alcázar by 1636). PARIS Louvre *Earth* (or *Earthly Paradise*) (with allegorical figures; from series *The Elements* painted for Cardinal Borromeo; taken from Milan by Napoleon and not returned; *cf.* Paris signed and Milan examples); *The Virgin and Child in a garland of flowers* (figures by Rubens; referred to (1621) in a letter by Brueghel to Cardinal Borromeo; in Milan Ambrosiana till taken by Napoleon 1796). VIENNA Kunsthist. *Bouquet of flowers* (Archduke Leopold Wilhelm inventory 1659). Seventeenth century inventories record landscapes with figures (some in collaboration with J. de Momper), flower pieces, and a *Flower garland round a Virgin and Child by H. van Balen*; the Antwerp collector Alexander Voet owned (1689) a *Quarrel* by him after his father ('Een stuck, crackeelders, van den fluweelen Bruegel, naer den ouden Bruegel, zyn vader) *cf.* P. B. the elder and P. B. the younger; J. B. Anthoine, Antwerp postmaster, whose collection was assessed by J. E. Quellinus *q.v.* and P. v. d. Willigen *q.v.*, owned (1691)

a *Temptation of S. Anthony* and a *Shipping with Antwerp in the distance*, also a *S. John preaching* by him after his father (*cf.* P. B. the elder and P. B. the younger) and a *Peasants' quarrel* by him after his father ('Een boerenstrijt van den Fluweelen Breugel naer zyn vader) *cf.* P. B. the elder and P. B. the younger. The Daybook of his son Jan Brueghel the younger *q.v.* records a *Battle of Sennacherib*, a *Pan and Syrinx* (*cf.* J. Jordaens), a *Diana fishing*, a *S. Jerome in the Desert*, a *Temptation of S. Anthony* (copied by J. B. the younger; *cf.* P.B. the younger) and a copy of a composition *Three figures with a fishing net and fishes*. His son Ambrosius B. *q.v.* records (1639) a *Christ on the Cross*. The Forchoudt firm of Antwerp dealers owned (1672) a *Triumph of Death* by him after his father (*cf.* P. B. the elder) and sent it to their Vienna branch. Houbraken (1718) records and highly praises a large *Flowered garden with a fig tree and Vertumnus and Pomona* the figures by Rubens, and a *Landscape with nymph and satyr* the figures also by Rubens. D'Argenville (1745) records a *Daniel in the lions' den* (*cf.* Vienna Daniel Painter) and *The burning of Sodom and Gemorrah* (*cf.* Brussels Sodom and Gemorrah Painter) both among his pictures in the Ambrosiana Library, a *Battle of Prague*, an *Orpheus in the Underworld* (*cf.* P. B. the younger), and *Woman caressing a dog* among pictures owned by the King of France, and, in the Palais Royal, '*La Transmigration de Babylone*' and a picture '*où il y a beaucoup de poissons*'. Descamps (1753) records a *Baptism of the Eunuch* among thirty-seven pictures owned by the Elector Palatine. Pictures presumed by some his work are in various museums.

[Fl. 559, Fl. 86, Fl. 425, Fl. 22, Fl. 215, Fl. 177, Fl. 107, Fl. 717, Fl. 90, Fl. 602, Fl. 892, Fl. 180, Fl. 212, Fl. 213, Fl. 214, Fl. 133 (1934), Fl. 787, Fl. 16, Fl. 678.]

*****Brueghel, Jan the younger.** Flemish Sch. *b* son of J. (Velvet) Brueghel *q.v.*, Antwerp 1601 *d* Antwerp 1678. *Landscapes, flowers, animals, religious subjects, allegories, battle pieces; copies of his father's pictures; also active as dealer.* Pupil of his father and A. Janssens *q.v.*; went Milan with introduction from his father to Cardinal Federigo Borromeo (*cf.* F. Snyders) 1622; visited Genoa where consorted with his cousin L. de Wael *q.v.* and Van Dyck; went with Van Dyck to Rome (*cf.* Philips de Momper, P. de Lignis, W. Backereel; also F. v. d. Kasteele) 1623; visited Malta and Palermo (*cf.* Van Dyck); left Palermo and went Milan (viâ Genoa) where stayed in Cardinal Borromeo's palace; thence to Turin, Lyons and Paris where met Peter Goetkint the younger (*cf.* P. Goetkint) and returned with him to Antwerp 1625; took over his father's studio; Master in Antwerp Guild 1625; married daughter of A. Janssens (a niece of the dealer Antoon Goetkint) 1626; became an Antwerp agent for his cousin C. van Immerseel, dealer in Seville, and ordered pictures for him from A. Janssens, C de Vos *q.v.*, J. v. Uden *q.v.* and 'de Momper' 1628; had large workshop where produced pictures and copies with assistants including two Germans who were paid by the hour; sent scores of pictures by himself and others to Immerseel (*cf.* J. Boots) 1628-36; quarrelled with one Vermeurs, another Immerseel agent; both agents superseded by A. Cossiers father of J. Cossiers *q.v.* 1636; made arrangements at various times for collaboration with Rubens, A. Janssens, J. de Momper, L. de Wael, H. v. Balen, T. v. Thulden. P. v. Avont, P. Gysels, G. Coques, H. van Kessel, D. Teniers, J. Fouquier, A. v. Diepenbeeck, F. Wouters, C. Cauwer, A. v. Stalbemt and others; patronized by Archduke Leopold Wilhelm (*cf.* J. B. v. Heil, J. v. d. Hoecke, E. Quellinus, J. A. v. d. Baren and D. Teniers the younger) 1651; with Ambrosius B., C. de Baellieur *q.v.*, E. Snayers *q.v.*, F. Francken III and others testified that the request of Jan Cossiers to be allowed to finish his picture for the Malines Béguinage *in situ* was in accordance with common usage 1656; lost an eye in a violent quarrel with one P. v. Breckevelt 1677; had eleven children of whom Jan Peter B. *q.v.*, Abraham B. *q.v.*, Philips B. *q.v.*, Ferdinand B. *q.v.* and Jan Baptiste B. *q.v.* were painters. P. Gysels was among his pupils. Many letters and documents concerning his activities,

and his own Daybooks 1625-51 are preserved. **Signed Examples:** (Brueghel or Breughel): DRESDEN *Landscape with village inn and man with three horses* 1641, *Wooded landscape with hunter and other figures* 1642. VIENNA Kunsthist. *Flora in a garden* (signature, no longer legible, was recorded on it 1796; also signed by P. van Avont *q.v.*). The numerous works recorded in his Daybooks and correspondence include a *Flora by a fountain with figures by van Balen* and a copy of the same, *Flora with figures by A. Janssens, The elements: Fire and Water* (*cf.* J. (Velvet) several sets of *The Five Senses* (*cf.* J. (Velvet) B.) including one set admired by crowds in his studio 1632; *Pan and Syrinx* (*cf.* J. (Velvet) B.), a *Series: The History of Adam* (mainly by himself), *Series of Months: May, June, July and August* (*cf.* P. B. the elder) for Archduke Leopold Wilhelm; a *Battle of Calloo* (*cf.* Bonaventura and Gillis Peeters and P. P. Rubens), and many *Flower garlands*. A letter (1631) to Immerseel refers to pictures which he has just inherited from his stepmother including a *S. Jerome in the Desert* and two others painted just before his death by J. (Velvet) B. for Cardinal Borromeo and not quite finished; these have been sent to Paris to be sold and for copies to be made of them (*cf.* Philips Brueghel and J. M. Picart); he adds that the pictures from his stepmother's collection included some done entirely by J. (Velvet) Brueghel and some done largely by himself which have been sold as by his father (alsoo myn stiefmoeder stervende veel stucen naer liet waer onder ettelyce van syn eygen handt als ooc sommige half meer ofte myn die ic hebbe voldaen ende woorden voor de syne verkocht). The Antwerp postmaster J. B. Anthoine whose collection was assessed on his death (1691) by E. Quellinus *q.v.* and P. v. d. Willigen contained an *Earthly Paradise* by him, G. Coques and J. Fouquier (Een paradys pineel van Gonzael ende Breugel met Fouqueel), and a *Christ with Mary and Martha* (*cf.* H. v. Steenwyck the younger) also in collaboration with G. Coques. Pictures presumed by some his work are in various museums.
[Fl. 177, Fl. 88, Fl. 107, Fl. 602, Fl. 892, Fl. 440, Fl. 715 (1926), Fl. 214, Fl. 678.]

Brueghel, Jan Baptist, called Meleager. Flemish Sch. *b* son of Jan B. the younger, Antwerp 1647 *d* Rome 1719. *Still life with fruit and flowers.* Van Gool (1750) records that he went with his brother Abraham B. *q.v.* to Rome where received his nickname in Flemish artists' colony; also that he worked Naples and was known as Brueghel of Naples; recorded Rome 1700.
[Fl. 353, Fl. 215, Fl. 612, Fl. 107, Fl. 892, Fl. 440, Fl. 798.]

Brueghel, Jan Peter. Flemish Sch. *b* eldest son of Jan B. the younger, Antwerp 1628 *d* Liège or Italy (?) after 1662. *Flowers; and garlands round pictures by other artists* (*cf.* A. and J. B. Brueghel and D. Seghers). Master in Antwerp Guild 1646; worked at one time in Liège with W. Damery *q.v.*
[Fl. 481, Fl. 107, Fl. 892, Fl. 440.]

Brueghel, Philips. Flemish Sch. *b* son of Jan B. the younger, Antwerp 1635 *d* place unknown after 1662. Master Antwerp Guild 1655; sent by his father to Paris to work for three years under his uncle Jan Valdor, engraver and art dealer, 1657; recorded in Antwerp as a painter 1662.
[Fl. 107, Fl. 892, Fl. 214.]

*****Brueghel, Pieter the younger** (known as Hell Brueghel). Flemish Sch. *b* son of P. Bruegel the elder, Brussels 1564 *d* Antwerp 1638. *Religious subjects, hell pieces and conflagrations* (*cf.* H. Bosch, J. (Velvet) Brueghel, P. Huys, L. J. v. d. Bosch, and P. Schoubroeck), *landscapes and genre;* Van Mander (1604) records him as skilful *copyist of his father's pictures.* After death of his father (1569) lived with his grandmother Marie Bessemers (?) *q.v.*; then Antwerp; presumed by some pupil of P. Goetkint *q.v.*; Van Mander records him pupil of G. van Coninxloo *q.v.*; Master Antwerp Guild (when van Coninxloo

had left Antwerp as a Protestant) 1585; remained Antwerp; had seven children one of whom Pieter B. III *q.v.* was a painter; had financial difficulties and sold his share in his grandmother's property to his brother J. (Velvet) Brueghel 1612; may have collaborated with A. van Stalbemt *q.v.* and J. de Momper; F. Snyders was his pupil. Van Dyck drew his portrait (engraved as 'pictor ruralium prospectuum'). **Signed Examples** (P. Brueghel or Breughel): AMSTERDAM *Adoration of the Magi* (*snow scene*) (version without snowflakes of picture by 'vieil Brugel' recorded owned by the banker Jabach 1695; *cf.* P. Bruegel the elder). ANTWERP *The road to Calvary* 1603 (*cf.* Copenhagen example), *The blind leading the blind* (two figures; variant of two front figures in picture by P. B. the elder), *The Misanthrope* (variant of picture by P. B. the elder). Some pictures in Antwerp signed P. Breughel are presumed by some by P. Breughel III. AUGSBURG *Village fair* 1616. BERLIN *Peasants quarrelling in a landscape.* BRUNSWICK *Nero and the burning of Rome.* BRUSSELS *The Massacre of the Innocents* (after P. B. the elder), *The numbering at Bethlehem* 1610 (after P. B. the elder). COPENHAGEN *The road to Calvary* (variant of Antwerp example). DUBLIN N.G. Ireland *Peasant wedding with guests bringing money* 1620 ('P. Breghel'; related to Van Mander's description of a picture by P. B. the elder). FLORENCE Uffizi *The road to Calvary* 1599 (variant of Antwerp and Copenhagen examples), *Dante and Virgil in the Underworld* 1594 (*cf.* J. (Velvet) B.). HAARLEM *The Blue Cape (Proverb)* ('P. Breugel. F.' after P. B. the elder). MADRID Prado *Winter landscape with skaters* (after a picture by P. B. the elder; *cf.* Vienna Kunsthist. example). MONTPELLIER *Peasants quarrelling over cards* 1620 (related to a picture of this subject by P. B. the elder, recorded by an engraving; *cf.* New York example and J. (Velvet) Brueghel). NARBONNE *Wooded landscape with dancing peasants* 1620. NEW YORK Met. *Peasants quarrelling over cards* 1619. ('P. Bruegel' *cf.* Montpellier example), *The Whitsun Bride.* PHILADELPHIA (Johnson) *Christ and the adulteress.* VIENNA Kunsthist. *Winter landscape with skaters* (*cf.* Madrid example); Liechtenstein *Triumph of Death* 1597 ('Bruegel'; variant of picture by Madrid Triumph of Death Painter *q.v.*; a picture so titled was recorded in an Antwerp inventory as by J. (Velvet) Brueghel *q.v.* 'after oude Bruegel' *cf.* P. B. the elder also J. (Velvet) B.); *S. John preaching in the wilderness* 1620 (copy with some changes of picture by his father; *cf.* P. B. the elder and J. (Velvet) B.). The signature 'Brueghel 1618' on a *Return of David with the head of Goliath* (*cf.* J. B. Saive) also signed by A. van Stalbemt *q.v.* in Madrid Prado is presumed his. The Antwerp collector P. v. Valckenisse owned 1614 a '*Winterken*' and a '*Boerenkermisse*' and pictures titled *Massacre of the Innocents, Children's games, Peasants' wedding, S. John preaching in the wilderness* and *The Blue Cape (Proverb)* (*cf.* P. B. the elder) all as by 'helschen Bruegel'; Susanna Willemsens, widow of an Antwerp cloth and silk merchant and dealer, owned (1657) a *Peasant dance;* Abraham van Lamoen, Dean of the Antwerp Old Cloth Merchants' Guild (*cf.* C. Cauwer) owned (1661) a *Shepherd;* other 17th cent. Antwerp inventories record a *Hurdygurdy player* and a *Numbering at Bethlehem.* D'Argenville (1745) writes; 'Il a peint chez le Grand Duc *Orphée jouant de la lire devant Pluton et Proserpine assis sur leur trône*' (*cf.* Florence Uffizi examples and J. (Velvet) B.) 'et *La tentation de S. Antoine avec un beau paisage*' (*cf.* J. (Velvet) B.).
[Fl. 559, Fl. 48, Fl. 22, Fl. 602, Fl. 120, Fl. 892, Fl. 13, Fl. 304, Fl. 212, Fl. 213, Fl. 345, Fl. 615, Fl. 16, Fl. 678.]

Brueghel, Pieter III. Flemish Sch. *b* son of P. Brueghel the younger *q.v.*, Antwerp 1589 *d* Antwerp (?) after 1634 (?). *Religious subjects, genre, proverbs in tradition of P. B. the elder and the younger.* Master Antwerp Guild 1608; G. Coques *q.v.* was his pupil. The following pictures signed P. Breughel are presumed by some his work: Antwerp *Three proverbs* (tondos), *Flemish fair, Adoration of the Magi, Wedding pro-*

cession, Massacre of the Innocents. Innsbruck *Peasant dance round a maypole* 1634. [Fl. 892, Fl. 13, Fl. 16.]

*Bruges Baptism of Christ Painter. Presumed Flemish Sch. 15th/16th cent. Name for painter of BRUGES Mus. (35-39) Triptych: centre: *Baptism of Christ, with S. John preaching in the wilderness* (*cf.* J. Patinir and P. Bruegel the elder); wings: *Donor Jean des Trompes with son and patron saint S. John the Evangelist: Elizabeth, first wife of J. de Trompes with four daughters and patron saint S. Elizabeth of Hungary;* exterior wings: *Virgin and Child; Madeleine second wife of J. des Trompes with daughter and patron saint S. Mary Magdalene,* presented to Bruges: S. Basile in 1520. Presumed by some identical with G. David *q.v.*

*Bruges Birth of the Virgin Painter. Presumed Flemish Sch. 16th cent. Name for painter of BRUGES Mus. (219) *Birth of the Virgin* (from Dixmude: S. Nicolas; centre of triptych of which Bruges (220) *Meeting of Joachim and Anne* from Dixmude S. Nicolas is the left wing). [Fl. 113, Fl. 114.]

Bruges *c* 1520 Master. Presumed Flemish Sch. 16th cent. Name for painter of ANTWERP Mus. (531) *Donor Abbot R. de Clercq,* exterior of panel Antwerp (530) by Bruges 1499 Master *q.v.* From Bruges Abbaye des Dunes where R. de Clercq was Abbot from 1519. [Fl. 13, Fl. 16.]

*Bruges Death and the Miser Painter. Presumed Flemish Sch. 15th/16th cent. Name for painter of BRUGES Mus. (218) *Compact between death and the miser.* Presumed by some identical with Jan Provoost *q.v.*

Bruges 1500 Master. Earlier name for Bruges Passion Scenes Master *q.v.*

Bruges 1499 Master. Presumed Flemish Sch. 15th cent. Name for painter of ANTWERP Mus. (255, 256, 530) *Virgin and Child in a church,* exterior: *Salvator Mundi* 1499; *Donor, Abbot C. de Hondt with a little dog.* From Bruges Abbaye des Dunes. Paintings presumed by some his work are in various museums (*cf.* Bruges *c.* 1520 Master). [Fl. 13, Fl. 316.]

Bruges Passion Scenes Master. Presumed Flemish Sch. 16th cent. Name for painter of BRUGES S. Sauveur *Scenes from the Passion* (*Christ carrying the Cross, Crucifixion, Deposition*). A metal panel nailed to the frame bears an inscription 'Meeren 1500' presumed by some to be false (*cf.* G. v. d. Meire). Presumed by some identical with London Passion Scenes Painter *q.v.* (*Cf.* also Bruges 1500 Master). [Fl. 316, Fl. 550.]

*Bruges Virgin with the Apple Painter. Presumed Flemish Sch. 15th cent. Name for painter of BRUGES Hôpital Saint Jean *Virgin and Child* (*with Nieuwenhove* arms) 1487. Left hand panel of a diptych with the arms of the donor Martin van Nieuwenhove in the window. Inscribed on original frame 'Hoc opus fieri fecit Martinus D. Newenhoven. anno D. M. 1487'. The donor's age, 23, is recorded on the frame of the right hand panel (also in Bruges Hôpital Saint Jean), which shows his portrait as adorant. Donated to Bruges Hospice de Saint Julien of which the donor was a guardian. Presumed by some identical with H. Memlinc *q.v.*

Brunin (Leon de Meutter) known as. Flemish Sch. *b* Antwerp 1861. *Genre, interiors, still life.* Began as a sculptor; pupil in Antwerp Academy; then of C. Verlat; member Als ik kan group (founded by H. Luyten *q.v.* 1885); visited Holland; teacher in Antwerp Academy; exhibited Paris Salon. Represented in ANTWERP *Meditation* 1891, *The geographer* 1891, *A fine blade, The restorer.* Pictures titled *Rembrandt painting* (*cf.* J. Senave), *Benvenuto Cellini* and *A sculptor's studio* are recorded. [Fl. 465, Fl. 73, Fl. 17.]

Brunswick Diptych Master. Presumed Flemish (Dutch) Sch. 15/16th cent. Name for painter of BRUNSWICK Mus. (13) *Virgin and Child with S. Anne, Carthusian monk as donor with female saint* (with *S. Bavo* on reverse). Pictures presumed by some his work are in various museums. [Fl. 316.]

Brunswick Monogrammist. Presumed Flemish or Flemish (Dutch) Sch. 16th cent. Name for painter of BRUNSWICK Mus. *Feeding of the Poor* signed with unidentified monogram. Paintings presumed by some his work are in various museums. [Fl. 358, Fl. 892, Fl. 316, Fl. 798.]

Bruselas, A. de, see **Wyngaerde.**

Brusselmans, Jean. Flemish Sch. *b* Brussels 1884. *Landscapes, marines, figure pieces, still life in Post Impressionist conventions; also engravings.* Pupil in Brussels Acad.; then studied Paris. Represented in ANTWERP *Sunny landscape, Snow landscape, Flower piece.* BRUSSELS *In the Garden* 1916. IXELLES *Still life.* [Fl. 388, Fl. 393, Fl. 568, Fl. 296.]

*Brussels Haneton Lamentation Painter. Presumed Flemish Sch. 16th cent. Name for painter of BRUSSELS Mus. (559) Triptych: centre: *Lamentation,* wings: *Philippe Haneton and his seven sons with patron saint S. Philip; Margaret, wife of Philippe Haneton and her five daughters with patron saint S. Margaret;* exterior wings: (grisaille) *Annunciation.* From Brussels S. Gudule. Presumed by some identical with B. v. Orley *q.v.*

*Brussels Icarus Painter. Presumed Flemish Sch. 16th cent. Name for painter of BRUSSELS Mus. (800) *Landscape with fall of Icarus.* Presumed by some identical with P. Bruegel the Elder *q.v.* (*cf.* also H. Bol).

*Brussels Kitchen Scene Painter. Presumed Flemish Sch. 16th cent. Name for painter of BRUSSELS Mus. (2) *Kitchen scene with cook and boy* presumed by some identical with P. Aertsen *q.v.*

*Brussels Man with a Rosary Painter. Presumed Flemish Sch. 15th/16th cent. Name for painter of BRUSSELS Mus. (538) *Man with a rosary and Tiburtine Sibyl* (*cf.* Tiburtine Sibyl Master and G. Rem). Presumed by some identical with J. Mostaert *q.v.*

*Brussels Micault Triptych Painter. Presumed Flemish Sch. 16th cent Name for painter of BRUSSELS Mus. (493) Triptych: centre: *Raising of Lazarus,* wings: *Jean Micault (Receiver General of the Emperor Charles V) and his three sons, Wife of Jean Micault and her four daughters with Segovia* (?) *aqueduct in background*); exterior wings: (grisaille) *Christ with Mary and Martha* (*cf.* P. Aertsen). From Micault family altar in Brussels S. Gudule. Presumed by some identical with J. C. Vermeyen *q.v.*

*Brussels Mystic Marriage Painter. Presumed Flemish Sch. 15th cent. Name for painter of BRUSSELS Mus. (545) *Mystic marriage of S. Catherine* (*Virgo inter Virgines*) Painted for the Bruges Confrérie des Trois Saintes (Bruges Notre Dame) 1489. Presumed by some identical with Lucy Legend Master *q.v.* (*Cf.* also Catherine (Mystic Marriage) Master). [Fl. 120, Fl. 892.]

*Brussels Piper Painter. Presumed Flemish Sch. 16th cent. Name for painter of BRUSSELS Mus. (676) *Bagpiper and woman.* Presumed by some identical with P. Huys *q.v.* and by others with J. S. v. Hemessen *q.v.* [Fl. 120, Fl. 124.]

*Brussels Prodigal Son Painter. Presumed Flemish Sch. 16th cent. Name for painter of BRUSSELS Mus. (34) *The Prodigal Son* (monogrammed Hb) (*cf.* Prodigal Son Master,

P. C. van Ryck and S. Vrancx). Presumed by some identical with J. Beuckelaer *q.v.* and by others referred to as Monogrammist Hb. [Fl. 120, Fl. 124.]

*Brussels Sodom and Gemorrah Painter.** Presumed Flemish Sch. 16th/17th cent. Name for painter of BRUSSELS Mus. (750) *Destruction of Sodom and Gomorrah.* (*cf.* L. J. v. d. Bosch, J. (Velvet) Brueghel, P. Schoubroeck, F. v. Oosten, F. and G. van Valkenborch). Presumed by some identical with G. Mostaert *q.v.* [Fl. 124.]

*Brussels Virgin with a Milk Bowl Painter.** Presumed Flemish Sch. 16th cent. Name for painter of BRUSSELS (666) *Virgin and Child with a bowl of milk.* Presumed by some identical with G. David *q.v.*

*Brussels Young Knight Painter.** Presumed Flemish Sch. 15th cent. Name for painter of BRUSSELS Mus. (720) *Young knight of the Golden Fleece.* Presumed by some identical with J. Gossaert *q.v.* and by others with the Magdalene Legend Master *q.v.* [Fl. 120, Fl. 121, Fl. 124.]

Brussels Zierickzee Master. Presumed Flemish Sch. 15th/16th cent. Name for painter of BRUSSELS Mus. (557) Triptych: centre: *Last Judgement,* wings: *Philip the Fair, Joanna the Mad,* exterior wings: (grisaille) *SS. Livin and Martin* from Zierickzee Hôtel de Ville. Presumed by some identical with Abbey of Afflighem Master *q.v.* [Fl. 120, Fl. 316, Fl. 124.]

Bruycker, Constant de. Flemish Sch. *b* Ghent 1823 *d* Ghent 1896. *Costume genre (especially 17th cent. scenes of cavaliers on horseback at inn doors).* Associated with a stained glass factory in Ghent. Represented in GHENT Library: Drawings and sketches. [Fl. 440.]

Bruycker, Frans Antoon de. Flemish Sch. *b* Ghent 1816 *d* Ghent 1882. *Genre and flower pieces.* Pupil in Ghent Academy and in Antwerp of F. de Braekeleer. Represented in ANTWERP *Afternoon coffee;* LEIPZIG and STUTTGART. Pictures titled *Waiting* 1851, *The lace maker* 1845 and *Young girls playing forfeits* are recorded. [Fl. 451, Fl. 440, Fl. 17.]

Bruycker, Jules de. Flemish Sch. *b* Ghent 1870 *d* Ghent 1945. *Contemporary genre, satirical and fantastic compositions, town and street scenes* (mainly in *w.*); *also engravings.* Pupil in Ghent Acad. of L. Tytgadt; teacher in Antwerp Higher Institute; described (1945) as 'à l'heure actuelle, avec James Ensor *q.v.* le plus grand aquafortiste de l'école Belge'. Represented in ANTWERP (Drawing). BRUSSELS *Preparing for the Friday market.* GHENT *The wood engraver, F. Masereel.* Illustrated C. de Coster's *Uylenspiegel* 1922. Pictures titled *Street sweepers, Ghent market* and *Damme Fair* (1907) are recorded. [Fl. 440, Fl. 296, Fl. 17.]

Bruyn, Theodor de. Flemish Sch. *b* Amsterdam (or Antwerp 1726? or Switzerland?) *d* London 1804. *Landscapes (some with cattle and others with views of mansions and parks, cf.* P. Tillemans); *allegorical groups in grisaille imitating sculpture* (*cf.* M. J. Geeraerts, A. M. van Reysschoot and F. Eisen). Pupil in Antwerp of N. v. d. Bergh *q.v.* 1753; Master Antwerp Guild 1758; citizen Antwerp 1759; Dean Antwerp Guild 1765; may have worked in Paris *c.* 1767 (*cf.* G. de Pélichy and J. B. Suvée); came London where living in Castle Street, Cavendish Square from 1769; exhibited Society of Artists, Free Society and Royal Academy; painted grisaille panels for Greenwich Hospital chapel. An H. and a John de B. exhibited portraits and drawings from the same address; a son was a student in the Academy Schools in 1804. Grisaille compositions titled *Allegory of Painting* and *Allegory of Sculpture* (painted for the Duke of Norfolk at Worksop Manor) and *Bacchanalian groups* were in the Free Society 1769, 1770 and 1771. Pictures titled *Views of the Mansion of Paris Hill, seat*

of *B. Bond Hopkins Esq.* (1790-1791), *View of Donnington Park, Leicestershire* (1799) and *View in Holland* (1788) and a number of landscapes were among his R.A. exhibits 1773-1803. [Fl. 612, Fl. 695, Fl. 223, Fl. 361, Fl. 362, Fl. 440.]

Bruyne (or Brun), Chrétien de. Flemish Sch. *b* Malines (?) before 1545 *d* Malines (?) after 1576. *Decorative paintings including processional banners; also restorations of pictures* (*cf.* L. Blondeel). Paid for restoring pictures in the Palais du Grand Conseil at Malines 1560; assisted Raphael Coxie *q.v.* in a painting commissioned 1571; recorded painting coats of arms 1576. [Fl. 613, Fl. 892, Fl. 440.]

Bruyne, Gustave de. Flemish Sch. *b* Malines 1914. *Landscapes and illustrations.* Pupil in Malines Acad. and in Antwerp of G. v. d. Woestyne. Teacher in Antwerp Acad. Represented in ANTWERP *July.* [Fl. 17.]

Bruyns (Bruns), Anna Françoise de. Flemish Sch. *b* Brussels (?) 1605 *d* after 1629 *Portraits, religious subjects.* Pupil of her uncle J. Francart; presented by Francart to the Infanta Isabella; married I. Bullart (author of L'Académie des Sciences et des Arts); went (?) with I. Bullart to Arras 1629. Houbraken (1718) records her as the best woman painter of her time (*cf.* G. v. Veen and M. Wautier also M. Bessemers). A *Portrait of J. Francart* 1622 is recorded by an engraving; a series *The fifteen Mysteries of the Rosary* commissioned by the Infanta as a present for the Pope (*cf.* J. Francart) is recorded by C. Weyerman (1749). [Fl. 425, Fl. 878, Fl. 892, Fl. 88, Fl. 440.]

*Buckingham Palace Mystic Marriage Painter.** Presumed Flemish Sch. 15th cent. Name for painter of LONDON Royal Collection: Buckingham Palace *Mystic marriage of S. Catherine (Virgo inter Virgines).* Presumed by some identical with the Lucy Legend Master *q.v.* [Fl. 736.]

Bueckelaer, J., see **Beuckelaer.**

Buisseret, Louis. Flemish Sch. *b* Binche (Hainault) 1888. *Compositions, portraits, still life.* Pupil in Brussels Academy Bergen. Represented in ANTWERP *Hellas.* [Fl. 17.]

*Buken (Beucken), Jan van.** Flemish Sch. *b* Antwerp 1635 *d* Antwerp 1694. *Market scenes* (*cf.* E. de Bie, P. v. Bredael, J. Broers, P. Gysels, N. Spalthof also S. Vrancx), *still life* (*cf.* T. Aenvanck, J. v. Es and C. Mahu). In Antwerp Guild (as Beucken) 1658; visited Italy. **Signed Examples:** SCHWERIN *Kitchen piece.* STOCKHOLM *Italian market with actors on a stage* (*cf.* A. v. d. Meulen, P. Bout and P. Spierinckx). [Fl. 107, Fl. 892, Fl. 440.]

Bundel, Willem van den. Flemish Sch. *b* Brussels 1577 *d* Delft 1655. *Landscapes* (*cf.* J. (Velvet) Brueghel). In Amsterdam 1600; in Delft 1623-1639; the Hague 1642. He had a son, also a painter, of the same name. **Signed Example:** AMSTERDAM Rijks. *Wooded landscape with horseman and peasants near a village* 1623. [Fl. 481, Fl. 631 (1890 and 1920), Fl. 892, Fl. 8.]

Burgh, Jacques van der. Flemish Sch. 18th cent. *Landscapes with figures.* Descamps (1768) saw in Lille Jacobins eight landscapes with figures; in Lille Dominicans nine large *landscapes* ('il y a quelque mérite pour la couleur, le reste est foible') and in Tournai Abbaye de S. Martin *landscapes with S. Benedict, S. Ambrose, and the Flight into Egypt* ('le paysage est largement fait et d'une bonne couleur'). [Fl. 216.]

Buschmann, Gustave (François Gustave). Flemish Sch. *b* Antwerp 1818 *d* Antwerp 1852. *Illustrative genre and religious subjects.* Pupil of I. J. v. Regemorter and F. de Braekeleer the elder. Pictures representing *Scenes from the Vicar of Wake-*

field and *Scenes from the novels of Walter Scott* are recorded. Religious pictures for churches in S. Nicolas and other towns in Flanders are also recorded.

[Fl. 451, Fl. 88, Fl. 892, Fl. 440.]

Bussche, Joseph Emmanuel van den. *b* Antwerp 1837 *d* Boitsfort (near Brussels) 1908. *Costume history compositions, also panoramas and dioramas* (*cf.* P. v. Engelen, L. v. Engelen, C. Verlat, R. Mols and P. Mathieu). Pupil in Antwerp Acad. of N. de Keyser; won Rome prize 1863; professor of perspective in Antwerp Acad. 1872; and in Antwerp Higher Institute 1886; commissioned by Government to paint series of large mural paintings *The circulation of letters through the ages* for Brussels Post Office 1896; chevalier of the Order of Leopold. Retrospective exhibition in Brussels 1909. A very large picture *The last of the Romans* (*c.* 1864) is recorded.

[Fl. 440.]

Buyle, Robert. Flemish Sch. *b* S. Nicolas (East Flanders) 1895. *Landscapes, figures, nudes, interiors, genre, still life; book illustrations.* Exhibited Paris (Salon d'Automne and Salon des Indépendants). Represented in ANTWERP *Corn, Bar interior.* NAMUR.

[Fl. 465, Fl. 17.]

Buys, Cornelis the elder. Flemish (Dutch Sch. *b* Alkmaar (?) before 1500 *d* Alkmaar (?) after 1519. *Religious subjects and decorative painting.* Van Mander (1604) records him a brother of J. Cornelisz van Oostanen *q.v.* A. Buchelius (*c.*1585) records him as first master of J. Scorel *q.v.* (*cf.* W. Cornelisz); worked in Alkmaar S. Laurentius (built 1470-98) 1516-19 (*cf.* Alkmaar Master, M. v. Heemskerck, and C.Buys the younger).

[Fl. 127, Fl. 559, Fl. 892, Fl. 631 (1930), Fl. 421.]

Buys, Cornelis the younger. Flemish (Dutch) Sch. *b* son of C. B. the elder, Alkmaar date unknown *d* Alkmaar 1546. Nephew of J. Cornelisz van Oostsanen *q.v. Landscapes with religious subjects.* Recorded as concerned in negotiations between M. v. Heemskerck *q.v.* and Alkmaar S. Laurentius (*cf.* C. Buys the elder) 1541. Amsterdam Rijks. has (666) *Meeting of Elieser and Rebecca at the well* (*cf.* C. v. d. Broeck and Dublin Penelope Painter) with monogram resembling that of J. Cornelisz van Oostsanen and C. B., presumed by some his work.

[Fl. 892, Fl. 7.]

Buys, Cornelis III. Flemish Sch. *b* Alkmaar (?) before 1522 *d* Antwerp (?) after 1560. *Religious subjects.* A *S. Paul holding a sword, behind a table with an open book* (signed Cornelius Buys 1560) in Venloo church is recorded.

[Fl. 892, Fl. 133 (1907).]

Buysse, Georges. Flemish Sch. *b* Ghent 1864 *d* Ghent 1916. *Landscapes* (*in Impressionist conventions*). Brother of the novelist C. Buysse and brother-in-law of A. Baertsoen. Pupil in Ghent of L. Tytgadt; also of J. Delvin and E. Claus; Member of 'Libre Esthétique' (which included A. Baertsoen, H. Evenepoel, A. J. Heymans, J. Montigny, F. Khnopff, T. v. Rysselberghe) 1900; founder member of 'Vie et Lumière' (*cf.* G. Morren); member Paris Salon de la Nationale and exhibitor also at Paris Salon d'Automne; had all his life an interest in an industrial firm. Represented in ANTWERP *Winter storm.* BARCELONA *September* 1904. BRUSSELS *Moonrise* 1900. GHENT *Red sail, Wondelgem church, Ghent canal* and nine others. PARIS State Collection.

[Fl. Bib. 19th cent. Fl. 178, Fl. 592, Fl. 388, Fl. 465.]

C

Caisne, (or **Decaisne**) **Henri de.** Flemish Sch. *b* Brussels 1799 *d* Paris 1852. *Costume history, allegories, religious subjects, genre, portraits.* Pupil in Brussels of P. J. François and helped by L. David (*cf.* H. Coene, M. G. Stapleaux, J. Paelinck and F. J. Navez); went Paris where pupil of A. L. Girodet 1819 and Baron Gros (*cf.* F. Simonau) 1820-3; remained Paris where exhibited Salons 1824-52; exhibited London R.A.: visited Italy and Holland; Inspecteur des musées nationaux in Paris 1848. His work was praised in the Revue des Deux Mondes by Alfred de Musset. Represented in AMIENS *Maternal joys.* ANTWERP *Mater Dolorosa* 1834, *The Guardian Angel* 1852, *Countess H.* BRUSSELS *Belgium crowning her illustrious children* (18 feet by 15 feet) 1837, *Giotto drawing the sheep* (*cf.* P. Kremer) 1839, *Self portrait* 1852. THE HAGUE *Venetian concert.* PARIS Luxembourg *Ceiling. Religious subjects* in N. D. de Lorette, S. Pierre de Gros Caillou and other Paris churches. VERSAILLES *Death of Louis XIII* 1831, *Entry of Charles VII into Rouen* 1838; *Institution of the Order of S. John of Jerusalem* 1842 and others. Pictures titled *Charles I taking leave of his children* 1829, *Milton dictating Paradise Lost to his daughter* 1828 and portraits *Alphonse de Lamartine* 1839, *The Queen of the Belgians* and *Madame Malibran Garcia as Desdemona* (London R.A. 1830) are recorded.
[Fl. 451, Fl. 612, Fl. 66, Fl. 126, Fl. Bib. 19th cent. Fl. 361, Fl. 296.]

Calcar, Jan Joest van, see **Joest.**

Calcar, Jan Stephen van (Giovanni di Calcker). Flemish Sch. *b* Calcar (Cleves) 1499 *d* Naples between 1546 and 1550. *Portraits and anatomical drawings.* Van Mander records (1604) that he left the Netherlands with a girl from Dordrecht whose parents kept an inn where travellers disappeared (een moord-herberg), that he took her to Italy *c.* 1537, knew there M. van Heemskerck *q.v.* and remained there (*cf.* J. van der Straet). Vasari (1550) records him as a pupil of Titian in Venice (*cf.* D. Barendsz and L. Toeput also H. Staben), as a wonderful portraitist (nei ritratti maraviglioso) who so successfully practised the Italian manner that his works were not recognised as those of a Fleming, and as the author of eleven engraved studies illustrating the anatomical writings of Andreas Vesalius; Vasari met him in Naples (*cf.* C. Pyp and A. Mytens) 1545, became his close friend and records that he died there. Van Mander records that the engraver Hendrik Goltzius (1558-1614) mistook portraits in Naples by C. for works by Titian and was told by local artists that all connoisseurs made the same error. **Signed Examples:** None. **Documented Examples:** None. Vienna K. (217) *Portrait of a bearded man* was recorded his work in Archduke Leopold Wilhelm's inventory 1659; J. B. Cachiopin, an Antwerp nobleman, owned a *Man's portrait* recorded in the inventory of his collection 1662; Paris Louvre has *Portrait of Melchior van Brauweiler* 1540 recorded as his work in 1683 (Glasgow has a replica). The anatomical drawings referred to by Vasari were published 1538-43 before Vesalius, condemned by the Inquisition to be burned alive as a sorcerer, made the pilgrimage to Jerusalem to which the sentence, at the instance of Philip II, was commuted (*cf.* G. Coxie).
[Fl. 818, Fl. 559, Fl. 892, Fl. 213, Fl. 530.]

Calvaert, Denys (known in Italy as **Dionisio Fiammingo**). Flemish Sch. *b* Antwerp *c.* 1540 *d* Bologna 1619. *Landscapes, religious subjects and 'history'.* Pupil in Antwerp of C. van den Queborne *q.v.* 1556; went Italy and remained there (*cf.* J. van der Straet); worked in Bologna under Prospero Fontana and then L. Sabbatini whom he accompanied to Rome, *c.* 1570, and assisted in Vatican Sala Regia (*Battle of Lepanto*) fresco (*cf.* P. de Witte) 1572-3; returned Bologna *c.* 1574 and directed there successful art school where his pupils (whom he bullied and cuffed) included the Italians F. Albani, Domenichino and Guido Reni; many of his pupils migrated to the art school of the Carracci. **Signed Examples:** GÖTSCHWILER *Descent from the Cross* 1609. ROME Capitoline Mus. (Palazzo die Conservatori) *Mystic marriage of S. Catherine* 1590. SAN LORENZO (Piacenza prov.) S. Lorenzo *Martyrdom of S. Lawrence* 1583. ZUG Capuchin church *Entombment* 1595. **Documented Examples:** (recorded by 17th cent. writers) include BOLOGNA Pinacoteca *Noli me tangere* from S. Maria Maddalena, *Flagellation* from S. Leonardo, *Moses and the Burning Bush* from demolished church S. Trinita; also works in Corpus Domini, S. Domenico (*Annunciation*), S. Maria dei Bulgari (*Annunciation* 1582), SS. Gregorio e Siro, S. Maria dei Servi (*Paradise* and *S. Onophrius* 1602), S. Maria della Vita (*S. Ursula* from S. Trinita), S. Petronio and IMOLA *Purgatory* from Bologna Mad. delle Grazie. Other paintings are recorded by engravings; small religious subjects on copper, painted for individual cells in Bolognese convents are also recorded.
[Fl. 557, Fl. 558, Fl. 642, Fl. 892, Fl. 305, Fl. 74, Fl. 75, Fl. 678.]

Cambier, Juliette (née **Ziane**). Flemish Sch. *b* Brussels 1879. *Landscapes, figures, still life.* Pupil of her husband L. G. Cambier and in Paris of the French painter Maurice Denis. Represented in ANTWERP *Flowerpiece.* [Fl. 17.]

Cambier, Louis Gustave. Flemish Sch. *b* Brussels 1874. *Landscapes, interiors, genre, portraits, occasional religious subjects, still life; also worked as sculptor.* Pupil Brussels Acad. of J. Portaels. Travelled France, Italy, Palestine and Near East. Member of Société des Artistes Français. Represented in BRUGES *The Golden Horn* (Constantinople) 1905. BRUSSELS *Russian pilgrims in Jerusalem* 1904. GHENT, LIÈGE and Belgian Royal Collection. [Fl. 114, Fl. 296.]

*Cambridge Veronica Draughtsman. Presumed Flemish Sch. 15th cent. Name for author of CAMBRIDGE Fitzwilliam *S. Veronica* drawing. Presumed by some identical with Flémalle Master *q.v.*

Camp, Camille van. Flemish Sch. *b* of rich family, Tongres 1834 *d* Montreux 1891. *Costume history, portraits, genre, animals; also worked as engraver and illustrator.* Pupil of F. J. Navez; friend and generous helper of H. Boulenger; member of Soc. libre des Beaux-Arts (*cf.* L. Dubois, L. Speeckaert and E. Lambrichs who included his portrait in his group picture of the members) 1868; a founder of the review L'Art Libre; and contributor to the London *Illustrated London News.* Represented in ANTWERP *Mme. van Camp.* BRUSSELS *Maria of Burgundy's fall from her horse 1482* 1878.
[Fl. 296, Fl. Bib. 19th cent.]

Campaña, P. de, see **Kempener.**

Campin, Robert. Flemish Sch. *b* place unknown *c.* 1378 *d* Tournai 1444. Working Tournai from 1406; received freedom of city 1410; Master Tournai Guild *c.* 1410 (?); J. de Stoevere

was his pupil from 1416; held offices in Guild 1423-8;
Jacques Daret *q.v.* was a member of his household from 1418
and his pupil 1427-32; Rogelet v. d. Weyden *q.v.* was also his
pupil 1427-32; other pupils (of whom nothing is known) were
'Haquin de Blandain' (1426) and 'Willemet' (1427); was fined,
sentenced to make a pilgrimage to S. Gilles en Provence, and
debarred from civic office 1429; banished for a year 'pour la
vie ordurière et dissolue qu'il menait depuis longtemps, lui,
homme marié, avec Laurence Polette' but sentence commuted
to fine at instance of Jacqueline of Bavaria, Countess of
Hainault and ex-Duchess of Gloucester, 1432; made cartoons
of *Scenes from the life of S. Peter* 1438. **Signed Examples:**
None. **Documented Examples:** None. Presumed by some
identical with Flémalle Master *q.v.* and/or Mérode Master *q.v.*
[Fl. 892, Fl. 316, Fl. 530.]

Candido, Pietro, see **Witte.**

Canneel, Théodore Joseph. Flemish Sch. *b* Ghent 1817 *d* Ghent
1892. *Religious subjects, murals (cf.* J. Swerts), *costume history,
genre, portraits.* Pupil in Ghent Acad. of P. van Hanselaere
q.v. 1838; Professor 1843; visited Rome and other Italian
cities 1848-50; director Ghent Acad. 1850-92; Inspector of
Belgian Academies and Art schools 1869. F. Cogen and F.
Willaert were among his pupils. Represented in ANTWERP
Studies for Ghent S. Anne murals; Self portrait. GHENT *Jan
Steen and Margareta van Goyen (cf.* P. Kremer), *Charles V
and Johanna v. d. Gheenst by the cradle of their child*; S. Anne
church *Scenes from the life of Christ* murals 1862-92 (completed by T. Lybaert). A *Cain after the murder of Abel* 1838
and a *Scene from the life of Van Dyck (cf.* G. Wappers) 1841
are recorded.
[Fl. 11 (1894), Fl. 160 (1892), Fl. 892, Fl. Bib. 19th cent.]

Cantelbeeck, Hendrick. Flemish Sch. 18th cent. Pupil in
Antwerp of J. van Hal 1709; Master Antwerp Guild 1717.
[Fl. 714.]

Cap, Constant Aimé Marie. Flemish Sch. *b* S. Nicolas (East
Flanders) 1842 *d* Antwerp 1915. *Anecdotic genre (including
scenes from daily life, many in drawing rooms and trains); old
Antwerp picturesque corners and interiors.* Pupil in Antwerp
Acad.; won gold medal at London Crystal Palace Exhibition
1873; Chevalier of the Order of Leopold 1881. Represented in
ANTWERP *Elegant company watching from a drawing room
window the Royal procession in the Fêtes Nationales 1880* 1880
(cf. L. H. Hendrickx). BELGIAN ROYAL COLLECTION
La Saint-Nicolas 1881. [Fl. 440, Fl. 17.]

Caracca, see **Kraek.**

Cardon, Antoine Alexandre Joseph. Flemish Sch. *b* Brussels
1739 *d* Brussels 1822. *Town views (?), portraits (?), contemporary history (?); but chiefly active as engraver.* Went Vienna
where pupil of H. de La Pegnia *q.v.*; sent Rome with stipend
from the Empress Maria Theresa; thence to Naples where
left painting for engraving *c.* 1763; returned Brussels 1769;
patronized by Count de Cobenzl *(cf.* L. Legendre) and the
Duke of Arenberg; Professor Brussels Acad. and member of
Institut Royal des Pays Bas. His engravings include *Views of
Naples* (1764), plates for Sir William Hamilton's *Etruscan,
Greek and Roman Antiquities* (1765) and *The Emperor Joseph
II* after W. J. Herreyns *q.v.*; and an original composition *Fête
donnée dans le Parc de Schoonenberg à Laeken par leurs
Altesses Royales les Gouverneurs Généraux des Pays Bas
(Marie-Christine et Albert de Saxe-Teschen) aux cinq sermens
de la ville de Bruxelles le 2 Août 1785 (cf.* F. B. Solvyns, P, J.
Sauvage, J. G. Sauvage, A. C. Lens, A. Plateau, P. J. Thys).
His son Antoine C. (1772-1813) went 1792 to London and had
much success there as engraver. [Fl. 612, Fl. 892, Fl. 440.]

Cardon, Charles Léon. Flemish Sch. *b* Brussels 1850 *d* after
1910. *Anecdotic genre and murals; also active as collector.*

Pupil in Brussels Acad.; exhibitor Paris Salon. Represented in
BRUSSELS Town Hall (Hall of marriages) *The Joys of
Marriage (presided over by the City of Brussels)* inscribed
'Hier bindt de liefde U bly te gader' 1881. Pictures titled
Flemish archers 1872 and *The present* 1874 are recorded.
[Fl. Bib. 19th cent., Fl. 119.]

Carings, A., see **Keirincx.**

Carlier, Jean Guillaume (Jan Willem). Flemish Sch. *b* Liège
1638 *d* Liège 1675. *Religious subjects for Liège churches (cf.*
J. B. P. Coclers and P. Coclers, G. Douffet, J. G. Delcour, E.
Fisen, M. Ponteau), *portraits.* Pupil of B. Flémalle *q.v.* and
followed him to Paris to work for Louis XIV *(cf.* W. Damery,
N. la Fabrique, A. F. v. d. Meulen, J. van Reyn and P. Mol)
1670; returned Liège where was painting the family of the
military commander when latter received orders to hand over
to French armies 1675; is said to have died from distress at
the incident. **Documented Examples:** BRUSSELS *Martyrdom of S. Denis* (oil sketch for painting in Liège S. Denis).
LIÈGE S. Denis *Martyrdom of S. Denis* 1666 (damaged and
repainted 1795); Cathedral *Baptism of Christ* (from Liège
Carmes Déchaussés). MAINZ *S. Joseph and the Christ Child.*
[Fl. 451, Fl. 612, Fl. 409, Fl. 892, Fl. 440.]

Carlier, Modeste. Flemish Sch. *b* son of a miner, Wasmuel
1820 *d* Ixelles 1878. *Costume history, genre, portraits, flower
still life.* Pupil in Mons Acad. and of the French flower
painter F. Picot in Paris. Rome prizewinner 1850; lived Italy 1850-5;
then Paris to 1870. Represented in BRUSSELS *Locusta ex-
perimenting with poison on a slave* 1853. GHENT, MONS.
[Fl. 839, Fl. 440.]

Carolus, Louis Antoine. Flemish Sch. *b* Antwerp 1814 *d*
Antwerp 1865. *Costume genre; also engravings.* Pupil of J.
Eeckhouts and F. de Braekeleer and in Paris of the French
painter E. Le Poitevin. Represented in BARNARD
CASTLE Bowes Mus. *The Reprimand.* [Fl. 481, Fl. 440.]

Carpentero, Henri Joseph Gommaire. Flemish Sch. *b* son of
J. C. C., Antwerp 1820 *d* Schaerbeek (Brussels) 1874. *Domes-
tic and rural genre.* Pupil of F. de Braekeleer and N. de
Keyser. Represented in BRUNSWICK *The oyster eater.*
KOENIGSBERG *Peasant interior.* [Fl. 440.]

Carpentero, Johannes Carolus (Jean-Charles). Flemish Sch. *b*
Antwerp 1784 *d* Antwerp 1823. *Landscapes with animals (cf.*
A. C. M. Engel and J. B. de Roy). Pupil of M. I. van Brée.
Was so close an imitator of B. P. Ommeganck *q.v.* that even in
his lifetime some of his pictures passed under that name. A
Mountainous and wooded landscape with sheep and cows is
recorded in Antwerp 1819 exhibition. [Fl. 451, Fl. 440.]

Carpentier, Evariste. Flemish Sch. *b* Cuerne (nr. Courtrai)
1845 *d* Liège 1922. *Anecdotic and rustic genre, costume history,
landscapes with figures.* Pupil in Antwerp Acad. under N. de
Keyser; lived some years in Paris; Professor Liège Acad.
1897-1919. Represented in ANTWERP, BERLIN,
BRUGES *The Foreigners* 1887, BRUSSELS, COURTRAI,
LIÈGE, MALINES, MONTPELLIER, NAMUR, TRI-
ESTE. [Fl. Bib. 19th cent. Fl. 440.]

Carpentiers, O. S. B. (Christian names unknown). Flemish
Sch. 18th cent. *b* Brussels. *Portraits.* **Signed Example:** ROME
S. Cecilia *Portrait of a Cardinal* 1736. [Fl. 305.]

Carrach, see **Kraek.**

Carte, Antoine. Flemish Sch. *b* Mons 1886. *Religious subjects,
genre, landscapes; also illustrations, engravings, applied arts.*
Pupil in Mons and Brussels Acads.; Member of Nervia group
of La Louvière which, founded 1928, included L. Devos,
P. Paulus, R. Strebelle and T. Wallet among its members.
Represented in BRUSSELS *Good Friday.* [Fl. 296.]

Casembrot, Abraham. Flemish Sch. 17th cent. *Religious subjects, landscapes; also active as engraver.* Left the Netherlands and settled Messina, where acted as consul for his fellow countrymen. Works by him recorded in Messina churches were destroyed in the earthquake of 1908.
[Fl. 481, Fl. 892, Fl. 305.]

Cassiers, Henri. Flemish Sch. *b* Antwerp 1858 *d* 1918. *Landscapes, marines, coast scenes, picturesque corners of Flemish and Dutch towns and villages* (many in *w.); also designs for posters and book illustrations* (including Camille Mauclair's *'Trois femmes de Flandres'*). Member of Soc. Int. de la peinture à l'eau, Paris 1906 (*cf*. F. Charlet); President of the Société Royale Belge des Aquarellistes. Represented in ANTWERP, BRUGES, BRUSSELS, DIJON, NAMUR, PARIS, ROME.
[Fl. Bib. 19th cent., Fl. 388, Fl. 254, Fl. 114, Fl. 296.]

Casteels, Alexander. Flemish Sch. *b* Antwerp (?) *c*. 1638 *d* *c*. 1681. *Battles and other military pieces* (*cf*. Pauwels C., P. Snayers and L. de Hondt the elder). Master Antwerp Guild 1658; painted many pictures in Antwerp for the Forchoudt firm of art dealers (*cf*. L. Achtschellinck, P. v. Avont, A. F. Baudewyns, A. Coppens, A. v. Ertvelt, B. Floquet, P. v. Lint, V. Malo, J. B. v. d. Meiren, P. Meulener, E. and J. E. Quellinus, L. Smout the elder, L. v. Uden, P. v. d. Velde, Jan Verhuyck, S. de Vos, G. de Witte, P. de Witte III, F. Wouters); a letter from the Forchoudt son in Vienna to his father in Antwerp (1671) asks urgently for 'small and big battles by Alexander and Pauwels Casteels', and a second letter repeats the request; the firm's records show many such pieces exported to Vienna, Frankfort and elsewhere (five being sold to the Bishop of Kremsmünster) 1668-71.
[Fl. 892, Fl. 212, Fl. 213.]

Casteels, Frans. Flemish Sch. *b* son of Peter C. II, Antwerp 1686 *d* Antwerp 1727. *Town views.* In Antwerp Guild 1714. Antwerp Mus. has *La Grand' Place en 1715* traditionally recorded as his work.
[Fl. 892.]

Casteels, Pauwels. Flemish Sch. *b* Antwerp (?) before 1638 *d* after 1673. Brother of Alexander C. (?). *Battles and other military pieces* (*cf*. P. Snayers and L. de Hondt the elder). In Antwerp Guild 1656; worked for Forchoudt firm of art dealers (*cf*. A. Casteels). **Signed Examples:** *Battle pieces* LEMBERG and SCHLEISSHEIM. Two pictures in Oldenburg Mus. signed P. Kasteels are presumed by some his work (*cf*. Peter C. II).
[Fl. 892, Fl. 212, Fl. 213.]

Casteels, Peter (I). Flemish Sch. *b* Antwerp (?) before 1615 *d* Antwerp 1683. Master Antwerp Guild 1629.
[Fl. 892.]

Casteels, Peter (II). Flemish Sch. Worked Antwerp 1673. *Picturesque military pieces* (*cf*. L. de Hondt the elder). F. X. H. Verbeeck was his pupil and later his son-in-law. Two pictures in Oldenburg Mus. *Cavalry skirmishes* signed P. Kasteels are presumed by some his work (*cf*. Pauwels C.).
[Fl. 892.]

*****Casteels, Peter (III).** Flemish Sch. *b* son of Peter C. (II), Antwerp 1684 *d* Richmond 1749. *Birds and animals* (*cf*. P. F. de Hamilton) *occasional portraits but chiefly still life with flowers and fruit* (*cf*. J. B. de Crépu and J. v. d. Borght); *also worked as draughtsman and engraver* (not to be confused with Robert Castell) *and textile designer.* Came London (*cf*. F. Breydel, Jan Peeters the younger and P. J. van Reysschoot) at invitation of a dealer with his brother-in-law Peter Tillemans *q.v.* 1708; foundation member of Kneller's Great Queen Street Acad. 1711; revisited Antwerp *c*. 1713 or 1716; published set of bird prints 1726; employed by calico printers in Tooting from 1735 and moved with them to Richmond. **Signed Examples:** BARNARD CASTLE Bowes Mus.

Flower piece on a terrace with parrot and monkey. Flower piece on a terrace with parrots and melons, figs, grapes and pomegranates. LÜBECK *Flower piece.* Twelve *Flower pieces in vases representing the months* painted 1730 and engraved for Robert Furber's 'Twelve months of Flowers' (*cf*. J. F. van Son) are recorded 1950 in a London sale.
[Fl. 826, Fl. 856, Fl. 892, Fl. 880, Fl. 133 (1950).]

Casteels, Peter Franz. Flemish Sch. *b* Antwerp (?) before 1675 *d* date and place unknown. *Religious subjects.* Pupil in Antwerp of G. P. Verbruggen the younger *q.v.* 1690; Master Antwerp Guild 1697. **Signed Examples:** BRUGES S. Sauveur *Annunciation; Holy Family in a garland of flowers* (*cf*. D. Seghers), both medallions dated 1694.
[Fl. 65, Fl. 871, Fl. 892.]

Castelein, Ernest Marie Félix. Flemish Sch. *b* Belgium 1882. Murdered in London July 26, 1945. [Fl. 809 (1945).]

Castello, F. de, see **Kasteele.**

Catherine Legend Master. Presumed Flemish Sch. late 15th cent. Name for painter of NEW YORK private coll. *Scenes from the life of S. Catherine.* Pictures presumed by some his work are in various museums (*cf*. Melbourne Miracles Painter). [Fl. 798, Fl. 316.]

Catherine (Mystic Marriage) Master. Wurzbach's name for painter of BRUSSELS (545) *Mystic marriage of S. Catherine cf*. Brussels Mystic Marriage Painter. [Fl. 892.]

Caullery (Coulery or Colori), Louis de. Presumed Flemish Sch. 16th-17th cent. *'History' and genre.* **Signed Examples:** HAMBURG Kunsthalle *Carnival* (Coulery). Philips van Valckenisse had, 1614, in Antwerp a *'Banquet'* (Banquet? Larger Still life?) after Loys Caulery in his collection which included many works by G. Mostaert, D. Vinckeboons and their contemporaries. A *Christ carrying the Cross*, a *Magdalena Amoreuse* and a *Triumph of Bacchus, Venus and Ceres* by Loys Colori are recorded in an Antwerp inventory of 1627; a *Burning of Troy* (*cf*. P. Schoubroeck) by Loys Colori is recorded in an inventory of 1652 and a *'Danschmerckt van Jouffrouwen'* (*Girls dancing?*) by Loys Celery in the collection of the Dean of the Antwerp Old Cloth Merchants' Guild (*cf*. C. de Cauwer) 1661; an invoice of 1676 records export from Antwerp of a *Peasant fair* by Loweis Collore with landscape by Jan (Velvet) Brueghel. [Fl. 212, Fl. 213, Fl. 16.]

Caussiers, J., see **Cossiers.**

Cauwenbergh, Robert van. Flemish Sch. *b* Ghent 1905. *Figures, genre, still life, decorative paintings.* Pupil in Ghent Acad. of J. Delvin and G. Minne and in Antwerp Higher Institute, of I. Opsomer. Represented ANTWERP *Jazz-band; Still life.* [Fl. 17.]

Cauwer (Cauver or Couwer), Charles (Carel) de. Flemish Sch. *b* Antwerp (?) before 1590 *d* before 1658. *Landscapes, religious subjects, still life.* Pupil of Juliaen Teniers the elder in Antwerp 1601; Master Antwerp Guild 1609; Jacques Snel, Antwerp wine taverner (wijntavernier) owned, 1623, an *Emmaus*, a *S. John baptising*, a *Picture with a large waggon* and other works by him in a collection which included works by Juliaen Teniers, J. de Momper, Pieter Bruegel and others; collaboration with J. de Momper and with Jan Brueghel the younger and A. van Stalbemt (in a large flower piece for the Spanish market) is recorded 1635; Susanna Willemsen widow of an Antwerp cloth and silk merchant had ten landscapes including a *Winter scene* in her large collection 1657. Abraham van Lamoen Dean of the Old Cloth Merchants' Guild owned a landscape 1661 (*cf*. L. de Caullery).
[Fl. 714, Fl. 213, Fl. 214.]

Cauwer, Émile P. J. de. Flemish Sch. *b* son of Joseph de C., Ghent 1827 *d* Berlin 1873. *Architectural pieces.* Represented in STETTIN *Antwerp, S. Jacques.* Others in BERLIN and COLOGNE. [Fl. 94, Fl. 892.]

Cauwer (Cauwer-Rousse), Joseph de. Flemish Sch. *b* Beveren-Waes 1779 *d* Ghent 1854. *Religious subjects, costume history, portraits.* Pupil in Antwerp and Ghent Acads. Professor Ghent Acad. 1807. Represented in BRUGES and GHENT Mus. and S. Bavon (*Baptism of Christ*) and Académie des Beaux Arts (*Portraits*). A *Belgian Humanity: episode of the Battle of Waterloo* is recorded.
[Fl. 126, Fl. 88, Fl. 612, Fl. 451, Fl. 892, Fl. 798.]

Cels, A. Flemish Sch. *b* Brussels 1883. *Portraits and drawings.* Nephew of Cornelis C. Pupil in Brussels Acad. and in Glasgow under J. Delville *q.v.*; then in Paris of the French painter J. É. Blanche. Member of the Société royale des Beaux Arts de Belgique. [Fl. 440.]

Cels, Cornelis. Flemish Sch. *b* Lierre 1778 *d* Brussels 1859. *Portraits, 'history', religious subjects, genre.* Pupil of A. Lens in Brussels and of J. Suvée *q.v.* in Paris; in Italy 1801-7; gold medal at Ghent with *Cincinnatus* (1803); Professor Accad. di San Luca Rome 1807; Antwerp 1808-14; The Hague 1815-19; director of Tournai Acad. 1820-7; then Brussels. Represented in AMSTERDAM *Swiss peasant girl* 1821; *C. v. d. Hoop.* ANTWERP Église des Augustins *Visitation*; S. Paul *Descent from the Cross* 1807. ROTTERDAM *Comte de Hogendorp.* Portraits of *William I King of United Netherlands* and his family and of the painter *B. P. Ommeganck* and religious subjects for churches in Bruges, Lierre and The Hague are recorded. [Fl. 451, Fl. 612, Fl. 440.]

Cephalus, see Bloemen, N. van.

Ceramano, Charles Ferdinand. Flemish Sch. *b* Thielt 1829 *d* Barbizon 1909. *Landscapes with animals.* Pupil of French artist C. E. Jacque and lived Barbizon from *c.* 1870. Represented in CHICAGO Art Inst. *Landscape with sheep,* TOULON and other collections. [Fl. 160 (1909).]

Ceustere, A. de, see Coster.

Ceustere (or Coster or Keuster), Jan (Hans) de. Flemish Sch. 17th cent. Pupil of Jan Snellinck in Antwerp 1599; Master Antwerp Guild 1606; a Hans (Jan) de Coster collaborated with J. Jordaens, under Rubens, on Pageant Entry into Antwerp of Cardinal Infante Ferdinand (*cf.* G. Weri) 1635. (*Cf.* Jan de Coster). [Fl. 714, Fl. 613, Fl. 892.]

Champaigne, Jean Baptist de. Flemish Sch. *b* Brussels 1631 *d* Paris 1681. *Religious subjects, 'history', portraits.* Brought Paris by his uncle Philippe de C. *q.v.* 1643; naturalized Frenchman 1655; visited Rome 1657-8; member French Acad. roy. des B.A. (*cf.* M. Plattenberg and P. Mol) 1663; assisted his uncle in decorative work in Val de Grâce and for Louis XIV at Vincennes, the Tuileries and Versailles. **Signed Example:** ROTTERDAM Boymans *Self portrait* (with self portrait by the French artist N. de Platte-Montagne signed by each) 1650. **Documented Examples:** MARSEILLES *Stoning of S. Paul* (painted for the Paris Goldsmiths' Guild as 'Mai' presentation to Notre Dame 1667). PARIS Louvre *Hercules crowned by Virtue* (Acad. reception piece 1663), *Education of Achilles* (two) begun by P. de C. and finished by J. B.. VERSAILLES Salon de Mercure *Alexander receiving submission of the Ethiopian ambassador; Ptolemy showing his library to the philosophers* both in Salon 1673; *Mercury in his chariot drawn by cocks.* RHEIMS Mus. has *Transfiguration* from Brussels Abbey of S. Thierry traditionally recorded as placed in position by the artist himself 1677. [Fl. 425, Fl. 287, Fl. 22, Fl. 66.]

*Champaigne, Philippe de. Flemish Sch. *b* Brussels 1602 *d* Paris 1674. *Religious subjects, decorative paintings, portraits.* Pupil in Brussels of M. de Bordeau (*cf.* A. Sallaert) and of J. Fouquier *q.v.* before 1621; declined, Félibien (1668) records, his father's offer to place him in the Rubens atelier 'et pour cela payer une bonne pension comme faisaient tous les jeunes gens qui travaillaient sous lui'; went Paris (*cf.* P. Franchoys, H. Staben and C. E. Biset); pupil there of French painter G. Lallemand (master of N. Poussin) and lived in Collège de Laon; became friend of Poussin and collaborated with him on decorations in Luxembourg apartments of Marie de Médicis; after visit to Brussels succeeded the French painter N. Duchesne as First Painter to Marie de Médicis (*cf.* P. P. Rubens) 1627; given studio in the Luxembourg 1628; married Duchesne's daughter 1628; citizen of Paris 1629; after flight of Marie de Médicis, entered service of Louis XIII (*cf.* J. Fouquier, J. van Egmont, F. Elle, F. Pourbus the younger) 1633; member of Acad. roy. des B.A. (*cf.* M. Plattenberg and P. Mol) 1648; visited Brussels and received commissions from Archduke Leopold Wilhelm (*cf.* G. Seghers and J. B. van Heil) *c.* 1654; worked for Cardinal Richelieu (in Palais Cardinal and the Sorbonne), for Anne of Austria (in Val-de-Grâce), for Louis XIV, for the Jansenists at Port Royal and for many Paris churches (*cf.* J. B. de C.). **Signed Examples:** BUDAPEST *Man's portrait* 1654. CARLSRUHE *Portrait of a Statesman* 1668. GRENOBLE *Crucifixion* 1655, *Louis XIV conferring the Order of the Saint Esprit on the Duc d'Anjou 1654* (commissioned by the King 1665 *cf.* Toulouse example). LONDON N.G. *Cardinal Richelieu* (full length); Wallace Coll. *Marriage of the Virgin.* PARIS Louvre *Président de Mesmes* 1653; *Arnauld d'Andilly* 1650; *Crucifixion* 1674. TOULOUSE *Louis XIII conferring the Order of the Saint Esprit on the Duc de Longueville 1633* commissioned by the king 1656. VIENNA K. *Adam and Eve with murdered Abel* 1656 (painted for the Archduke Leopold Wilhelm). **Documented Examples:** AIX-EN-PROVENCE *Pompone de Bellievre* (engraved 1633). BRUSSELS *Presentation in the Temple* (called by d'Argenville *Circumcision,* painted for Carmelite church rue S. Jacques Paris), *S. Ambrose, S. Stephen* (both painted for S. Germain l'Auxerrois, Paris), *S. Geneviève* (engraved), *S. Joseph* (both from S. Severin, Paris). CAEN *Louis XIII in adoration* (*Le vœu de Louis XIII*) (Ex-voto commissioned in 1634 for Notre Dame). DIJON *Presentation in the Temple* (d'Argenville records as painted for Paris S. Honoré). GRENOBLE *Duvergier de Hauranne, Abbot of S. Cyran* 1643 (engraved), *Raising of Lazarus, Assumption of the Virgin* (both from Carmelite church Faubg. S. Jacques, Paris, for which painted 1631-2). LENINGRAD *Moses* (engraved). LONDON N.G. *Cardinal Richelieu* (triple portrait for use by a sculptor; (engraved 1657); Wallace Coll. *Annunciation* (from church of Culture de S. Catherine, Paris, for which d'Argenville records that he painted this subject). LYONS *The finding of the relics of SS. Gervais and Protais* (tapestry cartoon from Paris, S. Gervais where d'Argenville records it). PARIS Louvre *The Last Supper* (from high altar of the Port Royal church of which community he was a member, 1648), *S. Philip* (presented by artist to Acad. roy. des B.A. 1649), *The dead Christ* (engraved), *Mother Catherine Agnes Arnauld and the artist's daughter Sister Catherine de S. Suzanne 1662* (Ex-voto painted as thank offering for his daughter's recovery from illness; given to Port Royal where it remained till 1793), *Louis XIII crowned by Victory, The Provost and sheriffs of Paris* (commissioned by the Paris magistrature), *Self portrait with view of Brussels in background* 1668 (engraved); The Sorbonne *Church fathers* (frescoes in dome). ROUEN Cathedral *Nativity* (in situ since 1644). TOULOUSE *Souls in Purgatory* bought by the poet Le Franc de Pompignan from the Capucins of Lille.
[Fl. 287, Fl. 373, Fl. 22, Fl. 27, Fl. 892, Fl. 578, Fl. 876, Fl. 553.]

Chappel, Édouard. Flemish Sch. *b* Antwerp 1859. *Still life* (*flowers, fruit*), *animals, landscapes with figures.* Lived for some time in London; visited Cornwall; exhibited London R.A.

1892-1903 and Paris Autumn Salon 1907; Member Antwerp group Als ik kan (*cf.* H. Luyten) 1885. Represented in ANTWERP *Fish shop, Still life.* [Fl. 361, Fl. 17.]

Charlerie, Hippolyte de la. Flemish Sch. *b* Mons 1827 *d* Paris 1867. *Landscapes, animals, genre, portraits; also drawings for illustrations.* Pupil of Brussels Acad. Lived much in Paris from 1860. Member of Brussels Soc. libre des B.A. (*cf.* E. Lambrichs who included his portrait in his picture of the group). Represented in BRUSSELS *Old man's head.*

Charlet, Franz. Flemish Sch. *b* Brussels 1862 *d* Paris 1928. *Landscapes, coast scenes, genre, portraits.* Pupil Brussels Acad., then Paris École des Beaux Arts. Travelled with T. van Rysselberghe in Spain and Morocco and with J. M. Whistler in Holland (1885); member of Brussels group Les Vingt (*cf.* J. Ensor) 1884; with H. Stacquet, H. Cassiers and F. Khnopff founded in Paris the Soc. Internationale de la peinture à l'eau 1906. Represented in ANTWERP *The Widower* 1900; *The Burgomaster's family.* BRUSSELS *Fisherman's wife.* GHENT *The Maisons dorées in Bruges.* PARIS State Coll. *Motherhood; Dordrecht; The Grandfather.* [Fl. Bib. 19th cent.]

Chauvin, August. Flemish Sch. *b* Liège 1810 *d* Liège 1884. *Costume history, portraits, genre, religious subjects.* Pupil in Düsseldorf Acad. Director Liège Acad. 1842; exhibited London 1851. Represented in LIÈGE Mus. *S. Lambert at the banquet of Pépin d'Herstal;* Town Hall *The Burgomasters Beeckman and Lamelle at Liège Town Hall 1631.* [Fl. 466 (1884), Fl. 361.]

*Chicago 1562 Painter. Presumed Flemish Sch. 16th cent. Name for painter of CHICAGO Art Inst. *Portrait of a lady* dated 1562.

*Chicago Man with a Pink Painter. Presumed Flemish Sch. 16th cent. Name for painter of CHICAGO Art Inst. *Man with a pink.* Presumed by some identical with Q. Massys *q.v.*

Chouette, Maître see Bles.

Christoph van Utrecht. Flemish (Dutch) Sch. *b* Utrecht (?) 1498 (?) *d* Lisbon (?) after 1565 (not 1557). *Portraits and religious subjects* (?) Went young to Portugal; documented working with Portuguese artist C. de Figueiredo in Lamego 1534; living in Lisbon when his wife denounced to the Inquisition a coal merchant who spoke disrespectfully of the King, the Pope and the Inquisition 1537; Examiner of Paintings 1556; mentioned in Lisbon Tax accounts 1565. Palomino (1724) states that he worked for King John III and was knighted in 1550. Count Raczynski (1846) records a signature XV on a *Jesus among the Doctors* in Evora Library.
[Fl. 637, Fl. 629, Fl. 153, Fl. 692, Fl. 774, Fl. 175.]

*Christus, Petrus (Pieter Cristus). Flemish Sch. *b* Baerle (near Limbourg?) before 1430 *d* Bruges *c.* 1472. *Religious subjects, portraits, genre.* Master Bruges Guild 1444; painted for the Comte d'Estampes three copies of a picture of the Virgin (brought from Rome 1451 to Cambrai and credited with miraculous powers) 1454; member of Fraternity of Our Lady of the Dry Tree, Bruges, by 1462; with one Pieter de Nachtegale painted a *Tree of Jesse* for procession of the Confraternity of the Holy Blood 1463; Dean of Guild 1471 and as such a prosecutor of P. Coustain *q.v.* **Signed Examples:** (usually in semi-Greek lettering xpi); BERLIN K.F. (pair of wings) *Annunciation and Nativity* and *Last Judgement* (related to panel by the New York Crucifixion and Last Judgement Painter *q.v.*) *s* on frame and dated 1452. FRANKFORT Staedel. *Virgin and Child with SS. Jerome and Francis* 14.7 (1457?). LONDON N.G. (loan) *Edward Grymeston, Ambassador from Henry VI to the Netherlands 1445-6* 1446. NEW YORK Met. *Portrait of a Carthusian* 1446. A private collec-

tion (U.S.A.) has *S. Eligius in his goldsmith's shop handing a ring to a young lady with her betrothed* (painted for Antwerp Goldsmiths' Guild) *s* and 1449. A *Young lady in a high black cap* in Berlin K.F. (532) is recorded as formerly inscribed on frame 'Opus Petri Christophori'. A *Young man with a book* in London N.G. (2592) with xpi (as signature?) in a hymn on a scroll on the wall is presumed by some his work and by others the work of the French painter Jean Fouquet. A *Portrait of a Frenchwoman* belonged to Lorenzo de' Medici and a *Christ in Glory* to the poet Sannazaro (1524). Paintings presumed by some his work are in various museums (*cf.* Detroit S. Jerome Painter, New York Virgin in a Tabernacle Painter and Washington Nativity in a Sculptured Porch Painter).
[Fl. 371, Fl. 818, Fl. 874, Fl. 892, Fl. 316, Fl. 530.]

Christus, Petrus the younger. Flemish Sch. *b* son of Sebastian C., Bruges 1479. Master Bruges Guild 1501. Perhaps identical with one Pedro de Christo recorded in Granada 1507, 1516, 1528 and 1530. [Fl. 892, Fl. 874.]

Christus, Sebastian. Flemish Sch. *b* Bruges (?) illegitimate son of P. C. *q.v.* date unknown *d* Bruges (?) 1500. *Religious subjects and ms. illustrations.* Master in Bruges Guild 1476. A *Virgin and Child* was recorded in the possession of Anne of Brittany on her marriage with Charles VIII of France 1491.
[Fl. 892, Fl. 874.]

Cierkens, Jean. Flemish Sch. *b* Bruges 1819 *d* Rome 1853. *Historical and genre subjects, nudes.* Pupil in Bruges and Antwerp Acads. and later Professor in Bruges Acad.; went Rome with a government grant. Represented in ANTWERP Acad. [Fl. 440.]

Civetta, see Bles.

*Claeissins (or Claessens), Antoine. Flemish Sch. *b* son of Pieter C. the elder, Bruges *c.* 1536 *d* Bruges 1613. *Religious subjects, allegories and decorative works.* Pupil of his father and of P. J. Pourbus; Master Bruges Guild 1570; city painter 1570-81 (*cf.* P. C. the younger); restored P. J. Pourbus' *Last Supper* in Bruges Notre Dame 1589. **Signed Examples** BRUGES Mus. *The Banquet of Ahasuerus* (*cf.* G. Geldorp) 1574, *Mars and the Fine Arts overcoming Ignorance* 1605; Notre Dame *Virgin and Child with donors* 1584; S. Gilles *Last Supper* 1593; S. Sauveur (triptych) *Descent from the Cross, Saints and Donor* 1609. A *Virgin and Child with S. Bernard in adoration* (monogrammed A.C.) in Bruges S. Sauveur is presumed by some his work. [Fl. 892, Fl. 113, Fl. 114.]

Claeissins (or Claessens or Claes), Gillis. Flemish Sch. *b* son of Pieter C. the elder, Bruges (?) *c.* 1545 *d* Bruges 1607. *Religious subjects, portraits.* Master Bruges Guild 1566; court painter to Alexander Farnese, Duke of Parma, Governor of the Netherlands (*cf.* P. C. the younger) and to his successors the Archduke Ernest (*cf.* G. Schoof, Cornelis Floris and J. de Momper), and the Archduke Albert and the Infanta Isabella (*cf.* G. de Crayer and D. van Alsloot). A signed *Trinity* and a *Portrait of the Infanta Isabella* (miniature 1607) are recorded. His son Gillis C. was also a painter. [Fl. 892, Fl. 798.]

Claeissins (or Claessens), Pieter the elder. Flemish Sch. *b* Bruges (?) *c.* 1500 *d* Bruges (?) 1576. *Religious subjects, portraits, but chiefly active as illuminator.* Master Bruges Guild 1530; in Booksellers' Guild as illuminator 1544. Collaborated with his son P. C. the younger *q.v.* in altarpiece for Bruges S. Sauveur 1572. **Signed Example:** OSLO *Portrait of a man* 1560. [Fl. 892, Fl. 316.]

*Claeissins (or Claessens or Claes), Pieter the younger. Flemish Sch. *b* son of P. C. the elder, Bruges *c.* 1550 *d* Bruges 1623. *Religious subjects, portraits, decorative works; also worked as cartographer* (*cf.* P. J. Pourbus). Master Bruges Guild 1571;

succeeded his brother Antoine *q.v.* as city painter 1581; worked on decorations for Pageant Entry into Bruges of Alexander Farnese, Duke of Parma 1584 (*cf.* Gillis C., J. Sons, J. B. Saive, O. van Veen, M. Coxie, J. van Winghe also D. v d. Queborne). **Signed Examples:** BRUGES Mus. *The Convention of Tournai* (*Allegory of the Spanish triumph and submission of Bruges to Parma 1584*); S. Sauveur (triptyx) *Ecce Homo* and on wings: *S. John the Evangelist* and *Jean van den Berghe, Donor* 1609; Musée des Hospices Civils *Christ bearing the Cross* 1616; Hospice de la Poterie *Notre Dame de l'arbre sec* (*Virgin in a landscape*) 1608; S. Walpurge (triptych) *Notre Dame de l'arbre sec* (*with Moses and Gideon*) and on wings *Sixteen nobles of the Confraternity* 1620 (on signing the contract for this picture (1606) the painter received three canettes of French wine and his wife a capon). **Documented Examples:** BRUGES S. Sauveur *SS. Crispin and Crispinian* and *Twenty-one members of the Shoemakers' Guild* 1608; *The Resurrection* (commissioned and painted with P. C. the elder 1572 and restored by P. C. the younger 1586); Town Hall *Map of the Franc de Bruges* (copy of work by P. J. Pourbus) 1601.   [Fl. 892, Fl. 133 (1911), Fl. 113, Fl. 114.]

Claes, A., P. and G. see Claeissins.

Claes, Constant Guillaume. Flemish Sch. *b* Tongres 1826 *d* Hasselt 1905. *Genre, and in later years, religious subjects* (murals *cf.* J. Swerts). Pupil in Antwerp Acad. of N. de Keyser. Represented in TONGRES Notre Dame. Pictures titled *The school master's birthday, Visit of the doctor* and *Le bon Curé* (popular in a lithograph) are recorded.   [Fl. 440.]

Claes, Jan Frans Floris. Flemish Sch. *b* Antwerp 1818 *d* Antwerp 1870. *Genre, portraits, religious subjects*. Pupil of N. de Keyser in Antwerp Acad. Represented in MELSELE Church *Seven Sorrows of the Virgin*. Collaborated with G. Guffens and J. Swerts *q.v.* on frescoes for Antwerp churches.   [Fl. 451, Fl. 837 (1870).]

Claes, Paul. Flemish Sch. *b* Antwerp 1866 *d* Antwerp 1940. *Portraits, figures, interiors, picturesque corners of towns and villages, still life*. Represented ANTWERP *Still life with tin can*.   [Fl. 17.]

Claessens (or **Claesz**), **Jacob** known as **Trajectensis** (i.e. 'of Utrecht'). Flemish (Dutch) Sch. *b* Utrecht before 1490 (?) *d* date and place unknown. *Portraits, religious subjects*. Presumed by some identical with Jacob of Utrecht *q.v.* and by others with Jacob of Lübeck mentioned by Dürer. **Signed Examples:** BERLIN *Man in large hat with river landscape in background* (Jacobus Traiectensis 1523); *Man at writing table* (Jacobus Traiectensis 1524) with arms of Lübeck and Stralsund families. PARIS Louvre *Girl with carnations* (Jacobus Claess. Trajectensis). STOCKHOLM *Man standing by dining table with little dog* (Jacob. Claes Traiectensis). RIGA *Virgin and Child with angels* and *Donors Councillor of Lübeck and his wife* (Jacobus Traiectensis 1520).   [Fl. 243, Fl. 421.]

Claesz (**Claeszoon**) **van Leyden, Aert**; also known as **Aert** or **Aertgen van Leyden** and **Aertgen de Volder** (the Fuller). Flemish (Dutch) Sch. *b* son of a fuller, Leyden 1498 *d* through fall into a canal by night, Leyden 1564 or 1568. *Religious subjects, many designs for glass painters* (*cf.* P. A. Cluyt), *genre* (?). Pupil of C. Engelbrechtsz. Van Mander (1604) records him as a 'Bohemian' badly paid for his work and content to live in poor conditions; on Mondays he did little or no work but took his pupils to a tavern 'though he was no drinker'; when he sold a picture he would pass the whole night with his friends, if one left him he would go on to another and out in the dark streets he would play his German flute; F. Floris went (1553) to Leyden from Delft to see him and invited him to Antwerp where he undertook to get him better prices for his work, but failed to persuade him to leave his humble hut

(nederig hutje). Van Mander describes his work as influenced by Engelbrechtsz then by J. Scorel (*cf.* J. Swart) and M. v. Heemskerck, as good in composition and appreciated by connoisseurs but characterized by natural talent (geest) rather than by knowledge (studie) and by tall figures not always harmoniously proportioned; and there was often something slovenly (slordig) and unpleasant (onbehaaglijk) about his productions. **Signed Examples:** None. **Documented Examples:** None. His *Self portrait* (with scar on his face resulting from a dagger attack by a drunkard related by Van Mander) and a *Four Evangelists writing* are recorded by engravings. Van Mander knew works titled *Crucifixion, Christ carrying the Cross, Abraham and Isaac, Nativity, Last Judgement* (*with portraits of the Montfoort family on the wings*) and a *Judgement of Solomon*; also a *Crossing of the Red Sea* (with many varied costumes, turbans and shawls (*cf.* M. Pepyn)) then owned by the engraver H. Goltzius; and a tempera painting on canvas *Mary with singing angels*. Rubens owned (1640) a *Nativity*, a *Brothel* (*cf.* M. van Cleve) and an *Epitaph with wings* by 'Artus van Leyden' and a *S. Hubert in a landscape* by 'Artus de Hollander'; the Antwerp dealer H. de Neyt owned (1642) a *Last Supper* by Aertssen van Leyden; Rembrandt owned a *Scene from the story of Joseph* (*cf.* Joseph Master). Paintings and drawings presumed by some his work are in various museums.   [Fl. 559, Fl. 892, Fl. 213, Fl. 421, Fl. 631 (1939).]

Claesz, Allaert. Flemish (Dutch) Sch. early 16th cent. (Not to be confused with A. C. van Leyden). *Portraits*. Worked Amsterdam where employed by the Doelen (shooting clubs) (*cf.* C. Anthonisz); P. Aertsen was his pupil before 1535.   [Fl. 559, Fl. 892.]

Claeys, Albert. Flemish Sch. *b* Eeke 1889. *Landscapes*. Pupil in Ghent Acad. of J. Delvin. Represented in ANTWERP.   [Fl. 17.]

Claret, Jan. Flemish Sch. *b* Brussels before 1600 *d* after 1641. *Religious subjects*. Travelled in France and Spain; went Italy; worked for churches in Turin (*cf.* F. Pourbus the younger, E. Dubois and J. Miel) and at Savigliano (Piedmont) where Lanzi (1796) records him as friend and associate of Italian artist G. Molinari. **Documented Examples** (recorded by Bartoli 1776): BRÀ (prov. Cuneo) S. Giovanni Battista *Beheading of S. John*. SAVIGLIANO S. Filippo Neri *Virgin of the Rosary with SS. Dominic, Catherine and others* (*cf.* A. Mytens and J. Francart), *Pietà*. A *Virgin with S. Anthony of Padua, S. Bernard and others* signed J. Claret was formerly in the no longer extant church Virgine del Suffragio in Turin.   [Fl. 138, Fl. 505, Fl. 84, Fl. 305.]

Claus, Émile. Flemish Sch. *b* sixteenth son of a grocer, Vive-St. Éloi (near Courtrai) 1849 *d* Astene (East Flanders) 1924. *Rural genre; then landscapes* (*some with figures and cattle*) *in Impressionist conventions; interiors, portraits*. Pupil in Antwerp Acad. of J. Jacobs; visited Spain and Morocco and worked for some years in Paris; member of Impressionist group De Dertien (XIII) (*cf.* E. Farasyn) *c.* 1891, Vie et Lumière (*cf.* G. Morren) 1914, and L'Art Contemporain (Kunst van Heden) (*cf.* R. Strebelle); worked Holland and Venice; Chevalier of the Légion d'Honneur; in London during 1914-18 German invasion (*cf.* L. de Smet). Represented in ANTWERP *Flax weeding in Flanders* 1887, *Summer* 1893, *Winter* 1900. BERLIN, BRUGES *River Lys at Astene*. BRUSSELS *Cows crossing the Lys* 1899, *Waterloo bridge* 1916 and others, COURTRAI, DOUAI, DRESDEN, GHENT, LIÈGE *The old gardener* 1885, MONS, PARIS State Coll. *Sunshine*. ROME, VENICE *Autumn*, VERVIERS.   [Fl. 517, Fl. 388, Fl. 296, Fl. Bib. 19th cent.]

Clays, Paul Jean. Flemish Sch. *b* Bruges 1819 *d* Brussels 1900. *Marines, estuaries and coast scenes* (*cf.* L. Artan). Went to sea in his young days; studied in Paris under the French painters

H. Vernet and Baron T. Gudin; lived Antwerp and Brussels (Schaarbeek); exhibited from 1839; visited London and Southampton; worked much in Holland. C. Tschaggeny *q.v.* collaborated with him in some pictures. Commander of the Order of Leopold; Officer of the Légion d'Honneur. Represented in ANTWERP *Calm waters, Dordrecht* 1876. BRUGES *Le port de Ferragendo* 1846, *Bruges: Bassin de Commerce* 1870, *Rough sea* 1875, *Estuary of the Scheldt.* BRUSSELS *Shipwreck off the Shetlands, Rough sea off Ostend* 1851, *Antwerp Harbour Roads* 1869. BELGIAN ROYAL COLLECTION *Arrival of Queen Victoria at Ostend* 1844. LEICESTER *Calm on the Kel, near Dordrecht,* 1870, LONDON Tate *Dutch shipping* 1870. LIÈGE *The North Sea* 1891, MUNICH, NEW YORK *Celebration of the Freedom of Port of Antwerp* 1863, SHEFFIELD, PHILADELPHIA Wilstach, CHICAGO.

[Fl. 451, Fl. 481, Fl. 89, Fl. 440, Fl. 114, Fl. Bib. 19th cent.]

Clé, Cornelis de. Flemish Sch. *b* Antwerp (?) before 1645 *d* Antwerp 1724. *Religious subjects.* Master in Antwerp Guild 1661. A *Christ in Gethsemane* and a *Christ before Pilate* painted for the Fraternity of Married Men are recorded. His son of the same name was also a painter.

[Fl. 714, Fl. 126, Fl. 798.]

Cleef (or Cleve), Jan van. Flemish Sch. *b* Venlo 1646 *d* Ghent 1716. *Religious subjects for churches and convents; occasional 'history'.* Pupil in Brussels of L. Cousin (Primo) and G. de Crayer; accompanied de Crayer to Ghent 1664; Master Ghent Guild 1668; assisted de Crayer in his later works and completed some after his death 1669; also completed tapestry cartoons ordered by Louis XIV from de Crayer for Versailles and took them to Paris where was fêted by French artists and the court (*cf.* P. Vleughels, B. Flémalle, P. Mol, C. E. Biset). V. Verspilt *q.v.* collaborated with him in some pictures for Ghent churches. R. v. Audenaerd *q.v.* was his pupil. **Documented Example:** GHENT Mus. *Holy family, with Infant Jesus crowning Joseph with a wreath of roses.* Descamps (1763) writes 'J'ai vu la plupart des ouvrages de ce grand peintre dont je crois faire l'éloge en assurant que quelques-uns m'ont paru avoir tant de rapport avec ceux de Poussin qu'on pourroit quelquefois s'y méprendre' and records (1769); GHENT S. Jacques *Miracle of the loaves* (with landscape by V. Verspilt), *S. Barbara* and others; S. Nicolas *S. Amandus baptizing the Dauphin* ('le costume est peu exact'), *Christ and the Magdalene, Virgin of Sorrows;* Notre Dame (S. Pierre) *Immaculate Conception* (with *Adam and Eve* below); Sœurs Noires Convent: *A sœur noire succouring victims of the plague with the Virgin and Saints above* ('C'est içi qu'il est possible de juger Van Cleef un des grands artistes de la Flandre; l'artiste même a jugé avant nous ce tableau son chef d'œuvre . . . on l'estime autant que les plus beaux de Van Dyck'); Jacobins *Rest on the Flight* ('bien dans la maniere de Pietre de Cortone'); Hôtel de Ville *Allegory of Charles II receiving the Homage of Flanders* (*cf.* F. Duchatel) and *Allegory of Ghent deploring sacrilege* ('bien dans la manière de Lairesse'); others in Ghent, Baudeloo Abbey (*cf.* R. v. Audenaerd) and other churches in Ghent, Alost and elsewhere.

[Fl. 215, Fl. 216, Fl. 451, Fl. 434, Fl. 386.]

Cleef, see **Cleve.**

*****Clerck, Hendrik de.** Flemish Sch. *b* Brussels 1570 *d* Brussels (?) *c.* 1629. *Religious and mythological subjects; also figures in landscapes by Denis van Alsloot q.v., and others* (?) Pupil of M. de Vos; Court painter of Archduke Albert and Archduchess Isabella 1606. **Signed Examples:** BRUSSELS triptych *Lineage of S. Anne* (*cf.* M. de Vos), with *Judgement of Solomon* (*cf.* G. de Crayer) and *S. Ives: Patron of lawyers* (*cf.* J. Jordaens) on wings (from Brussels Notre Dame de la Chapelle 1590 where recorded by Descamps 1769 as 'assez

bien composé'); *Suffer little children to come unto me* (from Brussels S. Gudule) 1592 *cf.* J. Snellinck and V. Sellaer). LOUVAIN Jesuit College *Jesus tempted in the Desert* (also signed by D. van Alsloot) 1611. MOSIGKAU (nr. Dessau) *Judgement of Paris.* SCHLEISSHEIM *Earthly Paradise* (also signed by D. van Alsloot) (*cf.* J. Velvet Brueghel, I. v. Oosten and R. Savery). VIENNA K. *Wooded landscape with Cephalus and Procris* 1608 (D. v. Alsloot's signature formerly visible has now disappeared), *Feeding of the five thousand.* **Monogrammed Examples:** BRUSSELS *Descent from the Cross* 1628. MADRID Prado *Earthly Paradise with the Four Elements.* The large collection of Antoinette Wiael who died Antwerp 1627 contained a *Crucifixion,* a *S. Jerome with angels* and a *Nativity.* The Forchoudt firm of Antwerp dealers exported (1672) a *Moses striking water from the rock* to Vienna. Descamps (1769) records pictures in Brussels: S. Jacques and Convent S. Elizabeth, Louvain: S. Pierre and other churches. A copy of M. Coxie's *Crucifixion* (now Escorial) painted by H. de C. and presented (1623) by Archduchess Isabella to S. Josse-ten-Noode is recorded.

[Fl. 86, Fl. 425, Fl. 576, Fl. 216, Fl. 481, Fl. 892, Fl. 212, Fl. 213.]

Clesse, Louis. Flemish Sch. *b* Elsene 1889. *Landscapes (many in neighbourhood of Brussels).* Represented in ANTWERP *The willow.* [Fl. 17.]

Cleve, Claes van see **Nicolas C.**

Cleve (or Cleef), Cornelis van. Flemish Sch. *b* son of Joos van C., Antwerp 1520 *d* England (?) after 1554 (?). *Religious subjects.* Not recorded as a painter in Guild records. Recorded as a painter from Antwerp in an inventory of Lord Lumley's pictures (*cf.* H. Ewouts and S. v. d. Meulen) 1590, and by Van Mander 1604. **Signed Examples:** None. **Documented Examples:** None. A triptych *The Descent from the Cross* and a *Virgin* are recorded owned by an Antwerp merchant Guillaume van Brecht (*cf.* Joos van C.) 1585. Presumed by some identical with Sotte Cleve *q.v.*

[Fl. 559, Fl. 892, Fl. 133 (1915), Fl. 213, Fl. 316.]

Cleve (or Cleef), Gillis van. Flemish Sch. *b* eldest son of Marten van C. the elder, Antwerp (?) *c.* 1557 *d* Paris 1597. Recorded in Paris (*cf.* W. Coebergher, G. v. Coninxloo, H. Francken the elder, J. de Wael, also L. Thiry and A. P. Crabeth), 1588. [Fl. 559, Fl. 107, Fl. 892.]

Cleve, Hendrik van, the elder. Flemish Sch. *b* Antwerp (?) before 1475 *d* date and place unknown. Master Antwerp Guild 1489; J. van Hemessen *q.v.* was his pupil 1519.

[Fl. 714, Fl. 107, Fl. 892.]

Cleve (or Cleef), Hendrik (or Arigo or Rigo) van. Flemish Sch. *b* son of Willem v. C. the elder, Antwerp 1525 *d* 1589. *Landscapes* (*cf.* F. Mostaert and M. de Cock), *religious subjects in landscape, Italian views and ruins* (*cf.* M. v. Heemskerck and M. Gast); *also active as draughtsman and engraver.* Pupil of Frans Floris and painted landscape backgrounds in some pictures by Floris and by Marten van C. *q.v.*; Master Antwerp Guild 1551 or 1553; visited Italy and other countries. Van Mander (1604) records that he did not visit all the places of which he made drawings and engravings but made use of material provided by the engraver Melchior Lorch (Lorich of Flensburg who had lived in Constantinople and also worked in Italy, the Netherlands, Austria and Germany, engraved Luther's portrait 1548 and died Rome 1586); he adds that P. Vlerick *q.v.* made pen drawings in his manner. Another H. v. C. Master Ghent Guild 1598 who died Ghent 1646 is presumed by some his son. VIENNA Albertina and BERLIN Print Room have monogrammed drawings. An Antwerp collection inventoried (1621) by P. Goetkint *q.v.*, H. v. Balen *q.v.* and A. v. Stalbemt *q.v.* contained a painted *Landscape;*

the Antwerp dealer H. de Neyt owned (1642) a *S. John on Patmos;* Jeremias Wildens *q.v.* inherited from his father (1653) a *View of Milan;* other 17th cent. Antwerp inventories record *Palace of a cardinal, Ruins* and a *Landscape with S. John baptizing.* Vertue (before 1754) records a *Prospect of Rome* by 'Arigo van Cleve' in the English Royal Collection Catalogue of 1687. [Fl. 559, Fl. 892, Fl. 826, Fl. 213.]

Cleve (or **Cleef**), **Jooris van.** Flemish Sch. *b* Antwerp (?) son of Marten van C. after 1557 *d* before 1604. *Religious subjects, genre including night pieces* (*cf.* G. Congnet, L. Blondeel, H. Jordaens, Joos v. Winghe, H. van Steenwyck the elder and younger, G. Mostaert). Van Mander (1604) records him as a painter of small pictures who died young from loose living (hij ging te veel naar de hoeren). A *Kermesse* (*Village fair*) by 'Jorken van Cleve' was inventoried, 1614, in the large collection of P. van Valckenisse of Antwerp who died that year. A *Christ appearing to S. Peter in the storm* and a *Night masquerade* were recorded in the Prague Imperial Inventory 1621. *Cf.* A. Brouwer. [Fl. 559, Fl. 456 (1895), Fl. 213.]

Cleve (or **Cleef**), **Joos van** (real name documented as **Joos van der Beke**). Flemish Sch. *b* Cleves (?) before 1495 *d* Antwerp *c.* 1540. *Religious subjects, portraits.* Master Antwerp Guild 1511; Dean 1519 and again 1525; pupils recorded 1516-36; made his will (witnessed by P. Coecke van Aelst *q.v.*) 1540; Guicciardini (*c.* 1567) records a 'Gios de Cleves' of Antwerp summoned to France (*cf.* C. Smets) by François I (*cf.* L. Thiry and J. van Scorel) to paint his portrait and those of the Queen and princes; Van Mander (1604) records that he often painted the Virgin surrounded by angels. **Signed Examples:** None. **Documented Examples:** None. An *Adoration of the Magi* (Dry Coninghen) is recorded owned by an Antwerp merchant Guillaume van Brecht (*cf.* Cornelis van C.) in 1585; Rubens owned a *Portrait* (on panel) 1640. Pictures presumed by some his work are in various museums (*cf.* Hampton Court Henry VIII *c.* 1536 Painter, Philadelphia Francis I Painter and Death of the Virgin Master). *Cf.* also Sotte C.
[Fl. 371, Fl. 559, Fl. 892, Fl. 44, Fl. 316, Fl. 213, Fl. 530.]

Cleve (or **Cleef**), **Joos van the younger.** Flemish Sch. 16th cent. Not recorded in the Guild records and presumed by some identical with Joos van C. the elder. Van Mander (1604) records him as son of Willem van C. the elder *q.v.* and as identical with Sotte C. *q.v.* This is presumed by some an error. (*Cf.* Cornelis van C.). [Fl. 559, F. 316.]

*****Cleve** (or **Cleef**), **Marten van.** Flemish Sch. *b* son of Willem van C. the elder, Antwerp 1527 *d* afflicted with gout, Antwerp 1581. *Some religious subjects but mainly peasant genre* (*cf.* F. Verbeeck, P. Aertsen, J. Beuckelaer, P. Bruegel the elder, P. Balten, P. C. van Ryck, Prodigal Son Master). Pupil of F. Floris. Master Antwerp Guild 1551; Van Mander records (1604) that he never left his own country, that he began by painting large pictures and later painted small ones which had success with amateurs; that he sometimes painted figures in landscapes by his brother Hendrick and G. van Coninxloo *q.v.* and that Hans Jordaens I and D. v. d. Laen were his pupils. **Monogrammed Examples:** VIENNA K. *The flayed ox* 1566 (*cf.* D. Teniers and A. v. d. Hecken). SCHLEISSHEIM *Peasant girl led to bridal bed* 1580. **Documented Examples:** VIENNA K. *Peasant household and cavalier* (Archduke Leopold Wilhelm inventory 1659), *The brawl* (Granvella inventory 1607). Rubens owned (1640) a *Brothel* (*cf.* A. Claesz van Leyden; also J. van Craesbeeck), the Antwerp dealer H. de Neyt owned (1642) a *Demolition of the Antwerp Citadel 1577* (*cf.* Worcester Destruction of Citadel Painter), also a *Landscape with Abigail* (*cf.* H. v. d. Goes) painted with 'Grimmer' and a *Twelfth Night* (*Le roi boit*) (*cf.* J. Jordaens); the painter S. Wils *q.v.* owned (1628) *Picking chestnuts from the fire.* Antwerp inventories record (1574) *S. John preaching in the wilderness* (*cf.* P. Balten, K. van Mander); (1614) *Land-*

scape with Paul (*cf.* K. Foort and P. Bruegel the elder) painted with 'Grimmer', and *Paul in prison*; (1621) two landscapes painted with J. Grimmer *q.v.* Other inventories record *Susanna and the Elders, A peasant bride going to bed* (*cf.* Schleissheim example) and *The Five Senses.* A *Satire on Calvin* is recorded by an engraving.
[Fl. 559, Fl. 107, Fl. 56, Fl. 892, Fl. 212, Fl. 213.]

Cleve (or **Cleef**), **Marten van, the younger.** Flemish Sch. *b* son of Marten van C. the elder, Antwerp *c.* 1560 *d* place unknown after 1604. Van Mander (1604) records him as a good painter who went to Spain (*cf.* A. Pupiler, F. Sturm, S. Pereyns and P. de Kempener) and from there to the Indies (naar Indië) (*cf.* Jan Mostaert). [Fl. 559, Fl. 107.]

Cleve (or **Cleef**), **Nicolas van.** Flemish Sch. *b* son of Marten van C., Antwerp after 1560 *d* Antwerp 1619. Master Antwerp Guild 1595 and working there 1604. An Antwerp inventory of 1623 records a *Tower of Babel* (*cf.* M. van Valkenborch) with landscape by J. de Momper and figures by Juliaen Teniers the elder and Claes (Nicolas) van Cleve.
[Fl. 559, Fl. 107, Fl. 213.]

Cleve, 'Sotte' (the Crazy). Flemish Sch. *b* Antwerp (?) after 1504 *d* England (?) after 1554. Recorded by Van Mander (1604) as identical with Joos van Cleve the younger *q.v.* and son of Willem van C. the elder *q.v.* Presumed by some identical with Cornelis van C. *q.v. Religious subjects, mythologies, portraits.* Van Mander records that he came to England at the time of Philip II's marriage with Queen Mary (*cf.* A. Mor and J. C. Vermeyen) 1554 and failed to sell his pictures to Philip who was then enamoured of the works of Titian; that he quarrelled with Mor for not helping him in this matter, abused him as an inferior artist and bade him return to Utrecht and protect his wife from the Canons (*cf.* J. van Scorel) 'en dergelijke lasterpraat', but collapsed completely ('kroop onder tafel') when Mor made threatening rejoinders; that he adopted strange behaviour appearing abroad in glittering varnished clothing (*cf.* L. van Leyden) and eventually went mad. **Signed Examples:** None. **Documented Examples:** None. The Royal Collection, Windsor Castle, has a *Portrait of a bearded man with gesticulating hands 'in a black cap and furred gown upon a greenish ground'* recorded in Charles I's inventory as *Self portrait of Sotto Cleve* and engraved 1572 as 'Justo Clivensi Antverpiano Pictori' with the following legend by Lampsonius

> Nostra nec artifices inter te musa silebit
> Belgas picturae non leve, Juste, decus.
> Quam propria, nati tam felix arte fuisses
> Mansisset sanum si misero cerebrum

presumed by Van Mander to mean that the sitter went mad and presumed by others to mean that his son went mad. The Royal Collection, Windsor Castle also contains a *Portrait of a woman* recorded in Charles I's inventory as '*Portrait of the wife of Sotto Cleve in a white linen head dress with two hands together wherein holding a Pater noster. Done by Sotto Cleve*'. Charles I's inventory also records a *Mars and Venus.* James II owned a *Judgement of Paris* and a *Birth of Christ with angels.* Sir Peter Lely owned a *Bacchanale.* Van Mander records him as a fine painter of figures, the best colourist of his time, who excelled in suggesting relief (zijn objecten mooi plastisch schilderde) and in the painting of natural flesh tints on which he concentrated the lights (de lichtpartijen met de vleeschkleur zelf aanbracht); he records a *Virgin* set in an exceptionally fine landscape background by Joachim Patinir (presumed by some a confusion with Joos van Cleve *q.v.* as Patinir *q.v.* died in 1524) and a *Bacchus* 'represented as a very fat old man with grey hair to suggest that old age loves drink or that excessive drinking causes premature old age'. Antwerp inventories 1614-89 record religious subjects (some after Italian painters), landscapes, portraits and mythologies. Rubens owned (1640) an '*Emmaus*', a *Landscape* and a *Judge-*

ment of Paris: Jeremias Wildens, *q.v.* owned (1653) a *Judgement of Paris* and Canon Guillaume van Hamme owned 1668 a *Genealogy of S. Anne.* The Forchoudt firm of Antwerp dealers exported (1672) to their Vienna branch a work 'by Sotto Cleef as fine as a Raphael', a *Children's dance* (1698) and two pictures sold to Prince Liechtenstein.

[Fl. 559, Fl. 826, Fl. 856, Fl. 892, Fl. 212, Fl. 213, Fl. 316.]

Cleve (or Cleef), Willem van, the elder. Flemish Sch. *b* Antwerp (?) before 1504 *d* after 1543. In Antwerp Guild 1518; S. van der Meulen *q.v.* was his pupil in Antwerp 1543. (*Cf.* Hendrick van C., Marten van C. and Joos van C. the younger), [Fl. 559, Fl. 107, Fl. 892.]

Cleve (or Cleef), Willem van, the younger. Flemish Sch. *b* son of W. van C. the elder, Antwerp *c.* 1530 *d* before 1564. In Antwerp Guild 1550. Van Mander (1604) records him as 'a good painter of large figures'. Gaspar Rem was his pupil.

[Fl. 559, Fl. 107.]

Clevenbergh, Antoine. Flemish Sch. *b* son of decorative painter Pieter C., Louvain 1755 *d* Louvain 1810. *Religious subjects* (including copies of works by P. J. Verhaghen), *landscapes and still life, also game pieces* (*cf.* D. de Coninck, A. de Gryef, J. B. Govaerts, P. A. Rysbraeck). Patronized by Louis Engelbert, Duke of Arenberg; visited Germany. **Signed Example:** HAMBURG Kunsthalle *Fox and poultry.*

[Fl. 271, Fl. 892, Fl. 296, Fl. 798.]

Clevenbergh, Charles Antoine. Flemish Sch. *b* son of Antoine C., Louvain 1791 *d* Louvain (?) date unknown. *Still life.*

[Fl. 271.]

Clevenbergh, Joseph. Flemish Sch. *b* son of Antoine C., Louvain 1796 *d* Louvain (?) date unknown. *Still life.* Professor in Louvain Acad. [Fl. 271.]

Cleynhens, Théodore J. Flemish Sch. *b* Antwerp 1841 *d* Antwerp 1916. *Genre and costume history.* Pupil of V. Lagye in Antwerp Acad. Represented in ANTWERP *The Market* 1876, *Interior.* [Fl. 17.]

Clite, Liévin van den. Flemish Sch. *b* Ghent (?) before 1386 *d* Ghent 1422. A *Last Judgement* painted for GHENT Château des Comtes de Flandre 1413 (and paid for by one Joos de Valmerbeque as a fine imposed by a judicial sentence) is recorded. [Fl. 481, Fl. 385, Fl. 892.]

Cluysenaar, Alfred J. A. Flemish Sch. *b* son of architect Jean P. C., Brussels 1837 *d* St. Gilles, nr. Brussels 1902. *Costume history, religious subjects, genre, portraits, murals.* Pupil Brussels Acad. and of the French artist L. Cogniet in Paris; visited Germany, Holland and Italy; Professor decorative painting Antwerp Higher Institute; Officer of the Order of Leopold and Chevalier of the Légion d'Honneur. J. de Lalaing was his pupil. Represented in ANTWERP *Mazeppa* 1875, *Two children* 1872. BRUSSELS *Henri IV at Canossa* 1878, *Vocation* (*child's portrait*) 1875. *Murals* in BRUSSELS Ministry Foreign Affairs and S. GILLES Hôtel de Ville (ceilings) (*cf.* André C.), GHENT University, and HOMBURG Kurhaus (built by his father). A *Riders of the Apocalypse* 1867 was exhibited in Paris 1868.

[Fl. 440, Fl. 296, Fl. Bib. 19th cent.]

Cluysenaar, André. Flemish Sch. *b* son of Alfred C., Brussels 1872. *Portraits; also active as sculptor.* Pupil of his father. Exhibited Paris Salon des Artistes Français; finished his father's ceilings in S. GILLES, Hôtel de Ville. In London during 1914–18 German invasion (*cf.* P. Paulus and L. de Smet). [Fl. 440.]

Cluyt, Adriaen Pietersz. Flemish (Dutch) Sch. Sch. *b* son of Pieter A. C. before 1567 *d* Alkmaar 1604. *Portraits.* Van

Mander (1604) records him among the pupils and assistants of A. Blocklandt (*cf.* C. Ketel); citizen of Alkmaar 1594.

[Fl. 559, Fl. 892, Fl. 631 (1909).]

Cluyt, Pieter Adriaensz. Flemish (Dutch) Sch. *b* Alkmaar (?) before 1560 *d* Alkmaar 1586. *Contemporary history; also worked as heraldic and glass painter* (*cf.* P. Crabeth, P. Cornelisz, H. Bosch, J. J. de Gheyn, J. Ramey, Jacques Floris, D. J. Velaert, M. v. Heemskerck, A. Claesz van Leyden) *and cartographer.* **Signed Example:** ALKMAAR Stedelijk Mus. *Siege of Alkmaar 1573* (*cf.* Antwerp Destruction of Citadel Painter) painted for the Civic Guard House 1580. Another version is monogrammed. [Fl. 559, Fl. 116, Fl. 892.]

Cnodder, C. de see **Knodder.**

Cnoop, Cornelia see **David.**

Cock, César de. Flemish Sch. *b* son of a tailor, Ghent 1823 *d* Ghent 1904. Brother of Xavier de C. *Landscapes; also worked as engraver and musician.* In Paris where earned living as violinist in Châtelet Theatre orchestra and as chorister in S. Roch church 1857; became deaf and gave up music for painting; worked at Barbizon and Gasny (Eure); settled Ghent 1882. Represented in ANTWERP *Near St. Germain-en-Laye* 1879, *Wooded landscape on the Epte near Gasny* 1882. GHENT, GRENOBLE *Watercress beds at Veules.* LONDON V. and A. *The Epte at Gasny.* NEW YORK Met. *Spring landscape* 1878. PARIS State Collections. PHILADELPHIA Wilstach *Landscape with men and river* 1869.

[Fl. 250, Fl. 422, Fl. 160 (1904).]

Cock, Franciscus de. Flemish Sch. *b* Antwerp 1643 *d* Antwerp 1709. *Portraits; also active as architect, draughtsman and collector.* Canon (*cf.* A. Bosman and J. A. v. d. Baren) and cantor of Antwerp Cathedral. Visited Italy; was witness at the baptism of a child of J. E. Quellinus 1675. When he died the chaplains of Antwerp recorded him as follows in their register:

Si Cocum cognovisses,
Non verè ut cocum, sed ut pictorem amasses.
Si Cocum mecum audisses,
Non cocum, sed cantorem dilexisses:
Nunc pictor, cantor, Cocus,
Coxit sibi cibos in œvum. Echo: verum!

Portraits of *Ferdinand van Beughem Bishop of Antwerp* and *Reginald Cools, Bishop of Antwerp* and *Count Kaunitz Imperial ambassador at the Peace of Ryswick* are recorded by engravings. Sir Godfrey Kneller painted his portrait (now Antwerp Museum). [Fl. 481, Fl. 892, Fl. 13.]

Cock, Hieronymus (Jeroon) Wellens de. Flemish Sch. *b* son of Jan W. de Cock, Antwerp *c.* 1510 (or 1507) *d* Antwerp (?) or Rome (?) 1570. *Landscapes; but chiefly active as engraver, publisher and dealer.* Master Antwerp Guild 1545; went Rome where met Vasari (*cf.* J. van der Straet, M. Coxie and J. S. van Calcar); in Antwerp working on Pageant Entry of Charles V and Philip II (*cf.* A. van Palerme and F. Floris and P. Coecke van Aelst) 1549; had handsome house 'Aux quatre vents' by 1560. Published prints after fantasias by H. Bosch; landscapes by himself and his brother M. de Cock; peasant genre, landscapes and social-satirical drawings by P. Bruegel the elder; 'Romanist' compositions by L. Lombard and Italian painters; Roman views by M. van Heemskerck; and perspectives of temples, palaces, gardens and interiors by J. V. de Vries; his widow published after his death (1572) a series of portraits of artists with verses by Lampsonius. This eclectic art publishing was referred to in a poem by himself beginning: 'Den Kock moet Koken om't volcx wil van als,/ D'een ghebraden, en het ander ghesoden'. Guicciardini (1567) describes him as 'inventore et gran divulgatore per via di stampa'; Van Mander (1604) says: 'He was a most inventive landscape painter who gave up art and became a dealer. He commis-

sioned paintings, engravings and etchings and bought oils and watercolours; he thus became rich and bought one house after another'. An engraving *Landscape with S. Christopher* inscribed 'Pictum J. Cock' is presumed by some to record a painting by his hand (*cf.* J. de C.).
[Fl. 371, Fl. 818, Fl. 559, Fl. 602, Fl. 892, Fl. 440, Fl. 316.]

Cock, Jan de (known as **Wellens**). Flemish Sch. *b* Antwerp (?) or Leyden (?) before 1490 *d* Antwerp *c.* 1527. Father of Mathys de C. *q.v.* and Hieronymus de C. *Religious subjects.* Recorded in Antwerp 1506; took Wouter Key *q.v.* as his pupil 1516; Dean in Antwerp Guild 1520. Presumed by some identical with Jan van Leyen recorded Master Antwerp Guild 1503. **Signed Examples:** None. An engraving *Landscape with S. Christopher* inscribed 'Pictum J. Cock' is presumed by some to record a painting by his hand (*cf.* Hieronymus de C.). Paintings presumed by some his work are in various museums (*cf.* Dublin Flight Painter). [Fl. 107, Fl. 892, Fl. 316.]

Cock (Cocq, Kock, Cocx), Jan Claudius de. Flemish Sch. *b* Antwerp *c.* 1668 *d* Antwerp 1736. '*History' and religious subjects; decorative paintings; drawings for engravings; also active as sculptor, engraver and poet.* Pupil of a sculptor 1682; Master Antwerp Guild (beltsnyder) 1688; worked under an architect on decorations of William III's palace in Breda 1696. The Albertina has signed drawings *Boreas and Oreithyia* 1709, *Abraham and Melchisedek;* Antwerp Mus. Plantin has illustrations to a breviary *s* 1704. Drawings of *Biblical subjects s* 1728 and an engraving *Martyrdom of S. Quirinus s* are recorded. [Fl. 878, Fl. 451, Fl. 612, Fl. 714, Fl. 892.]

Cock, Mathys Wellens de. Flemish Sch. *b* son of Jan de C., Antwerp *c.* 1509 *d* in poverty Antwerp 1548. *Landscapes (cf.* F. Mostaert and H. van Cleve). Visited Italy; Master Antwerp Guild 1540. Van Mander (1604) records him as an excellent (uitnemend) landscapist in oil and water colour who 'was the first to paint landscapes in a better way, with more variety, according to the new Italian or antique method, and was remarkably inventive in his compositions and grouping'; he adds that his pupils included J. Grimmer *q.v.* and Hans Keynooghe *q.v.*; and that his younger brother Hieronymus C. *q.v.* engraved a number of his works. His name was reported as noteworthy to Vasari before 1568. Lampsonius *q.v.* in a poem (published 1572) praised him as landscapist. After his death his mother maintained his illegitimate child aged seven who was left unprovided for. **Signed Examples:** None. **Documented Examples:** None. Drawings of mountainous and river landscapes with castles and villages signed 'Cock' and dated in his life time are presumed by some his work.
[Fl. 818, Fl. 559, Fl. 107, Fl. 892, Fl. 440, Fl. 316.]

Cock van Aelst, P., see **Coeke.**

Cock (or Cockq), Paul Joseph de. Flemish Sch. *b* Bruges 1724 *d* Bruges 1801. *Landscapes and 'history'; also worked as architect.* Pupil of M. de Visch; then studied Paris and Valenciennes; Professor Bruges Academy 1766; Director (*cf.* J. A. Garemyn) from 1775; G. de Pélichy and J. F. Ducq were his pupils. J. B. Suvée and J. A. v. d. Donckt painted his portrait. [Fl. 216, Fl. 114.]

Cock, Xavier de. Flemish Sch. *b* son of a tailor, Ghent 1818 *d* Deurle, East Flanders 1896. Brother of C. de C. *Animals, rural genre, landscapes.* Pupil Antwerp Acad. of F. de Braekeleer; visited Holland; in France (Paris and Barbizon) 1852-9; also frequently in Paris in later years. Represented in AMSTERDAM, BRUSSELS *Cattle returning.* GHENT, THE HAGUE, LIÈGE, LILLE, MONTPELLIER *Cattle at a pond.* PARIS State Coll. and U.S.A. NEW YORK Met. *Children calling the cows.* [Fl. 422, Fl. 264.]

Cockels, J. C. see **Cogels, J. C.**

Cocks, G. see **Coques.**

Cockx, Jan. Flemish Sch. *b* Antwerp 1891. *Marines, still life.* Represented in ANTWERP *Seapiece.* [Fl. 17.]

Cockx, Philibert. Flemish Sch. *b* Ixelles 1879. *Landscapes, figures, nudes, religious subjects, still life oil and w.* Influenced by French 'Fauve' movement (*cf.* C. Dehoy). Pupil Brussels Acad. Represented in ANTWERP *The horse, Spring.* BRUSSELS *Flemish landscape* 1924. [Fl. 123, Fl. 568, Fl. 296.]

Coclers, Jean Baptiste Pierre. Flemish Sch. *b* son of Philippe C., Maestricht 1696 *d* Liège 1772. *Religious subjects for Liège churches* (*cf.* J. B. Carlier, H. Deprez, O. Pirotte, E. Plumier and E. P. de Rendeux), '*history', portraits.* Went Italy where pupil of the Italian painter S. Conca and M. Benefial. Returned via Marseilles *c.* 1731; worked Maestricht 1732-7; court painter to Prince Bishops of Liège and painted decorations in Bishop's Palace (completed by P. J. Delcloche *q.v.*); had some children by a first wife and 15 more by a second, five of whom were painters. L. Defrance, M. Aubée, J. Latour and N. H. J. Fassin were his pupils. H. Deprez collaborated with him in decorative works.
[Fl. 275, Fl. 409, Fl. 462.]

Coclers, Jean Georges Christian. Flemish Sch. *b* Liège 1715. *d* Liège 1751 Brother of J. B. P. C. *Still life with flowers, fruit, birds and insects* (*cf.* R. J. Malaine, C. W. de Hamilton, S. Hardimé, P. Hardimé, P. Snyers, G. F. Ziesel also J. B. de Crépu and P. Faes). Official painter to city of Liège 1743; also acted as councillor and customs official.
[Fl. 409, Fl. 470, Fl. 798.]

*Coclers, Louis Bernard (baptised **Jean Baptiste Bernard**). Flemish Sch. *b* son of Jean Baptiste P. C., Liège 1741 *d* Liège 1817. *Portraits; genre in Dutch tradition; active as engraver, dealer and restorer.* Pupil of his father; in Rome (*cf.* E. P. de Rendeux, H. de La Pegnia, H. F. van Lint, J. X. Vermoelen) 1759-62; some years in Holland (Maestricht, Nymwegen, Dordrecht, Leyden); in London (*cf.* P. J. Lion, P. J. Tassaert, H. J. de Cort, P. J. Redouté and P. de Glimes) 1784; in Paris where was friend of Greuze 1787; sold contents of his studio and dealer's stock and left Paris in year of Revolution (*cf.* J. L. Malaine, J. F. Ducq, J. B. Suvée); went Amsterdam; returned Liège after union of Belgium and Holland 1816. **Signed Examples:** AMSTERDAM *Jan Bicker* 1776, *Catharina Six, wife of Jan Bicker seated by a table with trinket box and flowers* 1776, *Mother and child at a table* (the woman drinking from a glass through which the child's face is seen). His engravings include a *Young couple who have changed clothes,* a *Young woman drawing milk from her breast* and a version of F. Hals' *Hille Bobbe.*
[Fl. 275, Fl. 451, Fl. 612, Fl. 423, Fl. 892, Fl. 798.]

Coclers, Philippe. Flemish Sch. *b* Liège *c.* 1660 *d* Liège *c.* 1736. *Portraits, 'history' religious subjects* (*cf.* J. Carlier). Visited Italy; worked Maestricht and Liège; Court painter to Joseph of Bavaria, Prince Bishop of Liège.
[Fl. 275, Fl. 612, Fl. 423.]

Coclers, Philippe Henri (known as **Philippe van Wyck**). Flemish Sch. *b* son of Jean Baptiste C., Liège 1738 *d* Marseilles *c.* 1803. *Portraits, miniatures, still life* (*cf.* J. G. C. C.). Pupil of his father; travelled in Italy; settled Marseilles where later became Director of the Acad. royale de peinture. **Signed Example:** SCHWERIN *The stall* 1784. [Fl. 423. Fl. 462.]

*Coebergher (Koebergher), Wenzelas. Flemish Sch. *b* Antwerp 1557 or 1561 *d* Brussels 1634. *Religious subjects; also active as architect* (Montaigu, Notre Dame 1609-21. Antwerp, Église des Augustins; Bergues-Saint-Winoc, Mont-de-Piété), *engineer, numismatist, and director of first Flemish pawnshops.*

Pupil of M. de Vos 1573; went Paris (*cf.* G. van Cleve and H. Francken the elder) to cure passion for daughter of M. de Vos *c.* 1578; in Naples (*cf.* J. S. van Calcar, A. Mytens, J. van der Straet, L. Finson, F. Pourbus the younger, P. Schephen, D. Hendricksz and C. Smet) 1580 till after 1594; married in Naples; in Rome 1598-1603; after death of first wife, 1599, married sister of J. Francart *q.v.*; visited Antwerp 1601 (?); back in Antwerp and Master Antwerp Guild 1604; moved Brussels 1605; became painter, architect and engineer to Archduke Albert (*cf.* G. de Crayer); instructed the Archduke in mathematics and designed fountains for him at Tervueren and other palaces; was visited in Brussels by the antiquary and numismatist Claude Fabri de Peiresc (close friend of Rubens) who lived Aix-en-Provence; Van Dyck drew his portrait. **Signed Example:** NAPLES S. Domenico Maggiore *Resurrection* 1594. **Documented Examples:** ROME Sta Maria in Vallicella (Chiesa Nuova) *Pentecost* (contract 1598, receipt for payments 1603). BRUSSELS *Entombment* 1605 (from Brussels S. Géry; engraved; seen by Descamps 1768 and by Sir Joshua Reynolds who described it (1781) as 'equal to the best of Domenichino'). NANCY *Martyrdom of S. Sebastian* painted Rome or Naples for Crossbowmen's altar in Antwerp Cathedral where damaged by a rival or lunatic who cut the heads of two women which C. repainted 1601; seen by Descamps who described the repainted heads as 'ni belles ni agréables' and by Reynolds who says 'two women's heads are introduced very awkwardly in the bottom of the picture' and describes it as not equal to the Brussels *Entombment*; taken by the French for the Musée Napoléon, sent Nancy 1812 and not returned (*cf.* J. D. Odevaere) 1815; NAPLES S. Maria di Piedigrotta *Crucifixion*. An altarpiece *The Emperor Constantine adoring the True Cross recovered by the Empress Helena* painted for Antwerp S. Jacques is recorded. Philip van Valckenisse of Antwerp owned (1614) a *Caritas*, another Antwerp collector owned (1627) a *Magdalene*, and Jan Gillis, Antwerp silversmith, owned 1682 a *S. Catherine*.
[Fl. 168, Fl. 425, Fl. 215, Fl. 216, Fl. 702, Fl. 99, Fl. 759, Fl. 84, Fl. 375, Fl. 892, Fl. 440, Fl. 305, Fl. 213, Fl. 296, Fl. 678.]

Coecke van Aelst, Pauwels. Flemish Sch. *b* illegitimate son of P. Coecke van A., Antwerp *c.* 1530 *d* Antwerp date unknown. Van Mander (1604) records him as an excellent copyist of the works of Jan Mabuse (Gossaert) and as painter of flowers in small glasses (*cf.* A. Bosschaert and G. Congnet). His widow married G. van Coninxloo. [Fl. 559, Fl. 107.]

*Coecke van Aelst, Pieter. Flemish Sch. *b* Aelst (Alost) 1502 *d* Brussels 1550. *Religious subjects, designs for tapestries and glass; also worked as sculptor, architect and writer* (translator of the Bolognese architect Serlio's book on Vitruvius). Pupil in Brussels of B. v. Orley; Master Antwerp Guild 1527; visited Rome; in Constantinople for a year in connection with tapestry making and offered tapestry designs with human figures to the Sultan who as a Mohammedan declined them but otherwise received him well 1533; returned Antwerp 1534; married as second wife Marie Bessemers *q.v.* 1537; Court painter to Mary of Hungary (*cf.* J. C. Vermeyen) and Charles V; took leading part with F. Floris *q.v.* H. W. de Cock *q.v.*, A. van Palerme *q.v.*, J. V. de Vries *q.v.* and many others on decorations for Pageant Entry into Antwerp of Charles V and Philip II (when a giant polychrome Antigonus figure of his fashioning was a feature) 1549; published engravings of procession 1550; Willem van Breda (presumed by some Willem Key *q.v.*), N. v. Neufchatel and P. Bruegel the elder, who married his daughter, were among his pupils (*cf.* also Joos van Cleve). **Signed Examples:** None. **Semi-documented Example:** BRUSSELS *The Last Supper* 1531 (several versions exist of this picture which was engraved 1585 by H. Goltzius without painter's name; one extant print has the name written in by hand.) A series of woodcuts of Turkish subjects (*cf.* J. Swart) made from his drawings, was published by his widow

1553 (an edition titled '*The Turks in 1533*' was published by Sir W. Stirling Maxwell 1873). Drawings, signed or inscribed with his name, are in Rotterdam (Boymans) *Prodigal Son* (*cf.* Prodigal Son Master), Vienna (Albertina) *Paul before Agrippa*, *Passage of the Red Sea*, London (B.M.) *Orpheus* (*cf.* L. v. d. Borcht). Margareta Boge widow of an Antwerp Mintmaster owned (1574) a *Jupiter*; the Antwerp dealer H. de Neyt had (1642) in his very large collection an *Abraham* (grisaille), a *Moor with Tunis in the background* (*cf.* J. C. Vermeyen) and a *Portrait of a Moor*. Paintings presumed by some his work or from his studio are in various museums.
[Fl. 371, Fl. 559, Fl. 107, Fl. 213, Fl. 316, Fl. 530, Fl. 173.]

Coecke (or Cock) van Aelst, Pieter, the younger. Flemish Sch. *b* son of P. C. van Aelst, Antwerp (?) before 1527 *d c.* 1559. Recorded Antwerp 1552. First master of G. van Coninxloo *q.v.* [Fl. 892.]

Coelenbier (Koelombier), Jan. Flemish Sch. *b* Courtrai *c.* 1600 *d* Haarlem (?) after 1677. *Landscapes.* Went Haarlem where member of Guild 1632; in later life worked there as art dealer. **Signed Example:** COPENHAGEN *River landscape.*
[Fl. 892, Fl. 170.]

Coene, Constantin Fidèle. Flemish Sch. *b* Vilvorde 1780 *d* Brussels 1841. *Costume history, street scenes, genre.* Pupil of F. Faber; in Amsterdam 1800-2; Professor Brussels Acad. 1820. Represented in AMSTERDAM *Porte de Hal, Brussels, with market carts, many figures and two peasants fighting* (*cf.* J. B. de Jonghe) 1823. GHENT *Charles I knighting Rubens* (*cf.* P. Kremer) 1808. His *The Battle of Waterloo* was bought by George IV when Prince of Wales. A *Peasant family seated at the door of their cottage* (*cf.* H. Voordecker) is also recorded. [Fl. 451, Fl. 612, Fl. 440, Fl. 73.]

Coene, Henri (Jean-Henri) de. Flemish Sch. *b* Nederbrakel 1798 *d* Brussels 1866. *Indoor and outdoor genre.* Pupil (in Brussels) of L. David (*cf.* H. de Caisne, M. G. Stapleaux and F. J. Navez) and of J. Paelinck *q.v.* Professor Brussels Acad. Represented in AMSTERDAM *News from market with peasants meeting on country road* (*cf.* J. L. Demarne) 1827. BRUSSELS *The lacemaker*. LILLE A *Veterinary surgeon* in collaboration with E. Verboeckhoven 1834 is recorded.
[Fl. 451, Fl. 160 (1866), Fl. 440.]

Coetsiers, Jan see **Cossiers.**

*Coffermans (or Koffermans), Marcellus. Flemish Sch. *b* Antwerp before 1535 *d* after 1575. *Religious subjects.* Master Antwerp Guild 1549. His daughter Isabella was a painter. **Signed Examples:** FLORENCE Bargello *Christ in Purgatory.* MADRID Prado *Penitent Magdalene* 1568; S. Sebastian *Annunciation* 1575. Pictures presumed by some his work are in various museums (*cf.* M. Helmon).
[Fl. 892, Fl. 807, Fl. 668, Fl. 615.]

Cogels, Joseph Charles. Flemish Sch. *b* Brussels 1785 *d* Leitheim Castle, Donauwörth, Bavaria 1831. *Landscapes with canals, bridges and castles, marines; also lithographs and engravings.* Studied Düsseldorf; visited Paris; worked mainly in Munich where was patronized by the King and Queen and the Duke of Leuchtenberg. [Fl. 612, Fl. 892.]

Cogen, Félix. Flemish Sch. *b* St. Nicolas 1838 *d* Brussels 1907. *Genre, costume history, portraits.* Pupil of T. Canneel in Ghent Acad. Exhibited London Crystal Palace 1882 and Paris Salon. Chevalier of the Légion d'Honneur 1883. Represented in BRUGES *Distribution of bread to widows and orphans.* COURTRAI, GHENT, LIÈGE and MELBOURNE (Australia) *Fishergirl.* [Fl. Bib. 19th cent. Fl. 114.]

Coignet see **Congnet.**

Col, David (Jan David). Flemish Sch. *b* Antwerp 1822 *d* Antwerp 1900. *Anecdotic genre.* Pupil in Antwerp of N. de Keyser. Represented in ANTWERP *Shaving day* 1877. BRUGES *Politicians* (*cf* J. B. Madou). CHICAGO *Dispute in a tavern* 1874. CINCINNATI, MONTREAL. [Fl. Bib. 19th cent.]

Colijn of Brussels, see **Coter.**

Collart, Marie (Mme. Henrotin). Flemish Sch. *b* Brussels 1842 *d* 1911. *Animal pieces and landscapes (some with figures).* Pupil of A. Verwée. Worked mostly in Brabant; given Cross of the Order of Leopold 1880. Represented in ANTWERP *Courtyard of a Brabant farmhouse* 1890. BRUSSELS *Orchard in Flanders.* LOUVAIN Town Hall and Belgian royal collection. [Fl. Bib. 19th cent., Fl. 440.]

Collens, Charles. Flemish Sch. *b* Antwerp 1869 *d* Antwerp 1901. *Genre (street types), caricatures, illustrations.* Represented ANTWERP *Pilgrimage.* [Fl. 17.]

Colori, L., see **Caullery.**

Colsoulle, Gustave. Flemish Sch. *b* Bruges 1843 *d* Antwerp 1895. *Animals (mainly horses and stall interiors* (*cf.* J. Stobbaerts)), *landscapes.* Represented ANTWERP *Farm Horses.* [Fl. 17.]

****Congnet (or Coignet), Gillis,** known as Gillis with the Birthmark (met de Fleck). Flemish Sch. *b* son of a goldsmith, Antwerp *c.* 1535 *d* Hamburg 1599. *Portraits, mythological subjects with nudes, night pieces* (*cf.* Jooris van Cleve), *landscapes and religious subjects.* Pupil of and lived in house of A. van Palerme *q.v.*; Master Antwerp Guild 1561; went Sicily, Naples (*cf.* W. Coebergher) and Rome; painted frescoes at Terni with one 'Stello' who was killed by a rocket when watching fireworks in Rome; back in Antwerp 1570; Dean in Guild 1583; went Amsterdam on Parma's expulsions of Protestants (*cf.* F. Spierinx, D. v. d. Queborne, C. Ketel and C. v. d. Voort) 1586; Amsterdam citizen 1589; went Hamburg *c.* 1595 worked there for churches and recommended J. V. de Vries *q.v.* to visit Amsterdam; van Mander (1604) records him as a skilful painter of night pieces who used gold to obtain effects of torch and candle light and adds that he was censured for selling works almost wholly by his pupils as his own. C. Molenaer *q.v.* sometimes painted landscape and other backgrounds in his pictures. The Dutch painter Cornelis of Haarlem (*cf.* P. Pietersz) was among his pupils in Antwerp and painted, on his instruction, a striking flower piece, van Mander records, almost without verdure 'bijna zonder groen' (*cf.* P. Coecke van Aelst). **Signed Examples:** ANTWERP *Pierson la Hues, Drummer of the Crossbowmen* doc. 1581), *S. George* (*cf.* F. Pourbus the elder) 1581 (richly gilded). **Documented Example:** AMSTERDAM Rijks. *Drawing of a lottery in an Amsterdam Street 1592* (night scene by torchlight (*cf.* D. Vinckeboons). Works recorded by engravings include *Phryne and Aristotle* (*cf.* C. van Savoyen), *Bacchus and Venus, Cleopatra* and biblical subjects. Seventeenth century Antwerp inventories record a *Last Supper* and *Landscapes.* [Fl. 559, Fl. 892, Fl. 213.]

****Coninck (or Koninck), David de,** known as Rammelaer (Buck rabbit). Flemish Sch. *b* Antwerp 1636 *d* Brussels 1699. *Hunting scenes, animals, birds, game pieces* (*cf.* F. Snyders, P. de Vos, J. Fyt, N. Bernaerts, P. Boel, J. v. Kessel the elder, A. de Gryef, J. B. Govaerts, also A. Clevenbergh). Pupil of P. Boel; went Italy 1670; worked Rome where was given nickname in Flemish painters' colony and, with other members of the colony was arrested and interrogated by the Inquisition for alleged heretical practices; member of Accad. di S. Luca 1686; returned Antwerp 1687. **Signed Examples:** AMSTERDAM Rijks. *Stag hunt, Bear hunt, Hawk and dogs attacking waterfowl.* PRAGUE Nostitz. *Lion hunt, Bear hunt.* [Fl. 425, Fl. 892.]

Coninck, K. de see **Keuninck.**

****Coninxloo, Cornelis van** (real name **Scernir** or **Schernier**). Flemish Sch. 16th cent. Worked Brussels. **Signed Example:** BRUSSELS Mus. (588a) *Genealogy of the Virgin s* Cornelis va Conixlo Scernir 1526. Presumed by some identical with Abbey of Dilighem Master *q.v.* [Fl. 121.]

****Coninxloo, Gillis van.** Flemish Sch. *b* son of one G. or J. van C., Antwerp 1544 *d* Amsterdam 1607. *Landscapes* (*cf.* A. Mirou). Pupil of P. Coecke van Aelst the younger, L. Kroes and G. Mostaert (*cf.* J. Sons); visited Paris (*cf.* G. v. Cleve, B. Spranger and H. Francken the elder); in Antwerp Guild 1570; in Antwerp during patriot occupation (*cf.* F. Pourbus the elder) and siege by Parma and fled as Protestant to Zeeland after Parma's conquest (*cf.* D. v. d. Queborne) 1585; in Frankenthal (*cf.* J. v. Liere) 1587-96; returned Amsterdam where became citizen 1597 (*cf.* P. Stalpaert). Lampsonius *q.v.* refers to him as a pioneer landscapist. Van Mander (1604) who knew him in Amsterdam calls him the best landscape painter of the time and records his influence in Dutch landscape. Marten van Cleve, H. van Balen (?) and D. Vinckeboons painted figures in some of his landscapes. P. Brueghel the younger was his pupil. **Signed Example:** VIENNA Liecht. *Wooded landscape with huntsman crossing bridge* 1598. **Monogrammed Examples:** DRESDEN *Landscape with Judgement of Midas* 1588. GRAZ *Wooded landscape with staghunt* 1600. VIENNA K. *Wooded landscape* (monogram partly obliterated); Liecht. *Wooded landscape* 1604. BRUSSELS *Wooded scene* (drawing). [Fl. 559, Fl. 892, Fl. 659, Fl. 213, Fl. 691.]

Coninxloo, Hans van, the elder. Flemish Sch. *b* son of Jan van C. the younger, Antwerp *c.* 1540 *d* Emden 1595. '*History*'. As Protestant left Antwerp under Alva persecutions (*cf.* A. de Weerdt) and went Emden (where remained) 1571. **Signed Examples:** EMDEN *The Gods on Olympus* 1592. PRAGUE Rudolfinum *Hercules on Olympus* 1592 (*cf.* H. van C. the younger). [Fl. 892.]

Coninxloo, Hans van, the younger. Flemish Sch. *b* son of Hans van C. the elder, Antwerp *c.* 1565 *d* Emden *c.* 1620. Taken by his parents to Emden 1571; citizen Emden 1593; in Amsterdam as art dealer by 1603; van Mander (1604) records him as ordering pictures from D. Vinckeboons *q.v.*; returned Emden 1618. The signed pictures listed as by his father may be possibly his work. [Fl. 559, Fl. 892.]

Coninxloo, Hans van, the third. Flemish Sch. *b* son of Hans van C. the younger, Emden *c.* 1589 *d* Amsterdam after 1645. *Game, still life* (?). Led an irregular life as painter and dealer between Amsterdam and Emden. EMDEN has a *Game piece* signed H V Coninxloo presumed by some his work. [Fl. 892.]

Coninxloo, Isaak G. van. Flemish Sch. *b* son of Hans van C. the elder, Emden *c.* 1580 *d* Amsterdam 1634. In Antwerp 1607-13; then in Amsterdam. [Fl. 892.]

Coninxloo, Jan van, the elder. Flemish Sch. 15th cent. As 'Jan de Royaulme, called Scernier, son of Brussels painter' in Tournai 1483; in Brussels 1491. Presumed father of Jan van C. [Fl. 316.]

****Coninxloo, Jan van.** Flemish Sch. *b* son of J. v. C. the elder (?), Brussels 1489 *d* Antwerp (?) after 1555. *Religious subjects.* With his wife and his relation B. van Orley *q.v.* and others condemned for heresy for listening to Protestant sermons and punished with a fine and order to attend an equal number of Catholic sermons (*cf.* A. v. Overbeke and H. Tons) 1527; working Brussels 1541; in Antwerp Guild 1552 and citizen there 1555. **Signed Examples:** BRUSSELS Single panel *Nativity* 1530. Triptych centre: *The lineage of S. Anne*: wings:

Joachim's sacrifice rejected, Death of S. Anne 1546. Two wings: *Jesus among the Doctors, The Marriage Feast at Cana* with *Miracle of the loaves and fishes* on reverses. ROUEN *Circumcision.* [Fl. 892, Fl. 316.]

Coninxloo, Pieter van (Pierre de Royaulme). Flemish Sch. *b* Brussels (?) *c.* 1460 *d* Brussels (?) after 1513. *Portraits and decorative work.* Recorded in Brussels 1479; designed catafalque for Duke John of Cleve 1481; painted coaches for Duke Philip the Fair (*cf.* J. van Lathem) 1499; painted portrait of Margaret of Austria (*cf.* J. Schooff) sent by Duke Philip to Henry VII of England then negotiating a marriage with her 1505; painted Charles V and other members of the family (*cf.* J. v. Battel and J. C. Vermeyen) 1513. **Signed Examples:** None. **Documented Examples:** None.
[Fl. 316, Fl. 530.]

Coomans, Pierre Olivier Joseph. Flemish Sch. *b* Brussels 1816 *d* Boulogne-sur-Seine (Paris) 1889. *Costume history, Neo-Pompeian subjects, genre, book illustrations.* Pupil of P. van Hanselaere and N. de Keyser; illustrated his brother Joseph's 'Histoire de Belgique' 1836; visited Italy, N. Africa and Near East. Represented in BELGIAN Royal Coll. *Capture of Jerusalem by the Crusaders* commissioned 1841. CHICAGO *Pompeian lady* 1877. GOTHA *Phryne* 1857, STUTTGART *Roman Family* 1864, *Sappho* 1870. YORK *The Mask* 1870. Very large compositions painted in his early years including *Ossian and Malvina* 1836, *S. Peter* 1836 and *The Deluge* (described as influenced by the English painter John Martin) 1839 are recorded.
[Fl. 451, Fl. 481, Fl. 160 (1890), Fl. 440.]

Coornhuuse, Jacques van den. Flemish Sch. *b* Furnes before 1540 *d* after 1584. Master Bruges Guild 1556; worked Bruges. **Monogrammed and Documented Example:** BRUGES *Last Judgement* 1578 free copy of painting by J. Provoost *q.v.* commissioned by Prévôté of S. Donatian. (*cf.* J. de Backer).
[Fl. 65 (1864), Fl. 892, Fl. 114.]

★Coosemans, Alexander. Flemish Sch. *b* Antwerp 1627 *d* Antwerp 1689. *Still life with fruit, vessels and flowers* (*cf.* T. Aenvanck), *asparagus* (*cf.* F. Ijkens, F. Snyders, P. Snyers) and '*Vanitas*' *subjects* (*cf.* C. N. Gysbrechts). Pupil of flower painter J. D. de Heem in Antwerp 1642; Master Antwerp Guild 1645. **Signed Examples:** BORDEAUX *Flower garland* (*cf.* D. Seghers). BRUSSELS '*Vanitas*' (with skull, crucifix, candle and hour glass). COPENHAGEN *Fruit and flower garland round a wine glass* (*cf.* A. van Utrecht). MADRID Prado *Still life with fruit and asparagus.* NIORT *Fruit and crabs.* VIENNA K. *Still life with fruit and vessels.* Still life subjects with monogram A. C. in various museums are presumed by some his work. [Fl. 107, Fl. 892.]

Coosemans, Joseph Théodore. Flemish Sch. *b* Brussels 1828 *d* Schaerbeek nr. Brussels 1904. *Landscapes (mostly of Limbourg region).* Employed in commerce till *c.* 1860; then pupil of T. Fourmois, C. Tschaggeny and A. Verwée. Joined Tervueren group of artists (*cf.* H. Boulenger); worked at Fontainebleau and Barbizon; settled Louvain 1876; worked at Genck; Professor Antwerp Higher Institute 1887; E. Viérin was among his pupils. Memorial exhibition with two hundred pictures Brussels 1905. Represented in ANTWERP *Winter day* 1879. BRUGES *Sunshine after storm* BRUSSELS, GHENT, LIÈGE, LOUVAIN, NAMUR, ROUEN, TERMONDE. [Fl. 440, Fl. 296.]

★Coosemas, J. D. Presumed Flemish Sch. 17th cent. MADRID Prado has fully signed *Still life with peaches, grapes and glass of white wine* (*cf.* Joris v. Son and T. Aenvanck). [Fl. 555.]

Copman, Eugène Jean. Flemish Sch. *b* Bruges 1839 *d* Bruges 1930. *Portraits.* Pupil in Bruges of E. Wallays; then in Ant-

werp of N. de Keyser; also studied Paris and Rome. Curator Bruges Mus. 1892-1930. Represented in BRUGES *Dr. J. F. Isacq, Mme. Charles van Robays.* [Fl. 114.]

★Coppens, Augustin. Flemish Sch. *b* Brussels (?) *c.* 1668 (?) *d* after 1695. *Landscapes, topographic drawings and engravings, designs for tapestry backgrounds, portraits.* **Signed Example:** BRUSSELS *Self portrait with ruins of Brussels and steeple of town hall in background* (after Marshal Villeroi's 1695 bombardment, *cf.* Z. J. van Helmont, J. van Orley, R. van Orley, E. Pery and R. v. d. Weyden). An *Ovid subject* tapestry with figures by L. van Schoor *q.v.* and landscape by Coppens was exported to Vienna by the Forchoudt firm of Antwerp dealers (*cf.* L. Achtschellinck) 1702; landscape backgrounds in tapestries *Triomphes des dieux* with figures by J. van Orley and drawings for engravings of the 1695 destruction of Brussels are recorded. Descamps (1769) records landscapes in Brussels Église des Dominicains with figures (*Prodigal Son* other subjects) by 'J. Milé', and a landscape in S. Gudule (*cf.* F. Coppens). [Fl. 216, Fl. 612, Fl. 892, Fl. 212, Fl. 296.]

★Coppens, François. Flemish Sch. *b* Brussels (?) before 1635. *Wooded landscapes (forest of Soignes) with religious subjects* (*cf.* J. d'Arthois, L. Achtschellinck, I. v. d. Stock, D. v. Heil, A. Coppens). Master Brussels Guild 1650. **Signed Examples:** BRUSSELS Notre Dame de la Chapelle *Landscape with Holy Family, Landscape with Rest on the Flight.* [Fl. 301.]

Coppens, Omer. Flemish Sch. *b* Dunkirk 1864 *d* Ixelles 1926. *Landscapes and town scenes, genre; also coloured etchings.* Member of L'Essor group (*cf.* A. Hamesse); worked Morocco, France and Venice. Represented in BRUSSELS *Autumn day in Bruges* 1922, OSTEND. [Fl. Bib. 19th cent., Fl. 123.]

Coppieters, Alberic. Flemish Sch. *b* Ypres 1878 *d* Paris 1902. *Landscapes, figures, still life.* Represented ANTWERP *Flowers and lemons.* BRUSSELS *Dixmude farm, Chinese vase.* [Fl. Bib. 19th cent., Fl. 123, Fl. 17.]

Coppieters, Gustave. Flemish Sch. *b* Brussels *c.* 1840 *d* Brussels 1885. *Fantastic subjects* (*cf.* J. Ensor).
[Fl. Bib. 19th cent., Fl. 515.]

★Coques, Gonzales (b Cockx but adopted Spanish form). Flemish Sch. *b* son of P. W. C., Antwerp 1614 *d* Antwerp 1684. *Portraits and conversation pieces* (*cf.* P. Fruytiers and P. Meert) *mostly on small scale, genre, gallery interiors* (*cf.* H. Staben and W. van Haecht). Known as the Little van Dyck. Pupil of P. Brueghel III and of D. Ryckaert II (whose daughter was his mistress and later his wife); de Bie (1661) records a visit to England and patronage by Charles I (*cf.* C. de Neve); Master Antwerp Guild 1641; worked for Prince Frederick Henry (*cf.* D. Seghers) and the Princess of Orange; farmed out to A. v. Diepenbeeck *q.v.* most of a commission for a *Story of Psyche* series for Prince Frederick Henry 1647 and to T. v. Thulden *q.v.* most of a commission from Amalie van Solms for the Huis ten Bosch (*cf.* J. Jordaens) 1649; also patronized by Frederick William Elector of Brandenburg and the Governors Archduke Leopold Wilhelm (*cf.* G. Seghers, J. B. v. Heil and D. Teniers the younger), Don John of Austria (*cf.* H. Janssens and P. Snayers) and the Comte de Monterey (*cf.* A. Genoels); was member of Chamber of Rhetoric; married a second wife 1675; at one time had a liaison with a young lady who came to his studio disguised as a Polish young man and took lessons in painting. The architecture and landscapes in his pictures are sometimes by other hands. **Signed Examples:** CASSEL *A young man with a book and a young lady playing a painted harpsichord s* Gonsales 1640. LONDON Royal Coll. (Buckingham Palace) *The Verbiest family on a terrace s* Gonsales 1664. **Inscribed Example:** AMIENS *Execution of Charles I.* **Documented Examples:** THE HAGUE *Interior of a picture gallery* (painted

for and presented to an Antwerp lawyer by the Antwerp Guild for services rendered; many of the pictures shown bear signatures of the artists *cf*. C. E. Biset, T. Boeyermans, P. Bredael, J. Cossiers, J. de Duyts, A. Goubau, P. Gysels, J. v. d. Hecke, J. v. Kessel the elder, K. v. Opstal, J. Peeters the elder, E. Quellinus and P. Spierinckx; the architecture traditionally ascribed to W. S. van Ehrenberg (*cf*. also J. S. Saey)). LONDON N.G. *The painter R. v. d. Hoecke* (as *Sight* in *Five Senses* series) engraved. A genre piece titled *Early Vanity* (child with mirror) is among pictures recorded by engravings. Contemporary Antwerp inventories record many portraits including one with flower garland by D. Seghers, another with garland by N. v. Verendael, a *Group of the family of Geerard de Jode* (possibly with portrait of P. Spierinckx *q.v*.) and occasional religious and genre pieces. Portraits and conversation pieces presumed by some his work, are in many museums.
[Fl. 86, Fl. 425, Fl. 878, Fl. 22, Fl. 215, Fl. 770, Fl. 892, Fl. 213.]

Cordua (or **Corduba** or **Corduwa** or **Curta** or **Kurte**), **Joannes de.** Flemish Sch. *b* Brussels (?) before 1650 *d* Vienna or Prague 1702. *Genre and still life including 'Vanitas' pieces* (*cf*. C. N. Gysbrechts and J. Plasschaert). Went Vienna where worked for the Court (*cf*. J. B. Cordua, J. A. v. d. Baren, P. Evrard, R. Megan and J. Thomas (van Ypern)). Signed Examples: HERMANNSTADT *Vanitas* (J. de Cordua). VIENNA Harrach *Old woman counting money* (Joe de Corduba). Monogrammed Example: VIENNA Harrach *Peasant girl and young man.*
[Fl. 753, Fl. 612, Fl. 631 (1905) Fl. 892, Fl. 798.]

Cordua, Johan Baptist. Flemish Sch. *b* Brussels 1649 *d* Vienna 1698. Brother of Joannes de C. Worked in Vienna. [Fl. 892.]

Corkole, Auguste. Flemish Sch. *b* Ghent 1822 *d* Ghent 1875. *Anecdotic genre.* Represented in YPRES *The interrupted game of cards.* [Fl. 837 (1875).]

Cornelis van Gouda. Flemish (Dutch) Sch. *b* Gouda 1510 (?) *d* 1550 (?). *Portraits.* Pupil of M. v. Heemskerck. Van Mander (1604) writes: 'In his youth he detested drinking but after frequenting the Court and becoming acquainted with people of high rank he changed his habits so completely that even great drunkards stood in awe before him; he then became a dauber (een knoeier)'. *cf*. F. Floris. VIENNA Harrach has a *Portrait of a man* signed C G 1537 presumed by some his work. [Fl. 559, Fl. 892, Fl. 842.]

*Cornelis, Albert. Flemish Sch. *b* *c*. 1485 (?) *d* Bruges 1532. *Religious subjects.* Brought action against a man who had sold him bad colours 1513; had five stalls in Bruges market place for sale of pictures 1515-30; an assessor (vinder) in Bruges Guild 1518; worked for decorations for Pageant Entry into Bruges of Charles V (*cf*. J. Provoost) 1520. Signed Examples: None. Documented Example: BRUGES S. Jacques *Coronation of the Virgin with choirs of angels* commissioned 1517 by the Fullers' Guild who provided a detailed programme for the picture and who stopped payments before the picture was finished (1519) on ground that he had farmed out subsidiary parts; claimed successfully in the courts that he was entitled to do this by custom and the terms of his contract by which he was bound only to design the composition and paint the flesh parts himself; the picture (which formerly had wings not known to be extant) was finished by 1522 (*cf*. Brighton Assumption of the Virgin Painter).
[Fl. 892, Fl. 298, Fl. 113, Fl. 316.]

Cornelisz, Cornelis (called **Kunst**). Flemish (Dutch) Sch. *b* second son of Cornelis Engelbrechtsz, Leyden 1493 *d* 1544. *Religious subjects, portraits.* Pupil of his father; worked Leyden with visits to Bruges where he was successful. Van Mander (1604) records a dramatic *Christ bearing the Cross* (with the two thieves and the Virgin weeping) and a *Descent from the Cross*, also a *Portrait of the artist and his wife in a garden, with a city in the background* then owned by the artist's daughter. [Fl. 559, Fl. 892.]

*Cornelisz van Oostsanen, Jacob (sometimes called Jacob of Amsterdam). Flemish (Dutch) Sch. *b* Oostsanen nr. Amsterdam *c*. 1470 *d* Amsterdam 1533. Brother of Cornelis Buys the elder and father of Dirk Jacobsz. *Religious subjects, portraits; also worked as wood engraver.* Lived Amsterdam where owner of a house by 1500; painted works for the Oude Kerk mostly destroyed by iconoclasts (*cf*. P. Aertsen) 1566. Jan Scorel was his pupil or assistant between 1512 and 1517. Monogrammed Examples: (characteristic monogram) AMSTERDAM Rijks. *Portrait of a man* (presumed by some a self portrait) 1533, *Saul and the Witch of Endor* November 29, 1526 (*cf*. F. Francken). CASSEL Triptych *Worship of the Holy Trinity* 1523. THE HAGUE Mauritshuis *Salome with the head of John the Baptist* (*cf*. H. Memlinc) 1524. Van Mander (1604) records fragments of a *Seven Works of Mercy*, a *Circumcision* dated 1517, a *Descent from the Cross* with landscape by Jan Scorel and a *Crucifixion* which are not known to be extant. Van Mander records as among his wood engravings nine round *Scenes from the Passion* and a series of *Knights on horseback*. Paintings presumed by some his work are in various museums. [Fl. 559, Fl. 892, Fl. 316, Fl. 421.]

Cornelisz, Lucas (called **Kunst** and **de Kok**). Flemish (Dutch) Sch. *b* son of Cornelis Engelbrechtsz, Leyden *c*. 1495 *d* England (?) or Leyden (?) 1552. *Religious subjects, portraits* (?). Van Mander (1604) records that he became a cook and went with his wife and seven or eight children to England in the reign of Henry VIII (*cf*. L. Teerlinck and S. Bening) and adds 'when the Earl of Leicester came from England as Governor there were some Englishmen with him who were eager to buy his works which shows that they had known of him in England' (*cf*. D. Barendsz, C. Ketel and J. Savery the elder). Presumed by some identical with one Luca Cornelis recorded as tapestry designer in Ferrara 1535-47. Signed Example: VIENNA Acad. Drawing *Adoration of the Kings* signed Luijcas Kunst 1531. Van Mander records a *Women taken in Adultery.* Vertue (before 1756) saw at Penshurst Castle a portrait *T. Arundel, Archbishop of Canterbury* 'the posture like Bishop Warham' signed 'on the book the edges of the leaves' with a monogram which he guessed might represent this name. [Fl. 559, Fl. 826, Fl. 856, Fl. 892, Fl. 631 (1935 and 1936), Fl. 421.]

Cornelisz, Pieter (called **Kunst**). Flemish (Dutch) Sch. *b* eldest son of Cornelis Engelbrechtsz, Leyden *c*. 1490 *d* Leyden (?) after 1527. Van Mander records him as glasspainter (*cf*. D. J. Velaert, P. A. Cluyt and A. P. Crabeth) friendly with the youthful Lucas of Leyden who learned glass painting from him; recorded in Leyden Civic Guard 1514, 1519; was paid for glass paintings 1523, 1527. A drawing *Death scene* in Amsterdam Rijks. signed with monogram read as P. C. is presumed by some his work. (*Cf*. Hampton Court Cromatius Painter.)
[Fl. 559, Fl. 892, Fl. 316, Fl. 631 (1935), Fl. 421, Fl. 736.]

Cornelisz, Willem. Flemish (Dutch) Sch. 15/16th cent. Van Mander (1604) records him as the master of J. Scorel; he adds that he was often drunk (*cf*. Cornelis van Gouda), that he made money from Scorel's three years' apprenticeship because he had inserted a clause in the contract that he could fine the guarantors whenever the pupil failed to give satisfaction, and that one night when he was drunk Scorel stole the document tore it, and threw the pieces in the river. Presumed by some identical with Cornelis Willemsz *q.v*. and by others with C. Buys the elder or the younger. [Fl. 559.]

Corr, F. see Geefs.

Cort, Hendrik Joseph Frans de. Flemish Sch. *b* Antwerp 1742 *d* London 1810. *Landscapes and topographic paintings.* Pupil of W. J. Herreyns, then of H. J. Antonissen *q.v.* where B. P. Ommeganck (who painted figures in his early pictures *cf.* P. J. van Regemorter) was fellow pupil; in Antwerp Guild 1770; painter to Archduke Maximilian 1774; went Paris 1776; court painter to Prince de Condé; associate of Paris Acad. (*cf.* A. Ansiaux, J. L. Demarne, P. J. Lafontaine, P. J. Sauvage, J. B. Suvée) 1779; in Antwerp 1782; founded with B. P. Ommeganck and others the Antwerp Soc. of Artists (Kunstmaatschappij) 1788; went London after outbreak of Brabant revolution (*cf.* P. J. Tassaert, P. J. Redouté also P. Tillemans) 1790; exhibited R.A. views of castles, mansions and cathedrals in England and Wales including Windsor Castle, Cliveden Ruins, Fonthill, Corfe, Conway, and Ely, Exeter and Winchester Cathedrals 1790-1803; the English painter G. H. Harlow began as his pupil. **Signed Example:** VIENNA K. *View of Castle Temsch on the Schelde* 1774. **Documented Examples:** CHANTILLY Mus. Condé *Chantilly in 1781, seen from La Pelouse, Chantilly in 1781, seen from Le Vertugadin* (with the end of a staghunt) both pictures commissioned by the Prince de Condé 1776. London B.M. has line and wash drawings of English views.

[Fl. 451, Fl. 66, Fl. 361, Fl. 363.]

Cortbemde, Balthasar van. Flemish Sch. *b* son of an art dealer, Antwerp 1612 *d* Antwerp 1663. *Religious subjects; also active as art dealer.* Master Antwerp Guild 1632; Ignacio Raeth *q.v.* was his pupil. **Signed Example:** ANTWERP *The Good Samaritan* 1647 (painted for Antwerp Guild of Surgeons).

[Fl. 107, Fl. 892.]

Corvus, Joannes (Jan Raf or **Jan de Rave).** Flemish Sch. *b* Bruges (?) before 1495 *d* England (?) after 1544. *Portraits and topographic drawings.* Master in Bruges Guild 1512; in England before 1528 (*cf.* S. Bening, G. L. and S. Horenbout, L. Cornelisz, L. Teerlinck). A Jehan Raf painted for François I of France a map of England 1532 and 'ung portrait de la ville de Londres' 1534; a Jan Raven was naturalised English 1534. **Documented Example:** OXFORD Corpus Christi College *Richard Foxe: Bishop of Winchester, Founder of Corpus Christi College* (the sitter who went blind about 1518 and died in 1528 is shown blind in the picture; Vertue, who engraved the picture in 1723, records that the original frame was then inscribed 'Ionnes Corvus Flandrus faciebat'). A *Mary Tudor Countess of Suffolk* 1531 formerly signed on the frame is recorded.

[Fl. 826, Fl. 856, Fl. 665, Fl. 39, Fl. 40, Fl. 28.]

Cossier, Simon. Presumed Flemish Sch. 17th cent. Painter of PARIS Louvre (1952E) *Three smokers* (signed Simon Cossier 1626). Presumed by some identical with Jan Cossiers *q.v.*

[Fl. 639.]

*****Cossiers (or Coetsiers** or **Caussiers), Jan.** Flemish Sch. *b* son of a painter Antoon C., Antwerp 1600 *d* Antwerp 1671. *Religious subjects, 'history' also portraits and genre* (?). Fellow pupil with S. de Vos of C. de Vos 1615; Master Antwerp Guild 1629; member Chamber of Rhetoric 'De Violiere'; employed under Rubens on Pageant Entry into Antwerp of Cardinal Infante Ferdinand as Governor (*cf.* G. Weri) 1635; contributed to *Metamorphoses* pictures commissioned from Rubens by Philip IV of Spain for Torre de la Parada hunting lodge (*cf.* J. P. Gowi) 1636-8; also employed by Governor General Archduke Leopold Wilhelm (*cf.* G. Seghers, J. B. van Heil and D. Teniers the younger). C. van Savoyen *q.v.* was his pupil. **Signed Examples:** ANTWERP Sœurs Noires Convent *Adoration of the Magi* 1666. THE HAGUE Mauritshuis *Triumph of Bacchus* (*cf.* C. de Vos) 1671 (in *Interior of a picture gallery* by G. Coques *q.v.*). LILLE *Miracle of S.*

Nicholas 1666. LOUVAIN Town Hall *Adoration of the Shepherds* 1646. MADRID Prado *Narcissus* (*cf.* K. P. Spieringh), *Jupiter and Lycaon.* **Documented Examples:** MADRID Prado *Prometheus* (from a sketch by Rubens). MALINES Béguinage *Golgotha* (3 panels 29 feet high painted in Antwerp 1655-c. 62 because Malines Guild refused permission for an Antwerp artist to work in the city (*cf.* C. de Baellieur and E. Snayers). Houbraken (1718) described the Malines triptych as sufficient to 'trumpet his fame'; Descamps (1769) records other pictures in Malines, Ypres (Jesuit church), Bruges (Jesuit church), Brussels (Ursulines), and Louvain (S. Quentin). Pictures signed 'Cossiers' in Antwerp (*Portrait of a surgeon*) and Cassel *Two old beggars* are presumed by some his work (*cf.* S. Cossier). A genre piece *Young woman playing the lute, man singing and Death with a violin* (*cf.* J. van Craesbeeck) is recorded by an engraving. The Forchoudt firm of Antwerp dealers exported a *Judith with the head of Holofernes* (*cf.* A. de Coster) to their Vienna branch (1670) and two large 'history' pieces *Marcus Curtius* and *Horatius Cocles.* Erasmus Quellinus *q.v.* owned a *Bathsheba.*

[Fl. 86, Fl. 425, Fl. 215, Fl. 216, Fl. 613, Fl. 614, Fl. 107, Fl. 892, Fl. 212, Fl. 213.]

Coster (or Ceustere), Adam de. Flemish Sch. *b* Malines 1586 *d* Antwerp 1643. *Religious subjects, genre (some with artificial light effects* (*cf.* A. Mytens)). Master Antwerp Guild 1608; then Italy (?). Van Dyck drew his portrait which was engraved with legend 'pictor noctium Mecheliensis'. A picture presumed by some his work *Judith killing Holofernes* (*cf.* P. van Mol, F. Voet, J. B. Saive also M. Willems) is shown in a gallery interior by W. van Haecht *q.v.* (*cf.* also Hague Studio of Apelles Painter); pictures titled *Diogenes, Liberation of S. Peter* (*cf.* H. v. Steenwyck the younger), *Denial of S. Peter, Christ on the Cross, S. Francis at a table with books, S. Francis with an angel* were recorded by himself (1627) as painted within three months; other titles recorded are *Woman with a candle, Joseph's cup found in Benjamin's sack.* A *Men and women playing backgammon by candlelight* is recorded by an engraving. (*Cf.* Madrid Judith Painter.)

[Fl. 613, Fl. 612, Fl. 107, Fl. 892, Fl. 160 (1907), Fl. 213, Fl. 554, Fl. 555.]

Coster (or Costere), Jan (Hans) de. Flemish Sch. 17th cent. Pupil of J. B. Saive 1614. *cf.* J. de Ceustere. [Fl. 892.]

Coster, Pieter de. Flemish Sch. *b* Antwerp *c.* 1614 *d* Venice 1702. Nephew of A. de C. Went Italy *c.* 1633 and remained there (*cf.* J. Sutterman); worked in Venice. (*cf.* N. Regnier). VENICE S. Lazzaro dei Mendicanti has remains of *Religion presenting the Venetian Republic to the Virgin* traditionally recorded as his work. A ceiling recorded in Venice S. Giustina was lost when the church was rebuilt.

[Fl. 628, Fl. 594, Fl. 629, Fl. 892, Fl. 305.]

*****Coter, Colijn de.** Flemish Sch. *b* Brussels (?) before 1470 *d* after 1538 (?). Presumed the 'Colijn van Bruesele' Master in Antwerp 1493 who was commissioned to paint angels on ceiling of the Painters' Guild Chapel of N. Dame (destroyed by fire 1533) 1493; presumed also the 'Colyne de Coutere', painter, who (with his wife) mortgaged his house to Confrérie de S. Éloi, Brussels 1479 (interest on the mortgage was paid in C's name until 1538); presumed the 'Colijne de Coultere' who contracted to paint for the chapel of the S. Éloi Confrérie 1509-10. **Signed Examples:** PARIS Louvre Two parts of triptych: centre: *The Trinity with angels* right wing: *The Three Maries* grisaille on reverse: *S. Barbara and arms of Averhoult* (?) *family* from S. Omer, Church of S. Denis (Colijn de Coter pingit me in Brabancia Bruselle). VIEURE, nr. Moulins, Church *The Virgin and S. Luke* (Colijn de Coter pingit me in Brabancia). A *Virgin crowned by angels* (Colijn de

Coter pingit me in Bruccelle) is recorded in a private collection. Pictures presumed by some his work are in various museums.

[Fl. 892, Fl. 640, Fl. 316, Fl. 560.]

Cotsiers, J. see **Cossiers.**

Coudenberghe, Jan van. Flemish Sch. 15th cent. Master in Ghent Guild 1429; working with M. van Ghestele q.v. 1430.

[Fl. 135, Fl. 385.]

Coulery, L. de see **Caullery.**

Coulx, Servaes de. Flemish Sch. b before 1590. *Religious subjects.* **Signed Example:** MONS Cathedral S. Waudru *Last Supper* (full signature and letters L. B.) (cf. F. Saive). An *Adoration of the Magi* presented to Enghien Capucin church is recorded 1615. His son Lancelot was Master in Brussels Guild 1610.

[Fl. 892, Fl. 798.]

Courtens, Frans (Baron). Flemish Sch. b Termonde 1854 d Brussels 1943. *Outdoor genre; later landscapes with figures and animals in Impressionist conventions, also seapieces.* Pupil Termonde Acad. and Brussels; with H. Stacquet q.v., P. Pantazis and others worked in Patte de Dindon Free Academy; Professor Antwerp Higher Institute. Received many honours and medals and was made a baron. V. de Saedeleer was among his pupils. Represented in ANTWERP *Forest ride in sunshine* 1894, *Landscape with sheep, Autumn, Sunny lane* 1894 BRUSSELS *After early Mass* 1885, *Wooded landscape (Sunbeams), Woman and cow* 1896 BUDAPEST *Autumn (the Golden Rain)* LIÈGE *September sun* MUNICH N.P. *Field of hyacinths* NAMUR, TERMONDE, MELBOURNE (Australia).

[Fl. Bib. 19th cent., Fl. 737, Fl. 440, Fl, 388, Fl. 913, Fl. 296.]

Courtens, Herman. Flemish Sch. b son of Frans C., Brussels 1884. *Landscapes, genre, still life.* Pupil of his father and I. Verheyden. Visited Holland and Egypt; exhibited Paris Salon; Professor Antwerp Higher Institute. Represented in ANTWERP, BRUGES *The Surprise.* [Fl. 114.]

Cousin, Louis, known in Italy as **Luigi Primo** and nicknamed Gentile (Gentiel). Flemish Sch. b Brussels 1606 d Brussels or Rome c. 1667. *Religious subjects, portraits, decorative paintings and tapestry designs.* Went Rome (cf. J. Sutterman) via Paris (cf. P. Vleughels and J. Fouquier) c. 1626; protégé in Rome of the Brussels sculptor F. Duquesnoy; member of Rome Accad. di S. Luca 1638; a Princeps of the Academy 1651; member Rome Confrérie de Saint-Julien l'Hospitalier 1653; returned Brussels 1657; Master in Brussels Guild 1661; Jan van Cleef q.v. was his pupil in Brussels. The Confrérie de Saint Julien l'Hospitalier sent his heirs some property he had left in Rome 1668. **Signed Examples:** GHENT S. *Raymond of Peñafort adoring the Christ child.* POZZUOLI (prov. Naples) S. Procolo S. *Augustine founding his order.* **Documented Examples:** (recorded by 18th cent. writers): ANCONA Cathedral prebendaries' house S. *Margaret and the dragon* from Ancona church S. Margarita. PESARO Cappucini *Nativity* and *Saints.* ROME SS. Domenico e Sisto fresco S. *Dominic ordering the burning of the books;* S. Marco *Virgin with SS. John the Baptist and Anthony of Padua* S. Maria Magg. *Martyrdom of S. Catherine.* Other works recorded include altarpieces in Brussels S. Jacques and Ghent S. Michel (seen by Descamps 1768), portraits of *Pope Alexander VII* 1655 and various cardinals and *Clement IX* (engraved). The Archduke Leopold Wilhelm's inventory (1659) contained a *Venus and Adonis in a landscape* and two portraits; a *Woman's portrait* (Vrouwken) by 'Gentiel' was inventoried (1678) in the large collection of Erasmus Quellinus q.v.

[Fl. 86, Fl. 753, Fl. 800, Fl. 425, Fl. 878, Fl. 215, Fl. 216, Fl. 642, Fl. 505, Fl. 88, Fl. 892, Fl. 440, Fl. 798, Fl. 417, Fl. 617, Fl. 305, Fl. 213, Fl. 678.]

Coustain (Cousstens, Cousteyn), Pierre. Flemish Sch. b before 1430 d after 1477. Court painter to Philip the Good and Charles the Bold; succeeded H. de Boulogne q.v. as governor of Hesdin, with title of 'paintre des princes' c. 1449; work valued by R. van der Weyden and others, Brussels 1461; painted a *Crucifixion* and *Virgin and Child* placed on catafalque of Philip the Good 1467; employed on decorations for marriage of Charles the Bold (cf. D. de Rycke, J. Hennecart, J. Daret, H. van der Goes, V. van der Stoct) Bruges 1468; with assistant Jehan Hervy prosecuted for non-payment of guild dues (cf. P. Christus) but acquitted as ducal 'valet de chambre' Bruges 1471; made decorations for entry of Maria of Burgundy into Bruges 1477 (cf. B. van Battel and M. van Roden). [Fl. 490, Fl. 179, Fl. 892.]

Couwenberg, Thielen van see **Thielen.**

Couwer, C. de see **Cauwer.**

Coxie, Antoine. Flemish Sch. b Malines (?) after 1650 d Milan (?) 1720. *Portraits, portrait groups, landscapes, occasional religious subjects.* Worked Malines; in Amsterdam 1699-1704; in Berlin working for Frederick I 1705-13; later in Mainz and Milan. **Signed Example:** BRUGES S. Jacques *Large landscape with figures* 1698. A *Portrait of Charles II of Spain* painted for Malines Magistrates 1691 is recorded.

[Fl. 425, Fl. 613, Fl. 892, Fl. 113, Fl. 798.]

Coxie, Guillaume (Willem.) Flemish Sch. b son of M. Coxie the elder, Malines or Brussels after 1540 d 1597. Worked Antwerp and Malines; went Italy; was accused of heresy by the Inquisition and condemned to ten years in the galleys but was reprieved on intervention of Philip II whom his father had petitioned 1574 (cf. J. S. van Calcar and Philippe Vos).

[Fl. 613, Fl. 892.]

★Coxie (or Coxcie or Coxcyen), Michiel. Flemish Sch. b son of painter Michiel C., Malines 1499 d aged ninety-two, Malines 1592. *Religious subjects; also designs for tapestry.* Pupil in Brussels of B. van Orley; went Rome c. 1530 and worked there for Cardinal van Enckevoort in Sta. Maria dell'Anima (church of the Flemish and German Catholics); met Vasari (cf. H. de Cock) 1532; returned Flanders; in Malines and Master in Guild 1539; then Brussels where designed window for S. Gudule 1542-56; and directed Brussels tapestry factory (cf. P. de Kempener); became very successful and rich and won high favour with Spanish Catholic rulers; Charles V commissioned him to design tapestry of Battle of Mühlberg (cf. J. C. Vermeyen) and took four of his pictures with him to hang with his works by Titian and A. Mor at Yuste (1557); Philip II made him 'King's Painter' (cf. R. Coxie and R. Diriksen) commissioned him to copy H. and J. Van Eyck's *Altarpiece of the Mystic Lamb* in Ghent 1557-9 (cf. A. Pupiler) and granted his petition to intervene for release of his son Guillaume q.v. from his punishment for heresy; the Duke of Alva (cf. A. Mor, P. de Kempener, W. Key, C. v. d. Perre) exempted his Malines house from the billeting of troops 1572; the Duke of Parma (cf. P. Claeissins the younger and O. van Veen) paid him compensation for war damage (cf. Philippe Vos) 1589; he died from injuries received in a fall from a scaffold in Antwerp Town Hall where he was restoring a *Judgement of Solomon.* A portrait of him holding a skull is recorded in an Antwerp inventory 1628 (cf. S. Wils) **Signed Examples:** ANTWERP Triptych *Martyrdom of S. Sebastian* '1575 aetatis suae 76' (on wings *Scenes from the life of S. George*) from Cathedral, and *Christ in Glory on the tomb.* BRUSSELS S. Gudule Triptych *Scenes from the life of S. Gudule* 'pictor regius fecit anno salutis 1592 vero aetatis suae 92'; Mus. Triptych *Last Supper* 1567 (on wings *The Footwashing* (cf. J. Cransse) and *Agony in the Garden* and on reverse *Elijah in the wilderness*). LENINGRAD *Annunciation.* MADRID Prado S. *Cecilia.* MALINES S. Rombout Triptych *Martyrdom of S. George*

'pictor regius 1588 aetatis suae 89' Triptych *Martyrdom of S. Sebastian* 'pictor regius 1587 aetat. suae 88'. PRAGUE Rudolfinum *Martyrdom of S. John, S. John on Patmos* (wings of altarpiece by J. Gossaert *q.v.*) 'Mighel de Malino faciebat' and monogram. VIENNA Liechtenstein *Christ bearing the Cross*. **Documented Examples:** BRUSSELS S. Gudule Triptych *Crucifixion* (paid for in 1589) MADRID Escorial *Christ crucified between the Thieves* (Van Mander (1604) records that this, his first important work, was painted for Alsemberg near Brussels and sold during the troubles in the Netherlands by a dealer to Spain where Philip II acquired it from Cardinal Granvella). *The Descent from the Cross* (copy of picture by R. v. d. Weyden *q.v.* paid for by Philip II 1569), *David and Goliath* (recorded by Sigüenza 1605); Prado Triptych *Death of the Virgin*, on wings *Birth of the Virgin, Presentation in the Temple* (painted for Brussels S. Gudule, acquired by Philip II and sent to Escorial 1586). ROME Sta. Maria dell'Anima (fresco) *Trinity* (with *S. Barbara and Cardinal Enckevoort* and *SS. Martin and Lambert* 1531-4 (recorded by Vasari 1568, Van Mander 1604, Titi 1763)). A *Resurrection* painted for S. Pietro in Vaticana, recorded by Van Mander perished with the church. The pictures, owned by Charles V at Yuste were titled *Christ bearing the Cross, Crucifixion, The Virgin Mary* and *Mary meeting Christ on the Road to Calvary*. The copy of the Van Eyck altarpiece was in the Madrid Alcázar Palace till the Napoleonic wars when it was divided, portions going to Berlin and Brussels.
[Fl. 818, Fl. 767, Fl. 559, Fl. 148, Fl. 801, Fl. 216, Fl. 613, Fl. 892, Fl. 305, Fl. 751, Fl. 678.]

Coxie, Michiel the younger. Flemish Sch. *b* son of M. C. the elder *c.* 1569 (?) *d* 1616. *Religious subjects*. Master Malines Guild 1598. **Signed Example:** MALINES Notre Dame triptych *Temptation of S. Anthony, S. Paul the Hermit, S. Anthony* 1607. [Fl. 613, Fl. 892.]

Coxie, Raphael. Flemish Sch. *b* son of Michiel C. the elder, Malines *c.* 1540 *d* Antwerp (?) 1616. *Religious subjects, portraits*. Pupil of his father *q.v.*; Master Malines Guild 1562; Court Painter to Philip II of Spain by 1570 (*cf.* R. Diriksen, A. Pupiler, M. Coxie, S. Pereyns, F. Sturm and P. de Kempener); Master Antwerp Guild 1584; working in Ghent 1588-9; in Brussels 1594; lived an extravagant and disordered life but was able to charge high prices for his pictures; G. de Crayer was among his pupils. **Signed Example:** GHENT *Last Judgement* (commissioned by City Council 1588; A. Francken *q.v.*, G. Mostaert *q.v.*, B. de Ryckere *q.v.* and M. de Vos *q.v.* were assessors in a dispute about the price 1589). Recorded works include a *Resurrection* (painted for Ghent 1589), wings to an altarpiece for Antwerp Cathedral 1601 and portraits of the Spanish royal family. *Cf.* C. de Bruyne.
[Fl. 135, Fl. 613, Fl. 892.]

Crabbe van Espleghem, Frans. Flemish Sch. *b* son of an artist Jan C., Malines before 1480 *d* Malines 1553. *Religious subjects*. In Malines Guild 1501; Dean 1540 and 1549. Van Mander (1604) calls him a rich man and records tempera paintings *Scenes from the Passion* in the church of the Minnebroer (Franciscan) Monastery, Malines, the faces being very beautiful in the style of Quinten Massys; 'his works' he adds 'are much like those of Lucas van Leyden'. Presumed by some identical with the engraver known as the 'Maître à l'Écrevisse'; and by other with F. Minnebroer *q.v.*
[Fl. 559, Fl. 613, Fl. 892, Fl. 440, Fl. 296.]

Crabeels, Florent Nicholas. Flemish Sch. *b* Antwerp 1829 *d* Antwerp 1896. *Landscapes* (*some with figures and animals*), *occasional marines; also engravings* (*genre subjects*). Pupil of J. M. Ruyten. Member of Termonde Sch. (*cf.* A. J. Heymans). Represented ANTWERP *Spring landscape, Autumn landscape, Coalfield by moonlight*. BRUSSELS *The Season of Growth*. MONTREAL, NAMUR, VERVIERS.
[Fl. Bib. 19th cent., Fl. 296.]

Crabeth, Adriaen Pietersz. Flemish (Dutch) Sch. *b* son of glasspainter Pieter D. C., Gouda before 1515 *d* Autun 1553. Brother of glass painter Dirk and Wouter C. (*cf.* P. A. Cluyt). Pupil of J. Swart van Groningen *c.* 1525; went France (*cf.* G. van Cleve, Joos van Cleve and L. Thiry) and died there.
[Fl. 559, Fl. 425, Fl. 892.]

*****Craesbeeck (or Craesbeke), Joos van.** Flemish Sch. *b* Neerlinter (Brabant) *c.* 1606 *d* Brussels (?) before 1661. *Peasant genre* (*cf.* A. Wouwer, M. van Helmont, D. Teniers, A. Victoryns, D. Boone), *also bourgeois genre, studio interiors, landscapes, portraits*. Began life as a baker and was employed as such in Antwerp Castle and political prison *c.* 1631; met A. Brouwer *q.v.* who was imprisoned there 1633; took Brouwer to his house (*cf.* B. van Somer) and became his pupil and drinking and smoking companion (as recorded by Houbraken (1718) who adds that Brouwer fell in love with C's wife); Master Antwerp Guild as 'baker and painter' 1634; in Brussels where Master in Guild 1651. Houbraken's comment on his work is: 'Al wat uit zyn penceel kwam waren schyters, spouwers, dobbelaars, tuisschers, bordeelders, luizeknippers en diergelyke walgelyke drolligheden'. **Fully Signed Example:** CASSEL *Carouse outside an inn*. **Monogrammed Examples:** (C. B. or J. V. C. B.): ANTWERP *Peasants' brawl in a tavern, Soldiers and peasants in a tavern*. BRUSSELS Mus. *Meeting of Rhetoricians*; Pal. d'Egmont (Arenberg Coll.) *Studio interior*. GOTHA *Old couple at table with Death at the window* (*cf.* J. Cossiers). HERMANNSTADT *Quack doctor*. MADRID Prado *Boors' concert*. MUNICH A.P. *Village alehouse*. ORLÉANS *The pig killer*. PHILADELPHIA (Johnson) *Peasants drinking, The smokers*. VIENNA Kunsthist. *Peasant company in a tavern, Landscape with soldiers and women*; Liecht. *The lute player* (*Prodigal Son*), *Homecoming by night*. An Antwerp inventory (1657) records a *landscape* and a *portrait*; the Forchoudt firm of Antwerp dealers sold a *Night piece* to Prince Liechtenstein in 1674 and exported other works to Vienna including a *Schoolmaster*, a *Barber*, a *Brothel scene* (*cf.* M. van Cleve) and landscapes.
[Fl. 86, Fl. 425, Fl. 878, Fl. 215, Fl. 108, Fl. 892.]

Crahay, Albert. Flemish Sch. *b* Antwerp 1881 *d* Antwerp 1914. *Marines, beach scenes, landscapes, figures*. Pupil in Antwerp Acad. and of F. Hens. Exhibited L'Art Contemporain group (*cf.* R. Strebelle) 1907. Represented in ANTWERP *Shrimpfishers*.
[Fl. 388, Fl. 17.]

Cransse (Crans), Jan. Flemish Sch. *b* Antwerp (?) before 1510 *d* Antwerp (?) after 1561 (?). Master Antwerp Guild 1523; Dean 1535; recorded 1548. Van Mander (1604) records a large *Christ washing the Disciples' feet* (*cf.* M. Coxie) painted for the Chapel of the Sacrament in Antwerp Cathedral and describes it as remarkable (een zeer bijzonder werk). Antwerp Mus. has *Coats of Arms* of the 'Christus Oog', ('L'Œil du Christ') Chamber of Rhetoric of Diest and the 'Heibloemken' Chamber in Turnhout, showing *Christ Crucified* on the one and *S. Apolline* on the other, painted 1561, presumed by some his work. [Fl. 559, Fl. 892, Fl. 16.]

*****Crayer (or Craeyer), Gaspar (Jaspar) de.** Flemish Sch. *b* son of a schoolmaster, Antwerp 1582 *d* Ghent 1669. *Religious subjects, occasional 'history', portraits*. Pupil in Brussels of Raphael Coxie; Master in Brussels Guild 1607; patronised by Archduke Albert (*cf.* Gillis Claeissins, W. Coebergher, G. v. Deynum, J. Francart, H. v. Kessel, J. de Momper, J. Snellinck, A. de Succa, O. v. Veen) and bought works of art for him from *c.* 1612; after Archduke Albert's death (1621) given title of Archer de la Garde Noble by the Infanta Isabella (*cf.* D. v. Alsloot) and held offices of Collector of Canal dues and City Councillor; for Jacob Boonen, Archbishop of Malines painted pictures for Afflighem Abbey one of which was much admired by Rubens; in Ghent where visited by Van Dyck (who painted his portrait) *c.* 1634; worked on decor-

ations for the Pageant Entry into Ghent of the Cardinal Infante Ferdinand (*cf.* C. Schut, T. Rombouts also G. Weri) 1635; court painter to the Cardinal Infante (*cf.* P. Snayers) 1635; visited Spain (?) (*cf.* A. Smit); appointed King's Painter by Philip IV (*cf.* C. Luyckx and A. v. Utrecht) 1641; in Brussels where received a *S. Benedict* from Rubens' estate 1641; had large atelier with assistants on the Rubens model from which he supplied scores of altarpieces for churches and religious establishments; left Brussels and settled Ghent with his pupil Jan van Cleef *q.v.* 1664. **Signed Examples:** AMBERG *S.* Martin *Coronation of the Virgin* 1658. BRUSSELS *The Virgin and Child, with S. Dominic receiving the rosary, and other saints; SS. Paul and Anthony, hermits; Pietà with Burgomaster H. Dongelberghe and his wife as adorants* (from Brussels, Grand Béguinage church). GHENT *Martyrdom of S. Blaise* (dated 1668 aet 86). MADRID Prado *Cardinal Infante Ferdinand* (*cf.* P. P. Rubens) 1639 (sent to Philip IV the same year). MUNICH A. P. *The Virgin and Child enthroned with saints, and the artist and members of his family as adorants* 1646 (painted for Brussels Augustines church, seen (1781) in Düsseldorf Gallery by Sir Joshua Reynolds who wrote 'The composition is something on the plan of the great picture by Rubens in the St. Augustine in Antwerp' and comments on its 'dead and cold effect' and adds 'there is no union between the figures and the ground, the outline is everywhere seen which takes away the softness and richness of effect; the men are insipid characters and the women want beauty'). RENNES *Christ on the Cross* 1664. **Documented Examples:** ALOST S. Martin *Virgin with Saints* 1619 (painted for tomb of J. v. d. Meersche). ANTWERP *The Virgin succouring the religious orders with her milk* (painted for the Abbaye de Dames, Nazareth near Lierre where seen by Descamps (1768)). BRUSSELS *Assumption of S. Catherine* (from Louvain, church of Shod Carmelites where seen by Descamps), *S. Apolline* (from Brussels Augustine church where seen by Descamps), *SS. Roch, Anthony, Sebastian, Adriano, and Carlo Borromeo invoked against a plague* (commissioned for Anderlecht S. Guidon 1633-4), *Miraculous Draught of Fishes* (painted for Brussels Fishmongers' Guild), *The Virgin protecting the Brussels Crossbowmen's Guild* (from the Guild chapel in N. D. du Sablon, seen by Descamps) (*cf.* A. Sallaert), *S. Agapit, S. Florent* (from Brussels Capuchin church, seen by Descamps); Musée des Hospices *Christ on the Cross, with dignitaries of a hospital as adorants.* GHENT *Judgement of Solomon* (*cf.* H. de Clerck and M. Pepyn) *c.* 1620, *Decorative panels for Pageant Entry of Cardinal Infante Ferdinand* (*cf.* N. de Liemaker). LILLE *The Four Crowned Martyrs* (painted for Brussels Sculptors' Guild and seen by Descamps in Brussels S. Catherine). VIENNA Kunsthist. *Lamentation* (Inventory of Archduke Leopold Wilhelm 1659). Many other pictures were seen by Descamps in churches; some taken to France in 1794 were sent to French provincial museums and not returned 1815 (DIJON has a *Lamentation* and an *Assumption of the Virgin* acquired in this way). A copy of a *Nativity* by C. made by P. van Lint *q.v.* for the Forchoudt firm of Antwerp dealers was sent by them to Vienna in 1668 and a *Virgin and S. Anne and Joachim* was sold by this firm to Count Czernin in 1671. A portrait of C. by Van Dyck was in Alexander Voet's collection in Antwerp 1689.
[Fl. 86, Fl. 425, Fl. 878, Fl. 22, Fl. 215, Fl. 216, Fl. 702, Fl. 612, Fl. 107, Fl. 386, Fl. 556, Fl. 892, Fl. 204, Fl. 212, Fl. 213 Fl. 584, Fl. 296, Fl. 16.]

Crec, C. J. de. Flemish Sch. *b* before 1695 *d* after 1717. *Genre.* Pupil in Antwerp of G. J. van Opstal *q.v.* 1707. **Signed Example:** VALENCIENNES *Carnival scene* 1717 (*cf.* H. Goovaerts, A. F. Rubens). [Fl. 296.]

Crépin, Louis Joseph Désiré. Flemish Sch. *b* Fives (France) 1828 *d* Etterbeek (Brussels) 1887. *Landscapes and coastscenes, canals.* Pupil in Brussels Acad. Began as sculptor; painter from after *c.* 1860; associated with Tervueren school (*cf.* H. Boulenger). [Fl. Bib. 19th cent., Fl. 440, Fl. 296.]

Crépu, Jan Baptist de (not N.). Flemish Sch. *b* Antwerp (?) before 1642 *d* Brussels *c.* 1689. *Flowers* (*cf.* F. v. Aken, J. v. d. Borght, A. Bosman, J. B. Boschaert, P. Casteels III, S. Hardimé, J. v. d. Hecke, J. B. Morel, D. Seghers, C. de Somme, N. van Verendael, G. P. Verbruggen the elder). Officer in Spanish service till age of forty; then settled Antwerp; Master in Antwerp Guild where J. B. Boschaert and S. Hardimé were his pupils 1685. Lived last years in Brussels where going home one night in his cups he killed the governor's pet hind mistaking it for a footpad. No known works in public galleries. [Fl. 878, Fl. 215, Fl. 107, Fl. 892.]

Crespin, Adolphe. Flemish Sch. *b* Brussels 1859. *Decorative paintings; designs for posters and applied art.* Pupil of French painters Blanc-Garin in Brussels Acad. and of L. Bonnat in Paris. Teacher in Brussels S. Josse-ten-Noode art school; Professor Brussels École des Beaux-Arts. H. Evenepoel *q.v.* was among his pupils. Represented in GHENT and IXELLES. [Fl. Bib. 19th cent., Fl. 296.]

Creytens, Julien. Flemish Sch. *b* Wyngene (West Flanders) 1897. *Figures, landscapes, marines, still life, portraits.* Pupil in Antwerp Higher Institute of I. Opsomer, and later professor there himself. Won Prix de Rome 1925. Represented in ANTWERP *Fishing port, Still life with fish, The sculptor A. van Beurden* LIÈGE, LOUVAIN. [Fl. 17, Fl. Bib. 20th cent.]

Cristus, P. see **Christus.**

Croes, Jacques van. Flemish Sch. 17th cent. *Topographic draughtsman.* His drawings of *Rubens' house in Antwerp* are recorded by engravings. [Fl. 481, Fl. 717, Fl. 798.]

Crommelynck, Albert. Flemish Sch. 20th cent. *Portraits.* [Fl. 568, Fl. 296.]

Crommelynck, Robert. Flemish Sch. 20th cent. *b* Liège. *Landscapes, religious subjects.* [Fl. 296.]

★**Cronenburch, Adriaen van.** Flemish (Dutch) Sch. *b* Pietersbierum (Friesland) before 1540 *d* after 1604. *Portraits.* In Bergum near Leeuwarden 1567; connected with a monastery there 1570-80; recorded living Bergum with a daughter 1604. **Signed Examples:** MADRID Prado *Lady with a yellow flower, Young lady with a girl holding carnations (and a death's head on a table)* 1587 (or 1567?), *Lady in Dutch dress* (The signature Aaaa v. Cronenburch was formerly read as Anna v. C. till the discovery of a legal document (dated 1602) signed by Adriaen in this way.) [Fl. 860, Fl. 421, Fl. 555.]

Cronenburch, Anna van. Formerly believed to be a portrait painter on the strength of works now known to be by Adriaen van C. *q.v.* [Fl. 421.]

Croonenborgh, Steven. Flemish (Dutch) Sch. 16th century. Recorded by Van Mander as a native of The Hague and a pupil in Antwerp of F. Floris. [Fl. 559.]

Crussens (or **Krussens**), **Anton.** Flemish Sch. 17th cent. worked Brussels *c.* 1655. *Italianate landscapes with genre figures* (*cf.* J. F. Millet, J. F. Soolmaker, G. de Witte and J. B. Juppin) *and caricatures.* **Signed Example:** (drawing on parchment) VIENNA Albertina *Mountain landscape with soldiers and officer on horseback* (Crussens fec. Brux 1655) (*cf.* C. Breydel). A drawing on parchment *Attack on Valenciennes* 1656 (*cf.* P. Snayers and A. v. d. Meulen) is recorded in the collection of G. Huymans 1685. [Fl. 612, Fl. 892, Fl. 213.]

Cruyl, Liévin. Flemish Sch. *b* Ghent *c.* 1640 *d* Ghent after 1685. *Architectural drawings, some engraved by himself.* A priest who was also active as architectural designer in Ghent; worked in Rome and region where drew (and engraved) the Forum and other buildings *c.* 1666 (*cf.* A. Goubau); later in France; returned Ghent by 1684.

[Fl. 451, Fl. 481, Fl. 612, Fl. 892, Fl. 798.]

Curta, J. see **Cordua.**

Custodis (or **Custos**), **Hieronymus.** Flemish Sch. *b* Antwerp date unknown *d* London (?) *c.* 1592. *Portraits.* In London (*cf.* S. van der Meulen and F. Spierinx) 1589. His widow remarried in London 1593. **Signed Example:** HAMPTON COURT Royal Coll. *Sir John Parker* 'Jeronimo Custodis Antwerpien 10th August 1589'. An English private coll. has *Elisabeth Bruges* (*Brydges*) *age 14* 8th July 1589 (of which Walpole (1768) wrote 'the colouring is flat and chalky') and *Giles Bruges* (*Brydges*) *3rd Lord Chandos* 8th July 1589 both signed 'Hieronimo Custodis Anverpiensis'.

[Fl. 856, Fl. 730, Fl. 39.]

Custodis, P. see **Balten, Pieter.**

Cuyck de Mierhop (or **Myerhop**), **Jonkheer Frans van.** Flemish Sch. *b* descendant of noble family, Bruges (?) *c.* 1640 *d* Ghent 1689. *Still life with animals and fish* (*cf.* A. Adriaenssen); *also group portraits and decorations.* Worked at first as amateur; then moved Ghent and became professional artist; held high offices in Ghent Carpenters', Butchers' and Painters' Guilds. R. van Audenaerd *q.v.* was his pupil. **Signed Examples:** COPENHAGEN *Fish stall.* GHENT *Group portrait of members of the Butchers' Guild with Vision of S. Hubert* 1678 (given by C. de M. to the Guild). Descamps (1768) saw *Still life with fish, dogs, fruit and a Turkish carpet* (*cf.* J. Fyt and A. van Utrecht) as an over-door in Ghent Église des Alexiens. [Fl. 215, Fl. 216, Fl. 892, Fl. 386.]

D

*Dael, Jan Frans (Jean François), van. Flemish Sch. *b* Antwerp 1764 *d* Paris 1840. *Fruit and flower pieces* (*cf.* P. Faes and A. Damis). Apprenticed to an ornament and coach painter; then pupil in Antwerp Acad.; went Paris 1786; given studio in Louvre by Government of the Revolution (*cf.* P. J. Redouté) 1793; patronized by Napoleon and Josephine (*cf.* L. Gerbo, M. I. van Brée, B. P. Ommeganck); worked for Josephine at Saint Cloud; gold medals in Paris Salon 1810 and (under Louis XVIII) 1819; Legion of Honour from Charles X 1825; medal of honour from Leopold I of Belgium. **Signed Examples:** LYONS *La tubéreuse cassée* 1807. PARIS Louvre *Flowers and fruit* 1810. Three compositions painted for Josephine *Tombeau d'une jeune fille decoré par ses amies, Offrande à Flore* and *La Croisée* are recorded.
[Fl. 451, Fl. 612, Fl. 66, Fl. 296.]

Daelmans (or **Daleman**), **Hans.** Flemish Sch. 16th cent. In Antwerp Guild 1561. Van Mander records him as pupil of F. Floris. [Fl. 559, Fl. 892.]

Daems (or **Dams**), **Joannes.** Flemish Sch. 17th cent. Master in Antwerp Guild 1634. [Fl. 714.]

Daeye, Hippolyte. Flemish Sch. *b* son of a landowner, Ghent 1873. *Figures (often children), nudes, genre, landscape, portraits in Impressionist and later delicate Expressionist technique.* Pupil in Ghent Academy of J. Delvin 1896; in Antwerp Higher Institute 1899; member of Antwerp Group L'Art Contemporain (Kunst van Heden) *cf.* R. Strebelle; in London during 1914-18 German invasion (*cf.* E. Tytgat, C. Permeke, L. de Smet, G. v. d. Woestyne); visited Italy, Paris, Spain and Morocco; member of Salon des IX with W. Paerels, C. Permeke, Ramah, G. de Smet, E. Tytgat, G. v. d. Woestyne and the sculptor O. Jespers 1926; had large retrospective exhibition Brussels Palais des Beaux Arts 1945. Represented in ANTWERP *Nude, Child, Girl in brown* 1946, *Woman in a toque, Sérénité.* BRUSSELS *Rêverie, Expression de jeune fille* 1923. GHENT, GRENOBLE, LIÈGE, PARIS.
[Fl. 592, Fl. 388, Fl. 196, Fl. 296, Fl. 599, Fl. 172.]

Dalem (or **Daele**), **Cornelis van.** Flemish Sch. *b* before 1535 *d* after 1564. *Landscapes* (*cf.* Mostaert). Master Antwerp Guild 1556. Van Mander (1604) describes him as a nobleman whose parents had encouraged him to study painting for pleasure; he had a large library and painted rarely but when the spirit moved him he would paint a rocky scene or landscape; other artists such as Gillis Mostaert or Joachim Beuckelaer put in the little figures. B. Spranger was apprenticed to him 1560-4. An Antwerp inventory (1642) records a *landscape* (by 'van Daele') owned by the dealer H. de Neyt.
[Fl. 559, Fl. 212, Fl. 213.]

Dalen (or **Dalem**), **Jan van.** Flemish Sch. *b* Antwerp (?) before 1620 *d* after 1653. *Portraits and genre.* Master Antwerp Guild 1640. **Monogrammed Examples:** SCHLEISSHEIM *Portrait of a young painter.* VIENNA Kunsthist. *Bacchus with a wineglass* (in Archduke Leopold Wilhelm inventory 1659), *cf.* Léandre van D. [Fl. 892.]

Dalen, Léandre van. Presumed Flemish Sch. 17th cent. Painter of TOURNAI Mus. *Family group* (lady at spinet with husband and two children in landscape) *s* Léandre van Dalen 1649. Presumed by some a misreading for Jan van Dalen *q.v.*
[Fl. 434, Fl. 892.]

Damery, Jacques. Flemish Sch. *b* Liège 1619 *d* Rome 1685. *Flowers, fruit, ornaments.* Pupil of his brother Walther. In Rome 1657; and again 1671. His works are recorded by engravings made in Rome. [Fl. 26. Fl. 84, Fl. 409, Fl. 892.]

Damery, Simon. Flemish Sch. *b* Liège 1597 *d* Milan 1640. *Religious subjects.* In Rome where was concerned in picture dealing (*cf.* C. de Wael) 1616. Two paintings at one time in Liège Cathedral are recorded.
[Fl. 26, Fl. 84, Fl. 409, Fl. 892.]

Damery, Walther (Gauthier). Flemish Sch. *b* Liège 1610 *d* Liège 1672. *Religious subjects, 'history', portraits.* Visited England (*cf.* C. de Neve) *c.* 1635; then France and Italy (Rome); returned Toulon (after being kidnapped by Algerian pirates and rescued by Recollets) *c.* 1643; worked Paris *c.* 1644; then settled Liège. G. Hallet was among his pupils. **Signed Examples:** HERCK—S. LAMBERT Parish Ch. *Deposition* 1650. TOULON Cathedral *Altarpiece* 1644. **Documented Examples:** MAINZ *S. Simon Stock receiving the scapular from the Virgin* (painted for Liège Carmelite Church; taken Paris Musée Napoléon and thence to Mainz). PARIS Église des Carmes (Ceiling paintings): *Scenes from the lives of Elijah and Elisha.* [Fl. 86, Fl. 425, Fl. 289, Fl. 409, Fl. 892.]

Damis, Amedée, G. F. Flemish Sch. *b* Bruges 1811 *d* Bruges 1851. *Flowers, fruit.* Pupil in Paris of P. J. Redouté *q.v.*; exhibitor Paris Salon 1846-8. [Fl. 66.]

Damme, Frans van. Flemish Sch. *b* Waesmunster 1860. *Marines, coastscenes, landscapes.* [Fl. 798.]

Damme, Suzanne van. Flemish Sch. *b* Ghent 1901. *Town views, landscapes, portraits.* Represented in ANTWERP *View of the Tuileries.* [Fl. 17.]

Dammes, Lucas, see Hoey.

Dansaert, Léon Marie Constant. Flemish Sch. *b* Brussels 1830 *d* Ecouen 1909. *Costume genre.* Pupil in Paris of E. Frère. Exhibited Paris Salon 1868-89. Represented in BRUSSELS *The Diplomats.* PERIGUEUX, SHEFFIELD *Promenade in Versailles in time of Louis XV.* [Fl. Bib. 19th cent.]

Danzig Last Judgement Master. Flemish Sch. 15th cent. Name for painter of DANZIG Marienkirche, triptych *The Last Judgement* (centre), *The Blessed, The Damned* (wings), *Virgin and Child with Donor, S. Michael and Donor's wife* (exterior wings) commissioned by Jacopo Tani, Medici agent in Bruges until 1471; captured at sea on its way to Florence and brought to Danzig 1473. Presumed by some identical with H. Memlinc *q.v.* and by others with R. v. d. Weyden *q.v.*
[Fl. 892, Fl. 858, Fl. 316.]

Daret, Daniel (Danelet). Flemish Sch. *b* son of sculptor, Tournai (?) before 1420 *d* after 1449. Half-brother of Jacques D. whose pupil he became 1433; Master in Tournai Guild 1441; court painter and 'valet de chambre' to Philip the Good, Duke of Burgundy (*cf.* J. van Eyck) 1449. **Signed Examples:** None. **Documented Examples:** None.
[Fl. 359, Fl. 427, Fl. 892.]

Daret, Jacques. Flemish Sch. *b* son of woodcarver, Tournai before 1410 *d* after 1468. *Religious subjects, festival decora-*

tions; also worked as MS. illuminator. Member of household of R. Campin and in Holy Orders 1418; made pilgrimage to Aix-la-Chapelle 1426; formally apprenticed to R. Campin 1427; Master and Provost Tournai Guild 1432; received his step-brother Daniel D. as pupil 1433; went Arras where worked for Abbot of S. Vaast 1433-5; in Tournai where took pupil for illumination 1436; in Arras making tapestry cartoons 1441; worked again for Abbot of S. Vaast 1452; went Lille to work on decorations for 'Oath of the Pheasant' ceremonies when Philip the Good, Duke of Burgundy, swore to go on a crusade 1454; in Bruges designing decorations for Chapter of the Golden Fleece 1467 and, with many other artists, decorations for marriage of Charles the Bold and Margaret of York (*cf.* H. v. d. Goes and P. Bernart) 1468. **Signed Examples:** None. **Documented Example:** BERLIN K.F. *The Visitation, with Abbot Jean du Clerq of S. Vaast as donor* c. 1434 which delegates to the S. Vaast d'Arras Peace Conference saw there together with pictures representing *The Adoration of the Magi, The Presentation in the Temple* and *The Nativity* as shutters covering a sculptured altarpiece 1435. Pictures in Berlin K.F., Paris Petit Palais and a private collection in Switzerland are presumed by some the other three panels. A *Holy Ghost* altar painted for S. Vaast 1452, and a large *Resurrection* tapestry cartoon in tempera (also for S. Vaast) painted in Arras c. 1441 are recorded. The Berlin *Visitation* was formerly presumed by some the work of G. v. d. Meire *q.v.* [Fl. 427, Fl. 133 (1909), Fl. 892, Fl. 316.]

Daret, Jean. Flemish Sch. *b* Brussels 1613 *d* Aix-en-Provence 1668. *Religious, allegorical and mythological subjects, portraits; also worked as engraver.* Visited Italy; settled Aix-en-Provence 1637. His two sons Michel and Jean Baptiste are said to have been painters and to have collaborated in allegorical compositions. **Signed Examples:** AIX-EN-PROVENCE Cathedral *Crucifixion with the Virgin of the Seven Sorrows* 1640; S. Madeleine *Salvator de Horta healing the sick* 1637; *Virgin of the rosary* 1643, S. Theresa 1641. MARSEILLES *Portrait of a magistrate* 1638. [Fl. 66, Fl. 892.]

Dargent, see **Argent.**

Dargonne, see **Argonne.**

Dasnoy, Albert. Flemish Sch. *b* Lier 1901. *Rural, urban and poetic landscape, interiors, genre portraits.* Represented in ANTWERP *Town scene, The visit to the invalid.* [Fl. 17.]

Daverdoing, Charles A. J. Flemish Sch. *b* Arras 1813 *d* Averdoingt, nr. Calais 1895. *Religious subjects, portraits.* Pupil in Paris of Baron Gros. Exhibited Paris Salon from 1844. Represented in ARRAS, BOURGES, TROYES, VERSAILLES. [Fl. 66.]

David, Cornelia (née Cnoop). Flemish Sch. 15th-16th cent. *b* Bruges (?) daughter of Dean of Goldsmiths' Guild, date unknown. *Miniatures* (?). Married Gérard David c. 1496. **Signed Examples:** None. **Documented Examples:** None. [Fl. 872.]

*David, Gerard. Flemish Sch. *b* Oudewater, S. Holland before 1470 *d* Bruges 1523. *Religious subjects.* In Bruges Guild as foreign master 1484; decorated window bars of the house in which Bruges City Council held Maximilian of Austria prisoner 1488; received other commissions from Council 1491 and 1499; married Cornelia Cnoop daughter of Dean of Goldsmiths' Guild c. 1496; Dean of Painters' Guild 1501; joined the patrician confraternity, Société de Notre Dame de l'Arbre sec 1508; presumed by some the 'Meester Gheraet van Brugghe' admitted to Antwerp Guild 1515; recorded in Bruges 1521 and 1523; buried in Bruges Notre Dame. Presumed by some the 'Gherardo' recorded by Vasari (1551) and Guicciardini (1581) as an excellent miniature painter. Van Mander (born 1548) was unable to discover anything of his

life or work. A. Ysenbrandt was his pupil. **Signed Examples:** None. **Documented Example:** ROUEN *Virgin and Child with SS. Catherine, Agnes, Dorothy, Barbara and Lucy (Virgo inter Virgines)*, presented by D. to Sion Convent, Bruges 1509. A *Last Judgement* commissioned by Bruges Council for the Town Hall is not known to survive; extant receipts for other commissions from Bruges Council are presumed by some to refer to BRUGES *Judgement of Cambyses* 1498 and *The Flaying of the unjust Judge Sisamnes.* Many pictures presumed by some his work are in European and American museums (*cf.* Bruges Baptism of Christ Painter, Brussels Virgin with a Milk Bowl Painter, New York Rest on the Flight Painter and Philadelphia Lamentation Painter).
[Fl. 872, Fl. 93, Fl. 892, Fl. 316, Fl. 530, Fl. 615, Fl. 143.]

Death of the Virgin Master. Presumed Flemish Sch. 16th cent. (not to be confused with Amsterdam Death of the Virgin Master). Name for painter of COLOGNE Wallraf-Richartz Mus. Triptych: (centre) *Death of the Virgin*, (wings) *SS. Nicasius and George with donors, SS. Christine and Gudule with donors' wives*, (reverses) *Virgin with SS. Christopher, Sebastian and Roch* dated 1515 and inscribed J. x. b. (Larger version in Munich A.P.) The monogram J. x. b. is presumed by some to stand for Joos van der Beke (i.e. Joos van Cleve *q.v*); presumed by others identical with J. van Scorel *q.v.* Many pictures presumed by some his work are in European and American museums. [Fl. 892, Fl. 316, Fl. 530.]

Decaisne, H., see **Caisne.**

*Defrance, Léonard. Flemish Sch. *b* Liège 1735 *d* Liège 1805. *Contemporary genre, portraits.* Pupil of J. B. Coclers; in Italy 1753-c. 1760; in France working at Montpellier, Castres, Toulouse and Bordeaux c. 1761-3; returned Liège 1764; visited Holland with H. de Fassin 1773; director of Liège Acad. 1778; as a Francophil and anti-clerical collaborated in removal of works of art to France and destruction of S. Lambert Cathedral, Liège after occupation by French Revolutionary Armies 1794 (*cf.* J. Dreppe and J. Latour); in last years held post of professor in School of Design in Dept. of Ourthe under French administration (*cf.* S. P. d'Argonne, P. J. C. François, L. Moons, H. A. Myin and P. J. v. Regemorter). **Signed Examples:** BRUSSELS *Portrait of a member of the Jalheau family* 1768, *Interior of a glass factory.* NEW YORK Met. *The forge* (*cf.* J. F. Depelchin), *The rope dancer.* Pictures titled *Suppression of the monasteries by Joseph II* and *Interior of a prison during the Revolution* are recorded.
[Fl. 451, Fl. 63, Fl. 409, Fl. 198, Fl. 815, Fl. 537, Fl. 296.]

Degouve de Nuncques, William. Flemish Sch. *b* Monthermé 1866 *d* Stavelot 1934. *Religious subjects, symbolist allegories* (*cf.* A. Levêque), *landscapes, genre.* Exhibited with Brussels group Les Vingt (*cf.* J. Ensor); Member of La Libre Esthétique and later of Vie et Lumière; worked in Venice (1895), Spain and Majorca 1900-2. Represented in ANTWERP, OTTERLOO Kröller-Müller Mus. [Fl. 391, Fl. 296.]

Dehoy, Charles. Flemish Sch. *b* Brussels 1872 *d* 1940. *Landscapes, figure and still life compositions in Post Impressionist and Fauve conventions* (*cf.* P. Cockx, P. Maes, A. Oleffe, R. Parent, W. Paerels, Ramah, F. Schirren, R. Wouters). Represented in BRUSSELS *The Teatable* 1918. [Fl. 388, Fl. 296.]

*Deipara Virgo Master. Presumed Flemish Sch. first half of 16th cent. Name for painter of ANTWERP Mus. (262) *Virgin with Prophets and Sibyls (Deipara Virgo).* Presumed by some identical with A. Benson *q.v.*

Delaunois, Alfred Napoléon. Flemish Sch. *b* St.-Josse-ten-Noode, nr. Brussels 1876 *d* Louvain 1941. *Church interiors, landscapes, genre.* Pupil in Brussels Acad. then of C. Meunier. Director of Louvain Acad. Represented in ANTWERP

Interior Louvain S. Pierre. BRUSSELS *After Vespers* (w). BUENOS AIRES *Vespers.* GHENT *The tomb of Duke Henry of Brabant.* LIÈGE, LOUVAIN, NAMUR *The Angelus in the Béguinage.* PARIS State Coll. *The Ray of Sun (Interior Louvain S. Pierre).*
[Fl. 909, Fl. 178, Fl. 388, Fl. 296.]

Delbeke, Louis. Flemish Sch. *b* Poperinghe 1821 *d* Schaerbeek (Brussels) 1891. *Costume history, murals (cf.* J. Swerts), *genre, portraits.* Was commissioned (1884) by Ypres town to paint with A. Pauwels a series of murals in the Cloth Hall representing scenes of Ypres life in the 15th and 16th cents. (*cf.* H. Leys); these were destroyed with the building by the Germans in their 1914-18 invasion. Represented in BRUSSELS *Sketches for Ypres Cloth Hall murals.* PARIS (Faculté de Médecine).
[Fl. 435, Fl. Bib. 19th cent.]

Delcloche, Paul Joseph. Flemish Sch. *b* son of Pierre D., Namur 1716 *d* Liège 1755. *Contemporary warfare (cf.* P. J. v. Bredael), *religious subjects, decorative compositions, fêtes galantes, portraits.* Went Paris (*cf.* J. J. Spoede); pupil there of Perpète D. *q.v.* and Lancret; returned Liège 1740; painted decorations in Château Colonster for the de Horion family, in Bishops Palace (*cf.* J. B. Coclers), and in Palais de Justice; court painter to Prince Bishop 1753. **Documented Example:** LIÈGE Mus. d'Ansembourg *The family Horion.* A *Battle of Raucourt* 1746 and a *Battle of Lawfeld* 1747 commissioned by Marshal de Saxe and works in Liège churches are recorded.
[Fl. 63, Fl. 451, Fl. 409, Fl. 892.]

Delcloche, Perpète. Flemish Sch. *b* Dinant 1671 *d* Paris after 1734. Went Paris where became member of the old Acad. de Saint Luc (1723) and later Professor.
[Fl. 409, Fl. 410, Fl. 798.]

Delcloche, Pierre. Flemish Sch. *b* Dinant before 1680 *d* Namur 1729. *Religious subjects.*
[Fl. 73, Fl. 798.]

Delcour (or de la Cour), Jean Gilles. Flemish Sch. *b* Hamoir nr. Liège 1632 *d* Liège 1695. *Religious subjects for Liège churches, portraits; also copies after Italian painters.* Pupil of G. Douffet. Visited Rome, where worked under the Italian painter A. Sacchi (*cf.* J. Miel). **Monogrammed Example:** LIÈGE *Portrait of the painter's brother the sculptor J. Delcour* 1685.
[Fl. 451, Fl. 409.]

*Delff, Jacob Willemsz. Flemish (Dutch) Sch. *b* Gouda *c.* 1550 *d* Delft 1601. *Portraits, groups (cf.* D. Barendsz also C. Anthonisz) *and Old Testament subjects.* Citizen of Delft 1582; Cornelis J. D., the Dutch painter of kitchen pieces (*cf.* P. Aertsen) was his son. Pieter C. v. Ryck *q.v.* was his pupil. **Signed Examples:** AMSTERDAM Rijks. *Paulus Cornelisz van Berestyn* 1592. DELFT Town Hall *Group of Civic Guards* 1592 (thirty-one figures in two rows restored by his grandson J. W. D. II after it was damaged by an explosion 1654). ROTTERDAM *Baertje van Adrichem* 1593. VIENNA K. *The reconciliation of Jacob and Esau* 1584. **Documented Example:** AMSTERDAM Rijks. *Self portrait before an easel with his wife and three sons, Cornelis, Rochus and Willem* (in inventory of Willem's widow 1639). *Cf.* Amsterdam Little Girl with Dog Painter.
[Fl. 559, Fl. 215, Fl. 425, Fl. 892.]

Delfosse, Eugène. Flemish Sch. *b* Brussels 1825 *d* Brussels 1865. *Genre, portraits, costume history.* Exhibited London R.A. between 1849 and 1861. Represented in BRUSSELS *The Despatch Rider.* BUDAPEST *Family scene.* LIÈGE.
[Fl. 361, Fl. 892.]

Delft Master. Presumed Flemish (Dutch) Sch. early 16th cent. Name for painter of ROTTERDAM Mus. (loan) *Burgomaster van Beest with his four sons and S. John the Baptist,*

His wife and daughter with S. Mary Magdalene (two wings of an altarpiece) with *S. Jerome and lion in the desert* on exterior. Pictures presumed by some his work are in London N.G. (*cf.* London Delft Painter) and Amsterdam Rijks. (*cf.* Amsterdam Delft Painter and Amsterdam Cadaver Painter).
[Fl. 316, Fl. 530.]

Delhaze, J. B. Flemish Sch. 18th cent. **Signed Example:** LUXEMBOURG Wellin Church *S. Dominic receiving a rosary from the Virgin* 1717.
[Fl. 409.]

Delien (or Delyen or Deslyens or Lyen), Jacques (or Jean) François. Flemish Sch. *b* Ghent 1684 *d* Paris 1761. *Portraits and genre; also worked occasionally as engraver.* Pupil in Ghent of R. van Audenaerd; went Paris (*cf.* J. J. Spoede); pupil there of the French painter N. de Largillière; remained Paris; member of Acad. Royale 1725 (*cf.* P. Mol and J. van Bredael); and 'peintre du Roi' (*cf.* C. van Falens); exhibited Paris Salon between 1737-47 (*cf.* C. J. Redouté); dissatisfied with the appreciation of his work he engraved a plate representing the public as an ass examining his pictures and another of himself painfully ploughing the field of art. **Documented Examples:** TROYES *M. Berryer (Police lieutenant and protégé of Mme. de Pompadour).* VERSAILLES *The painter N. Bertin* and *G. Coustou (sculptor of the Chevaux de Marly at entrance of Champs Élysées)* both 1725 Acad. reception pieces. Works titled *La Lanterne Magique* (Salon 1740), *La Marmotte* (Salon 1741) are recorded by engravings. [Fl. 564, Fl. 229.]

Delmont (or van der Mont), Deodatus. Flemish Sch. *b* son of a silversmith, Saint-Trond (nr. Hasselt) 1582 *d* Antwerp 1644. *Religious subjects; also active as architect and engineer.* Pupil of Rubens and accompanied him to Italy 1600; Master Antwerp Guild 1608; as painter and architect worked for and was ennobled by Duke of Pfalz-Neuburg 1612-20; was given stipend as engineer (*cf.* W. Coebergher) by Philip IV of Spain. Rubens' first wife was godmother to his son; Rubens in an affidavit praised him as artist, friend and 'zealot of the true Catholic religion' 1628; his daughter married Rubens' son Albert; his portrait by Van Dyck is recorded by an engraving. **Documented Examples:** ANTWERP *Transfiguration* (painted for Antwerp Cathedral where recorded by C. de Bie (1661) and Descamps (1769)); Jesuit College *Christ bearing the Cross* (de Bie and Descamps).
[Fl. 86, Fl. 425, Fl. 215, Fl. 216, Fl. 892, Fl. 204.]

Delpérée, Émile. Flemish Sch. *b* Huy 1850 *d* Esneux 1896. *Costume history, genre, portraits.* Pupil and later Professor Liège Acad. Represented in COURTRAI *Charles V rehearsing his own Funeral in S. Yust.* LOUVAIN *Martin Luther at the Diet of Worms.* LIÈGE, NAMUR, MIDDELBURG.
[Fl. Bib. 19th cent.]

Delvaux, Édouard. Flemish Sch. *b* Brussels 1806 *d* Charleroi 1862. *Landscapes.* Pupil of H. van Assche *q.v.* Travelled in France, Germany, Italy and Switzerland. Represented in AMSTERDAM *Banks of the Sambre.*
[Fl. 451, Fl. 481, Fl. 798.]

Delvaux, Ferdinand M. Flemish Sch. *b* son of sculptor Laurent D., Brussels 1782 *d* Bologna 1815. *Religious subjects, genre, interiors of Italian buildings with costume-history figures.* Pupil of A. Lens; worked for a number of years in Italy. Represented in GHENT Acad. *David and Saul* 1806; Franciscan Monastery *Martyrdom of S. Stephen* 1809.
[Fl. 451, Fl. 49, Fl. 481, Fl. 84, Fl. 612.]

Delvaux, Paul. Flemish Sch. *b* Antheit-lez-Huy (Liège) 1897. *Expressionist and, then, neo-surrealist compositions.* Associated with Belgian neo-surrealist movement (*cf.* R. Magritte) from 1936. Professor of composition in Brussels Institut Supérieur des arts décoratifs 1950. Represented in GHENT

LIÈGE *L'homme de la rue* 1940. LONDON Tate Gallery: *Venus endormie* 1944.   [Fl. 327, Fl. 543, Fl. 786, Fl. 296.]

Delville, Jean. Flemish Sch. *b* Louvain 1867. *Symbolist allegories, murals, cartoons for mosaics.* Pupil Brussels Acad. Winner of Rome Grand Prix 1895; associated with Paris Rose-Croix symbolist movement and founded with A. Levêque *q.v.* a related group in Brussels. Professor first in Glasgow School of Art; later in Brussels Acad. Represented in ANTWERP. BRUSSELS *Treasures of Satan*; Palais de Justice *Murals.* LOUVAIN, PARIS Sorbonne *School of Plato.*   [Fl. 178, Fl. 592, Fl. 388, Fl. Bib. 19th cent.]

Delvin, Jean. Flemish Sch. *b* Ghent 1853 *d* Ghent 1922. *Animals, genre, portraits.* Pupil J. Portaels and A. Cluysenaar. Member of Brussels group Les Vingt (*cf.* J. Ensor) 1884; and later of L'Art Contemporain (Kunst van Heden) (*cf.* R. Strebelle) in Antwerp; worked at various times in Paris; Professor Ghent Academy from 1902. Represented in BRUSSELS *Bullfight* 1902. GHENT *Shrimpfishing at Coxyde* 1883, *Horses fighting* 1903 and others. LIÈGE *Fire in a stable* 1874. PARIS State Coll. *The Team* 1909. VENICE.
     [Fl. Bib. 19th cent.]

Delyen, J. F., see **Delien.**

*Demarne (or **Marne, de**), **Jean Louis,** called Demarnette (or Marnette, de). Flemish Sch. *b* son of officer in Austrian service, Brussels 1754 *d* Paris 1829. *At first costume history, then picturesque outdoor genre with figures and animals* (*cf.* C. v. Falens, N. H. J. Fassin and S. J. Denis), *later contemporary genre on roads and fairs; some ports and military pieces; also worked as painter for Sèvres factory.* Taken Paris as a child and became pupil of the French painter G. Briard; competed for Rome Prize but lost with Louis David (*cf.* J. B. Suvée) against P. C. Jombert 1772; Salon exhibitor from 1783; associate of Paris Acad. Royale (*cf.* P. J. Lafontaine and P. J. Sauvage also P. Mol) 1783; member during Revolution of Société Populaire et Républicaine des Arts (*cf.* A. Ansiaux); officially patronized and popular during Empire (*cf.* L. Gerbo); also patronized by Louis XVIII 1814; Legion of Honour from Charles X 1828. **Signed Examples:** BUDAPEST *Landscape with peasants and animals.* LENINGRAD *Fair by a river.* **Documented Examples:** CHERBOURG *Townsmen visiting a farm* (Salon 1814), *Sea shore with fishermen* (Salon 1817). GRENOBLE *Landscape with man and dancing dog* (Salon 1824). PARIS Louvre *A country road, Fair in front of an inn* (both Salon 1814, then coll. Louis XVIII). VERSAILLES *Napoleon and Pope Pius VII in Fontainebleau forest* (Salon 1808, landscape by the French painter A. H. Dunouy). Others in BORDEAUX, LYONS, MONTPELLIER and ORLÉANS. Among early works *Bravery rewarded; (scene from the American War of Independence)* 1781 and *Louis XV after the battle of Fontenoy c.* 1781 are recorded. A *Robinson dans son île* is also recorded.   [Fl. 451, Fl. 66, Fl. 197, Fl. 525, Fl. 73.]

Denayer, Félix. Flemish Sch. *b* Elsene 1875 *d* Paris 1934. *Genre, symbolist allegories* (*cf.* A. Levêque), *landscapes.* Pupil in Brussels Acad. of J. Portaels. Worked mainly in Paris. Represented in ANTWERP *Landscape.*   [Fl. 17.]

Deneve, F. see **Neve, F. de.**

Denis (or **Denys**), **Simon Joseph Alexander Clement,** called the Squinter (le Louche, de Schelen). Flemish Sch. *b* Antwerp 1755 *d* Naples 1813. *Picturesque landscapes with figures and animals* (*cf.* J. L. Demarne). Fellow pupil with B. P. Ommeganck of H. J. Antonissen *q.v.*; then worked Paris; went Italy and remained there (*cf.* H. F. Lint); in Rome 1786-1801; in Naples 1803; in Rome 1805; court painter in Naples to Joseph Bonaparte 1806. Known as Ridder (Knight) D. in

Naples. Goethe admired his pictures. **Signed Examples:** ANTWERP *Cascade* 1793, *Evening landscape with figures and dogs.* An *Eruption of Vesuvius* 1804 is recorded.
     [Fl. 275, Fl. 451, Fl. 612, Fl. 481, Fl. 107, Fl. 798.]

Denonne, Alex. Flemish Sch. *b* St. Josse-ten-Noode (Brussels) 1879. *Indoor and outdoor peasant genre, landscapes and town views, gardens with figures.* Pupil in Antwerp Acad. of H. Luyten. Represented in ANTWERP *My garden.*   [Fl. 17.]

Denys (or **de Nys**), **Frans.** Flemish Sch. *b* Antwerp *c.* 1610 *d* of fever, Mantua 1670. *Portraits and allegorical pieces.* Master Antwerp Guild 1632; left Antwerp *c.* 1656; visited Germany; then Italy where remained (*cf.* J. Miel and J. Sutterman) and was court painter to Ranuccio Farnese II in Parma; also worked in Mantua for Isabella Clara of Austria (*cf.* Jacob D. and D. van den Dyck) 1669-70. J. de Duyts was among his pupils. **Signed Examples:** VERSAILLES *Franz Paulin van Broeckhoven, lord of Vechel* 1652. VIENNA K. *A cleric* 1640. **Documented Examples:** NAPLES *Duke Ranuccio Farnese II, Isabella d'Este wife of Duke Ranuccio II* (both recorded Farnese inventory 1680). An *Allegory of the towns Parma and Piacenza handing over the town keys to Ranuccio* and portrait groups are among other pictures recorded in the same Farnese inventory.   [Fl. 892, Fl. 798.]

*Denys, (de Nys), Jacob. Flemish Sch. *b* son of Frans D., Antwerp 1644 *d* place unknown 1708 or later. *Portraits, religious subjects, 'history', allegories.* Pupil of E. Quellinus; in Antwerp Guild 1664; went Italy (*cf.* A. v. Goubau, J. Miel and J. F. v. Bloemen) *c.* 1666; worked in Mantua (*cf.* Frans D.) for Isabella Clara of Austria and painted portraits in Florence for Grand Duke Cosimo III; visited Venice (*cf.* L. de Deyster) 1674; returned Antwerp *c.* 1679; married widow with children 1691; fled from widow to destination never discovered 1695. **Documented Examples:** ANTWERP *Gregorius Martens, Director of Antwerp Guild* (presented by artist to Guild 1694), *Allegory of the Study of the Nude* (presented to Guild by artist 1693 *cf.* G. Neyts). Paintings commissioned by Isabella Clara for Mantua S. Maurizio and an *Ecce Homo* are recorded.
     [Fl. 753, Fl. 425, Fl. 215, Fl. 289, Fl. 107, Fl. 892, Fl. 305.]

Depelchin, J. F. Flemish Sch. *b* Velaines *c.* 1770 *d* Equerme 1835. *Landscapes, architectural views, genre.* In Paris *c.* 1792. Visited Italy; exhibited Paris Salon 1791, 1793 and 1795; professor Courtrai Acad. from 1800. In Equerme from 1833. Represented in COURTRAI *Interior of Notre Dame de Paris, Interior of a forge* (*cf.* L. Defrance).   [Fl. 66, Fl. 73, Fl. 798.]

Deprez, Henri. Flemish Sch. *b* Liège 1727 *d* Liège 1797. *Religious subjects, decorative paintings, portraits.* Pupil of R. Panhay de Rendeux *q.v.*; then Rome where pupil of the Italian painter Corrado Giaquinto 1746-51 (*cf.* J. Latour); returned Liège; worked often in collaboration with J. B. Coclers. Decorative paintings for houses and public buildings and pictures for Liège churches are recorded.   [Fl. 409.]

Depunder, Jacobus, see **Punder.**

Derickx, Louis. Flemish Sch. *b* Antwerp 1835 *d* Antwerp 1895. *Landscapes, genre.* Represented in ANTWERP *Stormy landscape.*   [Fl. 17.]

Derus, Lucas, see **Heere.**

Desubleo (**De Subleo, Sobleo**), **Michele,** known in Italy as Michele Fiammingo. Flemish Sch. *b.* Maubeuge (?) *c.* 1601 (?) *d* Parma (?) after 1676. *Religious subjects, portraits, allegories.* Went Italy and remained there (*cf.* J. Sutterman); in Bologna *c.* 1636; worked in Guido Reni's studio and for Bolognese churches; taught with F. Albani, Guercino and others in an academy founded by Count Ghisilieri in his own palace in Bologna; left Bologna c. 1655; worked in Venice and, later, in Parma. **Documented Examples** (recorded by contemporary writers): BOLOGNA Pinac. *Footwashing of S. Augustine and apparition of Christ, Virgin and Child* both from convent church of Gesù e Maria. CASTEL FRANCO D'EMILIA (nr. Bologna) S. Urbano *S. Urban.* VENICE S. Maria in Nazaretto *Virgin in glory with Carmelite saints*; S. Zaccaria *Agony in the Garden* (seen by Boschini in Sta. Croce della Giudecca). PARMA Cathedral *SS. Firmus, Rusticus and Proclus.* Parma inventories of 1690 and 1708 record a *Sacred and Profane Love*, a *Cain and Abel* and a *Portrait of Princess Caterina Farnese.* [Fl. 101, Fl. 558, Fl. 505, Fl. 305.]

Detilleux, Servais. Flemish Sch. *b* Stambert-lez-Verviers 1874. *Portraits, costume history, genre; also sculpture.* Pupil in Liège Acad. of E. Delpérée and in Brussels of J. Portaels. Exhibited Paris Salon from 1914. An *Equestrian portrait of King Albert* (1910) and a picture titled *Silent prayer* (exhibited 1929) are recorded. [Fl. 465.]

*Detroit Crucifixion Painter. Presumed Flemish Sch. 16th cent. Name for painter of DETROIT Institute of Arts (34.15) *Crucifixion.* Presumed by some identical with J. v. Scorel *q.v.*

*Detroit Mystic Marriage Painter. Presumed Flemish Sch. 15th cent. Name for painter of DETROIT Institute of Arts (26.387) *Mystic Marriage of S. Catharine (Virgo inter Virgines).* Presumed by some identical with Lucy Legend Master *q.v.*

*Detroit S. Jerome Painter. Presumed Flemish Sch. 16th cent. Name for painter of DETROIT Institute of Arts (25.4) *S. Jerome in his study.* Presumably by some identical with P. Christus *q.v.*

*Detroit Wedding Dance Painter. Presumed Flemish Sch. 16th cent. Name for painter of DETROIT Institute of Arts *The Wedding Dance*, 1566. Presumed by some identical with P. Bruegel the elder *q.v.*

Devos, Charles. Presumed Flemish Sch. 19th cent. *Still Life.* Represented in BRUGES *Trophée de Gibier* (*s* and 1869). [Fl. 114.]

Devos, Leon. Flemish Sch. *b* Klein Edingen 1897. *Genre, portraits, still life, landscapes.* In army during German invasion 1914-18. Pupil and later teacher in Brussels Acad.; Member of Nervia group (*cf.* A. Carte). Represented in ANTWERP *Girl with basket.* TOLEDO (U.S.A.) *Susanna.* [Fl. 17.]

Deweerdt, Armand. Flemish Sch. *b* Niel 1890. *Landscapes, still life.* Pupil of K. Mertens in Antwerp Acad. and of J. de Vriendt in Antwerp Higher Institute. Represented in ANTWERP *Flemish village.* [Fl. 17.]

Deynum, Guillaume (Willem) van. Flemish Sch. *b* Antwerp (?) before 1580 *d* Brussels (?) after 1618. *Miniatures.* Court painter in Brussels to Archduke Albert (*cf.* G. de Crayer and O. van Veen) and Archduchess Isabella (*cf.* D. van Alsloot) from 1614. [Fl. 656, Fl. 892.]

Deynum, Jan Baptist van. Flemish Sch. *b* Antwerp 1620 *d* Antwerp (?) 1668. *Portrait miniatures, also 'history' and landscapes in w.* Master Antwerp Guild 1647. [Fl. 86, Fl. 425.]

Deyster, Lodewyk (Louis) de. Flemish Sch. *b* Bruges c. 1656 *d* Bruges 1711. *Religious subjects for Bruges churches* (*cf.* N. Vleys); *also worked as an engraver.* Visited Rome and Venice (*cf.* J. Denys) with A. van Eeckhout *q.v.*; back in Bruges by 1688; married sister of van Eeckhout; in later life occupied himself without success with musical instrument building; van Eeckhout painted flowers in some of his pictures and L. Achtschellinck *q.v.* sometimes collaborated as landscapist.

His daughter Anna (*b c.* 1690 *d* 1747) was a painter. **Signed Examples:** VIENNA Liecht. *Landscape with the Carrying of the Cross, Deposition* (with night effect) both 1704. **Documented Examples:** BRUGES S. Jacques *Crucifixion, Resurrection, Death of the Virgin*; S. Sauveur three *Scenes from the Passion*; Notre Dame *Esther before Ahasuerus*; S. Anne *S. Sebastian.* Descamps who had information from Anna D. records (1760 and 1769) many examples in churches in and around Bruges and gives details of his technical procedures. [Fl. 215, Fl. 216, Fl. 207, Fl. 871, Fl. 892, Fl. 113.]

Diels, Herman. Flemish Sch. *b* Turnhout 1903. *Portraits, figures, landscapes.* Pupil in Antwerp Higher Institute of E. van Mieghem and I. Opsomer. Represented in ANTWERP *Portrait of a lady.* [Fl. 17.]

Diepenbeeck, Abraham Jansz. van. Flemish Sch. *b* son of a glass painter, Bois-le-Duc 1596 *d* Antwerp 1675. *Religious subjects, 'history', mythologies, portraits, animals; also active as glass painter and draughtsman for engravers.* In Antwerp Glassmakers' Guild 1623; worked in Rubens' studio; in England *c.* 1629 (?); visited Italy with J. Thomas; in Antwerp Painters' Guild 1638; painted most of the *History of Amor and Psyche* (commissioned 1647 from G. Coques *q.v.* by Prince Frederick Henry of Orange) from sketches after Raphael 1648; visited Paris where William Cavendish, Duke of Newcastle then in exile as Royalist was buying his Barbary horses 1645-8; made drawings for *Le Temple des Muses* (published Paris 1655); illustrated the Duke of Newcastle's book on Managed Horses possibly when the Duke was in Antwerp 1648-60; Vertue (before 1752) records a visit to England (*cf.* C. de Neve); drawings of the Duke's seats occur in the book which was published 1657. He married twice and had twelve children. **Documented Examples:** ANTWERP Cathedral *S. Norbert* (engraved 1634). DEURNE Church *S. Norbert consecrating the first abbot of S. Michel* (painted for S. Michel monastery). Frankfort (Staedel) has a *Young man in sporting costume* monogrammed A.D. presumed by some his work. Vertue saw large paintings of managed horses at Walbeck which he presumed to be his work. Descamps (1769) records glass paintings in Antwerp, Brussels and Lille churches; and *Elijah in Heaven* in Antwerp Carmes Chaussées. Antwerp inventories of 1689 record a *S. Roch in captivity* and many drawings.
[Fl. 86, Fl. 753, Fl. 652, Fl. 425, Fl. 878, Fl. 826, Fl. 22, Fl. 215, Fl. 216, Fl. 564, Fl. 856, Fl. 107, Fl. 892, Fl. 213, Fl. 899.]

Dierckx, Jacques (Pierre). Flemish Sch. *b* Antwerp 1855 *d* Brussels 1947. *Landscapes, interiors with genre figures o. and w.* Pupil in Antwerp Acad. of C. Verlat and in Paris École des B. A. of P. Baudry. Worked in Antwerp, Campine, Brittany, Holland and Italy. Represented in ANTWERP *Meditation, Sorrow, Brittany interior with lacemakers.* ADELAIDE (Australia) *Girl scouring.* BARCELONA, BRUGES, BRUSSELS *Women spinning* 1903. BUDAPEST, LIVERPOOL Walker *Knitting lesson* 1890. PARIS State Coll. *Reading the Bible* 1904. [Fl. 17.]

Dierckx, Matthew I. Flemish Sch. *b* Antwerp 1807 *d* Antwerp 1832. *Religious subjects.* [Fl. 451.]

Dierickx, A., see Rodriguez.

Diez (or Dietz), Gustave Adolph. Flemish Sch. *b* Malines 1801 *d* Malines or Schaerbeek 1844. *Decorative paintings, mythological subjects.* Pupil of J. Odevaere and later his assistant; worked for Tervueren Palace. Represented in AMSTERDAM Rijks. *Hebe.* A portrait of *J. Odevaere* is recorded by an engraving. [Fl. 451, Fl. 612, Fl. 798.]

Dijck, Henri van. Flemish Sch. *b* Bruges 1849 *d* after 1886. *Costume history, genre, town views, interiors.* Pupil in Antwerp Acad. of J. van Lerius. Represented in ANTWERP *Interior of Mutsaerdstraat Museum* 1886. [Fl. 17.]

Dilighem Abbey Master, see **Abbey.**

Dillens, Adolf Alexander. Flemish Sch. *b* Ghent 1821 *d* Brussels 1877. *Zeeland peasant scenes, costume anecdotes and engravings.* Pupil of his brother Hendrick D. and his uncle Julien D. sculptor. Represented in BRUGES, BRUSSELS *Recruiting scene, Zeeland skating scene.* A *Fair at Westcapelle* exhibited in Paris International Exhibition 1855 is recorded. *Cf.* F. Rops. [Fl. 440, Fl. Bib. 19th cent.]

Dillens, Hendrick. Flemish Sch. *b* Ghent 1812 *d* Elsene (Brussels) 1872. *Costume history, genre.* Represented in COURTRAI, LIÈGE, YPRES. A *Charles V and the swineherd* is recorded. [Fl. Bib. 19th cent.]

Dinant, Enrico da, see **Bles.**

Dircksz, Barent, known as Doove (Deaf) Barent. Flemish (Dutch) Sch. *b* Amsterdam (?) before 1520. Van Mander (1604) records that he painted in Amsterdam Town Hall 'pictures of a raving sect which tried to gain control of the city in 1535' and describes the subjects as 'strange and horrifying happenings'. Pictures in Amsterdam Town Hall representing punishments deemed appropriate for Anabaptists were destroyed by fire in 1652. Dirck Barendsz *q.v.* was the son of this artist. [Fl. 559, Fl. 892.]

Diriksen (Dirsen), Felipe. Flemish Sch. *b* son of Rodrigo D. *q.v.* and grandson of A. v. d. Wyngaerde, the Escorial, Madrid 1594 *d* Spain (?) after 1629. *Religious subjects, portraits.* Patronized by Philip III; applied unsuccessfully for post as his 'pintor de Cámara' 1617. **Signed Examples:** AVILA Capilla de Mosén Rubín *S. Jerome* 1629. A *Philip III making a state entry into Lisbon 1619* and a *S. Diego* painted for Toledo convent of Barefooted Carmelites are recorded. [Fl. 153, Fl. 95 (1915), Fl. 904.]

Diriksen (Dirsen or de Holanda), Rodrigo. Flemish Sch. *b* Oudenburg, nr. Bruges before 1550 *d* Spain (?) after 1599. *Religious subjects, decorative paintings; also worked as picture restorer.* In Spain and working for Philip II (*cf.* P. Kempener) in the Escorial by 1572; granted a retirement pension by Philip III 1599 (*cf.* L. Franchoys the elder); married the daughter of A. v. d. Wyngaerde *q.v.* **Documented Examples:** MADRID Escorial Sala de Batallas *Battle of Higueruela 1431* fresco (painted from his cartoons by Spanish artists F. Castelo and others) 1589; Lower Escorial Church of S. Bernabe *Christ* and a *S. Mary Magdalene* for tomb of Philip II's fool Miguel de Antona. An *Ecce Homo* left unfinished at his death by the Spanish painter J. F. Navarrete (El Mudo) was finished by D. in 1581. [Fl. 95 (1915), Fl. 904.]

Dobbelaere, Henri. Flemish Sch. *b* Bruges 1822 *d* Bruges 1885. *Costume history, religious subjects; also worked as glasspainter for public buildings in Ypres, Bruges and in Ghent S. Bavon.* Pupil in Bruges Acad. and of G. Wappers. Represented in BRUGES Town Hall *The finding of the body of Charles the Bold after the Battle of Nancy 1477. Seven Works of Mercy.* BRUSSELS *Memlinc painting the S. Ursula shrine* (*cf.* P. Kremer). [Fl. 160 (1885).]

Dolphyn, Victor. Flemish Sch. *b* Diest 1909. *Interiors, figures.* Pupil of I. Opsomer in Antwerp Higher Institute. Represented in ANTWERP *Interior of a fisherman's cottage, Near Perpignan.* [Fl. 17.]

Donck, G. (Gerard?) van. Presumed Flemish (or Dutch) Sch. *b* before 1627 *d* after 1640. *Portraits, genre.* **Signed Examples:** LONDON N.G. *J. van Hensbeeck and his wife Maria Koeck.* NEW YORK Hist. Soc. *Vegetable seller.* VIENNA Liecht. *Portrait of a woman aged 60* 1627, *Portrait of a man aged 57* 1627, *Mother and child* 1634; Czernin *The cooper.* [Fl. 892.]

Donck, Geerard. Flemish Sch. *b* before 1636 *d* after 1691.

Miniatures. Worked Antwerp where was Master in Guild 1652 and Dean 1687. [Fl. 892, Fl. 798.]

*****Donckt, Joseph Angelus van der.** Flemish Sch. *b* son of town clerk, Alost 1757 *d* Bruges 1821. *Portraits (some in pastel) and miniatures.* Pupil in Bruges of J. A. Garemyn before 1775; in Marseilles 1780; in Paris where copied pictures in the Orléans collection *c.* 1782-*c.* 1785; in Bruges *c.* 1786-89; Paris 1789; Italy 1789-91; returned Bruges 1791 and became director of Acad. till 1815 (*cf.* J. D. Odevaere and J. F. Ducq). **Documented Examples:** BRUGES *Self portrait, P. J. de Cock* (miniature), *Sylvie de la Rue and her dog.* [Fl. 451, Fl. 114.]

Donnay, Auguste. Flemish Sch. *b* Liège 1862 *d* Méry-sur-Ourthe 1921. *Landscape compositions, portraits, religious subjects, decorative panels, illustrations.* Pupil Liège Acad.; then Paris. Teacher decorative painting Liège Acad. 1901-5; settled Méry 1905. Represented in BRUSSELS *Annunciation* 1914. LIÈGE *Flight into Egypt, The River* and others; Hastière Church triptych *S. Walhère.* [Fl. 483, Fl. 296.]

Donny, Désiré. Flemish Sch. *b* Bruges 1798 *d* Brussels 1861. *Historical genre, marines, and harbour scenes (some by moonlight), portraits.* Pupil of J. D. Odevaere. Professor in Bruges Acad. Lived for some years in Frankfort. Represented in COURTRAI *William I of the Netherlands.* YPRES *Moonlight.* [Fl. 451, Fl. 798.]

Doormael, Theo van. Flemish Sch. *b* Standdaarbuiten (N. Brabant) 1871 *d* Antwerp 1910. *Figures, landscapes, still life (o., w.* and *pastel).* Represented in ANTWERP *The two friends, Soapbubbles* 1899, *Flowers* 1909. [Fl. 17.]

Doort, Everardus. Flemish Sch. 17th cent. *Religious subjects.* Went Italy and remained there (*cf.* J. Sutterman). **Signed Examples** (recorded but no longer *in situ*): PAVIA S. Epifanio *Coronation of the Virgin s* 'Everardus Doort Belga' 1614, *Death of S. Augustine* (similar signature) and frescoes 1616. [Fl. 138, Fl. 305.]

Dorizi (or Dorisy), Claude. Flemish Sch. *b* Malines (?) 1517 *d c.* 1565. In Malines Guild and citizen Malines 1536; employed J. Vredeman de Vries *q.v.* on pictures with architectural detail; organised an exhibition and lottery of pictures 1555. [Fl. 559, Fl. 613, Fl. 892.]

Dormagen Master (Holy Night Master). Presumed Flemish Sch. early 16th cent. Name for painter of COLOGNE Wallraf-Richartz Mus. Triptych *Nativity* (centre), *Virgin of Mercy, S. Ursula* (wings); *cf.* Milan Adoration Master. [Fl. 316.]

Dorne, François van. Flemish Sch. *b* son of Martin van D., Louvain 1776 *d* Louvain 1848. *Religious subjects for Louvain churches, portraits.* Pupil of P. J. Verhaghen and in Paris of Louis David 1806 (*cf.* F. J. Navez and M. G. Tieleman). [Fl. 269, Fl. 798.]

Dorne, Martin van. Flemish Sch. *b.* 1736 *d* 1808. *Fruit and flowers* (*cf.* A. Plateau). Worked at Louvain. *Cf.* F. van D. [Fl. 798.]

Douffet, Gérard. Flemish Sch. *b* Liège 1594 *d* Liège 1660. *Religious subjects, 'history', portraits.* Pupil of J. Taulier; went Antwerp; visited Italy (Rome and Venice) *cf.* P. de Lignis 1614; returned Liège 1623; painter to Prince Bishop of Liège. J. G. Delcour, B. Flémalle and G. Goswin were among his pupils. **Signed Examples:** AUGSBURG *Christ appearing to the Apostles.* MUNICH A. P. *The finding of the True Cross by the Empress Helena.* **Documented Examples:** LIÈGE *Vulcan's forge* (engraved). MUNICH A. P. *Pope Nicholas V opening the tomb of S. Francis in 1449* commissioned by Liège Franciscans 1627 (the French painter L. de la Hire painted the same subject in 1636). [Fl. 409, Fl. 464.]

Douw, Simon Johannes van. Flemish Sch. *b* place unknown *c.* 1630 *d* place unknown after 1677. *Picturesque military scenes* (*cf.* L. de Hondt the elder), *horse markets* (*cf.* S. Vrancx) *and landscapes with horsemen* (*cf.* J. d'Arthois and A. v. d. Meulen). Master in Antwerp Guild 1654; worked Middelburg *c.* 1656 and Rotterdam (?) 1666. P. van Bloemen was among his pupils. **Signed Examples:** *Cavalry skirmishes* in HERMANNSTADT, PRAGUE Rudolfinum (*Combat with Turks*), VIENNA Liecht. (*Combat with Turks*); and *Horsemarkets* in SCHWERIN, VIENNA Liecht.; *Landscapes with horsemen* in LILLE (1677) and TROYES (*Horseman and a peasant girl with cattle at a ford* 1661) *cf.* J. Siberechts. [Fl. 107, Fl. 481, Fl. 892, Fl. 212, Fl. 213.]

Dreppe, Joseph. Flemish Sch. *b* son of medallist Jean Noël D., Liège 1737 *d* Liège 1810. *Decorative works for churches and mansions, landscapes, marines, tapestry cartoons, book illustrations.* Pupil of Jan Latour *q.v.*; went Rome 1758; worked there under a pupil of the German R. Mengs (*cf.* F. J. Lonsing); returned Liège *c.* 1761; patronised by Prince Bishops and painted ceilings in chapel of Bishop's Palace; director of Liège Acad. 1784; collaborated with French in removing works of art from Liège after 1794 (*cf.* L. Defrance). [Fl. 409, Fl. 798.]

Dreux (de Rieue), Jehan. Flemish Sch. *b* Bruges (?) before *c.* 1420 *d* after 1464. *MS illustrations.* In service of Dukes of Burgundy, Philip the Good and Charles the Bold. [Fl. 490, Fl. 892.]

*Dublin Flight Painter. Presumed Flemish Sch. 15th/16th cent. Name for painter of DUBLIN N.G. of Ireland *Flight into Egypt.* Presumed by some identical with Jan de Cock *q.v.*

*Dublin Rebecca Painter. Presumed Flemish Sch. 16th cent. Name for painter of DUBLIN N. G. of Ireland (845) *Rebecca at the Well* (*cf.* C. Buys the younger). Presumed by some identical with Prodigal Son Master *q.v.* [Fl. 715, Fl. 236.]

*Dublin S. Augustine Painter. Presumed Flemish Sch. 15th cent. Name for painter of DUBLIN N.G. of Ireland (823) *Scenes from the life of S. Augustine* (catalogued as Silver Windows Master). Presumed by some identical with Augustine Master *q.v.* [Fl. 316, Fl. 236.]

*Dublin S. Nicholas Painter. Presumed Flemish Sch. 15th cent. Name for painter of DUBLIN N.G. of Ireland (360) *Two Miracles of S. Nicholas of Bari.* Presumed by some identical with Barbara Legend Master *q.v.*

*Dubois, Ambroise. Flemish Sch. *b* Antwerp *c.* 1543 (?) *d* Fontainebleau 1614. *'History', portraits, decorative work.* Went France *c.* 1568 (?) and remained there; employed by Henri IV *c.* 1594; J. de Hoey was godfather to his son 1595; naturalized French 1601; married (as second wife) the sister of J. de Hoey 1601; worked in Paris and at Fontainebleau (*cf.* Gillis v. Cleve, W. Coebergher, A. Francken, H. Francken the elder, P. Franchoys, L. de Heere, W. v. Haecht, J. de Hoey, C. Ketel, H. de Maier, H. v. d. Mast, D. Pietersz, J. de Wael; also L. Thiry and C. E. Biset); after death of French painter T. Dubreuil (1602) directed painting at Fontainebleau Château; painter to Queen Marie de Médicis 1606. **Documented Examples:** PARIS Louvre *Baptism of Clorinda by Tancred* (from series painted for Queen's apartments in Fontainebleau). FONTAINEBLEAU Château has remains of pictures (*Scenes from the story of Theagenes and Chariclea* and frescoes (repainted in the nineteenth century). A *Gabrielle d'Estrées as Diana* is recorded. [Fl. 287, Fl. 227, Fl. 440, Fl. 798.]

Dubois, Charles Sylva. Flemish Sch. *b* Brussels 1668 *d* Köpenick, Berlin 1753. *Landscapes.* Soldier, then opera dancer; appointed Court dancing master Berlin 1707; began to paint 1713; his friend the French artist Antoine Pesne (court painter to Frederick I, Frederick William and Frederick II (*cf.* A. Schoonjans)) and the German architect G. W. Knobelsdorff painted figures in some of his pictures. Examples are recorded in German collections and by engravings. *Cf.* S. P. d'Argonne. [Fl. 616, Fl. 612, Fl. 892, Fl. 798.]

Dubois (Du Bois, Du Booys), Eduard. Flemish Sch. *b* son of Hendrick D., Antwerp 1619 *d* London 1697. *Landscapes, portraits and 'history'.* Pupil in Holland of Dutch landscape painter P. A. van Groenewegen; in Haarlem Guild 1648; went Paris, then Italy with his brother Simon D. *c.* 1653; worked Turin for Charles Emmanuel II Duke of Savoy (*cf.* J. Miel) *c.* 1653-*c.* 1661; returned Holland; in London living with Simon D. *q.v.* from *c.* 1680. **Signed Example:** OXFORD Queen's College *Joseph Addison* s 'Du Bois pinx' (possibly therefore by S. D.). [Fl. 878, Fl. 826, Fl. 856.]

Dubois, Hendrik. Flemish Sch. *b* Antwerp (?) *c.* 1589 *d* Rotterdam 1646. Pupil in Antwerp of Jan de Wael 1602. Settled Rotterdam *c.* 1638; a document describes him as painter and art dealer. His son Simon D. *q.v.* bequeathed his portrait as by Van Dyck to Lord Somers. [Fl. 892.]

Dubois, Louis. Flemish Sch. *b* Brussels 1830 *d* Brussels 1880. *Animals, landscapes, genre, still life, portraits.* Pupil of T. Couture in Paris; friend of G. Courbet. Founded in Brussels the Société Libre des Beaux Arts of which the motto was 'naturism, individualism and colour' (*cf.* L. Artan, T. Baron, C. van Camp, H. de la Charlerie, C. de Groux, H. v. d. Hecht, E. Huberti, E. Lambrichs (who painted a group portrait of the members), C. Meunier, F. Rops, E. Smits, A. Verwée) 1868. Represented in BRUSSELS *Storks* 1858, *Dead deer* 1863, *Portrait of the artist's father* 1858, *Still life (fish)* 1874, *Landscape.* [Fl. 837 (1880), Fl. 296, Fl. Bib. 19th cent.]

Dubois, Pieter (Pierre), see **Lignis, P.**

Dubois, Simon (Du Bois, Du Booys). Flemish Sch. *b* son of Hendrick D., Antwerp 1632 *d* London 1708. *Portraits, picturesque landscapes with figures and animals, military pieces.* In Haarlem with his brother Eduard D. *q.v.* 1648; pupil there of the Dutch painters C. P. Berchem and P. Wouverman; went Italy via Paris with Eduard D. *c.* 1653; in Rome 1655; in Venice 1657; visited Haarlem 1661; returned Rome (?)—(Vertue (before 1721) says he lived there twenty-five years); with Eduard D. came London (*cf.* J. B. Medina, J. Peeters, S. Hardimé, J. B. Lantscroon, P. H. Lankrinck, A. Schoonjans, P. Tillemans, also C. de Neve, V. H. Janssens and P. Breydel) *c.* 1680; collaborated with Dutch marine painter W. v. d. Velde from *c.* 1698; at age of seventy-five married v. d. Velde's daughter 1707. Vertue (before 1731) records him as a great mimic of the Italians in his genre pictures abundance of which were sold by him during his life for capital Italian paintings. Weyerman (1729) records him as living in Covent Garden with his brother, and amassing money by portrait painting while living as a recluse without a servant. **Signed Examples:** AMSTERDAM *Emerentia van Citters, Josina v. C., Johanna v. C.* (daughters of Dutch ambassador to England) all 1693. CAMBRIDGE Fitz. *Man's portrait* (miniature) 1682. DULWICH *Sir William Jones (Solicitor-General), Lady Jones* 1682. OXFORD Queen's Coll. *Joseph Addison* ('Du Bois pinxit' possibly therefore by E. D.). **Documented Examples:** LAMBETH Palace *Archbishop Tenison* (mentioned by G. Vertue and J. Weyerman), AMSTERDAM *Arnout* and *Anna v. Citters* bequeathed by v. C. family. A *Tower of Babel* (*cf.* M. v. Valkenborch) and several battle pictures were bequeathed by him to his wife and portraits of his father and mother as by A. van Dyck to his patron Lord Somers (Lord Chancellor) whose portrait he had painted.

[Fl. 878, Fl. 826, Fl. 856, Fl. 38.]

*Duchatel (or du Chastel), François. Flemish Sch. *b* Brussels 1625 (or 1616) *d* Brussels 1694 (or 1679). *Portraits, official ceremonies* (*cf.* A. Sallaert), *and genre.* Served as soldier, then pupil of D. Teniers the younger; visited Paris (*cf.* C. E. Biset) where worked with A. F. v. d. Meulen *q.v.* 1668; Sir J. B. Medina was his pupil. **Signed Example:** GHENT *The Marquis of Castel-Rodrigo receiving on behalf of Charles II of Spain the allegiance of the states of Flanders 1666* 1668, large picture showing nearly 1,000 figures, from which 116 portraits were engraved (*cf.* J. de Hornes, J. v. Werden and E. Quellinus); seen by Descamps in Ghent Town Hall 1768. His *Marquis of Castel Rodrigo governor general Spanish Netherlands 1664-69* and *Duke of Villa Hermosa governor general Spanish Netherlands 1674-80* are recorded by engravings; a *Charles II of Spain 1676* commissioned by Brabant authorities (*cf.* P. Thys, P. Ijkens and R. Mol) is also recorded.

[Fl. 86, Fl. 425, Fl. 576, Fl. 216, Fl. 892.]

Duchêne, Charles, see Eycken.

Ducorron, Julien (Jules) Joseph. Flemish Sch. *b* Ath 1770 *d* Ath 1848. *Landscapes with animals and figures.* Pupil in Antwerp of B. Ommeganck. Founder of and Professor in Ath School of Art 1819. Represented in AMSTERDAM, CAMBRAI and ATH Townhall and church.

[Fl. 451, Fl. 612, Fl. 798, Fl. 296.]

Ducq, Joseph François. Flemish Sch. *b* son of village physician, Ledeghem 1762 *d* Bruges 1829. '*History*', *mythologies, portraits, Italian landscapes.* Pupil in Bruges Acad. of P. J. de Cock 1780 and in Paris of J. B. Suvée (*cf.* J. Odevaere) from 1786; to Bruges to escape from Paris conditions 1792; returned Paris 1795; given lodgings in Louvre under Consulate (*cf.* J. F. v. Dael and P. J. Redouté); successful Salon exhibitor under Empire (*cf.* L. Gerbo); commissioned to paint ceilings in St. Cloud Palace (destroyed 1870) 1799-1806; went Rome where given studio in Villa Medici 1807; returned Paris 1813; appointed Professor Bruges Acad. and court painter on establishment of Kingdom of United Netherlands 1815; restored Memlinc's *Virgin and Child with SS. Catherine, Barbara and John* (Bruges Hôpital S. Jean) 1817. A portrait *William, First King of the United Netherlands* is recorded. Pictures titled *Scipio receiving the Ambassadors of Antiochus* (1800) and *Meleager taking arms to free Calydon from the boar* (Salon 1804) were bought by Fouché, Napoleon's Chief of Police. Mythologies and Old Testament subjects painted 1807-12 for Eugène de Beauharnais Viceroy of Italy are also recorded. [Fl. 451, Fl. 66, Fl. 612, Fl. 114.]

Dujardin, Edward. Flemish Sch. *b* Antwerp 1817 *d* Antwerp 1889. *Religious subjects for churches, designs for stained glass costume history, portraits, illustrations.* Pupil in Antwerp Acad. of G. Wappers. Professor Antwerp Acad. 1841. Represented in ANTWERP *Adam and Eve finding Abel's corpse, Abel's corpse taken to Heaven by an Angel, Cain in the power of Satan.* [Fl. 451, Fl. 837 (1889), Fl. 17.]

Du Monceau de Bergendal, Countess Mathilde. Flemish Sch. *b* Schaarbeek (Brussels) 1877. *Landscapes in the mining districts, parks, gardens, flowers.* Pupil in Liège Acad. of A. de Witte and A. Donnay. Represented in ANTWERP *Mining village under snow.* [Fl. 17.]

Dumoulin, A. Flemish Sch. *b* nr. Liège 1675 *d* Liège *c.* 1740. *Religious subjects and 'history'* (*often with landscapes by his brother Lambert D. q.v.*). Worked for Liège churches.

[Fl. 409, Fl. 798.]

Dumoulin, Lambert. Flemish Sch. *b* nr. Liège 1665 *d* Liège

1743. Italianate landscapes (*cf.* J. B. Juppin) *some with figures by his brother A. D. q.v.* [Fl. 409.]

Dupagne, Adrien. Flemish Sch. *b* Liège 1889. *Peasant genre.* Travelled in Brittany, Spain, North Africa and near East. Represented ANTWERP *Acrobats in a Spanish village.*

[Fl. 17.]

Duvenede, Marcus van. Flemish Sch. *b* Bruges *c.* 1674 *d* Bruges 1730. *Religious subjects.* Pupil of J. B. Herregouts 1689. Master in Bruges Guild 1700; travelled in Italy and studied under the Italian painter Carlo Maratta (*cf.* R. v. Audenaerd and R. P. de Rendeux); returned Bruges; founder member of Bruges Acad. (*cf.* J. v. Kerckhove) 1717; married a rich lace dealer and gave up painting 1718. **Signed Example:** BRUGES S. Jacques *Assumption of the Virgin 1700*. Descamps (1769) records a *S. Clara* and a *S. Laurence* in Bruges churches. [Fl. 216, Fl. 451, Fl. 892.]

Duwée, Henri Joseph. Flemish Sch. *b c.* 1810 *d* after 1870. *Genre, religious subjects, costume history.* Pupil of F. J. Navez. Made illustrations for Ch. de Costers 'Uylenspiegel'. Represented in AMSTERDAM *Woman with tambourine 1858.*

[Fl. 451, Fl. 798.]

Duyts, Gustave den. Flemish Sch. *b* Ghent 1850 *d* Brussels 1897. *Landscapes (o. and w.) in Impressionist convention; also engravings.* Represented in ANTWERP *Felled trees* (w.) 1891, *Evening* 1894. BRUSSELS *The Thaw* 1890. GHENT *Snow landscape* 1889. PARIS State Coll. *Woodcutters.*

[Fl. 160 (1897), Fl. 296, Fl. Bib. 19th cent.]

Duyts, Jan de. Flemish Sch. *b* Antwerp 1629 *d* Antwerp 1676. *Religious and mythological subjects, portraits.* Pupil of F. Denys 1642; Master Antwerp Guild 1648. **Signed Examples:** BRUNSWICK *Diana, Venus and Amor*. LEIPZIG *Children's bacchanal*. *A Scene with nymphs* (*s* 1671) is shown in G. Coques' *Picture gallery* (Hague, Mauritshuis).

[Fl. 86, Fl. 107, Fl. 892.]

Dyck, Albert van. Flemish Sch. *b* Turnhout 1902. *Rural genre, portraits, animals, landscape.* Pupil of I. Opsomer in Antwerp Higher Institute. Contributor to Antwerp 'L'Art Contemporain' (Kunst van Heden) exhibitions (*cf.* R. Strebelle). Represented in ANTWERP *Peasant girl, Portrait of a woman.* [Fl. 568, Fl. 296, Fl. 17.]

*Dyck, Antoon (Sir Anthony), van. Flemish Sch. *b* son of a rich merchant, Antwerp 1599 *d* London and buried old S. Paul's 1641. *Portraits, religious subjects, mythologies; also some engravings.* Pupil of H. van Balen 1610; master in Antwerp Guild 1618; then pupil and assistant of P. P. Rubens; was living in Rubens' house and the only assistant named in Rubens' contract for Antwerp Jesuit church (to be painted from Rubens' sketches by his assistants) 1620; received first independent contract for an Antwerp church same year; went England (*cf.* C. de Neve) on invitation from the Earl of Arundel and granted yearly salary by James I Nov. 1620; paid £100 by the King for a special service and granted eight months leave of absence Feb. 1621; in Antwerp and Saventhem 1621; in Italy (except for a visit to Antwerp for his father's death Dec. 1622) from Nov. 1621 to 1626; visited Genoa (*cf.* J. Roos, C. and L. de Wael), Venice, Mantua (with the Countess of Arundel), Bologna, Turin, Florence (*cf.* J. Sutterman) and Rome (with J. Brueghel the younger) where stayed in the Palace of Cardinal Bentivoglio; unpopular with painters in Flemish colony in Rome (*cf.* P. de Lignis); made Genoa his headquarters and was popular with and much employed there by the rich families; visited Palermo 1624; back in Antwerp by 1627; joined Jesuit Bachelors' Fraternity; visited Holland and worked for Prince Frederick Henry of Orange; began an 'Iconography' (portrait drawings and grisailles of contemporary celebrities including artists, which were engraved, some by himself) and worked for a number of Antwerp churches; Court Painter to Archduchess Isabella (*cf.* D. v. Alsloot) 1630; was visited in his studio by Marie de Médicis 1631; went London and stayed for a time with Jorge Geldorp *q.v.* 1632; given by Charles I a yearly salary, a knighthood and residences in Blackfriars and Eltham, Kent; employed as portraitist by the court and English nobility; made much money which he spent in sumptuous living and elegant entertainment of his sitters, surrounded by 'lackeys, musicians, singers and fools'; used professional models for the hands of his portraits and employed assistants to lay in drapery and accessories; kept Margaret Lemon as his mistress; tried to balance his expenditure by establishing a laboratory for an alchemist who claimed to be able to make gold; visited Antwerp and Brussels 1634; married Mary Ruthven, one of the Queen's ladies 1639; submitted plans to Charles I for *History of the Order of the Garter* murals for Whitehall Banqueting Hall (where Rubens had painted the ceiling) but the King recoiled at his price 1639-40; went Antwerp with his family after death of Rubens; negotiated (without result) with Cardinal Infante Ferdinand for the continuation of the pictures supplied by the Rubens atelier for Philip IV's palaces (*cf.* J. P. Gowi); went Paris and negotiated (without result) with Louis XIII for the decoration of the Louvre (*cf.* J. Fouquier) 1641; went London to attend to some affairs; fell ill and the King offered £300 to his own physician if he could save his life; Houbraken (1718) records him 'burned by the flame of Cupid's torch', and subjected, in vain, to fantastic treatments by the doctors. His pupils and assistants in England included the Dutch painters David Beck and A. Hanneman, the Spaniard P. Moya and the Englishman William Dobson (*cf.* also J. van Belcamp, T. Boeyermans, R. v. Leemput and J. van Reyn). **Signed Examples:** ANTWERP *Crucifixion with SS. Catherine and Dominic* 1629 (painted for Antwerp Dominican church in fulfilment of promise to his father on his deathbed), *The painter Martin Pepyn* 1632. BERLIN K. F. *Thomas Francis de Carignan, Prince of Savoy* 1634, *SS. John the Baptist and John the Evangelist.* HAGUE Mauritshuis *Petrus Stevens* 1627, *Anna Wake, wife of Petrus Stevens* 1628. LENINGRAD *Charles I, Henrietta Maria, William Laud (Archbishop of Canterbury), Adriaen Stevens (Treasurer of Antwerp)* 1629. LONDON Royal Coll. *The Three Children of Charles I* 1635, *Charles I in State robes* 1636, *The Five Children of Charles I* 1637, *Thomas Killigrew and Thomas Carew* 1638, *The Mystic Marriage of S. Catherine*; Wallace *Philippe Le Roy* 1630. MADRID Prado *Diana Cecil (Countess of Oxford)* 1638, *Count Henri de Bergh.* MUNICH A.P. *The sculptor G. Petel.* PARIS Louvre *Charles I with horse, equerry and groom.* STOCKHOLM *S. Jerome.* VIENNA K. *Marqués Francesco de Moncada, A woman in a black dress* 1634. WASHINGTON *Philip, Lord Wharton* 1632. **Monogrammed Example:** DRESDEN *Drunken Silenus.* **Documented Examples** include AMSTERDAM Rijks. *Jan Caspar Gevaerts.* ANTWERP *Jan Malderus (Bishop of Antwerp), Christ dying on the Cross, Descent from the Cross, Lamentation over the dead Christ*; Augustine Church *S. Augustine in ecstasy*; S. Paul *The bearing of the Cross.* BERLIN K.F. *A Genoese nobleman, A Genoese lady, Christ mocked, Bathing nymphs surprised by satyrs.* BRUSSELS *The Jesuit J. C. della Faille, Alexander della Faille, S. Anthony of Padua, S. Francis of Assisi.* CASSEL *Joost de Hertoghe, Justus van Meerstraeten.* COURTRAI NotreDame *Raising of the Cross* 1632. DUBLIN N.G. Ireland *Frédéric de Marselaer.* EDINBURGH N.G. Scotland *The Lommelini Family.* FLORENCE Pitti *Cardinal Guido Bentivoglio*; Uffizi *Marguerite de Lorraine.* GENOA Palazzo Rosso *Marchesa Paola Adorno, Marchesa Geronima Brignole-Sale and her daughter, Equestrian portrait of Marquis Anton Giulio Brignole-Sale.* GHENT S. Michel *Crucifixion (Le Christ à l'éponge)* 1630 (restored). HAGUE Mauritshuis *The painter Quintin Simons* described by Sir J. Reynolds

(1781) as 'a perfect pattern of portrait painting'. LENINGRAD *The Rest on the Flight (The Virgin with the partridges), Sir Thomas Wharton* 1639, *Elizabeth and Philadelphia Cary as children* 1640, *Lady Jane Goodwin, Lord Wandesford* 1638, *Jan v. d. Wouver.* LONDON N.G. *Charles I on horseback, Marchese Cattaneo, Marchesa Cattaneo;* Royal Coll. *Charles I in three positions, Henrietta Maria (full face), Henrietta Maria (profile), Equestrian portrait: Charles I and M. de St. Antoine, Venetia Lady Digby as Prudence, Margaret Lemon, George and Francis Villiers as children.* MADRID Prado *The Crowning with Thorns, The Betrayal, The one armed painter Martin Ryckaert, S. Rosalia.* MALINES S. Rombaut *Christ crucified between the thieves* (seen in Recollets church by Sir J. Reynolds who wrote (1781) 'This, upon the whole, may be considered as one of the first pictures in the world'). MUNICH *Susanna and the Elders, Martyrdom of S. Sebastian, Rest on the Flight, The painter Jan de Wael and his wife, The organist H. Liberti.* NEW YORK Met. *James Stuart, Duke of Richmond and Lennox;* (Frick) *Marchesa Giovanna Cattaneo, James Earl of Derby, his Lady and child.* PALERMO Cathedral *The Virgin of the Rosary.* PARIS Louvre *Equestrian portrait of Francesco de Moncada, The Duke of Richmond and Lennox as Paris, Charles Louis Elector Palatine and Prince Rupert* 1637, *The Virgin with donors, The Virgin with Penitents, Venus and Vulcan, Rinaldo and Armida.* ROME Capitol *Cornelis and Lucas de Wael.* SAVENTHEM Church *S. Martin and the Beggar* (*cf.* J. I. de Roore). TERMONDE Notre Dame *Adoration of the Shepherds, Crucifixion with the Virgin and SS. Mary Magdalene and Francis of Assisi.* TURIN *Equestrian portrait: Prince Thomas of Savoy, Children of Charles I.* VIENNA K. *Samson and Delilah, The Blessed Herman Joseph before the Virgin* 1629, *S. Rosalia receiving a chaplet from the Infant Christ* 1629, *Venus and Vulcan, The Archduchess Isabella, Prince Charles Louis of the Palatinate, Prince Rupert.* WASHINGTON N.G. *Elena Grimaldi (Marchesa Cattaneo), Clelia Cattaneo aged 13, Filippo Cattaneo as a child.* Many English private collections have documented examples. Pictures presumed by some his work are in many collections (*cf.* London van der Geest Painter).

[Fl. 67, Fl. 773, Fl. 287, Fl. 425, Fl. 826, Fl. 856, Fl. 216, Fl. 702, Fl. 770, Fl. 585, Fl. 372, Fl. 181, Fl. 182, Fl. 591, Fl. 755, Fl. 715, Fl. 581, Fl. 346, Fl. 343, Fl. 678, Fl. 736.]

Dyck, Daniel van den. Flemish Sch. *b* Antwerp (?) *c.* 1615 *d* Mantua (?) 1670 (?). *Religious and mythological subjects; also worked as engraver.* Master Antwerp Guild 1633. Went Venice where married Lucretia, daughter of N. Regnier *q.v.* and herself a painter; went Mantua where appointed curator of Duke of Mantua's Gallery 1658 (*cf.* F. and J. Denys). **Documented Example:** VENICE S. Maria dell'Orto *Martyrdom of S. Laurence.* Works painted for Venice Frari, S. M. Mater Domini and S. M. dell'Anconetta are recorded.
[Fl. 101, Fl. 892, Fl. 536, Fl. 305.]

Dyck, J. A. Flemish Sch. Presumed 17th cent. **Signed Example:** CARLSRUHE *Throne of Venus.* [Fl. 798.]

Dyck, Justina (or Justiniana) van. Flemish Sch. *b* daughter of A. van Dyck, London 1641 *d* Antwerp (?) 1690. Married Sir J. B. Stepney; received a pension from Charles II. A *Christ on the Cross with four angels receiving the Holy Blood* is recorded. [Fl. 826, Fl. 107, Fl. 892.]

Dyckmans, Joseph Laurens. Flemish Sch. *b* Lierre 1811 *d* Antwerp 1888. *Genre and picturesque corners of old buildings.* Pupil in Lierre Acad. and of G. Wappers in Antwerp. Professor Antwerp Acad. 1841-54; exhibited London R. A. 1846-69. Represented in ANTWERP *Pump in the Old Antwerp Fishmarket, Façade in the Groenplaatztraat, Blind Beggar* 1852. LONDON Tate Gall. *Blind Beggar* 1853; Vic. & Alb. *Portrait group.*
[Fl. 837 (1888), Fl. Bib. 19th cent.]

E

Ecke, J. van den, see **Hecke.**

Eeckele (or Eecke or Heke), Jan van. Flemish Sch. *b* Bruges(?) before 1520 *d* Bruges 1561. *Religious subjects.* Master Bruges Guild 1534. BRUGES S. Sauveur *Mater dolorosa* (*s* JVE) and TOURNAI Mus. *Virgin with S. Bernard* (*s* JVE or JVP) have been presumed by some to be his work.
[Fl. 892, Fl. 113.]

Eeckhout, Anthonie van den. Flemish Sch. *b* Bruges 1656 *d* Lisbon 1695. *Fruit and flowers* (*cf.* D. Seghers, J. B. de Crépu, A. Bosman, J. P. v. Thielen, J. v. Son, J. v. d. Borght). Visited Italy with his brother-in-law L. de Deyster; in Bruges *c.* 1688-91; then Italy and Lisbon where made a rich marriage and was shot dead in his coach by a rival. L. de Deyster painted figures in some of his flowerpieces.
[Fl. 215.]

Eeckhout, Jacob Joseph. Flemish Sch. *b* son of goldsmith, Antwerp 1793 *d* Paris 1861. *Costume history, genre, portraits; also drawings for lithographs (portraits and costumes).* Pupil in Antwerp Acad.; worked as sculptor till 1821; in the Hague where became director of Acad. 1831-43; returned Belgium where member of Antwerp and Brussels Acads.; went Paris, gave up painting and entered a banking business 1859. Represented in AMSTERDAM *Marriage of Jacqueline of Bavaria and John IV* 1839. ANTWERP *Self-portrait.* BAYEUX, MONTPELLIER, YPRES. *Cf.* J. B. Berré.
[Fl. 451, Fl. 481, Fl. 892, Fl. Bib. 19th cent.]

Eertvelt, see **Ertvelt.**

***Egmont, Justus (Verus) van.** Flemish Sch. *b* son of a carpenter, Leyden 1601 *d* Antwerp 1674. *Portraits, religious subjects, 'history', tapestry designs.* Went Antwerp where pupil of Gaspar v. d. Hoecke 1615; visited Italy 1618; in Rubens studio in Antwerp (while Marie de Médicis pictures for Luxembourg were being painted) 1622-5; went Paris to help install them 1625; Master Antwerp Guild 1628; worked Paris with French courtpainter S. Vouet; became court portrait painter to Louis XIII (*cf.* J. Fouquier); and later to Louis XIV (*cf.* A. F. v. d. Meulen); a founder member of the French Académie royale (*cf.* P. Mol) 1648; in Brussels 1649; Antwerp 1653; worked for Archduke Leopold Wilhelm (*cf.* J. B. van Heil); in later life designed for Brussels tapestry factory (*History of Caesar, Anthony and Cleopatra, Aurelius and Zenobia*), became rich, owned a considerable collection of pictures (*cf.* V. Wolfvoet and Jeremias Wildens) and tried to establish his kinship with the family of the Counts of Egmont which he represented in a large genealogical picture including his own portrait. **Signed Examples:** None. **Documented Example:** VIENNA K. *Archduke Leopold Wilhelm.* Portraits *Louis XIII, Queen Anne of France, Louis XIV, Ludovica Gonzaga Queen of Poland* and *Queen Christina of Sweden in armour* (1654) are among his works recorded by engravings. Many portraits, allegorical figures and 'history' subjects are recorded in the inventory of his collection made on his wife's death 1685.
[Fl. 86, Fl. 425, Fl. 215, Fl. 107, Fl. 892, Fl. 204, Fl. 213.]

Egret (or Hegret), Peter. Flemish Sch. *b* Malines 1637. Master in Malines Guild 1663. Brother of Theodor E. *q.v.*

Egret (or Hegret), Theodor. Flemish Sch. *b* Malines 1640 *d* Malines 1722. *Landscapes and religious subjects.* Brother of

Peter E. Works acquired by Malines S. Catherine and other local churches are recorded (*cf.* G. van Beerings the younger).
[Fl. 613, Fl. 892.]

Ehrenberg, Peter Schubert van. Flemish Sch. *b* son of W. van Ehrenberg, Antwerp 1668 *d* Germany (?) date unknown. *Portraits.* Worked in Germany.
[Fl. 892.]

***Ehrenberg (or Aerdenberg), Wilhelm Schubert van.** Flemish Sch. *b* Antwerp 1630 (or Germany 1637) *d* Antwerp *c.* 1676. *Architectural interiors and views (with figures by other painters) cf.* H. van Steenwyck the younger. In Antwerp Guild 1663; member Chamber of Rhetoric 1666. **Signed Examples:** BRUSSELS *Interior of Antwerp Jesuit Church* 1667 (*cf.* S. Vrancx and A. G. Gheringh), *Interior of Malines S. Rombout with group of figures* 1673. HAMBURG Kunsthalle *Renaissance hall with staircase* 1667. VIENNA K. *Church interior* 1664. **Documented Examples:** ANTWERP *Cariclea before the King of Ethiopia.* BRUSSELS *The story of William Tell performed at Antwerp* (figures by C. E. Biset *q.v.*, landscape by P. A. Immenraet). The architecture in Gonzales Coques' *Interior of a Gallery* (The Hague Mauritshuis) is recorded as his work.
[Fl. 216, Fl. 892, Fl. 459.]

Eisen, François. Flemish Sch. *b* Brussels 1695 *d* Paris after 1778. *Religious subjects, genre and decorative pieces; also active as engraver after Rubens and others.* Worked for Valenciennes churches from 1716; in Brussels 1745; then settled Paris where painted small genre pieces for dealers. Charles E. the famous French engraver was his son. **Signed Examples:** DIJON *Cupids and flowers* (2 grisailles) *s* 'Eisen le père' (*cf.* M. J. Geeraerts, A. M. van Reysschoot and T. de Bruyn).
[Fl. 612, Fl. 892, Fl. 798.]

Elburcht (Elborch, Elsborch, Elbrucht), Jan van der, (known as Cleen-Hansken). Flemish (Dutch) Sch. *b* Elburg (Holland) before 1520 *d* Antwerp (?) after 1553. *Religious subjects.* Master Antwerp Guild 1535. Pupils entered 1540 and 1551. Van Mander (1604) records an *Altarpiece with the Miraculous Draught of Fishes* (Fishmongers' altar) in Antwerp Notre Dame and praises the painting of the sea. Descamps who saw it still there in 1769 said 'tout y est peint avec trop de sécheresse'.
[Fl. 559, Fl. 215, Fl. 216, Fl. 612, Fl. 892, Fl. 631 (1935).]

***Eliaerts, Jan Frans.** Flemish Sch. *b* Deurne, nr. Antwerp 1761 *d* Antwerp 1848. *Still life: flowers and fruit* (*cf.* P. Faes). Pupil Antwerp Acad.; then to Paris; exhibited Salon from 1899 (*cf.* L. Gerbo). Some of his pictures were used in the Gobelins factory. **Signed Examples:** ANTWERP *Flower piece.* A picture titled *L'amour aux aguets dans un buisson de roses* was in Paris Salon 1848.
[Fl. 451, Fl. 66, Fl. 798.]

Elias, Matthieu. Flemish Sch. *b* Peene 1658 *d* Dunkirk 1741. *Religious subjects, ecclesiastical genre, portraits, landscapes.* Went Paris *c.* 1678; member of Paris Acad. de S. Luc; rector 1709; then settled Dunkirk. **Signed Example:** DUNKIRK *Dunkirk harbour* ('Matheus Elyas Rector academiae pictorum Parisiennis 1709'). **Documented Examples:** DUNKIRK *Sacrifice of Abraham, Christ on the Cross.* PARIS Louvre *The sons of Scaeva* ('May' picture for Notre Dame 1702). Descamps (1769) records a *Group portrait of the Confrérie de S. Sébastien* painted for the Dunkirk Confrérie (*cf.* R. v. Audenaerd), religious pictures in Dunkirk churches including S. Eloi and S. Jean Baptiste (*The gathering of the Manna, Balthazar's feast, S. Winoc distributing bread*) and in Ypres Carmelite Church and Menin Capucins (*S. Felix reviving a dead man*). Vienna Albertina has signed drawings *Sermon in a church* 1707 and *Cistercian monks before the Pope* 1707. [Fl. 215, Fl. 216, Fl. 66, Fl. 892.]

Elle (Helle), Ferdinand. Flemish Sch. *b* Malines *c.* 1585 *d* Paris *c.* 1638. *Portraits.* Went Paris (*cf.* H. Francken the elder); changed his name to Ferdinand; commissioned to paint group of Paris Guild notables for the Hôtel de Ville 1609; the French painter N. Poussin was his pupil 1612; 'Peintre ordinaire' to Louis XIII (*cf.* P. de Champaigne, J. Fouquier, J. v. Egmont, R. Schoof, H. Staben, F. Pourbus the younger). Mariette (*c.* 1746) describes him as 'l'un des plus habiles peintres de portraits qui aient paru en France'. Two of his sons, Louis and Pierre, were painters. Recorded works include a *Portrait of Mademoiselle de Montmorency* painted for the King and smeared with butter that it might be rolled and conveyed secretly to him without damaging the pigment.
[Fl. 878, Fl. 564, Fl. 66, Fl. 892, Fl. 580.]

Elsen, Alfred. Flemish Sch. *b* Antwerp 1850 *d* Antwerp 1914. *Landscapes; also active as engraver.* Pupil of F. Lamorinière and E. Dujardin. Represented in ANTWERP *Wood in sunshine* and two others. [Fl. 17.]

*Engel, Adolphe Charles Maximilian. Flemish Sch. *b* Courtrai 1801 *d* (suicide) Ghent 1833. *Landscapes, some with cattle.* Pupil in Ghent Acad. and of J. B. de Noter; graduate of Ghent University; painted in regions of Dinant, Liège, Namur and the Ardennes; exhibited Ghent, Brussels, Lille and Douai from 1820; won Ghent Academy's landscape prize 1832; J. L. Geinaert painted figures in some of his works. J. B. de Vriendt was his pupil. Represented in AMSTERDAM *Wooded landscape with cattle* 1827 and COURTRAI. *Cf.* J. B. de Roy. [Fl. 451, Fl. 798.]

*Engelbrechtsz (Engelbrechtsen, Engebrechtsz, Engelbertsz), Cornelis. Flemish (Dutch) Sch. *b* son of carpenter, Leyden 1468 *d* Leyden 1533. *Religious subjects.* Recorded in Leyden Civic Guard 1499-1519; his sons Peter, Cornelis and Lucas (all called Kunst) were his pupils (*cf.* P., C. and L. Cornelisz); other pupils were Lucas van Leyden and A. Claesz. Van Mander (1604) states that many of his pictures were destroyed by the Iconoclasts (1566). **Documented Examples:** LEYDEN Triptych *Crucifixion* (centre), *Abraham's Sacrifice, The Brazen Serpent* (wings), *Christ stripped, Christ mocked* (reverse of wings), *Cadaver* (*cf.* Amsterdam Cadaver Painter) with the donor *Jacob Maertensz, SS. Martin, Augustine and five nuns* (predella); Triptych *Lamentation* (centre), *The donor Jacob Maertensz with SS. James and Martin, His wife with SS. Cecilia and Mary Magdalene* (wings), *SS. Apollonia and Gertrude, SS. Agatha and Agnes* (reverse of wings), both altarpieces formerly in Marienpoel Convent, and described by Van Mander who also records an *Adoration of the Virgin* and a memorial altarpiece painted for the Lockhorst family with portraits of the donors and 'a scene from the revelation of S. John in which the Lamb of God opens the book with the Seven Seals, the entire celestial Hierarchy being represented'. Paintings presumed by some his work are in various museums (*cf.* Munich S. Helena and Constantine Painter).
[Fl. 559, Fl. 238, Fl. 892, Fl. 330, Fl. 316.]

Engelen, Louis van. Flemish Sch. *b* Lierre 1856. *Landscapes and town views, genre, animals, panoramas.* Pupil in Antwerp Acad. Assistant with others to C. Verlat in his panorama *Battle of the Plevna.* Visited Italy and U.S.A. Represented in ANTWERP *Belgian emigrants* 1890, *Panorama of City of Antwerp* 1902. [Fl. 374, Fl. 17.]

Engelen, Piet van. Flemish Sch. *b* Lierre 1863 *d* Antwerp 1924. *Animals, hunting pieces, anecdotic genre, still life; also* panoramas. Pupil in Antwerp Acad. of C. Verlat. Member of Antwerp group The XIII (*cf.* E. Farasyn) 1891; painted with R. Mols *Diorama of the Congo* (*cf.* F. Jespers) for the Antwerp World Exhibition 1894; teacher in Antwerp Acad. 1897. Represented in ANTWERP *Cockfight* 1902. LIÈGE *Still life with game.* [Fl. 699 (1922-3), Fl. 17.]

Engelen, Pieter van. Flemish Sch. *b* Antwerp 1664 *d* Antwerp 1711. *Market and fair scenes.* Pupil of his uncle G. de Witte. **Signed Example** in MAINZ. A 1945 acquisition is catalogued in Antwerp Mus. [Fl. 107.]

Engelen, René. Flemish Sch. *b* Antwerp 1897. *Marines and landscapes.* Pupil in Antwerp Acad. of F. Gogo. Represented in ANTWERP *On the Lower Scheldt.* [Fl. 17.]

Enghelrams (or Ingelrams), Cornelis. Flemish Sch. *b* Malines *c.* 1527 *d* Malines 1580 or 1583. Master Malines Guild 1546; van Mander (1604) records a *Feeding the Poor* painted in *w.* on canvas for Malines S. Rombouts in which 'he differentiated between the truly poor and the professional fake beggars with their hurdy-gurdies and other instruments'; also a *Story of David* for the Prince of Orange (based on a composition by L. de Heere with architecture by J. Vredeman de Vries). A series of *Church fathers* is recorded by engravings.
[Fl. 559, Fl. 892.]

Ensor, James. Flemish Sch. *b* of English father and Flemish mother who kept a shop selling sea-shells and curios, Ostend 1860 *d* in house above the still-existing shop, Ostend 1949. *Indoor and outdoor genre, portraits, landscapes, marines, still life in Impressionist and Expressionist techniques; symbolical fantastic and satirical compositions (many with masks and skeletons); also worked as engraver and music composer.* Student in Brussels Acad. 1877; returned Ostend which remained his permanent headquarters 1881; founder-member of Brussels group Les XX (Les Vingt) (*cf.* A. Boch, F. Charlet, J. Delvin, H. de Groux, F. Khnopff, G. Lemmen, X. Mellery, P. Pantazis, F. Rops, T. Rysselberghe, F. Simons, G. v. Strydonck, I. Verheyden, T. Verstraete, R. Wytsman) 1883-4; his vast symbolic-satiric composition *Christ's entry into Brussels in 1889* was centre of controversy in Les XX exhibition 1889; won friendship of the writers E. Verhaeren and M. Maeterlinck; visited London 1892; sent ten pictures to Paris Salon des Indépendants 1901; painted little and spent much time composing music 1912-20; his ballet 'La Gamme d'amour', for which he wrote the music, devised the action and designed scenery and costumes, was produced in Brussels 1920; large retrospective exhibition of his works in Brussels Palais des Beaux-Arts 1929; from 1929-39 painted mainly light-coloured still life compositions; became a naturalized Belgian and was created Baron 1930; large exhibition of his works arranged by French Government in Paris Musée du Jeu de Paume 1931; London exhibition (Leicester Galleries) 1936; another at the National Gallery 1946. Ostend has a 'rue James Ensor'. Represented in ANTWERP *Girl with the snub nose* 1879, *Grey sea* 1880, *Woman with red parasol* 1880, *Afternoon at Ostend* 1881, *Woman with a blue shawl* (*the artist's mother*) 1881, *Music in the rue de Flandre* 1881, *Théo Hannon* 1882, *Still life with oysters* 1882, *Woman eating oysters* 1882, *The skate, The white cloud* 1882, *The expulsion from Paradise* 1887, *Mask comedy* (*Le théâtre des masques*) 1889, *Ostend harbour* 1890, *The intrigue* 1890, *Masks quarrelling about a hanged man* 1891, *Still life* (*chinoiseries*) 1891, *Masks and molluscs* 1891. BÂLE *Masques intrigués* 1929. BELGIAN Royal Collection *Skeletons warming themselves* 1892. BRUSSELS *Boy with a lamp* 1880, *Russian music* 1881, *The woman in the dark dress* (*La dame au parapluie*) 1881, *The skate* 1892, *Strange masks* 1892. LIÈGE *Masks and death* 1897 (formerly in Mannheim Museum whence sold as 'degenerate art' by the Nazis during A. Hitler's régime). OSTEND *The haunted Room* 1885. Others in Zurich and

other museums. *Christ's entry into Brussels 1889* (painted 1888) was still in the artist's possession when he died.
[Fl. 660, Fl. 211, Fl. 821, Fl. 521, Fl. 183, Fl. 704, Fl. 388, Fl. 760, Fl. 675, Fl. 294, Fl. 295, Fl. 296, Fl. 24, Fl. 290, Fl. 897.]

*****Ertvelt** (or **Eertveld**, wrongly **Artvelt**), **Andries van.** Flemish Sch. *b* Antwerp 1590 *d* Antwerp 1652. *Marines (many with warships)*. Master Antwerp Guild 1609; went Genoa where associated with C. de Wael *c*. 1628; back Antwerp by 1630. G. v. Eyck *q.v.* was among his pupils. Van Dyck painted his portrait with marine background. **Signed Examples:** GREEN-WICH Maritime Mus. *Spanish troops embarking from barges, Naval action between English and Spanish.* **Monogrammed Example:** VIENNA K. *Harbour with Spanish warships.* Antwerp inventories (1652-90) and the records of the Forchoudt firm of Antwerp exporting dealers mention a *Night sea piece* (with figures by V. Malo *q.v.*) several pictures titled *Sea storm* and *Fire at sea* and a *Whaling scene*. An angry letter from a Lisbon dealer (1643) complains that the *Ship pieces* by E. sent him by Forchoudt are very bad examples. Many of his pictures were also exported to Seville (*cf.* V. Wolfvoet).
[Fl. 86, Fl. 425, Fl. 564, Fl. 215, Fl. 892, Fl. 212, Fl. 213, Fl. 214.]

*****Es** (or **Essen**), **Jacob Foppens van.** Flemish Sch. *b* Antwerp *c*. 1596 *d* Antwerp 1666. *Still life with fish and fruit* (*cf.* A. Adriaenssen, O. Beet, J. v. Hulsdonck, Grenoble Artichoke Painter, Grenoble Strawberry Painter, H. Francken the elder, C. Peeters, C. Mahu, J. v. Son, F. Snyders, A. v. Utrecht also T. v. Aenvanck). Master Antwerp Guild 1617. Rubens owned '*Une petite pièce avec un verre et quelques tranches de jambon*' and '*Un bancquet sur fond de bois*'; V. Wolfvoet *q.v.* also owned a '*Déjeuner still life*' and J. Wildens *q.v.* inherited a *Fruit piece* from his father. A contemporary poet wrote: 'when he painted grapes you could count the pips through the skin'. J. Jordaens, C. Schut and D. Delmont were godfathers to his children. **Signed Examples:** ANTWERP *Still life with artichoke, oysters and salmon.* BARNARD CASTLE *Grapes.* FRANKFORT *Still life with fish.* LILLE, OXFORD, PRAGUE, STOCKHOLM and VIENNA Leicht (*cf.* V. Wolfvoet).
[Fl. 86, Fl. 425, Fl. 215, Fl. 892, Fl. 213.]

Evenepoel, Henri Jacques Édouard. Flemish Sch. *b* Nice of Belgian parents 1872 *d* of typhoid fever, Paris 1899. *Indoor and outdoor genre compositions (some of African subjects) portraits, landscapes*. Pupil in Brussels Acad., of the Frenchman E. Blanc-Garin, and of the decorative painter A. Crespin; went Paris 1892; worked there under Gustave Moreau as contemporary of the French painters H. Matisse and G. Rouault; acquainted with the French painter H. de Toulouse-Lautrec; elected Associé of the Salon de la Nationale (at the same time as H. Matisse) 1897; in Algeria during winter 1897-8; member of Brussels La Libre Esthétique (*cf.* G. Buysse). Represented in ANTWERP *La loge 1896, Sunday in the Bois de Boulogne, The Poultry stall, Interior, The errand girl.* BRUSSELS *The Man in red* (P. Baignères) 1894, *Selfportrait 1895, Child at play 1896, Eve, La Fête aux Invalides 1898, African orange market 1898, L'Annonce de la fête nègre à Blidah 1898, La Koubba de Sidi Jacomb à Blidah 1898, Henriette au grand chapeau.* FRANKFORT Städt. Inst. *Le Café d'Harcourt (Paris)* 1897. GHENT *L'Espagnol à Paris* (the painter Ytturino). LIÈGE *Sunday at St. Cloud.* PARIS State Collection *Charles Milcendeau.* VIENNA Mus. Mod. *Return from work.*
[Fl. 496, Fl. 160 (1900), Fl. 3 (1899), Fl. 388, Fl. 389, Fl. 397, Fl. 411, Fl. Bib. 19th cent.]

Everbroeck, Frans van. Flemish Sch. *b* Antwerp before 1645 *d* after 1672. *Flowers and fruit and flower garlands* (*cf.* D.

Seghers). Pupil of Joris van Son *q.v.* 1654; Master Antwerp Guild 1661. A *Flower piece* is recorded in LONDON Painters Stainers Hall. [Fl. 714, Fl. 533.]

Everen, Gillis van. Flemish Sch. *b* Antwerp before 1460 *d* Antwerp 1512. *Religious subjects.* Antwerp Master 1477. Worked for the Emperor Maximilian in Prague. A signed *Pietà* recorded in Nuremberg is not known to be extant.
[Fl. 612, Fl. 892.]

Evrard, Adèle. Flemish Sch. *b* Ath (Hennegau) 1792 *d* Ath 1889. *Fruit, game, flower still life.* Pupil of J. Ducorron. Represented in AMSTERDAM *Flowers and fruit.* Exhibited 1827 BRUSSELS. [Fl. 451.]

Evrard, Perpète. Flemish Sch. *b* Dinant (Liège) 1662 *d* The Hague 1727. *Portraits and miniatures.* Worked for court circles in Spain (*cf.* J. van Kessel the younger and A. Smit) and in Vienna (*cf.* P. F. de Hamilton and R. Megan). In The Hague by 1707. Charles of Lorraine, Governor of the Netherlands, owned a number of his miniatures (*cf.* J. P. Sauvage).
[Fl. 451, Fl. 409.]

Eworth, see **Ewouts.**

*****Ewouts** (called **Eworth** in England), **Hans.** Flemish Sch. *b* Antwerp before 1525 *d* London (?) after 1578. *Portraits, allegories and decorative paintings.* Master Antwerp Guild 1540. Came England *c*. 1545; worked for English nobility and for Queen Mary (*cf.* A. Mor); employed by Queen Elizabeth's Office of Revels on decorations for masques 1572-4. Records in Lumley Inventory (*cf.* S. van der Meulen) 1590 show that he signed with monogram HE (formerly presumed by some the monogram of Lucas de Heere). **Fully Signed Examples:** None. **Monogrammed Examples:** COPENHAGEN *The Wise and Foolish Virgins* 1570. LONDON Dulwich *Portraits in an Allegory* 1560. ROYAL COLL. *Queen Elizabeth eclipsing Juno, Minerva and Venus* 1569, *Henry Stuart, Lord Darnley with his brother Charles Stuart, later Earl of Lennox* 1563 (another version in Holyrood); Soc. of Antiquaries *Queen Mary* 1554. MILAN Mus. Poldi-Pozzoli *Man's portrait* 1559. OTTAWA N.G. Canada *Mary Nevill, Baroness Dacre.* Others in English private collections. *Cf.* C. v. d. Broeck.
[Fl. 826, Fl. 856, Fl. 39, Fl. 630, Fl. 28.]

*****Exhumation of S. Hubert Master.** Presumed Flemish Sch. 15th cent. Name for painter of LONDON N.G. (783) *The Exhumation of S. Hubert.* Presumed by some to be R. van der Weyden *q.v.* or a follower, and by others to be Rogier of Bruges *q.v.* [Fl. 892, Fl. 316, Fl. 530.]

*****Eyck, Gaspar** (or **Jasper**) **van.** Flemish Sch. *b* son of a collector N. van E. Antwerp 1613 *d* Brussels 1673. *Naval warfare and other marine subjects* (*cf.* A. v. Ertvelt, B. Flessiers, O. Grevenbroek, J. A. v. d. Leepe, A. and H. van Minderhout, A. Matthys, J. B. v. d. Meiren, B. Peeters the elder and the younger, J. Peeters, M. Plattenberg, L. Smout, P. v. d. Velde, C. de Wael, A. Willaerts). Pupil of A. v. Ertvelt. Master Antwerp Guild 1632; visited Italy (where worked with C. de Wael in Genoa) and Spain (*cf.* L. Franchoys the elder and A. Smit). Recorded as dissolute and as suffering from intermittent madness in later life when established Brussels. **Signed Example:** MADRID Prado *Naval battle between Turks and Maltese* 1649. Landscapes by him are recorded in the collection of his father from whom he inherited (1656) a *Virgin and Child* by A. Janssens, a *Sea storm* by A. v. Ertvelt and a *Vanitas* by his brother N. v. E. *q.v.* [Fl. 86, Fl. 878, Fl. 215, Fl. 892, Fl. 213.]

*****Eyck, Hubert van.** Flemish Sch. *b* Maeseyck (?) before 1400 *d* and buried in crypt of Ghent S. Bavon (then called S. Jean)

1426. *Religious subjects*. Presumed by some (1) the 'Hubert' recorded as painter of a picture bequeathed by Jan de Visch to his daughter 1413; (2) the 'meester Luberecht' paid by the Ghent magistrates for two sketches 1425; (3) the 'Ubrechts' to whose apprentices the Ghent Council paid gratuities 1425; (4) the 'meester Aubrechte' recorded, in the will of Robert Poortier and wife, as having in his hands a statue of S. Anthony and other parts of an altar, destined for Ghent, S. Sauveur 1426; (5) the 'Lubrecht van Heyke' deceased, whose estate tax was paid in Ghent 1426. Referred to as brother of Jan van Eyck *q.v.* by A. de Beatis (as Robert) 1517, by Lucas de Heere *q.v.* in a poem written 1559, by Guicciardini 1567, M. van Vaernewyck 1568, Vasari 1568 and Van Mander 1604. Vaernewyck transcribed the epitaph on a brass plate (since lost) on his tombstone which records the year and day of his death and contains the lines:

> Hubrecht van Eyck was ick ghenant
> Nu spyse der wormen, voormals bekant
> In Schilderye zeer hooghe gheert.

Signed Examples: None. **Inscribed and Documented Example**: Initial work on GHENT S. Bavon *Altarpiece of the Mystic Lamb* referred to as joint work of Hubert and Jan van Eyck by Beatis, de Heere, Vaernewyck, and Van Mander who records that it was opened out and shown to the public only on important feast days when there was usually such a crowd that it was difficult to get near it. Provided on its completion (or later) with an inscription (on the foot of the exterior of the wings and thus visible only when the altarpiece was not opened out) recording that Hubert van Eyck began the work and that Jan finished it at the request of Jodoc Vyt May 6, 1432. C. de Huerne (*d* 1629) recorded the text as: 'Pictor Hubertus eeyck major quo nemo repertus Incoepit. pondus quod Johannes arte secundus Frater perfectus Iudoci Vyd prece fretus. Vers Vse Xta Ma I Vos CoLLo Cata Cta t Ver I'. This inscription (with the first two words of the third line rubbed away) was found beneath green paint during cleaning operations in Berlin 1823, and the missing words are presumed by some to be 'frater perfecit'; the date when the inscription was first covered with green paint is not known; the altarpiece has suffered damage several times by fire, by concealment during riots and invasions, and through dismemberment and dispersal after sale of some panels; the first recorded restorations (and, it may be, renewal of the inscription) were by J. Scorel *q.v.* and L. Blondeel *q.v.* in 1550; A. van Heuvel *q.v.* restored parts in 1663; fire damage to parts in 1832 was made good by restorations in 1846 and 1859; panels (with the inscription) returned from Berlin to Ghent under the Treaty of Versailles (1919) had been restored in Berlin. (*Cf.* New York Crucifixion and Last Judgement Painter, Madrid Fountain of Grace Painter and M. Coxie).
[Fl. 405, Fl. 371, Fl. 811, Fl. 818, Fl. 812, Fl. 559, Fl. 853, Fl. 385, Fl. 725, Fl. 873, Fl. 898, Fl. 245, Fl. 875, Fl. 697, Fl. 316, Fl. 530, Fl. 615, Fl. 296, Fl. 185, Fl. 174, Fl. 754, Fl. 144.]

Eyck, Jacques van. Flemish Sch. *b* Antwerp 1601 *d* Antwerp 1648. Sold pictures to the Seville dealer C. van Immerseel (*cf.* J. Boots) 1636 and 1637. [Fl. 714, Fl. 214.]

***Eyck, Jan van.** Flemish Sch. *b* Maeseyck nr. Maastricht before 1420 *d* Bruges and buried S. Donatian 1441. *Religious subjects, portraits, genre*. Stated by Vasari to have invented oil painting; first recorded working in Hague Palace of John of Bavaria, Count of Holland, with apprentices on decorations 1422-4; Court painter and 'varlet de chambre' to Philip the Good, Duke of Burgundy (*cf.* D. Daret) 1425; moved from Bruges to Lille where lived in house rented by the Duke for two years from 1425; made a pilgrimage and secret journeys 'to certain distant places of which no mention is to be made' on Duke's behalf 1426; further special services and secret journeys (when visited Tournai and received 'wine of honour' from magistrates—*cf.* R. van der Weyden) 1427 and 1428;

accompanied mission to John I of Portugal to negotiate marriage of Philip and Isabella of Portugal (*cf.* J. Martins) which left Flanders and visited England 1428; toured Portugal and Spain and returned Flanders Christmas 1429; bought house in Bruges 1431-2; visited by the two Burgomasters and some Councillors, who saw works and left gratuity for apprentices 1432; visited by Duke Philip who also saw works and left gratuity 1433; paid for special services to Duke and Duchess 1434; Duke was godfather to his first child and presented six silver cups 1434; was granted life pension with increase of salary (partly charged on cloth tax) which the Ducal accountants, who protested, were ordered to pay in a letter stating that the Duke intended to employ the artist 'on certain great works and could find no other painter equally to his taste or of such excellence . . .' 1435; paid for polychroming and gilding six (of eight) statues of Counts and Countesses of Flanders for new Town Hall, Bruges 1435; paid for further secret journeys 1436; the Duke gave money to his widow Margaret 1441 and to his daughter Livina enabling her to enter a convent 1450. **Signed Examples**: ANTWERP S. *Barbara* (unfinished) *s* on frame 1437, *Virgin and Child by a fountain s* on frame with addition of words 'Als ich kan' (from Flemish proverb 'As I can, not as I would') 1439. BRUGES *Virgin and Child, with SS. Donatian and George and the donor, Canon van aer Paele* inscribed on frame 1436; *Margaret, wife of the painter s* on frame 1439. LONDON N.G. *A young man s* and inscribed 'Timotheos' and 'Leal Souvenir' 1432, *Man in a red turban s* and Als ich Kan 1433, *The Marriage of Giovanni Arnolfini and Giovanna Cenami s* 1434. MELBOURNE N.G. of Victoria *Virgin and Child* ('The Ince Hall Madonna') inscribed on frame and Als ich Kan 1433. VIENNA K. *Jan de Leeuwe*, goldsmith inscribed on frame 1436. **Inscribed and Documented Example**: Later work on GHENT S. Bavon *The Altarpiece of the Mystic Lamb* (polyptych) Interior, from left to right: Upper row *Adam, and Sacrifice of Cain and Abel, Singing Angels, The Virgin, God the Father (or Christ as Judge), S. John the Baptist, Musician Angels, Eve, and Cain killing Abel*. Lower row: *The Just Judges* (stolen 1933, replaced by modern copy), *The Knights of Christ, The Adoration of the Lamb, The Holy Hermits, The Holy Pilgrims*. Exterior, from left to right: Upper row: *Prophet Zechariah, Erythraean Sibyl, Cumaean Sibyl, Prophet Micah*. Centre row: *Archangel Gabriel, The Virgin's room* (two panels), *The Virgin Annunciate*. Lower row: *Jodoc Vyt, the donor, The two SS. John* (two panels in grisaille), *Elisabeth Borluut Vyt* 1432. A predella representing 'Hell' or 'Purgatory' was destroyed by bad cleaning before 1550 (*cf.* Hubert van Eyck). A portrait of *Isabella of Portugal* drawn in Portugal and sent to Duke Philip 1429, a *Portrait of a Portuguese lady* owned by Don Diego de Guevara who presented it and also *The Marriage of Giovanni Arnolfini* to Margaret of Austria, Governor of the Netherlands before 1516, a *Woman bathing with attendant, and a mirror on the wall* owned *c.* 1450 by Cardinal Ottaviano dei Medici (*cf.* W. van Haecht), a *Bathing scene* owned by Frederick I, Duke of Urbino (*cf.* Rogerius Gallicus) *c.* 1600, and *Deux portraits, le mari et la femme* owned by Rubens are recorded. Pictures presumed by some his work are in Paris Louvre and other museums (*cf.* Madrid Fountain of Grace Painter, New York Annunciation in a Porch Painter; Washington Annunciation in a Church Painter).
[Fl. 286, Fl. 818, Fl. 405, Fl. 811, Fl. 559, Fl. 725, Fl. 892, Fl. 873, Fl. 875, Fl. 213, Fl. 698, Fl. 316, Fl. 530, Fl. 615, Fl. 174, Fl. 296, Fl. 677, Fl. 143, Fl. 144, Fl. 145.]

Eyck (or **Aeyck**), **Jan** (**Hans**). Flemish Sch. *b* before 1615. *'History' and decorative paintings, mythological subjects, ceremonial decorations*. Master Antwerp Guild 1633; worked under Rubens on Pageant Entry into Antwerp of Cardinal Infante Ferdinand 1635 (*cf.* G. Weri), and on paintings commissioned from Rubens by Philip IV of Spain for the hunting lodge Torre de la Parada (*cf.* J. P. Gowi) 1636-8. **Signed**

Example: MADRID Prado *The Fall of Phaeton* (painted for Torre de la Parada from a sketch by Rubens now in Brussels Mus.). [Fl. 468, Fl. 555.]

Eyck, Jan Carel van. Flemish Sch. *b* son of Nicolaas van E. the elder, Antwerp 1649 *d* Italy (?) after 1685. *Landscapes with genre figures.* Pupil in Antwerp of J. E. Quellinus 1669; pictures signed 'Rome 1685' are recorded. [Fl. 107.]

Eyck, Margaret van. Flemish Sch. 15th cent. Sister of Hubert and Jan van E. Recorded (1559) by L. de Heere; M. v. Vaernewyck (1568) adds that her name was Margaret, that she remained a spinster, devoted herself to painting, lived with, and was buried beside Hubert. **Signed Examples:** None. **Documented Examples:** None. London N.G. (708) *The Virgin and Child* (now catalogued as by 'a follower of D. Bouts') was exhibited as her work at Kensington Palace in 1848; the triptych London N.G. (1085) *Mystic marriage of S. Catherine with angels and saints in a garden before a church with window lit from within* now catalogued as 'Netherlandish School' and formerly catalogued as 'School of the Lower Rhine' (1901) and 'by a follower of Geertgen tot Sint Jans' (1929) was presumed by some her work in 1831.
[Fl. 405, Fl. 811, Fl. 612, Fl. 528, Fl. 875, Fl. 529, Fl. 530.]

***Eyck, Nicolaas van.** Flemish Sch. *b* son of a collector N. van E., Antwerp 1617 *d* Antwerp 1679. *Official ceremonies* (*cf.* A. Sallaert), *contemporary warfare* (*cf.* P. Meulener), *picturesque military scenes* (*cf.* L. de Hondt the elder). Pupil in Antwerp of T. Rombouts 1633; in Guild by 1641; captain in civic guard 1658. **Signed Examples:** ANTWERP *The 1673 review of Antwerp guard* 1673. LILLE *A man on horseback followed by his servant.* MALINES *Occupation of Malines by Protestants 1580.* TURIN Pinac. *Soldiers crossing a river.* VIENNA K. *Soldiers camping in a village.* A portrait and a *Vanitas* are recorded in the collection of his father (*cf.* G. van Eyck).
[Fl. 425, Fl. 878, Fl. 215, Fl. 107, Fl. 892, Fl. 213.]

Eyck, Nicolaas van, the younger. Flemish Sch. *b* son of Nicolaas van E. Antwerp 1646 *d* Antwerp 1692. Master Antwerp Guild 1671. [Fl. 892.]

Eycke, J. van den, see **Hecke.**

Eycken, Charles van den (sometimes signed **Charles Duchêne**). Flemish Sch. *b* Brussels 1859. *Animals* (*mainly cats and dogs) and some interiors.* Pupil of J. Stevens. Patronised by Queen Henrietta of Belgium. Represented in ANTWERP *The busybody* 1911. [Fl. 17.]

Eycken, Charles van der. Flemish Sch. *b* Aershot (nr. Louvain) 1809 *d* after 1863. *Landscapes (including mountain.and river pieces).* Travelled in Holland, Germany and the Ardennes.
[Fl. 451, Fl. Bib. 19th cent.]

Eycken, Jean Baptiste van. Flemish Sch. *b* Brussels 1809 *d* Brussels 1853. *Religious subjects (some in fresco), costume history, portraits, genre.* Pupil of F. J. Navez; visited France, Italy 1837-9 and Germany where studied fresco technique with P. von Cornelius (*cf.* J. Swerts) 1848. Professor Brussels Acad. 1839. Represented in AMSTERDAM. *He wants to be a painter* 1827. BRUSSELS *Descent from the Cross* 1848, *Parmigiano surprised in his studio by Charles V's soldiers* (*cf.* P. Kremer) 1849; Bon Secours *Healing of Tobit* 1835; Chapelle de N.D. *Frescoes* 1840-53. COURTRAI.
[Fl. 451, Fl. 481, Fl. 798, Fl. Bib. 19th cent.]

Eyckens (or **Eykens**), see **Ijkens.**

Eyden, Jeremias van der. Flemish Sch. *b* Brussels before 1650 *d* Staplefort 1695. *Portraits, draperies.* Pupil in The Hague of A. Hanneman 1658; came London (*cf.* C. de Neve) and painted draperies for Sir P. Lely (*cf.* J. B. Gaspers); later went Northamptonshire and worked for Earls of Rutland and Gainsborough; then for Lord Sherard (in whose house in Leicestershire he died). [Fl. 856, Fl. 892.]

F

Faber, Frédéric Théodore. Flemish Sch. *b* Brussels 1782 *d* Brussels 1844. *Genre, landscapes, animals; also worked as painter on porcelain and engraver.* Pupil of B. Ommeganck; opened a porcelain factory 1819. Represented in BRUSSELS *Workman resting.* [Fl. 451.]

Fabrique, Nicolas La. Flemish Sch. *b* Namur 1649 *d* Liège 1733. *Religious subjects, figures pieces and still life.* Visited Rome and Paris. **Signed Example:** NAMUR *Raising of the Cross. A Self portrait in a feathered hat s* and 1685 is recorded. [Fl. 217, Fl. 88, Fl. 409, Fl. 463.]

Fabry, Émile. Flemish Sch. *b* Verviers 1865. *Murals with symbolist allegories (cf.* A. Levêque), *poster designs, portraits.* Pupil in Brussels Acad.; associated with group founded by J. Delville *q.v. c.* 1895; Professor Brussels Acad. Represented in ANTWERP *Portrait of the artist's mother.* BRUSSELS (Théâtre de la Monnaie) *Murals.* IXELLES *Child, Heaven, Roses.* [Fl. Bib. 19th cent.]

Fackere, Jef van der. Flemish Sch. *b* Bruges 1879. *Still life* (mainly flowers), *figures, portraits.* Pupil Bruges Acad. under E. van Hove. Professor Bruges Acad. from 1904. Represented in BRUGES *Peonies, Portrait* 1906. [Fl. 114.]

*Faes, Pieter. Flemish Sch. *b* Meir (province Antwerp) 1750 *d* Antwerp 1814. *Flowers and fruit (cf.* J. F. Eliaerts, M. v. Dorne, J. F. v. Dael, J. L. and R. J. Malaine, P. J. Thys, G. F. Ziesel). Patronized by Governor-General of Austrian Netherlands, Archduchess Maria Christina who took a number of his works, painted for Château Laeken (*cf.* J. Gilson, A. C. Lens, P. J. Verhaghen and F. B. Solvyns) to Vienna at outbreak of Brabant Revolution 1789. **Signed Examples:** BARNARD CASTLE Bowes Mus. *Flowers in Vase* (1796). BRUGES *Flowers and fruit* (1794). BRUSSELS *Flowers* (1791). [Fl. 451.]

Falange, Enrico. Flemish Sch. 17th cent. *Religious subjects.* Worked in Venice *c.* 1650. **Documented Examples:** VENICE Oratorio di S. Bartolommeo *Ten scenes from the life of the Virgin* (described 1664 by Boschini). A *Virgin with Saints* is recorded Venice, Ospedale dei Mendicanti. [Fl. 101, Fl. 594, Fl. 305.]

Falckenburg, see Valkenborch.

*Falens (or Valens), Carel van. Flemish Sch. *b* son of Antwerp Militia captain, Antwerp 1683 *d* Paris 1733. *Picturesque outdoor genre (cf.* N. H. J. Fassin). Pupil in Antwerp of C. Francken 1697; went Paris 1703 (*cf.* J. J. Spoede); court painter to Louis XV (*cf.* J. F. Delien) 1724; member of Acad. Royale (*cf.* P. Mol) 1726. **Signed Examples:** AMSTERDAM Rijks. *Hawking party.* DRESDEN *Heron-hawking party.* **Monogrammed Examples:** PARIS Louvre *Hunters assembling. Hunting interlude* (Acad. reception works). COURTRAI (1730); LENINGRAD. *Cf.* J. P. van Bredael. [Fl. 564, Fl. 107, Fl. 892.]

Farasyn, Edgard. Flemish Sch. *b* son of an artist, Antwerp 1858 *d* Antwerp 1938. *Genre, figures, animals, marines, coast scenes; murals.* Pupil and later professor Antwerp Acad. Founder member of Antwerp group De Dertien (XIII) 1891 (other members were L. Abry, L. van Aken, E. Claus, P. van Engelen, F. Hens, E. de Jans, E. Larock, R. Looymans, H. Luyten, C. Mertens, H. P. Rul, H. de Smeth,

P. Verhaert and T. Verstraete). Represented in ANTWERP *The old fish market* 1883, *Étaples Market, The Village doctor* 1908; Town Hall *Literature* (mural), *cf.* C. Boom, 1899. BERLIN; BRUSSELS *Shipwreck* 1903; COURTRAI; NAMUR. [Fl. 592, Fl. Bib. 19th cent.]

Fassin, Charles Victor. Flemish Sch. *b* Liège 1826 *d* Liège 1906. *'History', Italian landscapes and genre, portraits.* Went Italy and lived Rome, where met Alexandre Dumas, 1856-61; returned Liège 1861. Represented in LIÈGE *The Good Samaritan.* Pictures titled *Diana hunting* and *Messalina driven from Rome* are recorded. [Fl. Bib. 19th cent.]

Fassin (or Facin), Nicolas Henri Joseph, Chevalier de. Flemish Sch. *b* Liège 1728 *d* Liège 1811. *Picturesque landscapes with figures and animals (cf.* C. v. Falens, H. J. Antonissen, J. L. Demarne), *social genre (cf.* P. J. and J. J. Horemans), *portraits.* Pupil of J. B. Coclers. Went Paris and served as officer of 'mousquetaires gris du Roi' 1748-54; student in Antwerp Acad. 1762-8; visited Rome, Naples, Geneva and Ferney where was entertained by Voltaire; with his friend L. Defrance *q.v.* founded Liège Academy 1773; declined invitation to join court painters of Catherine II of Russia who bought some of his pictures and sent him a gold snuff box with her portrait thereon; lived for a time at Spa; many of his pictures are said to have been bought by English and German collectors. **Documented Examples:** BUDAPEST *Landscape with shepherds.* LIÈGE *Landscape with cattle.* A *Voltaire in his dressing gown* 1769, a *Lady drinking tea* (s) and *The Four Times of the Day* (s) are recorded. [Fl. 63, Fl. 432, Fl. 451, Fl. 409.]

Faydherbe, Rombaut. Flemish Sch. *b* son of architect and sculptor Luc F., Malines 1649, *d* Naxos or Constantinople of the plague 1673. Pupil of A. van Diepenbeeck and Jordaens. In Belgrade on establishment of Marquis de Nointel, French ambassador to the Sultan and wrote of conditions to Antwerp dealer Forchoudt 1670-2; had as colleague French draughtsman J. Carrey (who accompanied the Marquis to Athens 1673 and drew the Parthenon sculptures 1674). [Fl. 613, Fl. 798, Fl. 213.]

Felaert, see Velaert.

Felbier, Maurits. Flemish Sch. *b* Antwerp 1903. *Still life, figures, portraits.* Represented ANTWERP *Autumn fruit.* [Fl. 17.]

Felu (Felou), Charles François. Flemish Sch. *b* Waermaerde 1830 *d* Antwerp 1900. *Portraits.* Born without arms he painted with his feet, his brush held with his right foot and his palette with his left (*cf.* Cornelis Ketel). Visited London where made copies in Victoria and Albert Museum. A portrait *The African King Massala* (s Charles Felu pede pinxit) is recorded 1886. [Fl. 892, Fl. 73.]

*Female Half-Lengths Master. Presumed Flemish Sch. 16th cent. Name for painter of VIENNA Harrach *Trio of musician ladies.* Paintings presumed by some his work are in various museums. [Fl. 892, Fl. 316, Fl. 530, Fl. 798.]

Ferdinandus, Philips. Flemish Sch. 16th cent. BRÜNN (Mähren) has a votive picture *Christ crowned with thorns* (with portraits of Brünn citizens as donors) signed Phil. fernandus Antwerpensis 1593. [Fl. 117.]

Ferrer, Antoine. Presumed Flemish Sch. 16th or 17th cent. *Religious subjects.* Descamps (1769) records in Nieuport Parish Church: Triptych: centre *Hérodiade qui perce la langue de Saint Jean dont elle porte la tête,* wings: *S. Sebastien dont l'on perce le corps avec des flèches, S. Sebastien mourant* ('C'est un bon tableau, usé et gaté'). [Fl. 216.]

Fiammingo, see Borremans, W.

Fiammingo, see Calvaert, D.

Fiammingo, see Duquesnoy, F.

Fiammingo, Arrigo, see Broeck, H. van den.

Fiammingo, Ludovico, see Toeput, L.

Fiammingo, Paolo, see Franck.

Fierlants, Captain Nicolaas Marten. Flemish Sch. *b* 'S Hertogenbosch *c.* 1622 *d* Antwerp 1694. *Religious and allegorical subjects, architectural drawings; also worked as tapestry designer.* Master Antwerp Guild 1651; Captain in Civic Guard. A. Genoels was his pupil. **Signed Example:** NEERLINTER Church *S. Augustine between an angel and a nun* 1656. A *Pictura bewailing her fate to Jupiter* presented by him to the Antwerp Guild 1670 is recorded. [Fl. 425, Fl. 107.]

Fifteen Eighteen (1518) Master. Presumed Flemish Sch. 16th cent. Name for painter of *Life of the Virgin* altarpiece dated 1518, donated 1522 to LÜBECK Marienkirche. Presumed by some identical with Abbey of Dilighem Master *q.v.*
[Fl. 316, Fl. 530.]

Figdor Deposition Master. Presumed Flemish (Dutch) Sch. 15/16th cent. Name for painter of BERLIN K.F. *Descent from the Cross* (formerly in Figdor Collection, Vienna). Sometimes referred to as Pseudo-Geertgen. [Fl. 316, Fl. 798.]

Finson, David, see Finson, L.

Finson (Finsonius), Louis (Ludovicus). Flemish Sch. *b* son of painter, Bruges *c.* 1580 *d* Amsterdam *c.* 1618 or by drowning in the Rhone 1632. *Religious subjects, 'history', portraits.* Pupil in Rome of Caravaggio *c.* 1600; in Aix 1610; in Naples 1612 (*cf.* W. Coebergher); then mainly active in Provence (Aix and Arles); recorded Amsterdam where made will 1617; left his art collection to his nephew David F. (portrait painter *d* after 1629), and to the German-Dutch painter and copyist A. Vinck his part-ownership of Caravaggio's *Virgin of the Rosaries* (acquired by group of artists including Rubens, Jan (Velvet) Brueghel and H. van Balen and presented to Antwerp Dominican church whence bought by Emperor Joseph II 1781 (*cf.* A. Quertemont). **Signed Examples:** AIX-EN-PROVENCE Cathedral *The Incredulity of S. Thomas* 1613; S. Jean *Resurrection* 1610; Séminaire *Annunciation* 1612. ANDENNES Church *Massacre of the Innocents.* ARLES S. Trophime *Adoration of the Magi* 1614, *Martyrdom of S. Stephen* 1614. MARSEILLES Mus. *Self-portrait with bare chest and feathered cap* 1613. NAPLES *Annunciation* 1612 (small version of Aix picture). ROME Accad. di S. Luca *Man's portrait* 1613. Portraits of Aix Magistrates 1616 are recorded. [Fl. 892, Fl. 305, Fl. 678.]

Fisen, Englebert. Flemish Sch. *b* son of a barber, Liège 1655 *d* Liège 1733. *Religious subjects for Liège churches, 'history', portraits, designs for tapestry.* Pupil of B. Flémalle, then, in Rome, of Carlo Maratta (*cf.* S. v. Aken); in Liège 1679; kept diary from 1679-1729 recording 652 pictures including 146 portraits; E. Plumier was his pupil.
[Fl. 63, Fl. 451, Fl. 407, Fl. 409.]

Flamen (or Flamand), Albert. Flemish Sch. *b* Bruges (?) *c.* 1620 *d* Paris (?) after 1692. *Portraits, but mainly active as draughtsman and engraver of landscapes, topographic views, and natural history (fish and birds).* In Paris (*cf.* C. E. Biset) 1648-69; worked for Gobelins factory (*cf.* A. Baudewyns) *c.* 1650; 'peintre et dessinateur ordinaire de Monsieur, Frère du Roi' 1692. VIENNA Albertina and LONDON British Mus. have signed drawings. [Fl. 564, Fl. 612, Fl. 892.]

Flémalle (or Flemael), Bertholet (sometimes referred to as Bertholet). Flemish Sch. *b* son of a glass painter, Liège 1614 *d* Liège 1675. *Religious subjects, 'history', portraits; also active as architect and amateur singer and musician.* Pupil of G. Douffet; went Italy 1638; worked Rome, then Florence for Medici Grand duke Ferdinand II (*cf.* J. Sutterman); went Paris (*cf.* C. E. Biset) where patronized by Chancellor Séguier and worked for Paris churches; returned Liège 1647; painted *Allegory of Religion protecting France* (burned 1871) for Paris, Tuileries, went Paris to instal it, and was made member and professor of Paris Acad. (*cf.* P. Mol) 1670; returned Liège where was given canonry of Cathedral same year; suffered from melancholia in last years and is said to have been poisoned by the Marquise de Brinvilliers (then in Liège). His pupils included J. G. Carlier, E. Fisen and G. de Lairesse. **Signed Example:** DRESDEN *Aeneas leaving Troy.*
[Fl. 86, Fl. 287, Fl. 425, Fl. 22, Fl. 409, Fl. 892.]

*Flémalle Master. Presumed Flemish Sch. 15th cent. Name for painter of FRANKFORT Staedel. *S. Veronica with the Sudary, Standing Virgin and Child* and (grisaille) *The Trinity,* three panels alleged to have come from Flémalle (near Liège). *Cf.* Cambridge Veronica Draughtsman, London Woman in a Wimple Painter, London Virgin with a Fire-screen Painter, Madrid Werl Wings Painter and Mérode Master. Presumed by some identical with R. Campin *q.v.* and by others with R. v. d. Weyden *q.v. Cf.* J. van Battel the elder. [Fl. 316, Fl. 696, Fl. 530.]

Flessiers (or Flissier), Baltazar. Flemish Sch. *b* Ghent (?) before 1555 *d* The Hague *c.* 1626. *Portraits.* His portrait of *Eva Fliegen* (said to have lived for years without taking food) is recorded by an engraving. *Cf* J. Porcellis. [Fl. 892.]

Flessiers (or Flesshiers), Benjamin. Flemish Sch. *b* son of Baltazar F., The Hague (?) *c.* 1615 *d* London (?) after 1680 (?). *Marines* (*cf.* G. van Eyck), *Landscapes, portraits, still life.* Praised as a marine painter 1658; came London (*cf.* C. de Neve) where lived in later years near Fountain Tavern in the Strand. The English portrait painter Mary Beale wrote (1680) of 'Mr. Flessiere the framemaker' presumably B. F. or a brother. Vertue (before 1756) records *A Man and a Woman* signed 'B. Flesshier Fecitt 1670', and a landscape in the Royal Collection. Walpole (1786) records a still life in Sir P. Lely's collection and landscapes and marines at Ham House. [Fl. 826, Fl. 856.]

Flessiers (or Flesshier), Tobias. Flemish Sch. 17th cent. Son of Baltazar F. Painter and dealer. In London 1652-63.
[Fl. 892.]

Floquet, Bartholomeus. Flemish Sch. *b* before 1635 *d* Vienna 1690. *Religious subjects; also worked as engraver.* Recorded working for the Antwerp art dealers Forchoudt by 1652; in Antwerp Guild 1665; delivered paintings regularly to Forchoudt (*cf.* A. Casteels) 1666-72; set up for himself as an art dealer; as 'peintre et marchand' was godfather to the engraver G. Edelinck's child Paris 1685; left a collection of pictures at his death in Vienna. [Fl. 212.]

Floquet, Lucas. Flemish Sch. *b* Antwerp 1578 *d* Antwerp 1635. *Religious subjects and decorative murals.* In Antwerp Guild 1598; went Ghent where worked for churches; returned Antwerp 1618. His daughter married F. Ijkens; his three sons Lucas (*b* before 1602 *d* 1666), Pauwel and Simon were also painters. **Signed Example:** CALCKEN church (triptych) *Martyrdom of S. Denis* 1616. Descamps (1769) records an altarpiece in Ghent S. Michel.

[Fl. 216, Fl. 107, Fl. 386.]

***Florence (Poggio Imperiale) Crucifixion Painter.** Presumed Flemish (Dutch) Sch. late 15th cent. Name for painter of FLORENCE Uffizi (906) (1237) *Crucifixion.* Presumed by some identical with Virgo inter Virgines Master *q.v.* [Fl. 304.]

Floris, Baptiste. Flemish Sch. *b* son of Frans Floris the elder after 1547. Van Mander (1604) records that he was murdered by the Spaniards in Brussels. [Fl. 509.]

Floris (de Vriendt), Cornelis. Flemish Sch. *b* son of sculptor and architect Cornelis F., Antwerp 1551 *d* Antwerp 1615. *Religious and mythological subjects; also worked as sculptor.* Went Paris where pupil of H. Francken the elder *q.v.* 1568; Master Antwerp Guild 1577; with J. de Momper and others worked on Antwerp Pageant Entry of Archduke Ernest of Austria 1594 (*cf.* G. Schoof). H. van Kessel was his pupil. A *Temptation of Christ* is recorded in an Antwerp inventory of 1614 and a *Feast of Bacchus* in one of 1642.

[Fl. 559, Fl. 88, Fl. 892, Fl. 213.]

***Floris (de Vriendt), Frans.** Flemish Sch. *b* son of a sculptor, Antwerp *c.* 1516 *d* Antwerp 1570. *Religious and mythological subjects, portraits.* Pupil in Liège of L. Lombard *c.* 1536; Master Antwerp Guild 1540; visited Rome and copied Michelangelo's *Last Judgement* 1541; back in Antwerp by 1547; in charge of decorations for Pageant Entry into Antwerp of Charles V and Philip II, for which he painted seven figures a day for five weeks (*cf.* A. v. Palerme, J. v. Rillaert, P. J. Pourbus and P. Coecke v. Aelst) 1549; took picture commissioned by Delft Confraternity of the Holy Cross to Holland and visited A. Claesz. *q.v.* in Leyden 1553; directed decorations for Pageant Entry into Antwerp of Philip II for which he painted in one day a *Victory trampling fettered prisoners* 1556; at height of his success, patronised by the Prince of Orange and Counts Egmont and Hoorn (*cf.* W. Key); spent his substance on building himself a mansion with large figures in golden grisaille on the outer walls (*cf.* K. Foort); in later years had reputation of the stoutest drinker in Antwerp and was nightly helped to bed by two of his numerous pupils and assistants who included C. v. d. Broeck, M. v. Cleve, H. v. Cleve, L. de Heere, H. Francken the elder, A. Francken, F. Francken the elder, F. Pourbus the elder and M. de Vos. Both Lampsonius *q.v.* and L. de Heere extolled him in poems. **Signed Examples:** FLORENCE Uffizi *Adam and Eve* 1560. THE HAGUE *Venus mourning the dead Adonis.* **Monogrammed Examples:** ANTWERP *Fall of the Rebel Angels* 1554 (painted for the Fencers' altar in Antwerp Notre Dame and described by van Mander), *S. Luke painting* (from Painters' Guild) 1556 (*cf.* R. Aertsz). BERLIN *Mars and Venus in Vulcan's Net* 1547. BRUNSWICK *The Falconer* 1558. BRUSSELS *Last Judgement* (*cf.* J. de Backer), *Adoration of the Magi* (with monogram also of H. Francken who finished it 1571). CAEN *Portrait of an old lady* 1558. DRESDEN *Adoration of the Shepherds, The Emperor Vitellius, Laughing girl.* SCHWERIN *Head of Christ.* STOCKHOLM *Feast of the Sea gods* 1561. VIENNA K. *Last Judgement* 1565. **Documented Example:** TURIN *Allegory of the Muses asleep in wartime* (in 1612 inventory and mentioned by Van Mander). Van Mander records an *Assumption of the Virgin* destroyed by the iconoclasts (though some believed at the time that it was taken to the Escorial Madrid), a *Nativity* in Antwerp Cathedral, *Scenes from the life of S. Luke* (with donor and his spaniel), *S. Luke writing his gospel dictated by the Virgin. Luke preaching, The capture and death of S. Luke, Adam and Eve driven from Paradise, Adam and Eve mourning Abel, The story of Hercules* (ten pictures), *The Seven Liberal Arts, Christ blessing the children,* and as his

last work for the Grand Prior of Spain a *Crucifixion* and an *Ascension* (wings, left unfinished, painted by other artists).

[Fl. 371, Fl. 818, Fl. 559, Fl. 892, Fl. 908, Fl. 316.]

Floris, Frans, the younger. Flemish Sch. *b* son of F. F. the elder, Antwerp *c.* 1547 *d* Rome *c.* 1620. *Religious subjects, portraits.* Left Flanders before 1579; in Rome 1592; in financial distress there 1602; recorded by van Mander as painting there small pictures on copper 1604; married there before 1602, again in 1610 and again in 1620.

[Fl. 559, Fl. 107, Fl. 416, Fl. 417.]

Floris (de Vriendt), Jacques. Flemish Sch. *b* son of a sculptor (and brother of F. F. the elder) 1524 *d* 1581. Van Mander records him as a good glass painter who also painted pictures. P. Vlerick was his pupil *c.* 1551. [Fl. 559.]

Floris (de Vriendt), Jan. Flemish Sch. *b* Antwerp (?) *c.* 1530 *d* Spain after 1581. *Painter on faience.* As such in Antwerp Guild. Went Spain (*cf.* A. v. d. Wyngaerde) where employed by Philip II; Director of an Azulejos (painted tiles) factory Madrid 1563; Superintendant in Pardo Palace 1581; Van Mander says he painted 'charming little stories' on his pottery. [Fl. 559, Fl. 153.]

***Fogg S. Luke Painter.** Presumed Flemish Sch. 16th cent. Name for CAMBRIDGE (Mass.) Fogg Mus. (1910-16) *S. Luke painting the Virgin.* Presumed by some identical with Saint Sang Master *q.v.* (*cf.* also Boston S. Luke Painter).

Fonteyn, Adriaen Lucasz. Flemish Sch. *b* Ypres date unknown *d* Rotterdam 1661. *Peasant, social and gay life genre* (*cf.* J. van Winghe, H. Francken the elder, F. Francken II, G. Coques, H. Janssens, C. J. v. d. Lamen, G. v. Tilborgh, D. Teniers). Worked Rotterdam from 1626. **Signed Example:** AMSTERDAM Rijks. *Rotterdam mussel market* 1657. Signed pictures titled *Merry company* and *The music party* are recorded.

[Fl. 892, Fl. 798.]

Foort, Karel, called **Karel van Yperen.** Flemish Sch. *b* Ypres *c.* 1510 *d* Courtrai (Abbey de Groeninghem) 1562. *Religious subjects, some in fresco, and paintings on exteriors of houses* (*cf.* F. Floris); *also worked as designer for glass windows and as sculptor.* Went Italy and lived there for some time; back in Ypres where P. Vlerick *q.v.* was his pupil (*cf.* N. Snellaert) *c.* 1550. Van Mander (1604) records that always cranky and irritable he became melancholic, stabbed himself at a supper in the company of fellow artists in Courtrai, and was carried by his friends to the Abbey of Groeninghem where he died. Van Mander also records a grisaille *Conversion of S. Paul* (*cf.* P. Bruegel the elder), a *Resurrection* on a chest lid and a *Last Judgement* with a drawing for it, with Christ seated on the clouds and, below, the symbols of the Evangelists 'somewhat in the style of Tintoretto' (*cf.* L. Toeput).

[Fl. 559, Fl. 892, Fl. 440.]

***'Forties Master.** Presumed Flemish Sch. 16th cent. Name for painter of ANTWERP Mus. (696) *Gillis van Schoonbeke* dated 1544. Pictures presumed by some his work are in Antwerp (*cf.* Antwerp Forties Painter) and other museums.

[Fl. 316.]

Foué, see Voet, F.

***Fouquier (Fockeel, Foucquier, Fouquières, Foquier), Jacques.** Flemish Sch. *b* Antwerp *c.* 1585 *d* Paris 1659. *Landscapes.* Pupil of Jan (Velvet) Brueghel and of J. de Momper. D'Argenville (1745) records him as landscape assistant in tapestry designs to Rubens who liked him for 'his poetical ideas'; Master Antwerp Guild 1615; travelled Italy (Rome and Venice); went Heidelberg where employed by Elector Palatine on decorations of his castle; in Brussels where P. de

Champaigne was his pupil; went Paris (*cf.* C. E. Biset and P. Franchoys) 1621; commissioned by Louis XIII (*cf.* J. v. Egmont) to paint the principal towns of France between the windows of the Grande Galerie du Louvre (*cf.* V. Leckerbetien); in Toulon 1626; Marseilles 1629; ennobled by Louis XIII; Félibien (1666-88) records him as drinking heavily instead of working and as very pretentious; quarrelled with the French painter N. Poussin (lately returned from Rome and given charge of the Louvre decorations *cf.* A. van Dyck) 1641; died in indigence, his funeral being paid for by his pupil M. Platte-Montagne (Plattenberg). **Signed Examples:** CAMBRIDGE Fitzwilliam *Landscape.* COLOGNE *Wooded landscape* 1622. GHENT *Landscape with view of Avignon.* NANTES *River landscape* 1620. D'Argenville records five pictures in the possession of Louis XIII *Winter, Market with landscape, Horsemen at inn door, Hunting scene, Château on a rock.* Antwerp inventories record (1644):—*Landscape by Brueghel and F.*; (1668):—*Landscape by F. with figures by Rubens*; (1689):—*Landscape by F. and Brueghel with figures by Diepenbeeck* and *Landscape with chickens by F.*; (1691):—*Paradise* (*Garden of Eden?*) *by Brueghel, F. and Gonzales Coques. Wooded landscapes* are recorded by engravings.

[Fl. 287, Fl. 22, Fl. 289, Fl. 892, Fl. 213.]

Fourmois, Théodore. Flemish Sch. *b* Presles 1814 *d* Brussels 1871. *Landscapes* (*Antwerp Campine, Ardennes, France*); *also worked as lithographer and engraver.* C. P. Tschaggeny collaborated in some of his pictures (*cf.* J. B. Madou and E. J. Verboeckhoven). Represented in ANTWERP *Landscape near Dinant* 1854. BRUGES *The Valley* 1850. BRUSSELS, HAMBURG (with C. P. Tschaggeny), LIÈGE, MONS.

[Fl. Bib. 19th cent.]

Francart (or **Francquart**), **Jacques.** Flemish Sch. *b* son of a painter, Brussels or Antwerp *c.* 1582 *d* Brussels 1651. *Religious subjects and designs for ceremonial decorations; but mainly active as architect* (Brussels Église des Augustins now de la Trinité and Jesuit Church now destroyed and Malines Église du Béguinage now S. Alexis). Brother-in-law of W. Coebergher *q.v.*; visited Italy 1607; back in Antwerp 1613; court painter and architect to Archduke Albert (*cf.* G. de Crayer) and the Archduchess Isabella (*cf.* D. v. Alsloot); delivered paintings for Isabella's private chapel 1614-18; published fragment of a Livre d'Architecture (designs for doors, etc.) 1617; designed catafalques for funeral ceremonies of Archduke Albert 1622 and Archduchess Isabella 1634; continued as court architect to Cardinal Infante Ferdinand; invented an alarm clock which also struck a light; gave up professional work and devoted himself to culture of flowers from *c.* 1645. *The Mysteries of the Rosary* (*cf.* A. Mytens) a series of pictures painted for Isabella as present to Pope Paul V is recorded. (*Cf.* A. F. Bruns.)

[Fl. 85, Fl. 168, Fl. 425, Fl. 892, Fl. 617.]

Franceschi, Paolo, see **Franck.**

Franchoys (or **François**), **Lucas the elder.** Flemish Sch. *b* Malines 1574 *d* Malines 1643. *Portraits, religious subjects.* Master Malines Guild 1599; visited France (*cf.* A. Dubois) and Spain (*cf.* P. de Kempener, A. Smit, G. v. Keak and F. and R. Diriksen); back in Malines 1605. **Monogrammed Example:** GHENT S. Bavon *Pietà* 1610. **Documented Examples:** MALINES S. Jean *Pentecost* with wings by L. F. the younger *q.v.*; Town Hall *Burgomaster Philip Snoy 1619.* Antwerp Mus. has *S. Anne teaching the Virgin to read* recorded (1769) as by 'L. Franchoys' in Malines Carmes Déchaussés by Descamps who makes no distinction between father and son. [Fl. 425, Fl. 216, Fl. 613, Fl. 614, Fl. 892.]

Franchoys, Lucas the younger. Flemish Sch. *b* son of Lucas F. the elder *q.v.*, Malines 1616 *d* Malines 1681. *Religious subjects, 'history', portraits.* Pupil of his father in Malines, then in

Antwerp of Rubens; went Paris (*cf.* P. Mol) after 1640 and painted portraits at the court; Master Malines Guild 1655; worked for Malines and Tournai churches and religious houses (*cf.* S. v. Aken). **Signed Examples:** ANTWERP *S. Louis receiving Pierre de Corbie* (fragment of a large picture in Malines Carmes Déchaussés till Revolution when it was cut into sections). TOURNAI Cathedral *The Resurrection of Christ* 1657; S. Quentin *Beheading of S. John* 1650. **Documented Example:** AMSTERDAM Rijks. *François Vilain de Gand, Bishop of Tournai* (engraved). MALINES S. Jean has *S. Roch healing the plague-stricken* (large triptych with predella recorded by Descamps 1769). Antwerp Mus. has *The Virgin appearing to S. Simon Stock* recorded by Descamps as by 'L. Franchoys' in Malines Carmes Déchaussés (*cf.* L. F. the elder).

[Fl. 86, Fl. 425, Fl. 216, Fl. 613, Fl. 107, Fl. 614, Fl. 892.]

*Franchoys (or **François**), **Peeter.** Flemish Sch. *b* son of Lucas F. the elder, Malines 1606 *d* Malines 1654. *Portraits, genre figures, religious subjects, landscapes with small figures.* Pupil of his father then in Antwerp of G. Seghers. In Paris (*cf.* L. Franchoys, P. de Champaigne, P. Mol and C. E. Biset) and Fontainebleau (*cf.* A. Dubois and T. van Thulden) *c.* 1631; back in Malines by 1635; worked for Archduke Leopold Wilhelm (*cf.* J. v. Egmont, J. B. v. Heil and P. Thys). **Signed Examples:** BRUSSELS *Young man with wine glass* 1639. DRESDEN *Man in armour.* LILLE G. *Mutsaerts, Provost of Leliendael monastery* 1645. Descamps (1769) records in Lierre Collegiate Church *Christ on the Cross* (as by P. F. Pierre François) and in Antwerp Carmes Chaussés *The Institution if the Carmelite Order.*

[Fl. 86, Fl. 425, Fl. 216, Fl. 892.]

Franck, Laureys (Laurent). Flemish Sch. *b* Antwerp (?) before 1610 *d* Paris (?) after 1662. *Landscapes* (?). Pupil of Gabriel Francken Antwerp 1622. In Lyons 1645; in Paris 1659 where his nephew A. Genoels *q.v.* stayed in his house; J. Francisque Millet was his pupil and married his daughter.

[Fl. 425, Fl. 215, Fl. 714.]

Franck, Pauwels (known as **Paolo Fiammingo** or **Franceschi**). Flemish Sch. *b* Antwerp 1540 *d* Venice 1596. *Landscapes with religious, classical and allegorical subjects.* Master Antwerp Guild 1561; went Venice where became landscape assistant in Tintoretto's workshop (*cf.* L. Toeput, M. de Vos and P. Vlerick); under Tintoretto took part in repainting the Large Council Chamber of the Doges' palace after the 1577 fire; worked for Emperor Rudolph II (*cf.* B. Spranger), for Venetian palace of Pietro Gradenigo and for Hans Fugger. **Signed Example:** SCHLEISSHEIM *Pietà with SS. John and Joseph of Arimathea* ('Paulus Franceschi'). **Traditional Ascriptions:** VENICE Doges' Palace *Pope Alexander III blessing the Fleet 1176*; Accad. *S. John preaching.* A *Last Judgement* painted for Venice SS. Giovanni e Paolo was destroyed by fire 1867. An Antwerp inventory of 1649 records a series of panels showing 'Kinderkens' painted 'by Paolo Franchyon in Titian's house'. *Cf.* D. Barendsz.

[Fl. 709, Fl. 101, Fl. 536, Fl. 305, Fl. 213, Fl. 691, Fl. 798.]

Franck, Sebastian, see **Vrancx.**

Francken (or **Franck**), **Ambrosius the elder.** Flemish Sch. *b* son of painter Nicolaes, Herenthals 1544 *d* Antwerp 1618. Brother of Hieroymus F. the elder and Frans F. the elder. *Religious and allegorical subjects.* Pupil of F. Floris. In Tournai where met Van Mander 1569; in Fontainebleau (*cf.* H. F. the elder) 1570; Master Antwerp Guild 1573; married (1577) a rich widow who owned a stone and chalk enterprise; supplied materials for public buildings 1579-81; alderman 1585; member Antwerp Chamber of Rhetoricians ('Violiere') 1588; with M. de Vos directed decorations (*cf.* G. Schoof) for Antwerp Pageant Entry of Archduke Ernest 1594. **Signed Ex-**

ample: AIX (Provence) *Rape of Deianeira s* 'A. Franck' 1596. **Monogrammed Examples:** ANTWERP Triptych *Last Supper* (centre), *Disciples at Emmaus, SS. Paul and Barnabas.* GHENT Recollets *Carrying of the Cross* 1610. **Documented Example:** ANTWERP S. Jacques Two wings paid for 1611. Works recorded in 17th cent. Antwerp inventories include a 'very large' *The Preaching on the Sea* with landscape by T. van Haecht and J. de Momper, and a *Leda* (*cf.* V. Geldersman). [Fl. 559, Fl. 892, Fl. 213.]

Francken, Ambrosius the younger. Flemish Sch. *b* son of Frans F. the elder, Antwerp after 1581 *d* Antwerp 1632. *Religious subjects.* Master Antwerp Guild 1624; assisted M. van Nègre with paintings for Louvain S. Pierre 1620-5. [Fl. 107.]

*Francken, Constantyn. Flemish Sch. *b* son of painter Hieronymus F. III, Antwerp 1661 *d* Antwerp 1717. *Contemporary warfare* (*cf.* J. B. van der Meiren and J. P. v. Bredael), *and other outdoor subjects; and portraits.* Lived fifteen years Paris and Versailles (*cf.* C. E. Biset and A. F. v. d. Meulen) from c. 1680; in Antwerp and member Guild 1695; C. van Falens was his pupil 1697; involved in legal proceedings with the parents of his wife who had gone mad and run naked from his house 1707. **Signed Examples:** ANTWERP *The Battle of Eeckeren 1703* 1703 (*cf.* J. Broers), *M. van Rossem after the attempt on Antwerp 1542.* A *Siege of Namur 1695* with portraits of King William III of England and his generals, is recorded. [Fl. 451, Fl. 107, Fl. 892.]

Francken, Frans the elder. Flemish Sch. *b* son of a painter Nicolaes F. Herenthals, 1542 *d* Antwerp 1616. *Religious subjects, 'history', portraits.* Pupil of F. Floris 1565; citizen Antwerp and Master Guild 1567. A successful artist with many pupils (including Gortzius Geldorp, H. v. d. Mast and J. de Wael) and a large collection of pictures. From 1597 he signed Frans Francken D.o. (Den ouden, the elder) to distinguish himself from his son F. F. II (who later signed the same way to distinguish himself from F. F. III). **Signed Examples:** (Den ouden): DRESDEN *The road to Calvary* 1597. VIENNA K. *Croesus showing his treasures to Solon* (possibly by F. F. II). **Documented Examples:** ANTWERP Notre Dame Triptych *Jesus among the Doctors,* (*S. Ambrose baptizing S. Augustine* and *Miracle of Sarepta* on wings), for the Schoolmasters' Guild 1586 (Sir Joshua Reynolds (1781) wrote of this: 'there are some fine heads in this picture particularly the three men that are looking on one book; the Christ is but a poor figure'); S. André *Crucifixion* doc. by a receipt dated 1603. [Fl. 559, Fl. 425, Fl. 702, Fl. 892.]

*Francken (or Franck), Frans II (the younger). Flemish Sch. *b* son of Frans F. (I), Antwerp 1581 *d* Antwerp 1642. *Religious subjects, 'history', social scenes* (*cf.* J. v. Winghe), *interiors.* Master Antwerp Guild 1605. Signed Den jongen (the younger) during lifetime of F. F. I. then F. Francken, and finally D. o. (Den ouden, the elder) when his son Frans F. III began working. In the 17th cent. many of his works were exported to Vienna and elsewhere. **Signed Examples** include (Religious subjects): AMSTERDAM Rijks. (1616), ANTWERP *Works of Mercy* 1608. BARNARD CASTLE *The Flagellation.* BERLIN K.F., BRUNSWICK *The crossing of the Red Sea* (*cf.* H. Jordaens III and M. Pepyn). BRUGES N.D., BUDAPEST *Esther before Ahasuerus.* CAMBRIDGE Fitz. *Worship of the Golden Calf.* DRESDEN *Flight into Egypt.* HAMBURG, LENINGRAD, MADRID Prado *Ecce Homo.* MUNICH *Works of Mercy* 1630. PARIS Louvre *Prodigal Son* (centre picture surrounded by eight small grisaille narrative panels) 1633. VIENNA K. *Crucifixion* 1606. ('History' and mythology): BRUNSWICK *King Midas at table.* CASSEL *Apelles and the cobbler.* MADRID Prado *Neptune and Amphitrite.* PARIS Louvre *Achilles among the daughters of Lycomedes, Croesus*

showing his treasures to Solon 1633. VIENNA K. *Witches' Sabbath* 1607, *Croesus showing his treasures.* (Social scenes): THE HAGUE *Ball at the Court of Albert and Isabella* 1611. (Picture gallery interiors): (*cf.* W. v. Haecht): ANTWERP (1619) and ROME (Borghese). **Documented Example:** ANTWERP Triptych *The Four Crowned Martyrs* 1624. Some of the above may be by his father or his son. [Fl. 86, Fl. 892, Fl. 212, Fl. 213.]

*Francken (or Franck), Frans III, known as 'the Rubenist'. Flemish Sch. *b* son of Frans F. II *q.v.,* Antwerp 1607 *d* Antwerp 1667. *Religious subjects, church interiors* (in collaboration with L. and P. Neeffs the younger) *and interiors of picture galleries* (*cf.* W. v. Haecht). In later years active as linen merchant as well as painter. C. Luyckx and J. B. Seghers were among his pupils. **Signed Examples:** ANTWERP *Family group in a picture gallery.* AUGSBURG S. *John preaching in the wilderness, Moses striking the rock* 1654. DRESDEN *Interior of Antwerp Cathedral* (with L. Neeffs signed by both 1648). THE HAGUE Mauritshuis *Interior of Antwerp Cathedral* (with P. Neeffs the younger signed by both 1654). MADRID Prado *Church interior* (with L. Neeffs signed by both 1646). A *Salome with the head of John the Baptist* signed and dated 1664 is recorded. Some pictures catalogued under his father's name may be his work. [Fl. 107, Fl. 892.]

Francken, Gabriel. Flemish Sch. *b* Antwerp (?) before 1595 *d* Antwerp 1639. Pupil in Antwerp of G. Schoof *q.v.* Master Antwerp Guild 1620; member of Antwerp Chamber of Rhetoricians (Violiere); had many pupils; corresponded regularly with C. v. Immerseel, art dealer in Seville, who imported many of his works. *Cf.* G. Seghers and J. van Uden. [Fl. 86, Fl. 892, Fl. 212, Fl. 214.]

*Francken, Hieronymus (Jeroom) the elder. Flemish Sch. *b* son of painter Nicolas F., Herenthals 1540 *d* Paris 1610. *Religious subjects, social scenes* (*cf.* J. van Winghe and A. L. Fonteyn), *portraits, still life* (?). Pupil of his father then of F. Floris. Went Venice (?) then Fontainebleau and joined A. F. Houve (Franssen), H. de Maier and other Flemish artists (*cf.* L. Thiry, C. Ketel, D. v. Utrecht and A. Dubois) 1566; then to Paris (*cf.* J. de Wael) where Cornelis Floris (1568) and the Dutchman A. Bloemaert (1582) were his pupils; in Antwerp 1571; returned Paris (by 1585) where married a Frenchwoman and held rank of 'peintre du roy' in later years. His daughter was the mistress of F. Pourbus the younger. **Signed Examples:** ANTWERP *Still life* (may be by H. F. the younger) 1607. STOCKHOLM University *Evening Party* (figures presumed by some to represent Mary Stuart, Henri III and Catherine de Médicis). **Monogrammed Examples:** AIX LA CHAPELLE *Venetian Carnival* 1564. BRUSSELS *Adoration of the Magi* (F. F. and H. F.) 1571 (begun by F. Floris and finished by H. F.). DRESDEN *Beheading of S. John Baptist* 1600. **Documented Example:** AIX LA CHAPELLE *Self portrait* (?) (engraved). Recorded works include *Adoration of the Shepherds* painted for Paris Église des Cordeliers 1585 (disappeared after 1798) and *Group of Paris Sheriffs* painted for the Hôtel de Ville 1604. Some religious subjects are recorded by engravings. [Fl. 559, Fl. 107, Fl. 892, Fl. 16.]

Francken, Hieronymus the younger. Flemish Sch. *b* son of Frans F. the elder, Antwerp 1578 *d* Antwerp 1623. *Interiors, 'history', still life.* Pupil of his father, then of his uncle Ambrosius; Master Antwerp Guild 1607. **Signed Examples:** ANTWERP *Horatius at the Bridge* 1620 painted for the 'Serment des Escrimeurs'. DOUAI *Studio interior* with portraits of H. Francken and the flower painter D. Seghers (*s* I. Franck). An Inventory dated 1623 records a large picture by J. de Momper with figures by H. F. the younger (*cf.* H. F. the elder). [Fl. 107, Fl. 213.]

Francken, Jan (Hans). Flemish Sch. *b* Antwerp 1581 *d* Antwerp 1624. Pupil of his uncle Ambrosius F. Visited Paris 1607; Master Antwerp Guild 1611. [Fl. 107, Fl. 892.]

Francken (or Franck), Jan Baptist. Flemish Sch. *b* son of S. Vranckx, Antwerp 1599 *d* Antwerp 1653. Possibly a painter and the sitter for the portrait in Amsterdam Rijks. (855) catalogued as by Van Dyck. [Fl. 86, Fl. 425, Fl. 892, Fl. 114.]

Francken, P. H. (or H. P.). Flemish Sch. 17th cent. Name for painter of ANTWERP Mus. *S. Francis of Assisi, S. Louis the Crusader* and *S. Anthony of Padua* (1652) signed with monogram P. H. F. or H. P. F. all (with an unsigned fourth picture *S. James della Marca*) from Antwerp Recollets. [Fl. 216, Fl. 16.]

Francken, Thomas. Flemish Sch. *b* son of F. F. the elder, Antwerp after 1574 *d* after 1626. Master Antwerp 1601. Small pictures with figures are recorded in an Antwerp Inventory 1627. [Fl. 107, Fl. 892, Fl. 213.]

François, Lucas, see **Franchoys.**

François, Joseph (Pierre Joseph Célestin). Flemish Sch. *b* Namur 1759 *d* aged ninety-two Brussels 1851. *Religious subjects, 'history', portraits.* Pupil in Antwerp Acad. of A. C Lens; in Italy 1778-81 then Germany and Vienna; returned Antwerp and sold pictures to the Governors of Belgium for Château Laeken; sent *Judgement of Paris* to London Royal Academy 1788; in Italy 1789-92; thereafter Brussels where professor at Academy. A political composition during the French régime '*The Concordat of 1802*' (*cf.* L. Defrance) and another after the Union with Holland '*Allegory on the birth of the crown Prince of Orange 1817*' were engraved. H. de Caisne, J.-B. Madou and F. J. Navez were among his pupils. Represented in BRUSSELS Mus. *Marius among the ruins of Carthage*; Pal. Arenberg *Bacchante with bare breasts* (reputed portrait of Mme. Dubarry said to have been painted in Brussels); Égl. des Minimes *The Four Evangelists*; Notre Dame du Sablon *S. Germain blessing S. Geneviève.* GHENT S. Michel *The Assumption of the Virgin.* [Fl. 451, Fl. 361, Fl. 436, Fl. 612, Fl. 892, Fl. 798.]

Francquart, Jacques, see **Francart.**

*****Frankfort Master.** Presumed Flemish Sch. 15th-16th cent. Name for painter of FRANKFORT Staedelisches Inst. (81) Triptych *Crucifixion; Donor, Claus Humbrecht with three sons and S. Nicholas of Bari; Donor's wife with three daughters and S. Margaret;* on outside of wings *Allegory of Death.* Pictures presumed by some his work include Frankfort Städt. Mus. Triptych *Holy Kinship, Birth of the Virgin, Death of the Virgin* (painted for Dominican church). [Fl. 316, Fl. 16.]

Frankfort Sibyl Master, see **Tiburtine Sibyl Master.**

Franquinet, Willem Hendrik. Flemish Sch. *b* Maestricht 1785 *d* New York 1854. *Costume history, portraits, genre and worked as lithographer.* Pupil in Antwerp of W. Herreyns; in Maestricht 1804-15; visited Frankfort; settled Paris 1817; in London where exhibited *Mary Queen of Scots* and *Shylock* and other pictures (British Institution and R.A.) 1832-6; finally settled New York. [Fl. 451, Fl. 612, Fl. 361, Fl. 363, Fl. 798.]

Franssen (or Fransz), A., see **Houve.**

Frédéric, Léon. Flemish Sch. *b* son of a watchmaker Brussels 1856 *d* Brussels 1940. *Peasant and urban genre compositions with implicit social comment* (*cf.* E. Carpentier, C. de Groux, C. Hermans, E. Laermans, H. Luyten, C. Meunier, A. Struys) *also religious and symbolical compositions.* Pupil of J. Portaels; visited Italy. Member of 'Essor' group 1875 (*cf.* A. Hamesse) and Founder Member of Antwerp 'Kunst van Heden' (*cf.* R. Strebelle). Represented in ANTWERP *Two Walloon peasant girls.* BRUSSELS *The chalksellers* 1882, *The Ages of the Peasant* 1887, *Moonlight* 1900, *Return from the Procession* 1904. GHENT *Funeral repast* 1886, *Sunday before Mass.* LIÈGE *Burial of a peasant.* PARIS (State collection) *The old servant* 1885, *The Ages of the Workman, The Age of Gold.* Recorded works include *The People one Day will see the Sun* 1894, *The Vanity of Grandeur* 1892 and *Everything is dead* 1894. [Fl. Bib. 19th cent.]

Frey, Alice. Flemish Sch. *b* Antwerp 1895. *Portraits, poetic genre and religious subjects.* Studied in Antwerp Academy and under James Ensor in Ostend. Represented in ANTWERP *The Angel and the children, Portrait of a woman.* [Fl. 17, Fl. 568.]

Frutet, Francisco. Presumed Flemish Sch. 16th cent. *Religious subjects.* Worked Seville (*cf.* P. de Kempener). **Documented Example:** SEVILLE Mus. Triptych *Crucifixion, Christ bearing the Cross, Virgin and Child, Deposition* and *S. Bernard* (recorded in archives of the Seville Merced Calzada monastery as painted by this Flemish artist for the Hospital of SS. Cosmas and Damian (Las Bubas) in 1548; the record was seen by the art historian Ceán Bermudez 1800). An *Entombment* painted 1546 for the nuns of S. Maria de Gracia is recorded. [Fl. 153.]

Fruytiers, Philip. Flemish Sch. *b* Antwerp 1610 *d* Antwerp 1666. *Religious subjects, 'history' but chiefly small portrait groups and miniatures* (*cf.* G. Coques), *also active as portrait engraver.* Pupil of Rubens. Master Antwerp Guild 1632; employed in connection with inventory of Rubens' collection 1640. **Signed Example:** ANTWERP *Family group* 1642 (on parchment). Weyerman (1729) records a miniature group *Rubens and his family.* Vertue (1740) records a miniature 22 × 16 inches (after a drawing by Van Dyck) *Thomas Earl of Arundel and his family* (the sons handing him his armour) and a *woman dwarf* signed and dated 1643, later in Frederick Prince of Wales collection, and engraved by Vertue, who assumed it drawn in Antwerp when the family was there 1641. Descamps (1769) records (as by H. Fruitiers) a *Virgin and Child seated on a globe surrounded by the celestial choir* in Antwerp Abbaye de S. Michel. An *Assumption of the Virgin* painted for Antwerp S. Jacques is also recorded. [Fl. 86, Fl. 878, Fl. 826, Fl. 425, Fl. 216, Fl. 88, Fl. 892, Fl. 213.]

Fuchs, Louis Julien. Flemish Sch. *b* Lille 1814 *d* Antwerp 1873. *Landscapes.* Served in Dutch navy; retired and became painter 1846. Represented in ANTWERP. [Fl. 837 (1873).]

*****Fyt, Jan (Joannes).** Flemish Sch. *b* son of merchant, Antwerp 1611 *d* Antwerp 1661. *Animals* (*cf.* P. de Vos), *birds and still life* (*game, fruit, etc., some with cat, dog or peacock*); *also worked as engraver.* Pupil of F. Snyders; Master Antwerp Guild 1630; in Paris 1633; Italy 1635; Antwerp 1641; brought action against Antwerp dealer for selling a forged picture as his work 1656; J. Brueghel the younger, E. Quellinus and J. Peeters assessed his work worth 18 guilders a day 1660; T. Willeboirts (Bosschaert) and others painted figures in some of his pictures. P. Boel was among his pupils. **Signed Examples:** ANTWERP, BRUSSELS, BUDAPEST, CAMBRIDGE Fitz., COPENHAGEN, LENINGRAD, LONDON N.G. and Wallace, MADRID Prado *Dogs and waterfowl.* NEW YORK Met., PARIS Louvre, PHILADELPHIA Wilstach, STOCKHOLM, VIENNA K. *Diana returning from the Chase* 1650 (figures doc. by T. Willeboirts). Others in German galleries. [Fl. 86, Fl. 107, Fl. 892.]

G

Gabron, Guilliam (Willem). Flemish Sch. *b* son of an armorial coach painter G. G., Antwerp 1619 *d* Antwerp 1678. Nephew of Jan Cossiers. *Still life* (*cf.* T. Aenvanck). Visited Italy and returned Antwerp before 1660. **Signed Examples:** BRUNSWICK *Still life with table, globe, musical instruments and parrot* 1652. HANOVER *Still life with game.*
[Fl. 425, Fl. 481, Fl. 107.]

Gailliard (not **Gaillard**), **Frans.** Flemish Sch. *b* Brussels 1861 *d* 1932. *Naturalistic and (later) Impressionist portraits, landscapes, city views;* also worked as illustrator. Travelled France, Italy and Greece. Exhibited in Brussels, Paris, Venice, Berlin and Munich. Represented in BRUSSELS *Cardinal Mercier* (*s*) 1917-19. [Fl. 693.]

Gailliard, Jean Jacques. Flemish Sch. *b* son of F. Gailliard, Brussels 1890. *Symbolist and surrealist compositions, 'surimpressionist' genre, landscape and portraits.* Pupil of J. Delville and of the sculptor V. Rousseau; visited Paris and Greece 1909; influenced by Swedenborg from 1912; in Paris where acquainted with Isadora Duncan (*cf.* R. Wouters) Pavlova, Jean Cocteau 1920-4. Represented in BRUSSELS *The purple paradise* 1917, *The blue cathedral* 1941; Swedenborgian Church of the New Jerusalem *Murals*; Musée Charlier *Cyclone*; Conservatoire de Musique *Igor Stravinsky* 1923, *Orphée* 1924. BRYN-ATHYN (U.S.A.). [Fl. 843.]

Gain, see **Gheyn.**

Gallait, Louis. Flemish Sch. *b* Tournai 1810 *d* Brussels 1887. *Costume-history, allegory, religious subjects, genre, portraits.* Pupil in Tournai Acad. of C. Cels and the French painter P. Hennequin; in Antwerp 1832; went Paris with scholarship from Tournai municipality 1834; became friend of P. Delaroche; executed commissions for Versailles; achieved wide fame with *Abdication of Charles V* which was sent on exhibition to many European countries 1841; settled Brussels 1843; exhibited London and was Hon. Foreign Royal Academician. Represented in ANTWERP *The unhappy mother.* BALTIMORE (U.S.A.) *Peace and War.* BRUSSELS *Abdication of Charles V, The plague at Tournai, Joanna the Mad* (*cf.* W. Geets), *Art and Liberty, Portrait of Fétis*; Royal Palace *Pius IX.* GHENT *The tribute money* 1831, *Jewish family accused of concealment.* LIÈGE *The old beggar.* LILLE *Job tormented by his wife.* LONDON Wallace *The Duke of Alva administering an oath.* TOURNAI Mus. *Last honours to the decapitated Egmont and Hoorn* (*cf.* E. de Biefve and W. Key) 1850; Cathedral *Healing of the blind* (presented by Municipal Council 1833). VERSAILLES four pictures. YPRES *The broken bow* 1850.
[Fl. 784, Fl. 451, Fl. 434, Fl. 435, Fl. 296, Fl. 798, Fl. Bib. 19th cent.]

Galle, Hieronymus the elder. Flemish Sch. *b* son of an Antwerp courier, Antwerp 1625 *d* Antwerp (?) after 1679. *Still life* (*fruit, flowers and garlands*). Master Antwerp Guild 1645. **Signed Example:** DESSAU Schloss. An Antwerp inventory (1691) records flower pieces in a collection with others by J. (Velvet) Brueghel and D. Seghers *q.v.*
[Fl. 107, Fl. 213.]

*****Garemyn, Jan Anton.** Flemish Sch. *b* Bruges 1712 *d* Bruges 1799. *Religious subjects, outdoor genre, ceremonial designs, occasional portraits.* Pupil in Bruges Academy of J. van der Kerckhove and of L. Roons; also helped by J. Beernaert and M. de Visch; etched illustrations for Wyt's Chronyk van Vlandern 1736; designed decorations for Pageant Entry of Louis XV into Bruges during war of Austrian Succession (*cf.* J. F. van Bredael) 1745, and for Jubilee of S. Sang Chapel 1749; director-professor of Bruges Acad. 1765-75. J. A. v. d. Donckt, C. Noel and A. I. Steyaert were among his pupils. **Signed Example:** BRUGES *The vegetable market* 1778. **Documented Examples:** BRUGES Mus. *The building of the Ghent Canal* (two pictures officially commissioned in 1753), *The artist's mother* (miniature); S. Anne *S. Anne teaching the Virgin to read* 1768, *Six Old Testament subjects* 1760-1; S. Gilles *Scenes from the History of the Order of Trinitarians* 1777-82 (*cf.* J. I. de Roore); others in Notre Dame (1764), S. Sauveur (1760) and S. Walburga (1783). COURTRAI S. Martin *S. Roch interceding for the Plague Stricken* 1770. MALINES S. Rombaut *The Calling of S. Romualdus* 1775.
[Fl. 216, Fl. 451, Fl. 88, Fl. 113, Fl. 114.]

Garibaldo, Marc Antonio. Flemish Sch. *b* of Italian origin, Antwerp 1620 *d c.* 1678. *Religious subjects.* Presumed by some to have visited Italy. Master Antwerp Guild 1652. **Signed Examples:** ANTWERP *Flight into Egypt* (from Carpenters' Altar in Cathedral). BRUGES S. Gilles *S. Bernhard and William of Aquitania.* LONDON Hampton Court Royal Collection. *Christ falling beneath the Cross.* A picture titled *Disciples at Emmaus* taken from Antwerp Cathedral to the Louvre in 1794 was not recovered (*cf.* J. D. Odevaere) and is not known to be extant. A *Virgin as Queen of Martyrs* painted for Antwerp Jesuit Church 1658 is also recorded. [Fl. 216, Fl. 107.]

Garrard, M., see **Geeraerts.**

Garret, M., see **Geeraerts.**

Gaspers (Gaspars or **Jaspers), Jan Baptist,** known as 'Lely's Baptist'. Flemish Sch. *b* Antwerp (?) 1620 (?) *d* London 1691. *Portraits and 'postures' for other portrait painters* (*cf.* J. v. Aken), '*history*', also worked as engraver and tapestry designer. Pupil of T. Willeboirts (Bosschaert); in Antwerp Guild 1641; in England from *c.* 1649 (*cf.* C. de Neve); was present at sales of Charles I's pictures (*cf.* R. v. Leemput); worked for General Lambert; assistant to Sir P. Lely (*cf.* J. v. d. Eyden and P. H. Lankrink) after 1660, and later to John Riley and Sir G. Kneller. **Documented Example:** LONDON Painters Stainers Hall *Charles II* (a variant with mathematical instruments was painted for S. Bartholomew's Hospital). A *Catherine of Braganza, Queen of Charles II* and *Thomas Hobbes* are recorded by engravings. *A Cleopatra* was inherited by his widow. [Fl. 826, Fl. 865, Fl. 223, Fl. 38.]

*****Gassel, Lucas** (known as **Lucas van Helmont**). Flemish Sch. *b* Helmont *c.* 1500 *d* place unknown *c.* 1560. *Landscapes with figures* (*cf.* F. Mostaert). Worked mostly in Brussels; was a friend of D. Lampsonius *q.v.* Van Mander says he worked little but talked well. **Monogrammed Examples:** BRUSSELS *Mountainous landscape with mine workers* (*cf.* L. v. Valkenborch) 1544, *Landscape with religious subjects.* VIENNA K. *Landscape with Judah and Tamar* 1548. BERLIN Kupferstichkab. has a signed drawing dated 1560. A series of landscapes with saints and biblical figures are recorded by engravings. [Fl. 559, Fl. 892, Fl. 301, Fl. 318.]

Gast, Michiel de. Flemish Sch. *b* Antwerp (?) before 1520 *d* after 1575. *Roman landscapes with ruins.* Documented in Rome 1538 and 1556 (*cf.* M. van Heemskerck); Master Antwerp Guild 1558. [Fl. 559, Fl. 84.]

Gastemans, Émile. Flemish Sch. *b* Borgerhout (Antwerp) 1883. *Landscapes, figures (many painted in Spain and Morocco)* Represented ANTWERP *Panorama of Avila, Spanish figure.* [Fl. 17.]

Geedts, Josse Pierre. Flemish Sch. *b* Louvain 1770 *d* Louvain 1834. *Religious subjects and 'history'.* Pupil of W. J. Herreyns in Antwerp Acad.; Professor Louvain Acad. 1800-33. Recorded works include *The Archbishop of Cologne handing a miraculous host to the Prior of the Augustine Monastery* painted for Louvain S. Jacques 1824. [Fl. 88, Fl. 451, Fl. 269, Fl. 126.]

Geedts Pierre Paul. Flemish Sch. *b* son of J. P. G., Louvain 1793 *d* Louvain 1856. *Portraits and religious subjects; also worked as sculptor.* Pupil and assistant of his father. [Fl. 88, Fl. 451, Fl. 269.]

Geefs, Fanny née Corr. Flemish Sch. *b* of Irish origin, Brussels 1807 (not 1814) *d* Schaerbeek nr. Brussels 1883. *Religious subjects, genre, portraits.* Pupil of F. Navez. Married sculptor Willem G. 1836. Exhibited London R.A. *Portraits* 1847, *The Outcast* 1849; also exhibited Brussels, Paris and Amsterdam. BRUSSELS Hôp. S. Jean has *Virgin of Misericord.* Other examples in Belgian Royal collection. [Fl. 451, Fl. 481, Fl. 781.]

Geeraerts, Jan. Flemish Sch. *b* Antwerp 1818 *d* Antwerp 1890. *Architectural views, genre.* Represented ANTWERP *Antwerp S. Paulus church, Wedding chamber in Antwerp Town Hall* (w.). [Fl. 17.]

Geeraerts, Jasper, see **Gerardi.**

Geeraerts (or **Gheeraerts,** known in England as **Gerrard** or **Garret**), **Marcus the elder.** Flemish Sch. *b* son of an artist Egbert G., Bruges *c.* 1520 *d* London (?) before 1604. *Religious subjects, architectural and ornamental work, topographic and illustrative drawings with animals and birds, and landscapes into which (Van Mander (1604) relates) 'he introduced a little figure of a woman, squatting on a small bridge, passing water';* also *active as engraver and designer for glass painting.* Pupil of his father; Master Bruges Guild 1558; worked for Bruges churches 1561-5; came England (*cf.* S. v. d. Meulen) having escaped from Alva's persecutions of the Protestants (*cf.* A. de Weerdt) 1568; married into artist family de Critz 1571; baptised children (one of whom Sara married the miniature painter Isaac Oliver) 1573-6; went Antwerp where mentioned in Antwerp Guild records 1577 and 1585-6. Not mentioned in England after 1576. **Documented Examples:** BRUGES Notre Dame: Completion of *Passion Altarpiece* begun by B. van Orley *q.v., Decorative works on tombs of Charles the Bold and Mary of Burgundy* (railings and other furnishings and coverings for silver images) 1561; Archives: Drawings for a *Plan of Bruges* 1562. Engravings record drawings of bears (1559), *Illustrations to Aesop's Fables* 1567 and drawings of birds, butterflies and other animals; *The Labours of Hercules* and religious subjects; *Procession of the Sovereign and Knights of the Garter at the Feast of St. George c.* 1576 and ornaments for goldsmiths. London N.P.G. and other galleries have portraits presumed by some his work (*cf.* M. G. the younger). [Fl. 559, Fl. 857, Fl. 758, Fl. 798, Fl. 899.]

Geeraerts (or **Gheeraerts,** known in England as **Gerrard** or **Garret**), **Marcus the younger.** Flemish Sch. *b* son of M. G. the elder, Bruges 1561 *d* London 1635. *Portraits.* Brought England (*cf.* S. v. d. Meulen) by his father 1568; pupil of L. de Heere before 1577; later of Anglo-Dutch painter Jan de Critz; married Magdalena de Critz 1590. Court painter from *c.* 1611. Called 'Her Majestie's painter' 1617 and picture drawer to James I 1618. Listed among notable painters in England by F. Meres (Wit's Commonwealth) 1598. **Signed Examples:** OXFORD Bodleian *William Camden, Headmaster of Westminster Sch.* ('Marcus Gheeraedts'), *Sir Henry Savile* 'Marcus Garret' 1621 (signature no longer visible) presented to Lady Savile 1622; Trinity College *William Pope* ('Marcus Gherae Brugensis' on back). English private collections have *Elizabeth, Lady Russell* and *Mrs. Anne Hoskins* 1629. **Monogrammed Example:** OTTERLO Kröller Muller Mus. *Head and shoulders of a dead man* (M. G. F. 1607). An English private collection has an undated full length *Queen Elizabeth* with the same monogram. A *Self portrait* 1627 is recorded by W. Hollar's engraving 1644 which is the source for dates of birth and death. Paintings presumed by some his work include London N.P.G.: *Queen Elizabeth at Ditchley* (*cf.* London Queen Elizabeth at Ditchley Painter), Hampton Ct. Royal Coll. *Arabella Stuart* (?) *in a Persian Dress* (*cf.* Hampton Court Lady in Persian Dress Painter). [Fl. 857, Fl. 39, Fl. 758, Fl. 899, Fl. 28, Fl. 744.]

*****Geeraerts, Marten Joseph** (known as **Gerard of Antwerp**). Flemish Sch. *b* son of jeweller, Antwerp *c.* 1707 *d* Antwerp 1791. *Allegorical and religious subjects many in grisaille imitating stone and wood reliefs* (*cf.* F. Eisen). Pupil of A. Godyn 1723-4; in Antwerp Guild 1731; teacher without fee in Antwerp Acad. to forward interests of that institution (*cf.* P. Snyers) from 1741; was visited in his studio by Charles of Lorraine, governor general of Austrian Netherlands 1759. H. Gillis, J. Gillis, P. de Grée, F. J. Lonsing and P. J. Sauvage were among his pupils. **Signed Examples:** VIENNA Liecht. *Children and Amorini gathering fruit* (grisaille) 1752, *Allegory of Peace* 1753. **Documented Examples:** ANTWERP *Allegory of the Fine Arts* (grisaille) 1760. BRUSSELS *Seven scenes from the Old and New Testaments* (grisailles from Afflighem Abbey where seen by Descamps 1769). THE HAGUE *Autumn* (grisaille) and VIENNA K. (*cf.* B. Beschey). [Fl. 216, Fl. 451, Fl. 107.]

*****Geertgen tot Sint Jans** (**Geeraert** or **Gerrit van Haarlem** or **van Leyden**). Flemish (Dutch) Sch. 15th cent. *b* Leyden date unknown *d* aged about twenty-eight, Haarlem (?) *c.* 1495 (?). *Religious subjects.* Pupil of A. van Ouwater; worked for Brethren of S. John Haarlem (whence his name) but was not a member of the Order. **Signed Examples:** None. **Documented Examples:** VIENNA K. *Lamentation over the Dead Christ* and *Julian the Apostate burning the bones of S. John the Baptist with Members of the Order of S. John saving some of the bones from destruction,* originally back and front of right wing of *Crucifixion* triptych in monastery of S. John, described by Van Mander (1604) as dismembered and partly destroyed 'in the siege or by iconoclasts', given by Dutch to Charles I of England 1635, sold under Commonwealth 1649, and acquired by the Hapsburgs. HAARLEM Groote Kerk *View of the Groote Kerk* is presumed identical with a picture recorded by Van Mander. Pictures presumed by some his work are in London N.G. (*cf* London *Nativity by Night* Painter) and other museums. [Fl. 559, Fl. 316, Fl. 814, Fl. 421, Fl. 530.]

Geets, Willem. Flemish Sch. *b* Malines 1838 *d* Malines 1919. *Costume history, genre; also tapestry designs.* Pupil in Antwerp Acad. and of N. de Keyser; director Malines Acad. Represented in ANTWERP *Joanna the Mad* (*cf.* L. Gallait) 1876. BRUSSELS Town Hall *Tapestries with portraits of contemporaries in Renaissance costumes.* BIRMINGHAM *The Protestant Johanna van Santhoven buried alive* 1883. LIVERPOOL Walker *Awaiting an audience* LOUVAIN. [Fl. 17, Fl. Bib. 19th cent.]

Geirnaert, Joseph Lodewyck. Flemish Sch. *b* Eecloo 1791 *d* Ghent 1859. *Religious subjects, costume history, genre.*

Pupil in Antwerp of W. Herreyns and in Ghent of J. Paelinck. In The Hague 1830-6; professor in Ghent Acad. 1836. Represented, in BARNARD CASTLE Bowes *Phaedra and Hippolytus* 1819. COURTRAI, GHENT Mus. and S. Nichole, HAARLEM *The Doctor's Visit.* MALINES *The Schoolmaster* (*cf.* A. C. Engel).

[Fl. 451, Fl. 612, Fl. 88, Fl. 126, Fl. 798.]

Geldersman, Vincent. Flemish Sch. *b* Malines (?) *c.* 1515 (?) *d* place and date unknown. *Religious and mythological subjects with nudes* (*cf.* R. Aertsz). Worked Malines. Van Mander (1604) records: 'He painted a *Leda* a half length (*cf.* A. Francken the elder), with two eggs, a *Susanna* (*cf.* G. Geldorp), a *Cleopatra with the asp*; many copies were made of his pictures. A *Descent from the Cross* was in the Ridders Chapel of the S. Rombout church, in which "the Magdalene could be seen washing the feet of Our Lord amidst a crowd"' (*cf.* V. Sellaer). [Fl. 559, Fl. 613.]

*Geldorp, Gortzius. Flemish Sch. *b* Louvain 1553 *d* Cologne *c.* 1616. *Portraits, biblical subjects, nudes.* Pupil in Antwerp of F. Francken the elder from 1570 and of F. Pourbus the elder. Painter to Carlo d'Aragona, Duke of Terranova whom he accompanied to the Peace negotiations between the Walloon provinces and Spain at Cologne 1579; settled Cologne (*cf.* F. Hogenberg). **Signed Example:** BUDAPEST *Man's portrait* 1605. **Monogrammed Examples:** AMSTERDAM *Lucretia Pellicorne* (1608), *Hortensia del Prado* (two 1596 and 1599), *Jean Fourmenois 1590*, *Jeremias Boudinois* 1610, *Lucretia del Prado* 1610, *Catherina Fourmenois* 1604, *Her sister aged 6* 1606. COLOGNE, MILAN (Brera), LENINGRAD *Lucretia* (*cf.* J. S. v. Hemessen and J. Gossaert), TURIN and other galleries. Van Mander (1604) records a *Susanna* (*cf.* V. Geldersman) owned by the banker E. Jabach and a *Diana* (both engraved) and an *Esther and Ahasuerus* (*cf.* A. Claeissins). Religious subjects are also recorded by engravings. A nude *Magdalene* and a *Venus* are recorded by 17th cent. Antwerp inventories.

[Fl. 559, Fl. 88, Fl. 892, Fl. 213.]

Geldorp, Jorge (George). Flemish Sch. *b* son of Gortzius Geldorp (?), Cologne (?) after 1580 *d* London after 1660. *Portraits, occasional 'history' and copies after Van Dyck and others.* Master Antwerp Guild 1610; member of Antwerp chamber of Rhetoricians 'de Violiere' 1620; came London after 1623 (*cf.* C. de Neve); was patronized by Charles I and made a curator of Royal Collection; had large house and garden in Drury Lane; was 'mighty great with people of quality in his time' and 'used to entertain Ladies and Gentlemen with wine and hams and other curious eatables and carried on intreagues between them'; Van Dyck lived in his house on his second visit to London (after G's discovery that a painting offered to Charles I by his Brussels representative Sir B. Gerbier as by Van D. was a copy) 1632; commissioned by Cologne banker and patron Jabach to negotiate with Rubens for latter's *Martyrdom of S. Peter* (now Cologne SS. Peter and Paul) 1637; received P. Lely in his house when he first came to England 1641; at revolution stored some of King's pictures in his house. Portraits of *James Stuart, Duke of Richmond and Lennox* and *Robert Bertie, Earl of Lindsay* are recorded by engravings.

[Fl. 753, Fl. 826, Fl. 856, Fl. 223.]

Geldorp, Melchior, Flemish Sch. *Op.* 1609-37. *Portraits and religious subjects.* Active in Cologne. [Fl. 577, Fl. 892.]

Gelissen, Maximilian Lambert. Flemish Sch. *b* Brussels 1786 *d* Brussels 1867. *Landscapes.* Pupil of H. van Assche. Exhibited London British Institution 1833. **Documented Example:** GHENT *Sunset over a watermill* for which he received a prize 1820. [Fl. 451, Fl. 612, Fl. 360, Fl. 363, Fl. 892.]

Génisson, Jules Victor. Flemish Sch. *b* St. Omer 1805 *d* Bruges 1860. *Church interiors with figures, portraits.* Pupil Antwerp Acad. of M. and P. van Brée; travelled France, England, Italy and Germany 1829-34. Lived for some years in Louvain from 1835. Represented in ANTWERP *Church interior.* BRUSSELS *Archduke Albert and Archduchess Isabella visiting Tournai Cathedral in 1600.* COURTRAI *Interior of Brussels S. Gudule* 1835. DUBLIN *Interior of Antwerp S. Jacques* 1836. LIÈGE, MONTREAL.

[Fl. 451, Fl. 481, Fl. 360, Fl. 363, Fl. 126, Fl. 17, Fl. 75.]

*Genoels, Abraham (nicknamed Archimedes in Rome Flemish colony). Flemish Sch. *b* son of starch manufacturer, Antwerp 1640 *d* Antwerp 1723. *Picturesque landscapes (often with mythological figures); also worked as tapestry designer and engraver.* Pupil as a boy of J. Backereel and later for architectural drawing of N. M. Fierlants. Went Paris (*cf.* C. E. Biset) 1659; drew landscapes in tapestry cartoons commissioned from French painter G. de Seve by Marquis Louvois and Prince de Condé; and assisted French painter C. Le Brun in same way for 'Alexander' Gobelin tapestries for Louis XIV (*cf.* A. Baudewyns); member of French Acad. roy. (*cf.* P. Mol) 1665; visited Hainault with Baudewyns to make drawings of Château Mariemont commissioned by Louis XIV 1669; in Antwerp where Master in Guild by 1672; worked for Count de Monterey (Governor General 1670-4); went via Venice and Bologna to Rome (*cf.* J. Miel) where worked for Cardinal Rospigliosi and made drawings of ruins and Campagna landscapes (*cf.* A. Goubau) 1674-82; returned Antwerp via Paris 1682. His pupils included J. B. (Francisque) Millet in Paris and J. I. de Roore in Antwerp. **Signed Example:** AMSTERDAM Rijks. *Diana hunting.* **Documented Examples:** ANTWERP *Landscape with Minerva and the Muses* given by him to Antwerp Academy (*cf.* J. Jordaens). MONTPELLIER *Classical landscape* (engraved by himself).

[Fl. 425, Fl. 215, Fl. 892.]

Gentile, Luigi, see **Cousin.**

Gérard, Joseph. Flemish Sch. *b* Ghent 1821 *d* Brussels 1895. *Costume history, genre; also worked as engraver.* Assisted J. F. Portaels in mural paintings 1851; later assistant professor in Brussels Academy. [Fl. 892.]

Gérard, Théodore. Flemish Sch. *b* Ghent 1829 *d* Laeken, nr. Brussels 1902. *Decorative compositions; later genre.* Visited Germany; exhibited Brussels, Vienna, London and Philadelphia. Represented in ANTWERP *Guests at the Wedding Ball.* BRUSSELS *Swabian Peasants' wedding.* SYDNEY (N.S.W.) *Share and share alike.* Others in Courtrai, Ghent and Hull.

[Fl. 892, Fl. 17, Fl. Bib. 19th cent.]

Gérard van Gent, see **Meire.**

Gerardi (or Geerardi or Geeraerts), Jasper. Flemish Sch. *b* Antwerp (?) before 1620 *d* Amsterdam (?) *c.* 1654 (?). *Still life (tables with food, shell fish, fruit and vessels).* In Antwerp Guild 1634; Master 1644 (*cf.* C. Mahu). [Fl. 714, Fl. 798.]

Gerards, M., see **Geeraerts.**

Gerbo, Louis. Flemish Sch. *b* Bruges 1761 *d* Bruges 1818. *Religious and decorative subjects, portraits.* Professor in Bruges Acad.; visited Paris during the Empire (*cf.* A. Ansiaux, A. v. d. Berghe, J. B. Berré, M. I. v. Brée, J. F. v. Dael, J. L. Demarne, J. F. Ducq, J. F. Eliaerts, P. v. Huffel, F. J. Kinson, L. Moons, J. D. Odevaere, B. P. Ommeganck, A. F., P. J. and H. J. Redouté, M. Verstappen). **Documented Example:** GHENT S. Jacques *The Holy Family* 1810. Portraits of *The Empress Josephine* and *The Empress Marie Louise* are recorded by engravings. [Fl. 451, Fl. 798.]

Geudens, Albert. Flemish Sch. *b* Malines 1869. *Old town views, churches, cloisters, interiors, portraits and child studies.* Represented in ANTWERP *The Hall.* [Fl. 17.]

Geyn, J. de, see Gheyn.

Ghaeraedts, M., see Geeraerts.

*****Gheringh** (or **Gerinck**), **Anton Günther** (not Jan). Flemish Sch. *b* place and date unknown *d* Antwerp 1668. *Church interiors and other architectural subjects* (*cf.* H. van Steenwyck the younger). Master Antwerp Guild 1662; friend of P. Gysels; died in extreme poverty. **Signed Examples:** DRESDEN *Interior of Antwerp Jesuit Church* 1664 (church with decorations by Rubens and others burnt down 1718, *cf.* W. v. Ehrenberg, J. Peeters, S. Vrancx also C. Schut the elder). MUNICH A.P. *Same subject* 1663. VIENNA K. *Same subject* 1665; Acad. *Interior of a church* 1663. [Fl. 107, Fl. 892.]

Ghestele (**Gestele**), **Marc van.** Flemish Sch. *b* Ghent (?) before 1415 *d* after 1445. Master in Ghent Guild 1429; contracted to paint altarpieces for Ruyslede church 1430, and for Courtrai S. Martin 1445. (*Cf.* J. van Coudenberghe). [Fl. 135.]

Gheyn (or **Gain**), **Jacob Jansz de the elder.** Flemish Sch. *b* on a ship in Zuiderzee *c.* 1532 *d* Utrecht (?) 1582. *Miniatures, portraits, drawings for engravings; but chiefly active as glass-painter* (*cf.* J. de Gheyn the younger and J. Ramey). In Antwerp Guild 1558; made windows for Antwerp and Amsterdam churches; and for the Italian 'nation'; in Utrecht 1580. A *Demolition of the Spanish Citadel in Antwerp 1577* (signed Jac de Gain inv. et fec) is recorded by an engraving (*cf.* Worcester Destruction of Citadel painter). [Fl. 559, Fl. 892.]

*****Gheyn, Jacques de the younger.** Flemish Sch. *b* son of Jacob Janz de G., Antwerp 1565 *d* The Hague 1629. *Religious subjects, 'history', flowerpieces, horses; also active as engraver.* Began as a glass-painter, then pupil of Dutch engraver H. Goltzius in Haarlem 1585-7; in Amsterdam 1592; Master there and acted in Rhetoricians' play in honour of Prince Maurice (*cf.* D. v. d. Queborne) 1594; married into The Hague aristocracy 1595; in Leyden 1596; in The Hague from 1598; commissioned to paint flowerpiece to be given to Marie de Médicis 1606; designed gardens for palaces in The Hague; was friend of Dutch poet C. Huygens who ranked him as flower painter above J. (Velvet) Bruegel and A. Bosschaert *q.v*; with his son (engraver of same name) visited London (*cf.* P. V. Somer and C. de Neve) 1622. **Signed Examples:** AMSTERDAM Rijks. *A white Spanish warhorse* (the horse was captured from Archduke Albert at Battle of Nieuport (1600) by Prince Louis of Nassau who gave it to Prince Maurice; the picture is inscribed: 'His Spanish fatherland gave him to the Austrian and Flanders gave him to the victorious Maurice') 1603, *Venus and Amor.* THE HAGUE (Gemeente) *Flower piece* 1612. **Monogrammed Example:** ORLÉANS *Dead swan.* **Documented Example:** BRUGES Seminar *S. Helena and the True Cross* 1611 (from Dominican church where Deschamps saw it 1768). Van Mander (1604) records a flowerpiece and a book illuminated with animals both bought by the Emperor Rudolf II (*cf.* P. Stevens and B. Spranger), a *Sleeping Venus with Cupid and approaching satyrs* and a *Skull,* also a large window in Amsterdam Oude Kerk (*cf.* P. Aertsen). [Fl. 559, Fl. 216, Fl. 892, Fl. 798, Fl. 743, Fl. 146.]

Gheysels, P., see Gyse s.

Ghindermollen (**Ghindermeulen**), **P. V.** Presumed Flemish Sch. 17th cent. **Signed Example:** LONDON Bridgewater House (185) *Village wedding.* The signature 'P. V. Ghindermeulen' is painted over that of Matthys van Helmont (*q.v.*). [Fl. 527.]

Ghistelles Master, see New York Godelieve Legend Painter.

Ghuens, Jan the elder. Flemish Sch. *b* Malines before 1512 *d* after 1557. *Religious subjects.* A *Crucifixion* painted 1528 for Malines Town Hall is recorded. [Fl. 613.]

Ghuens (**Gheens**), **Jan the younger** called **Prins.** Flemish Sch. *b* son of Jan G. the elder, Malines 1557 *d* after 1618. *Topographical views, military pieces, decorative painting; picture restoration.* Witness in a trial for witchcraft 1601. **Documented Example:** MALINES Mus. *Bird's-eye view of Lierre: the 1595 relief of Lierre by Malines troops* 1596. His son Boudewyn specialised in the painting of sundials. [Fl. 613.]

Gietleughen (or **Gulleghem**), **Joos van.** Flemish Sch. 16th cent. Van Mander (1604) records him as a painter from Courtrai employed by Hubert Goltzius *q.v.* on the coloured wood blocks for his 'Portrait medals of the Roman Emperors' published 1557; his name ('Stream of lies') Van Mander adds, belied his character, as he was skilled and learned. [Fl. 559, Fl. 892.]

*****Giles Master.** Presumed Flemish or French Sch. 15th-16th cent. Name for painter of LONDON N.G. (1419) *S. Giles and the hind* (reverse: *Bishop* in grisaille). London N.G. (*cf.* London S. Giles Mass Painter) and other museums have pictures presumed by some his work. [Fl. 778, Fl. 530, Fl. 710, Fl. 798.]

Gillemans, Jan Pauwel the elder. Flemish Sch. *b* son of a gold beater, Antwerp 1618 *d* Antwerp *c.* 1675. *Still life, mainly shell fish, fruit and flowers* (*cf.* T. Aenvanck); *also portraits.* Master Antwerp Guild 1647; J. F. van Son was his pupil. **Signed Examples:** ANGERS, BRUSSELS *Oysters and fruit* 1662. INNSBRUCK, LILLE, LONDON V. and A. *Fruit and flowers round a landscape.* ROTTERDAM, SCHWERIN, VALENCIENNES. [Fl. 107, Fl. 892.]

Gillemans, Jan Pauwel the younger. Flemish Sch. *b* son of Jan Pauwel G. the elder, Antwerp 1651 *d* drowned in canal, Amsterdam 1704. *Fruit and flowers* (*cf.* T. Aenvanck, A. v. Utrecht and J. v. d. Borght); *also garlands and still life in works by other painters including J. I. de Roore and P. Rysbraeck.* Pupil of J. van Son; Master Antwerp Guild 1674; recorded in Middelburg 1675 and 1702. G. P. Verbruggen the younger was his friend. **Signed Examples:** BAMBERG, BARNARD CASTLE *Fruit and vegetables in architectural setting* (1674). FREDENSBORG Castle *Garland round portrait of Christian V.* RAUDNITZ (Lobkowitz) has *Fruit and flowers* in four landscapes by P. Rysbraeck *s* by both artists. [Fl. 878, Fl. 892.]

Gillemans, Peter Mathys. Flemish Sch. *b* presumed son of Jan Pauwel G. the elder, Antwerp date unknown *d* Antwerp 1692. *Fruit and flowers* (*cf.* T. Aenvanck). Master Antwerp Guild 1673. [Fl. 717.]

Gillis, Herman (**Armand**). Flemish Sch. *b* Antwerp 1733 *d* place unknown, after 1777. *Religious subjects, 'history', portraits.* Pupil of M. J. Geeraerts; in Antwerp Guild from 1751; in Vienna 1762; back in Antwerp by 1768; also worked in Louvain and Malines. Recorded works include *Scenes from the Legend of the Holy Blood* for church at Hoogstraeten (near Antwerp), *General Loudon* (Fieldmarshal in Seven Years War) painted Vienna 1762 (engraved). A *Portrait of the Emperor Joseph II* 1777 (*cf.* G. de Pélichy) is recorded painted for Louvain Town Hall (*cf.* W. J. Herreyns and P. J. Lion). [Fl. 768, Fl. 613, Fl. 798.]

Gillis, Josephus. Flemish Sch. Working Antwerp second half 18th cent. '*History*'; *also worked as sculptor*. Apprenticed to painter M. J. Geeraerts 1757. [Fl. 892.]

Gillon, J. F., see Legillon.

Gilson, Jean Henri (known as Brother Abraham d'Orval). Flemish Sch. *b* Habay-la-Vieille (nr. Arlon) 1741 *d* Florenville 1809. *Religious subjects, portraits*. Lived as a hermit in the Ardennes till the hermits were suppressed by the Emperor Joseph II; became lay brother in Orval Abbey; travelled France, Italy and Germany; was patronised by Archduchess Maria Christina, sister of Joseph II and Governor of Netherlands (*cf.* P. Faes) 1787; settled Florenville. An *Adam and Eve lamenting Abel* which won a prize in Düsseldorf Academy is recorded. His many paintings for Orval Abbey were destroyed by fire in 1793. [Fl. 88, Fl. 126, Fl. 798.]

Gilsoul, Victor Olivier. Flemish Sch. *b* Brussels 1867 *d* St. Lambrechts-Woluwe 1939. *Landscapes, coast scenes, town pieces*. Pupil of A. Courtens and L. Artan. Member of Brussels group Voorwaerts (*cf.* F. J. Laermans); visited Holland; member Paris Salon de la Nationale; lived France 1914-24; Professor Antwerp Higher Inst. 1924-30; chevalier of the Order of Leopold; painted panels for King of the Belgians' yacht. Represented in ANTWERP *Showery weather at Nieuport*. BARCELONA, BRUGES *The Porte des Maréchaux at Bruges*. BRUSSELS Mus. and Town Hall and BELGIAN Royal Coll. *Harbour scene near Nieuport*. His *Pond in Brabant* 1899 was acquired by the French State. [Fl. 573, Fl. Bib. 19th cent.]

Gilsoul-Hoppe, Mme. Ketty. Flemish Sch. *b* Düsseldorf 1868. *Flowers and landscapes* (*gouache o. and w.*). Pupil in Brussels of J. Portaels. Married V. O. Gilsoul 1894. Represented in BRUSSELS *Flower piece* (*w.*). [Fl. 775.]

Gingelen, Jacques van. Flemish Sch. *b* Borgerhout (nr. Antwerp) 1810. *Landscapes* (*some with figures in renaissance costume*), *marines, town views, animals; also worked as engraver and lithographer*. Pupil of J. J. Moerenhout in Antwerp; also studied Paris; visited Holland and England. [Fl. 451, Fl. 892.]

Gioncoy, see Joncquoy.

Gisler, Édouard. Flemish Sch. *b* Tournai (?) before 1820. *Religious subjects and costume history, portraits*. [Fl. 451, Fl. 892.]

Gisler, Lucien. Flemish Sch. *b* Tournai 1810. *Religious subjects*. Exhibited Paris Salon 1837 and 1841-4. [Fl. 66.]

Giusto da Guanto, see Justus.

*****Glasgow Saint and Donor Painter.** Presumed Flemish or French Sch. 15th-16th cent. Name for painter of GLASGOW Mus. (203) *Saint and donor*. Presumed by some identical with the presumed French Moulins Master (painter of Moulins Cathedral Triptych *Virgin in Glory* with *Pierre de Bourbon* and *Anne de Beaujeu* as adorants on wings). Presumed by others identical with H. v. d. Goes or H. Memlinc or J. Gossaert or the French painter J. Fouquet. [Fl. 342, Fl. 710.]

*****Glimes, P. de.** Flemish Sch. *b* before 1770 *d* after 1800. *Portraits and genre figures*. Worked in Brussels *c.* 1800; may have visited England before 1790. **Signed Examples:** CAMBRIDGE Fitzw. *A young man in a hat* 1793. GHENT *Four bathing shepherdesses*. A three-quarter length portrait *General Eliott* (*Lord Heathfield of Gibraltar*) is recorded by a

stipple engraving *c.* 1787; a portrait *Henri van der Noot* was also engraved. [Fl. 892, Fl. 612, Fl. 798.]

Godding, Émile Hendrik Karel. Flemish Sch. *b* Bruges 1841 *d* Antwerp 1898. *Genre*. Represented in ANTWERP *The Fluteplayer*. [Fl. 17.]

Goddyn (or Godyn), Pieter Matthias. Flemish Sch. *b* son of master mason, Bruges 1752 *d* Bruges 1811. '*History*' *and portraits*. Pupil in Bruges Acad.; to Paris 1772; then Italy; won prize in Parma competition 1782; returned Bruges where, to celebrate prizewinning, festive entry was staged with pealing church bells and cavalcade to Town Hall (*cf.* A. v. d. Berghe, J. D. Odevaere, P. J. Verhaghen, J. B. Suvée) 1784. **Documented Examples:** BRUGES Acad. *Allegories of Geometry and Mathematics* (presented to Acad. 1784). PARMA *Sinon advising Priam to admit the Wooden Horse* (prize picture 1782). [Fl. 451, Fl. 892.]

Godevaerts, A., see Govaerts.

Godyn, Abraham. Flemish Sch. *b* Antwerp (?) before 1663 *d* Antwerp after 1724. '*History*' *and decorative paintings*. Visited Italy; then worked Prague, where decorated Troja Castle, 1687-94; returned Antwerp and Master in Guild there 1711; member of Antwerp Romanists. M. J. Geeraerts was among his pupils. **Signed Example:** PRAGUE Rudolfinum *Jael and Sisera*. [Fl. 231, Fl. 107, Fl. 892.]

Godyn, Izaak. Flemish Sch. *b* Antwerp (?) before 1668. '*History*' *and decorative paintings*. Presumed brother of A. G. with whom he worked in Prague 1688-94. [Fl. 231.]

Godyn, P. M., see Goddyn.

Goebouw, A., see Goubau.

Goeimare, Joos. Flemish Sch. *b* Courtrai 1575 *d* Amsterdam (?) 1610. *Landscapes with figures and animals; interiors with religious subjects*. Married in Amsterdam into the Savery family (*cf.* J. Savery the elder) 1600. A *Christ in the house of Mary and Martha* with much still life (*cf.* A. Grimmer and H. van Steenwyck the younger), and an *Orpheus charming the animals* (*cf.* L. v. d. Borcht) are recorded by engravings. [Fl. 892, Fl. 798.]

Goes, Hugo van der. Flemish Sch. *b* Ghent (?) date unknown *d* insane, Rouge-Cloître monastery, nr. Brussels 1482. Stated by Van Mander (1604) to have been a pupil of J. van Eyck. Recorded as Master in Ghent Guild (sponsored by J. v. Wassenhove) 1467; painted ceremonial decorations in Ghent 1467-8; in Bruges working on decorations for marriage of Charles the Bold and Margaret of York (*cf.* P. Coustain, J. Daret, D. de Rycke, V. v. d. Stoct) 1468; returned Ghent and designed for ceremonies (including translation of the body of Philip the Good (*d* 1467) to Dijon) 1468-74; Dean of Ghent Guild 1473-4 and 1475; joined his brother in Rouge-Cloître (Roodendale) Augustinian monastery 1475; enjoyed special privileges in monastery where the Archduke Maximilian (later Emperor) was among his visitors; went Louvain to value pictures by D. Bouts *c.* 1478 and was then called 'most famous' and 'a native of Ghent'; went Cologne and was seized with madness on return journey *c.* 1481; his Prior met him at Brussels and tried to cure him with music; returned to monastery where was intermittently insane till his death. Dürer saw (1521) pictures by 'Meister Hugo' and refers to him and 'Rüdiger' (presumed R. v. d. Weyden) as 'both great masters'. **Signed Examples:** None. **Documented Examples:** None. Van Mander records a *Virgin and Child* (with little plants and stones on the ground), a *Legend of S. Catherine*, a *Meeting of David and Abigail* and a *Chris Crucified between the Thieves* (for Bruges S. Jacques). Florence Uffizi (*cf.* Hugo of Antwerp),[1] Vienna K. (*cf.* Vienna Cruciform Lamentation Painter and Vienna Adam and Eve Painter) and other museums have pictures presumed by some his work.

[Fl. 243, Fl. 559, Fl. 862, Fl. 179, Fl. 892, Fl. 219, Fl. 700, Fl. 316, Fl. 143.]

Goetkint (or **Goetkindt), Peter.** Flemish Sch. *b* Antwerp (?) *c.* 1540 *d* Antwerp 1583. *Landscapes with figures; also active as art dealer.* Pupil (and later son-in-law) of A. van Palerme (*cf.* Jacques de Backer and G. Congnet) 1555; Master Antwerp Guild 1561. Jan (Velvet) Brueghel was his pupil (*cf.* Marie Bessemers). His son Peter G. the younger was a painter; his son Antoon G. became a successful dealer in Paris where he changed his name to Bonenfant; his daughter Sara married A. Janssens *q.v.* (*Cf.* also Antwerp Destruction of Citadel Painter.) [Fl. 559, Fl. 214.]

Gogo, Félix. Flemish Sch. *b* Antwerp 1872. *Interiors, genre, religious subjects, landscapes, town views, still life.* Pupil in Antwerp Higher Institute. Director Termonde Acad.; teacher in Antwerp Acad. Represented in ANTWERP *Virgin and Child, Interior, Prayer.* [Fl. 17.]

Goltzius, Hubert. Flemish (Dutch) Sch. *b* son of a German painter, Venloo 1526 *d* Bruges 1583. *Pageant designs and portraits; but chiefly active as numismatist and archaeological writer, engraver and publisher.* Pupil in Liège of Lambert Lombard; then worked Antwerp where designed some of the pageantry for the Hanseatic League's Golden Fleece Pageant 1555; established his own printing press at Bruges 1558; visited Germany, France, Italy and Switzerland 1558-60; made an honorary citizen of Rome 'for his excellence and learning' 1567; A. Mor painted his portrait (now Brussels Mus.) in return for the gift of one of his books (*cf.* J. Gietleughen) 1576. Van Mander (1604) records a portrait *Brother Cornelis* presumed by some the *Cornelis Adriensen* 1573 now in Brussels Mus. [Fl. 559, Fl. 892, Fl. 798.]

Goovaerts, Abraham, see **Govaerts.**

*Goovaerts (or **Govaerts), Hendrick.** Flemish Sch. *b* Malines 1669 *d* Antwerp 1720. *Portraits, contemporary genre and 'history'.* Travelled Central Europe *c.* 1690-9; Master Antwerp Guild 1700. **Signed Examples:** ANTWERP *The Junior Crossbowmen's Guild inaugurating portrait of their Captain Jan Carel de Cordes* 1713. BRUSSELS *Carnival in a palace* 1714. BUDAPEST *The studio of a sculptor* (*cf.* D. Ryckaert III). HERMANNSTADT *Sick woman with her family* 1707, *Antony and Cleopatra.* Descamps saw and described (1769) a picture then called *Allegory of the Peace of Utrecht* in the Crossbowmen's Chamber of the Antwerp Town Hall.
[Fl. 216, Fl. 107, Fl. 613, Fl. 892.]

Gorge, Paul. Flemish Sch. *b* Antwerp 1856. *Interiors, landscapes.* Represented ANTWERP *Bakery.* [Fl. 17.]

Gortzius, G., see **Geldorp.**

Gorus, Jacques. Flemish Sch. *b* St. Gilles (East Flanders) 1901. *Portraits, figures, landscapes, town views, still life.* Pupil in Ghent Acad. of J. v. Delvin and in Antwerp Higher Institute of I. Opsomer. Teacher in Antwerp Acad. Represented in ANTWERP *Winter landscape.* [Fl. 17.]

*Gossaert (**Gossart), Jan** called **Mabuse** (Malbodius). Flemish Sch. *b* Slot Duurstede near Utrecht or Maubeuge in Hainault *c.* 1480 *d* Antwerp after *c.* 1534. *Religious subjects, 'history', portraits.* Referred to by Guicciardini (*c.* 1567) as Giovanni di Maubuge 'the first Netherlander to bring from Italy the art of painting history and poesy with nude figures'. Presumed by some the 'Jennyn van Hennegouwe' (Hainault) Master in

Antwerp 1503; as 'J. Cossardum Malbodium' entered service of Philip, Bastard of Burgundy (Admiral and Governor of Gelderland and Zutphen); went with his patron to Italy on mission from Margaret of Austria, Governor of the Netherlands to Pope Julius II 1508; drew antiquities in Rome; returned by 1510; worked mainly Middelburg where lived in Philip's palace for some years; designed car for mourning ceremonies in Brussels for Ferdinand of Spain, and was paid for two pictures of Leonore (sister of Charles V and wife of Manoel the Fortunate of Portugal and later of François I) 1516; went Utrecht when Philip was made Bishop of Utrecht 1517; Van Mander (1604) records that J. van Scorel was then his pupil; restored pictures for Margaret of Austria (*cf.* J. Schooff) 1523; after Philip's death (1524) entered service of his nephew Adolph of Veere, Lord of Beveren in Middelburg where he was visited by L. van Leyden with whom he made a tour (*cf.* L. van L.) *c.* 1527; L. Lombard was also his friend; designed monument for Isabella of Burgundy (*cf.* J. Horenbout) Queen of Christian II, refugee king of Denmark (guest of Adolph of Veere 1523) 1528 (*cf.* P. Tubach); made his will 1533. **Signed Examples** (all *s* with some form of Malbodius except where otherwise stated). BERLIN K.F. *Neptune and Amphitrite* 1516. LONDON N.G. *Adoration of the Magi s* Ienni Gossart and Iennin Gos. MUNICH A.P. *Danaë* 1527, *Virgin and Child* 1527. MÜNSTER Landesmus. *Virgin and Child.* NEW YORK Met. *Portrait of a man.* PARIS Louvre diptych *Virgin and Child, Jean Carondelet as donor* (*Arms* and *Skull* on reverses) 1517, *Benedictine Monk* 1526. PRAGUE Rudolfinum *S. Luke drawing the Virgin* recorded as by B. van Orley by Van Mander but signature 'Gossa . .' found on cleaning 1836; ordered by Malines Guild for cathedral; removed by Archduke Mathias 1580; returned Malines 1614; given to Prague cathedral by Ferdinand II (the wings are *s* M. Coxie *q.v.*). VENICE Bib. S. Marco 'The Grimani Breviary' has a *S. Catherine disputing s* Gosar Mabus. **Documented Examples:** MADRID Prado *The Virgin of Louvain* (an inscription dated 1588 on reverse states this picture by Johannes Mabeus was saved from the Iconoclasts and given to Philip II by Louvain town (*cf.* J. van Rillaert the younger). LONDON Royal Coll. *Children of Christian II of Denmark, Adam and Eve* (both from Henry VIII's coll.). Van Mander records (1) a *Descent from the Cross* an altar-piece in Middelburg Abbey 'a very large painting which needed extra supports when the wings were opened'; this was seen in December 1520 by Dürer who commented: 'better painted than constructed' ('nit so gut im Hauptstreichen als im Gemäl'): it was destroyed with the church by lightning 1568; (2) another *Descent from the Cross* (a rather large upright picture); (3) a *Lucretia* (*cf.* G. Geldorp); (4) an almost life-size *Adam and Eve*; (5) many fine portraits made in London including in Whitehall 'the heads of two young children of the nobility'. An Antwerp inventory (1574) records a *Mars and Venus* and another of (1585) records a *Story of Hercules s* and dated 1530. Paintings presumed by some his work are in varous museums.
[Fl. 243, Fl. 371, Fl. 559, Fl. 354, Fl. 868, Fl. 892, Fl. 877, Fl. 763, Fl. 316, Fl. 530.]

Goswin, Gérard. Flemish Sch. *b* Liège 1616 *d* Liège 1691. *Flowers* (*cf.* J. B. Crépu) *and tapestry designs.* Pupil of G. Douffet at same time as B. Flémalle *q.v.* Went Rome; then Paris (*cf.* C. E. Biset); member of Paris Acad. Roy. (*cf.* P. Mol) 1648; professor Paris Acad. 1659; returned Liège 1660.
[Fl. 63, Fl. 451, Fl. 409, Fl. 892.]

*Goubau (or **Goebouw** or **Goubay), Antoon.** Flemish Sch. *b* Antwerp 1616 *d* Antwerp 1698. *Picturesque military scenes* (*cf.* L. de Hondt the elder), *occasional religious pieces, but mainly Flemish and Italianate landscapes with genre figures, also tapestry cartoons.* Master Antwerp Guild 1636; visited Italy (*cf.* J. Miel and M. Sweerts); his pupils included J. F. v. Bloemen and the French painter N. de Largillière, *cf.* also

G. de Witte. **Signed Examples:** ANTWERP *Artists of the Flemish colony sketching Roman ruins* (dated 1662 and presented to Antwerp Guild), *Piazza Navona Rome* 1680. BRUNSWICK *Roman ruins with cavaliers, ladies and peasants.* DESSAU *Adoration of the Magi* 1670. DUBLIN *Farmyard with figures.* MEININGEN Schloss *Camp scene* 1639. PRAGUE Rudolfinum *Military scene.* Others in AUGSBURG and CARLSRUHE (1658). **Monogrammed Examples:** ANTWERP S. Jacques *Christ on the Cross* 1657. SCHWERIN *Soldiers playing cards.* G. Coques' *Interior of a gallery* (The Hague Mauritshuis) includes an *Italian landscape* depicted with Goubau's signature. A *Portrait of Jeremias Wildens in a landscape* is recorded with other pictures in the Jeremias Wildens collection 1653 (*cf.* J. Wildens).

[Fl. 86, Fl. 481, Fl. 107, Fl. 213.]

Goubau, Frans. Flemish Sch. *b* Antwerp 1622 *d* Antwerp 1678. *Religious subjects, portraits.* Master Antwerp Guild 1649; married (and was later separated from) a rich widow described by her first husband as a 'duyvel's wyf' 1657; in later years became a collector of wine taxes. **Signed Examples:** ANTWERP Mus. *S. Norbert adoring the Sacrament* 1650; S. Jacques *Entombment* 1655, *The priest F. van den Bossche* 1657. [Fl. 107, Fl. 892.]

Goubau, Laurent (or **Laureys**). Flemish Sch. 17th cent. Pupil of A. Goubau 1651; Master Antwerp Guild 1669. A signed *Girl holding a plate with half-peeled lemon in a window niche* (half length) is recorded. [Fl. 892.]

Gouweloos, Jean. Flemish Sch. *b* Brussels 1868. *Genre, nudes and portraits.* Represented in ANTWERP *Dreaming.* BRUSSELS *The Bath* 1907. LIÈGE *The Child.* [Fl. 17.]

Gouwi, see Gowi, J. P.

*****Govaerts** (or **Goyvaerts,** or **Godevaerts**), **Abraham.** Flemish Sch. *b* Antwerp 1589 (?) *d* Antwerp 1626. *Wooded landscapes (with small religious, mythological or genre figures sometimes by other painters (cf.* G. v. Coninxloo and A. Mirou). Master Antwerp Guild 1607; Dean 1623. **Signed Examples:** ANTWERP *Landscape with Rape of Europa* (1621). AUGSBURG *Sacrifice of Isaac, Landscape with cottage.* BORDEAUX *Diana and her nymphs* 1614. BRUNSWICK *Landscape with the Four Elements as nymphs* 1624. BRUSSELS *The Inn* 1626. GÖTTINGEN *Landscape with deer hunt.* THE HAGUE *Oakwood with gypsies* 1612. MILAN Brera *Wooded landscape with Abraham and Isaac* 1615. DOUAI Mus. has a *s* example with figures by F. Francken II (*cf.* J. v. d. Lanen and H. Jordaens III). **Documented Examples:** BUDAPEST *Landscape with fisherman, Landscape with river.* An Antwerp 1627 Inventory records a *Landscape with the Five Senses* with figures by F. Francken II. A *Five Senses* (signed and dated 1624) is recorded (1926) in a private collection. [Fl. 107, Fl. 892, Fl. 128, Fl. 301, Fl. 213.]

Govaerts, H., see Goovaerts.

*****Govaerts, Jan Baptist.** Flemish Sch. *b* Antwerp (?) 1701 (?) *d* Antwerp (?) 1746. *Kitchen scenes, still life, game pieces* (*cf.* P. Boel and B. de Bridt). Pupil in Antwerp of A. v. Bredael 1713-14; went Mainz where was court painter 1740-5. **Signed Examples:** BALTIMORE (U.S.A.) *Game piece with dead boar in a landscape.* HERMANNSTADT, WÜRZBURG University. [Fl. 612, Fl. 892, Fl. 798.]

*****Gowi** (**Gouwi** or **Gowy**), **Jacob Peter.** Flemish Sch. 17th cent. '*History*'. In Antwerp 1633; Master 1637; painted decorations from Rubens' sketches for Philip IV's hunting lodge La Torre de la Parada from 1636 (*cf.* J. B. Borkens, J. Cossiers, J. Eyck, J. Jordaens, E. Quellinus, J. v. Reyn, F. Snyders, P. Symons, T. v. Thulden, C. de Vos, P. de Vos, T. Wille-

boirts). **Signed Examples:** MADRID Prado *Hippomenes and Atalanta, The fall of Icarus* both from La Torre de la Parada. [Fl. 718, Fl. 296.]

Gowy, L. Presumed Flemish Sch. working 1644-61 (?) *Portraits.* Worked London (*cf.* C. de Neve) where W. Hollar engraved some portraits drawn by him. OXFORD Christ Church has *Thomas Wood* (*s* 'Gowy' and unclearly dated 1661). [Fl. 826, Fl. 892, Fl. 665.]

Graef, Jan de. Flemish Sch. *b* Antwerp 1877. *Landscapes, park scenes, still life.* Teacher in Antwerp Acad. Represented in ANTWERP. [Fl. 17.]

Grée, Pieter Jan Balthasar de. Flemish Sch. *b* Antwerp 1751 *d* Dublin 1789. *Grisaille compositions imitating bas-reliefs, some portraits.* Pupil of M. J. Geeraerts; in Antwerp Guild 1773; agent for Sir Joshua Reynolds in the purchase of Flemish pictures 1785; visited England; introduced by Reynolds to the Duke of Rutland; went Dublin *c.* 1786; employed there by the Lord Lieutenant (First Marquis of Buckingham) and by the Dublin Society which rewarded him with silver palette for a *Ceres and Triptolemus.* His funeral was organised with special pomp by Roman Catholic authorities in Dublin. [Fl. 742, Fl. 451, Fl. 333.]

Greef, Jan de. Flemish Sch. *b* Brussels 1851 *d* Auderghem 1894. *Landscapes (many of Soignes forest cf.* J. d'Arthois), *rural genre, portraits.* Pupil of J. Portaels and A. Verwée. Member of L'Essor group (*cf.* A. Hamesse) and of Les XX (*cf.* J. Ensor); settled in ruined monastery at Auderghem using granary as studio. Represented in ANTWERP *Little girl with sheep in a park, The S. Anna chapel.* BRUSSELS *Pond at Auderghem, Haystacks, Horses ploughing.* [Fl. 57, Fl. Bib. 19th cent.]

Gregorius, Albert Jacob Frans. Flemish Sch. *b* Bruges 1774 *d* Bruges 1853. *Portraits and occasional 'history'.* Pupil Bruges Acad.; went Paris and worked in school of L. David (*cf.* F. J. Navez) 1802; remained Paris where drew and painted portraits and made drawings of Old Masters in the Musée Napoléon for engravers; exhibited Paris Salon 1812-35; then returned Bruges where became Director Acad. **Signed Examples:** BRUGES Acad. sketch for *Prodigal Son* (unsuccessful composition for Prix de Rome 1805). LILLE and VERSAILLES have *Portraits.* Portraits of *Napoleon as Emperor, Louis XVIII, Charles X* and *Louis Philippe* are recorded. [Fl. 451, Fl. 88, Fl. 66, Fl. 73, Fl. 798.]

*****Grenoble Artichoke Painter.** Presumed Flemish Sch. early 17th cent. Name for painter of GRENOBLE Mus. *Still life with artichoke.* Presumed by some identical with Grenoble Strawberry Painter. *q.v.*

*****Grenoble Judith Painter.** Presumed Flemish Sch. 16th cent. Name for painter of GRENOBLE Mus. *Judith with head of Holofernes.* (*Cf.* M. Willems and Ottawa Judith Painter).

*****Grenoble Strawberry Painter.** Presumed Flemish Sch. early 17th cent. Name for painter of GRENOBLE Mus. *Still life with strawberries and flowers.* Presumed by some identical with O. Beet *q.v.* and by others with the French painter Louise Moillon, (*cf.* Grenoble Artichoke Painter).

Greuzen, Charles. Flemish Sch. worked Antwerp *c.* 1750-9. *Landscapes and marines (with blue predominating).* Represented in DIJON *Seaport* and six others. [Fl. 892, Fl. 254, Fl. 787.]

Grevenbroeck, Orazio. Flemish Sch. (?) *b* Milan (?) 1678 (?). **Signed Example:** VIENNA K. *Stormy sea.* [Fl. 903.]

Grief, see Gryef, A. de.

Grifoni, G., see Grisoni.

*Grimmer, Abel. Flemish Sch. *b* son of Jacob G., Antwerp after 1570 *d* Antwerp before 1619. *Landscapes with figures, Towers of Babel, interiors; also worked as architect.* Pupil of his father; in Antwerp Guild 1592. **Signed Examples:** ANTWERP *View of Antwerp* 1600, *View of the country round Antwerp, The Four Seasons* (based on prints after drawings by P. Bruegel and H. Bol) 1607. BRUSSELS *Christ in the house of Martha* (*cf.* J. Goeimare) 1614, *Landscape with castle* 1592, *Skating scene outside Antwerp* (partly copied from a print after P. Bruegel) 1602, *Summer* 1599, *Winter.* Other signed works in ABBEVILLE and PHILADELPHIA Johnson. Three versions of *The Tower of Babel* (*cf.* M. van Valkenborch) are recorded in invoices as exported from Antwerp in 17th cent.

[Fl. 892, Fl. 301, Fl. 212, Fl. 213.]

*Grimmer, Jacob. Flemish Sch. *b* Antwerp *c.* 1526 *d* Antwerp 1590. *Landscapes* (*cf.* F. Mostaert), *mainly in the region of Antwerp, some religious and genre subjects.* Pupil of G. Bouwens 1539, also of M. Cock and C. v. d. Queborne; Master Antwerp Guild 1547; also member Rhetoricians' Chamber and, van Mander (1604) says, 'a very good actor'. Guicciardini (1567) named him to Vasari as a good landscapist; Van Mander praised his skies and his fidelity to nature. **Signed Examples:** ANTWERP Mus. *Outskirts of Antwerp* 1578, *View on the Scheldt* 1587; Town Hall *Village* 1586. BUDAPEST *The Four Seasons* one *s* 1575. FRANKFORT Städt. Mus. *Landscape* 1588. VIENNA K. *Landscape with castle* 1583. **Monogrammed Example:** PRAGUE Rudolfinum *Festival in landscape* 1583. Recorded works include a set of *Months* in collection of the Archduke Ernest (*d* 1595), a *Landscape with the Woman of Samaria* (before 1588), a *Winter landscape* owned by Rembrandt, and a *Peasant fair* owned by Rembrandt's master P. Lastman.

[Fl. 371, Fl. 818, Fl. 559, Fl. 107, Fl. 892, Fl. 301, Fl. 213.]

Grisoni (or Grifoni), Giuseppe (real name **Pierre Joseph Grison**). Flemish Sch. *b* Florence 1692 or Mons 1699 *d* Rome 1769. *Religious subjects often in landscape, portraits and illustrations.* In Florence as a boy and pupil of T. Redi; came London (*cf.* F. Breydel) brought by J. Talman (first director of Soc. of Antiquaries) *c.* 1715; worked in van der Banck's S. Martin's Lane drawing Acad. 1720; returned Florence after London auction of pictures and portraits 1728; worked for Florentine churches; settled Rome after 1740. **Signed Examples:** LONDON B.M. *Doge in costume* 1719, *Pope in state robes* 1722 (both *w.*). **Documented Examples:** FLORENCE S. Annunziata *S. Barbara in a landscape* (painted 1740 in competition with V. Meucci for the Compagnia dei Tedeschi e Fiamminghi); Uffizi *Self portrait in a landscape.* LONDON Garrick Club *Colley Cibber in a star part* (engraved by contemporary J. Simon). Illustrations to Swift's *Gulliver's Travels* are recorded by engravings.

[Fl. 826, Fl. 856, Fl. 505, Fl. 221, Fl. 223.]

Groenendael, Cornelis. Flemish Sch. *b* Lierre 1785 *d* Antwerp 1834. *Portraits, religious subjects.* Pupil Antwerp Acad., then of L. David in Paris (*cf.* F. J. Navez); returned Antwerp 1814. **Signed Examples:** ANTWERP Mus. *M. van Doninck* 1810 and *Mme. van Doninck* 1810. An *Education of the Virgin* for a church in Lierre (*c.* 1818) is recorded.

[Fl. 451, Fl. 612, Fl. 88, Fl. 798.]

Groenning (or Groeningen), Gerard P. Flemish Sch. 16th cent. *Religious subjects and drawings for engravings; also worked as engraver.* [Fl. 53.]

Groote Adoration Master. Presumed Flemish Sch. early 16th cent. Name for painter of KITZBURG von Groote Coll.

Triptych *Adoration of the Kings, David and the Messengers, Queen of Sheba.* Pictures presumed by some his work are in various museums. [Fl. 316.]

Groux, Charles de. Flemish Sch. *b* son of ribbon manufacturer, Comines (France) 1825 *d* Brussels 1870. *Costume history, then peasant and working class genre with implicit social comment* (*cf.* L. Frédéric). Pupil of F. Navez 1843; and of J. B. van Eycken; then studied Rome and Düsseldorf; was helped by L. Robbe; Member of Soc. Libre des B.A. (*cf.* L. Dubois) 1866. Represented in ANTWERP *The Expulsion, The Pilgrimage.* BRUSSELS *Death of Charles V, Franciscus Junius preaching the Reformation* 1860, *Procession of S. Guidon, Saying Grace, The Conscript's Farewell, The Gleaners, The Drunkard, The Funeral, Cartoons for decoration Ypres Cloth hall* (which his death prevented him from executing). [Fl. 509, Fl. 466 (1870) Fl. Bib. 19th cent.]

Groux, Henri Jules Charles Corneille de. Flemish Sch. *b* Brussels 1866 *d* Paris 1930. *Religious and anti-war propaganda subjects* (*cf.* A. Wiertz), *historical compositions, genre; also worked in pastel and as lithographer* (*Apotheosis of Zola*) *and sculptor* (symbolical statues of Tolstoy, Wagner and Baudelaire). Pupil of J. Portaels in Brussels Acad., also of C. Meunier and F. Rops. Member of L'Essor group (*cf.* A. Hamesse) and Les XX (*cf.* J. Ensor) 1889; caused controversy by *Christ mocked* rejected from Paris Salon de la Nationale and shown in Union libérale des artistes français 1892; illustrated 'Sar' Péladon's 'Le livre secret' (*cf.* F. Knopff); lived many years in retirement in frontier village of Merveille; had large group of pictures and sculptures in Paris Salon d'Automne 1911; painted protests against horrors of 1914-18 German invasion. Represented in ANTWERP *Gypsies* (pastel). [Fl. 661 (1899), Fl. 465, Fl. Bib. 19th cent.]

*Gryef (Grief, Grief or Grif), Adriaen de. Flemish Sch. *b* place unknown *c.* 1670 *d* probably Brussels 1715. *Dogs and sporting trophies in landscapes, still life* (*fruit, flowers, vegetables, game*) *and landscapes with sporting and 'history' figures.* Master in Ghent Guild 1687; also worked Brussels and Antwerp. **Signed Examples:** BRUSSELS *Eagle attacking poultry.* CAMBRIDGE Fitz. *Spaniel and dead game.* OXFORD Ashmolean *Dogs and dead game in landscape.* PARIS Louvre *Huntsman and trophies in landscape.* SCHLEISSHEIM *Paradise, Orpheus and the animals* (*cf.* L. v. d. Borcht). PRAGUE *Vegetable seller.* AMSTERDAM Rijks., LENINGRAD, LILLE and ROUEN have signed *Still life* pieces. (*Cf.* B. de Bridt.) [Fl. 878, Fl. 892, Fl. 386.]

Gualdorp, see Geldorp.

Gudule Master, see View of Sainte G.

Guffens, Godefroid. Flemish Sch. *b* Hasselt 1823 *d* Schaerbeek 1901. *Costume history, religious subjects* (*including mural compositions*), *portraits.* Pupil Antwerp Acad. under N de Keyser; studied Paris; with J. Swerts *q.v.* travelled Germany where studied 'Nazarene' school. Represented in ANTWERP *Cartoons for murals.* BRUGES *The painter Euphrosina Beernaert* 1898. LIÈGE, PRAGUE *Return from the Sepulchre* and other museums. Murals (many in conjunction with J. Swerts) in ANTWERP S. Georges, COURTRAI Townhall, GHENT Notre Dame. Murals in Ypres townhall were destroyed in the 1914-18 German invasion.

[Fl. Bib. 19th cent.]

Guiette, René. Flemish Sch. *b* Antwerp 1893. *Landscapes* (*some in Southern France*). Represented in ANTWERP Mus. *Collioure in blue.* [Fl. 17.]

Güstrow Master. Flemish Sch. 16th cent. Name for painter of GÜSTROW (Mecklenberg) *Altarpiece* (in collaboration with the sculptor J. Borreman 1522).

[Fl. 120, Fl. 892, Fl. 316.]

*Gysaerts, Gualterus (Wouter).** Flemish Sch. *b* Antwerp 1649 *d* after 1674. *Flowers and garlands round grisaille panels by other painters (cf.* D. Seghers). Master Antwerp Guild 1670; entered Malines Franciscan monastery 1674. **Signed Example:** AMSTERDAM *Flower garland round grisaille portrait of H. van Weert* (also signed 'D. T.' presumed signature of David Teniers for the portrait). Descamps (1769) records a flower painting in Malines Recollets church.

[Fl. 216, Fl. 481, Fl. 892.]

*Gysbrechts, Cornelis Norbertus.** Flemish Sch. *b* Antwerp (?) before 1643 *d* after 1675. *'Trompe-l'œil' still life some with objects hanging on boards or walls and 'Vanitas' motifs (cf.* Amsterdam Cadaver Painter, H. Andriessen, A. Benedetti, J. B. Boel, Bruges Death and the Miser Painter, A. Coosemans, C. Engelbrechtsz, Frankfort Master, J. Gossaert, Hague Vanitas Painter, J. de Heem, J. v. d. Hoecke, Marinus v. Reymerswaele, J. Plasschaert). In Antwerp Guild 1659; court painter to King of Denmark from *c.* 1670. **Signed Examples:** AUGSBURG *Vanitas* 1662. COPENHAGEN *Vanitas* 1668, *Still life with letter carrier* 1668, *Still life with letter carrier on a wall* 1671, *Violin and documents on a wall, Still life with lobster* 1672 and others. **Documented Examples:** COPENHAGEN *Musical instruments on a wall* and others.

A *Vanitas* was recorded in the Vienna stock of the Forchoudt firm of Antwerp art dealers 1690.

[Fl. 714, Fl. 212, Fl. 170, Fl. 83.]

Gyselaer (or Giselaer), Philip. Flemish Sch. 17th cent. Pupil in Antwerp of A. v. Utrecht 1634. VIENNA Kunsthist. *Jupiter and Mercury entertained by Philemon and Baucis* (s Giselaer) is presumed by some his work. [Fl. 892.]

*Gysels (Gheysels or Gyzens), Pieter.** Flemish Sch. *b* Antwerp 1621 *d* Antwerp 1690. *Still life (cf.* A. v. Utrecht) *and landscapes, some with genre scenes.* Pupil of J. Boots 1641 and J. Brueghel the younger. Master Antwerp Guild 1650; De Bie described him as a taciturn recluse. **Signed Examples:** (Still life): AMSTERDAM Rijks. *Monkey, rabbits, fruit, flowers and vegetables in a loggia.* ANTWERP *Fruit, vegetables, swan, with live peacock, parrot and cupids in loggia with view of park* (large picture and last work), COPENHAGEN, DRESDEN, TURIN (1679). (Landscapes with figures): AMSTERDAM Rijks., ANTWERP *Village fair* (1687). DRESDEN *River valley.* G. Coques' *Interior of a gallery* (The Hague, Mauritshuis) shows a *Dead game* signed with his name. The still life pictures and the landscapes are presumed by some to be by different artists of the same name.

[Fl. 86, Fl. 425, Fl. 892.]

H

*Haecht (or **Verhaecht**), **Tobias van.** Flemish Sch. *b* son of an artist, Antwerp 1561 *d* Antwerp 1631. *Landscapes (some with ruins and some with figures by other artists).* Went young to Rome and Florence where worked for Grandduke of Tuscany; back in Antwerp where Master in Guild 1590; took Rubens as his pupil 1591; married a relative of Rubens 1592; worked on Pageant Entry into Antwerp of Archduke Ernest (*cf.* G. Schoof) 1594. **Monogrammed Examples:** AIX-LA-CHAPELLE *Landscape with horsemen* 1614. BRUSSELS *Landscape with hunting adventure of Archduke Maximilian* 1615. MUNICH A.P. *Mountain landscape* 1612. ST. OMER *Landscape.* A *Tower of Babel* (*cf.* M. van Valkenborch) with figures by Jan (Velvet) Brueghel was exported from Antwerp to Vienna 1690; C. de Bie records that he painted this subject in Rome as well as landscapes in fresco (*cf.* J. de Momper and A. Mirou). An Antwerp inventory (1627) records his collaboration with S. Vrancx *q.v.* in a *Diana hunting* and a *Conversion of S. Paul.*
[Fl. 559, Fl. 86, Fl. 753, Fl. 892, Fl. 212, Fl. 213.]

Haecht, Willem van. Flemish Sch. *b* son of Tobias van H. Antwerp 1593 *d* Antwerp 1637. *Interiors of picture galleries* (*cf.* C. de Baellieur, J. (Velvet) Brueghel, G. Coques, F. Francken the y., H. Jordaens III, H. Staben, D. Teniers the y., G. v. Tilborgh, C. de Vos), *also worked as reproducing engraver.* In Paris (*cf.* A. Dubois) 1615; in Italy 1619; back in Antwerp by 1628 and thereafter Keeper of picture gallery of Cornelius van der Geest (*cf.* London van der Geest Painter). **Signed Example:** NEW YORK private collection *Visit of Archduke Albert and the Infanta Isabella, Sovereigns of the Spanish Netherlands to the art gallery of C. van der Geest, Antwerp 1615* 1628; this shows *The Battle of the Amazons* (now Munich A.P.) painted by Rubens for C. van der Geest, a version of A. de Coster's *Judith killing Holofernes* and pictures in the styles of J. Beuckelaer, J. Wildens, Q. Massys and others; also a *Woman bathing with attendant, and a mirror on the wall* presumed by some the picture by Jan van Eyck recorded owned by Cardinal Ottaviano de' Medici *c.* 1455. Vertue (before 1754) records in England 'a large picture of the picture gallery of Archduke Albert and the Infanta Isabella' signed and dated 1621 (*cf.* Hague Studio of Apelles Painter). [Fl. 286, Fl. 826, Fl. 892, Fl. 875, Fl. 213.]

Haeck, Leopold. Flemish Sch. *b* Antwerp 1869 *d* Wijnegem 1928. *Portraits, genre, landscapes, religious subjects; also worked as etcher.* Pupil of C. Verlat. Founder Member of the 'Als ik kan' group (*cf.* H. Luyten). Represented ANTWERP *Evening in the meadows.* [Fl. 17.]

Haecken (or **Aken**), **Alexander van.** Flemish Sch. *b* Antwerp 1701 *d* London before 1758. *Portraits and drapery for other painters; also active as engraver.* Brother of, assistant to and heir of drapery painter Joseph van Aken *q.v.* in whose London house he lived; accompanied his brother, and others (including W. Hogarth) to France 1748; employed by the English painter T. Hudson for drapery after J. van A's death (1749) *cf.* P. J. Tassaert; engraved C. Lucy's portrait of the male soprano *Farinelli* and *The Five Senses* (female half lengths) after the Venetian painter P. Amigoni (in England 1729-36). His own portrait was painted by Hudson.
[Fl. 826, Fl. 481, Fl. 892, Fl. 223.]

Haert, Henri A. V. van der. Flemish Sch. *b* Louvain 1790 *d* Ghent 1846. *Portraits, some religious subjects; and murals*

for Tervueren Castle and Brussels Royal palace; also lithographs and engravings. Visited Paris; pupil in Brussels of L. David (*cf.* H. de Coene) 1817; professor in Brussels School of Engraving 1836; Director Ghent Academy 1846. Represented in BRUSSELS *The Terwagne Family.* GHENT *The Dismissal of Hagar.* [Fl. 451, Fl. 266, Fl. 892, Fl. 296, Fl. 798.]

Haes, Charles (**Carlos**) **de.** Flemish Sch. *b* Brussels 1829 *d* Madrid 1898. *Landscapes.* Spent childhood in Spain where his father had business interests. Worked Brussels as pupil of J. Quinaux *q.v.*; settled Madrid 1856; appointed Professor of Landscape Painting in Madrid Academia de San Fernando 1857. Painted in various parts of Spain, France and the Netherlands. Influenced the Spanish landscape painters J. Morera, A. de Beruete, D. de Regoyos and others. Represented in MADRID Museo Moderno (numerous paintings, sketches and drawings). [Fl. 626 (1910), Fl. 798.]

Haese (**Hase, Haase**), **Maximilien de.** Flemish Sch. *b* Brussels (?) after *c.* 1718 *d* Brussels 1787. *Religious subjects and tapestry designs.* Pupil of his uncle Jan van Orley. Master Brussels Guild 1726; Rome *c.* 1739 member Accad. S. Luca 1746. Denderleeuw Church has *Supper at Emmaus s* DHASE 1754 presumed by some his work. Descamps (1769) records in many Brussels churches and in Alost and Dilighem. Two *Scenes from the life of S. Romualdos* for Malines: S. Rombout are recorded. [Fl. 216, Fl. 613.]

Hageman, Victor. Flemish Sch. *b* Antwerp 1868 *d* Uccle 1938. *Genre (chiefly Antwerp harbour and Jewish types).* Represented in ANTWERP *Mother and child, The emigrants.* [Fl. 17.]

Hagemans, Maurice. Flemish Sch. *b* Liège 1852 *d* Brussels 1917. *Landscapes and marines, animals, genre (mainly w.).* Travelled in Germany and Scandinavia with F. Rops. Worked for King Leopold II. Represented in ANTWERP *Landscape with sheep.* BRUSSELS *The woodcutters* 1893. NAMUR, OSTEND. [Fl. Bib. 19th cent.]

Haghe, Louis. Flemish Sch. *b* son of architect, Tournai 1806 *d* Stockwell (London) 1885. *Interiors and other architectural motifs, and genre (w.); also worked as lithographer and illustrator.* Pupil of his father and in Tournai Acad. made drawings for topographic publications; settled London *c.* 1826; exhibited New Water Colour Soc. 1835; partner there in firm of lithographic publishers (Day and Haghe); vice-president, then president of the New Watercolour Society (later Royal Institute) 1873-84; travelled widely in Europe and Near East; his *Audience chamber at Bruges* in the Paris Exposition Universelle (1855) was highly praised by Théophile Gautier. Represented in BRUSSELS *Interior S. Peter's Rome* 1865. LONDON Bethnal Green *Interior Courtrai Town Hall*; V. and A. Twenty-two examples. LEICESTER, MANCHESTER (Whitworth) *Tournai Cathedral* 1869. SHEFFIELD, NEW YORK Met. *The Toast.* SYDNEY (Australia). [Fl. 451, Fl. 481, Fl. 329, Fl. 223, Fl. 798.]

*Hague Studio of Apelles Painter. Presumed Flemish Sch. 17th cent. Name for painter of HAGUE Mauritshuis (266) *The Studio of Apelles: Interior of a picture gallery* bought from King of Poland's collection 1765; this shows an imaginary collection including Q. Massys' *The Moneychanger and his wife*, a version of A. de Coster's *Judith with the head of*

Holofernes and recognisable works by Rubens, Van Dyck, Titian, Correggio, Albani, Domenichino and others. Presumed by some identical with W. van Haecht *q.v.* [Fl. 401.]

*Hague Vanitas Painter. Presumed Flemish Sch. 17th cent. Name for painter of HAGUE Mauritshuis (1694) *Vanitas* (*cf.* C. N. Gysbrechts).

Hal, Jacob (not Nicolas) **van.** Flemish Sch. *b* Antwerp 1672 *d* Antwerp 1750. *Religious and mythological subjects.* Master in Antwerp Guild 1692; the Dutch painter Jacob de Wit was among his pupils 1710; collaborated in some pictures with S. Hardimé *q.v.* **Signed Example:** POMMERSFELDEN *Esther and Ahasuerus.* **Documented Examples:** ANTWERP S. Jacques *The Collecting of the Manna* 1742 and *The Holy Sacrament adored by the Four Quarters of the World* 1743. Weyerman (1729) records a *Pygmalion* and Descamps (1769) a *Nativity* in Antwerp Jesuit College.
[Fl. 878, Fl. 216, Fl. 612, Fl. 481, Fl. 107, Fl. 892.]

Hal, Nicolas van. Presumed misnomer for Jacob van H. *q.v.*

Halen, Peter van. Flemish Sch. *b* son of an art dealer, Antwerp 1612 *d* Antwerp 1687. *Picturesque landscapes with small figures* (*religious, history and bacchanalian subjects*). Said to have been popular with English collectors in early 19th cent. **Signed Example:** CASSEL *The Flood.* Archduke Leopold Wilhelm owned a small *Ecce Homo* (1659 inventory). The Forchoudt firm of Antwerp dealers exported a number of his pictures to Vienna, and sold a *Diana sleeping* to Prince Carl von Liechtenstein *c.* 1674. [Fl. 86, Fl. 892, Fl. 212.]

Hallet (or **Alé**), **Gilles.** Flemish Sch. *b* Liège 1620 *d* Rome 1694. *Religious subjects.* Pupil of W. Damery; went Italy and settled there (*cf.* P. de Lignis and J. Sutterman). **Documented Examples:** ROME S. Isidoro *Scenes from the life of S. Anthony*; Sta. Maria dell' Anima *Nativity of the Virgin.*
[Fl. 800, Fl. 26, Fl. 892, Fl. 305, Fl. 678.]

Hallez, Germain Joseph. Flemish Sch. *b* Frameries, nr. Mons 1769 *d* Brussels 1840. *Portraits, landscapes, religious subjects, mythologies, genre.* Pupil Mons School 1781; France 1787; in Brussels as successful portrait painter 1790; returned Mons 1792; director Mons Acad. 1802-39. Signed some pictures 'Le petit Borain'. Represented in FRAMERIES Church *S. Barbara.* MONS *The devoted young mother* and portraits; Town Hall *Allegory of Napoleon's marriage to Marie Louise.* A portrait *The Emperor Leopold II* painted in Brussels in 1791 and an *Awakening of Jupiter* are recorded.
[Fl. 451, Fl. 612, Fl. 221, Fl. 88.]

Hals, Pieter. Flemish Sch. *b* Ghent (?) before 1620 *d* after 1649. *Religious and historical subjects, landscapes.* Member of Ghent Guild 1633. Restored Rubens' *S. Bavon renouncing worldly pleasures* in Ghent Cathedral 1648. Recorded works include Ypres Cathedral *The raising of the siege of Ypres s* 1649 (destroyed in German invasion 1914-18) and many works seen by Descamps in Ghent and Louvain churches.
[Fl. 216, Fl. 479, Fl. 892, Fl. 435.]

Hamen, Jan van der. Flemish Sch. *b* Brussels before 1576 *d* Madrid after 1621. *Flowers.* Went Madrid before 1596; practised as amateur painter; later an Archer of the Guard to Philip IV. His son Juan van der Hamen, born in Madrid in 1596, was a professional still life painter (who ranks in the Spanish Sch.). [Fl. 636, Fl. 153, Fl. 779, Fl. 555.]

Hamesse, Adolphe Jean. Flemish Sch. *b* Brussels 1849 *d* Ixelles (Brussels) 1925. *Landscapes.* Pupil of P. Lauters in Brussels Acad. Founder member of 'Essor' group (*cf.* L. Frédéric, L. Herbo, E. Hoeterickx, F. Khnopff, Clémence Lacroix, J. v. Leemputten, A. Lynen, who were joined later

by A. Baertsoen, E. de Biefve and O. Coppens) 1875; inspector of drawing in Ixelles state schools. Represented in BRUSSELS *Pond in the Campine s.* 1883, IXELLES.
[Fl. Bib. 19th cent. Fl. 296.]

Hamilton, Charles William de (called 'Thistle-Hamilton'). Flemish Sch. *b* son of Scottish still life painter James H., Brussels *c.* 1668 *d* Augsburg 1754. *Still life with plants* (*cf.* J. v. d. Borght, L. v. Heil and J. v. Kessel) *and insects; also animals and game.* In Baden 1699-1707; then Augsburg. **Signed Examples:** LYONS *Plants, insects and lizard.* SCHWERIN *Dead fox* 1739 and STUTTGART.
[Fl. 612, Fl. 798.]

Hamilton, Frans de. Flemish Sch. *b* Brussels (?) before 1650 *d* after 1695. *Animals, still life with game, also flora, insects and reptiles.* Presumed relative of Scottish still life painter James H.; went Germany where in service of Courts of Brandenburg, Hanover, Hesse-Cassel and Bavaria. **Signed Examples:** ASCHAFFENBURG *Hunting piece.* SCHWERIN *Trophies of the chase.* [Fl. 612, Fl. 892.]

*Hamilton, John George (Johann Georg) de. Flemish Sch. *b* son of Scottish still life painter James H., Brussels 1672 *d* Vienna 1737. *Animals and birds, hunting scenes, riding schools, still life* (*some with dead game*) *equestrian portraits.* In Vienna 1698; then Berlin where court painter to Frederick I; returned Vienna where worked for Prince von Liechtenstein, Prince von Schwarzenberg and the Emperor Charles VI (*cf.* P. F. de H.). **Signed Examples:** BUDAPEST *Riding school* 1735. DRESDEN *Horse portraits* 1703-9. STUTTGART *Bear hunt* 1712. VIENNA K. *The Imperial stables at Lipizza* 1727, *Grazing horses, Boar's head* 1718; Liechtenstein *The Imperial riding school with the future Emperor Charles VI on a white horse* 1702. [Fl. 451, Fl. 892.]

*Hamilton, Philip Ferdinand de. Flemish Sch. *b* son of Scottish still life painter James H., Brussels 1664 (?) *d* Vienna 1750. *Animals and birds, and still life* (*game, insects, fruit*). Went Vienna where worked as Court painter to Emperors Joseph I (*cf.* P. Evrard) and Charles VI and Empress Maria Theresa. **Signed Examples:** BUDAPEST *Still life* 1698. FRANKFORT Staedel. *Bunch of grapes with butterflies* 1696. LENINGRAD *Still lifes.* MUNICH A.P. *Larder with dead hare and birds.* VIENNA K. *Hound and dead hare* 1698, *Leopard defending prey against vulture* 1722, *Wolves and dead hind* 1720, *Deer and porcupine* 1724.
[Fl. 612, Fl. 481, Fl. 892.]

Hamman, Édouard Jean Conrad. Flemish Sch. *b* Ostend 1819 *d* Paris 1888. *Costume history, anecdotic genre, portraits; also worked as engraver and illustrator.* Pupil Antwerp Acad. of N. de Keyser. Went Paris 1846; exhibited Paris Salon 1847-87. Received Order of Leopold and Légion d'honneur. Represented in ANTWERP *Francis I starting for the hunt*, BRUSSELS *The Mass of Adriaen Willaerts.* BUDAPEST, THE HAGUE, LA ROCHELLE *Mary Stuart's farewell to France.* MARSEILLES, MINNEAPOLIS, MOSCOW, NEW YORK Public Lib., PARIS State Coll. *Erasmus and Charles V.*, REIMS, STRASBOURG.
[Fl. 481, Fl. Bib. 19th cent.]

Hamme, Alexis van. Flemish Sch. *b* Brussels 1818 *d* Brussels 1875. *Costume history, genre.* Pupil of N. de Keyser and F. Leys. Represented in BRUSSELS *The Lacemaker* 1847. BELGIAN ROYAL COLL. *Pageant Entry of the Archduke Albert and the Infanta Isabella into Brussels 1599.* NEW YORK Public Lib. *Dutch market scene.*
[Fl. 451, Fl. Bib. 19th cent.]

*Hampton Court Cromatius Painter. Presumed Flemish (Dutch) Sch. 16th cent. Name for painter of ROYAL COLLEC-

TION HAMPTON COURT (455) *Conversion of Cromatius* (catalogued in Charles I's collection as by Lucas van Leyden). Presumed by some identical with P. Cornelisz *q.v.* Two other panels in Hampton Court (*S. Sebastian before Diocletian* and *Martyrdom of S. Sebastian*) are presumed by some from the same series.

*Hampton Court Henry VIII *c.* 1536 **Painter.** Presumed Flemish Sch. 16th cent. Name for painter of ROYAL COLLECTION HAMPTON COURT (563) *Henry VIII holding a scroll* (the scroll quotes S. Mark 16 'Go ye into all the world . . .' presumed reference to 1536 Bible). Presumed by some identical with Joos van Cleve *q.v.*

*Hampton Court Lady in Persian Dress Painter. Presumed Flemish (or British) Sch. 16th cent. Name for painter of ROYAL COLLECTION HAMPTON COURT (349) *Arabella Stuart* (?) *in Persian dress with a stag* presumed by some to represent Queen Elizabeth and by others Lady Arabella Stuart. (*cf.* M. Geeraerts the younger).
[Fl. 730, Fl. 857, Fl. 734.]

Hannon, Théodore. Flemish Sch. *b* Brussels 1851. *d* Etterbeck nr. Brussels 1917. *Landscapes, genre, still life* (*w.*)*; also active as poet and art critic.* Represented in BRUSSELS *Winter, A Tragedy.*
[Fl. 626 (1917), Fl. Bib. 19th cent.]

Hannotiau, Alexandre A. Flemish Sch. *b* Brussels 1863 *d* Molenbeck, Brussels 1901. *Picturesque corners of Flemish towns and villages, some with genre figures; also worked as lithographer and poster artist.* Represented in BRUGES and BRUSSELS.
[Fl. Bib. 19th cent.]

*Hanselaere, Pieter van. Flemish Sch. *b* Ghent 1786 *d* Ghent 1862. *Costume history, religious subjects, portraits.* Pupil of P. van Huffel in Ghent Acad.; went Paris where pupil of L. David (*cf.* F. J. Navez) 1809; to Rome with Ghent scholarship 1816; member Rome Accad. di S. Luca on the sculptor Canova's recommendation; Naples *c.* 1823; court painter to the King and member of Academy; returned Ghent where professor in Acad. 1829. **Signed Examples:** AMSTERDAM *Selfportrait* 1824, *Susanna and the Elders* (Rome) 1820. Also represented in COURTRAI, GHENT Mus. and S. Sauveur.
[Fl. 451, Fl. 612, Fl. 798.]

Hardimé, Pieter. Flemish Sch. *b* Antwerp or The Hague *c.* 1677 *d* The Hague 1758. *Flowers and fruit* (*cf.* J. v. d. Borght) (*many for over-doors*). Pupil of his brother Simon H. in Antwerp; went The Hague 1697 where member of Guild 1700; married sister of abbot of S. Bernard (nr. Antwerp) 1709; employed (displacing G. P. Verbruggen the younger) by the Dutch decorative artist M. Terwesten to paint flowers and fruit in his allegorical compositions for ceilings and easel pictures. Four pictures *The Seasons* (flowers and fruit pieces) painted for S. Bernard Abbey 1718 are recorded.
[Fl. 878, Fl. 353, Fl. 215, Fl. 481.]

Hardimé, Simon. Flemish Sch. *b* Antwerp 1664 or 1672 *d* London 1737. *Flowers and fruit* (*sometimes with classical figures by J. van Hal or J. Leyssens*). Pupil of flower painter Guild 1688. His contemporary C. Weyerman states that he J. B. de Crépu 1685 (*cf.* J. Bosschaert). Master in Antwerp became embarrassed through overfrequenting taverns and went to The Hague to quarter himself on his brother Pieter H. 'where he was no more welcome than a dog at a game of skittles'; in England from *c.* 1700 (*cf.* S. Dubois and V. H. Janssens) and patronized by the Earl of Scarborough. **Signed Examples:** BORDEAUX *Flowerpieces.*
[Fl. 878, Fl. 223.]

Harembourg, G., see **Horenbout.**

Harp, Guilliam, see **Herp.**

Hase, Jacob de. Flemish Sch. *b* Antwerp 1575 or 1579 *d* Rome 1634. *Religious subjects and battle pictures.* Pupil in Antwerp of G. Schoof 1588; in Rome 1601; Paul Brill witnessed his marriage there 1602; Jan Snellinck the younger and the Dutch religious painter A. van Os were among his pupils 1603; member Rome Accad. di San Luca 1604. A weeping child-angel by the sculptor F. Duquesnoy marks his grave in Rome S. Maria in Campo Santo. An *Assumption of the Virgin* and a pendant formerly in S. Maria in Campo Santo are recorded. [Fl. 800, Fl. 892, Fl. 798, Fl. 305, Fl. 678.]

Hase, M. de, see **Haese.**

Havermaet, Pieter van. Flemish Sch. *b* St. Niklaas 1834 *d* Antwerp 1897. *Portraits, genre, landscapes.* Pupil in Antwerp Acad. Professor there 1886. Visited London and painted Lord Beaconsfield (exhibited R.A. 1881). Represented in ANTWERP *An Antwerp streetsweeper* 1890 and *portraits.* [Fl. 892, Fl. 361, Fl. 17.]

Hay, J., see **Hey.**

Hebbelynck, A., see **Hulle.**

Hecht, Henri van der. Flemish Sch. *b* Brussels 1841 *d* Brussels 1901. *Landscapes including river pieces.* Pupil of J. Portaels. Member of Tervueren Group (*cf.* H. Boulenger) and of Soc. Libre les B.A. (*cf.* L. Dubois). Exhibited in London R.A. Represented in ANTWERP *River scene.* BRUSSELS *The Rainbow, Rotterdam marshes* 1878 and other museums.
[Fl. 361, Fl. Bib. 19th cent.]

Hecke (Ecke, or Eycke), Jan van den. Flemish Sch. *b* Quaremonde (nr. Audenarde) 1620 *d* Antwerp 1684. *Landscapes with figures and animals, still life* (*including flower pieces, cf.* A. Bosschaert and J. B. de Crépu) *and garlands round other painters' pictures* (*cf.* D. Seghers). Visited Italy, back in Antwerp by 1659. His son Jan van den H. was mainly active as engraver. **Signed Examples:** SCHLEISSHEIM *Dead birds, trophies of the chase, and dogs* 1658. HAGUE Mauritshuis (in Gonzales Coques' *Interior of a Gallery*) *Landscape with cattle and shepherds* and *Men and horses bathing.* **Documented Example:** VIENNA K. *Flower garland round a portrait of Rembrandt* (?) *by the Dutch painter J. Lievens* (recorded in Archduke Leopold Wilhelm's Inventory 1659 'die Blumen von von Eckh'). An Antwerp inventory (1663) records a *Flowers in a pot* (by von Eycke) in the collection of Maria van der Goes.
[Fl. 86, Fl. 425, Fl. 892, Fl. 213.]

*Hecken (or Heck), Abraham van den. Flemish Sch. *b* son of Samuel van den H., Antwerp before 1618 *d* London (?) after 1655. *Interiors, religious subjects, genre, still life with flowers and portraits.* Worked Amsterdam and married sister of Dutch painter G. Lundens 1635; also worked at The Hague; carried on business as wine merchant as well as his painting; recorded in London (*cf.* C. de Neve) after 1655. **Signed Examples:** AMSTERDAM Rijks. *The Flayed ox, The engineer C. Meyer* (full length). BUDAPEST *Merry company.* LENINGRAD Hermitage *Repentance of Judas* 1654. [Fl. 892.]

Hecken, Samuel van den. Flemish Sch. *b* Antwerp (?) before 1600 *d* Amsterdam (?) after 1637. *Landscapes.* Master Antwerp Guild 1616; in Amsterdam 1635 and 1637. **Signed Example:** DESSAU Amalienstift *Landscape with the Four Elements.* [Fl. 714, Fl. 798.]

Heede, Vigor van. Flemish Sch. *b* Furnes 1661 *d* Furnes 1708. *Religious subjects.* Worked in Italy with his brother Willem.

Descamps records a *Prodigal Son* painted by him and Willem in Furnes S. Walburga. *cf.* V. Boucquet. [Fl. 215, Fl. 216.]

Heede, Willem van. Flemish Sch. *b* Furnes 1660 *d* 1728. *Religious subjects.* Travelled in France, Italy, Germany. Worked in the Imperial Palace, Vienna (*cf.* Vigor van H.).
[Fl. 215.]

*Heem, Cornelis de. Flemish Sch. *b* son of Jan Davidsz de H., Leyden 1631 *d* Antwerp 1695. *Still life, mainly fruit* (*cf.* T. Aenvanck). Brought Antwerp by his father 1636; pupil of his father; in Antwerp Guild 1660; made visits to The Hague (where he joined the Guild) 1676-81. **Signed Examples:** BERLIN, BRUSSELS (1671), CARLSRUHE (1659), DRESDEN, FRANKFORT (1657), THE HAGUE, OXFORD, PRAGUE, STOCKHOLM, VIENNA K. *Table with oysters, fruit and watch* (*cf.* J.-P. van Thielen).
[Fl. 425, Fl. 892.]

Heem, David Cornelisz de. Flemish Sch. *b* son of Cornelis de Heem, Antwerp 1663 *d* London (?) after 1718. *Flowers* (*cf.* J. v.d. Borght). Master in Antwerp Guild 1693; in The Hague 1697-1701; in London (*cf.* S. Hardimé) where Weyerman met him as a very sick man 1718. **Signed Example:** THE HAGUE Gemeente mus. *Vase with flowers* (*s* D De Heem). BRUSSELS has a *Fruit piece s* D. De Heem presumed by some the work of his Dutch uncle David Davidsz de H. (*b* Utrecht *c.* 1610). LONDON N.G. and OXFORD have *Fruit and flower pieces s* D de Heem presumed by some the work of his Dutch great-grandfather (1570-1632).
[Fl. 878, Fl. 632]

Heem, Jan Davidsz de. Flemish (Dutch) Sch. *b* son of Dutch still life painter David de H., Utrecht 1606 *d* Antwerp 1683 or 1684. *Still life: flowers, fruit, shell fish, silver and glass vessels* (*cf.* J. van Es, T. Aenvanck); '*Vanitas*' *with skull* (*cf.* C. N. Gysbrechts); *books.* In Leyden 1626; settled Antwerp and member of Antwerp Guild 1636; citizen of Antwerp 1637; visited Utrecht and joined the Utrecht Guild 1669; fled back to Antwerp before the French invasion 1672; Houbraken (1718) states that he worked on, and passed as his own, some paintings by his son Jan and by his German pupil A. Mignon (who lived with him for some years). Copies after his pictures were already being exported to Vienna by 1667. **Signed Examples:** 'Jan de Heem R' (it is presumed by some that R=retouchiert; i.e. touched up work of other artists): AMSTERDAM, DRESDEN, STOCKHOLM. **Signed in full without Addition of R.:** AMSTERDAM *Self portrait, Books.* ANTWERP *Flowers and insects.* BERLIN, BRUSSELS *Vanitas* and two others 1667. CAMBRIDGE Fitz. *Flowers.* CARLSRUHE, CASSEL, COPENHAGEN, DRESDEN, FLORENCE, THE HAGUE *Books and violin* 1628. LENINGRAD, LONDON Hampton Court, MADRID, MUNICH *Still life* 1653 and *Vanitas with flowers, skull and crucifix* (also signed by N. v. Verendael *q.v.*). NEW YORK Met., OXFORD, PARIS Louvre, ROTTERDAM, SCHLEISSHEIM, SCHWERIN, VIENNA Liecht., K. *Church vessels in flower garland* 1648 and others. **Monogrammed Example:** BRUSSELS *Flower garland round grisaille panel* 1668 (*cf.* C. Lambrechts and D. Seghers).
[Fl. 86, Fl. 753, Fl. 425, Fl. 215, Fl. 892, Fl. 212, Fl. 632, Fl. 146.]

Heem, Jan Jansz de. Flemish Sch. *b* son of Jan Davidsz de H., Antwerp 1650. Pupil and assistant of his father. Houbraken (1718) records that his father touched up and passed off as his own his son Jan's work. [Fl. 425.]

*Heemskerck, Marten van. Flemish (Dutch) Sch. *b* son of a farmer (J. W. van Veen), Heemskerk 1498 *d* Haarlem 1574. *Religious subjects, 'history', portraits; also worked as glass painter and engraver.* Pupil in Haarlem of Cornelis Willemsz;

assistant in Haarlem to Jan Scorel 1527; went Rome where drew monuments and buildings (*cf.* M. Gast) 1532; worked in team of Flemings and Germans engaged on triumphal arches for Emperor Charles V's Pageant Entry into Rome (described by Vasari as 'cose stupende' because the painters were always 'riscaldoti dal furor del vino' while at work 1536; back in Haarlem 1537; dean of Haarlem Guild 1540; exempted from taxation as a distinguished artist 1570; took refuge in Amsterdam with his Dutch pupil collector J. Rauwaert (*cf.* P. Aertsen, G. v. d. Meire, K. v. Mander) when Haarlem was besieged by Spaniards 1572; later returned Haarlem; van Mander describes him as wealthy but so obsessed with fear of poverty that he always carried money sewn into his clothes; he suffered much embarrassment from dishonest habits of his second wife; left in his will a property providing annual dowries for couples to be married on his grave (a provision executed till 1781). **Signed Examples:** AMSTERDAM Oudekerk *S. Nicholas* 1561; Mus. *The Erythrean Sibyl* with *donor and S. Paul in a landscape* on reverse 1564. BARNARD CASTLE *Christ on Sea of Tiberias* 1567. BERLIN K.F. *Momus ridiculing the work of the gods* 1561. BRUNSWICK *Baptism of Christ* 1563. BRUSSELS (triptych) *Entombment* (on wings *donor and S. Peter* and *donor's wife and S. Mary Magdalene*, on reverses *Isaiah* and *Jeremiah*) 1559 and 1560. CAMBRIDGE *Selfportrait with the Colosseum in background* 1553. DELFT *Lamentation* 1566 (?). GHENT *Man of Sorrows* 1532, *Crucifixion* 1543. HAARLEM *S. Luke painting the Virgin* 1532 (presented to Haarlem Guild before he left for Rome), *Aaron and Moses with the brazen serpent* 1551, *Ecce Homo* (triptych) 1559-60. HAMPTON COURT (Royal Collection) *Jonah under the Gourd* 1561, *Death and Judgement* 1565 (Van Mander records that he painted this subject for Jacob Rauwaert). LILLE *Bulls fighting in Roman amphitheatre* 1552. LINKOPPING (Sweden) triptych *Scenes from the Passion* with *Crucifixion* and *Resurrection* and *donor, Bishop of Utrecht* and *Martyrdom of S. Lawrence* 1540 (painted for Alkmaar Sint Laurenskerk (*cf.* C. Buys) and bought by Johann III for 1,200 tons of cheese 1581). NEW YORK Met. *Portrait of his father* (monog. and inscribed) 1532. RENNES *S. Luke painting the Virgin* TURIN Acad. *Last Judgement* 1554. VIENNA K. *Triumph of Silenus* (based on a drawing by Giulio Romano). **Documented Example:** HAGUE *Annunciation* (on wings of an altarpiece later attached to the *Massacre of the Innocents* by the Dutch painter Cornelis of Haarlem) 1546. Many of the above are described by Van Mander who also records a *Deluge*, a *Sol and Luna* and *Adam and Eve* with lifesize nudes 'painted from life'. Lifesize paintings titled *Venus and Vulcan* and *Venus and Mars* sold for a high price and described as 'equal to Raphael in beauty' are among many works recorded in Antwerp 17th cent. inventories.
[Fl. 818, Fl. 559, Fl. 671, Fl. 429, Fl. 212, Fl. 213, Fl. 316.]

Heere, Lucas de (Lucas Derus). Flemish Sch. *b* son of sculptor Jan de H. and miniature painter Anna de Smytere *q.v.*, Ghent 1534 *d* place unknown 1584. *Religious subjects, portraits (including portrait drawings from memory), tapestry and glass designs; also active as poet and humanist.* Pupil of F. Floris; went France and worked Fontainebleau (*cf.* L. Thiry and A. Dubois); returned Ghent where designed decorations for Chapter of Golden Fleece 1559; took van Mander as pupil *c.* 1566; banished as Protestant by Alva (*cf.* A. de Weerdt) 1568; went England (*cf.* S. v. d. Meulen) employed there by Lord High Admiral Edward Lord Clinton Earl of Lincoln to represent the habits of different nations and 'when he came to the English he painted a naked man, with cloth of different sorts and a pair of shears, as a satire on the fickleness of English fashions' 1570; returned Flanders after 'Ghent Amnesty' 1576; designed decorations for entry of Prince of Orange into Ghent 1577, for presumed betrothal of Queen Elizabeth and the Duc d'Anjou 1581, and for entry

of Anjou into Ghent 1582; fled again from Ghent during Parma's campaigns (*cf.* D. v. d. Queborne). His poems include 'Jardin et verger de poésie' (Den Hof en Boomgaerd . .) written *c.* 1559, published 1565 containing an Ode on the Ghent *Altarpiece of the Mystic Lamb* (*cf.* H., J. and M. van Eyck) and a description of a *David and Abigail* by H. van der Goes *q.v.*; he also wrote a 'Lives of Painters' in verse; he collected antiques, coins, bronzes (*cf.* L. Lombard) and possibly owned J. van Eyck's *S. Barbara* (Antwerp Mus.). **Signed Examples:** GHENT S. Bavon *Solomon and the Queen of Sheba* (Lucas Derus) 1559; Municipal Archives (water-colours of costumes) 'Théâtre de tous les peuples . . . par Luc. Dheere'. **Documented Example:** GHENT Univ. *View of the Abbey of S. Bavon.* Van Mander records an altarpiece in Ghent, S. Pierre destroyed by iconoclasts 1566. Pictures signed with monogram HE presumed by Vertue and others his work are now known to be by H. Ewouts *q.v.* (*Cf.* also Madrid Philip II (head) Painter.)
[Fl. 559, Fl. 856, Fl. 223, Fl. 892, Fl. 857, Fl. 39, Fl. 28, Fl. 744.]

Heesvelde, Hippoliet van. Flemish Sch. *b* Antwerp 1904 *d* Antwerp 1944. *Landscapes.* Pupil of R. Baseleer in Antwerp Institute. Represented in ANTWERP. [Fl. 17.]

*****Heil, Daniel van.** Flemish Sch. *b* Brussels (?) 1604 *d* Brussels after 1664. *Landscapes (often winter scenes), conflagrations* (*cf.* G. Mostaert and T. v. Heil). Brother of Jan Baptist and Leo van H.; patronized by Archduke Leopold Wilhelm (*cf.* J. B. v. Heil). **Monogrammed Examples:** BRUSSELS Collegiate SS. Michel et Gudule *Landscape with fantastic view of Antwerp and Flight into Egypt* (D.V.H. and doc. 1664); Mus. *Conflagration near Antwerp, Winter pleasures, Conflagration* (1655). **Documented Example:** VIENNA K. *Winter landscape* (Archduke Leopold Wilhelm 1659 inventory). Antwerp Mus. has a 1939 acquisition *Conflagration with fantastic view of Antwerp* presumed by some his work. De Bie (1661) and Houbraken (1718) admired pictures titled *The Destruction of Sodom* (*cf.* Brussels Sodom and Gemorrah Painter) and *The Fall of Troy* (*cf.* P. Schoubroeck).
[Fl. 86, Fl. 425, Fl. 878, Fl. 892, Fl. 301.]

Heil, Jan Baptist van. Flemish Sch. *b* Brussels 1609 *d* Brussels (?) after 1661. *Portraits; also worked as copyist and engraver.* Brother of Daniel and Leo van H.; patronized by Archduke Leopold Wilhelm, Governor General Spanish Netherlands 1647-55 (*cf.* D. v. H., J. A. v. Baren, J. v. Egmont, P. Franchoys, J. and R. v. d. Hoecke, N. v. Hoy, F. Luyckx, D. Ryckaert III, G. Seghers, P. Snayers, D. Teniers the younger, P. Thys). *Archduke Leopold Wilhelm* (1655), *Andreas Cantelemo, General of Spanish army in the Netherlands* (1646) and other portraits are recorded by engravings. [Fl. 86, Fl. 425, Fl. 892.]

Heil, Leo van. Flemish Sch. *b* Brussels 1605 *d* after 1661. Brother of Daniel and Jan Baptist van H. *Flowers, insects and other small animals* (*cf.* C. W. and F. de Hamilton, J. v. Kessel), *architectural drawings; also worked as architect to Archduke Leopold Wilhelm.* R. Megan was his pupil. A miniature *Large stag beetle with two unequal horns* was owned by Archduke Leopold Wilhelm (1659 inventory). Drawings of *Triumphal Arch for Archduke Leopold Wilhelm* 1648, *Bird's eye view of Tongerloo Abbey* 1650 and *View of Brussels town hall* are recorded by engravings.
[Fl. 86, Fl. 892.]

Heil, Théodore van. Flemish Sch. *b* son of D. van H., Brussels (?) before 1650. *d* Brussels (?) after 1692. *Panoramic town views, winter scenes, conflagrations* (*cf.* D. van H.). Master Brussels Guild 1668. **Monogrammed Examples:** BRUSSELS *Panorma of Brussels* (T. V. H. 1692), *Fire in the Brussels Palace 1674* (T.V.). [Fl. 301.]

Heinz, Richard. Flemish Sch. *b* Herstal lez Liège 1871 *d* Sy 1929. *Landscapes (many in the Belgian Ardennes)* in broad Impressionist technique. Pupil in Liège Acad.; visited Italy 1906. Represented in LIÈGE. [Fl. 102.]

Hele (or Helle), Abraham del. Flemish Sch. *b* Antwerp (?) 1534 *d* Augsburg 1598. '*History*' *and portraits.* Presumed brother of Izaak del H. Documented in Regensburg 1576. **Signed Example:** SCHLEISSHEIM *Penelope and her maidens* 1565. [Fl. 892, Fl. 798.]

Hele (or Helle), Izaak del. Flemish Sch. *b* son of sculptor, Antwerp *c.* 1536 *d* Antwerp after 1573. *Religious subjects.* Working in Spain (*cf.* P. de Kempener) 1562. Recorded works include wall paintings in Toledo Cathedral (replaced with frescoes by Spanish artists Fr. Bayeu and M. Maella in 18th cent.) and *Scenes from the life of Bishop Nicasius of Reims* (extant in Toledo Cath. 1800) 1568. [Fl. 153, Fl. 892.]

Hellemans, Pierre Jean. Flemish Sch. *b* Brussels 1787 *d* Brussels 1845. *Landscapes.* Pupil of J. B. de Roy. E. Verboeckhoven painted animals in some of his pictures (*cf.* J. B. de Jonghe, F. Keelhoff, P. L. Kuhnen, H. de Coene, P. de Noter, C. P. Tschaggeny). **Signed Examples:** BRUSSELS *Outskirts of the Forest of Soignes* 1830. HAMBURG Kunsthalle *Landscape with huntsmen and dogs* (signed also by E. Verboeckhoven). LEIPZIG *Wooded landscape* 1829.
[Fl. 451, Fl. 481, Fl. 88, Fl. 612, Fl. 798.]

*****Helmon, Marcel.** Presumed Flemish Sch. 16th cent. Signature on NEW YORK Met. (17.190.3) *Adoration of the Shepherds.* Presumed by some identical with Marcellus Coffermans *q.v.*

Helmont (or Hellemont), Jan van. Flemish Sch. *b* son of Matthys van H., Antwerp 1650 *d* Antwerp (?) after 1714. *Portraits.* Master Antwerp Guild 1676; worked for town authorities. **Signed Example:** ANTWERP Sœurs Noires Convent *Twelve nuns adoring the Cross* (life size).
[Fl. 107, Fl. 892.]

Helmont, Lucas van, see **Gassel.**

Helmont (or Hellemont), Matthys van. Flemish Sch. *b* Antwerp 1623 *d* Brussels (?) after 1674. *Peasant genre; interiors* (*cf.* D. Ryckaert III). In Antwerp Guild 1646; went Brussels 1674. **Signed Examples:** AIX-EN-PROVENCE, BRUNSWICK, BUDAPEST *The vegetable market.* COPENHAGEN *Peasant fair, The alchemist.* DOUAI, GHENT, LILLE, MANNHEIM, STOCHKOLM *Village wedding* (and others). [Fl. 215, Fl. 107, Fl. 892.]

Helmont (or Hellemont), Zeger (or Seger) Jacob van. Flemish Sch. *b* son of Jan van H., Antwerp 1683 *d* Brussels 1726. *Old and New Testament subjects, portraits and designs for tapestry.* Master in Brussels Guild 1711; painted for Brussels public buildings reconstructed after Marshal Villeroi's bombardment during Louis XIV's 1695 campaign (*cf.* R. v. d. Weyden, N. E. Pery, J. v. Orley, R. v. Orley, J. B. Morel; also A. Coppens, G. J. v. Opstal and V. Janssens). C. Breydel and P. K. Marissal were associated with him *c.* 1723. **Signed Example:** GHENT Mus. (formerly Carmelite Church) *Crucifixion.* **Documented Example:** BRUSSELS S. Nicolas *Christ and the Woman of Canaan* seen, 1768, by Descamps who saw others in Brussels churches and Town Hall.
[Fl. 878, Fl. 215, Fl. 216.]

Heme, Lowijs. Flemish Sch. 16th-17th cent. Van Mander (1604) records: 'When P. Vlerick was living at Courtrai, he had a pupil Lowijs Heme who came from this town; his work was very similar to that of his master, especially in architectural detail and in perspective; he is the best of the painters in Courtrai'. [Fl. 559.]

Hemelraet, P. A., see **Immenraet.**

*Hemessen, Catherina van. Flemish Sch. *b* daughter of Jan van H., Antwerp (?) 1528 *d* Spain (?) after 1566. *Portraits, landscapes with religious subjects.* Married musician (organist) Christian de Morien 1554; taken with her husband to Spain (*cf.* P. de Kempener) by Charles V's sister Mary of Hungary (*cf.* J. C. Vermeyen) who provided for them for life 1556. Her name was reported as noteworthy to Vasari. **Signed Examples:** AMSTERDAM *Lady's portrait* 1548. BAR-NARD CASTLE *Lady's portrait.* BRUSSELS *Man's portrait* 1549, *Lady's portrait* 1549. LENINGRAD *Self portrait* 1548 (aetatis suae 20). LONDON N.G. *Man's portrait* 1552, *Lady with a little dog* 1551. Signed landscapes with *Virgin and Child* and *Rest on the Flight* are recorded.
[Fl. 371, Fl. 818, Fl. 892, Fl. 530.]

*Hemessen, Jan Sanders van. Flemish Sch. *b* Hemishen nr. Antwerp *c.* 1500 *d* Haarlem 1566 or later. Father of Catherina van H. *Religious subjects, nudes and genre.* Pupil of H. v. Cleve the elder 1519; Master Antwerp Guild by 1524; Dean 1548; moved to Haarlem *c.* 1550/5. **Signed Examples:** BRUSSELS *Prodigal Son* 1536. HARTFORD (U.S.A.) *Prodigal Son* 1543. LENINGRAD Hermitage *S. Jerome* 1543. LISBON *S. Jerome* 1531. LONDON Royal Coll. (Hampton Court) *S. Jerome writing* 1545. MUNICH A.P. *Holy Family with SS. Elizabeth and John* 1541, *Calling of S. Matthew* 1536. NANCY *Christ and the money-changers* 1536. PARIS Louvre *Healing of Tobit* 1555. SCHLEISS-HEIM *Ecce Homo* 1544. STOCKHOLM *Virgin and Child* 1544. The triptych *Last Judgement* with (on wings) *donor A. Rokox with three sons and S. Andrew, and his wife with ten daughters and S. Catherine* in Antwerp S. Jacques is recorded as his work by Descamps (1769) and Sir J. Reynolds (1781). Van Mander (1604) records a *Christ and the Apostles on the way to Jerusalem.* Rubens owned a *Portrait of a man with a large nose* and paintings titled *Judith* (*cf.* M. Willems) and *Lucretia* (*cf.* G. Geldorp, J. Gossaert, G. v. d. Meire) were in other 17th cent. Antwerp Collections. Pictures presumed by some his work are in various museums (*cf.* Brussels Piper Painter and Worcester Girl at Clavichord Painter).
[Fl. 371, Fl. 559, Fl. 216, Fl. 702, Fl. 892, Fl. 358, Fl. 213, Fl. 316.]

Hemmelinck, J., see **Memlinc.**

Hendricksz, Dirck (known in Italy as Errico Fiammingo). Flemish (Dutch) Sch. *b* Amsterdam (?) *c.* 1550 *d* Amsterdam 1618. *Religious subjects.* Went Naples where was witness at wedding of Cornelis Smet *q.v.* 1574; worked for Naples churches 1578-1604. **Documented Examples** (recorded by 17th cent. writers): NAPLES S. Gregorio ceiling *Execution of S. John the Baptist, Assumption of the Virgin* and other panels; S. Maria Donnaromita ceiling, *Flagellation, Virgin in Glory, King Totila and S. Benedict;* S. Paolo Maggiore *Virgin of Purity.* VIBO VALENTIA (Cattanzaro) S. Spirito *Presentation of Jesus in the Temple.* An altarpiece painted for S. Gaudioso was burnt with the church 1578.
[Fl. 154, Fl. 766, Fl. 713, Fl. 305.]

Hendrickx, L. Henri. Flemish Sch. *b* Brussels 1817 *d* Brussels 1894. *Costume history; but mainly active as book illustrator.* Director of Acad. at Saint Josse ten Noode (Brussels); designed cars for Belgian Jubilee processions 1880.
[Fl. Bib. 19th cent.]

Hendrix, Louis. Flemish Sch. *b* Peer 1827 *d* Antwerp 1888. *Religious subjects, occasional portraits.* Pupil in Antwerp Acad. Represented in ANTWERP *The Holy Women* 1869. Also in Antwerp Cathedral (*cf.* F. Vinck), S. André, S. Joseph and N. D. de Grace.
[Fl. 837.]

Hennebicq, André. Flemish Sch. *b* Tournai 1836 *d* Brussels 1904. *Costume history, portraits, landscapes, genre, religious subjects, decorative panels for Mons and Louvain public buildings.* Pupil of J. Portaels in Brussels Acad.; then in Rome. Director Mons Acad. 1870-9. Represented in BRUS-SELS *Workers in the Campagna* 1870. MONS *Messalina insulted by the people.* NAMUR *The Doge Foscari.* TOUR-NAI *Jeremiah.* [Fl. Bib. 19th cent.]

Hennecart (Hennequart, Hannequart), Jan (Jehan). Flemish Sch. 15th cent. Recorded as *decorative painter and illuminator* to Philip the Good and Charles the Bold of Burgundy 1454-75; as Court painter and 'valet de chambre' collaborated with P. Coustain *q.v.* on decorations for marriage of Charles the Bold 1468. **Signed or Documented Works:** None.
[Fl. 490, Fl. 228, Fl. 150.]

Hennegouwe, J. van, see **Gossaert.**

Henrico da Dinant, see **Bles.**

Henricus Malinus, see **Broeck, H. v. d.**

Hens, Frans. Flemish Sch. *b* Antwerp 1856 *d* Antwerp 1928. *Rural and urban landscapes; rivers and marines; also worked as engraver and botanist.* Pupil in Antwerp Acad. of J. Jacobs. Visited the Congo 1886-8. Member of Antwerp group 'De XIII' (*cf.* E. Farasyn) 1891 and of 'Kunst van Heden' (*cf.* R. Strebelle). Represented in ANTWERP, BARCELONA, BRUSSELS, GHENT.
[Fl. 388, Fl. Bib. 19th cent.]

Her (Herbruggen), Charles van. Flemish Sch. *b* Brussels 1884. *Marines, still life, portraits.* Represented in ANTWERP *Still life.* [Fl. 17.]

Herbo, Léon. Flemish Sch. *b* Templeuve, nr. Tournai 1850 *d* Ixelles 1907. *Portraits, genre, costume history.* Co-founder L'Essor group (*cf.* A. Hamesse) 1875. Represented in BRUSSELS, COURTRAI, TOURNAI, YPRES.
[Fl. 497, Fl. Bib. 19th cent.]

Herdenberg, W. S. van, see **Ehrenberg.**

Herder, of Groningen. Flemish (Dutch) Sch. *b* Groningen 1550 *d* Groningen 1609. *'History' and allegories.* In Rome where he knew Van Mander *c.* 1575. Later, painter to François Verdugo, Spanish Governor of Friesland, in Groningen.
[Fl. 559, Fl. 451, Fl. 892.]

Herdt (Herde or Hert), Jan de. Flemish Sch. *b* Antwerp before 1626 *d* place unknown after 1668. *Religious subjects, 'history', portraits, genre.* Master Antwerp Guild 1647; visited Italy and worked Brescia *c.* 1660; went Vienna (where his brother had been jeweller to Ferdinand III) before 1670. **Signed Examples:** BRÜNN Augustinerstift *Four scenes from Tasso* 1667. CARLSRUHE *An old antiquary* 1663, *Old woman counting money* 1663. His *S. Elizabeth of Portugal* documented in Brescia, S. Francisco was removed 'in a deplorable condition' in 1920. A *Santiago in combat with the moors* was recorded in Brünn S. Jacob in 1835.
[Fl. 628, Fl. 612, Fl. 892, Fl. 305.]

Hermans, Charles. Flemish Sch. *b* Brussels 1835 *d* Mentone 1924. *Anecdotic genre* (some with social comment, *cf.* L. Frédéric), *later landscapes.* Went Paris where pupil in École des B.A. and of C. Gleyre (master of A. Renoir and C. Monet) 1858-61; visited Italy; returned Brussels 1866; in later years travelled in Southern France and Spain. Represented in BRUSSELS *At Dawn* (revellers and workers) 1875. BUDA-PEST, NAMUR, TERMONDE *Visit to the children's hospital.* PHILADELPHIA *Bal masqué.*
[Fl. Bib. 19th cent.]

Herp (or **Harp**), **Guilliam** (**Willem** not **Gerard**) **van**. Flemish Sch. *b* Antwerp 1614 *d* Antwerp 1677. *Genre*. Master Antwerp Guild 1638; lover and husband of A. Wolfordt's daughter. **Signed Examples:** BERLIN K.F. *Satyr and peasant family* (*Blowing hot and cold*), *cf*. J. Jordaens. VIENNA Harrach *Soldiers attacking a cottage* (*cf*. D. Ryckaert III) 1664. Mythologies (with nudes) and religious subjects by 'Van Herp' recorded by Houbraken and Descamps may be his work or that of some member of his family. Pictures presumed by some his work are in various museums.
[Fl. 425, Fl. 216, Fl. 892.]

Herp, Guilliam van (the younger). Flemish Sch. *b* son of G.H. the elder (?), Antwerp 1657 *d* Antwerp (?) after 1729. Recorded Antwerp 1680-1729. [Fl. 107, Fl. 892.]

Herregouts, David. Flemish Sch. *b* Malines 1603 *d* Ruremonde 1662. *Religious subjects.* Master Malines Guild 1624. Worked for Malines S. Catherine. [Fl. 613, Fl. 892.]

Herregouts, Henri, known as 'Le Romain'. Flemish Sch. *b* son of David H., Malines 1633 *d* Antwerp *c*. 1704. *Religious subjects, portraits, small pictures with nymphs.* Visited Italy and Germany (Cologne); worked Malines, Antwerp and Bruges. Descamps (1763) records Antwerp S. Paul *Martyrdom of S. Matthew.* Bruges S. Anne *Last Judgement* ('with nudes that might with advantage have been draped') and other pictures in Bruges churches.
[Fl. 215, Fl. 216, Fl. 613, Fl. 892.]

Herregouts, Jan Baptist. Flemish Sch. *b* son of David H. Termonde *c*. 1640 *d* Bruges 1721. *Religious subjects, portraits; also worked as engraver.* Visited Italy; worked Antwerp 1673-1682; Bruges from 1684; founder-member of Bruges Acad. (*cf*. J. van den Kerckhove) 1717. Descamps (1769) records BRUGES Carmes Déchaussés *Flight into Egypt, Presentation in the Temple, The Virgin and Saints kneeling to Christ* and other pictures in Bruges churches. [Fl. 215, Fl. 216, Fl. 892.]

Herremans, Lieven. Flemish Sch. *b* Bruges 1858 *d* Elsene 1886. *Landscapes, genre, nudes.* Represented in ANTWERP.
[Fl. 17.]

Herreyns, Daniel the younger. Flemish Sch. *b* son of Jacob and grandson of engraver D.H. the elder, Antwerp 1678. Deaf and dumb painter. [Fl. 107.]

Herreyns (or **Herryns**), **Jacob.** Flemish Sch. *b* son of engraver Daniel H. the elder, Antwerp 1643 *d* Antwerp 1732. *Religious and mythological subjects, also worked as tapestry designer for churches and as engraver.* His son and grandson both called Jacob, are also recorded as painters. [Fl. 481, Fl. 107.]

*Herreyns, Willem Jacob (**Guillaume Jacques**). Flemish Sch. grandson of Jacob H., *b* Antwerp 1743 *d* Antwerp 1827. *Religious subjects, 'history', portraits and festival decorations.* Pupil in Antwerp Acad.; professor when 23 years old 1766; went Malines 1771, where founded Acad. under patronage of Charles of Lorraine; appointed Court History Painter by Gustavus III of Sweden *c*. 1780 but declined invitation to settle Sweden; received Emperor Joseph II in his studio (*cf*. A. C. Lens) 1781; went Antwerp (then centre of Département des Deux-Néthes during French occupation) as director and professor of Acad. (*cf*. S. P. d'Argonne) 1798; active in recovering works of art requisitioned by the French (*cf*. J. D. Odevaere) 1815. **Signed Example:** ANTWERP. *Christ on the Cross* (about 1780). **Monogrammed Example:** ANTWERP. *The Priest J. J. de Brandt* 1790. **Documented Examples:** ANTWERP Notre Dame *The Disciples at Emmaus* 1808. BRUSSELS. *Adoration of the Magi.* MALINES S. Rombaut *Scenes from the life of S. Romualdus. A Portrait of Joseph II* (*cf*. G. de Pélichy) is recorded. (*Cf*. also F. M. Smits).
[Fl. 275, Fl. 612, Fl. 451, Fl. 613, Fl. 107, Fl. 332, Fl. 798.]

Heur, Cornelis Jozef d'. Flemish Sch. *b* son of a Liège sculptor, Antwerp 1707 *d* Antwerp 1762. *'History', interiors and book illustrations.* Pupil of J. J. Horemans the elder and P. Snyers. In Paris *c*. 1730; Professor of Perspective Antwerp Academy 1749. **Signed Example:** ANTWERP (grisaille) *The Teaching of Perspective* (1761). [Fl. 107, Fl. 892.]

Heuvel, Anton van den, known as 'Don Antonio'. Flemish Sch. *b* Ghent *c*. 1600 *d* Ghent 1677. *Religious subjects, portraits.* Pupil of G. de Crayer; went Rome after 1618; back in Ghent and Master Guild 1628; much employed by religious institutions; restored H. and J. van Eyck's Ghent *Altarpiece of the Mystic Lamb* 1663 (*cf*. L. Blondeel). **Signed Example:** GHENT Mus. *Adoration of the Magi.* Descamps (1768) saw many paintings in Ghent churches and in Brussels Égl. des Capucins *Martyrdom of a Female Saint.* [Fl. 216, Fl. 892.]

Heuvick (or **Huevick**), **Gaspar.** Flemish Sch. *b* Audenarde *c*. 1550 *d* after 1611. *Religious subjects.* Went Italy where worked with Lorenzo Costa in Mantua; met van Mander in Rome *c*. 1575; later worked in Bari; van Mander records; 'he was successful in the grain trade in the last period of the high cost of living in Italy' and describes him as 'a good master widely experienced in all branches of painting'. **Signed Example:** MOLFETTA (Bari prov.) S. Bernardo *Nativity* (*with donors*) 1596. A painting *Faith, Justice and Truth* recorded (1845) in Audenarde Town Hall is said to have had his signature and date 1589 on the frame.
[Fl. 559, Fl. 892, Fl. 305.]

*Hey (**Hay**), **Johannus** (**Jean**). Presumed Flemish (or French) Sch. 15th/16th cent. *Religious subjects.* **Signed Example:** BRUSSELS *Christ crowned with thorns* inscribed on reverse 'Magr . JO . cueillete . etat' . 64/annor . notari . et . secretari '/regis . Karoli . octam . hoc/opus . insigne . fieri . fecit . /per . m . Jo . hey . teutoni/cu . pictorem . egregiu . 14/94.'
[Fl. 512, Fl. 124, Fl. 710.]

Heymans, Adriaan Josef. Flemish Sch. *b* Antwerp 1839 *d* Schaarbeeck 1921. *Landscapes* (*some with figures*), *marines.* Studied in Paris 1856-7; then went Holland and England; associated with Termonde School (*cf*. F. Crabeels, I. Meyers and J. Rosseels); member of 'Libre Ésthetique' (*cf*. G. Buysse) *c*. 1900 and of the 'Vie et Lumière' group (*cf*. G. Morren) 1914; in later years worked in Impressionist conventions. Represented in ANTWERP *Brittany wood* 1901, *Moonlight* 1908, *Stall.* BRUSSELS *Spring, Moonlight* 1907, *The heath.* GHENT *Spring in the Campine, Sunset* 1875. LIÈGE *Campine landscape.* [Fl. 388, Fl. Bib. 19th cent.]

Hoecke, Gaspar (**Jasper**) **van den.** Flemish Sch. *b* place unknown before 1585 *d* place unknown after 1648. *Religious subjects, ceremonial decorations.* Pupil in Antwerp of Juliaen Teniers the elder 1595; Master Antwerp Guild 1603; J. v. Egmont was his pupil 1615; with his son Jan v. d. H. executed 'Ferdinand Arch' under supervision of Rubens (*cf*. G. Weri), for Pageant Entry into Antwerp of Cardinal Infante Ferdinand 1635. **Signed Example:** SPIRES *Mystic marriage of S. Catherine* 1624. An *Esther, Ahasuerus and Mordecai* and a *Beheading of S. John the Baptist* belonged to Archduke Leopold Wilhelm (1659 inventory). [Fl. 107, Fl. 892.]

*Hoecke, Jan van den. Flemish Sch. *b* son of first marriage of Gaspar van den H., Antwerp 1611 *d* Antwerp or Brussels 1651. *Religious, allegorical subjects, 'history', portraits and tapestry designs.* With his father worked under Rubens (*cf*. G. Weri) for Pageant Entry into Antwerp of Cardinal Infante Ferdinand 1635; in Italy *c*. 1637-44; visited Vienna and returned Antwerp as painter in ordinary to Archduke Leopold Wilhelm (*cf*. J. B. v. Heil) 1647; member of Soc. of Antwerp Romanists 1647. **Signed Example:** STOCKHOLM Univ. *Virgin and Child with S. Anne.* **Documented Examples:**

PRAGUE Rudolfinum *Jupiter and Mercury with Philemon and Baucis* (*cf.* J. Jordaens). VIENNA K. *Archduke Leopold Wilhelm on horseback, Vanitas: a philosopher in black, with a death's head, strewing ashes on the ground while two genii blow soap bubbles* (*cf.* C. N. Gysbrechts), *Archduke Leopold Wilhelm in prayer before the Virgin and Child, Amor vincit omnia* (with dogs by P. de Vos *s*). Designs for tapestries (extant in Vienna and Stockholm) include *The Four Elements and Time, Day, Night,* and a series of *Allegories of the Months* on which P. Thys, T. Willeboirts (Bosschaert), A. v. Utrecht and J. Brueghel the younger collaborated (Archduke Leopold Wilhelm inventory 1659). Several versions of his *Charles II of England as Prince* (painted Brussels 1649) are recorded by engravings. [Fl. 86, Fl. 425, Fl. 892.]

*Hoecke, Robert van den. Flemish Sch. *b* son of second marriage of Gaspar van den H., Antwerp 1622 *d* Antwerp (?) 1668. *Picturesque battle and camp pieces* (*cf.* L. de Hondt the elder), *winter landscapes, still life; also worked as engraver.* Master Antwerp Guild 1645; patronized by Governor General Archduke Leopold Wilhelm (*cf.* J. B. v. Heil). G. Coques depicted him with a painter's implements in *Sight* ('Five Senses' series, now London N.G.). **Signed Examples:** BERLIN K.F. *Encampment* 1659. DUNKIRK *Bivouac* 1665 (with several hundred figures). LENINGRAD *The storming of a fortress.* STRASBOURG *Winter landscape.* VIENNA K. *View of Ostend, Still life with kitchen utensils* 1645. **Monogrammed Example:** VIENNA K. *Skating on Brussels moat* (RVH 1649). **Documented Example:** VIENNA K. *Troops in a camp at night; Conflagration with Archduke Leopold Wilhelm as spectator* (Archduke Leopold Wilhelm inventory 1659).
[Fl. 86, Fl. 425, Fl. 481, Fl. 892.]

Hoefnagel, Jacob (not Jan). Flemish Sch. *b* son of Joris H. *q.v.*, Antwerp 1575 *d* Holland or Munich *c.* 1630. *Miniature paintings of landscape, animal and bird and allegorical subjects; also occasional portraits; but chiefly active as engraver.* At age of 17 engraved a collection of his father's plant and animal drawings 1592; court painter to the Emperor Rudolf II (*cf.* P. Stevens the younger) 1602; was paid for pictures of the Emperor's rare birds 1610; citizen of Prague 1614; accused of financial irregularities or seditious action; fled to Munich or Holland. **Signed Examples:** VALENCIA. Coloured miniature copy of Dürer's *Samson* (*s* Antwerp 1600). A *Portrait of Maria Eleonora of Brandenburg* 1629 is recorded by an engraving. An *Orpheus charming the animals* (*cf.* L. van der Borcht) is also recorded. [Fl. 559, Fl. 892, Fl. 798.]

Hoefnagel, Joris (George). Flemish Sch. *b* son of rich diamond merchant, Antwerp 1542 *d* Vienna 1600. *Miniature drawings, paintings and book illustrations (landscapes, town views, animals, birds, insects, flowers) also worked as engraver.* Pupil in Malines (?) of Hans Bol; travelled France and Spain (*cf.* P. de. Kempener) as artist and dealer in jewels 1561-1567; in England (*cf.* S. v. d. Meulen) 1569; in Antwerp where he married (*cf.* F. Pourbus the elder) 1571; when his father's fortune was destroyed by Spanish Fury in Antwerp 1576 (*cf.* F. Badens) went with geographer A. Ortelius to Augsburg and then to Venice where witnessed burning of Doge's Palace 1577 (*cf.* L. Toeput); went Rome where declined offer from Cardinal Farnese to take the place of the recently deceased Giorgio Clovio (*cf.* B. Spranger) as his miniaturist (because through an introduction from the banker Hans Fugger of Augsburg he had already contracted to serve Duke Albert V of Bavaria in Munich); in Naples 1578; then Munich where worked for Duke Albert, for his successor William V (*cf.* P. de Witte, F. de L. Sustris) and also for Duke Ferdinand of the Tyrol (*cf.* A. de Rye); entered service of Emperor Rudolf II in Vienna and Prague (*cf.* P. Stevens the younger) 1590. He signed sometimes with his full name and sometimes with initials and a rebus (a nail). **Signed Example:** BRUSSELS Bib. Roy. *View of Seville* Antwerp 1573. **Mono-**

grammed Examples: BRUSSELS *River scene.* VIENNA (Hofbibliothek) 'Missale Romanum' 500 miniatures and 100 decorated borders (described by Van Mander) painted for Ferdinand of Tyrol 1582-90; (K.) miniatures in G. Bocskay's 'Examples of Calligraphy' (1594 'aged 52') commissioned by Emperor Rudolf II. **Documented Examples:** ROTTERDAM Boymans *Allegory of Friendship* (dedicated to Jan Rademacker). ROUEN Library *Traité de la Patience* (dated London 1569). Van Mander speaks of four books with drawings *Natural History* (quadrupeds, reptiles, birds and fishes) done for Rudolf II. Drawings (including some of English towns) for G. Braun's 'Civitates orbis terrarum' engraved in collaboration with F. Hogenberg *q.v.* and S. Novellani, published Cologne 1572-1618 are recorded. The Archduke Leopold Wilhelm's inventory (1659) lists 41 miniatures used as decoration of a room. LILLE Mus. has two miniatures *Butterflies and insects* said to be monogrammed and dated 1591.
[Fl. 559, Fl. 88, Fl. 856, Fl. 892, Fl. 798, Fl. 899, Fl. 146.]

Hoese, Jean de la. Flemish Sch. *b* Molenbeek-St. Jean, nr. Brussels 1846 *d* 1917. *Portraits, genre.* Member of Soc. Libre des B.A. (*cf.* L. Dubois) 1868 and of Sillon Group (*cf.* A. Pinot) 1893. Represented in BRUSSELS, GOTHA.
[Fl. Bib. 19th cent.]

Hoeterickx, Emile. Flemish Sch. *b* Brussels 1853 *d* Brussels 1923. *Urban genre scenes, landscapes (some w.) and decorative paintings for Brussels and Lille theatres; also active as applied art designer.* Studied Paris; member of Brussels 'L'Essor' group (*cf.* A. Hamesse) 1880; worked for some years in England (Dover and London) and Holland; professor in Brussels École d'Art industriel from 1890. Represented in ANTWERP *Scene in a park w.* ABBEVILLE *Saturday afternoon in London.* LILLE *London view.*
[Fl. Bib. 19th cent.]

Hoeven van der, A., see Houve.

Hoey, Dammes Claesz de. Flemish (Dutch) Sch. *b* Utrecht before 1520 *d* Leyden (?) 1560. *Religious subjects and ceremonial designs.* Married daughter of Lucas van Leyden. Citizen Leyden 1542; worked on funeral ceremonies in Leyden S. Peter's on death of Charles V 1559. BREMEN Kunsthalle has *Daniel as Judge s* 'Hoey' (?) presumed by some his work. [Fl. 559, Fl. 892, Fl. 798.]

Hoey (Doe or Dhoe), Jan de. Flemish (Dutch) Sch. *b* son of painter Dammes Claesz de H. (and grandson of Lucas van Leyden), Leyden 1545 *d* Fontainebleau 1615. *Religious subjects.* Pupil of his brother Lucas D.; went France and lived in Troyes 1571-1585: entered service of Henri IV and his 'peintre et valet de chambre' before 1592; his son Claud granted right of eventual succession to this post 1603; working in Fontainebleau (*cf.* A. Dubois) where Keeper of the King's pictures 1608. An *Assumption of the Virgin* and a *Church militant* painted by him for Fontainebleau chapel (removed in 19th cent. when the chapel was rebuilt) and a *Last Judgement* in Paris Notre Dame (moved during the French Revolution) are recorded.
[Fl. 287, Fl. 425, Fl. 227, Fl. 892, Fl 798.]

Hoey, Lucas Dammes (or **Lucas Dammerts**) **de.** Flemish (Dutch) Sch. *b* son of D. C. H. *q.v.*, Leyden 1533 *d* Utrecht 1604. [Fl. 559, Fl. 892.]

Hoey, N. van, see Hoy.

*Hofstadt, Pieter van der (sometimes called **de Vocht**). Flemish Sch. *b* Louvain (?) before 1505 *d* after 1569. *Religious subjects, portraits.* Recorded working for Louvain S. Jacques 1523 and on other church commissions Louvain 1552. **Signed Examples:**

CONSTANCE Cathedral *Triptych: Christ as the Man of Sorrows, The Agony in the Garden, Christ carrying the Cross,* 1569. VIENNA Liecht. *An Old Man in prayer* 156.

[Fl. 269, Fl. 798.]

Hogenberg (or **Hoogenbergh**), **Frans.** Flemish Sch. *b* Malines before 1540 *d* Cologne 1590. Recorded as painter among the Protestants driven from Flanders by Alva 1567 but worked mainly (like his brother Remigius) as an engraver; in England (*cf.* S. v. d. Meulen) 1568; in Cologne (*cf.* G. Geldorp, Jerrigh and A. de Weerdt) 1570. Worked for *Theatrum Orbis Terrarum* (1570) of the geographer A. Ortelius and for the *Civitates Orbis Terrarum* of G. Braun (*cf.* J. Hoefnagel). His engravings also include *Queen Elizabeth, Robery Dudley Earl of Leicester* (*cf.* C. Ketel, D. Barendsz, J. Savery the elder, also L. Cornelisz) and *Battle of Carnival and Lent* published by H. W. de Cock *q.v.* 1558 (*cf.* P. Bruegel the elder).

[Fl. 826, Fl. 856, Fl. 612, Fl. 613, Fl. 88, Fl. 223, Fl. 892, Fl. 798.]

Holder, Frans van. Flemish Sch. *b* son of artist, Ixelles (Brussels) 1881 *d* Geneva 1919. *Portraits, genre, landscapes, costume history (decorative panels).* Visited Spain and Italy; member of Sillon group (*cf.* A. Pinot) 1893. Represented in ANTWERP *Landscape* (pastel). BRUGES *Symphony in white* 1910, *Portrait* 1912. BRUSSELS *Evening* (portrait group) 1912. GHENT. [Fl. 160 (1920).]

Hollander, Jan de. Flemish (Dutch) Sch. 16th cent. *b* Antwerp *d* Antwerp. *Landscapes* (*cf.* F. Mostaert). Van Mander (1604) records him as the first husband of the mother of G. van Coninxloo, and adds 'he used to spend much time leaning out of the window and looking at the sky in order to paint everything true to nature (*cf.* L. van Uden); he used to allow the ground tint on his panels to show through and be part of his pictures wherein he was followed by Bruegel; his wife travelled in Brabant and Flanders and made much money selling his pictures; he produced little but his landscapes are inferior to none of his time'. Lampsonius also extols him as a landscape painter: 'This Brabant artist chose rather to paint landscapes well than to paint portraits, figures and the Deity badly.' Presumed by some identical with Jan van Amstel *q.v.*

[Fl. 559.]

Hollanders, Johannes. Flemish Sch. *b* Oosterhout 1821. *Religious subjects.* Pupil in Antwerp of N. de Keyser.

[Fl. 451.]

Hollebeke, Bruno J. C. van. Flemish Sch. *b* Bruges 1817 *d* (blind) Brussels 1892. *Costume history, religious subjects, genre, portraits.* Pupil of Bruges Acad. and in Antwerp of G. Wappers. Represented in BRUGES *Last day of the condemned man* 1840, *The last consolation.* COURTRAI *Scenes from the life of S. Armand* 1846, *Portrait of an old man* 1850. OSTEND. [Fl. 160 (1892).]

Holy Blood Master, see **Saint Sang.**

Holy Night Master, see **Dormagen Master.**

Hon, Henri le. Flemish Sch. *b* Lez Pommereul 1809 *d* San Remo 1872. *Marines and coast scenes.* Army captain and drawing master in Brussels Military Acad. Visited the Isle of Wight. [Fl. 451.]

Hondecoeter (**Hondecoutre**), **Gillis Claesz de.** Flemish Sch. *b* Malines or Antwerp *c.* 1580 *d* Amsterdam 1638. *Landscapes, some with animals.* Taken Holland by his father to escape Spanish religious persecutions (*cf.* D. v. d. Queborne); in Utrecht 1602; in Amsterdam from *c.* 1610. He was father and grandfather respectively of the Dutch bird painters Gysbert and Melchior de H.; his daughter married J. B.

Weenix. **Monogrammed Examples:** AMSTERDAM *Wooded landscape with deer* 1620, *Landscape with sportsmen shooting waterfowl.* ANTWERP *Landscape with bridges and waterfall* 1613. BERLIN K.F. *Rocky landscape.* CASSEL *River landscape* 1618. DRESDEN *Village road with cowherd* 1629. SCHLEISSHEIM, STOCKHOLM *Orpheus charming the animals* (*cf.* L. v. d. Borcht). UTRECHT *Orpheus charming the animals* 1624. [Fl. 425, Fl. 892.]

Hondt, Jan de the younger. Flemish Sch. *b* son of painter Jan de H. the elder, Malines 1649 *d* Malines 1726. Nephew of Lambert de H. *Decorative works for Malines Hôtel de Ville and other buildings are recorded.* [Fl. 613.]

*Hondt (or **Honnt**), **Lambert de the elder.** Flemish Sch. *b* place unknown before 1620 *d* Malines before 1665. *Picturesque military scenes* (*cf.* S. Vrancx, C. de Wael, P. Meulener, N. van Eyck, A. Goubau, R. v. d. Hoecke, J. Verhuyck, S. J. v. Douw, A. F. v. d. Meulen, A. Casteels, Pauwels Casteels, Pieter Casteels the younger), *landscapes with figures and cattle.* Brother of Jan de H. the elder; worked in Malines. **Signed Examples:** BAMBERG *Landscape with figures s* L. D. Hondt F 1636. FRANKFORT *Horsemen in pursuit of baggage waggon s* L. D. Honnt F. (*cf.* also J. B. v. d. Meiren).

[Fl. 613.]

Hondt, Lambert de the younger. Flemish Sch. worked Brussels and Munich (?) 1679-1709. *Designer of tapestries with military subjects* (executed for Munich Residenz Palace).

[Fl. 612, Fl. 892.]

Hondt, Philippe de. Flemish Sch. 18th cent. *Religious subjects.* Descamps (1768) saw paintings by 'de Hondt' or 'de Hondt the younger' in Brussels Notre Dame de la Chapelle, and Carmes Déchaussés, and in the Abbaye de Ninove. [Fl. 216.]

Hooghe, Antoine. Flemish Sch. *b* son of a magistrate, Bruges 1630 *d* Bruges 1662. *Landscapes and miniatures.* [Fl. 451.]

Hooghe, Balthasar Richard d'. Flemish Sch. *b* son of a magistrate, Bruges 1636 *d* Bruges 1697. *Wooded landscapes.* He was a monk and lived in the Abbaye des Dunes (*cf.* D. Bogaerde) from 1656. **Signed Example:** BRUGES S. Anne *Landscape with flight into Egypt* 1691. **Documented Examples:** BRUGES Séminaire Épiscopal (formerly Abbaye des Dunes) *Landscapes* (*cf.* P. van Bredael). [Fl. 451, Fl. 892, Fl. 114.]

*Hoogstraeten Master. Presumed Flemish Sch. early 16th cent. Name for painter of ANTWERP Mus. (383-9) *Presentation in the Temple, Jesus in the Temple, Carrying of the Cross, Crucifixion, Entombment, Mater dolorosa, Donatrix with S. Otillia* from Hoogstraeten S. Catherine. Formerly presumed by some identical with G. v. d. Meire. Pictures presumed by some his work are in various museums.

[Fl. 316.]

*Horemans, Jan Joseph the elder. Flemish Sch. *b* son of lawyer, Antwerp 1682 *d* Antwerp 1759. *Genre and portraits.* Pupil of J. van Pee. Master Antwerp Guild 1706. **Signed Examples:** AIX-EN-PROVENCE *Card players.* BRUSSELS *The poacher denounced.* BRUNSWICK *Musical company* 1715. BUDAPEST *Card players, Skittle players.* DARMSTADT *Fighting peasants, Dancing peasants.* DRESDEN *Cobbler in workshop, Mother and sleeping child.* DUBLIN *Kitchen interior.* FLORENCE Uffizi *Card players.* ORLÉANS *The conjurer, The schoolmistress.* VIENNA K. *The shoemaker's shop* 1712, *Village school* 1712. **Documented Example:** ANTWERP *Reception of the Abbot of S. Michel by the Confraternity of Fencers at the entrance of their Headquarters* (commissioned from J. J. the elder and his son J. J. the younger 1746), *cf* F. X. H. Verbeeck.

[Fl. 878, Fl. 481, Fl. 107, Fl. 892.]

*Horemans, Jan Joseph the younger. Flemish Sch. *b* son of Jan Joseph H. the elder *q.v.*, Antwerp 1714 *d* Antwerp after 1790. *Conversation pieces, portraits, bourgeois genre scenes and contemporary history.* Dean Antwerp Guild 1769. In the mid-nineteenth century many of his works were said to be in English collections. **Signed Examples:** AMSTERDAM Rijks. *Music party, Interior with figures.* NEW YORK Met. *Autumn* (1762), *Winter* (1761), *A landlord and his tenant* (1764), *Returning from the hunt* (1761), *The fish market* (1762), *Rest after hunting.* **Documented Example:** ANTWERP *Triumphal Entry of Charles of Lorraine into Antwerp in 1749. Cf.* W. I. Kerricx. [Fl. 481, Fl. 107.]

Horemans, Pieter Jacob. Flemish Sch. *b* son of a lawyer, Antwerp 1700 *d* almost blind, Munich 1776. *Court festivals, conversation groups* (*cf.* I. v. d. Beken, and J. J. H. the younger and J. F. Nollekens) *and single portraits, genre scenes, fruit and flower pieces.* Pupil of his brother J. J. H. the elder; settled Munich 1725; court painter to Charles Albert, Elector of Bavaria (later Emperor Charles VII) 1727. **Signed Examples:** AUGSBURG *Fruit piece* (1768). NUREMBERG Germ. Mus. *Fruit piece* (1766). SCHLEISSHEIM *Two portraits of Court Musicians* (1774 and 1777), *Portrait of his friend, the sculptor W. de Grooft* (1766), *Self portrait* (1766). *A Carrousel celebrating birth of Kurfürst Max-Joseph* 1727, a *Concert, Quadrille and Coffee Party celebrating visit of Augustus III of Poland and his family* (with thirty-two portraits) 1761 and two hundred *Portraits of court ladies* painted for Nymphenburg (Amalienburg) are recorded. [Fl. 612, Fl. 107, Fl. 892.]

Horenbant, Joseph. Flemish Sch. *b* Ghent 1863. *Landscapes, genre.* Pupil in Ghent Acad. of T. Canneel. Represented in ANTWERP *Lacemakers.* GHENT *Happy old age.* NAMUR. [Fl. 17.]

Horenbout (or Hornebolt), Gerard. Flemish Sch. *b* son of a Ghent artist (?) before 1470 *d* London or Ghent after 1540. *Portraits and religious subjects in oil, book illustrations, designs for windows.* In Ghent Guild 1487; in service of Margaret of Austria, regent of the Netherlands 1516-21 (*cf.* J. Schooff); probably in Antwerp where Dürer met his daughter Susanna 1521; to England (*cf.* S. v. d. Meulen) with his daughter *c.* 1522; paid by Henry VIII for work from 1528 (*cf.* L. Teerlinck, L. Horenbout and S. Horenbout). **Semidocumented Example:** LONDON Royal Soc. of Antiquaries *Christian II of Denmark* (*cf.* J. Gossaert) 1521 presumed by some a portrait recorded as commissioned by Margaret of Austria from Gérard Harembourg with whom he is presumed by some to be identical. A *Flagellation* and a *Descent from the Cross* (with, in the background, the three Maries carrying lanterns as they approach the sepulchre), painted for Ghent S. Bavon and saved from the Iconoclasts (1566), and a tondo painted on both sides with *Christ crowned with thorns* and *Virgin and Child with angels* are recorded by Van Mander (1604).
[Fl. 243, Fl. 371, Fl. 559, Fl. 892, Fl. 223, Fl. 10 (1939), Fl. 28.]

Horenbout (or Hornebolt), Lucas. Flemish Sch. *b* son or brother or cousin of Gerard H. *q.v.*, presumably Flanders date unknown *d* London 1544. *Paintings and miniatures.* Worked at Court of Henry VIII from 1528 or earlier; King's Painter and naturalized 1534; gave Henry VIII a firescreen and received from the King 'a gilte cruse, with a cover' 1539; Van Mander (1604) records that before Holbein went into the service of King Henry VIII he had not done any miniature painting but learned the technique from one of the King's artists by the name of Lucas who was renowned for his miniatures, and whom he 'surpassed as much as the light of the sun surpasses that of the moon'. *Cf.* S. v. d. Meulen and L. Teerlinck. [Fl. 371, Fl. 818, Fl. 559, Fl. 223, Fl. 535, Fl. 28.]

Horenbout (or Hornebolt), Susanna. Flemish Sch. *b* daughter of Gerard H., Ghent *c.* 1503 *d* Worcester 1545. *Miniatures.* Met Dürer in Antwerp 1521 and D. wrote 'Master Gerard, the illuminator, has a daughter about 18 years old called Susanna she has illumined a little piece, a Saviour, for which I gave her one florin' 'ist ein gross Wunder dass ein Weibsbild also viel machen soll' (Dürer also states that he himself drew her portrait); to England with her parents *c.* 1522, where she had success at Henry VIII's Court (*cf.* L. Teerlinck), and married first John Parker Gentleman of the Robes and second a sculptor named Worsley attached to the Royal Household. *Cf.* S. v. d. Meulen. [Fl. 243, Fl. 371, Fl. 818, Fl. 535.]

Horion, Alexander de. Flemish Sch. *b* Liège *c.* 1590 *d* Liège (?) 1659. *Portraits, religious subjects.* City painter of Liège 1626. A *Resurrection* in Liège S. Clara and a signed *Dismissal of Hagar* 1646 are recorded. [Fl. 63, Fl. 451, Fl. 892.]

Horizonte, see Bloemen, J. F.

Hornes (or Dehorne or Horne), Jacques de. Flemish Sch. *b* Malines before 1620 *d* Malines 1674. *Religious and decorative paintings.* Pupil of G. Beerings the younger. Master in Malines Guild 1648; worked for Malines churches and on decorations for Malines allegiance ceremony to Charles II of Spain 1666 (*cf.* F. Duchatel and E. Quellinus). [Fl. 613, Fl. 614, Fl. 88.]

Horst, Nicolaus van der. Flemish Sch. *b* Antwerp 1587 or 1598 *d* Brussels 1646. *Portraits; but mainly worked as draughtsman of official ceremonies for engravers.* Pupil of Rubens. Travelled France, Italy and Germany, then settled Brussels where was halbardier to household of Archduke Albert and Infanta Isabella (*cf.* D. v. Alsloot). J. Meyssens (not Mytens) was his pupil. May have visited England. **Signed Example:** BRUSSELS Town Hall *Procession of the Infanta Isabella with four hundred nuns to N.D. de Laeken in 1623.* **Documented Drawings:** ANTWERP Plantin Mus. *Ceremonial entry of Marie de Médicis into Antwerp* 1631. Portraits of *Marie de Médicis* (*cf.* F. Pourbus the younger), *Charles I and Henrietta Maria of England* and *Octavio Piccolomini* are recorded by engravings. [Fl. 86, Fl. 425, Fl. 107, Fl. 892.]

Houben, Henri. Flemish Sch. *b* Antwerp 1858 *d* Antwerp (?) 1910. *Landscapes, genre* (some with Zeeland subjects), *murals.* Teacher in Antwerp Acad. Represented in ANTWERP Town Hall *The cultivation of music in Antwerp* (mural based on drawing by A. de Vriendt *q.v.*) (*cf.* also C. Boom). [Fl. 741, Fl. 73, Fl. 798.]

Houseman, Jacob, see Huysmans.

Houten, F. van. Flemish Sch. 17th cent. **Signed Example:** VIENNA Liecht. *Guard room.* [Fl. 892.]

Houten (or Hout or Houtter), T. van. Flemish Sch. 17th cent. Presumed *b* and working Brussels. *Landscapes and peasant genre.* [Fl. 892.]

Houve (or Hoeven), Aper Fransz. (Franssen) van der. Flemish Sch. *b* Delft (?) before 1550 *d* Delft *c* 1623. Pupil of Frans Floris; worked in Fontainebleau with H. Francken the elder, H. de Maier and Cornelis Ketel (*cf.* L. Thiry) 1566; later returned Delft where painted little and became a collector and brewer. [Fl. 559.]

Houwaert (Hovart), Jan Lambertsz; called in Italy Giovanni di Lamberto. Flemish Sch. *b* Antwerp *d* Genoa 1668. *Portraits, religious subjects.* Went Genoa where pupil of Cornelis de Wael before 1656; lived there till his death. **Documented Example:** GENOA S. Maria Maddalena *A saint with three nuns* (described by contemporary writer Soprani). [Fl. 773, Fl. 305.]

Houzé, Florentin. Flemish Sch. *b* Tournai 1812 *d* after 1860. *Costume history, religious subjects, genre.* Pupil of N. de Keyser; also studied in Paris; worked Tournai and Brussels. Represented in BRUSSELS *The last moments of Grethrys' daughter* 1860. TOURNAI *A Cardinal visiting Tournai Hospital*; and churches. [Fl. 451, Fl. 481.]

Hove, Edmond van. Flemish Sch. *b* Bruges 1851 *d* Bruges 1913. *Costume history, genre, religious subjects, portraits.* Pupil Bruges Acad. and in Paris of the French painter A. Cabanel; visited Italy. Represented in ANTWERP *The head of S. John the Baptist* 1879. BRUGES Mus. *Galilee* 1885, *The Savant*; S. Giles *Altarpiece* (polyptych). BRUSSELS *Jacques van Maerlandt* 1890. GLASGOW *The botanist.* [Fl. Bib. 19th cent.]

Hove, Victor F. G. van. Flemish Sch. *b* Renaix 1826 *d* Koekelbergh, nr. Brussels 1891. *Genre, portraits; but chiefly active as sculptor.* Pupil of sculptor F. Rude in Paris. Represented in BRUSSELS *Dutch girl, Selfportrait.* LIÈGE *Dutch girls on way to church.* [Fl. Bib. 19th cent.]

Hoy (or Hoey), Nicolas van. Flemish Sch. *b* Antwerp 1631 *d* Vienna 1679. *Religious and allegorical subjects, military pieces, genre, portraits; also worked as engraver.* Pupil of M. Matheussens; went Rome where became friendly with the Dutch artist J. v. Ossenbeeck; in Brussels where employed by Archduke Leopold Wilhelm (*cf.* J. B. v. Heil); contributed to D. Teniers' 'Theatrum Pictorium'; went Vienna where worked for Emperor Leopold I and Count Schwarzenberg. Pictures painted for Vienna and Graz churches are recorded. [Fl. 753, Fl. 892.]

Hubert, Alfred. Flemish Sch. *b* Liège 1830 *d* Brussels 1902. *Military genre, animals, landscapes; also active as illustrator and sculptor.* An artillery officer, he worked at first as amateur; later produced many sepia and other drawings; his oil paintings are rare; visited Spain and Morocco. Represented in BRUSSELS *Waterloo cuirassiers.* LIÈGE *After the battle, Circus horses.* [Fl. 264, Fl. 440.]

Huberti, Édouard J. J. Flemish Sch. *b* Brussels 1818 *d* Schaarbeek 1880. *Landscapes, flowers, still life.* Began as student of architecture in Antwerp Acad.; then active as composer (mainly of songs); influenced by T. Fourmois and the Tervueren School (*cf.* H. Boulenger); member of Brussels group 'Soc. Libre des B.A.' (*cf.* L. Dubois) 1868 (H. Lambrich included him in his picture of the group's members). Represented in ANTWERP *Marsh in the Campine.* BRUSSELS *Grey weather.* [Fl. 466 (1880), Fl. Bib. 19th cent.]

Huffel, Peter van. Flemish Sch. *b* Grammont 1769 *d* Ghent 1844. *Religious subjects, portraits.* Pupil in Malines of W. J. Herreyns; in Paris *c.* 1799 (*cf.* L. Gerbo); returned Ghent where Director of Academy (*cf.* A. I. Steyaert) in 1814. Worked for Prince and Princess of Orange. **Documented Example:** ANTWERP *Napoleon Bonaparte as First Consul* (miniature). Altarpieces for Dooreseele Abbey (1817), Ghent S. Bavon and S. Jacques and a *John Quincy Adams, American Ambassador to the Congress of Ghent 1814* are recorded. Portraits of prelates are also recorded. [Fl. 451.]

*****Hugo of Antwerp.** Flemish Sch. 15th cent. Painter of FLORENCE Uffizi (48, 49, 50) large triptych known as *The Portinari Altarpiece: Adoration of the Shepherds* (centre), *SS. Thomas and Anthony Abbot with donor Tommaso Portinari and his sons* (wing), *SS. Margaret and Mary Magdalene with Maria Baroncelli Portinari's wife, and daughter* (wing). Bought by the Italian State 1897 from Florence Church of the Hospital of S. Maria Nuova to which it was donated by Portinari (Medici agent sent to Bruges for Charles the Bold's wedding 1468, and married 1470). Presumed by some identical with H. v. d. Goes *q.v.* [Fl. 818, Fl. 371.]

Hulle (real name Hebbelynck), Anselmus van. Flemish Sch. *b* Ghent 1601 *d* Germany (?) after 1674. *Religious subjects, portraits.* Master Ghent Guild 1620; in service of Prince Frederick Henry of Orange in Holland after 1642; sent Münster to make portraits of delegates at peace conference concluding Thirty-Years-War 1648; later worked for Emperor Ferdinand III (who ennobled him) and visited other German courts. **Signed Example:** GHENT Mus. *Pietà.* Descamps (1768) saw Ghent (N.D.) *Coronation of the Virgin. Cf.* F. Luyckx. [Fl. 216, Fl. 892.]

Hulmans, Jan. Flemish Sch. 17th cent. *Landscapes.* Worked Antwerp. **Signed Example:** BERLIN *Vintagers in a rocky landscape with castle.* [Fl. 77, Fl. 787.]

Hulsdonck, Gillis van. Flemish Sch. *b* son of Jacob van H., Antwerp (?) *c.* 1625 *d* Antwerp (?) after 1669. *Still life.* [Fl. 107, Fl. 892.]

*****Hulsdonck, Jacob van.** Flemish Sch. *b* Antwerp 1582 *d* Antwerp 1647. *Still life* (*cf.* O. Beet, J. van Es, T. Aenvanck). Master Antwerp Guild by 1609. **Signed Examples:** BARNARD CASTLE *Basket of Fruit.* BONN, MUNICH A.P. *Lobster, orange, peeled lemon, bread, drinking vessels.* ORLÉANS and STOCKHOLM. [Fl. 107, Fl. 892.]

Hulsman (Holsman or Holtzman), Jan (Johann). Presumed Flemish Sch. *b* place unknown before 1615 *d* Cologne (?) after 1644. *Religious subjects, 'history', genre, portraits.* Worked Cologne. **Signed Examples:** COLOGNE Cathedral *Martyrdom of S. Stephen* 1639; Wallraf-Rich. *Martyrdom of S. Cecilia.* NUREMBERG *Feast in a park* 1644. An engraving with his signature depicts a *Troop of Gypsies in a landscape.* [Fl. 86, Fl. 753, Fl. 425, Fl. 892.]

Hulst, Jan Baptist van der. Flemish Sch. *b* Louvain 1790 *d* Brussels 1862. *Portraits and religious subjects for churches.* Pupil of J. P. Geedts. Visited Paris 1819; Rome 1825-6; in Louvain 1827; court painter to William I from *c.* 1828; **Signed Examples:** AMSTERDAM Rijks. *King William I* went The Hague 1830; later Court Painter to William II. 1833, *Queen Wilhelmina* 1833, *Count Adam v. d. Duyn* 1839. **Documented Example:** WANDERGEM Church *Nativity.* A *Miracle of the Holy Sacrament* for Louvain S. Jacques is also recorded. [Fl. 451, Fl. 481, Fl. 892, Fl. 440.]

Hulst (Verhulst), Pieter van der the elder. Flemish Sch. *b* Malines (?) before 1575 *d* 1628 (?). *Landscape.* Master Antwerp Guild 1589; Jan Wildens and P. de Witte the younger were his pupils 1596. Another P. v. d. H., presumed his son, is recorded in Antwerp 1623-37. Rubens had an assistant for landscapes called 'Verholst' who worked on his *View from the Escorial* (painted 1628 and sold by Rubens to Charles I in 1640 and now in a private collection) *cf.* L. v. Uden. **Signed Example:** BRUNSWICK *Village fair* (P. v. Hulst) 1628. *Cf.* V. Wolfvoet. [Fl. 892.]

Humbeeck, Pierre van. Flemish Sch. *b* Louvain 1891. *Figures, decorative compositions, religious subjects, book illustrations.* Pupil Brussels Acad. of J. Delville. Represented in ANTWERP *Girls of the Ardennes.* [Fl. 17.]

Hunin, Alouis P. P. Flemish Sch. *b* son of engraver Joseph H., Malines 1808 *d* Malines 1855. *Anecdotic genre.* Pupil in Antwerp Acad. of F. de Braekeleer the elder and in Paris of Ingres. Represented in BRUSSELS *Nuns distributing alms.* [Fl. 451, Fl. 481, Fl. 837 (1855).]

Huygens, François Joseph. Flemish Sch. *b* Brussels 1820 *d* 1908. *Flowers.* Represented in BRUSSELS *Hawthorn* 1875. LOUVAIN *Roses.* [Fl. 123.]

*Huys, Pieter. Flemish Sch. *b* 1519 (?) *d* 1581 (?). *Religious, fantastic* (*cf.* H. Bosch, P. Bruegel the elder, F. Francken, Madrid Triumph of Death Painter, J. Mandyn, F. Mostaert, G. Mostaert, J. Cornelisz van Oostsanen, D. Ryckaert III, F. Verbeeck) *and genre subjects; also worked as book-illustrator for Plantin Press and as engraver.* Master Antwerp Guild as painter 1545. **Signed Examples:** ANTWERP M. van den Bergh *Temptation of S. Anthony* 1577. BERLIN K. F. *Bagpiper and old woman* 1571. MADRID Prado *Battle of angels and demons; and torments of Hell* 1570. PARIS Louvre *Temptation of S. Anthony* 1547. Pictures presumed by some his work are in various museums (*cf.* Brussels Piper Painter). [Fl. 892, Fl. 615.]

Huysmans (Housmans), Cornelis, called 'Huysmans of Malines' (Van Mecheln), Flemish Sch. *b* son of an architect, Antwerp 1648 *d* Malines 1727. *Wooded landscapes* (*some with figures) also Italianate landscapes* (*cf.* J. B. Juppin). Pupil in Antwerp of G. de Witte and in Brussels of J. d'Arthois; assisted d'Arthois for two years in pictures of the forest of Soignes; then worked Malines; declined invitation from A. F. v. d. Meulen to establish himself in Paris; visited England (*cf.* C. de Neve, J. B. Medina and S. Hardimé) where had frames made by Grinling Gibbons and gave him pictures in exchange; back in Antwerp by 1702 and member of Guild there 1706; returned Malines 1716. Descamps (who saw a number of his pictures in his daughter's house) states that (1) he painted landscape background for 'history' painters, (2) 'retouched' landscapes by Minderhout, Achtschellinck and d'Arthois, (3) excelled in painting mountains and rocks and (4) that the colour in his foregrounds resembled Rembrandt's. **Documented Examples:** MALINES Notre Dame *The Road to Emmaus* (seen by Descamps 1768). COPENHAGEN *Wooded landscape with rocky foreground and figures* (bought 1763), *Wooded landscape with huts* (bought 1742). VIENNA K. *Wooded landscape* (catalogued 1783). Pictures presumed by some his work are in many museums.
[Fl. 878, Fl. 826, Fl. 215, Fl. 216, Fl. 856, Fl. 892.]

*Huysmans (called **Houseman** in England), **Jacob.** Flemish Sch. *b* Antwerp *c.* 1633 *d* London 1696. *Portraits, religious subjects and 'history'.* Pupil of G. Backereel and F. Wouters; came England (*cf.* C. de Neve) soon after 1660; Pepys wrote (1664): 'To see some pictures at one Huysman's . . . which is said to exceed Lely; and indeed there is both of the Queen's and Maids of Honour, particularly Mrs. Stuart's in a buff doublet like a soldier, as good pictures, I think, as ever I saw. The Queen is drawn in one like a Shepherdess, in the other like S. Catherine, most like and most admirably. I was mightily pleased with this sight indeed'; worked Chichester (Sussex) for a time after the Great Fire 1666; was witness in trial of the presumed Catholic murderers of Sir Edmund Berry Godfrey (Magistrate who had received deposition from Titus Oates) 1678; lived in Jermyn Street in later life. **Signed Example:** LONDON N.P.G. *Izaak Walton.* **Documented Examples:** LONDON Royal Coll. *Queen Catherine of Braganza as Shepherdess with Cupids, Frances Stuart Duchess of Richmond 'in a buff doublet like a soldier';* Painters Stainers Hall *Queen Catherine.* DULWICH *Head of a woman.* Vertue (before 1756) states that he painted an alterpiece in the Queen's Chapel St. James' (*cf.* W. de Keyser) and introduced the Queen's features into his religious and mythological pictures; he records two portraits of *Charles II, Bernard and Mrs. Granville* in Lord Lansdowne's collection and *Judge Jenner* at Hampton Court. Portraits recorded by engravings include *Queen Catherine as S. Catherine* and *Alexander Browne* (author of *Ars Pictoria*).
[Fl. 645, Fl. 878, Fl. 826, Fl. 856, Fl. 223, Fl. 38, Fl. 744.]

*Huysmans, Jan Baptist. Flemish Sch. *b* Antwerp 1654 *d* Antwerp 1716. *Italianate landscapes* (*cf.* J. B. Juppin) *some with wooded foregrounds and figures and animals.* Master Antwerp Guild 1677. **Signed Examples:** ANTWERP *Landscape with cattle* (1700). BRUSSELS *Landscape with cattle and two herdsmen* (1697). MUNICH A.P. (1695). [Fl. 892.]

Huysmans, Jan Baptist. Flemish Sch. *b* Antwerp 1826 *d* after 1890. *Costume and contemporary history, religious subjects, anecdotic genre* (*some of Near Eastern subjects), book illustrations.* Pupil Antwerp Acad., then studied Paris. Travelled widely in Europe and the Near East from 1854. Represented in ANTWERP *Leopold I laying Foundation Stone of Kattendyk docks 1856* (1866). [Fl. Bib. 19th cent.]

I

Ijkens, Catharina. Flemish Sch. *b* Antwerp 1659 *d* place and date unknown. *Still life: fruit and flower garlands round grisailles pictures* (*cf.* D. Seghers). In Antwerp Guild 1688.

[Fl. 481, Fl. 107, Fl. 892.]

*Ijkens (or Eykens or Ykens), Frans. Flemish Sch. *b* Antwerp 1601 *d* in poverty, Brussels (?) *c.* 1693. *Still life, flowers and garlands* (*cf.* D. Seghers), *also genre.* Pupil of his uncle O. Beet the elder 1614. In France (Aix-en-Provence and Marseilles) 1629; Master Antwerp Guild 1630; married daughter of L. Floquet 1635; in Brussels 1666. **Signed Examples** (Still life): BERLIN K.F., GHENT (1636), LENINGRAD Hermitage *Lady at market*, MADRID Prado *Hare, asparagus and dead game* 1646, VIENNA K. *Flowers in a glass vase*, ANTWERP Plantin, CARLSRUHE (1652), OXFORD Ashmolean (1646) and ROTTERDAM Boymans.

[Fl. 425, Fl. 878, Fl. 215, Fl. 892.]

*Ijkens (Ykens), Jan. Flemish Sch. *b* son of a sculptor, Antwerp 1613 *d c.* 1679. *Allegorical and religious subjects; also worked as sculptor.* In Antwerp Guild as sculptor 1640; learned painting from his friend D. Ryckaert. **Signed Example:** ANTWERP *Allegory in honour of the Birth of a Prince* 1659.

[Fl. 425, Fl. 892.]

Ijkens, Karel. Flemish Sch. *b* Antwerp 1682 *d* Brussels (?). *Religious subjects and 'history'.* Master Brussels Guild 1718.

[Fl. 584, Fl. 892.]

Ijkens, Karel the younger. Flemish Sch. *b* son of K.I., Brussels 1719 *d* Antwerp 1753. *Religious and allegorical subjects.* Pupil of P. Snyers in Antwerp. Master Antwerp Guild 1746; spent his last years in an Antwerp monastery; A. C. Lens was his pupil.

[Fl. 892.]

Ijkens (or Eykens or Ykens), Peter. Flemish Sch. *b* son of a painter and sculptor, Antwerp 1648 *d* Antwerp 1695. *Religious subjects, portraits.* Master Antwerp Guild 1673; married daughter of P. van Bredael and had thirteen children; contracted to paint for an Antwerp councillor for three years for fixed wage 1675. **Signed Examples:** ANTWERP Mus. *S. Catherine disputing with the heathen scholars* (1684); S. André *Last Supper* (1687). LILLE *Stigmatisation of S. Theresa.* **Documented Examples:** ANTWERP Mus. *J. B. Greyns* (painted for Guild for exemption from war service 1690). Descamps (1769) recorded in Malines, SS. Pierre et Paul *Two scenes from life of S. Francis Xavier.* A *Charles II of Spain* (*cf.*

F. Duchatel and P. Thys) painted for Antwerp Magistrates 1686 (seen by Descamps 1768 and later taken to Paris) and an *Abraham and Hagar* presented to Antwerp Guild 1689 are recorded. (*Cf.* J. d'Arthois and J. B. Wans). [Fl. 216, Fl. 892.]

Immenraet, Andries. Flemish Sch. *b* son of Philips Augustyn I., Antwerp 1662 *d* insane after 1699. *Landscapes.* Taken by amateur A. van Leyen (to whom De Bie's 'Gulden Cabinet' was dedicated) to France, Italy and Germany 'to draw everything his patron selected' 1685; Master Antwerp Guild 1687. A signed *View of Gaasbeck Castle* 1699 is recorded.

[Fl 107, Fl. 303, Fl. 892.]

Immenraet (or Imrath), Michiel Engel (or Michel Angelo). Flemish Sch. *b* son of a piano maker, Antwerp 1621 *d* Utrecht 1683. *Religious subjects, 'history', portraits.* Brother of P. A. I. and painted figures in some of his landscapes; Master Antwerp Guild 1663; recorded as ('Imrath') in Idstein (Hesse-Nassau) 1673-5; married three times and died in poverty. **Signed Examples:** THE HAGUE Gem. Mus. *Portraits of the Wassenaer sisters as Shepherdesses* 1661. A signed *Continence of Scipio* and a *Full length portrait of a young nobleman* 1662 are recorded. [Fl. 107, Fl. 892.]

Immenraet (or Emmelraet or Hemelraet), Philips Augustyn. Flemish Sch. *b* son of a piano maker, Antwerp 1627 *d* Antwerp 1679. *Italianate landscapes.* Pupil in Antwerp of L. v. Uden. Spent some years in Rome; back in Antwerp by 1655. The figures in his pictures were habitually by other artists including his brother Michiel E. I. and E. Quellinus. P. Rysbraeck was his pupil. **Signed Example:** AIX-EN-PROVENCE *Landscape with waterfall* 1676. **Documented Example:** BRUSSELS *Landscape in the Story of William Tell performed at Antwerp* (*cf.* C. E. Biset). Works in Antwerp Carmes Déchaussés are recorded by Houbraken (1718) and Descamps (1769). [Fl. 425, Fl. 216, Fl. 892.]

Impens, Josse. Flemish Sch. *b* Brussels 1840 *d* Brussels 1905. *Genre.* Pupil P. J. Portaels. Represented in BRUSSELS *Flemish Cabaret.* [Fl. 160 (1905).]

Isenbrant, see **Ysenbrandt.**

Iserentant, Mayou. Flemish Sch. *b* Liège 1903. *Landscapes, interiors, genre, portraits.* Represented in ANTWERP *House behind trees* 1939. [Fl. 17.]

Isselsteyn, A., see **Ysselsteyn.**

J

Jacob of Amsterdam, see **Cornelisz van Oostsanen.**

Jacob of Utrecht, see **Claessens, J.**

Jacob, Jansz (Jacob of Haarlem). Flemish (Dutch) Sch. *b* before 1454 *d* Haarlem 1509. *Religious subjects.* Documented in Haarlem from 1483; Jan Mostaert when very young was his pupil. A *Crucifixion* painted for the Carriers' Guild in Haarlem S. Bavo 1474 was extant till 1784 (*cf.* R. Aertsz).
[Fl. 559, Fl. 883.]

Jacobs, Gerard. Flemish Sch. *b* Antwerp 1865. *Marines.* Represented ANTWERP.
[Fl. 17.]

Jacobs, Jacob A. M. Flemish Sch. *b* Antwerp 1812 *d* Antwerp 1879. *Marines, landscapes, animals.* Pupil of M. van Brée and G. Wappers. Visited England, Russia and other European countries: also Egypt and the Balkans; teacher in Antwerp Acad. 1843; sold pictures to Queen Victoria and Prince Albert for their Osborne collection. Represented in ANTWERP *Waterfall in Norway* 1855. BERLIN, BRUSSELS, COURTRAI, CONSTANTINOPLE, MUNICH N.P. *Shipwreck of the Floridian on the Essex Coast 1848.*
[Fl. 451, Fl. 837 (1879), Fl. Bib. 19th cent.]

Jacobs, Pierre François. Flemish Sch. *b* Brussels 1780 *d* Rome 1808. *Costume history.* Pupil of A. Lens; also studied Paris and Rome. Represented in BRUSSELS *Pompey's head brought to Julius Caesar when he landed in Egypt.*
[Fl. 451, Fl. 481, Fl. 88.]

Jacobsz, Dirk. Flemish (Dutch) Sch. *b* son of Jacob Cornelisz v. Oostsanen, Amsterdam *c.* 1500 *d* Amsterdam 1567. *Portrait groups* (*cf.* C. Anthonisz and D. Barendsz). Van Mander (1604) records many pictures painted from life in the Amsterdam headquarters of the Civic Guards (Doelen); and a portrait with a hand especially admired. **Monogrammed Examples** (D. I. and his father's mark): AMSTERDAM *Seventeen members of the Civic Guard* 1529 (with wings containing other portraits presumed later additions), *Twelve members of the Civic Guard* (inscribed Vreede: Eendrachticheidt Behaecht: Gods Maiesteid 1563). LENINGRAD *Group of Guards* 1532, *Another* 1561.
[Fl. 559, Fl. 892, Fl. 316.]

Jacobsz (or Jacobszoon), Hughe. Flemish (Dutch) Sch. *b* Leyden before 1480 *d* before 1539. Father of Lucas van Leyden *q.v. Religious subjects.* In Leyden Civic Guard 1494; worked for Ghent S. Peter's Abbey. Van Mander records him as an excellent artist.
[Fl. 559, Fl. 811.]

Jacobsz, Lucas, see **Leyden.**

Jacobsz, Simon. Flemish (Dutch) Sch. *b* Gouda 1520 *d* fighting as a volunteer during the siege of Haarlem 1573. *Portraits.* Pupil of Karel Foort. Van Mander records a portrait of the Haarlem glass painter *Willem Tybout.*
[Fl. 559.]

Jacquin, François X. J. Flemish Sch. *b* Brussels 1756 *d* Louvain 1826. *Portraits, still life.* Pupil Brussels Acad. and of H. J. Antonissen in Antwerp. Founder-member and teacher Louvain Acad. 1800. A portrait *The Emperor Francis II* painted for Louvain Town Hall (burnt 1795) is recorded by an engraving; clerical portraits are recorded in Louvain churches and University.
[Fl. 269, Fl. 88.]

Jamar, Armand G. G. Flemish Sch. *b* Liège 1870 *d* 1947 *Landscapes, marines, interiors, industrial and peasant genre.* Pupil of E. Carpentier. Visited Brittany, U.S.A. and North Africa; worked much in the region of Bruges. Represented in ANTWERP *Steel works.* LIÈGE *Peasant interior.* LILLE and ROUEN.
[Fl. 465.]

Jambers, Theodorus (Thierry). Flemish Sch. *b* Brussels 1804 *d* after 1842. *Genre.* Represented in COURTRAI Mus. *The Smoker s* 1841.
[Fl. 451]

Jan de Bruxelles, see **Roome.**

Jans, Édouard de. Flemish Sch. *b* St. André-lez-Bruges 1855 *d* Antwerp 1919. *Portraits, figure subjects, murals.* Pupil of N. de Keyser and A. Verlat; went Paris where pupil of the French painter A. Cabanel; Rome prizewinner 1878; member of Antwerp group De Dertien (XIII) 1891 (*cf.* E. Farasyn); travelled Italy and central Europe. Represented in ANTWERP Mus. *Portraits*; Hôtel de Ville *Staircase painting.* BRUGES *Portrait, Departure of Prodigal Son* 1881, *Return of the Prodigal Son* 1878. BUCHAREST *Roman Scene* (two).
[Fl. 699 (1922/3).]

*Janssens (van Nuyssen), Abraham. Flemish Sch. *b* Antwerp 1575 *d* Antwerp 1632. *Religious subjects* (*some with torchlight effects, cf.* H. Jordaens I), '*history*', *portraits, allegories.* Pupil of Jan Snellinck. Visited Italy where recorded Rome 1598; Master Antwerp Guild and member Society of Romanists and of Antwerp Chamber of Rhetoric (Violiere) 1601; married daughter of P. Goetkint; G. Seghers and T. Rombouts were his pupils; his daughter married Jan Brueghel the younger; challenged Rubens to a competition which R. declined; said to have worked little in later years and spent his time in taverns. **Documented Examples:** ANTWERP Mus. *Allegory of Antwerp and the Scheldt* (painted for Antwerp Town Hall 1610); Maison de la Vieille Arbalètre *Allegory of Peace* 1614 (both seen by Descamps 1768). Descamps also records pictures in Ghent S. Bavon and S. Pierre Abbey (*The Crowning with Thorns by torchlight*) and in Bruges and Malines churches. A *Crucifixion* sold 1626 in Antwerp for 1000 guilders is recorded (1643). A *S. Thomas* exported (1643) from Antwerp to Lisbon was described by the recipient as 'stony and cold like most of his paintings'; works exported in the 17th cent. to central Europe included a *Vertumnus and Pomona.* A portrait of *The Humanist Justus Lipsius* is recorded by an engraving.
[Fl. 86, Fl. 753, Fl. 425, Fl. 215, Fl. 216, Fl. 892, Fl. 212, Fl. 213, Fl. 214.]

Janssens, Daniel. Flemish Sch. *b* Malines 1636 *d* Malines 1682. *Decorative paintings, designs for Ommegancks* (*cf.* D. van Alsloot) *and other processions.* Master Malines Guild 1660; in Antwerp Guild 1667. **Documented Example:** MALINES Mus. Communal *Portions of triumphal arch for Jubilee of S. Romualdus 1680.* Paintings and decorations for Malines churches (1680), and canvas ceiling paintings for Malines Town Hall (1681) are recorded.
[Fl. 451, Fl. 613.]

*Janssens, Hieronymus (or Jeroom). Flemish Sch. *b* Antwerp 1624 *d* Antwerp 1693. *Conversation pieces* (*cf.* P. Meert) *and social entertainments* (*cf.* A. L. Fonteyn) *especially during governor-generalship of Don John of Austria* (*cf.* P. Snayers)

1656-8. Called at the time '*Le Danseur et Peintre à la mode*'. Pupil of C. J. v. d. Lamen 1637; Master Antwerp Guild 1644; member of Antwerp Chamber of Rhetoric (Violiere). **Signed Examples:** BRUSSELS *La main chaude* 1656. DUNKIRK *Ladies and gentlemen in front of a palace* 1672. LILLE *Court Ball* 1658. PARIS Louvre *Cavaliers and Ladies*. VIENNA Liecht. *Family group*. Figures in some architectural paintings by W. v. Ehrenberg, G. A. Gheringh and P. Neeffs the younger are presumed by some his work. [Fl. 107, Fl. 892.]

Janssens, Jan (Joannes). Flemish Sch. *b* son of physician, Ghent 1590 *d* Ghent (?) after 1650. *Religious subjects*. Travelled Italy; Master Ghent Guild 1621; last recorded Ghent 1650. **Signed Examples:** BRUGES S. Sauveur *Resurrection* (bought Ghent 1640, restored by J. van Oost the elder 1645, described by Descamps (1769) as 'comme de Van Dyck'). GHENT Mus. *Annunciation*; S. Martin *Martyrdom of S. Adrian*. ROESELARE Church *The Crowning with Thorns*. **Documented Example:** GHENT S. Nicholas *S. Jerome* (presented to the church in memory of his father, inscribed 'proprio aere et penicillo' and recorded by Descamps). An *Assumption of the Virgin* (1634) painted for Ghent S. Michel is also recorded. [Fl. 216, Fl. 892, Fl. 386.]

Janssens, René Emmanuel. Flemish Sch. *b* Brussels 1870. *Church and other interiors, landscapes, genre*. Pupil of J. Portaels and in Paris of P. V. Galland. Represented in ANTWERP, BRUSSELS *The Staircase*. GHENT *The red room*. [Fl. 123, Fl. 337.]

*****Janssens, Victor Honoré.** Flemish Sch. *b* son of a tailor, Brussels 1658 *d* Brussels 1736 (or 1739). '*History*' *compositions and religious subjects* (*cf.* J. I. de Roore), *designs for tapestry* (*cf.* H. de La Pegnia). Pupil of L. Volders 1675; went Flensburg where worked as court painter to Duke of Holstein *c.* four years; then Rome; returned Brussels where Master Guild 1689; painted pictures and decorations for reconstructed buildings after Marshal Villeroi's bombardment during Louis XIV's 1695 campaign (*cf.* Z. J. van Helmont); visited Vienna *c.* 1718 and London *c.* 1722 (*cf.* C. de Neve, and S. Hardimé, D. C. de Heem, F. Breydel, S. Dubois). **Signed Examples:** BRUSSELS *Dido building Carthage, Lavinia's presentiment, S. Carlo Borromeo interceding for the plague stricken*. **Documented Examples:** BRUSSELS Mus. *Apparition of the Virgin to S. Thomas Aquinas* (from Dominican church); Town Hall *Allegory of the Year* 1708, *Olympus* (ceiling), *Allegory of the three Orders of the Estates of Brabant*; S. Nicholas *S. Roch healing the plague stricken, King David's repentance*; S. Madeleine *S. Mary Magdalene annointing Christ's feet*. MALINES S. Jean *Pietà* all seen 1768 by Descamps who records also other works. Brussels Town Hall has three tapestries *Inauguration of Philip of Burgundy as Duke of Brabant 1430, Abdication of Charles V 1555, Inauguration of Charles VI 1718* from his cartoons. [Fl. 878, Fl. 564, Fl. 576, Fl. 215, Fl. 216, Fl. 119, Fl. 892, Fl. 296.]

Jansz, Symon. Flemish (Dutch) Sch. 15th cent. Recorded as paid for portraits of Philip of Burgundy and Charles the Bold for Leyden Town Hall 1464. [Fl. 481, Fl. 892.]

Jaspers, see **Gaspers, J. B.**

Jefferys, Marcel. Flemish Sch. *b* Milan 1872 *d* Ixelles (Brussels) 1924. *Still life, landscapes and town views in Impressionist and Post-Impressionist conventions*. Visited Paris, London and Venice. Represented in ANTWERP *Tulips* (*w.*). BRUSSELS *The Seine*. [Fl. 388.]

Jerrigh. Flemish Sch. *b* of Walloon origin, place and date unknown *d* Cologne *c.* 1574. *Portraits*. Studied Antwerp. In

Cologne (*cf.* F. Hogenberg) where the German painter J. (Hans) van Aachen (*cf.* G. Rem) was his pupil 1568. [Fl. 559, Fl. 577.]

Jespers, Floris. Flemish Sch. *b* son of sculptor Émile J., Borgerhout (Antwerp) 1889. Brother of sculptor Oscar J. *Cubist, expressionist and decorative compositions* (*some on glass*), *landscapes, designs for tapestry* (*for 1937 Paris International exhibition*). Represented ANTWERP *Harlequinade, Clown*. BRUSSELS: Congo Pavilion (1958 International Exhibition) Large mural: *Congo life and fauna*. *Cf.* H. Kerels, A. Mambour, R. Mols. [Fl. 388, Fl. 568, Fl. 296.]

Joest, Jan. Flemish (Dutch) Sch. *b* Wesel (Holland) (?) *c.* 1450 *d* Haarlem 1519. *Religious subjects*. Living in Wesel and Calcar 1474-1508; settled Haarlem 1509. **Documented Example:** CALCAR Nicolaikirche High Altar wings to carved wooden centre, twenty panels, *Scenes from Life of Christ* with 2 Old Testament subjects (contract 1505; payment 1506-8). Presumed by some identical with Juan de Holanda *q.v.* [Fl. 892, Fl. 316.]

Jolly, Henri Jean Bapt. Flemish Sch. *b* Antwerp 1814 *d* Amsterdam 1853. *Genre and portraits*. Visited Germany and France; settled Holland 1848. Represented in THE HAGUE Gemeentemus. *Portrait*. Pictures titled *The gleaners* and *Young girl's secret* were in the Paris salon 1847 and 1848. Others titled *Lacemaking in the 17th cent.* and *Young girl tending a wounded soldier* are recorded. [Fl. 451, Fl. 88, Fl. 66.]

Joncquoy, Antoine. Flemish Sch. *b* nephew of Michel J., Tournai before 1570 *d* after 1607. *Portraits and decorative painting*. Painted large decorative portraits *Archduke Albert and Archduchess Isabella* used in their Pageant Entry into Tournai (*cf.* Michel J.) 1600. [Fl. 359.]

Joncquoy (Gioncoy), Michel. Flemish Sch. *b* son of Pierchon J., Tournai *c.* 1530 *d* Tournai 1606. *Religious subjects, portraits*. Went Rome where painted on copper many small crucifixions with black backgrounds repeated by means of stencils (which he sold to devout Spaniards); B. Spranger worked with him in 1567 and later; returned Tournai *c.* 1575; incensed P. Vlerick by adverse comments on his pictures; citizen of Antwerp 1584; given free lodging by City of Tournai to retain him there 1596; worked on arches for Pageant Entry into Tournai of Archduke Albert and Archduchess Isabella and painted their portraits 1600 (*cf.* Antoine J., P. v. d. Meulen, J. de Liemakere, and D. v. Alsloot). Tournai archives have inventory of pictures in his house at his death. [Fl. 559, Fl. 657, Fl. 163, Fl. 84, Fl. 359, Fl. 892.]

Joncquoy, Pierchon. Flemish Sch. *b* Tournai before 1495 *d* after 1544. *Religious subjects and designs for civic and church ornaments*. Master Tournai Guild 1513. Painted six *Crucifixions* to be carried before condemned criminals on the way to execution 1516; employed by Tournai city and churches 1516-44. [Fl. 359.]

Jones, Adolphe R. (Daniel A. R.). Flemish Sch. *b* son of carriage maker, Brussels 1806 *d* Schaerbeek 1874. *Animals, landscapes*. Pupil of E. Verboeckhoven. Visited Holland and England; exhibited London British Institution 1839. Represented in MAINZ *Cowstall*. [Fl. 451, Fl. 363.]

Jonghe, Gustave de. Flemish Sch. *b* son of J. B. J., Courtrai 1829 *d* blind, Antwerp 1893. *Genre*. Pupil Brussels Acad. of F. Navez and L. Gallait. Settled Paris as friend of A. Stevens *c.* 1855; returned Belgium *c.* 1884; exhibitor Paris Salon from 1855; in London where exhibited R.A., 1875. Represented in ANTWERP *Before the mirror*. BRUSSELS *The Visit, The Pilgrim*. COURTRAI *The Orphans* 1862, *Devotion* 1865. GHENT *The Beggar, Declaration of Love*. [Fl. 361, Fl. Bib. 19th cent.]

*Jonghe, Jan Baptist de. Flemish Sch. *b* Courtrai 1785 *d* Brussels 1844. *Landscapes, town views with figures; drawings for topographic publications; also engravings and lithographs.* Pupil of J. Depelchin (?) in Courtrai and of B. Ommeganck in Antwerp. Professor Courtrai Acad. 1826 and Antwerp Acad. 1841; visited Holland, France, England and Italy. E. J. Verboeckhoven painted animals in some of his pictures (*cf.* P. J. Hellemans). Represented in ANTWERP *In the Ardennes.* AMSTERDAM *Market day in Courtrai* 1828. BRUSSELS, COURTRAI, GHENT *Stream with cattle.* TOURNAI.
[Fl. 451, Fl. 481, Fl. 798.]

Jooris van Ghent. Flemish Sch. 16th cent. Van Mander (1604) records him as: 'A pupil of F. Floris who became painter to the King of Spain and later to the Queen of France'.
[Fl. 559.]

Joors, Eugène. Flemish Sch. *b* Borgerhout 1850 *d* Antwerp 1910. *Portraits, still life, landscapes, animals, genre.* Pupil of C. Verlat in Antwerp Acad. Represented in ANTWERP *Game still life* 1880, *Wild Fowl* 1892, *Portraits.*
[Fl. 264, Fl. Bib. 19th cent.]

Joos, see Cleve, Joos van.

Joos van Ghent, see Justus.

Jordaens (Joerdaens), Hans, I. Flemish Sch. *b* Antwerp (?) before 1556 *d* Delft 1630. *Genre and coast scenes, some with night and conflagration effects* (*cf.* Jooris v. Cleve). Pupil in Antwerp of M. van Cleve; Master in Antwerp Guild 1581; married widow of F. Pourbus the elder 1582; moved with his family to Holland when Parma expelled the Protestants from Antwerp (*cf.* D. v. d. Queborne) 1587; documented in Delft 1597-1629. **Signed Examples:** DRESDEN *Company at table with an ape* (H. Joerdaens). KIEV *Beach scene with whale and many figures* (H. Joerdaens) 1598. Van Mander (1604) records that he copied in oil for Prince Maurice of Nassau, tapestry cartoons *Equestrian Portraits of the House of Orange* by B. van Orley.
[Fl. 559, Fl. 892.]

Jordaens, Hans II. Flemish Sch. *b* (not son of Hans J. I) Antwerp 1581 *d* Antwerp 1653. Master Antwerp Guild 1600.
[Fl. 107, Fl. 892.]

Jordaens, Hans III (called **'Lange Jan'** or **'den Langen Jordaens'**). Flemish Sch. *b* son of Hans J. II (?), Antwerp *c.* 1595 *d* Antwerp 1643. *Old Testament and allegorical subjects, interiors of picture galleries* (*cf.* W. van Haecht). Master Antwerp Guild 1620; member Antwerp Chamber of Rhetoricians ('Violiere'); completed, with other painters, pictures left by A. Govaerts 1626. **Signed Examples:** BERLIN K.F. *The Passage of the Red Sea* (*cf.* F. Francken II) 1624. HAGUE Mauritshuis *Same subject.* DUNKIRK *Scenes from Genesis* (thirteen small pictures). VIENNA Kunsthist. *Interior of a picture gallery.* An *Orpheus* (*cf.* L. van der Borcht) is recorded in an Antwerp 1627 inventory. A signed *Road to Calvary* (with many figures) was recorded in the 19th cent.
[Fl. 481, Fl. 892, Fl. 213.]

*Jordaens, Jacob. Flemish Sch. *b* son of a dealer in painted linen wall hangings, Antwerp 1593 *d* of plague and buried Putte (Holland) Protestant Cemetery, 1678. *Religious and mythological subjects, genre, portraits, designs for tapestries and painted wall hangings.* Pupil of A. van Noort 1607; Master (watercolour) Antwerp Guild 1615; married his master's daughter 1616; associated with the Rubens atelier in capacity not precisely recorded from *c.* 1618; Sandrart (writing in J's lifetime) states that Rubens was jealous of his talents; visited Holland with Van Noort 1632; employed under Rubens with many other artists on decorations for Pageant Entry into Antwerp of Cardinal Infante Ferdinand

(*cf.* G. Weri) 1635; contributed a painting to the series provided (from Rubens' sketches) for Philip IV's Torre de la Parada (*cf.* J. P. Gowi) 1637; through Sir B. Gerbier and the Abbé Scaglia commissioned by Charles I to paint *The story of Cupid and Psyche* in a series of wall and ceiling pictures for the Queen's villa at Greenwich 1639; had a large atelier on the Rubens model and contracted to produce thirty-five large compositions for J. Silvercroon in The Hague, the pictures to be by himself and others but all worked on and signed by himself 1648; with other artists (*cf.* T. van Thulden) worked for Amalia van Solms (widow of Prince Frederick Henry of Orange) in the Hague Huis-ten-Bosch (House in the Wood) 1649-52; converted to Calvinism at a date not precisely recorded and fined for 'scandalous writings' *c.* 1651; member of Calvinist society 'De Brabantsche Olyfberg' which met secretly in his house (*cf.* B. v. Orley); but continued to work for Roman Catholic churches. **Signed Examples:** AMSTERDAM *Peter finding the coin, Allegory of Justice* 1663. ANTWERP Mus. *The Daughters of Cecrops finding Erichthonius* 1617, *The old sing and the young pipe* 1638, *Triumph of Fred. Henry of Orange* (sketch), *Human Law based on Divine Law* (given by the artist with *Pegasus* (ceiling painting) and *Allegory of Commerce and Industry* to the Antwerp Academy newly founded by Philip IV (*cf.* T. Boeyermans, A. Genoels and H. v. Minderhout) 1665; S. Jacques *S. Carlo Borromeo praying for the plague stricken* 1665. BERLIN K.F. *The old sing . . .* 1658. BRUSSELS *Allegory of Abundance; S. Martin curing a demoniac* 1630; *S. Yves, patron of lawyers* 1645. CASSEL *Jupiter nurtured by the goat Amalthea, A Moor displaying a horse to his master.* COPENHAGEN *Hercules and Deianira* 1649. FRANKFORT *Adoration of the Shepherds* 1653. GRENOBLE *Adoration of the Shepherds, Allegory: Truth and the Princes* 1658. MADRID Prado *Apollo and Marsyas* (from Rubens' sketch for Torre de la Parada) 1637. MAINZ *Christ among the doctors* (painted for Furnes S. Walpurga) 1663. MUNICH A.P. *The old sing . . .* 1646. STOCKHOLM *Adoration of the Shepherds* 1618. STRASBOURG *The Satyr and the Peasants* (*Blowing hot and cold*), (*cf.* G. van Herp) 1652. **Documented Examples:** AMSTERDAM *The piping satyr* (engraved Bolswert). ANTWERP Mus. *Triumph of Prince Frederick Henry* (sketch), *The Last Supper* (from Augustine church where seen by Descamps 1768); Augustine Church *Martyrdom of S. Apollonia* (engraved by Marinus before 1639 and seen by Descamps 1768); Béguinage Church *Descent from the Cross* (engraved by J. himself); Hospice Civil *Descent from the Cross* (bequeathed to the Hospice by J.); S. Paul *Christ on the Cross* (with the Virgin, S. John and S. Mary Magdalene) (commissioned 1617). BERLIN K.F. *Adam v. Noort* (engraved by H. Snyers). BRUSSELS *Triumph of Prince Frederick Henry* (sketch). COPENHAGEN *The ferry boat* (or *Peter finding the coin*) (mentioned by Sandrart 1675). THE HAGUE Huis-ten-Bosch *The Triumph of Prince Frederick Henry* (*cf.* T. Willeboirts), *Allegory of Time* 1649-52. PARIS Louvre *The Four Evangelists* (from the Dutch painter P. Lastman's collection 1632). VIENNA K. *Twelfth Night* (*Le roi boit*) (Archduke Leopold Wilhelm Inventory 1659).

Madrid (Prado) has a Portrait group (*The Painter and his Family* (?)) recorded as by 'Giarduns' in Philip V Inventory 1746. For the Greenwich commission J. delivered eight pictures but their present whereabouts is not known. A *Philemon and Baucis with Jupiter and Mercury* is among titles recorded by engravings. J's own engravings include a *Christ driving the traders from the Temple* 1652. Rubens' inventory (1640) records three pictures by J. (*Ulysses and Polyphemus, Nativity, The Virgin*) and Rubens' executors paid J. 240 florins for work done on a *Hercules* and an *Andromeda* sold to the King of Spain's agent. An Antwerp dealer's inventory of 1642 records a *Four Doctors of the Church* 'by Rubens and Jordaens'; other contemporary Antwerp inventories record works titled *Banquet of the Gods, Judgement of Midas, The*

story of Cleopatra (two pictures), *Callisto* and a series of thirty cartoons for tapestry bought at the sale of Jordaens' effects. Houbraken (1718) records twelve pictures (*The Passion*) painted for Charles Gustavus King of Sweden, a torchlight *S. Peter cutting Malchus' ear* and a *Pan and Syrinx* painted in six days; D'Argenville (1745) records a 'grande galerie' for Denmark. Paintings seen by Descamps (1768) in churches included: Antwerp Béguinage *Christ on the Cross* (*with the Virgin, S. John and the three Maries*) an epitaph for two Béguines; Carmes Chaussés *Carmelites receiving authority to build their establishments*; S. André *Christ holding the Cross flanked by the Virtues and S. Paul, a rainbow in the sky and sheep at the base, the whole set in a painted altar.* Ghent S. Pierre Abbey *The Woman taken in Adultery* and *Christ enjoining disputants to compose their enmity.* (*Cf.* Paris Expulsion of Traders Painter).
[Fl. 86, Fl. 753, Fl. 425, Fl. 22, Fl. 216, Fl. 702, Fl. 703, Fl. 134, Fl. 297, Fl. 461, Fl. 722, Fl. 892, Fl. 213.]

Jordaens, Jacob (not Jan) **the younger.** Flemish Sch. *b* son of Jacob Jordaens, Antwerp 1625. *d* Denmark (?) after 1650. **Signed Example:** AMIENS Mus. *Christ appearing to S. Mary Magdalene* 'Jacob Jordaens junior' 1650.
[Fl. 107, Fl. 892.]

Joseph Master. Presumed Flemish Sch. late 15th cent. Name for painter of BERLIN K.F. (539) *Scenes from the life of Joseph* four circular panels. (*Cf.* Abbey of Afflighem Master).
[Fl. 892, Fl. 316.]

Juan Flamenco. Flemish (or Hispano-Flemish) Sch. 15th cent. Recorded as painter of two altarpieces in the Miraflores Carthusian monastery (Burgos) 1496-9. MADRID Prado has five panels (706-10) *Birth of S. John the Baptist, S. John preaching, Baptism of Christ, S. John in Prison, Beheading of S. John* from the Miraflores Monastery presumed by some the pictures recorded there by A. Ponz (1794) and presumed by him the works of J. F. by reason of a document he had seen recording that J. F. painted a *Baptism of Christ* at Miraflores 1496-9.
[Fl. 664, Fl. 153, Fl. 668.]

Juan de Flandes. Flemish (or Hispano-Flemish) Sch. *b* before 1475 *d* Palencia (?) before the end of 1519. *Religious subjects.* Court painter in service of Queen Isabella of Spain 1496-1504; in Salamanca 1505; in Palencia 1506. **Documented Examples:** PALENCIA Cathedral High Altar *Twelve scenes from the Life of Christ and the Virgin* (which he contracted to paint within three years 1506). SALAMANCA University *Fragments of a retable* painted by him for University chapel 1505.

Some panels presumed to come from the *Polyptych or Oratorium of Isabella* (originally forty-seven panels) now in Madrid, Royal Palace and elsewhere are presumed by some his work.
[Fl. 153, Fl. 20 (1930, 1931), Fl. 529, Fl. 668.]

Juan de Holanda. Flemish or Hispano-Flemish Sch. early 16th cent. Documented as painter of PALENCIA Cathedral altarpiece *Virgin of Pity with scenes from the Life of Christ and the Virgin and donor Juan de Fonseca, Bishop of Palencia* (commissioned by Bishop Fonseca on his visit to Brussels to announce the death of Isabella to Philip the Fair and Joanna the Mad 1505). Presumed by some identical with Jan Joest *q.v.*
[Fl. 469, Fl. 316, Fl. 538, Fl. 668.]

Juppin, Jean Baptiste. Flemish Sch. *b* son of a merchant, Namur 1675 *d* Namur 1729. *Italianate landscapes* (*cf.* A. F. Baudewyns, J. F. van Bloemen, P. van Bloemen, A. Genoels, C. Huysmans, J. B. Huysmans, P. Rysbraeck, J. F. Soolmaker, P. Spierinckx). Travelled Italy where saw an eruption of Vesuvius 1712; in Liège and patronised by religious and town authorities from 1717. The figures in some of his pictures (religious subjects) are said to have been painted by E. Plumier. **Documented Examples** in LIÈGE S. Denis and S. Martin. An *Eruption of Vesuvius* painted for Liège Town Hall was destroyed by fire 1734.
[Fl. 63, Fl. 217, Fl. 451, Fl. 409, Fl. 892.]

Justus of Ghent (Giusto da Guanto, Joos van Ghent). Flemish Sch. 15th cent. Recorded in Urbino *c.* 1473-5; presumed by some the (unnamed) Netherlander invited to Urbino by Duke Federigo da Montefeltre to decorate his study with pictures of poets and philosophers. **Signed Examples:** None. **Documented Example:** URBINO Ducal Pal. *The Institution of the Eucharist* (painted for Corpus Domini Fraternity with a portrait of their president Duke Federigo 1473-4). Paris (Louvre) and Urbino (Ducal Pal.) each have fourteen *Heads of Learned Men* and Urbino also has a *Portrait of Duke Federigo and his son* all recorded (*c.* 1482) as by an unnamed Netherlander and presumed by some his work. London (N.G.) and Berlin (K.F.) each have two panels presumed allegories of *The liberal Arts* (presumed from the Duke's apartments at Urbino or from the Gubbio studiolo which has been acquired and reassembled by New York Met.) which are also presumed by some his work. Other pictures presumed by some his work are in various museums. Some of the painting in the Duke's apartments was recorded (1604) as by a Spanish artist (*cf.* J. van Wassenhove and G. v. d. Meire).
[Fl. 818, Fl. 156, Fl. 507, Fl. 316, Fl. 530.]

K

Karel van Yperen, see **Foort.**

Kasteele (or **Castello**), **Frans van den.** Flemish Sch. *b* Brussels of Spanish parentage (?) *c.* 1540 *d* Rome 1621. *Religious subjects for churches and paintings in miniature.* Went Italy and remained there (*cf.* J. v. d. Straet and P. de Lignis); in Rome Accad. di San Luca by 1577; principe of the Accad. 1600; Rubens knew him in Rome. **Signed Examples:** ORTE (prov. Rome) Capuchin ch. *Virgin in Glory with SS. Clara, Michael, Francis and Catherine.* PISA S. Francesco *S. Anthony Abbot with Antonio Campiglia as donor* ('Franciscus de Castello Flandriae Bruxellensis f. Romae 15 . .' last figures hidden by frame). SPELLO (prov. Perugia) S. Lorenzo *Christ and the Virgin receiving souls from Purgatory* '(Francesco di Castello f. Roma 1599'). **Documented Example:** ROME S. Maria di Monserrato *Assumption of the Virgin* (seen by contemporary Baglione in S. Giacomo dei Spagnuoli). A small parchment *Adoration s* 1584 is recorded. An altarpiece recorded in Rome S. Rocco is not known to be extant.
[Fl. 36, Fl. 417, Fl. 305, Fl. 678.]

Kasteels, see **Casteels.**

Kay, W., see **Key.**

Kaynoot, H., see **Keynooghe.**

Keelhoff, Frans. Flemish Sch. *b* Neerhaaren, nr. Maastricht 1820 *d* Brussels 1893. *Landscapes.* Visited France, Switzerland and Italy. E. Verboeckhoven painted animals in some of his pictures (*cf.* P. J. Hellemans). Represented in ANTWERP 1886. BRUSSELS 1873. GHENT.   [Fl. Bib. 19th cent.]

*****Keirincx** (**Keerincx, Kerrincx**), **Alexander** (known in England as Carings). Flemish Sch. *b* Antwerp 1600 *d* Amsterdam 1652. *Wooded landscapes* (*cf.* J. d'Arthois) *and views.* Master Antwerp Guild 1619; came England (*cf.* C. de Neve) and drew London views 1625; in Amsterdam 1636; in England painting 'prospects', and castles in Scotland for Charles I *c.* 1640; in Holland from 1643. The figures in some of his pictures are by the Dutchman C. van Poelenburgh (who was in England for some years after 1637) and in others by the Utrecht painter P. van Hillegaert. **Signed Examples:** ANTWERP *Oakwood with staghunt* 1630. BREMEN *Landscape* (with figures by C. van Poelenburgh *s* by both, 1633). BRUNSWICK (1621 and 1640). BRUSSELS *Landscape with shepherd.* COPENHAGEN (1630). DRESDEN (1620). THE HAGUE and MUNICH A.P. (1635). **Monogrammed Examples:** CAMBRIDGE Fitz. *River scene.* COPENHAGEN *Landscape with bathing women.* ROTTERDAM (Boymans) *Wood with huntsmen.* Vertue who saw (before 1756) a painting signed by Keirincx and Poelenburgh states that the Royal Collection had several of K's landscapes; one was owned by Horace Walpole.
[Fl. 425, Fl. 826, Fl. 856, Fl. 892.]

Keldermans, Hendrik. Flemish Sch. *b* son of Malines architect *c.* 1450 *d* after 1521. *Glass painter.* Had workshop in Louvain before 1486; in Antwerp Guild 1490; in Malines 1516; presumed by some identical with 'Henry the painter' who kept the Malines inn, the 'Golden Head' where Dürer stayed 1521.   [Fl. 243, Fl. 269, Fl. 613, Fl. 88.]

*****Kempener, Pieter de** (known in Spain as Pedro de Campaña). Flemish Sch. *b* Brussels 1503 *d* Brussels after 1580. *Religious subjects, portraits; also worked as tapestry designer.* Went Italy; employed on triumphal arch in Bologna for Coronation Pageant of Emperor Charles V 1530 (*cf.* M. v. Heemskerck); then Rome where patronised by Cardinal Grimani who took him to Venice; went Seville and employed by Cathedral 1537; assessed a painting by F. Sturm 1549; worked Spain till 1562 (*cf.* J. Floris, F. Frutet, I. del Hele, C. v. Hemessen, J. Hoefnagel, J. Kraeck, A. Mor, F. Sturm, J. C. Vermeyen, A. v. d. Wyngaerde and L. Franchoys the elder); returned Brussels where succeeded M. Coxie as Director of Tapestry factory 1563; later Master of Works to Duke of Alva (*cf.* M. Coxie). His *Self-portrait in winter clothes* was hung in Brussels Town Hall after his death. **Signed Examples:** BERLIN *Adoration of the shepherds* 'Petriz Campani'. SEVILLE Cathedral *Descent from the Cross* 'Petrus Campaniensis' (painted for chapel in Santa Cruz given by Hernando de Jaen 1548; the painter historian Pacheco (1649) declared himself terrified by this picture in the dark church; Murillo profoundly admired it: *cf.* Montpellier example); S. Isidoro *SS. Paul and Anthony*; S. Juan de la Palma *Crucifixion*; S. Catalina *Christ and S. Peter*; S. Pedro *Virgin of Peace* and S. Ana (Triana) *Burial of Lupez Cepero* and *Stigmatisation of S. Francis.* **Documented Examples:** MONTPELLIER Mus. Fabre *Descent from the Cross* (smaller version of Seville Cathedral picture commissioned by Diego de Herrera for Seville Regina Angelorum 1561). SEVILLE Cathedral *Mariscal altarpiece* with *Presentation in the Temple* and *Portraits of donor Mariscal Diego Caballero and his Family* with Spanish painter Antonio de Alfián) 1556; S. Ana (Triana) *Life of the Virgin* 15 panels recorded by Pacheco. Lanzi (1796) records *The Magdalene led by Martha to the Temple to hear Christ preaching* painted for Grimani in Venice which came to England; the London N.G. has a picture of this subject (1241) presumed by some this work. A *Portrait of Hernando de Jaen* painted for Santa Cruz disappeared 1810-14.
[Fl. 635, Fl. 636, Fl. 505, Fl. 335, Fl. 892, Fl. 20 (1937).]

Kerckhove, Joseph van den. Flemish Sch. *b* Bruges 1667 *d* Bruges 1724. *Religious subjects, 'history', portraits.* Pupil in Bruges of J. van Meunincxhove and in Antwerp of J. E. Quellinus 1685; visited France where worked Paris (*cf.* C. E. Biset), Angers and Nantes; returned Bruges where Master Guild 1695; founder member of Bruges Acad. (*cf.* J. B. Herregouts and M. van Duvenede) 1717; later director of Acad. Descamps (1763 and 1769) records in Bruges Carmes Déchaussés *Circumcision* and others in Jacobins church and S. Sauveur; and in Ostend Town Hall (ceiling) *Assembly of the gods* and Sœurs Noires *Martyrdom of S. Lawrence.*
[Fl. 215, Fl. 216, Fl. 237.]

Kerels, Henri. Flemish Sch. *b* St. Jans-Molenbeek (Brussels) 1896. *Figures, landscapes.* Pupil in Brussels Acad.; visited the Congo. Represented ANTWERP. *Cf.* F. Jespers.   [Fl. 17.]

Kernkamp, Anna. Flemish Sch. *b* Antwerp 1868. *Landscapes marines, interiors, town views, still life.* Pupil in Antwerp of French painter Blanc-Garin and of H. Rul. Represented in ANTWERP *S. Anthony's church in Antwerp.*   [Fl. 17.]

Kerricx, Katrina Klara. Flemish Sch. *b* daughter of sculptor Willem K., Antwerp 1684 *d* 1762. Copied other artists' works and in later years, when an invalid, painted watercolours.
[Fl. 451.]

Kerricx, Willem Ignatius. Flemish Sch. *b* son of a sculptor and poetess Barbe Ogier, Antwerp 1682 *d* Antwerp 1745. *Large religious compositions (cf. J. I. de Roore) and ceremonial designs; also worked as sculptor and architect and wrote plays performed by Antwerp Guild.* Pupil of G. Maes; Master Antwerp Guild 1703-4; designed decorations for Pageant Entry of Charles of Lorraine and Archduchess Maria Anna, Joint Governors-general of Austrian Netherlands (*cf.* J. J. Horemans the younger) April 1744. **Documented Examples:** ANTWERP *S. Luke* (presented to Guild 1718), *Passover in Egypt* and *Adoration of the Lamb* (both from Tongerloo Abbey 1725-31). Two paintings commissioned by the abbots of Tongerloo and S. Bernard for the jubilee of S. Gudule 1720 are recorded by engravings. Paintings in a convent at Lierre and in the Antwerp Jesuit Church were seen by Descamps (1768). [Fl. 216, Fl. 451, Fl. 481, Fl. 107, Fl. 798.]

Kessel, Ferdinand van. Flemish Sch. *b* son of Jan van K. the elder, Antwerp 1648 *d* Breda 1696. *Animals, bird and flower pieces (some with figures by G. J. van Opstal and others).* Worked Breda for William III and John Sobieski King of Poland who made him Court painter and ennobled him 1694. Left art collection to his nephew J. T. van K.; J. C. Weyerman, who was his pupil, records that pictures symbolising *The Four Quarters of the Globe* and the *Four Elements* sent to Warsaw were destroyed by fire and that K. then painted another series (*cf.* J. van K., the elder). [Fl. 878, Fl. 215.]

Kessel, Hieronymus (Jeroom) van. Flemish Sch. *b* Antwerp 1578 *d* Antwerp (?) after 1636. *Portraits.* Pupil of C. Floris. Worked Augsburg, Cologne and Innsbruck; visited Rome; returned Antwerp where patronised by Archduke Albert (*cf.* G. de Crayer); married daughter of Jan (Velvet) Brueghel 1624. **Signed Examples** in COLOGNE, HANOVER and SCHLEISSHEIM. [Fl. 107, Fl. 892.]

*Kessel, Jan van the elder. Flemish Sch. *b* son of Hieronymus van K., Antwerp 1626 *d* Antwerp 1679. *Still life, animals, birds and insects (cf. E. v. d. Broeck and L. van Heil). flower garlands (cf. D. Seghers) and town views.* Pupil of his uncle Jan Brueghel the younger and of S. de Vos; Master Antwerp Guild 1645 and Captain in Civic Guard; married daughter of F. van Apshoven. Many of his works were exported for high prices to Vienna and elsewhere during his lifetime. **Signed Examples:** AIX-LA-CHAPELLE, AIX-EN-PROVENCE, AMSTERDAM Rijks. *Fruit and insects.* BORDEAUX, BRUSSELS *Birds.* CAMBRIDGE Fitz. *Apple blossom, shells, butterflies and insects* (1661). DRESDEN *Still life with fruit and lobster* (1654). FLORENCE Uffizi *Interior with monkeys* 1660. HANOVER, LENINGRAD, MADRID Prado *Garland round a S. John with the Infant Jesus*; series of small pictures including *Birds and dead fox* 1660, *Fish with town view in background* 1656. MUNICH A.P., SCHLEISSHEIM series of small pictures constituting the *Four Quarters of the World (cf.* F. v. K.). STOCKHOLM *Birds attacking poultry.* STRASBOURG *Flower piece.* STUTTGART. [Fl. 86, Fl. 107, Fl. 892, Fl. 212.]

*Kessel, Jan van the younger. Flemish Sch. *b* son or nephew of J. van K. the elder, Antwerp 1654 *d* Madrid 1708. *Portraits, mythologies, landscape, animals, still life.* Went Spain (*cf.* A. Smit); said to have accompanied the Queen Mother Mariana of Austria to Toledo 1677; court painter (without salary) to Charles II of Spain 1683; paid for ten portraits 1684; on death of court painter J. Carreño de Miranda applied for his salary recalling his own services and those of his father and uncle who had served the King of Spain 'as captains' (*cf.* J. van K. the elder) 1685; after death of Charles II (1700) was patronised by his widow Queen Mariana of Neuburg but failed to please Philip V of whom he painted an unsuccessful portrait (*cf.* S. v. Aken). **Signed Example:** MADRID Prado *Family in a garden* (with portrait of the artist in a window)

dated 1680, described (1724) by Palomino who records the sitters as the family of a Flemish patron in Spain; the figure by the fountain is traditionally presumed a caricature of Charles II. [Fl. 637, Fl. 153, Fl. 612, Fl. 95 (1915).]

Kessel, Jan Thomas (wrongly as Nicolas) van. Flemish Sch. *b* son of a lawyer, Antwerp 1677 *d* in poverty, Antwerp 1741 (?). *Peasant genre and portraits.* Pupil of P. Ijkens 1691, and in Breda of his uncle F. van K. 1695; inherited property and art collection from his uncle; Master Antwerp Guild 1703; visited Paris; very successful artist who led life of dissipation with a wife who shared his tastes. [Fl. 878, Fl. 215, Fl. 107, Fl. 892.]

*Ketel, Cornelis. Flemish (Dutch) Sch. *b* Gouda 1548 *d* Amsterdam 1616. *Allegorical compositions (cf. C. Anthonisz), religious subjects, portraits, portrait groups (cf. D. Barendsz).* Pupil of his uncle, a glass-painter; then in Delft of A. Blocklandt 1565. Went Fontainebleau (*cf.* L. de Heere, H. Francken the elder, L. Thiry and A. Dubois) 1566; left France when Charles IX expelled recent Netherlandish immigrants; in Gouda 1568; went London (*cf.* S. v. d. Meulen) 1573; in London sold pictures to Hansa merchants and painted portraits of nobles and the Queen; returned Holland and established himself at Amsterdam 1581; with D. Barendsz painted decorations for entry of Earl of Leicester into Amsterdam 1587; experimented, after 1599, with painting without brushes using only his hand or his foot (*cf.* C. Felu). **Signed Example:** AMSTERDAM Rijks. *The Company of Capt. D. J. Rosencranz and Lieutenant Pauw* 1588. **Monogrammed Examples:** AMSTERDAM *Dirk Barendsz* 1590, *Admiral Jacobus van Neck* 1605, *Griete van Neck* 1605. OXFORD Bodleian *Martin Frobisher.* Van Mander who knew him personally records (1604) a *Christ and the Apostles* (including portraits of contemporary artists and collectors), pictures sold to Danzig including a *S. Paul, S. Mary Magdalene, Suicide of Saul (cf.* P. Brueghel), *Judas* and a life size *Danaë and the golden rain (cf.* J. Gossaert), a lifesize *Judith,* portraits of *Queen Elizabeth* ('from life'), the *Earl of Oxford* (recorded by Vertue before 1756 in a Yorkshire private collection), *Morosini a Venetian 'Magnifico', V. Jacobsen: wine-inspector, The sculptor-architect H. de Keyser,* a group of Amsterdam Civic Guardsmen *The Company of Captain Herman Rodenborgh Beths in a gallery with allegorical figures,* and many allegorical compositions including *Triumph of Virtue, Triumph of Vice, Force controlled by Wisdom* (acquired by Sir Christopher Hatton), *Youth, Art, Hope, Genius and Ambition, Desire has no rest, Naked Truth guarded by Virtue against Deceit, Intelligence disarmed by Wine, Venus and Avarice.* Of pictures painted without brushes or other tools Van Mander records—(by hand): *Self-portrait, Democritus and Heraclitus, S. John* and *Christ the Saviour*; (by foot): *Hippocrates God of Silence* and (partly by hand and partly by foot): *Allegory of Painting without Tools.* Vertue records 'a great piece representing the *Virtues and Vices* 46 by 7 ft. catalogued in the collection of the 1st Duke of Buckingham'. Walpole (1762) records portraits of the Earls of Arundel and Pembroke and Lord Admiral Lincoln. A *Self portrait* 'painted with fingers and thumb and the foot' was left to his wife in his will.
[Fl. 559, Fl. 826, Fl. 856, Fl. 892, Fl. 665.]

*Keuninck (or Koninck or Coninck), Kerstiaen de the elder. Flemish Sch. *b* Courtrai *c.* 1560 *d* Antwerp 1635 (?). *Landscapes (cf. A. Mirou).* Master Antwerp Guild 1580. **Signed Examples:** ANTWERP *Landscape with Diana and Actaeon.* BRUSSELS *Landscape.* COLOGNE *Wooded landscape with sportsmen* 1610. GHENT *Landscape with shipwreck and a saint.* **Documented Example:** VIENNA K. *Rocky landscape with figures* (Archduke Leopold Wilhelm inventory 1659). A signed *Jardins d'Armide* is recorded (1926).
[Fl. 892, Fl. 691, Fl. 440.

Keuninck (or **Coninck**), **Kerstiaen de the younger.** Flemish Sch. *b* son of K. de K. the e., before 1600 *d c.* 1642. Master Antwerp Guild 1613. [Fl. 892.]

*Key (**Keyen, Kay**), **Adriaen Thomas.** Flemish Sch. *b* Antwerp (?) *c.* 1544 *d* Antwerp (?) after 1589. *Religious subjects, portraits.* Presumed nephew and pupil of Willem Key; Master Antwerp Guild 1568. Presumed by some identical with an Adriaen de Keyn recorded in Venice *c.* 1566. **Signed Examples,** ANTWERP wings of triptych *Gillis de Smidt with seven children, His second wife Maria de Deckere and daughter,* and on reverse in two parts *Last Supper* 1575. **Monogrammed Examples:** BRUSSELS *Portrait of a man* 1580. COURTRAI, MUNICH and VIENNA K. [Fl. 107, Fl. 612, Fl. 892.]

*Key (or **Kay**), **Willem.** Flemish Sch. *b* Breda *c.* 1515 *d* Antwerp 1568. *Portraits, religious subjects.* Presumed the 'Willem van Breda' recorded pupil of P. Coecke the elder 1529; a pupil or assistant of L. Lombard, Liège 1540 (*cf.* F. Floris); Master Antwerp Guild 1542. Guicciardini (*c.* 1566) describes him as excelling in portraiture; Lampsonius (1572) praises him as second only to A. Mor in this field; Van Mander (1604) records that while painting a portrait of the Duke of Alva he noted an expression of great savagery on his face and overheard the decision to execute Counts Egmont and Hoorn which greatly distressed him; he died on the day on which the Counts were executed. His widow died a Protestant. J. V. de Vries painted a trompe-l'œil perspective for his garden. Rubens owned two paintings by him. **Signed Example:** AMSTERDAM Rijks. (loan) *Old woman* (*s* on back W. Kaij). A *Lamentation* (*s* W. Keien 1553) is recorded. **Semi-Documented Example:** HAMPTON COURT Royal Coll. *Lazarus Spinola* 1566 (recorded as 'by Will Key' in Charles I's Inventory, bought by Charles before 1625. Van Mander records a *Portrait of Cardinal Granvella* (*cf.* A. Mor) in Cardinal's robes, a *Come unto me . . .* (with portraits of many merchants) in Antwerp Notre Dame destroyed by iconoclasts 1566, an *Antwerp Councillors with Christ and angels above* in Antwerp Town Hall destroyed in the Spanish Fury 1576 and a *Triumph of Christ.* A *Lot and his daughters* is recorded (1682) in an Antwerp inventory. [Fl. 371, Fl. 818, Fl. 502, Fl. 559, Fl. 107, Fl. 892, Fl. 214, Fl. 316.]

Key, Wouter. Flemish Sch. *b* Breda *c.* 1500 *d* after 1544. Brother of Willem K.; Master Antwerp Guild 1531. Painter and art dealer. [Fl. 107, Fl. 892.]

Keynooghe (**Kaynoot**), **Hans,** called Den Dooven (the Deaf). Flemish Sch. *b* Malines (?) before 1510 *d* after 1570. *Landscapes* (*cf.* F. Mostaert). In Malines Guild 1527; associated with M. de Cock before 1548. Van Mander says: 'He followed markedly the style of J. Patinir'. [Fl. 559, Fl. 613, Fl. 715.]

Keyser, Nicaise de. Flemish Sch. *b* son of a farmer, nr. Antwerp 1813 *d* (and given semi-state funeral) Antwerp 1887. *Few religious subjects, then battle pictures, costume history, genre, murals, portraits* (*of royalty, social figures and successful artists, including the French painters Rosa Bonheur and Meissonier and the English painter J. E. Millais); also drew illustrations for books.* Pupil of J. Jacobs and M. van Brée; travelled Italy, France, Germany. Decorated by the king for his first battle picture, at 23, 1836; succeeded G. Wappers as director of Antwerp Academy 1855; had numerous pupils. Represented (Religious subjects): in MANCHESTER Catholic church, ANTWERP, LIMBURG, TIRLEMONT churches and GHENT Mus. (Costume history and genre) in AMSTERDAM, ANTWERP *Bravo Toro* 1880, *Good Friday Procession in Seville* 1885. BERLIN, BRUSSELS, MUNICH. (Battles): in BRUSSELS, COURTRAI, PRAGUE. (Portraits): in ANTWERP, BRUSSELS,

THE HAGUE. (Murals): in ANTWERP Mus. Vestibule (also cartoons for same). [Fl. 451, Fl. 481, Fl. 433, Fl. Bib. 19th cent.]

Keyser (or **Keisar**), **Willem de.** Flemish Sch. *b* Antwerp 1647 *d* London 1692. *Religious subjects and portraits in w., enamel and oils; also practised as a jeweller.* Painted altarpieces for Antwerp churches; then came England (*cf.* C. de Neve and J. B. Medina) where worked for James II's court *c.* 1687; ruined by the Revolution took to 'studying that folly the philosopher's stone'. A small *Self-portrait* (*w.*) and a *S. Catherine* commissioned by the Queen Dowager for Somerset House Chapel (*cf.* J. Huysmans) were among pictures seen by Vertue in possession of his daughter (an amateur painter) whom he knew. [Fl. 826, Fl. 856.]

Khnopff, Fernand. Flemish Sch. *b* son of Councillor of Court of Appeal, Grimbergen nr. Termonde 1858 *d* Brussels 1921. *Symbolist allegories* (*cf.* A. Levêque), *landscapes, indoor and outdoor genre, portraits some in w. and pastel; also worked as sculptor and illustrator.* Lived in youth at Bruges; then pupil of X. Mellery in Brussels Acad. 1877. Went Paris where pupil of J. J. Lefebre and influenced by G. Moreau; illustrated 'Sar' Péladan's 'Le vice suprême' (*cf* H. de Groux); member of Brussels L'Essor group (*cf.* A. Hamesse) 1881, of the Vingt (*cf.* J. Ensor) 1884 and Libre Esthétique (*cf.* G. Buysse) 1894 founded in Paris the Soc. Int. de la Peinture à l'eau (*cf.* F. Charlet) 1906; came often to London where friend of E. Burne-Jones; wrote articles for English periodicals. Represented ANTWERP *Self-portrait.* BRUSSELS *Memories* (English women with tennis racquets) pastel, *Child's portrait* 1883. BUDAPEST *Landscape.* GHENT *Landscape.* MUNICH N.P. *I lock my door upon myself.* Pictures titled *Interior: Listening to Schumann* 1883 and *Sleeping Medusa* 1896 are in private collections. [Fl. 820, Fl. 590, Fl. 242, Fl. Bib. 19th cent.]

Kierings, Alexander, see **Keirincx.**

Kindermans, Jean Baptiste. Flemish Sch. *b* Antwerp 1821 *d* Ixelles (Brussels) 1876. *Landscapes.* Pupil of F. Marinus. Visited England, Switzerland and the Ardennes. Represented in ANTWERP, BRUSSELS, RHEIMS. [Fl. 837 (1876), Fl. Bib. 19th cent.]

Kindt, Laurence (**Petronilla**). Flemish Sch. *b* Brussels 1805 *d* Charleroi 1863. Sister of Marie Adelaide K. and Claire K. (landscape painter). *Landscapes, genre.* Pupil of H. van Assche; married E. Delvaux *q.v.* 1838. [Fl. 451, Fl. 798.]

Kindt, Marie Adelaide. Flemish Sch. *b* Brussels 1804 *d* Brussels after 1884. *Portraits, genre and costume history.* Pupil of A. Cardon, L. David and F. J. Navez. Represented in BRUSSELS *Professor Baron* 1826. CAMBRAI *Woman tending vines.* COURTRAI *Van Dyck showing his picture of S. Martin to the peasant girl in Saventhem* 1841 (*cf.* P. Kremer). [Fl. 451, Fl. 798.]

*Kinson (or **Kinsoen**), **François Josèphe.** Flemish Sch. *b* son of an iron master, Bruges 1771 *d* Bruges 1839. *Portraits and 'history'.* Pupil in Bruges Acad.; worked as portraitist in Bruges, Ghent and Brussels; to Paris *c.* 1798 where was helped by J. B. Suvée *q.v.* and became a favourite painter in Imperial circles (*cf.* L. Gerbo); exhibited Salon from 1799; court painter to Jérôme Bonaparte, King of Westphalia (*cf.* S. J. Denis) and went Cassel 1810; left Cassel with retreating French 1813; returned Paris after fall of Empire 1814; court painter to Duc d'Angoulême 1817; received Legion of Honour from Louis XVIII; court painter to Charles X after 1824; on accession of Louis Philippe returned Bruges 1830. **Signed Examples:** BARNARD CASTLE Bowes Mus. *Jérôme Bonaparte.* BORDEAUX *Duke of Angoulême as Grand Admiral* *with part of Bordeaux in background* (Salon 1819). BRUGES *The blind Belisarius at the deathbed of his wife Antonina* (Salon 1817). **Documented Examples:** BARNARD CASTLE Bowes Mus. *Laetitia Bonaparte* (*Mme Mère*), *Portrait of a Lady*. BRUGES *Senator de Viry, Prefect of La Lys Département* (painted for Bruges Acad. 1806) and two *Portraits of ladies*; S. Sebastian Guild *King Leopold I of the Belgians* (Salon 1834). THE HAGUE Oranje Nassau Mus. *William Second King of the Netherlands and his wife when Prince and Princess of Orange* (painted Brussels 1821). VERSAILLES *General Charles Leclerc* (Salon 1804). *Portraits of Laetitia Bonaparte* (*Mme Mère*), *Joseph Bonaparte* and *Pauline Borghese* were exhibited in the Paris Salon 1808 (*cf.* M. G. Stapleaux). A *Duchess of Berry, with her infant daughter, mourning before the bust of her husband* (*murdered 1820*) (said by Immerzeel to have moved Louis XVIII to tears) and a *Lady Montgomerie* (exhibited London R.A. 1822) are recorded.

[Fl. 451, Fl. 612, Fl. 66, Fl. 361.)

Knodder (Cnodder), Christiaen de. Flemish Sch. *b* Antwerp (?) *c.* 1665. *Still life* (*flowers*). Master Antwerp Guild 1685. **Signed Examples:** TERMONDE Hospital Two *Flower pieces with grisaille bas-reliefs* (Ch. de Cnodder), *cf.* N. van Verendael. [Fl. 656, Fl. 892.]

Knyff, Alfred de. Flemish Sch. *b* Brussels 1819 *d* Paris 1885. *Landscapes* (*some with cattle*), *town scenes*. Settled France where worked at Fontainebleau (*cf.* H. Langerock) and was friend of Constant Troyon; exhibitor Paris Salon. Represented in AMIENS, ANTWERP, BRUSSELS, LIÈGE. [Fl. 837 (1885), Fl. Bib. 19th cent.]

Koebergher, see **Coebergher.**

Koninck, K. de, see **Keuninck.**

Kraeck (Caracca, Carrachio and in Spain **Juan Carraza), Jan.** Flemish (Dutch) Sch. *b* Haarlem *c.* 1538 *d* Turin where buried in Cathedral, 1607. *Portraits, religious subjects, landscapes, still life*. Went Turin where documented as a Flemish Court painter to Duke Emmanuel Philibert of Savoy 1568; appointment continued by Duke Charles Emmanuel I; citizen of Chambéry 1579; in Spain (*cf.* P. de Kempener) on affairs of his patron 1585 and 1591; for Duke of Savoy valued pictures in the collection left by the Spanish artist A. Ardente 1597; the Dutch marine painter H. C. de Vroom was his pupil in Turin. **Signed Examples:** ANNECY S. Maurice *Holy Family* (*s* Ih/ ancaraca harlemu/ hoc fecit 1578).

CHAMBÉRY Mus. *Margaret of Valois* (wife of Duke Emmanuel Philibert of Savoy) *s* on back 'Carrachio pinxit 1577', *Carlo Emmanuel* I *Duke of Savoy s* 'Carrachyo pinxit 1580', *Claude Millet and his wife* 1577. **Documented Example:** MADRID Prado *Philip of Savoy aged 5* 1591 (in Valladolid inventory 1615). Pictures titled *The Prodigal Son, Fruitpiece, Landscape* and *S. Mary the Egyptian* are recorded paid for by the Duke of Savoy 1586. [Fl. 559, Fl. 505, Fl. 157, Fl. 798.]

Kremer, Petrus. Flemish Sch. *b* Antwerp 1801 *d* Antwerp 1888. *Costume history, religious subjects, genre, portraits.* Pupil of W. Herreyns and M. van Brée; also studied in Paris; visited Germany and Italy; exhibited London (British Institution) 1829. Represented in ANTWERP (Cathedral and S. André), BRUSSELS *Count van der Marck swears vengeance for the deaths of Counts Egmont and Hoorn.* BRUGES *Children feeding a bird.* MONTREAL *Jan Brueghel's studio.* Scenes from the lives of *Brouwer, Craesbeek, Van Dyck, Rubens* and *Daniel Seghers* are recorded.

[Fl. 451, Fl. 481, Fl. 837 (1888), Fl. 798, Fl. Bib. 19th cent.]

Kroes, Lenaert. Flemish Sch. 16th cent. Recorded by van Mander as painter of figures and landscapes in oil and *w.*; and as second master of G. van Coninxloo. [Fl. 559.]

Kuhnen, Pierre Louis. Flemish Sch. *b* Aix-la-Chapelle 1812 *d* Schaerbeek nr. Brussels 1877. *Landscapes, portraits; also worked as lithographer.* Settled Brussels 1836; later patronised by royal family, and drawing master to Princess Charlotte. E. Verboeckhoven painted animals in some of his pictures (*cf.* P. J. Hellemans). Represented in BRUSSELS *Sunset.* FRANKFORT *Falls of the Rhine at Schaffhausen.*

[Fl. 451, Fl. 481, Fl. Bib. 19th cent.]

Kunst, see **Cornelisz.**

Kurte, Joannes de, see **Cordua.**

Kuyck, Frans van. Flemish Sch. *b* son of Louis van K., Antwerp 1852 *d* Antwerp 1915. *Landscapes, genre, portraits, decorative work, illustrations.* Represented in ANTWERP *The Woodcutter's return* (1888). [Fl. 17.]

Kuyck, Louis (Jean Louis) van. Flemish Sch. *b* Antwerp 1821 *d* Antwerp 1871. *Animals* (*mainly horses*) *and genre.* Pupil Antwerp Acad. of G. Wappers. Represented in ANTWERP *Stable interior* and others. BRUSSELS *Stable in a Flemish farm.* HAMBURG, MUNICH. [Fl. 264, Fl. 892.]

L

Lacroix, Antoine. Flemish Sch. *b* Wauré 1845 *d* Schaerbeek (near Brussels) 1896. *Genre, portraits.* [Fl. 892.]

Lacroix, Madame Clémence. Flemish Sch. *b* Charleroi 1849 *d* Schaerbeek 1925. Wife of A. L. *Marines, landscapes, interiors.* Member of L'Essor group (*cf.* A. Hamesse); founder member of Pour L'Art group. Represented in ANTWERP *Antwerp docks.* [Fl. 17.]

Ladam, Ghislain François. Flemish Sch. *b* Tournai before 1645 *d* Tournai 1708. *Religious subjects, portraits.* In Tournai Guild 1659; designed decorations for entry of Louis XIV into Tournai 1680 (cf. J. van Reyn). Tournai Cathedral has *Fall of the rebel Angels* and *Christ giving keys to S. Peter* and Tournai Mus. *An angel dictating the Apocalypse to S. John* referred to as his works. [Fl. 163, Fl. 359, Fl. 88.]

Laemen or **Laenen,** see **Lamen.**

Laen, Dirck van der. Flemish or Flemish-Dutch Sch. Van Mander (1604) records him as excelling in small pictures and as pupil of Marten van Cleve and F. Floris. [Fl. 559.]

Laermans, Eugeen Jules Joseph, Baron. Flemish Sch. *b* son of bank cashier, St-Jans-Molenbeek, Brussels 1864 *d* Brussels 1940. *Peasant and working class genre compositions with implicit social comment* (*cf.* L. Frédéric). Pupil of J. Portaels in Brussels Acad. Deaf and stammered from boyhood; lost sight 1924. Ennobled 1928. Represented in ANTWERP Triptych *The Emigrants, The Blind Man* 1898, *Storm* 1899, BRUSSELS *Death* 1904, *The Drunkard* 1894, *Drowned man* 1894, *The Return from the fields*; Belgian Royal Coll. *Peasant's funeral*; DRESDEN, GHENT, LIÈGE, PARIS (State Collection) and other galleries. [Fl. 910, Fl. Bib. 19th cent.]

Laet, Alois de. Flemish Sch. *b* Antwerp 1866. *Landscapes and genre.* Represented ANTWERP *Kermesse carts in the rain.* [Fl. 17.]

Laet, Peter de. Flemish Sch. *b* Antwerp 1820 *d* Antwerp 1865. *Costume history, religious subjects, genre.* Pupil of N. de Keyser. Represented in GHENT Couvent des Sœurs de l'Enfant Jésus. *Vision of Sister Emmanuella* 1861. [Fl. 837 (1765).]

Laethem, see **Lathem.**

La Fabrique, see **Fabrique.**

Lafontaine, Pierre Joseph. Flemish Sch. *b* Courtrai 1758 *d* Paris 1835. *Church and other interiors (with figures by J. L. Demarne q.v. or French artists); also active as dealer.* Went Paris where became associate of the Académie Royale (*cf.* P. Mol and J. L. Demarne) 1789. Represented in COURTRAI, ORLÉANS, PARIS (Carnavalet). May have been the Lafontaine (no initial) who exhibited in Paris Salon *Fire in a village near Beauvais* 1817, *S. Pierre at Beauvais* 1817 and *Interior of a Gothic church (artificial light effect)* 1827. [Fl. 451, Fl. 66, Fl. 88, Fl. 892.]

Lagye, Victor. Flemish Sch. *b* Ghent 1829 *d* Antwerp 1896. *Genre, costume history, murals, religious subjects and illustrations.* Pupil Ghent Acad. under T. Canneel, and in Antwerp of H. Leys; worked Paris; went Rome 1843; fought under

Garibaldi in Italy; returned Belgium 1849; assisted Leys on murals in his dining room; settled Antwerp where Professor in Inst. des B.A. 1891. Represented in ANTWERP *Johanna v. d. Gheynst at her child's bedside* 1861, *Gipsy* 1878; Town Hall (Salle du Mariage) *Marriage in the Olden Days* (murals); S. Antoine *Holy Family.* BRUSSELS *The Sorceress.* GHENT Mus. and University. [Fl. 837 (1896), Fl .Bib. 19th cent.]

Lairesse, Ernest. Flemish Sch. *b* son of Renier L., Liège 1636 *d* Bonn 1676 or Amsterdam 1718. *Flowers, birds and miniatures.* In Rome at expense of Prince Bishop of Liège 1662-4; later went Bonn. [Fl. 425, Fl. 409.]

*****Lairesse, Gérard de.** Flemish Sch. *b* son of Renier L., Liège 1641 *d* blind and a victim of syphilis, Amsterdam 1711. *'History', allegories, mythologies, religious subjects, occasiona portraits; also worked as engraver.* Pupil of his father and of B. Flémalle. Fled from Liège to Bois-le-duc after stabbing a girl 1664; in Utrecht 1665; settled Amsterdam at suggestion of art dealer Gérard van Uylenburg 1665; bought citizenship in Amsterdam 1667; much employed in decorative commissions for public buildings and private mansions; was a musician and man of parts and his house was a centre for literary reunions; in The Hague working on decorative paintings for the Courts of Justice 1684; went blind 1690; dictated to his son Abraham 'Het Groot Schilderboek' (lectures defending Academic art against Rembrandt and the naturalists); had many pupils including his two sons Abraham and Jan and collaborated in some works with the Dutch landscape painter and engraver J. Glauber. **Signed Examples:** AMIENS *Allegoric portrait with Amor and Abondantia* 1671. AMSTERDAM *Seleucus renouncing Stratonice, Antony and Cleopatra (The Pearl), Mars, Venus, Mercury and Amor, Allegory of Virtue* 1670. CASSEL *Bacchanal, Man's portrait* 1682. COPENHAGEN *Alexander and Roxane* 1664. DRESDEN *Parnassus.* HAGUE *Achilles discovered among the daughters of Lycomedes* (cf. E. Quellinus), *Apotheosis of William III, King of England.* LENINGRAD *Sacrificial feast, Solomon and the Queen of Sheba* 1683. STOCKHOLM *Achilles discovered among the daughters of Lycomedes, Achilles playing the lyre before Patroclus.* **Monogrammed Examples:** COPENHAGEN, VIENNA Liecht. **Documented Examples:** AIX-LA-CHAPELLE *Martyrdom of S. Ursula* 1660 (from Aix-la-Chapelle Cathedral). AMSTERDAM *Allegory of the healing of lepers and the insane* (painted for Leper Hospital). HAGUE Courts of Justice *Classical compositions* (painted there 1684). Descamps (1769) records in Liège, S. Ursule *Scenes from the life of S. Augustine.* D'Argenville (1745) records several pictures then in England.
[Fl. 494, Fl. 425, Fl. 22, Fl. 215, Fl. 702, Fl. 612, Fl. 892.]

Lairesse, Jacques. Flemish Sch. *b* son of Renier L., Liège after 1641 *d* Amsterdam 1690 or 1709. *Flowers, grisaille panels, portraits, religious subjects.* Joined Gérard de L. in Amsterdam 1680. [Fl. 425, Fl. 409, Fl. 892.]

Lairesse, Renier. Flemish Sch. *b* Liège c. 1597 *d* Vitry-le-Français 1667. *Religious subjects, 'history' and decorative painting (marbling).* Pupil and son-in-law of J. Taulier *q.v.* Worked for Liège churches and the Prince Bishop of Liège. A *Death of Seneca* is recorded by an engraving. [Fl. 425, Fl. 215, Fl. 409, Fl. 892.]

Lalaing, Count Jacques de. Flemish Sch. *b* son of Belgian diplomat, London 1858 *d* Brussels 1917. *Portraits, allegorical and costume history, murals; also worked as sculptor* (*Monument to British officers who fell at Waterloo* and *Fighting horsemen* Brussels, *Tigers* Ghent). Educated in England; served as junior officer in British navy; then pupil in Brussels of J. Portaels, A. Cluysenaar and E. Agneesens; exhibited with Brussels L'Essor group (*cf.* A. Hamesse) 1882; worked mainly at sculpture after 1884. Represented in ANTWERP *Portrait*. BRUSSELS *Prehistoric hunter* 1885. BRUGES *Portrait* 1907. GHENT *Equestrian portrait* (*Officer with Lancers*) 1883, *Village priest* 1883. LILLE *Prisoners of War*. Murals in BRUSSELS Senate house and Town Hall staircase *Costume history allegories* 1895.

[Fl. 497, Fl. 499, Fl. Bib. 19th cent.]

Lambeaux, Jules. Flemish Sch. *b* Antwerp 1858 *d* Antwerp 1890. Brother of sculptor Jef L. *Interiors, genre, costume history.* Represented in ANTWERP *Dispensary in Bruges Hôpital de S. Jean.* [Fl. 17.]

Lambert (Suster or Sustris) of Amsterdam. Flemish (Dutch) Sch. *b* Amsterdam (?) before 1520 *d* after 1568 (?). *Religious subjects in landscape, portraits.* Vasari records him as father of F. Suster (Sustris) and a good painter in the Italian manner who lived for many years in Venice. Presumed by some identical with Lamberto Tedesco *q.v.* F. di L. Sustris was his son. **Signed Examples:** CAEN *Baptism of Christ in landscape* 'Lambertus de Amsterdam'. COLOGNE Wallraf-Richartz *Erhard von Frickenhausen* (inscribed 'Durh Maister Lăpreht võ Asterdă besechĕ ŭd volĕdet') 1552.

[Fl. 818, Fl. 892, Fl. 305.]

Lamberto (Tedesco). Flemish (Dutch) Sch. 16th cent. Ridolfi (1648) records him as landscape assistant to Titian and Tintoretto (*cf.* L. Toeput). Presumed by some identical with Lambert (Sustris) of Amsterdam *q.v.*

[Fl. 709, Fl. 892, Fl. 305.]

Lambrechts, C. Presumed Flemish Sch. 17th cent. Painter of BRUSSELS Mus. (206) *Charity* (or *Fecundity*) grisaille signed 'C. Lambrechts pinxit' surrounded by flower garland monogrammed J. H. D. and dated 1668. (*cf.* J. D. de Heem).

[Fl. 120, Fl. 124.]

Lambrechts, Jan Baptist. Flemish Sch. *b* Antwerp 1680 *d* place unknown, after 1731. *Outdoor and indoor genre and conversation pieces.* Went France as art dealer 1703; in Lille 1704; returned Antwerp and Master in Guild 1709; member of Senior Crossbowmen 1721; left Antwerp before 1731 when trace is lost of him, but may have gone Vienna and South Germany where a Lambrechts is said to have worked Augsburg *c.* 1750. **Signed Examples:** FLORENCE Uffizi *Genre scenes* (two: 'Lambrechts'). **Monogrammed Examples:** BRUNSWICK Mus. *Conversation pieces* (two: monogram J. B. L.). **Documented Examples:** STOCKHOLM *At a meal* (two: from the coll. of Queen Louise Ulrique). Vienna (Liechtenstein) has pictures now presumed by some his work, formerly presumed by the French painter N. Lancret. Other pictures presumed by some his work are in various museums.

[Fl. 107, Fl. 296.]

Lambrichs, Edmond A. C. Flemish Sch. *b* Brussels 1830 *d* Brussels 1887. *Landscapes, portraits; also worked as engraver.* Pupil of C. de Groux. Member of Société Libre des Beaux Arts (*cf.* L. Dubois). Represented in BRUSSELS *Sixteen members of the Société Libre des B.A.* (including F. Rops, C. Meunier, E. Huberti and H. Charlerie).

[Fl. Bib. 19th cent.]

Lamen (or Laemen or Lanen), Christoffel Jacobsz van der. Flemish Sch. *b* son of Jacob van der L., Antwerp *c.* 1606 or Brussels *c.* 1615 *d* Antwerp before 1652. *Conversation pieces* (*cf.* P. Meert), *social entertainments* (*cf.* H. Janssens); *also peasant, lowlife and military genre.* Master Antwerp Guild 1637; H. Janssens was his pupil; Van Dyck drew his portrait. The Forchoudt firm of Antwerp dealers exported many of his pictures in the second half of the 17th century. **Signed Examples:** GOTHA *Dancing company* 1640. LUCCA Mansi Gall. *Elegant company in a park* 1641, *Company in a drawing room* 1641. STRASBOURG *Lady and four gentlemen making music and drinking.* VIENNA Liecht. *Lady and gentleman playing cards* (signature now illegible).

[Fl. 878, Fl. 107, Fl. 892, Fl. 212.]

Lamen (or Laemen), Jacob van der. Flemish Sch. *b* Antwerp 1584 *d* Brussels (?) after 1620. *Conversation pieces.* Master Antwerp Guild 1605; Master Brussels Guild 1616 (*cf.* C. v. d. L.). [Fl. 425, Fl. 107, Fl. 892.]

Lamoen, Abraham van. Flemish Sch. *b* Antwerp (?) before 1630 *d* Antwerp 1669. *Still life.* Master in Antwerp Guild 1647. **Signed Example:** YPRES *Fruit piece.* [Fl. 714.]

Lamorinière, François. Flemish Sch. *b* Antwerp 1828 *d* (blind) Antwerp 1911. *Landscapes.* Pupil of E. Noterman and J. Jacobs. Professor landscape Antwerp Acad. 1885; worked mainly in Antwerp Campine; visited Holland and England. Represented in ANTWERP, BRUSSELS, CHICAGO, CINCINNATI, GHENT, LIÈGE *Burnham Beeches.* LIVERPOOL Walker *Sunset, Landscape.*

[Fl. 160 (1911), Fl. Bib. 19th cent.]

Lampsonius, Domenicus. Flemish Sch. *b* Bruges 1532 *d* Liège 1599. *Art historian, humanist and painter.* In service of Cardinal Reginald Pole; then, in Liège, private secretary to a succession of bishops; pupil of Lambert Lombard *q.v.* and member Liège Guild; acquainted with many artists and supplied Vasari with material on Flemish painters; wrote biography of Lombard 1565 and poem on Netherlandish artists published by the widow of Hieronymus Cock *q.v.* 1572; O. van Veen was his pupil 1573. In a letter to Vasari 1564 L. wrote: 'I draw and occasionally paint in oil the natural objects before me, more particularly figures nude or draped, but I have not courage to go further and attempt such things as require a firmer and more practised hand, landscapes, trees, waters, clouds, conflagrations, etc. ... for the present I have contented myself with the limning of portraits' and he adds a reference to a *Self-portrait* painted in a mirror. Hasselt, S. Quentin has a *Crucifixion* presumed by some his work.

[Fl. 818, Fl. 559, Fl. 88, Fl. 892.]

Landois. Flemish Sch. (?) Painter of *Attack on the stage coach s* and dated 1714 exhibited Brussels 'Exp. du paysage Flamand' 1926. [Fl. 301.]

Landtsheer, Jan Baptiste de. Flemish Sch. *b* son of 'history' and genre painter Jan de L., Brussels 1797 *d* after 1851. '*History*', *genre and portraits.* Pupil of F. J. Navez. Teacher in Brussels Academy. **Signed Example:** COURTRAI *Obstinacy* 1840. [Fl. 451, Fl. 612.]

Lanen, C. J., see **Lamen.**

Lanen, Jasper (Gaspar) van der. Flemish Sch. *b* before 1600 *d* after 1626. *Landscapes with small figures.* Master Antwerp Guild 1615; friend of A. Govaerts *q.v.* and was one of several artists who completed some pictures left unfinished by G. at his death. A *Balaam and the Angel in a wood s* and dated 1624 was recorded (1948) in London commerce.

[Fl. 107, Fl. 892.]

Lange, Frans de. Flemish Sch. *b* Ghent (?) before 1745 *d* Ghent (?) after 1780. *Religious subjects.* In Ghent Guild

1759-66. Signed Example: GHENT S Jacques *Martyrdom of S. Cornelius* (F. de Lange fecit 1780). [Fl. 479, Fl. 386.]

Lange Jan (Langjean), see Boeckhorst.

Lange Peer (or Pier), see Aertsen.

Langerock, Henri. Flemish Sch. *b* Ghent 1830 *d* Paris 1885. *Landscapes.* Went Paris and worked much at Fontainebleau (*cf.* A. de Knyff). Represented in AMIENS and MULHOUSE [Fl. 466 (1883)]

Lankrink, Prosper Henricus. Flemish Sch. *b* son of a German officer serving with Spanish army, Antwerp 1628 *d* in poverty, London 1692. *Landscapes, decorative pieces, portraits; also active as dealer.* Studied Antwerp, visited Italy; came England (*cf.* C. de Neve and S. Dubois) with pictures for sale; painted in some noblemen's houses; assisted Sir Peter Lely with landscape backgrounds, flowers, ornaments and draperies (*cf.* J. B. Gaspers and R. van Leemput) and was a buyer of pictures at Lely's sale (1680); Vertue states that he signed P.HL and describes him as 'not only a good bottle companion and excellent company but also a great favourite with the ladies through his exceeding complaisance and comely appearance'. A *Nymph bathing her feet* and a portrait *Thomas Streater, brother of Serjeant painter Robert S.* are recorded. His *Narcissus* was celebrated in an epigram by J. Elsum 1700.
[Fl. 878, Fl. 826, Fl. 856, Fl. 223 (1892), Fl. 440.]

Lantscroon (or Lanscron or Lanscroon), Jean Baptiste (van den). Flemish Sch. *b* son of a sculptor, Malines 1653 *d* in poverty, London 1737. Came England 1677 (*cf.* C. de Neve and J. B. Medina) and worked as assistant to the Italian A. Verrio at Windsor and Hampton Court; also associated here with the French painter L. Laguerre.
[Fl. 826, Fl. 856, Fl. 613, Fl. 892.]

*La Pegnia (or Pegna or Peigne), Hyacinth de. Flemish Sch. *b* Brussels 1706 *d* Rome 1772. *Battle pieces* (*cf.* J. P. v. Bredael), *town views, designs for tapestries* (*cf.* V. Janssens); *also worked as engraver.* In Paris as 'ingénieur-dessinateur' (*cf.* C. J. Redouté) c. 1740-c. 1743; then Turin in service of Charles Emmanuel III of Savoy (*cf.* J. P. Verdussen); member of Rome Accad. di S. Luca (*cf.* H. F. van Lint) 1748; returned Turin 1749; in Brussels working for tapestry factory and 'peintre extraordinaire' to the Empress Maria Theresa (*cf.* P. J. Lion) 1755; in Vienna 1759-62; returned Rome 1762; patronized there by Cardinal Albani; Provisor of Flemish Foundation of S. Julien 1768 (*cf.* A. de Muynck). **Signed Examples:** TURIN Pinac. *The handing over of Milan to Charles Emmanuel III, King of Sardinia 1734* 1752, *The Siege of Tortona 1734* 1752. VIENNA K. *Paris, Pont Neuf from the Quai de l'Horloge* 1743, *Paris, Pont Neuf from the Quai de la Mégisserie.* The Austrian State Colls. own tapestry cartoons of military subjects 1756-7.
[Fl. 612, Fl. 892, Fl. 296.]

Laridon, Louise. Flemish Sch. *b* Liège 1868 *d* Antwerp 1943. Wife of E. Vloors. *Flowers, figures, landscapes.* Studied Paris (Acad. Julian). Represented in ANTWERP. [Fl. 17.]

Larock, Evert. Flemish Sch. *b* Kapellan-op-den-Bosch 1865 *d* Kapellan-op-den-Bosch 1901. *Genre, landscapes, portraits, interiors; also worked as engraver.* Member of Antwerp group De Dertien (XIII) (*cf.* E. Farasyn) 1891. Represented in ANTWERP *The idiot* 1892, *The cinder-sifter, The village church, The studio, Old woman.* [Fl. 837 (1901), Fl. 624.]

Lathem (Laethem, Lathim), Jacques (Jakob) van. Flemish Sch. *b* before 1480 *d* Brussels (?) after 1522. Master Antwerp Guild 1493; Court painter and 'valet de chambre' to Duke Philip the Fair by 1498; accompanied Duke to Spain 1501; collaborated with J. v. Battel *q.v.* 1505; retained posts under Emperor Charles V and accompanied him to Spain (*cf.* J. C. Vermeyen) 1517; worked Brussels where designer for Golden Fleece Chapter and for commemorative ceremonies on death of Isabella of Castile 1504 and Manoel of Portugal 1521.
[Fl. 892, Fl. 309, Fl. 316.]

Lathouwer, August de. Flemish Sch. *b* Louvain 1836 *d* Antwerp 1915. *Landscapes.* Pupil of J. Jacobs. Represented in ANTWERP. [Fl. 17.]

Latinis, Georges. Flemish Sch. *b* Brussels 1885. *Figures, still life, landscapes and town views.* Represented in ANTWERP and BRUSSELS. [Fl. 17.]

Latour, Alexandre de (signed **Delatour**). Flemish Sch. *b* Brussels 1780 *d* Brussels 1858. *Portrait miniatures and figures.* Pupil in Brussels of the French miniaturist L. M. Autissier and in Paris of J. B. Augustin; patronized by King William I. Represented in ANTWERP, BRUSSELS, LONDON (Wallace). [Fl. 451, Fl. 539.]

Latour, Édouard de. Flemish Sch. *b* son of Alexandre L., Brussels 1817 *d* Schaerbeek nr. Brussels 1863. *Portraits, mostly in miniature.* Represented in ANTWERP, BRUSSELS. [Fl. 892, Fl. 497.]

Latour, Jean. Flemish Sch. *b* Liège 1719 *d* Moislains (N. France) 1782. *Religious subjects and 'history'; also worked as sculptor.* Pupil in Liège of J. B. Coclers; and in Rome of the Italian painter Corrado Giaquinto 1740-5 (*cf.* H. Deprez); visited London and Paris. The French authorities (1798) did not take his pictures to Paris judging them unworthy of selection (*cf.* L. Defrance). [Fl. 409, Fl. 892.]

Lauters, Paul. Flemish Sch. *b* Brussels 1806 *d* Brussels 1875. *Landscapes, figures but chiefly active as engraver.* Professor Brussels School of Engraving 1836. Represented in BRUSSELS. [Fl. 451, Fl. 892.]

Lauwers, Balthasar. Flemish Sch. *b* Antwerp 1578 *d* Rome 1645. *Landscapes and decorative panels.* Pupil in Antwerp of F. Borsse. Went Italy and remained there (*cf.* J. v. d. Straet and J. Sutterman); worked as assistant to P. Brill; commissioned by Don Francesco Pacheco to paint twelve pictures (hunting pieces and hermit saints) 'in the style of Tempesta' 1604; painted decorative panels in Brill tradition for Roman palaces; visited Milan c. 1634. His sons Francesco and Filippo were also painters.
[Fl. 559, Fl. 48, Fl. 84, Fl. 440, Fl. 416, Fl. 617.]

Lauwers, Jacobus Johannes. Flemish Sch. *b* son of master cooper, Bruges 1753 *d* Amsterdam 1800. *Outdoor and indoor genre; also pastiches of works by G. Dou and other Dutch genre painters.* Pupil in Bruges Acad.; went, as a pilgrim, to Rome where arrived destitute and was assisted by J. B. Suvée and A. de. Muynck, before 1777; in Rome was employed in a workshop producing cheap portraits of the pope and cardinals for peasants; went Paris then Amsterdam with a rich Dutchman who befriended him. **Signed Example:** AMSTERDAM Rijks. *Flemish farmyard* 1799.
[Fl. 275, Fl. 451, Fl. 612, Fl. 440, Fl. 892.]

Leckerbetien, Vincent (known in Italy as Manciolla or Mozza d'Anversa, and in France as Le Manchole because he had lost his right hand and painted with his left). Flemish Sch. *b* Antwerp (?) c. 1600 (?) *d* Rome (?) 1650 (?). *Landscapes and battlepieces.* Went Rome; acquainted with the French painter N. Poussin who records him as invited to contribute to the decoration of the Louvre (*cf.* J. Fouquier) 1642. *The Battles* *of Alexander the Great* painted for Vincennes Château during Regency of Anne of Austria (1643-61) are recorded.

[Fl. 753, Fl. 287.]

Ledoulx, Pierre François. Flemish Sch. *b* son of an historian, Bruges 1730 *d* Bruges 1807. *Miniatures of flowers and insects, landscapes and views of Bruges in oil and w.; also worked as art historian.* Pupil of J. Garemyn and M. de Visch. His MS history of Bruges artists (now in Bruges Academy Archives) was used by Immerzeel.

[Fl. 207, Fl. 451, Fl. 88, Fl. 892.]

Leemans, Egidius F. Flemish Sch. *b* Antwerp 1839 *d* Antwerp 1883. *River scenes and other landscapes (many with moonlight effects).* Visited Holland. Represented in ANTWERP *Summer evening, Marine* and others.   [Fl. 837 (1883), Fl. 892.]

Leempoels, Jef. Flemish Sch. *b* Brussels 1867. *Symbolist allegories* (*cf.* A. Levêque), *portraits, genre, landscapes.* Pupil J. Portaels and J. Stallaert. Visited England, France and Germany. Represented in BUENOS AIRES *Friendship.* LEIPZIG, NAMUR, SANTIAGO (Chile). Pictures titled *Fate and Mankind, Young Sphinx* and *Horrific Vision* are recorded. [Fl. 465, Fl. Bib. 19th cent.]

Leemput (Lemput or Limpitt), Remigius (Remy) van, known as **Remee** (not to be confused with **G. Remeeus**). Flemish Sch. *b* son of a tailor, Antwerp 1607 *d* London 1675. *Portraits, but mainly active as copyist and dealer.* Master Antwerp Guild 1628; came England after 1630 (*cf.* C. de Neve and A. Keirincx); lived with Van Dyck and copied his pictures (*cf.* J. van Reyn); later worked as copyist for Lely; was a buyer in Commonwealth sales of Charles I's coll. (*cf.* J. B. Gaspers and J. v. Belcamp) and procured Van Dyck's *Charles I on horseback* (now English Royal Collection) for which was successfully sued by Crown after Restoration (1660). His sons Antonio (killed in a brawl in Rome 1667) and Giovanni were painters. His daughter, also a painter, married Thomas, brother of the English painter Robert Streater (*cf.* P. H. Lankrink). Signed Examples: LONDON Hampton Court *Henry VIII and Jane Seymour; Henry VII and Elizabeth of York* 1668 (full lengths, after Holbein's Whitehall fresco destroyed by fire 1698).

[Fl. 878, Fl. 826, Fl. 856, Fl. 84, Fl. 223, Fl. 440.]

Leemputten, Cornelis van. Flemish Sch. *b* Werchter nr. Louvain 1841 *d* Schaerbeek 1902. Brother of F. van L. *Landscapes with animals (mostly sheep).* Represented in ANTWERP *The Flock, Sunny day in March.* BUCHAREST, LOUVAIN, SHEFFIELD *Sheep and poultry.*

[Fl. Bib. 19th cent.]

Leemputten, Frans van. Flemish Sch. *b* Werchter nr. Louvain 1850 *d* Antwerp 1914. Brother of Cornelis van L. *Peasant genre, landscapes, animals.* Pupil in Brussels Acad. of P. Lauters. Member of L'Essor group (*cf.* A. Hamesse); professor Antwerp Institut des B.A. Represented in ANTWERP *Bread distribution in the village* 1892, *Sunday morning in winter* 1896, *Procession* triptych 1903-5. BARCELONA, BRUSSELS *Palmsunday in the Campine.* BUDAPEST, COURTRAI *Market day in the Campine.* DRESDEN, GHENT, LOUVAIN, NAMUR, PRAGUE.

[Fl. Bib. 19th cent., Fl. 440.]

Leepe, Jan Anthonie van der. Flemish Sch. *b* Bruges 1664 *d* Bruges (?) 1718. *Sea pieces* (*cf.* G. van Eyck), *landscapes (with figures of religious subjects by other artists)* in *o.* and *w.*; *occasional engravings;* but later active as state and town official (*Ranger of Flanders, Councillor and Sheriff of Bruges*). A series of pictures *Scenes from the life of Christ* and a *Flight into Egypt* painted for Bruges S. Anne are recorded.

[Fl. 451, Fl. 612, Fl. 126, Fl. 88, Fl. 892, Fl. 798.]

Le Febre (or Lefevre), Valentin, known as de Venise. Flemish Sch. *b* Brussels 1642 *d* London or Venice (?) after 1676. *Religious subjects and history, copies of works by P. Veronese; but chiefly active as engraver after Veronese, Titian, Tintoretto and others.* Lived many years in Venice. Vertue (possibly confusing him with the French painter Rolland L.) states (before 1752) that he came to England and 'had a particular excellence in staining marble which he did several times for Prince Rupert' and died London where buried S. Martin's in the Fields 1677. **Signed Example:** VENICE S. Giorgio Maggiore Monastery (ceiling) *Jacob's ladder.* A copy of Veronese's *Feast in the house of Simon* made 1664-5, when the Signoria presented the original to Louis XIV, is recorded.

[Fl. 101, Fl. 22, Fl. 564, Fl. 826, Fl. 505, Fl. 440, Fl. 536, Fl. 305.]

Legendre, Louis. Flemish Sch. *b* Paris (?) 1723 (?) *d* Brussels after 1780. *Portraits oil and miniature.* Court painter to Governor General Prince Charles of Lorraine (*cf.* J. P. Sauvage); also worked for Maria Theresa's minister in the Netherlands Count Cobenzl (*cf.* A. J. Cardon). Portraits of *Charles of Lorraine* and the actress *Eugénie d'Hannetaire* are recorded by engravings.   [Fl. 612, Fl. 296, Fl. 798.]

*Legillon (or Le Gillon or Gillon), Jean François. Flemish Sch. *b* son of French aristocrat, Bruges 1739 *d* Paris 1797. *Landscapes with figures and animals.* Pupil in Bruges Acad. of M. de Visch (*cf.* J. B. Suvée) *c.* 1755; went Rouen where pupil of French painter and art historian J. B. Descamps in Acad. 1759-60; in Marseilles 1769; Italy 1770; Bruges 1774; Switzerland 1780; settled Fontainebleau Forest 1783; member of French Acad. Royale 1789; domiciled Paris; visited Bruges during revolution; exhibited Paris Salons; was visiting a friend in Paris when he died; J. B. Suvée took charge of his effects and sent them to his relatives in Bruges. **Signed Examples:** BRUGES *Self-portrait in Rome* 1772, *A stable in Switzerland* 1780. *A derelict barn in sunlight with women and animals* (Acad. reception piece, Salon 1789) and *View of Fontainebleau Forest with figures and animals by a fountain* (Salon 1791) are recorded.

[Fl. 207, Fl. 451, Fl. 481, Fl. 66.]

Leickert, Charles H. J. Flemish Sch. *b* Brussels 1818 *d* Mainz 1907. *Landscapes, coast scenes, picturesque corners in towns and villages.* Pupil of Dutch painters J. B. van Hove and A. Schelfhout. Worked much in Holland and Mainz. Represented in AMSTERDAM *Winter landscape* 1867. MAINZ, ROTTERDAM, PHILADELPHIA Wilstach *Coast scene in Holland* 1859.

[Fl. 451, Fl. 481, Fl. Bib. 19th cent.]

Le Mayeur de Merprès, Adrien. Flemish Sch. *b* Boitsford 1844 *d* Brussels 1923. *Marines and coast scenes.* Represented in BRUSSELS *The Breakwater.* MONS, MUNICH, NAMUR. [Fl. 123.]

Lemens, Balthasar van. Flemish Sch. *b* Antwerp 1637 *d* London 1704. *'History' and landscape.* Came England at Restoration (*cf.* C. de Neve); mainly employed as assistant to other painters and as draughtsman for engravers. Compositions titled *Venus and Adonis, Vanitas* and *Diana and Actaeon* are recorded by engravings.   [Fl. 826, Fl. 856, Fl. 223.]

Lemmen, Georges. Flemish Sch. *b* Brussels 1865 *d* Uccle (Brussels) 1916. *Landscapes and coast scenes, interiors, figures, portraits, still life; also designs for posters, tapestry and mosaic.* Went Paris where influenced by French Impressionists and Seurat; used 'pointilliste' technique; member of Brussels groups 'Les Vingt' (*cf.* J. Ensor) and 'Libre Esthétique' (*cf.* G. Buysse); and later of the 'Vie et Lumière' group (*cf.* G. Morren) 1914. Represented in BRUSSELS *Sewing w., Reading w., Nude, Children's room w.* GHENT, IXELLES.

[Fl. Bib. 19th cent.]

*Lens, Andreas Cornelis. Flemish Sch. *b* son of Cornelis L., Antwerp 1739 *d* Brussels 1822. *Religious, mythological and allegorical subjects, occasional portraits.* Pupil of Karel Ijkens the younger, then of B. Beschey (fellow student with H. J. Antonissen) from 1753; professor in Antwerp Acad. when 24 years old 1763; 'peintre ordinaire' to Charles of Lorraine, Governor general of Austrian Netherlands (*cf.* J. P. Sauvage), who sent him to Italy (*cf.* F. J. Lonsing) 1764; worked Rome and visited Naples, returned Antwerp via France 1768; moving spirit in transferring power from the Antwerp Guild to the Academy 1769-73; published 'Le Costume, ou Essai sur les Habillements et les Usages de plusieurs Peuples de l'Antiquité prouvé par les monuments' 1776; conducted round Antwerp the Emperor Joseph II (*cf.* W. J. Herreyns) but declined his invitation to join Vienna Court 1781; resigned teaching at Acad. and settled Brussels 1781; worked for the new Governors Albert of Saxe-Teschen and the Archduchess Maria Christina at Château de Laeken (*cf.* P. Faes and F. B. Solvyns) 1782-4; appointed member of French Institut National after 1795 but unlike his pupil P. J. C. François *q.v.* and L. Defrance *q.v.* was unwilling to serve the French régime; published 'Du Bon Goût, ou de la Beauté de la Peinture' Brussels 1811; an inscription on his tomb reads 'Régénerateur de la Peinture de Belgique et parfait chrétien; il réunit la pratique de toutes les vertus à un talent enchanteur'. **Signed Examples:** ANTWERP *Hercules protecting the Muse of Fine Arts against Jealousy and Ignorance* 1763 (presented to Antwerp Acad. on appointment as professor-director), *The engraver Peter Frans Martenasie* 1762. **Documented Examples:** ANTWERP Augustins *Presentation in the Temple.* BRUSSELS *Ariadne consoled by Bacchus, Offering to Bacchus.* GHENT S. Michel *Annunciation* (clerical protests made the artist add wings to the angel originally wingless) 1809. LILLE S. Madeleine *Four scenes from the life of S. Mary Magdalene* 1777-8. MALINES Notre Dame d'Hanswyck *Marie Catherine de Villegas de Borsbeke* 1764 (*cf.* Cornelis L.). VIENNA K. *Jupiter, on Mount Ida, put to sleep by Juno* (from Château de Laeken).
[Fl. 451, Fl. 479, Fl. 356, Fl. 440, Fl. 341.]

Lens, Cornelis. Flemish Sch. *b* Tilff (nr. Liège) before 1725 *d* Antwerp after 1766. *Flowers and coach decorations.* In Antwerp from 1738; a Dean in Guild 1751; practised as a gilder and was prosecuted by the Guild. MALINES Notre Dame d'Hanswyck *Marie Catherine de Villegas de Borsbeke* (by his son A. C. Lens 1764) has flower passages recorded as his work.
[Fl. 614, Fl. 440.]

*Lens, Johannes Jacobus. Flemish Sch. *b* son of Cornelis L., Antwerp 1746 *d* S. Josse-ten-Noode 1814. *Religious subjects, 'history' and portraits.* Pupil in Antwerp Acad.; went Italy with his brother A. C. L. and returned with him via France 1764-9; then settled Brussels; worked for Prince Charles of Lorraine (*cf.* J. P. Sauvage and A. C. L.) 1779. **Signed Examples:** BRUSSELS *The Emperor Leopold II* 1791. RUHMANNSFELDEN (Bavaria) Church *Virgin and Child* 1793. Pictures titled *The Death of Abel, The Death of Cleopatra, The Birth of Venus* and *La marchande d'Amours* are recorded.
[Fl. 451, Fl. 107, Fl. 440.]

Lentzen (Lenzen), Jan Frans. Flemish Sch. *b* Antwerp *c.* 1790 *d* Antwerp 1840. *Landscapes and animals.* Pupil of H. A. Myin. Made many copies of pictures by B. Ommeganck. A picture titled *The Comet seen at 7 p.m. on October* 7 1811 was exhibited in the Antwerp Salon 1813.
[Fl. 451, Fl. 440.]

Le Pla, Jacques. Flemish Sch. *b* Malines *c.* 1650 *d* Malines after 1678. *Religious subjects.* Pupil of J. Saive the younger. Master Malines Guild 1675. **Signed Example:** MALINES N. Dame d'Hanswyck *Adoration of the shepherds* (J. Pla 1678).
[Fl. 613, Fl. 440.]

Le Plat, Gilles. Flemish Sch. *b* son of Pieter L., Ghent *c.* 1656 *d* Ghent 1724. *Religious subjects.* **Signed Example:** GHENT S. Jacques *S. Nicholas baptising an old woman* 1684. Descamps (1769) recorded works by Le Plat (without initial) in Ghent S. Bavon, S. Nicholas, Baudeloo Abbey (*cf.* R. v. Audenaerd) and elsewhere (*cf.* P. Le P.); a *Seven Works of Mercy* painted for Ghent Town Hall 1691 is also recorded.
[Fl. 216, Fl. 576, Fl. 479, Fl. 88.]

Le Plat, Pieter. Flemish Sch. *b* Ghent 1630 *d* Ghent after 1685. *Religious subjects.* In Ghent Guild 1655; worked for Ghent churches and city. **Documented Example:** GHENT University *Marc d'Aviano preaching in Ghent during plague epidemic of 1681 with members of Heynderickx family as donors.*
[Fl. 88, Fl. 338.]

Lerius, Joseph Henri François. Flemish Sch. *b* Boom 1823 *d* Malines 1876. *Portraits. costume history, genre; also lithographs.* Pupil of G. Wappers. Teacher Antwerp Acad. 1854. Represented ANTWERP *Woman's portrait* 1854, *Portrait of a child, Lady Godiva* 1870 (this picture toured England with great success), AMSTERDAM, BRUSSELS *Erasmus.*
[Fl. 88, Fl. Bib. 19th cent.]

Leroy, Joseph Anne Jules. Flemish Sch. *b* son of Pierre J. B. L., Brussels 1812 *d* Brussels 1860. *Genre, military scenes (some in w.) and portraits.* Pupil of E. Verboeckhoven; professor of drawing in the École Militaire.
[Fl. 440.]

Leroy, Pierre François Charles (known as **Leroy fils**). Flemish Sch. *b* son of P. J. B. L., Brussels 1803 *d* Brussels 1833. *Genre and costume history (some in w).* Collaborated with E. J. Verboeckhoven *q.v.* Visited Italy (?) and Spain; painted reconstructed scenes of guerilla fighting in the Peninsular War. *A young man preparing breakfast* 1823 and an *Italian shepherd nursing a lamb* (with Verboeckhoven) are among other subjects recorded.
[Fl. 451, Fl. 440.]

Leroy, Pierre Jean Baptiste. Flemish Sch. *b* son of sculptor Pierre François L., Namur 1784 *d* Brussels 1861. *Military and social genre with animals, contemporary history. landscapes (some in w.); also active as engraver.* Pupil of J. B. de Roy *q.v.* Exhibitor Antwerp during French régime from 1805 (*cf.* P. J. Regemorter) and under William I; left Brussels 1830 and visited Paris, London and Vienna. Represented in BRUSSELS *Entry of Napoleon into Brussels* 1810 w., *Fête at Brussels for the entry of William I of the Netherlands* 1815 w. A large drawing *Battle of Waterloo* with many portraits was exhibited in the Ghent Salon 1816. An *Interior of the 1812 Ghent Exhibition* (*cf.* A. de Baets) is recorded
[Fl. 451, Fl. 481, Fl. 442, Fl. 440.]

Leux, F. see **Luyckx.**

Levêque, Auguste. Flemish Sch. *b* Nivelles 1864 *d* Brussels 1921. *Symbolist allegories and decorative compositions* (*cf.* W. Degouve de Nuncques, J. Leempoels, X. Mellery, F. Khnopff, C. Montald, E. Motte, E. Fabry), *mythologies, portraits; also worked as sculptor.* Pupil of J. Portaels. Influenced by Paris Rose-Croix symbolist movement and founded with J. Delville *q.v.* a related group in Brussels *c.* 1895. Represented in ANTWERP *Triumph of Death* 1900, *Hymn of Love, Bacchanale* 1903. BRUSSELS *The tragic workmen* (triptych). IXELLES, LIÈGE, TOURNAI.
[Fl. Bib. 19th cent.]

*Leyden (Huygensz), Lucas van. Flemish (Dutch) Sch. *b* son of Huygh Jacobsz, Leyden 1494 *d* Leyden 1533. *Religious subjects, portraits; also active as glass painter and engraver.* Pupil of his father and of C. Engelbrechtsz. Learned glass painting from P. Cornelisz *q.v.* Unusually small in stature and precociously skilful both as painter and engraver; married into

rich Leyden family 1515; met Dürer who drew his portrait in Antwerp 1521; presumed by some the 'Lucas de Hollandere' in Antwerp Guild 1522; visited J. Gossaert (Mabuse) in Middelburg and accompanied him to Ghent, Malines and Antwerp, where Gossaert wearing cloth of gold and L. in yellow silk 'which looked like gold in the sunlight' entertained local artists at banquets c. 1527; in last years suffered from persecution mania and believing himself poisoned by rival spent most of his time in bed, working with specially made tools. **Signed Examples:** None. **Monogrammed Examples** (initial L.): AMSTERDAM Rijks. *Sermon in a loggia.* BRUSSELS *Temptation of S. Anthony* 1511. LENINGRAD *Healing of the Blind man at Jericho* (triptych, described by Van Mander as dated 1531). MUNICH A.P. *Virgin and Child with S. Mary Magdalene and donor, Annunciation* (formerly reverse of preceding) 1522 described by Van Mander. NUREMBERG German Mus. *Moses striking the Rock,* tempera, 1527. **Documented Example:** LEYDEN Mus. triptych *Last Judgement* (*cf.* J. de Backer) with *Hell* and *Paradise* on interior wings and *SS. Peter and Paul in landscapes* on exterior wings, originally in Leyden Town Hall and described by Van Mander who also described (1604) a diptych *The Children of Israel banqueting and dancing before the Golden Calf,* tempera paintings titled *Rebecca at the Well* and *Scenes from the Story of Joseph* and, on glass, *Girls dancing before King David.* Paintings presumed by some his work are in various museums.
[Fl. 818, Fl. 559, Fl. 52, Fl. 53, Fl. 272, Fl. 892, Fl. 64, Fl. 43, Fl. 316.]

Leys, Henri. Flemish Sch. *b* son of vendor of religious statuary, Antwerp 1815 *d* Antwerp and given public funeral 1869. *Costume history at first in Romantic but mainly in 'pre-Rubéniste' and neo-Gothic style; occasional portraits.* Pupil in Antwerp Acad. and of his brother-in-law F. de Braekeleer; in Paris where frequented studio of the French painter E. Delacroix 1835-9; visited Holland 1839; visited Germany 1852; created Baron 1862; commissioned to decorate Antwerp Town Hall 1863. His many pupils included the Anglo-Dutch painter L. Alma Tadema and the French painter J. Tissot (*cf.* also V. Lagye, J. Lies). Represented in ANTWERP *Rubens received in the Kolveniersgilde in Antwerp* 1851, *Flemish wedding in 17th cent.* 1839, *Entry of the Duke of Anjou into Antwerp* 1840, *Albert Dürer visiting Antwerp 1520* 1855, *The artist's daughter Lucie* 1865 and others; Town Hall *Series of scenes from Flemish history* 1863-9, *Scenes from Flemish history* (formerly in the artist's house). BRUSSELS Royal Collection *Institution of the Order of the Golden Fleece*; Mus. *The Spanish Fury in Antwerp, Restoration of the Roman Catholic worship in Antwerp 1585* 1845, *The Mass of Berthal de Haze* 1854, *Frans Floris' studio* 1866. Others in AMSTERDAM, BRUGES, CHANTILLY, COURTRAI, FRANKFORT, LEIPZIG, LILLE, LIVERPOOL (Walker), LONDON (Wallace), MONTREAL, MUNICH, NEW YORK Met., PHILADELPHIA Wilstach, STOCKHOLM and other museums.
[Fl. 88, Fl. 440, Fl. 914, Fl. 296, Fl. Bib. 19th cent.]

Leyssens (or **Lyssens**), **Jacques** (not **Nicolaas**). Flemish Sch. *b* Antwerp 1661 *d* Antwerp 1710. '*History*', *decorative pieces*; *also allegorical figures in pictures by contemporary flower painters* including J. B. Bosschaert, S. Hardimé and G. P. Verbruggen the younger. Pupil in Antwerp Guild 1674; went Rome where given nickname 'Nooten Kraaker' (Nut cracker) in Flemish artists colony; returned Antwerp where Master in Guild 1699 and much employed on interior decoration of Antwerp mansions.
[Fl. 878, Fl. 215, Fl. 903, Fl. 451, Fl. 892, Fl. 440.]

Lidts, Jacob. Flemish Sch. *b* Antwerp (?) before 1620 *d* Antwerp 1657. Master in Antwerp Guild 1643. **Signed Example:** DESSAU Amalienstift. *Church interior.* [Fl. 892.]

Liemakere, Jacques de. Flemish Sch. *b* Ghent (?) before 1580 *d* Ghent (?) after 1629. *Religious subjects and glass designs for Ghent churches.* Master Ghent Guild 1597; was among designers employed on decorations for entry into Ghent of Archduke Albert and the Infanta Isabella 1599 (*cf.* A. Joncquoy and D. van Alsloot). [Fl. 136, Fl. 386.]

Liemaker Nicolas de, known as 'Roose'. Flemish Sch. *b* son of Jacques de L., Ghent 1601 *d* Ghent 1646. *Religious subjects and 'history'.* In Ghent Guild 1624; worked on decorations for Pageant Entry into Ghent of Cardinal Infante Ferdinand (*cf.* T Rombouts) 1635. **Documented Examples:** GHENT Mus. d'Archéol. *Five decorative panels* (for Entry of Cardinal Infante Ferdinand); Mus. d. B.A. *SS. Bernard and Benedict in adoration of the Virgin.* Descamps (1768) saw in Ghent S. Bavon *The Virgin with her celestial court*; S. Jacques *Last Judgement*; S. Nicolas *Consecration of S. Nicholas, The fall of the rebel angels,* and others in Bruges and other Flemish churches.
[Fl. 215, Fl. 576, Fl. 216, Fl. 451, Fl. 155, Fl. 711, Fl. 712.]

Liere, Joos van. Flemish Sch. *b* Brussels before 1526 *d* Swyndrecht nr. Antwerp 1583. *Landscapes* (*oil and w.*); *also tapestry designs.* Dean Antwerp Guild 1546; left Netherlands to escape the Inquisition (*cf.* A. de Weerdt) and settled Frankenthal (*cf.* G. v. Coninxloo, A. Mirou, P. Schoubroeck) after 1562; citizen of Frankenthal 1574; town councillor 1576; returned Netherlands where active as Calvinist preacher at Swyndrecht. VIENNA Albertina has *s* landscape drawing.
[Fl. 559, Fl. 659, Fl. 892.]

Lies, Joseph Henri. Flemish Sch. *b* Antwerp 1821 *d* Antwerp 1865. *Costume history, portraits, landscape.* Pupil N. de Keyser; close friend of H. Leys. Represented in ANTWERP *The Misery of War, The enemy approaches* 1857, *Dürer travelling up the Rhine* 1855, *Episode in Rembrandt's life* (*cf.* J. Senave and P. Kremer) also *Landscapes* and *Portraits.* BRUSSELS *Baldwin Count of Flanders.* [Fl. 510, Fl. 88.]

***Lignis, Pietro de** (or **Dubois** or **del Legno**—presumed member of van den Houte artist family of Malines). Flemish Sch. *b* Malines (?) *c.* 1577 *d* Rome 1627. *Religious subjects.* Went Italy and remained there (*cf.* J. v. d. Straet, G. Hallet, F. v. Kasteele, W. Backereel and J. S. Sutterman); in Rome from 1599; member of Accad. di S. Luca by 1607. **Signed Example:** MADRID Prado *Adoration of the Magi s* 'Pietro de Lignis. Fiamengo in Roma 1616'. [Fl. 613, Fl. 84, Fl. 417.]

***Lille Path to Paradise Painter.** Presumed Flemish Sch. 15th cent. Name for painter of LILLE Mus. (747) *The Path to Paradise* (from Tongerloo Abbey). Presumed by some identical with D. Bouts, *q.v.*

Linnig, Egidius. Flemish Sch. *b* Antwerp 1821 *d* Antwerp 1860. *Landscapes, marines, coast and river scenes.* Represented in ANTWERP *Nightpiece* 1843. [Fl. 17.]

Linnig, Jan Theodor. Flemish Sch. *b* Antwerp 1815 *d* Antwerp 1891. Brother of Egidius and W.L. the elder. *Landscapes, marines, coast and river scenes; mainly active as engraver.* Represented in Antwerp *Landscape* 1875.
[Fl. 17.]

Linnig, Willem (Guillaume) the elder. Flemish Sch. *b* Antwerp 1819 *d* Antwerp 1885. *Costume history, interiors, genre, marines; also active as engraver.* Pupil of H. Leys. Worked in Weimar from *c.* 1876-*c.* 1883. Represented in ANTWERP *Workshop of the metalworker Geert de Winter in the 18th century, Studio interior of the 18th century* 1862, *The fortunate moment, The school* 1875, *The banquet* 1850, *The wardrobe* 1875, *The kitchen* 1883. STRASBURG *Little Savoyarde.* STUTTGART, WEIMAR. [Fl. 88, Fl. Bib. 19th cent.]

Linnig, Willem the younger. Flemish Sch. *b* son of W. L. the elder, Antwerp 1842 *d* Antwerp 1890. *Costume history, genre, interiors, landscapes, architecture views, murals; also worked as engraver.* Pupil of his father. Professor Weimar art school 1876-82. Represented in ANTWERP *An Antwerp wedding* 1867, *Vanitas* 1869, *Woman washing dishes* 1873, *The violin maker* 1878, *Storm landscape* 1875 and others.

[Fl. 9, Fl. Bib. 19th cent.]

★Lint, Hendrik Frans van, called 'Studio'. Flemish Sch. *b* son of Peter van L., Antwerp 1684 *d* Rome 1763. *Picturesque Italianate landscapes* (*cf.* J. B. Juppin). Pupil in Antwerp of P. v. Bredael. Went Rome and remained there (*cf.* J. F. v. Bloemen, S. J. Denis, also J. Miel); nicknamed 'Studio' in Flemish colony; was attacked as a sorcerer by villagers in the Campagna because a house collapsed when he was sketching it 1711; member of Rome Congregazione dei Virtuosi 1744, and regent thereof 1752 (*cf.* H. de La Pegnia and E. P. de Rendeux). His son J. v. L. was a painter and another, M. v. L., was a sculptor. **Signed Examples:** BRUNSWICK *Return from the chase: near Rome.* CAMBRIDGE Fitz. *Lake with boats and fishermen* 1756, *Landscape with figures and cattle* 1756, *Italian house* 1748. PRAGUE Rudolfinum *Group of trees with Nymph and Satyr* 1724. TURIN *Landscape with procession crossing a bridge* 1726.

[Fl. 425, Fl. 107, Fl. 440, Fl. 892, Fl. 678.]

★Lint, Peter van. Flemish Sch. *b* Antwerp 1609 *d* Antwerp 1690. *Religious subjects, 'history', portraits.* Pupil of A. Wolfordt 1624-9; Master Antwerp Guild 1632; visited Italy and worked for Cardinal Ginnasio (Bishop of Ostia) in Rome from 1633; returned Antwerp *c.* 1640; worked for Christian IV of Denmark (*cf.* Karel van Mander the younger). G. Maes was among his many pupils. **Signed Examples:** ANTWERP *The Miracle of S. John of Capistrano, Portrait of a baby* 1645, *Cardinal Ginnasio* 1639. BERLIN K.F. *Adoration of the Shepherds.* BRUSSELS *Self-portrait* 1646, *The pool of Bethesda* 1642. BUDAPEST *Man's portrait.* COPENHAGEN *Adoration of the Shepherds.* HERMANNSTADT *Allegory of Immortality.* VIENNA K. *The pool of Bethesda.* **Monogrammed Examples:** LENINGRAD *Return of Jeptha.* MONTPELLIER Fabre *The wise and foolish virgins.* **Documented Examples:** ROME S. Maria del Popolo *The Finding and Raising of the True Cross* (murals). Descamps (1768) saw works in Antwerp S. Jacques, Carmes Chaussés and Recollets. A monogrammed *Hercules and Omphale* 1542 was formerly in Vienna Liechtenstein. Pictures executed for the Antwerp dealer Forchoudt for whom he worked regularly 1665-78 (*cf.* A. Casteels) included *Six scenes from the life of Adam and Eve* and an *Escape of Lot.*

[Fl. 86, Fl. 753, Fl. 216, Fl. 892, Fl. 440, Fl. 212, Fl. 678.]

Lion (or Lyon), Pierre Joseph (or Jean Joseph). Flemish Sch. *b* Dinant 1729 *d* partly paralysed and ruined by Revolution, Dinant 1809 or 1814. *Portraits and landscapes, some in pastel.* Pupil of the French painter J. M. Vien in Paris from 1754; went Vienna; court painter to Empress Maria Theresa (*cf.* P. J. Verhaghen, J. B. Millé, H. de La Pegnia, J. P. Sauvage, G. Pélichy) from 1760; made portraits of members of the Esterhazy and Poniatowski families and drew series of landscapes in pastel for private apartments of the Empress; recorded in London where exhibited R.A. 1772; after death of Empress 1780 served Emperor Joseph II in Vienna; worked Château Sorinne nr. Dinant 1787. **Signed Examples:** YPRES *The Empress Maria Theresa, The Emperor Joseph II* (*cf.* H. Gillis) 1784. His *Daughters of General Carpenter* is recorded by a mezzotint.

[Fl. 451, Fl. 409, Fl. 361, Fl. 435, Fl. 440, Fl. 892.]

Lisaert, Philip. Flemish Sch. *b* Antwerp before 1530 *d* Antwerp (?) after 1588. Twenty-one of his pictures are recorded taken from Malines to Paris 1577. B. van somer was his pupil.

[Fl. 612, Fl. 892, Fl. 798.]

★Lisbon Alexander VI Painter. Presumed Flemish Sch. 15th-16th cent. Name for painter of LISBON Mus. (517) triptych *Virgin of Mercy with King Manoel the Fortunate and Pope Alexander VI*; on wings *S. Sebastian* and *S. Christopher.* Presumed by some identical with Jan Provoost *q.v.*

★Liverpool Entombment Painter. Presumed Flemish (Dutch) Sch. 15th cent. Name for painter of Liverpool Walker Mus. (Roscoe 81) *Entombment.* Presumed by some identical with Virgo inter Virgines Master *q.v.*

Loesen, see Rudolph of Antwerp.

Lombard, Lambert. Flemish Sch. *b* Liège *c.* 1506 *d* Liège 1566. *Religious subjects; also worked as architect, archaeologist and humanist.* Recorded (17th cent.) pupil of J. Gossaert (Mabuse) in Middelburg *c.* 1524 and of glass painter A. de Beer in Antwerp *c.* 1529; entered service of Erard de la Marck Prince Bishop of Liège before 1533; travelled Germany and France 1533-4; in Liège 1535-6; accompanied the English Cardinal Reginald Pole (*cf.* D. Lampsonius) to Italy to collect antiques for the Prince Bishop 1537; painted in Rome for Pope Paul III and for G. B. Pellegrini's villa between Moncelice and Ghioggia; returned and settled Liège 1539; had influential art school where F. Floris, Willem Key, H. Goltzius and D. Lampsonius (who wrote his biography 1565) were among his pupils; collected antique coins and sculpture (*cf.* L. de Heere, and H. Goltzius); wrote to Vasari giving information about Jan v. Eyck, R. v. d. Weyden and the German Martin Schongauer and asking for drawings or engravings after Margaritone, Gaddi and Giotto that he might compare them with glass paintings in Northern churches 1565. **Signed Examples:** None. **Documented Examples:** None. *A Last Supper* and other subjects are recorded by engravings. (*Cf.* L. Suavius.)

[Fl. 502, Fl. 818, Fl. 371, Fl. 559, Fl. 408, Fl. 409, Fl. 892 Fl. 316.]

★London Christ Appearing to His Mother Painter. Presumed Flemish Sch. 15th cent. Name for painter of LONDON N.G. (1086) *Christ appearing to His Mother.* [Fl. 530.]

★London Christ Mocked Painter. Presumed Flemish Sch. 16th cent. Name for painter of LONDON N.G. (4744) *The Crowning with Thorns.* Presumed by some identical with H Bosch *qv.* [Fl. 316, Fl. 530.]

★London Delft Painter. Presumed Flemish (Dutch) Sch. early 16th cent. Name for painter of LONDON N.G. (2922) triptych *Crucifixion, Christ presented to the people* and *Descent from the Cross.* Presumed by some identical with Delft Master *q.v.*

★London (Guicciardi) Entombment Painter. Presumed Flemish Sch. 15th cent. Name for painter of LONDON N.G. (664) *Entombment.* Presumed by some identical with D. Bouts *q.v.*

★London Lady in a Flat Cap Painter. Presumed Flemish Sch. 16th cent. Name for painter of LONDON N.G. (184) *Portrait of a young lady.* Presumed by some identical with N. de Neufchatel *q.v.*

★London (Layard) Virgin and Child Painter. Presumed Flemish Sch. presumed late 15th cent. or early 16th cent. Name for painter of LONDON N.G. (3066) *Virgin and Child* (Layard bequest). [Fl. 530.]

★London Magdalene Reading Painter. Presumed Flemish Sch. 15th cent. Name for painter of LONDON N.G. (654) *S. Mary Magdalene reading.* Presumed by some identical with R. v. d. Weyden *q.v.*

*London Nativity by Night Painter. Presumed Flemish Sch. 15th cent. Name for painter of LONDON N.G. (4081) *The Nativity by Night.* Presumed by some identical with Geertgen tot Sint Jans *q.v.*

*London Passion Scenes Painter. Presumed Flemish Sch. 16th cent. Name for painter of LONDON N.G. (1087) *Christ presented to the people.* Presumed by some identical with Bruges Passion Scenes Master *q.v.* [Fl. 530.]

*London Queen Elizabeth at Ditchley Painter. Presumed Flemish (or British) Sch. 16th cent. Name for painter of LONDON N.P.G. *Queen Elizabeth at Ditchley* (painted to commemorate the Queen's visit to Sir Henry Lee at Ditchley 1592). The Queen stands on a Sheldon tapestry map of Oxfordshire with her feet on Sir Henry's property. Presumed by some identical with Marcus Geeraerts the younger *q.v.*

*London S. Giles Mass Painter. Presumed Flemish or French Sch. 15th-16th cent. Name for painter of LONDON N.G. (4681) *Mass of S. Giles with view of interior of S. Denis near Paris.* Presumed by some identical with Giles Master *q.v.*

*London S. Luke Painter. Presumed Flemish Sch. 16th cent. Name for painter of LONDON N.G. (3092) *S. Luke painting the Virgin.* [Fl. 530.]

*London Tax Collectors Painter. Presumed Flemish Sch. 15th cent. Name for painter of LONDON N.G. (944) *Two tax collectors.* Presumed by some identical with Marinus van Reymerswaele *q.v.*

*London Van der Geest Painter. Presumed Flemish Sch. 17th cent. Name for painter of LONDON N.G. (52) *Cornelius van der Geest.* Presumed by some identical with A. van Dyck *q.v.*

*London Virgin with Brocade Screen Painter. Presumed 15th cent. Name for painter of LONDON N.G. (2595) *Virgin and Child before a brocaded screen.* Presumed by some identical with D. Bouts *q.v.*

*London Virgin with a Firescreen Painter. Presumed Flemish Sch. 15th cent. Name for painter of LONDON N.G. (2609) *Virgin and Child before a firescreen.* Presumed by some identical with Flémalle Master *q.v.* [Fl. 316, Fl. 530.]

*London Virgin with Nun Painter. Presumed Flemish Sch. 16th cent. Name for painter of LONDON N.G. (945) *Virgin and Child with a Cistercian nun.* [Fl. 530.]

*London (Wagner) Ecce Homo Painter. Presumed Flemish Sch. 16th cent. Name for painter of LONDON N.G. (3900) *Christ crowned with thorns.* Presumed by some identical with the Oultremont Master *q.v.*

*London (Wallace) Sleeping Boor Painter. Presumed Flemish Sch. 17th cent. Name for painter of LONDON Wallace Coll. (211) *Pipe Drunkard (Boor asleep).* Presumed by some identical with A. Brouwer *q.v.* [Fl. 534.]

*London Woman in a Wimple Painter. Presumed Flemish Sch. 15th cent. Name for painter of LONDON N.G. (653b) *Woman in wimple.* Presumed by some identical with Flémalle Master *q.v.*

*London Young Man in High Cap Painter. Presumed Flemish Sch. 15th cent. Name for painter of LONDON N.G. (943) *Young man in cap* dated 1462. Presumed by some identical with D. Bouts *q.v.* (*cf.* also Rogier of Brussels).

*London Young Woman in White Head-dress Painter. Presumed Flemish Sch. 15th cent. Name for painter of LON-DON N.G. (1433) *Young woman in white head-dress* (dateable by costume *c.* 1450). Presumed by some identical with Roger van der Weyden. *q.v.*

Longe, Robert la. Flemish Sch. *b* Brussels *c.* 1645 *d* Piacenza 1709. *Religious subjects.* Studied in Brussels; went Italy and remained there (*cf.* J. F. v. Bloemen, H. v. Lint, also J. Miel and J. Sutterman); worked mainly at Cremona and Piacenza. **Documented Examples** (recorded by 18th century writers): CREMONA S. Imerio *Preaching of S. John of the Cross*; S. Sigismondo *S. Theresa.* PIACENZA S. Antonino *Scenes from the life of S. Antoninus*; S. Giorgio sopra mura *The Virgin praying for souls in purgatory*; S. Giuseppe *Scenes from the life of S. Joseph*; S. Paolo *Execution of S. Blasius.* Others recorded in S. Pietro, S. Teresa, S. Vincenza and Oratorio della morte. [Fl. 305.]

Lonsing, François Joseph. Flemish Sch. *b* Brussels 1739 *d* Léognan nr. Bordeaux 1799. *Portraits, genre, 'history'; also worked as engraver.* Pupil in Antwerp Acad. and of M. J. Geeraerts till 1759 when Charles of Lorraine, Governor General of Austrian Netherlands, sent him with a scholarship to Italy (*cf.* A. C. Lens and J. P. Sauvage); in Rome pupil of the German, Rafael Mengs, till 1761; made drawings and engravings for Sir William Hamilton's 'Antiquités Étrusques, Grecques et Romaines' Naples 1766/67, and for Gavin Hamilton's 'Schola Italica Picturae', Rome 1773; in Lyons 1778; settled Bordeaux 1783 where remained and painted town notables. **Documented Examples:** BORDEAUX *Self-portrait, Duc de Duras, Maréchal de Mouchy.* BRUSSELS *J. S. de Larose.* A *Mirabeau on the rostrum* is recorded. [Fl. 451, Fl. 481, Fl. 892, Fl. 506, Fl. 296.]

Loo, Jean Floris Maria van der. Flemish Sch. *b* Boechout 1908. *Portraits, landscapes.* Pupil in Antwerp Higher Institute, of I. Opsomer. Represented in ANTWERP. [Fl. 17.]

Loon, Pieter van. Flemish Sch. *b* Antwerp 1600 *d* Antwerp 1660. *Architectural pieces, landscapes, 'history'.* A picture titled *The woman taken in adultery* was recorded in his will 1652. A *Desert* and an *Architectural piece with figure of the Viceroy of Naples* were recorded in Antwerp collections 1642 and 1689. [Fl. 86, Fl. 425, Fl. 107, Fl. 440, Fl. 212.]

Loon, Théodore van. Flemish Sch. *b* Brussels (?) or Louvain (?) *c.* 1585 *d* Louvain (?) *c.* 1660. *Religious subjects.* Went Italy 1604 (?); working Brussels 1609; Louvain 1623-8; Rome 1628-c. 1632. **Documented Examples** (seen and praised by Descamps 1768): BRUSSELS *Assumption of the Virgin* (from Brussels Béguinage church). MONTAIGU (near Aerschot) church *Scenes from the life of S. Anne and the Virgin.* Descamps also records works in other churches at Brussels and at Alost, Ghent, Louvain and Malines. A *S. Anne* painted for Rome S. Maria dell'Anima (paid for 1628 and 1629) is no longer in the church (unless it be the *Virgin and Child with SS. Joachim and Anne*). [Fl. 86, Fl. 425, Fl. 215, Fl. 576, Fl. 216, Fl. 892, Fl. 204, Fl. 305, Fl. 584, Fl. 678.]

Loose, Basile de. Flemish Sch. *b* son of J. J. L., Zele near Termonde 1809 *d* Brussels 1885. *Religious subjects, portraits, genre.* Pupil of his father and M. I. v. Brée. Represented in BERLIN and LEIPZIG. [Fl. 451, Fl. 892, Fl. 798.]

Loose, Joannes Josephus de. Flemish Sch. *b* Zele nr. Termonde 1770 *d* S. Nicolas 1849. *Religious subjects, portraits; also active as writer on art.* Pupil in Malines of W. J. Herreyns; painted portraits in The Hague 1815; professor in S. Nicolas Acad. Pictures painted for Ghent S. Jacques (*S. Cornelia*) and S. Nicholas and for churches at Hamme (*The traders in the Temple, Entry of Christ into Jerusalem*) and Lokenen (*Martyr-*

dom of *S. Barbara*) are recorded. His writings include a 'Treatise on the present state of Painting'.

[Fl. 451, Fl. 612, Fl. 892.]

Looymans, Romain. Flemish Sch. *b* Antwerp 1864 *d* Antwerp 1914. *Genre, interiors, portraits, landscapes, religious subjects; murals in churches.* Pupil of J. Portaels. Member Antwerp group De Dertien (XIII) (*cf.* E. Farasyn) 1891. Professor Antwerp Acad. Represented in ANTWERP *The kitchen, S. Augustine* and in Nymwegen Cathedral and church of the Grand Séminaire of Bois-le-duc. [Fl. 699 (1922/23).]

Lotyn (or **Lotten**), **Jan Christoph.** Flemish Sch. *b* Brussels or The Hague *d* Brussels after 1695. *Flowers and designs for tapestry* (*cf.* J. v. d. Borght). In Hague Guild 1685; in England during reign of William and Mary (*cf.* P. v. d. Meulen and N. Stramot) and in service of the Queen; in Brussels after 1695. [Fl. 878, Fl. 892.]

Loyer, Nicolas. Flemish Sch. *b* Antwerp 1625 *d* Antwerp (?) 1681 (?). *History.* [Fl. 86, Fl. 425, Fl. 612, Fl. 892.]

Loys, —. Flemish Sch. 16th cent. *b* Brussels. Pupil of F. Floris. Van Mander (1604) calls him a 'very good painter, luteplayer and harpist'. [Fl. 559.]

Lübeck Marienaltar Master, see **Fifteen Eighteen (1518) Master.**

Lucas van Leyden, see **Leyden.**

Lucidel, see **Neufchatel.**

Luckx, C., see **Luyckx.**

Luckx, Frans Joseph. Flemish Sch. *b* Malines 1802 *d* Brussels 1849. *Flowers, portraits, genre.* Studied Malines Acad. and Paris. Represented in BRUSSELS, MALINES, MUNICH. [Fl. 892.]

*Lucy Legend Master. Presumed Flemish Sch. 15th cent. Name for painter of BRUGES *S. Jacques Scenes from the Legend of S. Lucy* inscribed 'Dit was ghedaen int jaer MCCCCLXXX' (This was done in 1480). Pictures presumed by some his work are in London Royal Coll. (*cf.* Buckingham Palace Mystic Marriage Painter), Brussels (*cf.* Brussels Mystic Marriage Painter), Detroit (*cf.* Detroit Mystic Marriage Painter), Minneapolis (*cf.* Minneapolis *S.* Catherine Painter), New York (*cf.* New York *S.* Catherine Painter), Philadelphia (*cf.* Philadelphia *S.* Catherine Painter) and other museums. [Fl. 316.]

Luppen, Jozef van. Flemish Sch. *b* Antwerp 1834 *d* Antwerp 1891. *Landscapes.* Pupil of J. Jacobs and later in Paris of the French painter T. Rousseau. Visited Italy, Switzerland and Germany; teacher in Antwerp Acad. Represented in ANTWERP *Autumn* 1873 and two others. BRUSSELS, CARDIFF, GHENT and LIÈGE. [Fl. 17.]

*Luyckx (or **Luckx**), **Christiaan** (**Carstian** or **Kerstiaen**). Flemish Sch. *b* Antwerp 1623 *d* Antwerp (?) after 1653. *Still life, some with cats* (*cf.* A. Adriaenssen and A. v. Utrecht). Pupil of Frans Francken III; Master Antwerp Guild 1645;

went Spain (*cf.* A. Smit and J. v. Kessel the younger) and recorded as Court Painter to Philip IV 1646; signed document in Antwerp promising to paint a *Still life with fruit* as payment to a doctor 1648. **Signed Examples:** ANTWERP *Cat and birds.* BRUNSWICK *Still life with food and vessels.* BUDAPEST *Still life.* DRESDEN *Still life* (in kitchen piece with flowers by N. v. Verendael *s* and other parts by D. Teniers *m.*). MADRID Prado *Flower garland with three amoretti. Cf.* V. Wolfvoet. [Fl. 107, Fl. 262, Fl. 892, Fl. 213.]

Luyckx (or **Leux** or **Luycx**), **Frans** (**von Leuxenstein**). Flemish Sch. *b* son of a silk merchant, Antwerp 1604 *d* Vienna 1668. *Portraits, occasional religious subjects.* Master Antwerp Guild 1620; presumed by some assistant in Rubens' studio; Rome 1635; then went Vienna (where a brother became tutor to Princess Mariana, later Queen to Philip IV); court painter to Emperor Ferdinand III 1638; ennobled 1645; went to courts of Electors and painted their portraits 1648-50; visited Antwerp 1652; confirmed as court painter by Emperor Leopold I (*cf.* J. Thomas 'van Ypern') 1658; travelled with Archduke Leopold Wilhelm former Governor of the Netherlands (*cf.* J. B. v. Heil) and drew him on deathbed 1662. **Signed Example:** STOCKHOLM *Archduke Leopold Wilhelm* (full length). **Documented Examples:** PRAGUE Rudolfinum *Octavio Piccolomini, Annunciation.* VIENNA K. *Elector Friedrich Wilhelm of Brandenburg;* Liecht. *Christ and the Holy Women at the tomb.* Others in Swedish palaces (from Prague). *Cf.* G. Seghers. [Fl. 753, Fl. 425, Fl. 215, Fl. 262, Fl. 892.]

Luyten, Henri. Flemish Sch. *b* Roermond 1859 *d* Antwerp 1945. *Working class genre* (*some with implicit social comment, cf.* L. Frédéric), *landscapes with cattle, portraits.* Founder member of the Als ik kan group 1885 and of De Dertien (XIII) (*cf.* E. Farasyn) 1891. Represented in ANTWERP *Members of Als ik kan group* (including E. Chappel, C. Mertens, J. G. Rosier, H. Rul) 1885, *The Strike* 1891, *Children of the Sea* 1898. LIÈGE *Rêverie.* DÜSSELDORF and MUNICH (*cf.* L. Brunin). [Fl. Bib. 19th cent.]

Lybaert, Théophile M. F. Flemish Sch. *b* Ghent 1848 *d* Ghent 1927. *Costume history and religious subjects, portraits.* Pupil in Ghent Acad. and in Paris of L. Gérôme. Represented in BRUGES *Virgin and Child* 1883. BRUSSELS, BUENOS AIRES, COURTRAI; also in GHENT churches and ANTWERP Jesuit College (*cf.* T. J. Canneel). [Fl. 406, Fl. 129.]

Lyen, J. F. de, see **Delien.**

Lynen, Amédée. Flemish Sch. *b* St. Josse-ten-Noode 1852. *Illustrations, water colours, poster designs, engravings, lithographs.* Pupil of P. Lauters and J. Stallaert. Founder member of L'Essor group (*cf.* A. Hamesse) 1875. Represented in BRUSSELS and LIÈGE. [Fl. Bib. 19th cent.]

Lynen, André V. J. Flemish Sch. *b* Antwerp 1888. *Marines* (*Belgian and Brittany coasts*) *and landscapes.* Pupil of J. Michaux. Represented in ANTWERP *The North Sea.*

Lytens, Gysbrecht. Flemish Sch. *b* Antwerp (?) *c.* 1585 *d* place and date unknown. *Landscapes.* Master Antwerp Guild 1617. [Fl. 892.]

M

Mabuse, see Gossaert.

Madou, Jean Baptiste .Flemish Sch. *b* son of municipal employee, Brussels 1796 *d* Brussels 1877. *Anecdotic genre; also lithographs, etchings and illustrations.* Pupil in Brussels Acad. of J. François and later of I. Brice. Worked, through poverty, as clerk in soap factory, then as draughtsman in government map offices in Courtrai and Mons; entered lithographic studio in Brussels 1820; began successful career as painter *c.* 1842; Professor of drawing in École Militaire; drawing master to Belgian royal children 1850; C. P. Tschaggeny *q.v.* painted animals in some of his pictures (*cf.* T. Fourmois). Represented in AMSTERDAM, ANTWERP *Courtesy, Riders by an inn* 1856 (with C. P. Tschaggeny). BRUSSELS *The intruders at the fête, The Castle fête, Village politicians.* Others in Belgian Royal Collection.
[Fl. 451, Fl. 88, Fl. 440, Fl. Bib. 19th cent.]

*Madrid Fountain of Grace Painter. Presumed Flemish Sch. 15th cent. Name for painter of MADRID Prado (1511) *Fountain of Grace and Triumph of the Church over the Synagogue.* Presumed by some identical with or a follower or copyist of H. or J. van Eyck *q.v.* [Fl. 555.]

*Madrid Judith Painter. Presumed Flemish Sch. 17th cent. Name for painter of MADRID Prado (1466) *Judith and servant with the head of Holofernes* (*cf.* P. van Mol, F. Voet and M. Willems). Presumed by some identical with A. de Coster *q.v.* (Presumed by others (1772) identical with Murillo and by others (1794) with Rembrandt.) [Fl. 554, Fl. 555.]

*Madrid Philip II (Head) Painter. Presumed Flemish Sch. 16th cent. Name for painter of MADRID Prado (1949) *Philip II* (head). Presumed by some the picture referred to by Cardinal Granvella 1553 as then in progress by 'Lucas' (*cf.* L. de Heere). [Fl. 555.]

*Madrid Triumph of Death Painter. Presumed Flemish Sch. 16th cent. Name for painter of MADRID Prado (1393) *Triumph of Death*, presumed by some the picture 'where all kinds of remedies are used against death' recorded by Van Mander (1604) as by P. Bruegel the elder. *q.v. Cf.* also P. Brueghel the younger. [Fl. 559, Fl. 555.]

*Madrid Werl Wings Painter. Presumed Flemish Sch. *b* before 1425. Name for painter of MADRID Prado (1513) *Donor Henricus Werl with S John the Baptist* inscribed 'anno milleno centum quater decem ter et octo hic fecit effigiem . . . depingi minister henricus Werlis magister coloniensis'; (1514) *S. Barbara.* Two wings of triptych donated 1438. Presumed by some identical with the Flémalle Master *q.v.* [Fl. 555.]

Maes, Godfried. Flemish Sch. *b* son of painter Godfried M., Antwerp 1649 *d* Antwerp *c.* 1700. *Religious subjects, 'history', portraits; also worked as tapestry designer, and engraver.* Pupil of P. van Lint in Antwerp 1665. Master Antwerp Guild 1672, Dean 1682. Many works then in Flanders churches and religious institutions were seen by Descamps (1768). **Signed Examples:** ANTWERP *Martyrdom of S. George* 1684. GHENT *S. Nicholas* 1689. JAVIER (Navarre) Castle (Chapel) *S. Francis Xavier preaching* 1692. An *Allegory of Painting, Sculpture and Poetry* and a *Creation of Eve* are among subjects recorded by engravings.
[Fl. 878, Fl. 216, Fl. 892.]

Maes, Jacques. Flemish Sch. *b* Elsene (Brussels) 1905. *Domestic and outdoor genre, landscapes, portraits, still life and compositions.* Professor in S. Josse-ten-Noode Acad. Represented in ANTWERP *Georgette.* [Fl. 17.]

Maes (Maes-Canini), Jan Baptist Lodewyck. Flemish Sch. *b* Ghent 1794 *d* Rome 1856. *Religious subjects, portraits, Italian peasant genre.* Went Rome with scholarship from King William I of the Netherlands 1822; in Ghent 1826; returned Italy, married daughter of engraver Canini and remained Rome. Represented in AMSTERDAM *The Good Samaritan* 1825. BERLIN, GHENT (Mus., S. Michel and S. Nicholas), LEYDEN, MUNICH *Roman beggarwoman in prayer.* An *Allegory on the marriage of the Prince of Orange* 1816 is recorded.
[Fl. 451, Fl. 612, Fl. 481, Fl. 88, Fl. 798, Fl. Bib. 19th cent.]

Maes, Joseph. Flemish Sch. *b* Antwerp (?) before 1810 *d* after 1836. *Seascapes.* Exhibited in Antwerp 1828 and 1834 and in Brussels 1836. [Fl. 451.]

Maeterlinck, Louis. Flemish Sch. *b* Ghent 1846 *d* Ghent 1926. *Portraits, genre; also worked as art historian.* Keeper of Ghent Mus. Represented in GHENT *Cruel love.*
[Fl. 626 (1926), Fl. 699 (1926).]

Maeyer, Louis de. Flemish Sch. *b* Berchem (Antwerp) 1903. *Genre.* Pupil in Antwerp Higher Institute of I. Opsomer. Teacher in Berchem Acad. Represented in ANTWERP *Grandmother.* [Fl. 17.]

*Magdalene Legend Master. Presumed Flemish Sch. 15th-16th cent. Name for painter of PHILADELPHIA (Johnson) (402) *S. Mary Magdalene preaching.* Pictures presumed by some his work and part of the same altarpiece are in Budapest, Copenhagen and Schwerin (*cf.* Brussels Young Knight Painter and Melbourne Miracles Painter). [Fl. 316. Fl. 530.]

Magritte, René. Flemish Sch. *b* Lessines 1898. *Neo-Surrealist compositions.* Pupil in Brussels Acad.; in Paris where acquainted with French neo-surrealists P. Eluard and A. Breton 1927-1931; then settled Brussels; exhibited London Surrealist Exhibition (New Burlington Galleries) 1936 and N.Y. Mus. of Mod. Art (Fantastic Art, Dada, Surrealism Exhibition) 1936. Represented in ANTWERP *Vengeance.* NEW YORK Mus. Modern Art *The Path of the Air, The Eye.* [Fl. 563, Fl. 619, Fl. 296, Fl. 761, Fl. 762, Fl. 352.]

Mahu, Cornelis. Flemish Sch. *b* Antwerp *c.* 1613 *d* Antwerp 1689. *Still-life mainly tables with food* (*cf.* J. v. Es, J. Gerardi, M. Matheussens, A. v. Utrecht). Master Antwerp Guild 1638; G. P. Verbruggen the elder was his pupil 1645. **Signed Examples** in BERLIN K.F., GHENT and QUIMPER.
[Fl. 107, Fl. 440.]

Mahu, Guilliam. Flemish Sch. *b* Brussels 1517 *d* Brussels 1569. *Portraits.* [Fl. 86, Fl. 440, Fl. 88.]

Mahu, Victor. Flemish Sch. *b* son of Cornelis M., Antwerp before 1675 *d* Antwerp (?) 1700. *Genre.* **Signed Examples** in BERNE. [Fl. 440, Fl. 892.]

Maier (Mayer), Hans de. Flemish Sch. *b c.* 1543 *d* after 1610. Pupil in Antwerp of F. Floris 1559; in Fontainebleau 1566-9 (*cf.* L. Thiry, H. Francken the elder, C. Ketel and A. Dubois); back in Antwerp by 1575. [Fl. 559, Fl. 491, Fl. 892.]

Malaine, Joseph Laurent. Flemish Sch. *b* son of Regnier M., Tournai 1745 *d* Paris 1809 or 1815. *Still life, mostly flowers* (*cf.* P. Faes and Regnier M.); *also worked as tapestry designer.* Went Paris and worked at Gobelins factory; appointed flower painter to Louis XVI (*cf.* P. J. Sauvage and J. B. Suvée) 1787; fled from the Revolution to Alsace *c.* 1793; returned Paris 1798 or 1814; exhibited Paris Salon 1791 and 1808. **Signed Examples:** MADRID Prado *Flower pieces* (two; one with 'Cy devant peintre aux Gobelins' after signature). MÜHLHAUSEN *Flower pieces* (two). [Fl. 66, Fl. 440.]

Malaine (or **Malin** or **Malines**), **Regnier Joseph.** Flemish Sch. *b* Tournai 1711 *d* Tournai 1762. *Flowers* (*cf.* P. Faes and C. Bigée). P. J. Sauvage was his pupil. **Signed Examples:** TOURNAI *Flower pieces* (two). [Fl. 88.]

Malbodius, see **Gossaert.**

Maldeghem, Jean Baptiste. Flemish Sch. *b* elder brother of R. E. M., 1803 *d* Brussels 1841. *Landscapes.*
[Fl. 481, Fl. 88.]

Maldeghem, Romain Eugène van. Flemish Sch. *b* Denterghem, nr. Bruges 1813 *d* Ixelles 1867. *Religious subjects, costume history, portraits, landscapes.* Pupil in Bruges Acad. and of G. Wappers in Antwerp. Travelled France, Italy, Greece and the Near East 1838-43; Director Bruges Acad. 1852; settled Brussels 1854. Represented in ANTWERP Acad. *Hannibal's vow* 1838. BRUGES Hôtel de Ville *Leopold II.* BRUSSELS *Queen Louise* 1851 and GHENT; also BRUGES, BRUSSELS, DENTERGHEM and other churches. Recorded works include a *Charles V* which won a Ghent prize 1838 and a *Rubens at the death bed of his wife* (*cf.* P. Kremer) painted in Paris 1839, sent to the Brussels Salon and sold by lottery for the benefit of the poor of Denterghem.
[Fl. 451, Fl. 481, Fl. 88, Fl. 440.]

Malfait, Hubert. Flemish Sch. *b* 1898. *Rural and domestic genre* (*some in expressionist conventions*). [Fl. 568, Fl. 296.]

*****Malines Guild of S. George Master.** Presumed Flemish Sch. late 15th cent. Name for painter of ANTWERP Mus. (818) *S. George with two Bishops and members of the Malines Crossbowmen's Guild of S. George* (recorded 1589 in Malines Crossbowmen's Guild of S. George). [Fl. 316. Fl. 16.]

*****Malo, Vincent.** Flemish Sch. *b* Cambrai (?) *c.* 1600 *d* lunatic asylum, Gheel nr. Antwerp 1668 (not Rome 1649). *Religious subjects, 'history', landscapes and peasant genre.* Pupil of D. Teniers the elder and Rubens. Master Antwerp Guild 1623; went Genoa and stayed with Cornelis de Wael (*cf.* A. van Ertvelt); worked for Genoese churches; may have visited Florence and Rome; returned Antwerp where worked for the Forchoudt firm of art dealers (*cf.* A. Casteels); a letter (1668) from the head of the firm to his son in Vienna records M's madness and death as caused by rage at an insult. **Signed Examples:** LONDON Hampton Court *Conversion of Paul.* MAGDEBURG *Peasant scene* 1647. **Monogrammed Examples:** AMSTERDAM Rijks. *Peasants before an Inn, Christ in the House of Martha.* PRAGUE *Peasant Family.* **Documented Example:** GENOA S. Stephano *S. Ampelius.* Antwerp invoices record many works including *Samson and Delila* 'touched up by Van Dyck' sent Vienna 1668; a *S. John preaching*; a *Landscape* by C. de Wael with figures by V. M. and a *Battle of Amazons* (sent Graz 1675). Antwerp inventories record (1659) a *Kiss of Judas* after Van Dyck and (1689) a *Good Samaritan. Cf.* V. Armanno.
[Fl. 86, Fl. 773, Fl. 892, Fl. 212, Fl. 213.]

Malo, Vincent the younger. Flemish Sch. *b* son of V. M. the elder, Antwerp 1629 *d* Antwerp (?) after 1653.

Malpé, Jean. Flemish Sch. *b* Ghent 1764 *d* Ghent 1818. *Portraits and miniatures.* Worked in Paris for some time.
[Fl. 451, Fl. 892.]

Mambour, Auguste. Flemish Sch. *b* Liège 1896 *Expressionist and Surrealist compositions.* Pupil of E. Carpentier and A. de Witte. Worked for some time in Belgian Congo. Represented in AMSTERDAM, GRENOBLE, IXELLES and TER-VUEREN (Colonial Mus.); murals in LIÈGE Lycée du Boulevard d'Avroy. *Cf.* F. Jespers. [Fl. 524, Fl. 296.]

Manche, Édouard. Flemish Sch. *b* Brussels 1819 *d* Paris 1861. *Genre, costume history, religious subjects; worked mainly as engraver and lithographer.* Pupil of P. Lauters. [Fl. 892.]

*****Mander, Karel van.** Flemish Sch. *b* son of tax collector and bailiff, Meulebeke, nr. Courtrai 1548 *d* Amsterdam 1606. *Religious subjects, 'history', allegories, portraits, landscapes, nudes, occasional genre, drawings for engravers;* also active as playwright, poet and translator of 'The Iliad' and still famous as *author of 'Het Schilderboek'* (biographies of painters) which, first published in 1604, remains a basic source of information for the Flemish School in the 16th cent. Pupil of Lucas de Heere (till de H. was banished as a Protestant by Alva) *c.* 1566-8; then of P. Vlerick in Courtrai and Tournai 1568-9; returned Meulebeke where produced his play 'Noah and the Flood' (with scenery painted by himself and real water pumped upon the ark) and other plays called 'Nebuchadnezzar' and 'The Judgement of Solomon'; went Italy 1573; visited Florence and was employed at Terni to paint *Scenes from the Massacre of S. Bartholomew with Admiral Coligny thrown from the window* for a private villa; in Rome where he spent much time with B. Spranger *q.v.* 1574-5 and drew in the newly discovered catacombs; followed Spranger to Vienna and worked on decorations for Pageant Entry of Rudolf II 1577; returned Meulebeke via Nuremberg 1578; suffered loss of his property and destruction of his home by plundering soldiers when 'the burden of the armies of both sides was too heavy to be borne by the populace' and fled from Meulebeke; worked in Courtrai 1581-2; in Bruges 1582; then fled to Haarlem to escape from Parma's persecutions (*cf.* D. v. d. Queborne) 1583; painted grisaille pictures there for the collector J. Rauwaert (*cf.* M. v. Heemskerck) and founded an art school with the Dutch engraver Hendrick Goltzius and the Dutch 'history' painter Cornelis of Haarlem; the Dutch painter Frans Hals was his pupil in Haarlem; moved to Zevenbergen where prepared 'Het Schilderboek' for publication and wrote a play performed by his pupils 1603; settled Amsterdam 1604. **Signed Examples:** COURTRAI S. Martin *Martyrdom of S. Catherine* 1582, commissioned 1581 by the Cloth and Linenweavers' Guild of Courtrai. HAARLEM *Annunciation* 1593. HANOVER *S. John preaching in the wilderness* 1597. LENINGRAD *Village fair* 1600. VIENNA K. *Man's portrait* 1592. **Monogrammed Example:** VIENNA K. *Jesus leaving the Temple with his parents* 1598. Amsterdam, Paris Louvre and Vienna Albertina have monogrammed drawings. Recorded works include a *Fall of the Tower of Babel* (*cf.* M. v. Valkenborch), 'various' *Vases with wild flowers,* an *Amor omnibus idem,* an *Adam and Eve in the Garden of Paradise,* a *Deluge* (in grisaille) *The Crossing of the Jordan* (with self-portrait as a Levite carrying the Ark, mussels and snails in the bed of the river and a grey dog growling at a red one), *The Israelites dancing round the Golden Calf, The battle between Hannibal and Scipio,* and his last work *The Israelites committing whoredom with the Moabite women.* A *Judgement of Midas,* an *Allegory of a Wise King* and *Allegory of a Foolish King, The Four Times of the Day* (*Aurora, Phoebus, Venus, Morpheus*), a *Judgement of Solomon* and a *Repentant Magdalene* are among the drawings recorded by engravings.
[Fl. 559 (1617), Fl. 367, Fl. 892, Fl. 440, Fl. 813.]

Mander, Karel van the younger. Flemish Sch. *b* son of K. v. M. the elder, Courtrai *c.* 1579 *d* Delft 1623. *Tapestry designs.* Worked in tapestry factory of F. Spierinx in Delft 1604-14; directed a rival factory in Delft where tapestries from his designs were made for Christian IV of Denmark (*cf.* P. v. Lint) from *c.* 1615; visited Denmark. The King of Denmark's tapestries were destroyed in the Frederiksborg fire 1859. [Fl. 892, Fl. 440.]

Mandyn, Jan. Flemish (Dutch) Sch. *b* Haarlem *c.* 1500 *d* Antwerp, as pensioner of city, *c.* 1560. *Religious and satirical subjects.* Working Antwerp from 1530; P. Aertsen lived there with him *c.* 1535; G. Mostaert and B. Spranger were his pupils. Van Mander (1604) records that he worked in the style of H. Bosch (*cf.* P. Huys). **Signed Example:** HAARLEM *The Temptation of S. Anthony.*
[Fl. 559, Fl. 107, Fl. 892.]

Manisfeld, François Joseph. Flemish Sch. *b* Tournai 1742 *d* Tournai 1807. *Genre.* Master Tournai Guild 1772. Represented in TOURNAI Mus. [Fl. 359, Fl. 88.]

Manrique, Miguel (known in Spain as de Amberés). Flemish Sch. 17th cent. *b* of Spanish parents, Flanders *d* Malaga (?). *Religious subjects* (in Rubens tradition). Served in Spanish army in the Netherlands; went Spain *c.* 1650 and settled Malaga. **Documented Example:** MALAGA Cathedral *S. Mary Magdalene anointing the feet of Christ* (from Malaga Convent de la Victoria). [Fl. 153, Fl. 779, Fl. 575.]

Mansi Magdalene Master. Presumed Flemish Sch. 16th cent. Name for painter of BERLIN K.F. (574D) *S. Mary Magdalene* (ex-Mansi Coll.). Pictures presumed by some his work are in various museums. [Fl. 316.]

Marcette, Alexandre. Flemish Sch. *b* Spa 1853 *d* Brussels 1929. *Marines and landscapes* (many in w. and pastel). Represented in ANTWERP *Rain and sunshine at Nieuwpoort* w. BRUSSELS *Moonlight, In Holland* 1900, *Heavy weather.* GHENT, LIÈGE, OTTAWA *Rainy weather* (sea piece).
[Fl. Bib. 19th cent.]

Marcette, Henri. Flemish Sch. *b* Spa 1824 *d* Spa 1890. *Landscapes.* Represented in BRUSSELS. [Fl. 892.]

Marchin, Laurent. Flemish Sch. 17th cent. *Religious subjects.* **Signed Example:** MALINES Celliten convent Triptych *Crucifixion* (centre), *donors' portraits* (on wings) 1633.
[Fl. 613, Fl. 892.]

Marinus, Ferdinand. Flemish Sch. *b* Antwerp 1808 *d* Namur 1890. *Landscapes with figures, town views, genre.* Pupil of B. Ommeganck and M. van Brée. Director of Namur Acad. where J. Quinaux was among his pupils. Represented in ANTWERP *The Meuse at Poilvache* 1873. COURTRAI, NAMUR (Murals in Salle du Conseil). [Fl. 451, Fl. 892.]

*Marinus van Reymerswaele or **Roymerswaele** or **Romerswaele** (a place in Zeeland now engulfed by the sea). Flemish (Dutch) Sch. *b* son of painter Claes van Zierickzee (?) before 1500 *d* 1567 (?). *Religious subjects and genre.* Recorded (as 'Moryn Claessone, Zeelander') pupil in Antwerp of a glass painter 1509; Vaernewyck (*c.* 1570) records that 'Marin Claeszoon from Romerswaele' was sentenced (1567) to do public penance in a shirt, holding a candle, and to six years' banishment (*cf.* A. v. Overbeke and J. Massys) for taking part in the 1566 Iconoclast raid on Westminsterkerk Middelburg; Guicciardini (before 1567) wrongly (?) records a 'Marino di Sirissea' (Zierickzee) as dead. Van Mander (1604) records him as Marinus de Seeuw, painter of Romerswaelen, 'a contemporary of Fr. Floris'. **Signed Examples:** *The money changer and his wife* in COPENHAGEN, DRESDEN (1541), FLORENCE (1540), MADRID Prado (1537 and 1538), MUNICH (1538), NANTES (1538), S. *Jerome* in ANTWERP (1541), MADRID Prado ('Mdad me fecit 1521') and (1547). MUNICH A.P. has *Tax collector and peasants* 1542. Pictures presumed by some his work are in London N.G. (*cf.* London Tax Collectors Painter) and other museums. Copies of his pictures are known to have been made by B. de Ryckere *q.v.* Van Mander records a *Banker* (*tax collector?*) *in his office.* Forchoudt the Antwerp firm of art dealers exported (1668) a *Calling of Matthew.*
[Fl. 812, Fl. 818, Fl. 371, Fl. 559, Fl. 892, Fl. 316, Fl. 212.]

Marissal (or **Maresschal**), **Philips Karel.** Flemish Sch. *b* Ghent 1698 *d* Ghent 1770. *Religious and decorative paintings for Ghent churches and religious houses, also portraits.* Studied Ghent and Paris; in Brussels and associating with C. Breydel and Z. J. Helmont *q.v. c.* 1723; in Ghent with C. Breydel 1726; founded and directed art school (later Ghent Academy) 1751. [Fl. 215, Fl. 216, Fl. 451, Fl. 479, Fl. 88, Fl. 386.]

Markelbach, Alexandre. Flemish Sch. *b* Antwerp 1824 *d* Brussels 1906. *Costume history, genre.* Pupil of G. Wappers. Represented in ANTWERP *A 17th century potter* 1884. BRUSSELS *Antwerp Rhetoricians in the 16th century preparing for a competition* 1872. LIÈGE *Daniel Seghers studying botany* (*cf.* P. Kremer). [Fl. Bib. 19th cent.]

Marne, Jean Louis de, see **Demarne.**

Marneffe, Ernest. Flemish Sch. *b* Liège 1866 *d* Liège 1920. *Symbolist allegories* (*cf.* A. Levêque). Pupil of A. de Witte.
[Fl. 160 (1920).]

Marneffe, François de. Flemish Sch. *b* Brussels 1793 *d* Brussels 1877. *Genre, costume history and landscapes.* Represented in COURTRAI *Luderic and the hermit.*
[Fl. 451, Fl. 73, Fl. 892, Fl. 837 (1877), Fl. Bib. 19th cent.)

Marstboom, Anton. Flemish Sch. *b* Antwerp 1905. *Landscape, figures, theatre designs.* Teacher in Antwerp Acad. Represented in ANTWERP *Park, Gardens, Nude.* [Fl. 17.]

Martins (Martius, Martens), Jan. Flemish Sch. *b* Tournai (?) before 1410 *d* Ghent (?) after 1449. *Decorative works and religious subjects* (?). With W. van Axpoele *q.v.* contracted to paint about thirty *Counts and Countesses of Flanders* lifesize for Ghent Scepenenhuis (Sheriffs' Hall), to replace faded tempera portraits 1419-20; in Ghent Guild 1420. Worked with others on Pageant Entry into Ghent of Isabella of Portugal, third wife of Duke Philip the Good (*cf.* J. van Eyck) 1430. Possibly identical with Joao Martins who worked in Lisbon Cathedral 1441. Dean of Ghent Guild 1449. (Extensive falsifications in Ghent archives have been alleged.)
[Fl. 224, Fl. 179, Fl. 88, Fl. 385, Fl. 774, Fl. 892.]

Martins (Martius), Nabor (Nabur, Nabucadonozor). Flemish Sch. *b* son of J. Martins (?), Ghent before 1420 *d* Ghent 1454. *Decorative work and religious subjects.* Had decorative commissions from Ghent city 1433-49; Master Ghent Guild 1435; worked for churches in and near Ghent 1443-53; fined for delay in work for S. Walburga, Oudenarde 1446. (Extensive falsifications in Ghent archives have been alleged.)
[Fl. 179, Fl. 88, Fl. 385, Fl. 892.]

Martius, see **Martins.**

Martsen or **Martensz, Jacob** (not to be confused with Dutch painter Jan or Jacob M.). Flemish Sch. *b* Ghent 1580 *d* Holland (?) after 1630 (?). *Portraits.* Pupil of K. van Mander. Married sister of Dutch painter Es. v. d. Velde Haarlem 1608. ROTTERDAM Boymans *Portrait of a man* (*s* J. Ma. 1630) is presumed by some his work. [Fl. 728.]

Martyrdom of S. John Master. Presumed Flemish (Dutch) Sch. early 16th cent. Name for painter of PARIS Louvre (Schlichting) *Martyrdom of S. John the Evangelist.* [Fl. 316.]

Masereel, Frans. Flemish Sch. *b* Blankenbergh 1889. *Contemporary genre (including scenes of port and night life) in Cubist-Expressionist technique; wood engravings with implicit social comment and book illustrations.* Pupil in Ghent Acad. of J. Delvin. Worked Geneva during German 1914-18 invasion; illustrated R. Rolland's Pacifist fantasia 'Liluli' (1919), writings by Ch. Vildrac, M. Maeterlinck and others; published many collections of woodcuts and drawings in woodcut manner including *Figures et Grimaces* (1926), *Danse macabre* (1942), *Destins* (1943); worked much in Paris. Represented in BROOKLYN and DETROIT, U.S.A. and other galleries. [Fl. 87, Fl. 158, Fl. 403.]

Massaux (Massaulx), Léon. Flemish Sch. *b* Ghent 1845 *d* Ixelles 1926. *Landscapes, genre.* Pupil of A. Verwée. Worked at one time in Paris. Represented in BRUSSELS *Evening in the Polders.* MUNICH N.P. [Fl. 892, Fl. 123.]

***Massys (Metsys), Cornelis.** Flemish Sch. *b* son of Quinten M., Antwerp *c.* 1508 *d* after 1550. *Landscapes (cf. F. Mostaert) with genre and religious subjects; but chiefly active as engraver.* Pupil of his father; Master, with his brother Jan, in Antwerp Guild 1531. **Signed Example:** AMSTERDAM Rijks. *The return of the Prodigal Son* 1538. **Monogrammed Examples:** ANTWERP *S. Jerome in landscape* 1547. BERLIN K.F. *Arrival of the Holy Family in Bethlehem* 1543 (*cf.* J. van M.). Brussels Mus. has monogrammed drawing *Mountain landscape.* The subjects of his engravings include *Peasants and peasant women fighting, The beggars' meal, Judith with the head of Holofernes* and *The blind leading the blind (cf.* P. Bruegel). [Fl. 892, Fl. 316.]

***Massys (Matsys, Metsys), Jan.** Flemish Sch. *b* son of Quinten M., Antwerp *c.* 1509 *d* Antwerp 1575. Brother of Cornelis M. *Religious subjects, 'history', genre and low-life scenes.* Pupil of his father; Master Antwerp Guild, with his brother Cornelis, 1531; banished as suspected Protestant (*cf.* A. van Overbeke and Marinus van Reymerswaele) 1544; requested permission to return 1550; returned 1558. **Signed Examples:** ANTWERP *The Holy Family turned away from the Inn* 1558 (*cf.* C. van M.), *Healing of Tobit* 1564. BOSTON U.S.A. *Judith with the head of Holofernes* 1543 (*cf.* M. Willems). BRÜNN Landesmus. *Merry Company* 1562. BRUSSELS *Lot and his Daughters* 1565. CARLSRUHE *Elijah and the Widow* 1565. COPENHAGEN *The Procuress.* PARIS Louvre *David and Bathsheba* 1562. SCHLEISSHEIM *S. Paul* 1565. STOCKHOLM *Flora* 1561, *Procuress* 1566, *Merry Company.* VIENNA K. *Lot and his Daughters* 1563, *Merry Company* 1564. Antwerp inventories (1685 and 1692) record *A child and Death's Head in a Vanitas (cf.* Bruges Death and the Miser Painter, J. Gossaert, Frankfort Master and Hague Vanitas Painter) and a *Landscape with sheep.* (*Cf.* also Ottawa Judith Painter.) [Fl. 371, Fl. 559, Fl. 892, Fl. 316, Fl. 213.]

***Massys (or Matsys or Metsys), Quinten.** Flemish Sch. *b* son of a smith, Louvain, *c.* 1465 *d* Antwerp 1530. *Religious subjects, portraits.* Worked first as a smith; Master Antwerp Guild 1491; had many pupils (including Eduardo o Portugues and other Portuguese, *cf.* G. v. d. Weyden); with 250 other artists worked for Pageant Entry of Charles V into Antwerp (*cf.* J. Provoost) 1520; lived in striking house decorated outside with frescoes which Dürer was shown as one of the town's spectacles 1520; was friend of J. Patinir with whom he collaborated in some pictures. **Signed Examples:** BRUSSELS Triptych (*S.* Anne Altarpiece) *Holy Kinship, Annunciation to Joachim, Death of S. Anne*; (on outside wings) *Joachim and S. Anne dividing their goods among the poor, Joachim's sacrifice refused* 1507-9 (commissioned for and

originally in Louvain S. Pierre; damaged and restored in 17th cent.; taken Paris by French 1794, returned and suffered damage in transit 1816, restored again 1860. PARIS Louvre *The Banker and his Wife* 1514, *Virgin and Child* 1529; Mus. Jacquemart-André *Profile of an old man* 1513. **Documented Examples:** ANTWERP Triptych *Lamentation, Salome with S. John Baptist's head, Martyrdom of S. John Evangelist* 1508-11 (commissioned for Antwerp Cathedral by Cabinetmakers' Guild; after proposed sale to Queen Elizabeth (1577) bought by civic authorities at instance of M. de Vos 1582). MADRID Prado figures in *Temptation of S. Anthony* (landscape signed by Patinir q.v.) A diptych *Portrait of Erasmus* and *Portrait of Aegidius* painted 1517 is recorded by correspondence between Erasmus and Sir Thomas More to whom Erasmus sent it as a present (paintings in Rome (Corsini) and Longford Castle, of which there are other versions elsewhere, are presumed by some to be these portraits). Other paintings presumed by some his work are in various museums (*cf.* Chicago Man with a Pink Painter and Philadelphia Maria Egyptiaca Painter). The Antwerp dealer H. de Neyt owned 1642 '*An old man with a young girl and a Fool*' by 'Quinten' (*cf.* S. Wils). Descamps (1769) records a *Last Supper* in Louvain S. Pierre and, in a Brussels convent, an *Ecce Homo* (half-length with the people shown only by heads).
[Fl. 243, Fl. 371, Fl. 559, Fl. 216, Fl. 892, Fl. 316, Fl. 88, Fl. 111, Fl. 203, Fl. 213, Fl. 45.]

***Mast, Herman van der.** Flemish (Dutch) Sch. *b* Briel *c.* 1550 *d* Delft 1610. *Portraits and religious figures in landscape.* Pupil in Antwerp of F. Floris before 1570; then of F. Francken the elder; went Paris (*cf.* A. Dubois) where painted for Archbishop of Bourges, and was seven years in service of Attorney General and shield bearer to his wife a lady in waiting to the Queen Mother Catherine de Médicis, who knighted him at a Carnival ball; returned Holland *c.* 1580 and settled Delft. **Signed Example:** AMSTERDAM *Man's portrait* 1587. **Monogrammed Example:** *Woman's portrait* 1587. Van Mander records a *S. Sebastian* with realistic painting of the Archbishop of Bourges' mule and of recognisably different herbs 'some evidently stepped on'. [Fl. 559.]

Matheussens (or Mattheussens), Mathieu. Flemish Sch. *b* Malines (?) *c.* 1600 *d* Antwerp (?) 1677. *Kitchen pieces (cf.* C. Mahu). Pupil of Marten Pepyn in Antwerp 1613; Master Antwerp Guild 1629; N. de Hoy was his pupil 1636. A private collection (Denmark) has a *Kitchen piece* signed and dated 1648. [Fl. 613, Fl. 892.]

Mathieu, Lambert Joseph. Flemish Sch. *b* Bure nr. Namur 1804 *d* Louvain 1861. *Religious subjects, costume history, genre, portraits.* Pupil of W. J. Herreyns and M. de Brée. Worked for some time in Paris; Director of Louvain Acad. 1834. Represented in BRUSSELS *Descent from the Cross.* LOUVAIN *The Flood, Raphael and La Fornarina (cf.* P. Kremer) and churches in ANTWERP and LOUVAIN.
[Fl. 268, Fl. 451, Fl. 481, Fl. 88.]

Mathieu, Paul. Flemish Sch. *b* St. Josse-ten-Noode (Brussels) 1872. *Landscapes, still life, interiors.* Pupil of Marie Josephine Meyer. Teacher in Brussels Acad.; with A. Bastien painted *Panorama of the Congo* for Ghent International Exhibition (*cf.* F. Jespers) 1912. Represented in ANTWERP *Flemish coast scene.* BRUGES *Landscape in rain.* BRUSSELS *Snow.* COURTRAI, MAESEYCK.
[Fl. 806, Fl. 17, Fl. 114, Fl. 909.]

Matsys, see **Massys.**

Matthys (Matthysens), Abraham. Flemish Sch. *b* son of fish dealer (with interests in whale fisheries), Antwerp 1581 *d* Antwerp 1649. *Religious subjects, portraits, sea pieces (cf.* G. van Eyck). Pupil of T. van Haecht 1591. In Italy 1603;

Master Antwerp Guild 1619; on a voyage with the whaling fleet 1619-23; became a brother of the tertiary order of S. Francis; formed large collection of paintings including several by P. Brill and many copies of Italian pictures; also prints and drawings. **Documented Examples:** ANTWERP Notre Dame *Death of the Virgin* 1632; Recollets church *S. Francis before the Virgin* (painted for his own tomb). GREENWICH Maritime Mus. *Whalefishing* 1623. HOBOKEN Church *Bonaventura Peeters* (placed over Peeters' tomb by his brother Jan P.).

[Fl. 216, Fl. 107, Fl. 892, Fl. 440, Fl. 159, Fl. 364, Fl. 213.]

Maus, Eugène. Flemish Sch. *b* Ixelles 1847 *d* Ixelles 1881. *Landscapes, still life.* Worked in Holland from 1870. Represented in AMSTERDAM. [Fl. 892.]

Mechelen, Jan van. Flemish Sch. *b* Malines 1587 or 1589 *d* after 1629. *Chiefly active as dealer.* Pupil of G. Schoof in Antwerp 1600. Master Antwerp Guild 1609. Many transactions with Jan Brueghel the younger are recorded 1626-9.

[Fl. 613, Fl. 214.]

Medina, Sir John Baptist (Juan Bautista), known as 'the Kneller of the North'. Flemish Sch. *b* son of Spanish officer serving in Netherlands, Brussels before 1659 *d* Edinburgh 1710. *Portraits, 'history' and occasional landscapes; illustrations for books.* Pupil of F. Duchatel. Came England (*cf.* S. Dubois, C. Huysmans, W. de Keyser, P. v. d. Meulen the younger, J. B. Lantscroon, N. Stramot) 1686; patronized by David Melville third Earl of Leven who invited him to Scotland and procured for him £500 worth of commissions which 'he did in less than one year having beforehand provided postures painted for heads and half lengths that he should want'; settled Edinburgh with his wife; had twenty children 'which prevented his growing rich'; drew illustrations for Milton's 'Paradise Lost' published 1705, and for Ovid's 'Metamorphoses' (not published); knighted by Duke of Queensberry Lord High Commissioner of Scotland (last knight made before the Union) 1707. The Scottish portrait painter W. Aikman was among his pupils. A son and grandson (both called John Medina) were also painters. **Documented Examples:** EDINBURGH Surgeons' Hall *Fellows of the Royal College of Surgeons, Self-portrait* 1708. FLORENCE Pitti *Self-portrait* (presented 1716 by Duke of Gordon). Recorded portraits include *The Duke of Argyll with his two sons, in Roman habits, The Duke of Gordon with his son and daughter, The Earl of Leven and his family* (twenty portraits), *George Earl of Melville, Dr. Alex. Pitcairne* (at one time in Dr. Meade's collection) and *A son and a daughter of the artist.* The inventory of his studio, included in his will, contained *Adam and Eve expelled from Paradise, Venus and Adonis, Lucretia* and *Rosamond with a cup.*

[Fl. 826, Fl. 856, Fl. 779, Fl. 223.]

Meert (or Meerte or Merten), Peter (Pierre). Flemish Sch. *b* Brussels *c.* 1619 *d* 1669. *Portrait groups and conversation pieces (cf.* T. Boeyermans, G. Coques, P. Fruytiers, H. Janssens, C. J. v. Lamen, G. v. Tilborgh). Master Brussels Guild 1640; employed by Guilds and trade associations. **Monogrammed Example:** BRUSSELS *Portrait of a man* 1661, *Portrait of a woman* 1661. **Documented Example:** BRUSSELS *The Deans of the Fishmongers' Guild* (from Fishmongers' Guild). A *Conversation piece* and *The painter A. de Bie* are recorded by engravings.

[Fl. 86, Fl. 425, Fl. 216, Fl. 892.]

Meerts, Frans. Flemish Sch. *b* Ghent 1836 *d* Brussels 1896. *Genre.* Pupil of J. Portaels. Worked in Spain copying Flemish painters. Represented in BRUSSELS *The Avowal.*

[Fl. 892.]

Megan, R. Flemish Sch. Recorded in Brussels 1618. [Fl. 440.]

Megan (or Meganck or Meganet), Renier. Flemish Sch. *b* Brussels 1637 *d* Vienna 1690. *Landscapes.* Pupil of L. v. Heil 1656; in Vienna by 1670 where became court painter (*cf.* P. Evrard). **Signed Example:** VIENNA Harrach *Landscape.*

[Fl. 892, Fl. 440.]

Mehus (Meus), Lieven (Leven). Flemish Sch. *b* Audenarde 1630 *d* Florence 1691. *Religious subjects, 'history', also drawings of outdoor scenes with small figures.* Taken Milan by his parents as a boy; pupil in Florence of Pietro da Cortona; attempting to return to Milan fell into hands of Piedmontese recruiting officers and did military service for three years; returned Florence, obtained appointment at Medici court (*cf.* J. Sutterman), and painted cabinet pieces. Lanzi (1792-6) writes 'His tints are restrained, his attitudes lively, his shadows most beautiful and his inventions ingenious'. His cupola decoration in Florence S. Maria della Pace was destroyed when the church was burnt down in the 18th cent. Works recorded in Prato cathedral and other Prato churches have not been traceable since 1846. Fiorillo (1798-1804) describes a *Mystic Marriage of S. Catherine* then in a Bolognese private collection as 'one of the most charming pictures in the world'. *S. Barbara* in Siena Assunta and a *Bacchus and Ariadne* painted for Marquis Gerini were recorded in the eighteenth century as his work.

[Fl. 317, Fl. 505, Fl. 612, Fl. 892, Fl. 305.]

Meire, Gerard van der. Flemish Sch. *b* Ghent (?) before 1440 *d* Ghent 1512. Master Ghent Guild 1452; citizen Brussels 1467. **Signed Examples:** BRUGES S. Sauveur *Christ carrying the Cross, Crucifixion, Deposition* (signed on frame Meeren 1500). GHENT S. Bavon (Triptych) *Crucifixion* centre, *Moses striking water from the rock, The Brazen Serpent* wings (signed Ger van der Meeren). Both signatures are presumed by some to be false. Pictures formerly presumed by some his work are now known to be (*cf.* J. Daret and A. Bouts) or presumed to be (*cf.* Bruges Passion Scenes Master, Justus of Ghent, Hoogstraeten Master) by other artists. Van Mander records a *Lucretia* (*cf.* J. S. van Hemessen) owned (1604) by J. Rauwaert an Amsterdam collector and amateur painter (*cf.* M. van Heemskerck). [Fl. 559, Fl. 135, Fl. 385, Fl. 892.]

Meiren (not Moiron), Jan Baptist van der. Flemish Sch. *b* Antwerp 1665 *d* Antwerp (?) *c.* 1708. *Contemporary warfare and picturesque military pieces (cf.* P. van Bloemen, J. P. v. Bredael, C. Breydel, J. Broers, C. Francken, A. F. v. d. Meulen, D. Nollet, P. Tillemans, P. Verdussen, J. P. Verdussen also L. de Hondt the elder and P. Meulener), *occasional naval warfare (cf.* L. Smout the younger) *and outdoor genre.* Master in Antwerp Guild 1685. Collaborated as figure painter with A. F. Baudewyns. Some of his pictures were exported to Vienna by G. Forchoudt (*cf.* A. Casteels) the Antwerp dealer and a letter (1700) to Forchoudt from his brother-in-law in Vienna (referring presumably to pieces with Orientals) says 'The little figures by Van der Meiren with feathered headdresses and strange clothes do not please the gentlemen here, ordinary clothes of the Brueghel kind would go better'. **Signed Examples:** ANTWERP *Coblenz besieged by Turenne.* DRESDEN *Military camp in mountain landscape* 1698, *Oriental market* 1698. SCHLEISSHEIM *Oriental seaport* 1700. STOCKHOLM *Italian market* (two). VIENNA Liecht. *Seabattle with Barbary pirates* 1701.

[Fl. 88, Fl. 892, Fl. 212.]

*Melbourne Miracles Painter. Presumed Flemish Sch. 15th-16th cent. Name for painter of MELBOURNE N.G. of Victoria Triptych *Miracle of the loaves and fishes* (centre), *Marriage at Cana, Rest on the Flight* (front and back of left wing), *Raising of Lazarus, S. Peter* (front and back of right wing). The centre panel is presumed by some the work of the Catherine Legend Master *q.v.*; the left wing is presumed by some the work of the Magdalene Legend Master *q.v.*

[Fl. 316.]

Mellery, Xavier. Flemish Sch. *b* Laeken nr. Brussels 1845 *d* Laeken 1921. *Symbolist allegories* (*cf.* A. Levêque), *interiors, landscapes, genre* (*including Béguinage motifs*), *portraits also drawings and book illustrations.* Pupil of J. Portaels in Brussels Acad.; went Italy with Rome prize 1870; member of Brussels group Les XX (*cf.* J. Ensor) 1884. F. Khnopff was among his pupils. Represented in ANTWERP *Mother's pride, Inspiration, Peasants, Family group, The artist's mother, Self-portrait, P. de Vigne, sculptor.* BRUSSELS *Allegory 'La Delicatesse est fille de la Force', L'Ardenne* and others; Town Hall *Allegory of the virtues incumbent in a Burgomaster: Equity, Firmness and Kindness* 1894. GHENT *Fête in Doge's palace.* [Fl. Bib. 19th cent., Fl. 350, Fl. 670, Fl. 296.]

Melsen, Marten. Flemish Sch. *b* Brussels 1870 *d* Stabroek 1947. *Peasant genre and landscape.* Pupil in Brussels Acad. of J. Stallaert. Represented in ANTWERP *Winter (killing swine).* [Fl. 17.]

*Memlinc (Memling, Hemmelinck), Hans (Jean). Flemish Sch. *b* Seligenstadt near Frankfort-on-Main date unknown *d* Bruges 1494. *Religious subjects, portraits.* Presumed by some the 'Hausse' recorded by Vasari (1550) as pupil of Rogier of Bruges and by Guicciardini (*c.* 1567) and Vasari (1568) as pupil of Rogier van der Weyden; citizen of Bruges 1465; not recorded as Master in Bruges Guild but had as pupils two otherwise unknown artists Annekin Verhanneman (1480) and Paschier van der Mersch (1483); bought large house (domus magna lapidea) in Bruges 1480 (the miniature painter W. Vrelant *q.v.* was at one time his neighbour and the painter L. Boel *q.v.* acquired his house in 1509); married and had three sons all under twenty-five at his death. A 17th cent. tradition (not confirmed by documents so far discovered) records that he first came to Bruges as a wounded refugee soldier and was befriended by the brothers of the Hôpital S. Jean; Canon James de Damhouder (17th cent.) records that he painted a picture for the Hôpital in gratitude for services rendered. **Signed Examples:** None. **Documented (Inscribed) Examples:** BRUGES Hôpital S. Jean 'The Floreins Altar' Triptych *Adoration of the Magi* (centre), *Nativity, Presentation in the Temple* (wings), *SS. John Baptist and Veronica* (reverses) inscribed on original frame 'Opus Johannis Memlinc' and dated 1479; donated by Brother Jan Floreins. 'The S. John Altar' Triptych *Virgin and Child with SS. Catherine, Barbara, John the Baptist and John the Evangelist* (centre), *Beheading of S. John the Baptist, S. John on Patmos* (wings), *Four donors with patron saints* (reverses) inscribed on original frame 'opus Johannis Memling Anno 1479' (*cf.* J. F. Ducq). 'The S. Ursula Shrine' *S. Ursula and her companions, Virgin and Child with donors* (ends), *Scenes from the Legend of S. Ursula* (sides), consecrated 1489 and recorded (1604) as by Memlinc by Van Mander who states that the painter P. Pourbus *q.v.* went to admire it on certain saints days when it was exhibited to the public and never tired of praising its workmanship (*cf.* Ursula Legend Master). Morelli's 'Anonimo' (1521) saw a *Portrait of Isabella of Portugal, wife of Duke Philip the Good* by 'Zuan Memelin' and dated 1450 in Cardinal Grimani's collection in Venice (*cf.* J. van Eyck); Descamps (1768) saw in Bruges, Hospice S. Julien an *Altarpiece of SS. Christopher and Maur* 'painted in 1484 by Hemmelinck' and in Bruges Notre Dame, Tanner's Chapel, a 'tableaux curieux' with a *Series of scenes of Christ's Passion* ('les figures ont environ six pouces de hauteur; on ne peut rien de plus precieux pour le fini, la couleur belle est pleine de chaleur et de finesse: rien n'est plus ressemblant a l'émail le plus poli'). A number of pictures presumed by some his work are in various museums (*cf.* Bruges Virgin with Apple Painter, Danzig Last Judgement Master, New York Lady with a Pink Painter and Washington Man with an Arrow Painter). [Fl. 12, Fl. 371, Fl. 818, Fl. 559, Fl. 215, Fl. 216, Fl. 870, Fl. 892, Fl. 840, Fl. 316, Fl. 115, Fl. 62, Fl. 46, Fl. 143.]

Mensaert, Guillaume Pierre. Flemish Sch. *b* Brussels 1711 *d* Brussels after 1777. *Religious subjects, portraits; also active as art historian.* Pupil of V. H. Janssens. Master in Brussels Guild 1740. His paintings for the Brussels Jesuit and Dominican churches are recorded in his book 'Le Peintre-amateur et curieux' (1763) which describes the pictures in Belgian churches, etc. and served as a basis for Descamps' 'Voyages' (1769). His *Portrait of J. L. Krafft* (1736) is recorded by an engraving. [Fl. 576, Fl. 216, Fl. 440.]

Mera, Pietro (known in Italy as Il Fiammingo). Flemish Sch. *b* Brussels (?) before *c.* 1550 *d* Venice after 1611. *Religious subjects, 'history'.* Went Italy and remained there (*cf.* J. v. d. Straet); worked Florence and Venice (*cf.* L. Toeput). **Signed Examples:** CIVIDALE (Prov. Udine) Cathedral *SS. James the less, Lawrence and Stephen* painted in Venice 1611. VIENNA Liecht. *Nativity* painted in Florence 1570. **Documented Examples:** VENICE S. Maria dell'Orto *Trinity with Virgin and S. Francis*; SS. Giovanni e Paolo *Circumcision*; S. Nicolò di Lido *Nativity and Saints*; S. Salvatore *S. Theodore* (all recorded by Boschini 1664). [Fl. 709, Fl. 101, Fl. 612, Fl. 440, Fl. 892, Fl. 536, Fl. 305.]

Mérode Master (Mousetrap Master, Maître à la Souricière). Presumed Flemish Sch. 15th cent. Name for painter of WESTERLOO Mérode Coll. Triptych *Annunciation* (centre), *Donors: Man and woman kneeling* (left wing), *S. Joseph making mousetraps* (right wing). Presumed by some identical with Flémalle Master *q.v.* [Fl. 316, Fl. 530.]

Mertens, Charles. Flemish Sch. *b* Antwerp 1865 *d* Calverley (Yorkshire) 1919. *Genre, interiors, portraits, landscapes* (*some in pastel*), *cartoons for murals.* Pupil of C. Verlat in Antwerp Acad.; later Professor there; Member of Antwerp group 'Als ik kan' (*cf.* H. Luyten) 1884-92; founder member of 'De Dertien' (XIII) (*cf.* E. Farasyn) 1891, and 'L'Art Contemporain' (Kunst van Heden) (*cf.* R. Strebelle); came England during 1914-18 German invasion (*cf.* G. v. d. Woestyne) and stayed. Represented in ANTWERP *Singing children, F. van Leemputten artist* 1913, *Waffle seller, Evening at Royston, The spinner, Fishing by moonlight, Garden at Calverley, The bridal array*; Opera House *Ceiling* (*cf.* C. Boom). BRUSSELS *The studio* 1905, *Zeeland family* and others. [Fl. 17, Fl. Bib. 19th cent.]

Mertens, Jan (Joannes Martini, Martin of Antwerp). Flemish Sch. *b* before 1460 *d c.* 1509. *Religious subjects; but chiefly active as sculptor.* Master (as sculptor) in Antwerp Guild 1473. **Documented Example** (painting): LÉAU S. Léonard *Three Maries at the Sepulchre.* His son Jean M., a pupil of J. Gossaert, was master in Antwerp Guild 1505. [Fl. 893, Fl. 88, Fl. 892.]

Mets, Pieter de. Flemish Sch. *b* Antwerp 1880. *Landscapes, figures, still life* (*in Impressionist and Post-Impressionist conventions*). Represented in ANTWERP *Self-portrait.* [Fl. 17.]

Metsys, see Massys.

*Meulen, Adam Frans (Antoine François) van der. Flemish Sch. *b* Brussels 1632 or 1634 *d* Paris 1690. *Picturesque military pieces* (*cf.* L. de Hondt the elder), *contemporary warfare* (*cf.* P. Meulener), *ceremonial pieces, outdoor social genre; also worked as tapestry designer.* Pupil of P. Snayers in Brussels Guild 1648; went Paris (*cf.* C. E. Biset) where was recommended to Colbert by C. Le Brun; became court painter to Louis XIV (*cf.* J. v. Egmont, B. Flémalle, P. Spierincx, A. F. Baudewyns, A. Genoels) 1664; given lodgings in the Gobelins and a stipend 1667; accompanied the King on his travels and recorded his campaigns and progresses; member of Paris Acad. *cf.* P. Mol) 1673; married Le Brun's niece 1681; A. F.

Baudewyns (who married his sister), F. Duchatel and the French painters J. B. Martin (M. des Batailles) and R. Bonnart were among his pupils and assistants. **Signed Examples:** AUGSBURG *Baggage transport passing a village* 1660. BUDAPEST *Battlepiece.* CASSEL *Travelling suite of a princess* 1659, *A ceremonial entry into Brussels* 1659. LENINGRAD *Episode from Cromwell's invasion of Scotland 1650-1* 1657, *Episode from Louis XIV's invasion of Flanders* 1667, *Louis XIV travelling* 1664, *Siege of a town* 1677, *Cavalry skirmish.* LONDON N.G. *Hunting party* (*with coach*) 1662. MADRID Prado *A General in a coach with escort* 1660, *Cavalry skirmish* 1657. MONTPELLIER *Halt of horsemen.* NEW YORK Met. *Cavalry skirmish.* VIENNA Liecht. *Open air performance in the Grand Sablon Brussels* (*cf.* D. van Alsloot, A. Sallaert and D. Teniers). **Documented Examples:** GRENOBLE *Louis XIV approaching the Palace* (with many portraits; engraved). MUNICH A.P. *Louis XIV conquering Dôle* (*Franche Comté*) 1668, *The siege of Tournai, Louis XIV ordering the shelling of Audenarde, Louis XIV conquering Lille* (all engraved). PARIS Louvre *Victories and sieges of Louis XIV* (twenty paintings from Louis XIV collection; others in VERSAILLES. OXFORD: Ashmolean has a signed *Landscape with bandits attacking a convoy.*
[Fl. 425, Fl. 22, Fl. 215, Fl. 288, Fl. 88, Fl. 892, Fl. 519, Fl. 584.]

Meulen, Edmond van der. Flemish Sch. *b* Brussels 1841 *d* Brussels 1905. *Animals, still life, book illustrations.* Represented in AMIENS, BRUGES, *Dog,* BRUSSELS *Bulldog.* COURTRAI, DIJON, GHENT *The two friends.* HAGUE, LOUVAIN, MONS, MUNICH, NAMUR, OSTEND, PRAGUE, TOURNAI, VERVIERS.
[Fl. 264, Fl. 160 (1905).]

Meulen, Pierre van der the elder. Flemish Sch. *b* before 1585 *d* after 1619. *Decorative painter.* Worked on Pageant Entry into Ghent of Archduke Albert and Archduchess Isabella 1599 (*cf.* M. Joncquoy). [Fl. 136, Fl. 386.]

Meulen, Pierre van der the younger. Flemish Sch. *b* Brussels 1638 *d* Paris (?) after 1690. Brother of A. F. v. d. M. *q.v.* Recorded as painter and draughtsman of *contemporary warfare* (*cf.* P. Meulener), but began as a sculptor. Came London 1670 (*cf.* C. de Neve) and worked for William III 1689 (*cf.* J. B. Medina); then went Paris. Vertue (before 1756) records his portrait by the French painter N. de Largillière in London.
[Fl. 425, Fl. 826, Fl. 856, Fl. 612, Fl. 892.]

Meulen, Steven van der. Flemish Sch. *b* Antwerp (?) *c.* 1527 *d* England (?) after 1563 (?) *Portraits.* Pupil in Antwerp of W. van Cleve the elder 1543. Master Antwerp Guild 1552; fled, as a Protestant, from religious persecution (*cf.* A. de Weerdt) to London (*cf.* H. Custodis, H. Ewouts, M. Geeraerts the elder and the younger, L. de Heere, J. Hoefnagel, F. Hogenberg, G. Horenbout, L. Horenbout, S. Horenbout, C. Ketel), 1560; naturalized Englishman 1562; presumed the painter Stephens or Stevens who, Vertue (before 1756) records, painted signed portraits of the Lumley family like 'the pencil and manner' of Holbein but 'softer and tenderer'. An inventory of Lord Lumley's pictures dated 1590 mentions several portraits by 'Steven'. Unsigned portraits of *John Lord Lumley* dated 1563 and his wife *Joan Fitzalan Lady Lumley* are still at Lumley Castle. (*Cf.* also H. Ewouts.)
[Fl. 826, Fl. 857.]

*Meulener (or **Meulenaer** or **Molenaer**), **Pieter.** Flemish Sch. *b* Antwerp 1602 *d* Antwerp 1654. *Contemporary warfare* (*cf.* S. Vrancx, P. Snayers, G. Peeters, N. v. Eyck, J. v. Werden, A. F. v. d. Meulen, P. v. d. Meulen the y., also J. B. v. d. Meiren), *picturesque military pieces* (*cf.* L. de Hondt the elder) *and social scenes.* Pictures commissioned from him by the Forchoudt firm of Antwerp dealers (*cf.* A. Casteels) were

exported to Lisbon and Vienna. **Signed Examples:** AMSTERDAM Rijks. *Landscape with social scene* from a virginal's lid (*cf.* F. Borsse). BERLIN *Battle of Fleurus 1622 with Antwerp in background* 1650. BRUNSWICK *Battle of Fleurus* 1645. LENINGRAD, MADRID Prado *Attack on a convoy* 1644, *Cavalry skirmish* 1644. PRAGUE Nostitz, STOCKHOLM *Occupation of Magdeburg by Catholic troops under Tilly 1631* 1650 (*cf.* V. Wolfvoet).
[Fl. 86, Fl. 107, Fl. 892, Fl. 440, Fl. 212.]

Meunier, Charles (Karel). Flemish Sch. *b* son of Constantin M., St.-Josse-ten-Noode 1864 *d* Louvain 1894. *Landscapes and town pieces; also engravings from his father's drawings.* Represented in BRUSSELS (Triptych) *Louvain S. Pierre Hospital* 1892. [Fl. 123.]

Meunier, Constantin. Flemish Sch. *b* son of a rate collector, Etterbeek 1831 *d* Ixelles (Brussels) 1905. *Religious and other compositions, peasant and industrial genre, landscapes; but more widely known as sculptor of agricultural labourers and miners.* Pupil of F. J. Navez and C. de Groux *q.v.* Began as sculptor; turned for financial reasons to painting; joined 'Soc. Libre des B.A.' 1868 and with L. Dubois *q.v.* founded 'L'Art libre' *c.* 1872; sent to Spain by Belgian government to copy P. de Kempener's *Descent from the Cross* 1882-3; concentrated on sculpture from 1886. Represented as painter in ANTWERP *Martyrdom of S. Stephen* 1867, *The organ grinder, Steel works, Unloading a ship, Coming from the mines.* BRUSSELS *Episode of the Peasants War* 1878. *Spanish Tobacco Factory* 1889, *Coal-depot in snow, Red roofs.* COURTRAI *Burial of a Trappist monk* 1860. GHENT, LOUVAIN, PARIS (State Collection) *In the Black Country.*
[Fl. 513, Fl. 662, Fl. 308, Fl. Bib. 19th cent.]

Meunier, Georgette. Flemish Sch. *b* daughter of J. B. Meunier engraver, Brussels 1859. *Genre.* Pupil of A. Stevens. Represented in BRUSSELS *After the ball.* CANNES, IXELLES.
[Fl. 775, Fl. Bib. 19th cent.]

Meunincxhove, Jean Baptiste van. Flemish Sch. *b* Bruges *c.* 1620 *d* Bruges 1704. *Contemporary history, topographic paintings and religious subjects.* Pupil of J. van Oost the elder 1638; Master Bruges Guild 1644; Master Antwerp Guild 1677; J. v. d. Kerckhove was among his pupils. **Signed Examples:** BRUGES. *La Place du Bourg* 1682; *Hôtel de Ville Charles II of England and the Duke of York in Bruges* (dated 1671) and *Charles II at the Bruges Banquet*; N. D. des Aveugles *Shipwreck* (1677); S. Anne *Christ before Caiphas* (1691). Descamps (1769) records an *Adoration of the Magi* in Bruges church of the Jesuits and '*Landscapes and perspectives*' in the Church of the Abbaye des Dunes (*cf.* D. v. d. Bogaerde).
[Fl. 216, Fl. 440, Fl. 892, Fl. 114.]

Meus, L., see **Mehus.**

Meyer, Marie Josephine Valérie Constance. Flemish Sch. *b* Brussels 1835. *Landscapes. Also active as lithographer* (*cf.* P. Mathieu). [Fl. 481, Fl. 892.]

Meyers, Isidore. Flemish Sch. *b* Antwerp 1836 *d* Brussels 1917. *Landscapes, marines.* Pupil of J. Jacobs; worked Paris with J. Heymans 1855-7; member of Termonde Group and settled Termonde where Professor in Acad. Represented in ANTWERP *The Scheldt at Maria Kerke, At my neighbour's.* BRUSSELS *Winter morning.*
[Fl. 626 (1917), Fl. Bib. 19th cent.]

Meyssens, Joannes (Jan). Flemish Sch. *b* Brussels 1612 *d* Antwerp 1670. *Religious subjects, allegories, portraits, copies of pictures by Van Dyck; later active as engraver, draughtsman for engravers and publisher.* Pupil in Brussels of A. van Opstal and N. van der Horst. Visited Holland (?); in Antwerp

Guild 1640; founded publishing business in Antwerp and employed many engravers including Wenceslas Hollar (then driven from England by the Civil War); published de Bie's 'Gulden Cabinet'. Van Dyck painted his portrait. His *Hendrik Count of Nassau* and *Penitent Magdalene* are among works recorded by engravings. His drawings for 'Les Portraits des Souverains, Princes et Comtes de Hollande' were engraved by his son Cornelis M.

[Fl. 86, Fl. 481, Fl. 612, Fl. 440, Fl. 892.]

*Michau (Micho), Theobald. Flemish Sch. *b* Tournai 1676 *d* Antwerp 1765. *Landscapes and river scenes with genre figures and animals.* Pupil of L. Achtschellinck in Brussels; Master Brussels Guild 1698; in Antwerp Guild 1711. **Signed Examples:** AUGSBURG *River landscape, Market.* BRUNSWICK *Market.* BRUSSELS *Landscape with peasants' cart.* BUDAPEST *River landscape.* ROTTERDAM *Landscape with farm.* VIENNA K. *Market scene, Winter landscape.* **Documented Examples:** MADRID Prado *River scene with peasants and farm animals, River scene with peasants and cattle.* [Fl. 612, Fl. 892, Fl. 440.]

Michaux, John. Flemish Sch. *b* Antwerp 1876. *Landscapes, seapieces, figures, still life.* Pupil in Antwerp Higher Institute and of F. Hens. Represented in ANTWERP *Rising moon, Niewpoort harbour.* [Fl. 17.]

Michiel (Michel), 'Master Michel'. Presumed Flemish Sch. 15th/16th cent. Painter to Archduchess Margaret of Austria (*cf.* J. Schooff); her inventory (1516) records '*Ung visaige du controlleur de Madame, fait de la main de Michiel sur ung petit tableau*'; '*Une petite Nostre Dame disant ses heures, faicte de la main de Michiel que Madame appelle sa mignonne et le petit dieu dort*'; and '*Ung bien petit tableau à double feullet de la main de Michiel de l'ung des coustez de Nostre Dame . . . de l'autre costez d'ung sainct Jehan et de saincte Marguerite, faiz à la semblance du prince d'Espaigne et de Madame.*' (*cf.* Vienna Catherine Painter). [Fl. 810, Fl. 798.]

Mieghem, Eugeen van. Flemish Sch. *b* Antwerp 1875 *d* Antwerp 1930. *Landscapes and harbour scenes, figures; poster designs.* Teacher in Antwerp Acad. Represented in ANTWERP *Women on the harbour* (two), *The harmonica player.* [Fl. 17.]

*Miel, Jan (called in Italy Miele, Milo and Bicke, i.e. Beetje, The Little One, and in France Petit Jean). Flemish Sch. *b* Beveren near Antwerp 1599 *d* Turin 1663. *Italian genre scenes* (*cf.* A. Goubau, L. de Deyster, M. Sweerts, C. de Wael, J. B. Wolfordt). *religious subjects and frescoes; also worked as engraver.* Pupil of G. Seghers (?) and/or A. van Dyck (?); went Italy and remained there (*cf.* J. Sutterman); in Rome by 1636; presumed to have known the Dutch painter P. van Laer (Bamboche); painted figures in some pictures by the French painter Claude Lorrain; assisted the Italian painter A. Sacchi in the Barberini Palace (*cf.* J. G. Delcour) 1641-3; quarrelled with S. who complained that he introduced 'popular' figures; Member of Rome Congregazione dei Virtuosi and of Accad. de San Luca; worked for Pope Alexander VII 1656; court painter to Charles Emmanuel Duke of Savoy (*cf.* E. Dubois) from 1658. **Signed Examples:** CHIERI (Prov. Torino) Church of the Assunta *Virgin with saints* 1654. LONDON Royal Collection *Italian scene with cobbler and peasants.* MADRID Prado *Roman Carnival* (Rome 1653). TURIN *Charles Emmanuel after the hunt* 1660. **Documented Examples:** ROME S. Lorenzo in Lucina *Scenes from life of S. Anthony of Padua: The miracle of the ass* and *The healing of the child* (frescoes); S. Maria dell'Anima *Scenes from the life of S. Lambert* (frescoes); S. Martino di Monti *Baptism of S. Cyril* (frescoes); Quirinal *Crossing of the Red Sea* (paid for by Alexander VII 1656). PARIS Louvre *Soldiers resting, Travellers at dinner.* Allegorical composi-

tions and hunting pieces painted for Turin palaces are recorded.

[Fl. 48, Fl. 642, Fl. 22, Fl. 800, Fl. 505, Fl. 84, Fl. 417, Fl. 305, Fl. 83, Fl. 678.]

Mierhop, F. de, see Cuyck.

Milan Adoration Master. Presumed Flemish Sch. early 16th cent. Name for painter of MILAN Brera (620) Triptych *Adoration of the Magi* (centre), *Nativity, Rest on the Flight* (wings). Has been presumed by some identical with Dormagen Master *q.v.* [Fl. 316, Fl. 798.]

Millé, Jean Baptiste. Flemish Sch. *b* Brussels before 1710 *d* after 1766. *Religious subjects for Brussels churches; portraits.* Pupil of Z. G. van Helmont. In Brussels Guild 1729; teacher in Brussels School of Art; P. L. J. Spruyt was his pupil. **Documented Example:** BRUSSELS Town Hall *The Empress Maria Theresa on horseback* (*cf.* P. J. Lion and G. Pélichy). [Fl. 216, Fl. 451, Fl. 119, Fl. 88.]

Millet (Millé), Jean François called Francisque, Flemish Sch. *b* son of a Dijon ivory worker (later patronized by the Prince de Condé in Flanders), Antwerp 1642 *d* insane as result of poison (?) Paris 1679. *Picturesque landscapes* (*cf.* J. B. Juppin, P. Rysbraeck and G. de Witte) *with religious and other figures.* In Paris (*cf.* C. E. Biset) by 1659; pupil there of Laureys Franck and A. Genoels *q.v.*; married daughter of L. Franck *c.* 1662; copied paintings by Poussin in Jabach collection; Associate of French Académie des Beaux Arts (*cf.* P. Mol) and exhibited landscapes in Paris 1673; visited Holland and England (*cf.* C. de Neve). Genoels (in a letter to Houbraken) extolled M's exceptional visual memory. **Documented Examples:** BERLIN K.F. *River landscape with the Finding of Moses.* LONDON N.G. *Mountain landscape with lightning.* Antwerp inventories (1691 and 1694) record a *Winter landscape* and *Landscape with religious subjects.* D'Argenville (1745) records three landscapes in the Düsseldorf Gallery of the Elector Palatine; also a *Sacrifice of Abraham* and *Elisha in the desert* with landscape backgrounds in Paris, S. Nicolas du Chardonnet, and eleven landscapes in the king's collection. A series of twenty-six *Scenes from Ovid's Metamorphoses,* a *Baptism of Christ,* a *Baptism of S. John* and a *Virgin with S. Joseph* are also recorded.

[Fl. 168, Fl. 425, Fl. 22, Fl. 66, Fl. 892, Fl. 213.]

Milo, Jean. Flemish Sch. *b* Brussels 1906. *Landscapes, figures, genre, still life.* Pupil in Brussels Acad. of C. Montald. Represented in ANTWERP *Grey weather by the sea, Interior with flowers.* [Fl. 17.]

Minderhout, Antoon van. Flemish Sch. *b* son of Hendrik van M., Antwerp 1675 *d* Antwerp 1705. *Marines* (*cf.* G. van Eyck). Pupil in Antwerp Guild 1687. **Monogrammed Example:** PRAGUE Rudolfinum *Seaport.* [Fl. 892.]

*Minderhout, Hendrik van. Flemish Sch. *b* Rotterdam 1632 *d* Antwerp 1696. *Marines and port scenes* (*cf.* G. v. Eyck). In Bruges 1652, where Master in Guild 1662; settled Antwerp 1672. **Signed Examples:** ANTWERP *Levantine Port* 1675 (presented to Antwerp Acad. *cf.* J. Jordaens), *Antwerp fish market* 1695. BRUGES *Port of Bruges* 1653 (or 1663). DRESDEN *Oriental seaport* 1673. MADRID Prado *Disembarkation, Festival embarkation* both 1688. ROUEN *Oriental seaport.* [Fl. 216, Fl. 107, Fl. 892, Fl. 884.]

Minderhout, Willem Augustin van. Flemish Sch. *b* son of Hendrik van M., Antwerp 1680 *d* Moravia 1752. *Architectural views.* **Signed Example:** FRANKFORT Städt. Mus. (1705). [Fl. 107, Fl. 892, Fl. 88.]

Minguet, André Josef. Flemish Sch. *b* Antwerp 1818 *d* Antwerp 1860. *Church and other interiors, genre, still life.* Pupil of

G. Wappers. Figures in his pictures were sometimes painted by F. Pauwels. Represented in ANTWERP *Interior of Bruges Cathedral, The sacristy* 1857. A picture titled *Screen in Antwerp S. Jacques* was exhibited in London British Institute in 1855. [Fl. 451, Fl. 481, Fl. 363, Fl. 837 (1861).]

Minne, Jean Baptiste. Flemish Sch. *b* Wacken 1734 *d* Wacken 1817. *Religious subjects.* Pupil of M. J. Geeraerts (?). [Fl. 481, Fl. 892.]

*Minneapolis Adoration Painter. Presumed Flemish Sch. 15th cent. Name for painter of MINNEAPOLIS Inst. of Arts *Adoration of the Shepherds.*

*Minneapolis S. Catherine Painter. Presumed Flemish Sch. 15th cent. Name for painter of MINNEAPOLIS Inst. of Arts *S. Catherine of Alexandria.* Presumed by some identical with Lucy Legend Master *q.v.*

Minnebroer, Frans (Frans the Minorite). Flemish Sch. *b* Malines (?) *c.* 1500. *Landscapes with religious subjects (cf.* F. Mostaert). Working Malines *c.* 1540. F. Verbeeck was his pupil before 1531. Van Mander (1604) writes: 'He was a clever painter in oil colours. In a *Flight into Egypt* in Malines Onze Vrouwe Kerk the family travels through the wilderness; the figures and trees are excellent.' Van Mander also records an *Annunciation* and *Visitation* in the church at Hanswyck (near Malines). Presumed by some identical with F. Crabbe *q.v.* [Fl. 559, Fl. 440.]

*Mirou (not **Miron**), **Antonie.** Flemish Sch. *b* of Netherlandish parents, Antwerp or Frankenthal before 1587 *d* after 1653. *Landscapes with figures (cf.* P. Brill, G. van Coninxloo, A. Govaerts, W. van Nieulandt, T. van Haecht, K. de Keuninck, J. van Liere, J. de Momper, M. Ryckaert, J. Savery, R. Savery, P. Schoubroek, A. Stalbemt, F., G., L. and M. van Valkenborch, J. Tilens, L. Toeput; also D. van Alsloot, J. (Velvet) Brueghel and F. Mostaert). Recorded in Frankenthal 1602-20. **Signed Examples:** AMSTERDAM Rijks. *Village, wood and figures* 1608. BERLIN K.F. *Forest scene with duckhunters* 1653. COPENHAGEN *Village, wood and figures.* MADRID Prado *Landscape with Abraham and Hagar.* MAGDEBURG, PRAGUE Nostitz *Wooded landscape with huntsmen* 1611. VIENNA K. *Wooded landscape* 1612; Harrach *Wooded landscape* 1603. A series of landscapes in the region of Bad Schwalbach are recorded by engravings 1620. [Fl. 892, Fl. 659, Fl. 440.]

Moer, Jean Baptiste van. Flemish Sch. *b* Brussels 1819 *d* Brussels 1884. *Architectural pieces, interiors, landscapes.* Pupil of F. A. Bossuet *q.v.* Travelled in France, Italy, Spain and Portugal. Represented in AMIENS *Studio interior.* BRUSSELS Town Hall *Views of Old Brussels* (fifteen) 1875. [Fl. 892, Fl. 119.]

Moerenhout, Josephus Jodocus. Flemish Sch. *b* Eeckeren nr. Antwerp 1801 *d* Antwerp 1875. *Landscapes with figures and animals (especially horses); hunting and military pieces.* Pupil in Antwerp of H. J. F. v. d. Poorten 1817-20; in The Hague 1824; in Paris working with H. Vernet 1825. Worked in Holland 1831-54; and sometimes collaborated with the Dutch painter A. Schelfhout *(cf.* P. J. Hellemans). Represented in AMSTERDAM *Stable, Cossack advance-guard, Race course.* DORDRECHT, THE HAGUE *Race course at Scheveningen* 1846. MUNICH, PHILADELPHIA *Return from the chase* 1854.
[Fl. 451, Fl. 440, Fl. 88, Fl. Bib. 19th cent.]

Moerman, Albert Édouard. Flemish Sch. *b* Ghent 1808 *d* Ghent 1856. *Landscapes.* Pupil of P. F. de Noter. Represented in COURTRAI *Winter morning.* [Fl. 451, Fl. 892.]

Moermans, Jacques. Flemish Sch. *b* Antwerp 1602 *d* (drowned in canal) Antwerp 1653. *'History' but also active as engraver and art dealer.* Pupil of Rubens 1622; Master Antwerp Guild 1630. Mentioned in Rubens' will as executor with F. Snyders and J. Wildens for the sale of his effects 1640.
[Fl. 892, Fl. 213.]

Moiron, see **Meiren, J. B. van der.**

Mol, Pieter (Pierre) van. Flemish Sch. *b* Antwerp 1599 *d* Paris 1650. *Religious subjects, 'history', genre, portraits.* Master Antwerp Guild 1623; went Paris *(cf.* C. E. Biset, and L. Franchoys the younger) 1631; 'peintre ordinaire de la Reine' by 1640; original member of Paris Acad. Royale *(cf.* J. v. Egmont, C. v. Falens, B. Flémalle, A. Genoels, G. Goswin, A. F. v. d. Meulen, J. F. Millet, M. Plattenberg, P. J. Lafontaine, J. F. Voet) 1648. **Signed Examples:** MARSEILLES *Adoration of the Shepherds* 1642 or '43. PARIS Louvre *Entombment.* ROUEN *The Continence of Scipio.* RHEIMS *Descent from the Cross.* A *Young man in a mitre* (replica in Dijon Mus.) in Paris Louvre is presumed by some his work. Descamps (1769) records paintings in Groenendael Priory church, Antwerp *(Adoration of the Magi),* and Ghent S. Jacques. Portraits of *Robert de Sorbon confessor of S. Louis (IX) founder of the Maison de Sorbonne, 1201-74, Anne of Austria Queen of France and Navarre* and *Cardinal Mazarin 1602-61* are among works recorded by engravings. An Antwerp inventory (1654) records two genre subjects in the collection of Jeremias Wildens *(cf.* J. Wildens); others (1657 and 1685) record a *Four Seasons* and a *Judith (cf.* A. de Coster, also M. Willems). Mural paintings for Paris Carmelite Church (1631-5) are also recorded.
[Fl. 878, Fl. 216, Fl. 440, Fl. 213, Fl. 699 (1935).]

Mol, Robertus de. Flemish Sch. *b* son of Pieter van M., place and date unknown *d* place unknown *c.* 1680. *Portraits, also worked as engraver.* Went Rome where in Accad. di S. Luca 1674. Master Ghent Guild 1676. A *Charles II of Spain (cf.* F. Duchatel) is recorded in Rome, Accad. di S. Luca.
[Fl. 892, Fl. 417.]

Molenaer, Cornelis (known as Schele Neel, Cockeye). Flemish Sch. *b* son of an artist, Antwerp *c.* 1540 *d* Antwerp 1589? *Landscapes (cf.* F. Mostaert). Master Antwerp Guild 1564; worked with Gillis Congnet and for many other artists to whom he hired himself for a daily wage to paint landscape in their pictures. Van Mander (1604) says he could paint a landscape in a day, but took to drink and was unlucky in his home as his wife took his money. **Monogrammed Example:** BERLIN K.F. *Wooded landscape with the Good Samaritan (cf.* F. Mostaert). An Antwerp inventory (1614) records a 'Landscape with the Virgin and angel' by Mostaert and Schele Neele'. [Fl. 559, Fl. 88, Fl. 892, Fl. 213.]

Molenaer, P., see **Meulener.**

Mols, Robert C. G. L. Flemish Sch. *b* son of Florent F. (painter of oriental subjects) Antwerp 1848 *d* Antwerp 1903. *Marines (port scenes), landscapes, panoramas, town views, still life, murals (in Antwerp Town Hall).* Pupil in Antwerp Acad. and in Paris of J. F. Millet and J. Dupré. Worked at Fontainebleau; exhibited London R.A.; made *Diorama of the Congo* with P. van Engelen for Antwerp Exhibition 1894 *(cf.* P. Mathieu). Represented in ANTWERP *The south Arsenal quay at Antwerp in 1870* 1876, *Antwerp docks in 1870* 1878, *Flowers* 1879. CETTE *Bordeaux Port, Cette harbour, Shipwreck.* PRAGUE *Rouen docks.* His panoramas *The Port of Marseilles* 1879 and *President Carnot reviewing the fleet at Boulogne 1890* were bought by the French state.
[Fl. 160 (1903), Fl. Bib. 19th cent.]

Momper, Frans (François) de. Flemish Sch. *b* son of landscape painter Jan de M., Antwerp 1603 *d* Antwerp 1660.

Landscapes and views. Master Antwerp Guild 1629; worked at The Hague, Haarlem and Amsterdam. **Signed Examples:** BERLIN K.F. *Distant view of Amsterdam.* BRUSSELS *Peasants dancing.* CASSEL *Village by a river.* THE HAGUE *The Binnenhof at The Hague.* **Monogrammed Example:** INNSBRÜCK *Winter landscape* (F. d. m. F.).

[Fl. 892.]

Momper, Gaspard de. Flemish Sch. 17th cent. Son of Josse de M. and painted figures in some of his pictures. [Fl. 214.]

*Momper, Josse (Jodocus) de.** Flemish Sch. *b* son of painter and dealer Bartholomaeus de M., Antwerp 1564 *d* Antwerp 1635. *Landscapes (cf.* A. Mirou) *with figures often by others.* Master in Antwerp Guild (while his father was Dean) 1581; referred to in Antwerp inventory (1642) as pupil of Lodewyck van Tren (L. Toeput (?) *q.v.*); with C. Floris *q.v.* worked on Pageant Entry into Antwerp of Archduke Ernest 1594; designed tapestries for Archduke Albert (*cf.* G. de Crayer) 1596; Van Dyck painted his portrait. His pupils included his sons Philips and Gaspard. **Monogrammed Examples:** DRESDEN *Waterfall and bridge* (s I. D. M.) UTRECHT *Landscape with Grotto* (s M.) WÜRZBURG *Rocky landscape* (s J. M.) and unclear date. **Documented Example:** VIENNA K. *Mountain landscape* (in Archduke Leopold Wilhelm's 1659 Inventory as 'Original von Johannes de Momper, die Figuren von (Hans) Jordaens'. Drawings, signed in full, are in London, B.M. (1610), Orléans (1599) and Paris Louvre *Landscape with the Fall of Icarus* (1610). Jan Brueghel the younger records (1627) a landscape by de Momper with figures by Jan (Velvet) Brueghel and (1628) twelve pictures by de Momper with figures by himself sent to Van Immerseel of Seville; 17th cent. Antwerp inventories record landscapes with figures of *Daedalus and Icarus* and *Lot fleeing from Sodom* (*cf.* F. Mostaert), *The Preaching on the Sea* with T. van Haecht *q.v.* and figures by A. Francken, a *Tower of Babel* (*cf.* M. van Valkenborch) with figures by J. Teniers and N. van Cleve, *The woman of Samaria* with figures by J. Teniers, and some with figures by H. van Balen, S. Vrancx and other artists. Rubens owned a landscape with animals by 'Breugel'. Descamps (1768) saw examples in Bruges, Brussels, Malines and Tournai churches. OXFORD, Ashmolean, has a monogrammed *Winter landscape with the Flight into Egypt.* Pictures presumed by some his work are in many museums.

[Fl. 559, Fl. 86, Fl. 425, Fl. 216, Fl. 892, Fl. 213, Fl. 214.]

Momper, Philips de. Flemish Sch. *b* son of Josse de Momper before 1608 *d* Antwerp 1634. *Figures in his father's landscapes.* In Rome (at same time as Jan Brueghel the younger *q.v.*) 1623. Master Antwerp Guild 1624. Another Philips de M. (*d* Amsterdam 1675) is recorded. [Fl. 107, Fl. 892.]

Monogrammist Hb, see Brussels Prodigal Son Painter.

Mont (or Dal Monte), Gillis du. Flemish Sch. *b* Antwerp (?) before 1660 *d* Rome 1697. Recorded in Rome 'Bentbroeder-schap' (confraternity of artists) where nicknamed 'Brybergh'; sponsor for A. Genoels 1674. [Fl. 425.]

Montagne, M., see Plattenberg.

Montald, Constant. Flemish Sch. *b* Ghent 1862. *Symbolist allegories, decorative compositions (cf.* A. Levêque), *landscapes, still life, portraits.* Pupil of T. Canneel. Visited Italy 1886; later professor in Brussels Acad. Represented in BRUSSELS *Group of nudes* 1903. GHENT Pal. de Justice *The Struggle of Mankind.* LIÈGE *Apollo and the Muses* (sketch for mosaic decoration in Ghent Theatre).

[Fl. Bib. 19th cent., Fl. 296.]

Montfoort, A. B. van., see Blocklandt.

Montigny, Jenny. Flemish Sch. *b* Ghent 1875. *Genre and landscapes in Impressionist convention.* Pupil of E. Claus. Member of Brussels group 'La Libre Esthétique' (*cf.* G. Buysse) *c.* 1900 and of 'Vie et Lumière' group (*cf.* G. Morren) 1914. Frequent exhibitor in Paris Salon. Represented in GHENT *The Gardener.* LILLE.

[Fl. Bib. 19th cent., Fl. 337.]

Montigny, Jules Léon. Flemish Sch. *b* St. Josse-ten-Noode, Brussels 1847 *d* Tervueren 1899. *Animals and landscapes.* Associated with Tervueren Sch. (*cf.* H. Boulenger). Represented in BRUSSELS *Horses in winter scene* 1890. LIÈGE *Autumn evening after rain.* LOUVAIN.

[Fl. 264, Fl. 160 (1899), Fl. Bib. 19th cent.]

Moons (Moens), Louis Adrien François. Flemish Sch. *b* Antwerp 1769 *d* Antwerp 1844. *Religious subjects, 'history', portraits.* Pupil of A. B. de Quertenmont in Antwerp Acad. 1792; professor Antwerp Acad. after Quertenmont's refusal to serve under French occupation (*cf.* S. d'Argonne and L. Defrance) 1797; in Dresden 1798-1805; visited Paris (*cf.* L. Gerbo) 1801; Russia *c.* 1806; Antwerp 1817-20; Italy 1820-23. **Documented Example:** ANTWERP S. Jacques *The Disciples at Emmaus* (exhibited Antwerp 1822). An *Æschylus writing* (exhibited Malines 1822), *Isaac blessing Jacob* (exhibited Ghent 1823), *Job and his friends, Hagar and Ishmael* (exhibited Brussels 1824), and *The return of the dove to the Ark* (exhibited Antwerp 1834) are among recorded pictures of his later years. [Fl. 451, Fl. 612, Fl. 481.]

Moortele, Gheerolf van den. Flemish Sch. *b* Ghent before 1453 *d* after 1485. *Religious subjects.* Pupil of D. de Rycke; was made Master Ghent Guild at same time as Hugo van der Goes 1467; painted for Ghent S. Bavon 1478. (Extensive forgeries of the Ghent archives have been alleged.)

[Fl. 135, Fl. 385.]

*Mor (known in Spain as **Moro**; later took name **van Dashorst** from a property), **Antonis.** Flemish (Dutch) Sch. *b* Utrecht *c.* 1519 *d* Antwerp 1576. *Portraits and some religious subjects.* Pupil in Utrecht of Jan van Scorel; went Antwerp where Master in Guild 1547; appointed painter to Bishop, later Cardinal, Granvella 1549 and introduced by Granvella to Duke of Alva and Spanish court; in Rome 1550-1; went Spain and Portugal by order of Mary of Hungary (*cf.* J. C. Vermeyen) to paint her sister Queen Catherine of Portugal, King John III and the Infanta Maria of Portugal (then prospective bride for Philip II of Spain) 1552; in Brussels 1553; in Utrecht 1554; thence to England (*cf.* Sotte Cleve) to paint Queen Mary (*cf.* H. Ewouts) for Philip II 1554; knighted by the Queen; returned Netherlands and became King's painter to Philip II by 1558; and accompanied him to Spain 1559; worked Spain (*cf.* P. de Kempener) but left (van Mander states hurriedly believing himself in danger because he had touched with his maulstick the sacred person of the King who was visiting his studio) 1560 (?); settled Netherlands in spite of invitations from Philip to return to Spain; lived Utrecht, Brussels and Antwerp and worked in service of Duke of Alva (*cf.* M. Coxie) whose mistresses he painted and from whom he received preferment for his children; may have visited England again in 1568. **Signed Examples:** BERLIN *Cornelis van Horn and Antonis Taets* (Canons of Utrecht Cathedral carrying palms as Jerusalem pilgrims) 1544. CASSEL *Jean Lecoq* 1559. FLORENCE Uffizi *Self-portrait* 1558. HAGUE Mauritshuis *Man's portrait* (formerly called William of Orange) 1561. LONDON N.P.G. *Sir Henry Lee* 1568; Soc. of Antiquaries *Jan van Scorel* 1560. MADRID Prado *Queen Mary of England* 1554 (Charles V had this portrait with him in his retirement at Yuste), *Emperor Maximilian II* 1550, *Empress Maria of Austria* 1551. NEW YORK Hispanic Soc. *Duke of Alva* 1549. PARMA *Alexander Farnese* 1557. PARIS Louvre *Man's portrait*

1565. VIENNA K. *Bishop (later Cardinal) Granvella* 1549 (*cf.* J. van Scorel), *Anne of Austria, Queen of Spain* (4th wife of Philip II) 157?. WASHINGTON N.G. *Gentleman with a dog* 1569. **Inscribed Example:** BRUSSELS Mus. *Hubert Goltzius* 1576 (Van Mander records a portrait of Goltzius which M. painted in an hour). **Documented Examples:** MADRID Prado *Catherine of Austria, Queen of Portugal* (payment made 1552, in Alcazar inventory 1600). *Joanna of Austria, mother of King Sebastian of Portugal* (in Alcazar inventory 1600). Van Mander records a *Resurrection of Christ with angels and SS. Peter and Paul*, a copy of Titian's *Danaë* made for the King, and a *Circumcision* for Antwerp, Notre Dame, on which he was working at his death. An Antwerp inventory of 1574 records a *Nude Venus* and a *Nude Mars*. Many of his pictures were destroyed in the Pardo fire (1604). Paintings presumed by some his work are in many museums (*cf.* Paris Granvella's *Dwarf Painter*). *Cf.* also J. Beuckelaer, C. Schot and A. Pupiler.

[Fl. 559, Fl. 692, Fl. 892, Fl. 437, Fl. 566, Fl. 316, Fl. 213.]

Morel, Jean Baptiste (not **Nicholas**). Flemish Sch. *b* Antwerp 1662 *d* Brussels 1732. *Flower pieces* (*cf.* J. B. de Crépu) *and flower garlands round grisaille centres* (*cf.* D. Seghers). Pupil in Antwerp of N. van Verendael; in Brussels Guild 1699; worked for Maximilian of Bavaria, Governor of Netherlands and much employed by rich Brussels families on decoration of their new houses after Marchal Villeroi's bombardment (*cf.* Z. J. van Helmont and A. Coppens). Descamps (1768) saw in Ghent S. Pierre Abbey flower decorations on the doors of a cupboard where the Abbey's tapestries were kept. Pictures in Lille presumed by some his work may be by a flower painter of same name who died in Liège 1754.

[Fl. 878, Fl. 215, Fl. 216, Fl. 107, Fl. 409, Fl. 892, Fl. 440.]

Morren, Georges. Flemish Sch. *b* Eeckeren 1868 *d* Brussels 1941. *Figures, landscapes, still life in Impressionist conventions; also sculpture and applied arts.* Pupil of E. Claus and in Paris of A. Roll and E. Carrière; lived for some years at S. Germain-en-laye; Founder member of Brussels 'Vie et Lumière' group (which included A. Boch, G. Buysse, E. Claus, J. Heymans, G. Lemmen, Jenny Montigny, W. Paerels) 1914. Represented in ANTWERP *Interior.* BRUSSELS *Young woman at her toilet* 1903. LIÈGE *The Toilet.*

[Fl. 388, Fl. 296, Fl. Bib. 19th cent.]

Mortelmans, Frank. Flemish Sch. *b* Antwerp 1898. *Still life, landscapes, portraits* (*some in pastel*). Pupil Antwerp Acad.; later teacher there and in Berchem Acad. Represented in ANTWERP *Still life.* [Fl. 17.]

Mortelmans, Frans. Flemish Sch. *b* Antwerp 1865 *d* Antwerp 1936. *Still life* (*mainly flowers and fruit*) *some in w.* Represented in ANTWERP and COURTRAI. [Fl. 17.]

*****Mostaert, Frans.** Flemish Sch. *b* twin brother of Gillis M., Hulst nr. Antwerp *c.* 1534 *d* 1560. *Landscapes* (*cf.* J. de Hollander, C. Massys, M. de Cock, L. Gassel, C. v. Dalem, J. Grimmer, H. Keynooghe, F. Minnebroer, C. Molenaer, C. v. d. Queborne, J. Sons, A. de Weerdt, P. Bruegel the elder, P. Balten, also J. Patinir, C. Rogier and A. Mirou). Pupil of H. met de Bles. Master Antwerp Guild 1554; B. Spranger was his pupil 1560; Vasari (1568), informed by J. v. d. Straet *q.v.*, states that he painted landscapes in oil and fantastic compositions 'imitated by H. Bosch and P. Bruegel'. Van Mander (1604) records that the figures in his 'beautiful landscapes' were sometimes painted by others, *cf.* Gillis M. **Signed Example:** ANTWERP *Landscape with the Good Samaritan.* [Fl. 818, Fl. 559.]

*****Mostaert, Gillis (Egidius).** Flemish Sch. *b* son of an artist Hulst nr. Antwerp *c.* 1534 *d* Antwerp 1598. Twin brother of Frans M. *q.v. Religious subjects, landscapes with figures and*

moonlight effects, snow landscapes, conflagrations (*cf.* P. Schoubroeck, F. v. Oosten, D. v. Heil) *and peasant genre.* Pupil of Jan Mandyn; Master Antwerp Guild 1554; Van Mander describes him as a practical joker who used a medium that could later be removed to add scandalous details in his pictures to horrify his friends—e.g. himself and a friend playing backgammon in Hell in a *Last Judgement*, and a brawl in a *Last Supper*; valued with other artists R. Coxie's *Last Judgement* 1589; sold a *Landscape in moonlight* and a *Fire* to Archduke Ernest of Austria 1595. G. v. Coninxloo (*c.* 1564) and J. Sons were his pupils. **Signed Examples:** COPENHAGEN *Christ on the Cross.* STOCKHOLM *Landscape with Flight into Egypt* 1573. BREMEN *Peasant fair* 1576. PRAGUE Nostitz *Peasant fair* 1579. **Documented Example:** VIENNA K. *Landscape by moonlight* (1621 inventory). Van Mander records *Melchior Schetz* (*Treasurer-General of Philip II*) *and his brothers acclaimed Lords of Hoboken*, a *Christ carrying the Cross* and a *S. Peter delivered from prison* (*cf.* H. Steenwyck the younger and Jooris van Cleve). 17th cent. Antwerp inventories record many pictures (some as 'by Mostaert') including a *Lot fleeing from Sodom* and a *Massacre of the Innocents. A Christ mocked*, an *Et vidimus eum . . .*, an *Adam and Eve* and *Landscapes illustrating the months* are among works recorded by engravings. (*Cf.* C. v. Dalem.)

[Fl. 559, Fl. 753, Fl. 88, Fl. 892, Fl. 650, Fl. 213.]

Mostaert, Jan (Joannes Sinapius). Flemish (Dutch) Sch. *b* of distinguished local family, Haarlem *c.* 1475 *d* Haarlem *c.* 1556. *Religious, classical and genre subjects, portraits.* Pupil of Jansz Jacob of Haarlem. Presumed by some the artist who received a commission (as Jan Mostertsoen) for the Groote Kerk, Haarlem 1500; received payment (as Jehan Masturd) for a portrait of the late Duke of Savoy from Margaret of Austria, Regent of the Netherlands 1521; sold a house (as Jan Jansz Mostert) in Haarlem and asked permission of the Burgomaster to go to Hoorn to paint pictures for the high altar there 1549. Many of his pictures were destroyed in a fire at Haarlem when his house was burned down. R. Aertsz was his pupil. Van Mander (1604) records that he worked for Margaret of Austria for 18 years (*cf.* J. Schooff), that J. Gossaert vainly invited him to work with him at Middelburg and M. van Heemskerck highly praised him. **Signed Examples:** None. **Documented Examples:** None. Van Mander records a *Lineage of Saint Anne* and *Abraham, Sarah, Hagar, Ishmael* (life size half-lengths), and *Ecce Homo* (life size three-quarter-length) 'with portraits, painted from memory and from life, among them a guard well known in those days for his comical, mean face and his head done up with plasters', a *Banquet of the Gods* 'the company looking alarmed and Mars drawing his sword because Discordia enters with the apple of misunderstanding', a *West Indian landscape* 'with many nude figures and strangely constructed huts', and a *Self-portrait* with folded hands, a rosary before him, a naturalistic landscape background, and a *Last Judgement* in the sky. Pictures presumed by some his work are in Brussels (*cf.* Brussels *Man with a Rosary* Painter and Oultremont Master) and other museums.

[Fl. 559, Fl. 892, Fl. 316, Fl. 530.]

Motte, Émile. Flemish Sch. *b* Mons 1860. *Symbolist allegories* (*cf.* A. Levêque), *portraits, figure pieces*; also active as writer on art. Pupil in Mons Acad. of A. Hennebicq, and in Paris of the French painter J. P. Laurens. Later Director of Mons Acad. Represented in BRUSSELS *Portrait of a young girl* 1894. MONS *The Foolish Virgins.* PARIS State Coll. *Autopsychological study.* TOURNAI *The English Beauty.*

[Fl. Bib. 19th cent.]

Mous, Joseph. Flemish Sch. *b* Antwerp 1896. *Port scenes with figures.* Pupil in Antwerp Higher Institute of R. Baseleer. Represented in ANTWERP *Work at the docks.* [Fl. 17.]

Muelenbroec, Willem. Flemish Sch. 16th cent. Recorded as apprentice of Q. Massys 1501. [Fl. 316.]

Munich Adoration Master (Pseudo-Blesius). Presumed Flemish Sch. early 16th cent. Name for painter of MUNICH A.P. (708, formerly 146) *Adoration of the Magi* formerly signed 'Henricus Blesius fecit' (signature removed in cleaning 1911). Pictures presumed by some his work are in various museums. [Fl. 316.]

*Munich Duchess Magdalena Painter.** Presumed Flemish Sch. 16th-17th cent. Name for painter of MUNICH A.P. (2471) presumed portrait of *Duchess Magdalena, daughter of William V of Bavaria*. Presumed by some identical with P. de Witte (Candido) *q.v.* (*cf.* E. van Pee).

*Munich S. Helena and Constantine Painter.** Presumed Flemish (Dutch) Sch. 16th cent. Name for painter of MUNICH A.P. (1458) *S. Helena and the Emperor Constantine*. Presumed by some identical with C. Engelbrechtsz *q.v.*

*Munich Tobacco Den Painter.** Presumed Flemish Sch. 17th cent. Name for painter of MUNICH A.P. (2062) *Interior of a tobacco den*. Presumed by some identical with A. Brouwer *q.v.*

Musin, Auguste Henri. Flemish Sch. *b* son of F. M., Ostend 1852. *Marines*. Represented in COMPIÈGNE *Mouth of the Meuse at Meurenliet* 1874. RHEIMS *Moonlight on the Tamise*. [Fl. Bib. 19th cent.]

Musin, François Etienne. Flemish Sch. *b* Ostend 1820 *d* Brussels 1888. *Marines and port scenes*. Pupil of F. Bossuet. Received a medal at London Crystal Palace Exhibition 1884. Represented in BRISTOL *Mutiny at sea, Bad weather*. BRUSSELS *La Panne beach*. COURTRAI, MONTREAL *Calais port*. NICE, *Brighton*. OSTEND, RHEIMS *Rough weather off the Dutch coast*. SHEFFIELD *Naval battle*. YPRES *The Scheldt Estuary*. [Fl. Bib. 19th cent., Fl. 440.]

Muynck, Andreas Peter Victor de. Flemish Sch, *b* son of a gardener, Bruges 1737 *d* Rome 1813. '*History*' and copies of *works by Italian painters*. Pupil in Bruges Acad. of M. de Visch; to Paris with two sculptors and J. B. Suvée 1763; settled Rome where Provisor of Flemish charitable S. Julien Foundation 1772 (*cf.* J. J. Lauwers and H. de La Pegnia); sold many of his copies for high prices to rich English visitors. [Fl. 207, Fl. 451.]

Myin (or Mijin or Myn), Hendrik Aarnut. Flemish Sch. *b* Antwerp 1760 *d* Antwerp 1826. *Landscapes with animals*. Pupil of B. P. Ommeganck *q.v.* and married his sister Maria Jacoba O. herself a painter; professor in Antwerp Acad. when it was reorganised by the French as École Speciale de Peinture in 1796 (*cf.* L. Defrance). M. Verstappen and F. Lentzen were among his pupils. [Fl. 451, Fl. 481, Fl. 440.]

Myin, Maria Jacoba, née **Ommeganck.** Flemish Sch. *b* Antwerp 1769 *d* Antwerp 1849. *Landscapes with animals* (*cf.* her brother B. P. O.); in Antwerp Acad. 1784; married H. A. M. 1786. Not to be confused with Maria Baesten *q.v.* [Fl. 481, Fl. 440.]

Mytens, Aert (or Arnold), called in Italy Rinaldo fiammingo. Flemish Sch. *b* Brussels *c.* 1541 *d* Rome 1602. *Religious subjects, portraits*. Worked Brussels where stole a corpse from the gallows in order to study anatomy; went Italy and settled there (*cf.* J. v. d. Straet); worked Rome and Naples (*cf.* W. Coebergher); in Rome was employed by A. Santvoort, was friend of J. Speeckhaert and worked for St. Peter's; in Naples was associate of C. Pyp whose widow he married; later left his wife on account of her shameless 'misbehaviour' and went Abruzzo, Aquila and Rome. **Documented Examples:** AQUILA S. Bernardino *Crucifixion* (presumed the picture recorded by Van Mander). MERCOGLIANO (Avellino) S. Giovanni *Virgin of the Rosary* 1586. NAPLES S. Severino *Virgin of the Rosary with the fifteen mysteries* (*cf.* J. Francart) 1584. STOCKHOLM *Christ crowned with thorns* (night piece) presumed the picture recorded by Van Mander who also writes of a *S. Mary beating the devil with a club* and a *Torture of S. Catherine*, with a portion of the wheel wounding an executioner, painted for a Naples church. *Cf.* B. van Somer. [Fl. 559, Fl. 302, Fl. 892, Fl. 305].

N

Navez, Arthur. Flemish Sch. *b* Antwerp 1881 *d* Brussels 1931. *Landscapes, town views, figures, still life.* Pupil in Antwerp Higher Institute and of the French painter J. L. Gérôme in Paris. Represented in ANTWERP *The Montagne de la Cour in Brussels.* [Fl. 17.]

*Navez, François Joseph. Flemish Sch. *b* son of bourgeois family, Charleroi 1787 *d* deaf and almost blind, Brussels 1869. *'History', religious subjects, portraits, genre.* Pupil in Brussels of P. J. François; then in Paris of L. David (*cf.* J. B. J. Bastiné, H. de Caisne, H. de Coene, F. v. Dorne, A. Gregorius, C. Groenendael, H. v. d. Haert, P. v. Hanselaere, M. A. Kindt, J. D. Odevaere) 1813; followed David to Brussels 1816. In Rome with scholarships from Brussels Soc. des Beaux Arts and King William I 1817-21; friend in Rome of French painters Ingres and Léopold Robert; had many private pupils including J. Portaels, A. Robert, J. Stallaert; his correspondence with many contemporary French artists is preserved in the Brussels Bibliothèque Royale. Represented in AMSTERDAM *Elisha raising the Shunamite's son* 1821, *Meeting of Isaac and Rebecca* 1826. ANTWERP *Holy Family* 1848, *Self-portrait* 1854. BRUSSELS *The vow of Brutus, The Hemptinne Family* 1816, *Louis David* 1817, *Hagar in the desert c.* 1820, *Athaliah and Joash* 1830, *Judgement of Solomon* 1855 and others. GHENT *Virgil reading the Aeneid to Agustus* 1812. MUNICH *Spinning women of Fondi* 1845. Religious subjects in AMSTERDAM, BRUSSELS, CHARLEROI, MALINES and BOMBAY churches. A full-length *William I of the Netherlands* 1823 is recorded. [Fl. 451, Fl. 481, Fl. 6, Fl. 88, Fl. 440, Fl. Bib. 19th cent., Fl. 674, Fl. 387, Fl. 296.]

Neeffs, Lodewyck. Flemish Sch. *b* son of P. N. the elder, Antwerp 1617 *d* place unknown after 1648. *Church interiors* (*cf.* H. van Steenwyck the younger). Pupil of his father; became a monk before 1646. F. Francken III painted figures in some of his pictures. **Signed Examples:** DRESDEN *Interior of Antwerp Cathedral* ('Frater Lodevicus Neeffs 1648. D. j. ffranck'). MADRID Prado *Church interior* ('F. L. Neeffs 1646 ffranck'), *Church interior* P. L. Neeffs 1646. [Fl. 107, Fl. 892.]

*Neeffs (Neefs, Nefs), Peeter the elder. Flemish Sch. *b* Antwerp *c.* 1578 *d* Antwerp between 1656 and 1661. *Church interiors, some lit by tapers* (*cf.* H. van Steenwyck the younger). Master Antwerp Guild 1609; Houbraken (before 1718) records that he also painted 'palaces and galleries in perspective' (*cf.* J. Vredeman de Vries); figures in some pictures are by other artists. **Signed and Dated Examples:** AMSTERDAM *Antwerp Dominican church interior* 1636, *Church interior with candlelight effect* 1636. BOSTON (Mass.) *Interior of Antwerp Cathedral* 1638. BUDAPEST *Interior of Antwerp Cathedral* 1637. CASSEL 1636. DRESDEN 1605. FLORENCE Uffizi 1636. GHENT *Liberation of S. Peter* 1651. LONDON N.G. 1644. MADRID Prado *Mass in a Flemish church* 1618, *Ambulatory in a Gothic church,* 1636. **Signed Undated Examples:** AIX-EN-PROVENCE, AMSTERDAM, ANTWERP, BRUSSELS, CAMBRIDGE Fitz., FRANKFORT, LONDON (N.G., Dulwich and Wallace), MADRID Prado *Interior of a church with adoration of a relic (candle-light effect).* MARSEILLES, MUNICH, OXFORD Ashmolean *Interior of Antwerp Cathedral.* PARIS Louvre. Some of the above may be by his son P. N. the younger *q.v.* (*cf.* J. Lidts). [Fl. 425, Fl. 215, Fl. 107, Fl. 892, Fl. 459.]

Neeffs, Peeter the younger. Flemish Sch. *b* son of P. N. Antwerp 1620 *d* Antwerp after 1675. *Church interiors.* Pupil of his father *q.v.* F. Francken III painted figures in some of his pictures (*cf.* L. Neeffs). **Signed Examples:** BOSTON (Mass.) 1648. BRUSSELS (also signed D. j. FFranck). DRESDEN 1658. THE HAGUE (also signed F. Franck) 1654. GLASGOW, PRAGUE Nostitz 1659, SCHWERIN (also signed D. j. F. Franck) 1653, STRASBOURG 1654, TURIN 1658, VIENNA Liecht. 1675. Some of the above are possibly by P. Neeffs the elder *q.v.* [Fl. 107, Fl. 892, Fl. 459.]

Negre, Mathieu van. Flemish Sch. *b* Tournai (?) before 1610 *d c.* 1644. *Religious subjects.* TOURNAI Notre Dame has an altarpiece *Holy Family* and (wings) *Joachim's prayer, Birth of the Virgin, Marriage of the Virgin* and *Presentation in the Temple* 1623 recorded by Descamps (1769) as badly repainted. *Cf.* A. Francken the younger. [Fl. 215, Fl. 440.]

Neste, Alfred van. Flemish Sch. *b* Bruges 1874. *Landscapes, town views, figures, still life, poster designs, illustrations.* Pupil in Bruges and Antwerp Acads. Later teacher Antwerp Acad.; visited Venice. Represented in ANTWERP *View of Bruges.* [Fl. 17.]

Neufchatel (Nieucastell), Nicolas or Colyn, known as Lucidel. Flemish Sch. *b* Hainault *c.* 1530 *d* Nuremberg (?) 1590 or 1600. *Portraits.* Pupil in Antwerp of P. Coecke van Aelst 1539; then to Mons; went Nuremberg *c.* 1561; was paid for painting Emperor Maximilian II and his daughter Anna 1566; admonished for Calvinism by Nuremberg Council 1567. **Inscribed Example:** MUNICH A.P. *The Nuremberg mathematician J. Neudörfer and his son* (repainted inscription on frame 'autor Nicolaus de Novo Castello 1561'). Portraits presumed by some his work are in various museums (*cf.* London *Lady in a Flat Cap* Painter). [Fl. 753, Fl. 892, Fl. 440, Fl. 530, Fl. 296.]

Neufville, Louisa Charlotte. Flemish Sch. *b* daughter of miniature painter G. N. Ritter, Amsterdam after 1770 *d* after 1823. *Miniature portraits.* Member of Antwerp and Amsterdam Academies; worked mainly in Brussels; in London (where copied Rubens' *Chapeau de Paille*) 1823. [Fl. 481, Fl. 275, Fl. 612, Fl. 892.]

Neuhuys, Jan Antoon. Flemish Sch. *b* brother of Dutch painters A. and H. N., Haarlem 1832 *d* Antwerp 1891. *Costume history, genre.* Pupil of N. de Keyser. Represented in ANTWERP *Siesta, Interior.* [Fl. 837 (1891), Fl. 17.]

Neve, Cornelis de. Flemish Sch. *b* Antwerp *c.* 1612 *d* paralysed, Antwerp 1678. *Portraits.* In England 1637-64 (*cf.* P. v. Somer, J. de Gheyn the younger, H. v. Steenwyck the younger, A. v. Stalbemt, W. Damery, A. v. Diepenbeeck, A. van Dyck, F. Wouters, P. P. Rubens, R. v. Leemput, J. v. Reyn, J. Geldorp, J. Weesop, A. Keirincx, B. v. Lemens, J. Huysmans, J. B. Gaspers, T. Willeboirts, J. v. d. Eyden, P. Lankrink, L. Gowy, J. B. Lantscroon, W. de Keyser, B. Flessiers, P. Rysbraeck, J. F. Millet, C. Huysmans, J. F. v. Son). **Documented Examples:** OXFORD Ashmolean *Portrait of the artist* inscribed 'Mr. Le Neve, a famous painter' (from Tradescant Collection presented by Elias Ashmole 1683, seen by Vertue 1737). Vertue (1737) records full length portraits of *Richard Lord Buckhurst and Edward Sackville sons of the Earl of Dorset in a group 1637* at Knole; and he quotes an extract from E. Ashmole's memoirs 'my picture was drawn by Mr. Le Neve in my herald's coat 1664'.

[Fl. 826, Fl. 440, Fl. 744.]

Neve, Frans de the elder. Flemish Sch. *b* Antwerp 1606 *d* Salzburg (?) after 1688 (?). *Religious subjects, mythologies, landscapes with pastoral figures, portraits; also active as engraver.* Antwerp Master 1629; Rome where known in the Flemish colony as 'Bloosaerken' 1660-6, later in Salzburg, Vienna and other Austrian cities. **Signed Example:** SALZBURG Cathedral *Baptism of Christ.* A *Venus and Cupid* is among pictures recorded by engravings. Some paintings presumed by some his work may be by his son F. de N. the younger.

[Fl. 86, Fl. 425, Fl. 215, Fl. 612, Fl. 895, Fl. 799, Fl. 798.]

Neve, Frans de the younger. Flemish Sch. *b* son of F. N. the elder, Austria (?). Recorded Antwerp Guild 1691. [Fl. 892.]

*New York Adoration in a White Castle Painter. Presumed Flemish Sch. 15th cent. Name for painter of NEW YORK Met. (13.26) *Adoration of the Magi.* Presumed by some identical with H. Bosch *q.v.*

*New York Annunciation in a Porch Painter. Presumed Flemish Sch. 15th cent. Name for painter of NEW YORK Met. (32.100.35) *Annunciation.* Presumed by some identical with J. van Eyck *q.v.* 'and assistants'. [Fl. 615.]

*New York Christ Appearing to His Mother Painter. Presumed Flemish Sch. 15th cent. Name for painter of NEW YORK Met. (22.60.58) *Christ appearing to His Mother.* Presumed by some identical with R. van der Weyden *q.v.*

*New York Crucifixion and Last Judgement Painter. Presumed Flemish Sch. 15th cent. Name for painter of NEW YORK Met. (33.92.A.B.) diptych *Crucifixion and Last Judgement* Presumed by some identical with H. van Eyck *q.v.*

*New York d'Este Painter. Presumed Flemish Sch. 15th cent. Name for painter of NEW YORK Met. (32.100.43) *Portrait of a member of the d'Este family* (Leonello, Francesco or Méliaduse). Presumed by some identical with R. van der Weyden *q.v.*

*New York Godelieve Legend Painter. (Sometimes referred to as Master of Ghistelles.) Presumed Flemish Sch. late 15th cent. Name for painter of NEW YORK Met. (12.79) polyptych *The life and miracles of S. Godelieve of Ghistelles* (five panels), *Four saints with donors* (exterior wings).

[Fl. 892, Fl. 615.]

*New York Lady with a Pink Painter. Presumed Flemish Sch. 15th cent. Name for painter of NEW YORK Met. (L44.22.1) *Lady in a hennin with a pink.* Presumed by some identical with H. Memlinc *q.v.*

*New York Lamentation Painter. Presumed Flemish (Dutch) Sch. 15th cent. Name for painter of NEW YORK Met. (26.26) *Lamentation.* Presumed by some identical with Virgo inter Virgines Master *q.v.*

*New York Man in a High Cap Painter. Presumed Flemish Sch. 15th cent. Name for painter of NEW YORK Met. (14.40.644) *Portrait of a man.* Presumed by some identical with D. Bouts *q.v.*

*New York Rest on the Flight Painter. Presumed Flemish Sch. 15th/16th cent. Name for painter of NEW YORK Met. (L.44.23.21) *The Rest on the Flight.* Presumed by some identical with G. David *q.v.*

*New York S. Catherine Painter. Presumed Flemish Sch. 15th cent. Name for painter of NEW YORK Met. (44.105.2) *S. Catherine.* [Fl. 615.]

*New York Virgin in a Tabernacle Painter. Presumed Flemish Sch. 15th cent. Name for painter of NEW YORK Met. (89.15.24) *Virgin and Child.* Presumed by some identical with P. Christus *q.v.*

Neyts (or Nyts), Gillis (Aegidius). Flemish Sch. *b* Ghent 1623 *d* Antwerp 1687. *Landscapes and town views; mainly active as draughtsman and engraver.* Master Antwerp Guild 1647; presumed (from subjects of engravings) to have visited Lille and Italy. **Signed Examples:** DRESDEN *Wooded landscape with cavaliers and ladies* 1681, *Landscape with mountains and ruins.* STOCKHOLM *River landscape* 1641. VALENCIENNES *Landscape with castle.* VIENNA Schönborn *Landscape with huntsmen.* BRUSSELS Mus. has signed *w. Panorama of Brussels* and signed landscape drawings. Descamps (1769) records in Antwerp Acad. an *Academy School where painters and sculptors work after the living model* 'by Neyts'. *Cf.* J. Denys.

[Fl. 216, Fl. 612, Fl. 107, Fl. 520, Fl. 440, Fl. 892.]

Neyts, Leonardus. Flemish (Dutch) Sch. 16th cent. **Signed Example:** HAARLEM *The Four Evangelists* 1525. [Fl. 892.]

Nicolai (Nicolay), Frater Jacques. Flemish Sch. *b* 1605 *d* 1678. A Jesuit; worked for Jesuit church in Namur.

[Fl. 481, Fl. 892.]

Nicolié, Joseph Chrétien. Flemish Sch. *b* son of picture dealer, Antwerp 1791 *d* Antwerp 1854. *Church interiors (cf.* H. van Steenwyck the younger and P. F. de Noter). Studied architecture in Antwerp Acad.; later assisted F. van Ertborn to form collection bequeathed in 1840 to Antwerp Mus. His father sold many of his pictures to English visitors to Antwerp. Represented in ANTWERP *Interior of Antwerp S. Paul.* AMSTERDAM *Interior of Antwerp S. Jacques with tomb of Rubens* 1825. [Fl. 451, Fl. 892, Fl. 88, Fl. 440.]

Nicolié, Paul Emile. Flemish Sch. *b* son of J. C. N., Antwerp 1828 *d* Antwerp 1894. *Genre.* Was for many years expert to the Antwerp Museum. Represented in ANTWERP *Kitchen interior.* [Fl. 892, Fl. 440.]

*Nieulandt (or Nieuweland), Adriaen van. Flemish Sch. *b* brother of W. v. N., Antwerp 1587 *d* Amsterdam 1658. *Landscapes with religious, mythological and genre figures, portraits and still life.* Taken from Antwerp to Amsterdam by his Protestant parents (*cf.* D. v. d. Queborne) *c.* 1588. Pupil of F. Badens *q.v.* **Signed Examples:** AMSTERDAM Rijks. *Procession of the lepers on 'Kopper Maandag' in Amsterdam* 1633, *Allegory of the Peace of Münster* (1648) 1650, *Amphitrite* 1651. BRUNSWICK *Kitchen piece with swan, venison, lobster and figures* (*cf.* F. Snyders) 1616, *Landscape with huntsman* 1640, *Diana and nymphs* 1641, *Diana and Callisto* 1654. COPENHAGEN *Christ's entry into Jerusalem* 1655, *Triumph of Bacchus* 1652, *Elijah and the widow.* HAMBURG *Rape of Proserpina* 1649, *Rape of Europa* (*cf.* H. v. Balen) 1649. Others in DARMSTADT and LENINGRAD. **Documented Example:** THE HAGUE Mauritshuis *Stadtholder Maurice, Prince of Orange, with Prince Frederick Henry and his suite by the sea shore* (recorded in a 1644 inventory). The Brunswick still-life example which has an unusual signature may be the work of another artist of the same name. [Fl. 86, Fl. 425, Fl. 612, Fl. 892.]

Nieulandt, Jacob van. Flemish Sch. *b* younger brother of Adriaen and Willem van N., Amsterdam (?) 1592 *d* Amsterdam 1634. *Genre.* **Signed Example:** AMSTERDAM *Fishmonger's shop* 1617. [Fl. 892.]

*Nieulandt (or Nieuweland), Willem (Guillaume) van (known as Guglielmo Terranova in Italy). Flemish Sch. *b* Antwerp 1584 *d* Amsterdam *c.* 1635. *Italianate landscapes and views in*

611

Rome and region (with small figures). Taken by parents from Antwerp to Amsterdam (*cf.* D. v. d. Queborne) *c.* 1588; pupil of Jacques Savery the elder; went Rome where lived with his uncle (a painter of the same name) and was pupil of P. Brill *q.v.* 1602-3; back in Antwerp 1604-*c.* 1624; member Antwerp Chamber of Rhetoricians 'de Violiere' and wrote many tragedies (including an 'Antony and Cleopatra' 1624) for the 'Olyfetak' drama society; visited Rome again 1626; in Amsterdam from *c.* 1629. His daughter, Constance, a poetess, married A. v. Utrecht. **Signed Examples:** ANTWERP *View in Rome* 1611. BUDAPEST *The Forum, Rome* 1628. COPENHAGEN *Campo Vaccino, Rome* 1609. VIENNA K. *Campo Vaccino, Rome* 1612. BRUSSELS has signed drawings.

[Fl. 559, Fl. 86, Fl. 425, Fl. 106, Fl. 892, Fl. 678.]

Noël, C. Flemish Sch. 18th cent. *Portraits.* Pupil in Bruges of J. A. Garemyn. Exhibited Lille Acad. 1773-88. **Signed Example:** BRUGES *The painter J. A. Garemyn* 1777.

[Fl. 114.]

Noël, Julie Anne Marie. Flemish Sch. *b* Brussels 1812 *d* Brussels 1843. *Genre.* Pupil of F. J. Navez. Married J. B. van Eycken *q.v.* 1840.   [Fl. 451, Fl. 440.]

Noël, Paul Godefroid Joseph (Peter). Flemish Sch. *b* Waulsort, nr. Dinant 1789 *d* Sosoye 1822. *Anecdotic genre, costume history, landscape, animals.* Pupil in Antwerp of W. J. Herreyns and I. van Regemorter; then in Paris of J. Swebach 1814; in Brussels 1815-19, then Holland; visited London 1821. Represented in AMSTERDAM *Drunkards in Amsterdam market* 1821, *Wine harvester's flirtation.* BRUSSELS *Bavarian cavalry halting at a farm* 1817. Pictures titled *Painting moustaches on a girl* and *Crazy dancer with a dancing dog* were exhibited in 1816 and 1820.

[Fl. 716, Fl. 451, Fl. 481, Fl. 612, Fl. 88, Fl. 440.]

Nollekens, Jan Baptiste. Flemish Sch. *b* Antwerp 1665 *d* Roanne before 1748. *Conversation pieces and genre.* In Antwerp 1702; in Middleburg Guild 1718; was many years in England and then settled Roanne. Joseph Francis N. (Old Nollekens) was his son.   [Fl. 826, Fl. 771.]

Nollekens, Jean (or Jan). Flemish Sch. *b* son of J. B. N., Antwerp 1695 *d* Paris 1783. *Religious and allegorical subjects, genre scenes and portraits.* In Paris before 1731 (*cf.* C. J. Redouté); exhibited Paris Acad. de S. Luc *A drawing academy* 1752, *The woman taken in adultery* 1753, *Samson and Delilah* 1756, *The Four Seasons* 1774. Presumably the 'uncle' visited by the sculptor Joseph N. in Paris 1760.

[Fl. 771, Fl. 66, Fl. 440.]

Nollekens, Joseph Francis, called 'Old Nollekens'. Flemish Sch. *b* son of J. B. N., Antwerp 1702 *d* London 1748. *Conversation pieces* (*cf.* I. v. d. Beken and P. J. Horemans), *genre, decorative compositions and pastiches after Watteau and Panini.* Went Paris where pupil of Watteau before 1721; in London by 1733 and associated with P. Tillemans *q.v.*; employed by Lord Cobham on decorative work when Stowe was rebuilt; and by Lord Castlemain (Lord Tylney) at the Palladian mansion Wanstead House (now demolished); described by Vertue as 'a little spritely man' and by the sculptor T. Banks as a timorous miser who, as a Roman Catholic, was prostrated by fear lest his house should be looted in the anti-Catholic demonstrations after the 1745 Rebellion. The English sculptor Joseph N., also a miser, was his son. A private collection (England) has *Music party on a terrace* (documented).   [Fl. 826, Fl. 856, Fl. 771, Fl. 769, Fl. 296.]

Nollet, Dominique. Flemish Sch. *b* Bruges 1640 (?) *d* Paris 1736. *Landscape with figures (often religious) and military pieces* (*cf.* A. F. v. d. Meulen and J. B. v. d. Meiren). In

Bruges Guild 1687; court painter to Maximilian Emmanuel, Elector of Bavaria and governor-general Spanish Netherlands (1692-1701) for whom acted as curator of art collections; followed Elector to Munich in war of Spanish Succession (when his collections went to Schleissheim forming foundation of gallery there) 1701; accompanied Electress on visit to Venice 1706; after death of Elector (1726) went Paris where remained. **Documented Examples:** BRUGES S. Jacques thirteen *Landscapes with life of S. James* (1694); S. Anne *Landscape with Visitation* (1692) (all seen (1768) by Descamps who also saw in Bruges N. D. *Elijah on the Mountain* and in the Carmelite church *S. Louis embarking for the Holy Land*).

[Fl. 215, Fl. 216, Fl. 892, Fl. 440, Fl. 113.]

Noort, Adam van. Flemish Sch. *b* son of Lambert van N., Antwerp 1562 *d* 1641. *Religious and mythological subjects, portraits.* Travelled Italy; Master Antwerp Guild 1587; in Chamber of Rhetoric (Violiere) 1619; had large art school where his pupils included P. P. Rubens (before 1594), J. Jordaens (who married his daughter 1616), F. Apshoven the elder 1592, H. v. Balen the elder and S. Vrancx; visited Holland with Jordaens 1632. **Signed Example:** ANTWERP Mus. Rubens *S. John the Baptist preaching.* **Monogrammed Example:** BRUSSELS *Suffer little children....* Descamps (1769) records a *Nativity* in Brussels, Petit Béguinage, and a *S. Francis* in Courtrai, Capuchin church. *The Five Senses* (nudes), *Orpheus* and *Life of S. Clara* are recorded by engravings; two portraits are recorded in an Antwerp inventory (1655).

[Fl. 559, Fl. 86, Fl. 215, Fl. 216, Fl. 107, Fl. 892, Fl. 213, Fl. 296.]

*****Noort, Lambert van.** Flemish Sch. *b* Amersfoort *c.* 1520 *d* Antwerp 1571. *Religious subjects and 'history'; also worked as architect and glass designer (for Gouda and other churches).* Master Antwerp Guild 1549; citizen Antwerp 1550. **Signed Examples:** ANTWERP *Nativity* 1555, *Last Supper* 1558, *Entombment* 1565. **Monogrammed Examples:** ANTWERP *The Sibyl and the Church of Christ, The Agrippine Sibyl* (with five other *Sibyls* from the Guild of S. Luke for which they were painted), *The Agony in the Garden, The Crowning with Thorns,* and *Calvary* (all 1565). BRUSSELS *Adoration of the Shepherds* 1568. HAARLEM (Teyler Mus.) and VIENNA (Albertina) have signed cartoons for windows. An Antwerp inventory of 1642 records a *Marcus Curtius* and engravings record *Busts of Roman Emperors.*   [Fl. 88, Fl. 892, Fl. 213.]

Noter, David Emil Joseph de. Flemish Sch. *b* Ghent 1825 *d* after 1880. *Still life, Algerian scenes and landscapes.* Exhibited Paris Salon 1853-80. (His son Raphael de N. painted landscapes and town views). Represented in BRESLAU, COURTRAI, PRAGUE and PHILADELPHIA (Wilstach) *Fruit and flowers.*   [Fl. 837 (1856), Fl. 66.]

Noter, Herman August de. Flemish Sch. *b* son of architect Pierre François de N., Ghent 1806 *d* Ghent 1837 or 1838. *Landscapes.* (His sisters Annette and Josephine were flower painters).   [Fl. 451, Fl. 837 (1856), Fl. 88, Fl. 892, Fl. 73.]

Noter, Jean Baptiste de. Flemish Sch. *b* son of architect, Waelhem 1787 *d* Malines 1855. *Town views and architectural pieces.* Worked Ghent and Malines. A. C. M. Engel *q.v.* was his pupil.   [Fl. 613, Fl. 451, Fl. 892.]

Noter, Pierre François de. Flemish Sch, *b* son of architect, Waelhem 1779 *d* Ghent 1843. *Landscapes, marines, town views church interiors* (*cf.* J. C. Nicolié); *also worked as sculptor and engraver.* Pupil of sculptor J. F. v. Geel. Represented in AMSTERDAM *The Ghent 'Sassentor' with skaters* 1825, *Audenarde S. Walpurgis church* 1825, *The Altarpiece of the Mystic Lamb in Ghent S. Bavon* 1829; and in COURTRAI,

GHENT, HAARLEM and LIÈGE. A *Cattle market in Ghent* in collaboration with E. Verboeckhoven 1821 is recorded. *Cf.* P. J. Hellemans. [Fl. 451, Fl. 612, Fl. 88.]

Noterman, Emmanuel. Flemish Sch. *b* son of decorative painter J. B. N., Audernarde 1808 *d* Antwerp 1863. *Anecdotic genre, portraits, animals.* Pupil in Ghent of J. B. L. Maes (Canini) and in Antwerp of P. Kremer. Represented in AMSTERDAM Sted. Mus. *Dog seller.* BROOKLYN (U.S.A.), CHALONS-SUR-MARNE, MONTREAL *Secret pleasures.* A *Preparation for the masked ball* was exhibited in 1836.
[Fl. 451, Fl. 481, Fl. 837 (1863), Fl. 88, Fl. 440.]

Noveliers, Pierre. Flemish Sch. *b* before 1579 *d* old after 1618. Master Antwerp Guild 1599. Keeper of pictures in Archduchess Isabella's palaces in Brussels and Tervueren (*cf.* D. v. Alsloot) 1605; paid for pictures painted by her instructions 'd'après l'estimation de Rubens' 1617; asked to be relieved from his offices on account of his great age and infirmities 1618. No known extant works. [Fl. 440.]

Noveliers, Salomon. Flemish Sch. *b* son of Pierre N., before 1590 *d* after 1660. Master Antwerp Guild 1614. Succeeded his father as Keeper of the pictures in Brussels and Tervueren palaces and given title of 'peintre de l'hostel de la cour' with exemption from some taxes and right to receive certain duties on wine and beer 1618; testified that Rubens had authenticated as by Van Dyck a portrait which he sold to B. Gerbier for resale to Charles I as by Van Dyck but which Van Dyck disowned 1632; was paid for a *Procession of the dowered maidens to Notre Dame du Sablon* for Château de Tervueren (*cf.* A. Sallaert) 1641. [Fl. 440.]

Nys, de, see **Denys.**

Nyts, G., see **Neyts.**

O

Obeet, see **Beet.**

*Odevaere, Joseph Dionysius (Joseph Denis). Flemish Sch. *b* son of a town councillor, Bruges 1775 or 1778 *d* Brussels 1830. *Contemporary and costume history, religious subjects, portraits.* Pupil in Bruges Acad. of J. A. van der Donckt before 1796; then in Paris of J. B. Suvée (*cf.* J. F. Ducq) about 1799 and of L. David (*cf.* F. J. Navez) by 1802; won Prix de Rome, was received by Napoleon and given festive reception by Bruges authorities (*cf.* P. M. Goddyn) 1804; in Rome whence sent successful pictures to Paris Salons (*cf.* L. Gerbo) 1805-12; returned Paris till fall of Empire; in Bruges 1814; court painter to William I of United Netherlands who sent him to Paris to recover his family pictures taken for the Louvre by the French (*cf.* P. J. v. Regemorter and B. P. Ommeganck) 1815; welcomed Louis David in Brussels 1816; opened subscription for funeral monument in Brussels to David after French authorities had refused a burial in France 1826. **Signed Examples:** AMSTERDAM Rijks. *The last defenders of Missolonghi 22 April 1826* 1826. BESANÇON *Fountains in Villa Borghese* 1809. BRUGES *Self-portrait with F. J. J. Wynckelman, president of Bruges Acad., and the director J. A. van der Donckt* 1805, *Marquis de Chauvelin* 1805, *The artist's wife Sylvie de la Rue* 1830. BRUSSELS *The Union of Utrecht 1579* 1824. **Documented Examples:** BRUGES S. Walburga *Pietà* (Salon 1812). PARIS École d. Beaux Arts *Death of Phocion* (1804 Prix de Rome picture). ROME Quirinal *Romulus receiving booty; Greeks and Trojans fighting over Patroclus' corpse* (frescoes) 1811. A *Coronation of Charlemagne* (showing the Pope bending knee to the Emperor) sent to Paris Salon from Rome 1810 was much admired by Napoleon. *The Prince of Orange wounded at Waterloo* (commissioned on appointment as court painter 1815), *Louis David refusing to paint the Duke of Wellington, Raphael introduced by Bramante to Julius II, Iphigenia in Aulis* (Salon 1812) and a *Roman girl in her bath* are also recorded.
[Fl. 451, Fl. 612, Fl. 197, Fl. 66, Fl. 440, Fl. 680.]

Oleffe, Auguste. Flemish Sch. *b* St. Josse-ten-Noode, Brussels 1867 *d* Uccle 1931. *Landscapes, indoor and outdoor genre (some of fisherfolk), portraits, still life.* At age of 14 worked in a lithographer's studio; then pupil in St. Josse-ten-Noode Art School. Was helped by collector H. van Cutsem; worked much at Nieuwpoort *c.* 1897; adopted 'Fauve' conventions in later work (*cf.* C. Dehoy); had large retrospective group of pictures in Antwerp L'Art Contemporain (*cf.* R. Strebelle) exhibition 1925. Represented in ANTWERP *Spring* 1911, *Flowers, Woman at window, Sunset.* BRUSSELS *The lighthouse keeper* 1897, *The artist's mother* 1904, *Bouquet* 1907, *August* 1909, *Rijk Wouters* 1910, *Group at Evening.* GHENT *May.* IXELLES *Jehan Frison.* TOURNAI *Girl by the sea, Heavy weather, Study of a woman.*
[Fl. 388, Fl. 296, Fl. Bib. 19th cent.]

Oliviers, Antonius, known as **'De Schilder Antonie'** (the painter **Anthony**). Flemish (Dutch) Sch. 16th cent. *b* Mons or Brussels. Famous as a fighting hero at Bergen in Hennegau and Haarlem in the war against the Spaniards *c.* 1572.
[Fl. 892.]

*Ommeganck, Balthasar Paul. Flemish Sch. *b* son of a framemaker, Antwerp 1755 *d* Antwerp 1826. *Landscapes with animals and figures, and portraits.* Pupil of H. J. Antonissen (*cf.* H. J. F. de Cort); foundation member of Antwerp Soc. of Artists 1788; during French invasion arrested as a spy for sketching but soon released; professor Antwerp Acad. under French occupation (*cf.* W. J. Herreyns) from 1796; popular in Paris during Empire where known as 'Le Racine des moutons', and patronised by Empress Josephine (*cf.* M. I. v. Brée, J. F. v. Dael and L. Gerbo); appointed by Antwerp authorities to recover works of art taken for the Louvre by the French (*cf.* P. J. Regemorter, J. D. Odevaere and W. J. Herreyns) 1815; his many pupils and imitators included his sister and brother-in-law H. A. and M. J. Myin, his daughter M. Baesten, J. C. Carpentero and J. F. Lentzen. He sometimes painted animals in pictures by other artists (*cf.* H. v. Assche and E. J. Verboeckhoven). **Signed Examples:** AMSTERDAM Rijks. *Landscape with sheep and shepherdess* ANTWERP *Mountain landscape with sheep, Woman and animals at a ford, Landscape with animals.* LYONS *The return to the farmyard.* PARIS Louvre *Landscape with cattle, goats and sheep* (1781), *Landscape with cattle and peasants* (l'an 10). ROTTERDAM Boymans and other museums.
[Fl. 838, Fl. 451, Fl. 107, Fl. 341, Fl. 296, Fl. 680.]

Ommeganck, M., see **Baesten.**

Ommeganck, M. J., see **Myin.**

Ooms, Charles. Flemish Sch. *b* Desschel nr. Antwerp 1845 *d* Cannes 1900. *Costume history, murals, portraits, genre.* Pupil in Antwerp of N. de Keyser. Travelled widely in Europe and visited Palestine and Egypt; Chevalier of the Order of Leopold. Represented in ANTWERP *Philip II, Antonio Perez, Cardinal Granvella and the Duke of Alva paying the last honours to Don John of Austria* 1875, *Egyptian Fantasia, At twilight, On the terrace* 1894, *Self-portrait, Madame Ooms* 1895; Palais de Justice *De Wet protecting Innocence.* BRUSSELS *The forbidden book.* PRAGUE *The street dealer.*
[Fl. 892, Fl. Bib. 19th cent.]

Oortelmans (Ortelmans or **Wortelmans), Damiaen.** Flemish Sch. *b* before 1530 *d* after 1570. *Decorative paintings on musical instruments* (*cf.* F. Borsse). Master Antwerp Guild 1545; Paul Brill *q.v.* was his pupil *c.* 1570. His son Adrien was also an artist.
[Fl. 559, Fl. 892, Fl. 88.]

Oost, Dominique Joseph van. Flemish Sch. *b* son of Jacob van O. the younger, Lille 1677 *d* Lille 1738. *Religious subjects for Lille churches, portraits.* **Signed Example:** LILLE *The lawyer Paton.* *The Emperor Charles VI* and *Prince Eugène* painted for Tournai Council Chamber 1720 are recorded.
[Fl. 359, Fl. 701, Fl. 88, Fl. 440.]

*Oost, Jacob (Jacques) van the elder. Flemish Sch. *b* Bruges *c.* 1601 *d* Bruges 1671. *Religious subjects for Bruges churches, portraits and genre.* Master Bruges Guild 1621; visited Italy; back in Bruges by 1629 and remained there. **Signed Examples:** BERLIN K.F. *Portrait of a man* 1638. BRUGES *Christ crowned with thorns* 1661, *S. Martin dividing his cloak.* LENINGRAD *David as victor over Goliath* 1645. LYONS *Old woman giving a letter to a young man.* **Monogrammed Examples:** LONDON N.G. *Portrait of a boy* 1650. LYONS *Old man in meditation.* **Documented Examples:** BRUGES Mus. two *Scenes from the life of S. Anthony of Padua* formerly monastery of the Recollets; Cathedral (S. Sauveur) *Pentecost* (1658, with self-portrait and portrait of Jacob van O. the younger), *Annunciation* 1658 both formerly S. Trond

Abbey (cf. Jan Janssens). Descamps (1769) records a number of pictures in Bruges churches.

[Fl. 215, Fl. 216, Fl. 871, Fl. 88, Fl. 892, Fl. 113.]

*Oost, Jacob (Jacques) van the younger. Flemish Sch. *b* son of Jacob van O. the elder, Bruges 1639 *d* Bruges 1713. *Religious subjects, portraits.* Pupil of his father in Bruges; in Paris (*cf.* C. E. Biset) *c.* 1659-61, then Italy and lived Rome for some years; returned Bruges and worked for churches; in Lille (where settled and married) *c.* 1670; returned Bruges *c.* 1710. **Signed Examples:** BRUGES Mus. *Children drawing in a studio* 1666, *Portrait of a man* 1697; Cathedral (S. Sauveur) *The Virgin giving a stole to S. Hubert* 1668. BRUSSELS *Jacques Matyn, canon of S. Donatien at Bruges* (inscribed 'Nul soir sans matin'). LILLE S. André *The Christ Child with globe and cross before God the Father*; S. Maurice *S. Francis with the Christ Child* 1687. Descamps (1769) records *The Infant Jesus on the knees of the Virgin showing Angels the instruments of the Passion* (1680) in Lille S. Étienne and other pictures in Lille and Tournai churches.

[Fl. 215, Fl. 216, Fl. 701, Fl. 892.]

Oost, Willem (Guillaume) van. Flemish Sch. *b* son of Jacob van O. the elder, Bruges 1651 *d* Bruges 1686. *Religious subjects.* Entered Bruges Dominican Priory as lay brother 1671. **Documented Example:** BRUGES *Landscape with S. Dominic and angels* (landscape by L. Achtschellinck) from Dominican church where recorded by Descamps (1769).

[Fl. 216, Fl. 892, Fl. 440.]

Oosten (or Osten), Frans van. Flemish Sch. *b* Antwerp (?) before 1620 *d* Antwerp (?) *c.* 1680 (?). *Conflagration effects* (*cf.* D. and T. van Heil, G. Mostaert and P. Schoubroeck). Brother of Izaak van O. J. B. Wans was his pupil. **Signed Example:** POMMERSFELDEN *Destruction of Sodom* (*cf.* Brussels Sodom and Gemorrah Painter). [Fl. 107, Fl. 892.]

*Oosten, Izaak van. Flemish Sch. *b* son of an art dealer, Antwerp 1613 *d* Antwerp 1661. *Landscapes with small figures and animals.* Brother of Frans van O.; Master Antwerp Guild 1652. **Signed Examples:** ORLÉANS *Wooded landscape* 1650. VIENNA Liecht. *The Garden of Eden* (a similar picture presumed by some the work of J. (Velvet) Brueghel is in Royal Coll. Windsor Castle). [Fl. 892.]

Oostsanen, C. van, see **Cornelisz.**

Opsomer, Isidore. Flemish Sch. *b* Lierre 1878. *Religious subjects, then landscapes, marines, town views and corners (many of Lierre), still life, portraits, nudes.* Pupil in Antwerp Higher Institute of A. and J. de Vriendt. In London and Holland during 1914-18 German invasion (*cf.* L. de Smet); director Antwerp Higher Institute; visited Italy and Spain; successful as portrait painter from 1926; created baron by Leopold III 1939. Represented in AMSTERDAM *The Béguinage at Lierre.* ANTWERP *Camille Huysmans* 1926, *Felix Timmermans, A. Vermeylen* 1943, *Antwerp docks, Lierre market* BRUSSELS *Jules Destrée* 1935. GHENT, NAMUR, ROTTERDAM, FLORENCE Uffizi *Self-portrait.* PARIS Mus. d'Art moderne *Still life with eggs and plant* 1928.

[Fl. 184, Fl. 164, Fl. 906, Fl. 162, Fl. 80, Fl. 916.]

Opstal, Anton van. Flemish Sch. *b* Antwerp (?) *c.* 1590 *d* after 1624. *Portraits.* Worked for Archduke Charles of Austria in Silesia 1621-4; then Brussels for the Archduchess Isabella (*cf.* D. v. Alsloot); J. Meyssens was his pupil. His portrait by Van Dyck is known from an engraving inscribed 'Bruxellensis pictor iconum'. [Fl. 425, Fl. 88.]

Opstal, Gaspar Jacob van the elder. Flemish Sch. *b* Antwerp (?) before 1620 *d* Antwerp (?) after 1661. Pupil of S. de Vos 1632-3. Master Antwerp Guild 1644. [Fl. 107, Fl. 892.]

Opstal, Gaspar (Jasper) Jacob van. Flemish Sch. *b* son of G. J. van O. the elder, Antwerp 1654 *d* Antwerp 1717. '*History', religious subjects, portraits; also classical figures in pictures by F. v. Kessel and other flower and fruit painters.* Master Antwerp Guild 1677; Dean 1698; had large atelier which produced copies after Rubens, Van Dyck and Teniers (some said to have been sold as originals); his assistants included J. de Roore *q.v.* and his pupils included C. J. de Crec. **Signed Examples:** ANTWERP *A. E. van Valckenisse* 1699: S. Charles Borromée *Holy Family with angels* 1693. DARMSTADT *Holy Family with classical buildings* 1692. **Documented Example:** ANTWERP *J. K. van Hove President of the Corporation of S. Luke and of the Rhetoricians* 1699. A copy of Rubens' *Descent from the Cross* (Antwerp Cathedral) made for Marshal Villeroi 1705 and sent to Versailles, and a *Charles III* (Austrian nominee for Spanish succession) painted for town of Antwerp 1707 are recorded. THE HAGUE (Mauritshuis) has G. Coques' *Interior of a gallery* dated 1671 into which was later painted a *Venus and Adonis s* J. van Opstal, dated 1706. Descamps (1768) saw a *Four Fathers of the Church* in S. Omer Cathedral. An Antwerp inventory (1697) records a *Flight into Egypt.*

[Fl. 878, Fl. 215, Fl. 216, Fl. 612, Fl. 481, Fl. 892, Fl. 213.]

Orizonte, see **Bloemen, J. F.**

*Orley, Bernaert van. Flemish Sch. *b* Brussels before 1495 *d* Brussels 1541. *Religious subjects, portraits; also active as designer for tapestry* (*cf.* L. Blondeel) *and glass.* Visited Italy; commissioned to paint altarpiece for Furnes S. Walburga 1515; appointed Court painter to Margaret of Austria, Regent of the Netherlands (*cf.* J. Schooff) 1518; gave banquet in Brussels in honour of Dürer (who drew his portrait) 1520; was paid for various works and for 'certain agreeable services' which the Regent 'does not wish to be mentioned' 1521; with his family, other artists and tapestry workers including H. Tons *q.v.* accused by the Inquisition of hearing Protestant sermons in the houses of the painters Valentyn and Everaert van O. (*cf.* J. Jordaens); was acquitted but others were fined or ordered as penance to attend as many Catholic sermons in S. Gudule as they had heard Protestant sermons (*cf.* A. van Overbeke) 1527; valued religious pictures bequeathed by the Regent to Bourg-en-Bresse, Église de Brou, which were then bought in by her successor Mary of Hungary; appointed Court painter to Mary of Hungary (*cf.* J. C. Vermeyen) 1532; designed windows for Brussels S. Gudule 1537; buried in S. Géry; had nine children; several of his sons were painters; some of his descendants were Protestants. M. Coxie the elder and P. Coecke van Aelst the elder were among his pupils. **Signed Examples:** BRUSSELS *Dr. Georg de Zelle* 1519. Triptych: *The Virtue of Patience: The banquet of Job's children, Job's flocks stolen, Job's friends asking him to intercede for them with God, Lazarus at the rich man's door, Death of the rich man: the rich man in hell* 1521. MADRID Prado *Virgin and Child with S. Joseph and angels* 1522. PARIS Louvre *Holy Family* 1521. VIENNA K. *Scenes from the lives of SS. Thomas and Matthew.* **Documented Examples:** ANTWERP Mus. (in Notre Dame in 18th cent.) Triptych: *Last Judgement* with portraits of Luther (?) and Melancthon (?) presumed added *c.* 1550 (*cf.* J. v. d. Perre), *Works of Mercy, Saints,* commissioned by Antwerp Almoners 1518-19 and finished 1525, recorded by Van Mander (1604) who says O. gilded the ground before painting on it; Sir J. Reynolds (1781) wrote of this: 'It has no excellence of any kind to make amends for its extreme hardness of manner. I suspect it by one of his descendants'. BRUGES Notre Dame. Triptych *Crucifixion, Carrying of the Cross and Crowning with Thorns, Lamentation and Resurrection* commissioned by Margaret of Austria for Bourg-en-Bresse, Église de Brou, left unfinished and completed by M. Geeraerts the elder *q.v.* 1561; restored (after Iconoclast destructions) by F. Pourbus the younger 1589. A *Nativity* was placed at his death above his tomb in

Brussels S. Géry; payments for portraits of Margaret of Austria, of Prince Charles (Charles V), his brother and sister, Christian of Denmark and Mary of Hungary are recorded in documents. Paris Louvre has tapestries *Belles chasses de Maximilien* documented from his designs. Paintings presumed by some his work are in various museums (*cf.* Brussels Haneton Lamentation Painter).
[Fl. 559, Fl. 287, Fl. 702, Fl. 179, Fl. 864, Fl. 892, Fl. 316, Fl. 530, Fl. 296.]

Orley, Hieronymus (Jérôme) van. Flemish Sch. *b c.* 1595. Franciscan monk; recorded in Malines 1612.   [Fl. 613.]

Orley, Jean van. Flemish Sch. *b* son of Peter van O., Brussels 1665 *d* Brussels 1735. *Religious and allegorical subjects, 'history', portraits; also worked as tapestry designer and engraver.* Much employed by Brussels town authorities, and by churches and Guild Houses reconstructed after Marshal Villeroi's bombardment during Louis XIV's 1695 campaign (*cf.* Z. J. v. Helmont). **Documented Examples** (seen by Descamps 1768): ASCH Parish Church *Resurrection.* BRUGES S. Sauveur *Eight scenes from the life of Christ* (commissioned by Bishop van Susteren, who also had tapestries made after them). BRUSSELS Town Hall *Christ on the Cross* 1712, *Charles II on horseback* 1698, *Members of the Clothmakers' Guild* 1699, *Allegory with Genii and arms of Brussels, Antwerp and Louvain* (ceiling); S. Nicolas *Liberation of S. Peter.* DILIGHEM Abbey *Adoration of the Magi.* Liège Mus. has cartoons for *Telemachus* tapestries extant in Liège Pal-de Justice (*cf.* R. van O.).
[Fl. 878, Fl. 576, Fl. 216, Fl. 451, Fl. 88, Fl. 892, Fl. 119.]

Orley, Peter van. Flemish Sch. *b* Brussels 1638 *d* after 1708. *Landscapes.* Dean of Brussels Guild 1678 and 1688; worked also as tax-collector. **Signed Examples:** BÂLE two *Arcadian landscapes* 1702 (miniatures on parchment).
[Fl. 88, Fl. 892.]

Orley, Richard van. Flemish Sch. *b* son of Peter van O., Brussels 1652 or 1663 *d* Brussels 1732. *Religious subjects, 'history' and miniatures; also worked as engraver and (with his brother Jan van O.) as tapestry designer;* took over his father's post as tax collector. **Signed Example:** LONDON V. and A. *Pandora opening the box* 1692 (miniature in gouache). **Documented Example:** ANTWERP *The return to Rome of Pope Innocent II, 1133* (formerly Tongerloo Abbey). Signed gouaches, including two *Telemachus* subjects (*cf.* Jan van O.), are recorded. His engraved work included plates from drawings of Brussels ruins after Marshal Villeroi's bombardment (1695) by A. Coppens *q.v.*
[Fl. 878, Fl. 215, Fl. 88, Fl. 892, Fl. 857 (1916).]

Orley, Valentin van, see **B. van O.**

Ort (or Hort), Aert or Arnold van. Flemish Sch. *b* before 1500 *d* after 1538. *Glasspaintings.* Mentioned by Dürer in his Tagebuch.   [Fl. 243, Fl. 371.]

Os, Tony van. Flemish Sch. *b* Antwerp 1886 *d* Temsche (East Flanders) 1945. *Genre figures, landscapes, marines and some religious subjects.* Pupil in Antwerp of F. Courtens. Represented in ANTWERP *Old farmer.*   [Fl. 17.]

*Ottawa Judith Painter. Presumed Flemish Sch. 16th cent. Name for painter of OTTAWA N.G. of Canada (3695) *Judith with the head of Holofernes.* Presumed by some identical with J. van Scorel, by others with A. Benson and others with J. Massys (*cf.* M. Willems and Grenoble Judith Painter).   [Fl. 630.]

Ottevaere, Henri. Flemish Sch. *b* Brussels 1870. *Murals, poster designs and genre.* Pupil of J. Portaels. Represented in

BRUSSELS (nr.) S. Gilles Townhall, DRESDEN *Hymn to the setting sun.*   [Fl. 465.]

Oudenaerde, R. van, see **Audenaerd.**

Ouderaa, Pierre Jean van der. Flemish Sch. *b* Antwerp 1841 *d* Antwerp 1915. *Costume history, religious subjects in realistic Oriental settings, murals, landscapes, portraits.* Pupil of N. de Keyser. In Italy 1869; Professor in Antwerp Acad. from 1885; visited Palestine. Represented in ANTWERP *Legal episode in the olden days* 1879, *The return of the Holy Women, The painter David Col* 1897; Palais de Justice (murals). BRUSSELS *The Refuge (Episode of the Spanish Fury).*
[Fl. Bib. 19th cent.]

*Oultremont Master. Presumed Flemish (Dutch) Sch. 15th-16th cent. Name for painter of BRUSSELS Mus. (537) Triptych *Descent from the Cross* (centre), *The Crowning with Thorns* and *Ecce Homo* (wings), *Road to Calvary with S. Veronica, Road to Calvary with donor Count Albert of Adrichem and SS. Bavon and Catherine* (exterior of wings) acquired from the heirs of Count Florent d'Oultremont de Warfusée 1899 (and sometimes known as the Adrichem Triptych). Presumed by some identical with J. Mostaert *q.v.*

Oury, Jean Libert. Flemish Sch. *b* Liège 1833 *d* Dresden 1908. *Genre, portraits.* Pupil in Liège Acad. Visited Italy; settled Dresden 1876. Represented in DRESDEN *The Nun* and LIÈGE.   [Fl. Bib. 19th cent.]

Ouwater, Albert van. Flemish (Dutch) Sch. 15th cent. *b* Oudewater (near Haarlem) (?). Date and place of death unknown. *Religious subjects (some with figures in landscape).* His daughter (age unknown) was buried in Haarlem S. Bavon 1467. Van Mander (1604) records (1) that Geertgen tot Sint Jans was his pupil in Haarlem; (2) that an altarpiece by O. was in the Haarlem Groote Kerk on the Roman altar so-called because it was donated by pilgrims returned from Rome; the interior showed standing figures of *SS. Peter* and *Paul* below 'an interesting landscape in which many pilgrims were painted, some walking, others resting, eating or drinking; Albert painted the faces well; also the hands, feet, draperies and landscape'; (3) that he himself had seen a grisaille copy of a large, upright painting 'done by Albert' of *The Raising of Lazarus* showing in a temple with small columns, the figure of Lazarus nude, with apostles on one side and Christ on the other, and 'pleasing female figures' and in the background some people looking through a colonnade of the choir'; (4) that the original of this *Raising of Lazarus* was stolen from Haarlem and taken to Spain after the siege of Haarlem (1573); (5) that M. van Heemskerck (*q.v.*) never tired of looking at this painting and said to the owner who was his pupil 'son, what did these fellows *eat*?' (to acquire such skill). **Signed Examples:** None. **Documented Examples:** None. BERLIN K.F. (532A) *The Raising of Lazarus* is presumed by some the original of which Van Mander saw the grisaille copy (this picture was acquired 1889 in Italy and was said to have been given by Philip II to the Balbi family from whom it was inherited by the vendor; it is said to have the letters MIRIN on one of the mantles) (*cf.* G. v. d. Meire).   [Fl. 559, Fl. 892, Fl. 316, Fl. 77.]

Overbeke, Adriaen van. Flemish Sch. *b* before 1488 *d* after 1529. *Religious subjects and decorative work.* Presumed by some the 'Adriaen' apprenticed to Q. Massys 1495; Master Antwerp Guild 1508; was found guilty of listening to Protestant sermons and of publicly reading and expounding the Bible and sentenced to leave the town before nightfall and go on pilgrimage to Wilsenaken on pain of having his right hand cut off (*cf.* B. van Orley, Simon Pereyns, H. Tons, J. v.

Coninxloo the younger, Jan Massys) 1521. An altarpiece painted or procured for Lille Hôpital Comtesse 1510, and one painted for Kempen (nr. Crefeld) church 1529, and a commission to polychrome the sculptured altarpiece (extant) in Kempen church 1513 are recorded. [Fl. 892.]

Overlaet, Anton. Flemish Sch. *b* Antwerp 1720 *d* Antwerp 1774. *Pen drawings (mostly copies of engravings); also active as engraver.* **Signed Examples:** ANTWERP Hospital of S. Julian (1760), VIENNA Albertina *Diana and hounds* 1750. [Fl. 451, Fl. 88, Fl. 892.]

Overstraeten, War van. Flemish Sch. *b* Wetteren 1891. *Landscapes, interiors, genre figures and compositions.* Some works record travels in Spain and Southern France. Represented in ANTWERP. [Fl. 17, Fl. 296.]

P

Paelinck, Joseph. Flemish Sch. *b* Oostacker (near Ghent) 1781 *d* Brussels 1839. *Religious subjects, 'history', portraits.* Pupil in Paris of L. David (*cf.* F. J. Navez); Professor Ghent Acad. *c.* 1809; in Italy where worked for Napoleon in the Quirinal 1810-*c.* 1812; court painter to Queen of the Netherlands 1815; welcomed David to Brussels 1816; Professor Brussels Acad.; C. Picqué, E. Biefve *q.v.* and J. Geinaert were his pupils. Represented in AMSTERDAM *Psyche in Love's Palace* 1823. GHENT *Juno; Anthea on the way to Ephesus;* S. Michel *Finding of the True Cross by Empress Helena* 1811. MALINES S. Catherine *Flight into Egypt.* A *Judgement of Paris, The Empress Josephine, William I of the Netherlands, Queen Wilhelmina,* a *S. Colette obtaining permission to found a convent in Ghent,* and a *Battle of Waterloo* are recorded.
[Fl. 451, Fl. 612, Fl. 126, Fl. 892, Fl. 296, Fl. Bib. 19th cent.]

*Paepe (or **Pape**), **Josse (Joos) de.** Flemish Sch. *b* son of architect and goldsmith Simon de Pape, Audenarde before 1615 *d* Rome 1646. *Mythologies and drawings for engravings.* Went Italy and remained there (*cf.* W. Backereel and J. Sutterman); in Rome by 1634; in Rome Guild of S. Luke 1641. **Signed Example:** AMSTERDAM Rijks. *Venus and Adonis* 1629 (Amsterdam Cat. 1927 writes: 'Venus draped in a light red robe, is seated before a highly coloured landscape against a brown rock; Adonis, holding his arms round her waist, is filled with a secret longing to go hunting with his dogs'.).
[Fl. 84, Fl. 417, Fl. 715 (1926), Fl. 8.]

Paepe (or **Pape**), **Martin de.** Flemish Sch. *b* Malines before 1620 *d* Malines (?) before 1687. *Still life with fruit* (*cf.* T. Aenvanck).
[Fl. 613, Fl. 892.]

Paerels, Willem. Flemish Sch *b* Delft 1878. *Landscapes, marines and port scenes, figure and still life compositions (in Post-Impressionist and Fauve conventions cf.* C. Dehoy). Began as professional skater and then studied painting; worked in Paris and later in Brussels; member of Vie et Lumière group (*cf.* G. Morren) 1914 and of L'Art Contemporain (Kunst van Heden) (*cf.* R. Strebelle). Represented in ANTWERP *Woman in blue* 1921, *Boats in harbour, View of Brussels* AMSTERDAM, BRUSSELS.
[Fl. 388, Fl. 296, Fl. Bib. 20th cent.]

Palerme (or **Palermo**), **Antonio van.** Flemish Sch. *b* Malines 1503 or 1513 *d* Antwerp before 1589. *Decorative paintings, maps, but chiefly active as dealer.* In Malines till 1544; citizen of Antwerp and Master Antwerp Guild by 1547; worked on Pageant Entry into Antwerp of Charles V and Philip II 1549 (*cf.* P. Coecke van Aelst, H. de Cock and F. Floris); published a map of Antwerp 1565; Dean Antwerp Guild 1571; had Jacques de Backer *q.v.* as apprentice pupil in his house and exploited him; G. Congnet *q.v.* and P. Goetkint *q.v.* were also his pupils. His daughter Catharine married P. Goetkint and his daughter Lucretia married the father of V. Wolfvoet *q.v.* C. v. d. Queborne was his friend.
[Fl. 559, Fl. 613, Fl. 892, Fl. 214.]

Paludanus, see **Broeck, C. v. d.**

Panhay de Rendeux, see **Rendeux.**

*Panneels, Willem (Guillaume). Flemish Sch. *b* Antwerp 1600 *d* after 1640. *Mythologies; but chiefly active as engraver (sometimes after Rubens).* Pupil of Rubens 1623-8; Master Antwerp Guild 1628; was in charge of Rubens' house during the latter's absence in Spain and England, and Rubens testified (1630) to that effect; worked Cologne, Frankfort, Baden and Strasbourg 1630-2. **Signed Example:** NANTES *Diana and her nymphs* (signed P..els 1640).
[Fl. 612, Fl. 892, Fl. 204.]

Pannemaker, see **Pennemaecker.**

Pantazis, Péricles. Flemish Sch. *b* Athens 1849 *d* Brussels 1884. *Genre figures, landscapes, marines and coast scenes, still life and interiors.* Pupil in Paris of French painters G. Courbet and A. Chintreuil; then settled Brussels; worked there in Patte de Dindon Free Academy (*cf.* F. Courtens and H. Stacquet); member of Brussels group Les XX (*cf.* J. Ensor) but died a few days before opening of first exhibition. Represented in ANTWERP *Sulking, Man with a cap, Reconciliation, The rock, Man's head, Coast scene.* BRUSSELS *Child with a cock, Self portrait, Still life, Blankenberghe plage.*
[Fl. 388, Fl. 296, Fl. 17, Fl. 123.]

Paolo Fiammingo, see **Franck, P.**

Pape, Ferdinand C. F. J. de. Flemish Sch. *b* son of a goldsmith, Bruges 1810 *d* 1885. *Miniatures; also worked as illustrator.* Collaborated with his brother François (*b* Bruges 1814 *d* 1863). His son Charles de P., a miniature painter died in England 1915.
[Fl. 88.]

Pape, Gillis. Flemish Sch. *b* son of Simon de Pape, Audenarde (?) before 1677 *d* 1705. *Tapestry designs.* Worked at Audenarde.
[Fl. 892.]

Pape, J. de, see **Paepe.**

Pape (or **Paepe**), **Simon de.** Flemish Sch. *b* son of architect and goldsmith Simon de P., Audenarde 1623 *d* Audenarde 1677. *Religious subjects for Audenarde churches; also worked as tapestry designer and architect.* Pictures titled *The ransoming of Christian slaves* 1669 and *The finding of the True Cross by S. Helena* are recorded.
[Fl. 88, Fl. 798.]

Papeleu, Victor Eugène de. Flemish Sch. *b* Ghent 1810 *d* Ghent 1881. *Landscapes, marines.* Settled Paris where pupil of French painter J. Dupré and regular exhibitor in Salon; worked in France, Italy (Rome) and Holland; also visited the Orient. Represented in GHENT, LIMOGES, MARSEILLES, MONTAUBAN, NEUCHATEL.
[Fl. 66, Fl. 837 (1881), Fl. 126, Fl. 88.]

Parcelles, see **Porcellis.**

Parent, Roger. Flemish Sch. *b* Paris 1881. *Figure compositions, interiors, and still life in Fauve conventions* (*cf.* C. Dehoy). Settled Brussels. Represented BRUSSELS.
[Fl. 123, Fl. 388.]

*Paris Expulsion of Traders Painter. Presumed Flemish Sch. 17th cent. Name for painter of PARIS Louvre (2011) *Christ driving the traders from the Temple.* Presumed by some identical with J. Jordaens *q.v.*

*Paris Granvella's Dwarf Painter. Presumed Flemish Sch. 16th cent. Name for painter of PARIS Louvre (2470) *Cardinal Granvella's dwarf with dog.* Presumed by some identical with A. Mor *q.v.*

Parmentier, Georges. Flemish Sch. *b* Ostend 1870. *Landscapes.* Pupil of A. Verwée. [Fl. 892.]

Parrhasius, see **Schoonjans.**

Pasture, de le or **de la.** French form of van der Weyden *q.v.*

Patenir, Henri or **Herri de.** Flemish Sch. 16th cent. In Antwerp Guild 1535. Presumed by some a son or nephew of J. Patinir *q.v.*; presumed by some identical with H. met de Bles *q.v.* [Fl. 892, Fl. 316.]

*****Patinir** (or **Patinier** or **Patenier**), **Joachim.** Flemish Sch. *b* Dinant (or Bouvines) before 1500 *d* Antwerp 1524. *Landscapes with figures (cf.* H. Bosch, J. Swart van Groningen and F. Mostaert); *also landscapes in figure pictures by contemporaries.* Master Antwerp Guild 1515; visited by Dürer who drew his portrait, gave him a picture by the German painter H. Baldung Grien, and called him a 'good landscape painter' 1521; friend of Q. Massys *q.v.* who was a guardian to his children. Don Felipe de Guevara (in 'Comentarios de la Pintura' before 1560) names him and 'Johannes' (van Eyck) and 'Rugier' (van der Weyden) as the greatest painters of the Netherlands; Van Mander (whose account some presume to be partly a confusion with Herri de Patenir (*q.v.*)) records that his drunken habits were a strain on the loyalty of his pupil (sic) F. Mostaert (*cf.* J. van Scorel), that he painted a fine landscape in a picture by Sotte Cleve (*q.v.*) and that Hans Keynooghe (*q.v.*) painted in his manner; Van Mander adds: 'Hij had tot gewoonte in zyn landschappen ergens een mannetje te schilderen, dat zijn gevoeg deed'. **Signed Examples** (*s* 'Joachim D. Patinir or Patinier) ANTWERP *Landscape with Flight into Egypt.* CARLSRUHE *S. Jerome.* MADRID Prado *Temptation of S. Anthony* (figures documented 1574 as 'de mano maestre Coryntin' i.e. Quinten Massys), *Landscape with S. Jerome and the Lion.* VIENNA Kunsthist. *Baptism of Christ.* Van Mander records a *Battle scene* 'with little figures so well done that no illuminator could surpass it'; Sigüenza (1605) records a *Miracle of the Loaves and Fishes* (*cf.* Melbourne Miracles Painter). A *Lot and his daughters* owned by Dürer is also recorded. Cardinal Grimani owned (1521) a *Tower of Babel* (*cf.* M. van Valckenborch). Pictures presumed by some his work are in various museums. [Fl. 243, Fl. 12. Fl. 371, Fl. 370, Fl. 559, Fl. 767, Fl. 612, Fl. 892, Fl. 316, Fl. 530.]

Paul (surname unknown). Flemish (or Dutch) Sch. 17th cent. *Marines and moonlight effects (maneschyne).* Houbraken (1718) records him as a member of Flemish colony in Rome where he was given the nickname 'Wellust'. [Fl. 425.]

Paul, Bernard. Flemish Sch. *b* Ghent 1737 *d* Ghent 1820. *Religious subjects, 'history', social genre, portraits (including conversation pieces); also crayon portraits.* Recorded in The Hague 1763; in London where exhibited crayon portraits in Soc. of Artists 1766 and 1767 (*cf.* P. J. Tassaert and Louis P.); resettled Ghent by 1771. **Documented Example:** GHENT *Self portrait.* A *Venus and Adonis* and *Judith and Holophernes* are among subjects exhibited 1796 in Ghent. [Fl. 481, Fl. 362, Fl. 440, Fl. 88.]

Paul, Louis. Flemish Sch. *b* Ghent 1733 *d* Ghent 1817. *'History', mythologies, landscapes, portraits; also copies of pictures by 17th cent. Flemish painters.* In London with his brother Bernard P. *q.v.* 1766; exhibited portraits in London Soc. of Artists 1766 and 1767. An *Oedipus* and a *Venus crowned with flowers* were exhibited 1810 in Ghent. [Fl. 362, Fl. 440.]

Pauli, Charles F. H. Flemish Sch. *b* Ghent 1819 *d* Tübingen 1880. *Landscapes.* Represented in BRUSSELS and GHENT. [Fl. 88.]

Paulus, Pierre. Flemish Sch. *b* son of an ornamental sculptor, Châtelet (Hennegouw) 1881. *Landscapes (including snow-scenes, river scenes and night pieces), mining subjects (cf.* C. Meunier), *blast furnaces and iron foundries; genre, still life and portraits; worked also in pastel and as lithographer.* Pupil of C. Montald in Brussels Acad.; in London during 1914-18 German invasion (*cf.* A. Cluysenaer and L. de Smet); worked Brittany and Provence, Italy and Spain; member of the Nervia group (*cf.* A. Carte, L. Devos, R. Strebelle) 1929; professor in Antwerp Higher Institute. Represented in ANTWERP *Mine accident, Mother and child, Charleroi by night.* BRUSSELS *The mining village, Returning from work.* BRUSSELS Belgian Royal Collection *The Strike.* BUENOS AIRES *Mother and child,* BUFFALO, CARDIFF, GHENT, LIÈGE, MONS, NAMUR, TORONTO; also in CHARLEROI Town Hall *Youth* and Palais du Peuple. A film titled 'Le peintre du Pays Noir: Pierre Paulus' is recorded. [Fl. 626 (1915), Fl. 651, Fl. 328, Fl. 123, Fl. 70, Fl. 201, Fl. 561, Fl. 79, Fl. 672, Fl. 195, Fl. 82, Fl. 209, Fl. 296, Fl. 649.]

Pauly, Nicolas. Flemish Sch. *b* Antwerp *c.* 1660 *d* Brussels 1748. *Miniatures.* [Fl. 878.]

Pauw, René de. Flemish Sch. *b* Bruges 1887. *Coast scenes, compositions with fisher folk and other genre subjects.* Represented in BRUGES Railway station *Murals.* [Fl. 568.]

Pauwels, Ferdinand (Willem Ferdinand). Flemish Sch. *b* Eekeren, nr. Antwerp 1830 *d* Dresden 1904. *Costume history (including murals).* Pupil of G. Wappers and N. de Keyser; won Rome prize and studied Italy 1852-6; teacher in Weimar Academy 1862-72; and Dresden Academy from 1876. Represented in BRUSSELS, DRESDEN, EISENACH Wartburg *Scenes from the life of Luther,* MUNICH (Maximilianeum). His murals commissioned for Ypres Cloth Hall were destroyed by the Germans in their 1914-18 invasion (*cf.* L. Delbeke, G. Guffens and J. Swerts). [Fl. 160 (1904), Fl. Bib. 19th cent.]

Pauwels, Jean Baptiste (known as Pauwels van de Borre). Flemish Sch. *b* Brussels 1754 *d* Brussels 1832. *Religious subjects.* Pupil in Antwerp Acad. 1773-5; worked in Brussels under A. C. Lens *c.* 1781; visited Rome. Pictures painted for churches in Brussels (Saint Josse-ten-Noode) and Everberg (near Louvain) and a *Christ* for Pope Pius VI are recorded. [Fl. 440, Fl. 88.]

Pauwels, Joseph. Flemish Sch. *b* Sleydinge 1818 *d* Ghent 1876. *Religious subjects, portraits, genre.* Pupil of P. v. Hanselaere *q.v.* and G. Wappers. Represented in GHENT. Religious subjects for churches in Sleydinge, Waarschot and Wetteren are recorded. [Fl. 837 (1876), Fl. 88.]

Payen, Antoine A. J. Flemish Sch. *b* Tournai 1785 *d* Brussels 1853. *Landscapes.* Pupil of H. v. Assche *q.v.* Sent by Government to draw Batavian flora and landscapes 1815; in Java making drawings and studies 1815-27; after return Brussels (Etterbeek) painted oil pictures from his Javanese studies. A picture titled 'Vue du volcan de Gounong-Gountow à Java, avec divers végétaux de ces localités, tels que cocotiers, kamiri . . .' exhibited 1827 was acquired by the Government. [Fl. 612, Fl. 88, Fl. 440.]

*****Pearl of Brabant Master.** Presumed Flemish (Dutch) Sch. 15th cent. Name for painter of MUNICH Alt. Pin. (76-8) Triptych: centre: *Adoration of the Magi,* wings: *S. John the Baptist, S. Christopher,* exterior wings: *S. Catherine, S. Barbara* (grisailles); known as 'Pearl of Brabant Altar'. Presumed by some identical with D. Bouts the elder *q.v.* and by others with D. Bouts the younger *q.v.* [Fl. 316, Fl. 757.]

Pee, Emanuel van. Flemish Sch. 17th cent. *b* son or grandson of secretary to Margaret of Parma *d* Amsterdam where active as dealer, after 1656. Houbraken (1718) records him as compelled to give up painting because of his short sight (but able nevertheless to read the smallest handwriting in the dark, as he often proved in company). [Fl. 425, Fl. 892.]

Pee, Engelhart van. Flemish Sch. *b* Brussels before 1550 *d* Munich 1605. *Portraits.* Worked in Landshut 1570-77; then court painter in Munich to Duke William V (*cf.* J. Hoefnagel, F. di L. Sustris, P. de Witte); had difficulties with Munich Painters' Guild. Portraits of *The Elector Maximilian* 1600, *Duchess Magdalena* (*cf.* Munich Duchess Magdalena Painter) 1601 and the *Cardinal de Lorraine* 1604 are recorded. Portraits presumed by some his work are in the Bavarian State collections. [Fl. 612, Fl. 440, Fl. 798.]

Pee, Jan van. Flemish Sch. *b* son of Emanuel van P. *q.v.*, Amsterdam before 1640 *d* Antwerp 1710. *Genre.* Worked first as copyist for his father's business and for the dealer G. van Uylenburg (*cf.* G. de Lairesse) in Leyden where married 1657; played trick on his wife (recorded by Houbraken (1718)) to escape to Antwerp; copied pictures there by Rubens and Van Dyck that deceived the experts (*cf.* Jan Peeters the younger); fetched his wife and settled Antwerp before 1680. J. J. Horemans the elder was his pupil. **Monogrammed Example:** ANTWERP *Old woman baking cakes with her family round her.* A *Peasant with glass and pipe* is recorded by an engraving. [Fl. 425, Fl. 107, Fl. 440, Fl. 892.]

*****Peeters, Bonaventura.** Flemish Sch. *b* Antwerp 1614 *d* Hoboken 1652. *Marines with calm and stormy seas, and port scenes* (*cf.* G. v. Eyck, M. Plattenberg and J. Porcellis), *naval warfare* (*cf.* A. v. Ertvelt); also active as engraver and poet. Master Antwerp Guild 1634; with his brother Jan *q.v.* and his sister Catharina *q.v.* left Antwerp to escape enmity of Jesuits, whom he had satirized, and settled Hoboken (*cf.* A. Matthys); his pictures were much collected by the Antwerp bourgeoisie in the 17th cent. and also exported to Vienna and Seville (*cf.* M. Pepyn). Houbraken (1718) writes of his work 'Hy schilderde Zeestormen, en Schepen door velerhande droevige Zeerampen in nood van vergaan . . . en hoe de Schepen in die branding vervallen'; It is not known whether he sailed to foreign ports or used drawings or prints by others for the local features. **Signed Examples:** BRUNSWICK *River banks* 1636. BRUSSELS *Oriental port* 1651 (?). BUDAPEST *Arrival of a ship* 1637. DARMSTADT *View of Dordrecht* 1641 (?). DRESDEN *Oriental seashore with battle ships* ('Hoboken') 1652. SCHLEISSHEIM *Marines* (two). **Monogrammed Examples:** AMSTERDAM Rijks. *The Scheldt with shipping round a pier* AUGSBURG, BERLIN *War ships in a rough sea* 1636. BRUSSELS *Stormy sea and shipwreck.* CAMBRIDGE Fitz. *Beach scene with ship and fishing boat, River scene.* DRESDEN, GREENWICH Maritime Mus. *The 'Hercules' and the 'Eenhorn' in the port of Hoorn with heavy seas beyond* 1634. HARTFORD (U.S.A.) Wadsworth Atheneum *Dutch man of war off a West Indian coast* 1648 (the Forchoudt family of Antwerp dealers owned 1698 a picture by B. P. described as 'De Hollanders de eerste reys in Oost Indien comen en van de Indiaenen wel onthaelt worden' which they exported for sale to Vienna). LENINGRAD, SCHWERIN, STOCKHOLM *Oriental port.* VIENNA Kunsthist. *Turks storming a fortress* 1641 or 1645, *Mediterranean port scene with wounded Turks;* Liecht.; Academy. **Documented Example:** ANTWERP *Battle of Calloo 1638* (*cf.* Gillis P., J. Brueghel the younger, and P. P. Rubens) 1639. [Fl. 86, Fl. 425, Fl. 481, Fl. 892, Fl. 212, Fl. 213.]

Peeters, Bonaventura the younger. Flemish Sch. *b* son of Gillis P., Antwerp 1645 or 1648 *d* Antwerp 1702. *Wooded landscapes* (*cf.* J. d'Arthois), *marines and port scenes* (*cf.* G. v. Eyck and Bonaventura P.). **Signed Example:** ANTWERP

Wooded landscape with lake and fishing boats, man and dog 1684. [Fl. 107, Fl. 892, Fl. 88, Fl. 16.]

Peeters, Catharina. Flemish Sch. *b* Antwerp 1615 *d* Antwerp after 1676. *Marines.* Went Hoboken with her brothers Bonaventura P. *q.v.* and Jan P. the elder; returned Antwerp 1654. De Bie (1661) confused her with Clara P. *q.v.* **Signed Example:** VIENNA Liecht. *Sea battle* 1657.
[Fl. 86, Fl. 107. Fl. 892, Fl. 440.]

*****Peeters** (or **Pieters**), **Clara.** Flemish Sch. *b* Antwerp *c.* 1589 *d* place and date unknown. *Still life with food, fish, fruit, flowers and vessels* (*cf.* A. Adriaenssen, O. Beet, J. v. Es, H. Francken, Grenoble Artichoke Painter, Grenoble Strawberry Painter, J. v. Hulsdonck). Recorded in Amsterdam 1612 and The Hague 1617. **Signed Examples:** AMSTERDAM Rijks. *Still life with fish and shells.* ANTWERP *Still life with fish, lobsters and oysters.* MADRID Prado *Still life with fish and artichoke* 1611, *Still life with flowers, dried fruit and cakes* 1611, *Still life with dead birds and vessels* 1611, *Still life with chickens, cake, fruit and vessels.* OXFORD Ashmolean *Still life with vase of flowers, fruit, vessels, coins and shrimps.*
[Fl. 892, Fl. 859, Fl. 583.]

Peeters, Gillis. Flemish Sch. *b* elder brother of Bonaventura P. *q.v.* Antwerp 1612 *d* Antwerp 1653. *Landscapes, port scenes, contemporary warfare* (*cf.* P. Meulener and P. Snayers). Master in Antwerp Guild 1634. **Signed Examples:** AMSTERDAM Rijks. *Rocky landscape with watermill* 1633. DÜSSELDORF Acad. (also signed by Bonaventura P.). LENINGRAD *Landscape.* **Documented Example:** ANTWERP *Battle of Calloo* 1638 (together with Bonaventura P. commissioned 1639 for Hôtel de Ville where seen by Descamps 1768). A *Sea port* was recorded in an Antwerp collection 1676. A *Landscape with cottages, man and cows* in Dresden signed 'Peeters' is presumed by some his work.
[Fl. 216, Fl. 107, Fl. 892.]

Peeters (or **Peeter**), **Jacob.** Flemish Sch. *b* Antwerp (?) before 1660 *d* after 1721. *Church interiors* (*cf.* H. v. Steenwyck the younger, W. v. Ehrenberg and J. Saey). In Antwerp Guild 1672 or 1675, Master 1689. J. v. d. Straeten *q.v.* was his pupil. **Signed Examples:** ARRAS *Interior of the Jesuit church at Antwerp* (before 1718 when church was burnt down *cf.* A. G. Ghering). COPENHAGEN *Interior of a church in the Jesuit style* 1714. A *Church interior* dated 1721 is also recorded. [Fl. 481, Fl. 892.]

*****Peeters, Jan.** Flemish Sch. *b* Antwerp 1624 *d* Antwerp *c.* 1677. *Marines and naval battles* (*cf.* G. v. Eyck), *landscapes; town views; drawings for engravers;* also active as dealer. Pupil of his elder brothers Gillis P. and Bonaventura P.; Master Antwerp Guild 1645; went with Bonaventura P. *q.v.* and Catharina P. *q.v.* to Hoboken; returned Antwerp 1654; married 1655; in Holland 1669-70. A. Goubau and E. Quellinus were witnesses at his wedding; F. Denys was godfather to his son J. F. P. *q.v.*; his daughter Isabella was also a painter. Houbraken (1718) describes his work in terms similar to those applied to Bonaventura P. **Signed Examples:** DARMSTADT *Whale hunt.* HOBOKEN Church *S. Paul shipwrecked off Malta* (memorial to his brother Bonaventura P. the elder (*cf.* A. Matthys). **Monogrammed Examples:** BUDAPEST *Shipwreck.* CASSEL *Sea battle* 1667. THE HAGUE Mauritshuis *Ship entering rocky narrows in a storm* (in *Interior of a gallery* by G. Coques *q.v.*) SCHWERIN, STOCKHOLM, VIENNA Kunsthist. *Stormy sea and shipwreck, Rocky harbour with shipping.* **Documented Examples:** VIENNA Kunsthist. *Harbour with ship at anchor and crew lighting a fire on shore, Shipping in harbour in a storm* (both in Archduke Leopold Wilhelm inventory 1659). A *Constantinople* was recorded in an Antwerp collection 1686; drawings of Dutch towns and fortresses and Mediterranean and Near Eastern ports and cities are recorded by contemporary engravings; Descamps saw (1768) four marines 'foibles en tout' in Antwerp Jacobins church.

[Fl. 86, Fl. 425, Fl. 878, Fl. 215, Fl. 216, Fl. 612, Fl. 892.]

Peeters (or **Pieters**), **Jan the younger** (known as 'Dr. Peeters'). Flemish Sch. b Antwerp c. 1667 d London and buried in S. Martin's Westminster 1727. 'History'; but chiefly draperies, etc. for portrait painters; also active as restorer. Pupil in Antwerp of P. Ijkens; came England (cf. W. de Keyser, S. Dubois, J. B. Medina, P. v. Angellis, P. Casteels III, J. F. v. Bredael, W. de Ryck) c. 1685. Vertue, who knew him from before 1709, and had taken drawing lessons from him in his youth and had other help from him, records him (1727) as a relative of Bonaventura Peeters q.v., as pupil of Sir G. Kneller and his drapery assistant till 1712, and as 'a proper lusty man of a free open temper, a lover of good company and his bottle'. After leaving Kneller, Vertue records, he painted draperies for other leading artists 'but having great knowledge in the hands and manners of several famous Italian but especially Flemish Masters,' he chiefly employed himself in mending and restoring old pictures with such success that he was often called 'Doctor Peeters'; in restoring old drawings 'though poorly done he would give them the masterly stroak and Air of genuin drawings so that many of the Prime Connoisseurs or Vertuose purchased at great prices'; in his later years, Vertue adds, gout prevented him working and reduced him to great straits 'but being of a high spirit and a little of the Spanish blood in him, rather bore his misfortunes to himself than acquaint his friends to the last'. Descamps (1763) records that on arriving in England he found no market for his 'history' pictures and entered the service of the Papal Nuncio but remained there only one day, that his copies of works by Rubens were sold as originals (cf. J. van Pee), that he visited the Netherlands and bought pictures which he resold in England. Descamps also records a 'history' picture in the style of Rubens. His portrait was painted by A. Schoonjans q.v. [Fl. 826, Fl. 878, Fl. 215, Fl. 856.]

Peeters, Jan Frans. Flemish Sch. b son of Jan P., Antwerp 1655 d place and date unknown. VIENNA Albertina has a drawing Cattle and pigs under trees signed 'J. F. de Peters' presumed by some his work. [Fl. 892.]

Peigne (or **Pegna**), **H. de la**, see **La Pegnia**.

*****Pélichy, Gertrude de.** Flemish Sch. b daughter of J. P. de P. (Flemish Baron), Utrecht 1743 d Bruges 1825. Portraits, animals, landscapes. Taken Bruges by her father (who became sheriff there and later Burgomaster) 1753; pupil in Bruges of P. J. de Cock (cf. J. F. Ducq); also studied architecture; in Paris where lived in Pensionnat des Dames de l'Instruction Chrétienne 1767; pupil in Paris of J. B. Suvée q.v. c. 1770; back Bruges by 1777; honorary member of Imperial Vienna Academy. **Documented Examples:** BRUGES Town Hall The Empress Maria Theresa wearing a gown covered with Brussels lace (cf. B. Beschey, P. J. Lion and J. P. Sauvage) and The Emperor Joseph II (cf. W. J. Herreyns and H. Gillis, A. B. Quertenmont, J. J. de Soignie, F. van Stampart).

[Fl. 451, Fl. 440, Fl. 434, Fl. 114.]

Pennemaecker (or **Pannemaker**). **Pater.** Flemish Sch. 17th cent. Religious subjects. Franciscan monk who worked for his order. **Documented Example:** ANTWERP Ascension of Christ (from tomb of Justis Canis, Almoner of Antwerp (d 1664) in Antwerp Recollets church where recorded by Descamps (1769) as 'assez dans la manière de Rubens mais incorrect de dessein et d'une touche molle et indécise, peint par un Religieux Recollet').

[Fl. 216 ,Fl. 612, Fl. 892, Fl. 13.]

Pepyn, Catharina. Flemish Sch. b daughter of Marten P., Antwerp 1619 d Antwerp 1688. Portraits. 'Meesteresse' in Antwerp Guild 1654. **Signed Example:** ANTWERP Mus. N. van Couwerven, Abbot of S. Michel 1657 (from Tongerloo Abbey). Another signed portrait Abbot J. C. van der Sterre 1657 is recorded in Tongerloo Abbey.

[Fl. 481, Fl. 107, Fl. 892.]

*****Pepyn, Marten.** Flemish Sch. b son of painter and dealer Willem P., Antwerp 1575 d Antwerp 1643. Religious subjects (New and Old Testament). Houbraken (1718) records that he went to Italy where he was so conspicuously able that Rubens, hearing of his approaching return, was disturbed (was daar over verzet); but hearing a rumour that he had married and intended to remain in Rome, Rubens said 'Now that Pepyn is married, I have no fear that anyone will surpass me' (cf. F. Snyders); recorded in Antwerp Guild 1600; married there 1601; took pupils there 1602, 1613, 1620, 1625; Rubens' first wife Isabella Brant was godmother to one of his daughters 1615; Van Dyck painted his portrait. **Signed Examples:** ANTWERP Mus. Triptych: centre: S. Elizabeth giving her jewels to the poor; wings: Death of S. Elizabeth, S. Elizabeth received in Heaven; exterior wings (grisaille): Poor family going to hospital, S. Elizabeth tending the sick (from Antwerp S. Elizabeth Hospital where seen and admired by Descamps 1768); Triptych: centre: Baptism of S. Augustine; wings: Consecration of S. Augustine; S. Augustine healing; exterior wings: (grisaille): S. Augustine giving alms, Sick going to hospital 1626 (from Antwerp S. Elizabeth Hospital where seen and admired by Descamps 1768); Cathedral Notre Dame S. Norbert 1637; S. Paul Holy Family 1643. VIENNA Liecht. Entombment 1603. WIESBADEN Circumcision, Adoration of the Magi 1641. **Monogrammed Examples:** ANTWERP Passage of the Red Sea (cf. H. v. Balen, F. Francken, H. Jordaens III, J. Snellinck, C. de Wael also A. Claesz) 1626. STOCKHOLM Simeon in the Temple. A Susanna and the Elders inscribed 'Turpe senilis amor' is recorded by an engraving. The dealer C. Immerseel in Seville (cf. A. v. Ertvelt) imported from Antwerp (1632) a case of twelve paintings including an Adam and Eve, Joseph and Potiphar's wife (cf. J. Speeckaert and G. Seghers), Sarah and Hagar, Ahasuerus and Esther, The triumph of David (cf. J. B. de Saive), Bathsheba and the Judgement of Solomon (cf. G. de Crayer and H. de Clerck).

[Fl. 86, Fl. 425, Fl. 878, Fl. 216, Fl. 892, Fl. 213, Fl. 214.]

Pere (**Vandepere**), **Anton van de.** Flemish Sch. b Flanders before 1645 d Madrid (?) after 1676. Religious subjects. Went Spain (cf. A. Smit) c. 1650. **Signed Examples:** MADRID Colegio Sta. Isabel Adoration of the Shepherds; San Martin S. Theresa 1676. Mus. Cerralbo Annunciation 1667. Two holy bishops for the Carthusian church El Paular and pictures for Madrid Carmelite and Jeronymite establishments (one dated 1659) are recorded.

[Fl. 664, Fl. 153, Fl. 95 (1920), Fl. 807.]

Pere, J. van der, see **Perre.**

Pereyns, Simon. Flemish Sch. 16th cent. b Antwerp before 1550 d Mexico (?) after 1586. Religious subjects. Worked in Portugal and Spain (cf. M. v. Cleve the younger, A. Pupiler, F. Sturm and P. de Kempener); in Mexico 1566; sentenced there to paint an altarpiece for the Cathedral as penance for blasphemy (cf. A. v. Overbeke) 1586. [Fl. 61, Fl. 798.]

Perez (or **Peris** or **Peres**), **Henri.** Flemish Sch. b of Spanish family, Antwerp c. 1635 d Antwerp 1671. Portraits and landscapes with figures. Dean in Antwerp Guild 1662. A Portrait of Ambroise Capello Bishop of Antwerp is recorded by an engraving 1664. The Forchoudt firm of Antwerp dealers owned c. 1671 a S. Jerome by 'Peris' and in 1678 an 'Oferande van Venus' by 'Peres'. Two Landscapes with ruins and figures recorded in Antwerp 'Chapelle du Marché-aux-Souliers' are

presumed by some his work or that of his son, also named Henri (Master Antwerp Guild 1684).
[Fl. 481, Fl. 107, Fl. 440, Fl. 88, Fl. 212.]

Peris, Henri, see **Perez.**

Permeke, Constant. Flemish Sch. *b* son of landscape painter H. P., Antwerp 1886 *d* 1952. *Landscapes, marines, interiors, figure compositions in Impressionist and, later, Post-Impressionist and Expressionist conventions (cf.* C. Dehoy and H. Ramah), *nudes; also active (after 1936) as sculptor.* Pupil of J. Delvin in Ghent Acad.; worked in Laethem-St. Martin 1906-12 (*cf.* F. v. d. Berghe, A. Servaes, G. de Smet also A. v. d. Abeele and G. v. d. Woestyne); then Ostend till 1914; was wounded in German 1914-18 invasion and evacuated to England (*cf.* A. Baertsoen, E. Tytgat and L. de Smet); worked in Devonshire; returned Belgium after 1918; worked Antwerp, Ostend and Jabbeke (near Bruges); exhibited with Salon des IX (*cf.* H. Daeye) 1926; honorary member of L'Art Contemporain (*cf.* R. Strebelle). Represented in ANTWERP *Winter in Flanders* 1912, *Life of the peasant, Coffee drinkers, Fisher woman, Green sea, Snow landscape, Fair clouds, Autumn landscape.* BRUSSELS *The engaged couple, The stranger* (painted in England). GHENT *Landscape, Ostend Port.* PARIS Mus. d'Art Moderne *The stable.* PRAGUE *Peasant woman with bare breast;* also Bâle, Berne and London (Tate).
[Fl. 291, Fl. 147 (1930), Fl. 705, Fl. 783, Fl. 388, Fl. 390, Fl. 392, Fl. 504, Fl. 296.]

Perre (or Pere), Christiaen van den. Flemish Sch. *b* Brussels (?) before 1550 *d* Antwerp (?) after 1580. Painter to the Duke of Alva (*cf.* M. Coxie, W. Key, P. de Kempener, A. Mor) 1572; Master in Antwerp Guild 1580. [Fl. 440,]

Perre (Pere), Jan (Johann) van der. Flemish Sch. *b* son of Nicolas v. d. P., Antwerp before 1569 *d* Leipzig 1621. *Religious subjects, portraits.* Taken Leipzig by his father *q.v.* to escape Alva's persecutions 1569; Leipzig citizen 1595. Signed Example: LEIPZIG Mus. *Kurfürst Moritz* 1616. Signed religious subjects are recorded in Leipzig Paulinerkirche (1596 and 1603) and Johanneskirche (1616). Portraits of deceased notables including Luther and Melanchthon are also recorded. [Fl. 612, Fl. 376, Fl. 440, Fl. 892, Fl. 798.]

Perre (or Pere), Nicolas van der. Flemish Sch. *b* Antwerp (?) before 1550 *d* Leipzig 1595. *Portraits.* Driven as a Protestant from Antwerp by Alva's persecutions (*cf.* J. Hoefnagel, H. v. Steenwyck the elder and A. de Weerdt) 1569; in Leipzig with wife and child 1570; Leipzig citizen 1583. [Fl. 88, Fl. 440.]

Pery (or Perri), N. Emmanuel (Nicolas E.). Flemish Sch. *b* Alost before 1725 *d* after 1775 (?). *Religious subjects.* Master in Brussels Guild 1736. Descamps (1768) saw a *Birth of the Virgin* and *Assumption of the Virgin* ('tous deux médiocres') in Brussels Église des Cordeliers and pictures painted for Brussels Église des Jacobins reconstructed after Marshal Villeroi's bombardment during Louis XIV's 1695 campaign (*cf.* A. Coppens and Z. J. v. Helmont). An *Apotheosis of S. Romualdus* (1775) in Malines S. Rombout is also recorded.
[Fl. 216, Fl. 614.]

Pesser, Denis. Flemish Sch. 16th cent. Worked Liège 1589-98. Signed Example: LIÈGE S. Jacques fresco *Resurrection* 1598.
[Fl. 88, Fl. 892.]

Peters, François Luc. Flemish Sch. 18th cent. *b* Brussels. *Genre; also engravings and drawings for engravers.* Worked in France *c.* 1760 (*cf.* P. Spruyt). Compositions titled *L'amour maternel, La jeune dévideuse, La petite marchande de carpes, La jardinière en repos* and *Le vigneron galant* are recorded by engravings. Presumed by some identical with the German painter and engraver Johann Anton de P. [Fl. 612, Fl. 798.]

Peters (or Peeters), Frans Lucas. Flemish Sch. *b* Antwerp 1606 *d* Brussels 1654. *Landscapes with figures; also flowers (cf.* A. Bosschaert and D. Seghers). Pupil of G. Seghers; worked in service of Archduke Leopold Wilhelm (*cf.* J. v. d. Baren and J. B. v. Heil). Two *Flower pieces* are recorded in the Archduke's inventory 1659. [Fl. 440, Fl. 88, Fl. 892.]

Pez, Aimé. Flemish Sch. *b* Tournai 1808 *d* 1849. *Genre.* Pupil of M. v. Brée and F. de Braekeleer the elder. Represented in TOURNAI *The school.* MONTREAL *Children's dance.*
[Fl. 451, Fl. 612, Fl. 892.]

*****Philadelphia Adorant Painter.** Presumed Flemish Sch. 15th cent. Name for painter of PHILADELPHIA Mus. (Johnson) (327) *Young man in prayer.* Presumed by some identical with Ursula Legend Master *q.v.*

*****Philadelphia Adoration of Magi Painter.** Presumed Flemish Sch. 15th-16th cent. Name for painter of PHILADELPHIA Mus. (Johnson) (1321) *Adoration of the Magi.* Presumed by some identical with H. Bosch *q.v.*

*****Philadelphia Francis I Painter.** Presumed Flemish (or French) Sch. 16th cent. Name for painter of PHILADELPHIA Mus. (Johnson) (769) *King Francis I with a glove.* Presumed by some identical with Joos van Cleve *q.v.*

*****Philadelphia Lamentation Painter.** Presumed Flemish Sch. early 16th cent. Name for painter of PHILADELPHIA Mus. (Johnson) (328) *Lamentation.* Presumed by some identical with Gerard David *q.v.*

*****Philadelphia Maria Egyptiaca Painter.** Presumed Flemish Sch. 15th/16th cent. Name for painter of PHILADELPHIA Mus. (Johnson) (366) *S. Mary of Egypt penitent in the desert (cf.* E. Schayck the elder and J. Kraeck). Presumed by some identical with Q. Massys *q.v.*

*****Philadelphia Marriage of the Virgin Painter.** Presumed Flemish Sch. 15th cent. Name for painter of PHILADELPHIA Mus. (Johnson) (344) *Marriage of the Virgin, with scenes from the life of the Virgin in the background.* Presumed by some identical with the Tiburtine Sibyl Master *q.v.*

*****Philadelphia S. Catherine Painter.** Presumed Flemish Sch. 15th cent. Name for painter of PHILADELPHIA Mus. (Johnson) (326) *S. Catherine.* Presumed by some identical with the Lucy Legend Master *q.v.*

*****Philadelphia S. Christopher Painter.** Presumed Flemish Sch 15th cent. Name for painter of PHILADELPHIA Mus. (Johnson) (342) *S. Christopher.* Presumed by some identical with D. Bouts *q.v.*

Phillipet, Léon. Flemish Sch. *b* Liège 1843 *d* Brussels 1906. *Genre, portraits.* Pupil Liège Acad. and in Paris of the French painter W. A. Bouguereau; in Rome where founded and directed an Academy with financial help from Belgian government 1877-84. Represented in BRUSSELS *The murdered man* (painted in Rome). LIÈGE *Canzonetta* 1870, *Battle of women* 1870, *Cabaret in Rome* 1883 and others.
[Fl. 160 (1906), Fl. 296.]

Picart, Jean Michel. Flemish Sch. *b* Brabant *c.* 1600 (?) *d* Paris 1682. *Flowers and fruit (cf.* T. Aenvanck), *landscapes; also active as art dealer (cf.* P. Goetkint). Went Paris (*cf.* P. Vleughels and C. E. Biset); member there of Guild of S. Luc 1640; employed young artists to copy pictures which he sold as originals; his daughters married the French artists Jacques d'Agar and S. Bonnet. Houbraken records that the Dutch painter J. Glauber worked with him for a year 1671. The Prince of Liechtenstein asked the Antwerp Art dealer

Forchoudt to examine and return to 'the art dealer Picart' a *S. Jerome* sold him as by Van Dyck but not an original 1698. **Signed Example:** CARLSRUHE *Basket of fruit on a stone table.* [Fl. 425, Fl. 168, Fl. 612, Fl. 126, Fl. 892, Fl. 212.]

Picqué, Charles. Flemish Sch. *b* Deynze (near Ghent) 1799 *d* Brussels 1869. *Portraits, religious subjects, 'history', genre.* Pupil of J. Paelinck. Represented in AMSTERDAM *On the S. Bernard* (a *S. Bernard dog, and woman with unconscious child*) 1827. BRUSSELS Town Hall *The Provisional Government* 1830. GHENT *Hebe, Portrait of J. Paelinck, Self-portrait.* A *Tobit blessing Tobias* (1823), a *S. Roch healing the plague-stricken* (1836) and a *Capture of Naarden by the Spaniards 1572* (1842) are recorded.
[Fl. 451, Fl. 612, Fl. 837 (1869), Fl. 88, Fl. 296.]

Piéron (Pierron), Gustave Louis Marie. Flemish Sch. *b* son of a banker, Antwerp 1824 *d* Antwerp 1864. *Landscapes.* Pupil of J. Jacobs (with F. Lamorinière and J. van Luppen) in Antwerp Acad.; visited France and had contact with artists of the Barbizon School; exhibited London 1862. Represented in ANTWERP *The marsh* 1857, *Farm at Merxem* 1863. BRUSSELS *Landscape* 1847. An *Autumn morning in Fontainebleau forest* was in the Paris Salon 1854. [Fl. 88, Fl. 440.]

Pieters, Jan, see **Peeters, J. the younger.**

***Pietersz, Aert.** Flemish (Dutch) Sch. *b* son of P. Aertsen *q.v.,* Antwerp 1550 *d* Amsterdam 1612. *Portraits, portrait groups* (*cf.* D. Barendsz and C. Ketel) *and religious subjects.* Pupil of his father in Amsterdam. Van Mander (1604) records that P. Aertsen painted him as a boy in a kitchen scene that had an ox's head. **Monogrammed Examples:** (Monogram and woolcomb *cf.* P. Pietersz) AMSTERDAM Rijks. *The Company of Captain Jan Philipsz de Bischop and Lieutenant P. Ebgertsz Vinck* 1599, *Anatomy lecture of Dr. Egbertsz* 1603 (*cf.* H. Sporckmans), *Last Judgement.* COPENHAGEN *Man's portrait* (monogram only, 1573). [Fl. 559, Fl. 892, Fl. 421.]

Pietersz, Dirk. Flemish (Dutch) Sch. *b* son of P. Aertsen, Amsterdam 1558 *d* Fontainebleau before 1604. Van Mander (1604) records that he went France and worked Fontainebleau (*cf.* C. Ketel, R. Savery and A. Dubois) where he died in misery (rampspoedig) 'during the last war'. [Fl. 559.]

Pietersz, Gérard. Flemish Sch. *b* before 1546 *d* Ghent 1612. (Not to be confused with Dutch painter Gerrit P. brother of composer J. P. Sweelinck). *Decorative compositions.* Master Bruges Guild 1562; went with his two sons from Bruges to Ghent 1590; worked on Pageant Entry into Ghent of Archduke Albert and Infanta Isabella 1599 (*cf.* M. Joncquoy, J. de Liemakere, P. v. d. Meulen and D. v. Alsloot). One of his sons named Pieter is recorded as his assistant in the Ghent decorations. [Fl. 892, Fl. 88.]

***Pietersz, Pieter.** Flemish (Dutch) Sch. *b* son of P. Aertsen, Antwerp 1541 or 1543 *d* Amsterdam 1603. *Portraits; also occasional religious subjects and 'history'.* Pupil of his father *q.v.* in Amsterdam; in Haarlem 1572; withstood there the thirty-one weeks Spanish siege and protected the Dutch painter Cornelis of Haarlem (then a child of twelve whose parents had fled the town) 1572-3; later gave Cornelis his first instructions in painting (*cf.* G. Congnet); settled Amsterdam by 1585. He was a Protestant and Van Mander (1604) records him as a reserved, intelligent and cultivated man who was mainly employed on portraits because there were few commissions for large pictures at the time. . His son Pieter P. was also a painter. **Monogrammed Examples:** (Monogram and woolcomb *cf.* P. Aertsen) HAARLEM *Shadrach, Meshach and Abednego in the Fiery Furnace* 1575 (from Haarlem Bakers' Guild for which Van Mander records it painted). UTRECHT (loan) *The Miracle at Genesareth* and on reverse *Martyrdom*

of SS. Peter and Paul (from Gouda church for which it is recorded painted before 1569).
[Fl. 559, Fl. 892, Fl. 445, Fl. 421.]

Pigeon, Jean Baptiste. Flemish Sch. *b* Bure 1823 *d* 1868. *Religious subjects, portraits.* Pupil of H. v. d. Haert and L. J. Mathieu. Painted *Institution of the Rosary* for Anhée Church (near Dinant). [Fl. 768, Fl. 126, Fl. 892.]

Pindar, Jacques, Presumed Flemish Sch. 16th cent. Recorded (1590) in an inventory of Lord Lumley's pictures (*cf.* H. Ewouts and S. v. d. Meulen) as painter of a '*Portrait of the Duke of Savoy, Regent in Flaunders*' (i.e. Duke Emmanuel Philibert Lieutenant General 1556-9). Presumed identical with J. de Poindre *q.v.* and J. de Punder *q.v.*
[Fl. 857 (II and VI), Fl. 50 (1938), Fl. 631 (1942).]

Pinot, Albert. Flemish Sch. *b* St. Gilles, Brussels 1875. *Landscapes, portraits, genre.* Pupil Brussels Acad.; founder member of Brussels 'Sillon' group (*cf.* A. Bastien, F. v. d. Holder, J. de la Hoese, H. Thomas, F. Smeers, P. Swyncop and M. Wagemans) 1893. Represented in BRUGES *The blue river Oise.* IXELLES, RIGA. [Fl. 114, Fl. 296.]

Pirotte, Olivier. Flemish Sch. *b* Liège 1699 *d* Liège 1764. *Religious subjects for Liège churches* (*cf.* H. Deprez and J. B. Coclers). Pupil in Liège of R. P. de Rendeux *q.v.* 1716; went Rome (*cf.* J. La Tour) where pupil of the Italian artists B. Luti and P. Bianchi 1721-5; went Paris (*cf.* J. F. Delien) and worked under the French painters N. N. Coypel and F. Lemoyne (*cf.* P. J. v. Reysschoot) 1725-7. Paintings for churches in Wandre and Flores (nr. Namur) are recorded.
[Fl. 409, Fl. 892.]

***Plas** (or **Plaes**), **Pieter van der.** Flemish Sch. *b* Brussels (?) before 1600 *d* Brussels after 1647. (Not to be confused with Dutch artist David van der Plas). *Portraits and civic portrait groups* (*cf* A. Sallaert and G. de Crayer). Pupil in Brussels Guild 1610; Master Brussels Guild 1619. Highly praised by de Bie (1661) who records that his works were then to be found in Brussels and 'foreign towns'. **Signed Examples:** BRUSSELS *Virgin and Child with syndics of a Brussels guild 1647.* LONDON N.G. (on loan to N.P.G.) *Portrait of a man with hand on his breast and pilgrim's staff* (presumed by some to represent John Milton; presumed by some to represent John Bunyan). Designs for tapestry are recorded.
[Fl. 86, Fl. 425, Fl. 126, Fl. 892, Fl. 440, Fl. 88, Fl. 798.]

***Plasschaert, Jacobus.** Flemish Sch. *b* Bruges (?) before 1725 *d* Bruges 1765. *Trompe-l'œil still life including 'Vanitas' subjects* (*cf.*J. de Cordua, W. Vaillant and C. N. Gysbrechts). Master Bruges Guild 1739. **Signed Example:** BARNARD CASTLE Bowes Mus. *Still life with skull and engravings* ('Bruges 1741/42'). [Fl. 798.]

Plateau, Antoine. Flemish Sch. *b* Tournai 1759 *d* Tournai 1815. *Flowers* (*cf.* A. F. and P. J. Redouté and P. Faes) *also decorative paintings.* Worked for Château Laeken (built for Governors General Albert of Saxe-Teschen and Maria Christina 1782-4 and owned by Napoleon 1802-14) (*cf.* P. J. Sauvage and A. Cardon). Represented in TOURNAI *Flower piece.* [Fl. 451, Fl. 163, Fl. 88, Fl. 892.]

Platte-Montagne, see **Plattenberg.**

Plattenberg (or **Platten** or **Platte-Montagne**), **Mathieu van.** Flemish Sch. *b* Antwerp 1606 or *c.* 1608 *d* Paris 1660. Confused by some with his son the French painter N. de Platte-Montagne (*cf.* J. B. de Champaigne) and/or the Dutch (?) painter R. de la Montagne (Rinaldo de la Montagna) who worked in Italy (Venice, Florence, Rome). *Marines* (*cf.* G. v.

Eyck, A. v. Ertvelt, B. Peeters, J. Porcellis), *landscapes with figures; also engravings*. Pupil in Antwerp (?) of A. v. Ertvelt; went Italy (?); went Paris (*cf.* P. de Champaigne); earned living there at first (his son-in-law P. Vleughels *q.v.* records) by designing for embroidery; pupil there of J. Fouquier *q.v.* and befriended by J. v. Egmont *q.v.*; changed his name to French form; married sister of French engraver J. Morin; founder member of French Académie des Beaux Arts (*cf.* P. v. Mol) 1648; became 'Peintre du roy pour les mers'; paid for funeral of J. Fouquier 1659. Marines and landscapes with figures are recorded by engravings.
[Fl. 287, Fl. 564, Fl. 505, Fl. 249, Fl. 593, Fl. 612, Fl. 66 Fl. 440, Fl. 892.]

Plumier, Edmond (Théodore Aimond). Flemish Sch. *b* Liège 1694 *d* Liège 1733. *Religious subjects for Liège churches* (*cf.* J. B. Coclers), '*history*', *portraits.* Pupil of E. Fisen *q.v.* in Liège; went Paris; pupil there of the French painter N. de Largillière; visited Rome; back in Liège by 1719; said to have painted figures in some landscapes by J. B. Juppin *q.v.* His son Jacques Théodore was also a painter. **Signed Examples:** LIÈGE Mus. (drawings) *Beheading of S. John the Baptist* 1713, *Louis de Berg, Prince Bishop of Liège* 1728. **Documented Example:** LIÈGE S. Remacle-au-Pont *Descent from the Cross* (taken to Paris 1794 and returned 1815). *Portraits of the Oultremont family* and a *Rape of Proserpina* are recorded. [Fl. 409, Fl. 892.]

Plumot, André. Flemish Sch. *b* Antwerp 1829 *d* Antwerp 1906. *Animals, interiors, landscapes.* Pupil in Antwerp Acad. of J. v. d. Poorten. Represented in ANTWERP *Crossing the bridge* 1878, *Animal studies.* [Fl. 17.]

Poelman, Pierre J. Flemish Sch. *b* Ghent 1801 *d* Ghent 1826. *Architectural views, genre, portraits and interiors.* Worked Ghent, Bruges (*cf.* J. C. Verbrugge) and Mons; exhibited from 1820. A contemporary records: 'Le jeune artiste fut exploité par un speculateur dont il espérait épouser la fille; le projet ayant manqué le pauvre garçon en mourut de chagrin'. After his death his pictures were sought after by Ghent collectors. Represented in AMSTERDAM *Audenarde Town Hall with Cossacks by the fountain on the square* 1824. (*Cf.* J. Moerenhout). [Fl. 451, Fl. 440, Fl. 88.]

Poindre, Jacques de. Flemish Sch. *b* Malines 1527 *d* Germany (Oostland) or Denmark *c.* 1570. *Portraits, religious subjects.* Pupil and brother-in-law of Marcus Willems *q.v.* One W. de Vos is recorded as his pupil 1559. Van Mander records a *Crucifixion* with many portraits inserted and a *Portrait of an English captain* to which he added prison bars because the picture had been left unpaid for on his hands. Presumed identical with Jacques Pindar *q.v.* and with Jacobus de Punder *q.v.*
[Fl. 559, Fl. 451, Fl. 440, Fl. 50 (1938), Fl. 631 (1942).]

Ponteau, Michel (called **Pontiani** or **Ponciani**). Flemish Sch. *b* Liège *c.* 1588 *d* Liège (?) or Italy (?) *c.* 1650. *Religious paintings for Liège churches* (*cf.* J. G. Carlier). Went Italy; painted Roman Emperors on the windows of his house in Liège (*cf.* B. Spranger); presumed by some identical with one Ponthier who went to America.
[Fl. 26, Fl. 63, Fl. 126, Fl. 88, Fl. 892.]

Poorten, Henri Joseph François van der. Flemish Sch. *b* Antwerp 1789 *d* Antwerp 1874. *Landscapes with figures and animals, some with moonlight effects* (*cf.* P. v. Schendel); *also engravings and lithographs.* Pupil of W. J. Herreyns and H. A. Myin *q.v.*; worked in the region of Antwerp, in Germany and France; won landscape prizes in Ghent, Brussels and Antwerp exhibitions 1813-16; professor in Antwerp Academy J. Moerenhout and J. Rosseels were among his pupils. Represented in GHENT *Country road with figures* (*cf.* J. L. Demarne) 1814.
[Fl. 451, Fl. 612, Fl. 446, Fl. 440, Fl. 88, Fl. 892, Fl. 73.]

Popelier, A., see **Pupiler.**

Porcellis (Parcelles, Perseles), Jan. Flemish Sch. *b* of Spanish descent, Ghent before 1585 *d* Soeterwoude, nr. Leyden 1632. *Marines* (*cf.* B. Peeters); *also worked as engraver.* Houbraken (1718) records him as pupil in Haarlem of Dutch marine painter H. C. Vroom; in Rotterdam where married 1605; went Antwerp, contracted there with a dealer named Delen to paint (with the help of a pupil, one Hans Bogaert) forty marines with ships within twenty weeks, two to be delivered weekly and the proceeds to be shared (*cf.* A. Casteels and J. d'Arthois) 1615; Master in Antwerp Guild 1617; insolvent 1618; had natural son from a girl called Kerstiaensen 1620; married as second wife in Haarlem a daughter of Baltasar Flessiers *q.v.* (*cf.* also Benjamin and T. Flessiers) 1622; mainly at sea and visiting various Dutch ports 1624; citizen of Amsterdam 1625. E. Norgate (1650) ranks him above Vroom as a painter of the sea and adds 'he very naturally describes the beauties and terrors of that element in Calmes and tempests, soe lively exprest, as would make you at once in love with and forsweare the sea for ever'; Hoogstraaten (1678) describes him as the Raphael of seapainters and as winner in a contest against the Dutch painters F. Knibbergen and J. van Goyen when each painted a picture in a day. Both Rembrandt and Rubens owned examples of his work; others are recorded in the collections of V. Wolfvoet *q.v.* and Jeremias Wildens *q.v.* His brother Jonas P. was Master in Antwerp 1618; his son Julius P., who died Leyden 1645, was also a painter of marines. **Signed Examples:** BUDAPEST *Storm at sea* (Jan Por). MUNICH *Storm* (Joannes porsellis 1629). **Semi-documented Example:** HAMPTON COURT Royal Collection *Charles I leaving Santander 1623* (a picture of this subject, with different dimensions, was recorded as by 'Persellis' in Charles I's inventory). *Sea pieces* monogrammed J. P., presumed by some his work are in various museums (Jan Peeters *q.v.* and Julius Porcellis also monogrammed J. P.). Oxford Ashmolean has a *Sea piece* (*a fresh breeze*) with initials I. P. presumed by some his work.
[Fl. 618, Fl. 86, Fl. 447, Fl. 425, Fl. 88, Fl. 892, Fl. 884, Fl. 212, Fl. 213, Fl. 83.]

Portaels, Jean François. Flemish Sch. *b* Vilvorde 1818 *d* Schaerbeek (Brussels) 1895. *Portraits, costume history, religious subjects, contemporary genre.* Pupil of his father-in law F. Navez and in Paris of the French painter P. Delaroche (*cf.* A. Robert); also studied Rome 1844-7; Professor in Ghent Acad. 1847-50; in Brussels Acad. 1863-5; Director Brussels Acad. from 1878; travelled in Spain, Morocco, Egypt, Hungary, Norway. Had many successful pupils (*cf.* E. Agneessens, Léon Frédéric, A. Hennebicq, E. Laermans, J. de Lalaing, T. van Rysselberghe, I. Verheyden, E. Wauters). Represented in ANTWERP *The writer H. Cousience,* P. *Delaroche, Judith.* BRUSSELS *A box at Budapest theatre, Mignon, The Maid of Zion, Cercle Artistique, Woman with fan;* S. Jacques-sur-Coudenberg *Virgin of Mercy* (mural). LIÈGE *Gipsy girls.* PRAGUE *Christian maiden led to crucifixion.* SYDNEY (Australia) N.G. of New South Wales *Esther.* Portraits of *The singer Rose Caron* and *Paul Deroulède* are recorded. [Fl. 415, Fl. Bib. 19th cent.]

Portielje, Edward. Flemish Sch. *b* son of Dutch painter J. F. P., Antwerp 1861. *Interiors, genre.* Pupil in Antwerp Acad. of C. Verlat. Represented in ANTWERP *Teasing* 1891.
[Fl. 892, Fl. 17.]

Portielje, Gérard. Flemish Sch. *b* son of Dutch painter Jan P., Antwerp 1856 *d* Luxembourg 1929. *Anecdotic genre, interiors.* Pupil of J. van Lerius. Professor Antwerp Acad. Represented in ANTWERP *A victim* 1894. MELBOURNE *The old bachelor.* [Fl. 17, Fl. 296.]

Posenaer, Joseph. Flemish Sch. *b* Antwerp 1876 *d* Borgerhout 1935. *Landscapes, figures, decorative panels.* Pupil in Antwerp

Acad. of J. B. Michiels and F. Lauwers. Teacher in Antwerp Acad. Represented in ANTWERP *The birdcages* 1911; Academy *Murals*, MALINES. [Fl. 17.]

*Pourbus, Frans the elder. Flemish Sch. *b* son of Pieter J. P. *q.v.*, Bruges 1545 *d* of typhoid fever, Antwerp 1581. *Religious subjects, wooded landscapes with animals, portraits.* Pupil in Bruges of his father; then in Antwerp of F. Floris who, Van Mander (1604) records, much admired his talent; in Antwerp Guild 1564; in Ghent where met Van Mander in studio of L. de Heere *q.v.* 1566; contemplated journey to Italy but returned Antwerp for love of Susanna, daughter of architect-sculptor Cornelis Floris (brother of F. F.) who became his mistress; Master in Antwerp Guild (while retaining citizen rights in Bruges) 1569; married Susanna Floris 1569; completed with C. v. d. Broeck *q.v.* a Spanish commission left unfinished by Floris at his death (1570); married second wife 1578; ensign in Civic Guard during patriot occupation of Antwerp (*cf.* Antwerp Destruction of Citadel Painter and J. V. de Vries); Van Mander records that he caught his fatal fever after a Civic Guard exercise from resting near an open drain; he died a Protestant. His widow married H. Jordaens the elder *q.v.* G. Geldorp was among his pupils. **Signed Examples:** BERLIN K. F. *Portrait of a man, Portrait of a woman.* BRUSSELS *The family of Joris Hoefnagel* (painted 1571 on occasion of the marriage of Joris H. *q.v.*; recorded in an inventory of the contents of P's studio made by his father, his father-in-law and Gillis van Coninxloo *q.v.* 1581; in 1696 Constantin Huygens (son of the poet) records: 'This morning I called on cousin Hoefnagel and exchanged my English saddle horse and saddle, bought last year in London, for a picture by Pourbus of the Hoefnagel family, where grandmother Huygens is shown aged fifteen or sixteen with a parrot on her hand'). *S. Matthew inspired by the angel* 1573. DUNKIRK Triptych: *Martyrdom of S. George with the lancing of the dragon in a landscape background* (*cf.* G. Congnet) 1577; wings: *Scenes from the ordeals of S. George* (described by Van Mander who records it exhibited in the Bruges studio of P. J. P.; seen (1768) in S. Éloi by Descamps who records: 'Le tableau du milieu a souffert: un Anglois en le nettoyant y enleva quelques glacis, il a même repeint une ou deux têtes dans le milieu de la composition qui se distinguent par leur médiocrité). GHENT Mus. Triptych *Isaiah predicting the recovery of Hezekiah* 1576; wings: *Crucifixion, S. James of Compostella (S. Iago) as patron saint of donor Jacques del Rio, Abbot of Baudeloo*, exterior (grisaille); *Raising of Jairus' daughter;* Cathedral S. Bavon Triptych *Jesus among the doctors, with portraits of Charles V, Philip II, Alva and others* 1571; wings: *Circumcision, Baptism of Christ*, exterior: *Christ blessing; The donor Viglius ab Aytta President of the Privy Council and Coadjutor Abbot of S. Bavon aged sixty-four kneeling before Christ* (recorded by Van Mander; seen by Descamps; taken Paris for Musée Napoléon and returned 1815 (*cf.* J. D. Odevaere)). LONDON Wallace *The Duke of Alençon* (?) 1574 (*cf.* Pieter J. P.). TOURNAI Cathedral *Raising of Lazarus* 1573. VIENNA K. *Jan van Hembyze* 1567. **Monogrammed Example:** DRESDEN *An old lady with a lap dog* 1568 (*cf.* C. v. Hemessen and Amsterdam Little Girl with Dog Painter). Van Mander records an *Adoration of the Magi* in an Audenarde monastery and, as painted in his youth, a *Paradise* 'with many animals and trees painted from life in which one could distinguish pear, apple and nut trees' (*cf.* J. (Velvet) Brueghel and R. Savery). The Forchoudt firm of Antwerp dealers sent (1674) to Vienna an *Orpheus* (*cf.* L. v. d. Borcht) by 'Pourbus' which was sold in Graz, and (1675) a *Pomona* by 'Poerbus' with landscape by J. (Velvet) Brueghel (?). Descamps saw religious subjects in Bruges (S. Christophe), Courtrai (S. Martin) and Tournai (Abbaye de S. Martin). Compositions titled *Conversion of Saul* (*cf.* P. Bruegel the elder), *Martyrdom of S. Paul* and *Susanna and the elders* and a *Vanitas: Allegory of Death* (*cf.* Amsterdam Cadaver Painter and Hague Vanitas Painter)

are recorded by engravings. Pictures presumed by some his work are in various museums.
[Fl. 559, Fl. 216, Fl. 478, Fl. 440, Fl. 88, Fl. 892, Fl. 212, Fl. 213.]

*Pourbus, Frans the younger. Flemish Sch. *b* son of Frans P. the elder, Antwerp 1569 *d* Paris 1622. *Portraits (some in miniature); portrait groups, occasional religious subjects.* Studied Antwerp (?) and/or Bruges (?); inherited money from his grandmother wife of Pieter J. P. *q.v.* 1588; in Bruges where restored Iconoclast damage to altarpiece in Notre Dame by B. van Orley *q.v.* (*cf.* M. de Vos) 1589; Master Antwerp Guild 1591; working for Brussels Court of Archduke Albert and Infanta Isabella (*cf.* D. van Alsloot) 1599-1600; invited by Vincenzo Gonzaga, Duke of Mantua (in Brussels 1599) to become his court painter (*cf.* P. P. Rubens); went Mantua 1600; employed there as portrait painter and contributor to the Duke's gallery of pictures of beautiful women; visited Innsbruck at invitation of Emperor Rudolf II's chamberlain to paint portrait of Anna of Tyrol in place of the German painter Hans van Aachen whom he thought incompetent (*cf.* G. Rem, B. Spranger, J. V. de Vries and P. Stevens the younger). 1603; commissioned by Rudolf II to paint Margherita Gonzaga (Duke Vincenzo's daughter) with whom he contemplated marriage 1605; sent by the Duke to Turin to paint two daughters of Duke Charles Emmanuel I of Savoy (as his son Francesco Gonzaga contemplated marriage with one of them) and worked there 1605-6 (*cf.* J. Claret); visited Paris (to join Duchess Eleanora Gonzaga sister of Marie de Médicis who was there as godmother at the baptism of the Dauphin) with instructions to paint the Queen, the King and the Dauphin 1606; sent Naples (*cf.* A. Mytens and W. Coebergher) to buy pictures for Duke of Mantua and to paint some Neapolitan beauties 'of any rank' for the Duke's collection; reported to Duke from Naples that another Fleming had already painted most of the local beauties and recommended him to buy *Judith and Holofernes* and *Virgin of the Rosaries* by Caravaggio (*cf.* L. Finson and A. B. Quertenmont) 1607; returned Mantua with portraits of two Neapolitan beauties; went Turin with Duke for wedding of Francesco Gonzaga with Margaret of Savoy; met there the Italian painter F. Zuccaro who dedicated to him his account of the festivities 1608; in Innsbruck 1608; went Paris at invitation of Marie de Médicis 1609; wrote to Duke describing his success in Paris as due to the difference in his manner of painting from that of the French painters 1609; remained Paris; court painter to Marie de Médicis 1611 (*cf.* P. P. Rubens); worked for Petite Galerie du Louvre; Elisabeth daughter of H. Francken the elder *q.v.* was his mistress 1613; court painter to Louis XIII (*cf.* P. de Champaigne) by 1616; was naturalized French and had studio in the Louvre 1618. Died unmarried. Had many studio assistants; J. Sutterman *q.v.* was his pupil *c.* 1618. Van Mander (1604) records him as painter of 'goede portretten naar het leven'; Félibien (1688) wrote: 'il n'y ait pas dans ce que Pourbus a peint ni un grand feu ni une force de dessein, mais seulement une beauté de pinceau qui plait à tout le monde: il a fait de grandes compositions d'Histoires, mais c'étoit à faire des portraits qu'il réussissoit davantage'; Mariette (*c.* 1760) wrote: 'J'ai une tête d'Henri IV, faite par lui, qui peut aller de pair avec tout ce que Rubens et Van Dyck ont fait de plus beau'. **Signed Examples:** FLORENCE Pitti *Eleonora Gonzaga (daughter of Duke Vincenzo) as a child, Margherita Gonzaga (later Duchess of Lorraine)* 1605, *Isabella of Bourbon (daughter of Henri IV and later Queen of Spain)* 1611; Uffizi *A painter with brushes and palette* 1591. MADRID Prado *Marie de Médicis* 1617. MUNICH *Man with his hand on a chair* 1614. NANCY *Annunciation* 1619 from Paris Jacobins church, rue S. Honoré (recorded by Félibien and d'Argenville (1752)). PARIS Louvre *Henri IV in black* 1610, *Marie de Médicis in state robes* (from the Petite Galerie du Louvre), *Last Supper* 1618 from Paris: S. Leu et S. Gilles (recorded by Félibien and by d'Argenville: 'l'ordonnance et le

coloris sont admirables'). VALENCIENNES *Dorothée de Croy* 1615. VIENNA Harrach *Man in a black cap* 1613. **Monogrammed Examples:** FLORENCE Pitti *Henri IV* 1611, *Marie de Médicis* 1611; Uffizi *Louis XIII* 1617. HAMPTON COURT Royal Collection *Henri IV* 1610. PARIS Louvre *Stigmatisation of S. Francis* 1620 from Paris Jacobins church, rue S. Honoré. **Documented Examples:** MADRID Prado *Isabella of Bourbon (first Queen of Philip IV) with a little dog* (in Madrid Alcázar inventory 1621; wrongly referred to by some as representing Anne of Austria in mourning for her father Philip III). PARIS Louvre *Henri IV in armour* (recorded by d'Argenville). A *Portrait of Duke Vincenzo of Mantua* by 'Francesco Fiamingo' was taken by Rubens (1603) to Spain. Félibien and d'Argenville record two large pictures *The Provost and Sheriffs of Paris kneeling before Louis XIII as a child* and *The Majority of Louis XIII* painted for and then in Paris, Hôtel de Ville; d'Argenville also records *The making of Peace between the Archduke and Holland with a landscape setting* painted on wood and then in the King's collection. Portraits presumed by some originals or studio replicas are in various museums.
[Fl. 559, Fl. 287, Fl. 22, Fl. 564, Fl. 54 (1868), Fl. 478, Fl. 541, Fl. 440, Fl. 88, Fl. 892, Fl. 255, Fl. 798, Fl. 555.]

*Pourbus (or Poerbus), Pieter Jansz.** Flemish Sch. *b* Gouda before 1520 *d* Bruges 1584. *Religious subjects, allegorical genre, portraits; also active as cartographer (cf. M. Geeraerts the elder and J. Provoost).* Went Bruges where married daughter of L. Blondeel *q.v.*; in Bruges S. George Guild of Crossbowmen 1540; Master in Bruges Painters' Guild 1543; designed costumes for Rhetoricians in Pageant Entry into Bruges of Philip II (*cf.* L. Blondeel, P. Coecke van Aelst, J. V. de Vries, G. Schoof the elder, J. v. Rillaert, C. Anthonisz, J. Scorel) 1549; ordered by Bruges magistrates to paint out a cartload of churchmen shown among the damned in *Last Judgement* by J. Provoost 1550; worked as town planner and cartographer for Bruges magistrates and made maps of the coast with depths of the water for Charles V (*cf.* J. Bellegambe and J. C. Vermeyen) 1552; painted large birds' eye map of Franc de Bruges from sketches made in the Belfry (Tour des Halles) 1562; Dean of Bruges Guild 1569; made plans for the defence of Bruges by flooding 1578-9; in Antwerp 1581 and 1582; had large house in Bruges known as 'Rome'; Van Mander (1604) records: 'I have never seen a better equipped (beter ingerichte) studio than his' and adds that he went often to the Hôpital S. Jean to admire the *S. Ursula shrine* by H. Memlinc *q.v.* when it was on view on special occasions. His son Frans P. and A. Claeissins were among his pupils. **Signed Examples:** BRUGES Mus. *Jan Fernaguut with Bruges Place de la Grue and the crane seen through a window* 1551, *Wife of Jan Fernaguut with the Bruges house known as 'The Cock' (1542) seen through a window* 1551, Triptych; (grisaille) centre: *Descent from the Cross* 1570, wings: *Christ carrying the Cross, Resurrection*, predella (grisaille): *Adoration of the Shepherds* predella wings: *Annunciation, Circumcision*. Notre Dame *Last Supper* 1562 (restored by A. Claeissins 1589). Triptych; centre: *Adoration of the Shepherds* 1574; wings: *donor, his wife, their nine children and patron saints*, exterior: *Circumcision, Adoration of the Magi*. S. Sauveur Triptych; centre: *Last Supper* 1559; wings: *Abraham and Melchisedek, Elijah*, exterior: *Mass of S. Gregory*; S. Jacques Triptych; centre: *Seven Sorrows of the Virgin* 1556; wings: *donor, his wife and patron saints*. Confrérie du Saint-Sang *Thirty one members of the Confrérie* 1556. BRUSSELS *Jan van der Gheenste* 1583. EDINBURGH N. G. Scotland *Flemish lady* 1565. LONDON Wallace. *Allegorical Love-Feast* (on the table a sheet of music with the opening of a four part chanson by T. Crecquillon published 1543). PARIS Louvre *Resurrection* 1556. **Monogrammed Examples:** BRUGES Mus. *Last Judgement* 1551 (*cf.* J. de Backer); S. Sauveur *Pierre de Cuenync;* Notre Dame pair of wings: *donor, his wife and ten children* 1573; exterior: *SS. Anselm and John the Baptist;* S. Jacques

Resurrection 1578. Bruges Town Hall has damaged remains of the *Map of the Franc de Bruges* (*cf.* P. Claeissins the younger) of which Van Mander wrote: 'He made the priming too thick and as the map was often rolled and unrolled the paint flaked off'. Van Mander records a *Portrait of the Duke of Alençon* (*cf.* F. Pourbus the elder) painted in Antwerp (i.e. 1582); he also records a triptych in grisaille painted for Gouda Groote Kerk (later in Delft) with *Scenes from the legend of S. Hubert* ('*two persons being baptized by a bishop in a church*', '*The saint tempted by evil spirits and by women*' and *The Visitation*). Effigies of *Charles V* and *Philip II* tinted for Bruges Town Hall 1560 are also recorded. Pictures presumed by some his work are in various museums.
[Fl. 559, Fl. 478, Fl. 65, Fl. 126, Fl. 440, Fl. 892, Fl. 113, Fl. 534, Fl. 114, Fl. 10 (1939).]

Pozzoserrato and **Pozzo da Treviso, see Toeput.**

Praetere (Prater), Jules de. Flemish Sch. *b* Ghent 1879. *Portraits, still life; also worked as applied art designer and hand printer of éditions de luxe.* Pupil in Ghent Acad.; associated with Laethem St. Martin group (*cf.* G. v. d. Woestyne); taught in Crefeld and Düsseldorf; in Zurich where professor in Arts and Crafts school 1905-21; returned Belgium 1921. Represented in BRUSSELS *Flowers*. [Fl. 699 (1926).]

Pratere (Praetere), Edmond Joseph de. Flemish Sch. *b* Courtrai 1826 *d* Ixelles 1888. *Animals, landscapes, genre.* Studied Courtrai, Brussels and Paris; travelled in France, England, Scotland, Italy, Switzerland and Austria; worked chiefly in region of Furnes. Represented in BRUGES *Cows grazing.* BRUSSELS *Cattle market, Donkeys.* COURTRAI, GHENT (Palais de Justice), LILLE, SYDNEY (Australia) N.G. of New South Wales. Pictures titled *Dray horses* and *Scotch horses* are recorded. [Fl. 88, Fl. 434, Fl. 264, Fl. 114.]

Prévost, see Provoost.

Primo, Louis, see Cousin.

*Princeton Christ before Pilate Painter.** Presumed Flemish Sch. 15/16th cent. Name for painter of PRINCETON University (711) *Christ before Pilate.* Presumed by some identical with H. Bosch *q.v.*

*Prodigal Son Master.** Presumed Flemish Sch. 16th cent. Name for painter of VIENNA K. (773) *Story of the Prodigal Son* (*cf.* J. Beuckelaer, Brussels Prodigal Son Painter, P. Coecke van Aelst, J. S. v. Hemessen, Jan Kraek, C. Massys, J. Savery the elder and S. Vrancx.) Presumed by some identical with Dublin Rebecca Painter *q.v.*
[Fl. 831, Fl. 798.]

Proost, Alfons. Flemish Sch. *b* St. Nicholas 1880. *Genre and landscapes.* Pupil of F. Courtens. Teacher in Antwerp Acad. Represented in ANTWERP *Dancers, On the shore.*

*Provoost (or Provost or Prévost), Jan.** Flemish Sch. *b* Mons 1462 or *c.* 1465 *d* Bruges 1529. *Religious subjects; also worked as cartographer and architect.* Citizen of Valenciennes 1489 (?); married there widow of the French painter S. Marmion *c.* 1490; Master Antwerp Guild 1493; moved to Bruges 1494; assessor (vinder) in Bruges Guild 1501; commissioned to condition shields of the Knights of the Toison d'Or and do other decorative work in Bruges S. Donatien 1506; made topographic drawings for Bruges magistrates (*cf.* M. Geeraerts the elder and P. J. Pourbus) 1513; designed domed ceiling for the Choir of Bruges S. Jacques 1516; Dean in Bruges Guild 1519; worked on decorations for Charles V's Pageant Entry into Bruges (*cf.* A. Cornelis. A. Ysenbrandt also Q. Massys) 1520; entertained Dürer in his house and arranged a banquet in his honour in Bruges 1521;

called a good painter by Dürer who drew his portrait. His son Adriaen was a painter and his son Thomas was a glass painter. **Signed Examples:** None. **Documented Example:** BRUGES *Last Judgement* (commissioned by the Bruges Magistrates for their Council Chamber 1524; payments made 1525 and 1526; figures of priests depicted among the damned were removed by P. J. Pourbus; *cf.* J. v. d. Coornhuuse and J. de Backer). An altarpiece painted for Bruges S. Donatien 1524 is recorded. Paintings presumed by some his work are in various museums (*cf.* Bruges Death and the Miser Painter and Lisbon Alexander VI Painter).

[Fl. 243, Fl. 65 (1875), Fl. 431, Fl. 892, Fl. 440, Fl. 113, Fl. 114, Fl. 316, Fl. 530.]

'Pseudo-Blesius', see **Munich Adoration Master.**

Pseudo-Geertgen, see **Figdor Deposition Master.**

*****Punder, Jacobus de.** Presumed Flemish Sch. *b* before 1550 *d* after 1572. *Portraits, religious subjects.* Presumed by some identical with J. de Poindre *q.v.* and with Jacques Pindar *q.v.*

Signed Examples: BALTIMORE Walters Art Gall. *Portrait of a Bishop (or Abbot)* (ACOBUS EPUNDER ECIT 1563). LAUSA (nr. Dresden) Church *Resurrection of Christ* (JACOP DEPUNDER 1572).

[Fl. 440, Fl. 50 (1938), Fl. 631 (1942).]

Pupiler (Popelier), Antoni. Flemish Sch. *b* Antwerp (?) before 1535 *d* Spain (?) or Netherlands (?) after 1567. Master Antwerp Guild 1550; entered service of Philip II (*cf.* A. Mor) 1556; went Spain (*cf.* M. v. Cleve the younger, S. Pereyns and P. de Kempener); had his salary increased 1562; worked in Pardo Palace (destroyed by fire 1604); sent by Philip II to Louvain for nine months to copy a famous altarpiece there (by R. v. d. Weyden? or D. Bouts?) 1567. (*Cf.* M. Coxie).

[Fl. 153, Fl. 440, Fl. 88, Fl. 20 (1932).]

Pyp, Cornelis. Flemish Sch. In Naples *c.* 1560-70 (*cf.* J. S. van Calcar, W. Coebergher, H. v. d. Broeck, C. Smet, P. Schephen, J. v. d. Straet). A. Mytens *q.v.* worked there under him and married his widow with whom he found life intolerable.

[Fl. 559.]

Q

Quaedvlieg, Carel Max. Flemish Sch. *b* Valkenberg 1823 *d* Rome 1874. *Animals and genre.* Studied Antwerp; went Rome 1853. [Fl. 837 (1874), Fl. 88.]

Quartenmont, A. B. de, see **Quertenmont.**

Queborne (or **Queckborne**), **Christian van den.** Flemish Sch. *b* Antwerp *c.* 1515 *d* Antwerp 1578. *Landscapes and designs for ceremonial decorations.* Antwerp Master 1545; Official painter to Antwerp city 1560; close friend of A. v. Palerme *q.v.*; A. de Weerdt, J. Grimmer and D. Calvaert were among his pupils. [Fl. 559, Fl. 892, Fl. 88.]

Queborne (or **Queckborne**), **Daniel van den.** Flemish Sch. *b* son of Christian Q., Antwerp before 1560 *d* before 1618. *Portraits.* In Antwerp Guild 1577-84; with his wife the engraver Barbara v. d. Broeck fled from Antwerp after Duke of Parma's conquest (*cf.* Frans Boels, H. Bol, Gillis Congnet, G. v. Coninxloo, G. C. de Hondecoeter, H. Jordaens (I), K. v. Mander, A. and W. v. Nieulandt, H. v. Steenwyck the elder, G. Steynemolen, F. v. Valkenborch, D. Vinckeboons, C. v. d. Voort, J. V. de Vries, J. v. Winghe) and went Middelburg (*cf.* C. v. d. Broeck, A. v. Stalbemt) 1585; later went The Hague where became court painter to Prince Maurice of Nassau (*cf.* J. de Gheyn the younger). [Fl. 559, Fl. 892, Fl. 88.]

*Quellinus (or **Quellin**), **Erasmus.** Flemish Sch. *b* son of sculptor Erasmus Q., Antwerp 1607 *d* Antwerp 1678. *Religious subjects, 'history', mythological and allegorical compositions; also book illustrations (for Plantin Press) and engravings.* Applied himself to painting after literary studies; Master Antwerp Guild 1633; assistant in Rubens' atelier; worked under Rubens on Pageant Entry into Antwerp of Cardinal Infante Ferdinand (*cf.* G. Weri) 1635; also under Rubens on *Metamorphoses of Ovid* series for Torre de la Parada (*cf.* J. P. Gowi) and other commissions for Philip IV of Spain; succeeded Rubens as Antwerp City Painter; directed decorations for Pageant Entry of Archduke Leopold Wilhelm (*cf.* D. Teniers the younger and F. Snyders) 1648, for Proclamation of Peace of Münster 1648, for Don John of Austria's Antwerp Entry (*cf.* P. Snayers) 1657 and for the Marquis of Castel-Rodrigo's Entry (*cf.* F. Duchatel and J. v. Werden) 1665; his first wife was a sister of J. P. v. Thielen; his second wife was a sister-in-law of D. Teniers the younger; J. P. van Thielen and D. Seghers painted flower garlands round some of his pictures and P. A. Immenraet sometimes assisted him with landscapes (*cf.* also P. Boel and P. v. d. Velde); W. Vaillant and J. Denys were among his pupils. His large collection of pictures, sculpture, drawings and prints included works by Rubens, Van Dyck, Jan Fyt, L. de Vadder, P. Spierincx and other Flemish contemporaries, 'twee curieuses lantschapkens van Glaude' (Claude le Lorrain) and copies of Italian paintings by his son Jan Erasmus Q.; a number of his own works and a *Last Judgement* (sketch) by Tintoretto were shown in a room hung with gold leather; his library included a Rubens sketch book, Descartes' Principia Philosophiae, Van Mander's 'Schilderboek', the 'Pompa Introitus' book of engravings by T. van Thulden *q.v.*, a book of prints by M. v. Heemskerck, Ovid's Metamorphoses in French, The Legends of the Saints, and books on music, pharmacy, optics, coins, architecture and a number of dictionaries. Many copies of his pictures, and some originals, were exported in his lifetime to the Vienna branch of the Forchoudt firm of dealers for whom he under-

took (1670) to paint a picture, the time employed to be dependent on the price ('want men moet meer winnen of 2 maanden dan op eene'). **Signed Examples:** ANTWERP S. Jacques *The miraculous healing of S. Roch* 1660; Mus. *Holy Family.* AUGSBURG *Adoration of the Shepherds.* BUDAPEST *The Four Seasons* 1676. DUNKIRK *Holy Family* 1639. MALINES Cathedral *Adoration of the Shepherds* 1669. MADRID Prado *Bacchus and Ariadne, Death of Eurydice, Jason and the Golden Fleece* (from sketches by Rubens). VIENNA Liecht. *The Queen of Sheba before Solomon, Achilles discovered among the daughters of Lycomedes* (*cf.* P. P. Rubens, Jan Erasmus Q. and G. de Lairesse) 1643. **Monogrammed Examples:** THE HAGUE Mauritshuis *Allegory: The Earth* (in *Interior of a gallery* by G. Coques *q.v.*). PRAGUE Rudolfinum *Grisaille of Virgin with flower garland.* **Documented Examples:** ANTWERP Mus. Plantin-Moretus *Balthasar Moretus, printer* (contemp. engraving). VIENNA K. *Grisaille of Virgin with flower garland* (recorded 1659 Archduke Leopold Wilhelm inventory as by 'Erasmo Quillinio'; flowers by J. P. v. Thielen, *s*). His *Peace driving Mars and Bellona to Candia, The Marriage of Louis XIV of France and Infanta Maria Theresa of Spain, Philip IV and his son receiving allegiance of the Seventeen Provinces* and *Don Francisco de Moura, Marquis de Castel-Rodrigo, governor-general Spanish Netherlands, crowned by Mercury and Athene* are among many paintings recorded by contemporary engravings. Jan Gillis, Antwerp silversmith, owned (1682) a *Four Quarters of the World* with figures by him and the rest by 'Kessel' (*cf.* F. v. K. and J. v. K. the elder). Titles recorded in contemporary inventories and in the Forchoudt records include a *Mystic marriage of S. Catherine* (*cf.* O. v. Veen), *Suffer little children to come unto me* (*cf.* H. de Clerck, Jan Snellinck and V. Sellaer), *The Immaculate Conception, S. Sebastian, Pomona, Mercury and Argus, Jupiter and Callisto* and *Artemisia drinking the ashes of Mausolus.* Descamps (1769) saw many of his works in Flemish churches (some possibly by J. E. Q. *q.v.*) [Fl. 86, Fl. 425, Fl. 22, Fl. 215, Fl. 216, Fl. 107, Fl. 88, Fl. 892, Fl. 212, Fl. 213.]

*Quellinus (or **Quellin**), **Jan Erasmus,** called 'Sederboom'. Flemish Sch. *b* son of Erasmus Q., Antwerp 1634 *d* Malines 1715. *Religious subjects, 'history', still life, portraits.* Pupil of his father *q.v.*; travelled Italy visiting Venice, Florence and Naples; in Rome where received nickname 'Cedar tree' in Flemish colony 1660; returned Antwerp 1661; married a daughter of D. Teniers the younger; had eleven children; quarrelled with his father-in-law; went Vienna where court painter to Emperor Leopold I (*cf.* J. Thomas 'van Ypern') *c.* 1680; back in Antwerp where assessed the large art collection of the Antwerp Postmaster J. B. Anthoine 1691; spent last years, in financial distress, with a daughter in Malines. **Signed Examples:** ANTWERP *Christ in the house of Simon* 1692, *Nativity* 1689, *Miracle of S. Hugh, Bishop of Lincoln* 1685 (from Carthusian monastery at Lierre), *Christ at the Pool of Bethesda* 1672 (very large Picture from Antwerp Abbey of S. Michel *cf.* P. v. Lint). DUNKIRK *S. Helena finding the True Cross* 1692. MALINES S. Rombout *The Last Supper* 1690; Béguinage *S. Carlo Borromeo* 1694. **Documented Examples:** ANTWERP *The martyrs of Gorcum* (from Abbey of S. Michel). VIENNA K. *Coronation of Charles V as Roman Emperor by Clement VII, Bologna 1530* (from series of 15 ceiling paintings commissioned by Leopold I for Vienna Hofburg, painted 1687). Vienna (Albertina) has

signed pastels including *Vertumnus and Pomona* 1678 and *Achilles among the daughters of Lycomedes* (*cf*. Erasmus Q. and G. de Lairesse) 1660. The inventory of his father's collection (1678) records an *Apollo*, many *Fruit and flower pieces*, and copies of pictures by Bassano, Tintoretto and other Italians; Descamps (1769) records many pictures in Flemish churches; a series *The Four Feasts of Scripture* painted for the Refectory of the Abbey of S. Michel is recorded by engravings; records of the Forchoudt firm of dealers (1670) refer to an *Antony and Cleopatra* (*cf*. G. Seghers and G. de Lairesse).
[Fl. 425, Fl. 753, Fl. 216, Fl. 451, Fl. 107, Fl. 892, Fl. 212, Fl. 213.]

Quertenmont (or **Quartenmont**), **Andreas Bernardus de.** Flemish Sch. *b* Antwerp 1750 *d* Antwerp 1835. '*History*' *and portraits; also worked as portrait draughtsman and engraver.* Pupil in Antwerp Acad.; teacher there 1779; copied for Antwerp Dominicans Caravaggio's *Virgin of the Rosaries* (to replace original sold to Emperor Joseph II 1781 and now Vienna Kunsthist). (*cf*. L. Finson and F. Pourbus the younger);

drew portraits of members of the États de Brabant Meeting 1787 and of the 1790 Republican Government; Director Antwerp Acad. from 1791; lost post for refusal to serve under French occupation (*cf*. S. d'Argonne); his full-length portrait *Joseph II* (*cf*. G. de Pélichy), painted for Antwerp City 1784, was publicly burned as representing a 'çi-devant tyran' 1794; later had private art school in his own house. L. Moons, F. M. Smits, F. B. Solvyns and the Dutch portraitist A. de Lelie were among his pupils.
[Fl. 451, Fl. 107, Fl. 892, Fl. 440.]

Quinaux, Joseph. Flemish Sch. *b* Namur 1822 *d* Schaerbeek (Brussels) 1895. *Landscapes.* Pupil of F. Marinus in Namur Academy; also studied Antwerp and Louvain; member of Antwerp Academy; professor Brussels Academy; worked for some time in France. Represented in ANTWERP *Landscape in Savoy* 1867, *Landscape near Liège* 1864. BRUSSELS *In Dauphiné* 1869, *The Ford* 1875. SYDNEY (Australia) *Landscape nr. Dinant* and two others.
[Fl. Bib. 19th cent., Fl. 88, Fl. 296, Fl. 17.]

R

Raemaeker, Henri F., see **Ramah.**

Raemdonck, Georges van. Flemish Sch. *b* Antwerp 1888 *Portraits, landscapes, still life, book illustrations, caricatures.* Pupil in Antwerp Acad. of P. Verhaert and in Higher Institute of F. Courtens. Represented in ANTWERP *Portraits* (three). [Fl. 17.]

Raet, Arnould. Flemish Sch. *b* Louvain (?) before 1430 *d* Louvain after 1477. In early life practised as a baker in Louvain; worked for Léau church 1470-2; working Louvain from 1473 (*cf.* D. Bouts and H. Stuerbout). His father of the same name was also a painter. [Fl. 269, Fl. 88.]

Raet, Louis (known as **Louis de scildere**). Flemish Sch. *b* son of Arnould R. Louvain (?) before 1490. Recorded working for church of Léau 1505-7. [Fl. 88.]

Raeth (Rach, Raes), Ignacio. Flemish Sch. *b* Antwerp *c.* 1626 *d* Antwerp (?) or Germany (?) 1666. *Religious subjects, portraits.* Pupil of B. van Cortbemde; in Antwerp Guild 1641; Díaz del Valle (1659) records that he entered the Jesuit order and worked under D. Seghers *q.v.*, went Spain (*cf.* A. Smit) and was attached to Madrid Jesuit College 1655-8; Palomino (1725) adds that he went back to Flanders from Spain and visited Germany where he died. **Signed Examples:** None. **Documented Example:** MADRID Colegio Imperial (Jesuit College) *Portrait of Father J. E. Nierenberg* (recorded by Díaz as seen by him in the Corpus Christi day exhibition). Díaz and Palomino record *Thirty six scenes from the life of S. Ignatius Loyola* painted for Madrid Jesuit church before 1658. (*Cf.* A. Rodriguez). [Fl. 222, Fl. 637, Fl. 153, Fl. 612, Fl. 88, Fl. 892, Fl. 20 (1928), Fl. 807, Fl. 798.]

Raeymackers, Jules. Flemish Sch. *b* Laeken 1883 *d* Houffalize 1904. *Landscapes.* Associated with Tervueren Sch. (*cf.* H. Boulenger). Represented in LIÈGE. [Fl. 892, Fl. 160 (1905), Fl. 17.]

Raf, Jehan, see **Corvus.**

Ramah (pseudonym of **Raemaeker, Henri François**). Flemish Sch. *b* St. Josse-ten-Noode 1887 *d* Brussels 1947. *Landscape and figure compositions in Post Impressionist* (*cf.* C. Dehoy and C. Permeke) *and Cubist conventions; also still life and book illustrations.* Worked at various times in Provence; member of Antwerp group L'Art Contemporain (Kunst van Heden) (*cf.* R. Strebelle) and of Salon des IX (*cf.* H. Daeye) 1926. Represented in ANTWERP *Boule players* 1921. BRUSSELS *Mme. Ramah* 1921. GHENT *The harvest.* [Fl. 388, Fl. 296.]

Ramey (or **Ramaye**), **Jean.** Flemish Sch. *b* Liège *c.* 1530 *d* on journey back from France after 1602. *Religious subjects; also worked as glass painter* (*cf.* D. J. Velaert, J. de Gheyn the elder and the younger, P. Aertsen and P. A. Cluyt). Pupil of Lambert Lombard (*cf.* L. Suavius); took O. v. Veen as his pupil 1573; Dean of Liège Silversmiths' Guild 1585; went Paris (*cf.* L. Thiry and A. Dubois) and worked on decorations of Luxembourg Palace (?). **Signed Examples:** GLAIN nr. Liège, Ste Marie-des-Lumières *Adoration of the Shepherds.* LIÈGE Mus. de l'inst. arch. *S. Paul healing the lame* 1600. A *Last Supper* for Liège, S. Pierre 1576 and a signed *Raising of Lazarus* 1602 are recorded. [Fl. 409, Fl. 88, Fl. 892.]

Rammelaer or **Ramelaer,** see **Coninck, D. de.**

Ranieri, see **Regnier.**

Rassenfosse, Armand. Flemish Sch. *b* Liège 1862 *d* Liège 1934 *Genre, also engravings, illustrations and posters.* Pupil in Liège Acad. of A. de Witte; then pupil and collaborator of F. Rops *q.v.*; worked much in Paris; illustrated Baudelaire's 'Fleurs du Mal' 1899-1901. Represented in ANTWERP *Nude* (drawing). BRUSSELS *The Hungarian Cap* 1914, *Work girls* 1905. GHENT *Dancer* and drawings DORDRECHT and ROME. [Fl. 296, Fl. Bib. 19th cent.]

Rave, Jan de, see **Corvus.**

Reckelbus, Louis. Flemish Sch. *b* Bruges 1864. *Landscape, picturesque corners of Bruges, marines, still life, interiors (o. and w.).* Pupil Bruges Acad.; worked on the Belgian coast, in Holland and France; curator Bruges Mus. 1930. Represented in ANTWERP *Snowpiece (Bruges).* BRUGES *Old Bruges house in autumn. Fountain of the little faun* and others. BRUSSELS *Stormy night in Flanders* BUENOS AIRES, COURTRAI, DIXMUDE, NAMUR, VENICE. [Fl. 114, Fl. 296.]

***Redemption Master.** Flemish Sch. 15th cent. Name for painter of MADRID Prado (1888-92) Triptych; centre: *Crucifixion in a church,* wings: *Last Judgement, Expulsion from Eden,* exterior of wings: *The Tribute money.* Presumed by some identical with R. v. d. Weyden *q.v.* [Fl. 555, Fl. 798.]

Redig, Laurent. Flemish Sch. *b* 1822 *d* Antwrep 1861. *Landscapes (some with peasant genre figures); also worked as engraver.* Pupil of J. B. de Jonghe and J. Ruyten. Worked in the region round Antwerp and in Holland. Represented in COURTRAI. [Fl. 440, Fl. 88.]

Redouté, Antoine Ferdinand. Flemish Sch. *b* son of Charles J. R., S. Hubert 1756 *d* Paris 1809. *Flowers and fruit* (*cf.* P. Faes and A. Plateau), *decorative paintings.* Pupil of his father *q.v.*; in Paris from 1776; after the Revolution exhibited flower pieces in Salon 1793 and 1795 (*cf.* P. J. Redouté); officially patronized under Consulate and Empire (*cf.* L. Gerbo and J. F. v. Dael); decorations by him for the Salle du Tribunat in Palais-Royal (where Napoleon was declared Emperor 1804), for the Palais de l'Élysée (reconstructed for Caroline Murat 1805 and occupied by the Empress Josephine 1809), for Josephine's Château de Malmaison, for Compiègne and for the Salle de Spectacle at Bordeaux are recorded. [Fl. 451, Fl. 66.]

Redouté, Charles Joseph. Flemish Sch. *b* son of Jean Jacques R., Jamagne nr. Philippeville 1715 *d* S. Hubert 1776. *Religious subjects, landscapes, portraits.* Pupil of his father in Dinant; went Paris (*cf.* J. F. Delien, G. de Spinny, J. Nollekens and H. de La Pegnia) 1737; worked at Acad. of S. Luc and remained Paris till 1743; went S. Hubert where worked for the Abbey 1744; also painted for Benedictine Abbey at Liège, for the Abbey of Stavelot and for neighbouring country houses. [Fl. 451, Fl. 66.]

Redouté, Henri Joseph. Flemish Sch. *b* son of Charles J. R., S. Hubert 1766 *d* Paris 1852. *Drawings and watercolours of natural history.* Went Paris and became pupil and assistant of his brother Pierre J. R. *q.v.* 1785; after the Revolution painter and draughtsman to Musée d'histoire naturelle (Jardin des Plantes) 1793; exhibited drawings of fish in 1795 Salon; member of the Art and Science Commission which accompanied Napoleon on Egyptian campaign 1798; illustrated many publications including 'Collection de poissons des côtes de la Mediterranée' by Coquebert (*cf.* A. v. Aken).

[Fl. 451, Fl. 66.]

Redouté, Jean Jacques. Flemish Sch. *b* Dinant 1687 *d* Dinant 1752. The eldest of the painters of this name.

[Fl. 63, Fl. 451, Fl. 892.]

Redouté, Pierre Joseph. Flemish Sch. *b* son of Charles J. R., S. Hubert 1759 *d* Paris 1840. *Flower paintings (many in watercolour), botanical drawings and lithographs.* Pupil of his father; went Paris and joined his brother Antoine F. R. *q.v.*; began as stage designer for the Italian comedy; specialized in plant drawing after meeting the botanist C. L. Lhéritier de Brutelle for whose 'Stirpes novae . . .' (published Paris 1784) he drew plates; received his brother H. J. R. *q.v.* as pupil and assistant 1785; with Lhéritier visited London (*cf.* P. J. Tassaert, L. B. Coclers, H. J. de Cort, P. J. Lion and P. de Glimes) where made experiments in colour printing; returned Paris and worked for the Dutch flower painter G. van Spaendonck at the Jardin du Roi; dessinateur du cabinet to Queen Marie-Antoinette 1788, then flower painter to the nation (*cf.* J. F. van Dael and J. F. Ducq also A. Ansiaux and J. L. Demarne) 1793; exhibited Salon from 1796; natural science draughtsman at the Institute founded by Napoleon 1799, official painter to Jardin des Plantes 1800, flower painter to Empress Josephine (*cf.* L. Gerbo) 1805 and again court flower painter under the Restoration and Louis Philippe. His publications include 'La famille des Liliacées' (1802) given by Napoleon to all European sovereigns and leading scholars and artists to celebrate his coronation 1804; 'Les plantes du jardin de la Malmaison' 1803; 'Les Roses' 1817, 'Choix des plus belles fleurs . . .' 1827. **Documented Examples:** PARIS Jardin des Plantes, COMPIÈGNE, MONTPELLIER, NARBONNE.

[Fl. 210, Fl. 451, Fl. 97, Fl. 612, Fl. 66, Fl. 511.]

Reesbroeck (or Rysbroeck), Jacob van. Flemish Sch. *b* Antwerp 1620 *d* Hoogstraaten 1704. *Portraits; also worked as engraver.* Master Antwerp Guild 1642; in Hoogstraaten from 1682. Antwerp Mus. Plantin has portraits traditionally recorded as his work. A signed painting stated to represent '*William Hyde, Lord Clarendon*' is recorded.   [Fl. 892.]

Regemorter, Ignatius Josephus van. Flemish Sch. *b* son of P. J. van R., Antwerp 1785 *d* Antwerp 1873. *Landscapes; bourgeois, peasant and military genre; costume and contemporary history* (*cf.* M. v. Brée); *also active as engraver.* Pupil of his father, then of B. P. Ommeganck; to Paris where saw Musée Napoléon 1809; took part, with his father, in restoration of works of art recovered from Paris 1814-15; member of Netherlandish Institute and Amsterdam Acad. 1829; founder of Antwerp Kunstverbond. G. E. C. Wappers and J. M. Ruyten were among his pupils. Represented in AMSTERDAM Rijks. *Fishmarket in Antwerp, Jan Steen sending out his son to sell his pictures* 1828. ANTWERP *Cardplayers quarrelling* BRUSSELS, HAARLEM. Pictures titled *The visit of King Leopold I of the Belgians and of Queen Victoria of England to S. Jacques, Antwerp 1843; The marriage of Ferdinand Prince de Ligne and Princess Louise de Lorraine 1841* are recorded. Pictures titled *The old gallant* and *Jan Steen, having exhausted his finances and the contents of his cellar, by his generosity to his brother artists, ceases to sell beer and wine and resumes his profession of painter while Frans v. Mieris offers his disconsolate wife a portion of the last bottle* (*cf.* P. Kremer) were in the London R. A. 1828.

[Fl. 451, Fl. 481, Fl. 837 (1873), Fl. 361, Fl. 73.]

Regemorter, Petrus Johannes van. Flemish Sch. *b* Antwerp 1755 *d* Antwerp 1830. *Landscapes with figures (some by moonlight)* (*cf.* P. van Schendel), *peasant genre, interiors (some by candlelight); also active as restorer and pasticheur.* Pupil in Antwerp Acad.; painted figures in early views by H. J. F. de Cort *q.v.*; held offices in Antwerp Guild 1784-90; professor in Antwerp Acad. during French occupation (*cf.* B. P. Ommeganck, L. Defrance, S. P. Argonne and P. J. B. Leroy) from *c.* 1800; M. van Brée and M. Verstappen were his pupils; visited Rotterdam 1797 when the flower painter P. J. Thys *q.v.* describes him in a letter, as staying with an art dealer named Marneffe and producing pictures purporting to be by the Dutch painters Ruysdael, Pynacker, Both and others (*cf.* J. v. Bredael and J. I. de Roore); sent Paris by Antwerp authorities to assist B. Ommeganck *q.v.* in recovering works of art from the Musée Napoléon (*cf.* I. J. van R.) 1815. **Signed Example:** ANTWERP *Interior of Old S. Georges Church Antwerp* (figures by P. J. van R., architecture by A. Blom).

[Fl. 451, Fl. 612, Fl. 570.]

Regnier, Nicolas (known in Italy as **Ranieri** or **Reinieri**). Flemish Sch. *b* Maubeuge *c.* 1590 *d* Venice 1667. Half brother of M. Desubleo *q.v. Religious subjects, portraits.* Pupil in Antwerp of A. Janssens *q.v.*; went Italy and remained there (*cf.* F. v. d. Kasteele, P. de Lignis and J. Sutterman); pupil in Rome of Italian painter B. Manfredi; member of Congreg. dei Virtuosi 1623; in Venice and member of Venetian Guild 1626-41 (*cf.* P. de Coster); had four beautiful daughters Angelica, Anna, Clorinda and Lucretia (*cf.* D. v. d. Dyck) who served him as models and were also painters. **Documented Examples** (Recorded by contemporary writers): VENICE Acad. *Annunciation* (in 2 parts; formerly in Venice S. Teresia); S. Canciano *Virgin in Glory with S. Philip Neri*; S. Luca *SS. Louis of France, Cecilia and Margaret*; S. Salvadore *Baptism of Christ*; S. Teresia *Virgin in Glory with Senator Giov. Moro*; S. Maria of Carmel *S. Simon Stock and other saints.* Recorded works also in Venice S. Cassiano, S. Gregorio, S. Nicolò da Tolentino and other churches.

[Fl. 709, Fl. 101, Fl. 753, Fl. 612, Fl. 892, Fl. 844, Fl. 536, Fl. 305.]

Rem (or Rems), Gaspar. Flemish Sch. *b* Antwerp 1542 *d* Venice (?) after 1614. *Portraits, religious subjects.* Pupil in Antwerp of W. v. Cleve; went Italy and remained there (*cf.* J. v. d. Straet); in Venice by 1572 (*cf.* D. Barendsz, M. de Vos and L. Toeput); refused there to take the German painter Hans v. Aachen as a pupil on the ground that the 'Moffen' (Germans) had no capacity for art, but relented after seeing v. A.'s *Laughing self portrait* (*cf.* F. Pourbus the younger, B. Spranger and Jerrigh); presumed by some to have worked for Austrian court (*cf.* A. de Rye). **Signed Example:** VIENNA K. *Self portrait at age of 72* 1614. **Documented Example:** VIENNA K. *S. Jerome in the desert striking his breast with a stone* (engraved 1603 and dedicated by the painter to F. v. d. Kasteele *q.v.*). Pictures titled *The three Kings, Sibyl and Joseph* 'after Gaspar Rem' are recorded in Antwerp collections 1621, 1642, and 1663.

[Fl. 559, Fl. 753, Fl. 612, Fl. 892, Fl. 440, Fl. 213.]

Remaut, Pierre Joseph. Flemish Sch. *b* Bruges 1772 *d* Bruges 1826. *Portraits* (*cf.* J. v. d. Donckt, J. D. Odevaere, F. J. Kinson). Represented in BRUGES Hôpital S. Jean *Portrait of a Mother Superior.*   [Fl. 88.]

Remee (or Remy), see Leemput, R. van.

Remeeus, David. Flemish Sch. *b* Antwerp 1559 *d* Antwerp 1626. *Religious subjects; also worked as gilder.* Pupil of M. de Vos; Master Antwerp Guild 1581; Dean 1601; married niece of M. de Vos, then granddaughter of J. de Momper; his daughter married P. de Witte the younger; C. and P. de Vos were his pupils.   [Fl. 107, Fl. 892.]

Remeeus, Gillis. Flemish Sch. *b* son of David R., Antwerp (?) before 1630 *d* date unknown. *Genre.* Master in Antwerp Guild 1644. **Signed Example:** GRAZ *Lute player.*
[Fl. 107, Fl. 892.]

Remes, Charles. Flemish Sch. *b* Wetteren 1795 *d* Wetteren 1837. *Religious subjects for churches in Ghent region; and genre.* Pupil of P. v. Huffel. Teacher in Wetteren Art school. **Signed Example:** GHENT Grand Béguinage *S. Dominic receiving a rosary from the Virgin* 1820.
[Fl. 451, Fl. 479, Fl. 88.]

Remonde (or **Romunde** or **Rormonde**), **Everard van (de).** Presumed Flemish Sch. 17th cent. Commissioned by the Brabant Chambre des Comptes, together with P. van Somer *q.v.*, to paint portraits of the Archduke Albert and the Archduchess Isabella 1616; the portraits were paid for 1617.
[Fl. 440.]

Rendeux, Englebert Panhay de. Flemish Sch. *b* son of Renier P. de R. *q.v.*, Liège 1719 *d* Rome 1777. *Marines.* Pupil of his father in Liège; went Rome (*cf.* J. B. and L. B. Coclers) 1746; pupil there of the French painter Joseph Vernet; settled Rome (*cf.* H. F. van Lint and A. P. V. de Muynck); took religious orders. Was also known in his day as a violin virtuoso.
[Fl. 892.]

Rendeux, Renier Panhay de. Flemish Sch. *b* Liège 1684 *d* Liège 1744. *Religious subjects for Liège churches* (*cf.* J. and N. J. Riga and J. B. Coclers); *but mainly worked as sculptor.* Pupil in Rome of the Italian painter Carlo Maratta 1702 (*cf.* S. v. Aken, R. v. Audenaerd, M. v. Duvenede, N. Vleys); remained Italy till 1712; then settled Liège. O. Pirotte and H. Deprez were among his pupils. A *Last Judgement* (wall painting) for a convent, now demolished, is recorded.
[Fl. 409, Fl. 88.]

Reuille, Jules. Flemish Sch. *b* Lyons 1816 *d* after 1860. *Portraits.* Worked Brussels where his 'effigies féminines' described as 'gracieuses et d'un coloris éclatant' had a vogue in fashionable circles from *c.* 1850.
[Fl. 440.]

Reymerswaele, M. van, see **Marinus.**

*Reyn (or **Ryn**), **Jan van** (or **de**). Flemish Sch. *b* Dunkirk 1610 *d* Dunkirk 1678. *Portraits, religious subjects, 'history'.* Pupil of Van Dyck in Antwerp *c.* 1630; came England (*cf.* C. de Neve) lived with and worked under Van Dyck (*cf.* R. van Leemput) *c.* 1632-*c.* 1635; returned Antwerp and worked under Rubens on Torre de la Parada commission for Philip IV of Spain (*cf.* J. Gowi) 1636; went Paris at invitation of the Comte de Gramont (*cf.* W. Vaillant) but left in dudgeon because a shirt had been stolen from him; settled Dunkirk; painted festival decorations for Pageant Entry of Louis XIV (*cf.* J. G. Carlier and G. Ladam) into Dunkirk 1663. **Signed Examples:** BERGUES-ST-WINOC *The daughter of Herodias.* BRUSSELS *Portrait of a lady in a black dress with red ribbons* 1637. WULVERINGHEM Church *Adoration of the Shepherds* 1663. **Monogrammed Example:** MADRID Prado *Marriage of Peleus and Thetis* (I. R. 163 . .) presumed based on a sketch by Rubens. **Documented Examples:** DUNKIRK S. Éloi *The four Crowned Martyrs* (with portrait of the artist in a white hat); Mus. *S. Alexander freed from prison by an angel* with donor *Alexander Leys, his wife and children* (both seen in S. Éloi by Descamps, who writes of the second (1769): 'c'est l'ouvrage d'un artiste habile' and ranks it with 'les plus beaux ouvrages de Van Dyck'. Descamps also records a *Baptism of Totila* in Dunkirk Riches-Claires, *SS. Benedict, Scholastica and Agatha* in Bergues St. Winoc Abbey and a copy in Dunkirk S. Roch of Rubens' *S. Roch* ('cette copie pourra tromper un jour, tant elle approche de son modèle: la facilité et la fermeté de la touche n'y laissent nulles traces de gêne ni de tâtonnement').
[Fl. 215, Fl. 216, Fl. 612, Fl. 440, Fl. 88, Fl. 892.]

Reysschoot, Anna Maria van (Mme. Diegenant). Flemish Sch. *b* daughter of E. P. v. R., Ghent 1758 *d* Ghent 1850. *Genre and grisaille imitating bas reliefs* (*cf.* F. Eisen and M. J. Geeraerts). Married E. Diegenant.
[Fl. 451, Fl. 126, Fl. 798.]

Reysschoot, Emanuel Petrus van. Flemish Sch. *b* Ghent 1713 *d* Ghent 1772. Brother of P. J. v. R. *Religious subjects, history, portraits.* A series of pictures painted on the occasion of the sixth jubilee of S. Bernard celebrated at Baudeloo Abbey 1753 are recorded (*cf.* R. v. Audenaerd, J. v. Cleef and G. Le Plat).
[Fl. 451, Fl. 126, Fl. 892, Fl. 798.]

Reysschoot, Petrus Johannes van. Flemish Sch. *b* Ghent 1702 *d* Ghent 1772. Brother of E. P. v. R. *Religious subjects, portraits, genre; also active as engraver.* Presumed by some the 'Reyschoot' recorded pupil in Paris Acad. (*cf.* O. Pirotte) 1730; went England (*cf.* P. A. Rysbraeck and P. Casteels III); remained sometime and was known therefore on his return Ghent as 'the Englishman'. A series of paintings *The Twelve Apostles* (over life size) recorded painted for Ghent Augustine church were not seen there by Descamps (1768). A *Portrait of the Duchess of Norfolk* is recorded by an engraving 1746; a plate titled (in English) *The happy man* is among his own engravings.
[Fl. 451, Fl. 593, Fl. 386, Fl. 892.]

Reysschoot, Petrus Norbertus van. Flemish Sch. *b* son of E. P. v. R., Ghent 1738 *d* 1795. *Religious subjects; also landscapes with genre figures, decorative paintings for Ghent houses, mythologies and designs for applied arts.* Visited Italy where collected drawings; professor of architecture in Ghent Acad. 1770; had a library of art historical books. **Documented Examples:** GHENT S. Bavon (grisailles) *Scenes from the Old and New Testaments* 1774-91. A *Charles of Lorraine shooting down the popinjay* (*cf.* D. v. Alsloot, D. Teniers the younger and J. P. Sauvage) in Ghent Mus. is recorded.
[Fl. 451, Fl. 479, Fl. 481, Fl. 892, Fl. 296.]

Rheni (or **Rhen**), **Remigius van.** Flemish Sch. *b* Brussels *c.* 1560 *d* Brussels 1619. Went Germany and worked for Count Henry of Waldburg-Wolfegg whose castle was burned with the works of art which it contained; returned Brussels after the fire.
[Fl. 86, Fl. 425, Fl. 878, Fl. 215, Fl. 440, Fl. 88, Fl. 892, Fl. 798.]

Ribaucourt Master. Presumed Flemish Sch. 17th cent. Name for painter of BRUSSELS Mus. (605) *Family group* bought 1891 (as by Van Dyck) from the Comte de Ribaucourt.
[Fl. 892, Fl. 124.]

Richir, Herman J. J. Flemish Sch. *b* Ixelles 1866. *Portraits and figure pieces.* Pupil in Brussels Acad. of C. Hermans and A. Robert; Member of Paris Salon de la Nationale 1906; professor and director of Brussels Acad. Represented in ANTWERP (Academy) *The artist A. Robert.* BRUSSELS *The artist's wife.* LIVERPOOL Walker *Figure in white.* NAMUR *Black and White* (from Brussels) and SYDNEY (Australia) *After the bath.*
[Fl. Bib. 19th cent. Fl. 296.]

Ricquier (Riquier), Louis. Flemish Sch. *b* Antwerp 1792 *d* Paris 1884. *Costume history, genre, classical and occasional religious subjects.* Pupil of M. v. Brée; went Paris where worked with M. v. Brée's brother P. v. B.; in Italy with P. v. B. 1816-19; married daughter of M. v. Brée and settled Paris; in Italy 1832 and 1842. Represented in BRUSSELS *Family of brigands* 1833. HAARLEM *Rubens presenting Adrian Brouwer to his wife* (*cf.* P. Kremer) 1824. Pictures titled *Androcles and the lion* and *Virgil reciting the Aeneid to Augustus and Octavia* painted when he was twenty were exhibited in 1813; a *Fernando Cortez triumphing over Montezuma* exhibited in Paris Salon 1816 is also recorded.
[Fl. 451, Fl. 88, Fl. 440, Fl. 73.]

Rieue, J. de, see **Dreux.**

Riga, Jean. Flemish Sch. *b* Liège 1680 *d* Liège 1725. *Religious pictures for Liège churches* (*cf.* N. J. Riga); *allegories for murals.* A *Wedding Feast at Cana* for Liège S. Nicolas and ceiling paintings for Liège Town Hall (*Faith, Hope and Charity* in Council Chamber and *Justice, Prudence* and *Strength* in Hall of Marriages) are recorded. [Fl. 409, Fl. 440, Fl. 88.]

Riga, N. J. Flemish Sch. *b* Liège (?) 1653 *d* Liège 1717. *Religious subjects for Liège churches* (*cf.* J. Riga, R. P. de Rendeux and J. B. Coclers). A *S. Anthony of Padua kneeling before Christ with the Virgin and Trinity above and an old man as donor* is recorded. [Fl. 409, Fl. 440, Fl. 88.]

Rigouldts, see Thielen, J. P. van.

Rillaert (or Rillaer), Jan van. Flemish Sch. *b* Louvain (?) before 1510 *d* Louvain 1568. *Religious subjects and designs for official ceremonies; also worked as engraver.* Painter to Louvain city 1547; designed for 'Ommeganck' processions (*cf.* D. v. Alsloot) and for the Pageant Entry into Louvain of Charles V and Philip II 1549 (*cf.* C. Anthonisz, H. W. de Cock, P. Coecke van Aelst, F. Floris, A. v. Palerme, P. J. Pourbus, J. Scorel, J. V. de Vries and M. Willems); designed for ceremonies in Louvain S. Pierre on death of Charles V 1558. **Monogrammed Example:** BERLIN K. F. (grisaille) *Judgement of Solomon* (J v R 1528). Compositions recorded in Louvain Mus., Hôtel de Ville and S. Pierre are presumed by some his work. [Fl. 269, Fl. 440, Fl. 88, Fl. 892.]

Rillaert (or Rillaer), Jan van the younger. Flemish Sch. *b* son of Jan v. R. the elder, Louvain *c.* 1547 *d* 1592. *Religious subjects* (?) In Denmark 1580 (*cf.* K. v. Mander the younger); returned Louvain where valued *The Virgin of Louvain* by J. Gossaert *q.v.*, which was saved from the Iconoclasts (*cf.* P. Aertsen) and presented by the town to Philip II 1588. [Fl. 269, Fl. 440, Fl. 892, Fl. 88.]

Ritter, L. C., see Neufville.

Robbe, Henri. Flemish Sch. *b* Courtrai 1807 *d* Brussels 1899. *Flowers, fruit, occasional landscapes.* Pupil of his brother Louis R. Officer of the Order of Leopold. Represented in BRUSSELS, COURTRAI, GHENT, and NEW YORK Public Library. [Fl. 160 (1899), Fl. 440, Fl. 798, Fl. 73.]

Robbe, Louis M. D. Flemish Sch. *b* son of a barrister, Courtrai 1806 *d* Brussels 1887. *Animals in landscape* (*cf.* A. Engel, B. P. Ommeganck, H. Ronner, J. B. de Roy, J. Stevens, J. Stobbaerts, E. J. Verboeckhoven, C. Verlat). Began as a lawyer; pupil in Courtrai Acad.; thereafter of J. B. de Jonghe; practised both law and painting for some years from *c.* 1833-*c.* 1839; thereafter highly successful as painter in Brussels; friend and first patron of C. de Groux; exhibited Paris; Chevalier of the Légion d'honneur 1845; Commander of the Order of Leopold. Represented in ANTWERP *Cattle in pasture, Hay cart.* BRUSSELS *Campine with cattle, Cattle in pasture near Courtrai* (commissioned by Government 1842). BRUGES *Goat and sheep, Cattle in pasture* COURTRAI, GHENT, HAMBURG, LIÈGE, LILLE, MALINES, CINCINNATTI and WASHINGTON. A dog piece *La pâtée trop chaude* 1845 and *Bulls fighting* (*cf.* J. B. de Roy) 1851 are recorded. [Fl. 451, Fl. 329, Fl. 264, Fl. 440, Fl. Bib. 19th cent.]

Robert, Alexandre Nestor Nicolas. Flemish Sch. *b* son of a lawyer, Trazegnies (Hainault) 1817, *d* St. Josse-ten-Noode, Brussels 1890. *Religious subjects, costume history, genre, portraits.* Pupil of F. J. Navez; went with J. Portaels *q.v.* to Paris and Rome 1842; married daughter of J. B. Madou; professor Brussels Acad. (*cf.* J. Stallaert and J. v. Severdonck). Represented in ANTWERP *Singing lesson, The painter J. B. Madou.* BRUSSELS *Luca Signorelli painting his dead son* (*cf.* P. Kremer) 1848, *Sack of an Antwerp convent in the sixteenth century* 1866; Senate *The return from Calvary* 1847. BUENOS AIRES *Charles V contemplating death* 1854. GHENT *Head of a monk* 1849. COURCELLES Church *Martyrdom of S. Barbara.* TRAZEGNIES Church *Moses on the Mount* 1841. A portrait *M. Ad. van Soust* exhibited Paris 1855 was praised by Delacroix. [Fl. 440, Fl. 88.]

Roberti, Albert. Flemish Sch. *b* Brussels 1811 *d* Brussels 1864. *Costume history, portraits.* Pupil of F. J. Navez. Teacher Brussels Acad. 1854. Represented in BRUSSELS *Rachel mourning her children* 1851, *A nun.* [Fl. 88.]

Robie, Jean Baptiste. Flemish Sch. *b* Brussels 1821 *d* S. Gilles, Brussels 1910. *Still life* (*flowers and fruit*). Exhibited London R. A. 1875; frequent exhibitor in Paris Salon; Chevalier of the Légion d'honneur; Commander of the Order of Leopold. Represented in BRUSSELS, GHENT, LILLE, BOSTON, BROOKLYN, SYDNEY (Australia) *Flowers and fruit* and FLORENCE (Uffizi) *Self portrait.* [Fl. 361, Fl. 160 (1910), Fl. Bib. 19th cent.]

Roden, Matthys van. Flemish Sch. *b* Ghent *c.* 1450 *d* Ghent 1514. Master Ghent Guild 1475; worked on Pageant Entry into Ghent of Archduke Maximilian on his marriage with Maria of Burgundy 1477 (*cf.* P. Coustain and B. v. Battel). [Fl. 126, Fl. 88.]

Rodriguez, Adriano (real name **Adriaen Dierickx**). Flemish Sch. *b* Antwerp 1600 or 1618 *d* Madrid Jesuit College 1669. *Religious subjects.* Master Antwerp Guild 1629; went Spain aged 30 (*cf.* A. Smit); Palomino (1725) records that he changed his name because his own 'sounded so strangely in these parts'; entered Jesuit order (where known as 'Hermano Adriano') 1648. Paintings in Madrid S. Isidro (in collaboration with Ignacio Raeth *q.v.*) and pictures painted for the refectory of the Madrid Colegio Imperial (Jesuit College) are recorded. [Fl. 222, Fl. 637, Fl. 153, Fl. 612, Fl. 88, Fl. 892, Fl. 807.]

Roffiaen, François (**Jean François Xavier**). Flemish Sch. *b* Ypres 1820 *d* Ixelles 1898. *Landscapes* (*many of Swiss subjects*). Pupil in Brussels Acad. and of the Swiss painter A. Calame in Geneva. Represented in BRUGES *Evening on the Wallenstaat Lake,* BRUSSELS *Valley of the Aar* 1873, *Mont Rose* 1875, THE HAGUE, LOUVAIN Town hall, MONTREAL *Pilatus from Lake Lucerne,* NAMUR, YPRES. [Fl. 88, Fl. 296.]

Rogerius Gallicus. Flemish Sch. 15th cent. *b* date and place unknown *d* after 1450. *Religious subjects, compositions with nudes.* Pupil of 'Johannes' (presumed Jan van Eyck). B. Facio (1456) records him in Rome for the Jubilee Year 1450 where he admired Gentile da Fabriano's frescoes in the Lateran. **Signed Examples:** None. **Documented Examples:** None. Facio records (1) Genoa: *A woman sweating in a bath spied on by two laughing youths; a dog beside the woman* (*cf.* Jan van Eyck); (2) Ferrara: Palace of the Duke. Triptych: centre: *Lamentation,* on wings *The Expulsion from Paradise, Portrait of the donor;* (3) Naples: Palace of King Alfonso *Mater Dolorosa* and *Passion scenes;* (4) Brussels 'Aedes sacra'. Presumed by some identical with Rogier of Bruges *q.v.* and/or Rogelet van der Weyden *q.v.* [Fl. 286, Fl. 892.]

Rogier of Bruges. Flemish Sch. *b* Bruges (?) date unknown *d* Bruges (?) after 1470 (?). *Religious subjects, portraits and tempera paintings on wall hangings.* Pupil of Jan van Eyck; went Italy and was paid in Ferrara for work executed for Duke Leonello d'Este 1450; Vasari (1550) records 'Hausse' (presumed H. Memlinc) as his pupil. **Signed Examples:** None. **Documented Examples:** None. Cyriacus of Ancona (1449) was shown by Leonello d'Este in Ferrara an *Adam and Eve* and a

Lamentation by Rogier of Bruges (or Brussels) and pictures of similar subjects are recorded in the Duke of Ferrara's collection (as by 'Rogerius Gallicus pupil of Johannes') by B. Facio (1456); Dürer (1521) saw a chapel in the 'Kaiser Haus' in Bruges painted by 'Rudiger'; the Anonimo of Morelli (1530) records in the Vendramin collection in Venice a *Crowned and standing Virgin and Child in a church.* Don F. de Guevara (*c.* 1560) records a *Portrait of his father, Don Diego de Guevara* painted by 'Rogier' about ninety years earlier (i.e. *c.* 1470) 'still as perfect as though it were finished yesterday'; Vaernewyck (1568) records work in Bruges churches and private houses; Van Mander (1604) records wall hangings 'on large scale with tall figures' in old houses in Bruges and paintings in churches. Presumed by some identical with Rogerius Gallicus *q.v.* and/or Rogelet van der Weyden *q.v.* (*Cf.* also Rogier van der Weyden, Vienna Adam and Eve Painter, Vienna Cruciform Lamentation Painter and Exhumation of S. Hubert Master.)
[Fl. 286, Fl. 754, Fl. 12, Fl. 243, Fl. 818, Fl. 370, Fl. 812, Fl. 559, Fl. 892.]

Rogier of Brussels. Flemish Sch. 15th cent. Recorded (1531) by the Anonimo of Morelli (Marc Anton Michiel?) as painter of *Self portrait* (*bust length*) *dated 1462* then in possession of Zuanne Ram in S. Stefano (Venice). Presumed by some identical with London Young Man in High Cap Painter *q.v.*
[Fl. 12, Fl. 892.]

Rogier of Louvain. Flemish Sch. 15th or 16th cent. *Religious subjects.* Recorded by Molanus (*c.* 1575) as 'Magister Rogerius civis et pictor Lovaniensis'. Molanus also records him as painter of (1) Louvain: S. Pierre *Edelheer altarpiece;* this altarpiece still in situ and dated 1443 includes portraits of donor W. Edelheer and his two sons and a reduced version of the *Descent from the Cross* by R. v. d. Weyden. (2) Louvain Notre Dame *High altarpiece* which was acquired from the Louvain Archers' Guild by Mary of Hungary, Regent of the Netherlands, sent by her to Spain, shipwrecked but rescued on the way to Spain, and replaced in Notre Dame by a copy made by the court painter M. Coxie *q.v.* of Malines; (Van Mander (1604) describes the Coxie copy then in Louvain Notre Dame hors des murs (Onze Lieve Vrouwe daar buiten) as showing a *Descent from the Cross* and refers to the original, sent to Spain, as by Rogier van der Weyden of Brussels); (3) Brussels: Town Hall '*Justice*' pictures (Van Mander records these as by Rogier van der Weyden of Brussels). *Cf.* R. v. d. Weyden.
[Fl. 589, Fl. 559, Fl. 892, Fl. 316, Fl. 530.]

Rogier, Claes (Nicolas). Flemish Sch. *d* Malines 1534. Van Mander (1604) describes him as 'a good painter of landscapes' (*cf.* F. Mostaert). [Fl. 559.]

Roije (Roye), Jozef van de. Flemish Sch. *b* Antwerp 1861. *Still life.* Pupil in Antwerp Acad. of L. Schaefels. Worked at one time in Holland. Represented in ANTWERP *Fruit* 1894 MALINES, YPRES. [Fl. 73, Fl. 17.]

*Rombouts, Theodoor (sometimes referred to as **Roelands** or **Roelants**). Flemish Sch. *b* Antwerp 1597 *d* Antwerp 1637. *Religious subjects, 'history' and genre.* Pupil of A. Janssens; went Italy *c.* 1616; worked Florence (for Duke Cosimo II and/or Duke Ferdinand II (*cf.* J. Sutterman)) also in Rome and Pisa; back in Antwerp where Master in Guild 1625; married sister of J. P. v. Thielen *q.v.* 1627; Dean in Antwerp Guild 1628; commissioned by Ghent Magistrates to paint for Town Hall; worked on Pageant Entry into Ghent of Cardinal Infante Ferdinand (*cf.* G. de Crayer, N. de Liemaker, C. Schut, also G. Weri) 1635. Eighteenth century writers record that he claimed to equal Rubens in his art (*cf.* A. Janssens) and also in the grandeur of his house on which he squandered his substance. His widow married G. Weri a few weeks after his death. J. P. v. Thielen and N. v. Eyck were his pupils. Van

Dyck drew his portrait. D'Argenville referring to his genre pictures 'assemblées de charlatans, des tabagies, des cabarets' wrote 'son pinceau n'a jamais allarmé la vertu par des figures obscènes'. **Signed Examples:** ANTWERP *S. Augustine washing the feet of Christ as pilgrim* 1636 (from Malines Augustine Church where admired by Descamps 1768), *Christ driving the money changers from the Temple* (*cf.* Paris Expulsion of Traders Painter); S. Jacques *Mystic Marriage of S. Catherine* 1634. CARLSRUHE *S. Irene withdrawing the arrows from S. Sebastian's wounds.* GHENT *The Five Senses* (*cf.* D. Teniers the younger), *Allegory of Justice* (from Town Hall where 18th cent. writers record it much admired by Rubens). VIENNA Liecht. *S. Peter's denial, Death of Seneca.* **Documented Examples:** MADRID Prado *The quack dentist, Card players.* The Forchoudt firm of Antwerp dealers owned (1650) a *Christ and S. Mary Magdalene;* a *S. Peter's denial* is recorded (1657) in an Antwerp collection; D'Argenville records *S. Francis receiving the stigmata* and *Sacrifice of Isaac* (*cf.* D. Teniers the younger) in Ghent Town Hall and *Old Testament subjects* painted for a French patron; Descamps saw in Ghent, S. Bavon a *Descent from the Cross* ('la tête de notre Seigneur, en racourçi, est médiocre et mal dessinée'), in Ghent Recollets *The Angel appearing to S. Joseph in his dream,* in Ypres S. Martin *The Visitation* and other pictures in Brussels and Malines churches. A number of compositions are recorded by engravings. Genre pictures presumed by some his work are in various museums.
[Fl. 86, Fl. 425, Fl. 878, Fl. 22, Fl. 215, Fl. 216, Fl. 612, Fl. 107, Fl. 892, Fl. 212, Fl. 213, Fl. 214.]

Rommelaere, Émile. Flemish Sch. *b* Bruges 1873. *Landscapes, portraits, interiors, genre.* Pupil of Bruges and Antwerp Acads. Professor Bruges Acad. 1895. Represented in BRUGES *News from the Front, Garden of the Maison Dieu.* [Fl. 114.]

Ronner, Alfred. Flemish Sch. *b* son of Henrietta R., Brussels (?) 1852 *d* Brussels 1901. *Cats.* Pupil of his mother *q.v.* [Fl. 892.]

Ronner, Alice (Emma Alice). Flemish Sch. *b* daughter of Henrietta R., Brussels 1857. *Still life.* Pupil of her mother. Represented in ANTWERP *Flower piece* 1906. BRUSSELS *The pewter jug* 1887, *The turkey* 1902, *Poppies* 1909.
[Fl. 17, Fl. 123.]

Ronner (Ronner-Knip), Henrietta. Flemish Sch. *b* daughter of Dutch painter J. A. Knip, Amsterdam 1821 *d* Brussels 1909. *Animals (mostly cats)* (*cf.* Alfred R. and L. Robbe), *genre.* Pupil of her father; in Brussels by 1857; exhibited London Royal Academy 1891-1903; member London Royal Institute. Represented in AMSTERDAM *Cat and kittens* 1844. *Three against one* (*cat and dogs*). ANTWERP *Shameless* BRUSSELS, DIJON, LEEDS *A literary dispute, How funny.* TOLEDO (U.S.A.). Pictures titled *Amateurs of jewels, A cosy corner* and *Coaxing* were among those exhibited in London R.A. [Fl. 777, Fl. 264, Fl. 296, Fl. Bib. 19th cent.]

Roome (Roem, Romme), Jan van. Called Jan or Jean de Bruxelles. Flemish Sch. *b* before 1480 *d* after 1521. *Portraits, designs for tapestry, glass and sculpture.* Referred to by Margaret of Austria as 'Jean van Roome autrement dit Jean de Bruxelles' 1510; took part in the designing of the tapestry *The Miraculous Communion of Herkenbald* (now Brussels Musées Royaux) commissioned by the Confrérie du Saint-Sacrement of Louvain S. Pierre and finished 1513; employed by Margaret of Austria for her memorial Église de Brou, Bourg-en-Bresse (*cf.* J. Schooff) 1516. A portrait *Philibert II of Savoy* is recorded. Presumed by some identical with J. Gossaert *q.v.* or J. Mostaert *q.v.*
[Fl. 892, Fl. 88, Fl. 798, Fl. 296.]

Roons, Lodewyk. Flemish Sch. 18th cent. Worked Courtrai and Bruges where J. A. Garemyn *q.v.* was his pupil *c.* 1725.
[Fl. 451.]

Roore (or **Rore** or **Rorus**), **Jacques Ignatius de.** Flemish Sch. *b* son of an art dealer, Antwerp 1686 *d* The Hague 1747. *Large 'history' and religious compositions (cf.* R. P. de Rendeux, W. I. Kerricx, Z. J. v. Helmont, V. Janssens, also P. Verhaghen) *and mythological decorations; also worked as pasticheur, restorer and dealer.* Pupil of A. Genoels; then in Brussels of L. v. Schoor 1703; friend in Antwerp of H. v. Lint *q.v.*; Master Antwerp Guild 1707; assisted G. v. Opstal from 1706 on his copies of works by Rubens, Van Dyck, Teniers, Jan Steen and others for French and German markets (*cf.* C. J. de Crec, J. van Pee, J. Peeters the younger, and P. J. van Regemorter); executed decorative compositions for Antwerp authorities and rich private citizens; later similarly employed in Holland; as dealer in The Hague (in partnership with the Dutch painter G. Hoet) bought Van Dyck's *S. Martin* from Saventhem Church but was forced by a local riot in protest to return it 1739; a smaller version of Van Dyck's picture was in the very large collection of pictures dispersed on R.'s death. **Signed Examples:** ANTWERP S. Jacques *The liberation of Christian slaves by Trinitarian monks* 1709 (*cf.* J. A. Garemyn). HAMBURG *Self portrait* 1707, *Portrait of his mistress.* **Documented Examples:** ANTWERP Town Hall *Allegorical subjects* (ceiling in Salle du Conseil and Salle de la Trésorerie) 1715-17. Small pictures titled *Julius Caesar proclaimed Emperor, The burning of Caesar's corpse* and *The withering of Jeroboam's hand* are recorded in his testament.
[Fl. 353, Fl. 878, Fl. 215, Fl. 216, Fl. 451, Fl. 612, Fl. 440.]

Roos (or **Roosen**), **Jan** (known in Italy as Giovanni Rosa). Flemish Sch. *b* Antwerp 1591 *d* Genoa 1638. *Religious subjects, animals, still life (flowers and fruit).* Pupil of J. de Wael (1605) and Frans Snyders; went Italy and remained there (*cf.* J. Sutterman); in Rome 1614; in Genoa (*cf.* C. and L. de Wael) from 1616; friend of A. van Dyck and presumed by some to have painted animals in his Genoese pictures; Soprani (1674) relates that dogs mistook the hares in his pictures for live ones; some of his paintings were sold to Spain and France. **Documented Example:** GENOA SS. Cosma e Damiano *Entombment of Christ with the Virgin, S. Francis of Assisi and donors* (recorded by Soprani).
[Fl. 773, Fl. 505, Fl. 612, Fl. 440, Fl. 88, Fl. 305.]

Roose, see **Liemaker.**

Rooster, Jacques de. Flemish Sch. *b* Malines *c.* 1661 (?) *d* place and date unknown. *Italianate landscapes (cf.* A. Baudewyns and P. v. Bredael). D'Argenville (1745) records him as pupil (follower?) of the French painter Gaspard Poussin in Italy. Malines Mus. has *Landscape with classical ruins* presumed by some his work.
[Fl. 22, Fl. 613, Fl. 88, Fl. 892.]

Roover, Albert de. Flemish Sch. *b* Boom 1892. *Portraits, landscapes.* Pupil of J. de Vriendt and I. Opsomer in Antwerp Higher Institute. Teacher in Antwerp Acad. Represented in ANTWERP *Chimneys.*   [Fl. 17.]

Roover, Carlo de. Flemish Sch. *b* Boom 1900. *Genre, landscapes, still life.* Teacher in Antwerp Acad. Represented in ANTWERP *Bathing women.*   [Fl. 17.]

Rops, Félicien. Flemish Sch. *b* of rich family, Namur 1833 *d* (partially blind) Essonnes (France) 1898. *Social genre with implicit comment (cf.* L. Frédéric), *symbolic figures (cf.* X. Mellery, J. Delville, and A. Levêque), *landscapes, coast scenes; but chiefly active and notorious as lithographer and engraver of social-satirical genre (many with female nudes and half nudes).* Self taught; went Brussels where directed satirical journal 'Uylenspiegel' for which he drew many lithographs (other contributors being L. Artan, A. Dillens, C. de Groux, E. Smits) 1856-61; illustrated books for French publisher Poulet-Malassis (then in Brussels) from 1863; drew frontispiece for Baudelaire's 'Les épaves' 1866; met Baudelaire (then in Brussels) who addressed a poem to him (*cf.* J. Stevens) with the lines

'Ce tant bizarre Monsieur Rops,
Qui n'est pas un Grand-Prix de Rome
Mais dont le talent est haut comme
La pyramide de Chéops'.

Member of Brussels group Société Libre des Beaux Arts (*cf.* L. Dubois) 1868; included in the portrait group of the members by E. Lambrichs *q.v.*; launched without success in Brussels 'La Société Internationale des Graveurs' 1875; made frequent visits to Paris where drew in the Académie Julian; had studios in Paris and Brussels from 1876 and country house at Marlotte 1878; member of the Brussels group Les Vingt (*cf.* J. Ensor) 1884; drew titlepages for works by G. de Maupassant, Barbay d'Aurévilly, P. Verlaine, Catulle Mendès, J. ('Sar') Péladan and S. Mallarmé; visited Holland, Norway, the Tyrol and Spain; made many technical experiments in engraving some with A. Rassenfosse *q.v.*; A. Daudet describes him as 'un tzigane qui satanise' (he was suspected of Hungarian blood) and the painter A. Renoir as 'un Cabanel belge'. A retrospective exhibition of his painting was held in Brussels 1932. Represented in ANTWERP *Fishing port at Blankenberghe, Landscape in the Ardennes, Bridge over the Lesse, Barges at Dinant.* BRUSSELS *The beach, The quarrel* (*w.* 1877). OTTERLO (Kröller-Müller Mus.) *Death at the Ball.* Others in LIÈGE, MOSCOW Mus. Modern Western Art, PARIS State Collections. Paintings titled *Dimanche à Bougival, La Cantinière du pilotage* and *L'Espagnole de Cordova* are recorded.
[Fl. 681, Fl. 4, Fl. 694, Fl. 486, Fl. 516, Fl. 572, Fl. 307, Fl. 603, Fl. 277, Fl. 274, Fl. 484, Fl. 465, Fl. 296.]

Rosier, Jean Guillaume. Flemish Sch. *b* Lanaeken 1858 *d* Antwerp 1931. *Religious subjects, costume history and genre, portraits, interiors.* Pupil of M. Verlat in Antwerp Acad., then in Paris of the French painters J. L. Gérome and A. Cabanel in École des Beaux Arts. Member of Als ik Kan group (*cf.* H. Luyten) 1885; teacher in Antwerp Acad.; later director Malines Acad.; in London during 1914-18 German invasion (*cf.* L. de Smet). Represented in ANTWERP *The minuet, The music party.* MALINES Jesuit church *Altarpiece.* LANAEKEN Church *Stations of the Cross.*
[Fl. 889, Fl. 348, Fl. Bib. 19th cent.]

Rosseels (Rossells), Jacques. Flemish Sch. *b* Antwerp 1828 *d* Antwerp 1912. *Landscapes (mostly in regions round Antwerp, Limbourg and Upper Scheldt).* Pupil in Antwerp Acad. of H. v. d. Poorten *q.v.* Travelled Italy; member of Termonde School (*cf.* J. Heymans) and director Termonde Acad. Represented in ANTWERP *Near Waasmunster, Moonlight* and others BRUSSELS, GHENT, LIÈGE, NAMUR, TERMONDE.   [Fl. 160 (1912), Fl. Bib. 19th cent.]

Rottie, Pierre. Flemish Sch. *b* Antwerp 1895 *d* Antwerp 1946. *Portraits, still life, flowers, interiors.* Pupil in Antwerp Higher Institute of I. Opsomer. Teacher in Antwerp Acad. Represented in ANTWERP *Portrait of a lady.*   [Fl. 17.]

Roy, Jean Baptiste de, known as De Roy de Bruxelles. Flemish Sch. *b* son of an art dealer, Brussels 1759 *d* Brussels 1839. *Animals and landscapes (cf.* J. B. Berré, J. C. Carpentero, A. Engel, J. F. Legillon); *also active as engraver,* Went Holland in youth; tried to become a pupil of but was not accepted by B. P. Ommeganck *q.v.*; Louis David referred to him as the best Netherlandish colourist; another contemporary wrote (1827): 'De Roy nous a donné des foires de bestiaux, des parcs de bœufs, des combats de taureaux (*cf.* L. Robbe), des hardes dans des gras pâturages, des incendies, des coups de vent, des brouillards, là tout un troupeau qui quitte la ferme vers la prairie ou qui regagne l'étable, et toujours des sites spacieux et romantiques'. H. v. Assche, S. P. d'Argonne,

P. J. B. Leroy and H. Voordecker *q.v.* were among his pupils. **Signed Examples:** GOTHA, MAINZ Town Coll. and VIENNA Liecht. A life size *Bull standing in a meadow with Château of Laeken in the background* painted in emulation of the Dutch painter Paul Potter (*cf.* W. Spoor) 1803 is recorded.

[Fl. 451, Fl. 612, Fl. 440, Fl. 88, Fl. 892.]

Royalme, Pierre de, see **Coninxloo.**

Roye, see **Roije.**

Roymerswael, see **Marinus.**

*Rubens, Arnold Frans. Flemish Sch. *b* Antwerp 1687 *d* Antwerp 1719. *Outdoor genre and military scenes* (*cf.* P. van Bloemen), *some in Italianate landscapes* (*cf.* P. v. Bredael and M. Schoevaerdts). Master Antwerp Guild 1709. **Signed Examples:** COPENHAGEN *Skating scene, Dance round a Maypole, Carnival in Italian landscape, Merrymaking outside a tavern,* two *Camp scenes.* Others in HERMANNSTADT and STOCKHOLM Univ. **Documented Examples:** ROME Doria *Levantine Port, Battle piece* (18th cent. inventory).

[Fl. 612, Fl. 892, Fl. 88, Fl. 170, Fl. 678.]

Rubens, Joannes Baptist. Flemish Sch. *b* Brussels (?) before 1780 *d* after 1845. *Miniatures, genre.* Worked Brussels. P. J. Hellemans was his pupil. A snuff box with portrait of a woman signed 1792 is recorded.

[Fl. 612, Fl. 892.]

Rubens, Peter Paul. Flemish Sch. *b* son of Antwerp lawyer and alderman Jan R. (who had fled (1568), accused of Calvinism, from Alva's persecutions to Cologne (*cf.* A. de Weerdt and F. Hogenberg), where was imprisoned and later interned Siegen (1573–1578) for adultery with the drunken Princess Anna of Saxony, wife of William of Orange) Siegen 1577 *d* Antwerp 1640. *Religious subjects, 'history', mythologies, allegories; portraits; landscapes with animals, rural and social genre and mythological figures; designs for pageantry and tapestry; book illustrations for the Plantin Press; also active as collector, antiquary, humanist and diplomat.* Was not baptized a Catholic (as Jan R. and his wife Maria were Lutherans in Siegen though they again became Catholics some time after their return (1578) to Cologne where Maria kept a shop); taken by his mother after his father's death (1587) to Antwerp *c.* 1588; attended a school where Balthasar Moretus (grandson of Christopher Plantin of the Plantin Press) was fellow pupil; page in Audenarde to widow of Count Philip of Lalaing; pupil of Tobias van Haecht (Verhaecht) 1591; of Adam van Noort before 1594; of Otto van Veen 1596; Master in Antwerp Guild 1598; assistant to van Veen on Pageant Entry into Antwerp of the Archduke Albert and Infanta Isabella (*cf.* A. and M. Joncquoy, P. v. d. Meulen the elder, G. Pietersz, J. de Liemakere) 1599; had D. Teniers the elder *q.v.* as his pupil (?); with his pupil Deodatus Delmont *q.v.* went Venice (*cf.* H. Staben and P. Mera) 1600; introduced there to Vincenzo Gonzaga, Duke of Mantua, and appointed his Court Painter (*cf.* F. Pourbus the younger) 1600; taken by the Duke to Florence for the marriage by proxy of Marie de Médicis and Henri IV of France; in Rome (*cf.* F. v. d. Kasteele, P. de Lignis and P. Brill) where sent by the Duke to copy pictures 1601; in Mantua and Verona 1602; sent by the Duke (then a candidate for the office of Admiral in the Spanish service) to conduct a convoy of presents to Philip III (*cf.* F. and R. Diriksen, L. Franchoys the elder and G. Seghers) and his favourite the Duke of Lerma 1603; stayed four months in Valladolid, where the presents, (including a coach and seven horses, firearms, gold, silver and crystal vases and copies of pictures by Raphael and other Italians by the Italian painter P. Facchetti) were delivered by the Duke's resident agent; saw the pictures by Titian in the Royal Palaces and the Escorial and painted an equestrian portrait of the Duke of Lerma but was not presented to the King; declined suggestion from his employer that he should visit France and paint the court beauties for his gallery of beautiful women (*cf.* F. Pourbus the younger); returned Mantua 1604; still so little known in the Netherlands that Van Mander (1604) did not record him in the Schilderboek; in Rome (with visit to Genoa 1607) 1606-8; negotiated in Rome for purchase of Caravaggio's *Death of the Virgin* (now Paris, Louvre) for Duke Vincenzo; friend there of the German painter Adam Elsheimer and patronized by Cardinal Scipio Borghese; painted two versions of an altarpiece ordered for the 'New Church' Sta. Maria in Vallicella; gave his doctor a picture of a cock (sacred to Aesculapius) as a thank offering for his services (*cf.* C. Luyckx); returned Antwerp on learning that his mother was in extremis 1608; officially received into Antwerp Society of Romanists by the Dean, Jan (Velvet) Brueghel *q.v.* 1609; left Duke Vincenzo's service and settled Antwerp; appointed Court Painter to Archduke Albert and Infanta Isabella (*cf.* G. de Crayer and D. v. Alsloot) 1609; commissioned by Burgomaster Rockox and Antwerp magistrature to paint a picture for the Town Hall (*cf.* A. Janssens) 1609; assisted Jan (Velvet) Brueghel in his correspondence with Cardinal Borromeo; married Isabella Brant (daughter of Antwerp City Secretary) 1609; commissioned by the Guild of Crossbowmen to paint a picture for Antwerp Cathedral, payment to include a freehold site for his house and a pair of gloves for his wife, 1611; acquired a house and property in Antwerp, enlarged the house and gave it a palatial character with garden pavilions and loggias, a studio for himself forty-six by thirty-four feet and others above for his pupils and assistants 1611-15; established mass-production picture factory, with specialist assistants for figures, landscape, draperies, animals, still life and so forth (*cf.* A. v. Dyck, J. Jordaens, F. Snyders, L. v. Uden, J. Wildens, P. de Vos, J. Fouquier, V. Wolfvoet, T. v. Thulden, F. Wouters, J. Thomas (van Ypern), A. J. v. Diepenbeeck, M. v. d. Bergh, J. Moermans, L. Franchoys the younger, N. v. d. Horst, also P. de Champaigne); his wife stood godmother to a daughter of M. Pepyn *q.v.* and to a daughter of Jan (Velvet) Brueghel 1615; collaborated with Jan (Velvet) Brueghel in several pictures *c.* 1617; acquired a collection of marbles from Sir Dudley Carleton in exchange for a group of his pictures and a money payment to be expended on Brussels tapestries 1618; began series of paintings and sketches for tapestries (History of Decius Mus) *c.* 1618; commissioned to paint altarpieces for the new Jesuit church (*cf.* A. G. Gheringh and W. S. v. Ehrenberg); contracted to make thirty-nine sketches for ceiling panels for the church to be executed by A. v. Dyck and other assistants (*cf.* D. Seghers, G. Seghers and C. Schut) 1620; on death of Archduke Albert (1621) became increasingly the confidant of the Infanta Isabella who began to employ him on diplomatic tasks; commissioned by the Queen Mother Marie de Médicis to paint series of pictures for the Luxembourg Palace; went Paris to arrange details (taking with him a little dog and a necklace as presents to Marie de Médicis from the Infanta) 1622; directed execution of nine of the pictures in the Antwerp atelier (*cf.* J. v. Egmont) and took them to Paris where they were approved by Marie de Médicis and admired by Richelieu 1623; applied for and received patent of nobility from Philip IV 1624; appointed Gentleman of the Household by Infanta Isabella 1624; employed by Isabella on secret negotiations for a truce between the Spanish Netherlands and the United Provinces 1624; took remaining pictures for Luxembourg Palace to Paris and finished them in situ with J. v. Egmont as chief assistant 1625; present at the marriage of Charles, Prince of Wales (by proxy) with Henrietta Maria, sister of Louis XIII, in Paris; met there the Duke of Buckingham, and wrote of Prince Charles as 'the greatest lover of painting I know among princes' 1625; returned Antwerp where was visited in his studio by the Infanta Isabella who sat for her portrait (*cf.* A. v. Dyck) 1625; with C. Schut and H. v. Balen *q.v.* an executor of Jan (Velvet) Brueghel's estate and guardian of his children

1625; death of his wife 1626; engaged in discussions about the sale of many pictures and works of art to Buckingham conducted by the Duke's agent the painter-adventurer Balthasar Gerbier who also brought Rubens a secret letter from the Duke proposing negotiations for peace between England and Spain; empowered by the Infanta Isabella to negotiate in the matter (whereat Philip IV wrote to the Infanta 'I much regret that you have had recourse to a painter to treat of such important affairs'); went Holland to have diplomatic meetings and masked his mission by visiting the Dutch painters Gerard Honthorst, Abraham Bloemaert, and C. van Poelenburgh (*cf*. H. v. Steenwyck the younger) accompanied by the unsuspecting German art historian J. von Sandrart then a pupil of Honthorst; returned Brussels and Antwerp when Gerbier was recalled to England 1626-7; called to Spain by Philip IV in connection with the continuing secret negotiations with England 1628; left his house in charge of W. Panneels *q.v.* and went Spain 1628; remained Madrid for eight months and wrote 'I . . . have done an equestrian portrait of His Majesty much to his liking and satisfaction . . . my rooms are in the palace and he comes to see me nearly every day. I have also done, for my lady, the Serenissima Infanta, the heads of all the royal family who have sat to me'; copied pictures by Titian in the Spanish royal collections and went with Velázquez to the Escorial (*cf*. P. v. d. Hulst); appointed by Philip Secretary of the Netherlands Privy Council with right of succession for his eldest son; sent by Philip to England as diplomatic envoy to Charles I 1629; stayed England ten months and helped to arrange an exchange of ambassadors with a view to discussing peace; wrote there: 'This island seems to me worthy the consideration of a man of taste, not only because of the charm of the countryside and the beauty of the people, not only because of the outward show, which appears to me most choice and to announce a people rich and happy in the bosom of peace, but also by the incredible quantity of excellent pictures, statues and ancient inscriptions which are in this Court'; knighted by Charles I and given Hon. M.A. by the University of Cambridge 1630; went Brussels where reported to Infanta Isabella; returned Antwerp 1630; married as second wife Helena Fourment daughter of a rich Antwerp silk merchant 1630; employed as diplomatic envoy to Marie de Médicis on her arrival in the Netherlands 1631; reported on the matter to the Infanta and Philip's minister Olivarez; wrote later to a private friend: 'I was entrusted, alone, with the whole secret negotiation with France touching the flight of the Queen Mother and the Duke of Orléans from the Kingdom of France and the asylum granted to them here. I could furnish much matter to an historian and tell the real truth of this affair which is very different from what is generally believed'; was visited in his studio by Marie de Médicis (*cf*. A. v. Dyck) 1631; helped her to pawn her jewels (the Infanta had already pawned hers in 1629; *cf*. W. Coebergher) 1631; sent by the Infanta on secret missions to Prince Frederick Henry 1631 and 1632, to the indignation of the États Généraux (convened 1632) and the Flemish nobles who were also negotiating 1632 and 1633; obtained permission from the Infanta to be released from further missions; not further employed in diplomacy after the death of the Infanta 1633; directed the completion of decorations for the ceiling of Whitehall Banqueting House 1634; directed Pageant Entry into Antwerp of Cardinal Infante Ferdinand, Isabella's successor as Governo (*cf*. E. Quellinus, G. Seghers, C. de Vos, T. v. Thulden, G. Weri, also T. Rombouts), 1635; bought estate known as Château de Steen, where mainly lived thereafter, 1635; sent the Whitehall pictures to London 1635 and wrote: 'As I abhor court life I have sent my work to England by a third hand. My friends write that it has now been placed in position and that His Majesty is entirely satisfied with it. I have not yet been paid, but I should be a novice in the affairs of the world if that were to surprise me, for long experience has taught me that princes are slow where the financial interests of others are concerned' 1636; was

visited in his house and appointed Court Painter by the Cardinal Infante Ferdinand (*cf*. G. de Crayer and P. Snayers). 1636; witness at the wedding of J. B. Borkens *q.v.* with daughter of Jan (Velvet) Brueghel 1636 and of another daughter with D. Teniers the younger *q.v.* 1637; designed tapestries to be made for Philip IV's Minister the Count-Duke Olivarez; painted landscapes in the region of Steen; received final payment for Whitehall paintings and a gold chain from Charles I 1638; made sketches for series of paintings (mostly executed by his assistants and associates) for the Torre de la Parada and other royal residences of Philip IV (*cf*. J. v. Reyn, P. Symons, T. Willeboirts and J. P. Gowi) 1636-9; sold *Allegory of the outbreak of War* to J. Sutterman *q.v.* for Medici Duke Ferdinand II 1638; became increasingly afflicted with gout (the Infante Ferdinand reported to Philip IV 'Rubens has been paralysed in the hands for more than a month' April 1640); made his will dividing his property between Helena Fourment and his children (with agates and medals to his sons Albert and Nicholas, books to Albert and the painting *Het pelsken* i.e. *Helena Fourment nude with a fur coat* to Helena herself) and appointing F. Snyders and J. Wildens among the executors May 1640; buried in Antwerp S. Jacques May 1640.

The inventory of works in his studio (1640) records about eighty of his own paintings (of which ten were bought by Philip IV); his own copies of works by Titian and others; originals by Titian, Tintoretto, Veronese and other Italians and pictures by Dürer, Holbein and Elsheimer; *Two portraits, a man and wife* by Jan van Eyck, a *Portrait of a jeweller* by Master Quintinus (Massys), a *Virgin in a landscape* by H. Bles, a *Portrait of Granvella* by Schorre (J. v. Scorel), a *Portrait of Erasmus* by L. v. Leyden and works by 'Sotte' Cleve, 'Breugel' (Pieter and Jan (Velvet)) including a *Diana and her nymphs returning from the chase* by himself and Jan B., Joos van Cleve, J. S. v. Hemessen, A. Mor, F. Floris, W. Key, M. Coxie, M. v. Cleve, A. Claesz v. Leyden, B. de Ryckere and W. Tons; the paintings by his Flemish contemporaries included works by A. Adriaenssen, P. Brill, A. v. Dyck, J. F. v. Es, F. Ijkens, J. Jordaens, Jan Porcellis, D. Seghers, P. Snayers, F. Snyders, P. de Vos, S. de Vos, S. Vrancx, J. Wildens and sixteen by A. Brouwer; works by the Dutch painters C. van Poelenburgh and Cornelis Saftleven were also recorded. **Signed Examples:** ANTWERP *Venus frigida* 1614. CASSEL *Jupiter and Callisto* 1613, *Flight into Egypt* 1614. THE HAGUE *Adam and Eve in Paradise* (also *s* by Jan (Velvet) Brueghel). MUNICH *Cupid cutting his bow* 1614. PARIS Louvre *The flight of Lot* 1625. POTSDAM *The Emperor Augustus* 1619. STOCKHOLM *Susanna and the Elders* 1614. VIENNA K. *The Lamentation* 1614, *Self portrait* 'P. P. Rubins' (a signature nowhere repeated). **Documented Examples** (wholly by Rubens or partly or wholly the production of his atelier) include: ALOST S. *Martin S. Roch interceding for the plague stricken* (engraved by Pontius: Sir J. Reynolds wrote (1781): 'I suspect it has been in some picture cleaner's hands'). AMSTERDAM *Cimon and Pero* (*Roman charity*) (engraved with variations by W. Panneels). ANTWERP Mus. *Gaspar Gevartius* (engraved by Pontius), *Baptism of Christ* (from Mantua Jesuit church); Triptych: centre: *Lamentation* (*Christ à la Paille*) wings: *The Virgin and Child, S. John* (from Antwerp Cathedral: Reynolds wrote: 'The colouring of the Christ and the Virgin is of a most beautiful and delicate pearly tint'); *The Trinity* (from Antwerp Carmelite church); *The last Communion of S. Francis of Assisi* (extant receipt states 'exécuté par moi' 1619; from Antwerp Recollets church; Reynolds wrote: 'The Saint is nearly naked, without dignity, and appears more like a lazar'); *Crucifixion* (*Le coup de lance*) (commissioned by Burgomaster Nicolas Rockox a close friend of Rubens for Antwerp Recollets church 1620; discussed at length by Reynolds who concludes: 'It is certainly one of the first pictures in the world for composition, colouring and what was not to be expected from Rubens, correctness of drawing'); *S. Theresa interceding* *for souls in purgatory* (from Antwerp Carmes Dechaussés Reynolds wrote: 'In his best manner'); *The Education of the Virgin* (from Antwerp Carmes Dechaussés; Reynolds wrote: 'The white silk drapery of the Virgin is well painted but not historical; the silk is too particularly distinguished, a fault of which Rubens is often guilty in his female drapery'); Triptych: centre: *Incredulity of S. Thomas*, wings: donors *Nicolas Rockox and his wife* (commissioned by N. R. for his tomb in Antwerp Recollets church c. 1614), *Adoration of the Magi* (from Abbaye de S. Michel; paid for 1624); *The Prodigal Son* (in Rubens' possession when he died; seen by Reynolds in private collection in Antwerp); *The Virgin with the Parrot* (given by Rubens to S. Luke's Guild; Reynolds wrote: 'It is not by such pictures Rubens acquired his reputation'); *The Calloo Chariot* (design for a triumphal car to commemorate the victory of Calloo (*cf.* B. and G. Peeters) 1638: Rubens received a cask of French wine in payment); *Sketches for Triumphal Arches* (for Pageant Entry of Cardinal Infante Ferdinand into Antwerp 1635 (*cf.* Brussels, Cambridge (Mass.) and Leningrad examples)); *Chastity (Minerva) destroying Lust* (composition connected with Whitehall ceiling (*cf.* Brussels, Leningrad, Minneapolis and Vienna examples)). ANTWERP Cathedral: Triptych: *The Raising of the Cross* (painted for Antwerp S. Walpurgis 1610-11; Reynolds wrote: 'The blue drapery about the middle of the figure at the bottom of the Cross and the grey colour of some armour are nearly all the cold colours in the picture ... certainly not enough to qualify so large a space of warm colours'); Triptych: *The Descent from the Cross* (commissioned by the Guild of Crossbowmen 1611, finished 1614. Reynolds wrote: 'It is mortifying to see to what degree it has suffered by cleaning and mending ... Has more the manner of Rembrandt's disposition of light than any other of Rubens' works'); Triptych: *Resurrection* (commissioned by widow of J. B. Moretus 1612); *Assumption of the Virgin* (commissioned by Jan Delrio, Dean 1616; placed in position 1626; Reynolds: 'It is said to have been painted in sixteen days'); Augustins *The Virgin and Child worshipped by Saints* (painted for the church 1628; Reynolds wrote: 'As much animated and in motion as it is possible for a picture to be where nothing is doing ... Rubens' manner is often too artificial and picturesque for the Grand Style; Titian knew that so much formality and regularity as to give the appearance of being above all the tricks of art which we call picturesque is of itself grandeur'); S. Jacques *The Virgin and Child adored by SS. George, Jerome, Mary Magdalene and other saints* (selected by Rubens for his own tomb c. 1638; Reynolds wrote: 'As bright as if the sun shone on it'); S. Paul *Disputa* (engraved by Snyers; recorded in the church (then Antwerp Jacobins) by Descamps (1769) and Reynolds); *Flagellation* (engraved by Pontius; recorded in the church by Descamps and by Reynolds who wrote: 'some of the figures are awkwardly scourging with their left hand ... disagreeable to look at, the black and bloody stripes are marked with too much fidelity'). AUGSBURG Holy Cross *Assumption of the Virgin* (commissioned by Count Otto von Fugger). BAYONNE *Rape of Proserpina* sketch for picture for Torre de la Parada (*cf.* Brussels, Madrid and Rotterdam examples). BERLIN *Diana hunting* (in Rubens' possession when he died); *Diana and nymphs surprised by satyrs* (in Rubens' possession when he died); *Andromeda* (in Rubens' possession when he died); *S. Cecilia playing the organ* (in Rubens' possession when he died); *Landscape with shipwreck of Aeneas* (engraved by S. Bolswert; seen in Duke of Richelieu's collection by R. de Piles); *Capture of Paris by Henri IV* (sketch for second Luxembourg series *The History of Henri IV* commissioned by Marie de Médicis, begun c. 1628 and abandoned 1631 (*cf.* Florence Uffizi and London Wallace examples). BORDEAUX *Martyrdom of S. Just* (commissioned by Balthasar Moretus for Antwerp Annunciation Convent; Reynolds: 'S. Justus with two other figures who appear astonished at seeing him with his head in his hands ... Every part touched in such a style that it may be considered a

pattern for imitation'. Descamps: 'L'effet m'en a paru égal et monotone'). BOSTON U.S.A. *Queen Tomyris receiving the head of Cyrus* (engraved by Pontius; in Queen Christina of Sweden's collection); *Landscape with an avenue of trees* (in E. Jabach collection 1696). BRUSSELS *Dead Christ on the knees of the Virgin with S. Francis and other saints* (commissioned by Prince of Arenberg for Brussels Capucins 1620. Reynolds: 'The drapery of the Magdalene is execrable; the angels have been totally repainted'); *Road to Calvary* (commissioned for Afflighem Abbey c. 1636); *Martyrdom of S. Livin* (painted for Ghent Jesuit church); *The Virgin and S. Francis interceding to avert the Divine thunderbolts* (painted for Ghent Recollets; Reynolds: 'The Christ, which is ill drawn, in an attitude affectedly contrasted, is the most ungracious figure that can be imagined'); *Adoration of the Magi* (painted for Tournai Capucins); *Assumption of the Virgin* (commissioned for Brussels Carmes Dechaussés by Archduke Albert and the Infanta Isabella; dedicated 1614); *The adulteress before Christ* (engraved by Lauwers and others); *Coronation of the Virgin* (painted for Antwerp Recollets church); *Archduke Albert* and *Infanta Isabella* (connected with paintings for an arch in the Pageant Entry into Antwerp of Cardinal Infante Ferdinand 1635; *cf.* Antwerp, Cambridge (Mass.) and Leningrad examples); *Landscape with Atalanta hunting* (in Rubens' possession when he died); *The Fall of Icarus* (*cf.* J. P. Gowi), *Apotheosis of Hercules* (*cf.* J. B. Borkens), *The Fall of Phaeton* (*cf.* J. Eyck), *Jason and the Golden Fleece* (*cf.* E. Quellinus), *Birth of Venus* (*cf.* C. de Vos) and other sketches for pictures painted by his assistants for Madrid Torre de la Parada (*cf.* Bayonne, Madrid and Rotterdam examples); *Minerva driving War and Discord from the throne of James I* (composition connected with Whitehall ceiling; *cf.* Antwerp, Leningrad, Minneapolis and Vienna examples). CAEN *Abraham and Melchizedek* (engraved by Witdoek). CAMBRIDGE (Mass.) Fogg Mus. *Wrath of Neptune* ('*Quos ego*') (sketch for decoration in Pageant Entry into Antwerp of Cardinal Infante Ferdinand 1635; *cf.* Antwerp, Brussels and Leningrad examples). COLOGNE SS. Peter and Paul *Martyrdom of S. Peter* (in Rubens' possession when he died; commissioned by Cologne banker E. Jabach who died before it was finished (*cf.* J. Geldorp); Rubens wrote (1638): 'This subject interests me more than any other I have in hand'; and Reynolds commented on this dictum 'natural to such a mind as that of Rubens who was perhaps too much looking about him for the picturesque or something uncommon; a man with his head downward is certainly a more extraordinary object than in its natural place' and adds of the picture 'many parts are so feebly drawn and with so tame a pencil that I cannot help suspecting ... it was finished by some of his scholars'). COPENHAGEN *Judgement of Solomon* (engraved by Bolswert). DIJON *The entry into Jerusalem*, *The footwashing* (predella panels from altarpiece painted for Malines S. Rombout 1632 (*cf.* Milan example)). DRESDEN *Bathsheba receiving King David's letter from a negro page* (in Rubens' possession when he died); *Wild boar hunt* (sold by Rubens to Duke of Buckingham 1627); *Diana returning from the chase* (half length; engraved by Bolswert); *The drunken Hercules* (in 1722 inventory as 'original by Rubens'; another version in the gallery). DULWICH *Flight of S. Barbara* (sketch for a ceiling panel in Antwerp Jesuit church *cf.* Paris and Vienna examples); *Venus, Mars and Cupid* (engraved by Bolswert). DÜSSELDORF *Assumption of the Virgin* (from Brussels N. D. de la Chapelle). FLORENCE Pitti *Allegory of the Outbreak of War* (*cf.* J. Sutterman); *Landscape* (*Return from Work*) (engraved by Bolswert); Uffizi *The Three Graces* (grisaille) recorded 1671; *Henri IV at the Battle of Ivry* and *Entry of Henri IV into Paris* (sketches for the second Luxembourg series *cf.* Berlin and London, Wallace examples). GENOA Sant' Ambrogio *Miracles of S. Ignatius* (painted for the church). GHENT Cathedral *S. Bavon renouncing worldly pleasures* (commissioned 1612, executed 1624 (*cf.* P. Hals); Reynolds: 'For composition, colouring, richness of effect, and all those qualities in which Rubens particularly excelled ... among his greatest and best works'). GLASGOW *Nature adorned by the Graces* (engraved by van Dalen). GRENOBLE *Saints adoring a picture of the Virgin and Child* (painted for the Rome 'New Church' S. Maria in Vallicella 1607, exhibited but not placed there; offered by Rubens to Duke Vincenzo Gonzaga who would not buy it; placed by Rubens on his mother's tomb in Antwerp Abbaye S. Michel; taken Paris 1794 and sent Grenoble 1811 (*cf.* G. de Crayer and J. D. Odevaere). LENINGRAD *Bacchus holding a cup* (in Rubens' possession when he died); *Descent from the Cross* (painted for Lierre Capucins church); *Christ in the house of Simon* (engraved by Panneels; in Duke of Richelieu's collection); *Charles de Longueval Count of Bucquoy* (design for an engraving by Vorsterman); *The Virgin and Child* (engraved by Bolswert); *Ecce Homo* (engraved by Lauwers); *Virgin of the Rosaries* (engraved by Lommelin); *Landscape with a cart in mud* (engraved by Bolswert); *The Apotheosis of James I; James I enthroned and the infant Prince Charles crowned as heir by allegorical figures* (sketches for Whitehall ceiling; *cf.* Antwerp, Brussels, Minneapolis and Vienna examples); *Sketches for Triumphal Arches* (for Pageant Entry into Antwerp of Cardinal Infante Ferdinand 1635; *cf.* Antwerp, Brussels, Cambridge (Mass.) examples). LONDON N.G. *Triumph of Silenus* (in Duke of Richelieu's collection 1642); *The birth of Venus* (design for silver dish made for Charles I); *Susanna Fourment* (*Le chapeau de paille*) (in Rubens' possession when he died, then owned by Nicholas Lunden husband of Rubens' daughter Isabella); *Peace and War* (given by Rubens to Charles I 1630); *The Judgement of Paris* (in Cardinal Richelieu's collection); *Landscape at sunset; The watering place; The brazen serpent* (engraved by Bolswert). ROYAL COLLECTION (H.M. the Queen) *Summer* (sold by Rubens to the Duke of Buckingham 1627; E. Norgate (*c.* 1649) wrote: 'un poco ajutato as Rubens himself told me'); *Winter* (companion piece sold by Rubens to Duke of Buckingham 1627), *The Farm at Laeken* (in Antwerp collection of Lunden family (related to Rubens) before 1649; described by Descamps 1763); *S. George and the Dragon* (Charles I as S. George; Thames Valley in background; painted for Charles I 1629-30); *Assumption of the Virgin* (engraved by S. Bolswert); *Self portrait* 1623 (commissioned by Lord Danby for Charles I. Rubens wrote 1625: 'Through the English agent resident in Brussels he (the King) has so pressed me for my portrait that I could not refuse it, though I did not think it fitting to send my own portrait to a prince of his eminence, he finally overcame my modesty'); *Portrait of a young lady* (owned by Lunden family; described by Descamps 1753). LONDON Wallace *Defeat and death of Maxentius* (sketch for *History of Constantine* tapestries commissioned by Louis XIII 1621 *cf.* Philadelphia example); *Christ's charge to Peter* (commissioned for a chapel of Brussels S. Gudule (*c.* 1616); Reynolds suspected it a copy); *Holy Family with SS. Elizabeth and John the Baptist* (painted for Archduke Albert's oratory); *Adoration of the Magi* (sketch for Antwerp picture); *Entrance of Henri IV into Paris* (and two other sketches for the second Luxembourg series *cf.* Berlin and Florence examples); LONDON Whitehall *Apotheosis of James I* ceiling (completed 1634). LYONS *Virgin and Saints interceding for sinners* (from Antwerp Jacobins church; taken Paris 1794 and not returned *cf.* Grenoble example; Reynolds: 'much damaged, St. Sebastian in particular has been repainted by some ignorant person'). MADRID Prado *S. George and the dragon; Supper at Emmaus; Three nymphs with cornucopia; Nymphs and satyrs; Peasant dance; Marie de Médicis; Cardinal Infante Ferdinand at the battle of Nordlingen; The Garden of Love (Fête galante); The Three Graces* (all bought from Rubens' effects by Philip IV); *Twelve Apostles* (painted for the Duke of Lerma; referred to in letter from Rubens to Sir Dudley Carleton 1618); *Heraclitus weeping; Democritus laughing* (both painted for the Duke of Lerma); *Achilles*

among the daughters of Lycomedes (*cf.* F. Francken II, E. Quellinus and G. de Lairesse; offered by Rubens to Sir Dudley Carleton as 'done by my best pupil and the whole retouched by my hand, a most delightful picture and full of many beautiful girls' 1618; taken to Spain by Rubens 1628 and bought by Philip IV; *cf.* Rotterdam examples); *Adoration of the Magi* (commissioned by Burgomaster Rockox and Antwerp Magistrature for Antwerp Town Hall 1609; given by Magistrature to D. Rodrigo Calderón, Duke of Oliva 1612; acquired by Philip IV after the execution of the Duke 1621; enlarged and partly repainted by Rubens 1628); *Holy family and S. Anne; The Triumph of the Eucharist* (both sketches for tapestry cartoons commissioned by the Infanta Isabella for the Descalzas Reales in Madrid; paid for 1628); *Diana and Callisto* (in Alcázar 1666) *Perseus and Andromeda* (commissioned by Philip IV 1639; unfinished when Rubens died and finished by J. Jordaens); *Judgement of Paris* (painted for Philip IV 1639 and referred to in a letter by Cardinal Infante Ferdinand to the King: 'All painters call this his best work, the Venus is an excellent portrait of his wife who is without doubt the prettiest woman here' (lo mejor do lo que ahora hay aqui); *Atalanta and Meleager* (in Alcázar inventory 1636); *The rape of Hippodameia* (*Battle of Lapiths and Centaurs*); *The rape of Proserpina* (*cf.* Bayonne example; both painted for Torre de la Parada); also sketches: *Apollo and the Python* (*cf.* C. de Vos); *Prometheus* (*cf.* J. Cossiers); *Cephalus spied upon by Procris* (*cf.* P. Symons) and others (*cf.* Brussels and Rotterdam examples); *Adam and Eve* (copy by Rubens of picture by Titian also in Prado; painted 1628-9). MALINES Notre Dame Triptych: centre: *Miraculous draught of fishes*, wings: *The Tribute money, Tobias and the fish* (commissioned by Fishermen's Guild 1618 *cf.* Nancy examples); S. Jean Triptych: centre: *Adoration of the Magi*, wings: *Martyrdom of S. John the Baptist, Martyrdom of S. John the Evangelist* (commissioned 1616, *cf.* Marseilles examples). MANTUA Town Library and Academy (half each) *The Gonzaga family adoring the Trinity* (commissioned by Duke Vincenzo Gonzaga for Mantua Jesuit church *c.* 1604; sawn in half 1797, *cf.* Antwerp and Nancy examples). MARSEILLES *Adoration of the Shepherds, Resurrection* (predella panels from Malines S. Jean triptych; *cf.* Malines examples). MILAN Brera *Last Supper* (commissioned for Malines S. Rombout 1630, engraved Pontius and Bolswert; *cf.* Dijon example). MINNEAPOLIS *The infant Prince Charles crowned as heir by allegorical figures* (composition connected with Whitehall ceiling; *cf.* Antwerp, Brussels, Leningrad and Vienna examples). MUNICH A.P. *Rubens and Isabella Brant* (recorded in contemporary epigram by D. Baudius; seen in Düsseldorf by Reynolds: 'Rather in a hard manner ... the linen is grey, he was at this period afraid of white'); *Jan Brant* (in Rubens' possession when he died); *Helena Fourment in her wedding dress* (bought by Elector Max Emanuel from Gisbert van Ceulen 1698); *Helena Fourment with her son Frans* (bought by Elector Max Emmanuel from Gisbert van Ceulen 1698); *Rubens and Helena Fourment in a garden* (bought by Elector Max Emmanuel from Gisbert van Ceulen 1698); *Lion hunt* (painted for Maximilian of Bavaria and referred to in a letter by Rubens to Sir Dudley Carleton 1618); *Battle of the Amazons* (painted for C. van der Geest (*cf.* London van der Geest Painter, Hague Studio of Apelles Painter and W. van Haecht) and referred to in letter by Rubens to P. van Veen 1619); *Landscape with cattle* (bought by Elector Max Emmanuel from Gisbert van Ceulen 1698); *Fame (or Victory) crowning a hero* (in Rubens' possession when he died. Reynolds who saw it in Düsseldorf wrote 'The "Fame" is too red as well as the rest of the picture'); *Bacchanal with drunken Silenus* (in Rubens' possession when he died; then owned by Rubens' nephew Philip); *Shepherd embracing a woman* (in Rubens' possession when he died; then owned by Frederick Henry of Orange); *Fruit garland carried by cupids* (owned by Anton Triest, Bishop of Ghent before 1657; seen in Düsseldorf by Reynolds who presumed the fruit painted by

F. Snyders): *Rape of the daughters of Leucippus* (seen in Düsseldorf by Reynolds who wrote: 'A fine piece of colouring but the composition too artful'); *The Host of Sennacherib* (engraved by Soutman); *Fall of the rebel angels* (referred to in a letter by Rubens to Wolfgang Wilhelm von Neuburg 1619; finished 1622); *Last Judgement* (large version: painted for W. W. von Neuburg; referred to in letter by Rubens to Sir Dudley Carleton 1618); *Last Judgement* (small version: engraved by Suyderhoef 1642; Reynolds: 'Far superior to the large one in every respect'); *The Fall of the Damned* (referred to in letter from Rubens' nephew Philip R. to de Piles; Reynolds: 'It is impossible to form an adequate idea of the powers of Rubens without having seen this picture ... one of the greatest efforts of genius that ever the art has produced'); *Woman of the Apocalypse* (commissioned for Freising Cathedral); *Martyrdom of S. Lawrence* (from Brussels Notre Dame de la Chapelle; Reynolds wrote: 'The colouring appears raw'), *Pentecost, Nativity* (both commissioned by W. W. von Neuburg for Neuburg Jesuit church 1619); *Massacre of the Innocents* (in Paris collection 1642; then Duke of Richelieu; engraved Pontius); *Arrival of Marie de Médicis at Marseilles* and other sketches for the Luxembourg series, (*cf.* Paris examples). NANCY *Jonah thrown into the sea, Christ walking on the waters* (panels from predella of Fishermen's Guild altarpiece from Malines Notre Dame, *cf.* Malines examples); *The Transfiguration* (from Mantua Jesuit church whence taken by the French 1797 *cf.* Mantua examples). NANTES *Judas Maccabeus praying for the dead* (commissioned for Tournai Cathedral; where Descamps (1769) commented: 'belle composition; mal repeinte et entièrement perdu'). OLDENBURG (formerly) *Prometheus bound* (referred to by Rubens in letter to Sir Dudley Carleton (1618) 'original by my hand; the eagle done by Snyders'). PARIS Louvre *Adoration of the Magi* (given by widow of P. Pecquius to Brussels Annonciades; Descamps: 'd'une fraicheur de couleur et d'un transparent surprenant; tout a l'air d'être fait sans peine'); *Crucifixion* (from Bergues S. Winnocq Jesuit church); *The Virgin and Child in a garland of flowers* (painted for Cardinal Borromeo in collaboration with Jan (Velvet) Brueghel who wrote to the Cardinal (1621) 'the most rare and beautiful piece I have ever done. Master Rubens has also made his best efforts to show his powers in the centre panel which has a beautiful Virgin and Child. The birds and little animals are painted from life from specimens owned by the Infanta'); *The Virgin and Child surrounded by angels* (collection of Louis XIV); *Baron de Vicq, Netherlands ambassador to France* (engraved by Caukerken); *Landscape with ruins* (engraved by S. Bolswert and inscribed 'painted in Rome'); *Landscape with mill and bird catchers* (engraved by Bolswert); *Landscape with rainbow* (engraved by Bolswert); *Kermesse* (collection of Louis XIV); *Tournament before a castle moat* (in Rubens' possession when he died 'une pièce d'une Jouste dans un paysage' (een stuk van een Ridderspel met spiezen in een Lantschap)); *Four sketches for ceiling panels* (for Antwerp Jesuit church; *cf.* Dulwich and Vienna examples); *The History of Marie de Médicis* (Twenty-one panels painted for the Luxembourg Palace 1622-5). PAU *Thetis receiving arms from Vulcan for Achilles, Death of Hector* (compositions connected with designs for tapestries 'The History of Achilles', *cf.* Rotterdam examples). PHILADELPHIA (Johnson) *Christ's emblem appearing to Constantine* (composition connected with designs for 'History of Constantine' tapestries, *cf.* London Wallace example). PRAGUE Rudolfinum S. *Augustine and the child on the shore; Martyrdom of S. Thomas* (both commissioned for Prague Augustins and placed there 1639). ROME S. Maria in Vallicella *Angels adoring a picture of the Virgin and Child* (painted 1608 to replace the picture now in Grenoble, *cf.* Grenoble example); SS. *Gregory, Maurus and Papianus, SS. Domitilla, Nereus and Achilles* (painted for the church). ROTTERDAM Boymans *The Triumph of Bacchus* (composition connected with painting by C. de Vos *q.v.* for Torre

de la Parada *cf.* Bayonne, Brussels and Madrid examples); *Achilles dipped in the Styx by Thetis; Achilles among the daughters of Lycomedes* (and four other compositions connected with designs for tapestry 'The History of Achilles', *cf.* Madrid and Pau examples). VIENNA Academy *Six sketches for ceiling panels* (for Antwerp Jesuit church, *cf.* Dulwich and Paris examples); *The Good Government of James I with Minerva driving War and Discord from the throne* (sketch for Whitehall ceiling, *cf.* Antwerp, Brussels, Leningrad and Minneapolis examples). VIENNA Kunsthist. *Helena Fourment nude with a fur coat* (bequeathed to her by Rubens); *S. Ignatius Loyola healing the possessed* (painted for Antwerp Jesuit church 1619-20; shown over the high altar in pictures of the interior by A. G. Gheringh *q.v.* and W. v. Ehrenberg *q.v.*; sold to Empress Maria Theresa 1776); *S. Ignatius Loyola healing the possessed* (sketch for the above; hung in the choir of Antwerp Jesuit church (where seen by Descamps 1768) till acquired with the picture by the Empress); *Miracles of S. Francis Xavier* (painted for Antwerp Jesuit Church 1619-20; alternated with *S. Ignatius Loyola healing the possessed* on the high altar; sold to Empress Maria Theresa 1776); *Miracles of S. Francis Xavier* (sketch for the above; hung in the choir of Antwerp Jesuit church till acquired with the picture by the Empress); *Assumption of the Virgin* (bought from Antwerp Jesuit church by Empress Maria Theresa 1776); Triptych: centre: S. *Ildephonse receiving a cope from the Virgin*, wings: *Archduke Albert with S. Albert of Liège, Infanta Isabella with S. Elizabeth of Hungary*, exterior of wings: *Holy family under an apple tree* (commissioned for Brussels S. Jacques-sur-Coudenberg by the Fraternity of S. Ildefonso 1629 and paid for by the Infanta; completed 1632; sold to the Empress Maria Theresa to pay for repairs to the church 1776); *The Annunciation* (from Antwerp Jesuit church where seen by Descamps in the Salle de la Congrégation 'ouvrage du premier temps du maître'; engraved by Bolswert; bought from Jesuit church by Empress Maria Theresa 1776); *Cimon finding the sleeping Iphigenia* (sold by Rubens to the Duke of Buckingham); *Victory crowning a hero* (in Venetian collection 1642; in Archduke Leopold Wilhelm's inventory 1659 'as original by P. P. Rubens'); *Atalanta hunting* (Archduke Leopold Wilhelm's inventory as 'original by P. P. Rubens'); *Jupiter and Mercury as guests of Philemon and Baucis* (Archduke Leopold Wilhelm inventory); *Stormy landscape with Philemon and Baucis* (in Rubens' possession when he died; acquired by Archduke Leopold Wilhelm); *Young people disporting in a castle park* (engraved by S. Bolswert); *Head of Medusa* (in collection of the Duke of Buckingham sold 1648); SS. *Pipin and Bega* (in Duke of Buckingham's collection sold 1648 as 'The Dutchess of Brabant with her lover'; engraved by F. v. d. Steen as by Rubens 'after old paintings'). VIENNA Liecht. *Death in battle of Decius Mus, Obsequies of Decius Mus* (compositions for tapestry series 'The History of Decius Mus' referred to by Rubens in letter to Sir Dudley Carleton 1618; an Antwerp inventory of 1692 records 'ses stucken schilderye, geordonneert door den Heere Rubens ende opgeschildert door de Heere van Dyck, wesende de Historie van den Keyser Desius' and 'een groot stuck daer den Keyser Decius te paert gaet, geschildert door van Dyck'); *Landscape with girls and cows* (engraved by Bolswert). The engravers named above were contemporaries of Rubens and many of the plates were executed under his supervision. **Traditionally Ascribed Examples** include: BRUSSELS Mus. *Martyrdom of S. Ursula* (bought 1851). THE HAGUE *Michiel Ophovius Bishop of Bois le Duc* (from Antwerp Dominican Monastery; engraved in 18th cent. as portrait of Rubens' confessor). LONDON N. G. *The Château de Steen* (from Genoa Palazzo Balbi 1802); *The Rape of the Sabines* (seen in Antwerp by Reynolds in the collection of Madame Boschaert where it was then for sale); Wallace *Landscape with rainbow* (from Genoa Palazzo Balbi 1802). PARIS Louvre *Helena Fourment with two children* (collection Louis XVI.). VIENNA Kunsthist. *Feast of Venus*; Liecht. *Albert and*

Nicholas Rubens, Head of a fair haired child. Replicas of many pictures were made in the Rubens atelier. Many copies are recorded in Antwerp collectors' inventories of the 17th century. Copies intended to deceive were made in the 17th century by G. J. van Opstal, J. I. de Roore, J. van Pee, J. Peeters the younger and others. Pictures presumed by some his work are in many museums and collections. Conflicting dates for many pictures are given in the standard monographs when the dates of the pictures are, in fact, not known. [Fl. 21, Fl. 753, Fl. 652, Fl. 287, Fl. 425, Fl. 22, Fl. 215, Fl. 216, Fl. 826, Fl. 856, Fl. 702, Fl. 718, Fl. 581, Fl. 719, Fl. 720, Fl. 726, Fl. 426, Fl. 721, Fl. 226, Fl. 892, Fl. 625, Fl. 482, Fl. 85, Fl. 212, Fl. 213, Fl. 458, Fl. 787, Fl. 347, Fl. 273, Fl. 296, Fl. 676, Fl. 131, Fl. 132.]

Rudolph of Antwerp (full name presumed by some to be Rudolph Loesen). Flemish Sch. 16th cent. *Religious subjects, portraits* (?). Was paid for altarpiece in Church of S. Victor, Xanten nr. Crefeld 1553. Leyden Mus. has *The poet J. van der Does* (*Janus Dousa*) *with his wife and nine children* inscribed 'Rudolphi artifici quam bene picta manus' presumed by some his work. [Fl. 481, Fl. 892, Fl. 88.]

Ruel (Rüll), Jan Baptiste de. Flemish Sch. *b* Antwerp *c.* 1634 *d* Würzburg 1685. *Religious subjects, portraits.* Began career as singer in service of Prince Bishop of Mainz; pupil for painting there of J. Thomas (van Ypern) *q.v. c.* 1655; remained Germany where worked for a number of churches. **Signed Examples:** GOTHA *Adoration of the Christchild by the six penitents* 1678. LOERZWEILER Church *Assumption of the Virgin* (from Mainz Cathedral) 1684. SCHWEINFURT Church *Coronation of the Virgin* 1664. WOLFSBERG (Carinthia) Church *Legend of S. Cunegund* (painted for Prince Bishop of Bamberg) 1667. WÜRZBURG Cathedral *S. Elizabeth* 1659, *S. Mary Magdalene* 1661. **Monogrammed Example:** HEIDELBERG *Freiherr von Schönborn and his wife* (J B R.) [Fl. 753, Fl. 612, Fl. 481, Fl. 440, Fl. 891.]

Rul, Henry. Flemish Sch. *b* Antwerp 1862 *d* 1942. *Landscapes.* Studied in Middelburg; then pupil in Antwerp Acad. of J. v. Luppen; Member of Antwerp Group Als ik Kan (*cf.* H. Luyten) 1883 and of De Dertien (XIII) group (*cf.* E. Farasyn) 1891; exhibited London R.A. 1888-90. Represented in ANTWERP *Dunes, Spring time.* [Fl. 361, Fl. Bib. 19th cent. Fl. 17.]

Ruyten, Jan Michiel. Flemish Sch. *b* Antwerp 1813. *d* Antwerp 1881. *Landscapes, with figures, snow scenes, coast and river scenes, picturesque architectural pieces, costume history and genre, interiors.* Pupil of I. v. Regemorter; also studied in Holland 1837-8; Member of Antwerp Acad. 1840; F. Crabeels and H. Schaefels were among his pupils. Represented in ANTWERP *Antwerp Grand' Place in 1878, Antwerp Canal des Brasseurs 1875, Antwerp Canal au Charbon 1875* COURTRAI, STUTTGART *Cavalry halt before an inn* 1840 TOULOUSE *Corner of a street in Flanders.* A *Sack of Antwerp Cathedral by the Iconoclasts* is recorded. [Fl. 451, Fl. 612, Fl. 837 (1882), Fl. 440, Fl. 88.]

Ryck, Pieter Cornelisz van. Flemish Sch. *b* son of a brewer, Delft 1568 *d* Haarlem (?) after 1621. *Kitchen interiors with figures* (*cf.* P. Aertsen, J. Beuckelaer, M. v. Cleve); *portraits.* Van Mander (1604) records him as pupil of J. Willemsz Delff *q.v.* and of the Dutch painter Huybrecht Jacobsz (who was known as Grimani, worked in Venice (*cf.* D. Barendsz and M. de Vos) and was later associated with the tapestry works of K. v. Mander the younger *q.v.*); went Italy with his master; remained for fifteen years and worked for 'vorsten, heeren, prelaten, monniken, nonnen en allerlei anderen in de meeste plaatsen'; in Haarlem 1604; Van Mander adds that his manner of painting shows the influence of Bassano. **Signed Example:**

BRUNSWICK *Kitchen piece with dogs, figures and biblical scene in background* 1604. **Monogrammed Example:** HAARLEM *Kitchen piece with venison, poultry, fish, vegetables; man jesting with woman in background* 1621. **Documented Example:** AMSTERDAM Rijks. *Kitchen piece with meat, poultry, fish, vegetables; two maid servants in foreground and Lazarus and Dives in the background* (corresponds to the description by Van Mander who records it as then 'in the hospital outside Haarlem'). A *Prodigal Son wasting his substance* (*cf.* Brussels Prodigal Son Painter and J. v. Hemessen) monogrammed PVR and a *Nativity* are recorded by engravings. [Fl. 559, Fl. 612, Fl. 892, Fl. 445.]

Ryck (Deryke), Willem (Guillaume) de. Flemish Sch. *b* Antwerp 1635 *d* England 1697 or 1699. *Religious subjects, portraits, mythologies; also worked as engraver.* Trained as a goldsmith; recorded by Marshall Smith (before 1693) as 'disciple of Queline' (Erasmus or Jan Erasmus? Quellinus); Master Antwerp Guild 1673; came England (*cf.* Jan Peeters the younger) *c.* 1689; Smith records that his daughter Catherine 'comes behind none of her fair sex in the art.' **Recorded Works:** ANTWERP Notre Dame *Martyrdom of S. Matthew* (described by Smith as his first work; *cf.* B. de Ryckere); COURTRAI Cathedral *The King of Spain on horseback* (*cf.* F. Duchatel, J. van Orley and L. van Schoor, recorded by Smith). DUNKIRK *S. Michael* (*cf.* N. Ryckx), *S. Benedict.* Smith also records a *Judgement of Paris* and a *S. Mary Magdalene.* Vertue (before 1741) records *Conversation piece of Mr. Pittfield and all his family* and an engraving *S. Catherine before her judges* dedicated to Ferdinand van Beughem, Bishop of Antwerp 1684 (*cf.* F. de Cock); inventories of Antwerp collections (1685 and 1692) record *A figure holding a letter* and a *Flora.* Engravings *Mars and Venus* 1683 and *Susanna and the Elders* and a signed painting *Reclining nude woman* are also recorded. Nagler (*c.* 1840) records landscapes and 'bambochades'. [Fl. 826, Fl. 856, Fl. 612, Fl. 126, Fl. 223, Fl. 213, Fl. 892, Fl. 798.]

Ryckaert, see Aertsz, R.

Ryckaert, David (I). Flemish Sch. *b* Antwerp 1560 *d* Antwerp 1607. *Figures (mostly in compositions by other artists); also active as dealer and brewer.* Master Antwerp Guild 1585; married in a Protestant church 1585; remarried in a Catholic church 1589; father of D. R. (II). [Fl. 892.]

Ryckaert, David (II). Flemish Sch. *b* son of David R. (I), Antwerp 1586 *d* Antwerp 1642. *Landscapes with mountains; genre, portraits; also active as art dealer.* Master Antwerp Guild 1608; his daughter married G. Coques *q.v.* **Signed Example:** SCHWERIN *Peasant interior* (D. Ryc. F. 1617). An Antwerp inventory (1642) records a *Woman's portrait* by 'Old Ryckaert'. [Fl. 86, Fl. 892, Fl. 213.]

*Ryckaert, David (III). Flemish Sch. *b* son of David R. (II), Antwerp 1612 *d* Antwerp 1661. *Indoor and outdoor peasant genre* (*cf.* D. Teniers the younger, G. v. Tilborgh, F. and T. v. Apshoven, M. v. Helmont), *some social scenes* (*cf.* H. Janssens) *and some fantastic 'spook' pictures* (*cf.* P. Huys). Pupil of his father; Master Antwerp Guild 1637; brother-in-law to G. Coques *q.v.* 1643; patronized by Governor General Archduke Leopold Wilhelm (*cf.* J. B. v. Heil); Dean of Guild 1652. **Signed Examples:** ANTWERP *Peasants at table* 1641 or 1651, *Plundering soldiers* (*cf.* G. v. Herp, S. Vrancx). BRUSSELS *Chemist in his laboratory* 1648, *Family scene with dancing children* 1651. BUDAPEST *Peasants in a tavern* 1654. COPENHAGEN *Musical company* 1650, *Peasant feast* 1657. DRESDEN *Peasant interior* 1638, *The peasant family: 'As the old sing so the young cheep'* (*cf.* J. Jordaens) 1639, *Corner of a kitchen with still life and a cat* 1659. DUBLIN N. G. *Dinner at a farmhouse.* FRANK-

FORT Städel. *Butcher's shop with man offering beer to a woman* 1639. MADRID Prado *The alchemist* 1640. MONTPELLIER *The dentist*. MUNICH *Twelfth Night feast* (*cf.* J. Jordaens) 1648. NEW YORK Met. *Farmhouse*. PARIS Louvre *A painter in his studio* (*cf.* H. Goovaerts and G. Thomas) 1638. VIENNA K. *Peasants' pleasure* (*Kermesse*), *Peasants' distress* (*Soldiers plundering a village*) 1649; Czernin *Peasant company* 1650; Harrach *Soldiers plundering a house* 1656; Liecht. *Musical company* 1650. Houbraken (before 1718) records that R. changed his style at the end of his life and painted 'spook' pictures, (*Temptation of S. Anthony* and like subjects); the Forchoudt firm of Antwerp dealers (*cf.* A. Casteels) exported a *Temptation of S. Anthony* 'by David Ryckaert' to Vienna in 1669; Antwerp inventories of 1676 and 1678 record pictures titled *Supper at Emmaus* and *Bacchanal*.
[Fl. 425, Fl. 215, Fl. 612, Fl. 892, Fl. 212, Fl. 213.]

Ryckaert, Marten. Flemish Sch. *b* son of David R. (I), Antwerp 1587 *d* Antwerp 1631. *Italianate landscapes with rivers, rocks, waterfalls and small figures* (*cf.* P. Brill and A. Mirou). Pupil of his father and T. van Haecht *q.v.*; Master Antwerp Guild 1612; visited Italy; member of Antwerp artists' Chamber of Rhetoric (Violiere) 1620; Van Dyck painted his portrait (now in Madrid Prado); he was one-armed; Houbraken (before 1718) describes him as a follower of J. de Momper *q.v.* **Monogrammed Examples:** FLORENCE Uffizi *Waterfall at Tivoli* 1616. LENINGRAD *Landscape* 1616. MADRID Prado *Landscape with figures*. Paintings presumed by some his work are in various museums. A *Waterfall* by 'Ryckaert' is recorded in an Antwerp Inventory of 1642. A fully signed *River and mountain landscape with figures and goats* was recorded (1948) in commerce.
[Fl. 86, Fl. 425, Fl. 215, Fl. 878, Fl. 892, Fl. 83.]

Ryckaert, Pauwel. Flemish Sch. *b* son of David R. (I), Antwerp 1592 *d* 1650. Master Antwerp Guild 1618.   [Fl. 714.]

Rycke (or **Ryke**), **Daniel de.** Flemish Sch. *b* Ghent (?) before 1425 *d* after 1482. *Religious subjects, portraits, decorative works*. Master Ghent Guild 1440; Dean 1460; with many others worked on Bruges pageantry for Charles the Bold's marriage with Margaret of York and received much higher payment than the others (*cf.* H. v. d. Goes and V. v. d. Stoct) 1468; also decorated two triumphal arches for Charles the Bold's Pageant Entry into Ghent (*cf.* C. Spierinc) 1469.
[Fl. 135, Fl. 385, Fl. 892.]

Ryckere (or **Rycke**), **Abraham de.** Flemish Sch. *b* son of B. de R., Antwerp 1566 *d* 1599. *Religious subjects, portraits*. Pupil of his father. **Signed Examples:** ANTWERP S. Jacques *Jan Doncker and his wife* (wings of triptych) 1591. The central panel *Christ crucified between the thieves* disappeared from the church *c.* 1807.   [Fl. 481, Fl. 107, Fl. 892.]

Ryckere (**Rycke, van Rues**), **Bernaert de.** Flemish Sch. *b* Courtrai *c.* 1535 *d* Antwerp 1590. *Religious and mythological subjects; also active as copyist*. Master Antwerp Guild 1561; valued R. Coxie's *Last Judgement* in Ghent with M. de Vos, A. Francken the elder and G. Mostaert 1589; left a large collection of pictures including originals by Q. Massys and Marinus van Reymerswaele *q.v.* with his own copies from them and copies of works by F. Floris, M. de Vos, 'Sotte' Cleve, W. Key and others. Van Mander (1604) says: 'he changed his style in later life (after 1560) and in his own judgement improved it'. **Signed Examples:** BUDAPEST *Diana and Actaeon* (*cf.* A. Blocklandt) 1582. COURTRAI S. Martin, Triptych: centre: *Pentecost*, wings: *Baptism of Christ, Creation of Adam*, exterior of wings: *SS. Salvator and Martin;* painted without assistants 1587. *Carrying of the Cross* 1560 (recorded by van Mander). Descamps (1769) records (wrongly *cf.* W. de Ryck) *Martyrdom of S. Matthew* in Antwerp Notre Dame; Rubens owned a *Feast of the gods* (*cf.* F. Floris); the head of the Forchoudt firm of Antwerp dealers bought (1669) at a sale a *Finding of Moses* 'as fine as Pourbus' which his son recorded (1670) as 'Godt lof wel vercocht' (thank God well sold).
[Fl. 559, Fl. 216, Fl. 107, Fl. 892, Fl. 212, Fl. 213.]

Ryckx, Nicolas. Flemish Sch. *b* son of painter Jan R., Bruges 1637 *d* Bruges 1695. *Oriental views, landscapes, religious subjects*, Visited Spain (*cf.* A. Smit) and Palestine (*cf.* M. Sweerts); returned Bruges where Master in Guild 1667. Descamps (1763) wrote 'Presque tous ses tableaux représentent des caravannes et des vues de Palestine. Sa composition est abondante, les figures, les chameaux, les chevaux, etc. sont dessinés avec esprit'; and he records (1769) a *S. Michael in conflict with the Demon* in Dunkirk Riches-Claires (error (?) for W. de Ryck *q.v.*).
[Fl. 215, Fl. 216, Fl. 612, Fl. 88.]

Ryckx, Paul. Flemish Sch. *b* son of Jan R., Bruges 1612 *d* Bruges 1668. *Religious subjects for Bruges churches* (*cf.* J. v. Oost the elder, G. Vroilynck, L. de Deyster and N. Vleys). Master Bruges Guild 1635; designed doors of the tabernacle on the high altar of Bruges S. Sauveur 1643; Dean of Guild 1645. A younger brother of the same name was Master Bruges Guild 1672. **Signed Example:** BRUGES S. Sauveur *S. Jerome and the trumpets of the Last Judgement* 1644 (wings, with a portrait of the donor J. B. Croquet, not known to be extant are recorded).   [Fl. 892, Fl. 88, Fl. 113.]

Rye, Aegidius de. Flemish Sch. *b* Netherlands date unknown *d* Graz 1605. *Religious subjects, city views*. Went Graz where court painter to Archduke Ferdinand who granted him annual pension 'for long and loyal services' 1602 (*cf.* G. Rem); painted frescoes in Graz castle chapel and drew views of Cracow, Klausenboorg and Kaschau engraved in 'Civitates Orbis Terrarum' (*cf.* J. Hoefnagel). **Signed Example:** VIENNA K. *S. Catherine buried by angels* (on copper) 1597.
[Fl. 612, Fl. 289, Fl. 440, Fl. 88.]

Ryn, J. van, see **Reyn.**

Rysbraeck, Gérard. Flemish Sch. *b* son of Peter R., Antwerp 1696 *d* blind and in poverty. Antwerp 1773. *Hunting scenes, still life with fish and game* (*cf.* J. Spoede). Antwerp Master 1726; in Paris (*cf.* H. de La Pegnia and P. J. Lion) where employed by Court (*cf.* C. v. Falens, and J. F. Delien) 1747-54. **Signed Example:** COMPIÈGNE *Stag hunt*.
[Fl. 856, Fl. 107.]

Rysbraeck, Jacques (or **Jacob**) **Cornill.** Flemish Sch. *b* son of Peter R. (?), Antwerp 1685 *d* Paris 1765. Lived Paris from *c.* 1730 (*cf.* Gérard R.).   [Fl. 892.]

Rysbraeck, Ludovicus (**Louis**). Flemish Sch. *b* son of P. R. (?) before 1700 *d* date and place unknown. '*History*'. **Signed Example:** VIENNA Liecht. *Diana and her nymphs in wooded landscape with a temple* (*cf.* A. Genoels) 1716.   [Fl. 856.]

Rysbraeck, Peter. Flemish Sch. *b* son of Andreas R. an art dealer, Antwerp 1655 *d* Brussels 1729. *Italianate landscapes* (*cf.* A. Crussens, J. F. Millet, G. de Witte and J. B. Juppin), *often with figures or animals; also worked as engraver*. Pupil of P. A. Immenraet 1672; Master Antwerp Guild 1673; went England (*cf.* P. v. d. Meulen, J. Siberechts, C. de Neve) with the French painter N. de Largillière (*cf.* A. Goubau) *c.* 1674; Vertue (before 1754) records that as result of Titus Oates' anti-Catholic disturbances went with Largillière to Paris (*cf.* A. v. d. Meulen) *c.* 1678; returned Antwerp before 1692; director of Antwerp Acad. 1713; lived Brussels from 1720. Carel Breydel and J. Vervoort were his pupils. **Signed**

Examples: BAMBERG; BERLIN K.F. *Landscape with Baptism of Christ*; HAMBURG *Landscape with thunderstorm*; POMMERSFELDEN. **Documented Example:** ANTWERP *Large landscape* (from Antwerp Guild to which donated by artist 1692). Descamps (1768) saw 'four fine landscapes' in Afflighem Abbey.
[Fl. 878, Fl. 826, Fl. 215, Fl. 216, Fl. 856, Fl. 481, Fl. 612, Fl. 107, Fl. 892, Fl. 440.]

Rysbraeck, Peter Andreas, often called the younger. Flemish Sch. *b* son of Peter R., Paris 1685 *d* of consumption in his house near Bloomsbury Square and buried Marylebone churchyard London 1748. *Still life with game, fruit and fish, some in landscapes* (*cf.* A. Clevenbergh, D. de Coninck, A. de Gryef, J. B. Govaerts, G. Rysbraeck, J. J. Spoede), *landscapes* (?), *views of mansions* (?). Pupil of his father; Master Antwerp Guild *c.* 1709; Dean 1713; went London (*cf.* P. Casteels III, P. J. v. Reysschoot and P. Tillemans) with his brother the sculptor John Michael R., 1720; Vertue (before 1754) records that 'his works were paid for by Noblemen and Gentlemen at as high rate as any contemporary painter in that kind'; the English painter B. Dandridge painted his portrait. **Signed Example:** HERMANNSTADT *Dead birds and fruit in landscape.* [Fl. 826, Fl. 856, Fl. 440.]

Rysbroeck, J. van see **Reesbroeck.**

Rysselberghe, Théo van. Flemish Sch. *b* son of a rich business man, Ghent 1862 *d* S. Clair (Var, France) 1926. *Landscapes, figure compositions and portraits, many in Impressionist and 'Pointilliste' conventions.* Pupil in Ghent Acad., and in Brussels Acad. of J. Portaels; Member of Les XX group (*cf.* J. Ensor) 1884; visited Paris where saw Seurat's *Grande Jatte* 1886; member of Libre Esthétique (*cf.* G. Buysse); travelled widely in Europe; visited Morocco; after 1898 lived mainly in Paris and south of France. Represented in AMSTERDAM *Aquarium* BRUSSELS Bib. Roy. *Mme. E. Verhaeren* 1899; Mus. *The painter, Dario de Regoyos, playing the mandoline,* 1882, *Fantasia arabe* 1884, *Octave Maus* 1885, *E. Verhaeren writing* 1915, *Woman reading and a child* 1899, *La promenade* 1901, *Mdlle. Z.* 1910. GHENT *The reading* (with portraits of M. Maeterlinck, A. Gide, E. Verhaeren, F. Fénéon and others) 1903. OTTERLO Kröller Müller Mus. *Mme. T. van Rysselberghe.* PARIS Jeu de Paume *E. Verhaeren* 1890. WEIMAR *Noonday heat* (composition with nudes).
[Fl. 292, Fl. 562, Fl. 296, Fl. 388, Fl. Bib. 19th cent.]

S

Sacré, Émile. Flemish Sch. *b* St. Gilles, nr. Brussels 1844 *d* Ixelles 1882. *Portraits, genre.* Pupil A. Cluysenaer. Represented in BRUSSELS *Lady with fan, The artist's father, Self portrait* LIÈGE *Laundress.*
[Fl. 837 (1882), Fl. 296, Fl. Bib. 19th cent.]

Sacré, Joseph. Flemish Sch. *b* Ghent before 1815. *Genre and interiors.* Settled Paris 1837 where exhibited Salon till 1848. Represented in DOUAI *Return from market.*
[Fl. 451, Fl. 612, Fl. 66.]

Sadeler, Aegidius. Flemish Sch. *b* Antwerp 1570 *d* Prague 1629. May have worked as painter; but chiefly active as engraver; worked for the Emperor Rudolf II (*cf.* B. Spranger) in Prague.
[Fl. 86, Fl. 612, Fl. 892.]

Saedeleer, Valerius de. Flemish Sch. *b* Alost 1867 *d* Leupegem 1941. *Landscapes (at first in Impressionist and later in Post-Impressionist conventions).* Pupil of F. Courtens; lived Lisseweghe in a hut very simply 1900-3; visited Holland; in Laethem St Martin (*cf.* A. v. d. Abeele and G. v. d. Woestyne) 1904-10; in Wales with de Woestyne during German invasion 1914-18; returned Belgium and settled Etichove 1921; contributed tapestry designs for studio directed there by his daughters and L. and P. Haesaerts. Represented in ALOST, ANTWERP *Snow in Flanders* BRUSSELS *Landscape after storm.* GHENT *End of a grey day.*
[Fl. 568, Fl. 588, Fl. 707, Fl. 388, Fl. 296.]

Saey (Seys or **Saiss), Jacques (Jacob) Ferdinand.** Flemish Sch. *b* son of dealer Jan S., Antwerp 1658 *d* Vienna *c.* 1726. *Architectural views* (*cf.* Jacob Peeters). Pupil of his maternal uncle W. v. Ehrenberg *q.v.* in Antwerp; Master Antwerp Guild 1680; recorded as contributor (architecture?) to *Interior of a picture gallery* by Gonzales Coques *q.v.* (his signature is not on any of the pictures shown); in Malines 1684; in Vienna (*cf.* A. Schoonjans) 1694. **Signed Example:** HERMANNSTADT *Hall with columns and figures* 1725.
[Fl. 481, Fl. 613, Fl. 107, Fl. 892, Fl. 88, Fl. 440.]

*St. Louis Entombment Painter. Presumed Flemish (Dutch) Sch. late 15th cent. Name for painter of ST. LOUIS *Entombment.* Presumed by some identical with the Virgo inter Virgines Master *q.v.*

*Saint Sang Master (Holy Blood Master). Presumed Flemish Sch. 16th cent. Name for painter of BRUGES Confrérie du Saint Sang Triptych *Descent from the Cross, S. Mary Magdalene, S. Joseph of Arimathea.* Presumed by some identical with Fogg S. Luke Painter *q.v.* [Fl. 316, Fl. 615, Fl. 798.]

Saiss see **Saey.**

Saive (or Sayve, Le Saive or **Savio), Frans**; called Francisco de Namur. Flemish Sch. *b* before 1585 *d* after 1627. *Religious subjects.* Master Antwerp Guild 1599; recorded in Namur 1627; Van Mander (1604) records 'I hear good accounts of a certain Francisco Savio working at Mons in Hainault' (*cf.* S. de Coulx). **Signed Example:** SCHLEISSHEIM *Lamentation.*
[Fl. 559, Fl. 892, Fl. 88.]

Saive, Jean the younger. Flemish Sch. *b* son of J. B. S., Malines 1597 *d* Malines (?) after 1665. *'History', landscapes, genre, still life.* J. Le Pla was his pupil. [Fl. 612, Fl. 892.]

Saive (or Sayve), Jean Baptist called Jean de Namur. Flemish Sch. *b* Namur 1540 *d* Malines 1624. *Religious subjects, genre, portraits.* Worked Namur till 1578; in Brussels where court painter to Duke of Parma (*cf.* Joos van Winghe, and P. Claeissins the younger) and 'Concierge des Vignobles' 1590; in Malines 1597 (?) and after 1603. **Signed Examples:** BRUSSELS Ste. Catherine *Crucifixion.* MALINES N. D. au delà de la Dyle *S. Catherine altarpiece*; Cathedral S. Rombout *S. John the Baptist altarpiece.* PARMA R. Gall. *Alexander Farnese Duke of Parma with Scheldt landscape in background.* Recorded works include *Four Seasons* and *Market scene* painted for Archduke Ernest (*cf.* G. Schoof) 1594, a *Crucifixion* for Namur Town Hall 1597, and a triptych *David and Goliath* (*cf.* M. Pepyn, A. v. Stalbemt, A. Schoonjans), *Judith and Holofernes* (*cf.* A. de Coster) and *Sacrifice of Isaac* (*cf.* D. Teniers the younger) for Malines S. Rombout.
[Fl. 613, Fl. 409, Fl. 126, Fl. 892.]

Saligo, Charles Louis. Flemish Sch. *b* Grammont 1804 *d* S. Josse-ten-Noode 1874. *'History', religious subjects, portraits, still life.* Pupil of P. v. Huffel in Ghent and in Paris of the French painter Baron Gros (*cf.* J. v. d. Abeele and F. Simonau); remained Paris till 1848; thereafter Brussels, Lokeren and S. Josse-ten-Noode; exhibitor in Brussels and Paris Salons. Represented in AMSTERDAM *Self portrait* 1826. GRAMMONT Town Hall *Holy Family. A Briseis taken from Achilles' tent* 1827 is recorded.
[Fl. 451, Fl. 612, Fl. 481, Fl. 66, Fl. 440.]

*Sallaert (or Sallaerts), Antoine. Flemish Sch. *b* son of a patrician, Brussels *c.* 1590 *d* Brussels *c.* 1658. *Religious subjects, portraits and civic portrait groups* (*cf.* G. de Crayer and P. v. d. Plas), *ceremonies and processions* (*cf.* D. v. Alsloot, A. v. Bredael, F. Duchatel, N. v. Eyck, P. Snayers, D. Teniers the younger); *also designs for tapestry* (*cf.* J. v. d. Hoecke, C. Schut and P. Thys) *and for woodcuts.* Pupil in Brussels of M. de Bordeau (*cf.* P. de Champaigne) 1606; Master Brussels Guild 1613; patronized by the Infanta Isabella (*cf.* D. v. Alsloot) 1615; Dean in Guild 1633 and 1648. De Bie (1661) records him as a versatile artist of the first rank; Houbraken (1721) has barely heard of him; Mensaert (1763) records him as collaborator with Van Dyck; Kramm (1864) as friend and collaborator with Rubens on the wings of the Antwerp Cathedral *Raising of the Cross* (not confirmed elsewhere). **Signed Examples:** BRUSSELS Town Hall *Brussels magistrates presented to the Virgin by S. Michael* 1634. RELEGHEM Church *Beheading of S. John the Baptist* 1634 (*cf.* J. B. Sallaert). **Monogrammed Example** (A S interlaced): TURIN Mus. *Procession in the Place du Sablon with the six maidens dowered by the Infanta Isabella in commemoration of her success in shooting down the popinjay* 1615. **Documented Examples:** BRUSSELS *The Infanta Isabella shooting down the popinjay* 1615 (taken to Paris Louvre 1794 and reclaimed 1815; *cf.* J. D. Odevaere) and *The Procession with the maidens dowered by the Infanta Isabella* 1616 (variant of Turin picture) both formerly at Château de Tervueren where recorded in inventory of 1667 (*cf.* S. Noveliers). Compositions recorded by engravings include *Beatus Albertus Magnus blessing the founder of the Order of Predicants; Pope Innocent X extending his hand to weeping Religion; Funeral of the Infanta Isabella 1633* and a *Portrait of Archduke Leopold Wilhelm* (*cf.* J. v. Egmont, P. Thys, J. Thomas 'van Ypern'). Woodcuts from his drawings include an *Allegory of the transcience of Beauty* (*young woman with death's head and a snake round her throat*) and many religious subjects published in devotional books. An engraving *Two fools in caps* bears his own signature as engraver.

[Fl. 86, Fl. 425, Fl. 878, Fl. 576, Fl. 612, Fl. 481, Fl. 120, Fl. 892, Fl. 88, Fl. 440, Fl. 796, Fl. 204.]

Sallaert, Jan Baptist. Flemish Sch. *b* son of Antoine S., Brussels 1612 *d* place and date unknown, Pupil of his father in Brussels Guild 1629; Master 1644. Presumed by some assistant to his father on Releghem Church picture. [Fl. 88.]

Sammeling (or **Sameling**), **Benjamin.** Flemish Sch. *b* Ghent 1520 *d* after 1604. *Portraits, 'history' and decorative work*. Pupil in Antwerp of Frans Floris. Master Antwerp Guild 1555; Dean in Ghent Guild 1598. An *Allegory of Benevolence* in Ghent Mus. (Monogrammed B S 1589) is presumed by some his work. *Decorative work* painted in Ghent, S. Bavon for the festival of the Golden Fleece 1559 and *Portraits of members of Plantin family with S. John and S. Roch* on wings of the funeral monument of the printer Christ. Plantin (*cf.* J. de Backer) in Antwerp Cathedral painted 1591 are recorded. Possibly the unnamed artist recorded by Van Mander (1604) among the hundred and twenty pupils of Floris: 'First I will mention among them an old bachelor from Ghent who is still living and was born in 1520; he was a good colourist in his time as can be seen from his painting on the roodscreen in Ghent S. Jean (S. Bavon), which he carried out from drawings by L. de Heere, and from many other works: he also did very good portraits'.

[Fl. 559, Fl. 216, Fl. 135, Fl. 892, Fl. 88.]

Sanders, Frans. Flemish Sch. *b* Malines (?) before 1495 *d* after 1542. *Religious subjects*. Master Malines Guild 1511. A *Last Judgement* painted for Malines Council Chamber (1526) is recorded. Dürer owned an *Adam and Eve* by him, and Margaret of Austria (*cf.* J. Schoof) a *Virgin and Child*.

[Fl. 243, Fl. 613, Fl. 892.]

Sanders, Jan see **Hemessen.**

Santvoort, Anthoni (known as Groene Anthony or Antonio Verde). Flemish Sch. *b* Malines before 1555 *d* Rome 1600. *Religious subjects*. Went Italy and remained there (*cf.* J. van der Straet); in Rome employed A. Mytens *q.v.* to make many copies on copper of a *Virgin and Child* in S. Maria Maggiore; worked for a church with J. Speeckaert *q.v.* and was prosecuted with him for doing so without being member of Guild 1575; Member of newly-founded Accad. di S. Luca 1577; had German pupils including H. v. Aachen (*cf.* G. Rem and B. Spranger); inherited property from the engraver Cornelis Cort 1578. [Fl. 559, Fl. 84, Fl. 892, Fl. 416, Fl. 798.]

Santvoort, Philipp (Jacob Philipp) van. Flemish Sch. 17th/18th cent. *Interiors and contemporary social genre* (*cf.* J. J. Horemans). Presumed by some the Jacob Philipp van S. recorded pupil in Antwerp of G. J. v. Opstal 1711-12, and Master in Antwerp Guild 1721-2. A *Polish manners in the time of Augustus the Strong* (signed P. van Santvoort 1718) is recorded.

[Fl. 92.]

Sassenbrouck, Achille L. van. Flemish Sch. *b* Bruges 1886. *Landscape, marines, still life, genre*. Pupil in Bruges Acad. of E. van Hove, then in Antwerp of F. Courtens and F. v. Leemputten. Travelled widely in Europe and U.S.A. Represented in BRUGES *Ostend harbour* DIXMUDE, IXELLES.

[Fl. 114.]

Sauvage, Jean Pierre. Flemish Sch. *b* Brussels (?) or Lunéville (?) 1699 *d* Brussels 1780. *Portraits*. In Brussels Guild 1736; court painter to Governor General of Austrian Netherlands, Prince Charles of Lorraine (*cf.* P. Évrard, M. J. Geeraerts, J. J. Horemans the younger, L. Legendre, A. C.

Lens, J. J. Lens, F. J. Lonsing, P. N. van Reysschoot, J. G. Sauvage, F. Stampart, P. J. Tassaert, P. J. Verhaghen, and B. Verschoot), and to Empress Maria Theresa (*cf.* P. J. Lion, H. de La Pegnia, G. de Pélichy, P. J. Verhaghen). **Signed Examples:** BRUSSELS *Empress Maria Theresa* and *Emperor Francis I* 1765 (companion pieces). Signed pictures *Prince Charles of Lorraine as Grand Master of the Teutonic Order* 1776, and *Count F. J. B. de Coswarem, Chamberlain to the Empress, in the service of Charles of Lorraine Grand Master of the Teutonic Order* 1761 are recorded in German castles.

[Fl. 440, Fl. 88, Fl. 798.]

Sauvage, Joseph Grégoire. Flemish Sch. *b* son of Jean Pierre S., Brussels 1733 *d* probably in Brussels in or after 1787. *Portraits in miniature and enamel*. Court Painter to Prince Charles of Lorraine (*cf.* J. P. S.) 1763-80; his mother begged the Governors General Duke Albert of Saxe-Teschen and Maria Christina (*cf.* A. J. Cardon) to admit him to the newly founded S. Pierre Hospital in Brussels 'afin de terminer sa deplorable carrière aux frais de la caisse de religion' seeing that he was 'atteint d'une maladie nerveuse et incapable de tout travail' 1787; the request was at first refused but he was eventually admitted (*cf.* G. J. Smeyers). [Fl. 440.]

Sauvage, Piat Joseph. Flemish Sch. *b* Tournai 1744 *d* Tournai 1818. *Allegories, decorative subjects and still life, many in grisaille imitating reliefs* (*cf.* M. J. Geeraerts), *miniature portraits some imitating cameos; occasional religious subjects and history; also worked as porcelain painter and enamellist*. Pupil in Tournai of R. Malaine and in Antwerp of M. J. Geeraerts; began with religious paintings for churches; went Paris (*cf.* F. B. Solvyns) 1774; met there the (Dutch born) miniature and flower painter G. van Spaendonck; member of Académie de S. Luc 1774; member of Toulouse and Lille Academies 1776; member of Paris Acad. Royale (*cf.* J. L. Demarne, A. Ansiaux, P. J. Lafontaine; also P. Mol) 1783; court painter to Louis XVI (*cf.* J. L. Malaine and J. B. Suvée) and the Prince de Condé (*cf.* H. F. de Cort); frequent exhibitor in Paris Salons; visited Brussels 1781 (?); turned republican with Revolution (*cf.* A. Ansiaux, P. J. Redouté) and commanded a battalion of Paris National Guard 1795; returned Tournai 1808; professor there in Acad. 1810 and again painted for churches. His son C. G. S. painted still life pieces with flowers and insects. **Signed Examples:** CHANTILLY (miniatures) *Louis XVI, Marie Antoinette* 1792 (?). MONTPELLIER *Children's Bacchanal* (imitation bronze relief). **Documented Examples:** BRUSSELS S. Gilles *S. Carlo Borromeo and the plague-stricken* (*cf.* V. H. Janssens) 1765. COMPIÈGNE *Grisaille decorations, Justice, Prudence, Anacreon and Lycoris, Bacchus and Ariadne and others* 1785. FONTAINE-BLEAU *Still life (table, bronze vase, helmet and visor)* (Acad. Royale reception piece 1783), *Grisaille over-door decorations*. LILLE *Minerva patron of painting and sculpture* (grisaille). MONTARGIS *Children as soldiers* (grisaille). MONTAU-BAN *Amoretti* (grisaille). TOULOUSE *Children's Bacchanal* (Toulouse Acad. reception piece 1776). TOURNAI S. Marie Madeleine *Assumption of the Virgin*. VALENCIENNES *J. B. Rousseau* (engraved). His Salon exhibits included *The death of Germanicus* (imitation marble bas-relief), (Acad. de S. Luc reception piece 1774) and *Pageant Entry of the Archduchess Maria Christina and the Prince of Saxe-Teschen into Brussels 1781* (*cf.* A. Cardon). Grisaille medallions *Napoleon as First Consul* are recorded. Portraits of *William Beckford* the *Comte de Buffon*, the actor *La Rive* and others are recorded by engravings.

[Fl. 451, Fl. 612, Fl. 88, Fl. 66, Fl. 359, Fl. 892, Fl. 798, Fl. 73.]

*Savery, Jacques (Jacob) the elder. Flemish Sch. *b* Courtrai 1569 or 1570 *d* of plague, Amsterdam 1602. *Landscapes with religious and other figures* (*cf.* A. Mirou); *also worked as engraver*. Van Mander, a contemporary and also from Courtrai, records him as elder brother of Roelandt S. *q.v.* and the best pupil of H. Bol *q.v.*; went Holland at time of Parma campaigns (*cf.* D. v. d. Queborne) and recorded in The Hague 1585; Van Mander describes his work as delicate and patient in execution. The Dutch genre painter J. Savery the younger (*b* Amsterdam *c.* 1593) was his son. **Signed Examples:** AMSTERDAM Rijks. *Landscape with Jephthah's daughter* (miniature dated 158–). MILAN Brera *Landscape with Tobias and the angel* (*cf.* J. van Scorel, and Jan (Velvet) Brueghel) 1591. Works recorded by engravings include a *Landscape with S. John preaching*, *Landscape with the Prodigal Son among the swine* (*cf.* Prodigal Son Master) and *Pageant Entry of Robert Dudley Earl of Leicester in the Hague* 1586 (*cf.* C. Ketel, D. Barendsz and L. Cornelisz). His own engravings include landscapes with hunting subjects. Three landscapes (one with birds) were in a large collection of pictures by Jan (Velvet) Brueghel, J. Grimmer, M. v. Cleve, and many others, assessed in Antwerp by P. Goetkint, H. v. Balen and A. v. Stalbemt 1621. [Fl. 559, Fl. 425, Fl. 892, Fl. 798, Fl. 213.]

Savery, Jan see **Roelandt S.**

*Savery, Roelandt. Flemish Sch. *b* Courtrai *c.* 1576. *d* insane Utrecht 1639. *Landscapes with figures, animals and birds* (*some with Orpheus cf.* L. v. d. Borcht), *flowers* (*cf.* A. Bosschaert). Pupil in Holland of his brother Jacques S. the elder *q.v.*; visited France and worked for Henri IV (*cf.* A. Dubois); went Prague and worked for Emperor Rudolf II (*cf.* B. Spranger and P. Stevens) *c.* 1604; sent by Emperor to paint in the Tyrol 1606-8; painter to Emperor Matthias 1612; in Amsterdam 1613; Vienna 1614-16; Amsterdam 1616; Utrecht 1619; chosen to present personally to Amalia van Solms, wife of Prince Frederick Henry, a wedding gift of his own pictures on behalf of City of Utrecht 1626. Houbraken (1721) records him as a bachelor who in later years worked in the mornings and gave the rest of the day to pleasures. Norgate (*c.* 1649) refers to the 'blushing reflections' on clouds in his fair-weather landscapes; other early writers complain of an undue dominance of blue. His nephew the Dutch painter Jan (Hans) S. (1597-1654) and G. C. de Hondecoeter *q.v.* were among his pupils. **Signed Examples:** AMSTERDAM *Cowshed with milking* (and in the corners, witches on brooms) (*cf.* J. Cornelisz van Oostsanen, F. Francken II, J. Ghuens the younger, B. Spranger) 1615, *Stag hunt in a rocky landscape* 1620, *Coronation of Orpheus at feast of animals* 1623, *Elijah fed by ravens* 1634, *Fable of the Hart and the Cows*. ANTWERP *Birds in a forest*. BERLIN *Garden of Eden* (*cf.* D. v. Alsloot, H. de Clerck, J. (Velvet) Brueghel, F. Pourbus the elder, I. v. Oosten, A. Snellinck) 1626. BRUSSELS *Birds in a landscape* 1622, *Landscape with animals*. CAMBRIDGE Fitz. *Orpheus* 1622, *Creation of Birds* 1619. COPENHAGEN *Flowers* 1620. LONDON N.G. *Orpheus charming the animals* 1628; Victoria and Albert *Flowers* 1620; ROYAL COLLECTION Hampton Court *Landscape with lions* 1622. MUNICH *Landscape with wild boar hunt* 1609. NUREMBERG *Tower of Babel* (*cf.* M. v. Valkenborch) 1602. ROTTERDAM *A hen*. TURIN *Landscape with lions, tigers and leopards*. UTRECHT *Flowers* 1624, *Orpheus*. VERVIERS *Landscape with a white horse* 1624. VIENNA K. *Landscape with huntsmen* 1604, *Wooded landscape with fruitseller* 1609, *Landscape with woodmen* 1610, *Orpheus in the underworld, Landscape with birds* 1628, *Garden of Eden* 1623, *Rocky landscape*. Others signed in BRUNSWICK, BUDAPEST, DESSAU, DRESDEN, *Noah and the animals round the Ark* 1620, THE HAGUE, PRAGUE. [Fl. 559, Fl. 618, Fl. 86, Fl. 763, Fl. 425, Fl. 878, Fl. 22, Fl. 215, Fl. 265, Fl. 892, Fl. 146.]

Saverys, Albert. Flemish Sch. *b* Deynze 1886. *Landscapes, still life, marines*. Pupil of J. Delvin and the sculptor, G. Minne in Ghent Acad. Worked mainly in region round Deynze; had at one time a studio in a mill; in Bruges 1939-40;

teacher in Antwerp Higher Inst. Represented in ANTWERP *Landscape, Still life* BRUSSELS *Winter, Marine*. [Fl. 71, Fl. 568, Fl. 296.]

Savoyen (or **Savoy**), **Carel van.** Flemish Sch. *b* Antwerp before 1625 *d* Amsterdam 1665. *Mythologies* (*often with nude figures*), *religious subjects; portraits; occasional engravings*. Pupil in Antwerp of J. Cossiers *q.v.* 1635; went Amsterdam as a Protestant (?) (*cf.* P. van S.) and was married there 1649. Houbraken (1719) quotes the following by J. de Vos on a *Venus, Adonis and Diana*:

Diana word Adoon, in schyn van Blaau, ontschaakt:
Want Venus, vol van list ontziet geen slaapende oogen.
Op, Jagtgodin, eer u nog grooter ramp genaakt.
De zorgelooze slaap word ligtelyk bedroogen.

Nagler (before 1852) records him as a painter of frivolous subjects. **Signed Example:** LEIPZIG Greek Orthodox Chapel *Adoration of the Shepherds* (C. v. Savo ... 166 ...). A *Christ at Emmaus* (monogrammed K. v. S.) in Darmstadt is presumed by some his work. H. Bartels in Antwerp owned (1672) a *Diana bathing*. Others titles recorded are *Aristotle and Campaspe* (*cf.* G. Congnet), *Nymphs and satyrs in a wooded landscape, Offering to Priapus, Bacchanal, Venus and Cupid* and *Allegory of the Arts*. C. v. S. engraved his own portrait for de Bie's Gulden Cabinet 1662.
[Fl. 86, Fl. 425, Fl. 215, Fl. 612, Fl. 892, Fl. 88, Fl. 440, Fl. 213, Fl. 109 (1916 and 1917).]

Savoyen, Philip van. Flemish Sch. *b* Antwerp 1630 *d* Amsterdam 1664. Brother of Carel van S.; was married in a Protestant church in Amsterdam with his brother as a witness 1661. [Fl. 440.]

Schaefels, Henri François. Flemish Sch. *b* son of decorative painter H. R. S., Antwerp 1827 *d* Antwerp 1904. *Costume history, sea battles, marines and picturesque corners of old Antwerp*. Pupil of J. de Jonghe, J. Jacobs and J. Ruyten. Represented in ANTWERP *Old courtyard in the Antwerp Hôtel de Ville* 1870, *Courtyard in the Zilvermidstraat* 1871. *The 'Algeciras' at Trafalgar, Siege of Flushing in 1809* 1890. BRUSSELS *Storm over the Scheldt* 1901. COURTRAI *Seventeenth century fête at Antwerp* 1858. GHENT. [Fl. 88, Fl. Bib. 19th cent.]

Schaefels, Lucas. Flemish Sch. *b* son of decorative painter H. R. S., Antwerp 1824 *d* Antwerp 1885. *Decorative work for Antwerp churches, and still life*. Pupil of his father. Teacher in Antwerp Acad. 1857; worked at one time with V. Lagye. Represented in ANTWERP *Flower piece;* S. Antoine *Murals*. MONTREAL *Still life*. [Fl. 88.]

Schaep, Henri Adolphe. Flemish Sch. *b* place unknown 1826 *d* place unknown 1870. *Marines*. Represented in ANTWERP *Shipwreck* 1857. [Fl. 17.]

Schaepkens, Théodor. Flemish Sch. *b* Maestricht 1810 *d* Saint-Josse-ten-Noode 1883. *Contemporary and costume history, religious subjects, genre, portraits; also active as engraver and lithographer*. Pupil in Antwerp Academy of M. v. Brée; in Paris of the French painter L. Hersent 1829; returned Belgium and witnessed 1830 revolution; defeated in Rome prize by A. Wiertz 1832; invited Rome by Wiertz who wrote 'Le monde entier sera stupéfait de ce que nous ferons ensemble'; lived mainly Belgium with visits to Maestricht. Represented in BRUSSELS, LOUVAIN, MAESTRICHT (Hôtel de Ville) and Belgian churches. His brothers Alexander and Arnaud S. were mainly active as draughtsmen, engravers and archaeologists. Titles recorded include: *Columbus in chains, Columbus and his son seeking asylum at a monastery, Jeanne d'Arc on a white horse, Death of Count Frédéric de Mérode* (*cf.* F. de Braekeleer), *The Duke of Orléans at the siege of Antwerp, Massacre on Maestricht Bridge 1579, The*

assumption of S. Servatus (for Maestricht S. Servatus), *The death of Evrard t' Serclaes on the Brussels Grand' Place 1387* and a lithographed *Portrait of Pope Gregory XVI*.
[Fl. 451, Fl. 612, Fl. 892, Fl. 440, Fl. 88, Fl. 466 (1884).]

Schampeleer, Edmond de. Flemish Sch. *b* Brussels 1824 *d* Brussels 1899. *Landscapes, also worked as an engraver*. Pupil of E. de Block in Antwerp. Visited Munich and Holland. Represented in ANTWERP *Souvenir of the Zuiderzee* 1867, *Souvenir of Gouda* 1878, *Harvest*, BRUSSELS, COURTRAI, LIÈGE. [Fl. Bib. 19th cent., Fl. 17.]

Schaubruck see **Schoubroeck**.

Schavije, L. see **Stapleaux.**

Schayck, Ernest the elder. Flemish (Dutch) Sch. 16th cent. Presumed by some painter of Amsterdam Rijks. (55) altarpiece from Utrecht S. Peter's: *Stoning of S. Stephen, Allegory of Human Vanity* (cf. Amsterdam Cadaver Painter and Frankfort Master), *S. Mary Magdalene in the garden, S. Mary of Egypt in the desert* (cf. Philadelphia Maria Egyptiaca Painter) inscribed as donated 1554 by Ernest van Schayck, Canon of S. Peter's Utrecht (cf. J. Scorel and Sotte Cleve) who died 1564. A painter of this name son of Joachim S. (Schuyck) recorded by Van Mander was in Utrecht Guild 1569. [Fl. 559, Fl. 892, Fl. 7, Fl. 631 (1933).]

Schayck, Ernest the younger (Ernesto de Scaichis). Flemish (Dutch) Sch. *b* Utrecht before 1567 *d* Italy (?) after 1631. *Religious subjects*. Went Italy before 1600 and remained there (cf. J. van der Straet). Signed Examples: APPIGNANO S. Giov. Batt. *Marriage of the Virgin* 'Ernesto de Scaichis'. FILOTTRANO (Ancona) S. Maria Assunta *Virgin of Mercy* 'Ernesto de Scaychis' 1609, *SS. Anthony Abbot, Francis of Assisi, Benedict and Sebastian* 1609. LUGO S. Maria *Virgin in glory with saints* 'Ernestis de Schaichis Fiamengus 1615'; S. Rocco *Virgin in glory with saints and 5 donors* 'Ernestus de Schaichus Belga de Traiecto 1600'. RECANATI S. Placido *S. Carlo Borromeo*. SANSEVERINO S. Giuseppe *Virgin in glory with saints* 1631; SS. Marino e Giacomo *Virgin of the Rosary* 'Ernestus de Scaychis Flamingus 1625'. UTRECHT *SS. Sebastian and Roch* 1600. [Fl. 305.]

Schendel, Petrus van. Flemish Sch. *b* Terheyde nr. Breda 1806 *d* Brussels 1870. *Portraits, religious subjects (some with artificial light effects); but mainly market scenes, moonlight effects* (cf. H. J. v. d. Poorten, P. J. Regemorter, A. I. Steyaert, J. L. de Wouters) *and genre*. Pupil in Antwerp Acad. of M. v. Brée 1822-8; then Holland where famous before he was thirty; settled Brussels *c.* 1845. Represented in AMIENS *S. Mary Magdalene*. AMSTERDAM *Frisian marketplace by moonlight, Adriana Johanna van Wijck, wife of J. Ploos van Amstel* 1829. COURTRAI *Moonlight scene*. HARTFORD U.S.A. (Wadsworth Atheneum) *Marketplace at night with candlelight effects*. HAMBURG *Kitchen scene* 1831. MELBOURNE (Australia) *Poultry seller*. MONTREAL *Holy Family, Moonlight market scene in Antwerp*. NICE *Fruit seller*. STUTTGART *Vegetable seller*. YPRES *Fish seller*.
[Fl. 451, Fl. 612, Fl. 837 (1871), Fl. 892, Fl. Bib. 19th cent.]

Schephen (or Scheffer), Paul. Flemish (Dutch) Sch. 16th cent. *Religious subjects*. Went Italy; worked for Naples churches (cf. J. S. van Calcar, A. Mytens, J. van der Straet) 1560-7. Documented Example: NAPLES S. Severino frescoes (restored) *Pentecost, Evangelists, Saints* and *Church fathers* 1567. [Fl. 232, Fl. 892, Fl. 305.]

Schernier, see **Coninxloo, C. van.**

Schey, Philip. Flemish Sch. 17th cent. Signed Example: AMSTERDAM Rijks. *Riverside banquet* 1626 (painted on a spinet lid cf. F. Borsse). [Fl. 8.]

Schirren, Ferdinand. Flemish Sch. *b* Antwerp 1872 *d* Brussels 1943. *Figures, landscape and still life compositions in Post Impressionist and Fauve conventions* (cf. C. Dehoy and R. Wouters); *also worked as sculptor*. Pupil of the sculptors J. de Keyser and Jef Lambeaux. Worked much in the South of France. Represented in ANTWERP *Landscape* (w), *Still life* (w). BRUSSELS *Woman in blue* 1921. [Fl. 388, Fl. 296.]

Schneider, N (?). Flemish Sch. 18th cent. *Landscapes with birds and game* (cf. J. B. Govaerts, P. F. de Hamilton, J. Sloots also J. v. Kessel the elder). Recorded in The Hague 1753 and later in Amsterdam. [Fl. 481, Fl. 892.]

Schney, F. van. Flemish Sch. 17th cent. *Still life* (cf. F. Ijkens, C. Luyckx, F. Snyders and P. Boel). Signed Example: OSLO *Still life with dead birds and porcelain* 1610 (?). A *Still life with fruit* in Brunswick Mus. monogrammed and dated 1634 is presumed by some his work. [Fl. 798.]

*Schoevaerdts (or Schovaerdts), Mathieu. Flemish Sch. *b* Brussels (?) *c.* 1665 *d* Brussels (?) after 1694. *Landscapes (some Italianate) with genre figures* (cf. P. v. Bredael, A. F. Rubens) *and peasant gatherings* (cf. P. Bout, T. Michau, J. v. Bredael); *also worked as engraver*. Pupil in Brussels of A. F. Baudewyns *q.v.* 1682; Master Brussels Guild 1690, Dean 1692-4. His brother François and his nephew Pierre were also painters. Signed Examples: BRUSSELS *The procession of the Fat Ox in front of the Swan Inn, Fish market by the shore*. CAMBRIDGE Fitz. *Italianate landscape with mounted figures and peasants*. FLORENCE Uffizi *Village landscape*. PARIS Louvre *Landscape with figures and animals, Entrance to a wood*. STOCKHOLM *Vegetable market by a river*.
[Fl. 451, Fl. 612, Fl. 892, Fl. 88.]

Schoof, Gerard the elder. Flemish Sch. *b* Malines before 1504 *d* Malines 1586. *Decorative paintings; also active as sculptor*. Master Antwerp Guild 1518; Town Painter to Malines (cf. J. Schooff); designed 'Ommeganck' processions; worked on decorations for Philip II's Pageant Entry into Malines (cf. M. Willems and J. V. de Vries) 1549.
[Fl. 613, Fl. 88, Fl. 798.]

Schoof, Gerard. Flemish Sch. *b* Malines before 1560 *d* Antwerp 1624. *Religious subjects and decorative work*. Nephew of Gerard S. the elder. Master Antwerp Guild 1575; under M. de Vos and Ambrosius Francken and with C. Floris, T. v. Haecht, J. de Momper, A. v. Uden and others worked on Pageant Entry into Antwerp of Archduke Ernest 1594 (cf. G. Claeissins, J. Snellinck, J. B. Saive and G. v. Veen); became citizen of Antwerp 1597; gave a *Descent from the Cross* to Hoboken Church on condition he and his wife were taken every year by carriage to the Kermesse and given a good dinner 1612; J. de Hase and G. Francken and the painter-dealer J. v. Mechelen were among his pupils.
[Fl. 613, Fl. 126, Fl. 892, Fl. 88, Fl. 798.]

Schoof, Rudolf. Flemish Sch. 17th cent. *b* son of Gerard S. Went Paris where became painter to Louis XIII (cf. J. Fouquier, J. v. Egmont, P. de Champaigne also H. Staben). Adriaen de Bie *q.v.* was his pupil there 1612-14.
[Fl. 425, Fl. 892.]

Schooff (Schoef), Jean. Flemish Sch. *b* Malines (?) *c.* 1475 *d* after 1533. *Contemporary history and decorative work*. Town painter to Malines (cf. G. Schoof the elder) 1506; designed 'Ommeganck' processions; employed by Archduchess Margaret of Austria (cf. J. Gossaert, B. v. Orley, J. C. Vermeyen, J. Mostaert, P. Tubach, J. v. Roome, F. Sanders, G. Horenbout, P. v. Coninxloo and 'Michiel') 1519-28. Documented Example: MALINES Town Hall Archives *First Session of Malines Parlement presided over by Charles the*

Bold 1473 (commissioned by town authorities 1515; dated 1516 with barely legible signature). A smaller version is in Brussels. [Fl. 689, Fl. 120, Fl. 892.]

Schoonjans (or **Sevonyans**), **Anthoni**. Nicknamed 'Parrhasius' (sometimes referred to as Jean le Bel?). Flemish Sch. *b* Antwerp *c.* 1655 *d* Vienna 1726. *Religious subjects, 'history', portraits.* Pupil of E. Quellinus in Antwerp; in Rome at the same time as A. Genoels and received his nickname in Flemish colony 1674; went Vienna *c.* 1693; with his wife a singer had social success there; court painter to the Emperor Leopold I (*cf.* J. A. v. d. Baren, P. Evrard, J. v. Hoy, J. F. Saey and J. Thomas 'van Ypern') 1695; left Vienna suddenly for unknown reason; in Copenhagen *c.* 1696; in Berlin and working for Frederick I (*cf.* C. S. Dubois and J. G. de Hamilton) *c.* 1702; in Holland *c.* 1704-6; went London (*cf.* S. Dubois and P. Angellis); Vertue (1728) records a staircase painted by him in Little Montagu House (demolished); went Düsseldorf where worked for Elector Palatine Johann Wilhelm; returned Vienna *c.* 1716. Recorded as intolerably vain. **Signed Examples:** AUGSBURG *Job tormented by his wife* 1710. BERLIN Charlottenburg *Crown Prince Friedrich Wilhelm aged 14 as David, with Goliath and the Philistines in the background* (*cf.* J. B. Saive and A. v. Stalbemt) 1702. OTTNANG (Upper Austria) Parish church *Altar piece.* **Documented Examples:** BERLIN Charlottenburg *Ceilings.* BUDAPEST *Man playing mandoline.* FLORENCE Uffizi *Self portrait* (engraved). A *Joseph I on horseback with Fortuna and Justice in the clouds* is among works recorded by engravings. H. Walpole owned a *Self portrait.* Vertue records a *Portrait of Dr. Peeters of S. Martins Lane* (*cf.* Jan Peeters the younger). [Fl. 425, Fl. 353, Fl. 826, Fl. 215, Fl. 616, Fl. 451, Fl. 612, Fl. 892, Fl. 88, Fl. 798.]

*Schoor, Guillaume van. Flemish Sch. 17th cent. In Brussels Guild 1654. **Signed Example:** BRUSSELS *L'Hôtel de Nassau at Brussels* 1658 (the guitar held by one of the ladies is monogrammed T. B.). A *Landscape* by 'van Schoor' described (1689) as 'in the manner of J. Fouquier' *q.v.* was then in an Antwerp collection. [Fl. 301, Fl. 213, Fl. 296, Fl. 124.]

Schoor, Louis (or **Ludwig**, also referred to as **N.** and **Nicolas**) **van.** Flemish Sch. *b* Antwerp 1666 *d* Antwerp 1726. *Mythologies and allegories, mainly as cartoons for tapestry* (*cf.* A. Genoels, A. Baudewyns, V. H. Janssens, P. Spierinckx, also H. v. d. Hoecke and P. Thys). In Brussels where J. I. van Roore was his pupil 1703; collaborated with A. Coppens *q.v.,* J. B. Morel and P. Rysbraeck (or another member of that family). Tapestries from his designs representing *The Elements, The Seasons, The Months* and the *Quarters of the World* are recorded. A *Charles II of Spain aged eighteen on horseback* (*cf.* F. Duchatel) and a *Triumph of Louis XIV* (*tapestry imitation*) are also recorded. [Fl. 878, Fl. 215, Fl. 612, Fl. 481, Fl. 892, Fl. 212, Fl. 798, Fl. 296.]

Schoor, Lucas van. Flemish Sch. *b* Antwerp *c.* 1566 *d* Italy *c.* 1610. *Religious subjects.* Went Italy and remained there (*cf.* J. v. d. Straet). A *Crucifixion* recorded (1825) in Bergamo S. Maria Maggiore is no longer in that church. A *Virgin* (Mariebeelt) by 'Van Schoor' is recorded in an Antwerp inventory 1655. [Fl. 612, Fl. 892, Fl. 305, Fl. 213.]

Schot, Conrad. Flemish Sch. *b* Brussels 1527 *d* after 1553. Pupil in Brussels of A. Mor *c.* 1549; declined invitation from Mor to go with him to Portugal 1552; referred to in a testimonial by Mor (1553): 'à tous et à chacun soit certifié que maître Antoine Mor, natif d'Utrecht, habitant la ville de Bruxelles, peintre de Sa Majesté Impériale (Charles V), que Conrad Schot, de Bruxelles, a séjourné chez lui l'espace d'un an et demi environ pour s'initier à la peinture; qu'il a toujours été de bonne fâme et, en ma compagnie, a hanté journelle-

ment la Cour de Sa Majesté Impériale les appartements du prince d'Espagne (Philip II) et de Mgr. d'Arras (Cardinal Granvella), également des grandes et nobles maisons; qu'il s'est toujours conduit d'une manière honorable, agissant envers tous comme il sied à un bon compagnon; que jamais il n'a été articulé à sa charge rien qui soit contraire à l'honneur et à la vertu, ce que le prédit maître Antoine se déclare prêt à confirmer sous serment'; collaborated later with one Jean Maes in Malines and Antwerp. A *Portrait of Edward VI of England,* painted, with one Jean Maes, for the English Ambassador in Antwerp is recorded. [Fl. 440, Fl. 88, Fl. 892.]

*Schoubroeck (or **Schaubruck** or **Schubroeck**), **Pieter.** Flemish Sch. *b* son of Flemish emigré Protestant minister, Hessheim (nr. Frankenthal) before 1570 *d* Frankenthal 1607. *Landscapes with figures, conflagration effects* (*cf.* C. de Caullery, Brussels Sodom and Gemorrah Painter, F. v. Oosten, J. Sons, F. and G. v. Valkenborch). Recorded in Nuremberg (*cf.* N. Neuchatel); in Frankenthal (*cf.* G. v. Coninxloo and J. v. Liere) 1598 and from 1600. **Signed Examples:** BRUNSWICK *S. John preaching in the wilderness* (*cf.* K. v. Mander). CASSEL *Troy burning* 1606. COPENHAGEN *Village landscape* 1597. MUNICH A. P. *Wooded landscape with figures* 1604 VIENNA K. *Troy burning and Aeneas carrying his father* 1606. **Monogrammed Examples:** DRESDEN *Battle of the Amazons* 1603. VIENNA Harrach *Wooded landscape.* [Fl. 612, Fl. 892, Fl. 659.]

Schovaerdts, M. see **Schoevaerdts.**

*Schut, Cornelis. Flemish Sch. *b* Antwerp 1597 *d* Antwerp 1655. *Religious subjects, history, allegories; also active as engraver and tapestry designer* (*cf.* A. Sallaert). Recorded by early writers as pupil of Rubens; Master Antwerp Guild 1618; member of Chamber of Rhetoric and wrote verses; worked 1620 under Rubens with Van Dyck, D. and G. Seghers and others on ceiling panels for Antwerp Jesuit church (building begun 1614, burnt 1718, *cf.* A. Gheringh; executor with Rubens, H. v. Balen and others of Jan (Velvet) Brueghel's will 1625; worked under Rubens on decorations for Pageant Entry into Antwerp of Cardinal Infante Ferdinand (*cf.* G. Weri) 1635; and on Ghent Entry (*cf.* G. de Crayer and T. Rombouts) the same year; was commissioned to arrange with engravers to record the Ghent decorations (*cf.* T. v. Thulden); Spanish writers record a visit to Spain (*cf.* C. Luyckx and A. Smit) where his brother Pieter S. was engineer in Philip IV's service; returned Antwerp and was much employed after Rubens' death 1640; bought himself a country property (*cf.* D. Teniers the younger) 1652; D. Seghers *q.v.* painted flower garlands round some grisaille panels by his hand; his nephew Cornelis S. III and P. Vleughels were among his pupils. Van Dyck painted his portrait. **Signed Example:** ANTWERP Cathedral (ceiling in cupola) *Assumption of the Virgin* 1647. **Documented Examples:** ANTWERP Mus. *Martyrdom of S. George* (*the saint refusing to sacrifice to Apollo*) painted for Junior Crossbowmen's altar in Antwerp Cathedral in successful competition against T. Willeboirts *q.v.* 1643 (seen by Descamps (1768) and by Sir J. Reynolds (1781) who wrote: 'Well composed and well drawn but the saint has too much of that character which painters have fixed for Christ; there is a want of brilliancy from its having too much harmony; to produce force and strength, a stronger opposition of colours is required'.); *Purification* (from Malines, Augustins where seen by Descamps); *The granting of the Indulgentia Plenaria Portiuncula to S. Francis* (from Antwerp Recollets where seen by Descamps); S. Jacques *Christ on the knees of the Virgin* painted for the tomb of a member of his first wife's family (Descamps wrote: 'il est certainement beau comme de Van Dyck'; Reynolds wrote: 'Well drawn and coloured, something in the manner of Rubens'); S. Willebrord *The Trinity, Christ dead, Resurrection* above his own tomb and inscribed

'Godt is ons Schut'. EECKEREN *Last Supper* 1650. SANTA CRUZ DE MUDELA *S. Francis Xavier baptising 'Indians'* (from Madrid Colegio Imperial Staircase; painted on his visit to Spain). VIENNA K. *Allegory: The Triumph of Time; Bacchus and his train* (both in Archduke Leopold Wilhelm's inventory 1659 (*cf.* C. Schut the younger); others in COLOGNE S. Gereon and S. Peter (engraved by himself). His will (1654) left his daughter pictures titled *The Triumph of a Fair Name, The Seven liberal Arts* and *Daphne;* his son-in-law Guillelmo Huymans sold pictures by and after and touched up (geretocqueert) by him 1685; the Forchoudt firm of Antwerp dealers (*cf.* A. Casteels) sent a *Fame and Envy* to their Vienna branch in 1668 and an *Ecce Homo* to Graz in 1673; Descamps records a *Departure of a young lord for the Crusades* in Ghent Jesuit Church, a *Nativity* (je le crois un des beaux tableaux de ce maître) and a series of grisaille and coloured panels with garlands by D. Seghers in Antwerp Cordeliers, and pictures in Brussels and Lierre churches. Many pictures are recorded by his own and other engravings. D'Argenville (1752) records some characters in his drawings adding 'on reconnoitra toujours Corneille Schut à ses grosses têtes d'enfans et de femmes'. Cartoons for tapestry *The Seven Liberal Arts* are recorded.
[Fl. 86, Fl. 425, Fl. 878, Fl. 22, Fl. 215, Fl. 216, Fl. 702, Fl. 153, Fl. 612, Fl. 892, Fl. 712, Fl. 807, Fl. 204, Fl. 296.]

Schut, Cornelis the younger. Flemish Sch. 17th cent. *Religious subjects, 'history'.* In Rome where nickname 'Brotsack' in Flemish colony 1624-7. Presumed by some identical with an artist of this name recorded Antwerp Guild 1628 who died Rome 1636. Signed Example: BRUNSWICK (drawing) *Bacchus and his Train s* at back 'Brotsack' (*cf.* C. Schut). Descamps saw (1768) a *Conversion of S. Francis Borgia* and a *Presentation in the Temple* by 'C. Schut Le fils' in Ypres Jesuit church. *Cf.* C. Schut III.

[Fl. 216, Fl. 84, Fl. 416, Fl. 617, Fl. 798.]

Schut, Cornelis (III). Flemish Sch. *b* son of Pieter S. an engineer, Antwerp *c.* 1629 *d* Seville *c.* 1685. *Religious subjects, portraits, drawings.* Pupil of his uncle Cornelis S. *q.v.*; taken Spain by his father who entered service of Philip IV (*cf.* D. Delmont and A. Smit); in Seville by 1653; founder member, with Murillo, Francisco de Herrera, J. Valdés Leal and other Spanish painters, of Seville Acad. (where the students were fined for swearing or talking of anything not pertaining to their studies) 1660; treasurer of the Academy; then demonstrating professor using nude models often paid for by himself; president 1672, 1673; made his will 1685. His brother, a tailor, also lived in Seville. **Signed Examples:** CADIZ Cathedral *S. Theresa.* SEVILLE Prov. Mus. *The Dominican Fr. Domingo de Bruselas* 1665. MADRID Prado *Immaculate Conception* 1667. Signed paintings titled *The story of Cain and Abel* are recorded.
[Fl. 637, Fl. 22, Fl. 153, Fl. 612, Fl. 779, Fl. 335, Fl. 798.]

Scoenere, J. de see Stoevere.

*****Scorel (or Schoorel), Jan van.** Flemish (Dutch) Sch. *b* bastard of parish priest, Scorel nr. Alkmaar 1495 *d* Utrecht 1562. *Religious subjects, portraits;* also recorded as architect, engineer, poet, musician and humanist versed in Latin, Italian, French and German. Pupil of C. Buys *q.v.* in Alkmaar, of Willem Cornelisz *q.v.* in Haarlem, and of J. Cornelisz van Oostsanen in Amsterdam; also of J. Gossaert in Utrecht 1517 (of this Van Mander writes (1604): 'he stayed but a short time because Mabuse had an irregular life frequenting taverns where he became involved in drunken brawls and S. had to pay the bill and sometimes even risk his life' (*cf.* J. Patinir)); went Rhineland, Strasbourg, Bâle and Nuremberg where visited Dürer and heard his comments on Luther's activities 1518-19; went Styria and Obervellach in Carinthia 1520; thence to Venice (*cf.* J. Swart) where joined pilgrimage of

Netherlanders to Jerusalem (*cf.* B. v. d. Stoct, M. Sweerts) 1520-1; returned Venice via Rhodes; went Rome; made Keeper of Belvedere antiquities and nominated as a Canon of Utrecht by the Utrecht born Pope Adrian VI; back in Holland by 1523 (?); in Utrecht by 1525; fled from Utrecht's political troubles to Haarlem 1526; worked in Haarlem for Commander of the Knights of S. John (*cf.* Geertgen tot Sint Jans); returned Utrecht *c.* 1529; refused to join Utrecht Guild or pay subscription on ground—as Buchelius records (1585)—that he was exempt as a Canon; set up house with Agatha van Schoonoven as his mistress and had five children (*cf.* Sotte Cleve); visited France (?) (*cf.* L. Thiry); declined offer of François I to become his court painter (*cf.* Joos v. Cleve); worked in Breda Castle for Count Henry of Nassau and René de Châlons Prince of Orange 1541; painted picture for and recommended an architect to King Gustavus I of Sweden who replied with a signed letter announcing presents of 200 lbs of cheese, an ice sledge, a case of furs and a ring (but only the letter arrived) 1542; worked on Pageant Entry into Utrecht of Charles V and Philip II (*cf.* C. Anthonisz and J. v. Rillaert) 1549; with J. Vermeyen *q.v.* made plans for improving Harderwijk harbour and damming the Zype (executed a century later) 1549-51; went Ghent with L. Blondeel to clean H. and J. van Eyck's *Altarpiece of the Mystic Lamb* 1550 (*cf.* A. van Heuvel). Many of his pictures were destroyed by the iconoclasts 1566. D. Lampsonius *q.v.* praised him as a Romanist and Van Mander records that F. Floris and others looked upon him as a pioneer painter (lantaarndrager en baanbreker) in the Italian style. M. van Heemskerck and A. Mor *q.v.* were among his pupils. Mor painted his portrait for his tomb. **Signed Examples:** BONN *Crucifixion* ('Schoorle' 1530). HAARLEM Mus. *Twelve Jerusalem Pilgrims* (including self portrait of the artist described as Canon of Utrecht; originally owned by the Knights of S. John). OBERVELLACH Carinthia, Parish church, Triptych (centre): *The Holy Kinship* ('Joannes Scorel hollandius pictorie artis amator pingebat . . . 1520'), (wings): *S. Christopher, S. Apollonia* grisailles; (reverses presumed by some by another hand): *Carrying of the Cross, Flagellation.* ROME Doria *The painter's mistress Agatha van Schoonhoven* ('. . . 1529 per Scorelium pictorem'). A *Tobias and the Angel* (*cf.* J. Savery) signed and dated 1521 was recorded (1925) in a private collection. **Documented Examples:** HAARLEM *Baptism of Christ* (painted for S. Saen, Commander of the Order of S. John *c.* 1527 described by Van Mander), *Adam and Eve* (recorded archives of S. John Chapterhouse, Haarlem). UTRECHT *Christ on the road to Jerusalem* (corresponds to the picture described by Van Mander as painted for Deacon Lockhorst), Two wings and reverses *Donors and Saints* are presumed by some the completion of this altarpiece. VALENCIENNES *Martyrdom of S. Laurence* (presumed by some part of the picture from Marchiennes Abbey mentioned by Van Mander). VIENNA Kunsthist. *Presentation in the Temple* (presumed by some the picture described by Van Mander). Rubens owned (1640) a *Portrait of Cardinal Granvella* (*cf.* A. Mor and L. Suavius). Van Mander records an *Incredulity of S. Thomas* painted in Venice for Zion Monastery, Jerusalem, a sketch book with drawings of people, happenings and landscapes including mountains and castles done on his travels to Candia, Cyprus, on the Jordan and elsewhere, used in a painting *Joshua leading the Israelites across the Jordan;* a drawing of Jerusalem used in a number of his pictures including *Christ leaving the Mount of Olives* and the *Sermon on the Mount;* he also names a *Holy Sepulchre,* several versions of the *Crucifixion,* a *Last Supper* (with life size figures painted for Groot-Ower (Aduard) Abbey in Frisia), a *S. Ursula and the eleven thousand virgins,* a *Stoning of S. Stephen.* A *Sacrifice of Isaac* was bought by Philip II on his Netherlands tour 1549. A *Portrait of Pope Adrian VI* is recorded in a letter written by Scorel from Rome in 1524. Pictures presumed by some his work are in various museums (*cf.* Amsterdam Armed Arquebusiers Painter,

Death of the Virgin Master, Detroit Crucifixion Painter, Ottawa Judith Painter).

[Fl. 127, Fl. 559, Fl. 892, Fl. 418, Fl. 213, Fl. 316.]

Scrots, Guillaume. Flemish Sch. *d* after 1544. *Portraits.* Court painter to Mary of Hungary Governor of the Netherlands (*cf.* J. C. Vermeyen) 1537. Presumed by some identical with the Anglo-Dutch Guillim Stretes who worked in England 1546-53. [Fl. 892, Fl. 899, Fl. 28.]

Sederboom see Quellinus, J. E.

*Seghers (or Segers or Zeghers), **Daniel.** Flemish Sch. *b* son of Catholic silk merchant and Protestant Dutch mother, Antwerp 1590 *d* Antwerp 1661. *Still life, chiefly flower pieces and garlands round grisaille panels* (*cf.* J. v. d. Baren, J. v. d. Borght, A. Bosman, A. Bosschaert, A. Brueghel, J. (Velvet) Brueghel, P. F. Casteels, H. Galle, A. Goswin, G. Gysaerts, J. v. d. Hecke, J. D. de Heem, C. Ijkens, F. Ijkens, J. v Kessel, C. de Knodder, J. B. Morel, J. Seldenslach, F. Snyders, J. P. v. Thielen, G. P. Verbruggen, N. v. Verendael, P. Willebeeck). Educated as a Protestant by his mother in Holland; went Antwerp; pupil there of Jan (Velvet) Brueghel; rejoined Catholic church (*cf.* A. van Stalbemt); Master Antwerp Guild 1611; admitted into Jesuit Order 1614 (*cf.* I. Raeth); visited Rome (*cf.* J. de Hase, F. v. d. Kasteele and P. de Lignis); worked under Rubens (with Van Dyck, C. Schut and G. Seghers) on decorations for Antwerp Jesuit church (burnt 1718 *cf.* A. G. Gheringh) 1620; painted flower-piece for Prince Frederick Henry of Orange (*cf.* A. v. Utrecht, T. Willeboirts, G. Coques, A. Snellinck) for which he refused payment receiving in exchange a jewelled chain and permits for a group of Jesuits to travel Holland 1645; painted another for the Prince's widow Amalia van Solms (who gave him a gold palette and six gold brushes and also granted privileges for Jesuits); worked for Amalia van Solms in the Hague, Huis ten Bosch (*cf.* T. v. Thulden), for her son Prince William II and for the Archduke Leopold Wilhelm (*cf.* D. v. Heil, D. Teniers the younger, E. Quellinus, G. Seghers, P. Snayers). D'Argenville (before 1752) writes: 'Il ne vendoit pas ses ouvrages: mais les présens qu'étoient obligés de faire au Couvent ceux qui vouloient en avoir, étoient si considérables, que les particuliers ne pouvoient y atteindre; il n'y eut que les Princes ... qui par leurs liberalités en acquirent quelques-uns'; He generally signed his pictures with 'Society of Jesus' after his name or initials. The grisaille and other centres for which he painted garlands were sometimes the work of E. Quellinus, C. Schut, G. Seghers and others; in the Antwerp Jesuit church his garland surrounded a *S. Ignatius* by Rubens. The poets J. v. Vondel and Constantyn Huygens wrote poems on his work. **Signed Examples:** BERLIN K. F., BRUNS-WICK, BRUSSELS, COPENHAGEN *Flower garland round a sculptured shield* DULWICH, DRESDEN *Tulips, iris, lilies, roses in a glass vase with butterflies* THE HAGUE Mauritshuis *Garland of flowers round a statue of the Virgin* 1645 (presumed by some the picture painted for Prince Frederick Henry) LONDON Royal Collection Hampton Court, ROTTERDAM *Bust of Ceres surrounded by flowers* 1644 SCHLEISSHEIM *Roses in a glass vase* STOCK-HOLM. Jan Brueghel the younger owned (1626) a *Flowers in a small glass;* Rubens owned (1640) a *Flower garland;* Queen Christina of Sweden sent to Rome a *Flowerpiece* with other pictures and tapestries from her collection (*cf.* D. Teniers the younger and B. Spranger) 1656; Houbraken (1718) saw a whole chapel hung with his flower pictures in a Brabant Jesuit church; Descamps (1768) saw examples in Louvain Jesuit and Recollets churches, Antwerp Hôtel de Ville and elsewhere. *Cf.* J. F. Thys.

[Fl. 86, Fl. 425, Fl. 22, Fl. 215, Fl. 216, Fl. 480, Fl. 892, Fl. 213, Fl. 214.]

*Seghers (or Zegers), **Gerard.** Flemish Sch. *b* son of keeper of Antwerp tavern 'Le Rubis' (*cf.* F. Snyders), who had reverted

from Protestantism to Catholicism, Antwerp 1591 *d* Antwerp 1651. *Religious subjects, 'history', allegories, portraits and occasional genre; also active as dealer* (?). Pupil of H. van Balen (?) and A. Janssens; Master Antwerp Guild 1609; went Rome (*cf.* P. de Lignis and J. Snellinck the younger); patronized there by Cardinal Zapata y Mendoza (Spanish ambassador); thence to Madrid where worked for Philip III (*cf.* F. and R. Diriksen, L. Franchoys the elder and A. Smit); returned Antwerp 1620; member of Violiere Chamber of Rhetoric; worked under Rubens on decorations of new Jesuit Church (*cf.* A. van Dyck, C. Schut and A. G. Gheringh) 1621; worked also under Rubens on Pageant Entry into Antwerp of Cardinal Infante Ferdinand (*cf.* G. Weri) 1635; Court Painter to the Cardinal Infante (*cf.* G. de Crayer) 1637; and to Archduke Leopold Wilhelm (*cf.* G. Coques, J. Cossiers, P. de Champaigne, J. B. v. Heil, D. Seghers, D. Teniers the younger); sent a case of fourteen pictures (by himself and/or others) to the dealer C. Immerseel in Seville 1642; Dean of Guild 1646; died a rich man and left a large collection of pictures. Sandrart (1675) records that in order to make money he changed his style and used brighter colours in imitation of Rubens; d'Argenville (misreading Sandrart?) records (1752) a visit to England (*cf.* A. v. Stalbemt and C. de Neve) after the death of Van Dyck; Houbraken (1719) writes: 'Het geen hem wel meest beroemt gemaakt heeft is de natuurlyke verbeelding der lyden de hartstochten, die hy in zyne Passiestukken van Jesus Christus en Tafereelen van lydende Roomsche Kerk-heiligen zoodanig heeft weten te vertoonen dat het den aanschouwer de traanen uit de oogen perste'. His pupils included T. Willeboirts, J. Miel (?) and P. Franchoys. Van Dyck painted his portrait. **Documented Examples:** ANT-WERP *Marriage of the Virgin* (over life size figures), S. *Theresa* (seen by Descamps (1768) in Carmes Déchaussés), S. *Norbert receiving the habit from the Virgin* (seen by Descamps in Abbaye de S. Michel), S. *Louis de Gonzaga in Jesuit habit renouncing his marquisate* (seen by Descamps in Jesuit Collegiate church and described as 'A young lord renouncing his rank to become a Jesuit' *cf.* T. van Thulden). BRUGES Notre Dame *Adoration of the Magi* 1630 (seen by Descamps; 'la figure du roi placée sur le devant est de la plus grande beauté). Descamps also saw in Antwerp S. *Jacques* S. *Roch dying supported by angels,* S. *Yves comforting poor litigants* (*cf.* J. Jordaens); Abbaye de S. Michel S. *Anne teaching the Virgin to read;* Hotel de Ville *The nuptial bed* (ce tableau se place devant l'Hôtel de Ville lors du Mariage du Souverain ou de la Naissance d'un Duc de Brabant); Ghent Jesuit Church *Scenes from the life of S. Livin* and others in Ghent S. Bavon, Dunkirk, Tournai and elsewhere. Pictures titled *Infanta Isabella descending from heaven to advise Philip IV to appoint his brother Cardinal Infante Ferdinand Governor of Netherlands* (painted for Ferdinand's entry 1635 *cf.* G. Weri) and S. *Leopold of Austria* (presented to Archduke Leopold Wilhelm) are also recorded. The painter V. Wolfvoet *q.v.* had (1652) a *Cleopatra* (*cf.* G. de Lairesse), a S. *Francis* and others in his large collection; J. Wildens *q.v.* owned (1653) *A man with a cap. A Joseph and Potiphar's wife* (*cf.* M. Pepyn) is recorded in an Antwerp inventory of 1686; *Guard room scenes* and *Denial of S. Peter* with candle light effects (*cf.* Madrid Judith Painter, H. v. Steenwyck the younger and A. Mytens) and a portrait of Prince Octavio Piccolomini (*cf.* J. B. Seghers and P. Snayers) are among many works recorded by engravings.

[Fl. 86, Fl. 753, Fl. 425, Fl. 22, Fl. 576, Fl. 215, Fl. 216, Fl. 612, Fl. 892, Fl. 331 (1930), Fl. 213, Fl. 214.]

Seghers, Jan Baptist. Flemish Sch. *b* son of Gerard S., Antwerp 1624 *d* Antwerp (?) after 1670. Master Antwerp Guild 1646; visited Italy; went Vienna and worked for Prince Octavio Piccolomini (Duke of Amalfi) *c.* 1649 (*cf.* P. Snayers and F. Luyckx); recommended by the Prince to Archduke Leopold Wilhelm 1652; living Antwerp and Dean of Guild 1670. [Fl. 753, Fl. 425, Fl. 481, Fl. 107, Fl. 892, Fl. 212.]

Seldenslach, Jacob. Flemish Sch. *b* Breda 1652 *d* Antwerp 1735. *Flowers and garlands* (*cf.* D. Seghers and J. v. d. Borght). Pupil in Antwerp of G. P. Verbruggen the elder 1680. A *Flowers round a Christ* and *Flowers round a picture of the Virgin* both *s* and dated 1682 are recorded.

[Fl. 107, Fl. 892.]

Sellaer, Vincent. Flemish Sch. 16th cent. Recorded working Malines 1544. **Signed Example:** SCHLEISSHEIM *Christ blessing the children* 1538 (*cf.* H. de Clerck and J. Snellinck). Presumed by some identical with V. Geldersman *q.v.* Pictures presumed by some his work are in various museums.

[Fl. 613, Fl. 892, Fl. 885.]

Senave (or Sinave), Jacques Albert. Flemish Sch. *b* Loo (nr. Furnes) 1758 *d* Paris 1829. *Genre, landscapes and occasional 'history'.* Pupil of a Canon of Loo who procured him admission to Ypres Academy founded by Empress Maria Theresa. In Paris as pupil of J. B. Suvée 1781; settled Paris (*cf.* J. F. van Dael, J. L. Demarne); exhibited Paris Salon (*cf.* L. Gerbo) 1791; honorary director Ypres Academy 1821. Represented in BÂLE *Little girl feeding a cow in a shed* (*cf.* J. F. Legillon), *Little boy leading horse from a stable.* BRUSSELS *Parodies of Zeuxis and Apelles.* GOTHA *View of Paris* two (*cf.* H. de La Pegnia). LOO Church *Seven works of Mercy* (presented 1820). NANTES *Market on a square* (*cf.* C. F. Coene and J. B. de Jonghe), *Fruit market, Cottage interior.* YPRES Acad. had till *c.* 1915 when it disappeared *Rembrandt and other artists in his atelier* (*cf.* J. H. Lies) presented to the Academy 1821. A *View of Paris from above the Jardin de l'Arsenal* was in the Paris Salon 1791. A *Marriage vow* is recorded by an engraving. [Fl. 451, Fl. 612, Fl. 66.]

Serin, Harmen (or Hendrick) Jan. Flemish Sch. *b* son of Jan S., Ghent 1677 *d* The Hague after 1754. *Portraits.* Working in The Hague where entered Guild 1718. **Signed Example:** AMSTERDAM Rijks. *Dr. Louis Trip de Marez* 1743. A portrait signed and dated 1754 'aetatis 77' is recorded.

[Fl. 353, Fl. 878, Fl. 451, Fl. 359, Fl. 892, Fl. 798.]

Serin, Jan. Flemish Sch. *b* Ghent (?) before 1665 *d* The Hague after 1698. *Religious subjects for Ghent and Tournai churches.* Pupil of E. Quellinus. Descamps (1768) saw in Tournai Abbaye de S. Martin an *Assumption of the Virgin with an abbé of the Order at the base.* [Fl. 353, Fl. 216, Fl. 612, Fl. 359.]

Serrure, Auguste. Flemish Sch. *b* Antwerp 1825 *d* Brussels 1902. *Genre.* Pupil of F. de Braekeleer. Represented in BRUSSELS, NAMUR, NANTES. [Fl. 892, Fl. 123.]

Serruys, Louis. Flemish Sch. 19th cent. *Landscapes, marines, architectural views.* Worked at Ostend *c.* 1840. [Fl. 612.]

Servaes, Albert. Flemish Sch. *b* Ghent 1883. *Religious subjects, symbolic scenes of peasant life, landscapes; designs for stained glass.* Worked with Laethem St. Martin group (*cf.* C. Permeke and G. v. d. Woestyne) from 1904 and settled there; visited Italy (Venice), France and Holland; his religious paintings with Expressionist distortions caused protests from Rome. Represented in AMSTERDAM, ANTWERP *Life of the Peasant* (12 large compositions in 4 groups *Baptism, First Communion, Marriage, Death*). BRUSSELS *Peasants in the fields* 1909, *Crucifixion* 1927, *Pietà* 1920 and *Pietà* 1922 GHENT, THE HAGUE, ORVAL Abbey (Ardennes) *Stations of the Cross* (grisaille) 1930 UTRECHT *Death of S. Theresa of Avila* painted for Luythagen Carmelite Chapel but removed on instructions from Rome. A window in the Belgian Pavilion at the 1937 Paris exhibition was made from his design.

[Fl. 485, Fl. 69, Fl. 125, Fl. 296, Fl. Bib. 20th cent.]

Servaes, Herman. Flemish Sch. *b* Antwerp *c.* 1601 *d* Antwerp *c.* 1675. *Religious subjects.* First pupil of Van Dyck *c.* 1618

and copied his *Twelve Apostles;* in Malines 1630; in Antwerp Guild 1650. [Fl. 613, Fl. 892.]

★Seven Sorrows of the Virgin Master (Maître des sept douleurs de la Vierge). Presumed Flemish Sch. 16th cent. Name for painter of BRUGES Notre Dame *The Virgin with the Seven Sorrows* (*Mater Dolorosa*). Presumed by some identical with A. Ysenbrandt *q.v.*

[Fl. 444, Fl. 93, Fl. 120, Fl. 892, Fl. 316.]

Severdonck, Frans van. Flemish Sch. *b* Brussels 1809 *d* Brussels 1889. *Landscapes, architectural views, animals, genre.* Represented in MONTREAL *The pigeon house, Sheep.* ROUEN *Sheep.* A *View of Spa* is recorded. [Fl. 612.]

Severdonck, Joseph van. Flemish Sch. *b* Brussels 1819 *d* Brussels 1905. *Costume history, military genre, battle pieces.* Pupil of G. Wappers; teacher in Brussels Academy (*cf.* A. Robert). Represented in BRUSSELS *Lancers reconnoitring.* YPRES.

[Fl. 160 (1905), Fl. 776, Fl. bib. 19th cent.]

Sévin, Jean-Baptiste. Flemish Sch. 18th cent. Painted ceiling for Brussels, Notre Dame de la Chapelle (Sacristy) 1753. Descamps (1769) wrote of Antwerp, Le Cigne (Maison des Bouchers): 'Le plafond de la Salle d'Assemblée est peint par Sévin'. [Fl. 216, Fl. 798.]

Siberdt, Eugeen. Flemish Sch. *b* Antwerp 1851 *d* Antwerp 1931. *Costume history, portraits.* Pupil in Antwerp Acad. of N. de Keyser. Represented in ANTWERP *Erasmus and Quentin Massys* (*cf.* P. Kremer) 1908. [Fl. 17.]

Siberecht, Guillaume van. Presumed Flemish Sch. 17th cent. **Signed Examples:** BRUSSELS *The goatherds.* LIÈGE *Italianate landscape* 1666. [Fl. 301.]

★Siberechts, Jan (called Sybrecht in England). Flemish Sch. *b* son of sculptor Jan S., Antwerp 1627 *d* London 1703. *Wooded landscapes* (*cf.* J. d'Arthois), *with peasant girls, animals and often a ford* (*cf.* S. J. v. Douw), *occasional interiors; (later) views of mansions.* Houbraken (1718) records him as a follower of the Dutch Italianate (landscape with genre) painters A. Dujardin and N. Berchem (*cf.* J. F. Soolmaker and G. van Siberecht); in Antwerp Guild 1648; married in Antwerp 1652; Walpole (1786) records him brought to London (*cf.* D. Boone, P. Rysbraeck, P. v.ʲd. Meulen, S. Dubois, J. Lantscroon, P. H. Lankrink and C. de Neve) by 2nd Duke of Buckingham passing through Flanders on his way home from a Paris mission 1672; painted views and mansions (some in watercolour) for Dukes of Buckingham, Devonshire and others; signed, in London, document concerning an inheritance in Antwerp 1687. The French painter N. Largillière painted his portrait. **Signed Examples:** ANTWERP *The castle ford* 1661, *Two peasant girls (one footwashing) at a ford* 1665 (*cf.* Copenhagen examples), *S. Francis preaching to birds and animals* 1666, *Peasant girl with cart and cattle at a ford.* BERLIN K. F. *Italianate landscape with horsemen and animals* 1653, *Peasants at a ford* (Anvers) 1670, *The old willow* 1670, *River landscape with coach and six.* BORDEAUX *Landscape with two girls* 1678. BRUSSELS *Courtyard of a farm* 1660, *Start for the market (Ferme des Maraîchers)* 1664, *Huntsmen setting out* 1684. BUDAPEST *Canal with figures and cattle* 1661, *Ford with footwashing girl and mounted girl and cattle* 1672. COPENHAGEN *Two peasant girls (one footwashing) at a ford* (variant of Antwerp picture); *The cradle: domestic scene in the artist's house* (with the other Copenhagen picture on the wall) 'Anvers' 1671. DUBLIN N. G. I. *Market cart with animals at a ford* 1671. Others (signed) in Göteborg, Hanover, Lille and other museums. Amsterdam Rijks. has signed watercolour *Landscape near Chatsworth.* Paris: Louvre has *Toilette rustique*

(landscape with ford and young peasant woman examining a child's hair) recorded as traditionally once owned by Constable. Vertue (before 1752) records *Drawings of Chatsworth* 1686, also several landscapes, signed and dated 1676 'painted for the Earl of Portland, large and small not much esteemed or valued, I suppose done for furniture at that time'. Walpole (1786) records 'a prospect of Longleat not unlike the manner of Wouwerman' and a landscape 'in the style of Rubens' school' both owned by Lord Byron at Newstead, and a number of watercolour *Views on the Rhine.*
[Fl. 86, Fl. 425, Fl. 826, Fl. 856, Fl. 892, Fl. 88, Fl. 306, Fl. 899.]

Silver Windows Master see **Dublin S. Augustine Painter.**

Simonau, François. Flemish Sch. *b* Bornheim 1783 *d* London 1859. *Portraits and genre.* Went Paris where pupil of French painter Baron Gros (*cf.* H. de Caisne and C. L. Saligo); returned Belgium 1812; settled London 1815; introduced by Sir T. Lawrence to London society where known as 'the Flemish Murillo'; exhibited London R.A. and British Institution; made considerable money but died in poor circumstances. Represented in BRUSSELS *Young Italian in top hat playing a hand organ* (painted in England 1828 and shown B.I. 1829), *Man's portrait.* A *Brighton fisherman* was in B.I. 1841, a *Jewish Rabbi* in R.A. 1822, *J. Ancot, composer and professor of the pianoforte* in R.A. 1829 and '*A specimen of Nelson's invincibles pensioned off*' in R.A. 1860 (as by 'the late F.S.').
[Fl. 481, Fl. 360, Fl. 361, Fl. 363, Fl. 88, Fl. 126, Fl. 892, Fl. 296, Fl. Bib. 19th cent.]

Simonau, Gustave Adolphe. Flemish Sch. *b* son of a lithographer Pierre S. and nephew of F. S., Bruges 1810 *d* Brussels 1870. *Town views and architectural studies (w); also worked as lithographer.* Taken London by his father 1818; back in Brussels by 1829; made drawings and lithographs of Belgian Gothic buildings published as '*Monuments gothiques du Royaume des Pays Bas*'; another series depicted Brussels monuments damaged in the 1830 revolution; a third, after travels in Italy, Germany and again England was titled '*Recueil des principaux monuments gothiques de l'Europe*' and published from 1841 onwards. Represented in BRUSSELS.
[Fl. 612, Fl. 88.]

Simons, Frans. Flemish Sch. *b* Antwerp 1855 *d* Brasschaet 1919. *Portraits, landscape, animals, genre, still life.* Member of Brussels group 'Les XX' (*cf.* J. Ensor) 1884; exhibited in Paris Salon. Represented in ANTWERP *A drive between trees in sunshine, Antwerp roadstead.* TOURNAI *Convalescent.*
[Fl. 14, Fl. 388.]

Simons, Jean Baptiste. Flemish Sch. *b* before 1725 *d* after 1777. *Religious subjects and decorative paintings.* Worked in Paris (*cf.* G. de Spinny), Brussels and Ghent. A *Jesus and the Woman of Samaria* and a *Disciples at Emmaus* (signed and dated 1743) were recorded (1858) in Ghent S. Etienne (formerly part of Augustinian Monastery); overmantels for Mariemont (Royal Castle) are also recorded.
[Fl. 479, Fl. 749.]

Simons, Quintin. Flemish Sch. *b* Brussels 1592 *d* place unknown after 1634. '*History*'. His portrait by Van Dyck *q.v.* now in The Hague Mauritshuis was engraved with the legend 'pictor Historiarum' and was especially admired by Sir Joshua Reynolds. [Fl. 702, Fl. 612, Fl. 481, Fl. 401.]

Sisel, see **Ziesel.**

Sittow, Michel see **Vienna Catherine Painter.**

Sleenwegen, Gustave van. Flemish Sch. *b* Antwerp 1905. *Flowers, landscapes.* Pupil of A. Geudens. Represented ANTWERP *Flowers, Village.* [Fl. 17.]

Slingeneyer, Ernest. Flemish Sch. *b* Loochristi, nr. Ghent 1820 *d* Brussels 1894. *Costume history, religious subjects, genre, portraits.* Pupil in Antwerp of the Romantic painter G. Wappers *q.v.*; Member of Brussels Acad.; chevalier of the Order of Leopold. Represented in ANTWERP *Woman bathing* 1872, *The painter Gerard van der Ven* BRUSSELS *Battle of Lepanto;* Palais de l'Académie (Murals) *Scenes from the History of Belgium* LONDON Guildhall *A Christian martyr in the time of Diocletian* TOURNAI.
[Fl. 481, Fl. 892, Fl. 88, Fl. Bib. 19th cent., Fl. 296.]

Sloots, Jan. Flemish Sch. *b* Malines 1636 *d* Malines 1690. *Birds and animals* (*cf.* L. van Heil, J. van Kessel the elder and N. Schneider). Visited the Tyrol and Italy; back in Malines by 1684. [Fl. 614, Fl. 892, Fl. 88.]

Sloovere, Georges de. Flemish Sch. *b* Bruges 1873. *Landscapes portraits, figures.* Pupil in Bruges and Brussels Acads. Represented in BRUGES *Women scouring pots, Tree trunks by the river, Trees.* [Fl. 114.]

Sluyse, Charles Joseph Jean van der. Flemish Sch. *b* Heusden before 1755 *d* Antwerp (?) after 1784. Pupil in Antwerp Academy 1768; Director of Academy 1784 (*cf.* A. C. Lens).
[Fl. 481, Fl. 88.]

Smeers, Frans. Flemish Sch. *b* 1873. *Landscapes, marines.* Pupil Brussels Acad. under J. Portaels and J. Stallaert. Member of Sillon group founded 1893 (*cf.* A. Pinot). Represented in THE HAGUE (Gem. Mus) *Scheveningen pier, Boulevard in Scheveningen.* [Fl. 296.]

Smet, Cornelis (called Ferraro). Flemish Sch. *b* before 1560 *d* Naples *c.* 1592. *Religious subjects.* In Naples where Dirck Hendricksz *q.v.* was witness at his wedding 1574; friend of W. Coebergher *q.v.* in Naples from 1580. (*cf.* also J. v. Stinemolen). **Signed Example:** NAPLES San Eligio *Last Judgement* (copy after Michael Angelo; contract 1578). **Documented Examples:** NAPLES San Domenico Maggiore *Circumcision* (contract 1580). MERCATO SANSEVERINO (Salerno) S. Giovanni *Virgin of the Rosary* (contract 1579). MURO LUCANO (Potenza) *Virgin of the Rosary* (contract 1590), A '*Naked Christ under a wine press*' 1581 is recorded. [Fl. 302, Fl. 305.]

Smet, Frédéric de. Flemish Sch. *b* Ghent 1876. *Marine and coast pieces; worked mainly as sculptor and art critic.* Pupil in Ghent Acad. 1893-7 and of J. Delvin, A. de Vriendt and of sculptors L. Mast and V. der Stappen; visited Italy; in Paris 1905-10; then settled Ghent. Represented GHENT.
[Fl. 465.]

Smet, Gustave de. Flemish Sch. *b* Ghent 1877 *d* Deurle 1943. *Figure compositions (many of peasant themes), landscapes, still life at first in Impressionist and later in Post-Impressionist and Expressionist conventions.* Pupil Ghent Acad. 1888-95. Worked Laethem St. Martin (*cf.* C. Permeke and G. v. d. Woestyne); in Holland during 1914-18 German invasion (*cf.* F. v. d. Berghe); later lived mainly Deurle (on the Lys); exhibited in Salon des IX (*cf.* H. Daeye) 1926. Represented in AMSTERDAM. ANTWERP *The mussel eaters, Mme. van Spakenburg. Still life with herring, The girl in pink,* BRUSSELS *Beatrice.* GHENT *Porcelain in an interior.* GRENOBLE, THE HAGUE.
[Fl. 428, Fl. 394, Fl. 404.]

Smet, Léon de. Flemish Sch. *b* Ghent 1881. Brother of G. de S. *Portraits, nudes, still life, landscape, interiors in Impressionist and Neo-Impressionist conventions.* Pupil in Ghent Acad. of J. Delvin; travelled France and Italy; in England during 1914-18 German invasion (*cf.* A. Baertsoen, V. de Saedeleer, E. Tytgat, C. Mertens, I. Opsomer, J. G. Rosier, André

Cluysenaar, E. Claus, C. Permeke, H. Daeye and G. v. d. Woestyne). Represented in ANTWERP *Still life, Interior; Town hall Queen Astrid.* BRUSSELS *The white azalea* 1920. GHENT *Still life.* Portraits of *G. Bernard Shaw, John Galsworthy* and *Eden Philpots* are recorded.
[Fl. 705, Fl. 17.]

Smet, Wolfgang de. Flemish Sch. 17th cent. **Signed Example:** LOUVAIN *Interior Louvain S. Pierre* 1667. [Fl. 88.]

Smeth, Henri de. Flemish Sch. *b* Borgerhout 1865 *d* Brasschaet 1940. *Interiors, landscapes, genre, portraits, murals and illustrations.* Pupil of A. de Lathouwer and L. Hendrix. Member of Antwerp group The XIII (*cf.* E. Farasyn) 1891. Represented in ANTWERP *The Sacristy* 1878, *The dressmaker's bill* 1901. BRUSSELS *Consultation.* TOURNAI.
[Fl. 17.]

Smets, Chrétien. Flemish Sch. *b* Malines before 1530 *d* after 1557. Went France (*cf.* Joos v. Cleve and L. Thiry); worked for Court of Navarre at Pau 1550-6; returned Netherlands 1557. [Fl. 892, Fl. 88.]

Smets, Jacques. Flemish Sch. *b* Malines 1680 *d* Auch (France) 1764. *Religious subjects.* Pupil in Malines of J. Smeyers; went France (*cf.* J. Spoede) and worked for churches in Auch. His son Jean Baptiste S., a deaf mute, was also a painter who worked in Auch and the region. [Fl. 88.]

Smeyers, Gilles (Egide). Flemish Sch. *b* son of Nicolas S., Malines 1634 or 1635 *d* Malines 1710. *Religious subjects for Malines churches* (*cf.* S. van Aken) *and portrait groups* (*cf.* I. v. d. Beken and F. Verbeeck). Pupil in Malines of J. Verhoeven *q.v.*; married daughter of D. Herregouts; Dean of Malines Guild 1676; associated with L. Franchoys the younger. A group portrait *Directors of the Malines Tailors' Guild* (1695) in Brussels (Mus.) and *The Blessings of the Trinity* in Malines (S. Jean) are traditionally recorded as his work (*cf.* G. J. Smeyers).
[Fl. 451, Fl. 613, Fl. 614, Fl. 892, Fl. 88.]

Smeyers, Gilles (Egide) Joseph. Flemish Sch. *b* son of Jacques S. *q.v.*, Malines 1694 *d* Malines 1771 or 1774. *Religious subjects for churches in Malines and environs* (*cf.* S. van Aken), *portraits and portrait groups* (*cf.* B. v. d. Bossche). Pupil in Düsseldorf (*cf.* I. v. d. Beken) of Dutch portrait painter J. F. van Douven 1715-18; then to Rome (*cf.* H. F. van Lint and R. v. Audenaerd); returned Malines to support family after his father's blindness; worked also as art-historical writer; contributed information to J. B. Descamps for his 'Vies des Peintres' (*cf.* M. de Visch); passed his last years in poverty in Malines almshouse (*cf.* J. G. Sauvage). Descamps records (1769 in lifetime of the artist) *Assumption of the Virgin* in Malines S. Rombout and pictures in Asch Parish church, Malines (Recollets) and the Abbey of Ninove. A *Directors of the Malines Tailors' Guild* 1735 in Malines Mus. is traditionally recorded as his work. Two *Scenes from the life of S. Norbert* in Brussels Mus. are presumed by some his work and by others the work of Gilles S. *q.v.*
[Fl. 216, Fl. 451, Fl. 613, Fl. 614, Fl. 892.]

Smeyers, Jacques. Flemish Sch. *b* son of Gilles S. *q.v.* Malines 1657 *d* (blind) Malines 1732. *Genre; also religious and allegorical subjects for Malines and regional churches and public buildings.* Master Malines Guild 1688. His brothers Guillaume Juste S. (*b* 1669) and Jean Louis S. (*b* 1663) were also painters. (*cf.* Gilles Joseph S.). **Signed Example:** LIÈGE *Old man counting money and old woman* 1710.
[Fl. 613, Fl. 614, Fl. 892, Fl. 88.]

Smeyers, Nicolas. Flemish Sch. *b* son of a painter, Malines *c.* 1600 *d* Malines 1645. Pupil in Malines of L. Franchoys the elder 1630; Master Malines Guild 1632. [Fl. 451, Fl. 613.]

Smidt, Jacques de. Flemish Sch. *b* Bruges before 1740 *d* Bruges 1787. *Religious subjects for Bruges churches* (*cf.* J. A. Garemyn and M. de Visch). Master Bruges Guild 1754. An altarpiece for Bruges, S. Sauveur, Chapelle de Notre Dame des Sept Douleurs 1756-9 is recorded. [Fl. 151, Fl. 892.]

Smit, Andries. Flemish Sch. 17th cent. (confused by some with a Dutch marine painter Aernout S.). *Landscapes.* Went Italy (*cf.* M. Sweerts, M. Stom and J. Miel); worked in Rome where met Velázquez 1650; later recorded in Madrid (*cf.* S. v. Aken, G. de Crayer, F. and R. Diriksen, P. Evrard, G. v. Eyck, L. Franchoys the elder, J. van Kessel the younger, C. Luyckx, A. v. d. Pere, I. Raeth, A. Rodriguez, N. Ryckx, P. P. Rubens, C. Schut, C. Schut II, G. Seghers, P. Sperwer, D. Teniers III, A. van Utrecht, also P. de Kempener). [Fl. 153, Fl. 612.]

Smits, Eugène Joseph Henri. Flemish Sch. *b* Antwerp 1826 *d* Brussels 1912. *Allegorical, decorative and some religious compositions, genre, still life, landscape, portraits.* Pupil in Brussels of F. J. Navez and in Paris of the French painters J. F. Millet, E. Isabey and Gaston Ricard. Member of Soc. Libre des B.A. (*cf.* L. Dubois); visited Italy. His bust by the sculptor P. de Vigne is in Brussels Mus. Represented in ANTWERP *Grief and Joy.* BRUSSELS *The Four Seasons, Diana, Judgement of Paris, The Letter to Metella* and others. BELGIAN ROYAL COLLECTION *Roma.* GHENT *Pietà. Cf.* F. Rops. [Fl. 909, Fl. 498, Fl. 296.]

Smits, Frans Marcus. Flemish Sch. *b* Antwerp 1760 *d* in poverty in S. Elizabeth almshouse Antwerp 1833. *Portraits.* Pupil of A. B. de Quertenmont *q.v.*; friend of G. F. Ziesel Represented in ANTWERP *The painter W. J. Herreyns.* Portraits of the painters *B. P. Ommeganck* and *G. F. Ziesel* are recorded. [Fl. 481, Fl. 88.]

Smits, Jacob. Flemish Sch. *b* son of Jewish parents, Rotterdam 1855 *d* Mol (nr. Antwerp) 1928. *Landscapes and peasant genre compositions (many of the Campine region), religious subjects (some in modern setting), symbolic compositions, interiors, portraits.* Pupil in Rotterdam Acad. 1872-6; then in Brussels of J. Portaels and J. Stallaert; visited Munich, Vienna and Italy where copied Michael Angelo's frescoes in Sistine Chapel; returned Holland; earned his living for some years by work as decorative painter; executed ceiling for Rotterdam Boymans Museum; settled Mol in the Antwerp Campine 1889; naturalised Belgian 1900; went Holland during 1914-18 German invasion (*cf.* F. v. d. Berghe); spent last years in Mol. Represented in ANTWERP *Mill in the Campine, Evening, Interior, The Pilgrims at Emmaus, Pietà, The artist's mother, The sky weeping over the ruins* and others. BRUGES *Christ at the peasant's house.* BRUSSELS *The father of the condemned man, Mater Dolorosa, The potato harvest, End of the day, Symbol of the Campine, Golden dawn, Woman's portrait;* Palais de Justice *Crucifixion.* COURTRAI *Woman knitting.* GHENT *Pietà.* ROTTERDAM Boymans Mus. *Rotterdam as Protector of the Fine Arts* (ceiling), *The woman taken in adultery.*
[Fl. 68, Fl. 673, Fl. 100, Fl. 565, Fl. 388, Fl. 395, Fl. 400, Fl. 81, Fl. Bib. 19th cent.]

Smitsens, Arnold. Flemish Sch. *b* Liège *c.* 1681 or 1687 *d* Liège 1744. *Hunting scenes and still life* (*cf.* J. J. Spoede); *also religious subjects and designs for tapestry* (*cf.* A. F. Baudewyns). **Signed Examples:** LIÈGE Town Hall *Trophies of the chase* (seven panels), over-doors and overmantels 1721.
[Fl. 409, Fl. 88.]

Smitsens, Jean François. Flemish Sch. *b* Liège 1684 or 1719 *d* 1758. Brother of Arnold S. *Still life.* **Signed Example:** COLONSTER Castle (Tilff) *Still life* 1756.
[Fl. 409, Fl. 88.]

Smout, Lucas the elder. Flemish Sch. *b* Antwerp 1620 *d* Antwerp 1674. Step-brother of C. Mahu *q.v.*; *Religious subjects, portraits, genre.* Married into the Tyssens family of painters; sold two paintings (religious subjects) to the Forchoudt firm of Antwerp exporting dealers (*cf.* A. Casteels) 1666. Pictures inventoried in an Antwerp collection 1657 record an *Adoration of the Magi* and twelve fashionable portraits or tableaux de modes ('alemode tronien').

[Fl. 107, Fl. 892, Fl. 212, Fl. 213.]

*Smout, Lucas the younger. Flemish Sch. *b* son of Lucas S. the elder, Antwerp 1671 *d* Antwerp 1713. *Contemporary naval warfare* (*cf.* G. v. Eyck, and J. B. van der Meiren), *and other marine subjects and coast scenes, landscapes with figures.* Pupil in Antwerp of marine painter H. v. Minderhout *q.v.* 1686; worked little owing to gout. **Signed Examples:** ANTWERP *Beach scene at Scheveningen.* COPENHAGEN Royal Coll. *Sea battle at Kjogebucht 1710.* SCHWERIN *Marine.*

[Fl. 612, Fl. 107, Fl. 892, Fl. 88.]

Smytere (or **Smyters**), **Anna de.** Flemish Sch. *b* Ghent (?) before 1520 *d* after 1566. Wife of sculptor Jan de Heere and mother of Lucas de Heere *q.v.* *Miniature paintings.* Worked in Ghent; Van Mander (pupil of L. de Heere 1556) records (1604) 'She made a picture of a windmill, with every sail on the wings, and a miller in it, loaded with a bag, and climbing the mill; below on the knoll of the hill, were a horse and wagon and people walking. This entire picture could be covered by half an ear of wheat'. Guicciardini (1581) records her as 'grande illuminatrice' (*cf.* L. Teerlinck and S. Bening).

[Fl. 371, Fl. 559, Fl. 892.]

Snayers, Eduaert. Flemish Sch. *b* Antwerp (?) before 1600 *d* Antwerp (?) after 1659. Presumed by some brother of Peeter S. *Religious subjects; also battle pieces* (?). Master Antwerp Guild 1617; Dean 1632; With C. de Baellieur *q.v.* and others testified as ex-Dean in favour of J. Cossiers *q.v.* in matter of dispute with Malines Guild 1656. An Antwerp inventory of 1627 records a *Dying Magdalene.* A *Descent from the Cross* and *Four scenes from the life of Adam*, recorded in the day book of Jan Brueghel the younger 1629-31 as by 'Snayers', may refer to him or Peeter S. *q.v.*

[Fl. 714, Fl. 481, Fl. 88, Fl. 213, Fl. 214.]

*Snayers, Peeter. Flemish Sch. *b* son of an Antwerp-Brussels courier, Antwerp 1592 *d* Brussels after 1666. *Contemporary warfare* (*cf.* P. Meulener also C. Anthonisz, J. P. Verdussen, A. Casteels, L. de Hondt the elder, A. Crussens, J. Snellinck), *official ceremonies* (*cf.* A. Sallaert, F. Duchatel, D. Teniers the younger), *hunting scenes, landscapes, portraits and occasional religious subjects.* Pupil of S. Vrancx *q.v.* in Antwerp; Master Antwerp Guild 1613; married into the Schut family 1618; Court Painter to Archduke Albert (*cf.* W. Coebergher) *c.* 1620, and went Brussels where Master Guild 1628; Court Painter to Infanta Isabella (*cf.* D. van Alsloot) also to Governor general, Cardinal Infante Ferdinand 1634-41 (*cf.* G. de Crayer) who commissioned hunting pieces for Philip IV's hunting lodge the Torre de la Parada (*cf.* J. P. Gowi); to Archduke Leopold Wilhelm 1647-55 (*cf.* D. Seghers and J. B. v. Heil); and to Don John of Austria 1656-8 (*cf.* H. Janssens, E. Quellinus, D. Teniers, G. Coques); received order for twenty-one battle pieces from Prince Octavio Piccolomini, Imperial commander in Thirty Years War (*cf.* J. B. Seghers); directed decorations for Don John's Pageant Entry into Brussels 1656; Van Dyck painted his portrait; A. F. v. d. Meulen *q.v.* was his pupil. **Signed Examples:** BERLIN K.F. *Woodland lane with figures.* BRUSSELS *Spanish troops besieging the French in Courtrai 1648* 1650, *Archduke Leopold Wilhelm at the Popinjay shooting of the Guild of Crossbowmen at Notre Dame du Sablon 1651* (*cf.* D. van Alsloot and D. Teniers the younger). MADRID Prado *Hunting party of Cardinal Infante Ferdinand; Hunting*

scene: *Philip IV killing a wild boar; Philip IV hunting; Cavalry skirmish 1646, Night attack on Lille 1650, Conquest of Ypres 1649, Siege of Aire-sur-la-Lys 1641* 1653, *Relief of Lerida 1646.* VIENNA Liecht. *Skirmish near a wood 1657.* **Monogrammed Examples:** BRUSSELS *Pilgrimage of Infanta Isabella to healing waters of 'Fontaine S. Anne' 1623* with panorama of Brussels seen from Laeken. MADRID Prado *Capture of Breda 1625, Isabella at Breda 1650.* **Documented Examples:** MADRID Prado *Infanta Isabella and A. Spinola at Breda* (inventory 1636). VIENNA Kunsthist *Cavalry halt, Battlefield* (both collection Archduke Leopold Wilhelm). Rubens owned two landscapes and a *Night piece* (Een nagt). G. Huymans, son-in-law of Cornelis Schut *q.v.* owned (1685) a number of examples including sketches for *Don John's Pageant Entry* and a *Siege of Breda* painted from the print by the French draughtsman and engraver Jacques Callot. A *Don John on horseback* and a *Conversion of Paul* (*cf.* A. Snellinck, K. Foort, M. van Cleve and P. Bruegel the elder) are recorded by engravings.

[Fl. 86, Fl. 425, Fl. 612, Fl. 892, Fl. 88, Fl. 213.]

Snel (or **Snelle**), **Jan.** Flemish Sch. *b* before 1470 *d* 1504. Recorded Master in Antwerp Guild 1483.

[Fl. 612, Fl. 481, Fl. 892, Fl. 88.]

Snellaert, Jan. Flemish Sch. *b* before 1440 *d* after 1480. Held offices in Antwerp Guild between 1454 and 1480. Court Painter to Maria of Burgundy (?) (*cf.* P. Coustain and B. v. Battel) A painter of the same name was Master in Tournai 1453 and is recorded there between 1462 and 1476. Another was Master in Antwerp Guild 1483.

[Fl. 612, Fl. 481, Fl. 107, Fl. 359, Fl. 892, Fl. 88.]

Snellaert, Nicolas (**Claes**). Flemish Sch. *b* son of Willem S., Courtrai *c.* 1540 *d* Dordrecht 1602. *Portraits and architectural paintings.* In Dordrecht Guild 1586. Van Mander (1604) records him as pupil of K. Foort (Karel van Yperen) *q.v.* whom he assisted in a *Last Judgement.* [Fl. 559, Fl. 892.]

Snellaert, Willem. Flemish Sch. *b* Courtrai before 1545. Van Mander (1604) records him as a watercolour painter and first master of P. Vlerick *q.v.*, his own master. [Fl. 559.]

Snellinck, Abraham. Flemish Sch. *b* son of Jan S., Antwerp 1597 *d* Antwerp 1661. *Landscapes.* Received payment from Prince Frederick Henry of Orange for eleven pictures for Breda Castle 1647 (*cf.* D. Seghers). [Fl. 481.]

Snellinck, Andreas (**Andries**). Flemish Sch. *b* son of Jan S., *q.v.*, Antwerp 1587 *d* Antwerp 1653. *Landscapes, religious and mythological subjects; also active as dealer.* Pupil of his father; Master Antwerp Guild 1608; the painter V. Wolfvoet *q.v.* owned (1652) a *Garden of Eden* (Paradysken) (*cf.* J. (Velvet) Brueghel, R. Savery and J. Uytewael), a *Landscape* and a '*Simmen feeste*'. Invoices of the Forchoudt firm of Antwerp exporting dealers record a *Landscape* (with *Virgin and Child* by C. de Vos *q.v.*) a *Europa* (*cf.* H. v. Balen) and a *Conversion of S. Paul* (*cf.* G. Snellinck, P. Snayers and P. Bruegel the elder) all sent to Vienna 1671-8.

[Fl. 714, Fl. 892, Fl. 212, Fl. 213.]

Snellinck, C. Presumed Flemish Sch. 17th cent. *Landscapes and genre.* **Signed Examples:** PRAGUE Rudolfinum *Children in front of a fruit stall.* VIENNA Liecht. *Wooded landscape with lake.* [Fl. 892.]

Snellinck, Daniel. Flemish Sch. *b* son of Jan S., Antwerp 1576 *d.* Antwerp 1627. Master Antwerp Guild 1606. [Fl. 892.]

Snellinck, Geeraert. Flemish Sch. *b* son of Jan S., Antwerp 1577. *Religious subjects.* Master in Brussels Guild 1603; Master in Antwerp Guild 1608. A *Conversion of S. Paul* (*cf.* Andreas S.) and other religious subjects are recorded in an Antwerp collection in 1627. *Landscapes with horsemen* monogrammed G.Ss recorded in a private collection 1905 are presumed by some his work (*cf.* C. Snellinck.)

[Fl. 892, Fl. 213, Fl. 296.]

*Snellinck (or Snellincx), Jan. Flemish Sch. *b* son of a painter, Malines 1544 or 1549 *d* Antwerp 1638. *Religious subjects and 'history', designs for tapestry; also active as dealer.* Van Mander (1604) and Houbraken (1719) record him as successful painter of battle pieces (*cf.* P. Meulener and P. Snayers); In Antwerp by 1574; married daughter of engraver G. de Jode; remarried after 1581; Court Painter to Archduke Ernest, governor general of Netherlands (*cf.* G. Schoof and J. B. Saive) 1593-5; to Archduke Albert (*cf.* G. de Crayer) 1596-1621, and Infanta Isabella (*cf.* D. v. Alsloot); with O. van Veen *q.v.* made tapestry designs for Audenarde factory recording Archduke Albert's battles; also worked for Count Mansfeld, military commander between 1603 and 1609; of his thirteen children several of his sons were painters (*cf.* Abraham, Andreas, Daniel and Geeraert S.). His pupils included A. Janssens and J. de Ceustere. Van Dyck drew and painted his portrait; one version placed on his tomb in Antwerp S. George (demolished 1797) was seen there by Descamps (1768). **Signed Examples:** ANTWERP *Crucifixion* 1597. MALINES S. Rombout Cathedral *Triptych with the Resurrection* 1601; S. Catherine *Pentecost* 1606 (overpainted fragment). MAASTRICHT Franciscan Monastery *Allegory of the Franciscan Order* 1608. AUDENARDE Notre Dame de Pamele *Triptych with Creation and Fall of Man* 1608; S. Walburge *Transfiguration and Crowning of the Virgin* 1616. Frescoes painted in three days for the Confraternity of Married Men in 1610 and *Scenes from the Passion* painted in 1611 and 1612 are recorded; other religious subjects are recorded by engravings. Jacques Snel, wine taverner, owned (1623) in Antwerp a *Wedding Feast at Cana*, a *Crossing of the Red Sea* (*cf.* M. Pepyn) and a *Suffer little children* ... (*cf.* H. de Clerck) also an elaborate organ decorated by F. Borsse *q.v.*, O. van Veen and 'Snellincx'. The Forchoudt firm of Antwerp dealers bought pictures by P. de Vos and Sebastian Vrancx from the sale of his effects in 1638. Charles I owned an *Assumption of the Virgin* 'by Snellinx' which is still at Hampton Court.

[Fl. 559, Fl. 86, Fl. 425, Fl. 215, Fl. 216, Fl. 451, Fl. 612, Fl. 481, Fl. 613, Fl. 892, Fl. 212, Fl. 213.]

Snellinck (or Snellincx), Jan the younger. Flemish Sch. *b* son of Jan S., Antwerp 1580 *d* Holland (?) after 1627. *Landscapes with figures.* Went Rome (*cf.* P. v. d. Kasteele, P. de Lignis, G. Seghers); pupil there of J. de Hase *q.v.* 1603; Master Antwerp Guild 1606; went Holland and recorded in Rotterdam 1614 and Amsterdam 1627. [Fl. 481, Fl. 892.]

*Snyders, Frans. Flemish Sch. *b* son of keeper of tavern called 'Groote Bruyloft Kamere' frequented by Guild artists (*cf.* G. Seghers), Antwerp 1579 *d* Antwerp 1657. *Still life* (*cf.* A. v. Utrecht and F. Schney) *some with swans* (*cf.* A. v. Nieulandt, P. J. Snyers, D. Teniers the younger), *flowers and garlands* (*cf.* J. (Velvet) Brueghel and D. Seghers), *animals including hunting pieces* (*cf.* P. de Vos, J. Fyt, N. Bernaert, D. de Coninck). Pupil of P. Brueghel the younger and H. v. Balen; Master Antwerp Guild 1602; went Italy (Milan) with letter of introduction from Jan (Velvet) Brueghel to Cardinal Federigo Borromeo (nephew of S. Carlo B. and founder of Ambrosiana Library) 1608; back in Antwerp 1609; married sister of C. and P. de Vos 1611; worked as assistant to Rubens for still life and animals from *c.* 1613; Toby Matthew wrote (1617) to Sir Dudley Carleton about a picture by Rubens 'Concerning the causinge of anie part thereof to be made by Snyder, that other famous Painter, Y^r L^p and I had been in an errour, for I thought as y^u doe, that his hand had been in that Peece, but sincerley and certainly it is not soe.

For in this Peece the beasts are all alive, and in act eyther of escape or resistance, in the expressing whereof Snyder doth infinitlie come short of Rubens, and Rubens saith that he should take it in ill part, if I should compare Snyders wth him in that point (*cf.* M. Pepyn); The talent of Snyders, is to represent beasts but especiallie Birds altogether dead, and wholly wthout anie action; and that wch we liked soe well was a gruppo of dead birds ...' Was very successful and had bought his own house by 1620; Member of Antwerp 'Romanists' Society; painted picture for Antwerp Town Hall 1630; worked on some of the paintings commissioned from Rubens by Philip IV for Torre de la Parada (*cf.* J. P. Gowi) *c.* 1636; executor of Rubens' will (*cf.* J. Wildens) 1640; was friend of Van Dyck who painted his portrait with his wife. Houbraken (1719) records him as patronized by Archduke Leopold Wilhelm (*cf.* J. A. v. d. Baren, J. B. v. Heil and E. Quellinus) and adds of his hunting pieces 'Zietmen de Jagthonden draven naar't Wildt, zy schynen't oog voorby te gieren. Grypen zy't met hun gespitste tanden aan, 't vuur straalt hun ten oogen uit: een die verminkt of gebeten vertoond worden, drukken de pynlykheid van hun ontfangene wonden, door een gekromden rug, gewrongne buiging en wyt opgesparde muilen, zoo natuurlyk uit, dat men 'er deernis mee hebben zoude'. J. Jordaens, J. Boeckhorst (Lange Jan), A. Janssens, J. Wildens and others are referred to by some as his collaborators; P. de Vos, J. Fyt, N. Bernaert and the Swiss (or Dutch) animal painter Juriaen Jacobsen were among his pupils. Many of his works, and many copies, were exported in the seventeenth century to Spain and Vienna. **Signed Examples:** AMSTERDAM Rijks. *Still life with fruit and game.* BERLIN K.F. *Cock fight* 1615, *Still life with lobster, plucked chicken and a cat.* BRUSSELS *Stag hunt, Larder with swan and servant.* BUDAPEST *Fable of hawk and hen* 1646. COPENHAGEN *Still life with lobster, peacock, asparagus, young man carrying boar's head and dog.* LENINGRAD *Studies of cats' heads* 1609, *Market stalls with figures* (four pictures acquired by Catherine the Great 1770 from Walpole collection at Houghton Hall; originally commissioned by Bishop Triest of Bruges *cf.* P. v. Angellis). LONDON Royal Coll. (Hampton Court) *Boar's head.* MADRID Prado *Boar hunt, Fable of the hare and the tortoise* (*cf.* A. v. Stalbemt), *Decorative panel with waterbirds and ermines, Decorative panel with wild cat, monkey, fox and ermines, The fox and the cat* and others. MUNICH *Kitchen piece with young man, dog and cat.* OLDENBOURG *Still life* 1614. PARIS Louvre *Monkeys stealing fruit.* OTTAWA N.G. *Larder with swan, asparagus and young man in kitchen* (*cf.* A. Coosemans). PHILADELPHIA *Terms: and a fruit garland round a bust of Ceres.* ROTTERDAM *Boar hunt.* SCHLEISSHEIM *Garland round a picture of Jesus, S. John and angels.* STOCKHOLM *Dead game on kitchen table.* VIENNA Liecht. *Squirrel and fruit.* **Documented Example:** HARTFORD U.S.A. Wadsworth Ath. *The market stall.* Rubens owned (1640) a *Stag hunt* and still life pieces. A *Fruit piece with monkeys* and a *Hunting piece with dogs* are among pictures recorded in Antwerp 17th cent. inventories. The Forchoudt firm of Antwerp exporting dealers sold (1690) in Vienna to Count van Hoegen a *Kitchen piece with figures by Jan de Vos* (Simon de V.?). Some of the pictures painted for Philip IV's Torre de la Parada were destroyed in 1710; Descamps (1768) saw in Antwerp Hôtel de Ville (Cabinet des États) a *Still life with dead game, lobster, fruit and a woman* ('la femme semble demander des prunes qu'un perroquet mange; cette figure très belle est peinte par Rubens'). Paintings presumed by some his work are in many museums (*cf.* Vienna Daniel Painter and P. de Vos).

[Fl. 86, Fl. 425, Fl. 22, Fl. 215, Fl. 216, Fl. 612, Fl. 721, Fl. 892, Fl. 88, Fl. 204, Fl. 212, Fl. 213.]

*Snyers, Pieter called 'The Saint'. Flemish Sch. *b* Antwerp 1681 *d* Antwerp 1752. *Still life, mostly flowers and fruit* (*cf.* J. G. C. Coclers), *genre, portraits; also worked as engraver.* Pupil of

A. v. Bredael; Master in Antwerp Guild 1707; visited London (*cf.* P. Angellis and P. Tillemans) where painted portraits; back in Antwerp 1726; professor without fee in Antwerp Acad. to forward interests of that institution (*cf.* M. J. Geeraerts) from 1741; had large collection of works by Dutch and Flemish painters. **Signed Examples:** AMSTERDAM Rijks. *Market vendors with fruit, fish and ram.* ANTWERP *Landscape with duck pond and children pointing to a bird's nest; flowers and mushrooms in the foreground* (known as '*The nest*'; from Antwerp Acad. which bought it from the artist's widow for the Directors' Chamber 1763), *Still life with fruit, pheasant and partridge with landscape background* 1734. BRUSSELS *Fruit and plants.* LONDON N.G. *Still life with asparagus, fruit, flowers and shell fish* (*cf.* A. Coosemans). OXFORD *Fruit, flowers and ivory tankard.*
[Fl. 481, Fl. 107, Fl. 892, Fl. 13.]

Snyers, Pieter Jan. Flemish Sch. *b* son of diamond cutter and jeweller, Antwerp 1696 *d* Antwerp 1757. Nephew of Pieter S. *q.v. Animals and still life with game* (*cf.* J. J. Spoede); *but chiefly active as collector (and dealer?).* Pupil of his uncle Pieter S. 1713; Dean in Antwerp Guild 1733-4 and 1741-3. A *Swan and cygnets with dead game* (*cf.* F. Snyders and B. de Bridt) painted by him was among his effects (which included pictures ascribed to Rubens and Van Dyck) sold 1758.
[Fl. 481, Fl. 892.]

Soens, J. see **Sons.**

Soignie, Jacques Joachim de. Flemish Sch. *b* Mons 1720 *d* Mons 1783. *Religious subjects, portraits.* Studied Brussels, Antwerp and Paris (*cf.* G. de Spinny); returned Mons and worked for churches and religious institutions. Paintings titled *Scenes from the life of S. Jeanne Françoise de Chantal, founder of the Order of Visitants, Scenes from the life of S. Angela* and *The Emperor Joseph II* (*cf.* G. de Pélichy) are recorded. [Fl. 221, Fl. 126, Fl. 88, Fl. 798.]

Solemaker, see **Soolmaker.**

*****Solomon Master.** Presumed Flemish or Flemish (Dutch) Sch. early 16th cent. Name for painter of THE HAGUE Mauritshuis (433) Triptych; *Solomon worshipping the idol, The Queen of Sheba, Jehovah appearing to Solomon.*
[Fl. 316, Fl. 798.]

Solvyns, Frans Balthasar. Flemish Sch. *b* Antwerp 1760 *d* Antwerp 1824. *Marine and port scenes; but chiefly known for drawings and etchings of Indian types and costumes.* Pupil of A. B. de Quertenmont in Antwerp; then of French painter F. A. Vincent in Paris (*cf.* P. J. Sauvage); enrolled there as officer in 'corps du génie'; returned Antwerp and was appointed captain of Château Laeken by Archduchess Maria Christina (*cf.* A. C. Lens, P. Faes and A. A. Cardon); after outbreak of Brabant Revolution went with Sir Home Riggs Popham to India *c.* 1790; associated there with English artist T. Daniell then engaged on his 'Antiquities of India'; his own work '*Two hundred and fifty Etchings descriptive of the Manners, Customs and Dresses of the Hindoos*' sponsored by General Wellesley (later Duke of Wellington) as part of his efforts to make British officials acquainted with the characters and customs of the Indian peoples) was published Calcutta 1799; returned Paris 1806; prepared French and English editions of his book published (with preface complaining of piracy in England) Paris 1808-12; resettled Antwerp 1815; in last years held rank of an Antwerp harbour master but also practised as painter and was member of the academy. A *View of Ostend Harbour* (painted for the Archduchess) is known from engravings.
[Fl. 545, Fl. 451, Fl. 126 (1849), Fl. 612, Fl. 892, Fl. 88.]

Somer, (Someren), Bernaert (Barent) van. Flemish Sch. *b* Antwerp before 1575 *d* Amsterdam 1632. Brother of P. van S.

Religious subjects, mythologies with nudes, portraits; also active as innkeeper and art dealer. Pupil of P. Lisaert in Antwerp 1588; went Rome where married daughter of A. Mytens *q.v.*; in Amsterdam where Van Mander records him as a good portrait painter and owner of Mytens' *Christ crowned with thorns* 1604; friend of A. Brouwer (*cf.* J. v. Craesbeeck) who lived in his inn 'Het Schild van Frankrÿck' 1626; stood godparent with the Dutch painter Judith Leyster to a daughter of Frans Hals 1631. The Dutch painter Hendrik van S. was his son.
[Fl. 559, Fl. 892, Fl. 88.]

*****Somer (Someren), Paul (Pauwels) van.** Flemish Sch. *b* Antwerp 1576 *d* London and buried S. Martin in the Fields 1621. Brother of B. van S. *q.v. Portraits, mythologies, religious subjects* (?). In Amsterdam where Van Mander records him as a good painter of portraits and other types of picture including imaginative compositions (werk van eigen vinding) 1604; visited Leyden 1612-14; in Brussels 1616; went London (*cf.* J. de Gheyn the younger, C. de Neve, G. Coques, H. v. Steenwyck the younger, also S. v. d. Meulen) 1616; painter to James I and his Queen, Anne of Denmark; **Signed Example:** ENGLAND Royal Coll. (Windsor) *Anne of Denmark: Queen of James I, with horse, negro and dogs* 1617. **Documented Example:** ENGLAND Royal Coll. *James I in a black suit* (in Charles I's catalogue; sold by the Commonwealth, recovered at Restoration). Vertue (1727) records *James I in his Crown and robes with view of Whitehall Palace; Queen Anne in a farthingale with west façade of S. Paul's in background; The Earl of Ancrum* (signed and 1619) and other portraits in private collections; Walpole (1771) also records portraits then in private collections. Portraits of *The Archduke Albert and the Infanta Isabella* were painted for Brabant Chambre des Comptes 1616 (*cf.* E. v. Remonde and D. v. Alsloot). S. Wils *q.v.* owned a *Pan and Syrinx* (*cf.* J. Jordaens) in Antwerp 1628. A *Time unveiling Truth* is recorded by an engraving. Portraits presumed by some his work are still in English private collections.
[Fl. 559, Fl. 826, Fl. 856, Fl. 223, Fl. 612, Fl. 892, Fl. 38, Fl. 88, Fl. 39, Fl. 213, Fl. 899.]

Somers, Guillaume. Flemish Sch. *b* Antwerp 1819 *d* place and date unknown. *Bourgeois genre and interiors.* Pupil of G. Wappers. [Fl. 451.]

Somers, Louis Jean. Flemish Sch. *b* Antwerp 1813 *d* Antwerp 1880. *Costume history, genre, portraits.* Pupil of F. de Braekeleer; visited Paris and Italy. Represented in ANTWERP *The librarian, Reading proofs* BREMEN, LEIPZIG *Oliver Cromwell discovering a conspiracy* 1837 LIÈGE *Monks singing* MALINES *Expectation* STRASBOURG *Three drinkers.* His *The children of Jacques d'Armagnac Duke of Nemours tied to the scaffold while their father was beheaded 1477* was in the Brussels exhibition of 1845.
[Fl. 451, Fl. 612, Fl. 837 (1880), Fl. 88.]

Somme, Charles de. Flemish Sch. *b* Brussels 1637 *d* Paris 1673. *Flowers and fruit* (*cf.* T. Aenvanck, J. B. Crépu and J. v. Son). Félibien records him as famous in this field 'bien que ces sortes d'ouvrages ne soient pas les plus considérables dans l'art de peindre'. Worked in France where recorded as 'peintre de la reine'. A piece titled *Peaches and grapes* was engraved before 1735. [Fl. 287, Fl. 612, Fl. 798.]

Sommé, Félicité de. Flemish Sch. *b* Antwerp before 1810 *d* after 1849. *Genre, costume history, portraits.* Pupil in Antwerp Acad. Exhibited *Rubens and his family* (*cf.* P. Kremer) and portraits in Paris Salon 1831-49. [Fl. 451, Fl. 612, Fl. 66.]

Son (or Zoon), Jan Frans (Francis) van. Flemish Sch. *b* son of Joris van S. *q.v.*, Antwerp 1658 *d* London 1718 or earlier. *Still life (some very large) with fruit, flowers, vessels, carpets*

and damask gold-fringed draperies (cf. T. Aenvanck, P. Boel, P. Gysels, G. Gabron); also dead birds and game pieces (cf. F. Snyders, J. Fyt, J. B. Govaerts, A. Smitsen). Pupil of his father; came England when young (cf. G. Coques, J. B. Medina and C. de Neve); married niece of serjeant painter R. Streater the elder and lived Long Acre; worked for Lord Radnor's mansion in St. James', Lord Dover at Cheveley and Lord Ranelagh at Chelsea; began series of large paintings showing all the medicinal plants in the physic garden at Chelsea (cf. P. Casteels III) but abandoned project; R. Streater the younger (died 1711) owned about thirty of his paintings; J. C. Weyerman, in London, c. 1718, finished a number left unfinished at his death. Signed Examples (Jan van Son): LILLE Flowers and fruit, 1705. TOURNAI Still life. Vertue (before 1734) describes a large overmantel with dead fowl in Lord Radnor's house into which the French painter L. Laguerre has inserted a portrait of Van S. 'coming in with a hawk on his fist and his other hand on a spaniel dog'; he describes his earlier works as 'laboured' his later as 'broad' and painted with a 'loose, free and natural pencil as any master whatever'. Descamps (1763) writes: 'on apperçoit dans ses ouvrages cette abondance et cette vérité qui intéressent même ceux qui ne connoissent rien à notre art'. Walpole (1771) writes: 'He painted that medley of familiar objects that strike the ignorant vulgar'. Some pictures signed J. v. S. are presumed by some his work and by others his father.
[Fl. 878, Fl. 215, Fl. 826, Fl. 856, Fl. 612, Fl. 892, Fl. 223, Fl. 88.]

*Son (or Zoon), Joris van. Flemish Sch. b Antwerp 1623 d Antwerp 1667. Still life with fruit, flowers, shellfish, tortoises, tablevessels (cf. J. D. Coosemas, A. Coosemans, A. Brueghel, A. v. d. Eeckhout, J. v. Es, T. Aenvanck, C. de Heem, M. Verhoeven, C. de Somme) also fruit and flower garlands (cf. D. Seghers and A. v. Utrecht). Master Antwerp Guild 1644; married his mistress 1656; E. Quellinus drew his portrait. J. P. Gillemans the younger and F. van Everbroeck were among his pupils. Signed Examples: CAMBRIDGE Fitz. Table with fruits (including peeled lemon), shrimps and lobster. 1660. COPENHAGEN Fruit and flowers 1665. GOTHA Shellfish with fruit and flowers 1658. MADRID Prado Fruit garland with insects round a S. Michael 1657, Still life with oyster, fruit and flowers 1664. Still life with oysters, fruit and butterfly 1664. SCHLEISSHEIM Fruit garland 1656. Monogrammed Example: STOCKHOLM. The collection of the painter V. Wolfvoet q.v. inventoried 1652 included a Fruit piece. A Vanitas (cf. C. Gysbrechts) is recorded in an Antwerp inventory of 1666. Cf. Jan Frans van S. who also signed 'J. van Son'.
[Fl. 86, Fl. 425, Fl. 878, Fl. 215, Fl. 612, Fl. 892, Fl. 88, Fl. 213.]

Sons (or Soens), Jan. Flemish Sch. b Bois-le-Duc 1548 or 1533 d Parma 1611 or Cremona 1614. Landscapes with roads, trees, fields, crops and small figures including 'droleries' (cf. P. Stevens, J. Grimmer and P. Bruegel the elder); also wide landscapes in fresco; conflagrations (cf. P. Huys and P. Schoubroeck) and religious subjects. Pupil in Antwerp of Gillis Mostaert q.v.; copied landscapes by F. Mostaert q.v.; went Italy where remained (cf. J. v. d. Straet); worked in Vatican Sala Ducale with M. Brill q.v. 1573-5; met Van Mander in Rome (cf. B. Spranger) and took him to inspect his Vatican frescoes; went Parma where became court painter to Duke Ottavio Farnese 1575 and his successors Alexander (cf. P. Claiessens the younger) and Ranuccio I; married in Parma 1596. Signed Examples: PARMA Pinacoteca Resurrection 1590 (from S. Francesco del Prato); S. Maria della Steccata Holy Family 1607. ROME Vatican Landscape with a cock in foreground (fresco; recorded by Van Mander). A S. Augustine and the child by the seashore also recorded by Van Mander in the Vatican is not now traceable. Work by him in

the (no longer extant) S. Maria Bianca in Parma was much admired by Annibale Carracci.
[Fl. 559, Fl. 800, Fl. 505, Fl. 612, Fl. 892, Fl. 715 (1927 and 1928), Fl. 305, Fl. 678.]

*Soolmaker (or Solemaker), Jan Frans. Flemish Sch. b Antwerp 1635 d Italy (?) after 1665. Italianate landscapes with animals and figures (cf. A. Crussens, G. de Witte, J. F. Millet, P. Spierincx, P. Rysbraeck, J. Spalthof, and J. B. Juppin). Master Antwerp Guild 1654; went Amsterdam and recorded by early writers as pupil there of Dutch painter N. Berchem (cf. J. Siberechts) made will in Amsterdam with intention of travelling by sea to Portugal and thence to Italy 1665. Signed Examples: BRUSSELS Italianate landscape with the reconciliation of Jacob and Esau (cf. J. W. Delff); Italianate landscape with Esau selling his birthright. BUDAPEST, DUBLIN Cattle in a hilly landscape. THE HAGUE Landscape with road among ruins in Roman Campagna and peasants, sheep, goats and a horseman with attendants. SCHLEISSHEIM, VALENCIENNES and VIENNA Acad.
[Fl. 22, Fl. 612, Fl. 107, Fl. 892.]

Soutman, Pieter. Flemish (Dutch) Sch. b Haarlem before 1600 d Haarlem 1657. Religious subjects, 'history' portraits; but chiefly active as engraver. Pupil of Rubens. In Antwerp 1620-8 then back to Haarlem. Court Painter to Vladislaus Sigismund, King of Poland (who was in the Netherlands 1624). Signed Examples: BRUSSELS Jonkheer A. F. de Kies van Wissen 1649. STOCKHOLM The Four Evangelists. Documented Examples: HAARLEM Meeting of Arquebusier Archers 1642, Meeting of Civic Guard Officers 1644. THE HAGUE Huis Ten Bosch Triumph of Prince Frederick Henry (cf. J. Jordaens). Paintings presumed by some his work are in various museums.
[Fl. 86, Fl. 425, Fl. 451, Fl. 612, Fl. 892, Fl. 798.]

Spaden, Jan. Flemish Sch. b Louvain (?) before 1394 d Louvain (?) after 1424. Worked in Louvain 1414-24. His father (same name) known as Olieput (Oil pot) was town painter in Louvain 1364-c. 1394. [Fl. 267, Fl. 269, Fl. 892.]

Spalthof (Joannes Philip?). Flemish Sch. b Flanders (?) c. 1636 (?) d Antwerp (?) after 1700 (?). Italian and Flemish market scenes, Roman and other landscapes (cf. A. F. Baudewyns, P. v. Bloemen, P. v. Bredael, J. v. Buken, A. Goubau, P. Gysels, M. Schoevaerdts, P. Spierinckx, J. F. Soolmaker, G. de Witte also S. Vrancx) and 'history'. Houbraken (1718) records him without christian name and adds that he went three times on foot to Rome (cf. N. van Bloemen). Presumed by some identical with J. P. S. recorded Antwerp Guild 1700.
[Fl. 425, Fl. 878, Fl. 215, Fl. 612, Fl. 892.]

Speeckaert (or Specart), Jan (Hans). Flemish Sch. b son of an embroiderer, Brussels before 1550 d Rome c. 1577 or c. 1582. Religious subjects, 'history', portraits. Went Italy and remained there (cf. J. v. d. Straet); Van Mander (1604) records: 'When I was in Rome (1575-7) there was still there an exceptionally clever young painter Hans Speeckaert who painted and drew very well; on a journey to the Netherlands he was taken ill in Florence and returned Rome ... A. Mytens (q.v.) often went about with him'. Worked with and was prosecuted with A. Santvoort q.v. 1575; Van Mander records his death in Rome 'about 1577'; Nagler (1835-52) records it in or soon after 1582. Signed Examples: VIENNA Kunsthist. The engraver Cornelis Cort. A Joseph and Potiphar's wife (cf. M. Pepyn) and Scenes from the life of the Virgin are recorded by engravings. [Fl. 559, Fl. 612, Fl. 892, Fl. 416, Fl. 88.]

Speeckaert, Léopold. Flemish Sch. b Brussels 1834 d Brussels 1915. Figures. Member of Brussels Société Libre des Beaux Arts (cf. C. van Camp). [Fl. 296.]

Speeckaert (or **Speckaert**), **Michel Joseph.** Flemish Sch. *b* Louvain 1748 *d* Brussels 1838. Represented in LA FÈRE *The nest* and *The mouse.* Presumed identical with a J. Speeckaert (1748-1838) recorded painter in Malines of fruit and flowers. His grandson Gustave S. (1843-87) was also a painter.
[Fl. 451, Fl. 612, Fl. 837 (1887), Fl. 73, Fl. 798.]

Sperwer, Peter (Signor Pedro). Flemish Sch. *b* Antwerp 1662 *d* Antwerp 1727. *Portraits; religious subjects* (?). Went Paris (*cf.* A. v. d. Meulen and C. E. Biset); married in Paris; worked Brussels; Master Antwerp Guild 1700. A *Philip V of Spain* for Antwerp Hôtel de Ville was paid for by town authorities 1703. Descamps (1769) records a work in the Salle de la Congrégation of Antwerp Jesuit Church.
[Fl. 216, Fl. 107, Fl. 892, Fl. 88.]

Spey, Martinus. Flemish Sch. *b* Antwerp 1771 or 1777 *d* place unknown after 1818. *Portraits, still life with flowers* (*cf.* J. F. Eliaerts); *still life with game* (*cf.* J. B. Berré); *also genre* (?). Worked in Paris under the Empire (*cf.* J. F. Dael and L. Gerbo). [Fl. 275, Fl. 451, Fl. 612, Fl. 798.]

Spierinc (Spirinc), Clay (Nicolas). Flemish Sch. 15th cent. *Manuscript illustrations, calligraphic and heraldic work.* Employed by Charles the Bold Duke of Burgundy 1469 (*cf.* J. Hennecart and J. de Boulogne).
[Fl. 385, Fl. 892, Fl. 248, Fl. 88.]

Spierinckx (or **Spiering** or **Spirinx**), **Pieter** (not Nicolas). Flemish Sch. *b* son of a tapestry worker or woodcutter, Antwerp 1635 *d* Antwerp 1711. *Italianate landscapes, some with figures illustrating religious and mythological subjects* (*cf.* A. Crussens, J. F. Millet, G. de Witte, J. B. Juppin), *others with genre scenes* (*cf.* P. v. Bredael, M. Schoevardts, J. P. Spalthof), *conflagrations* (?) *and marines* (?); *also designs for tapestry.* Master Antwerp Guild 1655; in Italy *c.* 1660; then Lyons and Paris (*cf.* C. E. Biset); worked for Louis XIV (*cf.* A. v. d. Meulen); in Antwerp 1666. **Signed Examples:** HAGUE Mauritshuis *Landscape with village fair and tight rope walker on a stage* (*cf.* P. Bout, J. v. Buken and L. Defrance) in *Interior of a picture gallery* by Gonzales Coques *q.v.* RENNES *Landscape with nymphs* 1659 SCHLEISSHEIM. Descamps saw (1768) a ceiling panel in Antwerp Academy, a *Landscape with scenes from the life of S. Augustine* in Antwerp Church of the Augustines and others in Carmelite church. Erasmus Quellinus *q.v.* owned a number of his pictures; the Forchoudt firm of Antwerp dealers sent tapestries from his designs in 1686 and 1708 (*Orpheus*) to their Austrian branch (*cf.* L. Schoor).
[Fl. 215, Fl. 216, Fl. 612, Fl. 107, Fl. 892, Fl. 88, Fl. 212, Fl. 213, Fl. 296.]

Spieringh (or **Spierincks**), **Karel Philips.** Flemish Sch. *b* Brussels 1609 *d* Rome 1639. *Religious subjects, 'history'.* Went Italy and remained there (*cf.* J. Sutterman); pupil in Rome of Paul Brill (?); worked for Galleria Giustiniani 1631; was painting frescoes in Flemish-German colony's church S. M. dell'Anima when he died. Pictures titled *Narcissus* (*cf.* J. Cossiers) and *Satyr* are recorded.
[Fl. 612, Fl. 84, Fl. 892, Fl. 416, Fl. 417, Fl. 617.]

Spierinx (or **Spiering**), **Frans** (known in England as Francis Spirinx). Flemish Sch. *b* Antwerp 1551 *d* Delft 1630. *Drawings; but chiefly active as tapestry worker.* In Antwerp where suffered damage during Spanish Fury (*cf.* F. Badens and J. Hoefnagel) 1576; fled from Parma's edicts against Protestants (*cf.* G. Congnet) to Holland *c.* 1590; founded a tapestry factory in Delft where Karel van Mander the younger *q.v.* was his associate; produced tapestry titled *The Defeat of the Armada 1588* for Earl of Nottingham (Admiral Lord Howard of Effingham) from cartoons by the Dutch marine painter C. Vroom (destroyed by fire London 1834).

A tapestry *The Battle of Bergen-op-Zoom* made in his factory for Middleburg is extant. [Fl. 559, Fl. 612, Fl. 892.]

Spilliaert, Leon. Flemish Sch. *b* Ostend 1881 *d* Brussels 1946. *Marines and coast scenes, landscapes, tree studies, interiors, still life, figures (mainly w. or pastel).* Worked much at Ostend. Represented in BRUSSELS *Carnival, The Masts, Washing day,* (all *w.*) *The Port* (drawing). [Fl. 123, Fl. 296.]

*Spinny, Guillaume de. Flemish Sch. *b* Brussels 1721 *d* Eik en Duimen (The Hague) 1785. *Portraits.* In France during War of Austrian Succession and the early Pompadour period (*cf.* J. F. Delien, P. J. Delcloche, P. J. Lion, Jean Nollekens, C. J. Redouté, J. B. Simons, J. J. de Soignie, J. J. Spoede, P. L. J. Spruyt; also J. F. v. Bredael, J. A. Garemyn); went The Hague *c.* 1756; became a favourite portrait painter in Dutch court circles. **Signed Examples:** AMSTERDAM Rijks. *Vice-admiral H. Lijnslager, Baron S. P. Collot d'Escury 1758, Anna Magdalena Della Faille, A lady with a rose 1762.* THE HAGUE Mauritshuis *Frederika Sophia Wilhelmina of Prussia, wife of Stadholder William V 1769*; Geemente Mus. *Members of The Hague town council in 1759.* ROTTERDAM Boymans. *Jacob van der Heine 1775.*
[Fl. 481, Fl. 892, Fl. 88.]

Spoede, Jean Jacques. Flemish Sch. *b* Antwerp *c.* 1680 *d* Paris 1757 (or 1760). *Animals and still life with game* (*cf.* A. de Gryef, J. B. Govaerts, G. Rysbraeck, A. Smitsens, P. J. Snyers, A. Verhoeven, J. X. Vermoelen). *mythologies and allegorical pieces; caricatures (in black and red chalk); also active as dealer.* Pupil in Antwerp Acad.; went Paris (*cf.* P. J. Delcloche, J. F. Delien, C. van Falens, H. de La Pegnia, J. Smets, G. de Spinny); associated with Confrérie Flamande de S. Germain des Prés (*cf.* P. Vleughels); friend of Watteau and introduced him to the dealer Sirois 1709; exhibited in Exposition de la Jeunesse, Place Dauphine and in the Society of S. Luc's exhibitions; rector of the Society of S. Luc from 1748; the French pastellist M. Quentin de la Tour was apprenticed to him as a pupil *c.* 1721. **Documented Example:** ORLÉANS Portrait-caricature *Bolureau Doyen des maîtres peintres.* Pictures exhibited (in addition to *game pieces* included *The Triumph of Neptune and Amphitrite* (*cf.* F. Francken the younger and A. v. Nieulandt) 1751, *Bacchanal* 1751, *Spring* and *Autumn* 1752. [Fl. 612, Fl. 66, Fl. 51.]

Spoor, W. J. L. Flemish Sch. *b* Budel (N. Brabant) date unknown *d* after 1810. *Landscapes with animals* (*cf.* J. B. de Roy); *also drawings and copies.* Pupil of H. J. Antonissen in Antwerp after 1755. A man of means and steward to Prince William V at Eindhoven; copies of pictures by the Dutch animal painter Paul Potter and other paintings in the Prince's collection, are recorded. [Fl. 451, Fl. 612, Fl. 892.]

*Sporckmans (or Sporkmans), Huybrecht (Hubertus). Flemish Sch. *b* son of a lawyer, Antwerp 1619 *d* Antwerp 1690. *Religious subjects, allegories, portrait groups.* Master Antwerp Guild 1640; a Dean of the Chamber of Rhetoric (Violieren) 1658; Dean of the Guild 1659; was rich and owned several houses; one of his daughters married A. v. Bredael *q.v.* Another painter of the same name working as copyist and restorer 1651 is recorded. **Signed Example:** ANTWERP *The city of Antwerp begging the Emperor to re-open the Scheldt* (date 1677 visible in 1883. *cf.* A. Janssens). Descamps (who records him without christian name as pupil of Rubens) saw (1768) a *S. Carlo Borromeo interceding for the plague stricken* (*cf.* V. H. Janssens) and *The Order of the Carmelites confirmed by the Pope* 'tableau bien composé mais mal drapé, sans aucunes formes naturelles' in Antwerp Carmelite Church. Antwerp Mus. catalogues an *Anatomy lesson* (*cf.* A. Pietersz) from Antwerp College of Surgeons. [Fl. 216, Fl. 892.]

*Spranger (van den Schilde), Bartholomaeus. Flemish Sch. *b* Antwerp 1546 *d* Prague 1611. *Landscapes, then religious sub-*

jects and mythologies with nudes. Pupil of J. Mandyn *q.v.* for eighteen months 1558-9; then, for a fortnight before his death of landscape painter F. Mostaert *q.v.* 1560 and thereafter apprentice to C. v. Dalem *q.v.* Went Paris (*cf.* C. Ketel and G. v. Coninxloo) 1565; thence via Milan to Parma 1566; worked there for B. Gatti (Il Sojaro: a Correggio follower) and on decorations of Pageant Entry of Alexander Farnese and Maria of Portugal (*cf.* P. Claeissens the younger); went Rome 1567; worked there with M. Joncquoy *q.v.*; met the miniaturist G. Clovio (*cf.* Joris Hoefnagel) who recommended him to Cardinal Farnese (as three years later he recommended El Greco) 1567; worked in Caprarola (Villa Farnese) under direction of F. Zuccaro (*cf.* O. v. Veen); became Papal Court painter to Pius V (S. Michele Ghislieri) who lodged him in the Belvedere in spite of Vasari's attempts to discredit him, 1570; took painting *Christ in the Garden of Olives* to Pope's bedside in his last illness 1572; worked for Roman churches and met Van Mander (*cf.* J. Sons); recommended by sculptor Giovanni da Bologna to Emperor Maximilian II and went Vienna 1575; with Van Mander and others decorated a huge triumphal arch with allegorical figures for entry of Emperor Rudolf II to Vienna (the whole work done in twenty-eight days 'in spite of heavy rain') 1577; took house in Prague and painted the outside with figures imitating copper reliefs (*cf.* Q. Massys, F. Floris, K. Foort, M. Ponteau); accompanied the Emperor to Augsburg Diet 1582; worked in Vienna palace 1583; Court Painter to Rudolf II (*cf.* P. Stevens and H. V. de Vries) 1584; in Prague and Vienna worked exclusively for Emperor and had studios in his private apartments where the Emperor often watched him at work (*cf.* P. V. de Vries); given gold chain by Emperor at public banquet 1588; acquainted with German painters J. Heintz the elder and H. von Aachen (*cf.* G. Rem and F. Pourbus the younger); ennobled as 'van den Schilde' 1595; visited Netherlands (Antwerp and Haarlem) where was fêted by the artists including Van Mander 1602. **Signed Examples:** NÜREMBERG Germ. Mus. *Venus, Mercury and Cupid* 1597. VIENNA K. *Self portrait, Hercules and Omphale, Parnassus.* **Monogrammed Example:** VIENNA K. *Allegory on the virtues of Rudolf II* 1592. **Documented Examples:** CAPRAROLA Villa Farnese *Landscapes* (fresco) 1570. ROME S. Giovanni alla Porta Latina *Martyrdom of S. John the Evangelist in burning oil* (recorded by Van Mander). VIENNA K. *Vulcan and Maia, Venus and Mars, Odysseus and Circe* and others. Subjects recorded by engravings include: *The Birth of the Virgin, The Marriage of Cupid and Psyche* and *Apollo's contest with Marsyas.* Van Mander records a *Landscape with witches on broomsticks flying round a ruin like the Colosseum* (*cf.* J. Cornelisz van Oostsanen, F. Francken the younger, J. Ghuens the younger, R. Savery), *Christ triumphing over Death and the Devil*, a *Last Judgement* (painted for Pius V 1572), *Venus and Mercury teaching Cupid to read* and others; he further records a portrait of a lady, done from memory, in Rome for her lover (*cf.* A. Mor). The Forchoudt firm of Antwerp dealers sent (1668) to their Vienna branch a *Venus and Amor with several cupids* formerly owned by Rudolf II, then by the Queen of Sweden and sold by her agents (?) 'domistiken' in Antwerp (*cf.* D. Seghers and D. Teniers the younger).

[Fl. 559, Fl. 612, Fl. 892, Fl. 225, Fl. 419, Fl. 305, Fl. 678.]

Spruyt, Charles. Flemish Sch. *b* son of P. L. J. S., Brussels 1769 *d* Brussels 1851. *Religious subjects, costume history, architectural subjects (Rome), landscape, genre.* Pupil of his father and of Ghent Acad.; in Rome (*cf.* P. v. Hanselaere) 1815-20; returned Brussels 1821; published 'Lithographies d'après les principaux tableaux de la coll. de Mons. le Prince Auguste d'Arenberg' with 54 plates, Brussels 1829. A *Dying man receiving the consolations of the Church* was recorded (1845) in Ghent S. Nicolas. Other titles recorded include *S. Theresa begging the Virgin to redeem certain souls from purgatory; John, Duke of Brabant, rescuing his sister from prison; Francesco Francia dying in contemplation of a painting*

by his friend *Raphael* 1829 (*cf.* P. Kremer); *The Supper at Emmaus* (sold to North America before 1843); and *Girl and her lover with a fortune-teller* 1845.

[Fl. 451, Fl. 612, Fl. 479, Fl. 617, Fl. 88.]

Spruyt, Jacob Philips. Flemish Sch. *b* Ghent before 1750 *d* Ghent (?) date unknown. *Genre and portraits.* Recorded in The Hague 1764; also worked Delft; returned Ghent. [Fl. 481.]

Spruyt, Philippe Lambert Joseph. Flemish Sch. *b* son of an army contractor and tax collector, Ghent 1727 *d* Ghent 1801. *Religious subjects, 'history', conversation pieces; also active as engraver (after Rubens and others), restorer and dealer.* Pupil of J. B. Millé in Brussels; went Paris (*cf.* F. L. Peters and G. de Spinny) where pupil of the French painter C. van Loo; then Rome, worked under German painter Rafael Mengs (*cf.* J. Dreppe and F. J. Lonsing) 1757-60; visited Naples 1760; in Brussels 1761-70; professor in Ghent Acad. from 1770; contributed engravings for inventory of works of art in churches and monasteries of Austrian Netherlands commissioned by Empress Maria Theresa (*cf.* F. Stampart) before 1780; published book on elements of drawing ('Beginselen der Teeken Kunst') Ghent 1792, and a miscellany on art ('Konstlievende Mengelingen') 1794.

[Fl. 451, Fl. 892, Fl. 88, Fl. 617.]

*Staben, Henri. Flemish Sch. *b* Antwerp 1578 *d* Paris 1658. *Social scenes* (*cf.* F. Francken II, A. L. Fonteyn, C. J. v. d. Lamen, J. v. d. Lamen, P. Meert, J. v. Winghe, also H. Janssens), *interiors including picture galleries* (*cf.* W. v. Haecht). Went young to Venice (*cf.* D. Barendsz, J. S. van Calcar, L. Toeput) and worked in atelier of Domenico Tintoretto which continued that of his father Jacopo Tintoretto (*cf.* P. Franck, P. Vlerick, M. de Vos); probably in Antwerp before 1621; worked in Paris (*cf.* J. Fouquier, P. de Champaigne, J. v. Egmont, R. Schoof, P. Vleughels, J. de Wael; also G. v. Cleve, L. Thiry, A. Dubois, and C. E. Biset). Félibien (1688) recording a picture by him in the collection of M Le Nôtre writes: 'La composition vous surprendra pour le grand travail qu'on y voit; ce tableau n'est que d'une médiocre grandeur; il représente la galerie d'un curieux dans laquelle sont disposez des cabinets, des meubles, mais sur tout plusieurs tableaux si delicatement faits et si finis, qu'on y voit distinctement tous les sujets qu'ils traitent, et qui cependant ne laissent pas d'être diminuez de force et de teintes selon leurs diverses situations et les degrez d'éloignement, avec une entente admirable'. **Signed Example:** BRUSSELS *Visit of the Archduke Albert and Infanta Isabella to Rubens' studio.*

[Fl. 287, Fl. 168, Fl. 892, Fl. 88, Fl. 124.]

Stacquet, Henri. Flemish Sch. *b* Brussels 1838 *d* (Schaerbeek) Brussels 1906. *Landscape, marines (and coast scenes), interiors, genre, mainly in w.* Worked in Brussels Acad. Libre (Patte de Dindon) (*cf.* F. Courtens and P. Pantazis); President Soc. Roy. Belge des Aquarellistes 1901; foundation member of 'La Chrysalide'; member of Soc. int. de la peinture à l'eau (*cf.* F. Charlet) Paris 1906. Represented in ANTWERP *Woman reading*, (w.) *The Chapel* (w.) BRUSSELS, COURTRAI *Winter landscape* GHENT *Fishing boats in a storm* MALINES, OSTEND, PARIS State Coll. *Interior* BOSTON U.S.A. *Winter landscape.* [Fl. Bib. 19th cent.]

*Stalbemt (or Stalbempt, known in England as Stalband), Adriaen van. Flemish Sch. *b* of Protestant parents, Antwerp 1580 *d* Antwerp and buried in Putte Protestant cemetery 1662. *Landscapes some with religious, mythological and genre scenes* (*cf.* A. Keirincx, A. Mirou, P. Stalpaert, P. Stevens, J. Sons); *also worked as engraver.* Taken as a child to Middelburg after Parma's capture of Antwerp (*cf.* D. v. d. Queborne) 1585; returned Antwerp and became Catholic (*cf.* D. Seghers); Master in Antwerp Guild 1610; dean in Antwerp 'Violiere' 1618; with H. v. Balen *q.v.* and P. Goetkint the younger assessed an Antwerp art collection 1622; in England for ten months (*cf.* C. de Neve) 1632-3; returned Antwerp; worked there for the dealers A. Goetkint (Bonenfant) and C. Immerseel of Seville (both associated in business with J. Brueghel the younger) 1635-9 (*cf.* G. Seghers); reverted to Protestantism in last years (?). Van Dyck drew his portrait for his Iconography; C. de Bie, author of the Gulden Cabinet, was his friend. **Signed Examples:** AMSTERDAM Rijks. *Wooded landscape with hunters and dogs.* ANTWERP *Landscape with fables: the fox and the eagle, the rabbits and the frogs, the frogs and the stork, the two men and the bear and others.* (*Cf.* F. Snyders) 1620. BERLIN K.F. *Grotto with Adoration of the Shepherds* 1622. CASSEL *Kermesse in a village.* DRESDEN *Wooded landscape with feast of gods* (*cf.* F. Floris and Vienna Feast of the Gods Painter). FRANKFORT Staedel. *Kermesse with peasants and gentry on a village square* (*cf.* D. Teniers the younger). MADRID Prado *Return of David with the head of Goliath* 1619 (*cf.* J. B. Saive and A. Schoonjans) also signed by 'Brueghel 1618' *cf.* P. Brueghel the younger. A *Virgin and Child* in a flower piece (in collaboration with C. de Cauwer *q.v.*), a *Five senses*, a *Morality in thirty-two scenes* (Morael ofte die Histori van den Geltduvel), twenty-two *Emblems of love*, twenty-one scenes *Pallas as Goddess of Wisdom*, and *Figures for a church interior by P. Neeffs the elder* are recorded among works painted for Immerseel; works painted for Goetkint included a series of *Pastorals* and *Scenes from Ovid* for Cabinets (*cf.* F. Borsse). The collectors Sara Schut (1644) and V. Wolfvoet *q.v.* (1652) owned *Church interiors* in collaboration with P. Neeffs the elder. V. Wolfvoet also owned *The Good Samaritan, S. Mary Magdalene, The Story of Achilles, Pyramus and Thisbe, Pan and Syrinx, Winter landscape, Night landscape* and other landscapes. A. v. Lamoen, Antwerp cloth merchant (*cf.* L. de Caullery) owned (1661) a *Feast of the gods*. The Forchoudt firm of Antwerp exporting dealers sent many of his works to Vienna between 1640 and 1700 (a letter to them from a Seville dealer 1653 asks for a pair of his pictures, the same size, 'landscapes with some nice little figures of little dancers and shepherds and satyrs'). Vertue (before 1756) refers to a *Landscape of Greenwich* in the sale of Charles I's pictures 1649-51, possibly a picture signed A. v. Stalbent in WINDSOR Royal collection (*cf.* J. v. Belcamp). Walpole (1771) records an *Octagonal landscape with the story of the Centurion* 'something in the manner of Paul Brill but the colours exceedingly bright and glaring' seen by him in a 1764 sale. [Fl. 86, Fl. 425, Fl. 826, Fl. 856, Fl. 612, Fl. 892, Fl. 212, Fl. 213, Fl. 214.]

Stallaert, Joseph. Flemish Sch. *b* Merchtem 1825 *d* Brussels 1903. '*Classical*' *subjects, murals and ceiling paintings, portraits.* Pupil in Brussels Academy of F. J. Navez; Rome prizewinner 1847; then studied Paris and Italy; Director Tournai Acad. 1852-65; professor 1865 and finally director Brussels Acad. (*cf.* A. Robert); Represented in ANTWERP *Polyxena sacrificed on the pyre of Achilles* (another version in GHENT), *Portrait of Constant Wauters.* BRUSSELS *Death of Dido* and *Ceiling painting;* National Bank *Ceiling painting;* Town Hall (Burgomaster's office) *Love of Justice, Benevolence and Perseverance.* Others in LIÈGE and TOURNAI. [Fl. 160 (1903), Fl. 218, Fl. 88, Fl. Bib. 19th cent.]

Stalpaert, Pieter. Flemish Sch. *b* son of a tapestry worker, Brussels 1572 *d* Amsterdam *c.* 1637. Father of Dutch architect Daniel S. *Landscapes* (*cf.* A. v. Stalbemt, P. Stevens and A. Mirou). In Amsterdam by 1599 (*cf.* F. Badens, G. v. Coninxloo, G. C. de Hondecoeter, A. v. Nieulandt). **Signed Example:** AMSTERDAM Rijks. *Rural landscape with trees, farmhouses and a horseman* 1635. *Marines* are also recorded. [Fl. 892.]

Stampart, Frans van. Flemish Sch. *b* Antwerp 1675 *d* Vienna (Minorite Monastery) 1750. *Portraits; also worked as engraver.*

Pupil of A. Tyssens the younger; Master in Antwerp Guild 1692; went Vienna where Court Painter to Leopold I (*cf.* J. A. v. d. Baren, A. Schoonjans and J. Thomas 'van Ypern') to Joseph I (*cf.* P. Evrard), Charles VI (*cf.* P. F. and J. G. de Hamilton) and the Empress Maria Theresa (*cf.* G. de Pélichy). Descamps 1763 writes: 'Lorsqu'il peignoit des personnes de considération qui n'avoient ni le temps ni la patience d'attendre, il dessinoit leur tête aux crayons noir, blanc et rouge; d'après ce dessein il peignoit et il ne se servoit plus de la nature que pour finir'. Descamps saw (1768) a *Portrait of Prince Charles of Lorraine* (*cf.* L. Legendre, and J. P. Sauvage) in the apartments of the Antwerp Academy (in Antwerp Bourse). Portraits of *Leopold I, of Charles VI in armour* and of Austrian and German nobility are recorded. He contributed plates to an engraved repertoire (Prodromus . . .) of works of art in the Vienna Imperial collections, 1735 (*cf.* P. L. J. Spruyt). [Fl. 215, Fl. 216, Fl. 612, Fl. 892, Fl. 798.]

Standaart see **Bloemen, P. van.**

Stapleaux, Michel Ghislain. Flemish Sch. *b* Brussels 1799 *d* Gien (Loiret) 1881. *Portraits, 'history', costume history, religious subjects, genre.* Pupil of L. David in Brussels (*cf.* H. v. d. Haert, H. de Caisne, J. Paelinck and F. J. Navez). Visited France, Italy and Switzerland; worked Stuttgart for King of Würtemberg 1834-6; later professor Brussels Acad. His wife Louiza Schavije was painter of flowers and portraits. Represented in SOISSONS *White poodle.* WIESBADEN *Portraits.* Portraits of members of the Bonaparte family, including *The children of Jérôme Bonaparte* (*cf.* S. J. Denis and F. J. Kinson) and a *Return of the Prodigal* are recorded. [Fl. 451, Fl. 837 (1882), Fl. 88, Fl. 798.]

Star Master (D. van Star) see **Velaert, D. J.**

Staynemer, ——. Flemish Sch. (?) 16th cent. *Topographic drawings.* **Signed Example** (drawing): EDINBURGH N. G. Scotland *View of Ponza with ruin in clouds* (*s* 'Monte Zerzello, staynemer: Fec: Isola Pons') presumed by some identical with J. van Stinemolen *q.v.* [Fl. 276.]

Steenwinkel, Antonie van. Flemish Sch. 17th cent. *d* Copenhagen 1688. *Portraits and figures.* Member of Flemish painter family. Court painter of Christian V of Denmark 1670 (*cf.* P. v. Lint). **Signed Example:** ANTWERP *Portrait of a philosopher* (*with books and a skull*). [Fl. 17.]

*Steenwyck, Hendrik van the elder. Flemish Sch. *f* Steenwijck (Overyssel) *c.* 1550 *d* Frankfort 1603. *Architectural pieces* (*interiors of Gothic churches, palaces and other buildings*) (*cf.* P. Neeffs and H. v. S. the younger) *some with torch light effects* (*cf.* J. v. Cleve) *also market scenes* (*cf.* D. Vinckeboons, A. v. Nieulandt, S. Vrancx); *figures sometimes by other artists.* As Protestant went Aix-la-Chapelle to escape Alva's persecutions (*cf.* N. and P. v. d. Perre); pupil there of J. V. de Vries *q.v.*; married there daughter of M. v. Valkenborch *q.v. c.* 1573; in Antwerp and Master in Guild 1577; had Jacques de Backer in his house; left Antwerp again to escape from Parma's campaigns (*cf.* D. v. d. Queborne) and settled Frankfort (*cf.* J. v. Winghe); citizen of Frankfort 1586. **Signed Examples:** AMSTERDAM *Night scene in a crypt.* BRUNSWICK *Market place* 1598. BUDAPEST *Interior of Antwerp Cathedral* 15.5. DESSAU Amalienstift *Palace room with musicians* (Frankfort 1588). **Monogrammed Example:** SCHLEISSHEIM *Aix-la-Chapelle Cathedral* 1573. [Fl. 559, Fl. 826, Fl. 612, Fl. 892, Fl. 459, Fl. 213, Fl. 907.]

*Steenwyck, Hendrik van the younger. Flemish Sch. *b* son of H. v. S. the elder, Antwerp (?) or Frankfort (?) *c.* 1580 *d* London (?) *c.* 1649. *Architectural scenes, interiors of churches* (*cf.* H. v. S. the elder, P. Neeffs, L. Neeffs, Jacob Lidts,

W. v. Ehrenberg, J. Peeters, S. Vrancx, W. de Smet) *some by torchlight* (*cf.* J. v. Cleve, A. de Coster, A. Mytens), *palace courtyards* (*cf.* J. V. de Vries); *architectural backgrounds for figures by other artists*. In London (*cf.* P. v. Somer, H. v. d. Borcht the younger, and C. de Neve) by 1617; worked much with Dutch painter C. van Poelenburgh who came London 1637; patronized by Charles I; friend of E. Norgate to whom he complained that other artists could complete a picture in the time he needed to set down his perspective lines. Van Dyck drew his portrait. **Signed Examples:** BRUSSELS *Church interior* 1645. BUDAPEST *Liberation of S. Peter* (*cf.* C. de Wael) 1620. CAMBRIDGE Fitz. *Liberation of S. Peter* 1626. DRESDEN three *Church interiors* dated 1609, 1611, 1614; architecture in picture titled *Charles I of England beneath a triumphal arch* 1637. LENINGRAD *Sacristy interior* 1634, *Court of a Renaissance Palace with figures* 1623. LONDON N.G. *The Palace of Dido* 1610; two *Church interiors* 1603 and 1615. PARIS Louvre *Christ in the house of Martha* (*cf.* J. Goeimare and A. Grimmer) 1620. TURIN Architecture in *Charles I of England in a portico* 1627. VIENNA Kunsthist. *Interior of a Gothic church* 1605, *Liberation of S. Peter* night piece (*cf.* G. Mostaert) 1621, *Same subject* 1604; Czernin *Liberation of S. Peter* 1638. Others signed in CASSEL, COPENHAGEN, PRAGUE, SCHWERIN. **Monogrammed Examples:** CAMBRIDGE Fitz. *Prison scene with sleeping guards* 1618. DETROIT *Christ in the house of Martha* 1620. THE HAGUE *Open square with figures* 1614. **Documented Examples** in English Royal Coll. (Hampton Court) and MADRID Prado. Vertue (before 1756) records an ebony cabinet decorated by C. Poelenburgh and Steenwyck, an architectural background to a portrait of G. Frobenius 1629 and other works in English collections. *Cf.* J. van Belcamp.
[Fl. 559, Fl. 618, Fl. 753, Fl. 826, Fl. 215, Fl. 856, Fl. 612, Fl. 730, Fl. 892.]

Steenwyck, N. (Nicholas?). Flemish Sch. 17th cent. Descamps (before 1763) records him as painter of *Vanitas still life compositions* (*cf.* J. B. Boel and C. N. Gysbrechts) who lived in Breda and was frequently confused with H. v. Steenwyck the younger; he adds: 'ce peintre si moral, si grave dans ses pensées, étoit très déréglé dans sa conduite; livré pendant toute sa vie à la crapule la plus honteuse, il mourut dans la plus grande misère, On estimoit autant ses ouvrages de son vivant qu'on les estime aujourd'hui'. Walpole (1771) records a Nicholas van S. son of H. v. S. the younger who 'was in England, painted for Charles I and probably died here'. Presumed by some a confusion with one of the Dutch still life painters Abraham Steenwyck or Herman S.
[Fl. 878, Fl. 215, Fl. 856, Fl. 892.]

Steenwyck, Susanna van (née **Gaspoel**). Flemish Sch. 17th cent. *Architectural views*. Wife of Hendrik v. S. the Younger. Recorded in Leyden 1642; settled Amsterdam after her husband's death in England *c.* 1649. **Signed Examples:** DESSAU *Gothic church* 1639; ZWOLLE *Church interior* 1651. **Documented Example:** LEYDEN *The Lakenhal (cloth hall) of Leyden* (bought by town authorities 1642). [Fl. 612, Fl. 892.]

Stella (or **Stellaert**), **François.** Flemish Sch. *b* son of painter Jean S., Malines 1563 *d* Lyons 1605. *Religious subjects, landscapes, portraits*. Went Rome *c.* 1576; later settled Lyons (*cf.* J. v. d. Straet) where worked for churches. The French painters Jacques Stella and François Stella the younger were his sons. **Signed Example:** PARIS Louvre *Cascade at Tivoli* 1587. An *Entombment* in Rome, S. Pietro in Montorio was engraved in the eighteenth century as 'd'après le tableau de F. Stellart'.
[Fl. 559, Fl. 287, Fl. 66, Fl. 892, Fl. 88, Fl. 678.]

Stephani, see **Stevens, P.**

Stevens, Alfred. Flemish Sch. *b* son of picture dealer and restaurant keeper, Brussels 1823 *d* Paris 1906. Brother of Joseph S. *Costume history, then anecdotic and social genre subjects (especially figures of Second Empire Parisiennes, many with the Japanese accessories fashionable at the period); later, landscapes and seascapes*. Pupil in Brussels of F. J. Navez; then in Paris of Florent Willems and the French painters J. D. Ingres and C. Roqueplan; lived mainly in Paris; visited London where friend of the French painter J. Tissot 1863; regular exhibitor at Paris Salons; received many medals and decorations; Commander of the Légion d'Honneur 1878. Represented in ANTWERP *Authorised begging, Parisian Sphinx, Despair*. BRUSSELS *Lady in pink, Maternal Bliss, Studio interior, The road from Cap St. Martin to Mentone* and others LIÈGE, LONDON Tate *The Present, Seascape* MARSEILLES, MUNICH, NANTES *Seapiece* PARIS State Coll. *The Passionate song, Home from the ball* STOCKHOLM, TOURNAI; also in BOSTON, CHICAGO, DETROIT, NEW YORK, PHILADELPHIA *Shall we go out Fido?*. ST. LOUIS, WORCESTER.
[Fl. 23, Fl. 495, Fl. 518, Fl. 103, Fl. 296, Fl. Bib. 19th cent.]

Stevens, Gustave Max. Flemish Sch. *b* Brussels 1871. *Figures, landscapes, portraits, flowers*. Pupil in Brussels of J. Portaels and in Paris of F. Cormon. Represented in BRUSSELS *Winter landscape* 1908. IXELLES *Last rays*. PARIS State Coll. *The Curve of the Seine (Paris)* 1920. [Fl. Bib. 19th cent.]

Stevens, Jacob. Flemish Sch. *b* son of painter Anton S., Malines *c.* 1565 *d* Antwerp before 1630. *Allegorical subjects*. Master Antwerp Guild 1589. In Malines 1590-1614; painted panels on arch for a pageant entry into Malines of Archduke Albert and Archduchess Isabella (*cf.* A. and M. Joncquoy and D. v. Alsloot). His sons Jacob S. the younger (1593-1662) and Jan S. (1595-1627) also worked at Malines. [Fl. 612, Fl. 88.]

Stevens, Joseph (Joseph-Édouard). Flemish Sch. *b* Brussels 1816 or 1819 *d* Brussels 1892. Brother of Alfred S. and the art critic Arthur S. *Anecdotic animal genre, mainly dogs; occasional horses; (cf.* J. Stobbaerts) *also monkey pieces* (*cf.* D. Teniers the younger and N. v. Verendael). Pupil of L. Robbe *q.v.* but largely self taught; worked Brussels and Paris; regular exhibitor Paris Salons; Chevalier of the Légion d'Honneur 1861; Officer of the Order of Leopold 1863. The French poet Baudelaire inscribed to him his prose poem *Les bons chiens (Le Spleen de Paris)* (*cf.* F. Rops). Represented in ANTWERP *Dog and tortoise*; BRUSSELS *The Paris dogmarket* 1857, *The dog and the mirror, Brussels in the morning* 1848, *Episode at the Paris dogmarket 1857* and others. MARSEILLES, NEW YORK, PARIS State Coll. *The torments of Tantalus*; ROUEN *Métier de chien*; TOURNAI *Dog with a bone*. Other titles recorded include *The prisoner's dog* and *Flemish bull pursued by a dog*.
[Fl. 264, Fl. 452, Fl. 292, Fl. 915, Fl. 296, Fl. Bib. 19th cent.]

Stevens, Léopold. Flemish Sch. *b* son of Alfred S., Paris 1866 *d* Paris 1935. *Landscape, marines, genre, portraits*. Pupil of his father. Regular exhibitor in Paris Salon de la Nationale. Represented in BRUSSELS *The Demolition* 1896. [Fl. 123.]

Stevens (known as **Stephani**), **Pieter the elder.** Flemish Sch. *b* Malines *c.* 1540. *Religious subjects*. In Malines Guild 1560; in Rome 1566 (?). An *Adoration of the Magi* signed Pet. Stephani, Rome 1566 is recorded by an engraving. Presumed by some identical with P. S. the younger *q.v.*
[Fl. 892, Fl. 88.]

***Stevens** (called **Stephani**), **Pieter the younger.** Flemish Sch. *b* *c.* 1567 *d* Prague (?) after 1624. *Landscapes with figures* (*cf.* J. (Velvet) Brueghel, J. Sons, A. v. Stalbemt, P. Stalpaert and A. Mirou). Master Antwerp Guild 1589; went Prague *c.* 1590; painter to Rudolf II (*cf.* K. v. Mander, B. Spranger, F.

Pourbus the younger, J. V. de Vries, P. V. de Vries, J. Hoefnagel, P. Bruegel the elder, J. de Gheyn, R. Savery) 1594-1612; presumed to have visited Rome and Venice (*cf.* H. v. Cleve). **Monogrammed Examples:** ANTWERP *Village fair* 1596. BRUNSWICK *Landscape with hermitage* 1609. A *Landscape with figures* (inscribed 'Vervulling van wyn, baert twist en pyn'), a *Lovers and Death*, a series of *Roman ruins* and others of *The Four Seasons*, *The Four times of the Day* and *The Twelve Months* are among works recorded by engravings. Presumed by some identical with P. S. the elder *q.v.*

[Fl. 559, Fl. 612, Fl. 613, Fl. 892, Fl. 88.]

Steyaert, Antoine Ignace. Flemish Sch. *b* Bruges 1761 *d* Bruges 1841. *Religious subjects, genre scenes, some with candle and lamp light effects, landscapes in moonlight* (*cf.* P. van Schendel); *copied old masters in gouache and worked as colour lithographer.* Pupil of J. A. Garemyn and P. de Cock in Bruges Acad.; settled Ghent; teacher in Acad. 1802; director 1809-14; later in Bruges. **Documented Example:** GHENT S. Nicolas *S. Anthony preaching in Limoges* 1809. Recorded titles include *Two young people working in a room by lamp light, Girl by a window with candle light effect* 1814, *Ceres, Rest on the Flight* 1830, *Moonlight landscape* 1834, *Children coming from school* 1834. [Fl. 451, Fl. 612, Fl. 88, Fl. 798.]

Steyaert, Antoine Pierre. Flemish Sch. *b* son of A. I. S., Bruges 1788 *d* Ghent 1863. *Landscapes.* Teacher in Ghent Acad.

[Fl. 837 (1863), Fl. 88.]

Steynemolen (or Stinemolen), Godefroid van. Flemish Sch. *b* Malines before 1550. Dean Malines Guild 1581. Had to leave the town for taking part in rising against the Spaniards (*cf* J. v. Winghe) 1586. [Fl. 613.]

Stinemolen (or Steynemolen), Jan van. Flemish Sch. 16th cent. *b* Malines (?). *Topographic drawings.* Worked Naples (?) (*cf.* C. Smet). **Signed Example:** VIENNA Albertina *Panorama of Naples* (Jan van Stinemolen . . . 1582). Presumed by some identical with Staynemer *q.v.* [Fl. 798.]

Stobbaerts, Jan (Jean Baptiste). Flemish Sch. *b* son of cabinet maker, Antwerp 1838 *d* Brussels 1914. *Peasant genre, animals* (*cf.* Joseph Stevens, G. Colsoulle, A. Verwée, C. Verlat, H. Ronner, L. Robbe, J. B. de Roy, I. Stocquart, A. C. M. Engel; also B. P. Ommeganck and E. J. Verboeckhoven) *including stable interiors with cattle, pigs and horses; landscapes; later studio interiors with nudes and 'classical' subjects; occasional portraits.* Apprenticed at eight to a cabinet maker; then to a housepainter, then to a decorator; taught himself to read and write; began to study painting in Antwerp Acad. under E. Noterman *q.v.* met H. de Braekeleer and was helped by H. Leys; settled Brussels 1886; foundation member of L'Art Contemporain (Kunst van Heden) (*cf.* R. Strebelle); Knight of Légion d'Honneur 1900. Represented in ANTWERP *Leaving the stable, Haywain, Butcher's shed, The slaughterhouse, Dogs, Horse stall, Kiel Mill, Interior of a mill, Dredging in the Woluwe, The sculptor R. Fabri, Diana resting* and others. BRUSSELS *Stable at Cruyninghen* 1884, *Kitchen, Stable interior* and others; THE HAGUE, NAMUR, TOURNAI *Making pancakes, Pigs, Cows* and others. [Fl. 626 (1906), Fl. 264, Fl. 569, Fl. 388, Fl. 296, Fl. Bib. 19th cent.]

Stobbaerts, Marcel. Flemish Sch. *b* grandson of J. B. S., Vorst near Brussels 1898. *Urban and rural landscapes, portraits, genre, religious subjects.* Pupil of C. Montald in Brussels Acad. Represented in ANTWERP *Mother and Child.*

[Fl. 17.]

Stock, B. and V. van der see Stoct.

*Stock, Ignatius van der. Flemish Sch. *b* Brussels (?) before 1640 *d* after 1665. *Wooded landscapes (Forest of Soignes cf.*

J. d'Arthois, D. v. d. Bogaerde and F. Coppens) *with figures and animals; also worked as engraver.* Pupil in Brussels of L. de Vadder 1653; Master Brussels Guild 1660; A. F. Baudewyns was his pupil. **Signed Example:** BRUSSELS S. Gudule *Wooded landscape with figures* 1661 paid for in 1664 (*cf.* L. Achtschellinck); Ministry of Agriculture *Plan of the Forest of Soignes.* **Monogrammed Example:** MADRID Prado *Wooded landscape with figures* 1660. Engravings by him after his own pictures and those of J. Fouquier are recorded.

[Fl. 612, Fl. 892, Fl. 301, Fl. 88.]

Stocquart, Henry. Flemish Sch. *b* Antwerp *c.* 1815. *Landscapes with animals and figures; architectural pieces.* Presumed by some identical with Ildephonse S. *q.v.*

[Fl. 612, Fl. 481, Fl. 892.]

Stocquart, Ildephonse. Flemish Sch. *b* Grammont 1819 *d* Brussels 1889. *Landscapes with animals* (*cf.* J. Stobbaerts). Pupil of H. v. d. Poorten. Presumed by some identical with Henry S. *q.v.* Represented in BRUSSELS *Landscape with animals.* YORK *Cattle.* [Fl. 892, Fl. 264.]

Stoct (Stock). Bernaert van der. Flemish Sch. *b* son of Vrancke van der S. *q.v.*, Brussels (?) before 1469 *d* after 1538. Went Jerusalem (*cf.* J. v. Scorel) 1505; Brussels Town Councillor 1532; made will 1538. **Signed Examples:** None. **Documented Examples:** None. Presumed by some a painter of Münster, Landesmus. *Annunciation* with reverse *Nun as Donor* inscribed 'S^{or} KA^{na} Vand Stoct. P'FSSIE NONE A^o XV, XX. DIE. XXIII JUNII' (Katherina v. d. S. was Bernaert's daughter).

[Fl. 530, Fl. 798.]

Stoct (Stock), Vrancke (Franck) van der. Flemish Sch. *b* son of painter, perhaps Brussels before 1430 *d* Brussels 1495. Assistant to his father 1444; succeeded R. van der Weyden *q.v.* as painter to city of Brussels 1464; member of Town Council between 1465 and 1475; employed on decorative works for marriage festivities of Charles the Bold, Bruges 1468 (*cf.* P. Coustain, J. Daret, H. v. d. Goes, D. de Rycke, J. Hennecart); bequeathed some contents of his studio to his son Bernaert v. d. S. *q.v.* in will dated 1489. **Signed Examples:** None. **Documented Examples:** None. [Fl. 88, Fl. 316, Fl. 555.]

Stoevere (or Scoenere), Jean de. Flemish Sch. 15th cent. *Religious subjects and decorative paintings for Ghent churches.* Pupil of R. Campin *q.v.* in Tournai 1416; Dean of Ghent Guild 1431; contracted with B. van Wytevelde *q.v.* to work for Ghent Nieuwenboss Abbey 1443. His son J. de S. the younger was Dean in Ghent Guild 1480 and 1493. **Signed Examples:** None. **Documented Examples:** None.

[Fl. 385, Fl. 892, Fl. 88.]

Stoevere (or Scoenere), Saladin. Flemish Sch. *b* before 1414 *d* after 1458. *Religious subjects, portraits and decorative paintings.* In Ghent Guild 1434; worked for churches in Ghent, Audenarde and Bruges; painted portraits of donors on wings of altarpiece for Ghent Nieuwenboss Abbey (*cf.* J. de S. and B. van Wytevelde). **Signed Examples:** None. **Documented Examples:** None. [Fl. 385, Fl. 126, Fl. 892, Fl. 88, Fl. 798.]

Stom (or Stomer), Matthias. Flemish Sch. *b* Amersfoort 1600 *d* Sicily (?) after 1651. *Religious subjects.* A contemporary inventory describes him as pupil of the Dutch painter G. Honthorst; went Italy and remained there (*cf.* J. Sutterman); recorded Rome 1630 (fiamengo pittore di anni 30) (*cf.* A. Smit); in Naples after 1632; in Sicily 1641-51. **Signed Examples:** CACCAMO (Palermo) S. Augustine *Miracle of S. Isidore* 1641. MESSINA Capuchin Church *S. Cecilia* ('Flandriae Stomus coloribus exprexit') destroyed in earthquake 1908. **Documented Examples:** NAPLES Pinacoteca *Holy Family, Supper at Emmaus, Liberation of S. Peter, Adoration of the Shepherds, Arrest of Christ* all from church of

Immacolata Concezione: recorded by Celano (1692). Orlandi (1704) records a son of same name who painted landscapes and battle pictures and died aged 59, Verona 1702. An Antwerp inventory 1672 records a *Landscape* by de Stom. [Fl. 154, Fl. 628, Fl. 612, Fl. 892, Fl. 631 (1929), Fl. 305, Fl. 213.]

Stradanus (or **della Strada**) see **Straet**.

Straet, Jan van der (called Stradanus, della Strada or Straetensis). Flemish Sch. *b* of noble family, Bruges 1523 *d* Florence 1605. *Religious subjects, 'history', decorative genre scenes, tapestry designs (including hunting scenes with birds, fish and animals cf. M. Geeraerts the elder and J. Hoefnagel).* Pupil in Antwerp of P. Aertsen; Master Antwerp Guild 1545; went Lyons (*cf.* F. Stella) and worked there with the portrait painter Cornelis de la Haye (Corneille de Lyon) *c.* 1548; went Italy and remained there (*cf.* H. v. d. Broeck, M. Brill, P. Brill, J. S. v. Calcar, D. Calvaert, F. v. d. Kasteele, P. Mera, A. Mytens, G. Rem, A. Santvoort, E. Schayck the younger, L. v. Schoor, J. Sons, K. P. Spieringh, J. Speeckaert also J. Sutterman); visited Venice (*cf.* D. Barendsz, H. v. Staben and L. Toeput); then Florence where met Vasari; in Rome with Vasari (*cf.* H. de Cock) *c.* 1551; assisted Vasari on Vatican frescoes; visited Reggio; worked in Vatican Belvedere with the Italians Daniele da Volterra and Salviati; assisted Vasari in Florence Palazzo Vecchio 1561-2; and made many tapestry designs for Duke Cosimo I dei Medici; worked on Michael Angelo's catafalque in Santa Croce 1564; took part in designing pageantry for Francesco dei Medici's marriage with Joanna of Austria (*cf.* F. di L. Sustris) 1565; member of Florence Accad. del Disegno; at invitation of Don John of Austria (*cf.* A. de Succa) went Naples (*cf.* P. Schephen) and worked in S. Anna dei Lombardi; followed Don John to Netherlands (?) 1576; in Naples 1579; in Florence and working on decorations for wedding of Duke Ferdinand dei Medici with Christina of Lorraine 1589. **Signed Examples:** AUGSBURG *Pietà.* FLORENCE S. Annunziata *Crucifixion* 1569; Santa Croce *Ascension* 1569. **Inscribed Examples:** FLORENCE Palazzo Vecchio *Chemists at work* 1570, *Mineworkers* 1570. **Documented Examples:** FLORENCE S. Maria Novella *Baptism of Christ*; S. Spirito *Expulsion of the money changers*; Palazzo Vecchio, Eleanora di Toledo's apartments, ceilings. Vienna (Albertina) has signed drawings (*Battle of the Amazons*) 1564 and (*Battle of Saul and the Philistines*) Naples 1579. Of his tapestry cartoons for Duke Cosimo, Vasari writes (1568): 'Made following the Duke's ideas ... they show such a variety of animals, birds, fish, landscapes and costumes, with hunters on foot and on horseback, and fowlers ... and nude fisherman, that the designer is proved a truly able artist (*veramente valent uomo*) who has well acquired the Italian manner'. Van Mander (1604) records *Studies of different breeds of horses* (*cf.* J. de Gheyn and A. J. v. Diepenbeeck) and the continuation of a series *Acts of the Apostles* begun by M. v. Heemskerck *q.v.* Many of his cartoons for tapestry and other works are recorded by engravings. Paintings presumed by some his work are in various museums (*cf.* Vienna Feast of the Gods Painter). [Fl. 818, Fl. 98, Fl. 559, Fl. 48, Fl. 612, Fl. 627, Fl. 892, Fl. 305.]

Straeten, Jan van der (also called **Verstraeten**). Flemish Sch. *b* Antwerp (?) before 1670 *d* Antwerp (?) 1729. *Architectural subjects* (*cf.* W. v. Ehrenberg) some as backgrounds in works by contemporaries including B. van den Bossche *q.v.* and F. X. H. Verbeeck *q.v.* Pupil of Jacob Peeters *q.v.* [Fl. 126, Fl. 296.]

Stramot, Nicolas. Flemish Sch. *b* Diest 1637 *d* Montaigu nr. Diest 1709. *Portraits, religious subjects; also architectural views for topographic publications.* Worked at Louvain; visited England *c.* 1695 (*cf.* D. Boone, J. C. Lotyn, J. B. Medina and S. Hardimé); settled Montaigu 1706. His uncle Nicolas S., his brother Pierre (represented by signed pictures in Diest Town Hall) and his nephew Nicolas Etienne were also painters. **Signed Examples:** ANTWERP *Frans van Sterbeeck* (*architect and botanist*) 1693. DIEST Monastery of the Cross Bearers *Samson killing the lion* 1677. LOUVAIN S. Gertrude *The members of All Souls Brotherhood of S. Gertrude at the Mass in celebration of their 50th anniversary* 1682. [Fl. 267, Fl. 271, Fl. 892, Fl. 647, Fl. 88, Fl. 798.]

Strebelle, Rodolphe. Flemish Sch. *b* Tournai 1880. *Decorative compositions, portraits, still life; designs for tapestry and glass; also water colours and wood cuts.* Pupil in Brussels Acad. of J. Delville and G. v. Strydonck; Member of Nervia group founded at La Louvière (*cf.* A. Carte, L. Devos, P. Paulus) 1929; and L'Art Contemporain (Kunst van Heden) (*cf.* R. Baseleer, E. Claus, A. Crahay, H. Daeye, J. J. Delvin, A. v. Dyck, J. Ensor, L. Frédéric, V. Hageman, F. Hens, C. Mertens, A. Oleffe, W. Paerels, Ramah, J. Stobbaerts, W. Vaes, E. Vloors, G. v. d. Woestyne, R. Wouters); designed tapestry *Le Doudou de Mons* for Belgian Pavilion in Paris Exhibition (*cf.* F. Jespers and S. Wynants) 1937. Represented in ANTWERP *Self portrait.* GRENOBLE, IXELLES, LIÈGE, NAMUR, VENICE. [Fl. 764 (1921), Fl. 296.]

Strick, Henri. Flemish Sch. *b* Borgerhout 1892. *Genre, portraits, religious subjects, landscapes.* Pupil in Antwerp Higher Institute of J. de Vriendt and I. Opsomer. Visited Holland; fought in 1914-18 German invasion. Professor in Antwerp Institut Notre Dame. Represented in ANTWERP *The blonde lady.* BORGERHOUT Institut S. Agnès *The twelve apostles.* [Fl. 17.]

Stroobant, François. Flemish Sch. *b* Brussels 1819 *d* Brussels 1916. *Architectural views (some of old Brussels cf. J. B. v. Moer), landscapes, drawings and lithographs for topographic publications; also active as engraver.* Pupil of F. J. Navez and P. Lauters; Director of Molenbeek Academy. Represented in BRUSSELS *Old guild houses on Brussels Grand' Place.* LONDON Guildhall *Brussels Hôtel de Ville, Liège Bishop's Palace.* Drawings for 'Les splendeurs de l'Art en Belgique' (to which L. H. Hendrickx also contributed) were published 1844; worked also on publications recording buildings in Ostend, Spa and Cracow. [Fl. 612, Fl. 626 (1916), Fl. 88, Fl. 798, Fl. 296.]

Struys, Alexander Théodore Honoré. Flemish Sch. *b* son of glasspainter, Antwerp 1852 *d* Uccle 1941. *Working class and peasant genre with implicit social comment* (*cf.* L. Frédéric), *portraits.* Pupil in Antwerp Academy of J. v. Lerius; visited Paris and London; began with anti-clerical picture *Birds of Prey* representing Jesuits at bedside of dying man 1874, but many of his later works show benevolent priests. Professor in Weimar School of Art 1878-82; settled Malines 1884: member Belgian Acad. 1897-1922. Represented in ANTWERP *The breadwinner* 1887, '*Peut-être*' BRUSSELS *Priest visiting the sick* 1893 DORDRECHT *Abandoned* 1874 GHENT *Despair* LIÈGE, PHILADELPHIA, TOURNAI *Trust in God, Starving, The Rest* WEIMAR and other museums. [Fl. Bib. 19th cent. Fl. 741, Fl. 17.]

Strydonck, Guillaume van. Flemish Sch. *b* of Flemish parents, Namsos, Norway 1861 *d* St. Gilles (Brussels) 1937. *Landscapes, portraits, genre, still life, religious subjects.* Pupil in Brussels Acad. of J. Portaels and in Paris of the French painter L. Gérome; won Godecharle scholarship (*cf.* P. Swyncop) 1884; Member of Brussels Impressionist group Les Vingt (*cf.* J. Ensor) 1884; visited Holland, Italy, the West Indies and Florida; worked in England and South of France; teacher in Brussels Acad. Represented in ANTWERP *Stephanie in white* BRUGES Triptych *Story of Tobias* 1884 BRUSSELS *The sculptor Ch. v. d. Stappen* 1884 IXELLES. LOUVAIN,

PARIS, TOURNAI *Les Canotiers, Mme. van Cutsem, Déjeuner at Blankenberghe, The Ayah.*
[Fl. Bib. 19th cent., Fl. 114, Fl. 17.]

Stuerbout (or **Sturbout**), **Hubert (Hubrecht)**. Flemish Sch. *b* Louvain (?) before 1430 *d* Louvain *c.* 1483. *Religious subjects and decorative designs for ceremonies; also active as carver.* Recorded Louvain 1439; painter to the town (*cf.* D. Bouts the elder) 1454; designed 250 bas-reliefs for Louvain Town Hall, the subjects being selected by Maître Jean v. d. Phalizen, Priest of Louvain, S. Pierre and Dr. Jacques a Dominican, 1449-51; concerned with pageant and processional decorations Louvain 1452 and 1463; confused with D. Bouts the elder in Louvain archives 1468; carved frame for a picture by D. Bouts 1481. His eldest son Hubert S. worked with him on an Ommeganck procession in Louvain 1463; his son Frans (Frissen) worked on these processions in 1487 and 1492; his son **Gillis (Egidjus)** was town painter in Louvain 1482. (*cf.* A. and L. Raet). Some fragments of bas-reliefs in Louvain Mus. are presumed by some from his Town Hall series.
[Fl. 179, Fl. 892, Fl. 757.]

Sturm (or **Stormius** or **Stormio**, known in Spain as Esturme or Desturme), **Ferdinand**. Flemish (Dutch) Sch. *b* Ziriksee before 1510 *d* Spain (?) after 1557. *Religious subjects.* In Spain and citizen of Seville 1537; worked for Seville and Cadiz churches (*cf.* M. v. Cleve the younger, S. Pereyns, R. Coxie and P. de Kempener) 1539-57; godfather at baptism in Seville of Canon Majorga's slave 1545; worked for Count of Ureña (later Duke of Osuna); valued a picture by the Spanish artist A. de Zamora 1552; valued pictures for the Chapter of Seville Cathedral 1554; took a Flemish apprentice who could speak no Spanish 1554. **Signed Example:** SEVILLE Cathedral: (Capella de los Evangelistos) Polyptych with predella *Mass of S. Gregory, Saints, Resurrection of Christ* 1555. **Documented Examples:** OSUNA Capella del Instituto: Polyptych *Annunciation, Nativity, Adoration of the Magi* and *Church Fathers* (contract from Count de Ureña 1547). OSUNA Colegiata (Osuna burial chapel) *Immaculate Conception* 1555. Works executed 1539-42 with two Spanish artists for S. Pedro in Arcos de la Frontera (Cadiz) are recorded.
[Fl. 153, Fl. 779, Fl. 335, Fl. 575.]

Suavius (real name **Zutman**, also known as Le Doux), **Lambert**. Flemish Sch. *b* son of H. Zutman, Liège *c.* 1510 *d* Frankfort (?) after 1562. *Religious subjects, portraits; but chiefly active as architect and engraver.* Pupil of Lambert Lombard (*cf.* J. Ramey) who married his sister; then studied Rome; worked Liège, Antwerp and Frankfort. **Signed Examples:** None. **Documented Examples:** None. The Antwerp dealer H. de Neyt owned 1642 a *Judgement of Paris* catalogued as 'by Lambertus or Lombardus Swavus'. A *Portrait of Cardinal Granvella* (*cf.* A. Mor and J. v. Scorel) is recorded.
[Fl. 371, Fl. 818, Fl. 612, Fl. 892, Fl. 88, Fl. 213.]

Succa, Antonio de. Flemish Sch. *b* of noble Italian family, Antwerp before 1582 *d* Antwerp 1620. *Portraits.* Master Antwerp Guild 1598; official genealogical portrait painter to Archduke Albert and Infanta Isabella (*cf.* G. de Crayer and D. v. Alsloot) 1600; travelled Netherlands and copied old portraits of ruling and famous personalities (his copies preserved in Antwerp Town hall till 1685 are not now traceable). BRUSSELS Mus. has a book of drawings titled 'Memoriaux d'Antoine de Succa'. Madrid, Prado (1148) *Don John of Austria and his Lion* has been presumed by some his copy of a lost original presumed by the Spanish painter Sanchez Coello (*cf.* J. van der Straet). [Fl. 892, Fl. 13, Fl. 88.]

Sustermans see **Sutterman.**

Sustris, Federico di Lamberto. Flemish (Dutch) Sch. *b* son of Lambert (Sustris) of Amsterdam *q.v.*, Italy (?) *c.* 1540 *d* Munich 1599. *Religious and 'classical' subjects, portraits; also worked as architect.* Married daughter of a Paduan playing card designer 1564; worked under Vasari in Florence on Michael Angelo's catafalque in Santa Croce (*cf.* J. v. d. Straet) 1564 and on pageantry for wedding of Francesco dei Medici with Joanna of Austria 1565; designed tapestries for Eleanora di Toledo's apartment in Florence Palazzo Vecchio 1565; Councillor of the Florence Accad. del Disegno 1567; went Augsburg to work for the banker Hans Fugger 1569 and later to Munich to work for Duke William V (*cf.* Joris Hoefnagel, Engelhart v. Pee, P. de Witte and Munich Duchess Magdalena Painter). Religious and 'classical' subjects are recorded by engravings. [Fl. 818, Fl. 612, Fl, 892, Fl. 643, Fl. 798.]

Sutterman (or **Susterman** or **Zetterman**), **Justus**. Flemish Sch. *b* son of a cloth weaver, Antwerp 1597 *d* Florence 1681. *Portraits; also occasional allegories and religious subjects.* Pupil as a boy of W. de Vos; went Paris (*cf.* J. Fouquier) 1616; pupil there of F. Pourbus the younger *q.v.* 1617-19; went Italy with a company of French tapestry workers travelling Florence to work for Medici Duke Cosimo II (*cf.* T. Rombouts); remained Italy (*cf.* W. Backereel, P. de Coster, L. Cousin, F. Denys, E. Doort, M. Desubleo, D. van den Dyck, G. Hallet, B. Lauwers, P. de Lignis, J. Miel, L. Mehus, N. Regnier, J. Roos, M. Stom, C. de Wael also Jan van der Straet, S. Denis and R. la Longe); in Florence where painted the doyen of the French tapestry workers which impressed Duke Cosimo II who made him Court Painter 1620; Court painter in Florence to Duke Ferdinand II 1621-70 and thereafter to Duke Cosimo III (*cf.* J. Denys); had headquarters Florence but also worked elsewhere; in Vienna where the Emperor Ferdinand II allowed him to paint seated and covered in his presence and ennobled him 1623-4; was visited in Florence by Van Dyck who drew his portrait before 1626 and sent him his own portrait later; in Rome where Pope Urban VIII gave him special privileges 1627; bought (for Duke Ferdinand II) Rubens' *Allegory of the Outbreak of War* (now Florence Uffizi) described in a letter to him from Rubens who asked him to repair it if damaged in transit 1638; painted notables in Parma, Piacenza, Milan, Rome, Modena, Ferrara, Mantua, Genoa and Innsbruck 1640-54; many details of his life are recorded by his friend the art historian Baldinucci whom he helped with the Flemish section of his 'Notizie dei professori...' (published 1681-1728). **Signed Examples:** None. **Documented Examples:** FLORENCE Uffizi *Homage of the Florentine Senate to Grand Duke Ferdinand II as a child* (commissioned by the Duke's mother Maria Magdalena of Austria, widow of Cosimo II 1621), *Galileo Galilei* (commissioned by the sitter 1636). Florence Uffizi and Pitti galleries have originals, replicas and copies of many *Portraits of the Medici Family.* Portraits presumed by some his work are also in other museums. He is known to have painted *The Emperor Ferdinand II, Pope Urban VIII, Pope Innocent X* and *Francesco d'Este* (triple portrait for use by a sculptor, *cf.* P. de Champaigne).
[Fl. 48, Fl. 612, Fl. 892, Fl. 59, Fl. 357.]

*Suvée, Joseph Benoît. Flemish Sch. *b* Bruges 1743 *d* Rome 1807. *Religious subjects, 'history', portraits, designs for tapestry.* Pupil in Bruges Acad. of M. de Visch (*cf.* J. F. Legillon and A. de Muynck); went Paris 1763; pupil of French painter J. Bachelier; teacher in Acad. Royale 1767; won first Prix de Rome (defeating L. David (*cf.* J. L. Demarne)) 1771; visited Bruges, where to celebrate Prix de Rome, the city was illuminated, and S. drove in coach and six followed by 27 other coaches to Town Hall ceremony (*cf.* A. v. d. Berghe, P. M. Goddyn, J. D. Odevaere and P. J. Verhaghen) 1771; worked French Acad. Rome under French painter C. J. Natoire 1772-5 and the French painter J. M. Vien, with Louis David (who referred to him as 'l'ignare Suvée') as fellow student, 1775-7; visited Naples and Sicily and returned Paris 1778; member of Académie Royale (*cf.* H. F. de Cort, P. J. Sauvage, also P. Mol) 1780; 'peintre du Roy' (*cf.* J. L.

Malaine); had studio in the Louvre where directed an art school for young ladies (*cf*. G. de Pélichy); assistant professor Acad. where J. A. Senave was his pupil 1781; nominated director of French Acad. in Rome 1792; imprisoned in S. Lazare under Terror (when Louis David suppressed Paris and Rome Academies) 1793-4; painted fellow prisoners including Trudaine-Montigny (who was taken away to guillotine while sitting to S.), and the poet André M. Chénier; released on collapse of Terror (when Louis David was imprisoned) 1794-5; took up Rome directorship when French Acad. was reopened under Consulate (*cf*. A. Ansiaux) 1801; moved French Acad. from Palazzo Mancini to Villa Medici 1804. **Signed Example:** PARIS L'Assomption *Birth of the Virgin* 1779. **Documented Examples:** BESANÇON *Cornelia Mother of the Gracchi* (Salon 1795). BRUGES *The daughter of Butades drawing the shadow of her lover* (given by artist to Bruges Acad. 1799), *Self portrait* (given by artist in return for festive entry 1772), *P. J. de Cock* (gift of subject's brother); S. Walpurga Church *Resurrection* (Salon 1783). DIJON *Death of Coligny* (tapestry design: Salon 1787). DOUAI *Aeneas in the ruins of Troy* (Salon 1785). LILLE *Combat of Minerva and Mars* (1771 Prix de Rome). PARIS Maisons-Laffitte *The vestal Emilia maintaining her innocence* (Salon 1781); Ste. Marguérite *Visitation* (Salon 1781) ROUEN *Fête à Palès* (Salon 1783). Recorded works include *Freedom restored to the Arts by Louis XVI, 1777, through the good offices of M. d'Angiviller* (reception work French Acad. Roy. 1779), a *Death of Cleopatra* (Salon 1779) and portraits of *Napoleon as First Consul* and *Josephine* (*cf*. F. J. Kinson).

[Fl. 451, Fl. 612, Fl. 66, Fl. 434, Fl. 785, Fl. 525, Fl. 296.]

Swart of Groningen, Jan (also known as Swart Jan (Dark Jan) and Giovanni da Frisia). Flemish (Dutch) Sch. *b* Groningen before 1500 *d* place unknown after 1523. *Landscapes with figures* (*cf*. J. Patinir, F. Mostaert), *nudes* (*cf*. J. Gossaert); *also worked as engraver*. Van Mander (1604) records him as 'one of the high points in our art' and adds: 'He lived some years in Gouda about the time that Scorel came back from Italy that is about 1522 or 1523; his way of painting landscapes, nudes and figures was much like that of Scorel (*cf*. A. Claesz van Leyden); he travelled in Italy, was some time in Venice (*cf*. D. Barendsz) and brought from Italy, as Scorel did, a way of working different from the ugly (onschoone) manner prevailing here and more like the Italian' (*cf*. J. van Scorel). Van Mander had seen no paintings by him but describes two woodcuts *Turks on horseback* (*cf*. P. Coecke van Aelst) and *Christ preaching from the ship*. A. P. Crabeth *q.v.* was his pupil. **Signed Examples:** None. **Documented Examples:** None. Prints from a wood block *Christ preaching from the ship* monogrammed J. S. and corresponding to Van Mander's description, are extant (Amsterdam Rijks. Mus. print room). Paintings, drawings and engravings presumed by some his work are in various museums.

[Fl. 526, Fl. 559, Fl. 892, Fl. 316, Fl. 421, Fl. 798.]

*Sweerts (Suars, Suerts), Michael (known as Cavaliere). Flemish Sch. *b* son of merchant, Brussels 1624 *d* Goa 1664. *Interiors with genre figures, portraits, some religious subjects; also active as engraver*. Went Rome (*cf*. A. Smit) where recorded as Roman Catholic and associate of Accad. di San Luca (*cf*. J. Miel) 1646; in Brussels where tried to found an academy for drawing from the nude 1656 (*cf*. D. Teniers the younger and J. Denys); in Amsterdam where successful as portrait painter 1661; joined a French missionary society and followed the Bishop of Heliopolis to Palestine (*cf*. J. van Scorel and N. Ryckx) 1662; began journey with mission to Cochin China but left it before reaching destination. **Signed Examples:** AMSTERDAM *Young men playing draughts* 'Roma 1652'. DETROIT Inst. of Art *In the studio: Young artists with plaster casts* (*cf*. J. v. Oost the younger, W. Vaillant, A. Goubau) 'Roma 1652'. LENINGRAD *Young man holding his head in his hands* 1656. Munich A. P. has *Interior of an inn: four youths by a fire* presumed by some the picture sold as by 'Cav. Swartz' Amsterdam 1783. Other pictures presumed by some his work are in various museums. Works recorded by engravings include a *Lamentation over the Dead Christ* and *Smoker with a boy beside him*.

Fl. 451, Fl. 612, Fl. 631 (1907 and 1916), Fl. 892, Fl. 798.]

Swerts, Jan. Flemish Sch. *b* Antwerp 1820 *d* Marienbad 1879, *Religious subjects, costume history, murals* (*cf*. F. v. Acker. T. J. Canneel, C. C. and J. F. Claes, J. B. v. Eycken), *portraits*. Pupil in Antwerp Acad. of N. de Keyser; travelled with G. Guffens *q.v.* in Italy and Germany where studied 'Nazarene' school 1850-2; director Prague Acad. Represented in ANTWERP *Cardinal Prince van Schwarzenberg, Episode from life of G. van Schoonbeke* and *Cartoons* for costume history frescoes in Antwerp Bourse (burnt 1858); S. George (with G. Guffens) *Scenes from the Life and Passion of Christ*. BRUSSELS Mus. *Cartoon* for frescoes in Antwerp S. George. COURTRAI Town hall *Murals* (with G. Guffens). PRAGUE Cathedral *Frescoes from his cartoons*. His *Murals* painted with G. Guffens for Ypres Cloth Hall were destroyed by the Germans with the building in their 1914-18 invasion (*cf*. L. Delbeke). [Fl. 88, Fl. 435.]

Swyncop, Philippe. Flemish Sch. *b* Brussels 1878. *Portraits, landscapes, figures, decorative paintings (murals), illustrations to books* (including Blasco Ibanez *'La femme nue de Goya'*). Pupil in Brussels Acad. of C. Montald; worked for a time as commercial artist in Paris and London; won Godecharle travelling scholarship (*cf*. G. v. Strydonck) 1900; visited Italy and Spain; member of the Sillon group (*cf*. A. Pinot); exhibitor Paris Salon de la Nationale; worked much in Granada. His brother Charles S. also a painter, worked in Spain and the Congo (*cf*. P. Mathieu, P. v. Engelen, R. Mols). Represented in BRUSSELS (on loan at Acad. roy. de langue et lit. franç.) *Brand Whitlock U.S.A. Ambassador* 1921. OSTEND Casino *Decorative paintings*. SPA Casino *Decorative paintings*.

[Fl. Bib. 19th cent., Fl. 465, Fl. 798, Fl. 296, Fl. 73.]

*Symons (Symen or Simons), Peeter. Flemish Sch. *b* Antwerp before 1615 *d* after 1637. *Mythologies; still life* (?). Master Antwerp Guild 1629; Van Dyck drew his portrait. **Signed Example:** MADRID Prado *Cephalus spied upon by Procris* painted for the Torre de la Parada (*cf*. J. P. Gowi) from a sketch recorded as by Rubens (Prado 2459) *c*. 1636. A *Still life with fish* (Stuck met visschen) by Peeter Symons was in the Antwerp collection of Sarah Schut 1644.

[Fl. 612, Fl. 88, Fl. 213, Fl. 555.]

T

Taelemans, Jean François. Flemish Sch. *b* Brussels 1851 *d* after 1909. *Landscapes and decorative painting.* Lived at one time in Paris; exhibited Liverpool; teacher in Brussels Acad. Represented in ANTWERP *Brabançon village under snow* 1909. BRUSSELS *Village in winter* 1897.
[Fl. Bib. 19th cent., Fl. 17.]

Tassaert, Jean Pierre. Flemish Sch. *b.* son of a painter Antwerp 1651 *d* Antwerp 1725. *Religious subjects, 'history', interiors, portraits.* Antwerp Master 1690; in Munich 1717. *Scenes from the lives of SS. Peter and Paul* (8 large panels) painted for the Antwerp Guild of Diamond Polishers are recorded. [Fl. 88.]

Tassaert, Philip Joseph. Flemish Sch. *b* Antwerp 1732 *d* London 1803. *Landscapes with animals, religious and allegorical subjects, banditti and other genre scenes, portraits; also active as engraver after old masters, pasticheur and dealer.* Came England (*cf.* P. Tillemans); became pupil of Th. Hudson's drapery painter A. van Haecken *q.v.*; returned Antwerp where Master in Guild 1756; court painter to Prince Charles of Lorraine (*cf.* J. P. Sauvage); back in London by 1769; member Soc. of Artists, and president in 1775; quarrelled with Soc. of Artists 1777; exhibited London R.A.; in Rome 1785-90; agent for Christie's in Paris in connection with project to buy the Orléans collection *c.* 1791.
[Fl. 263, Fl. 612, Fl. 695, Fl. 361, Fl. 362, Fl. 880, Fl. 88, Fl. 617.]

Taulier (or Tauler), Jean. Flemish Sch. *b* Brussels before 1590 *d* Liège *c.* 1640. *Religious subjects for Liège churches; also worked as engraver and woodcarver.* Was secretly a Protestant. Renier Lairesse, his son-in-law, and G. Douffet were his pupils. [Fl. 63, Fl. 451, Fl. 26, Fl. 409, Fl. 140, Fl. 88.]

Teerlinck (née Bening or Benninck), Livina. Flemish Sch. *b* daughter of Simon B. *q.v.* date and place unknown *d* London (Stepney) 1576. *Miniature portraits and 'limnings'.* To London with her husband G. Teerlinck 1545; salaried as artist and 'nurse' by Henry VIII (*cf.* G., L. and S. Horenbout) and three succeeding sovereigns; presented Queen Mary with a limning *The Holy Trinity* as a New Year's gift 1556, and Queen Elizabeth with 'The Queen's picture painted finely on a card' as a New Year's gift 1558 for which she was rewarded by the present of 'one casting bottell guilt weighing 2¾ ounces'; referred to among Flemish miniaturists by Vasari (1568). **Signed Examples:** None. **Inscribed Examples:** LONDON V. and A. (p. 145-1910) *Little Girl with apple* and (p. 146-1910) *Little Girl with red carnation*; these had formerly old parchment labels reading 'fynely painted by Lavinia Teerlinck in 1590 (*sic*) at Greenwich' seen by Dr. G. C. Williamson but since lost. Payment for a *Princess Elizabeth* 1551 is recorded.
[Fl. 818, Fl. 826, Fl. 881, Fl. 892, Fl. 882, Fl. 535, Fl. 887, Fl. 28.]

Tency, Jan Baptist. Flemish Sch. 18th cent. *Marines.* Sent pictures from Brussels to Ghent exhibition 1792. **Signed Example:** ANTWERP *Storm at sea.* [Fl. 16.]

Teniers, Abraham. Flemish Sch. *b* son of David T. the elder, Antwerp 1629 *d* Antwerp 1670. *Peasant genre; also active as art dealer and engraver for his brother David T. the younger.* Master Antwerp Guild 1646; patronised by the Archduke

Leopold Wilhelm (*cf.* J. B. van Heil and David T. the younger). **Signed Examples:** ANTWERP *Country fête.* DRESDEN *Kitchen scene.* VIENNA Harrach *Monkey comedies* (*cf.* David T. the younger and N. van Verendael).
[Fl. 107, Fl. 892.]

Teniers, David the elder. Flemish Sch. *b* son of a linen draper, Antwerp 1582 *d* Antwerp 1649. *Religious subjects, mythologies, peasant genre; also active as dealer.* Pupil of his elder brother Juliaen T. then of Rubens (in Antwerp 1599 or Italy); went Rome where pupil of the German painter A. Elsheimer (a friend of Rubens); returned Antwerp where Master in Guild 1606; worked for Antwerp churches; married a rich wife 1608; bought three houses in Antwerp with borrowed money 1615; later imprisoned for raising second mortgage and other financial frauds; rescued by sales of his own and his son David T. the younger's pictures organised by his sons 1629; visited Paris S. Germain fair (*cf.* C. de Vos) where sold pictures by himself and his sons David and Juliaen 1635. **Signed Examples:** MADRID Prado *Scenes from Tasso's 'Gerusalemme Liberata'.* VIENNA K. *Mercury and Argus* 1638, *Pan with nymphs and satyrs* 1638, *Vertumnus and Pomona* 1638. **Documented Example:** BERLIN K.F. *Temptation of S. Anthony* (engraved). A *Seven Works of Mercy* and a *Jesus among the Doctors* for Antwerp S. Paul are recorded; a *Triumph of King David* is referred to in a legal dispute as to its value 1621; a *Village wedding* is recorded by Descamps (1763) in a Paris collection. Some pictures signed with name or monogram catalogued as by David Teniers the younger *q.v.* may be wholly or in part his work.
[Fl. 86, Fl. 425, Fl. 753, Fl. 215, Fl. 892, Fl. 646, Fl. 214.]

★**Teniers, David the younger.** Flemish Sch. *b* son of David T. the elder, Antwerp 1610 *d* Antwerp 1690. *Indoor and outdoor peasant genre* (*cf.* A. Brouwer, D. Boone, J. van Craesbeeck, A. Victoryns, D. Ryckaert III, G. van Tilborgh the younger and the elder, F. and T. van Apshoven, J. van Kessel, M. van Helmont, A. Teniers, J. Teniers the younger, A. Wouwer, also B. Beschey), *guard room and military pieces* (*cf.* L. de Hondt the elder, J. Verhuyck and S. Vrancx), *monkey pieces* (*cf.* A. Teniers and N. van Verendael), *Temptation of S. Anthony and other 'spook' pieces* (*cf.* P. Huys and F. Francken II), *official ceremonies* (*cf.* D. van Alsloot, F. Duchatel, E. Quellinus, A. Sallaert, A. F. v. d. Meulen, J. van Werden, C. E. Biset, N. van Eyck), *gallery interiors* (*cf.* W. van Haecht), *occasional religious pieces and portraits; also active as copyist and dealer.* Pupil of his father *q.v.*; copied pictures by many artists sold to ease his father's financial difficulties; Master Antwerp Guild 1633; met the dealer Immerseel in Dover and contracted to paint on copper twelve religious subjects and an A. Brouwer pastiche to be sent to Seville 1636; married Anna, daughter of Jan (Velvet) Brueghel and a ward of P. P. Rubens (the contract signed in house of H. van Balen's widow was witnessed by Rubens, Jan Brueghel the younger and others) 1637; his first son David baptised, with D. Teniers the elder and Helena Fourment (Rubens' second wife) as godparents 1638; rented country house the Dry Toren (three towers) Château at Perck (near Rubens' Château de Steen); Dean in Antwerp Guild 1644; court painter to Archduke Leopold Wilhelm (*cf.* J. B. van Heil also J. van der Hoecke and E. Quellinus) 1647; went London (*cf.* C. de Neve and F. Wouters) to buy Italian pictures for the Conde de Fuensaldaña; moved to Brussels where curator of the Archduke's picture gallery (*cf.* J. A. van der Baren) 1651;

made small copies of Italian pictures in the Archduke's gallery used by engravers for the 'Theatrum Pictorium' known as 'the Teniers Gallery' showing 244 of the Italian pictures (published 1660); given a gold chain and a medal with her portrait by Christina of Sweden (on her way to Rome after her abdication) 1654; applied to Philip IV for title of nobility and received reply that any selling of pictures (his own or other people's) must be renounced as a condition 1655; on departure of Archduke Leopold Wilhelm to Vienna reappointed court painter by Don John of Austria (cf. H. Janssens, E. Quellinus, P. Snayers) 1656; married as second wife the richly dowered Isabella de Fren, daughter of a Secretary to Council of Brabant 1656; visited by Prince Charles of England in exile 1658; at baptism of his third child, by his second wife, the Marquis of Fromista and Caraçena (successor to Don John as governor-general) stood godfather; bought the Dry Toren Château 1662; active in obtaining patronage of Philip IV for founding of Antwerp Academy (cf. J. Jordaens, T. Boeyermans, A. Genoels, H. v. Minderhout) 1660-65; his continuous dealing in pictures and the announcement of an auction in his house caused protests by Brussels Guild and legal actions against him 1660-83; involved in later years in legal disputes with the children of his first wife, one of whom Cornelia married J. E. Quellinus. His pupils included F. Duchatel. His assistants and copyists included his brothers Abraham and Juliaen T. q.v. His pictures were much imitated by Dutch and other foreigners as well as by Flemish genre painters. Sir Joshua Reynolds wrote: 'His works are worthy the closest attention of a painter who desires to excel in the mechanical knowledge of his art. His manner of touching, or what we call handling, has perhaps never been equalled; there is in his pictures that exact mixture of softness and sharpness which is difficult to execute.' Voltaire wrote: 'Louis XIV traitait les fables de la Fontaine comme les tableaux de Teniers dont il ne voulait voir aucun dans ses appartements; il n'aimait pas le petit, en aucun genre . . .' and records that Louis XIV said of some examples shown to him 'Ôtez ces magots de mes yeux'. **Signed Examples:** include AMSTERDAM *Guard room* 1641, *Dice players*, *Temptation of S. Anthony* and others. ANTWERP *Peasants drinking before an inn*, *Temptation of S. Anthony*, *Old woman cutting tobacco*, *Hunstmen before an inn*, *Duet*, *The singer*, *Landscape with figure and six dogs* 1670. BERLIN K.F. *The dinner party* 1634, *Tric-trac players* 1641, *Temptation of S. Anthony* 1647 and others. BOSTON U.S.A. *The flayed ox*. BRUNSWICK *At the barber's* (*monkey piece*). BRUSSELS *Temptation of S. Anthony*, *The five senses*, *The village doctor*, *Archduke Leopold Wilhelm in his picture gallery at Brussels* 1651, *Lady and gentleman at a village fête* 1652. BUDAPEST *Village barber*, *Tric-trac players*. CAMBRIDGE Fitz. *Old woman peeling apples* (cf. Juliaen T.). CARLSRUHE *Peasants in a barn* 1634, *Consulting the doctor* 1640. CASSEL *Ecce Homo* 1646, *The entrance of the Archduchess Isabella into Brussels* and others. CHANTILLY *Louis II, Prince de Bourbon* (*Le Grand Condé*). CHICAGO *Guard room*. DRESDEN *Halbmond village fête* 1641, *Interior of an inn with self-portrait* 1646, *Dice players* 1646, *Peasants at a meal* 1648, *Landscape by moonlight*, *River landscape*, *Peasants smoking in an inn*, *The lesson in smoking*, *Bleaching linen*, *Liberation of S. Peter*, *Lady and gentleman visiting a village fête*, *Temptation of S. Anthony* and others. DUBLIN *Hustle Cap*. DULWICH *Brickmaking in a landscape*, *The chaff cutter*, *Sow and litter* and others. EDINBURGH *Peasants playing at skittles*. FRANKFORT *Milking* (*landscape with shepherd boy, peasant girl, sheep, goat and cow*), *Smokers' den* and others. GLASGOW *S. Jerome*, *A surgical case*, *Temptation of S. Anthony*, *Jealousy*, *Huntsmen and dogs*, *Peasants before a fire*. THE HAGUE *Kitchen scene with swan pâté* 1644, *The alchemist*. HARTFORD (Wadsworth Ath.) *Exterior of a guard room* (*with armour and a drum*). LENINGRAD *Rocky landscape* 1640, *Guard room* 1642, *Fête of the Crossbowmen of S. Sebastian on Antwerp Grande Place* (260 figures) 1643,

Landscape 1644, *Kitchen interior* 1646, *Village fête* 1648, *Wedding feast* 1650, *Village fête* 1654, *Monkeys in a kitchen* and others. LONDON N.G. *The artist's Château at Perck with figures and greyhound*, *Village fête with cauldrons* (*Fête aux chaudrons*) 1643, *Dives in Hell*, *Jealousy* (*La surprise fâcheuse*), *Music Party*, *Money changers*, *Tric-trac players* and others; Royal Collection *Villagers dancing outside a manor house* 1645, *Village merrymaking* 1649, *Rustics playing cards in a tavern*, *Peasants smoking and drinking before an inn*, *Drummer beating a call* (*Le Tambour battant*) and others; Wallace *Boors carousing* 1644. MADRID Prado *Wedding feast* 1637, *Archduke Leopold Wilhelm in his picture gallery at Brussels with the Conde de Fuensaldaña, the artist and others*, *Archduke Leopold Wilhelm at a village fête* 1647 and others. MINNEAPOLIS *The Prodigal Son*. MONTPELLIER *The Château*. MUNICH *Interior of an inn* 1643, *Dancers at an inn with portrait of the artist* 1645, *Archduke Leopold Wilhelm in his picture gallery in Brussels*, *The alchemist* 1680, *Witchcraft* and others. NEW YORK Met. *Peasant wedding*, *Merrymaking in a village*, *Temptation of S. Anthony*. PARIS Louvre *The smoker* 1643, *The Prodigal Son at table outside an inn* 1644, *Cabaret interior* 1645, *The denial of S. Peter* 1646, *Lady and gentleman at a village fête* 1652, *Archduke Leopold Wilhelm at a heron hunt*. PHILADELPHIA (Johnson) *The alchemist* 1649, *Soldiers departing*, *Violinst in a tavern*. STOCKHOLM *Tavern scene* 1661. SCHWERIN *Daniel in the lions' den* 1649. VIENNA K. *The goat herd*, *Peasant wedding* 1646, *Soldiers plundering a village* 1648, *Shooting at the Popinjay in Brussels 1651* 1652, *Sacrifice of Isaac* 1653, *The Archduke Leopold Wilhelm in his picture gallery in Brussels with the dwarfish court chaplain, Canon J. A. van der Baren and others*, *Peasants dancing* and others (all in Archduke Leopold's inventory 1659). **Monogrammed Examples** include BERLIN K.F. *The artist playing the violoncello with his family on the terrace at Perck*. DOUAI *Witches*. PARIS Louvre *Hockey players* 1661. (Cf. also L. van Uden and N. van Verendael.)

More than 2,000 pictures are catalogued under his name in public and major private collections. Many were acquired in his lifetime by Philip IV and scores alleged to be his work were imported for the Spanish tapestry factories (cf. D. Teniers III) in the XVIIIth century, especially by A. Calleja. Some pictures signed with name or monogram may be wholly or in part the work of his father.

[Fl. 86, Fl. 425, Fl. 22, Fl. 215, Fl. 770, Fl. 824, Fl. 825, Fl. 107, Fl. 865, Fl. 727, Fl. 892, Fl. 646, Fl. 95 (1915), Fl. 440, Fl. 88, Fl. 214, Fl. 544.]

Teniers, David III. Flemish Sch. *b* son of David T. the younger, Antwerp 1638 *d* Brussels 1685. *Religious subjects, designs for tapestry, portraits.* Went Spain (cf. A. Smit) 1661; in Brussels by 1666; in Termonde 1671; Brussels Master 1675; worked for Brussels tapestry factories. **Signed Examples:** BOORTMEERBEEK (near Malines) Church *Temptation of S. Anthony* (David Teniers Junior fecit 1666). PERCK Church *S. Dominic adoring the Virgin and Child* (David Teniers Junior fecit). Tapestries with mythologies signed D. Teniers Jun. Pinxit, dated 1680 and 1683, are recorded. Cf. A. Baudewyns. [Fl. 824, Fl. 892.]

Teniers, Juliaen the elder. Flemish Sch. *b* son of a linen draper, Antwerp 1572 *d* Antwerp (?) 1615. *Religious and mythological subjects, flowerpieces.* Master Antwerp Guild 1594. His brother D. T. the elder and G. v. d. Hoecke were his pupils. Antwerp inventories of 1623 record a *Balthasar*, the figures in a *Woman of Samaria* by J. de. Momper, and figures by him and N. van Cleve q.v. in a *Tower of Babel* (cf. M. van Valkenborch) by J. de Momper.

[Fl. 107, Fl. 213, Fl. 214.]

*Teniers, Juliaen the younger. Flemish Sch. *b* son of David T. the elder, Antwerp 1616 *d* Antwerp 1679. *Peasant genre.*

Master Antwerp Guild 1636. **Signed Example:** COPEN-HAGEN *Old woman peeling apples* (*cf.* D. T. the younger).
[Fl. 892.]

Terlinden, Félix. Flemish Sch. *b* Lodelinsart 1836 *d* Brussels 1912. *Genre, portraits, landscapes.* Represented in BRUS-SELS *The Captives* 1893. [Fl. Bib. 19th cent.]

Tetar van Elven, Jean Baptiste. Flemish Sch. *b* Amsterdam 1805 *d* Amsterdam after 1879. Brother of engraver Paul Constantin T. van E. (*b* Antwerp 1823). *Genre, portraits, interiors, landscapes; but worked chiefly as engraver and lithographer.* Pupil in Antwerp of W. Herreyns and M. van Brée; and for engraving of J. Meulemeester; also worked Brussels. Visited Portugal and Egypt. Represented in BRUSSELS *Church interior.* THE HAGUE *Self-portrait.*
[Fl. 451, Fl. 481, Fl. 892.]

Tetar van Elven, Pierre Henri T. Flemish Sch. *b* son of J. B. T. van E., Amsterdam or Antwerp 1831 *d* Milan 1908. *Landscapes, architectural pieces and contemporary history.* Pupil in Hague Acad. Went Turin where became court painter to Victor Emmanuel II and fought against the Austrians; later worked in Venice, Naples and Paris where exhibited in Salon; visited Spain and N. Africa; exhibited London R.A. 1865. Represented in ALGIERS *Venice: St. Mark's Square.* AMSTERDAM *Peter the Great's house in Zaandam* 1851. BERNAY, FLORENCE, MILAN (Mus. Risorgimento), NICE, ROUEN, TURIN *The First Italian Parliament.*
[Fl. 481, Fl. 66, Fl. 361, Fl. 798.]

Teunissen, C., see **Anthonisz.**

Thevenet, Louis. Flemish Sch. *b* Bruges 1874 *d* of apoplexy, Halle 1930. *Interiors, genre, still life, marines.* Self-taught painter who began life as a sailor; lived quietly in Nieuport, Halle and Brussels suburbs without connection with official art circles; little known till after his death. Represented in ANTWERP *Interior, Silver wedding.* Other titles recorded include *The Invitation* (*La lettre de faire part*), *The Man with the map, Kitchen with cat, The hat and coat stand, Chest of drawers with top hat.* [Fl. 388, Fl. 568, Fl. 296.]

Thevenet, Pierre. Flemish Sch. *b* Bruges 1870 *d* Brussels 1937. Brother of Louis T. *Landscapes, town pieces, still life.* Studied Paris and settled there. Represented in ANTWERP *Montmartre.* [Fl. 17.]

Thielen, Anna Maria van. Flemish Sch. *b* daughter of J. P. van T. *q.v.*, Antwerp 1641 *d* place and date unknown. *Flowers and garlands round grisaille pictures.* [Fl. 88.]

Thielen, Frances Catharina van. Flemish Sch. *b* daughter of J. P. van T. *q.v.*, 1645 (or 1647) *d* place and date unknown. *Flowers.* [Fl. 88.]

*****Thielen (Thielen-Rigouldts** or **Thielen van Couwenberg), Jan Philip van.** Flemish Sch. *b* son of a Lord of Couwenberg (mother's name Rigouldts), Malines 1618 *d* Boisschot 1667. *Flower pieces and garlands* (*cf.* M. T. van T. and A. M. van T. and D. Seghers). Went Antwerp 1632 where pupil of his brother-in-law T. Rombouts and of D. Seghers; Master in Antwerp Guild 1642; an assessor of the art collection of N. van Eyck 1656; Master in Malines Guild 1660; added garlands round grisaille panels by his brother-in-law Erasmus Quellinus and other artists; his pictures were much admired by the Spanish court; V. Wolfvoet *q.v.* owned examples. **Signed Examples:** AMSTERDAM Rijks. *Flower garland round a bust of Flora* 1665. ANTWERP (1667), BRUS-SELS (1650), HERMANNSTADT (1661), MADRID Prado (1651), MILAN (1648), OXFORD *Flowers and a watch.* VIENNA K. *Flowers round a statue of the Virgin*

(1648), and Liecht. (1657). Descamps saw (1768) in the church of S. Bernard Abbey (nr. Antwerp) two *Flower garlands* with *S. Bernard* and *S. Agatha* in the centres.
[Fl. 86, Fl. 425, Fl. 216, Fl. 892, Fl. 88, Fl. 213.]

Thielen, Maria Theresa van. Flemish Sch. *b* daughter of J. P. van T. *q.v.*, Antwerp 1640 *d* 1706. *Flowers.* Pupil of her father. **Signed Example:** MALINES Town Hall *Garland of flowers round a bas relief* 1664. [Fl. 892, Fl. 88.]

Thielens, Jan. Flemish Sch. Worked Antwerp 1694. *Interiors of studios, alchemist's kitchens and other genre scenes* (*cf.* G. Thomas). [Fl. 612.]

Thiry, Léonard. Flemish Sch. *b* Deventer before 1520 *d* Antwerp after 1550. *Allegorical and mythological compositions, drawings for engravers.* Went Fontainebleau (*cf.* J. van Cleve, G. van Cleve, H. Francken the elder, L. de Heere, J. de Hoey, A. v. d. Houve, C. Ketel, H. de Maier, J. Ramey, D. van Utrecht, A. J. Verburcht, also A. Dubois); worked there under the Italians Rosso and Primaticcio.
[Fl. 818, Fl. 892, Fl. 227.]

Thomas, Alexandre Joseph. Flemish Sch. *b* Malmédy 1810 *d* Brussels 1898. *Religious subjects.* Pupil of Düsseldorf Acad. and of M. van Brée in Antwerp. Represented in BRUSSELS *Judas on the night of the Crucifixion, Barabbas at the foot of Calvary* 1857. Others recorded in Malmédy, Dunkirk and Ypres. [Fl. 88, Fl. 798, Fl. 73, Fl. 296.]

*****Thomas, Gérard.** Flemish Sch. *b* son of painter Pieter T., Antwerp 1663 *d* Antwerp 1720. *Studio interiors, alchemist's kitchens and other genre* (*cf.* H. Goovaerts and D. Ryckaert III, J. Thielens, F. X. H. Verbeeck). Pupil in Antwerp of G. Maes 1680; Master Antwerp Guild 1688; B. van den Bossche *q.v.* was among his pupils before 1697. **Signed Examples:** ANTWERP *Painter's studio.* VIENNA Liecht. *An alchemist* (initial in signature uncertain).
[Fl. 440, Fl. 88, Fl. 296.]

Thomas, Henri J. Flemish Sch. *b* Molenbeek-saint-Jean 1878. *Genre, portraits, flowers; also worked as sculptor and engraver and illustrator.* Represented in BARCELONA *Venus.* BRUGES *The reserved table* 1914. LIÈGE *Dancer*; and PARIS State Collection. [Fl. 178, Fl. 465, Fl. 114, Fl. 73.]

Thomas, Jan (or **Joannes**) called 'van Ypern'. Flemish Sch. *b* Ypres 1617 *d* Vienna 1678. '*History*', *religious subjects, genre and portraits; also worked as engraver and became famous as one of the first mezzotinters.* Pupil of Rubens; visited Italy with A. van Diepenbeeck; back in Antwerp where Master in Guild 1640; went Mainz where became court painter to Prince Bishop (*cf.* J. B. de Ruel) *c.* 1654; then Vienna where court painter to Leopold I (*cf.* J. E. Quellinus, F. Luyckx, J. and W. Vaillant, J. A. v. d. Baren); accompanied Leopold to Frankfort for coronation ceremonies 1658. **Signed Examples:** ENNS Schloss Fürstenberg *Triumph of Silenus* 1677, *Perseus and Andromeda.* HERMANN-STADT *Alexander the Great and Diogenes* 1672. OLMÜTZ Gall. *Three children with a lamb* 1672. PRAGUE Nostitz *A family of satyrs* 1665; Strahow Monastery *Christ on the Cross with the Virgin, S. John and S. Mary Magdalene* 1663, *A satyr, woman and child under a tree* 1665. VIENNA K. *A bacchanal* 1656, *Emperor Leopold I receiving the homage of his provinces* (symbolized by female figures) 1663; Hofburg *Archduke Leopold Wilhelm with red sash* (*cf.* J. v. d. Hoecke, J. v. Egmont, P. Thys, D. Teniers the younger) 1658; Harrach *Old man with young woman trying to rob his pocket* 1661 and companion piece *Old woman with young man* 1661. YPRES Mus. *Virgin and Child with penitent sinners*; S. Martin *Francisco de Mannez before the Virgin* 1645, *A Saint inter-*

ceding with the Virgin for souls in purgatory was seen 1768 by Descamps in Antwerp Carmelites Church.
[Fl. 86, Fl. 753, Fl. 425, Fl. 878, Fl. 216, Fl. 612, Fl. 107, Fl. 435, Fl. 892, Fl. 88.]

Thonet, Victor. Flemish Sch. *b* Antwerp 1885. *Landscapes.* Pupil of F. Hens. Teacher in Antwerp Acad. Represented in ANTWERP *Old garden* and others. [Fl. 17.]

*Thulden (or **Tulden**), **Theodor van.** Flemish Sch. *b* Bois-le-Duc (Hertogenbosch) 1606 *d* there 1669. *Religious subjects, 'history', peasant genre (fairs, weddings); also worked as engraver.* Pupil in Antwerp of A. Blyenberch and Rubens; Master Antwerp Guild 1626; worked Paris and Fontainebleau from *c.* 1631 (*cf.* P. Franchoys and P. Mol); returned Antwerp and collaborated, under Rubens, on decorations for Pageant Entry of Cardinal Infante Ferdinand as Governor-General (*cf.* G. Weri) 1635; married godchild of Rubens, daughter of H. van Balen the elder; assisted Rubens (in Antwerp) in pictures for Philip IV's hunting lodge Torre de la Parada (*cf.* J. P. Gowi) 1636-8; worked in the Huis ten Bosch (House in the Wood) at The Hague (with G. Coques, J. Jordaens and the Dutchmen G. Honthorst, P. F. de Grebber, C. van Everdingen, S. de Bray, J. Lievens and P. Soutman) 1649-51; later worked for Malines and Bruges churches. **Signed Examples:** BRUSSELS *Love and Music* 1652, *Young lord renouncing the world.* LENINGRAD *Time and Truth.* PARIS Louvre *Christ appearing to his Mother* (from Bruges Jesuit Church). VIENNA K. *The Netherland provinces worshipping the Virgin* 1654, *Allegory of Return of Peace* 1655 **Documented Examples:** ANGERS, GRENOBLE and LE MANS *Pictures painted for Trinitarian Church Paris* 1647. THE HAGUE Huis ten Bosch (Orange Saloon) *Allegories of the life of Prince Frederick Henry* (including *Charles I of England as Marcus Curtius, Prince Maurice and Prince Frederick Henry at the battle of Nieuport 1600, The Conquest of Brazil by Count John Maurice of Nassau, The Liberation of the Netherlands*). MADRID Prado *Orpheus, Discovery of the Purple* (painted for Torre de la Parada 1636-8). VIENNA Acad. *Allegory of the Union of the Netherlands.* BRUSSELS Mus. Cinquantenaire *Cartoons for glass paintings* for Brussels S. Gudule. As engraver T. copied the now no longer extant pictures at Fontainebleau (Ulysses Gall.) by the Italian painters Primaticcio and N. del Abbate (*cf.* L. Thiry and A. Dubois) and recorded the arches erected for Infante Ferdinand. A *Christ on the Cross* was owned by Erasmus Quellinus *q.v.*
[Fl. 86, Fl. 425, Fl. 892, Fl. 204, Fl. 88, Fl. 213, Fl. 296.]

Thys, A., see **Tyssens.**

Thys (or **Thyssens**), **Father.** Flemish Sch. Presumed 18th cent. A Dominican painter of *religious subjects.* **Documented Example:** ANTWERP Mus. *Descent from the Cross* (from Église des Sœurs Noires). [Fl. 16.]

Thys, Gysbrecht. Flemish Sch. *b* Antwerp *c.* 1616 *d* in poverty, Antwerp 1684. *Landscapes, figure pieces and portraits.* Master Antwerp Guild 1637; member of Antwerp Chamber of Rhetoric (Violiere) 1639. Houbraken (1719) states that his portraits were often taken for the work of van Dyck. An Antwerp inventory 1678 records a *Europa*, and pictures exported by the Forchoudt firm of Antwerp dealers included a *Pyramus and Thisbe* and a *Sleeping woman.*
[Fl. 86, Fl. 425, Fl. 215, Fl. 892, Fl. 88, Fl. 212, Fl. 213.]

Thys, Jean François. Flemish Sch. *b* son of P. J. T., Brussels 1780 or 1783 *d* Brussels 1865. *Decorative painting, 'history', costume history, genre, portraits.* Pupil of his father, of J. Cardon and of Brussels Acad.; visited Paris and Italy. A *Battle of Waterloo* and a *D. Seghers painting a garland round*

a picture of the Virgin and presented with a golden palette sent him by the Prince of Orange (*cf.* P. Kremer) 1821 are recorded.
[Fl. 451, Fl. 481, Fl. 612, Fl. 892, Fl. 88.]

*Thys (or **Thijs** or **Tyssens**), **Peter.** Flemish Sch. *b* Antwerp 1624 *d* Antwerp 1677. *Religious subjects, 'history', portraits.* Master Antwerp Guild 1645; member of the Olyftak artists' confraternity; patronized by Archduke Leopold Wilhelm (*cf.* J. B. v. Heil); went Holland to paint Stadholder William II of Orange and other portraits *c.* 1649; commissioned by Antwerp authorities to paint Charles II of Spain (*cf.* F. Duchatel and J. v. Werden) for Town Hall 1672. **Signed Examples:** ANTWERP *Apparition of the Virgin to S. William Duke of Aquitaine.* GHENT *S. Sebastian and the angels, Temptation of S. Anthony.* WÖRLITZ Castle *Mercury and Herse* 1664. **Documented Examples:** TERMONDE Church *The Virgin, SS. Roch and Anna with the plague-stricken* (declared by himself to have been painted for this church 1661), *The martyrdom of S. Catherine* (commissioned 1665). MUNICH A.P. *The painter David Teniers the younger* (engraved). VIENNA K. *Archduke Leopold Wilhelm, governor-general Spanish Netherlands (1647-55)* (*cf.* J. Thomas). Tapestry cartoons: *The Months of November and December, Allegory of Day, Allegory of Night* (*cf.* J. v. d. Hoecke) all in Archduke L.W. inventory 1659. Descamps (1768) saw pictures in Alost (S. Martin) Antwerp (S. Jacques) and Malines (Leliendael Church) and other Belgian churches. A *Venus and satyr* was exported to Vienna in 1674; a *Man in a helmet* and an *Ecce Homo* were in the Alexander Voet collection in Antwerp 1689.
[Fl. 86, Fl. 216, Fl. 612, Fl. 892, Fl. 88, Fl. 212, Fl. 213.]

Thys, Peter Pauwel. Flemish Sch. *b* son of Peter T., Antwerp 1652 *d* Antwerp 1679. Undertook 1677 to complete his father's *Group portrait of Antwerp 'Kolveniers' Guild.*
[Fl. 107, Fl. 892, Fl. 88.]

Thys, Pierre Joseph. Flemish Sch. *b* Lierre 1749 *d* Brussels 1825. *Flowers* (*cf.* J. B. de Crépu, P. Casteels, J. F. Eliaerts, P. Faes); *also worked as restorer* (*cf.* P. J. Regemorter). Pupil Antwerp Acad.; went Paris with the Dutch flower painter G. van Spaendonck. In Brussels from *c.* 1780; visited Rotterdam 1797. His decorative paintings in Château Laeken Orangerie disappeared during the French invasion 1792.
[Fl. 275, Fl. 612, Fl. 88, Fl. 570.]

*Tiburtine Sibyl Master (sometimes called Frankfort Sibyl Master). Presumed Flemish Sch. late 15th cent. Name for painter of FRANKFORT Staedel. (97) *The Virgin appearing to the Tiburtine Sibyl and the Emperor Augustus.* (*Cf.* Philadelphia *Marriage of the Virgin Painter*). [Fl. 316.]

*Tiel (or **Tilens**), **Justus.** Flemish Sch. 16th cent. *'History', portraits, landscapes.* **Signed Example:** MADRID Prado *Allegory of the Education of Philip III* (the gauntlets worn by the Prince are now in New York Met.). Portraits of Popes Urban VII and Clement VIII were recorded in the Escorial 1593. A landscape is recorded among Philip II's pictures (*cf.* O. van Veen). [Fl. 95 (1914), Fl. 555.]

Tieleman, Melchior Gommar (also called **Maerten Frans**). Flemish Sch. *b* Lierre 1784 *d* Lierre 1864. *Religious subjects, portraits.* Pupil in Antwerp Acad. of W. J. Herreyns and in Paris of L. David (*cf.* F. J. Navez). Visited England; in Hanover as court painter to Duke of Cambridge after 1816; Director Lierre Acad. 1829-64. Represented in LIERRE Cathedral *The Pilgrims to Emmaus*; Town Hall *Napoleon as First Consul* (*cf.* F. J. Kinson and L. Gerbo).
[Fl. 451, Fl. 892, Fl. 88, Fl. 798.]

Tierendorf, Jeremias van. Flemish Sch. *b* before 1600. *Religious subjects.* Worked Ypres and neighbourhood.

Descamps (1768) saw in Loo parish church an *Adoration of the Shepherds* dated 1621, and other pictures in Ypres not traceable since the German invasion 1914-18.   [Fl. 216.]

Tilborgh, Gillis van the elder. Flemish Sch. *b* Antwerp 1578 *d c.* 1632. *Peasant genre.* Lille Mus. has *Village Fête* dated 159 . . and signed with a monogram presumed by some to be his work.   [Fl. 215, Fl. 892.]

★Tilborgh (or **Tilborch**), **Gillis** (or **Egidius**) **van.** Flemish Sch. *b* son of G. van T. the elder (?), Brussels (?) *c.* 1625 *d* Brussels *c.* 1678 (?). *Portrait groups, interiors, conversation pieces* (*cf.* P. Meert), *peasant genre* (*cf.* D. Teniers the younger, D. Ryckaert III), *occasional religious subjects.* Traditionally pupil of D. Teniers the y. at the same time as F. Duchatel; Master Antwerp Guild 1654. **Signed Examples:** ANTWERP *Adoration of the shepherds.* BOSTON *Peasants outside an inn.* BRUSSELS *Family group, The five senses* (series) 1658. COPENHAGEN *Artist painting in a picture gallery* (*cf.* W. v. Haecht), *Cobbler's family at a meal.* DARMSTADT *Man robbed by a boy while offered drink by a woman.* DRESDEN *Flemish peasant wedding feast.* THE HAGUE *Family group.* HAMBURG *Inn with peasants* 1657. LENINGRAD *Interior with peasant smoking, woman and man in background* 1658. MUNICH A.P. *Peasant reading letter to a woman.* PHILADELPHIA Wilstach *Guard room.* PRAGUE Rudolfinum *Interior of inn with peasants* 1660. ROME Borghese *Conversation piece.* SCHLEISSHEIM *Inn with peasants.* VIENNA K. *Peasant company with cardplayers and children*; Liecht. *Guard room* 1669; Czernin *Old woman with hand basket.* A *Peasants fighting* was sold to Prince von Liechtenstein by the Forchoudt firm of Antwerp dealers in 1671.
          [Fl. 86, Fl. 425, Fl. 215, Fl. 612, Fl. 892, Fl. 88, Fl. 212.]

Tilens, see Tiel.

★Tilens (or **Tielens**), **Jan** (or **Hans**). Flemish Sch. *b* Antwerp 1589 *d* Antwerp 1630. *Landscapes* (*cf.* A. Mirou). Master Antwerp Guild 1612. The figures in his landscapes are presumed by some by other hands. **Signed Examples:** BERLIN K.F. *Valley landscape with figures.* CASSEL *Landscape with Diana and Actaeon.* VIENNA K. *Landscape near Tivoli.*
          [Fl. 86, Fl. 892, Fl. 88.]

Tillemans, P. J. Flemish Sch. 19th cent. *Hunting scenes and peasant genre in Dutch tradition.* Worked in Antwerp. Represented in ROSTOCK *Return from hunting s* 1845.
          [Fl. 612.]

★Tillemans (not **Tilmans**), **Peter.** Flemish Sch. *b* son of a diamond cutter, Antwerp *c.* 1684 *d* Norton, Suffolk 1734. *Military pieces* (*cf.* C. Francken, A. v. d. Meulen, C. Breydel), *landscapes, views of mansions with figures and animals, portraits in oil and w.* Came London (*cf.* J. v. Aken, P. V. Angellis, P. A. Breydel, T. de Bruyn, S. Dubois, J. B. Nollekens, P. A. Rysbraeck, P. J. Tassaert) with his brother-in-law Peter Casteels (III) *q.v.* at invitation of a dealer who employed him to copy battlepieces by the French painter Jacques Courtois and Flemish genre pictures 1708; foundation member of Kneller's Acad. 1711; drew views for Bridges' 'History of Northamptonshire' published 1719; patronized by the Dukes of Devonshire and Kingston, Lord Derby and the fourth Lord Byron (who took drawing lessons from him); with the French painter J. Goupy painted scenery for Haymarket opera house; a member of the Virtuosi of S. Luke (Van Dyck's Club) and its steward 1725; had studio at Richmond and frequented Lord Radnor's house at Twickenham where the poet Alexander Pope, in his absence, made alterations to one of his pictures then in progress; employed by Dr. Cox Macro, chaplain to King George II, to decorate the staircase at Little Haugh, Norton, near Bury S. Edmunds and to draw in London (1730) the handless and footless

dwarf Buchinger (who himself drew, danced and played the hautboy); had (possibly) the English painter Arthur Devis as a pupil, and befriended J. F. (Old) Nollekens *q.v.* when he came to England. **Signed Examples:** BRUSSELS *Attack on a convoy.* CAMBRIDGE Fitz. *View of the walls of a town and a castle, with figures* 1709. Recorded paintings include *Little Haugh, Norton, with Dr. Macro and his family, Richmond Hill with Lord Radnor and other local residents* and *Thoresby Hall with the Duke of Kingston and shooting party* (signed and dated 1725 and engraved).
          [Fl. 826, Fl. 856, Fl. 223, Fl. 880, Fl. 88, Fl. 744.]

Timmermans, Jean. Flemish Sch. *b* Brussels 1899. *Urban and rural landscapes* (*many in w.*), *genre* (*many of peasants and fisher folk*). Some works record travels in Holland and Southern France. Represented in ANTWERP *Children playing in a park, Street in Marseilles.*   [Fl. 568, Fl. 17.]

Titz, Louis. Flemish Sch. *b* Bruges 1859. *Decorative paintings, theatre designs, genre, urban landscapes* (*mainly in w.*); *also illustrations and engravings.* Teacher in Brussels Acad. Represented in ANTWERP *Quay at Bruges* 1911. BRUSSELS *Bagpipe player* 1881, *The painter* 1883.
          [Fl. Bib. 19th cent., Fl. 17.]

Toeput, Lodewyck (called in Italy Pozzoserrato, and Pozzo da Treviso). Flemish Sch. *b* Antwerp or Malines *c.* 1550 *d* Treviso after 1604. *Landscapes* (*cf.* F. Mostaert and A. Mirou) *some with small figures, gardens and Venetian pieces, religious subjects, also social genre and portraits.* Went Italy with the Dutch painter of still life and kitchen pieces D. de Vries and worked in Venice (*cf.* K. Foort, Lamberto (Tedesco), P. Mera, P. Stevens, P. Vlerick, M. de Vos, D. Barendsz and P. Franck (Fiammingo)) 1577; visited Rome and Florence and established himself at Treviso. Van Mander (1604) described him as good at landscape and composition and a poet; Ridolfi (1648) praises the effects of distance and of changing light and weather in his landscapes. J. de Momper *q.v.* was possibly his pupil. **Monogrammed Examples:** MILAN Brera *Mountain landscape.* HANOVER *Mountain landscape with fall of Phaeton* (1599). A *Tower of Babel* (*cf.* M. van Valkenborch) monogrammed 1584 is recorded (1939) in a private collection. **Monogrammed Drawings** in VIENNA Albertina. Some drawings engraved in Civitates Orbis Terrarum published by F. Hogenberg *q.v.* are recorded. Ridolfi records a *Fire in the Doge's Palace* 1577 (*cf.* J. Hoefnagel), a *State Barge on the Venetian Canal* and a *Fireworks in Florence* Portraits of *Tintoretto* and *Giovanni da Bologna*, a *Masked Ball on a Terrace* and a *View of S. Mark's, Venice* are recorded by engravings. Some paintings in Italian churches and museums are presumed by some his work.
[Fl. 559, Fl. 709, Fl. 505, Fl. 612, Fl. 892, Fl. 644, Fl. 305, Fl. 88, Fl. 691.]

★Toledo Marriage of Henry VI Painter. Presumed Flemish Sch. late 15th cent. Name for painter of TOLEDO (Ohio) *Marriage of Henry VI with Margaret of Anjou* (formerly owned by Horace Walpole).   [Fl. 856, Fl. 802.]

Tons, Hans (Jan). Flemish Sch. *b* son of Willem T., *c.* 1467 *d* after 1533. *Landscapes in distemper and designs for tapestry.* Visited Italy (date unknown); friend and assistant of B. van Orley *q.v.* in designs for *Belles Chasses de Maximilian* tapestries (now Paris Louvre); with B. van Orley and others accused by Inquisition of listening to Protestant sermons and fined (*cf.* B. van Orley and A. van Overbeke) 1527; worked for Brussels S. Pierre Hospital 1529; again arrested for heresy by order of Mary of Hungary, Regent of the Netherlands, but soon released 1533.   [Fl. 559, Fl. 287, Fl. 179, Fl. 88.]

Tons, Hubert. Flemish Sch. *b* son of Willem T., before 1580 *d* of plague Rotterdam 1620. *Religious subjects, landscapes* *with animals and small figures.* In Antwerp Guild 1596; worked for Rotterdam churches from 1604.

[Fl. 892, Fl. 88.]

Tons, Willem (Guillaume) the elder. Flemish Sch. 16th cent. Van Mander (1604) records: 'Not so long ago there lived in Brussels an old and good master called Willem Tons. He was excellent at making watercolours and at designing tapestry cartoons containing all kinds of trees, bushes, animals, birds, eagles and similar subjects, which he did from life well and pleasingly.' Rubens owned a watercolour by him or his son of the same name. [Fl. 559, Fl. 213.]

Tons, Willem (Guillaume) the younger. Flemish Sch. 16th-17th cent. Van Mander (1604) records: 'Guillaume Tons, son of Willem Tons, painted very well in oil—small pictures of figures in brothels and kindred subjects. He went to Italy, where now he is supposed to be.' [Fl. 559.]

Toussaint, Pierre Joseph. Flemish Sch. *b* Brussels 1822 *d* Brussels 1888. *Genre.* Represented in AMSTERDAM *The young artist.* [Fl. 7.]

Trachez (or Trachy), Jacques André Joseph (or Jacob Andries). Flemish Sch. *b* Antwerp 1746 *d* Antwerp 1820. *Landscapes and town views (mainly in w.); also worked as engraver.* Pupil of H. J. Antonissen *q.v.*; worked for some years in Ghent; Master in Antwerp Guild 1771; had to abandon painting owing to eye trouble. A *Winter landscape in Holland s* 1780 is recorded. [Fl. 451, Fl. 88.]

Trajectensis, see **Claessens.**

Troyer, Prosper de. Flemish Sch. *b* 1880. *Religious, allegorica and satirical subjects, landscapes, genre, portraits, still life.* Living at Malines 1942. [Fl. 568.]

Tschaggeny, Charles Philogène. Flemish Sch. *b* Brussels 1815. *d* St. Josse-ten-Noode 1894. *Animals (chiefly horses) and genre.* Pupil of E. Verboeckhoven. N. de Keyser and H. Leys 1839-40. In London 1848-9; painted animals in pictures by T. Fourmois, J. B. Madou and others (*cf.* E. Verboeckhoven). Represented in ANTWERP *Horsemen by an inn* (with J. B. Madou), BRUGES, BRUSSELS *Mail coach in the Ardennes.* COURTRAI, LONDON Tate Gall. *Incident in a battle.*

[Fl. 481, Fl. 612, Fl. Bib. 19th cent., Fl. 892, Fl. 264, Fl. 88.]

Tschaggeny, Edmond Jean Baptiste. Flemish Sch. *b* brother of Charles T., Brussels or Neuchatel 1818 *d* Brussels 1873. *Animals (mainly cattle and horses); also worked as engraver and illustrator of animal anatomy books.* Pupil of E. Verboeckhoven. Travelled in Algeria; exhibited London R.A. 1850. Represented in BRUSSELS *A bull.* LILLE, MELBOURNE *Sheep.* NEUCHATEL *Bull pursuing a woman and child.*

[Fl. 451, Fl. 612, Fl. 481, Fl. 837 (1873), Fl. 264, Fl. 88.]

Tschaggeny, Frédéric Pierre. Flemish Sch. *b* son of C. T., Brussels 1851 *d* Brussels 1921. *Portraits, genre.* Exhibited London R.A. Represented in ANTWERP *Portrait of Charles Tschaggeny.* NEUCHATEL *The sorceress.* [Fl. 88.]

Tubach (or Tuback), Paul (known as Paul l'Archer). Flemish Sch. *b* Malines (?) *c.* 1485 *d* after 1534. *Decorative paintings,*

ceremonial and glass designs. Master Malines Guild 1510; 'Archer de corps' to Margaret of Austria, governor of the Netherlands (*cf.* J. Schooff); worked on decorations in her palaces from 1512; carried out decorations in rooms occupied by the children of King Christian II of Denmark (*cf.* J. Gossaert) 1529; with J. van Battel *q.v.* designed catafalque of Margaret of Austria 1530. [F. 613, Fl. 892, Fl. 88.]

Turin Adoration Master. Presumed Flemish Sch. 15th-16th cent. Name for painter of TURIN Gall. (193) *Adoration of the Magi.* [Fl. 316.]

Tyn, Lambrecht den. Flemish Sch. *b* Antwerp 1770 *d* 1816. *Interiors by candlelight, landscapes by moonlight.* Pupil of P. van Regemorter *q.v.* [Fl. 275, Fl. 88.]

Tyssens, Augustyn. Flemish Sch. *b* Antwerp (?) before 1620 *d* Antwerp 1675. *Landscapes; also active as dealer.* In Antwerp Guild 1654; was an assessor of Anna de Schot's Antwerp collection 1663. A landscape by him is recorded in Anna Jordaens' Antwerp collection 1668. His own collection inventoried after his death included pictures by J. B. Tyssens *q.v.* [Fl. 892, Fl. 213.]

Tyssens (or Thys), Augustyn. Flemish Sch. *b* Antwerp 1662 *d* 1722. Director of Antwerp Acad. 1691. [Fl. 451, Fl. 892.]

Tyssens, Jan Baptiste. Flemish Sch. *b* Antwerp (?) before 1660 *d* date and place unknown. *Genre, still life with armour, 'history', religious subjects.* **Signed Examples:** HERMANN-STADT *The suicide of Varus, Venus in Vulcan's forge.* PRAGUE *Still life with armour.* The Antwerp collection of Augustyn Tyssens *q.v.* contained (1675) a *Prodigal Son* and a *Virgin.* [Fl. 213, Fl. 83.]

Tyssens, Peter, see **Thys.**

Tytgadt, Louis. Flemish Sch. *b* Lovendegem 1841 *d* Ghent 1918. *Religious subjects, genre.* Pupil in Ghent Acad. of T. Canneel and in Paris of A. Cabanel. Director Ghent Acad. 1892. Represented in GHENT *Martyrdom S. Sebastian, After Mass in the Ghent Béguinage* and others. LIÈGE *Ghent Béguinage.* [Fl. 338.]

Tytgat, Edgard. Flemish Sch. *b* son of lithographer, Brussels 1879 *d* Brussels 1957. *Interiors, landscapes, poetic fantasies, genre (including circus and fair pieces) in impressionist and later naif-expressionist conventions; book illustrations, woodcuts.* Worked first as draughtsman in father's lithographic studio in Bruges; then pupil of C. Montald in Brussels; friend of R. Wouters; in England during 1914-18 German invasion (*cf.* L. de Smet) and published in London albums with text and illustrations *Le petit chaperon rouge, Quelques images de la vie d'un artiste, Carrousels et baraques*; exhibited with Salon des IX (*cf.* H. Daeye); visited Portugal 1936; illustrated 'Triptych de Noël' by F. Timmermans 1936, 'Fables de La Fontaine' 1947 and other books. Represented in ANTWERP *The sketch, Child's portrait.* BRUSSELS *Sunday afternoon, Snow scene through a window* 1940, *The Temptation of Father Benedict* 1943. GRENOBLE *Eastern tales.*

[Fl. 586, Fl. 764 (1929), Fl. 587, Fl. 388, Fl. 598, Fl. 739, Fl. 296.]

U

Uden, Artus van. Flemish Sch. *b* son of a tapestry designer and manufacturer, Antwerp 1544 *d* after 1627. *Landscapes and decorative paintings.* Master Antwerp Guild 1587; official town painter; employed on Pageant Entry into Antwerp of Archduke Ernest (Governor-General Spanish Netherlands 1593-5) 1594. *Cf.* G. van Veen and G. Schoof. [Fl. 107.]

Uden, Jacob van. Flemish Sch. *b* son of Artus v. U. (?), Antwerp *c.* 1600 *d* after 1641. *Landscapes.* Supplied pictures in large quantities for export to the dealer C. van Immerseel in Seville 1627-30; some commissioned by Jan Brueghel the younger 1628; offered to supply fruit and flower pieces from his workshop 1629; in Antwerp Guild 1641. *Cf.* J. Boots and G. Francken. [Fl. 892, Fl. 214.]

*Uden, Lucas van. Flemish Sch. *b* son of Artus van U., Antwerp 1595 *d* Antwerp *c.* 1672. *Landscapes with figures by other artists* (*cf.* J. B. v. d. Meiren)*; also worked as engraver.* Employed by Rubens for landscape backgrounds from *c.* 1615 (*cf.* P. v. d. Hulst and J. Wildens); Master Antwerp Guild 1627; was accustomed (Houbraken (before 1718) records) to rise before dawn to study sunrise effects (*cf.* L. de Vadder also J. de Hollander). Many of his works were exported to Spain and Austria by the Forchoudt firm of dealers (*cf.* A. Casteels); P. A. Immenraet and J. B. Bonnecroy were his pupils. His daughter Maria v. U. also a painter, married C. E. Biset *q.v.* **Signed Examples:** BARNARD CASTLE *Rocky landscape with Ulysses and Nausicaa.* BUDAPEST *Wooded landscape.* DRESDEN. DUBLIN *Wooded landscape with peasants dancing* (figures by D. Teniers). FRANKFORT *Flat landscape with peasants returning from* (*or going to?*) *work.* MUNICH *Rocky coast landscape* 1635 and others. STUTTGART *Landscape with the Rest on the Flight* 1654 and another. VIENNA K. *Flat landscape with peasants.* **Monogrammed Examples:** ANTWERP *Landscape with sunset.* DRESDEN *The forest brook* 1656. LENINGRAD, VIENNA Liechtenstein. Pictures presumed by some his work are in various museums. (*Cf.* V. Wolfvoet.) [Fl. 86, Fl. 425, Fl. 22, Fl. 878, Fl. 215, Fl. 107, Fl. 892, Fl. 212, Fl. 88.]

*Ursula Legend Master. Presumed Flemish Sch. 15th cent. Name for painter of BRUGES Sœurs Noires Convent *Eight scenes from the life of S. Ursula* (*cf.* H. Memlinc). Pictures presumed by some his work are in various museums (*cf.* Philadelphia Adorant Painter). [Fl. 316.]

*Utrecht, Adriaen van. Flemish Sch. *b* Antwerp 1599 *d* Antwerp 1652 or 1653. *Poultry yards; but chiefly still life with game, birds, shellfish and fruit* (*cf.* A. Adriaenssen, T. Aenvanck, P. Boel, A. Brueghel, J. v. Es, F. Fyt, J. Gillemans, P. Gysels, C. Luyckx, C. Mahu, F. Snyders, I. Wigans, P. Willebeeck, A. Ysselsteyn), *some with figures by other artists.* Travelled France, Italy and Germany; Master in Antwerp Guild 1624; patronised by Philip IV of Spain (*cf.* A. Smit) and by Frederick Henry of Orange (*cf.* T. Willeboirts); his wife, a poetess, was daughter of W. van Nieulandt; his sister married S. de Vos; P. Gyselaer was his pupil. **Signed Examples:** AMSTERDAM Rijks. *Still life with food, musical instruments, monkey, parrot and dog* 1644. BRUNSWICK *Fruit piece, Fruit and vessels.* BRUSSELS *Still life with parrot* 1636, *Fruit garland* 1640, *Dead birds, game and fruit* 1648. CASSEL *Kitchen piece with figures* 1629. COPENHAGEN *Fruit with squirrel* 1647. DRESDEN *Still life with dog and cat* 1647. LENINGRAD *Fruit piece.* MADRID Prado *Larder* 1642, *Garland of fruits and flowers* 1638. MUNICH A.P. *Dead hares and birds with fruit and vegetables* 1648. OXFORD *Lobster, fruit and game* 1645. VIENNA K. *Fruit garland round still life with Italian wine bottle* 1644. **Monogrammed Examples:** BRUSSELS *Food stall with three figures* 1637. COPENHAGEN and GHENT. Pictures presumed by some his work are in various museums (*cf.* J. v. d. Hoecke and V. Wolfvoet). [Fl. 86, Fl. 753, Fl. 425, Fl. 215, Fl. 892, Fl. 88.]

Utrecht, Denys van. Flemish (Dutch) Sch. 16th cent. Went Fontainebleau where worked with other young artists from the Netherlands (*cf.* H. Francken the elder, C. Ketel also L. Thiry and A. Dubois) 1566. [Fl. 559.]

Utrecht, Jacob of. Flemish (Dutch) Sch. *b* Utrecht (?) before 1490. Recorded Antwerp Guild 1506; took pupils 1512. Presumed by some identical with Jacob Claessens (Trajectensis) *q.v.* [Fl. 714, Fl. 892.]

*Uytewael (or Wtewael), Joachim. Flemish (Dutch) Sch. *b* son of a glass painter, Utrecht 1566 *d* Utrecht 1638. *Religious and mythological subjects, kitchen genre, portraits; designs for glass windows;* also active in Utrecht as a flax merchant. Pupil of his father and of Joos de Beer *q.v.*; then went Italy *c.* 1587; travelled Italy and then France (*cf.* A. Dubois) with the Bishop of St. Malo (whom he had met in Padua) 1587-91; returned Utrecht where member Saddlers' Guild 1592; councillor in Utrecht and member of the newly founded Painters' Guild (*cf.* A. Willaerts) 1611. **Signed Examples:** AMSTERDAM Rijks. *David and Abigail* 1597, *The Annunciation to the Shepherds* (referred to by Van Mander 1604). BERLIN K.F. *Kitchen scene with parable of the great supper* 1605, *Lot and his daughters* (small version of large picture recorded by Van Mander). BRUNSWICK *Feast of the Gods* 1602 (referred to by Van Mander). COPENHAGEN *S. John preaching* 1618. DRESDEN *Apollo and the Muses on Parnassus* 1598 or 1599. GATESHEAD Shipley Art Gall. *Adam and Eve* (*s* 'inventor' 1614). THE HAGUE Mauritshuis *Mars and Venus surprised by Vulcan* (Van Mander records two pictures of this subject) and *portraits.* LENINGRAD *Christ blessing Children* 1621. MADRID Prado *Adoration of the Shepherds* 1625. OXFORD *Adoration of the Shepherds.* UTRECHT *Self-portrait* (Aetatis 34.1601), *The artist's wife* (Aetatis 33. 1601) and other *portraits.* VIENNA K. *Diana and Actaeon* (*cf.* A. Blocklandt) 1607, *The Adoration of the Shepherds* 1607. [Fl. 559, Fl. 892, Fl. 523.]

Uytterschaut, Victor. Flemish Sch. *b* Brussels 1847 *d* Boulogne 1917. *Landscapes, marines, still life mostly in w.* Pupil in Brussels Acad. of P. Lauters. Represented in ANTWERP *Brabant landscape w.* BRUGES *Orchard in blossom w.* BRUSSELS *Stranded ships w., Liukebeeck w.* IXELLES. [Fl. 806, Fl. 160 (1917-19), Fl. 114, Fl. 17.]

V

*Vadder, Lodewyk de. Flemish Sch. *b* Brussels 1605 *d* Brussels 1655. *Wooded landscapes* (*cf.* A. Keirincx and J. d'Arthois) *sometimes with horsemen and genre figures by others; also worked as engraver and designer for tapestry.* Master in Brussels Guild 1628. Early writers including Houbraken (1718) record that he especially studied effects of mists disappearing at dawn (*cf.* L. v. Uden). L. Achtschellinck and I. v. d. Stock were his pupils. **Monogrammed Examples:** BARNARD CASTLE *Wooded landscape with peasants.* STOCKHOLM *Road in a wood.* WÜRZBURG University two *Landscapes.* A *S. Hubert* (with figures by G. de Crayer, animals by P. Boel and landscape by L. de V.) was seen by Descamps (1768) in Louvain S. Jacques. The Alexander Voet collection (1689) had a *Landscape with genre figures* (a man playing the flute and another passing water).
[Fl. 86, Fl. 425, Fl. 878, Fl. 216, Fl. 892, Fl. 213.]

Vaenius, O., see **Veen.**

Vaes, Walter. Flemish Sch. *b* Borgerhout (Antwerp) 1882. *Figure pieces, portraits, still life, landscapes; also engravings; worked sometimes in pastel.* Pupil in Antwerp of his maternal uncle P. Verhaert and A. de Vriendt. Won Rome prize and travelled Italy, Spain, Central Europe and Palestine; went Holland (*cf.* R. Wouters) during 1914-18 German invasion; founder member of L'Art Contemporain (Kunst van Heden) group (*cf.* R. Strebelle) 1905; teacher in Antwerp Higher Institute. Represented in ANTWERP *The artist's father, the architect R. Vaes, The red fish, Zinnias, Still life with sucking pig.* BRUSSELS *Still life with ham.* ROTTERDAM Boymans *Girl in green.* UTRECHT *Petunias.* Also in AMSTERDAM, GHENT, LIÈGE and STOCKHOLM.
[Fl. Bib. 19th cent., Fl. 17, Fl. 171, Fl. 206.]

Vaillant, Bernard. Flemish Sch. *b* half-brother of Wallerant V., Lille 1632 *d* Leyden 1698. *Portraits (oil and pastel); also worked as mezzotint engraver* (*cf.* Wallerant V.). Accompanied Wallerant V. to Germany and Paris 1656-9; worked Amsterdam from 1664; Rotterdam from 1675, Nymwegen where drew envoys to the Peace Conference 1677-9. Houbraken (1718) records him as famous for his crayon drawings. **Signed Examples:** AMSTERDAM *Joh. Parker, Sheriff of Middelburg* 1670, *Thomas Parker* (pastel) 1695. LEYDEN Cloth Hall and NYMWEGEN Mus.
[Fl. 425, Fl. 88, Fl. 816.]

Vaillant, Jacques, called **'Leewerik'** (lark). Flemish Sch. *b* brother of Wallerant V., Lille *c.* 1625 *d* Berlin 1691. *Portraits, 'history', religious subjects; also worked as mezzotinter.* In Rome where received his nickname in Flemish colony 1664-6; then Holland; court painter to Frederick William 'the Great Elector' in Berlin 1672; visited Vienna to paint Emperor Leopold I (*cf.* J. Thomas 'van Ypern'). **Signed Examples:** PRAGUE Nostitz *Moses striking the rock* and *Moses and the Brazen Serpent* both 1666. **Documented Examples:** WILHELMSHÖHE Schloss *The Great Elector* 1686 (engraved by his brother Andries V.) and others in other German castles.
[Fl. 425, Fl. 616, Fl. 892, Fl. 402, Fl. 88, Fl. 816.]

Vaillant, Jean. Flemish Sch. *b* brother of Wallerant V., Lille 1627 *d* place unknown after 1668. *Landscapes and portraits; also active as engraver,* and in later years in commerce. In Frankfort 1660; in Frankenthal 1668.
[Fl. 425, Fl. 892, Fl. 88, Fl. 816.]

*Vaillant, Wallerant. Flemish Sch. *b* son of a linen manufacturer, Lille 1623 *d* Amsterdam 1677. *Portraits (oil and pastel), genre, still life; also active as early mezzotint engraver.* Pupil of Erasmus Quellinus; worked Antwerp, Holland and Heidelberg; went Frankfort where met Prince Rupert of the Palatine with whom he collaborated in the new technique of mezzotint *c.* 1656; in Frankfort painted the Emperor Leopold I (*cf.* J. Thomas 'van Ypern') and notables at his coronation 1658; went Paris with Marquis de Grammont (*cf.* J. van Reyn) and had success at French Court; Vertue (1713) records a visit to England of some years; settled Amsterdam 1665. **Signed Examples:** AMSTERDAM Rijks *Jacoba Bicker, wife of P. de Graeff* 1674, *Maria van Oosterwyck, Dutch flower painter* 1671; Walenweeshuis *Reception of a child by the Women Guardians* 1671. DRESDEN *Letter carrier on a board* (*trompe-l'œil still life*) 1658 (*cf.* C. N. Gysbrechts and J. Plasschaert). LILLE *Young artist drawing.* **Documented Examples:** AMSTERDAM Rijks. *P. de Graeff, A lady with three children* (engraved by V.). DRESDEN Print Room (pastel) *Portraits of notables at Leopold I's coronation.* LONDON N.G. *Young artist drawing from sculpture* (mezzotinted by V.). *Leopold I on horseback* is recorded by an engraving.
[Fl. 753, Fl. 425, Fl. 826, Fl. 215, Fl. 856, Fl. 612, Fl. 66, Fl. 892, Fl. 816.]

Valckenborch, Lodewyck J. van, see **Bosch, L. J.**

Valens, C, see **Falens.**

Valescart, see **Walschartz.**

*Valkenborch (or Falckenburg), Frederick van. Flemish Sch. *b* son of Martin van V., Antwerp *c.* 1570 *d* Nuremberg 1623. *Landscapes with figures* (*cf.* A. Mirou). With his brother Gillis and his father fled when Parma expelled Protestants from Antwerp (*cf.* D. v. d. Queborne) to Frankfort (*cf.* J. v. Winghe) 1586; in Rome 1591; proposed by his father for Frankfort citizenship and accepted after examination in Lutheran doctrine 1597; settled Nuremberg 1602; designed triumphal arch for Emperor Matthias' entry into Nuremberg 1612. **Signed Example:** AMSTERDAM Rijks. *Mountain landscape with robbers* 1605. **Monogrammed Examples:** PRAGUE Nostitz. *Burning city* (*cf.* P. Schoubroeck and Brussels Sodom and Gemorrah Painter) 1607. VIENNA K. *Village feast* 1595. **Signed Drawings:** BERLIN Kupferstichkab. *Bacchanal* (Nuremberg 1613). VIENNA Albertina *Fantastic landscape* 15 . 7.
[Fl. 753, Fl. 233, Fl. 892, Fl. 907, Fl. 691, Fl. 83, Fl. 798.]

Valkenborch (or Falckenburg), Gillis (Egidius) van. Flemish Sch. *b* son of Martin van V., Antwerp *c.* 1570 *d* Frankfort 1622. *Landscapes with figures* (*cf.* A Mirou). With his father and brother Frederick *q.v.* fled from Parma's persecutions in Antwerp (*cf.* D. van den Queborne) to Frankfort (*cf.* J. v. Winghe) *c.* 1586; in Rome with Frederick 1590-1; citizen of Frankfort after examination in Lutheran principles 1597. **Signed Example:** BRUNSWICK *Defeat of Sennacherib* 1597. **Monogrammed Drawing:** VIENNA Albertina *Landscape with ruins and figures.* Recorded works include a *Burning of Troy* (*cf.* P. Schoubroeck and Brussels Sodom and Gemorrah Painter).
[Fl. 86, Fl. 892, Fl. 907.]

Valkenborch, Lodewyck J. van, see **Bosch, L. J.**

*Valkenborch (or **Falckenburg**), **Lucas van.** Flemish Sch. *b* Malines or Louvain before 1535 *d* Frankfort 1597 (not 1625). *Landscapes with genre and occasional religious subjects (cf.* A. Mirou), *portraits.* In Malines Guild 1560; in Antwerp 1565; as Protestant fled to Aix-la-Chapelle with his brother Martin to escape Spanish persecutions (*cf.* A. de Weerdt) 1566; returned *c.* 1578; worked for Archduke Matthias and accompanied him to Linz 1581; settled Frankfort (*cf.* J. v. Winghe) 1593; citizen there 1594. Was a good flautist. **Signed Example:** MUNICH A.P. *Tower of Babel* (*cf.* M. van V.) 1568. **Monogrammed Examples:** AMSTERDAM Rijks. *Mountain landscape* 1582. BERLIN K.F. *Mountain landscape* 1567. BRUNSWICK *Rocky landscape with huntsman* 1595, *A Healing Spring* 1596. BRUSSELS *Landscape with village* 1570, *The Gergesene demoniacs* 1597, *Landscape with inn and peasants* 1577 (gouache). COPENHAGEN *Landscapes with peasant scenes* 1574 (two circular pictures, a third in same series in GOTHA). FRANKFORT Staedel. *View of Linz with man painting* 1593, *Skating scene with view of Antwerp* (?) 1590. MADRID Prado *Landscape with ironworks* (*cf.* L. van Gassel). PARIS Louvre *Tower of Babel* 1594. VIENNA K. *Mountain landscape* 1580, *Wooded landscape with man fishing* 1590. *Archduke Matthias as a Roman General* 1580, *Autumn* (*fruit gathering*) 1585, *Autumn* (*vintage*) 1585, *Summer* (*harvest*) 1585, *Winter landscape* (*village in snowstorm*) 1586, *Spring* (*picnic with elegant company*) 1587, *Archduke Matthias* 1579. *Cf.* F. Boels. [Fl. 127, Fl. 559, Fl. 753, Fl. 892, Fl. 88, Fl. 691, Fl. 907, Fl. 798.]

*Valkenborch (or **Falckenburg**), **Martin van.** Flemish Sch. *b* Malines or Louvain 1535 *d* Frankfort 1612. *Landscapes with religious subjects and genre (cf.* A. Mirou). In Malines Guild 1559; in Antwerp 1565; with his brother Lucas van V. went Aix-la-Chapelle to escape Spanish persecution of Flemish Protestants (*cf.* A. de Weerdt) 1566; citizen there 1573; returned Antwerp *c.* 1579 (?); in Guild 1584; after Antwerp's surrender to Parma emigrated to Frankfort (*cf.* F. van V.) 1586; citizen there 1586; in Venice 1602; in Rome 1604. **Signed Examples:** DRESDEN *Tower of Babel* (*cf.* L. van V. and P. Bruegel the elder, R. Savery, N. van Cleve, T. v. Haecht, A. Grimmer, L. Toeput, J. V. de Vries, K. v. Mander, J. de Momper, S. Dubois, C. Anthonisz) 1595. GOTHA *Landscape* 1566. **Monogrammed Examples:** VIENNA K. *February: Flight into Egypt* and ten other months illustrated by scenes from the New Testament. [Fl. 559, Fl. 892, Fl. 907, Fl. 88.]

Vanaise, Gustave. Flemish Sch. *b* Ghent 1854 *d* Brussels 1902. *Costume history, portraits, nudes, landscapes.* Pupil in Ghent Acad. and of T. Canneel; worked much in Paris where friend of J. van Beers and A. Stevens. Member of Brussels Group Les Vingt (*cf.* J. Ensor) 1884; visited Italy and Spain before 1888 when settled in Brussels. Represented in ANTWERP *Allegory of Happiness, Nude, Two portraits.* BRUSSELS *Prince Baudoin of Belgium* 1893, *Bacchante, Self-portrait with his wife.* GHENT *Peter the Hermit preaching for the First Crusade* and others. LIÈGE *Lady in red.* [Fl. Bib. 19th cent., Fl. 296.]

Vanaken, see **Aken.**

Vanderlinck, Armand. Flemish Sch. *b* S. Jean-Molenbeek 1897. *Still life, figure pieces, landscapes.* Pupil in Brussels of C. Montald. Represented in ANTWERP *Still life.* [Fl. 17.]

Veen (or **Vaenius**), **Gertrude van.** Flemish Sch. *b* daughter of Otto van V., Antwerp 1602 *d* Antwerp 1643. *Portraits.* **Documented Example:** BRUSSELS *The painter Otto van Veen* (engraved). *Cf.* A. F. de Bruyns. [Fl. 481.]

Veen, Gysbert van. Flemish (Dutch) Sch. *b* son of Burgomaster, Leyden *c.*1562 *d* Antwerp 1628. *Portraits, but chiefly active as engraver and gem-cutter.* Taken with his brother Otto v. V. *q.v.* to Antwerp 1572; visited Rome and Venice 1588-9; worked for Archduke Ernest 1594 (*cf.* G. Schoof) and then for Archduke Albert and Archduchess Isabella in Brussels and Antwerp. Engraved *Alexander Farnese Duke of Parma* and other pictures by his brother. [Fl. 559, Fl. 612, Fl. 892.]

Veen, Marten van, see **Heemskerck.**

*Veen (**Vaenius, Voenius, Venius**), **Otto van.** Flemish (Dutch) Sch. *b* son of Burgomaster, Leyden 1556 *d* Brussels 1629. *Religious subjects, 'history', portraits; designs for tapestries* (*cf.* J. v. Snellinck the elder) *and engravings; also active as writer.* Pupil in Leyden of the Dutch painter I. C. Swanenburgh; taken by his father (partisan of the Spaniards) to Antwerp 1572; pupil Liège of D. Lampsonius; and of J. Ramey 1573; went Italy where pupil of the Italian painter F. Zuccaro *c.* 1576; returned via Germany to Liège and became page to Prince Bishop Ernest *c.* 1583; went Prague with Embassy to Emperor Rudolf II 1584; in Brussels as Court Painter to Alexander Farnese Duke of Parma (*cf.* P. Claeissins the younger and J. van Winghe) from 1586; in Antwerp from 1593; Rubens was his pupil and assistant 1596-1600; worked on Pageant Entry into Antwerp of Albert and Isabella (*cf.* M. Joncquoy) 1599; Court Painter to Archduke Albert (*cf.* G. de Crayer) and Archduchess Isabella (*cf.* D. v. Alsloot); settled Brussels 1620; declined invitation of Louis XIII to go to France. **Signed Examples:** BRUNSWICK *Assumption of the Virgin* (*s* on reverse). BRUSSELS *Mystic Marriage of S. Catherine* 1589. PARIS Louvre *Self-portrait with his family* (inscribed with names of persons and dated 1584). **Monogrammed Example:** STOCKHOLM *Allegory of the Temptations of Youth* (*cf.* J. Tiel and C. Ketel). **Documented Examples:** AMSTERDAM Rijks. twelve *Scenes from the revolt of the Batavians against the Romans* (including *Brinio acclaimed Chief of the Caninifates* and *Supper in the wood*) paid for 1613. ANTWERP *The Charity of S. Nicholas.* HAMPTON COURT Royal Coll. *Archduchess Isabella* (recorded by Van Mander (1604) and in James I's Cat., artist unnamed). Portraits of *Albert and Isabella as hermits* painted for the Chartreuse de Marlagne 1621 are also recorded. Van Mander mentions a *Triumph of Bacchus* dated 1604 and a *Zeuxis with five nude women.* An *Alexander Farnese, Duke of Parma,* other portraits, and allegorical subjects are recorded by engravings (*cf.* Gysbert van V.); Descamps (1769) records religious subjects in Flemish churches. [Fl. 559, Fl. 141, Fl. 425, Fl. 86, Fl. 215, Fl. 216, Fl. 612, Fl. 384, Fl. 892, Fl. 416, Fl. 88.]

Veen, Pieter van. Flemish (Dutch) Sch. *b* son of Burgomaster, Leyden 1563 *d* Hague 1629. *Landscapes, seascapes, still life, contemporary history;* but chiefly active as successful lawyer in Leyden and The Hague where he held official posts because unlike the other members of family (*cf.* O. van V.) he belonged to anti-Spanish party. **Documented Example:** LEYDEN *Relief of Leyden by Admiral Boisot and the 'Beggars' Fleet* 1574 presented by him to the City 1615. [Fl. 559, Fl. 892.]

Veerendael, see **Verendael.**

*Veken, J. van der. Flemish Sch. 20th cent. Copied the panel of *Just Judges* in *Altarpiece of the Mystic Lamb* by Hubert and Jan van Eyck *q.v.* The profile of the rider, last but one in the group in the background, has been changed to a portrait of King Leopold III of Belgium. The original was stolen from Ghent S. Bavon in 1934. Restored the *Adam and Eve* panels 1936. *Cf.* L. Blondeel. [Fl. 174.]

Velaert (or **Felaert** or **Vellert**), **Dirck Jacobz.** Flemish Sch. *b* Antwerp (?) before 1500 *d* after 1550. *Drawings and possibly paintings of religious subjects, 'history' and allegory; but chiefly active as glass painter and engraver.* Formerly

referred to as D. van Staren (or Star) because he signed with his initials and a star. Master in Antwerp Guild as glass painter 1511; Dean 1518. Presumed by some the 'Meister Dietrich Glasmaler' who entertained Dürer in Antwerp 1521; executed window for Antwerp Cathedral 1540; Guicciardini (1581) records him as 'maestro excellentissimo e di grande inventione'. **Signed Example:** BRUSSELS *The Triumph of Time* 1517 (glass panel). **Monogrammed Examples:** LONDON B.M. and VIENNA Albertina (drawings with D and V and star between). Some windows in Cambridge King's College Chapel (1516-26) are presumed by some his work.
[Fl. 243, Fl. 371, Fl. 612, Fl. 456, Fl. 626 (1908), Fl. 892, Fl. 316, Fl. 296.]

Velde, Henry van de. Flemish Sch. *b* Antwerp 1863. *Genre and other compositions; but chiefly active after 1890 as architect and applied art designer* (*L'Art Nouveau building Paris 1896 and Théâtre des Champs Élysées 1913; Gallery for Kröller-Müller Collection Holland 1921*). Pupil in Antwerp Acad. of C. Verlat and in Paris of Carolus Duran; Director Decorative Art Institute Weimar 1902-14 and of Brussels Higher Decorative Art Institute from 1926. Represented in ANTWERP *Woman at a window, The Laundress.*
[Fl. 152, Fl. 841, Fl. 296, Fl. 17.]

Velde, Nicolas van de. Flemish Sch. 17th cent. *Religious subjects.* Descamps (1769) records a *S. Martin*, a *Triumph of the Church* and a *Holy Family* in Ypres S. Martin (church destroyed in 1914-18 German invasion) and a *Trinity* in Dunkirk S. Éloi.
[Fl. 216.]

Velde, Peter van de. Flemish Sch. *b* son of a gold beater, Antwerp 1634 *d* after 1687. *Marines (some off Antwerp and Rotterdam) and naval warfare* (*cf.* G. van Eyck); *figures in his pictures often by others.* Master Antwerp Guild 1654; worked for Forchoudt firm of dealers (*cf.* A. Casteels) who exported many of his pictures to their branch in Vienna. **Monogrammed Examples:** ANSBACH Residence *Marines* (two). AMSTERDAM Ned. Mus. voor Gesch. *The burning of the English fleet off Chatham, Battle between the Dutch and Swedish fleets in the Sund* 1658. HERMANNSTADT *Marines* (two). STOCKHOLM *Wood by the sea with figures, Castle with stormy sea.* A *Loevestein Castle, prison of Hugo Groot,* with warships fully *s* P. v. d. Velde f. 1666 is recorded. Erasmus Quellinus (father of the artist) owned five seapieces with figures by Erasmus Q. and three with figures by 'Teniers'.
[Fl. 892, Fl. 884, Fl. 212, Fl. 213.]

Vellert, see Velaert.

Venius, O., see Veen.

Venneman, Charles Ferdinand. Flemish Sch. *b* son of carpenter, Ghent 1802 *d* St.-Josse-ten-Noode 1875. *Peasant scenes, interiors, anecdotic genre, some early portraits and landscapes.* Worked first at father's trade and as decorative painter; then pupil of F. de Braekeleer in Antwerp 1836; his son Camille V. (1827-68) was also a painter. Represented in ANTWERP *Flemish fair.* GHENT *Card players.* MONTREAL *Mesmerising.* MUNICH, WASHINGTON Corcoran *Village doctor.*
[Fl. 451, Fl. 612, Fl. 88.]

Venneman, Rosa. Flemish Sch. *b* daughter of Charles V., Antwerp after 1818. *Landscapes, animals, genre.* Represented in CAMBRAI *The fishermen's return.* COMPIÈGNE *Cattle in a meadow.* LIÈGE *Cow.*
[Fl. 88.]

Verbeeck, Anne. Flemish Sch. *b* Antwerp 1727 *d* place and date unknown. Daughter and pupil of F. X. H. V. *q.v.*
[Fl. 481.]

Verbeeck, Elizabeth. Flemish Sch. *b* Antwerp 1720 *d* place and date unknown. Daughter and pupil of F. X. H. V. *q.v.*
[Fl. 481.]

Verbeeck (or Verbeck), François Xavier Henri. Flemish Sch. *b* Antwerp 1686 *d* Antwerp 1755. *Conversation pieces, portrait groups* (*cf.* R. v. Audenaerd, B. v. d. Bossche, J. v. d. Beken), *studio interiors* (*cf.* G. Thomas), *peasant and social genre* (*cf.* T. Michau, C. Falens, H. Goovaerts, A. F. Rubens). Pupil and later son-in-law of P. Casteels (II); Master Antwerp Guild 1710, several times Dean in Guild; director of Antwerp Acad.; Melchior Brassauw was his pupil. **Signed Examples:** ANTWERP (Vieille Boucherie Mus.) *Reception of J. B. Vermoelen, abbot of S. Michel, by the Confraternity of Fencers* 1713 (*cf.* J. J. Horemans the elder. The architecture is presumed by some to be by J. v. d. Straeten *q.v.*). HERMANNSTADT *Party after the hunt, Music party.*
[Fl. 481, Fl. 107, Fl. 892, Fl. 296.]

Verbeeck, Frans. Flemish Sch. *b* Malines before 1515 *d* Malines 1570. Pupil of F. Minnebroer *q.v.*; Master Malines Guild 1531. Van Mander (1604) records him as painter of *landscapes* (*cf.* F. Mostaert), *peasant genre* (*cf.* P. Aertsen), *and fantastic pictures in the manner of H. Bosch* (*cf.* P. Huys); he names a *Winter fog scene* (with bare trees but without snow), a *S. Christopher* with 'many spooks', a *Parable of the Vineyard* also with spooks, and a comic *Peasants' Wedding* (*cf.* P. Bruegel). *Cf.* also S. Wils.
[Fl. 559, Fl. 613, Fl. 213.]

*★**Verboeckhoven, Eugène Joseph.** Flemish Sch. *b* son of sculptor Barthélemy V., Warneton 1799 *d* Brussels 1881. *Animals (cattle, sheep, horses), landscapes, marines, portraits; also lithographs and some animal sculpture.* Pupil of his father and the sculptor A. Voituron; then of B. P. Ommeganck. Visited France before 1824, England 1826, and Italy after 1840; painted animals in pictures by other artists (*cf.* L. P. Verwée, B. P. Ommeganck, P. J. Hellemans, P. F. C. Leroy, P. F. de Noter and C. P. Tschaggeny); received French, Belgian and other decorations; exhibited London R.A. 1845 and 1856 (*Portrait of King Leopold I of Belgium*). Represented in AIX-EN-PROVENCE, AMSTERDAM *Boy and cattle in a field* 1824, *Horses and riders attacked by wolves in Poland* 1836. ANTWERP *Rising tide* 1839 (with his brother L. V. the elder) and three *Cattle pieces.* BRUSSELS *Cattle surprised by a storm, Cattle in the Roman Campagna.* GHENT, THE HAGUE, HAARLEM, LIÈGE, LONDON Wallace *Sheep and cows* and V. and A., NANTES, STOCKHOLM, TOURS, UTRECHT and many American and English provincial galleries.
[Fl. 451, Fl. 481, Fl. 612, Fl. 837 (1881), Fl. Bib. 19th cent., Fl. 361, Fl. 264, Fl. 88, Fl. 73, Fl. 798.]

Verboeckhoven, Louis the elder (Charles Louis). Flemish Sch. *b* son of sculptor Barthélemy V., Warneton (W. Flanders) 1802 *d* Brussels 1889. *Marines, animals.* Pupil of his father and of his brother E. J. V. Worked on the coasts of Holland, France and England. Represented in AIX-EN-PROVENCE *Seapiece with shipping* 1834. ANTWERP *Rough sea, Cows.* CAMBRAI, CHERBOURG, COURTRAI, HAARLEM, YPRES.
[Fl. 451, Fl. 612, Fl. Bib. 19th cent., Fl. 17.]

Verboeckhoven, Louis the younger. Flemish Sch. *b* son of Louis (Charles Louis) V. the elder, date and place unknown *d* Ghent 1884. *Landscapes, still life.* [Fl. 837 (1884).]

Verbrugge, Jean Charles. Flemish Sch. *b* Bruges 1756 *d* Bruges 1831. *Topographic drawings and genre scenes.* Pupil of J. A. Garemyn and J. F. Legillon. **Signed Examples:** BRUGES *Farm interior* 1790, also drawings of Bruges (*cf.* S. F. Vermote) including *Porte d'Ostende* 1780, *Porte Sainte-Croix* 1780, *Porte Saint-Léonard* 1780.
[Fl. 114, Fl. 892.]

*★**Verbruggen (or Verbrugghen), Gaspar Pieter the elder.** Flemish Sch. *b* Antwerp 1635 *d* Antwerp 1681 (not 1687).

Flowers (*cf.* J. B. de Crépu), *garlands* (*cf.* D. Seghers) *and vases with allegorical figures.* Pupil of C. Mahu 1645; Master Antwerp Guild 1650; the Forchoudt firm of Antwerp dealers exported examples in his life time to their branch in Vienna. **Signed Examples:** ANTWERP *Vase of flowers with allegorical figures* 1668. HERMANNSTADT (1675), INNSBRÜCK (1654), LYONS (1670), SCHLEISSHEIM (1679 and 1680), WÜRZBURG University (1654). Pictures dated after 1677 may be G. P. V. the younger *q.v.*

[Fl. 878, Fl. 353, Fl. 892, Fl. 212.]

*Verbruggen, Gaspar Pieter the younger. Flemish Sch. *b* son of G. P. V. the elder, Antwerp 1664 *d* Antwerp 1730. *Flowers and fruit* (*cf.* J. v. d. Borght and N. Verendael) *some with allegorical figures* (*cf.* J. Leyssens), *many as decorations for ceilings and overdoors.* In Antwerp Guild 1677; Dean 1691; much employed during Governor-Generalship of Maximilian Emmanuel of Bavaria 1692-9; worked in The Hague with the Dutch decorator M. Terwesten but lost employment through irresponsibility and idleness (*cf.* P. Hardimé) 1706-22; returned in poverty to Antwerp 1723; worked there as servant of the Guild in his last years. **Signed Examples:** ANTWERP *Vase of flowers with allegorical figures* 1696, *Flower garland round Apollo* 1694. ARRAS *Children adorning a statue of Pan with flowers* 1695. BERLIN, COPENHAGEN, LYONS, STOCKHOLM and TURIN (*cf.* G. P. V. the elder). *Cf.* J. B. Morel.

[Fl. 353, Fl. 215, Fl. 451, Fl. 107, Fl. 892.]

Verburcht, Augustin Jorisz. Flemish (Dutch) Sch. *b* son of a brewer, Delft 1525 *d* drowned in a well, Delft 1552. *Religious subjects, allegories; also worked as an engraver.* Studied Malines; was five years in Paris (*cf.* L. Thiry); then made reputation in Delft with five striking pictures including a *Lineage of S. Anne.* An *Allegory of the transcience of Life* (child and skull) (*cf.* Amsterdam Cadaver Painter) is recorded by an engraving. [Fl. 559, Fl. 892.]

Verdussen, Jan Peter (or **Jean Pierre**). Flemish Sch. *b* son of Peter V., Antwerp *c.* 1700 *d* Avignon 1763. *Contemporary warfare and picturesque military pieces* (*cf.* J. B. v. d. Meiren and C. Francken); *also other outdoor genre scenes* (*cf.* A. F. Rubens). Went Provence and lived Marseilles till 1744; called to Turin by Charles Emmanuel III of Savoy, King of Sardinia (*cf.* H. de La Pegnia) 1744 and accompanied him on his campaigns (*cf.* J. C. Vermeyen, P. Snayers, A. v. d. Meulen); returned South of France and became member of Marseilles Acad. by 1759. **Signed Examples:** CARLSRUHE *Italian mountain landscape with cattle and herdsmen.* MARSEILLES *Cavalry battle* (1759 Acad. reception piece). METZ *Horse market* (*cf.* S. Vrancx), *Cattle market.* SCHLEISSHEIM *Attack on a convoy, Horse market.* **Documented Examples:** TURIN Pinac. *The Franco-Sardinians defeat the Imperial Austrian army at Guastalla 1734.* VERSAILLES *Siege of S. Guilhain* 1746. AVIGNON Mus. Calvet has signed drawing *Battle of Piacenza.*

[Fl. 612, Fl. 66, Fl. 25 (1921), Fl. 296.]

Verdussen, Peter. Flemish Sch. *b* son of a painter, Jacob V., Antwerp 1662 *d* place unknown, after 1710. *Landscapes and contemporary warfare* (*cf.* J. B. van der Meiren). Father (?) of J. P. V. *q.v.* Master Antwerp Guild 1697. **Signed Examples:** ANTWERP Plantin *Landscape with wood.* PRAGUE Rudolfinum *Forest landscape* 1689. **Documented Example:** ANTWERP *Battle of Eeckeren* 1703 (*cf.* C. Francken and J. Broers). [Fl. 107, Fl. 25.]

Verdyen, Eugène. Flemish Sch. *b* Liège 1836 *d* Brussels 1903. *Landscapes, animals and genre.* Pupil of J. Portaels. Professor Brussels Acad. Represented in BRUSSELS, LIÈGE.

[Fl. 264, Fl. Bib. 19th cent.]

Verellen, Jan Joseph. Flemish Sch. *b* Antwerp 1788 *d* Antwerp 1856. *Religious and mythological subjects.* Pupil of W. J. Herreyns. [Fl. 107, Fl. 613.]

*Verendael (or **Veerendael**), **Nicolas van.** Flemish Sch. *b* son of a painter Willem van V., Antwerp 1640 *d* Antwerp 1691. *Flowers and insects* (*cf.* G. P. Verbruggen the elder and the younger), *garlands round grisaille panels by other painters* (*cf.* D. Seghers), *other still life including 'Vanitas' subjects* (*cf.* C. N. Gysbrechts) *and monkey pieces* (*cf.* D. Teniers the younger). Master Antwerp Guild 1677; lived and died in poverty. An Antwerp inventory (1686) records a *Flower piece* with two children by J. Boeckhorst (Lange Jan) and a *Garland* round figures by Gonzales Coques. Descamps (1763) describes pictures in contemporary collections and adds: 'Quoi qu'en dise Weyerman il n'était ni stupide ni singulier; son grand talent lui tenait lieu de tout; il était renfermé vis-à-vis des fleurs qu'il copiait'. **Signed Examples:** BERLIN K.F. *Flower garland* (round a *Virgin and Child*) 1670. BRUSSELS *Flowers round an antique bust, Happy meeting* (monkeys). DRESDEN *Monkeys round a table* 1686, *Flower piece, Flowers in kitchen piece* (with still life by C. Luyckx *s* and figures by D. Teniers the younger *m*). MONTPELLIER *Flower piece* 1672. LONDON V. and A. *Swag of fruit.* MUNICH A.P. *Flowers in 'Vanitas'* (composition also signed by J. D. de Heem). VENICE (Accademia) *'Vanitas' still life.* Others in SCHWERIN and VIENNA Liecht. *Cf.* J. B. Morel.

[Fl. 878, Fl. 215, Fl. 451, Fl. 107, Fl. 892, Fl. 213.]

Verhaecht, Tobias, see **Haecht.**

Verhaeren, Alfred. Flemish Sch. *b* Brussels 1849 *d* Ixelles 1924. *Church and other interiors, still life.* Cousin of the poet Émile V. Pupil of L. Dubois. Exhibited Paris; Officer of the Légion d'honneur; vice president Belgian Royal Museums Commission. Represented in ANTWERP *Still life.* BRUSSELS *Church interior* 1897, *Studio interior, Still life* 1888, *Pig stye.* GHENT *Studio props.* HAGUE (Mesdag). PARIS State Coll. [Fl. Bib. 19th cent., Fl. 388.]

Verhaert, Piet. Flemish Sch. *b* Antwerp 1852 *d* East Dunkirk 1908. *Historical and other genre, urban landscapes, interiors, portraits, murals; also worked as an engraver.* Pupil of J. van Lerius. Member of Brussels group Les Vingt (*cf.* J. Ensor) 1884, of Antwerp group The XIII (*cf.* E. Farasyn) 1891 and Paris Soc. des art. français; teacher in Antwerp Acad. Represented in ANTWERP *The artist's mother* 1880, *The prison bridge* 1880, *Old Antwerp slaughter house* 1882 and others; Town Hall *Murals* (*cf.* C. Boom). BRUSSELS *Girl reading* 1901. CHICAGO Art Inst. TOURNAI.

[Fl. Bib. 19th cent.]

Verhaghen, Jean Joseph (known as 'Pottekens V.'). Flemish Sch. *b* Aerschot 1726 *d* Louvain 1795. *Still life with kitchen utensils; also peasant interiors and religious subjects.* Pupil in Antwerp Acad. and of his brother Pierre Joseph V. *q.v.,* in whose studio he worked. Religious pictures for LOUVAIN S. Quentin and PARC Abbey (nr. Louvain) are recorded.

[Fl. 451, Fl. 88.]

*Verhaghen, Pierre Joseph. Flemish Sch. *b* son of a physician, Aerschot 1728 *d* Louvain 1811. *Religious subjects and 'history'.* Pupil in Antwerp Acad. from 1741 and of B. Beschey while working as lace designer 1744-7; settled Louvain 1749 where carried out decorative work and copied pictures by G. de Crayer, Rubens and van Dyck; married 1753 and continued painting while wife kept draper's shop; attracted attention of Count de Cobenzl, minister plenipotentiary to Austrian Netherlands and of Prince Charles of Lorraine, Governor-General, who appointed him 'peintre ordinaire' (*cf.* A. C. Lens) and sent one of his pictures to Empress Maria Theresa in Vienna 1770; went Italy with funds provided by

the Empress 1771; works painted in Rome for her (*Ecce Homo* and *Disciples at Emmaus*) attracted favour of Pope Clement XIV; visited Vienna where was appointed 'premier peintre de la cour' (*cf.* P. J. Lion and G. de Pélichy) and presented a *S. Theresa* to Empress who hung it in her bedroom 1773; returned Louvain with snuff box of massive gold from the Empress and was given triumphal reception by city (*cf.* P. M. Goddyn) 1773; painted many works for local churches; was visited in his studio by new Governor-General of Austrian Netherlands, Archduchess Maria Christina (*cf.* P. Faes) 1784; worked only for private patrons after the suppression of religious houses (1783) and the French occupation 1794; but became honorary president of newly founded Louvain art school 1800. F. van Dorne was among his pupils. **Signed Examples:** ANTWERP *The Dismissal of Hagar* 1781. BRUSSELS *The Supper at Emmaus* 1779, *Belshazzar and Daniel* 1784. GHENT *The presentation in the Temple* 1767. VIENNA K. *S. Stephen, King of Hungary, receiving the Pope's ambassadors 1003* 1770 (sent Vienna to Maria Theresa). Others recorded include AVERBODE Church *Abraham and Melchisedek* 1765, *The Last Supper* 1766. BOIS-LE-DUC S. Catherine *The Wedding Feast at Cana, Christ in the house of Simon* and seven other large religious panels (from Tongerloo Abbey). LOUVAIN Mus. *Adoration of the Magi* 1781, *The continence of Scipio* 1803; S. Quentin *Purgatory* 1753, and pictures in Louvain (Hôtel de Ville, S. Jacques, S. Pierre, Parc Abbey and other churches in environs) and Malines (S. Rombout).
[Fl. 216, Fl. 451, Fl. 658, Fl. 612, Fl. 270, Fl. 269, Fl. 601, Fl. 88, Fl. 296.]

Verhas, François. Flemish Sch. *b* son of E. V. (painter and draughtsman) Termonde 1826 *d* Schaerbeek (Brussels) 1897. *Interiors, bourgeois genre.* Represented in GHENT.
[Fl. 160 (1897), Fl. Bib. 19th cent.]

Verhas, Jean François. Flemish Sch. *b* son of E. V. (painter and draughtsman), Termonde 1834 *d* Schaerbeek (Brussels) 1896. *Genre (many child subjects), portraits and (in early life) 'history'.* Pupil of his father in Termonde Acad. and in Antwerp of N. de Keyser; visited Italy (Venice); frequent exhibitor at Paris Salon. Represented in ANTWERP *Donkey race at Heyst* 1884, *Two children, Inconsolable.* BRUSSELS *March past of the school children before the King and Queen of Belgium on their silver wedding 1878* 1880 (with many portraits of contemporary notables). GHENT *Children watching a baby painting.* LIÈGE *The fisherman's daughter.*
[Fl. Bib. 19th cent.]

Verheyden, François. Flemish Sch. *b* Louvain 1806 *d* Brussels 1888. *Genre, portraits.* Pupil in Brussels of L. David (*cf.* H. de Coene) and in Paris of J. Langlois. Represented in BRUSSELS, LIÈGE *Peeling onions.* NICE *The rain has stopped!* BROOKLYN Inst. Arts *Schoolgirl in rainstorm.* MONTREAL *The school teacher's birthday.*
[Fl. 451, Fl. 481, Fl. 296, Fl. Bib. 19th cent.]

Verheyden, Isidore. Flemish Sch. *b* son of François V., Antwerp 1846 *d* Brussels 1905. *Landscapes and outdoor genre (some in Impressionist conventions), portraits, still life.* Pupil of J. Quinaux and J. Portaels. Member of Brussels group Les Vingt (*cf.* J. Ensor) 1884; director Brussels Acad. 1904. Represented in ANTWERP *Pilgrimage in the Campine.* BRUSSELS *The painter E. Agneesens* 1867, *Constantin Meunier* 1885, *F. P. v. d. Eeckhoudt* 1900, *Orchard in spring, Gathering wood, Clearing in the forest* and others. GHENT *The chapel.* LIÈGE *Winter in Brabant.* LOUVAIN *Oyster fishing.*
[Fl. Bib. 19th cent., Fl. 909, Fl. 388, Fl. 88.]

Verhoeven, Andries. Flemish Sch. 17th-18th cents. Master Antwerp Guild 1687; went Rome where was nicknamed Distelbloem (Thistleflower) in Flemish colony. A *Hunting*

trophies in landscape (*cf.* A. de Gryef, J. B. Govaerts and J. X Vermoelen) signed 'Andreas Verhoeven alias distelbloem F. Romae 1716' is recorded.
[Fl. 425, Fl. 798.]

Verhoeven, Jan (or Hans). Flemish Sch. *b* son of a sculptor and painter Gillis V., Malines *c.* 1600 *d* after 1676. *Religious subjects for Malines churches* (*cf.* L. Franchoys the younger and S. van Aken). Master Malines Guild 1642; Dean 1669. **Documented Example:** MALINES S. Jean *S. Hyacinth* (from Church of Dominicans where seen by Descamps 1768).
[Fl. 216, Fl. 613, Fl. 614.]

Verhoeven, Martin. Flemish Sch. *b* son of painter and sculptor Gillis V., Malines (?) before 1610 *d* date and place unknown. *Fruit pieces* (some with grapes, *cf.* J. F. van Es and J. van Son). Master Malines Guild 1623.
[Fl. 613, Fl. 892.]

Verhulst, Charles Pierre. Flemish Sch. *b* son of landscape and marine painter P. A. V., Malines 1775 *d* Brussels 1820. *Portraits, 'history', genre.* Settled Brussels and taught in Academy; Court painter to Prince of Orange. Represented in BRUSSELS *Prince of Orange* (later William II of Holland), *Prince Frederick of Nassau, The sculptor G. L. Godecharle.* MALINES *William First King of United Netherlands, The musician Tuerlinckx.*
[Fl. 451, Fl. 612, Fl. 613, Fl. 892.]

Verhulst, Mayken, see **Bessemers.**

Verhuyck (or **Verhayck**), **Jan.** Flemish Sch. *b* son of landscape and marine painter Willem V., Malines 1622 *d* Malines (?) after 1681. *Marines* (*cf.* G. v. Eyck), *picturesque battle scenes* (*cf.* L. de Hondt the elder), *hunting, conversation and village genre pieces* (*cf.* D. Teniers the younger). Dozens of his pieces were commissioned by the Antwerp exporting dealer Forchoudt (*cf.* A. Casteels). His son Michiel V. was also a painter.
[Fl. 613, Fl. 212.]

Verlat, Charles (Michel Charles). Flemish Sch. *b* Antwerp 1824 *d* Antwerp 1890. *Religious subjects, costume history animals, Near Eastern genre pieces, portraits.* Pupil of N. de Keyser, G. Wappers and J. Lies in Antwerp, and of the French painters A. Scheffer, H. Flandrin and T. Couture in Paris. Lived Paris for 18 years and was friend of Courbet 1859-68; teacher Weimar School of Art 1869-74; travelled Egypt, Syria and Palestine 1875-7; teacher in Antwerp Acad. 1877; director 1885. Represented (religious subjects and costume history) in ANTWERP *Pietà* 1866, *The Mother of the Messiah and the four Evangelists* (triptych) 1873, *Vox Dei* (triptych) 1877, *Destruction of Alva's statue in Antwerp 1577* (*cf.* Antwerp Destruction of Citadel Painter) 1888. BRUSSELS *Godfrey de Bouillon attacking Jerusalem.* (Animals, portraits and other subjects in AMSTERDAM, ANTWERP *Defence of the herd (buffalo attacking lion)* 1878, *King of the poultry yard* 1857, *Hen with chickens, Plough oxen with fellah* 1877, *Portraits of the painters L. Derrickx and F. Lamorinière.* BRUSSELS *Sheep dog defending flock against an eagle, Ducks.* WEIMAR *Portrait of Liszt.* Panoramas of *The Battle of Waterloo* and *The Battle of Plevna* (assisted by L. van Engelen and others) are recorded.
[Fl. Bib. 19th cent., Fl. 264, Fl. 823.]

Verlinde, Pierre Antoine. Flemish Sch. *b* Bergues-Saint-Winoc (France) 1801 *d* Antwerp 1877. *Religious subjects, 'history', genre, portraits.* Pupil in Bruges of J. F. Ducq, in Antwerp Acad. of M. van Brée, and Paris of P. Guérin. Teacher Antwerp Acad. 1829; resigned 1830; left collection of pictures to the town of Bergues-Saint-Winoc; his daughters Adelaide and Eugénie were also painters. Represented in ANTWERP *Sketch for Triumphal Arch for Rubens Bicentenary in Antwerp* 1840. BERGUES-SAINT-WINOC *The Woman of Samaria.*
[Fl. 451, Fl. 892, Fl. 837 (1877), Fl. 88.]

Verlinden, Pierre Simon. Flemish Sch. *b* Malines before *c.* 1665 *d* after 1725. *Decorative paintings (allegories) and religious subjects.* Pupil of L. Franchoys the younger (*cf.* S. van Aken) 1677; Master Malines Guild 1690. Allegories painted for Malines Townhall (ceiling) and religious subjects for Malines Couvent des Sœurs Noires and Jesuit church are recorded. [Fl. 613, Fl. 614.]

Vermeersch, Ivo Ambros. Flemish Sch. *b* Maldeghem, nr. Ghent 1810 *d* Munich 1852. *Architectural subjects and picturesque corners.* Pupil of P. de Noter in Ghent Acad. Travelled Germany, Austria, Italy and Sicily; settled Munich 1841. Represented in COURTRAI *Bacharach church.* MUNICH, PRAGUE, STUTTGART, YPRES. [Fl. 451, Fl. 612, Fl. 481, Fl. 88.]

*Vermeyen (in Latin **Maius**, known in Spain as **Juan de Barbalonga), Jan Cornelisz.** Flemish (Dutch) Sch. *b* Beverwijck *c.* 1500 *d* Brussels 1559. *Religious subjects, contemporary history, portraits, designs for tapestry; also worked as engraver.* Court Painter to Margaret of Austria, Governor of the Netherlands (*cf.* J. Schooff) 1525-9; sent by her to Augsburg to paint Charles V, his sister Mary of Hungary and other portraits; 1530; reappointed Court portrait painter by Mary of Hungary (*cf.* B. van Orley, P. Coecke van Aelst G. Scrots, A. Mor, C. v. Hemessen) 1531; then Court Painter to Charles V (*cf.* M. Coxie, and J. v. Lathem) whom he accompanied on Tunis expedition (*cf.* C. Anthonisz, A. v. d. Meulen and J. P. Verdussen) 1535; visited Spain (*cf.* P. de Kempener and Philippe Vos) 1539; was friend of J. Scorel *q.v.* and associated in his Zype damming schemes 1549-51; visited England (*cf.* Sotte Cleve and H. Ewouts); was famous for his beard which reached his feet and was extolled by Lampsonius in a poem. Most of his religious pictures were destroyed by the iconoclasts 1566. **Signed Example:** BRUSSELS Bib. Roy. (coloured gouache) *Punishment of Ghent* 1540 (*cf.* A. F. L. de Vriendt). A signed *Holy Family* and a *Tourney at Toledo* 1539 signed 'ut presens viderat Joannus Maius pictor' are recorded. **Documented Examples:** VIENNA K. Cartoons for tapestry *Siege and battles in Tunisian campaign* (tapestries in Madrid). Van Mander, who knew his daughter, records (1604) a *Self-portrait painting, with Tunisian background and an allegorical female figure*; a *Portrait of his daughter in Turkish costume* (which she wore for an Ommeganck procession), a *Portrait of the artist's second wife* (born with six fingers on her hands and the stumps of the amputated fingers visible in the picture); also a *Victory at sea* (with nudes), *Resurrection, Nativity,* a *Standing Christ* (nude, his hand on his breast); and works at one time in the Abbey of S. Vaast at Arras. Views of London, Naples, Valladolid and Madrid were destroyed in the Pardo Palace fire 1604. His engravings include a *Portrait of Philip II* inscribed 'Rex Anglorum' 1555 and another recording Philip's Pageant Entry into Brussels that year (*cf.* F. Floris). Paintings presumed by some his work are in various museums (*cf.* Brussels Micault Triptych Painter). [Fl. 503, Fl. 559, Fl. 564, Fl. 867, Fl. 892, Fl. 416, Fl. 316, Fl. 631 (1942), Fl. 530.]

Vermeylen, Alphonse. Flemish Sch. *b* Borgerhout (Antwerp) 1882 *d* Antwerp 1939. *Figure pieces, landscapes, marines, interiors, portraits.* Pupil in Antwerp Acad. of C. Mertens. Represented in ANTWERP *On the balcony, Entrance to Zeebrugge harbour.* [Fl. 17.]

Vermoelen, Jacob X. Flemish Sch. *b* Antwerp *c.* 1714 *d* Rome 1784. *Still life with game* (*cf.* A. Verhoeven). In Antwerp Guild 1733; went Rome and remained there (*cf.* J. F. van Bloemen and H. van Lint). **Signed Examples:** SCHLEISSHEIM (Rome 1754). STUTTGART (Rome 1753). WÜRZBURG University (Rome 1754). [Fl. 892, Fl. 617.]

Vermote, Seraphin F. Flemish Sch. *b* Moorseele 1788 *d* Courtrai 1837. *Architectural subjects, landscapes and genre.* Commissioned by Baron van Huerne (Bruges) to draw monuments of Flanders 1812-14; went Paris 1815; then worked Ypres and Bruges; Professor Courtrai Acad. 1832. Represented in BRUGES *Notre Dame* 1816 (grisaille) and others of Bruges buildings (*cf.* J. C. Verbrugge). BRUSSELS, COURTRAI *Arrival of the Post on Ypres Grand' Place, Interior of a ruined church, Landscape with church.* [Fl. 451, Fl. 481, Fl. 88, Fl. 114.]

Verpoorten, Oscar. Flemish Sch. *b* Antwerp 1895 *d* Antwerp 1948. *Figure pieces, landscapes.* Pupil in Antwerp Higher Institute (under F. Lauwers, C. Mertens and I. Opsomer). Teacher in Berchem Drawing School. Represented in ANTWERP *Harbour scene.* [Fl. 17.]

Verryck (or **Vereyk), Theodor.** Flemish Sch. 18th cent. *Topographic drawings.* In Malines *c.* 1765. Visited Holland. [Fl. 481, Fl. 613.]

Verschaeren, Jean Antoine. Flemish Sch. *b* Antwerp 1803 *d* Antwerp 1863. *Religious subjects, portraits, landscapes.* Pupil of W. J. Herreyns, Visited France, England, Germany and Italy where friend of the German 'Nazarenes' P. van Cornelius and J. Overbeck (*cf.* J. Swerts) 1830-8; professor Antwerp Acad. 1842. Represented in ANTWERP *The painter W. J. Herreyns.* BOIS-LE-DUC, BRUSSELS *The sculptor M. Kessels.* LOUVAIN *Descent from the Cross.* [Fl. 451, Fl. 837 (1863).]

Verschoot (Verschooten), Bernard. Flemish Sch. *b* Bruges 1728 *d* Brussels 1783. *Portraits, decorative paintings.* Pupil of J. A. Garemyn in Bruges Acad.; in Paris 1754-7; then Rome, Naples; Court Painter in Brussels to Charles of Lorraine (*cf.* J. P. Sauvage) 1765; director of Brussels Acad. 1768 (*cf.* J. B. Millé); decorative paintings for Château Mariemont are recorded. [Fl. 88, Fl. 740 (1936), Fl. 798.]

Verspilt (or **Versplit), Victor.** Flemish Sch. *b* Ghent 1646 *d* Ghent 1722. *Landscapes.* Master Ghent Guild 1679; collaborated with J. van Cleef *q.v.* Descamps (1769) records a landscape in Ghent S. Jacques. [Fl. 216, Fl. 386, Fl. 479.]

Verstappen, Martin. Flemish Sch. *b* Antwerp 1773 *d* Rome 1853. *Picturesque landscapes with figures and animals; views of Rome and environs.* Pupil of P. J. van Regemorter and H. A. Myin in Antwerp, then of J. C. Klengel in Dresden; travelled the Rhine and Switzerland; settled Rome; friend of S. Denis *q.v.* by 1805; professor in Accad. di S. Luca; patronized by King of Naples and foreign collectors visiting Rome; successful Paris exhibitor (*cf.* L. Gerbo and M. G. Tieleman) and gold medallist 1810; sent paintings also to exhibitions in United Netherlands 1815-40. V. was left-handed. Represented in BESANÇON and MONTPELLIER [Fl. 451, Fl. 612, Fl. 84, Fl. 617.]

Verstraete, Théodore. Flemish Sch. *b* son of an actress and a musician, Ghent 1850 *d* insane, Antwerp 1907. *Peasant genre, landscapes, seapieces.* Pupil in Antwerp Acad. of J. Jacobs. Member of Brussels group Les XX (*cf.* J. Ensor) 1884; helped by the collector H. van Cutsem; worked in Holland 1886-90; member of Antwerp group XIII (*cf.* E. Farasyn) 1891; member Paris Salon de la Nationale 1889. Represented in ANTWERP *The visit to the house of the dead, After rain, Meadow landscape, Moonrise.* BRUSSELS *After the funeral.* GHENT *Ploughing.* LIÈGE, TOURNAI (formerly van Cutsem collection) *The haystacks, Funeral in the Campine, Spring in Zeeland, The organ grinder.* [Fl. Bib. 19th cent., Fl. 772, Fl. 592, Fl. 72, Fl. 388.]

Verstraeten, Edmond. Flemish Sch. *b* Waesmunster 1870. *Landscapes (in Impressionist conventions).* Represented in

ANTWERP *Winter* 1919. BRUSSELS, GHENT *The harvest.* BUENOS AIRES. [Fl. 592, Fl. 388.]

Verstraeten, J., see **Straeten.**

Vervloet, François. Flemish Sch. *b* Malines 1795 *d* Venice 1872. *Architectural subjects (mainly interiors); also lithographs.* Pupil of his brother J. J. V. in Malines Acad. In Rome 1822; settled Naples 1825; travelled many parts of Italy and visited Constantinople. His wife or sister-in-law Augustina V. painted *flowers, fruit and game pieces.* Represented in AMSTERDAM *Interior of S. Peter's Rome* 1824. BRUSSELS *Naples S. Maria la Nuova* 1826, *Certosa di S. Martino (interior)* 1852. [Fl. 451, Fl. 612, Fl. 613, Fl. 798.]

Vervloet, Jean Joseph. Flemish Sch. *b* Malines 1790 *d* Malines 1869. *Religious subjects, contemporary and costume history, genre, portraits.* Professor Malines Acad. 1818-69. Possibly the husband of Augustina V.
[Fl. 451, Fl. 613, Fl. 837 (1869).]

Vervoort, Joseph. Flemish Sch. *b* Antwerp 1676 *d* after 1716. *Landscapes.* Pupil of P. Rysbraeck *q.v.* [Fl. 894, Fl. 798.]

Verwée, Alfred Jacques. Flemish Sch. *b* son of L. P. V., St. Josse-ten-Noode 1838 *d* Schaerbeek (Brussels) 1895. *Animals (chiefly cattle and horses) in landscape, genre.* Pupil of his father and in Brussels of E. Verboeckhoven. Worked in Paris where friend of the Barbizon painters and Manet; visited London 1867 and 1868; also Holland and Italy; member of Brussels Soc. Libre des B.A. (*cf.* L. Dubois); received Belgian and French decorations. Represented in ANTWERP *Colts in a meadow, Cows in pasture.* BRUSSELS *Cattle and shipping at the mouth of the Scheldt, A Zeeland team, Cattle on a river bank, In the fine Flemish land* and others. COURTRAI, GHENT, THE HAGUE (Mesdag) *Morning in the dunes.* LIÈGE *Bull in stormy landscape.* MONTREAL *Cattle returning from pasture.*
[Fl. Bib. 19th cent., Fl. 892, Fl. 264, Fl. 912, Fl. 88, Fl. 296.]

Verwée, Louis Pierre. Flemish Sch. *b* Courtrai 1807 *d* Schaerbeek (Brussels) 1877. *Landscapes.* Pupil of J. B. de Jonghe in Courtrai Acad. and in Brussels of E. Verboeckhoven who sometimes painted animals in his pictures (*cf.* P. J. Hellemans). Represented in BRUSSELS, COURTRAI, DIJON, YPRES *The river Lys in winter.*
[Fl. 451, Fl. 466 (1877), Fl. 892.]

Vianen, Cornelis van. Flemish Sch. *d* Malines (?) *c.* 1560. *Perspectives.* Van Mander (1604) records: 'H. Vredeman de Vries was employed in Malines to finish a perspective picture begun by one Cornelis de Vianen who died while at work on it. Vianen was proficient in this kind of painting but his procedures were over laborious (moeizaam); de Vries developed a lighter and more fluent manner' (*cf.* J. (H.) V. de Vries).
[Fl. 559.]

***Victoryns, Anthoni.** Flemish Sch. *b* Antwerp (?) before 1620 *d* Antwerp before 1656. *Peasant genre* (*cf.* A. Brouwer, D. Teniers the younger and D. Boone). Master Antwerp Guild 1640. **Signed Examples:** COPENHAGEN *Peasant interior.* COURTRAI Hospital Notre Dame *Interior of an inn.* 1637.
[Fl. 714, Fl. 170.]

Vieillevoye, Joseph Barthélemy. Flemish Sch. *b* Verviers 1798 *d* Liège 1855. *Portraits, religious subjects, 'history', genre.* Pupil in Antwerp Acad.; also studied Paris. Director Liège Acad. Represented in ANTWERP *Portraits.* LIÈGE Mus. *The poacher, Murder of the Burgomaster S. Laruelle, Portraits;* S. Gervais *Christ appearing to the founder of the Jesuit Order.* [Fl. 451, Fl. 892, Fl. 88, Fl. 798, Fl. 296.]

***Vienna Adam and Eve Painter.** Presumed Flemish Sch. 15th cent. Name for painter of VIENNA K. (631) *Adam and Eve (The Fall)* (*cf.* Vienna Cruciform Lamentation Painter). Presumed by some identical with H. v. d. Goes *q.v.* and by others with Rogier of Bruges *q.v.*

***Vienna Catherine Painter.** Presumed Flemish (or French or Esthonian) Sch. 15/16th cent. Name for painter of VIENNA K. (1489) *Portrait of a lady with a necklace* presumed by some a portrait of Catherine of Aragon (with halo a later addition). Presumed by some identical with Michiel ('Master Michel') *q.v.* who is presumed by some identical with the Talinn (Reval) born Michel Sittow (Sithium or Zittow); presumed by others identical with the (presumed French) Moulins Master.
[Fl. 668, Fl. 20 (1933), Fl. 457 (1940), Fl. 798.]

***Vienna Cruciform Lamentation Painter.** Presumed Flemish Sch. 15th cent. Name for painter of VIENNA K. (629) *Lamentation* (recorded (1659) in Archduke Leopold Wilhelm's Inventory as 'original by Jan van Eyck' and catalogued as half of a diptych with an *Adam and Eve* (*cf.* Vienna Adam and Eve Painter)). Presumed by some identical with H. v. d. Goes *q.v.* and by others with Rogier of Bruges *q.v.*

***Vienna Daniel Painter.** Presumed Flemish Sch. 16th-17th cent. Name for painter of VIENNA K. (1078) *Daniel in the lions' den.* Presumed by some identical with F. Snyders *q.v.*

***Vienna Feast of the Gods Painter.** Presumed Flemish Sch. 16th cent. Name for painter of VIENNA K. (800) *Feast of the gods.* Presumed by some identical with J. v. d. Straet (Stradanus) *q.v.*

Viérin, Emanuel. Flemish Sch. *b* Courtrai 1869. *Landscapes and picturesque corners of old Flemish towns.* Pupil in Courtrai Acad. and in Antwerp of J. Coosemans. Director Courtrai Acad. Represented in ANTWERP *Flemish town* 1911. BARCELONA, BRUGES *The Béguinage at Bruges* 1911, *Old grange.* BRUSSELS *A clear night* 1920. COURTRAI, MALINES. [Fl. 178.]

Vierpyl, —. Flemish Sch. 17th-18th cent. *Group portraits and conversation pieces.* Pupil of B. van den Bossche *q.v.* Perhaps identical with the Dutch social genre painter J. C. Vierpyl, or with Gregorius Vierpyl, Master Antwerp Guild 1702.
[Fl. 892, Fl. 296.]

***View of Sainte Gudule Master.** Presumed Flemish Sch. 15th cent. Name for painter of PARIS Louvre *A preacher with Brussels Sainte Gudule Cathedral in background* (one tower unfinished and picture therefore datable *c.* 1490). Pictures presumed by some his work are in various museums.
[Fl. 316, Fl. 530, Fl. 798.]

Vigne, Édouard de. Flemish Sch. *b* son of decorative painter I. de V., Ghent 1808 *d* Ghent 1866. *Landscapes and drawings.* Pupil in Ghent Acad. Studied Italy 1836-8; in London 1841. Represented in GHENT *Woods at Alife, Monastery at Cava.* YPRES *Wooded landscape in Italy.* [Fl. 451, Fl. 892.]

Vigne, Félix de. Flemish Sch. *b* son of decorative painter I. de V., Ghent 1806 *d* Ghent 1862. *Costume history, religious subjects, genre, portraits, drawings and engravings of 'moyen âge' costumes.* Pupil of J. Paelinck. Professor Ghent Acad. Represented in ANTWERP *Picking hops.* BRUSSELS *Winter evening.* COURTRAI *The first bouquet, Mediaeval butcher's shop.* GHENT *Mediaeval Ghent fair* and others; Bishop's Palace Chapel *Religious subjects.* He published a book on mediaeval costume with a thousand illustrations.
[Fl. 451, Fl. 612, Fl. 466 (1862), Fl. 892.]

Vinas, A. de las, see **Wyngaerde.**

Vinck, Frans. Flemish Sch. *b* Antwerp 1827 *d* Berchem 1903. *Costume history, religious subjects, oriental and other genre.* Pupil of Baron Leys. Visited France, Italy and Egypt (*cf.* A. de Vriendt); teacher in Antwerp Acad.; worked with L. Hendrix in Antwerp Cathedral 1865. Represented in ANTWERP *Protestants before Margaret of Parma.* LIÈGE *Cairo genre piece.* [Fl. 892, Fl. 17.]

Vinck, Josef. Flemish Sch. *b* Berchem (Antwerp) 1900. *Suburban and other landscapes; figures and animals.* Pupil of F. Hens. Teacher in Antwerp Higher Inst. Represented in ANTWERP *Country house* and two others. [Fl. 17.]

★Vinckeboons, David. Flemish (Dutch) Sch. *b* son of water-colour painter Philipp V., Malines 1576 *d* Amsterdam *c.* 1630. *Landscapes with peasant genre and religious subjects, occasional night scenes; also worked as engraver.* Taken by his father to Antwerp 1580 and thence after Parma's conquest (*cf.* D. v. d. Queborne) to Amsterdam *c.* 1586. **Signed Examples:** DARMSTADT *Landscape.* THE HAGUE *Village Fête* 1629. MUNICH *Christ bearing the Cross* 1604 and 1611. NANTES *Wooded landscape with robbers* 1603. SCHLEISSHEIM *S. John preaching* 1621. **Monogrammed Examples:** ANTWERP *Flemish fair* 1610. BERLIN *Landscape with two peasants* 1620. LENINGRAD *Wooded landscape with figures* 1618, *Christ at Gennesareth* 1623. SCHLEISSHEIM *Landscape with staghunt* 1624. SCHWERIN *Pair of lovers fishing* 1629. **Documented Example:** AMSTERDAM *Oude Mannen Gasthuis Night scene: the drawing of a lottery* (*cf.* G. Congnet) 1603 (described by Van Mander 1604 as very large and painted for this almshouse). Other works are recorded by Van Mander, contemporary engravings and 17th cent. Antwerp inventories. Pictures in various museums including BRUSSELS *Wooded scene with Diana hunting* (with a finch on a tree presumed by some his mark) are presumed by some his work. [Fl. 559, Fl. 425, Fl. 215, Fl. 892, Fl. 213, Fl. 124, Fl. 377.]

Vinckenborch, Arnold. Flemish Sch. 16th-17th cent. *Religious subjects.* Recorded painter of ANTWERP S. Paul *Assumption of the Virgin, Coronation of the Virgin, Resurrection* (*cf.* M. Voet). [Fl. 107, Fl. 296.]

Vinson, L., see **Finson.**

★Virgo inter Virgines Master. Presumed Flemish (Dutch) Sch. late 15th cent. Name for painter of AMSTERDAM Rijks. (43) *The Virgin and Child in a Hortus Conclusus with SS. Barbara, Cecilia, Catherine and Ursula.* Pictures presumed by some his work are in Florence Uffizi (*cf.* Florence (Poggio Imperiale) Crucifixion Painter), Liverpool (*cf.* Liverpool Entombment Painter), New York Met. (*cf.* New York Lamentation Painter), St. Louis (*cf.* St. Louis Entombment Painter) and other galleries. [Fl. 892, Fl. 316, Fl. 798.]

Visch, Mathias de. Flemish Sch. *b* Reninghe 1702 *d* Bruges 1765. *Religious subjects, 'history', portraits.* Pupil of J. v. d. Kerckhove in Bruges Academy; visited Paris 1723; went Rome, then Venice where studied under the Italian painter Piazzetta; returned Bruges 1732; opened art school in which J. A. Garemyn was his pupil; became director of the Bruges Academy where J. B. Suvée and J. F. Legillon were among his pupils; wrote notes on the lives and work of Flemish artists which were used by J. B. Descamps in 'La Vie des Peintres'. **Documented Examples:** BRUGES S. Jacques *Adoration of the Shepherds, Christ washing the disciples' feet* (both seen 1768 by Descamps who also records in Bruges Carmes Déchaussés *The Four Evangelists, Elijah's Offering, S. Joseph supporting the Christ child on a globe,* an *Adoration of the Magi* and pictures in Ypres churches). [Fl. 215, Fl. 216, Fl. 451, Fl. 612, Fl. 88, Fl. 113.]

Visscher, Cornelis. Flemish (Dutch) Sch. *b* Gouda *c.* 1520 *d* at sea returning from Hamburg 1586. *Portraits.* Van Mander records him as 'sometimes out of his mind'. **Monogrammed Example:** VIENNA K. *Portrait of an elderly man* 1574. Amsterdam Rijks. has *William I of Orange* inscribed 'painted by M. v. Miereveld after the original by Cornelis de Visscher'. Charles I of England's pictures included a *Portrait of a scholar, without a beard, in black habit and cap looking down at a letter* 'done by Cornelis Visscher'. [Fl. 559, Fl. 892, Fl. 842.]

Vissenaken, Jérome van. Flemish Sch. *b* The Hague (?) before 1565 *d* Antwerp (?) after 1617. Pupil of Frans Floris. Master Antwerp Guild 1579. [Fl. 559, Fl. 892.]

Vlerick, Pieter. Flemish Sch. *b* son of a lawyer, Courtrai 1539 *d* of plague, Tournai 1581. *Religious subjects, portraits; architectural pieces often in tempera.* Pupil in Ypres of K. Foort *c.* 1554; worked Malines; then Antwerp, with glass painter Jacques Floris; went through France to Venice (*cf.* L. Toeput) where worked under Tintoretto (*cf.* P. Franck (Fiammingo) and M. de Vos); in Rome where painted figures in (no longer extant) landscape frescoes executed by Girolamo Muziano for Cardinal Ippolito d'Este in Villa d'Este at Tivoli (between 1560-6); visited Naples; travelled in Germany; in Courtrai 1567; in Tournai where K. van Mander was his pupil 1568; member (after much opposition from local craftsmen) of Tournai Guild 1575; quarrelled with M. Joncquoy *q.v.*; Van Mander (1604) says large and deformed feet figured in some of his pictures, that he was always badly paid for his work and died in poverty. Pictures described by Van Mander include a *Massacre of the Innocents,* a *Christ in the tomb with instruments of the Passion, The Brazen Serpent, The Maccabees suffering tortures, Susanna and the Elders, Judith with the head of Holofernes* (*cf.* M. Willems) and a *Crucifixion* (triptych) in dramatic lighting in the manner of Tintoretto with one of the thieves in a cart with his confessor. [Fl. 559, Fl. 892.]

Vleughels (or **Wleughels**), **Philippe.** Flemish Sch. *b* Antwerp 1619 *d* Paris 1694. *Religious subjects, 'history', portraits.* Father of Nicholas V. (Watteau's friend). Pupil of C. Schut; frequented atelier of Rubens to whom his mother was related; visited London (*cf.* F. Wouters) 1641; then settled Paris; introduced there by P. van Mol *q.v.* to Flemish colony's club 'La Chasse', where met J. Fouquier *q.v.* and M. van Plattenberg *q.v.* whose daughter he married; became a naturalized Frenchman; member of Paris Acad. Royale (*cf.* F. Voet) from 1663. Forty pictures painted for the S. Denis Carmelites, and others for S. Jacques du Haut-Pas are recorded. [Fl. 249, Fl. 593, Fl. 892, Fl. 229.]

Vleys, Nicolas. Flemish Sch. *b* Bruges before 1670 *d* Bruges 1703. *Religious subjects for Bruges churches* (*cf.* G. Vroilynck). Pupil in Rome of the Italian painter C. Maratta (*cf.* R. P. de Rendeux); Master Bruges Guild 1694. **Signed Example:** BRUGES S. Jacques *Nativity of the Virgin* 1700. Two *Views of Rome* (dated 1695) in Bruges Hospice S. Esprit are recorded. [Fl. 892, Fl. 113.]

Vloors, Émile. Flemish Sch. *b* Borgerhout 1871. *Still life, interiors, portraits, decorative paintings; also worked as sculptor.* Pupil in Antwerp Higher Inst. of A. de Vriendt and in Paris of Léon Bonnat. Member of L'Art Contemporain (Kunst van Heden) group (*cf.* R. Strebelle); director of Antwerp Acad. 1924. Represented in ANTWERP *The blue thistle, The mirror;* Opera house *Ceiling decoration.* BRUSSELS. [Fl. 592, Fl. 17.]

Vobere, see **Wobeck.**

Voenius, O., see **Veen.**

Voet (Vouet or Foué), Ferdinand (Jacob Ferdinand). Flemish Sch. *b* Antwerp 1639 *d* Antwerp *c.* 1700. *Portraits, 'history', landscapes.* Went Paris (*cf.* C. E. Biset) and became member Acad. Roy. (*cf.* P. Mol and P. Vleughels) 1664, but later expelled; went Rome where frescoed the headquarters of the Flemish colony with portraits of the members; Court Portrait Painter to Christina of Sweden (then in Rome) 1670; expelled from Rome 1678; went Turin; returned Antwerp 1684. **Documented Examples:** BERLIN K.F. *Cardinal Dezio Azzolini.* FLORENCE Uffizi *Self-portrait.* Portraits of *Pope Clement IX, Federico, Cardinal Colonna* and *Livio Odescalchi* are recorded by engravings. Vienna Kunsthist has a picture recorded in Archduke Leopold Wilhelm's inventory (1659) as 'Judith with bare breasts in a red and gold dress and green mantle, holding a sword in her right hand and the head of Holofernes by the hair in her left, original by monsieur Voet' (*cf.* Ottawa *Judith* Painter and M. Willems)—possibly a confusion with the French painter Simon Vouet.
[Fl. 425, Fl. 892, Fl. 678, Fl. 798.]

Voet, Mathieu. Flemish Sch. 16th-17th cent. *Religious subjects.* Recorded painter of ANTWERP S. Paul *Jesus in the Temple, Pentecost* (*cf.* C. de Vos and A. Vinckenborch).
[Fl. 296.]

Vogels, Guillaume. Flemish Sch. *b* Brussels 1836 *d* Ixelles (Brussels) 1896. *Landscapes, village and wood motifs, marines and coast pieces (many with rain or mist effects), still life.* Began as a decorator specialising in painted blinds; saved money and painted easel pictures from *c.* 1881; member of Brussels group Les XX (*cf.* J. Ensor) 1884. Represented in ANTWERP *The fishpond, Faded roses, Rainbow, Corn, Harbour entrance at night, Ostend, My garden, Roses, Road under snow, Coast scene.* BRUSSELS *Snow scene, Clearing, Still life, Ixelles in rain, La rue des Chanteurs, Twilight, Ostend.*
[Fl. Bib. 19th cent., Fl. 822, Fl. 388, Fl. 88, Fl. 296.]

Volders, Jan. Flemish Sch. 17th cent. *Portraits.* Perhaps identical with Louis and/or Lancelot V. [Fl. 481, Fl. 798.]

Volders, Lancelot. Flemish Sch. *b* Brussels (?) before 1637 *d* date and place unknown. *Religious subjects.* Master Brussels Guild 1657; V. H. Janssens was his pupil 1675. Descamps (1769) records an *Entombment* in Brussels, Riches Claires, and a *SS. Roch, Sebastian and Anthony* in Anderlecht church both as by 'Volders' (*cf.* Louis and J. V.).
[Fl. 216, Fl. 481, Fl. 267.]

Volders, Louis. Flemish Sch. 17th-18th cents. *Portraits.* Court painter to Jan Willem Friso. **Signed Examples:** THE HAGUE *Hendrik Casimir II* (L. Volders pinxit Bruxelles 1691). LEEUWARDEN Palace *Prince J. W. Friso* (Louis Volders pinxit 1710). [Fl. 631 (1946).]

Volsum, Jan Baptist van. Flemish Sch. *b* Ghent 1679 *d* Ghent after 1734. *Religious subjects, contemporary history.* Pupil of R. van Audenaerd; in Ghent Guild 1706. **Documented Examples:** GHENT *Emperor Charles VI proclaimed Count of Flanders* 1717 (commissioned 1718; completed 1728). ALOST S. Martin *S. Nicholas overthrowing the idols* (seen by Descamps 1768). [Fl. 216, Fl. 88.]

Voordecker, Henri. Flemish Sch. *b* Brussels 1779 *d* Brussels 1861. *Landscapes with animals, rural genre, portraits.* Pupil of J. B. de Roy; friend of Louis David in Brussels from 1816. Represented in AMSTERDAM Rijks. *A hunter and his family with fowls and doves at entrance to his house* 1826. BRUSSELS *Dovecot* (*cf.* C. F. Coene). [Fl. 451, Fl. 481.]

Voort, Cornelis van der. Flemish Sch. *b* Antwerp *c.* 1576 *d* Amsterdam 1625. *Portraits, including groups* (*cf.* D. Barendsz). Taken by his father to Amsterdam after Duke of Parma's capture of Antwerp (*cf.* G. Congnet, C. Ketel, D. v. d. Queborne) 1586; worked Amsterdam; had collection of contemporary pictures which included *Justice protecting Innocence against Tyranny* by Joos van Winghe *q.v.* and works by F. Badens and the Dutch painter A. Bloemaert. **Monogrammed Example:** AMSTERDAM Rijks. *The Guardians of the Old Men's and Women's Almshouse* 1618. **Documented Examples:** AMSTERDAM Rijks. *Burgomaster Cornelis Hooft* 1622, *Captain Witsen's Company of Archers* and *Lieutenant Hasselaer's Company* 1623.
[Fl. 559, Fl. 892, Fl. 88.]

Voort, Michiel Frans van der. Flemish Sch. *b* son of decorative painter Joseph v. d. V., Antwerp 1714 *d* insane, Antwerp 1777. *Allegories and decorative pieces with cupids some in grisaille* (*cf.* M. J. Geeraerts). Dean in Antwerp Guild 1752; Director Antwerp Academy 1752-62. **Documented Examples:** ANTWERP Mus. two *Allegories with cupids* (grisaille) from Antwerp Abbey of S. Michel. Descamps (1768) saw *Apollo and the Muses* in the Antwerp 'Salle de Concert'. A signed engraving representing *Five children playing musical instruments* is recorded. [Fl. 216, Fl. 892, Fl. 16.]

***Vos, Cornelis de.** Flemish Sch. *b* Hulst 1585 *d* Antwerp 1657. *Religious subjects, 'history', portraits.* Pupil in Antwerp of D. Remeeus (*cf.* his brother P. de V.); then abroad; Master Antwerp Guild 1608; bought right to trade as art dealer Antwerp 1616; sold pictures in foreign artists section of S. Germain Fair, Paris (*cf.* D. Teniers the elder) 1619; had workshop and certified that six portraits exported to Spain were by him and his assistants 1627; worked under Rubens on Pageant Entry into Antwerp of Cardinal Infante Ferdinand (*cf.* G. Weri) 1635; and on pictures commissioned from Rubens for Philip IV's Torre de la Parada (*cf.* J. P. Gowi) 1637; made a fortune from portrait commissions some of which were passed on to him by Rubens. Van Dyck painted his portrait. J. Cossiers and S. de V. were his pupils. **Signed Examples:** ANTWERP triptych *Adoration of the Magi, Donor and wife, S. Norbert recovering the Sacred Vessels* 1630, *Abraham Grapheus, servant of Antwerp Guild* 1620, *Family group* 1631. BERLIN K.F. *Married couple on a terrace* 1629. BRUNSWICK *Allegory of the futility of wealth.* BRUSSELS *The artist and his family* 1621, *Anne Frédérique van der Bouckhorst* 1622. CASSEL *Solomon Cock, warden of Antwerp orphanage and a boy.* COLOGNE Wallraf-Rich. *Family group* 1626. GRAZ *Diana with her nymphs.* MADRID Prado *Triumph of Bacchus* also *Birth of Venus* and *Apollo and the Python* (from sketches by Rubens). PHILADELPHIA *Family group* 1631. **Monogrammed Example:** BUDAPEST *Family group.* **Documented Examples:** ANTWERP S. Paul *Adoration of the Shepherds* (*cf.* M. Voet and A. Vinckenborch). VIENNA K. *The anointing of Solomon* (Archduke Leopold Wilhelm inventory 1659). Portraits of *Henri IV* and *Marie de Médicis, Louis XIII,* the *Archduke Albert and Infanta Isabella* and *Philip IV of Spain* were exported to Spain in 1627; an Antwerp invoice (1671) records a *Virgin and Child* in a landscape by Andreas Snellinck *q.v.* exported to Austria; other titles recorded *Venus and Adonis* and *Jacob wrestling with the angel.*
[Fl. 86, Fl. 892, Fl. 597, Fl. 366, Fl. 212, Fl. 213, Fl. 214.]

Vos, Daniel de. Flemish Sch. *b* son of Marten de V., Antwerp 1568 *d* Antwerp 1605. An Antwerp inventory (1623) records a clavichord painted by Marten de V. and 'his son Daniel' (*cf.* Marten de V.). [Fl. 213.]

Vos, Jan de. Flemish Sch. *b* son of Ghent goldsmith J. de V., Ghent (?) 1460 (?) *d* place unknown 1533 (?). *Religious subjects.* Master Antwerp Guild 1489. Visited Germany (Cologne 1508, Frankfort 1512). In Antwerp 1514 and 1521.
[Fl. 253, Fl. 16.

*Vos, Marten de. Flemish Sch. *b* son of Pieter de V. the elder. Antwerp *c.* 1531 *d* Antwerp 1603. *Religious subjects, 'history' portraits, designs for tapestry; also many drawings (religious and 'history' subjects) for engravers.* Pupil of his father and F. Floris; went Italy 1552; visited Rome, Florence and Venice (*cf.* L. Toeput) where worked as assistant to Tintoretto (*cf.* P. Franck (Fiammingo) and P. Vlerick); back in Antwerp where Master in Guild 1558; much employed to replace church pictures destroyed by iconoclasts 1566 (*cf.* F. Pourbus the younger); Dean of Guild 1572; intervened with magistrates when Cabinetmakers' Guild proposed to sell Q. Massys' *Lamentation* triptych (now Antwerp Mus.) to Queen Elizabeth of England (1577) and secured its purchase for the town 1582; in charge of decorations for Antwerp Pageant Entry of Governor-General Archduke Ernest (*cf.* G. Schoof) 1594. His pupils included his brother Pieter the younger, his nephew Willem, his sons Daniel *q.v.* and Marten, W. Coebergher and H. de Clerck. **Signed Examples:** AMSTERDAM Rijks. *The Antwerp shipowner Gilles Hoffman and his wife* 1570. ANTWERP triptych *Triumph of Christ* (centre), *Baptism of Constantine* 1590 (right wing), *Constantine building a church to S. George* (left wing), *S. George delivering S. Margaret* (reverse of both wings); from the altar of the Old Crossbowmen's fraternity in Antwerp Cathedral where seen by Descamps (1768); *S. Luke painting the Virgin* 1602. BRUSSELS *S. Paul at Ephesus* (*the burning of the books*) 1568, *Antoine Anselmo with his wife and children* 1577, *Apollo and the Muses.* GHENT *The Lineage of S. Anne* (*cf.* H. d. Clerck) 1585. GRAZ *Self-portrait.* ROUEN *Meeting of Isaac and Rebecca at the well* 1562. VALENCIENNES *Presentation in the Temple* 1593. VIENNA Liecht. *Raising of Lazarus* 1593. **Monogrammed Examples:** ANTWERP triptych *Render unto Caesar* 1601, *S. Peter finding the tribute money* (right wing), *The widow's mite* (left wing), *Abraham at Hebron* (reverse of both wings) from the altar of the Minters' Guild, Antwerp S. André where seen by Descamps (1768). BERLIN *Christ on the sea of Tiberias,* (reverse) *Jonah swallowed by the whale* 1589. **Documented Examples:** ANTWERP Mus. *Temptation of S. Anthony* (paid for 1594; from Antwerp Cathedral where seen by Descamps); triptych *The Incredulity of S. Thomas* 1574 from the altar of the Furriers' Guild in Antwerp Cathedral where seen by Descamps; *Nativity* from Malines Capuchin church where seen by Descamps; Cathedral (Notre Dame) *The Wedding Feast at Cana* seen there by Descamps who also records other pictures in Flemish churches. An *Immaculate Conception* in Rome S. Francesco a Ripa is referred to as his work by 17th cent. writers. A 1588 Antwerp inventory records a *Suffer little children . . .*; other inventories 1588-1649 record many works including a *Prodigal Son* (*cf.* S. Vrancx) and other paintings on clavichords (*cf.* F. Borsse). Paintings presumed by some his work are in various museums.
[Fl. 371, Fl. 127, Fl. 559, Fl. 709, Fl. 753, Fl. 48, Fl. 215, Fl. 425, Fl. 216, Fl. 892, Fl. 416, Fl. 230, Fl. 401, Fl. 213, Fl. 678.]

*Vos, Paul (Pauwel) de. Flemish Sch. *b* Hulst *c.* 1596 *d* Antwerp 1678. *Animals* (*cf.* J. Fyt, P. F. de Hamilton, J. v. Kessel the elder, J. Roos, F. Snyders), *hunting scenes, still life with game, trophies, etc.* Pupil of D. Remeeus; Master Antwerp Guild 1620; assistant to Rubens by 1626; worked on pictures commissioned from Rubens for Philip IV's Torre de la Parada (*cf.* J. P. Gowi) 1637; sold works to many Flemish and Spanish notables; Cornelis de V. was his brother; F. Snyders married his sister; Rubens stood godfather to one of his children; Van Dyck painted his portrait and that of his wife. **Signed Examples:** BRUSSELS *Staghunt.* LENINGRAD *Leopard hunt.* MADRID Prado *Kitchen piece with cats fighting, Deerhunt, Staghunt, Greyhound in flat landscape, Fox* and others; Acad. S. Fernando *Dogs chasing hare.* MUNICH Residenz. *Bull fight.* VIENNA K. *Still life and dogs* in *Amor vincit omnia* (figures documented L. W. inventory 1659 as by J. van den Hoecke). Rubens owned four of his pictures:

Kitchen piece with cats fighting, Peasants with venison and fruit, Concert of birds, Fruit and birds. Antwerp inventories record (1657) *Wolf hunt*; (1659) *Dogs and cats fighting* and others. Many pictures presumed by some the work of F. Snyders are presumed by others to be his work.
[Fl. 425, Fl. 892, Fl. 837 (1927), Fl. 213.]

Vos, Philippe. Flemish Sch. *b* Brussels before 1550 *d* after 1588. Recorded in service of Emperor Charles V (*cf.* M. Coxie); went Spain (*cf.* J. C. Vermeyen); Philip II granted him the release of his property in the Netherlands which had been sequestered under Parma in his absence 1588. [Fl. 892.]

Vos, Pieter de the elder. Flemish Sch. *b* Leyden or Gouda 1490 *d* Antwerp 1567. Worked Antwerp where was Master in Guild 1519. A signed portrait is recorded (*cf.* P. de V. the younger). [Fl. 559, Fl. 892, Fl. 798.]

Vos, Pieter de the younger. Flemish Sch. *b* son of Pieter the elder, Antwerp (?) before 1538 *d* Antwerp after 1580. *'History'.* Worked as assistant to his brother Marten. An Antwerp inventory of 1661 records an *'Abigail* by Peeter de Vos'. [Fl. 559, Fl. 612, Fl. 892, Fl. 213.]

*Vos, Simon de. Flemish Sch. *b* Antwerp 1603 *d* Antwerp 1676. *Religious subjects, 'history', genre, portraits.* Pupil of C. de Vos (not a relative) 1615; Master Antwerp Guild when 17 years old 1620; worked under Rubens and contributed to his Marie de Médicis series (*cf.* J. van Egmont) 1622-5; married sister of A. van Utrecht 1628; supplied many pictures to the Forchoudt firm of Antwerp art dealers (*cf.* A. Casteels) and received from them a Rubens sketch *Last Supper* as a gift 1662; also worked for the Seville dealer C. van Immerseel. The Dutchman A. de Vries painted his portrait (Antwerp Mus. formerly presumed his self-portrait). **Signed Examples:** ANTWERP *The beheading of S. Paul* 1648, *Gipsy woman telling a young man his fortune* 1639. AVIGNON *The Prodigal son* (*cf.* S. Vrancx). BARNARD CASTLE *A Flemish lady with a dish of fruit.* LENINGRAD *Abigail offering presents to King David, The Queen of Sheba before Solomon* 1641 (companion pieces). MALINES Hermitage chapel *Adoration of the Shepherds* 1644. PRAGUE Nostitz *Allegory: Sine Baccho et Cerere friget Venus* (*cf.* Jan Miel) 1635. Rubens owned a *Prodigal son.* Pictures titled *The Four Elements* (*cf.* J. (Velvet) Brueghel) are recorded. *Cf.* J. Boots, G. v. Opstal, J. v. Kessel the elder.
[Fl. 86, Fl. 216, Fl. 107, Fl. 892, Fl. 212.]

Vos, Vincent de. Flemish Sch. *b* Courtrai 1829 *d* Courtrai 1875. *Animals* (*mainly dogs and monkeys*). Pupil of E. Woutermaertens. Visited Italy 1870. Represented in BRUGES *Monkeys and dogs.* COURTRAI, LILLE *Caught in the trap.* MULHOUSE *Dogs.* TOURCOING *Two dogs.*
[Fl. 466 (1875), Fl. 837 (1875), Fl. 114.]

Vos, Willem de. Flemish Sch. *b* son of Pieter de V. the younger, Antwerp before 1580 *d* after 1629. Pupil of his uncle M. de V.; Master Antwerp Guild 1593. Van Dyck drew his portrait. [Fl. 86, Fl. 892.]

Vouet, J. F., see Voet.

Vrancx (or Vranx), Adriaen. Flemish Sch. 16th-17th cent. Pupil in Antwerp of J. Snellinck the elder *q.v.* 1582. DRESDEN *Southern mountain landscape with figures and animals* signed AVRanx is presumed by some his work. [Fl. 234.]

*Vrancx, Sebastiaan. Flemish Sch. *b* son of a merchant, Antwerp 1573 *d* Antwerp 1647. *Picturesque military scenes* (*cf.* L. de Hondt the elder), *contemporary warfare* (*cf.* P. Meulener), *horse markets* (*cf.* S. J. van Douw and J. P. Verdussen), *other outdoor genre; also occasional 'history' and*

religious subjects and figures in pictures by other artists. Pupil of A. van Noort and brother-in-law of T. van Haecht; went Italy *c.* 1597; back in Antwerp by 1601; held offices in Guild of Crossbowmen, Civic Guard and Antwerp Chamber of Rhetoric 'de Violiere' (for which he wrote comedies and poems); P. Snayers was among his pupils. The Antwerp dealer Goetkint wrote (1624) 'Sebastian Vrancx is making six paintings; he refuses all help and will not have his pictures copied'. **Signed Examples:** LONDON Royal Coll. *An ambush* 1616, *Attack on a convoy* 1616. MADRID Prado *Attack on a convoy.* PARMA *S. John preaching* 1600, *Battle of Centaurs and Lapiths* 1600. ROTTERDAM *Sack of a village.* VIENNA K. *Interior of the Jesuit Church at Antwerp* (*cf.* W. van Ehrenberg and A. G. Gheringh). **Monogrammed Examples:** AMSTERDAM Rijks. *Woman and bandit* (also titled *The Robber robbed*), *Market place with flogging, Winter games on the Scheldt* 1622. ANTWERP *Winter scene, Leckerbetken's battle* 1601, *Plundering a village* (*cf.* D. Ryckaert III). BRUNSWICK, BRUSSELS *Horse market, Flemish proverbs.* GOTHA, HANOVER *Landscape with Roman ruins* and *Works of Mercy.* MUNICH, NAPLES and PARIS Louvre. Collaborated with J. (Velvet) Brueghel and H. van Balen the elder. A *Prodigal son* (*cf.* Prodigal Son Master, J. V. de Vries, M. de Vos, S. de Vos, J. B. de Wael) is recorded by an engraving. Descamps (1769) records pictures in Brussels Chartreuse. Rubens owned a *Bataille du roi Sebastien de Portugal* and a *Blind leading the blind.* V. Wolfvoet *q.v.*, Jeremias Wildens *q.v.* and other 17th cent. Antwerp collectors owned examples. Copies by him of the *Twelve Months* by L. van der Borcht *q.v.* and figures in a landscape by J. de Momper are recorded in an inventory of 1623. Collaboration with T. van Haecht (the sister of whose second wife he married in 1613) is also recorded.
[Fl. 559, Fl. 425, Fl. 215, Fl. 216, Fl. 107, Fl. 892, Fl. 542, Fl. 213, Fl. 214.]

Vrelant (Vredelant, Wyelant), Willem (Guillaume). Flemish (Dutch) Sch. *b* Utrecht date unknown *d* Bruges 1481-2. *Manuscript illustrations.* In Bruges where founder member of Guild of S. John (scribes, illuminators, book-sellers) 1454; citizen of Bruges 1456; at one time neighbour and friend of H. Memlinc *q.v.*; gave the Guild of S. John an altarpiece *Passion of Christ, with Vrelant and his wife as donors* (the wings painted by Memlinc) 1478. **Documented Examples:** BRUSSELS Bib. Roy. (no. 9243). Sixty miniatures in 'Chroniques de Hainault' paid for by Duke Philip the Good of Burgundy before 1467. Manuscript illustrations presumed by some his work are in various museums and libraries.
[Fl. 892, Fl. 248, Fl. 886, Fl. 150.]

Vriendt, see Floris.

Vriendt, Albert F. L. de. Flemish Sch. *b* son of Jan de V., Ghent 1843 *d* Antwerp 1900. *Costume history, some religious subjects, genre, murals.* Pupil of his father and in Ghent and Antwerp Acads. Visited Germany with his brother Juliaan de V.; visited Egypt (*cf.* F. Vinck) and Palestine (*cf.* C. Ooms and P. van der Ouderaa); director of Antwerp Acad. 1891-1900; received Belgian decorations and the French Légion d'honneur. Represented in ANTWERP *Pope Paul III before Luther's portrait* 1883, *Cartoons for murals in Bruges Town Hall.* BRUSSELS *Homage of Ghent citizens to Charles V* (*cf.* J. C. Vermeyen) 1886, *Excommunication of Bouchard d'Avesnes* 1877. MUNICH, BRUGES Town Hall *Murals* (finished by his brother). LIÈGE *Egyptian dancer, Jacqueline of Bavaria imploring Philippe-le-bon to pardon her husband.* *Cf.* H. Houben. [Fl. Bib. 19th cent.]

Vriendt, Jan Bernard de (also known as **Devriendt**). Flemish Sch. *b* Ghent 1809 *d* Ghent 1868. *Landscapes, genre, flower pieces and decorative paintings.* Pupil of A. C. M. Engel *q.v.*

1830. Travelled in France and the Ardennes. Worked on *murals* in Ghent University from 1860.
[Fl. 451, Fl. 837 (1868), Fl. 798.]

Vriendt, Juliaan (Julien) de. Flemish Sch. *b* son of Jan de V., Ghent 1842 *d* Oude-God 1935. *Religious subjects, costume history, genre, murals, illustrations.* Pupil in Ghent and Antwerp Acads. Visited Germany with his brother A. de V. 1869; director Antwerp Acad. 1901-24; finished his brother's murals in Bruges Town Hall. Represented in ANTWERP Mus. *Raising of the daughter of Jairus* 1888; Academy *Suffer little children to come unto me*; Palais de Justice *Murals* (with C. Ooms and P. v. d. Ouderaa). BRUSSELS *Christmas song, Portrait of Marie de Vriendt.* LIÈGE *S. Elizabeth of Hungary rejected by the inhabitants of Eisenach.* NEW YORK Met. *Chapel scene: Old Antwerp.*
[Fl. Bib. 19th cent., Fl. 699 (1935).]

*Vries, Jan (Hans) Vredeman de. Flemish (Dutch) Sch. *b* Leeuwarden 1527 *d* Holland after 1604. *Architectural scenes with figures, tromp-l'œil decorative perspectives* (*cf.* C. de Vianen, P. Neeffs the elder, H. v. Steenwyck the younger); *also worked as an architect-engineer and as illustrator and compiler of architectural books.* Studied P. Coecke van Aelst's translation of Serlio's book on Vitruvius; went Malines; then Antwerp; worked on triumphal arches for Pageant Entries into Malines and Antwerp of Charles V and Philip (II) 1549 (*cf.* P. Coecke van Aelst, J. van Rillaert, M. Willems and P. J. Pourbus); in Malines working for C. Dorizi *q.v.* and completing work by C. de Vianen 1561; returned Antwerp 1563; designed triumphal arch for Anne of Austria's visit to Antwerp (*cf.* A. Mor) 1570; fled from Antwerp to Aix-la-Chapelle (*cf.* M. van Valkenborch) with his sons Salomon and Paul *q.v.*, when Alva's 'General Amnesty' excepted all guilty or suspected of heresy (*cf.* A. de Weerdt) 1570; took H. van Steenwyck as his pupil; in Liège 1574; returned Antwerp 1575; acted as engineer in charge of Antwerp fortifications from 1577; fled again when Antwerp fell to Duke of Parma (*cf.* D. v. d. Queborne) 1586; worked Frankfort (*cf.* J. van Winghe), Brunswick, Hamburg, Danzig; followed his son Paul de V. to Prague where worked for Emperor Rudolf II (*cf.* P. Stevens the younger) 1596-7; went Amsterdam as suggested by G. Congnet *q.v.* 1601. **Signed Examples:** HAMPTON COURT *Christ with Mary and Martha* 1566 (figures recorded in Charles I's catalogue as by A. Blocklandt). VIENNA K. *Elegant company and a dwarf, with table for a banquet, in a forecourt; Musical party in a loggia* 1596, *Marble pillared hall with cavaliers and lady* (signed by him and his son Paul 1596). AMSTERDAM *Renaissance palace with Lazarus* (indistinct signature). Van Mander (1604) records *Orpheus charming the animals* (*cf.* L. v. d. Borcht) and a series of *Allegories* painted for Danzig city council and a *Christ driven from the Temple* and *Christ driving out the money changers* (with trompe-l'œil perspectives) painted for Hamburg, S. Peter's (burnt 1842); also a *Tower of Babel* (*cf.* M. van Valkenborch), a perspective for W. Key *q.v.*, a summer house into which P. Bruegel the elder inserted (in his absence) a lovemaking couple behind a door, and a garden perspective in a room painted for the Antwerp shipowner Gilles Hoffman (*cf.* M. de Vos) which deceived the Prince of Orange. Antwerp inventories (1614-85) record a *Prodigal son in a perspective* (*cf.* S. Vrancx), other perspectives, and a *Tower of Babel.*
[Fl. 559, Fl. 892, Fl. 213, Fl. 798.]

Vries, Paul Vredeman de. Flemish (Dutch) Sch. *b* son of Jan V. de V., Antwerp 1567 *d* Amsterdam (?) after 1630. *Architectural scenes with figures and trompe-l'œil perspectives.* Worked with his father for Danzig City Council 1594; went thence to Prague where decorated rooms for Emperor Rudolf II who often watched him at work (*cf.* P. Stevens the younger); in Amsterdam 1601. **Signed Example:** VIENNA K. *Marble pillared hall s* in collaboration with his father *q.v.* Van Mander (1604) and Descamps (1769) record a *Last*

Supper by J. van Winghe with architecture by P. V. de V. in Brussels S. Géry. [Fl. 559, Fl. 216, Fl. 892.]

Vries, Salomon Vredeman de. Flemish (Dutch) Sch. *b* son of Jan V. de V., Antwerp (?) 1566 *d* The Hague 1604. *Architectural perspectives*. Pupil and assistant of his father *q.v.* [Fl. 559, Fl. 892.]

Vroilynck (or **Vroylinck**), **Ghislain.** Flemish Sch. *b* Bruges (?) before 1600 *d* Hondschoote 1635 (or Bruges 1625). *Religious subjects for Bruges churches* (*cf.* J. van Oost the elder, P. Ryckx the elder, L. de Deyster and N. Vleys). Travelled France and Italy; Master Bruges Guild 1620. **Signed Examples:** BERGUES *Entombment* and two wings of triptych *The Creation* and *Two praying donors*. BRUGES Mus. *Three saints* 1613; Notre Dame *Descent from the Cross* 1620. **Documented Example:** BRUGES S. Sauveur *S. Eligius* (altar piece commissioned 1621). [Fl. 892, Fl. 114, Fl. 798.]

Vroom, Matheus. Flemish Sch. 17th cent. Master Antwerp Guild 1620. DRESDEN (1113) *Arrival of Marie de Médicis in Antwerp* 1631 signed 'VM in et fec. 1632' is presumed by some his work. (Antwerp has an unsigned variant.) [Fl. 234, Fl. 16.]

W

Wael, Anton de. Flemish Sch. *b* illegitimate son of Lucas de W., Antwerp 1629 *d* struck by lightning in his bed, Rome *c.* 1672. Pupil in Antwerp of J. Boots (*cf.* P. Gysels). Went Rome where lived with his uncle C. de W. *q.v.* and later with brother L. de W. *q.v.* and painted figures in landscapes by B. Torreggiani. [Fl. 48, Fl. 612, Fl. 892, Fl. 617, Fl. 715.]

Wael (or Waal), Cornelis de. Flemish Sch. *b* son of Jan de W., Antwerp 1592 *d* Rome 1667. *Picturesque military scenes* (*cf.* L. de Hondt the elder), *marines* (*cf.* G. van Eyck), *Italian genre and religious subjects; also active as engraver and art dealer in Italy* (*cf.* S. Damery). With his brother Lucas de W. *q.v.* went Italy and settled there (*cf.* G. Hallet, P. de Lignis, J. Miel, J. Sutterman); worked Genoa (*cf.* A. van Ertvelt, V. Malo the elder, J. Roos and A. v. Dyck) 1613-56; then Rome where lived with his nephew Anton; Van Dyck a friend of the family (*cf.* J. de Wael) stayed with him at one time in Genoa and painted his portrait with his brother Lucas (now Rome Capitol). Houbraken (1719) states that he worked for Philip III (Philip IV?) of Spain and describes in detail a *Siege* with storm troops climbing ladders, etc. **Signed Examples:** KOENIGSBERG *The Halt.* BERLIN K.F. (drawing) *Camp scene.* STOCKHOLM has signed drawings. **Documented Example:** VIENNA K. *Crossing of the Red Sea* (in Archduke Leopold Wilhelm 1659 inv.) *cf.* M. Pepyn. Seventeenth century Antwerp inventories record works of the types named above, and a *Seven Works of Mercy*, a *Noah's Ark* and an *Ash Wednesday* are among pictures exported by the Forchoudt firm of dealers to Vienna 1673-6. A series *The Seasons*, another *The Senses* and *Views of the Port of Genoa* are recorded by engravings (*cf.* J. B. de W.). A *S. Peter in prison* (*cf.* H. van Steenwyck the younger) in Genoa S. Ambrogio (with the head worked on by Van Dyck) was destroyed with the church 1917. *Cf.* P. Boel. [Fl. 86, Fl. 773, Fl. 425, Fl. 892, Fl. 715 (1915), Fl. 212, Fl. 213, Fl. 305, Fl. 678.]

Wael, Jan de. Flemish Sch. *b* Antwerp 1558 *d* Antwerp 1633. *Religious subjects.* Pupil of F. Francken I. Visited Paris (*cf.* L. Thiry, G. v. Cleve, H. Francken the elder, C. Ketel, A. Dubois); Master in Antwerp Guild 1583. Van Dyck painted his portrait with his wife Gertrude, daughter of the engraver Gérard de Jode (now Munich A.P.). [Fl. 86, Fl. 425, Fl. 892.]

Wael, Jan Baptist de. Flemish Sch. *b* illegitimate son of Lucas de W., Antwerp 1632 *d* Italy (?) after 1669. *Italian genre pieces; also active as engraver.* Pupil in Genoa of his uncle Cornelis de W. *q.v.*; recorded in Rome living with his brother Anton 1669; engraved a series *Story of the Prodigal Son* (*cf.* S. Vrancx) from drawings by C. de W. 1658. [Fl. 612, Fl. 107, Fl. 892.]

Wael (or Waal), Lucas de. Flemish Sch. *b* son of Jan de W., Antwerp 1591 *d* Antwerp 1661. *Landscapes with mountains, waterfalls and weather effects.* Pupil of his father and of his uncle Jan (Velvet) Brueghel; with his brother Cornelis de W. *q.v.* went through France to Italy and worked Genoa; friend in Genoa of Jan Brueghel the younger (*cf.* A. Van Dyck); back in Antwerp and Master in Guild 1628. [Fl. 425, Fl. 892, Fl. 678.]

Wagemaekers, Victor. Flemish Sch. *b* Ganshoren (Brabant) 1876. *Landscapes* (*many of Brabant and Antwerp Campine motifs*), *interiors, genre* (*many in w.*). Represented in ANTWERP *The old castle in autumn w.* [Fl. 17.]

Wagemans, Maurice. Flemish Sch. *b* Brussels 1877 *d* Breedene-sur-mer 1927. *Marines, landscapes, genre, portraits, still life.* Pupil of J. Portaels and J. Stallaert. Founder member of Sillon group (*cf.* A. Pinot) 1893. Represented in ANTWERP *Still life.* BRUSSELS *The violinist, Nude in the open air, War cemetery at Loo.* GHENT. [Fl. 296, Fl. 17, Fl. Bib. 19th cent.]

Walckiers, Gustave. Flemish Sch. *b* Brussels 1831 *d* Brussels 1891. *Landscapes and town views.* Worked mainly in Brussels. Represented in ANTWERP, BRUSSELS, COURTRAI, GHENT, TOURNAI. [Fl. 17.]

Walescart, see **Walschartz.**

Wallays, Édouard Auguste. Flemish Sch. *b* Bruges 1813 *d* Bruges 1891. *Costume history, religious subjects, interiors.* Pupil of Geirnaert; in Paris 1835-9 Director Bruges Acad. 1855-86. Represented in BRUGES *Memlinc painting S. Ursula's shrine* (*cf.* P. Kremer), *La cheminée du Franc in Bruges Palais de Justice* (*cf.* L. Blondeel), *Prometheus bound* and others; Séminaire Épiscopal *Stations of the Cross.* [Fl. 451, Fl. 892, Fl. 114.]

Wallet, Taf. Flemish Sch. *b* La Louvière 1902. *Still life, marines, decorative compositions.* Represented in ANTWERP *Still life.* [Fl. 17.]

Walschartz (or Walescart), François (not Jean). Flemish Sch. *b* son of a goldsmith, Liège *c.* 1595 *d* Liège 1665 or 1675. *Religious subjects for Liège and Namur churches, and decorative paintings.* Pupil of Rubens (?) in Antwerp; working Liège 1618; visited Rome; back in Liège 1635; in Westphalia 1655. **Signed Examples:** FOY-NOTRE-DAME nr. Dinant *Adoration of the Shepherds.* MALMÉDY, Capuchin church *Holy Family.* An *Immaculate Conception* for Palermo S. Anne, an *Adoration of the Kings* for Liège Minorites church and decorative paintings for Raesfeld Castle (Westphalia) are recorded. [Fl. 63, Fl. 26, Fl. 409, Fl. 892, Fl. 305.]

Wans, Jan Baptist. Flemish Sch. *b* Antwerp 1628 *d* Antwerp 1684. *Landscapes.* Known as the Captain because in command of Civic Guard. Pupil of F. van Oosten; Master Antwerp Guild 1657. Descamps (1769) records a *Landscape with Elisha carried up to heaven* with figures by P. Ijkens in Antwerp Carmes Déchaussés. [Fl. 216, Fl. 892.]

Wante, Ernest. Flemish Sch. *b* Ghent 1872. *Religious subjects* (*some in fresco*). Pupil in Antwerp Higher Institute of A. de Vriendt. Teacher in Antwerp Acad. Represented in ANTWERP *Death of S. Godelieve* 1911; S. Antoine *The Road to Calvary.* BRUSSELS S. Joseph, *The Road to Calvary.* MOL Church *The Entry into Jerusalem.* [Fl. 17.]

Wappers, (Baron) Gustave. Flemish Sch. *b* Antwerp 1803 *d* Paris 1874. *Contemporary and costume history, religious subjects, genre, portraits.* Pupil of I. van Regemorter, W. Herreyns and M. van Brée. Failed to get Rome Scholarship in 1821 and 1823; in Holland 1824; Paris 1826 and 1829; Leader of Romantic movement in opposition to F. J. Navez *q.v.* by 1830; patriotic painter of the new Belgian state 1835; ennobled by King Leopold 1845; commissioned by King Louis Philippe to paint a picture for Versailles (*cf.* A. Ysendyck) visited by Queen Victoria and Prince Albert who commissioned a picture and presented him with an inscribed silver vase 1852; director Antwerp Acad. 1840-53; his many pupils included the English painter Ford Madox Brown; lived mainly in Paris from 1853. Represented in AMSTERDAM *Van Dyck making love to his model* 1827. ANTWERP *Portrait of a lady, Young artist in meditation, The brothers de Wit in prison, Young mother and her child* 1854; Jesuit church *Presentation in the Temple*. BRUSSELS *Episode of the September Days of 1830 in Brussels* (with portraits of E. Verboeckhoven, F. Bossuet, H. Leys and other contemporaries) 1835, *Charles I on the way to the scaffold*; Royal Palace *Charles I taking leave of his children*. LOUVAIN S. Michel *Entombment* 1833. UTRECHT *Patriotism of the Burgomaster of Leyden during the siege by the Spaniards* (50 lifesize figures) 1830. VERSAILLES *Defence of Rhodes by the Knights of S. John of Jerusalem*. NEW YORK Met. *The artist's daughters*.

[Fl. 451, Fl. 612, Fl. 540, Fl. 440, Fl. Bib. 19th cent.]

*Washington Annunciation in a Church Painter. Presumed Flemish Sch. 15th cent. Name for painter of WASHINGTON, N.G. (39) *Annunciation* (formerly in Leningrad Hermitage). Presumed by some identical with J. van Eyck *q.v.*

*Washington Man with Arrow Painter. Presumed Flemish Sch. 15th cent. Name for painter of WASHINGTON, N.G. (42) *Young man with an arrow*. Presumed by some identical with H. Memlinc *q.v.*

*Washington Nativity in Sculptured Porch Painter. Presumed Flemish Sch. 15th cent. Name for painter of WASHINGTON, N.G. (40) *Nativity*. Presumed by some identical with P. Christus *q.v.*

Wassenhove, Joos van. Flemish Sch. 15th cent. Master in Antwerp Guild 1460; Master in Ghent Guild 1464; sponsored H. v. d. Goes *q.v.* in Ghent Guild 1467; left for Rome before 1475. **Signed Examples:** None. Presumed by some identical with Justus of Ghent *q.v.*   [Fl. 316.]

Wauquier, Étienne Omer. Flemish Sch. *b* Cambrai 1808 *d* Mons 1869. *Genre and portraits; also worked as a sculptor.* Pupil and finally director of Mons Acad. Represented in BRUSSELS *The painter A. Wiertz* 1866.   [Fl. 221.]

Wauters, Camille. Flemish Sch. *b* Temsche 1856 *d* Lokeren 1919. *Landscapes.* Pupil in Antwerp Acad. and in Paris (Acad. Julian). Visited Holland, Scandinavia, Italy, Spain, Egypt; also worked at Barbizon. Represented in ANTWERP *View of Cairo*.   [Fl. 17.]

Wauters, Charles Augustin. Flemish Sch. *b* Boom, nr. Antwerp 1811 *d* Malines 1869. *Costume history, religious subjects, genre portraits.* Visited Paris and Rome. Represented in MALINES *The reading of the death sentence on Montigny;* S. Jean *Crucifixion;* S. Rombout *Last Supper.* YPRES *S. Clotilde giving alms.* Others in MALINES Town Hall and BRUSSELS Palais de la Nation.
[Fl. 451, Fl. 612, Fl. 892, Fl. 614, Fl. 837 (1869).]

Wauters, Émile. Flemish Sch. *b* Brussels 1846 *d* Paris 1933. *Costume history, portraits, oriental scenes and landscapes.* Pupil in Brussels of J. Portaels and in Paris of the French painter J. L. Gérome. Visited Italy, Spain, Morocco and Egypt; received Belgian and other decorations including the Légion d'honneur; frequent exhibitor in Paris Salon and London R.A.; lived mainly in Paris after 1890. Represented in ANTWERP *The bridge of Kasr-el-Nil at Cairo, Spring.* BRUSSELS *The madness of Hugo van der Goes* (*cf.* P.

Kremer) 1872, *Sobieski before Vienna* (very large picture), *Princess Clémentine of Belgium, The actress Mme. Judic, M. Solvay and dog* and others; Parc du Cinquantenaire *Panorama of Cairo*. LIÈGE *Marie de Bourgogne imploring mercy for her councillors*. THE HAGUE (Mesdag), PHILADELPHIA. A portrait of the art critic *M.H. Spielman* was in the London R.A. in 1890.

[Fl. Bib. 19th cent., Fl. 361, Fl. 331 (1933), Fl. 699.]

Wautier (or Woutiers), Charles. Flemish Sch. working 1652-1685. *Religious subjects, 'history', portraits.* **Signed Examples** BRUSSELS *Portrait of a young man* 1656, *Portrait of a man* 1660. PRAGUE Nostitz. *Bacchus crowned with vine leaves* 1652. Descamps (1769) records a *Visitation* in Antwerp Église des Augustins and *Christ handing the Keys to Peter* 1685 in Louvain S. Pierre. His *A. Pimentel de Prado, Spanish Ambassador to Paris 1659* is among portraits recorded by engravings.
[Fl. 216, Fl. 892.]

Wautier (or Woutiers), Michaelina. Flemish Sch. *b* Mons (?) before 1627. *Portraits and religious subjects.* **Signed Example:** BRUSSELS *Portrait of a man* (half length) 1646. **Documented Examples:** VIENNA K. *S. Joachim reading, S. Joseph with a lily* (both half lengths and in Archduke Leopold Wilhelm's inventory 1659). A half length *Don Andrea Cantelmo* (*General in service of Charles I of England*) *in armour* is recorded by an engraving 1643. *Cf.* A. F. de Bruyns.
[Fl. 221, Fl. 892.]

Weerdt, Adriaen de. Flemish Sch. *b* Brussels *c.* 1510 (?) *d* Cologne *c.* 1590 (?). *Landscapes, religious subjects; allegories; also worked as engraver.* Pupil in Antwerp of C. v. d. Queborne *q.v.* Went Italy; returned Flanders but fled from Spanish persecutions under Alva (*cf.* H. v. Coninxloo, L. de Heere, M. Geeraerts, J. v. Liere, S. v. d. Meulen, N. Neufchatel, N. v. Perre, M. and L. v. Valkenborch, J. V. de Vries) to Cologne (*cf.* F. Hogenberg) *c.* 1567. Van Mander states that he painted landscapes 'in the style of Frans Mostaert' and after his Italian visit, pictures in the style of Parmigianino, and worked as engraver in Cologne. Vienna Albertina has *s* drawings for engravings *The Story of Ruth* (mentioned by Van Mander).   [Fl. 559, Fl. 892.]

Weesop (or Wesop). Flemish Sch. 17th cent. *Portraits.* Came England (*cf.* C. de Neve) shortly before Van Dyck's death 1641; left in protest against execution of the King *c.* 1649. Vertue wrote (*c.* 1718): 'Many pictures painted by him pass for Van Dyck'. One John W. buried S. Martin in the Fields 1652 was perhaps his son. A signed *Execution of Charles I* is recorded.   [Fl. 826, Fl. 856, Fl. 899.]

Werden (or Weerden), Jacques van. Flemish Sch. *b* before 1647 *d* after 1696. *Drawings (for engravers) of contemporary warfare* (*cf.* P. Meulener), *official ceremonies* (*cf.* D. Teniers the younger), *town and architectural views, portraits.* Went Paris (*cf.* C. E. Biset) where 'archer de garde de corps' of Louis XIV. Drawings of *The inauguration of Charles II of Spain at Ghent 1666* (*cf.* F. Duchatel and Jan van Cleef), *The siege of Armentières, The siege of Landrécy* are among those recorded by engravings.   [Fl. 612, Fl. 481, Fl. 892.]

Weri (or Verry), Geeraard. Flemish Sch. *b* Antwerp 1605 *d* Antwerp 1644. *Religious subjects and decorative work.* Pupil of Rubens; married widow of T. Rombouts; employed under Rubens on decorations for Pageant Entry of Cardinal Infante Ferdinand as Governor into Antwerp 1635 (*cf.* A. Adriaenssen, J. Boeckhorst, J. Ceustere, J. Cossiers, J. Eyck, G. and J. van den Hoecke, J. Jordaens, E. Quellinus, T. Rombouts, C. Schut, G. Seghers, T. van Thulden, C. de Vos, J. Wildens, A. Wolfordt, F. Wouters). **Documented Example:** VERREBROEK Church *Adoration of the Magi* (commissioned 1639). A painting *The Virgin handing a sword to Cardinal Infante Ferdinand* commissioned for Calloo Church is recorded by an engraving. [Fl. 107, Fl. 892.]

Weyden, Goswin (Goosen, Gosewyn) van der. Flemish Sch. *b* son of Pieter and grandson of Rogier van der W., Brussels (?) *c.* 1465 *d* Antwerp (?) *c.* 1538. *Religious subjects.* In Lierre 1497; in Antwerp *c.* 1498; Master in Antwerp Guild by 1504; his pupils included the Portuguese Simon Portugalois (*cf.* Q. Massys); Dean of Guild 1514 and 1530; worked for Tongerloo Abbey. **Signed Examples:** None. **Documented Example:** BERLIN K. F. *Virgin and Child with donors bearing trees* ('The Calmpthout Altar') 1511-15 from Tongerloo. A triptych *Scenes from the life of the Virgin* painted when he was 70 in 1535 is recorded. [Fl. 892, Fl. 457 (1913), Fl. 316.]

Weyden, Pieter (Peter, Pierre) van der. Flemish Sch. *b* son of R. v. d. Weyden, Brussels 1437 *d* Brussels (?) 1514. Recorded Brussels 1459-84. **Signed Examples:** None. **Documented Examples:** None. [Fl. 892, Fl. 220, Fl. 316.]

Weyden, Rogelet (or Rougelet)—diminutive of Rogier—**van der (or de la Pasture).** Flemish Sch. *b* Tournai before 1414 *d* place and date unknown. Apprenticed as Rogelet de la Pasture native of Tournai, to Robert Campin *q.v.* in Tournai at the same time as J. Daret *q.v.* 1427; finished his studies with Campin 1432; presumed by some the Rogier de la Pasture, native of Tournai, who became master in Tournai Guild 1432 (*cf.* Rogier van der Weyden); presumed by some the 'Rogier le peintre' who received three commissions in Tournai 1436 and 1437. **Signed Examples:** None. **Documented Examples:** None. Presumed by some identical with Rogier of Bruges *q.v.* and/or Rogier van der Weyden. [Fl. 892.]

*Weyden, Rogier van der (or de la Pasture). Flemish Sch. *b* son of a cutler, Tournai *c.* 1400 *d* Brussels 1464. *Religious subjects, portraits, 'Justice' scenes.* As 'Maistre Rogier de le Pasture' twice given Wine of Honour by Tournai Council (*cf.* J. van Eyck) 1426; was married to a Brussels girl and had a son by 1427; presumed by some the 'Maister Rogier de le Pasture, natif de Tournay' who became Master in Tournai Guild 1432 (*cf.* Rogelet v. d. Weyden); was living Brussels when money invested in Tournai was paid to 'maistre Roger de le Pasture, peintre . . . à Bruxelles . . .' 1435; recorded as painter to Brussels city 1436; directed colouring of sculpture ordered by Duke Philip the Good for Brussels Recollets church and other decorative work 1439 and 1440; recorded as 'portrateur' in Brussels 1437-49; may have visited Italy (*cf.* Rogier of Bruges and Rogerius Gallicus); as 'Rogier de la Pasture' made contract with Abbot of S. Aubert, Cambrai, for eleven unknown subjects 1455; this work delivered by his wife and workmen with cart and three horses 1459; member of Confrérie de la Ste-Croix; at request of Bianca Sforza, Duchess of Milan, accepted as pupil the Italian painter Zanetto Bugatti 1460; was thanked by her as 'Maestro Rugerio de Tornay pictori in Burseles' 1463; buried in Ste. Gudule, Brussels; candles were placed on the S. Luke's Guild altar in Tournai in memory of 'Master Rogier de la Pasture born in Tournai but resident in Brussels' 1464. **Signed Examples:** None. **Documented Examples:** MADRID Prado (formerly Escorial) *Descent from the Cross* (from Louvain, Notre Dame hors des Murs, Archers' Chapel, with Archers' Guild stamp upon it; engraved as by 'Rogier' in 1563; in Philip II's inventory as by 'Rogier' 1574; recorded by Van Mander (1604) as by Rogier v. d. Weyden of Brussels (*cf.* Rogier of Louvain). **Semi-documented Example:** MADRID Escorial *Crucifixion with the Virgin and S. John* placed in the Escorial by Philip II and recorded in Escorial inventory as by 'Rogier' and from Brussels 'Cartuja' (Charterhouse) 1574.

The archives of Burgos, Miraflores Charterhouse 1445

(copied by A. Ponz 1783) record the gift by John II of Castile of a triptych *Nativity, Descent from the Cross*, and *Christ appearing to His Mother* by 'Master Rogel, great and famous Flemish painter'. A. Ponz saw the triptych and added that Pope Martin V (who died 1431) had given it to King John; A. Conca (1793) who also saw the triptych there, records elaborately carved arches round the scenes (pictures corresponding to these descriptions are extant in Granada Cathedral Capilla Real (bequeathed by Isabella the Catholic 1504), in New York Metropolitan Mus. and in Berlin K.F.). Dürer (1521) saw in the Golden Chamber of the Brussels Town Hall 'the four painted scenes done by the great Master Rudiger', Guicciardini (1567), Vasari (1568) and Van Mander (1604) described them as 'Justice' scenes (*cf.* Rogier of Louvain) and they were extant till 1695 when they were destroyed in Marshal Villeroi's bombardment of the city (*cf.* Z. J. van Helmont and A. Coppens). An inventory (1516-33) of Margaret of Austria, Governor of the Netherlands records a Pietà with *Christ in the arms of the Virgin* and *Angels* on the wings, the picture by 'Rogier' and the wings by 'Master Hans' (presumed by some H. Memlinc).

Rogier v. d. Weyden is presumed by some identical with some or all of the following: Rogelet v. d. Weyden *q.v.*, Rogier of Bruges *q.v.*, Rogier of Brussels *q.v.*, Rogier of Louvain *q.v.*, Rogerius Gallicus *q.v.* Pictures presumed by some his work are in various museums (*cf.* Antwerp Philippe de Croy Painter, Beaune Last Judgement Painter, Boston S. Luke Painter, Exhumation of S. Hubert Master, London Magdalene reading Painter, London Young Woman with White Headdress Painter, Madrid Werl wings Painter, New York Christ appearing to his Mother Painter, New York d'Este Painter, Redemption Master, Flémalle Master and Danzig Last Judgement Master). [Fl. 243, Fl. 371, Fl. 818, Fl. 559, Fl. 179, Fl. 754, Fl. 892, Fl. 220, Fl. 696, Fl. 316, Fl. 88, Fl. 467 (1940), Fl. 798, Fl. 530, Fl. 615.]

Weyden, Rogier van der the younger. Flemish Sch. *b* son of Goswin v. d. W., before 1516 *d* Antwerp (?) before 1543. Master in Antwerp Guild 1528. [Fl. 892, Fl. 457 (1913).]

Wiertz, Antoine Joseph. Flemish Sch. *b* son of a gendarme, Dinant 1806 *d* Brussels 1865. *Large religious and 'history' compositions and didactic allegories, portraits; also worked as sculptor.* Pupil in Antwerp Acad. under W. J. Herreyns and M. van Brée; given a small scholarship by King William of the Netherlands 1821; living Paris in poverty 1829-32; Rome prizewinner 1832; in Italy 1833-38; returned Belgium 1839; asked permission to paint a large picture in Antwerp Cathedral with Rubens' *Descent from the Cross* within sight; on refusal obtained allocation of a disused church in Liège; moved to Brussels where used an empty factory as a studio 1848; refused to sell his religious and didactic pictures and painted portraits for his livelihood; designed house with vast studio in form of a ruined temple which the Government erected for him in Ixelles (Brussels) on condition that his large compositions already painted should remain there 1850-53; left, on his death, all works in this house and studio (now Musée Wiertz) to the nation. Represented in LIÈGE *Greeks and Trojans fighting for the body of Patroclus* (painted in Rome 1835-6, exhibited Rome, Paris and Brussels 1837-9). ANTWERP *Portrait*, Sketch for Liège '*Patroclus*'. BRUSSELS Mus. Wiertz (a) Anti-war compositions: *The last cannon* 1855, *Napoleon in Hell, Civilization.* Plea for unmarried mothers: *Hunger, Folly, Crime.* Protest against capital punishment: *Visions and reflections of a decapitated head.* Protest against danger of premature burial: *The precipitate burial.* Religious and 'history' subjects: *Revolt of the Angels, Triumph of Christ* 1848, *Beacon of Golgotha, Polyphemus devouring the companions of Ulysses* and replica of *Fight for the body of Patroclus* 1860 and many others. [Fl. 118, Fl. 489, Fl. 5, Fl. 137, Fl. 300, Fl. 669, Fl. 817, Fl. 296, Fl. Bib. 19th cent.]

Wiethase, Edgard. Flemish Sch. *b* Antwerp 1881. *Landscapes, animals, genre and still life.* Pupil in Antwerp Acad. and Higher Institute. Represented in ANTWERP *Head of a woman.* [Fl. 17, Fl. 568.]

Wigans, Isaac. Flemish Sch. *b* Antwerp 1615 *d* 1662. *Still life, including tables with provisions* (*cf.* A. v. Utrecht). Pupil of V. Malo; Master Antwerp Guild 1651. [Fl. 892.]

*****Wildens, Jan.** Flemish Sch. *b* Antwerp 1584 or 1586 *d* Antwerp 1653. *Landscapes* (*with figures generally by others*). Pupil of P. van der Hulst 1596; Master Antwerp Guild 1604; in Italy 1613-18; married in Antwerp (Rubens, described in the contract as 'his good friend', being a witness) 1619; contributed landscapes (some from Rubens' drawings) for pictures by Rubens and other painters in the Rubens entourage (J. Jordaens, F. Snyders, C. Schut, T. Rombouts, J. Boeckhorst, and C. and P. de Vos to whom he was related by marriage); his wife's niece Helena Fourment married Rubens 1630; provided views of Antwerp for Pageant Entry of Cardinal Archduke Ferdinand (*cf.* G. Weri) 1635; an executor with Snyders of Rubens' will (*cf.* J. Moermans) 1640; left collection of 700 paintings when he died (*cf.* Jeremias W.). Both Rubens and Van Dyck painted his portrait. **Signed Examples:** AMSTERDAM *View of Antwerp from the countryside* 1636. ANTWERP *Landscape with dancing peasants* 1631; Mayer van den Bergh *Mountain landscape, The Plain with peasants.* BERGEN *Landscape.* BERLIN K. F. *Rainbow landscape* 1621. DRESDEN *Winter landscape with huntsman* 1624 (shown in *van der Geest's Gallery interior* by W. van Haecht *q.v.*). VIENNA K. *Landscape with huntsmen* 1649. **Monogrammed Example:** AUGSBURG *Stormy landscape* 1640. London Royal Coll. (Buckingham Palace) has a *Pan and Syrinx* presumed by some the work recorded as by Rubens and W. in the inventory of Jeremias W. 1653. A series of landscapes symbolising *The months* 1614 are known from engravings. [Fl. 425, Fl. 892, Fl. 204, Fl. 213, Fl. 88.]

Wildens, Jeremias. Flemish Sch. *b* son of Jan W., Antwerp 1621 *d* Antwerp 1653. *Roman landscapes, hunting pieces, flower pieces, religious subjects.* Visited Rome *c.* 1646; inherited his father's collection of 700 paintings three months before his own death (*cf.* A. Goubau, V. Wolfvoet, J. van Egmont, P. Mol and P. Bruegel). [Fl. 107, Fl. 892, Fl. 213.]

Willaert, Ferdinand. Flemish Sch. *b* Ghent 1861 *d* Ghent 1938. *Landscapes, picturesque corners of old Flemish towns, portraits.* Pupil Ghent Acad. under T. Canneel; travelled Spain and Morocco; member and later Associate of Paris Soc. Nat. B.A.; Director of Termonde Acad. Represented in ANTWERP *The Béguinage church.* BRUGES *Malines Béguinage.* BRUSSELS *Fisherman awaiting the tide.* BUENOS AIRES, GHENT *View of Ghent.* MONS, NAMUR, OLDHAM, PARIS (State Collection), PAU, SANTIAGO (Chile). [Fl. 338, Fl. 114, Fl. 17.]

*****Willaerts, Adam.** Flemish Sch. *b* Antwerp 1577 *d* Utrecht 1664. *Marines, battles and coast scenes* (*cf.* G. van Eyck). In Utrecht by *c.* 1603; took part in organizing new painters' and sculptors' guild from Saddlers' Guild to which they formerly belonged (*cf.* J. Uytewael) 1611; Dean of new guild 1620; may have visited England. The Dutch marine and portrait painter Abraham W. and the Dutch marine painter Isaac W. were his sons (*cf.* also Cornelis W.) The Dutch fish painter W. Ormea sometimes painted still life in the foreground of his pictures. **Signed Examples:** AMSTERDAM *Dutch defeat of Spaniards off Gibraltar* 1607 (two pictures dated 1617 and 1639), *Fishmarket on the Coast* 1621, *Coast scene* 1628, *Storm at sea with whale* 1614. BARNARD CASTLE Bowes Mus. *An Embarkation* 1626. BERLIN K.F. *Coast scene* 1635. BRUSSELS *Departure of a Battle Fleet* 1623. COPENHAGEN *Naval Battle* 1641. DRESDEN *Dutch ships in a*

rocky harbour 1620. GREENWICH Maritime Mus. *Dutch ships and a whale, Elector Palatine leaving England with his bride* 1613 (in the Prince Royal, largest ship of her time: near her, the Disdain, a miniature ship built 'for the young Prince Henry to disport himself in about London Bridge'), *Return of Sir E. Michelbourne from the East Indies to Portsmouth 1606* 1640. HAARLEM *Battle off Gibraltar 1607* 1639. OXFORD Ashmolean *Fleet in harbour, Fishmarket on the shore.* Others in MARSEILLES, ROTTERDAM, VIENNA K. and Liechtenstein, WÜRZBURG (1651). **Monogrammed Examples:** AUGSBURG *Calm sea with ships.* FRANKFORT *Coast scene with stormy sea and ships* 1638. NEW YORK Met. *River with ships* 1643. (His son Abraham also monogrammed A. W.) [Fl. 86, Fl. 425, Fl. 892, Fl. 884.]

Willaerts, Cornelis Adamsz. Flemish Sch. *b* son of Adam W., Antwerp (?) before 1611 *d* Utrecht 1666. *Landscapes with allegorical figures.* **Signed Example:** LENINGRAD *Bacchus and Ariadne.* [Fl. 892, Fl. 798.]

Willebeeck, Peter. Flemish Sch. *b* Antwerp (?) before 1620 *d* after 1647. *Flowers and fruit and garlands* (*cf.* A. v. Utrecht and D. Seghers). Master Antwerp Guild 1646. **Signed Example:** VIENNA Harrach *Garland round head of Christ* (in grisaille) 1647. [Fl. 612, Fl. 892.]

*****Willeboirts, Thomas** (known as **Bosschaert**). Flemish Sch. *b* Bergen-op-Zoom 1613 *d* Antwerp 1654. *'History', religious subjects, portraits, also designs for tapestries* (*cf.* J. v. d. Hoecke and P. Thys) *and copies of pictures by Rubens and Van Dyck.* Pupil of G. Seghers in Antwerp; employed by Rubens on Torre de la Parada commission (*cf.* J. P. Gowi) 1636; Master in Antwerp Guild 1637; worked for Stadholder Frederick Henry (*cf.* A. v. Utrecht) and his son Prince William; was defeated by C. Schut the elder *q.v.* in competition for a *Beheading of S. George* for Antwerp Cathedral 1643; collaborated with J. v. d. Hoecke and J. Fyt *q.v.*; D. Ryckaert III and G. Coques were his friends. J. B. Gaspers (Lely's Baptist) was his pupil. Houbraken (1719) states that he exhibited his art in Rome, Germany, Spain and England (*cf.* C. de Neve). **Signed Examples:** AMSTERDAM Rijks. *Venus arming Mars* (allegory of Prince Frederick Henry 1644 *cf.* J. Jordaens). THE HAGUE Mauritshuis *Venus and Adonis.* NUREMBERG *Venus and Cupid* 1653. SCHLEISSHEIM *Angel removing arrows from S. Sebastian's wounds.* **Documented Examples:** ANTWERP Plantin Mus. *Balthasar Moretus I dead and other portraits.* VIENNA K. *Elijah fed in his sleep, Diana returning from the chase* (both in Archduke Leopold Wilhelm's inventory 1659; animals in the second by J. Fyt). Descamps (1769) records in Bruges S. Jacques *Martyrdom of S. James* and Brussels Égl. des Capucins *Martyrdom of S. Basil* and comments 'La finesse de dessein et celle de la couleur peuvent être égalée aux bons ouvrages de Van Dyck'. [Fl. 425, Fl. 216, Fl. 892.]

Willems, Florent. Flemish Sch. *b* Liège 1823 *d* Neuilly (Paris) 1905. *Anecdotic and costume genre; also worked as restorer.* Pupil in Malines Acad.; settled Paris 1844; restored the Louvre *S. John the Baptist in the desert* then ascribed to Raphael; A. Stevens was his pupil and friend. Represented in AMSTERDAM, ANTWERP *A seventeenth century market.* BRUGES *Woman at a mirror.* BRUSSELS *La fête chez la Duchesse, Toilet of the bride, The widow, The print collector.* LIÈGE, NEW YORK Met. *Preparing for the promenade.* PHILADELPHIA Wilstach *Interior, Signed and sealed.* VIENNA Czernin *Lady with little dog.* [Fl. Bib. 19th cent., Fl. 892, Fl. 114.]

Willems, Marcus. Flemish Sch. *b* Malines *c.* 1527 *d* 1561. *Religious subjects, 'history', portraits* (?) *also designed for windows and tapestries.* Pupil of M. Coxie. Painted triumphal arch with *Story of Dido* for entry of Philip II into Malines

(cf. J. V. de Vries) 1549; married sister of J. de Poindre q.v. **Signed Examples:** None. **Documented Examples:** None. Van Mander records *Beheading of John the Baptist* with foreshortened arm of executioner thrusting forward the head, painted for Malines S. Rombout and a *Judith and Holofernes* (cf. Grenoble Judith Painter, Ottawa Judith Painter, D. Barendsz, J. Massys, P. Vlerick, J. v. Hemessen, C. Ketel, F. Badens, F. Voet also P. v. Mol and A. de Coster). Vertue (before 1721) saw in the Somerset House Collection a *Portrait of Queen Elizabeth* (or Edward VI?) 'aged nine 1546' in the Holbein manner 'on a long board for a sylinder' with 'Guilhelmus pingebat' on the frame and suggested it might be Willems' work (others have assumed that Guilhelmus stood for English painter Guillaume Stretes); Walpole (1771) describes the picture as representing *Edward VI* 'on a long board to be discerned only by the reflection of a cylindric mirror', a landscape 'not ill done' by the side of the head.
[Fl. 559, Fl. 826, Fl. 856.]

Willemsz, Cornelis. Flemish (Dutch) Sch. *b* Haarlem (?) before 1466 (?) *d* Haarlem (?) date unknown. *Religious subjects and decorative work.* Documented working Haarlem 1481-1552 (?). Van Mander (1604) records him as master of M. van Heemskerck and adds that he had two sons Lucas and Floris, also painters who went to Rome. Presumed by some identical with Willem Cornelisz q.v.
[Fl. 559, Fl. 883, Fl. 892, Fl. 421.]

Willigen, Pieter van der. Flemish Sch. *b* Bergen-op-Zoom c. 1635 *d* Antwerp 1694. *Still life (some with 'Vanitas' emblems* (cf. J. B. Boel, P. Boel and C. N. Gysbrechts). Went Antwerp where pupil of T. Willeboirts 1653; Master Antwerp Guild 1655; with J. E. Quellinus assessed the large collection of the Antwerp Postmaster J. B. Anthoine (cf. J. (Velvet) Brueghel and A. Brouwer) 1691. His brother Jan v. d. W. (Master in Antwerp Guild 1662) was his pupil. A *Children blowing soap bubbles, with a skull* is recorded.
[Fl. 612, Fl. 107, Fl. 892, Fl. 213.]

Wils, Steven. Flemish Sch. *b* Antwerp(?) before 1600 *d* Antwerp 1628. *Religious subjects, 'history', mythologies and allegories.* Pupil of A. Janssens. Master Antwerp Guild 1615; Dean 1625. An inventory made on his death records among works by him in his studio *Justice asleep, Justice triumphant, Pan and Apollo, Satyr admiring the beauty of Diana, David offering the head of Goliath to Saul, S. Francis, S. John preaching in the wilderness* (cf. M. van Cleve) and other religious subjects. He owned a number of pictures including *A young woman taking an old man's purse* by 'Meester Quinten' (Massys?), a *Taking chestnuts from the fire* by Marten van Cleve, a *Portrait of Michiel Coxie with a death's head in his hand,* a *Judith with the head of Holofernes* (cf. Madrid Judith Painter) and a *Temptation of S. Anthony* by F. Verbeeck q.v.
[Fl. 631 (1910), Fl. 213.]

Winder, F. J. Flemish Sch. 18th cent. **Signed Example:** BRUGES *Portrait of a man,* 1723. Presumed by some (before the signature was discovered) the work of the French painter Hyacinthe Rigaud.
[Fl. 114.]

Winghe, Jeremias van. Flemish Sch. *b* son of Joos van W., Brussels 1578 (not Frankfort 1587) *d* Frankfort 1645. *Portraits.* Pupil of his father in Frankfort and of F. Badens in Amsterdam. Visited Rome; returned Frankfort and married a rich lady. **Signed Example:** FRANKFORT Städel. *Maria Stalburg* 1611.
[Fl. 559, Fl. 892, Fl. 907.]

★**Winghe, Joos van.** Flemish Sch. *b* Brussels 1542 or 1544 *d* Frankfort 1603. *'History', religious subjects, allegories and interiors with social scenes* (cf. H. Francken the elder, F. Francken II, F. Badens, A. L. Fonteyn, H. Staben). Spent four years in Rome; visited Paris (cf. C. Ketel); returned

Brussels; appointed Court painter to Alexander Farnese. Duke of Parma (governor of the Netherlands from 1578); was among burghers of Brussels sent to negotiate the surrender of the city to Parma 1585; resigned to Otto van Veen his post as Duke's painter and emigrated (cf. D. v. d. Queborne) to Frankfort (cf. F. van Valkenborch, J. V. de Vries, H. van Steenwyck the elder) 1586. **Signed Examples:** VIENNA K. *Apelles painting Campaspe* (two versions). **Documented Examples** (mentioned by Van Mander and engraved): AMSTERDAM Rijks. *Night banquet and masquerade* (cf. Jooris v. Cleve). DÜSSELDORF *Samson and Delila.* Recorded by Van Mander: *Andromeda, The story of Pyneas, Belgica's Ordeal (Tyranny trampling on religion)* (allegory of the suffering Netherlands after Parma's conquest), *Conversion of S. Paul, Last Supper* (with architecture by P. V. de Vries painted for Brussels S. Géry where seen by Descamps 1769) and *Justice protecting Innocence against Tyranny* owned by C. v. d. Voort q.v. Many others recorded by engravings.
[Fl. 559, Fl. 216, Fl. 892, Fl. 907, Fl. 419.]

Winne, Liévin de. Flemish Sch. *b* Ghent 1821 *d* Brussels 1880. *Some religious subjects, then mainly portraits; occasional genre.* Pupil in Ghent Acad. and of F. de Vigne; in Paris 1853; in Italy 1870. Represented in ANTWERP *The architect L. J. A. Roelandt* 1859, *Capt. v. d. Woestyne.* BRUSSELS *Leopold I of Belgium* and other portraits. GHENT *Lady in green* and other portraits.
[Fl. 139, Fl. 160 (1880), Fl. 892, Fl. Bib. 19th cent., Fl. 738, Fl. 296.]

Witte, Adrien de. Flemish Sch. *b* Liège 1850 *d* 1935. *Still life, genre, portraits; also active as engraver.* Pupil in Liège Acad.; lived for some years in Rome; Professor, then Director Liège Acad. Represented in BRUSSELS *The laundresses* (Rome) 1880. LIÈGE *Woman putting on her shoe, Man with a pipe, The laundress.*
[Fl. 892, Fl. 123.]

Witte, Cornelis de. Flemish Sch. *b* son of bronzecaster Elias de W. (and brother of P. de W. q.v.), Bruges before 1550 *d c.* 1615. *Landscapes.* Went Florence where served in Duke's Guard and began painting 1573; later went Munich and served in the Ducal Guard there. Vienna Liechtenstein has *Landscape* signed C. de Witte presumed by some his work.
[Fl. 559, Fl. 892.]

★**Witte, Gaspar (Jasper) de.** Flemish Sch. *b* son of Pieter de W. the younger, Antwerp 1624 *d* Antwerp 1681. *Italianate landscapes* (cf. J. F. Millet and P. Rysbraeck), *with religious and other figures; designs for tapestry, also active as artists' colourman.* G. Seghers was his godfather. Visited Italy and France; back in Antwerp by 1651; worked for Antwerp art dealer Forchoudt (cf. A. Casteels) from 1665; and sold many landscapes (some in collaboration with his brother P. de W. III q.v.) for export to Vienna and elsewhere. C. Huysmans was his pupil. **Signed Examples:** ANTWERP *Landscape with fortune teller* 1667, *Landscape with Christ healing the blind* 1671. Others in TURIN, VIENNA K. and Liechtenstein. An Antwerp inventory (1666) records *Two landscapes* with figures by A. Goubau q.v. The Forchoudts owned four pictures by H. v. Balen the younger with landscapes by G. de W.
[Fl. 86, Fl. 892, Fl. 212, Fl. 213.]

Witte, L. de. Presumed Flemish Sch. 18th cent. Painter of BUDAPEST. *Riding School* signed and dated 1737.
[Fl. 892.]

Witte, Pieter de (known in Italy as Pietro Candido and in Germany as Candid). Flemish Sch. *b* son of bronzecaster Elias de W., Bruges c. 1548 *d* Munich 1628. *Religious and allegorical subjects (oil and fresco), portraits; also modelled and worked as tapestry and architectural designer.* Went Italy with his father and worked Florence and Rome; assisted Vasari in

Sala Regia of the Vatican (*cf.* H. v. d. Broeck, D. Calvaert) 1572 and with his paintings for the cupola in Florence Cathedral 1573-4; met Van Mander in Italy; worked for Duke Albert of Bavaria; went Munich 1586; worked there for William V (*cf.* E. van Pee) and for Maximilian I who made him Court Painter for life and superintendent of all artists employed in the building of his palace. His daughter married the engraver P. Sadeler. **Signed Examples:** BRESCIA Carmelite Ch. *Annunciation* (P. Candidus pictor Ducis Bavariae) 1595. SCHLEISSHEIM *Holy Family* (P. Candidus) 1623. **Documented Examples:** MUNICH Frauenkirche *Assumption of the Virgin* 1620 (engraved); Jesuit Ch. *Annunciation*. *S. Ignatius Loyola* (engraved by Sadeler). A *Virgin with SS. Nicholas and Jerome* (fresco) was recorded in Florence S. Niccolo in 1591. (*Cf.* Munich Duchess Magdalena Painter.)

[Fl. 559, Fl. 612, Fl. 892, Fl. 798, Fl. 305, Fl. 600, Fl. 457 (1937).]

Witte, Pieter de, the younger. Flemish Sch. *b* Antwerp 1586 *d* Antwerp 1651. *Landscapes and religious subjects*. Pupil in Antwerp of P. v. d. Hulst. Master in Antwerp Guild 1610; an *Agony in the Garden* for Antwerp Townhall 1632 and eleven paintings for Audenarde Notre Dame are recorded. Gaspar de W. and P. de W. III were his sons.

[Fl. 86, Fl. 216, Fl. 107, Fl. 892.]

Witte, Pieter de III. Flemish Sch. *b* illegitimate son of P. de W. the younger, Antwerp 1617 *d* Antwerp 1667. *Landscapes, hunting scenes; and with his brother Gaspar de W. q.v. designer for tapestry.* Pupil of his father; then visited Italy; Master in Antwerp Guild 1647; worked Antwerp for Forchoudt firm of exporting art dealers (*cf.* A. Casteels) from 1652; letters from the Vienna branch of the firm record excellent sales of his work and lament his death.

[Fl. 215, Fl. 892, Fl. 212, Fl. 213.]

Wobeck (Wobrck or Vobere), Simon de. Flemish (Dutch) Sch. *b* Haarlem (?) before 1530 *d* after 1586. *Religious subjects.* Working in Sicily by 1557. **Signed Examples:** CATANIA Mus. *Adoration of the Kings* (Simon Wobeck) painted for Palermo Oratorium dei Tre Re 1585. PALERMO Orat. di S. Nicolò del Borgo *Assumption of the Virgin with Trinity, Apostles and S. Nicholas* (Simon Vobre me fecit 1581); Pinac. (depot) *Virgin of the Rosary* (copy of picture by V. de Pavia) from Partanna (Simon de Wobrck de Haarle f. 1585). Recorded works include *The Feast in the House of Simon* commissioned 1557. [Fl. 305.]

Woestyne, Gustave van de. Flemish Sch. *b* Ghent 1881 *d* Uccle 1947. *Religious and symbolist subjects, landscapes, portraits, still life.* Pupil in Ghent Acad.; went with his brother the poet Charles v. d. W. to Laethem St. Martin (nr. Ghent) (*cf.* V. de Saedeleer, A. Servaes, G. de Smet, J. de Praetere, C. Permeke, F. van den Berghe) 1899; left Laethem and lived Brussels and Louvain 1909-12; visited Italy 1912; went England and worked in Wales during German invasion (*cf.* D. Baertsoen, H. Daeye, C. Mertens, L. de Smet, E. Tytgat, V. de Saedeleer, C. Permeke) 1914-18; on return, appointed professor in Antwerp Higher Institute; later director Malines Acad.; member of L'Art Contemporain (Kunst van Heden) *cf.* R. Strebelle; exhibited with Salon des IX 1926 (*cf.* H. Daeye); in Italy 1927-8; returned Laethem 1942; his son Maximilien v. d. W. (*b* 1911) is also a painter. Represented in AMSTERDAM, ANTWERP *Christ showing his wounds* 1921, *The two Spring times, The blind man, Azure.* BRUSSELS *Sunday afternoon* 1914, *Still life* 1925, *Christ offering his blood* 1925, *Flowers from my garden* 1921, *Decorative landscape, The kiss of Judas* 1937. GHENT *The artist's wife, Head of a peasant, The answer.* LAETHEM St. MARTIN Church *S. Dominic receiving the rosary.* LIÈGE *The blind fiddler* 1920.

[Fl. 388, Fl. 888, Fl. 568, Fl. 708, Fl. 296.]

*Wolfordt (or Wolfaert), Artus. Flemish Sch. *b* Antwerp 1581 *d* Antwerp 1641. *Religious and 'history' subjects, some in landscape or garden settings (cf.* P. van Avont); *also genre.* Pupil of F. Francken the younger 1616; employed under Rubens on decorations for Pageant Entry of Cardinal Infante Ferdinand into Antwerp 1635 (*cf.* G. Weri); his daughter married G. van Herp *q.v.* P. van Lint was his pupil; Van Dyck painted his portrait. **Monogrammed Examples:** MADRID Prado *Flight into Egypt, Rest on the Flight.* A large *House of Simon* was exported (1669) to Vienna by the Forchoudt firm of Antwerp dealers (*cf.* A. Casteels); Erasmus Quellinus *q.v.* owned a *Judgement of Solomon.*

[Fl. 86, Fl. 425, Fl. 892, Fl. 440, Fl. 212, Fl. 213.]

Wolfordt (or Wolfaert), Jan Baptist. Flemish Sch. *b* son of Artus W., Antwerp 1625 *d* after 1658. *Italianate landscapes with genre figures (cf.* J. Miel) *and animals, hunting scenes.* Visited Italy; in Haarlem after 1647; in Rome 1658. **Signed Examples:** AMSTERDAM Rijks. *Italianate landscape with shawm player* 1646. ANTWERP Mus. Plantin *Hunting scene.* LILLE *Mountainous landscape with figures* 1650.

[Fl. 107, Fl. 892, Fl. 715 (1938).]

Wolfvoet, Victor. Flemish Sch. *b* son of a painter and art dealer of the same name, Antwerp 1612 *d* Antwerp 1652. *Religious subjects and 'history', also active as art dealer.* Pupil of Rubens; Master in Antwerp Guild 1644. His mother was a daughter of the painter A. v. Palerme *q.v.* and sister of Catherine v. Palerme wife of the painter and dealer P. Goetkint *q.v.* The inventory of his possessions after his death records over 500 pictures (*cf.* Jeremias Wildens) by contemporary Flemish painters including pictures, sketches and drawings by Rubens, landscapes by J. d'Arthois, 'Brueghel' 'Momper', and 'Grimmer', T. van Haecht, P. v. d. Hulst, A. v. Stalbemt, L. van Uden, battlepieces by P. Meulener, seapieces by A. van Ertvelt, still life by A. Adriaenssen, A. Bosschaert, J. van Es, C. Luycx, C. Mahu, J. v. Son, J. P. v. Thielen, A. v. Utrecht and various works by P. v. Avont, G. Seghers, D. Teniers, F. Wouters and others. **Signed Example:** DRESDEN *Head of Medusa* (recalling picture by Rubens). **Monogrammed Example:** THE HAGUE Mauritshuis *Meeting of Abraham and Melchisedech* (VW). **Documented Example:** ANTWERP S. Jacques *The Visitation* 1639. A fully signed *Satyr and Bacchante* is recorded, and a *S. Catherine* figures in his own inventory.

[Fl. 216, Fl. 481, Fl. 892, Fl. 213.]

Wollés, Lucien. Flemish Sch. *b* Schaerbeek 1862. *Portraits.* Studied in Düsseldorf, and in Brussels Acad. Represented in BRUSSELS *Woman's portrait* 1891, *The painter A. J. Heymans, The art historian C. Lemonnier* 1905 (drawing), *The poet E. Verhaeren* 1905 (drawing). [Fl. 123.]

Wolvens, Henri. Flemish Sch. *b* Brussels 1896 *Figure pieces, interiors, landscapes, marines.* Pupil of H. Ottevaere; worked Paris and Prague; visited Italy; a leader of 'Animiste' group in Bruges and Brussels. Represented ANTWERP *Old lady, The window* and LIERRE.

[Fl. 567, Fl. 396, Fl. 208, Fl. 296, Fl. 17.]

*Worcester Destruction of Citadel Painter. Presumed Flemish Sch. late 16th cent. Name for painter of WORCESTER (Mass.) *Demoliton of the Spanish Citadel in Antwerp 1577* inscribed 'Antwerps Kasteel den 23 Augustus 157(7)'. Cf. M. van Cleve, J. de Gheyn the elder and Antwerp Destruction of Citadel Painter.

*Worcester Girl at Clavichord Painter. Presumed Flemish Sch. 16th cent. Name for painter of WORCESTER (U.S.A.) *Girl playing the clavichord*, Presumed by some identical with J. S. van Hemessen *q.v.*

*Worcester Saint and Donor Painter. Presumed Flemish (or French) Sch. 15th cent. Name for painter of WORCESTER (Mass.) *Saint and donor.* Presumed by some a portrait of Claude de Toulongeon with his patron saint S. Claude.
[F. 778, Fl. 710.]

Wortelmans, D., see Oortelmans.

Woutermaertens, Édouard. Flemish Sch. *b* Courtrai 1819 *d* Courtrai 1897. *Animals (mostly sheep).* Pupil of L. Robbe. Represented in BRUGES *Sheep returning.* COURTRAI.
[Fl. 114.]

*Wouters, Frans. Flemish Sch. *b* son of furniture maker, Lierre 1612 *d* Antwerp through accident with a pistol, 1659. *Landscapes with mythological, religious and genre figures; also active as engraver and art dealer.* Pupil of P. v. Avont in Antwerp 1629; Master Antwerp Guild 1634; joined Rubens' workshop 1634; worked under Rubens on Pageant Entry into Antwerp of Cardinal Infante Ferdinand (*cf.* G. Weri) 1635; went Vienna and became painter to Emperor Ferdinand II; came England (*cf.* C. de Neve, P. Vleughels and D. Teniers the younger) with Emperor's ambassador and wrote the Antwerp dealer Forchoudt (*cf.* A. Casteels) 'I can't complain because I ride here daily in a carriage with six horses and dine at the ambassador's table with twenty-one footmen behind' 1636; appointed painter to Charles Prince of Wales; returned Antwerp and took part in valuing Rubens' pictures at Château de Steen, in fulfilment of latter's will, 1641; helped the second Duke of Buckingham to raise money on his collection evacuated to Antwerp; married a rich lady 1644; collaborated with J. Brueghel the younger and P. v. Avont; sold works to Antwerp dealers for export to Vienna and Seville. J. Huysmans was among his pupils. **Signed Examples:** DOLE *Conversation piece in a landscape* 1654. OLMÜTZ *Diana and Callisto.* VIENNA K. *Landscape with Diana resting* 1630 or 1636. **Monogrammed Examples:** BUDAPEST *Juno in the Underworld.* COPENHAGEN *Landscape with Venus and Adonis.* GOTHA *The Rape of Europa.* LONDON N.G. *Landscape with nymphs and satyrs.* NANCY *Andromeda.* **Documented Examples:** LONDON Royal Coll. (Hampton Court) *Landscape with rainbow and man at plough* (Commonwealth inventory, sold 1650). VIENNA K. *Triumph of Silenus, Wooded landscape with Hagar and Ishmael, Landscape with Holy Family with S. Anthony of Padua, Triumph of Time* (all in Archduke Leopold Wilhelm inventory 1659). A ceiling (*Hercules on Olympus*) for one of the London Royal Palaces, a *S. Sebastian* and a *Landscape with man on a watercart* (Charles I coll.) are recorded by Vertue (before 1756); a small painting *Entry into Antwerp of Cardinal Infante Ferdinand as Governor General* and a '*Conversatie*' were among pictures owned by V. Wolfvoet *q.v.* 1652. A *Pan and Syrinx* and copies of works by Rubens are recorded in an inventory 1644.
[Fl. 86, Fl. 425, Fl. 215, Fl. 826, Fl. 105, Fl. 892, Fl. 212, Fl. 213, Fl. 214, Fl. 899.]

Wouters, Gomar. Flemish Sch. *b* Antwerp *c.* 1649 or 1658 *d* Rome (?) after 1696. '*History*' *also worked as engraver.* Settled in Rome 1680. [Fl. 425, Fl. 612, Fl. 84.]

Wouters (Wauters), Jan Lodewick de. Flemish Sch. *b* Ghent 1731 *d* after 1777. *Landscapes; also active as an engraver.* **Signed Examples:** CASSEL *Moonlight landscape* (two).
[Fl. 892.]

Wouters, Rik. Flemish Sch. *b* son of cabinet maker, Malines 1882 *d* Amsterdam 1916. *Figure pieces, interiors, landscapes, still life, portraits in Fauve conventions* (*cf.* C. Dehoy); *also worked as sculptor* (*Portrait of E. Tytgat* 1910; *La vierge folle* inspired by the dancer Isadora Duncan 1912). Left school at 12; began as wood carver in his father's workshop; pupil in Malines and Brussels Acads.; exhibited first with Antwerp

'L'art Contemporain' (Kunst van Heden) *cf.* R. Strebelle 1909; friendship with E. Tytgat *c.* 1910; in Paris 1912; made arrangement with French dealer in Brussels which enabled him to work without financial worries; in army and interned in Holland during German invasion (*cf.* F. v. d. Berghe) 1914; died after a series of operations at age of thirty-three. Represented in AMSTERDAM, ANTWERP *Woman ironing* 1912, *Education, Still life, Self portrait with a cigar, Interior with embroiderer, Woman in white, Dining table, Woman resting, The Chapel, Woman at the window* 1915. BRUSSELS *Apples in a bowl, Woman with yellow necklace, Landscape at Boitsfort, Simon Lévy* 1913, *The flautist, Still life.* PARIS Jeu de Paume *Mme. Wouters* 1912.
[Fl. 202, Fl. 388, Fl. 890, Fl. 296, Fl. 252.]

Woutiers, C., see Wautier.

Wouwer, Abraham. Flemish Sch. *b* Antwerp before 1610. *Peasant genre* (*cf.* D. Teniers the younger and J. van Craesbeeck). **Signed Example:** DESSAU *Peasants making music.*
[Fl. 892.]

Wraghe, Johannes. Flemish Sch. *b* Antwerp before *c.* 1550 *d* place unknown after 1592. Master in Antwerp Guild 1571; assistant to Hendrik v. d. Broeck *q.v.* in Perugia 1580-92. **Signed Example:** MONGIOVINO (nr. Perugia) Church *Visitation* (Johannes Wraghe de Anversa). [Fl. 305.]

Wtewael, see Uytewael.

Wueluwe, Hendrik van. Flemish Sch. *b* Antwerp (?) before 1470 *d* Antwerp 1533. Master Antwerp Guild 1483; Dean 1523. [Fl. 16.]

Wueluwe, Jan van. Flemish Sch. *b* presumed son of H. van W., Antwerp (?) before 1490 *d* Antwerp (?) after 1556. Master Antwerp Guild 1503; recorded in other offices 1521-43. His portrait by an unknown artist is in Antwerp Mus. (No. 968).
[Fl. 16.]

Wyct, van der see Battel, van.

Wyelant, see Vrelant.

Wynants, Sander. Flemish Sch. *b* Malines 1903. Nephew of sculptor Ernest W. Designed tapestry for Belgian Pavilion in Paris Exhibition 1937 (*cf.* F. Jespers and R. Strebelle).
[Fl. 296.]

Wynckelman, François Jacques Jean. Flemish Sch. *b* Bruges 1762 *d* Bruges 1844. *Landscapes.* Went Paris where pupil of J. B. Suvée *q.v. c.* 1781; Italy 1784-9; returned Bruges 1790. President of the Council of Administration of Bruges Academy 1805 and painted as such by J. D. Odevaere *q.v.* A *Neapolitan landscape is recorded.* [Fl. 112, Fl. 892, Fl. 798.]

Wyngaerde, Antonio van den (presumed by some identical with Antonio de Bruselas and de las Viñas). Flemish Sch. *b* Antwerp or Brussels before 1510 *d* Spain (?) after 1572. *Lansdcapes and city views, in pen and w.* (some published by Plantin). Visited Rome and London (*cf.* S. v. d. Meulen); visited Spain *c.* 1558; requested Margaret of Parma Regent of the Netherlands for permission to emigrate there with his family and property and enter service of Philip II 1561; settled Spain (*cf.* J. Floris, R. Diriksen, P. de Kempener) and worked Madrid and neighbourhood; was granted a disability pension by the king because both his hands were crippled 1572; his daughter married R. Diriksen. **Signed Examples:** LONDON Vic. and Alb. *Views of Spanish cities* (thirty-one leaves, many signed and annotated and dated 1558-70). OXFORD Bodleian Library *Hampton Court, Oatlands* 1559, *Richmond* 1562. VIENNA Hofbib. *Views of Spanish cities*

1563-70 (some inscribed 'Wingarde' and some Hoefnagel *q.v.*). A series of *Dutch and Flemish views* signed Antonio de las Viñas was recorded in the Pardo Palace, Madrid 1582.

[Fl. 153, Fl. 481, Fl. 892, Fl. 95 (1914), Fl. 857 (1947).]

Wytevelde (Witevelde), Baldwin van. Flemish Sch. *b* Ghent (?) before 1420 *d* after 1457. *Religious subjects.* A *Temptation of S. Anthony* (*cf.* H. Bosch) for Ghent S. Bavon 1439 (*cf.* Hubert and Jan van Eyck) and an altarpiece for Ghent, Nieuwenbossche Abbey are recorded.

[Fl. 135, Fl. 385, Fl. 88.]

Wytsman, Juliette, Mme. (*née* **Trulemans.**) Flemish Sch. *b* Brussels 1866 *d* Brussels 1925. *Flowers, landscapes (in Impressionist conventions), genre.* Pupil of P. Hendrickx. Exhibited in Liverpool 1909. Represented in ANTWERP *Summer* (*Evening on the Meuse*). BRUSSELS *Broom in flower.* GHENT *Apple blossom.* [Fl. 296, Fl. 17.]

Wytsman, Rodolfe. Flemish Sch. *b* Termonde 1860 *d* Linkebeek 1927. *Landscapes (in Impressionist conventions) mainly of Brabant motifs.* Student in Ghent and Brussels Acads.; member of Brussels group 'Les Vingt' (Les XX) (*cf.* J. Ensor) 1884. Represented in AMSTERDAM, ANTWERP *Equinoctial storms.* BRUSSELS *Saint Éloi farm.* GHENT *Orchard.* LIÈGE *Winter at La Hulpe.* [Fl. 388, Fl. 17.]

Y

Ykens, see Ijkens.

Yperen, Karel van see Foort.

Ypern, J. Thomas van see Thomas.

Ysenbrandt (Isenbrant, Ysenbaert), Adriaen. Flemish Sch. *b* place unknown before 1500 *d* Bruges 1551. *Nudes and portraits.* Pupil of G. David; Master (as 'foreigner') Bruges Guild 1510; held various offices in Guild 1516-48; collaborated on decorations for Pageant Entry of Charles V into Bruges (*cf.* J. Provoost) 1520. **Signed Examples:** None. **Documented Examples:** None. Pictures presumed by some his work are in various museums (*cf.* Seven Sorrows of the Virgin Master).

[Fl. 752, Fl. 93, Fl. 892, Fl. 316, Fl. 530, Fl. 615, Fl. 678.]

Ysendijck, Antoon van, Flemish Sch. *b* Antwerp 1801 *d* Brussels 1875. *Costume history, religious subjects, genre, portraits.* Pupil in Antwerp Acad. of M. v. Brée. Rome prizewinner 1823; in Italy *c.* 1825-8; in Paris during reign of Louis Philippe (*cf.* G. Wappers); Director Mons Acad. 1840. His son Léon Jean van Y. was also a painter. Represented in Belgian churches and in ANTWERP *The painter M. v. Brée, Self portrait, Judith.* MONS *Aristomenes.* VERSAILLES *Capture of Ypres 1744* 1837 and *Proclamation of Peace between France and England 1783* 1837.

[Fl. 451, Fl. 612, Fl. 892, Fl. 221.]

Ysselsteyn (or Isselsteyn), A. Flemish or Dutch Sch. *b* before 1630 *d* Utrecht 1684. *Still life* (*cf.* A. van Utrecht). In Utrecht where married daughter of A. Bloemaert the younger 1653. Presumed by some identical with Dutch portrait painter Adriaen van Essestein recorded Rome 1647. **Signed Example:** SCHLEISSHEIM *A dead cock and small birds on a table.* (*cf.* C. Luyckx). [Fl. 892, Fl. 798.]

Z

*Zeeu (or **Zeeuw**), **Cornelis de.** Flemish (Dutch) Sch. *b* Zeeland (?) before 1545 *d* after 1570. *Portraits.* Master Antwerp Guild 1558. **Signed Examples:** AMSTERDAM Rijks. *Bearded man in cap* 1563. BRUSSELS *Jacques della Faille* 1569. MUNICH A.P. *Portrait of a man* 1570. OXFORD S. John's College *Man in a red chair* 1565. Brussels (1079) *Marie Gammels wife of Jacques della Faille* is presumed by some a companion piece to the Brussels signed example. (*Cf.* also Amsterdam Moucheron Family Painter).
[Fl. 826, Fl. 665, Fl. 798.]

Zeghers see **Seghers.**

Zevenbergen, Georges van. Flemish Sch. *b* S. Jean-Molenbeek 1877. *Figure pieces, still life.* Pupil in Molenbeek and Brussels Acads. Represented ANTWERP *The etcher.*
[Fl. 17.]

Zierickzee, Thomas van. Flemish (Dutch) Sch. 16th cent. Pupil of F. Floris.
[Fl. 559.]

Ziesel (or **Sisel**), **Georges** (**Joris**) **Frédéric.** Flemish Sch. *b* Hoogstraeten 1756 *d* Antwerp 1809. *Flowers and fruit, sometimes on glass or in miniature.* Worked mainly in Antwerp but lived some time in Paris (*cf.* J. F. Dael and J. F. Eliaerts); was friend of flower painter P. Faes *q.v.*, B. P. Ommeganck and F. M. Smits who painted his portrait. **Signed Example:** ANTWERP *Flowers with insects and fruit on marble table and fish in bowl reflecting window and houses opposite.*
[Fl. 451, Fl. 481, Fl. 892.]

Zittow, M. see **Vienna Catherine Painter.**

Zoon see **Son.**

Zutman, L. see **Suavius.**

BIBLIOGRAPHIC INDEX TO THE DICTIONARY

Books and other publications referred to by code numbers at the end of the entries in the DICTIONARY can be identified by this INDEX. The books referred to under the signs Fl. Bib. 19th cent. and Fl. Bib 20th cent. will be found in NOTES ON THE LITERATURE on pp.725–759

Fl. 1	A. de A. (contributors)	L'Amour de l'Art.	*Paris*	from 1891
Fl. 2	A. F. E. H. (contributors)	L'Art flamand et hollandais.	*Antwerp and Paris*	from 1896
Fl. 3	A. M. (contributors)	L'Art Moderne.	*Brussels*	1881–1914
Fl. 4	Alexandre, A. and Champsaur, F.	Félicien Rops et son temps.	*Brussels*	1897
Fl. 5	Alvin, L.	Antoine Wiertz, sa vie et ses œuvres, analyse des documents laissés par l'auteur.	*Brussels*	1869
Fl. 6	Alvin, L.	F. J. Navez: Vie, Œuvres, Correspondance.	*Brussels*	1870
Fl. 7	Amsterdam	Amsterdam Rijksmuseum Catalogue (Riemsdijk).	*Amsterdam*	1920
Fl. 8	Amsterdam	Amsterdam Rijksmuseum Catalogue. (Schmidt-Degener). *Supplement*	*Amsterdam* *Amsterdam*	1927 1934
Fl. 9	André, P.	Le Peintre Willem Linnig Jun.	*Brussels*	1907
Fl. 10	Annuaire	Annuaire des Musées royaux des beaux-arts de Belgique. (Edited by L. van Puyvelde). 2 vols.	*Brussels*	1938–1939
Fl. 11	Annuaire (contributors)	Annuaire de l'Académie royale de Belgique.	*Brussels*	
Fl. 12	Anonimo.	Notizie d'opere di disegno.		1512–1543
	(Anonimo of Morelli. Marc Anton Michiel?)	*Published by J. Morelli.* *Edited Frimmel*	*Bassano*	1800 1888
Fl. 13	Antwerp	Musée Royal des Beaux-Arts d'Anvers. Catalogue descriptif. Maîtres Anciens. (Pol de Mont and Wappers, J.).	*Antwerp*	1920
Fl. 14	Antwerp	Antwerp Museum Catalogue. Modern Painters.	*Antwerp*	1930
Fl. 15	Antwerp	Maîtres Anciens du Musée Royal d'Anvers. (A. H. Cornette).	*Antwerp*	1939
Fl. 16	Antwerp	Koninklijk Museum voor Schone Kunsten.—Antwerpen. Beschrijvende Catalogus. Oude Meesters. (Delen).	*Antwerp*	1948
Fl. 17	Antwerp	Koninklijk Museum voor Schone Kunsten.—Antwerpen. Berchrijvende Catalogus. Moderne Meesters. (Buschmann van Rijswijck).	*Antwerp*	1948
Fl. 18	Apollo (contributors)	Apollo.	*London*	from 1925
Fl. 19	Annales (contributors)	Annales de la Société Royale des Beaux-Arts de Gand.		
Fl. 20	Archivo (contributors)	Archivo Español de Arte y Arqueologia.	*Madrid*	1925 in progress
Fl. 21	Arents, P.	Geschriften van en over Rubens.	*Antwerp*	1948
Fl. 22	Argenville, D. d'	Abrégé de la vie des Plus Fameux Peintres. 3 vols.	*Paris*	1745–1752

Fl. 23	Armstrong, W.	Alfred Stevens.	*Paris and London*	1881
Fl. 24	Avermaete, R.	James Ensor.	*Antwerp*	1947
Fl. 25	Annales (contributors)	Annales de l'Académie royale d'archéologie de Belgique.	*Antwerp*	1843–1930
Fl. 26	Abry, L.	Les hommes illustres de la nation liégeoise.	*Liège*	1867
Fl. 27	Argenville, D. d'	Voyage pittoresque de Paris.	*Paris*	1749
		6th edition	*Paris*	1778
Fl. 28	Auerbach, E.	Tudor Artists.	*London*	1954
Fl. 36	Baglione, G.	Le vite dei pittori, scultori et architetti, dal pontificato di Gregorio XIII del 1572 in fino al tempi di Papa Urbano Ottavo nel 1642.	*Rome*	1642
Fl. 37	Baglione, G. and Passari, G. B.	Le Vite dei pittori, scultori architetti ed intagliatori. Con la vita di Salvator Rosa Napoletano scritta da Giovanni Batista Passari.	*Naples*	1733
		Modern edition	*Rome*	1935
Fl. 38	Baker, C. H. Collins	Lely and the Stuart Portrait Painters.	*London*	1912
Fl. 39	Baker, C. H. Collins and Constable, W. G.	English painting of the 16th and 17th centuries.	*Florence and Paris*	1930
Fl. 40	Baker, C. H. Collins	British Painting.	*London*	1933
Fl. 41	Baldass, L.	Die Niederländische Landschaftsmalerei von Patinier bis Bruegel.	*Vienna*	1918
Fl. 42	Baldass, L.	Die Anfänge des Niederländischen Sittenbildes.	*Vienna*	1918
Fl. 43	Baldass, L.	Die Gemälde des Lucas van Leyden.	*Vienna*	1923
Fl. 44	Baldass, L.	Joos van Cleve.	*Vienna*	1925
Fl. 45	Baldass, L.	Gotik und Renaissance im Werke des Quentin Metsys.	*Vienna*	1933
Fl. 46	Baldass, L.	Hans Memling.	*Vienna*	1942
Fl. 47	Baldass, L.	Hieronymus Bosch.	*Vienna*	1943
Fl. 48	Baldinucci, F.	Notizie dei professori del disegno da Cimabue in quà . . . 6 vols.	*Florence*	1681–1728
		Later edition: 'Opere di F.B.'		
		Annotated by D. M. Manni.	*Milan*	1808–1812
Fl. 49	Balkema, C. H.	Biographie des peintres flamands et hollandais . . . depuis Jean et Hubert van Eyck jusqu'à nos jours.	*Ghent*	1844
Fl. 50	Baltimore	Walters Art Gallery Journal.	*Baltimore (U.S.A.)*	1938
Fl. 51	Barker, G. W.	Antoine Watteau.	*London*	1939
Fl. 52	Bartsch, A.	Catalogue raisonné de toutes les estampes de Lucas de Leyde.	*Vienna*	1798
Fl. 53	Bartsch, A.	Le Peintre-Graveur.	*Vienna*	1803–1821
		21 vols.		
		Supplements	*Leipzig*	1843
Fl. 54	Baschet, A.	F. Pourbus. Peintre de portraits à la cour de Mantoue. *in* Gazette des Beaux Arts.	*Paris*	1868
Fl. 55	Bastelaer, R. van	Les estampes de Peter Bruegel l'ancien.	*Brussels*	1907
Fl. 56	Bastelaer, R. van and Hulin de Loo G.	Peter Bruegel l'Ancien, son œuvre et son temps. 2 vols.	*Brussels*	1907 1906–
Fl. 57	Bastien, A.	Jan de Greef.		1932

Fl. 58	Bautier, P.	Lancelot Blondeel.	*Brussels*	1910
Fl. 59	Bautier, P.	Juste Suttermans, peintre des Médicis.	*Brussels and Paris*	1912
Fl. 60	Bax, D.	Ontcijfering van Jeroen Bosch.	*The Hague*	1949
Fl. 61	Baxter, S.	Spanish colonial architecture in Mexico.		1902
Fl. 62	Bazin, G.	Memling.	*Paris*	1939
Fl. 63	Becdelièvre, Comte de	Biographie liégeoise.	*Liège*	1836
Fl. 64	Beets, N.	Lucas de Leyde.	*Brussels*	1913
Fl. 65	Beffroi	Le Beffroi (Edited by W. H. J. Weak).	*Brussels*	1865–1876
Fl. 66	Bellier de la Chavignerie, E. and Auvray, L.	Dictionnaire général des artistes de l'école française. 2 vols.	*Paris*	1882–1887
Fl. 67	Bellori, G. P.	Le vite dei pittori, scultori ed architetti moderni. *Later edition* *Modern edition*	*Rome* *Rome* *Rome*	1672 1728 1931
Fl. 68	Bendère, R. de	Jacob Smits.	*Brussels*	1923
Fl. 69	Bendère, R. de	Albert Servaes.	*Brussels*	1927
Fl. 70	Bendère, R. de	Pierre Paulus.	*Paris and Brussels*	1929
Fl. 71	Bendère, R. de	Albert Saverys.	*Paris*	1929
Fl. 72	Bénédite, L.	Great Painters of the Nineteenth Century.	*London*	1910
Fl. 73	Bénézit, E.	Dictionnaire ... des peintres, sculpteurs, dessinateurs et graveurs de tous les temps et de tous les pays. 3 vols. *New edition* 8 vols.	*Paris* *Paris*	1911–1913 1948–1954
Fl. 74	Bergmans, S.	D. Calvart: Catalogue critique.	*Brussels*	1931
Fl. 75	Bergmans, S.	Denis Calvart, peintre anversois.	*Brussels*	1934
Fl. 76	Berlin	Die Gemäldegalerie des Kaiser-Friedrich-Museums: Die Germanischen Länder. (W. Bode).	*Berlin*	1911
Fl. 77	Berlin	Beschreibendes Verzeichnis der Gemälde im Kaiser-Friedrich-Museum ...	*Berlin*	1931
Fl. 78	Bernard, C.	Pierre Breughel l'Ancien.	*Brussels*	1908
Fl. 79	Bernard, C.	Pierre Paulus.	*Brussels*	1935
Fl. 80	Bernard, C.	Opsomer.	*Antwerp*	1947
Fl. 81	Bernard, C.	Jacob Smits.	*Brussels*	1948
Fl. 82	Bernier, A.	Pierre Paulus.	*Brussels*	1939
Fl. 83	Bernt, W.	Die Niederländischen Maler des 17. Jahrhunderts. 3 vols.	*Munich*	1948
Fl. 84	Bertolotti, A.	Artisti belgi ed olandesi a Roma nei secoli XVI e XVII. *Supplement*	*Florence* *Rome*	1880 1885
Fl. 85	Bertram, A.	The life of Sir Peter Paul Rubens.	*London*	1928
Fl. 86	Bie, C. de	Het gulden Cabinet ...	*Antwerp*	1661
Fl. 87	Billiet, J.	Frans Masereel.	*Paris*	1925

Fl. 88	B. N. de B. (contributors)	Biographie Nationale de Belgique.	*Brussels*	from 1866
Fl. 89	Blanc, C.	Les artistes de mon temps.		1876
Fl. 90	Bleynié, L.	Jean Brueghel de Velours.	*Toulon*	1886
Fl. 91	Bode, W.	Adriaen Brouwer.	*Berlin*	1923
Fl. 92	Bode, W. von	Das Flämische Sittenbild in der ersten Hälfte des XVIII Jahrhunderts. (P. van Angellis und P. van Santvoort). *in* Zeitschrift für bildenden Kunst.	*Munich*	1924–1925
Fl. 93	Bodenhausen, E. von	Gerard David und seine Schule.	*Munich*	1905
Fl. 94	Boetticher, F. von	Malerwerke des 19ten Jahrhunderts. *Later edition*	*Dresden*	1891 1898
Fl. 95	Boletín (contributors)	Boletín de la Sociedad Española de Excursiones.	*Madrid*	from 1892
Fl. 96	Bom, E. de	H. de Braekeleer.	*Antwerp*	1941
Fl. 97	Bonafons, N.	Pierre Joseph Redouté.	*Paris*	1846
Fl. 98	Borghini, R.	Il Riposo in ciu della Pittura e della Scultura ...	*Florence*	1584
Fl. 99	Bortier, P.	Coebergher, peintre, architecte, ingénieur.	*Brussels*	1875
Fl. 100	Bosch, E. van der	Jacob Smits.	*Antwerp*	1930
Fl. 101	Boschini, M.	Le Minere della Pittura ... *Enlarged edition* Le Ricchi Minere della Pittura Veneziana. *Later edition* Descrizione di tutti le pubbliche pitture della Città di Venezia ...	*Venice* *Venice*	1664 1674 1733
Fl. 102	Bosmant, J.	Richard Heinz.	*Antwerp*	1948
Fl. 103	Boucher, F.	Alfred Stevens.	*Paris*	1930
Fl. 104	Branden, F. J. van den	Geschiedenis der Academie van Antwerpen.	*Antwerp*	1864
Fl. 105	Branden, F. J. van den	Frans Wouters.	*Antwerp*	1872
Fl. 106	Branden, F. J. van den	Willem van Nieuweland.	*Ghent*	1875
Fl. 107	Branden, F. J. van den	Geschiedenis der Antwerpsche Schilderschool. 3 vols.	*Antwerp*	1878–1883
Fl. 108	Branden, F. J. van den	Adriaan de Brouwer en Joos van Craesbeeck.	*Antwerp*	1882
Fl. 109	Bredius, A.	Künstler Inventare vom 16–18 Jahrhundert. 7 vols. and Index.	*The Hague*	1915–1922
Fl. 110	Brion, M.	Breughel.	*Paris*	1939
Fl. 111	Brising, H.	Quentin Metsys und der Ursprung des Italianismus in der Kunst der Niederlände.	*Leipzig*	1908
Fl. 112	Bruges	Catalogue du Musée de l'Académie de Bruges. (W. H. J. Weale).	*Bruges*	1861
Fl. 113	Bruges	La peinture à Bruges. (H. Fierens-Gevaert).	*Brussels and Paris*	1922
Fl. 114	Bruges	Catalogue illustré du Musée Communal des Beaux-Arts à Bruges. (Hosten and Strubbe).	*Bruges*	1935
Fl. 115	Bruges	Exposition Memlinc (Catalogue).	*Bruges*	1939
Fl. 116	Bruinvis, C. W.	Levensschetsen ... over beeld. Kunstenaars te Alkmaar.		1905

Fl. 117	Brünn	Brünn Museum Catalogue.		1899
Fl. 118	Brussels	Catalogue raisonné du Musée Wiertz: Précédé d'une Biographie du Peintre. (L. Watteau).	*Brussels*	1861
Fl. 119	Brussels	Brussels Town Hall (Guide).	*Brussels*	1896
Fl. 120	Brussels	Catalogue des tableaux anciens du Musée de Bruxelles. (A. J. Wauters).	*Brussels*	1908
Fl. 121	Brussels	The Brussels Gallery of Old Masters. (H. Fierens-Gevaert).	*Brussels and Paris*	1914
Fl. 122	Brussels	Catalogue de la Peinture ancienne: Musée de Bruxelles. (H. Fierens-Gevaert and A. Laes).	*Brussels*	1927
Fl. 123	Brussels	Catalogue de la peinture moderne: Musée de Bruxelles.	*Brussels*	1928
Fl. 124	Brussels	Catalogue de la peinture ancienne: Musée de Bruxelles. (P. Fierens).	*Brussels*	1949
Fl. 125	Bruyne, E. de	Albert Servaes.	*Brussels and Amsterdam*	
Fl. 126	Bryan, M.	Dictionary of Painters and Engravers. 2 vols.	*London*	1816
		Later editions (*Stanley*)	*London*	1849
		(*Graves and Armstrong*)	*London*	1884– 1889
		(*Williamson*)	*London*	1903– 1904
		(*reprint*)	*London*	1930
Fl. 127	Buchelius, A.	Res Pictoriae . . .	*MS.*	*c.* 1585
		Modern edition (*edited by G. J. Hoogewerff*).	*The Hague*	1928
Fl. 128	Budapest	Catalogue of the Old Masters in the Budapest Museum of Fine Arts. (G. de Tèrey).	*Budapest*	1924
Fl. 129	Buet, C.	T. Lybaert.	*Paris*	1902
Fl. 130	Bulletin (contributors)	Bulletin de l'Académie Royale de Belgique.	*Brussels*	from 1832
Fl. 131	Burchard, L.	Catalogue of Rubens exhibition. (Wildenstein Gall.).	*London*	1950
Fl. 132	Burckhardt, J.	Erinnerungen aus Rubens. *English translation* Recollections of Rubens. (Edited by H. Gerson).	*Bâle* *London*	1898 1950
Fl. 133	Burlington (contributors)	The Burlington Magazine.	*London*	from 1903
Fl. 134	Buschmann, P.	J. Jordaens.	*Antwerp and Brussels*	1905
Fl. 135	Busscher, E. de	Recherches sur les peintres Gantois, des XIVe et XVe siècles.	*Ghent*	1859
Fl. 136	Busscher, E. de	Recherches sur les peintres et les sculpteurs à Gand aux XVIIe et XVIIIe siècles.	*Ghent*	1866
Fl. 137	Brussels	Catalogue du Musée Wiertz.	*Brussels*	1909
Fl. 138	Bartoli, F.	Notizie delle pitturi, sculture ed architetture che ornano le chiese e gli altri luoghi pubblici di tutte le piú rinomate città d'Italia. 2 vols.	*Venice*	1776– 1777
Fl. 139	Breton, J.	Liévin de Winne.	*Ghent*	1880
Fl. 140	Brassine, J.	L'Art Mosan.	*Liège*	1911
Fl. 141	Bullart, I.	Académie des sciences et des arts.	*Brussels*	1682

Fl. 142	Blanc, C.	Histoire des peintres de toutes les écoles. 14 vols.: École flamande.	*Paris*	1861– 1876
Fl. 143	Bisthoven, A. J. de and Parmentier, R.A.	Les Primitifs Flamands. Le Musée Communal de Bruges.	*Antwerp*	1951
Fl. 144	Baldass, L.	Jan van Eyck.	*London*	1952
Fl. 145	Brockwell, M.	The Pseudo-Arnolfini Portrait.	*London*	1952
Fl. 146	Bergström, Ingvar.	Dutch still life painting in the 17th century.	*London*	1956
Fl. 147	Cahiers (contributors) Cahiers de Belgique.		*Brussels*	from 1928
Fl. 148	Carducho, V.	Diálogos de la Pintura *in* Sánchez Cantón: Fuentes Literarias. . . . vol. II	*MS.* *Madrid*	1633 1933
Fl. 149	Cary, M. (and others)	The Oxford Classical Dictionary.	*Oxford*	1949
Fl. 150	Cartellieri, O.	Am Hofe der Herzöge von Burgund. *English edition* The Court of the Dukes of Burgundy.	*Bâle* *London*	1926 1929
Fl. 151	Casteele, D. van de	Keuren 1441–1774. Livres d'admission 1453–1574 et autres documents inédits concernant la Ghilde de St. Luc de Bruges suivis des keuren de corporation des peintres, sculpteurs et verriers de Gand 1541–1575. *Bruges*		1867
Fl. 152	Casteels, M.	Henry van de Velde.	*Brussels*	1932
Fl. 153	Ceán Bermúdez, J. A.	Diccionario . . . de las bellas artes en España. 6 vols.	*Madrid*	1800
Fl. 154	Celano	Notizie . . . di Napoli.		1692
Fl. 155	Cellis, G.	N. de Liemacker.	*Ghent*	1910
Fl. 156	Cespedes, P. de	Discurso de la Comparacion . . . *in* Sánchez Cantón: Fuentes Literarias. . . . vol. II.	*MS.* *Madrid*	1604 1933
Fl. 157	Chambéry	Chambéry Museum Catalogue. (J. Carotti).	*Chambéry*	1911
Fl. 158	Charles, G.	Frans Masereel, peintre.	*Paris*	1929
Fl. 159	Chatterton, E.	Old Sea Paintings.	*London and New York*	1928
Fl. 160	C. des A. (contributors)	La Chronique des Arts . . .	*Paris*	1874– 1922
Fl. 161	Clemen, P. (contributors)	Belgische Kunstdenkmäler vom neunten bis zum Ende des achtzehnten Jahrhunderts. 2 vols.	*Munich*	1923
Fl. 162	Clijmans, F.	Opsomer.	*Antwerp*	1942
Fl. 163	Cloquet, H.	Tournai et Tournaisis.	*Bruges*	1884
Fl. 164	Colin, P.	Opsomer.	*Brussels*	1933
Fl. 165	Colin, P.	Hippolyte Boulenger.	*Brussels*	1934
Fl. 166	Colin, P.	Brueghel le Vieux.	*Paris*	1936
Fl. 167	Combe, J.	Jérôme Bosch.	*Paris*	1946
Fl. 168	Comte, F. Le	Cabinet des Singularitez . . .	*Paris*	1699
Fl. 169	Conca, A.	Descrizione . . . . della Spagna.	*Parma*	1793
Fl. 170	Copenhagen	Katalog Statens Museum for Kunst. (L. Swane).	*Copenhagen*	1946
Fl. 171	Corbet, A.	Walter Vaes.	*Antwerp*	1948

Fl. 172	Corbet, A.	Hippolyte Daeye.	*Antwerp*	1949
Fl. 173	Corbet, A.	Pieter Coecke van Aelst.	*Antwerp*	1950
Fl. 174	Coremans, P. and Bisthoven, J. de	Van Eyck. The Adoration of the Mystic Lamb	*Antwerp*	1948
Fl. 175	Correia, V.	Pintores Portugeses dos seculos XV e XVI	*Coimbra*	1928
Fl. 176	Courtrai	Catalogue du Musée de Courtrai. (M. G. Caullet).	*Courtrai*	1912
Fl. 177	Crivelli, G.	Giovanni Brueghel, pittor fiamingo e sue lettere e quadretti esistensi presso l'Ambrosiana.	*Milan*	1868
Fl. 178	Croquez, A.	Les peintres flamands d'aujourd'hui.		1910
Fl. 179	Crowe, J. A. and Cavalcaselle, G. B.	Early Flemish painters. 3rd edition.	*London*	1879
Fl. 180	Crucy, F.	Les Brueghel.	*Paris*	1928
Fl. 181	Cust, L.	Anthony Van Dyck.	*London*	1900
Fl. 182	Cust, L.	The Van Dyck sketchbook at Chatsworth.	*London*	1905
Fl. 183	Cuypers, F.	James Ensor, l'homme et l'œuvre.	*Paris*	1925
Fl. 184	Colin, P.	Opsomer.	*Paris*	1931
Fl. 185	Clark, Sir K.	Landscape into Art.	*London*	1949
Fl. 186	Clement and Hutton	Art of the 19th century. *Later edition*	*London*	1879 1893
Fl. 194	Daniel, H.	Hieronymus Bosch.	*New York*	1947
Fl. 195	Danigrand, J.	Pierre Paulus.	*Brussels*	1937
Fl. 196	Dasnoy, A.	H. Daeye.	*Brussels*	1937
Fl. 197	David, J.	Louis David. 2 vols.	*Paris*	1880
Fl. 198	Defrance, L.	Autobiographie d'un Peintre Liégeois.	*Liège*	1906
Fl. 199	Dehaisnes, C.	Documents et extraits divers concernant l'histoire de l'art dans la Flandre, l'Artois et le Hainaut avant la XVe siècle. 2 vols.	*Lille*	1886
Fl. 200	Dehaisnes, C.	La vie et l'œuvre de Jean Bellegambe.	*Lille*	1890
Fl. 201	Delahaut, J. R.	Pierre Paulus.	*Brussels*	1933
Fl. 202	Delen, A. J. J.	Rik Wouters.	*Antwerp*	1922
Fl. 203	Delen, A. J. J.	Quentin Metsys.	*Brussels*	1926
Fl. 204	Delen, A. J. J.	De Vlaamsche Kunst, voor, tijdens en na Rubens. *in* Kryn, L. J.: Rubens en zijne eeuw.	*Brussels*	1927
Fl. 205	Delen, A. J. J. and Leclercq, R.	Guide des Musées Belges. *Later editions and English edition*	*Antwerp* *Antwerp and London*	1927 before 1935
Fl. 206	Delen, A. J. J.	Walter Vaes.	*Antwerp*	1942
Fl. 207	Delepierre, J. O.	Galerie d'artistes brugeois.	*Bruges*	1840
Fl. 208	Delevoy, R.	La Jeune Peinture Belge.	*Brussels*	1946
Fl. 209	Delruelle, J.	Pierre Paulus.	*Paris and Brussels*	1946
Fl. 210	Delsart, A.	P. J. Redouté.	*Valenciennes*	1841

Fl. 211	Demolder, J. E.	James Ensor.	*Brussels*	1892
Fl. 212	Denucé, J.	Art Export in the 17th century in Antwerp. The firm Forchoudt.	*Antwerp*	1931
Fl. 213	Denucé, J.	Inventories of the Art Collection in Antwerp in the 16th and 17th centuries.	*Antwerp*	1932
Fl. 214	Denucé, J.	Letters and documents concerning Jan Breughel I and II.	*Antwerp*	1934
Fl. 215	Descamps, J. B.	La Vie des Peintres Flamands, Allemands et Hollandois. 4 vols.	*Paris*	1753– 1763
Fl. 216	Descamps, J. B.	Voyage Pittoresque de la Flandre et du Brabant. *Annotated edition* (*C. Rochu*).	*Paris* *Paris*	1769 1838
Fl. 217	Descamps, A. I.	Jean Baptiste Juppin et N. La Fabrique.	*Namur*	1873
Fl. 218	Desmons, F.	Joseph Stallaert.	*Tournai*	1905
Fl. 219	Destrée, J.	Hugo van der Goes.	*Brussels and Paris*	1914
Fl. 220	Destrée, J.	Roger de la Pasture van der Weyden. 2 vols.	*Paris and Brussels*	1930
Fl. 221	Devillers, L.	Le passé artistique de la ville de Mons.	*Mons*	1885
Fl. 222	Díaz del Valle,	Epílogo y nomenclatura de algunos artífices. *in* Sánchez Cantón: Fuentes Literarias. . . . vol. II	*Madrid*	1656– 1659 1933
Fl. 223	D. N. B. (contributors)	Dictionary of National Biography. 63 vols. and supplements.	*London*	from 1885
Fl. 224	Diericx	Mémoires de la ville de Gand.		1813
Fl. 225	Diez, E.	Der Hofmaler Bartholomaeus Spranger. *in* Jahrbuch der Kunsthistorischen Sammlungen des Allerhöchsten Kaiserhauses.	*Vienna*	1909– 1910
Fl. 226	Dillon, E.	Rubens.	*London*	1909
Fl. 227	Dimier, L.	French Painting in the XVI century.	*London*	1904
Fl. 228	Dimier, L.	La miniature flamande.	*Paris*	1921
Fl. 229	Dimier, L. (editor)	Les peintres français du XVIIIe siècle. 2 vols.	*Paris and Brussels*	1928– 1930
Fl. 230	Dirksen, V. A.	Die Gemälde des Marten de Vos.	*Berlin*	1914
Fl. 231	Dlabacz	Kunstlerlexikon für Böhmen.		1815
Fl. 232	Dominici, B. de	Vite de' pittori, scultori ed architetti napolitani. 4 vols. *Later edition*	*Naples* *Naples*	1742– 1763 1840– 1846
Fl. 233	Doppelmayr, J. G.	Historische Nachrichten von den Nürnbergischen Mathematicis und Küstlern.	*Nuremberg*	1730
Fl. 234	Dresden	Katalog der Königlichen Gemäldegalerie zu Dresden. (K. Woermann).	*Dresden*	1887
Fl. 235	Dresden	Die Staatliche Gemäldegalerie zu Dresden: Katalog der Alten Meister. (H. Posse).	*Dresden*	1930
Fl. 236	Dublin	National Gallery of Ireland Catalogue. (T. Bodkin).	*Dublin*	1932
Fl. 237	Duclos, A.	Bruges. Histoire et Souvenirs.	*Bruges*	1910

Fl. 238	Dülberg, F.	Die Leydener Malerschule.	*Berlin*	1890
Fl. 239	Dülberg, F.	Niederländische Malerei der Spätgotik und Renaissance.	*Berlin*	1929
Fl. 240	Dulwich	Dulwich Gallery Catalogue.	*London*	1926
		Supplements	*London*	
Fl. 241	Dulwich	Some Pictures from the Dulwich Gallery. (Exhibited London National Gallery 1947).	*London*	1947
Fl. 242	Dumont-Wilden, L.	Fernand Khnopff.	*Brussels*	1907
Fl. 243	Dürer, A.	Tagebuch der Reise in die Niederlande.	*MS.*	1521
		in Conway, Sir M.: Literary remains of Albrecht Dürer.	*London*	1889
Fl. 244	Durrieu, Comte P.	La Peinture en France: Débuts de la Renaissance. *in* Michel, A.: Histoire de l'Art. vol. III part I.	*Paris*	1907
Fl. 245	Durrieu, Comte P.	Heures de Turin.	*Paris*	1891
		Another edition	*Paris*	1911
Fl. 246	Durrieu, Comte P.	Les très riches Heures de Jean de France, Duc de Berry	*Paris*	1904
Fl. 247	Durrieu, Comte P.	A. Bening et les Peintres du Bréviaire Grimani. *in* Gazette des Beaux-Arts.	*Paris*	1903
Fl. 248	Durrieu, Comte P.	La Miniature flamande au temps de la cour de Bourgogne 1415–1530.	*Paris and Brussels*	1921
		Later edition	*Paris and Brussels*	1927
Fl. 249	Dussieux, L. (and others)	Mémoires inédits sur la vie et les ouvrages des Membres de l'Académie Royale de Peinture et de Sculpture publiés d'après les manuscrits conservés à l'École Impériale des Beaux-Arts. 2 vols.	*Paris*	1854
Fl. 250	Dutry, A.	César de Cock.	*Ghent*	1895
Fl. 251	Dvoràck, M.	Pieter Brueghel l'Angien.	*Vienna*	1926
Fl. 252	Delen, A. J. J.	Rik Wouters.	*Antwerp*	1948
Fl. 253	Detroit.	Art Quarterly.	*Detroit*	1945
Fl. 254	Dijon	La peinture au musée de Dijon. (J. Magnin).	*Besançon*	1933
Fl. 255	Dimier, L.	Histoire de la peinture de portrait en France au XVI siècle.	*Paris*	1924
Fl. 256	Dupont, J.	Primitifs français.	*Paris*	1937
Fl. 257	Dvoràck, M.	Kunstgeschichte als Geistgeschichte.	*Munich*	1923
Fl. 262	Ebenstein, E.	Der Hofmaler Frans Luyckx.	*Vienna*	1907
Fl. 263	Edwards, E.	Anecdotes of painters who have resided or been born in England . . . intended as a Continuation to the Anecdotes of Painting by the late Horace, Earl of Orford.	*London*	1808
Fl. 264	Eekhoud, G.	Les peintres animaliers belges.	*Brussels*	1911
Fl. 265	Erasmus, K.	R. Savery, sein Leben und sein Werke.	*Halle*	1908
Fl. 266	Even, E. van	Henri van der Haert.	*Diest*	1847
Fl. 267	Even, E. van	Louvain monumental.	*Louvain*	1860
Fl. 268	Even, E. van	Le peintre Lambert Mathieu.	*Paris*	1862
Fl. 269	Even, E. van	L'ancienne école de peinture de Louvain.	*Brussels*	1870
Fl. 270	Even, E. van	De Schilder P. J. Verhaghen.	*Louvain*	1875
		Later edition	*Antwerp*	1903

Fl. 271	Even, E. van	Louvain dans le passé et dans le présent.	*Louvain*	1895
Fl. 272	Evrard, W.	La vie et l'œuvre de Lucas de Leyde.	*Brussels*	1884
Fl. 273	Evers, H. G.	Peter Paul Rubens.	*Munich*	1942
Fl. 274	Exteens, E.	Félicien Rops, peintre.	*Brussels*	1933
Fl. 275	Eynden, R. van and Willigen, A. van der	Geschiedenis der Vaderlandsche Schilder-Kunst, sedert de Helft de XVIII Eeuw. *Haarlem* 4 vols.		1816– 1842
Fl. 276	Edinburgh	Catalogue National Gallery of Scotland.	*Edinburgh*	1946
Fl. 277	Exteens, E.	L'œuvre gravé et lithographié de Félicien Rops.	*Paris*	1928
Fl. 286	Facio, B.	De viris illustribus Liber. *MS.* *Published Florence*		1454– 1456 1745
Fl. 287	Félibien des Avaux, A.	Entretiens sur les vies et les ouvrages des plus excellens peintres anciens et modernes. *Paris* 5 vols. *Later edition* *London*		1666– 1688 1705
Fl. 288	Fétis, E.	Les artistes belges à l'Étranger.	*Brussels*	1857– 1865
Fl. 289	Fidière, O.	État Civil de peintres et sculpteurs de l'Académie Royale de 1648–1745. *Paris*		1883
Fl. 290	Fierens, P.	James Ensor.	*Paris*	1929
Fl. 291	Fierens, P.	C. Permeke.	*Paris*	1930
Fl. 292	Fierens, P.	Joseph Stevens.	*Brussels*	1930
Fl. 293	Fierens, P.	Théo van Rysselberghe.	*Brussels*	1937
Fl. 294	Fierens, P.	James Ensor.	*Paris and Brussels*	1943
Fl. 295	Fierens, P.	Les dessins d'Ensor.	*Brussels*	1944
Fl. 296	Fierens, P. (editor)	L'Art en Belgique du moyen âge à nos jours.	*Brussels*	1947
Fl. 297	Fierens-Gevaert, H.	Jacques Jordaens.	*Paris*	1905
Fl. 298	Fierens-Gevaert, H.	Les primitifs flamands. *Brussels* 4 vols.		1909– 1912
Fl. 299	Fierens-Gevaert, H.	Albert Baertsoen.	*Brussels*	1910
Fl. 300	Fierens-Gevaert, H.	Antoine Wiertz.	*Turnhout*	1920
Fl. 301	Fierens-Gevaert, H.	Catalogue de l'Exposition rétrospective du paysage Flamand. *Brussels*		1926
Fl. 302	Filangieri, G.	Documenti per la storia, le arti . . . della provincia Napolitana. 6 vols. *Naples*		1883– 1891
Fl. 303	Floerke, H.	Studien zur Niederländischen Kunst und Kulturgeschichte. (Die Formen des Kunsthandels, das Atelier und die Sammler . . . vom 15–18 Jahrhundert). *Munich and Leipzig*		1905
Fl. 304	Florence (Uffizi)	R. Gallerie degli Uffizi. Catálogo dei Dipinti.	*Florence*	1926
Fl. 305	Fokker, T. H.	Die Werke niederländischer Meister in den Kirchen Italiens. *The Hague*		1931
Fl. 306	Fokker, T. H.	Jan Siberechts.	*Brussels and Paris*	1931
Fl. 307	Fontainas, A.	Rops.	*Paris*	1925

Fl. 308	Fontaine, A.	Constantin Meunier.	*Paris*	1923
Fl. 309	Foronda y Aguilera, M.	Estancias y Viajes del Emperador Carlos V.	*Madrid*	1914
Fl. 310	Foster, J. J.	A dictionary of painters of miniatures (1525–1850).	*London*	1926
Fl. 311	Fourcaud, L. de	La peinture dans les Pays-Bas XVe siècle. *in* Michel, A.: Histoire de l'Art. vol. III part 1.	*Paris*	1907
Fl. 312	Fourcaud, L. de	La peinture dans les Pays-Bas depuis les successeurs des Van Eyck … jusque dans la seconde moitié du XVIe siècle. *in* Michel, A.: Histoire de l'Art. vol. V part 1.	*Paris*	1926
Fl. 313	Fraenger, W.	Der Bauern Bruegel und das deutsche Sprichwort.	*Munich and Leipzig*	1923
Fl. 314	Fraenger, W.	Hieronymus Bosch. (Das Tausendjaehrige Reich). *English edition* The Millennium of Hieronymus Bosch.	*Coburg* *London*	1947 1951
Fl. 315	Friedländer, M. J.	Die Antwerpener Manieristen von 1520. *in* Jahrbuch der Preussischen Kunstsammlungen.	*Berlin*	1915
Fl. 316	Friedländer, M. J.	Die Altniederländische Malerei. 14 vols.	*Berlin and Leyden*	1924–1937
Fl. 317	Fiorillo, J. D.	Geschichte der zeichnenden Künste von ihrer Wiederauflebung bis auf die neuesten Zeiten. Geschichte der Mahlerey. 5 vols.	*Göttingen*	1798–1804
Fl. 318	Friedländer, M. J.	Landscape, Portrait, Still life. Their origin and development.	*Oxford*	1949
Fl. 319	Fourcaud, L. de	Hieronymus van Aken dit Jérome Bosch.	*Paris*	1912
Fl. 327	Gaffé, R.	Paul Delvaux.	*Brussels*	1945
Fl. 328	Gailly, D. H.	Pierre Paulus.	*Gembloux*	1927
Fl. 329	Gautier, T.	Les Beaux Arts en Europe.	*Paris*	1855
Fl. 330	Gavelle, E.	Engelbrechtsz.	*Lyons*	1929
Fl. 331	G. des B. -A. (contributors)	Gazette des beaux-arts.	*Paris* *New York*	1859 1942
Fl. 332	Génard, P.	Anvers à travers les âges. 2 vols.	*Brussels*	1886–1892
Fl. 333	Génard, P.	Levensschets van Pieter-Jan Balthasar de Grée.	*Antwerp*	1858
Fl. 334	Germain, A.	Les Neerlandais en Bourgogne.	*Brussels*	1909
Fl. 335	Gestoso y Pérez, J.	Ensayo de un diccionario de los artífices que floreceiron en Sevilla. 3 vols.	*Seville*	1899–1900
Fl. 336	Gerrits, L.	Levensbeschryving van M. I. van Brée.	*Antwerp*	1852
Fl. 337	Ghent	Ghent Museum Catalogue.	*Ghent*	1930
Fl. 338	Ghent	Catalogue de l'exposition de l'art ancien.	*Ghent*	1913
Fl. 339	Gillet, L.	La peinture dans les Pays-Bas à la fin du XVIe siècle. *in* Michel, A.: Histoire de l'Art. vol. V part 2.	*Paris*	1925
Fl. 340	Gillet, L.	La peinture dans les Pays-Bas au XVIIe siècle. *in* Michel, A.: Histoire de l'Art. vol. VI part 1.	*Paris*	1921

Fl. 341	Gillet, L.	La peinture dans les Pays-Bas au XVIIIe siècle. *in* Michel, A.: Histoire de l'Art. vol. VII part 1.	*Paris*	1923
Fl. 342	Glasgow	Glasgow Art Gallery Masterpiece Series No. 2.	*Glasgow*	1938
Fl. 343	Glück, G.	Van Dyck. *in* Klassiker der Kunst series.	*Stuttgart*	1931
Fl. 344	Glück, G. and Haberditzl, F. M.	Handzeichnungen von Rubens.	*Berlin*	1928
Fl. 345	Glück, G.	Brueghels Gemälde. *Second edition with L. Burchard's additions* *English translation by E. Byam Shaw*	*Vienna* *Vienna* *London*	1932 1934 1937
Fl. 346	Glück, G.	Rubens, van Dyck und ihr Kreis.	*Vienna*	1933
Fl. 347	Glück, G.	De Landschappen van Rubens.	*Amsterdam*	1940
Fl. 348	Godenne, L.	Malines, jadis et aujourd'hui.	*Malines*	1908
Fl. 349	Goffin, A.	Bouts.	*Brussels*	1907
Fl. 350	Goffin, A.	Xavier Mellery.	*Brussels*	1925
Fl. 351	Goffin, A.	Memling.	*Brussels and Paris*	1926
Fl. 352	Gomez-Correa, E.	El espectro de René Magritte.	*Santiago de Chile*	1948
Fl. 353	Gool, J. van	De Nieuwe Schouburg der Nederlantsche Konstschilders en Schilder- essen. 2 vols.	*The Hague*	1750
Fl. 354	Gossart, M.	Jean Gossaert de Maubeuge.	*Lille*	1902
Fl. 355	Gossart, M. G.	Jérôme Bosch, 'le faizeur de diables' de Bois-le-Duc.	*Lille*	1907
Fl. 356	Goswin, J. A.	A. C. Lens.	*Liège*	1846
Fl. 357	Götz, M.	Justus Suttermans, ein flämischer Bildnismaler im Italien d. 17. Jahrhunderts.	*Günzburg*	1928
Fl. 358	Graefe, F.	Jan Sanders van Hemessen.	*Leipzig*	1909
Fl. 359	Grange, A. de la and Cloquet, L.	Études sur l'art à Tournai et sur les anciens artistes de cette ville.	*Tournai*	1888– 1889
Fl. 360	Graves, A.	A Dictionary of Artists who have exhibited in London from 1760– 1893.	*London*	1895
Fl. 361	Graves, A.	The Royal Academy of Arts. A Complete Dictionary of Contributors and their work from its foundation in 1769 to 1904.	*London*	1905– 1906
Fl. 362	Graves, A.	The Society of Artists of Great Britain, 1760–1791 and The Free Society of Artists 1761–1783.	*London*	1907
Fl. 363	Graves, A.	The British Institution 1806–1867.	*London*	1908
Fl. 364	Greenwich	Macpherson Exhibition Catalogue. (G. Callender).	*London*	1928
Fl. 365	Greenwich	National Maritime Museum, Greenwich, Catalogue.	*Greenwich*	1937
Fl. 366	Greindl, E.	Corneille de Vos.	*Brussels*	1944
Fl. 367	Greve, H. E.	De Bronnen van Carel van Mander.	*The Hague*	1903
Fl. 368	Gramm, J.	Die Ideale Landschaft. 2 vols.	*Freibourg*	1912
Fl. 369	Grosse, R.	Holländische Landschaftskunst 1600–1650.	*Berlin and Leipzig*	1925

Fl. 370	Guevara, F. de	Comentarios de la Pintura.	*MS.*	before 1563
		First published (A. Ponz)	*Madrid*	1788
		Modern edition in Sánchez Cantón: Fuentes Literarias...	*Madrid*	1923– 1941
Fl. 371	Guicciardini, L.	Descrittione di tutti i Paesi Bassi...	*Antwerp*	1567
		Revised edition	*Antwerp*	1581
		English edition	*London*	1795
Fl. 372	Guiffrey, J.	Antoine Van Dyck, sa vie et son œuvre.	*Paris*	1882
		English edition	*London*	1896
Fl. 373	Guillet de Saint-Georges	*In* Memoires inédits sur la vie et les ouvrages des Membres de l'Académie Royale de Peinture...		1690
		Published by L. Dussieux and others 2 vols.	*Paris*	1854
Fl. 374	Graef, G. de	Nos Artistes Anversois.	*Antwerp*	1898
Fl. 375	Gheyn, J. van den	Peiresc et Coebergher.	*Antwerp*	1905
Fl. 376	Geyser, G. W.	Geschichte der Malerei in Leipzig.	*Leipzig*	1858
Fl. 377	Goossens, K.	David Vinckbooms	*Antwerp and Amsterdam*	1954
Fl. 378	Genaille, R.	Bruegel l'Ancien	*Paris*	1953
Fl. 383	Hausenstein, W.	Der Bauern Bruegel.	*Munich*	1920
Fl. 384	Haberditzl, F. M.	Otto van Veen. *in* Jahrbuch der Kunsthistorischen Sammlungen der Allerhöchsten Kaiserhauses.	*Vienna*	1907
Fl. 385	Haeghen, V. van der	Mémoire sur les documents faux relatifs aux anciens peintres... flamands.	*Brussels*	1899
Fl. 386	Haeghen, V. van der	La Corporation des Peintres et Sculpteurs de Gand.	*Brussels*	1906
Fl. 387	Haesaerts, L.	Histoire du Portrait de Navez à Ensor.	*Brussels*	1942
Fl. 388	Haesaerts, L. and P.	Flandre: Essai sur l'art flamand depuis 1880: L'Impressionnisme.	*Paris*	1931
Fl. 389	Haesaerts, L. and P.	H. Evenepoel.	*Brussels*	1932
Fl. 390	Haesaerts, L. and P.	Le mouvement expressionniste.	*Ghent*	1935
Fl. 391	Haesaerts, L. and P.	W. Degouve de Nuncques.		1935
Fl. 392	Haesaerts, P.	C. Permeke.	*Antwerp and Amsterdam*	1938
Fl. 393	Haesaerts, P.	Jean Brusselmans.	*Brussels*	1939
Fl. 394	Haesaerts, P.	Gustave de Smet.	*Antwerp and Amsterdam*	1940
Fl. 395	Haesaerts, P.	Jakob Smits.	*Brussels*	1942
Fl. 396	Haesaerts, P.	Retour à l'humain. L'animisme.	*Brussels*	1942
Fl. 397	Haesaerts, P.	Les Dessins d'Henri Evenepoel.	*Brussels*	1943
Fl. 398	Haesaerts, P.	H. de Braekeleer.	*Brussels*	1943
Fl. 399	Haesaerts, P.	L'École de Laethem Saint Martin.	*Brussels*	1945
Fl. 400	Haesaerts, P.	Jacob Smits.	*Antwerp*	1948
Fl. 401	Hague (Mauritshuis)	Musée royal de La Haye: Catalogue. (W. Martin).	*The Hague*	1914
Fl. 402	Hall, H. van and Wolterson, B.	Repertorium voor de geschiedenis der Nederlandsche schilder en graveerkunst.	*The Hague*	1936

Fl. 403	Havelaar, J.	Frans Masereel.	*The Hague*	1930
Fl. 404	Hecke, P. and Langui, E.	Gustave de Smet.	*Brussels*	1945
Fl. 405	Heere, L. de	Ode on the Ghent Altarpiece of the Mystic Lamb.	*MS.*	1559
		Published with other poems by him in Der Hof en Boomgaerd der Poësien.	*Ghent*	1565
Fl. 406	Hekema, V.	T. Lybaert.	*Munich*	1889
Fl. 407	Helbig, J.	Les papiers de famille d'Englebert Fisen. *in* Bull. Soc. dioc. de Liège.	*Liège*	1881
Fl. 408	Helbig, J.	Lambert Lombard, peintre et architecte.	*Brussels*	1892
Fl. 409	Helbig, J.	La peinture au pays de Liège et sur les bords de la Meuse.	*Liège*	1903
Fl. 410	Helbig, J.	L'Art Mosan. 2 vols.	*Brussels*	1906– 1911
Fl. 411	Hellens, F.	Henri Evenepoel.	*Antwerp*	1947
Fl. 412	Hind, A. M.	Drawings by Rubens, Van Dyck and other artists of the Flemish School of the XVIIth century. Vol. 2 of British Museum Catalogue of drawings by Dutch and Flemish Artists.	*London*	1915– 1932
Fl. 413	Hofstede de Groot, C.	Catalogue raisonné of the Works of . . . Dutch Painters of the XVIIth century. 8 vols.	*London*	1907– 1927
Fl. 414	Hollanda, F. de	De Pintura Antiga.	*MS.*	1548– 1549
		French translation in: Raczynski: Les Arts en Portugal.	*Paris*	1846– 1847
		Spanish translation in: Sánchez Cantón: Fuentes Literarias.	*Madrid*	1923– 1941
		English translation by A. F. G. Bell.	*London*	1928
Fl. 415	Hondt, P. d'	Jan Frans Portaels.		1895
Fl. 416	Hoogewerff, G.	Nederlandsche Schilders in Italie in de XVIe eeuw.	*Utrecht*	1912 and 1913
Fl. 417	Hoogewerff, G. J. and Orbaan, J. A. F.	Bescheiden in Italie omtrent Nederlandsche kunstenaars en geleerden. 3 vols.	*The Hague*	1911– 1917
Fl. 418	Hoogewerff, G. J.	Jan van Scorel.	*The Hague*	1923
Fl. 419	Hoogewerff, G. J.	Vlaamsche Kunst en Italiaansche Renaissance.	*Malines and Amsterdam*	1936
Fl. 420	Hoogewerff, G. J.	Nederlandsche Kunstenaars te Rome, 1600–1725	*The Hague*	1924
Fl. 421	Hoogewerff, G. J.	De Noord-Nederlandsche Schilder-Kunst. 5 vols.	*The Hague*	1937– 1947
Fl. 422	Hoorde, J. van	De Gebroeders Xaveer en César de Cock.		
Fl. 423	Hora Siccama, W.	Louis Bernard Coclers.	*Amsterdam*	1895
Fl. 424	Hosten, E. and Strubbe, E. I.	Het leven van Jan Garemyn. *in* Annales de la Société d' Émulation de Bruges.	*Bruges*	1931
Fl. 425	Houbraken, A.	De Groote Schouburgh der Nederlantsche Konstschilders en Schilder-essen. 3 vols.	*Amsterdam*	1718– 1721
		Later edition	*The Hague*	1753

Fl. 426	Hourticq, L.	Rubens.	*Paris*	1906
Fl. 427	Houtart, M.	Jacques Daret, peintre tournaisien du XVe siècle.	*Tournai*	1907
Fl. 428	Hübner, F. M.	Gustave de Smet.	*Amsterdam* *Leipzig*	1921 1923
Fl. 429	Huelsen, C. and Egger, H.	Die Römischen Skizzenbücher von Martin van Heemskerck. 2 vols.	*Berlin*	1913– 1916
Fl. 430	Hulin de Loo, G.	Aelbrecht Bouts et le Maître de l'Assomption.	*Ghent*	1902
Fl. 431	Hulin de Loo G.	Jean Prévost.	*Ghent*	1902
Fl. 432	Hulst, F. van	N. H. J. de Fassin.	*Liège*	1837
Fl. 433	Hymans, H.	Nicaise de Keyser.	*Brussels*	1889
Fl. 434	Hymans, H.	Gand et Tournai.	*Paris*	1902
Fl. 435	Hymans, H.	Bruges et Ypres.	*Paris*	1903
Fl. 436	Hymans, H.	Die belgische Kunst des neunzehnten Jahrhunderts.	*Leipzig*	1906
Fl. 437	Hymans, H.	Antonio Moro, son œuvre et son temps.	*Brussels*	1910
Fl. 438	Hymans, H.	Bruxelles. *Later edition*	*Paris* *Paris*	1910 1926
Fl. 439	Hymans, H.	Anvers.	*Paris*	1914
Fl. 440	Hymans, H.	Œuvres: vol. 2: Près de 700 Biographies d'artistes Belges.	*Brussels*	1920
Fl. 441	Hymans, H.	Œuvres: vol. 1: Études relatives à l'histoire de l'art dans les Pays-Bas: La gravure.	*Brussels*	1884
Fl. 442	Hippert, T. and Linnig, J.	Le peintre-graveur Hollandais et Belge du XIXe siècle. 2 vols.	*Brussels*	1874
Fl. 443	Heinecken, C. H. von	Nachrichten von Künstlern ind Kunstsachen. 2 vols.	*Leipzig*	1768– 1769
Fl. 444	Hulin de Loo, G.	Catalogue Critique de l'Exposition de Bruges.	*Ghent*	1902
Fl. 445	Haarlem	Frans Hals Gallery of Art Catalogue.	*Haarlem*	1914
Fl. 446	Havard, H.	Animaux et paysages par H. J. F. van der Poorten.	*Paris*	1874
Fl. 447	Hoogstraten, S. van	Inleydinge tot de Hooge schoole der Schilderkunst.		1678
Fl. 448	Hecke, P. G. van	Peintres Belges contemporains.	*Brussels*	1947
Fl. 449	Hecke, P. G. van	Frits van den Berghe.	*Antwerp*	1948
Fl. 450	Huebner, F. M.	Hieronymus Bosch.	*Berlin*	1938
Fl. 451	Immerzeel, J.	De Levens en Werken der Hollandsche en Vlaamsche Kunstschilders …	*Amsterdam*	1843
Fl. 452	Inghuem, A. d'	Joseph Stevens.	*Brussels*	1905
Fl. 456	Jahrbuch (contributors)	Jahrbuch der Kunsthistorischen Sammlungen der Allerhöchsten Kaiserhauses. *Continued as* Jahrbuch der Kunsthistorischen Sammlungen in Wien.	*Vienna* *Vienna*	from 1883 1926
Fl. 457	Jahrbuch (contributors)	Jahrbuch der Preussischen Kunstsammlungen.	*Berlin*	from 1880
Fl. 458	Jamot, P.	Rubens.	*Paris*	1936

Fl. 459	Jantzen, H.	Das Niederländische Architekturbild.	*Leipzig*	1910
Fl. 460	Jedlicka, G.	Pieter Bruegel: der Maler in seiner Zeit.	*Zurich*	1938
Fl. 461	Jordaens (exhibition)	Catalogue of Jacob Jordaens Exhibition.	*Antwerp*	1905
Fl. 462	Jorissenne, G.	J. B. P. Coclers, peintre wallon.		1908
Fl. 463	Jorissenne, G.	Nicolas La Fabrique.	*Liège*	1908
Fl. 464	Jorissenne, G.	Douffet, peintre mosan, catalogue de ses œuvres.	*Liège*	1910
Fl. 465	Joseph, E.	Dictionnaire Biographique des artistes contemporains. 3 vols and supplement.	*Paris*	1930– 1936
Fl. 466	J. de B. -A. (contributors)	Journal des Beaux Arts et de la littérature. (Edited by A. Siret).	*Brussels*	1859– 1887
Fl. 467	J. W. and C. I. (contributors)	Journal of the Warburg Institute. *Continued as* Journal of the Warburg and Courtauld Institute.	*London* *London*	1937– 1938 from 1939
Fl. 468	Justi, C.	Velázquez and his century. *Later edition* Velázquez und sein Jahrhundert.	*London* *Zurich*	1899 1933
Fl. 469	Justi, C.	Aus drei Jahrhunderten spanischen Kunstlebens. 2 vols.	*Berlin*	1908
Fl. 470	Jorissenne, G.	J. G. Christian Coclers.	*Liège*	1908
Fl. 476	Kahn, G.	Rops.	*Paris*	1904
Fl. 477	Kalcken, G. van and Six, J.	Peintures ecclésiastiques du moyen-âge en Hollande. 5 vols. *Haarlem and the Hague*		1903– 1919
Fl. 478	Kervyn de Volkaersbeke	Les Pourbus.	*Ghent*	1870
Fl. 479	Kervyn de Volkaersbeke	Les Églises de Gand. 2 vols.	*Ghent*	1857– 1858
Fl. 480	Kieckens, J. F.	Daniel Seghers de la Compagnie de Jésus, Peintre des Fleurs.	*Ghent*	1845
Fl. 481	Kramm, C.	De Levens en werken der hollandsche en vlaamsche Kunstschilders ... *Amsterdam* 7 vols.		1857– 1864
Fl. 482	Kryn, L. J. (editor)	Rubens en zijne Eeuw: in 5 parts. Rubens' Antwerpen (F. Prims). Het Geestesleven te Antwerpen in Rubens' tijd (M. Sabbe). Het Volksleven in Rubens' tijd. (V de Meyere). De Vlaamsche Kunst, voor, tijdens en na Rubens (A. J. J. Delen). Rubens' Leven en Werk. (P. Lambotte).	*Brussels*	1927
Fl. 483	Kunel, M.	Auguste Donnay.	*Liège*	1923
Fl. 484	Kunel, M.	Félicien Rops.	*Brussels*	1943
Fl. 485	Kwakman, T.	Kruiswegstaties door A. Servaes.	*Amsterdam*	1922
Fl. 486	Klein, R.	Félicien Rops.	*Paris*	1906
Fl. 489	Labarre, L.	Antoine Wiertz.	*Brussels*	1867
Fl. 490	Laborde, L. de	Les Ducs de Bourgogne. 3 vols.	*Paris*	1849– 1851
Fl. 491	Laborde, L. de	La Renaissance des arts à la cour de France.	*Paris*	1850

Fl. 492	Lacomblé, A.	De l'état actuel de la Peinture en Belgique.	*Mons*	1847
Fl. 493	Lafond, P.	Hieronymus Bosch.	*Brussels and Paris*	1914
Fl. 494	Lairesse, G. de	Het Groot Schilderboek.	*Amsterdam*	1707
		Later editions	*Amsterdam*	1712
			Amsterdam	1720
			Amsterdam	1745
		French translation (with biography by J. H. Jansen).	*Paris*	1787
Fl. 495	Lambotte, P.	Alfred Stevens.	*Brussels*	1907
Fl. 496	Lambotte, P.	Henri Evenepoel.	*Brussels*	1908
Fll 497	Lambotte, P.	Les peintres de portraits.	*Brussels*	1913
Fl. 498	Lambotte, P.	Eugène Smits.	*Brussels*	1913
Fl. 499	Lambotte, P.	Jacques de Lalaing.	*Nymwegen*	1918
Fl. 500	Lambotte, P.	Rubens' Leven en Werk. *in* Kryn, L. J.: Rubens en zijne Eeuw.	*Brussels*	1927
Fl. 501	Lambotte, P.	Hippolyte Boulenger.	*Brussels*	1931
Fl. 502	Lampsonius, D.	Lamberti Lombardi . . . pictoris celeberrimi vita.	*Bruges*	1565
Fl. 503	Lampsonius, D.	Pictorum aliquot celebrium germaniae inferioris effigies: . . .	*Antwerp*	1572
Fl. 504	Langui, E.	Permeke.	*Brussels*	1947
Fl. 505	Lanzi, L.	Storia pittorica della Italia.	*Florence*	1792–1796
		Revised by author 6 vols.	*Bassano*	1809
		English translation by T. Roscoe. 3 vols.	*London*	1847
Fl. 506	Lapouyade, M. de	Un maître flamand à Bordeaux: Joseph Lonsing.	*Paris*	1911
Fl. 507	Lavalleye, J.	Juste de Gand, peintre de Frédéric de Montefeltre.	*Louvain*	1936
Fl. 508	Laver, J.	D. van Alsloot. Isabella's Triumph. (Faber Gallery).	*London*	1947
Fl. 509	Leclercq, E.	Charles de Groux.	*Brussels*	1871
Fl. 510	Lefèvre, E.	Joseph Lies.	*Antwerp*	1888
Fl. 511	Leger, C.	Redouté et son temps.	*Paris*	1945
Fl. 512	Lemaire de Belges, J.	La Couronne Margaritique.	*MS.*	1504–1511
		Published	*Lyons*	1549
Fl. 513	Lemonnier, C.	L'œuvre de Constantin Meunier.	*Brussels*	1896
Fl. 514	Lemonnier, C.	Henri de Braekeleer et son œuvre.	*Brussels*	1905
Fl. 515	Lemonnier, C.	L'École belge de Peinture 1830–1905.	*Brussels*	1906
Fl. 516	Lemonnier, C.	F. Rops, l'homme et l'artiste.	*Paris*	1908
Fl. 517	Lemonnier, C.	Émile Claus.	*Brussels*	1908
Fl. 518	Lemonnier, C.	Alfred Stevens et son œuvre.	*Brussels*	1910
Fl. 519	Lemonnier, H.	L'art au temps de Louis XIV.	*Paris*	1911
Fl. 520	Lerius, T. van	Biographies d'artistes anversois.	*Antwerp and Ghent*	1880
Fl. 521	Le Roy, G.	James Ensor.	*Brussels*	1928
Fl. 522	Leurs, Stan (editor)	Geschiedenis van de vlaamsche Kunst.	*Antwerp and The Hague*	1937

Fl. 559	Mander, K. van	Het Schilderboek. *2nd edition*	*Haarlem* *Haarlem*	1604 1616– 1618
		French translation H. Hymans. *English translation* C. van der Wall. *Modern Dutch edition* A. F. Mirande and G. S. Overdiep.	*Paris* *New York* *Amsterdam*	1884 1936 1943
Fl. 560	Maquet-Tombu, J.	Colijn de Coter.	*Brussels*	1937
Fl. 561	Marchi, M. de	Pierre Paulus.	*Brussels*	1934
Fl. 562	Maret, F.	Théo van Rysselberghe.	*Antwerp*	1948
Fl. 563	Marien, M.	Magritte.	*Brussels*	1943
Fl. 564	Mariette, P. J.	Abecedario. *Published by P. de Chennevières and A. de Montaiglon. 6 vols.*	*MS.* *Paris*	*c.* 1760 1851– 1860
Fl. 565	Marlier, G.	Jacob Smits.	*Brussels*	1931
Fl. 566	Marlier, G.	Anthonis Mor.	*Brussels*	1933
Fl. 567	Marlier, G.	Vingt-cinq Années de Peinture et de Sculpture en Belgique. (La Génération de l'Entre-deux Guerres).	*Brussels*	1942
Fl. 568	Marlier, G.	Flämische Malerei der Gegenwart. *Flemish edition*	*Jena* *Brussels*	1943 1944
Fl. 569	Marlier, G.	J. Stobbaerts.	*Brussels*	1943
Fl. 570	Martin, W.	Alt-Holländische Bilder.	*Berlin*	1921
Fl. 571	Marzo, G. de	Guglielmo Borremans di Anversa.	*Palermo*	1912
Fl. 572	Mascha, O.	Félicien Rops und sein Werk.	*Munich*	1910
Fl. 573	Mauclair, C.	Victor Gilsoul.	*Brussels*	1909
Fl. 574	Mayer, A.	Matthäus und Paul Bril.	*Leipzig*	1910
Fl. 575	Mayer, A. L.	Historia de la Pintura española. *3rd edition*	*Madrid*	1947
Fl. 576	Mensaert, G. P.	Le Peintre Amateur et Curieux . . . 2 vols.	*Brussels*	1763
Fl. 577	Merlo, J. J.	Nachrichten von dem Leben und Werken Kölnischer Künstler.	*Düsseldorf*	1895
Fl. 578	Meunier, S.	Philippe de Champaigne.	*Paris*	1924
Fl. 579	Micha, A.	Les peintres célèbres de l'ancien pays de Liège.	*Liège*	1911
Fl. 580	Michel, A. (editor)	Histoire de l'Art depuis les premier temps jusqu'à nos jours. 9 vols.	*Paris*	1905– 1929
Fl. 581	Michel, E.	Rubens, sa vie, son œuvre et son temps.	*Paris*	1900
Fl. 582	Michel, E.	Bruegel.	*Paris*	1933
Fl. 583	Michel, E.	Flemish Painting in the XVIIth Century.	*London*	1939
Fl. 584	Michiels, A.	Histoire de la peinture flamande depuis ses débuts jusqu'en 1864. 10 vols.	*Paris*	1865– 1876
Fl. 585	Michiels, A.	Van Dyck et ses élèves.	*Paris*	1882

Fl. 586	Milo, J.	Tytgat.	*Paris*	1920
Fl. 587	Milo, J.	E. Tytgat.	*Paris*	1931
Fl. 588	Milo, J.	V. de Saedeleer.	*Brussels*	1934
Fl. 589	Molanus, J.	Historiae Lovanensium libri XIV ... *First published*	*MS.* *Brussels*	*c.* 1575 1861
Fl. 590	Mont, Pol de	Fernand Khnopff.	*Amsterdam*	1901
Fl. 591	Mont, Pol de	Antoon van Dijck	*Haarlem*	1906
Fl. 592	Mont, Pol de	De Schilderkunst in Belgie van 1830–1921.	*The Hague*	1921
Fl. 593	Montaiglon, A. de	Procès-verbaux de l'Académie Royale (1648–1792).	*Paris*	1875–1892
Fl. 594	Moschini, G	Guida per la città di Venezia. 4 vols.	*Venice*	1815
Fl. 595	Mosmans, J.	Jheronimus Anthoniszoon van Aken alias Hieronymus Bosch.	*Bois le Duc*	1947
Fl. 596	Muls, J.	Bruegel.	*Brussels*	1923
Fl. 597	Muls, J.	Cornelis de Vos.	*Antwerp*	1932
Fl. 598	Muls, J.	E. Tytgat.	*Brussels*	1943
Fl. 599	Muls, J.	Hippolyte Daeye.	*Hasselt*	1947
Fl. 600	Munich	Katalog der Älteren Pinakothek. (E. Buchner).	*Munich*	1936
Fl. 601	Munter, V. de	Pierre Joseph Verhaghen.	*Brussels*	1932
Fl. 602	Michel, E.	Les Brueghel.	*Paris*	1892
Fl. 603	Maus, M. O.	Trente Années de Lutte pour l'Art 1884–1914.	*Brussels*	1926
Fl. 604	Mosmans, J.	De St. Janskerk te 's Hertogenbosch.	*'s Hertogenbosch*	1931
Fl. 605	Mont-Louis, R. de	Adrien Brawer (Brouwer).	*Limoges*	1895
Fl. 612	Nagler, G. K.	Neues Allgemeines Künstlerlexikon. 25 vols.	*Leipzig*	1835–1852
Fl. 613	Neeffs, E.	Histoire de la peinture et de la sculpture à Malines. 2 vols.	*Ghent*	1876
Fl. 614	Neeffs, E.	Inventaire historique des tableaux, sculptures et objets d'art conservés dans les édifices religieux et civils de Malines.	*Malines*	1891
Fl. 615	New York	Catalogue of Early Flemish, Dutch and German Paintings in the Metropolitan Museum New York. (H. B. Wehle and M. Salinger).	*New York*	1947
Fl. 616	Nicolai, F.	Nachrichten von Baumeistern ... in Berlin.	*Berlin*	1786
Fl. 617	Noack, F.	Das Deutschtum in Rom. 2 vols.	*Berlin and Leipzig*	1927
Fl. 618	Norgate, E.	Miniatura or the Art of Limning. *First published with Introduction by M. Hardie*	*MS.* *Oxford*	1648–1650 1919
Fl. 619	Nougé, P.	Magritte.	*Brussels*	1943
Fl. 624	Offel, van E.	E. Larock.	*Antwerp*	1901

Fl. 625	Oldenbourg, R.	P. P. Rubens. *in* Klassiker der Kunst series.	*Stuttgart and Leipzig*	1921
Fl. 626	Onze Kunst (contributors)	Onze Kunst.		1902– 1929
Fl. 627	Orbaan, J. A. F.	Stradanus te Florence.	*Rotterdam*	1903
Fl. 628	Orlandi, P. A.	L'Abecedario pittorico ... *Later edition* *Later edition:* Edited by P. M. Guarienti.	*Bologna* *Bologna* *Venice*	1704 1719 1753
Fl. 629	Orlandi, P. A.	L'Abecedario pittorico ... (edited by P. M. Guarienti). *Later edition: in* Raczynski 'Les Arts en Portugal'.	*Paris*	1846
Fl. 630	Ottawa	National Gallery of Canada. Catalogue of Paintings.	*Ottawa*	1948
Fl. 631	Oud Holland (contributors)	Oud Holland.	*Amsterdam*	from 1883
Fl. 632	Oxford	Catalogue of Dutch and Flemish still life paintings. (Ward Collection) in Oxford Ashmolean Museum. (J. G. van Gelder).	*Oxford*	1950
Fl. 635	Pacheco, F.	El Libro de Retratos. *in:* Sánchez Cantón: Fuentes Literarias ...	*Seville* *Madrid*	1599– 1616 1923– 1941
Fl. 636	Pacheco, F.	El Arte de la Pintura. *Later edition* *Modern edition in* Sánchez Cantón: Fuentes Literarias ...	*Seville* *Madrid* *Madrid*	1649 1866 1923– 1941
Fl. 637	Palomino de Castro y Velasco, A.	El Museo pictórico y Escala óptica *in* Sánchez Cantón: Fuentes Literarias ... vol. III.	*Madrid* *Madrid*	1715– 1724 1934
Fl. 638	Paris (Louvre)	Le Musée National du Louvre. (G. Lafenestre and E. Richtenberger) 4th edition.	*Paris*	1907
Fl. 639	Paris (Louvre)	Musée National du Louvre: Catalogue des Peintures: Écoles Flamande, Hollandaise, Allemande et Anglaise. (L. Demonts).	*Paris*	1922
Fl. 640	Paris (Louvre)	La Peinture au Musée du Louvre: École Flamande. (E. Michel). 	*Paris*	c. 1926
Fl. 641	Paris (Louvre)	La Peinture au Musée du Louvre: École Hollandaise. (C. Misme). 	*Paris*	1922
Fl. 642	Passeri, G. B.	Vite de' pittori, scultori ed architetti, che anno lavorato in Roma morti dal 1641 fino al 1673. *Modern edition* (Hess)	*Rome* *Leipzig*	1772 1934
Fl. 643	Peltzer, R. A.	Lambert Sustris. *in* Jahrbuch der Kunsthistorischen Sammlungen der Allerhöchsten Kaiserhauses.	*Vienna*	1913
Fl. 644	Peltzer, R. A.	Niederländisch-venezianische Landschaftsmalerei.	*Munich*	1924
Fl. 645	Pepys, S.	Memoirs of Samuel Pepys. Edited by Lord Braybrooke.	*MS.* *London*	1659– 1669 1825
Fl. 646	Peyre, R.	David Teniers.	*Paris*	1911
Fl. 647	Philippen, L.	Les Peintres Stramot.	*Antwerp*	1913
Fl. 648	Pierard, L.	Le peintre wallon Nicolas de Neufchatel dit Lucidel.	*Brussels*	1913
Fl. 649	Pierard, L.	Pierre Paulus.	*Antwerp*	1948
Fl. 650	Pierron, S.	Les Mostaert.	*Brussels*	1912
Fl. 651	Pierron, S.	Pierre Paulus.	*Brussels*	1922

Fl. 652	Piles, R. de	Dissertation sur les ouvrages des plus fameux peintres avec la vie de Rubens.	*Paris*	1681
Fl. 653	Piles, R. de	Cours de peinture par principe. *English edition*	*Paris* *London*	1708 1743
Fl. 654	Pilkington, M.	A Dictionary of Painters. (Edited by H. Fuseli).	*London*	1805
Fl. 655	Pilkington, M.	A General Dictionary of Painters. 2 vols.	*London*	1829
Fl. 656	Pinchart, A. (editor)	Archives des Arts . . . 3 vols.	*Ghent*	1860– 1863
Fl. 657	Pinchart, A.	Quelques Artistes de Tournai.	*Tournai*	1883
Fl. 658	Piot, C.	Notice biographique sur le peintre Verhaghen.	*Ghent*	1839
Fl. 659	Plietzsch, E.	Die Frankenthaler Maler.	*Leipzig*	1910
Fl. 660	La Plume	James Ensor, peintre et graveur. *in* special number of La Plume.	*Paris*	1899
Fl. 661	La Plume	L'œuvre de Henry de Groux. *in* special number of La Plume.	*Paris*	1899
Fl. 662	Poinsot, M. C.	Constantin Meunier.	*Paris*	1910
Fl. 663	Poirier, P.	Initiation à la peinture flamande.	*Brussels*	1950
Fl. 664	Ponz, A.	Viage de España. 18 vols.	*Madrid*	1776– 1794
Fl. 665	Poole, Mrs. R. L.	Catalogue of Oxford Portraits. 3 vols.	*Oxford*	1925
Fl. 666	Popham, A. E.	Dutch and Flemish drawings of the XVth and XVIth centuries. Vol. 5 of British Museum: Catalogue of Drawings by Dutch and Flemish Artists.	*London*	1915– 1932
Fl. 667	Popham, A. E.	Drawings of the Early Flemish School.	*London*	1926– 1927
Fl. 668	Post, C. R.	A History of Spanish Painting. *Cambridge* (*Mass.*) and London 12 vols.		1930– 1958
Fl. 669	Potvin, J.	Antoine Wiertz.	*Brussels*	1920
Fl. 670	Potvin, J.	Xavier Mellery.	*Brussels*	1925
Fl. 671	Preibisz, L.	Martin van Heemskerck.	*Leipzig*	1911
Fl. 672	Prist, P.	Pierre Paulus.	*Brussels*	1936
Fl. 673	Pulings, G.	Jacob Smits.	*Brussels*	1929
Fl. 674	Puyvelde, L. van	F. J. Navez.	*Brussels*	1931
Fl. 675	Puyvelde, L. van	L'ardente peinture d'Ensor.	*Paris*	1939
Fl. 676	Puyvelde, L. van	The sketches of Rubens.	*Brussels*	1947
Fl. 677	Puyvelde, L. van	The Mystic Lamb.	*London*	1948
Fl. 678	Puyvelde, L. van	La Peinture Flamande à Rome. (XVe-XVIIIe siècles).	*Brussels*	1950
Fl. 679	Pevsner, N.	Academies of Art, Past and Present.	*Cambridge*	1940
Fl. 680	Piot, C.	Rapport à Mr. le Ministre de l'Intérieur sur les tableaux enlevés à la Belgique en 1794 et restitués en 1815.	*Brussels*	1883
Fl. 681	La Plume	Felicien Rops. *in* special number of La Plume.	*Paris*	1896

Fl. 689	Quinsonas, E. de	Matériaux pour servir à l'histoire de Marguerite d'Autriche.		1860
Fl. 691	Raczynski, Count J. A.	Die flämische Landschaft vor Rubens.	*Frankfort*	1937
Fl. 692	Raczynski, Count A.	Les Arts en Portugal.	*Paris*	1846
Fl. 693	Ramaekers, G.	Frans Gailliard.	*Brussels*	1911
Fl. 694	Ramiro, E.	Rops.	*Paris*	1905
Fl. 695	Redgrave, S.	A Dictionary of Artists of the English School.	*London*	1878
Fl. 696	Renders, É.	La solution du problème Van Der Weyden—Flémalle—Campin.	*Bruges*	1931
Fl. 697	Renders, É.	Hubert van Eyck, personnage de légende.	*Paris and Brussels*	1933
Fl. 698	Renders, É.	Jean van Eyck.	*Bruges*	1935
Fl. 699	Revue (contributors)	La revue d'art.	*Antwerp*	from 1922
Fl. 700	Rey, R.	Hugo van der Goes.	*Paris*	1936
Fl. 701	Reybourbon, L. Q.	Les Peintres Van Oost à Lille.	*Paris*	1898
Fl. 702	Reynolds, Sir J.	A Journey to Flanders and Holland. *in* The Literary Works of Sir J. Reynolds, edited by E. Malone.		1781
			London	1798
		Later edition	*London*	1819
		(Edited by H. W. Beechey).	*London*	1852
Fl. 703	Reynolds, Sir J.	Discourses.		1769– 1790
		Edited by R. Fry.	*London*	1905
Fl. 704	Ridder, A. de	James Ensor	*Paris*	1930
Fl. 705	Ridder, A. de	La jeune peinture belge. (De l'impressionnisme à l'expressionnisme).	*Antwerp*	1930
Fl. 706	Ridder, A. de	H. de Braekeleer.	*Brussels*	1931
Fl. 707	Ridder, A. de	Valerius de Saedeleer.	*Antwerp*	1938
Fl. 708	Ridder, A. de	Laethem St. Martin colonie d'artistes.	*Brussels*	1945
Fl. 709	Ridolfi, C.	Le Maraviglie dell'arte . . . le vite degli . . . pittori veneti	*Venice*	1648
		Later editions	*Padua*	1835– 1837
			Berlin	1914– 1924
Fl. 710	Ring, G.	A century of French Painting 1400–1500.	*London*	1949
Fl. 711	Roggen, D.	N. de Liemaker.	*Ghent*	1924
Fl. 712	Roggen, D.	Les Arcs de Triomphe de la Joyeuse Entrée de 1635	*Ghent*	1925
Fl. 713	Rolfs, W.	Geschichte der Malerei Neapels.	*Leipzig*	1910
Fl. 714	Rombouts, P. and Lerius, T. van	Les Liggeren et autres Archives Historiques de la Gilde Anversoise de de Saint-Luc. 2 vols.	*Antwerp and The Hague*	1864– 1876
Fl. 715	Rome	Bulletin de l'Institut historique belge de Rome. (Mededeelingen van het Nederlandsch Historisch Instituut te Rome).	*Brussels and Rome*	from 1919
Fl. 716	Roosen, J. P. de	P. Noël, peintre de genre.	*Liège*	1845

Fl. 717	Rooses, M.	Geschiedenis der Antwerpsche Schilderschool. *Later edition*	*Ghent* *Ghent*	1879 1889
Fl. 718	Rooses, M. and Ruelens, C.	L'œuvre de Rubens. 5 vols.	*Antwerp*	1886– 1892
Fl. 719	Rooses, M. and Ruelens, C.	Rubens: Leven en Werken.	*Antwerp*	1903
Fl. 720	Rooses, M.	Rubens. *English translation* by H. Child. 2 vols.	*London*	1904
Fl. 721	Rooses, M. and Ruelens, C.	Correspondance de Rubens. 6 vols.	*Antwerp*	1887– 1908
Fl. 722	Rooses, M. and Ruelens, C.	Jacques Jordaens.	*Amsterdam*	1905
Fl. 723	Rooses, M.	Jordaens, sa vie, ses œuvres.	*Paris*	1906
Fl. 724	Rooses, M.	Life and Works of Jordaens.	*London*	1908
Fl. 725	Rosen, F.	Die Natur in der Kunst.	*Leipzig*	1903
Fl. 726	Rosenberg, A. (editor)	Rubens. *in* Klassiker der Kunst series.	*Stuttgart*	1906
Fl. 727	Rosenberg, A.	Teniers der Jüngere.	*Leipzig*	1901
Fl. 728	Rotterdam	Rotterdam: Boymans Museum. Catalogue.	*Rotterdam*	1921
Fl. 729	Rouquet, A.	L'état des arts en Angleterre.	*Paris*	1755
Fl. 730	Royal Collection	The Royal Gallery at Hampton Court. (E. Law.) *Abridged*	*London* *London*	1898 1915
Fl. 731	Royal Collection	Catalogue of Paintings and Drawings in Buckingham Palace. (L. Cust). *London*		1909
Fl. 732	Royal Collection	Catalogue Raisonné of Pictures . . . at Buckingham Palace. (L. Cust). *London*		1920
Fl. 733	Royal Collection	Catalogue Raisonné of the Pictures . . . at Windsor Castle. (L. Cust). *London*		1922
Fl. 734	Royal Collection	Catalogue of the pictures at Hampton Court. (C. H. Collins Baker). *London*		1929
Fl. 735	Royal Collection	Catalogue of the pictures at Windsor Castle. (C. H. Collins Baker). *London*		1937
Fl. 736	Royal Collection	Exhibition of the King's Pictures. Burlington House 1946–1947. Catalogue. (A. Blunt). *London*		1947
Fl. 737	Ruhemann, A.	Frans Courtens.	*Brussels*	1909
Fl. 738	Roelandt, O.	Liévin de Winne.	*Ghent*	1930
Fl. 739	Roelants, M.	Edgard Tytgat.	*Antwerp*	1948
Fl. 740	Revue (contributors)	Revue Belge d'Archéologie et d'Histoire de l'Art.	*Brussels*	from 1931
Fl. 741	Rooses, M.	Art in Flanders.	*London*	1914
Fl. 742	Reynolds, Sir J.	Letters. (Edited by F. W. Hilles.)	*Cambridge*	1927
Fl. 743	Regteren Altena J. G.	Jacques de Gheyn's drawings.	*Amsterdam*	1935
Fl. 744	Royal Academy (Contributors).	British Portraits Exhibition Catalogue.	*London*	1956
Fl. 748	Sainsbury, W. N.	Original unpublished papers illustrative of the life of Sir Peter Paul Rubens.	*London*	1859

Fl. 774	Sousa Viterbo, Marquis of	Noticia de alguns pintores portuguezes e de outros que sendo estrange-iros execeram a sua arte em Portugal.	Lisbon	1902–1913
Fl. 775	Sparrow, W. S.	Women Painters of the World.	London	1905
Fl. 776	Sparrow, W. S.	Memories of life and art through sixty years.	London	1925
Fl. 777	Spielmann, H.	Henriette Ronner, the painter of cat life.	New York	1893
Fl. 778	Sterling, C.	La Peinture Française. (Moyen âge).	Paris	1942
Fl. 779	Stirling-Maxwell, Sir W.	Annals of the Artists of Spain. 4 vols.	London	1891
Fl. 780	Stockholm	Catalogue descriptif des peintures. Musée National: Maîtres Étrangers. (O. Sirén).	Stockholm	1928
Fl. 781	Strickland, W. G.	Dictionary of Irish Artists. 2 vols.	Dublin	1913
Fl. 782	Strutt, J.	A Biographical Dictionary: containing an historical account of all the Engravers from the earliest period of the art of engraving to the present time. 2 vols.	London	1785–1786
Fl. 783	Stubbe, R. P.	Constant Permeke.		1930
Fl. 784	Sulzberger, M.	Louis Gallait.	Brussels	1889
Fl. 785	Suvée, J. B.	Correspondance de Suvée en 1778. in Gazette des Beaux-Arts.	Paris	1903
Fl. 786	Spaak, C.	Paul Delvaux.	Antwerp	1948
Fl. 787	Sterling, C.	Catalogue of 'Rubens et son Temps' Exhibition held in Musée de l'Or-angerie.	Paris	1936
Fl. 788	Schmidt, W.	Adriaen Brouwer.		1873
Fl. 796	Terlinden, C.	Notes et Documents relatifs à la Galerie de Tableaux conservée au Château de Tervueren aux XVIIe et XVIIIe siècles. in Annales de l'Académie Royale d'Archéologie de Belgique.	Antwerp	1922
Fl. 797	Terlinden, C.	P. Bruegel le Vieux et l'Histoire. in Revue Belge d'Archéologie et d'Histoire de l'Art.	Brussels	1942–1946
Fl. 798	Thieme, U. and Becker, F.	Allgemeines Lexikon der Bildenden Künstler von der Antike bis zur Gegenwart. 37 vols.	Leipzig	1907–1950
Fl. 799	Tietze, H. and others	Oesterreichische Kunst-Topographie. 17 vols.	Vienna	1907–1919
Fl. 800	Titi, F.	Studio di pittura . . . nelle chiese di Roma. Second edition Nuova studio di pittura. Composite edition Descrizione delle pitture . . . esposte . . . in Roma.	Rome Rome Rome	1675 1685 1708 1763
Fl. 802	Toledo (Ohio)	Catalogue of European Paintings in Toledo Museum. (Blake-More Godwin).	Toledo (Ohio)	1939
Fl. 803	Tolnay, C. de	Die Handzeichnungen P. Bruegels.	Munich	1925
Fl. 804	Tolnay, C. de	Pierre Bruegel l'Ancien.	Brussels Paris	1935 1936
Fl. 805	Tolnay, C. de	Hieronymus Bosch.	Bâle	1937

Fl. 806	Tombu, L.	Peintres et sculpteurs belges a l'aube du 20e siècle.	*Liège*	1907
Fl. 807	Tormo y Monsó, E.	Las Iglesias del antiguo Madrid.	*Madrid*	1927
Fl. 808	Tovell, R. M.	Flemish Artists of the Valois Courts.		1950
Fl. 809	The Times (contributors)	The Times.	*London*	from 1785
Fl. 810	Tremayne, E. E.	The First Governess of the Netherlands, Magaret of Austria.	*London*	1908
Fl. 811	Vaernewyck, M. van	Den Spieghel der Nederlandscher Audtheyt. *Later edition:* called Historie van Belgis.	*Ghent* *Ghent*	1568 1574
Fl. 812	Vaernewyck, M. van	Die Beroerlyke Tyden in die Nederlanden en voornamelyk in Ghendt 1566–68 *in* Annales des Bibliophiles Gantois.	*MS.*	1569 *c.* 1884
Fl. 813	Valentiner, E.	Karel van Mander als Maler.	*Strasbourg*	1930
Fl. 814	Valentiner, W. R.	The Art of the Low Countries. (The Haarlem School of Painting).	*London*	1920
Fl. 815	Vallery-Radot, J.	Léonard Defrance.	*Paris*	1924
Fl. 816	Vandalle, M.	Les frères Vaillant. *in* Revue belge d'archéologie et d'histoire de l'art.	*Antwerp*	1937
Fl. 817	Vanderpyl, F.	Antoine Wiertz.	*Brussels*	1931
Fl. 818	Vasari, G.	Le Vite de' piu eccellenti pittori, scultori et architettori. *Revised by author* *Later edition* (G. Milanesi) 8 vols. *English translations* Edited Foster. 5 vols. Edited G. de Vere. 10 vols.	*Florence* *Florence* *Florence* *London* *London*	1550 1568 1877–1885 1910 1912–1915
Fl. 819	Vasari, G.	Le Vite de' piu eccellenti pittori, scultore et architettori. *Illustrated edition:* edited with notes by P. Pecchiai. 3 vols.	*Milan*	1928–1930
Fl. 820	Verhaeren, E.	L'œuvre de Fernand Khnopff 1881–1887.	*Brussels*	1887
Fl. 821	Verhaeren, E.	James Ensor.	*Brussels*	1906
Fl. 822	Verlant, E.	Guillaume Vogels.	*Brussels*	1921
Fl. 823	Verlat, C. and V.	Charles Verlat.	*Antwerp*	1926
Fl. 824	Vermoelen, J.	Teniers le jeune.	*Antwerp*	1865
Fl. 825	Vermoelen, J.	Notes historiques sur David Teniers et sa famille.	*Paris*	1870
Fl. 826	Vertue, G.	Notebooks. 6 vols. Walpole Soc., XVIII, Vertue I. Walpole Soc., XX, Vertue II. Walpole Soc., XXII, Vertue III. Walpole Soc., XXIV, Vertue IV. Walpole Soc., XXVI, Vertue V. Walpole Soc., XXIX, Vertue Index.	*MS.* *Oxford*	1713–1754 1930 1932 1934 1936 1938 1947
Fl. 827	Vienna	Inventar der Kunstsammlung des Erzherzogs Leopold Wilhelm von Österreich (J. A. v. d. Baren and others). *in* Jahrbuch der Kunstsammlungen des Allerhöchsten Kaiserhauses. (A. Berger).	 *Vienna*	1659 1883
Fl. 828	Vienna	Führer durch die Gemälde-Galerie. Vol. II. Niederländische und Deutsche Schulen. (H. Dollmayr). *New edition* *English translation*	*Vienna* *Vienna* *Vienna*	1896 1906 1912

Fl. 829	Vienna	Die Gemäldegalerie des Kunsthistorischen Museums in Wien. (G. Glück).	*Vienna*	1925
Fl. 830	Vienna	Führer durch die Gemäldegalerie. (E. H. Buschbeck).	*Vienna*	1928
Fl. 831	Vienna	Katalog der Gemäldegalerie. (G. Glück).	*Vienna*	1928
Fl. 832	Vienna	Katalog der Gemäldegalerie: Kunsthistorisches Museums. (L. Baldass, E. Buschbeck and others).	*Vienna*	1938
Fl. 833	Vienna (Albertina)	Vienna: Albertina. Die Zeichnungen der Niederländischen Schulen des 15. und 16. Jahrhunderts. (O. Benesch).	*Vienna*	1928
Fl. 834	Vienna (Albertina)	Vienna: Albertina. Handzeichnungen vlämischer and holländischer Meister der XV-XVII Jahrhunderts. (J. Meder). *English edition:* (C. Dodgson).	*Vienna* *Vienna*	1923 1930
Fl. 835	Vienna	Führer durch die Fürstlich Liechtensteinsche Gemäldegalerie in Wien. (A. Kronfeld).	*Vienna*	1931
Fl. 836	Vienna	Katalog der Graf Czernin'schen Gemäldegalerie in Wien. (K. Wilczek).	*Vienna*	1936
Fl. 837	Vlaamsche School (contributors)	De Vlaamsche School.	*Antwerp*	1855–1901
Fl. 838	Voisin, A.	Éloge du peintre B. P. Ommeganck.	*Ghent*	1826
Fl. 839	Voituron, H.	M. Carlier.	*Mons*	1907
Fl. 840	Voll, K.	Memling.	*Stuttgart and Leipzig*	1909
Fl. 841	Voort, J. van de	Gedenkboek H. van de Velde. *French edition*	*Ghent* *Brussels*	1933 1933
Fl. 842	Vries, A. B. de	Het Noord-Nederlandsche Portret in de tweede helft van de 16de eeuw.	*Amsterdam*	1934
Fl. 843	Valentin, S.	Jean Jacques Gailliard.	*Antwerp*	1949
Fl. 844	Voss, H.	Die Malerei des Barock in Rom.	*Berlin*	1924
Fl. 853	Waagen, G. F.	Die Gemäldesammlung in der Kaiserlichen Eremitage zu St. Petersburg nebst Bemerkungen über andere dortige Kunstsammlungen.	*St. Petersburg*	1864 and 1870
Fl. 856	Walpole, H.	Anecdotes of Painting in England. 5 vols. *Later edition* *Later edition* (edited J. Dallaway). 5 vols. *Revision of Dallaway edition* (edited R. N. Wornum). 3 vols.	*Strawberry Hill* *London* *London* *London*	1762–1771 1786 1826–1828 1876
Fl. 857	Walpole Society	Publications Vols. I-XXXIII. (Index up to date in vol. XXXI). (Vertue Index vol. XXIX).	*London*	1912–1947
Fl. 858	Warburg, A.	Gesammelte Schriften.	*Leipzig and Berlin*	1932
Fl. 859	Warner, R.	Dutch and Flemish Flower and Fruit painters of XVII and XVIII centuries.	*London*	1928
Fl. 860	Wassenbergh, A.	L'art du portrait en Frise au XVIe siècle.	*Leyden*	1934
Fl. 861	Wauters, A.	Thierry Bouts et ses Fils.	*Brussels*	1863
Fl. 862	Wauters, A.	Hugues van der Goes, sa vie et ses œuvres.	*Brussels*	1872
Fl. 863	Wauters, A.	Le Testament de Thierry Bouts. *in* Bulletin de l'Académie royale de Belgique.	*Brussels*	1883

Fl. 864	Wauters, A.	Bernart van Orley.	Paris	1893
Fl. 865	Wauters, A.	David Teniers et son fils.	Brussels	1897
Fl. 866	Wauters, A. J.	Denis van Alsloot, peintre des archiducs Albert et Isabelle.	Brussels	1896
Fl. 867	Wauters, A. J.	Jan Cornelisz Vermeyen : peintre de Charles V.	Brussels	1901
Fl. 868	Wauters, A. J.	Jean Gossaert et Antoine de Bourgogne.	Brussels	1903
Fl. 869	Weale, W. H. J.	Documents authentiques concernant Memlinc. in Journal des Beaux-Arts.	Brussels	1861
Fl. 870	Weale, W. H. J.	Hans Memlinc. Later edition	London London	1865 1901
Fl. 871	Weale, W. H. J.	Bruges et ses environs.	Bruges	1884
Fl. 872	Weale, W. H. J.	Gerard David.	London	1895
Fl. 873	Weale, W. H. J.	Hubert and John van Eyck.	London	1908
Fl. 874	Weale, W. H. J.	Peintres brugeois, Les Cristus.	Bruges	1909
Fl. 875	Weale, W. H. J. and Brockwell, M. W.	The van Eycks and their art.	London	1912
Fl. 876	Weisbach, W.	Französische Malerei des XVII Jahrhunderts.	Berlin	1932
Fl. 877	Weiss, E.	Jan Gossart genannt Mabuse.	Parchim	1913
Fl. 878	Weyerman, J. C.	De Levensbeschryvingen der Nederlantsche Konstschilders en Konstschilderessen. 4 vols.	The Hague	1729–1749
Fl. 879	Wilenski, R. H.	Dutch Painting. Revised edition	London London	1928 1945
Fl. 880	Whitley, W. T.	Artists and their Friends in England, 1700-1799. 2 vols.	London and Boston	1928
Fl. 881	Williamson, G. C.	History of Portrait Miniatures. 2 vols.	London	1904
Fl. 882	Williamson, G. C.	The Miniature Collector.	London	1921
Fl. 883	Willigen	Artistes de Haarlem.		1870
Fl. 884	Willis, F. C.	Die Niederländische Marinemalerei.	Leipzig	1911
Fl. 885	Winkler, F.	Die altniederländische Malerei: die Malerei in Belgien und Holland von 1400–1600.	Berlin	1924
Fl. 886	Winkler, F.	Die Flämische Buchmalerei des XV und XVI Jahrhunderts.	Leipzig	1925
Fl. 887	Winter, C.	Elizabethan Miniatures.	London	1943
Fl. 888	Woestyne, K. van de	Gustave van de Woestyne.	Brussels	1931
Fl. 889	Wouters de Bouchot, Chevalier de	Jean Guillaume Rosier.	Malines	1911
Fl. 890	Wouters, N.	La vie de Rik Wouters à travers son œuvre.	Brussels	1944
Fl. 891	Wulff, M.	Ruel, ein Barockmaler.	Strasbourg	1930
Fl. 892	Wurzbach, A. von	Niederländisches Künstler-Lexikon. 3 vols.	Vienna	1906–1911
Fl. 893	Wauters, A.	Recherches sur l'histoire de l'école flamande de peinture.		1882

NOTES ON THE LITERATURE

The books listed below in categories may be of service as introduction to later specialist writings as and when they appear.

The latest specialist writings on any painter must be sought in periodic publications—(such as Museum Bulletins and Year Books. Annals and Proceedings of academic bodies, and art journals, magazines and reviews)—some of which are only accessible in specialist libraries. Most of these publications publish indices. Many have been indexed since 1933 in the ART INDEX (New York). The RÉPERTOIRE D'ART ET D'ARCHÉOLOGIE, published in Paris since 1910, is another index of professional writings. Both the RÉPERTOIRE and the ART INDEX record writings containing new information discovered by researchers, conjectures (including style ascriptions and putative datings) and comment.

Monographs on individual painters are not included in the books listed below because they can be found by the code numbers placed at the end of each entry in the DICTIONARY OF FLEMISH PAINTERS in this volume; the code numbers refer to the BIBLIOGRAPHIC INDEX TO THE DICTIONARY which follows the DICTIONARY before these NOTES.

BIBLIOGRAPHIES

FLEMISH

There are bibliographic references at the end of all the entries in A. VON WURZBACH's fundamental NIEDERLÄNDISCHES KÜNSTLER LEXIKON (1906–1911). The following can also be consulted:

Someren, J. F. van	Essai d'une Bibliographie de l'Histoire spéciale de la peinture et de la gravure en Hollande et en Belgique 1500–1875. *Amsterdam*	1882
Hall, H. van, and Wolterson, B.	Repertorium voor de geschiedenis der Nederlandsche schilder en graveerkunst. (12th century to 1932). *The Hague*	1936
Pirenne, H.	Bibliographie de l'histoire de Belgique. *Brussels*	1931

GENERAL

There are bibliographic references at the end of all the entries in ULRICH THIEME and FELIX BECKER'S ALLGEMEINES LEXIKON DER BILDENDEN KÜNSTLER (1907–1950). The following books give information indicated by their titles:

Compilation	Universal Catalogue of Books on Art. 2 vols. *London* / *Supplement* *London 1877*	1870
Compilation	Gazette des Beaux Arts (Tables générales des cinquantes années de la Gazette des Beaux Arts), *Paris*	1859–1908
Compilation	Repertorium für Kunstwissenschaft. *Stuttgart, later Berlin*	from 1876
Compilation	Internationale Bibliographie der Kunstwissenschaft. *Berlin*	1903–1920
Schlosser, J.	Die Kunstliteratur. *Vienna*	1924
McColvin, E. R.	Painting. A guide to the best books... *London*	1934
Lucas, E. L.	Books on Art (Foundation List). *Cambridge Mass. (Fogg Museum)*	1938

NOTES ON THE LITERATURE

HISTORICAL OUTLINES

For those seeking a general account of Flemish art (including architecture, sculpture, and tapestry, as well as MS. illustrations, paintings and engravings) I recommend MAX ROOSES: ART IN FLANDERS (Ars Una series, London 1914) and PAUL FIERENS: L'ART EN BELGIQUE DU MOYEN ÂGE À NOS JOURS 1947. The following may also be found informative or of interest:

Taine, H.	Philosophie de l'art dans les Pays-Bas.	*Paris*	1869
Michiels, A.	Histoire de la peinture flamande depuis ses débuts jusqu'en 1864. 10 vols.	*Paris*	1865–1876
Riegel, H.	Beiträge sur Niederländischen Kunstgeschichte. 2 vols.	*Berlin*	1882
Ysendyck, J. J. van	Documents classés de l'art dans les Pays-Bas du Xe au XVIIIe siècle. 6 vols.	*Antwerp*	1880–1889
Bredius, A.	Künstler Inventare vom 16–18 Jahrhundert. 7 vols. and Index.	*The Hague*	1915–1922
Catalogue	Exposition de l'art belge ancien et moderne . . . au musée du Jeu de Paume à Paris.	*Paris and Brussels*	1923
Lambotte, P. (and others)	Flemish and Belgian Art in the Burlington House Exhibition 1927.	*London*	1927
Lambotte, P.	Flemish painting before the 18th century.	*London*	1927
Conway, Sir M. (and others)	Flemish and Belgian Art at Burlington House 1927. Memorial volume. (Painting: T. Borenius.) (Drawings: C. Dodgson.) (Tapestries: A. F. Kendrick.)	*London*	1927
Leurs, Stan (editor)	Geschiedenis van de vlaamsche Kunst. 2 vols.	*Antwerp and The Hague*	1937
Gelder, H. E. van (editor)	Kunstgeschiedenis der Nederlanden.	*Utrecht*	1938
Fansler, R. M. and Scherer, M. R.	Painting in Flanders.	*New York*	1945

For the setting of the Flemish School in relation to European art as a whole the reader may consult C. BLANC: HISTOIRE DES PEINTRES DE TOUTES LES ÉCOLES (14 vols., Paris 1861–1876), A. MICHEL: HISTOIRE DE L'ART DEPUIS LES PREMIERS TEMPS JUSQU'À NOS JOURS (9 vols., Paris 1905–1929), the PROPYLAEAN KUNSTGESCHICHTE (16 vols., Berlin from 1925) and above all ÉLIE FAURE: HISTOIRE DE L'ART (5 vols., Paris 1921–1927) a series of brilliant interpretative essays by a writer of fine sensibility. For the general history of Belgium there is the great book H. PIRENNE: HISTOIRE DE BELGIQUE 1909–1926.

ICONOGRAPHY

For the mythological subjects in Flemish paintings the reader whose acquaintance with ancient literature is slight will find the later edition of SMITH'S SMALLER CLASSICAL DICTIONARY (London 1928), T. BULLFINCH'S THE AGE OF FABLE (London and New York 1910) and E. VÉRON: LA MYTHOLOGIE DANS L'ART ANCIEN ET MODERNE (Paris 1878) more helpful than the OXFORD CLASSICAL DICTIONARY (Oxford 1949), which is designed for professional classical scholars. In the same way, for the meaning of the Christian subjects outside the Old and New Testaments and the Apocrypha, the general reader will more often find the answers in J. DE VORAGINE: LA LEGENDE DORÉE (Paris: Garnier Edition) and A. BUTLER: THE LIVES OF THE FATHERS, MARTYRS AND OTHER PRINCIPAL SAINTS (2 vols. London 1833) than in the BENEDICTINE BOOK OF SAINTS (London 1947). A handy book is L. MENZIES: THE SAINTS IN ITALY (London 1924). The following may also be helpful for the meaning of some subjects:

Molanus, J.	De picturis et imaginibus sacris	*Louvain*	1570
Waters, C. E. C.	Handbook of Christian symbols and stories of the saints as illustrated in art.	*Boston*	1886
Waters, C. E. C.	Handbook of legendary and mythological art.	*Boston*	1892
Jameson, Mrs. A. M. and Eastlake, Lady	The History of Our Lord, as exemplified in works of art . . . 2 vols.	*London*	1892

NOTES ON THE LITERATURE

Jameson, Mrs. A. M.	Legends of the Madonna as represented in the fine arts ...	*London*	1899
Jameson, Mrs. A. M.	Sacred and legendary art: containing legends of the Angels and Archangels, the Evangelists, the Apostles and Doctors of the Church and St. Mary Magdalene, as represented in the fine arts. 2 vols.	*London*	1900
Jameson, Mrs. A. M.	Legends of the Monastic Orders as represented in the fine arts.	*London*	1900
Mâle, E.	L'art religieux de la fin du moyen âge en France.	*Paris*	1908
Mâle, E.	L'art religieux de XIIe siècle en France.	*Paris*	1922
Mâle, E.	L'art religieux du XIIIième siècle en France.	*Paris*	1925
Künstle, K.	Iconographie der christlichen Kunst. 2 vols.	*Freiburg*	1926–1928
Webber, F. R.	Church symbolism.	*Cleveland*	1927
Sabbe, M.	Het geestesleven te Antwerpen in Rubens' Tijd. *in* Kryn, L. J. 'Rubens en zijne Eeuw'.	*Brussels*	1927
Brehier, L.	L'art chrétien: son développement iconographique des origines à nos jours.	*Paris*	1928
Mâle, E.	L'art religieux après le Concile de Trente.	*Paris*	1932
Smits, K.	De iconografie van de Nederlandsche Primitieven.	*Amsterdam*	1933
Hastings, J.	Dictionary of the Bible.	*London*	1936
Panofsky, E.	Studies in Iconology.	*New York*	1939
Rudrauf, L.	L'Annonciation.	*Paris*	1943
Benesch, O.	The Art of the Renaissance in Northern Europe.	*Cambridge (Mass.)*	1947
Fraenger, W.	Hieronymus Bosch (Das Tausendjaehrige Reich). *English edition* The Millennium of Hieronymus Bosch.	*Coburg* *London*	1947 1951
Contributors	Journal of the Warburg Institute. *Continued as* Journal of the Warburg and Courtauld Institutes.	*London* *London*	1937–1938 from 1939 in progress

LANDSCAPES, MARINES AND ARCHITECTURAL PAINTINGS

Readers interested in Flemish landscape painting will find much in the monographs on the individual landscape painters referred to beneath the entries in the DICTIONARY. The following books (some of which are also referred to in the entries) may be of use.

Wurzbach, A. von	Die Niederländischen Landschafts-, See-, Thier-, und Schlachtenmaler des XVII Jahrhunderts.	*Vienna*	1876
Levieux, F.	Essai sur le développement de la peinture de paysage et sur les voyages d'artistes aux XVe et XVIe siècles, dans leurs rapports avec l'histoire de l'art en Belgique.	*Brussels*	1891
Rosen, F.	Die Natur in der Kunst.	*Leipzig*	1903
Plietzsch, E.	Die Frankenthaler Maler. Ein Beitrag zur Entwickelungsgeschichte der Niederländischen Landschaftsmalerei.	*Leipzig*	1910
Jantzen, H.	Das Niederländische Architekturbild.	*Leipzig*	1910
Michel, E.	Great Masters of Landscape Painting.	*London*	1910
Willis, F. C.	Die Niederländische Marinemalerei.	*Leipzig*	1911

Gramm, J.	Die Ideale Landschaft. 2 vols.	*Freibourg*	1912
Baldass, L. von	Die Niederländische Landschaftsmalerei von Patinier bis Bruegel. *Vienna*		1918
Puyvelde, L. van	De Belgische Schilders in Holland, hoe zij Holland zagen.	*Leyden*	1919
Peltzer, R. A.	Niederländisch-Venezianische Landschaftsmalerei.	*Munich*	1924
Grosse, R.	Holländische Landschaftskunst 1600–1650.	*Berlin and Leipzig*	1925
Fierens-Gevaert, H.	Catalogue de l'Exposition rétrospective du paysage Flamand.	*Brussels*	1926
Callender, G.	Greenwich Museum: Macpherson Collection of Maritime paintings and prints.	*London*	1928
Sterling, C.	Les Paysages de Rubens.	*Paris*	1928
Havelaar, J.	De Nederlandsche Landschapskunst (tot het einde der XVIIe eeuw).		1931
Fritz, R.	Das Stadt- und Strassenbild in der Niederländischen Malerei des XVII Jahrhunderts.	*Stuttgart*	1932
Raczynski, Count J. A.	Die flämische Landschaft vor Rubens.	*Frankfort*	1937
Thiery, Y.	Histoire du paysage flamande au XVIIe siècle.	*Brussels*	1937
Callender, G.	Greenwich: National Maritime Museum Catalogue.	*Greenwich*	1937
Preston, L.	Sea and river painters of the Netherlands in the seventeenth century. *London and Oxford*		1937
Wetering, C. van de	Die Entwicklung der Niederländischen Landschaftsmalerei (XV und XVI Jahrhunderts). *Berlin*		1938
Glück, G.	De Landschappen van Rubens.	*Amsterdam*	1940
Clark, Sir K.	Landscape into Art.	*London*	1949
Friedländer, M. J.	Landscape, Portrait, Still life. Their Origin and Development.	*Oxford*	1949
Thiery, Y.	Le paysage Flamand	*Paris and Brussels*	1953

GENRE

The references to monographs beneath the DICTIONARY entries on the individual genre painters may be supplemented by the following books.

Franck, Seb.	Sprichwörter, Schöne, Weise herrliche Klugreden u Hoffsprüche. *Frankfort*		1541
Goedthals, F.	Les proverbes anciens Flamengs.	*Antwerp*	1568
Harrebomée, P. J.	Spreekwoordenboek der Nederlandsche Taal. 3 vols.	*Utrecht*	1858–1870
Maeterlinck, L.	Le Genre satyrique dans la Peinture Flamande. *Later edition*	*Brussels* *Brussels*	1901 1907
Cock, J. de and Teirlinck	Kinderspel en Kinderlust in Zuid-Nederland.	*Ghent*	1905
Drost, N. P.	Het Nederl. Kinderspel voor de XVIIe eeuw.	*The Hague*	1914
Baldass, L. von	Die Anfänge des Niederländischen Sittenbildes.	*Vienna*	1918
Manteuffel, K. Z. von	Das Flämische Sittenbild des XVII Jahrhunderts.	*Leipzig*	1921
Veth, C.	Geschiedenis van de Nederlandsche caricatuur en van de scherts in de Nederlandsche beeldende Kunst.	*Leyden*	1921
Brieger, L.	Das Genrebild. Die Entwicklung der Bürgerlichen Malerei.	*Munich*	1922

Baldass, L. von	Sittenbild und Stilleben.	*Vienna*	1923
Fraenger, W.	Der Bauern Bruegel und das deutsche Sprichwort.	*Munich and Leipzig*	1923
Meyere, V. de	Het Volksleven in Rubens' Tijd. *in* Kryn, L. J.: Rubens en zijne Eeuw.	*Brussels*	1927
Heurck, E. H. van	Les livres populaires flamands.	*Antwerp*	1931
Sudeck, E.	Bettlerdarstellungen vom Ende des XV Jahrhunderts bis zu Rembrandt. 	*Strasbourg*	1931
Friedländer, M. J.	Landscape, Portrait, Still life. Their Origin and Development.	*Oxford*	1949
Edwards, R.	Early Conversation Pictures	*London*	1954

FIFTEENTH AND SIXTEENTH CENTURIES

Readers who approach the subject by special periods will find a copious recent literature on the Flemish and Flemish (Dutch) painters of the fifteenth century, though few facts are known about the painters and extant pictures known to be by particular artists are extremely rare. Most of the recorded facts were already known by 1911 when A. VON WURZBACH completed his NIEDERLÄNDISCHES KÜNSTLER LEXIKON. Since that date some further information from archives and early writings has been published. But the major part of the recent specialist literature is conjecture—which explains of course the profusion of this literature, since about facts there can be no argument, whereas in the field of conjecture guesses and counter-guesses can be made until some factual knowledge proves the one guess or the other to be right or wrong. No one who cares for the pictures surviving from this period can resist the temptation to make conjectures about authorship and dates; we all do it in front of the originals and from photographs; we all 'confirm', or 'reject', or 'doubt' the specialists' guesses by our own experience. No harm is done by this parlour game which groups together pictures and reproductions of pictures that seem to belong together and gain in interest by the grouping—no harm that is, so long as the parlour game is recognised as such. But confusing levity begins when 'ascriptions' and 'chronologies' by the best reputed specialist style students of the moment are recorded by those students or by others as though they were statements of fact; and confusion takes charge when pictures are reproduced in books with 'By So-and-so' and a date beneath them, when both statements are conjectures, and when labels of this character appear upon the frames in our museums.

We have more knowledge of Flemish and Flemish (Dutch) painting in the 16th century. We know the names of more painters and more about them; and more signed and documented pictures have survived. But here again most of the recorded facts were already known by 1911, and the recent literature again is largely speculative. For this century we stand nevertheless on firmer ground because contemporary writings have come down to us—especially the basic book by KAREL VAN MANDER, who was born in 1548, wrote his book at the end of the century and published it in 1604. Researches in archives have confirmed a very large number of Van Mander's statements and revealed only very occasional mistakes; and scores of pictures named or described by him survive to prove the extent of his knowledge, the accuracy of his memory, and the quality of his perception.

The following list of books may give the reader some idea of the growth of the literature on this period. I have included a few books on the MS. painters and on drawings, though each of these subjects has its own literature which those concerned can separately explore. As elsewhere I have not included monographs, as these are recorded beneath my DICTIONARY entries.

Facio, B.	De viris illustribus Liber. *Published Florence 1745*	*MS.*	1454–1456
Lemaire de Belges, J.	La Couronne Margaritique. *Published Lyons 1549*	*MS.*	1504–1511
Dürer A.	Tagebuch der Reise in die Niederlande. *English translation in* Conway, Sir M.: Literary remains of Albrecht Dürer. *London 1889*		1521

Vasari, G.	Le Vite de' piu eccellenti Pittori, Scultori et Architettori. *Florence*
	Revised by author *Florence*
	Later edition: G. Milanesi. 8 vols. *Florence 1877–1885*
	English translations
	   Edited Foster. 5 vols. *London 1910*
	   Edited G. de Vere. 10 vols. *London 1912–1915*
	Modern Italian edition Edited P. Pecchiai 3 vols. *Milan 1928–1930*
			1550
			1568

Guevara, F. de	Comentarios de la Pintura. *First published (A. Ponz) Madrid 1788.* *Modern edition in* Sánchez Cantón: Fuentes Literarias. *Madrid 1923–1941.*		before 1563
Guicciardini, L.	Descrittione di tutti i Paesi Bassi... *Antwerp* *Revised edition* *Antwerp 1581* *English Edition* *London 1795*		1567

Vaernewyck, M. van	Den Spieghel der Nederlandscher Audtheyt. *Later edition called* Historie van Belgis.	*Ghent* 1568 *Ghent*	1574
Vaernewyck, M. van	Die Beroerlyke Tyden in die Nederlanden en voornamelyk in Ghendt 1566–1568. *in* Annales des Bibliophiles Gantois	*MS.* *c.* 1884.	1569
Lampsonius, D.	Pictorum aliquot celebrium germaniae inferioris effigies; una cum doctis. Dom. Lampsonii hujus artis peritissimi elogiis.	*Antwerp*	1572
Molanus, J.	De picturis et imaginibus sacris *2nd edition*	*Louvain* *Louvain* 1594	1570
Molanus, J.	Historiae Lovanensium libri XIV ... *First published*	*MS.* *Brussels* 1861	*c.* 1575
Lomazzo, G. P.	Trattato dell' Arte della Pittura, diviso in VII libri, nei quali si contiene tutta la Teoria e la practica di essa Pittura. *Later edition*	*Milan* *Rome* 1844	1584
Buchelius, A.	Res Pictoriae ... *Modern edition Edited G. J. Hoogewerff.*	*MS.* *The Hague* 1928	*c.* 1585

Mander, K. van	Het Schilderboek.
	2nd edition
	French translation
	    H. Hymans.
	English translation
	    C. van der Wall.
	Modern Dutch edition
	    A. F. Mirande and G. S. Overdiep.
		Haarlem
		Haarlem 1616–1618
		
		Paris 1884
		
		New York 1936
		
		Amsterdam 1943
			1604

Sigüenza, Fray J. de	Historia de la orden de San Jerónimo. *Modern edition in* Sánchez Cantón: Fuentes Literarias. *Madrid* 1923–1941	*Madrid*	1600–1605
Sanderus, A.	Flandria illustrata ... *2 vols.* *Dutch translation* Verheerlykt Vlaandre ...	*Cologne* *Leyden* 1735	1641
Bie, C. de	Het gulden Cabinet van de edele vry Schilder-Const inhoudende den lof van de vermarste Schilders, ... van dese eeuw.	*Antwerp*	1661
Bastard, Comte A. de	Peintures et Ornements des Manuscrits.		1832–1869
Haseloff, A.	Catalogue des manuscrits de la Bibliothèque des Ducs de Bourgogne.	*Brussels*	1842
Denis, F.	Le Monde enchanté: Cosmographie et histoire naturelle et fantastique du moyen âge.	*Paris*	1843
Rathgeber, G.	Annalen der Niederländischen Malerei, Formschneide—und Kupferstecherkunst.	*Gotha*	1844
Laborde, L. de	Les Ducs de Bourgogne, études sur les lettres, les arts et l'industrie pendant les XVe siècle et plus particulièrement dans les Pays-Bas et le Duché de Bourgogne. *3 vols.*	*Paris*	1849–1851
Dehaisnes, C.	L'Art chrétien en Flandre.	*Douai*	1860
Pinchart, A.	Miniaturistes, Enlumineurs et Calligraphes employés par Philippe le Bon et Charles le Temeraire.	*Brussels*	1865
Delisle, L.	Le Cabinet des manuscrits de la Bibliothèque Nationale.	*Paris*	1868–1881
Hymans, H.	Les Images populaires flamandes au XVIe siècle.	*Liège*	1869
Crowe, J. A. and Cavalcaselle, G. B.	Early Flemish painters. *3rd edition.*	*London*	1879
Rooses, M.	Geschiedenis der Antwerpsche Schilderschool. *Later edition*	*Ghent* *Ghent* 1889	1879

Wauters, A.	Art ancien en Belgique.	*Brussels*	1880
Branden, F. J. van den	Geschiedenis der Antwerpsche Schilderschool.	*Antwerp*	1878–1883
Wauters, A.	Les Commencements de l'ancienne école flamande de Peinture antérieurement à Van Eyck. *in* Bulletin de l'Académie royale de Belgique.	*Brussels*	1883
Wauters, A.	Recherches sur l'Histoire de l'École Flamande de peinture pendant la seconde moitié du XVe siècle. *in* Bulletin de l'Académie royale de Belgique.	*Brussels*	1882–1884
Venturi, A.	Zur Geschichte der Kunstsammlungen Kaiser Rudolf II. *in* Repertorium für Kunstwissenschaft.	*Stuttgart*	1885
Dehaisnes, C.	Documents et extraits divers concernant l'histoire de l'art dans la Flandre, l'Artois et le Hainaut avant le XVe siècle. 2 vols.	*Lille*	1886
Conway, Sir M.	Early Flemish Artists and their predecessors on the Lower Rhine.	*London*	1887
Durrieu, Comte P.	Heures de Turin.	*Paris*	1891
Ewerbeck, F.	Die Renaissance in Belgien und Holland. 3 vols.	*Leipzig*	1888–1891
Dülberg, F.	Die Leydener Malerschule.	*Berlin*	1899
Tulpinck, C.	Étude sur la peinture murale en Belgique jusqu'à l'époque de la Renaissance.	*Brussels*	1900
Gheyn, J. van den	Catalogue des manuscrits de la Bibliothèque royale de Belgique.	*Brussels*	1901
Puyvelde, L. van	Les Arts Anciens de Flandre; l'évolution de la conception artistique chez les peintres de la Renaissance Septentrionale.	*Bruges*	1902
Hymans, H.	L'Exposition des primitifs flamands à Bruges.	*Paris*	1902
Hulin de Loo, G.	Catalogue Critique de l'Exposition de Bruges.	*Ghent*	1902
Weale, W. H. J.	Catalogue de l'exposition des primitifs flamands.	*Bruges*	1902
Friedländer, M. J.	Meisterwerke der Niederländische Malerei des XV und XVI Jahrhunderts auf der Ausstellung zu Brügge 1902.	*Munich*	1903
Greve, H. E.	De Bronnen van Carel van Mander.	*The Hague*	1903
Durrieu, Comte P.	Les très riches Heures de Jean de France, Duc du Berry.	*Paris*	1904
Dalbon	Les Procédés des Primitifs.	*Paris*	1904
Moes, E. W.	Original drawings of the Dutch and Flemish schools in the print room of the State Museum (Amsterdam).	*Amsterdam*	1904
Fierens-Gevaert, H.	La Renaissance septentrionale et les premiers maîtres flamands.	*Brussels*	1905
Bruinvis, C. W.	Levensschetsen . . . over beeld. Kunstenaars te Alkmaar.		1905
Voll, K.	Die Altniederländische Malerei von Jan van Eyck bis Memling. *Leipzig* *New edition* *Leipzig* 1932		1906
Durrieu, Comte P.	La Peinture en France: Débuts de la Renaissance. *in* Michel, A.: Histoire de l'Art.	*Paris*	1907
Fourcaud, L. de	La peinture dans les Pays-Bas, XVe siècle. *in* Michel, A.: Histoire de l'Art.	*Paris*	1907
Mont, Pol de	Exposition de la Toison d'Or à Bruges 1907.	*Bruges*	1907
Kervyn de Lettenhove, H. (editor)	Les chefs-d'œuvre d'art ancien à l'exposition de la Toison d'Or à Bruges en 1907.	*Brussels*	1908

Pierron, S.	Chefs-d'œuvre de l'art flamand à l'exposition de la Toison d'Or.	*Bruges*	1908
Tremayne, E. E.	The First Governess of the Netherlands, Margaret of Austria.	*London*	1908
Waetzold, W.	Die Kunst des Porträts.	*Leipzig*	1908
Germain, A.	Les Neerlandais en Bourgogne.	*Brussels*	1909
Mont, Pol de	La peinture néerlandaise des frères Van Eyck à Pieter Breughel. 3 vols.	*Brussels*	1909
Hulin de Loo, G.	Les Heures de Milan.	*Brussels*	1911
Fierens-Gevært, H.	Les primitifs flamands. 4 vols.	*Brussels*	1909–1912
Schlosser, J. von	Der burgundische Paramentenschatz des Ordens von Goldenen Vliesse.	*Vienna*	1912
Ring, G.	Beiträge zur Geschichte niederländischer Bildnismalerei im 15. und 16. Jahrhunderts.	*Leipzig*	1913
Foronda y Aguilera, M.	Estancias y Viajes del Emperador Carlos V.	*Madrid*	1914
Mont, Pol de	La Peinture Ancienne au Musée Royal des Beaux-Arts d'Anvers.	*Brussels and Paris*	1914
Fierens-Gevaert, H.	The Brussels Gallery of Old Masters.	*Brussels and Paris*	1914
Fierens-Gevaert, H.	Histoire de l'art flamand. Vol. 1: XVIe et XVIIe siècles.	*Brussels*	1917–1918
Kalcken, G. van and Six, J.	Peintures ecclésiastiques du moyen-âge en Hollande. 5 vols.	*Haarlem and The Hague*	1903–1919
Valentiner, W. R.	The Art of the Low Countries.	*London*	1920
Conway, Sir M.	The Van Eycks and their followers.	*London*	1921
Friedländer, M. J.	Von Eyck bis Bruegel.	*Berlin*	1921
Dimier, L.	La miniature flamande.	*Paris*	1921
Durrieu, Comte P.	La miniature flamande au temps de la cour de Bourgogne 1415–1530. *Later edition* *Paris and Brussels* 1927	*Paris and Brussels*	1921
Misme, C.	La Peinture au Musée du Louvre: École Hollandaise. (L'Illustration).	*Paris*	1922
Faure, É.	L'Art Renaissant (Le Cycle Franco-Flamand) vol. III of Histoire de l'Art. *English translation* (W. Pach) *New York and London* 1923	*Paris*	1922
Fierens-Gevaert, H.	La Peinture à Bruges.	*Brussels and Paris*	1922
Casier, J.	L'art ancien dans les Flandres. 3 vols.	*Brussels*	1914–1922
Baldass, L. von	Der Kunstlerkreis Kaiser Maximilians.	*Vienna*	1923
Meder, J.	Vienna: Albertina. Handzeichnungen vlämischer und holländischer meister des XV–XVII Jahrhunderts. *English edition* C. Dodgson *Vienna* 1930	*Vienna*	1923
Verlant, E.	La Peinture Ancienne à l'Exposition de l'Art Belge à Paris en 1923.	*Paris and Brussels*	1924
Heidrich, E.	Alt-niederländische Malerei.	*Jena*	1924

NOTES ON THE LITERATURE

Byvanck, A. W. and Hoogewerff, G. J.	Noord-Nederlandsche Miniaturen in handschriften der 14, 15 en 16 eeuwen. *The Hague*		1921–1925
Winkler, F.	Die altniederländische Malerei; die Malerei in Belgien und Holland von 1400–1600. *Berlin*		1924
Winkler, F.	Die Flämische Buchmalerei des XV und XVI Jahrhunderts. *Leipzig*		1925
Fourcaud, L. de	Le peinture dans les Pays-Bas depuis les successeurs des Van Eyck... jusque dans la seconde moitié du XVIe siècle. *in* Michel, A.: Histoire de l'Art. *Paris*		1925
Gillet, L.	La peinture dans les Pays-Bas à la fin du XVIe siècle. *in* Michel, A.: Histoire de l'Art. *Paris*		1925
Burger, W.	Die Malerei in den Niederländen 1400 bis 1550. *Munich*		1925
Cartellieri, O.	Am Hofe der Herzöge von Burgund. *Bâle*		1926
	English edition The Court of the Dukes of Burgundy. *London* 1929		
Michel, Éd.	La Peinture au Musée du Louvre: École Flamande. (L'Illustration). *Paris*		c. 1926
Riegl, A.	Das Holländische Gruppenporträt. *Vienna*		1926
Delen, A. J. J.	De Vlaamsche Kunst, voor, tijdens en na Rubens. *in* Kryn, L. J.: Rubens en zijne Eeuw. *Brussels*		1927
Popham, A. E.	Drawings of the early Flemish School. *London*		1926–1927
Benesch, O.	Vienna: Albertina. Die Zeichnungen der Niederländischen Schulen des 15 und 16 Jahrhunderts. *Vienna*		1928
Glück, G.	Die Kunst der Renaissance in Deutschland, den Niederlanden, Frankreich... *Berlin*		1928
Dülberg, F.	Niederländische Malerei der Spätgotik und Renaissance. *Berlin*		1929
Fierens-Gevaert, H. and Fierens, P.	Histoire de la peinture flamande des origines à la fin du XVe siècle. 3 vols. *Paris and Brussels*		1927–1929
Catalogue	Catalogue de l'exposition internationale, Anvers, 1930. Section d'art flamand ancien. Peintures. *Brussels*		1930
Denucé, J.	Inventories of the Art Collections in Antwerp in the 16th and 17th centuries. *Antwerp*		1932
Popham, A. E.	Dutch and Flemish drawings of the XVth and XVIth centuries. (Vol. 5 of British Museum Catalogue of Drawings by Dutch and Flemish Artists). *London*		1915–1932
Lyna, F.	De Vlaamsche Miniatuur van 1200 tot 1530. *Brussels*		1933
Warburg, A.	Gesammelte Schriften. *Leipzig and Berlin*		1932
Lugt, F.	Les dessins du Musée du Louvre: Écoles des Pays-Bas des origines jusqu'aux maîtres nés avant 1550. *Paris*		1932–1934
Vries, A. B. de	Het Noord-Nederlandsche Portret in de tweede helft van de 16de eeuw. *Amsterdam*		1934
Wassenbergh, A.	L'art du portrait en Frise au XVIe siècle. *Leyden*		1934
Troche, E. G.	Niederländische Malerei des funfzehnten und sechszehnten Jahrhunderts. *Berlin*		1935
Tolnay, C. de	Le Maître de Flémalle et les Frères van Eyck *Brussels*		1936
Lederle, U.	Gerechtigkeitsdarstellungen in deutschen und niederländischen Rathausern. *Philippsburg*		1937
Friedländer, M. J.	Die Altniederländische Malerei. 14 vols. *Berlin and Leyden*		1924–1937

Lavalleye, J.	De Vlaamsche Schilderkunst tot ongeveer 1480. *in* Stan Leurs: Geschiedenis van de Vlaamsche Kunst. *Antwerp and The Hague*		1937
Lavalleye, J.	De Vlaamsche Schilderkunst, van Memling tot Metsijs. *in* Stan Leurs: Geschiedenis van de Vlaamsche Kunst. *Antwerp and The Hague*		1937
Vermeylen, A.	Van Bosch tot Bruegel. *in* Stan Leurs: Geschiedenis van de Vlaamsche Kunst. *Antwerp and The Hague*		1937
Gabriels, J.	Vroeg-Renaissance in de Schilderkunst. De Schilderkunst der Laat-Renaissance. De Manieristen van het tweede geslacht. *in* Stan Leurs: Geschiedenis van de Vlaamsche Kunst. *Antwerp and The Hague*		1937
Baldass, L. von	Niederl. Maler d. spätgot. Stiles (16 Jahrhundert).	*Vienna*	1937
Gaspar, C. and Lyna, F.	Les principaux manuscrits à peintures de la Bibliothèque Royale de Belgique.	*Paris*	1937
Fierens, P.	La peinture flamande. Des origines à Quentin Matsys.	*Paris*	1938
Schoene, W.	Die grossen Meister der niederländischen Malerei des XV Jahrhunderts. Hubert van Eyck bis Quentin Massys.	*Leipzig*	1939
Puyvelde, L. van	La Renaissance flamande. *in* Annuaire des musées royaux ... de Belgique.	*Brussels*	1939
Puyvelde, L. van	Les primitifs flamands. *English edition*	*Paris* *London* 1948	1941
Gaspar, C. and Lyna, F.	Philippe le Bon et ses beaux livres.	*Brussels*	1942
Sterling, C.	La Peinture Française (Moyan Age).	*Paris*	1942
Toth, K.	Die alten Niederländer: Van Eyck bis Bruegel.	*Bielefeld and Leipzig*	1943
Michel, É.	L'école flamande du XVe siécle au musée du Louvre.	*Brussels*	1944
Lavalleye, J.	Le Portrait (XVe siècle).	*Brussels*	1945
Davies, M.	Early Netherlandish School: National Gallery Catalogue.	*London*	1945
Bodkin, T.	Flemish Paintings. (Faber Gallery).	*London*	1945
Catalogue	Van Jan Eyck tot Rubens. Tentoonstelling van meesterwerken uit de Belgische Museen en Kerken; Amsterdam.	*Amsterdam*	1946
Terlinden, Vicomte C.	P. Bruegel le Vieux et l'Histoire. *in* Revue Belge d'Archéologie ...	*Brussels*	1942–1946
Hoogewerff, G. J.	De Noord-Nederlandsche Schilderkunst. 5 vols.	*The Hague*	1937–1947
Wehle, H. B. and Salinger, M.	Catalogue of Early Flemish, Dutch and German Paintings in the Metropolitan Museum New York.	*New York*	1947
Fierens, P. (editor)	L'art en Belgique: La peinture et l'enluminure des origines à la fin du XVe siècle. (J. Lavalleye) *and* La peinture au XVIe siècle (J. Maquet-Tombu).	*Brussels*	1947
Tovell, R. M.	Flemish artists of the Valois Courts.		1950
Bisthoven, A. J. de and Parmentier, R. A.	Les primitifs flamands. Le Musée Communal de Bruges.	*Antwerp*	1951
Panofsky E.	Early Netherlandish Painting	*Cambridge (Mass.) and Oxford*	1953

SEVENTEENTH CENTURY

The literature about Flemish painters working in the 17th century can be divided into writings about Rubens and his entourage and writings about other painters of the period. A selection of the vast literature on Rubens (including some writings after 1939) is given beneath my DICTIONARY entry; a copious bibliography up to 1939 is contained in GESCHRIFTEN VAN EN OVER RUBENS by P. ARENTS (Antwerp 1940). A few books dealing specifically with the Rubens entourage are included in my list below; the other books named there deal mainly with the other painters. It has been the custom of writers on this period to describe the whole century as dominated—swamped indeed—by Rubens (who died in 1640); but, as made clear in my text in this volume, this seems to me a misconception of the development of Flemish painting, which was continuous from the sixteenth to the nineteenth century apart from and in spite of the Rubens interlude. We have a number of contemporary books about the other painters: DE BIE'S GULDEN CABINET (1661) shows the repute of many at that date; J. VAN SANDRART records some first-hand contacts in his TEUTSCHE ACADEMIE (1675–1679), ARNOLD HOUBRAKEN (1660–1719), who set out to continue Van Mander's book, gives a highly interesting and entertaining series of records and comments, based largely on personal knowledge and first-hand information, in his GROOTE SCHOUBURGH (published partly in his lifetime and partly just after his death) and, as in the case of Van Mander's book, researches in archives have confirmed a great many of his statements. J. CAMPO WEYERMAN (1677–1747), who makes some additions to Houbraken in his LEVENSBESCHRYVINGEN, has always been regarded as rather unreliable, though he actually had contact with a number of painters at the end of the century and up to 1739 when his habit of writing libellous lampoons and poems landed him in gaol. D. D'ARGENVILLE in his ABRÉGÉ (1745–1752) records some pictures known to him in French collections; JEAN BAPTISTE DESCAMPS (1706–1791) in LA VIE DES PEINTRES (begun 1738 and finished 1763) repeats Van Mander, Houbraken and Weyerman, adds some information given him by the descendants of certain artists, and locates some paintings he had personally seen; G. P. MENSAERT in LE PEINTRE AMATEUR (1763), and DESCAMPS in VOYAGE PITTORESQUE (1769), give first-hand records of pictures by 17th century painters then in Belgian churches and religious houses. SIR JOSHUA REYNOLDS' JOURNEY TO FLANDERS AND HOLLAND (1781) is, of course, a precious document both as objective record and as subjective choice and comment. Information on the range of subjects painted by the 17th century artists (and by some in earlier periods) and on the taste of 17th century Antwerp collectors in different social spheres is given in the contemporary inventories published by J. DENUCÉ in INVENTORIES OF THE ART COLLECTIONS IN ANTWERP IN THE 16TH AND 17TH CENTURIES (Antwerp 1932); contemporary dealers' documents are published in the same author's ART EXPORT IN THE 17TH CENTURY IN ANTWERP (Antwerp 1931) and in his LETTERS AND DOCUMENTS CONCERNING JAN BREUGHEL I AND II (Antwerp 1934).

Bie, C. de	Het gulden Cabinet van de edele vry Schilder-Const inhoudende den lof van de vermarste Schilders . . . van dese eeuw.	*Antwerp*	1661
Sandrart, J. von	Teutsche Academie der Edlen Bau-Bild-und-Mahlerey Künste. 2 vols. *Later edition* 8 vols. *Modern edition* (A. R. Peltzer) *with notes.*	*Nuremberg* *Nuremberg* 1769–1775 *Munich* 1926	1675–1679
Piles, R. de	Dissertation sur les ouvrages des plus fameux peintres avec la vie de Rubens.	*Paris*	1681
Félibien des Avaux, A.	Entretiens sur les vies et les ouvrages des plus excellens peintres anciens et modernes. 5 vols. *Later edition*	*Paris* *London* 1705	1666–1688
Lairesse, G. de	Het Groot Schilderboek. *Later editions* *French translation* (*with biography by* J. H. Jansen).	*Amsterdam* *Amsterdam* 1712 *Amsterdam* 1720 *Amsterdam* 1745 *Paris* 1787	1707
Piles, R. de	Cours de peinture par principe. *English edition*	*Paris* *London* 1743	1708
Houbraken, A.	De Groote Schouburgh der Nederlantsche Konstschilders en Schilderessen. 3 vols. *Later edition*	*Amsterdam* *The Hague* 1753	1718–1721
Weyerman, J. C.	De Levensbeschryvingen der Nederlantsche Konstschilders en Konstschilderessen. 4 vols.	*The Hague*	1729–1749
Gool, J. van	De Nieuwe Schouburg der Nederlantsche Konstschilders en Schilderessen. 2 vols.	*The Hague*	1750
Argenville, D. d'	Abrégé de la vie des Plus Fameux Peintres. 3 vols.	*Paris*	1745–1752

Mensaert, G. P.	Le Peintre Amateur et Curieux; ou description générale des tableaux des plus habiles maîtres, qui font l'ornement des églises, couvents, abbayes, . . . dans l'étendue des Pays-Bas Autrichiens. 2 vols.	*Brussels*	1763
Descamps, J. B.	La Vie des Peintres Flamands, Allemands et Hollandois. 4 vols.	*Paris*	1753–1763
Descamps, J. B.	Voyage Pittoresque de la Flandre et du Brabant. *Annotated edition* (C. Rochu).	*Paris* *Paris* 1838	1769
Reynolds, Sir J.	A Journey to Flanders and Holland. 1781 *in* The Literary Works of Sir J. Reynolds (*edited* E. Malone) *Later edition* (*edited* H. W. Beechey)	*London* *London* 1819 *London* 1852	1798
Smith, J.	A Catalogue raisonné of the works of the most eminent Dutch, Flemish and French painters. 9 vols.	*London*	1829–1842
Voorhelm-Schneevoogt, C. G.	Catalogue des Estampes gravées d'après Rubens.	*Haarlem*	1873
Rooses, M.	Geschiedenis der Antwerpsche Schilderschool. *Later edition*	*Ghent* *Ghent* 1889	1879
Fidière, O.	État Civil des peintres et sculpteurs de l'Académie Royale de 1648–1745.	*Paris*	1883
Branden, F. J. van den	Geschiedenis der Antwerpsche Schilderschool. 3 vols.	*Antwerp*	1878–1883
Rosenberg, A.	Die Rubensstecher.	*Vienna*	1893
Glück, G.	Aus Rubens' Zeit und Schule.	*Vienna*	1903
Moes, E. W. (editor)	Original drawings of the Dutch and Flemish Schools in the print room of the State Museum. (Amsterdam).	*Amsterdam*	1904
Rooses, M. and Ruelens, C.	Correspondance de Rubens. 6 vols.	*Antwerp*	1887–1908
Waetzold, W.	Die Kunst des Porträts.	*Leipzig*	1908
Lemonnier, H.	L'art au temps de Louis XIV.	*Paris*	1911
Heidrich, E.	Flämische Malerei.	*Jena*	1913
Fierens-Gevaert, H.	The Brussels Gallery of Old Masters.	*Brussels and Paris*	1914
Mont, Pol de	La Peinture Ancienne au Musée Royal des Beaux-Arts d'Anvers.	*Brussels and Paris*	1914
Oldenbourg, R.	Die Flämische Malerei des XVII Jahrhunderts. *Second edition*	*Berlin* *Berlin* 1922	1918
Fierens-Gevaert, H.	Histoire de l'art flamand. Vol. I, XVIe et XVIIe siècles.	*Brussels*	1917–1918
Faure, É.	Histoire de l'art: L'art moderne (La Flandre) vol. IV. *English translation* (W. Pach)	*Paris* *New York and London* 1924	1921
Hymans, H.	Œuvres: L'art au 17e et au 19e siècle dans les Pays-Bas. (vol. IV).	*Brussels*	1920–1921
Gillet, L.	La peinture dans les Pays-Bas au XVIIe siècle. *in* Michel, A.: Histoire de l'art.	*Paris*	1921
Weisbach, W.	Der Barock als Kunst der Gegenreformation.	*Berlin*	1921
Fierens-Gevaeart, H.	La Peinture à Bruges.	*Brussels and Paris*	1922

Meder, J.	Vienna: Albertina. Handzeichnungen vlämischer und holländischer Meister des XV-XVII Jahrhunderts. *Vienna*		1923
	English edition (C. Dodgson) *Vienna* 1930		
Michel, Éd.	La Peinture au Musée du Louvre: École Flamande. (L'Illustration). *Paris*		c. 1926
Drost, W.	Die Barockmalerei in den Germanischen Ländern. *Berlin*		1926
Champier, V.	L'art dans les Flandres françaises aux XVIIe et XVIIIe siècles, après les conquêtes de Louis XIV. *Roubaix*		1926
Riegl, A.	Das Holländische Gruppenporträt. *Vienna*		1926
Muchall-Viebrook, T.	Flemish drawings of the seventeenth century. *London*		1926
Kryn, L. J. (editor)	Rubens en zijne Eeuw: in 5 parts.		
	Rubens' Antwerpen. (F. Prims.)		
	Het Geestesleven te Antwerpen in Rubens' tijd. (M. Sabbe.)		
	Het Volksleven in Rubens' tijd. (V. de Meyere.)		
	De Vlaamsche Kunst, voor, tijdens en na Rubens. (A. J. J. Delen.)		
	Rubens' Leven en Werk. (P. Lambotte.) *Brussels*		1927
Glück, B. and Haberditzl, F. M.	Handzeichnungen von Rubens. *Berlin*		1928
Warner, R.	Dutch and Flemish Flower and Fruit Painters of XVIIth and XVIIIth centuries. *London*		1928
Denucé, J.	Art Export in the 17th century in Antwerp. The Firm Forchoudt. *Antwerp*		1931
Denucé, J.	Inventories of the Art Collections in Antwerp in the 16th and 17th centuries. *Antwerp*		1932
Hind, A. M.	Drawings by Rubens, Van Dyck and other artists of the Flemish School of the XVIIth century.		
	Vol. 2 of British Museum Catalogue of drawings by Dutch and Flemish artists. *London*		1915–1932
Glück, G.	Rubens, van Dyck und ihr Kreis. *Vienna*		1933
Denucé, J.	Letters and documents concerning Jan Breughel I and II. *Antwerp*		1934
Lugt, F.	Les dessins du Musée du Louvre: École flamande depuis les maîtres nés après 1550 jusqu'à la fin du XVIIe siècle. *Paris*		1932–1934
Grosse, R.	Niederlaendsche Malerei des 17 Jahrhunderts.		1936
Sterling, C.	La peinture flamande: Rubens et son temps. (Catalogue of exhibition in the Musée de l'Orangerie). *Paris*		1936
Hannema, D. and Schendel, A. van	Noord en Zuid Nederlandsche schilderkunst der XVII eeuw. *Amsterdam*		1936
Michel, Éd.	Flemish Painting in the XVIIth century. *London*		1939
Cornette, A. H.	De Vlaamsche Schilderkunst in de XVIIe eeuw. *Antwerp*		1939
Arents, P.	Geschriften van en over Rubens. *Antwerp*		1940
Fierens, P.	La peinture flamande de Bruegel au XVIIIe siècle. *Paris*		1942
Delen, A. J. J.	Teekeningen van Vlaamsche Meesters. *Antwerp*		1943
Arschot, Comte d'	Le Portrait aux XVIIe et XVIIIe siècles. *Brussels*		1945
Fierens, P. (editor)	L'Art en Belgique: La peinture au XVIIe siècle. (A. J. J. Delen). *Brussels*		1947
Bernt, W.	Die Niederländischen Maler des 17 Jahrhunderts. *Munich*		
	3 vols.		1948
Gelder, J. G. van	Ashmolean Museum: Catalogue of the Dutch and Flemish still life pictures (Ward Collection). *Oxford*		1950

EIGHTEENTH CENTURY

Flemish painting in the 18th century has not yet received the attention it deserves. Information about many painters who began in the 17th century can be found in the books by HOUBRAKEN, WEYERMAN, D'ARGENVILLE and DESCAMPS which figure in my 17th century list; both MENSAERT and DESCAMPS record works by some 18th century painters in their travel books, and J. VAN GOOL in his NIEUWE SCHOUBURG continues Houbraken. For the painters working after 1750 the contemporary or near-contemporary books include VAN EYNDEN AND WILLIGEN'S GESCHIEDENIS (1816–1842), and J. IMMERZEEL'S LEVENS EN WERKEN (1843), continued and corrected by C. KRAMM in DE LEVENS EN WERKEN DER HOLLANDSCHE EN VLAAMSCHE KUNST-SCHILDERS (Amsterdam 1857–1864). Contemporary records for this period also include the newspapers and journals of the time, for we have here reached the point where much enlightening information can be gathered not only from the annals of academic bodies but also from contemporary gossips, critics, diarists and other journalists.

Houbraken, A.	De Groote schouburgh der Nederlantsche Konstschilders en Schilderessen. 3 vols. *Later edition*	*Amsterdam* *The Hague* 1753	1718–1712
Weyerman, J. C.	De Levensbeschryvingen der Nederlantsche Konstschilders en Konst-schilderessen. 4 vols.	*The Hague*	1729–1749
Argenville, D. d'	Abrégé de la vie des Plus Fameux Peintres. 3 vols.	*Paris*	1745–1752
Gool, J. van	De Nieuwe Schouburg der Nederlantsche Konstschilders en Schilderessen. 2 vols.	*The Hague*	1750
Descamps, J. B.	La Vie des Peintres Flamands, Allemands et Hollandois. 4 vols.	*Paris*	1753–1763
Mensaert, G. P.	Le Peintre Amateur et Curieux; ou description générale des tableaux des plus habiles maîtres, qui font l'ornement des églises, couvents, abbayes . . . dans l'étendue des Pays-Bas Autrichiens. 2 vols.	*Brussels*	1763
Descamps, J. B.	Voyage Pittoresque de la Flandre et du Brabant. *Annotated edition (C. Rochu)*	*Paris* *Paris* 1838	1769
Anon.	Le voyageur dans les Pays-Bas autrichiens ou Lettres sur l'état actuel de ces Pays.	*Amsterdam*	1783
Fiorillo, J. D.	Geschichte der zeichnenden Künste von ihrer Wiederauflebung bis auf die neuesten Zeiten. Geschichte der Mahlerey. 5 vols.	*Göttingen*	1798–1804
Delepierre, J. O.	Galerei d'artistes brugeois.	*Bruges*	1840
Eynden, R. van and Willigen, A. van der	Geschiedenis der Vaderlandsche Schilder-Kunst, sedert de Helft der XVIII Eeuw. 4 vols.	*Haarlem*	1816–1842
Nagler, G. K.	Neues allgemeines Künstler-Lexikon. 25 vols.	*Leipzig*	1835–1852
Immerzeel, J., C. and C. H.	De Levens en werken der hollandsche en vlaamsche Kunstschilders . . . van het begin der vijftiende tot op de helft der negentiende eeuw. 3 vols.	*Amsterdam*	1843
Fétis, E.	Les artistes belges à l'étranger.	*Brussels*	1857–1865
Kramm, C.	De Levens en werken der hollandsche en vlaamsche Kunstschilders. 7 vols.	*Amsterdam*	1857–1864
Rooses, M.	Geschiedenis der Antwerpsche Schilderschool. *Later edition*	*Ghent* *Ghent* 1889	1879
Branden, F. J. van den	Geschiedenis der Antwerpsche Schilderschool. 3 vols.	*Antwerp*	1878–1883

Fidière, O.	État Civil des peintres et sculpteurs de l'Académie Royale de 1648–1745.	*Paris*	1883
Dujardin, J.	L'art flamand. (Vol. IV).	*Brussels*	1894–1900
Helbig, J.	La peinture au pays de Liège et sur les bords de la Meuse.	*Liège*	1903
Micha, A.	Les Peintres Célèbres de l'Ancien Pays de Liège.	*Liège*	1911
Gillet, L.	La peinture dans les Pays-Bas au XVIIIe siècle. *in* Michel, A.: Histoire de l'art.	*Paris*	1923
Bode, W. von	Das Flämische Sittenbild in der ersten Hälfte des XVIII Jahrhunderts. (P. van Angellis und P. van Santvoort). *in* Zeitschrift für bildenden Kunst.	*Munich*	1924–1925
Champier, V.	L'art dans les Flandres françaises aux XVIIe et XVIIIe siècles, après les conquêtes de Louis XIV.	*Roubaix*	1926
Warner, R.	Dutch and Flemish Flower and Fruit painters of XVII and XVIII centuries.	*London*	1928
Donnet, F. and Rolland, P.	L'influence artistique d'Anvers au XVIIIe siècle. *in* Annales de l'Académie royale d'archéologie de Belgique.	*Antwerp*	1929
Catalogue	Exposition d'œuvres choisies d'artistes Belges du XVIIIe siècle. (Musée de Bruxelles).	*Brussels*	1930
Lavalleye, J.	La Peinture en Belgique du XVIIIe siècle.	*Brussels*	1930
Bautier, P.	Peintres flamands du XVIIIe siècle.	*Stockholm*	1933
Lavalleye, J. and Anciaux, S.	Notes sur les peintres de la cour de Charles de Lorraine. *in* Revue belge d'archéologie et d'histoire de l'art.	*Brussels*	1936
Huebner, F. M.	Nederlandsche en Vlaamsche Rococo-schilders.	*The Hague*	1943
Arschot, Comte d'	Le Portrait aux XVIIe et XVIIIe siècles.	*Brussels*	1945
Bautier, P.	La peinture en Belgique au XVIIIe siècle.	*Brussels*	1945
Fierens, P. (editor)	L'Art en Belgique: La Peinture au XVIIIe siècle. (P. Bautier).	*Brussels*	1947

NINETEENTH CENTURY

For the period between 1800 and 1830 near-contemporary books include those by VAN EYNDEN AND WILLIGEN, by IMMERZEEL, KRAMM and NAGLER, all named in my eighteenth century list.

As my DICTIONARY OF FLEMISH PAINTERS (1430–1900) in this volume contains entries for many nineteenth century painters and some working in the twentieth century, I add here some books relating to those periods.

Cross references in my DICTIONARY entries show the contacts of the painters with various art societies and exhibiting groups. Monographs on individual painters are referred to in the DICTIONARY entries.

Eynden, R. van and Willigen, A. van der	Geschiedenis der Vaderlandsch Schilder-Kunst, sedert de Helft der XVIII Eeuw. 4 vols.	*Haarlem*	1816–1842
Immerzeel, J.	De Levens en Werken der hollandsche en vlaamsche Kunstschilders, ... van het begin der vijftiende tot op de helfte der negentiende eeuw. 3 vols.	*Amsterdam*	1843
Kramm, C.	De Levens en werken der hollandsche en vlaamsche Kunstschilders ... van den vroegsten tot op onzen Tijd. 7 vols.	*Amsterdam*	1857–1864
Nagler, G. K.	Neues Allgemeines Künstlerlexikon. 25 vols.	*Leipzig*	1835–1852
Lacomblé, A.	De l'état actuel de la Peinture en Belgique.	*Mons*	1847
Joly, V.	Les Beaux-Arts en Belgique.		1857

NOTES ON THE LITERATURE

Contributors	Biographie Nationale de Belgique.	*Brussels*	from 1866
Hippert, T. and Linnig, J.	Le peintre-graveur Hollandais et Belge du XIXe siècle. 2 vols.	*Brussels*	1874
Blanc, C.	Les artistes de mon temps.		1876
Vapereau, L. G.	Dictionnaire Universelle des Contemporains. *6th edition*	*Paris* 1892–1895	1858–1859
Lemonnier, C.	Histoire des Beaux-Arts en Belgique.	*Brussels*	1881
Riegel, H.	Geschichte de Wandmalerei in Belgien seit 1856.	*Berlin*	1882
Boetticher, F. von	Malerwerke des 19ten Jahrhunderts. *Later edition*	*Dresden* 1898	1891
Rooses, M.	Oude en nieuwe Kunst.	*Ghent*	1896
Græf, G. de	Nos artistes anversois.	*Antwerp*	1898
Rooses, M.	Les Peintres belges du XIX siècle.	*Paris*	1900
Dujardin, J.	L'art flamand.	*Brussels*	1894–1900
Muther, R.	Die belgische Malerei im 19ten Jahrhundert.	*Berlin*	1904
Zype, G. van	Nos peintres.	*Brussels*	1903–1905
Lemmonier, C.	L'École belge de Peinture 1830–1905.	*Brussels*	1906
Hymans, H.	Die belgische Kunst des neunzehnten Jahrhunderts.	*Leipzig*	1906
Tombu, L.	Peintres et sculpteurs belges à l'aube du 20e. siècle,	*Liège*	1907
Bénédite, L.	Great Painters of the Nineteenth Century.	*London*	1910
Croquez, A.	Les peintres flamands d'aujourd'hui.		1910
Eekhoud, G.	Les peintres animaliers belges.	*Brussels*	1911
Lambotte, P.	Les peintres de portraits (19e siècle).	*Brussels*	1913
Puyvelde, L. van	De Belgische Schilders in Holland, hoe zij Holland zagen.	*Leyden*	1919
Hymans, H.	Œuvres: vol. II: Près de 700 Biographies d'artistes Belges.	*Brussels*	1920
Hymans, H.	Œuvres: vol. IV: L'art au 17e et au 19e siècle dans les Pays-Bas.	*Brussels*	1920
Mont, Pol de	De Schilderkunst in Belgie van 1830–1921.	*The Hague*	1921
Zype, G. van	L'art belge du XIXe siècle.	*Brussels*	1923
Fontaine, A.	L'art belge.	*Paris*	1925
Maus, M. O.	Trente années de lutte pour l'art 1884–1914.	*Brussels*	1926
Styns, M.	De beeld. Kunsten in Belgie.	*Bruges*	1927
Focillon, H	La peinture au XIXe siècle.	*Paris*	1928
Gillet, L.	La peinture belge et hollandaise au XIXe siècle. *in* Michel, A.: Histoire de l'art.	*Paris*	1929
Bosmant, J.	La peinture et la sculpture au Pays de Liège 1793–1930.	*Liège*	1930
Colin, P.	La peinture belge depuis 1830.	*Brussels*	1930
Haesaerts, L. and P.	Flandre: Essai sur l'art flamand depuis 1880. L'Impressionnisme.	*Paris*	1931
Muls, J.	Schilders van Gisteren uit Noord en Zuid Nederland.	*Utrecht*	1939

Wilenski, R. H.	Modern French Painters. *Revised editions*	*London and New York* *London 1947 qnd 1954*	1941
Haesaerts, L.	Histoire du Portrait de Navez à Ensor.	*Brussels*	1942
Fierens, P. (editor)	L'Art en Belgique: La peinture au XIXe siècle. (P. Fierens).	*Brussels*	1947

TWENTIETH CENTURY

Some of the later books named in my nineteenth century list are concerned with the early phases of modern Belgian painting and are thus informative also about living men; TRENTE ANNÉES DE LUTTE POUR L'ART 1884–1914 by M. O. MAUS, and FLANDRE: IMPRESSIONNISME by L. and P. HAESAERTS are examples of such books helpful for both periods; my MODERN FRENCH PAINTERS records the relations of some French painters with the Brussels exhibiting society Les Vingt (whose members are recorded in my DICTIONARY entry on James Ensor). Some of the other books named below, though mainly concerned with 20th century painters, may throw light also on some 19th century men. Monographs on individual painters are referred to in the DICTIONARY entries.

Maus, M. O.	Trente années de lutte pour l'art 1884–1914.	*Brussels*	1926
Ridder, A. de	La jeune peinture belge. (De l'impressionnisme à l'expressionnisme).	*Antwerp*	1930
Haesaerts, L. and P.	Flandre: Essai sur l'art flamand depuis 1880. L'Impressionnisme.	*Paris*	1931
Marlier, G.	Bilan de l'Expressionnisme flamand.	*Antwerp*	1934
Haesaerts, L. and P.	Le mouvement expressionniste.	*Ghent*	1935
Huyghe, R.	Histoire de l'art contemporain.	*Paris*	1935
Barr, A. H. (editor)	Fantastic Art—(Dada, Surrealism). Catalogue of Museum of Modern Art Exhibition, New York.	*New York*	1937
Wilenski, R. H.	Modern French Painters. *Revised editions*	*London and New York* *London 1947 and 1954*	1941
Haesaerts, P.	Retour à l'humain. L'Animisme.	*Brussels*	1942
Marlier, G.	Vingt-cinq années de peinture et de sculpture en Belgique. (La Génération de l'Entre-deux-Guerres).	*Brussels*	1942
Marlier, G.	Hedendaagsche Vlaamsche Schilderkunst.	*Brussels*	1944
Haesaerts, P.	L'École de Laethem Saint Martin.	*Brussels*	1945
Ridder, A. de	Laethem Saint Martin colonie d'artistes.	*Brussels*	1945
Delevoy, R.	La Jeune Peinture Belge.	*Brussels*	1946
Hecke, P. G. van	Peintres Belges contemporains.	*Brussels*	1947
Fierens, P. (editor)	L'Art en Belgique: L'art contemporain. (P. Fierens).	*Brussels*	1947
Mesens, E. L. T.	Peintres belges contemporains.	*Brussels*	1948

REGIONAL

For those approaching the subject from a regional angle I have already named the books by the eighteenth century travellers G. P. MENSAERT and J. B. DESCAMPS; and it may help to note here that MENSAERT went to Alost, Antwerp, Assche, Bergues-Saint-Winnocq, Bruges, Brussels, Courtrai, Dixmude, Enghien, Furnes, Ghent, Grammont, Hérinnes, Léau, Lille, Lierre, Louvain, Malines, Mons, Namur, Ninove, Termonde, Tournai and Villers, and that DESCAMPS who visited the same towns (with the exception of Léau, Namur and Villers) also went to Aerschot, Afflighem, Ath, Dilighem, Dunkirk, Loo, Menin, Nieuport, Ostend, Rupelmonde, Saint-Omer and Ypres. When the subject is approached in a regional way the local records and writings are always fruitful. Much has already been extracted from such sources, but as local writings survive from all periods and are continually produced, the reader on the spot is always likely to gain something from the publications of the local academic bodies (past and present), from local books and pamphlets and articles in the local press by local patriots and antiquaries, and from guide books to the town, its churches and its monuments, easily come by in the local shops and libraries but only with difficulty obtainable elsewhere. There are also, of course, the catalogues to the museums (the earlier catalogues being often more complete and more informative than the latest editions on sale). For Belgium as a whole, in addition to the standard guide books, there is DELEN and LECLERCQ: GUIDE DES MUSÉES BELGES (1927 and later editions); and the books named in the following lists may also be helpful in some way:

FLANDERS AND BRABANT

Monconys, de	Journal des voyages de Monsieur de Monconys, conseiller du roy.	*Lyon*	1666
Mensaert, G. P.	Le Peintre Amateur et Curieux; ou description générale des tableaux des plus habiles maîtres, qui font l'ornement des églises, couvents, abbayes . . . dans l'étendue des Pay-Bas Autrichiens. 2 vols.	*Brussels*	1763
Descamps, J. B.	Voyage Pittoresque de la Flandre et du Brabant. *Annotated edition (C. Rochu)*	*Paris* *Paris 1838*	1769
Anon.	Le voyageur dans les Pays-Bas autrichiens ou Lettres sur l'état actuel de ces Pays.	*Amsterdam*	1783
Passavant, J. D.	Kunstreise durch England und Belgien. *English edition*	*Frankfort* *London 1836*	1833
Schnaase, K.	Niederländische Briefe.	*Stuttgart*	1834
Contributors	Annales de la Société d'émulation pour l'étude de l'histoire et des antiquités de la Flandre. *continued as:* Handelingen van het Genootschap voor Geschiedenis.	*Bruges* *Bruges*	from 1839 in progress
Burckhardt, J.	Die Kunstwerke der belgischen Städte.	*Düsseldorf*	1842
Couvez	Inventaire . . . des objets d'art . . . de la Flandre occidentale.		1852
Fromentin, E.	Les maîtres d'autrefois.	*Paris*	1876
Lafenestre, G. and Richtenberger, E.	La Belgique: Catalogue raisonné des œuvres principales conservées dans les musées, collections, édifices civils et religieux.	*Paris*	1895
Nothomb, P.	Villes de Flandres: Audenarde, Bruges, Courtrai, Dixmude, Ghent, L'Yser, Nieuport, Poperinghe, Termonde, Ypres.	*Paris and Brussels*	1917
Clemen, P. (and others)	Belgische Kunstdenkmäler vom neunten bis zum Ende des achtzehnten Jahrhunderts 2 vols.	*Munich*	1923
Cammaerts, É.	The Treasure House of Belgium.	*London*	1924
Delen, A. J. J. and Leclercq, R.	Guide des Musées Belges. *Later edition and English edition Antwerp and London before 1935*	*Antwerp*	1927

NOTES ON THE LITERATURE

ANTWERP

Berbie, G.	Description des principaux tableaux, sculptures et autres raretés . . . dans les églises et couvents de la ville d'Anvers.	*Antwerp*	1755
Contributors	Bulletin des Archives d'anvers.	*Antwerp*	from *c.* 1850
Mertens, F. H. and Torfs, K. L.	Geschiedenis van Antwerpen. 8 vols.	*Antwerp*	1845–1854
Straelen, J. B. van der	Jaerboek der vermaerde en kunstryke Gilde van Sint Lucas binnen de stad Antwerpen.	*Antwerp*	1855
Branden, F. J. van den	Geschiedenis der Academie van Antwerpen.	*Antwerp*	1864
Rombouts, P. and Lerius, T. van	Les Liggeren et autres Archives Historiques de la Gilde Anversoise de Saint Luc. 2 vols.	*Antwerp and The Hague*	1864–1876
Rooses, M.	Geschiedenis der Antwerpsche Schilderschool. *Later edition*	*Ghent* *Ghent* 1889	1879
Lerius, T. van	Biographies d'artistes anversois. 2 vols.	*Antwerp and Ghent*	1880
Branden, F. J. van den	Geschiedenis der Antwerpsche Schilderschool. 3 vols.	*Antwerp*	1878–1883
Génard, P.	Anvers à travers les âges. 2 vols.	*Brussels*	1886–1892
Kintsschots, L.	Anvers et ses faubourgs.	*Bruges*	1894
Graef, G. de	Nos Artistes Anversois.	*Antwerp*	1898
Donnet, F.	Het Jonstich Versaem der Violieren.	*Antwerp, Ghent, The Hague*	1907
Hymans, H.	Anvers.	*Paris*	1914
Mont, Pol de and Wappers, J.	Musée Royal des Beaux-Arts d'Anvers. Catalogue descriptif. Maîtres Anciens.	*Antwerp*	1920
Guides illustrés Michelin	Anvers.	*Clermont-Ferrand*	1921
Kryn, L. J. (editor)	Rubens en zijne Eeuw. (in 5 parts): Rubens' Antwerpen (F. Prims) Het Geestesleven te Antwerpen in Rubens tijd. (M. Sabbe) Het Volksleven in Rubens' tijd. (V. de Meyere) De Vlaamsche Kunst, voor, tijdens en na Rubens. (A. J. J. Delen) Rubens' Leven en Werk. (P. Lambotte)	*Brussels*	1927
Donnet, F. and Rolland, P.	L'influence artistique d'Anvers au XVIIIe siècle. *in* Annales de l'Académie royale d'archéologie de Belgique.	*Antwerp*	1929
Pirenne, H.	Le rôle économique et moral d'Anvers à l'époque de Plantin.	*Brussels*	1930
Denucé, J.	Art Export in the 17th century in Antwerp. The Firm Forchoudt.	*Antwerp*	1931
Denucé, J.	Inventories of the Art Collections in Antwerp in the 16th and 17th centuries.	*Antwerp*	1932
Delen, A. J.	Koninklijk Museum voor Schone Kunsten. Antwerpen. Beschrijvende Catalogus. Oude Meesters.	*Antwerp*	1948
Buschmann van Rijswijck, E.	Koninklijk Museum voor Schone Kunsten. Antwerpen. Beschrijvende Catalogus. Moderne Meesters.	*Antwerp*	1948

NOTES ON THE LITERATURE

BRUGES

Delepierre, J. O.	Galerie d'artistes brugeois.	*Bruges*	1840
Gaillard, J.	Ephémérides brugeoises . . .	*Bruges*	1847
Gaillard, J.	Revue pittoresque des monuments qui décoraient autrefois la ville de Bruges.	*Bruges*	1850
Weale, W. H. J.	Catalogue du Musée de l'Académie de Bruges.	*Bruges*	1861
Weale, W. H. J. (editor)	Le Beffroi. (Periodical)	*Brussels*	1865–1876
Casteele, D. van de	Keuren 1441–1774. Livres d'admission 1453–1574 et autres documents inédits concernant la Ghilde de St. Luc de Bruges suivis des keuren de la corporation des peintres, sculpteurs et verriers de Gand 1541–1575. *Bruges*		1867
Weale, W. H. J.	Bruges et ses environs.	*Bruges*	1884
Woestyne, K. van de	De Vlaamsche primitieven te Brugge.	*Ghent*	1892
Verkest, M.	Studien over Brugsche Kunstenaars.	*Tongeren*	1900
Verkest, M.	Guide illustré du touriste à Bruges.	*Bruges*	1903
Hymans, H.	Bruges et Ypres.	*Paris*	1903
Velde, A. van de	Het Schildersgild te Brugge.	*Bruges*	1905
Duclos, A.	Bruges. Histoire et Souvenirs.	*Bruges*	1910
Haute, C. van den	La Corporation des peintres de Bruges.	*Bruges and Courtrai*	1913
Fierens-Gevaert, H.	La Peinture à Bruges.	*Brussels and Paris*	1922
Hosten, E. and Strubbe, E. I.	Catalogue illustré du Musée communal des beaux-arts à Bruges. *Bruges* *Flemish edition* *Bruges* 1938		1935
Parmentier, R. A.	Bronnen voor de geschiedenis van het Brugsche schilders-milieu in de XVIe eeuw. *in* Belgisch tijdschrift voor Oudheidkunde en Kunstgeschiedenis. *Antwerp*		1941 and 1942
Bisthoven, A. J. de and Parmentier, R. A.	Les Primitifs Flamands. Le Musée Communal de Bruges.	*Antwerp*	1951

BRUSSELS

Hymans, L.	Bruxelles à travers les âges. 2 vols.	*Brussels*	1882–1884
Hymans, H.	Bruxelles. *Later edition* *Paris* 1926	*Paris*	1910
Dumont-Wilden, L.	Bruxelles et Louvain.	*Brussels and Paris*	1916
Saintenoy, P.	L'art et les artistes à la cour de Bruxelles.	*Brussels*	1932
Duverger, J.	Brussel als Kunstcentrum in de XIV en de XV Eeuw.	*Ghent*	1935
Terlinden, Vicomte C.	L'Archiduchesse Isabelle.	*Brussels*	1943

GHENT

Vaernewyck, M. van	Die Beroerlyke Tyden in die Nederlanden en voornamelyk in Ghent 1566–1568. *MS.* *in* Annales des Bibliophiles Gantois. *c.* 1884		1569

NOTES ON THE LITERATURE

Kervyn de Volkaersbeke	Les églises de Gand. 2 vols.	*Ghent*	1857–1858
Contributors	Annales de la Société Royale des Beaux-Arts de Gand.		
Busscher, E. de	Recherches sur les peintres Gantois, des XIVe et XVe siècles.	*Ghent*	1859
Pinchart, A. (editor)	Archives des Arts, Sciences et Lettres, etc. vols. I-III.	*Ghent*	1860–1863
Busscher E. de	Recherches sur les peintres et les sculpteurs à Gand aux XVIe, XVIIe et XVIIIe siècles.	*Ghent*	1866
Casteele, D. van de	Keuren 1441–1774. Livres d'admission 1453–1574 et autres documents inédits concernant la Ghilde de St. Luc de Bruges suivis des keuren de la corporation des peintres, sculpteurs et verriers de Gand 1541–1575.	*Bruges*	1867
Claeys, P.	Les expositions d'œuvres d'art à Gand.	*Ghent*	1892
Claeys, P.	Mélanges historiques . . . sur la ville de Gand.	*Ghent*	1895
Haeghen, V. van der	Mémoire sur les documents faux relatifs aux anciens peintres . . . flamands.	*Brussels*	1899
Pauw, N. de	Les premiers peintres et sculpteurs Gantois.	*Ghent*	1899
Gheyn, J. van den	La Cathédrale de Saint Bavon à Gand.	*Ghent*	1901
Inventaire	Inventaire archéologique de Gand. (Société d'Histoire et d'Archéologie de Gand.)	*Ghent*	before 1902
Hymans, H.	Gand et Tournai.	*Paris*	1902
Potter, F. de	Geschiedkundige Beschrijving der Stad Gent.	*Ghent*	*c.* 1902
Haeghen, V. van der	La Corporation des Peintres et des Sculpteurs de Gand.	*Brussels*	1906
Commissie der Monumenten van Gent	Gids voor Gent.	*Ghent*	*c.* 1912
Catalogue	Catalogue de l'exposition de l'art ancien.	*Ghent*	1913
Contributors	Gentsche Bijdragen tot de Kunstgeschiedenis.	*Ghent*	from 1934

OTHER TOWNS

Vyvere, P. v. d.	Audenarde et ses monuments.	*Ghent*	1912
Molanus, J.	Historiae Lovanensium libri XIV . . . *First published*	*MS.* *Brussels* 1861	*c.* 1575
Even, E. van	Louvain monumental.	*Louvain*	1860
Even, E. van	L'ancienne école de peinture de Louvain.	*Brussels*	1870
Even, E. van	Louvain dans le passé et dans le présent.	*Louvain*	1895
Linden, H. van der	Geschiedenis van de Stad Leuven.	*Louvain*	1899
Malines Congrès Archéologique	Malines, S. Nicolas, Hulst, Louvain.	*Malines*	1911
Neeffs, E.	Histoire de la peinture et de la sculpture à Malines. 2 vols.	*Ghent*	1876
Neeffs, E.	Inventaire historique des tableaux, sculptures et objets d'art conservés dans les édifices religieux et civils de Malines.	*Malines*	1891
Godenne, L.	Malines, jadis et aujourd'hui.	*Malines*	1908

Peereboom, A. van den	Ypriana, notices, études, notes et documents sur la ville d'Ypres. 7 vols.	*Ypres*	1878–1881
Hymans, H.	Bruges et Ypres.	*Paris*	1903

WALLOON REGIONS

Cloquet, L.	Les artistes Wallons.	*Brussels and Paris*	1913
Destrée, J.	Les Villes Wallonnes: Antoing, Beloeil, Charleroi, Chimay, Dinant, Liège, Mons, Namur, Spa, Tournai, Verviers.	*Brussels and Paris*	1917
Becdelièvre, Comte de	Biographie Liégeoise.	*Liège*	1836
Abry, L.	Les hommes illustres de la nation liégeoise.	*Liège*	1867
Renier, J. S.	Inventaire des objets d'art renfermés dans les monuments civils et religieux de la ville de Liège.	*Liège*	1893
Catalogue	Catalogue de l'exposition de l'art ancien de Liège.	*Liège*	1881
Helbig, J.	La peinture au pays de Liège et sur les bords de la Meuse.	*Liège*	1903
Catalogue	Catalogue de l'exposition de l'art ancien de Liège.	*Liège*	1905
Defrance, L.	Autobiographie d'un peintre liégeois.	*Liège*	1906
Helbig, J.	L'Art Mosan. 2 vols.	*Brussels*	1906–1911
Micha, A.	Les peintres célèbres de l'ancien Pays de Liège.	*Liège*	1911
Catalogue	Catalogue de l'exposition de l'art ancien au pays de Liège.	*Paris*	1924
Bosmant, J.	La peinture et la sculpture au Pays de Liège 1793–1930.	*Liège*	1930
Devillers, L.	Le passé artistique de la ville de Mons.	*Mons*	1885
Bezière, A.	Tournai, ancien et moderne.	*Tournai*	1864
Pinchart, A.	Quelques artistes de Tournai.	*Tournai*	1883
Cloquet, H.	Tournai et le Tournaisis.	*Bruges*	1884
Grange, A. de la and Cloquet, L.	Études sur l'art à Tournai et sur les anciens artistes de cette ville.	*Tournai*	1888–1889
Hymans, H.	Gand et Tournai.	*Paris*	1902
Rolland, P.	Les primitifs tournaisiens, peintres et sculpteurs.	*Brussels*	1932

FLEMISH PAINTERS ABROAD

FRANCE

Flemish painting at all periods has found nurture in the art of France. In the 14th and early 15th centuries the stories of Flemish and French painting (in manuscripts, on panels and on walls) are indeed so intertwined that records of all the earliest Flemish painters, as well as of those then living in France or working for French patrons, must be sought in books about French as well as about Flemish 'Primitives'.

Félibien des Avaux, A.	Entretiens sur les vies et les ouvrages des plus excellens peintres anciens et modernes.	*Paris*	1666–1688
	5 vols.		
	Later edition	*London* 1705	
Comte, F. Le	Cabinet des singularitez d'Architecture, Peinture etc.; ou introduction à la connaissance des plus beaux-arts etc.		
	2 vols.	*Paris*	1699–1700
Argenville, D. d'	Abrégé de la vie des plus fameux peintres.		
	3 vols.	*Paris*	1745–1752
Mariette, P. J.	Abecedario.	*MS.*	*c.* 1760
	Published by P. de Chennevières *and* A. de Montaiglon. 6 vols.		
		Paris 1851–1860	
Waagen, G. F.	Kunstwerke und Künstler in Paris.	*Berlin*	1839
Dussieux, L. (and others)	Mémoires inédits sur la vie et les ouvrages des Membres de l'Académie Royale de Peinture et de Sculpture, publiés d'après les manuscrits conservés à l'École Impériale des Beaux-Arts.	*Paris*	1854
	2 vols.		
Laborde, L.	La Renaissance des arts à la cour de France.	*Paris*	1850
Fétis, E.	Les artistes belges à l'Etranger.	*Brussels*	1857–1865
Michiels, A.	L'art flamand dans l'est et le midi de la France.	*Paris*	1877
Bellier de la Chavignerie, E. and Auvray, L.	Dictionnaire général des artistes de l'École Française.	*Paris*	1882–1887
Montaiglon, A. de	Procès-verbaux de l'Académie Royale (1648–1792).	*Paris*	1875–1892
Fidière, O.	État civil des peintres et sculpteurs de l'Académie Royale de 1648–1745.	*Paris*	1883
Hébert, F.	Extraits d'actes concernant les artistes de Fontainebleau.	*Paris*	1901
Dimier, L.	Les primitifs français.	*Paris*	1910
Dimier, L.	Fontainebleu, Ville d'Art.	*Paris*	1911
Lemonnier, H.	L'art au temps de Louis XIV.	*Paris*	1911
Locquin, J.	La peinture d'histoire en France de 1747 à 1785.	*Paris*	1912
Rauch, C.	Douai. Kultur und Kunstgeschichtliche Studien in Nord-Frankreich.	*Heidelberg*	1917
Faure, É.	L'Art Renaissant: Fontainebleau, La Loire et Les Valois.		
	in Histoire de l'Art.	*Paris*	1922
Martin, H.	La miniature française du XIIIe au XVe siècle.	*Paris*	1923
Dimier, L.	Histoire de la peinture de portrait en France au XVI siècle.	*Paris*	1924
Wilenski, R. H.	French Painting.	*London and Boston*	1931
	Revised edition	*London* 1949	
Lesmoine, P. A.	Gothic Painting in France.		1932

Weisbach, W.	Französische Malerei des XVII Jahrhunderts im Rahmen von Kultur und Gesellschaft.	*Berlin*	1934
Dupont, J.	Primitifs français.	*Paris*	1937
Sterling, C.	La Peinture Française. (Moyen âge).	*Paris*	1942
Ring, G.	A Century of French Painting 1400–1500.	*London*	1949

ENGLAND

Weyerman, J. C.	De Levensbeschryvingen ...	*The Hague*	1729–1749
Rouquet, A.	L'État des arts en Angleterre.	*Paris*	1755
Vertue, G.	Notebooks. *in* Walpole Soc. 6 vols. *Oxford* 1930, 1932, 1934, 1936, 1938, 1947	*MS.*	1713–1754
Walpole, H.	Anecdotes of Painting in England. 5 vols. *Later editions* (J. Dallaway) 5 vols. (R. N. Wornum) 3 vols.	*Strawberry Hill* *London* 1786 *London* 1826–1828 *London* 1876	1762–1771
Passavant, J. D.	Kunstreise durch England und Belgien. *English edition*	*Frankfort* *London* 1836	1833
Smith, J.	Catalogue raisonné of the works of the most eminent Dutch, Flemish and French painters.	*London*	1829–1842
Waagen, G. F.	Kunstwerke und Künstler in England. 2 vols. *English translation* Works of Art and Artists in England.	*Leipzig* *London* 1838	1837
Waagen, G. F.	Treasures of Art in Great Britain. 3 vols. *Supplement* Galleries and Cabinets of Art in Great Britain. Summary and Index to Waagen (A. Graves).	*London* *London* 1857 *London* 1912	1854
Burger, W. (T. Thoré)	Trésors d'art en Angleterre.	*Paris*	1865
Contributors	Dictionary of National Biography. 63 vols. and supplements.	*London*	from 1885
Graves, A.	A Dictionary of Artists who have exhibited in London from 1760–1893.	*London*	1895
Law, E.	The Royal Gallery at Hampton Court. *Abridged*	*London* *London* 1915	1898
Graves, A.	The Royal Academy of Arts. A complete Dictionary of Contributors and their work from its foundation in 1769 to 1904.	*London*	1905–1906
Williamson, G. C.	History of Portrait Miniatures. 2 vols.	*London*	1904
Graves, A.	The Society of Artists of Great Britain, 1760–1791 and the Free Society of Artists 1761–1783.	*London*	1907
Graves, A.	The British Institution 1806–1867.	*London*	1908
Baker, C. H. Collins	Lely and the Stuart Portrait Painters.	*London*	1912
Williamson, G. C.	The Miniature Collector.	*London*	1921
Poole, Mrs. R. L.	Catalogue of Oxford Portraits. 3 vols.	*Oxford*	1925
Whitley, W. T.	Artists and their Friends in England, 1700–1799. 2 vols.	*London and Boston*	1928

Baker, C. H. Collins	Catalogue of the pictures at Hampton Court.	*London*	1929
Long, B.	British Miniaturists 1520–1860.	*London*	1929
Baker, C. H. Collins and Constable, W. G.	English painting of the 16th and 17th centuries.	*Florence and Paris*	1930
Baker, C. H. Collins	Catalogue of the pictures at Windsor Castle.	*London*	1937
Winter, C.	Elizabethan Miniatures.	*London*	1943
Walpole Society	Publications Vols. I-XXXIII. (Index in Vol. XXXI).	*London*	1912–1953
Waterhouse, E. K.	Painting in Britain 1530–1790.	*London*	1953
Auerbach, E.	Tudor Artists.	*London*	1954

SPAIN

Sigüenza, Fray J. de	Historia de la orden de San Jerónimo. *in* Sánchez Cantón: Fuentes Literarias ... *Madrid* 1923–1941	*Madrid*	1600–1605
Pacheco, F.	El Libro de Retratos. *in* Sánchez Cantón: Fuentes Literarias ... *Madrid* 1923–1941	*Seville*	1599–1616
Carducho, V.	Diálogos de la Pintura. *in* Sánchez Cantón: Fuentes Literarias ... vol. II. *Madrid* 1933	*MS.*	1633
Pacheco, F.	El Arte de la Pintura. *Later edition* *Madrid* 1866 *Modern edition in* Sánchez Cantón: Fuentes Literarias ... *Madrid* 1923–1941	*Seville*	1649
Palomino de Castro y Velasco, A.	El Museo pictórico y Escala óptica. *in* Sánchez Cantón: Fuentes Literarias ... vol. III *Madrid* 1934	*Madrid*	1715–1724
Ponz, A.	Viage de España. 18 vols.	*Madrid*	1776–1794
Ceán Bermudez, J. A.	Diccionario .. de las bellas artes en España.	*Madrid*	1800
Stirling-Maxwell, Sir W.	Annals of the Artists of Spain. 4 vols.	*London*	1891
Gestoso y Pérez, J.	Ensayo de un diccionario de los artífices que floreceiron en Sevilla. 3 vols.	*Seville*	1899–1900
Justi, C.	Velázquez and his century. *Later edition* Velázquez und sein Jahrhundert. *Zurich* 1933	*London*	1899
Justi, C.	Aus drei Jahrhunderten spanischen Kunstlebens. 2 vols.	*Berlin*	1908
Sánchez Cantón, F.	Los Pintores de Cámara de los Reyes de España. *in* Boletín de la Sociedad Española de Excursiones.	*Madrid*	1914–1916
Tormo y Monsó, E.	Las Iglesias del antiguo Madrid.	*Madrid*	1927
Bertaux, E.	La fin de la Renaissance en Espagne. *in* Michel, A.: Histoire de l'Art.	*Paris*	1925
Post, C. R.	A History of Spanish Painting. 12 vols. *Cambridge (Mass.) and London*		1930–1958
Lafuente Ferrari, E.	Breve Historia de la Pintura Española. *3rd edition, revised and enlarged.*	*Madrid*	1946
Mayer, A. L.	Historia de la Pintura española. *3rd edition.*	*Madrid*	1947

NOTES ON THE LITERATURE

GERMANY AND AUSTRIA

Baren, J. A. van der and others	Inventar der Kunstsammlung der Erzherzogs Leopold Wilhelm von Österreich. *MS* *in* Jahrbuch der Kunstsammlungen des A. H. Kaiserhauses vol. 1. (edited A. Berger) *Vienna 1883*	1659
Doppelmayr, J. G.	Historische Nachrichten von den Nürnbergischen Mathematicis und Künstlern. *Nuremberg*	1730
Heinecken, C. H. von	Nachrichten von Künstlern und Kunstsachen. 2 vols. *Leipzig* *Supplement* Neue Nachrichten. *Leipzig 1786*	1768–1769
Nicolai, F.	Nachrichten von Baumeistern . . . in Berlin. *Berlin*	1786
Waagen, G. F.	Kunstwerke und Künstler in Deutschland. 2 vols. *Leipzig*	1843–1845
Geyser, G. W.	Geschichte der Malerei in Leipzig. *Leipzig*	1858
Venturi, A.	Zur Geschichte der Kunstsammlungen Kaiser Rudolf II. *in* Repertorium fur Kunstwissenschaft vol. VIII.	1885
Merlo, J. J.	Nachrichten von dem Leben und Werken Kölnischer Künstler. *Düsseldorf*	1895
Plietzsch, E.	Die Frankenthaler Maler. Ein Beitrag zur Entwickelungsgeschichte der Niederländischen Landschaftsmalerei. *Leipzig*	1910
Zülch, W. K.	Frankfurter Künstler 1223–1700. *Frankfort*	1935
Tietze, H. (and others)	Oesterreichische Kunst-Topographie. *Vienna* 17 vols.	1907–1919

ITALY

Anonimo. (Anonimo of Morelli. Marc Anton Michiel?)	Notizie d'opere di disegno. *Published by* J. Morelli. *Bassano 1800*	1512–1543
Hollanda, F. de	De Pintura Antiga. *MS.* *French translation in:* Raczynski: Les Arts en Portugal. *Paris 1846–1847* *Spanish translation in:* Sánchez Cantón: Fuentes Literarias . . . *Madrid 1923–1941* *English translation:* A. F. G. Bell. *London 1928*	1548–1549

Vasari, G.	Le Vite de' piu eccellenti Pittori, Scultori et Architettori. *Florence*
	Revised by author. *Florence 1568*
	Later edition (G. Milanesi)
	8 vols. *Florence 1877–1885*
	English translations
	  Edited Foster. 5 vols. *London 1910*
	  Edited G.de Vere. 10 vols. *London 1912–1915*
	Modern Italian edition
	  Edited P. Pecchiai 3 vols. *Milan 1928–1930*
		1550

Borghini, R.	Il Riposo in ciu della Pittura e della Scultura . . . *Florence*	1584
Lomazzo, G. P.	Trattato dell' Arte della Pittura. *Milan* *Later edition* *Rome 1844* *English edition:* (R. Heydock) *1598*	1584
Mander, K. van	Het Schilderboek *Haarlem*	1604
Baglione, G.	Le vite dei pittori, scultori et architetti, dal pontificato di Gregorio XIII del 1572 in fino al tempi di Papa Urbano Ottavo nel 1642. *Rome*	1642
Ridolfi, C.	Le Maraviglie dell'arte . . . le vite degli . . . pittori veneti . . . *Venice* *Later editions* *Padua 1835–1837* *Berlin 1914–1924*	1648

Boschini, M.	Le Minere della Pittura ...	*Venice*	1664
	Enlarged edition		
	Le Ricchi Minere della Pittura Veneziana.	*Venice 1674*	
	Later edition		
	Descrizione di tutti le pubbliche pitture della Città di Venezia ...	1733	
Bellori, G. P.	Le vite dei pittori, scultori ed architetti moderni.	*Rome*	1672
	Later edition	*Rome 1728*	
	Modern edition	*Rome 1931*	
Soprani, R.	Le Vite dei pittori, scultori et architetti Genovesi e dei forestieri che in Genova operarono.	*Genoa*	1674
	Later edition: Edited by and with notes by C. J. Ratti.	*Genoa 1768–1769*	
Titi, F.	Studio di pittura ... nelle chiese di Roma.	*Rome*	1675
	Second edition	1685	
	Nuova studio di pittura.	*Rome 1708*	
	Composite edition		
	Descrizione delle pitture ... esposte ... in Roma.	*Rome 1763*	
Malvasia, C. C.	Felsina Pittrice. Vite de Pittori Bolognese.	*Bologna*	1678
	2 vols.		
	Later edition	*Bologna 1842*	
Sandrart, J. von	Teutsche Academie der Edlen Bau-Bild-und-Mahlerey Künste.		
	2 vols.	*Nuremberg*	1675–1679
	Later edition 8 vols.	*Nuremberg 1769–1775*	
	Modern edition with notes (A. R. Peltzer)	*Munich 1926*	
Malvasia, C. C.	Le Pitture di Bologna ...	*Bologna*	1686
	Later edition: (C. Bianconi)	*Bologna 1792*	
Orlandi, P. A.	L'Abecedario pittorico ...	*Bologna*	1704
	Later edition	*Bologna 1719*	
	Later edition (*edited* P. M. Guarienti)	*Venice 1753*	
Baldinucci, F.	Notizie dei professori del disegno da Cimabue in quà ...	*Florence*	1681–1728
	6 vols.		
	Later edition: Opere di F. B. *annotated by* D. M. Manni.		
		Milan 1808–1812	
Zanetti, A. M.	Descrizione di tutte le pubbliche pitture della città di Venezia e isole ...		
		Venice	1733
Houbraken, A.	De Groote Schouburgh ...	*Amsterdam*	1718–1721
Baglione, G. and Passeri, G. B.	Le Vite dei pittori, scultori, architetti ed intagliatori. Con la vita di Salvator Rosa Napoletano scritta da Giovanni Batista Passeri.	*Naples*	1733
	Modern edition	*Rome 1935*	
Dominici, B. de	Vite de' pittori, scultori ed architetti napolitani.	*Naples*	1742–1763
	Later edition	*Naples 1840–1846*	
Passeri, G. B.	Vite de' pittori, scultori ed architetti, che anno lavorato in Roma morti dal 1641 fino al 1673.	*Rome*	1772
	Modern edition: (Hess)	*Leipzig 1934*	
Bartoli, F.	Notizie delle pitturi, sculture ed architetture che ornano le chiese e gli altri luoghi pubblici di tutte le più rinomate città d'Italia.	*Venice*	1776–1777
	2 vols.		
Sigismondo, G.	Descrizione della città di Napoli e suoi borghi.	*Naples*	1788–1789
Lanzi, L.	Storia pittorica della Italia.	*Florence*	1792–1796
	Revised by author. 6 vols.	*Bassano 1809*	
	English translation		
	(T. Roscoe) 3 vols.	*London 1847*	
Moschini, G.	Guida per la città di Venezia.	*Venice*	1815
	4 vols.		
Zani, P.	Enciclopedia metodica ... delle belle arti.		
	28 vols.	*Parma*	1817–1828

NOTES ON THE LITERATURE

Fétis, E.	Les artistes belges à l'Étranger.	*Brussels*	1857–1865
Bertolotti, A.	Artisti belgi ed olandesi a Roma nei secoli XVI e XVII. *Supplement*	*Florence* *Rome* 1885	1880
Filangieri, G.	Documenti per la storia, le arti . . . delle provincie Napolitane. 6 vols.	*Naples*	1883–1891
Lafenestre, G. and Richtenberger, E.	La peinture à Florence.	*Paris*	1895
Warburg, A.	Flandrische Kunst und florentinische Frührenaissance.	*Berlin*	1902
Orbaan, J. A. F.	Stradanus te Florence.	*Rotterdam*	1903
Brising, H.	Quentin Metsys und der Ursprung des Italianismus in der Kunst der Niederlände.	*Leipzig*	1908
Lohninger, J.	S. Maria dell'Anima in Rome.	*Rome*	1909
Aschenheim, C.	Der Italienische Einfluss in der Flämischen Malerei der Frührenaissance.	*Strasbourg*	1910
Rolfs, W.	Geschichte der Malerei Neapels.	*Leipzig*	1910
Hoogewerff, G. J.	Nederlandsche Schilders in Italie in de XVIe eeuw.	*Utrecht*	1912 and 1913
Hoogewerff, G. J. and Orbaan, J. A. F.	Bescheiden in Italie omtrent Nederlandsche kunstenaars en geleerden. 3 vols.	*The Hague*	1911–1917
Contributors	Bulletin de l'Institut historique belge de Rome. (Mededeelingen van het Nederlandsch Historisch Instituut te Rome).	*Brussels and Rome*	from 1919 in progress
Hoogewerff, G. J.	Nature Morte italiane del seicento e del settecento.	*Milan and Rome*	1924
Voss, H.	Die Malerei des Barock in Rom.	*Berlin*	1924
Peltzer, R. A.	Niederländisch-venezianische Landschaftsmalerei.	*Munich*	1924
Noack, F.	Das Deutschtum in Rom. 2 vols.	*Berlin and Leipzig*	1927
Lorenzetti, G.	Venezia e il suo estuario.	*Milan*	1927
Fokker, T. H.	Die Werke niederländischer Meister in den Kirchen Italiens.	*The Hague*	1931
Schneider, A. v.	Caravaggio und die Niederländer.	*Marburg*	1933
Hoogewerff, G. J.	Vlaamsche Kunst en Italiaansche Renaissance.	*Malines and Amsterdam*	1936
Kroenig, W.	Der italienische Einfluss in der flämischen Malerei in ersten Drittel des 16. Jahrhunderts.	*Würzburg*	1936
Inventories	Inventario degli Oggetti d'Arte d'Italia. 9 vols.	*Rome*	1931–1938
Hoogewerff, G. J.	Nederlandsche Kunstenaars te Rome, 1600–1725.	*The Hague*	1942
Puyvelde, L. van	La peinture flamande à Rome. (XVe-XVIIIe siècles).	*Brussels*	1950
Hoogewerff, G. J.	De Bentvueghels		1952
Mahon, D., and Sutton, D.	Artists in 17th century Rome. (*Catalogue of Wildenstein Gallery Exhibition*)	*London*	1955

MISCELLANEOUS

The following books may be found useful in ways indicated by their titles.

Füssli, J. R.	Allgemeines Künstler Lexicon. *Later editions*	*Zurich* 1779 and 1806	1763
Pilkington, M.	The Gentleman's and Connoisseur's Dictionary of Painters. Containing a complete collection and account of the most distinguished artists who have flourished ... from 1250–1767. To which are added two catalogues; the one ... of the Disciples of the most famous Masters ... The other ... of those Painters who imitated the works of the eminent masters so exactly, as to have their copies frequently taken for originals.	*London*	1770
	Later editions (*with essay by* James Barry R.A.) (Fuseli) 2 vols (Cunningham) (Davenport)	*London* 1798 1805 and 1829 1840 1852 and 1857	
Heinecken, C. H. von	Dictionnaire des Artistes dont nous avons des Estampes, avec une notice détaillée de leurs ouvrages gravés. (A-DIZ). 4 vols.	*Leipzig*	1778–1790
Strutt, J.	A Biographical Dictionary ... of Engravers ... to the present time. 2 vols.	*London*	1785–1786
Fiorillo, J.	Geschichte der Zeichnenden Künste ... bis auf die neuesten Zeiten. Geschichte der Mahlerei. 5 vols.	*Göttingen*	1798–1808
Contributors	Biographie Nationale de Belgique.	*Brussels*	from 1866
Nagler, G. K.	Die Monogrammisten. 5 vols.	*Munich*	1871–1879
Jal, A.	Dictionnaire critique de biographie et d'histoire.	*Paris*	1872
Siret, A.	Dictionnaire Historique et Raisonnée des Peintres. 2 vols.	*Paris*	1883
Bartsch, A.	Le Peintre-Graveur. 21 vols. *Supplements*	*Vienna* *Leipzig*	1803–1821 1843
Balkema, C. H.	Biographie des peintres flamands et hollandais qui ont existé depuis Jean et Hubert van Eyck jusqu'à nos jours.	*Ghent*	1844
Bryan, M.	Dictionary of Painters and Engravers. 2 vols.	*London*	1816
	Later editions (Stanley).. (Graves and Armstrong) (Williamson) (*reprint*)	*London* 1849 *London* 1884–1889 *London* 1903–1904 *London* 1930	
Mireur, Dr. H.	Dictionnaire des Ventes d'Art. 7 vols.	*Paris*	1911–1912
Bénézit, E.	Dictionnaire ... des peintres, sculpteurs, dessinateurs et graveurs de tous les temps et de tous les pays. 3 vols. *New edition*	*Paris* *Paris* 1948–1953	1911–1913
Erréra, I.	Répertoire des peintures datées. 2 vols.	*Brussels*	1920–1921
Mallet, D. T.	Index of Artists: international—biographical. *Supplement*	*New York* *New York* 1940	1935

College Art Association	Index of Twentieth Century Artists.	*New York*	1933 in progress
Drugulin, W. E.	Allgemeiner Porträt-Katalog. 2 vols.	*Leipzig*	1859
Lemberger, E.	Meisterminiaturen aus fünf Jahrhunderten.	*Stuttgart*	1911
Gruenstein, L.	Die Bildnisminiatur und ihre Meister. 16 vols.	*Vienna*	1925–1928
Baes, E.	La peinture flamande et son enseignement sous le régime des confréries de S. Luc.	*Antwerp*	1882
Pevsner, N.	Academies of Art, Past and Present.	*Cambridge*	1940
Floerke, H.	Studien zur Niederländischen Kunst und Kulturgeschichte. (Die Formen des Kunsthandels, das Atelier und die Sammler . . . vom 15–18 Jahrhundert).	*Munich and Leipzig*	1905
Buchanan, W.	Memoirs of the Importation of Pictures . . . into England since the French Revolution. 2 vols.	*London*	1824
Martin, W.	Alt-Holländische Bilder. (Sammeln-Bestimmen-Konservieren).	*Berlin*	1921
Taylor, F. H.	The Taste of Angels. (A History of Art Collecting).	*London*	1948
Wilenski, R. H.	The Study of Art.	*London*	1933
Friedländer, M. J.	Art and Connoisseurship.	*London*	1942
Kurz, O.	Fakes.	*London*	1948
Contributors	Répertoire international des archives photographiques d'œuvres d'art. (Unesco).	*Paris*	1950
Contributors	Catalogue de reproductions en couleurs de la peinture (avant 1860 et de 1860 à 1949). 2 vols. (Unesco).	*Paris*	1949 and 1950

PERIODICALS

Intelligent and/or sensitive interpretative comments on Flemish, as on other, paintings can be found all over the general press of Europe and America since the eighteenth century, and for this reason no 'priorities' in such comment can ever properly be claimed by a professional art historian; and it may be indeed that the most enlightening comments have always been made verbally in museums by artists, near-artists, general visitors and professional students at moments of uninhibited contact with the actual paintings. But, as stated above, for the recording of factual information and of conjectures the professional art historians everywhere have long used specialist periodicals, and though most of the information and some of the conjectures are eventually incorporated into accessible books, the place of first publication is often referred to in bibliographies or footnotes. I make no attempt here to name these countless professional periodic publications since the early eighteenth century. Many are no longer published and others have been continued or revived under different titles. But the following list supplemented by the use of the New York ART INDEX and the Paris RÉPERTOIRE D'ART ET D'ARCHÉOLOGIE may be of use.[1]

[1] Swiss and Scandinavian publications, and, I imagine, some in Russian, should also be consulted.

ENGLISH AND AMERICAN

Proceedings of the Society of Antiquaries.	*London*	
The Studio	*London*	from 1893
Illustrated London News.	*London*	from 1842
The Connoisseur.	*London*	from 1901
Country Life.	*London*	from 1897

NOTES ON THE LITERATURE

The Burlington Magazine.	*London*	from 1903
Apollo.	*London*	from 1925
Walpole Society Publications. Vols. I-XXXIII.	*London*	1912–1953
Journal of the Warburg Institute. *Continued as* Journal of the Warburg and Courtauld Institutes.	*London* *London*	1937–1938 from 1939
Museums Journal.	*London*	
The Listener.	*London*	from 1929
The Art Index.	*New York*	from 1933
Art News.	*New York*	from 1902
Art in America and elsewhere.	*New York*	from 1912
The Art Bulletin.	*Providence and New York*	from 1913
American Magazine of Art. *Later:* Magazine of Art.	*Washington D.C.*	
Art Quarterly.	*Detroit*	
Art Digest.	*New York*	from 1926
Parnassus (College Art Association of America).	*New York*	from 1929
Museum News (American Association of Museums).	*Washington D.C.*	
Speculum (Mediaeval Academy of America).	*Cambridge (U.S.A.)*	
The Magazine of Art.	*Washington and New York*	from 1935
The Art Quarterly.	*New York*	from 1938
Museum Bulletins.		

BELGIAN AND DUTCH

Mémoires de l'Académie royale des sciences, des lettres et des beaux-arts de Belgique.	*Brussels*	1820–1904
Bulletins de l'Académie royale des sciences, des lettres et des beaux-arts de Belgique.	*Brussels*	1832–1898
Bulletin de l'Académie royale de Belgique.	*Brussels*	from 1832
Annales de la Société d'émulation pour l'étude de l'histoire et des antiquités de la Flandre. *Continued as* Handelingen van het Genootschap voor Geschiedenis.	*Bruges* *Bruges*	from 1839
Mémoires couronnés et autres mémoires publiés par l'Académie royale des sciences, des lettres et des beaux-arts de Belgique.	*Brussels*	1840–1904
Annales de l'Académie royale d'archéologie de Belgique.	*Antwerp*	1843–1930
De Vlaamsche School.	*Antwerp*	1855–1901
Journal des beaux-arts et de la littérature. (edited A. Siret).	*Brussels*	1859–1887
Archives des Arts, Sciences et Lettres etc. (edited A. Pinchart). vols. I-III	*Ghent*	1860–1863
Bulletin des Commissions royales d'art et d'archéologie.	*Brussels*	from 1862
Le Beffroi. (edited by W. H. J. Weale).	*Brussels*	1865–1876
Bulletin de l'Académie royale d'archéologie de Belgique.	*Antwerp*	1868–1930
La Chronique des Arts . . .	*Paris*	1874–1922

Archief voor Nederlandsche Kunstgeschiedenis. (edited by Fr. D. O. Obreen). Vols. I–VII.		1877–1890
L'Art Moderne.	*Brussels*	1881–1914
Oud Holland.	*Amsterdam*	from 1883
Annales de la Société d'archéologie de Bruxelles. Mémoires, rapports et documents.	*Brussels*	from 1887
L'Art flamand et hollandais.	*Antwerp and Paris*	from 1896
Bulletins de la Classe des lettres et de la Classe des beaux-arts de l'Académie royale de Belgique.	*Brussels*	from 1899
Bulletin des Musées royaux d'art et d'histoire.	*Brussels*	from 1901
Revue de Belgique.	*Brussels*	
Onze Kunst.		1902–1929
De Vlaamsche Gids.	*Antwerp*	from 1905
Mémoires de l'Académie royale de Belgique. Classe des lettres et des sciences morales et politiques et classe des beaux-arts.	*Brussels*	1906–1912
Bulletin des Musées royaux du Cinquantenaire.		
L'Art Belge: Revue périodique des mouvements artistiques.	*Brussels*	
Bulletins de la Classe des beaux-arts de l'Académie royale de Belgique.	*Brussels*	from 1919
Mémoires de l'Académie royale de Belgique. Classe des beaux-arts.	*Brussels*	from 1921
La revue d'art.	*Antwerp*	from 1922
La revue belge.	*Brussels*	from 1924
Maandblad voor Beeldende Kunsten.	*Amsterdam*	from 1925
Bulletin des musées royaux des beaux-arts de Belgique.	*Brussels*	from 1928
Cahiers de Belgique: Peinture, sculpture, architecture, arts décoratifs, musique, cinéma.	*Brussels*	from 1928
Maandblad voor oude en jonge Kunst.	*Ghent*	from 1930
De Kunst der Nederlanden. Maandblad voor oude en nieuwe beeldende Kunst.	*Amsterdam and Brussels*	from 1930–1931
Revue Belge d'archéologie et d'histoire de l'art.	*Brussels*	from 1931
Gentsche bijdragen tot de Kunstgeschiedenis.	*Ghent*	from 1934
Historia: Maandschrift voor Geschiedenis en Kunstgeschiedenis.	*Utrecht*	from 1935
Annuaire des Musées royaux des beaux-arts de Belgique. (edited by L. van Puyvelde).	*Brussels*	from 1938
Bulletin de la Société royale d'archéologie de Bruxelles.		in progress
Phoenix. Maandschrift voor Beeldende Kunst.	*Amsterdam*	from 1945
Proceedings of regional academic bodies.		

FRENCH

Répertoire d'art et d'archéologie.	*Paris*	from 1910
Revue des Deux Mondes.	*Paris*	from 1829
Journal des Artistes.	*Paris*	
Gazette des beaux-arts.	*Paris*	from 1859
	New York	from 1942

NOTES ON THE LITERATURE

La Chronique des Arts et de la Curiosité.	*Paris*	1874–1922
L'Art.	*Paris*	1875–1907
Courier de l'art.	*Paris*	
Mercure de France. Série moderne.	*Paris*	from 1890
L'Amour de l'art.	*Paris*	from 1891
Revue de l'art ancien et moderne.	*Paris*	from 1897
Revue archéologique.	*Paris*	
Bulletin de l'art ancien et moderne.	*Paris*	from 1899
La Plume.	*Paris*	
Les Arts. Revue mensuelle des Musées, Collections, Expositions.	*Paris*	1902
L'Art et les Artistes.	*Paris*	from 1905
Bulletin de la Société de l'Histoire de l'Art Français.	*Paris*	
L'Illustration.		
Beaux-arts.	*Paris*	from 1923
Art et Style.	*Paris*	from 1924
Cahiers d'art.	*Paris*	
Formes.	*Paris*	
L'art vivant.	*Paris*	from 1925
La Renaissance de l'Art.	*Paris*	
Mouseion (L'office International des Musées).	*Paris*	
Bulletin des Musées de France.	*Paris*	from 1929
Verve.	*Paris*	
Arts de France.	*Paris*	1946
Proceedings of Parisian and provincial academic bodies and museums.		

SPANISH

Boletín de la Sociedad Española de Excursiones.	*Madrid*	from 1892
Archivo Español de Arte y Arqueologia.	*Madrid*	from 1925
Anales y Boletín de los museos de Arte de Barcelona.	*Barcelona*	
Arte en España.	*Barcelona*	
Museum. Revista . . . de Arte español . . .	*Barcelona*	from 1911
Arte Español (Sociedad de Amigos del Arte).	*Madrid*	
Arbor.	*Madrid*	
Goya: Revista de Arte.	*Madrid*	
Spanish Cultural Index. (Cultural Relations Department).	*Madrid*	
Proceedings of provincial museums and academic bodies.		

NOTES ON THE LITERATURE

ITALIAN

Archivio storico dell'Arte.	*Rome*	from 1888
Emporium. Rivista Mensile d'Arte e di Cultura.	*Bergamo*	from 1895
L'Arte.	*Rome* *later Turin*	from 1898
Rassegna d'Arte.	*Milan*	from 1901
Rivista d'Arte.	*Florence*	
Bolletino d'Arte del Ministero della P. Instruzione.	*Rome*	from 1907
Bulletin de l'Institut historique belge de Rome. (Mededeelingen van het Nederlandsch Historisch Instituut te Rome).	*Brussels and Rome*	from 1919
Diana.	*Siena*	
Dedalo	*Milan*	
Aevum.	*Milan*	from 1932
Miscellanea d'Arte.		
Critica d'Arte.	*Florence*	from 1935
Le Arti.	*Florence*	from 1938
Documenti e Commenti per la Storia dell' Arte.		
L'Illustrazione Italiana.		
Museum bulletins, proceedings of academic bodies, local inventories and other local publications.		

GERMAN AND AUSTRIAN

Zeitschrift für Bildende Kunst.	*Leipzig*	from 1866
Repertorium für Kunstwissenschaft.	*Stuttgart, later Berlin*	from 1876
Jahrbuch der Preussischen Kunstsammlungen.	*Berlin*	from 1880
Jahrbuch der Kunsthistorischen Sammlungen der Allerhöchsten Kaiserhauses. *Continued as*	*Vienna*	from 1883
Jahrbuch der Kunsthistorischen Sammlungen in Wien.	*Vienna*	from 1926
Kunstchronik, Wochenschrift für Kunst und Kunstgewerbe.	*Munich*	from 1890
Münchner Jahrbuch der Bildenden Kunst.	*Munich*	from 1906
Monatshefte für Kunstwissenschaft.	*Leipzig*	from 1908
Der Cicerone.	*Leipzig*	from 1909
Die Kunst.	*Munich*	
Berliner Museen, amtliche Berichte aus den Preussischen Kunstsammlungen.	*Berlin*	from 1908
Marburger Jahrbuch für Kunstwissenschaft.	*Marburg*	
Museumskunde.	*Berlin*	
Städel Jahrbuch.	*Frankfort*	from 1921
Belvedere.	*Vienna*	from 1922
Graphischen Kunst.	*Vienna*	

NOTES ON THE LITERATURE

Wiener Jahrbuch für Kunstgeschichte.	*Vienna*	
Zeitschrift für Kunstgeschichte.	*Berlin*	
Jahrbuch für Kunstwissenschaft.	*Leipzig*	from 1923
Pantheon.	*Munich*	from 1928
Regional publications and proceedings of academic bodies.		

GENERAL INDEX (SELECTIVE) TO PART I

(Pages 1-477)

[N.B. For Index of Painters' names see below pp. 769–83]

GENERAL INDEX (SELECTIVE) TO PART I

GENERAL INDEX (SELECTIVE) TO PART I

INDEX TO PART I

(Pages 1-477)

ARTISTS

INDEX TO PART I